P9-CRB-161

History of the American Economy

Tenth Edition

Gary M. Walton
University of California, Davis

Hugh Rockoff
Rutgers University

Australia · Canada · Mexico · Singapore · Spain · United Kingdom · United States

History of the American Economy, **10e**
Gary M. Walton and Hugh Rockoff

VP/Editorial Director:
Jack W. Calhoun

VP/Editor-in-Chief:
Michael P. Roche

Publisher:
Michael B. Mercier

Sr. Acquisitions Editor:
Peter Adams

Developmental Editor:
Sarah K. Dorger

Sr. Marketing Coordinator:
Jenny Fruechtenicht

Production Editor:
Amy McGuire

Technology Project Editor:
Peggy Buskey

Sr. Media Editor:
Pam Wallace

Manufacturing Coordinator:
Sandee Milewski

Production House/Compositor:
DPS Associates, Inc.

Printer:
Thomson/West
Eagan, MN

Design Project Manager:
Rik Moore

Internal Designer:
Creatives on Call

Cover Designer:
John Robb,
JWR Design Interaction, LLC

Cover Images:
© PhotoDisc, Inc.

Photography Manager:
John Hill

Photo Researcher:
Seidel Associates

Printed in the United States of America
1 2 3 4 5 07 06 05 04

Package ISBN: 0-324-25969-7
Text ISBN: 0-324-22636-5

Library of Congress Control Number:
2003115115

For more information contact South-Western,
5191 Natorp Boulevard,
Mason, Ohio 45040.
Or you can visit our Internet site at: http://www.swlearning.com

Douglass C. North

Robert W. Fogel

In honor of our dissertation advisors,
Douglass C. North and Robert W. Fogel,
Nobel Laureates in Economics, 1993

Brief Contents

Contents

Preface

This new edition of *History of the American Economy* was made necessary by the brisk advance of research in economic history and the rapid changes unfolding in the economy. The struggle of many nations to convert from centrally planned to market-led economies after the collapse of communism, the rapid economic expansion of India and China, and the growing economic integration in Europe invite new perspectives on the historical record of the American economy. Moreover, the terrorist attacks of September 11, 2001, on the World Trade Center and the Pentagon and the subsequent wars in Afghanistan and Iraq have spread a blanket of uncertainty on the future of the United States. These events have heightened the importance of understanding the sources of economic growth and change.

To properly convey the speed of change of American lifestyles and economic well being, chapter 1 begins with a focus on twentieth-century American life, mostly but not entirely economic. The purpose is to show how dramatically different the way we live today is compared to the times of our grandparents and great-grandparents. The remarkable contrasts in living standards, length of life, and how we work and consume from 1900 to 2000 provide a "wake-up call" for all of us on the changes soon to unfold in our lives and in the lives of generations to come. This wake-up call serves a vital purpose: preparation for the future. As Professor Deirdre McCloskey admonishes us in her book *Second Thoughts*, in preparing for the future we best arm ourselves with a good understanding of the past. We better control our future by mastering the lessons of the past.

Entirely new to this edition are "New Views," boxed discussions that draw explicit analogies between current issues and past experiences—drug prohibition today and alcohol prohibition in the 1920s, and war finance today and war finance in the past, to name two. Economic historians, of course, have always made these connections for their students, but we believe that by drawing attention to them in the text we reinforce the lesson that history has much to teach us about the present, and the perhaps equally important lesson that detailed study of the past is needed to determine both the relevance and the limits of historical analogies.

We have retained the presentation of material in chronological order, albeit not rigidly. Part One, "The Colonial Era: 1607–1776," focuses on the legacies of that era and the institutions, policies, economic activities, and growth that brought the colonies to a point where they could challenge the mother country for their independence. Part Two, "The Revolutionary, Early National, and Antebellum Eras: 1776–1860," and Part Three, "The

Reunification Era: 1860–1920," each begin with a chapter on the impact of war and its aftermath. The other chapters in these parts follow a parallel sequence of discussion topics—land, agriculture, and natural resources; transportation; product markets and structural change; conditions of labor; and money, banking, and economic fluctuations. Each of these parts, as well as Part Four, closes with a chapter on an issue of special importance to the period: Part One, the causes of the American Revolution; Part Two, slavery; and Part Three, domestic markets and foreign trade. Part Four closes with a discussion of World War II. All the chapters have been rewritten to improve the exposition and to incorporate the latest findings. Part Five, "The Postwar Era: 1946 to the Present" moreover, has been extensively revised to reflect the greater clarity with which we can now view the key developments that shaped postwar America.

All five parts explicitly emphasize and illustrate five grand themes that provide the foundation of the book: (1) economic growth, (2) markets and the role of government, including monetary and fiscal policy, (3) the quest for security, (4) international trade and finance, and (5) demographic forces. These themes reflect the research of scholars, past and present, who have contributed to the revision of the historical record. We have stressed these themes to excite the readers' interest in economic history and, we hope, to place current problems in historical perspective. We believe that presenting specific policy issues in their web of economic, political, and demographic forces provides convincing evidence of the relevance of economic history to contemporary events and to our personal lives.

The tenth edition retains and increases the strong emphasis from earlier editions on the importance of institutions and the influence, both positive and negative, of government policies. It gives special note to the economic consequences of legal change, of government intervention and regulation of business practices and markets, and of policies affecting Native Americans and others placed at disadvantage. The book provides evidence on the distributions of income prevailing in each of the major periods. This should encourage students to draw their own conclusions on matters of economic justice and to appreciate that economic change produces both winners and losers. Similarly, this edition highlights slavery and the failures of Reconstruction to increase our understanding of the racial issues we face today.

Finally, the tenth edition further develops the pedagogical features used in earlier editions. We outline five basic principles of economic history, or "Economic Reasoning Propositions," in chapter one. We repeatedly draw attention in the text to these propositions with explicit text references and a new marginal icon for easy reference. A list of historical and economic perspectives precedes each of the five parts of the book, providing a summary of the key characteristics and events that gave distinction to each era. Furthermore, each chapter still ends with a reference list of articles, books, and websites. Each list is at once the basis of much of the scholarship underlying the chapter and a source of suggested readings. In addition to these pedagogical aids, each chapter begins with a brief overview and summary of the key lesson objectives and issues. In addition to the "New Views" boxed feature described above, we have retained the "Economic Insights" boxes that utilize explicit economic analysis to reveal the power of economic analysis in explaining the past and to show economic forces at work on specific issues raised in the chapters. We have also retained the "Perspectives" boxes that discuss policies and events impacting disadvantaged groups.

We are pleased to introduce an improved technology supplement with this edition: *Economic Applications* (**http://econapps.swlearning.com**). This site offers dynamic Web features: EconNews Online, EconDebate Online, and EconData Online. Organized by pertinent economic topics, and searchable by topic or feature, these features are easy to integrate into the classroom. EconNews, EconDebate and EconData deepen a student's understanding of theoretical concepts through hands-on exploration and analysis of the latest economic news stories, policy debates, and data. These features are updated on a regular basis. The *Economic Applications* Web site is complimentary via an access card included with each new edition of *History of the American Economy*. Used book buyers can purchase access to the site at **http://econapps.swlearning.com**.

David Mustard and Myra Moore have authored a test bank to accompany *History of the American Economy*, tenth edition, which is available to qualified instructors through the Web site (**http://walton.swlearning.com**).

We are especially grateful to the reviewers of this edition: Phil Coelho, Martha L. Olney, David Mitch, Michael R. Haines, Daniel Barbezat, and David Mustard.

This edition, moreover, reflects the contributions of many other individuals who have helped us with this and previous editions. Here we gratefully acknowledge the contributions of Hugh G.J. Aitken, Lee Alston, Terry Anderson, Fred Bateman, Diane Betts, Stuart Bruchey, Colleen Callahan, Ann Carlos, Susan Carter, Phil Coelho, Raymond L. Cohn, James Cypher, Paul A. David, Lance Davis, William Dougherty, Richard A. Easterlin, Barry Eichengreen, Stanley Engerman, Dennis Farnsworth, Price Fishback, Albert Fishlow, Robert W. Fogel, Andrew Foshee, Claudia Goldin, Joseph Gowaskie, Phil Graves, George Green, Robert Higgs, John A. James, Stewart Lee, Gary D. Libecap, James Mak, Deirdre McCloskey, Russell Menard, Lloyd Mercer, Pamela Nickless, Douglass C. North, Anthony O'Brien, Jeff Owen, Edwin Perkins, Roger L. Ransom, David Rasmussen, Joseph D. Reid Jr., Paul Rhode, Elyce Rotella, Barbara Sands, Don Schaefer, R. L. Sexton, James Shepherd, Mark Siegler, Austin Spencer, Richard H. Steckel, Paul Uselding, Jeffrey Williamson, Richard Winkelman, Gavin Wright, and Mary Yeager. The length of this list (which is by no means complete) reflects the extraordinary enthusiasm and generosity that characterizes the discipline of economic history.

Gary Walton is grateful to the Foundation for Teaching Economics for research assistance and clerical support and to his colleagues at the University of California, Davis for advice and encouragement, especially Alan Olmstead, Alan Taylor, Greg Clark, and Peter Lindert.

Hugh Rockoff thanks his colleagues at Rutgers, especially his fellow economic historians Michael Bordo and Eugene White. He is greatly indebted to Deepa Bhat for her careful statistical work. Hugh owes his largest debt to his wife, Hope Corman, who provided instruction in the subtleties of labor economics and unflagging encouragement for the whole project. Hugh also owes a special debt to his children, Jessica and Steven, who have now reached an age where they no longer provide a plausible excuse for not finishing the revision on time.

GARY WALTON
HUGH ROCKOFF

About the Authors

Gary M. Walton became the Founding Dean of the Graduate School of Management at the University of California, Davis in 1981 and is currently Professor of Economics at the University of California, Davis. In addition, he is President of the Foundation for Teaching Economics where he has designed and administered highly acclaimed economics and leadership programs (domestically and internationally) for high school seniors selected for their leadership potential, and to high school teachers.

He credits much of his personal success to his coach at UC Berkeley, the legendary Brutus Hamilton (U.S. Head Coach of Track and Field in the 1952 Olympics), and his success as an economist to his Ph.D. dissertation advisor, Douglass C. North (1993 Nobel Laureate in Economics).

Hugh Rockoff is Professor of Economics at Rutgers University and a research associate of the National Bureau of Economic Research. He has written extensively on banking and monetary history and wartime price controls. He enjoys teaching economic history to undergraduates, and credits his success as an economist to his Ph.D. dissertation advisor, Robert W. Fogel (1993 Nobel Laureate in Economics).

Chapter One

GROWTH, WELFARE, AND THE AMERICAN ECONOMY

AMERICANS 1900–2000

When Rutgers and Princeton played the first intercollegiate football game in 1869, it is doubtful any person alive could have foreseen the impact football would have on twenty-first-century American life. From the weekly money and passion fans pour into their favorite teams, to the media hype and parties linked to season-ending bowl games, football is truly big business, both in college and in the pros. And how the game has changed!

By the turn of the twentieth century, some of the land grant colleges of the Midwest were also fielding teams, one of the earliest being the University of Wisconsin–Madison. The Badgers, as they are popularly called today, enjoy a long-standing sports tradition, and thereby provide some historically interesting facts. As shown in Figure 1.1 on page 2, in 1902, UW's football team was made up of players whose average size was 173 pounds. Most of the athletes played "both sides of the ball," on offense as well as defense, and substitutions were infrequent. Economists today would say they were short on specialization. By 1929, the average size had increased modestly to 188 pounds, and players were increasingly, though not yet exclusively, specializing on offense or defense. By 1999, the average weight of Wisconsin football players was 234 pounds, and players routinely specialized not just on defense or offense, but by particular positions and by special teams, and sometimes by types of formations. Even more dramatic size changes are revealed by comparing the weight of the five largest players. UW's five biggest players in 1902 averaged 184 pounds, hardly more than the average weight of the whole team. As shown in Figure 1.2 on page 2, in 1929 the five biggest players averaged 199 pounds. By 1999, they averaged an amazing 309 pounds, a 53 percent jump over 1929.

UW alumni and students have also been big-time basketball enthusiasts, favoring players with speed, shooting and jumping skills, and height. In 1939, the Badgers starting five had a considerable range of heights by position just as they do today. Figure 1.3 on page 3 conveys not only the consistent differences among guards, forwards, and the centers but also the dramatic gains in height by players at every position taking the court today. The 1999 guards had an average height equal to the height of the 1939 center. Such dramatic height gains, from 4 to 7 inches, are partly a result of the growing college entrance opportunities

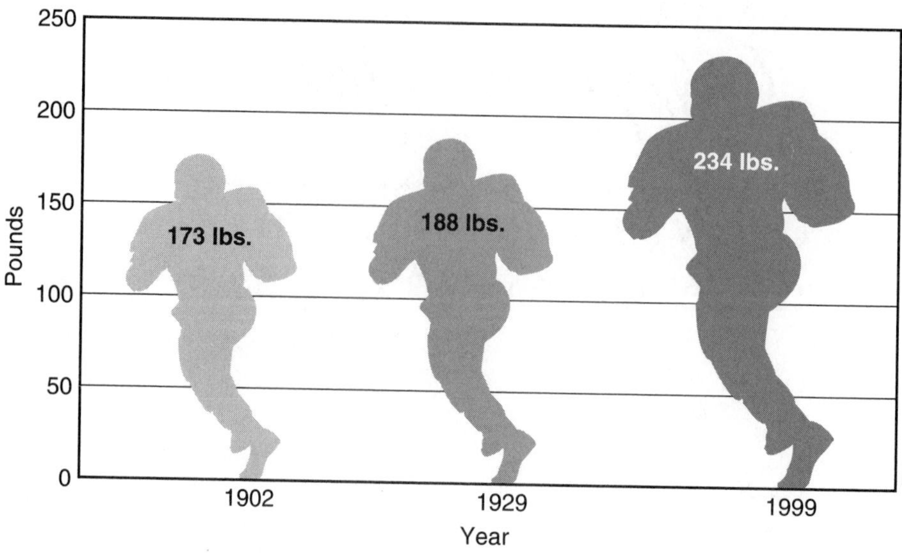

FIGURE 1.1 University of Wisconsin Football Players' Average Weight

Source: Sport Information Office, University of Wisconsin–Madison

that exceptionally talented players enjoy today compared to young players long ago. But the height gains also reflect more general increases in average heights for the U.S. population overall, and these gains in turn indicate improvements in diet and health.

Changes in average height tell us quite a lot about a society; nations whose people are becoming taller, as they have in Japan over the last 50 years, are becoming richer and eating better. Because of genetic differences among individuals, an individual woman who is short can't be considered to be poor. Such a conclusion would not be unreasonable, however, especially along with other evidence, for a society of short people. Adult heights reflect the accumulative past nutritional experience during the growing years, the disease environment,

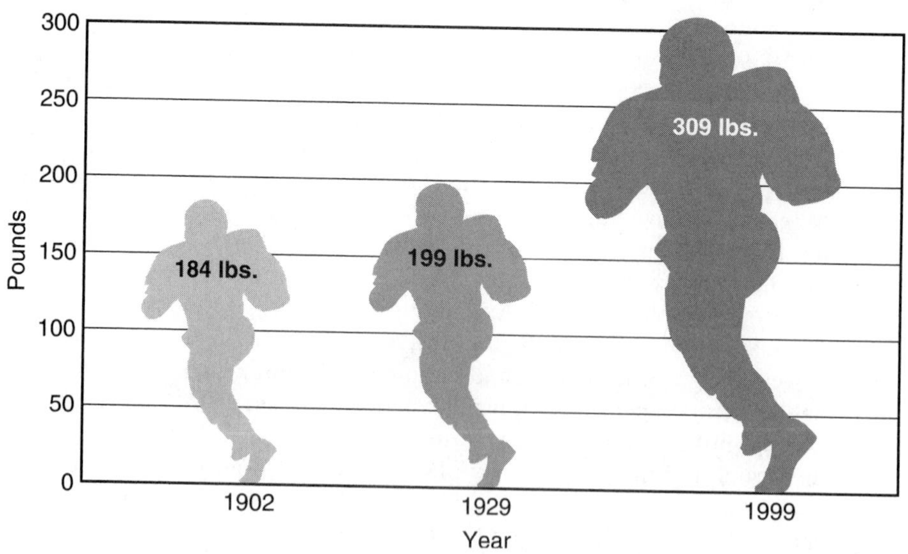

FIGURE 1.2 University of Wisconsin Football: Average Weight of Five Largest Players

Source: Sport Information Office, University of Wisconsin–Madison

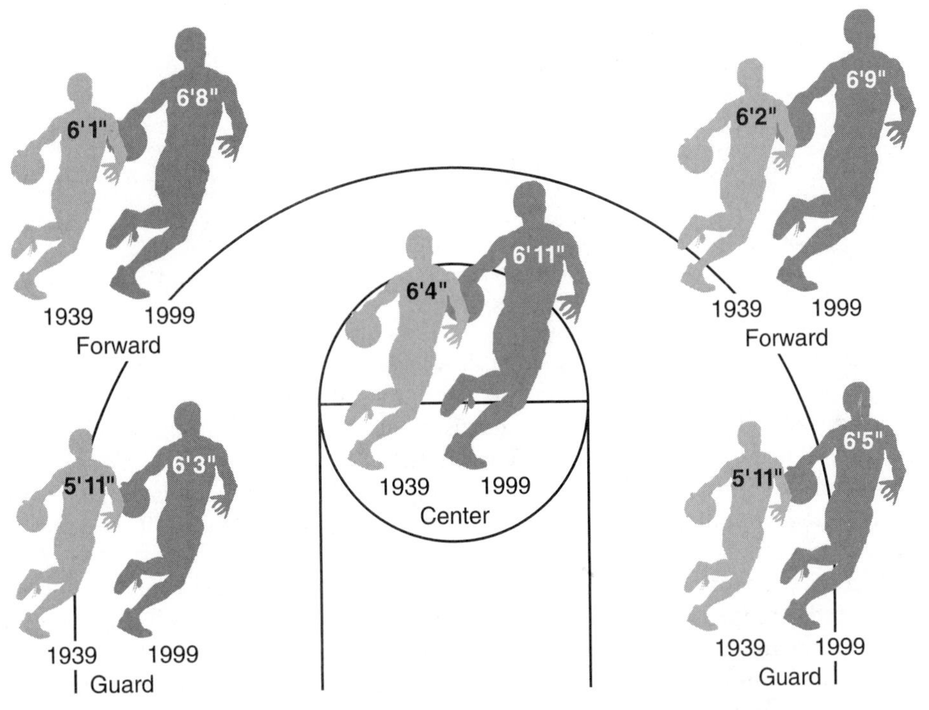

FIGURE 1.3 University of Wisconsin Basketball Players' Heights

Source: Sport Information Office, University of Wisconsin–Madison.

health care, as well as genetic factors (which change very slowly.)[1] Americans are the largest people in the world; the Germans are second. Americans today, with adult males averaging 5'10" and 172 pounds, are nearly 2 inches taller than their grandparents. The average height gain of Americans during the twentieth century was a little more than 3 inches. We are richer and eat more and better than Americans did 100 years ago.

Another, and arguably even better measure of a society's vitality and well-being is the length of life of its citizens. Throughout most of history, individuals and societies have fought against early death. The gain in life expectancy at birth from the low 20s to nearly 30 by around 1750 took thousands of years. Since then, life expectancy in advanced countries has jumped to 75, or 150 percent, and in 2001 in the United States it was 77 years. This phenomenal change is not merely a reflection of decline in infant mortality; as Table 1.1 on page 4 shows for the United States, the advances in length of life are spread across all age groups. As a consequence, in 2000, 290 million people were living in the United States, up from 76 million in 1900.

The gains in population size and in length of life stem primarily from economic growth, because these lead to better diets and cleaner water, to sewage disposal, and other health-enhancing changes. The broadest and most commonly used measures of overall economic performance are the levels and the rise in real gross domestic product (GDP). The U.S. real GDP increased from $0.5 trillion in 1900 to about $9.5 trillion in 2000, measured in constant real purchasing power of 1998 dollars. From Figure 1.4 on page 4 we see that when divided by the population, GDP per capita averaged $4,800 (in 1998 constant dollars) in

[1]See, for example, Dora L. Costa and Richard H. Steckel, "Long-Term Trends in Health, Welfare, and Economic Growth in the United States," in *Health and Welfare during Industrialization*, eds. Richard H. Steckel and Roderich Floud (Chicago: University of Chicago Press, 1995), 5.

TABLE 1.1 Life Expectancy by Age in the United States

AGE	1901	1954	1977	2000
0	49	70	73	77
15	62	72	75	78
45	70	74	77	79
65	77	79	81	83
75	82	84	85	86

Sources: Data for 1901, U.S. Life Tables, 1890, 1901, and 1901–1910, *Department of Commerce (Washington: U.S. Government Printing Office, 1921), 52–53; and data for 1940–1996,* Vital Statistics of the United States *(Hyattsville, Md.: National Center for Health Statistics, DHEW, selected years).*

1900. In 2000 it was $34,000, about seven times higher. Average yearly increases of 2.0 percent, which for any given year appear small, have compounded year after year to realize this sevenfold advance. These gains have not been just for the few, the middle class, or the very rich.

The rise in material affluence in the United States in this century has been so great that citizens whom the government labels "officially poor" currently have incomes surpassing those of average middle-class Americans in 1950 and higher than all but the richest Americans (top 5 percent) in 1900. The official poverty income level in the United States is based on the concept of meeting basic needs. The measure starts with a minimum amount of money needed to feed a person properly. This amount is then multiplied by 3 to meet needs for shelter, clothing, and other essentials. This widely used poverty threshold measure for Americans was about $8,500 at the end of the century, almost exactly one-quarter the income of the average American, but higher than average incomes for most of the rest of the world, and above the world average per capita income.

Another way to show how widespread the gains have been from economic growth is to show the availability of things we take for granted today but that were rather special in 1950. Figure 1.5 provides comparisons of items owned or used by average households in the United States in 1950 with those used by Americans below the poverty threshold today. Indeed, American households listed below the poverty level today are more likely to own a color television set than an average household in Italy, France, or Germany. Air-conditioned

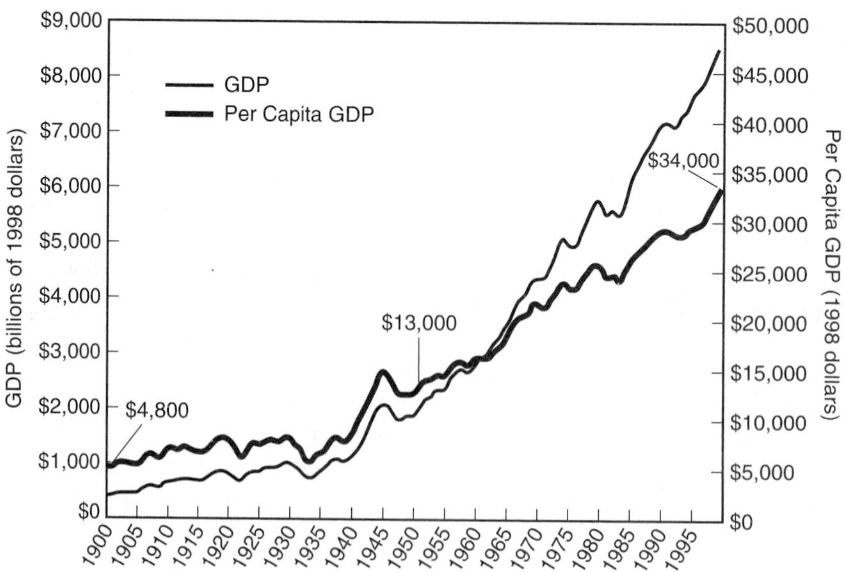

FIGURE 1.4 Gross and Per Capita Domestic Product

Sources: Historical Statistics of the United States, *Series F1, and U.S. Department of Commerce, Bureau of Economic Analysis, http://www.bea.doc.gov/bea/dn/gdplev.htm.*

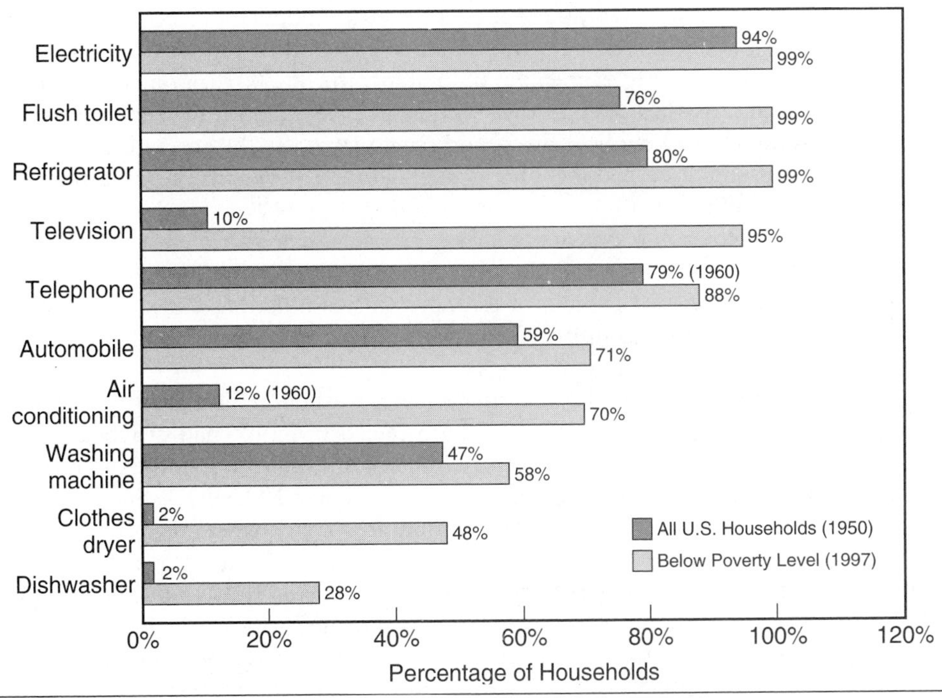

FIGURE 1.5 Ownership of Poor Households (1997) versus Ownership of All U.S. Households (1950)

Sources: U.S. Bureau of the Census, American Housing Survey for the United States in 1997*; U.S. Bureau of the Census, "Housing Then and Now," http://www.census.gov/hhes/www/housing/census/histcensushsg.html; and* Historical Statistics of the United States, *Series Q175.*

homes with electricity, a refrigerator, a flush toilet, a television, and telephones are common even among poor Americans (Figure 1.5).

Despite these gain for people labeled "poor" in the United States, the gap between the rich and the poor remains wide. This gap is an important element in drawing conclusions about the success or failure of an economic system. It bears on the cohesion, welfare, and security of a society. A useful starting point from which to consider this issue is to view a snapshot of the division of income in the United States. Figure 1.6 shows this distribution in fifths for all U.S. households for 2001. As in other years, a large gap existed between the

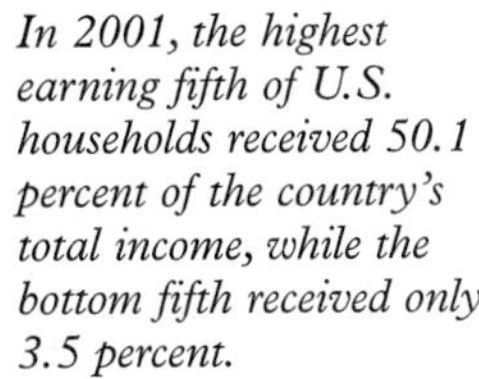

In 2001, the highest earning fifth of U.S. households received 50.1 percent of the country's total income, while the bottom fifth received only 3.5 percent.

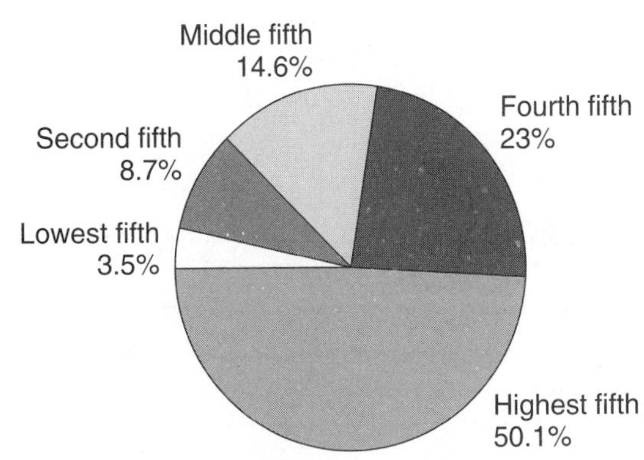

FIGURE 1.6 The American Income Pie by Fifths, 2001

Source: "The Changing Shape of the Nation's Income Distribution, 1747–2001," U.S. Census Bureau, http://www.census.gov

top fifth and the bottom fifth. In fact, the richest fifth of the population received half the income (50.1 percent), about the amount the remaining four-fifths received. The poorest fifth U.S. households received only 3.5 percent of total income on 2001 (not including food stamps, assisted housing, Medicaid, and other such assistance). Figure 1.7 shows changes in average real income received by these five groups since 1966. By the end of the century, the top fifth of the households earned incomes averaging over 13 times the average incomes of those in the bottom fifth.

In Figure 1.7, the income gap appears to have grown in recent years: The two top lines drift upward, while the lower three remain level. In percentage terms, for example, for 1975 the lowest fifth received 4.2 percent of total income; as noted, in 2001 it was down to 3.5 percent. In 1975 the top group received 43.7 percent but claimed 50.1 percent of the total in 2001.

The question begging, however, is whether the people in the bottom fifth in 1975 were also in that category in 2001? If all of the people in the top category in 1975 had switched places by 2001 with all the people in the bottom category (the bottom fifth rising to the top fifth by 2001), no change would be observed in the data shown in Figures 1.6 and 1.7. Surely such a switch would be considered a huge change in the distribution of income among people.

The best available data on the movement of people in these classifications come from a study undertaken by the University of Michigan Panel Survey on Income Dynamics covering 1975–1991. The conventional view of widening income disparity suggested by Figures 1.6 and 1.7 stands in sharp contrast to the evidence in Table 1.2. Reading along the bottom line, we find only 5.1 percent of those in the bottom quintile in 1975 were there in 1991; 29 percent had moved into the top fifth. Reading along the top line indicates that 0.9 percent of those in the top fifth in 1975 had fallen into the bottom fifth by 1991; 62.5 percent remained in the top category.

Further analysis of the data has shown that the rise in income and upward movement into higher categories were frequently swift. In any given year, many of those identified in the bottom fifth were young and in school. With gains in education and job opportunities, many advanced readily into higher rankings.

Another perspective on the economic gains that Americans experienced during the twentieth century comes from looking at the availability, ownership, and use of new goods. Figure 1.8 shows a virtual explosion in the array of goods routinely owned and used in U.S. homes. Most of the items shown were not even available to the richest Americans alive in

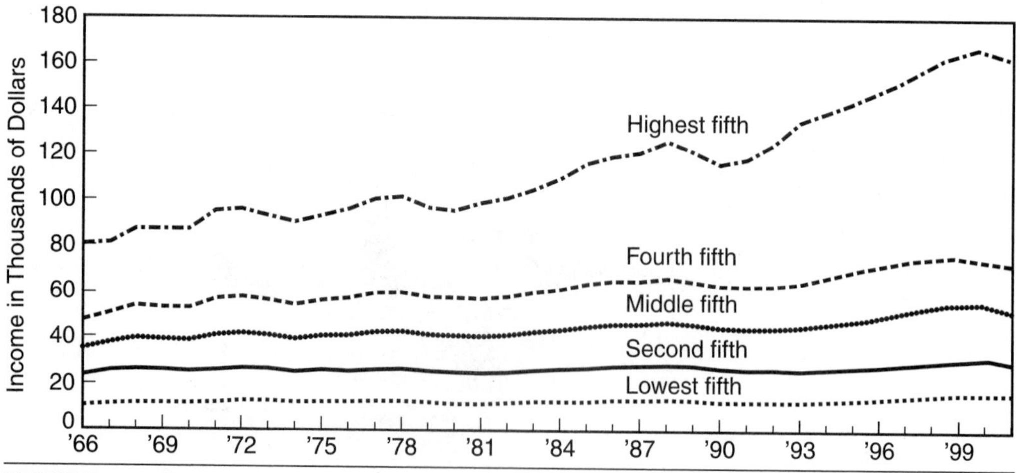

FIGURE 1.7 The Income Gap, 1966–2001

Source: http://www.census.gov/hhes/income/histinc/f03.html

TABLE 1.2 Changes among Income Rankings

INCOME QUINTILE IN 1975	PERCENTAGE IN EACH QUINTILE IN 1991				
	1ST	2ND	3RD	4TH	5TH
5th (highest)	0.9	2.8	10.2	23.6	62.5
4th	1.9	9.3	18.8	32.6	37.4
3rd (middle)	3.3	19.3	28.3	30.1	19.0
2nd	4.2	23.5	20.3	25.2	26.8
1st (lowest)	5.1	14.6	21.0	30.3	29.0

In 1991, only 5.1 percent who were in the lowest income quintile in 1975 were still there. Of the lowest quintile in 1975, 29 percent had progressed to the top one-fifth by 1991.

Source: *W. Michael Cox and Richard Alm, "By Our Own Bootstraps: Economic Opportunity and the Dynamics of Income Distribution." (Federal Reserve Bank of Dallas, 1995).*

1900, so invention is a necessary cause of availability. Nevertheless, the extraordinarily high percentage of households having these items as the twentieth century drew to a close raises this question: How could they afford them? To answer this question, we compare prices in 1900 with those today and wages in 1900 with those today to measure how long a worker in 1900 had to work to get an item compared to the length of time an average worker today must work to get the same item.

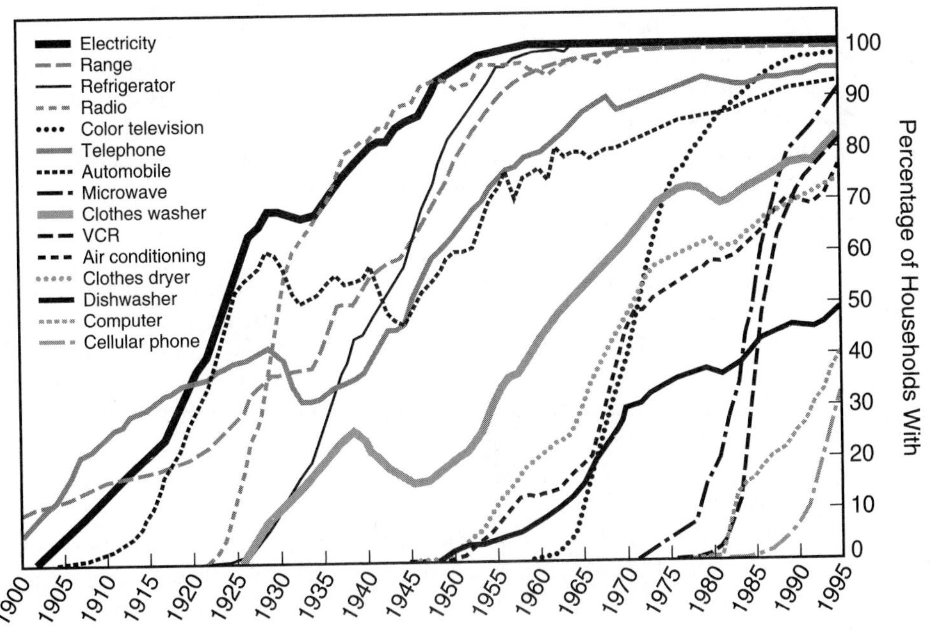

FIGURE 1.8 Household Ownership and Use of Products
The past 100 years have brought a virtual explosion in the array of goods Americans routinely enjoy. At the turn of the century, nobody—not even society's wealthiest—could travel by air, wear comfortable tennis shoes, or even take an aspirin, yet the majority of modern-day Americans regularly do so. From cars to computers to cell phones, our ancestors would gawk at the products we take for granted.

Source: *W. Michael Cox and Richard Alm, "Time Well Spent: The Declining Real Cost of Living in America." (Federal Reserve Bank of Dallas, 1997)*

TABLE 1.3 Share of Income Spent on Food, Clothing, and Shelter

	1901	1995
Food	46%	14%
Clothing	14%	5%
Shelter	15%	18%
Share of Total	76%	38%

Source: *W. Michael Cox and Richard Alm, "Time Well Spent: The Declining Real Cost of Living in America." (Federal Reserve Bank of Dallas, 1997).*

In 1900, an average hourly wage in manufacturing for non-supervisory employees was $0.15, or $8.88 per week. Manufacturing wages were then the highest in the nation; today they roughly equal earnings in other sectors such as services. To repeat, how long did a typical U.S. worker have to work to pay for the basics of food, clothing, and shelter in 1900 compared to the length of time for a worker today?

The shares of total income Americans have spent on these basic items, in 1900 and in 1995, are shown in Table 1.3. The dramatic drop in the proportion of income spent on these basic categories means that more income has become available for other types of goods and services.

First, consider food costs. Table 1.4 shows a list of food item and how long workers had to work in 1919 to be able to buy them and how many minutes workers today must spend on the job to be able to buy them. In the early part of the twentieth century, most U.S. children looked forward with great anticipation to Christmas morning in the hope of finding oranges in their stockings. Table 1.4 data indicate that it took more than an hour of relatively highly paid work to pay for a dozen oranges. For many Americans in 1919, oranges were a luxury, a dozen costing more than twice the cost of a pound of ground beef.

The comparisons in Table 1.4 indicate that to pay for a pound of ground beef took half an hour of work in 1919 but only 6 minutes in 1997. Early in the twentieth century, a family meal of chicken was special. Indeed, in 1928, one of Herbert Hoover's presidential promises was "a chicken in every pot." In 1919, a 3-pound chicken cost $1.23, or 2 hours and 37 minutes in real work time. In 1997, at $3.15 for a 3-pounder, the real work time cost was only 14 minutes.

Because of changes in the size and amenities in houses, it is more difficult to compare housing costs than food cost changes over time. In 1920, a rather typical new house, small by today's standards, cost $4,700, or 7.8 hours of work per square foot of space. Table 1.5 shows the costs of typical new houses in dollars and the percentage of new houses with various amenities. Note that most of the amenities in new houses today were found in new houses in 1956 in much smaller percentages. Despite the increases in amenities and home sizes, as well as higher costs, the work time needed per square foot was 6.5 hours in 1956 and fell to 5.6 hours by 1996.

Turning from shelter to clothes, consider just one item: jeans. Levi Strauss sold his first pair of jeans to California gold miners in 1853, and his 501s® and other variations have been popular ever since. A pair of Levi's in 1900 cost about 7 hours of work for a typical manufacturing employee. Today the work time cost to buy a pair of Levi's is about half of that.

We conclude this analysis with a long list of items by date and the percentage of work time a manufacturing employee must work in America today compared to the labor time needed to pay for the item at the date shown (see Figure 1.9 on page 10). For example, color TVs today cost only 4 percent of the labor time needed to acquire one in 1954, soon after they first appeared. Electricity costs less than 1 percent of what it took in labor time to acquire it in 1900.

TABLE 1.4 The Cost of 12 Food Items, in Minutes of Work

FOOD	1919	1997
Tomatoes, 3 lb.	101	18
Eggs, 1 dozen	80	5
Sugar, 5 lb.	72	10
Bacon, 1 lb.	70	12
Oranges, 1 dozen	68	9
Coffee, 1 lb.	55	17
Milk, half-gallon	39	7
Ground beef, 1 lb.	30	6
Lettuce, 1 lb.	17	3
Beans, 1 lb.	16	3
Bread, 1 lb.	13	4
Onions, 1 lb.	9	2

These figures are computed by dividing the prices of the items by the hourly wage rate. The results show how long people had to work to earn their "daily bread" in 1900 and 1997.

Source: W. Michael Cox and Richard Alm, "Time Well Spent: The Declining Real Cost of Living in America." (Federal Reserve Bank of Dallas, 1997).

TABLE 1.5 The Cost of Housing

	1956	1996
Median price	$14,500	$140,000
Median square footage	1,150	1,950
Median price per square foot	$12.61	$71.79
Average hourly wage	$1.95	$12.78
Hours of work per square foot	6.5	5.6
PERCENTAGE OF NEW HOUSES EQUIPPED WITH . . .		
Garage	50%	86%
Three or more bedrooms	78%	87%
Two or more bathrooms	28%	91%
One or more fireplaces	35%	62%
Two stories or more	6%	47%
Insulation in the walls	33%	93%
Storm windows	8%	68%
Central heat and air	6%	81%
Range	1%	94%
Dishwasher	11%	93%
Refrigerator	5%	18%
Microwave	0%	85%
Garbage disposal	34%	90%
Garage door opener	<1%	78%

Source: W. Michael Cox and Richard Alm, "By Our Own Bootstraps: Economic Opportunity and the Dynamics of Income Distribution" (Federal Reserve Bank of Dallas, 1995).

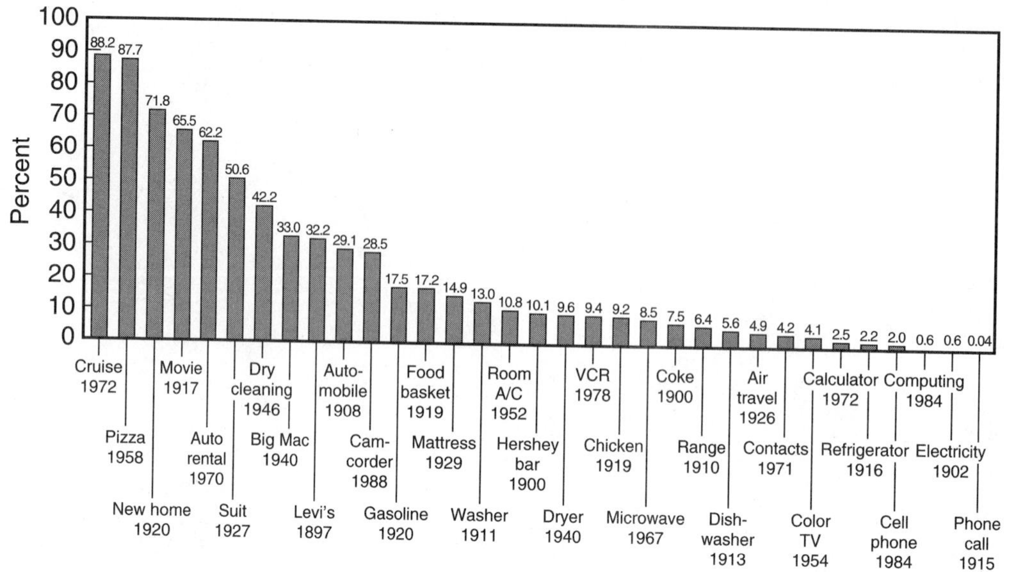

FIGURE 1.9 Time Cost of Items Today Compared with Their Cost at Introduction

Source: W. Michael Cox and Richard Alm, "Time Well Spent: The Declining Real Cost of Living in America." (Federal Reserve Bank of Dallas, 1997).

A STUDY WITH A PURPOSE

Why should you study economic history? One straightforward answer is to better prepare you for the future. Economic history provides you with a clear perspective on the forces of change and a good understanding of the lessons of the past. The study of economic history also provides lessons on nation building and how analyzing policies and institutions that impact the nation as well as you personally.

One hundred years ago, citizens of Great Britain enjoyed the highest standards of living in the world, and the British Empire was the leading world power. In 1892, the dominant European powers upgraded the ranks of their diplomats in Washington, D.C., from ministers to ambassadors, thereby elevating the United States to first-division status among nations. On economic grounds, this upgrading should have occurred much earlier, because in 1892, output per capita in the United States was much higher than in France and Germany and not far below that in Great Britain.

In 1950, the United States was the most powerful nation in the world, and Americans enjoyed standards of living higher, by far, than those of any other people. Another "super power," however, was intensely challenging this supremacy. As the cold war unfolded and intensified after World War II, nations became divided into two clusters; communist nations emphasizing command, control, and central planning systems, and free nations emphasizing markets, trade, competition, and limited government. This division into clusters was especially apparent in Europe and Asia, and many other nations sat on the sidelines pondering their futures and which system to follow. By all appearances, the Soviet Union displayed levels of economic, technological, and military strength, rivaling those of the United States. It launched its space satellite, called Sputnik, in 1957, placing the first vehicle constructed on Earth in space. The cold war ended in 1989, and many satellite nations of the Soviet Union (e.g. Eastern Germany, Czechoslovakia, etc.) broke free. By the mid-1990s, Russia desperately needed aid just to feed its people. The life expectancy of men in Russia plummeted from the low 60s (mid-1980s) to 56 (mid-1990s). The economic and political collapse of the

Soviet Union and the overwhelming relative success of market-driven systems provide another example of the importance of studying economic history.

Such swings in international power, status, and relative well-being are sobering reminders that the present is forever changing and slipping into the past. Are the changes that all of us will see and experience in our lifetimes inevitable, or can destinies be steered? How did we get where we are today?

It is unfortunate that history is often presented in forms that seem irrelevant to our everyday lives. Merely memorizing and recalling dates and places, generals and wars, presidents and legislative acts misdirects our attention to what happened to whom (and when) rather than the more useful focus on how and why events happened. One of the special virtues of the study of economic history is its focus on how and why. It provides us a deeper understanding of how we developed as a nation, how different segments of the population have fared, and what principal policies or compelling forces brought about differential progress (or regress) among regions and people. In short, the study of economic history holds great promise for us. It not only enriches our intellectual development and provides an essential perspective on contemporary affairs, but also it offers practical analytical guidance on matters of policy. The study of economic history is best suited for those who care about the next 1 to 1,000 years and who want to make the future better than the past.

This is no empty claim! Surely one of the primary reasons students major in economics or American history is to ultimately enhance the operation and performance of the American economy and to gain personally. Certainly instructors hope their students will be better-informed citizens and more productive businesspeople, politicians, and professionals. "If this is so," as Gavin Wright recently properly chastised his economic colleagues,

> "if the whole operation has something to do with improving the performance of the U.S. economy, then it is perfectly scandalous that the majority of economics students complete their studies with no knowledge whatsoever about how the United States became the leading economy in the world, as of the first half of the twentieth century. What sort of doctor would diagnose and prescribe without taking a medical history?"[2]

Too often, students are victims of economics textbooks that convey no information on the rise and development of the U.S. economy. Rather, textbooks convey the status quo of American preeminence as if it just happened, as if there were no puzzle to it, as if growth were more or less an automatic, year-by-year, self-sustained process. Authors of such textbooks need an eye-opening sabbatical in Greece, Russia, or Zaire.

Economic history is a longitudinal study but not so long and slow as, say, geology, in which only imperceptible changes occur in one's lifetime. In contrast, the pace of modern economic change is fast and accelerating in many dimensions. Within living memory of most Americans, nations have risen from minor economic significance to world prominence (Hong Kong, Japan, South Korea) while others have fallen from first-position powers to stagnation (Russia in the 1990s and Argentina after 2002). Whole new systems of international economic trade and payments have been developed (North American Free Trade Agreement, European Union). New institutions, regulations, and laws (1990 Clean Air Act, 1996 Welfare Reform Act) have swiftly emerged; these sometimes expand and sometimes constrain our range of economic choices.

The role of government in the economy is vastly different from what it was only 60 or 70 years ago; undoubtedly, it will be strikingly different 50 years from now. The study of economic history stresses the role of institutional change, how certain groups brought about

---

[2]Gavin Wright, "History and the Future of Economics," in *Economic History and the Modern Economists,* ed. William N. Parker (New York: Blackwell, 1986), 81.

economic change, and why. The study of history, then, is more than an activity to amuse us or sharpen our wits. History is a vast body of information essential to making public policy decisions. Indeed, history is the testing grounds for the economic theory and principles taught in economics classes, and the theories taught in other subjects.

To simplify the vast range of economic theory, we rely primarily on five Economic Reasoning Propositions, as given in Economic Insight 1.1. These Economic Reasoning Propositions can be summarized for referral purposes throughout the text, as follows:

1. Choices matter.
2. Costs matter.
3. Incentives matter.
4. Institutions matter.
5. Evidence matters.

Next time you are in a discussion or argument, recall Economic Reasoning Proposition 5. Evidence comes from history and tests the soundness of an opinion. An opinion is a good way to start a discussion but it should not end one.

As Economic Reasoning Proposition 5 (evidence matters) emphasized, not all opinions are equal, not when we want to understand how and why things happen. Two of the great advantages of economic history are its quantitative features and use of economic theory to give useful organization to historical facts. In combination, use of theory and evidence enhances our ability to test (refute or support) particular propositions and recommendations. This helps us choose among opinions that differ.

Consider, for instance, a recommendation for mandatory wage and price controls as a means to combat inflation. Figure 1.10 traces a decade of inflation and reveals our experience with wage and price controls during the Nixon years. President Nixon's opinion at the time was that the controls would benefit the economy.

As shown in Figure 1.10, Nixon's controls (a choice made by his administrators) were imposed in August 1971, when the inflation rate was 3.5 percent. The precontrol peak rate of inflation was 6 percent in early 1970 and was actually falling at the time controls were imposed. The rate of inflation continued to drift downward and remained around 3 percent throughout

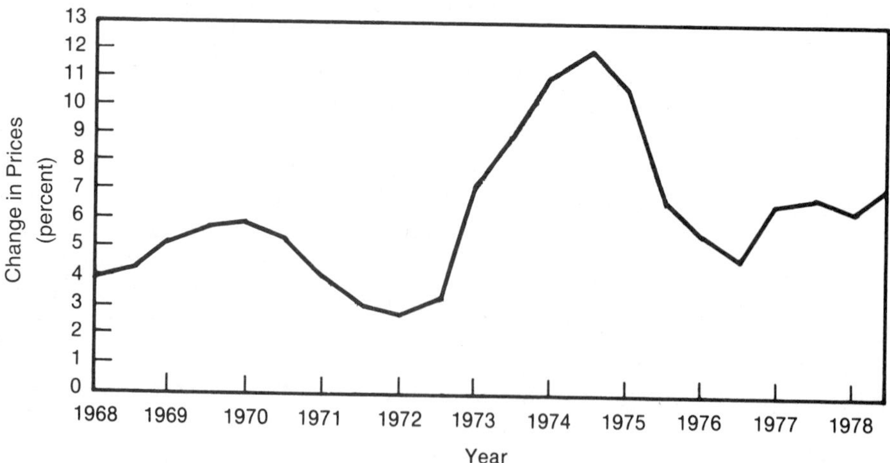

FIGURE 1.10 Inflation and Nixon's Price Controls

Source: U.S. Department of Commerce, Statistical Abstract, *1978, 483.*

Economic Insight 1.1

Five Propositions for Economic Reasoning

As John M. Keynes has said:

> [E]conomics does not furnish a body of settled conclusions immediately applicable to policy. It is a method rather than a doctrine, an apparatus of the mind, a technique of thinking which helps its possessor to draw correct conclusions.

This "apparatus of the mind," or economic way of thinking, follows logically from *five basic propositions* of human nature and well-accepted truths.

1. *People choose, and individual choices are the source of social outcomes.* Scarcity compels us to compete in some form and it necessitates choice. People make choices based on their perceptions of the expected costs and benefits of alternatives. Choices involve risk; outcomes cannot be guaranteed because the consequences of choices lie in the future.
2. *Choices impose costs.* People incur costs when making decisions. Choices involve trade-offs among alternatives. People weigh marginal gains against marginal sacrifices. Ultimately, the cost of any decision is the next-best alternative that must be forgone. Reasoned decision making leads to an increase in any activity in which expected benefits exceed expected costs, and a decrease in any activity in which expected costs exceed expected benefits.
3. *Incentives matter.* Incentives are rewards that encourage people to act. Disincentives discourage actions. People respond to incentives in predictable ways; when incentives change, behavior changes in predictable ways.
4. *Institutions matter, and the "rules of the game" influence choices.* Laws, customs, moral principles, ideas, and cultural institutions influence individual choices and shape the economic system.
5. *Understanding based on knowledge and evidence imparts value to opinions.* The value of an opinion is determined by the knowledge and evidence on which it is based. Statements of opinion should initiate the quest for economic understanding, not end it.

1972; it started to rise in 1973, and by the time the controls were completely lifted in early 1974, the rate was 10 percent and rising.

On the face of it, controls did little to stop inflation. But what explains this dismal record? Were the controls themselves to blame, or were other factors responsible? Only a careful study of the period can identify the role of controls in the acceleration of inflation. A contrast between Nixon's price controls and those imposed during the Korean War (which were not followed by a price explosion after controls were lifted) suggests two important things to look at: monetary and fiscal policies.

Economic Reasoning Proposition

Price controls, moreover, disrupted the smooth functioning of the economic system. For example, to circumvent the Nixon controls, the U.S. lumber industry regularly exported lumber to Canada and then reimported it for sale at higher prices. (Refer to Economic Reasoning Proposition 4: institutions (rules) matter.) As fertilizers and chemical pesticides

became more profitable to sell abroad than at home, agricultural production suffered for want of these essential inputs. (Recall Economic Reasoning Proposition 3: incentives matter.) These and many other similar disruptions to production decreased the growth rate of goods and services less and, therefore, the inflation worse than it would have been otherwise. We cannot explore this issue in depth here. Our point is simply that to evaluate policy proposals, we must inevitably turn to the historical record.[3]

The use of wage and price controls during World War II provides another example adding to our understanding of their effectiveness. One important lesson this episode teaches is the need to supplement quantitative studies with historical research. An economist cannot naively assume that price statistics always tell the truth. During the war, controls were evaded in numerous ways that were only partly reflected in the official numbers despite valiant efforts by the Bureau of Labor Statistics. One form of evasion was quality deterioration. Fat was added to hamburger, candy bars were made smaller and had inferior ingredients substituted, coarser fabrics were used in making clothes, maintenance on rental properties was reduced, and so on. Sometimes whole lines of low-markup, low-quality merchandise were eliminated, forcing even poor consumers to trade up to high-markup, high-quality lines or go without any new items. And, of course, black markets developed, just as current ones in controlled substances, such as marijuana, have done. The job of the economic historian is to try to assess the overall effect of these activities.[4]

Many students ask: Granted that economic history is important to the professional economist or economic policymaker, is there any practical reason for studying it if I have other long-term goals? The answer is yes. (See Black, Sanders, and Taylor, who show that undergrad economics majors do better financially than do business, math, or physics majors). The skills developed in studying economic history—critically analyzing the economic record, drawing conclusions from it based on economic theory, and writing up the results in clear English—are valuable skills in many lines of everyday work. The attorney who reviews banking statutes to determine the intent of the law, the investment banker who studies past stock market crashes to find clues on how to foretell a possible crash, the owner-operator of a small business who thinks about what happened to other small businesses that were sold to larger firms—are all taking on the role of economic historian. It will help them if they can do it well.[5]

Besides the importance of historical study for its vital role in deliberating private and public policy recommendations, knowledge of history has other merits. For one thing, history can be fun—especially as we grow older and try to recapture parts of our lives in nostalgic reminiscence. For another, history entertains as well as enriches our self-consciousness, and, often, because of TV, the historical account is provided almost instantly (e.g., news coverage of the 2003 war in Iraq). A sense of history is really a sense of participation in high drama—a sense of having a part in the great flow of events that links us with people of earlier times and with those yet to be born.

We conclude this section with the reminder that two of the principal tasks of economic historians are to examine a society's overall economic growth (or stagnation or decline) and to find out what happens to the welfare of groups within the society as economic change occurs. Our primary purpose in the following pages is to explain how the American economy grew and changed to fit into an evolving world economy. We study

---

[3]An attempt to compare and contrast American experiences with wage and price controls is presented in Hugh Rockoff, *Drastic Measures: A History of Wage and Price Controls in the United States* (New York: Cambridge University Press, 1984).

[4]For one exploration of this issue, see Hugh Rockoff, "Indirect Price Increases and Real Wages in World War II," *Explorations in Economic History* 15 (1978): 407–420.

[5]For further insights into the gains of studying economic history, see Donald N. McCloskey, "Does the Past Have Useful Economics?" *Journal of Economic Literature* 14 (1976): 434–461.

the past to better understand the causes of economic change today and to learn how standards of living can be affected by policies and other forces stemming from technological, demographical, and institutional change.[6]

The Long Road out of Poverty

Before diving into the chronology of American economic history emphasizing the forces of economic growth, it is very important to place the present day circumstances of Americans and others in proper historical perspective. As Winston Churchill is credited with saying, "The longer back you look, the farther into the future you can see." However, we don't see the distant past clearly, let alone the future.

Reflecting on some historical episode, perhaps from the Bible, or from Shakespeare, or some Hollywood epic is an interesting exercise. For most of us, the stories we recall are about great people, or great episodes, tales of love, war, religion, and other dramas of the human experience. Kings, heroes, or religious leaders . . . in castles, palaces, or cathedrals . . . engaging armies in battles, or discovering inventions or new worlds—-readily come to mind, often glorifying the past.[7]

To be sure, there were so called golden ages, as in Ancient Greece and during the Roman Era, the Sung Dynasty (in China), and other periods and places in which small fractions of societies lived in splendor and reasonable comfort, and in which small portions of the population sometimes rose above levels of meager subsistence. But such periods of improvement were never sustained.[8] Taking the long view, and judging the lives of almost all of our distant ancestors, their reality was one of almost utter wretchedness. Except for the fortunate few, humans everywhere lived in abysmal squalor. To capture the magnitude of this deprivation and sheer length of the road out of poverty, consider this time capsule summary of human's history from Douglass C. North's 1993 Nobel address:

> Let us represent the human experience to date as a 24-hour clock in which the beginning consists of the time (apparently in Africa between 4 and 5 million years ago) when humans became separate from other primates. Then the beginning of so-called civilization occurs with the development of agriculture and permanent settlement in about 8000 B.C. in the Fertile Crescent—**in the last 3 of 4 minutes of the clock** (emphasis added). For the other 23 hours and 56 or 57 minutes, humans remained hunters and gatherers, and while population grew, it did so at a very slow pace. Now if we make a new 24-hour clock for the time of civilization—the 10,000 years from development of agriculture to the present—the pace of change appears to be very slow for the first 12 hours. . . . Historical demographers speculate that the rate of population growth may have doubled as compared to the previous era but still was very slow. The pace of change accelerates in the past 5,000 years with the rise and then decline of economies and civilization. Population may have grown from about 300 million at the time of Christ to about 800 million by 1750—a substantial acceleration as compared to earlier

[6]For examples of institutional change, see Lee J. Alston, "Institutions and Markets in History: Lessons for Central and Eastern Europe," in *Economic Transformation in East and Central Europe: Legacies from the Past and Policies for the Future,* ed. David F. Good (New York: Routledge, 1994), 43–59; and Jan Siniecki, "Impediments to Institutional Change in the Former Soviet System," in *Empirical Studies in Institutional Change,* eds. Lee J. Alston, Thrainn Eggertsson, and Douglass C. North (New York: Cambridge University Press, 1996), 35–59.

[7]Such glorification has a long tradition: "The humour of blaming the present, and admiring the past, is strongly rooted in human nature, and has an influence even on persons endued with the profoundest judgment and most extensive learning," from David Hume, "Of the Populousness of Ancient Nations," in 1777/1987, 464.

[8]For example, see Winston Churchill's description of life in Britain during and after the Roman Era: *A History of the English Speaking People,* Vol. 1 (New York: Dorsett Press, 1956).

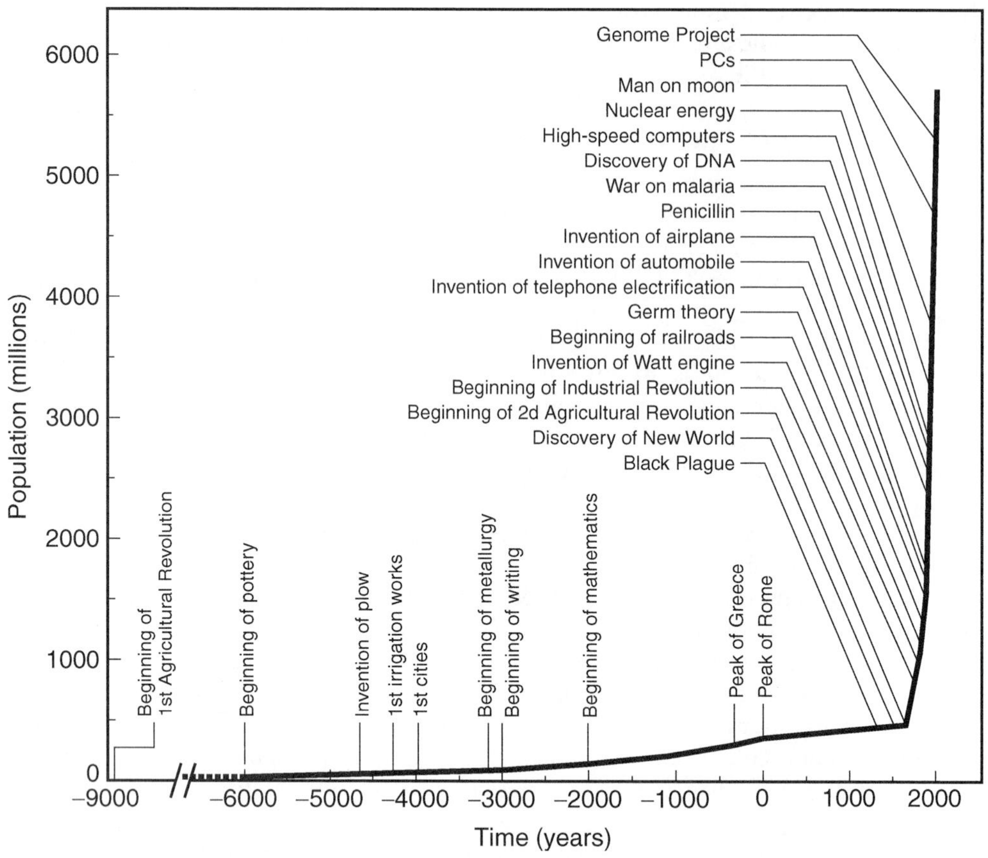

Figure 1.11 World Population and Major Inventions and Advances in Knowledge

Source: Robert W. Fogel, "Catching Up with the Economy," The American Economic Review *89 (1999).*

> rates of growth. The last 250 years—**just 35 minutes on our new 24-hour clock** (emphasis added)—are the era of modern economic growth, accompanied by a population explosion that now puts world population in excess of 5 billion (1993). If we focus on the last 250 years, we see that growth was largely restricted to Western Europe and the overseas extensions of Britain for 200 of those 250 years.[9]

Evidence supporting North's observation that 1750 was a major turning point in the human existence is provided in Figure 1.11.

This graph of the world population over the past 11,000 years, along with noteworthy inventions, discoveries, and events, conveys its literal explosion in the mid-eighteenth century. Just a few decades before the United States won its independence from Britain, the geographical line bolts upward like a rocket, powering past 6 billion humans alive. The advances in food production from new technologies, commonly labeled the second Agricultural Revolution, and from the utilization of new resources (e.g., land in the New World) coincide with this population explosion. Also noteworthy is the intense acceleration in the pace of change in vital discoveries. Before 1600, centuries elapsed between them. Improvements in and the spread of the use of the plow, for example, first introduced in the Mesopotamian Valley around 4000 B.C., changed very little until around 1000 A.D.

[9]Douglass C. North, "Economic Performance Through Time," *The American Economic Review* 84 (1994): 364–365.

TABLE 1.6 Years of Life Expectancy at Birth

PLACE	MIDDLE AGES	SELECT YEARS	1950-1955	1975-1980	2000
France		30 (1800)	66	74	78
United Kingdom	20-30	36 (1799-1803)	69	73	77
India		25 (1901-1911)	39	53	63
China		25-35 (1929-1931)	41	65	70
Africa			38	48	54
World	20-30		46	60	67

Sources: J. Lee and W. Feng "Malthusian Models and Chinese Realities: The Chinese Demographic System, 1700-2000," Population and Development Review *25(1999); E. A. Wrigley and R. S. Schofield* The Population History of England, 1541-1871: A Reconstruction *(Cambridge, Mass: Harvard University Press, 1981); World Resources Institute; and United Nations Development Program,* Human Development Report *(New York: Oxford University Press, 1999).*

Contrast this with air travel. The Wright brothers were responsible for the first successful motor-driven flight, in 1903. In 1969, a mere 66 years later, Neil Armstrong became the first human to step foot on the moon. In short, the speed of life's changes many of us take for granted has been accelerating, especially in the last two and a half centuries.

Before 1750, chronic hunger, malnutrition, disease, illness, and resulting early death were the norm for almost all people everywhere. Even wealthy people ate poorly; as Nobel Laureate Robert Fogel reports:

> Even the English peerage, with all its wealth, had a diet during the sixteenth and seventeenth centuries that was deleterious to health. Although abundant in calories and proteins, aristocratic diets were deficient in some nutrients and included large quantities of toxic substances, especially alcoholic beverages and salt.[10]

Exceedingly poor diets and chronic malnutrition were the norm because of the absence of choices, or the fact of scarcity. Food production seldom rose above basic life sustaining levels. People were caught in a food trap: Meager yields severely limited energy for all kinds of pursuits, including production. Inadequate diets were accompanied by high rates of disease and low rates of resistance to them.

The maladies of malnourishment and widespread disease are revealed in evidence regarding height and weight. As late as 1750, the average height of adult males in England, the world's most economically advanced nation, was about 4′ 7″, and less in France and Norway.[11] The average U.S. man today stands 15 inches taller. In the 1750s, typical weight was 130 pounds for an Englishman and 110 pounds for a Frenchman. Compare this to the weight of U.S. males today at about 175 pounds. It is startling to see the suits of armor in the Tower of London that were worn for ancient wars; they vividly remind us of how small, even the supposedly largest people of long-ago really were.

The second Agricultural Revolution, beginning in the mid-eighteenth century, soon followed by the Industrial Revolution (first in England, then France, the United States and other Western countries), initiated and sustained the population explosion, lifting birth rates and lowering death rates. Table 1.6 summarizes research findings on life expectancy at birth for various nations, places, and times. From this and other empirical evidence we find that for the world as a whole, the gain in life expectancy at birth took thousands of years to rise from the low 20s to approximately 30 around 1750.[12] Nations of Western Europe led the breakaway

---

[10]Robert W. Fogel, "Catching Up with the Economy," *The American Economic Review* 89 (1999).
[11]Robert W. Fogel, "Economic Growth, Population Theory, and Physiology: The Bearing of Long-Term Processes on the Making of Economic Policy," *The American Economic Review* 84 (1994), 369–395.
[12]S. H. Preston, "Human Mortality Throughout History and Prehistory," in *The State of Humanity*, ed. Julian L. Simon (Cambridge, Mass.: Blackwell, 1995), 30–36.

TABLE 1.7 Real Gross Domestic Product per Capita (1990 Dollars)

AREA	1000	1500	1700	1820	1952	1995
Europe	$400	$640	$870	$1,130	$ 4,370	$13,950
United States			$600	$1,260	$10,650	$23,380
India			$530	$ 530	$ 610	$ 1,570
China	$450	$600	$600	$ 600	$ 540	$ 3,200
Africa	$400	$400	$400	$ 400		$ 1,220
World	$420	$550	$600	$ 670	$ 2,270	$ 5,190

Source: Maddison (1998, 1999).

from early death and the way out of the malnutrition, poor diet, chronic disease, and low human energy of the past. Data in Table 1.6 for example, indicate that by 1800, life expectancy in years in France was just 30, and in the United Kingdom about 36. By comparison, India's rate was still under 25 in the first decade of the twentieth century, and China's ranged between 25 and 35 two decades later. By 1950, life expectancy in the United Kingdom and France was in the high 60s, while in India and China it was 39 and 41, respectively, comparable to rates in other low income, developing countries.

In the period before 1750, children and infants especially experienced high death rates everywhere. At least 20 to 25 percent of babies died before their first birthday. By 1800, infant mortality in France, the United States, and probably England had broken through the 20 percent level, comparable to rates that prevailed in China and India and other low-income, developing nations in 1950. For Europe, the United States, and other advanced economies, this rate is currently under 1 percent, but is 4 percent in China, 6 percent in India, and 9 percent in Africa.[13]

To provide another long-term perspective on the escape from poverty, Tables 1.7 and 1.8 provide evidence, albeit very inexact, on real income per person, for various periods. Europe led the gradual rise of real income over a 1,000 year period. By 1700, it had risen above the

TABLE 1.8 GDP per Capita for 56 Countries in 1990 Dollars

	1820	1870	1900	1913	1950	1973	1992
TWELVE WESTERN EUROPEAN COUNTRIES							
Austria	$1,295	$1,875	$2,901	$3,488	$3,731	$11,308	$17,160
Belgium	$1,291	$2,640	$3,652	$4,130	$5,346	$11,905	$17,165
Denmark	$1,225	$1,927	$2,902	$3,764	$6,683	$13,416	$18,293
Finland	$ 759	$1,107	$1,620	$2,050	$4,131	$10,768	$14,646
France	$1,218	$1,858	$2,849	$3,452	$5,221	$12,940	$17,959
Germany	$1,112	$1,913	$3,134	$3,833	$4,281	$13,152	$19,351
Italy	$1,092	$1,467	$1,746	$2,507	$3,425	$10,409	$16,229
Netherlands	$1,561	$2,640	$3,533	$3,950	$5,850	$12,763	$16,898
Norway	$1,004	$1,303	$1,762	$2,275	$4,969	$10,229	$17,543
Sweden	$1,198	$1,664	$2,561	$3,096	$6,738	$13,494	$16,927
Switzerland	—	$2,172	$3,531	$4,207	$8,939	$17,953	$21,036
United Kingdom	$1,756	$3,263	$4,593	$5,032	$6,847	$11,992	$15,738
Arith. average	$1,228	$1,986	$2,899	$3,482	$5,513	$11,694	$17,412
FOUR WESTERN OFFSHOOTS							
Australia	$1,528	$3,801	$4,299	$5,505	$7,218	$12,485	$16,237
Canada	$ 893	$1,620	$2,758	$4,213	$7,047	$13,644	$18,159
New Zealand	—	$3,115	$4,320	$5,178	$8,495	$12,575	$13,947
United States	$1,287	$2,457	$4,096	$5,307	$9,573	$16,607	$21,558
Arith. average	$1,236	$2,748	$3,868	$5,051	$8,083	$13,828	$17,475

continued

[13]World Resources Institute 1999 and UNDP 2000

TABLE 1.8 *Continued*

	1820	1870	1900	1913	1950	1973	1992
FIVE SOUTH EUROPEAN COUNTRIES							
Greece	—	—	—	$1,621	$1,951	$ 7,779	$10,314
Ireland	$ 954	$1,773	$2,495	$2,733	$3,518	$ 7,023	$11,711
Portugal	—	$1,085	$1,408	$1,354	$2,132	$ 7,568	$11,130
Spain	$1,063	$1,376	$2,040	$2,255	$2,397	$ 8,739	$12,498
Turkey	—	—	—	$ 979	$1,299	$ 2,739	$ 4,422
Arith. average	—	$1,194*	$1,676*	$1,788	$2,259	$ 6,770	$10,015
SEVEN EAST EUROPEAN COUNTRIES							
Bulgaria	—	—	—	$1,498	$1,651	$ 5,284	$ 4,054
Czechoslovakia	$ 849	$1,164	$1,729	$2,096	$3,501	$ 7,036	$ 6,845
Hungary	—	$1,269	$1,682	$2,098	$2,480	$ 5,596	$ 5,638
Poland	—	—	—	—	$2,447	$ 5,334	$ 4,726
Romania	—	—	—	—	$1,182	$ 3,477	$ 2,565
U.S.S.R.	$ 751	$1,023	$1,218	$1,488	$2,834	$ 6,058	$ 4,671
Yugoslavia	—	—	—	$1,029	$1,546	$ 4,237	$ 3,887
Arith. average	—	$ 876*	$1,174*	$1,527*	$2,235	$ 5,289	$ 4,627
SEVEN LATIN AMERICAN COUNTRIES							
Argentina	—	$1,311	$2,756	$3,797	$4,987	$ 7,970	$ 7,616
Brazil	$ 670	$ 740	$ 704	$ 869	$1,673	$ 3,913	$ 4,637
Chile	—	—	$1,949	$2,653	$3,827	$ 5,028	$ 7,238
Colombia	—	—	$ 973	$1,236	$2,089	$ 3,539	$ 5,025
Mexico	$ 760	$ 710	$1,157	$1,467	$2,085	$ 4,189	$ 5,112
Peru	—	—	$ 817	$1,037	$2,263	$ 3,953	$ 2,854
Venezuela	—	—	$ 821	$1,104	$7,424	$10,717	$ 9,163
Arith. average	—	$ 783*	$1,311	$1,733	$3,478	$ 5,017	$ 5,949
ELEVEN ASIAN COUNTRIES							
Bangladesh	$531	—	$ 581	$ 617	$ 551	$ 478	$ 720
Burma	—	—	$ 647	$ 653	$ 393*	$ 589	$ 748
China	$523	$523	$ 652	$ 688	$ 614	$ 1,186	$ 3,098
India	$531	$558	$ 625	$ 663	$ 597	$ 853	$ 1,348
Indonesia	$614	$657	$ 745	$ 917	$ 874	$ 1,538	$ 2,749
Japan	$704	$741	$1,135	$1,334	$1,873	$11,017	$19,425
Pakistan	$531	—	$ 687	$ 729	$ 650	$ 981	$ 1,642
Philippines	—	—	$1,033	$1,418	$1,293	$ 1,956	$ 2,213
South Korea	—	—	$ 850	$ 948	$ 876	$ 2,840	$10.010
Taiwan	—	—	$ 759	$ 794	$ 922	$ 3,669	$11,590
Thailand	—	$717	$ 812	$ 846	$ 848	$ 1,750	$ 4,694
Arith. Average	$609*	$638*	$ 775	$ 872	$ 863	$ 2,442	$ 5,294
TEN AFRICAN COUNTRIES							
Côte d'Ivoire	—	—	—	—	$ 859	$ 1,727	$ 1,134
Egypt	—	—	$ 509	$ 508	$ 517	$ 947	$ 1,927
Ethiopia	—	—	—	—	$ 277	$ 412	$ 300
Ghana	—	—	$ 462	$ 648	$1,193	$ 1,260	$ 1,007
Kenya	—	—	—	—	$ 609	$ 947	$ 1,055
Morocco	—	—	—	—	$1,611	$ 1,651	$ 2,327
Nigeria	—	—	—	—	$ 547	$ 1,120	$ 1,152
South Africa	—	—	—	$1,451	$2,251	$ 3,844	$ 3,451
Tanzania	—	—	—	—	$ 427	$ 655	$ 601
Zaire	—	—	—	—	$ 636	$ 757	$ 353
Arith. Average	—	—	—	—	$ 893	$ 1,332	$ 1,331

*Hypothetical average: Assumes that the average movement of GDP per capita in countries of the group with data gaps was the same as the Average for the countries remaining in the sample.

Source: Angus Maddison, Monitoring the World Economy 1820–1992 *(Paris Development Centre of the Organisation for Economic Co-Operation and Development, 1995), 23–24.*

lower level of per capita income it had shared with China (the most advanced empire/region around 1000.) While the rest of the world slept and remained mostly unchanged economically, Europe continued to advance. By the early 1800s, the United States had pushed ahead of Europe, and by the mid-1900s, U.S. citizens enjoyed incomes well above those of people residing in Europe and many multiples above those of people living elsewhere. One thousand years ago, even just 500 years ago, Europe and the rest of the world lived at levels of income similar to today's poorest nations: Zaire, Ethiopia, Tanzania, Burma, and Bangladesh (see Table 1.8).

An Institutional Road-Map to Plenty

From the preceding per capita income estimates, other evidence, and North's fascinating time capsule summary of human existence, the road out of poverty clearly is new. Few societies have traveled it; Western Europe, the United States, Canada, Australia, and New Zealand (Britain's offshoots), Japan, Hong Kong, Singapore, and a few others. What steps did Western Europe and Britain's offshoots take to lead humanity along the road to plenty? Why is China, the world's most populous country (almost 1.3 billion), now far ahead of India (second with 1 billion) when merely 50 years ago both nations were about equal in per capita income and more impoverished than most poor African nations today? Is there a road map leading to a life of plenty, a set of policies and institutional arrangements that nations can adopt to replicate the success of the United States, Europe, and other advanced economies? An honest answer to this question is disappointing. Economic development organizations such as the International Monetary Fund and the World Bank, as well as countless scholars who have committed their professional lives to the study of economic growth and development are fully aware of the limited theoretical structure yet pieced together.

The fact is well known that a nation's total output is fundamentally determined (and constrained) by its total inputs—its natural resources, labor force, stock of capital, entrepreneurial talents—and by...the productivity of its inputs, measured as the output or service produced by a worker (or unit of capital, or acre of land, etc.). To measure standards of living, however, we rely on output (or income) per capita, rather than total output. For changes in income per capita, productivity advance dominates the story. For example, if a nation's population increases by 10 percent, and the labor force and other inputs also increase by 10 percent, output per capita remains essentially unchanged unless productivity increases. Most people (80 to 90 percent of the labor force) everywhere 250 years ago were engaged in agriculture, with much of it being subsistence, self-sufficient, noncommercial farming. Today that proportion is under 5 percent in most advanced economies (3 percent in the United States). During this transition, people grew bigger, ate more, and worked less (and lived in more comfort). The sources of productivity advance that have raised output per farmer (and per acre) and allowed sons and daughters of farming people to move into other (commercial) employments and careers and into cities include advances or improvements in the following:

1. Technology (knowledge)
2. Specialization and division of labor
3. Economies of scale
4. Organization and resource allocation
5. Human capital (education and health)

These determinants are especially useful for analyzing a single nation's rate and sources of economic growth, but are less satisfactory for explaining the reasons that productivity advances and resource reallocations have been so apparent and successful in some parts of the world but not in others.

To explain why some nations grow faster than others, we need to look closely at the way nations apply and adapt these sources of productivity change. To use this perspective, we need to assess the complex relationships of a society's rules, customs, and laws (the institutions) and its economic performance. For clarification, consider just one source of productivity change, technology. A new technology can introduce an entirely new product or service such as the airplane (and faster travel) or a better product such as a 2004 BMW automobile compared to a 1930 Model A Ford. A new technology can also lead to new materials, such as aluminum, that affect the cost of production. Aluminum provided a relatively light but strong material for construction of buildings and equipment.

In short, technological changes can be thought of as advances in knowledge that raise (improve) output or lower costs. They often encompass both invention and/or modifications of new discoveries, called *innovation*. Both require basic scientific research, trial and error, and then further study to adapt and modify the initial discoveries to put them to practical use. The inventor or company pursuing research bears substantial risk and cost, including the possibility of failure and no commercial gain. How are scientists, inventors, businesses, and others encouraged to pursue high-cost, high-risk research ventures? How are these ventures coordinated and moved along the discovery-adaptation-improvement path into commercially useful applications for our personal welfare?

This is how laws and rules—or institutions as we call them—help us better understand the causes of technological change. Institutions provide a society's incentive framework (Economic Reasoning Proposition 3: Incentives Matter), including the incentives to invent and innovate. Patent laws, first introduced in 1789 in the U.S. Constitution, provided property rights and exclusive ownership to inventors for their patented inventions. This pathbreaking law spurred creative and inventive activity. Importantly, this exclusive ownership right includes the right to sell it, usually to people specialized in finding commercial uses of new inventions. The keys here are the laws and rules—the institutions that generate dynamic forces for progress in some societies and stifle creativity and enterprise in others. In advanced economies, laws provide positive incentives to spur enterprise and help forge markets using commercial legal and property right systems that allow new scientific breakthroughs (technologies) to realize their full commercial-social potential. Much more that could be added to describe in detail the evolving and intricate connections among universities, other scientific research institutions, corporations, and various business entities (and lawyers and courts), all of which form interrelated markets of production and exchange, hastening technological advances.[14]

Developing and sustaining institutional changes that realize gains for society as a whole are fundamental to the story of growth. The ideologies and rules of the game that form and enforce contracts (in exchange), protect and set limits on the use of property, and influence people's incentives in work, creativity, and exchange are vital areas of analysis, according to Douglass C. North, Mancur Olsen, Jr. and other leading scholars of institutional change.

North admonishes that, "it is adaptive rather than allocative efficiency which is the key to long-term growth."[15] The ability or inability to access, adapt, and apply new technologies and the other sources of productivity advances points directly to a society's institutions. Institutional change often come slowly (customs, values, laws, and constitutions evolve), and established power centers sometimes deter and delay changes conducive to economic progress. How accepting is a society to risk and change when outcomes of actions create losers as well as winners?[16]

---

[14]Nathan Rosenberg and L.E. Birdzell, Jr., *How the West Grew Rich* (New York: Basic Books, 1986).
[15]Douglass C. North, "Economic Performance through Time," *The American Economic Review* 84 (1994): 359–368.
[16]Joseph A. Schumpeter, *The Theory of Economic Development* (Cambridge, Mass.: Harvard University Press, 1934).

The following is a partial list of key institutional determinants that allow markets to form and strengthen, and that explain the road out of poverty and early death experienced by Europe, the United States, and other modern economies:

- The rule of law
- Clear specification of property rights
- Enforcement of contracts
- Access to information and low transaction costs
- Open competition with freedom of entry and exit
- Access to capital
- Mobility of inputs
- Education and health
- Political participation
- Limited government
- Individual freedom

In the following pages, we retrace the history of the American economy, not simply by updating and recounting old facts and figures, but also by emphasizing the forging of institutions (customs, values, laws, and the Constitution). The end of the cold war and the growing body of knowledge about the importance of institutions to economic progress give solid reasons for recasting the historical record and bearing witness to the strengths and shortcomings of an emerging democracy operating within the discipline of markets constrained by laws and other institutions.

SELECTED REFERENCES AND SUGGESTED READINGS

Atack, Jeremy. "Long-Term Trends in Productivity." In *The State of Humanity,* ed. Julian L. Simon. Boston: Basil Blackwell, 1995, 161–170.

Avery, Dennis. "The World's Rising Food Productivity." In *The State of Humanity,* ed. Julian L. Simon. Boston: Basil Blackwell, 1995, 379–393.

Black, Dan A., Seth Sanders, and Lowell Taylor. "The Economic Reward for Studying Economics." *Economic Inquiry* 41 (3), (July 2003): 365–377.

Blank, Rebecca M. "Trends in Poverty in the United States." In *The State of Humanity*, ed. Julian L. Simon. Boston: Basil Blackwell, 1995, 231–240.

Burnette, Joyce and Joel Mokyr. "The Standard of Living Through the Ages." In *The State of Humanity*, ed. Julian L. Simon. Boston: Basil Blackwell, 1995, 135–148.

Churchill, Winston S. *A History of the English Speaking People.* Vols 1–4. New York: Dorset Press, 1956.

Fogel, Robert W. "Economic Growth, Population Theory, and Physiology: The Bearing of Long-Term Processes on the Making of Economic Policy." *The American Economic Review* 84 (1994): 369–395.

Fogel, Robert W. "The Contribution of Improved Nutrition to the Decline of Mortality Rates in Europe and America." In *The State of Humanity*, ed. Julian L. Simon. Boston: Basil Blackwell, 1995, 61–71.

______. "Catching Up with the Economy." *The American Economic Review* 89 (1999): 1–21.

Haines, Michael R. "Disease and Health through the Ages." In *The State of Humanity*, ed. Julian L. Simon. Boston: Basil Blackwell, 1995, 51–60.

Harberger, Arnold C. "A Vision of the Growth Process." *The American Economic Review* 88 (1998): 1–32.

Kennedy, Paul. *The Rise and Fall of the Great Powers*. New York: Random House, 1987.

Lee, J., and W. Feng, "Malthusian Models and Chinese Realities: The Chinese Demographic System, 1700-2000." *Population and Development Review* 25 (1999): 33–65.

Lindert, Peter H. and Jeffery G. Williamson. "The Long-Term Course of American Inequality: 1647–1969." In *The State of Humanity*, ed. Julian L. Simon. Boston: Basil Blackwell, 1995, 188–195.

North, Douglass C. *Institutions, Institutional Change and Economic Performance*. Cambridge: Cambridge University Press, 1990.

Preston, S. H. "Human Mortality throughout History and Prehistory." In *The State of Humanity*, ed. Julian L. Simon. Boston: Basil Blackwell, 30–36.

Rector, Robert. "Increasing Returns and Long-Run Growth." *Journal of Political Economy* 94(5), (October 1986), 1002–1037.

______. "Endogenous Technological Change." *Journal of Political Economy* 98(5), (October 1990), S71–S102.

______. "The Origins of Endogenous Growth." *Journal of Economic Perspectives* 8(1), (Winter 1994), 3–22.

______. "New Goods, Old Theory, and the Welfare Costs of Trade Restrictions." *Journal of Developmental Economics* 43(1), (February 1994), 5–38.

______. "How "Poor" Are America's Poor?" In *The State of Humanity*," ed., Julian L. Simon. Boston: Basil Blackwell, 1995, 241–256.

Rosenberg, Nathan, and L. E. Birdzell, Jr. *How the West Grew Rich*. New York: Basic Books, Inc., 1986.

Schumpeter, Joseph A. *The Theory of Economic Development*. Cambridge: Harvard University Press, 1934.

Simon, Julian L. and Rebecca Boggs. "Trends in the Quantities of Education—USA and Elsewhere." In *The State of Humanity*, ed. Julian L. Simon. Boston: Basil Blackwell, 1995, 208–223

United Nations Development Program. *Human Development Report 1999*. New York: Oxford University Press, 1999.

Wrigley, E. A., and R. S. Schofield. *The Population History of England, 1541–1871: A Reconstruction*. Cambridge: Harvard University Press, 1981.

Zakaria, Farred. *The Future of Freedom*. New York: W. W. Norton, 2003.

The Colonial Era: 1607–1776

ECONOMIC AND HISTORICAL PERSPECTIVES *1607–1776*

1. The American colonial period was a time when poverty was the norm throughout the world and wars among nations were frequent. The earliest English settlements in North America were costly in terms of great human suffering and capital losses.
2. The nations and city states of Europe that emerged from the long, relatively stagnant period of feudalism rose to prominence in wealth and power relative to other leading empires in Islam and the Orient and quickly dominated those in the Americas.
3. Spain, Portugal, Holland, England, and France each built international empires, and England and France especially further advanced their relative economic and military strength by successfully applying mercantilist policies. Great Britain ultimately dominated the colonization of North America and was the nation that launched the Industrial Revolution, beginning in the second half of the eighteenth century.
4. Innovations in trade and commerce, the spread of practical learning, new and expanding settlements that added land and adapted it to best uses, and falling risks in trade and frontier life raised living standards in the New World. By the time of the American Revolution, the material standards of living in the colonies were among the highest in the world and comparable to those in England. However, the distribution of wealth and human rights among the sexes, races, and free citizens was vastly unequal.
5. Although Americans sustained their long English cultural and institutional heritage, even after independence, their strong economic rise ultimately placed them in a position of rivalry with the mother country. The period from 1763 to 1776 was one of confrontation, growing distrust, and, ultimately, rebellion. Throughout the colonial era, the Native American population declined through disease, dislocation, and war.

Chapter Two

FOUNDING THE COLONIES

Chapter Theme

From the perspective of European colonists in America, the New World was a distant part of a greatly expanded Europe, a western frontier, so to speak. The New World presented new opportunities and challenges for settlers, but their language and culture, laws and customs, and basic institutions were fundamentally derived and adapted from the other side of the Atlantic. In the colonies that would first break free of Europe and become the United States, these ties were primarily to Great Britain, for in the race for empire among the European nation-states, it was ultimately Britain that prevailed in North America. Britain dominated because of its institutions and its liberal policies of migration and colonization. Accordingly, our legacy as Americans is principally English—if not in blood, at least in language, law, and custom.

To understand this legacy it is important to have at least a brief background in the rise of western Europe, the voyages of discovery, and key developments of empire building in the New World. This will help to place in clearer perspective the demographic transition that led to British domination of North America relative to the native population and to other colonists from rival European nation-states.

EUROPEAN BACKGROUND TO THE VOYAGES OF DISCOVERY

More than ten centuries passed from the fall of Rome to the voyages of discovery that led to the European expansion into the "New World." Toward the end of that period the feudal age had passed, and by the late 1300s many nation-states had emerged throughout Europe. In Russia, Sweden, England, France, and Spain, national rulers held the allegiance of large citizenries, and sizable groups of German-speaking peoples were ruled by their own kings and nobles.

The center of European wealth and commerce rested in the Mediterranean. That economic concentration was based primarily on long-distance trade among Asia (mainly Persia), the Middle East, and Europe. Because of their locational advantage and superior production and commercial skills and knowledge, the Italian city-states of Milan, Florence, Genoa, and Venice had dominated most of the Old World's long-distance trade for centuries.

European Roots and Expanding Empires

By the end of the fifteenth century, however, northern Europe had experienced substantial commercial growth, especially in the Hanse cities bordering the North Sea and the Baltic.

Greater security of persons and property, established in law and enforced through courts and recognized political entities, spurred commerce and economic investments. Growing security in exchanges and transactions opened up whole new trades and routes of commerce, especially in the northern and western regions of Europe. This rise often augmented the old trades in the Mediterranean, but the new trades grew faster than the old.

Noteworthy as well was the rapid increase in Europe's population, which was recovering from the famines of the early fourteenth century and most importantly from the Black Death of 1347 and 1348. In England, for example, the population had fallen from 3.7 million in 1348 to less than 2.2 million in the 1370s; France probably lost 40 percent of its population; and losses elsewhere vary in estimates from 30 to 50 percent. During the fifteenth and sixteenth centuries, the demographic revival from that catastrophe added to the commercial growth and shifting concentrations of economic activity. The rapid growth of populations and growing commercialization of Europe's economies were significant building blocks in the strengthening of Europe's fledgling nation-states. Expansion in Europe and elsewhere—including, ultimately, America—was also part of the nation-building process.

It is important to understand that for centuries Catholic Europe had been pitted in war against the Muslim armies of Islam with one Crusade following another. By the fifteenth century, the age of Renaissance, Europe forged ahead in many political, commercial (and seagoing), and military areas. This century was a turning point, speeding the pace of an arms race among competing nations and empires. The year 1492 is as celebrated in Christian Spain for its capture of Granada from the Moors, ending seven centuries of Muslim rule there, as for Christopher Columbus's voyage to America.

PORTUGAL AND THE FIRST DISCOVERIES

It was somewhat of a historical accident that Christopher Columbus—a Genoese sailor in the employ of Spain—made the most vital and celebrated of the landfalls. Neither Spain nor the great Italian city-states were the world's leaders in long-distance exploration. Tiny, seafaring Portugal was the great Atlantic pioneer, and by the time Columbus embarked, Portugal could claim more than seven decades of ocean discoveries.

Having already driven the Muslims off Portuguese soil in the thirteenth century, Portugal initiated Europe's overseas expansion in 1415 by capturing Cuenta in North Africa. Under the vigorous and imaginative leadership of Prince Henry the Navigator, whose naval arsenal at Sagres was a fifteenth-century Cape Canaveral, Portugal—from 1415 to 1460—sent one expedition after another down the western coast of Africa. The island of Madeira was taken in 1419 and the Canary Islands shortly thereafter. The Portuguese colonized the Azores from 1439 to 1453 and populated most of these islands with slaves imported from Africa to grow sugar. These ventures had commercial as well as military aims. Europeans had first become familiar with sugar during the early Crusades, and the Mediterranean islands of Cypress, Crete, and Sicily had long been major sugar-producing areas. The commercial development and sugar plantations of the Iberian-owned islands reflected the fifteenth-century western shift of economic strength and activity. In addition, the Portuguese and others sought to circumvent the Turk-Venetian collusion to control trade and prices over the eastern Mediterranean trade routes. Europeans hungered for Asian goods, especially spices. In an age before refrigeration, pepper, cloves, ginger, nutmeg, and cinnamon were used with almost unbelievable liberality by medieval cooks, whose fashion it was to conceal the taste of tainted meat and embellish the flavor of monotonous food. Accompanying the discoveries of new places and emergence of new trades was the accumulation of knowledge. New methods of rigging sails and designing ships (from one- to three-masted vessels) and other navigational advancements were learned by trial and error. These new technologies were vital in overcoming the difficult prevailing winds of the mighty Atlantic.

Commercial Splendor: Venice (rendered here by Caneletto) was almost as much an eastern as a western city, and for hundreds of years its commercial and naval power was a great sustaining force of western civilization.

PORTUGAL AND SPAIN: EXPANDING EMPIRES

As shown in Map 2.1, the greatest of the sea explorations from Europe took place within a little less than thirty-five years. The historical scope of it is astonishing. In 1488, Bartholomeu Dias of Portugal rounded the Cape of Good Hope and would have reached India had his mutinous crew not forced him to return home. In September 1522, the *Vittoria*—last of Ferdinand Magellan's fleet of five ships—put in at Seville; in a spectacular achievement, 18 Europeans had circumnavigated the globe. Between these two dates, two other voyages of no less importance were accomplished. Columbus, certain that no more than 2,500 miles separated the Canary Islands from Japan, persuaded the Spanish sovereigns Ferdinand and Isabella to finance his first Atlantic expedition. On October 12, 1492, his lookout sighted the little island of San Salvador in the Bahamas. Only a few years later,Vasco da Gama, sailing for the Portuguese, reached Calicut in India via the Cape of Good Hope, returning home in 1499. Following Dias's and Columbus's discoveries, Portugal and Spain, with the pope's blessing, agreed in the treaty of Tordezillas (1494) to grant Spain all lands more than 370 leagues (1,100 miles) west of the Cape Verde Islands (a measurement accident that ultimately established Portugal's claim to Brazil). Thus, the sea lanes opened, with Portugal dominant in the East (to East Africa, the Persian Gulf, the Indian Ocean, China, and beyond) and Spain supreme in the West.

By the early sixteenth century, the wealth and commerce of Europe had shifted to the Atlantic. The Mediterranean leaders did not decline absolutely; they were simply overtaken and passed by. In an international context, this was a critical first phase in the relative rise and eventual supremacy of key Western nation-states.

After Spain's conquest of Mexico by Hernando Cortez in 1521, American silver and gold flowed into Spain in ever-increasing quantities.When the Spanish king Philip II made good his claim to the throne of Portugal in 1580, Spanish prestige reached its zenith. By royal decree, Spain simply swallowed Portugal, and two great empires, strong in the Orient

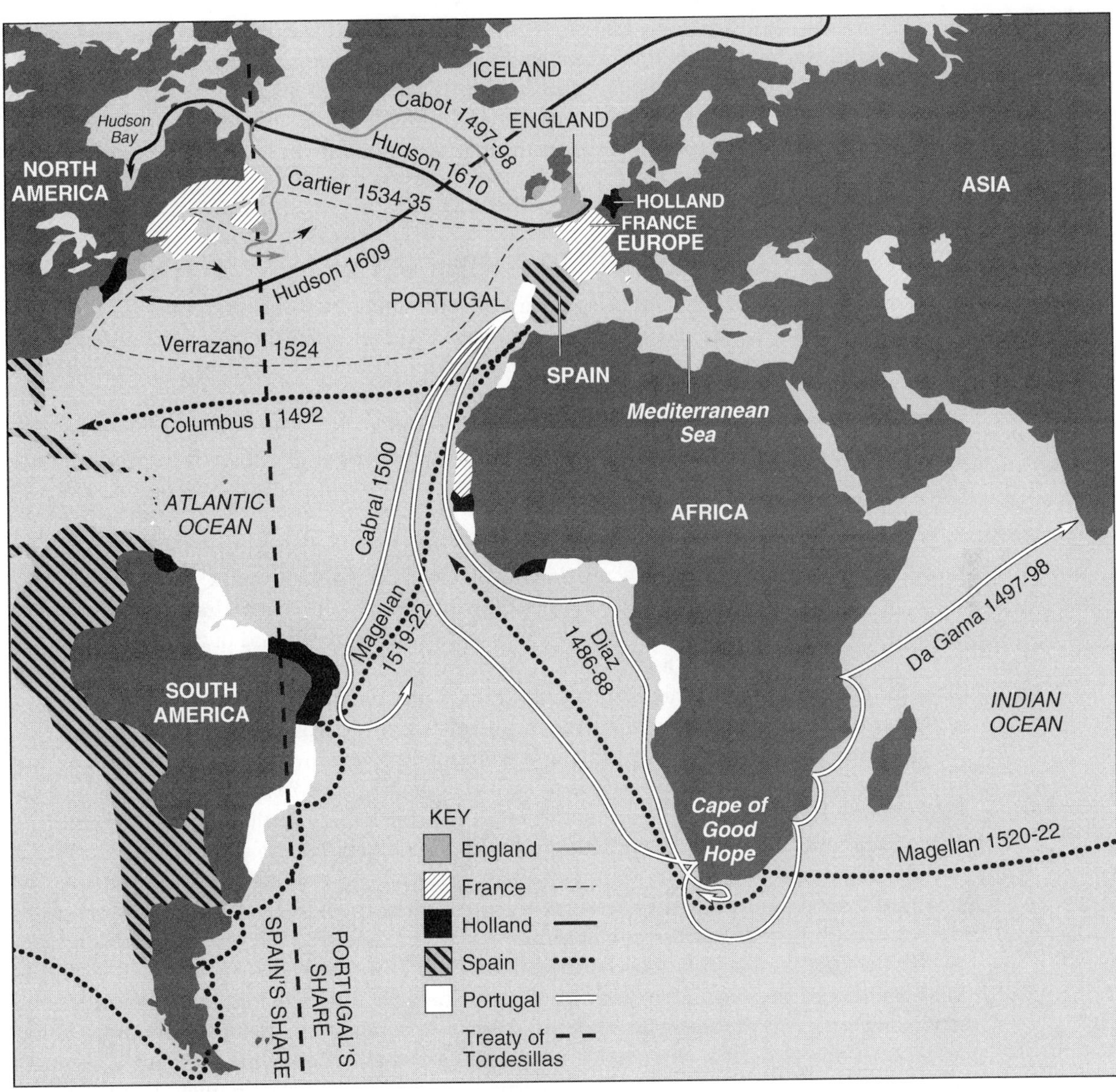

MAP 2.1 Exploration *Spain and Portugal came first; then France, Holland, and England. All these nations explored vast amounts of territory in North America, giving rise to new economic opportunities, but England's exploration gave rise to the most extensive permanent settlements in the New World.*

and unchallenged in the Americas, were now joined. When we reflect that no other country had as yet established a single permanent settlement in the New World, it seems astonishing that the decline of Spanish power was so imminent.

Although Spain was a colonizer, Spanish attempts to settle in the Americas lacked a solid foundation. Spain's main interests, for both the conquistadors and the rulers at home, were treasures from America's mines (especially silver) and Christianity for the conquered. To be sure, attempts were made to extend agriculture and to establish manufacturing operations in the New World, but the Spaniards remained a ruling caste, dominating the natives who did the work and holding them in political and economic bondage. Their religious, administrative, military, and legal institutions were strong and lasting, but the Spanish were more like occupying rulers than permanent settlers.

Meanwhile, the Protestant Reformation radically altered the nature of European nation building and warfare. When, toward the end of the sixteenth century, Spain became involved in war with the English and began to dissipate its energies in a futile attempt to bring the Low Countries (Holland and Belgium) under complete subjection, Spain lost the advantage of being the first nation to expand through explorations in America. Also harmful to Spain was the decline in gold and silver imports after 1600 as the mines of better-grade ores became exhausted.

THE LATECOMERS: HOLLAND, FRANCE, AND ENGLAND

Holland, France, and England, like Spain, all ultimately vied for supremacy in the New World (see Map 2.2). English and Dutch successes represented the commercial revolution sweeping across northern and western Europe in the 1600s. Amsterdam in particular rose to preeminence in shipping, finance, and trade by midcentury. But Holland's claim in North America was limited to New York (based economically on furs), and for the most part its interest lay more in the Far East than in the West. Moreover, the Dutch placed too much emphasis on the establishment of trading posts and too little on colonization to firmly establish their overseas empire.

As it turned out, France and England became the chief competitors in the centuries- long race for supremacy. From 1608, when Samuel de Champlain established Quebec, France successfully undertook explorations in America westward to the Great Lakes area and had pushed southward down the Mississippi Valley to Louisiana by the end of the century. And in the Orient, France, though a latecomer, competed successfully with the English for a time after the establishment of the French East India Company in 1664. In less than a century, however, the English defeated the French in India, as they would one day do in America. The English triumphed in both India and America because they had established the most extensive permanent settlements. It is not without significance that at the beginning of the French and Indian War in 1756, some 60,000 French had settled in Canada and the Caribbean compared with two million in the English North American colonies.

For our purposes, the most important feature of the expansion of Europe was the steady and persistent growth of settlements in the British colonies of North America. Why were the English such successful colonizers?

To be sure, the English, like the French and the Dutch, coveted the colonial wealth of the Spanish and the Portuguese, and English sailors and traders acted for a time as if their struggling outposts in the wilderness of North America were merely temporary. They traded in Latin America, while privateers such as Francis Drake and Thomas Cavendish plundered Spanish galleons for their treasures as they sailed the Spanish Main. English venturers, probing the East for profitable outposts, gained successive footholds in India as the seventeenth century progressed. Yet, unlike the leaders of some western European countries, Englishmen such as Richard Hakluyt advocated permanent colonization and settlement in the New World, perceiving that true colonies would eventually become important markets for manufactured products from the mother country as well as sources of raw materials.

It was not enough, however, for merchants and heads of states to reap the advantages of the thriving colonies: commoners had to be persuaded of the benefits of immigrating to the New World to themselves and their families. The greatest motivations to immigrate were a desire to own land—still the European symbol of status and economic security—and to strive for a higher standard of living than could be attained at home by any but the best-paid artisans. These economic motivations were often accompanied by a religious motivation. Given the exorbitant costs of the transatlantic voyage (more than an average person's yearly income), the problem remained how to pay for moving people to the New World.

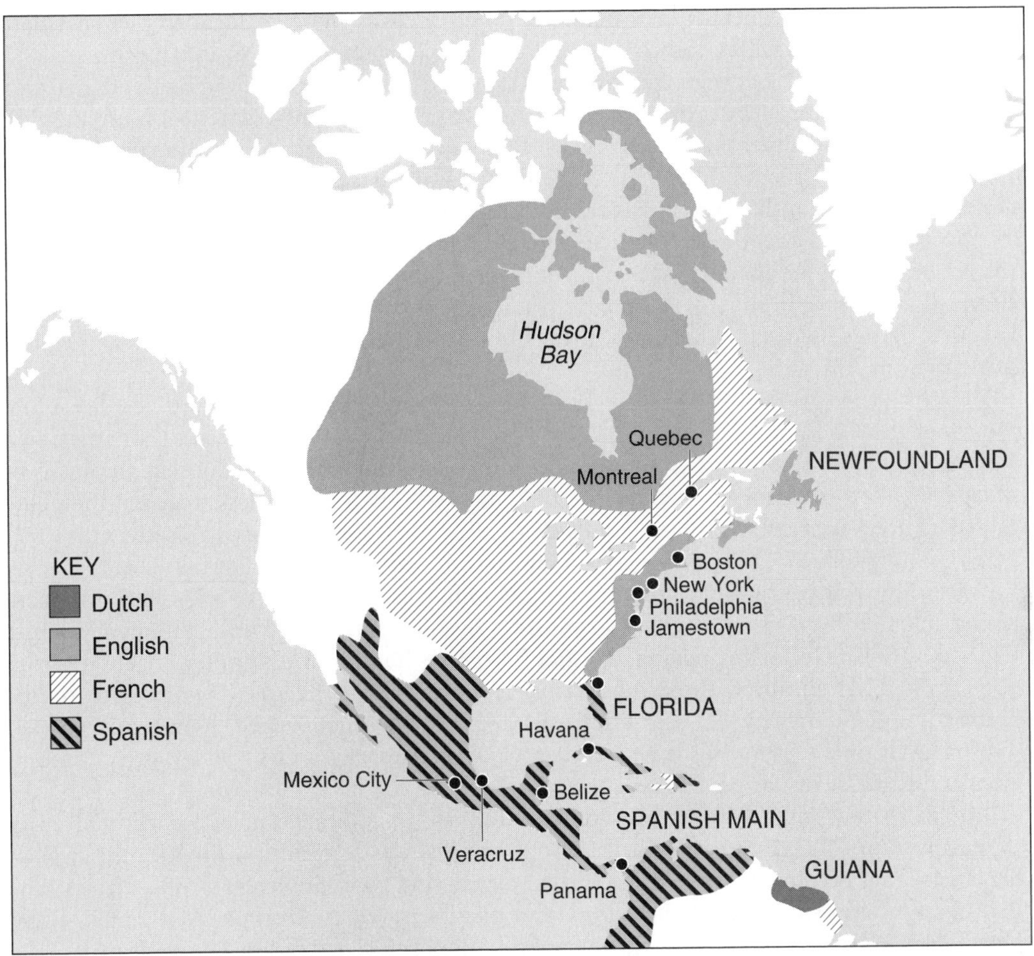

MAP 2.2 European Colonies *European possessions and claims in America fluctuated. Shown here are those territories and the major cities toward the end of the seventeenth century.*

FIRST BRITISH SETTLEMENTS IN NORTH AMERICA

Perilous Beginnings

Two half-brothers, Sir Humphrey Gilbert and Sir Walter Raleigh, were the first Englishmen to undertake serious ventures in America. Gilbert, one of the more earnest seekers of the Northwest Passage, went to Newfoundland in 1578 and again in 1583 but failed to colonize the territory either time and lost his life on the return voyage to England after the second attempt. Raleigh, in turn, was granted the right to settle in "Virginia" and to have control of the land within a radius of nearly 600 miles from any colony that he might successfully establish. Raleigh actually brought two groups of colonists to the new continent. The first landed on the island of Roanoke off the coast of what is now North Carolina and stayed less than a year; anything but enthusiastic about their new home, these first colonists returned to England with Sir Francis Drake in the summer of 1586. Undaunted, Raleigh solicited the financial aid of a group of wealthy Londoners and, in the following year, sent a second contingent of 150 people under the leadership of Governor John White. Raleigh had given explicit instructions that this colony was to be planted somewhere on the Chesapeake Bay, but Governor White disregarded the order and landed at Roanoke. White went back to

England for supplies; when he returned after much delay in 1590, the settlers had vanished. Not a single member of the famed "lost colony" was ever found, not even a tooth.

After a long war between England and Spain from 1588 to 1603, England renewed attempts to colonize North America. In 1606, two charters were granted—one to a group of Londoners, the other to merchants of Plymouth and other western port towns. The London Company received the right to settle the southern part of the English territory in America; the Plymouth Company received jurisdiction over the northern part.

So two widely separated colonies were established in 1607: one at Sagadahoc, near the mouth of the Kennebec River, in Maine; the other in modern Virginia.[1] Those who survived the winter in the northern colony gave up and went home, and the colony established at Jamestown won the hard-earned honor of being the first permanent English settlement in America.

Hard earned indeed! When the London Company landed three tiny vessels at the mouth of the Chesapeake Bay in 1607, 105 people disembarked to found the Jamestown Colony. Easily distracted by futile "get-rich-quick" schemes, they actually sent shiploads of mica and yellow ore back to England in 1607 and 1608. Before the news reached their ears that their treasure was worthless "fool's gold," disease, starvation, and misadventure had taken a heavy toll: 67 of the original 105 Jamestown settlers died in the first year.

The few remaining survivors (one of whom was convicted of cannibalism) were joined in 1609 by 800 new arrivals, sent over by the reorganized and renamed Virginia Company. By the following spring, frontier hardships had cut the number of settlers from 838 to 60. That summer, those who remained were found fleeing downriver to return home to England by new settlers with fresh supplies, who encouraged them to reconsider. This was Virginia's "starving time," to use Charles Andrews's vivid label, and a time of environmental degradation (Earle 1975).

Inadequately supplied and untutored in the art of colonization, the earliest frontier pioneers routinely suffered and died. In 1623, a royal investigation of the Virginia experience was launched in the wake of an Indian attack that took the lives of 500 settlers. The investigation reported that of the 6,000 who had migrated to Virginia since 1607, 4,000 had died. The life expectancy of these hardy settlers upon arriving was two years.

The heavy human costs of first settlement were accompanied by substantial capital losses. Without exception, the earliest colonial ventures were unprofitable. Indeed, they were financial disasters. Neither the principal nor the interest on the Virginia Company's accumulated investment of more than £200,000 was ever repaid (approximately $22 million in today's values). The investments in New England were less disappointing, but overall, English capitalists were heavy losers in their quest to tame the frontier.

EARLY REFORMS

The economic and institutional lessons of these first settlements, though negative, proved useful in later ventures, and colonization continued with only intermittent lapses throughout the seventeenth and eighteenth centuries. Because North America rendered no early discoveries of gold or silver mines or ancient populations prepared to exchange exotic wares, trading post establishments characteristic of the European outposts in South America and the Orient proved inadequate. North America's frontier demanded a more permanent form of settlement. For this to result without continuous company or Crown subsidization, the discovery of "cash crops" or other items that could be produced in the colonies and exchanged commercially was essential. Consequently, the production of tobacco and rice and the expansion

---

[1]At this time, the name *Virginia* referred to all the territory claimed by the English on the North American continent. Early Charters indicate that the area lay between the thirty-fourth and forty-fifth parallels, roughly between the southern portion of the Carolinas and the northernmost boundary of New York.

of many other economic activities we will discuss in chapter 3 proved vital in giving deep roots and permanent features to British settlement in North America. In addition, substantial organizational changes were made to increase production efficiency. The joint-stock company arrangement, which facilitated the raising of capital and which had served the British well in other areas of the world, faltered when forced to conform to the conditions in North America. Modeled after such great eastern trading companies as the East India Company, new companies—including the London Company, the New Plymouth Company, the Massachusetts Bay Company—must receive credit for establishing the first British settlements in the New World. But their success was limited merely to securing a colonial foothold. With the exceptions of the Hudson Bay Company (founded in 1670 and still in operation today) and the unique Georgia experiment in the late colonial period, the joint-stock company (with absentee direction from England) survived less than two decades in British North America.

The ordeals of the Jamestown experience forcefully accent the difficulties encountered and the adjustments required by the early settlers. The early Jamestown settlers were brought over by the company and given "planter shares," with profits to be divided five years later. Meanwhile, they were to live at the company's expense and work wholly for the company. In effect, the colony originally operated as a collective unit, in which both production methods and consumption were shared. But collectivity encouraged individuals to work less and resulted in much discontent. Unmarried men complained of working without recompense for other men's wives and children. Stronger, more able workers were embittered when they did not receive larger amounts of food and supplies than others who could or would not work as hard. In addition, common ownership stifled incentives to care for and improve lands and to make innovations in production.

In addition, absentee direction from England created problems, because successful production required local managerial direction. Futile insistent demands from England for quick profits sidetracked productive efforts and added to the settlers' discouragement.

Jamestown residents gained greater control over local matters in 1609 when small garden plots of land were given to individuals and again in 1612 when various institutional reforms were undertaken. To generate more flexible leadership and local autonomy in that hostile environment, a deputy governor was stationed in Virginia. Steadily thereafter, centralized direction from England became less and less frequent.

As private landholdings replaced common ownership, work incentives improved; the full return for individual effort became a reality, superseding output-sharing arrangements. In 1614, private landholdings of 3 acres were allowed. A second and more significant step toward private property came in 1618 with the establishment of the headright system. Under this system, any settler who paid his own way to Virginia was given 50 acres and another 50 acres for anyone else whose transportation he paid. In 1623—only 16 years after the first Jamestown settlers had arrived—all landholdings were converted to private ownership. The royal investigation of that year also ushered in the dissolutions of the corporate form of the colony. In 1625, Virginia was converted to a Crown colony.

Many of the difficulties experienced in early Jamestown were also felt elsewhere in the colonies. But the Puritan settlements of New England, first at Plymouth (the Plymouth Company, 1620) and then at Boston (the Massachusetts Bay Company, 1630), avoided some of the problems faced by the Jamestown settlers. For instance, because the Massachusetts Bay Company actually carried its own charter to the New World, it avoided costly direction and absentee control from England. Stronger social and cultural cohesion and more homogeneous religious beliefs may have contributed to a greater success of communal arrangements there, but as noted in Economic Insight 2.1, the Plymouth colonies also reverted to private holdings. Town corporations prolonged the use of common landholdings, but private landholdings steadily replaced land held in common. By 1650, privately owned family farms were predominant in New England.

Economic Insight 2.1

Property Rights and Incentives

The problems of collective ownership and equally shared consumption have existed from ancient times to today. Colonial America and communist Russia attempted such organizational forms of production and distribution, and these attempts ultimately failed. Some have termed the problem the "tragedy of the commons" (common property), which leads to overuse and speedy exhaustion of a resource commonly owned.

You are encouraged at this point to briefly review the 5 Economic Reasoning Propositions in Economic Insight 1.1 in chapter 1. These propositions help explain how collective ownership and shared (equal or fixed-share) consumption of the output create a "free rider" problem. To illustrate this, consider 10 workers who share ownership of the land and who collectively produce 100 bushels of corn, averaging 10 bushels each for consumption. Suppose that one worker begins to shirk and cuts his labor effort in half, reducing output by 5. The shirker's consumption, like the other workers', is now 9.5 (95 ÷ 10) bushels thanks to the shared arrangement. Though his effort has fallen 50 percent, his consumption falls only 5 percent. The shirker is free riding on the labors of others. The incentive for each worker (Economic Reasoning Proposition 3), in fact, is to free ride, and this lowers the total effort and total output.

Conversely, suppose that one worker considers working longer daily hours (12 instead of 10) to raise total output from 100 to 102. The gain in consumption to each individual is 0.2 bushels, a 2 percent consumption increase for each person based on a 20 percent effort increase by one. Would you make the extra effort?

With private property for each, there is no free riding. Any effort cut is borne in proportion by the individual's output decline. Any effort increase places all the rewards of the extra effort in the lap of the one working harder (or smarter). More generally, with private property for each, any change in output (ΔQ) from more effort goes to the person extending the extra effort. With common property, the gain is not ΔQ but ΔQ divided by the number in the group. The larger the group, the less the gainfrom working harder and the less the loss from working less—from the individual's perspective. In other words, the larger the group, the greater the incentive to free ride. These incentive effects (Proposition 3) are telling, as Governor Bradford noted in 1623 at the Plymouth Colony in New England:

> So they begane to thinke how they might raise as much corne as they could, and obtaine a beter crope then they had done, that they might not still thus languish in miserie. At length, after much debate of things, the Governor . . . gave way that they should set corne every man for his owne perticuler, and in that regard trust to them selves; in all other things to goe on in the generall way as before. And so assigned to every family a parcell of land, according to the proportion of their number for that end, only for present use (but made no devission for inheritance), and ranged all boys & youth under some familie. This had very good success; for it made all hands very industrious, so as much more corne was planted then other waise would have bene by any means the Governor or any other could use, and saved him a great deall of trouble, and gave farr better contente. The women now wente willingly into the feild, and tooke their litle-ons with them to set corne, which before would aledg weaknes, and inabilitie; whom to have compelled would have bene thought great tiranie and oppression. The experience that was had in this commone course and condition, tried sundrie years, and that amongst godly and sober men, may well evince the vanitie of that conceite of Platos & other ancients, applauded by some

Economic Insight 2.1

Property Rights and Incentives, continued

of later times;—that the taking away of propertie, and bringing in communitie into a comone wealth, would make them happy and flourishing; as if they were wiser then God. For this comunitie (so farr as it was) was found to breed much confusion & discontent . . . For the yong-men that were most able and fitte for labour & service did repine that they should spend their time & streingth to worke for other mens wives and children, with out any recompence. The strong, or man of parts, had no more in devission of victails & cloaths, then he that was weake and not able to doe a quarter the other could; this was thought injuestice . . . Let none objecte this is men's corruption, and nothing to the course it selfe. I answer, seeing all men have this corruption in them, God in his wisdome saw another course fiter for them.[2]

Clearly, getting the institutional arrangements right (Proposition 4) is very important.

Another noteworthy colony established by a joint-stock venture was New York, first settled by the Dutch West India Company (1620) but taken in a bloodless confrontation in 1664 by the British. Maryland and Pennsylvania were initiated through proprietary grants, respectively to Lord Baltimore in 1634 and to William Penn in 1681. The former's desire was to create a haven for Roman Catholics, profitably if possible, and the latter's was the same for Quakers and other persecuted religious groups. Rhode Island's settlement was also religiously motivated due to Roger Williams's banishment from Puritan Massachusetts in 1644. These, the Carolinas, and the last mainland colony to be settled, Georgia (1733), benefited from the many hardships and lessons provided by the earlier settlements. Despite each colony's organizational form, the Crown assured all settlers except slaves the rights due English citizens. The British empire in North America extended from French Canada to Spanish Florida and through to the sugar plantation islands of the Caribbean.

Bringing in Settlers

The Atlantic Ocean posed a great barrier to settlement in North America. In the early seventeenth century, the cost of the Atlantic passage was £9 to £10 per person, more than an average English person's yearly income. Throughout most of the later colonial period, the peacetime costs of passage were £5 to £6. Consequently, in the seventeenth century, a majority of British and European newcomers could not and did not pay their own way to America. By 1775, however, more than half a million English, Scotch, Irish, German, and other Europeans had made the transatlantic voyage. More than 350,000 of them paid their way by borrowing and signing a unique IOU, an indenture contract.

The indenture contract was a device that enabled people to pay for their passage to America by selling their labor to someone in the New World for a specified future period of time. Often mistakenly referred to today in the press as quasi-slavery, indenture opportunities were really an expansion of individual freedoms. These contracts were written in a variety of forms, but law and custom made them similar. Generally speaking, prospective immigrants would sign articles of indenture binding them to a period of service that varied from three to seven years, although four years was probably the most common term. Typically,

[2] *William Bradford, of Plymouth Plantation* (New York: Capricorn, 1962), 90–91.

an indentured immigrant signed with a shipowner or a recruiting agent in England. As soon as the servant was delivered alive at an American port, the contract was sold to a planter or merchant. These contracts typically sold for £10 to £11 in the eighteenth century, nearly double the cost of passage. Indentured servants, thus bound, performed any work their "employers" demanded in exchange for room, board, and certain "freedom dues" of money or land that were received at the end of the period of indenture. This system provided an active trade in human talent, and the indenture system should be viewed as an investment in migration as well as in job training (or apprenticeship).

The first indentured immigrants were sent to Jamestown and sold by the Virginia Company: about 100 children in their early teens in 1618, a like number of young women in 1619 for marital purposes, and a young group of workers in 1620. Soon thereafter, private agents scoured the ports, taverns, and countryside to sign on workers for indenture. The indentured servants were drawn from a wide spectrum of European society, from the ranks of farmers and unskilled workers, artisans, domestic servants, and others. Most came without specialized skills, but they came to America voluntarily because the likelihood of rising to the status of landowner was very low in Britain or on the Continent. They were also willing to sign indenture contracts because their opportunity cost, the next best use of their time, was typically very low—room and board and low wages as a rural English farm worker, a "servant in husbandry." Children born in English cottages usually went to work at the age of ten, moving among families and farms until good fortune (often inheritance or gifts) allowed them to marry. For many, a period of bondage for the trip to America seemed worth the risk.

Whether the life of a servant was hard or easy depended primarily on the temperament of the taskmaster; the courts usually protected indentured servants from extreme cruelty, but the law could also be applied quickly to apprehend and return servants who ran away. The usual punishment for runaways was an extension of the contract period.

Studies by David Galenson, Robert Heavener, and Farley Grubb reveal many of the intricacies of this market in bonded labor. For example, the indentured period for women was originally shorter than for men because of the greater scarcity of women in the colonies, but by the eighteenth century, the periods of service were comparable for both sexes. The indentured servants' work conditions and duration of service also depended on location. Generally, the less healthful living areas, such as the islands of the Caribbean, offered shorter contractual periods of work than did the mainland colonies. Skilled and literate workers also obtained shorter contracts, as a rule. Overall, it was a highly competitive labor market system steeped in rational conduct.

Immigrants from continental Europe, mainly Germans, usually came as redemptioners, immigrants brought over on credit provided by ship captains. Sometimes the redemptioners prepaid a portion of the costs of passage. After arrival, they were allowed a short period of time to repay the captain, either by borrowing from a relative or a friend or by self-contracting for their services. Because they usually arrived with no ready contacts and typically could not speak English, the contract period for full cost of passage was sometimes longer than for indentures, up to seven years. In addition, German immigrants usually came over in families, whereas English immigrants were typically single and more likely to enter into indentured servitude. The longer period of service for German redemptioners also was in part a consequence of their preference to be highly selective in choosing their master-employers, a right indentured servants did not have. Migrating in family groups encouraged this preference, and most Germans settled in Pennsylvania. Alternatively, when the families had paid a portion of their passage costs before disembarking, their redemptioners' time could be much shorter.

As the decades passed, the percentage of European immigrants arriving as indentured servants or redemptioners declined. By the early nineteenth century, the market for indentures had largely disappeared, done in by economic forces rather than legislation. Alternative sources of financing, according to Farley Grubb, largely from residents in the United States paying for their relatives' passage from the Old World, were the main cause of this market's disappearance.[3]

Also helping it disappear were the drop in the costs of passage over this time and the rise of earnings of workers in Europe. In addition, slavery was a viable cost-cutting alternative labor source compared with indentured servants or free labor.

The counterpart to white servitude or free labor, namely slavery, did not become an important source of labor until after 1650, although slaves were imported in increasing numbers after 1620. By 1700, slavery had become a firmly established institution from Maryland southward.[4] Slaveholding was not unknown in New England and the Middle colonies, but it was less popular there for several reasons. Rarely was a slave in the South unable to work due to the rigors of bad weather, whereas working outdoors in the North could be impossible for days at a time. Also important was the fact that tobacco, then rice, and finally indigo were the staple crops of the South. Because raising them required much unskilled labor that could be performed under limited supervision in work groups, these cash crops were especially suited to cultivation by slaves. Although not nearly as large as the huge sugar plantations of the Caribbean islands, large-scale farm units made slavery particularly profitable, and the size of farms became much larger in the South than in the Middle or New England colonies. The crops, especially rice and indigo, and the slave system itself generated economies of scale and fostered larger production units of team labor under supervision. Economies of scale occur when output expands relative to inputs (land, labor, and capital) as the production unit gets larger. As we have learned from Christopher Hanes, another advantage of slavery compared with free labor, and to a lesser extent indentured servants, was the reduction in turnover costs.[5] Slave owners did not face the possibility of slaves leaving the fields at planting or harvest times or switching to other employers for higher pay. Finally, the mere momentum of the growth of slavery in the South was accompanied by moral and institutional adaptations to strengthen and sustain it. For example, the purchase of imported slaves in the South triggered the headright to land of 50 acres per slave purchased, reinforcing the growth in the size of farm units there. Also, primogeniture, a form of inheritance in which the land is transferred to the oldest son, prevailed in the southern colonies. In the Middle and New England colonies (except in Rhode Island and New York), multigeniture was typically followed, with an equal division of property among the sons. Over time, primogeniture perpetuated and built comparatively larger estates.

Unlike the indentured whites, African slaves were not protected in the colonies as British subjects. Terms of service were for life, and children of female slaves were born slaves, regardless of who fathered the children. Only by self-purchase or benevolence could a slave become free. In 1774, there were nearly half a million blacks in the colonies, 18,000 of whom were free.

As we have emphasized, those coming to America through their own resources received 50 acres of land from headright land grants in most colonies. However, not only land but also relatively high wages attracted workers to the colonies. Especially in the seaports,

---

[3]Farley Grubb, "The End of European Immigrant Servitude in the United States: An Economic Analysis of Market Collapse 1772–1835," *Journal of Economic History* 54 (1994): 794–824.

[4]For an economic analysis of the transition from indentures to slavery in the Chesapeake, see Farley Grubb and Tony Stitt, "The Liverpool Emigrant Servant Trade and the Transition to Slave Labor in the Chesapeake, 1697–1707: Market Adjustments to War," *Explorations in Economic History* 31 (1994): 376–40

[5]Christopher Hanes, "Turnover Cost and the Distribution of Slave Labor in Anglo-America," *Journal of Economic History* 56 (1966): 307–329.

craftsmen and artisans of all sorts, merchants and seamen, and even scholars gave vibrance to the commercial life on western Atlantic shores. Finally, prisoners, too—perhaps as many as thirty thousand—avoided death sentences or indefinite imprisonment in England by voluntarily transporting themselves to the New World. After 1718, it was customary for convicts to serve seven years of indenture for minor crimes and fourteen years for major ones.

DEMOGRAPHIC CHANGE

Underpopulation Despite High Rates of Population Growth

One major fact of American economic life—underpopulation and labor scarcity—persisted throughout the entire colonial period. Another extremely important aspect of British colonization and a crucial factor in securing and maintaining Britain's hold on the North American frontier was the extremely high rate of population growth in the colonies. What generated the characteristic of apparent underpopulation was the vast amount of available land, which "thinned" the population spatially and established high population densities in only a few major port towns. This occurred despite the exceptionally high rate of growth, which was so high—the population approximately doubled every 25 years—that Thomas Malthus worrisomely referred to it as "a rapidity of increase, probably without parallel in history." Malthus and others pointed to the American colonies as a prime example of virtually unchecked population growth. Wouldn't such a rate of increase, which was twice the population growth rate in Europe, ultimately lead to famine, pestilence, and doom?

Such European polemics were far from the minds of the colonists. Indeed, Benjamin Franklin wrote an essay in 1751 extolling the virtues of rapid population increases in the colonies. Overpopulation never occurred in the colonies, despite the various methods that were used to encourage or force (in the case of African captives) population relocation to the New World. Nor did the high natural rate of population increase create population pressures in the colonies; population growth was generally viewed as a sign of progress and a means of reducing the uncertainties, risks, and hazards of a sparsely populated frontier region.

Population Growth in British North America

The population growth from both migration and natural causes is illustrated by region and race in Table 2.1. Note the remarkable similarity in the timing, rise, and levels of the total populations in New England and the Upper South. The latecomers—the Middle colonies and the Lower South—displayed slightly higher growth rates, which allowed them to catch up somewhat. The rate of population expansion was quite steady for the colonies as a whole, slightly over 3 percent per year. From 300 settlers in Virginia in 1610, 1.7 million people of European origin and half a million of African origin resided in the 13 colonies by 1770.

The period of greatest absolute migration occurred in the eighteenth century—particularly after 1720, when between 100,000 and 125,000 Scotch-Irish and about 100,000 Germans arrived in North America. Most immigrants in the seventeenth century were British, and there was another strong surge of British migration between 1768 and 1775. Perhaps as many as 300,000 white immigrants came to the New World between 1700 and 1775, and a somewhat smaller number of blacks came as well. Plenty of highly fertile land and a favorable climate attracted Europeans and provided motives for securing African slaves. Nevertheless, migration was the dominant source of population growth in only the first decades of settlement in each region.

In New England, immigration virtually halted in the late 1640s, and natural causes became the source of population growth after 1650. For areas settled later, such as Pennsylvania, the forces of migration remained dominant later, but natural forces swiftly took over even there. Even the enslaved black population grew swiftly and predominantly from natural sources after 1700. On the eve of the Revolution, only one white in ten was foreign born; the figure for blacks was between two and three in ten.

Commercial successes, favorable economic circumstances, and the high value of labor powered a high rate of reproduction in the colonies. White birthrates in North America per 1,000 women ranged between 45 and 50 per year, compared with near 30 in Europe or 12 in the United States today. The colonial population was exceptionally young. By the 1770s, 57 percent of the population was under the age of 21. Moreover, a higher percentage of the colonial population was of childbearing age. Typically, colonial women tended to marry rather early, between the ages of 20 and 23, which was a couple of years younger than the average marriage age of European women. The cheapness of land encouraged early marriage in the colonies, and it was generally easier for colonists than for Europeans to strike out on their own, acquire land, and set up a household. Childbearing was a major cause of death for women, and many men remarried to sustain their families. The average European

TABLE 2.1 Population by Region for the Thirteen North American Colonies (in thousands)

	NEW ENGLAND			MIDDLE COLONIES		
YEAR	WHITES	BLACKS	TOTAL	WHITES	BLACKS	TOTAL
1620	0.1	0.0	0.1	0.0	0.0	0.0
1640	13.5	0.2	13.7	1.7	0.2	1.9
1660	32.6	0.6	33.2	4.8	0.6	5.4
1680	68.0	0.5	68.5	13.4	1.5	14.9
1700	90.7	1.7	92.4	49.9	3.7	53.5
1710	112.5	2.6	115.1	63.4	6.2	69.6
1720	166.9	4.0	170.9	92.3	10.8	103.1
1730	211.2	6.1	217.3	135.3	11.7	147.0
1740	281.2	8.5	289.7	204.1	16.5	220.5
1750	349.0	11.0	360.0	275.7	20.7	296.4
1760	436.9	12.7	449.6	398.9	29.0	427.9
1770	565.7	15.4	581.1	521.0	34.9	555.9
1780	698.4	14.4	712.8	680.5	42.4	722.9

	UPPER SOUTH			LOWER SOUTH			TOTAL OF 13 COLONIES		
YEAR	WHITES	BLACKS	TOTAL	WHITES	BLACKS	TOTAL	WHITES	BLACKS	TOTAL
1620	0.9	0.0	0.9	0.0	0.0	0.0	1.0	0.0	1.0
1640	8.0	0.1	8.1	0.0	0.0	0.0	23.2	0.5	23.7
1660	24.0	0.9	24.9	1.0	0.0	1.0	62.4	2.1	64.6
1680	55.6	4.3	59.9	6.2	0.4	6.6	143.2	6.7	149.9
1700	85.2	12.9	98.1	13.6	2.9	16.4	239.4	21.1	260.4
1710	101.3	22.4	123.7	18.8	6.6	25.4	296.0	37.8	333.8
1720	128.0	30.6	158.6	24.8	14.8	39.6	412.0	60.2	472.2
1730	171.4	53.2	224.6	34.0	26.0	60.0	551.9	97.0	648.9
1740	212.5	84.0	296.5	57.8	50.2	108.0	755.6	159.2	914.7
1750	227.2	150.6	377.8	82.4	59.8	142.2	934.3	242.1	1,176.5
1760	312.4	189.6	502.0	119.6	94.5	214.1	1,267.8	325.8	1,593.6
1770	398.2	251.4	649.6	189.4	155.4	344.8	1,674.3	457.1	2,131.4
1780	482.4	303.6	786.0	297.4	208.8	506.2	2,158.7	569.2	2,727.9

Source: Compiled from Tables 5.1, 9.4, 6.4, and 8.1 on the respective regions in John J. McCusker and Russell Menard, The Economy of British America 1607–1789 *(Chapel Hill: University of North Carolina Press, 1985), 103, 203, 136, and 172.*

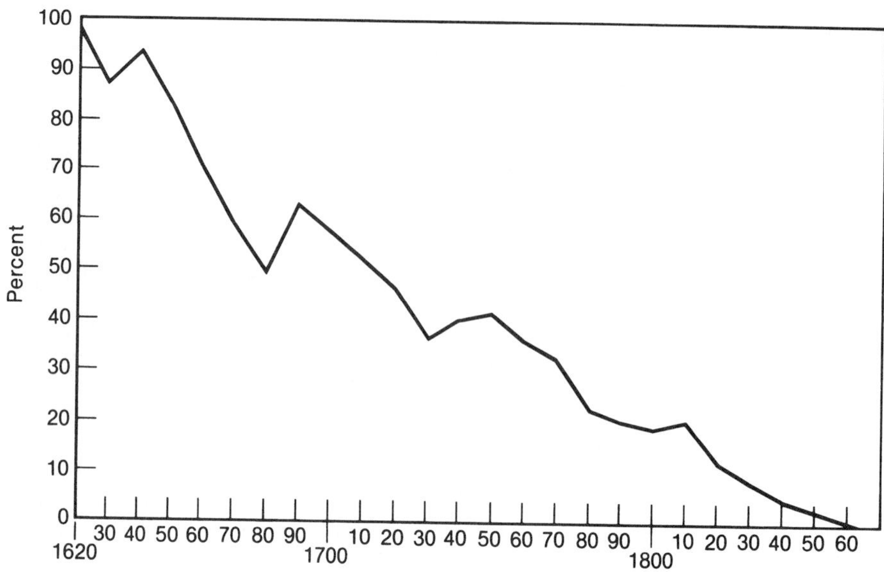

FIGURE 2.1 Foreign-Born Blacks as a Percentage of the U.S. Black Population, 1620–1860

Source: from TIME ON THE CROSS: The Economics of American Negro Slavery *by Robert William Fogel and Stanley L. Engerman, 23. Copyright © 1974 by Robert William Fogel and Stanley L. Engerman. Used by permission of W.W. Norton & Company, Inc.*

married man produced four or five children, but earlier marriages and higher proportions of mothers in their childbearing years resulted in an average colonial family of about seven to eight children. Greater emphasis on rural economic activity also encouraged higher birthrates in the colonies. Children were more costly to raise in urban areas, and their labor contribution tended to be less there.

Also of great significance was the fact that once the first few years of starvation had passed, the colonies experienced rather low mortality rates. The annual death rate in Europe was about 40 per 1,000 people; in the colonies, it was 20 to 25 per 1,000.

The lower age structure of the colonial population accounts in part for this, but the exceptionally low rate of child mortality was an even more impressive statistic. On the average, white mothers in the colonies were better fed and housed than mothers in Europe. Consequently, colonial babies were healthier. The harsh winters of North America and the inferior medical technology of the frontier were more than offset by plentiful food supplies, fuel, and housing. And because the population was predominantly rural, epidemics were rare in the colonies. Once past infancy, white colonial males typically lived to be 60 or older. Due to the hazards of childbirth, however, the comparable age for early colonial women was normally slightly over 40.[6]

The Racial Profile

Six percent of all slaves imported into the New World came to areas that became the United States. As shown in Figure 2.1, migration was the initiating force of population growth of blacks. By the eighteenth century, however, natural forces dominated the growth of the black population. By midcentury, the birthrate of blacks, like that of whites, was near the biological maximum. Death rates were also similar to those of whites in North America. Because the natural rate of increase was comparable for both races—which resulted in a doubling of the population nearly every 20 to 25 years—and because

[6]Although perhaps atypical, evidence presented by Philip Graven in "Family Structure in Seventeenth Century Andover, Massachusetts," *William and Mary Quarterly* (April 1966): 234–256, shows women also living into their sixties in that area.

the actual number of imported slaves practically equaled the number of white immigrants, the proportion of the total population that was black increased significantly after 1700. We see from Table 2.1 that in 1680, only about 3 percent of the total population was black. A century later, this proportion had increased to about 20 percent, and the black population was near half a million. Of course, regional differences were great, and more than 90 percent of the slaves resided in southern regions. As Figure 2.2 indicates, however, relatively small proportions of the total population of the mainland colonies were composed of blacks, compared with the Caribbean islands. In New England, the proportion of blacks was in the neighborhood of 2 percent; in the Middle colonies, 5 percent. In Maryland in the late colonial years, 32 percent of the total population comprised blacks; in Virginia, 42 percent. The more limited commercial development in North Carolina, due to inadequate harbors, generated a black population proportion of only 35 percent. In contrast, South Carolina contained the largest concentration of blacks—60 percent. This especially high proportion in South Carolina resulted from the special advantages of slave labor and economies of scale in rice and indigo production. Consequently, the social profile of South Carolina suggested by its high concentration of enslaved blacks was similar to the profiles of the British and French West Indies sugar islands. Although Virginia's population profile did approach this proportion, South Carolina's profile of a majority of slaves controlled by a minority of plantation owners was unique among the mainland colonies. In contrast to their Caribbean counterparts, blacks typically remained a minority race on the mainland of North America.

Finally, the pattern of change for the Native American population was in sharp contrast to that of whites and blacks. At the time Jamestown was founded, it was likely that as many as 300,000 native American Indians lived within 150 miles of the Atlantic seaboard. By the mid–eighteenth century, the impact of battle, and especially the devastation of communicable diseases such as smallpox and measles, against which the natives had developed no immunity, reduced their population to between 50,000 and 100,000. This depopulation aspect was unique among mainland North Americans, whatever their origin. This topic is further discussed in Economic Insight 2.2.

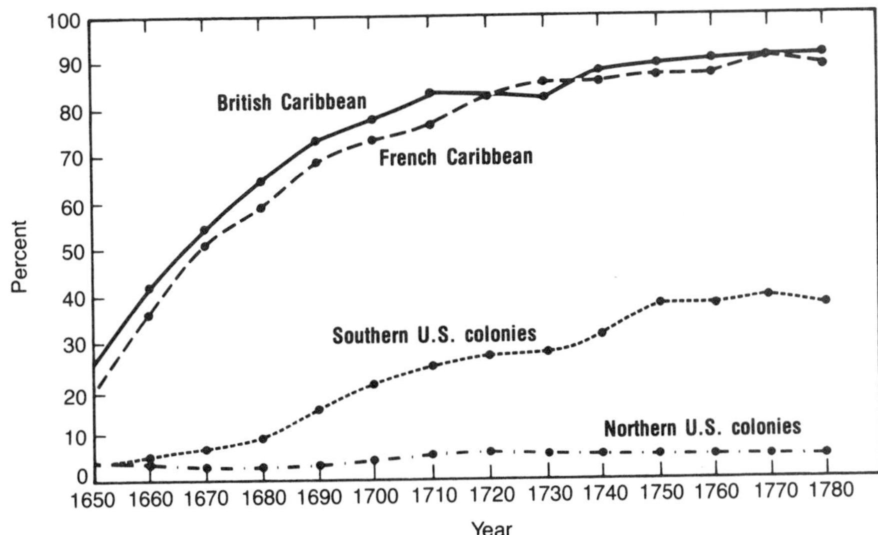

FIGURE 2.2 Blacks as a Percentage of the Total Population, 1650–1780
The population profile was much different on the North American continent from that on the islands of the Caribbean. Only in South Carolina did the black population outnumber the resident white population.

Source: from TIME ON THE CROSS: The Economics of American Negro Slavery *by Robert William Fogel and Stanley L. Engerman, 23. Copyright © 1974 by Robert William Fogel and Stanley L. Engerman. Used by permission of W.W. Norton & Company, Inc.*

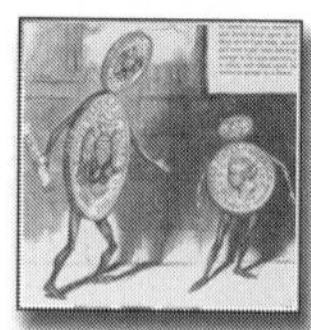

Economic Insight 2.2

Early European—American Economic Relations and Demographic Changes

The population data on native Indians in North America in early periods are more speculative and less accurate than population data on new settlers from Europe and slaves from Africa. Table 2.2 gives the best current estimates available of the total population of Native Americans in North America at the time of arrival of Europeans and of the population sizes of several northeastern regions and tribes. In the northern regions, the French formed political and economic alliances with the Huron and Algonquian tribes early in the seventeenth century. The early Dutch, mostly fur traders like the French, also linked themselves to the native Americans, soon after arriving in 1620. After the British took over New York in 1644, they also took over the economic and political relations with the Iroquois Confederacy (the "Six Nations" of the Cuyuga Mohawk, Oneida, Onondaga, Seneca, plus the Iroquois) that the Dutch traders had formed. Similar relationships were formed in the southeast: French-Choctaw, and British-Chickasaw. Beaver furs were the key economic element of these relationships in the Northeast, deer skins in the southeast. Indians specialized in hunting and skinning, and the Europeans bought wholesale trading cloth, gun powder, and other manufactured items.

These early relationships were fundamental to the first settlements, and the long-standing hostilities between the Huron and Mohawk tribes added force to the longtime rivalry between the French and the British (see Roback 1992, 14–16).

The economic gains from these relationships were soon overwhelmed by the effects of disease (epidemics against which the native Indians had no natural resistance), violence, and dislocation. Figure 2.3 shows the approximate timings of the demise of the Native American population relative to the rise of Europeans and Africans. In the Southeastern regions the nonindigenous population became the majority before 1715 (see Wood 1989). In all likelihood the crossover to a nonindigenous majority had occurred by a similar early date in the northeastern British colonies.

TABLE 2.2 Population Estimates for Various Regions or Tribes at Time of Arrival of First Europeans in North America

REGION OR TRIBE (NOT MUTUALLY EXCLUSIVE)	POPULATION ESTIMATE	SOURCE(S)
North America (excluding present-day Mexico)	3,790,000	Denevan, Table 1
New England	72,000–144,000	Cook (1976b), Snow (1980), Salisbury (1982)
Mohawk	13,700–17,000	Snow (1980) Virginia
Algonquian	14,300–22,000	Feest (1973)
Arikara	30,000	Holder (1970)
Iroquoi	20,000–110,000	Trigger (1976), Englebrecht (1987), Clermont (1980)
Huron	23,000–30,000	Trigger (1985), Dickinson (1980)
Micmac	12,000–50,000	Snow (1980), Miller (1976, 1982)

Source: Summarized from William Denevan, ed. The Native Population of the Americans in 1492, *2d ed. (Madison: University of Wisconsin Press, 1992), xix–xx and xxviii; Table 1 as given in Barrington (1992, 2).*

Economic Insight 2.2

Early European—American Economic Relations and Demographic Changes, continued

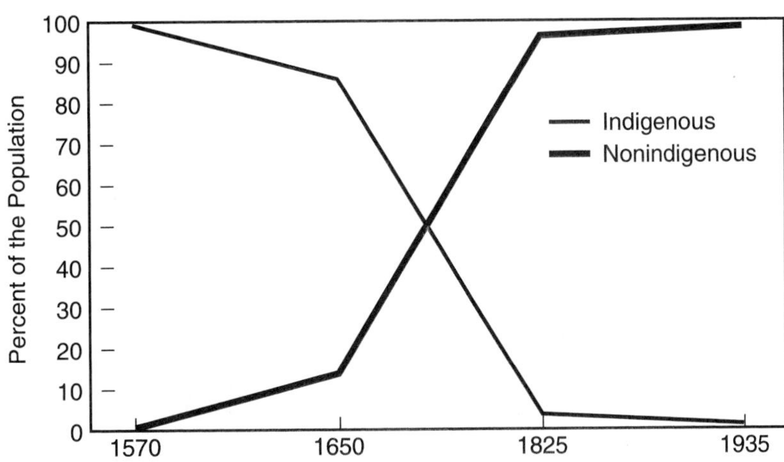

FIGURE 2.3 Indigenous and Nonindigenous Composition of Population, United States and Canada

Source: Population data from Angel Rosenblot, La Poblacion Indigena yel Mestizaje en America *(Buenos Aires: Nova, 1954), 1:21, 37, 59, 88, as given in Barrington (1999, 2).*

Spatial Distribution of the Population

Although the settlement of British North America continued steadily after Jamestown's founding, most of the population remained clustered around a few Atlantic ports. It took fifty years to secure a firm hold on the new continent, and at the end of the first century of colonial history, settlement of the eastern seaboard was far from complete. By 1660, Virginia, Maryland, and Massachusetts were established commonwealths, but the first settlers in Georgia did not arrive there for almost another 75 years. In 1640, about 24,000 people inhabited the English colonies on the mainland. By 1660, there were 65,000 colonists; by 1700, 260,000. From one-third of a million people in 1710, the colonial population had increased to nearly 2.5 million at the time of the Revolution.

Map 2.3 on page 44 shows the extent of settlement as of 1660, 1700, and 1760. Before 1660, there was nothing to speak of south of Norfolk, and at the turn of the century, a wilderness still separated Charleston and its environs from the major inhabited area in upper North Carolina. By 1760, the land-hungry rich and poor had spread over nearly all the coastal plain and into the Piedmont areas. As early as 1726, Germans and Scotch-Irish had begun moving into the Shenandoah Valley, and down this and the other great valleys in ever-increasing numbers, settlers sought the cheap land to the west. Through gaps in the mountains some turned east into the Piedmont area of Virginia and the Carolinas; only a few years later, pioneers began to trickle westward, particularly through the Cumberland Gap into Kentucky and Tennessee.

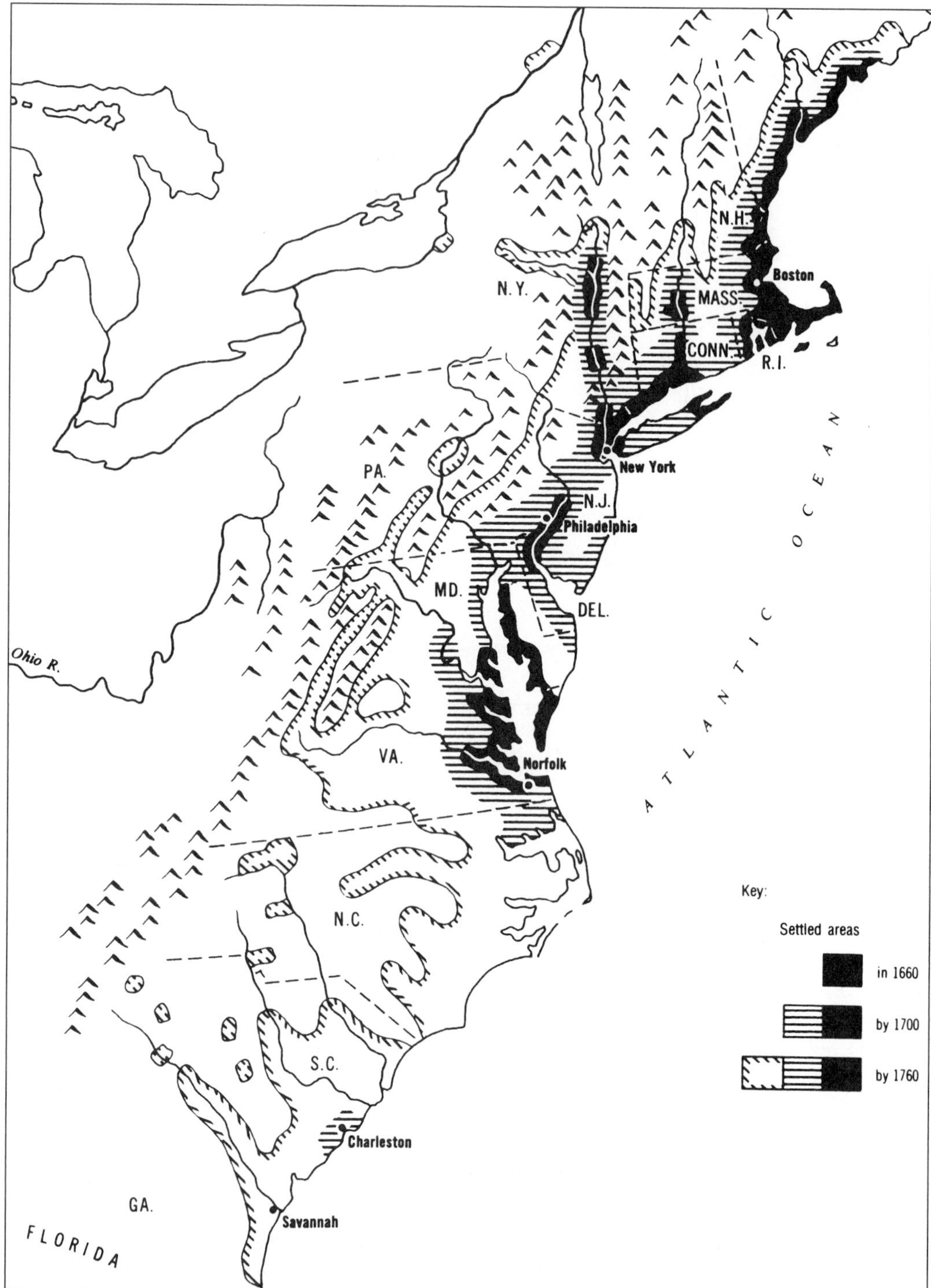

MAP 2.3 Settlement Shifts *Easily accessible coastal regions and river valleys provided the first sites for settlements, but settlers soon moved into the Piedmont areas, the great valleys of the Appalachians, and the inviting country of the mountains.*

Imperial Rivalries in North America

The rivalry of empires persisted for a long time, and the growth in population and the colonization of new territory were not restricted to the eastern coast of North America (see Map 2.4). During the sixteenth century, Spain had occupied northern Mexico and Florida, and while English settlement was taking place, the Spanish were moving northward into Texas, southern Arizona, and southern California. As we have already mentioned, in the seventeenth century, France established bases in the Lesser Antilles and in Canada; from Canada, French explorers and traders pushed into the Mississippi Valley and on to the Gulf of Mexico. The three rival states were bound to clash in America, even if they had not been enemies in other parts of the world. To the general historian we must leave the descriptions of these bitter rivalries and of the resulting complex, if small-scale, wars. Following intermittent conflict between the French and the English in the Northeast and along most of the western frontier, the French and Indian War resulted in the temporary downfall of the French in North America. By the treaty of Paris in 1763, only Spain and England were left in possession of the North American continent. Spain took all the territory west of the

MAP 2.4 Territorial Claims *Territorial possessions and claims in North and Central America toward the end of the eighteenth century.*

Mississippi, and England secured everything to the east, with the exception of certain fishing rights and small islands retained by the French off Newfoundland. According to this agreement, England acquired all of Florida, thereby settling perennial disputes with Spain that had long disturbed the colonies of South Carolina and Georgia. It is difficult to remember that Spain, not France, harassed the pioneers who moved out of the original 13 colonies and into the southern interior. Not until 1800 did France again own the Territory of Louisiana and its vital port of New Orleans, and that control did not last long.

Two institutional arrangements particularly favored British dominance in North America. First was the open labor market of indentured servitude, used by the British but not by the Spanish or French, to facilitate migration. Of the 500,000 British immigrants (1610–1775), 350,000 came as indentured servants. Second was the establishment of permanent British settlements, which fostered privately owned farms and families and, ultimately, towns. Thanks largely to these two institutions, British settlers in North America outnumbered the French nearly twenty to one by 1750. High levels of English migration, encouraged by wide-ranging economic opportunities, forged the beginnings of an American identity cloaked in English law, language, and customs.[7]

SELECTED REFERENCES AND SUGGESTED READINGS

Alston, Lee J., and Morton O. Shapiro. "Inheritance Laws Across the Colonies: Causes and Consequences." *Journal of Economic History* 44 (1984): 277–287.

Anderson, Terry, ed. *Property Rights and Indian Economics: The Political Economy Forum.* Lanham, Md.: Rowman & Littlefield, 1992.

Anderson, Terry, and Robert P. Thomas. "White Population, Labor Force, and Extensive Growth of the New England Economy in the Seventeenth Century." *Journal of Economic History* 33 (1973): 634–667.

______. "The Growth of Population and Labor Force in the 17th-Century Chesapeake." *Explorations in Economic History* 15 (1978): 290–312.

Andrews, Charles M. *The Colonial Period of American History.* New Haven: Yale University Press, 1934.

Bancroft, George. *History of the United States of America from the Discovery of the Continent*, 6 vols. Boston: Little, Brown, 1879.

Barrington, Linda, ed. *The Other Side of the Frontier.* Boulder: Westview, 1999.

Boorstin, Daniel. *The Americans: The Colonial Experience.* New York: Vintage Books, 1958.

Bradford, William. *Of Plymouth Plantation.* New York: Capricorn Books, 1962.

Bruce, Philip A. *Economic History of Virginia in the Seventeenth Century*, 2 vols. New York: Macmillan, 1896.

Bruchey, Stuart. *The Roots of American Economic Growth 1607–1861: An Essay in Social Causation.* London: Hutchinson University Library, 1965.

Curtin, Philip. *The Atlantic Slave Trade: A Census.* Madison: University of Wisconsin Press, 1969.

Earle, Carville. *The Evolution of a Tidewater Settlement System: All Hallow's Parish, 1650–1783.* Chicago: University of Chicago Press, 1975.

Ekirch, A. Roger, *Bound for America: The Transportation of British Convicts to the Colonies, 1718–1775.* Oxford: Oxford University Press, 1990.

Fogel, Robert, and Stanley Engerman. Chapter 1 in *Time on the Cross: The Economics of American Negro Slavery.* Boston: Little, Brown, 1974.

[7]For further analysis and comparisons of the differential paths of development among regions in the New World, see Stanley L. Engerman, and Kenneth L. Sokoloff, "Factor Endowments, Institutions, and Differential Paths of Growth Among New World Economics: A View From Economic Historians of the United States," in *How Did Latin America Fall Behind?* ed. Stephen Haber (Palo Alto, Calif.: Stanford University Press, 1996).

Franklin, Benjamin. "Observations Concerning the Increase of Mankind." Philadelphia, 1751. In *The Papers of Ben Franklin*, ed. Leonard Laberee. New Haven: Yale University Press, 1961.

Galenson, David W. "Immigration and the Colonial Labor System: An Analysis of the Length of Indenture." *Explorations in Economic History* 14 (1977): 361–377.

______. "British Servants and the Colonial Indenture System in the Eighteenth Century." *Journal of Southern History* 44 (1978): 41–66.

______."The Market Evaluation of Human Capital: The Case of Indentured Servitude." *Journal of Political Economy* 89 (1981): 446–467.

______. *White Servitude in Colonial America*. Cambridge: Cambridge University Press, 1981.

______."The Rise and Fall of Indentured Servitude in the Americas: An Economic Analysis." *Journal of Economic History* 44 (1984): 1–26.

______."The Settlement and Growth of the Colonies: Population, Labor, and Economic Development." In *The Cambridge Economic History of the United States*,Vol. I, eds. Stanley L. Engerman and Robert E. Gallman. Cambridge: Cambridge University Press, 1996, 135–207.

Gemery, Henry. "Emigration from the British Isles to the New World, 1630–1700." In *Research in Economic History*, Vol. 5, ed. Paul Uselding. New York: Johnson, 1980, 179–232.

Grubb, Farley. "The End of European Immigrant Servitude in the United States: An Economic Analysis of Market Collapse 1772–1835." *Journal of Economic History* 54 (1994): 794–824.

______. "Colonial Labor Markets and the Length of Indenture: Further Evidence." *Explorations in Economic History* 24 (1987): 101–106.

Grubb, Farley, and Tony Stitt. "Immigrant Servant Labor: Their Occupational and Geographic Distribution in the Late Eighteenth-Century Mid-Atlantic Economy." *Social Science History* 9 (1985): 249–275.

———. "The Incidence of Servitude in Trans-Atlantic Migration, 1771–1804." *Explorations in Economic History* 22 (1985): 316–339.

______."The Market for Indentured Immigrants: Evidence on the Efficiency of Forward-Labor Contracting in Philadelphia, 1745–1773." *Journal of Economic History* 45 (1985): 855–868.

______."Redemptioner Immigration to Pennsylvania: Evidence on Contract Choice and Profitability." *Journal of Economic History* 46 (1986): 407–418.

_______. "The Liverpool Emigrant Servant Trade and the Transition to Slave Labor in the Chesapeake, 1697–1707: Market Adjustments to War." *Explorations in Economic History* 31 (1994): 376–405.

Hanes, Christopher. "Turnover Cost and the Distribution of Slave Labor in Anglo-America." *Journal of Economic History* 56 (1966): 307–329.

Heavener, Robert. "Indentured Servitude: The Philadelphia Market, 1771–1773." *Journal of Economic History* 38 (1978): 701–713.

Higgs, Robert, and Louis Stettler. "Colonial New England Demography: A Sampling Approach." *William and Mary Quarterly* 27, no. 2 (1970): 282–294.

Hughes, Jonathan R. T. "William Penn and the Holy Experiment." Chapter 2 in *The Vital Few: American Economic History and Its Protagonists*. New York: Oxford University Press, 1973 (reprint).

Jones, E. L. "The European Background." In *The Cambridge Economic History of the United States*, Vol. I, eds. Stanley L. Engerman and Robert E. Gallman. Cambridge: Cambridge University Press, 1996, 95–133.

Kulikoff, Allan. "A 'Prolifick' People: Black Population Growth in the Chesapeake Colonies, 1700–1790." *Southern Studies* (1977): 391–428.

Lemon, James. *The Best Poor Man's Country: A Geographical Study of Early Southeastern Pennsylvania.* Baltimore: Johns Hopkins University Press, 1972.

Menard, Russell. "From Servants to Slaves: The Transformation of the Chesapeake Labor System." *Southern Studies* (1977): 355–390.

Morgan, Edmund S. *The Puritan Family: Religion and Domestic Relations in Seventeenth-Century New England.* New York: Harper & Row, 1966.

———. "The First American Boom: Virginia 1618 to 1630." *William and Mary Quarterly* 28 (1971).

———. *American Slavery, American Freedom: The Ordeal of Colonial Virginia.* New York: Norton, 1975.

Morison, Samuel E. *The Oxford History of the American People.* New York: Oxford University Press, 1964.

Morris, Richard. *Government and Labor in Early America.* New York: Columbia University Press, 1946.

Nash, Gary. *Red, White, and Black: The Peoples of Early America.* Englewood Cliffs: Prentice Hall, 1974.

North, Douglass C., and R. P. Thomas. *The Rise of the Western World.* New York: Cambridge University Press, 1973.

Perkins, Edwin J. Chapter 1 in *The Economy of Colonial America*, 2d ed. New York: Columbia University Press, 1988.

Potter, Jim. "The Growth of Population in America, 1700–1860." In *Population in History: Essays in Historical Demography*, eds. D. V. Glass and B. E. C. Eaversley. Chicago: Aldine, 1960.

Powell, Sumner C. *Puritan Village: The Formation of a New England Town.* Middletown, Conn.: Wesleyan University Press, 1963.

Rink, Oliver. *Holland on the Hudson: An Economic and Social History of New York.* Ithaca: Cornell University Press, 1986.

Roback, Jennifer. "Exchange Sovereignty, and Indian-Anglo Relations." In *Property Rights and Indian Economies: The Political Economy Forum*, ed. Terry Anderson. Lanham: Rowman & Littlefield, 1992.

Rosenberg, Nathan, and L. E. Birdzell, Jr. Chapter 3 in *How the West Grew Rich.* New York: Basic Books, 1986.

Salisbury, Neal. "The History of Native Americans from Before the Arrival of the Europeans and Africans Until the American Civil War." In *The Cambridge Economic History of the United States,* Vol. I, eds. Stanley L. Engerman and Robert E. Gallman. Cambridge: Cambridge University Press, 1996, 1–52.

Smith, Abbot E. *Colonists in Bondage: White Servitude and Convict Labor in America, 1607–1776.* Chapel Hill: University of North Carolina Press, 1947.

Smith, Billy G. "Death and Life in a Colonial Immigrant City: A Demographic Analysis of Philadelphia." *Journal of Economic History* 38 (1977): 863–889.

Smith, Daniel S. "The Demographic History of Colonial New England." *Journal of Economic History* 32 (1972): 165–183.

______. "The Estimates of Early American Historical Demographers: Two Steps Forward, One Step Back, What Steps in the Future." *Historical Methods* (1979): 24–38.

Thomas, Robert P., and Richard Bean. "The Adoption of Slave Labor in British America." In *The Uncommon Market: Essays in the Economic History of the Atlantic Slave Trade,* eds. H. Genery and J. Hogendorn. New York: Academic Press, 1978.

Thornton, John K. "The African Background to American Colonization." In *The Cambridge Economic History of the United States*, Vol. I, eds. Stanley L. Engerman and Robert E. Gallman. Cambridge: Cambridge University Press, 1996, 53–94.

Ver Steeg, Clarence. *The Formative Years, 1607–1763.* New York: Hill & Wang, 1964.

Walton, Gary M., and James F. Shepherd. Chapter 2 in *The Economic Rise of Early America*. Cambridge: Cambridge University Press, 1979.

Weeden, William B. *Economic and Social History of New England, 1620–1789*, 2 vols. Boston: Houghton Mifflin, 1890.

Wells, Robert V. *The Population of the British Colonies in America before 1776: A Survey of Census Data*. Princeton: Princeton University Press, 1975.

Wood, Peter. "The Changing Population of the Colonial South: An Overview by Race and Region, 1685–1760." In *Powhatan's Mantle: Indians in the Colonial Southeast,* eds. Peter Wood, Gregory A. Waselkov, and Tomas M. Hartley. Lincoln: University of Nebraska Press, 1989.

Chapter Three

COLONIAL ECONOMIC ACTIVITIES

Chapter Theme

After the discovery of "cash crops" such as tobacco, market production and trade grew rapidly and gave permanent features to the English settlements in North America. In this chapter, we present the economic activities of the colonists in terms of their regional and occupational specializations.

These specializations were fundamentally determined by comparative advantages in production, and the advantages varied significantly among the colonies. Overwhelmingly, however, the abundance of land and natural resources determined the path of development and particular economic activities in the various colonies. The regional specializations based on land (and natural resource) abundance relative to capital and labor contrasted sharply with the much higher labor-to-land and capital-to-land ratios in Britain and Europe. The colonial specializations that emerged, for market trade in particular, also enabled the young economy to grow and fit itself into the British imperial economy and the world economy.

LAND AND NATURAL RESOURCE ABUNDANCE, LABOR SCARCITY

Throughout the colonial period, most people depended on the land for a livelihood. From New Hampshire to Georgia, agriculture was the chief occupation, and what industrial and commercial activity there was revolved almost entirely around materials extracted from the land, the forests, and the ocean. Where soil and climate were unfavorable to cultivating commercial crops, it was often possible to turn to fishing or trapping and to the production of ships, ship timbers, pitch, tar, turpentine, and other forest products. Land was seemingly limitless in extent and, therefore, not highly priced, but almost every colonist wanted to be a landholder. When we remember that ownership of land signified wealth and position to the European, this is not hard to understand. The ever-present desire for land explains why, for the first century and a half of our history, many immigrants who might have been successful artisans or laborers in someone else's employ tended instead to turn to agriculture, thereby aggravating the persistent scarcity of labor in the New World. A shortage of workers with highly developed skills was most notable because artisans and trained craftsmen in great demand in Europe were too content at home to be tempted into a life of hardship at the very bounds of civilization even by substantially higher wages. But all types of labor were generally scarce because the high ratio of land to labor assured independent farmers fairly comfortable material standards of living after many of the early frontier hazards had been overcome. (However, there were some exceptions, as shown in Economic Insight 3.1 on page 52).

CAPITAL SCARCITY

Items of physical capital for production were in limited supply in the aggregate, especially during the first century of settlement. Particular forms of capital goods that could be obtained from natural resources with simple tools were in apparent abundance. For instance, so much wood was available that it was fairly easy to build houses, barns, and workshops. Wagons and carriages were largely made of wood, as were farm implements, wheels, gears, and shafts. Shipyards and shipwares were also constructed from timber, and ships were built in quantity from an early date.

Alternatively, finished metal products were especially scarce, and mills and other industrial facilities remained few and small. Improvements of roads and harbors lagged far behind European standards until the end of the colonial period. Capital formation was a primary challenge to the colonists, and the colonies always needed much more capital than was ever available to them. English political leaders promoted legislation that hindered the export of tools and machinery from the home country. Commercial banks were nonexistent, and English or colonials who had savings to invest often preferred the safer investment in British firms. Nevertheless, as we shall see in chapter 5, residents of the developing American colonies lived better lives in the eighteenth century than most other people, even those living in the most advanced nations of the time.

THE DOMINANCE OF AGRICULTURE

At the end of the eighteenth century, approximately 90 percent of the American people earned a major portion of their living by farming (compared with about 3 percent today). Generally, high ratios of land and other natural resources to labor generated exceptionally high levels of output per worker in the colonies. Most production in the New World was for the colonists' own consumption, but sizable proportions of colonial goods and services were produced for commercial exchange. In time, each region became increasingly specialized in the production of particular goods and services. Areas of specialization were largely determined by particular soil types, climate, and natural bounties of the forests and ocean.

The Southern Colonies

In terms of value of output, southern agriculture was dominant throughout the colonial period and well into the nineteenth century. The southern colonies present a good example of the comparative advantage that fertile new land can offer. Almost at the outset, southern colonials grew tobacco that was both cheaper to produce and of better quality than the tobacco grown in most other parts of the world. Later, the South began to produce two other staples, rice and indigo (a blue dye native to India). For nearly two centuries, the southern economy was to revolve around these few export staples because the region's soil and climate gave the South a pronounced advantage in the cultivation of crops that were in great demand in the populous industrializing areas of Europe.[1]

---

[1] There were failures, too. For example, every effort was made to encourage the production of wines then being imported from France and Spain, but the quality of American wines was so poor that serious attempts to compete with established wine-producing areas were abandoned. Similarly, it was hoped that silk and hemp could be produced in quantity, and bounties and premiums were offered for their production; but again, quality was inferior, and high wage rates resulted in a high-cost product.

Economic Insight 3.1

Social Engineering and Economic Constraints in Georgia

In 1732, plans for the last British colony to be settled in North America were being made. The colonization of Georgia provides a vivid example of good intentions pitted against the economic realities of opportunities and restraints. Here again, we observe the impact of relative factor (input) scarcities of abundant land (and natural resources) relative to labor and capital as well as observing the importance of institutions.

Like Pennsylvania and Massachusetts, Georgia was founded to assist those who had been beset with troubles in the Old World. General James Edward Oglethorpe persuaded Dr. Thomas Bray, an Anglican clergyman noted for his good works, to attempt a project for the relief of people condemned to prison for debt. This particular social evil of eighteenth-century England cried out to be remedied because debtors could spend years in prison without hope of escape except through organized charitable institutions. As long as individuals were incarcerated, they were unable to earn any money with which to pay their debts, and even if they were eventually released, years of imprisonment could make them unfit for work. It was Oglethorpe's idea to encourage debtors to come to America, where they might become responsible (and even substantial) citizens.

In addition to their wish to aid the "urban wretches" of England, Bray, Oglethorpe, and their associates had another primary motivation: to secure a military buffer zone between the prosperous northern English settlements and Spanish Florida. Besides their moral repugnance to slavery, they believed that an all-white population was needed for security reasons. It was doubtful that slaves could be depended on to fight, and with slavery, rebellion was always a possibility. Therefore, slavery as an institution was prohibited in Georgia—initially.

In 1732, King George II obligingly granted Dr. Bray and his associates the land between the Savannah and Altamaha Rivers; the original tract included considerably less territory than occupied by the modern state of Georgia. By royal charter, a corporation that was to be governed by a group of trustees was created; after 21 years, the territory was to revert to the Crown. Financed by both private and public funds, the venture had an auspicious beginning. Oglethorpe himself led the first contingent of several hundred immigrants—mostly debtors—to the new country, where a 50-acre farm awaited each colonist. Substantially larger grants were available to free settlers with families, and determined efforts were made, both on the Continent and in the British Isles, to secure colonists.

Unfortunately, the ideals and hopes of the trustees clashed with economic reality and the institutions used in Georgia. Although "the Georgia experiment" was a modest success as a philanthropic enterprise, its economic development was to prove disappointing for many decades. The climate in the low coastal country—where the fertile land lay—was unhealthful and generated higher death rates than in areas farther north. As the work of Ralph Gray and Betty Wood has shown, it was impossible without slavery to introduce the rice and indigo plantations in Georgia that were so profitable in South Carolina, and the 50-acre tracts given the charity immigrants were too small to achieve economies of scale and competitive levels of efficiency for commercial production.

Failing to attract without continuous subsidy a sufficient number of whites to secure a military buffer zone and given the attractive potential profits of slave-operated plantation enterprises, the trustees eventually bowed to economic forces. Alternatively stated, the opportunity costs of resources (Economic Reasoning Proposition 2) were too high under the nonslave small farm institutional structure to attract labor and capital

Economic Insight 3.1

Social Engineering and Economic Constraints in Georgia, continued

without continued subsidies. By midcentury, slavery was legalized, and slaves began pouring into Georgia, which was converted to a Crown colony in 1751. By 1770, 45 percent of the population there was black.

This particular example of social-economic engineering reveals a wider truth. The most distinctive characteristic of production in the colonies throughout the entire colonial period was that land and natural resources were plentiful, but labor and capital were exceedingly scarce relative to land and natural resources and compared with the input proportions in Britain and Continental Europe. This relationship among the factors of production explains many institutional arrangements and patterns of regional development in the colonies.

Tobacco

Virginia exported tobacco to England within a decade after the settlement of Jamestown. The weed had been known in Europe for more than a century; sailors on the first voyages of exploration had brought back samples and descriptions of the ways in which natives had used it. Despite much opposition on moral grounds, smoking had increased in popularity during the sixteenth century; thus, even though James I viewed it "so vile and stinking a custom," it was a relief to the English to find a source of supply so that tobacco importation from the Spanish would be unnecessary. Tobacco needed a long growing season and fertile soil. Furthermore, it could be cultivated in small areas, on only partly cleared fields, and with the most rudimentary implements. All this suited the primitive Virginia community. But tobacco production had two additional advantages in the colonies: As successive plantings exhausted the original fertility of a particular plot, new land was readily available, and ships could move up the rivers of the Virginia coast to load their cargoes at the plantation docks. One challenge that lingered for most of the seventeenth century was that the colonists had much to learn about the proper curing, handling, and shipping of tobacco, and for many years the American product was inferior to tobacco produced in Spain. Nevertheless, colonial tobacco was protected in the English market, and the fact that it was cheaper led to steady increases in its portion of the tobacco trade. The culture of tobacco spread northward around Chesapeake Bay and moved up the many river valleys. By the end of the seventeenth century, there was some production in North Carolina.

The highly productive American tobacco regions swelled the supply of tobacco in British and European markets and, as will be discussed in great detail in chapter 5, tobacco prices fell precipitously until the last quarter of the seventeenth century. By the turn of the eighteenth century, it was apparent that the competition in colonial tobacco production would be won by large plantations and that if the small planters were to succeed at all, they would have to specialize in high-quality tobacco or in the production of food and other crops. From the work of David Klingaman we have learned that in the eighteenth century, substantial areas around the Chesapeake (especially in Maryland) turned to the production of wheat.

Larger production units were favored in tobacco cultivation because slaves worked in groups and could be supervised and driven. To achieve the best results, a plantation owner had to have enough slaves to ensure the economical use of a plantation manager. Supervision costs did not grow in proportion to the number of slaves owned and used;

therefore, per-unit costs fell as plantations grew in size (at least up to a point). A plantation with fewer than 10 slaves intermittently prospered, but only larger units earned substantial returns above cost, provided they were properly managed and contained sufficient acreage to avoid soil exhaustion. Thus, the wealthy or those who were able to secure adequate credit from English and Scottish merchants attained more efficient scales of tobacco production and, in so doing, became even wealthier and improved their credit standing further. We should not conclude that slaves were held only by the largest plantation owners, however; the crude statistics available today indicate that in pre-Revolutionary times, as later, large numbers of planters owned fewer than 10 slaves. Nonetheless, there was persistent pressure in the southern colonies to develop large-sized farms favored by lower per-unit costs.

Rice

Around 1695, the second of the great southern staples was introduced. Early Virginia colonists had experimented with rice production, and South Carolina had tried to cultivate the staple in the first two years after settlement, but success awaited the introduction of new varieties of the grain.[2] By the early 1700s, rice was an established crop in the area around Charleston, although problems of irrigation still remained.

It is possible to grow rice without intermittent flooding and draining, but the quality of the grain suffers. Rice was first cultivated in the inland swamps that could be flooded periodically from the rivers, but the flooding depended on uncertain stream flows. Besides, such a growing method could not be used on the extremely flat land that lay along the coast itself. Before long, a system of flooding was devised that enabled producers to utilize the force of tidal flows. Water control, originally a Dutch specialty, had grown in importance and sophistication in England (to drain marshes), and this knowledge was transferred to America. Dikes were built along the lower reaches of the rivers, and as the tide pushed back the fresh water, it could be let through gates into irrigation ditches crossing the fields.

Proper flooding remained hazardous to crops because no salt water could be let in, and proper drainage demanded painstaking engineering. But the heavy investment of capital was worthwhile because proper engineering permitted the two major tide-propelled floodings to occur at precisely the right times and the water could be removed just as accurately. Such fixed costs added to the prospects of scale economies in rice production, and much labor was needed to build the dikes and to plant and harvest.

Slaves were imported in great numbers during the eighteenth century for these purposes. The "task" system of working slaves, which gave each slave a particular piece of ground to cultivate, was utilized. The work was back breaking, similar to the "gang system" used in sugar production in the Caribbean, and it was carried out in hot, mosquito-infested swamps. Although contemporary opinion held that Africans were better able to withstand the ravages of disease and the effects of overexertion than were Europeans, the mortality rate among blacks in this region was high. Recent scholarship provides evidence that bears out this contemporary view. Blacks had disproportionately high rates of mortality in the northern mainland colonies, and whites as disproportionately higher death rates in the far southern and Caribbean colonies. Phil Coelho and Bob McGuire explain these differences in terms of the races coming into contact with pathogens for which they had little or no prior geographic exposure. Tropical diseases were particularly devastating to Europeans, less so to Africans.[3] Despite production difficulties, rice output steadily increased until the end of the colonial period, its culture finally extending from below Savannah up into North Carolina.

---

[2]Lewis C. Gray, *History of Agriculture in the Southern United States to 1860*, Vol. I (Washington, D.C.: Carnegie Institution of Washington, 1933), 278.

[3]Philip R. Coelho and Robert A. McGuire, "African and European Bound Labor in the British New World: The Biological Consequences of Economic Choices," *Journal of Economic History* 37 (1997): 83–115.

The cultivation of rice required advanced engineering techniques and much slave labor, but it remained a profitable crop for South Carolina and Georgia during the colonial period.

Indigo

To the profits from rice were added those from another staple—indigo, so named from a plant native to India. The indigo plant was first successfully introduced in 1743 by Eliza Lucas, a young woman who had come from the West Indies to live on a plantation near Charleston. Indigo almost certainly could not have been grown in the colonies without special assistance because its culture was demanding and the preparation of the deep blue dye required exceptional skill. As a supplement to rice, however, it was an ideal crop, both because the plant could be grown on high ground where rice would not grow and because the peak workloads in processing indigo came at a time of year when the slaves were not busy in the rice fields. Indigo production, fostered by a British subsidy of sixpence a pound, added considerably to the profits of plantation owners, thereby attracting resources to the area.

In emphasizing the importance of tobacco, rice, and indigo, we are in danger of overlooking the production of other commodities in the southern colonies. Deerskins and naval stores were exported from the Carolinas, and iron in quantity was shipped from the Chesapeake region. Throughout the South, there was a substantial output of hay and animal products and of Indian corn, wheat, and other grains. These items, like a wide variety of fruits and vegetables, were grown mostly to make the agricultural units as self-sufficient as possible. Yet upland farmers, especially in the Carolinas and Virginia, raised livestock for commercial sale and exported meat, either on the hoof or in cured form, in quantity to other colonies. In all the colonies, food for home consumption was a main economic activity.

Colonial agriculture depended heavily on such cash crops as indigo—shown here being processed in South Carolina from freshcut sheaves to final drying—and rice, shown previously in a plantation setting.

The Middle Colonies

The land between the Potomac and the Hudson Rivers was, on the whole, fertile and readily tillable and therefore enjoyed a comparative advantage in the production of grains and other foodstuffs. As the seventeenth century elapsed, two distinct types of agricultural operations developed there. To the west, on the cutting edge of the frontier, succeeding generations continued to encounter many of the difficulties that had beset the first settlers. The trees in the forests—an ever-present obstacle—had to be felled, usually after they had been girdled and allowed to die. The felled trees were burned and their stumps removed to allow for the use of horse-drawn plows. The soil was worked with tools that did not differ much from the implements used by medieval Europeans. A living had literally to be wrested from the earth. At the same time, a stable and reasonably advanced agriculture began to develop to the east of the frontier. The Dutch in New York and the Germans in Pennsylvania, who brought skills and farming methods from areas with soils similar to those in this region, were encouraged from the first to cultivate crops for sale in the small but growing cities of New York, Philadelphia, and Baltimore. Gradually, a commercial agriculture developed.

Wheat became the important staple, and although there was also a considerable output of corn, rye, oats, and barley, the economy of the region was based on the great bread grain. During the latter part of the seventeenth century, a sufficient quantity of wheat and flour was produced to permit the export of these products, particularly to the West Indies.

The kind of agricultural unit that evolved in the Middle colonies later became typical of the great food belts of the midwestern United States. Individual farms, which were considerably smaller in acreage than the average plantation to the south, could be operated by the farmer and his family with little hired help. Slaveholding was rare (except along the Hudson in New York and in Rhode Island) because wheat production was labor intensive only during planting and harvest periods and because there were no apparent economies of large-scale production in wheat, corn, or generalized farming as there were in the southern plantation staples, especially rice. It was normally preferable to acquire an indentured servant as a hand; the original outlay was not great, and the productivity of even a young and inexperienced servant was soon sufficient to return the owner's investment. The more limited growing season in the North also lowered the economic gains of slave labor in the fields. Finally, as Coelho and McGuire show, the northern climates had negative biological consequences for blacks relative to whites.

New England

Vital as the agriculture of New England was to the people of the area, it constituted a relatively unimportant part of commercial output for sale. Poor soils, uneven terrain, and a severe climate led to restricted commercial farming. The typical farm emphasized subsistence farming, growing only those crops necessary for family maintenance. Because it could be produced almost anywhere and because its yield even on poor land was satisfactory, Indian corn was the chief crop. Wheat and the other cereal grains, along with the hardier vegetables, were grown for family use. Due partly to climate and partly to the protection from wild predators that natural barriers furnished, the Narragansett region, including the large islands off its coast, became a cattle- and sheep-raising center. By the eve of the Revolution, however, New England was a net importer of food and fiber. Its destiny lay in another kind of economic endeavor, and from a very early date, many New Englanders combined farming with other work, thereby living better lives than they would have had they been confined to the resources of their own farms. Homecraft employments of all varieties were common features of rural life in all the colonies, especially in New England. Shipping and fishing were also major economic activities of this region.

THE EXTRACTIVE INDUSTRIES

Although most colonial Americans made their livings from agriculture, many earned their livelihoods indirectly from the land in what we will call *extractive pursuits*. From the forest came the furs and wild animal skins, lumber, and naval stores. From the coastal waters came fish and that strange mammal, the whale. From the ground came minerals, though only in small quantities during the early colonial years. From the various industries that were built around these products came an output second in value only to that of agriculture.

Furs, Forests, and Ores

The original 13 colonies were a second-rate source of furs by the late colonial period because the finest furs along the seaboard were processed quickly and the most lucrative catches were made long before the frontier moved into the interior.[4] It was the French, with their strong trade connections to Native Americans (who did most of the trapping), not the English, who were the principal furriers in North America (see Perspective 3.1 on 58). Nonetheless, farmers trapped furs as a sideline to obtain cash, although they caught primarily muskrats and raccoons, whose pelts were less desirable then, as now.

The forest itself, more than its denizens, became an economically significant object of exploitation. The colonials lived in an age of wood. Wood, rather than minerals and metals, was the chief fuel and the basic construction material. Almost without exception, the agricultural population engaged in some form of lumbering. Pioneers had to fell trees to clear ground, and used wood to build houses, barns, furniture, and sometimes fences. Frequently, they burned the timber and scattered the ashes, but enterprising farmers eventually discovered that they could use simple equipment to produce potash and the more highly refined pearlash. These chemicals were needed to manufacture glass, soap, and other products and provided cash earnings to many households throughout the colonies.

From the forests also came the wood and naval stores for ships and ship repair. White pine was unmatched as a building material for the masts and yards of sailing ships, and white and red oak provided ship timbers (for ribbing) of the same high quality. The pine trees that grew abundantly throughout the colonies furnished the raw material for the manufacture of naval stores: pitch, tar, and resin. In the days of wooden vessels, naval stores were indispensable in the shipyard and were used mostly for protecting surfaces and caulking seams. These materials were in great demand in both the domestic and British shipbuilding industries.

---

[4]Carl Bridenbaugh, *Cities in the Wilderness* (New York: Oxford University Press, 1971), 43, 191.

Perspective 3.1

American Indian Hunters and the Depletion of the Beaver

Early forms of territorial hunting rights (property rights) among North American tribes sustained stocks of game, because hunters, especially in forested areas, had incentives (Economic Reasoning Proposition 3: incentives matter) to limit their takings. In forested areas, game generally remained in a fixed area, so tribes or groups established rules, giving hunting areas to particular tribes or groups. Only in the case of exceptional circumstances, such as famine, fire, or the like, would hunters from another tribe be allowed to hunt in another's territory. When the English-owned Hudson Bay Company was established early in the seventeenth century, its demand for beaver furs for the markets of England and Europe encouraged Indian hunters to harvest larger quantities of beaver pelts. The French, along with the Hudson Bay Company, competed to set prices for furs and for axes, cloth, and other manufactures exchanged for the furs.

When the French entered the market in competition with the English, fur prices moved upward, encouraging more intensive hunting. Figures 3.1 and 3.2 show an index of prices at two major English trading forts, 1700 to 1763, and regional beaver population estimates. Greater competition alone did not deplete the beaver population, which, though declining, remained above self-sustaining levels.

The maximum sustained yield (the horizontal Pmsy line in the figures) indicates the amounts that could be taken consistent with the forest habitat being able to sustain the population. In the 1720s and 1730s, this maximum yield, just consistent with a sustained beaver population, was maintained, as shown in Figures 3.1 and 3.2. In the 1740s, however, a rise in demand and prices for furs in Europe plus greater competition between the French posts and England's Hudson Bay Company forts, combined to deplete the stock. Higher prices encouraged greater takings and overharvesting (Proposition 3), and because of increasing tribal migrations and dislocations, the Native American groups were unable to generate communally based or closed access property rights systems.

The tragedy of the commons arose with all its negative consequences. Intense and growing competition in the absence of appropriate property rights fails (Economic Reasoning Proposition 4: institutions matter). By the late colonial period, the colonies contained few beavers, and even farther west the beaver population was moving toward extinction.

(For more analysis, see Carlos and Lewis, 1999).

Considerable skilled labor was required to produce naval stores, and only in North Carolina, where slaves were specially trained to perform the required tasks, were these materials produced profitably without British subsidy.

The only mineral obtained by the colonials in any significant quantity was iron. The methods used in the colonial iron industry did not differ greatly from those developed in the late Middle Ages, although by the time of the Revolution, furnace sizes had increased greatly. In the seventeenth century, the chief source of iron was bog ore, a sediment taken from swamps and ponds. When this sediment was treated with charcoal in a bloomery or forge until the charcoal absorbed the oxygen in the ore, an incandescent sponge of metal resulted. The glowing ball of iron was removed from the forge and in a white-hot condition was hammered to remove the slag and leave a substantial piece of wrought iron.

Rich rock ores were discovered as the population moved inward, and during the eighteenth century, a large number of furnaces were built for the reduction of these ores. Pig iron could

Perspective 3.1

American Indian Hunters and the Depletion of the Beaver, continued

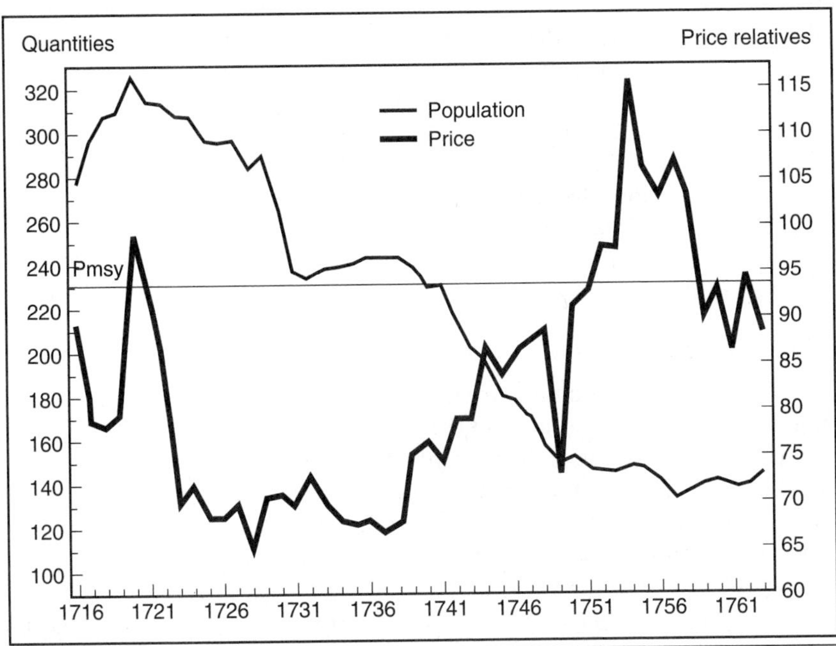

FIGURE 3.1 Fur Prices and Simulated Beaver Population: York Factory, 1716–1763

Source: Carlos and Lewis, 1999.

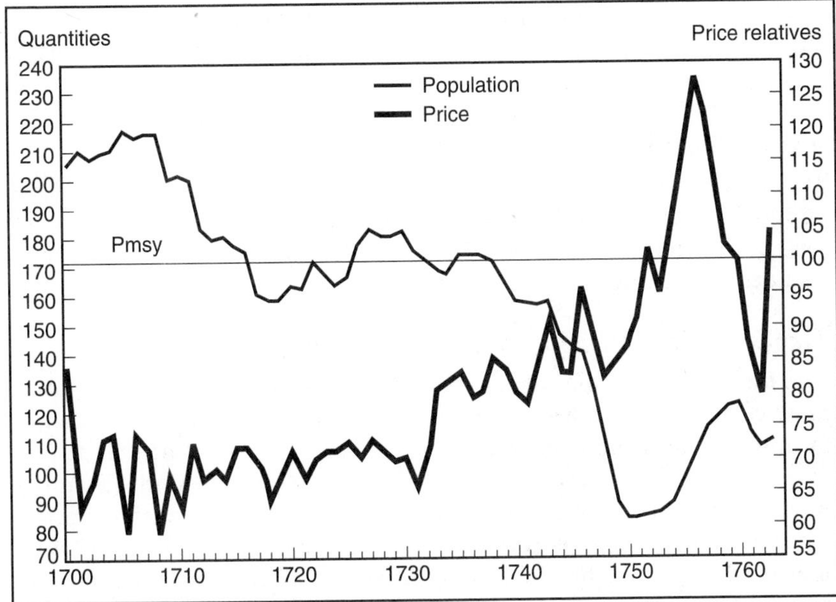

FIGURE 3.2 Fur Prices and Simulated Beaver Population: Fort Albany, 1700–1763

Source: Carlos and Lewis, 1999.

then be produced in quantity. A mixture of rock ore, charcoal, and oyster shells or limestone was placed in a square or conical furnace and then ignited. Under a draft of air from bellows worked by water power, the iron ore was reduced to a spongy metal, which as it settled to the bottom of the furnace alloyed itself with large amounts of carbon, thereby becoming what we call "cast iron." Poured into molds called "pigs" or "sows," the resulting metal could be either remelted and cast into final form later or further refined and reworked in a mill or blacksmith shop. The discussion of these rudimentary processes provides an important background that will help us understand the later development in the American iron and steel industry.

It is also worth noting that because of the simple processing required and an abundance of charcoal, the colonial iron industry was able to compete with that of the British Isles in the sale of bars and pigs. There is agreement that the number of forges and furnaces in the colonies just before the Revolution probably exceeded the number in England and Wales combined, and the annual output of wrought and cast iron by then was about 30,000 tons, or one-seventh of the world's output. But the colonies remained heavy net importers of finished iron products.

Sea Products

Although restricted primarily to the northern colonies, the occupations of fishing and whaling were of major importance in the development of the entire early colonial economy. The sea provided New Englanders a commodity for which there was a ready market, and there were also many splendid harbors to house small fishing vessels and plenty of timber with which to build them. But most important was the sizable market for the magnificent cod. The large, fat, hard-to-cure cod were consumed at home. The best cod were exported to Catholic Europe; the poorer grades were sent to the West Indies, where they were fed to slaves. Gloucester, Salem, Boston, and Marblehead became the chief home ports for the great fishing fleets.

In colonial times, whale oil was highly prized as both an illuminant and a lubricant, ambergris as a base for perfumes, and whalebone as a material for stays. Whaling was, therefore, a profitable and vigorous, if small, industry. Before 1700, whalers operated near the New England coast, but their take was small. During the eighteenth century, however, whalers ranged far and wide, and by 1775, more than 300 vessels of all sizes sailed from the Massachusetts ports, of which Nantucket was the great whaling center.

THE MANUFACTURING INDUSTRIES

The abundance of land and natural resources in the colonies and the sparse and scattered populations there discouraged manufacturing. Nevertheless, household production, mostly for self-sufficiency and outside the market, was pervasive, and craftshops, mills, and yards also deserve mention.

Household Manufacture and Craftshops

The first concern of the colonial household was the manufacture of food and clothing, and most colonial families had to produce their own. Wheat, rye, or Indian corn grown on the farm was ground into flour at the local gristmill, but the women of the family made plentiful weekly rations of bread and hardtack. Jellies and jams were made with enough sweetening from honey, molasses, or maple syrup to preserve them for indefinite periods in open crocks. The men of the family were rarely teetotalers, and the contracts signed by indentured servants indicate that nearly a third of the feeding costs of indentures was for alcoholic beverages. Beer, rum, and whiskey were easiest to make, but wines, mead, and an assortment of brandies and cordials were specialties of some households.

Making clothing—from preparing the raw fiber to sewing the finished garments—kept the women and children busy. Knit goods such as stockings, mittens, and sweaters were the

Whaling was a hazardous but profitable industry in early America and an important part of New England's seafaring tradition. New Bedford, where Captain Ahab started his quest for Moby Dick, and Nantucket were the main whaling centers of New England.

major items of homemade apparel. Linsey-woolsey (made of flax and wool) and jeans (a combination of wool and cotton) were the standard textiles of the North and of the pioneer West. Equally indestructible, though perhaps a little easier on the skin, was fustian, a blend of cotton and flax used mostly in the South. Dress goods and fine suitings had to be imported from England, and even for the city dweller, the purchase of such luxuries was usually a rare and exciting occasion.

Early Americans who had special talents produced everything from nails and kitchen utensils to exquisite cabinets. Everywhere the men of the family participated in the construction of their own homes, although exacting woodwork and any necessary masonry might be done by a specialist. Such specialists, of widely varying abilities, could be found both in cities and at country crossroads. Urban centers especially exhibited a great variety of skills, even at a rather early date. In 1697, for example, 51 manufacturing handicrafts, in addition to the building trades, were represented in Philadelphia.

The distinction between the specialized craftsman and the household worker, however, was not always clear in colonial America. Skilled slaves on southern plantations might devote all their time to manufacture; this made them artisans, even though their output was considered a part of the household. On the other hand, the itinerant jack-of-all-trades, who moved from village to village selling reasonably expert services, was certainly not a skilled craftsman in the European sense. Because of the scarcity of skilled labor, individual workers often performed functions more varied than they would have undertaken in their native countries; a colonial tanner, for example, might also be a currier (leather preparer) and a shoemaker. Furthermore, because of the small local markets and consequent geographic dispersal of nearly all types of production, few workers in the same trade were united in any particular locality.

For this reason, few guilds or associations of craftsmen of the same skill were formed. As an exception, however, we note that as early as 1648, enough shoemakers worked in Boston

The spinning wheel, the starting tool for homemade clothing, was a common utensil in the homes of colonial America.

to enable the General Court to incorporate them as a guild, and by 1718, tailors and cordwainers were so numerous in Philadelphia that they, too, applied for incorporation.[5]

Mills and Yards

To colonials, a mill was a device for grinding (grains), cutting (wood), or forging (iron). Until around the middle of the eighteenth century, most mills were crude setups, run by water power that was furnished by the small streams found all along the middle and north Atlantic coast. Throughout most of this period, primitive mechanisms were used; the cranks of sawmills and gristmills were almost always made of iron, but the wheels themselves and the cogs of the mill wheels were made of wood, preferably hickory. So little was understood about power transmission at this time that a separate water wheel was built to power each article of machinery. Shortly before the Revolution, improvements were made in the application of power to milling processes, and the mills along the Delaware River and Chesapeake Bay were probably the finest in the world at that time. In 1770, a fair-sized gristmill would grind 100 bushels of grain per day; the largest mills, with several pairs of stones, might convert 75,000 bushels of wheat into flour annually.

[5]Ibid

We can only suggest the variety of the mill industries. Tanneries with bark mills were found in both the North and the South. Paper-making establishments, common in Pennsylvania and not unusual in New England, were called "mills" because machinery was required to grind the linen rags into pulp. Textiles were essentially household products, but in Massachusetts, eastern New York, and Pennsylvania, a substantial number of mills were constructed to perform the more complicated processes of weaving and finishing. The rum distilleries of New England provided a major product for both foreign and domestic trade, and breweries everywhere ministered to convivial needs.

Shipbuilding

Although large-scale manufacturing was not characteristic of colonial economic activity, shipbuilding was an important exception. As early as 1631, barely a decade after the Pilgrims landed at Plymouth, a 30-ton sloop was completed in Boston.

During the seventeenth century, shipyards sprang up all along the New England coast, with Boston and Newport leading the way. New York was a strong competitor until the Navigation Act of 1651 (see chapter 4) dealt its Dutch-dominated industry a crippling blow, but the shipbuilding industry in New York again grew rapidly after 1720. By this time, Philadelphia boasted a dozen large shipyards along the banks of the Delaware River, and of the five major towns, only Charleston relied on ships produced by others. In the first half of the eighteenth century, the output of colonial shipyards reached its peak.

By 1700, the New England fleet exceeded 2,000 exclusive of fishing boats. American industry not only furnished the vessels for a large domestic merchant fleet, it also sold a considerable number of ships abroad, chiefly to the English. An uncontradicted estimate attributes nearly one-third of the ships in the British Merchant Marine in 1775 to American manufacture.[6]

Many of the ships constructed were small. But whether they were building a square-rigged, three-masted vessel of several hundred tons or a fishing boat of 10 tons, Americans had a marked and persistent advantage. The basis for success in colonial shipbuilding was the proximity of raw materials, mainly lumber. Although labor and capital costs were lower in England, the high costs of transport of bulky materials from the Baltic—or the colonies—made shipbuilding more expensive in England. Higher wages encouraged sufficient numbers of shipwrights and artisans to migrate from Holland and England to the colonies, where they built colonial vessels with low-cost materials for about two-thirds of British costs. Consequently, shipbuilding in the colonies was exceptional: Though most other manufacturers did not generate raw material cost savings enough to offset the much higher labor costs in the colonies, in this case, the high costs of transport of the bulky raw materials assured a comparative advantage of production in favor of the colonies. In addition, the Navigation Acts (discussed in chapter 4) equally encouraged shipbuilding, both in the colonies and in England. However, an important distinction arose between England and North America in the first century of manufacturing development. In England, raw materials were typically imported or brought to the craftsmen, but in the New World, workers located near raw materials.

The Merchant Marine

Finally, as the sizable New England fleet suggests, shipping services and other distribution services associated with the transportation, handling, and merchandising of goods were important commercial activities in the colonies. The merchant marines in New England and the Middle colonies, which employed thousands of men, were as efficient as the Dutch and English merchants in many trades throughout the world. Indeed, by the end of the

---

[6] Jacob Price, "A Note on the Value of Colonial Exports of Shipping," *Journal of Economic History* 36 (1976): 704–724.

Thanks to their ready supplies of first-class timber and naval stores, colonial shipbuilders enjoyed an early comparative advantage in shipbuilding.

colonial period, the colonies could boast of a sizable commercial sector, and as a source of foreign exchange earnings, monies earned from the sale of shipping services were second only to those earned from tobacco exports. Shipping and overseas trade as commercial activities were vital to the colonial economy.

OCCUPATIONAL GROUPS

Although the colonies established a rich diversity of economic activities, from a functional occupational standpoint, daily life was fairly stable. Occupational roles changed little over the years in settled areas; from today's perspective, occupational opportunities remained narrow and rigid. Most people expected the future to replicate the past, and most young people followed in the employment footsteps of their parents. Perspective 3.2 shows the traditionalism in the Native American culture.

The male population generally fit into one of several employment categories, the most predominant being family farmers. Other significant categories or classes were slave, indentured servant, unskilled laborer, and seaman. Upper middle classes included artisans, merchants, and landowning farmers, but the richest occupational groups included merchants in New England and the Middle colonies and large landholding planters in the South. As Edwin Perkins and Alice Jones inform us, the very wealthy were classified as esquires, gentlemen, or officials.

Most women participated in work to complement the work of the male head of the household. Child care, domestic service, livestock tending, and household production-dominated women's duties. Family farm life in particular, the most typical lifestyle of the period, had women and children engaged in handicraft production within the home. During harvest times, they usually turned to outdoor work to help the men. In seventeenth-century Maryland, for instance, Louis G. Carr and Lorena Welsh have shown that wives routinely spent the spring and summer months in the tobacco fields. In the Middle colonies, according to Joan Jensen, women typically helped in the easier tasks of spreading hay to dry, digging for potatoes, gathering flax, and picking fruit. Most away-from-home work for women, especially younger women, was in other people's homes. Such domestic service for extra income was common for women under the age of 25.

Perspective 3.2

Native American Family Structure

In contrast to the patriarchical family, social-economic structure of European settlers, the Iroquois and other eastern tribes developed a matrilinear family structure. As hunters, men were frequently absent from the household for long periods, often for months and sometimes even years at a time.This disengaged them from fatherly (and husband) responsibilities; therefore, the husband–wife relationship was not the most basic social relationship. Instead, the most fundamental foundation of the family was mother–daughter.

Women were the planters and harvesters, with corn the primary food source. Although all land was commonly owned by the nation, or tribe, loose ownership rights to individual plots could occur. From Anthony Wallace (1970, 24), we learn:

> An individual woman might, if she wished, "own" a patch of corn, or an apple or peach orchard, but there was little reason for insisting on private tenure: the work was more happily done communally, and in the absence of a regular market, a surplus was of little personal advantage, especially if the winter were hard and other families needed corn. In such circumstances hoarding led only to hard feelings and strained relations as well as the possibility of future difficulty in getting corn for oneself and one's family. (24)

The long-term relationships of mothers, daughters, granddaughters, and neighbors living communally minimized shirking and bad behavior, and the sharing provided a form of insurance against poor individual harvests and bad times.

It is important, as Alice Hanson Jones reminds us, to take special note of the inferior legal and political status of women and the fact of male dominance and patriarchal authority within the family. A woman was expected to be obedient to her husband, and marriage was accepted unquestionably as her proper destiny, regardless of class or status. For those who did not marry, the outlook for work was bleak.

To spin fiber or help in the household tasks of parents or relatives was likely for an unmarried woman (hence the term *spinster*, meaning an unmarried woman). Some, with education and special connections, might teach music, reading, or other skills.

Children began helping their parents at about the age of 7 or 8; by the age of 12, they were usually important apprentice-type workers in the home or fields. Child labor was very important, and maintaining the allegiance of children to labor on behalf of parents was a special problem for parents in the nonslave areas. Indeed, the problem was reflected even in the law. The laws of inheritance varied among the colonies but were consistent with the goals of economic efficiency and the maintenance of a reliable rural labor force. Southern colonies used primogeniture (oldest son inherits) because slaves supplied labor on the plantations, while the Middle and New England colonies typically used multigeniture (splitting estates among the sons) to better ensure work allegiance by sons.

SELECTED REFERENCES AND SUGGESTED READINGS

Adams, Donald. "Prices and Wages in Maryland 1750–1850." *Journal of Economic History* 46 (1986): 625–645.

Alston, Lee, and Morton Owen Shapiro. "Inheritance Laws Across Colonies: Causes and Consequences." *Journal of Economic History* 44 (1984): 277–287.

Bailyn, Bernard. *The New England Merchants in the Seventeenth Century*. Cambridge: Harvard University Press, 1955.

Bridenbaugh, Carl. *The Colonial Craftsman*. New York: New York University Press, 1950.

______. *Cities in the Wilderness: The First Century of Urban Life in America, 1625–1742*. New York: Oxford University Press, 1971.

Bruchey, Stuart. *The Colonial Merchant: Sources and Readings*. New York: Harcourt, Brace & World, 1966.

Carlos, Ann M., and Frank D. Lewis. "Indians, the Beaver, and the Bay: The Economics of Depletion in the Lands of the Hudson Bay Company 1700–1763." *Journal of Economic History* 53 (1993): 465–494.

______. "Property Rights and Competition in the Depletion of the Beaver: Native Americans and the Hudson Bay Company." In *The Other Side of the Frontier,* ed. Linda Barrington. Boulder: Westview, 1999, 131–149.

Carr, Louis G., and Lorena Walsh. "The Planting Wife: The Experience of White Women in Seventeenth Century Maryland." *William and Mary Quarterly* 34 (1977): 542–571.

Carroll, Charles. *The Timber Economy of Puritan New England.* Providence, R.I.: Brown University Press, 1973.

Clark, Victor S. *History of Manufacturers in the United States 1607–1860.* Washington, D.C.: Carnegie Institution of Washington, 1916.

Coelho, Philip R., and Robert A. McGuire. "African and European Bound Labor in the British New World: The Biological Consequences of Economic Choices." *Journal of Economic History* 37 (1997): 83–115.

Coon, David. "Eliza Lucas Pinckney and the Reintroduction of Indigo Culture in South Carolina." *Journal of Southern History* (1976): 61–76.

Doerflinger, Thomas. "Commercial Specialization in Philadelphia's Merchant Community 1750–1791." *Business History Review* 57 (1983): 20–49.

Goldenberg, Joseph. *Shipbuilding in Colonial America.* Charlottesville: University Press of Virginia, 1976.

Gray, Lewis C. *History of Agriculture in the Southern United States to 1860.* Washington, D.C.: Carnegie Institution of Washington, 1933.

Gray, Ralph, and Betty Wood. "The Transition From Indentured Servant to Involuntary Servitude in Colonial Georgia." *Explorations in Economic History* 13 (October 1976): 353–370.

Greenberg, Michael. "William Byrd II and the World of the Market." *Southern Studies* (1977): 429–456.

Hedges, James. *The Browns of Providence Plantation: The Colonial Years*. Cambridge: Harvard University Press, 1952.

Henretta, James. "Economic Development and Social Structure in Colonial Boston." *William and Mary Quarterly* 22 (1965).

Jensen, Joan. *Loosening the Bonds: Mid-Atlantic Farm Women 1750–1850.* New Haven: Yale University Press, 1986.

Jones, Alice Hanson. "The Wealth of Women, 1774." *Strategic Factors in Nineteenth Century American Economic History*, eds. Clauda Goldin and Hugh Rockoff. Chicago: University of Chicago Press, 1992.

Klingaman, David. "The Significance of Grain in the Development of the Tobacco Colonies." *Journal of Economic History* (1969): 267–278.

Menard, Russell R. "Economic and Social Development of the South." In *The Cambridge Economic History of the United States*, Vol. I, eds. Stanley L. Engerman and Robert E. Gallman. New York: Cambridge University Press, 1996, 249–295.

McCusker, J. J., and R. R. Menard. Part II and Chapters 14 and 15 in *The Economy of British America, 1607–1789*. Chapel Hill: University of North Carolina Press, 1985.

McManis, Douglas. *Colonial New England: A Historical Geography*. New York: Oxford University Press, 1975.

Norton, Thomas. *The Fur Trade in Colonial New York, 1686–1766*. Madison: University of Wisconsin Press, 1974.

Paskoff, Paul. *Industrial Evolution: Organization, Structure, and Growth of the Pennsylvania Iron Industry, 1750–1860*. Baltimore: Johns Hopkins University Press, 1983.

Perkins, E. J. Section 1 in *The Economy of Colonial America*, 2d ed. New York: Columbia University Press, 1988.

Price, Jacob. "A Note on the Colonial Exports of Shipping." *Journal of Economic History* 36 (1976): 704–724.

Schweitzer, Mary. *Custom and Contract: Household Government, and the Economy in Colonial Pennsylvania*. New York: Columbia University Press, 1987.

Shammas, Carol. "The Female Social Structure of Philadelphia in 1775." *Pennsylvania Magazine of History and Biography* (1983): 69–138.

Stackpole, Edward. *The Sea-Hunters: The New England Whalemen During Two Centuries, 1635–1835*. Philadelphia: Lippincott, 1953.

Vickers, Daniel. "The First Whalemen of Nantucket." *William and Mary Quarterly* 40 (1983): 560–583.

______. "The Northern Colonies: Economy and Society, 1600–1775." In *The Cambridge Economic History of the United States*, Vol. I, eds. Stanley L. Engerman and Robert E. Gallman. New York: Cambridge University Press, 1996, 209–248

Wallace, Anthony C. *The Death and Rebirth of the Seneca*. New York: Knopf, 1970.

Chapter Four

The Economic Relations of the Colonies

Chapter Theme

The economic relations of the colonies with England and other overseas areas are a central part of the story of economic progress in the colonies. Overseas areas were economically important as markets for colonial products, as sources of manufactured goods and other items demanded by American consumers, and as sources of labor and capital. Additional investment came from England for provision of defense. This chapter analyzes the commercial relations and commodity exchanges of the colonies, the legal and business aspects of their shipping and trade, and the special problems of money, capital, and debt in overseas and domestic commerce. It shows how the colonies fit into the world economy and into the English trading realm.

ENGLISH MERCANTILISM AND THE COLONIES

In the long period from 1500 to 1800, western European nation-states were all influenced by a set of ideas known as the mercantile system or mercantilism. Mercantilist doctrine and institutions were not created by a particular group of thinkers, nor were they ever set forth in systematic fashion by a "school" of economists, but the ideas were important because they were held by practical businesspeople and heads of state who—at different times in different countries—strongly influenced public policy and institutional change.

The primary aim of mercantilists, as John McCusker (1996) reminds us, was to achieve power and wealth for the state. Spain's experience in the sixteenth century had led most observers to conclude that an inflow of gold and silver was a potent help in attaining needed goods and services and in prosecuting wars. To generate an inflow of gold or silver through trade, the value of exports should exceed the value of imports. The gold or silver paid for the differences between exports and imports. With such additions to amounts of money, called *specie*, domestic trade would be more brisk and tax revenues higher. It was further held that the state could attain great power only if political and economic unity became a fact. In a day when productivity depended so greatly on the skills and knowledge of workers, it was crucial to keep artisans at home. If all the materials necessary to foster domestic industry were not available, they could best be obtained by establishing colonies or friendly foreign trading posts from which such goods could be imported. A strong merchant marine could carry foreign goods, thereby helping to secure favorable trade balances, and merchant ships could be converted for war if the need arose.

Mercantilists believed that these means of achieving national power could be made effective by the passage and strict enforcement of legislation regulating economic life. England had begun to pass such laws by the end of the fifteenth century, but its mercantilist efforts did not fully flower until after the British, together with the Dutch, had successfully turned back Spanish power. Indeed, it was largely a consequence of England's desire to surpass Holland—a nation that had reached the zenith of its power during the first half of the seventeenth century—that British legislation was passed marking the beginning of an organized and consistent effort to regulate colonial trade.

Adherence to mercantilist principles was implicit in the colonizing activity that the English began in the early 1600s. Almost as soon as Virginia tobacco began to be shipped in commercial quantities to England, King James I levied a tax on it while agreeing to prohibit the growth of competing tobacco in England. Taxes, regulation, and subsidies were all used as mercantile policies, but the primary ones that affected the colonies were the Navigation Acts.

The Early Navigation Acts

During the English Civil War, which began in 1642 and ended in 1649, the British had too many troubles of their own to pay much attention to regulating trade with the colonies. In this period, Americans had slipped into the habit of shipping their goods directly to continental ports, and the Dutch made great inroads into the carrying trade of the colonies. In 1651, Parliament passed the first of the so-called Navigation Acts, directed primarily at prohibiting the shipping of American products in Dutch vessels. Not until after the Restoration, however, was England in a position to enforce a strict commercial policy, beginning with the Navigation Acts of 1660 and 1663.

These acts were modified from time to time by hundreds of policy changes; at this point, it is sufficient to note the three primary categories of trade restriction:

1. All trade of the colonies was to be carried in vessels that were English built and owned, commanded by an English captain, and manned by a crew of whom three-quarters were English. English was defined as "only his Majesty's subjects of England, Ireland, and the Plantations." Of great importance to colonists was the fact that colonists and colonial ships were both considered "English" under the law.
2. All foreign merchants were excluded from dealing directly in the commerce of the English colonies. They could engage in colonial trade only through England and merchants resident there.
3. Certain commodities produced in the colonies could be exported only to England (or Wales, Berwick-on-Tweed, or other English colonies—essentially any destination within the Empire). These "enumerated" goods included sugar, tobacco, cotton, indigo, ginger, and various dyewoods (fustic, logwood, and braziletto). The list was later amended and lengthened, and Scotland was added as a legal destination after 1707.

It is important to keep these three categories of restrictions firmly in mind. Although they were the cause of occasional protests on the part of the colonists, they caused practically no disruption of established trade patterns during the remaining decades of the seventeenth century. Indeed, the acts were only loosely enforced throughout most of the seventeenth century. When in 1696 a system of admiralty courts was established to enforce the Navigation Acts, their impact became somewhat more pronounced. Indeed, from the beginning of the

TABLE 4.1 Top Ten Commodity Exports from the 13 Colonies (average annual values, 1768–1772, in thousands of pounds sterling)

Tobacco	£766
Bread and flour	410
Rice	312
Fish	154
Wheat	115
Indigo	113
Corn	83
Pine boards	70
Staves and headings	65
Horses	60

Source: Derived from Gary M. Walton and James F. Shepherd, The Economic Rise of Early America *(Cambridge, England: Cambridge University Press, 1975), Table 21, 194–195.*

eighteenth century, most spheres of colonial commercial activity were regulated. One relaxation of the regulations in the 1730s is noteworthy. At that time, some enumerated goods were allowed to be shipped directly to ports south of Cape Finisterre, in Northern Spain.

EXPORTS, IMPORTS, AND MARKETS

The enumeration of certain products requiring direct shipment to England suggests their special importance from the perspective of the mother country. Table 4.1 confirms this importance also from the perspective of the colonies. Tobacco, rice, and indigo accounted for more than half the value of the top 10 exports, and these were predominantly from southern soils. The dominance of the southern staples as a proportion of total colonial exports was greater in the seventeenth century than in the eighteenth, but their lead and importance were maintained right up to the decade of independence. These top ten exports made up 77 percent of the total commodity exports on average between 1768 and 1772.

Miscellaneous manufactured goods of all varieties composed the lion's share of imports from England; a Philadelphia merchant provided a contemporary description of his import trade from Britain:

> . . . all kinds of British manufactories in great abundance and India goods, etc. In the last of the winter or early spring [we] choose to import our linens and other things fit for summer, the latter end of which we should have our woolen goods of all kinds ready for fall sale to use in winter. The spring is the best time for iron mongery, cutleryware, furniture for furnishing houses, and all other brass and iron work. Our imports of those articles are very large, the people being much employed in agriculture, husbandry, clearing and improving lands, but slow progress is made in the manufactories here.[1]

Wine and salt came from southern Europe, and sugar, molasses, and rum imports from the West Indies.

A useful summary of the relative importance of the various trading partners of the colonies is shown in Figure 4.1. Great Britain was the main overseas region to receive colonial exports (56 percent of the total) and to supply colonial imports (80 percent of the

[1] Letter from Thomas Clifford, Philadelphia, to Abel Chapman, Whitby, England, July 25, 1767, as quoted from Ann Bezanson et al., *Prices in Colonial Pennsylvania* (Philadelphia: University of Pennsylvania Press, 1935), 263.

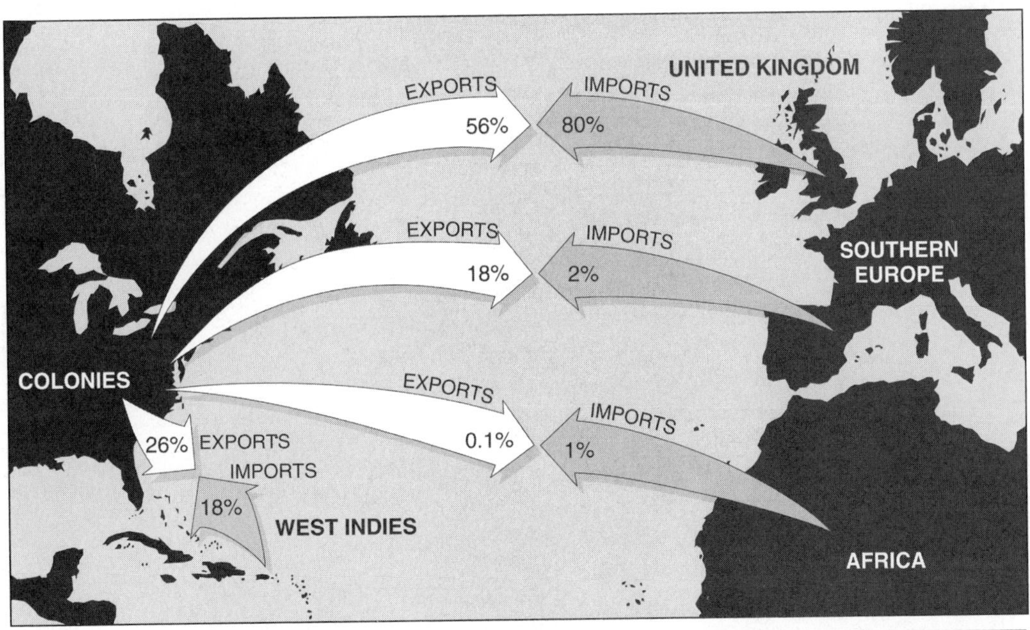

FIGURE 4.1 Percentage Distribution of Total Colonial Trade *The United Kingdom was colonial America's dominant trading partner in exports and imports, followed by the West Indies and southern Europe.*

Source: James F. Shepherd and Gary M. Walton, Shipping, Maritime Trade, and the Economic Development of North America *(Cambridge, England: Cambridge University Press, 1972), 160–161.*

total).[2] Nevertheless, the West Indies and southern Europe were important trading partners, especially as markets for American exports.

Another feature of colonial trade is revealed in Figure 4.2 (page 72). Here we see the sharp difference among the regions' ties to various overseas markets. Commerce in the southern regions was overwhelmingly dominated by the trades to Great Britain. Alternatively, the trades of the Middle colonies were more evenly balanced among Great Britain, southern Europe, and the West Indies. New England's most important trading partner was the West Indies. Colonial imports in each region arrived predominantly by way of Great Britain. Few products were imported from southern Europe, and commodity trade with Africa was insignificant.

OVERSEAS SHIPPING AND TRADE

Although urban residents numbered little more than 5 percent of the total population in the late colonial period, the major port towns with safe harbors and accessible productive hinterlands became key locations for trade and commerce. Map 4.1 (page 73) shows the 10 most populated towns in 1776. Philadelphia, with 40,000 people, was second only to London in population within the Empire, slightly less in number than Davis, California, or Iowa City, Iowa, today. New York (25,000), Boston (16,000), Charleston (12,000), and Newport (11,000) were the only other towns in excess of 10,000 residents. Note that all of the top 10 urban centers were port towns. Because these were both readily accessible and points of change in transportation modes, from sea- to rivercraft or land vehicles and animals, they were greatly advantaged as trade centers. In an age when bluff-bowed sailing ships typically took six weeks to cross the Atlantic and relaying news to the interior took

[2] Because of reshipment allowed by the Navigation Acts, not all of these amounts were actually consumed or produced in the British Isles.

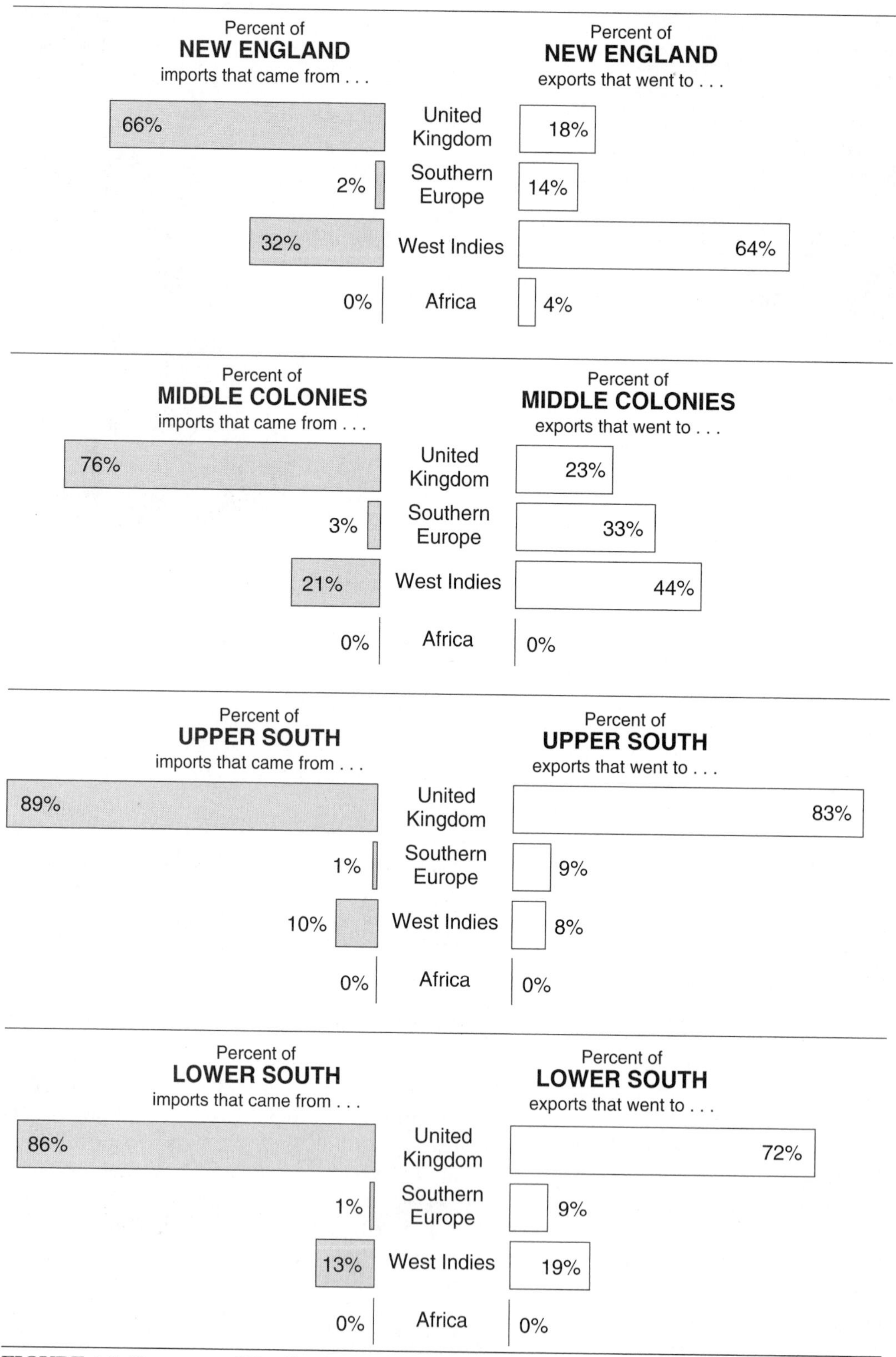

FIGURE 4.2 Percentage Distribution of Colonial Trade by Region

Source: James F. Shepherd and Gary M. Walton, Shipping, Maritime Trade, and the Economic Development of North America *(Cambridge, England: Cambridge University Press, 1972), 160–161.*

MAP 4.1 *Safe harbors and productive hinterlands were the conditions favoring these 10 leading urban centers in the colonies.*

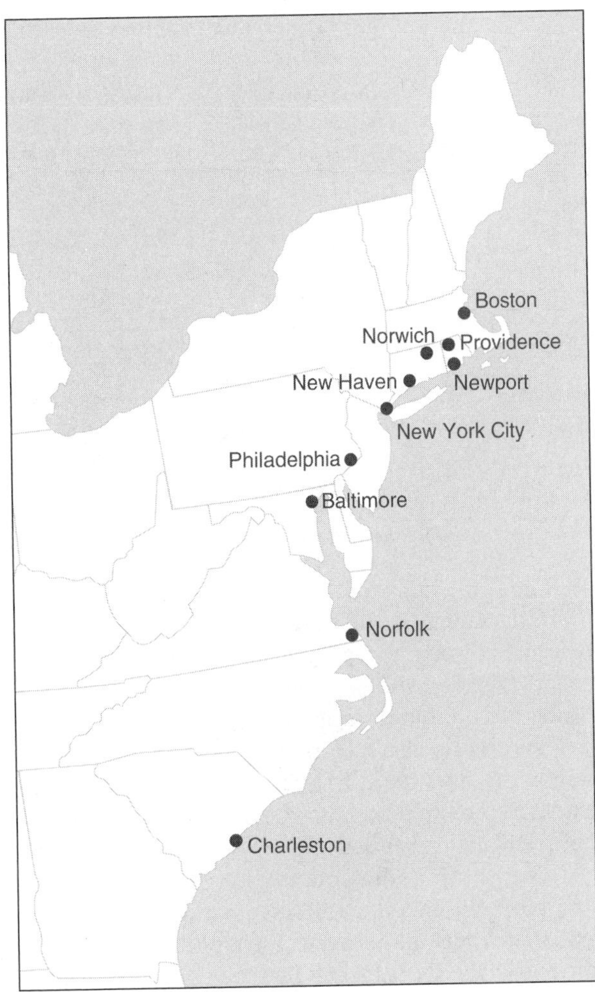

additional weeks, the port towns also had a special communication advantage. Lastly, travel and shipment were always much less expensive by water than by land, especially for bulky, weighty items typical of the colonies. Landlocked cities were a rarity in history before the railroad age.

Advantages of location and communication also went far in determining overseas shipping and trade patterns. For example, British ships almost completely dominated the trades of the southern colonial regions, whereas New England shippers dominated the New England–West Indies trade route.

Table 4.2 on page 74 shows ownership proportions of shipping on several key routes of commerce. It is clear that neither British nor colonial shippers dominated or had a comparative advantage in shipping on all routes. For example, colonists owned 96 percent of the tonnage clearing New England to the West Indies and 85 percent to Great Britain, but only 12 percent of the tonnage clearing the Upper South to Great Britain. Why did British shippers dominate the southern trades to England but get left behind in the trades between New England and Great Britain, and between New England and the West Indies? Three critical factors provide the answer: (1) the high risks of maritime trade, (2) the problems of acquiring and responding to information about markets (prices and trade opportunities), and (3) the opportunities to lower labor costs by discharging crews in home ports.

TABLE 4.2 Mid-Eighteenth Century Ownership, Proportions of Shipping

SHIPS CLEARING	TO GREAT BRITAIN			TO SOUTHERN EUROPE			TO WEST INDIES		
	Colonial Owned	British Owned	West Indian Owned	Colonial Owned	British Owned	West Indian Owned	Colonial Owned	British Owned	West Indian Owned
From New England	85	15	0	93	7	0	96	3	1
From Middle Colonies	72	28	0	75	25	0	80	20	0
From Upper South	12	88	0	88	12	0	85	0	15
From Lower South	23	77	0	0	100	0	51	23	26
SHIPS ENTERING	**FROM GREAT BRITAIN**			**FROM SOUTHERN EUROPE**			**FROM WEST INDIES**		
Into New England	68	32	0	84	16	0	96	1	3
Into Middle Colonies	63	37	0	76	24	0	84	16	0
Into Upper South	9	91	1	33	67	0	61	23	16
Into Lower South	12	88	0	20	80	0	30	43	27

Source: Gary M. Walton, "New Evidence on Colonial Commerce," Journal of Economic History *28 (September 1968): 368.*

Consider first the problem of trading and marketing goods. New England and other colonial merchants typically consigned their goods either to ship captains or selling agents, called factors, who were stationed in overseas markets and took delivery of the goods. Since these relationships necessitated placing a high degree of trust in a third party, it is not surprising that colonial merchants favored colonial ship captains. After all, greater familiarity and more frequent contact between merchant and agent lowered the risks of trade. So colonial merchants most often favored colonial shippers to gain trust and better ensure higher revenues in their exchanges.

Due to the rudimentary forms of communication and transportation at the time, geographical closeness to a market was an important advantage. For example, British shippers and merchants in the tobacco trade could acquire information about changing market conditions in the Chesapeake Bay area and in Europe more easily than New England shippers could. However, in trades to and from the West Indies, colonial shippers and merchants were nearer to their markets and could respond more quickly to fluctuations in them. Being close to a market reduced the time and cost of obtaining market information, allowing merchants to respond with more timely cargo arrivals and reduce the risks of trade. As British shipowner Michael Atkins stated in a 1751 letter to his colonial colleague, "Traders at the Northern Colonies have all the West India business to themselves, Europeans can have no encouragement for mixing with them in the commodities of provisions and lumber. You time things better than we and go to market cheaper."[3]

Finally, the efficient use of labor time was always an important factor. It was general practice in colonial times for crews to be paid while a vessel was docked in foreign ports, and crews were normally discharged only at the end of the voyage in the home port. This meant that British crews in the tobacco trade were paid for the time they spent at sea and in southern colonial ports, but not for their port time in England. Therefore, New England shippers were at a disadvantage on this trade route, because they paid wages both in British ports and in the Chesapeake Bay. Conversely, colonial shippers faced lower labor costs on trade routes between their home ports and the Caribbean.

These same considerations played a large role in determining the routes of trade. It was not too long ago that students of American colonial history were taught that shuttle routes (out and direct return) were common and typical of the southern colonial trades—

[3]See Richard Pares, *Yankees and Creoles* (Cambridge, Mass.: Harvard University Press, 1956), 8.

mainly to England—but that the New England and Middle colonial shippers usually engaged in triangular and other more complex patterns.[4] It has been shown, however, that shuttle patterns were the dominant pattern for all colonial regions.[5] For most trades, shuttle patterns cut costs. Although the desire to keep vessels as fully loaded as possible encouraged "tramping" from port to port to take advantage of differences in demand and cargo availability, such a practice often incurred major offsetting costs. For example, a New England ship captain in the West Indies trade, acting on behalf of his merchant, would attempt to locate the best markets for the commodities he carried. This might require several voyages among the islands before agreeing on prices, the medium of exchange, and even the question of past debts. Transactions were often complex, even when the merchants and captains were acquainted with each other. Of course, in unfamiliar markets, poor communications, credit limitations, and other vexatious details compounded the difficulties. For all these reasons, arrivals at strange ports often resulted in delays and costly extensions of port times; therefore, captains usually maintained regular runs between a limited number of familiar destinations. The practice of discharging crews only in their home ports further supported the growth of shuttle trade routes because such routes increased the percentage of total port time that was home port (wage-free) time.

INTERCOLONIAL COMMERCE

For similar reasons, colonials dominated the great volume of coastwise commerce. Early in the seventeenth century, the Dutch of New Amsterdam had anticipated the profit potential in distributing European products along the colonial coast in exchange for tobacco, furs, grain, and fish, which were then sent to Holland. After the Dutch lost power in North America in 1664, their hold on these trades declined, and New Englanders—together with enterprising merchants in New York and Philadelphia—dominated the coastal trades of North America.

In terms of the money value of products exchanged, coastal commerce was less than overseas trade with either Britain or the West Indies, but it was equal to each of these major trade branches in physical volume. As James Shepherd and Samuel Williamson have shown, just before the Revolution, coastwise trade comprised about one-third of the volume of total overseas trade. Compared with the North, the coastwise commerce of the South was much less important, but even there it contributed perhaps one-fifth of the tonnage that entered and cleared southern ports.[6]

With regard to commerce within the interior and between the countryside and towns, we can say little in quantitative terms. Thanks to recent work by a host of scholars, including James A. Henretta, Winifred B. Rothenberg, and Thomas M. Doerflinger, much of it based on probates, tax lists, and other original sources, we know much more about the rich diversity of rural trade and activity.[7] Statistical estimates of volume still elude us, however.

---

[4] American history college textbooks in the 1960s and before commonly emphasized these descriptions. Some high school history texts still do. Famous triangles included New England–Africa–West Indies (to New England); New England–southern Europe–England (to New England); and New England–West Indies–England (to New England). For examples, see Dudley Dillard, *Economic Development of the North Atlantic Community* (Englewood Cliffs: Prentice Hall, 1967), 197–198; Ross M. Robertson, *History of the American Economy*, 2d ed. (New York: Harcourt, Brace & World, 1964), 80–81; Harold F. Williamson, ed., *The Growth of the American Economy*, 2d ed. (Englewood Cliffs: Prentice Hall, 1951), 50–51; Edward Kirkland, *A History of American Economic Life* (New York: Appleton-Century-Crofts, 1960), 111–112; and Chester W. Wright, *Economic History of the United States* (New York: McGraw-Hill, 1941), 153–154.

[5] See Table 4.2 and its source (Gary M. Walton, "New Evidence on Colonial Commerce").

[6] E. R. Johnson et al., *History of Domestic and Foreign Commerce of the United States* (Washington, D.C.: Carnegie Institution of Washington, 1915), 171–172.

[7] For examples, see their chapters in Ronald Hoffman et al., eds., *The Economy of Early America: The Revolutionary Period, 1763–1790* (Charlottesville: University Press of Virginia, 1988).

Boston's natural endowments helped the city attain a place of prominence as a trading and shipping center; but the mountains to the west inhibited access to the hinterland, and Boston ultimately fell behind New York in the commercial rivalry between these two great ports.

Back-country people traded their small agricultural surpluses for goods they could not produce themselves—salt, medicines, ammunition, cotton yarn, tea or coffee, and the like. In the villages and towns, households were less self-sufficient, although even the wealthiest homes produced some goods for everyday consumption.

In the complex of colonial domestic trade between country and town, it became common practice for the town merchant to extend credit to farmers, either directly or through the so-called country traders who served as intermediaries. Advances were made for the purposes of obtaining both capital equipment, such as tools and building hardware, and the supplies necessary for day-to-day existence. At the end of the growing season, farmers brought their produce to town to discharge their debts.

MONEY AND TRADE

One of the most persistent problems in the colonies was establishing and maintaining an acceptable currency. Among friends and acquaintances especially, barter trade and exchanges on account were common. Money was needed for general commerce, however, to facilitate exchange among merchants and farmers. Money also served as a unit of account and as a liquid form of wealth.

Commodity Money

One of the earliest forms of money, borrowed from the Indians, was wampum, black and white polished beads made from clam shells. Wampum circulated as legal tender for private debts in Massachusetts until 1661 and was used as money in New York as late as 1701. In Maryland and Virginia, tobacco was initially the principal medium of exchange, while other colonies designated as "country pay" (acceptable for taxes) such items as hides, furs, tallow, cows, corn, wheat, beans, pork, fish, brandy, whiskey, and musket balls. Harried public officials were often swindled into receiving a poor quality of "country pay."

Clearly, one of the major problems in using commodity money, besides inconvenience, spoilage, and storage difficulties, was quality control because it was in an individual's self-interest to make payments whenever possible with low-quality goods.

One of the earliest domestically initiated regulations, the Maryland Tobacco Inspection Act of 1747, addressed this issue. The act was mainly designed to increase the value of tobacco exports from Maryland.[8] This move toward quality control ultimately did raise the value of Maryland's tobacco exports, but it also set firm standards of quality control for tobacco as money. In fact, because paper certificates called inspection notes were given on inspected tobacco, the circulation of money became easier. A Maryland planter in 1753 reported on

> . . . the Advantage of having Tobacco Notes in my pocket, as giving me credit for the quantity mentioned in them wherever I went, and that I was thereby at large to dispose of them when, to whom, and where I pleased; whereas, before this Act, my credit could not be expected to go beyond my own Neighborhood, or at farthest, where I might be known.[9]

Despite the problems, commodity money was extensively used in the colonies in the seventeenth century. By the early eighteenth century, however, both specie (gold or silver) and paper currency were common in the major seaboard cities, and by the end of the colonial period, commodities—particularly furs—were accepted only in communities along the western frontier.

Coins, Specie, and Paper Money

Because of the sizable colonial trades with many overseas areas, the gold and silver coins of all the important commercial countries of Europe and their dependencies in the Western Hemisphere were freely exchanged throughout the eastern seaboard. More important than English coins, which could not be legally exported from Britain to the colonies, were the silver coins of the Spanish mint. These were struck for the most part in Mexico City and Lima and introduced into the colonial economy via vigorous trading with the Spanish colonies. English-speaking people referred to the "piece of eight" (as the old Spanish peso was called) as a "dollar," probably because it was about the size of the German thaler. Spanish dollars were so common in the colonies that the coin was eventually adopted as the monetary unit of the United States. The fractional coin, known as the "real" or "bit," was worth about $12\frac{1}{2}$ cents, or one-eighth of a Spanish dollar, and was important in making change.[10]

Although Massachusetts first attempted to mint coins of low bullion content as early as 1652, the colonies eventually turned to paper to increase their meager and undependable money supply. The promissory notes of well-known individuals and bills of exchange drawn on English merchants readily exchanged hands for several months. In addition, treasurers of the various colonies began to issue promissory notes in advance of tax collection and issue written orders to town officers requiring the payment of obligations from local stores; like other negotiable instruments, these pieces of paper were exchanged on endorsement as money.[11]

---

[8] For an excellent analysis of the impact of the act and evidence on tobacco prices, see Mary McKinney Schweitzer, "Economic Regulation and the Colonial Economy: The Maryland Tobacco Inspection Act of 1747," *Journal of Economic History* 40 (1980): 551–570.

[9] *Maryland Gazette*, April 5, 1753, as reported in Schweitzer (1980), 564.

[10] The "piece of eight" was so called in colloquial language because of the numeral VIII impressed on one side to indicate its value of eight reales. In many parts of the United States, the expressions *two bits*, *four bits*, and *six bits* are still used today.

[11] See Curtis P. Nettels, *The Money Supply of the American Colonies Before 1720* (Madison: University of Wisconsin Press, 1934), 250–251.

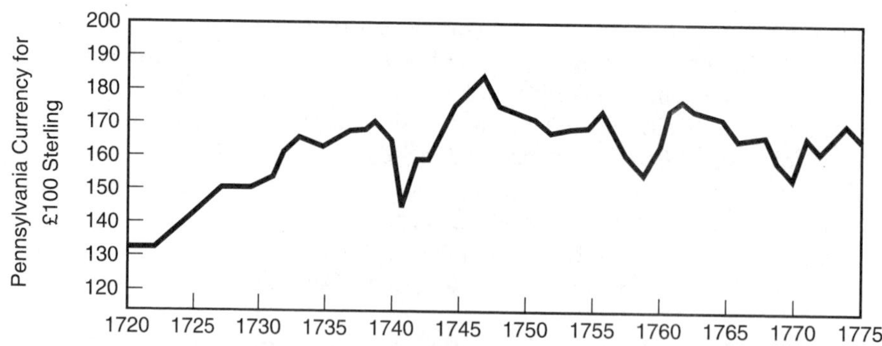

FIGURE 4.3 Annual Rate of Exchange in London for Pennsylvania Currency. *The exchange rates between English sterling and Pennsylvania's paper currency moved upward between 1720 and 1739, taking more Pennsylvania money to buy an English pound. In later periods, the sterling rate fell.*

Source: Historical Statistics *(Washington: Government Printing Office, 1976), Series Z585.*

In 1690, Massachusetts issued the first bills of credit to pay soldiers. During the next 65 years, at least eight other colonies followed this example to meet financial emergencies, especially payments of war-related efforts. Bills of credit were issued with the proviso that they were to be redeemed in specie at some future date; in the meantime, they were accepted for taxes by the issuing colony. Such redemption provisions, although restricted, facilitated the free circulation of these bills as money. In some states—notably Rhode Island, Massachusetts, Connecticut, and South Carolina—the bills were commonly overissued, thereby depreciating their value relative to specie. The same difficulty was encountered with the paper of the publicly owned "banks" established by colonial governments. These institutions, unlike anything we call a bank today, issued "loan bills" to individuals, usually based on the security of land or houses. Borrowers used the bills to meet their obligations and were usually required to repay the debt, with interest, in annual installments.

Occasionally, despite public issues of paper, private remedies were still undertaken, as exemplified by one merchant's April 1761 announcement in the *Maryland Gazette*:

> As I daily suffer much inconvenience in my Business for Want of small Change, which indeed is a universal Complaint of almost everybody in any Sort of Business, I intend to . . . Print . . . a Parcel of small Notes, from Three Pence to Two Shillings and Six Pence each, to pass Current at the same Rate as the Money under the Inspecting Law, and to be Exchanged by me . . . for good Spanish Dollars at Seven Shillings and Six Pence each Dollar.[12]

In this fashion, transaction costs were lowered, especially on retail and small-lot exchanges.

MONEY, DEBTS, AND CREDITORS

Historically, most paper issues in the colonies invited little attention from England, but over time, debtors more frequently attempted to pay off old obligations with depreciated paper. Using paper currency as legal tender, not only in tax payments but in private transactions as well, became well established by custom and law in New England.

Figure 4.3 illustrates the problem and traces the exchange rate of Pennsylvania paper currency for English sterling in London. In the late 1740s, nearly £180 Pennsylvania currency was needed to equal £100 sterling. The discrepancy between the currency's face value

[12]From Joseph A. Ernst, *Money and Politics in America, 1755–1775* (Chapel Hill: University of North Carolina Press, 1973), 154–155. For more on this issue, see John R. Hanson II, "Small Notes in the American Colonies," *Explorations in Economic History* 17 (1980): 411–420.

STOCK MONTAGE, INC.

Crowded prisons in seventeenth-century England held many debtors. The colonization of Georgia, in part, had a purpose of relieving debtor-filled jails.

and its market value was the source of the conflict between colonial debtors and English creditors. English merchants were normally willing to accept currency at market value, but debtors pointed to colonial laws stating that creditors had to accept paper money at face value (£1 colonial currency for £1 debt in English sterling). Ultimately, the Crown and Parliament were forced into the controversy. In response to complaints by British creditors, the Currency Act of 1751 restricted New England colonies to new bills of credit of no more than two years' duration and for no private transactions. Furthermore, existing paper note issues were to be retired as they fell due. More important from the point of view of its ultimate political consequences was the Currency Restraining Act of 1764. This act extended the provisions of the Currency Act of 1751 to all the colonies. Precipitated by events in Virginia, which after 1755 had issued £250,000 in bills of credit with full legal tender provisions, the act brought loud protests from residents in the southern colonies. Meanwhile, British merchants, who objected that debts due in specie were being paid in paper money issued in great quantity during the French and Indian War, nodded approval. Coming as it did during a postwar recession, the Currency Restraining Act aroused much animosity. By 1773, amid growing antagonism, Parliament relented and permitted the colonies to use currency issues as legal tender at face value for public payments but not for private ones.

Note that paper money at that time was uniquely American. Although invented and used in ancient China, paper money was not used anywhere in the world after 1500 until reintroduced by the mainland colonists. A paper currency that was widely acceptable stands as one of the great legacies of the colonists.

TRADE DEFICITS WITH ENGLAND

It is important to reemphasize here that mercantilist measures were implemented by the Crown to regulate trade and generate favorable trade balances for England. In addition, because European manufactured goods were in great demand in the New World, colonists

TABLE 4.3 Values and Balances of Commodity Trade Between England and the American Colonies (annual averages by decade, in thousands of pounds sterling)

	IMPORT	EXPORT	DEFICIT
1721–1730	£ 509	£ 442	£ 67
1731–1740	698	559	139
1741–1750	923	599	324
1751–1760	1,704	808	896
1761–1770	1,942	1,203	739

Source: James F. Shepherd and Gary M. Walton, Shipping, Maritime Trade, and the Economic Development of North America *(Cambridge, England: Cambridge University Press, 1972), 42.*

TABLE 4.4 Average Annual Commodity Trade Balances of the 13 American Colonies, 1768–1772 (in thousands of pounds sterling)

	GREAT BRITAIN AND IRELAND	SOUTHERN EUROPE	WEST INDIES	AFRICA	ALL TRADES
New England	£–0,609	£+048	£–36	£+19	£–0,577
Middle Colonies	–0,786	+153	–10	+01	–0,643
Upper South	–0,050	+090	–09	00	+0,031
Lower South	–0,023	+048	+44	0	+0,069
Total	£–1,468	£+339	£–11	£+20	£–1,120

Notes: (1) A plus sign denotes a surplus (exports exceed imports); a minus sign, a deficit (imports exceed exports). (2) Values are expressed in prices in the mainland colonies; thus, import values include the costs of transportation, commissions, and other handling costs. Export values are also expressed in colonial prices and, therefore, do not include these distribution costs.

Source: James F. Shepherd and Gary M. Walton, Shipping, Maritime Trade, and the Economic Development of North America *(Cambridge, England: Cambridge University Press, 1972), 115.*

faced chronic deficits, especially in their trade with England. Trade deficits in the colonies resulted in a continual drain of specie from colonial shores and encouraged the use of paper money substitutes. Table 4.3 shows the size and trend of these trade deficits with England over much of the eighteenth century. As highlighted in Table 4.4, most of these deficits were incurred by New England and the Middle colonies, but even the Southern colonies frequently faced deficits in their commodity trade with England.

How did the colonists pay for their trade deficits? Benjamin Franklin's reply to a Parliamentary committee in 1760 explaining Pennsylvania's payment of its trade deficit with England was the following:

> The balance is paid by our produce carried to the West Indies, and sold in our own islands, or to the French, Spaniards, Danes, and Dutch; by the same carried to other colonies in North America, as to New England, Nova Scotia, Newfoundland, Carolina and Georgia; by the same carried to different parts of Europe, as Spain, Portugal and Italy: In all which places we receive either money, bills of exchange, or commodities that suit for remittance to Britain; which, together with all the profits of the industry of our merchants and mariners arising in those circuitous voyages and the freights made by their ships, center finally in Britain to discharge the balance and pay for British manufactures continually used in the province or sold to foreigners by our traders.[13]

As emphasized by the esteemed Franklin, colonial trade deficits to Britain could be paid by surpluses earned in trades to other overseas areas as well as by earnings from shipping and other mercantile services.

[13]Quoted in Harold U. Faulkner, *American Economic History*, 8th ed. (New York: Harper & Row, 1960), 81.

Other sources of foreign exchange, such as payments by the British forces stationed in the colonies, also affected the inflow of sterling. To determine the relative importance of these and other sources of exchange earnings (and losses), we need to assess the various components of the colonies' overall balance of payments. (See Economic Insight 4.1 on page 82.)

Interpretations: Money, Debt, and Capital

Having assessed the colonies' balance of payments, we turn now to its impact on the colonial economy. The estimated remaining annual colonial deficit of £20,000 to £40,000 was paid either by an outflow of specie or by growing indebtedness to Britain. Temporary net outflows of specie undoubtedly did occur, thereby straining trade and prices in the colonies. Certainly, contemporary complaints of money scarcity, especially specie, indicate that this often happened. But no significant part of this normal deficit could have been paid with precious metals. The colonists could not sustain a permanent net outflow of specie because gold and silver mines were not developed in colonial North America. Typically, then, the outflow of specie to England was matched by an inflow from various sources of colonial exchange earnings. Nevertheless, the erratic pattern of specie movement and the issuance of paper money of uncertain value caused monetary disturbances, as reflected in price movements and alterations in rates of exchange among the currencies. But most colonists preferred to spend rather than to accumulate a stock of specie. After all, limited specie was simply another manifestation of a capital-scarce economy. To the colonists, it was more desirable to receive additional imports—especially manufactures—than to maintain a growing stock of specie.

The final remaining colonial deficits were normally financed on short-term credit, and American merchants usually purchased goods from England on one-year credit. This was so customary, in fact, that British merchants included a normal 5 percent interest charge in their prices and granted a rebate to accounts that were paid before the year ended. And in Virginia, Scottish firms generally established representatives in stores to sell or trade British wares for tobacco and other products. Short-term credit was a normal part of day-to-day colonial exchanges in these instances.

The growth of short-term credit reflected the expanding Atlantic trades and represented a modest amount of increasing colonial indebtedness to Britain. Sizable claims against southern planters by British merchants after the Revolution[14] have encouraged some historians to argue that the relationship between London merchants and southern planters was disastrous at that time and even to argue that increasing colonial indebtedness to Britain provided impetus for the Revolution. But was this, in fact, so?

By adding the "invisible" earnings and ship sales to the regional commodity trade deficits (and surpluses), we obtain these rough averages of the regional deficits (–) and surpluses (+) in the colonies:[15]

New England –£50,000   Middle colonies –£350,000   Southern colonies +£240,000

---

[14]Of the approximately £5,000,000 claimed by British merchants in 1791, more than £2,300,000 was owed by Virginia, nearly £570,000 by Maryland, £690,000 by South Carolina, £380,000 by North Carolina, and £250,000 by Georgia. However, nearly one-half of these amounts represented accumulated interest on deficits that had been in effect since 1776. Moreover, Aubrey Land argues that these claims were exaggerated by as much as 800 percent and that the Americans honored only one-eighth of such claims. See Aubrey C. Land, "Economic Behavior in a Planting Society: The Eighteenth Century Chesapeake," *Journal of Southern History* 32 (1967): 482–483.

[15]The regional division of shipping earnings and other "invisibles" is derived from James F. Shepherd and Gary M. Walton, *Shipping, Maritime Trade, and the Economic Development of North America,* chapter 8 (Cambridge, England: Cambridge University Press, 1972). Because the ownership of vessels is not given separately for the Upper South and Lower South, we have combined these two regions here, but undoubtedly, the Upper South earned the greater portion of the combined £240,000 surplus. All ship sales have been credited to the northern regions; £100,000 to New England and £40,000 to the Middle colonies.

Economic Insight 4.1

A Balance of Payments for the 13 Colonies

A balance of payments study clarifies many critical issues. It can determine how the deficits to England were paid and show the size of net specie drains from the colonies or indicate the magnitude of growing indebtedness of colonists to British creditors. It can show the inflows of capital into the colonies and suggest the magnitude of possible British subsidization of colonial economic development. A balance of payments is an accounting framework in which debits and credits always balance. In short, one way or another, things get paid for, with goods, money, or IOUs (debt).This is true for people and true for nations (and colonies) as well.

Surviving information on the myriad of exchanges for the years from 1768 to 1772 gives us a reasonably clear picture of the colonies' balance of payments in the late colonial period. A breakdown of the colonies' commodity trade balances with the major overseas areas during this period is provided in Table 4.4.These data confirm the findings presented earlier in Table 4.3, indicating that sizable deficits were incurred in the English trade, especially by New England and the Middle colonies. Somewhat surprisingly, even the colonies' commodity trade to the West Indies was unfavorable (except for the trade of the Lower South). However, trades to southern Europe generated significant surpluses (augmented slightly by the African trades), which were sufficient to raise the southern colonial regions to a surplus position in their overall commodity exchanges.

Although commodity exchanges made up the lion's share of total colonial exchanges, the colonies did have other sources of foreign exchange earnings (and losses) as well. Table 4.5 begins with colonial commodity exchanges indicating the £1,120 aggregate deficit in that category.

The most important source of foreign exchange earnings to offset that average deficit was the sale of colonial shipping services. Shipping earnings totaled approximately £600,000 per year in the late colonial period. In addition, colonial merchants earned more than £200,000 annually through insurance charges and commissions. Together, these "invisible" earnings offset more than 60 percent of the overall colonial commodity trade deficit. Almost 80 percent of these invisible earnings reverted to residents of New England and the Middle colonies. Thus, the mercantile activities of New Englanders and Middle colonists, especially in the West Indian trade, enabled the colonies to import large quantities of manufactured goods from Great Britain. When all 13 colonies are considered together, invisible earnings exceeded earnings from tobacco exports—the single most important colonial staple export.

Another aspect of seafaring, the sale of ships, also became a persistent credit item in the colonies' balance of payments. As Jacob Price (1976) has shown, colonial ship sales averaged at least £140,000 annually from 1763 to 1775, primarily to England. Again, the lion's share of these earnings went to New England shipbuilders, but the Middle colonies also received a portion of the profits from ship sales. Taken together, ship sales and "invisible" earnings reduced the colonies' negative balance of payments to only £160,000.

In contrast to these earning sources, funds for the trade of human beings were continually lost to foreign markets. An average of approximately £80,000 sterling was spent annually for the 5,000 to 10,000 indentured servants who arrived each year during the late colonial period. Most of these servants were sent to Pennsylvania and the Chesapeake Bay area. A more sizable amount was the nearly £200,000 spent each year

Economic Insight 4.1

The Balance of Payments for the 13 Colonies, continued

to purchase approximately 5,000 slaves. More than 90 percent of these slaves were sent to the southern colonies, especially to the Lower South in the later colonial period.

Finally, expenditures made by the British government in the colonies on defense, civil administration, and justice notably offset the remaining deficits in the colonists' current account of trade. Table 4.5 does not indicate the total amount of these costs to Great Britain. Instead, it shows how much British currency was used to purchase goods and services in the colonies and how much was paid to men stationed there. The net inflow for these expenditures averaged between £440,000 and £460,000 from 1768 to 1772, reducing the net deficit in the colonial balance of payments for these years to £40,000 per year at most, and probably less.

TABLE 4.5 Balance of Payments for the 13 Colonies, 1768–1772 (in thousands of pounds sterling)

	DEBITS	CREDITS
Commodities		
Export earnings		£2,800
Imports	£3,920	
Trade deficit	1,120	
Ship sales to foreigners		140
Invisible earnings		
Shipping cargoes		600
Merchant commissions, insurance, etc.		220
Payments for human beings		
Indentured servants	80	
Slaves	200	
British collections and expenditures		
Taxes and duties	40	
Military and civil expenditures[a]		440–460
Payments deficit financed by specie flows and/or increased indebtedness		£20–40

[a]*Gwyn's estimates of total expenditures for military and civil purposes for 1768–1772 are £365, but Thomas's study suggests higher arms payments by nearly £100,000 yearly for the same period. Neither accounts for savings by men stationed in the colonies who returned some of their earnings home; thus, the £440–460 range; £460 assumes no savings sent home.*

***Sources:** Data compiled from Gary M. Walton and James F. Shepherd,* The Economic Rise of Early America *(Cambridge, England: Cambridge University Press, 1979), Table 9, 101; Julian Gwyn, "British Government Spending and the North American Colonies, 1740–1775," in* The Atlantic Empire before the American Revolution, *ed. Peter Marshall and Glyn Williams (London: Cass, 1980), 74–84, fn. 7, and in* Journal of Imperial and Commonwealth History *(1980): 74–87, fn. 7; and Peter D. G. Thomas, "The Cost of the British Army in North America, 1763–1775,"* William and Mary Quarterly *(1988): 510–516.*

Clearly, the major deficit regions were north of the Chesapeake Bay area, primarily in the Middle colonies. The southern regions were favored with more than a sufficient surplus in their current accounts of trade to pay for their purchases of slaves and indentured servants.

A fair number of planters availed themselves of greater credit from abroad. Nevertheless, it appears there was no growing indebtedness on average in the South at this time, and British expenditures for military and administrative purposes eliminated the negative New England balance and reduced most of the Middle colonies' balances as well.[16]

Nevertheless, England's claims were real enough, even if exaggerated. But remember that British merchants and their colonial representatives normally extended credit to southern planters and accepted their potential harvests as collateral. Usually, of course, the harvests came in, and the colonists' outstanding debts were paid. But with the outbreak of the Revolution, this picture changed radically. Colonial credit normally extended throughout the year was still outstanding at the end of the year because agents or partners of British firms had retreated home before the crops were harvested and the debts were paid. But the mere existence of these debts did not indicate growing indebtedness—nor did it provide motivation for colonial revolt.

The capital inflows that did occur were rarely channeled directly into long-term investments in the colonies, and British merchants held few claims on such investments. Nevertheless, it is important to realize that because commercial short-term credit was furnished by the British, colonial savings were freed for other uses: to make long-term investments in land improvement, roads, and such physical capital as ships, warehouses, and public buildings. For the purposes of colonial development, British short-term credit represented a helping hand, and its form was much less important than its amount.

However, with the highly important exception of military and civil defense, the colonies apparently were not subsidized by Britain to any great extent. For the most part, the formation of capital in the New World depended on the steady accretion of savings and on investment from the pockets of the colonists themselves. It is impossible to determine precisely how much was annually saved and invested during the late colonial period. According to our estimates, which will be elaborated in chapter 5, annual incomes probably averaged at least £11 sterling per person in the colonies. Because nearly 2.5 million people were living in the colonies on the eve of the Revolution, if we assume a savings rate of not less than 9 percent (£1 out of £11), total capital accumulation per year would have exceeded £2.5 million at that time. Thus, the capital inflow from Britain probably accounted for 1 or 2 percent of capital formation in the colonies.

The sizable estimates of British military expenditures in North America between 1763 and 1775 (by Peter Thomas, 1988) and of civil and military expenditures for the longer period from 1740 to 1775 (by Julian Gwyn, 1984) support these general conclusions of small net deficits in the colonies' balance of payments throughout much of the late colonial period. Only the substantial British expenditures for military and administrative purposes reveal a form of British subsidization or colonial dependency in the decades just prior to the Revolution.

---

[16]Further alteration of the regional deficits and surpluses would have resulted from coastal trade among the regions. Surprisingly, however, the major regions in the 13 colonies appear to have earned surpluses in coastal trade. Florida, the Bahamas, and the Bermuda Islands and the northern colonies of Newfoundland, Nova Scotia, and Quebec were the deficit areas in coastal trade. See James F. Shepherd and Samuel H. Williamson, "The Coastal Trade of the British North American Colonies, 1768–1772," *Journal of Economic History* 32 (1972): 803.

SELECTED REFERENCES AND SUGGESTED READINGS

Andrews, Charles M. *The Colonial Period of American History.* Vol. 4 of *England's Commercial and Colonial Policy* (New Haven: Yale University Press, 1938).

Barrow, Thomas. *Trade and Empire: The British Customs Service in Colonial America, 1660–1775* (Cambridge: Harvard University Press, 1967).

Becker, Robert A. *Revolution, Reform, and the Politics of Taxation in America: 1763–1783* (Baton Rouge: Louisiana State University Press, 1980).

Beer, George L. *British Colonial Policy, 1754–1765* (Gloucester: Smith, 1958).

Bernstein, M. L. "Colonial and Contemporary Monetary Theory." *Explorations in Entrepreneurial History* 3, no. 3, 2d series (Spring 1966).

Breen, Timothy H. *Tobacco Culture: The Mentality of the Great Tidewater Planters on the Eve of the Revolution* (Princeton: Princeton University Press, 1985).

Brock, Leslie. *The Currency System of the American Colonies, 1700–1764* (New York: Arno, 1975).

Bruchey, Stuart. *The Roots of American Economic Growth 1607–1861: An Essay in Social Causation* (London: Hutchinson University Library, 1965).

———. *The Colonial Merchant: Sources and Readings* (New York: Harcourt, Brace & World, 1966).

Coleman, D. C., ed. *Revisions in Mercantilism* (London: Methuen, 1969).

Dickerson, Oliver M. *American Colonial Government 1696–1765* (Cleveland: Clark, 1912).

———. *The Navigation Acts and the American Revolution* (Philadelphia: University of Pennsylvania Press, 1951).

Ernst, Joseph. *Money and Politics in America, 1755–1775* (Chapel Hill: University of North Carolina Press, 1973).

Evans, Emory. "Planter Indebtedness and the Coming of the Revolution in Virginia, 1776 to 1796." *William and Mary Quarterly* 19, 2d series (1962): 511–533.

Greene, Jack P., and Richard M. Jellison. "The Currency Act of 1764 in Imperial-Colonial Relations, 1764–1776." *William and Mary Quarterly* 18 (4), 2d series (October 1961).

Gwyn, Julian. "British Government Spending and the North American Colonies, 1740–1775." *Journal of Imperial and Commonwealth History* 8 (1984): 74–84.

Hacker, Louis M. "The First American Revolution." *Columbia University Quarterly,* part 1 (September 1935). Reprinted in Gerald D. Nash. *Issues in American Economic History* (New York: D. C. Heath, 1972).

Hanson, John R. "Money in the Colonial American Economy: An Extension." *Economic Inquiry* (1979): 281–286.

———. "Small Notes in the American Economy." *Explorations in Economic History* 21 (1984): 411–420.

Harper, Lawrence A. *The English Navigation Laws* (New York: Columbia University Press, 1939).

———. "Mercantilism and the American Revolution." *Canadian Historical Review* (March 1942). Reprinted in Gerald D. Nash. *Issues in American Economic History* (New York: Heath, 1972).

Hughes, J. R.T. *Social Control in the Colonial Economy* (Charlottesville: University Press of Virginia, 1976).

Kulikoff, Allan. "The Economic Growth of the Eighteenth-Century Chesapeake Colonies." *Journal of Economic History* 39 (1979): 275–288.

Lester, Richard A. "Currency Issues to Overcome Depressions in Pennsylvania, 1723 and 1729." *Journal of Political Economy* 71 (1963): 324–375.

McCusker, John J. *Monetary Experiments: Early American and Recent Scandinavian* (Princeton: Princeton University Press, 1939).

———. "British Mercantilist Policies and the American Colonies." In *The Cambridge Economic History of the United States*, Vol. I, eds. Stanley L. Engerman and Robert E. Gallman (New York: Cambridge University Press, 1996), 337–362.

Neal, Larry. "Interpreting Power and Profit in Economic History: A Case Study of the Seven Years' War." *Journal of Economic History* 37 (1977): 20–35.

Nettels, Curtis P. "British Policy and Colonial Money Supply." *Economic History Review* 3 (1931).

———. *The Money Supply of the American Colonies Before 1720* (Madison: University of Wisconsin Press, 1934).

Perkins, Edwin J. Chapters 2 and 7 in *The Economy of Colonial America*, 2d ed. (New York: Columbia University Press, 1988).

Price, Jacob. "The Economic Growth of the Chesapeake and the European Market, 1697–1775." *Journal of Economic History* 24 (1964): 496–511.

———. "Economic Function and the Growth of American Port Towns in the Eighteenth Century." In *Perspectives in American History*, Vol. 8, eds. D. Fleming and B. Bailyn (Cambridge: Harvard University Press, 1974).

———. "A Note on the Value of Colonial Exports of Shipping." *Journal of Economic History* 36 (1976): 704–724.

———. *Capital and Credit in British Overseas Trade: The View from the Chesapeake, 1700–1776* (Cambridge: Harvard University Press, 1980).

Rosenberg, Nathan, and L. E. Birdzell, Jr. Chapter 4 in *How the West Grew Rich* (New York: Basic Books, 1986).

Schweitzer, Mary McKinney. "Economic Regulation and the Colonial Economy: The Maryland Tobacco Inspection Act of 1747." *Journal of Economic History* 40 (1980): 551–570.

Shepherd, James F., and Gary M. Walton. *Shipping, Maritime Trade and the Economic Development of Colonial North America* (Cambridge: Cambridge University Press, 1972).

Shepherd, James F., and Samuel Williamson. "The Coastal Trade of the British North American Colonies 1768–1772." *Journal of Economic History* 32 (1972): 783–810.

Smith, Bruce. "Some Colonial Evidence on Two Theories of Money: Maryland and the Carolinas." *Journal of Political Economy* 93 (1985): 1178–1211.

Studenski, Paul, and Herman Krooss. *Financial History of the United States* (New York: McGraw-Hill, 1952).

Thomas, Peter D. G. "The Cost of the British Army in North America, 1763–1775." *William and Mary Quarterly* 45 (1988): 510–516.

Ver Steeg, Clarence. *The Formative Years, 1607–1763* (New York: Hill & Wang, 1964).

Walton, Gary M., and James F. Shepherd. *The Economic Rise of Early America* (Cambridge, England: Cambridge University Press, 1979).

Weiss, Roger. "The Issue of Paper Money in the American Colonies, 1720–1774." *Journal of Economic History* 30 (1970): 770–785.

———. "The Colonial Monetary Standards of Massachusetts." *Economic History Review* 27 (4), 2d series (November 1974).

Wicker, Elmus. "Colonial Monetary Standards Contrasted: Evidence from the Seven Years' War." *Journal of Economic History* 45 (1985): 860–884.

Chapter Five

ECONOMIC PROGRESS AND WEALTH

Chapter Theme

Because of high levels of migration and rapid population growth, total output in the colonies grew at high rates throughout the colonial period. Standards of living for the average colonist also grew at rates that were high by contemporary standards and comparable to gains in Britain, Holland, and France. The sources of growth of per capita income form an important part of the story of economic development, because these sources of progress lifted the colonial economy to a position where it could become independent from England. These sources are found principally in case (or sectoral) studies of productivity change. Although the economy grew and prospered, people and regions did not gain equally, and already, substantial inequality of wealth (and income) existed among people and places as settlements in the wilderness grew into towns and centers of trade.

GROWTH AND CHANGE IN THE COLONIAL ECONOMY

The many local and regional economies that composed the total colonial economy were always in a state of flux. Because the colonies began literally as settlements in the wilderness, and because war and other frontier disturbances were frequent, it is particularly difficult to systematically portray the economic growth of the colonies. The data are simply too scant to provide any systematic and comprehensive measures of economic growth.

In 1964, George R. Taylor triggered a debate that has not yet run its course. In his presidential address to the Economic History Association, Taylor argued that before 1710, very little economic growth, in terms of sustained increases in real per capita income, occurred in the colonies (it was "slow and irregular"), but that then, between 1710 and 1775, it averaged "slightly more than 1 percent per annum."[1] A handy rule of thumb, known as the Rule of 70, shows the impact of annual growth rates. If r is the rate of growth in percentage terms and t is the number of years that the growing quantity takes to double, then $r \times t = 70$. Taylor's assertion of 1 percent implies a doubling of income per capita in 70 years: $t = 70/1$, or 70 years. Did Taylor's claim of an early eighteenth-century acceleration really take place, and did per capita incomes really almost double between 1710 and 1775, as the 1 percent rate implies? Did such economic advances continue indefinitely thereafter, or did periods of stagnation reappear?

[1] George R. Taylor, "American Economic Growth before 1840: An Exploratory Essay," *Journal of Economic History* 24 (1964): 437.

Because of data limitations on real per capita income, firm answers elude us.[2] Through recent scholarly efforts, however, fragments of information have appeared to significantly advance our understanding of the pace and main sources of growth in the colonies.

Productivity Change in Agriculture

The major economic activity in the colonies was agriculture, and progress in this sector had a particularly strong bearing on total colonial production. Because agriculture was such a significant part of total output, total average gains were significantly influenced by advances (or lack of advances) in this sector. Moreover, it is important to remember that economic progress in real per capita terms stems primarily from human efforts to raise productivity—the increase of output relative to the inputs of labor, capital, and land. Therefore, we will devote particular attention to periods of change in productivity and to the causes of the agricultural improvements that were introduced.

Tobacco in the Upper South

An obvious starting point is the dominant colonial staple, tobacco. Information on tobacco prices in the Chesapeake Bay area, as shown in Figure 5.1, suggests that most of the increases in the productivity of tobacco occurred very early in the colonial period. Ranging between 20d. and 30d. sterling per pound in the early 1620s, tobacco prices fell to less than 3d. per pound around 1630. A second phase, lasting approximately four decades, followed that precipitous decline. This time, the average price decreased to about a penny per pound. Of course, short-term periods of cyclical variations occurred, but tobacco prices stayed at that low price throughout most of the remaining peacetime years.

Little doubt exists that these two early periods of declining tobacco prices represented major surges in productivity. According to Allan Kulikoff (1979), tobacco output per worker doubled between 1630 and 1670. The demand for tobacco in Europe was persistently growing, and the costs of the labor and land required to produce tobacco did not decrease over these years. Declining wages or rents cannot explain the lower costs of tobacco, so these must have been largely caused by increases in output per unit of input (land, labor, and capital in combination)—that is, by gains in productivity. Terry Anderson and Robert Thomas (1978) also estimate very high productivity advances in tobacco: over the last three-quarters of the seventeenth century, the advance was nearly 1.5 percent per year on average. Very little productivity advance occurred in tobacco in the eighteenth century, however, and undoubtedly, the major period of progress in tobacco cultivation was during the seventeenth rather than the eighteenth century.

This characteristic of rapid early gains and subsequent periods of slower advance has always been common to the growth patterns of production in firms and industries. In colonial times, before the age of widespread technological advances, productivity gains stemmed primarily from trial and error and learning by doing. In agriculture, the fruits of these efforts generally materialized within a few decades of crop introduction. Sometimes, as in the case of tobacco, the introduction of a new seed type generated a surge of crop productivity. Also, in the early phases of experimentation, the colonists found ways to combine and adjust soils, seeds, labor implements, and other agricultural inputs to their optimum uses. In later stages of agricultural development, improvements were more gradual, based on a slower-paced accumulation of knowledge about the most productive uses of available soils and resources. In some instances, such as the colonists' futile attempts at wine production and silk cultivation, these efforts ceased in the experimentation phase.

[2]It is important to remember that in measuring changes of income, we often neglect other factors that affect the quality of life, such as the amount of leisure time enjoyed, conditions of health, environment, personal attributes, and even the distribution of wealth.

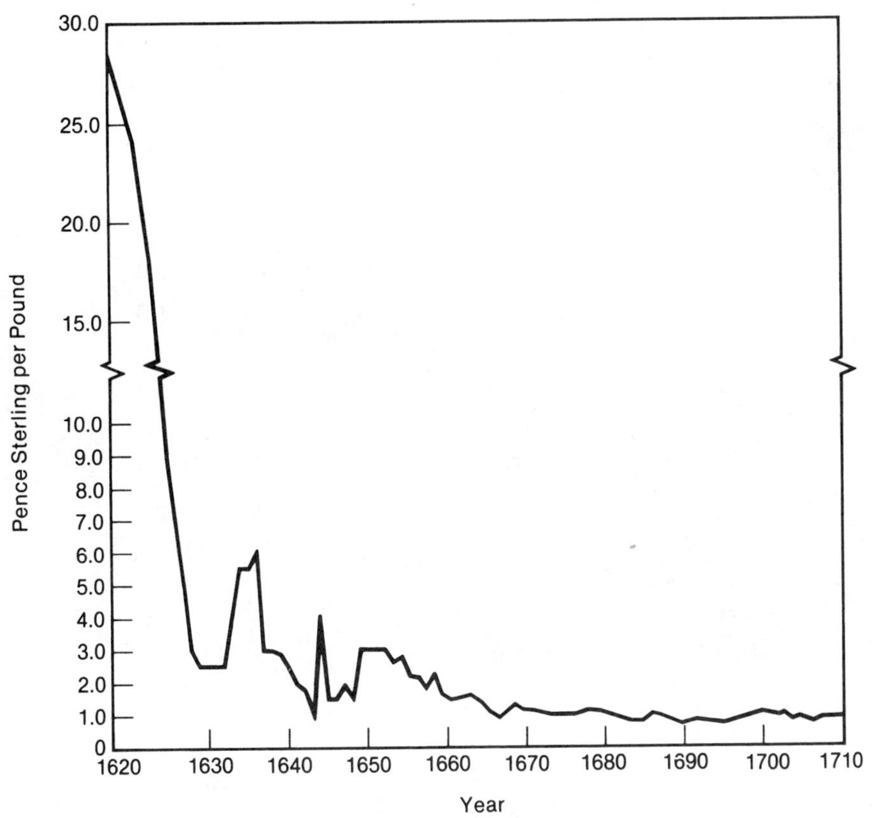

FIGURE 5.1 Chesapeake Farm Tobacco Prices, 1618–1710

Sources: Compiled from Russell R. Menard, "A Note on Chesapeake Tobacco Prices, 1618–1660," Virginia Magazine of History and Biography *(1976): 401–410; and Menard, "Farm Prices of Maryland Tobacco, 1659–1710,"* Maryland Historical Magazine *58 (Spring 1973): 85.*

Grain and Livestock in the Middle Colonies

In grain and livestock production, as in tobacco, gains in productivity appear to have been modest, indeed low, throughout most of the eighteenth century. The most visible change in Pennsylvania farms was the sharp decline in average farm size, from about 500 acres in 1700 to about 140 acres at the end of the century. But this decrease did not indicate a fall in the "effective land"–to–labor ratio. Instead, it was the consequence of population expansion and the subdivision of uncleared acres as new farms evolved. Because the amount of uncleared land per farm exceeded the minimum needs for fuel and timber, these acreage reductions had no noticeable effect on agricultural output. Because the average number of cleared acres per farm changed little, the effective input of land per farm remained almost constant throughout the entire eighteenth century.

Alternatively, additional implements, structures, and accumulated inventories raised the amount of capital inputs per farm. Meanwhile, average family size was shrinking. Consequently, in the predominantly family farm areas such as Pennsylvania, the amount of labor per farm decreased. Therefore, both the capital–labor ratio and the cleared land–labor ratio rose. Given the increase of inputs per worker, we would expect output per worker to expand.

Indeed, the evidence reveals that output per farm was increasing (See Ball and Walton, 1976). Not only were farms producing more livestock and grains (mainly wheat and maslin,

The tranquility of this eighteenth-century rural colonial setting belies the hard work and varied daily tasks of family farming.

a combination of wheat and rye), but also by the late colonial period, a small but growing portion of farm labor time was being diverted to nonagricultural production, including milling, smithing, cabinet making, chair making, and tanning. Overall, average output per farm increased by about 7 percent between the first and third quarters of the eighteenth century. When the gain in output is compared with the change in total input,[3] it appears that total productivity advanced approximately 10 percent during these decades. Expressed in terms of rates of change, total productivity expanded by 0.1 to 0.2 percent per year, with the most rapid change (0.3 percent) occurring in the first decades of the eighteenth century. Finally, the growth of output per worker was somewhat higher (approximately 0.2 to 0.3 percent per year) over the first three quarters of the century.[4]

Specific evidence on the precise sources of these advances is almost entirely lacking. The low measured rate of advance, however, does reinforce historical descriptions. For instance, in their classic study of agriculture, Bidwell and Falconer assert that in the colonies north of the Chesapeake, "The eighteenth century farmers showed little advance over the first settlers in their care of livestock," and "little if any improvement had been made in farm implements until the very close of the eighteenth century."[5] Another study of Pennsylvania agriculture specifically concludes that "economic conditions throughout the century prohibited major changes and encouraged a reasonably stable and uniform type of

[3]With land per farm nearly constant, labor per farm declining, and capital per farm rising, total input per farm changed according to the relative importance of labor and capital and the relative degree of change of each. Because labor comprised such a high percentage of total costs, total combined input per farm actually declined by a few percentage points during the eighteenth century.
[4]It should be noted that labor productivity (output per worker) increased more than total productivity (output per total combined input) because the amounts of capital and cleared land per worker increased during this period. Increases in these other inputs enabled labor to produce more.
[5]P.W. Bidwell and J. I. Falconer, *History of Agriculture in the Northern United States, 1620–1860* (Washington, D.C.: Carnegie Institution of Washington, 1925), 107, 123.

Additions of capital and the specialization of tasks raised productivity per worker in colonial tobacco production.

mixed farming that involved fairly extensive use or superficial working of the land."[6] It seems reasonable to conclude that farmers were probably beginning to learn to use the soil and their implements more effectively. But there is little indication of input savings, either from technological improvements or from economies of scale in terms of larger farms. Better organized and more widespread market participation, however, may have contributed somewhat to gains in agricultural productivity.

These findings and conclusions come as no surprise when examined in the light of agricultural developments in later periods. For instance, investigations by Robert Gallman indicate total productivity gains of approximately 0.5 percent per year over the nineteenth century.[7] However, in the first half of the century, combined output per unit of land, labor, and capital advanced at a rate of 0.1 to 0.2 percent. In the second half of the century, the productivity rate rose to 0.8 percent. Undoubtedly, the lower-paced first half of the nineteenth century—before the transition to animal power and increased mechanization—would be more suggestive of the eighteenth-century experience. In short, agricultural progress throughout most of the colonial period was sporadic, limited, and slow paced.

---

[6]James T. Lemon, *Best Poor Man's Country: A Geographical Study of Early Southwestern Pennsylvania* (Baltimore: Johns Hopkins University Press, 1972), 150–151.

[7]See Robert E. Gallman, "Changes in Total U.S. Agricultural Factor Productivity in the Nineteenth Century," *Agricultural History* 46 (1972): 191–210; and Gallman, "The Agricultural Sector and the Pace of Economic Growth: U.S. Experience in the Nineteenth Century," in *Essays in Nineteenth Century Economic History*, eds. David C. Klingaman and Richard K. Vedder (Athens: Ohio University Press, 1975), 35–76.

TABLE 5.1 $\frac{\text{Price in Europe} - \text{Price in America}}{\text{Price in Europe}}$

YEARS	
1720–1724	82%
1725–1729	76
1730–1734	82
1735–1739	77
1740–1744	77
1745–1749	76
1750–1754	67
1755–1759	72
1760–1764	70
1765–1769	65
1770–1774	51

Productivity Gains in Transportation and Distribution

Although productivity advances in agriculture were slow and gradual, substantially higher gains were registered in the handling and transportation of goods. Such gains were extremely important because transportation and other distribution costs made up a large portion of the final market price of products. This was especially true of the bulky colonial products, which were normally low in value relative to their weight or volume (displaced cargo space). For example, transportation and handling costs would double the value of a barrel of pitch between Maryland and London. Even the distribution costs of expensive lightwares represented a significant fraction of their value.

During the eighteenth century, the differential between English and colonial prices for manufactures shipped to the colonies was declining at a fairly steady rate. In the early decades of the century, it was not uncommon for English goods to sell for 80 to 140 percent more in the colonies than in England. By midcentury, prices on British wares were 45 to 75 percent higher in the colonies. Finally, just prior to the Revolution, this price spread had been reduced to a range of only 15 to 25 percent. However, as late as the 1770s, colonial staples such as pitch, tar, lumber, rice, and other space-consuming exports were still commanding more than double their domestic price in normal English and European markets.

Table 5.1 shows evidence of improvements in the marketing and distribution of transatlantic tobacco shipments. The average differential between the Amsterdam and the colonial price of tobacco (given as a percentage of the Amsterdam price) declined.[8]

A series of advances in transatlantic tobacco distribution stemmed from improvements in packaging and merchandising, from declining costs of information on prices and markets, and from reductions of risk in trade. However, by far the most important improvements were in shipping. Although freight rates fluctuated and varied according to route, and between periods of war and peace, the long-run trend was persistently downward. During the 100 years preceding the Revolution, the real costs of shipping were almost halved. Expressed in terms of productivity gains, shipping advanced at a rate of approximately 0.8 percent per year. For that period—and specifically compared with changes in agriculture—these increases suggest that shipping was a strategic factor in the overall economic advance of the colonies.

Sources of Productivity Change in Shipping

What caused these productivity gains? Where trades were well organized and markets reasonably large and safe, economies of scale in shipping were usually realized. In the Baltic timber trades, for instance, the use of larger vessels generated labor savings per ton shipped.

[8]James F. Shepherd and Gary M. Walton, *Shipping, Maritime Trade, and the Economic Development of Colonial North America* (Cambridge: Cambridge University Press, 1972), 60.

Although larger ships necessitated larger crews, the increased cargo capacity more than compensated for the additional labor costs. As vessels increased in size, their carrying capacity per unit of labor also increased. In other words, on larger ships, fewer men were needed to transport a given volume of goods.

Despite these possibilities, the average size of vessels employed in the western Atlantic and in the Caribbean failed to increase significantly over the 100-year period. The potential labor savings of the larger ships were offset by greater occurrences of low utilization in these waters. In fact, in those numerous small and scattered markets, the port times of large vessels were usually as much as twice as long as those for small vessels. Therefore, in colonial waters, schooners and sloops normally traveled a larger number of miles per ton than did large ships or brigs. Nevertheless, the number of tons per man increased because crew sizes decreased as vessels remained unchanged in size. For example, a Boston vessel of 50 tons employed an average of seven men early in the eighteenth century, but by the late colonial period, the same ship required only five crew members. Over this same time span, the crew size of a typical New York vessel of 50 tons decreased from 11 to 7 members. Paralleling this reduction in labor was the reduction or elimination of armaments on vessels that traded in colonial waters. Guns had been commonplace on seventeenth-century vessels trading in the western Atlantic, but cannons had all but disappeared on ships there by the end of the colonial period.

Although the average useful life of vessels changed little over the period, insurance rates decreased due to the declining risks in ocean travel. In contrast to earlier times, insurance rates for most one-way transatlantic passages had reached the rock-bottom common peacetime level of 2 percent by 1720. Of course, rates for voyages into pirate-infested waters were quite another matter. Between New York and Jamaica, for example, the prevailing rate of 5 percent in 1720 had dropped to 4 percent by the 1770s. On routes from New England to various other islands in the West Indies, peacetime insurance rates were halved between 1700 and 1775.

Faster ship speed was not a positive force in raising productivity. Vessels from New England and the Middle colonies that sailed to the West Indies and back showed no gains in speed on either leg of the journey during this period, as shown in Figure 5.2. Nevertheless, round-trip voyage times declined from 1700 to 1775. As Figure 5.3 shows, with the single exception of Boston, layover times fell markedly in many key ports in the New World. Because a very large portion of a sailing ship's life was spent in port, such declines contributed greatly to higher productivity. For example, in the Chesapeake trade, vessels were in port more than twice as long at the end of the seventeenth century as they were in the 1760s. An important contributor to this change was the introduction of Scottish factors (representatives of Scottish merchant firms) into the Chesapeake Bay area after

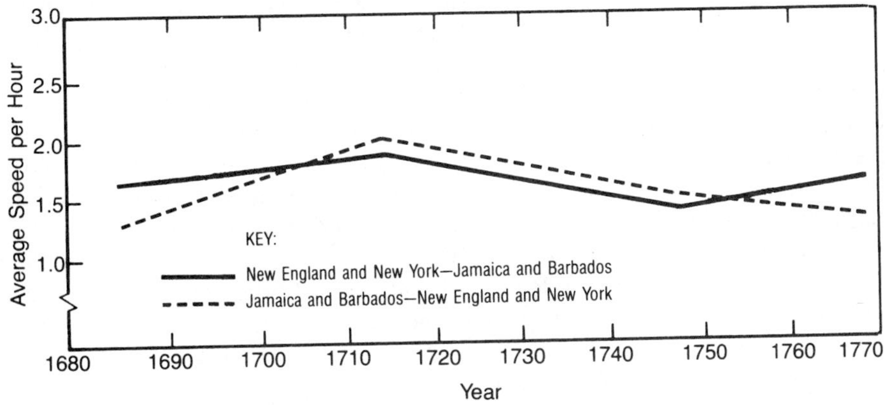

FIGURE 5.2 Average Ship Speeds (knots)

Source: Gary M. Walton, "Sources of Productivity Change in American Colonial Shipping," Economic History Review *20 (April 1967): 74.*

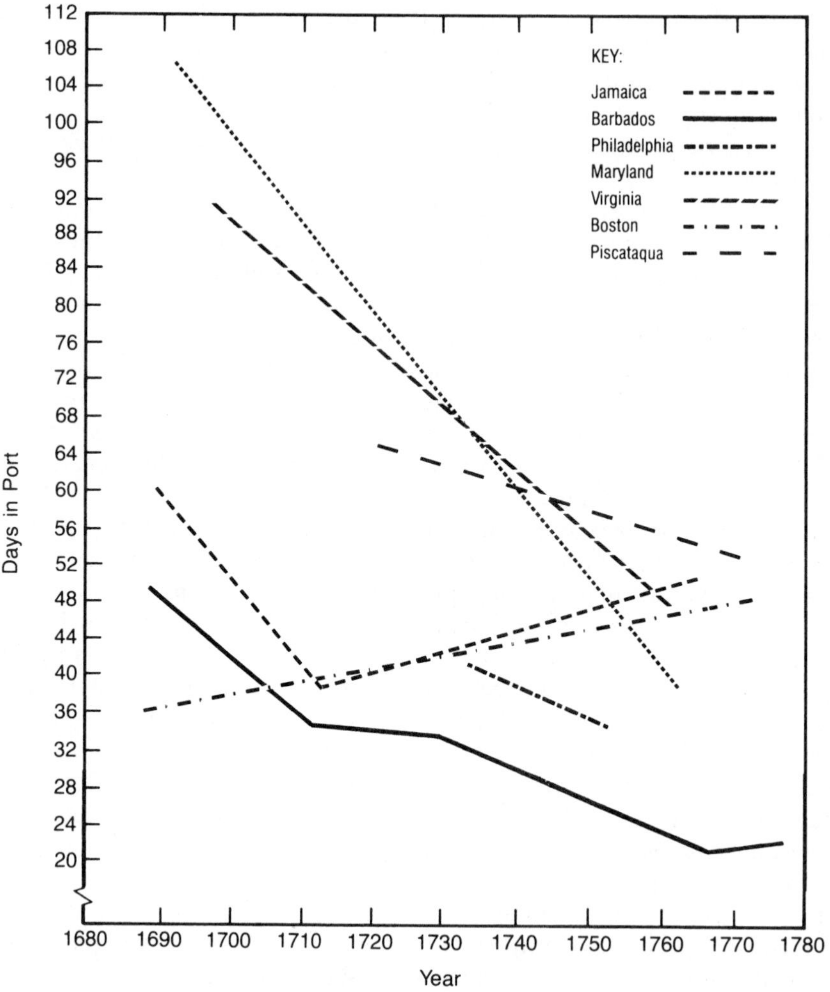

FIGURE 5.3 Average Port Times

Source: Gary M. Walton, "Sources of Productivity Change in American Colonial Shipping," Economic History Review *20 (April 1967): 75.*

1707. Undoubtedly, their methods of gathering and inventorying the tobacco crop in barns and warehouses for quick loading significantly shortened port times in the Chesapeake Bay.

Similarly, port times in Barbados were halved during this period. In the early colonial days, port times were extraordinarily long because exchanges were costly to transact. The many scattered markets were small and remote, and prices varied widely among islands and even within the same island. The shipmaster, acting on behalf of a merchant, might have to visit several islands on one trip to find the best market for his cargo. Difficulties in negotiating prices and determining the medium of exchange, as well as possibly settling past debts, all tended to lengthen the transaction period. Often, bartering was practiced, but even when money was used, prices were not easy to determine because different currencies and bills of exchange (with varying degrees of risk) were afforded no set value. Finally, the problem of collecting cargoes extended port times, especially when harvests were poor.[9] As a more systematic market economy and other institutional changes evolved, long layovers in the Caribbean became less common.

[9]As discussed in chapter 4, many of these factors also explain the generality of shuttle patterns of shipping and of route dominance by the colonists vis-à-vis the British on particular routes.

Perspective 5.1

The Horse and Institutional Change in Indian Culture

Like an invention, the northward diffusion of the horse, 1601 to 1740, first introduced in the New World by the Spanish in the sixteenth century, imposed dramatic changes on the daily lives of North American Indians. This was especially true of Indians living on the Great Plains. Before the horse, they were seminomadic, living much of the year in communal earthen lodges and cultivating gardens of beans, squash, and corn. Summers and falls found them on the move, on foot with dogs dragging teepees, following and hunting buffalo, thereby adding meat to their diet.

On foot and with dogs, a good day's journey was about 5 miles. In winter a few hunters could succeed in stalking a few bison; in good weather, larger bands of hunters used tactics of surrounding small herds and killing them with arrows. Given appropriate terrain, the "pedestrian drive" was used where herds were driven into traps or over cliffs.

The most immediate impact of the horse was to reduce the amount of agricultural work plains Indians had done. This changed the balance of their diet. It also led to more extensive killing and less intensive use of the meat on the carcass—"light butchering," as it was called.

From 5 miles a day, the hunting groups on horses could cover 20. Instead of a 50-mile hunting area in a season, they were soon able to extend their range to 500 miles. Hunting groups became smaller and more independent since communal schemes (a type of insurance) were less needed: Less time was spent in fixed locations in communal earthen lodges, and horse power enabled the movement of larger teepees that dogs could pull on travois (wheelless carts).

Pasturage and water sources took on greater importance, intensifying the problem of campsite selection. Prior to the horse, intertribal warfare was rare; afterward, intertribal alliances were few and warfare was frequent.

Finally, like land to the Europeans, the horse became the symbol of wealth and prestige for Native Americans. It was a form of personal property (including right to inheritance, trade, use, and exclusion of use). Especially on the plains, the institutional changes brought about by the horse were so great that the number of horses owned often meant the difference between survival, starvation, and conquest. (See Anderson 1999 for elaboration.)

Note that decreasing port times produced savings not only in capital but also in labor costs, since crews were customarily fed and paid while they were in foreign ports. Such savings more than offset other sources of cost increases. Although wages and ship repair costs remained fairly constant over the period, the costs of shipbuilding and victualing (obtaining food for the crew) increased. Overall, however, the productivity gains countervailed, and freight costs were cut in half between 1675 and 1775.

TECHNOLOGICAL CHANGE AND PRODUCTIVITY

Among the most powerful engines of modern economic growth have been technological changes that raise output relative to inputs. But compared with those of the nineteenth century, technological changes remained minor and sporadic in the colonial period. It preceded the era of the cotton gin, steam power, and the many metallurgical advances that vastly increased the tools available to workers. Even in iron production, we hear from Paul Paskoff, learning by doing and adapting remained the key source of labor and fuel savings

Acts of piracy in the western Atlantic, the Caribbean, and elsewhere thrived before 1720. The long-term effects of actions by the Royal Navy to eliminate piracy were to change the characteristic of ships and reduce freight rates on ocean transport.

in the late colonial period. In the decade preceding the Revolution, iron output per man increased nearly 50 percent, and charcoal use per ton decreased by half. Learning to reduce the fuel input to minimal levels saved on labor needed to gather charcoal and work the forges. Technology remained static and forge sizes constant, however. The evidence in agriculture also indicates no significant leaps in technology.

In shipping, the same conclusion is reached. This period preceded the era of iron ships and steam, and both ship materials and the power source of ships remained unchanged. Even increasingly complex sails and rigs and the alterations of hull shapes failed to increase ship speed and, in any case, did not represent fundamental advances in knowledge.

Of course, it might be argued that crew reductions stemmed from advances in knowledge. However, during the early seventeenth century, Dutch shipping had already displayed many of the essential characteristics of design, manning, and other input requirements that were found on the most advanced vessels in the western Atlantic in the 1760s and 1770s. In fact, the era's most significant technological change in shipping had occurred in approximately 1595, when the Dutch first introduced the flyboat, or flute, a specialized merchant vessel designed to carry bulk commodities. The flyboat was exceptionally long compared with its width, had a flat bottom, and was lightly built (armament, gun platforms, and reinforced planking had been eliminated). In addition, its rig was simple, and its crew size was small. In contrast, English and colonial vessels were built, gunned, and manned more heavily to meet the dual purpose of trade and defense. Their solid construction and armaments were costly—not only in materials but also in manpower. Larger crews were needed to handle the more complex riggings on these vessels as well as their guns.

New Views

Contemporary Issues and Lessons from History: Piracy and Terrorism

When terrorists hijacked planes from Boston's Logan Airport on the morning of September 11, 2001, and crashed them into the twin towers of the World Trade Center in New York and the Pentagon in Washington, D.C., American commercial life dramatically changed. The immense loss of life and property has been assessed at values ranging between 30 and 50 billion dollars, but added to those first round losses have been the growing costs of preventing other terrorist acts. Over 6,000 commercial airplanes in the United States carrying nearly 700 million people are now intensely scrutinized before each of the 11 million yearly takeoffs. Federal checkpoints for passengers and baggage increase the time costs of travel for each passenger. Federal employees, bomb-sniffing dogs, and air marshals add further to the cost of air travel, domestically and internationally. The Homeland Security Act of 2002 has created a federal conglomeration of intelligence and enforcement that adds still further to the cost of preventing and combating terrorism. It is, indeed, like a war.

Piracy and terrorism are not identical but their effects and the benefits of their elimination are similar. Nevertheless, the parallel effects of piracy and terrorism on trade and commercial life are striking. When the Royal Navy eliminated piracy in the western Atlantic and Caribbean in the 1720s and 30s, the cost of moving people and goods fell. Cannons, crew sizes, ship building costs, insurance premiums, and more all declined. Because of terrorism, these types of protection and combatant costs are once again rising, albeit in different specific forms. Ours is an age where the world is less safe and less wealthy because of terrorism, just as it was with piracy nearly 300 years ago. When (or if) terrorism subsides and commercial life becomes safer, trade and wealth will increase as in the days of piracy's demise.

It quickly became evident that the flyboat could be used advantageously in certain bulk trades where the danger of piracy was low. However, in the rich but dangerous trades into the Mediterranean and the West Indies, more costly ships were required. In general, high risks in all colonial waters led to one of the most notable features of seventeenth-century shipping—the widespread use of cannons and armaments on trading vessels. Such characteristics were still observed in certain waters throughout much of the eighteenth century. Until about 1750 in the Caribbean, especially near Jamaica, vessels weighing more than 100 tons were almost always armed, and even small vessels usually carried some guns.

The need for self-protection in the Caribbean was self-evident:

> There the sea was broken by a multitude of islands affording safe anchorage and refuge, with wood, water, even provision for the taking. There the colonies of the great European powers, grouped within a few days' sail of one another, were forever embroiled in current European wars which gave the stronger of them excuse for preying on the weaker and seemed to make legitimate the constant disorder of those seas. There trade was rich, but settlement thin and defense difficult. There the idle, the criminal, and the poverty-stricken were sent to ease society in the Old World. By all these conditions piracy was fostered, and for two centuries throve ruinously, partly as an easy method of individual enrichment and partly as an instrument of practical politics.[10]

[10]Violet Barbour, "Privateers and Pirates in the West Indies," *American Historical Review* 16 (1911): 529.

Privateering also added to the disorder. As a common practice, nation-states often gave private citizens license to harass the ships of rival states. These privateering commissions or "letters of marque" were issued without constraint in wartime, and even in peacetime they were occasionally given to citizens who had suffered losses due to the actions of subjects from an offending state. Since privateers frequently ignored the constraints of their commissions, privateering was often difficult to distinguish from common piracy.

Other government policies also tended to aggravate existing sea hazards. Adding to the supply of privateers and pirates, some of the islands were deliberately peopled with convicts. Even as late as 1718, the governor of Jamaica complained of this policy:

> Several People have been lately sent over out of the gaols [jails] in England, upon the Encouragement of An Act of Parliament pass'd the last sessions . . . those people have been so farr from altering their Evil Courses and way of living and becoming an Advantage to Us, that the greatest part of them are gone and have Induced others to go with them a Pyrating and have Inveglied and Encouraged Severall Negroes to desert from their Masters and go to the Spaniards in Cuba, the few that remains proves a wicked Lazy and Indolent people, so that I could heartily wish this Country might be troubled with no more of them.[11]

Earlier in 1700, Colonel Quary of Virginia wrote to the Council of Trade and Plantations that "all the news of America is the swarming of pirates not only on these coasts, but all the West Indies over, which doth ruin trade ten times worse than a war."[12]

Of course, piracy was not confined to the Caribbean. Pirates lurked safely in the inlets of North Carolina, from which they regularly raided vessels trading at Charleston. In 1718 it was exclaimed that "every month brought intelligence of renewed outrages, of vessels sacked on the high seas, burned with their cargo, or seized and converted to the nefarious uses of the outlaws."[13] Local traders, shippers, and government officials in the Carolinas repeatedly solicited the Board of Trade for protection. In desperation, Carolina's Assembly appropriated funds in 1719 to support private vessels in the hope of driving the pirates from their seas. These pleas and protective actions were mostly in vain, but finally, as the benefits of ensuring safe trade lanes rose relative to the costs of eliminating piracy, the Royal Navy took action. By the early 1740s, piracy had been eliminated from the western Atlantic.

The fall of piracy was paralleled by the elimination of ship armaments and the reduction of crew sizes. As such, this was a process of technical diffusion. Without piracy, specialized cargo-carrying vessels similar to the flyboat were designed, thereby substantially reducing the costs of shipping.

If the world today succeeds in eliminating or substantially reducing terrorism, the lessons from the Royal Navy's elimination of piracy in the western Atlantic and Caribbean in the 18th century can provide insights into the future. The falling costs of moving people and goods and the growing safety of property and people will bolster trade and spur the growth of income and wealth. The potential of this improving institutional framework reminds us again of the myriad sources of economic growth and the importance of Economic Reasoning Proposition 4.

★★★ *Economic Reasoning Proposition*

In summary, the main productivity advances in shipping during the colonial period resulted from institutional changes associated with the growth of markets, leading to (1) economies of scale in cargo handling, which reduced port times, and (2) the elimination of

[11] Letters to the Board of Trade (September 1, 1718, C. O. 137:13, 19), printed in Frank W. Pitman, *The Development of the West Indies, 1700–1763* (New Haven: Yale University Press, 1917), 55–56.

[12] Barbour, "Privateers and Pirates," 566.

[13] S. C. Hughson, "The Carolina Pirates and Colonial Commerce," *Johns Hopkins University Studies in Historical and Political Science* 12 (1894): 123.

piracy, which had stood as an obstacle to technical diffusion, permitting the use of specialized low-cost cargo vessels.[14]

SPECULATIONS ON EARLY GROWTH RATES

All such measures of productivity advance suggest that while improvements in colonial standards of material well-being occurred, the pace was slow and irregular, as George Taylor proposed. However, the measures do not support his assertion of an acceleration of growth of real income per capita to 1 percent annually between 1710 and 1775 (recall Economic Reasoning Proposition 5). Before the modern age of rapid technological change and widespread investments in schooling to generate a highly skilled and adaptive labor force, the effective sources of growth were much more limited. This is revealed in the analysis of sources of productivity advance, emphasizing the importance of learning by doing, adapting and utilizing economies of scale where possible, and diffusing existing technologies.

Wealth Holdings

Additional evidence, based on probated wealth holdings of deceased colonists, also portrays slow and irregular growth rates throughout the period from 1630 to 1775. Per capita wealth included land, buildings, physical possessions, money, debts receivable minus debts owed, and, often, slaves and indentured contracts. Allan Kulikoff 's analysis of wealth holdings in Maryland over the eighteenth century suggests a long-run trend rate of growth of 0.4 percent per year.[15] His evidence shows contrasting periods: a slight fall in the first quarter of the century, a sharper decline in the second, and a very strong advance in the third quarter. Recalling the strong productivity growth period of 1630 to 1670 in the tobacco colonies, with little or no change in the late seventeenth century, it appears that most of the growth bracketed a long period of no growth (or possibly some decline) in per capita well-being in the Upper South. Work by Terry Anderson on New England also shows very strong advances in wealth holdings per person from 1650 to 1680, and then very little growth up to 1710. The trend from 1650 to 1710 was unusually high, perhaps 1.6 percent per year.

Recent evidence provided by Gloria and Jackson Main on southern New England between 1640 and 1774 is shown in Table 5.2 on page 100. This evidence of growth in total wealth per male indicates a trend in yearly average income advance of 0.35 percent in this region. Note, however, the spurt following the 1638–1654 period, relative stagnation until the turn of the century, then another 20-year spurt followed by another 20-year flat period, and finally another rapid spurt. This evidence further supports the view that regions differed greatly in the timing of their growth phases. Over a very long period, however, the trend growth rates of regions were probably fairly similar.

---

[14]Other similar productivity gains deserve at least a brief mention here. As port times decreased, so did inventory times. This reduced the time in which a planter's capital (crop) lay idle in storage barns or warehouses. Decreased inventory times saved colonial capital. Similarly, declining risks and insurance rates reduced the costs to owners of insuring their shipments or bearing the risks of personal shipments. And considerable progress was made in packaging, as tobacco and sugar hogsheads, rice barrels, and other containers increased in size. Although larger hogsheads and barrels demanded more input in construction, their carrying capacity grew relatively more because the surface area of such containers expanded less in proportion to their capacity. Finding the point at which increased difficulties in handling roughly offset the productivity gains from using larger containers provides us with a good example of the learning-by-doing, trial-and-error procedure.

[15]Deceased people's wealth exceeded average wealth per capita substantially, but not everyone who died had an estate probated. However, if the distribution of wealth did not change dramatically over the period, trends of probated wealth holdings probably reflected the trend in wealth holdings per person. Furthermore, if the ratio of output (or income) to physical nonhuman wealth (capital) stayed fairly consistent, trends in such wealth per person would mirror trends in income per person.

TABLE 5.2 Male per Capita Probate Wealth in Southern New England, 1638–1774

YEARS	TOTAL WEALTH
1638–1654	£227.3
1655–1674	251.9
1675–1694	263.5
1695–1714	248.9
1715–1734	272.4
1735–1754	275.8
1765–1774	364.7

Note: For estates of males only; weighted for age and area. Estates from 1755 to 1764 are not included due to incomplete sample for area weighting.

Source: Adapted from Gloria L. Main and Jackson T. Main, "Economic Growth and the Standard of Living in Southern New England, 1642–1774," Journal of Economic History *48 (1988): 27–46.*

It seems reasonable to conclude that over the last 100 to 150 years of the colonial period, the growth rate trend was slightly below 0.5 percent per year. Based on evidence of wealth gathered from samples of probated estates for all the colonial regions, Alice Hanson Jones concludes:

> Despite possible local or regional spurts or lags or even declines in some subperiods after 1650, it seems likely that, for all regions combined, fairly steady intensive growth accompanied accumulating experience in the New World, learning by doing, increasing knowhow in shipping within the Atlantic community, and the enlargement in size of the market that came with growth of population and trade.[16]

By her calculations, Jones suggests growth rates for three distinct periods: 0.3 percent, 1650–1725; 0.4 percent, 1725–1750; and 0.5 percent, 1750–1775.[17] Although the acceleration of growth implied by her figures may be challenged, the range seems reasonable in light of the improvements we have already noted and in light of England's estimated annual economic growth rate of 0.3 percent throughout most of the eighteenth century.[18]

PER CAPITA WEALTH AND INCOME, 1774

Reflection upon the ordeals of first settlement, such as "the lost colony" at Roanoke and the "starving time" in early Jamestown, projects stark contrast to the economic conditions of colonial life on the eve of the Revolution. From distant Scotland in 1776, Adam Smith declared in his *Wealth of Nations*:

> There are no colonies of which the progress has been more rapid than that of the English in North America. Plenty of good land, and liberty to manage their affairs their own way, seem to be the two great causes of the prosperity.

Contemporaries in the colonies also supported this view. As early as 1663, the Reverend John Higginson of Boston could observe, "We live in a more plentifull and comfortable manner than ever we did expect." By the 1740s, Benjamin Franklin could remark, "The first drudgery of settling new colonies, which confines the attention of people to mere necessities, is now pretty well over; and there are many in every province in circumstances that set them at ease."[19] Indeed, by most any standards of comparison, the quality of life and standards of

[16] Alice Hanson Jones, *Wealth of a Nation to Be* (New York: Columbia University Press, (1980), 305.
[17] Ibid., 78.
[18] See Phyllis Deane and W. A. Cole, *British Economic Growth, 1688–1959: Trends and Structure* (London: Cambridge University Press, 1964), 80.
[19] Stuart Bruchey, ed., *The Colonial Merchant: Sources and Readings* (New York: Harcourt Brace Jovanovich, 1966), 1.

material well-being were extraordinarily high for free Americans by the end of the colonial period. They lived longer and better than populations of other nations and places at the time, and better than most people throughout the world today.

THE DISTRIBUTION OF INCOME AND WEALTH

As Economic Insight 5.1 and Tables 5.3 and 5.4 on page 102 illustrate, the high levels of material well-being for colonial Americans were not equally distributed regionally. By far the richest area was the South, where wealth and incomes per free capita were far above those in the Middle colonies and in New England.

Evidence from probate records of the time also permits us to estimate the distribution of wealth among individuals. It is widely believed that wealth and income in North America were fairly equitably distributed until the onset of industrialization in the early nineteenth century. However, the estimates in Table 5.5 on page 103 (which includes holdings in slaves and indentured contracts) suggest that widespread inequalities of wealth and income existed much earlier. For instance, the wealthiest 20 percent of all New Englanders owned 66 percent of the total wealth there. In the Middle colonies, the wealthiest 20 percent held 53 percent of the total wealth. In the South, 70 percent of the wealth was held by the top fifth. In short, the South had the most concentrated distribution of wealth, and the Middle colonies had the least. The greater southern concentration was due primarily to the dominance of wealthy plantations enjoying advantages of economies of scale in production. Slavery also added to the South's high concentrations of wealth, but note that New England had concentrations almost as high, and wealth inequalities were notably high in the port towns. It also merits emphasis that the degree of inequality reflected in these numbers was minor by comparison with the gaping wealth inequalities in the sugar islands of the Caribbean and throughout Brazil and Spanish America.

Thanks to the pioneering efforts of Jackson T. Main and James Henretta, we have learned that a growing inequality in wealth and income accompanied the very process of colonial settlement and economic maturity. As development proceeded, frontier areas were transformed into subsistence farming areas with little specialization or division of labor, then into commercial farming lands, and finally, in some instances, into urban areas. In Main's opinion, this increasing commercialization resulted in greater inequality in the distribution of colonial wealth and income.[20]

Other studies by James Henretta and Bruce D. Daniels also suggest a growth in the inequality of colonial wealth distribution within regions over time.[21] Comparing two Boston tax lists, Henretta found that the top 10 percent of Boston's taxpayers owned 42 percent of its wealth in 1687, whereas they owned 57 percent in 1771.[22] Daniels surveyed many New England probate records and, therefore, was able to tentatively confirm Main's contention that as economic activity grew more complex in the colonies, it tended to produce a greater concentration of wealth. Apparently, as subsistence production gave way to market production, the interdependence among colonial producers generated (or at least was accompanied by) a greater disparity in wealth. This was true both in older and in more

[20]Jackson T. Main, *The Social Structure of Revolutionary America* (Princeton: Princeton University Press, 1965).

[21]James Henretta, "Economic Development and Social Structure in Colonial Boston," *William and Mary Quarterly* 22 (1965): 93–105; and Bruce D. Daniels, "Long-Range Trends of Wealth Distribution in Eighteenth-Century New England," *Explorations in Economic History* 11 (1973–1974): 123–135.

[22]Henretta's 1771 estimate was later revised downward to 48 percent by Gerard Warden, who found historical inconsistencies in the evaluation of assets in the tax lists on which Henretta's study was based. This adjustment modifies substantially the argument for rapidly rising inequality in Boston but not the overall picture of substantial inequality of wealth holdings there.

Economic Insight 5.1

Per Capita Income Estimate, 1774

The quantitative basis for accepting the sweeping conclusions reported previously also stems from the work of Alice Jones. Her wealth estimates for 1774 are shown in Table 5.3. These are nonhuman physical wealth holdings (excluding financial debts and slavery and indenture contracts) per capita and per free person in the separate regions. Table 5.4 shows several income estimates per capita and per free person derived from the wealth figures in Table 5.3 by using capital–output ratios. Actual incomes estimated from wealth holdings would depend on the prevailing ratio of capital to output, but the range of ratios (3 to 1, 3.5 to 1, and 4 to 1) used is likely to bracket the true incomes earned in 1774.

Using a capital–output ratio of 3.5:1 generates an estimate of income per free person in 1774 of £13.8, or £12.1 if the ratio was 4:1. These estimates compare approximately with $1,500 and $1,300 in 2000 prices, less than half the official U.S. poverty level, but obviously, the range of goods and other conditions of life and the errors of estimation make any such comparisons extremely crude. Nevertheless, we can safely guess that free colonials enjoyed surprisingly high standards of living for the world at that time. Because taxes in the colonies were much less than in England, after-tax incomes of free persons in the colonies were probably above those in the mother country on the eve of the Revolution.

Even today, relatively few countries generate average income levels that approach the earnings of free Americans on the eve of the Revolution. In fact, more than one-half the current world population lives in countries where the average income is below the level of the typical free American's income of more than 200 years ago. This is true of most people of the "Third World," including India, Pakistan, Indonesia, and large parts of Africa and South America. Relatively speaking, free colonial Americans lived very well, both by today's standards in many areas of the world and in comparison with the most advanced areas of the world in the late eighteenth century.

TABLE 5.3 Private Nonhuman Physical Wealth, 1774 (in pounds sterling)

REGION	PER CAPITA	PER FREE CAPITA
New England	£36.4	£38.0
Middle colonies	40.2	44.1
Southern colonies	36.4	61.6
Thirteen colonies	37.4	48.4

Source: Adapted from Alice Hanson Jones, Wealth of a Nation to Be *(New York: Columbia University Press, 1980), 54, 58.*

TABLE 5.4 Estimates of Regional Incomes, 1774 (in pounds sterling)

	CAPITAL OUTPUT RATIOS					
	PER CAPITA			PER FREE CAPITA		
REGION	(3:1)	(3.5:1)	(4:1)	(3:1)	(3.5:1)	(4:1)
New England	£12.1	£10.4	£ 9.1	£12.7	£10.9	£ 9.5
Middle colonies	13.4	11.5	10.0	14.7	12.6	11.0
Southern colonies	12.1	10.4	9.1	20.5	17.6	15.4
Thirteen colonies	12.5	10.7	9.4	16.1	13.8	12.1

Note: These estimates of income per capita and for the free population are derived from Alice Hanson Jones's wealth estimates by using her assumption of a capital–income ratio of 3.5:1 and two others (3:1 and 4:1) to widen the analysis somewhat. It bears remembering that these income estimates are only approximate. Estimates of wealth stocks can be converted into income flows by dividing the wealth estimates by a capital–output ratio, but the relationship between capital and output (the capital–output ratio) is influenced by many factors and varies both over time and among countries and regions. Nevertheless, under normal peacetime conditions, the capital–output ratio is seldom lower than 3 or higher than 5.

Source: Adapted from Alice Hanson Jones, Wealth of a Nation to Be *(New York: Columbia University Press, 1980), 63.*

TABLE 5.5 Total Physical Wealth, 1774: Estate Sizes and Composition for Free Wealth Holders (in pounds sterling)

	ALL COLONIES	NEW ENGLAND	MIDDLE COLONIES	SOUTH
Mean average	£252.0%	£161.2%	£189.2%	£394.7%
Median average	108.7	74.4	152.5	144.5
Distribution				
Bottom 20%	0.8	1.0	1.2	0.7
Top 20%	67.3	65.9	52.7	69.6
Composition				
Land	53.0	71.4	60.5	45.9
Slaves and servants	22.1	0.5	4.1	33.6
Livestock	9.2	7.5	11.3	8.8
Consumer-personal	6.7	11.2	8.4	5.1

Source: Adapted from Alice Hanson Jones, American Colonial Wealth: Documents and Methods, *2d ed., 3 vols. (New York: Arno, 1978); presented in Edwin Perkins,* The Economy of Colonial America, *2d ed. (New York: Columbia University Press, 1988), 219.*

recently settled agricultural areas. Alternatively, large established urban areas such as Boston and Hartford exhibited a fairly stable distribution of wealth throughout the eighteenth century until 1776.These urban centers also reflected the greatest degree of wealth inequality in the colonies. Smaller towns showed less inequality, but as towns grew, their inequality also increased.

Particularly high levels of affluence were observed in the port towns and cities, where merchant classes were forming and gaining an economic hold. Especially influential were the merchant shipowners, who were engaged in the export–import trade and who were considered to be in the upper class of society. In addition, urbanization and industrialization produced another class group: a free labor force that owned little or no property.

Probably one-third of the free population possessed few assets (according to estate records and tax rolls), but as Jackson Main has argued and Mary Schweitzer's work supports, these were not a permanent underclass of free poor people. These were mostly young people in their twenties, still dependent on parents or relatives. Through gifts, savings, and other sources, marriage usually tripled household wealth almost immediately. Without evidence on upward mobility to higher income levels, we cannot discern, as was shown in chapter 1, how frequently people moved up the economic ladder, escaping the poverty trap. Our speculation, because of land availability and less rigid social constraints in the colonies, is that free people in the colonies had much greater "class mobility" than did people in the Old World.

Not only occupation, marriage, and property ownership but also circumstances determined by birth greatly influenced a person's social standing. Race and sex were major factors. Some women were wealthy, but typically they owned far less property than men, and very few owned land. The rise of slave labor after 1675 furthered the overall rise of wealth inequality in the colonies.

Throughout most of the colonial period up to 1775, growing wealth concentration did not occur among free whites in the 13 colonies as a whole. Although growing inequality occurred within specific regions and localities, this did not occur in the aggregate. This is because the lower wealth concentration areas, the rural and especially the new frontier areas, contained more than 90 percent of the population. These grew as fast, or faster than, the urban areas, therefore offsetting the modest growth of inequality of the urban centers.[23] As an added statistical oddity, although rural wealth holdings (per free person) were less than urban holdings within each region, in the aggregate, rural wealth holdings averaged above urban holdings. This reversal in order happened because of the very high wealth holdings per free person in the South, which actually exceeded the average wealth holdings of northern

[23]Jeffrey G. Williamson and Peter H. Lindert, *American Inequality: A Macroeconomic History* (New York: Academic Press, 1980), 21–31.

The urban wealth portrayed here stands in stark contrast to the mud huts of Virginia's first English settlers.

urban residents. In any case, despite these peculiarities of aggregation, substantial wealth inequality was a fact of economic life long before the age of industrialization and the period of rapid and sustained economic growth that occurred in the nineteenth century. The absence of growing inequality of wealth among free Americans implies that the growth of per capita income and wealth was shared widely among these nearly 1.8 million people. On the eve of the Revolution, their sense of well-being and economic outlook was undoubtedly positive. British interference and changing taxation policies were threats that a powerful young emerging nation was willing and able to overcome.

SELECTED REFERENCES AND SUGGESTED READINGS

Anderson, Terry. *The Economic Growth of Seventeenth-Century New England: A Measurement of Regional Income* (New York: Arno, 1975).

———. "Economic Growth in Colonial New England: 'Statistical Renaissance.'" *Journal of Economic History* 39 (1979): 243–257.

Anderson, Terry, and Steven LaCombe. "Institutional Change in the Indian Horse Culture." In *The Other Side of the Frontier*, ed. Linda Barrington (Boulder, Colo.: Westview, 1999).

Anderson, Terry, and Robert Paul Thomas. "White Population, Labor Force, and Extensive Growth of the New England Economy in the Seventeenth Century." *Journal of Economic History* 33 (1973): 634–661.

———. "Economic Growth in the Seventeenth Century Colonies." *Explorations in Economic History* 15 (1978): 368–387.

Ball, Duane, and Gary M. Walton. "Agricultural Productivity Change in Eighteenth-Century Pennsylvania." *Journal of Economic History* 36 (1976): 102–117.

Carr, Lois G., and Lorena S. Walsh. "Changing Life Styles in Colonial St. Mary's County." In *Economic Change in Chesapeake Colonies*, eds. G. Porter and W. Mulligan (Greenville: Regional Economic History Research Center, 1978).

Daniels, Bruce. "Long Range Trends of Wealth Distribution in Eighteenth-Century New England." *Explorations in Economic History* 11 (1973–1974): 123–135.

———. "Economic Development in Colonial and Revolutionary Connecticut: An Overview." *William and Mary Quarterly* 37 (1980): 427–450.

Doerflinger, Thomas. *A Vigorous Spirit of Enterprise: Merchants and Economic Development in Revolutionary Philadelphia* (Chapel Hill: University of North Carolina Press, 1986).

Egnal, Marc. "The Economic Development of the Thirteen Continental Colonies, 1720 to 1775." *William and Mary Quarterly* 32 (1975): 191–222.

Galenson, David, and Russell Menard. "Economics and Early American History." *Newberry Papers,* No. 77-4E. (Chicago, 1978).

Hanson, John R. "The Economic Development of the Thirteen Colonies, 1720 to 1775: A Critique." *William and Mary Quarterly* 37 (1980): 165–172.

Jones, Alice H. *American Colonial Wealth: Documents and Methods,* 3 vols. (New York: Arno, 1978.)

———. *Wealth of a Nation to Be: The American Colonies on the Eve of the Revolution* (New York: Columbia University Press, 1980).

Jones, Douglas L. "The Strolling Poor: Transiency in Eighteenth-Century Massachusetts." *Journal of Social History* (1975): 28–54.

Kulikoff, Allan. "The Economic Growth of the Eighteenth-Century Chesapeake Colonies." *Journal of Economic History* 39 (1979): 275–288.

———. *Tobacco and Slaves: The Development of Southern Cultures in the Chesapeake, 1680–1800* (Chapel Hill: University of North Carolina Press, 1986).

Maddison, Angus. "A Comparison of Levels of GDP per Capita in Developed and Developing Countries, 1700–1980." *Journal of Economic History* 43 (1983): 27–41.

Main, Gloria. *Tobacco Colony: Life in Early Maryland.* (Princeton, N. J.: Princeton University Press, 1982).

———. "The Standard of Living in Colonial Massachusetts." *Journal of Economic History* 43 (1983): 101–108.

Main, Gloria, and Jackson T. Main. "Economic Growth and the Standard of Living in Southern New England, 1640–1774." *Journal of Economic History* 48 (1988): 27–46.

Main, Jackson T. "Standard of Living and Life Cycle in Colonial Connecticut." *Journal of Economic History* 43 (1983): 159–165.

McCusker, John J., and Russell R. Menard. Chapters 3 and 12 in *The Economy of British America, 1607–1789* (Chapel Hill: University of North Carolina Press, 1985).

Paskoff, Paul. "Labor Productivity and Managerial Efficiency against a Static Technology: The Pennsylvania Iron Industry, 1750–1800." *Journal of Economic History* 40 (1980): 129–135.

Pencak, William. "The Social Structure of Revolutionary Boston: Evidence from the Great Fire of 1760." *Journal of Interdisciplinary History* (1979): 267–278.

Perkins, Edwin. "The Material Lives of Laboring Philadelphians, 1750 to 1800." *William and Mary Quarterly* 38 (1981): 163–202.

———. Chapter 1 in *The Economy of Colonial America,* 2d ed. (New York: Columbia University Press, 1988).

Schweitzer, Mary. *Custom and Contract: Household Government and the Economy in Colonial Pennsylvania* (New York: Columbia University Press, 1987).

Smith, Billy G. "Inequality in Late Colonial Philadelphia: A Note on Its Nature and Growth." *William and Mary Quarterly* 41 (1984): 629–645.

Walsh, Lorena S. "Urban Amenities and Rural Sufficiency: Living Standards and Consumer Behavior in the Colonial Chesapeake, 1643–1777." *Journal of Economic History* 43 (1983): 109–117.

Chapter Six

THREE CRISES AND REVOLT

Chapter Theme

At the close of the French and Indian War (also called the Seven Years' War), when the French were eliminated as a rival power in North America, Britain's mainland colonies were on the brink of another wave of economic growth and rising prosperity. In accordance with British practices of colonization, the colonists remained English citizens with all rights due the King's subjects under the laws of England. For financial, administrative, and political reasons, the Crown and Parliament in 1763 launched a "new order" (Economic Reasoning Proposition 4). Misguided policies, mismanagement, and ill timing from England added political will to the economic circumstances of the colonies to steer an independent course. The American Revolution was the outcome.

Economic Reasoning Proposition

THE OLD COLONIAL POLICY

Being part of the British Empire, and in accord with English laws and institutions, colonial governments were patterned after England's governmental organization. Although originally there were corporate colonies (Connecticut and Rhode Island) and proprietary colonies (Pennsylvania and Maryland), most eventually became Crown colonies, and all had similar governing organizations. For example, after 1625, Virginia was a characteristic Crown colony, and both its governor and council (the upper house) were appointed by the Crown. But only the lower house could initiate fiscal legislation, and this body was elected by the propertied adult males within the colony.

Although the governor and the Crown could veto all laws, power gradually shifted to the lower houses as colonial legislative bodies increasingly tended to imitate the House of Commons in England. The colonists controlled the lower houses—and, therefore, the purse strings—thereby generating a climate of political freedom and independence in the colonies. Governors, who were generally expected to represent the will of the Empire and to veto legislation contrary to British interests, were often not only sympathetic to the colonists but also depended on the legislatures for their salaries (which were frequently in arrears). Consequently, the actual control of civil affairs generally rested with the colonists themselves, through their representatives.

Of course, the power that permitted this state of affairs to exist rested in England, and the extent of local autonomy was officially limited. After the shift in power in England from the Crown to Parliament in 1690, the Privy Council reviewed all laws passed in the colonies as a matter of common procedure. According to official procedure, colonial laws were not in effect until the Privy Council granted its approval, and sometimes the council vetoed legislation passed in the colonies. Time, distance, and bureaucratic apathy, however, often permitted colonial laws and actions to become effective before they were even reviewed in England; and if the colonists highly desired a vetoed piece of legislation, it could be reworded and resubmitted.

In short, British directives influenced day-to-day events in the colonies only modestly. Indeed, government activity—whether British or colonial—was a relatively minor aspect of colonial affairs. The burdens of defense, for example, fell on the shoulders of those in Britain, not on those in the colonies, and colonists were among the most lightly taxed people in the world. Furthermore, the colonists themselves held the power to resolve issues of a local nature. They had no central or unifying government,[1] but the colonial governments had organized themselves to the point in the early eighteenth century where they appointed officials, granted western lands, negotiated with the Indians, raised taxes, provided relief for the poor, and the like. In this way, British subjects in the New World enjoyed extensive freedom of self-determination throughout most of the colonial period (Economic Reasoning Proposition 1).

The main provisions of the early Navigation Acts, which imposed the most important restrictions on colonial economic freedom, formed the basis of the old colonial policy. Recall that these laws epitomized British mercantilism and that their aim was threefold: (1) to protect and encourage English and colonial shipping; (2) to ensure that major colonial imports from Europe were shipped from British ports; and (3) to ensure that the bulk of desired colonial products—the enumerated articles—were shipped to England.

The first Acts of Trade and Navigation (in 1651, 1660, and 1663) introduced these concepts concerning the colonies' relationship with the Empire. Colonial settlers and investors had always been aware of the restrictions on their economic activities. Rules were changed gradually and, until 1763, in such a way that American colonists voiced no serious complaints. Articles were added to the enumerated list over a long period of time. At first, the list consisted entirely of southern continental and West Indian products, most importantly tobacco, sugar, cotton, dyewood, and indigo. Rice and molasses were not added until 1704, naval stores until 1705 and 1729, and furs and skins until 1721. Whenever enumeration resulted in obvious and unreasonable hardship, relief might be granted. For example, the requirement that rice be sent to England added so much to shipping and handling costs that the American product, despite its superior quality, was priced out of southern European markets. Consequently, laws passed in the 1730s allowed rice to be shipped directly to ports south of Cape Finisterre, a promontory in northwestern Spain.

Commodities were enumerated if they were especially important to English manufacturers or were expected to yield substantial customs revenue. However, the requirements of shipping listed items to English ports were less onerous than we might initially suppose. First, because the Americans and the English shared general ties of blood and language (and, more specifically, because their credit contacts were more easily established), the colonists would have dealt primarily with English merchants anyway. Second, duties charged on commodities that were largely re-exported, such as tobacco, were remitted entirely or in large part to the colonies. Third, bounties were paid on some of the enumerated articles. Fourth, it was permissible to ship certain items on the list directly from one colony to another for the purpose of furnishing essential supplies. Finally, the laws could be evaded through smuggling; with the exception of molasses, such evasion was probably neither more nor less common in the colonies than it was in Europe during the seventeenth and eighteenth centuries.

With respect to colonial imports, the effect of the Navigation Acts was to distort somewhat—but not to influence materially—the flows of trade. The fact that goods had to be funneled through England added to costs and restricted trade to the colonists. Again, however,

[1] Ben Franklin had proposed a new unified colonial administration in 1754, but his idea was rejected.

traditional ties would have made Americans the best customers of British merchants anyway. Furthermore, hardship cases were relieved by providing direct shipment of commodities such as salt and wine to America from ports south of Cape Finisterre.

If English manufacturers were to be granted special advantages over other European manufacturers in British American markets, should restrictions also be placed on competing colonial manufacturers? Many British manufacturers felt that such "duplicate production" should be prohibited and tried to convince Parliament that colonial manufacturing was not in the best interest of the Empire. In 1699, a law made it illegal to export colonial wool, wool yarn, and finished wool products to any foreign country or even to other colonies. Later, Americans (many of Dutch origin) were forbidden to export hats made of beaver fur. Toward mid-century, a controversy arose in England over the regulation of iron manufactures; after 1750, pig and bar iron were admitted into England duty free, and the colonial manufacture of finished iron products was expressly forbidden. The fact that these were the only prohibitive laws directed at colonial manufacturing indicates Britain's lack of fear of American competition.

After all, England enjoyed a distinct comparative advantage in manufacturing, and the colonies' comparative advantage in production lay overwhelmingly in agriculture and other resource-intensive products from the seas and forests. Note that the important shipbuilding industry in the colonies was not curtailed by British legislation; indeed, it was supported by Parliament. Therefore, any piecemeal actions to prevent colonial manufacturing activities appear to have been taken largely to favor particular vested interests in England, especially those with influence and effective lobbying practices.

The laws prohibiting colonial manufactures were loosely enforced; they were restrictive and a cause of annoyance, but they did not seriously affect the course of early American industrial development or the colonial quest for independence. Also, the economic controls that England imposed on the colonies were less strict than the colonial controls other European countries imposed, and these controls were less harsh for America than for Ireland and other colonies within the Empire. We should not, however, misapprehend the trend of enforcement of the old colonial policy. Regulation of external colonial trade was progressively strengthened. Beginning in 1675, governors were supplied with staffs of officials to aid in enforcing trade regulations; after the general reorganization of 1696, the powers of these officials were sufficient to provide considerable surveillance and commercial regulation.

The only trade law flaunted with impunity was the Molasses Act of 1733—an act that, if enforced, would have disrupted one of the major colonial trades and resulted in serious repercussions, especially in New England. Before 1700, New England had traded primarily with the British possessions in the West Indies. In time, however, British planters failed to provide a sufficient market for northern colonial goods, and sugar and molasses from the increasingly productive French islands became cheaper than the English staples. During the same period, British planters in the sugar islands were hurt by the requirement that cane products be shipped to England before being re-exported. In an effort to protect British West Indian holdings, Parliament imposed high duties on foreign (predominantly French) sugar, molasses, and rum imported to the English colonies. The strict levying of these duties and the prevention of smuggling would have suppressed the market of northern staples in the West Indies and would have seriously curtailed all trade involving rum. New Englanders felt they had no feasible alternative because they had to sell their fish, provisions, lumber, and rum to pay for their imports. Rather than accept such hardships, the New Englanders continued to trade as usual; instead of facing the issue resolutely, English officials, many of whom were routinely bribed (10 percent being the custom for "looking the other way"), made no serious attempts to enforce trade regulations (Economic Reasoning Proposition 4). Some 30 years later, after the matter had been raised time after time, the Sugar Act of 1764 ruled against the American colonists in

favor of the British West Indian planters. This decision to impose and collect the tax was a key factor in bringing on the first crisis leading to revolution.

THE NEW COLONIAL POLICY AND THE FIRST CRISIS

The events that led to the American Revolution are more clearly understood if we repeat and keep in mind their central underlying theme: New and rapid changes in the old colonial policy that had been established and imposed on an essentially self-governing people for 150 years precipitated a series of crises and, ultimately, war. These crises were essentially political, but the stresses and strains that led to colonial fear and hatred of British authority had economic origins. Britain's "new" colonial policy was only an extension of the old, with one difference: The new enactments were adopted by a Parliament and enforced by bureaucratic oversight that had every intention of enforcing them to the letter of the law, thereby sharply changing the atmosphere of freedom in the colonies. Furthermore, high British officials insisted—at almost precisely the wrong moments—on taking punitive actions that only compounded the bitterness they had already stirred up in the colonies.

The series of critical events that generated the first crisis began with the English victory over the French in 1763. The Seven Years' War had been a struggle for empire, of course, but it had also been a fight for the protection of the American colonies. And the colonials had been of only limited help in furnishing England with either troops or materials—to say nothing of the hurtful trade they intermittently carried on with the French in both Canada and the West Indies. The English were in no mood to spare the feelings of an upstart people who had committed the cardinal sin of ingratitude. Besides, the war had placed a heavy burden on the English treasury, and British taxes per capita in the mid-1760s were probably the highest in the world.[2] Interest on the national debt had soared to £5 million annually (nearly $500 million in today's values), and land taxes in England had doubled during the war. To many of the English, especially taxpayers, it seemed only fair that American colonists be asked to contribute to the support of the garrisons still required on their frontier. Despite their substantial wealth, the colonists at this time were still free riders of protection, receiving British defense at almost no cost. Taxes per capita in the colonies were among the lowest in the world, only 20 to 25 percent of taxes paid by the average English resident.

George Grenville, England's prime minister, proposed stationing a British force of some 10,000 men in the North American possessions. Although the actual number realized was closer to 6,000, their costs were more than £350,000 annually. To help meet these costs, Parliament passed two laws to generate approximately one-tenth of this revenue. Of the two laws, the Sugar Act of 1764 had more far-reaching economic implications for the colonists because it contained provisions that served the ends of all major English economic interests and threatened many American businesses in the colonies. But the Stamp Act of 1765, although actually far less inclusive, incited political tempers to a boil that in a very real sense started the first step toward rebellion.

The most important clauses of the Sugar Act levied taxes on imports of non-British products of the West Indies. Although the duty on foreign molasses was actually lowered from 6d. to 3d. a gallon—a marked reduction from the rate set by the old Molasses Act—provision was made for strict collection of the tax in the belief that the smaller tax, if strictly enforced, would produce a larger revenue. (A similar argument is characteristic of today's supply-side economics.) A more important goal, however, was the protection of British West Indian planters—who were well represented in Parliament—from the competition of New England rum makers. Actually, more than half the molasses imported by colonists was used

---

[2]Lance E. Davis and Robert A. Huttenback, "The Cost of Empire," in *Explorations in the New Economic History*, eds. Roger L. Ransom, Richard Sutch, and Gary M. Walton (New York: Academic Press, 1982), 42.

in homes to make Boston baked beans, shoofly pie, apple pandowdy, and molasses jack (a kind of homebrewed beer); but the chief fear of the English sugar planters was that cheap molasses imports from the French West Indies would enable the New England rum distilleries to capture the rum market on the mainland as well as in the non-British islands.[3] And their concern was probably justified, despite the alleged inferiority of the New England product. Moreover, the Sugar Act added to the list of enumerated articles several raw materials demanded by British manufacturers, including some important exports of the Northern and Middle colonies. Finally, this comprehensive law removed most of the tariff rebates (drawbacks) previously allowed on European goods that passed through English ports and even placed new duties on foreign textiles that competed with English products. Nevertheless, the Sugar Act, in form and substance, was much like earlier acts passed to restrict and control trade.

The Stamp Act, on the other hand, was simply designed to raise revenue and served no ends of mercantile policy. The law required that stamps varying in cost from half a penny to several pounds be affixed to legal documents, contracts, newspapers and pamphlets, and even playing cards and dice.

According to Benjamin Franklin's argument to Parliament against the tax, the colonists objected on the grounds that the act levied an "internal" tax, as distinguished from the traditional "external" taxes or duties collected on goods imported to the colonies. When English ministers refused to recognize this distinction, the colonists further objected that the tax had been levied by a distant Parliament that did not contain a single colonial representative. Thus was born the colonial rallying cry, "No taxation without representation!" Colonists complained that both the Sugar Act and the Stamp Act required the tax revenues to be remitted to England for disbursement, a procedure that further drained the colonies of precious specie and constantly reduced the amount of goods that could be imported to America. When it became apparent that strict enforcement would accompany such measures, severe resistance arose in the colonies. Lawyers and printers—who were especially infuriated by the Stamp Act—furnished articulate, able leadership and communication for anti-British agitation.

The decade of trouble that followed was characterized by alternating periods of colonial insubordination, British concession, renewed attempts to raise revenues, further colonial resistance, and, at last, punitive action—taken by the British in anger at what was felt to be rank disloyalty. The so-called Stamp Act Congress met in New York in 1765, passed resolutions of fealty, and organized a boycott of English goods. "Nonimportation associations" were established throughout the colonies, and the volume of imports from Britain declined dramatically as docks and warehouses bulged with unsold British goods.

A concerted effort to boycott English goods did not develop in all regions. The Middle colonies—where the boycotts first centered—exhibited the greatest decrease in trade with England. The Upper South contributed effectively to the boycott, largely because of the Restraining Act of 1764 curtailing Virginia's paper money issues (see chapter 4). New England gave only slight support to these first nonimport agreements, and the lower South failed to join the boycott. Yet overall, colonial efforts to boycott British imports were highly effective (Economic Reasoning Proposition 2). In fact, English merchants were so sharply affected that they demanded the repeal of the Stamp Act. They were joined by such political leaders as Edmund Burke and William Pitt, whose sympathies lay with the colonists. Parliament promptly responded, repealing the Stamp Act and reducing the duty on foreign molasses from 3d. to 1d. per gallon. Thus, the first major confrontation between America and England ended peacefully, and a profound lesson had been learned. In the mercantilist scheme of things, the Empire had tilted. The American mainland colonies ultimately had

★★★ *Economic Reasoning Proposition*

[3]For the details of this controversy, see Gilman M. Ostrander, "The Colonial Molasses Trade," Agricultural History 30 (1956): 77–84. See also Stuart Bruchey, *The Colonial Merchant* (New York: Harcourt Brace Jovanovich, 1966), 67–78.

become as important a market for English wares as they and the West Indian planters were a source of raw materials. Americans as consumers had found a new and powerful economic weapon—the boycott.

MORE CHANGES AND THE SECOND CRISIS

Although Parliament had responded to economic pressure from America by repealing the Stamp Act, England angrily and obstinately maintained its right to tax the colonies. The other sugar duties remained, and the Declaratory Act of 1766 affirmed the right of Parliament to legislate in all matters concerning Americans. Nevertheless, there was rejoicing both in the colonies and in England, and it was generally believed that the English and American differences would be reconciled. But even then, the Quartering Act of 1765 had been on the statute books a year, with its stipulations that the colonial assemblies provide barracks, some provisions, and part of the costs of military transport for British troops stationed within the colonies. This law was to prove especially problematic in New York, where soldiers were to be concentrated on their way to the West. Much worse was to come, however. George Grenville had been dismissed from the British ministry in 1765, largely because King George III (aged 25) disliked him. Grenville was replaced as chancellor of the exchequer by Charles Townshend. Because the great English landowners were persistently clamoring for relief from their heavy property taxes, Townshend tried once again to raise revenues in America. He felt that if the colonials objected to "internal" taxes, he would provide them with some "external" duties levied on such important articles of consumption as tea, glass, paper, and red and white lead (pigments for paint). By 1767, the Townshend duties were imposed.

Although these duties items were definitely important to colonial life, the colonists might have accepted their taxation calmly had the British not adopted measures to put real teeth into the law. One of the Townshend Acts provided for an American Customs Board, another for the issuance by colonial courts of the hated general search warrants known as writs of assistance, and another for admiralty courts in Halifax, Boston, Philadelphia, and Charleston to try smuggling cases. With a single stroke, the British ministry succeeded once again in antagonizing a wide cross-section of the American populace, and again resistance flared—this time in the form of both peaceful petitions and mob violence, culminating in the 1770 Boston Massacre, which left five colonials dead (Economic Reasoning Proposition 4). Once more the nonimportation agreements, especially effective in the port towns (see page 73, Map 4.1), were imposed. Only in the Chesapeake colonies—the one major colonial region spared a court of admiralty—was this boycott fairly unsuccessful.[4] Nevertheless, by late 1769, American imports had declined to perhaps one-third of their normal level. The value of lost English sales in the colonies exceeded £1 million in 1768 and 1769 combined, and once again English merchants exerted pressure to change trade policy. For the second time, Parliament appeared to acquiesce to colonial demands. In 1770, all the Townshend duties except the duty on tea were repealed, and although some of the most distasteful acts remained on the books, everyone except a few colonial hotheads felt that a peaceful settlement was possible. Trade was resumed, and a new level of prosperity was reached in 1771.

THE THIRD CRISIS AND REBELLION

Reasonable calm prevailed until 1773, when resistance flared up again over what now seems to have been an inconsequential matter. The English East India Company, in which many politically powerful people owned an interest, was experiencing financial difficulties. Parliament had granted the company a loan of public funds (such as Congress gave the

[4]Another contributing factor may have been that trade in the Chesapeake region was relatively decentralized, thereby reducing the possibility of blacklisting or boycotting colonial importers and others who failed to join the effort.

Angered colonists, disguised as Indians, invited themselves to a "tea party" to show the British how they felt about English mercantile policies. The damage to property was nearly £9,000 (about $1,000,000 in 2004 values).

Chrysler Corporation in 1981) and had also passed the Tea Act of 1773, which permitted the company to handle tea sales in a new way. Until this time, the company, which enjoyed a monopoly on the trade from India, had sold tea to English wholesalers, who, in turn, sold it to jobbers, who sent it to America. There the tea was turned over to colonial wholesalers, who at last distributed it to American retailers. Overall, many people had received income from this series of transactions; besides, duties had been collected on the product when it reached English ports and again when it arrived in America. The new Tea Act allowed the East India Company to ship tea directly to the colonies, thereby eliminating the British duty and reducing handling costs. Consumers were to benefit by paying less for tea, the company would presumably sell more tea at a lower price, and everybody would be happy. But everybody was not happy. Smugglers of Dutch tea were now undersold, the colonial tax was still collected (a real sore point), and, most important, the American importer was removed from the picture, thus alarming American merchants. If the colonial tea wholesaler could be bypassed, couldn't the business of other merchants also be undercut? Couldn't other companies in Great Britain be granted monopoly control of other commodities, until eventually Americans would be reduced to keeping small shops and selling at retail what their foreign masters imported for them? Wouldn't just a few pro-British agents who would handle the necessary distribution processes grow rich while staunch Americans grew poor? The list of rhetorical questions grew, and the answers seemed clear to almost every colonist engaged in business. From merchants in Boston to shopkeepers in the hamlets came a swift and violent reaction. Tea in the port towns was sent back to England or destroyed in various ways—the most spectacular of which was the Boston Tea Party, a well-executed three-hour affair involving 30 to 40 men (Economic Reasoning Proposition 1). Many colonists were shocked at this wanton destruction of private property, estimated at nearly £9,000 (or nearly $1,000,000 in 2004 prices), but their reaction was mild compared with the indignation that swelled in Britain.

The result was the bitter and punitive legislation known as the Intolerable Acts. Passed in the early summer of 1774, the Intolerable Acts (1) closed the port of Boston to all shipping

This illustration emphasizes the political antagonisms launched by the Intolerable Acts of 1774.

until the colonists paid the East India Company for its tea; (2) permitted British officials charged with crimes committed in an American colony while enforcing British laws to be tried in another colony or in Britain; (3) revised the charter of Massachusetts to make certain cherished rights dependent on the arbitrary decision of the Crown-appointed governor; and (4) provided for the quartering of troops in the city of Boston, which was especially onerous to the citizens after the events of the Boston Massacre four years earlier. In the ensuing months, political agitation reached new heights of violence, and economic sanctions were again invoked. For the third time, nonimportation agreements were imposed, and the delegates to the First Continental Congress voted not to trade with England or the British West Indies unless concessions were made. On October 14, 1774, the Continental Congress provided a list of grievances:

1. Taxes had been imposed upon the colonies by the "British" Parliament.
2. Parliament had claimed the right to legislate for the colonies.
3. Commissioners were set up in the colonies to collect taxes.
4. Admiralty court jurisdictions had been extended into the interior.
5. Judges' tenures had been put at the pleasure of the Crown.
6. A standing army had been imposed upon the colonies.
7. Persons could be transported out of the colonies for trials.
8. The port of Boston had been closed.
9. Martial law had been imposed upon Boston.
10. The Quebec Act had confiscated the colonists' western lands.[5]

[5]Jonathan Hughes, *American Economic History*, 3d ed. (Glenview: Scott, Foresman, 1990), 59.

The Congress ultimately went on to demand the repeal of all the major laws imposed on the colonies after 1763.[6] By this time, however, legislative reactions and enactments were of little importance. The crisis had become moral and political. Americans would not yield to the British until their basic freedoms were restored, and the British would not make peace until the colonists relented. The possibilities for peaceful reconciliation ebbed as the weeks passed. Finally, violence broke out with the shots of April 19, 1775, which marked a major turning point in the history of the world. On July 4, 1776, independence was declared. The Empire that had tilted in 1765 had now cracked.

Support in the Countryside

Although the events leading to the Revolution centered primarily on the conflicts between British authority and colonial urban commerce, the vast rural populace played an essential supporting role in the independence movement. How can we explain the willingness of wealthy southerners and many poor farmers to support a rebellion that was spearheaded by an antagonized merchant class? Though certainly no apparent allied economic interests were shared among these groups, each group had its own motives for resisting British authority. In rural America, antagonisms primarily stemmed from English land policy (Economic Reasoning Proposition 2).

Before 1763, British policy had been calculated to encourage the rapid development of the colonial West. In the interest of trade, English merchants wanted the new country to be populated as rapidly as possible. Moreover, rapid settlement extended the frontier and thereby helped strengthen opposition to France and Spain. By 1763, however, the need to fortify the frontier against foreign powers had disappeared. As the Crown and Parliament saw it, now was the time for more control on the frontier. First, the British felt it was wise to contain the population well within the seaboard area, where the major investments had been made and where political control would be easier. Second, the fur trade was now under the complete control of the British, and it was deemed unwise to have frontier pioneers moving in and creating trouble with the Indians. Third, wealthy English landowners were purchasing western land in great tracts, and pressure was exerted to "save" some of the good land for these investors. Finally, placing the western lands under the direct control of the Crown was designed to obtain revenues from sales and quitrents for the British treasury.[7]

In the early 1760s, events on the frontier served to tighten the Crown's control of settlement. Angry over injustices and fearful that the settlers would encroach on their hunting grounds, the northern Indians rebelled under the Ottawa chief Pontiac. Colonial and British troops put down the uprising, but only after seven of the nine British garrisons west of Niagara were destroyed. Everyone knew that western settlement would come under continuing threat unless the native Indians were pacified. Primarily as a temporary solution, the king issued the Royal Proclamation of 1763, which, in effect, drew a line beyond which colonials could not settle without express permission from the Crown (see Map 6.1). Governors could no longer grant patents to land lying west of the sources of rivers that flowed into the Atlantic; anyone seeking such a grant had to obtain one directly from the king. At the same time, the fur trade was placed under centralized control, and no trader could cross the Allegheny Mountains without permission from England.

A few years later, the policy of keeping colonial settlement under British supervision was reaffirmed, although it became apparent that the western boundary line would not remain rigidly fixed. In 1768, the line was shifted westward, and treaties with the Indians made large

[6] *Documents Illustrative of the Formation of the American States.* (Washington: Government Printing Office, 1927), 1–4.

[7] Quitrents were an old form of feudal dues seldom paid in any of the colonies except Virginia and Maryland. In Virginia, the quitrents went to the Crown (about £5,000 annually after 1765); in Maryland, they went to Lord Baltimore, the proprietor.

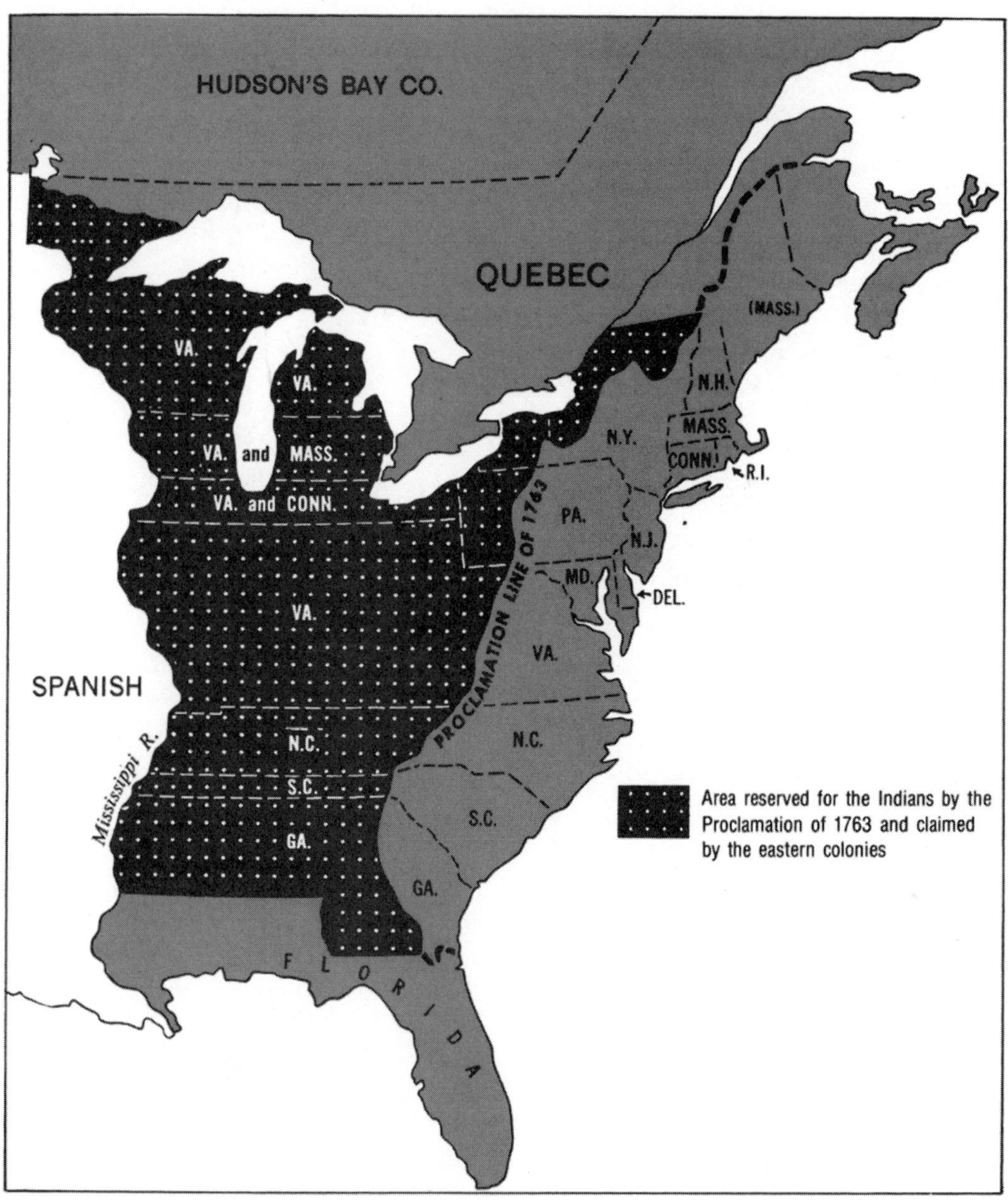

MAP 6.1 **Colonial Land Claims** *The colonial appetite for new land was huge, as colonial land claims demonstrated. The Royal Proclamation of 1763 was designed to stop westward movement.*

land tracts available to speculators. In 1774, the year in which the Intolerable Acts were passed, two British actions demonstrated that temporary expedients had evolved into permanent policies. First, a royal proclamation tightened the terms on which land would pass into private hands. Grants were no longer to be free; instead, tracts were to be sold at public auctions in lots of 100 to 1,000 acres at a minimum price of 6d. per acre. Even more serious was the passage of the Quebec Act in 1774, which changed the boundaries of Quebec to the Ohio River in the East and the Mississippi River in the West (see Map 6.2 on page 116). More important, the act destroyed the western land claims of Massachusetts, Connecticut, and Virginia. The fur trade was to be regulated by the governor of Quebec, and the Indian boundary line was to run as far south as Georgia. Many colonists viewed the act as theft.

MAP 6.2 Reassignment of Claims *The Quebec Act of 1774 gave the Indians territories that had earlier been claimed by various colonies and, at the same time, nearly doubled the area of Quebec.*

Not all colonists suffered from the new land policy. Rich land speculators who were politically powerful enough to obtain special grants from the king found the new regulations restrictive but not ruinous. Indeed, great holders of ungranted lands east of the mountains, such as the Penns and the Calverts, or of huge tracts already granted but not yet settled, stood to benefit from the rise in property values that resulted from the British embargo on westward movement. Similarly, farmers of old, established agricultural areas would benefit in two ways: (1) the competition from the produce of the new lands would now be less and (2) because it would be harder for agricultural laborers to obtain their own farms, hired hands would be cheaper.

Although many of the restrictions on westward movement were necessary, at least for a time because of Indian resistance on the frontier, many colonists resented these restrictions. The withdrawal of cheap, unsettled western lands particularly disillusioned young adults who had planned to set out on their own but now could not. Recall that from 1720 to 1775, about 225,000 Scotch-Irish and Germans had immigrated to America, mostly to the Middle colonies. These were largely men of fighting age with no loyalties to the English Crown. Now many had been denied land they saw as rightfully theirs. Similarly, even established frontier farmers usually took an anti-British stand because they thought that they would be more likely to succeed under a government liberal in disposing of its land. Although poor agrarians did not have dollar stakes in western lands that were comparable to those of large fur traders, land speculators, and planters, they were still affected. Those who were unable to pay their debts sometimes lost their farms through foreclosure; a British policy that inhibited westward movement angered the frontiersmen and tended to align them against the British and with the aristocratic Americans, with whom they had no other affiliation. The Currency Act (Restraining Act) of 1764 also frustrated and annoyed this debtor group because although prices actually rose moderately in the ensuing decade, farmers were persuaded that their lot worsened with the moderate contraction of paper money that occurred (Economic Reasoning Proposition 4).

★★★ *Economic Reasoning Proposition*

Economic Exploitation Reconsidered

It is sometimes alleged that the American Revolution was the result of the inevitable clash of competing capitalisms and of England's exploitation of the colonies. In the long run, such conjectures defy empirical testing. After all, how can one judge whether independence or British rule offered more promise for economic progress in North America?

Of course, the short-term consequences of independence can be assessed—a task that awaits us in chapter 7. But at this point, it is important to reconsider the question of colonial exploitation as a motive for revolt. Did British trade restrictions drain the colonial economy?

First, manufacturing restrictions had been placed on woolens, hats, and finished iron products. Woolen production in the colonies was limited to personal use or local trade, so this imposed no significant hardship. The colonists were quite satisfied to purchase manufactures from England at the lower costs made possible by the large-scale production methods employed there. This situation continued even after independence was achieved, and American woolens provided no competition for imported English fabrics until the nineteenth century.

A small portion of colonial manufacturing activity (predominantly New York producers) was hurt by the passage of the Hat Act in 1732. This one-sided legislation benefited London hatters by prohibiting the colonial export of beaver hats. For the overall American economy, however, the effects of the Hat Act were negligible. Similarly, parliamentary restrictions on iron proved moderately harmless. Actually, the colonial production of raw pig and bar iron was encouraged, but the finishing of iron and steel and the use of certain types of equipment were forbidden after 1750. Nevertheless, like the Molasses Act of 1733, restrictions on the manufacture of colonial iron were ignored with impunity: 25 iron mills were established between 1750 and 1775 in Pennsylvania and Delaware alone. Furthermore, the legislative freedom enjoyed by the colonists was amply displayed when the Pennsylvania assembly, in open defiance of the law, appropriated financial aid for a new slitting mill (nail factory). No matter how distasteful these British regulations were to the colonists, they were superfluous (woolen restrictions), ignored (the slitting mill), or inconsequential (hat production).

The generally liberal British land policy was designed to encourage rapid settlement. Only after the war with Chief Pontiac and the resulting Royal Proclamation of 1763 did land policy suddenly become less flexible. When land controls were tightened again by the

Quebec Act of 1774, important political issues emerged. Western lands claimed by Massachusetts, Connecticut, and Virginia were redistributed to the Province of Quebec, and land was made less accessible. Territorial governments were placed entirely in the hands of British officials, and trials there were conducted without juries.

We have already assessed the economic implications of these land policies. Some people gained; others lost. But clearly, the climate of freedom changed swiftly, and the political implications of these new policies were hard for the colonists to accept. The major issue appears to have been who was to determine the policy rather than what the policy itself was to be. In fact, the British land policies proved to be largely necessary, and the same basic restraints were prescribed and adopted by the federal government after American independence was achieved. It seems unlikely that the new government would have adopted these restraints had they been economically burdensome (Economic Reasoning Proposition 2).

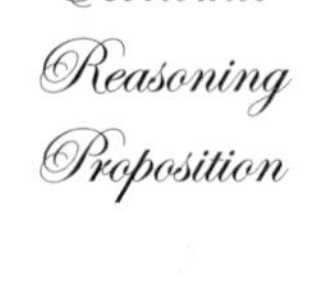

The same thing was true of currency restrictions. After independence, the new government adopted measures similar to those England had imposed earlier. For instance, in 1751, Parliament passed the Currency Act, which prohibited New England from establishing new public banks and from issuing paper money for private transactions. A similar and supplemental Restraining Act appeared in 1764, in the wake of events in the Chesapeake area. Planters there were heavily in debt because they had continued to import goods during the Seven Years' War even though their own exports had declined. When Virginia issued £250,000 in bills of credit, to be used as legal tender in private transactions as well as for public sector payments (mainly taxes), British creditors stood to lose. When the planters began to use cheap money to repay debts they had incurred in hard sterling, Britain countered by extending the original Currency Act to all the colonies. This extension certainly hurt the hard-pressed Chesapeake region and stimulated its unusual support for the boycott of English imports in 1765. But the adoption of similar controls after independence indicates that the economic burden of currency restriction could not have been oppressive overall. The real point at issue was simply whether England or the colonists themselves should hold the reins of monetary control.

It appears that only with respect to the Navigation Acts was there any significant exploitation in a strict economic sense, as illustrated in Economic Insight 6.1. In the words of Lawrence A. Harper:

> The enumeration of key colonial exports in various Acts from 1660 to 1766 and the Staple Act of 1663 hit at colonial trade both coming and going. The Acts required the colonies to allow English middlemen to distribute such crops as tobacco and rice and stipulated that if the colonies would not buy English manufactures, at least they should purchase their European goods in England. The greatest element in the burden laid upon the colonies was not the taxes assessed. It consisted in the increased costs of shipment, transshipment, and middleman's profits arising out of the requirement that England be used as an entrepot.[8]

While these burdens of more costly imports and less remunerative colonial exports amounted to nearly 1 percent of total colonial income, there were also benefits to the colonies: They were provided with bounties and other benefits such as naval protection and military defense at British expense.

In any case, the colonists had lived with these restrictions for more than a century. Even those hardest hit—the producers of tobacco and other enumerated products—almost never mentioned the restrictions in their lists of grievances against England. It is especially noteworthy that the acts of trade are not even mentioned in the Declaration of Independence.

[8]Lawrence A. Harper, "The Effect of the Navigation Acts on the Thirteen Colonies," in *The Era of the American Revolution*, ed. Richard B. Morris (New York: Columbia University Press, 1939).

Economic Insight 6.1

The Supply and Demand Effects of the Navigation Acts

Supply-and-demand analysis is useful to illustrate explicitly the burdens on the colonists caused by the Navigation Acts. The requirement that England be used as an "entrepot" burdened the colonists with extra handling and shipping costs—costs over and above those that would have occurred had commodities been shipped directly from continental Europe. A graph using supply-and-demand curves illustrates the case for imports:

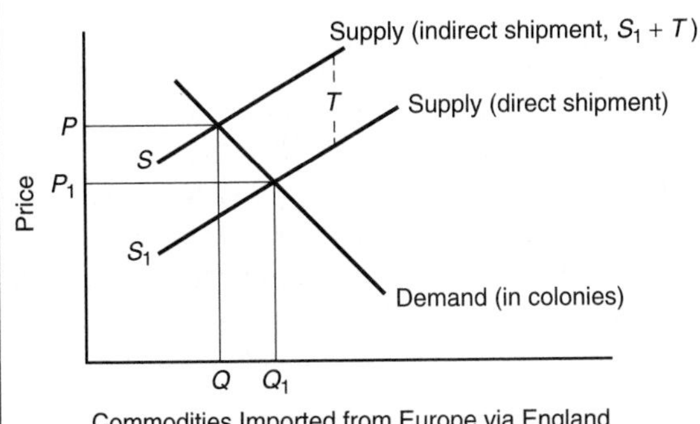

Let T represent these extra indirect routing costs on colonial imports from continental Europe. These extra costs may be viewed as a shift in the supply curve from S_1 to S. The effect of the higher transport costs is to cause prices of the affected imports to be higher in the colonies, at P rather than P_1, and quantities to be less, Q rather than Q_1.

The change in price $(P - P_1)$ times the quantities traded (Q) gives a lower bound to the burden on colonial imports from Europe. $(P - P_1)(Q_1)$ gives an upper-bound measure. A similar approach can illustrate the burdens of the laws on colonial exports to continental Europe. In this case, the export price in the colonies is lower because of the law. As the work of Roger Ransom has shown, these burdens were disproportionately large on southerners. Overall, however, the burdens on imports and exports from indirect routing were less than 1 percent of colonial income.[9]

Rather than exploitation, it was the rapidly changing and severely administered new colonial policies that precipitated the American Revolution. Before 1763, the colonists had been free to do pretty much as they pleased. An occasional new enactment or a veto of colonial legislation by Britain had caused little or no discord. After the Seven Years' War, however, conditions suddenly changed. A host of new taxes and regulations were effected and strictly enforced by Britain. The new taxes were light, but their methods of collection borne heavily.

Collectively, the acts after 1763 gave almost every colonist a grievance: Debtors objected to the Currency Act; shippers and merchants to the Sugar Act; pioneers to the Quebec Act; politicians, printers, and gamblers to the Stamp Act; retailers and smugglers to the Tea Act. As colonial resentments flared, Committees of Correspondence pressed forward to formally claim the rights they had long held de facto before 1763 (Economic Reasoning Proposition 4).

★★★ *Economic Reasoning Proposition*

In many ways, it appears that the growing economic maturity of the colonies would soon have made American independence inevitable. Indeed, the gross product of the

[9] For an assessment of the several studies and estimates of these costs, see Gary M. Walton, "The New Economic History and the Burdens of the Navigation Acts," *Economic History Review* 24, 2d series (1971): 533–542. Also, for a more recent article and counterargument, see Larry Sawyers, "The Navigation Acts Revisited," *Economic History Review* 45 (2), (May 1992): 262–284.

colonies was nearly £25 million at the time, or nearly one-third of England's gross national product, as compared with only about one-fourth at the beginning of the eighteenth century. Clearly, the colonies had matured economically to a point where an independent course was feasible.

But was Revolution necessary to break away from the Empire? After all, other English colonies subsequently gained independence without resorting to armed warfare. By 1775, according to Charles Andrews, the colonies had reached a point where they were

> qualified to cooperate with the mother country on terms similar to those of a brotherhood of free nations, such as the British world is becoming today (1926). But England was unable to see this fact, or to recognize it, and consequently America became the scene of a political unrest which might have been controlled by a compromise, but was turned to revolt by coercion. The situation is a very interesting one, for England is famous for her ability to compromise at critical times in her history. For once, at least, she failed.[10]

The nature of that "failure" is nicely summarized by Lawrence Harper:

> As a mother country, Britain had much to learn. Any modern parents' magazine could have told George III's ministers that the one mistake not to make is to take a stand and then to yield to howls of anguish. It was a mistake which the British government made repeatedly. It placed a duty of 3d. per gallon on molasses, and when it encountered opposition, reduced it to 1d. It provided for a Stamp Act and withdrew it in the face of temper tantrums. It provided for external taxes to meet the colonial objections and then yielded again by removing all except one. When finally it attempted to enforce discipline, it was too late. Under the circumstances, no self-respecting child—or colonist—would be willing to yield.[11]

It would appear that the lessons the English learned from their failures with the American colonies served them well in later periods because other English colonies subsequently won their independence without wide-scale bloodshed. This colonial legacy was of paramount importance in the centuries to follow.

SELECTED REFERENCES AND SUGGESTED READINGS

Barrow, Thomas. *Trade and Empire: The British Customs Service in Colonial America, 1660–1775* (Cambridge, Mass.: Harvard University Press, 1967).

Becker, Robert A. *Revolution, Reform, and the Politics of Taxation in America: 1763–1783* (Baton Rouge: Louisiana State University Press, 1980).

Beer, George L. *The Old Colonial System 1660–1754* (New York: Macmillan, 1912).

Davis, Lance E., and Robert A. Huttenback. "The Cost of Empire." In *Explorations in the New Economic History,* eds. Roger L. Ransom, Richard Sutch, and Gary M. Walton (New York: Academic Press, 1982).

Ernst, Joseph, and Marc Egnal. "An Economic Interpretation of the American Revolution." *William and Mary Quarterly* 29 (1972): 3–32.

---

[10] Charles Andrews, "The American Revolution: An Interpretation," *American Historical Review* 31 (1926): 232.

[11] Lawrence A. Harper, "Mercantilism and the American Revolution," *Canadian Historical Review* 25 (1942): 14.

Hacker, Louis M. "The First American Revolution." *Columbia University Quarterly*, part 1 (September 1935). Reprinted in Gerald D. Nash. *Issues in American Economic History* (New York: Heath, 1972).

Harper, Lawrence. "The Effects of the Navigation Acts on the Thirteen Colonies." In *The Era of the American Revolution*, ed. Richard Morris (New York: Columbia University Press, 1939).

Matson, Cathy. "Mercantilism and the American Revolution." *Canadian Historical Review* (March 1942). Reprinted in Gerald D. Nash. *Issues in American Economic History* (New York: Heath, 1972).

———. "The Revolution, the Constitution, and the New Nation." In *The Cambridge Economic History of the United States,* Vol. I, eds. Stanley L. Engerman and Robert E. Gallman (New York: Cambridge University Press, 1996), 363–401.

McClelland, Peter D. "The Cost to America of British Imperial Policy." *American Economic Review: Papers and Proceedings* 59 (7), (May 1969): 370–381.

Miller, John C. *Origins of the American Revolution* (Stanford: Stanford University Press, 1959).

Morgan, Edmund S. *The American Revolution: A Review of Changing Interpretations* (Washington, D.C.: Service Center for Teachers of History, 1958).

Morgan, Edmund, and Helen Morgan. *The Stamp Act Crisis: Prologue to Revolution* (Chapel Hill: University of North Carolina Press, 1963).

Nash, Gary. *The Urban Crucible* (Cambridge: Harvard University Press, 1979).

Nettels, Curtis P. "British Mercantilism and the Economic Development of the Thirteen Colonies." *Journal of Economic History* 12 (1952): 105–114.

Ostrander, Gilman M. "The Colonial Molasses Trade." *Agricultural History* 30 (1956): 77–84.

Perkins, Edwin J. Chapters 7 and 8 in *The Economy of Colonial America*, 2d ed (New York: Columbia University Press, 1988).

Ransom, Roger. "British Policy and Colonial Growth: Some Implications of the Burdens of the Navigation Acts." *Journal of Economic History* 27 (1968): 427–435.

Reid, Joseph D. "On Navigating the Navigation Acts with Peter D. McClelland." *American Economic Review* 60 (1970): 949–955.

———. "Economic Burdens: Spark to the American Revolution?" *Journal of Economic History* 38 (1978): 81–120.

Sawyers, Larry. "The Navigation Acts Revisited." *Economic History Review* 45 (2), (May 1992): 262–284.

Thomas, Robert P. "A Quantitative Approach to the Study of the Effects of British Imperial Policy on Colonial Welfare: Some Preliminary Findings." *Journal of Economic History* 25 (1965): 615–638.

———. "British Imperial Policy and the Economic Interpretation of the American Revolution." *Journal of Economic History* 28 (1968): 436–440.

Tucker, Robert W., and David Hendrickson. *The Fall of the British Empire: Origins and the Fall of the British Empire* (Baltimore: Johns Hopkins University Press, 1982).

Ver Steeg, Clarence. "The American Revolutionary Movement Considered as an Economic Movement." *Huntington Library Journal* 20 (1957).

Walton, Gary M. "The New Economic History and the Burdens of the Navigation Acts." *Economic History Review* 24 (4), 2d series, (1971): 533–542.

Walton, Gary M., and James F. Shepherd. Chapter 8 in *The Economic Rise of Early America* (Cambridge: Cambridge University Press, 1979).

Part Two

The Revolutionary, Early National, and Antebellum Eras: 1776–1860

ECONOMIC AND HISTORICAL PERSPECTIVES 1776–1860

1. Industrializing Great Britain and the newly revolutionized France under Napoleon stood as the world's two leading powers. Britain was dominant in naval forces and led in per capita income; France was dominant in land forces, strong in total output, and larger in population.
2. War broke out between Britain and France in 1793 and lasted until 1815. To help finance his war, Napoleon sold the Louisiana Territory to the United States in 1803, doubling the land size of the new nation. Trade and commerce soared in American ports as U.S. shippers served as neutrals to the belligerents. The suppression of U.S. shipping entangled the United States in a second war with Britain in 1812.
3. The Northwest Land Ordinances of 1785 and 1787 ensured that new U.S. territories could progress toward statehood and enter the Union having full equality with the older states.
4. The U.S. Constitution, adopted in 1789, is a landmark document, historically unprecedented for its scope and simplicity, for its constraint on government power, and as a model of political compromise. It provided assurances of protection of property consistent with individual freedoms (with the telling exception of slavery, which persisted in the South).
5. The cotton gin, invented in 1793 by Eli Whitney, allowed the seeds of short staple cotton to be economically removed. Thereafter, U.S. cotton production as a share of world production increased from 0.5 percent in 1791 to 68 percent in 1850. Southern slavery became increasingly entrenched and a growing threat to the Union as western migrations brought the proslavery and antislavery forces into continual dispute.
6. As the Industrial Revolution spread from England to the United States in the early nineteenth century, a transportation revolution also unfolded to create a strong national market linking the industrializing Northeast with the agrarian Midwest and the southern cotton kingdom.
7. By 1860, the United States was the second leading industrial power in the world.

Chapter Seven

Hard Realities for a New Nation

The years from 1776 to 1815 consisted of four distinct periods: first was war (the Revolution), then peace and independence followed by war again (Napoleonic wars) with the new United States acting as a neutral, and, finally, the young nation's second war with England. These events caused economic fluctuations and imposed significant shocks on the economy, pressing resources into new areas of production as trade lanes opened and closed. Years of war generally reduced American trade and economic activity. However, during the years of war when U.S. neutrality gave American shipping and commerce the opportunities to fill the void of others who were engaged in combat, times were especially prosperous.

Even during peacetime, great economic adjustments occurred because the new nation was now outside the British Empire; severe peacetime trade restrictions added to the nation's difficulties.

Finally, the new nation faced the problems of paying the debts accumulated during the Revolutionary War years and of forging agreements among the states on how to form a government based on constitutional limitations (Economic Reasoning Propositions 1, 2, and 4).

Economic Reasoning Proposition

THE WAR AND THE ECONOMY

The Revolutionary War, which began officially on April 19, 1775, dragged on for more than six bitter years. From a vantage point more than two centuries later, we can see that the war foreshadowed a massive upheaval in the Western world—a chain reaction of revolutions, great and small, that would transform the world. But to the embattled colonials, it was simply a conflict fought for the righteous cause of securing freedom from intolerable British intervention in American affairs. Paradoxically, the Revolution was never supported by the substantial popular majority. Perhaps one-third of the colonists remained loyal to England; another third did little or nothing to help the cause, often trafficking with the enemy and selling provisions and supplies to American troops at profitable prices. In varying numbers and in widely scattered theaters, foot soldiers slogged wearily back and forth in heartbreaking campaigns that produced no military gains. Although there were relatively few seamen and sea battles were, for the most part, militarily indecisive, it is an irony of history that the Revolutionary War was finally won with naval strength, as the French fleet under its admiral, the Comte de Grasse, drove off the British men-of-war and bottled up Cornwallis at Yorktown.

Of course, maritime commerce was always an important factor in the war effort, and trade linkages were vital to the supply of arms and ammunitions. When legal restrictions were implemented by both the British and the colonists in 1775, nearly all American overseas commerce abruptly ceased. By mid-1775, the colonies faced acute shortages in such military essentials as powder, flints, muskets, and knives. Even salt, shoes, woolens, and linens were in short supply. Late in 1775, Congress authorized limited trade with the West Indies, mainly to procure arms and ammunitions, and trade with other non-British areas was on an unrestricted basis by the spring of 1776.

Nevertheless, the British maintained a fairly effective naval blockade of American ports, especially during the first two years of the war. Boston was pried open late in 1776, but most of the other major ports in New England and the Middle colonies were tightly sealed until 1778. As the British relaxed their grip on the North, they tightened it on the South. Savannah was taken late in 1778, Charleston in 1780.

Yet the colonies engaged in international trade despite the blockade. Formal treaties of commerce with France in 1778 and with Holland and Spain shortly thereafter stimulated the flows of overseas trade. Between 1778 and early 1782, American wartime commerce was at its zenith. During those years, France, Holland, Spain, and their possessions all actively traded with the colonies. Even so, the flow of goods in and out of the colonies remained well below prewar levels. Smuggling, privateering, and legal trade with overseas partners only partially offset the drastic trade reductions with Britain. Even the coastal trades were curtailed by a lack of vessels, by blockades, and by wartime freight rates. British-occupied ports, such as New York, generated some import activity but little or nothing in the way of exports.

As exports and imports fell, import substitution abounded, and the colonial economy became considerably more self-sufficient. In Philadelphia, for instance, nearly 4,000 women were employed to spin materials in their homes for the newly established textile plants. A sharp increase also occurred in the number of artisan workshops with a similar stimulus in the production of beer, whiskey, and other domestic alcoholic beverages. The rechanneling of American resources into import competing industries was especially strong along the coast and in the major port cities (Economic Reasoning Propositions 1 and 2). Only the least commercialized rural areas remained little affected by the serpentine path of war and the sporadic flows of wartime commerce.

Overall, the war imposed a distinct economic hardship on the new nation. Most goods rose in cost and were more difficult to obtain. High prices and severe commercial difficulties encouraged some investors to turn from commerce to manufacturing. Then, once the trade lanes reopened with the coming of peace, even those who profited from the war were stung by the tide of imports that swept into American ports and sharply lowered prices. Although many Americans escaped the direct ordeals of war, few Americans were untouched by it—at least indirectly.

The strains of war and economic decline were complemented by the critical problem of forming a government. The thirteen colonies were bound together by the Articles of Confederation; established initially for the pressing issue of uniting to engage the enemy, it took from 1777 to 1781 for the individual states to ratify them. The Articles had merit and were effective as a source of early political agreement among the colonies, but they were inadequate as a permanent framework for national government. For example, the power to tax was left to the individual states, thus allowing any state to free ride on revenues supplied by others. Furthermore, after the colonies won independence, the great powers treated the

Perspective 7.1

Native Americans and the Revolution

The American Revolution was not entirely a war of colonial fighters against soldiers and sailors of the mother country. During the war, the Iroquois confederation (Six Nations) initially strained to maintain a neutral status. Eventually, however, most Iroquois tribes joined in fighting alongside the British. After the war, many Americans viewed the Iroquois as a people conquered and some wanted them banished west. In addition, Indian lands were greatly desired as a means to pay colonial soldiers for their services and help pay down the debts the colonists had built up during the war.

Despite refusing to accept a conquered status, the Iroquois' power was greatly weakened by the war and further reduced and broken in subsequent forest wars soon to follow. Many Iroquois moved to Canada, and much of their land was taken by the United States through purchase and treaties. By 1794, the remaining Iroquois were confined to a small set of reservations in the state of New York.

new nation with a disdain that bordered on contempt. Britain, annoyed because Americans refused to pay prewar British creditors or restore confiscated Tory property as provided in the peace treaty, excluded the United States from valuable commercial privileges and refused to withdraw troops from its frontier posts on American soil. Spain tried to close the lower Mississippi to American traffic. Even France refused to extend the courtesies traditionally offered a sovereign government. These and other problems too great to be surmounted by the states acting individually pressed inexorably for a strong rather than weak union. Under the Articles, the national government appeared too weak to negotiate improvements in its economic or military relations.

Internally, the most pressing problems were financial. Between 1775 and 1781, the war was financed by the issue of paper money in amounts great enough to result in a galloping inflation—the only one ever experienced in America except in the Confederate South. Nearly $400 million (at face value) in continental money, quartermaster and commissary certificates of the central government, and paper money of the states was issued to defray wartime expenses. For all practical purposes, these various issues were repudiated by the middle of 1783, the effect being a tax on those who held the depreciating currency while it declined in value. Only a relatively small foreign and domestic debt totaling less than $40 million remained, but the question of responsibility for its repayment remained a thorny issue because political leaders assumed that the states that paid the debt would ultimately hold the balance of power politically. More important was the fact that Congress had no independent income and had to rely for funds on catch-as-catch-can contributions from the states, made roughly in proportion to their individual populations. Nor were the states without their own fiscal problems. By 1786, no fewer than seven states were issuing their own paper, and debtor groups in the other six states were clamoring for similar issues. Although the issuing states (except Rhode Island) acted responsibly, perhaps no other course of events so frightened conservatives as the control of the money supply by the states. Indeed, the legacy of hyperinflation left a general distrust of government monetary management.[1]

[1] See Charles W. Calomiris, "Institutional Failure, Monetary Scarcity, and the Depreciation of the Continental," *Journal of Economic History* 48 (1988): 47–68.

American leaders remained divided over the kind of government that should ultimately be adopted. One group wanted no stronger central government than the Articles provided, preferring to cast its lot and fortune with the individual states. Another group, made up on the whole of less fiery revolutionaries, took the view that a strong central government, with power to coerce the states, should be quickly established. This clash of perspectives on the nation's basic institutions and jurisdictions, on states rights vis-à-vis federal mandates (or local or state regulations rather than federal ones), has remained a perennial political issue and has manifested itself in many forms, as will be emphasized. Until the end of the war, those who preferred a strong government were largely in control of the nation's affairs; but when news of a favorable peace arrived in 1783, many of the strongest leaders went home to their own pursuits, leaving the administration largely in the charge of weak-central government advocates.

Even as early as 1783, however, supporters of a weak central government had begun to make concessions that would strengthen the power of Congress, and by 1786, most of the vehement opponents of a strong central government knew that genuine union was inevitable. That year Virginia called the Annapolis Convention, ostensibly to settle questions of trade regulations among the states; however, the only action taken by the delegates was to recommend to Congress that another convention be called to examine a broader range of problems.

It was clear that American leadership was moving toward agreement. The convention that met in Philadelphia in 1787 was able to ignore its instructions to amend the Articles of Confederation and to create a new government instead only because the great constitutional questions debated so heatedly since 1775 were at least settled in the minds of the majority. In a little more than four months after the first meeting of the delegates, George Washington, president of the convention, sent the completed document to the states for ratification.[2] Delaware ratified it almost immediately, on December 7, 1787; on June 21, 1788, New Hampshire cast the crucial ninth vote in favor (Economic Reasoning Propositions 1 and 4). Congress declared the Constitution in effect beginning March 4, 1789, and two years later the Bill of Rights was passed and put into effect.

★★★ *Economic Reasoning Proposition*

THE CONSTITUTION

With the adoption of the Constitution, the power to tax was firmly delegated to the federal government, which was empowered to pay off past debts, even those incurred by the states. The assurance that public debts will be honored has proven critical to the development of a sound capital market in the United States. There have been failings—as in the late 1830s, when several states defaulted on loans—but even today, the United States benefits from this institutional heritage and is viewed as a haven by major investors seeking safety for their capital (Economic Reasoning Proposition 3).

★★★ *Economic Reasoning Proposition*

The Constitution also gave the central government the sole right to mint coins and regulate the money supply. Such rights were not allowed the states. Having just emerged from monetary chaos and hyperinflation, a stable dollar was highly desired and viewed as an answer to the conflicting interests of creditors and debtors.

Both these powers, to tax and to regulate money, brought into sharp focus the founders' concerns over conflicting factions, the limits of majority rule, and the ability to redistribute

---

[2]For an analysis assessing the economic vested interests of the delegates, see Robert A. McGuire and Robert L. Ohsfeldt, "An Economic Model of Voting Behavior over Specific Issues at the Constitutional Convention of 1787," *Journal of Economic History* 46 (1986): 79–82.

wealth and income by governmental means.[3] Consequently, federal taxes had to be uniform among all the states and, of course, U.S. dollars had to be exchangeable throughout the states. The concerns urging barriers to prevent significant and radical changes in the distribution of wealth through government formed the basis for a major section of the Fifth Amendment: "nor shall any person . . . be deprived of life, liberty, or property, without due process of law; nor shall private property be taken for public use without just compensation."

Another matter of great political and economic significance was the regulation of trade among the states. Although no substantial barriers to interstate commerce had emerged in the 1780s, the possibility for them was evident. Under the Constitution, the states were forbidden to enact tariffs, thus ensuring the toll-free movement of goods. The important "interstate clause" established a great national common market that reduced the potential of local monopolies and increased the gain from regional specialization and trade; in later decades, it also permitted the extension of federal authority to many areas of interstate economic activity.

The Constitution promoted trade and economic specialization in other ways. It authorized the federal government to maintain an army and navy, establish post offices and roads, fix standards of weights and measures, and establish uniform bankruptcy laws. It also gave Congress the authority to set laws on patents: "To promote the progress of science and useful arts by securing for limited times to authors and inventors the exclusive right to their respective writings and discoveries." With greater assurances to the gains of their own ideas and creations, creative people would hasten technical change.

Another transfer of authority to the federal government was that of foreign affairs. The federal government alone could negotiate treaties or set tariffs. The power to regulate tariffs became a powerful lever in negotiations with foreign nations to reduce or eliminate duties on American goods abroad, as it remains today in the global negotiations within the World Trade Organization (WTO). Before this shift of power, competition among the states minimized the possibility of this leverage, and U.S. tariffs were very low. Once they were centralized, however, tariffs became the chief source of federal revenues throughout most of the nineteenth century.

For the delegates at the Philadelphia convention (and the individual states) to voluntarily release such powers to the central government was unprecedented—made possible only through compromise, which was epitomized in the question of slavery. The Constitutional compromise allowed slavery to continue but limited the importation of slaves to only 20 years,

---

[3]In Paper 10 of the *Federalist Papers*, James Madison demonstrates his preoccupation with these important matters:

> The most common and durable source of factions has been the various and unequal distribution of property. Those who hold and those who are without property have ever formed distinct interests in society. Those who are creditors, and those who are debtors, fall under a like discrimination. A landed interest, a manufacturing interest, a mercantile interest, a money interest, with many lesser interests, grow up of necessity in civilized nations, and divide them into different classes, actuated by different sentiments and views. The regulation of these various and interfering interests forms the principal task of modern legislation, and involves the spirit of party and faction in the necessary and ordinary operations of the government. . . . The inference to which we are brought is, that the causes of faction cannot be removed, and that relief is only to be sought in the means of controlling its effects.
>
> If a faction consists of less than a majority, relief is supplied by the republican principle, which enables the majority to defeat its sinister views by regular vote. It may clog the administration, it may convulse the society; but it will be unable to execute and mask its violence under the forms of the Constitution. When a majority is included in a faction, the form of popular government, on the other hand, enables it to sacrifice to its ruling passion or interest both the public good and the rights of other citizens. To secure the public good and private rights against the danger of such a faction, and at the same time to preserve the spirit and the form of popular government, is then the great object to which our inquiries are directed.

This painting of the formal closing of the Philadelphia convention and sending the Constitution to the states for ratification highlights the hot work of the delegates through the months of late July, August, and September before the age of air conditioning.

ending in 1808. A tax of up to $10 per imported slave was allowed. Furthermore, each state was ordered to recognize the laws and court orders of other states; thus, runaway slaves escaping to another state were to be returned, like stolen property (Economic Reasoning Proposition 3). Was a slave merely property, or was a slave a person? Oddly, the Constitution viewed slaves in two respects: first and foremost, slaves were property, just as in colonial times; second, each slave was counted as three-fifths of a person for the purpose of determining each state's membership in the House of Representatives, which was based on population.

The debates of the convention focused carefully on the question of state versus national interests, and it was temporarily left implicit that powers not delegated to the federal government or forbidden to the states were reserved to the states (or the people). To strengthen these reserved rights, the Tenth Amendment was added to the Bill of Rights, ensuring the states' powers to set local and state laws such as licensing, regulation of business, taxes, zoning laws, civil conduct, and the like, and to use police powers to enforce them.

In respect to relations among people, the new nation preserved the treasured English Common Law. This long string of rules based on court decisions had worked well for centuries, and the First Continental Congress of 1774 had formally proclaimed the Common Law of England as the right of Americans.[4] Many states repeated this claim, and legal interpretations were left to the states as long as their legal statutes and interpretations were consistent with the Constitution, the supreme law of the land. Any conflict or challenge was to be adjudicated by the courts and, if necessary, ultimately by the Supreme Court.

---

[4]For the origins, development, and significance of the Common Law and trial by jury as contrasted with Roman law, see Chapter 13 in Winston S. Churchill, *A History of the English-Speaking Peoples: Vol. I. The Birth of Britain* (New York: Dorset, 1990).

The Constitution laid the foundation of the private property rights we enjoy today. It curbed the arbitrary powers of government and fostered personal security required for the pursuit of all varieties of productivity-enhancing activities. Amazingly brief and clear, the Constitution has proven flexible through court interpretation and, on sixteen occasions since the Bill of Rights, through amendment.

Probably no single original source exists from which the essential concepts of the Constitution were derived. And yet, in 1776, the same year that the Declaration of Independence rang its message of political freedom around the world, an odd-looking Scot, whose professorial mien belied his vast knowledge of economic affairs, offered a clarion rationale of economic freedom. *The Wealth of Nations* ultimately became a best-seller, and Adam Smith became admired and famous. Educated people everywhere, including American leaders, read his great work, marveling at the lucid language and its castigation of mercantilist constraints on economic processes. It does not diminish Adam Smith's great influence to say that he was the articulate commentator on forces that existed long before he began to write. Chief among these forces were a growing regard for the advantages of private property arrangements and an abiding conviction that law and order were essential to the preservation of property rights and to the opportunity for all people to acquire the things of this world. It follows, therefore, that matching the political guarantees of the Constitution with their ultimate assurance of personal freedoms would be norms, customs, and other laws establishing fundamental economic guarantees of protection of private property and enforcement of contracts, essential to a viable market economy. The United States was especially well tailored to Smith's concept of an economic order, directed by self-interest, that limited governmental rules and regulations but ensured the domestic tranquility and freedom from foreign interference that only a strong central government could provide.

AMERICAN INDEPENDENCE AND ECONOMIC CHANGE

The adoption of the Constitution in 1789 and the emergence of a stronger federal government did not have dramatic immediate effects. The crucial political decisions of that time were matched by challenging economic problems. The central problem was independence itself. All at once the young nation found itself outside the walls of the British Empire, and soon even the wartime trade alliances with France and Spain began to crumble.

In the Caribbean, U.S. ships were excluded from direct trade with the British West Indies. American merchants who tried to evade the law faced possible seizure by officials. Spain added to American woes by withdrawing the wartime privilege of direct U.S. trade with Cuba, Puerto Rico, and Hispaniola. In addition, Spain re-instituted its traditional policy of restricting trade with its possessions, permitting them to import goods only from Spain. U.S. trade with the French West Indies increased, but this was not enough to offset the declines in commercial trade with other Caribbean islands. Even in its lively trade with the French, the United States was not allowed to carry sugar from French islands, and only in times of severe scarcity did the French import American flour. In addition, the French imposed high duties on U.S. salted fish and meat, and these products were banned entirely from the British islands.

Restrictions and trade curtailments were not limited to the Caribbean. Now Americans were also cut off from direct trade with the British fisheries in Newfoundland and Nova Scotia. As a result, the New England states suffered severe losses in trade to the north in provisions, lumber, rum, and shipping services. To the east and into the Mediterranean, American shipping faced harassment by the Barbary pirates because the United States was no longer protected by the British flag and by British tribute to the governments of Tunis, Tripoli, and Algeria.

While American shipping rocked at anchor, American shipbuilding and the supporting industries of lumber and naval stores also remained unengaged. Britain now labeled all American-built vessels as foreign, thereby making them ineligible to trade within the Empire even when they were owned by British subjects. The result was the loss of a major market for American shipbuilders, and after 1783, U.S. ship production declined still further because American whale oil faced prohibitively high British duties. In fact, nearly all the activities that employed American-built ships (cod fishing, whaling, mercantile, and shipping services) were depressed industries, and New England—the center of these activities—suffered disproportionately during the early years of independence.

The states of the former Middle colonies were also affected. Pennsylvania and New York shared losses in shipbuilding. Moreover, their levels of trade in wheat, flour, salted meat, and other provisions to the West Indies were well below those of colonial peacetime years. By 1786, the Middle colonies had probably reached the bottom of a fairly severe business downturn, and then conditions began to improve as these products were reaccepted into the traditional West Indian and southern European markets.

Similar problems plagued the South. For instance, British duties on rice restricted the planters of South Carolina and Georgia primarily to markets in the West Indies and southern Europe. As the price of rice declined, further setbacks resulted from the loss of bounties and subsidies on indigo and naval stores. Having few alternative uses of their productive capacity, the Carolinas and Georgia faced special difficulties. Their economic future did not look bright. Similarly, Virginia and Maryland faced stagnating markets for their major staple—tobacco. In Britain, a tax of 15d. sterling was imposed on each pound of foreign tobacco. In France, a single purchasing monopoly, the Farmers-General, was created to handle tobacco imports. Meanwhile, Spain and Portugal prohibited imports of American tobacco altogether. These economic changes were the results of the colonies' choice to become independent (Economic Reasoning Propositions 1, 2, and 4).

Offsetting these restrictions were a few positive forces. Goods that previously had been "enumerated" could now be traded directly to continental European ports. This lowered the shipping and handling costs on some items such as tobacco, thereby having an upward effect on their prices. Meanwhile, the great influx of British manufactures sharply reduced prices on these goods in American ports. Although American manufacturers suffered, consumers were pleased: Compared with the late colonial period, the terms of trade—the prices paid for imports relative to the prices paid for exports—had improved. This was especially true in 1783 and 1784, when import prices were slightly below their prewar level and export prices were higher. Thereafter, however, the terms of trade became less favorable, and by 1790, there was little advantage in the adjustments of these relative prices compared with the prewar period.

A QUANTITATIVE ANALYSIS OF ECONOMIC CHANGE

To convey these many changes more systematically and in a long-run perspective, it is essential to compare the circumstances of the late colonial period and the years immediately following independence. Of course, this does not entirely isolate the impact of independence on the economy because forces other than independence contributed to the shifting magnitudes and patterns of trade and to the many other economic changes that occurred. Nevertheless, comparisons of the late colonial period with the early 1790s provide important insights into the new directions and prospects for the young nation.

Table 7.1 on page 132 shows that by 1790, the United States had taken advantage of its new freedom to trade directly with northern European countries. Most of this trade was in tobacco to France and the Netherlands, but rice, wheat, flour, and maize (Indian corn) were also shipped there in large amounts. Despite the emergence of this new trade pattern, the lion's share of American exports continued to be sent to Great Britain, including items that were then re-exported to the Continent. Many have speculated on the reasons for this

TABLE 7.1 Average Annual Real Exports to Overseas Areas from the 13 Colonies, 1768–1772, and the United States, 1790–1792 (in thousands of pounds sterling, 1768–1772 prices)

DESTINATION	1768–1772	PERCENTAGE OF TOTAL	1790–1792	PERCENTAGE OF TOTAL
Great Britain and Ireland	1,616	58%	1,234	31%
Northern Europe	—	—	643	16
Southern Europe	406	14	557	14
British West Indies } Foreign West Indies }	759	27	402	10
Foreign West Indies			956	24
Africa	21	1	42	1
Canadian Colonies	n.a.	—	60	2
Other	—	—	59	2
Total	2,802	100%	3,953	100%

Source: James F. Shepherd and Gary M. Walton, "Economic Change after the American Revolution: Prewar and Postwar Comparisons of Maritime Shipping and Trade," Explorations in Economic History *13 (1976): 397–422.*

renewal of American-British ties. Part of the explanation may be that Britain offered the greatest variety of goods at the best price and quality, especially woolens, linens, and hardware. Moreover, British merchants enjoyed the advantages of a common language, established contacts, and had a knowledge of U.S. markets. Because American imports were handled by British merchants, it was often advantageous to use British ports as dropping-off points for U.S. exports, even those destined for the Continent.

At the same time, new patterns of trade were emerging in the Caribbean. Before the Revolution, trade with the British West Indies had been greater than trade with the foreign islands, but by 1790 the situation was reversed, largely due to the exclusion of American shipping from the British islands. Undoubtedly, many American ships illegally traversed British Caribbean waters, and Dutch St. Eustatius remained an entrepot from which British islands were supplied as they had been during the war. Consequently, the statistics in Table 7.1 exaggerate this shift. Nevertheless, it would appear that U.S. trade with non-British areas of the Caribbean grew substantially during these years. This trend had been underway before the Revolution, but postwar restrictions on American shipping undoubtedly hastened it.

Lastly, it is worth noting that no new trades to romantic, faraway places emerged in any significant way during this period of transition. The changes in trade patterns were actually rather modest.

As trade patterns changed, so did the relative importance of the many goods traded. For instance, the most valuable export by the early 1790s was no longer tobacco, but bread and flour. Tobacco production grew slowly, but rising tobacco prices aided the recovery of the tobacco-producing areas of Virginia and Maryland. Other important southern staples, such as pitch, tar, rice, and indigo, fell both in value and in quantities produced. The decline of indigo was aggravated by the loss of bounties and by increased British production of indigo in the West Indies after the war. The most striking change of the period, however, was the increase in the export of foodstuffs such as salted meats (beef and pork), bread and flour, maize, and wheat. Of course, this increase accompanied the relative rise of the trades to the West Indies. Because the uptrend in food shipments to the West Indies was underway before the Revolution, not all of this shift in commodities can be attributed solely to independence.

Because of these changing patterns and magnitudes of trade, some states improved their economic well-being, while others lost ground. Table 7.2 shows exports per capita for each state during this period, after adjusting for inflationary effects. Compared with prewar levels, New England had returned to about the same per capita position by the early 1790s. The Middle Atlantic region showed improvement despite the depression felt so sharply in Pennsylvania in the mid-1780s. As indicated in Table 7.2, the trade of the southern regions

TABLE 7.2 Average Annual Exports from the 13 Colonies, 1768–1772, and the United States, 1791–1792 (in thousands of pounds sterling, 1768–1772 prices)

	1768–1772			1791–1792		
ORIGIN	TOTAL EXPORTS	PERCENTAGE OF TOTAL	PER CAPITA EXPORTS	TOTAL EXPORTS	PERCENTAGE OF TOTAL	PER CAPITA EXPORTS
New England	477	17%	0.82	842	22%	0.83
New Hampshire	46	2	0.74	33	1	0.23
Massachusetts	258	9	0.97	542	14	1.14
Rhode Island	81	3	1.39	119	3	1.72
Connecticut	92	3	0.50	148	4	0.62
Middle Atlantic	560	20	1.01	1,127	30	1.11
New York	187	7	1.15	512	14	1.51
New Jersey	2	—	0.02	5	—	0.03
Pennsylvania	353	13	1.47	584	16	1.34
Delaware	18	1	0.51	26	1	0.44
Upper South	1,162	41	1.79	1,160	31	1.09
Maryland	392	14	1.93	482	13	1.51
Virginia	770	27	1.72	678	18	0.91
Lower South	604	22	1.75	637	17	0.88
North Carolina	75	3	0.38	104	3	0.27
South Carolina	455	16	3.66	436	12	1.75
Georgia	74	3	3.17	97	3	1.17
Total, all regions	2,803	100%	1.31	3,766	100%	0.99

Source: James F. Shepherd and Gary M. Walton, "Economic Change after the American Revolution: Prewar and Postwar Comparisons of Maritime Shipping and Trade," Explorations in Economic History *13 (1976): 397–422.*

did not keep pace with a growing population. Although the South's prewar absolute level of exports had been regained by the early 1790s, its per capita exports were significantly below those in colonial times, with the Lower South most severely affected. However, once again, this decline was caused not so much by independence as by a decline in growth of demand in Europe for southern staples.

The wide variety of changes among the states makes it extremely hazardous to generalize nationally. Overall, a 30 percent decline in real per capita exports (per year) occurred. Total exports had climbed by 40 percent, but this fell far short of the 80 percent jump in population. Accompanying this change was a slowing in urbanization. The major cities of Philadelphia, New York, and Boston grew only 3 percent over this period, despite the large increase in the total population of the states. Both of these adjustments—the decline in per capita exports and the pause in urban growth—were extremely unusual peacetime experiences. Yet, as emphasized, such aggregate figures hide as much as they reveal. The southern declines were sharp; only New York and the New England states (except New Hampshire) fully recovered from trade disruptions.

WAR, NEUTRALITY, AND ECONOMIC RESURGENCE

As we have seen, the economic setbacks experienced by the United States throughout the late 1770s and most of the 1780s were followed by years of halting progress and incomplete recovery. Then, in 1793, only four years after the beginning of the French Revolution, the French and English began a series of wars that lasted until 1815.[5] During this long struggle, both British and French cargo vessels were drafted into military service, and both nations relaxed their restrictive mercantilist policies. Of all nations most capable of filling the shipping void created by the Napoleonic wars, the new United States stood at the forefront.

[5]The Treaty of Amiens, signed late in 1801, provided a year and a half of uneasy peace.

Due to these developments, the nation's economy briskly rebounded from the doldrums of the preceding years. The stimulus in U.S. overseas commerce is graphed statistically in Figure 7.1. As indicated, per capita credits in the balance of payments (exports plus other sources of foreign exchange earnings) more than tripled between 1790 and the height of war between the French and English. Overseas trade as a proportion of national income during these years is discussed in Economic Insight 7.1. There can be little doubt that these were extraordinary years for America—a time of unusual prosperity and intense economic activity, especially in the eastern port cities. It was a time characterized by full employment and sharply rising urbanization, at least until 1808. Famed entrepreneurs of New England and the Middle Atlantic region, such as Stephen Girard, Archibald Gracie, E. H. Derby, and John Jacob Astor, amassed vast personal fortunes during this period. These and other capital accumulations added to the development of a well-established commercial sector and eventually contributed to the incipient manufacturing sector.

It is important to recognize the significance of the commercial sector of the economy as well as the role of the merchant class during these decades. The growing merchant class, of course, had played an active role in helping to spearhead the move for national independence. Now the merchant class supplied the entrepreneurial talents required to take full advantage of the new economic circumstances. As the spreading European war opened up

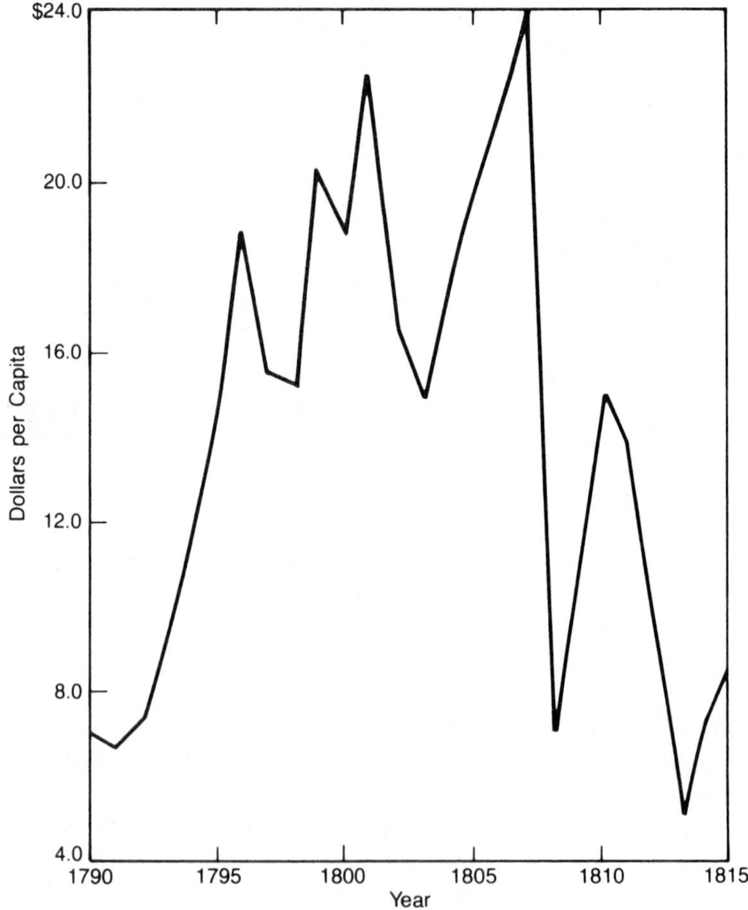

FIGURE 7.1 Per Capita Credits in the U.S. Balance of Payments, 1790–1815

Source: Douglass C. North, "Early National Income Estimates of the United States," Economic Development and Cultural Change 9 *(1961): 390. Reprinted by permission of the University of Chicago Press.*

Economic Insight 7.1

Overseas Trade and Total Income

How big was overseas trade as a proportion of national income? Was overseas trade large enough to merit the emphasis it has been given here? To answer these crucial questions, some calculations are in order.

Taking 1774 as a benchmark year, we see from Table 2.1 (page 41) that there were about 2.4 million people in the colonies. From Table 5.4 (page 104), we determine that average yearly incomes were about £10.7 (using the 3.5-to-1 capital output ratio). Total income was therefore £25.7 million (£10.7 × 2.4 million).

From Table 4.5 (page 85), we can sum commodity exports, plus ship sales, plus invisible earnings (but excluding British expenditures on military personnel) to show the average yearly values (1768–1772) of incomes from overseas trade and shipping activities. These were probably slightly below 1774's earnings, so we have a lower bound of £2,800,000 (exports) + £140,000 (ship sales) + £880,000 (invisible earnings) equaling £3.82 million. We can conclude, therefore, that income from overseas trade and shipping was nearly 15 percent of total incomes.

An added argument for stressing overseas economic activities is that these were market activities, ones that led the way in moving resources from lesser- to higher-valued uses. It was this commercial sector—not subsistence farming, hunting, woodcutting, and the like—that provided the chief stimulus to market expansion, economic specialization, technology transfer, capital accumulation, and advancing productivity and standards of living. Finally, if the coastal intercolonial trades are added to the overseas trade and shipping earnings (15 percent of total income), the combined proportion approaches one-fifth of total income.

The result of this quantitative analysis of the magnitudes of overseas (and coastal) trade, along with the arguments advanced here based on economic growth theory, urges our emphasis on this sector as a leading one for the economic progress of the colonies.

The western movement and the persistence of self-sufficient activities cushioned the downfall of incomes per capita. Undoubtedly, per capita internal trade did not decline to the same extent as per capita exports. (Unfortunately, we have no statistics on domestic trade during that hectic period.) Thus, the external relations probably exaggerated the overall setbacks of the period. It is safe to conclude, however, that the political chaos of the early national era was accompanied by severe economic conditions. Indeed, the problems of government contributed to the weakness of the economy, and economic events in turn clarified government failings under the Articles of Confederation.

These were the circumstances entering 1793, the year in which the Napoleonic wars erupted and Eli Whitney invented the cotton gin. The sweeping consequences of those events could never have been foreseen in colonial times. The colonies, however, had already developed a commercial base that now would prove crucial to further development. Because of its early efforts at overseas trade, the new nation was ready to take quick advantage of the economic opportunities available to a neutral nation in a world at war.

exceptional trade opportunities, America's well-developed commercial sector provided the needed buildings and ships as well as know-how. In short, both the physical and human capital were already available, and in many ways, the success of the period stemmed from developments that reached back to colonial times. It was exactly that prior development that singled out the United States as the leading neutral nation in time of war. Rather than the ports of the Caribbean, Latin America, or Canada, those of the United States emerged as the entrepots of trade in the western Atlantic.

The effects of war and neutrality on U.S. shipping earnings are shown in Figure 7.2. In general, these statistics convey the same picture that we saw in Figure 7.1, namely, that these were exceptionally prosperous times for the commercial sector.

Although the invention of the cotton gin stimulated cotton production and U.S. cotton supplies grew in response to the growth of demand for raw cotton in English textile mills, commercial growth was by no means limited to products produced in the United States. As Figure 7.3 shows, a major portion of the total exports from U.S. ports comprised re-exports, especially in such tropical items as sugar, coffee, cocoa, pepper, and spices. Because their commercial sectors were relatively underdeveloped, the Caribbean islands and Latin America depended primarily on American shipping and merchandising services rather than on their own.

Of course, such unique conditions did not provide the basis for long-term development, and (as Figures 7.1, 7.2, and 7.3 all show) when temporary peace came between late 1801 and 1803, the U.S. commercial boom quickly evaporated. When hostilities erupted again, the United States experienced another sharp upswing in commercial activity. This time, however, new and serious problems arose with expansion. In 1805, the British imposed an antiquated ruling, the Rule of 1756, permitting neutrals in wartime to carry only those goods that they normally carried in peacetime. This ruling, known as the Essex Decision, was matched by Napoleon's Berlin Decree, which banned trade to Britain. As a result, nearly 1,500 American ships and many American sailors were seized, and some were forcefully drafted into the British Royal Navy. The Congress and President Thomas Jefferson, fearful of entangling the United States in war, declared the Embargo Act of 1807, which prohibited U.S. ships from trading with all foreign ports.

Basically, this attempt to gain respect for American neutrality backfired, and as the drastic declines in Figures 7.1, 7.2, and 7.3 convey, the cure was almost worse than the disease. As pressures in the port cities mounted, political action led to the Non-Importation

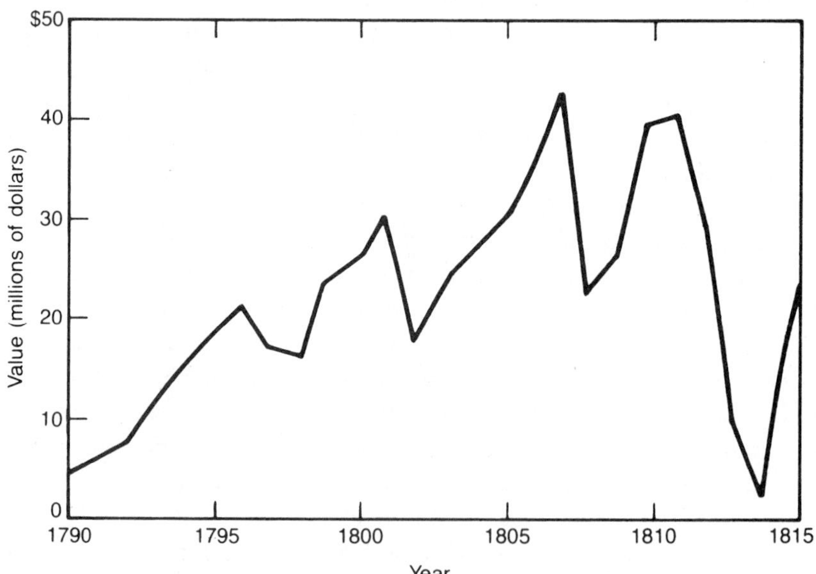

FIGURE 7.2 Net Freight Earnings of U.S. Carrying Trade, 1790–1815

Source: Douglass C. North, The Economic Growth of the United States, 1790–1860 *(Englewood Cliffs, N.J.: Prentice Hall, 1961): 26, 28.*

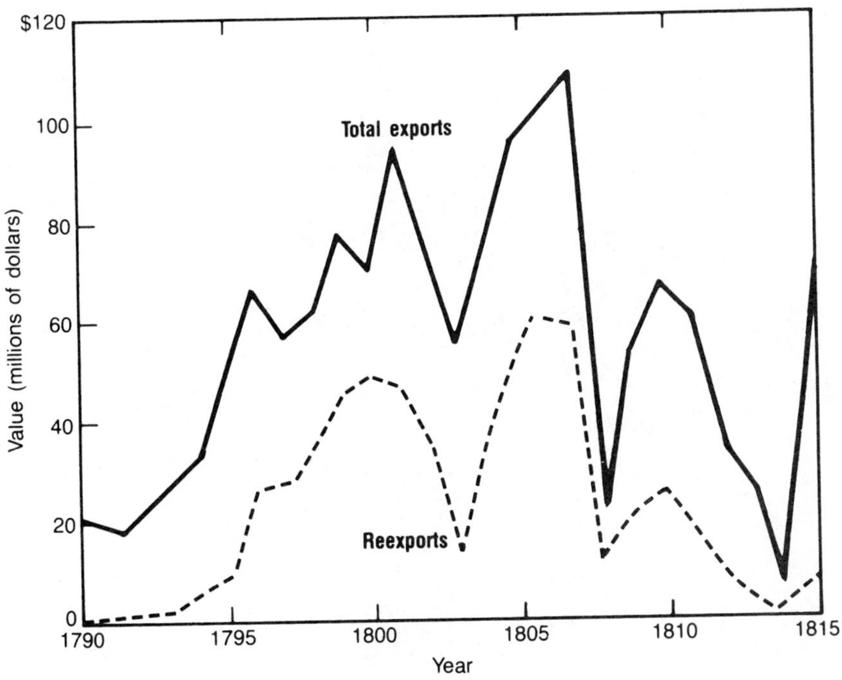

FIGURE 7.3 Values of Exports and Re-exports from the United States, 1790–1815

Source: Douglass C. North, The Economic Growth of the United States, 1790–1860 *(Englewood Cliffs, NJ: Prentice Hall, 1961): 28.*

Act of 1809. This act partially opened up trade, with specific prohibitions against Great Britain, France, and their possessions.

Nevertheless, continuing seizures and other complications between the United States and Britain along the Canadian border finally led to war—the second with England within 30 years. The War of 1812 was largely a naval war, during which the British seized more than 1,000 additional ships and blockaded almost the entire U.S. coast.

As exports declined to practically nothing, new boosts were given to the tiny manufacturing sector. Actually, stirrings there had begun with the embargo of 1807, which quickly altered the possibilities for profits in commerce relative to manufactures. As prices on manufactures rose, increasing possibilities for profits encouraged capital to flow into manufacturing. From 15 textile mills in 1808, the number rose to almost 90 by 1809. Similar additions continued throughout the war period, but when the Treaty of Ghent in 1814 brought the war to a close, the textile industry faltered badly. Once again, British imports arrived in massive amounts and undercut prices, which had been temporarily inflated by supply shortages resulting from the embargo and the war. Only large-scale U.S. concerns weathered the competitive storm, and there were few of these—most notably the Lowell shops using the Waltham system of cloth weaving (see chapters 10 and 11). Nevertheless, the war-related spurts in manufacturing provided an important basis for further industrial expansion, not only in textiles—the main manufacturing activity of the time—but also in other areas. This marked a time when the relative roles of the various sectors of the economy began to shift. Agriculture was to dominate the economy for most of the century, but to a lesser and lesser degree as economic growth continued.

The economic surge of the early Napoleonic war period (1793–1807) was unique, not so much by comparison with later years as by its striking reversal and advance from the two decades following 1772. Work by Claudia Goldin and Frank Lewis shows that during the

This bustling dockside scene in New York City in the mid-1800s mirrored the United States' emergence as a center of trade.

decade and a half after the beginning of the Napoleonic wars, the growth rate of per capita income averaged almost 1 percent per year, with the foreign sector accounting for more than 25 percent of the underlying sources of growth.[6]

In contrast, during the two decades preceding 1793, per capita exports fell (Table 7.2). Goldin and Lewis estimate that per capita income declined by a rate of 0.34 percent annually from 1774 to 1793.[7] Wealth holdings per capita also declined substantially over this period.[8]

There is little doubt that the several decades following independence were exceptionally unstable, not merely two decades of bust and then one and a half of boom. There were ups and downs within these longer bust and boom periods. Because of the importance of foreign trade at the time, export instability had strong leverage effects throughout the economy. Although external forces were always an important factor in determining economic fluctuations, as the influence of OPEC reminded U.S. consumers, workers, and businesses in the 1970s, their almost total dominance was now beginning to wane. By the turn of the century, internal developments—especially those in the banking sector—had assumed a more pivotal role in causing economic fluctuations. As we shall see in chapter 12, both external forces (acting through credit flows from and to overseas areas) and internal forces (acting through changes in credit availability and the money stock) came to bear on the economy during the early nineteenth century. And some of the biggest challenges and opportunities for young Americans were settling and working new lands in the West.

---

[6]Claudia D. Goldin and Frank D. Lewis, "The Role of Exports in American Economic Growth during the Napoleonic Wars, 1793–1807," *Explorations in Economic History* 17 (1980): 6–25, especially p. 22. For an alternative interpretation of the role of neutrality, see Donald R. Adams, Jr., "American Neutrality and Prosperity, 1793–1808: A Reconsideration," *Journal of Economic History* 40 (1980): 713–738.

[7]Goldin and Lewis, "The Role of Exports," 22–23.

[8]Alice H. Jones, *Wealth of a Nation to Be* (New York: Columbia University Press, 1980), 82.

SELECTED REFERENCES AND READINGS

Adams, Donald R., Jr. "American Neutrality and Prosperity, 1793–1808: A Reconsideration." *Journal of Economic History*, 40 (1980): 713–738.

Beard, Charles A. *An Economic Interpretation of the Constitution* (New York: Macmillian, 1913).

Bjork, Gordon C. "The Weaning of the American Economy: Independence, Market Changes and Economic Development." *Journal of Economic History* 24 (1964): 541–560.

Calomiris, Charles W. "Institutional Failure, Monetary Scarcity, and the Depreciation of the Continental." *Journal of Economic History* 48 (1988): 47–68.

Gilbert, Geoffery. "The Role of Breadstuffs in American Trade, 1770–1790." *Explorations in Economic History* 14 (1977): 378–387.

Goldin, Claudia D., and Frank D. Lewis. "The Role of Exports in American Economic Growth during the Napoleonic Wars, 1793–1807." *Explorations in Economic History* 17 (1980): 6–25.

Jensen, Merrill. *The New Nation: A History of the United States during Confederation* (New York: Knopf, 1958).

Jones, Alice H. *Wealth of a Nation to Be* (New York: Columbia University Press, 1980).

Matson, Cathy. "The Revolution, the Constitution, and the New Nation." In *The Cambridge Economic History of the United States.* Vol. 1, eds. Stanley L. Engerman and Robert E. Gallman (Cambridge University Press, 1996), 363–401.

McGuire, Robert A., and Robert L. Ohsfeldt. "Economic Interests and the American Constitution: A Quantitative Rehabilitation of Charles A. Beard." *Journal of Economic History* 44 (June 1984): 509–519.

———. "An Economic Model of Voting Behavior over Specific Issues at the Constitutional Convention of 1787." *Journal of Economic History* 46 (1986): 79–112.

Nettels, Curtis P. Chapters 3 and 4 in *The Emergence of a National Economy, 1775–1815* (New York: Holt, Rinehart & Winston, 1962).

North, Douglass C. *American Economic Growth 1790–1860* (Englewood Cliffs, N.J.: Prentice Hall, 1960).

———. "Early National Income Estimates of the United States." *Economic Development and Cultural Change* 9 (3), (April 1961).

Shepherd, James F., and Gary M. Walton. "Economic Change after the American Revolution: Pre-War and Post-War Comparisons of Maritime Shipping and Trade." *Explorations in Economic History* 13 (1976): 397–422.

Chapter Eight

Land and the Early Westward Movements

Chapter Theme

The Treaty of Versailles, signed in September 1783, granted the Americans independence and the western lands they claimed by the ancient right of conquest. The western lands, first claimed by individual states but soon ceded to the federal government, were a valuable asset, collectively owned. How to use them best for the collective good was the problem and the challenge.

For the most part, the great Land Ordinances of 1785 and 1787 determined land policy through the guiding spirit of Thomas Jefferson. Throughout his career, Jefferson had three main goals for land policy: (1) to provide revenues to the federal government through sales, but not perpetual taxes; (2) to spread democratic institutions; and (3) to ensure clear property rights to the land owned by individuals, thereby enhancing their liberty and freedom and providing incentives (Economic Reasoning Proposition 3) to utilize and make improvements on the land. Individual rights to buy, improve, work, and sell the land also inevitably created opportunities to speculate.

Economic Reasoning Proposition

Fearing the potential threat of an excessively powerful, land-rich national government, Jefferson argued that the land should be transferred in a swift but orderly manner to the people. He advocated a process of privatization. First, surveys would be made and boundaries clearly marked. Sales from the federal government to private persons would transfer title completely. The federal government would not tax the land. As populations and settlements spread west, territories would be formed and then through application become states, entering the Union on an equal footing with the existing states. All this was fundamentally Jefferson's vision, part of his legacy that remains with us today.

THE ACQUISITION OF THE PUBLIC DOMAIN

One of the first truly national issues for the new government, after waging war and financing it, was the disposition of new lands in the West. The Articles of Confederation held that western lands could not be unwillingly taken from the states by the central government, and seven states held claims on western lands. These claims were based on the colonies' original grants from England and from dealings with the Native Americans. Many people argued, however, that the new western territories should belong to the national government and held or disposed in the national interest. Maryland, a state without western claims, brought the issue to a head by refusing to ratify the Articles until the land issue was resolved. In 1781, Maryland finally signed, after New York voluntarily gave its claims, based on treaties with the Iroquois, to the national government. Virginia promptly followed suit and relinquished its claims on western lands. The other five states having claims soon followed their lead.

What the new nation obtained from the British in 1783 is portrayed in the darkened area of Map 8.1. The United States began with a solid mass of land extending from the Atlantic coast to the Mississippi River and from the Great Lakes to, but not including, Florida.

Between 1802, when Georgia became the last state to relinquish its rights to western land, and 1898, when the formal annexation of Hawaii occurred, the United States very nearly assumed its present physical form as the result of eight main acquisitions (shown in Map 8.1):

1. The Territory of Louisiana, acquired in 1803 by purchase from France.
2. Florida, acquired in 1819 by purchase from Spain. A few years earlier, the United States had annexed the narrow strip of land that constituted western Florida.
3. The Republic of Texas, annexed as a state in 1845. The Republic of Texas had been established in 1836 after the victory of the American settlers over the Mexicans.
4. The Oregon Country, annexed by treaty with Great Britain in 1846. Spain and Russia, the original claimants to this area, had long since dropped out. By the

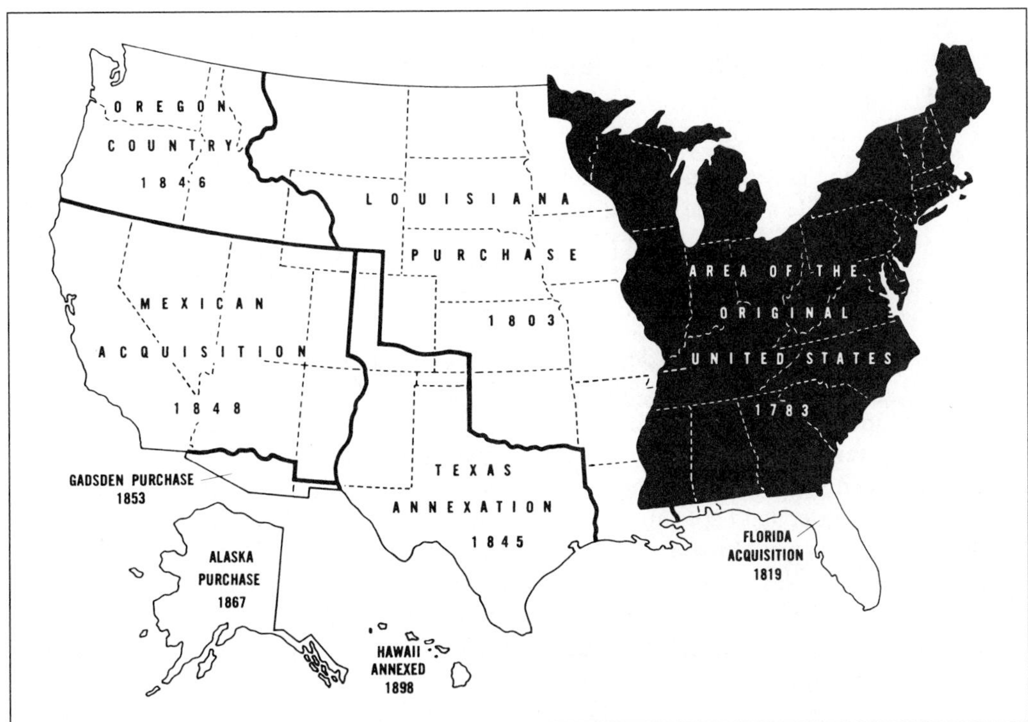

MAP 8.1 Land Growth *The purchase of Louisiana marked the beginning of the continental expansion of the United States, which culminated in the purchase of Alaska in 1867 and the annexation of Hawaii in 1898.*

Treaty of 1818, the United States and Great Britain agreed to a joint occupation of the Oregon Country and British Columbia; the Treaty of 1846 established the dividing line at the forty-ninth parallel.

5. The Mexican Cession, acquired by conquest from Mexico in 1848.
6. The Gadsden Purchase, acquired from Mexico in 1853.
7. The Alaskan Purchase, acquired from Russia in 1867.
8. The Hawaiian Annexation, formally ratified in 1898.

National acquisition of new land came either by a process of conquest and treaty or by purchase. The right of conquest was part of America's European heritage, rights claimed by the sovereigns of Europe and unquestioned by Christian societies when levied against non-Christian societies. This is seen clearly in early times in Europe, repeatedly against the Muslims, through the Crusades, and in Spain in 1492 against the Moors. The European belief in the right to conquer and rule non-Christian native societies in North America passed into American hands with independence. This legacy was ultimately extended in the nineteenth century, when the remaining Native Americans were forced onto reservations. These acts and their accompanying treaties are targets of continual challenge in the courts by Native Americans today.

In half a century (1803–1853), the United States obtained a continental area of 3 million square miles, of which 1.4 billion acres, or 75 percent, constituted the public domain.[1] In 1862, two-thirds of this vast area was still in the possession of the government, but the process of disposal had been agreed on long before.

Disposing of the Public Domain

With rare exceptions, the land was valueless until settled. To give the land value, the Congress of the Confederation had addressed three questions:

1. How were land holdings and sales to be administered?
2. Should the government exact high prices from the sale of land, or should cheap land be made available to everyone?
3. What was to be the political relationship between newly settled areas and the original states?

Two major land systems had developed during the colonial period. The New England system of "township planning" provided for the laying out of townships, for the subdivision of townships into carefully surveyed tracts, and for the auction sale of tracts to settlers. In the eighteenth century, it was usual to establish townships, which often were 6 miles square, in tiers. The opening of new townships proceeded with regularity from settled to unsettled land, gaps of unsettled land appeared infrequently, and no one could own land that had not been previously surveyed. In contrast, the southern system provided for no rectangular surveys. In the South, a settler simply selected what appeared to be a choice plot of unappropriated land and asked the county surveyor to mark it off. Settlers paid no attention to the relationship of their tracts to other pieces of property, and the legal description of a tract was made with reference to more or less permanent natural objects, such as stones, trees, and streams.

---

[1] Of the two later acquisitions, Alaska contained more than 586,400 square miles, most of it still in the public domain, and Hawaii added 6,423 square miles, none of it in the public domain.

Thomas Jefferson, the nation's third president, 1801–1809, had an earlier profound influence on the country for many of his leadership acts including his contribution to the momentous land ordinances of 1785 and 1787.

The Northwest Land Ordinance of 1785

No pressure was put on the Congress of the Confederation to provide a system for regulating public lands until 1784, after Virginia and New York had relinquished their claims to the southern part of the territory lying northwest of the Ohio River. In that year, a congressional committee of five, headed by Thomas Jefferson, proposed a system based on a rectangular survey. It is noteworthy that three of the five members were southerners who, despite their origins, recognized the value of the New England method of settlement. No action was taken, but a year later another committee, composed of a member from each state, reworked the 1784 report and offered a carefully considered proposal. With minor changes, this proposal was passed as the Northwest Land Ordinance of 1785.

Insofar as the ordinance set a physical basis for disposing of the public lands, its effects were permanent. Government surveyors were to establish on unsettled land horizontal lines called base lines and vertical lines called principal meridians, as shown in Map 8.2 on page 144. The first of the principal meridians was to be in what is now the state of Ohio, and the first surveys covered land north of the Ohio River. Eventually, all the land in the United States was included in the surveys except the original 13 states and Vermont, Kentucky, Tennessee, parts of Ohio, and Texas. These were literally celestial surveys, mappings by the stars.

As the surveys moved westward, other principal meridians were established—the second in what is now Indiana, the third in what is now Illinois, and so on. Map 8.2 on indicates the other principal meridians and the base lines perpendicular to them. The insets show how tiers of townships, called ranges, were laid out to the east and west of each principal meridian. The ranges were designated by a number and a direction from the meridian, and the townships within each range were numbered north and south from the base line. Each township, being 6 miles square, contained 36 square miles numbered as shown in Map 8.2. In the Ordinance of 1785, a square mile was called a *lot*, but in later acts, the term *section* was used. Each square-mile section contained 640 acres, an acre being about

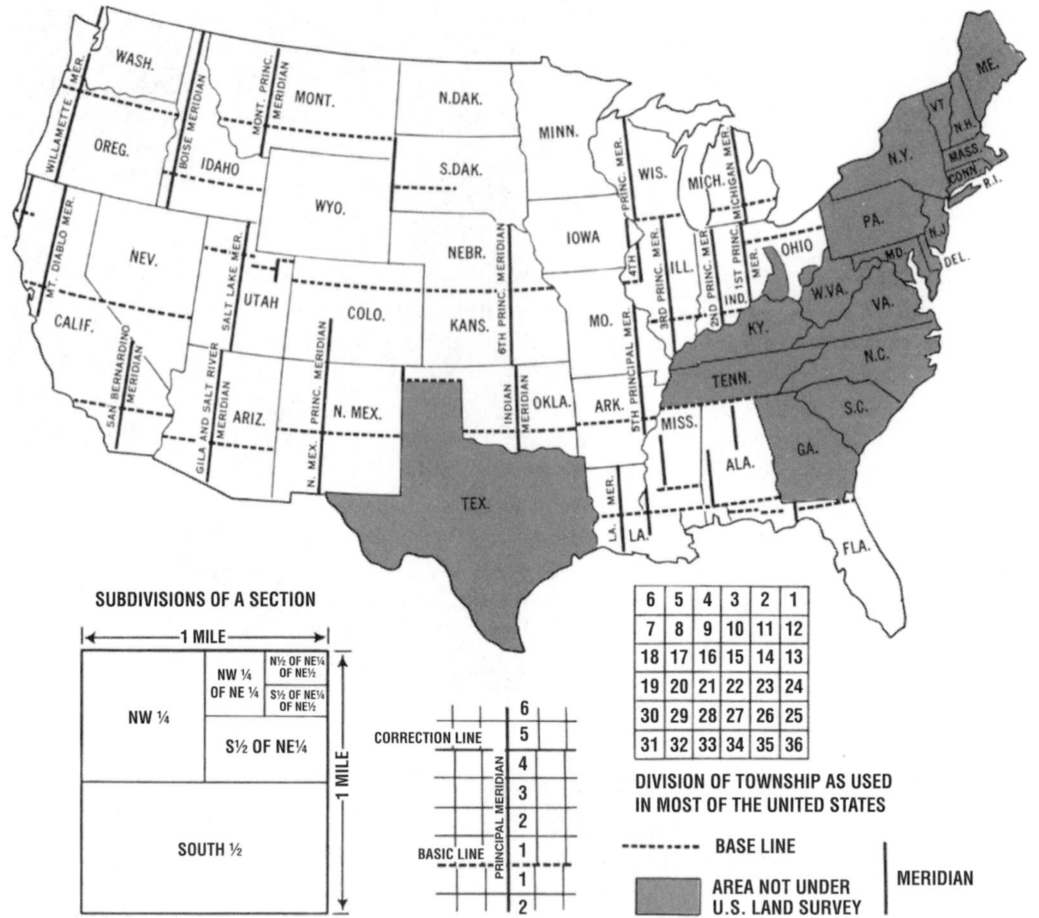

MAP 8.2 **Land Survey** *Principal meridians and base lines made possible precise apportioning of newly opened territories into sections and easily described subdivisions of sections, thus simplifying later property transfers.*

the size of a football field (70 yards by 70 yards). In flying over the United States on clear days, you can see these checkerboard squares endlessly over the ground.

Two fundamentally different points of view emerged about the terms on which land should be made available, and a debate ensued that was not to end for several decades. Those who advocated a "conservative" policy were in favor of selling the public lands in large tracts at high prices for cash. The proponents of a "liberal" policy were in favor of putting land within the reach of almost everyone by making it available in small parcels at low prices on credit terms.

The Land Ordinance of 1785 reflected the prevalent conservative view that public land should be a major source of revenue, though in fact revenues from land sales never became a major source of federal revenues. Provisions relating to minimum size of tracts, prices, and terms were severe. Alternate townships were to be sold as a whole; the other half of the townships were to be sold by sections. All sales at public auction were to be for a minimum price of $1 per acre in cash. Thus, the smallest possible cash outlay was the $640 necessary to buy a section—an expenditure beyond the means of most pioneers. Moreover, a square mile of land was more than small farmers could normally utilize and work; they could barely clear and cultivate 10 acres in their first year, and a quarter section was the most a settler could handle without the aid of grown children. Only individuals of means and land companies formed by large investors could purchase land under the first law.

The Northwest Ordinance of 1787

The decision regarding the status of areas to be settled in the future also involved a great political principle. Were these areas to remain in colonial dependence, subject to possible exploitation by the original 13 states? Or were they to be admitted into a union of states on a basis of equality? The answers to these questions would test the foresight and selflessness of Americans, who had themselves escaped the dominance of a ruling empire (Economic Reasoning Propositions 1, 3, and 4).

★★★ Economic Reasoning Proposition

In 1787, Congress addressed the problems of establishing the political principles for western settlement. The Ordinance of 1787 provided that the Northwest Territory should be organized as a district to be run by a governor and judges appointed by Congress. As soon as it contained 5,000 male inhabitants of voting age, a territorial legislature was to be elected, and a nonvoting delegate was to be sent to Congress. At least three and not more than five states were to be created from this territory; when any one of the established divisions of the territory contained a population of 60,000 inhabitants, it was to be admitted to the Union as a state on a basis of complete equality with the older states. Contained in the ordinance were certain guarantees of civil and religious liberties, proper treatment of Native Americans, together with a prohibition of slavery in the territory.[2] *The main principle, however, was the eventual equality of status for the new areas.* The age-old source of trouble between colony and ruling country was thus removed by a simple, although unprecedented, device—making the colonies extensions of the empire that would be allowed to become socially and politically equal. Recall Economic Reasoning Proposition 4.

The Later Land Acts, 1796–1862

For a decade after the passage of the Land Ordinance of 1785, pioneering in the area north of the Ohio River was restricted as much by Indian troubles as by the high price of government land. The British, who persisted in maintaining posts on American territory in the Northwest, for years encouraged the Native Americans to make war on American settlers. By a treaty of 1794, the British agreed to evacuate the posts in the Northwest, and in August of that year, "Mad Anthony" Wayne and his forces defeated the Native Americans at the Battle of Fallen Timbers. The time was then ripe for the establishment of new land policies by the Congress of the United States.

The Land Act of 1796 represented another victory for the conservatives. A system of rectangular surveys substantially the same as the one established by the Ordinance of 1785 was made permanent. The minimum purchase allowed by the Act of 1796 was still 640 acres, but the minimum price per acre was raised to $2, the only concession to the cheap-land advocates being a credit provision that permitted half the purchase price to be deferred for a year. Only a small amount of land was sold under this act before Congress changed the minimum acreage to 320 in 1800 and permitted the buyer, after a cash payment of one-half the value, to pay one-fourth the value in two years and the final fourth in four years. A law of 1804 further lowered the minimum purchase to 160 acres. By 1820, the liberal forces had clearly won the battle: the minimum purchase was reduced to 80 acres and the price per acre to $1.25, but the credit provisions, which had

---

[2]Here again it is to Jefferson, who wanted slavery prohibited in all the western territories and states (even south of the Northwest Territory), that we owe these guarantees. See Jonathan Hughes, "The Great Land Ordinances: Colonial America's Thumbprint on History," in *Essays on the Emerging of the Old Northwest*, ed. David C. Klingaman and Richard K. Vedder (Athens: Ohio University Press, 1987).

resulted in losses to the government, were repealed. Twelve years later, the minimum purchase was reduced to 40 acres, so in 1832, a pioneer could purchase a piece of farmland for $50 (less than two months' wages for a common laborer). It merits emphasis that these prices were government-set prices. Actual prices paid by many settlers were undoubtedly less than these "list prices." This happened because military veterans were often paid in "land warrants" to help them buy land at a discount. Because these warrants were transferable and were typically sold at discount, others as well as veterans paid less in cash than the official list prices suggest.

Settlers who were brave enough to risk their lives in a pioneering venture were not usually deterred from action by legal niceties. From the beginning, pioneers tended to settle past the areas that had been surveyed and announced for sale. As the decades passed and the West became "crowded," this tendency increased. Unauthorized settlement, or "squatting," resulted from the attempts of the pioneers to find better soils and the hope that they could settle on choice land and make it a going proposition before they were billed for it.

Squatting was illegal, of course, but it was an offense that was hard to police. Moreover, there were those who argued that by occupying and improving the land, a squatter gained the rights to it—"cabin rights," "corn rights," or "tommyhawk rights," as they were variously called on the frontier. At first, federal troops tried to drive squatters from unsurveyed land, but successes were only temporary. Gradually, the government came to view this pioneer lawbreaking less and less seriously. Against those who would purchase the squatter's land when it became available for public sale, informal but effective measures were taken by the squatters themselves, who formed protective associations as soon as they settled in a particular locality. When the public auction of land in that locality was held, the members of the protective association let it be known that there was to be no competitive bidding for land preempted by them. The appearance of well-armed frontiersmen at the auction ordinarily convinced city slickers and big land buyers that it would be unwise to bid. Even in places where there was no organized action, squatters who found their farms bought out from under them could often charge handsomely for the "improvements" they had made, and frontier courts were inclined to uphold their "rights."

As early as 1820, Congress began to give relief to squatters, and scarcely a year went by after 1830 in which preemption rights were not granted to settlers in certain areas. In 1841, a general Preemption Act, called the "Log Cabin Bill" by its proponents, was passed. This law granted, to anyone settling on land that was surveyed but not yet available for sale, the right to purchase 160 acres at the minimum price when the auction was held. No one could outbid the settler and secure the land, provided the squatter could raise the $200 necessary to buy a quarter section. Technically, squatting on unsurveyed land was still illegal; because of this and because there was still no outright grant of land, the westerner (and anyone else who could make money by buying land and waiting for it to rise in value) was not satisfied. Nevertheless, the land policy of the country was about as liberal as could be consistent with the demand that the public domain be a continuing source of revenue.

Pressure remained on Congress to reduce the price of "islands" of less desirable land that had been passed over in the first surges to the West. In 1854, the Graduation Act provided for the graduated reduction of the minimum purchase price of such tracts, to a point where land that remained unsold for 30 years could be purchased for as little as 12.5 cents an acre. Settlers quickly purchased these pieces of land, attesting to the fact that people were willing to gamble a little on the probable appreciation of even the most unpromising real estate.

In the 1850s, as agitation for free land continued, it became apparent that the passage of a homestead law was inevitable. Southerners, who had at one time favored free grants to actual settlers, became violently opposed to this as time went on. The 160-acre farm usually proposed by homestead supporters was not large enough to make the working of slaves economical, and it seemed obvious to southern congressmen that homesteading would fill the West with antislavery people. On the other hand, many northern congressmen who might normally have had leanings toward a conservative policy joined forces with the westerners; they, too, knew that free land meant free states.

In 1860, a homestead act was passed, but President James Buchanan, fearing that it would precipitate secession, vetoed it. Two years later, with the Civil War raging and the southerners out of Congress, the Homestead Act of 1862 became law. Henceforth, any head of a family or anyone older than 21 could have 160 acres of public land on the payment of small fees. The only stipulation was that the homesteader should either live on the land or cultivate it for five years. An important provision was that settlers who decided not to meet the five-year requirement might obtain full title to the land simply by paying the minimum price of $1.25 an acre.

Although much land was to pass into private hands under the Homestead Act of 1862, it was not the boon that it was expected to be. Most of the first-class land had been claimed by this time. Furthermore, it was so easy to circumvent the provisions of the law that land grabbers used it, along with the acts that still provided for outright purchase, to build up great land holdings. By 1862, the frontier had reached the edge of the dry country, where a 160-acre farm was too small to provide a living for a settler and his family.

THE MIGRATIONS TO THE WEST

In discussing the colonial period, we noted that pioneers were moving across the Appalachian Mountains by the middle of the eighteenth century. By 1790, perhaps a quarter of a million people lived within the mountain valleys or to the west, and the trickle of westward movement had become a small stream. In the eighteenth century, there were two routes to the West. The more important one passed through the Cumberland Gap and then into either Kentucky or Tennessee; the other ran across southern Pennsylvania to Pittsburgh and on down the Ohio River. Even as the movement to the West was gaining momentum, pioneers were still settling in Pennsylvania and New York and to the north in Vermont, New Hampshire, and Maine.

An overview of population growth and the distributional impact of western migration and other demographic effects are shown in Table 8.1, page 148, and Figure 8.1, page 149. In 1812, on the eve of the second war with Great Britain, just over 1 million people (about 15 percent of the nation's total) lived west of the Appalachians. From this 15 percent, the western population grew to almost half of the total by 1860. On the eve of the Civil War, the center of the population was near Chillicothe, Ohio. The western population grew from 1.0 to nearly 13.0 million as the total grew from 7.2 to 31.4 million. In short, the rate of population growth was twice as high west of the Appalachian Mountains as in the East, more than 5.0 percent annually compared with 2.2 percent.

As the population expanded and pushed westward, the nation's frontier was pressed outward. The frontier, as technically defined in the census reports, was any area containing more than two and less than six people per square mile. In Map 8.3, page 150, the frontier lines for 1800, 1820, 1840, and 1860 have been drawn from census data. The line for 1800 indicates a wedge driven into the West, with its point in western Kentucky. Sixty years later, the line ran in a southerly direction from a point in the middle of Minnesota, with a noticeable bulge into the Nebraska and Kansas territories and a definite drift into Texas.

The Northwestern Migration and Hogs, Corn, and Wheat

As shown in Table 8.1 on page 148 and in Map 8.3 on page 150, during the early 1800s the movement across the top of the country gained momentum and an initial lead over migration from the southern states. During the first quarter of the century, people from the New

TABLE 8.1 Population in the Trans-Appalachian States[a]

STATE	1810	1850	1860
Ohio	231	1,980	2,340
Michigan	5	398	749
Indiana	25	988	1,350
Illinois	12	852	1,712
Minnesota	—[b]	6	172
Wisconsin	—	305	776
Iowa	—	192	675
Kansas	—	—	107
Kentucky	407	982	1,156
Tennessee	262	1,003	1,110
Alabama	9	772	964
Mississippi	31	607	791
Louisiana	77	518	708
Arkansas	1	210	435
Missouri	20	682	1,182
Texas	—	213	604
Total	1,080	9,708	14,831
Total U.S.	7,224	23,261	31,513
Trans-Appalachia Percentage of Total U.S.	15.0%	41.7%	47.1%

[a]*Figures given in thousands of persons; excludes Far West and West Coast.*
[b]*No data.*

Source: Historical Statistics *(Washington, D.C.: Government Printing Office, 1960), derived from Series A, 123–180.*

In the nineteenth century, wagon trains brought a steady stream of migrants to western America and its expansive lands.

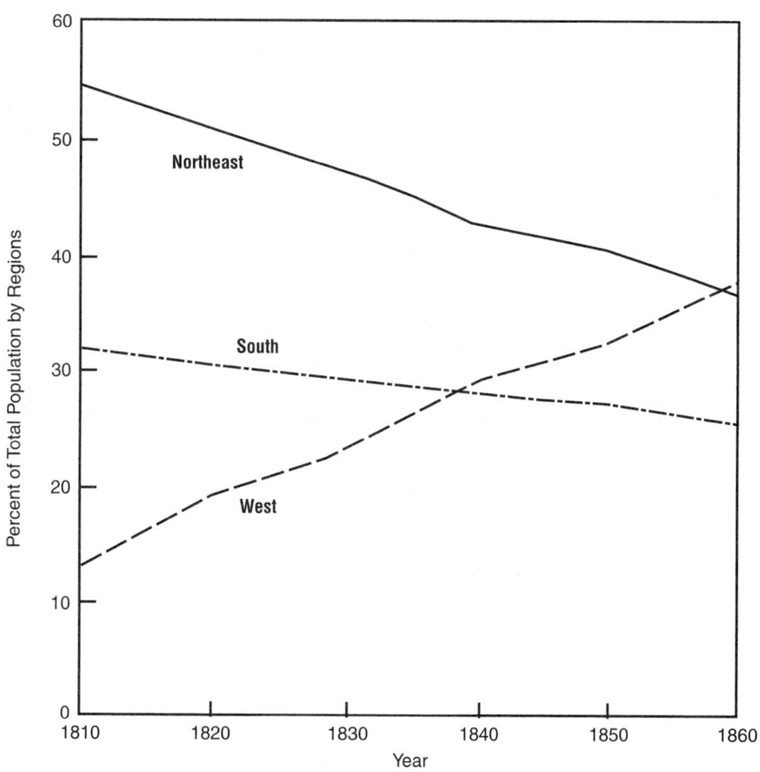

FIGURE 8.1 Population Distribution by Regions, 1810–1860

Note: South—Alabama, Arkansas, Florida, Georgia, Louisiana, Mississippi, North Carolina, Texas, and Virginia; West—Illinois, Indiana, Iowa, Kansas, Kentucky, Michigan, Minnesota, Missouri, Nebraska, Ohio, Tennessee, Wisconsin, California, Nevada, and Oregon; Northeast—Connecticut, Delaware, Maine, Maryland, Massachusetts, New Hampshire, New Jersey, New York, Pennsylvania, Rhode Island, and Vermont.

Source: U.S. Census Bureau, A Compendium of the Ninth Census, June 1, 1870, *by Francis A. Walker, Superintendent of Census (Washington, D.C.: 1872): 8–9. Reprinted from Douglas C. North,* The Economic Growth of the United States 1790–1860 *(Englewood Cliffs, N.J.: Prentice Hall, 1961), 121.*

England and Middle Atlantic states were pouring into the northern counties of Ohio and Indiana and later into southern Michigan. By 1850, lower Michigan was fairly well settled, and the best lands in northern Illinois and southern Wisconsin had been claimed. On the eve of the Civil War, pioneers were pushing the northwestern tip of the frontier into central Minnesota, most of Iowa was behind the frontier line, and the handsome country of eastern Kansas was being settled. Only in Texas did the frontier line of 1860 bulge farther to the west than it did in Kansas. By this time, California had been a state for a decade and Oregon had just been admitted, but the vast area between the western frontier and the coast was not to be completely settled for another half-century.

Southerners moving across the Ohio River were the chief influence in the lower part of the old Northwest. New Englanders, after the Erie Canal made transportation easier, were dominant in the Great Lakes region, but they were joined by another stream that originated in the Middle Atlantic states. For the most part, families moved singly, although sometimes as many as 50 to 100 would move together. As the frontier pushed westward, the pioneers on the cutting edge were frequently the same people who had broken virgin soil a short way back only a few years before. Others were the grown children of men and women who had once participated in the conquest of the wilderness.

MAP 8.3 Moving Frontier *Census data from 1800 onward chronicled the constant westward flow of population. The "frontier," its profile determined by natural attractions and a few man-made and physiographic obstacles, was a magnet for the venturesome.*

Throughout this early period of westward expansion was an ever-increasing influx of land-hungry people from abroad. From 1789 to the close of the War of 1812, not more than a quarter million people emigrated from Europe. With the final defeat of Napoleon and the coming of peace abroad, immigration resumed. From half a million people in the 1830s, the flow increased to 1.5 million in the 1840s and to 2.5 million in the 1850s. For the most part, the newcomers were from northern Europe; Germans and Irish predominated, but there were many immigrants from England, Scotland, Switzerland, and the Scandinavian countries. Of these peoples, the Germans tended more than any others to go directly to the lands of the West. Some immigrants from the other groups entered into the agricultural migration, but most were absorbed into eastern city populations. The timing of the western migration is discussed in Economic Insight 8.1.

Agricultural Specialization and Regional Dislocation

The resulting surges in production in the Northwest (the Midwest as we know it today) did not immediately dislocate agriculture in the older states. Over the decades, however, the leading producers of hogs, corn, and wheat became western states.

Early in the 1800s, western hog production was greatly limited by high transportation costs; hogs were driven overland from Ohio to the urban centers of the East or were sent

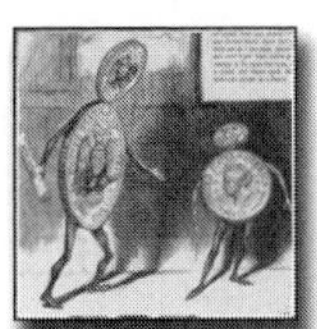

Economic Insight 8.1

Migration Waves and Economic Opportunity

Is there an economic explanation to the timing of the western migrations? Although the absolute numbers of western migrants from the eastern states and from abroad continued to swell, the decades of greatest western expansion, in terms of percentages, were the 1810s and 1830s. In absolute terms, the 1850s were the greatest. From Table 8.1 (see page 149) we can calculate percentage rates of increase of the western population for the five decades from 1810 to 1860: These were 6.9, 4.9, 5.6, 4.2, and 4.1 percent. Also from Table 8.1 we see the greatest increase in absolute numbers coming in the 1850s: nearly 4.3 million people.

As Douglass C. North has argued, in large measure, these surges are explained by the exceptional economic opportunities in the West.[3] Hogs, corn, and wheat became the great northwestern staples, and as shown in Figure 8.2, page 154, corn and wheat prices were unusually high in these decades. People came to the new lands in response to the profits to be made in the production of these great staples.

Critics of North's "market opportunity response" argument have countered that land sales during these periods were based on pervasive speculation, not settlement and production for market.[4] Much of the land, however, was being put to use. The decades of greatest growth in "improved land" (for grazing, grass, tillage, or lying fallow) were also the 1810s, 1830s, and 1850s. (The percentage rates of change in improved acres from 1810 to 1860, by decade, were 23.5, 6.5, 7.1, 5.4, and 7.8.[5]) In short, North's critics were wrong.

The only variable slightly out of step with North's general argument is the western population growth rate for the 1850s. This slowdown would be expected, however, from the general slowing of growth for the total population, the rise in the number of improved acres per person, and the rise in agricultural productivity—all of which occurred. The supply response to high staple prices is observed in terms of both population and improved acres in the 1810s and 1830s, but the supply response to the boom years of the 1850s was dominated more by improved acres than by population.

continued

south by boat for sale to the plantations. Cattle, too, were driven in great herds to the East, where they were sold for immediate slaughter or for further fattening. But it was not long before pioneer farmers could market their hogs fairly close to home. Slaughtering and meat-packing centers arose in the early West, and by the 1830s, Cincinnati, nicknamed Porkopolis, was the most important pork-processing city in the country.

Commercial hog raising required corn growing. For a while, hogs were allowed into the forests to forage on the mast (acorns and nuts that fell from the trees). But regular feeding is necessary to produce a good grade of pork, and corn is an ideal feed crop. Corn can be grown almost anywhere, provided there is adequate rainfall. It had been cultivated in all the original colonies and throughout the South. As late as 1840, Kentucky, Tennessee, and Virginia led the

---

[3]See Douglass C. North, *The Economic Growth of the United States 1790–1860* (Englewood Cliffs, N.J.: Prentice Hall, 1961).

[4]See, for example, Albro Martin's review of David H. Fischer's *Historians' Fallacies: Toward a Logic of Historical Thought* (New York: Harper & Row, 1971), in *Journal of Economic History* 32 (December 1972): 968–970, and in Peter Temin's *The Jacksonian Economy* (New York: Norton, 1969), 93–112.

[5]Eric F. Haites, James Mak, and Gary M. Walton, *Western River Transportation: The Era of Early Internal Improvements* (Baltimore, Md.: Johns Hopkins University Press, 1975), 113.

Economic Insight 8.1

Migration Waves and Economic Opportunity, continued

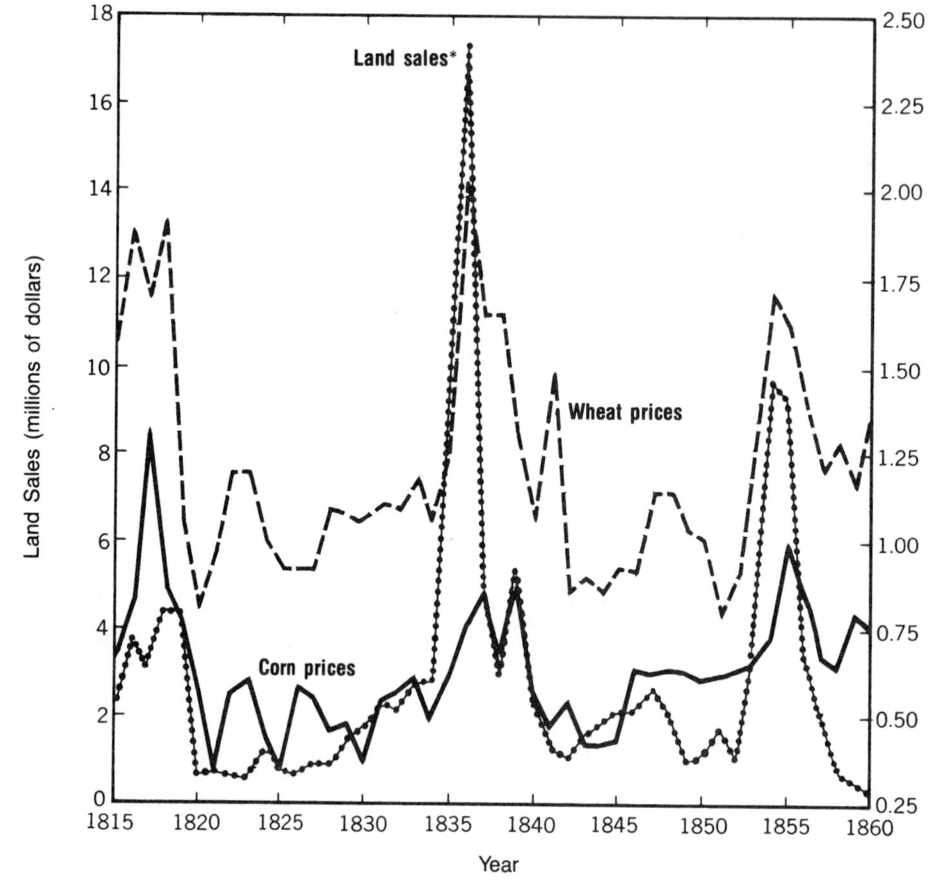

Land sales*
Wheat prices
Corn prices
Land Sales (millions of dollars)
Dollars per Bushel
Year
0 2 4 6 8 10 12 14 16 18
0.25 0.50 0.75 1.00 1.25 1.50 1.75 2.00 2.25 2.50
1815 1820 1825 1830 1835 1840 1845 1850 1855 1860

FIGURE 8.2 U.S. Public Land Sales in Several Western States* and Wheat and Corn Prices, 1815–1860

**Ohio, Illinois, Indiana, Michigan, Iowa, Wisconsin, and Missouri.*

***Source:** Douglas C. North,* The Economic Growth of the United States 1790–1860 *(Englewood Cliffs, N.J.: Prentice Hall, 1961), 137.*

nation in corn production. But within 20 years it was apparent that the states to the northwest would be the corn leaders.[6] On the eve of the Civil War, Illinois, Ohio, Missouri, and Indiana led in corn production, and it appeared that Iowa, Kansas, and Nebraska would one day rank ahead of Kentucky and Tennessee, then in fifth and sixth place, respectively.

The attraction of new lands for wheat was also tremendous. Western wheat could not come into its own until facilities were available for transporting it in quantity to the urban centers of the East; even as late as 1850, Pennsylvania and New York ranked first and third, respectively, in wheat production nationally. Ohio, which had become a commercial producer in the 1830s, ranked second. During the next decade, the shift of wheat production

[6] For the advantages of corn growing to the western pioneer, see Paul W. Gates, *The Farmer's Age: Agriculture, 1815–1860* (New York: Holt, Rinehart & Winston, 1960), 169. A single peck of seed corn, yielding as much as 50 bushels, planted an acre and could be transported far more easily than 2 bushels of wheat seed, which weighed 120 pounds but might bring in only 15 to 18 bushels per acre.

The morning of the opening of the Oklahoma Land Rush, April 22, 1889. The people shown here are waiting for the gun that will signal their right to enter and claim land formerly held by Native Americans. Those who jumped the gun were known as "sooners."

to the West was remarkable. By 1860, Illinois, Indiana, and Wisconsin were the leading producers, and the five states carved from the Northwest Territory produced roughly half the nation's output. The major wheat-growing areas were still not finally established, however; further shifts to the West in the production of this important crop were yet to come.

Ultimately, the western migration forced changes on the agriculture of the northeastern states. For a quarter of a century after the ratification of the Constitution, agriculture in New England, except in a few localities, remained relatively primitive; the individual farm unit produced practically everything needed for the household. With the growing industrialization of New England after 1810, production for urban markets became possible. Between 1810 and 1840, farmers in the Middle Atlantic states continued to grow the products for which their localities had traditionally been suited, and, as noted, Pennsylvania and New York remained major wheat producers until midcentury. But the arrival of the steamboat in the West in 1811, the opening of the Erie Canal in the 1820s, and the extension of the railroads beyond the Alleghenies in the 1840s meant that products of the rich western lands would flow in ever increasing amounts to the East. Western competition caused the northeastern farmer to reduce grain cultivation, and only dairy cattle remained important in animal production. Specialization in truck gardens and dairy products for city people and hay for city horses came to characterize the agriculture of this region, and those who could not adapt to the changing market conditions moved to the city or went west.

THE SOUTHWESTERN MIGRATION AND COTTON

As discussed in chapter 7, the Lower South suffered serious setbacks during the early years of independence. Even the market for tobacco stagnated, especially after the Embargo Act of 1807 and again after the War of 1812 allowed tobacco from other regions to enter and gain greater shares of the world market.

The hope of the South was in cotton. Obtaining their supplies of raw cotton from the Orient, the English had increasingly turned to the manufacture of cotton cloth instead of wool in the late seventeenth century. The inventions that came a century later—the steam engine, the spinning jenny, the water frame, the spinning mule, and the power loom—all gave rise to an enormous demand for cotton fiber. The phase of the Industrial Revolution that made it possible to apply power to textile manufacturing occurred at just the right time to stimulate and encourage the planting of cotton wherever it could be grown profitably. In the southern United States, the conditions for a profitable agriculture based on cotton were nearly ideal. Only some way of separating the green seed from the short-staple "upland cotton" had to be devised. One of the contributions of Yankee genius Eli Whitney was the invention of a gin that enabled a good worker to clean 50 pounds of cotton per day instead of only 1 pound by hand. With the application of power to the gin, the amount of fiber that could be produced appeared almost limitless.

On the humid coasts of Georgia and South Carolina, planters who had grown indigo turned to cotton. Even some rice fields were recultivated to produce the new staple. The culture moved up to North Carolina and Virginia and over the mountains to the beautiful rolling country of middle Tennessee. In the early 1800s, the piedmont of Georgia and South Carolina became the important cotton center; these states were vying for first place by 1820, with South Carolina slightly in the lead.

With the end of the War of 1812, the really important shift in cotton production to the west began (see Map 8.4). Almost unerringly, the settlers first planted the loamy, fertile soils that extended in an arc from Georgia through Alabama into northeastern Mississippi. A second major cotton-growing area lay in the rich bottom land of the lower Mississippi River and its tributaries. In this extremely fertile soil, the cotton even tended to grow a longer fiber. The culture spread into western Tennessee and eastern Arkansas. A jump into Texas then foretold the trend of cotton production.

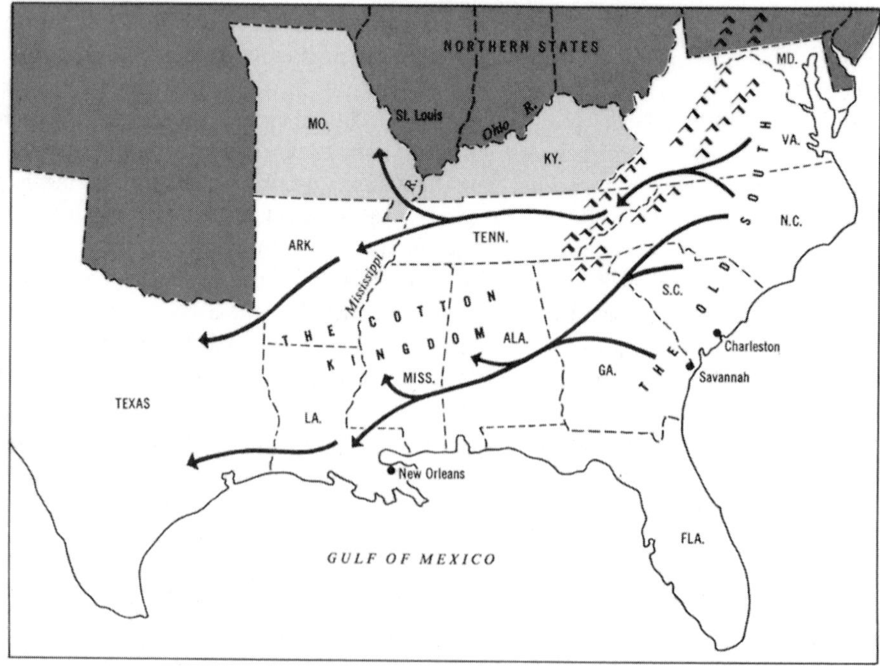

MAP 8.4 Shifts in Cotton Cultivation *The tremendous growth of the world demand for cotton propelled the westward movement of cotton cultivation after the War of 1812 and up to the onset of the Civil War.*

Perspective 8.1

Forced Immigration of Native Americans in the Southeastern United States

Part of Jefferson's vision of western settlement as portrayed in the Northwest Land Ordinance was the fair and proper treatment of Native Americans. Except for the prohibition of slavery clause, southwestern settlement also followed the 1785–1787 ordinances, including Article 3 (1787):

> The utmost good faith shall always be observed toward the Indians; their land and property shall never be taken from them without their consent; and in their property, rights, and liberty, they shall never be invaded or disturbed, unless in just and lawful wars authorized by Congress, but laws founded in justice and humanity shall from time to time be made, for preventing wrongs being done to them, and for preserving peace and friendship with them.

Along the southwestern path of expansion lay the lands (see Maps 8.4 and 8.5) of the Cherokee, Creek, Choctaw, Chickasaw, and Seminole tribes. In spite of Jefferson's words, many whites, both north and south, began calling for the removal of tribes to land farther west. White cravings for Cherokee lands, in particular, were intensified by the discovery of gold on Cherokee lands in 1828. President Andrew Jackson and other supporters of removal argued that the Cherokee would not be able to survive in the East because the game on which they mainly depended for food was disappearing. It was an opinion only (Economic Reasoning Proposition 5). Research by David Wishart (1999) confirms that the Cherokee had achieved a remarkable degree of success beyond hunting and skinning deer and other animals. In fact, most Cherokee were farmers, practicing a diversified agriculture. Productivity in corn production was comparable with that on similar white lands. Other Cherokee earned their livings in market activities such as weaving and spinning, inn keeping, operating ferryboats, and so on. A minority engaged in large-scale plantation agriculture based on slavery. In economic terms, the Cherokee were similar to their white neighbors, but the facts were of no

continued

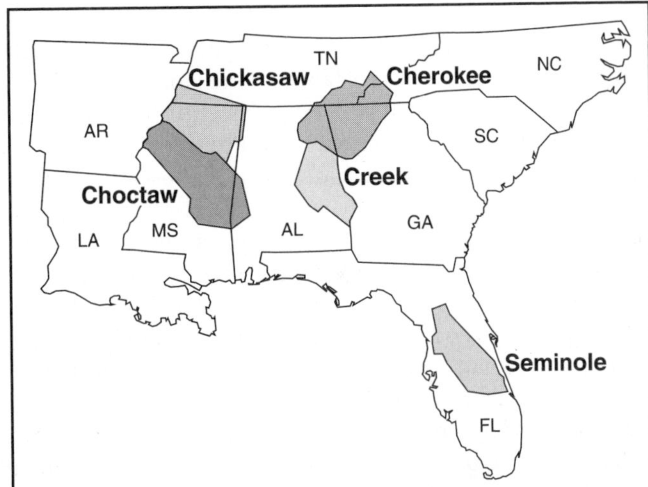

MAP 8.5 Tribal Lands of the Chickasaw, Cherokee, Choctaw, Creek, and Seminole before 1830.

Source: Philip Weeks, Farewell My Nation: The American Indian and the United States, 1820–1890 *(Wheeling, Ill.: Harlan Davidson, 1990), 20, as given in Barrington, 1999, 17.*

Perspective 8.1

Forced Immigration of Native Americans in the Southeastern United States, continued

avail. Indeed, the improvements they had made on their land increased white demands for removal. In 1830, Congress passed the Indian Removal Act. The Choctaw, Chickasaw, and Creek signed treaties ceding their holdings for new lands west of the Mississippi, while the Cherokee resisted until finally forced, eight years later, to march in severe winter weather to what is now Oklahoma. An estimated 4,000 people, nearly one-fourth of the Cherokee, died on the "Trail of Tears." A few Cherokee remained in North Carolina through assimilation and special assistance. Approximately 50 families forsook their Cherokee citizenship to become citizens of North Carolina; other families from the Snowbird community bought back 1,200 acres of their land. State law prohibited Indians from owning land (until after 1864), but the purchase was made using names of sympathetic whites.

Farther south, in Florida, the Seminoles resisted both assimilation and removal. Ten thousand federal troops, 30,000 citizen soldiers, and $40 million in war expenditures finally prevailed (with 14 percent losses of life by action and disease over seven years). Nearly 3,000 Seminoles were removed to lands west of the Mississippi.

By 1840, the early cotton-producing states had been left behind. In 1860, Alabama, Mississippi, and Louisiana were far in the lead, with Mississippi alone producing more cotton than Georgia and South Carolina combined. This shift in the realm of King Cotton was to have the most far-reaching consequences on the economy of the South.

Just before the Civil War, there could be no doubt that cotton was indeed king. As Douglass North has remarked, it is difficult to exaggerate the role of cotton in American economic growth between 1800 and 1850.[7] The great staple accounted for more than half the dollar value of U.S. exports—a value nearly 10 times as great in U.S. foreign trade as its nearest competitor, the wheat and wheat flour of the North. At home, cotton planters furnished the raw materials for textile manufacturers in the North, who by 1860 were selling half again as much cotton cloth as wool cloth. As we will see in chapter 10, cotton goods were the leading manufacture in the United States in 1860 when ranked by value added (second when ranked by employment). It was not surprising that even as antislavery forces strengthened in the late antebellum period, southerners could scarcely envisage a North, or even a world, without their chief product.

There was both a slight push and a major pull to the new lands of the South. The push had begun in colonial times as tidewater lands began to lose the natural fertility that staples grown there required. The small farmer, impelled by hardship, had moved into the piedmont. The shift had been especially pronounced in Virginia and North Carolina, from which struggling families tended to sift through the Cumberland Gap into Tennessee and Kentucky. The frontiersman—the professional pioneer —was then pulled into the rich new cotton country, mostly from Georgia and South Carolina, but partly from Tennessee and even Kentucky. Following closely came the yeoman farmer; almost simultaneously—and this is what clearly distinguishes the southern migration—came the planter, the man of substance, with his huge household establishment and his slaves.

As with the surges in the Northwest, the 1810s, the 1830s, and the 1850s were the boom decades for the new southwestern areas. It was, of course, the favorable returns expected on

[7] See North, *The Economic Growth of the United States 1790–1860.*

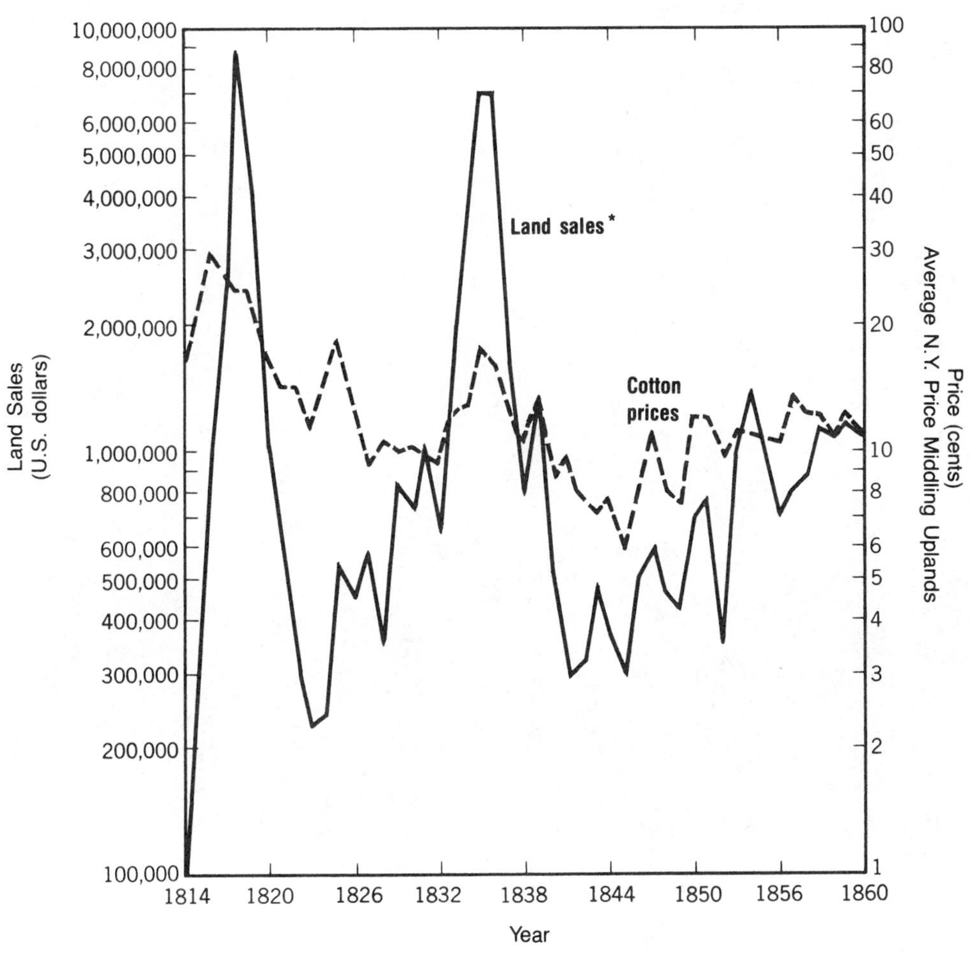

FIGURE 8.3 U.S. Public Land Sales and Cotton Prices, 1814–1860

**Alabama, Florida, Louisiana, Mississippi, and Arkansas.*

Source: Douglass C. North, The Economic Growth of the United States 1790–1860 *(Englewood Cliffs, N.J.: Prentice Hall, 1961), 124.*

cotton cultivation that brought the great, irregular surges of movement toward the southwest. As shown in Figure 8.3, there is close correlation between the price of cotton on the one hand and the volume of public land sales in Alabama, Florida, Louisiana, Mississippi, and Arkansas on the other. Here again, we observe the responsiveness of individuals to favorable economic opportunities.

THE FAR WESTERN MIGRATION

Although of only minor economic importance when compared with the southern and northwestern migrations, the California Gold Rush was one of the most widely discussed and emotionally charged of all the migrations in response to economic opportunity.[8] On January 24,

[8]Another fascinating western migration was that of the Mormons, driven by mob violence from Ohio, Missouri, and Illinois in the late 1830s and 1840s, plus the later gathering of the "saints" at Zion (Utah). For descriptions of this special migration, see Wallace Stagner, *The Gathering of Zion* (New York: McGraw-Hill, 1964); Leonard J. Arrington and Davis Bitton, *The Mormon Experience* (New York: Knopf, 1979); Gary M. Walton, *Chills along the Sweetwater* (Salt Lake City, Utah: Origin Book Sales, 1999): and Scott A. Carson, "Industrial Migration in America's Great Basin," *Journal of Interdisciplinary History* 33 (3), (2002), 387–404.

Land speculation—"holding for a rise"—became a lively offshoot of the westward population surge. Here, a Kansas land office provides a center for speculative activity.

1848, only nine days before the war with Mexico ended, James W. Marshall discovered gold while building a sawmill for John Sutter on the South Fork of the American River.

Sutter and Marshall attempted to keep the discovery a secret while trying to secure for themselves stronger property rights on the area. However, a young boy told of the discovery to a man bringing supplies to the mill, and, coincidentally, the boy's mother gave the driver a small nugget as a present. When the man later used the nugget to buy a drink back at "Fort Sutter," the word was out.

As gold fever swept the land, people poured across the country and "around the Horn." In the first several months of 1849, almost 20,000 left the East Coast by boat destined for California, and nearly 40,000 arrived in San Francisco throughout 1849. From a population of about 107,000 near the end of 1849, California grew to more than 260,000 within three years.

Among the most fascinating aspects of the California Gold Rush was the initial absence of property rights to land and of a government capable of enforcing law and order. Despite stiff penalties for desertion, for instance, U.S. soldiers in California left their posts in droves to hunt for gold. (Enlisted men, who typically earned $7 a month plus room and board, numbered almost 1,059 in 1847 but only 660 in 1848.) Yet despite an initial absence of law and order, violence in the gold fields was surprisingly low. As John Umbeck, one of the leading authorities on the Gold Rush, reports:

> During 1848, . . . nearly 10,000 people rushed to mine gold on property to which no one had exclusive rights. Furthermore, although nearly every miner carried a gun, little

violence was reported. In July, when Governor Mason visited the mines, he reported that the miners were respecting Sutter's property rights and that "crime of any kind was very infrequent, and that no thefts or robberies had been committed in the gold district . . . and it was a matter of surprise, that so peaceful and quiet a state of things should continue to exist."[9]

Only after new waves of miners entered the fields did gold land become troublingly scarce, thereby urging exclusive property rights or claims. Several firsthand accounts indicate the nature of those rights:

> When the mines in and around Nevada City were first opened they were solely in the ravines . . . and there was no law regulating the size of a miner's claim, and generally a party that first went into a ravine had the exclusive right there too. . . . As population increased that rule did not long maintain. The miners saw that something must be done, and therefore a meeting was called and a rule was established that each miner could hold thirty feet square as a mining claim.
>
> All these bars on the Middle Fork of the American River, from Oregon Bar upwards, after the lowest estimate, employed in the summer of 1850 not less than 1,500 men; originally working on shares, and the assessment on the share paid out daily, so that those who had been drunk or absent did not get any part of it; but this after a while caused dissatisfaction and was the reason of breaking up the co-operative work and commencing work on claims. A claim was a spot of ground fifteen feet wide on the river front.
>
> In a comparatively short time we had a large community on that creek, which led to rows and altercations about boundaries, that eventuated in an agreement, entered into by unanimous agreement, that each person should have 10 square feet.
>
> Wood's Creek was filled up with miners, and I here for the first time after the discovery of gold, learned what a miner's claim was. In 1848, the miners had no division of the ground into claims—they worked where it was richest, and many times four or five could be seen at work in a circle of six feet in diameter; but . . . here they were now measuring the ground off with tape measures so as to prevent disputes arising from the division.[10]

It was at the "miners' meetings" that contract specifications (Economic Reasoning Proposition 4) were determined to establish and enforce claims and prevent claim jumping. Each "field" held its own meetings, and afterward, each miner marked his claim boundary with wooden stakes and frequently a notice such as this:

> All and everybody, this is my claim, fifty feet on the gulch, cordin to Clear Creek District Law, backed up by shotgun amendments.
>
> Any person found trespassing on this claim will be persucuted to the full extent of the law. This is no monkey tale butt I will assert my rites at the pint of the sicks shirter if legally necessary to taik head and good warnin.[11]

In this fashion, property rights and other institutions first emerged in the gold fields of California, and with them an outpouring of millions of dollars in gold.

---

[9] See John Umbeck, "The California Gold Rush: A Study of Emerging Property Rights," *Explorations in Economic History* 14 (1977).This does not mean there was an absence of violence in the Far West; indeed, there were ample brawls, shootings, and killings in saloons and bars.
[10] As quoted in Umbeck, 215.
[11] As quoted in Umbeck, 216.

The great California Gold Rush had effects far beyond the bossless mass employment and wealth creation it generated.[12] It was a tidal wave of hope to people who no longer were forced to know their place and be resigned to it. And the timing! Ireland's potato famine, China's Taiping Rebellion, political uprisings in France and Germany—all added great numbers to young Americans, many discharged from service at the end of the Mexican War, who sought their fortunes in the gold fields. Not everyone struck it rich like Leland Stanford, formerly a failed lawyer, or Lucius Fairchild, a store clerk from Wisconsin who returned home rich and became Wisconsin's governor. But the Gold Rush did guarantee dreams and adventure to match the towering Sierra.

SELECTED REFERENCES AND SUGGESTED READINGS

Arrington, Leonard J. and Davis Bitton. *The Mormon Experience* (New York: Knopf, 1979).

Atack, Jeremy, Fred Bateman, and William N. Parker. "Northern Agriculture and the Westward Movement." In *The Cambridge Economic History of the United States*, vol. II, *The Long Nineteenth Century*, eds. Stanley L. Engerman and Robert E. Gallman (New York: Cambridge University Press, 2000), 285–328.

Barrington, Linda, ed. *The Other Side of the Frontier* (Boulder: Westview, 1999).

Berry, Thomas. *Western Prices before 1861* (Cambridge, Mass.: Harvard University Press, 1943).

Bidwell, Percy, and John Falconer. *History of Agriculture in the Northern United States 1620–1860* (Washington, D.C.: Carnegie Institution of Washington, 1925).

Billington, Ray A. "The Origin of the Land Speculator as a Frontier Type." *Agricultural History* 9 (October 1945).

———. *Westward Expansion: A History of the American Frontier* (New York: Macmillan, 1949).

Bogue, Allan C. "Farming in the Prairie Peninsula 1830–1890." *Journal of Economic History* 23 (March 1963).

———. *From Prairie to Cornbelt: Farming on the Illinois and Iowa Prairies in the Nineteenth Century* (Chicago: University of Chicago Press, 1963).

Bogue, Allan C., and Margaret Bogue. "Profits and the Frontier Land Speculation." *Journal of Economic History* 37 (March 1957).

Carstensen, Vernon, ed. *The Public Lands: Studies in the History of the Public Domain* (Madison: University of Wisconsin Press, 1963).

Carson, Scott A. "Industrial Migration in America's Great Basin," *Journal of Interdisciplinary History* 33 (3), (2002): 387–403.

Cole, Arthur H. "Cyclical and Sectional Variations in the Sale of the Public Lands, 1816–1860." *Review of Economics and Statistics* 9 (1927). Reprinted in Vernon Carstensen, ed. *The Public Lands* (Madison: University of Wisconsin Press, 1963).

Danhof, Clarence."Farm Making Costs and the Safety Valve, 1855–60." In *The Public Lands*, ed. Vernon Carstensen (Madison: University of Wisconsin Press, 1963).

———. *Change in Agriculture: The Northern United States, 1820–1870* (Cambridge, Mass.: Harvard University Press, 1969).

Freund, Rudolf. "Military Bounty Lands and the Origin of the Public Domain." *Agricultural History* 20 (1946). Reprinted in Vernon Carstensen, ed. *The Public Lands* (Madison: University of Wisconsin Press, 1963).

Gates, Paul W. "The Role of the Land Speculator in Western Development." *Pennsylvania Magazine of History and Biography* 66 (1942). Reprinted in Vernon Carstensen, ed. *The Public Lands* (Madison: University of Wisconsin Press, 1963).

[12]For the longer term effects of the gold rush, with emphasis on California history, see J. S. Holiday, *Rush for Riches: Gold Fever and the Making of California* (Berkeley: University of California Press, 1999).

———. "Charts of Public Land Sales and Entries." *Journal of Economic History* 24 (March, 1964).

———. *History of Public Land Law Development.* (Washington, D.C.: Public Land Law Review Commission, 1968).

Holiday, J. S., *Rush for Riches: Gold Fever and the Making of California* (Berkeley: University of California Press, 1999).

Hughes, Jonathon R.T. "The Great Land Ordinances: Colonial America's Thumb Print on History." In *Essays on the Economic Significance of the Old Northwest*, eds. David C. Klingaman and Richard K.Vedder (Athens: Ohio University Press, 1987), 1–18.

Lebergott, Stanley. "'O Pioneers': Land Speculation and the Growth of the Midwest." In *Essays on the Economy of the Old Northwest,* ed. David C. Klingaman and Richard K. Vedder (Athens: Ohio University Press, 1987), 37–58.

Merk, Frederick. *History of the Westward Movement* (New York: Knopf, 1978).

North, Douglass C. *Economic Growth of the United States 1790–1860* (Englewood Cliffs, N.J.: Prentice Hall, 1961).

North, Douglass C., and Andrew R. Rutten. "The Northwest Ordinance in Historical Perspective." In *Essays on the Economy of the Old Northwest*, ed. David C. Klingaman and Richard K.Vedder (Athens: Ohio University Press, 1987), 19–36.

Parker, William. "Agriculture." Chapter 11 in *American Economic Growth: An Economist's History of the United States*, ed. Lance E. Davis et al. (New York: Harper & Row, 1972).

Parker, William, and Judith Klein. "Productivity Growth in Grain Production in the United States." In *Output, Employment and Productivity in the United States after 1800*, vol. 30, ed. Dorothy Brady. *National Bureau of Economic Research, Studies in Income and Wealth* (New York: Columbia University Press, 1966).

Primack, Martin. "Land Clearing under 19th Century Techniques." *Journal of Economic History* 22 (December 1962).

Riegel, Robert E., and Robert G. Athearn. *America Moves West* (New York: Holt, 1964).

Rohrbough, Malcolm. *The Land Office Business: The Settlement and Administration of American Public Lands, 1789–1837* (New York: Oxford University Press, 1968).

Rothenberg, Winifred B. "The Market and Massachusetts Farmers, 1750–1855." *Journal of Economic History* 41 (1981): 283–314.

Stagner, Wallace. *The Gathering of Zion* (New York: McGraw-Hill, 1964).

Steckel, Richard. "The Economic Foundations of East-West Migration during the 19th Century." *Explorations in Economic History* 20 (1983): 14–36.

Treat, Payson J. "Origin of the National Land System under the Confederation." *American Historical Association Report* (1905). Reprinted in Vernon Carstensen, ed. *The Public Lands* (Madison: University of Wisconsin Press, 1963).

Turner, Frederick Jackson. *The Frontier in American History* (New York: Holt, Rinehart & Winston, 1921).

Umbeck, John. "The California Gold Rush: A Study of Emerging Property Rights." *Explorations in Economic History* 14 (1977): 192–226.

Walton, Gary M. *Chills along the Sweetwater* (Salt Lake City, Utah: Origin Book Sales, 1999).

Weiman, David F. "Peopling the Land by Lottery? The Market in Public Lands and the Regional Differentiation of Territory on the Georgia Frontier." *Journal of Economic History* 51 (1991): 835–860.

Wishart, David M. "Could the Cherokee Have Survived in the Southeast?" In *The Other Side of the Frontier*, ed. Linda Barrington (Boulder, Colo.: Westview, 1999), 165–189.

Wyman, Walker D., and Clifton B. Kroeber, eds. *The Frontier in Perspective* (Madison: University of Wisconsin Press, 1957).

Chapter Nine

TRANSPORTATION AND MARKET GROWTH

Chapter Theme

The economic growth of the United States in the nineteenth century was strategically influenced by the spread of a market economy, by the shifting of resources from lower-valued (subsistence) to higher-valued uses (production for market), and by the growth of specialization and divisions of labor in production. As Adam Smith and early nineteenth-century contemporaries knew, levels of productivity were vitally dependent on the size of the market, especially in manufacturing. Of course, market size was limited by the costs of moving goods and negotiating exchanges. In this early era, transportation costs were the most important component of these costs. For these many reasons, special concentration on transportation, mode by mode, is warranted and, indeed, vital to our understanding of long-term economic growth and the location of people and economic activity. A viable transportation system was key to forming a national market (as discussed in Economic Insight 9.1, on page 179). In combination, the improvements in transportation from 1800 to 1860 were so striking as to merit the description "a transportation revolution." The effects of this revolution are seen in the falling costs of obtaining information and moving people and goods, in settlement and production patterns, and in the forging of a national economy. There are many parallels to those effects and what we are observing today with the information revolution.

THE ANTEBELLUM TRANSPORTATION REVOLUTION

Once the western migrations were unleashed, the demand for improved transportation systems grew dramatically. Investments in steamboats, canals, and railroads were the most important internal transportation developments of the antebellum era. There can be little doubt that the host of improvements in transportation and the precipitous decline in freight rates (as shown in Figure 9.1) were truly revolutionary in impact as well as in form. Not only did they directly propel the process of westward expansion and the relocation of agriculture and mining discussed in chapter 8, but also they greatly altered various regions' comparative advantages in production. For example, they set the stage for New England to concentrate increasingly in manufacturing and to further the advance and application of new technologies and organizational forms of production in a factory setting (chapter 10). In turn, these changes set the stage for urbanization and heightening urban problems and labor

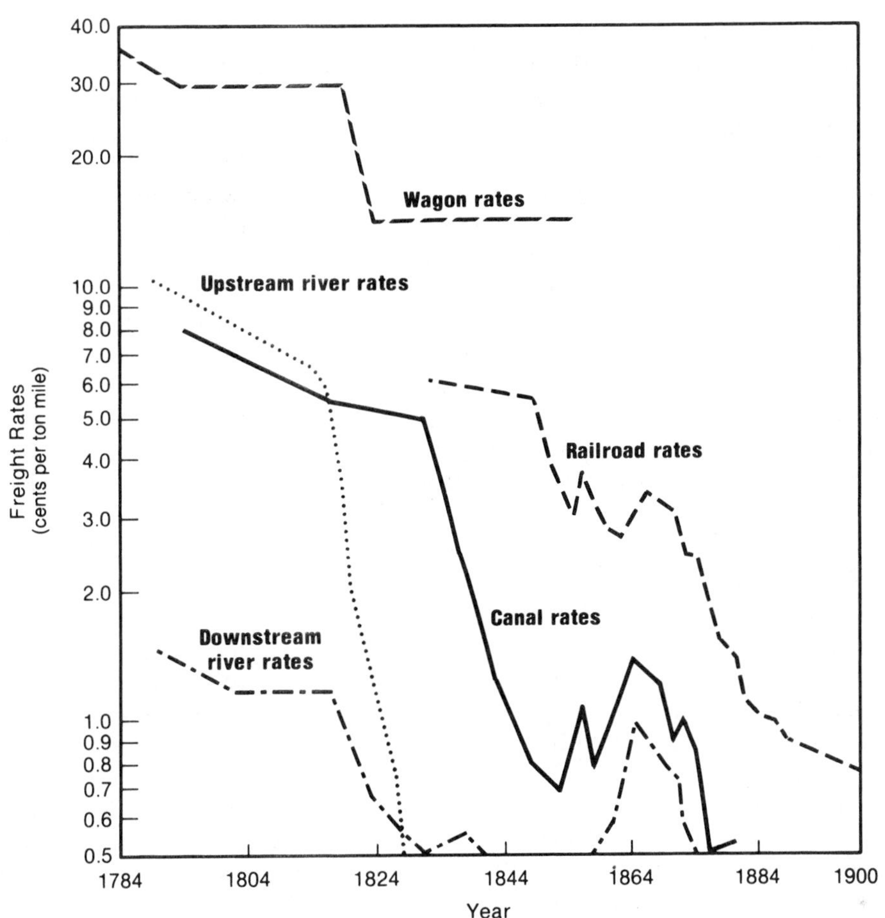

Freight rates declined dramatically during the nineteenth century.

FIGURE 9.1 Inland Freight Rates, 1784–1900

Sources: Douglass C. North, Growth and Welfare in the American Past *(Englewood Cliffs, N.J.: Prentice Hall, 1973), 108; and "The Role of Transportation in the Economic Development of North America," a paper presented to the International Congress of the Historical Sciences, Vienna, August 1965, and published in* Les Grandes Voies Maritimes dans le Monde *XV*[e]*–XIX*[e] *Siecles, ©1965 by Ecole des Hautes Etudes en Sciences Sociales, Paris.*

unrest (chapter 11). The falling costs of transport—and communication—boosted market size and efficiency and forged a national market for many goods and services. Whereas the pattern of general price declines in the western markets of Cincinnati and St. Louis had followed those in New York and Philadelphia by 12 months near the turn of the century, the lag was reduced to only 3 or 4 months by the 1830s. By the 1850s, this lag had fallen even further to a mere week or so. Lastly, the transportation linkage by water and rail between the East and West would prove significant in binding these two regions—politically as well as economically—as interregional tensions mounted in the years preceding the Civil War. The term *transportation revolution* consequently implies far more than a mere series of new technological forms rapidly introduced.

An important part of the transportation story is the role of private versus public initiative during this critical period of growing economic unification. In England, private entrepreneurs built and operated railroads and canals, and government participation was slight. In the United States, however, there was a mixture of private and public enterprise. Government investments in canals and railroads as a percentage of total investment in these modes were large. Public investments were a smaller proportion in roads, and they were minimal for the natural waterways. A strong, active role in transportation for government had been planned as early as 1807, when Treasury Secretary Albert Gallatin was asked to develop "a plan for the application of such means as are within the power of Congress, to the purpose of opening roads and making canals."[1] Gallatin's ingenious plan had a projected total cost of $20 million, but questions of legality—and politics, as always—prevented the federal government from undertaking it. Many viewed the Constitution as an agreement among sovereignties (the sovereign states), and "strict constructionism" throughout most of the antebellum period held the federal government to only a few projects, mainly those passing through several states at a time. Nevertheless, Gallatin's plan was carried out, not by the federal government but by private entrepreneurs and by state and local and private enterprise mixtures. Sheer size of the capital requirements often necessitated these collaborations. Both public officials and private citizens promoted government intervention in transport investment. In some cases, private operators succeeded in obtaining public credit and special assistance just as special interest groups (such as farmers) do today. In other cases, local politicians who wanted transportation improvements for their town or region took advantage of private entrepreneurs.

THE ROUTES OF WESTERN COMMERCE

During the antebellum period, three natural gateways linked the western territories and states with the rest of the nation and other countries. The first ran eastward, connecting the Great Lakes to New York. The main arteries feeding this Northern Gateway were down the St. Lawrence River or along the Hudson or Mohawk river valleys. Major investments on this route included the Erie Canal, which opened in 1825, and the New York Central and New York and Erie Railroads, completed in 1852.

The second gateway, the Northeastern Gateway, was a network of roads, canals, and, later, rail systems that connected the river launching points at Pittsburgh (on the Ohio River) to Philadelphia and Wheeling (also on the Ohio River) to Baltimore. The National Road was completed west to Wheeling in 1817, and the Pennsylvania Turnpike—a toll road—reached Pittsburgh the next year. Competing canals on these two links created a rivalry in the 1830s. Then, in the 1850s, the rivalry of these cities was boosted again through rail linkages.

The Southern Gateway, at New Orleans, was the main southern entrepot. The key event on the trunk rivers of the Mississippi, Missouri, Ohio, and other western river arteries to this gateway was the introduction of the steamboat in 1811.

Figure 9.2 shows the volume of shipments from the western interior to the East and abroad by each gateway.[2] The growth of total outbound shipments, from 65,000 tons in 1810 to nearly 4.7 million tons in 1860, documents the impressive development that was taking place in the West. We also see that the Northeastern Gateway played only a minor role, typically carrying less than 5 percent of the shipments from the West. The Northern Gateway was far more significant, but not until the late 1830s. Prior to 1825 and the opening of the Erie Canal, this gateway handled no outbound shipments. Even in the early 1830s, most of the shipments on the Erie Canal were from upstate New York. Therefore, it was primarily the Southern Gateway that handled western produce shipments, at least until the last few decades of the antebellum period. The dominance of the natural waterways, encompassing 16,000 miles of western rivers, led the contemporary James Lanman to say in 1841:

---

[1] Carter Goodrich, *Government Promotion of American Canals and Railroads* (New York: Columbia University Press, 1960), 27.

[2] The evidence on inbound shipments is more fragmentary and less complete, but it does not change the relative positions of each gateway in the movement of freight.

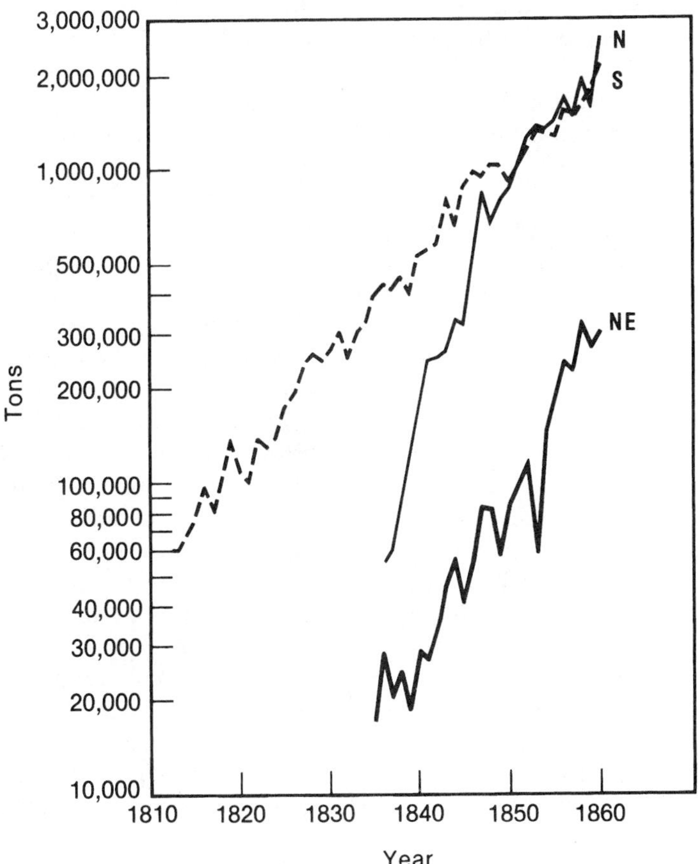

FIGURE 9.2 Freight Shipments from the Interior by the Western Gateways, 1810–1860

Source: Erik F. Haites, James Mak, and Gary M. Walton, Western River Transportation: The Era of Early Internal Development, 1810–1860 *(Baltimore: Johns Hopkins University Press, 1975), 7 and Appendix A.*

> Steam navigation colonized the west! It furnished a motive for settlement and production by the hands of eastern men, because it brought the western territory nearer to the east by nine tenths of the distance. . . . Steam is crowding our eastern cities with western flour and western merchants, and lading the western steamboats with eastern emigrants and eastern merchandise. It has advanced the career of national colonization and national production, at least a century![3]

STEAMBOATS AND THE NATURAL WATERWAYS

Before the coming of the steamboat in the West, river travel was especially difficult, hazardous, and costly. Rafts and flatboats allowed downriver passage at reasonable cost, but the return upriver on foot or horseback was time consuming and dangerous. Typical voyages of 1,000 miles took one month downstream and three to four months to return. The keelboat, which made upstream journeys possible, was based on labor-intensive, back-breaking work. As shown in Figure 9.1, upstream travel costs were typically more than five times downstream travel costs.

[3]James H. Lanman, "American Steam Navigation," *Hunt's Merchants' Magazine and Commercial Review* 4 (1841): 124.

In 1807, Robert Fulton, with the assistance of Robert R. Livingston, built the steamboat *Clermont,* which completed a historic voyage up the Hudson River from New York to Albany, a distance of 150 miles, in 32 hours. Following the initial trip, regular passenger service from New York to Albany was inaugurated, and the dependability of the steamboat was quickly demonstrated. A new era of transportation on the rivers of America had begun.

The steamboat's beginning in the West came at the northern terminus of Pittsburgh, where the junction of the Allegheny and the Monongahela forms the Ohio River and where plentiful supplies of timber and the local iron industry fostered a flourishing shipbuilding industry. Nicholas Roosevelt, under the Fulton-Livingston patents, constructed in Pittsburgh the first steamboat to ply the inland waters. Named the *New Orleans,* it left Pittsburgh on October 20, 1811, and completed its voyage to the Gulf of Mexico in a little over two and one-half months, despite an earthquake en route at New Madrid, Missouri. Six years passed before regular services upstream and downstream were established, but (as shown in Table 9.1) the tonnage of steamboats in operation on the western rivers by 1819 already exceeded 10,000. This figure grew to almost 200,000 tons by 1860. The periods of the most rapid expansion were the first two decades following 1815, but significant gains occurred throughout each decade. Not until the 1880s did steamboating on the western rivers register an absolute decline.

The appearance of the steamboat on inland waterways did not, by any means, solve all problems of travel. Variations in the heights of the rivers still made navigation uncertain, even dangerous. Ice in the spring and sand bars in the summer were ever present hazards; snags (trees lodged in rivers), rocks, and sunken vessels continually damaged and wrecked watercraft. In addition to these problems, the steamboat exposed westerners to some of the earliest hazards of industrialization; high-pressure boilers frequently exploded, accidentally killing thousands over the decades. This prompted the federal government to

Inland shipping points like Cincinnati soon became major markets for an increasing variety of goods and services.

TABLE 9.1 Annual Construction (gross and net) and Tonnage of Steamboats in Operation on Western Rivers, 1811–1868

SHIPS IN OPERATION			SHIPS IN OPERATION		
YEAR	NUMBER	TONNAGE	YEAR	NUMBER	TONNAGE
1811	1	400	1840	494	82,600
1812	1	400	1841	504	85,200
1813	2	400	1842	458	76,500
1814	3	700	1843	449	80,000
1815	7	1,500	1844	509	90,300
1816	11	2,300	1845	538	96,200
1817	16	3,000	1846	578	106,300
1818	30	5,800	1847	638	122,400
1819	59	13,000	1848	666	133,400
1820	69	14,200	1849	648	130,100
1821	73	14,500	1850	638	134,600
1822	71	13,400	1851	660	142,900
1823	74	12,500	1852	676	152,900
1824	67	10,500	1853	711	169,300
1825	80	12,500	1854	696	169,000
1826	107	17,300	1855	696	172,700
1827	120	19,700	1856	761	188,100
1828	118	18,900	1857	800	199,600
1829	140	22,300	1858	779	196,400
1830	151	24,600	1859	779	192,800
1831	183	28,700	1860	817	195,000
1832	227	35,200	1861	665	165,100
1833	239	36,800	1862	666	157,300
1834	270	41,000	1863	778	160,200
1835	324	50,100	1864	919	193,200
1836	374	57,400	1865	1,006	228,700
1837	399	63,600	1866	1,028	238,400
1838	391	65,300	1867	976	232,300
1839	480	78,200	1868	874	212,200

Source: *Erik F. Haites, James Mak, and Gary M. Walton,* Western River Transportation: The Era of Early Internal Development, 1810–1860 *(Baltimore: Johns Hopkins University Press, 1975), 130–131.*

intervene: in 1838 and again in 1852, some of the first U.S. laws concerning industrial safety and consumer protection were legislated. The 1852 steamboat boiler inspection law was especially effective, significantly reducing boiler explosions and loss of life. Refer to Economic Reasoning Proposition 4. Also, the federal government sporadically engaged in the removal of snags and other obstacles from the rivers. This also reduced losses of cargo, vessels, and people.

★★★ *Economic Reasoning Proposition*

Competition, Productivity, and Endangered Species

One of the most significant characteristics of western river transportation was the high degree of competition among the various craft. This meant that the revolutionary effects of the steamboat, which were critical to the early settlement of the West, were transfused through a competitive market. Fulton and Livingston attempted to secure a monopoly via government restraint to prevent others from providing steamboat services at New Orleans

Robert Fulton's steamboat the Clermont, *built in 1807, started a transportation revolution on America's rivers.*

and throughout the West.[4] Their quest for monopoly rights was ultimately defeated in the courts, reminding us again of the importance of Economic Reasoning Proposition 4. These and other associations failed to limit supply and block entry; and without government interference, the modest capital requirements needed to enter the business assured a competitive market.

Following an early period of bonanza profits (30 percent and more) on the major routes, a normal rate of return on capital of about 10 percent was common by 1820. Only on the remote and dangerous tributaries, where trade was thin and uncertain, could such exceptional returns as 35 or 40 percent be obtained.

Because the market for western river craft services was generally competitive, the savings from productivity-raising improvements ushered in by the steamboat were promptly passed on to consumers. And the cost reductions were significant, as the evidence in Table 9.2 illustrates.

Of course, a major cause of the sharp decline in freight costs was simply the introduction of steam power. However, the stream of modifications and improvements that followed the maiden voyage of the *New Orleans* provided greater productivity gains than the initial application of steam power. This assertion is verified in the fall of rates. The decrease in rates after 1820 was greater, both absolutely and relatively, than the decline from 1811 to 1820, especially in real terms. For example, in the purchasing power of 1820 dollars, the real-cost decline upstream on the New Orleans–Louisville run was from $3.12 around 1815 to $2.00 in 1820 to $0.28 in the late 1850s. Downstream, the real cost changes were from $0.62 around 1815 to $0.75 in 1820 to $0.39 in the late 1850s.

[4]See Gary M. Walton, "Fulton's Folly," in *Second Thoughts: Learning from American Social and Economic History*, ed. Donald McCloskey (London: Oxford University Press, 1992), 145–150.

TABLE 9.2 Average Freight Rates (per 100 pounds of cargo) by Decade between Louisville and New Orleans, 1810–1859

	UPSTREAM	DOWNSTREAM
Before 1820	$5.00	$1.00
1820–1829	1.00	0.62
1830–1839	0.50	0.50
1840–1849	0.25	0.30
1850–1859	0.25	0.32

Source: Erik F. Haites, James Mak, and Gary M. Walton, Western River Transportation: The Era of Early Internal Development, 1810–1860 *(Baltimore: Johns Hopkins University Press, 1975), 32.*

Major modifications were made in the physical characteristics of the vessels. Initially resembling seagoing vessels, steamboats evolved to meet the shallow-water conditions of the western rivers. These boats became steadily lighter in weight, with many outside decks for cargo (and budget-fare accommodations for passengers), and their water depth (or draft) became less and less despite increased vessel size. Consequently, the amount of cargo carried per vessel ton greatly increased. In addition, the season of normal operations was substantially extended, even during shallow-water months. This, along with reductions in port times and passage times, greatly increased the number of round trips averaged each year. It is noteworthy that the decline in passage times was only partially due to faster speeds. Primarily, this decline resulted from learning to operate the boats at night. Shorter stopovers at specified fuel depots instead of long periods spent foraging in the woods for fuel contributed as well. Lastly, as noted earlier, government activity to clear the rivers of snags and other natural obstacles added to the available time of normal operations and made river transport a safer business, as evidenced by a decline in insurance costs over the decades.

On reflection, it is clear that most of the improvements did not result from technological change. Only the initial introduction of steam power stemmed from advances in knowledge about basic principles. The host of modifications evolved from the process of learning by doing and from the restructuring of known principles of design and engineering to fit shallow-water conditions. In effect, they are a tribute to the skills and ingenuity of the early craftsmen and mechanics.

In sum, the overall record of achievement gave rise to productivity advances (output per unit of input) that averaged more than 4 percent per year between 1815 and 1860. Such a rate exceeded that of any other transport medium over a comparable length of time in the nineteenth century.[5]

With the steamboat's success, other forms of river transport either evolved or disappeared. The labor-consuming keelboat felt the strongest sting of competition from the new technology and was quickly eliminated from the competitive fray on the main trunk river routes. The keelboat made nearly 90 percent of its revenues on the upriver leg, where men labored to pole, pull, or row with backbreaking effort against the currents. As shown in Table 9.2, the steamboat's greatest impact was on the upstream rates. Only on some of the remote, hazardous tributaries did the keelboat find temporary refuge from the chugging advance of the steamboat.

Surprisingly, quite a different destiny evolved for the flatboat, which showed a remarkable persistence throughout the entire antebellum period. Because the reductions in downstream rates were more moderate, the current-propelled flatboat was less threatened. In addition, spillover effects from steam boating aided flat boating. First, there was the

[5] See Erik F. Haites, James Mak, and Gary M. Walton, *Western River Transportation: The Era of Early Internal Development, 1810–1860* (Baltimore: Johns Hopkins University Press, 1975), 60–63.

tremendous savings in labor that the steamboat generated by providing quick upriver transport to returning flatboat men. Not only were they saved the long and sometimes perilous overland journey, but access to steamboat passenger services led to repetitive journeys and, thus, to the acquisition of skills and knowledge. This led to the adoption of larger flatboats, which economized greatly on labor per ton carried. Because of these gains, there were more flatboats on the western rivers near the middle of the nineteenth century than at any other time.

In combination, these western rivercraft gave a romantic aura to the drudgery of day-to-day freight haulage and commerce. Sumptuously furnished Mississippi riverboats were patronized by rich and poor alike. Yeomen farmers also contributed their adventuresome flat boating journeys. However, such developments were regional in character, and their impact was mainly on the Southern Gateway. On the waterways of the East or on the Great Lakes, the steamboat never attained the importance that it did in the Midwest. Canals and turnpikes furnished alternative means of transportation, and the railroad network had an earlier start in the East. Steamboats in the East were primarily passenger carriers—great side-wheelers furnishing luxurious accommodations for people traveling between major cities. On the Great Lakes, contrary to what might be expected, sailing ships successfully competed for freight throughout the antebellum years. Where human comfort was a factor, however, the steamship gradually prevailed. Even so, the number and tonnage of sailing vessels on the Great Lakes in 1860 were far greater than those of steamboats.

PUBLIC VERSUS PRIVATE INITIATIVE ON THE NATURAL WATERWAYS

Transportation developments on the natural waterways, especially on the rivers through the Southern Gateway, but along the Northern Gateway avenues as well, were predominantly a product of private initiative. Government investments as a proportion of total investments in vessels and river improvements were minuscule. Private entrepreneurs owned and operated the craft, and state and local government rendered few improvements in the rivers because many of the benefits to users could not be captured within state boundaries. Why should state or local governments appropriate funds for river improvements if most of the benefits went to vessel owners (and users) passing by? Calls for federal action to improve the rivers often went unheeded because of strict constitutional interpretations. With the exception of sporadic but highly beneficial snag-removal programs, the public sector provided very little capital to transportation on the natural waterways, no more than 1 or 2 percent of the total expenditures.

THE CANAL ERA

Although the natural waterways provided a substantial web of transport facilities, many productive areas remained regionally and economically disconnected until the canals were built and other internal improvements were made to link the areas together. The first major undertaking began in 1816, when the New York legislature authorized the construction of the Erie and Champlain canals. With powerful canal commissioner DeWitt Clinton as its guiding spirit, the Erie Canal was promoted with enthusiasm, and sections were opened to traffic as they were completed. It quickly became apparent that the canal would have great success, and even before its completion in 1825, "canal fever" seized promoters throughout the country. In the tremendous building boom that followed, canals were constructed to link three types of areas. Some ran from the "back country" to the tidewater regions; some traversed, or attempted to traverse, the area between the older states and the Ohio valley; and some, the western canals, linked the Great Lakes with the waterways running to the East. The principal canals of the antebellum period are shown in Map 9.1. They were vital in developing the Northern and Northeastern gateways.

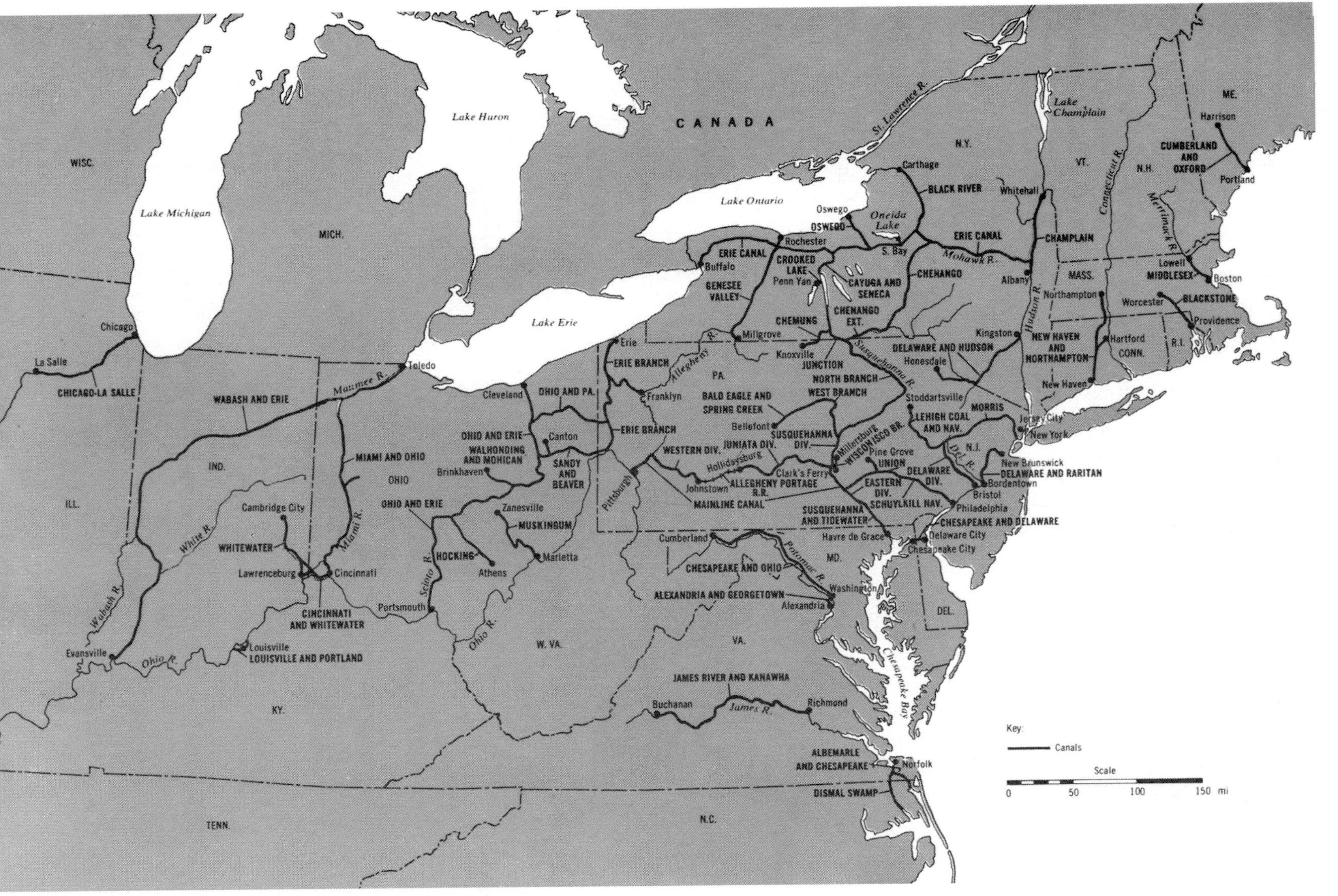

MAP 9.1 Principal Canals of the Antebellum Period, 1800–1860

Source: Carter Goodrich, ed., Canals and American Economic Development *(New York: Columbia University Press, 1961), 184–185.*

The Erie was the most important of the early canals, though by no means the only profitable one. This system, which still exists in an expanded and improved form as the New York Barge Canal, was a massive undertaking. Beginning at Albany on the Hudson River, it traversed the state of New York westward to Buffalo on Lake Erie, covering a distance of 364 miles. The work cost approximately $7 million and took about nine years to complete. The builders overcame countless difficulties, not the least of which was their own ignorance. Hardly any of the engineers had ever worked in canal construction, and much experimentation was necessary in the process. Some sections of the canal did not hold water at first and had to be lined with clay after work had been completed. The locks presented a special difficulty, but ingenuity and the timely discovery of water-resistant cement helped solve the problems of lock construction.

In its final form, the Erie system reached a fair portion of New York state. The Cayuga and Seneca, the Chemung, and the Genesee extensions connected important territory to the south with the canal. A branch to Oswego provided access to Lake Ontario, and the Champlain Canal gave access to the North. The system not only furnished transportation to much of the state but also tapped the Great Lakes areas served by the St. Lawrence route and the vast Ohio Territory. Beginning about 1835, a large part of the traffic from the West that had formerly traversed the Ohio and Mississippi rivers to New Orleans was diverted over the Erie Canal to the port of New York. This explains much of the convergence (catching up) of the Northern Gateway with the Southern Gateway revealed in Figure 9.2. Lumber, grain, and meat products were the chief commodities to move eastward; textiles, leather goods, machinery, hardware, and imported foods and drugs went west in exchange. Passengers, too, rode the horse-drawn boats in great numbers, with speeds of 100 miles in a 24-hour day compensating in part for the discomfort of cramped and poorly ventilated cabins.

Pennsylvania's answer to the competition of the Erie Canal was the Mainline of the Pennsylvania Public Works—a system of railroads and canals chartered in 1826 by the state legislature. But the fate of Pennsylvania's canals stood in sharp contrast with those in New York. A major disadvantage of the Pennsylvania canals was geographic. The terrain traversed by the Erie to reach the western frontier had been difficult enough for canal construction, rising as much as 650 feet above the Hudson at Albany and requiring many locks to raise the water. But the terrain of western Pennsylvania proved to be insurmountable by canal. The Mainline crossed the mountains, lifted passengers and freight to an altitude of more than 2,000 feet, and deposited both travelers and goods, westbound from Philadelphia, at Pittsburgh some 400 miles away. All this was accomplished by as fantastic a combination of transport as the country had ever seen. From Philadelphia, at tidewater, to Columbia, 81 miles westward on the Susquehanna River, a horse-drawn railroad carried both passengers and freight.[6] At Columbia the railroad joined the Juniata, or Eastern Division of the Pennsylvania Canal, from which passengers and freight were carried up a river valley by canal 173 miles to the Portage Railroad at Holidaysburg. Here, intrepid passengers saw their boat separated into front and rear sections, which were mounted on cars and run on underwater rails into the canal. A 36-mile trip on the Portage Railroad then began. The inclined tracks, over which cars were pulled by stationary steam engines winding cables on drums, accomplished a lift of 1,399 feet on the eastern slope to the summit and a descent of 1,172 feet on the western slope to another canal at Johnstown. From Johnstown to Pittsburgh, a distance of 105 miles, the water journey was comparatively easy.

The completion of this colossal work in 1834 was heralded by a celebration at Liberty Hall in Philadelphia. An old print depicts one of the halfboats decked with bunting and flags being drawn away from the hall by teams of prancing horses. In the sense that it carried all

[6]Although the steam locomotive was not employed in the United States until 1829, rails to permit smooth haulage had been used in both America and Europe for several years.

This painting shows the junction of the Champlain Canal and the Erie Canal—an important point on the trade route that was to become the preeminent link between Midwest and East Coast urban centers.

the traffic it could, the Mainline was successful, but the bottleneck of the Portage Railroad plus the fact that the system had twice as many locks as the Erie kept it from becoming a serious competitor for western business. Over the years, the Mainline carried 5 to 10 percent of the traffic volume of the Erie Canal, to the great disappointment of the people of a state that had spent more on waterways than any other.

Other states as well expended large sums of money on canals to draw the trade of the new West. The Chesapeake and Ohio Canal was projected up the valley of the Potomac to Cumberland, Maryland, and on to the Ohio River. The canal company was chartered by the state of Virginia with the assent of the Maryland legislature, and the federal government contributed heavily to the venture. However, despite the political blessings of two states and the federal government, the generous financial backing of all three, and the aid of some local governments, due to technical difficulties the project was completed only to Cumberland.

The dazzling success of the Erie Canal and the competitive rivalry among cities and regions for commercial traffic generated many unprofitable investments in canals. The great canal-building era (1815–1843) totaled $31 million in investments, nearly three-quarters from government sources, mostly state governments. Despite the lack of profitability and the arrival and practical demonstration of the railroads, regional competitiveness spurred a second wave of investment in canals, totaling $66 million between 1843 and 1860. Nearly two-thirds of the financing was from the government, again mainly from state treasuries. More might have been invested. However, the commercial crises of 1837 and 1839 and the deep depression of the early 1840s caused financial chaos, and nine states had to suspend payments on their debts (mainly bonds, many sold to foreigners). Major canals in Pennsylvania, Maryland, Indiana, and Illinois never recovered.

Although most of the canal investments were financial failures and could not be justified by comparisons of benefits and costs, they did support the natural waterways in opening up the West. Some that have been considered preposterous mistakes might have turned out to be monuments to human inventiveness if the railroad had not developed at almost the same time. The canals posed problems, it is true. The limitations on horse-drawn vehicles for cargo transport were great except with regard to a few commodities. Canals were supposed to provide a system of waterways, but as often as not, the boats of larger canals could not move through the smaller canals. Floods and droughts often made the movement of the barges uncertain. Yet the chief reason for the eventual failure of the canals was the railroad, which could carry people and a wide variety of commodities at a much greater speed—and speed was requisite to a genuine transportation revolution.

THE IRON HORSE

Despite the clear-cut technological advantages of the railroad, natural waterways remained the primary means of transportation for nearly 20 years after the first pioneering American railroads were introduced in the early 1830s. Besides the stiff competition of water transport, an important hindrance to railroad development was public antipathy, which had its roots in ignorance, conservatism, and vested interest. People thought that speeds of 20 to 30 miles per hour would be physically harmful to passengers. At least one city in Massachusetts directed its representatives in the state legislature to prevent "so great a calamity to our town as must be the location of any railroad through it." Many honestly believed that the railroad would prove to be impractical and uneconomical and would not provide service as dependable as that of the waterways.

Unsurprisingly, the most vigorous opposition to railroads came from groups whose economic interests suffered from the competition of the new industry. Millions of dollars had been spent on canals, rivers, highways, and plank roads, and thousands of people depended on these transportation enterprises for their livelihood. Tavern keepers feared their businesses would be ruined, and farmers envisioned the market for hay and grain disappearing as the "iron horse" replaced the flesh-and-blood animal that drew canal boats and pulled wagons. Competitive interests joined to embarrass and hinder the railroads, causing several states to limit traffic on them to passengers and their baggage or to freight hauled only during the months when canal operations ceased. One railroad company in Ohio was required to pay for any loss in canal traffic attributed to railroad competition. Other railroads were ordered to pay a tonnage tax to support the operation of canals.

Despite the opposition of those who feared the railroads (recall Economic Reasoning Proposition 5), construction went on. In sections of the country where canals could not be built, the railroad offered a means of cheap transportation for all kinds of commodities. In contrast to the municipality that wished to exclude the railroad, many cities and towns, as well as their state governments, did much to encourage railroad construction. At the time, the federal government was restrained by the prevailing political philosophy of strict constitutionalism from financially assisting and promoting railways. The government did, however, make surveys to determine rights of way and provided tariff exemptions on railroad iron.

By 1840, railroad mileage in the United States was within 1,000 miles of the combined lengths of all canals, but the volume of goods carried by water still exceeded that transported by rail. After the depression of the early 1840s, rail investments continued, mostly government assisted, and by 1850, the country had 9,000 miles of railroads, as shown in Table 9.3. Referring back to Figure 9.2, we see that by the late 1840s, the Northern Gateway had surpassed the Southern, and by the 1850s, the railroad's superiority was clear.

With the more than 20,000 miles of rails added to the transportation system between 1850 and 1860, total trackage surpassed 30,000 miles at the end of the decade, and the volume of freight traffic equaled that of canals.[7] All the states east of the Mississippi were connected during this decade. The eastern seaboard was linked with the Mississippi River system, and the Gulf and South Atlantic states could interchange traffic with the Great Lakes. Growing trunk lines such as the Erie, the Pennsylvania, and the Baltimore and Ohio completed construction of projects that had been started in the 1840s, and combinations of short lines provided new through routes. By the beginning of the Civil War, the

[7] Railroads had won from canals almost all passenger business (except that of poor immigrants coming across New York state) and the carriage of nearly all light, high-value goods.

TABLE 9.3 Miles of Railroad in Operation, 1830–1860

YEAR	MILEAGE
1830	23
1835	1,098
1840	2,818
1845	4,633
1850	9,021
1855	18,374
1860	30,626

Source: Historical Statistics (*Washington, D.C.: Government Printing Office, 1960), Series Q 15.*

TABLE 9.4 Productivity Change in Railroads, 1839–1859 (1910 = 100)

		INPUTS				
YEAR	(1) OUTPUT	(2) LABOR	(3) CAPITAL	(4) FUEL	(5) TOTAL INPUT[a]	(6) TOTAL FACTOR PRODUCTIVITY[b]
1839	0.08	0.3	0.8	0.07	0.5	16.0
1859	2.21	5.0	10.1	1.50	6.6	33.5

[a] *Weighted average of labor, capital, and fuel; weights are proportions of costs*
[b] *(column 1 ÷ column 5) 100.*

Source: Adapted from Albert Fishlow, "Internal Transportation," in American Economic Growth, *ed. Lance E.* Davis et al. (New York: Harper & Row, 1972), 499.

eastern framework of the present rail transportation system had been erected, and it was possible to travel by rail the entire distance from New York to Chicago to Memphis and back to New York.

But the United States was still a long way from establishing an integrated railroad system. Although the "Stephenson gauge" of 4 feet 8 inches (distance between the rails) was preponderant in 1860, its final selection as the "standard gauge" for the country was still a quarter-century away. Because locomotives and cars were built for one gauge only, a multitude of gauges prevented continuous shipment, as did the lack of agreement among companies on such matters as the interline exchange of rolling stock, through bills of lading and passenger tickets, the division of through rates, and standard time.[8]

Many modifications and improvements occurred, however, and, as shown in Table 9.4, total factor productivity in railroads more than doubled in the two decades before the Civil War. Alternately stated, railroad output grew relative to inputs by a factor of 2. Technological advances, according to Albert Fishlow, were reflected in the fact that the average traction force of locomotives more than doubled in these two decades. Freight car sizes also increased, with eight-wheel cars being common by 1859. Most of the productivity rise, however, resulted from increased utilization of existing facilities. The stock of capital—and other inputs—grew, but output grew much faster as the initial inputs became more fully utilized.

ROADS

Though technologically undramatic, roads and trails were part of the transportation network. Thanks to Hollywood and western movies, we are familiar with the trails followed by western settlers. These "highways" of long-distance land travel are shown in Map 9.2 on page 176. The overland routes of westward migration, settlement, and commerce usually

[8] George R. Taylor and Irene Neu, *The American Railway Network, 1861–1890* (Cambridge, Mass.: Harvard University Press, 1956), 6–7, 12–14.

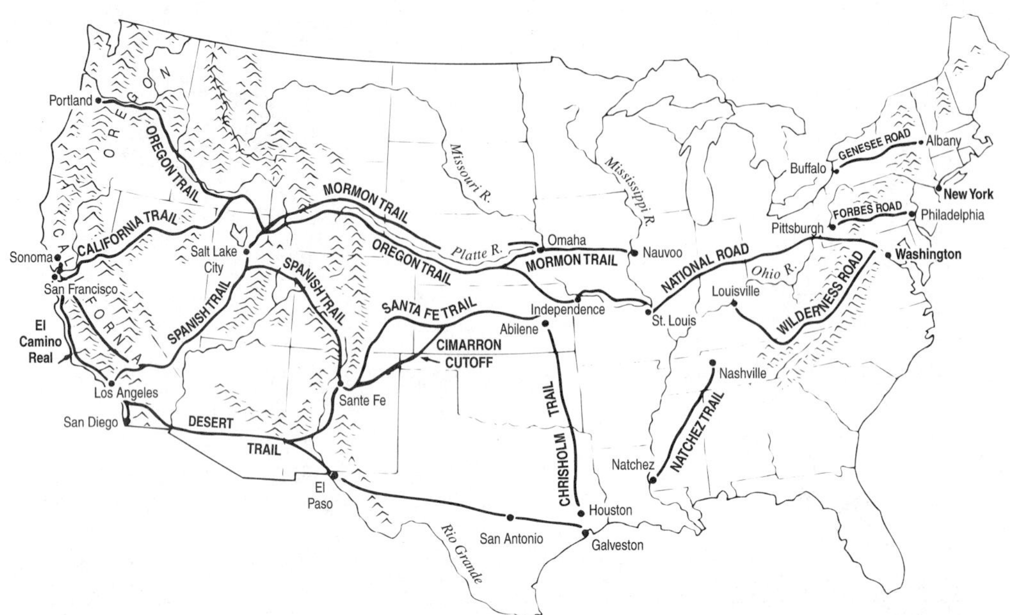

MAP 9.2 Westward Travel *The massive physical barriers faced by the pioneers could be minimized by following such famous routes as the Oregon, Mormon, or Santa Fe Trails. Note that the Mormons deliberately went north of the Platte River to avoid wagon trains hostile to them on the Oregon Trail south of the river.*

followed the old Indian hunting and war paths, which in turn had followed stream valleys providing the easiest lines of travel. One of the most important was the Wilderness Road, pioneered by Daniel Boone. Penetrating the mountain barrier at Cumberland Gap, near present-day Middlesboro, Kentucky, the road then went north and west into the Ohio Territory. Over this road, which in many places was only a marked track, poured thousands of emigrants.[9] Although most of the overland roads turned into quagmires in the rainy season and into billowing dust clouds in the dry season, some of them were well constructed and well maintained through portions of their length.

The most notable surfaced highway was the Cumberland Road, or "National Road," as it was often called, built by the federal government after much controversy. Begun at Cumberland, Maryland, in 1811, the road was opened to Wheeling on the Ohio River in 1818 and was later completed to St. Louis. This major government undertaking was part of Albert Gallatin's 1808 proposed plan for a system of federal roads. Despite support from many people for a comprehensive program of internal improvements, that was the only major road built in this early period by the federal government. Opposition to federal projects like this was based ostensibly on the assertion, that federal participation in such an activity was unconstitutional. Recall Economic Reasoning Propositions 1, 2, and 4. Sectional rivalries played a major role in blocking the proposed construction. The West, in particular, persistently and loudly called for a national road system, and at first, the Middle Atlantic states were inclined

9 This same type of road or marked track appeared during the overland migration to the West Coast. The Oregon Trail, over which travel began in the early 1840s, was 2,000 miles long and carried settlers to the Pacific Northwest and California. The Mormon Trail, broken by Brigham Young in the late 1840s, paralleled the Oregon Trail along the south bank of the Platte for some distance. Earlier trails marked by the Spaniards, such as the Santa Fe Trail into present-day New Mexico and Arizona and El Camino Real (the King's Highway) in California, were valuable to early explorers and traders.

to agree. But after New York and Pennsylvania developed their own routes to the West, they did not wish to promote federally financed competition elsewhere. New Englanders, with fairly good roads of their own, were even less inclined to encourage further population drains or to improve the commercial positions of Boston's rivals. The South, although mired in the mud, was bitterly antagonistic to any program that would add to the government's financial needs or facilitate access to nonslave portions of the West. Despite all the opposition, Congress could not avoid appropriating increasing sums for post and military roads, but sectional rivalries over the geographic allocation of internal improvements permitted an incredibly primitive road system to survive well into the twentieth century.

Turnpikes

In many areas, especially where other transport modes were unavailable, roads were built by private turnpike companies. These companies collected tolls and used gates consisting of pikes or spears to let the toll payer pass to and from the road at selected points. The turnpike era began in 1789 with the construction of the Philadelphia and Lancaster Turnpike; it ended about 1830, after which only a few private highways were attempted as business ventures. During this period, Pennsylvania chartered 86 companies that built more than 2,000 miles of road. By 1811, New York had 1,500 miles of highways constructed by 135 companies, and New England had granted some 180 companies the right to build turnpikes. Despite toll collections, few of the companies that constructed roads for public use were profitable ventures; in fact, it is doubtful that even one earned close to the going rate of return on its capital. Teamsters avoided the tolls if at all possible, and dishonest gatekeepers often pocketed the receipts. But the chief difficulty—one unforeseen by most promoters—was that the only long-distance trade the roads attracted was stagecoach passengers and emigrants. Freight would not, for the most part, stand the cost of land carriage over great distances, and without freight traffic, turnpikes simply could not earn a profit. They eventually faced extensive competition from steamboats, canals, and railroads, but by this time returns on invested capital had already proved disappointing. Some turnpikes were abandoned and later acquired by the states for the rapidly growing public road system; others were purchased by local governments and made into toll-free highways.[10]

A special kind of toll road was the plank road, developed shortly after the decline in turnpike construction. Plank roads were built by laying wide, heavy planks or "rails" on stringers or ties placed in the direction of travel and were superior for all-weather use. The first plank road in the United States was built at Syracuse in 1837, and over the next 20 years, several thousand miles of plank roads were built, the heaviest concentration being in timber-abundant New York and Pennsylvania. Some were subsidized by the states, although most were privately and locally financed.[11]

THE ANTEBELLUM INTERREGIONAL GROWTH HYPOTHESIS

The antebellum interregional growth hypothesis provides another perspective on the importance of falling transportation costs to the early growth of a national market. Douglass C. North advanced the argument with quantitative evidence derived from earlier works and added theoretical specifications and structure. Briefly stated, North argues

---

[10] A few private roads continued into the twentieth century, but all that now remains of them is the name "turnpike" given to some important arteries of the highway system. These throughways differ from the older turnpikes in that the modern enterprises are owned by public corporations.

[11] For an excellent analysis of the building boom of plank roads, see John Majewski, Christopher Baer, and Daniel B. Klein, "Responding to Relative Decline: The Plank Road Boom of Antebellum New York," *Journal of Economic History* 53 (1993): 106–122.

that U.S. growth from 1815 to 1843 was propelled primarily by the growth of British demand for southern cotton, which encouraged southern regional specialization in cotton. In turn, this raised the demand in the South for western foodstuffs and cheap northeastern manufactures, mainly boots, shoes, and coarse-fiber clothing for slaves. Growth in the size of the national market, through falling transport costs, realized economies of large-scale productions and greater regional economic specialization. As the Northeast became more specialized in manufacturing and more urbanized, the growing demand of the South for western foodstuffs was reinforced. Each region advanced along lines dictated by its respective comparative advantage in production, and each demanded goods produced in the other regions in greater and greater amounts. After 1843, the primary initiating role of foreign demand for cotton diminished, and internal market forces ascended in importance. The railroad linking the West to the North also contributed to the lessening initiating forces of the South. The evidence on the timing and waves of western migrations and land sales and prices of key regional staples supports North's argument. Evidence on Southern food productions, however, for the years after 1840—the only years providing us with reliable food-production data—suggests that the South was relatively self-sufficient in food.[12] Yet, as Lloyd Mercer has shown, pockets of food deficits in the South may have been sufficient to have a significant impact on western food production for market, especially before 1840.[13] Furthermore, the magnitude of self-sufficiency may hinge critically on how one defines "the South". For example, should the border states of Kentucky and Tennessee, with their large meat surpluses, be considered southern or northern states?[14] Despite the inconclusiveness of this lively debate, the hypothesis provides a useful framework of analysis and an international perspective on the advances and linkages of the regions and of the formation of a national economy during that vital period of the transportation revolution.

OCEAN TRANSPORT

In addition to the many developments in internal transportation, great strides were being made in the long-traditional merchant marine. Thanks to bold entrepreneurship, the Black Ball line of New York instituted regularly scheduled transatlantic sailings in 1818. Beginning with only four ships, the line had a vessel sailing from New York for Liverpool the first week of each month, and a ship began the Liverpool–New York passage at the same time. Considerable risk was involved in pledging ships to sail "full or not full," as the line's advertising declared, because a ship might make three round trips a year (instead of the usual two made by the regular traders) with its hold far from full.[15] But by specializing in passengers, specie, mail, and "fine freight," the packets managed to operate successfully for more than 100 years. In the 1820s, the Black Ball line increased its trips to two a month each way, and other packet lines between New York and European ports were soon established. Henceforth, passengers could count on sailing at a particular hour on a given day, and merchants could book freight with something more than a vague hope that it would arrive in time to permit a profitable transaction. By ensuring a set schedule, the Black Ball line reduced risks and uncertainties in overseas commerce.

---

[12] Albert Fishlow, "Antebellum Interregional Trade Reconsidered," *American Economic Review* 54 (May 1964): 352–364; also see the "Discussion," by Robert W. Fogel, in the same source, 377–389. In addition, see Robert E. Gallman, "Self-Sufficiency in the Cotton Economy of the Antebellum South," *Agricultural History* 44 (1970): 5–23.

[13] Lloyd Mercer, "The Antebellum Interregional Trade Hypothesis: A Reexamination of Theory and Evidence," in *Explorations in the New Economic History*, eds. Roger L. Ransom, Richard Sutch, and Gary M. Walton (New York: Academic Press, 1982), 71–96.

[14] Robert Sexton, "Regional Choice and Economic History," *Economic Forum*, 16 (1), (Winter 1987).

[15] Robert G. Albion, *The Rise of New York Port 1815–1860* (Hamden, Conn.: Archon, 1961), 4.

Economic Insight 9.1

A National Market Forms

Surges of internal transportation developments solidly linked the interior western regions to the seaboard and abroad. Also contributing to market unification and falling costs of trade was the telegraph, invented by Samuel F. B. Morse in the 1840s. Telegraph wires were strung parallel to the railroads across the nation. By 1852, 23,000 miles of wire were in operation, speeding communications and reducing uncertainties. In 1866, an undersea cable was laid to Europe, further integrating the U.S. and European economies.

Although economic unification was far from complete, dramatic gains had been realized by the eve of the Civil War. As stated earlier, regional price movements portrayed these strides toward economic unification. As Thomas Berry states:

> It is difficult to point to any consistent lag of the West behind the East during this early period (1788–1817) because of such diversity in general behavior; it is safe to state, however, that in such first magnitude movements as those of 1793–1797 and 1810–1817 there was a lag measuring somewhat more than a year in length. . . . Taking a later interval (1816–1860) weighted general indices of monthly prices in New York, New Orleans, and Cincinnati show agreement with each other to a surprising degree. . . . Cincinnati prices lagged the greater part of a year in their decline in 1819–1820, but they were only three or four months behind the seaboard markets in the turning-point of 1839 and reacted simultaneously at the time of the panic of 1857.[16]

A viable transportation system was vital in perfecting a national market and linking regions. First the steamboats on the western rivers, then the canals, and finally the railroad revolutionized the costs of transport between the West and the seaboard. As Table 9.5 shows, western prices as a percentage of eastern prices grew dramatically. The figure here provides an analytical framework for interpreting the evidence in Table 9.5 on page 180.

Let S_1 represent the costs of production plus any local (short-distance) transportation costs of western wheat. Let S_2 reflect S_1 plus the cost of interregional transport in the early nineteenth century and S_3 equal S_1 plus these costs for the mid-1800s. Consumer costs P_2C fell to P_3C for a bushel of wheat, and farmers, receipts per bushel rose from P_2F to P_3F. Both consumers and producers gained.

Farmers gained larger and larger shares of the selling price of their crops. Moreover, consumers paid decreasing shares of the purchase price for transportation and other marketing costs. As freight costs fell, new unsettled areas were profitably cleared and added to the nation's economic activity. As Peter Lindert has shown, average land prices, adjusted for quality, more than doubled and possibly tripled from 1810 to 1860.[17] Improvements in transportation increased economic specialization and raised living standards dramatically. Today's "information revolution," globally, is realizing similar changes on the world in our time.

continued

[16]Thomas S. Berry, *Western Prices Before 1861* (Cambridge, Mass.: Harvard University Press, 1943), 97–99.
[17]Peter H. Lindert, "Long-Run Trends in American Farmland Values," *Agricultural History* (Summer 1988): 60.

Economic Insight 9.1

A National Market Forms, continued

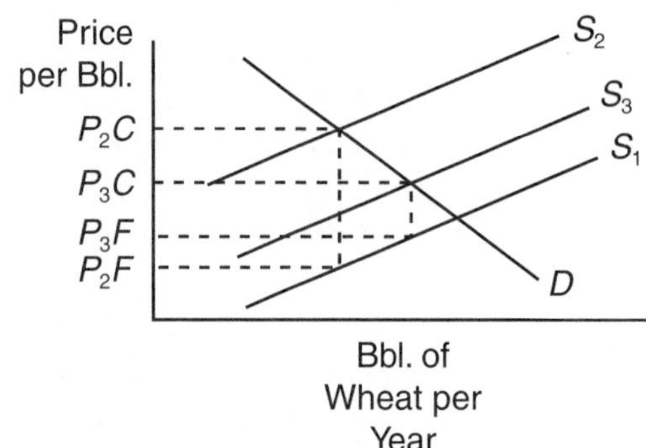

TABLE 9.5 Cincinnati Wholesale Prices as a Percentage of Philadelphia, New York, and New Orleans Wholesale Prices, 1816–1860[a]

	COMMODITY											
	FLOUR (bbl.)			WHEAT (bu.)			CORN (bu.)			MESS PORK (bbl.)		
PERIOD	PHIL	N.Y	N.O.	PHIL.	N.Y.	N.O.	PHIL.	N.Y.	N.O.	PHIL.	N.Y.	N.O.
1816–1820	63	66	72	45	48	—	51	48	—	56	58	63
1821–1825	52	52	56	39	38	—	38	32	30	63	67	76
1826–1830	68	67	67	50	48	—	49	41	29	67	68	78
1831–1835	73	74	76	57	56	—	55	49	36	77	77	85
1836–1840	73	73	77	59	61	—	56	51	47	87	85	86
1841–1845	77	73	86	68	65	90	53	47	65	82	79	84
1846–1850	78	71	87	68	63	88	51	48	62	81	90	88
1851–1855	82	79	90	73	61	90	61	59	74	85	90	92
1856–1860	88	95	89	79	70	86	70	66	72	91	94	93

[a] *The "spreads" between prices in Cincinnati and the port cities narrowed dramatically between 1816–1820 and 1856–1860.*

Source: Erik F. Haites, James Mak, and Gary M. Walton, Western River Transportation: The Era of Early Internal Development, 1810–1860 *(Baltimore: Johns Hopkins University Press, 1975), 7 and Appendix A.*

The transatlantic packets fully established New York as the predominant port in the United States. Coastal packets, running primarily to New Orleans but also to Charleston, Savannah, and Mobile, brought cotton to New York for eastbound ocean shipment and carried southward a considerable portion of the European goods brought from England and the Continent. In fact, trade between the cotton ports and New York was greater in physical and dollar volume than the ocean trade during most of the antebellum period.[18] These packets significantly complemented developments in the western rivers, which funneled produce from the interior through New Orleans, the Southern Gateway.

Between 1820 and 1860, remarkable design changes in sailing ships led to increases in tonnage and efficiency. From an average size of 300 tons in the 1820s, American sailing ships increased to 1,000 tons in the 1850s, and vessels of 1,500 tons' burden were not uncommon. There was a marked increase in length-to-beam ratios and spread of sail for the ordinary

[18] Robert G. Albion, *Square-Riggers on Schedule* (Princeton, N.J.: Princeton University Press, 1938), 49–50.

packet ship, and the centuries-old practice of making the widest part of the vessel forward of the center was abandoned. Borrowing from French designers, Yankee shipbuilders produced a special type of ship that was to dominate the seas for the three decades before the Civil War. This was the famed clipper ship, which, at some sacrifice of carrying capacity, attained unheard-of speeds. The clipper was a graceful ship with three masts, square-rigged but equipped with abundant fore-and-aft sails that gave it a great advantage going into the wind, thus increasing its speed. Manned by fewer hands than vessels of foreign register, a clipper was to be driven 24 hours a day, not put to bed for 7 or 8 hours at night.

The first American (or "Baltimore") clipper was the *Ann McKim*, launched in 1832. Its builder, Donald McKay, became a legendary figure, and some ships of his design bore names that are remembered even now: the *Flying Cloud*, the *Sovereign of the Seas*, the *Great Republic*, and the *Lightning* were spectacularly beautiful, with concave sides and bow and sails towering 200 feet above the deck. On its maiden voyage across the Atlantic, the *Lightning* logged a record 436 miles in one day with an average speed of 18 miles an hour. Even today, many ocean vessels do not approach this speed.

Clippers were designed for the express purpose of carrying passengers and high value cargo long distances. On the Atlantic runs, they were not profitable due to their limited capacity. But they dominated the China trade, and after 1849, they made fortunes for their owners by carrying passengers and freight during the gold rushes to California and Australia. On the New York–San Francisco trip around Cape Horn, a distance of 16,000 miles, the *Flying Cloud* set a record of just over 89 days, at a time when 100 days was about par for the clipper voyage.[19] This represented a time saving over ordinary ocean travel of up to three months, for which some merchants and travelers would pay a good price.

Clippers, however, were not the only vessels in the American merchant fleet. Broad-beamed and full-bowed freighting ships, much slower vessels than the clippers, were the backbone of the nation's merchant marine. Officered by men to whom seafaring was a tradition and a career of considerable social prestige, manned by crews of Americans bred to the sea, and owned by merchants of vision and daring like Stephen Girard of Philadelphia, the cheaply and expertly built ships from the marine ways of New York, Boston, and the Maine coast were the great ocean-freight carriers until the Civil War.

In the meantime, the British were making technical advances that enabled them to challenge American maritime supremacy and, finally, to overcome it. The major British innovation was the adaptation of the steamboat, originally invented for use on rivers and protected waters, to navigation on the open sea. The two principal changes made by the British were the use of iron instead of wood for the hull and the employment of the Archimedes' screw principle for propulsion instead of paddles. Iron hulls were necessary to transport the heavy machinery of the early steam era safely, but they also had greater strength, buoyancy, and durability than wood. From the 1830s on, the British rapidly solved the problems of iron ship construction. The composite ship, with a frame of iron and a hull of wood, was tried for a while, but the acid in the oak timber corroded the iron. Once the British had perfected the techniques of riveting and working with sheet iron and steel, they had an absolute advantage in the construction of iron ships—as great an advantage as the United States had enjoyed in the making of wooden ones.

The inefficiency and slow speeds of early steam engines were a source of unending difficulty. For a long time, steamships had to carry a greater weight of coal than of cargo, and low engine speeds made the inefficient paddle wheel necessary despite its theoretical inferiority. After nearly 20 years of development, however, transatlantic steamships were making six voyages a year—twice as many as their sailing-packet competitors. Ten years later, Samuel Cunard's success in starting a line service was not entirely fortuitous; by 1848,

[19]This record by sail was not broken until 1988.

engines were designed that could maintain higher speeds. The screw propeller was then rapidly adopted, and fuel consumption was cut greatly. During the 1850s, both the number and registered tonnage of steamships increased by leaps and bounds, and they almost entirely captured the passenger and high-value freight business.

In 1860, sailing ships still carried the greater part of the world's international freight. Yet by this time, the shape of the future was clear to all except die-hard American entrepreneurs, who—unable to comprehend the rapid obsolescence of their beautiful wooden ships—failed to take vigorous steps to compete with Britain. Recall Economic Reasoning Proposition 5. Although government subsidies to American steamship builders began as early as 1845, these were both insufficient and poorly administered. Under the most favorable circumstances, however, builders in the United States could scarcely have competed on a cost basis with the vastly superior British iron industry. The signs were there for those who chose to read them. During the 1820s, American ships had carried close to 90 percent of the foreign trade of the United States; by the 1850s, this figure had declined to about 70 percent. The times had changed, and fortune's hand was laid on other shoulders.

SELECTED REFERENCES AND SUGGESTED READINGS

Albion, Robert G. *Square-Riggers on Schedule*. Princeton, N.J.: Princeton University Press, 1938.

———. *The Rise of the New York Port, 1815–1860*. Hamden, Conn.: Archon, 1961.

Berry, Thomas S. *Western Prices before 1861*. Cambridge, Mass.: Harvard University Press, 1943.

Chandler, Alfred D., Jr. *The Railroads*. New York: Harcourt Brace Jovanovich, 1965.

Cootner, Paul. "The Role of the Railroads in the United States Economic Growth." *Journal of Economic History* 23 (1963).

David, Paul. "Transport Innovation and Economic Growth; Professor Fogel On and Off the Rails." *Economic History Review* 22 (3), 2d series, (1969).

Fishlow, Albert. "Antebellum Interregional Trade Reconsidered." *American Economic Review* 54 (May 1964): 352–364.

———. *American Railroads and the Transformation of the Antebellum Economy*. Cambridge, Mass.: Harvard University Press, 1965.

———. "Internal Transportation in the Nineteenth and Early Twentieth Centuries." In *The Cambridge Economic History of the United States,* Vol. II, *The Long Nineteenth Century*, eds. Stanley L. Engerman and Robert E. Gallman. New York: Cambridge University Press, 2000, 543–642.

Gallman, Robert E. "Self-Sufficiency in the Cotton Economy of the Antebellum South." *Agricultural History* 44 (1970): 5–23.

Goodrich, Carter H. *Government Promotion of American Canals and Railroads, 1800–1890*. New York: Columbia University Press, 1960.

———. *The Government and the Economy, 1783–1861*. Indianapolis: Bobbs Merrill, 1967.

———. "Internal Improvements Reconsidered." *Journal of Economic History* 30 (June 1970): 289–311.

Goodrich, Carter H., et al. *Canals and American Economic Development*. New York: Columbia University Press, 1961.

Haites, Erik F., James Mak, and Gary M. Walton. *Western River Transportation: The Era of Early Internal Development, 1810–1860*. Baltimore: Johns Hopkins University Press, 1975.

Hunter, Louis. *Steamboats on the Western Rivers*. Cambridge, Mass.: Harvard University Press, 1949.

Jenks, Leland H. "Railroads as a Force in American Development." In *Enterprise and Secular Change,* ed. Frederic C. Lane and Jelle Riemersma. Homewood, Ill.: Irwin, 1953.

Lindert, Peter H. "Long-Run Trends in American Farmland Values." *Agricultural History* (Summer 1988): 60.

Lindstrom, Diane L. "Demand, Markets and Eastern Economic Development, Philadelphia, 1815–1840." *Journal of Economic History* 25 (1975): 271–273.

Lindstrom, Diane L., and John Sharpless. "Urban Growth and Economic Structure in Antebellum America." In *Research in Economic History*, Vol. 3. Greenwich, Conn.: JAI, 1978.

Majewski, John. "Who Financed the Transportation Revolution? Regional Divergence and Internal Improvements in Antebellum Pennsylvania and Virginia." *Journal of Economic History* 56 (1996): 763–788.

Majewski, John, Christopher Baer, and Daniel B. Klein. "Responding to Relative Decline: The Plank Road Boom of Antebellum New York." *Journal of Economic History* 53 (1993): 106–122.

Mak, James, and Gary Walton. "Steamboat and the Great Productivity Surge in River Transportation." *Journal of Economic History* 33 (1972): 619–640.

McIlwraith, Thomas F. "Freight Capacity and Utilization of the Erie and Great Lakes Canals before 1850." *Journal of Economic History* 36 (December 1976).

Mercer, Lloyd. "The Antebellum Interregional Trade Hypothesis: A Reexamination of Theory and Evidence." In *Explorations in the New Economic History*, eds. Roger L. Ransom, Richard Such, and Gary M. Walton. New York: Academic Press, 1982, 71–96.

Niemi, Albert W., Jr. "A Further Look at Regional Canals and Economic Specialization: 1820–1840." *Explorations in Economic History* 7 (1970): 499–522.

———. "A Closer Look at Canals and Western Manufacturing in the Canal Era: A Reply." *Explorations in Economic History* 9 (1972): 423–426.

North, Douglass C. *The Economic Growth of the United States, 1790–1860.* Englewood Cliffs, N.J.: Prentice Hall, 1961.

———. "The Role of Transportation in the Economic Development of North America." A paper presented to the International Congress of the Historical Sciences, Vienna, August 1965, and published in *Les Grandes Voies Maritimes dans le Monde XVe–XIXe Siecles.* Paris: Ecole des Hautes Etudes en Sciences Sociales, 1965.

Ransom, Roger L. "Canals and Development, A Discussion of the Issues." *American Economic Review* 54 (1964): 365–376.

———. "Interregional Canals and Economic Specialization in the Antebellum United States." *Explorations in Economic History* 5 (1), 2d series, (Fall 1967).

———. "Social Rates of Return from Public Transport Investment: A Case Study of the Ohio Canal." *Journal of Political Economy* 78 (1970): 1041–1060.

———. "A Closer Look at Canals and Western Manufacturing in the Canal Era." *Explorations in Economic History* 8 (1971): 501–510.

Scheiber, Harry. *Ohio Canal Era.* Athens: Ohio University Press, 1969.

Stover, John F. "Canals and Turnpikes: America's Early-Nineteenth-Century Transportation Network." In *An Emerging Independent American Economy, 1815–1875,* eds. J. R. Frese and J. Judd. Tarrytown, N.Y.: Sleepy Hollow Press, 1980.

Taylor, George R. *The Transportation Revolution, 1815–1860.* New York: Holt, Rinehart & Winston, 1951.

Taylor, George R., and Irene Neu. *The American Railway Network, 1861–1890.* Cambridge, Mass.: Harvard University Press, 1956.

Thompson, Robert. *Wiring a Continent: The History of the Telegraph Industry in the United States, 1832–1866.* Princeton, N.J.: Princeton University Press, 1947.

Walton, Gary M. "River Transportation and the Old Northwest Territory." In *Essays on the Economy of the Old Northwest*, eds. David C. Klingaman and Richard K. Vedder. Athens: Ohio University Press, 1987, 225–242.

Chapter Ten

MARKET EXPANSION AND INDUSTRY IN FIRST TRANSITION

Between the adoption of the Constitution and the outbreak of the Civil War, the economy of the United States was structurally transformed, and a solid foundation was laid for the United States to become an industrial power. Beginning with only a few small factories, mostly lumber mills, the new nation emerged by 1860 with a manufacturing sector second only to that of Great Britain. Yet in 1860, the sizes of industrial firms were small by today's standards, and the United States was still predominantly an agricultural country. Nevertheless, many important changes had occurred that marked the advent of industrialization. Most significant was the evolution of new ways of combining factors of production, resulting in the substitution of capital for labor and requiring new forms of business organization. Business interests as a political force became evident, and New England and the Middle Atlantic states led the way in developing the industrial sector. Improvements in transportation played the main role in increasing regional specialization, and in many ways, transportation developments were instrumental to economic unification. What made the westward movement, the rise of King Cotton, and industrialization all the more remarkable is that all were unfolding simultaneously.

EARLY CHANGES IN U.S. MANUFACTURING

The Decline of Household Production

When Alexander Hamilton delivered his *Report on Manufacturers* to Congress in 1791, he estimated that from *two-thirds to four-fifths of the nation's clothing was homemade*. Most food processing was also done in the home. Water power had not yet been harnessed for textile production and was used mainly for milling grain, cutting lumber, and other uses. Artisans in the towns worked by hand, producing shoes, hats, pots, pans, and tools.

By 1830, however, household manufacture had exhibited a marked decline in the East and, thereafter, home manufacture and small artisan shops serving local markets continued to decline dramatically in all but the least accessible places. The major causes of this decline were the progress of industrial organization and modern means of transportation. Wherever steamboats ran or canals, highways, and railroads were built, home and artisan manufactures declined quickly. Even on the frontier, most households had access to the products of

American or European factories after the middle of the nineteenth century. Map 10.1 shows the influence of transportation on homemade versus factory-made manufactures. The shaded areas in the two maps of New York show the one-third of the counties in the state having the highest per capita output of woolen goods made in the home in two different years, 1820 and 1845. Note that in 1820, no county lying along the Hudson below Albany was in the top third. In 1845, the counties lying along the Erie Canal had similarly dropped in amount of home manufacture. In contrast, as late as 1865, nearly all the country people of Tennessee, especially those living in the mountain areas, wore clothing made at home. Primitive transport prolonged the wearing of homemade clothes. Recall Economic Reasoning Propositions 1 and 2.

★★★ *Economic Reasoning Proposition*

Craftshops and Mills

Until approximately 1850, the substantial increases in manufacturing output were effected by craftspeople operating independently or in craftshops. Craftspeople did "bespoke" work, making commodities only to order, maintaining the highest standards of quality, and selling through their own small retail outlets. But production by independent craftspeople declined rapidly after 1815. More important at that date and for some time afterward was the craftshop run by a master who employed several journeymen and apprentices. Sometimes, as in the case of the hatters of Danbury, Connecticut, an agglomeration of craftshops sold a quantity output to merchant wholesalers for distribution over wide market areas.

As in colonial days, the small mill was to be found in nearly all localities, and the national census of 1860 reported nearly 20,000 sawmills and 14,000 flour mills in the country. With few exceptions, tanneries, distilleries, breweries, and iron forges also produced for local markets. The decentralization of American industry before 1860, favored by the use of water power and commonly protected by high short-haul transport costs, produced small firms that often constituted effective local monopolies.

Before 1860, however, some mills had achieved large-scale production using methods of manufacture typical of the factory. Furthermore, large mills in two industries tended to concentrate in certain rather well-defined areas. Flour milling, which even in colonial days had been attracted to the Chesapeake area, continued to cluster there as farmers in Maryland and Virginia substituted wheat for tobacco. As cities grew larger and the demand for building

MAP 10.1 Canal Impact *Household manufacture of woolen cloth (an index of isolation from commercial routes) underwent a drastic change between 1820 and 1845 along the Erie Canal. The shaded areas indicate the one-third of the counties with the highest home production of woolen goods during this period.*

Source: Reprinted by permission of the publisher from American Wool Manufacture, *Volume 1, by Arthur H. Cole, Cambridge, Mass.: Harvard University Press, p. 280, copyright 1926 by the President and Fellows of Harvard College.*

materials increased, it became profitable for large lumbering firms to exploit timber areas located some distance from the markets. Typical were those situated by 1850 on the upper reaches of streams flowing through New England, New York, and Pennsylvania.

The Emergence of U.S. Factories

The term *factory* has been applied customarily to manufacturing units with the following characteristics:

1. A substantial output of a standardized product made to be sold in a wide, rather than a strictly local, market.
2. Complex operations carried on in one building or group of adjacent buildings. A considerable investment in fixed plant, the mechanization of processes, and the use of power are implied.
3. An assembly of workers under a definite organizational discipline.

In the United States, the factory developed first in the cotton textile industry. The mill of Almy, Brown, and Slater, in operation by 1793, is usually considered the first American factory. Moses Brown and William Almy were men of wealth in the New England mercantile tradition. Like many other American enterprisers, they had tried and failed to duplicate English spinning machinery. In 1789 a young mechanical wizard, Samuel Slater, came to Rhode Island after working for years in the firm of Arkwright and Strutt in Milford, England. Having memorized the minutest details of the water frames, Slater joined with Almy and Brown and agreed to reproduce the equipment for a mechanized spinning mill. Although small, the enterprise served as a training ground for operatives and as a pilot operation for managers.

A number of small cotton mills like the Slater mill soon followed, but most failed by the turn of the century because their promoters did not aim for a wide market. Not until the Embargo Act of 1807 and the consequent scarcity of English textiles that stimulated demand for domestic manufactures did spinning mills become numerous. Between 1805 and 1815, 94 new cotton mills were built in New England, and the mounting competition led Almy and Brown to push their markets south and west. By 1814, 70 percent of all consignments were to the Midwest via Philadelphia. Only two decades after Arkwright machinery was introduced into this country, the market for yarn was becoming national, and the spinning process was becoming a true factory operation as it was in England.

The Lowell Shops and the Waltham System

Two events propelled these changes. One was the successful introduction of the power loom into American manufacture; the other was the organization of production so that all four stages of the manufacture of cotton cloth could occur within one establishment. These stages were spinning, weaving, dying, and cutting.

After closely observing the workings of textile machinery in Great Britain, Francis Cabot Lowell, a New England merchant, gained sufficient knowledge of the secrets of mechanized weaving to enable him, with the help of a gifted technician, to construct a power loom superior to any that had been built to date. It was as an enterpriser, however, that Lowell made a more significant contribution. He persuaded other men of means to participate with him in establishing a firm at Waltham that had all the essential characteristics of factory production (Economic Reasoning Proposition 1). This was the famed Boston Manufacturing Company, the forerunner of several similar firms in which the so-called Boston Associates had an interest. Specializing in coarse sheetings, the Waltham factory sold its product all over America. Consolidating all the steps of textile manufacture in a single

The complexity of mechanized factories and the substantial economies of scale related to them are illustrated here with a cotton manufacturing plant (circa 1839) where cotton is being carded, drawn, and roven (twisted into strands).

Economic Reasoning Proposition

plant lowered production costs (Economic Reasoning Proposition 2). A large number of specialized workers were organized into departments and directed by executives who were not necessarily technical supervisors. The factory, by using power-driven machinery, produced standardized commodities in quantity.

At Lowell, where the Merrimack Manufacturing Company followed the Waltham pattern, and at Manchester and Lawrence, the factory system gained a permanent foothold. In the second leading center of New England textile manufacture—the Providence-Pawtucket region—there was a similar trend, although the factories there were fewer and smaller. The third great district, located about Paterson and Philadelphia, contained mainly small mills that performed a single major process and turned out finer weaves. But by 1860, New England's industry had nearly four times as many spindles as the Middle Atlantic industry and accounted for nearly three-fourths of the country's output of cotton goods. The factory had demonstrated its superiority in the textile field.

It was simply a matter of time until other industries adopted the same organization. Because technological changes in wool production were slower, the production of woolen cloth tended to remain in the small mill longer than cotton production did. But after 1830, woolen factories began to adopt the Waltham system, and by 1860, the largest textile factories in the United States were woolen factories. Again, New Englanders far surpassed the rest of the country in combining factors of production in large units; two-thirds of America's woolen output in 1860 was made in New England.[1]

[1]It merits emphasis also that cottage manufacture or putting-out system, where raw materials were taken to homes for processing (wool or cotton to be spun or yarn to be woven) and then to market, was prevalent in England but seldom used in the United States. U.S. manufactures for market came overwhelmingly from centralized plants. See Kenneth L. Sokoloff and David R. Dollar, "Agricultural Seasonality and the Organization of Manufacturing in Early Industrial Societies: The Contrast between England and the United States," *Journal of Economic History* (1997).

Technological advances in iron and steel production, such as the blast furnace and rolling mill shown here, epitomized the "modern" nineteenth-century factory.

Iron and Other Factories

In most other industries as well, the decade of the 1830s was one of expansion and experimentation with new methods. In the primary iron industry, establishments by the 1840s dwarfed those of a quarter-century earlier. By 1845, for instance, the Brady's Bend Iron Company in western Pennsylvania owned

> nearly 6,000 acres of mineral land and 5 miles of river front upon the Allegheny. It mined its own coal, ore, limestone, fire-clay, and fire-stone, made its own coke, and owned 14 miles of railway to serve its works. The plant itself consisted of 4 blast furnaces, a foundry, and rolling mills. It was equipped to perform all the processes, from getting raw materials out of the ground to delivering finished rails and metal shapes to consumers, and could produce annually between 10,000 and 15,000 tons of rails. It housed in its own tenements 538 laboring families. This company, with an actual investment of $1,000,000, was among the largest in America before the Civil War, though there were rival works of approximately equal capacity and similar organization.[2]

In the anthracite region to the east, factory operation of furnaces and rolling mills had been achieved by 1850. Also by the 1850s, American factories were manufacturing arms, clocks and watches, and sewing machines.

How one industry could adopt new methods as a consequence of progress in another is shown by the fact that once the sewing machine was produced on a quantity basis, the

[2] Victor S. Clark, *History of Manufactures in the United States, 1607–1860* (Washington, D.C.: Carnegie Institution of Washington, 1916), 446.

boot and shoe industry developed factory characteristics. Carriages, wagons, and even farm implements were eventually produced in large numbers. Finally, where markets were more extensive, where there was a substantial investment in fixed plant, and where workers were subjected to formal discipline, some firms in the traditional mill industries other than the textile and iron industries achieved factory status. The great merchant flour mills of Baltimore and Rochester fell into this category, as did some of the large packing plants in New York, Philadelphia, Baltimore, and (after 1840) Cincinnati.

The Rise of Corporate Organization

In addition to size and organization, changes were also taking place in the legal concept of the business firm—the change from sole proprietorship and partnership organization to corporate organization (Economic Reasoning Proposition 4). The corporation gained prominence chiefly because some businesses required more capital than one person or a few people could provide. The corporate form was commonplace for banks, insurance companies, and turnpike companies by 1810; in ensuing decades, canals and railroads could be financed only by tapping various sources of funds, from small merchants and professionals along proposed routes, to English capitalists thousands of miles away.

When it first appeared in the United States, the corporation lacked many of its present-day characteristics. Charters were granted by special acts of legislatures, and the question of the liability of stockholders was far from settled. Nevertheless, the corporation had a number of advantages over the sole proprietorship and the partnership, and its legal status came to be better defined than that of the joint-stock company. Of its unquestioned advantages, the most notable—in addition to the obvious one of attracting greater numbers of investors—were permanence and flexibility. The partnership and the sole proprietorship have one inescapable drawback: If one partner or the proprietor dies, the business is dissolved. The business can go on, of course, under a new partnership or proprietorship, but continuity of operation is contingent on the lives of particular individuals. The shares of a corporation, however, can be transferred, and investors, whether small or large, can enter and leave the business without destroying the structure of the corporation.

Early corporations did not have certain advantages that corporations have today, such as limited liability. Stockholders of the English joint-stock companies typically assumed "double liability"—that is, the stockholders were liable to the extent of their investment plus a like amount—and some states experimented with charters specifying either double liability or unlimited liability. After 1830, however, various states passed statutes providing for limited liability, and by 1860, this principle was generally accepted. Under limited liability, stockholders of a failed corporation could lose only the money they had invested in the venture.

The early requirement that incorporators of banks, insurance companies, canals, and railroads obtain their charters by the special act of a state legislature was not always a disadvantage. For those who had the political connections, this involved little uncertainty and expense, and there was always the possibility of obtaining a charter with exceptionally liberal provisions. Nevertheless, the politically unfavored could spend years lobbying futilely for corporate charters. As early as 1800, those who looked on incorporation by special act as "undemocratic" were agitating to secure "general" acts of incorporation—laws making it possible for any group, provided it observed and met prescribed regulations and requirements, to obtain a charter. Others, fearful that the corporation would spread too rapidly if their elected representatives did not review each application for charter, opposed general acts. In 1837, Connecticut passed the Connecticut General Incorporation Act, the first general act that made incorporation the right of anyone.

From that date, permissive general acts (acts allowing, but not requiring, incorporation under their provisions) were gradually placed on the statute books of most of the chief manufacturing states, and before 1861, the constitutions of 13 states required incorporation

TABLE 10.1 United States Manufactures, 1860

ITEM	(1) NUMBER OF EMPLOYEES	(2) COST OF RAW MATERIAL	(3) VALUE OF TOTAL PRODUCT	(4) (3)–(2) VALUE ADDED BY MANUFACTURE	RANK BY VALUE ADDED
Cotton goods	114,955	$ 52,666,701	$107,337,783	$54,671,082	1
Lumber	75,595	51,358,400	104,928,342	53,569,942	2
Boots and shoes	123,026	42,728,174	91,889,298	49,161,124	3
Flour and meal	27,682	208,497,309	248,580,365	40,083,056	4
Men's clothing	114,800	44,149,752	80,830,555	36,680,803	5
Iron (cast, forged, rolled, and wrought)	48,975	37,486,056	73,175,332	35,689,276	6
Machinery	41,223	19,444,533	52,010,376	32,565,843	7
Woolen goods	40,597	35,652,701	60,685,190	25,032,489	8
Carriages, wagons, and carts	37,102	11,898,282	35,552,842	23,654,560	9
Leather	22,679	44,520,737	67,306,452	22,785,715	10

Source: Eighth Census of the United States: Manufactures, 1860.

under general laws. In those states where permissive legislation had been enacted, incorporators continued until about 1870 to obtain special charters, which enabled the incorporators to secure more liberal provisions than they could under general laws.[3]

Leading Industries, 1860

The decline of household production and the rise in craftshops, mills, and factories changed the structure and location of manufacturing dramatically. By 1860, the total manufacturing labor force was nearly 1,530,000 (compared with almost 5,880,000 in agriculture). More than 96 percent of those engaged in manufacturing work in 10 industries. These ten are ranked in Table 10.1 by value added (value of total product minus raw material costs). Cotton goods ranked at the top, having grown from infancy 50 years earlier. Lumbering was a close second to cotton textiles. Looking now at ranking by number of employees, we see that boots and shoes (third by value added) was the top employer, and men's clothing (fifth by value added) was nearly tied with cotton goods as the next highest employer. Note that if iron products and machinery had been combined in a single category, their value added would have been the highest. Between 1850 and 1860, the doubling of the output of primary iron products and machinery forecast the shape of America's industrial future.

These industries were centered primarily in the Northeast. Cotton manufactures were located predominantly in New England, as were boots and shoes. Lumbering moved west and south but stayed strong in New England and the Middle Atlantic states. An overview of the location of industry, given in Table 10.2, testifies to the primacy of the East in early manufacturing. Because the census counted even the smallest sawmills and gristmills as "manufacturing establishments," the large numbers for the West and the South are misleading. By any other criterion, New England and the Middle Atlantic states were the leading regions. The figures for the Midwest reflect in part the rapid antebellum industrial growth of the Ohio Valley and the burgeoning of the Chicago area.

During the period from 1810 to 1860, the total value of manufactures increased from about $200 million to just under $2 billion, or roughly tenfold. Farming was still in first

[3]In 1811, New York had passed a law that permitted incorporation, without special act, of certain manufacturing concerns with capitalization of less than $100,000.

TABLE 10.2 Manufacturing, by Sections, Census of 1860

SECTION	NUMBER OF FIRMS	CAPITAL INVESTED	EMPLOYMENT		ANNUAL VALUE OF PRODUCTS	VALUE ADDED BY MANU-FACTURE
			MALE	FEMALE		
New England	20,671	$ 257,477,783	262,834	129,002	$ 468,599,287	$223,076,180
Middle Atlantic	53,287	435,061,964	432,424	113,819	802,338,392	358,211,423
Midwest	36,785	194,212,543	194,081	15,828	384,606,530	158,987,717
South	20,631	95,975,185	98,583	12,138	155,531,281	68,988,129
West	8,777	23,380,334	50,137	67	71,229,989	42,746,363
Territories	20,282	3,747,906	2,290	43	3,556,197	2,246,772
Totals	140,433	$1,009,855,715	1,040,349	270,897	1,885,861,676	$854,256,584

Source: Eighth Census of the United States: Manufactures, 1860.

place as a means of earning a livelihood: the value added by manufacture in 1860 was markedly less than the value of three of America's major crops—corn, wheat, and hay—and capital investment in industry totaled less than one-sixth the value of farm land and buildings. However, as already stated, the United States was even then second only to Great Britain in manufacturing.[4] Soon it would be the world's industrial leader as well as its agricultural leader. How was this remarkable achievement accomplished?

PREREQUISITES TO FACTORY PRODUCTION

The development of high-speed mass production required the introduction of machines and technology, standardization of items, continuous-process assembly lines of production, and new sources of power and energy. Advances in these areas increasingly led to the displacement of home manufactures, the putting-out system, and the craftshop. It was an evolutionary process, but in the longer view of history it has been called the Industrial Revolution.

Machines and Technology

Not until after 1845 did it become clear that the old methods of production listed above would soon be outmoded. Yet the developments of the 1850s were such that even the most casual contemporary observer could not fail to be impressed by the rapid advance of the "factory system."

The Industrial Revolution that had begun in England in the late eighteenth century by no means guaranteed the immediate establishment of the factory system in America. In fact, the English sought to prevent dissemination abroad of the details of the new inventions. Parliament passed laws in 1774 and 1781 prohibiting the export of new industrial machinery, not unlike later laws that prohibited high-tech exports to Soviet bloc countries during the Cold War. In 1782, a law was passed to prevent labor pirating, the luring abroad of highly skilled British mechanics. Although these efforts possibly slowed the introduction of new machines and technologies in the United States, technology transfers occurred anyway. For example, on the eve of the Napoleonic wars, the Scofield brothers arrived in New England from Yorkshire and built water-powered wool-carding machinery. They were preceded by Samuel Slater, who, as described earlier, came to the United States in 1789 and, in cooperation with Moses Brown and William Almy of Providence, Rhode Island, built the first American spinning mill powered by water. More than a dozen small prototypes of their mill were built during the next decade in New England.

[4]The *Twelfth Census of the United States*, quoting Mulhall's *Industries and Wealth of Nations*, placed the United States in fourth place after Great Britain, France, and Germany. But Douglass C. North shows convincingly that the United States ranked second; see *The Economic Growth of the United States, 1790 to 1860* (Englewood Cliffs, N. J.: Prentice Hall, 1961), v.

Largely because of the relatively high cost of labor in the United States, American managers always tended to use the most nearly automatic machines available for a particular application. More importantly, they successfully innovated ways of organizing production that saved labor expense per unit of output. Their chief contributions—the two basic ideas that led to American preeminence in nineteenth-century manufacturing—were interchangeable parts and continuous-process manufacture. Both advances were allied with the development of machine tools and with changes in techniques of applying power.

Standardized Interchangeable Parts

The idea of standardizing a product and its various parts originated in Sweden in the early eighteenth century and before 1800 had been tried in France, Switzerland, and England. Through standardization, the parts of one product could be interchanged for the parts of a like product, facilitating manufacture and repair. The first permanently successful application of the idea in an important use was made in the American armament industry. At the turn of the nineteenth century, Eli Whitney and Simeon North almost simultaneously obtained contracts from the government to manufacture firearms by the interchangeable-parts method. It has long been customary to credit Whitney with the first successful manufacture by interchangeable parts, but the evidence does not substantiate his claim. Records suggest that North was using the "uniformity principle" as early as 1807 in making his pistols. Perhaps the first application of the idea in a way that would be followed later was made by John H. Hall, inventor and engineer at the Harper's Ferry Armory, who by 1817 was installing his system using metal-cutting and woodworking machines.[5] In any case, it took more than two years to make the essential innovations in the arms industry. Captain Hall's pattern turning greatly reduced the number of hours needed to shape asymmetrical rifle stocks. Drop-forging with dies was successfully introduced in about 1827. By 1855, Samuel Colt, who had invented his six-shooter years earlier, established an armory in which machine work of a high degree of accuracy was accomplished by skilled operators. From approximately mid-century on, the ultimate precision tool was no longer the hand file.

Continuous-Process and Assembly Lines

Although milling processes did not require assembly operations, continuous-process manufacture—production in which the raw materials move continuously through the factory—had its first successful application in the mills. One of the first to succeed was the American inventor Oliver Evans. In 1782, he built a flour mill in Philadelphia run by gravity, friction, and water power that moved grain through its processing with no human intervention other than guiding and monitoring. Continuous-process manufacture in its most significant form today, with motor-driven moving assemblies like those introduced by Henry Ford for automobile production, was an outgrowth of the successful interchangeable-parts production of firearms, clocks and watches, sewing machines, and agricultural implements. In the 1850s, agricultural implement companies actually used conveyor belts to assemble the parts of major subassemblies in sequence, thus foreshadowing the mass production techniques of the early twentieth century.

Power and Energy

During the early years of manufacturing in the United States, water wheels furnished most of the motive power. Plentiful steadily moving rivers and streams assured this dependable source of power, and readily available water power was further enhanced by technological improvements in water wheels.

---

[5]See Robert S. Woodbury, "The Legend of Eli Whitney and Interchangeable Parts," *Technology and Culture* Vol. 2 (1), (1960): 235–253. In Woodbury's view, interchangeable-parts manufacture involves four elements: (1) precision machine tools, (2) precision gauges or other measuring instruments, (3) uniform measurement standards, and (4) techniques of mechanical drawing.

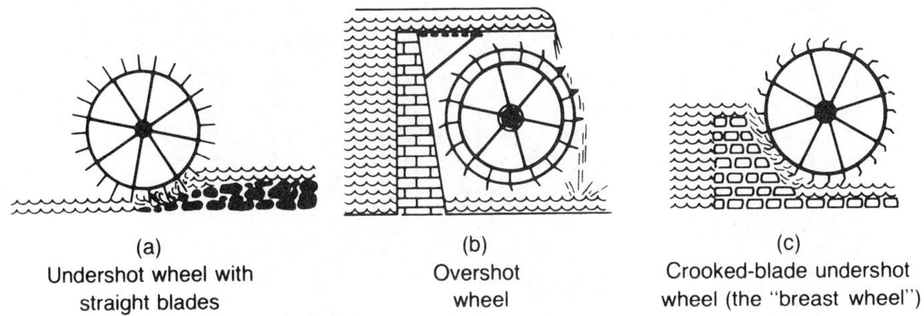

FIGURE 10.1 **Water Wheel Designs** The three main engineering designs of water wheels that powered early textile and woodworking machinery are displayed here.

A water wheel is always placed in a vertical position on a horizontal shaft and is moved at a comparatively low speed by direct action of the water. Wheels are classified by the way water is applied to turn them (see Figure 10.1). The kind used in colonial times and for a while thereafter in frontier areas was the undershot wheel, which was placed in the stream so that its blades were moved by the water passing underneath it. The undershot wheel, although easy to install, was inefficient, transmitting no more than 40 percent of the power applied to it. The overshot wheel was moved by water running from a flume across the top of the wheel into buckets covering its surface; the weight of the water in the buckets moved the wheel in the direction of the stream flow. The overshot wheel was more efficient, easy to install, and satisfactory wherever there was a good head of water, but the power it developed was not great enough for heavy industrial purposes. Consequently, the large manufacturing concerns almost invariably used the breast wheel. This type, too, was equipped with buckets, but the water struck the wheel short of its axle so that it rotated in an upstream direction; both the impulse of the water and its weight in the buckets enabled the wheel to utilize up to 75 percent of the power applied to it. Installed in multiples, the breast wheel developed sufficient horsepower to serve the largest early nineteenth century industrial firms. The machinery of the Merrimack Manufacturing Company, for example, was run by eight breast wheels, each 30 feet in diameter with buckets 12 feet long.

The slow-moving and cumbersome water wheels could develop several thousand horsepower, but they had marked disadvantages. Power from a wheel was transmitted by wooden shafts and cogwheels and was limited by the strength of the entire mechanism. Furthermore, industrial location was restricted to stream sites, and the problem of finding sites, especially in industrialized areas, became a serious one. The first difficulty was partially overcome by making wheels and transmission parts of metal, the second by the improved engineering of dams and canals. The water turbine, which revolved on a vertical shaft, was much more efficient than a wheel and by the 1850s was adding rapidly to the power potential of the country.

Finally came steam power, although its introduction into U.S. manufacturing was slow for several reasons. In the beginning, the steam engine was extremely costly to operate. Breakdowns were frequent, and expert repair technicians were rare. In transportation, the steam engine could pull such heavy loads at such increased speeds that these disadvantages were more than offset, but in industry, water power remained cheaper than steam power for a long time. It has been estimated that in 1812, only 11 engines of the high-pressure type developed by Oliver Evans were in use in this country.[6]

During the next two decades, steam engines became more common in the South and West, but most of them were used in ironworks and glass factories that required fuel for

[6] Clark, *History of Manufactures in the United States, 1607–1860,* 409.

This fairly typical overshot water wheel was one used in the 20,000 sawmills and 14,000 flour mills reported in the 1860 national census.

© H. ARMSTRONG ROBERTS

other purposes or in mills that could not conveniently be located near water. Around 1840, manufacturers in New England and the Middle Atlantic states estimated the annual cost per horsepower of steam to be five or six times that of water. Within the next 20 years, improvements in metalworking technology lowered the cost of steam engines and improved both their efficiency and reliability. By the 1850s, steam engines were replacing water wheels in the heat-using industries and wherever stream flows were highly variable, as they were along the Ohio River. In New England, steam engines were being installed to power textile mills due to the serious lack of adequate power sites. As of 1860, water was still the chief source of power, but the years of the water wheel were clearly numbered.

Paralleling the rise of steam power, with a lag, was coal, which eventually became a major new source of energy. Because wood and, hence, charcoal were so cheap in the United States, however, the increase in coal use was slowed in comparison with its rapid adoption in England. Coal, like water, had a major impact on the location of manufacturing. With adequate transportation facilities, coal power increasingly allowed factories to be built in urban centers, and after 1830, coal-powered factories increasingly became a feature of the rise of manufacturing in the United States.

Factor Proportions and Borrowing and Adapting Technology

Britain's head start in making machines gave the British a great advantage in manufacturing. Their machines typically embodied specific technological forms that reflected British relative costs of labor, capital, and raw materials. The relative costs of these inputs were different in the United States. Nineteenth-century Americans were short on labor and capital but long on raw materials and natural power sources (water). American industrialists had not only to copy English machines but to adapt them to economize on labor, perhaps at the sacrifice of raw material usage. One example of their success is reflected in the comparison of the textile industries in each country. English textile firms averaged 17,000 spindles and 276 looms compared with 7,000 spindles and 163 looms in the United States. Robert Zevin's study of textiles reveals that the American cotton textiles industry had only 20 percent of Britain's spindles and 25 percent of its workers but processed 40 percent as much cotton. Clearly, the Americans had successfully adapted their equipment to save on scarce labor and capital.

The works of Lars Sandberg and later William Lazonick on the choice of techniques and their adoption reveals that there was not a uniform technology on both sides of the Atlantic. In textiles, the British became increasingly labor intensive and lowered the quality of their raw material inputs. Americans conserved labor by upgrading machinery and adopting higher grades of raw cotton or wool materials. Because Americans did not unionize as did British workers and were more mobile than British workers, American management could more easily substitute new machines to reduce its labor dependence and labor costs. Claudia Goldin and Kenneth Sokoloff add another consideration: Early manufacturers depended primarily on women and children. Where the opportunity costs of this labor were low, as in New England where farming produced a poor livelihood, women and children were relatively more available to supply factory labor. This encouraged the location of manufacturing there and supplied a labor force accepting of technological changes. These propositions by Goldin and Sokoloff have been scrutinized, tested, and supported by Lee Craig and Elizabeth Field-Hendry.[7]

In textiles, firearms, clocks and watches, and many other items, the ideas of standardization, interchangeable parts, and division of labor in assembly production processes were being widely applied. In 1851, at the Great Exhibition in London (in many ways like the World's Fair today), American products were a primary attraction. Though simple in design and not elegant or long lasting, they were practical, cheap, and functional. After all, they reflected the characteristics demanded by a population dominated by masses of farmers, pioneers, and workers who were, for the most part, unpretentious, practical people. Recall Economic Reasoning Proposition 1. In 1855, a British parliamentary committee visited the United States to determine the secret of the "American system," as it became known. They found, to their surprise, that American machinery was often technologically more sophisticated than its British counterpart. "Yankee Ingenuity" had become the wonder of the world.

But a paradox remains. Capital was relatively scarce in the United States—interest rates were high compared with those in Britain. Why, then, was it the Americans who built the ingenious machines, not the British? The answer is that skilled labor was even scarcer in the United States. In those industries that required skilled labor (firearms), it paid the Americans to substitute capital and natural resources (water power) for skilled labor. In industries that used less skilled labor, American industries used less capital per worker than their British counterparts.

PRODUCTIVITY ADVANCES IN MANUFACTURES

The collective effects of the many and varied sources of productivity advance just discussed dramatically raised labor productivity in manufactures in the American Northeast. Estimates of the annual rates of growth of labor productivity by type of manufacture are given in Table 10.3 on page 196. These are ranges of percentage rates of advance and are divided between capital-intensive industries and typically smaller sized firms of non-capital-intensive industries.

[7]See Lee A. Craig and Elizabeth B. Field-Hendry, "Industrialization and the Earnings Gap: Regional and Sectoral Tests of the Goldin-Sokoloff Hypothesis," *Explorations in Economic History* 30 (1993): 60–80.

TABLE 10.3 Annual Growth Rates of Value Added per Worker in Selected Manufactures in the Northeast, 1820–1860

CAPITAL-INTENSIVE INDUSTRIES	% CHANGE OF LABOR PRODUCTIVITY
Cotton textiles	2.2–3.3%
Iron	1.5–1.7
Liquors	1.7–1.9
Flour/grist mills	0.6–0.7
Paper	4.3–5.5
Tanning	1.2–1.7
Wool Textiles	2.7–2.8
OTHER INDUSTRIES	
Boots/shoes	2.0–2.1
Coaches/harnesses	2.0–2.4
Furniture/woodwork	2.9–3.0
Glass	2.5
Hats	2.4–2.5
Tobacco	0.1–2.4

Source: Kenneth L. Sokoloff, "Productivity Growth in Manufacturing during Early Industrialization: Evidence from the American Northeast, 1820–1860," in Long-Term Factors in American Economic Growth, *ed. Stanley L. Engerman and Robert E. Gallman (Chicago: University of Chicago Press, 1986), 698.*

The comparable rates of advance of labor productivity by both categories of industries strongly suggest that capital deepening was not a prerequisite to higher output per worker, nor were there high rates only for a few select industries. A wide range of manufacturing industries exhibited high productivity rates, even shops, mills, and small firms with limited mechanization and primitive power sources. This reinforces the perspective of economic growth as the cumulative impact of many incremental advances throughout the economy, similar to the pattern we observed in chapter 9 in our analysis of productivity advance in steamboating.

PROTECTION FROM FOREIGN COMPETITION

After the peace of 1815, imports of English manufactured goods reached alarming proportions from the viewpoint of American businesses. Before 1815, duties on foreign goods had been set at rates that, although originally intended to protect, maximized governmental revenues in a hit-or-miss fashion. Growing protectionist sentiment in the Northeast gained enough support from the West and South to secure passage of the Tariff Act of 1816.

The tariff of 1816 levied ad valorem duties of 20 to 25 percent on most manufactured goods and 15 to 20 percent on raw materials. In general, the level of duties on manufactures did not prevent the entry of many goods at that time, although cheap cottons were shut out of the home market by specific duties (i.e., duties of so much per yard). Moreover, the tax on raw materials, particularly raw wool, lowered the expansion potential of domestic industries using raw wool inputs.

From 1816 until 1832, the protectionist tide rose; American producers of cottons, woolens, glass, and iron products received the greatest favors, with raw wool and hemp garnering their shares. Figure 10.2 traces the history of U.S. tariffs measured as rates, namely, duties collected as percentages of the values of dutiable imports. It shows the Tariff Act of 1828 realizing a record high, not to be matched again until the Smoot-Hawley Tariff of 1930.

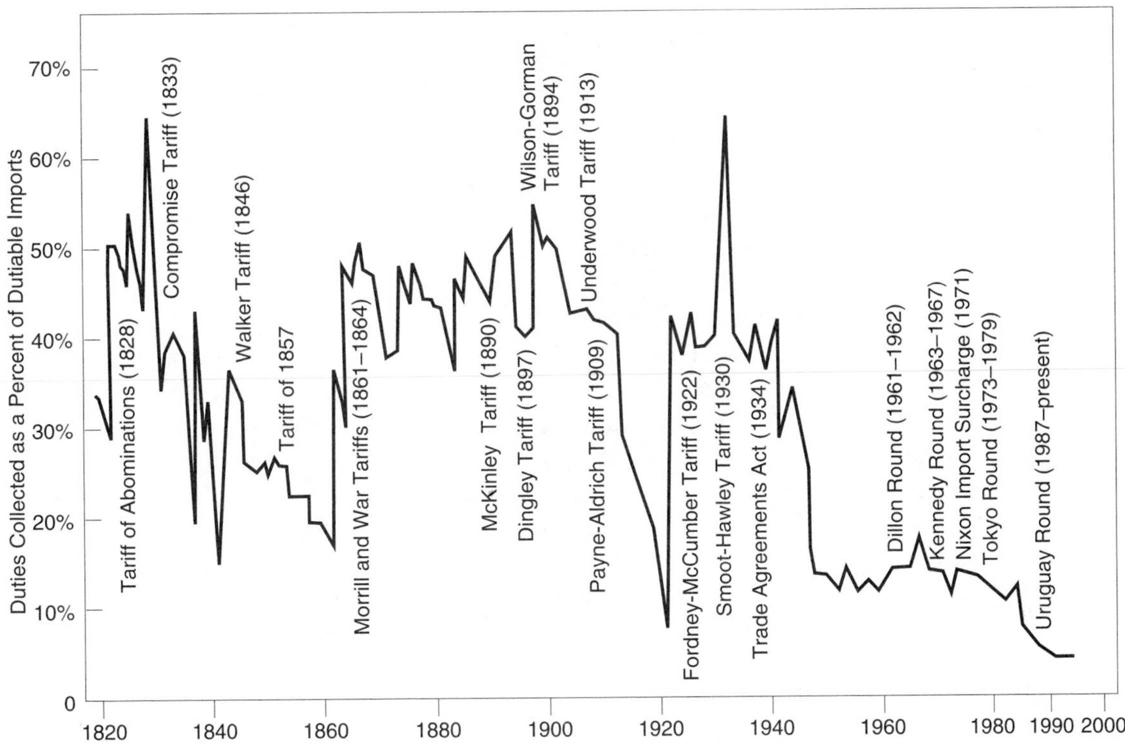

FIGURE 10.2 Tariff Rates in the United States Since 1820 *Tariff rates in the United States have bounced up and down, suggesting that in Congress, tariffs are a political football. Import-competing industries prefer high tariffs. The highest tariffs we have had were the Smoot-Hawley Tariff of 1930 and the "Tariff of Abominations" of 1828.*

Source: U.S. Department of Commerce.

In general, the Northeast and Middle Atlantic states favored high tariffs; the South did not. The political shenanigans leading to the high tariff of 1828—the "Tariff of Abominations"—precipitated agitation in the South and necessitated a compromise within only a few years. In fact, a severe threat to the Union was South Carolina's Nullification Ordinance, which was legislated even after downward revisions in import duties had been made in 1832.The Compromise Tariff of 1833 provided that all duties would be reduced to a maximum of 20 percent ad valorem within a decade.

But only two months after the 20 percent maximum level was reached in 1842, the Whigs (who had just gained control of the White House) passed a bill in which rates reverted to about the protective level of 10 years before, and President John Tyler, even though a southerner, accepted it because he felt this action would provide more revenue for the government. With the return of the Democrats to power in 1845, more moderate tariffs were rapidly secured, and the Walker Tariff of 1846 set an example that was followed until 1861.

The good times of the 1850s and the consequent increase in imports so swelled the revenues from tariffs that the government achieved great surpluses. The piling up of cash in U.S. Treasury vaults led to a general reduction in rates, and many items were placed on the free list. Just before the Civil War, it appeared that the United States might join the United Kingdom as a free-trade country. As shown in Figure 10.2, tariffs in 1860 averaged less than 20 percent of the value of dutiable imports (15 percent of the value of all imports), levels that had only moderate protective significance.

Economic Insight 10.1

The Incidence of the Tariff

As indicated by South Carolina's Nullification Ordinance in reaction to the "Tariff of Abominations" (1828), the South had no enthusiasm for high tariffs. It fought against high tariffs just as the Northeast and Middle Atlantic states fought for them, with clear economic gains in mind.

The figure below illustrates the effect of a duty (d) on foreign cotton textiles. First, we derive total supply (S) as the horizontal sum of New England's supply (S_{NE}) and Great Britain's (S_{GB}). At price P, the quantity supplied by New England is Q_{NE}, equal to the line distance ab. And the amount supplied by Britain is Q_{GB}, equal to the line distance aa^1. Total supply (s) at P is Q, the sum of Q_{NE} and Q_{GB} and equal to the line distance ab^1, where the segment a^1b^1 is equal to ba^1. Now we include the demand curve (D) and determine equilibrium at price P and quantity Q, where S and D intersect.

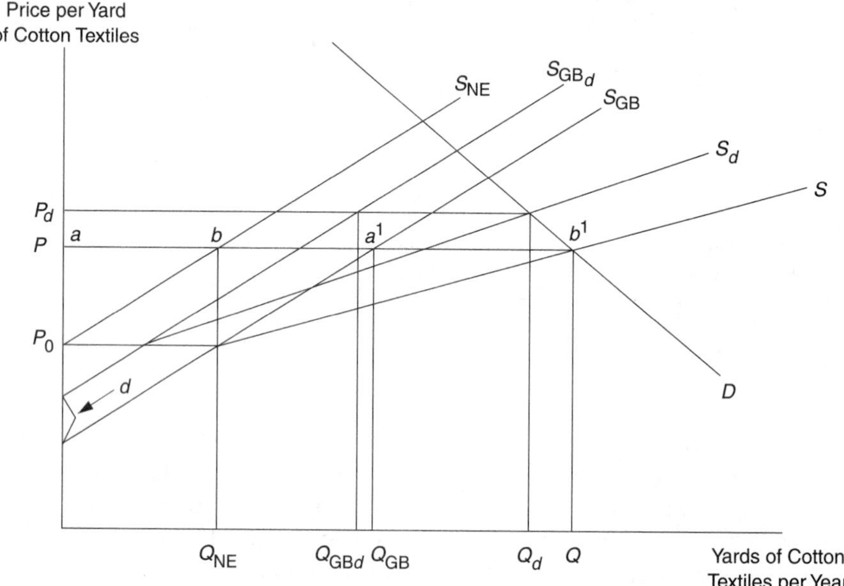

To see the effect of a duty (d) on British cotton textiles, we add it to S_{GB} to get a new, higher-cost supply curve S_{GBd} inclusive of the tax. The tax, in effect, adds to the costs of going to the U.S. market for British producers. The result is a new supply schedule S_d above S by the amount of the duty. The new equilibrium quantity is Q_d at price P_d. The government receives $Q_{GBd} \times d$ in revenues. Now we shall relate this changed equilibrium to the historical issues.

A *tariff* is a tax paid in part by consumers on dutiable imported goods. The tariff raised the price of all goods whether imported or not (P to P_d) and lowered the real income of consumers of these taxed goods. Since the dutied items were largely imported manufactures such as textiles, consumers had to pay more for manufactures when tariffs rose. Northeastern manufacturers, however, gained market shares and profits. (Check this by determining along the price line P_d the post duty quantities supplied by New England and Great Britain.) The losses of consumers outweighed the gains of manufacturers. But the manufacturers were better organized and could influence legislators.

The South lost because of high tariffs in another way. When the United States imported less, it placed fewer dollars in foreigners' hands. For example, with the English receiving fewer dollars for their textile exports to the United States, they had less foreign exchange (dollars) with which

Economic Insight 10.1

The Incidence of the Tariff, continued

to purchase American exports. What was the leading U.S. export, and to whom? Cotton, to England.

Sending more cotton to New England only partially offset the reduction to England. Higher-priced cotton textiles meant lower quantities demanded overall (Q_d rather than Q), which, in turn, meant lower quantities demanded of raw cotton materials. Southern planters simply lost customers abroad faster than they gained them at home.

We see that the tariff transfers money to the protected industries, helping the owners of capital and the workers employed there. It takes money away from consumers and from foreign producers. The government gains from the tax revenues collected. In short, tariffs take money from one group and give it to another. As John James (1978) has shown, the high antebellum tariffs redistributed wealth and resources from the South to northeastern industries, a transfer southerners abhorred. From the southern perspective, the terms of trade deteriorated; prices of their exports fell, and prices of their imports rose.

Tariffs are noteworthy for their political popularity. They are often advocated, for example, by politicians to protect American workers from "cheap" foreign labor. But these were not the original arguments for U.S. tariffs. The political economy of tariffs was first expressed in the first Tariff Act in 1789:

> Whereas it is necessary for the support of the government, for the discharge of the debts of the United States, and the encouragement of manufactures, that duties be laid on goods, wares, and merchandise imported.

So the original purposes of the tariff were clear: to generate government revenues and to protect infant American industry. Initially, tariffs successfully added revenue to government coffers. In 1790, 99.9 percent of total federal revenue was derived from tariffs. In 1860, it was still 94 percent. (Today, it is less than 1 percent of federal revenues, and accordingly, we never hear this argument—or seldom do.) What about the other purpose, to protect infant industries? Success in that area appears dubious.

When peace came in 1815, ending the protection from foreign competition caused by war, low-grade British textiles flooded U.S. markets. In 1816, Francis Lowell went to Congress asking for a tariff on low-grade textiles competing with the ones his established mills produced. High-grade cotton cloth like that made in the infant firms in Rhode Island received no protection. In short, the Lowell mills gained, but Rhode Island's infant industry did not. The protection received was primarily a political matter. Who primarily paid the higher prices on the tariff-protected low-grade cloth? Again, it was the South, primarily for textiles going to slaves.

Were later higher tariffs a necessary condition for the rise of manufacturing? We note that in 1830, when the nullification controversy raged, the tariff rate on dutied items exceeded 60 percent. By 1860, the tariff rate was just below 20 percent. In short, when manufacturing was growing rapidly (albeit faster in the 1830s and 1850s than in the 1840s), it did so over three decades while tariff protection was falling. But tariffs appear to have been important to U.S. cotton textiles. According to Mark Bils, Peter Temin, and Knick Harley, in independent studies, much of the U.S. cotton manufactures would have been competed away by the English without high tariffs.[8]

[8] See Mark Bils, "Tariff Protection and Production in the Early U.S. Cotton Textile Industry," *The Journal of Economic History* 44 (1984): 1033–1045; Peter Temin, "Product Quality and Vertical Integration in the Early Cotton Textile Industry," *Journal of Economic History* 48 (1988): 891–907; and C. Knick Harley, "International Competitiveness of the Antebellum American Cotton Textile Industry," *Journal of Economic History* 52 (1992): 559–584.

SELECTED REFERENCES AND SUGGESTED READINGS

Ames, Edward, and Nathan Rosenberg. "Changing Technological Leadership and Industrial Growth." *Economic Journal* 13 (1963).

Atack, Jeremy. "Returns to Scale in Antebellum United States Manufacturing." *Explorations in Economic History* 14 (1977): 337–359.

———. "Fact or Fiction? The Relative Costs of Steam and Water Power: A Simulative Approach." *Explorations in Economic History* 16 (1979): 409–437.

Atack, Jeremy, Fred Bateman, and Thomas Weiss. "The Regional Diffusion and Adoption of the Steam Engine in American Manufacturing." *Journal of Economic History* 40 (June 1980).

Bateman, Fred, and Thomas Weiss. "Comparative Regional Development in Antebellum Manufacturing." *Journal of Economic History* 35 (1975).

Bateman, Fred, James Foust, and Thomas Weiss. "Profitability in Southern Manufacturing: Estimates for 1860." *Explorations in Economic History* 12 (1975): 211–232.

Bils, Mark. "Tariff Protection and Production in the Early U. S. Cotton Textile Industry." *Journal of Economic History* 44 (1984): 1033–1045.

Brito, D. L., and Jeffrey G. Williamson. "Skilled Labor and Nineteenth Century Anglo-American Managerial Behavior." *Explorations in Economic History* 10 (1973): 235–252.

Broadberry, S. N. "Manufacturing and the Convergence Hypothesis: What the Long-Run Data Show." *Journal of Economic History* 53 (December 1993): 772–788.

Chandler, Alfred D. "Anthracite Coal and the Beginnings of the Industrial Revolution in the United States." *Business History Review* (1972): 141–181.

Clark, Victor S. *History of Manufactures in the United States 1607–1860.*Washington, D.C.: Carnegie Institution of Washington, 1929.

Cochran, Thomas. *Frontiers of Change: Early Industrialism in America.* New York: Oxford University Press, 1981.

"A Collection of Historical Documents Relating to the Steam Engine." **http://www.history.rochester.edu/steam/**.

Craig, Lee A., and Elizabeth B. Field-Hendry. "Industrialization and the Earnings Gap: Regional and Sectoral Tests of the Goldin-Sokoloff Hypothesis." *Explorations in Economic History* 30 (1993): 60–80.

David, Paul. "Learning by Doing and Tariff Protection: A Reconsideration of the Case of the Antebellum United States Textile Industry." *Journal of Economic History* 30 (1970): 521–601.

———. "The Horndal Effect in Lowell, 1834–1856: A Short-Run Learning Curve for Integrated Cotton Textile Mills." *Explorations in Economic History* 10 (1973): 131–150.

Davis, Lance E. "Sources of Industrial Finance: The American Textile Industry, A Case Study." *Explorations in Economic History*, 60 (4), 1st series (1957).

———. "The New England Textile Mills and the Capital Markets: A Study of Industrial Borrowing, 1840–1860." *Journal of Economic History* 20 (1960): 1–30.

Engerman, Stanley L., and Kenneth Sokoloff. "Technology and Industrialization, 1790–1914." In *The Cambridge Economic History of the United States*, Vol. II, *The Long Nineteenth Century*, eds. Stanley L. Engerman and Robert E. Gallman. Cambridge: Cambridge University Press, 2000, 367–401.

Field, Alexander James. "Sectoral Shift in Antebellum Massachusetts: A Reconsideration." *Explorations in Economic History* 15 (1978): 146–171.

Fogel, Robert. "The Specification Problem in Economic History." *Journal of Economic History* (September 1967).

Goldin, Claudia, and Kenneth Sokoloff. "Women, Children, and Industrialization in the Early Republic: Evidence from the Manufacturing Censuses." *Journal of Economic History* (December 1982).

———. "The Relative Productivity Hypothesis of Industrialization: The American Case, 1820 to 1850." *Quarterly Journal of Economics* 69 (August 1984).

Habakkuk, H. J. *American and British Technology in the Nineteenth Century: The Search for Labor Saving Inventions*. New York: Cambridge University Press, 1962.

Halsey, Harlan I. "The Choice between High Pressure and Low Pressure Steam Power in America in the Early Nineteenth Century." *Journal of Economic History* 61 (1981): 723–744.

Harley, C. Knick. "International Competitiveness of the Antebellum American Cotton Textile Industry." *Journal of Economic History* 52 (1992): 559–584.

Hounshell, D. *From the American System to Mass Production*. Baltimore, Md.: Johns Hopkins University Press, 1984.

Hughes, Jonathan. *Industrialization and Economic History: Theses and Conjectures*. New York: McGraw-Hill, 1970.

———. *The Vital Few: American Economic Progress and Its Protagonists*. New York: Oxford University Press, 1986.

James, John. "The Welfare Effects of the Ante-Bellum Tariff: A General Equilibrium Analysis." *Explorations in Economic History* 15 (1978): 231–256.

Lazonick, William H. "Production Relations, Labor Productivity, and Choice of Technique: British and U.S. Cotton Spinning." *Journal of Economic History* 41 (1981): 491–516.

Lindstrom, Diane. *Economic Development in the Philadelphia Region, 1810–1850*. New York: Columbia University Press, 1978.

Livesay, Harold. "Marketing Patterns in the Antebellum American Iron Industry." *Business History Review* (1971): 269–295.

Livesay, Harold, and Glen Porter. "The Financial Role of Merchants in the Development of U.S. Manufacturing, 1815–1860." *Explorations in Economic History* 9 (1971): 63–88.

North, Douglass C. *The Economic Growth of the United States 1790–1860*. Englewood Cliffs, N. J.: Prentice Hall, 1961.

Passell, Peter, and Marie Schmundt. "The Financial Role of Merchants in the Development of U.S. Manufacturing, 1815–1860." *Explorations in Economic History* 9 (1971): 35–48.

Pope, Clayne. "The Impact of the Antebellum Tariff on Income Distribution." *Explorations in Economic History* 9 (1972): 375–422.

Rosenberg, Nathan. "Factors Affecting the Diffusion of Technology." *Explorations in Economic History* 10 (1972): 3–34.

———. *Technology and American Economic Growth*. New York: Harper & Row, 1972.

Sokoloff, Kenneth L. "Inventive Activity in Early Industrial America: Evidence from Patent Records, 1790–1846." *Journal of Economic History* 48 (1988): 813–850.

Sokoloff, Kenneth L., and David R. Dollar. "Was the Transition from the Artisanal Shop to the Nonmechanized Factory Associated with Gains in Efficiency? Evidence from the U.S. Manufactures Censuses of 1820 and 1850." *Explorations in Economic History* 21 (1984): 351–382.

———. "Agricultural Seasonality and the Organization of Manufacturing in Early Industrial Societies: The Contrast between England and the United States." *Journal of Economic History* (1997).

Temin, Peter. "Steam and Water Power in the Early 19th Century." *Journal of Economic History* 26 (1966): 187–205. Reprinted in Robert Fogel and Stanley Engerman, ed. *The Reinterpretation of American Economic History*. New York: Harper & Row, 1971.

———. "Product Quality and Vertical Integration in the Early Cotton Textile Industry." *Journal of Economic History* 48 (1988): 891–907.

Terrill, Tom E. "Eager Hands: Labor for Southern Textiles, 1850–1860." *Journal of Economic History* 36 (1976): 84–99.

Uselding, Paul. "Factor Substitution and Labor Productivity Growth in American Manufacturing, 1839–1899." *Journal of Economic History* 32 (1972): 670–681.

Uselding, Paul, and W. Douglas Morgan. "Technical Progress at the Springfield Armory." *Explorations in Economic History* 9 (1972): 269–290.

Williamson, Jeffrey. "Urbanization in the American Northeast." *Journal of Economic History* 25 (1965): 592–608.

Williamson, Jeffrey, and Joseph Swanson. "The Growth of Cities in the American Northeast, 1820–1870." *Explorations in Entrepreneurial History* 4, 2d series, (Supplement) (1966).

Zevin, Robert B. "The Growth of Cotton Textile Production after 1815." In *The Reinterpretation of American Economic History*, eds. Robert Fogel and Stanley Engerman. New York: Harper & Row, 1971.

———. *The Growth of Manufacturing in Early Nineteenth-Century New England.* New York: Arno, 1975.

Chapter Eleven

LABOR DURING THE EARLY INDUSTRIAL PERIOD

Before 1860, most of the U.S. population lived in rural areas, and most workers were self-employed on farms and in craftshops. Nevertheless, after the War of 1812, rapid industrialization and urbanization, especially in the Northeast and Middle Atlantic states, transformed the working conditions and living standards of many Americans who depended on their labor for a living. Real wages—monetary wages adjusted for the cost of living—rose between 1820 and 1860; unskilled workers' earnings fell relative to those of skilled workers as the supply of unskilled labor swelled through immigration; and working conditions became less personal as more and more workers changed from self-employment to working for an employer. It was a period when the first stirrings of a labor movement began in the United States and when the right to vote spread in the Western world. These changes occurred as economic growth increased and industrialization advanced and spread.

THE GROWTH OF THE POPULATION AND THE LABOR FORCE

The population of the United States grew rapidly during the first half of the nineteenth century. In 1800, there were 5,308,000 Americans; by 1860, there were 31,443,000, a growth rate of about 3.0 percent per year, an extremely high rate in comparison with other countries. Population grew rapidly because both the rate of natural increase and the rate of immigration were high.

Families were large in the early republic. Although the evidence is fragmentary, it indicates that the average woman in 1800 would marry rather young, before age 20, and would give birth to about seven children. Few men or women would remain unmarried. Fertility declined during the first half of the nineteenth century, a trend that began in rural areas well before industrialization and urbanization became the norm. Economic historians have offered a number of hypotheses to explain this rather puzzling decline in fertility. Yasukichi Yasuba, who was one of the first to examine the problem, suggests the "land availability" hypothesis: as population and land prices rose, the cost to farmers of endowing their children with a homestead rose, and so parents chose to have smaller families to ensure a good life for their children. William A. Sundstrom and Paul A. David have described an interesting variation. The growth of nonfarm employment in rural areas forced farmers to provide more economic opportunities for their children to keep them "down on the farm." Maris A. Vinovskis notes that more conventional factors—especially the growth of urbanization, industrialization, and literacy—also played a role.

Mortality was also high in the early republic, near the 20 percent level for white infants below the age of one. Nevertheless, birthrates were so high that the increase in the population due to natural factors continued to be strongly positive despite declining fertility and high mortality.

Although the high birthrate dominates the story of rapid total population growth, immigration also had a significant impact, especially on labor markets because the flow of immigrants was rich in unskilled male workers in their prime working years. This is illustrated in Figure 11.1, which shows the number of workers coming to the United States. The huge increase toward the end of the period was created by events in Europe: the potato famine in Ireland (which also affected the continent of Europe, although to a lesser extent) and political unrest in Europe. While immigration accounted for only 3 percent of the total U.S. population growth from 1820 to 1825, it accounted for between 25 and 31 percent from 1845 to 1860. We will discuss various impacts of rapid immigration later.

THE CHANGING LABOR FORCE DISTRIBUTION AND COMPOSITION

Table 11.1 shows the continued dominance of agriculture throughout the period. It also shows how differently labor was allocated in 1860 compared with 1810. Mining took the biggest jump, largely because of the California Gold Rush, but more important is the twenty-fold increase of workers in manufacturing. On the eve of the Civil War, 1.5 million workers labored in manufacturing, most of them in the Northeast and Middle Atlantic states. In absolute numbers, agricultural workers grew the most, but manufacturing workers grew relatively. The economy was changing its structure from one of agriculture to one of manufacturing, a normal pattern of modern economic growth and development.

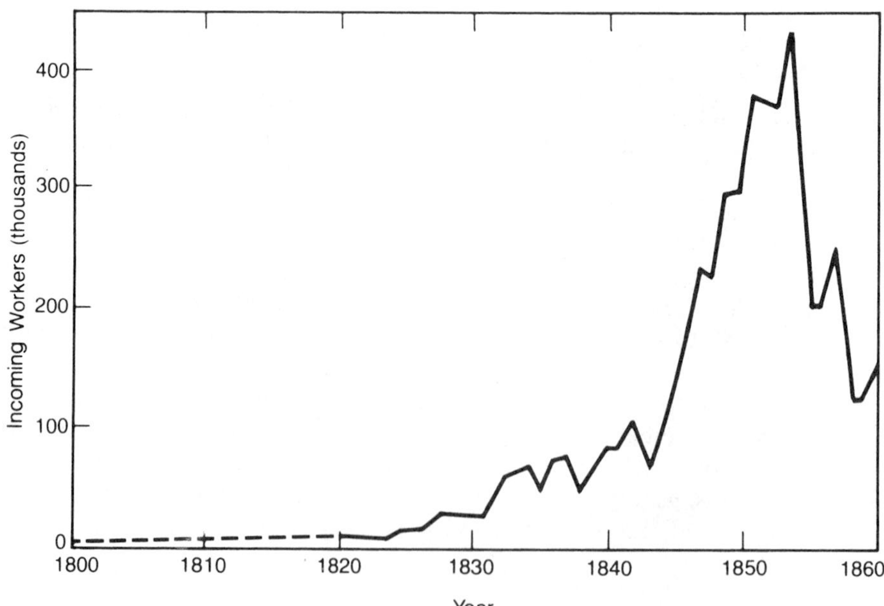

FIGURE 11.1 Additions to the U.S. Labor Force from Migration, 1800–1860 *Laborers came in huge numbers during the post-1845 period to a nation rich in land and rapidly increasing its stock of capital.*

TABLE 11.1 Labor Force Distribution, 1810 to 1860 (in thousands)

YEAR	TOTAL	AGRI-CULTURE	FISHING	MINING	CON-STRUCTION	MANU-FACTURES	TRANS-PORTATION	TRADE	SERVICES
1810	2,330	1,950	6	11	—	—	60	—	82
1820	3,135	2,470	14	13	—	—	50	—	130
1830	4,200	2,965	15	22	—	—	70	—	190
1840	5,660	3,570	24	32	290	500	112	350	285
1850	8,250	4,520	30	102	410	1,200	155	530	430
1860	11,110	5,880	31	176	520	1,530	225	890	715

Source: Adapted from Stanley Lebergott, Manpower in Economic Growth: The American Record Since 1800 *(New York: McGraw-Hill, 1964), 510.*

Factories and Workers

As the economy and especially urban centers grew, and as economic unification progressed, output was sold in larger, more integrated markets. In addition, as shown in Table 11.2, the size of firms grew, as reflected in the number of employees per firm. For example, the number of workers per firm in cotton textiles nearly tripled and more than doubled in wool textiles and in hats and caps between 1820 and 1850. Pressures were great to achieve volume at the expense of artistry, and the small artisanal shops were increasingly giving way to the factory. This change in firm size was apparent both in mechanized or mechanizing industries (cotton and wool textiles) and in nonmechanized industries (hats, books, and shoes). So mechanization was only part of the story of this trend toward larger production units. Another key change was the greater division of labor, diminishing the proportion and role of workers with general skills. A more intense workplace under careful supervision aimed for standardized products, an early form of quality control. Such a transition in a nonmechanized shop is described in a study by B. E. Hazard:

TABLE 11.2 Employees per Firm in Northeastern Manufacturing, 1820 and 1850

	1820		1850		
	EMPLOYEES PER FIRM	NUMBER OF FIRMS OBSERVED	EMPLOYEES PER FIRM	NUMBER OF FIRMS OBSERVED	RATIO OF FIRM SIZE IN 1850 TO THAT IN 1830
Boots and shoes	19.1	15	33.6	72	1.76
Cotton textiles	34.6	92	97.5	5,856	2.82
Flour and grist milling	2.4	90	1.8	5,128	0.75
Glass	56.9	8	64.6	76	1.14
Hats and caps	8.4	32	17.0	812	2.02
Iron and iron products	19.5	73	24.2	1,562	1.24
Liquors	2.7	165	5.0	633	1.85
Paper	14.3	33	22.4	12	1.57
Tanning	3.8	126	4.2	3,233	1.11
Wool and mixed textiles	10.6	107	24.5	1,284	2.31

Source: Adapted from the 1820 and 1850 Census of Manufactures, as provided in Kenneth L. Sokoloff, "Was the Transition from the Artisanal Shop to the Nonmechanized Factory Associated with Gains in Efficiency? Evidence from the U.S. Manufactures Censuses of 1820 and 1850," Explorations in Economic History *21 (1984): 354.*

> He [Gideon Howard, a manufacturer of shoes in South Randolph, Massachusetts] had a "gang" over in his twelve-footer who fitted, made and finished: one lasted, one pegged and tacked on soles, one made fore edges, one put on heels and "pared them up," and in cases of handsewed shoes, two or three sewers were needed to keep the rest of the gang busy. . . . These groups of men in a ten-footer gradually took on a character due to specialization demanded by the markets with higher standards and need of speed in output. Instead of all the men working there being regularly trained shoemakers, perhaps only one would be, and he was a boss contractor, who took out from a central shop so many cases to be done at a certain figure and date, and hired shoemakers who had "picked up" the knowledge of one process and set them to work under his supervision. One of the gang was a laster, another a pegger, one an edge-maker, one a polisher. Sometimes, as business grew, each of these operators would be duplicated. Such work did away with the old seven-year apprenticeship system.[1]

Another characteristic of this transition to larger firms, at least initially in most manufacturing firms, was the increase in the proportion of the labor force composed of women and children. Larger firms typically exhibited a proportionately large share of simple and relatively narrowly defined tasks, such as machine tending, starting materials in machines, carrying materials, and other simple tasks. A key problem for many firms was hiring unskilled but able workers. In New England, these were mostly women, especially before the large waves of immigration in the late 1840s and 1850s.

The Rhode Island and Waltham Systems

Mill and factory owners in the textile industry generally solved their employment problems in one of two ways. Under the *Rhode Island system,* they hired whole families, assigned father, mother, and children to tasks suitable to their strength and maturity, and housed the families in company-constructed tenements. South of Boston, the Rhode Island system was used almost exclusively, partly because child labor was first introduced there in imitation of English methods, and partly because the mule spinning typical of the area required both heavy and light work. A second system, called the *Waltham system,* was introduced in Waltham, Massachusetts, by Francis Cabot Lowell and the Boston Associates. It employed women in their late teens and early twenties who worked in large factories. Housed in dormitories or boarding houses, they remained under the careful supervision of matrons who kept any taint of disreputability from the young women (Economic Reasoning Proposition 1).

A key impetus to the Waltham system was the low female-to-male wage ratio in agriculture in the New England area. This argument was introduced by Claudia Goldin and Ken Sokoloff, and it has been buttressed by Lee Craig and Elizabeth Field-Hendry.[2] By contrast, the female-to-male wage ratio was higher and more steady in the South, which did not industrialize until much later. In the North, using the Waltham system, rapid advances in productivity in the mills raised the value and earnings of the women working there. The initially low female-to-male wage ratio rose as industries dominated by female labor experienced above-average productivity increases from 1815 to 1860. During these 45 years, female earnings rose from about one-third to nearly one-half of male wages. In short, low-cost female labor contributed significantly to the initiation of industrialization, and in turn, women's earnings in New England rose relative to men's in the antebellum period because

---

[1] From Kenneth L. Sokoloff, "Was the Transition from the Artisanal Shop to the Nonmechanized Factory Associated with Gains in Efficiency? Evidence from the U.S. Manufactures Censuses of 1820 and 1850," *Explorations in Economic History* 21 (1984): 357.

[2] See Lee A. Craig and Elizabeth B. Field-Hendrey, "Industrialization and the Earnings Gap: Regional and Sectoral Tests of the Goldin-Sokoloff Hypothesis," *Explorations in Economic History* 30 (1993): 60–80.

Child labor in spinning was common, especially in areas south of Boston; a family-based labor system known as the Rhode Island system *developed there.*

of industrialization. Moreover, by drawing women away from agriculture in the North, the Waltham system and other female work opportunities in industry increased the relative value and earnings of women who remained in farming. The weekly wage of farm women and hired farm "girls" more than doubled from 1830 to 1860.

Hours of work in the early factories were unbelievably long. A 12-hour day was considered reasonable, and half an hour off for meals was standard. From sunrise to sunset, it was possible to operate machinery without artificial light, and in wintertime, candles furnished enough illumination to permit operation into the evening. Because of the slow speeds of the early machines, the work pace was not great; for this reason, women and children could work 72 hours per week without physical breakdown.

The life of a New England textile worker was tiresome and drab, although it was not noticeably worse than the life of a poor New England farmer, whose dawn-to-dusk regimen left little time for pleasure and other pursuits. As noted, the factory offered young women an escape from the low pay, boredom, and isolation of farm life. Their next best alternative for work (Economic Reasoning Proposition 2) was typically farm work or to join their mothers in handweaving or making straw hats, palmleaf hats, or shoes. Taking another perspective, New England factory workers generally escaped the harshness subjected to English workers during the first decades of the factory system. Undoubtedly, largely because of greater labor scarcity, American manufacturers were compelled to maintain a certain standard of decency

TABLE 11.3 Average Yearly Immigration by Origin, 1845–1860 (in thousands)

YEAR	TOTAL	GREAT BRITAIN	IRELAND	GERMANY	OTHER
1845–1850	233	34	107	66	26
1851–1855	350	47	139	129	35
1856–1860	170	38	44	61	27

Source: Historical Statistics *(Washington, D.C.: Government Printing Office, 1958), Series C, 88–114.*

to attract and hold the labor they wanted. Nor does evidence show that American factory owners were as cruel to children as some English employers.

It was in the cities that the most negative aspects of industrialization were first witnessed, both in England and the United States. The worst conditions were in the so-called sweatshops, where workers worked 14 to 16 hours a day in the garment industries of New York, Philadelphia, and Boston. And common laborers who sold their services to transportation companies, urban building contractors, or factory and mill owners found themselves in an unenviable position when stiff competition from immigrant labor retarded the growth of real wages. For most workers, however, the antebellum period was one of rising wages and higher standards of material well-being.

THE IMPACT OF IMMIGRATION

Similar to current changes in the labor force, mainly from Asian and Hispanic immigrants, further composition changes came from immigration. As shown in Table 11.3, the large waves of immigrants who arrived in the 1840s and 1850s came principally from three countries: England, Ireland, and Germany. A steady stream of immigrants from England flowed into the United States until the decade of the Civil War; the Irish and the Germans came in ever-increasing numbers through the mid-1850s, repelled by conditions at home and attracted by economic opportunities in a new land. The tragic potato famine of 1845 to 1847 precipitated the heavy Irish emigration. Fleeing starvation and the oppression of hated absentee landlords, the Irish found employment as common laborers and factory hands. (As many American laborers moved west to join the gold rush, opportunities opened up for the new arrivals.) The census of 1850 reported nearly one million Irish in the United States, 40 percent of them in large cities, where their "shanty towns" became the notorious slums of the era. The Germans came a little later, following the failure of the democratic and nationalistic revolutions of 1848. Within 15 years, 1.3 million had arrived. Most Germans, having a little capital, settled on farms in the Midwest, but almost one-third of them swelled the populations of booming cities such as Cincinnati, Chicago, Milwaukee, and St. Louis. Immigration was also having its effects on the sexual composition of the labor force. By 1860, women constituted only one-fifth of the manufacturing labor force, indicating the lessening relative importance of textile manufacture and the competition of cheap immigrant labor, most of which was male. As it is today, this was a period of significant change in women's social roles, but then the trend was toward domestic pursuits. The cotton textile industry still employed the most females (many of whom were children); the clothing and shoe industries were second and third in this respect, ahead of woolen textiles. Nevertheless, as Pamela Nickless has shown, despite the transition in the late 1840s from predominantly women workers to male Irish workers, the advance of labor productivity in the textile mills remained high and steady, averaging 4.5 percent annually between 1836 and 1860.[3] Moreover, the slums and initial poor labor opportunities for Irish and other immigrants did not lock them into poverty. Upward

[3]Pamela J. Nickless, "Changing Labor Productivity and the Utilization of Native Women Workers in the American Cotton Textile Industry, 1825–1860," *Journal of Economic History* 38 (1978): 288.

TABLE 11.4 Indexes of Real Wages for Adult Males in Northeastern Manufacturing by Geographic Area, Urbanization, and Size of Firm, 1820 to 1860

WEIGHTED[a]	1820	1832	1850	1860	PER ANNUM GROWTH RATE, 1820–1860
Middle Atlantic	100	122–143	159–202	157–188	1.2–1.6
Rural	90	118–139	131–166	166–199	1.6–2.1
Urban	111	150–176	165–209	154–185	0.8–1.3
Major urban	115	—	171–217	151–180	0.7–1.2
Small	81	93–108	129–163	140–168	1.4–1.9
Medium	106	128–151	142–180	163–195	1.1–1.6
Large	110	123–144	171–216	159–190	0.9–1.2
New England	101	131–154	149–188	164–197	1.3–1.7
Rural	95	133–156	143–181	156–187	1.3–1.8
Urban[b]	110	130–153	150–190	165–198	1.2–1.5
Major urban	122	170–200	154–195	182–218	1.0–1.5
Small[c]	90	125–147	159–201	172–206	1.7–2.2
Medium	99	127–149	152–193	163–195	1.3–1.8
Large	110	133–157	146–185	164–196	1.0–1.5
Total	101	128–150	155–197	159–191	1.2–1.6

[a] *Weighted averages are weighted by number of employees in each group.*
[b] *Urban firms are those located in counties with a city of 10,000 or more; major urban, the same for 25,000 or more.*
[c] *Small firms, 1 to 5 workers; medium, 6 to 15; large, 16 or more.*

Source: *Kenneth L. Sokoloff and Georgia C. Villaflor, "The Market for Manufacturing Workers during the Early Industrialization: The American Northeast, 1820 to 1860," in* Strategic Factors in Nineteenth Century American Economic History: A Volume to Honor Robert W. Fogel, *eds. Claudia Goldin and Hugh Rockoff (Chicago: University of Chicago Press, 1992), 36.*

mobility and wealth accumulation accompanying changes in jobs and location by the immigrants improved their well-being.[4]

THE WAGES OF MALE LABOR IN MANUFACTURING

Although female earnings rose relative to men's in the antebellum period, the average wages of adult males working in manufacturing concerns in New England and the Middle Atlantic states grew dramatically between 1820 and 1860. Annual wage earnings of these workers averaged $267 in 1820, $292 in 1832, $341 in 1850, and $360 in 1860.[5] In today's money it would take about $7,400 to purchase the same amount of goods and services with the 1860 earnings.

Consumer prices fell between 1820 and the mid-1830s; then they rose, passing slightly above the 1820 level by the late 1830s. By the mid-1840s, prices had fallen below the mid-1830s floor. Then they rose again in the early 1850s.To account for these fluctuations, we must adjust the money wages by a consumer price index; this will show the changes in wages of constant purchasing power. Table 11.4 provides these adjustments and shows indexes of real wages for adult males by geographic area, level of urbanization, and firm size. For all workers together (bottom row), real wages grew between 60 and 90 percent (101 to 159 or 191) from 1820 to 1860; on average, wages rose between 1.2 and 1.6 percent per year.

[4]See Joseph P. Ferrie, "The Wealth Accumulation of Antebellum Immigrants to the U.S., 1840–60," *The Journal of Economic History* 54 (1994): 1–33.

[5]See Kenneth L. Sokoloff and Georgia C. Villaflor, "The Market for Manufacturing Workers during the Early Industrialization, the American Northeast 1820–1860," in *Strategic Factors in Nineteenth Century American Economic History: A Volume to Honor Robert W. Fogel,* ed. Claudia Goldin and Hugh Rockoff (Chicago: University of Chicago Press, 1992), 36.

LIBRARY OF CONGRESS

Women, whose wages were far below men's, made up a large portion of the early industrial labor force. Women's earnings began to close that gap by the end of the antebellum era.

Close inspection of Table 11.4 reveals many important features of workers' earnings. The period of fastest growth of real wages was between 1820 and 1832—a range of 2.2 to 3.7 percent per annum, depending on place and firm size. Between 1832 and 1850, the pace of advance slowed to between 1.1 and 1.5 percent. Little gain in real wages in manufacturing occurred during the 1850s.

Wages were at about the same levels in New England as in the Middle Atlantic states, and they grew at about the same rate. This reveals a labor market of workers and employers who were responsive (as sellers and buyers at the margin) and who moved and/or offered terms that arbitraged away geographic wage differences. In monetary (not real) terms, annual manufacturing wages in New England were only about 1 percent higher than in the Middle Atlantic states in 1820. This difference was still only 5 percent by 1860.

From Table 11.4, we see that in 1820, manufacturing workers in rural areas earned less than those in urban areas, who in turn earned less than those in major urban areas. A similar relation for 1820 is seen in the earnings among workers by size of firm: the larger the firm, the more the pay. But this was no longer true by 1860. Rural manufacturing real wages grew faster than urban wages, and the earnings in smaller firms rose faster than in larger firms.

Here again we see the erosion of wage gaps. Improvements in transportation enhanced labor mobility and made both product and labor markets more competitive. As navigable waterways spread and improved and railroads advanced, markets became more integrated, and wage rates converged. These market forces had disproportionately large effects on the rural areas and outlying hinterlands, pulling them into the market and affording them opportunities for specialization.

English–American Wage Gaps

Although wage gaps among the industrializing states were low, transportation costs sustained significant wage gaps between England and the United States. When American industry started to develop in the early nineteenth century, the wages of adult laborers were much higher in the United States than in England or other countries. Table 11.5, based on work by Nathan Rosenberg, shows pay differentials classified by various skills for the years 1820 through 1821. Across all skill categories listed, wages were higher in the United States than in England.

By and large, these pay differentials are attributable to the fact that a floor under the remuneration of labor in industry was set by rewards in agriculture. Well into the 1800s, there were no insuperable obstacles, either of distance or expense, to obtaining a fertile farm in the United States. Output per worker in agriculture was relatively high, and the course of agricultural technology in the early nineteenth century increased output per person. Moreover, farmers in America, who ordinarily owned their own land, received, in addition to their own wages and those of their families, elements of rent and profit that in England went to the landlord. Therefore, U.S. land abundance added to the apparent wage gap between American and English workers, making the income and/or wealth gap between typical workers larger than the wage gap.

International labor mobility, at least in the early nineteenth century, failed to close these observed wage differentials. Sharp increases in immigration in the late 1830s and throughout the 1840s and 1850s led to a narrowing of the wage differential between American and English labor; even so, the floor for U.S. industrial wages was, according to a consensus of voluminous testimony, still relatively high in 1860.

Skilled–Unskilled Wage Ratios

More important perhaps, from the perspective of free American workers, was the change in relative wages among various "grades" or skill levels. During the first decades of the nineteenth century, as throughout most of the colonial period, the premiums paid for artisan skills in the United States were typically less than those paid in England. By "premiums" we mean the extra amounts paid to skilled labor above wages paid to unskilled labor. Skilled American workers typically earned more than skilled British workers, but the skilled-to-unskilled U.S. wage ratio was lower than the skilled-to-unskilled English wage ratio. However, the evidence in Table 11.5 shows that this was not uniformly true. The lower ratio is most clearly evident in the machine makers skill category when compared with common or farm labor.

TABLE 11.5 Wage Differentials by Skill between England and the United States, 1820 to 1821 (English wage = 100)

WORKERS	U.S. WAGES
Skilled	
Carpenter	150
Mason	147
Best machine makers, forgers, etc.	77 to 90
Ordinary machine makers	114 to 129
Unskilled	
Common laborer	135
Farm laborer	123 to 154
Servant, maid	149 to 224
Common mule spinners in cotton mills	106 to 137
Common mule spinners in woolen mills	115
Weavers on hand looms	122
Women in cotton mills	102 to 153
Women in woolen mills	128
Boys 10 to 12 years old	115

Source: Adapted from Nathan Rosenberg, "Anglo-American Wage Differences in the 1820s," Journal of Economic History *27 (1967): 226.*

TABLE 11.6 Ratios of Daily Wages of Machinists to Common Laborers in Urban Massachusetts, 1825–1860

YEAR	PERCENT
1825	150%
1831–1840	156
1837	185
1845	169
1841–1850	190
1851–1860	220

Source: C. D. Wright, Comparative Wages, Price, and Cost of Living *(Boston: Wright & Potter, 1889), 22, 54, and 55. As quoted in Jeffrey G. Williamson and Peter H. Lindert,* American Inequality: A Macroeconomic History *(New York: Academic Press, 1980), 71.*

The relatively low premium paid for skilled labor in early nineteenth-century America resulted primarily from the greater pulling power of agricultural expansion on unskilled labor and the higher proportion of skilled British immigrants entering the United States before mass immigration began.[6]

By the 1820s, however, this skill premium began to advance. For example, Table 11.6 shows the ratio of machinists' daily wages to those of common laborers in urban Massachusetts during the antebellum period. See Economic Insight 11.1 on page 214 to explore questions raised by this trend. Although these widening pay differentials may have varied somewhat regionally, they generally represented a broad pattern of advance.[7]

GROWING INEQUALITY OF INCOME

Advancing pay differentials may have contributed to a growing sense of class consciousness. They certainly contributed to increased inequality of income and wealth. According to evidence on wealth trends provided by Jeffrey Williamson and Peter Lindert, we find that between 1774 and 1860 wealth concentrations grew significantly. Growing inequality was a sharp break with the stable (but unequal) pattern of aggregate wealth concentration prevalent during the colonial period. In 1774, 12.6 percent of total assets were held by the top 1 percent of free wealth holders, and the richest 10 percent held slightly less than half of total assets. By 1860, the wealthiest 1 percent held 29 percent of U.S. total assets, while the top 10 percent held 73 percent.[8] In short, the share held by the richest 1 percent more than doubled, and that of the top decile jumped by almost half of its previous level. Williamson and Lindert emphasize their broad impact: "the movement toward wealth concentration occurred within regions, just as it seems to have occurred within given age groups, among native and foreign born, and within rural and urban populations."[9] Further work by Jeremy Atack and Fred Bateman adds to this perspective, demonstrating that in 1860, wealth was more equally distributed in northern rural areas than in the cities or in the rural South.

Thomas Jefferson's egalitarian dream of a strong, free democratic nation of contented individualistic small farmers was a vision shared by others. But the forces of the Industrial Revolution had leaped the Atlantic from Great Britain. The famed traveler and

[6]See H. J. Habakkuk, *American and British Technology in the Nineteenth Century* (Cambridge: Cambridge University Press, 1962).

[7]For further evidence on this point, see Jeffrey G. Williamson and Peter H. Lindert, *American Inequality: A Macroeconomic History* (New York: Academic Press, 1980), 70–75. For work challenging this view and based on labor contracts at military installations, see Robert A. Margo and Georgia C. Villaflor, "The Growth of Wages in Antebellum America: New Evidence," *Journal of Economic History* 47 (1987): 837–896.

[8]Williamson and Lindert, *American Inequality*, 36.

[9]Ibid., 46.

commentator Alexis de Tocqueville warned in 1839 of the growing concentrations of wealth. He feared that the rise of an industrial elite would destroy the basis of American egalitarianism:

> I am of the opinion . . . that the manufacturing aristocracy which is growing up under our eyes is one of the harshest that ever existed . . . the friends of democracy should keep their eyes anxiously fixed in this direction; for if a permanent inequality of conditions and aristocracy . . . penetrates into [America] it may be predicted that this is the gate by which they will enter.[10]

American egalitarianism in terms of economic end results (income or wealth) was only a dream, then as now. But the Industrial Revolution and advance in the rate of economic growth before the Civil War were engines of opportunity for many, albeit not equally. As with other economies undergoing the transformation from an agrarian to an industrializing society, the U.S. transition generated greater inequality. The poor did not get poorer, but their advance was slower than the gains of the richer members of society.

THE EARLY UNION MOVEMENT

The rise in the numbers of workers in manufacturing paralleled growing activities by workers to organize for their benefits. Some have argued that the origin of the labor movement and the original labor–management problem sprang from the separation of workers from their tools. It is claimed that artisans, who owned their trade implements, lost their identity and independence when employer capitalists furnished the equipment. Like most generalizations, this one has its uses, but it may lead to false inferences. Economic Reasoning Proposition 5 applies here. The Industrial Revolution placed great numbers of laborers in a position of uncertainty and insecurity, making them depend on the vagaries of economic fluctuations and the mercy of employers. Yet the first impetus to a genuine labor movement was furnished by workers who were by no means separated from their tools. Craftsmen in Philadelphia, New York, and Boston founded craft labor societies in the 1790s, the prototypes of modern unions. Most of these societies were established in the hopes of securing increases in real wages (i.e., of pushing up monetary wages faster than the prices of consumer goods), although attempts were also made to gain shorter working hours, to establish and maintain a closed shop, and to regulate the conditions of apprenticeship. Invariably, there was considerable fraternal motivation as well to these societies, as people who made a living in the same way easily forged a social bond. In nearly all the major cities, shoemakers (cordwainers) and printers were among the first to form "workingmen's societies"; carpenters, masons, hatters, riggers, and tailors also found it worthwhile to organize. Again, these organizations were separated by craft and initiated by skilled workers (Economic Reasoning Proposition 1).

Legal Setbacks and Gains

The early craft societies were typically transitory, the longest-maintained union being the Philadelphia Cordwainers (1794–1806). Cyclical economic downturns routinely dissolved worker collective actions, and wage reductions, though resisted, were common during downturns in the economy. A more steady deterrent to unionization came from court actions. Conservative judges, in their instructions to juries, contended that union action per se was illegal. Societies of workers were considered conspiracies under English common law, a conspiracy being defined as "a confederacy of two or more, by indirect means to injure an individual or to do any act, which is unlawful or prejudicial to the community."

[10]As quoted in Ibid., 37–38.

Economic Insight 11.1

The Antebellum Labor Market

Two features of the antebellum labor market beg for more explicit economic analysis: first, why did the rapid rise in early nineteenth-century real wages in U.S. manufacturing slow to nearly zero in the 1850s (Table 11.4). Second, why did skilled wages rise relative to unskilled wages between 1830 and 1860 (Table 11.6). Supply and demand will serve as our analytical guide, and we can add demographic evidence to support the hypotheses empirically.

Figure 11.2 addresses the first question. Before 1850, demand shifts exceeded the supply shifts, and wages rose. After 1850, the supply increase was larger than normal. The supply shift was approximately the same as the demand shift, and wages changed little if at all.

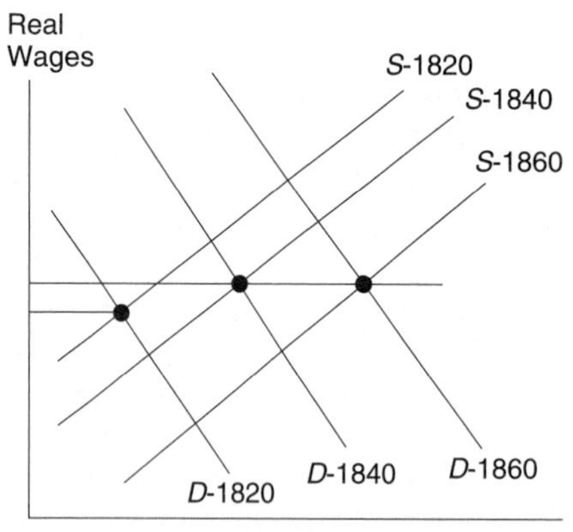

FIGURE 11.2 The Market for Manufacturing Workers

Figure 11.3 addresses the second question. While both the supply and demand for skilled and unskilled labor grew dramatically over the period, the growth in the supply of unskilled labor (*S*-1840 to *S*-1860, Fig. 11.3B) accelerated in the 1840s and 1850s and grew relative to the supply of skilled labor (*S*-1840 to *S*-1860, Fig. 11.3A). This lowered the wages of unskilled workers relative to those of skilled workers.

We now turn to the demographic evidence. The population data given in Table 11.7 reveal dramatic gains. The underlying rate of advance in the totals is 3.3 percent per annum. No European nation at the time showed anything like this rate of advance, not even by half. In addition, the bulge in immigration occurred after 1840 (see Figure 11.1, page 204). From Table 11.7 we see that immigration accounted for only 3.0 percent per annum of population growth, 1820–1825, but was 25–31 percent 1845–1860.

The combined effects of natural increases and immigration raised the average (median) age of the population from 16 to 19 and swelled the proportion of people in their working years and in the labor force. Between 1820 and 1860, the ratio of gainfully employed to total population grew from 33 to 36 percent—a gain of 9 percent (3/33rds). Moreover, the proportion of people

Economic Insight 11.1

The Antebellum Labor Market, continued

living in urban places more than doubled between 1820 and 1850 and nearly doubled between 1840 and 1860 (Table 11.7).The demographic evidence is consistent with the wage changes observed. Consistency, however, is not proof of causation. Other hypotheses may also explain the record. Recall Economic Reasoning Proposition 5.

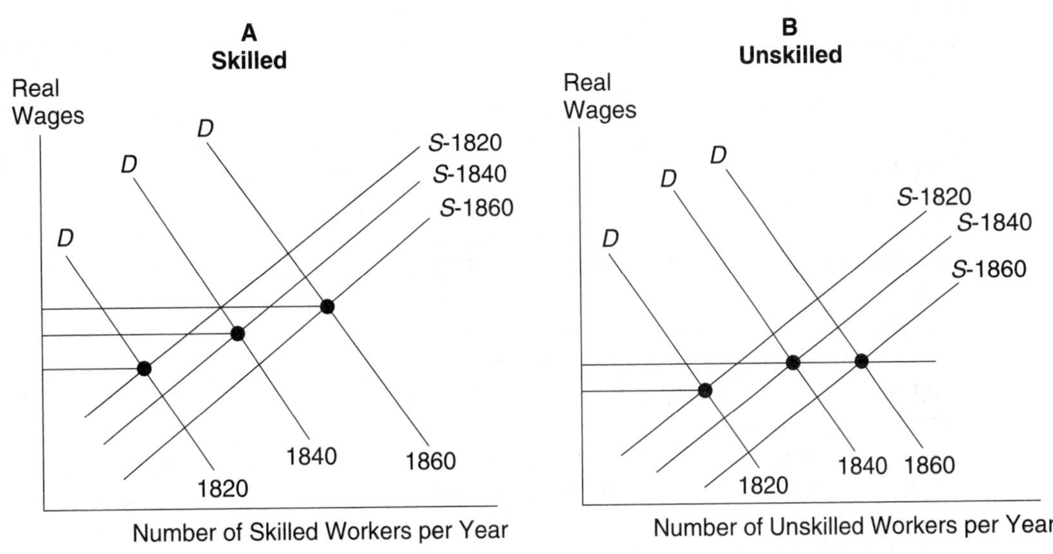

FIGURE 11.3 The Market for Manufacturing Workers Separated by Skill

TABLE 11.7 Basic Population Data, 1790–1860

YEAR	POPULATION (IN MILLIONS) TOTAL	WHITE	NONWHITE	PERCENTAGES NONWHITE	URBAN	NET IMMIGRANTS' SHARE OF POPULATION CHANGE IN PREVIOUS DECADE
1790	3.9	3.2	0.7	17.9	5.2	n.a.
1800	5.3	4.3	1.0	18.9	6.1	n.a.
1810	7.2	5.9	1.3	18.1	7.3	3.3
1820	9.6	7.9	1.8	18.8	7.2	2.1
1830	12.9	10.5	2.3	17.8	11.7	3.8
1840	17.1	14.2	2.9	17.0	10.8	11.7
1850	23.3	19.6	3.6	15.5	15.2	23.3
1860	31.5	26.9	4.5	14.3	19.4	31.1

Source: Historical Statistics *(Washington, D.C.: Government Printing Office, 1960), series A2, 45, 46, and 195.*

A doctrine developed in England during the late Middle Ages was thus applied some 500 years later to restrict the unionization of craftspeople. In the famous case of the Pittsburgh Cordwainers in 1815, the judge contended that both the master shoemakers and the journeymen were coerced:

> No shoemaker dare receive one who worked under price, or who was not a member of the society. No master workman must give him any employment, under the penalty of losing all his workmen. Moreover, a conspiracy to prevent a man from freely exercising his trade, or particular profession, in a particular place, is endictable. Also, it is an endictable offense, to conspire to compel men to become members of a particular association, or to contribute towards it.[11]

The jury in this case agreed that the master shoemakers, the journeymen, and the public were endangered by the association of journeymen and returned a verdict of guilty of conspiracy, although the court fined the defendants only $1 each, plus prosecution costs.

Later judgments sustained this legal perspective until the famous case of *Commonwealth v. Hunt.* In the fall of 1840, Hunt and other members of the Boston Bootmakers' Society were hauled into municipal court for attempting to enforce a closed shop. Again, after a strict charge from a judge who felt that such union activities could lead only to a "frightful despotism," the accused were convicted. The case was appealed to the supreme court of the Commonwealth of Massachusetts, and in 1842, Chief Justice Lemuel Shaw handed down a monumental decision that set a precedent on one point and opened the way to more liberal decisions on another. First, he held that a combination of union members was not criminal unless the object of the combination was criminal; the mere fact of organization implied no illegal conspiracy. Second, he asserted the doctrine that union members were within their rights in pressing for a closed shop and in striking to maintain union security. Justice Shaw was not a radical, nor was he particularly sympathetic with labor's cause, but he was well aware of the economic realities that were pressing labor to act collectively. This decision did not mean that trade unions were free from further court confrontations, but there were no more serious efforts to make the mere fact of organization a criminal offense, and there would henceforth be some reticence about presuming that the use of any and all weapons of the trade unions were socially harmful.

Organizational Gains

Judge Shaw's decision brought no immediate revival of unions, however; the long, deep slump from the late 1830s through the early 1840s had wiped out most of the societies that had formed in the craft union resurgence of 1824 to 1837. Workingmen's societies made a comeback in the 1850s (with setbacks in the recession years of 1854 and 1857), but it is important to remember that before 1860, union members never exceeded 1 percent of the total labor force. Factory workers, field hands, slaves, and domestic workers were almost completely outside the union movement. The primary early beneficiaries of workingmen's organizations were labor's minority elite, the craftsmen. Their unions were important, however, in that they established two concrete organizational advances for labor as a movement, as well as a series of political advances.

First, labor learned the technique of bargaining collectively, and aggressive unions began to use the weapons of the strike and boycott with skill and daring. The closed shop—an agreement whereby membership in a recognized union is made a condition of employment—was

---

[11] Quoted in J. R. Commons, *A Documentary History of American Industrial Society*, Vol. 4 (Glendale, Calif.: Clark), 82, 83.

soon tested as an instrument for maintaining union security. The benevolent and protective aims of labor organizations tended to disappear, and militancy replaced early hesitance and reluctance to act.

Second, the rapidly increasing number of individual societies began to coalesce. Local federations and then national organizations appeared. In 1827, unions of different crafts in Philadelphia federated to form a "city central" or "trades' union," the Mechanics' Union of Trade Associations. Six years later the societies in New York established a General Trades' Union. In the next three years, city centrals were formed in several major cities—not, as might be supposed from the modern functions of such organizations, to exchange information or engage in political activities, but for the more pressing purpose of aiding individual unions engaged in battle with employers. Attempts at organization on a national scale followed. In 1834, the General Trades' Union, New York's city central, called a national convention of these city federations, which resulted in the foundation of a National Trades' Union. At the same time, some of the craft societies began to see the advantages to be gained from a national organization along strict craft lines, and in 1835 and 1836, no less than five national unions of this type were established. The strongest of these were formed by the shoemakers and the printers.

POLITICAL GAINS FOR COMMON WORKING PEOPLE

Suffrage

As discussed in Perspective 11.1 on page 218, one of the most significant political gains for workers was the broadening of suffrage, the right to vote. In the first decades of U.S. history, a person had to own a minimum amount of real property or pay a certain amount in taxes in order to have a voice in political affairs. The struggle for voting privileges took place in the original 13 states; only 4 of the new states entering the Union placed no property or tax payment qualifications on the right for an adult male to vote. By the late 1820s, suffrage had been extended sufficiently to enable working men to participate in the elections of the populous states. First to disappear was the property-owning requirement; by 1821, only five states retained it. Five states still set a tax-paying restriction 30 years later, but it was purely nominal.[12] Generally speaking, by 1860, white male citizens of the United States could vote, black males could vote in New York and New England, and alien males could vote in the agricultural Northwest.

Public Education

Although she could not vote herself, Fanny Wright effectively worked tirelessly for reforms in education. Except in New England, children of the poor received little or no education; and even in New England the early training was of poor quality and exhibited a religious slant that many opposed. Wright and her followers proposed that the state establish boarding schools for the education of rich and poor children alike, where class distinction would be eliminated. Others, less radical, proposed a simple plan of free public schools. By the mid-1830s, progress had been made to broaden educational opportunity; Albert Fishlow (see his J. E. H. article from 1966) has shown that by midcentury, nearly 1 percent of GNP was spent on education (compared with almost 8 percent today). Public common schools were most prevalent in the North, where political concern and efforts were greatest. Recall Economic Reasoning Proposition 1.

[12] Comparing the votes for president with the total population, we find that there were two large jumps in the electorate: from 1824 to 1828 (3.2 percent to 9.3 percent) and from 1836 to 1840 (9.6 percent to 13.6 percent).

Perspective 11.1

Gains in the Right to Vote

The gains in the right to vote being won by American male adults were also being won elsewhere, notably in France and England, two other nations leading in the path to industrialization. France led the way, as shown in Table 11.8, partly due to forces stemming from the French Revolution near the turn of the century. France was the first democracy to grant the secret ballot and 100 percent adult male suffrage, with Germany and the United States following by a couple of decades. France also was the leader in women's suffrage (1845), all others lagging by three-quarters of a century or more.

TABLE 11.8 Laws on Suffrage

	SECRET BALLOT OBTAINED	WOMEN GAIN VOTE	100% MALE SUFFRAGE	PROPORTION OF POPULATION VOTING IN 1900
United States	1849	1920	1870	18.4
United Kingdom	1872	1918	1948	16.2
Germany	1848	1919	1872	15.5
France	1831	1845	1848	28.2
Argentina	1912	1947	1912	1.8
Brazil	1932	1932	1988	3.0
Chile	—	1949	1970	4.2
Peru	1931	1955	1979	—
Venezuela	1946	1945	1946	—
Costa Rica	1925	1949	1913	—

Debts, Military Service, and Jail

In the minds of the working people, the most needed reform, next to that of the educational system, was the abolition of imprisonment for debt. Thousands of citizens were jailed annually for failure to meet obligations of a few dollars, and there was understandably fierce resentment against this injustice. The unfairness of the militia systems of the several states, which favored the rich, rankled in the hearts of the poor who were faced with the alternatives of a term in the service or a term in jail. These and other objectives—removing the competition of convict labor and obtaining the right to file liens on the property of employers for back wages—inflamed the spirits of great numbers of laborers, small businessmen, and professional people with a high degree of social consciousness. The militia system did eventually become less onerous, mechanics' lien laws were passed in many states, and imprisonment for debt was outlawed in most jurisdictions. Recall Economic Reasoning Propositions 1, 2, and 4. But this first movement lost momentum after 1832, as labor turned its energies during the ensuing period of prosperity to advancing the cause of unionization, which in turn collapsed in 1837.

The Ten-Hour Day

Although later movements and colorful episodes of the 1840s and 1850s were characterized by impractical utopian schemes (proposed and led by Robert Owen, Charles Fourier, and George Henry Evans), one movement of the mid-century gained quick relief for workers:

the struggle for the 10-hour day. That goal was set as early as 1835, but there was then no serious prospect of attaining it. Hope rose in 1840 when Martin Van Buren set a 10-hour day for federal employees. Craftspeople in some trades already worked no longer than 10 hours, but factory operatives still labored 12 to 14 hours a day. In the mid-1840s, New England factory workers added to the agitation for shorter hours. In 1847, the New Hampshire legislature passed the first regulatory law setting a 10-hour upper limit for a day's work, but there was a loophole in it. The law provided that if workers agreed to work longer hours, the 10-hour limit might be exceeded. Threatened with discharge if they did not agree, factory hands found themselves no better off. Statutes passed by other state legislatures followed the same pattern, except that laws limiting the workday of children to 10 hours did not contain the hated "contract" clause.

Perhaps the most important effect of the agitation for regulatory acts was the pressure of public opinion thereby exerted on employers. Many large factories voluntarily established 11-hour days. By 1860, a 10-hour day was standard in all the craft trades, and already a new standard of 8 hours was being timorously suggested.

SELECTED REFERENCES AND SUGGESTED READINGS

Adams, Donald R., Jr. "Wage Rates in the Early National Period: Philadelphia, 1785–1830." *Journal of Economic History* 28 (1968): 404–426.

———. "Wage Rates in the Iron Industry: A Comment." *Explorations in Economic History* 11 (Fall 1973): 89–94.

Craig, Lee A., and Elizabeth B. Field-Hendrey. "Industrialization and the Earnings Gap: Regional and Sectoral Tests of the Goldin-Sokoloff Hypothesis." *Explorations in Economic History* 30 (1993): 60–80.

Crowther, Simon J. "Urban Growth in the Mid-Atlantic States, 1785–1850." *Journal of Economic History* 36 (1976): 624–644.

Dawley, Allan. *Class and Community: The Industrial Revolution in Lynn.* Cambridge, Mass.: Harvard University Press, 1976.

Dublin, Thomas. *Women at Work: The Transformation of Work and Community in Lowell, Massachusetts, 1826–1860.* New York: Columbia University Press, 1979.

Dunlevy, James A., and Henry A. Gemery. "Economic Opportunity and the Responses of Old and New Migrants to the United States." *Journal of Economic History* 38 (1978): 901–917.

Fishlow, Albert. "The Common School Revival: Fact or Fancy?" In *Industrialization in Two Systems*, ed. Henry Rosovsky. New York: Wiley, 1966.

———. "Levels of Nineteenth-Century American Investment in Education." *Journal of Economic History* 26 (1966): 418–436.

Goldin, C. *Understanding the Gender Gap: An Economic History of American Women.* New York: Oxford University Press, 1990.

Goldin, C., and K. Sokoloff. "Women, Children, and Industrialization in the Early Republic: Evidence from the Manufacturing Censuses." *Journal of Economic History* 42 (1982): 741–774.

Gutman, Herbert. *Work, Culture, and Society in Industrializing America.* New York: Knopf, 1977.

Habakkuk, H. J. *American and British Technology in the Nineteenth Century.* Cambridge: Cambridge University Press, 1962.

Haines, Michael R. "The Population of the United States, 1790–1920." In *The Cambridge Economic History of the United States*, Vol. II, *The Long Nineteenth Century*, eds. Stanley L. Engerman and Robert E. Gallman, 143–205. New York: Cambridge University Press, 2000.

Higgs, Robert. "Mortality in Rural America." *Explorations in Economic History* 10 (Winter 1973): 177–196.

Lebergott, Stanley. *Manpower in Economic Growth: The American Record since 1800.* New York: McGraw-Hill, 1964.

———. "Labor Force." In *American Economic Growth: An Economist's History of the United States*, ed. Lance E. Davis et al. New York: Harper & Row, 1972.

Leet, Don R. "The Determinants of the Fertility Transition in Antebellum Ohio." *Journal of Economic History* 36 (1976): 359–378.

———. "Interrelations of Population Density, Urbanization, Literacy, and Fertility." *Explorations in Economic History* (October 1977): 388–401.

Lindstrom, Diane. "American Economic Growth before 1840: New Evidence and New Directions." *Journal of Economic History* 39 (1979): 289–302.

Margo, Robert A. "The Labor Force in the Nineteenth Century." In *The Cambridge Economic History of the United States*, Vol. II, *The Long Nineteenth Century*, eds. Stanley L. Engerman and Robert E. Gallman. New York: Cambridge University Press, 2000, 207–243.

———. *Wages and Labor Markets in the United States, 1820–1860.* Chicago: University of Chicago Press for the NBER, 2000.

Margo, Robert A., and Georgia C. Villaflor. "The Growth of Wages in Antebellum America: New Evidence." *Journal of Economic History* 47 (1987): 873–896.

Neal, Larry, and Paul Uselding. "Immigration: A Neglected Source of American Economic Growth: 1790 to 1912." *Oxford Economic Papers* 24, 2d series (March 1972).

Nickless, Pamela J. "Changing Labor Productivity and the Utilization of Native Women Workers in the American Cotton Textile Industry, 1825–1866." *Journal of Economic History* 38 (1978): 287–288.

Pessen, Edward. *Most Uncommon Jacksonians: The Radical Leaders of the Early Labor Movement.* Albany: State University of New York Press, 1967.

Potter, J. "The Growth of Population in America, 1700–1860." In *Population in History*, eds. D. V. Glass and D. E. C. Eversley. New York: Aldine, 1965.

Rosenberg, Nathan. "Anglo-American Wage Differences in the 1820s." *Journal of Economic History* 27 (1967): 221–229.

Ross, Steven J. *Workers on the Edge: Work, Leisure, and Politics in Industrializing Cincinnati, 1788–1890.* New York: Columbia University Press, 1985.

Rostow, W.W. *The Stages of Economic Growth.* Cambridge: Cambridge University Press, 1961.

Rothenberg, Winifred B. "The Emergence of Farm Labor Markets and the Transformation of the Rural Economy: Massachusetts, 1750–1855." *Journal of Economic History* 48 (1988): 537–566.

Smith, Merritt R. *Harpers Ferry Armory and the New Technology: The Challenge of Change.* Ithaca, N.Y.: Cornell University Press, 1977.

Sokoloff, Kenneth L. "Was the Transition from Artisanal Shop to the Nonmechanized Factory Associated with Gains in Efficiency? Evidence from the U.S. Manufactures Censuses of 1820 and 1850." *Explorations in Economic History* 21 (1984): 351–382.

Soltow, Lee. "Economic Inequality in the United States in the Period from 1790 to 1860." *Journal of Economic History* 31 (1971): 822–839.

Steckel, Richard H. "Antebellum Southern White Fertility: A Demographic and Economic Analysis." *Journal of Economic History* 40 (1980): 331–350.

Sundstrom, William A., and Paul David. "Socioeconomic Determinants of Interstate Fertility Differentials in the United States in 1850 and 1860." *Journal of Interdisciplinary History* 6 (1976): 375–396.

———. "Old-Age Security Motives and Farm Family Fertility in Antebellum America." *Explorations in Economic History* 25 (1988): 164–197.

U.S. Bureau of the Census is a source of historical statistics on population, **http://www.census.gov**.

Uselding, Paul. "Conjectural Estimates of Gross Human Capital Inflow to the American Economy." *Explorations in Economic History* 9 (Fall 1971): 49–62.

Vinovskis, Maris. "Mortality Rates and Trends in Massachusetts before 1860." *Journal of Economic History* 32 (1972): 184–213.

Williamson, Jeffrey. "American Prices and Urban Inequality since 1820." *Journal of Economic History* 36 (June 1976).

Williamson, Jeffrey G., and Peter H. Lindert. *American Inequality: A Macroeconomic History.* New York: Academic Press, 1980.

Yang, Donghvu. "Notes on the Wealth Distribution of Farm Households in the United States, 1860: A New Look at Two Manuscript Census Samples." *Explorations in Economic History* 21 (January 1984): 88–102.

Yasuba, Yasukichi. *Birth Rates of the White Population of the United States, 1800–1860: An Economic Analysis.* Baltimore: Johns Hopkins University Press, 1962.

Zabler, Jeffrey F. "Further Evidence on American Wage Differentials, 1800–1830." *Explorations in Economic History* 10 (Fall 1972): 109–118.

———."More on Wage Rates in the Iron Industry: A Reply." *Explorations in Economic History* 11 (Fall 1973): 95–99.

Chapter Twelve

Money and Banking in the Developing Economy

After the Constitution was ratified, the new nation faced the problem of establishing a legal framework for its monetary system. But there was little agreement on how best to achieve the ultimate goals of a monetary unit of stable purchasing power and a banking system that was sound yet liberal in supplying credit. This chapter describes the many experiments tried by the young republic in the pursuit of these elusive goals. These experiments had at the time important consequences for the economy, and they permanently influenced Americans' beliefs about how the financial system should be regulated. The chapter also describes the macroeconomic fluctuations—inflation, depressions, and financial crises—that affected the course of economic development.

THE AMERICAN MONETARY UNIT

Because international trade had made the dollar (a common name for the Spanish peso) and its subdivisions more plentiful than any other coins in the commercial centers along the American seaboard, it became customary to reckon accounts in terms of dollars (although some merchants used pounds, shillings, and pence and continued to do so long after independence). The dollar, therefore, was adopted as the unit of account and, fortunately for all of us, a decimal system of divisions was adopted rather than the arithmetically troublesome old English system of pounds, shillings (20 = 1 pound), and pence (12 = 1 shilling). Thomas Jefferson, who along with Robert Morris and Alexander Hamilton was most responsible for our adopting the decimal system, made the following cogent argument in his 1783 report to Congress:

> The easiest ratio of multiplication and division, is that by ten. Everyone knows the facility of Decimal Arithmetic. Everyone remembers, that, when learning Money-Arithmetic, he used to be puzzled with adding the farthings, taking out the fours and carrying them on; adding the pence, taking out the twelves and carrying them on; adding the shillings, taking out the twenties and carrying them on; but when he came to the pounds, where he had only tens to carry forward, it was easy and free from error. The bulk of mankind are schoolboys through life.[1]

[1] Paul Leicester Ford, ed., *The Writings of Thomas Jefferson* (New York: Putnam's, 1894), 446–447.

More important than the decision to decimalize the currency was the question of a standard. Would the currency's value be based on paper? Gold? Silver? Gold and silver? There was no interest in a paper standard. The inflationary experiences of the United States during the Revolution, and in some of the states under the Articles of Confederation, showed that paper standards were liable to abuse: The government could print too much. But it was harder to choose between the two great monetary metals, gold and silver. Ultimately it was decided to use both. Gold would add its prestige to the monetary system and serve in higher-denomination coins; silver would serve for smaller denominations.

Alexander Hamilton, the first Secretary of the Treasury, pointed out that the dollar was, in fact, in general use in the states and that people everywhere would readily accept it as the monetary unit. The only difficulty, he said, was that Spanish dollars varied in their content of pure silver. He suggested that the pesos in circulation be assayed (tested) to see how much silver they contained. The number of grains of silver in the new U.S. dollar would simply be the average of that in the Spanish coins then circulating. Because gold was about 15 times as valuable as silver, gold coins need contain only one-fifteenth as much metal as silver coins of the same denomination. These ideas were ultimately translated into the Coinage Act of 1792. This decision for a bimetallic standard (both gold and silver) proved controversial over the three-quarters of a century during which it was maintained.

THE BIMETALLIC STANDARD

It is one thing to adopt a bimetallic standard and quite another to maintain it. The problem is that the relative values of gold and silver fluctuate. Thus, even though a mint ratio of 15 to 1 closely approximated the prevailing market ratio in 1792, world supplies of and demands for gold and silver were such that the ratio in the market rose gradually during the 1790s to about 15.5 to 1; by 1808, it was 16 to 1. A market ratio of 16 to 1 and a mint ratio of 15 to 1, technically, is a relationship in which gold is "undervalued" at the mint. Under such circumstances it paid to export gold coins, exchange them for silver in Europe, import the silver, and convert it into new coins at the mint.

For centuries, observers had noted this tendency for undervalued coins to be hoarded for export. One naturally paid out debased coins whenever it was possible to pass them off at their nominal value and held on to the undervalued coins. Popular sayings to the effect that "bad money drives out good money" or "cheap money will replace dear" thus came into use in various languages. Sir Thomas Gresham, Elizabeth I's master of the mint, is credited with analyzing this phenomenon, which has become known as *Gresham's law*. For our purposes, we may best state the law as follows: Money overvalued at the mint tends to drive out of circulation money undervalued at the mint, providing that the two monies circulate at fixed ratio.

In a well-known paper entitled "Gresham's Law or Gresham's Fallacy?" Arthur Rolnick and Warren Weber pointed out that if people were willing to use coins at their market values, there would be no reason for one coin to drive another out of circulation. For example, if people were willing to value one gold dollar at, say, $1.05 in silver coins, reflecting the market values of the metallic contents of the coins, both gold and silver could circulate side by side, even though gold was undervalued at the mint. But as Robert Greenfield and Hugh Rockoff, and George Selgin show, legal tender laws, custom, and convenience are powerful forces that tend to force the exchange of coins at their face (mint) values. In early nineteenth century America, it was easier for holders of gold coins to hoard them for export rather than to try to use them in everyday transactions at more than their face values. Recall Economic Reasoning Propositions 1 through 4.

The idea of Gresham's law incidentally is used (often somewhat loosely) in a wide variety of other situations. For example, some college professors worry that students will want to take easy courses because an A in an easy course counts just as much toward their grade point average as an A in a hard course: "Bad Courses Drive out Good." Gresham's law applies to college courses because of the difference between the way students and colleges value courses, just as it applies to coins when there is a difference between the way the market and the mint values the metal in the coins.

In June 1834, two acts were passed that changed the mint ratio to just a fraction over 16 to 1. Gold was then overvalued at the mint, and gold slowly began to replace silver, which was either hoarded or exported. The discovery of gold in California in 1848 accelerated the trend toward a pure gold circulation.

The international flows of metal under the bimetallic standard were a nuisance. Often coins in convenient denominations could not be had, and the coins that were available were badly worn. But the bimetallic standard also provided a major, if often overlooked, benefit. A change in the market ratio could reflect the slow growth of one metal, say, gold, relative to demand. If the country were tied solely to that metal, the general price level would fall. But under a bimetallic standard, the cheaper metal can replace the dear metal, thus helping to maintain the stock of money and the price level.

BANK NOTES AS PAPER MONEY

Although the Constitution forbade the states from issuing paper money, they did retain the power to create corporations. After the commercial boom beginning in 1793, special state charters established a large number of banks. These were entirely new institutions on the American scene, for commercial banks had not existed in the colonies. Before 1790 there had been only 3 banks, but by 1800, there were 20, and by 1811 there were 88. All but two were private, state-chartered banks empowered to issue their own paper money, redeemable in gold or silver.

In many ways, a bank note was similar to a bank deposit. When a bank made loans to its customers, it gave them the proceeds either in the form of its own notes, which then circulated as cash, or as a deposits on which they could write checks. Today, of course, banks no longer issue notes, and the Federal Reserve issues the paper money that passes from hand to hand; moreover, whenever a firm borrows money today, it takes the proceeds as a credit to its account. But during the years before the Civil War, and even for some time after that in rural areas, a bank issued notes much more frequently than it made credits to customers' accounts.

Typically, only bank notes issued by nearby banks were accepted at par. People arriving from a distant city would have to exchange their "foreign" bank notes for local money, and typically they would be charged a discount. They might get only $.97 in local money for each dollar of foreign money, a 3 percent discount. Note-brokers specialized in buying notes from distant banks, and "bank note reporters," publications that listed the discounts, aided them and other local merchants. Gary Gorton and Howard Bodenhorn have studied these discounts and found that the notes were priced much like short-term bonds in today's money market. Distance from the point of issue was the main determinant of the discount, but other factors also played a role. Typically, the notes of new banks were discounted more, as might be expected, with the discount falling as the bank established a reputation for soundness.

The system encouraged counterfeiting. By 1860, more than fifteen hundred state banks were issuing, on an average, six different denominations of notes. Therefore, not fewer than 9,000 different types of notes were being passed. Some counterfeiters issued spurious counterfeits that imitated the notes of no particular bank; others concentrated on careful imitations of genuine bills. Perhaps the most successful ways of counterfeiting were to alter the notes of a broken bank to make them appear to be the issue of a solvent bank or to change bills from lower to higher denominations. Some counterfeiters specialized in the manufacturing end of the business; others, called utterers, were adept at passing the bogus money. To combat counterfeiters, banks formed anticounterfeiting associations, hiring men called snaggers to ferret out makers of spurious bills.

Clearly, it was often difficult determining the genuineness of a bill and the discount at which a valid note should be accepted. If a bill was much worn, or if it was perforated many times by the bank teller's needlelike staple, one might presume it to be genuine. Anyone who regularly took in paper money, however, usually had more assistance in the form of a "bank-note reporter" and a "counterfeit detector." *Thompson's Bank Note and Commercial Reporter*, a weekly, contained alphabetical listings, by states, of the notes of banks and the discounts at which they should be received, together with descriptions of all known counterfeited bills. *Thompson's Bank Note Descriptive List*, published at irregular intervals, contained word descriptions of genuine bills of banks in the United States and Canada. *Nicholas' Bank Note Reporter* at one time listed 5,400 counterfeits. Only a small fraction of these were actually in circulation at any one time, but any of them might be. *Hodges' Bank Note Safeguard* contained 360 pages of facsimile reproductions of genuine notes.

Although this system seems strange to us today because our currency has the same value everywhere, it is easy to exaggerate the difficulties. Today, merchants must still contend with bad checks and stolen credit cards, and using an automated teller machine (ATM) often means paying a service charge analogous to the charge once made by note brokers. Indeed, today many individuals rely on check-cashing services, which perform an economic service quite similar to that performed by the note brokers before the Civil War. There can be little doubt, however, that many people of this period were dissatisfied with the currency and hankered for federal action to provide a uniform national currency.

THE FIRST BANK OF THE UNITED STATES

Robert Morris established and organized the first American bank in 1781, with Congress's approval, to help finance the war effort and provide financial organization in those troubled times. However, we usually think of the nation's first central bank as being established 10 years later. See a discussion of the definition of a central bank in Economic Insight 12.1 on page 228.

Shortly after becoming Secretary of the Treasury, Alexander Hamilton wrote a *Report on a National Bank* in which he argued for a Bank of the United States. Hamilton's report shows remarkable insight into the financial problems of the young republic. He argued that a "National Bank" would augment "the active or productive capital of a country." By this, he meant that the notes issued by the Bank would replace some of the gold and silver money in circulation, which could then be exported in exchange for real goods and services. Normally, moreover, the stock of money must grow from year to year to accommodate increased business activity. With a note-issuing national bank in place, the United States would not be forced in future years to export simply in order to increase its stock of money.

LOUISIANA.

Bank of Louisiana—New Orleans—Wm. W. Montgomery, Pres.; R. M. Davis, Cash . . . .

5s, alter.d from a broken bank, "Louisiana" defective.

20s, description hereafter, as we have not seen these bills.

50s, new plate, altered from 5s.

500s, let. A. Nov. 1, 1839—vig. Cybele & Mercury—on the right an Indian—the bank has issued nothing like it.

Citizens' Bank—New Orleans—E. W. Moise, Pres 3

Exchange Bank—New Orleans—H. Beard, Manager; J. E. Armor, Cash . . . 3

Louisiana State Bank—New Orleans—Samuel J. Peters, Pres.; Richard Relf, Cash 3

10s, L. Bihl cash., C. Clement, pres.—engraved by the "Western Bank note Company."

20s, v.g. a female, agricultural implements &c., her left hand rests on the figure 2, and her right hand on the 0—on the left, a view of the place d'arms and cathederal—not like genuine.

50s, the female in her right hand holds a sword, and her left arm rests on a sheaf of wheat—a bridge, train of cars, &c., on her right:—a broad, dark colored band on right and left margin, one having the figure 50, and the other the word FIFTY upon it. The note reads the "Louisiana State Bank will pay Fifty Dollars to the bearer on demand." All these particulars are different from the genuine note, although in their general appearance they are much the same.

100s, vig. locomotive and cars—Franklin on one end and Roman head on the other—not like genuine, and poorly done.

Louisiana State Bank—(Branch.) Wm. H. Avery, Pres.; R. J. Palfrey, Cash 3

Mech. & Trad. Bank—New Orleans—U. H. Dudley, Pres.; Gustavus Cruzat, Cash 3

5s, let. A. vig. steamboat, &c.—pay A. Brown Jan. 1, 1843.

10s, filling up in boy's hand, very bad—officers both in the same hand, in blue ink—engraving rather coarse.

100s, altered from tens—very well done.

New Orleans Canal & Banking Co.—R. W. Montgomery, Pres.; S. C. Bell, Cash 3

Union Bank—New Orleans—C. Adams, Pres.; F. Frey, Cash 3

50s, said to be in circulation—we have not seen this counterfeit.

An excerpt from Sheldon's North American Bank Note Detector and Commercial Reporter, *Chicago, July 2, 1853. Notes of Louisiana banks were at a 3 percent discount in Chicago. Descriptions of counterfeit notes are listed under the banks.*

Source: Newberry Library in Chicago.

Alexander Hamilton (1775–1804), shown here in a portrait by John Trumbull, was one of the chief architects of the Constitution and the economic policy of the new nation. He was killed in a duel with Aaron Burr.

YALE UNIVERSITY ART GALLERY

As important to Hamilton as its salutary effects on the economy was the assistance the bank could give the government by lending money to the U.S. Treasury. Moreover, the bank could serve as a fiscal agent for the government by acting as a depository of government funds, making transfers of funds from one part of the country to another and (Hamilton hoped) serving as a tax collection agency. Finally, because the government and private shareholders were to jointly own the bank, it would cement the relationship between the fledgling government and leading men of business.[2]

The bill creating the bank followed Hamilton's report closely. It had substantial opposition, even in the predominantly Federalist Congress, on the grounds that (1) it was unconstitutional, (2) it would create a "money-monopoly" that would endanger the rights and liberties of the people, and (3) it would be of value to the commercial North but not to the agricultural South. The bill was carried on a sectional vote, and President Washington signed it on St. Valentine's Day in 1791. The banks charter was limited to 20 years, so further battles lay ahead.

The notes of the Bank of the United States and its branches were soon circulating widely throughout the country at, or very close to, par.[3] In other words, $1.00 notes of the bank were always worth $1.00 in silver. Many state banks developed the habit of using notes or deposits issued by the Bank of the United States as part of their reserves, thus economizing on the use of silver, as Hamilton had predicted. At all times, the bank held a considerable portion of the silver in the country; its holdings during the last three years of its existence were probably close to $15 million, which practically matched the amount held by all state banks.

The bank followed a conservative lending policy compared with those of the state banks. As a result, it continually received a greater dollar volume of state-bank notes than state banks received of its obligations. It became, to put it differently, a creditor of the state

[2]The federal government bought one-fifth of the $10 million initial capital stock. The government paid for its shares with the proceeds of a $2 million loan extended by the bank on the security of its own stock; the loan was to be repaid in ten equal annual installments. At the start of operations, then, the government participated in the earnings of a privately financed venture without contributing a penny to the original capital.

[3]By 1800, the bank had branches in Boston, New York, Baltimore, and Charleston. Branches were added in Washington and Savannah in 1802 and in New Orleans in 1805.

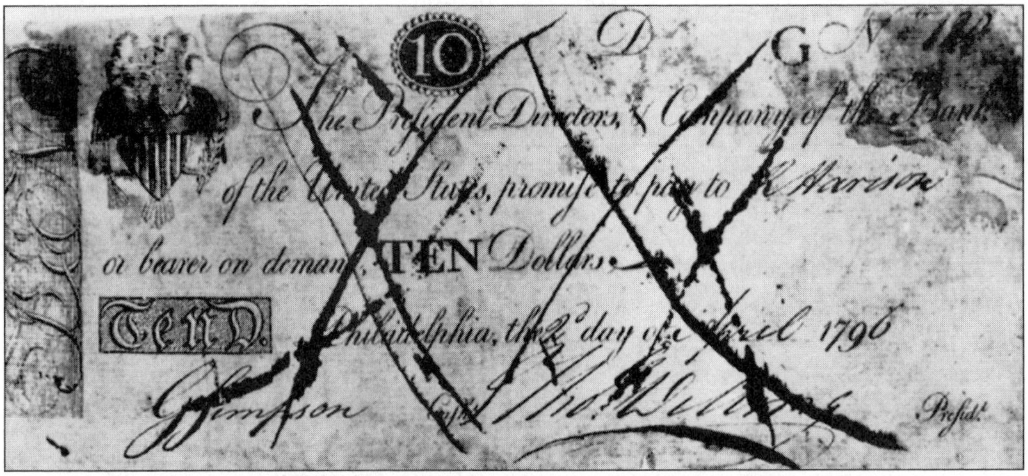

COURTESY OF JP MORGAN CHASE

The first Bank of the United States issued these 10-dollar notes, which were canceled by inking three or four Xs on their faces after they became worn. They were promises to pay dollars (most likely Mexican or American silver dollars) on demand immediately when brought to an office of the bank.

banks. The bank was, therefore, in a position to present the notes of the state banks regularly for payment in specie, discouraging them from issuing as many notes as they would have liked.

Although there was no obligation on its part, legal or customary, to assist other banks in need, in practice, the Bank of the United States (like the Bank of England, which was also a private bank) became a lender of last resort. The bank also acted as fiscal agent for the government and held most of the U.S. Treasury's deposits; in return, the bank transmitted government funds from one part of the country to another without charge. After 1800, the bank helped collect customs bonds in cities where it had branches. It further facilitated government business by effecting payments of interest on the public debt, carrying on foreign-exchange operations for the U.S. Treasury, and supplying bullion and foreign coins to the mint. All in all, we can conclude that the bank was well on its way to being a central bank when Congress refused to recharter it in 1811.

In retrospect, the reasons for the continued operation of the Bank of the United States seem compelling. During the two decades of the bank's existence, the country enjoyed a well-ordered expansion of credit and a general stability of the currency. Compared with the difficulties before 1791, the money problems of the 1790s and early 1800s were insignificant. The first Bank of the United States helped to give the nation a better monetary system than it had any reason to hope for in 1791.

Political arguments based on economic facts are rarely as effective, however, as those based on appeals to emotion and prejudice. Those who opposed the recharter of the bank made the same points that had been advanced when the matter had been originally debated nearly 20 years earlier. They argued that the bank was unconstitutional and that it was a financial monster so powerful it would eventually control the nation's economic life and deprive the people of their liberties. To these contentions was added a new objection: The bank had fallen under the domination of foreigners, mostly British. Foreign ownership of stock was about $7 million, or 70 percent of the shares. This was not unusual; foreigners owned about the same percentage of U.S. bonds. The bank's charter, moreover, attempted to prevent foreigners from exercising much influence over its policies: Only shareholding American citizens could be directors, and foreign nationals could not vote by proxy. Nevertheless, many people felt that the influence of English owners was bound to make itself felt through those American directors with whom they had close business contacts.

Economic Insight 12.1

A Central Bank

There is no precise definition of a central bank that all experts would agree to and, hence, no exact moment at which a big bank becomes a central bank. Typically, when speaking of central banking, economists have one or more of the following criteria in mind: (1) the bank serves as a lender of last resort to other banks or financial institutions by lending them money during crises. The idea is that by preventing a few major financial institutions from closing, the central bank can prevent a panic from taking hold. This function was analyzed by Walter Bagehot in his famous book *Lombard Street* (1873), in which he urged the Bank of England to declare its determination to be the lender of last resort and to acquire a gold reserve commensurate with that responsibility. *Bagehot's rule* is that during financial crises, the central bank should lend freely but at high interest rates (to encourage prompt repayment after the crisis). (2) The bank has considerable control over the stock of money and uses this control to moderate fluctuations in credit conditions, prices, or other aspects of the economy. If the country is on a metallic standard, the case we are examining here, the central bank cannot issue as much money as it might like because of the risk to its own metallic reserves. (3) The bank regulates other banks, punishing those whose behavior it considers imprudent. (4) Finally, we come to the modern definition of a central bank: It lends lots of money to the government.

Personal politics also mattered. On a number of occasions, Thomas Jefferson had stated his conviction that the bank was unconstitutional and a menace to the liberties of the people. Although Jefferson was no longer president when the issue of recharter arose, his influence was still immense, and many of his followers doubtlessly were swayed by his view. But the decisive votes were cast against the bank as a result of personal antagonism toward Albert Gallatin, who, although having served as Jefferson's Secretary of the Treasury, was a champion of the bank. In the House, consideration of the bill for renewal of the charter was postponed indefinitely by a vote of 65 to 64. In the Senate, Vice President George Clinton, enemy of both President James Madison and Gallatin, broke a 17–17 tie with a vote against the bank.

THE SECOND BANK OF THE UNITED STATES

Difficulties in financing the War of 1812 and the sharp inflation following the suspension of specie payments in 1814 convinced many people of the need for a second Bank of the United States. It took two years of congressional wrangling and consideration of no less than six separate proposals before a bill to charter such a bank was passed. The bank was finally chartered in 1816, again for a period of 20 years. And again, the renewal clause set the stage for future battles.

The charter of the second Bank of the United States resembled that of its predecessor. The capital was set at $35 million, four-fifths of it to be subscribed by individuals, firms, or states and the remaining one-fifth by the federal government. Most of the capital was to consist of government bonds, but one-fourth of the private subscription ($7 million) was to be paid in coin. The bank was to have 25 directors, 20 elected by private stockholders and 5 appointed by the president of the United States. The main office of the bank was to be located in Philadelphia, with branch offices to be established on the initiative either of the directors or of Congress.

President of the second Bank of the United States, archfoe of Andrew Jackson, and advocate of central-bank controls was Philadelphia aristocrat Nicholas Biddle (1780–1844). Some argued that his hauteur cost the bank its charter; others believed that Wall Street would have done in Chestnut Street anyway.

The greatest contributions of the second Bank of the United States came after 1823, the time of the appointment of Nicholas Biddle as its third president. Sophisticated, widely traveled, and well-educated, Biddle typified the early American aristocrat. He had wealth, power, and a mind that enabled him to successfully run the nation's largest enterprise. He was also arrogant and out of touch with the fears and aspirations of the average citizen.

Under Biddle, a conscious attempt was made to regulate the banking system according to certain preconceived notions of what ought to be done. In the first place, the bank soon became the lender of last resort to the state banks. State banks did not keep their reserves as deposits with the Bank of the United States, but they did come to depend on the second bank in times of crisis, borrowing specie from it to meet their obligations. The bank was able to meet such demands because it kept a much larger proportion of specie reserve against its circulation than other banks did. The second bank also assisted in times of stress by lending to business firms when other banks could not or would not. Because of these practices, many came to regard the bank as the holder of ultimate reserves of the banking system.

The bank developed a policy of regularly presenting the notes of state banks for payment. By presenting the notes of state banks for payment in specie, it kept their issues moderate. The bank not only furnished a currency of its own of uniform value over the entire country, but it also reduced to a nominal figure the discount at which the notes of state banks circulated. By the late 1820s, the paper money of the country was in a very satisfactory state. Biddle also tried to affect the general economic climate of the United States by alternate expansion and contraction of the bank's loans. Furthermore, he made the bank the largest American dealer in foreign exchange and was able to protect the country from severe specie drain when a drain would have meant a harmful contraction of monetary reserves. In the 1820s, the problem of making payments over considerable distances within the country was not much different from the problem of effecting remittances between countries. There was a flourishing business in "domestic exchange," and the bank obtained a large portion of it.

By 1829, the position of the second Bank of the United States seemed secure. It had grown and prospered. In many ways, it had become a central bank. It had attained a shining reputation abroad—so much so that when the Bank of Spain was reorganized in 1829, the Bank of the United States was explicitly copied. Although the bank had made enemies, the idea of a "national institution" was widely accepted, and even those who persistently opposed "the monster" grudgingly admitted that it had been good for business. Congress had made sporadic attacks on the bank, but these had been ineffective. Yet the apparent permanence of the bank was illusory.

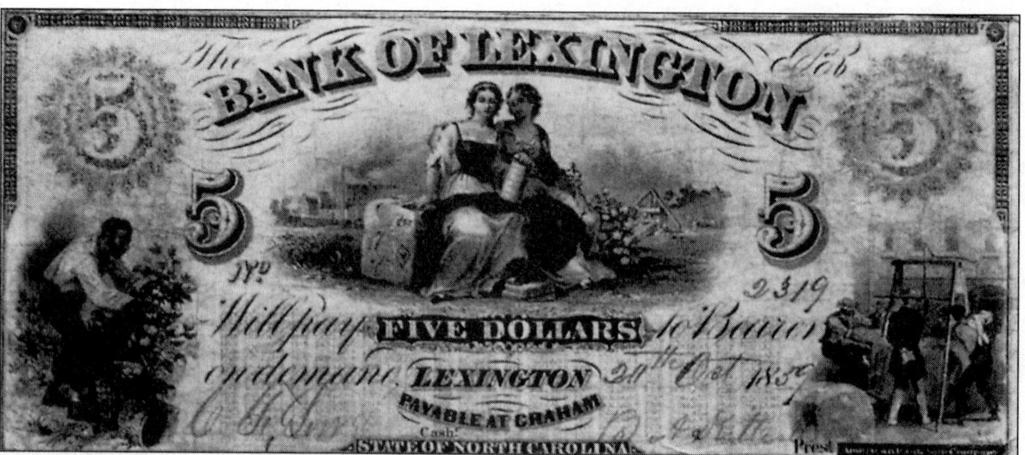

A bank note issued by a private bank before the Civil War. Notes like this one circulated from hand to hand as money.

In 1828, Andrew Jackson was elected to the presidency. Beloved by the masses, Jackson had the overwhelming support of the people during two terms in office. Long before taking office he had decided against supporting banks in general and "The Bank" in particular. As a young man in Tennessee, Jackson had taken the notes of a Philadelphia merchant that passed as currency in payment for 6,000 acres. When he tried to use these notes, he found that they were worthless because the merchant had failed. To make his obligations good, Jackson suffered years of financial difficulty in addition to the loss of his land. Later, he and his business partners often found themselves victims of exorbitant charges by bankers and bill brokers in both New Orleans and the eastern cities.[4] On one occasion, Jackson bitterly opposed the establishment of a state bank in Tennessee, and as late as 1826, he worked against the repeal of a law prohibiting the establishment of a branch of the Bank of the United States in his home state.

In his first annual message to Congress, seven years before the charter of the bank was to expire, Jackson called attention to the date of expiration, stated that "both the constitutionality and the expediency of the law creating this bank are well questioned by a large portion of our fellow citizens," and speculated that

> If such an institution is deemed essential to the fiscal operations of the Government, I submit to the wisdom of the Legislature whether a national one, founded upon credit of the Government and its revenues, might not be devised which would avoid all constitutional difficulties and at the same time secure all the advantages to the Government and country that were expected to result from the present bank.

We have the great Democrat's word for it that his statement was toned down by his advisers. It was the beginning of the "Bank War."

Biddle initially tried to win Jackson's support, but his efforts were unsuccessful. Henry Clay, charming and popular presidential candidate of the National Republicans (Whigs), finally persuaded Biddle to let him make the question of recharter a campaign issue in the election of 1832. During the summer there was enough support in Congress to secure passage of a bill for recharter—a bill that Jackson returned, as expected, with a sharp veto message prepared by presidential advisers Amos Kendall and Roger Taney. In the veto, the president contended that (1) the bank was unconstitutional, (2) there was too much foreign

[4] Claude A. Campbell, *The Development of Banking in Tennessee* (self-published, 1932), 27–29.

In this cartoon, Andrew Jackson (left) attacks the many-headed serpent (the second Bank of the United States) with his walking stick (his veto). The largest head is Nicholas Biddle, the bank's president. The remaining heads represent other officials of the bank and its branches. Jackson is assisted by Martin Van Buren (center).

ownership of its shares, and (3) domestic ownership was too heavily concentrated in the East. A central theme ran through the message: The bank was an instrument of the rich to oppress the poor; an institution of such power and so little responsibility to the people could undo democracy itself and should be dissolved.

Agrarians of the West and South felt that the bank's conservative policies had restricted the supply of credit to agriculture.[5] But Wall Street also opposed the bank; it wanted to supplant Philadelphia (where the home office of the bank was located) as the nation's financial center. Economics makes for strange bedfellows.

After a furious presidential campaign, Jackson emerged the victor by a substantial margin. He considered his triumph a mandate from the electorate on the bank question, and the acclaim he was receiving due to his masterful handling of the problem of nullification strengthened his resolve to restrict the bank's activities at once.[6] In the fall of 1833,

[5]The conviction in the West and South that interest rates are unnaturally high and that the government ought to do something about it is one of the hardy perennials of American politics. It would blossom again during the Populist era, as we will see in chapter 19. Indeed, politicians have continued to cultivate this issue to the present day.

[6]The principle of nullification, first enunciated by John C. Calhoun in 1828, was that any state could refuse to be bound by a federal statute it considered unjust until three-quarters of the states had agreed to the statute. South Carolina tried to apply the principle in 1832–1833 during a dispute over a tariff bill. Jackson's strong stand defeated the attempt.

the government discontinued making deposits with the bank, and editor Greene of the *Boston Post* was moved to write its epitaph: "Biddled, Diddled, and Undone."

Biddle was not through, however. Beginning in August 1833 and continuing into the fall of 1834, the bank contracted its loans sharply and continued its policy of presenting the notes of state banks for payment in specie. Biddle maintained that contraction was necessary to prepare the bank for liquidation, although there was doubtlessly a punitive motive in the vigor of his actions. In any case, his actions contributed significantly to the brief but definite financial stringency of 1834.

The administration, however, remained firm in its resolve to end the bank, which became a state bank chartered under the laws of Pennsylvania in 1836. Although stripped of its official status, the United States Bank of Pennsylvania remained the most powerful financial institution in America for several years. With its resources alone, Biddle engineered a grandiose scheme to support the prices of cotton and other agricultural staples during the nation's economic troubles of 1837 and 1838. Biddle, in other words, bet the bank on a final gamble that the price of agricultural products would rise. If they had, the bank would have made a tremendous amount of money, farmers would have credited the bank with raising farm incomes, and Biddle would have been a hero. But this last convulsive effort started a chain of events that led to the bank's failure in 1841, two years after Biddle's retirement.

ECONOMIC FLUCTUATIONS AND THE SECOND BANK

During the early years of Biddle's reign, the economy followed a relatively smooth course with no deep recessions or periods of significant inflation. As shown in Figure 12.1, during the 1820s, the price level slipped downward as the amount of specie in the economy remained roughly constant and the amount of money (specie plus bank notes plus bank deposits) rose modestly. Undoubtedly, the growth in the stock of money was less than the growth of the volume of goods exchanged.

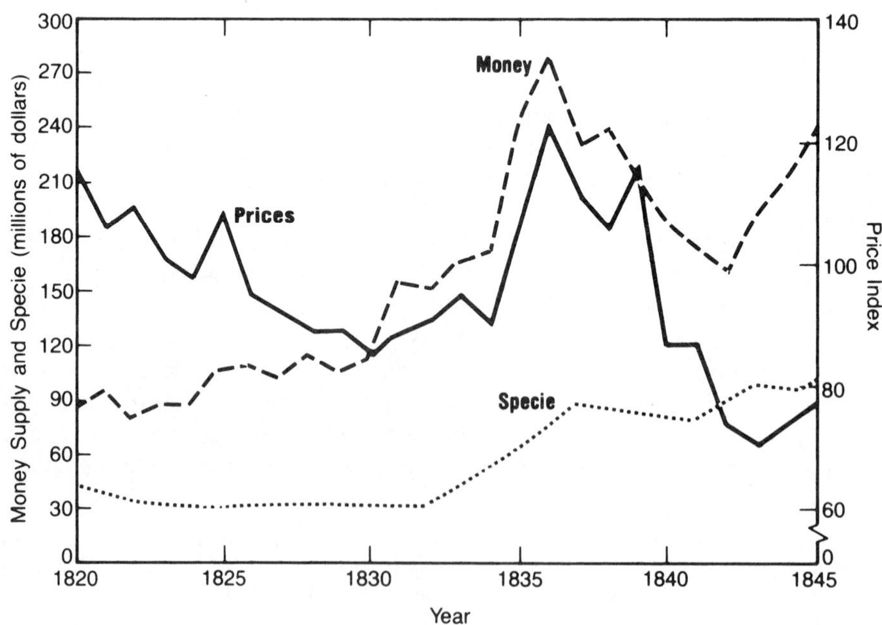

FIGURE 12.1 U.S. Prices, Money, and Specie, 1820–1845

Source: Hugh Rockoff, "Money, Prices, and Banks in the Jacksonian Era," in The Reinterpretation of American Economic History, *eds. Robert W. Fogel and Stanley l. Engerman (New York: Harper & Row, 1971), Table 1, 45.*

Then entirely new conditions began to prevail: first inflation in the mid-1830s and then the great depression of 1839–1843. At one time, historians blamed these disturbances on the demise of the second bank. The argument was that the absence of the second bank unleashed irresponsible banking, that increases in the money supply and the price level were a direct result, and that the crashes of the late 1830s and the depression of the early 1840s were the inevitable result of the previous excesses. A glance at the upper two lines in Figure 12.1 seems to support this argument: The stock of money (remember that this includes bank notes and deposits as well as specie) rose sharply, as did prices.

Shortly after President Jackson vetoed the bank's recharter, he began withdrawing government funds from the second bank and placing them in so-called pet banks, which the states charted. Allegedly, as Biddle's power to present the notes of state banks for redemption ebbed, many banks began to expand their paper note issues recklessly. Owners interested only in making a quick profit formed new banks. These disreputable banks came to be called "wildcat banks," and the name stuck. The origin of the term is somewhat obscure. One story, probably apocryphal, is that the banks were located in remote areas, wildcat country, to discourage people from trying to convert their notes into specie.

Subsequent research by George Macesich and Peter Temin showed, however, that Jackson's attack on the second bank deserves very little of the blame for the inflation. It must be remembered that the United States was still greatly influenced by external events. Coincidentally, at the time of the demise of the second bank, the United States began to receive substantial amounts of silver from Mexico, which was undergoing its own political and economic turmoil. These and other flows into the United States from England and France sharply raised the amount of specie in the United States. In addition, a steady outflow of specie to China substantially declined at this time. Historically, China had run balance-of-payments surpluses with the rest of the world, but as opium addiction spread in China, China's balance-of-payments surplus disappeared, and Chinese merchants began to accept bills of credit instead of requiring payment in specie.[7]

As shown in Figure 12.1, the stock of specie substantially increased in between 1833 and 1837. Because the amount of money banks could issue was limited mainly by the amount of specie they could keep in reserve, the amount of paper money and deposits increased, step by step, with the new supplies of specie. To a considerable extent, the influx of specie explains the increase in money and prices. The ratio of paper money and bank deposits to specie actually increased only slightly. The banking sector, in other words, does not appear to have acted irresponsibly during the 1830s, even after Jackson's veto.[8]

This episode shows that facts that seem to fit one interpretation on the surface may support an altogether different conclusion when thoroughly analyzed. It seems natural to blame Jackson for the inflation that occurred on his watch, but the real sources of the inflation were very different. We have another illustration of the fifth Economic Reasoning Proposition, "Evidence matters," and further explanation in Economic Insight 12.2 on page 234.

★★★ *Economic Reasoning Proposition*

Though the attack on the second bank was not the cause of the inflation, it did influence the economy in other ways. During Biddle's reign throughout the 1820s and early 1830s, people placed an increasing trust in banks, largely because of the leadership and sound banking practices of the second bank. As a result, the proportion of money that people normally held in specie declined.[9] Their confidence in paper money reached unusually high levels in the 1820s and early 1830s. Then events changed. First came Jackson's veto in

---

[7] China's attempts to restrict foreign trade, particularly the opium trade, led to the Opium War with Britain (1839–1842).

[8] For this evidence and a pathbreaking reinterpretation of the Bank War, see Peter Temin, *The Jacksonian Economy* (New York: Norton, 1969), 71.

[9] Ibid., 159.

Economic Insight 12.2

Hume's Price-Specie-Flow Mechanism

According to Hume's *Price-Specie-Flow mechanism* (named after the eighteenth-century Scottish philosopher David Hume), our story makes sense. A sudden increase in the stock of money in one country will raise prices in that country relative to those the rest of the world, but it will then set in motion forces that will ultimately restore the initial equilibrium. Imports will increase relative to exports as prices rise because imports become relatively cheaper and exports relatively more expensive, and specie will flow to the rest of the world. The loss of specie will reduce the stock of money and prices, and this will continue until prices fall back to a level consistent with balance in international trade.

Since Hume's day, economists have developed many qualifications and alternatives to his prediction. Advocates of the monetary theory of the balance of payments, for example, believe that prices of internationally traded goods will be kept in equilibrium at all times by commodity arbitrage (buying something where it is cheap and selling where it is expensive). They would expect to find the explanation for the U.S. inflation in a general inflation in countries on the bimetallic standard. They would expect the stock of money to increase during an inflation but only because a larger stock of money was demanded at a higher price level.

New theories force the historian to look at information that might have been ignored (here, the world price level and the lags between changes in money and prices). At the same time the examination of historical episodes can help economists choose among and refine their theories.

1832. This was followed by the Specie Circular in 1836, which required that most federal land sales be paid in specie. As prices rose and confidence in paper monies waned, more and more people returned paper for specie at their banks. When large numbers of noteholders attempted to do this, the banks were unable to make the exchanges, and banking panics occurred. (A strong second bank might have been able to nip these panics in the bud by acting as a lender of last resort.) The result was a sharp but temporary recession in 1837 and, finally, one of the worst depressions of the century from 1839 to 1843.[10]

EXPERIMENTS IN STATE BANKING CONTROLS

The variety of banking systems that the states established during the antebellum era is simply astonishing. Some prohibited banking, some established state banks, some permitted "free banking," and this list could easily be extended. For this reason economic historians have been drawn to this era to learn what sorts of banking systems work well and which do not.

The Suffolk System and the Safety Fund

Country bank note issues circulated widely in Boston. In 1824, six Boston banks joined with the Suffolk Bank of Boston to create a system for presenting country banks with their notes in volume, thus forcing them to hold higher reserves of specie. Soon after, the country banks agreed to keep deposits in the Suffolk Bank, resulting in the first arrangement of a clearing house for currencies of remote banks.

[10] In addition, the Bank of England, concerned over the continuing outflow of specie to the United States, began to call in specie (sell back bonds) in 1837.

A note issued by one of New Jersey's free banks. The bank's name stresses the point that the note is backed by government bonds (stocks).

These deposits, a costless source of funds, helped make the Suffolk Bank one of the most profitable in the country. The other Boston banks shared in this profit through their ownership of Suffolk stock, so the arrangement was hardly altruistic. As result, however, the prevailing discounts on country bank notes fell. By 1825, country notes passed through the "Suffolk System" at par. Consequently, New England was blessed with a uniform currency.

The Suffolk Bank continued as the agency for clearing New England notes until 1858, when some new Boston banks and country banks that resented the dictatorial policies of the Suffolk organized a rival institution. Shortly afterward, national banking legislation did away with state bank notes and the need for such regional systems, but the Suffolk System was the predecessor to the modern practice of requiring reserve deposits of member banks in the Federal Reserve System.

In addition to this private regulatory effort, New York in 1827 invoked state regulatory power. To increase protection for depositors and noteholders, the state passed a law holding bank stockholders responsible for debts equal to twice the value of their stock holdings. In 1827, New York passed the Safety-Fund Act, requiring new banks and those being rechartered to hold 3 percent of their capital stock in a fund to be used as reserves for banks that failed. This first state deposit insurance scheme failed in the panic of 1837, but others were tried again and again. State deposit insurance schemes, although generally unsuccessful, were the forerunner of Federal Deposit Insurance initiated in the 1930s.

Free Banking

The most important of the bank experiments was the free banking law. The New York Assembly passed the first such law in 1838. Actually, between the beginning of the agitation for the New York system and final passage of the act establishing it, a Michigan statute provided for a similar plan, but the chief influence on American banking derives from the New York law. The adjective *free* indicates the most important provision of the law, under which any individual or group of individuals, upon compliance with certain regulations, could start a bank. Under the old rule, the privilege of starting a bank had to be granted by a special legislative act. Increased competition promised improved services and a reduction of legislative corruption.

To protect noteholders and sometimes to boost the state's credit, the free banking laws required the banks to deposit bonds, usually federal bonds or those issued by the state where the bank was located, with the state banking authority. If a bank refused to redeem a note in specie, the holder could protest to the state banking authority, which would then sell the bonds and redeem all of the bank's notes. The rules governing the amount and type of bonds that had to be deposited had a great deal to do with the success or failure of the system. If too much backing was required for each note issued, no banks would be set up. If too little backing was required, the way might be opened for wildcat banking. If the required backing protected note holders while permitting the bankers a reasonable profit, however, the system would work well.

In New York, to take the most important example, free banking was successful. The system expanded rapidly, and there were few failures. Indeed, the free banking systems of New York and Ohio were probably the models for the national banking system adopted during the Civil War. But Michigan's free banking law of 1837 produced a famous episode of wildcat banking. Despite apparent safeguards, including a safety fund, the law permitted dubious securities to be put up as a guarantee of note redemption.

Under the Michigan law, all a bank had to do to start operation was to show that it had specie on hand. Enterprising bankers showed an amazing ingenuity in outwitting examiners. Moreover, specie payments at the time were suspended nationwide because of a banking crisis, so the would-be wildcat banker did not even have to fear immediate withdrawals. Two bank commissioners noted a remarkable similarity in the packages of specie in the vaults of several banks on their examination list and later discovered that a sleigh drawn by fast horses preceded them as they went from bank to bank. Specie, they said, flew about the backwoods of Michigan with the "celerity of magic." Nearly all banks operating on such a basis failed and disappeared by 1840, but not before a victimized public had been stuck with their worthless notes.

The Forstall System

Reasonably sound banking systems usually developed in states that had reached a degree of economic maturity. It was not by chance that Louisiana law of 1842 set up a system, called the *Forstall System*, that became a model of sound and conservative banking. With a port second only to that of New York, Louisiana had economic ties with both a great productive hinterland and the rest of the world.

The most notable feature of the Louisiana law required banks chartered under it to keep a specie reserve equal to one-third of their combined note and deposit liabilities. Before 1863, several states came to require specie reserves against notes, ranging variously from 5 to 33 percent, but except for Louisiana and Massachusetts, they did not require reserves against deposit liabilities as well. The notion that deposits as well as bank notes were money was not universally recognized. Partly as a result of the Forstall System, New Orleans banks developed a well-deserved reputation for soundness, and their notes circulated widely. According to one possibly apocryphal theory, the South became known as the Land of Dixie because $10 notes issued in New Orleans bore the French word *dix* (ten) on the back.

The financial upheavals that we have discussed so far were the work of politicians and businessmen. The financial upheaval that began in 1848 had a very different origin, however.

THE ECONOMIC CONSEQUENCES OF THE GOLD RUSH

In 1848, gold was discovered in California. Soon men (almost no women) from all over the world were on their way to California (see Holiday, 1999). Initially, the methods used to take the gold were simple. The gold was found in riverbeds. The gravel was scooped up and washed in a pan; the heavier gold remained, and the lighter elements washed away. If no gold was found, it was said that the gravel didn't "pan out." The miners, however, began to build machines that could wash larger and larger amounts of gravel. They realized,

TABLE 12.1 Money, Income, and Prices, 1849–1859

YEAR	MONEY	GDP	COMMODITY PRICES	ALL FARM PRICES	CHEMICAL AND DRUG PRICES
1849	100	100	100	100	100
1850	120	113	112	115	101
1851	129	114	101	115	101
1852	143	120	107	124	103
1853	160	135	118	134	111
1854	161	148	132	150	114
1855	169	161	134	158	117
1856	182	168	128	135	116
1857	151	181	135	153	113
1858	173	163	113	123	111
1859	179	174	116	132	111

Sources: Money: Milton Friedman and Anna J. Schwartz, Monetary Statistics of the United States *(Chicago: University of Chicago Press, 1970), Table 14, column 3, 232. GDP: Thomas Senior Berry,* Production and Population since 1789 *(Richmond: Bostwick, 1988), Table 9, 26. The numbers shown here are actually for GNP. In theory GNP differs from GDP by including income earned by Americans abroad and excluding income earned by foreigners in the United States. In this period the difference was probably very small and difficult to measure. Prices: U.S. Bureau of the Census,* Historical Statistics of the United States Colonial Times to 1970 *(Washington D.C.: U.S. Government Printing Office, 1976), series E52 (all commodities), E53 (farm products), and E60 (chemicals and drugs).*

moreover, that still larger deposits must lie in the mountains crossed by the streams they worked. Where, they asked, was the "mother lode"? Soon the source of gold was found, and conventional mining began.

Because gold was the basis of much of the world's monetary system, the outpouring of gold from California (and from Australia, where discoveries were soon made) increased the world's money supplies. Table 12.1 shows the results in the United States. An index of the stock of money in the United States rose from 100 in 1849 to a peak of 182 in 1856, a rate of increase of about 8.5 percent per year.[11] The result was a long economic boom, as indicated by the increase in GDP shown in column 3 of Table 12.1, and a substantial increase in prices, as shown in column 4.

How do we know that the increase in the stock of money caused the inflation, not some other factor? We cannot know for sure: Correlation does not prove causation. In this case, however, we have a "natural experiment." We know that the increase in the stock of money was mostly due to luck. Either the inflation that followed occurred by chance, or it was caused by the increase in the stock of money; the inflation could not have caused the increase in the amount of gold. Recall Economic Reasoning Proposition 5.

★★★ *Economic Reasoning Proposition*

All prices did not rise at the same rate during the inflation. An example is shown in the last two columns of Table 12.1. Farm prices rose sooner and further than the prices of chemicals and drugs. By 1855, farm prices had risen 58 percent compared to 17 percent for chemical and drug prices; chemical and drug prices had *fallen* 41 percent relative to farm prices. Why were there such disparities? Factors specific to individual markets are likely to affect relative prices: Good or bad harvests, technological progress, changes in consumer tastes, and so on, must be brought into the story when we discuss relative prices. The monetary expansion may also have played a role. It may have been true, as the great British economist William Stanley Jevons suggested, that prices in more competitive markets, such as agriculture, responded faster to the monetary expansion.

[11]The actual values were divided by the actual value in 1849 and multiplied by 100.

The long expansion came to an end in the Crisis of 1857, which is clearly visible in Table 12.1 as a sudden decline in money and (a year later) in prices. The crisis seemed to come like a bolt from the blue. The failure of the Ohio Life Insurance and Trust Company, a large bank with a reputation for sound investing (whose main branch was in New York despite its origins in Ohio) that had invested heavily in western railroad bonds, shocked the financial community. Distrust of banks spread. Soon there were runs, and the banks, desperate to protect themselves, called in loans and refused to make new ones. The result was a sharp recession. Unemployment rose, and New York experienced bread riots. The crisis, moreover, aggravated the tensions that were already pulling the country apart. In the North, the newly formed Republican Party argued that the crisis showed that traditional parties did not know how to manage the economy. In the South, advocates of secession argued that the relatively mild impact of the crisis on the South proved that cotton was king and that the South would be better off without the North.

SELECTED REFERENCES AND SUGGESTED READINGS

Adams, Donald R. "The Role of Banks in the Economic Development of the Old Northwest." In *Essays in Nineteenth Century Economic History: The Old Northwest*, eds. David C. Klingaman and Richard K. Vedder. Athens, Ohio: Ohio University Press, 1975.

Bodenhorn, Howard. "Capital Mobility and Financial Integration in Antebellum America." *Journal of Economic History* 52 (1992): 585–610.

———. *A History of Banking in Antebellum America: Financial Markets and Economic Development in an Era of Nation-building.* Cambridge, England: Cambridge University Press, 2000.

Bodenhorn, Howard, and Hugh Rockoff. "Regional Interest Rates in Antebellum America." In *Strategic Factors in Nineteenth Century American Economic History: A Volume to Honor Robert W. Fogel*, eds. Claudia Goldin and Hugh Rockoff, 159–187. Chicago: University of Chicago Press, 1992.

Bordo, Michael, and Anna J. Schwartz. "Money and Prices in the Nineteenth Century: An Old Debate Rejoined." *Journal of Economic History* 40 (1980): 61–67.

Calomiris, Charles W., and Charles M. Kahn. "The Efficiency of Self-regulated Payments Systems: Learning from the Suffolk System." *Journal of Money, Credit & Banking* 28 (1996): 766–797.

Calomiris, Charles W., and Larry Schweikart. "The Panic of 1857: Origins, Transmission, and Containment." *Journal of Economic History* 51 (1991): 807–834.

Catterall, Ralph. *The Second Bank of the United States.* Chicago: University of Chicago Press, 1903.

Davis, Lance E., and Jonathan R.T. Hughes. "A Dollar-Sterling Exchange 1803–1895." *Economic History Review* 13 (August 1960).

Engerman, Stanley. "A Note on the Economic Consequences of the Second Bank of the United States." *Journal of Political Economy* 78 (July/August 1970): 725–728.

Fenstermaker, J. van. *The Development of American Commercial Banking, 1782–1837.* Kent, Ohio: Kent State University Press, 1965.

Ferguson, E. James. *The Power of the Purse: A History of American Public Finance*, 1776–1790. Chapel Hill: University of North Carolina Press, 1961.

Fraas, Arthur. "The Second Bank of the United States: An Instrument for an Interregional Monetary Union." *Journal of Economic History* 34 (1974): 447–467.

Gorton, Gary. "Reputation Formation in Early Bank Note Markets." *Journal of Political Economy* 104 (1996): 346–397.

———. "Pricing Free Bank Notes." *Journal of Monetary Economics* 44 (1999): 33–64.

Green, George D. "The Louisiana Bank Act of 1842: Policy Making During Financial Crisis." *Explorations in Economic History* 7 (Summer 1970): 399–412.

Greenfield, Robert L. and Hugh Rockoff. "Gresham's Law in Nineteenth-Century America." *Journal of Money, Credit & Banking* 27 (November 1995): 1086–1098.

Hammond, Bray. *Banks and Politics in America from the Revolution to the Civil War.* Princeton, N. J.: Princeton University Press, 1957.

Holiday, J. S. *Rush for Riches: Gold Fever and the Making of California.* Berkeley: University of California Press, 1999.

Kahn, James A. "Another Look at Free Banking in the United States." *American Economic Review* 75 (1985): 881–885.

Knodell, Jane. "The Demise of Central Banking and the Domestic Exchanges: Evidence from Antebellum Ohio." *Journal of Economic History* 58 (1998): 714–730.

Macesich, George. "Sources of Monetary Disturbances in the U.S., 1834–1845." *Journal of Economic History* 20 (1960): 407–434.

Martin, David A. "1853: The End of Bimetallism in the United States." *Journal of Economic History* 33 (1973): 825–844.

———. "The Changing Role of Foreign Money in the United States, 1782–1857." *Journal of Economic History* 37 (1977): 1009–1027.

Museum of American Financial History at **http://www.financialhistory.org/**.

Neu, Irene D. "Edmund Jean Forstall and Louisiana Banking." *Explorations in Economic History* 7 (Summer 1970): 383–398.

Ng, Kenneth. "Free Banking Laws and Barriers to Entry in Banking, 1838–1860." *Journal of Economic History* 48 (1988): 877–889.

North, Douglass C. *The Economic Growth of the United States, 1790–1860.* New York: Norton, 1961.

Olmstead, Alan L. "Investment Constraints and New York City Mutual Savings Bank Financing of Antebellum Development." *Journal of Economic History* 32 (1972): 811–840.

Redlich, Fritz. *The Molding of American Banking: Men and Ideas.* 2 Vols. New York: Hafner, 1947 and 1951.

Rockoff, Hugh T. "Money, Prices and Banks in the Jacksonian Era." Chapter 33 in *The Reinterpretation of American Economic History*, eds. R.W. Fogel and Stanley Engerman. New York: Harper & Row, 1971.

———. *The Free Banking Era: A Reexamination.* New York: Arno, 1975.

———. "Banking and Finance, 1789–1914." In *The Cambridge Economic History of the United States*, Vol. II, *The Long Nineteenth Century*, eds. Stanley L. Engerman and Robert E. Gallman. New York: Cambridge University Press, 2000, 643–684.

Rolnick, Arthur J., and Warren E. Weber. "New Evidence on the Free Banking Era." *American Economic Review* 73 (1983): 1080–1091.

———. "The Causes of Free Bank Failures: A Detailed Examination of the Evidence." *Journal of Monetary Economics* 14 (1984): 267–291.

———. "Gresham's Law or Gresham's Fallacy?" *Journal of Political Economy* 94 (February 1986): 185–199.

———. "Explaining the Demand for Free Bank Notes." *Journal of Monetary Economics* 21 (1988): 47–71.

Scheiber, Harry N. "The Pet Banks in Jacksonian Politics and Finance, 1833–1841." *Journal of Economic History* 33 (1963): 196–214.

Selgin, George. "Salvaging Gresham's Law: The Good, the Bad, and the Illegal." *Journal of Money, Credit & Banking* 28 (1996): 637–649.

Smith, Walter B., and Arthur H. Cole. *Fluctuations in American Business 1790–1860.* Cambridge, Mass.: Harvard University Press, 1935.

Sylla, Richard. "Early American Banking: The Significance of the Corporate Form." *Business and Economic History* 14 (1985): 105–123.

Sylla, Richard, John B. Legler, and John J. Wallis. "Banks and State Public Finance in the New Republic: The United States, 1790–1860." *Journal of Economic History* 47 (1987): 391–404.

Taylor, George R., ed. *Jackson and Biddle: The Struggle over the Second Bank of the United States*. Boston: Heath, 1949.

Temin, Peter. *The Jacksonian Economy*. New York: Norton, 1969.

———. "The Anglo-American Business Cycle, 1820–1860." *Economic History Review* 27 (May 1974): 207–221.

Timberlake, Richard H., Jr. *The Origins of Central Banking in the United States*. Cambridge, Mass.: Harvard University Press, 1978.

Trescott, Paul B. *Financing American Enterprise: The Story of Commercial Banking*. New York: Harper & Row, 1963.

Willett, Thomas D. "International Specie Flows and American Monetary Stability." *Journal of Economic History* 28 (1968): 28–50.

Chapter Thirteen

THE ENTRENCHMENT OF SLAVERY AND REGIONAL CONFLICT

Slavery, as an economic and social organization, was morally and legally accepted by peoples everywhere for thousands of years. However, once abolitionist forces took effect, slavery collapsed in the Americas in approximately a century, between 1776 and 1888. First in the Caribbean and then throughout South America, politicians yielded to abolitionists' arguments and pressures to free the enslaved. In the southern United States, however, slavery based on race became increasingly entrenched in the decades leading to the Civil War. Investments in slaves had proved profitable, slave labor productivity and plantation efficiency were high, and wealthy planters who dominated southern politics saw clearly the wealth loss implications to them from abolitionists' aims. The clash of abolitionists' moral objectives and southern economic interests persisted, with noted intensity as the country grew westward, until the force of arms resolved the issue on the battlefield.

AFRICAN SLAVERY IN THE WESTERN HEMISPHERE

In the 1860s, the African slave trade ended, bringing to a close three and a half centuries of forced migrations of nearly 10 million Africans across the Atlantic. Their dominant economic activity, overwhelmingly, was sugar production. As Figure 13.1 on page 242 shows, most of the slaves were destined for Brazil (36 percent) and the Caribbean islands (40 percent), areas economically based on sugar production. The United States received only 6 percent of the total numbers crossing the Atlantic. By 1825, the distribution of slaves was noticeably different from the pattern of arrivals. As revealed in Figure 13.2 on page 242 , in 1825 the United States was the leading slave nation, housing 36 percent of all slaves in the Western Hemisphere. Differences in natural rates of population growth, negative in Brazil and in the Caribbean for long periods and positive and high in the United States, account for this significant demographic adjustment. Although having only a peripheral role in the Atlantic slave trade, the United States ultimately became the bulwark of resistance to the abolition of slavery in the Western world. This resistance was almost entirely in the southern United States.

In one sense at least, it is astonishing how quickly slavery collapsed in the Americas. For thousands of years, statesmen, philosophers, theologians, and writers had accepted uncritically the legitimacy and utility of slavery as a "time-honored" form of economic and social

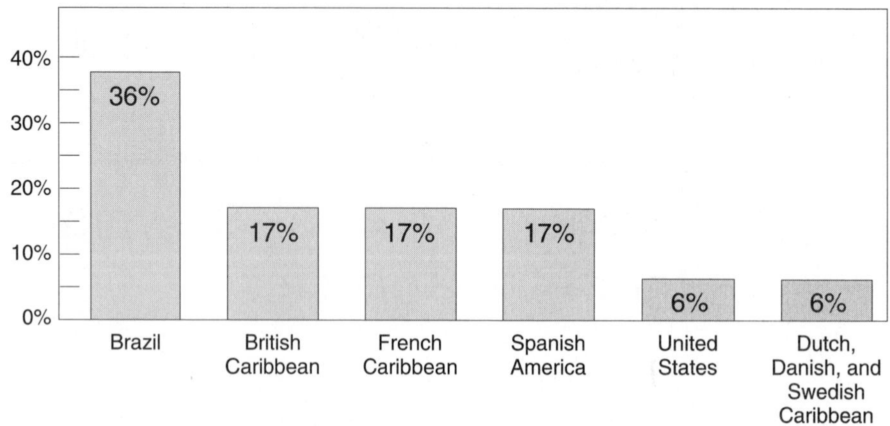

FIGURE 13.1 The Distribution of Slaves Brought into the New World, 1500–1870.

Source: Robert W. Fogel and Stanley L. Engerman, Time on the Cross: The Economics of American Slavery *(Boston: Little, Brown, 1974), 14. ©1974 by Robert W. Fogel and Stanley L. Engerman. Used by permission of W. W. Norton & Company, Inc.*

organization. Popes and queens and commoners alike accepted it. Early voices against it, such as the Germantown Quakers (Society of Friends), who in 1688 condemned it as a violation of the Golden Rule, were ridiculed. No actions compelling conformity to abolitionist arguments were taken until 1758, when the Quakers in Philadelphia condemned both the slave trade and the owning of slaves. Members in violation were to be excluded from positions of responsibility in the Society of Friends.

Across the Atlantic, the English Society of Friends voted in 1774 to expel any member engaging in the slave trade. As shown in Table 13.1, a year later slavery was abolished in Madeira; the abolition fever strengthened and spread until Brazil, the last American bastion of slavery, abolished it in 1888.

FIRST U.S. CONSTRAINTS ON SLAVERY

In 1780, the enslaved populations in the United States totaled nearly 575,000. Nine percent of these resided north of the Chesapeake; the remainder lived in the South. As part of one of the great constitutional compromises, the nation's forefathers agreed in 1787 to permit

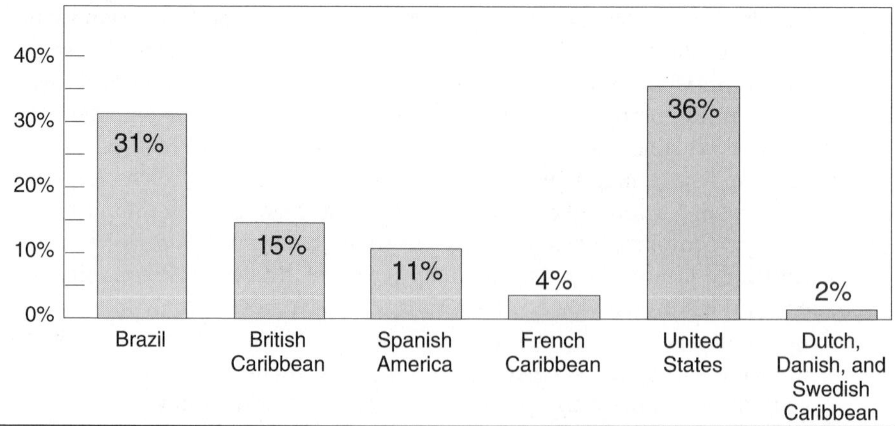

FIGURE 13.2 The Distribution of Slaves in the Western Hemisphere, 1825.

Source: Robert W. Fogel and Stanley L. Engerman, Time on the Cross: The Economics of American Slavery *(Boston: Little, Brown, 1974), 28. ©1974 by Robert W. Fogel and Stanley L. Engerman. Used by permission of W. W. Norton & Company, Inc.*

TABLE 13.1 A Chronology of Emancipation, 1772–1888

1772	Lord Chief Justice Mansfield rules that slavery is not supported by English law, thus laying the legal basis for the freeing of England's 15,000 slaves.
1774	The English Society of Friends votes the expulsion of any member engaged in the slave trade.
1775	Slavery abolished in Madeira.
1776	The Societies of Friends in England and Pennsylvania require members to free their slaves or face expulsion.
1777	The Vermont Constitution prohibits slavery.
1780	The Massachusetts Constitution declares that all men are free and equal by birth; a judicial decision in 1783 interprets this clause as having the force of abolishing slavery. Pennsylvania adopts a policy of gradual emancipation, freeing the children of all slaves born after November 1, 1780, at their twenty-eighth birthday.
1784	Rhode Island and Connecticut pass gradual emancipation laws.
1787	Formation in England of the "Society for the Abolition of the Slave Trade."
1794	The French National Convention abolishes slavery in all French territories. This law is repealed by Napoleon in 1802.
1799	New York passes a gradual emancipation law.
1800	U.S. citizens barred from exporting slaves.
1804	Slavery abolished in Haiti. New Jersey adopts a policy of gradual emancipation.
1807	England and the United States prohibit engagement in the international slave trade.
1813	Gradual emancipation adopted in Argentina.
1814	Gradual emancipation begins in Colombia.
1820	England begins using naval power to suppress the slave trade.
1823	Slavery abolished in Chile.
1824	Slavery abolished in Central America.
1829	Slavery abolished in Mexico.
1831	Slavery abolished in Bolivia.
1838	Slavery abolished in all British colonies.
1841	The Quintuple Treaty is signed, under which England, France, Russia, Prussia, and Austria agree to mutual search of vessels on the high seas in order to suppress the slave trade.
1842	Slavery abolished in Uruguay.
1848	Slavery abolished in all French and Danish colonies.
1851	Slavery abolished in Ecuador. Slave trade ended in Brazil.
1854	Slavery abolished in Peru and Venezuela.
1862	Slave trade ended in Cuba.
1863	Slavery abolished in all Dutch colonies.
1865	Slavery abolished in the United States as a result of the passage of the Thirteenth Amendment to the Constitution and the end of the Civil War.
1871	Gradual emancipation initiated in Brazil.
1873	Slavery abolished in Puerto Rico.
1886	Slavery abolished in Cuba.
1888	Slavery abolished in Brazil.

Source: Robert W. Fogel and Stanley L. Engerman, Time on the Cross: The Economics of American Slavery *(Boston: Little, Brown, 1974), 33–34. ©1974 by Robert W. Fogel and Stanley L. Engerman. Used by permission of W. W. Norton & Company, Inc.*

the existence of slavery but not to allow the importation of slaves after 20 years. (In 1807, therefore, Congress prohibited the foreign slave trade, effective the following year.) Also in 1787, the Northwest Land Ordinance forbade slavery in the Northwest Territory. It merits notice that the timing of the debates and discussions leading to the slavery restrictions in the Constitution and land ordinances coincided within days. In this way, the growth of slavery in the United States was limited and regionally restricted. Of course, the smuggling of human cargo was not uncommon, and various estimates suggest that as many as a quarter of a million blacks were illegally imported into the United States before 1860. But illicit human importation was only a minor addition to the total numbers held in bondage, and by 1860 foreign-born blacks were a small percentage of the enslaved population. Indeed, most blacks were third-, fourth-, and fifth-generation Americans. As mentioned earlier, natural sources of population expansion, averaging 2.4 percent per year between 1800 and 1860, were predominant in increasing the number of slaves. In 1863, the slaves numbered almost 4 million—all residing in the South.

Northern Emancipation at Bargain Prices

Even before the writing of the Constitution, some states had progressed toward the elimination of slavery. Between 1777 and 1804, the eight northeastern states individually passed measures to provide for the emancipation of their slave populations. In Vermont, Massachusetts, and New Hampshire, vague constitutional clauses left emancipation to the courts. Unfortunately, little is known about the results of this process; but in any case, these three states domiciled only a very small fraction of the northern blacks—probably 10 to 15 percent in 1780. As shown in Table 13.2, Pennsylvania, Rhode Island, Connecticut, New York, and New Jersey each passed laws of emancipation well before the year prohibiting slave importations. The process of emancipation used in these states was gradual, and the living population of slaves was not freed. Instead, newborn babies were emancipated when they reached adulthood (and were referred to as "free-born").

This form of emancipation demonstrates that many—perhaps most—of those who were politically dominant were more concerned with the political issue of slavery than with the slaves themselves. Besides not freeing the living slaves, there were no agencies in any of these states to enforce the enactments. In addition, the enactments themselves contained important loopholes, such as the possibility of selling slaves to the South.

The emancipation process, however, did recognize the issues of property rights and costs. These "gradual emancipation schemes" imposed no costs on taxpayers, and owners were not directly compensated financially for emancipated slaves. But curiously enough, owners were almost entirely compensated indirectly by maintaining the free-born in bondage until they had repaid their owner for their rearing costs. In most cases, these slaves were freed when they reached their mid-twenties. In the first several years after birth, a slave's maintenance cost was determined to be in excess of the value of his or her services (or output). Near the age of 10, the value of the slave's annual output usually just about matched the costs of food, clothes, and shelter. Thereafter, the value of output exceeded yearly maintenance costs, and normally by the age of 25 or 26, the slave had fully compensated the owner.

TABLE 13.2 Slave Emancipation in the North for the Free-Born

		AGE OF EMANCIPATION	
STATE	DATE OF ENACTMENT	MALE	FEMALE
Pennsylvania	1780[a]	28	28
Rhode Island	1784[b]	21	18
Connecticut	1784[c]	25	25
New York	1799[d]	28	25
New Jersey	1804[e]	25	21

[a] *The last census that enumerated any slaves in Pennsylvania was in 1840.*
[b] *All slavery was abolished in 1842.*
[c] *The age of emancipation was changed in 1797 to age 21. In 1848, all slavery was abolished.*
[d] *In 1817, a law was passed freeing all slaves as of July 4, 1827.*
[e] *In 1846, all slaves were emancipated, but apprenticeships continued for the children of slave mothers and were introduced for freed slaves.*

Source: *Robert W. Fogel and Stanley L. Engerman, "Philanthropy at Bargain Prices: Notes on the Economics of Gradual Emancipation,"* Journal of Legal Studies *3 (2), (June 1974): 341.*

TABLE 13.3 The Southern Population by Race, 1800–1860 (in millions)

YEAR	WHITE	BLACK		SLAVE AS A PERCENTAGE OF FREE
		SLAVE	FREE	
1800	1.70	0.86	0.06	49%
1810	2.19	1.16	0.11	50
1820	2.78	1.51	013	52
1830	3.55	1.98	018	53
1840	4.31	2.43	0.21	54
1850	5.63	3.12	0.24	53
1860	7.03	3.84	0.26	53

Note: Amounts rounded.

Source: Historical Statistics, *1960 (Washington, D.C.: U.S. Government Printing Office, 1960), Series A, 95–122.*

Thus, the slaves themselves bore nearly all the costs of emancipation in the North. Newborn slaves who were eventually freed fully paid back their owners for their rearing costs. Owners of males who were born before the dates of enactment suffered no wealth loss. Owners of females who were born before the enactments and who could or eventually would reproduce incurred some minor wealth losses in that they lost the value of their slaves' offspring. About 10 percent of the value (price) of a young female slave was due to the value of her offspring, and perhaps as many as 30 percent of the total enslaved population comprised females in their fertile or prefertile years.[1] Consequently, only 3 percent (10 percent of 30 percent) of the total slave wealth was lost to northern owners by abiding by these enactments, but the percentage was probably much closer to zero because of the loopholes of selling slaves to the South, working the slaves harder, and reducing maintenance costs.

The Persistence of Southern Slavery

Despite the constitutional restrictions on slave imports and the "gradual emancipation schemes" of the northern states, slavery did not die. Table 13.3 profiles the growth of the southern population, showing the slave population increasing slightly more rapidly than the free southern population. The proportion enslaved grew from about 49 percent in 1800 to 53 percent in 1860.

After Eli Whitney's invention of the cotton gin in 1793, mechanical means replaced fingers in the separation of seed from short-staple cotton varieties. The soils and climate of the South, especially the new Southwest, gave it a comparative advantage in supplying the massive and growing demand for raw cotton by the British and later by New England textile firms. Cotton quickly became the nation's highest-valued commodity export, and output expanded as the southwestern migrations discussed in chapter 8 placed an army of slaves on new southwestern lands. According to estimates by Robert Fogel and Stanley Engerman, nearly 835,000 slaves moved out of the old South (Maryland, Virginia, and the Carolinas, primarily), most of them going to the cotton-rich lands of Alabama, Mississippi, Louisiana, and eastern Texas. Three surges of movement and land sales occurred: the first in the years right after the end of the War of 1812, the second in the mid-1830s, and finally, the third in the early 1850s. (These are graphically shown in Figure 8.2, page 152). The plantation based on slave labor was the organizational form that ensured vast economical supplies of cotton.

[1] Female slaves of all ages represented 37 percent of the total slave population.

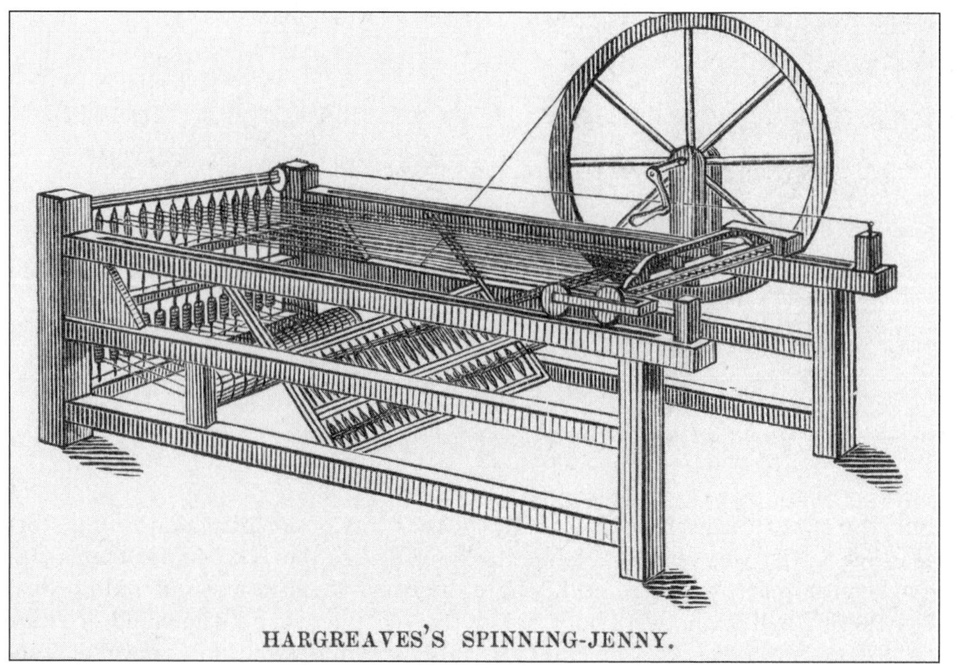

While the traditional method of spinning thread, the spinning wheel, produced only one thread at a time, Hargreave's spinning jenny (1764) allowed an individual spinner to produce eight threads at once. Soon, as the engraving shows, the machine was improved so that even more threads could be spun at one time by one worker.

PLANTATION EFFICIENCY

In the heyday of King Cotton, the growth in the number and size of plantations in the South was dramatic. Of course, many small family farm units produced cotton and related items for market, but the really distinguishing characteristic of southern agriculture in the antebellum period was the plantation. Based on forced labor, the plantation represented both the economic grandeur and the social tragedy of the southern economy.

Although most of the condemnation of slavery was confined to moral and social issues, some of the damnation was extended to strictly economic aspects. In some instances, the forced labor of blacks was condemned as inefficient, either on racial grounds or because slavery per se was considered economically inefficient and unproductive. For example, the white contemporary observer Cassius M. Clay noted that Africans were "far less adapted for steady, uninterrupted labor than we are."[2] Another contemporary, Frederick Law Olmsted, reported that "white laborers of equal intelligence and under equal stimulus will cut twice as much wood, split twice as many rails, and hoe a third more corn a day than Negroes."[3]

★★★ *Economic Reasoning Proposition*

There are sound reasons and growing evidence to reject these contemporary assertions and illustrate Economic Reasoning Proposition 5. For example, Gavin Wright has shown that 86 percent of the South's cotton crop was grown on farm units of more than 100 acres and owning 90 percent of the slaves.[4] Moreover, cotton production increased by 1,100 to 1,200 percent between 1820 and 1860, while the slave population grew by 250 percent, reflecting a four- to fivefold increase in cotton output per slave. Clearly, there was ample growth in agricultural productivity based on slave labor. See Also Economic Insight 13.1.

[2] C. M. Clay, in *The Writings of Cassius Marcelius Clay: Including Speeches and Addresses*, ed. H. Greeley (*The New Yorker*, 1848), 204.

[3] F. L. Olmsted, in *The Cotton Kingdom*, ed. A. M. Schlesinger (New York: Knopf, 1953), 467–468.

[4] Gavin Wright, *The Political Economy of the Cotton South: Households, Markets, and Wealth in the Nineteenth Century* (New York: Norton, 1978), 28.

Economic Insight 13.1

Capital Asset Value of a Slave

Writing in the first decade of this century, noted historian Ulrich Phillips claimed that antebellum southern slavery had become unprofitable by the 1840s and 1850s. This led some to believe, incorrectly, that slavery eventually would have died out because of market economic forces.

Phillips based his analysis on two time series: the price of prime field hands like that shown in the figure on the next page, and the trend of cotton prices. Cotton prices varied year to year, with $0.09 being typical in the 1840s and $0.10 being the average in the 1850s. With slave prices rising, especially between 1845 and 1859, but cotton prices hardly increasing, Phillips reasoned that investments in slaves increasingly were realizing losses. He further asserted that these losses surely occurred because slaves worked no harder in 1860 than in 1820 or 1830.

These conclusions were widely accepted until two economists, Alfred Conrad and John Meyer, took the pains in the late 1950s to actually measure the rates of return on investments in slaves. Their asset pricing model in its simplest form took into account the yearly expected output values (the price of cotton [P_c] times the marginal physical product of the slave [MP_s], minus yearly maintenance costs (M) summed over the expected remaining length of life of the slave (t = 0 . . . 30 years). This sum was discounted by (r) to equalize the price paid for the slave (P_s). Expressed as an equation,

$$P_s = \sum_{t=0}^{30} \frac{(P_c \times MP_s - M)_t}{(1+r)^t}$$

As the equation illustrates, if the price of cotton should rise, or output per worker rise, or maintenance costs fall, profits would rise, sending the price of the slave upward. These calculations and a host of other estimates that followed showed a range of returns, typically 8 to 12 percent, that were competitive or above normal compared with returns on alternative investments at that time.

But how, then, did the prices of slaves rise if cotton prices did not? We now know the answer: more output per slave. Phillips erred in overlooking the productivity gains that arose over the period—from economies of scale as plantations grew, from other organizational advances such as assigning tasks, from moving into more productive areas (the southwestern migrations), and from other sources. Phillips's observation, perhaps correct, that slaves worked no harder in 1860 than earlier and used the same technology, overlooked other sources of productivity advance.

Furthermore, there is no evidence to suggest that slavery would have died out. Not even temporary periods of overcapitalization of slaves—that is, when prices of slaves were being bid too high—would support such a conclusion. Indeed, slave prices were apparently overcapitalized in the years from 1818 to 1820 and in the mid-1830s, and prices readjusted to lower levels, reducing losses on "overpriced slaves" to normal rate of return levels. The facts are that slaves produced more, much more, than it cost to rear and maintain them throughout the entire antebellum period. Only if the value of slave output had fallen below subsistence costs would owners have gained by setting slaves free.

continued

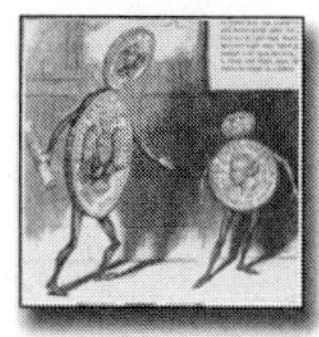

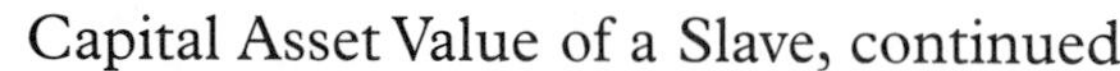

Economic Insight 13.1

Capital Asset Value of a Slave, continued

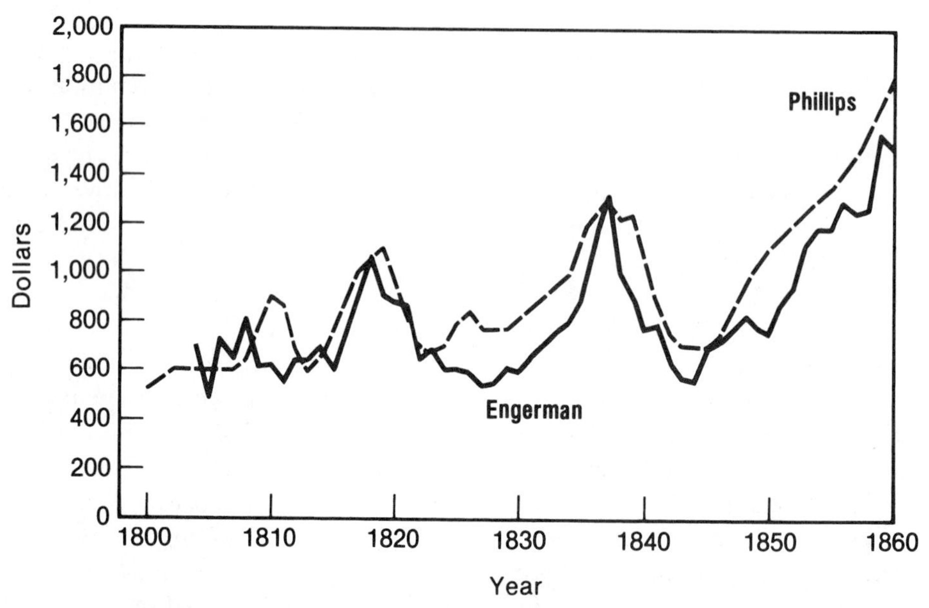

Price of a Prime Male Slave, New Orleans, 1800–1860

Source: Roger L. Ransom and Richard Sutch, "Capitalists without Capital: The Burden of Slavery and the Impact of Emancipation," Agricultural History *(Summer 1988): 155. As reported there, the original sources to these two series are Phillips and Engerman, as follows. Phillips: Prices for 1800, 1801, and 1812 are estimated visually from Ulrich Bonnell Phillips,* Life and Labor in the Old South *(Little, Brown, 1929), p. 177. All other figures are from Alfred H. Conrad and John R. Meyer, "The Economics of Slavery in the Antebellum South,"* Journal of Political Economy *66 (April 1958), reprinted in Alfred H. Conrad and John R. Meyer,* The Economics of Slavery and Other Studies in Economic History *(New York: Aldine, 1964), Table 17, column 6, p. 76. Engerman: Data were supplied by Stanley Engerman. They are mean values of the prices included in a sample of invoices of slave sales held in New Orleans. The sample size for each year ranged between 2.5 and 5 percent. The prices averaged refer to "males ages 18 to 30, without skills, fully guaranteed as without physical or other infirmity." Engerman "utilized only those cases in which there was an individual price listed for a separate slave." For most years, about 15 to 20 observations were used in preparing the averages given.)*

Another perspective is to compare plantations directly with free farms. Were plantations worked by masses of slaves more or less efficient than free-family farm units? Did the South face increasing economic retardation as slavery became more and more entrenched?

Before diving into the evidence, we must acknowledge certain caveats. The problems of measuring efficiency comparatively have been a source of intense scholarly debate. The agricultural output comparisons are really valued outputs rather than strictly physical output comparisons. Variations in soil type and location also pose problems of measurement.

Of course, because of their size, plantations produced more cotton and other goods and foodstuffs than the southern free-family farms. But when comparing output per unit of input (capital, labor, and land in combination), and after adjusting at least in part for variations in land quality, location, length of workday and work year, and other factors, it is clear that the large plantations were considerably more productive than the small or slaveless farms.[5] Table 13.4 shows these productivity comparisons for southern farms and plantations as well as for

[5]For a lively but highly technical debate on the issues of measuring the relative efficiency of slavery, see the exchanges in the March 1979 and September 1980 issues of the *American Economic Review* between Paul David and Peter Temin; Gavin Wright, Donald Schaefer, and Mark Schmitz; and Robert Fogel and Stanley Engerman.

TABLE 13.4 Comparisons of Efficiency in Southern Agriculture by Farm Type and Size (Index of Free Southern Farms = 100)

NUMBER OF SLAVES	INDEX OUTPUT PER UNIT OF TOTAL INPUT
0	100
1–15	101
16–50	133
51 or more	148

Source: Robert W. Fogel and Stanley L. Engerman, "Explaining the Relative Efficiency of Slave Agriculture in the Antebellum South," American Economic Review *67 (June 1977): 285.*

plantations worked by different numbers of slaves. By far the most efficient units were those using 50 or more slaves. Small-scale farming was less productive per unit of input employed, and there was little difference in efficiency between southern free-family farms and small farms employing only a few slaves. Therefore, it appears that racial factors had an insignificant effect on productivity. Black workers with their complementary but white-owned capital and land were about as productive in small units as white workers on single-family farms. Alternatively, plantations with sizable numbers of slaves were extraordinarily efficient. Clearly, economies of scale or some other sources of productivity gains provided advantages for large-sized plantations.

Final answers to why such differences existed still elude us. By and large, however, the main difference appears to be the organization of slaves into production units called *gangs*, the careful selection of slaves by skill for particular uses, and the intensity per hour with which the slaves were worked.

In many ways, the large antebellum plantations were more like factories than farms, and this distinction was even more clearly evident for the much larger sugar plantations in the Caribbean and in South America (see Fogel, 1989). In sugar production, the gang system was pervasive and particularly harsh and life shortening. The organization of slave labor resembled that of assembly-line workers. Contemporary reports, even on cotton, stress these characteristics:

> The cotton plantation was not a farm consisting, as the farm does, in a multiplicity of duties and arrangements within a limited scope, one hand charged with half a dozen parts to act in a day or week. The cotton plantation labor was as thoroughly organized as the cotton mill labor. There were wagoners, the plowmen, the hoe hands, the ditchers, the blacksmiths, the wheelwrights, the carpenters, the men in care of work animals, the men in care of hogs and cattle, the women who had care of the nursery . . . the cooks for all . . . [n]o industry in its practical operation was moved more methodically or was more exacting of a nice discrimination in the application of labor than the Canebrake Cotton plantation.
>
> When the period for planting arrives, the hands are divided into three classes: 1st, the best hands, embracing those of good judgment and quick motion; 2nd, those of the weakest and most inefficient class; 3rd the second class of hoe hands. Thus classified, the first class will run ahead and open a small hole about seven to ten inches apart, into which the 2nd class [will] drop from four to five cotton seeds, and the third class [will] follow and cover with a rake.[6]

[6]These quotations by contemporaries are in reference to the Canebrake Plantation and the McDuffie Plantation, respectively. See Jacob Metzer, "Rational Management, Modern Business Practices, and Economies of Scale in Antebellum Southern Plantations," *Explorations in Economic History* 12 (April 1975): 134–135, for complete citations and other examples.

Perspective 13.1

The Slave Family

In the 1930s the Works Projects Administration and Fisk University compiled nearly 2,200 interviews with ex-slaves. This unique source of information about life under slavery, though undoubtedly biased to various degrees, allows us valuable insights into the slave family (for greater detail and discussion, see Crawford, 1992, the source of the following evidence).

Table 13.5 gives the distribution of family structure under slavery, showing more than half of those interviewed being children of two-parent families living together. Another 12 percent had two parents in their lives, but with the father resident in another plantation and normally allowed weekly visits. Official passes were given for those "approved visits," but many reported that dads often risked being whipped by sneaking other visits. Within the mother-headed households (33 percent) between 15 and 25 percent were formed because the father was white. Death of fathers and separation by sale account for the rest of these single-mother families. Sexual contact between female slaves and whites was much more frequent on small than on large plantations. Once broken by death, desertion, or sale, slaves seldom remarried (stepfathers were very seldom mentioned in the narratives).

The average numbers of children per slave family are shown in Table 13.6 and the large numbers are consistent with the view that white owners preferred slaves in family formations.

Though slaves were sold, thus breaking marriages, such disruptions to the family were not costless to owners. The numbers of fathers being sold away are not known, but children were undoubtedly sold away more frequently than fathers or mothers. Table 13.7 shows the probability by age of a child's being sold away from the family. A child by the age of 16 had typically faced the risk of a 20 percent chance of being sold away from the family. Prudence, if not sensitivity, led to few small children being sold.

TABLE 13.5 Distribution of Family Type for Slave's Family of Origin

FAMILY TYPE	ABSOLUTE FREQUENCY	PERCENTAGE WITHIN SAMPLE
Two-parent, consolidated	694	51.1%
Two-parent, divided residence	168	12.4
One-parent, female headed	451	33.2
One-parent, male headed	24	1.8
Orphan	20	1.5
Total	1,357	100.0%

Note: Family of origin is given by the structure at the time the slave was sold from the family or at emancipation.

Source: Stephen Crawford, "The Slave Family: A View from the Slave Narratives," in Strategic Factors in Nineteenth Century American Economic History: A Volume to Honor Robert W. Fogel, *eds. Claudia Goldin and Hugh Rockoff (Chicago: University of Chicago Press, 1992), 331–350.*

TABLE 13.6 The Average Number of Children per Slave Family

FAMILY TYPE	NUMBER OF CHILDREN
Two-parent, consolidated	7.2
Two-parent, divided residence	8.0
One-parent, female headed	5.7

Source: Stephen Crawford, "The Slave Family: A View from the Slave Narratives," in Strategic Factors in Nineteenth Century American Economic History: A Volume to Honor Robert W. Fogel, *eds. Claudia Goldin and Hugh Rockoff (Chicago: University of Chicago Press, 1992), 331–350.*

Perspective 13.1

The Slave Family, continued

TABLE 13.7 Probability of a Child's Sale from the Family of Origin, by Age

AGE	PERCENTAGE SOLD[a] (1)	EXPECTED NUMBER SOLD[b] (2)	CUMULATIVE NUMBER SOLD (3)	SLAVES AT GIVEN AGE OR OLDER[c] (4)	CUMULATIVE PROBABILITY OF SALE[d] (5)
3	4.8%	5.23	5.23	1,833.6	.0028
4	7.1	7.74	12.97	1,764.6	.0073
5	7.1	7.74	20.71	1,695.6	.0122
6	7.1	7.74	28.45	1,599.9	.0178
7	14.3	15.59	44.04	1,519.4	.0290
8	14.3	15.59	59.63	1,423.6	.0419
9	2.4	2.62	62.25	1,308.6	.0476
10	9.5	10.36	72.61	1,222.4	.0594
11	11.9	12.97	85.58	1,118.9	.0765
12	2.4	2.62	88.20	1,021.2	.0864
13	4.8	5.23	93.43	915.8	.1020
14	4.8	5.23	98.66	785.6	.1256
15	4.8	5.23	103.89	705.1	.1473
16+	4.8	5.23	109.12	561.4	.1944
Total	100.0%	109.0			

[a]*Derived from the percentage of ex-slaves who reported being sold at that age among all who gave age at sale.*
[b]*Derived by multiplying the percentages in column 1 by 109, the total number of ex-slaves in the entire sample sold from their families.*
[c]*Derived by applying the age distribution of the subsample of ex-slaves who gave their exact age, 1,167, to the entire sample, 1,916.*
[d]*Column 3 divided by column 4.*

Source: Stephen Crawford, "The Slave Family: A View from the Slave Narratives," in Strategic Factors in Nineteenth Century American Economic History: A Volume to Honor Robert W. Fogel, *eds. Claudia Goldin and Hugh Rockoff (Chicago: University of Chicago Press, 1992), 331–350.*

The profitable exploitation of slave labor in the antebellum period was made possible principally by speeding up the work and demanding greater work intensity, not longer hours, and the efficiency gains stemmed primarily from worker-task selection and the intensity of work per hour. In fact, slaves on large plantations typically took longer rest breaks and worked less on Sundays than their white counterparts did. Indeed, these conditions were needed to achieve the levels of work intensity imposed on the slaves. It is apparent that these productivity advantages were not voluntary. Essentially, they required slave or forced labor. No free-labor plantations emerged during the period. And as we will see, a significant reduction occurred in labor participation, work intensity, and organization after emancipation.[7]

[7]Recent work on disease incidence differences between whites and blacks in the American South suggests another possible contributing factor to the productivity explanation. Blacks in adulthood had much less incidence of malaria and hookworm (the most common debilitating disease in the South) than whites (see Philip R.P. Coelho and Robert A. McGuire, "Biology Diseases, and Economics: An Epedemiological History of Slavery in the American South," *Journal of Economics* 1 (1999), 151–190.). This difference likely affected the productivities of white versus black laborers, but by how much is not clear. The closeness of the productivity measures for free southern white farms and small plantations suggests these effects were small.

An invoice of ten negroes sent this day to John B Williamson by Geo Kremer named & cost as fol-lows

To wit .. Betsey Kackley $410.00
Nancy Aulick 515.00
Harry & Helen Miller . . 1200.00
Mary Kootz 600.00
Betsey Ott 560.00
Isaac & Fanny Brent . . 992.00
Lucinda Luckett 467.50
George Smith 510.00
Amount of my traveling expences & boarding 5254.50
of lot No 9 not included in the other bills . . 39.50
Kremers expences transporting lot No 9 to Richd 51..00
Carryall hire . . 6.00
$5351.00

I have this day delivered the above named negroes costing including my expences and other expences five thousand three hundred & fifty dollars this May 26th 1835

John W. Pittman

I did intend to leave Nancy child but she made such a damned fuss I had to let her take it I could of got fifty Dollars for so you must add forty Dollars to the above

Invoice of a sale of slaves, 1835. The last two sentences are of special interest.

ECONOMIC EXPLOITATION

It hardly needs to be stressed that black slaves were exploited. They had no political rights, and the law of the plantation and the whim of the taskmaker was the web of confinement the slave directly faced. Owners did not carelessly mistreat their slaves, for obvious reasons. By our measure, a prime male field hand was worth close to $300,000 in 1999 prices (see Economic Insight 13.2).

Various forms of punishments and rewards pressured slaves to be obedient workers. Few failed to witness or feel the sting of the lash and fear combined with the hopelessness of escape in maintaining control. Slaves standards of living were low but self-sustaining; these certainly would have been much higher if the value of their total output had been returned to them. However, because the property rights to their labor and their product resided with the white owner, their output accrued to the owner.

Richard Vedder has attempted to measure the economic exploitation of slaves in the South. His measure is based on the fundamental economic proposition that workers in competitive industries such as cotton production tend to be paid amounts that are equal to what labor contributes at the margin. An additional worker adds a certain value of output. Any sustained difference between the value of output the worker adds and what he or she receives may be reasonably termed economic exploitation.

Economic Insight 13.2

1860 Slave Prices in Today's Values

In 1860 a prime unskilled male field slave cost about $1,800. But how much is that in today's money? One way of answering the question is by using a cost of living index (consumer price index).

A good estimate is that in 2000 the consumer price index was about 20.6 times the level in 1860. So using the consumer price index to inflate (to use the economist's term) the cost of a slave gives a figure in today's money of about $37,000 ($1,800 × 20.6). There are other ways, however, of putting historical values into today's money. Wages of unskilled labor in 1860 were perhaps $0.10 per hour. Today the wage of unskilled labor, at least in some areas of the country, would be about $7 per hour. Using wages to inflate yields a figure in the neighborhood of $125,000 ($1,800 × [$7/$0.10]). A third way of putting $1,800 in 1860 into today's money is by using per capita income. In 1860, per capita income was about $128; in 1999, per capita income was about $21,181. Therefore, using per capita income to inflate the value of a slave yields a value in today's money of about $300,000.

As this example illustrates, there is no unique way of putting things into today's money. The best method to use in a particular circumstance depends on the reason for asking the question. Inflating by the consumer price index tells us what kind of consumption someone was forgoing by owning a slave. For example, if we wanted to get an idea of how much of a sacrifice someone made by freeing a slave, rather than selling him, the first calculation would be appropriate. The other calculations tell us something about how much power a slaveholder had within the society in which he lived, about how much "noise" (political, economic, and social leverage) slaveholders made in the world, to use Deirdre McCloskey's term. If we want to know how valuable an asset a slave was in the production process, perhaps the high figure of $300,000 is most appropriate.

For the average slave, this difference (the value of output added minus maintenance costs) divided by the value of the output added was at least 50 percent and may have been as high as 65 percent.[8]

Of course, there was much more to the exploitation issue than simply taking one-half of each worker's earnings. The mere entrapment of workers blocked their advance materially and otherwise by taking away their incentive for self-improvement and gain.

Perhaps the best thing that can be said about the economic conditions of American slavery is that they were not typically as bad as the conditions of slavery elsewhere. The drastic relative declines in the slave population in the Caribbean and in Brazil testify to the especially brutal conditions there. By comparison, the southern United States offered treatment that was life sustaining. Slaves in the antebellum South experienced standards of material comfort that were low by today's standards but well above those of the masses in many parts of their contemporary world.

---

[8] For further elaboration, see Richard Vedder, "The Slave Exploitation (Expropriation) Rate," *Explorations in Economic History* 12 (October 1975): 453–458. As Vedder notes, in New England cotton textile mills (a sample of 71 firms) in 1820, the comparable exploitation calculation was 22 percent; for iron workers in 1820 (101 firms), the rate was 28 percent. Similar levels of exploitation (24 and 29 percent, respectively) have been computed in Roger L. Ransom and Richard Sutch, *One Kind of Freedom* (Cambridge: Cambridge University Press, 1977), 3.

ECONOMIC ENTRENCHMENT AND REGIONAL INCOMES

Although the slave system proved efficient on the plantation, its economic advantages were not widely applicable elsewhere. As a result, the South experienced little structural change during the antebellum years. For instance, the South was slow to industrialize, partly because of the slave system. Some slaves did become skilled craftsmen, and slaves were employed in cotton factories, coal mines, ironworks, lumber mills, and railroads. There was little point in incurring the costs of training slaves for industrial occupations on a large scale, however, when they could readily and profitably be put to work in agriculture.

In addition, the South experienced very little immigration from Europe or elsewhere. It was not the South's "peculiar institution" that kept European migrants away; immigration did not increase after emancipation. Europeans tended to settle in latitudes where the climate was like that of their former home. The main deterrent to locating in the South, however, was that outsiders perceived a lack of opportunity there; immigrants feared that they would become "poor whites." By 1860, only 3.4 percent of the southern population was foreign born, compared with 17 percent in the central states and 15 percent in New England.

There can be no doubt that plantation slavery when viewed as a business was profitable. Extremely high net returns in parts of the cotton belt and rewards at least equal to those of alternative employments of capital in most areas of the Deep South were the rule. Nor were there economic forces at work making the slave economy selfdestructive. There is simply no evidence to support the contention that slave labor was overcapitalized, and slaves clearly reproduced sufficiently to maintain a growing work force. In addition, internal migration from the older southern states to the new cotton belt illustrated the flexibility of the southern economy.

This flexibility, exhibited in the western migrations, was especially important to the South. Table 13.8 shows income figures for various regions in 1840 and 1860. Note that the nearly 44 percent growth in income for the entire free South, from $105 to $150, was higher than the internal growth of any subregion in the South (about one-third for the old South, about 15 percent for the new South). The southern migrations, in contrast to those in the north, were from poorer to richer areas on average, and this leveraged up the income growth for the South as a whole. As we shall see, the South was vitally concerned, for apparently sound economic reasons, with the right to extend slavery into western lands. Also noteworthy is the relative position of the West South Central region, where King Cotton and sugar reigned supreme. This was by far the highest income region in the country. And these high relative standings remain whether or not slaves are included in the population figures. When the incomes per capita of only the free population are compared,

TABLE 13.8 Per Capita Income Before the Civil War (in 1860 prices)

	TOTAL POPULATION		FREE POPULATION	
	1840	1860	1840	1860
National Average	$ 96	$128	$109	$144
North	109	141	110	142
Northeast	129	181	130	183
North Central	65	89	66	90
South	74	103	105	150
South Atlantic	66	84	96	124
East South Central	69	89	92	124
West South Central	151	184	238	274

Source: *Robert W. Fogel and Stanley L. Engerman, "The Economics of Slavery," in* The Reinterpretation of American Economic History *(New York: Harper & Row, 1971), Table 8, 335.*

TABLE 13.9 Total Value of Slaves in the United States, 1810–1860 (in millions of dollars)

YEAR	TOTAL VALUE
1810	$ 316
1820	610
1830	577
1840	997
1850	1,286
1860	3,059

Source: Roger L. Ransom and Richard Sutch, "Capitalists without Capital: The Burden of Slavery and the Impact of Emancipation," Agricultural History *(Summer 1988): 150–151.*

even the older, less wealthy southern areas show levels that were quite high.[9] There can be little doubt that on the eve of the Civil War, the South was a very rich area indeed.

From the moral, social, and political viewpoints, however, southern slavery imposed a growing source of selfdestruction on the American people. The system epitomized a great barrier to human decency and social progress that was contrary to deeply felt ideals in many quarters. With almost religious fervor, abolitionist elements grew in strength, and national disunity grew proportionately.

As the moral arguments against slavery gained a greater hearing, the economic costs of emancipation grew as well. Table 13.9 shows the wealth held in slaves in the South by decade. After 1830, the rise in value was dramatic, reaching almost $3.1 billion in 1860. According to Ransom and Sutch, slaves represented 44 percent of the total wealth in the major cotton-growing states in 1859, and real estate comprised another 25 percent.[10] Could $3.1 billion in taxes be raised to compensate owners for slaves emancipated? Would owners give up such wealth voluntarily? As an additional consideration, southerners had witnessed, in the late 1830s, the outcome of rapid emancipation in the British West Indies. There, land values plummeted when the gang system disappeared and labor was withdrawn from the fields. The prospect of land value losses adding to the wealth losses of uncompensated emancipations stiffened the resolve of the South's slaveholding oligarchy. Laws were passed in the southern states increasing the punishment for insurrection and for assisting runaways: Eleven imposed the death penalty on slaves participating in insurrection, and 13 made it a capital crime for free men to incite slave insurrection. Several states began requiring legislative consent for manumission on a case-by-case basis. Seven required newly freed slaves to leave their territory. Freedoms to bear arms, assemble in public meetings, and sell liquor were frequently denied free blacks. In these and other ways, slavery became more entrenched, both economically and legally.

POLITICAL COMPROMISES AND REGIONAL CONFLICT

For a majority of Americans living at the time of slavery, the most significant issue was its containment, not its eradication. Indeed, the basis of political compromise on this issue was first established in the Northwest Ordinance, passed unanimously by Congress in 1787. Article six reads: "there shall be neither slavery nor involuntary servitude in the said territory . . . provided always, that any person escaping into the same, from whom labor or service is claimed in any of the original states, such fugitive may be lawfully reclaimed and

[9]Robert W. Fogel and Stanley L. Engerman, (1974), used $20 per year as the average income of slaves to estimate the incomes of only the free population. Later work by them and others raised the yearly average values of slave consumption (income). Therefore, modest downward adjustments in the free population in the South are required, but they do not change significantly the conclusions given here.

[10]Roger L. Ransom and Richard Sutch, "Capitalists without Capital: The Burden of Slavery and the Impact of Emancipation," *Agricultural History* (Summer 1988): 138–139.

A familiar scene—slaves picking cotton as white overseers look on. Costs of supervision were higher in northern agriculture because the labor force often had to be dispersed.

conveyed to the person claiming his or her labor or service as foresaid." The 1787 ordinance, in effect, outlawed slavery in lands that became the states of Ohio, Indiana, Michigan, Illinois, Wisconsin, and Minnesota. This set the stage for controlling the expansion of slavery in other territories, allowing some new regions at least to be nonslave, but this important legislation did not provide a final solution.

The western migrations, both north and south, continued to bring the issue of slavery to a head. The key problem for the South, as a political unit, was to maintain at least equal voting power in the Senate. The South accomplished this objective and won a series of compromises that enabled it to extend the institution of slavery and counter abolitionist threats.

In 1819, the Senate was balanced: There were 11 slave and 11 free states. By the Missouri Compromise of 1820 (see Map 13.1), Missouri was admitted as a slave state and Maine as a free state on the condition that slavery should thereafter be prohibited in the territory of the Louisiana Purchase north of 36 × 30′. For nearly 30 years after this, states were admitted to the Union in pairs, one slave and one free, and by 1850, there were 15 free and 15 slave states. As of that year, slavery had been prohibited in the Northwest Territory, in the territory of the Louisiana Purchase north of 36 × 30′, and in the Oregon Territory—vast areas in which an extensive slave system would not have been profitable anyway. Violent controversy arose over the basis of admission for prospective states in the area ceded to the United States by Mexico. The terms of the Mexican Cession required that the territory remain permanently free, yet Congress in 1848 had rejected the Wilmot Proviso, which would have prohibited slavery in the Southwest, where its extension was economically feasible. In the end, California was admitted as a free state in 1850. In the territories of Utah and New Mexico, however, slaveholding could be permitted. The final decision on slavery was to be made by the territorial populations on application for admission to the Union.

Further events of the 1850s for a time appeared to portend ultimate victory for the South. The Kansas-Nebraska Act of 1854 (see Map 13.2 on page 258) in effect repealed the

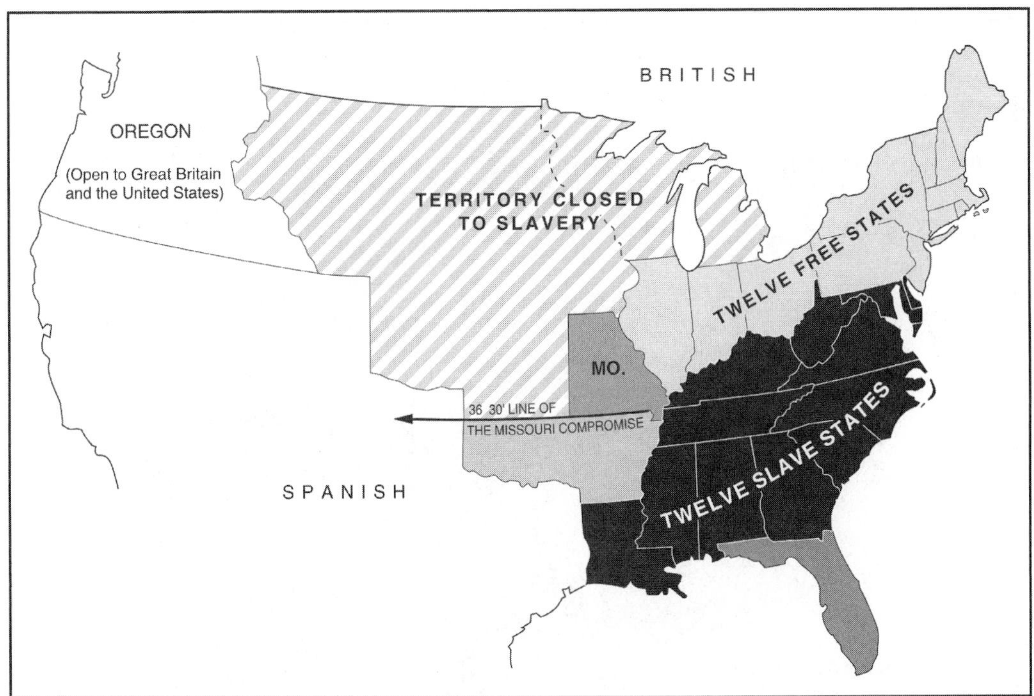

MAP 13.1 The Missouri Compromise of 1820 *After this enactment, growing sectional acrimony was supposed to be a thing of the past. For a time, a truce did prevail.*

Missouri Compromise by providing for "popular sovereignty" in the hitherto unsettled portions of the Louisiana Purchase. The result was gunfire and bloodshed in Kansas. In the *Dred Scott* decision (1857), the Supreme Court went even further, declaring that Congress could not prohibit slavery in the territories. And during this time, southerners, desperately eager to inhibit the movement of small farmers into territories where slavery could not flourish, successfully resisted passage of a homestead act that would have given free land to settlers.

Yet legislative successes could be achieved only as long as Democrats from the North and Northwest were willing to ally themselves with the South. Toward the end of the 1850s, the antislavery movement in the North became irresistible. In large part, the movement was led by those who opposed the servitude of anyone on purely ethical grounds, but altruistic motives were reinforced by economic interests. Northwest farmers resisted the extension of the plantation system because they feared the competition of large units with their small ones. And as transportation to eastern centers improved, especially through the Northern Gateway, the products of the Northwest increasingly flowed into the Middle Atlantic states and Europe. In this way, the people of the Northwest found their economic interests more closely tied to the eastern industrialists than to the southern planters. The large migrations of Irish and Germans, who had no stake in slavery, added to the shift in economic and political interests near midcentury. The Republican party, founded in the mid-1850s, capitalized on the shift in economic interests. As old political alignments weakened, the Republican party rapidly gained strength, chiefly from those who opposed the extension of slavery into the territories.

In the opening speech of his sixth debate with Stephen A. Douglas on October 13, 1858, in Quincy, Illinois, Abraham Lincoln elaborated on slavery:

> We have in this nation the element of domestic slavery. . . . The Republican party think it wrong—we think it is a moral, a social, and a political wrong. We think it is a

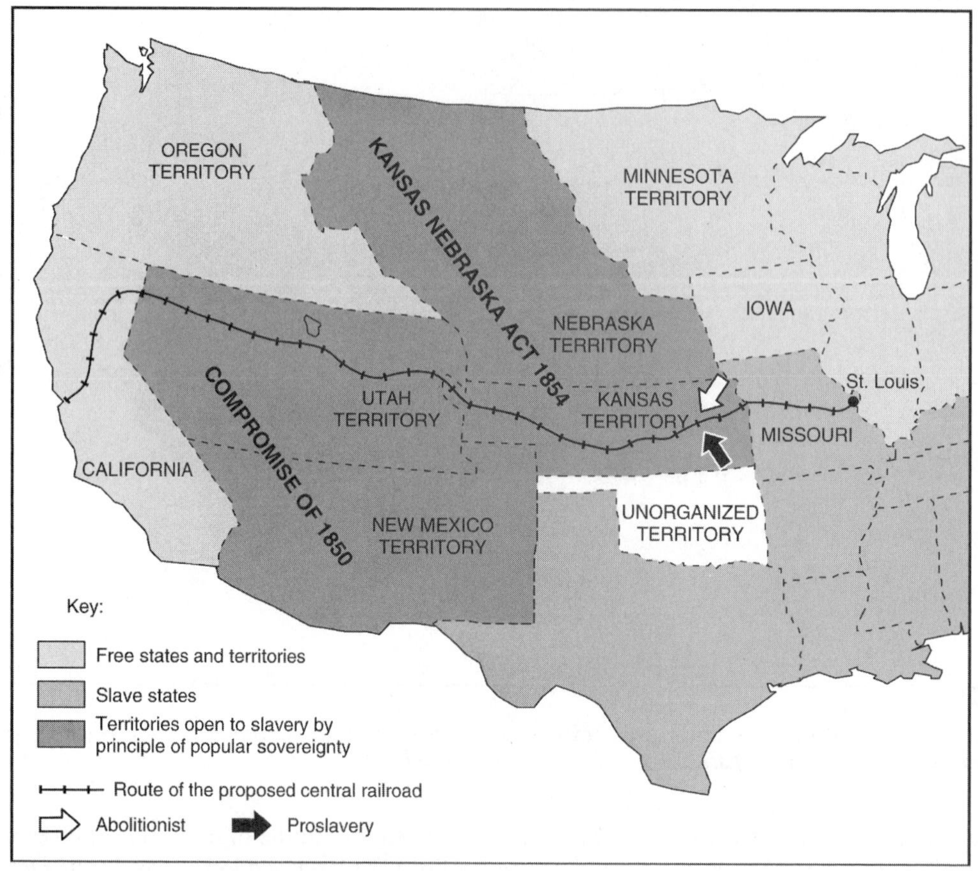

MAP 13.2 New Settlements *The Compromise of 1850 and the Kansas-Nebraska Act of 1854 were further attempts to keep sectional strife from erupting into war. The concept of "popular sovereignty" introduced in this act led to conflict in Kansas.*

> wrong not confining itself merely to the persons or the State where it exists, but that it is a wrong which in its tendency, to say the least, affects the existence of the whole nation. . . . I suppose that in reference both to its actual existence in the nation, and to our constitutional obligations, we have no right at all to disturb it in the States where it exists, and we profess that we have no more inclination to disturb it than we have the right to do it. . . . We also oppose it as an evil so far as it seeks to spread itself. We insist on the policy that shall restrict it to its present limits. . . . We oppose the Dred Scott decision in a certain way. . . . We propose so resisting it as to have it reversed if we can, and a new judicial rule established upon this subject.

Lincoln's advocacy of fencing in slavery as the South saw it violated the federal Constitution. Cotton was already flourishing in Texas. California and Arizona boded well for the extension of cotton cultivation. These promising lands had been acquired from Mexico in the 1840s. Were southerners to be excluded from them?

From the southern perspective, the election of Lincoln in 1860 presented only two alternatives: submission or secession. To a wealthy and proud people, submission was unthinkable.[11] To Lincoln, alternatively, the Union had to be preserved.

[11] Recall the prewar scene from *Gone With the Wind* when eager southern warriors were predicting a short war and a decisive southern victory. Rhett Butler, alone, cautioned to the contrary.

The holocaust that maintained the Union cost the country more lives and human suffering than any other war in the history of the United States. Although initially, emancipation was not an objective of the northern war effort, it became the ultimate moral justification for the war.

SELECTED REFERENCES AND SUGGESTED READINGS

The American Memory Historical Collections of the Library of Congress Web site provides access to the WPA Slave Narratives, the African American pamphlet collection, and other valuable sources. **http://memory.loc.gov/.**

Aufhauser, R. Keith. "Slavery and Technological Change." *Journal of Economic History* 34 (1974): 36–50.

Blassingame, John. *The Slave Community: Plantation Life in the Antebellum South.* New York: Oxford University Press, 1972.

Canarella, Georgio, and John A. Tomaske. "The Optimal Utilization of Slaves." *Journal of Economic History* 35 (1975): 621–629.

Coelho, Philip R. P., and Robert A. McGuire. "Biology Diseases, and Economics: An Epidemiological History of Slavery in the American South." *Journal of Bionomics* 1 (1999): 151–190.

Conrad, Alfred, and John Meyer. "The Economics of Slavery in the Antebellum South." *Journal of Political Economy* 66 (1958): 95–130.

Crawford, Stephen. "The Slave Family: A View from the Slave Narratives." In *Strategic Factors in Nineteenth Century American Economic History: A Volume to Honor Robert W. Fogel*, eds. Claudia Golden and Hugh Rockoff. Chicago: University of Chicago Press, 1992, 331–350.

Curtin, Philip D. *The Atlantic Slave Trade: A Census.* Madison: University of Wisconsin Press, 1969.

David, Paul, Herbert Gutman, Richard Sutch, Peter Temin, and Gavin Wright. *Reckoning with Slavery.* New York: Oxford University Press, 1976.

Douglass, Frederick. *Narrative of the Life of Frederick Douglass.* New York: New American Library, 1968.

Elkins, Stanley M. *Slavery: A Problem of American Institutional and Intellectual Life.* New York: Grosset & Dunlap, 1959.

Eltis, David. "Free and Coerced Transatlantic Migrations: Some Comparisons." *American Historical Review* 88 (1983): 251–280.

Engerman, Stanley L. "Slavery and Its Consequences for the South in the Nineteenth Century." In *The Cambridge Economics History of the United States*, Vol. II, *The Long Nineteenth Century*, eds. Stanley L. Engerman and Robert E. Gallman. New York: Cambridge University Press, 2000, 329–366.

Engerman, Stanley, and Eugene Genovese. *Race and Slavery in the Western Hemisphere: Quantitative Studies.* Princeton, N. J.: Princeton University Press, 1978.

Fleisig, Heywood. "Slavery, the Supply of Agricultural Labor, and the Industrialization of the South." *Journal of Economic History* 36 (1976): 572–597.

Fogel, Robert W. "Three Phases of Cliometric Research on Slavery and Its Aftermath." *American Economic Review* 65 (May 1975): 37–46.

———. *Without Consent or Contract: The Rise and Fall of American Slavery.* New York: Norton, 1989.

Fogel, Robert W., and Stanley L. Engerman. "The Relative Efficiency of Slavery: A Comparison of Northern and Southern Agriculture in 1860." *Explorations in Economic History* 8 (Spring 1971): 353–367.

———. *Time on the Cross: The Economics of American Slavery,* 2 vols. Boston: Little, Brown, 1974.

———. "Explaining the Relative Efficiency of Slave Agriculture in the Antebellum South." *American Economic Review* 67 (June 1977): 275–296.

———. "Explaining the Relative Efficiency of Slave Agriculture in the Antebellum South: A Reply." *American Economic Review* 70 (September 1980): 672–690.

Genovese, Eugene. *Roll, Jordan, Roll: The World the Slaves Made.* New York: Vintage Books, 1976.

———. *From Rebellion to Revolution: Afro-American Slave Revolts in the Modern World.* BatonRouge: Louisiana State University Press, 1979.

Goldin, Claudia. *Urban Slavery in the American South.* Chicago: University of Chicago Press, 1976.

Gray, Lewis. *History of Agriculture in the Southern United States to 1860*, 2 vols. Washington, D.C.: Carnegie Institution of Washington, 1933.

Gunderson, Gerald. "The Origins of the American Civil War." *Journal of Economic History* 34 (1974): 915–950.

Gutman, Herbert. *The Black Family in Slavery and Freedom.* New York: Pantheon Books, 1976.

Hutchinson, W. K., and Samuel H. Williamson. "The Self-Sufficiency of the Ante-Bellum South: Estimates of the Food Supply." *Journal of Economic History* 31 (1971): 591–612.

Kotlikoff, Laurence J., and Sebastian E. Pinera. "The Old South's Stake with Inter-Regional Movement of Slaves, 1850–1860." *Journal of Economic History* 37 (1977): 434–450.

Metzer, Jacob. "Rational Management, Modern Business Practice, and Economies of Scale in the Antebellum Plantations." *Explorations in Economic History* 12 (April 1975): 123–150.

Olmsted, Frederick L. *The Cotton Kingdom: A Traveler's Observations on Cotton and Slavery in the American Slave States.* New York: Knopf, 1953.

———. *The Slave States*. New York: Capricorn Books, 1959.

Parker, William, ed. *The Structure of the Cotton Economy of the Antebellum South.* Washington, D.C.: Agricultural History Society, 1970.

Passell, Peter. "The Impact of Cotton Land Distribution on the Ante-Bellum Economy." *Journal of Economic History* 31 (1971): 917–937.

Phillips, Ulrich B. "The Economic Cost of Slaveholding in the Cotton Belt." *Political Science Quarterly* (June 1905).

Ransom, Roger L. *Conflict and Compromise: The Political Economy of Slavery, Emancipation, and the American Civil War.* New York and London: Cambridge University Press, 1989.

Ransom, Roger L., and Richard Sutch. "Capitalists without Capital: The Burden of Slavery and the Impact of Emancipation." *Agricultural History* (Summer 1988): 133–160.

Schmitz, Mark D., and Donald F. Schaefer. "Slavery, Freedom, and the Elasticity of Substitution." *Explorations in Economic History* 15 (July 1978): 327–337.

Steckel, Richard H. "A Peculiar Population: The Nutrition, Health, and Mortality of American Slaves from Childhood to Maturity." *Journal of Economic History* 46 (1986): 721–741.

Steckel, Richard H., and Richard A. Jensen. "New Evidence on the Causes of Slave and Crew Mortality in the Atlantic Slave Trade." *Journal of Economic History* 46 (1986): 57–77.

Sutch, Richard. "The Treatment Received by American Slaves: A Critical Review of the Evidence Presented in Time on the Cross." *Explorations in Economic History* 12 (October 1975): 335–438.

Thomas, Robert P., and Richard N. Bean. "The Fishers of Men: The Profits of the Slave Trade." *Journal of Economic History* 34 (1974): 885–914.

Vedder, Richard K. "The Slave Exploitation (Expropriation) Rate." *Explorations in Economic History* 12 (October 1975): 453–458.

Washington, Booker T. *Up from Slavery.* New York: Bantam Books, 1963.

Wright, Gavin. "Slavery and the Cotton Boom." *Explorations in Economic History* 12 (October 1975): 439–452.

———. *The Political Economy of the Cotton South: Households, Markets, and Wealth in the Nineteenth Century*. New York: Norton, 1978.

Part Three

THE REUNIFICATION ERA: 1860–1920

ECONOMIC AND HISTORICAL PERSPECTIVES *1860–1920*

1. For nearly 100 years following 1815, there were no major wars between national coalitions. The U.S. Civil War, our bloodiest war ever, was a violent exception in this long period of global peace.
2. After the Civil War, rapid industrialization in the North and renewed western expansion sustained a high overall growth rate for the nation. The large absolute fall in output in the South due to the war and emancipation and the slow pace of growth in the cotton belt ushered in an era of southern backwardness and regional disparity.
3. Emancipation redistributed wealth and incomes sharply from white slave owners to blacks but created a legacy of slavery that sustained black poverty, especially in the Deep South.
4. By the mid-1890s, the United States had become the world's leading industrial power, and by 1910 it was out producing by nearly twice the nearest industrial rival, Germany, while England had slipped into third place.
5. Technological change, economies of scale, and mass production methods became the main engines of modern economic growth.
6. The path of growth was far from smooth. Periods of deflation, financial crises, and fears of the concentration of wealth led to demands for reform of the economic and financial systems.
7. The U.S. population topped 100 million during World War I; 48 states were in the Union; and federal, state, and local expenditures combined reached a record high of nearly 10 percent of GNP.

Chapter Fourteen

War, Recovery, and Regional Divergence

Chapter Theme

The Democratic party split in mid-1860, permitting the Republican candidate for President, Abraham Lincoln, to win the November election with a mere 40 percent of the popular vote. Lincoln carried the North and West solidly, but his name did not even appear on 10 state ballots in the South. The South's political strategy had been to control the Senate and the presidency. Both were lost in 1860.

By the time of Lincoln's inauguration on March 4, 1861, 10 southern states had followed South Carolina's decision to secede. One of Lincoln's first tasks was to counter threats to Fort Sumter in Charleston Harbor. His order to reinforce the fort gave South Carolinians the excuse they sought to begin shooting.

Slavery was the root cause of the Civil War. The United States had equivocated on the slave issue both in 1776 and in 1790. The last "slavery truce," in 1850, was based on popular sovereignty in the western territories, and it ended within a decade. By 1860, the South was prepared to fight to save its social order, based on plantation slavery. The North was prepared to fight to save the Union and to save the Republican victory that "finally had contained the slave power within the political framework of the United States."[1] Permitting independence to the southern states would have divided the nation and allowed the South to pursue a separate foreign policy committed to the expansion of slavery.

Lincoln's key miscalculation, like the South's, was his belief that a strong show of force would bring the fighting to a speedy end. The South's victory at Bull Run, the first great battle of the Civil War, added to southern confidence and resolve to maintain the course of rebellion.

Economic Reasoning Proposition

The war proved to be longer and more destructive than anyone in power imagined at its start. An estimated 620,000 American soldiers and sailors would lose their lives, nearly as many as in all the rest of America's wars combined. By the time the war ended, America's society and economy had been radically transformed. The most important change was the freeing of 4 million slaves. Moreover, the institutional framework (Economic Reasoning Proposition 4) of nearly every aspect of economic life—

[1] Roger Ransom, *Conflict and Compromise: The Political Economy of Slavery, Emancipation, and the American Civil War* (New York and London: Cambridge University Press, 1989), 177.

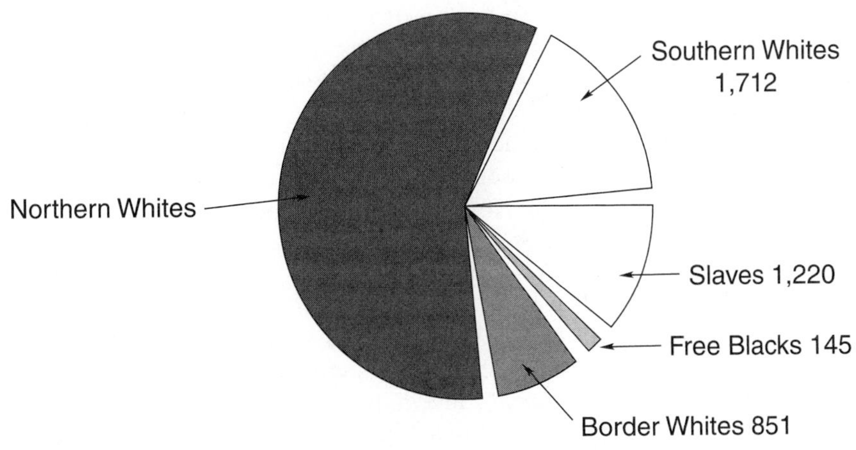

FIGURE 14.1 Population of Males 10-49 Years of Age in 1860 (in thousands)

Source: Roger Ransom, Conflict and Compromise: The Political Economy of Slavery, Emancipation, and the American Civil War *(New York and London: Cambridge University Press, 1989), Figure 6.2.*

including finance, education, land policies, and tariff policies—was altered in some way. In the North and parts of the South, recovery from the war was rapid. But in parts of the South, the institutional framework that developed after the Civil War prevented the former slaves and poor whites from being rapidly integrated into the mainstream of the American economy.

THE ECONOMICS OF WAR

Despite ample pride, talent, and faith in its cause, the South was woefully unprepared for a protracted war. Figure 14.1 provides a rough portrayal of the available human resources that each side possessed for potential combat. The reality of the situation, moreover, was that the 1.2 million military-aged slaves in the South could not be used for fighting on the front, and probably fewer than 30 percent of eligible whites in the Border States sided with the southern cause.[2]

Indeed, the South had to use some of its precious manpower to repress its slave labor force. And, when circumstances permitted, slaves and free blacks joined the Union forces, further tipping the balance in favor of the North. By the end of the war, blacks in the Union army alone outnumbered the Confederate forces. Conventional military wisdom of the day calculated a ratio of two to one for an attacking army to overcome a defending army. Ultimately, those calculations proved valid: The North could outman the South three or more to one.

In industrial capacity, the comparisons are even more lopsided. Value added in manufacturing in the North, according to Fred Bateman and Thomas Weiss, totaled $1.6 billion in 1860.[3] It was merely $193 million in the South, half of it in Virginia. Richmond, Virginia, was also the site of the only cannon manufacturer in the South. (The original buildings are still there along the James River.) Initially, neither side had a significant advantage in arms production, and both depended heavily on imported arms. But the North was able to increase production quickly. The South was much less able to do this, and its lack of domestic manufacturing bore down heavily after the federal naval blockade during 1863 and 1864 shut off foreign supplies.

[2]Ibid., 196.

[3]Fred Bateman and Thomas Weiss, *A Deplorable Scarcity* (Chapel Hill: University of North Carolina Press, 1981).

Particularly troubling to the South, especially after the North took control of the Mississippi River, was the lack of a transport network sufficient to move food and supplies to the troops. The South's limited rail network was strained to capacity, but the primary shortage was of horses and mules. Because the fighting was largely on southern soil, the South's animal stocks fell relative to the North's as the war wore on.

These comparisons, however, do not mean that the South's decision to fight was irrational. The South's hope was that the North would eventually tire of the enormous human costs of the war and agree to let the South go its own way. The Revolutionary War had provided a forceful example of a nation winning independence from an economically and militarily more powerful foe. (For Robert E. Lee, that example was part of the family history: His father, "Light-Horse Harry" Lee, had been an outstanding cavalry commander in the Revolution.) In the summer of 1864, even after numerous southern defeats, it still seemed possible that war weariness might defeat Lincoln in his bid for reelection—indeed, Lincoln himself doubted that he would win—and that Lincoln's successor might negotiate a peace that preserved slavery. However, General William Tecumseh Sherman's capture of Atlanta in September rekindled Lincoln's fortunes, and Lincoln's reelection sealed the South's fate.

Trade and Finance Policies South and North

With the exception of two new government-built and -operated munitions factories, the South maintained its emphasis on agriculture. The South's early confidence in the power of King Cotton and the likelihood of a quick end to fighting, moreover, encouraged it to adopt trade policies that reinforced its poor preparation for war.

The northern naval blockade did not become really effective until 1863. Thus, for nearly two years the South could produce and export specialty crops, particularly cotton, to England in exchange for munitions and manufactures. The Confederate government, however, discouraged exports in the hope of forcing England to support the southern effort; during 1861 and 1862, the South exported only 13,000 bales of cotton from a crop of 4 million bales. The southern government also imposed a ban on sales of cotton to the North. Although the "cotton famine" imposed severe costs on British employers and workers, England could not be moved from neutrality. In hindsight, it is clear that these policies weakened the southern war effort.

Besides production and trade problems, the South also faced financial difficulties. Although a few bonds backed by cotton were sold in Europe, foreigners for the most part were unwilling to lend to the Confederacy, especially after the North's naval blockade became effective. It also proved difficult, for both political and economic reasons, to develop an effective administrative machinery for collecting taxes. The South's war materials and support, therefore, were financed primarily by inflationary means—paper note issues. Only 40 percent of its expenditures were backed by taxes or borrowing.

Indexes of prices and money in the South given in Figure 14.2 show clearly that prices rose further and faster than the stock of money and that the final months were ones of hyperinflation. There were two reasons for the gap that opened between prices and money: the decline in southern production and the decline in confidence in the southern currency.

A diary account of an exchange in 1864 reveals the decline in confidence in the Confederate paper money:

> She asked me 20 dollars for five dozen eggs and then said she would take it in "Confederate." Then I would have given her 100 dollars as easily. But if she had taken my offer of yarn! I haggle in yarn for the million the part of a thread! When they ask for Confederate money, I never stop to chafer. I give them 20 or 50 dollar cheerfully for anything.[4]

[4]Dated March 7, 1864, from *Mary Chesnut's Civil War*, ed. C. Vann Woodward, (New Haven, Conn.: Yale University Press, 1981), 749.

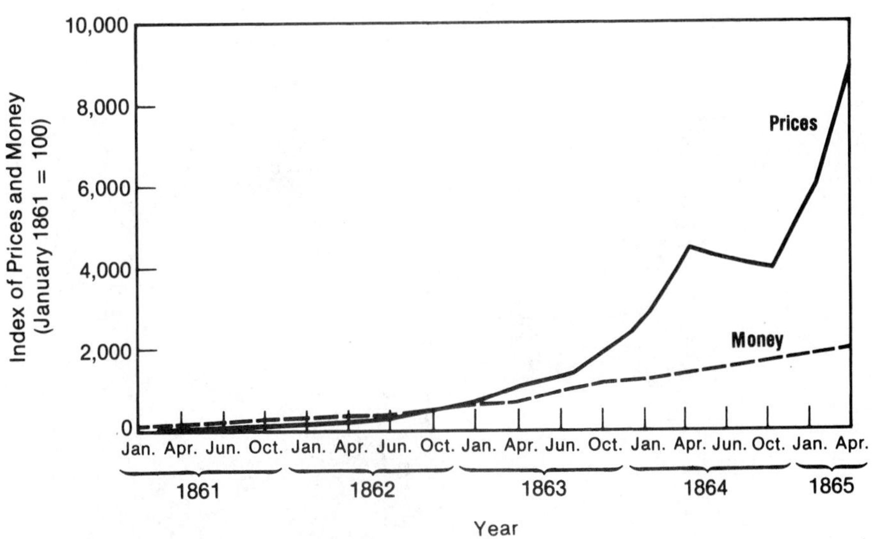

FIGURE 14.2 INFLATION IN THE CONFEDERACY
The rate of inflation was not very great in the beginning of the Civil War, but the value of a Confederate dollar had depreciated to about 1 percent of its original value by the end of the war.

Source: E. M. Lerner, "Money, Wages, and Prices in the Confederacy, 1861–1865," Journal of Political Economy *63 (February 1955): 29.*

Despite the heroism and daring displayed by the Confederates, Union troops increasingly disrupted and occupied more and more southern territory. By late 1861, Union forces controlled Missouri, Kentucky, and West Virginia; they took New Orleans in the spring of 1862, cutting off the major southern trade outlet. By 1863, thanks to the brilliant campaigning of Ulysses S. Grant, the entire Mississippi River basin was under Union control. Sherman's march through Georgia in 1864, in which he followed a deliberate policy of destroying the productive capacity of the region, splintered the Confederacy and cut off Lee's Army of Northern Virginia from an important source of supplies.

Once a Union victory appeared likely, confidence declined even more sharply, producing the astronomical rates of inflation experienced in the final months of the war.

The economic strain of the war was not as severe in the North as it was in the South, but the costs of the war were extremely high even there. A substantial portion of the labor force was reallocated to the war effort, and the composition of production changed with the disruption of cotton trade and the growing number of defaults on southern debts. At the outset, in 1861, a sharp financial panic occurred, and banks suspended payments of specie. With the U.S.Treasury empty, the government quickly raised taxes and sold bonds. The tax changes included the first federal taxes on personal and business incomes. But the most significant increases were in tariffs and internal taxes on a wide range of commodities—including specific taxes on alcohol and tobacco (which are still with us) as well as on iron, steel, and coal—and a general tax on manufacturing output. Despite these increases, however, bond sales brought in nearly three times the revenues of taxes.

The Union government also resorted to inflationary finance. Paper notes, termed "greenbacks" because of their color (and because they were backed by green ink rather than gold or silver), were issued. They circulated widely but declined in value relative to gold.[5]

[5]The greenbacks were legal tender for paying private debts (including the obligations of banks to their depositors), but they were not legal tender for paying tariffs—these had to be paid in gold.

The South could not match the vast amount of munitions produced by northern industry.

In 1864, one gold dollar was worth two and one-half greenbacks, and the northern price level in 1864 in terms of greenbacks was twice what it had been in 1860. Nevertheless, the North escaped the near hyperinflation that confounded the South.

THE CIVIL WAR AND NORTHERN INDUSTRIALIZATION

Writing in the years between World War I and World War II, Charles Beard and Louis Hacker provided a captivating economic interpretation of the Civil War—namely, that the war spurred northern industrial expansion. The *Beard-Hacker thesis* emphasized the transfer of political power from southern agrarians to northern industrial capitalists. With new power in Congress, northern legislators passed laws intended to unify markets and propel industrialization. The range of new programs established during the war was remarkable, including the establishment of the national banking system, an increase in tariffs (to protect American industry from foreign competition), the land-grant college act, and grants of land to transcontinental railroads. We will discuss the impact of these pieces of legislation at

TABLE 14.1 Average Annual Rate of Growth of Commodity Output, 1840–1899

YEARS	U.S. ECONOMY	MANUFACTURING SECTOR
1840–1859	4.6%	7.8%
1860–1869	2.0	2.3
1870–1899	4.4	6.0

Source: Robert E. Gallman, "Commodity Output, 1839–1899," in Trends in the American Economy in the Nineteenth Century, *24, Series on Income and Wealth (Princeton, N. J.: Princeton University Press, 1960).*

length in later chapters; it is sufficient to note here that subsequent research, while not denying important effects on individuals and regions, has questioned the overall impact of these changes. Total output of the economy would probably have been much the same in any case.

The Beard-Hacker thesis also emphasized that the war stimulated the economy and increased investment. This part of the thesis, too, has been rejected in subsequent research, based on estimates of economic activity that were not available when the thesis was formulated (Economic Reasoning Proposition 5). Perhaps this is less surprising when we realize that nearly 1 million men—or almost 15 percent of the labor force of 7.5 million—were normally involved in the fighting each year. Of these working-age soldiers, 259,000 Confederate men and 360,000 Union men were killed and another 251,000 southerners and 356,000 northerners were wounded. One person was killed and another wounded for every six slaves freed and for every 10 southerners kept within the Union. Claudia Goldin and Frank Lewis have assessed these permanent losses of labor and human capital (Economic Reasoning Proposition 2) to have had economic values approaching $1.8 billion ($1.06 billion in the North and $787 million in the South—all lost). In addition, the North spent $2.3 billion directly on the war effort; the South spent $1 billion through direct government outlays. Another $1.5 billion worth of property was destroyed, most of this in the South. These combined sums of $6.6 billion were probably more than twice the size of our national income in 1860 and exceeded eight times the value added of total U.S. manufacturing that year.

The tragedy of the Civil War is compounded by the fact that in 1860, the total market value of slaves was approximately $3.06 billion.[6] The costs of the war were more than twice the cost of purchasing the slaves. This does not mean that peaceful abolition was realistic before the war. After 1845, peaceful abolition like that undertaken by the British in the West Indies was viewed in the South as a complete disaster. Southerners were convinced that the economy of the West Indies was in shambles and that slave owners there had lost fortunes in the process of emancipation.

The work of Stanley Engerman and Robert Gallman provides further ground for rejecting the Beard-Hacker thesis that the Civil War stimulated postwar industrialization. As shown in Table 14.1, growth rates of total commodity output and manufacturing output were no higher, and possibly lower, after the Civil War than they were before the War.

Even within the various war industries of the North, there was no great spurt; by and large, the new dimensions of output in the North were modest adjustments in the various sectors. In fact, the most startling aspect of the war years was the minute stimulus to manufacturing. Iron production for small arms increased, but iron production for railroads declined. Although the demand for clothes and boots for servicemen stimulated manufactures, the loss of the southern market more than offset this. For example, in Massachusetts—

[6]Roger L. Ransom and Richard Sutch, "Capitalists without Capital: The Burden of Slavery and the Impact of Emancipation," *Agricultural History* 62 (3), (Summer 1988): 151.

the center of boot and shoe production—employment and output in that important industry decreased almost one-third during the war. Similarly, without raw cotton, the textile mills were underutilized. True, the enlistment and conscription of men ameliorated unemployment, and speculation offered opportunities for enrichment for a select few. Overall, however, expenditures by the federal government did not spur rapid industrialization or economic expansion.

We have considered the debate over the Beard-Hacker thesis in detail because it illustrates so clearly the importance of quantitative evidence. An argument may be persuasive, and it may be supported by numerous illustrative examples, but it can still be wrong (Economic Reasoning Proposition 5).

Economic Reasoning Proposition

ECONOMIC RETARDATION IN THE SOUTH

The economic outcome of the war was a distinct reversal in the relative positions of the North and South. As shown in Table 14.2, in 1860 the North's real commodity output per capita was slightly less than the South's ($74.8 compared with $77.8). By 1870, the North's per capita output exceeded the South's by nearly two-thirds ($81.5 compared with $47.6). This advantage remained in 1880. The major source of this reversal was not the northern and midwestern advance, but the dramatic absolute decline in southern output during and shortly after the war.

It would be an error, however, to conclude that the entire southern economy remained stagnant. The commodity output per capita figures for 1870 and 1880 show that the South's growth rate was initially rapid and close to the North's growth rate of almost 2.6 percent yearly. Such high rates were not sustained, however, nor were they distributed evenly across the South. Table 14.3 shows estimates of the rate of growth of personal income per capita in real terms for the five most cotton-dependent states of the Deep South (Louisiana, Georgia, Mississippi, South Carolina, and Alabama) and for the remaining eight southern states from 1879 to 1899. Clearly, there was great variation among the southern states, with several growing more than twice as fast as those making up the Deep South.

As this evidence suggests, southern manufacturing rebounded from the war more quickly than southern agriculture. Southern manufacturing output had approached prewar levels by the early 1870s, and the South's transportation network (based on steamboats, roads, and railroads) had been completely revitalized. This revitalization was accomplished with reasonable ease, requiring little more than repairs and replacements and modest additions of capital. In fact, as John Stuart Mill had noted shortly before the Civil War, rapid postwar recoveries have been quite common throughout history:

> An enemy lays waste a country by fire and sword, and destroys or carries away nearly all the movable wealth existing in it; all the inhabitants are ruined, and yet in a few years after, everything is much as it was before. . . .The possibility of a rapid repair of their disasters, mainly depends on whether the country has been depopulated. If its effective population have not been extirpated at the time, and are not starved afterwards; then, with the same skill and knowledge which they had before, with their land and its permanent improvements undestroyed, and the more durable

TABLE 14.2 Commodity Output per Capita by Region (in 1879 prices)

YEARS	OUTSIDE THE SOUTH	SOUTH
1860	$ 74.8	$77.7
1870	81.5	47.6
1880	105.8	61.5

Source: Stanley Engerman, "The Economic Impact of the Civil War," Explorations in Economic History *3 (Spring 1966): 181.*

TABLE 14.3 Annual Rates of Growth in Constant–Dollar Values of per Capita Personal Income by State between 1879 and 1899

STATE	ANNUAL PERCENTAGE RATES OF GROWTH PER CAPITA PERSONAL INCOME
Louisiana	0.44%
Georgia	0.81
Mississippi	0.96
South Carolina	0.98
Alabama	1.14
Five cotton states	**0.86**
North Carolina	1.38
Kentucky	1.42
Arkansas	1.43
Tennessee	1.89
Virginia	2.15
West Virginia	2.26
Texas	2.53
Florida	2.64
Total, 13 southern states	**1.54**
United States	**1.59%**

Source: Derived from Richard Easterlin, "Regional Growth of Income: Long-Term Tendencies, 1880–1950," in Population Redistribution and Economic Growth, United States 1870–1950, *vol. 2,* Analyses of Economic Change, *eds. S. Kuznets, A. R. Miller, and R. A. Easterlin (Philadelphia: American Philosophical Society, 1960), 185.*

buildings probably unimpaired, or only partially injured, they have nearly all the requisites for their former amount of production.[7]

Rapid regeneration is propelled by eliminating bottlenecks. For example, the South's railroad network had almost ceased to function by the war's end, largely due to the lack of rolling stock and partially destroyed track; the roadbed, specialized labor expertise, and considerable track remained in good condition but were unusable. Prompt investment in the essential complementary resources (rolling stock and damaged track) reemployed the other existing resources (labor, roadbed, and usable track). This initiated a regenerative spurt, and other similar spurts in combination led to a temporary high-growth period. When these unusual investment opportunities had been fully exploited, the long-run slower rate of growth resumed.[8]

In agriculture, however, the prospects for southern recovery were quite different. Lincoln's Emancipation Proclamation altered the whole makeup of the South's agricultural society for both whites and blacks. The results were great reductions in agricultural output, especially during the late war years and the immediate postwar years. In the absence of emancipation, the South's agricultural sector surely would have restored itself within a few years; but the political, social, and economic adjustments stemming from emancipation delayed regenerative growth for many years.

[7]J. S. Mill, *Principles of Political Economy*, 1848, Book I, chapter 5, section 7, http://socserv2.socsci.mcmaster.ca/~econ/ugcm/3113/mill/prin/index.html.

[8]For elaboration on the theory of regenerative growth, see Donald F. Gordon and Gary M. Walton, "A New Theory of Regenerative Growth and the Post-World War II Experience of West Germany," in *Explorations in the New Economic History: Essays in Honor of Douglass C. North*, ed. Roger L. Ransom, Richard Sutch, and Gary M. Walton (New York: Academic Press, 1982), 171–192.

RECORDS OFFICE OF THE CHIEF SIGNAL OFFICER: NATIONAL ARCHIVES

Richmond, Virginia, after the destruction caused in the Civil War.

The decline in southern output, especially in the cotton states of the Deep South, was much deeper than that precipitated by war destruction alone. Indeed, the growth of agricultural output in the Deep South averaged negative 0.96 percent per year from 1857 to 1879.

Decline in the Deep South

The five key cotton states of the Deep South—South Carolina, Louisiana, Georgia, Alabama, and Mississippi—have been shown to have experienced the greatest setbacks (Table 14.3). This precipitous decline occurred for three principal reasons.

First, the highly efficient plantation system was destroyed, and attempts to resurrect plantation methods proved futile. Free blacks shunned assembly-line methods employing gangs driven intensively from dawn to dusk, as they always had been by free whites. In place of the plantations, there arose smaller units—some owned, many rented, and many sharecropped (the owner of the land and the tenant split the crop). Table 14.4 shows the alteration in farm sizes between 1860 and 1870 in the Deep South. Whereas 61 percent of the farms had been less than 100 acres in 1860, 81 percent were under 100 acres in 1870. Economies of scale based on the intense driving of slave labor were lost.

A second closely related reason was the significant withdrawal of labor from the fields, especially labor by women and children. This reallocation of human effort undoubtedly raised household production and improved the quality of life, but it nevertheless contributed to the decline in measured per capita agricultural output in the Deep South by 30 to 40 percent between 1860 and 1870.

TABLE 14.4 Farm Size Distribution in Five Major Cotton States

	PERCENTAGE OF FARMS IN SIZE CLASS		PERCENTAGE OF LAND IN SIZE CLASS	
IMPROVED ACRES	1860	1870	1860	1870
3–49	36.9%	60.9%	7.4%	20.2%
50–99	24.2	19.8	12.0	19.6
100–499	32.0	17.2	47.6	49.1
500+	6.9	2.1	33.0	11.0

Source: Roger Ransom and Richard Sutch, One Kind of Freedom: The Economic Consequences of Emancipation *(Cambridge, England: Cambridge University Press, 1977), 71.*

Finally, the growth of the demand for southern cotton slowed because of competition from India, Brazil, and Egypt, and because the growth of world demand slowed. The U.S. South had dominated the world cotton market in 1860, commanding 77 percent of English imports.[9] During the war years, however, when the door to the new competition was opened, only 10 percent of England's cotton came from the South. The South's market share rebounded well in the late 1870s, but it never reached its 1860 high mark.

The decline in the Deep South immediately after the Civil War was to be expected. The tragedy was that southern agricultural production remained depressed for decades afterward. The most puzzling aspect of the decline in the Deep South was the increased concentration on cotton. Unlike small prewar southern farms, small postwar farms, especially those operated by former slaves, became highly specialized in cotton. In the five main cotton-growing states, 82 percent of nonslave farms (85 percent of all farms) had grown cotton in 1860 compared with 97 percent of all farms there in 1870.[10] Moreover, a greater proportion of the land on each farm was devoted to cotton production in 1870 than in 1860. Indeed, whereas many slave plantations had been self-sufficient in food before the Civil War, the Deep South now became a food-importing region. Black farmers were the most cotton dependent, with 85 percent of their crop in cotton compared with 60 to 70 percent for white farmers. White owners placed the smallest proportion of their land in cotton; white tenant farmers produced nearly twice that of white owners, and black tenants nearly four times that of white owners. Increased dependency on cotton occurred despite declining cotton prices in the 1870s.

Concentration on cotton production was not irrational. Stephen DeCanio has shown that the South had a comparative advantage in cotton production and that southern cotton farmers were about as responsive to price changes as northern wheat farmers were to wheat prices (Economic Reasoning Proposition 3).[11] Nevertheless, the limited economic alternatives provided by the cotton economy sentenced many former slaves to a life of grinding poverty. To see why this happened, we must explore the transition from slavery to freedom and the new economic institutions that replaced the old.

The Inequities of War

Men from lower-income groups primarily waged fighting in the Civil War. Once the need for mass mobilization was evident, both sides turned to the draft to acquire men, and both

[9]See Thomas Ellison, *The Cotton Trade of Great Britain* (Augustus Kelley, 1968), cited in Gavin Wright, "Cotton Competition and the Post-Bellum Recovery of the American South," *Journal of Economic History* 34 (1974): 611. Also see Gavin Wright, *The Political Economy of the Cotton South* (New York: Norton, 1978), and *Old South, New South: Revolutions in the Southern Economy* (New York: Basic Books, 1986).

[10]These figures are from Ransom, *Conflict and Compromise,* Table 7–3, 257.

[11]Stephen DeCanio, *Agriculture in the Postbellum South* (Cambridge, Mass.: MIT Press, 1974).

sides allowed conscripts to buy out their service by paying another to go in their place. From this time on, the war was widely and correctly viewed as a "rich man's war and a poor man's fight." While this policy shifted the burden of fighting to the poor, it arguably had efficiency advantages. The exchanges were voluntary, and if those with higher labor opportunity costs were replaced by those with lower opportunity costs, the overall costs of the war effort were reduced. The inequities, however, remained.

In the North, the cities witnessed the most heated discontent, especially New York, where large numbers of immigrants lived. The Irish, especially, felt that the burden of the draft was falling on them. In July 1863, mobs stormed through the streets of New York for four days; 20,000 federal troops were needed to quell the riots, which resulted in 105 deaths.

The recruitment and drafting of large numbers of men might have been expected to raise the real wages of those working on the homefront by reducing the available supply of labor, but this did not happen.

As shown in Figure 14.3, prices rose more rapidly than wages in the North. Thus, real wages (wages/prices), the amount of goods and services that could be bought with an hour's work, fell. Wesley C. Mitchell, who first studied this problem, thought that workers bargained ineffectively because they (and their employers) were influenced by customary notions about wages. The wage lag, he believed, had produced a surge in profits that could be invested after the war, another reason for thinking that the war accelerated industrialization.[12] Reuben Kessel and Armen Alchian, however, pointed out that the fall in real wages could also be explained by rising taxes, rising prices of imported goods, and other real factors.[13] Subsequently, Stephen DeCanio and Joel Mokyr showed that failure to anticipate inflation explains about two-thirds of the fall in real wages and real factors about one-third.[14] Northern labor, in other words, would have experienced a substantial decline in its income in any case, but the inability of labor markets to adapt rapidly to the inflation made things a lot worse than they otherwise would have been.

Inequality was even more glaring in the South. In October 1862, the southern draft law was altered to allow an exemption for anyone owning 20 or more slaves. Although this exemption benefited small numbers, it created great resentment. Small farmers were infuriated to see their farms, dependent on their own labor, deteriorate while rich plantations were maintained. R. M. Bradford of Virginia wrote the Confederate Secretary of War in October 1864:

> The people will not always submit to this unequal, unjust, and partial distribution of favor and wholesale conscription of the poor while able-bodied and healthy men of property are all occupying soft places.[15]

The South did not use slaves for fighting because both masters and slaves knew the enemy provided a route to freedom.[16] Ironically, the efforts of slaves to grow cotton, spurred by the exceptionally high prices in the early 1860s, was negated by the South's trade policies to England. Most of this vital labor was simply wasted as high stockpiles of cotton rotted in the countryside and on the docks.

---

[12]Wesley C. Mitchell, *A History of the Greenbacks* (Chicago, 1903), 347.
[13]"Real Wages in the North during the Civil War: Mitchell's Data Reinterpreted," in *The Reinterpretation of American Economic History*, eds. Robert W. Fogel and Stanley L. Engerman (New York: Harper & Row, 1971).
[14]"Inflation and Wage Lag during the American Civil War," *Explorations in Economic History* 14 (1977): 311–336.
[15]R. M. Bradford to James Seddon, quoted in Paul Escott, *After Secession: Jefferson Davis and the Failure of Confederate Nationalism* (Baton Rouge: Louisiana State University Press, 1978), 119.
[16]At the very end of the war, the South considered plans to employ slaves as soldiers.

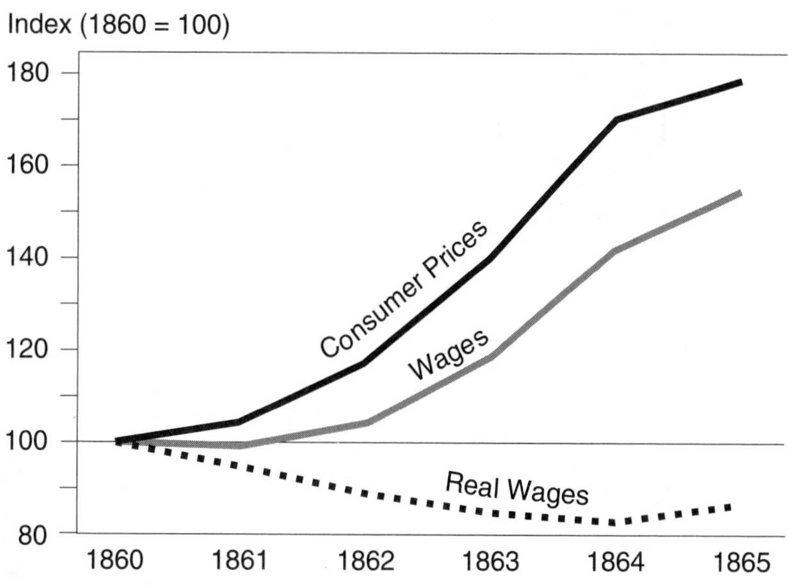

FIGURE 14.3 The Wage Lag in the Civil War

Source: Reuben A. Kessel and Armen A. Alchian, "Real Wages in the North During the Civil War: Mitchell's Data Reinterpreted," in The Reinterpretation of American Economic History, *eds. Robert W. Fogel and Stanley L. Engerman (New York: Harper & Row, 1971), 460.*

THE LEGACY OF SLAVERY

The Thirteenth Amendment to the Constitution freed all slaves; the Fourteenth Amendment ensured that no "state shall deprive any person of life, liberty or property, without due process of law" and guaranteed that "the right of citizens to vote shall not be abridged." These amendments were passed soon after the war but were not sufficient to ensure sustained progress for blacks. The first effects of the new freedoms surely helped blacks dramatically. Just as surely, many southern whites suffered in the late 1860s. The redistribution and changing levels of income by race are shown in Figure 14.4 on page 276. In addition, average wealth holdings of whites in the Deep South in 1860 had been \$81,400 for plantation owners, \$13,300 for slave-owning small farmers, and \$2,400 for nonslave-owning farmers. In 1870, the average for all white farmers in the Deep South was \$3,200. Resentment against Yankees and blacks reflected the whites' slide in wealth and hatred of the northern occupation.

Land reform that broke up the plantations and gave the land to former slaves was pushed by radical Republicans in Congress. This might have set the South, and ultimately the whole country, on a different course. The House and Senate each passed a bill to give black heads of households 40 acres but President Andrew Johnson vetoed it. Except in a few isolated areas such as the Sea Islands of Georgia and on the former plantation of Confederate President Jefferson Davis, where land reform proved to be a success in promoting stable farming communities, most of the land remained in the hands of the same people who had owned it before the war. Roger Ransom and Richard Sutch show that the wealthiest fifth of the population still owned 73 percent of the land in 1870, a drop of only 2 percent from 1860.[17] Moreover, the power of northern Republicans to ensure a solid political base in the South by protecting the civil rights of the former slaves was limited by economic

[17]Roger L. Ransom and Richard Sutch, *One Kind of Freedom: The Economic Consequences of Emancipation* (New York: Cambridge University Press, 1977), 79.

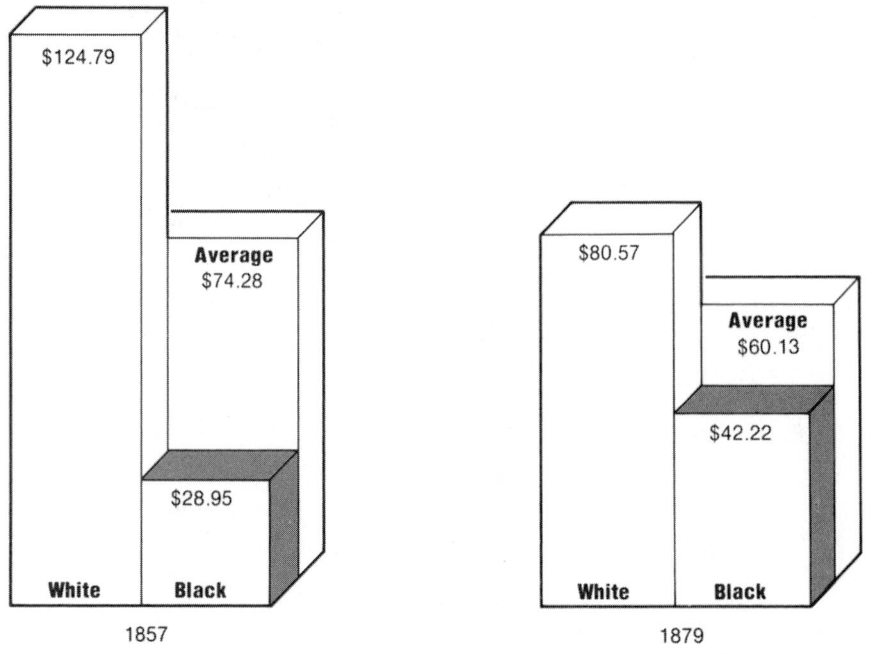

FIGURE 14.4 Distribution of Agricultural Output per Capita by Race in the Deep South, 1857 and 1879

Source: Richard Sutch, "Growth and Welfare in the American South," in Market Institutions and Economic Progress in the New South 1865–1900, *eds. Gary M. Walton and James F. Shepherd (New York: Academic Press, 1981), 145.*

conditions nationally and by an absence of effective local support in the South. When the courts upheld President Johnson's executive order of total amnesty to anyone willing to take an oath of allegiance, the old Confederates began to take power—aided by violence, including that of the newly formed Ku Klux Klan. The Constitutional amendments protecting black rights were subverted, and blacks ultimately became disenfranchised.

In the immediate aftermath of the war, there was considerable interstate migration of former slaves. Much of this movement can be explained by the efforts of former slaves to reunite families broken up during slavery. Perhaps also, many former slaves wanted to see a bit of the country in which they lived, a privilege denied to them by slavery. From 1870 to 1890, however, black migration within the South, as shown by Philip E. Graves, Robert L. Sexton, and Richard K. Vedder, was reduced compared with migration during the antebellum period.[18] While slaveowners would generally move or sell slaves whenever economic considerations dictated, the former slave could also weigh the costs of leaving behind family, friends, and familiar institutions (Economic Reasoning Propositions 1 and 2). Black migration to the North did not become truly large until after 1910, when a combination of rising northern wages, rising expectations of a better life, and the information provided by earlier generations of migrants encouraged a mass exodus. This important wave of northern migration also opened new occupational opportunities for blacks and spurred their mobility into higher earnings categories.[19]

[18]Philip E. Graves, Robert L. Sexton, and Richard K. Vedder, "Slavery, Amenities, and Factor Price Equalization: A Note on Migration and Freedom," *Explorations in Economic History* 20 (1983): 156–162.

[19]Thomas N. Maloney, "Migration and Economic Opportunities in the 1920s: New Evidence on African-American Occupational Mobility in the North," *Explorations in Economic History* 38 (1), (2001): 147–165.

Economic Insight 14.1

The Labor Market in the North during the Civil War

This figure shows why real wages would have declined in the North during the Civil War even if inflation had been held in check. *S*-1860 is the supply of labor before the war, and *D*-1860 the demand.

The expansion of the armed forces reduced the supply of labor to *S*-1864. Other things being equal, this would have raised real wages. But the demand for labor is derived from the demand for final products. Rising taxes on production (excise taxes) and rising costs of imported products reduced profits and the demand for labor from *D*-1860 to *D*-1864. The shift in demand was greater than the shift in supply and lowered equilibrium real wages from *W*-1860 to *W*-1864.

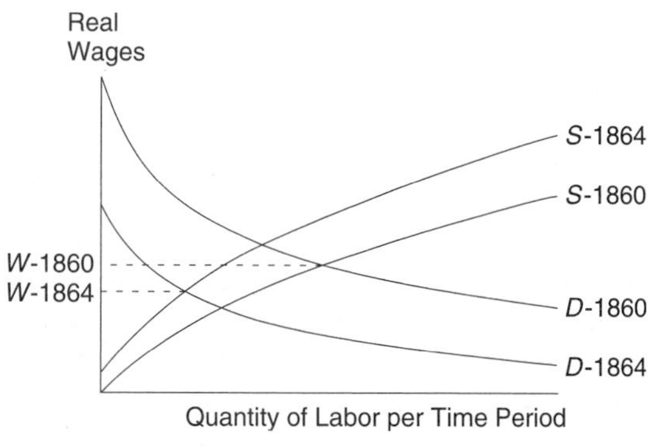

Nevertheless, before 1910 most African Americans had to make their living in southern agriculture. Most were simply hired hands earning abysmally low wages. Many, however, worked the land as tenant farmers or in a small but surprising number as owners.

As shown in Figure 14.5 on page 278, blacks worked about 30 percent of the land in crops, and whites worked 70 percent. Blacks were close to 70 percent of the agricultural work force in 1880 but owned less than 10 percent of the land. (As can be seen in the figure, if 30 percent was occupied by blacks and 32 percent of that land was owned by blacks, then 0.3 × 0.32, or 9.6 percent, of all land was owned by blacks.) Given the resistance and hostility of white southerners and the absence of any federal redistribution program, it is a wonder that blacks owned even this much land. Of the two-thirds of the land that was tenanted by blacks, two-thirds was sharecropped.

The basic idea of sharecropping, as we noted above, was simple. Instead of paying a fixed annual sum in dollars for the use of the land, the sharecropper split the crop with the land owner after the harvest. Standard yearly contracts gave a 50-50 split to owner and tenant. Economic historians have hotly debated the benefits and costs of sharecropping. To Ransom and Sutch, tenant farming, sharecropping in particular, was a disaster that forced the former slaves into dependency on cotton, and in some cases into a condition similar to slavery known as "debt peonage."

Other students of sharecropping, however, have concluded that it offered a number of advantages, at least compared with the available alternatives. Former slaves and poor whites

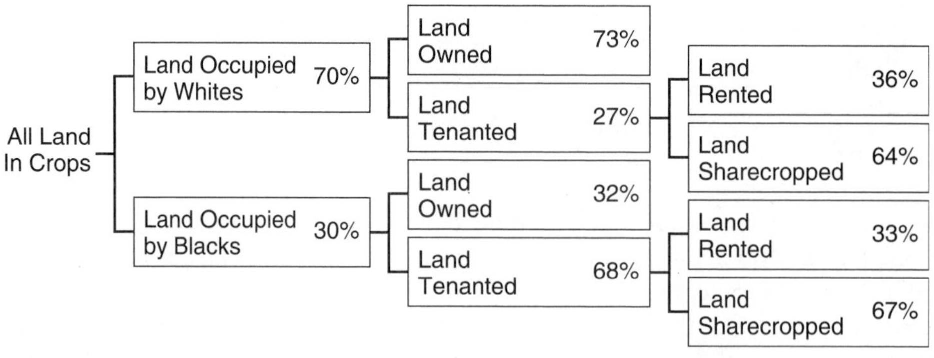

FIGURE 14.5 Ownership and Use of Farm Land in Crops in the Deep South by Race, 1880

Source: Adapted from Roger L. Ransom and Richard Sutch, One Kind of Freedom: The Economic Consequences of Emancipation *(New York: Cambridge University Press, 1977), 84.*

were provided independence from day-to-day bossing and given a chance to earn a living. The risk of a very bad year—due perhaps to poor growing conditions or unusually low prices—was shared with the owner. The sharecropping contract, moreover, as Joseph Reid has pointed out, also gave the owner an incentive to remain interested in the farm throughout the growing season and to share information such as changing crop prices with the tenant.[20] On large plantations where such information sharing was difficult, renting predominated.[21] Just as the sharecropper shared part of the risk of a bad harvest with the owner, he also shared part of any gain from his own hard work. Tenant farmers had an incentive to sleight long-term investments. Competition among tenants and incentives built into rental contracts partially but only partially offset the negative effects of renting on long-term investment.

Meanwhile, the credit system added to the cropper's burden. The source of rural credit was the white-owned country store. Here the farmer bought most of his supplies, including food. Typically, two sets of prices were common in country stores, one for goods bought for cash and one for goods bought on time to be paid after the harvest. The markups were steep, often implying an interest rate of 40 to 70 percent per annum for buying on time. The cropper who could not pay his debts after harvest often had to mortgage the next year's crop to receive continued credit. This transaction was made possible by "crop lien" laws passed in many states. The crop lien was a powerful means of control, and storekeepers (nearly eight thousand throughout the rural South) soon learned that by insisting on payment in cotton, they could maintain long-term control over their debtors. The tenant was thus "locked in" to cotton.[22]

High interest rates were the result of the high costs of credit to the storeowner, the risks faced by the storeowner, and the exploitation of local monopoly power possessed by the storeowner. The slow recovery of southern banking in rural areas after the Civil War contributed to the storeowner's costs of doing business and protected his local monopoly. The National Banking Act had set a minimum capital requirement that made it hard to establish

[20]Joseph Reid, "Sharecropping as an Understandable Market Response: The Postbellum South," *Journal of Economic History* 33 (1973): 106–130.

[21]Lee Alston and Robert Higgs, "Contractual Mix in Southern Agriculture since the Civil War: Facts, Hypotheses, and Tests," *Journal of Economic History* 42 (1982): 327–353.

[22]For further discussion of these and other issues in the postwar South, see *One Kind of Freedom* by Ransom and Sutch (1977) and the collection of papers in their book; Gary M. Walton and James F. Shepherd, eds., *Market Institutions and Economic Progress in the New South 1865–1900* (New York: Academic Press, 1981); and the special issue of *Explorations in Economic History* 38 (January 1, 2001) in *One Kind of Freedom.*

TABLE 14.5 Incomes of Slaves and Sharecroppers

	SLAVE ON A LARGE PLANTATION IN 1859	SHARECROPPER IN 1879	ANNUAL RATE OF GROWTH (PERCENT PER YEAR)
Income (1879 dollars)	$27.66	$40.24	1.87%
Value of the increase in leisure time	—	33.90[a]	—
Total	$27.66	74.14	4.93%

[a] *The average of the high and low estimates.*

Source: Kenneth Ng and Nancy Virts, "The Value of Freedom," Journal of Economic History *49 (December 1989): 959.*

national banks in small towns and very hard to establish more than one.[23] Banking legislation had also made it impossible for state chartered banks to issue bank notes and directed the funds that national banks received by issuing notes into federal bonds rather than local loans. After the turn of the century, the development of deposit banking, along with the easing of state and federal banking regulations, helped bring southern interest rates into line with those in other parts of the country. There is some dispute about how much of the storeowner's high interest charges reflected his monopoly power and how much reflected his own high costs of supplying credit. In either case, the result for the farmer caught in the trap of debt peonage was extreme poverty and very little freedom of choice.

Table 14.5 shows estimates of the real income of slaves in 1859 and of sharecroppers in 1879. Evidently, in terms of real spendable income (available for food, clothing, shelter), emancipation was only a moderate boon. Sharecroppers had more freedom to choose how they would spend their limited income, but between 1859 and 1879, blacks' real disposable income increased at an average rate of only 1.87 percent per year. The 1879 figures, moreover, apply to all black sharecroppers. For some of those caught most firmly in the vise of debt peonage, the gains were even smaller. Only when an allowance is made for the monetary value of increased leisure time (the reduction in hours spent working multiplied by the wage of agricultural labor) does the material gain from emancipation appear to be truly large.[24]

The problem of debt peonage was not endemic to the entire South. To recall the evidence from Table 14.3, such states as Virginia, West Virginia, Texas, and Florida showed remarkable recoveries and sustained advances following the war. Research by Price Fishback has shown that Georgia sharecroppers, on average in the 1880s, were able to pay off their debts after the harvest, and that their debt burdens were declining.[25] Research by Robert Higgs and Robert Margo has shown that in some areas blacks, despite the enormous difficulties they faced, were able to move up the agricultural ladder and become owners of their own farms.[26]

---

[23]As late as 1880, there were only 42 national banks in the Deep South of 2,061 in the nation as a whole (126 in the 12 former Confederate states).

[24]One way to increase our understanding of postbellum southern poverty is to use data and methods drawn from other disciplines. For an excellent example, see Jerome C. Rose, "Biological Consequences of Segregation and Economic Deprivation: A Post-Slavery Population from Southwest Arkansas," *Journal of Economic History* 49 (1989): 351–360. Rose uses skeletal remains to identify disease and nutritional problems in the black population.

[25]Price V. Fishback, "Debt Peonage in Postbellum Georgia," *Explorations in Economic History* 26 (1989): 219–236.

[26]Robert Higgs, "Accumulation of Property by Southern Blacks before World War I," *American Economic Review* 72 (1982): 725–735; Robert A. Margo, "Accumulation of Property by Southern Blacks Before World War One: Comment and Further Evidence," *American Economic Review* 74 (1984): 768–776; and Higgs, "Reply," *American Economic Review* 74 (1984): 777–781.

Typical of many blacks in the postwar South, the couple in this photograph taken in 1875—12 years after emancipation—remained entrapped in poverty.

A variety of factors gradually weakened the grip of debt peonage. One, surprisingly enough, was the boll weevil, an insect that attacked cotton and gradually spread throughout the Deep South after the turn of the century. The boll weevil could be a tragedy for the individual farmer whose crop was ruined and who could not get credit on the basis of his infested land. In some areas, however, the long-run consequences were favorable: The boll weevil forced farmers to switch to other crops, which proved to be profitable. Improved roads and the automobile also eroded the monopoly power of the local storeowner. And the growth of the great mail-order houses in Chicago provided increased competition in the supply of certain kinds of merchandise. Nor, to look at things from the other direction, was being a sharecropper necessarily the lowest rung on the agricultural ladder. In the Mississippi Delta, as James R. Irwin and Anthony Patrick O'Brien have shown, moving from agricultural laborer to tenant was a source of considerable economic progress. That it was indicates how low wages were in this region.[27]

More important than these factors, however, were increasing urbanization and industrialization throughout the nation, which provided alternatives to agriculture. Southern industrialization was the goal of the "New South" movement proclaimed by southern politicians, newspapermen, and church leaders. There were some successes—a steel industry developed in Birmingham, the cigarette industry developed in North Carolina, and the cotton textile industry moved to the South—but the southern effort to industrialize progressed slowly. Ultimately, it was northern industrialization and its growing demand for labor that allowed many southern blacks to escape from tenant farming.[28]

---

[27]James R. Irwin and Anthony Patrick O'Brien, "Economic Progress in the Postbellum South? African-American Incomes in the Mississippi Delta, 1880–1910," *Explorations in Economic History* 38 (2001): 166–180.

[28]See Fred Bateman and Thomas Weiss, *A Deplorable Scarcity* (Chapel Hill: University of North Carolina Press, 1981).

The Monument to the Boll Weevil. When the boll weevil destroyed their cotton, farmers near Enterprise, Alabama, turned to peanuts, which proved profitable. The partly ironic plaque reads as follows: "In profound appreciation of the boll weevil and what it has done as the herald of Prosperity, this monument is erected by the citizens of Enterprise, Coffee County, Alabama, Dec. 11, 1919."

SERIES VII.1, PHOTOGRAPHS, BOX 7.1/3, FILE "II PHOTOGRAPHS - BOLL WEEVIL MONUMENT, ALABAMA," USDA HISTORY COLLECTION, SPECIAL COLLECTIONS, NATIONAL AGRICULTURAL LIBRARY.

Despite a modest exodus of labor and limited advance of industrialization, the southern economy, especially that of the Deep South, remained a distinctive low wage economy until the 1940s. Gavin Wright's book *Old South, New South* explains the slow pace of progress toward regional parity. In Wright's view, the South remained a separate labor market. Many people left, and few came in, but rapid natural increase kept labor abundant.[29] Cotton became increasingly labor intensive as farm sizes fell. By the late nineteenth century, most southern farms were smaller than northern farms, the reverse of the situation during the antebellum years. Mechanization was slowed, and wages and earnings kept low.

Southern whites attempted to protect their position by keeping blacks even lower on the economic ladder. By the turn of the century, "black codes" and "Jim Crow" laws segregated blacks and maintained their impoverishment. Such laws determined where blacks could work, live, eat and drink, ride on public transport, and go to school. Northerners, as Wright emphasizes, shunned investments in the South. The result was that a striking wage gap remained between the North and South.[30] A considerable part of the South's relative

---

[29]See Richard Vedder, Lowell Gallaway, Philip E. Graves, and Robert Sexton, "Demonstrating Their Freedom: The Post-Emancipation Migration of Black Americans," *Research in Economic History* 10 (1986): 213–239.

[30]For the importance of these initial institutions on twentieth-century developments, see Lee J. Alston and Joseph P. Ferrie, *Southern Paternalism and the Rise of the Welfare State: Economics, Politics, and Institutions in the U.S. South 1865–1965* (Cambridge, England: Cambridge University Press, 1998).

backwardness can surely be attributed to its educational system. Public expenditures per pupil remained a mere fraction of those in the North. Wealthy southerners argued that educating the poor, especially blacks, merely encouraged their migration north in pursuit of higher wages. The Supreme Court held in *Plessy v. Fergusson* (1896) that separate education for blacks was constitutional as long as it was equal. "Separate" was adhered to religiously, but "equal" was not. As Robert Margo shows in his *Race and Schooling in the South*, far more money was spent on white students than on black students. Margo found, for example, that in 1910, spending on black pupils relative to white pupils ranged from 17 percent in Louisiana to 75 percent in Delaware.[31]

Part of this discrepancy can be explained by discrimination against black school teachers; but other measures of the quality of schooling, such as class size, show similar differentials. Lack of spending on education may have served the interest of some wealthy southerners, but the result was a labor force ill prepared to participate in modern economic growth.

---

[31]Robert A. Margo, *Race and Schooling in the South*, 1880–1950 (Chicago: University of Chicago Press, 1990), 21–22.

Selected References and Suggested Readings

Aldrich, Mark. "Flexible Exchange Rates, Northern Expansion, and the Market for Southern Cotton, 1866–1879." *Journal of Economic History* 33 (1973): 399–416.

Alston, Lee, and Robert Higgs. "Contractual Mix in Southern Agriculture since the Civil War: Facts, Hypotheses, and Tests." *Journal of Economic History* 42 (1982): 327–353.

Alston, Lee J., and Kyle D. Kauffman. "Competition and the Compensation of Sharecroppers by Race: A View from Plantations in the Early Twentieth Century." *Explorations in Economic History* 38 (2001): 181–194.

Andreano, Ralph, ed. *The Economic Impact of the Civil War*. Cambridge, Mass.: Schenkman, 1964.

Bateman, Fred, and Thomas Weiss. *A Deplorable Scarcity*. Chapel Hill: University of North Carolina Press, 1981.

Cochran, Thomas. "Did the Civil War Retard Industrialization?" *Mississippi Valley Historical Review* 48 (September 1961).

DeCanio, Stephen. *Agriculture in the Postbellum South*. Cambridge, Mass.: MIT Press, 1974.

———. "Productivity and Income Distribution in the Post-Bellum South." *Journal of Economic History* 34 (1974): 422–446.

DeCanio, Stephen, and Joel Mokyr. "Inflation and Wage Lag during the American Civil War." *Explorations in Economic History* 14 (1977): 311–336.

Engerman, Stanley. "The Economic Impact of the Civil War." In *The Reinterpretation of American Economic History*, eds. Robert W. Fogel and Stanley L. Engerman. New York: Harper & Row, 1971.

———. "Some Economic Factors in Southern Backwardness in the Nineteenth Century." In *Essays in Regional Economics*, eds. John F. Kain and John R. Meyer. Cambridge, Mass.: Harvard University Press, 1971.

Fishback, Price V. "Debt Peonage in Postbellum Georgia." *Explorations in Economic History* 26 (1989): 219–236.

Fogel, Robert W. *Without Consent or Contract: The Rise and Fall of American Slavery*. New York: Norton, 1989.

Goldin, Claudia, and Frank Lewis. "The Economic Cost of the American Civil War." *Journal of Economic History* 35 (1975): 294–326.

Graves, Philip E., Robert L. Sexton, and Richard K.Vedder. "Slavery, Amenities, and Factor Price Equalization: A Note on Migration and Freedmen." *Explorations in Economic History* 20 (1983): 156–162.

Hacker, Louis. *The Triumph of American Capitalism*. New York: Columbia University Press, 1940.

Higgs, Robert. "Race, Tenure, and Resource Allocation in Southern Agriculture." *Journal of Economic History* 33 (1973): 149–169.

———. "Patterns of Farm Rental in the Georgia Cotton Belt, 1880–1900." *Journal of Economic History* 34 (1974): 468–482.

———. *Competition and Coercion: Blacks in the American Economy, 1865–1914*. New York: Cambridge University Press, 1977.

———. "Accumulation of Property by Southern Blacks before World War I." *American Economic Review* 72 (1982): 725–735.

———. "Accumulation of Property by Southern Blacks before World War I: Reply." *American Economic Review* 74 (1984): 777–781.

Kauffman, Kyle D. "The U.S. Army as a Rational Economic Agent: The Choice of Draft Animals during the Civil War." *Eastern Economic Journal* 22 (1996): 333–343.

Kessel, Reuben A., and Armen A. Alchian. "Real Wages in the North during the Civil War: Mitchell's Data Reinterpreted." In *The Reinterpretation of American Economic History*, eds. Robert W. Fogel and Stanley L. Engerman. New York: Harper & Row, 1971.

Lebergott, Stanley. "Through the Blockade: The Profitability and Extent of Cotton Smuggling, 1861–1865." *Journal of Economic History* 41 (1981): 867–888.

Lerner, Eugene. "Money, Wages, and Prices in the Confederacy, 1861–1865." *Journal of Political History* 63 (February 1955).

Maloney, Thomas N. "Migration and Economic Opportunity in the 1910s: New Evidence on African-American Occupational Mobility in the North." *Explorations in Economic History* 38 (1), (2001): 147–165.

Mandle, Jay R. "The Plantation States as a Sub-Region of the Post-Bellum South." *Journal of Economic History* 34 (1974): 732–738.

Margo, Robert A. "Accumulation of Property by Southern Blacks before World War One: Comment and Further Evidence." *American Economic Review* 74 (September 1984): 768–776.

———. *Race and Schooling in the South,1880–1950*. Chicago: University of Chicago Press, 1990.

McGuire, Robert A., and Robert Higgs. "Cotton, Corn, and Risk in the Nineteenth Century: Another View." *Explorations in Economic History* 14 (1979): 167–182.

———. "A Portfolio Analysis of Crop Diversification and Risk in the Cotton South." *Explorations in Economic History* 17 (1980): 342–371.

Ransom, Roger L. *Conflict and Compromise: The Political Economy of Slavery, Emancipation, and the American Civil War*. New York: Cambridge University Press, 1989.

Ransom, Roger L., and Richard Sutch. "The Ex-Slave in the Post Bellum South." Journal of Economic History 33 (1973): 131–148.

———. "The Impact of the Civil War and of Emancipation on Southern Agriculture." *Explorations in Economic History* 12 (January 1975): 1–28.

———. *One Kind of Freedom: The Economic Consequences of Emancipation*. New York: Cambridge University Press, 1977.

———. "Capitalists without Capital: The Burden of Slavery and the Impact of Emancipation." *Agricultural History* 62 (Summer 1988): 133–160.

Reid, Joseph. "Sharecropping as an Understandable Market Response: The Postbellum South." *Journal of Economic History* 33 (1973): 106–130.

Rose, Jerome C. "Biological Consequences of Segregation and Economic Deprivation: A Post Slavery Population from Southwest Arkansas." *Journal of Economic History* 49 (1989): 351–360.

Sellers, James L. "The Economic Incidence of the Civil War in the South." *Mississippi Valley Historical Review* 14 (September 1927).

Temin, Peter. "The Post-Bellum Recovery of the South and the Cost of the Civil War." *Journal of Economic History* 36 (1976): 898–907.

Vedder, Richard, Lowell Gallaway, Philip E. Graves, and Robert L. Sexton. "Demonstrating Their Freedom: The Post-Emancipation Migration of Black Americans." *Research in Economic History* 10 (1986): 213–239.

Walton, Gary M., and James F. Shepherd. *Market Institutions and Economic Progress in the New South, 1865–1900*. New York: Academic Press, 1981.

Wright, Gavin. *The Political Economy of the Cotton South*. New York: Norton, 1978.

———. *Old South, New South: Revolutions in the Southern Economy*. New York: Basic Books, 1986.

Wright, Gavin, and Howard Kunreuther. "Cotton, Corn, and Risk in the Nineteenth Century." *Journal of Economic History* 35 (1975): 526–551.

Chapter Fifteen

Agriculture's Western Advance

Chapter Theme

During the 25 years following the Civil War, the American frontier moved steadily west. So dense was settlement by 1890 that people claimed the frontier had virtually disappeared. Spearheading the drive into the western territories were miners and cowboys. The miners were drawn by discoveries such as the famed Comstock Lode of silver in Nevada and the gold in the Black Hills of South Dakota. Though remembered in legend as hard-drinking tellers of tall tales, the miners were first of all businessmen who were able to evolve precise sets of efficient property rights from their crude mining camp rules.[1]

The cowboys came to spur cattle on the long drives to market. Cattle drives from Texas began in 1866, and by the 1880s, cattle baronies of great wealth occupied the territories from Texas to Montana. The cattle drives were destined for the nearest railheads: in the earliest years Sedalia, Missouri, but later Abilene (the destination of the famous Chisholm Trail) and then Dodge City, Kansas (for transport to Chicago). The rise and decline of the great long-distance cattle drives is fascinating history and superb folklore.[2] *The long drives ended abruptly in 1885, not because of the advent of barbed wire (as popularly believed) but because northern cattlemen organized and created new institutions to curb the overstocking of the northern ranges. The passage and enforcement of quarantine laws kept out the distant Texas herds.*[3]

However important miners and cattlemen were as path breakers, the families who settled down to farm set the abiding economic pattern of the West. This chapter tells their economic history: how they got title to their land, what they grew and how

---

[1]See Gary D. Libecap, "Economic Variables and the Development of the Law: The Case of Western Mineral Rights," *Journal of Economic History* 38 (1978): 338–362.

[2]The movie classic *Red River* starring John Wayne and Montgomery Clift and the 1989 CBS TV special "Lonesome Dove" are recommended. Also see Lewis Atherton, *The Cattle Kings* (Bloomington: Indiana University Press, 1961). Although the scions of wealthy eastern families such as Richard Trimble and Teddy Roosevelt could not resist the West, the men who started from scratch and became fabulously successful were, for the most part, country boys from the Midwest and South or cowboys only a few years away from the hard-drinking, roistering life of Newton or Dodge City.

[3]For an in-depth account of the reasons long drives were abruptly ended in 1885, see David Galenson, "The End of the Chisholm Trail," *Journal of Economic History* 24 (2), (June 1974): 350–364.

they grew it, what prices they were paid for their products, and why many farmers became disillusioned with the economic system and demanded help from state governments and, ultimately, from Washington, D.C.

THE EXPANSION OF LAND UNDER CULTIVATION

Most of the participants in the final opening of new land came from places that only a few years before had been the object of settlement. People who moved into Kansas, Nebraska, the Dakotas, and, later, Montana and Colorado more often than not traveled only short distances to get there. Some had settled previously in Missouri or Iowa, Minnesota or Wisconsin, Indiana or Illinois; others were sons and daughters of the pioneers of a previous generation. It was not uncommon for settlers to move from place to place within one of the new states. No matter how bitter previous pioneer experiences or how monotonous and unrewarding the life on virgin land, the hope persisted of better times if only new soil could be broken farther west.

Table 15.1 shows the total number of farms and farm acres by decade from 1860 to 1920. The decades of sharpest advance were the 1870s and 1890s. The addition of land input in these decades was extraordinary: Total land under cultivation more than doubled between 1870 and 1900.[4] (Refer to Economic Reasoning Propositions 2 and 3 concerning choices and costs). This was made possible by a policy of rapidly transferring ownership of land to farmers and other users—by rapidly "privatizing" government land, to use modern jargon.

FEDERAL LAND POLICY

During the Civil War, the absence of southern Democrats allowed the Republican Congress to pass the Homestead Act of 1862. Recall from chapter 8 that this act, which provided 160 acres per homestead (320 per married couple), continued the liberalization of the federal government's land policy. At the time of the act, prime fertile lands remained unclaimed in western Iowa and western Minnesota and in the eastern parts of Kansas, Nebraska, and the Dakotas; these were soon taken, however, leaving little except the unclaimed lands west of the hundredth meridian in the Great Plains (an area of light annual rainfall) or in the vast mountain regions. In most of these plains and mountain regions, a 160-acre homestead was impractical because the land, being suitable only for grazing livestock, required much larger farms. Consequently, between 1870 and 1900, less than one acre in five added to farming belonged to homesteads.

Mining and timber interests also pressed Congress to liberalize land policy, winning four more land acts:

1. *The Timber-Culture Act of 1873.* Passed ostensibly to encourage the growth of timber in arid regions, this law made available 160 acres of free land to anyone who would agree to plant trees on 40 acres of it.
2. *The Desert Land Act of 1877.* By the terms of this law, 640 acres at $1.25 an acre could be purchased by anyone who would agree to irrigate the land within three years. One serious defect of this act was its lack of a clear definition of irrigation.
3. *The Timber and Stone Act of 1878.* This statute provided for the sale at $2.50 an acre of valuable timber and stone lands in Nevada, California, Oregon, and Washington.

[4]During the 1860s, the number of farms increased sharply but total acreage not at all. As discussed in chapter 14, the 1860s were unusual because of the breakup of southern plantations.

TABLE 15.1 Total Number of Farms and Acres by Decade, 1860–1920

YEAR	NUMBER OF FARMS (in millions)	PERCENT INCREASE	NUMBER OF ACRES (in millions)	PERCENT INCREASE
1860	2.0		407	
1870	2.7	35%	408	0.2%
1880	4.0	48	536	31
1890	4.6	15	623	16
1900	5.7	24	839	35
1910	6.4	11	879	5
1920	6.5	2	956	9

Source: Historical Statistics *(Washington, D.C.: Government Printing Office, 1975), Series K4 and J51.*

4. *The Timber-Cutting Act of 1878.* This law authorized residents of certain specified areas to cut trees on government lands without charge, with the stipulation that the timber be used for agricultural, mining, and domestic building purposes.

The transfer of public lands into private hands also included purchases at public auctions under the Preemption Act. This act, as noted in chapter 8, encouraged "squatting" by allowing first rights of sale to settlers who arrived and worked the land before public sales were offered.[5] Furthermore, huge acreages granted by the government as subsidies to western railroads and to states for various purposes were in turn sold to settlers. Nearly 100 million acres from the Indian territories were opened for purchase by the Dawes Act of 1887 and subsequent measures, ignored promises made to Native Americans.

Although steps were taken in the 1880s to tighten up on the disposition of public lands, Congress did not pass any major legislation until the General Revision Act of 1891, which closed critical loopholes. In addition, the Preemption Act, and provisions defining irrigation added to the Desert Land Act of 1877. Congress also repealed the Timber-Cutting Act of 1878, removing from the books one of the most flagrantly abused of all the land laws. Finally, the president was authorized to set aside forest preserves—a first milestone in the conservation movement, which had been gaining popular support.

After the turn of the century, the Homestead Act itself was modified to enable settlers to obtain practical-sized farms. Beginning in 1904, a whole section (one square mile, or 640 acres) could be homesteaded in western Nebraska. A few years later, the Enlarged Homestead Act made it possible to obtain a half-section in many areas free of charge. Still later, residence requirements were reduced to three years, and the Stock-Raising Homestead Act of 1916 allowed the homesteading of 640 acres of land suitable only for grazing purposes. Whereas only 1 acre in 5 added to farming before 1900 came from homesteading, the ratio jumped to 9 in 10 between 1900 and 1920.

From the findings of a commission that reported to President Theodore Roosevelt on the pre-1904 disposition of public lands, we may see how the land had been distributed. The total public domain in the United States from 1789 to 1904 contained 1,441 million acres. Of this total, 278 million acres were acquired by individuals through cash purchase. Another 273 million acres were granted to states and railroads, about which more will be said in chapter 16. Lands acquired by or available to individuals free of charge (mostly via the Homestead Act) amounted to 147 million acres. The rest of the public domain, aside from miscellaneous

---

[5]As late as 1891, an individual could buy a maximum of 1,120 acres at one time under the public land acts. Unlimited amounts of land could be purchased from railroad companies and from states at higher, although still nominal, prices.

grants, was either reserved for the government (209 million acres) or unappropriated (474 million acres). Between 1862 and 1904, acres homesteaded exceeded government cash sales to individuals. If, however, we count purchases from railroads and states, ultimate holders of land bought twice as much between 1862 and 1904 as they obtained free through homesteading.

After 1904, U.S. land policy became less generous, but by that time, nearly all the choice agricultural land, most of the first-rate mineral land, and much of the timber land located close to markets had been distributed. Between 1904 and 1920, more than 100 million new acres of land were homesteaded in mainly dry and mountainous areas. During this same short period, the government reserved about 175 million acres. Of the original public domain, 200 million acres of land that remained to be disposed of were "vacant" in 1920.[6]

THE IMPACT OF FEDERAL LAND POLICY

The principal goals of federal land policy—namely, government revenues, wide accessibility (or fairness), and rapid economic growth—varied in importance over time, with the latter two gaining. Clearly, the most outstanding feature of American land policy was the rapidity with which valuable agricultural, mineral, and timber lands were transferred into private hands. In addition, the goal of making land widely accessible was largely achieved, especially in the second half of the nineteenth century. But by no means was the process, or the result, egalitarian. As we just emphasized, large tracts of lands went to corporations and wealthy individuals. Special interests were favored, and for a time, the granting of land to railroads was considered normal public policy. In addition, large grants to the states were rationalized as growth enhancing, either to support transportation ventures or for educational purposes (the land-grant universities). See Economic Reasoning Proposition 2.

Economic Reasoning Proposition

Frequently, good land was fraudulently obtained by mining and lumber companies or speculators. Aided by the lax administration of the land laws, large operators could persuade an individual to make a homesteading entry or a purchase at a minimum price and then transfer the title. With the connivance of bribed land officials (Economic Reasoning Proposition 3) entries were occasionally made for people who did not even exist. As Gary Libecap and Ronald Johnson have shown convincingly, fraud ultimately served a positive economic purpose: it helped transfer resources to large companies that could take advantage of economies of scale. Resource laws that recognized economic realities and permitted sales of large acreages directly to final users would have reduced fraud and corruption.[7]

Until the 1970s, the consensus among American historians was that federal land policy was economically inefficient and reduced total output. Because people of all sorts and circumstances settled on the land, there was a high rate of failure among the least competent—settlers who eventually lost their holdings and became either poor tenants or low-paid farmworkers. More importantly, it is alleged that the rapid distribution of the public domain laid the groundwork for modern agricultural problems by inducing too much capital and labor into agriculture, thereby impeding the process of industrialization.

Little doubt exists that specific errors were made and inefficiencies were imposed, yet it is difficult to make the case that federal policies were generally inefficient. Partially as a result of this rapid addition of resources, the new West produced crops at such a rate that consumers of foodstuffs and raw materials enjoyed 30 years of falling prices. Furthermore, according to Robert Fogel and Jack Rutner, average rates of return on investments in land improvements, livestock, farm buildings, and machinery equaled or exceeded returns on

---

[6]Homestead entries were substantial in the 1920s and 1930s but fell to practically zero by midcentury. Some homesteading continues today in Alaska.

[7]Gary D. Libecap and Ronald N. Johnson, "Property Rights, Nineteenth-Century Federal Timber Policy, and the Conservation Movement," *Journal of Economic History* 39 (1979): 129–142.

Economic Insight 15.1

A National Market

What price for federal land would have maximized real GNP? Surprisingly, the answer, in many areas, would have been zero. In the figure below, the vertical axis shows the price of land and the horizontal axis the quantity, arranged from high quality to low. In effect, ACF is the demand for farmland in a region of new settlement, and the federal government initially owned all the land.

The government might set a relatively high price for federal land, BD, to maximize the government's revenues (BCED). This might seem the best policy because the revenues could then be redistributed fairly to the people—assuming, of course, that special interests did not get there first. But setting a price of BD reduces the land in production from a maximum of DF to DE. How do we measure the loss associated with keeping EF out of production? The distance between a point on the horizontal axis and the demand curve tells us the maximum that some farmer will pay for a piece of land, presumably because the farmer's resources would produce this much wealth in alternative uses. Therefore, the triangular area CEF measures the value of the future incomes that are lost if the price for the land is set at BD and EF is kept out of production. Setting the price at zero will eliminate the welfare loss triangle.

Concerns about fairness, about the rationality of farmers, or about the effect on the environment may lead one to reject the GNP-maximizing policy. But one should at least recognize the powerful economic argument that the right policy (Economic Reasoning Proposition 5) was the one followed: getting federal land rapidly into the hands of those who could use it productively.

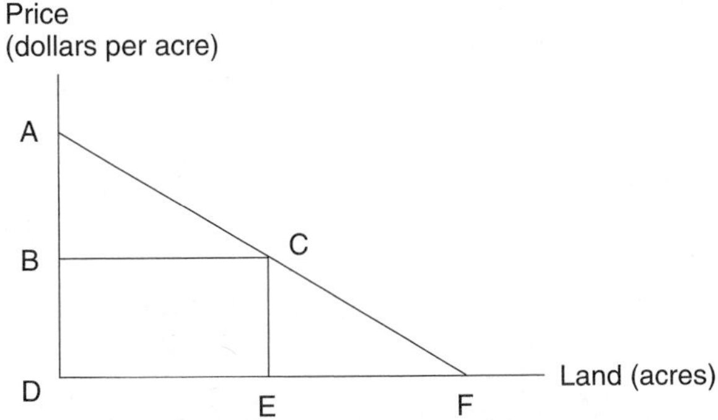

other contemporary investments, and real incomes in the new agricultural areas outside the South grew at rates comparable with those in manufacturing.[8] Once again we see the importance, as emphasized in Economic Reasoning Proposition 5, of quantitative evidence. Instances of hard times in rural America were numerous, and political unrest characterized certain sections of the Midwest and the Plains in the late nineteenth century, but these should not be permitted to dominate our judgment of federal land policy.[9]

[8]For the evidence and more discussion of these issues, see Robert Fogel and Jack Rutner, "Efficiency Effects of Federal Land Policy, 1850–1900," in *Dimensions of Quantitative Research in Economic History*, ed. William Aydelotte et al. (Princeton, N.J.: Princeton University Press, 1972); and Susan Previant Lee and Peter Passell, *A New Economic View of American History* (New York: Norton, 1979), 318–322.

[9]For an assessment of the politics of federal land policy, see Paul Gates, "An Overview of American Land Policy," in *Two Centuries of American Agriculture*, ed. Vivian Wiser. (Washington, D.C.: Agricultural History Society, 1976), 213–229.

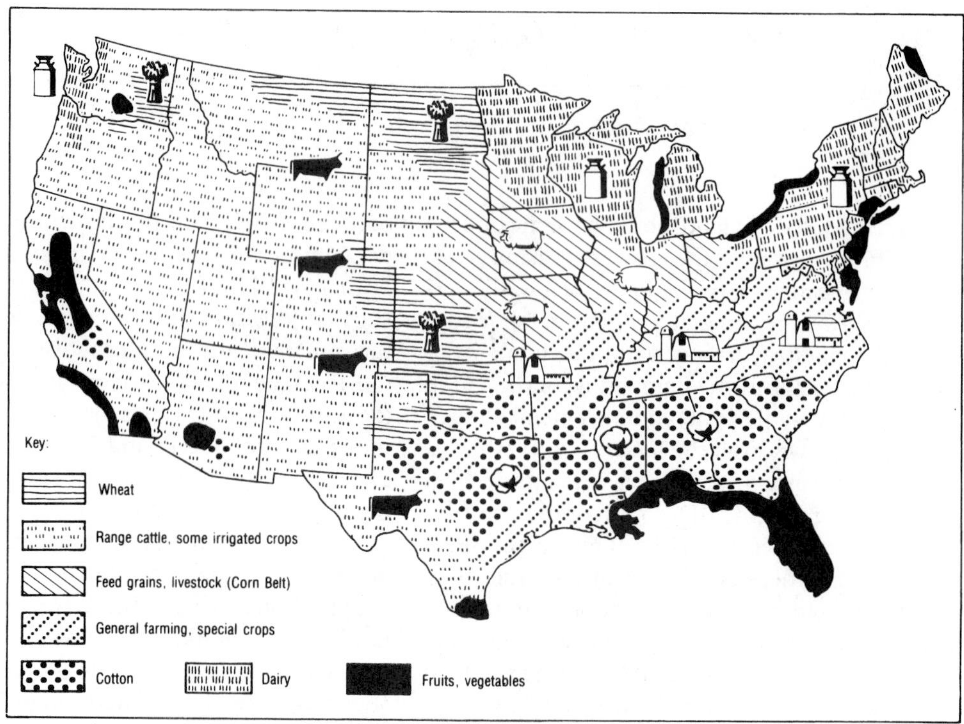

MAP 15.1 Geographic Areas of Specialization in Major Cash Crops in the Late Nineteenth Century *Note that the boundaries between sections did change and that many crops were and still are grown within various belts.*

GROWTH AND CHANGE IN AGRICULTURE

New Areas and Methods of Cultivation

As areas became settled, they tended to specialize in certain crops. These areas of geographic specialization are depicted for the principal crops in Map 15.1. The wheat and corn belt continued its western advance over the century, with spring wheat leading in western Minnesota and the Dakotas and winter varieties dominating the southern Midwest and Nebraska, Kansas, and Oklahoma.[10]

Though tobacco remained tied to the old South, cotton production leapfrogged the Mississippi River. By 1900, Texas was the leading cotton producer as well as a major source of cattle. Farmers around the Great Lakes found it profitable to turn from cereals to dairy farming, following a path traveled previously by farmers in New England. In California, Florida, and other warm-climate areas, fruits, vegetables, and specialty crops became important—especially after the refrigerated railcar, introduced in the 1880s, created a national market.

In addition, and contrary to conventional wisdom (as revealed in numerous writings including earlier editions of *History of the American Economy*), the nineteenth and early twentieth centuries witnessed a stream of biological innovations, many of which successfully modified the planting and growing environment. Thanks to the research of Olmstead and Rhode we have a greater appreciation of changes in plant varieties, irrigation systems,

[10]Winter wheat is sown in the fall and harvested in late spring or early summer, depending on the latitude. Where the climate is too cold, spring wheat is grown. Modern varieties of winter wheat are hardy enough to be grown in the southern half of South Dakota, at least as far north as Pierre.

TABLE 15.2 Cereals Output and Land Input, 1870–1910

YEAR	CORN[a]	LAND IN CORN[b]	BUSHELS OF CORN PER ACRE	WHEAT	LAND IN WHEAT	BUSHELS OF WHEAT PER ACRE
1870	1,125	38.4	29.3	254	20.9	12.1
1890	1,650	74.8	22.1	449	36.7	12.2
1910	2,853	102.3	27.9	625	45.8	13.7

[a]*In millions of bushels.*
[b]*In millions of acres harvested.*

Source: Historical Statistics *(Washington, D.C.: Government Printing Office, 1975), Series K502, K503, K506, and K507.*

fertilizers, and other biological inventions that greatly impacted the use of land for planting.[11] These changes worked along two lines: (1) the discovery of new wheat varieties (and hybrids), that allowed the North American wheat belt to push hundreds of miles northward and westward and (2) researchers and farmers who found new methods of combating insects and diseases, some of which came from experimentation with new varieties (seeds) from Europe and elsewhere. This is a good example of the positive and negative effects of globalization in an earlier era. Table 15.2 shows the growth of corn and wheat outputs and acreage harvested in each crop between 1870 and 1910. The evidence shows very little, if any, growth in land productivity as measured in bushels per acre. Nonetheless, labor productivity grew dramatically in wheat and corn over these decades. According to Robert Gallman, labor productivity in these two crops grew at a rate of 2.6 percent annually between 1850 and 1900.[12] In the first half of the nineteenth century, the comparable figure was 0.4 percent. Further evidence of output growth relative to inputs is shown in Figure 15.1 on page 292, which plots total agricultural output relative to all inputs (land, labor, and capital). Figure 15.1 clearly shows the "miracles" of the scientific chemical and biological advances that came in the 1920s and after. It also reveals the effects of mechanization that had such important influences, as Gallman's nineteenth-century findings reveal.

In 1848, Cyrus Hall McCormick, who had received a patent in 1834 for his reaper, boldly moved his main implement plant to Chicago, thereby ensuring a steady supply of his harvesting machines to the Midwest. The day of the hand scythe and the one-horse plow had passed, as this editorial from an 1857 *Scientific American* suggests:

> Every farmer who has a hundred acres of land should have at least the following: a combined reaper and mower, a horse rake, a seed planter, and mower . . . a thresher and grain cleaner, a portable grist mill, a corn-sheller, a horse power, three harrows, a roller, two cultivators, and three plows.[13]

Increased amounts of capital per worker, along with new technologies embodied in the capital equipment, raised labor's productivity. Even though yields per acre changed little,

[11]Alan L. Olmstead and Paul W. Rhode, "The Red Queen and the Hard Reds: Productivity Growth in American Wheat, 1800–1940," *Journal of Economic History* 62 (2002): 929–966.
[12]Derived from Robert E. Gallman, "The Pace of Economic Growth: U.S. Experience in the Nineteenth Century," in *Essays in Nineteenth Century History*, eds. David C. Klingaman and Richard K. Vedder (Athens: Ohio University Press, 1975).
[13]Quoted in C. Danhof, "Agriculture," in *The Growth of the American Economy*, ed. H. F. Williamson (New York: Prentice Hall, 1951), 150.

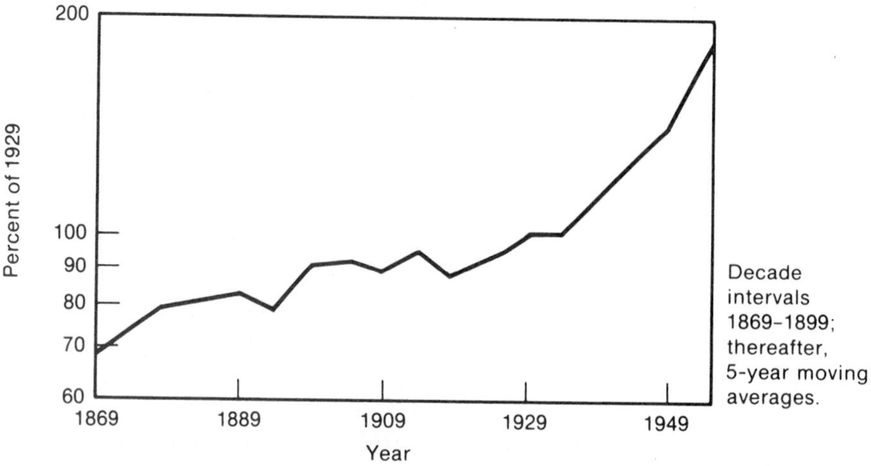

FIGURE 15.1 Total Factor Productivity in Agriculture, 1869–1955
This figure shows a ratio of agricultural output relative to a price weighted average of land, labor, and capital inputs.

Source: John W. Kendrick, Productivity Trends in the United States *(Princeton, N.J.: Princeton University Press, 1961), 362–364.*

mechanization allowed farmers to add more acres to their farms, thus expanding output per farm. Mechanized farming, however, did not replace traditional farming instantaneously but the advances were relentless.[14] After the Civil War, wages paid to grain cradlers (hand harvesters) increased, and acres per farm devoted to grains increased, hastening the introduction of mechanical reapers.

By 1857, John Deere's new plant in Moline, Illinois, was annually producing 10,000 steel plows, eclipsing the iron plow, which had proved ineffectual in the tough clay sod of the prairies as Olmstead and Rhode report:

> Between the censuses of 1850 and 1860, the number of firms producing reapers and mowers increased from roughly 20 to 73, and annual output rose about tenfold to roughly 25,000 machines. This expansion set the stage for an explosion in sales during the war years. By 1864 approximately 200 firms were making reapers and mowers with a total output of about 90,000 machines."[15]

Seed drills, cultivators, mowers, rakes and threshing machines, and myriad attachments and gadgets for harvesting machines added to the mechanization of farming in the second half of the century. Between 1860 and 1920, the number of mouths fed per farmer nearly doubled, freeing labor for industry, but not without economic dislocations and personal hardships.

[14]Paul David argues that this was due in part to the large minimum size of farm needed to employ a reaper profitably. But Alan Olmstead adduced evidence to show that farmers could hire the services of reapers or share them with neighbors. See, Paul David "The Mechanization of Reaping in the Antebellum Midwest," in *Technical Choice, Innovation and Economic Growth, Essays on American and British Experiences in the Nineteenth Century* (Cambridge, England: Cambridge University Press, 1975); and Alan Olmstead, "The Mechanization of Reaping and Mowing in American Agriculture, 1833–1870," *Journal of Economic History* 35 (June 1975).

[15]Alan R. Olmstead and Paul W. Rhode, "Beyond the Threshold: An Analysis of the Characteristics and Behaviors of Early Reaper Adapters," *Journal of Economic History* 55 (1995): 27–57.

TABLE 15.3 Trends in Farm Income and Productivity (average annual percentage change)

YEARS	REAL INCOME PER CAPITA	REAL INCOME PER WORKER
1849–1859	2.0%	2.0%
1859–1869	0.8	0.9
1869-1879	0.8	0.3
1879–1889	0.7	0.3
1889–1899	2.2	2.1
1849–1899	1.3	1.0
1869–1899	1.2	0.7

Source: Robert Fogel and Jack Rutner, "Efficiency Effects of Federal Land Policy, 1850-1900," in The Dimensions of Quantitative Research in History, *eds. W. O. Aydelotte, A. G. Bogue, and R. W. Fogel, © 1972 by the Center for Advanced Study in the Behavioral Sciences. Table 2, 396, adapted by permission of Princeton University Press.*

HARD TIMES ON THE FARM, 1864–1896

The years from the close of the Civil War to the end of World War I comprise two contrasting periods in agricultural history. The first of these, from 1864 to 1896, was characterized by agricultural hardship and political unrest; the second, from 1896 until about 1920, represented a sustained period of improvement in the lot of the farm population. This improvement is reflected quantitatively in Table 15.3, which traces average annual percentage growth rates in real farm income over the last half of the nineteenth century. Note that real incomes did rise from 1864 to 1896, but the rate of increase seemed painfully slow, and the averages obscure the hardships suffered by many western farmers in the 1870s and 1880s who claimed, "In God we trusted; in Kansas we busted."

American farmers, from the mid-1860s to the mid-1890s, knew that their lives were hard without being shown data to prove it. Conditions were especially hard on the frontier, where the combination of dreary surroundings and physical hardship compounded the difficulties of economic life, which included declining prices, indebtedness, and the necessity of purchasing many goods and services from industries in which there appeared to be a growing concentration of economic power.

All prices were falling between 1875 and 1895, but as Table 15.4 on page 294 shows, the price of farm products was falling relative to other prices. To put it slightly differently, the farmer's terms of trade—the price of the things the farmer sold divided by the price of things the farmer bought—were worsening. This did not mean that real farm income was falling (recall that Table 15.3 shows that it was rising), because the terms of trade refer only to price and do not take productivity into account.[16] It does mean, however, that the farmer had to run faster just to avoid losing ground. By 1895, to take the low point in Table 15.4, the farmer had to produce about 16 percent more than in 1870 just to offset the fall in his terms of trade.

Why were the farmer's terms of trade worsening? Part of the explanation is the rapid increase in the supply of agricultural products. All over the world, new areas were entering the competitive fray. In Canada, Australia, New Zealand, and Argentina as well as in the United States, fertile new lands were becoming agriculturally productive. In the United States alone (as Table 15.1 indicates), the number of acres in farming more than doubled between 1870 and 1900. Reinforcing this trend was the increased output made possible by mechanization.

Notable changes occurred, too, on the demand side. One favorable influence on the domestic demand was the continued rapid increase in the population. After 1870, the rate of population growth in the United States fell, but until 1900, it was still high. In the

[16]For alternative definitions and more data, see John D. Bowman and Richard H. Keehn, "Agricultural Terms of Trade in Four Midwestern States, 1870–1900," *Journal of Economic History* 34 (1974): 592–609.

TABLE 15.4 The Farmer's Terms of Trade, 1870–1915

YEAR	WHOLESALE FARM PRICES	CONSUMER PRICES	TERMS OF TRADE
1870	100	100	100
1875	88	87	102
1880	71	76	94
1885	64	71	90
1890	63	71	89
1895	55	66	84
1900	64	66	97
1905	71	71	100
1910	93	74	127
1915	90	80	112

Source: Historical Statistics *(Washington, D.C.: Government Printing Office, 1975), Series E42, E53, and E135.*

decades of the 1870s and 1880s, the increase was just over 25 percent, and in the 1890s, it was more than 20 percent—a substantial growth in the number of mouths to feed. There was an offsetting factor, however: In 1870, Americans spent one third of their current per capita incomes on farm products. By 1890, they were spending a much smaller fraction, just over one-fifth, and during the next few years this proportion dropped further. Thus, although the real incomes of the American population rose during the period, and although Americans did not spend less on food absolutely, the proportion of those incomes earned by farmers declined. (In technical terms, the income elasticity of demand was less than 1 for most agricultural crops.) This observation is discussed in terms of the Engel Curve in Economic Insight 15.2 on page 296.

Offsetting these effects in part was the rise in the demand abroad for U.S. crops. Export demand for farm products increased steadily until the turn of the century. Wheat and flour exports reached their peak in 1901, at which time nearly one-third of domestic wheat production was sold abroad. Likewise, meat and meat products were exported in larger and larger quantities until 1900, when these exports also began to decline. Overall, the value of agricultural exports rose from $297 million in 1870 to more than $840 million in 1900. Exports of farm products during these decades helped expand agricultural markets, but they were far from sufficient to alleviate the hard times on the farm.

Farmers were not inclined to see their difficulties as the result of impersonal market forces. Instead, they traced their problems to monopolies and conspiracies: bankers (some thought that Jewish bankers were particularly to blame) who raised interest rates, manipulated the currency, and then foreclosed on farm mortgages; grain elevator operators who charged rates farmers could not afford; industrialists who charged high prices for farm machinery and consumer goods; railroads that charged monopoly rates on freight; and so on.

The evidence of these alleged sources of distress is largely unsupported, suggesting that farmers were attacking symptoms rather than causes. Figure 15.2 shows that the prices of industrial items in the West fell relative to the prices of farm products; Figure 15.3 shows that freight costs also fell as a percentage of farm prices. This does not mean, of course, that every complaint of every farmer was baseless. Although long-haul railroad rates fell dramatically relative to agricultural prices over the period, for example, certain monopolized sections of railroad permitted discriminatory monopoly pricing on short hauls.[17]

[17]For more on this, see Robert Higgs, "Railroad Rates and the Populist Uprising," *Agricultural History* 44 (July 1970).

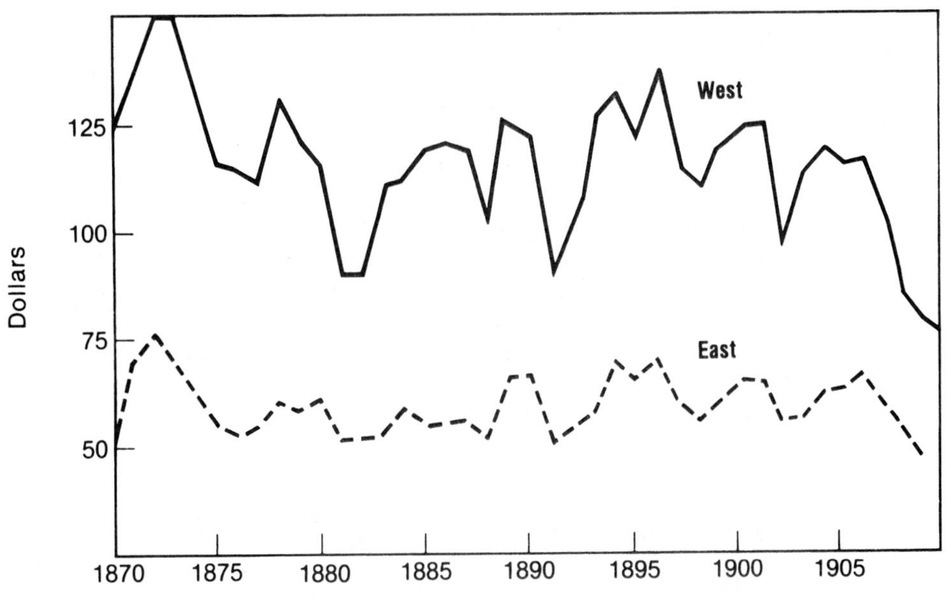

FIGURE 15.2 Price of Industrial Goods in Terms of Farm Products, West and East. 1870-1910

Source: Derived from Jeffrey G. Williamson, Late Nineteenth Century American Development, A General Equilibrium History *(Cambridge, England: Cambridge University Press, 1974), 149.*

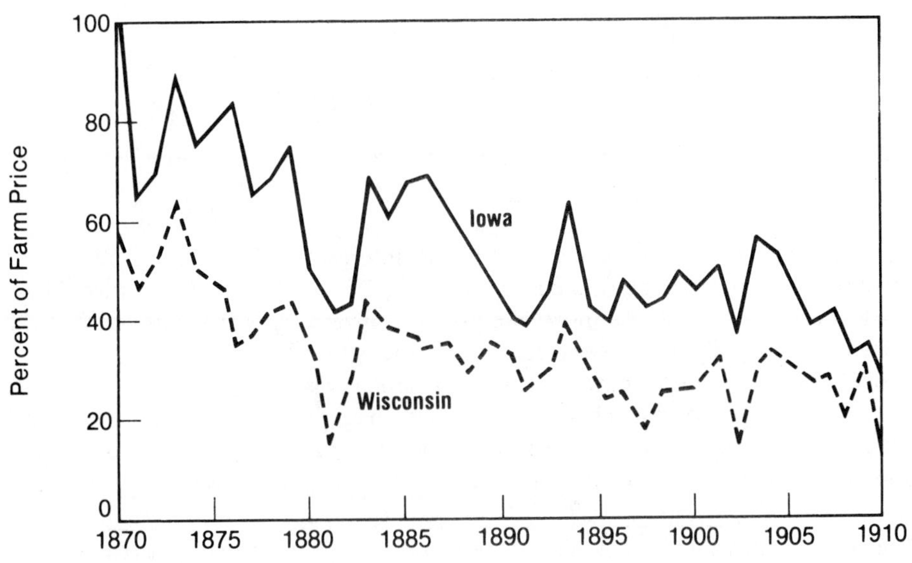

FIGURE 15.3 Freight Costs on Wheat from Iowa and Wisconsin in New York as Percentage of Farm Price, 1870-1910

Source: Derived from Jeffrey G. Williamson, Late Nineteenth Century American Development, A General Equilibrium History *(Cambridge, England: Cambridge University Press, 1974), 261.*

Economic Insight 15.2

The Engel Curve

The slow growth of demand for farm products reflected the slope of the Engel curve, named for nineteenth-century Prussian statistician Ernst Engel. Engel curves are usually based on samples of family budgets and show average expenditures on food (or other goods and services) at each level of income. Economic growth lifts the average family to higher income levels, but expenditures on food rise less rapidly, and the share spent on food falls. The farmer could retain his share of total spending only if the slope of the Engel curve for farm products were equal to the slope of the 45° line bisecting the figure.

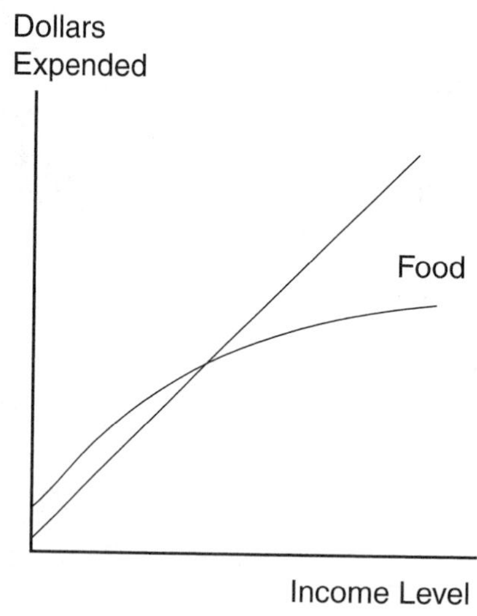

Finally, both in nominal and in real terms, interest rates charged on midwestern farm mortgages declined over the decades, as shown in Table 15.5. Such rates were higher than n the East, where capital was more plentiful and investments typically less risky, but they declined more rapidly in the West. Indeed, to the extent that farmers were suffering from monopoly prices in credit markets, it was the small western bank rather than the eastern financier who was to blame. This point was first made by Richard Sylla and John James.[18] Even here, however, subsequent research has narrowed the potential role of local bank monopolies in the credit problems of farmers.[19] Farm mortgage rates, as well as short-term

[18] Richard Sylla, "Federal Policy, Banking Market Structure, and Capital Mobilization in the United States, 1863–1913," *Journal of Economic History* 29 (1969): 657–686, and John James, "The Development of the National Money Market," *Journal of Economic History* 36 (1976): 878–897.

[19] See Gene Smiley, "Interest Rate Movements in the United States, 1888–1913," *Journal of Economic History* 35 (1975): 591–662; Richard Keehn, "Market Power and Bank Lending: Some Evidence from Wisconsin, 1870–1900," *Journal of Economic History* 35 (1975): 591–620; and John J. Binder and David T. Brown, "Bank Rates of Return and Entry Restrictions, 1869–1914," *Journal of Economic History* 51 (1991): 47–66.

THE GRANGER COLLECTION, NEW YORK

The mechanial reaper, developed by Robert McCormick and his son Cyrus Hall McCormick, revolutionized the American wheat harvest and created a major industry.

TABLE 15.5 Real (Nominal) Interest Rates on Midwestern Farm Mortgages, 1870–1900

YEAR	ILLINOIS	WISCONSIN	IOWA	NEBRASKA
1870	17.0 (9.6)%	15.4 (8.0)%	16.9 (9.5)%	17.9 (10.5)%
1880	11.4 (7.8)	10.8 (7.2)	12.3 (8.7)	12.7 (9.1)
1890	7.6 (6.9)	6.6 (5.9)	7.7 (7.0)	8.5 (7.8)
1910	4.3 (5.8)	3.4 (4.9)	4.0 (5.5)	4.8 (6.3)

Note: The real rate is the nominal rate plus the rate of deflation or minus the rate of inflation.

Source: Derived from Jeffrey G. Williamson, Late Nineteenth Century American Development: A General Equilibrium History *(Cambridge, England: Cambridge University Press, 1974), 152.*

rates, were high, especially in the 1870s, but appear to have been a product of high lending risks and other causes rather than monopoly power.[20]

Part of the explanation for agricultural discontent in this era was the process of commercialization and globalization that created a world in which the farmer was subject to economic fluctuations that he could neither control nor even fully comprehend. As emphasized by Ann Mayhew, to keep abreast of progress, the farmer needed more equipment—reapers, planters, harrows—as well as more land and irrigation facilities. This often meant

[20]For more on this issue, see Barry Eichengreen, "Mortgage Interest Rates in the Populist Era," *American Economic Review* 74 (1984): 995–1015, and Kenneth Snowden, "Mortgage Rates and Capital Market Development in the Late Nineteenth Century," *Journal of Economic History* 48 (1987): 671–692.

© CULVER PICTURES

High horsepower was possible before the advent of steam- and gasoline-powered tractors.

greater indebtedness.[21] When agricultural prices fell, foreclosures or cessation of credit extensions brought ruin to many farmers. Farm prices, moreover, were increasingly subject to international forces. Farm prices could rise despite good weather and abundant crops in the United States and fall despite bad weather and poor crops. Everything might depend on events abroad, which the farmer could not directly observe. Robert A. McGuire has shown a strong correlation between political agitation in various western states and the economic instability of these states, and that price fluctuations had a particularly important bearing on the income instability of farmers.[22]

Even though modern research has rejected many of the analyses put forward in the late nineteenth century, we need to take a close look at the political forces spawned by the farmers' discontent, for the reforms proposed by the agrarian protesters helped shape the institutional framework of the American economy.

AGRARIAN POLITICAL ORGANIZATIONS

In what has been called the "Thirty Years' War" against the princes of privilege, a number of organizations, large and small, were formed to fight for the farmers.[23] Urban industrial labor influenced some organizations and many of the ideas of the agrarians originated in the urban radicalism of the East.[24] Farmers in the West and South dominated—if not entirely motivated—four rather clearly distinguishable movements.

[21]See Ann Mayhew, "A Reappraisal of the Causes of Farm Protest in the United States, 1870–1900," *Journal of Economic History* 32 (1972): 464–475.

[22]See Robert A. McGuire, "Economic Causes of Late Nineteenth Century Agrarian Unrest," *Journal of Economic History* 41 (1981): 835–849.

[23]For a most informative article providing a longer perspective on farm movements and political activity, see Morton Rothstein, "Farmers' Movements and Organizations, Numbers, Gains, Losses," *Agricultural History* 62 (3), (Summer 1988): 161–188.

[24]See Chester McArthur Destler, "Western Radicalism, 1865–1901: Concepts and Origins," *Mississippi Valley Historical Review* 31 (December 1944): 335–368.

The Grangers

The first farm organization of importance was the National Grange of the Patrons of Husbandry. Formally organized in 1867, the order grew rapidly. By 1874, it had 20,000 local branches and a membership of about 1.5 million. After seven years of ascendancy, a decline set in, and by 1880, membership had largely disappeared except in a few strongholds such as the upper Mississippi valley and the Northeast.

Although the organization's bylaws strictly forbade formal political action by the Grangers, members held informal political meetings and worked with reform parties to secure passage of regulatory legislation. In several western states, the Grangers were successful in obtaining laws that set an upper limit on the charges of railroads and of warehouse and elevator companies and in establishing regulation of such companies by commission, a new concept in American politics. The Supreme Court, in *Munn v. Illinois* (1877), held that such regulation was constitutional if the business was "clothed with the public interest." However, in 1886, the Court held that states could not regulate interstate commerce, so reformers had to turn to the federal government to regulate the railroads. The Interstate Commerce Commission (which will be discussed in chapter 16), established in 1887, was the result.

The Grangers developed still another weapon for fighting unfair business practices. If businesses charged prices that were too high, then farmers, it was argued, sensibly enough, ought to go into business themselves. The most successful type of business established by the Grangers was the cooperative, formed for the sale of general merchandise and farm implements to Grange member owners. Cooperatives (and conventional companies that sold stock) were established to process farm products, and the first large mail-order house, Montgomery Ward and Company, was established to sell to the Grangers.

In Granger Movement meetings like this one in Scott County, Illinois, members focused their discontentment on big-city ways, monopoly, the tariff, and low prices for agricultural products. From such roots grew pressures to organize support for agriculture.

The Greenback Movement

Some farmers, disappointed in the Grange for not making more decisive gains in the struggle to bolster farm prices, joined forces with a labor element to form an Independent National Party, which entered candidates in the election of 1876. This group was hopelessly unsuccessful, but a "Greenback Labor" party formed by the same people made headway in the election of 1878. To finance the Civil War, the government had resorted to the issue of paper money popularly known as "greenbacks," and the suggestion that a similar issue be made in the late 1870s appealed to poor farmers. The "Greenback Labor" platform, more than any other party program, centered on demands for inflationary (they would have said "reflationary") action. Although Greenback Labor candidates were entered in the presidential campaign of 1880, they received a very small percentage of the popular vote because labor failed to participate effectively. Greenback agitators continued their efforts in the elections of 1884 and 1888 but with little success.

The movement is worth remembering for two reasons. First, Greenback agitation constituted the first attempt of farmers to act politically on a national scale. Second, the group's central tenets later became the most important part of the populists' appeal to the electorate in the 1890s.

The Alliances

At the same time that the Granges were multiplying, independent farmers' clubs were being formed in the West and South. Independent clubs tended to coalesce into state "alliances," which, in turn, were consolidated into two principal groups—the Northwestern Alliance and the Southern Alliance. In 1889, an attempt to merge the Alliances failed, despite the similarity of their aims. The Alliances advocated monetary reforms similar to those urged by the Greenback parties and, like the Grangers, favored government regulation and cooperative business ventures. Alliance memberships, moreover, favored government ownership of transportation and communication facilities.

Each Alliance offered a proposal that had a highly modern ring. The Southern Alliance recommended that the federal government establish a system of warehouses for the storage of nonperishable commodities so that farmers could obtain low-interest loans of up to 80 percent of the value of the products stored. The Northwestern Alliance proposed that the federal government extend long-term loans in greenbacks up to 50 percent of the value of a farm. Because of their revolutionary nature, such ideas received little support from voters.

The Populists

After mild periods of prosperity in the late 1880s, economic activity experienced another downturn, and the hardships of the farmer and the laborer again became severe. In 1891, elements of the Alliances met in Cincinnati with the Knights of Labor to form the People's Party. At the party convention of 1892, held in Omaha, famed agrarian and formidable orator General James Weaver was nominated for the presidency. Weaver, an old Greenbacker, won 22 electoral votes in the election of 1892. Two years later, the party won a number of congressional seats, and it appeared that greater success might be on the way. Populism thus emerged from 30 years of unrest—an unrest that was chiefly agricultural but that had urban connections. To its supporters, populism was something more than an agitation for economic betterment: it was a faith. The overtones of political and social reform were part of the faith because they would help to further economic aims. The agitation against monopoly control—against oppression by corporations, banks, and capitalists—had come to a head. Along with the key principle of antimonopolism ran a strongly collectivist doctrine. Populists felt that only through government control of the monetary system and through government ownership of banks, railroads, and the means of communication could the evils of monopoly be put down. In fact, some populists advocated operation of government-owned firms in basic industries so that the government would have the information to determine whether or not monopolistic prices were being charged. The government-owned firm would, in other words, provide a "yardstick" by which to measure the performance of private firms.

In older parts of the country, the radicalism of the People's Party alienated established farmers. Had the leaders of the 1896 coalition of populists and Democrats not chosen to stand or fall on the issue of inflation, there is no telling what the future of the coalition might have been. But inflation was anathema to property owners with little or no debt, and when the chips were down, rural as well as urban property owners supported "sound" money.

THE BEGINNINGS OF FEDERAL ASSISTANCE TO AGRICULTURE

Although attempts by farmers to improve their condition through organization were unsuccessful as far as immediate goals were concerned, the way had been opened for legislation and federal assistance. Of course, the land acts of the nineteenth century had worked to the advantage of new farmers, but they can scarcely be considered part of an agricultural "program." Similarly, much regulatory legislation passed in the late nineteenth and early twentieth centuries, although originating in agrarian organizations, produced effects that were not restricted to agriculture. Federal assistance to agriculture before World War I was designed to compile and disseminate information in order to help the individual farmer to increase productivity; it was not designed to alleviate distress, as was later New Deal legislation.

The Department of Agriculture

As early as 1839, an Agricultural Division had been set up in the Patent Office. Congress created a Department of Agriculture in 1862, but its head, who was designated the Commissioner of Agriculture, did not have Cabinet ranking until 1889.

Until 1920, the Department of Agriculture performed three principal functions: (1) research and experimentation in plant exploration, plant and animal breeding, and insect and disease control; (2) distribution of agricultural information through publications, agricultural experiment stations, and county demonstration work; and (3) regulation of the quality of products through the authority to condemn diseased animals, to prohibit shipment in interstate commerce of adulterated or misbranded foods and drugs, and to inspect and certify meats and dairy products in interstate trade. Pressure always fell on the department to give "practical" help to the farmers, as evidenced by the fact that throughout this period, the department regularly distributed free seeds. In retrospect, it seems that the chief contribution of the Department of Agriculture in these early years lay in its ability to convince farmers of the value of "scientific" farming.

Agricultural Education

Attempts to incorporate the teaching of agricultural subjects into the educational system began locally, but federal assistance was necessary to maintain adequate programs. Although colleges of agriculture had been established in several states by 1860, it was the Morrill Act of 1862 that gave impetus to agricultural training at the university level. The Morrill Act established "land-grant" colleges that gradually assumed statewide leadership in agricultural research. The Hatch Act of 1887 provided federal assistance to state agricultural experiment stations, many of which had already been established with state funds. The Hatch Act also provided for the establishment of an Office of Experiment Stations in the Department of Agriculture in order to link the work of the department with that of the states. After 1900, interest in secondary schools began to develop. The Smith-Hughes Vocational Education Act of 1917 provided funds to states that agreed to expand vocational training at the high-school level in agriculture, trades, and home economics.

These and other measures advanced by reformers nurtured the beginnings of federal involvement in the agricultural sector. As we shall see, such involvement would grow dramatically in the decades after 1920. Similarly, calls to "end the waste" of natural resources advanced the role of government in the control and use of land, timber, and other natural resources.

NATURAL RESOURCE CONSERVATION: THE FIRST STAGES

The waste of natural resources in North America as perceived by Europeans, contemporaries, and others dates as far back as colonial times. For instance, many colonial farmers ignored "advanced" European farming methods designed to maintain soil fertility, preferring to fell trees and plant around stumps and then move on if the land wore out. Because land was abundant, their concern was not with soil conservation but with the shortage of labor and capital.

Similarly, in the early nineteenth century, lumber was in great abundance, especially in the eastern half of the nation, where five-sixths of the original forests were located. Indeed, in most areas of new settlement, standing timber was often an impediment rather than a valued resource. As late as 1850, more than 90 percent of all fuel-based energy came from wood.

By 1915, however, wood supplied less than 10 percent of all fuel-based energy in the United States, and in the Great Plains and other western regions, timber grew increasingly scarce.[25] The western advance of the railroad (which devoured nearly one-quarter of the timber cut in the 1870s) and the western shift of the population brought new pressures on limited western and distant eastern timber supplies. Moreover, the price of uncut marketable timber on public lands was zero for all practical purposes. This fact and the lack of clear legal rights to timber on public lands provided incentive to cut as fast as possible on public lands (Economic Reasoning Proposition 3). As a result, much waste occurred, and various environmental hazards were made more extreme. These included the loss of watersheds, which increased the hazard of floods and hastened soil erosion. More importantly, the buildup of masses of slash (tree branches and other timber deposits) created severe fire hazards. In the late nineteenth century, large cutover regions became explosive tinderboxes. For example, in 1871, the "Peshtigo fire" in Wisconsin devoured 1.28 million acres and killed more than 1,000 people. Similar dramatic losses from fire occurred in 1881 in Michigan and in 1894 in Wisconsin and Minnesota. These and other factors, such as fraudulent land acquisitions, demanded legislative action and reform.[26]

Land, Water, and Timber Conservation

The first major step toward reform was the General Revision Act of 1891. As noted earlier, this law repealed measures that had been an open invitation to land fraud, making it more difficult for corporations and wealthy individuals to steal timber and minerals. Prevention of theft scarcely constitutes conservation, but one section of the 1891 act, which empowered the president to set aside forest reserves, was a genuine conservation measure. Between 1891 and 1900, 50 million acres of valuable timberland were withdrawn from private entry, despite strong and growing opposition from interest groups in the western states. Inadequate appropriations made it impossible for the Division of Forestry to protect the reserves from forest fires and from depredations of timber thieves, but a start had been made.

---

[25]For an excellent account of the responsive process in the form and use of natural resources to changes in their costs and supplies, see Nathan Rosenberg, "Innovative Responses to Material Shortages," *American Economic Review* 63 (May 1973).

[26]For further detail, see Alan L. Olmstead, "The Costs of Economic Growth," in *The Encyclopedia of American Economic History*, Vol. 2, (New York: Scribner's, 1980), 863–881; and Marion Clawson, "Forests in the Long Sweep of American History," *Science* 204 (June 15, 1979).

Theodore Roosevelt and naturalist John Muir at Yosemite. An enthusiastic outdoorsman, Roosevelt expanded the role of the federal government in preserving America's wilderness and natural resources.

When Theodore Roosevelt succeeded to the presidency in 1901, there was widespread concern, both in Congress and throughout the nation, over the problem of conservation. With imagination, charm, and fervor, Roosevelt sought legislation during both his terms to provide a consistent and far-reaching conservation program. By 1907, he could point to several major achievements:

1. National forests comprised 150 million acres, of which 75 million acres contained marketable timber. In 1901, a Bureau of Forestry was created, which became the United States Forest Service in 1905. Under Gifford Pinchot, Roosevelt's able chief adviser in all matters pertaining to conservation, a program of scientific forestry was initiated. The national forests were to be more than just preserves; the "crop" of trees was to be continually harvested and sold such that ever-larger future crops were assured.
2. Lands containing 75 million acres of mineral wealth were reserved from sale and settlement. Most of the lands containing metals were already privately owned, but the government retained large deposits of coal, phosphates, and oil.
3. There was explicit recognition of the future importance of waterpower sites. A policy of leasing government-owned sites to private firms for a stipulated period of year was established, while actual ownership was reserved for the government.
4. The principle was accepted that it was a proper function of the federal government to implement a program of public works for the purpose of controlling stream flows. The Reclamation Act of 1902 provided for the use of receipts from land sales in the arid states to finance the construction of reservoirs and irrigation

works, with repayment to be made by settlers over a period of years. In reality, however, it was overwhelmingly taxpayers generally, rather than only western settlers, who paid for these water projects.

Although such achievements seem modest, it should be recalled that in the first decade of the twentieth century, many people bitterly opposed any interference with the private exploitation of the remaining public domain. Much of the growth of government expenditures in water control, dams, and irrigation systems awaited a second Roosevelt in the 1930s. But the precedents set by Theodore Roosevelt's administration set the stage for the engineering marvels of the present era, which freed western agriculture from the shackles of dry-land farming of basic grains and livestock feeding—at considerable cost to the taxpayer. They also set a new direction, however haltingly, toward more conservation of natural space, minerals, forests, and water.

Selected References and Suggested Readings

Arrington, Leonard. *Great Basin Kingdom.* Cambridge, Mass.: Harvard University Press, 1958.

Atack, Jeremy. "Tenants and Yeomen in the Nineteenth Century." *Agricultural History* 62 (3), (Summer 1988): 6–32.

Atack, Jeremy, and Fred Bateman. *To Their Own Soil: Agriculture in the Antebellum North.* Ames: Iowa State University Press, 1987.

Atack, Jeremy, Fred Bateman, and William N. Parker. "Northern Agriculture and the Westward Movement." In *The Cambridge Economic History of the United States,* Vol. II, *The Long Nineteenth Century,* eds. Stanley L. Engerman and Robert E. Gallman. New York: Cambridge University Press, 2000, 285–328.

Bateman, Fred. "Improvements in American Dairy Farming, 1850–1910: A Quantitative Analysis." *Journal of Economic History* 23 (1968): 255–273.

Bogue, Allan. *From Prairie to Cornbelt: Farming on the Illinois and Iowa Prairies in the Nineteenth Century.* Chicago: University of Chicago Press, 1963.

Bowman, John D. "An Economic Analysis of Midwestern Farm Land Values and Farmland Income, 1890 to 1900." *Yale Economic Essays* (Fall 1965).

Bowman, John D., and Richard H. Keehn. "Agricultural Terms of Trade in Four Midwestern States, 1870–1900." *Journal of Economic History* 34 (1974): 592–609.

Carstensen, Vernon. *Farmer Discontent, 1865–1900.* New York: Wiley, 1974.

Coelho, Philip, and James Shepherd. "Differences in Regional Prices: The United States, 1851–1880." *Journal of Economic History* 34 (1974): 551–591.

Craig, Lee A. *To Sow One Acre More: Childbearing and Farm Productivity in the Antebellum North.* Baltimore: Johns Hopkins University Press, 1993.

Cronon, William. *Nature's Metropolis: Chicago and the Great West.* New York: Norton, 1992.

Danhof, Clarence H. *Change in Agriculture: the Northern United States, 1820–1870.* Cambridge, Mass.: Harvard University Press, 1969.

David, Paul. "The Mechanization of Reaping in the Antebellum Midwest." In *Technical Choice, Innovation and Economic Growth, Essays on American and British Experience in the Nineteenth Century.* Cambridge, England: Cambridge University Press, 1975.

Eichengreen, Barry. "Mortgage Interest Rates in the Populist Era." *American Economic Review* 74 (December 1984): 995–1015.

Galenson, David. "The End of the Chisholm Trail." *Journal of Economic History* 24 (1974): 350–364.

Gallman, Robert E. "Changes in Total U.S. Agricultural Factor Productivity in the Nineteenth Century." *Agricultural History* (January 1972).

———. "The Agricultural Sector and the Pace of Economic Growth: U.S. Experience in the Nineteenth Century." In *Essays in Nineteenth Century Economic History*, eds. David Klingaman and Richard Vedder. Athens: Ohio University Press, 1975.

Gates, Paul Wallace. *The Farmer's Age: Agriculture, 1815–1860.* New York: Harper & Row, 1968.

Guilloches, Zvi. "Hybrid Corn and the Economics of Innovation." *Science* 132 (July 29, 1960).

Harley, C. Knick, "Western Settlement and the Price of Wheat, 1872–1913." *Journal of Economic History* 38 (1978): 865–878.

Hays, Samuel P. *Conservation and the Gospel of Efficiency: The Progressive Conservation Movement, 1890–1920.* Cambridge, Mass.: Harvard University Press, 1959.

Hicks, John D. *The Populist Revolt.* Lincoln: University of Nebraska Press, 1961.

Higgs, Robert. *The Transformation of the American Economy, 1865–1914: An Essay in Interpretation.* New York: Wiley, 1971.

Jones, Lewis. "The Mechanization of Reaping and Mowing in American Agriculture: A Comment." *Journal of Economic History* 37 (1977): 451–455.

Kantor, Shawn Everett. *Politics and Property Rights: The Closing of the Open Range in the Postbellum South.* Chicago: University of Chicago Press, 1998.

Libecap, Gary D. "Economic Variables and the Development of the Law: The Case of Western Mineral Rights." *Journal of Economic History* 38 (1978): 338–362.

———. "Bureaucratic Opposition to the Assignment of Property Rights: Overgrazing on the Western Range." *Journal of Economic History* 41 (1981): 151–158.

———. "Property Rights in Economic History: Implications for Research." *Explorations in Economic History* 23 (1986): 227–252.

Libecap, Gary D., and Ronald N. Johnson. "Property Rights, Nineteenth-Century Federal Timber Policy, and the Conservation Movement." *Journal of Economic History* 39 (1979): 129–142.

Lindert, Peter H. "Long-Run Trends in American Farm Values." *Agricultural History* 62 (3), (Summer 1988): 45–85.

Mayhew, Anne. "A Reappraisal of the Causes of Farm Protest in the United States, 1870–1900." *Journal of Economic History* 32 (1972): 464–475.

McGuire, Robert A. "Economic Causes of Late Nineteenth Century Agrarian Unrest." *Journal of Economic History* 41 (1981): 835–849.

Merk, Frederick. *History of the Westward Movement.* New York: Knopf, 1978.

Olmstead, Alan. "The Mechanization of Reaping and Mowing in American Agriculture, 1833–1870." *Journal of Economic History* 35 (June 1975).

Olmstead, Alan L. and Paul W. Rhode. "Beyond the Threshold: An Analysis of the Characteristics and Behaviors of Early Reaper Adopters." *Journal of Economic History* 55 (1995): 27–57.

———. "The Red Queen and the Hard Reds: Productivity Growth in American Wheat, 1800–1940." *Journal of Economic History* 62 (2002): 929–966.

Parker, William. "Agriculture." In *American Economic Growth: An Economist's History of the United States*, eds. Lance E. Davis et al. New York: Harper & Row, 1972.

Petulla, Joseph M. *American Environmental History: The Exploitation and Conservation of Natural Resources.* San Francisco: Boyd & Fraser, 1977.

Rasmussen, Wayne D. "The Impact of Technological Change on American Agriculture, 1862–1962." *Journal of Economic History* 22 (December 1962).

Rothstein, Morton. "Farmers' Movements and Organizations: Numbers, Gains, Losses." *Agricultural History* 62 (3), (Summer 1988): 161–181.

Shannon, Fred A. *The Farmer's Last Frontier*, 1860–1897. New York: Harper & Row, 1968.

Snowden, Kenneth A. "Mortgage Rates and American Capital Market Development in the Late Nineteenth Century." *Journal of Economic History* 47 (1987): 771–791.

Swierenga, Robert P. *Pioneers and Profits: Land Speculation on the Iowa Frontier.* Ames: Iowa State University Press, 1968.

Turner, Frederick Jackson. *The Frontier in American History.* New York: Holt, 1921.

U.S. Department of Agriculture. A history of American agriculture provided at **http://www.usda.gov/history2/**.

Williamson, Jeffrey G. "Greasing the Wheels of Sputtering Export Engines: Midwestern Grains and American Export Growth." *Explorations in Economic History* 17 (1980): 189–217.

Winters, Donald L. "Tenancy as an Economic Institution: The Growth and Distribution of Agricultural Tenancy in Iowa, 1850–1900." *Journal of Economic History* 37 (1977): 382–408.

Chapter Sixteen

Railroads and Economic Change

Few developments have captured the attention of historians and contemporary observers quite like the railroad. Fast and powerful, reaching everywhere, the railroad came to dominate the American landscape and the American imagination. Trains became the symbol of modern America, epitomizing America's economic superiority in an industrializing world.

To stipulate the many important influences of the railroad would soon generate a list of unmanageable proportions. We will constrain our attentions to four main questions:

1. Were these continent-spanning investments built ahead of demand, or were railroads followers in the settlement process?
2. How did the builders get their capital? Large land grants, both federal and state, and other means of financial assistance were given. Were these land grants needless giveaways or prudent uses of empty spaces? How important were they in the overall picture?

3. Another factor of great importance was the growth of government intervention in the economy as manifested in railroad regulation, both at the state and federal levels (Economic Reasoning Proposition 4). Key legal interpretations paved the way for new economic controls by government. Was there a capture of the regulatory process by railroad management, or did regulation primarily benefit users?
4. Finally, what impact did the railroad have on the overall growth rate of the economy? Was it only marginally superior to other modes of transport, or was it indispensable to American prosperity? Was the pace of productivity advance that we observed for the railroad in chapter 9 during the antebellum period sustained during the postbellum period?

Economic Reasoning Proposition

These questions have been asked by every generation of economic historians since the railroads were built. As we shall see, the answers have sometimes changed as new sources of data have been exploited and as new tools of analysis have been applied (Economic Reasoning Proposition 5).

THE TRANSCONTINENTALS[1]

The Gold Rush of 1849 yielded knowledge about the riches of the Pacific Coast and about the vast spaces that separated East from West. There were three ways to get there, all difficult. Wagon trains along trails to California and the Pacific Northwest were beset with blizzards in winter, thirst in summer, and Indian attacks in all seasons. The shorter sea route via the Isthmus of Panama could cut the six to eight month trip around Cape Horn to as little as six weeks. But from Chagres, the eastern port on the isthmus, to Panama City was a five-day journey by native dugout and muleback, and at Panama City, travelers might have a long wait before securing passage north. For those who could afford it, the best way to California was by clipper ship, which made the passage around the Horn in about 100 days. (The record between New York and San Francisco was 88 days, set in 1854 by the clipper *Flying Cloud*.[2]) Thus, it is hardly surprising that a safe rail connection with the Pacific Coast was eagerly sought.

From the outset, government participation was viewed as essential. It was assumed that while the profits to the nation would be enormous, the profits to private investors would be insufficient to compensate for the enormous uncertainty surrounding such a project. By 1853, Congress was convinced of the feasibility of a railroad to the West Coast and directed government engineers to survey practical routes. The engineers described five, but years passed before construction began because of rivalry for the eastern terminus of the line. From Minneapolis to New Orleans, cities along the Mississippi River vied for the position of gateway to the West, boasting of their advantages while deprecating the claims of their rivals. The outbreak of the Civil War removed the proponents of the southern routes from Congress, and in 1862, the northern Platte River route was selected because it was used by the pony express, stages, and freighter wagons.

By the Pacific Railway Act of 1862, Congress granted a charter of incorporation to the Union Pacific Railroad, which was authorized to build a line from Council Bluffs, Iowa, to the western boundary of Nevada. The Central Pacific, incorporated under the laws of California in 1861, was at the same time given authority to construct the western part of the road from Sacramento to the Nevada border. The government agreed to furnish financial assistance in two ways: Ten sections of public land (five alternate sections on each side of the right-of-way) were granted for each mile of track laid. The government agreed further to lend the companies certain sums per mile of construction; the loans were to be secured by first-mortgage bonds. Because the act of 1862 failed to attract sufficient private capital, the law was amended in 1864 to double the amount of land grants and to provide second-mortgage security of government loans, thus enabling the railroads to sell first-mortgage bonds to the public. To encourage speed of construction, the Central Pacific was permitted to build 150 miles beyond the Nevada line; later it was authorized to push eastward until a junction was made with the Union Pacific.

The last two years of construction were marked by a storied race between the two companies to lay the most track. With permission to build eastward to a junction with the Union Pacific, the directors of the Central Pacific wished to obtain as much per mile subsidy as possible. The Union Pacific, relying on ex-soldiers and Irish immigrants, laid 1,086 miles of track; the Central Pacific, relying on Chinese immigrants, laid 689 miles, part of it through the mountains. The joining of the Union Pacific and the Central Pacific occurred amid great fanfare and celebration on May 10, 1869, at Promontory Summit (commonly called Promontory Point), a few miles west of Ogden, Utah. By telegraph, President Ulysses S. Grant gave the signal from Washington to drive in the last spike. The hammer blows that drove home the golden spike were

[1]Astute readers will note that we sometimes use the term loosely to cover railroads that might be better designated as *western railroads*.

[2]This record was not broken until 1989, when a small, high-tech sailboat named *Thursday's Child*, with a crew of two, made the passage in 80 days.

echoed by telegraph to waiting throngs on both coasts. The hope was expressed that the fruits of the toil of farmer and laborer could now be transported swiftly and cheaply from coast to coast or from the interior to either coast. The continent had at last been spanned by rail; although transcontinental train travel was not without discomfort and even danger, the terrible trials of the overland and sea routes were over. See Perspective 16.1 on page 310.

TOTAL CONSTRUCTION: PACE AND PATTERNS

As the first transcontinentals pushed toward completion and others were added, settled regions were crisscrossed with rails for through traffic (see Map 16.1). All major lines tried to secure access to New York in the east and to Chicago and St. Louis in the west. On the more northerly routes, the New York Central completed a through line from New York to Chicago by 1877, and the Erie did the same only a few years later. After the mid-1880s, the trunk lines filled the gaps, gaining access to secondary railroad centers and building feeder lines in a north-south direction.

From 1864 to 1900, the greatest percentage of track, varying from one-third to nearly one-half of the country's total annual construction, was laid in the Great Plains states. Chicago became the chief railroad terminus, the center of a web of rails extending north, west, and south. St. Louis, Kansas City, Minneapolis, Omaha, and Denver became secondary centers.

The Southeast and the Southwest lagged both in railroad construction and in the combination of local lines into through systems. Sparseness of population and war-induced poverty accounted in part for the backwardness of the Southeast, but the competition of coastal shipping was also a deterrent to railroad growth. The only southern transmountain crossing utilized before 1880 was the Chesapeake and Ohio, and, except for the Southern, no main north-south line was completed until the 1890s.

Keeping in mind that the rate of growth of the main-line railroad network varied in different regions, we turn to Table 16.1 on page 311, which shows the expansion of total line mileage nationally. One feature is unsurprising: the eventual slowing in percentage jumps in

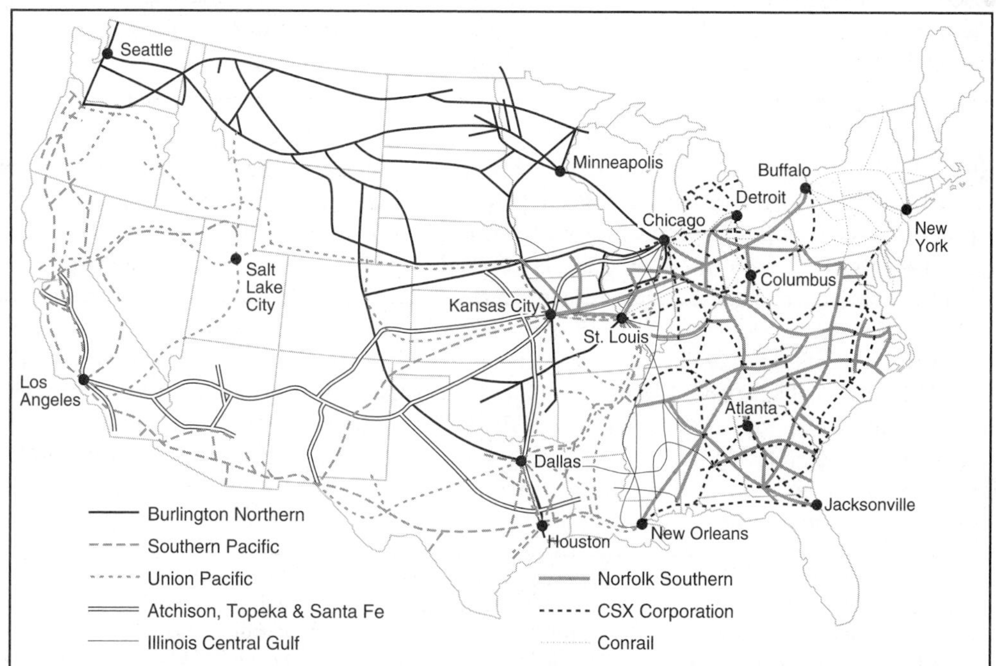

MAP 16.1 Today's Basic Railroad Network *The modern railroad network of the United States reflects the great waves of railroad building that occurred in the nineteenth century.*

Perspectives 16.1

The Railroad and Mormon Handcarters

When the Pacific Union hooked up with the Central Pacific Railroad at Promontory Point, May 10, 1869, to form the first transcontinental railroad line, the nation was at last united by rail. In addition, the linkage ended the long-distance mail-passenger stage lines, the pony express, and one of the most unique forms of migration in U.S. history.

Even before the Mormon pioneers, fleeing from persecution in Illinois, first entered the Great Basin of Utah in 1847 and relocated their church there (Salt Lake City today), Mormon missionaries were laboring in Great Britain and northern Europe to recruit new members into the church. Before 1854, Mormons, moving west to their Land of Zion, came in wagon trains.

From 1854 to 1868, most new Mormon arrivals in Utah came from European shores to the United States by ship, then by train to the western railhead of Iowa City (later to Omaha), and then by foot, walking the last 1,000 miles. Known as *handcarters*, they carried their belongings on hand-pulled flatbed carts resembling Chinese rickshaws. Too poor to afford animal-drawn wagons, they walked west under the direction and financial assistance of the church. A momentous disaster struck in early November 1856 when two handcart companies of nearly 500 each, under the direction of Captain Willie and Captain Martin, left Iowa City "late in the season." These two separate companies hit early winter storms at nearly 8,000 feet near the great divide in western Wyoming. News of the storms and knowledge of the numbers of people exposed and worn down on the trail motivated a rapid dispatch of an advance rescue party. Twenty-nine men galloped east from Salt Lake. Most of the 1,000-plus people stranded were saved, but between 200 and 300 perished from starvation and freezing.

Today, two coves in Wyoming where the companies held up and waited for a break in the weather are museums open to the public in remembrance of the greatest disaster of voluntary western migration in U.S. history. Though later handcart companies learned and avoided the risks that bore down so harshly on the Willie and Martin Companies, the long walks of handcarters were not ended until the railroad's advantage eclipsed them in the spring of 1869.

mileage added. Nobel laureate Simon Kuznets and Arthur Burns each revealed this typical feature of rapid industry expansion followed by a tapering off in the growth rate (and speed of productivity advance) in pioneering work done a half century ago.[3] All great innovations and industry growth patterns show these features, as we observed earlier in tobacco production, in cotton, and in steamboating, to name a few. It is interesting to note, however, that the total absolute mileage doubled in the 25 years preceding 1910. Work by Albert Fishlow reveals three major waves in the late nineteenth-century pattern of main track construction: 1868–1873, 1879–1883, and 1886–1892.[4] These construction booms ended promptly with each of the major financial crises of the period: 1873, 1882, and 1893. As J. R.T. Hughes has argued, this is not terribly surprising when we recall that railroad construction depended heavily on borrowed money.[5] Railroad construction had a strong influence on aggregate demand and business cycles. It accounted for 20 percent of U.S. gross capital formation in

[3]Simon Kuznets, "The Retardation of Industrial Growth," *Journal of Economic and Business History* (August 1929), and Arthur F. Burns, chapter 4, "Retardation in the Growth Industries" in *Production Trends in the United States Since 1870* (New York: National Bureau of Economic Research, 1934).
[4]Albert Fishlow, "Internal Transportation," in *Economic Growth: An Economist's History of the United States*, ed. Lance E. Davis et al. (New York: Harper & Row, 1972), 500.
[5]See his elegant and sophisticated book, *Industrialization and Economic History: Theses and Conjectures* (New York: McGraw-Hill, 1970), 120.

TABLE 16.1 Main Line Railroad Track in Operation (in thousands of miles)

YEAR	MILES	PERCENTAGE CHANGES (in five-year intervals)
1860	31	
1865	35	13
1870	53	63
1875	74	42
1880	93	26
1885	128	38
1890	167	30
1895	180	8
1900	207	15
1905	238	15
1910	266	12

Source: Derived from Historical Statistics *(Washington, D.C.: Government Printing Office, 1960), Series Q15, 49-50.*

TABLE 16.2 Productivity in the Railroad Sector, 1870–1910 (1910 = 100)

YEAR	OUTPUT	LABOR	CAPITAL	FUEL	TOTAL INPUT	TOTAL FACTOR PRODUCTIVITY
1870	7	14	17	5	14	47
1880	14	25	32	12	26	54
1890	33	44	62	29	49	67
1900	55	60	72	46	63	87
1910	100	100	100	100	100	100

To link these measures to similar ones before the Civil War, see Table 9.4 in chapter 9.

Source: Adapted from Albert Fishlow, "Internal Transportation," in Economic Growth: An Economist's History of the United States, *ed. Lance E. Davis et al. (New York: Harper & Row, 1972), 508.*

the 1870s, 15 percent of the total in the 1880s, and 7.5 percent of the total in each of the remaining decades until 1920. These investments reinforced and responded to swings in the business cycle. In 1920, railroad employment reached its peak, about 1 worker in 20.

Productivity Advance and Slowdown

The rapid but slowing pace of growth in construction is also seen in the gains in railroad productivity. As shown in Table 16.2, total factor productivity of the railroad somewhat more than doubled in the 40 years between 1870 and 1910. As in other maturing sectors and industries, the railroad experienced a continued but slowing advance. As observed in chapter 9, the pace of total factor productivity advance was so rapid between 1840 and 1860 that it doubled in this early 20-year period.

The sustained rapid growth of output relative to inputs was due primarily to two sources of productivity advance. First, as shown by Fishlow, were additional gains from economies of scale in operation, accounting for nearly half of the productivity advance of the railroads at that time. The other half resulted from four innovations. In order of importance, these were (1) more powerful locomotives and more efficient freight cars, which tripled capacity; (2) stronger steel rails, permitting heavier loads; (3) automatic couplers; and (4) air brakes—these latter two facilitating greater speed and safety.[6]

[6]See Albert Fishlow, *American Railroads and the Transformation of the Ante-bellum Economy* (Cambridge, Mass.: Harvard University Press, 1965), 509–510, and Fishlow's "Internal Transportation" for a more detailed analysis of these sources of productivity advance.

Despite the expected slowing of the railroad's productivity advance, it continued throughout the period up to World War I. It averaged 2 percent annually and exceeded the pace of productivity advance for the economy as a whole, which was approximately 1.5 per unit per annum. The railroads were not, in themselves, the cause of America's rapid economic progress in the nineteenth century, but for several generations of Americans, they symbolized the ceaseless wave of entrepreneurial energy and technological advance that was the cause of progress.

RAILROAD BUILDING AND RAILROAD DEMAND

Joseph Schumpeter, one of the leading economists of the early twentieth century, argued that many midwestern railroad projects "meant building ahead of demand in the boldest sense of the phrase" and that "Middle Western and Western projects could not be expected to pay for themselves within a period such as most investors care to envisage."[7] The implication of Schumpeter's argument was that government aid to the railroads was necessary in order to open the West.

To test Schumpeter's assertion, Albert Fishlow analyzed profit rates on railroad investments in the antebellum period. He specified and tested the Schumpeter thesis rigorously, drawing the praise of fellow economists.[8] Fishlow reasoned that if railroads were built in unsettled regions, the demand for the railroad's services must have been low initially, with prices below average costs. As settlement occurred, the demand curve would shift upward so that average revenues would eventually exceed average costs. This provided him with three tests: (1) government aid should be widespread; (2) profit rates initially should be less than profit rates in alternative investments and should grow as the railroad aged; and (3) the number of people living near the railroad should initially be low compared with the number living near eastern railroads.

On all three tests, Fishlow's findings failed to support Schumpeter's assertion that the railroads were built ahead of demand. Government aid to the railroads was often minimal, directed more at getting a railroad that was already under construction to go through one particular town rather than another. Profit rates often started out relatively high and then fell over time. And the number of people living near the railroads when they began operations was typically similar to the number living near railroads in eastern rural areas.

What could explain such a paradoxical result? After all, it seems self-evident that farmers wouldn't move into an area before the railroads and that railroads couldn't be built until the farmers were in place. How could the market coordinate economic development in the Midwest? Fishlow discovered what he called "anticipatory settlement." Farmers and businessmen were well informed about the new territories being opened up by the railroads. They moved into a region, cleared the land, planted crops, and opened up ancillary businesses while a railroad was being constructed. By the time it was completed, crops were waiting to go to market. Fishlow concluded, however, that "a similar set of criteria casually applied to post–Civil War railroad construction in states farther West suggest that this constituted a true episode of building before demand."[9]

The work to determine whether or not Fishlow's tentative answer was right about the post–Civil War's transcontinentals was done by Robert Fogel and Lloyd Mercer. Using Fishlow's criteria, they showed that indeed, the railroads were built ahead of demand; they had relatively low initial profit rates, and their profit rates grew over time. Finally, Fogel and Mercer tested for another interpretation of the notion of the railroads being built ahead of demand. Did the transcontinentals eventually earn high enough profit rates on operations

---

[7]Quoted in Fishlow, *American Railroads and the Transformation of the Ante-bellum Economy*, 165, 167.
[8]See Robert W. Fogel, "The Specification Problem in Economic History," *Journal of Economic History* 27 (1967): 296; and Meghnad Desai, "Some Issues in Econometric History," *Economic History Review* 21, 2d series (1968): 12.
[9]Fishlow, *American Railroads and the Transformation of the Ante-bellum Economy*, 204.

to justify private investment without government subsidy? Alternatively stated, was their average rate of return (excluding revenues from land sales) over several decades above or below average rates of return on alternative investments? Mercer's findings showed mixed results. The Central Pacific and the Union Pacific (which formed the first transcontinentals) and the Great Northern (the last) had private rates of return above rates on alternative investments in the long run. Had private investors anticipated this result, they would have been willing to finance the railroads without government assistance. Three others—the Texas and Pacific, the Santa Fe, and the Northern Pacific—did not. These findings show that the postbellum transcontinentals were all built ahead of demand, in the sense that initial profits were low. However, the necessity of government subsidies for the three high profit railroads could be questioned, since in the long run these railroads made enough extra profits to compensate investors for their low early returns.[10]

LAND GRANTS, FINANCIAL ASSISTANCE, AND PRIVATE CAPITAL

It is noteworthy that before the Pacific Railway Act of 1862, America's largest manufacturing plants rarely had more than $500,000 invested in capital or as many as 1,000 employees. In contrast, five railroads at that time each had more than $20 million invested and tens of thousands of employees. Building the transcontinentals was a huge undertaking, and the indivisibility of the fixed plant needed for operation added to the problems of attracting capital.

As we observed with canals and antebellum railroads, subsidies were common for major transportation projects. States and municipalities, competing with one another for lines they thought would bring everlasting prosperity, continued to help the railroads, though on a smaller scale than in the early days. They purchased or guaranteed railroad bonds, granted tax exemptions, and provided terminal facilities. Several states subscribed to the capital stock of the railroads, hoping to participate in the profits. Michigan built three roads, and North Carolina controlled the majority of the directors of three roads. North Carolina, Massachusetts, and Missouri took over failing railroads that had been liberally aided by state funds. Outright contributions from state and local units may have reached $250 million—a small sum compared with a value of track and equipment of $10 billion in 1880, when assistance from local governments had almost ceased.

In contrast to the antebellum period, subsequent financial aid from the federal government exceeded the aid from states and municipalities, although by how much we cannot be sure. Perhaps $175 million in government bonds was loaned to the Union Pacific, the Central Pacific, and four other transcontinentals, but after litigation, most of this amount was repaid. Rights-of-way, normally 200 feet wide, together with sites for depots and terminal facilities in the public domain and free timber and stone from government lands, constituted other forms of assistance. But the most significant kind of federal subsidy was the grant of lands from the public domain.

In this form, Congress gave a portion of the unsettled lands in the public domain to the railroads in lieu of money or credit. Following the precedent set by grants to the Mobile and Ohio and to the Ohio and Illinois Central in 1850, alternate sections of land on either side of the road, varying in size from 6 to 40 miles, were given outright for each mile of railroad that was constructed. The alternate-section provision was made in the expectation that the government would share in the increased land values that were expected to result from the new transportation facilities. Land-grant subsidies to railroads were discontinued after 1871 because of public opposition, but not before 79 grants amounting to 200 million

[10]Lloyd Mercer, "Building Ahead of Demand: Some Evidence for the Land Grant Railroads," *Journal of Economic History* 34 (1974): 492-500. Also see Robert Fogel, who anticipated the issue, *The Union Pacific Railroad: A Case of Premature Enterprise* (Baltimore: Johns Hopkins Press, 1968).

acres, reduced by forfeitures to just over 131 million acres, had been given.[11] This amounted to about 9 percent of the U.S. public domain accumulated between 1789 and 1904 and was slightly less than the amounts granted to the states.

Note, however, that aid to the railroads was not given unconditionally. Congress required that companies that received grants transport mail, troops, and government property at reduced rates. (In 1940, Congress relieved the railroads of land-grant rates for all except military traffic; in 1945, military traffic was removed from the reduced-rate category.) While land-grant rates were in effect, the government obtained estimated reductions of more than $500 million—a sum several times the value of the land grants when they were made and about equal to what the railroads received in land grants with an allowance for the long-run increase in the value of the land. The land grants, moreover, were in some ways a better incentive than alternative subsidies. A railroad could best realize the value of a land grant by quickly building a good track. In contrast, cash subsidies based on miles of track completed or similar criteria encouraged shoddy construction (Economic Reasoning Proposition 3). Subsidies added to the profits and, thus, to the incentives of railroad builders until the early 1870s, but the great bulk of both new and replacement capital came from private sources. The benefits of railroad transportation to farmers, small industrialists, and the general public along a proposed route were described in glowing terms by its promoters. Local investors responded enthusiastically and sometimes recklessly, their outlay of funds prompted in part by the realization that the growth of their communities and an increase in their personal wealth depended on the new transportation facility. Except in the industrial and urban Northeast, however, local sources could not provide sufficient capital, so promoters had to tap the wealth of eastern cities and Europe.

Thus, as the first examples of truly large corporations, railroad companies led the way in developing fundraising techniques by selling securities to middle-class investors. Even before 1860, railroads had introduced a wide range of bonds secured by various classes of assets.[12] After the Civil War, these securities proliferated as railroads appealed to people who had been introduced to investing through purchases of government debt during the war. Although conservative investors avoided the common stock of the railroads, the proliferation of such issues added tremendously to the volume of shares listed and traded on the floor of the New York Stock Exchange.

The modern investment banking house appeared as an intermediary between seekers of railroad capital in the South and the West and eastern and European investors, who could not easily estimate the worth of the securities offered them. From the 1850s on, the investment banker played a crucial role in American finance, allocating capital that originated in wealthy areas among those seeking it. J. Pierpont Morgan, a junior partner in the small Wall Street firm of Dabney and Morgan, joined forces in 1859 with the Drexels of Philadelphia to form Drexel, Morgan and Company. Along with Winslow, Lanier and Company and August Belmont and Company, Morgan's house grew rich and powerful by selling railroad securities, particularly in foreign markets. European interests eventually owned a majority of the stock in several railroads; English, Dutch, and German stockholders constituted important minority groups in the others. In 1876, European holdings amounted to 86 percent of the common stock of the Illinois Central, and at one time, two directorships of the Chicago and Northwestern were occupied by Dutch nationals. By 1914, Europeans, mostly English, owned one-fifth of all outstanding American railroad securities.

---

[11]Five great systems received about 75 percent of the land-grant acreage. These were the Union Pacific (including the Denver Pacific and Kansas Pacific); the Atchison, Topeka, and Santa Fe; the Northern Pacific; the Texas and Pacific; and the Central Pacific system (including the Southern Pacific Railroad).
[12]For a detailed treatment of financial innovation by railroad promoters, see Alfred D. Chandler Jr., *The Railroads—The Nation's First Big Business* (New York: Harcourt Brace Jovanovich, 1965), 43–94.

UNSCRUPULOUS FINANCIAL PRACTICES

Railroad promoters sometimes indulged in questionable, even fraudulent, practices. Typically, these schemes involved the construction companies that built the railroads and worked like this.

The railroad contracted with a construction company to build a certain number of miles of road at a specific amount per mile. The railroad then met the costs by paying cash (acquired by selling bonds to the public) and issuing common stock to the construction company. In addition, government subsidies (land grants, state and local bonds, etc.) were passed on to the construction company. Under one complicated but widely used system, common stock was transferred to permit its sale below par value, which was prohibited by law in some states. As long as the railroad corporation originally issued the securities at par, they could be sold at a discount by a second party, the construction company, without violating the law. The contract price was set high enough to permit the construction company, when selling the stock, to offer bargains to the investing public and still earn a profit.[13] This method of financing, although cumbersome, provided funds that might not have been obtained otherwise, given the restrictions on the railroads' issue of common stock.

So far so good, but the system was easily abused. The owners of the construction company were often "insiders"—that is, officers and directors of the railroad corporation. The higher the price charged by the construction company, the lower the dividends paid to shareholders in the railroad (and the greater the risk of bankruptcy), but the greater would be the profits that the insiders made on their investment in the construction company.

Although not all railroad construction was financed through inside construction companies, this device was common—especially during the 1860s and 1870s—and all the transcontinentals used it. It was not unusual for the proceeds of security issues, plus the value of the subsidies, to exceed twice the actual cost of constructing a railroad. The most notorious inside company was the Crédit Mobilier of America, chartered under Pennsylvania statutes, which built the Union Pacific. During President Grant's second term, this company's operations caused a national scandal. Certain members of Congress bought (at favorable prices) or were given shares. It was a clear conflict of interest. By voting for grants of land and cash for the railroad, they were enriching themselves. Two Congressmen were censured, and the careers of others (including outgoing Vice President Schuyler Colfax) were tarnished. Representative James A. Garfield was also implicated, but he denied all wrongdoing and was subsequently elected president. Huge profits accrued to the Crédit Mobilier. A congressional committee reported in 1873 that over $23 million in cash profits had been realized by the company on a $10 million investment—and this cash take was over and above a $50 million profit in securities. By inflating the cost of construction, the insider construction companies saddled the railroads with large debt burdens that came back to haunt them, especially in the depressed 1890s.

RATE SETTING AND REGULATION IN RAILROAD MARKETS

Before 1870, each railroad usually had some degree of monopoly power within its operating area. However, as the railway network grew, adding more than 40,000 miles in the 1870s and 70,000 miles in the 1880s, the trunk lines of the East and even the transcontinentals of the West began to suffer the sting of competition. To be sure, major companies often faced no competition at all in local traffic and therefore had great flexibility in setting prices for relatively short

[13]Rank-and-file investors quickly became accustomed to receiving $2,500 or more (at par value) in stocks and bonds for every $1,000 they paid out in cash. (To convert to 2000 prices, multiply by 20.6.) For 50 years or more after 1860, it was next to impossible to convince individuals to buy common stock in a new venture without sweetening the deal with a bond or two.

Public land granted to the railroads as a subsidy and in turn sold to settlers was a continuing source of capital funds. Ads like this one appeared in city newspapers, luring thousands of Americans and immigrants westward. Note that each region of the state is carefully described so that farmers can buy land suitable for crops with which they have some experience.

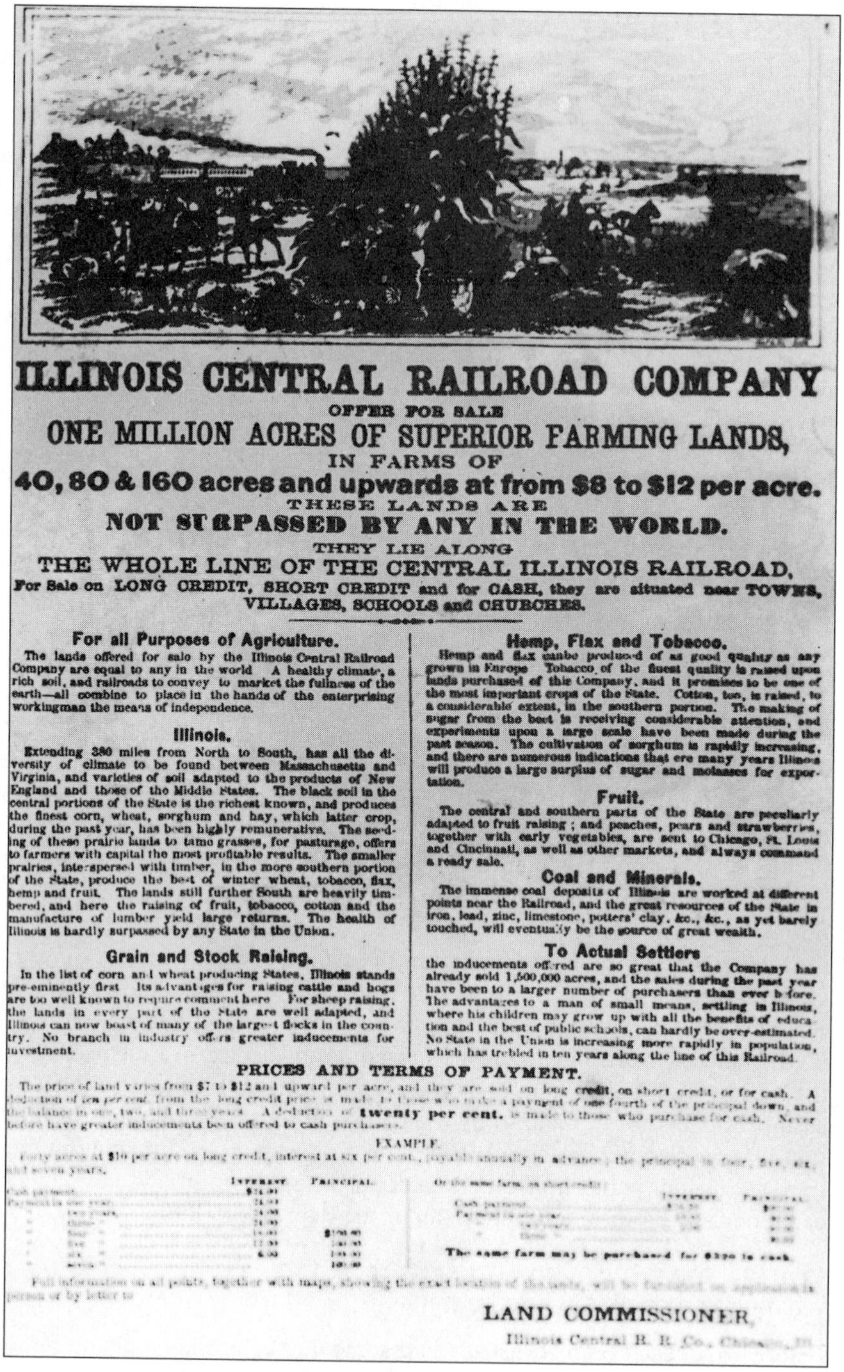

ILLINOIS CENTRAL RAILROAD COMPANY

OFFER FOR SALE

ONE MILLION ACRES OF SUPERIOR FARMING LANDS,

IN FARMS OF

40, 80 & 160 acres and upwards at from $8 to $12 per acre.

THESE LANDS ARE

NOT SURPASSED BY ANY IN THE WORLD.

THEY LIE ALONG

THE WHOLE LINE OF THE CENTRAL ILLINOIS RAILROAD,

For Sale on LONG CREDIT, SHORT CREDIT and for CASH, they are situated near TOWNS, VILLAGES, SCHOOLS and CHURCHES.

For all Purposes of Agriculture.

The lands offered for sale by the Illinois Central Railroad Company are equal to any in the world. A healthy climate, a rich soil, and railroads to convey to market the fullness of the earth—all combine to place in the hands of the enterprising workingman the means of independence.

Illinois.

Extending 380 miles from North to South, has all the diversity of climate to be found between Massachusetts and Virginia, and varieties of soil adapted to the products of New England and those of the Middle States. The black soil in the central portions of the State is the richest known, and produces the finest corn, wheat, sorghum and hay, which latter crop, during the past year, has been highly remunerative. The seeding of these prairie lands to tame grasses, for pasturage, offers to farmers with capital the most profitable results. The smaller prairies, interspersed with timber, in the more southern portion of the State, produce the best of winter wheat, tobacco, flax, hemp and fruit. The lands still further South are heavily timbered, and here the raising of fruit, tobacco, cotton and the manufacture of lumber yield large returns. The health of Illinois is hardly surpassed by any State in the Union.

Grain and Stock Raising.

In the list of corn and wheat producing States, Illinois stands pre-eminently first. Its advantages for raising cattle and hogs are too well known to require comment here. For sheep raising, the lands in every part of the State are well adapted, and Illinois can now boast of many of the largest flocks in the country. No branch in industry offers greater inducements for investment.

Hemp, Flax and Tobacco.

Hemp and flax canbe produced of as good quality as any grown in Europe. Tobacco of the finest quality is raised upon lands purchased of this Company, and it promises to be one of the most important crops of the State. Cotton, too, is raised, to a considerable extent, in the southern portion. The making of sugar from the beet is receiving considerable attention, and experiments upon a large scale have been made during the past season. The cultivation of sorghum is rapidly increasing, and there are numerous indications that ere many years Illinois will produce a large surplus of sugar and molasses for exportation.

Fruit.

The central and southern parts of the State are peculiarly adapted to fruit raising; and peaches, pears and strawberries, together with early vegetables, are sent to Chicago, St. Louis and Cincinnati, as well as other markets, and always command a ready sale.

Coal and Minerals.

The immense coal deposits of Illinois are worked at different points near the Railroad, and the great resources of the State in iron, lead, zinc, limestone, potters' clay, &c., &c., as yet barely touched, will eventually be the source of great wealth.

To Actual Settlers

the inducements offered are so great that the Company has already sold 1,500,000 acres, and the sales during the past year have been to a larger number of purchasers than ever before. The advantages to a man of small means, settling in Illinois, where his children may grow up with all the benefits of education and the best of public schools, can hardly be over-estimated. No State in the Union is increasing more rapidly in population, which has trebled in ten years along the line of this Railroad.

PRICES AND TERMS OF PAYMENT.

The price of land varies from $7 to $12 and upward per acre, and they are sold on long **credit**, on short credit, or for cash. A deduction of *ten per cent.* from the long credit price is made to those who make a payment of one fourth of the principal down, and the balance in one, two, and three years. A deduction of **twenty per cent.** is made to those who purchase for cash. Never before have greater inducements been offered to cash purchasers.

EXAMPLE.

Forty acres at $10 per acre on long credit, interest at six per cent., payable annually in advance; the principal in four, five, six, and seven years.

	INTEREST.	PRINCIPAL.
Cash payment	$24.00	
Payment in one year	24.00	
" two years	24.00	
" three "	24.00	
" four "	[illegible]	$100.00
" five "	12.00	[illegible]
" six "	6.00	[illegible]
" seven "		100.00

Or the same farm, on short credit:

	INTEREST.	PRINCIPAL.
Cash payment	[illegible]	[illegible]
Payment in one year	[illegible]	[illegible]
" two years	[illegible]	[illegible]
" three "		[illegible]

The same farm may be purchased for $320 in cash.

Full information on all points, together with maps, showing the exact location of the lands, will be furnished on application in person or by letter to

LAND COMMISSIONER,

Illinois Central R. R. Co., Chicago, Ill.

COURTESY ILLINOIS CENTRAL RAILROAD ARCHIVES, THE NEWBERRY LIBRARY, CHICAGO

hauls, but for long hauls between major cities there were usually two or more competing carriers. The consequence was a variance in the rates per mile charged between short and long hauls. Increasingly, these practices of price discrimination brought cries of outrage.

Railroad managers were in charge of firms with high fixed costs, so they tried to set rates in ways that would ensure the fullest possible use of plant and equipment. Where it was possible to separate markets, managers set rates in a discriminating way; recall Economic Reasoning Proposition 2. For example, rates per ton were set much lower on bulk freight such as coal and ore than on manufactured goods. If traffic was predominantly in one direction, shipments on the return route could be made at much lower rates because receiving any revenue was better than receiving nothing for hauling empty cars. For shippers, this common problem is called the "backhaul problem," yet lower charges per hundred pounds for hauling cars completely full rather than smaller piecemeal shipments were justified on the ground that it cost no more to move a loaded car than one that was half full.

Another form of rate discrimination arose when the same railroad was in a monopolistic position with respect to certain customers (a producer of farm machinery in the Midwest, for example) and a competitive position with respect to others (a favorably located producer of coal who could turn to water transport). Shippers not favored by these discriminatory rates or by outright rebates were naturally indignant at the special treatment accorded their competitors. Railroads also discriminated among cities and towns, a practice especially resented by farmers and merchants of one locality who watched those in another area enjoy lower rates for the same service.

There is a possible economic justification for these practices: By discriminating among customers, the railroad may have been able to increase its total output and lower its costs. The low-cost service provided some users, in other words, could have depended on the revenues generated by the high prices charged to others. Indeed, if forced to charge one price to all, the railroad may not have been able to cover its costs and remain in business. But the person paying the higher price generally doesn't see things that way, and the pressure to regulate such practices grew rapidly. Refer to Economic Reasoning Proposition 4.

Opposition to the railroads was heightened by the trend toward price fixing. By 1873, the railroad industry was plagued by tremendous excess capacity. One line could obtain business by cutting rates on through traffic, but only at the expense of another company, which then found its own capacity in excess. Rate wars during the depressed years of the 1870s led to efforts to stop "ruinous competition" (as railroad owners and managers saw it). Railroads responded by banding together on through-traffic rates. They allocated shares of the business among the competing lines, working out alliances between competing and connecting railroads within a region. More often than not, though, these turned out to be fragile agreements that broke under the pressure of high fixed costs and excess capacity. To hide the rate cutting, shippers might pay the published tariff and receive a secret rebate from the railroad. Sooner or later, word of the rebating would leak out, with a consequent return to open rate warfare.

To provide a stronger basis for maintaining prices, Albert Fink took the lead in forming regional federations to pool either traffic or profits. The first was the Southern Railway and Steamship Association, which was formed in 1875 with Fink as its commissioner. Then, in 1879, the trunk lines formed the Eastern Trunk Line Association. But the federations eventually came unglued as weak railroads or companies run by aggressive managers or owners such as Jay Gould broke with the pool and began price cutting.[14] Shippers and the general public naturally resented pooling as well as price discrimination. The result was widespread support for government regulation of the railroads.

State Regulation

★★★ Economic Reasoning Proposition

The first wave of railroad regulations came in the early 1870s, largely in response to increasing evidence of discrimination against persons and places (Economic Reasoning Propositions 2 and 3). As the decade progressed, agrarian tempers rose as farm incomes declined. As emphasized in Chapter 15, farmers in the Midwest blamed a large measure of their distress on the railroads. Many farmers had invested savings in railroad ventures on the basis

---

[14]Chandler, *The Railroads—The Nation's First Big Business*, 161. Also see Chandler's *The Visible Hand: The Managerial Revolution in American Business* (Cambridge, Mass.: Belknap Press of Harvard University Press, 1977), especially chapter 4.

of extravagant promises of the prosperity sure to result from improved transportation. When the opposite effect became apparent, farmers clamored for legislation to regulate rates. Prominent in the movement were members of the National Grange of the Patrons of Husbandry, an agrarian society founded in 1867. Thus, the demand for state passage of measures regulating railroads, grain elevators, and public warehouses became known as the *Granger movement*, the legislation as the *Granger laws*, and the review of the laws by the Supreme Court as the Granger cases.

Between 1871 and 1874, Illinois, Iowa, Wisconsin, and Minnesota passed regulatory laws. Fixing schedules of maximum rates by commission rather than by statute was a feature of both the Illinois and Minnesota laws. One of the common practices that western farmers could not tolerate was charging more for the carriage of goods over a short distance than over a longer distance in the same direction and by the same line. The pro rata clause contained in the Granger laws, which prohibited railroads from charging short shippers more than their fair share of the costs, was intended to rectify this alleged injustice and was the forerunner of the current long- and short-haul clause of the Interstate Commerce Act. Both personal and place discrimination were generally outlawed, although product discrimination was not. Finally, commissions were given the power to investigate complaints and to institute suits against violators.

Almost as soon as the Granger laws were in the statute books, attempts were made to have them declared unconstitutional on the ground, among others, that they were repugnant to the Fifth Amendment to the Constitution, which prohibits the taking of private property without just compensation. It was argued, for example, that limitations on the prices charged by the grain elevators restricted their earnings and deprived their properties of value. Six suits were brought to test the laws. The principal one was *Munn v. Illinois*, an action involving grain elevators. This case was taken to the U.S. Supreme Court in 1877 after state courts in Illinois found that Munn and his partner Scott had violated the state warehouse law by not obtaining a license to operate grain elevators in the city of Chicago and by charging prices in excess of those set by state law. From a purely economic point of view, the argument made by the grain elevator operators makes some sense. The loss of wealth may be the same whether the government takes a piece of land to build a road (the classic case requiring compensation) or imposes a maximum price.

But the Supreme Court saw the case (and five similar railroad cases before it) in a different light: it upheld the right of a state to regulate these businesses. Chief Justice Morrison Remick Waite stated in the majority opinion that when businesses are "clothed with a public interest," their regulation as public utilities is constitutional.[15] The *Munn* case settled the constitutionality of the state regulation of railroads and certain other enterprises within the states—but not between states.

In 1886, a decision in the case of *Wabash, St. Louis and Pacific Railway Company v. Illinois* made a critical delineation of the sphere of state control as distinguished from that of federal control. The state had found that the Wabash was charging more for a shorter haul from Gilman, Illinois, to New York City than for a longer haul from Peoria to New York City and had ordered the rate adjusted. The U.S. Supreme Court held that Illinois could not regulate rates on shipments in interstate commerce because the Constitution specifically gave the power to regulate interstate commerce to the federal government. This view was an extension of the opinion of the Court in the Granger cases, in which one contention of the railroads had been that the Granger laws interfered with interstate commerce and, therefore,

[15]Associate Justice Stephen Johnson Field, in the dissenting opinion, objected to the vague language of the majority; he went on to say that the public is interested in many businesses and that to extend the reasoning of the majority might bring "calico gowns" and "city mansions" within the scope of such regulation. As it turned out, Justice Field was simply ahead of his time.

with the powers of the U.S. government. In the absence of federal legislation, the *Wabash* case left a vast area with no control over carrier operation; regulation would have to come at the national level or not at all.

Federal Regulations[16]

Early in 1887, Congress passed and President Grover Cleveland signed the Act to Regulate Commerce. Its chief purpose was to bring all railroads engaged in interstate commerce under federal regulation. The Interstate Commerce Commission (ICC), consisting of five members to be appointed by the president with the advice and consent of the Senate, was created, and its duties were set forth. First, the commission was required to examine the business of the railroads; to this end, it could subpoena witnesses and ask them to produce books, contracts, and other documents. Second, the commission was charged with hearing complaints that arose from possible violations of the act and was empowered to issue "cease and desist" orders if unlawful practices were discovered. The third duty of the commission was to require railroads to submit annual reports based on a uniform system of accounts. Finally, the commission was required to submit to Congress annual reports of its own operations.

The Act to Regulate Commerce seemingly prohibited all possible unethical practices. Section 1 stated that railroad rates must be "just and reasonable." Section 2 prohibited personal discrimination; a lower charge could no longer be made in the form of a "special rate, rebate, drawback, or other device." Section 3 provided that no undue preference of any kind should be accorded by any railroad to any shipper, any place, or any special kind of traffic. Section 4 enacted, in less drastic form, the pro rata clauses of the Granger legislation by prohibiting greater charges "for the transportation of passengers or of like kind of property, under substantially similar circumstances and conditions, for a shorter than for a longer distance, over the same line, in the same direction, the shorter being included in the longer distance." Pooling was also prohibited.

The ICC was the first permanent independent federal regulatory agency. Its formation represented the beginning of direct government intervention in the economy on an expanding scale. The first decade and a half of the ICC, however, was filled with court challenges by the railroads. To clarify certain powers delegated by Congress, both the ICC and the railroads sought new legislation, especially regarding issues of price discrimination.

The Elkins Act

The Elkins Act of 1903 dealt solely with the practice of personal discrimination. The act made any departure from a published rate a misdemeanor and authorized the courts to enjoin railroads from (1) continuing to depart from published rates and (2) making unlawful discriminations. Convincing evidence suggests that the Elkins Act represented the wishes of a large majority of the railroad companies because it protected them from demands for rebates by powerful shippers and brought the government to their aid in enforcing the cartel prices set by the trunk line associates. The act stated that railroad corporations should be liable for any unlawful violation of the discrimination provisions. Up to this time, only officials and employees of a company had been liable for discriminatory actions; henceforth, the corporation itself would also be responsible. A second provision made the receiver of rebates guilty of violating the law, even when the rebate had been offered voluntarily by the carrier. But the most important provision of the act dealt with the practice of departing from published rates. Until this time, the courts had overruled the commission in the enforcement of published rates by requiring that discrimination against or injury to other shippers of similar goods had to be proved.

---

[16]For an excellent survey of the issues of regulation, see Thomas K. McCraw, "Regulation in America: A Review Article," *Business History Review* 49 (1975): 159–183.

The Hepburn Act

To close remaining loopholes, especially regarding other discriminatory pricing practices, Congress passed the Hepburn Act of 1906. This act extended the jurisdiction of the ICC to private-car companies that operated joint express, tank, and sleeping cars. Such services as storage, refrigeration, and ventilation, if furnished by the railroads in connection with transportation, were also made subject to the control of the commission. The extension of ICC jurisdiction over these phases of railroad transportation was inevitable because the management of the railroads could use such services to discriminate among shippers. For example, railroads normally charged for storage or refrigeration; if any shippers were not charged for these services, discrimination resulted. Perhaps even more important than this extension of authority was the change in the procedures for enforcement of the ICC's orders. Until 1906, the ICC had to prove before the court the case it had adjudicated. The Hepburn Act put the burden of proof on the carriers. Disobedience of commission orders carried a penalty of $5,000, and each day of violation constituted a separate offense. The right of judicial review was recognized, but the railroads—not the commission—had to appeal, and the presumption was for—not against—the commission.

Capturing the Regulators

Initially, the ICC clearly endeavored to protect consumers from abuses, and, also initially, the railroad industry was clearly not pleased with the ICC. In 1892, Charles E. Perkins, president of the Chicago, Burlington and Quincy Railroad, wrote a letter to his lawyer Richard Olney (who later became attorney general of the United States) recommending that the embryonic five-year-old commission be abolished. Olney's shrewd reply is worth quoting:

> My impression would be that looking at the matter from the railroad point of view it would not be a wise thing to undertake. . . . The attempt would not be likely to succeed; if it did not succeed, and were made on the grounds of the inefficiency and uselessness of the Commission, the result would very probably be giving it the power it now lacks. The Commission, as its functions have been limited by the courts, is, or can be made of great use to the railroads. It satisfies the public clamor for a government supervision of railroads, at the same time that the supervision is almost entirely nominal. Further, the older such a commission gets to be, the more inclined it will be found to take the business and railroad view of things. It thus becomes a sort of protection against hasty and crude legislation hostile to railroad interests. . . . The part of wisdom is not to destroy the Commission, but to utilize it.[17]

Economic Reasoning Proposition

To what extent did Olney's analysis (Economic Reasoning Proposition 5) prove to be an accurate prediction? Did the railroads capture the ICC and use it for their own ends? In 1965, the noted historian Gabriel Kolko suggested that railroad managers did use the ICC as a way of stabilizing profit rates and securing other advantages of cartel management.[18]

Although railroad managers openly supported the Elkins Act to ensure through regulation similar pricing among competing carriers, the scholarship of Albro Martin, which we find convincing, shows that the work of the ICC was largely for the benefit of users—shippers and passengers.[19] When the long period of falling prices reversed itself in 1896, the

---

[17] Robert C. Fellmeth, *The Interstate Commerce Commission* (New York: Grossman, 1970), xiv–xv.

[18] Gabriel Kolko, *Railroads and Regulation, 1877–1916* (Princeton, N.J.: Princeton University Press, 1965). For one of the first critiques of the Kolko thesis, see Robert Harberson, "Railroads and Regulation, 1877–1916: Conspiracy or Public Interest?" *Journal of Economic History* 27 (1967): 230–242.

[19] Albro Martin, *Enterprise Denied: Origins of the Decline of American Railroads, 1897–1917* (New York: Columbia University Press, 1971).

ICC disallowed rate increases sufficient to match rises in the general price level. Railroads reacted by slowing their repair and replacement of capital stock and equipment. This helped to some extent to slow the rising costs of railroad operations. By the outbreak of World War I, the railroads were physically decayed and financially strapped. If there was a management capture of the regulatory process, it is difficult to find in the events preceding the 1920s. Indeed, in 1917, the federal government scored the critical capture by nationalizing the railroads in the interests of the war effort. After the war, the railroads were returned to private ownership. As we shall see in later chapters, the "capture thesis" applies to other situations, but managers did not initially capture and control the regulation process in the case of early ICC activities. One reason the railroads failed to capture the ICC may be that many large shippers had nearly as much incentive to monitor the ICC and as much clout in Washington as the railroads had. The capture thesis is most likely to apply when the costs of a decision favoring the regulated industry are widely diffused.

RAILROADS AND ECONOMIC GROWTH

Joseph Schumpeter, whose argument that the railroads were built ahead of demand was noted earlier in this chapter, also believed that railroads had led the transition to modern economic growth.[20] Schumpeter argued that growth was a dynamic process of applying major technological advances, both invention and innovation, and that the railroad epitomized these growth-generating forces. Walt Rostow later added to this view by arguing that the railroad was a leading sector in the nation's takeoff to modern economic growth.[21]

Within a year of each other in the mid-1960s, Albert Fishlow and Robert Fogel produced books that generated an avalanche of debate.[22] Their objective was to pin down with actual numbers the contributions of the railroad to nineteenth-century U.S. economic growth. Although their classic works differed in style and approach, their goals were essentially the same: to measure the social savings of the railroad (amount of additional real GNP that could be attributed to the railroad) in 1859 (Fishlow) and in 1890 (Fogel). See Economic Insight 16.1 on page 322 concerning social savings from rail transport. Fogel's work particularly drew fire, perhaps because of his charged rhetoric and his willingness to explore what might have been.[23]

Fogel began his study by reviewing the evolution of the "axiom of indispensability," a term that became widely accepted in describing the role of the railroad. It was primarily in the late nineteenth-century battles over government control that "the indispensability of railroads to American economic growth was elevated to the status of an axiomatic truth."[24] Until Fishlow's and Fogel's books were published, the most widely used texts in American economic history courses portrayed the railroads as having "the power of life and death over the economy" or as "essential to the development of Capitalism in America."[25] Because of the efforts of Fishlow and Fogel and other scholars, those views are gone.

Fishlow measured the cost of moving all freight and passengers carried by rail in 1859 by the next best alternative to railroads. In other words, the cost of carrying freight or passengers in 1859 was estimated as if the railroads had suddenly vanished and shippers had to rely on water or wagon. The higher costs of carrying railroad passengers and freight by these

[20]Joseph Schumpeter, *The Theory of Economic Development* (Cambridge, Mass.: Harvard University Press, 1949).
[21]W.W. Rostow, *The Stages of Economic Growth: A Non-Communist Manifesto* (Cambridge, England: Cambridge University Press, 1960).
[22]Fishlow, *American Railroads and the Transformation of the Ante-bellum Economy*; and Robert W. Fogel, *Railroads and American Economic Growth* (Baltimore: Johns Hopkins University Press, 1964).
[23]See Donald McCloskey, *The Rhetoric of Economics* (Madison: University of Wisconsin Press, 1985), chapter 6.
[24]Fogel, *Railroads and American Economic Growth*, 7.
[25]See ibid., 9, for various examples.

Economic Insight 16.1

Social Savings from Rail Transport

The figure below illustrates the measurement of social savings. The quantity of transport (measured, say, in a standardized ton-mile) is measured on the horizontal axis; the price charged is measured on the vertical axis. *D* is the demand curve. P_W is the price of transport via water, and P_R is the price of transport via the railroad. Q_R is the amount of transport actually supplied with railroads predominant. Q_W is the amount of transport that would be carried by the waterways in the counterfactual world in which railroads did not exist. For simplicity, it is assumed that over the relevant range, the costs of supplying water transport and rail transport are constant.

The social savings from the railroad are given by the shaded area P_W-A-B-P_R. Why? The area under the demand curve is derived from the demand for goods and services and represents the value of the transport used in producing those final products. With the higher costs of water transport, some use of transport either must be abandoned (the area A-B-C) or be produced by using more resources and thus reducing output in other sectors (the area P_W-A-C-P_R).

The trick, of course, is to estimate the position and elasticities of the actual curves. Only points near B are likely to be observed directly; others must be estimated in some way. Controversy over the shape of the supply curve of water transport, for example, has been heated. But simply putting the issue in this way takes some of the steam out of the axiom of indispensability. Total railroad revenues were less than 10 percent of GNP in 1890, so it would take some extreme assumptions about the elasticity of demand and the increased costs of water transport to push the social saving to a significant share of GNP.

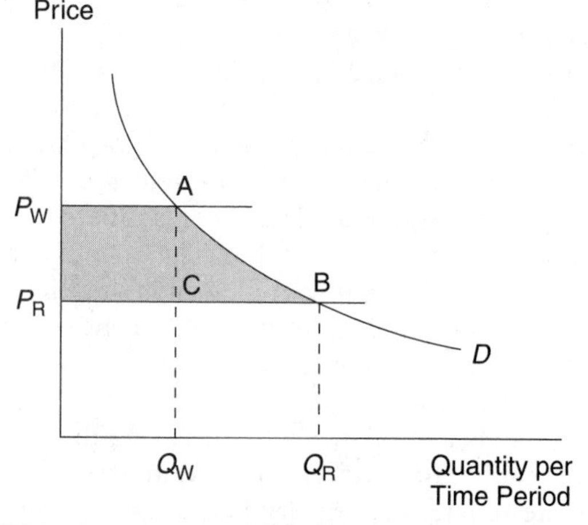

older technologies were figured to be about 4 percent of gross national product in that year. Fogel selected 1890 to make his social savings estimate, picking a year in which the cost advantage of railroads over alternatives and the mix of output produced by the economy were particularly favorable to the railroads. He wanted an upper-bound estimate of the social saving so that if the estimate nevertheless turned out to be small, there would be little argument that the axiom of indispensability had to go.

Fogel concentrated on the shipment of agricultural products. Surprisingly, when looking only at direct transport costs, one finds that the costs of shipping goods by water were often lower than shipping them by rail. In shipping wheat from Chicago to New York, for example, the average all-rail rate was $0.52 per ton-mile, while the average all-water rate was only $0.14 per ton-mile! Obviously, other costs made the total cost of shipping by water higher. Some of these were relatively easy to measure from existing commercial data. For example, grain shipped by water from Chicago to New York had to be shifted from lake steamers to canal barges at Buffalo; this cost must be added in to get the total cost of shipping by water.

The most important additional cost of shipping by water, however, was that it was slower in all seasons and not available at all in winter. How does one measure the cost of slowness? The answer is that with water transport, eastern merchants would be forced to keep larger inventories of grain. The advantage of fast, all-weather transport can be measured by estimating the reduction in eastern inventories.

Fogel also pointed out that in computing the true social savings, it is a mistake to assume that the same goods would have been shipped between the same places in the absence of the railroads. Instead, production would have been intensified in certain areas and cut back in others. Investments that were made in railroads would have gone into improving the canal and water network as well as into other areas of the economy. The true social savings compare actual real GNP with real GNP that has adjusted completely to the absence of the railroads. In one of the most creative parts of his research, Fogel investigated the effects of likely substitutes for rail services such as an extension of the canal network and improvements in the road network, particularly on the rents on agricultural land. This was possible because the Army Corps of Engineers had made extensive plans to extend the canal network, and the Bureau of Public Roads had made similar studies. Fogel did find that the "boundary of feasible agriculture" had been pushed outward by the railroads. Some land would not have been farmed had the rail systems not been developed, but the theoretical reduction in the land under cultivation was much smaller than suggested by some of the rhetoric surrounding the railroads. The prairies would have been farmed even if the railroads had never been invented.

Fogel's "counterfactual" world, in which canals are built and filled with water, roads improved, and the development of trucks and automobiles accelerated, proved to be an especially lively part of the debate and analysis that followed. Traditional historians did not like the idea of historians patiently investigating "imaginary" worlds. But a younger generation of economic historians trained in economics were enthusiastic about evaluating historical developments in terms of the relevant alternatives.

Overall, Fogel found that the railroad had saved about 1.6 percent of GNP in the production and transportation of agricultural products. He did not launch a full-scale effort to measure the social savings for other types of freight or for passengers. His preliminary estimate for total freight, an estimate that did not allow for full adjustment to a nonrail world, was quite similar to Fishlow's measure: about 4.7 percent of 1890 GNP. Subsequently, others calculated the social savings of 1890 rail passengers, including the value of their time saved.[26] The total extra costs of having rail passengers travel by water or stage figured to 2.6 percent of 1890 GNP.

This measure of the direct effects of the railroad (which probably overstates the effect) suggests that output per capita would not have reached its 1890 level until 1892 without the railroad. In short, the railroad accounted for about two years of growth, or alternatively stated, failure to build the railroads would simply have postponed growth for two years. Fishlow's and Fogel's pioneering classics debunked long-held myths about the indispensability of the railroad. Though it is difficult to think of any other single innovation that rendered economic gains of a similar magnitude, the railroads were nevertheless merely one among many developments that contributed to America's economic growth.[27]

As students of this lively professional debate quickly learn, however, it was not so much the final calculations that were Fishlow's and Fogel's main contributions, significant though these were; rather, it was their ability to focus the argument, to specify a testable hypothesis and bring forth the evidence that narrowed the range of disagreement. In short, they advanced the level of analysis and the profession's understanding of an important issue in economic growth generally and in American economic history in particular.

---

[26]J. Hayden Boyd and Gary M. Walton, "The Social Savings from Nineteenth Century Rail Passenger Services," *Explorations in Economic History* 9 (1972): 233–255.

[27]For a challenge to Fishlow's and Fogel's studies, one that addresses various indirect effects such as greater scale economics in industry and higher rates of capital formation, see Jeffrey G. Williamson, *Late Nineteenth Century American Economic Development* (Cambridge, England: Cambridge University Press, 1974), chapter 9. For Fogel's response, see "Notes on the Social Savings Controversy," *Journal of Economic History* 39 (1979): 1–55.

Selected References and Suggested Readings

Boyd, J. Hayden, and Gary M. Walton. "The Social Savings from Nineteenth-Century Rail Passenger Services." *Explorations in Economic History* 9 (1972): 233–254.

Central Pacific Railroad Photographic Museum, historical section. **http://cprr.org/**.

Chandler, Alfred D. *The Railroads: The Nation's First Big Business*. New York: Harcourt Brace Jovanovich, 1965.

Cochran, Thomas C. *Railroad Leaders, 1845–1890, The Business Mind in Action*. Cambridge, Mass.: Harvard University Press, 1953.

Coelho, P. R. P., R. P. Thomas, and D. Shetter. "Comment." *American Economic Review* 58 (1968): 184–189.

David, Paul. "Transport Innovation and Economic Growth: Professor Fogel On and Off the Rails." *Economic History Review* 2, 2d series (1969): 506–525.

Dick, Trevor J. O. "United States Railroad Inventions, Investment since 1870." *Explorations in Economic History* 11 (1974): 249–270.

Engerman, Stanley. "Some Economic Issues Relating to Railroad Subsidies and the Evaluation of Land Grants." *Journal of Economic History* 32 (1972): 443–463.

Fishlow, Albert. *American Railroads and the Transformation of the Ante-bellum Economy*. Cambridge, Mass.: Harvard University Press, 1965.

———. "The Dynamics of Railroad Extension into the West." In *Reinterpretation of American Economic History*, eds. Robert Fogel and Stanley Engerman. New York: Harper & Row, 1971.

———. "Internal Transportation in the Nineteenth and Early Twentieth Centuries." In *The Cambridge Economic History of the United States*, Vol. 2, *The Long Nineteenth Century*, eds. Stanley Engerman and Robert Gallman. Cambridge, England: Cambridge University Press, 2000, 543–642.

Fleisig, Heywood. "The Central Pacific Railroad and the Railroad Land Grant Controversy." *Journal of Economic History* 35 (1975): 552–566.

Fogel, Robert W. *The Union Pacific Railroad: A Case of Premature Enterprise*. Baltimore: Johns Hopkins University Press, 1960.

———. *Railroads and American Economic Growth*. Baltimore: Johns Hopkins University Press, 1964.

———. "Notes on the Social Saving Controversy." *Journal of Economic History* 39 (1979): 1–54.

Fogel, Robert W., and Stanley Engerman. *The Reinterpretation of American Economic History*. New York: Harper & Row, 1971.

Gates, Paul W. *The Illinois Central Railroad and Its Colonization Work*. Cambridge, Mass.: Harvard University Press, 1934.

Greeves, William S. "A Comparison of Railroad Land Grant Policies." *Agricultural History* (1951).

Grodinsky, Julius. *Transcontinental Railway Strategy*. Philadelphia: University of Pennsylvania Press, 1962.

Harbeson, Robert. "Railroads and Regulation, 1877–1916: Conspiracy or Public Interest?" *Journal of Economic History* 27 (1967): 230–242.

Heath, Milton. "Public Railroad Construction and the Development of Private Enterprise in the South before 1861." *Journal of Economic History* 9 (1949).

Hidy, Ralph, and Muriel Hidy. "Anglo-American Merchant Bankers and the Railroads of the Old Northwest, 1848–1860." *Business History Review* 34 (1960).

Hughes, Jonathan. *The Vital Few: American Economic Progress and Its Protagonists*. 2d ed. New York: Oxford University Press, 1987.

Hunt, E. H. "Railroad Social Savings in Nineteenth Century America." *American Economic Review* 57 (1967): 909–910.

Jenks, Leland. "Railroads as an Economic Force in American Development." Reprinted in Thomas Cochran and Thomas Brewer, eds. *Views of American Economic Growth*, Vol. 2. New York: McGraw-Hill, 1966.

Kolko, Gabriel. *Railroads and Regulation, 1877–1916*. Princeton, N.J.: Princeton University Press, 1965.

Lebergott, Stanley. "United States Transport Advance and Externalities." *Journal of Economic History* 26 (1966): 437–461.

———. "United States Transport Advance and Externalities: A Reply." *The Journal of Economic History* 28 (1968): 635.

MacAvoy, Paul. *The Economic Effects of Regulation*. Cambridge, Mass.: MIT Press, 1965.

Martin, Albro. *Enterprise Denied: Origins of the Decline of American Railroads, 1897–1917*. New York: Columbia University Press, 1971.

———. *James J. Hill and the Opening of the Northwest*. New York: Oxford University Press, 1976.

McClelland, Peter D. "Railroads, American Growth, and the New Economic History: A Critique." *Journal of Economic History* 28 (1968): 102–123.

McCraw, Thomas K. *Prophets of Regulation*. Cambridge, Mass.: Belknap Press of Harvard University Press, 1984.

Mercer, Lloyd. "Land Grants to American Railroads: Social Cost or Social Benefit?" *Business History Review* 43 (1969): 134–151.

———. "Rates of Return for Land Grant Railroads, The Central Pacific System." *Journal of Economic History* 30 (1970): 602–626.

———. "Taxpayers or Investors: Who Paid for the Land Grant Railroads?" *Business History Review* 46 (1972): 279–294.

———. "Building Ahead of Demand: Some Evidence for the Land Grant Railroads." *Journal of Economic History* 34 (1974): 492–500.

Ripley, W. Z. *Railroads: Rates and Regulations*. New York: Longmans, Green, 1912.

Rostow, W.W. *The Stages of Economic Growth: A Non-Communist Manifesto*. New York: Cambridge University Press, 1960.

Stover, John. *American Railroads*. Chicago: University of Chicago Press, 1961.

Ulen, Thomas S. "The Market for Regulation: The I.C.C., from 1887 to 1920." *American Economic Review* 70 (1980): 306–310.

———. "Railroad Cartels before 1887: The Effectiveness of Private Enforcement of Collusion." In *Research in Economic History*. Greenwich, Conn.: JAI, 1986.

Union Pacific Web site, historical section. **http://www.uprr.com/aboutup/history/**.

Weiss, Thomas. "United States Transport Advance and Externalities: A Comment." *Journal of Economic History* 28 (1968): 631–634.

Chapter Seventeen

INDUSTRIAL EXPANSION AND CONCENTRATION

Chapter Theme

During the half-century that lay between the Civil War and World War I, the American economy assumed many of its modern characteristics. The most impressive changes were the shift from an agricultural to an industrial economy and the speed of productivity advance, especially in manufactures. Although this shift had been underway throughout the entire nineteenth century, agriculture remained the chief generator of income in the United States until the 1880s. The census of 1890, however, reported manufacturing output greater in dollar value than farm output, and by 1900, the annual value of manufactures was more than twice that of agricultural products.

Social and political transformations accompanied industrial and economic progress, but our main concern here is with the primary technological and other productivity advances of the period, the expanding size and concentration of business enterprises, and the threat of monopoly that spurred new waves of government intervention and legal and institutional change. In short, we are looking primarily at changes on the supply side, in production, in business organization, and in the public policy responses. The issues of product distribution, urbanization, and other market changes are assessed in chapter 20.

STRUCTURAL CHANGE AND INDUSTRY COMPOSITION

Like the English Industrial Revolution before it, the rise of the industrial (manufacturing) sector in the United States was a key feature of modern economic growth and development. One striking set of numbers is the exact flip-flop between agriculture and manufactures in the percentage distribution of commodities produced in 1869 and in 1899: In 1869, this distribution was 53 percent agriculture, 33 percent manufactures, and 14 percent mining and construction combined. Thirty years later, it was 33 percent, 53 percent, and 14 percent.[1]

---

[1]Robert E. Gallman, "Commodity Output, 1839–1899," in *Trends in the American Economy in the Nineteenth Century*, National Bureau of Economic Research, Conference on Research in Income and Wealth (Princeton, N.J.: Princeton University Press, 1960), 26.

As emphasized in chapter 15, agriculture expanded greatly in these years but fell relatively because of more rapid increases elsewhere. Table 17.1 shows the 1910 labor force in several employments as multiples of their 1860 employment level. For example, in 1910, the total labor force of 37.5 million was approximately 3.4 times the 1860 level of 11.1 million. Agriculture's labor force grew only by a factor of 2, however, from 5.9 million to 11.8 million between 1860 and 1910. By comparison, total labor in manufacturing grew by a multiple of 5.4, and in railroads by 23.2, in these 50 years.

Table 17.2 on page 328 shows multiples of output in several categories. The output multiples are far larger than the labor multiples in comparable categories. For example, total manufactures output in 1910 was 10.8 times that of 1860, whereas the labor force in manufactures had grown by a multiple of only 5.4.The coal and cement multiples suggest the vast devouring of natural resources needed to industrialize the nation; they were far larger than the mining labor multiple. All of these selected categories reveal output multiples higher than the total labor force or sector labor multiples (Table 17.1).

Relative to the rest of the world, American gains in manufacturing output were also phenomenal. In the mid-1890s, the United States became the leading industrial power, and by 1910, its factories poured forth goods of nearly twice the value of those of its nearest rival, Germany. In 1913, the United States accounted for more than one-third of the world's industrial production.

Table 17.3 on page 328 lists the top 10 manufactures (by value added) in 1860 and again 50 years later. It is clear from this evidence that the "make-up" of manufactures altered significantly as industrial expansion unfolded over the period. The push and tug of market forces and a high degree of resource mobility rendered such change possible. In addition, the industrial products of the United States were sold in markets that were expanding both at home and abroad, as we shall see in detail in chapter 20. Most American manufacturers, however, did not aggressively seek major foreign outlets until late in the nineteenth century because the nation itself provided an expanding free trade arena. For every dollar purchase in 1860 there were nearly six (in real terms) by World War I.

A vast social transformation underlaid the changes shown in Table 17.3. Four new industries—printing and publishing, malt liquor, tobacco, and railroad cars—made the top 10 list in 1910, whereas flour and meal, woolens, wagons and buggies, and leather goods had slipped into lower positions. The low income elasticity of demand for flour products and woolens, plus new technologies (railroad cars instead of wagons) and other sources of productivity advance, explain much of this transition (Economic Reasoning Propositions 1 and 2). Also, tastes were changing as cottons and linens, cigars and cigarettes, and store-bought alcoholic beverages added to or replaced other items, many previously homemade.

TABLE 17.1 Labor Force Expansion, 1860–1910: Select 1910 Multiples of 1860

Agriculture	2.0
Cotton textiles	3.0
Construction	3.7
Teaching	5.2
Total manufacturing	5.4
Trade	6.0
Mining	6.7
Primary iron and steel	7.1
Railroads	23.2
Total labor force	**3.4**

Source: Derived from Stanley Lebergott, Manpower in Economic Growth: The American Record Since 1800 *(New York: McGraw-Hill, 1964), 510.*

TABLE 17.2 Output Expansion, 1860–1910: Select 1910 Multiples of 1860

Food and kindred products	3.7
Textiles and their products	6.2
Total manufacturing products	10.8
Iron and steel and their products	25.2
Bituminous coal	46.1
Cement	70.7
Railroad passenger miles[a]	17.1
Railroad freight ton miles[a]	98.1

[a] *The railroad multiples are for 1859 to 1910.*

Sources: Derived from Historical Statistics *(Washington, D.C.: Government Printing Office, 1960), Series M, 178, Part 1; Edwin Frickey,* Production in the United States, 1860–1914 *(Cambridge, Mass.: Harvard University Press, 1947), 38–43, 54; and Albert Fishlow, "Productivity and Technological Change in the Railroad Sector, 1840–1910," in* Output, Employment and Productivity in the United States after 1800, Studies in Income and Wealth, *Vol. 30, National Bureau of Economic Research (New York: Columbia University Press, 1966), 585.*

New Technologies

Technological changes, investments in human capital, new energy sources that widened markets and brought new organizational business structures and economies of scale, and structural shifts in resources from lower- to higher-productivity uses (agricultural to manufacturing) all combined to cause these exceptional long-term trends.

Technological changes particularly helped revolutionize industry after industry. No single industry is distinctly representative of the whole, but the advance of each was based on invention and innovation, the dual components of technological change. Invention signifies the discovery of something new, such as steam power or electricity. Innovation denotes the many ways found to use and adapt the new ideas to existing products and services.

The avalanche of technological change, especially in the 1870s and 1880s, was pervasive. The following sample of new technologies during these decades is by no means exhaustive: the roller mill to process oatmeal and flour; refrigerated cars for meat packing; can sealing for canned meat, vegetables, and soup; steel-bottomed stills, long-distance pipelines, and steel tank cars for the petroleum industry; advances in Bessemer and open-hearth processes for steel making, (see Table 17.4 on page 331); advances in electrometallurgy for

TABLE 17.3 The Ten Largest Industries, 1860 and 1910 (by value added)

1860 VALUE ADDED (IN MILLIONS OF DOLLARS		1910 VALUE ADDED (IN MILLIONS OF DOLLARS)	
Cotton goods	$ 55	Machinery	$ 690
Lumber	54	Lumber	650
Boots and shoes	49	Printing and publishing	540
Flour and meal	40	Iron and steel	330
Men's clothing	37	Malt liquors	280
Iron	36	Men's clothing	270
Machinery	33	Cotton goods	260
Woolen goods	25	Tobacco manufactures	240
Carriages and wagons	24	Railroad cars	210
Leather	23	Boots and shoes	180
All manufacturing	815	All manufacturing	8,529

Source: U.S. Bureau of the Census, Census of the United States: 1860, *vol. 3 (Washington, D.C.: Government Printing Office, 1861), 733–742; and U.S. Bureau of the Census,* Census of the United States: 1910, *Vol. 8 (Washington, D.C.: Government Printing Office, 1913), 40.*

Completed in 1883 at a cost of $15.1 million (about $2 billion today), the Brooklyn Bridge was a symbol of America's industrial and technological preeminence.

aluminum production; new varieties of machines and high-speed tools of all sorts; the typewriter, electrical streetcar, and so on.[2] Economic Insight 17.1 on page 330, including Table 17.4, discusses the two new steel processes in more detail. These new technologies permitted mass production and generated lower per-unit costs through economies of scale. Adding to these advances in plant size and productivity were the infrastructure of a transcontinental railroad and a national telegraph network. The outcome was a distribution system, by 1880, that was truly continental in scope.

The effects of these new technologies, economies of mass scale production, and other sources of advances in labor productivity are shown in Table 17.5 on page 331, which lists the growth in value added per worker in those 6 industries that were among the 10 largest in both 1860 and 1910.The cotton industry, which showed the slowest growth except for lumber in output per worker, was already maturing by 1860, and in no other field had power-driven machines already been so successfully applied. Therefore, most of the post–Civil War period was merely one of innovation and greater automaticity in cotton textiles. The industry listed in Table 17.5 with the most rapid advance per worker is men's clothing. During the Civil War, mechanization of the men's clothing increased rapidly as standardized sizes were derived from measurements taken by the army for soldiers' uniforms. Beginning in the 1870s, rotary cutting machines and reciprocating knives made it possible to cut several thicknesses of cloth at once. By 1895, sewing machines had been improved to the point that, power driven, they could operate at speeds of 1,600, 2,200, and 2,800 stitches per minute.

The boot and shoe industry, the second fastest growing in terms of value added per worker, was also markedly changed by invention and product-standardizing innovations. Only in the decade or so before the Civil War were manufactured shoes shaped for the left and the right foot; consequently, many ladies and gentlemen had their footwear custom made and continued to do so for a long time. Manufacturers eventually realized that design, finish, and attention to size and fit were necessary to secure a broad market for factory-made shoes. In

[2]For greater elaboration, see Anthony P. O'Brien, "Factory Size, Economies of Scale, and the Great Merger Wave of 1898–1902," *Journal of Economic History* 48 (1988): 648–649.

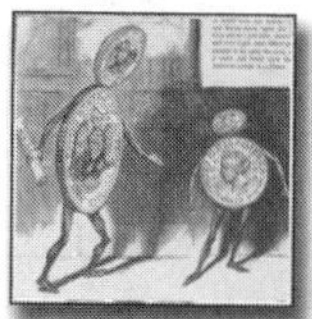

Economic Insight 17.1

Steel Industry Innovations of the 1860s

It is important to realize that new technologies often diffuse slowly; that is, their adoption after invention is not immediate but gradual. Here we analyze the steel industry in terms of two new and competing technologies—the Bessemer process and the open-hearth process—and link these to other technological advances raising productivity and reducing per-unit costs in steelmaking.

The first successful method of making steel in quantity was invented in the late 1850s and early 1860s almost simultaneously by an Englishman, Henry Bessemer, and by an American ironmaster, William Kelly. Only a little while after Bessemer and Kelly invented substantially the same process, the open-hearth method reached experimental status. Inventors were trying to find a way of making cheap steel without infringing on Bessemer's patents. They were also trying to overcome some of the deficiencies of Bessemer's process—including the fact that the method was so quick there was not sufficient time to test the steel for carbon content, so the manufacturer could never be certain for what purposes a given batch would be suitable. The best work in this new direction was accomplished by William and Friedrich Siemens in England and Emile and Pierre Martin in France. By 1868, the main features of the open-hearth or Siemens-Martin process had been developed. Instead of a cylindrical converter that could be tipped like a huge kettle, the open-hearth method employed a furnace with a shallow, open container holding a charge of molten pig iron, scrap iron, limestone, and even some iron ore.

Several considerations made the open-hearth process more economical than the Bessemer process. A large charge required about 12 hours, compared with 10 to 15 minutes for a Bessemer "blow," but during the long refining period, open-hearth steel could be sampled and its chemical composition adjusted to exact requirements. The open-hearth furnace also had a cost advantage over the Bessemer converter in that scrap iron and iron ore could be charged with the more expensive molten pig iron. The regeneration principle, by which the open-hearth furnace used hot gases drawn from nearby coke ovens or blast furnaces to melt and refine the charge, was highly efficient.

Increases in furnace size and efficiency of operation followed these changes. In 1860, good blast furnaces produced 7 to 10 tons of pig iron a day; 25 years later, 75 to 100 tons a day was the maximum; and by 1900, a daily output of 500 tons or more, with markedly less coke consumption, was common. During these years, methods of handling material improved greatly, regenerative heating of the blast was developed, blowing equipment was strengthened, and coke entirely superseded anthracite and bituminous coal as a fuel.

Another major accomplishment was the integration of processes that led to great savings in heat. Coke ovens were eventually placed close to blast furnaces to avoid heat loss. Blast furnaces, in turn, were placed near steel furnaces (either Bessemer or open hearth) so that molten pig iron could be delivered directly to them. Finally, converters and open hearths were situated near the roughing mills so that the first rolling could be accomplished as quickly as possible with a minimum of reheating.

There were, to be sure, other economies resulting from integration—notably, a savings in the handling of materials and in the administration of the entire process.

As shown in Table 17.4, by 1870 more than half of the steel was produced by the new methods. By 1880, the old methods of producing in pots and crucibles were fully eclipsed. Table 17.4 also indicates that, although introduced shortly

Economic Insight 17.1

Steel Industry Innovations of the 1860s (continued)

TABLE 17.4 Steel Production, 1870–1910

				PERCENTAGE	
YEAR	TOTAL[a]	BESSEMER[a]	OPEN-HEARTH[a]	BESSEMER	OPEN-HEARTH
1870[b]	69	38	1	55	2
1880	1,247	1,074	101	86	9
1890	4,277	3,689	513	87	12
1900	10,188	6,685	3,398	66	33
1910	26,095	9,413	16,505	36	63

[a]*Calculations are rounded in thousands of long tons.*
[b]*In 1870, a substantial proportion of steel was still made by old technologies in pots and crucibles.*

Source: Historical Statistics *(Washington, D.C.: Government Printing Office, 1960), Series P203-207.*

after the Bessemer method, the open-hearth steel method lagged far behind until 1900. Bessemer steels were eminently satisfactory for rails, which constituted one of the first great demands for the new product. Eventually, however, as engineers grew familiar with the characteristics of steel, they became convinced that plates and structural shapes made of Bessemer steel contained defects that did not appear in the open-hearth product. Because of this preference, some rolling mills had to build open-hearth furnaces to meet the new demand. Furthermore, the costs of open-hearth processing were much lower than those of the Bessemer process, not only because scrap could be used but also because small operators could build and operate plants far smaller than were needed for a Bessemer operation. Moreover, small owners did not have to fear being "held up" by the large companies that controlled the Bessemer ores. By 1910, the open hearth had clearly won out over the Bessemer converter: Of the 26 million tons of steel produced in that year, the open-hearth process accounted for 63 percent and the Bessemer process for only 36 percent; from this time on, the annual output of the Bessemer method decreased steadily.[3]

[3]For details of iron and steel output changes, see Peter Temin, *Iron and Steel in Nineteenth-Century America* (Cambridge, Mass.: MIT Press, 1964).

TABLE 17.5 Value Added per Worker in Leading Select Industries, 1860 and 1910

	1860	1910	PERCENT CHANGE
Lumber	$710	$ 930	31%
Cotton goods	480	680	42
Machinery	810	1,290	59
Iron and steel	720	1,370	90
Boots and shoes	400	910	128
Men's clothing	320	1,180	269

Note: Value added measures the total value of output minus material costs; therefore, value added per worker reflects both labor and capital productivity.

Source: Simon Kuznets, "Changes in the National Incomes of the United States of America Since 1870," Income and Wealth Series II *(London: Bowes & Bowes, 1952), 30. Used by permission of the publisher.*

1875, they introduced the Goodyear welt process, which enabled soles to be attached to uppers without allowing nails and stitches to penetrate the inside of the shoe. Within the next 20 years or so, machines were devised to do the work of lasting, eyeleting, heeling, and so on. By 1914, the industry was highly mechanized.

Improvements in steel processing and in nonferrous metals, especially copper and aluminum, made possible rapid advances in metalworking machinery, which jumped between 1860 and 1910 from the seventh largest to the largest manufacture. Metalworking machinery consists of two main types of power-driven machines: (1) shaping or forming machines, which press, forge, hammer, and the like, and (2) machines that cut metal, such as gear-cutting, grinding, and milling machines. During the 1890s, there were two major technical advances: (1) machine tools became automatic or semiautomatic, and (2) compressed air and electricity were used to drive high-speed cutting tools and presses. The demands of the automobile industry and of the armament and aircraft industries during World War I brought the machine industry to maturity. Victor S. Clark (1928) reports that between the end of the Civil War and the end of World War I, precision in metalworking increased from a tolerance limit of 0.01 inch to 0.001 inch, and tolerances of 0.0001 inch had been achieved in small-scale production. By 1919, metalworking machinery had increased in power as well as precision. Electrically driven shears could cut steel slabs 12 inches thick and 44 inches wide, and huge presses could stamp out parts of automobile bodies rapidly enough to make "mass" production possible. Moreover, the industry played the central role in diffusing technical knowledge from its point of origin to other sectors of the economy. As Nathan Rosenberg has so cogently observed:

> The machine-tool industry was a center for the acquisition and diffusion of the skills and techniques uniquely required in a machinofacture type of economy. Its role was a dual one: (1) new skills and techniques were developed here in response to the demands of specific customers, and (2) once acquired, the machine-tool industry served as the main transmission center for the transfer of new skills and techniques to the entire machine-using sector of the economy.[4]

New Forms and Sources of Energy

Between 1860 and World War I, there was a remarkable transition from reliance on the power of wind and water and the physical exertion of humans and animals to other sources of energy. This transition had begun in the first half of the nineteenth century but dramatically gained momentum in the second half. In 1850, more than three-quarters of all power was furnished by animal energy, and human energy produced more power than machines did. On the eve of the Civil War, water power was far more important than steam power in the United States. During the 1870s, steam surpassed water as a source of power. Then two major additional influences hastened the final phasing out of the ancient water wheel and the more recently developed water turbine: (1) the ever-increasing efficiency of the steam engine, along with the increased safety of high-pressure boilers and (2) the opening up of vast and apparently inexhaustible supplies of coal as a result of the transportation revolution. This instance portrays the interdependence of resource availability and technological advances. By 1890, relatively few factories—mostly in the textile and paper industries—used direct water power, although gristmills and sawmills were still powered by this source.

Another way of utilizing the force of water flow was to be devised. At the time when steam engines had gained an unquestioned ascendancy, electricity appeared on the scene as a form of power. Like steam, electricity was not a new energy source; it was a new means

[4]Nathan Rosenberg, *Technology and American Economic Growth* (New York: Harper & Row, 1972), 98.

Steel manufacture required unprecedented amounts of capital in the form of great furnaces and mechanical aids as well as skilled workers who were able to judge when the time was ripe to tap Bessemer converters such as these.

of using energy generated either by the flow of water or the burning of fuel. But electricity brought about a remarkable improvement in the utilization of the older sources of energy. Because electric power is flexible and divisible, the power plant could be separated from the manufacturing establishment by long distances, and the cumbersome devices required to change the to-and-fro motion of the steam engine into rotary motion and then to transmit this motion were no longer necessary. Furthermore, the energy required to turn either a small or large motor was readily "on tap."

By World War I, one-third of the nation's industrial power was provided by electricity, far more than in any other country. Nearly one-half of all urban dwellings had electric lights, although more than 98 percent of all farm families were burning kerosene lamps after dark.

The growing importance of electricity should not, however, divert our attention from the importance of other fundamental sources of energy. In 1890, coal was the source of 90 percent of the energy furnished to manufacturing; in the years just before 1920, coal remained the source of at least 80 percent of all industrial energy. But petroleum was rapidly growing more important, and hydropower was recovering. Within 25 years, petroleum and natural gas would become strategic fuels, although the transportation and manufacturing industries were planted squarely in the age of coal as late as 1920.

Managerial Changes

Technological changes, new power sources, development of the corporation based on multiple ownership of stock, and other forces brought forth the modern big business firm. Prior to the huge railroad companies, most businesses, even the largest, were typically managed by single owners or partners on a day-to-day basis. Oftentimes supervisors were added, but owners usually oversaw the business operations and made key managerial decisions. The railroads led the change.

Faced with unmanageable size and complexity, the railroads developed a host of new management practices and concepts. Managerial innovations and organizational changes were essential to better coordinate the activities of thousands of employees who ran the trains, sold the tickets, loaded freight, repaired track and equipment, and performed endless other tasks. In the 1850s, Daniel McCallum of New York, president of the Erie Railroad, proposed a series of new management principles—with wide potential application. First, managers' authority to make decisions should match their level of responsibility. Internal reporting systems (accounting) should be used to identify trouble spots and allow prompt solutions. Performance evaluations, for employees and managers alike, should be routine. Other large businesses in the late nineteenth century soon adopted these and other management systems, and today, McCallum's concepts are routine in virtually all large business organizations.[5]

Two relatively new ideas spread like wildfire after the Civil War: mass production and scientific management. Mass production implies two basic production procedures: continuous flow and interchangeable parts. Scientific management implies business procedures with a laboratory-like exactness. Entrepreneurs were constantly seeking more advanced production methods. Physically, it was necessary to devise mechanical means of systematically transporting materials from one stage of production to another. Intellectually, detailed planning and ordering of the assembly process by the managers were required. It was essential that management's goal be the minimization of the time consumed by workers in assembling a complex product.

Ever since Oliver Evans's first attempts at continuous-flow milling in the 1780s, entrepreneurs had understood the advantages of moving materials continuously through the production process. Applications in meat processing and cigarettes demonstrated the potential

---

[5]For more on the early leadership of the railroads in these areas, see Alfred D. Chandler, *The Railroads: The Nation's First Big Business* (New York: Harcourt, Brace & World, 1965).

THE GRANGER COLLECTION, NEW YORK

Mass production helped change the face of industry in the early part of the twentieth century.

profitability, but it was Henry Ford, the great automobile entrepreneur, who devised the first progressive, moving assembly-line systems for large, complex final products. In 1914, a chassis that had formerly been assembled in 12 hours could be put together along a 250-foot line in a little over one and one-half hours. Before 1920, motor-driven conveyors were moving motors, bodies, and chassis at optimum heights and speeds to workers along greatly lengthened lines. By this time, the moving assembly had spread throughout the automobile industry, the electrical industry, and the budding household-appliance industry.

With increases in size of plant and complexity of layout, the problems of efficiently handling a large labor force became apparent. Frederick W. Taylor, ultimately the most famous contributor in this regard, argued that worker efficiency could be improved by (1) analyzing in detail the movements required to perform a job, (2) carrying on experiments to determine the optimum size and weight of tools and optimum lifts, and (3) offering incentives for superior performance. From such considerations, Taylor went on to develop certain principles pertaining to the proper physical layout of a shop or factory, the correct routing of work, and the accurate scheduling of the production of orders.[6]

These productivity-enhancing improvements helped push real wages upward, softening somewhat workers' resentment to change and faster product processing. But competition kept the changes coming and the size of business growing.

ECONOMIES OF SCALE AND INDUSTRY CONCENTRATION

Central to the discussion of the rise of big business has been the debate over whether big business came about in response to technological changes and other advantages of

[6]For a full account of the timing and dimensions of Taylor's influence on the managerial revolution, see the important book by Daniel Nelson, *Frederick W. Taylor and the Rise of Scientific Management* (Madison: University of Wisconsin Press, 1980). For a critical assessment of "Taylorism," see David F. Noble, *America by Design: Science, Technology & the Rise of Corporate Capitalism* (New York: Knopf, 1977).

economies of scale, or whether the pursuit of monopoly power and market control was also a fundamental force.

Early Business Combinations

The first attempts at combination were two simple devices: (1) "gentlemen's agreements," usually used for setting and maintaining prices, and (2) "pooling"—dividing a market and assigning each seller a portion. In pooling, markets could be divided on the basis of output (with each producer free to sell a certain number of units) or on a territorial basis (with each producer free to sell within his own protected area). Or sellers could form a "profits pool," whereby net income was paid into a central fund and later divided on a basis of percentage of total sales in a given period. Although pools had been formed even before the Civil War, they did not become common until after 1875. During the 1880s and 1890s, strong pooling arrangements were made in a number of important industries: producers of whiskey, salt, coal, meat products, explosives, steel rails, structural steel, cast-iron pipe, and certain tobacco products achieved great success with pooling agreements, as did the railroads in trunk-line territory. The pool corresponded to the European cartel; it differed from its European counterpart chiefly because such agreements were considered illegal in this country (a heritage of English common law) and were not enforceable in the courts.

Although gentlemen's agreements and pooling both worked temporarily, they typically were not durable. First, insofar as they were successful in raising prices and achieving a "monopoly" profit, they encouraged new firms to enter the field. Second, the temptation to cheat was strong. Individual managers could profit by exceeding their assigned outputs and encroaching on another's territory, and there was no legal recourse against violators.

Trusts and Holding Companies

To overcome these deficiencies, a new combination device was created: the trust, a perversion of the ancient fiduciary device whereby trustees held property in the interest of either individuals or institutions. Under a trust agreement, the stockholders of several operating companies formerly in competition turned over their shares to a group of trustees and received "certificates of trust" in exchange. The trustees, therefore, had voting control of the operating companies, and the former stockholders received dividends on their trust certificates. This device (Economic Reasoning Proposition 4) was so successful as a means of centralizing control of an entire industry and so profitable to the owners of stock that trusts were formed in the 1880s and early 1890s to control the output of kerosene, sugar, whiskey, cottonseed oil, linseed oil, lead, salt, rubber boots and gloves, and other products. But the trust form had one serious defect: Agreements were a matter of public record. Once their purpose was clearly understood, such a clamor arose that both state and federal legislations were passed outlawing them, and some trusts were dissolved by successful common-law suits in the state courts.

Alert corporate lawyers, however, thought of another way of linking managerial and financial structures. Occasionally, special corporate charters had permitted a company to own the securities of another company, such provisions having been inserted to allow horizontal expansion. In 1889, the New Jersey legislature revised its general incorporation statutes to allow any corporation so desiring to hold the securities of one or more subsidiary corporations. When trusts were declared illegal in several states, many of them simply obtained charters in New Jersey as "holding companies."[7] The prime objective of centralizing control while leaving individual companies free to operate under their several charters

[7] "Charter mongering" was also profitable for New Jersey, which derived a substantial proportion of its revenues from corporate fees. Later, other states—Delaware, in particular—undercut New Jersey's monopoly.

could, therefore, be achieved by a relatively simple device. Theoretically, the holding company had to own more than 50 percent of the voting stock of its several subsidiaries. In practice, especially as shares became widely dispersed, control could be maintained with a far smaller percentage of the voting stock. The holding company was here to stay, although it would have to resist the onslaughts of Justice Department attorneys from time to time.

THE TWO PHASES OF THE CONCENTRATION MOVEMENT

Whatever the path to combination and whatever the form of organization finally selected, the large firm was typical of the American manufacturing industry by 1905. Why was bigness inevitable? How can we account for the major transformation that occurred in the last few decades of the nineteenth and the early years of the twentieth centuries? We have suggested that one reason for the concentration of industry was a natural movement, encouraged by competitive pressures, toward larger, more efficient sizes and that another reason was a conscious aiming for monopoly power. We now have to examine the forces that impelled entrepreneurs toward the control of a large part of the output of many major industries, for it is clear that a rapacious, overweening desire for monopoly profits did not suddenly sweep American entrepreneurs into great combinations.

Thanks to Alfred Chandler, we find clues to the motivation toward combination in the reflection that the movement in this period occurred in two major phases. The first phase (1879–1893) was the predominantly horizontal combination of industries that produced the old staples of consumption. The second (1898–1904) was the predominantly vertical combination, mostly in the producer-goods industries, but also in a few consumer-goods industries that manufactured new products for growing urban markets.[8]

Phase 1: Horizontal Mergers (1879–1893)

During the 1870s and 1880s, as the railroads extended the formation of a national market, many existing small firms in the consumer-goods industries experienced a phenomenal increase in the demand for their products. This was followed by an expansion of facilities to take advantage of the new opportunities. Then, in many areas, there was great excess capacity and "overproduction." When this occurred, prices dropped below the average per unit production costs of some firms. To protect themselves from insolvency and ultimate failure, many small manufacturers in the leather, sugar, salt, whiskey, glucose, starch, biscuit, kerosene, and rubber boot and glove industries (to name the most important) combined horizontally into larger units.[9] (*Horizontal mergers* are the combining of firms that produce identical or very similar products.) They then systematized and standardized their manufacturing processes, closing the least-efficient plants and creating purchasing, marketing, finance, and accounting departments to service the units that remained. By 1893, consolidation and centralization were well under way in those consumer-goods industries that manufactured staple household items that had long been in use. Typical of the large firms created in this way were the Standard Oil Company of Ohio (after 1899, the Standard Oil

[8]The following analysis is based closely on the path-breaking work of Alfred D. Chandler, Jr., to whom we are indebted for a new interpretation of the concentration movement. For the initial version of the Chandler thesis at various stages and in alternative sources, see "The Beginnings of 'Big Business' in American Industry," *Business History Review* 33 (Spring 1959): 1–31; "Development, Diversification and Decentralization," in *Postwar Economic Trends in the United States*, ed. Ralph E. Freeman (New York: Harper & Row, 1960), 235–288; and *Strategy and Structure* (Cambridge, Mass.: MIT Press, 1962). For Chandler's more recent interpretation, see *The Visible Hand*, Part 4 (Cambridge, Mass.: Harvard University Press, 1977).

[9]As we have already observed, in the various industries, pools and other loose forms of organization often preceded combination into a single large company.

John D. Rockefeller, archetype of the nineteenth-century businessman, brought discipline and order to the unruly oil industry, parlayed a small stake into a fortune estimated at more than $1 billion (about $20 billion in today's money), and lived in good health (giving away some of his millions) until 96 on a regimen of milk, golf, and river watching.

Company of New Jersey), the Distillers' and Cattle Feeders' Trusts, the American Sugar Refining Company, and the United States Rubber Company.

Of the firms that became large during the first wave of concentration, the most spectacular was the Standard Oil Company. From its beginnings in 1860, the petroleum-refining business had been characterized by a large number of small firms. By 1863, the industry had more than 300 firms, and although this number had declined by 1870 to perhaps 150, competition was vicious, and the industry was plagued by excess capacity. "By the most conservative estimates," write Harold Williamson and Arnold Daum, "total refining capacity during 1871–1872 of at least twelve million barrels annually was more than double refinery receipts of crude, which amounted to 5.23 million barrels in 1871 and 5.66 million barrels in 1872."[10] An industry with investment in fixed plant and equipment that can turn out twice the volume of current sales is one inevitably characterized by repeated failures (usually in the downswing of the business cycle) and highly variable profits in even the most efficient firms.

John D. Rockefeller's firm—organized in 1869 as the Standard Oil Company of Ohio—was perhaps the best managed, with two great refineries, a barrel-making plant, and a fleet of tank cars.[11] Standard's holdings grew steadily during the 1870s, largely through the acquisition of refineries in Pittsburgh, Philadelphia, and New York, as well as in Ohio. Demanding and receiving rebates on oil shipments (and even drawbacks on the shipments of competitors), Standard made considerable progress in absorbing independent refining

[10]Harold F. Williamson and Arnold R. Daum, *The American Petroleum Industry* (Evanston, Ill.: Northwestern University Press, 1959), 344.

[11]John D. Rockefeller got his start in business at the age of 19, when he formed a partnership with Maurice B. Clark to act as commission merchants and produce shippers. Moderately wealthy even before the end of the Civil War, Rockefeller entered the oil business in 1862, forming a series of partnerships before consolidating them as the Standard Oil Company.

competition. By 1878, Standard either owned or leased 90 percent of the refining capacity of the country. The independents that remained were successful only if they could produce high-margin items, such as branded lubricating oils, that did not require high-volume, low-cost manufacture.

To consolidate the company's position, a trust agreement was drawn in 1879 whereby three trustees were to manage the properties of Standard Oil of Ohio for the benefit of Standard stockholders. In 1882, the agreement was revised and amended; stockholders of 40 companies associated with Standard turned over their common stocks to nine trustees. The value of properties placed in the trust was set at $70 million, against which 700,000 trust certificates (par value $100) were issued.

The agreement further provided for the formation of corporations in other states having the name Standard Oil Company of New Jersey, and of New York, and so on. After the Supreme Court of Ohio ordered the Standard Oil trust dissolved in a decree in 1892, the combination still remained effective for several years by maintaining closely interlocking directorates among the major refining companies. Threatened by further legal action, company officials changed the Standard Oil Company of New Jersey from an operating to a holding company, increasing its capitalization from $10 million to $110 million so that its securities might be exchanged for those of the subsidiaries it held. It secured all the advantages of the trust form, and, at least for the time being, incurred no legal dangers. Thus, Standard went from a trust to a holding company after successful combination had long since been achieved.

Phase 2: The Vertical Mergers (1898–1904)

A vertically integrated firm is one in which each stage of the production process, from the production of raw materials to the marketing of the final product, is managed by different departments within one firm. In the latter part of the nineteenth century, industry after industry came to be dominated by giant vertically integrated firms. For example, Gustavus F. Swift and his brother Edwin, after experimenting with the shipment and storage of refrigerated meat, formed a partnership in 1878 that grew over the next two decades into a huge, integrated company. Its major departments—marketing, processing, purchasing, and accounting—were controlled from the central office in Chicago. Other meatpackers, such as Armour and Morris, built similar organizations, and by the late 1890s, a few firms dominated the meatpacking industry with highly centralized, bureaucratic managements. In a similar manner, James B. Duke set out in 1884 to establish a national, even worldwide, organization to market his machine-made cigarettes. In 1890, he merged his company with five competitors to form the American Tobacco Company. Less than 15 years later, American Tobacco, after a series of mergers, achieved a monopoly in the cigarette industry.

In steel, the Carnegie Company had by the early 1890s consolidated its several manufacturing properties into an integrated firm that owned vast coal and iron deposits. As the Carnegie interests grew, other businesspeople were creating powerful steel companies. In 1898, the Federal Steel Company was formed under the auspices of J. P. Morgan and Company. Its integrated operations and products greatly resembled those of the Carnegie Company, but it had the further advantage of having a close alliance with the National Tube Company and the American Bridge Company, producers of highly finished products. The National Steel Company, created by W. H. Moore, was the third-largest producer of ingot and basic steel shapes and was closely connected with other Moore firms that made finished products: the American Tin Plate Company, the American Steel Hoop Company, and the American Sheet Steel Company. When Carnegie, strong in coal and (through his alliance with Rockefeller) iron ore, threatened to integrate forward into finished products, he precipitated action toward a merger by the Morgan interests. The result was the United States Steel Corporation, organized in March 1901 with a capital stock of over $1 billion

Andrew Carnegie, a great salesman, built an integrated steel firm that combined with the Morgan and Moore interests to form the United States Steel Corporation in 1901. At that time, he sold out and became one of the world's leading philanthropists.

and, by a substantial margin, the largest corporation in the world. Controlling 60 percent of the nation's steel business, United States Steel owned, in addition to its furnaces and mills, a large part of the vast ore reserves of the Lake Superior region, 50,000 acres of coking-coal lands, more than 1,100 miles of railroad, and a fleet of lake steamers and barges. While protecting its position in raw materials, the corporate giant was then able to prevent price warfare in an industry typified by high fixed costs.

The severe depression of 1893 brought acts of combination of all kinds to a virtual standstill. With the return of prosperity late in 1896, however, a new momentum developed. Between 1898 and 1904, more than 3,000 mergers were effected. In the four years before 1903, companies accounting for almost one-half of U.S. manufacturing capacity took part in active mergers, most of them vertically integrating.

Why did these giant, vertically integrated firms come to dominate so much of American manufacturing? Why, to use the provocative terms of Alfred D. Chandler, did the *visible hand* of the giant corporation replace the *invisible hand* of the market in so many lines of business? Chandler's answer starts with technology. Factories constructed to take advantage of continuous-flow technologies minimized costs of production when they could operate continuously; any interruption of the inflow of raw materials or the sale of the final products sent costs upward. Thus, to minimize costs, managers needed to schedule flows with meticulous care. Having raw materials and the process of distributing the final product under their complete control allowed them to minimize costs. When a continuous-flow technology did not exist, the profits expected from vertical integration often proved chimerical. American Tobacco is a good example. A new machine, the so-called Bonsack machine, could produce good cigarettes with a continuous-flow technology. As a result,

American Tobacco was able to build a vertically integrated firm that monopolized the industry. On the other hand, no machine could be constructed that could produce good cigars on continuous-flow basis, and American Tobacco's efforts to monopolize the cigar industry failed. Of course, minimizing costs was not the whole story. If a firm was successful in building a monopoly position in an industry, it could increase its profits further by restricting output and raising prices. As Naomi Lamoreaux has shown, monopoly profits were an important part of the story. (Lamoreaux, 1985)[12]

Why was it that the United States led the way in the development of giant corporations? Continuous-flow facilities were being built elsewhere, but the process went further and faster in the United States. Part of the answer was the huge internal market in the United States, a market that was continually expanding due to the population growth and urbanization. Another part of the answer, as by Gavin Wright stressed, is that the successful new technologies required abundant natural resources: coal, iron, copper, petroleum, agricultural products, and so on. And abundant natural resources were America's great comparative advantage.[13]

LEGISLATION AND LEGAL ACTIONS

Also critical to the second wave of the concentration movement was the passage of legislation to control monopoly power. The clamor from agrarian interests for legal action against monopolies is discussed in chapter 15. Gary Liebcap has persuasively argued that cattlemen's associations provided the political muscle leading to the Sherman Antitrust Act of 1890.[14] Their quarrel was with the "Chicago meat packing monopolists," the Swift brothers and Armour and Morris, who they believed soaked up all their profits from cattle raising. Small slaughterhouses selling fresh meat and other small businesses and farmers joined the cattlemen in urging antimonopoly legislation. A complementary argument to Liebcap's, by Thomas Hazlett, focuses on Senator John Sherman (brother of General William Tecumseh Sherman), a high-tariff advocate who "traded" legislative votes with antimonopolists to secure the McKinley Tariff Bill of 1890, with its high average 51 percent rate on dutied goods. It seems that votes supporting anticompetitive practices (the higher tariffs) were being traded for votes supporting procompetitive policies (stronger antitrust legislation).[15]

As interesting as the Sherman Act's origins were its effects. As a legal statute, the Sherman Antitrust Act of 1890 seemed simple enough. It declared illegal "every contract, combination in the form of trust, or otherwise, or conspiracy in restraint of trade among the several states." It prescribed punishment of a fine or imprisonment or both for "every person who shall monopolize, or attempt to monopolize, or combine or conspire . . . to monopolize any part of the trade or commerce among the several states." The attorney general was charged with enforcing the act by bringing either civil or criminal proceedings in the federal courts. Thus, how the law should be interpreted was left to federal judges.

The Supreme Court did much to discourage enforcement of the act by its decision, in 1895, in the case of *United States v. E. C. Knight Company*. The American Sugar Refining Company had acquired the stock of the E. C. Knight Company along with that of three other

---

[12] Naomi R. Lamoreaux, *The Great Merger Movement in American Business, 1895–1904* (Cambridge, England: Cambridge University Press, 1985).

[13] Gavin Wright, "The Origins of American Industrial Success, 1879–1940," *American Economic Review* 80 (1990).

[14] Gary D. Liebcap, "The Rise of the Chicago Packers and the Origins of Meat Inspection and Antitrust," in a symposium: Economics and 100 Years of Antitrust, eds. George Bittlingmayer and Gary M. Walton, *Economic Inquiry* 30 (2), (April 1992): 242–262.

[15] Thomas W. Hazlett, "The Legislative History of the Sherman Act Re-examined," in a symposium: Economics and 100 Years of Antitrust, eds. George Bittlingmayer and Gary M. Walton, *Economic Inquiry* 30 (2), (April 1992): 263–276.

This 1890 drawing depicts a meeting of a company's board of directors—perhaps discussing how to deal with the passage of the Sherman Act.

sugar refiners in the Philadelphia area, raising American's shares of the refining market from 65 to 98 percent. The attorney general brought an action against the sugar trust; but the Court would not apply the Sherman Act on the grounds that the company was engaged in manufacture—not in interstate commerce—and that Congress intended the prohibitions to apply only to interstate commerce. The business of sugar refining, the Court held, "bore no direct relation to commerce between the states or with foreign nations. . . . Commerce succeeds to manufacture, and is not a part of it." The Court further implied that the Sherman Antitrust Act did not preclude the growth of large firms by purchase of property— that is, by merger or consolidation.

Consequently, after 1895, mergers were widely viewed as legal and as the safer way to effectively eliminate cutthroat price competition. The post-1898 merger wave was launched in part by the 1898 ruling in the case of *United States v. Addyston Pipe and Steel Company*. Here the Court made it clear that the Sherman Act did apply to collusive agreements among firms supposed to be in competition with each other. But mergers were still apparently legal. George Bittlingmayer reports:

> The trade publication for the iron, steel, and hardware industry, *Iron Age*, ran a full-column editorial on the decision and concluded that merger might now replace price fixing. "The new decision is one which may gravely affect some of the arrangements now in force among manufacturers in different lines, in which some control over prices is sought by concerns otherwise acting independently in the conduct of their business. At first sight it looks as though this decision must drive them to actual consolidation, which is really more apt to be prejudicial to public interests than the losses and temporary agreements which it condemns." [February 17, 1898] A month later *Iron Age* reported that "quite a number of meetings of manufacturers have been held

> during the past week all looking to some scheme to take off the keen edge of unbridled competition." [March 17, 1898][16]

As this trade publication suggests, the interest of the law and the effect of the law are not always consistent. The law itself, in this instance, was a strong force in bringing about the combinations—through merger—that people abhorred. Ironically, the available evidence strongly suggests that the first phase of the concentration movement (1879–1893), which led to the 1890 Sherman Antitrust Act, was less spurred by monopoly power seeking than was the second phase (1898–1904). As Anthony O'Brien informs us, factories grew in size much more rapidly in the 1870s and 1880s than in later decades.[17] This was so because the pace of technological change was so exceptional in those decades. Naomi Lamoreaux's research concludes that the great merger wave, the second phase, was propelled mainly by the desire to suppress price competition.[18] O'Brien also concludes: "Increases in concentration during the merger wave were motivated more by the desire to reduce price competition than by the desire to exploit scale economies."[19] Whatever its primary source of motivation, the great merger wave of the turn of the century became an inviting political target. See Economic Insight 17.2 on page 344.

Legal Refinements

In two decisions handed down at the close of World War I, large companies formed by merger were effectively freed from the threat of dissolution, provided that the actions of the dominant firm were not calculated to exclude competitors from the market. In the case of *United States v. United Shoe Machinery Company of New Jersey, et al.*, Justice Joseph McKenna took as the basis for his decision the finding of the trial court that the constituent companies had not been competitors—that they had performed supplementary rather than identical functions in making shoes. The Court did not deny the monopoly power of the United Shoe Machinery Company; it simply held that the company's power was not illegal because the constituent companies had never been competitive. The decision in *United States v. United States Steel Corporation* made the position of merged companies even safer. Justice McKenna, who again spoke for the Court, found that the corporation possessed neither the power nor the intent to exert monopoly control. The majority of the Court was impressed by the fact that examination of the history of United States Steel revealed none of the predatory practices complained of in the oil and tobacco cases. The Court took cognizance of the splendid relations of the steel company with its rivals, noting that United States Steel's power "was efficient only when in cooperation with its competitors, and hence it concerted with them in the expedients of pools, associations, trade meetings, and finally in a system of dinners inaugurated in 1907 by the president of the company, E. H. Gary, and called 'The Gary Dinners.'"[20] But the corporation

> resorted to none of the brutalities or tyrannies that the cases illustrate of other combinations. . . . It did not have power in and of itself, and the control it exerted was only in and by association with its competitors. Its offense, therefore, such as it was,

---

[16]George Bittlingmayer, "Did Antitrust Policy Cause the Great Merger Wave?" *Journal of Law and Economics* (April 1985): 90–91.
[17]O'Brien, "Factory Size, Economies of Scale, and the Great Merger Wave of 1898–1902," 639–649.
[18]Naomi R. Lamoreaux, *The Great Merger Movement in American Business, 1895–1904*, especially chapter 4.
[19]O'Brien, "Factory Size," 649.
[20]40 Sup. Ct. 251 U.S. 417, 295.

Economic Insight 17.2

The Supreme Court as Trust Buster

As early as 1902, Theodore Roosevelt sensed the political value of trust busting, and in the campaign of 1904 he promised vigorous prosecution of monopolies. During his administration, bills were filed against several great companies, notably the American Tobacco Company and the Standard Oil Company of New Jersey. These firms were the archetypes of monopoly in the public mind, and the judgment of the Supreme Court in the cases against them would indicate the degree of enforcement that might be expected under the Sherman Act.

In decisions handed down in 1911, the Supreme Court found that unlawful monopoly power existed and ordered the dissolution of both the Standard Oil Company and the American Tobacco Company. But it did so on rather narrow grounds. First, it gave great weight to evidence of intent to monopolize. The Court examined the predatory practices that had occurred during each company's growth period and the manner in which the companies exercised their monopoly power. The oil trust, so it was asserted, had achieved its powerful position in the market by unfairly obtaining rebates from the railroads and by acquiring refining companies brought to terms after price wars. Similarly, the tobacco trust was accused of bringing competing companies to heel by price wars, frequently closing them after acquisition by purchase. Moreover, the record showed that the old American Tobacco Company exerted a strong monopsonistic (single-buyer) power, beating down the prices of tobacco farmers when the crop was sold at the annual auctions. Second, the Court adopted a "rule of reason" with respect to restraints of trade; since action against all possible violators was obviously impossible, it became necessary for the Court to exercise judgment:

> Under this principle, combinations which restricted competition were held to be lawful as long as the restraint was not unreasonable. Since there is no precise economic standard by which the reasonableness of a restriction on competition can be measured, the courts examined the practices pursued by a corporate giant in achieving and maintaining its position in the market. Predatory practices were indicative of an intent to monopolize the market, and a corporate combination which achieved dominance by indulging in them might be dissolved. Those which behaved in a more exemplary manner, even though their size gave them power over the market, did not transgress the law.[21]

Standard Oil and American Tobacco were the only companies that the Supreme Court dissolved, but even if the courts had continued ordering dissolution or divestiture, it is unlikely that competition in the classical sense would have been restored. The four major successor companies to the American Tobacco Company constituted a tight oligopoly with respect to cigarette manufacture. Stock in the 33 successor companies of the Standard Oil Company was ordered distributed pro rata to the stockholders of the holding company, but whatever the benefits of dissolution, an increase in price competition was not an obvious outcome.[22]

---

[21]George W. Stocking, "The Rule of Reason, Workable Competition, and the Legality of Trade Association Activities," *University of Chicago Law Review* 21 (4), (Summer 1954): 532–533.

[22]For an interesting account of growing price rigidity during these decades, see Austin H. Spencer, "Relative Downward Industrial Price Flexibility 1870–1921," *Explorations in Economic History* 14 (1977): 1–19.

> was not different from theirs and was distinguished from theirs only in the leadership it assumed in promulgating and perfecting the policy. This leadership it gave up and it had ceased to offend the law before this suit was brought.[23]

Justice McKenna held that United States Steel had not achieved monopoly power, despite its control of 50 percent of the industry's output. He decided that the pattern of regular price changes over time, clearly shown by the evidence, could have emerged from a competitive market just as easily as from collusion. The government's assertion that the size of the corporation made it a potential threat to competition in the industry was denied. On the contrary, said the Court, "the law does not make mere size an offense, or the existence of unexerted power an offense." After such a decision, only the most optimistic Justice Department attorneys could see any point in bringing action against a firm simply because it was big.

The Federal Trade Commission

In 1914, during Woodrow Wilson's first term, Congress passed the Clayton Act, which was intended to remove ambiguities in existing antitrust law by making certain specific practices illegal. Price discrimination among buyers was forbidden, as were exclusive selling and tying contracts if their effect was to lessen competition. Firms could not acquire the stock of a competitor, and interlocking directorates among competing firms were forbidden—again, if the effect was to lessen competition. A newly established Federal Trade Commission (FTC) of five appointive members was to enforce the act, and decisions of the FTC were to be appealed to the circuit courts. The commission could also carry out investigations, acting on its own initiative or on the complaint of an injured party. If a violation was found, the commission could issue a "cease and desist" order; offenders then had the right to appeal to the federal courts.

The Clayton Act was so weakly drawn that it added little to the government's power to enforce competition. Once the existence of listed illegal practices was determined, the courts still had to decide whether their effect was to lessen competition or to promote monopoly. As we have just observed, by 1920, about the only practice the courts would consistently consider in restraint of trade was explicit collusion among independent producers or sellers. "Reasonable" monopoly practices of huge firms on one hand and "weak" forms of collusion on the other were not subject to punishment. The useful functions of the Federal Trade Commission became the compiling of a massive amount of data helpful to economists and the elevation of the ethics of competition by acting against misbranding and misleading advertising. Not until it could take action on the basis of injury to consumers instead of on the basis of injury to a competitor would the public gain much advantage from the FTC's efforts.

Thus, the one great pre-1920 experiment in the social control of business achieved little. By the time a vigorous enforcement of the antitrust laws was undertaken late in the 1930s, it was too late to do much about the problem of bigness in industry. But by then, it was clear that a kind of competition not envisioned by the framers of the Sherman Act protected consumers. The fall in communication and transportation costs wedded regional markets into national and international markets, thereby reducing local monopoly powers.[24] The effectiveness of these new competitive sources is examined in chapter 20.

---

[23] 40 Sup. Ct. 251 U.S. 417, 295–296.

[24] See Jeremy Atack, "Industrial Structure and the Emergence of the Modern Industrial Corporation," *Explorations in Economic History* 22 (1985): 29–52.

Selected References and Suggested Readings

Aduddell, Robert M., and Louis P. Cain. "Public Policy toward the 'Greatest Trust in the World.'" *Business History Review* 55 (Summer 1981): 2.

Allen, Robert C. "The Peculiar Productivity History of American Blast Furnaces, 1840–1913." *Journal of Economic History* 37 (1977): 605–633.

Asher, Ephraim. "Industrial Efficiency and Biased Technical Change in American and British Manufacturing: The Case of Textiles in the Nineteenth Century." *Journal of Economic History* 32 (1972): 431–442.

Atack, Jeremy. "Industrial Structure and the Emergence of the Modern Industrial Corporation." *Explorations in Economic History* 22 (1985): 29–52.

Berck, Peter. "Hard Driving and Efficiency: Iron Production in 1890." *Journal of Economic History* 38 (1978): 879–900.

Bittlingmayer, George. "Did Antitrust Policy Cause the Great Merger Wave?" *Journal of Law and Economics* (April 1985): 90–91.

Cain, Louis P., and Donald G. Paterson. "Factor Biases and Technical Change in Manufacturing: The American System, 1850–1919." *Journal of Economic History* 41 (1981): 341–360.

Chandler, Alfred D., Jr. *The Visible Hand: The Managerial Revolution in American Business.* Cambridge, Mass.: Harvard University Press, 1977.

———. *Scale and Scope: The Dynamics of Industrial Capitalism.* Cambridge, Mass.: Belknap, 1990.

Chandler, Alfred D., and Louis Galambos. "The Development of Large-Scale Economic Organizations in Modern America." *Journal of Economic History* 30 (1970): 201–217.

Clark, V. S. *History of Manufactures in the United States 1607–1914,* 2 vols. Washington, D.C.: Carnegie Institution of Washington, 1928.

Feller, Irwin. "The Urban Location of United States Invention, 1860–1910." *Explorations in Economic History* 8 (1971): 284–304.

Floud, R. C. "The Adolescence of American Engineering Competition, 1860–1900." *Economic History Review* 37 (1), (February 1974).

Frederick W. Taylor project, **http://atilla.stevens-tech.edu/intro.html**.

Frickey, Edwin. *Production in the United States, 1860–1914.* Cambridge, Mass.: Harvard University Press, 1947.

Galambos, Louis. *The Public Image of Big Business in America, 1880–1940.* Baltimore: Johns Hopkins University Press, 1975.

Gallman, Robert. "Gross National Product in the United States, 1834–1909." *Studies in Income and Wealth,* vol. 30. National Bureau of Economic Research. New York: Columbia University Press, 1966.

Gallman, Robert, and Edward S. Towle. "Trends in the Structure of the American Economy Since 1840." In *The Reinterpretation of American Economic History,* eds. Robert Fogel and Stanley Engerman. New York: Harper & Row, 1971.

Hughes, Jonathan. "Industrialization: Economic Aspects." In *International Encyclopedia of the Social Sciences,* 1968 edition, ed. David Sills, vol. 7. New York: Macmillan, 1968, 252–270.

———. *Industrialization and Economic History: Theses and Conjectures.* New York: McGraw Hill, 1970.

———. *The Governmental Habit: Economic Controls from Colonial Times to the Present.* New York: Basic Books, 1977.

———. *The Vital Few: American Economic Progress and Its Protagonists.* New York: Oxford University Press, 1986.

Hurst, James Willard. *The Legitimacy of the Business Corporation in the United States, 1780–1970.* Charlottesville: University Press of Virginia, 1970.

Josephson, Matthew. *The Robber Barons: The Great American Capitalists, 1861–1901*. New York: Harcourt Brace, 1934.

Kirkland, Edward. *Industry Comes of Age: Business, Labor, and Public Policy, 1860–1897*. New York: Holt, Rinehart & Winston, 1961.

Lamoreaux, Naomi R. *The Great Merger Movement in American Business, 1895–1904*. Cambridge, England: Cambridge University Press, 1985.

———. "Entrepreneurship, Business Organization, and Economic Concentration." In *The Cambridge Economic History of the United States*, vol. II, *The Long Nineteenth Century*, eds. Stanley L. Engerman and Robert E. Gallman. New York: Cambridge University Press, 2000, 403–434.

Livesay, Harold. *Andrew Carnegie and the Rise of Big Business*. Boston: Little, Brown, 1975.

McCurdy, Charles W. "American Law and the Marketing Structure of the Large Corporation, 1875–1890." *Journal of Economic History* 38 (1978): 631–649.

McGee, John. "Predatory Price Cutting: The Standard Oil (N.J.) Case." *Journal of Law and Economics* (1958): 137–169.

Mulligan, William H., Jr. "Mechanization and Work in the American Shoe Industry: Lynn, Massachusetts, 1852–1883." *Journal of Economic History* 41 (1981): 59–63.

O'Brien, Anthony P. "Factory Size, Economies of Scale, and the Great Merger Wave of 1898–1902." *Journal of Economic History* 48 (1988): 639–649.

Porter, Glenn. *The Rise of Big Business, 1860–1910*. New York: Crowell, 1973.

Pratt, Joseph A. "The Petroleum Industry in Transition: Antitrust and the Decline of Monopoly Control in Oil." *Journal of Economic History* 40 (1980): 815–837.

Romer, Christina D. "The Prewar Business Cycle Reconsidered: New Estimates of Gross National Product, 1869–1908." *Journal of Political Economy* 97 (February 1989): 1–37.

Rosenberg, Nathan. *Technology and American Economic Growth*. New York: Harper & Row, 1972, 98.

———. "American Technology: Imported or Indigenous?" *American Economic Review* 67 (1977): 21–26.

Stocking, George W. "The Rule of Reason, Workable Competition, and the Legality of Trade Association Activities." *University of Chicago Law Review* 21 (4),(Summer 1954): 532–533.

Troesken, Werner. "Antitrust Regulation before the Sherman Act: The Break-up of the Chicago Gas Trust Company." *Explorations in Economic History* 32 (1995): 109–136.

Wright, Gavin. "The Origins of American Industrial Success, 1879–1940." *American Economic Review* 80 (1990): 651–668.

Chapter Eighteen

THE EMERGENCE OF AMERICA'S LABOR CONSCIOUSNESS

Between the Civil War and World War I, the conditions of working Americans changed dramatically. The supply of labor grew rapidly because of immigration and natural increase. The demand for labor grew even faster because of capital accumulation and technological and other productivity advances in industry, agriculture, and the service sector. Real wages rose. But unemployment and real incomes rose and fell during the recessions that punctuated the era, and the gains for unskilled workers appeared to be agonizingly slow, bringing demands from labor and from the middle class for legislation to protect and improve the lot of the common worker.

Class consciousness was never as deeply felt in the United States as in Europe. Nevertheless, in the 50 years following the Civil War, the first national unions emerged and labor slowly developed a degree of political influence. The result was legislation and court decisions that gave greater weight to "labor's perspective."

DEMOGRAPHIC CHANGE AND THE SUPPLY OF LABOR

One reason that laborers as an organized group became more important was simple arithmetic. In 1860, there were about three farmers per manufacturing worker; by 1910, the ratio was one to one. Moreover, the number of workers as a percentage of the total population was rising, from 33 to 40 percent. Table 18.1 shows this relative growth: the population grew by a factor of 2.7 between 1870 and 1920, and the labor force grew by 3.2. Immigrants, as Table 18.1 shows, added substantially to the population and even more to the labor force since immigrants tended to be concentrated in the prime working years. But the main source of growth was the natural increase of the native and immigrant populations.

Birth and Death Rates

Fertility was high by modern standards, but the trend was down, as shown in Table 18.2, continuing the trend that had begun early in the nineteenth century. Live births per 1,000 people fell by almost half over the nineteenth century, from 55 (for whites; data for blacks before 1860 are not yet available) in 1800 to 30.1 in 1900. By the turn of the century,

TABLE 18.1 Population and Labor Force (in millions), 1870–1920

YEAR	POPULATION	PERCENT INCREASE	TOTAL IMMIGRATION	LABOR FORCE	PERCENT INCREASE
1870	39.9			12.9	
1880	50.3	26	2.8	17.4	35
1890	63.1	25	5.2	23.3	34
1900	76.1	21	3.7	29.1	25
1910	92.4	21	8.8	37.5	29
1920	106.5	15	5.7	41.6	10

Source: Historical Statistics *(Washington, D.C.: Government Printing Office, 1975), Series A6, C89, and D167.*

TABLE 18.2 Birthrate and Expected Life, 1800–1990

YEAR	WHITE BIRTHRATE (per 1,000)	BLACK BIRTHRATE (per 1,000)	WHITE EXPECTATION OF LIFE AT BIRTH	BLACK EXPECTATION OF LIFE AT BIRTH
1800	55.0	na	na	na
1830	51.0	na	na	na
1850	43.3	na	38.9	na
1860	41.4	56.8	40.9	na
1870	38.3	55.2	44.1	na
1880	35.2	53.7	39.6	na
1890	31.5	48.1	45.7	na
1900	30.1	44.4	49.6	na
1910	29.2	38.5	51.9	na
1920	26.9	35.0	57.4	47.0
1930	20.6	27.5	60.8	48.5
1940	18.6	26.7	65.0	53.9
1950	23.0	33.3	69.6	60.8
1960	22.7	32.1	70.7	63.6
1970	17.4	25.1	71.7	65.2
1980	14.9	22.1	74.4	68.1
1990	15.0	23.1	76.0	70.3

Sources: Statistical Abstract of the United States *(Washington, D.C.: Government Printing Office, 1992), 65, 76; and Michael R. Haines, "Birthrate and Mortality," in* The Readers' Encyclopedia of American History, *eds. Eric Foner and John Garraty (New York: Houghton Mifflin), 104.*

Americans were increasingly viewing two children as the "normal" family.[1] This trend has continued, and in the 1990s, the birthrate is less than half that of 1900. Urbanization has been a major source of this decline because the costs of raising an additional child are much higher in the city. Also playing their part was declining infant mortality (which reduced the number of births needed to reach a desired family size), rising female employment (which increased the opportunity cost of additional children), and compulsory schooling (which lengthened the time in which children depended economically on their parents).

[1]Paul A. David and Warren C. Sanderson, "The Emergence of a Two-Child Norm among American Birth Controllers," *Population and Development Review* 13 (1987): 1–41.

Even this list of factors, however, cannot fully explain the fertility decline. Urbanization was important, but fertility dropped in rural areas as well as urban areas in the nineteenth century. Rising land prices that forced families to accumulate greater financial reserves or do with less land may be the answer. Fertility was generally lower, moreover, in the United States than in Europe (other than France), a surprising contrast if urbanization and restrictions on child labor were the crucial factors explaining the decline in fertility.[2] Meanwhile, death rates—indicated in Table 18.2 by the expectation of life at birth—began a long decline dating from the 1870s. Surprisingly, specific medical treatments were probably not a major quantitative factor until well into the twentieth century. Instead, the key factor in the first phase of mortality reduction was improved sanitation, especially better water supplies and sewage disposal.[3] America's biggest cities had been particularly unhealthful; but beginning in the 1890s, they began large-scale projects to provide piped water, filtration and chlorination of water, sewer systems, and public health administration. These improvements brought down the death rates from cholera, typhoid fever, gastrointestinal infections, and other diseases.

Immigration

Figure 18.1 traces the arrivals of immigrants in the context of economic fluctuations. Major waves began in the early 1880s and late 1890s. Between 1880 and 1920, more than 23 million immigrants came to make their homes in the United States. Their impact on labor markets was substantial. In 1920, immigrants accounted for 33 percent of railroad laborers, 22 percent of railroad foremen, 33 percent of jewelers and watchmakers, and 17 percent of policemen. More generally, immigrants accounted for 25 percent of the labor force in manufacturing, 35 percent in mining, 18 percent in transportation, and substantial shares in most other sectors.[4]

As shown in Figure 18.1, the number of immigrants rose in good times and fell in bad times. In times of rising economic activity and employment, the tug on immigrants increased tremendously; as depressions ensued and jobs disappeared, the attractiveness of American opportunity receded. Peak years of inflow coincided with or immediately preceded the onset of severe depressions. Peaks were reached in 1873, 1882, 1892, 1907, and 1914. For obvious reasons, immigration declined greatly during the World War I years as shipping lanes were cut and people went about sterner business.[5]

The work of Brinley Thomas in the 1950s clarified underlying patterns. The inflow of immigrants—coupled with foreign capital inflows—helped push the American economy in its upswings and slowed the growth phase in the countries of departure. In effect, the growth surges in the United States coincided with slow expansion phases in much of

---

[2]Michael R. Haines, "American Fertility in Transition: New Estimates of Birth Rates in the United States, 1900–1910," *Demography* 26 (1989): 137–148; and "Western Fertility in Mid-Transition: Fertility and Nuptiality in the United States and Selected Nations at the Turn of the Century," *Journal of Family History* 15 (1990): 23–48. These are advanced scholarly papers, but perusing them will give a taste of demography, an important discipline with many ties to economic history.

[3]Edward Meeker, "The Improving Health of the United States, 1850–1915," *Explorations in Economic History* 9 (1972): 353–374; Robert Higgs, "Cycles and Trends of Mortality in 18 Large American Cities, 1871–1900," *Explorations in Economic History* 16 (1979): 381–408; and Michael R. Haines, "Inequality and Childhood Mortality: A Comparison of England and Wales 1911, and the United States, 1900," *Journal of Economic History* 45 (1985): 885–912.

[4]Albert W. Niemi, Jr., *U.S. Economic History*, 2d ed. (New York: University Press of America, 1980), 262.

[5]The ratio of foreign born to the total U.S. population rose only from 13.1 in 1860 to 14.6 in 1920. This curious fact is explained by the high rate of increase in the native population, the substantial emigration during depressions, and possibly by a bias in the statistics because persons for whom place of birth was not reported were counted as native born.

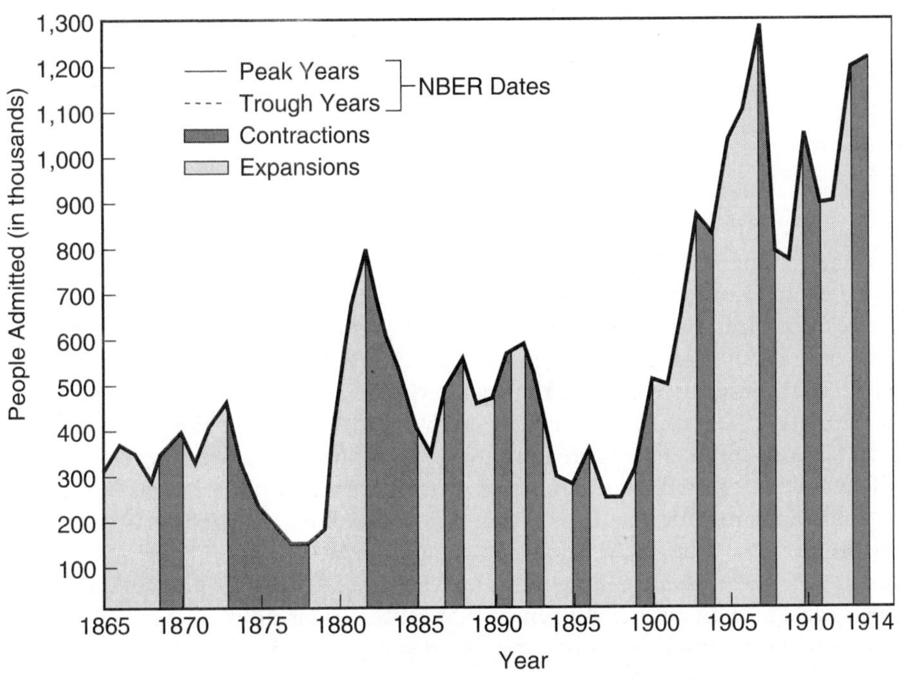

FIGURE 18.1 U.S. Immigration and Business Cycles, 1865–1914

Sources: Derived from Historical Statistics *(Washington, D.C.: Government Printing Office, 1960), Series C88; business cycle dates from A. F. Burns and W. C. Mitchell,* Measuring Business Cycles *(New York: National Bureau of Economic Research, 1947), 78.*

Europe, and growth surges in Europe coincided with slower expansion periods in the United States.

IMMIGRATION, POLITICS, AND ECONOMIC EFFECTS

Table 18.3 on page 352 shows a striking alteration in the origins of immigrants from 1820 to 1920. In the 1880s, there was a decreasing influx of people from northern and western Europe and an increasing influx from southern and eastern Europe. It is usual to speak of the immigration from Great Britain, Ireland, Germany, and the Scandinavian countries as the "old" immigration, as distinguished from the "new" immigration comprised of Hungarians, Poles, Russians, Serbs, Greeks, and Italians. In the 1870s, more than 80 percent of the immigrants came to America from northern and western Europe; by 1910, 80 percent of the total was arriving each year from southern and eastern Europe. The year 1896 is reckoned to mark the point at which a majority of those arriving annually were of the "new" nationalities.

Much was once made of the presumed economic significance of this geographic shift in the sources of immigration. In cultural characteristics, the Swedes and Germans of the old immigration were not unlike the Anglo-Saxons who colonized America. Slovaks and Magyars, on the other hand, along with Russians, Italians, and other people from the new areas, had unfamiliar customs, practiced strange religions, and spoke odd languages—and they looked different. To many native-born citizens of turn-of-the-century America, the new immigrants seemed inferior in skills, in cultural background, and in potential. The prejudice often went undisguised. Each immigrant group in its period of peak arrivals was deemed inferior: the "shanty Irish" and "dumb Swedes" of a previous generation were scorned as much as the "crazy Bohunks" who came later. Twentieth-century Americans seized on the assumed "inferiority" of southern and eastern Europeans as an argument for excluding them.

TABLE 18.3 Origins of Immigrants, 1820–1920 (in percent)

	NORTHERN AND WESTERN EUROPE	CENTRAL, EASTERN, AND SOUTHERN EUROPE	OTHER
1821–1890	82%	8%	10%
1891–1920	25	64	11

Source: Historical Statistics *(Washington, D.C.: Government Printing Office, 1960), Series C88-114.*

The new immigrants supplanted the old for two reasons. As economic opportunity grew in England, Germany, and Scandinavia, America became less attractive to the nationals of these countries. Also important was the rapid improvement in transportation during the 1860s and 1870s.The steamship put the Mediterranean much closer to America, and railroads from the interior of eastern Europe to Mediterranean ports gave mobility to southeastern Europeans. Vast differences existed between the economic opportunities offered an American laborer—even an unskilled one—and those available to the European peasant at home. The suction created by the removal of transportation barriers was irresistible; railroads, steamship companies, and American mill and factory managers hastened the movement by promotional advertising and financial assistance.

We can only guess whether immigrants arriving just after 1880 were less skilled and educated than earlier immigrants had been. It may be that their different political and cultural histories made their assimilation into American democracy and into the labor force more difficult. Nevertheless, the economic effects of the old and the new immigrations were roughly the same. New arrivals, whatever their national origins, usually filled the ranks of unskilled labor. Slovaks, Poles, and Italians replaced Irish, Germans, and Swedes in the coal fields and steel mills and, like their predecessors, took the lowest positions in the social strata.

Foreign Workers and American Labor

What was the impact of these foreigners on the American economy? The great majority of immigrants entered the labor markets of New England, the Middle Atlantic states, and the states of Ohio, Michigan, and Illinois, where they concentrated in the great industrial cities. Working for low wages in crowded factories and sweatshops and living in unsanitary tenements, immigrants complicated such urban social problems as slums, crime and delinquency, and municipal corruption.

For the most part, the difficulties of predominantly European immigrants did not result from discrimination in hiring or in wages. The relative earnings of native and foreign-born workers were approximately equal after adjusting for differences in schooling, experience, skills, and similar factors. Unskilled immigrants, in other words, earned about the same as unskilled American-born workers, and skilled immigrants about the same as skilled American-born workers.[6]

American business profited greatly from an inexhaustible supply of unskilled and semiskilled workers. The steamship companies that brought these immigrants to America and the railroads that took them to their destinations were the first to benefit. Manufacturing and mining companies profited most of all: Immigration enabled them to expand their operations to supply growing markets. The influx of immigrants also meant more customers for American retailers, more buyers of cheap manufactured goods, and a greatly enlarged market for housing. American consumers benefited from the increased supplies of goods and services.

[6]Martha Norby Frauendorf, "Relative Earnings of Native and Foreign-Born Women," *Explorations in Economic History* 15 (1978): 211–218; Peter J. Hill, "Relative Skill and Income Levels of Native and Foreign-Born Workers in the United States," *Explorations in Economic History* 12 (1975): 47–60; and Peter R. Shergold, "Relative Skill and Income Levels of Native and Foreign-Born Workers: A Re-examination," *Explorations in Economic History* 13 (1976): 451–461.

New Views

Contemporary Issues and Lessons from History

In the 1980s more than 7 million immigrants entered the United States; in the 1990s nearly 8 million more arrived, most of them from Mexico and Latin America. They are the latest waves of people into a nation that is most certainly a land of immigrants. Less than 1 percent of the U.S. population is Native American today. Current citizens complain about new immigrants, their oddities, their differences from established residents, and, most often, their supposed inferiorities. Many pundits and critics argue that these new immigrants, legal and illegal, have not made the kinds of advances that past European immigrants made because of their resistance to assimilation (e.g. demands for bilingual education) frequent return trips to their native countries, and discrimination against them. The first and third of these arguments are perennial to the issue, no different than those expressed against the Irish (1840s and 50s), the Italians, and others of southern European origin (1880s-1910s).

The perception that Mexican and other Latin immigrants have assimilated into society and into the economy less effectively than did Europeans should not rest on opinion. This claim is a testable proposition, and as we assert in Economic Reasoning Proposition 5, evidence is needed to prove or refute a hypothesis. Using census data from the recent century, James Smith of the Rand Corporation has found that male immigrants from Mexico born between 1905 and 1910 had an average of 4.3 years of formal schooling. Their sons had 9.4 years, and their grandsons more than 12.0. European immigrants in the same period started with higher levels of formal schooling, nearly 9.0 years, with their grandsons having nearly 13.5 years. Salaries for Latino male immigrants around 1900 were about 55 percent of the salaries of native white males, but their grandsons comparable earnings were nearly 90 percent of that of white males. In most respects, Latino immigrants have shared the same pattern of experiences with earlier immigrants, whether Irish, Italian, or eastern/southern European.

The rapidly increasing supply of unskilled labor, however, kept wage levels for great numbers of workers from rising as fast as they would have otherwise. Therefore, some established American workers who could not escape from the unskilled ranks were adversely affected. See Economic Insight 18.1 on page 354. But supervisory jobs and skilled jobs were given to native white Americans, and the number of better jobs available increased as the mass of unskilled new immigrants grew. As William Sandstrom has shown, by the turn of the century, U.S. firms methodically recruited and trained existing employees for more advanced and skilled positions. Promotion ladders were common, especially in large firms.[7] Moreover, the wages of craftsmen engaged in making equipment to be used by the unskilled and semi-skilled masses doubtlessly rose. Native-born American workers gained as consumers of the lower-priced manufactured products made possible by cheap labor.

Perspective 18.1 on page 355 discusses campaigns to restrict immigration, especially of the Chinese.

[7]William Sundstrom, "Internal Labor Markets before World War I: On the Job Training and Employee Promotion," *Explorations in Economic History* 25 (1988): 424–445.

Economic Insight 18.1

Immigration in Terms of Supply and Demand

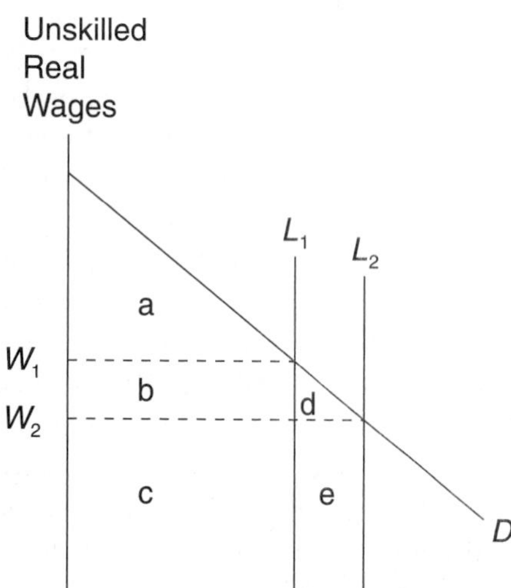

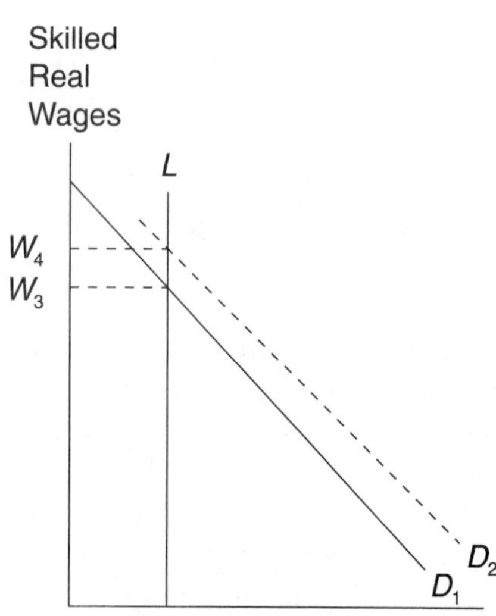

Supply and demand models help to clarify the effects of immigration on the economy. Figures A and B display models of the market for unskilled and skilled labor in the late nineteenth century. In Figure A, we assume that all immigrants are unskilled and when immigration shifts the supply of labor to the right (L_1 to L_2), the real wage of unskilled labor (in the absence of any effect on demand) falls from W_1 to W_2. Area b is the income (the change in wage rate multiplied by the amount of labor) lost by the existing supply of workers. This amount is transferred to other factors of production (owners of land and capital and skilled labor), and their share is further augmented by d as total production increases by e + d.

Is there no way to escape from the logic that immigration reduced the real wage of existing American workers? Figure B shows one possibility. If skilled labor was a complement to unskilled labor, then an influx of unskilled immigrants could actually raise the demand for skilled labor (D_1 to D_2). As drawn in Figure B, this effect raises the real wage of skilled labor to W_4, in contrast to the reduction in real wages of unskilled labor produced by immigration. An opposite wage effect occurs, however, when unskilled labor is a substitute for skilled labor. Probably most workers, skilled and unskilled, opposed immigration because they presumed that skilled and unskilled workers were substitutes in production.

GAINS FOR WORKERS IN THE POSTBELLUM PERIOD

Hours and Wages

Despite the rapid growth in the supply of labor, workers made considerable progress between the end of the Civil War and the end of World War I. In 1860, the average number of hours worked per day in nonagricultural employment was close to 10.8. By 1890, the

Perspective 18.1

Restricting Immigration

From the Civil War to the end of World War I, there was a constant struggle between the proponents and adversaries of immigration restriction. In 1864, when labor was in short supply because of the war, Congress passed the Contract Labor Law at the behest of the manufacturing interests. The new law authorized contracts made abroad to import foreign workers and permitted the establishment of the American Emigrant Company to act as an agent for American businesses. The Contract Labor Law had the practical effect of bringing in laborers whose status could scarcely be distinguished from that of indentured servants, their cost of passage being repaid out of their earnings in the United States. The law failed, however, and was repealed in 1868. Few Europeans volunteered to work on contract; ocean passages had become much less costly, and many who did sign contracts left their employment early. Wage earners fought effectively for the repeal of the Contract Labor Law and continued to struggle for additional restrictions on immigration.

The first to feel the effects of the campaign for immigration restriction were the Chinese. Their influence on the labor market was localized on the West Coast, where nearly 300,000 Chinese had arrived between 1850 and 1882. Facing long-distance passage fares four times their annual wage, most of those laborers arrived in debt. Six large Chinese owned and Chinese-controlled companies held title to most of the debts and used or rented out the immigrants' labor, taking systematically from the workers wages to ensure repayment. These immigrants typically worked in gangs (e.g., railroad building) under a foreman who oversaw repayment. Even if workers left the gangs, the six companies had agreements with the steamboat companies not to sell a return ticket to any migrant without a certificate from the companies declaring him free of debt. Threats of boycotts by the companies enforced the compliance of the steamship owners who handled the immigrants' passages coming and going. It was just short of actual indentureship, but no formal contracts existed or were exchanged. These informal but carefully controlled arrangements were legal, a peculiar system combining freedom and coercion that worked.[8]

Other laborers, especially in California, feared and despised this cheap labor competition, and the Workingman's Party (also known as the "sand lotters") urged the exclusion of all Asians. With the Chinese Exclusion Act of 1882, the first victory of the restrictionists was won, and this unique system of bringing in Chinese workers stopped. Successful in their first major effort, the restrictionists pressed on to make illegal the immigration of anyone who could neither read nor write English. Acts requiring literacy tests passed Congress, but President Grover Cleveland, and later President William Howard Taft, vetoed them. For many years, labor had to be content with whittling away at the principle of unrestricted immigration. In succeeding laws, further restrictions were imposed on the immigration of the physically and mentally ill, vagrants, and anarchists. In 1917, Congress finally passed a literacy requirement—this time over President Woodrow Wilson's veto—and permanent bars to the free flow of migrants into the United States were erected in 1920.

[8]For a fascinating account of this labor market, see Patricia Cloud and David W. Galenson, "Chinese Immigration and Contract Labor in the Late Nineteenth Century," *Explorations in Economic History* 24 (1987): 22–42.

Densely packed ships brought millions of workers to America, often under contracts that specified no wage increases during the first year of employment.

average workday in manufacturing was 10.0 hours, and people normally worked a six-day week.[9] There were, of course, deviations from the average. Skilled craftsmen in the building trades worked a 10.0-hour day in 1860 and probably no more than an average of 9.5 hours per day by 1890. On the other hand, in the textile mills outside New England, 12- to 14-hour days were still common in 1890, and workers in steel milling, paper manufacturing, and brewing stayed on the job 12 hours a day, seven days a week.

By 1910, the standard work week was 55 hours in all industries; by 1920, it had dropped to about 50. A widespread standard week consisted of five 9-hour days and 4 to 5 hours on Saturday morning. Again, the skilled trades fared better, having achieved a 40-hour week by 1920. Unskilled laborers, on the other hand, were still working 9-hour days, six days a week, and the 12-hour day persisted in the metal-processing industries.

Both daily wages and annual earnings in manufacturing increased by about 50 percent between 1860 and 1890. Prices rose so rapidly during the Civil War that real wages fell drastically between 1860 and 1865. But from then on, the cost of living declined, not steadily but persistently, eventually returning the dollar to its prewar purchasing power. So real wages and earnings also increased by about 50 percent between 1860 and 1890.[10] Daily wages in manufacturing rose from just over $1.00 in 1860 to $1.50 in 1890, and annual earnings increased from slightly less than $300 in 1860 to more than $425 in 1890. In the

[9]Clarence D. Long, *Wages and Earnings in the United States, 1860–1890* (Princeton, N. J.: Princeton University Press, 1960), especially 3–12 and 109–118.
[10]Data on average wages here and in the remainder of the paragraph are from Long, 1960, 109.

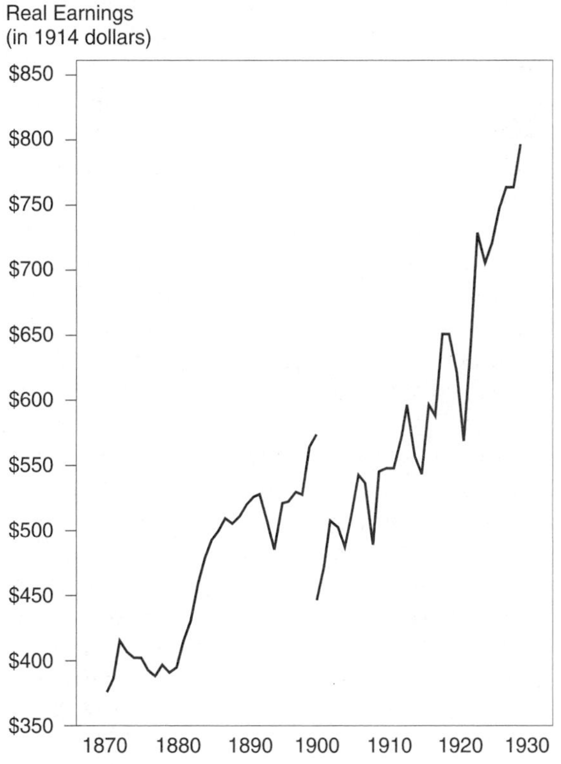

FIGURE 18.2 Real Earnings of Nonfarm Employees

Source: Stanley Lebergott, Manpower in Economic Growth: The American Record Since 1800 *(New York: McGraw-Hill, 1964), 524.*

building trades, both real wages and real earnings rose a little higher, perhaps by 60 percent. If we take into account the shortening of the work week by about 7 percent, the net increase in hourly money or real wages over the 30-year period was about 60 percent, or 1.6 percent compounded annually.

It should be noted that wage differentials among industries were great in both 1860 and 1890: the highest-wage industries paid more than twice as much as the lowest. These differentials reflected differences in skills and differences in the terms and conditions of work. Soft-coal miners, for example, earned a higher hourly wage than other industrial workers to compensate for the danger and disagreeable working conditions in the mines.[11]

In the decades after 1890, real wages continued to march upward. The real earnings of manufacturing workers advanced 37 percent (an annual compound rate of 1.3 percent) between 1890 and 1914.[12] Further gains were made during the war years, so the overall annual growth rate between 1891 and 1920 was only slightly less than that recorded during the preceding 30 years.

Figure 18.2 summarizes the growth of average real incomes of nonfarm workers—propelled by growing productivity in industry, agriculture, and the service sector—after the Civil War. The series beginning in 1870 assumes that the laborer worked a full year; the series beginning in 1900 takes unemployment into account. For that reason, the latter series shows the effects of the business cycle more clearly. But even the pre-1900 series is sharply

[11]Price V. Fishback, *Soft Coal, Hard Choices* (New York: Oxford University Press, 1992), chapter 6.

[12]Albert Rees, *Real Wages in Manufacturing, 1890–1914* (Princeton, N. J.: Princeton University Press, 1961), 3–5.

marked by the severe depressions of the 1870s and the 1890s. Keep in mind that these averages for all nonfarm workers conceal the difficulties of unskilled laborers competing in markets constantly augmented by fresh immigrants.

Women and Children

The role of women in society and in the labor force changed considerably over the period. Near mid-century, state after state passed laws giving women clearer title to property, the right to engage in business, secure rights to their earnings, and property rights to patents and intellectual property. As Zorina Kahn's research on patents and commercial activities of nineteenth-century women shows, American women were highly responsive to legal and institutional changes that elicited their creativity and commercial and market participation.[13] By 1880, 2.5 million women, constituting 15 percent of the workforce, were at work outside the home. By 1900, 5.3 million women, constituting 18 percent of the workforce, were at work outside the home. By 1920, 8.5 million women, or one-fifth of the gainfully employed, were involved in some pursuit other than homemaking.

Sales work in city stores and professional work, particularly teaching, became attractive alternatives to domestic service. The typewriter, which was introduced shortly after the Civil War, ushered in an office revolution that took hold in the 1890s. By the turn of the century, the typewriter and other office equipment had created a major field of employment for young women. As Elyce Rotella has shown, clerical workers as a percentage of the nonagricultural workforce grew from 1.2 to 9.2 percent between 1870 and 1920, while women as a percentage of all clerical workers grew from 2.5 to 49.2 percent over these 50 years.[14]

The office workforce, however, remained segregated by sex. Women were confined to routine clerical jobs, while personal secretaries and other decision-making jobs remained a male province. (The new clerical jobs were also segregated by race: black women were rarely hired.) Segregation of the office workforce by sex maintained the norm of the industrial workforce. Milliners (hatmakers) were generally women, whereas meatpackers were generally men; in cotton textiles, an industry in which about 50 percent of the workforce was female, spoolers (who transferred thread from the bobbins on which it was wound) were almost all women. The segregation of the labor force had some roots in economic differences between men and women: The labor force attachment of women was often less than for men, so some firms that did not want to invest as much in training workers who would soon leave found it convenient to treat women and men as separate classes, even though they made errors by doing so. But the main sources of sex and race segregation were powerful social norms that dictated the work opportunities for women and blacks.

These social norms, however, were being gradually eroded by economic forces and political opposition. Typing and sales work, for example, even as they confined women to subsectors of the labor force, changed traditional thinking about the role of women. World War I, moreover, further shook the ideologies that underlay segregated hiring: urged to employ women as replacements for men lost to the armed services, employers discovered that women performed a wide range of occupations as satisfactorily as men and that in some jobs their performance was often superior. It would take another half century, however, for the ideologies that segregated the workplace to begin to crumble on a major scale.

Statutes prescribing maximum hours and minimum wages for women were common by 1920. These were motivated in part by growing concerns about the physical surroundings in

---

[13]Zorina Kahn, "Married Women's Property Laws and Female Commercial Activity: Evidence from United States Patent Records 1790," *Journal of Economic History* 56 (1996): 356–388.

[14]Elyce J. Rotella, "The Transformation of the American Office: Changes in Employment and Technology," *Journal of Economic History* 41 (1981): 52.

In 1886, limited demand and financial difficulties forced Philo Remington to sell his typewriter company. By 1890, the boom was on, remaking the office and bringing large numbers of women into the paid labor force.

which women worked and the effects on their health and their ability to care for their children. The statutes were also supported by trade union leaders, who hoped that limiting the hours women could work would limit competition with male workers and might limit, in some cases, the hours of male workers whose jobs were complementary with those of female workers. Indeed, empirical studies reveal that wage and hour restrictions for women served to limit the hours worked by both male and female workers. The effect on women's employment, moreover, was negligible: few employers decided not to hire women simply because their hours were regulated.[15]

In the pre–World War I years, concerns about the employment of children also increased sharply. In 1880, 1 million boys and girls between the ages of 10 and 15 were "gainfully occupied," and the number rose to a high of nearly two million by 1910. In 1910, one-fifth of all youngsters between 10 and 15 had jobs, and they constituted 5.2 percent of the workforce. But in 1920, the total number employed in this market was again less than 1 million; children made up only 2.6 percent of the workforce, and only one-twelfth of the 10- to 15-year age group was at work. True, the proportion of children who worked was always small, except on the farm, and it was probably lower in the United States than in other industrial countries. But the conditions in which children worked were sometimes unsafe and harsh by modern standards.

---

[15]Claudia Goldin, *Understanding the Gender Gap: An Economic History of American Women* (New York: Oxford University Press, 1990), 195–199.

When publicized, bad working conditions like these among very young slate pickers in Pennsylvania at the turn of the century won middle-class sympathy for labor's cause.

The employment of children decreased primarily because various advocates, including religious groups and trade unions, worked to obtain protective legislation at the state level. Massachusetts had a long history of ineffective child labor legislation, and the first stringent state regulation did not appear until 1903, when Illinois passed a law limiting child labor to an eight-hour day. State laws limiting hours of work, requiring minimum wages, and setting age limits were common by 1920, but additional protection was needed in certain states, such as in the cotton belt and some industrial states in the mid-South and East. In these states especially, the fight against child labor was waged indirectly through increases in compulsory education ages. Federal legislation that outlawed child labor was passed in 1916 but the Supreme Court struck it down on the grounds that the federal government had no power to regulate intrastate commerce. Child labor would not be effectively controlled by the federal government until the 1930s, when the Supreme Court reversed itself.

UNIONS, EMPLOYERS, AND CONFLICT, 1860–1914

Following the Civil War, local unions stagnated and then grew in number until 1872, when memberships totaled nearly 300,000 nationally. Defeats at the polls in 1872 reduced union strength, but a new national union, the Knights of Labor, reached the unprecedented total of 750,000 members in 1885. When a general strike in May 1886 against the railroads failed to achieve an eight-hour day, members lost faith, and membership slipped to 100,000 by 1890. By then, the American Federation of Labor (AFL) had captured the leadership of

These pickets are helping to dramatize the case for labor's legislative agenda.

most union workers. The AFL was an amalgamation of two federations: the Federation of Organized Trades and Labor Unions (printers, glassworkers, iron and steel workers, welders, and cigar makers) and the American Federation of Labor (composed of several national unions spun off from the Knights). Under Samuel Gompers, the AFL's first president, membership rose to 1.5 million in 1905.

The AFL's one unifying principle was to control job opportunities and job conditions in each craft. This principle implied an organizational unit composed of workers who performed the same job and who, in the absence of collective action, would have competed with one another to their economic detriment. Thus, the craft union could act quickly to exert economic pressure on the employer.

It also merits emphasis that labor's organizational gains were not won without a serious and prolonged struggle, which was still unresolved by 1920. Strikes, though frequent even in the late nineteenth century, were not sanctioned legally nor were they always instigated by unions. Sometimes strikes erupted as simply the spontaneous responses of unorganized workers, and on certain occasions, successful strikes resulted in the formation of a union. In any case, employers, supported by middle-class opinion and by government authorities, took the position that their rights and the very institution of private property were threatened by the growing strength of the unions.

The most violent conflicts between management and labor occurred in the last quarter of the century. During the depressed years of the mid-1870s, much blood was shed when strikes were broken by force. The climax of this series of conflicts occurred in 1877, a zenith of turmoil that had begun with railroad strikes in Pittsburgh and had spread throughout the country. In the anthracite regions of Pennsylvania, a secret society of Irish American miners known as the "Molly Maguires" (named for the leader of an Irish antilandlord organization) was blamed for numerous murders and other outrages. What they did and didn't do is still a matter of heated dispute. Their power was finally broken after a

Labor leadership eventually became concentrated in the hands of Samuel Gompers, who sat on the first executive council of the American Federation of Labor in 1881.

trial that led to the hanging of 20 men on the basis of testimony provided by a Pinkerton agent who claimed to have infiltrated the organization.[16]

The brutality was not all on one side. Often it was the laborer who had to fend off the physical assaults of paid thugs, state militiamen, and federal troops. Three incidents, purposely spaced over time, it would seem, to do the maximum damage to labor's cause stand out as symbols of the most severe disputes.

The infamous Haymarket affair on May 4, 1886, was the tragic climax of efforts of the Knights of Labor to secure a general strike of workers in the Chicago area. A bomb thrown at police officers attempting to break up a mass meeting at Haymarket Square resulted in several deaths. The authorities and the press demanded action. Seven men, who were probably innocent, were executed for murder. Although the injustice of the punishment aroused great resentment among labor's sympathizers, antilabor agitators used the incident as a horrible example of what radicals and anarchists would do to undermine American institutions by violence.

---

[16]Recommended readings on the relative absence of radicalism in the American labor movement include Gerald Friedman, "Strike Success and Union Ideology: The United States and France, 1880–1914," *Journal of Economic History* 48 (1988): 1–25; Sean Wilentz, "Against Exceptionalism: Class Consciousness and the American Labor Movement," *International Labor and Working Class History* 26 (Fall 1984): 1–24; Werner Sombart, *Why Is There No Socialism in America?* (1906; 1st English ed., White Plains, 1976); Selig Perlman, *A Theory of the Labor Movement* (New York: 1928); and Seymour Martin Lipset, "Radicalism or Reformism: The Sources of Working Class Protest," *American Political Science Review* 77 (March 1983): 1–18.

Simultaneous strikes by various Chicago unions were met by strong police action, resulting in the Haymarket Riot of May 4, 1886.

Six years later, just as antilabor feeling was subsiding, the management of the Carnegie Homestead Works at Pittsburgh decided to oust the Amalgamated Association of Iron and Steel Workers, which was trying to organize the Homestead laborers. A strike was called, ostensibly because the company refused to come to an agreement on wage matters. Henry Frick, a close associate of Carnegie, brought in 300 Pinkerton detectives to disperse the strikers and maintain order. Turning the tables, the striking mob won a heated battle with the detectives, capturing several and injuring many severely. The state militia was called out to restore order, and the union suffered a defeat that set the organization of labor in steel mills back several decades.

The adverse publicity received by the Homestead episode was exceeded only by that of the Pullman strike of 1894. Although the Pullman strike was led by the mild mannered Eugene V. Debs, who had not yet embraced socialist doctrines, the strife was attributed to the un-American ideology of other radical leaders. Rioting spread over the entire Chicago area, and before peace was restored—this time by federal troops sent on pretext of protecting the U.S. mails—scores of people had been killed or injured. Again the seriousness of the labor problem became a matter for widespread concern and the basis of much immoderate opposition to labor's cause. On the other hand, the Pullman strike served as a warning to conservative union leaders that violence would only disrupt unions and damage them in the public regard. Furthermore, the dispatch with which Debs and other labor leaders were jailed on contempt proceedings for disobeying a court injunction against inciting union members to strike was a sobering blow. Any long-term strategy would have to include efforts both to pacify voters and to strengthen labor's position in the courts. Pre-1920 successes along both lines were limited, to say the least.

Beginning in 1902, employers changed their tactics. They began a serious drive to sell Americans on the benefits—to employers, workers, and the public—of the open shop. To further their propaganda, several organizations were formed. The most prominent were the National Association of Manufacturers and the American Antiboycott Association, both of which were assisted materially by employers' trade associations. So effective were the employers' efforts that even conservative labor leaders experienced increasing pressure from their constituents to fight back.

In response, Samuel Gompers and others favored a counteroffensive against the employers through education and propaganda. Affiliating with the National Civic Federation—an association that included wealthy eastern capitalists, corporate officers, editors, professionals, and labor representatives—AFL leaders sought to elicit a more favorable attitude from the electorate. The National Civic Federation maintained a division for the mediation and conciliation of disputes, tried to secure wider acceptance of collective-bargaining agreements, and preached the doctrine that greater labor responsibility would mean fewer work stoppages and a better livelihood for all. How much good the National Civic Federation did is difficult to say. It doubtlessly served in part to offset the organized efforts of employers, but the alliance may have lulled job-conscious unionists into ultraconservatism at a time when more aggressive policies were called for. At any rate, the core of employer opposition remained almost as solid as ever, particularly among industrialists of the Midwest.

Union activity in the United States, however, especially in comparison with labor efforts in Europe, was largely apolitical, at least at the national level. No national labor party emerged as a political entity, and unions were seldom united in their stand on national issues. Instead, the main confrontation lay outside the political arena and was predominantly between employers and employees. For that reason, perhaps, strikes were longer in the United States than in Europe, even without the sanction of law.[17]

Unionization and the Courts

By the end of the nineteenth century, the right of labor unions to exist had been established; yet the right of employers to force employees to enter into antiunion contracts was upheld to the very end of this period. In this way, many employers maintained nonunion status as a condition of employment. For example, in the case of *Coppage v. Kansas* (1912), the Court overturned a state law passed to outlaw antiunion contracts—called at the time by workers "yellow-dog contracts." Coppage, a railroad employee, had been fired for refusing to withdraw from a union. Because his withdrawal would have cost him $1,500 in insurance benefits, the Kansas Supreme Court held that the statute protecting him prevented coercion and was valid. But the U.S. Supreme Court reversed this decision, holding that an employer had a constitutional right to require an antiunion contract from employees; a statute contravening this right, the Court held, violated the Fourteenth Amendment in that it abridged the employer's freedom of contract.

As late as 1917, the U.S. Supreme Court decided that antiunion contracts, whether oral or written, could be protected by injunction, a court order. The Hitchman Coal and Coke Company, after winning a strike, had hired back miners on the condition that they could not be members of the United Mine Workers while in the company's employ. Later, union organizers tried to convince the miners to promise that after a certain time had elapsed, they would again join the union. In a U.S. district court, the company asked for and obtained an injunction stopping further efforts to organize. The Supreme Court affirmed the decision, holding that, even though the miners had not yet joined the union, they were being induced by organizers to break a contract with the employer and that the employer was entitled to injunctive protection.

State and federal governments typically stood firmly on the side of business against labor unions. Calling out troops to break strikes was considered a legitimate use of police power. Such actions were condoned by the state and federal courts, which proved to be invaluable allies of management in the struggle to suppress collective action on the part of the laboring class. The injunction was especially effective as a device for restraining union action. Employers could go to court to have labor leaders enjoined from calling or continuing a strike. Failure to comply with an injunction meant jail for the offenders, and "government by injunction" proved to be one of the strongest weapons in the antiunion arsenal.

---

[17]For an analysis of these and other historical features of strikes in the United States, see P.K. Edwards, *Strikes in the United States 1881–1974* (New York: St. Martin's, 1981).

TABLE 18.4 Union Membership, Selected Years

YEAR	TOTAL UNION MEMBERSHIP (thousands)	TOTAL MEMBERSHIP AS A PERCENT OF TOTAL LABOR FORCE	TOTAL MEMBERSHIP AS A PERCENT OF NONFARM LABOR FORCE
1860	5	0.1%	n.a.
1870	300	2.4	4.6%
1880	50	0.3	0.5
1886	1,010	4.8	8.2
1890	325	1.4	2.3
1900	791	2.8	4.7
1905	1,918	5.9	9.3
1910	2,116	5.8	8.6
1917	2,976	7.4	10.0
1920	5,034	12.2	16.7
1929	3,625	7.6	9.7

Sources: Stanley Lebergott, "The American Labor Force," in American Economic Growth: An Economist's History of the United States, *ed. Lance E. Davis et al. (New York: Harper & Row, 1963), 220; and* Historical Statistics *(Washington, D.C.: Government Printing Office, 1975), Series D4, D7, D8, D12, D17, D940, D943.*

LABOR'S GAINS AND THE UNIONS

In 1920, the American factory worker could look back on 66 years of substantial improvement. Real wages had risen, hours were shorter, and laborers, children, and (to some extent) women were protected by law. The fundamental ideas of social security were being more generally discussed, and clear-cut legislative victories had been won to reduce the hardships caused by industrial accidents. In addition, urban dwellers of all kinds saw vast improvements that brought about sharp long-term reductions in mortality.

How many of these gains should be attributed to the labor movement? Clearly, the unions' ability to control the supply of labor and, thus, the conditions and terms of work, was limited throughout the period from the Civil War to the Great Depression by the inability of the labor movement, despite valiant efforts, to organize more than a small fraction of the labor force. The crucial figures are given in Table 18.4. At the nineteenth-century peak in 1886, unions had organized about 8 percent of the nonfarm labor force. Even at the peak after World War I, unions could claim only 17 percent of the nonfarm labor force. Hence, unions could do little directly to raise the average level of real wages or improve the typical conditions of work. Unions could raise wages in unionized sectors; but by restricting the supply of labor in those sectors, they had the undesired effect of increasing the supply of labor and lowering wages in nonunionized sectors.

On the eve of World War I, however, unions could lay claim to some other important gains for their members. As direct owner supervision declined and management became impersonal, the power of foremen indulging their personal whims increased. Unions helped offset and reduce arbitrariness in hiring and firing and other harsh treatment by supervising personnel. In addition, some particularly strong unions gained substantial wage differentials for their members. For example, a substantial differential was obtained in the bituminous (soft) coal industry, where union workers received wages some 40 percent higher than those of nonunion workers.[18] For most unskilled work, though, the wages of union members were only slightly higher than those of nonunion workers, perhaps a few percentage points.

[18] H. G. Lewis, *Unionism and Relative Wages in the United States* (Chicago: University of Chicago Press, 1963).

Finally, trade unions had become an important voice for labor in the political system. Labor Day as a national holiday was first celebrated in 1894; in 1913, cabinet level status was given to the Department of Labor. One aspect of the growing political power of labor was the change in rules governing compensation to workers for injuries received on the job. Historically, an employer who was sued by an injured worker had three legal defenses: (1) that the worker had known and accepted the risk, (2) that the worker had not been reasonably careful, and (3) that the worker had been injured because of the negligence of a fellow worker.[19] Between 1910 and 1930, labor won changes in state laws that eliminated these defenses, clearly an instance of the fourth Economic Reasoning Proposition: Rules matter. Finally, insurance programs were eventually established; employers and employees contributed to a common pool that compensated injured workers. The result was that injured workers received more compensation. But, as Price Fishback has pointed out, the side effects sometimes differed from what was intended. It was hoped that putting the burden on employers would make for a safer workplace, and often it did. The rate of fatal accidents in bituminous coal mining increased, however, because workers had a smaller incentive to avoid accidents and because employers found it cheaper to pay the additional claims than to try to reduce accident rates.

The power of organized labor's support for favorable legislation was destined to grow and, as we shall see, flower during the Great Depression. For labor as a whole, however, it is fair to conclude that labor's nineteenth-century progress owed more to economic growth and rising productivity than to the unions' strength.

---

[19]These defenses were less effective in the southern states. In fact, southern slave law helped speed the evolution of law for non-slave accident victims because, under slavery, compensation to slave owners for injured slaves rented by others was well established in southern courts. See Jenny B. Wahl, "The Bondsman's Burden: An Economic Analysis of the Jurisprudence of Slaves and Common Carriers," *The Journal of Economic History*, 53 (1993): 495–526.

Selected References and Suggested Readings

"Between a Rock and a Hard Place: A History of American Sweatshops, 1820–Present." A virtual exhibit created by the Smithsonian Institute. **http://americanhistory.si.edu/sweatshops**.

Bernstein, Irving. *The Lean Years: A History of the American Worker, 1920–1933*. Boston: Houghton Mifflin, 1960.

Brody, David. *Steelworkers in America*. Cambridge, Mass.: Harvard University Press, 1960.

———. *Labor in Crisis: The Steel Strike of 1919*. Philadelphia: Lippincott, 1965.

Carlson, Leonard A. "Labor Supply, the Acquisition of Skills and the Location of Southern Textile Mills, 1880–1900." *Journal of Economic History* 41 (1981): 65–71.

Commons, John R., et al. *History of Labour in the United States*. New York: Kelly, 1921.

Dubofsky, Melvyn. *Industrialism and the American Worker, 1865–1920*. Arlington Heights, Ill.: Harlan Davidson, 1975.

Dunlevy, James A., and Henry A. Gemery. "Economic Opportunity and the Responses of the 'Old' and 'New' Migrants to the United States." *Journal of Economic History* 38 (1978): 901–917.

Easterlin, Richard. "Economic-Demographic Interactions and Long Swings in Economic Growth." *American Economic Review* (1966): 1063–1104.

———. *Population, Labor Force, and Long Swings in Economic Growth: The American Experience*. New York: Columbia University Press, 1968.

———. "Population." In *American Economic Growth: An Economist's History of the United States*, ed. Lance E. Davis et al. New York: Harper & Row, 1972.

———. "Population Issues in American Economic History: A Survey and Critique." In *Research in Economic History*, ed. Robert Gallman. Greenwich, Conn.: JAI, 1977, supplement.

Erickson, Charlotte. *American Industry and the European Immigrant 1860–1885*. New York: Russell & Russell, 1967.

Ermisch, John, and Thomas Weiss. "The Impact of the Rural Market on the Growth of the Urban Workforce, U.S., 1870–1900." *Explorations in Economic History* 11 (Winter 1973–1974): 137–154.

Fishback, Price V. "Workplace Safety during the Progressive Era: Fatal Accidents in Bituminous Coal Mining." *Explorations in Economic History* 23 (1986): 269–298.

———. *Soft Coal, Hard Choices: The Economic Welfare of Bituminous Coal Miners, 1890–1930*. New York: Oxford University Press, 1992.

Frauendorf, Martha Norby. "Relative Earnings of Native and Foreign-Born Women." *Explorations in Economic History* 15 (1978): 211–220.

Galloway, Lowell, and Richard Vedder. "Emigration from the United Kingdom to the United States, 1860–1913." *Journal of Economic History* 31 (1971): 885–897.

———. "Population Transfers and the Post-Bellum Adjustments to Economic Dislocation, 1870–1920." *Journal of Economic History* 40 (1980): 143–150.

Galloway, Lowell, Richard Vedder, and Vishwa Shukla. "The Distribution of the Immigrant Population in the United States: An Economic Analysis." *Explorations in Economic History* 11 (1974): 213–226.

Goldin, Claudia. "The Work and Wages of Single Women, 1870–1920." *Journal of Economic History* 40 (1980): 81–88.

———. *Understanding the Gender Gap: An Economic History of American Women*. New York: Oxford University Press, 1990.

Gompers, Samuel. Papers at **http://www.inform.umd.edu/EdRes/Colleges/ARHU/Depts/History/Gompers/web1.html**.

Grob, Gerald. *Workers and Utopia: A Study of the Ideological Conflict in the American Labor Movement, 1865–1900*. New York: Quadrangle Books, 1969.

Harber, Samuel. *Efficiency and Uplift: Scientific Management in the Progressive Era, 1890–1920*. Chicago: University of Chicago Press, 1964.

Higgs, Robert. "Race, Skills and Earnings: American Immigrants in 1909." *Journal of Economic History* 31 (1971): 420–428.

———. "Mortality and Rural America, 1870–1920." *Explorations in Economic History* 10 (1973): 177–196.

———. "Landless by Law: Japanese Immigrants in California Agriculture to 1941." *Journal of Economic History* 38 (1978): 205–225.

———. "Cycles and Trends of Mortality in 18 Large American Cities, 1871–1900." *Explorations in Economic History* 16 (1979): 381–408.

Hill, Peter. "Relative Skill and Income Levels of Native and Foreign-Born Workers in the United States." *Explorations in Economic History* 12 (1975): 47–60.

Jenks, Jeremiah, and Jeff Lauck. *The Immigration Problem*. New York: Funk & Wagnalls, 1926.

Jerome, Harry. *Migration and Business Cycles*. New York: National Bureau of Economic Research, 1926.

Kirk, Gordon W., and Carolyn J. Kirk. "The Immigrant, Economic Opportunity, and Type of Settlement in Nineteenth-Century America." *Journal of Economic History* 38 (1978): 226–234.

Kuznets, Simon. "Notes of the Pattern of U.S. Economic Growth." In *The Reinterpretation of American Economic History*, eds. Robert Fogel and Stanley Engerman. New York: Harper & Row, 1971.

———. "Two Centuries of Economic Growth: Reflections on U.S. Experience." *American Economic Review* 67 (1), (1977): 1–14.

Kuznets, Simon, and Ernest Rubin. *Immigration and the Foreign Born.* New York: National Bureau of Economic Research, 1954.

Lebergott, Stanley. "The American Labor Force." In *American Economic Growth*, ed. Lance E. Davis et al. New York: Harper & Row, 1972.

Livesay, Harold. *Samuel Gompers and Organized Labor in America.* Boston: Little, Brown, 1978.

McGouldrick, Paul F., and Michael B. Tannen. "Did American Manufacturers Discriminate against Immigrants before 1914?" *Journal of Economic History* 37 (1977): 723–746.

Margo, Robert A. "The Labor Force in the Nineteenth Century." In *The Cambridge Economic History of the United States*, vol. II, *The Long Nineteenth Century*, eds. Stanley L. Engerman and Robert E. Gallman. New York: Cambridge University Press, 2000, 207–243.

Meeker, Edward. "The Improving Health of the United States, 1850–1914." *Explorations in Economic History* 9 (1972): 353–374.

Neal, Larry, and Paul Uselding. "Immigration, A Neglected Source of U.S. Economic Growth, 1790–1913." *Oxford Economic Papers* 24 (1), 2d series, (March 1972).

Nelson, Daniel. *Managers and Workers: the Origins of the New Factory System in the United States, 1880–1920.* Madison: University of Wisconsin Press, 1975.

———. *Frederick W. Taylor and Scientific Management.* Madison: University of Wisconsin Press, 1980.

Nevins, Allan, and Frank Hill. *Ford: The Times, the Men, and the Company.* New York: Scribner's, 1954.

Niemi, Albert W. "The Role of Immigration in United States Commodity Production, 1869–1929." *Social Science Quarterly* 52 (1), (June 1971).

Rosenbloom, Joshua L. "Was There a National Labor Market at the end of the Nineteenth Century? New Evidence on Earnings in Manufacturing." *Journal of Economic History* 56 (1996): 626–656.

———. "Strikebreaking and the Labor Market in the United States, 1881–1894." *Journal of Economic History* 58 (1998): 183–205.

———. "The Extent of the Labor Market in the United States, 1870–1914." *Social Science History* 22 (1998): 287–318.

Rotella, Elyce J. *From Home to Office.* Ann Arbor, Mich.: UMI Research Press, 1981.

———. "The Transformation of the American Office: Changes in Employment and Technology." *Journal of Economic History* 41 (1981): 51–57.

Taylor, Philip. *The Distant Magnet: European Emigration to the United States.* New York: Harper & Row, 1971.

Thomas, Brinley. *Migration and Economic Growth.* Cambridge, England: Cambridge University Press, 1954.

Wahl, Jenny B. "The Bondsman's Burden: An Economic Analysis of the Jurisprudence of Slaves and Common Carriers." *The Journal of Economic History* 53 (3) (1993): 495–526.

Chapter Nineteen

Money, Prices, and Finance in the Postbellum Era

The 50-year span between the Civil War and World War I was one of continuous, intense public controversy over the American monetary system. Two issues—deflation and banking panics—overshadowed all others and produced repeated attempts to reform the monetary system.

Deflation began after the Civil War and persisted with brief interruptions for three decades. Debtors suffered from the protracted deflation, and farmers were particularly hard hit. As one popular folksong from the 1880s put it: "The farmer is the man, lives on credit till the fall, with interest rates so high, it's a wonder he don't die, for the mortgage man's the one who gets it all."[1] *Farmers and other debtors were vocal in their opposition to deflation and supported a number of inflationary schemes. Many Americans had learned lessons, however, they would not soon forget, from the high inflations of Revolutionary times and the Civil War. Leaders in politics and finance insisted on "sound money." They were generally successful in resisting inflationary changes in the monetary system.*

This was the era of the classical gold standard. It was almost an article of faith, at least in certain circles, that a nation's currency should be convertible into a fixed weight of gold. The leading industrial nations, the United States included, followed this policy. The benefits were clear: fixed exchange rates and confidence in the long-run value of money. But there were also costs: It was difficult to adjust the money supply in response to adverse trends in prices or income.

The deflation and rise in standards of living for most Americans were punctuated by financial crises in which banks closed, factories and railroads went bankrupt, and millions lost their jobs. The depressions of the mid-1870s and mid-1890s were especially severe. In April 1894, "Coxey's Army" of the unemployed arrived in Washington to demand federal relief. It portended a different future for the nation, one in which the government provided direct aid to the unemployed. Prices began rising after the depression of the mid-1890s, but another bank panic occurred in 1907.

[1]Pete Seeger, *American Favorite Ballads* (New York: Oak, 1961), 57.

Although the problems in the financial system were easy to identify, reaching agreement on solutions was far harder. Special interests used every means at hand to forestall change or force it in directions favorable to themselves. Silver producers, for example, jumped on the antideflation bandwagon and helped direct its course. Lobbying by country bankers shielded a system of thousands of isolated local banks, perpetuating a system that was vulnerable to banking panics.

These legal restrictions had an important impact on the growth of industrial firms hungry for financial capital. Investment bankers, essentially brokerage houses specializing in stocks and bonds, emerged to fill the void and take positions of dominance in the world of U.S. finance. This situation was quite different from the one in England, where large banking conglomerates were allowed and grew large enough to meet most of the financial needs of the industrializing nation.

Despite the conflicts among interest groups, by the end of 1913, the United States once again had a central bank based on arrangements different from those of earlier versions. These were codified in the Federal Reserve Act signed by President Woodrow Wilson. As the Great Depression of the 1930s proved, however, the Federal Reserve System was not a foolproof answer to the nation's hard-earned lessons about deflation and panics.

NEW FORMS OF CURRENCY

Before the Civil War, the amount of money in circulation was determined by flows of specie (money in the form of coin) into and out of the country through foreign trade and by flows from U.S. mines. By 1862, gold was flowing out of the country so fast that the government and banks were forced to suspend gold specie payments. Silver, which had been undervalued at the mint ever since the Currency Act of 1834, had virtually no circulation.[2]

Because sufficient revenues to wage the war were not obtained from sales of U.S. Treasury bonds (at least at interest rates the government was willing to pay), the Treasury in 1862 issued a new fiat currency, U.S. notes, nicknamed "greenbacks." In addition, in 1863 the National Bank Act was passed, creating a new set of banking institutions (national banks) and another new money (national bank notes). This avalanche of new paper money is shown in Figure 19.1, and the results are reflected in Figure 19.2 on page 372, which shows the upward zoom of prices during the war years. Collectively, greenbacks, national bank notes, and silver and gold specie or their certificates, plus small subsidiary coins, made up the currency. As shown in Figure 19.1, however, greenbacks supplied the monetary increases that sent prices skyrocketing during the Civil War years. Later, gold supplied increases in hand-to-hand money. These types of currency provided the base of the money supply. As shown in Figure 19.3 on page 372, however, most of the increase in the total money supply was created by the growth of bank deposits—savings and checking deposits created by loans. The new currency, however, was critical to the total because it constituted the reserves of the banking system. The growth of these reserves allowed the growth of bank deposits and the total money supply.

The greenbacks solved two problems: the immediate problem of providing additional revenue for the government during the war and the longer-run problem of providing a currency of uniform value throughout the country. In many parts of the country, especially in the West, where the state banks were having difficulties, "Lincoln Green" was very popular. Why then did Congress create the National Banking system? Conservative Republicans worried that making the greenbacks permanent would create a temptation for weak

[2]The mint set a price at which it would convert silver into money. If silver could be sold for a higher price on the bullion market, then the mint was said to *undervalue silver*. See chapter 12 for more discussion.

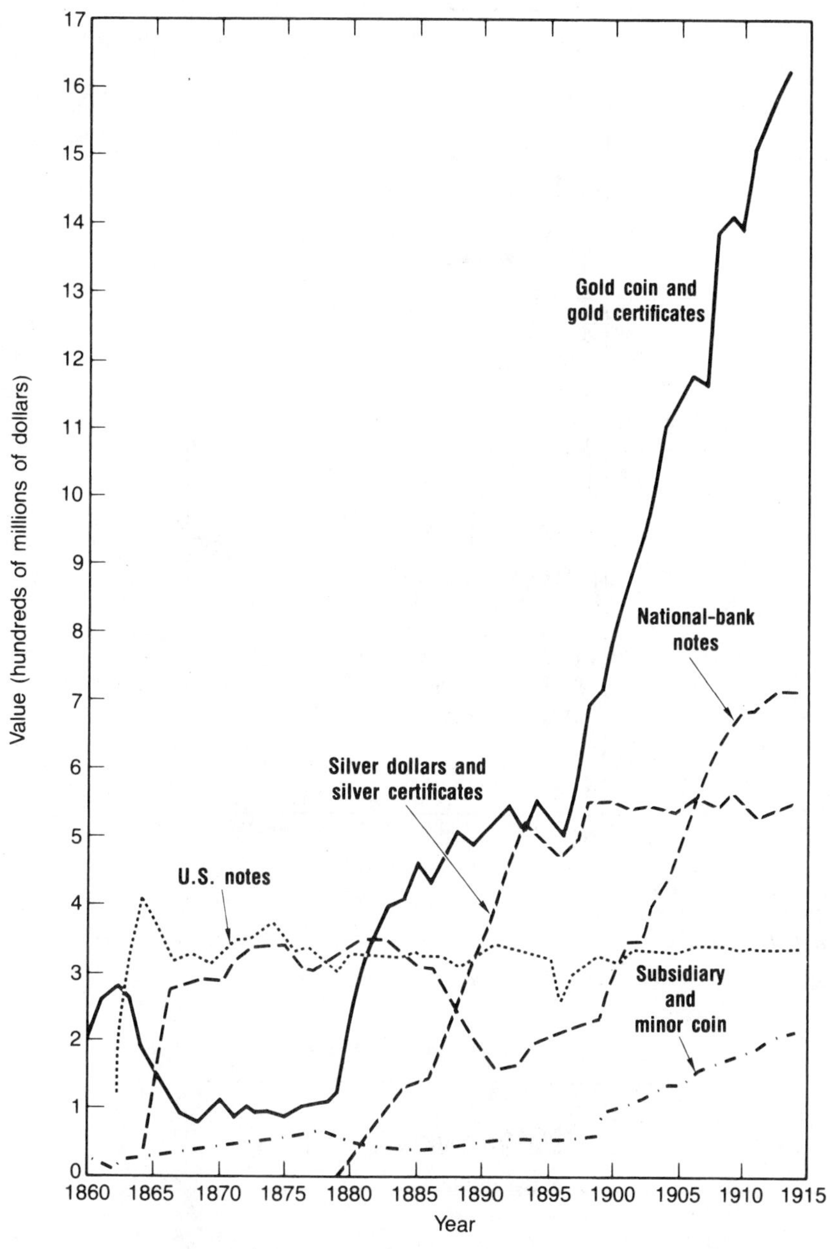

FIGURE 19.1 Forms and Values of Currency in the United States, 1860–1915
From the late 1870s to the early 1890s, substantial additions were made to the nation's monetary stocks of gold and silver, but it was not enough to prevent deflation. After 1895, however, the increase in the stock of gold became even more rapid, and deflation became inflation.

Source: Board of Governors of the Federal Reserve System.

administrations to issue too many notes. Hence, they created a new institution whose notes would be backed up by government bonds and would have uniform value throughout the country, thus solving the same problems that the greenback had solved. However, the issue of national bank notes would be in private hands, thus eliminating the danger of overissue.

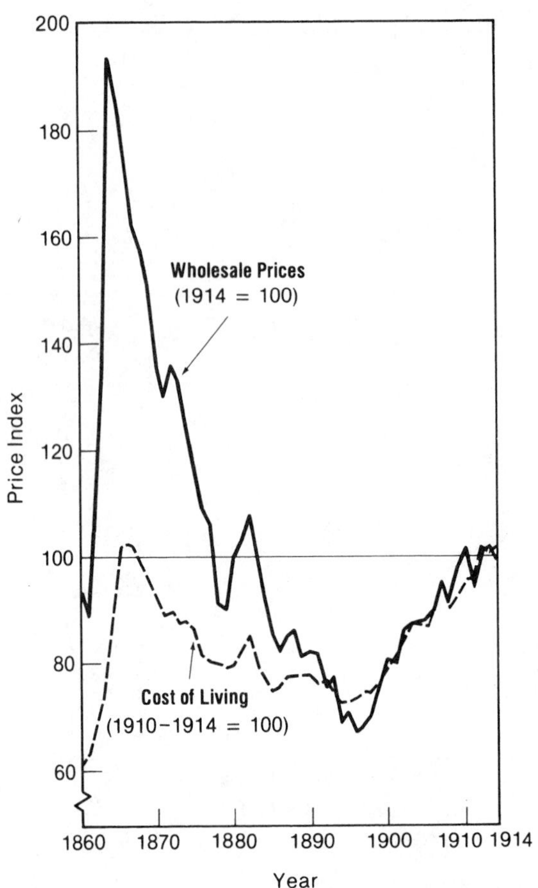

FIGURE 19.2 Prices, 1860–1914
Prices generally fell from the end of the Civil War until the 1890s and then rose until WWI.

Source: Historical Statistics *(Washington, D.C.: Government Printing Office, 1960), Series E1, 101, 157.*

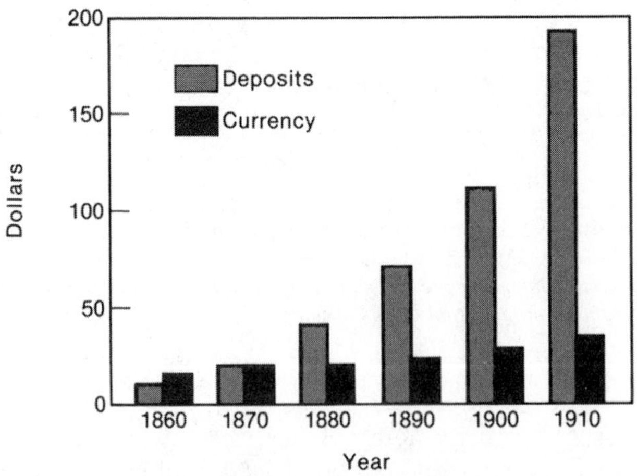

FIGURE 19.3 Per Capita Deposits and Currency in Circulation

Source: Data from Historical Statistics of the United States, 1789–1945 *(Washington, D.C.: Government Printing Office, 1947), 25, 262, 263, and 274.*

To secure its note issue, each national bank was required to buy U.S. government bonds equal to one-third (later one-quarter) of the dollar amount of its paid-in capital stock, with the provision that no bank would have to buy more than $50,000 worth of bonds. Each bank was to deposit its bonds with the U.S. Treasurer and was to receive notes, engraved in a standard design but with the name of the issuing bank on the obverse side, in the amount of 90 percent of the par or market value (whichever was lower) of the bonds deposited. A national bank could have any amount of government bonds in its portfolio, but the amount of its notes outstanding could not exceed its capital in dollar amount.

A Dual Banking System

Although the National Bank Act of 1863 created a new type of bank, it did not eliminate the older institutions chartered by the states. To make the national banks appear more sound than state banks, stiff legal reserve requirements were mandated, and double liability was imposed on the stock of national banks.

Because the early pace of conversion from state to national status was slow, a tax of 2 percent was levied against state bank notes in June 1864, and this was raised to 10 percent in March 1865. Then the pace of conversion soared. A majority of the state banks immediately shifted to federal jurisdiction; in 1866, fewer than 300 state banks remained.

At that point it might well have been assumed that the state banking system would soon wither and die, an assumption that proved to be spectacularly wrong. It was no longer necessary for a bank to issue notes to succeed; it could do quite well issuing only deposits. Often, moreover, the rules governing the operations of state banks were less onerous than those governing national banks. The revival in state banking began in about 1870. By 1914, as Table 19.1 shows, there were more state banks than national banks, and the state banks' total assets were larger. The United States ended up with a *dual banking system*. Bankers weighed the advantages of membership in the national system (prestige that

TABLE 19.1 Commercial Banks in the United States, 1860–1914

YEAR	NUMBER OF STATE BANKS[a]	ASSETS OF STATE BANKS[a] (millions of dollars)	NUMBER OF NATIONAL BANKS	ASSETS OF NATIONAL BANKS (millions of dollars)
1860	1,562	$ 1,000	0	$ 0
1863	1,466	1,192	66	17
1864	1,089	721	467	252
1865	349	231	1,294	1,127
1866	297	197	1,634	1,476
1867	272	180	1,636	1,494
1868	247	164	1,640	1,572
1869	259	171	1,619	1,564
1870	325	215	1,612	1,566
1880	1,279	1,364	2,076	2,036
1890	4,717	3,296	3,484	3,062
1900	9,322	6,444	3,731	4,944
1910	18,013	13,030	7,138	9,892
1914	20,346	15,872	7,518	11,477

[a]*Includes mutual savings banks.*

Source: U.S. Bureau of the Census, Historical Statistics of the United States, Colonial Times to 1957 *(Washington, D.C.: Government Printing Office, 1960), series X20, X21, X42, X43, X64, and X65.*

attracted depositors and the right to issue notes) against the costs (stricter regulations) and chose the charter that promised the most profits. Legislators and regulators also had to choose. Should they make stricter rules with respect to reserves, capital, and so on? This would protect depositors and increase the prestige of their system, but it also would encourage bankers to choose a different charter. (As Economic Reasoning Proposition 2 reminds us, choices must be made by weighing costs and benefits.)

GOLD, GREENBACKS, OR BIMETALLISM?

Between the Civil War and the end of the nineteenth century, Americans engaged in a long-running debate over their monetary system. Some people favored retention of the greenback, the paper money of the Civil War. Some favored a gold standard in which the dollar would be convertible into a fixed amount of gold. Others favored a bimetallic system in which the dollar would be convertible into a fixed amount of either gold or silver. Which system would solve the problems of deflation and banking instability?

Returning to the Gold Standard after the Civil War

During the Civil War, as noted, the United States was on the greenback standard. Greenbacks, which were legal tender, were not backed by either gold or silver. Indeed, as Americans liked to joke, they were "backed" only by the green ink on the back of the notes. Many people wanted to return to the situation that had existed before the war when the United States was on the gold standard and every dollar could be converted into 23.22 grains (a little less than 1/20th of an ounce) of pure gold. This was easier said than done, however.

Prices in the United States had risen substantially during the war relative to prices in Britain. In fact, as shown in columns (1) and (2) of Table 19.2, prices had risen 76 percent in the United States between 1861 and 1865 compared with only 5 percent in Britain. At the same time, the price of a British pound had risen, as shown in column (3), from $4.77 to $7.69, about 61 percent. This increase offset much of the attractiveness of British goods. Suppose the U.S. Treasury in 1865 decided to make the dollar convertible into gold at the prewar rate? This decision would have reestablished the prewar exchange rate or "prewar parity" of about $4.85 per British £ because $4.85 could be converted into an amount of gold that could be converted into £ at the Bank of England. This exchange rate would cause a rush to convert dollars into gold and the gold into pounds to buy the relatively cheaper British goods. The Treasury would soon find its stock of gold exhausted, and the United States would find that its gold coins were being exported.

Prices in the United States evidently had to come down before the United States could successfully resume the exchange of gold for greenbacks. Many Democrats, along with members of radical groups such as the Greenback Party, argued that returning to gold was not worth the economic pain that was sure to result. Debtors would suffer during the deflation, and working people would suffer from unemployment.

Republicans, who held the upper hand politically, argued, however, that resumption was necessary for several reasons. First, it was only fair that creditors, especially those who had lent to the government, be paid in gold. Bond prices had remained strong during the war, and, it was said, this was because bondholders had received an implicit promise that they would be repaid in gold.[3] Second, to leave the monetary base tied permanently to paper money would be dangerous because the government could not be trusted with this power. Third, and perhaps most important, returning to the prewar gold parity was necessary to maintain the credibility of the United States abroad and access to foreign capital markets, especially London.

---

[3]This policy was confirmed by the Public Credit Act of 1869.

TABLE 19.2 Returning to the Gold Standard

YEAR	(1) U.S. PRICES (GDP Deflator)	(2) BRITISH PRICES (GDP Deflater)	(3) PRICE IN U.S. DOLLARS OF A BRITISH POUND
1861 Beginning of the Civil War	100	100	$4.77
1865 End of the Civil War	176	105	7.69
1873 The Crime of 1873	129	113	5.55
1879 Resumption	104	96	4.85

Sources: (1) Louis Johnston and Samuel H. Williamson, "The Annual Real and Nominal GDP for the United States, 1789–2002," Economic History Services, March 2003 at http://www.eh.net/hmit/gdp; (2) Lawrence H. Officer, "The Annual Real and Nominal GDP for the United Kingdom, 1086–2000," Economic History Services, June 2003, at http://www.eh.net/hmit/ukgdp, and (3) Lawrence H. Officer, "Exchange Rate between the United States Dollar and the British Pound, 1791–2000," Economic History Services, 2001, at http://www.eh.net/hmit/exchangerates/pound.php.

Treasury officials had recourse to two courses of action over the price level:

1. The price level could be forced down rather quickly by contracting the supply of paper money. This could be done by running a surplus and burning up the greenbacks as they came in.
2. A slower, less painful decline in prices could be achieved by holding the money supply constant and allowing the growth of the economy to bring about a gradual decline in prices.[4]

The first alternative, a severe monetary contraction, was initiated by Hugh McCulloch, Secretary of the Treasury during the Andrew Johnson administration. Congress approved this strategy in December 1865 by passing of the Contraction Act. But the deflationary medicine was too bitter, and Congress ended contraction in February 1868. President Grant's Secretary of the Treasury, George S. Boutwell, followed a much easier policy: a general easing of the money markets rather than a tightening of them.[5] After Boutwell's resignation in 1873, Assistant Secretary William Richardson pursued a still more passive policy. The idea was that the price level would fall as the country "grew up" to its currency. See Economic Insight 19.1 on page 376.

After the Democrats won control of Congress in the election of 1874, lame-duck Republicans hurriedly passed an act providing for a return to gold payments in four years. Continued deflation, as shown in the last row of Table 19.2, restored (approximately) the

[4]Other alternatives included devaluation of metal dollars, abandoning the specie standard, and simply hoping and praying for a fortuitous increase in the supply of the money metals. See Richard H. Timberlake Jr., "Ideological Factors in Specie Resumption and Treasury Policy," *Journal of Economic History* 24 (1964). See also James K. Kindahl, "Economic Factors in Specie Resumption: The United States, 1865–1879," *Journal of Political Economy* 69 (February 1961): 30–48.

[5]It was Boutwell who broke the dramatic corner on gold attempted by James Fisk and Jay Gould by selling $4 million of the money metal in the "Gold Room" of the New York Stock Exchange. See Larry Wimmer, "The Gold Crisis of 1869: Stabilizing or Destabilizing Speculation under Floating Exchange Rates," *Explorations in Economic History* 12 (1975): 105–122.

Economic Insight 19.1

The Quantity Theory of Money

The quantity theory of money can be expressed by the following equation:

$$M = kPy$$

M stands for money (greenbacks, bank deposits, and so on); k for the proportion of income held as money, usually assumed to be fairly stable; P for the price level; and y for real output. The question during the greenback era was how to lower P to bring it into line with other countries. One policy was to lower M by the necessary amount. The alternative was to hold M constant and allow the increase in y to gradually lower P, letting the "country grow up to the currency."

When gold fluctuated wildly in 1869, The Gold Room of the New York Stock Exchange was the nerve center of speculation. In its center, a bronze Cupid sprayed water quietly; on the dais, the secretary of the room had to cup his ears to hear and record transactions.

The changing face of the American dollar—it reflected the search for a sound banking system and a stable price level.

1861 relationship between U.S. and British prices, and made it possible to resume conversion of greenbacks into gold on the appointed day. For a technical reason to be discussed presently, the United States was not finally and legally committed to a gold standard and would not be for another 21 years. Nevertheless, between 1879 and 1900, the government did, in fact, maintain parity of all forms of money with gold, and, during these years, America was on a de facto gold standard.

The Crime of '73

Large denomination silver coins had gone out of circulation in the 1890s. During the Civil War and for several years afterward, even small denomination silver coins had gone out of circulation, having been replaced at first by ungummed postage stamps and later by fractional currency—paper notes issued by the government in denominations of 5, 10, 25, and 50 cents. It is not surprising, then, that when Congress sought to simplify the coinage in 1873, the silver dollar was omitted from the list of coins to be minted. Some farseeing officials feared an increase in the supply of silver that would flood the mint, increasing the money supply, raising prices, and thus delaying resumption. Most of the Congress took little notice of the omission at the time because at the mint ratio of approximately 16 to 1, silver was worth more on the market than at the mint. Scarcely three years later, the failure to include the silver dollar in the act of 1873 began a furor that was to last for a quarter century.[6]

The reason for the subsequent agitation over the "demonetization" of silver lay in the fact that the price of silver began falling in international markets. The increasing output of western silver mines in the United States and a shift of the bimetallic countries of western Europe to the gold standard had led to a growing surplus of silver. When the market value of the silver contained in a dollar actually fell below a dollar, silver producers took silver to the mint for coinage. To their dismay, they discovered that the government would take only as much silver as the Treasury needed for small subsidiary coins. The cry from the silver producers was horrendous.

A relatively small group such as the silver producers would not appear to have much power. But during the 1870s and 1880s, a number of western states were being admitted to the Union, each having two U.S. senators to represent their small populations, and silver producers concentrated in these states acquired political representation out of all proportion to their numbers. Opponents of deflation joined the silver producers in a clamor for the free and unlimited coinage of silver at the old mint ratio of 16 to 1. Silver advocates knew that at such a ratio, silver would be brought to the mint in great quantities and that the monetary reserves of the country, the total money supply, and the general price level would rise.

The opposition's cry that gold would be driven out of circulation meant nothing to the advocates of free silver except relief to the unemployed and lighter burdens for oppressed debtors. To the supporters of the free coinage of silver, the act that had demonetized silver became the "Crime of '73."

Ultimately, Congress passed a compromise between the positions of the "sound-money" and free-coinage forces. The first of several major silver bills was the Bland-Allison Act of 1878. This law provided for the coinage of silver in limited amounts. The Secretary of the Treasury was directed to purchase not less than $2 million and not more than $4 million worth of silver each month at the current market price. The conservative secretaries in office during the next 12 years purchased only the minimum amount of silver, but by 1890, the Treasury's monetary silver (not counting subsidiary coins) amounted to almost $380 million.

The silver question was by no means settled. In 1878, the average market value of the silver contained in a dollar was just over 89¢. For the next 12 years, silver prices, despite the purchases, consistently fell. Neither the producers of silver nor the debtors who wanted inflation were appeased. A new bill, the Sherman Silver Purchase Law of 1890, was carefully prepared to avoid President Benjamin Harrison's veto. The Secretary of the Treasury was directed to make a monthly purchase, at the market price, of 4.5 million ounces of silver. To pay for this bullion, he was to issue a new type of paper money to be known as Treasury notes, which were to be redeemable in either gold or silver at his discretion. At the silver prices prevailing in 1890, the new law authorized the purchase of

[6]Inevitably, some critics of the "Crime of 1873" charged that Congress had been corrupted by foreign bankers. There was nothing to it, although some of the officials drafting the legislation may have been trying to protect a future commitment to gold.

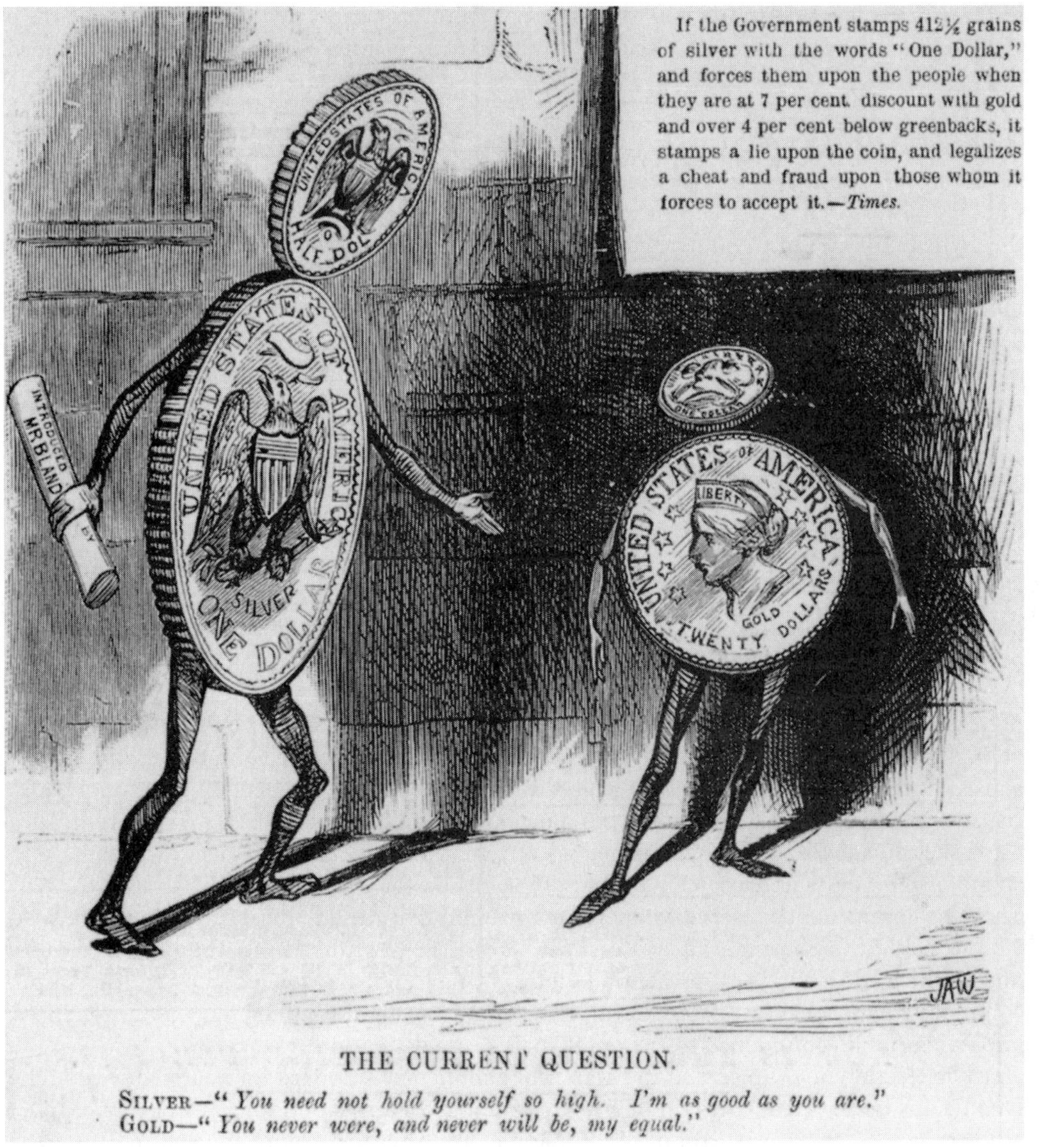

Friends of silver saw in its monetization relief from depression and persistent grief and agony if gold continued to reign as the sole monetary metal in America.

almost double the monthly amount of silver taken in under the previous law. Silver supplies kept expanding so rapidly that its market price resumed further sharp declines almost immediately.

Within three years, the dollar amount of silver being purchased was little more than it had been under the old act. In 1893, at the insistence of Democratic president Grover Cleveland—a "sound-money" man at odds with his party on this issue—the Sherman Act was repealed. President Cleveland believed that the act had undermined confidence in the dollar and produced a financial panic. In more than three years of purchasing under this law, more than $150 million of the Treasury notes of 1890 were issued; overall, between 1878 and 1893 (as shown in Figure 19.1), $500 million was added to the currency by silver purchases. This was a victory of sorts for the silver forces. But the Treasury's silver purchases were insufficient to prevent silver prices from falling, and the general price level continued its deflationary spiral (as shown in Figure 19.2 on page 372). Economic Insight 19.2 discusses the tendency of interest rates to reflect inflation and deflation.

The Commitment to the Gold Standard

As Figure 19.2 shows, prices continued to fall from resumption of gold payment in 1879 to the mid-1890s. This was true not only in the United States but also in other countries on the gold standard. Only countries on the silver standard experienced rising prices.

Why did prices fall? The basic problem was that the demand for money (and ultimately for gold, which was the base of the monetary system) was growing faster than the supply. The rapid increase in economic activity, growing financial sophistication, and the addition of more countries to the gold standard all increased the demand for gold. Meanwhile, the supply, although growing at a good rate by historical standards, could not keep pace.

Although the silver acts of 1878 and 1890 made silver certificates redeemable in either gold or silver, in practice, Treasury authorities redeemed them in gold if it were demanded. After 1879, Treasury secretaries and the public came to believe that a minimum gold reserve of $100 million was necessary to back up the paper circulation. Just when the Treasury notes of 1890 were authorized, the government's gold reserve began declining toward the $100 million mark as the public presented Treasury notes and greenbacks for payment in gold. By early 1893, the gold drain had become serious, and the gold reserve actually dipped below $100 million toward the middle of the year.

Several times during the next three years it appeared certain that the de facto gold standard would have to be abandoned. Two kinds of drains—"external" (foreign) and "internal" (domestic)—plagued the Treasury from 1891 to 1896. Recall that in the middle 1890s, conservatives considered going off the gold standard equivalent to declaring national bankruptcy. The difficulty was that when the danger of abandoning gold became apparent, people rushed to acquire gold, thus making it even more likely that the Treasury would have to abandon the gold standard. Chiefly by selling bonds for gold, the administration replenished the government's reserve whenever it appeared that the standard was about to be lost. The repeal of the Sherman Silver Purchase Law of 1893 reduced the number of Treasury notes, which the public was presenting along with greenbacks, for redemption. Increasing commodity exports at last brought an influx of gold from abroad in the summer of 1896, improving public confidence to the point that the gold standard was saved.

The election of 1896 settled the matter of a monetary standard for nearly 40 years. The Democrats, under the leadership of William Jennings Bryan, stood for free coinage of silver at a ratio of 16 to 1—even though the market ratio was then more than 30 to 1. At the Democratic national convention, Bryan inspired the inflationists and won the party's nomination with his famous "Cross of Gold" speech, which ended with this stirring call to arms:

> Having behind us the producing masses of this nation and the world, supported by the commercial interests, the laboring interests and the toilers everywhere, we will answer their demand for a gold standard by saying to them: You shall not press down upon the brow of labor this crown of thorns, you shall not crucify mankind upon a cross of gold.[7]

The Republicans, with William McKinley as their candidate, stood solidly for the gold standard.[8] The West and the South supported Bryan; the North and the East supported

---

[7]Speech is available at http://www.tntech.edu/history/crosgold.html.

[8]McKinley did, however, promise to call a conference to consider an international bimetallic standard, a promise he honored.

Economic Insight 19.2

The Fisher Effect

As debtors, farmers would benefit from inflation, but perhaps not by as much as they hoped. Farm mortgages, particularly on the frontier, were for short durations, often five years or less. If a mortgage was renewed after silver inflation was expected, lenders would demand and get higher interest rates. American economist Irving Fisher published a detailed study of the relationship between price level changes and interest rates in 1894 in response to the debate over silver. He found that interest rates did go up after inflation and down after deflation, but with a long lag. In his honor, the tendency of interest rates to reflect inflation is known as the "Fisher effect." It can be expressed by the following equation:

$$i = r + p$$

where i is the market rate of interest, r is the real rate of interest, and p is the rate of price change. Critics of the silverites maintained that an increase in p would produce an increase only in i, leaving r unchanged.

McKinley. In the East, industrial employers brought every possible pressure, legitimate or not, to bear on employee voters. One genuine issue was the tariff. Bryan, like many of his supporters in the farm states, opposed a high tariff, but workers may have been persuaded that the tariff protected jobs. In any event, Bryan did not draw the great urban vote, as

William Jennings Bryan on the political stump. Bryan was more than just a political leader; he also had a lively awareness of the need for economic and political reform. Although he was defeated on the money issue, Bryan's monetary prescriptions had a solid New Deal ring.

Franklin Roosevelt was to do 36 years later, and when well-to-do farmers in the older agricultural states deserted Bryan, the cause was lost.[9]

The Republican victory of 1896 was not followed immediately by legislation ending the controversy because free-silver advocates still held a majority in Congress. The return of prosperity, encouraged by new supplies of gold, however, made Congress receptive to definitive gold legislation. The new supplies of gold, although partly the result of the high real price for gold (the price paid by the mint relative to prices in general), were largely unanticipated. New gold fields were opened in many areas of the world, including the immensely rich gold fields of South Africa, and a new method for processing gold through the use of cyanide was developed. Ironically, the increase in the supply of gold accomplished the goal of the silverites: Expansion of the money supply and inflation. Figure 19.1 clearly shows the rapid increase in monetary gold after 1896.

Under the Gold Standard Act of 1900, the dollar was defined solely in terms of gold, and all other forms of money were to be convertible into gold. The Secretary of the Treasury was directed to maintain a gold reserve of $150 million, which was not to be drawn on to meet current government expenses. To prevent a recurrence of the difficulties of the 1890s, a provision was made to keep redeemed silver certificates and greenbacks in the Treasury during times of stress for borrowing to meet deficits that might occur from time to time. The United States had at last committed itself by law to the gold standard.

Who was right, Bryan and the silverites or McKinley and the "gold bugs"? Economist Milton Friedman has provided the most convincing answer. He argues that eliminating the silver dollar in 1873 was a mistake that produced an unnecessary deflation, but that by Bryan's time it was probably too late to do much about it.[10] Friedman and Anna J. Schwartz have also pointed out that a firm commitment to either standard would have been better than the long, drawn-out battle that took place.[11] The lessons to be drawn from this unique experience with deflation are discussed further in the accompanying New View 19.1.

The International Gold Standard

The years between 1896 and World War I were the heyday of the gold standard. As data in Figure 19.2 indicates, prices rose at a moderate rate, about 2 percent per year. International exchange rates among the industrial countries were fixed because most were on the gold standard. Indeed, it could well be said that there was really only one international currency, gold; it simply had a different name in each country. Fixed exchange rates and mildly rising prices encouraged the free flow of goods and capital across international borders. London was the financial center of the world. Bonds sold there sent streams of capital into the less-developed parts of the world. No wonder many economists still look to this period as a model for the world's monetary system.

However, the gold standard had costs as well as benefits. Resources were used to mine gold in South Africa and the Klondike and to dredge gold from the rivers of California. A

---

[9]The battle over the standards was reflected, it has been argued, in L. Frank Baum's contemporary *The Wonderful Wizard of Oz*. Dorothy represents America; the Scarecrow, the farmer; the Tin Man, the working man; the Cowardly Lion, William Jennings Bryan; and so on. Dorothy seeks wisdom by following the yellow brick road (the gold standard) to the Emerald City (Washington). But in the end, she discovers that she had the power to solve her problems with her the entire time, her silver shoes (the ruby slippers were added by MGM). See Hugh Rockoff, "The Wizard of Oz as a Monetary Allegory," *Journal of Political Economy* 98 (August 1990): 739–760.

[10]Milton Friedman, "The Crime of 1873," *Journal of Political Economy* 6 (December 1990): 1159–1194.

[11]Milton Friedman and Anna J. Schwartz, *A Monetary History of the United States* (Princeton, N.J.: Princeton University Press, 1963), 134.

New View 19.1

Deflation

For most of the years after World War II, inflation was the main worry of monetary economists. Today, the United States, as well as other industrial countries such as Japan, faces the prospect of deflation. Is deflation always a bad thing? Many people assume so, perhaps because of the correlation between falling prices and hard times during the 1930s. The experience of the United States after the Civil War shows that deflation, at least a mild form of it, may not be such a bad thing. Between 1865 and 1896, the price level in the United States fell at an annual rate of about 2.10 percent per year, but real GDP per capita rose at an annual rate of 1.35 percent per year, and total industrial production rose at 4.76 percent per year. Iron and steel production rose an astonishing 6.38 percent per year as the United States became the world's leader. Of course, deflation did not affect everyone the same way. If a lender and a borrower entered into a contract without factoring in the deflation, the lender would receive an unanticipated profit at the expense of the borrower. And while the period as a whole was one of rapid economic growth, there were shorter periods of hard times, especially in the mid-1870s and early 1890s. Still, a look back at this period helps put the simple equation of deflation and economic stagnation into richer perspective.

Sources: Prices and Real GDP per capita: Louis D. Johnston and Samuel H. Williamson, "Source Note for US GDP, 1789–Present" Economic History Services, March 2003, at http://www.eh.net/hmit/gdp/GDPsource.htm. Industrial production and iron and steel: Historical Statistics *(Washington D.C.: Government Printing Office, 1975), series P17 and P270.*

paper standard would have permitted those resources to be used elsewhere. The rates of growth of the world's money supplies, moreover, were determined by the individual decisions of miners and chemists and by the forces of nature that had sewn the rare seams of gold into the earth. During the years after 1896, the net result was that the world's stock of monetary gold grew at a satisfactory rate. But this was not true for the years before 1896. During financial crises, moreover, adherence to the gold standard made it difficult to supply additional money to financial markets. In any case, there was always the hope that central bankers backed by reams of scientific analysis could do a better job of controlling the money supply than an automatic mechanism such as the gold standard.

The debate over the net benefits of the gold standard continues unabated. Historical comparisons, however, can narrow the range of debate. Michael D. Bordo has shown that along many dimensions (most importantly, average unemployment), the performance of the gold standard was inferior to modern monetary standards. Only with respect to long-term price stability could the gold standard be declared clearly superior. Once again we see the value of testing conjectures with evidence (Economic Reasoning Proposition 5).

Economic Reasoning Proposition

FINANCIAL CAPITAL, INVESTMENT BANKING, AND THE NATIONAL DEBT

As we have seen, taxes on state bank notes protected national banks from competition from state banks. Barriers formed by high capital requirements of national banks, restrictions on mortgage loans, and limits on their note issues before 1875 also protected many country national banks from competition from new national banks. This allowed many rural national banks to price discriminate: to restrict loans and charge higher interest rates to local borrowers. Rural national banks also sent their reserves to city banks. This practice, in combination with slower banking expansion rurally, helped finance urban-industrial growth. Richard E. Sylla, one of the leading writers on the banking history of the period, has concluded that the national banking system "raised barriers to entry into banking, and these had differential geographic impact which, when coupled with the increased mobility the National Banking System gave to interbank transfers of funds, worked very much to the advantage of industrial finance."[12]

Rural banks' discrimination created regional differences in lending rates that persisted, narrowing gradually, from the Civil War to 1900. The differences narrowed for a number of reasons. The recovery of the southern financial system after the Civil War gradually brought rates in that region into line with those in other regions. The spread of the commercial paper market (in which short-term business loans were sold directly to private investors) provided additional competition for the state banks. And, as John James has pointed out, the introduction of free banking in a number of states increased competition among the state banks.[13] To some extent, as shown in recent work by Howard Bodenhorn and Hugh Rockoff, the postwar integration of the capital market marked a return to the pre–Civil War status quo. This was especially true for the South.

The Rise of Investment Banking

As Lance Davis has pointed out, British financial markets were very different from American markets.[14] British industrialists could visit their local branch banks—Lloyd's, or Westminster's or Barclays—and draw capital from a huge international system. American firms, on the other hand, faced banks with more restricted resources.

Because of this limitation, investment banking in the United States emerged to serve the expansion of railroads, mining companies, and large-scale manufacturers. Unlike commercial banks, investment banks did not have the power to issue notes (money) or create deposits. Instead they acted as intermediaries, bringing together lenders (stock and bond buyers) and borrowers (firms). J. P. Morgan and Company was a pioneer in investment banking, earning $3 million for services in advising and selling stocks for Vanderbilt and his New York Central Railroad in 1879. Charles Schwab, an employee of Andrew Carnegie, carried a note to Morgan in 1900 with an asking price of more than $400 million for Carnegie's steel holdings. Morgan promptly replied, "I'll take it"—thus giving birth to the United States Steel Corporation; it was by far the largest merger up to that time. Forty years earlier, when Carnegie tried to raise financial capital of only a fraction of the sum Morgan promptly gave him in 1900, Carnegie had to go to England because no U.S. banks could supply his capital needs.

The close links between investment bankers and big business were forged even more strongly by the practice of placing representatives of the large investment houses on the boards of directors of the firms. Critics of the investment bankers complained that this practice stifled competition. Morgan and a few smaller investment banking firms such as Kuhn Loeb and Company in New York and Kidder Peabody and Company in Boston seemed to control both the distribution of securities and (through interlocking directorates) the business decisions of the major industrial firms themselves. In 1912, Congress subjected this "money trust" to a detailed and highly critical examination by the Pujo committee. J. Bradford DeLong's recent research has shown that there was also a positive side to Morgan's links with industrial firms: Investment bankers

---

[12]Richard E. Sylla, "The United States, 1863–1913," in *Banking and Economic Development: Some Lessons of Economic History*, ed. Rondo Cameron (New York: Oxford University Press, 1972), 236.

[13]See John James, *Money and Capital Markets in Postbellum America* (Princeton, N.J.: Princeton University Press, 1978), for a thorough discussion of these issues.

[14]Lance E. Davis, "Capital Immobilities and Financial Capitalism: A Study of Economic Evolution in the United States," *Explorations in Entrepreneurial History* 1 (1), (Fall 1963): 88–105.

Investment banker J.P. Morgan ruled the world of finance. In 1901 he formed the United States Steel Corporation, the world's first billion-dollar corporation. When asked what the market would do, he answered, "It will fluctuate."

helped inform investors about how best to invest their funds (Economic Reasoning Proposition 5, evidence matters).

Another important force helping finance industrial growth was the rapid, steady retirement of the national debt. The federal debt had been retired completely by 1835 (for the first and only time in our history), and only a small debt existed on the eve of the Civil War. By 1865, the debt was $2.32 billion, about 25 percent of GDP; it was reduced to $648 million by 1877 before increasing for several years. By 1893, $1.73 billion had been retired. Sizably, collections of tariffs supplied government with continued surpluses that permitted the debt retirement. This inflow of government funds to buy up old bonds—a type of crowding in, as John James has called it—lowered yields on private assets and stimulated capital formation in the private sector.[15]

BANK PANICS AND THE ESTABLISHMENT OF THE FEDERAL RESERVE SYSTEM

Despite the increased flexibility, the panic of 1893 and the depression of the mid-1890s were followed by the severe panic of 1907 and the ensuing depression. Once again, the American people were aroused to the need for basic reforms. One of the most painful aspects of

[15]John A. James, "Public Debt and U.S. Economic Growth," *Explorations in Economic History* 21 (April 1984): 192–217.

economic crisis before World War I was the rush by individuals and business firms, as they became apprehensive about the economic future, to the banks to convert their deposits into cash. The banks, which operated on the "fractional reserve" principle, could not immediately meet the demands for their total deposit liabilities. Given time, any sound bank could be liquidated in an orderly fashion, and its depositors and stockholders could be paid in full. In periods of panic, on the other hand, an orderly shifting of assets into cash was difficult, if not impossible. As many harried banks tried to sell bonds (their most liquid assets) at the same time, the prices of bonds fell drastically. For some banks, the consequent losses on bonds proved disastrous, even though "runs" were stopped. If, instead of selling its securities, a bank called in its loans or refused to renew ones as they came due, it transferred pressure to its customers. If these customers could not meet their obligations, the banks were forced into insolvency.

A common way to mitigate these difficulties was to suspend cash payments during crises. After the Civil War, suspension meant that banks ceased to pay out cash in any form: gold or gold certificates, silver or silver certificates, greenbacks, national bank notes, or subsidiary coins. As another option, a bank might restrict cash payments to a certain maximum sum per day or per withdrawal. During the panic of 1907, such suspensions were more general and for longer time periods (over two months in some cities) than ever before. In the Southeast and Midwest, the resulting shortage of cash was so serious that local clearinghouses issued emergency notes against collateral pledged by cooperating banks so that people could carry on business. These small-denomination "clearinghouse certificates" were not issued much elsewhere, but banks in cities all over the United States used large-denomination certificates to make up balances due one another. The issue of clearinghouse loan certificates, as Gary Gorton (1985) and Richard Timberlake have shown, went a long way toward softening the effects of a crisis, but it could not prevent them.[16]

A related, although less severe, problem occurred almost every year. The demand for money would rise in the fall because money was needed to pay harvest workers and purchase commodities from farmers and during the winter because extra money was needed during the Christmas buying season. Because the supply of money, and especially cash, was "inelastic," the result was an increase in interest rates in the fall and winter. To farmers, this seemed grossly unfair: Interest rates rose just when the farmers had the greatest need to borrow. Seasonal fluctuations in the demand for money were inherent in an agricultural economy, but they were aggravated by the National Banking System, which made it hard for banks to accommodate changes in the desired ratio of deposits to bank notes. George Selgin and Lawrence H. White have shown that in Canada, where banks had more freedom to convert deposits into notes, seasonal fluctuations in interest rates were much less severe. Thus, the farmers' demand that something be done about seasonal fluctuations in interest rates was added to the general demand that something be done about banking panics.

National Monetary Commission

Suspending cash payments and issuing clearinghouse certificates were better than allowing a panic to continue, but the public wanted a reform that would prevent suspensions altogether. In response, the Aldrich-Vreeland Act of 1908 provided for the organization of "national currency associations" to be composed of no fewer than 10 banks in sound financial condition. The purpose of these associations was to enable the banks that formed them to issue emergency bank notes against the security of bonds and commercial paper in their portfolios. Another provision established the National Monetary Commission, whose report in 1912 blasted the American banking system:

---

[16]See Gorton, "Clearinghouses and the Origin of Central Banking in the U.S.," *Journal of Economic History* 45 (1985), 277–283; and Timberlake, *The Origins of Central Banking in the United States* (Cambridge, Mass.; Harvard University Press, 1978).

> The methods by which our domestic and international credit operations are now conducted are crude, expensive and unworthy of an intelligent people. . . .The unimportant part which our banks and bankers take in the financing of our foreign trade is disgraceful to a progressive nation. . . . The disabilities from which our producers suffer in our foreign trade also apply largely to domestic transactions.[17]

The Commission's key recommendation was a new central bank; Commissioners believed that what was needed was a central institution to hold the reserves of the commercial banks and with the power to increase the commercial bank's reserves through its own credit-granting powers. A central bank was also needed to help the Treasury. After the demise of the Second Bank of the United States, the federal government had to maintain its own fiscal agent in the form of the Independent Treasury, which was by law required to remain aloof from the banking system. Impossibly antiquated methods of handling government funds resulted. By 1912, the need for a modern, central fiscal agent was too great to be postponed further.

Federal Reserve Act

Two days before Christmas in 1913, President Wilson signed the bill that established the Federal Reserve System. The system was composed of 12 Federal Reserve Banks, one in each of 12 districts in the country, to protect the interests of different regions. Unlike the 20-year charter of the first and second Banks of the United States, the charter of the Federal Reserve was permanent.

The system was to be headed by a Federal Reserve Board composed of seven members, including the Secretary of the Treasury, the comptroller of the currency ex officio, and five appointees of the president. Each Federal Reserve Bank was to be run by a board of nine directors. The Federal Reserve Board was to appoint three of the directors representing the "public"; the member banks of the district were to elect the remaining six. Three of the six locally elected directors could be bankers; the remaining three were to represent business, industry, and agriculture. Thus, the banking community had a minority representation on the Reserve Bank directorates in each district.

The Federal Reserve Act made membership in the system compulsory for national banks. Upon compliance with federal requirements, state banks might also become members. To join the system, a commercial bank had to purchase shares of the capital stock of the district Federal Reserve Bank in the amount of 3 percent of its combined capital and surplus. Thus, the member banks nominally owned the Federal Reserve Banks, although the annual return they could receive on their stock was limited to a 6 percent cumulative dividend. A member bank also had to deposit with the district Federal Reserve Bank a large part of the cash it had previously held as reserves. After 1917, all legal reserves of member banks were to be in the form of deposits with the Federal Reserve Bank.[18]

It was hoped that if the Federal Reserve Act were carefully followed, monetary disturbances would be very nearly eliminated. As we will see in the next part, however, despite the high hopes held for the Federal Reserve System, periods of inadequate leadership and lack of understanding at the "Fed" permitted catastrophic monetary disturbances, bank panics, and sharp business cycles. Indeed, the Great Depression—America's darkest economic period—was partly a result of failure at the Fed.

---

[17] *Report of the National Monetary Commission* (Washington, D.C.: Government Printing Office, 1912), 28–29.

[18] All required reserves were held on deposit with Federal Reserve Banks from June 1917 until late 1959, when, after a series of transitional steps, member banks could once again count vault cash as reserves.

Selected References and Suggested Readings

Bodenhorn, Howard. "Capital Mobility and Financial Integration in Antebellum America." *Journal of Economic History* 52 (1992): 585–610.

Bodenhorn, Howard, and Hugh Rockoff. "Regional Interest Rates in Antebellum America." In *Strategic Factors in Nineteenth Century American Economic History: A Volume to Honor Robert W. Fogel*, eds. Claudia Goldin and Hugh Rockoff. A National Bureau of Economic Research Conference Report. Chicago: University of Chicago Press, 1992, 159–187.

Bordo, Michael D. "The Classical Gold Standard: Some Lessons for Today." *Federal Reserve Bank of St. Louis Review* 63 (1981): 1–17.

———. *The Gold Standard and Related Regimes: Collected Essays*. Cambridge, England: Cambridge University Press, 1999.

Bordo, Michael D., and Anna J. Schwartz, eds. *A Retrospective on the Classical Gold Standard, 1821–1931*. Chicago: University of Chicago Press, 1984.

Calomiris, Charles, and Glenn Hubbard. "Price Flexibility, Credit Availability, and Economic Fluctuations: Evidence from the United States, 1894–1909." *Quarterly Journal of Economics* 104 (1989): 429–452.

Carosso, Vincent P. *Investment Banking in America, A History*. Cambridge, Mass.: Harvard University Press, 1970.

———. *The Morgans: Private International Bankers, 1854–1913*. Cambridge, Mass.: Harvard University Press, 1987.

Chernow, Ron. *The House of Morgan: An American Banking Dynasty and the Rise of Modern Finance*. New York: Simon & Schuster, 1991.

Davis, Lance E. "Capital Immobilities and Finance Capitalism: A Study of Economic Evolution in the United States." *Explorations in Entrepreneurial History* 1 (1), (Fall 1963): 88–105.

———. "The Investment Market, 1870–1914: The Evolution of a National Market." *Journal of Economic History* 25 (1965): 355–399.

DeLong, J. Bradford. "Did J. P. Morgan's Men Add Value? A Historical Perspective on Financial Capitalism." In *Inside the Business Enterprise*, ed. Peter Temin. Chicago: University of Chicago Press, 1991.

Federal Reserve Bank of Minneapolis, **http://minneapolisfed.org/info/sys/history**, posted by the Federal Reserve Bank of Minneapolis. Also, see the Web site of the Museum of American Financial History, **http://www.financialhistory.org,** for a history of the Federal Reserve System.

Friedman, Milton. "The Crime of 1873." *Journal of Political Economy* 6 (1990): 1159–1194.

Friedman, Milton, and Anna J. Schwartz. *A Monetary History of the United States, 1867–1967*. Princeton, N.J.: National Bureau of Economic Research, Princeton University Press, 1963.

Garber, Peter M., and Vittorio U. Grilli. "The Belmont-Morgan Syndicate as an Optimal Investment Banking Contract." *European Economic Review* 30 (June 1986): 649–677.

Gorton, Gary. "Clearinghouses and the Origins of Central Banking in the U.S." *Journal of Economic History* 45 (1985): 277–283.

Hawtrey, R. G. *The Gold Standard in Theory and Practice*. London: Longmans, Green, 1939.

James, John A. "The Development of a National Money Market, 1893–1911." *Journal of Economic History* 33 (1976): 878–897.

———. "Cost Functions of Post-bellum National Banks." *Explorations in Economic History* 15 (1978): 184–195.

———. *Money and Capital Markets in Postbellum America*. Princeton, N.J.: Princeton University Press, 1978.

———. "Public Debt Management Policy and Nineteenth-Century American Economic Growth." *Explorations in Economic History* 21 (1984): 192–217.

Jenks, Leland H. *The Export of British Capital to 1875.* London: Cape, 1938.

Keehn, Richard H. "Market Power and Bank Lending: Some Evidence from Wisconsin, 1870–1900." *Journal of Economic History* 40 (1980): 45–52.

Kindahl, James K. "Economic Factors in Specie Resumption: The United States, 1865–1879." In *The Reinterpretation of American Economic History*, eds. Robert W. Fogel and Stanley L. Engerman. New York: Harper & Row, 1971.

Livingston, James. *Origins of the Federal Reserve System: Money, Class, and Corporate Capitalism, 1890–1913.* Ithaca, N.Y.: Cornell University Press, 1986.

Myers, Margaret. *The New York Money Market.* New York: Columbia University Press, 1931.

Officer, Lawrence H. "The Remarkable Efficiency of the Dollar-Sterling Gold Standard, 1890–1906." *Journal of Economic History* 49 (1989): 1–41.

Rockoff, Hugh. "The Wizard of Oz as a Monetary Allegory." *Journal of Political Economy* 98 (1990): 739–760.

———. "Banking and Finance, 1789–1914." In *The Cambridge Economic History of the United States*, Vol. II, *The Long Nineteenth Century*, eds. Stanley L. Engerman and Robert E. Gallman. New York: Cambridge University Press, 2000, 643–684.

Selgin, George A, and Lawrence H. White. "Monetary Reform and the Redemption of National Bank Notes, 1863-1913." *Business History Review* 68 (1994): 205–243.

Smiley, Gene. "Interest Rate Movements in the United States, 1888–1913." *Journal of Economic History* 35 (1975): 591–620.

Snowden, Kenneth. "American Stock Market Development and Performance, 1871–1929." *Explorations in Economic History* 24 (1987): 327–353.

Sobel, Robert. *The Big Board: A History of the New York Stock Market.* New York: Free Press, 1969.

Sylla, Richard. "Federal Policy, Banking Market Structure, and Capital Mobilization in the United States, 1863–1913." *Journal of Economic History* 29 (1969): 657–686.

———. "American Banking and Growth in the Nineteenth Century: A Partial View of the Terrain." *Explorations in Economic History* 9 (Winter 1971–1972): 197–228.

———. *The American Capital Market, 1846–1914.* New York: Arno, 1975.

Timberlake, Richard. *The Origins of Central Banking in the United States.* Cambridge, Mass.: Harvard University Press, 1978.

Unger, Irwin. *The Greenback Era.* Princeton, N.J.: Princeton University Press, 1964.

West, Robert Craig. *Banking Reform and the Federal Reserve 1863–1923.* Ithaca, N.Y.: Cornell University Press, 1977.

White, Eugene N. "The Political Economy of Banking Regulation, 1864–1933." *Journal of Economic History* 42 (1982): 33–42.

Wicker, Elmus. *Banking Panics of the Gilded Age.* New York: Cambridge University Press, 2000.

Williamson, Jeffrey G. *Financial Intermediation, Capital Immobilities and Economic Growth in Late Nineteenth Century American Development: A General Equilibrium History.* Cambridge, England: Cambridge University Press, 1974.

———. "Watersheds and Turning Points: Conjectures on the Long-Term Impact of Civil War Financing." *Journal of Economic History* 34 (1974): 636–661.

Wimmer, Larry T. "The Gold Crisis of 1869: Stabilizing or Destabilizing Speculation under Floating Exchange Rates?" *Explorations in Economic History* 12 (1975): 105–122.

Zecher, J. Richard, and D. N. McCloskey. "How the Gold Standard Worked, 1880–1913." In *The Monetary Approach to the Balance of Payments*, eds. Jacob A. Frenkel and Harry G. Johnson. London: Allen & Unwin, 1976. Reprinted in B. Eichengreen, ed. *The Gold Standard in Theory and History*. London: Methuen, 1985.

———. "The Success of Purchasing Power Parity: Historical Evidence and Its Implications for Macroeconomics." In *A Retrospective on the Classical Gold Standard 1821–1931*, eds. Michael Bordo and Anna J. Schwartz. Chicago: University of Chicago Press, 1984.

Chapter Twenty

Commerce at Home and Abroad

Chapter Theme

Between 1880 and 1920, the United States became the leading manufacturer in the world in terms of total production and output per worker. Both the quality and the quantity of goods and services increased. Rather than buying commodities in bulk for further processing within the home, as they had done in an earlier and simpler time, Americans increasingly relied on finished products. Dependable brand-name products, heavily promoted through advertising, played an increasingly important role in the distribution of goods. The new styles and number of goods lifted the material well being of greater and greater proportions of the population. These developments resulted from underlying trends in urbanization and, as emphasized in chapters 16 and 17, from advances in transportation and technology.

URBANIZATION

The choice of city life over rural life was largely a nineteenth century (and later) phenomenon. The long march to city dominance of where most Americans live is revealed in Table 20.1 on page 392, which shows that the percentage of the population living in urban centers nearly doubled between 1800 and 1840, doubled again between 1840 and 1860, and then again from 1860 to 1900. By 1910, nearly 10 percent of the total population lived in three cities—New York, Chicago, and Philadelphia—each having a million-plus residents.

Before 1860, the rapid pace of urbanization resulted primarily from the rapid growth of interregional trade spurred by the transportation revolution. Urban centers emerged as "entrepots" of trade, and trade more than industry was the magnet pulling people into cities and towns.[1] As Eric Lampard has shown, the 15 greatest cities in the nation in 1860 employed relatively small shares of their population in manufactures.[2] What the cities in this early period provided was primarily transport and commercial and banking services for expanding long-distance trades.

[1] V. S. Clark, *History of Manufactures in the United States*, Vol. 2 (New York: McGraw-Hill, 1929), 2.
[2] Eric Lampard, "The History of Cities in the Economically Advanced Areas," *Economic Development and Cultural Change* 3 (January 1955): 119.

TABLE 20.1 Urban Percentages of the Population, 1800–1910

YEAR	POPULATION IN TOWNS OVER 2,500	POPULATION IN TOWNS OVER 100,000
1800	6%	0%
1840	11	3
1860	20	8
1880	28	12
1900	40	19
1910	46	22

Source: Historical Statistics, 1975 *(Washington, D.C.: Government Printing Office, 1976), Series A2 and A57-72.*

Urbanization after the Civil War was different. Early industrial complexes, which had been tied to primary resources in city hinterlands, shifted to the city. The railroad and other advances in transportation and communication made factories and cities nearly synonymous by the late nineteenth century.

People, many from abroad, poured into the centers of trade and industrial activities. Between 1860 and 1910, over half of new city residents came from overseas. About 10 percent of the urban growth resulted from natural increase, and a little over one-third came from domestic rural areas.

Cities in the Midwest and the South, long established as distributing centers for the manufactures of the East and now developing industry of their own, grew phenomenally as

CHICAGO HISTORICAL SOCIETY (STEREO BY J. CARBUTT)

There were urban traffic jams long before automobiles were important, as this picture of mid-nineteenth century Chicago shows.

industrial workers flocked to them. Chicago and Detroit, Cleveland and Cincinnati, St. Louis and Kansas City, Memphis and New Orleans, and Atlanta and Birmingham originated shipments that went far beyond their own trade areas. By 1910, the West and the South originated half as much railroad tonnage of manufactures carried as the East did. Meanwhile, smaller cities within the trade areas of the metropolises and cities in the thinly populated region west of the Mississippi specialized in the mercantile functions. As automobiles came into common use after 1910, large towns and cities gained business at the expense of small towns and villages; by 1920, retailers in urban centers were attracting customers from distances that had been unimaginable just a few years earlier. These changes were reflected in new ways of distributing goods and in new marketing institutions, as Martha Olney has emphasized.[3]

MARKETING AND SELLING

On the eve of the Civil War, the typical store was more devoted to processing sales orders than to promoting and selling goods. Advertising was limited largely to local newspapers and some national magazines, with occasional outdoor ads in a few large cities. "Attracting customers" was not a purpose of advertisements; the information conveyed was simple and direct. Newspaper ads wasted no space, listing the items for sale and the location, but usually not prices. Installment buying was known but uncommon until after the turn of the century. See Perspective 20.1 on page 394. Cyrus McCormick sold his reaper "on time" at 20 percent down and four months to pay. Edward Clark of the Singer Sewing Machine Company had innovated consumer credit in 1856, selling $125 sewing machines for $5 down and $3 per month. McCormick and Singer, pioneers for direct sales to consumers before the Civil War, were rare exceptions. Most manufacturers sold directly to wholesalers or to commission agents who marketed the wares. Many wholesalers, in turn, hired "drummers," traveling salesmen who "drummed up" trade and solicited orders in the towns and countryside.

Wholesaling

The full-service wholesale houses that evolved after 1840 bought goods on their own account from manufacturers and importers to sell to retailers, frequently on credit. In the growing cities of the Midwest, successful retailers began to perform some wholesale functions along with the business of selling to consumers. As these houses grew, they sometimes dropped their retailing activities altogether and concentrated on handling the output of manufacturing centers in the East. A few wholesale firms, especially those located in major distributing centers such as Chicago and St. Louis, offered several lines of merchandise, but more often they specialized in a single "full line," such as hardware or dry goods.

From 1860 to 1900, full-line, full-service wholesale houses were without serious competitors in the business of distributing goods from manufacturers to retailers. Beginning in the 1880s and increasingly after 1900, however, they faced competition from the marketing departments of large manufacturers.[4] Wholesale houses did not decline absolutely between 1900 and 1920—in fact, their sales continued to increase—but they handled an ever-smaller proportion of goods in the channels of distribution.

The reason for the relative decline in wholesaling lay in the structure of emerging large-scale producers. Firms in many industries were adopting "continuous process" technologies, in which raw materials moved in a steady flow through the factory rather than being

---

[3]Martha L. Olney, *Buy Now-Pay Later* (Chapel Hill: University of North Carolina Press, 1991).

[4]For further discussion, see Alfred D. Chandler, Jr., *The Visible Hand: The Managerial Revolution in America* (Cambridge, Mass.: Belknap Press of Harvard University Press, 1977); and Harold Livesay and Glenn Porter, *Merchants and Manufacturers* (Baltimore: Johns Hopkins University Press, 1971).

Perspective 20.1

Credit, Installment Purchases, and Race

Although purchase on credit from country stores was common in the nineteenth century, buying on installment was uncommon until the early twentieth century. Thanks to the research of Martha Olney, an interesting racial profile has emerged on the use of store credit and installment payment for the purchase of goods. The purchase of merchandise (not homes or land) by borrowing money from banks was rare in the years before 1918. By then, less than 5 percent of families used bank loans to purchase goods. Table 20.2 shows the percentage of families who used merchant credit or installments to buy merchandise, and the relative uses of these debt forms by race. Blacks took on more debt than whites to acquire goods, and blacks were much more likely to use installment payments compared to whites, who relied mostly on merchant credit. Table 20.3 shows the use of installment payments for various common "durables." Although there is little difference between the races in the percentage of families buying each item listed (the first set of columns), blacks often nearly doubled their use of installment purchases compared to whites. Olney's analysis strongly suggests that this heavy reliance on installment purchases by blacks was because merchants (mostly white) were more reluctant to give blacks merchant credit. Such credit was informal and not tied to specific items that could be repossessed. Installment contracts were formal and could be used legally for repossession. Given high information costs about ability to pay and perhaps racial profiling, merchants reduced their risks of default by using installment methods. Especially for durables, Olney concludes (p. 427):

> Down payments were typically 10 to 25 percent of the goods' price. Contract maturities were typically 12 to 18 months, much shorter than the goods' expected service life. The value of the collateral therefore often exceeded the balance due, especially in the first few months of the installment contract. Whatever concerns a durable good merchant might have had regarding the creditworthiness of a family were easily allayed by the knowledge that valuable collateral could be repossessed if the family defaulted on the installment contract.

TABLE 20.2 Joint Use of Installment and Merchant Credit

	WHITE	BLACK
Percentage of families using installment or merchant credit	38.6%	48.9%
Of families using installment or merchant credit:		
Percentage using only installment credit	35.2	55.6
Percentage using only merchant credit	45.6	24.3
Percentage using both installment and merchant credit	19.2	20.2

Source: Martha Olney "When Your Word Is Not Enough: Race, Collateral, and Household Credit," Journal of Economic History *58 (2), (1998): 412.*

Perspective 20.1

Credit, Installment Purchases, and Race, continued

TABLE 20.3 Goods Families Purchased on Installment

	PERCENTAGE OF FAMILIES BUYING PRODUCT		PERCENTAGE OF PURCHASES MADE ON INSTALLMENT		PERCENTAGE OF FAMILIES BUYING GOODS ON INSTALLMENT	
GOODS BEING PURCHASED	WHITE	BLACK	WHITE	BLACK	WHITE	BLACK
Pianos and musical instruments	5.9%	5.5%	80.8%	93.6%	4.8%	5.2%
Phonographs	7.9	6.6	48.0	53.6	3.8	3.6
Furniture	45.9	47.9	20.7	52.8	9.5	25.6
Chair	21.0	24.6	26.5	56.2	5.6	14.0
Bedstead	18.4	21.7	26.6	57.3	4.9	12.6
Mattress	20.3	21.7	23.2	56.4	4.7	12.5
Table	13.8	18.5	31.2	59.5	4.4	11.2
Bureau	8.6	14.8	38.1	66.7	3.3	10.0
Couch	8.6	11.9	35.1	63.7	3.0	7.7
Buffet	5.4	5.4	38.6	67.4	2.1	3.7
Kitchen cabinets	3.4	4.8	38.9	65.8	1.3	3.2
Appliances	62.8	69.0	14.6	23.8	9.2	16.6
Stove	24.5	24.7	20.1	40.3	4.9	10.1
Sewing machine	8.0	8.0	45.3	72.1	3.6	5.8
Refrigerator	6.2	8.4	19.8	40.3	1.2	3.4
Washing machine	3.0	0.6	15.9	40.0	0.5	0.2
Vacuum	5.1	1.2	7.7	20.0	0.4	0.2

Source: Martha Olney "When Your Word Is Not Enough: Race, Collateral, and Household Credit," Journal of Economic History *58 (2), (1998): 413.*

processed in separate batches. This meant that any interruption in the distribution of the final product would cause a steep increase in production costs. These firms then sought to gain control over their distribution channels in some cases by dealing directly with retailers. James B. Duke's marketing of cigarettes illustrates the point. In 1884, Duke installed two Bonsack cigarette-making machines in his factory. Each machine could turn out 120,000 cigarettes per day, compared with the 3,000 that a skilled worker could produce by hand. Duke's machines, working continuously, easily could have saturated the cigarette market that existed in 1884. To create and maintain the market for these cigarettes, and to ensure that his output moved steadily to the consumer, Duke built an extensive sales network that kept an eye on local advertising and worked closely with other departments in the firm to schedule the flow of cigarettes from machine to consumer.

Brand Names

The marketing departments of firms like Duke's also helped to establish and maintain the brand name of the product, particularly by stressing better quality or unique services. For example, producers requiring controlled temperatures during shipment, such as the Chicago meatpackers Armour and Swift, wanted to be certain that consumers would identify their product as the one that reached the market at the right temperature. Others, such as John H. Patterson, founder of National Cash Register, needed to ensure that consumers knew that NCR provided adequate instruction in how the product worked, proper service, and credit. Manufacturers urged buyers to ask specifically for their brand. Brand names were the way the market protected consumers, far removed from producers, from inferior merchandise. They were an alternative market-generated substitute to consumer protection legislation.

Retailing

In rural areas, where retail units characteristically remained small and independent, the wholesale house kept its customers. The "general store" was rapidly disappearing elsewhere, however, as retailers in towns with a surrounding trade area began to specialize in particular lines, but, interestingly, this specialization of retail functions did not bring a reduction of the traditional wholesaler's business. What transpired instead was the development of new types of retail outlets, usually large ones, and the increasing ability of manufacturers to establish strong consumer preferences through advertising.

Department Stores

Of the new retailing organizations that had gained definite acceptance by World War I, the department store ran counter to the trend of greater specialization in handling merchandise. As cities became bigger and more congested, the convenience of being able to shop for all personal necessities in a single store had an increasing appeal. Furthermore, department stores offered delivery services and credit. The early department stores in large cities evolved after the Civil War from the efforts of drygoods stores to replace business lost to the growing ready-to-wear trade. There was a definite division of the store into separate departments, each with its own manager, buyers, and clerks; the separation was once so distinct that departments were frequently leased to individuals or companies.

At first, department stores bought merchandise through wholesalers. However, larger stores such as Macy's in New York, John Wanamaker's in Philadelphia, and Marshall Field's in Chicago took advantage of their growing size to obtain price reductions by going directly to manufacturers or their selling agents. Because of the size of their operations, large stores with numerous clerks had to set one price for all customers, and the old practice of haggling with merchants over the price of an article was soon a thing of the past. So successful was the department store concept that by 1920, even small cities could usually boast one. Small department stores purchased merchandise through regular wholesale channels, and their departmentalization was so indistinct that they were very similar to the general store of an earlier day.

Chain Stores

It soon became apparent to some enterprisers that the costs of distributing goods in certain lines could be reduced by performing agency and brokerage functions in their own departments and by buying directly from manufacturers and processors. Examples currently are Borders Books, Home Depot, and Toys "R" Us. To achieve the bargaining power that would enable them to buy directly, enterprisers had to have retail sales of considerable magnitude. Such sales could be obtained by combining many spatially separate outlets in "chains" with a centralized buying and administrative authority. Additional savings could be made by curtailing or eliminating the major services of credit and delivery.

One of the early chains, still with us today, was the Great Atlantic and Pacific Tea Company, founded in 1859. From an original line restricted to tea and coffee, the company expanded in the 1870s to include a general line of groceries. In 1879, F.W. Woolworth began the venture that was to make him a multimillionaire when he opened variety stores

F. W. Woolworth—a pioneer in chain-store merchandising—opened his first store in 1879 in Lancaster, Pennsylvania. At today's prices, it would be a one and two dollar store.

carrying articles that sold for no more than a dime. By 1900, tobacco stores and drugstores were often organized in chains, and hardware stores and restaurants soon began to fall under centralized managements. By 1920, grocery, drug, and variety chains were firmly established as a part of the American retail scene. A few companies then numbered their units in the thousands, but the great growth of the chains was to come in the 1920s and 1930s—along with innovations in physical layout and the aggressive selling practices that would incur the wrath of the independents.

Mail-Order Houses

Although e-commerce has propelled a tremendous resurgence of ordering goods by mail in the United States, it is probably difficult for the modern urban resident to imagine the thrill that "ordering by mail" once gave Americans. Indeed, for many American families in the decades before World War I, simply the annual arrival of a catalog from Montgomery Ward or Sears, Roebuck and Company was an event awaited with great anticipation. Although Montgomery Ward started his business with the intention of selling only to Grangers, he soon included other farmers and many city dwellers among his customers. Both Montgomery Ward and Sears, Roebuck experienced their great growth periods after they moved to Chicago—a vantage point from which they could sell, with optimum economies of shipping costs and time, to eager Midwestern farmers and to both coasts as well. Rural

COURTESY OF LEVI STRAUSS AND CO. ARCHIVES

Measurements of American male sizes for Civil War uniforms marked the beginning of standardized clothing, and U.S. manufacturers of boots and shoes steadily improved the quality and fit of their product. Economies resulting from mass-production techniques drove down the cost of clothing, and mail-order solicitation helped to broaden markets.

free delivery and the establishment of a parcel post system were godsends to mail-order houses. By 1920, however, towns were readily accessible to farmers, who could now make their own purchases. If the mail-order houses were to remain important merchandisers, they would have to modify their selling methods.

PRODUCT DIFFERENTIATION AND ADVERTISING

Merchants had advertised long before the Civil War, but as long as durable and semidurable goods were either made to order for the wealthy or turned out carelessly for the undiscriminating poor, and as long as food staples were sold out of bulk containers, the field of the advertiser was limited. In fact, the first attempts at advertising on more than a local level were directed largely toward retailers rather than consumers. Notable exceptions were patent medicine manufacturers, the first sellers in America to advertise on a national scale.[5]

After the Civil War, advertising on a national scale finally became a widely accepted practice. With the trusts came truly national firms whose brand names and trademarks became impressed on the minds of consumers. Economic Insight 20.1 on page 402 discusses monopolistic competition resulting from the growth of brand names, advertising, and product differentiating. Wherever products such as tobacco, whiskey, kerosene, or shoes could be differentiated in terms of buyer thinking, the trusts attempted an institutional advertising designed to reassure householders about the quality of the goods being purveyed. As the quality of nondurables improved, particularly in the case of clothing, manufacturers of leather shoes, hosiery, underwear, and men's suits and overcoats found that a loyal, nationwide following could be won through brand-name advertising. By 1920, advertising was a billion-dollar industry. In some fields, the increasing size of a firm was an important factor in the growth of its national advertising, but advertising itself helped many firms to attain large sizes.

It became a well-accepted fact that a firm had to advertise to maintain its share of an industry's sales. It was also realized that as competing firms carried on extensive campaigns, the demand for a product might increase throughout the entire industry. Yet only a beginning had been made. Two changes were to loom large in the future of American advertising. One was the radio, which within a decade was to do the job of advertising far more effectively than it had ever been done before. The second was the change in the kind of consumer durables people bought. In 1869, half the output of consumer durables consisted of furniture and house furnishings; 30 years later, the same categories still accounted for somewhat more than half of the total. But after 1910, as first the automobile and then electrical appliances revolutionized American life, the share of furniture and household furnishings in the output of consumer durables declined rapidly. Household furnishings were articles that could not be differentiated in people's minds with any remarkable degree of success, although efforts were continually made to do so. On the other hand, automobiles and household appliances could be readily differentiated, presenting a wonderful challenge to the American advertising account executive.

THE FIRST STEPS TOWARD CONSUMER PROTECTION

The Meat Inspection Act of 1891 and the Pure Food and Drug Act of 1906 were dramatic interventions by the federal government into the economy to ensure quality standards of products for unwary customers. In 1906, Upton Sinclair's novel *The Jungle* was published and received the personal attention of President Theodore Roosevelt. Sinclair's descriptions of unsanitary production facilities for meat and his allegations of occasional processing of diseased animals stirred up sensational media and public reactions.

---

[5]There is a suspicion that the popularity of patent medicines resulted in good part from their high alcohol content. Many, if not most, customers would not have touched liquor, and they may not have realized that the immediate sense of well-being derived from such medicines arose from alcohol instead of from other "beneficial ingredients."

Economic Insight 20.1

Monopolistic Competition

The growth of brand names, advertising, and product differentiation led economists to develop a new theory: monopolistic competition. In 1933, two books were published describing the new theory, Edward Chamberlin's *The Theory of Monopolistic Competition: A Re-orientation of the Theory of Value* and Joan Robinson's *Economics of Imperfect Competition*. The figure illustrates the famous "Chamberlinian tangency solution." The demand curve facing the firm, *dd*, is downward sloping, showing that the firm has some monopoly power. Even if it raises its price, it will not lose all of its customers because it produces a differentiated product. Some customers will remain loyal, for example, to Levi Strauss's overalls or Dr. C.V. Girard's ginger brandy even when the prices of these products are raised relative to alternatives. These firms will not be able to earn extraordinary profits for long. New entrants to the industry will capture some of the market, reducing demand, and force the existing firms into more advertising, raising costs. The long-run equilibrium price will be at *p*. Price will be equal to average cost, which includes only a normal profit.

There is, in one sense, excess capacity in a monopolistically competitive industry. If product differentiation could be eliminated, say, by prohibiting advertising and requiring firms to produce a simple, standardized product, the resulting competitive price would be lower, approximately at p^* (only approximately because cost curves would be affected as well as demand). There would be fewer firms in the industry, each producing more output. Critics of the theory of monopolistic competition have pointed out, however, that variety may be of real value to consumers. Although it is easy to make fun of Dr. Girard's ginger brandy, Levi Strauss's riveted overalls are another matter.

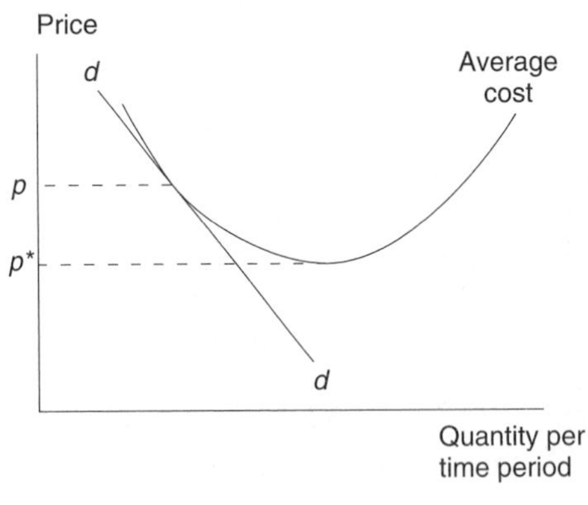

Sinclair's book was timely, coming on the heels of the 1898 "embalmed beef" scandal, an event of the Spanish-American War in which adulterated beef was allegedly provided to the army. Although Sinclair's allegations and those from the scandal ultimately were found baseless in congressional testimony, the acts were promptly passed.

The Pure Food and Drug Act was initially trivial in effect, calling simply for federal regulation of the content and labeling of certain food and medicinal products. The sum of

Advertising helped to expand the consumer demand for new products such as this all-purpose potion.

$174,180 was allocated to the Bureau of Chemistry for its enforcement. In contrast the 1906 Meat Inspection Act increased the Bureau of Animal Husbandry's budget for inspection purposes from $0.8 million to $3.0 million.

The 1906 meat act was not new. It was merely an amendment to the Meat Inspection Act of 1891, which had been passed in response to allegations by small local butchers and their organizations that dressed meat sent to distant markets by refrigerated railroad cars was unwholesome.[6] Chicago meatpacking companies such as Armour, Swift, Morris, and Hammond dominated the interstate dressed-beef trade. In 1890, their market shares of cattle slaughtered in Chicago were 27, 26, 24, and 12 percent, respectively. Because the new refrigeration technology dramatically lowered the costs of shipments (dressed beef was roughly one-third of the weight of whole beef), these companies vastly undercut local butchers' prices. To fight back, local butchers attempted to discredit refrigerated beef, claiming it was unwholesome. As Gary Libecap informs us, although these claims were unfounded, the big packers welcomed the governmental response.

The large Chicago packers had private quality controls for dressed beef and a substantial stake in protecting their brand-name reputations. They welcomed federal inspection of beef in interstate markets, first because federal inspection augmented their own quality

[6]Gary D. Libecap, "The Rise of the Chicago Packers and the Origins of Meat Inspection and Antitrust," *Economic Inquiry*, 30 (2), (April 1992): 242–262.

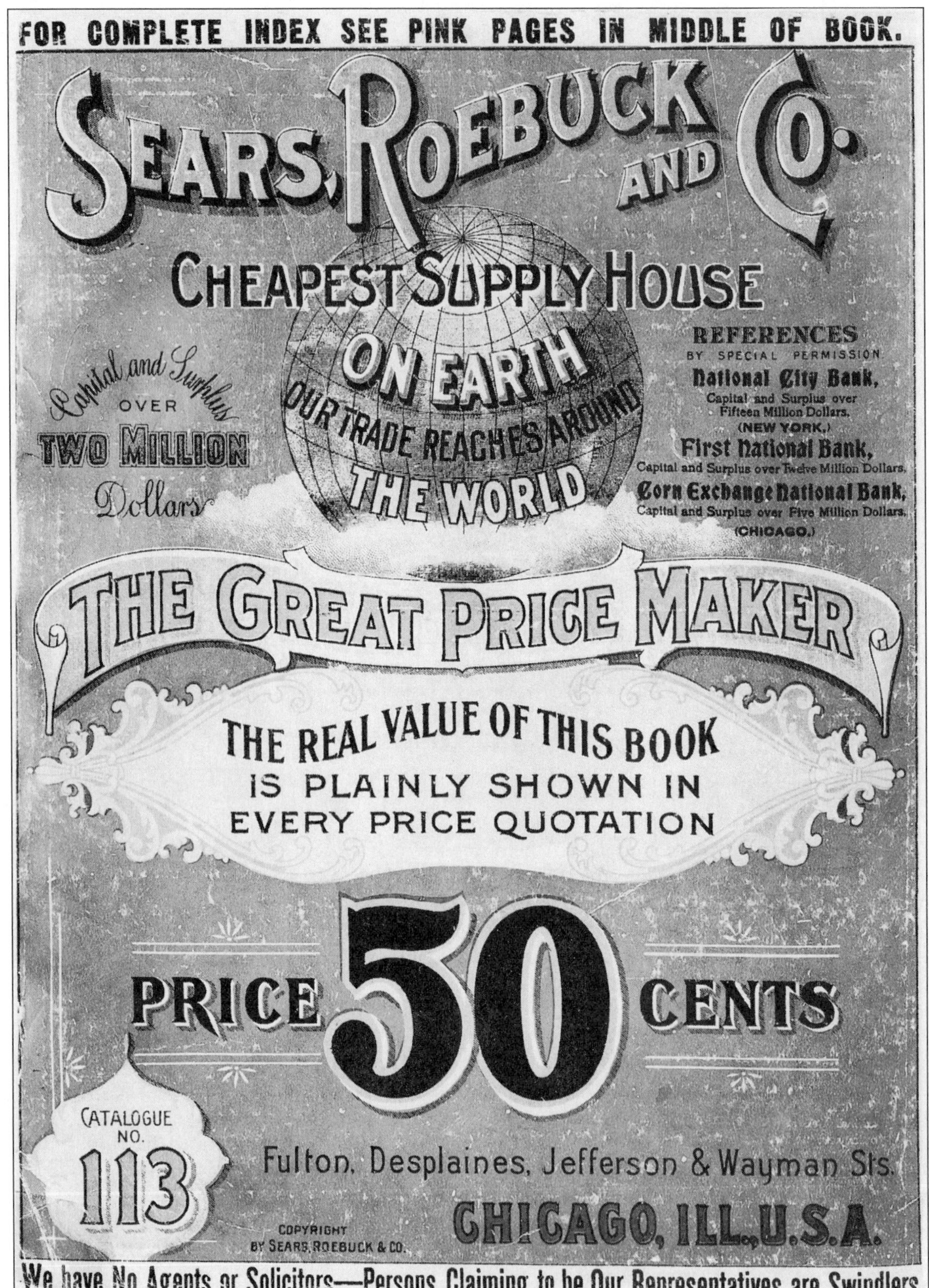

The famous Sears, Roebuck, and Co. catalog, and that of its rival, Montgomery Ward, brought access to an abundance of reasonably priced merchandise to every farmer's door.

assurances, and second because it gave each firm clear and accurate public information on the shipments of every other firm. This publicly provided inspection system allowed the firms to engage in pooling and market-sharing arrangements with excellent assurances that no firm could cheat on sale-share agreements.

The 1891 Meat Inspection Act for interstate trade was similar to an 1890 act on meat for export. Both acts largely benefited the producers by reinforcing each firm's quality control standards for shipment to markets at home and abroad. Whether or not consumers benefited from the acts is unsubstantiated, but the grounds and precedents for consumer protection were established by these first inspection acts, ostensibly on the consumers' behalf.

FOREIGN TRADE

By 1900, the United States had become the leading manufacturing country in the world in terms of total production. Great Britain (the world's first industrial nation) was second, and Germany was third. By 1913, the United States lead had increased, and Britain's position had fallen to third. The United States forged to the front in iron and steel production, and Germany and the United States became leaders in the electrical, chemical, and machine tool industries. This does not mean, we hasten to add, that output had declined in Britain. To the contrary, British output continued to increase. In terms of industrial output per capita, Britain was still the leader in 1900 and was only slightly below the United States in 1913 when the United States took over the lead. What had happened to Britain was simply that two large nations, well endowed with natural resources and possessing economic systems conducive to growth, had expanded their output more rapidly.

During this period, the network of international trade assumed its modern characteristics. From the industrial countries—the United States, Germany, Great Britain, and later several others—went the manufactured and semimanufactured products. In exchange, the less-industrialized nations sent an ever-swelling flow of foodstuffs and raw materials to support the growing industrial populations and feed the furnaces and fabricating plants of industry.

Rapid improvement in methods of communication and transportation was the key to this system. Several examples follow. The first successful transatlantic cable began operations in 1866, a railroad line spanned the American continent in 1869, the Suez Canal was opened in the same year, and dramatic productivity gains in ocean transportation occurred over the last half of the nineteenth century. An extremely important improvement was the development of railroads in various parts of the world, making possible a flood of cheap grain from Canada, Australia, Argentina, Russia, and the Danube valley, as well as from the midlands of the United States. In the late 1870s and early 1880s, refrigeration on vessels made possible the shipments of meats, then dairy products, and finally fruits. To these were added the products of the tropics: rice, coffee, cocoa, vegetable oils, and tapioca. However, the shipment of grains was also of great importance in stimulating the worldwide distribution of foods.

Changing Composition of Exports and Imports

Figure 20.1 on page 404 shows the changing composition of U.S. foreign trade between 1850 and 1900. This transition portrays the shift in U.S. comparative advantage internationally, away from agriculture and toward manufactures. On the export side, Figure 20.1 shows that the most striking change was the decline of raw materials (such as cotton) from three-fifths to one-fourth of the total. Crude foodstuffs, which had swelled from about 1 percent in 1850 to nearly one-quarter of all exports in the late 1870s (reflecting the piercing of the West by the railroad), declined to 17 percent by 1900 and continued to fall until 1915. Manufactured foodstuffs, which also had climbed to about 25 percent of the total, held fairly steady. As shown, another important trend was the rise of semimanufactures and finished manufactures. (By the period between 1915 and 1920, these would account for almost half the total value of exports.)

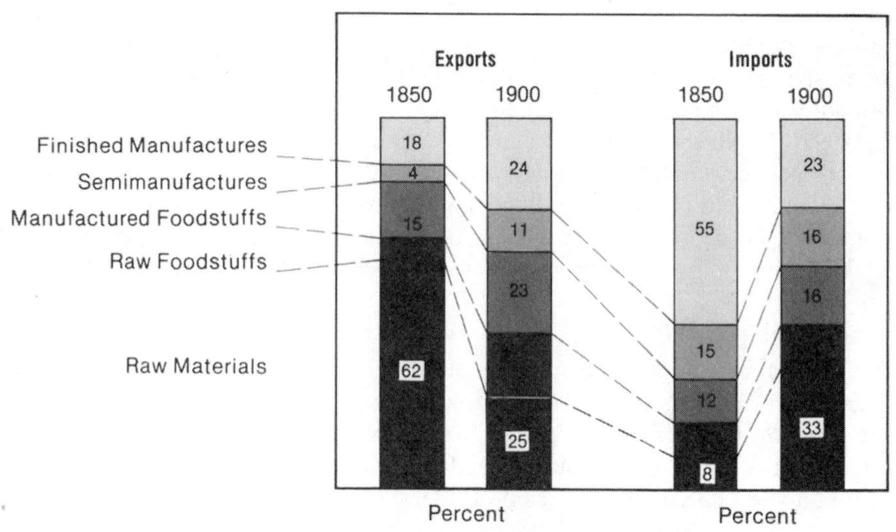

FIGURE 20.1 Composition of U.S. Foreign Trade, 1850 and 1900

Source: U.S. Department of Commerce.

Opposite movements, although not as remarkable, can be seen on the import side. Crude materials rose from one-twelfth the value of imports in 1850 to one-third by 1900. The chief crude materials imported—those that were necessary to a great industrial structure but that could not be found in the United States—were rubber, tropical fibers, and metals such as nickel and tin. Crude foodstuffs showed uneven ups and downs but did not change materially over the half-century as Americans imported coffee, tropical fruits, and olive and coconut oils, which could be produced domestically only at great cost, if at all. Imports of semimanufactures increased somewhat, but finished manufactures declined greatly in importance as American productive capacity grew.

Trade linkages altered as well. Although Europe became a more important customer of the United States after the Civil War than ever before, American exports to Europe began to decline relatively about 1885. During the 1870s and 1880s, Europeans were the recipients of more than four-fifths of all U.S. exports; by 1920, this share had dropped to three-fifths. In the meantime, the United States remained Europe's best customer. The sharp decline in the proportion of American imports from Europe between 1915 and 1920, a result of wartime disruption, permanently injured this trade.

In the first 20 years of the twentieth century, Americans found new customers in Asia and Canada, and their interest in the Latin American market was just beginning. On the import side, the Asian countries and Canada were furnishing a great part of the crude materials that were becoming typical U.S. imports. South America had already achieved a substantial position as a purveyor of coffee and certain key raw materials to the United States.

What was the source of the American preeminence in manufacturing achieved by 1900? As Gavin Wright's research has shown, America's preeminence resulted not so much from a relative abundance of capital or skilled labor or technological knowledge but from the relative abundance of nonreproducible natural resources.[7] In 1913, the United States produced 65 percent of the world's petroleum, 56 percent of the copper, 39 percent of the

[7]Gavin Wright, "The Origins of American Industrial Success, 1879–1940," *American Economic Review* 80 (September 1990): 651–668.The data on mineral output that follow are from p. 661.

coal, 37 percent of the zinc, 36 percent of the iron ore, and 34 percent of the lead, and the country was the world's leader in the production of each of these materials. It was the leader, or among the leaders, in the production of many other minerals. America's abundance of nonreproducible resources did not result from a series of lucky accidents of nature. The large and stable internal market for manufactures, combined with a flexible system for establishing property rights, promoted intensive exploration for and exploitation of natural resources.

It merits emphasis that this preeminence, founded in raw material abundance, did not lead to prosperity based on raw material dependence as it does in many oil rich countries in the world today. The expansion of materials and institutions favoring many diverse production and distribution forms sustained growth even as national resources were being used up and dependence on oil and other raw material imports increased.

Changes in Balance of Trade

A good way to summarize the history of American foreign trade is to examine a series of international balance-of-payments statements to see what changes occurred in the major accounts. As Table 20.4 shows, Americans paid out a net total of $1.8 million (columns 2 & 3) between 1850 and 1873. Residents of the United States could enjoy this net inflow of goods and services and pay interest and dividends on existing foreign investments largely because foreign nationals continued to make new investments in American businesses (column 4), especially in railroads. Another balancing item during this period was the $200 million in foreign currencies brought or sent to the United States and changed into dollars by immigrants and their families. Such payments are called *unilateral transfers* (column 5).

From 1874 to 1895, American agricultural commodities were available to the world market in rapidly increasing quantities. When we consider that the manufacturing industries of the United States were also becoming progressively more efficient, reflecting America's growing comparative advantage in the production of goods dependent on mineral resources, it is hardly surprising to find that exports increased as they did. During these years, the favorable trade balance was reduced by the growing tendency of Americans to use the services of foreigners. Even so, Americans had net credits on current account of $1.7 billion (column 2), and foreign investors poured another $1.5 billion into this country (column 4). Offsetting the credits were more than $2 billion in interest and dividend payments to foreigners, and on balance, unilateral transfers began to reverse themselves as immigrants sent substantial sums back to friends and relatives in their countries of origin. To make up the balance, the United States imported $400 million in gold (column 6).

During the prosperous years of 1896 to 1914, the United States came into its own as an economic power. The trade surplus shot up to more than $9 billion, although this figure was cut to less than $7 billion by purchases of services from foreigners. This surplus was

TABLE 20.4 United States International Payments, by Periods (in billions of dollars)

(1) PERIOD	(2) NET GOODS AND SERVICES	(3) NET INCOME ON INVESTMENT	(4) NET CAPITAL TRANSACTIONS	(5) UNILATERAL TRANSFERS	(6) CHANGES IN MONETARY GOLD STOCK[a]	(7) ERRORS AND OMISSIONS
1850–1873	–0.8	–1.0	1.6	0.2	–0.0	
1874–1895	1.7	–2.2	1.5	–0.6	–0.4	
1896–1914	6.8	–1.6	–0.7	–2.6	–1.3	–0.6

[a]*A minus sign indicates an addition to the U.S. monetary gold stock.*

Source: Historical Statistics, Colonial Times to 1970 *(Washington, D.C.: Government Printing Office, 1971), 865–869.*

offset by interest and dividend payments to foreign investors, remittances of immigrants to their families, foreign investments, and an inflow of gold. The reversal in the international capital flows, though small compared with domestic investment in the United States, nevertheless had considerable symbolic value. The United States had become a lender rather than a borrower, a sign of economic maturity.

THE ACCEPTANCE OF PROTECTIONIST DOCTRINES

The United States, which had long been protectionist (as had most of Europe, but not Great Britain), became more so beginning with the Civil War. Setting up ever-higher tariff walls, Americans sought to control trade with other countries in the interests of national policy. Figure 20.2 traces a 100-year history of tariffs, or customs duties, as a percentage of the value of (1) total imports and (2) dutiable imports. As revealed there, on the eve of the Civil War, protection was limited compared with earlier times.

In 1861, maximum U.S. tariffs were not more than 24 percent and averaged less than 20 percent on dutiable commodities. The national prosperity of the last 15 years before the Civil War seemed to refute protectionists' arguments that a healthy economy required high duties. Yet by 1864, the trend of nearly three decades was reversed sharply and positively to put the United States on a high protective-tariff basis for nearly three-quarters of a century. There was no widespread demand for such a change in policy; only in the manufacturing centers were the old arguments for protection advanced with enthusiasm. To win the votes of the industrial East, the Republicans advocated higher tariffs during the campaign of 1860. After the returns were in but before Lincoln's inauguration, Congress passed the Morrill Act of 1861, the first in a long series of laws levying ever-higher taxes on imports. Thus, Congress took the first step actually before the war but after the southern opponents of the tariff had left the Congress. The requirements of Civil War financing, at a time when import duties and domestic excises furnished the principal revenues, provided an excuse for raising tariffs to unprecedented highs. By 1865, the average level of duties was 48 percent, and protection was granted to nearly any commodity for which it was requested.

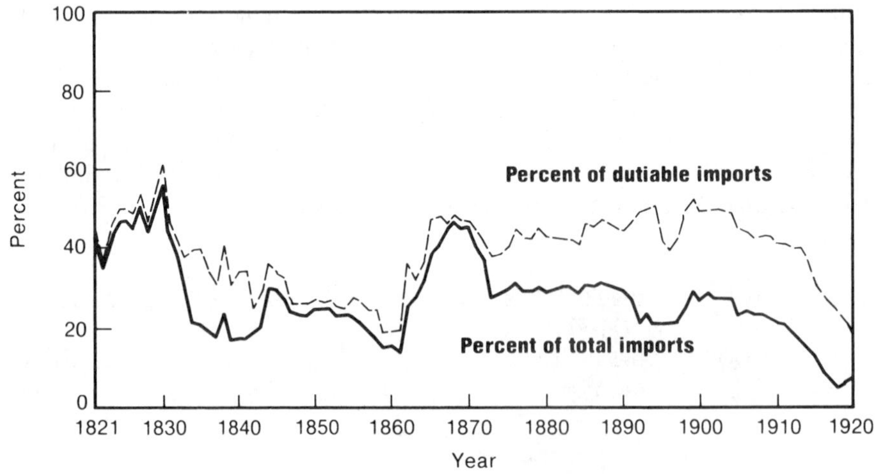

FIGURE 20.2 Customs Duties as a Percentage of (1) Total Imports and (2) Dutiable Imports, 1821–1920

Tariffs slid steadily until the Civil War; then the new politics produced a sharp increase and new level that was maintained until the turn of the century.

Source: Historical Statistics, Colonial Times to 1970 *(Washington, D.C.: Government Printing Office, 1981), 888.*

For 25 years after the war, a few leaders in both political parties attempted to reduce the "war tariffs." In 1872, to ward off drastic downward reductions that appeared imminent, protectionist forces in Washington agreed to a flat 10 percent decrease in all protective duties. In 1875, however, the earlier levels were restored, and it appeared for a time that consumers and the electorate were resigned to permanently high import rates. Yet people were increasingly persuaded that protective tariffs were, in effect, a tax that raised consumer-goods prices—and there was a growing suspicion that high levels of protection fostered the rapid growth of business combinations. During his first administration, President Grover Cleveland placed the Democrats squarely on the side of greater freedom of trade, but two Democratic assaults on the protective system produced disappointingly modest results. Cleveland's defeat in 1888 blasted hopes of genuine reform. The McKinley tariff of 1890 raised the average level of protection to 50 percent, increased the articles on the dutiable list, and reaffirmed the Republican commitment to the support of high tariffs. Following insignificant reductions during Cleveland's second term (1893–1897), the Dingley Act of 1897 raised duties above 50 percent. More goods, by value, were then taxed as imports than were admitted free. As might be expected, free goods were mostly raw and semifinished commodities requiring further processing, but even some farm products, raw wool, and hides were placed in a protected category.

The prosperity between 1897 and 1914 made it easy to defend high-tariff policies. Protectionists argued that the country was experiencing a high level of employment and economic activity because tariffs were high. Yet by 1900, American industry had obviously come of age. American manufacturers were competing in the markets of Europe; it was apparent, especially in the metal-processing industries, that most American firms needed no protection. The textile industries, which had enjoyed the benefits of high tariffs for a century, paid the lowest wages, had the highest unemployment, and suffered from the rigors of competition more than any other class of producers. Moreover, it was readily demonstrable by this time that import duties usually raised the prices of protected articles to consumers. As the populace felt the pressures of rising living costs in the first decade of the century, voters blamed the tariffs, and Democratic politicians exploited this political unrest. When the Payne-Aldrich bill of 1909 failed to bring any relief from high tariffs, widespread political protest resulted.

In the campaign of 1912, the Democrats promised a downward revision of import duties, which was carried out in the Underwood-Simmons bill of 1913. It placed iron and steel on the free list, and sharply reduced duties on cost-of-living items such as cotton and woolen textiles. The result was a simplified tariff structure, still of protective significance, with average duties about half of what they had been for several decades. During President Woodrow Wilson's administration, the average level of the tariffs was slightly below 25 percent—almost the level that had prevailed just before 1860.

Economists have long accepted the idea that protection may be beneficial in the case of an "infant" industry. When a firm is first starting out, its productivity will be low because workers and managers do not have much on-the-job training, and the firm may not be able to survive competition from experienced foreign firms. Tariff protection will buy the domestic firm time to mature. Eventually, tariff protection can be removed. In the long run, the gains to the consumer from having a vigorous domestic producer may offset the short-term costs of protection.

The problem with the infant-industry argument, revealed in the long history of tariff protection after the Civil War, is that the "infants" never grow up. As Bennett Baack and Edward Ray have shown, the structure of tariffs and subsequent levels of protection throughout the late nineteenth century were explained largely by the profit motives of established special interest groups rather than by a scientific determination of which infants needed protection based on costs and benefits to the economy as a whole.[8]

[8]Bennett D. Baack and Edward J. Ray, "The Political Economy of Tariff Policy: A Case Study of the United States," *Explorations in Economic History* 20 (1983): 73–93.

Although we are justified in criticizing tariff protection for established industries, we should not exaggerate the costs to the American people. In many protected industries, vigorous domestic competition was a close substitute for foreign competition. At the turn of the century, imports were a little over 6 percent of GNP, and it is hard to imagine that this figure would have increased dramatically even if all tariffs had been removed. Indeed, it was because the costs to individual consumers were relatively small that Congress was so open to persuasion by special interests seeking tariff protection.

The Income Tax

Opposition to the tariff was strong, particularly in the South and West. But if tariffs were cut, where would federal revenues come from? The answer, according to the Populists and other reformers, was from an income tax. The income tax was not a new idea. Income taxes had been used sporadically before the Civil War at the state level and sometimes proposed for the federal level. The Civil War income tax had been a successful moneymaker. In 1894, Congress passed income tax legislation, but it was declared unconstitutional in 1895. Overcoming the Supreme Court decision would require an amendment to the Constitution which became possible because support for the income tax continued to grow.

Two categories of spending proved extremely popular and increased support for a tax to fund them: more generous army pensions and increased military spending, particularly on the navy. Support for the naval buildup in turn is explained by the growing role of the United States in the world competition for colonies (which we will discuss later), and for naval supremacy. By 1907, when President Theodore Roosevelt sent the Great White Fleet of the United States around the world, the U.S. fleet, measured in battleship strength, was already second only to Britain's. Some states, moreover, that had opposed the income tax earlier saw that they would benefit from expenditures for naval construction.

In 1909, Congress passed an amendment to the Constitution providing for an income tax; it was ratified in 1913. The income tax, as Bennett Baack and John Ray conclude in their classic study, did not cause the great expansion of government spending that occurred later in the century, but it did make it possible.[9]

THE UNITED STATES IN AN IMPERIALIST WORLD

In the early 1880s, western Europeans became obsessed with a desire to own more of the earth's surface.[10] Africa's interior, which before 1875 had been almost entirely unexplored and unmapped by Europeans, was partitioned among the major European powers, with only Liberia and Ethiopia remaining independent. In Asia, the French took over all of Indochina, British India annexed Burma, and Britain extended its hold over the Malay states. Although it avoided physical disintegration, China nevertheless had to make humiliating economic concessions to the major European powers. By the end of the nineteenth century not much of the world was left to colonize.

A detailed study by Lance Davis and Robert Huttenback has shown that the costs of the British Empire to the British people outweighed the economic benefits, although some citizens and enterprises benefited.[11] Nevertheless, a combination of special interests, fears of other European powers, and exaggerated claims about potential economic gains kept the competition for colonies going full tilt.

---

[9]Bennett D. Baack and Edward J. Ray, "Special Interests and the Adoption of the Income Tax in the United States," *Journal of Economic History* 45 (1985): 607–625.

[10]For a most interesting reinterpretation of the issue of American imperialism, see Stanley Lebergott, "The Return to U.S. Imperialism, 1890–1929," *Journal of Economic History* 40 (1980): 229–252.

[11]Lance Davis and Robert Huttenback, *Mammon and the Pursuit of Empire: The Economics of British Imperialism* (New York: Cambridge University Press, 1988).

Through most of the nineteenth century, the United States remained apart from the race to acquire colonies in other parts of the world. Before the Civil War, southern politicians had looked to Central and South America for colonies that might be incorporated as slaveholding areas within the United States, but these efforts came to naught. Americans concentrated on westward expansion in North America, wresting control when necessary from the European powers and from Native Americans. It was imperialism, to be sure, but not what Americans of that day had in mind when they debated the merits of an empire.

The only territory outside the continental limits that the United States acquired before 1898 was Alaska (1867), which was presumed at the time to be almost worthless. In 1893, agitation to annex Hawaii began, but the American people balked at the highhanded methods used to depose the existing Hawaiian government, and the islands were not finally annexed until 1898. As explained at the end of this chapter, business interests generally opposed the needless and tragic Spanish-American War, despite the chauvinist campaign of the Hearst and Pulitzer newspapers, and there was little popular enthusiasm for the conflict until a martial spirit was whipped up by the destruction of the U.S. battleship *Maine* in Havana Harbor on February 15, 1898. The quick and favorable outcome of that "splendid little war" (as Secretary of State John Hay described it to Theodore Roosevelt) forced Americans to make decisions regarding expansion outside their continental borders.

The first decisions concerned disposition of the former Spanish colonies of Cuba, Puerto Rico, and the Philippines. Cuba was given nominal independence, and Puerto Rico received territorial status, but the Platt Amendment of 1901 so restricted Cuban independence that Cuba, in effect, became a protectorate of the United States. Instead of granting independence to the Philippines, the United States claimed that country as a colonial possession. An insurrection followed, which the United States put down with brutal force. With these islands in the Pacific and a growing interest in trade with the Orient, the United States insisted on an "open-door" policy in China and, in general, on economic opportunities in East Asia equal to those of the European powers. In the western hemisphere, the United States in 1903 acquired a perpetual lease of the Panama Canal Zone from the newly independent Republic of Panama, and the completion of the canal in 1914 ensured a lasting American interest in the Caribbean and Central America.

Indeed, two years before construction of the canal began, the policy known as the "Roosevelt Corollary" to the Monroe Doctrine had been pronounced. In a message to Congress in 1904, President Theodore Roosevelt had enunciated a principle that was to make the Monroe Doctrine an excuse for intervention in the affairs of Latin American countries. Roosevelt had argued that because chronic weakness of a government might require some "civilized" nation to restore order and because, according to the Monroe Doctrine, European interference would not be tolerated, the United States might be forced to exercise police power in "flagrant cases of wrongdoing or impotence." Europeans were not disturbed by such an assumption of international police power, but Latin Americans were—and they had reason to be apprehensive.

The United States did not wait long to apply the Roosevelt Corollary. When the Dominican Republic could not meet its financial obligations, certain European states threatened to collect payments by force. Roosevelt's new doctrine required American intervention to forestall such moves. A treaty was signed in 1905, giving the United States authority to collect customs duties, of which 55 percent was to be paid to foreign creditors. In 1916, the Dominican government tried to escape American domination, and U.S. marines were sent in to quell the rebellion. In 1914, Haiti was made a protectorate of the United States, again with the aid of the marines. American forces landed so often in Nicaragua that the succession of episodes became a standing joke.

After the 1910 Mexican revolution against the country's dictator, Porfirio Diaz, American and other foreign investors, who were heavily committed in railroads and oil, pressed for intervention and the restoration of order. For a time, President Wilson encouraged Latin Americans by declining to invade Mexico. But "watchful waiting" could last just so long amid the cries of outrage at the destruction of American property, and U.S. politicians were unable to tolerate these repeated affronts to American honor. Troops crossed onto Mexican soil in 1914 and 1917—the second time, under the leadership of General John "Black Jack" Pershing—to seize the "bandit" Pancho Villa. With the adoption of the Mexican constitution in 1917, the turmoil subsided temporarily, only to begin again in the early 1920s.

★★★ *Economic Reasoning Proposition*

Economic motives have been invoked to explain America's imperialist adventures. Recall Economic Reasoning Propositions 2 and 4. America sought foreign colonies, it is said, to provide an outlet for American capital and a cheap source of raw materials. Little evidence backs up such an explanation, however. Only a small fraction of U.S. foreign investment went to areas under U.S. political control, and only a small fraction of raw materials imported from the rest of the world came from these areas.[12] J. P. Morgan and other leaders of big business and finance opposed the Spanish-American War. Among other things, they were worried about the value of Spanish securities held by American banks and the value of American investments in the Cuban sugar industry. A more satisfying economic explanation could be based on the role of special interests anxious to collect debts or protect other interests.

Clearly, however, noneconomic motives were the prime movers of U.S. imperialism. It was widely believed that the United States had to play a role in the "great game" of international power politics, and that to do so, the United States needed overseas bases and colonies, especially coaling stations for its fleets.

Many Americans, however, remained unconvinced. The years from 1898 to 1918 were marked by an uncomfortable conviction that euphemisms such as "manifest destiny" and "extending the areas of freedom" could not long cover up the highhanded methods used to acquire America's growing empire. Nor would it be possible to maintain approval for a diplomacy that was devoted largely to promoting or protecting private financial or commercial interests. Critics of imperialism contended that investors seeking profits in the countries of Central America and the Caribbean should be willing to take the risks of venturing under unstable governments. As Economic Reasoning Proposition 4 states, "rules of the game" influence choices.

The economic consequences of America's imperialistic ventures were relatively small, but the diplomatic consequences were important. These adventures forced the United States to turn its attention outside itself and increase its military strength. Offsetting these gains were the fears and hatreds built up among natural allies in central and South America, with whose aspirations Americans should have sympathized. It would take a new generation of Americans and a second world war to remove part of this emotional conflict. Even so, the harm of two decades of harsh diplomacy could not be easily undone. As the fires of world revolution were kindled among the disadvantaged peoples of the world in the 1950s, it was not hard to perceive the long-term injury to U.S. international relationships by America's early experiments with imperialism had inflicted.

[12]Robert B. Zevin, "An Interpretation of American Imperialism," *Journal of Economic History* 32 (March 1972): 316–370, and Stanley Lebergott, "The Return to U.S. Imperialism, 1890–1929," *Journal of Economic History* 40 (June 1980): 229–252.

Selected References and Suggested Readings

Baack, Bennett D., and Edward John Ray. "Tariff Policy and Comparative Advantage in the Iron and Steel Industry, 1870–1929." *Explorations in Economic History* 11 (1973): 3–24.

———. "The Political Economy of Tariff Policy: A Case Study of the United States." *Explorations in Economic History* 10 (1983): 73–93.

———. "Special Interests and the Adoption of the Income Tax in the United States." *Journal of Economic History* 45 (1985): 607–625.

Chandler, Alfred D., Jr. *The Visible Hand: The Managerial Revolution in America*. Cambridge, Mass.: Belknap Press of Harvard University Press, 1977.

Clark, V. S. *History of Manufacturers in the United States*, Vol. 1. New York: McGraw-Hill, 1929.

Davis, Lance, and Robert Huttenback. *Mammon and the Pursuit of Empire: The Economics of British Imperialism*. New York: Cambridge University Press, 1988.

The Thomas Alva Edison Papers, **http://edison.rutgers.edu/**.

Galloway, Lowell E., and Richard K. Vedder. "The Increasing Urbanization Thesis: Did 'New Immigrants' to the United States Have a Particular Fondness for Urban Life?" *Explorations in Economic History* 8 (1971): 305–320.

Hawke, G. R. "The United States Tariff and Industrial Protection in the Late Nineteenth Century." *Economic History Review* 28 (1975).

Irwin, Douglas A. "Could the United States Iron Industry Have Survived Free Trade after the Civil War?" *Explorations in Economic History* 37 (2000): 278–299.

———. "Did Late-Nineteenth Century U.S. Tariffs Promote Infant Industries? Evidence from the Tinplate Industry." *Journal of Economic History* 60 (2000): 335–360.

Lebergott, Stanley. "The Return to U.S. Imperialism, 1890–1929." *Journal of Economic History* 40 (1980): 229–252.

Libecap, Gary D. "The First Consumer Quality Guarantees by the Federal Government: The Meat Inspection Acts of 1890 and 1891." Working Paper 88–12, Karl Eller Center, University of Arizona, 1988.

Lipsey, Robert. "Foreign Trade." In *American Economic Growth: An Economist's History of the United States*, ed. Lance E. Davis et al. New York: Harper & Row, 1972.

Livesay, Harold, and Glenn Porter. *Merchants and Manufacturers*. Baltimore: Johns Hopkins University Press, 1971.

Olney, Martha L. *Buy Now–Pay Later*. Chapel Hill: University of North Carolina Press, 1991.

———. "When Your Word Is Not Enough: Race, Collateral, and Household Credit." *Journal of Economic History* 58 (2), (June 1998): 408–431.

O'Rourke, Kevin H., and Jeffrey G. Williamson. *Globalization and History: The Evolution of a Nineteenth-Century Atlantic Economy*. Cambridge, Mass.: MIT Press, 1999.

Simon, Matthew. "The United States Balance of Payments, 1861–1900." In *Studies in Income and Wealth*, Vol. 24. National Bureau of Economic Research. Princeton: Princeton University Press, 1960.

Smolensky, Eugene. "Industrial Location and Urban Growth." In *American Economic Growth: An Economist's History of the United States*, ed. Lance E. Davis et al. New York: Harper & Row, 1972.

Stone, Irving. *The Global Export of Capital from Great Britain, 1865–1914: A Statistical Survey*. New York: St. Martin's, 1999.

Taussig, Frank W. *The Tariff History of the United States*. New York: Putnam's, 1932.

Weiher, Kenneth. "The Cotton Industry and Southern Urbanization, 1880–1930." *Explorations in Economic History* 14 (1977): 120–140.

Weiss, Thomas. "Urbanization and the Growth of the Service Workforce." *Explorations in Economic History* 8 (1971): 241–259.

———. "The Industrial Distribution of the Urban and Rural Workforces: Estimates for the United States, 1870–1910." *Journal of Economic History* 32 (1972): 919–937.

Wilkins, Mira. *The History of Foreign Investment in the United States to 1914*. Cambridge, Mass.: Harvard University Press, 1989.

Williamson, Jeffrey G. *American Growth and the Balance of Payments*. Chapel Hill: University of North Carolina Press, 1964.

———. "Globalization, Convergence, and History." *Journal of Economic History* 56 (1996): 277–306.

Wright, Gavin. "The Origins of American Industrial Success, 1879–1940." *American Economic Review* 80 (1990): 651–668.

Zevin, Robert B. "An Interpretation of American Imperialism." *Journal of Economic History* 32 (March 1972): 316–370.

Part Four

War, Depression, and War Again: 1914–1946

STOCK MONTAGE

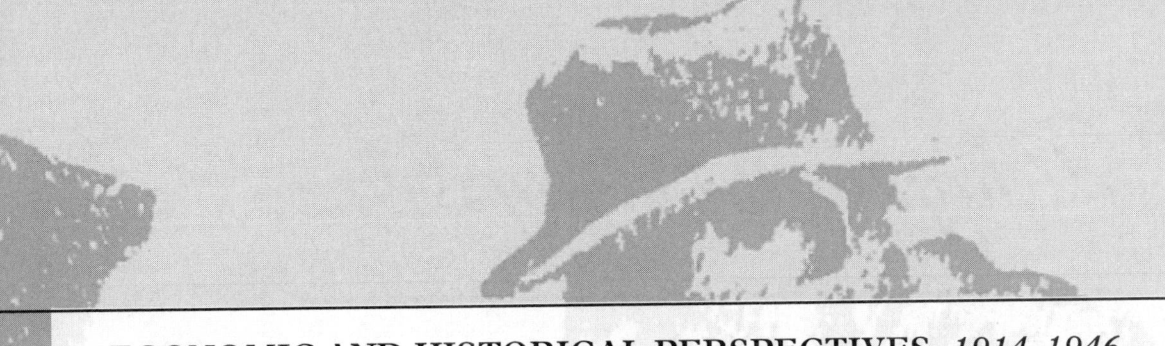

ECONOMIC AND HISTORICAL PERSPECTIVES *1914–1946*

1. Two world wars engulfed the industrial nations, producing enormous costs in terms of labor, capital, and human suffering. The United States emerged from each conflict with its domestic capital intact and with an enhanced position relative to that of its economic rivals.
2. A communist government came to power in Russia. The Soviet Union engaged in a long rivalry, first with Germany and then with the United States that dominated worldwide big-power politics for most of the century.
3. The stock market boom of the late 1920s was based on widespread expectations that a new age of continuous prosperity had dawned. The great crash of 1929 dashed those hopes and ushered in a severe economic contraction.
4. The Great Depression of the 1930s was a cataclysm of unparalleled magnitude. The banking system collapsed, farm prices fell, and industrial production plummeted. At the lowest point, in 1933, one worker in four was unemployed.
5. As a result of the depression, the federal government took a much larger role in the economic life of the nation. Regulation of the private sector and expenditures for social welfare increased. In 1929, federal spending amounted to 3 percent of GNP; in 1947, it amounted to 15 percent.
6. The nation's financial system was changed radically as a result of the depression. Deposit insurance was introduced, the payment of interest on deposits was prohibited, and the Securities and Exchange Commission was set up to regulate the stock market. The world's monetary system, moreover, was radically altered. The gold standard disappeared, and at the end of World War II, a new system was established in which the dollar was given the central role.

Chapter Twenty-One

World War I, 1914–1918

Chapter Theme

The United States entered World War I in April 1917. Although the United States was actively engaged for only 19 months, labor and capital were quickly mobilized on an impressive scale. The armed forces increased from 180,000 in 1916 to nearly 3 million in 1918. Scores of new agencies attempted to regulate prices, set priorities, and allocate resources. When the war ended, most wartime controls were abandoned, and most wartime agencies were dismantled. Nevertheless, the war provided a precedent for the federal government's increased role in the economy that emerged in the 1930s; the lesson that many people drew from the war, that the government could play a powerful positive role in meeting crises, would be remembered when the nation faced the Great Depression.

THE ORIGINS OF THE WAR

By 1914, Europe's armed forces had been built up in a sustained arms race, and her nations had been linked together in military alliances. Nationalistic and imperialistic rivalries had combined to produce a dangerous state of affairs. In France, for example, many still sought revenge for the territory and reparations that France had been forced to give Germany as a result of the Franco-Prussian War of 1870–1871. In Austria-Hungary, fear of the restive Slavic minorities had increased. In Britain, Germany's attempt to challenge British naval supremacy had produced heightened tensions. Germany was fearful about being surrounded by hostile military alliances. And this list of fears and conflicts could be greatly expanded.

Even on the eve of war, there was still considerable optimism that the peace would hold. Europe had experienced several decades without a major war, and in the meantime, industrialization and relatively free international trade had produced rapidly rising standards of living. A war that would destroy the fruits of this progress seemed irrational. Many people believed, moreover, that the rising international solidarity of the labor movement would undermine support for a war entered into by imperialistic capitalist powers. The optimists were wrong.

The assassination of Austrian Archduke Ferdinand by a Serb on June 28, 1914, set off a chain reaction that soon engulfed Europe in the bloodiest war the world had yet seen. On one side were the Allies: Britain, France, Russia, and several smaller nations. On the other side were the Central Powers: Germany, Austria-Hungary, and their associates. Many believed that the war would end quickly as the Franco Prussian War had done. But on the western front, a German advance into France became bogged down in trench warfare, producing a stalemate that could not be broken even with the loss of incredible numbers of lives. By one conservative estimate, 10 million people died in the war and another 20 million were wounded.[1]

The first economic reaction in the United States was a financial panic. The stock market was temporarily closed, and banks were under considerable pressure as depositors tried to convert their money into gold. But the crisis soon passed. Under the Aldrich-Vreeland Act, passed after the crisis of 1907, banks had been authorized to issue emergency currency as a temporary substitute for gold, and the issue of this currency put an end to the crisis. At one point, this currency amounted to nearly one-quarter of the currency in the hands of the public.[2]

During the period of American neutrality (from 1914 until 1917), it became clear that this period would be immensely profitable for American business. German imports from the United States fell to practically nothing because of the British naval blockade; but Britain, France, and other European countries began to purchase large amounts of munitions and food at ever-rising prices from the United States. A wide gap opened between America's soaring exports to Europe and her declining imports. The Europeans paid for these exports by extinguishing holdings of American debt, by shipping gold, and by incurring new debts. When the war began, the United States was a debtor, the normal status for a developing country. When the war ended, the United States was a creditor that held much of the world's stock of monetary gold. Before the war, the world's financial center was London; after the war, it was New York. With the fighting so far away and so bloody, sentiment in the United States initially favored keeping out of the war, but eventually, many forces and events combined to push the United States toward active involvement on the side of the Allies. Partly it was the close cultural and linguistic ties between Britain and the United States. But the crucial factor in turning public opinion against Germany was Germany's use of submarine warfare. In 1915, after the sinking without warning of the British ship Lusitania (with the loss of 1,198 lives, including 124 Americans), President Woodrow Wilson sent a series of strongly worded warnings to Germany. For a time, Germany moderated its use of submarines. In early 1917, however, the Germans returned to a policy of unrestricted submarine warfare in a desperate gamble to starve Britain into submission before intervention by the United States could turn the tide.

America's involvement in the war would be brief but decisive. The United States declared war on April 17, 1917. The armistice with Germany was signed on November 11, 1918, 17 months later. American forces were instrumental in winning a number of important victories. But it was not the victories themselves so much as the prospect of enormous American reinforcements that forced the Germans, exhausted by years of war and blockade, to come to terms. Indeed, when the war ended, the Central Powers still controlled large amounts of Allied territory from France to Crimea.

U.S. INVOLVEMENT

The armed forces of the United States, as noted in the chapter introduction, increased from 179,000 in 1916 to nearly 3 million in 1918. Some 2 million served overseas in the American Expeditionary Force, and about three-quarters of them saw combat. A military draft was instituted in April 1917, with a system of deferments for skilled workers.

---

[1]Roger Chickering and Stig Forster, *Great War, Total War* (Cambridge, England: Cambridge University Press 2000), 6.

[2]Milton Friedman and Anna J. Schwartz, *A Monetary History of the United States* (Princeton, N.J.: Princeton University Press, 1963), 172.

Americans took part in bitter fighting, and 117,000 Americans died in military service, more than half from disease. The United States produced vast amounts of arms and weapons, and launched a great shipbuilding program.

The financial reflection of the military effort was a tremendous increase in spending by the federal government, from 1.5 percent of GNP in 1916 to 24.2 percent in 1918. American involvement began with the country operating at close to full employment: the unemployment rate in 1916 was 5.1 percent. (This was in marked contrast to World War II, which America entered with reserves of underutilized labor and capital.) Therefore, it was not possible to increase the production of weapons and other military supplies greatly without reducing civilian consumption.

Financing the War

Governments obtain the resources needed to fight a war in four basic ways: (1) commandeering, including drafting soldiers, confiscating food and other raw materials, and appropriating living quarters for soldiers; (2) taxing; (3) borrowing, which could be broadened to include the sale of existing assets such as land and claims to future payments; and (4) printing money. We could add a fifth category, voluntary contributions to the war effort. The point here is to identify the ways that governments can acquire resources beyond the amounts that are forthcoming voluntarily. The latter three methods—taxing, borrowing, and printing money—are often called the three ways of *financing* wars because they are by far the main ways that modern governments acquire the money required to support war efforts.

In 1916 Congress levied an estate tax to help finance rearmament. Populist reformers who wanted to redistribute the wealth of the "Robber Barons" had long advocated this tax. The federal level had successfully resisted the tax on the grounds that it was needed only in wartime. (World War I was the first since the Spanish American War.) After its passage in 1916, however, the estate tax became a permanent but small part of the federal revenue system.

On October 3, 1917, after considerable wrangling, Congress passed the War Revenue Act. This act increased corporate and personal income taxes (the rate in the top bracket was raised to 70 percent) and established excise, excess profits (for business), and luxury taxes. Table 21.1 shows the total financial cost of the war and how it was distributed among various sources of finance. Taxation was important, but borrowing was far more important, accounting for 61 percent of total financing.

Why did Congress prefer to borrow? One reason may be that borrowing concealed some of the costs of the war. When taxes are raised, it is altogether too clear who is doing what to whom. It could also be argued that the war was an investment—"to make the world safe for democracy," in President Wilson's phrase. Since future generations would benefit, why should the current generation bear all the burden of the war? Raising taxes high enough to finance all of the war, moreover, would have reduced work effort. It is better, many economists now believe, to use borrowing to "smooth" taxes over time.

TABLE 21.1 Financing World War I, 1917–1919

	TOTAL (billions)	PERCENT
War expenditures	$31.0	100.0
Taxes	7.6	24.5
Borrowing from the public	19.0	61.4
Creating new money	4.4	14.1

Note: Total wartime expenditures were calculated as the sum of federal government expenditures in 1917 through 1919 less three times average expenditures in 1916.

Source: Historical Statistics *(Washington, D.C.: Government Printing Office, 1976), Series Y336 (expenditures), Y335 (taxes), X594 (U.S. government obligations held by commercial banks), and X800 (U.S. government obligations held by the Federal Reserve).*

TABLE 21.2 Money and Prices in World War I

YEAR	STOCK OF MONEY (billion $S)	MONEY PER UNIT OF REAL NNP[a] (1914 = 100)	PRICES IMPLICIT NNP[a] DEFLATOR (1914 = 100)
1914	$16.39	100.0	100.0
1915	17.59	104.1	103.1
1916	20.85	105.2	116.5
1917	24.37	126.3	143.9
1918	26.73	126.1	165.5
1919	31.01	140.5	168.0
1920	34.80	166.0	191.7

[a]*Net National Product*

Source: Milton Friedman and Anna J. Schwartz, Monetary Trends in the United States and the United Kingdom *(Chicago: University of Chicago Press, 1982), 123–124.*

Wilson's Secretary of the Treasury William Gibbs McAdoo studied the financing of the Civil War and concluded that Salmon Chase, the Treasury secretary, had erred in not linking the purchase of war bonds more closely to patriotism. McAdoo launched an aggressive program to market bonds in World War I, to "capitalize patriotism."[3] Huge bond rallies were held, and the crowds were exhorted to buy war bonds by celebrities such as Mary Pickford and Douglas Fairbanks. Charlie Chaplin made a film showing how the purchase of war bonds helped finance the war. How much all of this helped is open to question. Despite all the hoopla and the considerable, often vicious anti-German propaganda, the government found that it could not sell bonds that paid much below the going market rate.[4] Economic Reasoning Proposition 3 (economic incentives matter) applies in war as well as in peace.

The government also relied on creating new money. In earlier wars, the mechanism had been simple. In the Revolutionary War, the government had printed Continental dollars; in the Civil War, greenbacks. Now the mechanism was more complicated. When the Federal Reserve bought bonds on the open market, it did so by creating deposits that had not existed before. When lodged in the banking system, those deposits became the basis for a further expansion of money and credit by the banks. All told, as Table 21.1 shows, the Federal Reserve and the commercial banking system acquired over $4 billion worth of government bonds, about 14 percent of total war finance. Even this figure understates the effect of money creation to some extent because the banks made personal loans, secured by government bonds, to purchasers of bonds. Although this transaction appeared on the books of the bank as a personal loan, it was really the indirect purchase of a government bond.

The net result of financing part of the war by creating money was a substantial increase in the stock of money and the price level. As Table 21.2 shows, the stock of money about doubled between 1914 and 1920, as did the level of prices. Note, however, that prices did not rise in the exact proportion as money per unit of real output, as a naïve version of the quantity theory of money would predict. See Economic Insight box 19.1 on page 376. Prices rose more rapidly than money per unit of output (K fell) between 1915 and 1918, more slowly from 1918 to 1919, and then more rapidly from 1919 to 1920. This pattern can be given a fairly straightforward explanation. During the years of threatened and actual

[3]David M. Kennedy, *Over Here: The First World War and American Society* (Oxford, England: Oxford University Press, 1980), 105.

[4]Margaret G. Myers, *A Financial History of the United States* (New York: Columbia University Press, 1970), 280–283, and William J. Schultz and M. R. Caine, *Financial Development of the United States* (New York: Prentice-Hall, 1937), 533–539.

Movie star Charlie Chaplin selling War bonds.

war, the fear of inflation encouraged people to spend their money. The end of the war created expectations of a return to price stability, which reduced inflation. Finally, an unexpected postwar boom rekindled economic activity and expectations of inflation.

When the real value of the cash in your pocket goes down in value because the government acquires real resources and drives up prices, inflation occurs, and inflation is a tax on money. Inflation due to money creation has the attractive political property of being a hidden tax. The public will blame profiteers rather than monetary policy for the inflation. All of this does not mean that there is no justification for finance through money creation. If the government can tax houses, tobacco, and alcohol, why not money? It does suggest, however, that money creation is likely to be overused because policymakers will not be held accountable to the same degree as with more visible taxes.

Paying the Human Costs of the War

The major part of the war's cost was borne by the soldiers, sailors, and airmen, and their families. To some extent, we can think of these costs in economic terms. The draft can be thought of as a tax. The amount of the tax was the difference between what the government would have had to pay a soldier to get him to volunteer for military service and what it actually paid. When a soldier received a nonmortal wound (204,000) or died (117,000), there was a further loss: the discounted value of the lost future income.[5]

These losses, it was widely recognized, created an obligation of the United States to the veterans and their families. Partly, these obligations were made good through veterans' benefits paid after the war. The adequacy of compensation, however, was debated. The "fair" amount of compensation for death or dismemberment is hard enough to agree on, and the idea that war entails heavy psychological costs, shell shock, for example, was just gaining acceptance. There also were more subtle psychological effects, a disillusionment with American life and culture, that nonetheless sometimes affected the capacity of the veteran to earn a living. The writers who gave voice this disillusionment with war and traditional American values, such as Ernest Hemingway, John Dos Passos, and F. Scott Fitzgerald, became known as the "Lost Generation."

Payments to veterans or their families, do not change the loss of resources and output that the economy as a whole sustained. These payments merely redistribute the burden of the losses.[6] All of these calculations and the inevitable debate about whether compensation was adequate should not be allowed to obscure the reality that in the end, it is impossible to put dollar signs on all of the human costs, costs that were high for the United States and staggering for the European belligerents.

REPLACEMENT OF THE MARKET WITH A COMMAND SYSTEM

During World War I (unlike the Civil War), attempts were made to direct the economy from the top. This effort arose from the ideological temper of the times. The battle between those who favored and those who opposed organizing the economy through the market was sharp just prior to the war, and there were strong antimarket factions in both the Democratic and Republican parties. There was also the example of Germany, which was widely perceived to be both powerful and organized along centralizing lines. Perhaps the most daring departure from the tradition of laissez-faire was the nationalization of the nation's railroads. By the end of the war, Washington was bulging with agencies set up to cope with a vast array of economic problems: A Capital Issues Committee designed to limit issues of securities by the private sector, a War Trade Board with powers over imports and exports, a War Shipping Board and an Emergency Fleet Corporation designed to produce ships and to control their use, and about 150 others. Existing agencies, moreover, were often given new powers. How did the control and command system actually work?

The Food and Fuel Administrations

In August 1917, Congress passed the Lever Food and Fuel Control Act, establishing a wartime Food Administration and a Fuel Administration. Herbert Hoover was appointed the food administrator. Hoover enjoyed a reputation as a brilliant administrator—he was then serving as the director of the Commission for the Relief of Belgium—and his reputation grew with his performance as food administrator. His job was to maintain an adequate supply of food to the domestic market and to our allies while preventing excessive increases in prices. The tools given to Hoover were limited, and his philosophy of government—which emphasized voluntary cooperation—discouraged him from seeking greater authority. Direct control of prices, with penalties for violation, was generally avoided, as was formal rationing. But the food administrator was given the power to license food dealers. This license could be revoked if the dealer failed to go along with Food Administration price policies. Economic Insight 21.1 on page 422 discusses the role of rationing in a competitive market.

---

[5]*Historical Statistics* (Washington, D.C.: Government Printing Office, 1976), Series Y879, Y880, Y882.
[6]These issues are explored in John Maurice Clark, *The Cost of the War to the American People* (New Haven, Conn.: Yale University Press, 1931).

Economic Insight 21.1

The Role of Rationing

This figure illustrates the role of rationing. The government has fixed the price at *P*. But at this price, the quantity demanded exceeds the quantity supplied by *AB*. This reduces output (compared with letting the price rise to the free market equilibrium, *P**. Some consumers will be frustrated by empty shelves. Time may be wasted waiting in line. The scramble among consumers may lead to bribes and various forms of concealed price increases such as reductions in quality.

Instead, consumers can be issued ration tickets. With each purchase, a consumer must turn over a ration ticket along with the money price. The ration tickets in this case reduce the effective demand curve from *D*1 to *D*2. Because the government has guessed exactly right in this example (issued neither too few nor too many tickets), no excess demand occurs, and the problems created by price controls are reduced. Formal rationing was used for sugar (after long waiting lines became intolerable), but in many cases, the government permitted "socially desirable" forms of hidden price increases, such as the tie-in sales intended to promote the baking of Victory bread described in the text. The result was to move the true price toward the free market equilibrium, *P**.

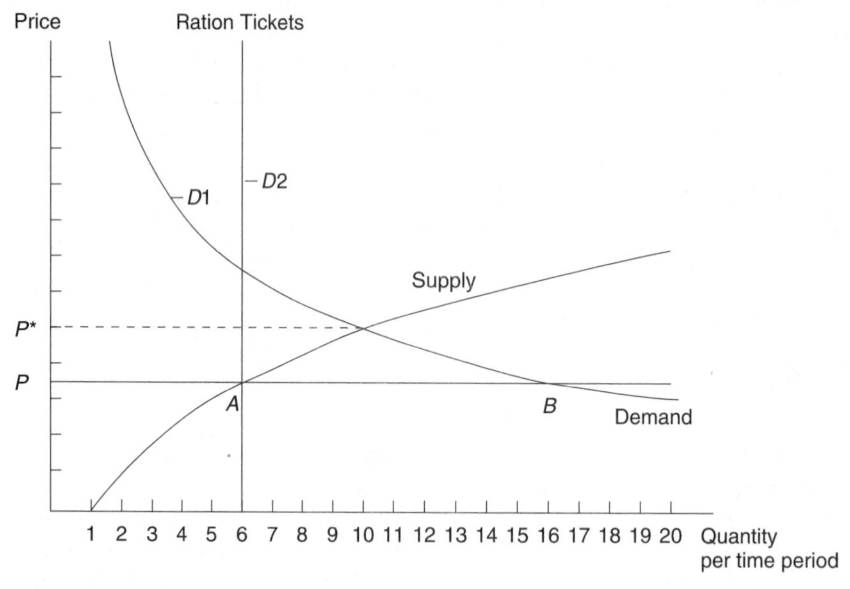

In place of formal rationing, Hoover called for voluntary conservation. "Meatless Mondays" and "Wheatless Wednesdays" were promoted as ways of reducing domestic demand and leaving more for exports. Hoover clearly believed that appeals to moral principles could influence behavior (Economic Reasoning Proposition 4: Institutions matter). Retailers were encouraged (or permitted, depending on how you look at it) to sell wheat flour along with less desirable substitutes such as rye or potato flour. The resulting mixture could be baked into a loaf of "Victory bread." Of course, this was really a hidden price increase. The true price of the wheat flour was the direct amount paid plus the difference

The Food Administration used appeals to patriotism to relieve the pressure on the prices of commodities in short supply.

between what the buyer paid for the less desirable flour and what he would voluntarily have paid for it. By such half-measures, food prices were controlled and output rationed.

The War Industries Board

In March 1918, responding to the mounting criticism of the war effort, Wilson reorganized the most ambitious of the war agencies, the War Industries Board, and placed at its head Bernard Baruch. Baruch was a successful Wall Street speculator, but as a southern Jewish Democrat, he was something of an outsider on the Street and an ideal candidate to manage the War Industries Board in a Democratic administration. Baruch went to work immediately, negotiating prices of key industrial products. Other industrial prices were set by a separate Price-Fixing Committee, which used a system called bulkline pricing. Under this system, firms reported their costs of production, and the committee then set a price that would bring forth the "bulk" (say, 80 percent) of the maximum possible output. This system was designed to balance the need for raw materials against the need for overall price stability while limiting the profits of low-cost producers. Baruch also set up a system of priorities to guide business in filling the mounting volume of war contracts. Each contract was given a government priority rating: AA, A, B, C, or D. If a conflict arose, a producer had to

Bernard Mannes Baruch in a less trying moment. A successful Wall Street investor and speculator and strong supporter of the Democratic Party, Wilson named him to head of the War Industries Board in 1918.

fill an AA order before an A order, and so on. It sounds good. Why rely on the market when a government planner could determine priorities on subcontracts in line with national values? But when firms were given their own power to set priorities on subcontracts in order to save administrative resources, industry soon became choked with high-priority contracts. The natural tendency was to give everything the highest priority. (In World War II, "priorities inflation" wrecked the system.)

Baruch's stint at the War Industries Board was brief—about eight months—but he drew strong conclusions from his experience. In subsequent years, he repeatedly argued that the example of the War Industries Board pointed the way toward cooperation between business and industry in peacetime and centralized administration (doing away with the market) in wartime.

LABOR DURING THE WAR

The demand for labor was increased by government contracts and the supply of labor was reduced by the cutoff of immigration and by the drafting of men into the armed forces. By 1918, as Table 21.3 shows, real earnings were considerably above the level of 1914. Adjustments in the labor market, however, were far from smooth. In 1917 in particular, money incomes were up 14.5 percent over 1916, but consumer prices were up 16.1 percent—real wages had fallen. The situation was reminiscent of the Civil War. In the long run, we expect real wages to be determined by the productivity of labor, but in the short run, some wages may prove to be sticky. It is not surprising, then, that 1917 was a year of strikes—4,450 of them, a record. Strikes were particularly acute west of the Mississippi, where a combination of low wages, harsh working conditions, uncompromising employers, and radical unions produced bitter labor disputes.

The Wilson administration's response was pragmatic. In a few cases, it threatened strikers through the draft and in other ways, but in most cases, it was more accommodating. War contracts generally included provisions calling for higher wages and better working conditions, though they did not provide the goal dearest to the heart of organized labor: the closed shop. When a strike of railroad workers threatened to disrupt the industry that was at the heart of the war effort, the administration nationalized the railroads. Under government control, the railroads provided improved working conditions and higher wages while raising shipping costs only modestly. The result was an operating deficit made up by the government. The railroads were finally returned to private ownership in 1920. According to Table 21.3, money earnings leaped upward in 1918 by some 22.6 percent, outrunning the cost of living (although it is difficult to be certain about these because price controls distorted the meaning of price indexes); real earnings probably reached an all-time high.

Organized labor was extremely optimistic in the immediate postwar period. Labor union membership was up, and the public's view of the conservative wing of the labor movement (under the leadership of Samuel Gompers, who had served on a government board during the war) was also high. But the hopes of many labor leaders for a new era in labor relations soon came to an end. An industrial conference called by the president in 1919—with representatives from labor, management, and the public under Baruch's leadership—ended in failure. More important, an attempt to organize the steel industry, then the bellwether of American industry, was beaten back after a long and bitter strike.

Women were one potential source of labor tapped during the war. Some women served with the armed forces in Europe, usually as nurses or telephone operators. Women also made important contributions in industry, with about a million taking up war work. However, the war did not mean a breakthrough in the economic role of women. Few took jobs in heavy industry. First-time hires were relatively few. Many married women who entered the labor force had been previously employed while single; they returned temporarily to help their families cope with war. When the war ended, the role of women in the labor force returned to what it had been before the war. Partly this was the result of

TABLE 21.3 Annual Earnings, 1914–1920

YEAR	MONEY EARNINGS OF ALL EMPLOYEES AFTER DEDUCTION FOR UNEMPLOYMENT	REAL EARNINGS OF ALL EMPLOYEES AFTER DEDUCTION FOR UNEMPLOYMENT (1914 dollars)
1914	$ 555	$555
1915	547	541
1916	647	595
1917	748	586
1918	972	648
1919	1,117	648
1920	1,236	619

Source: Historical Statistics *(Washington, D.C.: Government Printing Office, 1976), Series D723, D725.*

pressure from labor unions and other sectors for women to make room for returning veterans; partly it was the result of older economic pressures. The labor force participation rates for married and single women were both a bit lower in 1920 than they had been in 1910. On the political front, the Wilson administration strongly supported the right of women to vote, calling their contributions "vital to the winning of the war."[7] As a result, the Nineteenth Amendment to the Constitution, giving women the right to vote, was finally adopted in 1920.

Perhaps no group of workers seized the opportunities provided by the war more eagerly than African Americans. With factories operating at full capacity and deprived of a steady stream of immigrants from Europe, northern industry at last looked to African Americans for a supply of labor. Beginning in 1914, agents for northern industries fanned out across the South to recruit workers, who were often given free transportation north. There began a mass exodus of African American workers from the rural South: New York, Detroit, St. Louis, Cleveland, Chicago, and other industrial cities saw a steady stream of newcomers. In a few places in the South, the new shortage of labor actually led to improved race relations; but elsewhere, the South reacted in the old way, with harassment, detentions, and beatings. Some southerners also tried to prevent northern agents from recruiting black workers, but nothing could stem the tide: Northern industry provided higher wages, and northern cities a greater measure of freedom.

White workers, however, reacted negatively, sometimes violently, to the immigrants from the South. Competition between African American and white workers soon exploded in violent race riots: in East St. Louis in July 1917, 9 whites and a larger but undetermined number of African Americans were killed; in Chicago in July 1919, 13 whites and 23 African Americans were killed. But the result was not always so negative. In Cincinnati, we know, thanks to the work of Warren Whateley (1990), that the employment of African Americans during the War led to permanent changes in employment practices—the war provided the chance for African Americans to "get a foot in the door."

THE LEGACIES OF WORLD WAR I

Demobilization followed the simplest possible path after the Armistice. Soldiers were mustered out of the army as fast as possible. War contracts were canceled. Government bureaus were closed. Despite the rapid demobilization, things never returned to where they had been before.

The International Legacies: The Treaty of Versailles

Some of the most important changes were in the international sphere. Shortly after the war ended, Wilson sailed for Europe to take part in the Paris peace conference that would negotiate the Treaty of Versailles to end the war. Ultimately, a treaty was hammered out by the Big Four: Britain, France, the United States, and Italy. The United States, however, never ratified the treaty. It was bottled up in the Senate, where Republicans insisted on changes that Wilson would not agree to. John Maynard Keynes, who attended the conference as part of the British delegation, wrote a brilliant analysis of the Treaty of Versailles in *The Economic Consequences of the Peace*.[8]

Keynes clearly showed that the Allied demands for reparations went far beyond any that could be reasonably calculated on the basis of the understanding that had produced the Armistice. He also argued that Germany lacked the capacity to pay the reparations and would have to run a large surplus of exports over imports in order to pay them. Moreover, Keynes's

---

[7]As quoted in Kennedy, *Over Here*, 284.

[8]John Maynard Keynes, *The Economic Consequences of the Peace* (New York: Harcourt, Brace & World, 1919). This is one of the most powerful tracts ever written by an economist. It is still well worth your time. A powerful answer was provided later by Etienne Mantoux, *The Carthaginian Peace: Or the Economic Consequences of Mr. Keynes* (Oxford, England: Oxford University Press, 1946).

close study of Germany's prospects for expanding her exports and diminishing imports convinced him that changes on the order implied by the treaty were impossible. The treaty, in other words, was punitive and imposed severe penalties on Germany and Austria. Keynes's argument started a long debate among economists over the "transfer problem," as it came to be called, a debate that has still not been resolved. Perhaps Germany did have the capacity to make the required transfers if sufficient political will could be mustered. But few would argue today with Keynes's plea for a less punitive peace. The German belief that the peace was unjust contributed to what then seemed unthinkable—a second world war.

The Domestic Legacies

The war also left many domestic legacies, as shown by Robert Higgs in his book *Crisis and Leviathan.*[9] Some were financial, such as increased federal spending for interest on the national debt, veterans' benefits, and other long-term costs. More important was the ideological legacy. Though most Americans were more than willing to return to the old patterns after the war, some, such as Bernard Baruch, concluded that the economy would work better if the government played a major role in coordinating economic activity. In retrospect, we can see that American involvement in the war was too brief to draw strong conclusions about the short-term effects of government interventions, let alone the long-term effects. But the glow of success that surrounded wartime government programs made them powerful examples in the debate over the appropriate role of government in the economy. The idea that an activist government could improve the functioning of the economy lay dormant during the prosperous twenties but would become important as the Great Depression took form. The New Deal's National Recovery Administration, for example, was modeled on Baruch's War Industries Board. The New Deal's Commodity Credit Corporation was modeled on the United States Grain Corporation and controls exercised under the Agricultural Adjustment Acts, passed in the 1930s, were modeled on those exercised by the Food Administration. These are only a few examples; the complete list is much longer. Many of the individuals who were chosen to run New Deal programs, moreover, had worked for government agencies during the war. General Hugh S. Johnson, for example, who headed the National Recovery Administration in 1933, had served under Baruch at the War Industries Board.

Reformers undoubtedly would have won many changes in the economy in the 1930s even if World War I had never occurred. But the perception in the 1930s that federal programs controlling and regulating markets had been a success in World War I increased the pace and depth of reform.

The Postwar Recession

The immediate effect of the Armistice was a slowdown in the economy. Prices remained roughly level for some months. Then, in 1919, a vigorous boom began, and prices began to rise rapidly. The Federal Reserve realized that the policy of holding its discount rate below market rates was adding to inflationary pressures: Banks found it profitable to borrow from the Federal Reserve and then expand their own lending. The Federal Reserve, however, was reluctant to raise its rates. One reason was that higher interest rates might have depressed the values of the large amount of government war loans in the market.

Finally, possibly because its own reserves of gold were becoming depleted, the Federal Reserve acted. In late 1919 and early 1920, the Federal Reserve raised its discount rate. The increase in January 1920 from 4.75 percent to 6 percent was the sharpest single increase in the short history of the system. On June 1, the discount rate was raised again,

---

[9]Robert Higgs, *Crisis and Leviathan: Critical Episodes in the Growth of American Government* (New York: Oxford University Press, 1987), chapter 7.

to 7 percent. These increases sent a strong signal to the market that credit would soon be tight. In addition, there were sharp breaks in other sectors of the economy. Agricultural prices, for example, fell throughout much of the world as European production recovered. As a result, the economy went into a severe recession. From 1920 to 1921, nominal net national product fell 18 percent, and real net national product fell 4 percent. But the recession was also very brief: it resembled what has come to be called a "V-shaped" recession, straight down and straight back up again. One reason, perhaps, is that even though the number of bank failures rose substantially, there was no financial panic. (As we shall see, the sharp contraction during 1929 to 1930, which appeared at first to be a repeat of that in 1920 to 1921, produced a financial panic that drove the economy far deeper into depression.) After the economy recovered from the recession of 1920 to 1921, it entered a long period of economic expansion. So vigorous was this expansion that many people came to believe that a new age of continuous prosperity had arrived. The "roaring twenties" are the subject of the next chapter.

Selected References and Suggested Readings

Ayres, Leonard P. *The War with Germany: A Statistical Summary.* Washington, D.C. Government Printing Office, 1919. **http://www.lib.byu.edu/~rdh/wwi/memoir/docs/statistics/statstc.htm**.

Brandes, Stuart. *Warhogs: A History of War Profits in America.* Lexington: University Press of Kentucky, 1997.

Chambers, John Whiteclay II. *To Raise an Army: The Draft Comes to Modern America.* New York: Free Press, 1987.

Clark, John Maurice. "The Basis of War-Time Collectivism." *American Economic Review* 7 (1917): 772–790.

———. *The Costs of the War to the American People.* New Haven, Conn.: Yale University Press, 1931.

Clarkson, Grosvenor B. *Industrial America in the World War.* Boston: Houghton Mifflin, 1923.

Coit, Margaret L. *Mr. Baruch.* Boston: Houghton Mifflin, 1957.

Cuff, Robert D. *The War Industries Board: Business-Government Relations during World War I.* Baltimore: Johns Hopkins University Press, 1973.

———. "We Band of Brothers—Woodrow Wilson's War Managers." *Canadian Review of American Studies* 2 (1974): 135–148.

Cuff, Robert D., and Melvin I. Urofsky. "The Steel Industry and Price Fixing during World War I." *Business History Review* 44 (Autumn 1970): 291–306.

Edelstein, Michael. "War and the American Economy in the Twentieth Century." In *The Cambridge Economic History of the United States*, Vol. III, The Twentieth Century, eds. Stanley L. Engerman and Robert E. Gallman. New York: Cambridge University Press, 2000, 329–405.

Ferguson, Niall. *The Pity of War.* London: Penguin Press, 1998.

Friedman, Milton. "Price, Income, and Monetary Changes in Three Wartime Periods." *American Economic Review* 42 (May 1952). Reprinted in *The Optimum Quantity of Money and Other Essays.* Chicago: Aldine, 1969.

Friedman, Milton, and Anna J. Schwartz. *A Monetary History of the United States.* Princeton, N.J.: Princeton University Press, 1963.

Fussell, Paul. *The Great War and Modern Memory.* New York: Oxford University Press, 1975.

Gilbert, Martin. *The First World War: A Complete History.* New York: H. Holt, 1994.

Glaser, Elisabeth. "Better Late than Never. The American War Effort, 1917–1918." In *Great War, Total War: Combat and Mobilization on the Western Front 1914–1918.* eds. Roger Chickering and Sig Forster. New York: Cambridge University, Press, 2000, 389–407.

Higgs, Robert. *Crisis and Leviathan: Critical Episodes in the Growth of American Government.* New York: Oxford University Press, 1987.

Johnson, James P. "The Wilsonians as War Managers: Coal and the 1917–1918 Winter Crisis." *Prologue* 9 (1977): 193–208.

Kennedy, David M. *Over Here: The First World War and American Society*. Oxford, England: Oxford University Press, 1980.

Keynes, John Maynard. *The Economic Consequences of the Peace.* New York: Harcourt, Brace & World, 1919.

Koistinen, Paul A. C. "The 'Industrial-Military Complex' in Historical Perspective: World War I." *Business History Review* 41 (1967): 378–403.

Leuchtenburg, William E. "The New Deal and the Analogue of War." In *Change and Continuity in Twentieth-Century America*, ed. John Braeman et al. New York: Harper & Row, 1966.

Litman, Simon. *Prices and Price Control in Great Britain and the United States during the World War*. New York: Oxford University Press, 1920.

Mantoux, Etienne. *The Carthaginian Peace: Or the Economic Consequences of Mr. Keynes.* Oxford: Oxford University Press, 1946.

Rockoff, Hugh. *Drastic Measures: A History of Wage and Price Controls in the United States.* New York: Cambridge University Press, 1984.

Romer, Christina. "World War I and the Postwar Depression: A Reinterpretation Based on Alternative Estimates of GNP." *Journal of Monetary Economics* 22 (July 1988): 91–115.

Scheiber, Jane Lang, and Harry N. Scheiber. "The Wilson Administration and the Wartime Mobilization of Black Americans, 1917–1918." *Labor History* 10 (1969): 433–458.

Taussig, Frank W. "Price Fixing as Seen by a Price Fixer." *Quarterly Journal of Economics* 33 (1919): 205–241.

Urofsky, Melvin. *Big Steel and the Wilson Administration: A Study in Business Government Relations*. Columbus: Ohio State University Press, 1969.

Whateley, Warren C. "Getting a Foot in the Door: Learning, State Dependence, and the Racial Integration of Firms." *Journal of Economic History* 50 (March 1990): 43–66.

World War I Document Archive. **http://www.lib.byu.edu/~rdh/wwi/**.

Chapter Twenty-Two

THE ROARING TWENTIES

After World War I, the American public hoped for a "return to normalcy," as President Warren G. Harding put it. Wartime controls were removed, taxes were cut back, and the Republican administrations of the 1920s generally returned to market forces to produce economic growth. After a severe but brief recession in 1920 and 1921, the economy moved into a long expansion. A new American middle-class lifestyle emerged that relied on consumer durables, especially the automobile. The stock market surged, and the belief took hold that the economy had moved into a new era of continuous growth and prosperity that would eventually eliminate poverty. But the stock market crash in October 1929 and the fall into the depths of an unprecedented depression in the early 1930s made pessimists out of the most determined optimists.

A central question faced by economic historians is whether the disasters of the 1930s were the inevitable outcome of the prosperity of the 1920s and its reliance on a free-market economy, or whether they were the result of shocks and policy mistakes in the 1930s. Was there, to put it differently, a fatal cancer growing in the economy of the 1920s that brought disaster ever closer, even as the economic physicians of the day continued to pronounce the patient in good health? Economic historians have suggested numerous problems carried over from the 1920s to the 1930s—changes in the distribution of income, the ongoing problems in agriculture, the stock market boom and bust, and so on. The vast research on this period shows, however, that the depression could have been prevented or at least ameliorated if the right policies had been followed in the early 1930s. The prestige of the market economy peaked with the stock market. In the depression, the nation turned from the free-market model of 1920s to the central-planning model of the war years to restore prosperity and growth.

SOCIAL CHANGES IN THE AFTERMATH OF WAR

When World War I ended, a promising young songwriter named Harry Donaldson cast his lot with the just-organized Irving Berlin Music Company. His smash 1919 hit was at once a question and a prophetic answer: "How ya gonna keep 'em down on the farm after they've seen Paree?" How, indeed? Millions of young Americans had been wrested from the boredom of country life to serve in the war, marking the beginning of the end of an agrarian society. To be sure, only a fraction of them ever saw Paris, and some got no farther than Camp

Funston. But country boy, small-town bookkeeper, and city millworker alike developed a taste for travel and adventure.

Lured by the availability of jobs, the excitement of city life, and advances in transportation, nearly 15 million people were added to the number of American urbanites between 1920 and 1930. Sometime near the end of World War I, the number of Americans living in urban centers of 2,500 people or more passed the 50 million mark. As the census of 1920 was to report, for the first time, more than 50 percent of the population, over 54 million people, were urban dwellers. Leading the migration to the city were southern African Americans, who had begun migrating northward in large numbers during the war. Especially magnetic to African Americans were New York, Philadelphia, Washington, Chicago, St. Louis, and Los Angeles. By 1930, Harlem was the concentration point of nearly 300,000 African Americans. The term *Harlem Renaissance* refers to a remarkable flowering in literature and the arts, but its backbone was industrial jobs. This wave of migration was tied to the end of free immigration discussed later in the chapter. Unable to rely on a steady flow of unskilled and low-skilled immigrants from Europe, employers turned to immigrants from the South.

In a "dreadful" intrusion on the rights of the individual, a minority secured passage of the Eighteenth Amendment, prohibiting the manufacture, sale, or transport of "intoxicating liquors" and taking away a basic comfort of field hands, factory workers, and others, on the grounds that drinking was sinful and that poor people were not entitled to such a luxury anyway.[1]

A swell of fear and hate was rising that would crest in the activities of the Ku Klux Klan, and by 1924, that organization's anti-African American, anti-Jewish, and anti-Roman Catholic persecutions had become a national scandal.

The future nevertheless held a bright promise of prosperity and more leisure time. Women had gained the right to vote, but their emancipation was broader than that. Young women in particular began to chisel away at the double standard of morality that had been typical of pre-1914 relations between the sexes; the "flapper" of the 1920s was already emerging in 1919 as the girl who could smoke men's cigarettes, drink men's whiskey, and play men's games.

It might have been expected that these changes would be matched by changes in the workplace, especially among older married women.[2] Increased education, a reduced birthrate, smaller families, the emergence of the clerical sector, and the demonstration effect of World War I all worked toward greater female participation in the labor force. Indeed, looking at the purely economic factors, one might have expected a rapid increase in the number of two-earner households of the sort that actually arrived in the 1980s. But this development was prevented by "marriage bars," policies followed by public and private employers that prohibited the hiring of married women and that forced female employees to leave when they married. In part, these bars simply reflected broader social norms maintaining that married women belonged at home with their children. They became more widespread in the 1920s with the growth of large firms that relied on personnel departments to make hiring and firing decisions and that preferred bureaucratic rules for making decisions to individualized hiring and firing.

NEW GOODS AND THE RISE OF THE MIDDLE CLASS

Also in the 1920s, the modern American standard of living became available to a broad segment of the middle class. Mass production, mass marketing, and spectacular advances in the production of consumer durables, electric power, new appliances, suburban housing, and city skyscrapers highlighted the decade.

---

[1]The authors confess their prejudice on the issue.

[2]Claudia Goldin, *Understanding the Gender Gap: An Economic History of American Women* (New York: Oxford University Press, 1990), chapter 6.

The extent of that revolution is indicated by the figures in Table 22.1, which were compiled by Stanley Lebergott. At the beginning of the decade, only a little more than a third of American families lived in homes and apartments that were lit with electricity; by the end of the decade, only a little under a third lacked electric lighting. At the beginning of the decade, the automobile could still be regarded as a plaything of the wealthy; by the end of the decade, it had become a necessity for the middle class.

The Automobile

In many ways, the automobile was the economic symbol of the 1920s. Annual production rose from 1.5 million cars in 1921 to 4.8 million in 1929. By 1930, 60 percent of America's families owned an automobile (Table 22.1).

One consequence of the automobile was the great construction boom of the 1920s. The automobile changed the location of residences, portending the heyday of suburbia. The automobile combined travel with entertainment and spotted the countryside with motels, hot dog stands, road signs, and gas stations. This remaking of the American landscape was largely unplanned and unregulated by government. As shown by Alexander Field (1992), it also left a residual of legal tangles that made recovery from the depression more difficult in the late 1930s.

The automobile also enlarged the demands on government for paved roads, as automobile clubs and especially farmers pressed for assistance to get out of the mud. With the passage of the Federal Aid Road Act of 1916, the development of a nationwide highway system began. Under the act, the government committed itself to spending $75 million to build rural post roads, with the money to be expended by the Department of Agriculture over a period of five years. The national contribution was not to exceed 50 percent of the total construction cost, exclusive of bridges and other major structures, and was conditional on the organization of state highway departments with adequate personnel and sufficient equipment to initiate the work and carry out subsequent maintenance. The Federal Highway Act of 1921 amended the original law by requiring the secretary of agriculture to give preference to states that had designated a system of highways to receive federal aid. The designated system was to constitute the "primary" roads of the state and was not to exceed 7 percent of the state's total highway mileage. Incidentally, in the Highway Act of 1921, Congress appropriated as much money for a single year's construction (1922) as it had for all of the preceding five years.

TABLE 22.1 Percentage of American Families Owning Various Appliances, 1920 and 1930

	1920	1930
Inside flush toilets	20%	51%
Central heating	1	42
Home lighting with electricity	35	68
Mechanical refrigerators	—[a]	8
Washing machines	8	24
Vacuum cleaners	9	30
Radios	—[a]	40
Automobiles	26	60

[a]*Less than 1 percent*

Source: Stanley Lebergott, The American Economy: Income, Wealth and Want *(Princeton, N.J.: Princeton University Press, 1962), 248–299,* passim.

Henry Ford began mass production of the Model T in 1908; by 1916, he was producing 2,000 per day. In the 1920s, however, the Model T lost market share to more stylish, although more expensive, competitors. Production of the Model T was discontinued in 1926.

Buy Now, Pay Later

Another major growth sector was electric appliances such as ranges, vacuum cleaners, radios, and refrigerators. Over the decade, annual refrigerator production, for example, expanded by almost 50 times, reaching nearly 1 million units in 1930. Although only 8 percent (Table 22.1) of American families relied on mechanical refrigeration in 1930, the days of the "ice man" were numbered. Perhaps most spectacular was the rapid adoption of the radio. In 1920, when station KDKA in Pittsburgh became the first to broadcast commercially, radio was still a toy for the gadget minded; by the end of the decade, 40 percent of American families owned radios (Table 22.1), which had transformed the cultural and political life of the nation.

The growth in the market for consumer durables was brought about by developments on both the supply side and the demand side. Mass production and technological advances lowered the cost for a given quality of service of many consumer durables. Henry Ford, for example, had pioneered the mass production of low-cost automobiles using the moving assembly line before the war. In the twenties, to meet stiff competition from General Motors, he introduced improved models that incorporated the self-starter, the windshield wiper, and improved brakes.

Thanks to the work of Martha Olney, we now know that important developments also occurred on the demand side. One was the development of consumer credit— "buy now, pay later."[3] Rather than saving up cash or interest-earning assets to buy a consumer

[3]This advertising slogan became popular in the twenties. Olney chose it as the title for her definitive study of consumer behavior during the period. See Martha Olney, *Buy Now, Pay Later: Advertising, Credit, and Consumer Durables in the 1920s* (Chapel Hill: University of North Carolina Press, 1991).

AAA WESTERN AND CENTRAL NEW YORK

When Americans driving their new cars ended up stuck in the mud, they launched a national roadbuilding program.

durable, a consumer could make a down payment, take immediate possession of the durable, and pay for it on the installment plan. The finance company that made the loan was protected because it had a claim on the durable and could repossess it if the buyer failed to make the requisite payments. Originally, automakers established finance companies to help dealers purchase cars for inventories during the slow seasons and thus smooth the annual demand for automobiles. But the practice was quickly extended to the financing of automobile purchases by consumers.

The purchase of consumer durables was also promoted by the rapidly growing volume of advertising, which touted the benefits of the new life-style based on time and labor-saving consumer durables and pointed out how these improvements in one's standard of living could be realized immediately by buying on the installment plan. Advertising relied on newspapers and magazines, particularly those aimed at women, such as the *Ladies Home Journal*, but some advertising also relied on the new medium of radio. The National Broadcasting Company (NBC) was formed in 1926, and the Columbia Broadcasting System (CBS) in 1927. Predictably, a proliferation of radio stations resulted. Polling systems by telephone were used to determine program ratings, and programs with low rating were canceled. Certain goods became tied to particular programs as producers sought any and all means to address the desires, fads, and fancies of the American public.

Government policies toward business did not cause these fundamental changes in the consumption patterns of Americans, but they did accommodate them. In the 1920s, the administrations of Presidents Warren G. Harding and Calvin Coolidge were openly dedicated to the principle that business should be free to grow without government's meddling or interfering. With little hindrance from government, businesses became even more consolidated than in earlier decades. Secretary of Commerce Herbert Hoover, among others, encouraged consolidations for reasons of efficiency; competing firms were allowed to form trade associations, not just to standardize tools and share technical information but also to set prices. Both Harding and Coolidge appointed men to the Federal Trade Commission who had little intention of enforcing the antitrust laws, either in letter or in spirit. As the years passed, banking, manufacturing, distribution, electronics, iron and steel, automobiles, and mining all became increasingly controlled by large conglomerates. Mass consumption, mass production, and the giant corporation thus became the trademark of the 1920s.

Mass production of consumer durables, often purchased with credit, characterized the boom of the 1920s.

Prohibition

Calls to prohibit the consumption of alcohol date from the nineteenth century. The Prohibition Party, in particular, although never large, waged a long and militant campaign. But it was not until 1917 that legislation was finally passed at the national level to prohibit consumption of alcohol. This was a wartime measure. Giving up alcohol was seen as a temporary sacrifice that would free resources in the brewing and distilling industries and keep workers at peak efficiency. Enforcement of the law was tightened in the Volstead Act of 1919, and prohibition was made permanent, or as permanent as such things can be, in 1920 when the Eighteenth Amendment to the Constitution was ratified.

Initially, prohibition had wide middle-class support. This included one of the leading economists of the era, Irving Fisher, who believed that prohibition had increased the savings of the working class and had raised industrial productivity. As is well known, however, opinions changed when crime soared despite an increase in the amount spent on enforcement from $6.3 million in 1921 to $13.4 million in 1930. Bootlegging became a major industry, and gangsters such as Al Capone and Legs Diamond became household names. Spectacular stories could be backed up with cold statistics: The homicide rate rose, and prohibition cases swamped the federal courts. By the time the Twenty-First Amendment to the Constitution ending prohibition was ratified in 1933, a majority of Americans had become disillusioned with the results of the "Noble Experiment." See New View 22.1.

THE LABOR FORCE IN THE TWENTIES

America Goes to High School

Another component of the modern American standard of living that arrived in the 1920s was the American high school, complete with 45-minute periods, diverse curricula, academic tracking, and, of course, bands and athletic teams. The increase in enrollment and graduation rates during the 1920s and 1930s was astonishing, as shown in Table 22.2. In 1910, less than 10 percent of American 17-year-olds had graduated from high school. By 1938, almost half were graduates. Graduating from high school had become a standard rite of passage. The United States, moreover, led the way internationally. By the middle of the twentieth century, a large gap in years of secondary schooling per capita had opened between the United States and the rest of the industrial nations.

Why did the "High School Movement" have so much success in the United States? Recent research by Claudia Goldin and Larry Katz has clarified the underlying forces. First, the rate of return from going to high school was extremely high (the extra income earned after graduation compared with the earnings forgone). In addition, communities were willing to build and staff high schools so that the children and grandchildren of the people living there would have more economic and social opportunities. The kinds of communities that had the most social cohesion, and therefore were most likely to vote for high taxes to finance high schools, were not located in the big cities with their diverse immigrant populations. Instead, it was the farming communities of the Middle West—in Iowa and Nebraska, for example—that led the way in establishing high schools. The high school movement provides a further illustration of Economic Reasoning Propositions 3 and 4: incentives matter (high rates of return encouraged young people to stay in school), and institutions matter (local finance and control of public schooling encouraged the early adoption of the high school in the Middle West).

The Paycheck Rises

The consumer durables revolution produced a strong demand for industrial labor and, as a result, improvements in hours and wages. During World War I, many manufacturing industries accepted the 48-hour workweek, and by 1920, some agreements granted a half-holiday on Saturday. Not until the very end of the decade, however, did a 48-hour week become standard for most occupations. Nevertheless, advance in leisure for many American workers was one of the important gains of the period.

Another gain was the relative absence of cyclical unemployment. Except for the hard years of 1921 and 1922, the 1920s were generally free of mass joblessness. Unemployment averaged

TABLE 22.2 High School Graduation Rates

	HIGH SCHOOL GRADUATES (as a percentage of children age 17)	
	48 STATES	32 NONSOUTHERN STATES
1910	8.6%	11.1%
1920	16.2	19.9
1928	27.0	32.1
1938	48.2	55.9

Source: Derived from Claudia Goldin, "How America Graduated from High School: 1910 to 1960," NBER Working Paper No. w4762, 1994, Table 1.

New View 22.1

Prohibition

What happens when a society outlaws drugs such as marijuana, cocaine, heroin, anabolic steroids, and so on? The Noble Experiment can tell us a good deal about the potential costs and benefits of this action.

As a result of Prohibition, consumption of alcohol fell, although perhaps not as much as its advocates had hoped. Prohibition reduced supply because producers faced the risk of legal prosecution. Prohibition probably reduced demand because of respect for the law, although there is some uncertainty about this because demand might have been increased as a result of the "forbidden fruit" effect. Statistics on alcohol production are incomplete, of course, because so much was produced illegally. Economists such as Clark Warburton and, more recently, Jeffrey Miron and Jeffrey Zweibel use related variables, such as deaths from cirrhosis of the liver, to infer consumption. According to their work, consumption of alcohol fell drastically at first but then rose to 60 or 70 percent of its preprohibition level. With both supply and demand falling, it is not clear what the impact on the price would be. Evidence on prices is extremely sketchy but is consistent with the view that prices may have risen but not a great deal.

Crime increased. Participants in the "black market" could not use the legal system to settle disputes between buyers and sellers or among competing sellers. Hence, sellers turned to crime, sometimes violent crime, to protect their property. Because their business was already illegal, moreover, the marginal costs of violence aimed at potential competitors was lower than it otherwise would have been. The homicide rate rose during this era by an amount that cannot be explained by other factors.

Deaths from overdose and accidental poisoning increased. Producers tended to make highly concentrated alcoholic beverages in order to better conceal their product from authorities. This increased the risk of accidental overdoses. Quality, moreover, tended to vary widely because producers could not establish and protect brand names and therefore had little incentive to maintain the quality of their product. In one case, an adulterant used to disguise alcohol as medicine led to thousands of poisonings.

Sources: Clark Warburton, The Economic Results of Prohibition *(New York: Columbia University Press, 1932); and Jeffrey Zwiebel and Jeffrey Miron, "The Economic Case against Drug Prohibition,"* Journal of Economic Perspectives *9 (Autumn 1995): 175–192.*

only 3.3 percent between 1923 and 1929.[4] In short, the threat of unemployment was usually low, thereby contributing, along with added leisure, to the growing sense of prosperity.

Real annual earnings of nonfarm employees rose between 1919 and 1929 by about 23 percent; the increase over 1914 was about 33 percent. Overall, labor's advance, at least for those in the city and in industry, was substantial. Not all sectors, however, fared as well. Later in the chapter, we look at agriculture, which had a tough time in the twenties. And when workers compared their gains with those of people higher on the economic ladder, they saw less reason to be content with the gains they had made.

[4]These unemployment rates from Stanley Lebergott, *Manpower in Economic Growth: The American Record since 1800* (New York: McGraw-Hill, 1964), were challenged and revised upward to 5.1 percent by R.M. Coen in "Labor Force Unemployment in the 1920s and 1930s: A Re-examination Based on Postwar Experience," *Review of Economics and Statistics* 55 (1973): 46–55. Such an adjustment, if accepted, would alter the level but not the trend in the progress of labor in the 1923–1929 period.

The Unions Decline

Despite (or perhaps because of) the surge in the demand for industrial labor, the 1920s were not years of advance for organized labor. As Table 22.3 shows, the number of workers holding union membership fell from more than 12 percent of the civilian labor force in 1920 to less than 8 percent at the end of the decade. This fall is especially surprising in light of the rapid growth of manufacturing and the concentration of the population in urban areas. It is true that throughout the 1920s, employers continued their effective use of the antiunion instruments developed before World War I. They discriminated in hiring and firing against employees who joined or organized unions. They used the hated yellow-dog contract, in which new employees promised not to join a union, to prevent union membership and to serve as a basis of civil suits against unions that persuaded employees to violate the contracts. But the employers' most useful weapon was the injunction, by which a court could forbid, at least temporarily, such practices as picketing, secondary boycotts, and the feeding of strikers by the union. During the 1920s, except for legislation applying to railroads, government generally did not interfere with labor relations. Although such policies slowed organized labor's progress, it is difficult to accept such actions as the primary cause of an absolute decline in union membership.

It seems most likely that the upsurge in union membership associated with World War I had not been firmly established. The wartime increase in membership resulted in part from agreements by the unions to a nonstrike pledge in return for lessened opposition to union organization. The sharp recession of 1921 and 1922, which raised levels of unemployment to 11 percent, undermined labor's bargaining power. It is pertinent to note in Table 22.3 that most of the membership decline had occurred by 1923, after which there was only minor attrition. In addition, beginning with the important strike against U.S. Steel in 1916, a host of strikes failed—except to anger employers. Company welfare programs designed to entice workers away from their own organizations also took their toll, but the inertia between 1924 and 1929 must be attributed primarily to two other causes. First, the increase in real wages left the greater part of the labor force generally satisfied. More important, the powerful AFL unions, whose members especially benefited from the building boom, took no interest in organizing the growing mass production industries. Added to this was a generally tired and unimaginative labor leadership.

TABLE 22.3 Union Memberships, 1919–1929

YEAR	TOTAL UNION MEMBERSHIP (in thousands)	TOTAL MEMBERSHIP AS A PERCENTAGE OF TOTAL LABOR FORCE	TOTAL MEMBERSHIP AS A PERCENTAGE OF NONFARM LABOR FORCE
1919	4,046	10.2%	14.8%
1920	5,034	12.2	16.3
1921	4,722	11.2	15.0
1922	3,950	9.3	12.4
1923	3,629	8.4	11.1
1924	3,549	8.0	10.6
1925	3,566	7.9	10.3
1926	3,592	7.9	10.3
1927	3,600	7.8	10.0
1928	3,567	7.6	9.7
1929	3,625	7.6	9.7

Source: Historical Statistics *(Washington, D.C.: Government Printing Office, 1975), Series D4, D7, D8, D940.*

Immigration Is Restricted

Labor did, however, finally achieve one of its most cherished objectives in the 1920s—limiting immigration. The restrictions on immigration imposed in the 1920s were part of a long-term trend. In 1882, for example, Chinese immigration was banned for 10 years, a restriction that was later renewed and strengthened. In 1885, the practice of prepaying the cost of an immigrant's voyage in exchange for future labor services was made illegal. In 1907, a financial test for immigrants was imposed, and in 1917, a literacy test. This trend, which was common in other countries receiving large numbers of immigrants such as Argentina and Australia, reflected the growing assertiveness of labor, which believed that free immigration was slowing the growth of the real wages of relatively unskilled labor. In the United States, sectional interests, as Claudia Goldin has shown, also played a role. The South, for example, believed that its political power was being weakened by rapid population growth in other regions based on immigration. Until World War I, the door was still open; in 1921 legislation was finally passed that effectively limited immigration.

The Emergency Immigration Act of 1921 restricted the number of people to be admitted from any country each year to 3 percent of the number of people of that nationality residing in the United States in 1910. In 1924, a new law limited immigration to 2 percent of a nationality's 1890 U.S. population. This change further restricted immigration from southern and eastern Europe. Immigration from East Asia, moreover, was completely eliminated, reinforcing President Theodore Roosevelt's earlier "gentleman's agreement" with the Japanese. The law also set a maximum limit of slightly more than 150,000 immigrants with quotas based on 1920 to become effective in 1929. The effects of these restrictions on the flow of immigrants can be seen in Table 22.4. The contrast between the prewar years (the war in Europe began in 1914) and the 1920s is obvious. The limit on immigration was clearly effective in cutting the number of legal immigrants.

Why were drastic restrictions placed on immigration at this time? In part, the restrictions were the result of growing hostility to the "new immigrants" from southern and eastern Europe who had constituted the bulk of the large influx of immigrants in the years leading up to the war. Racism, including the activities of the Ku Klux Klan, was on the rise, excited partly by wartime propaganda and patriotism. Sometimes racism was given a pseudoscientific veneer by writers who claimed that the new immigrants were less able and intelligent than native-born Americans.

The war, moreover, had created the specter of a large influx of labor that would erode the real wages of unskilled labor. In the years preceding World War I, the economy of central Europe had grown rapidly; afterward it lay in ruins, saddled for years with heavy reparation payments. Farther east, the Russian economy had also been exhausted by years of war and

TABLE 22.4 Immigration, 1910–1929

YEAR	NEW ARRIVALS	YEAR	NEW ARRIVALS
1910	1,041,570	1920	430,001
1911	878,587	1921	805,228
1912	838,172	1922	309,556
1913	1,197,892	1923	522,919
1914	1,218,480	1924	706,896
1915	326,700	1925	294,314
1916	298,826	1926	304,488
1917	295,403	1927	335,175
1918	110,618	1928	307,255
1919	141,132	1929	279,678

Source: Historical Statistics *(Washington, D.C.: Government Printing Office, 1976), Series C89.*

revolution; now the communists controlled the economy, and no one could be sure what that would mean. The war, moreover, had created a vast new supply of shipping that could easily bring immigrants to the United States. Would not the country be swamped with immigrants from continental Europe once the war was over? These fears seemed to be confirmed by the resumption of a high level of immigration immediately after the war. Slightly more than 800,000 immigrants entered the United States between June 1920 and June 1921.

ON THE LAND

The period between 1896 and 1914, sometimes called the "Golden Age of Agriculture," was one of rapid improvement in the economic position of the American farmer. Then the surge in international demand for American farm products during World War I amplified the rise in farm incomes.

Economic Distress in Agriculture

In mid-1920, however, farm prices began a precipitous drop. By the end of 1921, despite a slight recovery, wheat that 18 months previously had sold for $2.58 per bushel was selling for $0.93, and corn was down to $0.41 from $1.86. Many commodities did not suffer quite as severe a decline, but prices seriously decreased in all lines of production. From an index of 234 in June 1920 (1909–1914 = 100), prices received by farmers fell to an index of 112 a year later. A gradual recovery followed, and the farm index stood at 159 in August 1925. After a small decline during 1926 and 1927, prices remained stable until the end of 1929.

The deflation of 1920 and 1921 was severe in the industrial sector and overall economy, too, but not as great as in the agriculture sector. Prices paid by farmers fell until the end of 1921 and then remained stable until the close of the decade. The terms of trade (the ratio of the prices received by farmers to the prices they paid) ran against agriculture during the break in prices and then recovered, so that by 1925, they were not much below the 1920 level. This index fell a little during the next few years, but in 1929, it was still not far from the level of prosperous prewar years. On the whole, then, it does not seem that agriculture should have suffered much in the middle and late 1920s. Moreover, research by Charles F. Holt suggests a rise in income for the average farmer in the 1920s. Yet great agitation for remedial farm legislation occurred during these years. Why?

The answer seems to be that many farmers, especially in the Midwest, had incurred fixed indebtedness at what turned out to be the wrong time. Land values had risen sharply between 1910 and 1920; at the height of the boom, the best lands in Iowa and Illinois sold for as much as $500 an acre—a fantastically high figure for the time. In those 10 years, many high-grade farms doubled in value. To buy such high-priced properties, farmers borrowed heavily. Long-term debt rose from $3.2 billion in 1910 to $8.4 billion in 1920 and reached a high of nearly $11 billion in 1923. Deflation in the early 1920s turned farm debts into crushing burdens. Although a majority of American farmers may not have been burdened with fixed debt payments during these years, a large and extremely vocal minority were pushed toward bankruptcy. The number of farm mortgage foreclosures advanced sharply at the turn of the decade and then remained high throughout the 1920s. According to H. Thomas Johnson, the rate increased from 2.8 per 1,000 mortgaged farms foreclosed in 1918 to 3.8 in 1920, to 6.4 in 1921, to 11.2 in 1922, and to between 14 and 17 per 1,000 for the remainder of the decade.[5]

First Steps toward Farm Subsidies

Violent protests from farmers in late 1920 led Congress to create the Joint Commission of Agricultural Inquiry in 1921. The commission reported the obvious—that farm troubles

---

[5]H. Thomas Johnson, "Postwar Optimism and the Rural Financial Crisis of the 1920s," *Explorations in Economic History* 11 (Winter 1973–1974): 176.

were the result of general business depression and a decline in exports—and recommended measures to help cooperative marketing associations, improve credit facilities, and extend the Department of Agriculture's research activities.

A more radical approach was advocated at the National Agricultural Conference, convened early in 1922 by Secretary of Agriculture Henry C. Wallace.[6] Despite President Harding's view that "the farmer must be ready to help himself," many radical proposals were heard at this conference. In its report, the idea of parity for agriculture was first made explicit, and the slogan "Equality for Agriculture" was offered. It was argued that agriculture was entitled to its fair share of the national income and that this would be achieved if the ratio of the prices farmers received to the prices they paid was kept equal to the ratio that had prevailed from 1910 to 1914.

Throughout the 1920s, various ideas were proposed aimed at securing "parity prices" or "fair-exchange values" for agricultural products. Most acceptable to professional farm supporters and politicians were the McNary-Haugen bills, which sought to determine the fair-exchange value of each farm product. The fair value was to be a price that would have preserved pre–World War I purchasing power and was to be maintained in two ways: first, a tariff was to protect the home market from imports, and second, a private corporation chartered by the federal government was to buy a sufficient amount of each commodity to force its price up to the computed fair value. The corporation could in turn sell the acquired commodities. It was proposed, moreover, that the surpluses be sold abroad at the world price, which would presumably be lower than the supported American price. Administrative expenses and operating losses would be shared among the producing farmers. For every bale of cotton or bushel of wheat sold, a tax called an "equalization fee" would be charged to the grower. These taxes would be used to defray all expenses of operating the price support plan. The farmer would gain insofar as the additional amount of income resulting from higher prices exceeded the tax. Refer to Economic Reasoning Propositions 1, 2 and 4: choices, costs, and institutions matter.

The McNary-Haugen bills were twice passed by Congress and twice vetoed by President Calvin Coolidge. Despite this setback, the agitation of the 1920s did secure some special privileges for agriculture. For one, the Capper-Volstead law of 1922 exempted farmers' cooperatives from the threat of prosecution for violation of antitrust laws. The following year, the Federal Intermediate Credit Act provided for 12 intermediate credit banks that would rediscount agricultural paper for commercial banks and other lending agencies.[7]

To achieve the broader aims of price and income maintenance, there were two major efforts. A naïve belief in the tariff as a device to raise the prices of farm products (which had been traditionally exported, not imported!) led to "protection" for agriculture, culminating in the high duties of the Smoot-Hawley Tariff Act of June 1930. More significant was the Agricultural Marketing Act of 1929, which was passed to fulfill Republican campaign promises of the previous year. This law, the first committing the federal government to a policy of stabilizing farm prices, worked as much as possible through nongovernment institutions. The act established a Federal Farm Board to encourage the formation of cooperative marketing associations and to establish "stabilization corporations" to be owned by the cooperatives, which would use a $500 million fund to carry on price support operations.

---

[6]His son, Henry A. Wallace, one of the developers of hybrid corn, would serve as secretary of agriculture and vice president under Roosevelt and as commerce secretary under Truman.

[7]Nonemergency short-term farm credit needs were fairly well taken care of with the passage of this act; the Federal Farm Loan Act of 1916 had already established 12 Federal Land Banks to provide long-term loans to farmers through cooperative borrowing groups.

Periods of distress in agriculture had occurred before. Why on a limited scale in the twenties were direct efforts made to aid farmers? Several things, as shown by Elizabeth Hoffman and Gary D. Libecap, had changed. First, the experiments with price controls in World War I had convinced farmers and their advocates that more direct controls would work. The federal government, moreover, had become far stronger than it had earlier been—in part because the passage of the income tax had given it a new source of revenue—and this made direct aid to farmers seem more realistic. Finally, the integration of national markets had made it clear that only federal intervention could help farmers.

Ultimately, the farm programs adopted in the 1920s provided only limited help to farmers. The supply of farm output was highly elastic. Without the means to control output, or buy it on a massive scale, federal legislation could not significantly alter farm incomes, especially those of poor farmers. Nevertheless, the policy discussions of the 1920s set the stage for the massive government intervention in agriculture that was to follow in the 1930s.

WERE THE RICH GETTING RICHER WHILE THE POOR GOT POORER?

Images of the wealthy during the 1920s often portray these people as self-satisfied and self-indulgent, drinking champagne and ignoring the growing misery around them. Some historians, moreover, have seen a direct link between a growing concentration of income during the 1920s and the depression of the 1930s. Too much income, goes the argument, was going to the rich, who were not spending it fast enough to maintain aggregate demand. Early studies of the distribution of income to some degree confirmed that the rich had grown relatively richer. In his pioneering work published in 1953, Simon Kuznets showed that the share of disposable income received by the top 1 percent of the population increased from 11.8 percent in 1920 to 18.9 percent in 1929.[8] Charles Holt, working from Kuznets's data, argued that all of the increases in real income in the 1920s went to upper-income groups.[9]

More recent research, however, counters this view. Gene Smiley points out that the upward trend in the share of income going to the richest fractions of the population was biased upward because it was based on tax returns.[10] Tax rates for the rich were lowered substantially in the 1920s, encouraging people to shift their wealth into assets yielding taxable income and to report income that had previously gone unreported.

Jeffrey Williamson and Peter Lindert, in a landmark study of American inequality, drew attention to the long-term dimension of the problem.[11] A long trend toward increased inequality had been interrupted by World War I, so some increase in inequality in the 1920s was to be expected. Whatever the increase in inequality, it probably represented a return to conditions that were prevalent before the war. The distribution of income was far from equal in 1929, but little evidence exists that something drastic and unexpected had occurred that could explain the depression that was to follow.

---

[8]*Historical Statistics* (Washington, D.C.: Government Printing Office, 1975), Series G341. These series are drawn from Simon Kuznets, *Shares of Upper Income Groups in Income and Savings* (New York: National Bureau of Economic Research, 1953). Kuznets, the father of national income accounting, was later awarded the Nobel Prize.

[9]Charles Holt, "Who Benefitted from the Prosperity of the Twenties?" *Explorations in Economic History* 14 (1977): 277–289.

[10]Gene Smiley, "Did Incomes for Most of the Population Fall from 1923 through 1929?" *Journal of Economic History* 42 (1983): 209–216. Kuznets himself had warned against putting too much weight on the date.

[11]Jeffrey Williamson and Peter Lindert, *American Inequality: A Microeconomic History* (New York: Academic Press, 1981), chapter 12.

When discussing the distribution of income in the 1920s, moreover, it is good to keep in mind the point Stanley Lebergott made on the basis of figures such as those in Table 22.1 (page 432): However much certain groups suffered, there were improvements in the standard of living of a large segment of the American people that can be seen in such statistics as the percentage of families with electric lighting, the percentage of families with washing machines, and even the percentage of families with inside flush toilets. Economic Reasoning Proposition 5 (evidence matters) is appropriate here.

MACROECONOMIC POLICIES

Fiscal Policy

Fiscal policy in the late 1920s is best viewed as a long, drawn-out postwar readjustment. Although certain costs of the war, such as veterans' benefits and interest on the increase in the national debt, continued into the postwar period, demobilization nevertheless created considerable scope for cutting the high level of taxes imposed during wartime.

The debate over taxes in the twenties covered the same ground as the debate that began in the 1970s (under the banner of supply side economics) and continues to the present day. The White House favored reducing taxes by removing the steep progression in rates introduced during the war. Secretary of the Treasury Andrew Mellon argued that reducing high tax rates would encourage savings and growth and that the effects on tax revenues would be relatively small. The wealthy would shift their assets from tax-exempt municipal bonds to taxable assets, thus minimizing the effect on total revenues. Liberals in Congress did not oppose cutting taxes altogether. However, they favored reducing taxes by increasing exemptions for those in lower-income groups. The outcomes of this fight—the revenue acts of 1924, 1926, and 1928—swept away the system of wartime excise taxes, reduced the rates for personal and corporate taxes, and reduced estate duties. On the whole, the pride in their fiscal policies taken by successive administrations during the 1920s is understandable. Tax rates were cut, but revenues grew, and a budget surplus was maintained. Perhaps even more important for the long run, a federal budget system was introduced in 1921 that would make it possible to cope, to some degree, with the massive expansion of the federal government that was to come in later decades.

Table 22.5 shows that federal spending was relatively small compared with the whole economy in the 1920s. Indeed, in 1927, the federal government was spending only 3.5 percent of GNP, most accounted for by the traditional categories of national defense, the postal service, veterans' services, and interest on the national debt. Although more funds were being spent on health and welfare, these were still minor categories. The revolution in the budget would come in the thirties.

TABLE 22.5 Government Spending and Distribution of Expenditures by Level of Government, 1922 and 1927 (in percent)

	1922	1927
Share of GNP		
Total government	12.6%	1.6%
Federal	4.9	3.5
State and local	7.7	8.1
Expenditure distribution by level		
Federal	39.2	30.4
State	11.7	12.9
Local	49.1	56.7

Source: Albert W. Niemi, U.S. Economic History *(Chicago: Rand McNally, 1975), 117; as derived from* Historical Statistics *(Washington, D.C.: Government Printing Office, 1960), 484–516.*

TABLE 22.6 Money, Prices, and Real Income, 1920–1929

YEAR	STOCK OF MONEY (in billions of dollars)	IMPLICIT PRICE DEFLATOR (1929 = 100)	REAL NATIONAL INCOME (in billions of 1929 dollars)
1920	$34.80	121.7	$62.208
1921	32.85	103.7	59.567
1922	33.72	98.6	63.859
1923	36.60	100.9	73.460
1924	38.58	99.6	75.559
1925	42.05	101.6	77.343
1926	43.68	102.1	82.807
1927	44.73	99.4	83.623
1928	46.42	100.1	84.918
1929	46.60	100.0	90.308

Source: Milton Friedman and Anna J. Schwartz, Monetary Trends in the United States and the United Kingdom *(Chicago: University of Chicago Press, 1982), 125.*

Monetary Policy

The period of the 1920s was one of growing prestige for the Federal Reserve System. Table 22.6 shows that after the sharp but brief recession of 1920 and 1921, the economy advanced smoothly. Real income rose steadily year after year, as did the stock of money. Prices, judging by the net national product (NNP) deflator, were stable.

What influenced the Fed's policy during these years? Surprisingly, one fact that did not influence policy was the large number of bank closings. Suspensions numbered in the hundreds each year, reaching a peak of 975 banks in 1926. The Federal Reserve concluded that these banks (mostly in rural areas) were plagued by bad management, unrealistic loans to farmers made during the war boom, and increased competition due to the rise of the automobile. (The automobile increased the ability of borrowers and depositors to shop for favorable terms.) It followed that simply allowing these banks to close strengthened the banking system as a whole. Although it is difficult to imagine the Fed taking such a callous position in today's political climate, its analysis probably contained a good deal of truth. Unfortunately, this policy was carried into the 1930s when high numbers of bank failures under very different economic conditions undermined confidence in the banking system.

An important series of papers by Eugene White clarifies the nature of the weakness in the rural banking system and its role in the breakdown of the banking system in the early 1930s. To a large extent, the problem stemmed from legislation that prohibited branch banking. Small unit banks were unable to diversify their loan portfolios and had no resources to draw on during periods of temporary illiquidity. The states tried various deposit insurance schemes to protect their systems, but these ended in failure. Eventually, most states began to eliminate crippling prohibitions against branch banking, but by then the damage had been done, and it was too late to build a system that could withstand the deflation of the 1930s.[12]

[12]Eugene N. White, "State-Sponsored Insurance of Bank Deposits in the United States," *Journal of Economic History* 41 (1981); "A Reinterpretation of the Banking Crisis of 1930," *Journal of Economic History* 44 (1984); and "Before the Glass-Steagall Act: An Analysis of the Investment Banking Activities of National Banks," *Explorations in Economic History* 23 (1986).

The Fed, moreover, was deeply concerned about the growing speculation on Wall Street that we will take up later in more detail. Speculation, the Fed believed, diverted capital from more-productive investments, and the inevitable retrenchment might cause widespread disturbances in the economy. But it was not clear how to slow the flow of funds to the stock market without simultaneously restricting the total supply of credit, thus risking a recession. At first, the Fed tried "moral suasion," pressuring the New York City banks into making fewer call loans. This policy was partly effective, but other lenders quickly moved into the gap left by the banks.

Finally, frustrated by its inability to cool the market in any other way, the Fed raised its discount rate from 4.5 to 5.5 percent on August 9, 1929.The discount rate was still well below the call loan and other bank lending rates, so the increase itself did not remove the incentive to borrow, but it signaled the Fed's intention to restrict the supply of credit. Other central banks were taking similar actions: the Bank of England raised its discount rate from 5.5 to 6.5 percent in September. Perhaps as a result of these widespread harbingers of tighter credit, American stock prices reached their peak early in September. The exact role of the Fed's policy in subsequent events is a matter of considerable debate, as we will see in the next chapter. During the 1930s, however, the Fed was given the power to set margin requirements because it was recognized that the Fed's monetary policy had been distorted in the late 1920s by its efforts to control the stock market.

INTERNATIONAL DEVELOPMENTS

During the 1920s, the problems of Europe seemed far away to most Americans and unrelated to their lives. In retrospect, we can see that such an attitude was naïve and counterproductive. The future might have been different if Americans had given more thought to its role in the world economy. Nevertheless, America could not completely ignore two problems that dominated the international scene: German war reparations (and Allied war debts to the United States) and the reestablishment of the international gold standard.

The Treaty of Versailles, which formally ended World War I, called for Germany to make large payments to France and the other Allies to compensate for damages caused by German forces during the war. It quickly became apparent that Germany lacked the economic strength and political cohesion to make its payments on schedule. Part of the problem was that Germany would need to run large surpluses to make the reparations payments, but tariffs and other economic policies in the United States and elsewhere limited German exports. Germany did benefit, however, from the willingness of Americans to lend heavily to Germany in the twenties. In 1924, under the Dawes plan, German debts were scaled down, and a large loan, mostly from the United States, was floated to help Germany restore its currency following its disastrous hyperinflation of 1923. Further reductions in payments were made under the Young plan of 1929. Most historians now agree that trying to extract reparations from Germany was a mistake and that a wiser policy would have aimed at restoring the German economy as rapidly as possible, the policy followed after World War II.[13]

It was taken for granted in the 1920s that restoration of the gold standard was necessary to achieve lasting prosperity. If each country made its currency convertible into gold, exchange rates would be fixed, and monetary authorities would be forced to be circumspect in the amount of money they created (to avoid an outflow of gold), and inflation would be prevented. British bankers were particularly anxious to return to the gold standard at the prewar parity (that is, the prewar price of pounds in terms of dollars) in order to help restore the position of London as the world's leading financial center. Britain finally did

---

[13]John Maynard Keynes warned of the dangers of trying to extract reparations from Germany in *The Economic Consequences of the Peace* (New York: Harcourt, Brace & World, 1920).

TABLE 22.7 The Stock Market, 1922–1929

YEAR	(1) STANDARD & POOR'S COMMON STOCK INDEX (all stocks)	(2) RATIO OF STOCK PRICE TO DIVIDEND
1922	100	17.24
1923	102	16.84
1924	108	17.04
1925	133	19.27
1926	150	18.80
1927	182	20.96
1928	237	25.13
1929	309	28.74

Source: Historical Statistics *(Washington, D.C.: Government Printing Office, 1976), Series X479 and X495.*

return to the gold standard in 1924, but it appears that the pound was overvalued at the prewar rate. (The rate was $4.86 per £1.00, but the equilibrium price where supply and demand for pounds would balance was probably less, say, $4.40.) The high rate made it difficult to export British goods and contributed to a long period of hard times in Britain.[14]

The pressure on British exports would have been lessened had the United States been willing to let the resulting influx of gold increase its price level, but the Federal Reserve chose instead to "sterilize" the gold inflows. In retrospect, considerable difficulties might have been avoided had American policymakers seen the importance of taking into account the international repercussions of their actions. American monetary and fiscal policies during the 1920s, however, were influenced primarily by domestic considerations, and (except in the agricultural sector) things seemed to be moving smoothly.

THE GREAT BULL MARKET

One event dominates the social memory of the twenties: the great stock market boom. Stock prices rose steadily in the early 1920s, but in 1928 and the first three-quarters of 1929, they rocketed upward. Table 22.7 shows what happened to stock prices between 1922 and 1929: In seven years, prices more than tripled. Between 1928 and 1929, the average stock (column 1) rose 26.5 percent in value. It seemed that getting rich was easy—just put money in the stock market and sit back and wait. Typical of the times was an article by financier John Jacob Raskob in the *Ladies Home Journal* with the optimistic title, "Everybody Ought to Be Rich."[15]

What caused the great bull market? One cause was the rise in earnings of and dividends paid by corporations in the 1920s, reflecting the great surge in the demand for automobiles and other consumer durables. General Motors, as a result of its strong earnings resulting from its successful challenge to Ford, was a market favorite.

But stock prices rose even faster than earnings. Consider column 2 of Table 22.7, which shows the ratio of stock prices to dividends. In 1922, an investor had to pay $17.24 for each dollar of current dividends; by 1929, that figure had climbed to $28.74. Of course, people do not invest on the assumption that dividends will remain the same forever. One of the favorites of the bull market was Radio Corporation of America (RCA), which had never

[14]Once again, Keynes warned against a mistaken policy. See *The Economic Consequences of Mr. Churchill* (London: Woolf, 1925).

[15]As quoted in John Kenneth Galbraith, *The Great Crash of 1929* (Boston: Houghton Mifflin, 1961), 57.

paid a dividend. People bought RCA stock on the assumption (a valid one) that it would pay large dividends in the future.

George Sirkin, in an interesting comment on the bull market, argues that if earnings growth in the years immediately preceding the stock market crash were projected forward, then only relatively few stocks could be considered overvalued at the market's peak. But Eugene White points out that Sirkin's result depends on projecting earnings from a very favorable period of years.[16] In White's view, this begs the question: Why did the market choose to base its projections on the most favorable years rather than on a long run of experience? See Economic Insight 22.1 on page 448. Part of the explanation, some historians have conjectured, is that people convinced themselves that a "New Age" had dawned. Science and technology would produce much faster earnings growth than had been possible in the past.

If earnings did not drive the market, did credit conditions do so? At that time, much stock was bought on margin. The buyer would put down, say, 50 percent of the value of the stock in cash and borrow the remaining 50 percent from the broker. Leveraging in this way means that when stock prices go up by, say, 10 percent, the speculator makes 20 percent on the initial investment. But what is true going up is also true going down. If stocks fall 10 percent, the speculator loses 20 percent. It is sometimes assumed that the margin requirements became very low—5 or 10 percent—but most brokers required 45 or 50 percent down.[17] Where did the brokers get the money to lend to speculators? The brokerage houses borrowed the money from banks in the form of call loans—loans that had to be repaid on demand, when "called."

Sometimes an assumption is made that the boom arose because banks became more willing to make these loans. This also appears not to be the case, however. See Economic Insight 22.2 on page 449.

It does appear then, that there was a "bubble" in the stock market in the late 1920s—March 1928 is often suggested as the date when the bubble began—in the sense that the prices of stocks diverged from what would be expected on the basis of "fundamentals" such as expected earnings and interest rates on alternative investments. The institutions that supplied credit to the market and perhaps many investors especially, expected a decline in prices. Money kept pouring into the market, even many investors who believed that the market was overvalued thought that they could beat the crowd out the door before the market began to tumble.

The true explanation for the boom, if there ever is one, will have to be provided by social psychologists. It was an optimistic age. Business was booming. There seemed to be no reason that it could not keep on booming, providing an ever-higher standard of living for the average American. The stock market reflected that optimism.

Should They Have Known Better?

In the uncommonly pleasant summer of 1929, Americans were congratulating themselves for having found a way to unending prosperity. The flow of U.S. goods and services had reached an all-time high, industrial production having risen 50 percent in a decade. Most businesses were satisfied with their profits, and workers were content with the gains in wages and earnings that enabled them to enjoy the luxury of automobiles and household appliances. Farmers grumbled about prices, but it was traditional that they should; anyone could see that mechanical inventions had made life on the farm easier and more productive than ever before. Besides, anyone who really wanted to become rich had only to purchase common stock. The

---

[16]Eugene White, "When the Ticker Ran Late: The Stock Market Boom and Crash of 1929," in *Panics and Crashes in Historical Perspective*, ed. Eugene N. White (Homewood, Ill.: Dow Jones-Irwin, 1989).

[17]John Kenneth Galbraith, *The Great Crash of 1929*, (Boston: Houghton-Mifflin, 1961), 37.

Economic Insight 22.1

Projection of Future Dividend Growth

Economic theory concludes that if investors are rational, the value of a stock (or group of stocks) will equal the discounted value of expected future dividends.

The formula is

$$(1)\quad P = \frac{D_1}{(1+i)} + \frac{D_2}{(1+i)^2} + \frac{D_3}{(1+i)^3} + \ldots$$

where P is the price of a stock or group of stocks; D_1, D_2, D_3, and so on, are the dividends expected next year, two years from now, three years from now, and so on; and i is the rate of interest at which investors discount the future.

If we make the additional assumption that dividends are expected to grow at the constant rate g, the equation reduces to:

$$(2)\quad P = \frac{D_1}{i-g}$$

In 1922, as shown in Table 22.7 the price-dividend ratio was 17.24. Suppose investors were using the prewar (1900–1914) rate of growth of dividends of 2.72 percent per year to project future dividend growth. This assumption would imply (from equation 2) a discount rate of about 8.52 percent per year. Let us suppose that in 1929 investors used the same discount rate but that they now used the postwar (1919–1929) rate of growth of dividends, 5.84 percent per year, to project the future growth of dividends. Then from equation 2, the expected price-dividend ratio would be 37.34, considerably above the actual market price-dividend ratio of 28.74. On these assumptions, stocks were still *undervalued* in 1929. But if we assume that a more reasonable rate of growth of dividends was 4.28, the average of the prewar and postwar growth rates, then the price-dividend ratio should have been around 23.58; stocks were *overvalued* in 1929.

political climate was favorable to the business venturer, then held high in public esteem as the provider of material well-being. Herbert Hoover, a successful businessman and a distinguished public servant, had been elected to the presidency, people generally expected him to be a temperate and judicious leader. Equally reassuring was the stability of the economies of western Europe. War damage had been repaired, the gold standard had been restored, and the problem of reparations seemed to be near solution.

The greatest American economist of the day was Irving Fisher. A remarkable figure, Fisher made important theoretical and empirical contributions in areas of economics ranging from index numbers to monetary theory. His invention of a card index system made him a fortune, and his book on how to eat a healthy diet was a best seller. When journalists wanted to know whether the popular song title "Yes, We Have No Bananas" was good English, they asked Irving Fisher.[18]

Fisher was not shy in making predictions about the stock market. Just weeks before the crash, he argued that "stock prices have reached what looks like a permanently high plateau," adding that "there might be a recession in stock prices, but not anything in the nature of a crash." Even after the crash, Fisher wrote that for "the immediate future, at least, the outlook is bright."[19]

---

[18]The answer was yes, if the question was "Have you no bananas?"

[19]As quoted in Galbraith, *The Great Crash*, 91, 99, 151.

Economic Insight 22.2

Call Loans and the Bull Market

Some historians have thought that an increased willingness on the part of the New York banks to supply call loans caused the bull market. Eugene White's study of the market shows, however, that this was not the decisive factor.[20] His analysis is illustrated in the following figure.

The amount of call loans rose dramatically in the 1920s, but it also rose from 4.36 percent in 1922 to 7.74 percent in 1929.[21] Evidently, as the figure illustrates, the market equilibrium moved toward the upper right, indicating that the demand for loans increased more than the supply. Had supply increased more than demand, the equilibrium call loan rate would have fallen. Credit, to put it somewhat differently, was being pulled into the stock market by the rising interest rate on call loans.

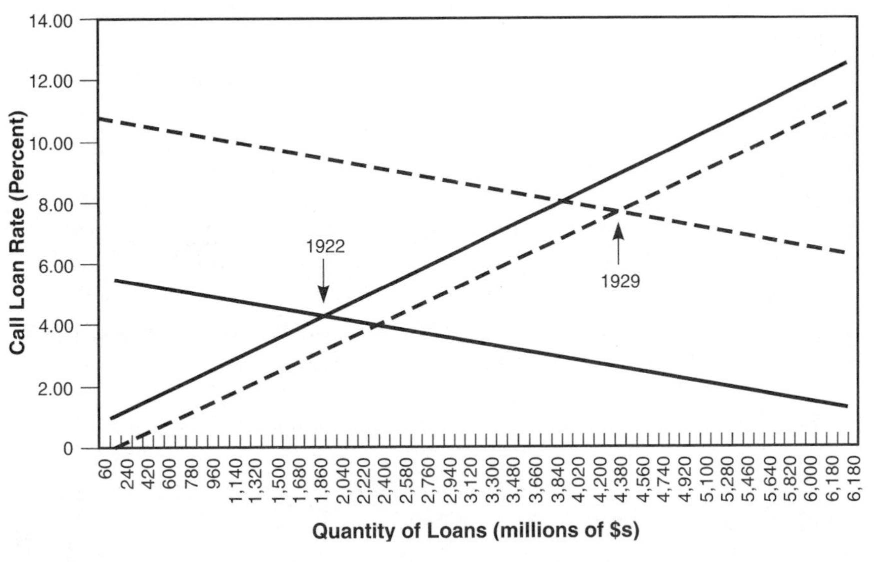

It is easy now to laugh at such optimism. But should Fisher and others have known better? Were there signs of the impending disaster that should have been heeded? The long history of panics and crises in U.S. history (which Fisher knew well) should, perhaps, have given pause. There also were, of course, weaknesses in the economy, such as the banking system and the agricultural sector, but the economy had expanded rapidly for years despite these weaknesses. Ultimately, whether we believe that Fisher and other optimists were unwise or merely incredibly unlucky depends on what we believe caused the Great Depression, the subject of the next chapter.

[20]See Galbraith, *The Great Crash*, 37.

[21]White, "When the Ticker Ran Late."

Selected References and Suggested Readings

American Stock Exchange, "History and Timeline." **http://www.amex.com.**

Field, Alexander J. "A New Interpretation of the Onset of the Great Depression." *Journal of Economic History* 45 (June 1984).

———. "Uncontrolled Land Development and the Duration of the Depression in the United States." *Journal of Economic History* 52 (December 1992): 785–805.

Fisher, Irving. *Prohibition Still at Its Worst*. New York: Alcohol Information Committee, 1928.

Galbraith, John Kenneth. *The Great Crash of 1929*, reissued with a new introduction. Boston: Houghton Mifflin, 1961.

Goldin, Claudia. *Understanding the Gender Gap: An Economic History of American Women*. New York: Oxford University Press, 1990.

———. "The Political Economy of Immigration Restriction in the U.S., 1890 to 1921." In *The Regulated Economy: A Historical Approach to Political Economy*, eds. Claudia Goldin and Gary Libecap. Chicago: University of Chicago Press, 1994.

———. "America's Graduation from High School: The Evolution and Spread of Secondary Schooling in the Twentieth Century." *Journal of Economic History* 58 (1998): 345–374.

———. "Egalitarianism and the Returns to Education during the Great Transformation of American Education." *Journal of Political Economy* 107, part 2, no. 6 (December 1999), S65–94.

———. "The Human Capital Century and American Leadership: Virtues of the Past." *Journal of Economic History* 61 (2001): 782–818.

Goldin, Claudia, and Lawrence F. Katz. "Education and Income in the Early Twentieth Century: Evidence from the Prairies." *Journal of Economic History* 60 (2000): 782–818.

Hawley, Ellis W. *The Great War and the Search for a Modern Order: A History of the American People and Their Institutions, 1917–1933*. New York: St. Martin's, 1979.

Holt, Charles. "Who Benefitted from the Prosperity of the Twenties?" *Explorations in Economic History* 14 (1977): 277–289.

Hughes, Jonathan. *The Vital Few*. New York: Oxford University Press, 1986.

Keynes, John Maynard. *The Economic Consequences of the Peace*. New York: Harcourt, Brace & World, 1920.

Keller, Robert. "Factor Income Distribution in the United States during the 1920s: A Reexamination of Fact and Theory." *Journal of Economic History* 33 (1973): 252–273.

Lampman, Robert. *The Share of Top Wealth-Holders in National Wealth, 1922–1956*. Princeton, N.J.: Princeton University Press, 1962.

Lebergott, Stanley. *The American Economy: Income, Wealth and Want*. Princeton, N.J.: Princeton University Press, 1976.

Leuchtenburg, William E. *The Perils of Prosperity, 1914–1932*, 2d ed. Chicago: University of Chicago Press, 1993.

Libecap, Gary D. "The Political Allocation of Mineral Rights: A Reevaluation of Teapot Dome." *Journal of Economic History* 14 (1984): 381–393.

Lorant, John H. "Technological Change in American Manufacturing During the 1920s." *Journal of Economic History* 27 (1967): 243–246.

Mercer, Lloyd, and Douglas Morgan. "Alternative Interpretations of Market Saturation: Evaluation for the Automobile Market in the Late 1920s." *Explorations in Economic History* 9 (Spring 1972): 269–290.

———. "The American Automobile Industry: Investment Demand, Capacity, and Capacity Utilization 1921–1940." *Journal of Political Economy* 80 (November–December 1972): 214–231.

———. "Housing Surplus in the 1920s: Another Evaluation." *Explorations in Economic History* 10 (Spring 1973): 295–304.

Metzer, Jacob. "How New Was the New Era? The Public Sector in the 1920s." *Journal of Economic History* 45 (March 1985): 119–126.

Miron, Jeffrey A. "Violence and the U.S. Prohibitions of Drug and Alcohol." *American Law & Economics Review* 1 (1999): 78–114.

Miron, Jeffrey A., and Jeffrey Zwiebel. "Economics of Drugs: Alcohol Consumption during Prohibition." *American Economic Review* 81, Papers and Proceedings (1991): 242–247.

———. "The Economic Case against Drug Prohibition." *Journal of Economic Perspectives* 9 (Autumn 1995): 175–192

New York Stock Exchange. "Historical Perspective." **http://www.nyse.com**.

Olney, Martha. "Credit as a Production-Smoothing Device: The Case of Automobiles, 1913–1938." *Journal of Economic History* 49 (June 1989): 377–391.

———. "Consumer Durables in the Interwar Years: New Estimates, New Patterns." In *Research in Economic History*, Vol. 12, eds. Roger Ransom, Peter Lindert, and Richard Sutch. Greenwich, Conn.: JAI, 1989, 119–150.

———. "Demand for Consumer Durable Goods in 20th Century America." *Explorations in Economic History* 27 (July 1990): 322–349.

———. *Buy Now Pay Later: Advertising, Credit, and Consumer Durables in the 1920s.* Chapel Hill: University of North Carolina Press, 1991.

Sirkin, Gerald. "The Stock Market of 1929 Revisited: A Note." *Business History Review* 49 (Summer 1975): 223–231.

Smiley, Gene. "Did Incomes for Most of the Population Fall from 1923 through 1929?" *Journal of Economic History* 42 (1983): 209–216.

Smiley, Gene, and Richard Keehn. "Margin Purchases, Brokers' Loans, and the Bull Market of the Twenties." *Business History Conference* 17 (1988): 129–142.

Soule, George. *Prosperity Decade: From War to Depression, 1917–1929.* New York: Holt, Rinehart and Winston, 1947.

Swanson, Joseph, and Samuel Williamson. "Estimates of National Product and Income 1919–1941." *Explorations in Economic History* 10 (Fall 1972): 53–73.

Timmer, Ashley S., and Jeffrey G. Williamson. "Racism, Xenophobia or Markets? The Political Economy of Immigration Policy Prior to the Thirties." *NBER Working Paper No. 5867.* Cambridge, Mass.: National Bureau of Economic Research, December 1996.

Vatter, Harold G. "Has There Been a Twentieth-Century Consumer Durables Revolution?" *Journal of Economic History* 27 (1967): 1–16.

Warburton, Clark. *The Economic Results of Prohibition.* New York: Columbia University Press, 1932.

White, Eugene N. "Before the Glass-Steagall Act: An Analysis of the Investment Banking Activities of National Banks." *Explorations in Economic History* 23 (1986): 33–53.

———. "A Reinterpretation of the Banking Crisis of 1930." *Journal of Economic History* 44 (1984): 119–138.

———. "State-Sponsored Insurance of Bank Deposits in the United States, 1907–1929." *Journal of Economic History* 41 (Sept. 1981): 537–557.

———. "When the Ticker Ran Late: The Stock Market Boom and Crash of 1929." In *The Stock Market Crash in Historical Perspective*, ed. Eugene Nelson White. Homewood, Ill.: Dow Jones–Irwin, 1989.

White, Eugene N., and Peter Rappoport. "Was There a Bubble in the 1929 Stock Market?" *Journal of Economic History* 53 (September 1993): 549–574.

———. "Was the Crash of 1929 Expected?" *American Economic Review* 84 (March 1994): 271–281.

Williamson, Jeffrey, and Peter Lindert. *American Inequality: A Macroeconomic History.* New York: Academic Press, 1981.

Chapter Twenty-Three

THE GREAT DEPRESSION

As the 1920s drew to a close, Americans were confident in their well-being and in the prospects of even better times ahead. On the election trail in the summer of 1928, presidential candidate Herbert Hoover boasted of America's optimism with these words:

> *We in America today are nearer to the final triumph over poverty than ever before in the history of any land. The poorhouse is vanishing from among us. We have not yet reached the goal, but, given the chance to go forward with the policies of the last eight years, we shall soon, with the help of God, be in sight of the day when poverty will be banished from this nation.*

Hardly a voice in the wilderness, Hoover's words were typical of the confidence of the times; nearly everyone missed the emerging signs of a faltering economy. Indeed, many failed to recognize the magnitude of the decline even after the Great Depression was erupting in full force.

The Great Depression was the most important economic event of the twentieth century. Between 1929 and 1933, the economy of the United States collapsed. It is almost impossible to convey the sheer terror and misery that the depression produced, but numbers can suggest the dimensions. Real GDP fell 30 percent. Unemployment rose from 3.2 percent of the labor force in 1929 to 24.9 percent in 1933. Hunger and fear paralyzed the nation.

The central questions for economic historians are these: What caused this unprecedented collapse? Why did the economy remain depressed for so long? How can a repetition be avoided? As we shall see, scholars are still far from full agreement on all the issues. A consensus has been reached, however, on the key factors that contributed to the severity of the crisis, in particular the breakdown of the financial system. In this chapter, we concentrate on the dimensions and causes of the crisis. In the next chapter, we focus on the response of the Roosevelt administration to the depression and on the long-term consequences, particularly the emergence of the modern "mixed" economy in which the central government plays a major role in the allocation of resources.

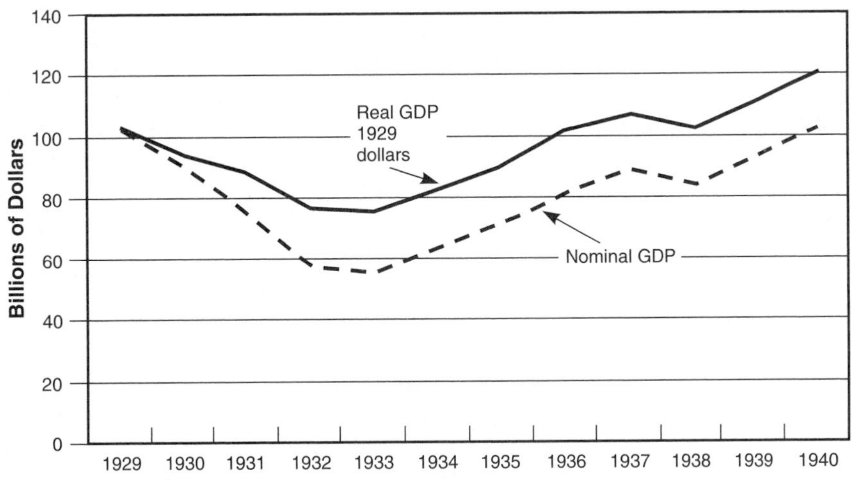

FIGURE 23.1 Gross Domestic Product, 1929–1940

Source: U.S. Bureau of Economic Analysis, http://www.bea.gov/.

DIMENSIONS OF THE DEPRESSION

It is utterly remarkable, even in hindsight, that an economic catastrophe of such magnitude could have occurred. In the four years from 1929 to 1933, the American economy simply disintegrated. The U.S. gross domestic product in current prices declined 46 percent, from $104.4 billion to $56 billion. As shown in Figure 23.1, in constant (1929) prices, the decline was 27 percent. Industrial production declined by more than one-half, and gross investment, as indicated in Figure 23.2, essentially collapsed. By 1933, gross investment was below levels of capital depreciation. The nation's capital stock was actually declining. In the process, wholesale prices dropped one-third and consumer prices one-quarter. At the trough of the depression in March 1933, output of durables had fallen 80 percent. Nondurables had fallen 30 percent.

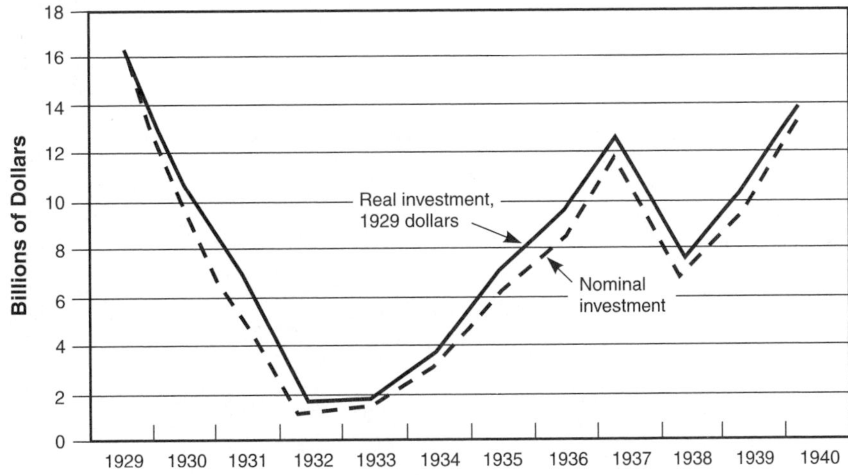

FIGURE 23.2 Gross Private Domestic Investment, 1929–1940

Source: U.S. Bureau of Economic Analysis, http://www.bea.gov/.

The most horrible statistics were those for unemployment. Figure 23.3 graphically illustrates how unemployment soared. The number of unemployed rose from 1.5 million to 11.5 million. One-quarter of the civilian workforce was unemployed or had to get by on emergency "make work" jobs created by the federal government in 1933. Fully half the nation's breadwinners were either out of work or in seriously reduced circumstances.

The intensity of the Great Depression was agonizing, and its seeming endlessness brought frustration and despair. The depression of 1920 and 1921 had been sharp and nasty, with a decline in durables output of 43 percent, but it had behaved as a depression should, coming and going quickly. In the Great Depression, on the other hand durable-goods production did not regain the 1929 peak until August 1940, more than 11 years after the beginning of the depression. Unemployment, as shown in Figure 23.3, remained stubbornly high a decade after the depression began.

It is difficult to overemphasize the deep imprint registered by the duration and depth of the collapse. The revolutionary impact—economically, politically, socially, and psychologically—of the events of that fateful decade were matched only by those of the Civil War.

CAUSES OF THE GREAT DEPRESSION

A satisfactory explanation of the Great Depression requires us to distinguish between the forces that brought a downturn in economic activity and those that turned a downturn into an utter disaster.

Hindsight enables us to detect two drags on the economy that prepared the way for a decline in economic activity. The most important was the decline from 1925 onward in both residential and nonresidential construction. The boom in building activity that began in 1918 had doubtlessly helped the economy out of the slump of 1920 and 1921; the downward phase of the same building cycle, coinciding as it did with other economic weaknesses, was a major depressing influence. What began as a gentle slide in construction from 1925 to 1927 became a marked decline in 1928.

The second drag on the economy came from the agricultural sector, which was still important enough in the 1920s to exert a powerful influence on the total economy. As noted

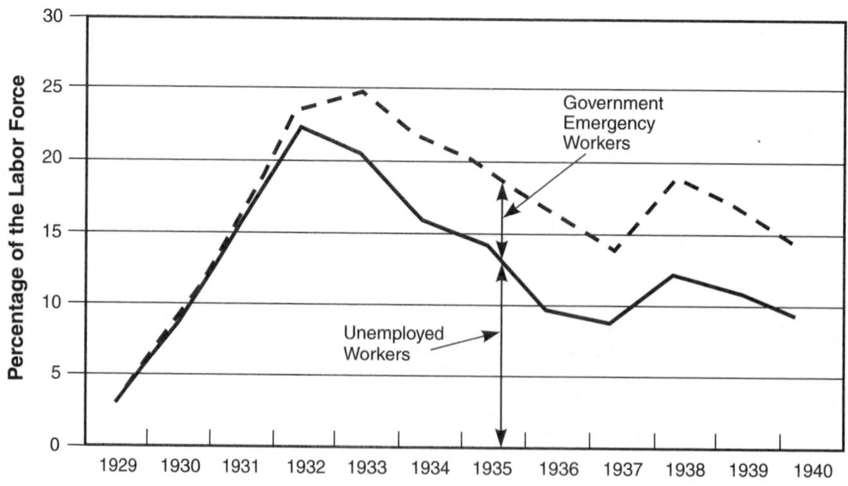

FIGURE 23.3 Percentage of the Labor Force Unemployed, 1920–1940

Source: Michael Darby, "Three and a Half Million U.S. Employees Have Been Mislaid: Or an Explanation of Unemployment, 1934–41," Journal of Political Economy *84 (1976): 7, 8.*

Wall Street on Black Thursday, October 24, 1929. Investors and the curious milled around in confusion in the planked street (subway construction was going on) as the extent of the disaster inside the New York Stock Exchange (at right) became clear.

in chapter 22, farmers struggled throughout the decade with falling world prices and heavy indebtedness. In the great agricultural midlands, few manifestations of boom psychology appeared after 1926.

A mild downturn in durables output in the spring of 1929 and a drop in nondurable production in the summer of that year could well have been expected—but nothing catastrophic was forecasted. A series of devastating blows that turned a recession into the Great Depression then hit the economy.

The Stock Market Crash

The first blow was the break in the stock market during the last week in October 1929. Declines in the stock market, even substantial ones, do not inevitably cause declines in business. The 1987 crash is an example of one that did not. The 1929 break, however, significantly accelerated the mild downturn then under way because of the catastrophic magnitude of the decline and the uncertainty it created about the future course of the economy.

The *New York Times* index of 25 industrial stocks, which early in 1924 had stood at 110, had climbed by January 1929 to 338, and by September to 452. It was almost impossible to buy a common stock that did not rise rapidly in value, and investors quickly

w York Times.

THE WEATHER
Rain today and probably tomorrow; somewhat colder tomorrow.

pyright, 1929, by The New York Times Company.

YORK, TUESDAY, OCTOBER 29, 1929. TWO CENTS

STOCK PRICES SLUMP $14,000,000,000 IN NATION-WIDE STAMPEDE TO UNLOAD; BANKERS TO SUPPORT MARKET TODAY

Sixteen Leading Issues Down $2,893,520,108; Tel. & Tel. and Steel Among Heaviest Losers

A shrinkage of $2,893,520,108 in the open market value of the shares of sixteen representative companies resulted from yesterday's sweeping decline on the New York Stock Exchange.

American Telephone and Telegraph was the heaviest loser, $448,905,162 having been lopped off of its total value. United States Steel common, traditional bellwether of the stock market, made its greatest nose-dive in recent years by falling from a high of 202½ to a low of 185. In a feeble last-minute rally it snapped back to 186, at which it closed, showing a net loss of 17⅛ points. This represented for the 8,131,055 shares of common stock outstanding a total loss in value of $142,293,446.

In the following table are shown the day's net depreciation in the outstanding shares of the sixteen companies referred to:

Issues.	Shares Listed.	Losses in Points.	Depreciation.
American Radiator	10,096,289	10⅜	$104,748,997
American Tel. & Tel.	13,203,093	34	448,905,162
Commonwealth & Southern	30,764,468	3⅛	96,138,962
Columbia Gas & Electric	8,477,307	22	186,500,754
Consolidated Gas	11,451,188	20	229,023,760
DuPont E. I.	10,322,481	16⅜	169,030,625
Eastman Kodak	2,229,703	41⅞	93,368,813
General Electric	7,211,484	47½	342,545,490
General Motors	43,500,000	6¾	293,625,000
International Nickel	13,777,408	7⅞	108,497,088
New York Central	4,637,086	22½	104,334,071
Standard Oil of New Jersey	24,843,643	8	198,749,144
Union Carbide & Carbon	8,730,173	20	[illegible]

EUROPE IS DISTURBED BY AMERICAN ACTION ON OCCUPATION DEBT

London Urges an Explanation of Move for Direct Payments by Germany.

BANK'S PRESTIGE INVOLVED

Britain and Continent Feel That We Do Not Have Faith in Young Plan Institution.

SCHEME IS LAID TO HOOVER

President Is Said to Wish to Avoid Clash in Congress Over Linking of Reparations and War Debts.

By EDWIN L. JAMES.

Special Cable to The New York Times.

LONDON, Oct. 28.—There appears to exist in London a certain absence of understanding as to the significance of the conversations between Washington and Berlin which now are about to ripen into diplomatic negotiations in the German capital for the preparation of a ...

PREMIER ISSUES HARD HIT

Unexpected Torrent of Liquidation Again Rocks Markets.

DAY'S SALES 9,212,800

Nearly 3,000,000 Shares Are Traded In Final Hour—The Tickers Lag 167 Minutes.

NEW RALLY SOON BROKEN

Selling by Europeans and "Mob Psychology" Big Factors in Second Big Break.

Memory Honored Day Fete on Ships

...ea and in port offi... ted Navy Day yester... igh major land cele... held on Sunday, the ... of the birth of Theo... ...lt, similar ceremonies ... were reserved for ...

... was kept by ships ... he public was invited ... Flags appropriate ... were broken out on all ships, and even some craft in the harbor ... ennants in honor of ...

...ngeles and the new ... irigible and other air craft at Lake... were ordered out and ... along the Atlantic ... over this city and ...

T. E. BURTON, DIES AT 77

...man Had Served in ... 41 Years—First to the House.

...VOCATE OF PEACE

Newspapers reported in sterile statistics the painful details of Wall Street's collapse.

accumulated fortunes. The optimism engendered by these gains permeated the business community and led to the conclusion that permanent prosperity had arrived. Many investors had become uneasy, however, about the dizzying heights to which prices had risen. President Hoover and officials at the Federal Reserve worried about excessive speculation and the danger of a crash. In August, the Federal Reserve raised the discount rate (the rate at which it lent to member banks) to 6 percent in an attempt to stem the flow of credit into the stock market. The Bank of England and other central banks took similar actions for the same reasons. For a short time, at least, these actions had no effect: Stock prices continued upward.

On September 5, investment adviser Roger Babson warned that a crash was coming, and the market staggered through the "Babson break." Prices declined through September, but as yet, there was no sign of panic. Then a sharp break occurred on October 23 and October 24 ("Black Thursday"), when a record 13 million shares traded (3 million was normal). Massive organized buying by banks and investment houses prevented a complete rout, but on October 28 ("Black Monday") and October 29 ("Black Tuesday"), the panic resumed. The slide continued until mid-November. By that time, stock prices had fallen to about one-half of what they had been in August.

Well into 1930, however, share prices remained above the levels reached in 1926. If all that was involved had been the loss of the extraordinary capital gains made by stock market investors in 1927 and 1928, it would be hard to blame the depression on the stock market crash—after all, "easy come, easy go." The unique psychological trauma produced by the crash was more significant than the direct effects of the loss of wealth. Many Americans had come to believe in the 1920s that the economy had entered a "new era" of continuous and rapid progress that would carry them to higher and higher standards of living. The spectacular rise in the stock market was taken as proof that this view was widely shared by knowledgeable investors. When the market crashed, this optimistic view of the future crashed with it; almost overnight, uncertainty and pessimism about the future gripped the public. Purchases of consumer durables, in particular, which depended on consumer confidence about the future and which had increasingly been bought on the installment plan, declined drastically.[1] See New View 23.1 on page 458 on lessons the stock crash could teach.

The Smoot-Hawley Tariff

In June 1930, Congress passed and the President signed the Smoot-Hawley Tariff, which raised tariffs on a wide array of goods, especially agricultural products. There were vigorous protests against the bill, and 1,000 economists, including all leaders of the profession, signed a petition urging President Hoover to veto it on the grounds that high tariffs would reduce imports, thus making it more difficult for other countries to earn the money needed to buy our exports. It also was believed that high tariffs would provoke retaliation by other countries. Every country would raise its tariffs, and trade would decline. Soon, in fact, other countries did raise their tariffs, for example, Great Britain in 1932. It is difficult to say, however, whether other countries raised their tariffs in retaliation for the American tariffs or for other reasons, such as simply to raise revenues during the depression because normal sources of funds were drying up.

The Smoot-Hawley tariff, although unwise, was, however, not a major cause of the depression. Exports were only 6 percent of GNP in 1930, and imports only 4.9 percent. The increases in the tariffs, moreover, applied only to a portion of the total array of our imports; many goods were exempted.[2] The increased tariffs did have some positive employment benefits in import-competing sectors. So at most, Smoot-Hawley made a bad situation slightly worse. Perhaps the greatest effect of the tariff was psychological: Controversy over the bill added to pessimism about the future, and dampened willingness to invest.

For many other countries more dependent on trade than the United States, the rounds of tariff increases that followed Smoot-Hawley in the thirties were more significant. Most experts at the time, and since, viewed the tendency to raise tariffs in the thirties as a self-defeating "beggar thy neighbor" policy. Partly as a result, the United States became a champion after World War II (although not always a consistent one) of lower tariffs and freer trade. The Smoot-Hawley tariff turned out to be the last of America's high "protective" tariffs.

The Banking Crises

The devastating impact of the stock market collapse came in the early stages of the depression. Morale might have improved, and the stock market and the economy might have regained some buoyancy had it not been for the structural weaknesses of the banking system.

The economy was repeatedly buffeted in the early 1930s by waves of bank failures. The first of these, as shown in Table 23.1 on page 459, began in October 1930 with the failure of banks in the South and Midwest. Although losses were heavy, these failures drew little attention from the Federal Reserve or the national media, perhaps because they were similar to the failures that had occurred in the 1920s.[3] Then on December 11, the Bank of the

---

[1]This point is developed in Christina Romer, "The Great Crash and the Onset of the Great Depression," *Quarterly Journal of Economics* CV (1990): 597–624.

[2]Many taxes on imports were fixed in nominal terms (so many cents per pound of an imported product). Deflation raised the burden of these taxes, which added to the increases called for by Smoot-Hawley.

[3]See Eugene N. White, "A Reinterpretation of the Banking Crisis of 1930," *Journal of Economic History* 44 (1984): 119–138; and Elmus Wicker, *The Banking Panics of the Great Depression* (New York: Cambridge University Press, 1996), chapter 2.

New View 23.1

Lessons from History for Investing in the Stock Market

The following figure shows prices on the New York Stock Exchange from January of 1926 to December 1938, and, by way of comparison, from January 1996 to August 2003. Evidently, the rise in stock prices during the second half of the 1990s was similar to the rise during the second half in the 1920s. This parallel encouraged many investors (including a number of economic historians!) to sell stocks near the peak in 2000. Does knowledge of financial history make one a better investor? Certainly, the study of financial history increases our understanding of the forces at work in the present, but financial markets do not mechanically follow past patterns. Note that so far, the recent decline in stock prices has not been as severe as the decline in the early 1930s, perhaps because there was no counterpart in the early 2000s to the banking crises and international financial crises that undermined confidence in the early 1930s.

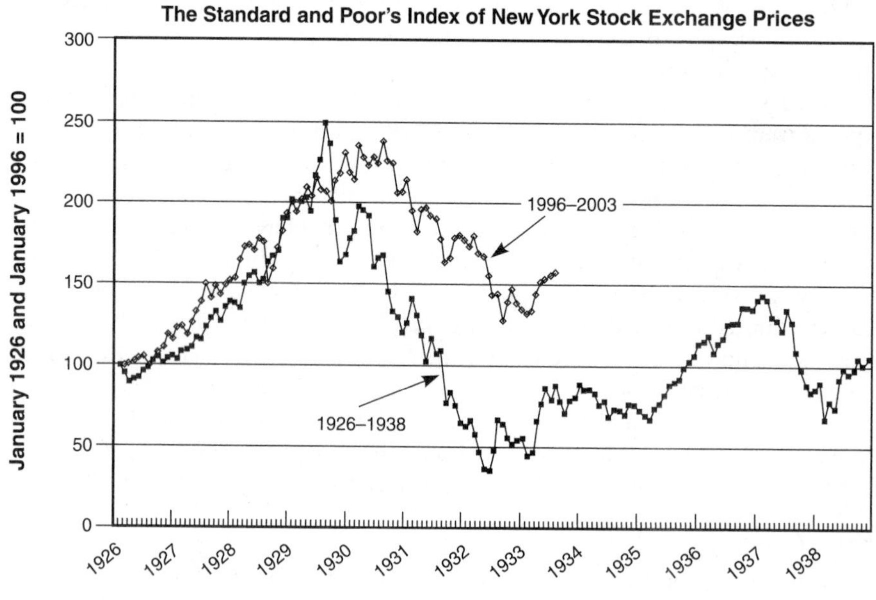

United States in New York failed. This failure was significant for several reasons. It was the largest failure, measured by deposits, in the history of the United States up to that time. Although it was an ordinary bank (chartered by the state of New York), its name may have led some people to believe that a bank having a particularly close association with the government had failed.

The Federal Reserve at this point, most economic historians agree, should have acted as a *lender of last resort*. It should have lent generously to the Bank of United States and other failing banks to break the cycle of fear that was undermining the banking system. For a variety of reasons that we will discuss later in detail, however, it did not do so. To the Federal Reserve it seemed that the banks that were failing were simply badly managed banks that should be eliminated to make the system more efficient. At times a rumor that a bank was in trouble would send people running to the bank to try to get their money out before the

TABLE 23.1 A Chronology of the Financial Meltdown, 1929–1933

DATE	EVENT	COMMENT
October 1929	The stock market crash	Optimism about the future becomes pessimism. Consumer durable purchases fall.
October 1930	Onset of the first banking crisis in the United States	Bank failures mount in the South and Midwest.
December 11, 1930	Failure of the Bank of the United States in New York City	The ratio of currency to deposits begins to rise.
March 1931	Onset of the second banking crisis in the United States	Bank failures reach new highs, and deposits fall.
May 1931	Failure of the Kreditanstalt, Austria's largest private bank.	The crisis has become international
July 1931	Closing of the German banks	Capital flows to the United States, but short-term obligations of U.S. banks are frozen.
September 1931	Britain's departure from gold standard	Is nothing sacred? Drain of gold from the United States.
April 1932	Beginnings of large-scale open-market purchases	Too little, too late.
March 1933	The banking panic of 1933	State bank holidays occur. President Roosevelt declares a national holiday on March 6.

Source: Derived from Milton Friedman and Anna J. Schwartz, A Monetary History of the United States *(Princeton, N.J.: Princeton University Press, 1965), 301–324, and other histories of the period.*

bank closed its doors, the classic sign of a panic. More generally, the fear of bank failures led people to convert deposits into cash, depriving the banks of reserves. The banks, moreover, refused to make new loans or renew old ones to build up their reserves. The result was shrinkage in the amount of deposits and bank loans available. In retrospect, we can see that it was important to end this downward spiral, but the Federal Reserve did not recognize it at the time.

For a few months, things seemed calmer, but a second, more intense crisis began in March 1931. This time events abroad reinforced the crisis. In May 1931, the Kreditanstalt, a major bank in Vienna, failed. Because gold was the base of the money supply in most industrial countries, failures such as this one convinced people worldwide that it was time to convert paper claims to gold into the real thing. In September 1931, Britain, still one of the world's financial centers and a symbol of financial rectitude, left the gold standard. The British pound would no longer be convertible on demand into gold. This, in turn, increased the pressure on the dollar, which was still convertible into gold.

The final banking panic began in 1933. Between 1930 and 1932, more than 5,000 banks containing more than $3 billion in deposits (about 7 percent of total deposits in January 1930) had suspended operations. In 1933, another 4,000 banks containing more than $3.5 billion in deposits would close. The banks' weakened condition after years of deflation, uncertainties about how the new administration of Franklin D. Roosevelt would handle the crisis, and the general atmosphere of distrust and fear—all contributed to the final crisis. By the time that Roosevelt took office on March 4, 1933, the financial system had ceased to function.

One of President Roosevelt's first acts was to announce a nationwide bank holiday beginning on March 6, 1933. This action, which followed a number of state bank holidays, closed all of the banks in the country for one week. How could such an action improve things? The public was told that during this period, the banks would be inspected and only the sound ones allowed to reopen. Questions have been raised about the way this was handled. Probably many sound banks were closed and unsound ones allowed to remain open. But the medicine seemed to work, even if it was only a placebo; the panic subsided.

In addition to the bank holiday, the federal government took a number of other actions that helped to restore confidence in the financial system. Gold hoarding was ended by the simple expedient of requiring everyone to turn monetary gold over to the Federal Reserve in exchange for some other currency. Perhaps most important, the Federal Deposit Insurance Corporation (FDIC) was established to insure bank deposits. The insurance took effect on January 1, 1934, and within six months, almost all of the nation's commercial banks were covered. Deposit insurance dramatically changed the incentives facing depositors. No longer would a rumor of failure send people rushing to the bank to try to be first in line because they now knew that they would eventually be paid their deposits in any case. Together these policies drastically changed the rate of bank failures. The number of bank failures fell from 4,000 in 1933 to 61 in 1934 and remained at double-digit levels through the rest of the 1930s. (By way of contrast, the lowest number of bank failures in any year from 1921 to 1929 was 366 in 1922.) Although the Great Depression was to drag on for the remainder of the decade, the banking crisis had been surmounted.

THE ROLE OF THE FINANCIAL CRISIS

The banking and financial crisis were clearly a disaster of major proportions. What was their role in the Great Depression? Were they the cause of the depression or only a consequence of it?

The Monetarist Interpretation

To monetarists such as Milton Friedman and Anna J. Schwartz, the primary cause of the Great Depression was the decline in the stock of money produced by the withdrawal of currency from the banking system and the decisions of banks to hold more reserves. The only way banks could maintain or increase their reserves was by decreasing their lending, a decision that led to a multiple contraction of bank credit and deposits. According to the quantity theory of money, when the stock of money contracts, people try to restore the relationship between their money balances and their incomes by spending less. The result is a fall in net national product. Thus, monetarists believe that the fall in the stock of money from $47 billion in 1929 to $32 billion in 1933, as shown in Table 23.2, was a major *cause* of the fall in net national product from $90 billion to $43 billion. They blame the Federal Reserve for not acting as a lender of last resort to prevent the decline in the stock of money.

Monetarists do not claim that the fall in the stock of money was the only factor at work. Note that the ratio of money to net national product (column 3 of Table 23.2) rose, showing that people were hoarding rather than spending. During the first year of the depression, in particular, the ratio of money to net national product rose dramatically, probably because of the stock market crash, while the money supply fell only slightly. Nevertheless, monetarists insist that any decline in the money supply is significant. (See page 462 for more discussion of the ratio and the Quantity Theory of Money.)

It is difficult to believe that the collapse of the stock of money did the economy any good, and most economic historians now follow the monetarists in assigning at least some role to the monetary collapse. There has been some controversy, however, over exactly how much weight to assign to the banking crisis compared with other causes such as the stock market crash. The most skeptical view has been expressed by Peter Temin, whose interpretation of the data in Table 23.2 is just the reverse of that proposed by the monetarists.[4]

Net national product fell, according to Temin, because of a collapse in consumer spending brought on partly by the stock market crash. As a result, profits fell, workers were laid

[4]Peter Temin, *Did Monetary Forces Cause the Great Depression?* (New York: Norton, 1976).

TABLE 23.2 Money and Income, 1929–1933

YEAR	(1) MONEY SUPPLY (billions)	(2) NET NATIONAL PRODUCT (billions)	(3) RATIO OF MONEY TO NNP	(4) COMMERCIAL PAPER RATE (percent)	(5) REAL RATE OF INTEREST (percent)
1929	$46.6	$90.3	0.52	5.78%	5.88%
1930	45.7	76.9	0.60	3.55	8.15
1931	42.7	61.7	0.69	2.63	15.46
1932	36.1	44.8	0.81	2.72	14.99
1933	32.2	42.7	0.76	1.67	3.03

Source: Milton Friedman and Anna J. Schwartz, Monetary Trends in the United States and the United Kingdom *(Chicago: University of Chicago Press, 1982),124.*

off, and many firms and individuals could no longer repay their bank loans. This triggered the waves of bank failures and the decline in the money stock shown in Column (1) of Table 23.2. This was a tragedy, to be sure, but it was a symptom, in Temin's view, of the depression analogous to the problems in agricultural, consumer durables production, and other sectors of the economy.

The key piece of evidence, according to Temin, is the behavior of the rate of interest. He contends that if the decline in the money stock were the initiating factor, we would have seen interest rates rising. People would have begun selling financial assets to acquire money, and the prices of those assets would have fallen while the returns they yielded (relative to their prices) would have risen. If there is a shortage of wheat, we expect the price of wheat to rise, and if there is a shortage of money, we expect the rate of interest to rise. But we observe just the opposite: Short-term interest rates, Column (4) fell from 5.78 percent in 1929 to 1.67 percent in 1933. Therefore, Temin concludes, there was no shortage of money during the contraction from 1929 to 1933.

Temin's analysis, however, did not end the debate. Monetarists countered that the interest rate is the price not of money but of credit. (See Economic Insight 23.1 on page 462). The demand for credit declined because of the general decline in economic activity caused by the decline in the money supply. To the monetarists, the price of money is the inverse of the price level, the purchasing power of money. That variable rose from 1929 to 1933, showing that the supply of money was contracting faster than demand. Monetarists also pointed out that what really matters to business is the real interest rate: the market rate plus the expected rate of deflation. Column (5) of Table 23.2 shows a simple measure of the real rate, the rate on commercial paper minus the percentage change in prices since the previous year. Real rates were clearly very high in the early years of the depression.

Nonmonetary Effects of the Financial Crisis

Recent research, moreover, has identified additional channels through which the financial crisis reinforced the decline in economic activity. The seminal research was done by Ben Bernanke, who argued on the basis of a wide range of evidence that bank failures made it difficult for firms, particularly smaller firms, to get the credit they needed to remain in operation.[5]

Bernanke's interpretation stressed the problem of "asymmetric information." When a borrower and lender negotiate, their access to key information differs. The lender cannot

[5]Ben Bernanke, "Nonmonetary Effects of the Financial Crisis in the Propagation of the Great Depression," *American Economic Review* 73 (1983): 257–276.

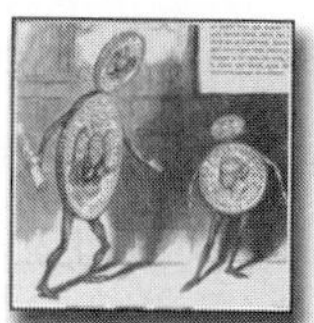

Economic Insight 23.1

Temin's Critique of the Monetarist Interpretation of the Great Depression

These figures illustrate Peter Temin's famous critique of the monetarist interpretation of the Great Depression. They depict the supply of and demand for money, with the interest rate as the price of holding money. Temin's rendering of the monetarist interpretation is in Figure A and the Keynesian interpretation is in Figure B. If the monetarists were correct (according to Temin), the dominant shift would have been the supply curve to the left (Figure A). If the Keynesians were right, the dominant shift would have been the demand curve to the left (Figure B). Because interest rates fell during the depression—as shown in column (4) of Table 23.2—Temin concluded that the Keynesians were right.

Monetarists countered that Temin neglected intermediate and longer-term effects of the decline in the quantity of money on the demand for money. Falling real income (caused by past decreases in the supply of money) reduced the demand for money. So part of the shift in the demand curve in Figure B could be attributed to the fall in the stock of money. Moreover, lower market rates were consistent with higher real rates.

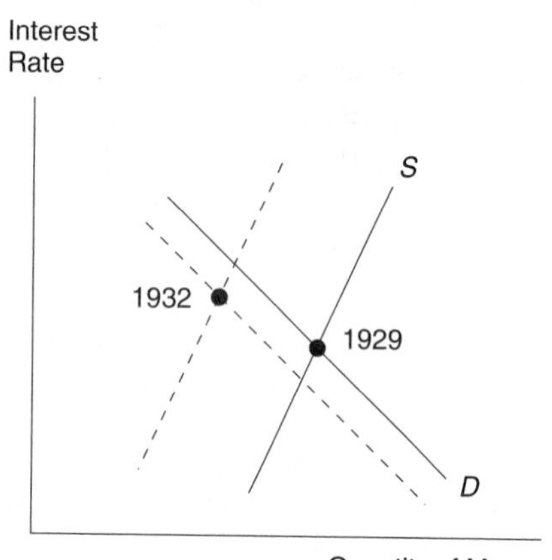

A. If the monetarists were right.

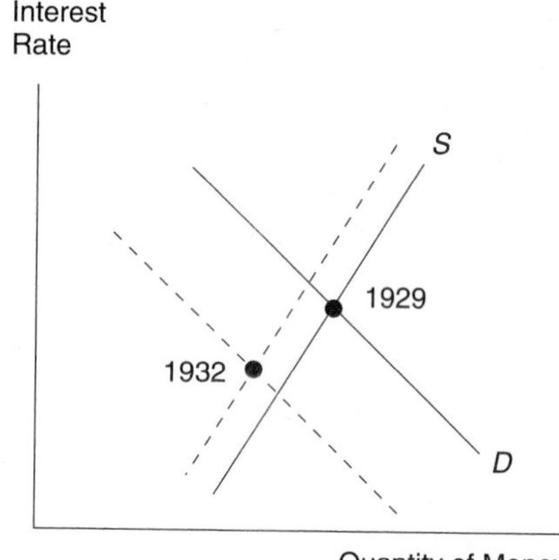

B. If the Keynesians were right.

see into the mind of the borrower to learn the borrower's determination to repay. Normally, this problem can be overcome by forging long-term relationships between borrowers and lenders or through the use of collateral. When a bank failed, however, the long-term relationships between the bank and its borrowers was severed. A borrower could approach another lender, but how would another lender know that in the past the borrower had struggled to faithfully repay loans or that the borrower was regarded by other members of the community as a good risk? Bernanke's analysis also helps explain why the depression lasted so long: it took time to forge new relationships.

In addition, Bernanke pointed out that the ongoing deflation increased the burden of debt carried by businesses and consumers and so reduced their ability to qualify for credit. The decline in the value of stocks and land, both urban and rural, had a similar effect. Businesses and individuals did not have assets that they could offer as collateral.

When the banking holiday ended in March 1933, thousands of people stood in line to withdraw cash.

Although the role of nonmenetary effects of the crisis has received considerable attention in recent years, it has been thought about for a long time. In 1933 Irving Fisher blamed the depression on the rising real value of debt and its effect on spending.

In short, controversy continues over the exact role of the financial crisis in the Great Depression, but most economic historians now agree that the financial crisis was important, and the Federal Reserve deserves considerable blame for the disastrous path along which events unfolded.[6] Refer to Economic Reasoning Proposition 5: Evidence matters.

★★★ *Economic Reasoning Proposition*

WHY DIDN'T THE FEDERAL RESERVE SAVE THE BANKING SYSTEM?

The Federal Reserve had been created in the wake of the Panic of 1907 for the purpose of preventing future crises by acting as a lender of last resort. For a number of reasons, however, it failed to do so.

---

[6]Even Peter Temin, in his later work, assigned some blame to the Federal Reserve for the tight money regime it initiated in the late twenties. See Peter Temin, *Lessons from the Great Depression* (Cambridge, Mass.: MIT Press, 1989).

One reason is that the members of the Federal Reserve Board simply failed to appreciate the magnitude of the crisis and the actions needed to combat it. In his diary entries during August 1931, Charles S. Hamlin, then a member of the Federal Reserve Board, tells us that the Open Market Committee voted 11 to 1 against open-market purchases of $300 million of government bonds—which would have pumped reserves into the banking system as sellers of bonds deposited their checks on the Federal Reserve—substituting $120 million instead. The governors of the regional banks, who were still in control, simply could not grasp the magnitude of the crisis, and Governor Meyer of the Federal Reserve Board was even worried about inflation.

To some extent, the failure to appreciate the magnitude of the collapse was the result of the tendency at the Federal Reserve to look at the wrong indicators of monetary policy. Many officials at the Federal Reserve believed that low nominal interest rates—Column (4) of Table 23.2—were a certain sign that financial markets were awash with money and that trying to pump in more would do little good. Had they looked at real interest rates—Column (5) of Table 23.2—they would have reached a different conclusion. The Federal Reserve also paid no heed to the fall in the stock of money. The data were available to them, but Fed officials viewed the decline in the stock of money merely as a sign that the need for money had fallen.

In its 1932 annual report, the Federal Reserve Board argued that its power to purchase bonds was limited by the requirement that Fed notes be backed 40 percent by gold and 60 percent by either gold or eligible paper (loans sold by the banks to the Federal Reserve). The only "free gold" the Federal Reserve owned, to use the technical term, was the amount of gold that it held in excess of the amount it was legally required to hold. This amount, it argued, was simply too small to permit substantial open-market purchases. Such purchases would have led banks to cut their borrowing from the Fed (why borrow reserves at interest if reserves are already adequate?), depriving the Fed of loans that it could count against notes. The result would be that the Fed's free gold, then about $416 million, would disappear, violating the rules that committed the United States to the gold standard.

Friedman and Schwartz advance a number of arguments to show that the free gold problem was merely a rationalization, not the real reason for the Federal Reserve's reluctance to expand the stock of money. For one thing, when the rules defining what the Fed had to hold in reserve against notes were eased by the Glass-Steagall Act in February 1932, the Federal Reserve did not respond by increasing its open-market purchases of bonds commensurately. Concern about the maintenance of the gold standard, however, as Barry Eichengreen has shown, rather than technical concerns about the amount of free gold, may have been an important psychological constraint on Federal Reserve actions. Indeed, in his view, central banks throughout the world made the mistake of putting the maintenance of the gold standard above expanding the stock of money to fight the depression.

A power struggle within the Federal Reserve system identified by Friedman and Schwartz was another important factor. In the 1920s, the Federal Reserve Bank of New York, under its charismatic president Benjamin Strong, had dominated the system. After Strong's death in 1928, the Federal Reserve Board in Washington tried to assert its authority by resisting pressures from New York. This power struggle took its toll in the 1930s, when the New York bank pushed for more expansionary monetary policies and the Federal Reserve Board in Washington resisted for internal political reasons.

The precise weight to be put on each of these factors is a matter of debate, but the important point is that as a result of them, the Federal Reserve system, although created in 1913 to protect the nation's banking system in times of crisis, failed 20 years later to stop the greatest banking crisis in American history.

TABLE 23.3 Governmental Expenditures and Revenues, 1927–1940 (billions of dollars)

	FEDERAL		STATE AND LOCAL		
YEAR	EXPENDITURES	REVENUES	EXPENDITURES	REVENUES	PRIVATE INVESTMENT
1927	$2.9	$4.0	$ 7.8	$ 7.8	$14.5[a]
1932	4.8	2.0	8.4	7.9	3.4
1934	6.5	3.1	7.8	8.4	4.1
1936	7.6	4.2	8.5	9.4	7.2
1938	7.2	7.0	10.0	11.1	7.4
1940	9.6	6.9	11.2	11.7	11.0

[a] *This is the 1929 figure.*

Source: Historical Statistics *(Washington, D.C.: Government Printing Office, 1976), Series F53, Y335, Y336, Y339, Y340, Y652, Y671.*

FISCAL POLICY IN THE 1930s

The popular belief that the Hoover administration did nothing to combat the depression is erroneous. In January 1932, he set up the Reconstruction Finance Corporation to borrow money by issuing securities guaranteed by the federal government and to relend it to banks, insurance companies, railroads, and other businesses experiencing financial difficulties. The very formation of such an agency in peacetime (a revival of the War Finance Corporation of World War I) marked a sharp break with tradition. Support of agricultural prices with production controls by the Federal Farm Board was equally revolutionary. The Hoover administration's major deficiencies were its persistent refusal to establish a desperately needed federal program of work relief, even if it meant deficits, and its failure to press the Federal Reserve to expand money and credit. Orthodox Keynesians would add that the administration should have deliberately raised spending for whatever purpose and cut taxes to generate "multiplier effects." Virtually all economic historians agree that too much reliance was placed on maintaining confidence through the public testimonials of business and government leaders but not enough on measures to raise incomes and correct the deflation.

Franklin D. Roosevelt and his staff were uncomfortable with deficits. During the campaign of 1932, Roosevelt promised to cut spending 25 percent and balance the budget. But once in office, the Roosevelt administration was willing to run large deficits by historical standards to finance its many new programs. How large were these deficits? Why did they not lift the country out of the depression, as Keynesian economic theory predicts?[7]

The relevant numbers are given in Table 23.3. The federal budget was steadily in deficit during the depression. Relative to the traditional size of the federal government, the level of spending and the deficits seemed large indeed. Note that by 1938, federal spending was two and one-half times as high as it had been in 1927. Taxes had also been increased (despite the depression!) by 75 percent from $4 billion to $7 billion.

The resulting deficit of $0.2 billion ($7.2 – $7.0) in 1938 was more than offset by a surplus at the state and local levels of $1.1 billion ($10.0 – $11.1).

Keynesian theory suggests that the role of government spending is to offset decreases in autonomous private spending such as investment or consumption. It is clear that the fall in private investment spending, $7.1 billion between 1929 and 1938 (Table 23.3) was far greater than the increase in federal spending or the federal deficit. No wonder, then, that Keynesian economist E. Cary Brown concludes that "fiscal policy . . . seems to have been

[7]The famous book by John Maynard Keynes, *The General Theory of Employment, Interest and Money*, was not published until 1936. Many economists, however, favored increased government spending financed by deficits. Some thought that increased spending would "prime the pump" and stimulate the natural expansionary powers of the economy.

Farm and home foreclosures and unemployment created a growing mass of homeless people during the depression. Shantytowns, like this one in New York's Central Park, were called "Hoovervilles."

an unsuccessful recovery device in the thirties—not because it does not work, but because it was not tried."[8]

PARTIAL RECOVERY AND THEN A NEW DOWNTURN

Climbing Out of the Abyss

Net national product rose from a low of $42.7 billion in 1933 to $75.1 billion in 1937, still well below the level of 1929 but sufficient to alleviate much hardship and to demonstrate the potential of the economy to recover. Over the same period, the implicit price deflator rose from 73.3 to 81.0 (1929 = 100). This boom was stimulated, orthodox Keynesians would argue, by the expansion of government spending for relief of the unemployed and for other New Deal programs to be described in chapter 24. Recovery was also stimulated by the expansion of the money stock from $32.2 billion in 1933 to $45.7 billion in 1937.

The monetary expansion was not the result of a deliberate Federal Reserve policy of increasing the money stock. Rather, as confidence in the banking system took hold, people began to redeposit currency in the banking system. This led to an increase in the money

[8]Cary E. Brown, "Fiscal Policy in the Thirties: A Reappraisal." *American Economic Review* 46 (December 1956): 879. Work by Larry Peppers strengthened Brown's original conclusions; see "Full Employment Surplus Analysis and Structural Changes: The 1930s," *Explorations in Economic History* 10 (Winter 1973): 197–210.

Campaign promises to balance the budget and cut spending met head-on with the economic realities of the Great Depression. Some in the media chastised FDR for deficit spending to pay for his new programs.

stock because banks would create several dollars of loans and deposits on the basis of each additional dollar of currency redeposited. The fractional reserve system that had worked to destroy the monetary system from 1930 to 1933 now ran in reverse. Even more important, however, was an increase in the monetary base, primarily because of purchases of gold by the U.S. Treasury.

The Price of Gold and the Stock of Money

During the bank holiday and the weeks that followed, the Roosevelt administration prohibited transactions in gold. On April 5, 1933, it took the extraordinary step of ordering all holders of gold to deliver their gold (rare coins and other specialized holdings were exempt) to the Federal Reserve. These actions took the United States off the gold standard. For several months, the price of gold, and therefore of foreign currencies still linked to gold, fluctuated according to the dictates of supply and demand. The federal government, however, made a determined effort to increase the price of gold by purchasing gold. The idea was to raise the dollar price of commodities, particularly agricultural commodities, set on world markets. To some extent, the policy was successful; some of the inflation that occurred in this period, otherwise surprising because of the depressed state of the economy, can be attributed to the manipulation of the exchange rate.

On January 31, 1934, the United States recommitted itself to a form of the gold standard by fixing a price of $35 per ounce (the predepression price had been $20 per ounce) at which the Treasury would buy or sell gold. The new form of the gold standard, however, was only a pale reflection of the classical gold standard because ordinary citizens were not allowed to hold gold coins. As a result of these policies, production of gold in the United States and the rest of the world soared in the 1930s. World production rose from 25 million ounces in 1933 to 40 million ounces in 1940. After all, costs of production such as wages had fallen, but the price at which gold could be sold to the U.S. Treasury had risen. The result was a rapid increase in the Treasury's stock of gold. When the government sets prices, it changes incentives and influences production. This is explained in Economic Reasoning Proposition 3: Incentives matter. In addition, the rise of fascism in Europe created a large outflow of capital, including gold, seeking a safe haven, further augmenting U.S. gold holdings.

When the Treasury purchased gold, it created gold certificates that it could use as cash or deposit with the Federal Reserve. In effect, if the Treasury bought gold, it was allowed to pay for it by printing new currency. The result was a rapid increase in the monetary base, which, in conjunction with the redeposit of currency in the banking system, produced a rapid increase in the money supply.

The Recession within the Depression

By early 1937, total manufacturing output had exceeded the rate of 1929, and the recovery, though not complete, seemed to be going well. At that point, however, the expansion came to an abrupt halt. Industrial production reached a post-1929 high in May 1937 and then turned downward. Commodity prices followed, and the weary process of deflation began again. Retail sales dropped, unemployment increased, and payrolls declined. Adding to the general gloom, the stock market started a long slide in August that brought prices in March 1938 to less than half the peak of the previous year. The important setbacks of 1937 are revealed graphically in Figures 23.1 through 23.3.

What had happened? Then, as now, many attributed the renewed onslaught of depression to the reform measures introduced and passed in 1935 and 1936. Social Security and the new freedom granted to labor came in for some harsh words. Most of the criticism was directed toward the antibusiness political climate created by the Roosevelt administration, which, it was asserted, made vigorous business expansion impossible. In his state of the union message of 1936, President Roosevelt had castigated "the royalists of the economic order" who, he said, opposed government intervention in economic affairs and received a disproportionate amount of national income. People of means especially resented the tax legislation in 1935 and 1936, directed at preventing tax avoidance and making the tax structure more progressive. In addition, estate and gift taxes were increased, as were individual surtaxes and taxes on the income of large corporations. The undistributed profits tax of 1936—a surtax imposed on corporations to make them distribute profits instead of holding them so that individual stockholders could avoid personal taxation—was also resented. Why would business undertake long-term investments, critics of the administration wondered, when the profits might all be taken away by future legislation?

Whatever merit there is in this argument, it is clear that fiscal and monetary policy also played a role in causing the downturn. Government officials were convinced in early 1937 that full employment and inflation were just around the corner. Expenditures for relief and public works were cut, and new taxes such as the Social Security tax (discussed in the next chapter) were imposed. The result was that the projected deficit for 1937 dropped significantly. Keynesian economists would not be surprised to find a recession.

Monetary policy also worked to create a recession. The excess reserves of the banks, as noted, had risen steadily after the banking crises of the early 1930s. The Federal Reserve interpreted these reserves simply as money piling up in the banks because it could not be profitably invested at the low interest rates then prevailing. The Fed then decided to raise legal reserve ratios to lock up the excess reserves and prevent them from being put into use during the anticipated not-too-distant inflation. This policy proved, however, to be a disastrous mistake. In fact, these reserves were not unwanted by the banks, which had been deliberately building up a cushion in the event of a replay of the banking crises. Their response to the Federal Reserve's decision to raise legal reserve ratios was to restore their margin of safety by acquiring more reserves. To do this, they reduced their loans and deposits. The money supply fell once again, although only slightly, in 1937.

The contraction from 1937 to 1938 was not as deep or as persistent as the contraction from 1929 to 1933. One reason is that the banking system did not collapse. The protection created by deposit insurance, along with the cautious behavior of the banks that survived the debacle of the early 1930s, prevented a repetition. The numbers of banks suspended operations in 1937 was only 82 and in 1938 only 80, compared with 1,350 in 1930 and 2,293 in 1931. Nevertheless, the result of the recession within the depression was that the economy was still far from fully employed in 1939.

CAN IT HAPPEN AGAIN?

No one, unfortunately, can say for certain that such a depression cannot happen again. There are many reasons for thinking that a collapse on the scale of the Great Depression is a remote possibility under modern circumstances.

One reason is that we are not likely to repeat the same mistakes. The Federal Reserve, with better data at hand and with the experience of the Great Depression laid out in many books and articles, is unlikely to permit a complete collapse of the banking system. Moreover, because we are no longer on a gold standard, the Fed's ability to create dollars during a crisis is virtually unlimited.

The same is true of fiscal policy, although here we cannot be quite so confident. Faith in a balanced budget seems to be hard to shake, even under very dire circumstances. Nevertheless, it seems likely that conditions similar to those of the early 1930s would be met today with tax cuts and increased spending on a substantial scale. Many sorts of spending—the so-called automatic stabilizers—such as unemployment benefits would increase even without specific congressional actions.

The private economy, too, is less vulnerable to economic collapse. The industrial sector, particularly producers of consumer durables, seems to be the most vulnerable to sudden shifts in demand that lead to massive layoffs. This sector is now relatively much smaller compared with the service sector, however, than it was in the 1930s. The rapid increase in two-earner households, moreover, has reduced the probability for many families that an economic downturn will completely deprive them of an income.

Finally, there exists a vast network of government programs that would alleviate suffering and, simply by being there, reduce the chance of a paralyzing fear. These include the Federal Deposit Insurance Corporation, the Pension Guarantee Corporation, and others. However much we may be aware of these facts, it is nevertheless true that the nightmare of the Great Depression comes back to haunt us time and again when conditions in one sector or another take a turn for the worse.

WHAT DOES THE DEPRESSION TELL US ABOUT CAPITALISM?

Rexford Tugwell, a member of President Roosevelt's "brain trust" (a group of advisers who suggested many new programs to combat the depression), remarked:

> The Cat is out of the Bag. There is no invisible hand. There never was. If the depression has not taught us that, we are incapable of education. . . . We must now supply a real and visible guiding hand to do the task which that mythical, nonexistent, invisible agency was supposed to perform, but never did.[9]

Tugwell's forthright remark addresses a fundamental question raised by the Great Depression: Doesn't the depression prove that unguided by government, a free-market economy has the potential to run off the rails and produce an economic disaster? Why should we leave the allocation of capital to a stock market that goes through ridiculous boom-and-bust cycles? And why should we leave the allocation of agricultural products to Adam Smith's "invisible hand" when it drives farmers off the land while people in cities go hungry? To many thoughtful observers in the 1930s, the clear answer to these questions was the one given by Tugwell: Do not leave things to the free market; common sense tells us that government regulation makes things better.

Most mainstream economists and economic historians, however, have not been entirely persuaded. John Maynard Keynes, who agreed that the depression revealed fundamental weaknesses in the economic system, nevertheless concluded that it did not justify across-the-board intervention in the market. He believed that the depression was a problem of aggregate demand and that this was separate from the problem of individual markets. As he wrote:

> To put the point concretely, I see no reason to suppose that the existing system seriously misemploys the factors of production which are in use. There are, of course, errors of foresight; but these would not be avoided by centralizing decisions. When 9,000,000 men are employed out of 10,000,000 willing and able to work, there is no evidence that the labor of these 9,000,000 men is misdirected. The complaint against the present system is not that these 9,000,000 men ought to be employed on different tasks, but that tasks should be available for the remaining 1,000,000 men. It is in determining the volume, not the direction, of actual employment that the existing system has broken down.[10]

More conservative economists have given the most negative answer to Tugwell. In their view, the Great Depression was a monetary-financial crisis. Government regulation had produced a weak, crisis-prone banking system. The Federal Reserve, the agency created to prevent banking crises, failed to save it when confidence in the banking system collapsed. Eliminate these weaknesses by allowing the banking system to strengthen itself through competition and by forcing the Fed to maintain the stock of money, and a recurrence of the Great Depression could be prevented. All government programs introduced in the 1930s, in their view, served merely to undermine confidence, discourage private investment, and delay recovery. During the 1930s, Tugwell's position prevailed. As we shall see in the next chapter, the depression led to a vast increase in the extent to which the federal government attempted to influence individual markets.

---

[9]Quoted in Rebecca Gruver, *An American History* (New York: Appleton-Century-Crofts, 1972), 936.
[10]John Maynard Keynes, *The General Theory of Employment, Interest and Money* (New York: Harcourt, Brace & World, 1964 [reprint of 1936 edition]), 379.

Selected References and Suggested Readings

Bernanke, Benjamin. "Nonmonetary Effects of the Financial Crisis in the Propagation of the Great Depression." *American Economic Review* 73 (1983): 257–276.

———. *Essays on the Great Depression*. Princeton, N.J.: Princeton University Press, 2000.

Bordo, Michael D., Ehsan Choudhri, and Anna J. Schwartz. "Could Stable Money Have Averted the Great Contraction?" *Economic Inquiry* 33 (1995): 484–505.

Bordo, Michael D., Christopher Erceg, and Charles L. Evans. "Money, Sticky Wages, and the Great Depression." *American Economic Review* 90 (2000): 1447–1463.

Brown, E. Cary. "Fiscal Policy in The Thirties: A Reappraisal." *American Economic Review* 46 (December 1956): 857–859.

Brunner, Karl., ed. *The Great Depression Revisited*. Boston: Martinus Nijhoff, 1981.

Calomiris, Charles W. "Financial Factors in the Great Depression." *Journal of Economic Perspectives* 7 (Spring 1993): 61–85.

Calomiris, Charles W., and Joseph R. Mason. "Contagion and Bank Failures during the Great Depression: The June 1932 Chicago Banking Panic." *American Economic Review* 87 (1997): 863–883.

Dighe, Ranjit S. "Wage Rigidity in the Great Depression: Truth? Consequences?" In *Research in Economic History*, Vol. 17, eds. Gregory Clark and William A. Sundstrom. Greenwich, Conn.: JAI, 1997, 85–134.

Eichengreen, Barry. "Central Bank Cooperation under the Interwar Gold Standard." *Explorations in Economic History* 21 (1984): 64–87.

———. "The Political Economy of the Smoot-Hawley Tariff." In *Research in Economic History*, Volume 12, eds. Roger Ransom, Peter H. Lindert, and Richard Sutch, Greenwich, Conn.: JAI, 1989, 1–43.

———. *Golden Fetters: The Gold Standard and the Great Depression, 1919–1939*. New York: Oxford University Press, 1992.

Epstein, Gerald, and Thomas Ferguson. "Monetary Policy, Loan Liquidation, and Industrial Conflict: "The Federal Reserve and the Great Contraction." *Journal of Economic History* 44 (1984): 957–984.

Farm Security Administration. **http://lcweb2.loc.gov/ammem/fsowhome.html**. Famous collection of photographs taken during the Great Depression.

Ferderer, J. Peter, and David A. Zalewski. "To Raise the Golden Anchor? Financial Crises and Uncertainty during the Great Depression." *Journal of Economic History* 59 (1999): 624–658.

Field, Alexander. "Asset Exchanges and the Transactions Demand for Money, 1919–1929." *American Economic Review* 74 (1984): 43–59.

———. "A New Interpretation of the Onset of the Great Depression." *Journal of Economic History* 44 (1984): 489–498.

Fisher, Irving. *Booms and Depressions*. New York: Adelphi, 1932.

———. "The Debt Deflation Theory of Great Depressions." *Econometrica* 1 (1933): 337–357.

Franklin D. Roosevelt Presidential Library and Museum. **http://www.fdrlibrarymarist.edu**.

Friedman, Milton. "Why the American Economy Is Depression-Proof." In *Dollars and Deficits*. Englewood Cliffs, N.J.: Prentice Hall, 1968.

Friedman, Milton, and Anna J. Schwartz. *A Monetary History of the United States*. Princeton, N.J.: Princeton University Press, 1965, 299–545.

Galbraith, John Kenneth. *The Great Crash*. Boston: Houghton Mifflin, 1972.

Gandolfi, Arthur, and James Lothian. "Review of 'Did Monetary Forces Cause the Great Depression.'" *Journal of Money Credit and Banking* 9 (1977): 679–691.

Higgs, Robert. "Regime Uncertainty: Why the Great Depression Lasted So Long and Why Prosperity Resumed after the War." *Independent Review* 1 (Spring 1997): 561–590.

Keynes, John Maynard. *The General Theory of Employment, Interest and Money*. New York: Harcourt, Brace & World, 1964 (reprint of 1936 edition).

Kindleberger, Charles P. *Manias, Panics, and Crashes*. New York: Basic Books, 1978.

Mayer, Thomas. "Money and the Great Depression: A Critique of Professor Temin's Thesis." *Explorations in Economic History* 15 (1978): 127–145.

———. "Consumption in the Great Depression." *Journal of Political Economy* 86 (1978): 139–145.

Meltzer, Allan H. "Monetary and Other Explanations of the Start of the Great Depression." *Journal of Monetary Economics* 2 (1976): 455–471.

Olney, Martha L. "Avoiding Default: The Role of Credit in the Consumption Collapse of 1930." *Quarterly Journal of Economics* 114 (1999): 319–335.

Peppers, Larry C. "Full Employment Surplus Analysis and Structural Changes: The 1930s." *Explorations in Economic History* 10 (Winter 1973): 197–210.

Romer, Christina. "The Great Crash and the Onset of the Great Depression." *Quarterly Journal of Economics* 105 (1990): 597–624.

———. "What Ended the Great Depression?" *Journal of Economic History* 52 (December 1992): 757–784.

———. "The Nation in Depression." *Journal of Economic Perspectives* 7 (Spring 1993): 19–39.

Rosenbloom, Joshua L., and William A. Sundstrom. "The Sources of Regional Variation in the Severity of the Great Depression: Evidence from U.S. Manufacturing, 1919–1937." *Journal of Economic History* 59 (1999): 714–747.

Temin, Peter. *Did Monetary Forces Cause the Great Depression*? New York: Norton, 1976.

———. *Lessons from the Great Depression*. Cambridge, Mass.: MIT Press, 1989.

———. "The Great Depression." In *The Cambridge Economic History of the United States,* Vol. III, *The Twentieth Century*, eds. Stanley L. Engerman and Robert E. Gallman. New York: Cambridge University Press, 2000, 301–328.

Temin, Peter, and Barrie A. Wigmore. "The End of One Big Deflation." *Explorations in Economic History* 27 (October 1990): 483–502.

Trescott, Paul. "Federal Reserve Policy in the Great Contraction: A Counterfactual Assessment." *Explorations in Economic History* 19 (1982): 211–220.

———. "The Behavior of the Currency-Deposit Ratio during the Great Depression." *Journal of Money, Credit and Banking* 16 (1984): 362–365.

Wheelock, David C. *The Strategy and Consistency of Federal Reserve Monetary Policy, 1924–1933*. Cambridge, England: Cambridge University Press, 1991.

White, Eugene N. "A Reinterpretation of the Banking Crisis of 1930." *Journal of Economic History* 44 (1984): 119–138.

White, Eugene N., and Peter Rappoport. "Was the Crash of 1929 Expected?" *American Economic Review* 84 (March 1994): 271–281.

Wicker, Elmus. "A Reconsideration of the Causes of the Banking Panic of 1930." *Journal of Economic History* 40 (1982): 435–445.

———. "Interest Rate and Expenditure Effects of the Banking Panic of 1930." *Explorations in Economic History* 19 (1982): 435–445.

———. *The Banking Panics of the Great Depression*. New York: Cambridge University Press, 1996.

Chapter Twenty-Four

The New Deal

The presidential campaign of 1932 was fought in an atmosphere of fear and discontent. Herbert Hoover, nominated for a second term, blamed events in Europe for the nation's troubles and promised that prosperity would soon return. Tampering with our basic economic institutions, Hoover argued, could only lead to even worse disasters. Franklin D. Roosevelt, the warm and yet forceful Democratic candidate, was generally not specific about what measures he would take if elected, although he did promise to balance the budget. There was no mistaking his willingness to use the power of the government to try to solve the nation's problems. In his acceptance speech at the Democratic convention, Roosevelt promised a "New Deal" if he were elected. Few people at the time realized how fully these words would be put into practice in the years to come.

Between Roosevelt's election and his inauguration, economic conditions deteriorated. No president since Abraham Lincoln had faced a greater crisis at the moment he assumed power. One-quarter of the nation's workers were unemployed. In his inaugural address, delivered on March 4, 1933, Roosevelt rallied the nation's spirits, declaring, "Let me assert my firm belief that the only thing we have to fear is fear itself—nameless, unreasoning, unjustified terror which paralyzes needed efforts to convert retreat into advance."

The New Deal unfolded in two phases. The First New Deal (1933–1934), in particular the first "100 days," consisted of the passage of a wide range of legislation designed both to provide immediate relief and to promote recovery. It was a time of experimentation in which any idea that offered hope might get a trial. The Civilian Conservation Corps (March 1933), the Agricultural Adjustment Act (May 1933), and the National Industrial Recovery Act (June 1933) were among the landmarks that we will discuss created in this phase of the New Deal. The Second New Deal (1935–1941) was marked by a more conscious turn toward the political left. Although it continued the relief and recovery measures, the administration pushed for reforms that it believed would permanently improve the standard of living of the working class. The Social Security Act (1935) and The Fair Labor Standards Act (1938) are among the major achievements of the Second New Deal. Although the New Deal occupied only a short span of time, we must consider it in detail because it is the origin of many of the institutions and ideas that shape our daily lives today.

THE FIRST NEW DEAL: RELIEF AND RECOVERY

Helping Those in Need

The most pressing problem for the new administration was to provide relief for destitute families. The Federal Emergency Relief Agency (FERA), directed by Harry Hopkins, pumped a half billion dollars into bankrupt state and local relief efforts. In 1935, the federal government set up the Works Progress Administration, later the Works Projects

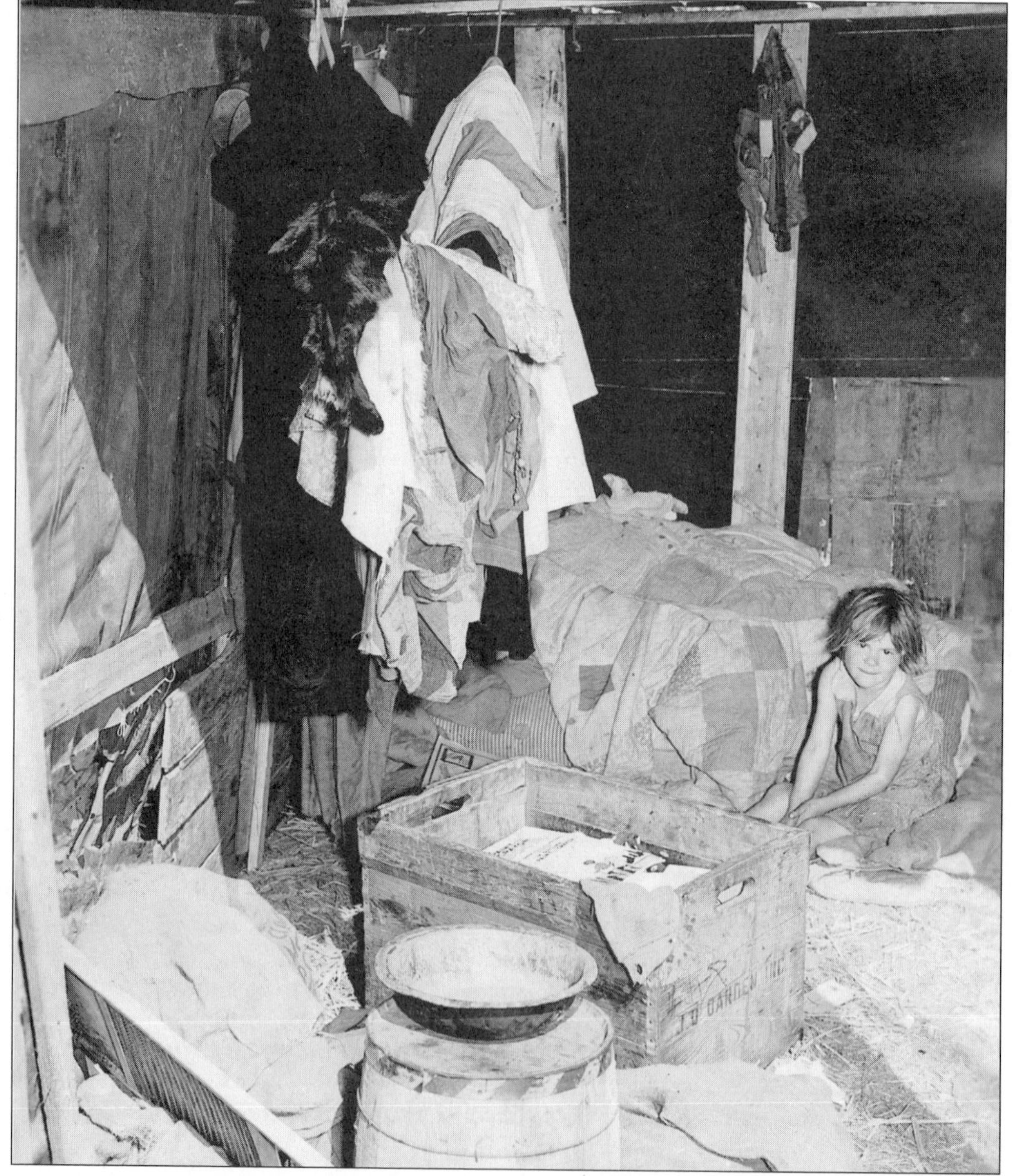

NATIONAL ARCHIVES, MARION POST WOLCOTT, FSA

Photographers for the Works Progress Administration took now classic pictures of poverty stricken Americans to build support for the New Deal.

Administration (WPA), also under Hopkins's direction. This agency employed millions of people in road building, flood control projects, and similar programs. Its most famous and controversial projects employed writers, photographers, and other creative artists. Critics complained, with some justice, that these projects often had strong left-wing political messages. Some of the projects, however, such as recording the recollections of the last generation of former slaves, also had lasting value. Under Hopkins's direction, the main emphasis of the WPA was creating employment; the contribution of these projects to the infrastructure of the economy was secondary. Another well-known agency with a similar purpose was the Civilian Conservation Corps.

The Public Works Administration undertook larger construction projects. It spent more than $6 billion over the course of the depression on dams, low-cost housing, airports, warships, and other projects. Its director, Harold Ickes, earned an enviable reputation for honesty and for his efforts to secure employment for African Americans, but he was sometimes criticized for taking too much time to plan projects. The most ambitious and controversial of all was the Tennessee Valley Authority, a multifaceted project designed to promote economic development in a large region that had been poverty stricken for decades. The Authority built dams in a seven-state area (see Map 24.1), supplied low-cost electric power to farmers (a policy that created considerable opposition from private power companies), engaged in flood control, created inland navigation routes, and promoted farmer education and related projects.

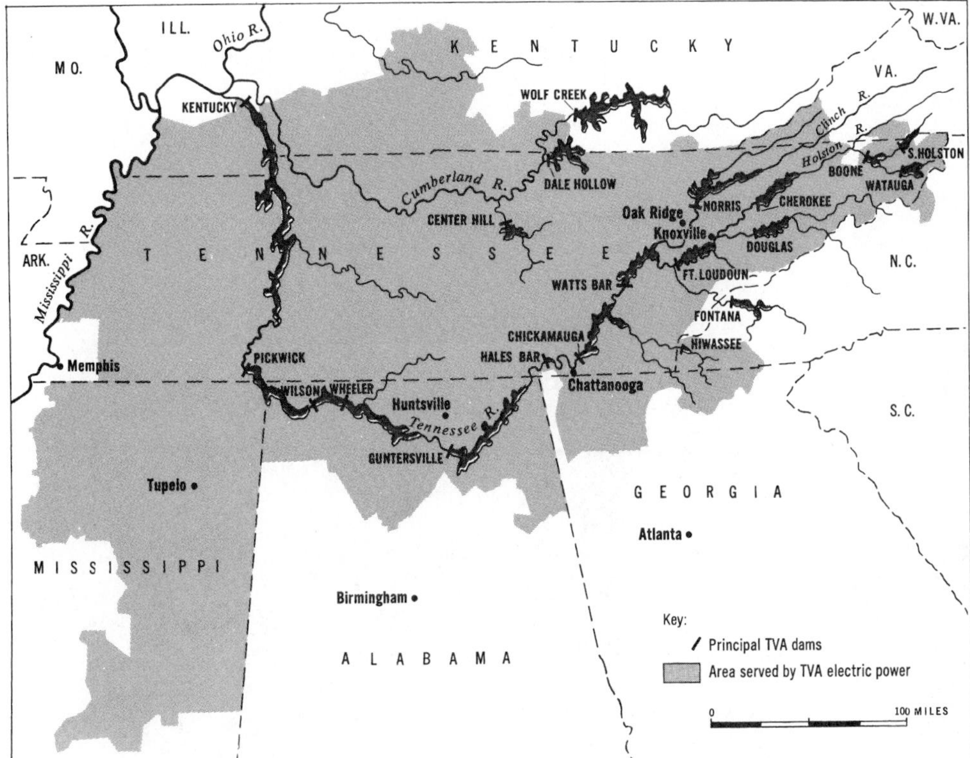

MAP 24.1 Public Power

The Tennessee Valley Authority—the New Deal's major experiment in publicly financed power—ranges through portions of seven states. Its supporters call it a splendid monument to "regional planning"; its foes denounce it as a noxious example of "creeping socialism."

New View 24.1

Should the Government Be the Employer of Last Resort?

When the unemployment rate rises, should the federal government step in and hire the unemployed? After all, if the banks can have a lender of last resort to bail them out, why can't the workingman or woman have an employer of last resort? Supporters of this proposal argue that the government has a moral obligation to relieve the enormous suffering caused by unemployment. Critics of this proposal warn that such a policy would be enormously expensive, would undermine the work ethic of the unemployed, and might well become political patronage, the breeding ground of corruption. The text discusses historical examples that one could study to see how such a system might work. The New Deal instituted a number of job creation programs. One of the most famous and most controversial was the Civilian Conservation Corps. Modeled on the army, the Corps, at its peak in 1935, employed 500,000 men in building national park facilities, cleaning and enlarging reservoirs, planting trees (as shown in the photo), and similar activities. The study of economic history, as Economic Reasoning Proposition 5 reminds us, can illuminate the most important policy issues of today.

The overall impact of the emergency relief measures is shown in Table 24.1. In 1933, the first year of the New Deal, federal, state, and local emergency work programs employed more than 2 million workers (4.3 percent of the labor force). The peak year was 1936, when 3.7 million people (7 percent of the labor force) were employed in such programs. To put the point somewhat differently, had the relief programs not existed, and had the workers not been able to find employment in the private sector, the percent of the labor force without jobs would have been not 9.9 percent in 1936 (in itself a very high rate) but 16.9 percent. Indeed, the official figures, the ones you are likely to see quoted in history textbooks or the newspaper, listed 16.9 percent of the work force as unemployed because it was believed that these workers would be unemployed in the absence of these jobs.

Reconstruction and Reform of the Financial System

The financial system lay in ruins after the contraction from 1929 to 1933. The Roosevelt administration, with allies in both parties, set out to revive and reform the system during the First New Deal. Profound changes occurred in four main areas: the banking system, the Federal Reserve System, the securities markets, and the international financial system. Let us consider each.

(1) Reconstruction of the Commercial Banking System: The Glass-Steagall Act of 1933

Perhaps the most important change was deposit insurance. The Federal Deposit Insurance Corporation (for commercial banks) and the Federal Savings and Loan Insurance Corporation (for savings banks) were established in 1934. Roosevelt was somewhat skeptical about deposit insurance, fearing that it would encourage lax banking practices, but he bowed to strong pressure in Congress. Initially, deposit insurance appeared to be an unalloyed success because bank failures fell to low levels once deposit insurance was in place. During the savings and loan crisis of the 1970s, however, a number of economists pointed out that deposit insurance had come with a long-run cost: Depositors no longer had an

TABLE 24.1 Emergency Workers During the Great Depression

YEAR	UNEMPLOYED (in thousands)	UNEMPLOYED (percent of labor force)	EMERGENCY WORKERS (in thousands)	EMERGENCY WORKERS (percent of labor force)
1929	1,550	3.2%	0	0.00%
1930	4,320	8.7	20	0.04
1931	7,721	15.3	299	0.6
1932	11,468	22.5	592	1.2
1933	10,635	20.6	2,195	4.3
1934	8,366	16.0	2,974	5.7
1935	7,523	14.2	3,087	5.8
1936	5,286	9.9	3,744	7.0
1937	4,937	9.1	2,763	5.1
1938	6,799	12.5	3,591	6.6
1939	6,225	11.3	3,255	5.9
1940	5,290	9.5	2,830	5.1
1941	3,351	6.0	2,209	3.9
1942	1,746	3.1	914	1.6
1943	985	1.8	85	0.2

Source: Michael Darby, "Three and a Half Million U.S. Employees Have Been Mislaid: Or, an Explanation of Unemployment, 1934–1941," Journal of Political Economy *84 (1976): 7, 8.*

incentive to regulate the banking system by withdrawing funds from risky banks and placing them in safer banks. Important changes to the banking system included separating commercial banking (taking deposits and making short-term loans) from investment banking (selling securities). The payment of interest on deposits was prohibited. Recent research by Barrie Wigmore suggests that this may have been important in eliminating the immediate financial problems of the banks. Both of these restrictions have since been removed on the grounds that they inhibited competition.

(2) Regulation of Securities Markets

The collapse of the stock market left many investors broke and with a strong suspicion they had been duped by Wall Street. A Congressional investigation led by Ferdinand Pecora seemed to provide the evidence for widespread fraud. The result was the establishment of the Securities and Exchange Commission in 1934. This agency was given wide powers to supervise the stock exchanges, their trading practices, and the issue of new securities. Joseph P. Kennedy, father of the future U.S. President, was its first chairman.

(3) Withdrawal from the Gold Standard

The most dramatic action was an executive order issued on April 5, 1933, that required that all holders to turn their gold (except for rare coins) into the Federal Reserve in exchange for Federal Reserve Notes. The gold standard was discarded for two reasons. First, it was thought that the attempt to convert assets into gold was undermining the banking system. Second, by breaking the fixed link to other currencies that were on the gold, the United States could devalue the dollar (make it standard, cheaper in terms of foreign currency) and so make U.S. exports, particularly of farm products, more attractive. Although an attempt was made to reestablish fixed exchange rates and a role for gold after World War II, Americans would never again hear the jingle of gold coins.

(4) Centralization of Monetary Power in the Federal Reserve Board

The Federal Reserve system clearly had failed to stem the tide of bank closures and failures. The response of the Roosevelt administration was to centralize power in Washington. (This was, to say the least, somewhat ironic, because the board in Washington had done the most to resist calls from some of the district banks for more vigorous action.) In 1935 the Federal Reserve Board became the Board of Governors, all of whose members the president appointed. The Board of Governors was given control of the system's most powerful economic tool, the ability to buy or sell securities on the open market. Marriner S. Eccles, a Utah banker, who believed strongly in using federal deficit spending and monetary policy to stimulate the economy, was the first chairman of the newly empowered board. Beginning in the 1930s, the district banks would serve only an advisory role in making monetary policy.

Although some of the financial reforms introduced by the New Deal were later abandoned, many others such as the Federal Deposit Insurance Incorporation and the Securities and Exchange Commission continue to the current day. There are few better examples of how institutions created in the heat of an emergency may continue to influence economic actions for decades to come, Economic Reasoning Proposition 5: Institutions matter.

The National Industrial Recovery Act

One of the most dramatic advances in government intervention came with the National Industrial Recovery Act (NIRA). Its chief purposes were to raise prices and wages, spread work by reducing hours, and prevent price cutting by competitors trying to maintain volume. The National Recovery Administration (NRA), under the direction of General Hugh Johnson, supervised the preparation of a "code of fair practice" for each industry. These

Roosevelt's broad grin, in evidence above, center, at the 1936 Democratic convention, made his theme song, "Happy Days Are Here Again," believable to a shaken nation. His charm and buoyancy did much in itself to soften the Great Depression's psychological impact.

were really agreements among sellers to set minimum prices, limit output, and establish minimum wages and maximum hours of work. Pending the approval of basic codes, the president issued a "blanket code" in July 1933. Sellers signing the blanket code agreed to raise wages, shorten the maximum work week, and abstain from price cutting. In return, they could display a "blue eagle" and avoid being boycotted for not doing their part.

By 1935, 557 basic codes had been approved. Although in theory the codes were supposed to be the product of labor, consumer, and employer representatives, in practice, labor representatives participated in the construction of fewer than 10 percent of the codes, and consumer representation was negligible. Employer representatives worked through their national trade associations and manufacturers' institutes, with the consequence that prices were set to maximize profits. The possibility of such an outcome was recognized in the NIRA by suspending the antitrust laws.

Was the NIRA effective? It appears that for the most part, the codes redistributed rather than expanded incomes. Manufacturing output jumped after the institution of the NRA as merchants added to their inventories in anticipation of price increases. Industrial production lapsed again, however, and by midsummer 1935, the index was no higher than it had been after the first NRA spurt. Unemployment, although reduced, was still incredibly high, and most manufacturing firms were operating at far less than capacity.

Early in 1935 there was a growing awareness that the lift the economy had experienced had come chiefly from income injections via deficit spending and money creation. It was with little regret, then, that New Dealers saw the passing of the NRA, which the Supreme Court declared unconstitutional on the grounds that Congress had illegally delegated legislative powers to the president.

AGRICULTURE AND THE NEW DEAL

The Farm Crisis

With the onset of the Great Depression, farm people began to suffer a severity of economic distress that only a few would have believed possible. In three years the average price of corn at central markets fell from $0.77 to $0.19 per bushel, and the average price of wheat dropped from $1.08 to $0.33 per bushel. Table 24.2 on page 480 shows the key averages. Between

TABLE 24.2 Farm Prices and Incomes in the Depression, Selected Years

YEAR	PRICES RECEIVED BY FARMERS	PRICES RECEIVED BY FARMERS RELATIVE TO PRICES PAID	TOTAL NET INCOME OF FARM OPERATORS FROM FARMING (millions)	NET INCOME OF FARM OPERATORS 1929 PRICES (millions)
1929	100	100	$6,152	$6,152
1932	44	63	2,032	2,956
1937	82	101	6,005	7,206
1938	66	85	4,361	5,509
1939	64	83	4,414	5,726

Sources: Historical Statistics *(Washington D.C.: Government Printing Office, 1975), Series K344, K347, K352, and K137.*

1929 and 1932, prices received by farmers declined 56 percent. True, prices farmers paid declined as well. Even taking this into account leaves the farmer's "terms of trade"—prices received by farmers divided by prices paid—down 37 percent. The net income of farm operators fell from a total of $6.2 billion in 1929 to $2.0 billion in 1932. Again, adjusting for the price change helps a little, but net real income fell from $6.2 billion to $3.0 billion in constant 1929 dollars.

Farmers with fixed indebtedness were particularly hard hit: In 1932, 52 percent of all farm debts were in default. The threat of foreclosure reached an all-time high and marred the lives of rural people everywhere.

From the previous record high of 15.0 farm foreclosures per thousand farms in 1929, foreclosures jumped to 18.0 per thousand farms in 1930 and 27.8 per thousand in 1931, finally peaking at 38.1 per thousand in 1932.[1] Mortgage foreclosures sometimes reduced the owners of farms that had been in the family for generations to the status of tenants or, in the depths of the depression, forced them on to relief rolls. Many states, under aggressive pressure from farm organizations and concerned about threats of violence by farmers, imposed moratoriums on foreclosures.

The foreclosures have often been blamed on the overexpansion of agriculture in World War I. Farmers went into debt to acquire land, it is said, and ended up defaulting when the postwar economy failed to sustain the high prices of the war years. A careful study by Lee J. Alston shows, however, that this problem, although important in the 1920s, had been worked out by 1929. The high levels of foreclosures in the early 1930s were mainly the result of the fall in agricultural prices.[2]

It also did not help that most farm mortgages at that time were relatively short-term "balloon" mortgages: The entire principal was due back after the end of, say, five years. This worked as long as prices were stable and banks were willing to "roll over" loans, that is replace maturing loans with new ones. If the bank was in trouble and demanded its money, and prices were low, there might be little a farmer could do to avoid bankruptcy. The replacement of short-term balloon mortgages with long term "amortized" mortgages, in which a little bit of the principal was paid off each year, became a high priority of the Roosevelt administration, one that it achieved through a variety of measures.

Before the 1930s, most devices to help raise farm prices had aimed at price parity or "fair exchange" values, as Senator George Norris had called them. Most acceptable to politicians had been the traditional device of high tariffs, as imposed by the Smoot-Hawley

[1]H. Thomas Johnson, "Postwar Optimism and the Rural Financial Crisis of the 1920s," *Explorations in Economic History* 11 (Winter 1973–1974): 176.

[2]Lee J. Alston, "Farm Foreclosures in the United States during the Interwar Period," *Journal of Economic History*, 43 (1983): 885–903.

Agricultural poverty sent thousands fleeing from the Midwest to California, with belongings piled in the family jalopy. A nation that "drove to the poor house in an automobile," as Will Rogers said, had to change some of its babies' diapers on the miserable highways of the time.

Act of 1930. Far more important, however, was the passage of the Agricultural Marketing Act of 1929, which was the outcome of Republican campaign promises of 1928. This pre-depression law committed the government to a policy of farm price stabilization and established the Federal Farm Board to encourage the formation of cooperative marketing associations. The board was also authorized to establish "stabilization corporations" to be owned by the cooperatives and to use an initial fund of $500 million for price support operations.

With the onset of serious depression in 1930, the Federal Farm Board strove valiantly to support farm prices, but between June 1929 and June 1932, the board's corporations bought surplus farm products only to suffer steadily increasing losses as prices continued to decline. The board itself took over the operation and accepted the losses, expending some $676 million. Meanwhile, however, farmers faced with catastrophically falling prices increased output. At the time, it seemed that prices could not be supported without production controls.

The End of the Free Market in Agriculture, 1933–1941

By the time of Franklin D. Roosevelt's inauguration, theories about farm policy had undergone fundamental changes. It was clear that supports through purchases and loans would require enormous outlays, which the New Deal was still reluctant to undertake. Consequently, the Agricultural Adjustment Act, passed in May 1933, provided for an Agricultural Adjustment Administration, the AAA, which was given the responsibility of raising farm prices by restricting the supply of farm commodities. The AAA's most important weapon was "acreage allotment." The AAA would determine a total acreage of certain major crops to be planted in the next growing season. The total acreage would then be subdivided into state totals, which were in turn to be allotted to individual farms on the basis of each farm's recent crop history. For example, the base acreage for each wheat farm was to be the average acreage in wheat from 1928 to 1932. To secure the cooperation of the individual farmer, a direct "benefit payment," later called an "adjustment payment," was made. The payment was made by check from the federal Treasury, but in these early New Deal days, it still seemed a little too much to expect the taxpayer to foot the bill—at least directly. The benefit payments were financed, therefore, by taxes paid by the first processor of any product (millers, for example, had to pay a tax for each bushel of wheat that was ground into flour), although it was assumed that the tax would be shifted forward the consumer.

The original AAA scheme experienced a setback in 1936 when the Supreme Court, in the *Hoosac Mills* case, declared the Agricultural Adjustment Act unconstitutional because it attempted to regulate agricultural production—a power reserved to the states. The decision, however, did not end acreage allotments. The administration quickly found a way around the decision by basing allotments on the need for soil conservation.

The severe drought of 1936, with its attendant dust bowl conditions that led to the migration of the "Okies" to California, provided the rationale. The dust bowl focused attention on the need for soil conservation, and the result was passage of the Soil Conservation and Domestic Allotment Act.[3] Under this act, the secretary of agriculture could offer benefit payments to farmers who would reduce their acreage planted in soil-depleting crops and take steps to conserve or rebuild the land withheld from production.

Farm production in 1937 was very high, and there was pressure to supplement acreage reduction with even more vigorous measures to raise prices. In 1938 Congress passed a new Agricultural Adjustment Act, which placed more emphasis on supporting prices by increasing demand. Since 1933, the Commodity Credit Corporation (CCC) had performed the minor function of "cushioning" the prices of corn, wheat, and cotton by making loans to farmers on the security of their crops. Most of these loans were made "without recourse." If the CCC extended a loan against a commodity and the price of that commodity fell, the farmer could let the CCC take title to the stored product and cancel the debt. If the price of the commodity rose, the farmer could sell the commodity, pay back the loan, and keep the profit. Thus, CCC support prices became minimum prices in the marketplace. See Economic Insight 24.1.

The Agricultural Adjustment Act of 1938 increased the role of the CCC by making it mandatory that the directors extend loans on corn, wheat, and cotton at "parity" prices. These prices were defined as farm prices adjusted to have the same purchasing power as those prevailing in 1910–1914, a time when farm prices relative to other prices were exceptionally high. The Populist dream of "fair" prices determined by the government had become a reality.

Two other means of raising farm prices were used during the 1930s: (1) marketing agreements and (2) surplus removal programs. Marketing agreements, which became important

---

[3]The migration of the "Okies" from the dust bowl of the Midwest to California is eloquently described by John Steinbeck in *The Grapes of Wrath.* A superb 1940 movie based on the novel stars Jane Darwell and Henry Fonda.

Economic Insight 24.1

Effects of Commodity Credit Corporation Price Supports

The figure illustrates the effects of CCC price supports. In the absence of government intervention, the price would be P_0 and the quantity produced Q_0. Intervention raises the price to P_1 and the quantity produced to Q_1. The higher price reduces consumption to Q_2 and leads to the accumulation of $Q_1 - Q_2$ stocks by the government. Farm incomes (net of production costs) are raised by the sum of areas $A + B + C$. Total expenditures by the government are $(Q_1 - Q_2) \times P_1$. Area A is paid directly by consumers in the form of higher prices. $B + C + D$ are paid by consumers indirectly through taxes. The change in direct expenditures by consumers is $Q_2 \times P_1 - Q_0 \times P_0$. (Whether consumers spend more or less than before depends on the elasticity of demand.)

A number of losses are associated with this program. First, the resources used to produce $Q_1 - Q_2$ are wasted. Storage costs for the surplus (not shown) are also incurred. Second, consumers are deprived of farm products that they value more than the costs of production. Their loss on this account is measured by area B. The attempt to minimize these losses then leads to other programs described in the text: production quotas, surplus removal programs, and export subsidies.

Economists often recommend direct income supplements to farmers combined with a free market in agricultural products as a way of helping farmers without incurring these losses. For a number of reasons, however, farmers usually prefer price supports. Three are worth noting: (1) direct income supplements may be viewed as demeaning, (2) direct income supplements may go mostly to poor farmers, and are therefore opposed by rich and influential farmers, and (3) direct income supplements tend to remain fixed over time. The subsidy delivered through price supports may grow as technological advances shift the supply curve to the right.

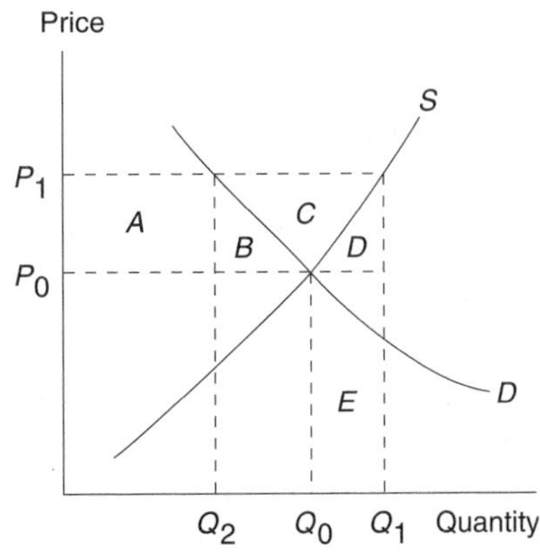

for milk and certain fruits and vegetables, are contracts (which require the approval of the Department of Agriculture) between an association of producers and the processors of a product. These agreements may set minimum prices, total quantities to be marketed, and allotments of marketings among processors. In other words, firms in the industry may legally set up cartels to reduce output and raise prices.

Adding to the farmer's woes during the depressed 1930s were several years of unprecedented heat and drought. The subsequent blowing of previously eroded land created dust storms like this one in the Texas panhandle. Government land policies also contributed, as Gary Libecap has shown, by limiting homesteaders to small plots.

The most acceptable and enduring surplus removal programs proved to be the nutrition programs, such as the food-stamp plans, low-cost milk distribution plans, and school lunch programs. The Food Stamp Plan, in operation from 1939 to 1942, won enthusiastic support. Stamps given to low-income families were used to purchase food from regular retail outlets. Thus, surplus commodities were given to those who presumably had the greatest need for them. In addition they helped offset the effect on the poor of artificially high prices created by the crop restrictions. In 1961 advocates finally secured reactivation of this program.

The Impact on Farmers

By 1937, thanks to the recovery of the economy and to the New Deal's farm programs, the farmer's terms of trade were back to where they had been in 1929 and total net real income of farmers was above the 1929 level (Table 24.2). The farmer was then hit by the "recession within the depression." In 1939 the farmer's terms of trade and total real net income were again well below the levels of 1929.

The most concrete steps taken by government to raise farm incomes during the 1930s were production controls. Of course, to restrict output in agriculture and raise prices of food and fiber when the major national problems were massive unemployment and hunger was a mistake. Far better ways were available to help farmers. This is easy to see now, but was not so easy to see at the time. Many of Roosevelt's early advisers were convinced that restoring the "balance" among the sectors of the economy would restore full employment. In truth, the primary outcome of the New Deal's farm policies, as with other types of New Deal legislation aimed at helping particular groups, was to redistribute income rather than end the depression.

Clearly, Roosevelt's New Deal for farmers was far removed from President Harding's policy advice that "the farmer must be ready to help himself." The acceptance by the American people of the principle that the government ought to bolster the economic fortunes of particular occupational groups or classes was momentous. Farmers have not been the only beneficiaries of this philosophy, but we cannot find a better example of the way in which legislation, passed at first in an effort to relieve emergency distress, has become accepted as a permanent part of the economic system. Again we see in action one of our Economic Reasoning Propositions, number 4—Institutions matter.

★★★ *Economic Reasoning Proposition*

LABOR AND THE NEW DEAL

The New Deal transformed the relationship between the American worker and the federal government. Before the New Deal, the dominant assumption was that most of the time the labor market would provide adequate opportunities for the poor to advance. If they failed to do so, it was because of individual failure: laziness, a fondness for drink, and so on. The Great Depression changed this attitude. The dominant assumption came to be that the opportunities provided by the market were inadequate. It was up to the federal government to make sure that those able to work could find work, and with decent wages and working conditions.

Why Was Unemployment So High for So Long?

Unemployment, persisted throughout the depression years. Many economists have argued that this was the result of the "sticky" wages. As you can see in Table 24.3, real wages (wages divided by prices) did remain high. Of course, this was cold comfort for those who had lost their jobs or had their weekly hours cut.

Why did real wages remain so high? Government policy is part of the explanation. In the first two years of the depression, as Anthony Patrick O'Brien has shown, the Hoover administration successfully pressured large corporations to maintain wages, a policy that the administration and business leaders thought would help maintain demand. During the early years of the New Deal, the National Industrial Recovery Act continued the policy of maintaining wages. Economic forces were also at work keeping real wages high. Unemployed workers are not likely to suddenly slash their "reservation wage" (the minimum they will take) to the bone. Instead, they are likely to slowly adjust their reservation wage as they search the market for jobs. (Recall Economic Reasoning Proposition 1.) The adjustment process therefore took a considerable time. During the latter part of the New Deal, the Wagner and Fair Labor Standard Acts and the associated growth of labor unions (discussed later) helped maintain wages.

★★★ *Economic Reasoning Proposition*

Would a policy of encouraging competition in labor markets have helped restore full employment? Even today, economists are far from a consensus on this contentious issue. Economists working in the neoclassical tradition, in particular Michael Bordo, Christopher J. Erceg, Charles L. Evans, Harold L. Cole, and Lee E. Ohanian, have argued that New

TABLE 24.3 Wages During the Great Depression

YEAR	NOMINAL WAGE (the hourly wage in manufacturing)	GROSS NATIONAL PRODUCT DEFLATOR	REAL WAGE
1929	$0.56	100	100
1930	0.55	97	101
1931	0.51	89	103
1932	0.44	79	99
1933	0.44	78	101
1939	0.63	85	132

Notes and Sources: *The real wage is the nominal wage divided by the gross national product deflator. The result was set equal to 100 in 1929 so that the trend could be observed easily. From* Historical Statistics *(Washington, D.C.: Government Printing Office, 1975), 169–170, D802; 197, E1.*

Deal policies that promoted high real wages, ironically, inhibited adjustment in the labor market and prolonged high unemployment. Neo-Keynesians have tended to follow John Maynard Keynes, who argued in his famous book *A General Theory of Employment, Interest, and Money* published in 1936, that wage cuts would have simply fed a downward spiral of expectations, investment, national income, and employment. In Keynes's view, only government spending on a massive scale could have cured the depression.

Whatever the impact of government programs on real wages, the establishment of government relief agencies and the new powers given to labor unions created a strong bond between labor and the New Deal. Most important of the elements creating that bond were the right to strike and to organize free of employer interference. Union membership had declined sharply from more than 5 million in 1920 to 3.5 million in 1923. It remained steady around this level until 1930, when it began falling again before reaching bottom in 1933. Before the new administration had been in power a year, the more vigorous union leaders sensed that the government would encourage organization and that the attitude of the nation toward unions had changed because people were disillusioned with business.

Especially successful were the powerful and able leaders of the industrial unions that had evolved within the AFL: John L. Lewis of the United Mine Workers, Sidney Hillman of the Amalgamated Clothing Workers, and David Dubinsky of the International Ladies Garment Workers. By the mid-1930s, a conflict within the union movement between the older craft unions and the newer industrial unions had grown to major proportions. The drive to organize the mass production industries (steel, automobiles, rubber, and electrical equipment) was inevitable, but the older unions hampered the effort by insisting that their craft jurisdictions remain inviolate and by raiding the membership of the new industrial unions. In 1935, eight industrial unions formed the Committee for Industrial Organization (CIO) within the AFL. In 1936 these unions were suspended from the federation; three years later, the CIO became a separate entity, the Congress of Industrial Organizations.

Relations between these two great federations were bitter. CIO leaders made no secret of their contempt for the AFL's lack of militancy, and AFL leaders viewed the CIO's violent break with conservative unionism with concern. However, complacency and inertia no longer beset the labor movement.[4]

Union membership increased rapidly in the 1930s (Table 24.4). Government's new prolabor attitude, clearly revealed in the labor legislation of the New Deal, played an important role. Between 1930 and 1939 union membership increased from 6.8 to 15.8 percent of the labor force.

A New Framework for Labor Relations

Except for legislation that applied only to the railroad industry, Congress had seldom interfered with labor relations before 1932. The Norris-LaGuardia Act of 1932 was the first step toward removing barriers to free organization. Largely procedural in character, the act greatly restricted the ability of the courts to issue labor injunctions. The yellow-dog contract—an employment contract in which a worker agrees not to join a union—was eliminated by making it nonenforceable in federal courts. Moreover, nonemployee boycotting and picketing was permitted. The Norris-LaGuardia Act granted workers the opportunity to organize but did not intercede to ensure that they could secure the benefits of collective bargaining.

The first positive assertion of the right of labor to bargain collectively was in Section 7a of the National Industrial Recovery Act, but no means of enforcing the statement of principle were provided. Two years later, when the NIRA was declared unconstitutional,

---

[4]In 1955, the AFL and the CIO, prodded into unity by hostile public opinion and labor legislation, merged to form the AFL-CIO. Roughly 50 percent of the total membership was in AFL affiliates, 30 percent in CIO unions, and the remainder in unaffiliated unions.

TABLE 24.4 Union Membership, 1930–1955

YEAR	NUMBER (in thousands)	PERCENT OF LABOR FORCE	YEAR	NUMBER (in thousands)	PERCENT OF LABOR FORCE
1930	3,401	6.8%	1943	13,213	20.5%
1931	3,310	6.5	1944	14,146	21.4
1932	3,050	6.0	1945	14,322	21.9
1933	2,689	5.2	1946	14,395	23.6
1934	3,088	5.9	1947	14,787	23.9
1935	3,584	6.7	1948	14,300	23.1
1936	3,989	7.4	1949	14,300	22.7
1937	7,001	12.9	1950	14,300	22.3
1938	8,034	14.6	1951	15,900	24.5
1939	8,763	15.8	1952	15,900	24.2
1940	8,717	15.5	1953	16,948	25.5
1941	10,201	17.7	1954	17,022	25.4
1942	10,380	17.2	1955	16,802	24.7

Source: Historical Statistics *(Washington, D.C.: Government Printing Office, 1975), 178, Series D948-949.*

Congress replaced Section 7a with a much more elaborate law, the National Labor Relations Act, usually called the Wagner Act after its sponsor, Senator Robert F. Wagner of New York.

The Wagner Act established the principle of collective bargaining as the cornerstone of industrial relations and stated that it was management's obligation to recognize and deal with a bona fide labor organization in good faith. The act further guaranteed workers the right to form and join a labor organization, to engage in collective bargaining, to select representatives of their own choosing, and to engage in concerted activity. In addition, the Wagner Act outlawed a list of "unfair" managerial practices.

Henceforth, employers could not:

1. Interfere with, restrain, or coerce employees in the exercise of their rights of self-organization and collective bargaining.
2. Dominate or interfere with the formation or administration of any labor organization or contribute financial or other support to it.
3. Encourage or discourage union membership by discrimination in regard to hiring or tenure of employment or condition of work, except such discrimination as might be involved in a closed-shop agreement with a bona fide union enjoying majority status.
4. Discharge or otherwise discriminate against an employee for filing charges or testifying under the act.
5. Refuse to bargain collectively.

The Wagner Act was more than a mere statement of principles. It established a National Labor Relations Board (NLRB) with powers of enforcement. When the Supreme Court declared the Wagner Act constitutional in 1937, there were no remaining legal barriers to the rapid organization of labor. Before the question of constitutionality was settled, however, many employers openly violated the act, producing increasing turbulence in labor relations. Animosity between the suspended CIO unions and the AFL grew, leading to jurisdictional conflicts that the NLRB had to spend much time settling. As industrial strife seemed to be increasing rather than decreasing, there were public demands for amendments to the act, and employers complained bitterly of the one-sidedness of the law. From labor's view, however, the Wagner Act was its Magna Carta.

The Fair Labor Standards Act

The Fair Labor Standards Act of 1938, which replaced and extended provisions of the National Industrial Recovery Act (NIRA), was the beginning of federal regulation of the work place. Among other things, the law set a minimum wage of $0.25 per hour (scheduled to rise eventually to $0.40), fixed a maximum work week of 44 hours (scheduled to fall to 40) with extra pay for overtime work, and prohibited the employment of children under 16 years of age.[5] The Wages and Hours Division of the Department of Labor was created to enforce the act. Agriculture was exempt, and other exemptions reduced the share of nonagricultural workers initially covered by the law to about 44 percent. The goal was to protect workers and to increase employment. The hope was, for example, that requiring extra pay for overtime would encourage firms to hire more workers at the lower rate that applied up to 44 hours.

Any assessment of the NIRA's long-term effects would be controversial. Even today, for example, economists have not reached agreement on the employment and income effects of the minimum wage. The minimum wage has been criticized by many economists for increasing unemployment among low-skilled workers. Why hire workers if what they add to the firm's income is less than their wage? Other economists maintain, however, that the employment losses are small and that the gains for those workers who would otherwise receive less than the minimum are more important. What is clear is that the Fair Labor Standards Act left an enduring imprint on the institutional structure of the labor market and created a presumption that the federal government would help set the terms and conditions of work.

THE SUPREME COURT AND THE NEW DEAL

Many opponents of the New Deal hoped that the Supreme Court would declare much of Roosevelt's legislation unconstitutional. Among other things, opponents were hopeful that the Fifth and Fourteenth Amendments to the Constitution, which prohibit the taking of private property without due process, would be invoked to limit the expansion of economic regulation. After all, whenever the government imposes controls, as in minimum wages or maximum prices, the value of someone's property is reduced. If each such taking must be adjudicated in court and properly compensated (substantive due process), there would be little practical scope for regulation.

The Supreme Court itself was deeply split about the New Deal. As a result, some early New Deal legislation won the Court's approval. Other New Deal legislation, including its most ambitious initiatives, were struck down. In *A.L.A Schechter Poultry Corp. et al. v. United States* (1935), the Supreme Court unanimously ruled the National Recovery Act unconstitutional on the grounds that the law delegated too much arbitrary authority to the executive branch and that it attempted to regulate intrastate commerce.[6] In *United States v. Butler* (1936), the Agricultural Adjustment Act was ruled unconstitutional on the grounds that it was financed by improper taxes.

Buoyed by his landslide victory in 1936, Roosevelt tried to change the Court's direction by proposing legislation that would permit him to appoint additional justices. Opposition to Roosevelt's attempt to "pack" the Court, however, was widespread, and he

---

[5]Average hourly earnings in manufacturing were then about $0.62 per hour.

[6]This famous case was known as the "sick chicken case" because among other violations of the code the firm, allegedly, had sold diseased chickens.

suffered one of his few political defeats. Nevertheless, in the end he got what he wanted. The moderates on the Court, perhaps reading the election returns, shifted to the left. Over the next few years, a number of conservative justices retired, permitting Roosevelt to appoint additional liberals. In *United States v. Darby* (1941), the Court ruled in favor of the Fair Labor Standards Act; in *Wickard v. Fillburn* (1942), it ruled in favor of the new Agricultural Adjustment Act.

Thus, legal doctrines that had stood in the way of federal (and state) control of the economy, such as the idea that the federal government could regulate only what was clearly interstate commerce, and the idea that federal and state governments could not interfere arbitrarily with private contracts, were overturned. The legal path to increased government regulation of the economy had been cleared.

THE SECOND NEW DEAL: THE WELFARE STATE

The American welfare state was launched in the 1930s with the establishment of national unemployment insurance and Social Security.

Social Security

Before 1932, a worker's loss of income from any cause other than industrial accident posed a great hardship. Workers had to rely on their savings, or help from friends and relatives, organized charities, and state and local government. The burden of relief during the Great Depression overwhelmed charitable organizations, state and local governments, and the federal government. This experience with federal relief convinced the majority of Americans, on both economic and ethical grounds, of the necessity of a permanent plan for coping with severe losses in income.

A few leaders in government, business, and academia had long argued that a comprehensive program of social insurance, including old age pensions and unemployment insurance, was needed. Such programs had long been common in Europe, Canada, and Australia, and learned journals contained glowing reports about these programs. Yet as late as 1930, there was little public sentiment in favor of social legislation in the United States. Americans believed that the individual ought to be self-reliant and objected to compulsory government support. Various interest groups voiced their opposition. Private insurance companies, as no surprise, sought to prevent, or at least modify, government insurance of social risks. In agriculture where the need for social insurance was not so pronounced, there was opposition to additional taxes for such insurance. The most astonishing fact is that organized labor itself did not support social insurance (except worker compensation) before the Great Depression: as late as 1931, a national AFL convention refused to endorse unemployment insurance legislation.

Four years of economic disaster removed all serious obstacles to major legislation. The Social Security Act of 1935 provided for a federal old-age and survivors' insurance program based on workers' payments of 1 percent of earnings up to $3,600. It further provided for assistance to the needy aged, dependent children, and blind. Subsequent amendments have added other groups.

The act was structured as an "insurance" plan in which the worker "contributed" half and the employer "contributed" half of the insurance premium. The language in which a bill is written does not determine its economic effect. The premium payment is part of its wage cost. Therefore, over time, this resulted in lower wages to workers. In the long run, it seems likely employers shifted most of the premiums to employees. By presenting Social Security as an insurance program rather than as a welfare program financed by a tax on workers, the administration hoped to overcome the negative image of welfare and build long-run support for the program. Roosevelt famously remarked that "we put those payroll contributions there so as to give contributors a legal, moral, and political right to collect their pensions. . . . With those taxes in there no damn politician can ever scrap my social security program."

The insurance idea, however, didn't last long. Pressure by seniors to start paying benefits as soon possible led to an amendment in 1939 that converted the system into one in which payments were not saved but instead promptly transferred to those receiving Social Security checks, a "pay as you go" system. Although highly controversial at the time, the American people quickly accepted Social Security. Controversies continued over who should be covered, what the level of benefits should be, and how the system should be financed, but the existence of the system itself was not challenged.

Unemployment Insurance

The program of unemployment insurance was less extensive in its aim than Social Security, but it has been a powerful short-run help to discharged workers. Largely to circumvent legal difficulties, unemployment insurance is provided through state systems. The Social Security Act of 1935 secured state action by levying a 3 percent tax on the first $3,000 of wages paid by employers in all except a few business occupations. Similar to changes in Social Security, recent trends have been to make unemployment insurance laws more liberal—partly in recognition of the fact that unemployment compensation is a highly dependable automatic stabilizer. This automatic stabilizing effect occurs through the timely increase in unemployment compensation payments when unemployment increases.

THE CRITICS OF THE NEW DEAL

Then, as now, the New Deal was heavily criticized. Its conservative critics complained that Roosevelt was creating an "alphabet soup" of new programs and agencies that was turning the United States into a bureaucratic state. They also complained that the jobs created by the Civilian Conservation Corps and other agencies were merely "leaf-raking jobs" that undermined the character of America's worker.

Critics also complained that funds were not being spent simply with the idea of providing relief for the destitute but also to maximize political support for the New Deal. This criticism has received considerable attention from economic historians because it is subject to empirical investigation. Leonard Arrington was the first to study the issue systematically. He found that New Deal per capita spending was higher in the West even though the program claimed that the South was the region in greatest need. Later, others, including Don Reading, Gavin Wright, Gary Anderson, and Robert Tollison confirmed that the New Deal appeared to be allocating funds to maximize its political support. John Wallis pointed out that some of what appeared to be political allocation could be explained by the provision in many New Deal programs that required matching grants from the states. This provision tended to reward people living in wealthier states. Nevertheless, it appears that even when considering matching grants, some evidence supports the political allocation theory. Of course, even if the most needy were not always the major beneficiaries, they may have benefited nonetheless. For example, recent research by Price V. Fishback, Michael R. Haines, and Shawn Kantor showed that in the South, New Deal programs lowered the infant mortality rates for both whites and African Americans, even though some, but not all programs seemed to be administered in a way that favored whites.

Perhaps the most damning criticisms were those that claimed that the Roosevelt administration's policies, although intended to help the poor, actually served to prolong the depression. We have already seen that some economists today, echoing a criticism made at the time, blame the prolongation of high rates of unemployment on New Deal labor policies designed to keep wages high and strengthen organized labor. Many critics, including Joseph Schumpeter, one of the leading economists of the day, argued more generally that Roosevelt's antibusiness rhetoric and his constant addition of new regulations and taxes had discouraged private investment, and that this had inhibited recovery. Without this break on private investment they argued, the economy might have recovered quickly as it had in 1921 under conservative Warren Harding and his regime of tax cuts and laissez-faire. In other words, far from curing the depression, the net effect of Roosevelt's policies had been to prolong it. This criticism remains controversial because determining the effect of the political regime on private investment is extremely difficult.[7]

Although Roosevelt's conservative critics were the most influential, the New Deal also came in for a good deal of criticism from radical leftists and populists who claimed that his attempts to help the poor did not go far enough. Dr. Francis E. Townsend, a California physician, attracted a considerable support for his plan to give everyone over the age of 60 a federal pension of $150 per month ($5,000 in today's money). Reverend Charles E. Coughlin, a radio priest, advocated populist monetary reforms. Perhaps the most influential of the radicals was Huey Long, the political boss and senator from Louisiana. His "Share-the-Wealth" plan would have presented every American family with a $5,000 house, a $2,000 annual income (about $67,000 in today's money), and other benefits, financed by a capital levy on great fortunes.

The critics from both the right and the left, as vociferous as they were, were in the minority, however. There can be no doubt that a large majority of the public approved of the administration's aggressive and experimental yet constrained response to the crisis, as revealed by Roosevelt's overwhelming reelection victories in 1936 and 1940.

THE LEGACY OF THE NEW DEAL

The New Deal, as we have seen, was a melange of sometimes conflicting programs, some aimed at relieving distress, others aimed at preventing a recurrence of the Great Depression. In retrospect, the New Deal might have done better had it followed Keynes's advice and concentrated on relieving distress and maximizing the aggregate monetary and fiscal stimulus rather than trying to reform markets. In any case, the New Deal left an indelible imprint. First, it created a wide array of institutions and programs that continue to regulate our economic life: the Securities and Exchange Commission, the Federal Deposit Insurance Corporation, minimum wages and other work place regulations, Social Security, Unemployment Compensation, and so on. Second, it created an idealistic spirit among young New Dealers that would bear fruit in the form of additional legislation passed during the Kennedy-Johnson years. Third, it created the presumption that people could look to Washington for solutions to their economic difficulties. True, people had often turned to Washington for help before 1929: to reduce foreign competition, to subsidize railroad construction, to relieve the victims of fire, and so on. All potential reforms had to overcome the presumption that the existing political and economic institutions, including the free market, were fundamentally sound. The Great Depression and the New Deal reversed the burden of proof, leaving it up to defenders of the status quo to show that market forces could solve a problem to which the attention of the public had been drawn by a crisis.

---

[7]See Joseph Schumpeter, *Business Cycles: A Theoretical, Historical, and Statistical Analysis of the Capitalist Process* (New York: 1939), vol. 2, 1044–1045; Thomas Mayer and Monojit Chatterji, "Political Shocks and Investment: Some Evidence from the 1930s" *Journal of Economics History* 45 (December 1948): 936–941; Anthony Patrick O'Brien, "Were Businessmen Afraid of FDR? A Comment on Mayer and Chatterji," *Journal of Economic History* 50 (December 1990): 936–941; "Reply to O'Brien," *Journal of Economic History* 50 (December 1990): 942–944; and Robert Higgs, 1997.

The fourth and perhaps most important legacy of the New Deal is, paradoxically, what it did not do: It did not try to overthrow capitalism. With the nation in turmoil and its economy in ruins, socialism or at least widespread nationalization of commerce and industry might have been instituted in 1933. The basic instinct of the New Deal was to reform and conserve the system. Americans like to think of themselves as good poker players. In 1932 they did not want to stop playing, they just wanted to change the rules and to get a New Deal.

Selected References and Suggested Readings

Allen, Frederick Lewis. *Since Yesterday: The Nineteen Thirties in America*. New York: Harper, 1940.

Alston, Lee J. "Farm Foreclosures in the United States during the Interwar Period." *Journal of Economic History* 43 (1983): 885–903.

———. "Farm Foreclosure Moratorium Legislation: A Lesson from the Past." *American Economic Review* 74 (1984): 445–457.

Alston, Lee J., and Randal R. Rucker. "Farm Failures and Government Intervention: A Case Study of the 1930's." *American Economic Review* 77 (September 1987): 724–730.

Anderson, Gary M., and Robert D. Tollison. "Congressional Influence, and Patterns of New Deal Spending." *Journal of Law and Economics* 34 (April 1991): 161–175.

Bernstein, Michael. "A Reassessment of Investment Failure in the Interwar American Economy." *Journal of Economic History* 44 (1984): 479–488.

———. *The Great Depression: Delayed Recovery and Economic Change in America*. New York: Cambridge University Press, 1988.

Bordo, Michael D., Claudia Goldin, and Eugene N. White, eds. *The Defining Moment: The Great Depression and the American Economy in the Twentieth Century*. Chicago: University of Chicago Press, 1998.

Bordo, Michael D., Christopher J. Erceg, and Charles L. Evans, "Sticky Wages, and the Great Depression." *American Economic Review* 90 (December 2000): 1447–1463.

Brunner, Karl, ed. *The Great Depression Revisited.* Boston: Martinus Nijhoff, 1981.

Chandler, Lester V. *America's Greatest Depression, 1929–1941*. New York: Harper & Row, 1970.

Cole, Harold L., and Lee E. Ohanian. "Re-examining the Contributions of Money and Banking Shocks to the U.S. Great Depression." In *NBER Macroeconomics Annual 2000*, eds. Ben S. Bernanke and Kenneth Rogoff. Cambridge, Mass.: MIT Press, 2001, 183–227.

Costa, Dora L. *The Evolution of Retirement: An American Economic History, 1880–1990*. Chicago: University of Chicago Press, 1998.

Darby, Michael. "Three and a Half Million U.S. Employees Have Been Mislaid: Or, an Explanation of Unemployment, 1934–1941." *Journal of Political Economy* 84 (February 1976): 1–16.

Farm Security Administration and Office of War Information photographs. **http://rs6.loc.gov/fsowhome.html**.

Franklin and Eleanor Roosevelt Institute Web site devoted to New Deal public works and art projects. **http://newdeal.feri.org**.

Franklin D. Roosevelt Library. **http://www.fdrlibrary.marist.edu/**.

Fishback, Price V., and Shawn Everett Kantor. *A Prelude to the Welfare State: The Origins of Worker's Compensation*. Chicago: University of Chicago Press, 2000.

Fishback, Price V., Michael R. Haines, and Shawn Kantor. "The Impact of the New Deal on Black and White Infant Mortality in the South." *Explorations in Economic History* 38 (January 2001): 93–122.

Hawley, Ellis W. *The New Deal and the Problem of Monopoly: A Study in Economic Ambivalence*. Princeton, N.J.: Princeton University Press, 1966.

Higgs, Robert. *Crisis and Leviathan: Critical Episodes in the Growth of American Government*. New York: Oxford University Press, 1987, chapter 8.

———. "Regime Uncertainty: Why the Great Depression Lasted So Long and Why Prosperity Resumed after the War." *Independent Review* 1 (Spring 1997): 561–590.

Kindleberger, Charles P. *The World in Depression 1929–1939*. Berkeley: University of California Press, 1973.

Leuchtenberg, William E. *Franklin D. Roosevelt and the New Deal, 1932–1940*. New York: Harper Colophon, 1963.

———. "The New Deal and the Analogue of War." In *Change and Continuity in Twentieth Century America*, eds. John Braeman, Robert H. Bremner, and Everett Walters. Columbus: Ohio State University Press, 1964.

Libecap, Gary D. "The Great Depression and the Regulating State: Federal Government Regulation of Agriculture, 1884–1970." In *The Defining Moment: The Great Depression and the American Economy in the Twentieth Century*, eds. Michael D. Bordo, Claudia Goldin, and Eugene N. White. Chicago: University of Chicago Press, 1998, 181–224.

Margo, Robert. "The Microeconomics of Depression Unemployment." *The Journal of Economic History* 51 (June 1991): 333–342.

Mayer, Thomas, and Monojit Chatterji. "Political Shocks and Investment: Some Evidence from the 1930s." *Journal of Economic History* 45 (December 1985): 913–924

———. "Reply to O'Brien" *Journal of Economic History* 50 (December 1990): 942–944.

O'Brien, Anthony Patrick. "A Behavioral Explanation for Normal Wage Rigidity during the Great Depression." *Quarterly Journal of Economics* 104 (1989): 719–735.

———. "Were Businessmen Afraid of FDR? A Comment on Mayer and Chatterji." *Journal of Economic History* 50 (December 1990): 936–941.

Public Broadcasting System Web site describing the Dust Bowl. **http://www.pbs.org/wgbh/amex/dustbowl**.

Schumpeter, Joseph. *Business Cycles: A Theoretical, Historical, and Statistical Analysis of the Capitalist Process*, New York: McGraw-Hill, 1939.

Smiley, Gene. "Recent Unemployment Rate Estimates for the 1920s and 1930s." *Journal of Economic History* 43 (1983): 487–493.

Social Security Administration Web site, history section. **http://www.ssa.gov/history**.

Temin, Peter. "The Great Depression." In *The Cambridge Economic History of the United States*, Vol. III, The Twentieth Century, eds. Stanley L. Engerman and Robert E. Gallman. New York: Cambridge University Press, 2000, 301–328.

Tennessee Valley Authority Web site, history section. **http://www.tva.gov/abouttva/history.htm**.

Wallis, John Joseph. "The Birth of the Old Federalism: Financing the New Deal, 1932–1940." *Journal of Economic History* 44 (1984): 139–159.

———. "Employment, Politics, and Economic Recovery during the Great Depression." *Review of Economics and Statistics* 64 (1987): 516–520.

Wallis, John Joseph, and Daniel K. Benjamin. "Public Relief and Private Employment in the Great Depression." *Journal of Economic History* 41 (1981): 97–102.

Walton, Gary M., ed. *Regulatory Change in an Atmosphere of Crisis: Current Implications of the Roosevelt Years*. New York: Academic Press, 1979.

Weinstein, Michael M. "Some Macroeconomic Impacts of the National Industrial Recovery Act, 1933–1935." In *The Great Depression Revisited*, ed. Karl Brunner. Boston: Martinus Nijhoff, 1981.

Wright, Gavin. "The Political Economy of New Deal Spending: An Econometric Analysis." *Review of Economics and Statistics* 56 (1974): 30–38.

Chapter Twenty-Five

WORLD WAR II

Only 21 years after the end of World War I, the world was once more engulfed in war. The war took an enormous human toll. The United States suffered 405,000 deaths in World War II, 292,000 in battle. In addition, 671,000 suffered nonmortal wounds. The death toll was four times that of World War I and two-thirds that of the Civil War. For the other belligerents, the tolls were much higher. All told, about 40 million people died in World War II. The loss of "human capital," to use the economists' term, was staggering.

America's primary economic goal was to supply sufficient arms to her own military forces and to those of her allies to overwhelm the Axis (Germany, Japan, and their allies), to become, as President Roosevelt put it, the "Arsenal of Democracy." This goal was achieved brilliantly. In a few short years, the factories of the United States were turning out more weapons than any other nation and more than all the Axis powers combined, even though the Axis had begun converting to a war footing years before the United States.

In the short run, the war effort alleviated the need for many of the New Deal's emergency measures. Work relief was no longer necessary because the nation's factories were humming at full capacity; emergency funds were no longer needed to bail out firms faced with bankruptcy because profits were surging. In the long run, the war effort reinforced the restructuring of the economy that had taken place in the 1930s. The association of large federal deficits and low unemployment convinced many economists and public of the effectiveness of Keynes's cure for unemployment. The government's management of the mobilization convinced economists and the public at large that the federal government had the ability to successfully manage large-scale projects.

MOBILIZING FOR WAR

World War II began in September 1939, when German forces attacked Poland.[1] Britain and France, who had guaranteed Poland's independence, then declared war on Germany. In the

[1]The best general survey of the American economy during the war is Harold G. Vatter, *The U.S. Economy in World War II* (New York: Columbia University Press, 1985).

United States, a brief surge occurred in industrial production as manufacturers anticipated a repeat of the heady days of 1916 when a neutral America had made enormous profits by supplying a Europe at war. Industrial production sagged during the "phony war," however, when it appeared that Britain, France, and Germany, although officially at war, would avoid a major clash of arms. The phony war ended in May 1940 when Germany launched a blitzkrieg (lightning war) attack against the Low Countries, swept around France's supposedly impenetrable Maginot Line, and conquered France. American manufacturers began building up inventories in anticipation of future shortages, Britain and her remaining allies began placing large orders for American war materials, and the United States launched a vastly expanded program of military procurement.

Initially, Britain was asked to pay for arms on a "cash and carry" basis. It paid by transferring gold and by requisitioning American bank deposits and securities owned by British nationals. (This policy stripped Britain of much of its overseas investment.) When these sources of funds began to run out, President Roosevelt succeeded in establishing the Lend-Lease program in March 1941.The name "Lend-Lease" was calculated to deflect attention from the simple fact that the United States government would now be paying for the arms sent to Britain and our other allies.

At first, prices remained relatively stable because millions of American workers were still unemployed and underemployed and because industrial capacity was much underutilized. The United States had not yet reached the production possibilities curve, to use the economist's term. By the autumn of 1940, however, supply had become less inelastic and wholesale prices had begun to rise. In 1941, the American economy was moving into high gear despite some pockets of unemployment. Production of steel ingots and castings, for example, had already reached 59.8 million long-tons in 1940, exceeding the previous peak of 56.4 million reached in 1929; in 1941, production reached 74.0 million long-tons. Sulfuric acid, a chemical having a wide variety of industrial applications, was also being produced in unprecedented quantities: 6.8 million short-tons in 1941 compared with 5.3 million in 1929. The Federal Reserve Board's index of industrial production reached a level of 139 in 1941 compared with 100 in 1929. Although American industry was moving into high gear, many Americans still doubted the wisdom of aid to Britain and its allies. All doubts vanished, however, on December 7, 1941. To quote President Roosevelt's famous war message:

> Yesterday, December 7, 1941—a date which will live in infamy—the United States of America was suddenly and deliberately attacked by the naval and air forces of the Empire of Japan. . . . The facts of yesterday speak for themselves. The people of the United States have already formed their opinions and well understand the implications to the very life and safety of our nation.

America was now fully committed to war against the Axis powers (Germany had quickly declared war against the United States after the Japanese attack and the United States reciprocated), but many military and economic questions still had to be answered.

Under President Roosevelt's leadership, the United States adopted a bold plan of economic mobilization. America would use its vast industrial might to mass-produce arms and overwhelm the Axis with sheer firepower. Characteristically, President Roosevelt called for the unheard-of total of 50,000 airplanes, although at the time no one knew how such a vast number of planes could be produced. Economic mobilization involved many trade-offs. The most important question was how far to reduce civilian consumption—the choice, as it was often put, between "guns and butter."[2] See Economic Insight 25.1 on page 496.

---

[2]Civilian consumption of butter did fall during the war, but this appears to have been simply part of a long-term trend toward lower consumption. Consumption of ice cream, on the other hand, was higher during the war than it had been before, also part of a long-term trend.

Economic Insight 25.1

"Guns or Butter" 1939–1949

The production possibilities curve shows the trade-off between guns (military spending), measured on the horizontal axis, and butter (civilian spending), measured on the vertical axis. The figure shows the actual combinations of guns and butter produced annually during the war years and a hypothetical curve drawn through the combinations achieved in 1944 and 1948. Some of the combinations lie inside the production possibilities curve (1939, 1940, 1941, and 1942, in particular); these points indicate that the economy was still operating below its maximum possible output. Thus, in general, the United States increased its war output mainly by moving horizontally toward the production possibilities curve rather than moving along it. (The term "guns or butter" is usually attributed to German Field Marshal Hermann Goering who in the 1930s demanded "Cannon instead of butter.")

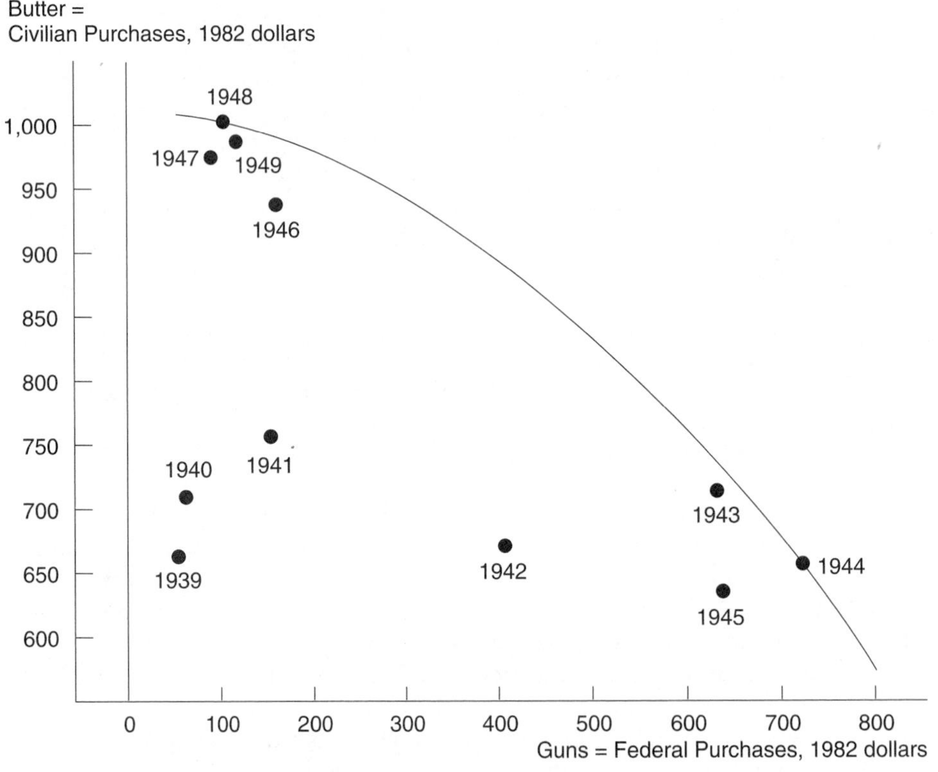

Table 25.1 shows, in very broad terms, how America allocated its resources to the war effort: In 1929, the federal government was spending a small fraction of GNP, 2.6 percent. Even in 1940, after years of expansion in the role of the federal government under the New Deal, the federal government was spending about 8.2 percent of GNP. The war changed things dramatically. The maximum effort occurred in 1944, when the federal government spent some $722.5 billion (at 1982 prices), about 52.3 percent of total GNP.

Another way of analyzing these figures is also of interest. Between 1940 and 1944, total real federal spending increased by $658.9 billion (722.5 – 63.6), while total real GNP increased by $607.7 billion (1,380.6 – 772.9). Thus, 92.2 percent of the increase in military spending (607.7 ÷ 658.9) can be accounted for by the increase in real GNP; only 7.8 percent of the increase had to be offset by a decline in production for the civilian sector. The great bulk of the resources for the war effort were obtained by employing previously unemployed resources and by using already employed resources more intensively. Remarkably enough, Germany was also able to sustain civilian consumption well into the war, although not throughout. In other countries, though, where the capacity to expand was less, the need to sacrifice current consumption or investment to make available resources for the military effort was correspondingly greater.

Trade-Offs

While the decision about how much to reduce civilian consumption and investment was the most important, other more subtle trade-offs were also involved in wartime mobilization (Economic Reasoning Proposition 2, which stresses the importance of trade-off, applies in war as well as in peace). One was in the area of industrial safety. Industrial accidents, often resulting in serious injury or death, increased dramatically during the war. To some extent this was to be expected, with so many more men and women working so many more hours in dangerous jobs. It also appears that the rate at which accidents occurred increased, at least in manufacturing. The official figures show an increase in the number of disabling injuries per million hours worked in manufacturing from 15.3 in 1940 to 20.0 in 1943, the all-time peak.

Should greater efforts have been made to maintain safety? Possibly, but the problem was always one of the trade-off between safety and production. Well-rested workers are safer

TABLE 25.1 Real Gross National Product (in billions of 1982 dollars)

YEAR	GNP	TOTAL FEDERAL PURCHASES OF GOODS AND SERVICES	PREVIOUS COLUMN AS A PERCENTAGE OF GNP	TOTAL CIVILIAN PURCHASES OF GOODS AND SERVICES[a]	PREVIOUS COLUMN AS A PERCENTAGE OF GNP
1929	$ 709.6	$ 18.3	2.58%	$ 691.3	97.42%
1939	716.6	53.8	7.51	662.8	92.49
1940	772.9	63.6	8.23	709.3	91.77
1941	909.4	153.0	16.82	756.4	83.18
1942	1,080.3	407.1	37.68	673.2	62.32
1943	1,276.2	638.1	50.00	638.1	50.00
1944	1,380.6	722.5	52.33	658.1	47.67
1945	1,354.8	634.0	46.80	720.8	53.20
1946	1,096.9	159.3	14.52	937.6	85.48
1950	1,203.7	116.7	9.70	1,087.0	90.30

[a]*Includes state and local government spending.*

Source: Economic Report of the President, 1987 *(Washington, D.C.: Government Printing Office, 1987), 246–247.*

TABLE 25.2 Combat Munitions Produced by the Major Belligerents (in billions of dollars at 1944 U.S. munitions prices)

	1933-1939	1940	1941	1942	1943	1944
United States	$ 1.5	$1.5	$4.5	$20	$38	$42
United Kingdom	2.5	3.5	6.5	9	11	11
U.S.S.R.	8	5	8.5	11.5	14	16
Germany	12	6	6	8.5	13.5	17
Japan	2	1	2	3	4.5	6

Source: Mark Harrison, "Resource Mobilization for World War II: The U.S.A., U.K., U.S.S.R., and Germany, 1938–1945," Economic History Review *41 (1988): 172.*

workers, but more rest breaks may mean lower output. More work space in shipping yards reduces the risk of accidents, but more work space means higher construction costs and fewer resources available for building other facilities.

Another subtle trade-off lay between the quality and quantity of arms produced. Changing technology and battlefield experience were constantly suggesting modifications of existing weapons. Making these modifications often meant tearing down and rebuilding an assembly line, thereby losing valuable production time. This trade-off was often a bone of contention between military leaders, who would argue for the most sophisticated weapon possible, and the civilians in charge of military production, who were more mindful of the potential loss in production. When Hitler's troops attacked the allied invasion force in the Battle of the Bulge, Germany's tanks, the famous panzers, were as good as or better than any tank in the hands of the Allies, but they were vastly outnumbered.

On the whole, America's decision to mass-produce the weapons of war turned out to be a brilliant success. America by itself produced more arms than the Axis countries combined. Not only were supplies such as small arms and ammunition mass-produced, but also planes and even ships to carry the arms to the theaters of war. At Henry Kaiser's shipyards in Portland, Oregon, where some of the most innovative techniques were used, one of the famous Liberty ships was produced in a record eight days. To some extent, as Henry A. Gemery and Jan S. Hogendorn have shown, mass-production techniques were used even in producing destroyers.[3]

Overwhelming Firepower

Table 25.2 shows the annual production of munitions (cumulatively for 1933–1939) by the five major powers. By 1939, Germany and Japan had accumulated considerable stocks of munitions. They hoped to win against countries with greater long-term economic capacities by employing these munitions in blitzkrieg attacks before their opponents had time to arm. Although they won numerous initial battles, eventually their paths of expansion were blocked, and the war became one of attrition. The United States launched a huge program to build both arms and the means of producing them, and its production surged. The result can be seen in Table 25.2. By 1942,U.S. munitions production exceeded that of Germany and Japan combined. Despite the ability of Germany and Japan to increase their production in the face of heavy air attacks, and despite the advantage of fighting behind defensive lines, the final outcome was no longer in doubt. The enormous weight of the combined munitions production of the United States and her allies meant that Germany and Japan would be defeated sooner or later.

[3]Henry A. Gemery and Jan S. Hogendorn, "The Microeconomic Bases of Short-Run Learning Curves: Destroyer Production in World War II," in *The Sinews of War: Essays on the Economic History of World War II*, eds. Geofrey Mills and Hugh Rockoff (Ames: Iowa State University Press, 1993).

Production of automobiles for civilian use ended in February 1942. The industry then turned to the mass production of tanks, machine guns, aircraft engines, and other weapons of war, including the jeep, shown here on a Ford assembly line.

Several agencies, the most important being the War Production Board, tried to manage the vast expansion of munitions production. One tool was the priority, essentially a rating placed on contracts to guide manufacturers in scheduling production. The reallocation of resources was so rapid and was so huge the volume of new contracts—at one point the total value of outstanding contracts was said to exceed the gross national product—that munitions production was reaching its peak when the War Production Board finally solved the problems such as "priority inflation" (too many contracts having the highest priority) that had developed soon after mobilization began. In the end, the profit motive was the primary allocator of resources.[4]

FISCAL AND MONETARY POLICY

As noted in previous chapters, four basic ways to obtain the resources needed to fight a major war are available for a country's use: (1) simply commandeering the resources, (2) taxing income or wealth, (3) borrowing, and (4) printing money. In World War II, the U.S. government relied on all four. The draft, of course, was the most important example of commandeering. The government also relied on taxation. The war radically changed the

[4]On the profitability of wartime contracts and the persistence of lavish profits for military contractors after the war, see Robert Higgs, "Private Profit, Public Risk: Institutional Antecedents of the Modern Military Procurement System in the Rearmament Program 1940–1941," in *The Sinews of War: Essays on the Economic History of World War II*, eds. Geofrey Mills and Hugh Rockoff (Ames: Iowa State University Press, 1993).

The Liberty ship, mass produced during World War II, helped the United States multiply the total tonnage of its merchant marine fleet by a factor of 5.

income tax. The exemptions for single and married persons were lowered. In 1943, the payroll deduction system for collecting income taxes was introduced, and the term *take-home pay* entered the language. Together, these innovations meant that the income tax had become a mass tax for the first time. Corporate tax rates were also increased, and an excess profits tax was introduced. As a result of these tax increases and the rapid increase in the tax base, the United States was able to finance about 40 percent of the war with taxes. (See Table 25.3.) This was a larger share than taxes had financed in the Civil War or World War I. Nevertheless, the United States still had to borrow large sums to help finance the conflict. Refer to New View 25.1.

TABLE 25.3 Financing World War II

	BILLIONS OF DOLLARS, 1941–1946	PERCENTAGE OF EXPENDITURES
Total federal expenditures for war[a]	$320.2	100.0%
Tax revenues	129.8	40.5
Borrowing from the public	115.8	37.0
Creating new money	74.6	22.5

[a] *Total expenditures 1941–1946, less six times 1940 expenditures.*

Sources: Historical Statistics *(Washington, D.C.: Government Printing Office, 1960), 711; and Milton Friedman and Anna J. Schwartz,* Monetary Statistics of the United States *(New York: National Bureau of Economic Research, 1970), 33–37.*

New View 25.1

How Should Wars Be Financed?

The World War II debate over whether to rely mainly on taxes or debt to finance the war (no one thought that relying on printing money was a good idea) continues to be relevant when the United States goes to war. The Roosevelt administration, reflecting one school of thought, proposed financing the greater part of the war by raising taxes. According to the administration, doing so would avoid burdening the younger generation (including those doing the fighting) with having to pay the interest and principal on a large debt in future years. Getting Congress to raise taxes, however, is never easy. Republican congressmen complained that high tax rates discouraged work, and they supported only partial financing through increased taxation. Today many neoclassical economists agree that "smoothing taxes"—raising them only a bit during wars and relying mainly on debt—is the most efficient way to finance a war. Supporters of deficit finance can also point to the fact that the federal debt reached $259 billion in 1945, 121 percent of gross domestic product, without causing an obvious crisis, as evidence that the economy can tolerate very high levels of debt.

In thinking about this debate, it is perhaps relevant to remind ourselves of what Adam Smith, a proponent of tax finance had to say (*The Wealth of Nations*, The Glasgow Edition, 925):

> Wars [if financed by taxes rather than debt] would in general be more speedily concluded, and less wantonly undertaken. The people feeling, during the continuance of the war, the complete burden of it, would soon grow weary of it, and the government, in order to humor them, would not be under the necessity of carrying it on longer than it was necessary do so.

Conceivably, all wartime deficits could have been financed by sales of securities to the general public, but (despite highly publicized war bond drives) it is likely that the interest rates required to market those bonds would have been very high by historical standards. Therefore, the Federal Reserve took the extraordinary step of "pegging" the rate of interest on government securities. It accomplished this by pledging to buy government securities whenever their price fell below predetermined support levels.[5] On the surface, selling bonds to the Fed seems to be a free ride because it minimizes the future interest costs that the government incurs. The fly in the ointment (or rat in the soup, depending on one's view of things) is that the Federal Reserve must create new money to purchase these securities, and this adds to the inflationary pressures facing the economy.

In 1939, unemployment remained at the stubbornly high level of 11.3 percent of the labor force. Keynesians claimed that unemployment could be cured with a sufficient increase in government spending, particularly deficit-financed spending. True, the deficit was 3.07 percent of GNP in 1939. What was needed, according to the Keynesians, was simply a much bigger deficit. By 1944 the deficit had been vastly increased, to 22.5 percent of GNP, and unemployment was virtually gone (1.2 percent), one of the lowest rates on record. Most economists, particularly those of the younger generation such as future Nobel Prize winners Paul Samuelson and James Tobin, found this demonstration of the effectiveness of the

[5]The interest rate paid on a government security is determined by the relationship between the fixed annual payments on the security and its market value; low market values imply high interest rates.

When the war began, the United States was producing only small amounts of synthetic rubber for specialty uses. By 1944, plants like this one in Baton Rouge assured the nation an adequate supply.

Keynesian remedy for unemployment convincing. To see why, consider Table 25.4 which shows the key figures.

A number of economists at the time, as well as a growing number since, were still skeptical about Keynes's cure. For one thing, the data are also consistent with the monetarist claim that a large increase in the money supply would cure the depression. Consider the last column of Table 25.4.The stock of money in 1939 was only slightly higher than that of 1929, but by 1944, it had more than doubled. Some economists have also pointed out that the drafting of large numbers of young men into the armed forces removed many individuals who had a high probability of being unemployed from the labor force. As in so many cases, the lessons of history are ambiguous because in the natural experiments of history, other factors are seldom as constant as we would like. Whatever reservations economists may now entertain about this demonstration of the Keynesian message, there is no doubt

TABLE 25.4 Deficit Spending and the Fall in Unemployment

YEAR	UNEMPLOYMENT (percent of the labor force)	GNP (in billions of dollars)	FEDERAL BUDGET DEFICIT (in billions of dollars)	DEFICIT AS A PERCENTAGE OF GNP	STOCK OF MONEY (in (in billions of dollars)
1929	3.2%	$103.9	$ 0.7	0.67%	$ 46.6
1933	20.6	56.0	–2.6	–4.64	32.2
1939	11.3	91.3	–2.8	–3.07	49.2
1944	1.2	211.4	–47.6	–22.52	106.8

Sources: Economic Report of the President, 1987 *(Washington, D.C.: Government Printing Office, 1987), 244, 280, and 331; and Michael R. Darby, "Three and a Half Million U.S. Employees Have Been Mislaid: Or, an Explanation of Unemployment, 1934–41,"* Journal of Political Economy *84 (1976): 8. The last column is derived from Milton Friedman and Anna J. Schwartz,* Monetary Trends in the United States and the United Kingdom *(Chicago: University of Chicago Press, 1982), 124–125.*

that it had a profound impact on economic policy making during the war. Even at the time, however, some Keynesians worried that the inflationary pressures produced by wartime policies of deficit spending had been checked only by a set of wage and price controls that would be unacceptable in peacetime.

WAGE AND PRICE CONTROLS

Early in the war, the Roosevelt administration decided that it would combat rising prices with direct controls. It would try to persuade firms not to raise prices by appealing to their patriotism; if persuasion failed, it would simply make price increases illegal.

In May 1940, President Roosevelt set up the National Defense Advisory Committee and chose Leon Henderson, a crusty, cigar-smoking New Dealer, to head its Price Stabilization Division. Henderson sought voluntary agreements from producers in key areas of the economy not to raise prices, a policy that met with little success. Prices continued to rise. In April 1941, Roosevelt strengthened Henderson's hand by creating the Office of Price Administration and Civilian Supply. Eventually, OPA would become the civilian agency most familiar to the average American because it set the prices and determined the quantities of the goods and services consumed every day. Of special interest to economists was the creation of the Price Division of OPA under the direction of John Kenneth Galbraith. In the postwar period, Galbraith would become a leading advocate of the liberal view that America's social and economic problems could be solved by expanding the role of the federal government. Undoubtedly, his experience at the OPA, with its enormous (and, in his view, favorable) effect on the economy, profoundly influenced his thinking.

Initially, the OPA hoped to control the general price level by applying controls in only selected sectors, but uncontrolled prices continued to rise, and at an increasing pace. In April 1942, this OPA issued the General Maximum Price Regulation, affectionately known as General Max, which put a ceiling on most prices. Even this measure was only partially successful, however; one problem was that each seller was responsible for setting his own prices according to the rules set up by the government. It was altogether too easy for a firm to justify the price it charged by pointing to an unusually high base period price or an unusually high price set by a competitor. Effective price control required that the OPA set specific dollars-and-cents prices that its employees or its boards of volunteer price watchers could check.

In April 1943, President Roosevelt issued his famous "hold-the-line" order requiring OPA to refuse all requests for price increases except in extremely limited circumstances. This approach, economically suspect because it did not provide for the adjustment of relative prices, but easy to defend in the court of public opinion, worked surprisingly well for the remainder of the war. The official consumer price index rose only 1.6 percent per year from April 1943 until February 1946, when the policy began to come apart.

Hidden Price Increases and the Black Market

The official index alone, however, does not tell the whole story. A basic proposition of economics is that if a price ceiling is set below the free-market equilibrium, a scramble for supplies will occur that will produce attempts to evade the ceiling. There were innumerable examples during the war. In some cases, evasion took the form of quality deterioration: Fat was added to hamburger, coarse fabrics were substituted for finer ones, and maintenance on rent-controlled apartments was reduced. Quality deterioration could be limited by regulations that specified the exact content of a product, such as the specified butterfat content of milk, but such regulations tended to get longer and longer and became a problem in themselves. In one famous case, Lou Maxon, an OPA official, resigned in 1943, complaining about what he saw as the antibusiness atmosphere at OPA. Many of Maxon's charges were exaggerated, but the six-page regulation specifying the content of fruit cakes, which he used to dramatize his charges, spoke to a real problem.

"Forced uptrading" was another problem caused by price controls. Before the war, manufacturers often offered buyers a choice between low-priced, low-quality items and high-priced, high-quality items. Typically, the high-priced lines carried higher profit margins but sold in smaller volumes. With wartime demand in all lines exceeding supply, manufacturers eliminated the lower-priced lines. This was fine for those consumers who wished to move up to the higher-priced item anyway, but for those who were forced to trade up, the difference between what they would have voluntarily paid for the high-priced line and what they were forced to pay because the low-priced line was eliminated was a hidden price increase.

The most startling form of evasion, although not the most frequent, was the black market. Here, buyers willing to pay more than the official price and sellers willing to sell for more would meet away from the prying eyes of the OPA. The black market took many forms, depending on the product and the enforcement effort being made by the OPA. In New York, there were "meat-easys," much like the speakeasys that had flourished during prohibition, where one could buy extra meat but at prices much higher than those set by the OPA. After production of automobiles resumed at the end of the war, evasion of automobile price controls was widespread. Some of it occurred in the dealer's showroom, where cash payments were often made on the side while official documents showed that the car had been sold at the OPA ceiling. A true black market also developed. At Leesville, South Carolina, for example, to a huge lot cars recently purchased from dealers were brought from all over the country to be resold at black-market prices.

Rationing

Rationing is one way to reduce evasion when prices are held below their free-market equilibrium. A consumer who is assured at least a bare minimum is less likely to enter the black market than a consumer who is in danger of being left without anything in a mad scramble for supplies. Moreover, a company that must be able to show the authorities ration tickets corresponding to the output it has sold will find it more difficult to divert supplies to the black market. In some cases, rationing was undertaken to achieve particular policy goals. Gasoline was rationed, for example, to reduce the use of automobile and truck tires, which were in short supply because of the rubber shortage.[6]

The simplest form of rationing was a ticket entitling the holder to buy a certain quantity of a certain good that was surrendered when the good was purchased. Tires, the first commodity rationed, were handled in this way. Under the red-point system for meats and fats, however, the consumer was periodically supplied with a certain number of points. Each good was assigned a point price, and the consumer could choose among rationed items as long as he or she had enough ration points.

Balancing the supply of goods and the number of ration tickets or points was no easy matter. To make the red-point system operate more smoothly, the OPA issued red-point tokens that could be taken as change and stored for use at a later date. By late 1944, surveys showed that consumers had stored up large quantities of these tokens, and the OPA feared a run on the stores that would leave shelves bare and confidence in the rationing program shaken. To regain control, OPA canceled all outstanding ration tokens, a move that

[6]In a few cases, the goals of the rationing program were debatable. A well-publicized fat salvage program led consumers to believe that the fat was needed to make a chemical crucial to the war effort. The real motive was the fear on the part of soap manufacturers that a shortage of fat would lead to rationing soap and that consumers accustomed to economizing on soap during the war would continue to buy less afterward.

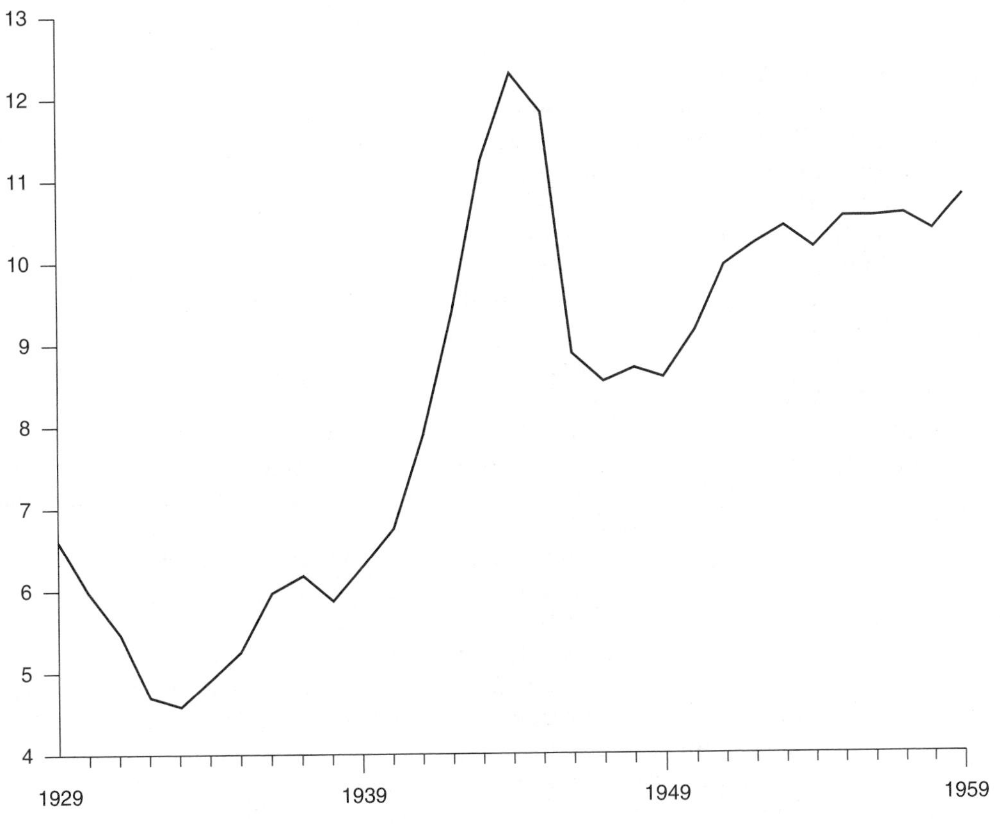

FIGURE 25.1 Real per Capita Income in 1987 Dollars

Official estimates of real GDP per capita reached an extraordinary peak in 1944. But can we really compare the output of the economy during the war with the output before or after?

Source: U.S. Bureau of Economic Analysis, National Income and Product Accounts of the United States, *Volume 2, 1959–1988.*

cost the agency a great deal of public support. In 1945, as the war came to a close, most of the rationing programs were discontinued, a highly popular decision.

When legislation authorizing price controls expired in June 1946, Congress passed a new law. It was so riddled with loopholes that President Truman vetoed it in the hope that a strong dose of inflation would force Congress to pass a stiffer measure. Eventually, legislation was passed that permitted the recontrol of selected prices. When meat prices were recontrolled, ranchers withheld their animals from the market—after all, it was clear that price controls were on the way out and that prices could only go higher—and the result was a meat shortage. Faced with outraged consumers on one hand and recommendations that he nationalize the nation's cattle herds on the other, Truman decided to terminate price controls for good.

WARTIME PROSPERITY?

If we look at a graph of real GDP per capita, as shown in Figure 25.1, the war years stand out as a unique achievement. Apparently, real per capita income was higher during the war than it was before or after. The statistics are matched by personal memories of the war and by historical accounts that single out the war years as a uniquely prosperous period.[7] Robert Higgs, however, has recently challenged this view of the war and claimed, for several reasons,

[7]Studs Terkel, *The Good War: An Oral History of World War Two* (New York: Pantheon Books, 1984), insightfully compiles war memories from an eclectic group of Americans.

that the war was not a period of unique prosperity but that in fact, it was a period of continued depression and that real prosperity did not come until after the war. In other words, Higgs asserts that the story told so eloquently in Figure 25.1 is spurious. Economic Reasoning Proposition 5 (evidence matters) is appropriate here.

First, Higgs points out that many problems created by price controls and rationing, as mentioned, make measurement of output and especially civilian consumption during the war problematic. If price indexes are understated because they miss hidden price increases or because the price of rationed goods understates the difficulty of acquiring them, output will be overstated. Higgs also points out that war output didn't contribute directly to consumption, either at the time or in the future. In his view, war production should be omitted altogether from GDP.

One can take issue with Higgs's arguments. Any measurement of the extent of hidden price increases during the war is bound to have a large margin of error. Price increase designed to go unseen by the prying eyes of the tax collector or price controller can only be guessed at or estimated in roundabout ways. Higgs's claim that war output should be omitted from GDP is also debatable. After all, we include categories, such as medical care, that raise many of the same issues in GDP. An operation for cancer, like fighting a battle against a determined enemy, is costly and painful. Indeed, we often use the same language: "He is battling for his life against cancer." Cancer operations and battles are good investments because they protect our ability to enjoy life in the future.

Nevertheless, Higgs's arguments do help us understand the nature of "wartime prosperity." For many people, the war did mean an increase in their current real consumption compared with that during the grinding poverty of the depression. For others, the important thing was not consumption during the war but the availability of jobs for the asking through which one could earn money that would be valuable in the years to come, even if it couldn't be spent during the war because of shortages and rationing.

LABOR RELATIONS DURING THE WAR

The war put labor relations on hold. The Roosevelt administration had been supporting labor's efforts to organize, bargain collectively, and strike; now labor was expected to cooperate with the effort to maximize production. Labor took a no-strike pledge, paralleling management's no-lockout pledge. For the most part, labor kept its pledge. The major exception was the United Mine Workers, under their charismatic leader John L. Lewis. As the result of public indignation over strikes in the coalfields, Congress passed the Smith-Connally War Labor Disputes Act in 1943, which provided for government takeover of plants in essential war industries that were hampered by strikes. Despite this case, however, the conflict between labor and management was generally kept in check during the war by labor's patriotism and by the government's extraordinary powers.

The real crunch came at the end of the war. As workers' overtime disappeared and real earnings were eroded by rising prices, labor leaders were under pressure to secure wage increases, which were not to be forthcoming without a struggle. Meanwhile, the widespread work stoppages of 1945 and 1946, shown vividly in Figure 25.2, alienated large segments of the electorate.

During this period employers complained that they were being caught in the jurisdictional disputes of rival unions and that labor itself was guilty of unfair practices. A belief was growing that union power was being used to infringe on the rights of individual workers. In fact, employers often used strikes to pressure the OPA to grant a price increase. Labor, of course, realized that this avenue was open to employers, and this entered into their strike calculations. The OPA, in many cases, claimed that higher wages could be paid without granting higher prices, but the path of least resistance often was to grant a round of wage and price increases in an industry experiencing a strike.

FIGURE 25.2 Five-Year Moving Average of Number of Strike Days per Thousand Nonagricultural Employees, 1929–1973

Source: P. K. Edwards, Strikes in the United States, 1881–1974 *(New York: St. Martin's Press, 1981), 18.*

After the Republicans won control of Congress in 1946, they lost no time in drawing up a long, technical bill that significantly amended the Wagner Act. The new law, passed in 1947 over President Truman's veto, was officially called the Labor Management Relations Act but became known familiarly as the Taft-Hartley Act. The act reflected the belief that individual workers should be protected by public policy not only in their right to join a labor organization but also in their right to refrain from joining. The closed-shop agreement, under which the employer hires only union members, was outlawed. Union shop agreements, which permit nonunion members to be employed but require them to join the union within a certain time period after starting to work, were permitted. However, the enforcement of union security provisions was limited to cases of nonpayment of dues. More important, the law permitted the states to outlaw all forms of union security, including the union shop.

The Taft-Hartley Act, unlike the Wagner Act, assumed that the interests of the union and individuals in the union were not identical, taking the view that many union members were "captives" of the labor bosses—a position offensive to a great part of organized labor.

The most important features of the Taft-Hartley Act were those purporting to regulate unions in the "public" interest. A union seeking certification or requesting an investigation of unfair labor practices had to submit to a scrutiny of its internal affairs by filing statements, and its officers were required to sign affidavits stating that they were not members of the Communist party. The right to strike was modified by provision of a cooling-off period after notice of termination of contract, and the president of the United States was given authority to postpone strikes for 80 days by injunction. More significant was the outlawing of certain unfair union practices. Since 1947, it has been unfair for a union to do the following:

1. Restrain or coerce employees regarding their right to join or refrain from joining a labor organization, or restrain or coerce employers in the selection of employer representatives for purposes of collective bargaining or adjustment of grievances.
2. Cause or attempt to cause an employer to discriminate against an employee.
3. Charge, under a valid union shop agreement, an excessive initiation fee.
4. Refuse to bargain collectively with an employer when the union involved is the certified bargaining agent.
5. "Featherbed" the job—that is, cause an employer to pay for services that are not performed.
6. Engage in, or encourage employees to engage in, a strike where the object is to force one employer to cease doing business with another employer (the secondary boycott).

After 12 years of almost complete freedom, labor found the Taft-Hartley Act harshly restrictive. Dire warnings were voiced about the coming decline of trade unionism in America. Labor's leadership was incensed at the offensive language and punitive spirit of the act. Many of the provisions looked worse in print, however, than they proved in practice. The injunction clause, for example, stirred memories of the days when the courts granted injunctions at the request of private parties; however, in the hands of a president of the United States, acting in an emergency, the injunction was no longer a destructive weapon. Moreover, although union problems persist today, they have arisen primarily from sources other than the Taft-Hartley Act.

WARTIME MINORITY EXPERIENCES

World War II had a significant effect on all Americans in one way or the other. It affected several specific groups in a certain way. Women, for example, entered the workforce to fill job vacancies left by soldiers. See Perspective 25.1 on page 510. The internment of Japanese Americans caused them enormous hardships. The wartime boom accelerated the long-term movement of poor whites and African Americans out of southern agriculture. Both groups responded to similar economic facts of life. Altogether, almost a million African Americans moved from southern farms to industrial centers in the South, the Northeast, the Midwest, and the Pacific Coast.[8]

The movement of the African American population had dramatic social and political consequences. In 1940, the African American population was about evenly divided between urban and rural areas; in 1950, it was predominantly urban. This rural exodus continued in the 1950s and 1960s. By 1970, three-quarters of the African American population lived in urban areas. The urbanization of the African American population contributed importantly to the Civil Rights movement and to the ending of legal discrimination. To some extent, that movement began during the war.

The military forces remained segregated for the duration of the war, but in 1940, officer's candidate schools (except those for the air force) were desegregated. Moreover, the outstanding record compiled by African American fighters, along with the growing demand by the African American community for equal justice, contributed to President Harry S. Truman's decision to issue an executive order desegregating the armed forces in 1948. Progress was also made on the homefront. In February 1941, A. Philip Randolph, head of the Brotherhood of Sleeping Car Porters, organized a march on Washington to protest discrimination in defense industries. The Roosevelt administration prevailed on

---

[8]Harold G. Vatter, *The U.S. Economy in World War II* (New York: Columbia University Press, 1985), 127.

the Randolph group to call off the march in exchange for an executive order forbidding discrimination in defense work and the establishment of the Federal Committee on Fair Employment Practices. The committee, although lacking in enforcement powers, worked with employers to end discrimination. Recent research by William Collins shows that these efforts had a positive impact on African American employment levels in war-related industries, and that continued employment in such industries was associated with a significant wage premium for blacks. The Committee on Fair Employment had to work, moreover, within a context in which violence was always possible. White–African American violence was not as frequent during World War II as in World War I, but in the early summer of 1943, a violent outburst near Detroit left 25 African Americans and 9 whites dead.

One of the worst examples of racial bigotry occurred in 1942. Some 110,000 Japanese Americans (75,000 of them citizens) were forced to leave their homes on the West Coast and were placed in internment camps until 1945. Many were forced to sell farms and other businesses at "fire-sale" prices, thus being deprived of property built up over decades. Meanwhile, Japanese Hawaiians and Japanese Americans distinguished themselves in the armed forces, fighting valiantly on the Italian front and serving as interpreters and translators in the Pacific theater. In 1988, Congress formally apologized and granted each of the survivors of the internment $20,000 as compensation.

AGRICULTURE DURING THE WAR

As demand expanded, agricultural production, aided by exceptionally good weather, climbed at the remarkable rate of 5 percent per year. This figure may be compared with the average during World War I, when agricultural production increased at 1.7 percent per year. Price controls during the war were purposely made less effective for agricultural than for nonagricultural commodities; consequently, the prices of farm products rose more rapidly during the war than the prices of the things that farmers had to buy.

During 1942, emphasis was placed on the necessity of stimulating particular kinds of output, notably meats and the oil-bearing crops, and avoiding a repetition of the price collapse that followed World War I. Legislation of October 1942 set final policy for the war period and for two postwar years. The 1942 act provided minimum support rates of 90 percent of parity for basic commodities; the supports were to remain in effect for two full years, beginning with the first day of January following the official end of the war. Price ceilings on farm products were set at a maximum of 110 percent of parity.

Cotton supports, however, were set at 92.5 percent of parity. Draft exemptions were provided for workers producing long-fiber cotton, which was demanded for a number of war-related uses.[9] The secretary of agriculture, at his discretion, could leave wheat and corn supports at 85 percent of parity if he felt that higher prices would limit available quantities of livestock feed. It is not entirely beside the point to note that cotton and beef interests were strongly represented by congressmen, some of whom had reached powerful positions through their seniority.

Over the war period and during the first two postwar years, price supports were not generally required. Because of the great demand for most products, agricultural prices tended to push against their ceilings. For some meats and dairy products, it was even necessary to roll back retail prices in an effort to "hold the line" against inflation. In such cases, to prevent a reduction in the floor prices received by farmers, meatpackers and creameries were paid a subsidy equal to the amount of the rollback on each unit sold.

---

[9]Rachel Maines, "Twenty-Nine Thirty-Seconds or Fight: Goal Conflict and Reinforcement in U.S. Cotton Policy, 1933–1946," in *The Sinews of War: Essays on the Economic History of World War II*, eds. Geofrey Mills and Hugh Rockoff (Ames: Iowa State University Press, 1993).

Perspective 25.1

Rosie the Riveter

One of the most dramatic developments during the war was the change in the role of women in the labor force. Some 200,000 women entered the military services. Mainly they served in the Women's Army Corps (WAC) and Women Accepted for Volunteer Emergency Services (WAVES), with smaller numbers in the Marine Corps, Coast Guard, and the Women's Auxiliary Ferrying Service. Women also entered the civilian labor force in large numbers. Many entered jobs that women had filled before the war, but many others, as symbolized by "Rosie the Riveter," entered jobs traditionally filled by men. Women became toolmakers, crane operators, lumberjacks, and stevedores. About 14 percent of the women who had been out of the paid labor force before Pearl Harbor went to work.[a]

High wages and a desire to serve their country encouraged women to take jobs. Government propaganda urged women to work in industry and to help supply the weapons needed to defeat the Axis. This propaganda also encouraged women to think of these jobs as temporary, to be turned back to returning soldiers after the war was over.

Women's participation in the labor force had seen a long-term upward trend throughout the twentieth century, but the war decade stands out as a period of especially rapid growth. In 1940, only 13.8 percent of married women participated in the paid labor force. In 1950, that figure stood at 21.6 percent, an increase in the participation rate of 5.65 percent per year, a higher rate of increase than in any other decade. This was partly the result of changes in attitudes brought about by the war. Women who went to work temporarily (or so they or others may have thought) developed a taste for working in the paid labor force, as well as useful skills, which encouraged them to remain in the labor force after the war was over. Some employers, moreover, after seeing women performing well in jobs traditionally reserved for men, may have revised their ideas about the productivity of working women.

© H. ARMSTRONG ROBERTS

"Debbie the Driller" helped keep production lines moving during the war.

We should not jump to the conclusion that all of the changes that occurred during the war or in subsequent decades were the result of women working in war production plants. Recent research by Claudia Goldin has shown that fundamental changes in the labor market were even more important than the changes in attitudes brought about by the war.[b]

---

[a]Surprisingly, about 34 percent of the women who had been working prior to Pearl Harbor left the labor force during the war. Increased wages earned by husbands or other family members, and a decline in the availability of household workers explain this phenomenon.

[b]Claudia D. Goldin, "The Role of World War II in the Rise of Women's Employment," *American Economic Review* 81 (1991): 741–756.

Perspective 25.1

Rosie the Riveter, continued

Investigating a sample of women workers over the war decade, Goldin found that more than half of the Rosies who had entered the paid labor force between 1940 and 1944 (the peak year) had dropped out by 1950. Many lost their jobs as a result of seniority rules and social pressures that favored returning servicemen. Others chose to leave because economic circumstances permitted them to do so.

Although many of the Rosies left the labor force after the war ended, many other women decided to enter in the late 1940s. Overall, Goldin found that about half of the women who entered the labor force between 1940 and 1950 were Rosies who had entered during the war and continued to work afterward, and about half were women who had not worked during the war but who had entered the labor force between the end of the war and 1950.

What factors brought women into the labor force in the immediate postwar years? One was the growing demand for women workers. Full employment meant more demand for all types of labor, and the clerical sector, which employed many women, was growing especially rapidly.

Table 25.5 shows the increase in jobs held by women between 1940 and 1950.The importance of clerical and sales jobs, which accounted for 47 percent of the increase, is evident.

Increased education also helped fit women for more jobs. The supply of younger unmarried women was shrinking as a result of low birthrates of the 1930s, and the supply of younger married women was also declining due to the increase in family formation during the postwar period.

These changes opened the market for older married women. By 1950, these fundamental forces had pushed the labor force participation of women, and especially that of older married women, above the wartime peak.

TABLE 25.5 Jobs Held by Women in 1940 and 1950 (in thousands)

OCCUPATION	1940	1950	INCREASE	PERCENTAGE OF TOTAL INCREASE
Professional, technical	1,608	2,007	399%	8.25%
Managers, officials, proprietors	414	700	286	5.91
Clerical	2,700	4,502	1,802	37.26
Sales	925	1,418	493	10.19
Manual	2,720	3,685	965	19.95
Craftswomen, forewomen	135	253	118	2.44
Operatives	2,452	3,287	835	17.27
Laborers	133	145	12	0.25
Service workers	3,699	3,532	–167	–3.45
Farm workers	508	601	93	1.92

Source: Historical Statistics *(Washington, D.C.: Government Printing Office, 1975), 132.*

The war enabled the CCC to unload heavy inventories that had built up between 1939 and 1941. From 1944 to 1946, loans extended by the CCC were small, although egg purchases became so great in 1944 as to cause embarrassment. Foreign demand through the United Nations Relief and Rehabilitation Administration and military governments and an unexpectedly high domestic demand led to highly favorable postwar prices and lightened CCC loan and purchase commitments. Indeed, contrary to the predictions of many experts, the demand for food, feed, and fiber was exceptionally high after the war. The removal of price controls in the summer of 1946 permitted all prices to shoot up, but the rise in agricultural prices was steeper than the price rise in other areas. Most production restrictions on crops were canceled before or during World War II, and by the spring of 1948, only tobacco and potatoes were still controlled.

DEMOBILIZATION AND RECONVERSION

Will the Depression Return?

The Great Depression was widely expected to return once the war was over. After all, it seemed as if the enormous level of government spending during the war was the only thing that had gotten the country out of the depression; cut spending and the economy would sink back into depression. Many, perhaps most, economists agreed with this analysis. Economists and policymakers therefore pressed for a commitment by the government to maintain the high level of employment after the war. The result was the Employment Act of 1946.

The federal government's responsibility was to "promote maximum employment, production and purchasing power." The adjective *maximum* was purposely ambiguous, but the entire statement was generally understood to mean that the government would act quickly to shore up the economy if a severe recession threatened. The Council of Economic Advisers, with an adequate professional staff, was added to the Executive Office of the President. The president, assisted by the council, was directed to submit to Congress at least annually a report on current economic conditions, with recommendations for legislative action. The statute further provided that the House and the Senate were to form a standing Joint Economic Committee, which would study the report of the president and the Council of Economic Advisers, hold hearings, and report, in turn, to Congress. Although no "investment fund" was provided, a watchdog agency was established to keep Congress and the president systematically informed of economic change. A compromise piece of legislation, the act acknowledged the government's role in maintaining full employment but did not say how the government would prevent depressions.

The expected depression did not materialize. During the war, people had accumulated large stores of financial assets, especially money and government bonds. They did so partly because they could not buy consumer durables during the war and partly because they were saving for the bad times they thought lay ahead. Once the war was over, these savings created a surge in demand that contributed to a postwar rise in prices and to the reintegration of workers from the armed forces and from defense industries into the peacetime labor force.

The GI Bill of Rights

Government policy also played a role in smoothing the transition of servicemen into the workforce. The so-called GI Bill of Rights provided returning servicemen a number of benefits. This legislation delayed the reentry of many former servicemen into the labor force and provided them with improved skills.

Planning for veterans started in a serious way when President Roosevelt appointed the Postwar Manpower Committee, which issued a report in June 1943 recommending a generous package of benefits for veterans, Pushed by the Veterans of Foreign Wars and the

American Legion, Congress was also inclined to be generous for a number of reasons beyond the simple gratitude that Americans felt toward the people who had sacrificed to defend them. There was a general perception that demobilization had gone badly after World War I and that veterans had not been treated well. There were also the examples of generous veterans' packages emphasizing education that had been provided by Wisconsin after World War I and by Canada during World War II. Finally, there was the fear that the depression would return after the war and that without an adequate package of veterans benefits, returning servicemen and -women would go straight from "the battle lines to the bread lines." The resulting legislation, the Servicemen's Readjustment Act of 1943, has generally been known since by its popular name: the GI Bill of Rights. The GI Bill provided a wide range of benefits, including mustering-out pay; health care; assistance with job placement; low-interest loans to buy a home, farm, or business; unemployment benefits; reemployment rights; employment preferences; and educational benefits.

The GI Bill's educational provisions have been considered the most revolutionary of the legislation. Among other educational benefits, the GI Bill provided money for tuition, fees, and living expenses for veterans enrolling in colleges and universities. Partly as a result of the GI Bill, enrollment in higher education boomed after the war. The peak year in terms of the influence of the original GI Bill was 1947, when about 1.7 million veterans were enrolled, making up 71 percent of the student body. (The Vietnam Era peak in 1977 was about 2.0 million.) The GI Bill cannot be given all the credit for increasing the percentage of young Americans attending colleges and universities in the postwar period. Enrollment continued to grow, and the percentage of young people attending colleges and universities continued to rise, long after the veterans of World War II had moved on. The emphasis on higher education was a natural outgrowth of the high school movement that had occurred earlier in the century. The GI bill did play a role in jump-starting the postwar expansion of higher education, however. It demonstrated that Americans from all sorts of backgrounds could succeed on the college campus. It also transformed many colleges and universities. Rutgers, now the State University of New Jersey, for example, had to hire professors and learn to "mass-produce" education, to accommodate the veterans.

Under the GI Bill, the veteran chose the school he or she wished to attend, and the school decided whether to admit the veteran. Schools had to be accredited, but the bill specifically prohibited the government from exercising any direct control over the admissions process or other aspects of education. It was, in short, a "voucher" system. Contemporary advocates of educational vouchers have cited the success of the GI Bill as evidence for the soundness of educational vouchers. It is undoubtedly a positive example. The situation, of course, was unusual because the veterans were an unusually mature population: This example can't be ignored, but it can't by itself make the case for educational vouchers.

Birth of the Consumer Society

The postwar surge in demand ushered in a new consumer-oriented society that to some represented the fulfillment of the American dream and to others represented the creation of an unthinking, materialistic culture. Builders such as Levitt and Sons utilized mass-production techniques developed during the war to provide housing for war workers, adapting them to mass-produce suburban homes, even creating entire new communities such as Levittown, New York. Aided by advances from the Federal Housing Administration and the Veterans Administration, the Levitts offered attractive terms to returning servicemen and other buyers.

Balladeer Malvina Reynolds expressed the feelings of many critics of the new "tract" housing in a popular folksong:

Little Boxes on the hillside, little boxes made of ticky tacky,
Little Boxes on the hillside, little boxes all the same.
There's a green one and a pink one and a blue one and a yellow one,
And they're all made of ticky tacky and they all look just the same.[10]

Defenders of the new construction techniques argued that by achieving the economies of long production runs, builders were able to lower the unit cost of housing and permit people to buy homes who could not otherwise afford them. No one, however, was able to put that into an enduring folksong. These years witnessed the beginning of the "baby boom" as birthrates surged in the late 1940s and 1950s. The image of a baby boom following shortly after the reuniting of soldiers with their loved ones is romantic and undoubtedly valid in many individual cases, but the baby boom was a much broader phenomenon that continued into and peaked in the late 1950s.

The war, in short, ushered in a period in which millions of Americans could take part for the first time in a middle-class lifestyle. Government programs for veterans such as the GI bill helped, but the key factor was the thing that did not happen—a return to the depressed economic conditions of the 1930s.

Selected References and Suggested Readings

Barro, Robert J. "The Neoclassical Approach to Fiscal Policy." In *Modern Business Cycle Theory*, ed. Robert J. Barro. Cambridge, Mass.: Harvard University Press, 1989, 178–235.

Blum, John Morton. *V was for Victory: Politics and American Culture during World War II.* New York: Harcourt Brace Jovanovich, 1977.

Bowles, Chester. *Promises to Keep.* New York: Harper & Row, 1971.

Broom, Leonard, and Ruth Reimer. *Removal and Return: The Socio-economic Effects of the War on Japanese-Americans.* Berkeley: University of California Press, 1949.

Buchanan, A. Russell. *Black Americans in World War II.* Santa Barbara, Calif.: Clio, 1977.

Cain, Louis, and George Neumann. "Planning for Peace: The Surplus Property Act of 1944." *Journal of Economic History* 41 (March 1981): 129–135.

Caruana, Leonard, and Hugh Rockoff. "A Wolfram in Sheep's Clothing: Economic Warfare in Spain, 1940–1944." *Journal of Economic History* 63 (March 2003): 100–126.

Catton, Bruce. *War Lords of Washington.* Washington, D.C.: Government Printing Office, 1948.

Chandler, Lester Vernon. *Inflation in the United States, 1940–1948.* New York: Harper, 1951.

Clinard, Marshall B. *The Black Market: A Study of White Collar Crime.* New York: Rinehart, 1952.

Collins, William J. "African-American Economic Mobility in the 1940s: A Portrait from the Palmer Survey." *Journal of Economic History* 60 (September 2000): 756–781.

———. "Race, Roosevelt and Wartime Production: Fair Employment in World War II Labor Markets." *American Economic Review* 91 (March 2001): 272–286.

Conrat, Maisie, and Richard Conrat. *Executive Order 9066: The Internment of 110,000 Japanese- Americans.* San Francisco: California Historical Society, 1972.

Eiler, Keith E. *Mobilizing America: Robert P. Patterson and the War Effort, 1940–1945.* Ithaca, N.Y.: Cornell University Press, 1997.

The Dwight D. Eisenhower Library and Museum. **http://www.eisenhower.utexas.edu**.

[10]Malvina Reynolds, "Little Boxes," in *The Ballad of America: The History of the United States in Song and Story*, ed. John Anthony Scott (Carbondale: Southern Illinois University Press, 1983), 378–380.

Friedman, Milton. "Price, Income and Monetary Changes in Three Wartime Periods." *American Economic Review* (May 1952): 612–625.

Friedman, Milton, and Anna J. Schwartz. *A Monetary History of the United States, 1867–1960.* Princeton, N.J.: Princeton University Press, 1963, chapter 10.

Galbraith, John Kenneth. *A Theory of Price Control.* Cambridge, Mass.: Harvard University Press, 1952.

———. *A Life in Our Times*. Boston: Houghton Mifflin, 1981.

Gemery, Henry A., and Jan S. Hogendorn. "The Microeconomic Bases of Short-Run Learning Curves: Destroyer Production in World War II." In *The Sinews of War: Essays on the Economic History of World War II*, eds. Geofrey Mills and Hugh Rockoff. Ames: Iowa State University Press, 1993.

Glenn, Norval D. "Changes in the American Occupational Structure and Occupational Gains of Negroes during the 1940's." *Social Forces* 41 (1962): 188–195.

Goldin, Claudia D. "The Role of World War II in the Rise of Women's Employment." *American Economic Review* 81 (1991): 741–756.

Goldin, Claudia, and Robert A. Margo. "The Great Compression: The Wage Structure in the United States at Mid-century." *Quarterly Journal of Economics* 107 (February 1992): 1–34.

Gordon, David L., and Royden Dangerfield. *The Hidden Weapon: The Story of Economic Warfare*. New York: Harper, 1947.

Gordon, Robert J. "45 Billion of U.S. Private Investment Has Been Mislaid." *American Economic Review* 59 (June 1969): 221–238.

Government Publications from World War II. **http://www2.smu.edu/cul/ww2/title.htm**.

Harrison, Mark, ed. *The Economics of World War II: Six Great Powers in International Comparison*. Cambridge, England: Cambridge University Press, 1998.

Higgs, Robert. *Crisis and Leviathan: Critical Issues in the Emergence of the Mixed Economy*. New York: Oxford University Press, 1986.

———. "Wartime Prosperity. A Reassessment of the U.S. Economy in the 1940s." *Journal of Economic History* 52 (1992): 41–60.

———. "Private Profit, Public Risk: Institutional Antecedents of the Modern Military Procurement System in the Rearmament Program 1940–1941." In *The Sinews of War: Essays on the Economic History of World War II*, eds. Geofrey Mills and Hugh Rockoff. Ames: Iowa State University Press, 1993.

Hoopes, Roy. *Americans Remember: The Homefront: An Oral Narrative*. New York: Hawthorne, 1977.

Janeway, Eliot. *The Struggle for Survival: A Chronicle of Economic Mobilization in World War II*. New Haven, Conn.: Yale University Press, 1951.

Kuznets, Simon. "National Product War and Prewar." New York: National Bureau of Economic Research, Occasional Paper 17, 1944.

Lane, Frederick C. *Ships for Victory: A History of Shipbuilding under the U.S. Maritime Commission in World War II*. Baltimore: Johns Hopkins University Press, 1951.

Maines, Rachel. "Twenty-Nine Thirty-Seconds or Fight: Goal Conflict and Reinforcement in the U.S. Cotton Policy, 1933–1946." In *The Sinews of War: Essays on the Economic History of World War II*, eds. Geofrey Mills and Hugh Rockoff. Ames: Iowa State University Press, 1993.

Mills, Geofrey, and Hugh Rockoff, eds. *The Sinews of War: Essays on the Economic History of World War II*. Ames: Iowa State University Press, 1993.

Millward, Alan S. *War, Economy and Society, 1939–1945*. Berkeley: University of California Press, 1977.

National Archives and Records Administration exhibit "A People at War." **http://www.nara.gov/exhall/people/people.html**.

National Historic Chemical Landmarks Program of the American Chemical Society, The United States Synthetic Rubber Program, 1939–1945 **http://www.acs.org/landmarks/rubber**.

Numerous documents related to the war maintained by The Avalon Project at the Yale Law School. **http://www.yale.edu/lawweb/avalon/avalon.htm**.

Nelson, Donald M. *Arsenal of Democracy: The Story of American War Production.* New York: Harcourt Brace, 1946.

Novick, D., M. Ashen, and W. C. Truppner, *Wartime Production Controls.* New York: Columbia University Press, 1949.

Overy, Richard J. *Why the Allies Won.* London: Jonathan Cape, 1995.

Polenberg, Richard, ed. *America at War: The Homefront, 1941–1945.* Princeton, N.J.: Princeton University Press, 1968.

Rockoff, Hugh. "The Response of the Giant Corporations to Wage and Price Controls in World War II." *Journal of Economic History* 41 (March 1981): 123–128.

———. *Drastic Measures: A History of Wage and Price Controls in the United States.* New York: Cambridge University Press, 1984.

Rupp, Leila J. *Mobilizing Women for War: German and American Propaganda, 1939–1945.* Princeton, N.J.: Princeton University Press, 1978.

Smith, T. Lynn. "The Redistribution of the Negro Population of the United States, 1910–1960." *Journal of Negro History* 51 (1966): 257–263.

Terkel, Studs. *The Good War: An Oral History of World War Two.* New York: Pantheon, 1984.

U.S. Bureau of the Budget, War Records Section. *The United States at War: The Development and Administration of the War Program by the Federal Government.* Washington, D.C.: Government Printing Office, 1946.

University of San Diego Department of History, time line of World War II, **http://history.sandiego.edu/gen/WW2Timeline/start.html**.

Vatter, Harold G. *The U.S. Economy in World War II.* New York: Columbia University Press, 1985.

Wilcox, Walter W. *The Farmer in the Second World War.* Ames: Iowa State College Press, 1947.

Young, Roland. *Congressional Politics in the Second World War.* New York: Columbia University Press, 1956.

Part Five

The Postwar Era: 1946 to the Present

ECONOMIC AND HISTORICAL PERSPECTIVES
1946 TO THE PRESENT

1. The depression that was widely expected after World War II failed to materialize. Economists credited Keynesian fiscal policy with the maintenance of high employment. For the first time in the nation's history, however, inflation became a chronic peacetime problem.
2. The role of the federal government in the economy continued to expand, especially during the first three decades of the postwar era. In 1949, federal spending amounted to 15 percent of GNP; in 1993, it amounted to 22 percent.
3. The structure of the economy changed dramatically in the postwar era: manufacturing and agriculture declined relative to the service sector.
4. In the 1960s, a civil rights revolution shook the nation. Efforts were made through the government, and through direct action, to secure greater economic progress for women, African Americans, and other disadvantaged groups.
5. The pace of economic growth was the subject of only minor complaints in the first two decades after the war; but in the 1970s, concern mounted as productivity growth slowed and troubling signs of social deterioration emerged.
6. In the late 1970s and early 1980s, a reaction to government involvement in the economy set in. The airlines, the banks, and other sectors were deregulated; and marginal tax rates were cut. In 1996, an attempt was made to reform the welfare system.

Chapter Twenty-Six

THE CHANGING ROLE OF THE U.S. GOVERNMENT

Chapter Theme

One of the most profound changes in the American economy in the first three decades after World War II was the continued growth in the size and influence of government at all levels, especially at the federal level. Government grew not only in dollars spent but also in power to control the private sector through legal regulations and bureaucratic decisions. Liberal economists thought that this was all to the good. The unstable free market economy of the past had been replaced by the "modern mixed economy" that combined the flexibility of markets and the stability of government controls. This growth was sustained until the late 1970s, when growing dissatisfaction with big government, as well as the growing menace of inflation, led to successful calls by conservatives for reduced spending and deregulation. This chapter discusses in broad terms the dimensions of the growth in government, the causes, and the eventual disillusionment.

Economic Reasoning Proposition

THE SIZE OF GOVERNMENT IN THE POSTWAR ERA

As Economic Reasoning Proposition 5 stresses, opinions about important historical issues such as the growth of the federal government must be based on evidence. Here we explore three measures of the growth of the federal government: (1) total federal spending relative to GDP, (2) federal purchases of goods and services relative to GDP, and (3) federal employment relative to the total labor force. Looking at all three is necessary to provide a nuanced answer to the question of how much government grew in the postwar era.

Federal Spending

Total spending by the federal government relative gross domestic product (GDP) is shown in Figure 26.1. Evidently, federal spending grew relative to the size of the economy until 1980, when it reached one-fifth of GDP. This is the most commonly used measure of the size of government, but it tells only part of the story. In the 1980s, however, this ratio leveled off, and in the 1990s it declined. This is the most commonly used measure of the size of government, but it tells only part of the story.

Government spending includes not only purchases of goods and services (such as paper clips, tanks, dams, and the salaries of Supreme Court justices and army privates) but also transfer payments (such as welfare expenditures and subsidies for state and local

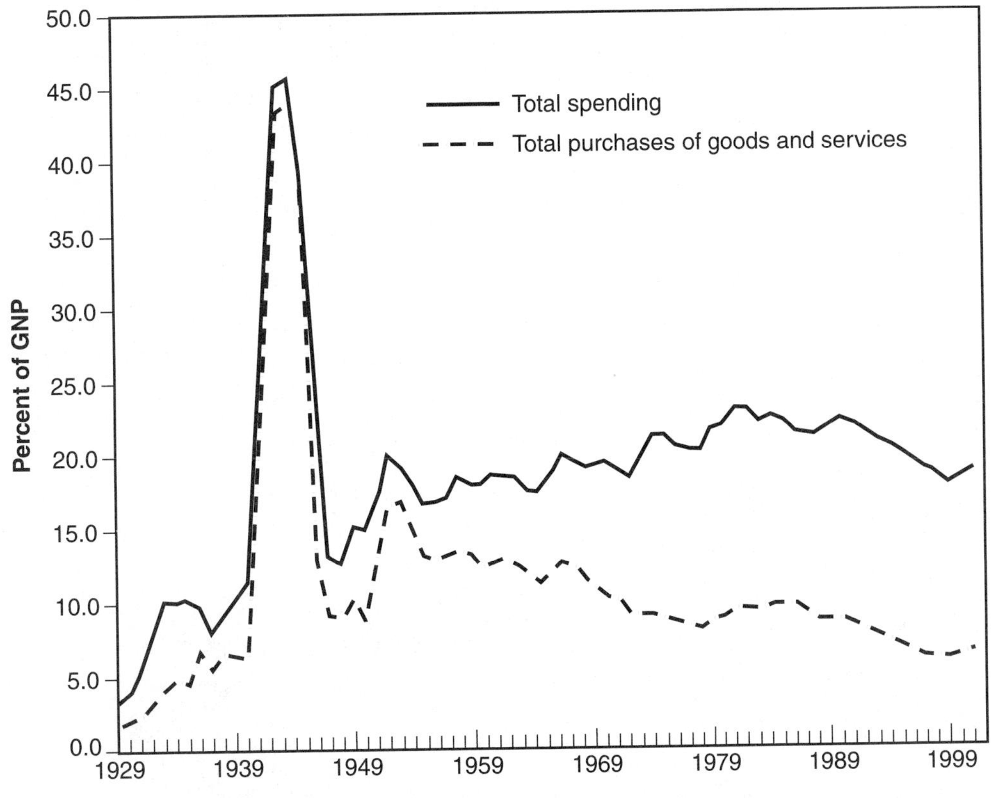

FIGURE 26.1 Two Measures of the Size of the Federal Government

Source: Historical Statistics of the United States *(1976) and various issues of the* Economic Report of the President.

governments). The dotted line in Figure 26.1 excludes transfer payments and reflects only purchases of goods and services relative to GDP. This measure of the size of the federal government generally trended downward after the Korean War. The only noticeable interruptions came during the Vietnam War and during the military build-up pushed by President Ronald Reagan. Because considerable economic activity takes place at the state and local levels, it is important to compare the trends at these levels with the trends at the federal level. As the upper panel of Table 26.1 on page 522 indicates, purchases of goods and services at the state and local levels (mostly for police, fire, and education) exceeded purchases of goods and services at the federal level in recent decades. When we look at the trend in total government spending at all levels relative to GDP in the lower panel (thus adding transfers to purchases of goods and services), we see that the ratio increased until about 1980 but then leveled off.

Transfer payments, in the first instance, do not use up GDP. People on welfare can buy more goods and services, but people who pay more taxes buy less. Indeed, because most of us receive subsidies and pay taxes, there is really no upper limit to the ratio of government spending to GDP; it could exceed 100 percent. In any one year, the government could tax and transfer the same dollar many times over. Each time the government imposes a tax, however, it affects incentives to work and invest, and those incentives, in turn, affect GDP. People who receive as much in government subsidies as they pay in taxes nevertheless have an incentive to reduce their taxes. If they do so by working less hard or by investing their capital in less productive uses, the total product of the economy will be reduced. (Never forget Economic Reasoning Proposition 3; incentives matter, even for a moment!)

TABLE 26.1 Spending at All Government Levels

YEAR	FEDERAL	STATE AND LOCAL	TOTAL
	PURCHASE OF GOODS AND SERVICES RELATIVE TO GDP		
1940	6.3%	8.6%	14.9%
1950	8.8	7.1	15.9
1960	12.5	9.1	21.6
1970	11.2	11.6	22.8
1980	8.8	11.6	20.4
1990	8.8	11.6	20.4
2001	6.2	12.2	18.4
	TOTAL SPENDING RELATIVE TO GDP		
1940	9.9%	11.1%	20.2%
1950	15.2	9.5	23.9
1960	18.4	11.6	28.7
1970	20.0	14.2	32.0
1980	20.6	11.0	29.1
1990	21.2	11.4	30.6
2001	19.2	12.8	29.3

Note: Grants from the federal government to state and local governments are deducted from the grand total to avoid double counting.

Sources: Historical Statistics of the United States Colonial Times to 1970 *(Washington D.C.: 1975), series Y533, Y590, Y671, and the* Economic Report of the President, *various years. See http://www.access.gpo.gov/eop.*

Most economists agree with this analysis of the direction of the effects of tax and transfer policies, but one of the major controversies of the postwar period concerns the magnitude of these effects. Some experts argued that the disincentive effects were not important and pointed out that total taxes in the United States, measured as a fraction of GDP, appeared relatively low compared with other developed countries, where work effort and savings seem to be satisfactory. For example, one comparison showed that total taxes at all levels of government in the United States in 1989 were 30.1 percent of GDP. This was about the same as in Australia (also 30.1 percent), Japan (30.6 percent), and Switzerland (31.8 percent), but it was lower than in Canada (35.1 percent), West Germany (38.1 percent), and France (43.8 percent).[1] Such comparisons are never conclusive, however, because many other things are not held constant. Perhaps the most important point to be learned from such comparisons is simply that the trend toward big government was not unique to the United States. It was common to all developed nations.

Federal Employment

Another frequently used measure of the size of the federal government is the share of federal employment in total employment, shown in Figure 26.2, which plots the ratio of federal employees (excluding the military and the postal service) to the total civilian labor force. This series ratchets upward dramatically in the 1930s and again in the 1940s (largely because of the expansion of the Veterans Administration). The share of the federal labor force in the total labor force then fluctuated, falling after 1980. Recall that dynamic element in the growth of the federal government was transfer payments. This source of growth did not imply an equally large expansion of the federal bureaucracy.

[1] *Statistical Abstract of the United States: 1992* (Washington, D.C.: U.S. Bureau of the Census, 1992), 836.

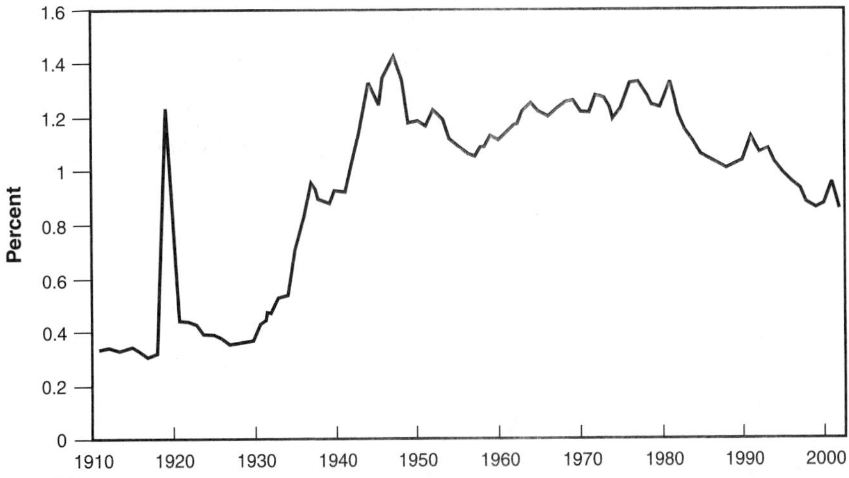

FIGURE 26.2 The Ratio of Federal Civilian Employment to the Total Labor Force, 1910–2001.

Note: From 1950 to 1980, the federal labor force grew slightly faster than the total labor force; but, since 1980, the federal labor force has grown less rapidly.

Source: The Statistical Abstract of the United States, *various issues.*

Winners and Losers in the Federal Budget

The big winners in the federal budget process between 1949 and 1989 were income security (social security, federal employee retirement and disability insurance, housing assistance, and so on), which grew at 11.6 percent per year between 1949 and 1989; education, which grew at 13.0 percent per year; and health (Medicare, health care services, health research, etc.), which grew at an astonishing 16.3 percent per year. During the same period, consumer prices rose about 4.2 percent per year, so all of these categories grew rapidly in real as well as nominal terms. Indeed, of all the major budget categories, only veterans' benefits and international affairs, which were high in 1949 due to the after-effects of the war, failed to grow faster than prices during the postwar period. The expansion of spending for income security, health, and education resulted from new programs designed (partly) to protect and expand the choices of the less well off.

Figure 26.3 provides a bird's-eye view of how budget priorities changed in the postwar period. It shows spending for defense, income security, and health as shares of the federal budget. Military spending increased primarily in three major buildups. The first was associated with the Korean War in the early 1950s, the second with the Vietnam War in the late 1960s, and the third with the Reagan administration's buildup in the 1980s. Expenditures on income security captured a larger share of the budget in the 1970s as eligibility for benefits was expanded. Spending on health, including Medicare and Medicaid, which was less than $1 billion in 1959, increased rapidly in the 1970s and 1980s as eligibility for various benefits expanded.[2]

In looking at Figure 26.3 on page 524, keep in mind that the total budget was expanding, so the long-term fall in the *share* of defense spending in the budget was not equivalent to a fall in real defense spending. In dollars of constant purchasing power (1982 dollars), defense spending fell from $166 billion in 1953 to $137 billion in 1960; then, after recovering to $204 billion in 1970, it fell to $152 billion in 1980, the eve of the Reagan military buildup. By 1991, real defense spending was up to $251 billion. These

[2]Although, as the late Senator Everett Dirksen of Illinois is credited with saying, "A billion here, a billion there, and pretty soon you are talking about real money."

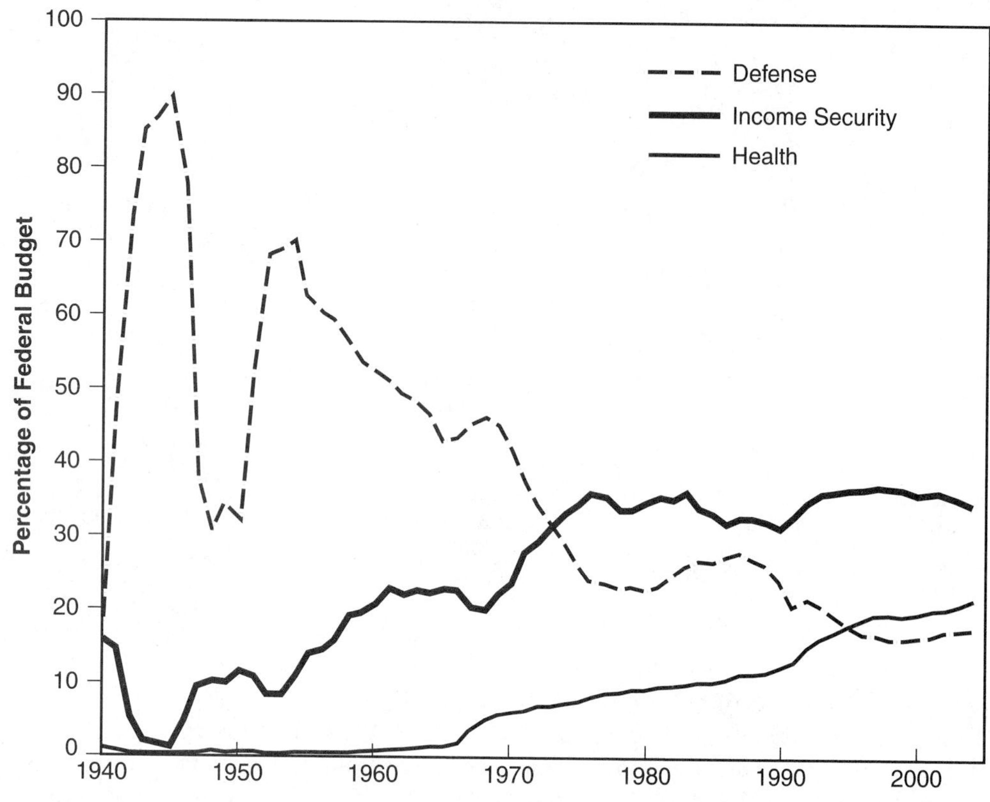

FIGURE 26.3 The Federal Budget, 1940–2004

Source: Economic Report of the President, *http://www.access.gpo.gov.*

enormous expenditures (in 1991, about 5.7 percent of GDP) were the legacy of the Cold War, America's ultimately successful attempt to contain communism.

What was the impact of the Cold War on the economy? The answer to this difficult question depends on which categories of spending had to be reduced to maintain a high level of defense spending. Did the decrease come in other kinds of government spending? Private consumption? Private investment? Careful studies by Michael Edelstein and Robert Higgs show that increases in defense spending came at the expense of private consumption rather than investment or nonmilitary government spending, suggesting that the long-term effects of defense spending on growth were small.[3]

THE LIBERAL ERA, 1945–1976: CONTINUED EXPANSION

What explains the growth of the federal government, especially transfers, in the first three decades after World War II? Changes in public attitudes about the appropriate role of government appear to have been the key factor.

In retrospect, we can divide the period after the war into two distinct ideological eras. No precise dividing line can be given. Nevertheless, it is clear that the period from the end of the war to, say, 1976 was a liberal era, one in which arguments to expand government received a sympathetic hearing from the general public, one in which even Republican presidents had to

[3]Robert Higgs, "The Cold War Economy: Opportunity Costs, Ideology, and the Politics of Crisis," *Explorations in Economic History* 31 (July 1994): 283–312; and Michael Edelstein, "What Price Cold War? Military Spending and Private Investment in the US, 1946–1979," *Cambridge Journal of Economics* 14 (1990): 421–437.

accommodate themselves to a dominant liberal ideology. Then, for a variety of reasons—the war in Vietnam, the slowing of economic growth, and the acceleration of inflation—sentiment turned toward the conservatives. Politicians, whether Democrats or Republicans, had to respond to the public's concern about the costs of expanding government.

During liberal era, Democrats pressed hard for an expansion of the welfare state and other New Deal reforms while conservatives fought a rear guard action, delaying the advance of the welfare state when they could and retreating to new positions when they could not. The first postwar president, Democrat Harry S. Truman, favored a major expansion of the New Deal. Truman's program, which he named the Fair Deal, called for a wide range of economic legislation, including repeal of the Taft-Hartley Act, increased Social Security benefits, a higher minimum wage, federal subsidies for housing, compulsory federal health insurance, and authority to build industrial plants to overcome "shortages."[4]

Some parts of his program, those that were extensions and modifications of existing programs, were enacted—Social Security benefits were extended, and the minimum wage was raised—but new programs were blocked by a congressional coalition of Republicans and southern Democrats. Special interest groups played an important role in lobbying Congress to oppose legislation they considered contrary to their interests. The American Medical Association, for example, lobbied vigorously against Truman's health insurance proposals, which they denounced as the forerunner of "socialized medicine."

The philosophy of Republican Dwight D. Eisenhower's administration generally opposed new initiatives in the economic sphere. The administration's motto, "less government in business and more business in government," summed up its philosophy, but existing programs around which a consensus had formed continued to expand. For example, Social Security benefits increased and extended to more workers, the minimum wage was raised from $0.75 to $1.00 per hour, more money was provided for housing, and a greatly expanded program of highway building was introduced: The replacement of America's congested single-lane highways with two-lane interstate "super highways."

The "Little New Deal"

The breakthrough in welfare legislation occurred during the presidencies of Democrats John F. Kennedy and Lyndon B. Johnson. Kennedy's New Frontier was similar to Truman's Fair Deal, but in many ways it did not go as far. Kennedy's narrow victory over Vice President Richard Nixon hardly seemed a mandate for radical change.

The program called for federal medical insurance for the elderly, aid to education, and more federal money for housing and "urban renewal." As in previous administrations, existing programs were expanded. Social Security benefits were increased, the minimum wage was raised from $1.00 to $1.25 (over a four-year period) and was made applicable to more workers, and, as promised, more money was made available for federal housing projects.

There were also new initiatives. Concern over poverty in Appalachia and other depressed areas led to the Area Redevelopment Act, which provided low-cost loans for businesses and money for training workers. Other legislation provided aid for medical education, college construction projects, and relief for areas adversely affected by federal projects. Kennedy's proposals for medical care for the aged and federal aid for public schools were defeated, however.

The civil rights movement, moreover, was drawing attention to the plight of African Americans and other disadvantaged groups. On college campuses, students were drawn to

---

[4]The tradition is for each administration to sum up its legislative programs in a single grand phrase. Franklin Roosevelt gave us the New Deal; Harry S. Truman, the Fair Deal; Dwight D. Eisenhower, the Great Crusade; John F. Kennedy, the New Frontier; and Lyndon B. Johnson, the Great Society. "Roosevelt gave us the New Deal, Truman gave us the Fair Deal, but Johnson gave us the Ordeal." William Morris and Mary Morris, *Morris Dictionary of Word and Phrase Origins* (New York: Harper & Row, 1971), 397.

Kennedy's faith in big government. For a time it seemed that Joseph Schumpeter's prediction that capitalism would be undermined by the children of the bourgeoisie, who would lose faith in the system that had created the basis for their own high standard of living, had at last begun to come true.[5]

When Lyndon B. Johnson took office in 1963 after the assassination of President Kennedy, he proclaimed his intention of fighting a "War on Poverty." The result was the Economic Opportunity Act of 1964, which established training camps in rural and urban areas, provided grants for farmers and small businesses, and helped communities fund their own antipoverty programs. In 1964, President Johnson was reelected by a large majority; this mandate, and Johnson's long experience in Washington, helped him in pushing for the programs that then were seen as the basis for the "Great Society."

A wide range of important legislation followed. Indeed, there had been nothing like it since the New Deal, and in some respects, it was even more radical. A medical care program (Medicare) for those aged 65 or over was at last added to Social Security. A billion dollars was voted for Appalachia to improve land and highways and to provide health centers. A Department of Housing and Urban Development was created, and its head was made a cabinet-level secretary. A new housing act provided, among other things, for federal rent subsidies for the poor, a new departure in welfare legislation. The minimum wage, a familiar part of liberal Democratic programs, was raised and extended to cover farm laborers, workers in small retail shops, and hospital workers. A mass transportation act provided money to improve rail transportation, and the Department of Transportation, the twelfth cabinet-level department, was created. These and other reforms substantially expanded the role of government in American life.

The New Regulation

During the nineteenth century, and with a few exceptions until World War II, federal regulation was designed to deal with specific problems in specific industries. The Interstate Commerce Commission was concerned mostly with regulation of prices charged by railroads, trucks, and water carriers; the Federal Reserve system regulated banks; and so on. In the postwar period, however, agencies were set up with the power to regulate a broad range of industries and in relation to a broad array of problems. For example, in 1970, Congress established the Occupational Safety and Health Administration to set standards for working conditions throughout the workplace. Presidential candidate Ronald Reagan later cited this agency's penchant for issuing irritating (to business) regulations as a prime example of how "government is the problem."

One of the most dramatic developments of the postwar period was the passage of major pieces of legislation designed to protect the consumer from the purchase of dangerous or otherwise unsatisfactory goods and services. Consumer protection is by no means unique to the postwar period. As early as 1838, Congress created the Steamboat Inspection Service to check the safety of steamboats, but as Table 26.2 makes clear, the rate of passage of such legislation accelerated in the postwar period.

The Steamboat Inspection Service was enacted after a series of explosions killed many passengers and crew. The Food, Drug, and Cosmetic Act of 1938 followed the Elixir Sulfonamide tragedy. The form in which this drug was sold proved to be toxic and left more than 100 dead, many of them children. But the producer was held, under existing law, to be guilty of no more than mislabeling his product.

The Kefauver-Harris amendments to the Food, Drug, and Cosmetic Act (1962) followed in the wake of the thalidomide tragedy. In Europe this drug produced severe birth defects when given to pregnant women. Similar outcomes were largely avoided in the

[5]Joseph Schumpeter, *Capitalism, Socialism, and Democracy,* 3d ed. (New York: Harper & Row, 1950), 415–424.

TABLE 26.2 Major Consumer Safety Laws of the United States, 1900–1980

YEAR	LAW	MAIN PROVISIONS
1906	Food and Drug Act	Prohibits misbranding and adulteration of foods and drugs. Requires listing of medicine ingredients on product labels.
1906	Meat Inspection Act	Provides for federal inspection of slaughtering, packaging, and canning plants that ship meat interstate.
1938	Food, Drug, and Cosmetic Act	Defines as "adulterated" any food or drug that contains a substance unsafe for human use. Requires application for introduction of new drugs supported by tests of safety.
1938	Wheeler-Lea Amendment to Federal Trade Commission Act (1914)	Extends prohibitions of FTC Act to "unfair or deceptive acts or practices."
1953	Flammable Fabrics Act	Prohibits manufacture, import, or sale of products so "flammable as to be dangerous when worn by individuals."
1958	Food Additives Amendment to Food, Drug, and Cosmetic Act (1938)	Prohibits use of food additives shown to cause cancer in humans or animals.
1960	Hazardous Substances Labeling Act	Requires labeling of hazardous household substances.
1962	Kefauver-Harris Amendments to Food, Drug, and Cosmetic Act (1938)	Requires additional tests of both safety and efficacy for new drugs.
1965	Cigarette Labeling and Advertising Act	Requires use of health warnings on cigarette packages and in advertising.
1966	Fair Packaging and Labeling Act	Requires listing of product contents and manufacturer.
1966	Child Protection Act (Amendment to Hazardous Substances Labeling Act of 1960)	Prohibits sale of hazardous toys and other items used by children.
1966	National Traffic and Motor Vehicle Safety Act	Provides for establishment of safety standards for vehicles and parts, and for vehicle recalls.
1967	Amendments to the Flammable Fabrics Act (1953)	Extends federal authority to establish safety standards for fabrics, including "household" products.
1970	Public Health Cigarette Smoking Act	Prohibits broadcast advertising of cigarettes.
1970	Poison Prevention Packaging Act	Provides for "child-resistant" packaging of hazardous substances.
1972	Consumer Product Safety Act	Establishes the Consumer Product Safety Commission, with authority to set safety standards for consumer products and to ban products that present undue risk.
1977	Saccharin Study and Labeling Act	Requires use of health warnings on products containing saccharin; postpones saccharin ban.
1980	Comperehensive Environmental Response Compensation and Liability (Superfund) Act	Provides funds for cleaning up toxic waste sites.

United States, mainly because of the resolute behavior of one public official, Dr. Frances Kelsey of the Food and Drug Administration, who had resisted enormous pressure to license the drug. It was believed that without additional legal safeguards, future situations might emerge in which the absence of such a resolute regulator would lead to tragedy.

The Flammable Fabrics Act of 1953 is another example. This act also followed in the wake of a number of accidents. The industry, it should be noted, did not resist this legislation. By being able to show that their fabrics met federal safety standards, manufacturers hoped to increase demand and provide a basis for defense in lawsuits.

Tragic events, however, are not the whole story. The passage of consumer protection legislation was also related to swings in public opinion between liberal and conservative views. Notice in Table 26.2 that eight major pieces of consumer-protection legislation were passed between 1965 and 1972, including the Fair Packaging and Labeling Act, the National Traffic and Motor Vehicle Safety Act, and the Consumer Product Safety Act. This burst of legislative activity was related not so much to individual tragedies as to a general lack of faith in the market. Later, however, the liberal faith in government's ability to improve on the outcome of market forces was placed on the defensive. The "Reagan Revolution" consistently opposed extensions of federal authority, and no major pieces of consumer legislation were passed during the administrations of Ronald Reagan or George Bush. More recently, during the first administration of Bill Clinton, however, a massive overhaul of the health care system was planned, but despite the administration's backing, the overhaul failed to achieve the level of public support needed to overcome opposition to it.

Weighing the costs and benefits of regulatory legislation is a difficult task, and economists are far from agreement even on individual regulations, let alone the whole trend. The benefits of regulation are relatively easy to see: consumers may be protected from consuming a dangerous food, using a dangerous drug, or driving a dangerous car, but regulation also has costs: It may raise prices by requiring expensive additions to a product or by requiring a firm to amass evidence that its product is safe. Regulation may also have the effect of limiting competition by preventing price competition or stifling innovation by raising the costs of introducing new products. It has been contended, for example, that regulation of the drug industry has limited the number of new drugs being brought to market.[6]

THE CONSERVATIVE ERA: 1976–2000

The 1960s were exciting times. To liberals it seemed that at last the promise of the New Deal would be realized, that a rapidly growing economy would provide the resources to solve the problems of poverty and inequality of opportunity. The 1960s were especially exciting times for liberal economists: the economy would be managed according to Keynesian full-employment policies. Even though new welfare and regulatory legislation would continue to be passed for the remainder of the decade and into the early 1970s, there were signs, as early as 1966, that the "Little New Deal" was losing momentum.

After Jimmy Carter's election in 1976, new federal initiatives would be few and far between. The underlying reasons were the disillusionment with government produced by the long and futile war in Vietnam, the failure of some liberal programs to deliver benefits consistent with optimistic forecasts, and the deterioration in the performance of the economy. Productivity growth slowed, inflation accelerated, and unemployment remained at high levels. The belief that the economy could easily generate a large surplus with which the government could do good works now appeared naïve.

Deregulation

In previous years, the 1976 election of Democrat Jimmy Carter would have signaled a new round of New Deal legislation, but the Carter administration, although it supported many traditional Democratic programs, emphasized economy and efficiency in government and, surprisingly, deregulation in a number of areas of the economy. The administration argued

---

[6]See Peter Asch, *Consumer Safety Regulation: Putting a Price on Life and Limb* (New York: Oxford University Press, 1988), chapter 7, for a fair-minded review of the literature on this question.

that these regulations were no longer needed or that the original intent of the legislation had been subverted by the very groups that the legislation was intended to control.

Academic circles had long recognized that regulatory agencies were often "captured" by a regulated industry. The public would become aroused by the revelation of an abuse in a certain industry and a regulatory agency would be created, staffed initially by people responsive to the public interest or at least highly critical of the industry. Eventually, however, public attention would turn to other problems, and only the regulated industry itself would maintain an interest in who was appointed to the agency and what decisions it rendered. The result, naturally enough, would be that in the long run, people sympathetic to the regulated industry would be appointed to the regulatory agency, and rulings would be made in the interest of the industry rather that of the public. Partly as a result of such ideas, President Carter supported decontrol of natural gas prices and deregulation of the airlines, trucking, railroads, and the financial services industry, including the elimination of ceilings on deposit interest rates.

Alfred E. Kahn, whom Carter chose to deregulate the airlines, was both symbolic of the new era and a major player in it.[7] Kahn was a liberal Democrat by upbringing and sentiment, but he had come to believe that the general interest would best be served if regulators put more emphasis on increasing competition and marginal cost pricing. (To take a simple example, marginal cost pricing held that airline seats should be priced at the cost of actually carrying one more passenger rather than at a high average cost.) At a time when many airline seats were going unfilled, important segments of the industry welcomed Kahn's emphasis on marginal cost pricing.

Reaganomics

Although the Carter administration undertook a number of reforms aimed at freeing markets from excessive regulation, it was Republican Ronald Reagan, first elected in 1980, who attempted to alter the basic ideological thrust of the postwar period. Reagan put it simply in his inaugural address: "Government is not the solution to our problems; government is the problem." His economic policy, often referred to as "Reaganomics," had several elements. One was the reduction in taxes, particularly the reduction of marginal rates (the rates applied to additional income). The Reagan administration claimed that such cuts were necessary to create incentives to work and invest. Its critics complained that such cuts were a giveaway to the rich.

The Reagan administration wanted to alter budget priorities radically, increasing defense expenditures and reducing civilian expenditures. It had little trouble increasing defense spending. Between 1980 and 1983, defense expenditures rose from $134 billion to $210 billion, but spending cuts on the civilian side, although some were made, were harder to get through Congress. Between 1980 and 1983, all spending other than national defense increased from $457 billion to $598 billion. Prices were rising over the same period (the rise in civilian expenditures was 27 percent, while the rise in the GNP deflator was 19 percent), and certain areas of the civilian budget were hit hard (the budget category of "education, training, employment, and social services" fell from $32 billion to $27 billion). On the whole, however, it was extremely difficult to make cuts, particularly after Reagan's initial "honeymoon" with Congress ended. Reagan's budget director, David Stockman, was in charge of proposing the cuts to be made and selling them to Congress. His book, *The Triumph of Politics,* describes in case after case how difficult it was to cut programs, even those having little justification, once the affected interests and their allies in Congress and the government bureaucracy were alerted for battle.

---

[7]See Thomas K. McCraw, *Prophets of Regulation* (Cambridge, Mass.: Harvard University Press, 1984), chapter 7, for an absorbing account of Kahn's role in the regulatory revolution.

The 1988 election of George Bush, a moderate Republican, promised a slowdown if not a reversal of the Reagan policies, especially on the regulatory front. Bush did say, in his speech accepting the Republican nomination, "Read my lips: no new taxes," thus laying claim to the most popular part of the Reagan legacy. Two years later, however, under intense pressure to do something about the mounting federal deficit, Bush accepted tax increases. The resulting loss of political capital far outweighed any effect on the deficit.

In 1992, Democrat Bill Clinton was elected president after promising to reverse the Reagan-Bush approach by raising taxes on the wealthy, spending more on the poor and on urban areas, spending less on defense, and increasing the federal government's role in health care. After his health initiative failed and a conservative Congress was elected in 1994, however, he retreated from attempts to expand the welfare state. In 1996, he became the first Democrat since Franklin Roosevelt to win reelection, but in the course of the campaign, he supported legislation that limited welfare and that in some cases would cut off benefits, a far cry from his initial goal of preserving and extending the New Deal. In 2000, George W. Bush, a conservative Republican, won a narrow and controversial election. His first legislative victory, a substantial tax cut, showed that the conservative tide had not yet run its course.

To see the liberal and conservative eras more clearly, we review two sectors of the economy that show the changes with particular clarity: agriculture and the environment.

AGRICULTURE

The Relative Decline of Agriculture

A decline in the number of agricultural workers relative to the total workforce is a common feature of economic development It is estimated that in 1800 about three-fourths of the workforce was employed in agriculture. By 1850, that proportion had fallen to 55 percent. In 1920, it was 26 percent, and by 1950, it had fallen to 12 percent.

The trend continued in the postwar period. In 1960, the percentage of the labor force employed in agriculture was 8 percent; in 1970, 4.4 percent; in 1980, 3.4 percent; and in 1994, only 2.8 percent. Similar declines were recorded throughout the industrial world. Indeed, the declines were larger in countries undergoing rapid industrialization. In Italy, for example, agricultural employment, measured as a share of the total labor force, fell from more than 30 percent in 1960 to about 9 percent in 1990; in Japan, the change was similar, a fall from just less than 30 percent in 1960 to about 7 percent in 1990. In the United States, it hasn't been a matter, simply, of the farm sector's holding its own while other sectors expanded. The number of farm workers actually declined from 9,926,000 in 1950 to 2,767,000 in 1994.

The decline in the agricultural workforce is the result of two phenomena. First, the demand for agricultural products generally did not grow as rapidly as real income. The income elasticity of demand for agricultural products, to use the technical term (the percentage change in the demand for an agriculutural product produced by a given percentage change in real income), is typically less than 1. Second, rapid technological progress in agriculture reduced the number of workers it took to produce a given amount of agricultural product. Technological progress came on several fronts. Farm machinery evolved rapidly. Tractors became larger, and sensitive electronic equipment was added that could monitor plowing, seeding, and harvesting. New herbicides and pesticides were developed, and scientific breeding of plants and animals and genetic modification further expanded output. In some cases, these developments were linked. Chemicals were used to defoliate cotton plants to make mechanical harvesting easier, and new strains of tomatoes were developed with tough skins that could withstand mechanical harvesting and cross-country—eventually international—transport.

Large farms with heavy investments in modern technology increasingly dominated the farm sector. Compare the grain harvester shown here with McCormick's reaper shown on page 297.

These innovations came from private companies producing farm machinery, chemicals, and seeds, and from federal and state laboratories and experiment stations. So successful were federal and state agencies in finding ways to increase output that liberals used the agricultural sector as an example of how the federal government could produce important technological advances. Liberals wanted to start similar federal programs in manufacturing, but the debate didn't end there; conservatives pointed out that whereas one part of the federal government was working to raise farm output, other federal farm programs, as we will see later, were working to reduce it.

Not only did the number of farm workers decline but so did the number of farms. This is shown in Table 26.3 on page 532, which includes some earlier years for comparison. In 1950, there were 5,388,000 farms in the United States; by 2002, that number had fallen to 2,158,000, fewer than in 1870. The amount of land in farms also fell, but at a much slower rate, from 1,161,000,000 acres in 1950 to 941 million acres in 2002. The result was that average farm size, shown in the final column of Table 26.3, rose from 216 acres in 1950 to 436 acres, an all-time high, in 2002. It was the farmer working a small or medium-sized farm who gave up the business. Much of the land went into larger farms owned by individual owner-operators or corporations. Indeed, the rise of corporate farm ownership was a striking and controversial feature of the postwar period, although many corporate farms were simply family farms converted to corporate status for tax purposes.

What had provoked these changes? The operators of small and medium-sized farms were both pushed and pulled from the farm. Typically, only those farm operators who could farm on a large scale and achieve the high productivity possible through massive investments in farm equipment could make farming pay. Alan Olmstead and Paul Rhode estimate that the tractor alone accounted for the disappearance of 956,000 farms between 1910 and 1960.[8] In the cotton-growing South, for example, many landholders terminated small tenancies and consolidated their land so that they could make use of large-scale

[8]Alan L. Olmstead and Paul W. Rhode, "Reshaping the Landscape: The Impact and Diffusion of the Tractor in American Agriculture, 1910–1960," *Journal of Economic History* 66 (September 2001): 663–980.

TABLE 26.3 Changing Structure of U.S. Agriculture

YEAR	FARMS (IN THOUSANDS)	TOTAL LAND IN FARMS: MILLIONS OF ACRES	TOTAL LAND IN FARMS: AVERAGE FARM SIZE IN ACRES
1850	1,449	294	203
1870	2,660	408	153
1880	4,009	536	134
1900	5,740	841	147
1920	6,454	959	149
1940	6,109	1,065	175
1950	5,388	1,161	216
1960	3,962	1,177	297
1970	2,954	1,108	373
1980	2,440	1,039	426
1990	2,140	987	461
2000	2,172	943	434
2002	2,158	941	436

Note: The definition of a farm changed in 1993 to include some smaller farm operations, so later figures are not strictly comparable to earlier figures.

Sources: 1850–1970: Historical Statistics; *1980–1990:* Statistical Abstract of the United States; *2000–2002: National Agricultural Statistics Service at http://www.nass.usda.gov.*

machinery. People were also pulled from agriculture by the possibility of earning higher incomes elsewhere. Tenant farmers in the South, for example, moved to industrial centers in the Mississippi Valley, the Midwest, and the Pacific Coast. While leaving farming generally meant earning more money, it was not a decision taken lightly, for it meant leaving family and friends behind and giving up a cherished way of life.

Why did farmers continue to leave the land despite substantial efforts by the federal government to aid them? Partly, this was because the lion's share of assistance went to those who were already at the top of the heap. When the government supported farm prices, those with the most bushels or bales to sell received the chief benefits; when acreage restrictions were put into effect, those who were in a position to reduce acreage the most received the largest checks. In 1989, for example, the top 15 percent of farm families by income received 62 percent of all government payments.

After World War II, the major agricultural problem was how to deal with the large farm surpluses created by farm price supports. To correct this problem, in 1949, Secretary of Agriculture C. F. Brannan announced the plan of compensatory payments to which the press and public quickly attached his name, although its central ideas had been developing for many years in academic writings. The Brannan plan would have allowed prices to seek their own level in the marketplace, with the difference between the market price and a "modernized" parity price to be paid to the farmer (up to a maximum amount) with a check from the Treasury. The potential benefits of the Brannan plan were obvious. Surpluses would be eliminated, saving storage costs; and the public, the poor in particular, would be able to buy food cheaply. See Economic Insight 26.1.

After months of heated debate, during which the National Grange and the American Farm Bureau Federation opposed the plan, the House of Representatives refused to give the Brannan plan a trial run. Typical of political debates at the time, opponents of the Brannan plan won by castigating it as "socialism." Of course, if the Brannan plan was socialism, so was the existing system. The real objection to the Brannan plan was that unconcealed subsidies might be more difficult to defend in the court of public opinion.

Economic Insight 26.1

Economics of the Brannan Plan

This figure illustrates the economics of the Brannan plan. In a free market, the price of an agricultural product would be P and output produced would be Q, determined as usual by the intersection of the supply and demand curves. This price is considered, however, to be unfair to farmers.

Under the traditional support system, the government wishes to raise the price to P^*, the modernized parity price. At this price, consumers are willing to buy only Q^*; but farmers produce Q^{**}. To hold the price in the market at P^*, the government must purchase the excess supply, $Q^{**} - Q^*$. This will cost the government (the taxpayer) $P^* \times (Q^{**} - Q^*)$. The surplus, $Q^{**} - Q^*$, will have to be stored, so storage costs will be incurred in future years. The gain to farmers (compared with the free-market equilibrium) will be the area P^*BCP.

Under the Brannan plan, the government simply allows the surplus to be sold in the marketplace. The price falls to P^{**}, the price at which Q^{**} can be sold. The Treasury then writes a check to each farmer for the difference between the parity price P^* and the new market price P^{**}. In this case, the total cost to the government is given by the area $Q^{**} \times (P^* - P^{**})$.

Consumers clearly benefit from switching to the Brannan plan: They pay a lower price for farm products. No resources are wasted simply producing food and then storing it in government warehouses. Even under the Brannan plan, however, there is an efficiency loss given by the triangle CBE: Resources are employed in farming that could better satisfy consumer demands elsewhere in the economy.

The impact on the government budget depends on whether area $Q^{**} \times (P^* - P^{**})$, the costs under the Brannan plan, exceed or fall short of area $P^* \times (Q^{**} - Q^*)$, the costs under the traditional purchase-for-storage system plus the storage costs. In general, this will depend on the elasticities of the supply and demand curves. The more elastic the supply and demand curves, the less costly will be the Brannan plan compared with the purchase-for-storage plan.

Financially, farmers fare the same under the two plans. They produce Q^{**} output and receive P^*Q^{**} total income. Under the Brannan plan, however, farmers receive a part of the income in the form of a "welfare" check. Some farmers will find this demeaning. Direct payments also will be obvious to the public and make it more difficult for farmers to defend and increase their subsidies.

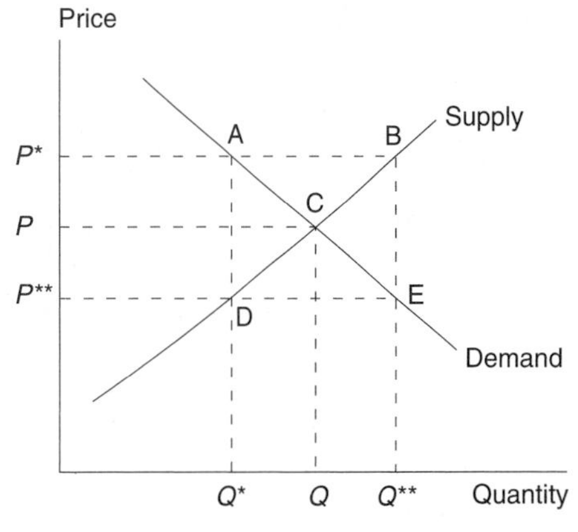

After the Brannan plan's failure, reformers turned their attention to less radical measures. For example, with surpluses still at controversial levels, Congress turned again to a Depression-era solution. The Soil Bank Act of 1956 was devised to reduce supplies of basic commodities by achieving a 10 to 17 percent reduction in plowland through payments to farmers who shifted land out of production into the "soil bank." The diversion payments were based on the old formula of multiplying a base price for the commodity by normal yield per acre by the numbers of acres withdrawn. Although the soil bank idea had been linked at its creation in the 1930s with the dust bowl in the Plains states, the plan remained what it had always been: an attempt to raise farm prices thinly disguised as a conservation program.

The results were unexpected but easy to understand in retrospect. Farmers placed their least productive land in the soil bank and cultivated the remainder more intensively. Surpluses went right on mounting, reaching astronomical heights in 1961 after nine consecutive years of increase.[9]

The Emergency Feed Grain Bill of 1961 encouraged drastic reductions in acreages devoted to corn and grain sorghums by offering substantial payments to farmers who reduced their acreage by 20 percent; even higher payments were offered for the diversion of an additional 20 percent of feed-crop acreage. On the whole, this plan worked because the reduction was large enough to offset attempts by farmers to minimize its effects. For the first time in a decade, feed grain carryover dropped.

This modest success encouraged the Kennedy and Johnson administrations to attack surpluses of wheat with a similar, but incredibly expensive, plan. Wealthy farmers and their organization, the Farm Bureau Federation, although at first opposed, quickly saw the error of their ways and joined wholeheartedly in forging the Food and Agriculture Act of 1965. A monstrous giveaway, this act cost the U.S. taxpayer $5 to $6 billion a year to make rich farmers richer while allowing a little to trickle down to poor farmers.

As inflation and concern about government spending mounted in the 1970s, Congress found it more difficult to respond unilaterally to farm interests. The Democratic Congress and President Jimmy Carter, who was well versed in agricultural subsidies (he was a prosperous peanut farmer from Georgia), made an effort to lower support prices in the Food and Agriculture Act of 1977. This monument to complication set support prices within specified ranges on wheat, cotton, feed grains, and many other commodities. Farmers, however, protested bitterly and crowded into Washington, D.C., to make known their opposition to lower prices. In the winter of 1978, they obtained higher support prices through the Emergency Act of 1978.

President Ronald Reagan's Farm Bill, passed in late 1981, exceeded $22.6 billion in expenditures, with more than $10 billion of it being allocated for the foodstamp program; price supports were continued on peanuts, sugar, wheat, feed grains, rice, soybeans, cotton, and wool though these supports were reduced from their levels during the Carter years. As expected, both Democratic and Republican farm interests claimed that the administration dictated the cutbacks, leaving no effective protection for farmers facing severely depressed incomes.

In subsequent years, the incentives offered farmers improved somewhat. Under the deficiency payments system used for grains, which had elements of the Brannan plan discussed earlier, farmers received a subsidy based on the difference between a "target" price and the market price or support price, whichever of the latter two was higher. The quantity to which this deficiency payment was applied was based on historical yields and acreages under cultivation, so farmers could not increase their deficiency payment by cultivating their land more intensively. An important change also occurred in the acreage restriction system. In 1985, the Conservation Reserve Program was set up, allowing farmers to enter into long-term contracts with the Agriculture Department to retire land from production. This program was designed to combine the goal of protecting the environment by retiring environmentally sensitive land (a point system determined the importance of the land for this purpose) with the goal of restricting output.

---

[9]Deirdre McCloskey has pointed out another unintended consequence of the soil bank program: Iowa farms were once wooded on the edges of their fields, but the wooded borders (a habitat for animals and birds and a source of lumber) were cut down in an effort to get around the acreage restrictions.

It seemed in the early 1990s that farming would escape deregulation. Even agriculture, however, could not hold out forever against the free-market tide. In 1996 Congress passed the Federal Agriculture Improvement and Reform Act, known colloquially as the "Freedom to Farm Bill." This legislation swept away the government's policy of setting a floor under agricultural prices in return for controls over production or acreage. As compensation, farmers were guaranteed annual payments through 2002 to aid the transition to free-market agriculture. Although many farmers were opposed to the measure, others supported it. Prices for many agricultural products were at historical highs, and it seemed to many farmers that the stream of assured payments under the transition program would be higher than what might be forthcoming under traditional programs. Once the act was passed, however, agricultural prices began to fall for a variety of reasons, including increased production in the rest of the world. In 1998 and again in 1999, Congress provided emergency payments to help farmers cope with the sudden fall in their incomes.

The Farm Security and Rural Investment Act of 2002 continued the subsidies tied to prices, which by 2002 made up the major share of transfers to farmers, although it did preserve the idea that in some circumstances farmers should receive direct subsidies because these are less likely to distort production decisions. Thus, for the foreseeable future, U.S. agriculture, like agriculture in other industrial economies, will be heavily subsidized.

Why are farmers so heavily subsidized in the United States and other developed countries? The sympathy that most of us feel for people who attempt to maintain a cherished way of life in the face of hard economic realities is part of the explanation. The main part of the explanation, however, is the political economy of farming. Farmers are a well-organized special interest with considerable influence in the House of Representatives and especially in the Senate (where representation is independent of a state's population). The subsidies farmers receive, moreover, while crucial to them, are only a minor irritant to the average taxpayer. Consumers, even when they are aware of the effects of U.S. farm policies, do not find it worthwhile to take the time to fight hard against price-increasing policies and tax-raising subsidies that reduce their incomes by only a small amount.[10]

THE ENVIRONMENT AND THE LEGACY OF THE CONSERVATION MOVEMENT

Yellowstone, the first and largest national park, was established in 1872 to preserve its natural wonders.[11] There was little fear at the time that the land in Yellowstone would be exploited for agricultural purposes if transferred to private hands. Rather, the concern in Congress was that if a private entrepreneur controlled access to Yellowstone, its natural beauties would be degraded by access roads and advertising.

A major change in policy took place under President Theodore Roosevelt, who believed that natural resources would be depleted too rapidly if the rate of depletion were left to the market and that the federal government should, therefore, take an active role in preserving depletable resources, particularly timber and minerals. Roosevelt publicized the cause of conservation and, aided by Gifford Pinchot, the dynamic head of the Forest Service (then the Divison of Forestry of the Department of Agriculture), converted some 150 million acres of western land in the public domain into national forests so that access could be controlled by the Forest Service.

---

[10]Gary Libecap has pointed out to us that in some cases there are "consumers" who have a large financial stake in reforming agricultural policies. Candymakers, for example, have a strong interest in reducing sugar prices. Nevertheless, in most cases, it doesn't pay the consumer to get involved in farm policy reform.

[11]A federal "reservation" had been established at Hot Springs, Arkansas, in 1832 to protect its mineral springs.

The conservation movement languished in the 1920s but surged under the administration of Franklin D. Roosevelt. In general, New Deal environmental policies can be classified into three categories: (1) government pursuit of the traditional plan of withdrawing public land from production and conserving it for future generations, (2) government introduction of the new policy of paying farmers to keep privately held land out of production, although, as noted earlier, the main reason for the "soil bank" was to raise farm prices and, (3) government insistence that, in some cases, conservation required the simultaneous protection of many resources within an entire region and major projects such as the Tennessee Valley Authority (TVA) were necessary.

In addition, during the New Deal era the first systematic efforts were made to conserve agricultural land. These efforts began in 1933 with the establishment of the Soil Erosion Service in the Department of the Interior. (In 1935, as the Soil Conservation Service, it became part of the Department of Agriculture.) Originally, contracts were made with individual farmers; the service furnished technical assistance and some materials, and the farmers furnished labor and the remaining materials. Early in 1937, President Roosevelt wrote the state governors requesting that their legislatures pass acts enabling landowners to form soil conservation districts. By 1954, about 2,500 soil conservation districts, including 80 percent of all U.S. farms, had been organized.

The New Deal also attempted conservation through its efforts to control water distribution in river valleys in programs of great scope, such as the TVA. Again, the main goals were providing construction jobs and cheap power that would lead to economic development, but conservation was also a goal. Some supporters of such programs argue that nothing less can produce permanently successful conservation. The evidence is not conclusive. The TVA has unquestionably done a remarkable job of upgrading an entire region, but the costs of building this huge project were also substantial.

Technical advances have made possible the reclamation of arid land once considered useless. Only water is needed to transform most deserts into croplands. For example, pumps driven by 65,000-horsepower motors have been installed at the Grand Coulee Dam in Washington state to lift water 280 feet from the Columbia River into the Grand Coulee chasm, from which it can then be diverted to irrigate vast areas. The Bureau of Reclamation estimates that 50 million acres west of the Rockies could be converted to fertile land.

As impressive as such achievements are from a technical point of view, they actually amount to nothing more than outlays to increase present production. These outlays could be made now or 100 years from now and produce no deterioration in our natural resources. Thus, irrigation and drainage projects do not ordinarily prevent diminution of future production. A piece of Arizona desert land can be irrigated at any time in the future, and the resultant increase in production will be just as great had the improvement been now. Reclamation, in other words, is not the same as conservation. Estimates of the full cost of producing crops on irrigated western land show that the effort is seldom worth it. Farmers can stay in business only because the water they use is highly subsidized.

The Rise of the Environmental Movement

During the 1960s, the public became convinced that the environment had become polluted with numerous dangerous by-products of industry. Making the environment whole again, many argued, was more important than rapid economic growth. The environmental movement did not break completely with the earlier emphasis on conservation, but the two movements had important differences. The conservationists had emphasized the management of resources to sustain long-term yields of timberland, farmland, water, and mineral resources; the environmentalists put more emphasis on the preservation of natural resources for future aesthetic enjoyment. The conservationists emphasized individual resources; the environmentalists emphasized the interdependence of different parts of the

Marine biologist Rachel Carson. Her book, Silent Spring, *published in 1962, spelled out the dangers of certain insecticides and helped launch the modern environmental movement.*

environment. It was not sufficient, in their view, simply to preserve patches of the environment in national parks; the whole environment had to be protected from the destructive side effects of economic development.

The growing concern about the environment was not confined to the United States; other industrialized countries, particularly those in western Europe, experienced the same phenomenon. Countries just beginning the process of industrialization often displayed what appeared to more developed countries to be a frustrating and cavalier attitude toward the environment. A clean and well preserved environment appears to be a luxury good: As income rises, consumers wish to spend a larger fraction of their income on it.

Although concern about the environment remained a constant, public attention in the United States shifted from problem to problem, depending on the events of the day. In the early 1960s, Rachel Carson's book *Silent Spring* heightened concern about the danger of indiscriminate pesticide use, and, as a result, the Department of Agriculture banned the use of DDT completely in 1969.That same year, a major oil spill off the coast of Santa Barbara, California, raised concerns about the danger of offshore oil drilling, and similar fears were raised about the impact of the proposed Alaska Pipeline.

Responding to these and other environmental concerns, Congress passed the Clean Air Act and Water Quality Improvement Act in 1970 and established the Environmental Protection Agency (EPA). Since then, the EPA has produced a flood of regulations. Typically, it sets a maximum level of pollution allowed based on the "best available technology." In many cases, the EPA must set literally hundreds of standards for each pollutant. For example, the EPA works out a separate standard for each model of automobile. Measuring the costs versus benefits of the EPA standards is exceedingly difficult and controversial, but no one doubts that the direct costs of complying with EPA standards are very high. By one estimate, these were $100 billion in 1988, about 2 percent of GNP.[12]

Concern about the "greenhouse effect" illustrates the environmental movement's emphasis on the way in which environmental problems are linked. The accumulation of certain gases (carbon dioxide, methane, and chlorofluorocarbons among them) produces the greenhouse effects in the atmosphere. These gases absorb infrared radiation being reflected from the earth (much as does the glass over a greenhouse) and thus raise temperatures worldwide. The greenhouse effect illustrates, once again, the problem of externalities. Individual producers, even entire nations, have no incentive to control the gases they release into the atmosphere because the costs will be shared worldwide and may be concentrated on the other side of the earth.

The effects to be expected from global warming are uncertain and controversial. They are likely to be greatest for the developing countries, where agriculture (which is a large share of GNP) might be adversely affected and where debilitating parasitic diseases might become more widespread. The melting of polar ice, moreover, might raise ocean levels and cause extensive shore damage. On the other hand, some areas that would experience longer growing seasons might actually improve their agricultural productivity.

Various solutions to the problem of global warming have been proposed. As usual, there are two approaches. Liberal economists favor explicit emission targets reached through international negotiations and detailed government plans for reaching those targets. Market-oriented economists favor taxes on emissions, and some favor creating tradeable rights, the usual solution to the problem externalities. Countries would be assigned maximum emission levels, and if they exceeded their assigned level, they would have to buy the right to emit more from other countries that had managed to hold their emissions below their targets. Perhaps the main issue to be resolved in years to come is whether environmental protection will rely more heavily on market mechanisms (taxes and the creation of tradeable rights) or on direct government controls.

CAN THE PRINCIPLES OF ECONOMICS EXPLAIN THE GROWTH OF GOVERNMENT?

We have seen that the growth of government in the postwar period was the outcome of an ongoing battle between liberal and conservative philosophies of political economy. Beneath these changing tides, however, a number of historians and economists have pointed to more fundamental forces that determine the size of government.

Wagner's Law

Writing in the 1880s, German economist and economic historian Adolph Wagner wrote that the growth of modern industry would produce increasing political "pressure for social

[12]In addition, a number of other programs to improve the quality of the environment have been introduced. Perhaps the most famous is Superfund, established in 1980 and charged with cleaning up hazardous waste dumps.

progress" and thereby continuous expansion of the public sector. In part, this would happen because competitive nation-states would find it in their interest to appease labor and to meet, at least partially, its demands for social justice. Wagner's prediction has proved accurate in a number of cases, and the idea that the public sector will inevitably expand relative to the private sector has come to be known as Wagner's Law.

A number of American economists have accepted Wagner's Law but emphasized a different underlying force: the increase of real per capital income. Governmental programs that help the disadvantaged, protect the environment, and the like may be luxury goods: we buy disproportionately more of them when income rises. The slowdown in the growth of the demand for government after 1969 is consistent with this thesis. To the extent that voting patterns reflect views about long-term incomes, the belief that productivity growth had slowed produced a substantial decrease in the demand for government expenditures. Other long-term trends may also influence the demand for government. Population growth and urbanization, for example, may have increased the demand for programs to preserve the environment or provide mass transportation.[13]

What about pure transfer payments? A poor person could be expected to vote for heavy taxes on the rich. We might expect, therefore, that in a democracy in which the rule of one adult, one vote was followed, income tax rates would be highly progressive, and after-tax incomes would tend toward equality. Indeed, the surprising thing about most industrial democracies is not that they have progressive income taxes but that those taxes are not even *more* progressive. Economists Allan H. Meltzer and Scott F. Richard have devised a rational theory of transfer payments. In their model, people vote for programs that redistribute income in their favor but take into account the disincentive effects of higher taxes—the tendency of high marginal tax rates to discourage work and savings. The poor do not automatically vote for "soak-the-rich" taxes because they think that as a result, the whole economy will be less productive and that they will end up with less than they had before.[14]

Economist Sam Peltzman has developed a related theory. Based on international comparisons, he argues that a more-equal distribution of income generated by the market, paradoxically, accelerates the growth of government because it increases the political strength of the group that favors further redistribution through the government. When the poor are very poor, they are not able to produce political pressures that advance their interests. Economic growth empowers the poor and makes them a political force to be reckoned with.[15]

Government Growth: Competing Interpretations

Liberal historian Arthur Schlesinger, Jr., stresses an alternation in the dominant ideology between "public purpose" and "private interest." In the long run, according to Schlesinger, government will tend to grow because programs initiated by liberal administrations are seldom eliminated by the conservatives who follow. The appropriate image is of government as a spiral that widens during periods of liberal dominance but that never contracts.[16] In Schlesinger's view, the alternation between liberalism and conservatism is perpetual. Politically active young people adopt the ideology dominant in their formative years. As time goes by, they reach higher and higher levels of influence in government, the private sector, academia, and the media. Eventually, they take power and attempt to reimpose the

---

[13]See Solomon Fabricant, *The Trend in Government Activity in the United States since 1900* (New York: National Bureau of Economic Research, 1952), for an early statement of this view.

[14]Allan H. Meltzer and Scott F. Richard, "A Rational Theory of the Size of Government," *Journal of Political Economy* 89 (October 1981): 914–927.

[15]Sam Peltzman, "The Growth of Government," *Journal of Law and Economics* 23 (October 1980): 220–285.

[16]Arthur Schlesinger, Jr., *The Cycles of American History* (Boston: Houghton, Mifflin, 1986), chapter 2. His father, also a distinguished historian, created the theory.

liberal or conservative ideology of their youth. The rise of Bill Clinton to the presidency is a clear illustration of Schlesinger's theory: Clinton and many of his close advisers were college students and antiwar activists during the liberal Kennedy-Johnson era. To take Schlesinger's point a step further, and perhaps a bit too literally, we can predict that in about 2016, a conservative administration will take power, reflecting the political and economic philosophies dominant in the early 1980s!

Economists Milton Friedman and Rose D. Friedman have emphasized the tendency of new reforms to survive subsequent administrations, libreal or conservative. Programs resist attempts to eliminate them because of the "tyranny of the status quo." An "iron triangle" of bureaucrats, (see Economic Insight 26.2) politicians, and private sector beneficiaries of government programs protect programs even when it has been shown that these programs are detrimental to the public interest. Measured across all voters, the gain from eliminating a given program may be large; but for each voter separately, the gain may be too small to make fighting for it worthwhile.[17]

In his book, *Crisis and Leviathan*, Robert Higgs agrees that the dominant ideology is the crucial factor determining the growth rate of government but emphasizes the role of economic or social crises in making the liberal interventionist ideology acceptable.[18] A mild recession in 1931 might have led to a Democrat's replacing Herbert Hoover, but the Great Depression made people eager to accept a wide range of new programs. John F. Kennedy and Lyndon B. Johnson would have pushed for new programs in any case, but the social and political crises of the 1960s made the public willing to accept a much broader range of new legislation and programs, particularly those designed to solve the problems of poverty and racial discrimination.

It is common for an academic writer to push his or her own theory as if it were the one and only cause of the trends observed. Product differentiation is as useful to academics as it is to producers of automobiles, insurance policies, and chickens. It seems to us, however, that the theories of the growth of government we have examined complement one another. Schlesinger's emphasis on the nostalgia of political leaders for the ideologies of their youth, Higgs's emphasis on the role of crises, and Friedmans' emphasis on the rational voter's concerns all contribute to our understanding of the complex process that produced first an expansion and later a retrenchment in the role of government in the postwar era.

[17]Milton and Rose D. Friedman, *Tyranny of the Status Quo* (San Diego: Harcourt Brace Jovanovich, 1983), 41–51.

[18]Robert Higgs, *Crisis and Leviathan: Critical Episodes in the Growth of American Government* (New York: Oxford University Press, 1987). "Leviathan" was a sea monster in the Bible. The term has come to stand for a totalitarian, bureaucratic state.

Economic Insight 26.2

Why Does Bureaucracy Have Negative Connotations?

Why do government bureaucracies often seem so big and inefficient? Why, to put it somewhat differently, does the term *bureaucracy* carry such negative connotations? Economist William Niskanen provides one still-controversial answer based on the relationship between Congress and the bureaus. The S curve in the figure represents a government bureau's cost of supplying units of "output"—acres of land irrigated, recommendations made to farmers, grants awarded, power plants inspected, or the like. The D curve shows the marginal valuation of each additional unit of output. The efficient output would be OG at that level of output; every unit would be produced for which the marginal value exceeded the marginal cost. At OG, the cost of producing the last unit, BG, would exactly equal the value placed on it. This is, of course, what would happen if the product were produced by private firms and sold in a competitive market.

Niskanen believes, however, that the budget-making process in Congress works differently.[19] Bureaucrats are not interested in minimizing costs or maximizing profits. Their goal is to preside over as large a budget as possible—whence comes prestige in Washington. Because they are likely to be a monopoly and to have all available information about costs of producing a somewhat difficult-to-measure output, they will make it extremely difficult to judge the shape of the S curve. Instead, they will provide the congressional committee overseeing the bureau a single request for the money needed to carry out the bureau's "mission." The congressional committee is also likely to be happy with an output larger than OG because committee members will be receiving campaign contributions from the interest groups that benefit from the bureau's work. If, however, the agency's total costs were to grow to the point where they exceeded the total benefits, questions would be raised by other members of Congress on other committees, by the press, and by the executive branch, which takes the heat when total taxes are raised. The result is that the bureau will produce output OF at a total cost of OCF and that these costs will be equal to total benefits of OAEF. The bureau will be too big.

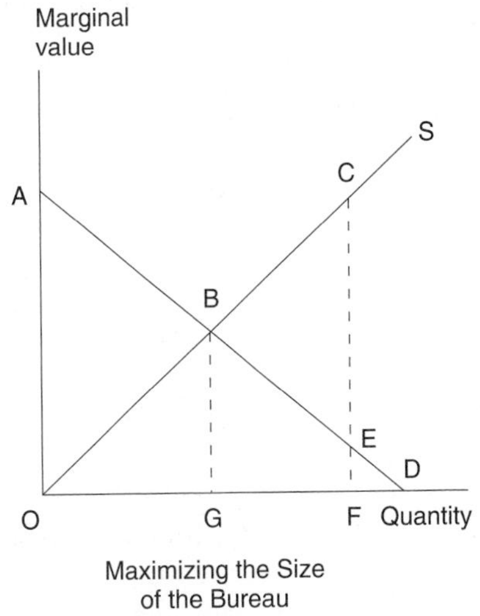

Maximizing the Size of the Bureau

[19] William A. Niskanen, *Bureaucracy and Representative Government* (Chicago: Aldine-Atherton, 1971), chapter 5.

SELECTED REFERENCES AND SUGGESTED READINGS

Aaron, Henry J. *Politics and the Professors: The Great Society in Perspective*. Washington, D.C.: Brookings Institution, 1978.

Anderson, Terry L. *Political Environmentalism: Going behind the Green Curtain*. Stanford, Calif.: Hoover Institution Press, 2000.

Asch, Peter. *Consumer Safety Legislation: Putting a Price on Life and Limb.* New York: Oxford University Press, 1988.

Bennett, James T., and Manuel H. Johnson. *The Political Economy of Federal Government Growth, 1959–1978*. College Station, Tex.: Center for Education and Research in Free Enterprise, 1980.

Borcherding, Thomas E. "The Sources of Growth of Public Expenditures in the United States, 1902–1970." In *Budgets and Bureaucrats: The Sources of Government Growth*, ed. Thomas E. Borcherding. Durham, N.C.: Duke University Press, 1977.

Buchanan, James M. *Public Finance in Democratic Process: Fiscal Institutions and Individual Choice*. Chapel Hill: University of North Carolina Press, 1967.

Economic Report of the President. The annual tables in the appendix are an excellent source of data on the postwar era. **http://www.access.gpo.gov/eop/**.

Edelstein, Michael. "What Price Cold War? Military Spending and Private Investment in the US, 1946–1979." *Cambridge Journal of Economics* 14 (1990): 421–437.

Fabricant, Solomon. *The Trend of Government Activity in the United States since 1900*. New York: National Bureau of Economic Research, 1952.

Friedman, Milton, and Rose D. Friedman. *Tyranny of the Status Quo.* San Diego: Harcourt Brace Jovanovich, 1983.

Galbraith, John K. *The Affluent Society.* Boston: Houghton, Mifflin, 1969.

Glasner, David. *Politics, Prices, and Petroleum: The Political Economy of Energy.* Cambridge, Mass.: Ballinger, 1985.

Hardin, Garrett. "The Tragedy of the Commons." *Science* 162 (1968): 1243–1248.

Heller, Walter. *New Dimensions of Political Economy.* Cambridge, Mass.: Harvard University Press, 1969.

Higgs, Robert. *Crisis and Leviathan: Critical Episodes in the Growth of American Government.* New York: Oxford University Press, 1987.

———. "The Cold War Economy: Opportunity Costs, Ideology, and the Politics of Crisis." *Explorations in Economic History* 31 (July 1994): 283–312.

Higgs, Robert, and Anthony Kilduff. "Public Opinion: A Powerful Predictor of U.S. Defense Spending." *Defence Economics* 4 (1993): 227–238.

Hughes, Jonathan R.T. *The Governmental Habit.* New York: Basic Books, 1977.

Kahn, Alfred E. "Surprises of Airline Deregulation." *American Economic Review, Papers and Proceedings* 78 (1988): 316–322.

Lilley, William, III, and James C. Miller, III. "The New 'Social Regulation.'" *The Public Interest* 47 (1977): 49–61.

Lowery, David, and William D. Berry. "The Growth of Government in the United States: An Empirical Assessment of Competing Explanations." *American Journal of Political Science* 27 (1983): 665–694.

McCraw, Thomas K. *Prophets of Regulation*. Cambridge, Mass.: Harvard University Press, 1984.

Meltzer, Allan H., and Scott F. Richard. "Why Government Grows (and Grows) in a Democracy." *Public Interest* 52 (Summer 1978): 111–118.

———. "A Rational Theory of the Size of Government." *Journal of Political Economy* 89 (October 1981): 914–927.

———. "Tests of a Rational Theory of the Size of Government." *Public Choice* 41 (1983): 403–418.

Niskanen, William A. *Bureaucracy and Representative Government.* Chicago: Aldine-Atherton, 1971.

Olmstead, Alan L., and Paul Rhode. "The Transformation of Northern Agriculture." In *The Cambridge Economic History of the United States,* Vol. III: *The Twentieth Century,* eds. Stanley L. Engerman and Robert E. Gallman. New York: Cambridge University Press, 2000, 693–742.

———. "Reshaping the Landscape: Impact and Diffusion of the Tractor in American Agriculture, 1910–1960." *Journal of Economic History* 61 (September 2001): 663-980.

Peltzman, Sam. "The Growth of Government." *Journal of Law and Economics* 23 (October 1980): 220–285.

Schlesinger, Arthur M., Jr. *The Cycles of American History.* Boston: Houghton, Mifflin, 1986.

Schumpeter, Joseph. *Capitalism, Socialism, and Democracy,* 3d ed. New York: Harper & Row, 1950.

Statistical Abstract of the United States, one of the best sources of current annual data. **http://www.census.gov/prod/www/statistical-abstract-us.html**.

Stockman, David A. *The Triumph of Politics: How the Reagan Revolution Failed.* New York: Harper & Row, 1986.

Stone, Alan. *Economic Regulation and the Public Interest: The Federal Trade Commission in Theory and Practice.* Ithaca, N.Y.: Cornell University Press, 1977.

Tanzi, Vito, and Ludger Schuknecht. *Public Spending in the 20th Century: A Global Perspective.* Cambridge: Cambridge University Press, 2000.

United States Environmental Protection Agency, the history of the Environmental Protection Agency. **http://www.epa.gov/history/**.

U.S. Department of Agriculture, the history of American Agriculture. **http://www.usda.gov/history2/front.htm**.

Vietor, Richard H. K. "Government Regulation of Business." In *The Cambridge Economic History of the United States,* Vol. III: *The Twentieth Century*, eds. Stanley L. Engerman and Robert E. Gallman. New York: Cambridge University Press, 2000, 969–1012.

Wildavsky, Aaron. *The Politics of the Budgetary Process.* Boston: Little, Brown, 1964.

Chapter Twenty-Seven

GOVERNMENT AND THE BUSINESS CYCLE AFTER WORLD WAR II

In the immediate aftermath of World War II, there was considerable fear that the Great Depression would return, but fear gave way to optimism when the expected economic collapse failed to materialize. Academic economists were especially optimistic because of the belief that John Maynard Keynes, the famous English economist, had shown how a modern industrial economy could be kept on an even keel through the judicious use of fiscal policy. The confidence of economists that the business cycle could be tamed reached its peak during the Kennedy-Johnson years, but then, the weakness of the Keynesian regimen (as it was applied in practice), its bias toward inflation, began to make itself felt.

Depression-level unemployment rates were never approached, even in the most severe postwar recessions after World War II. Instead, inflation became the primary problem. Inflation (see Figure 27.1) tended to fall and unemployment (see Figure 27.2 on page 546) tended to rise in each recession, but inflation did not fall as much in each recession as it had risen in the previous expansion, so that the core, or base, rate of inflation moved steadily upward during the 1960s and 1970s. Similarly, the unemployment rate did not fall as much in each expansion as it rose in each recession; the core, or natural, rate of unemployment, as some called it, also increased during these years. By the late 1970s, "stagflation" seemed to be as perplexing as depression had been to an earlier generation.

Stagflation presented a fundamental challenge to Keynesian economics. As a result, economists and policymakers began to pay more attention to the ideas of Milton Friedman, the free market economist at the University of Chicago. Friedman stressed several points that had a profound influence on policy from the 1970s through the remainder of the twentieth century: (1) The trade-off between inflation and unemployment was temporary, (2) inflation was a monetary problem best solved by increasing the stock of money at a slow and stable rate, and (3) freely floating exchange rates worked better than fixed exchange rates. The attempt to apply monetarist ideas (as the school of thought established by Friedman came to be called), although not always faithful to the original doctrine, became the basis for monetary and fiscal policy in the 1980s and early 1990s. Inflation was arrested in the early 1980s, but at the cost of a severe recession. Although inflation was never reduced to zero, it was kept under control for the remainder of the century.

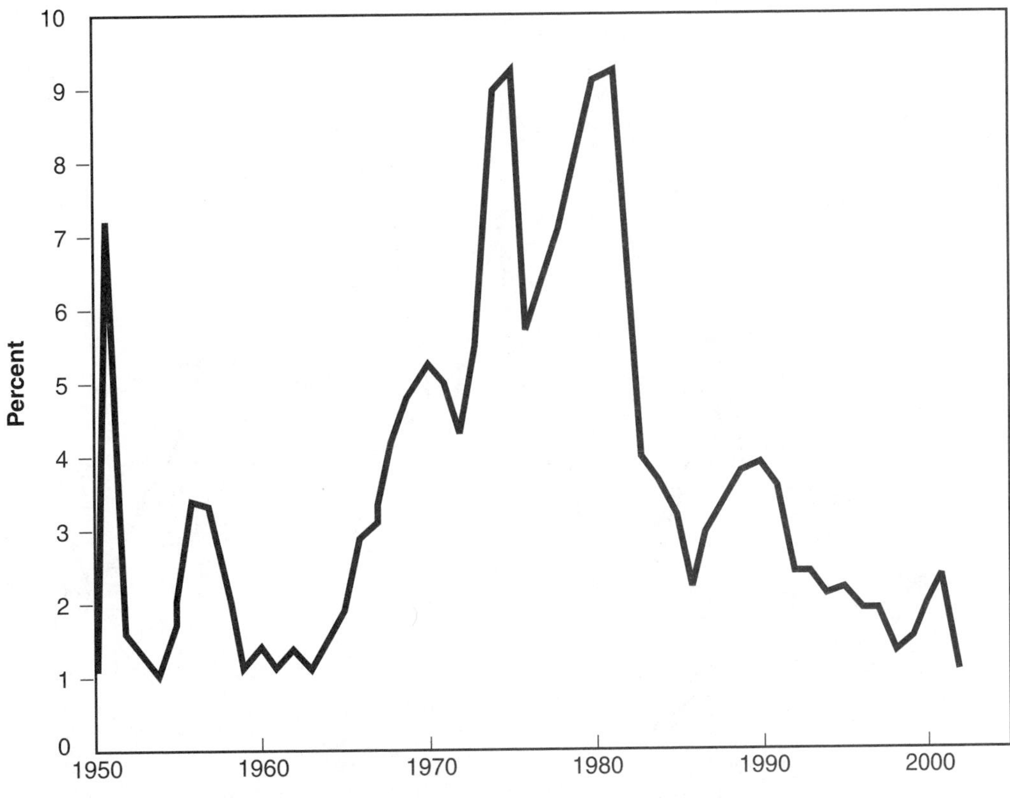

FIGURE 27.1 The Rate of Inflation in the United States, 1950–2002

Source: Bureau of Economic Analysis at http://www.bea.doc.gov.

THE KEYNESIAN ERA

Keynes's masterwork, *The General Theory of Employment, Interest, and Money*, appeared in 1936 and is often listed among the most influential books of the twentieth century. For more than three decades, the ideas advanced in *The General Theory* dominated macroeconomic policymaking in the United States and other industrialized countries. *The General Theory* is a complex book, and considerable controversy exists about how to interpret it.

Several key points, however, come through clearly: (1) No natural tendency exists for the economy to return to full employment after a recession; investment demand might be insufficient to soak up all the savings that people wish to accomplish at full employment income; (2) monetary policy is unlikely to be effective in restoring investment and full employment when the economy is below full employment; and (3) to restore full employment after a recession, it may be necessary to control private investment and supplement it with government spending on public works. The last point—stressed by Keynes's American disciples such as Alvin Hansen, Abba Lerner, and Paul Samuelson—was taken to mean that the economy could be kept on an even keel by increasing government spending, or cutting taxes, or both during recessions and by reversing these actions when, after reaching full employment, inflation threatened.

The success of deficit spending in eliminating unemployment during World War II confirmed (or so it seemed) the value of the Keynesian medicine for treating severe depressions. This mood of optimism was strengthened by the handling of the first postwar

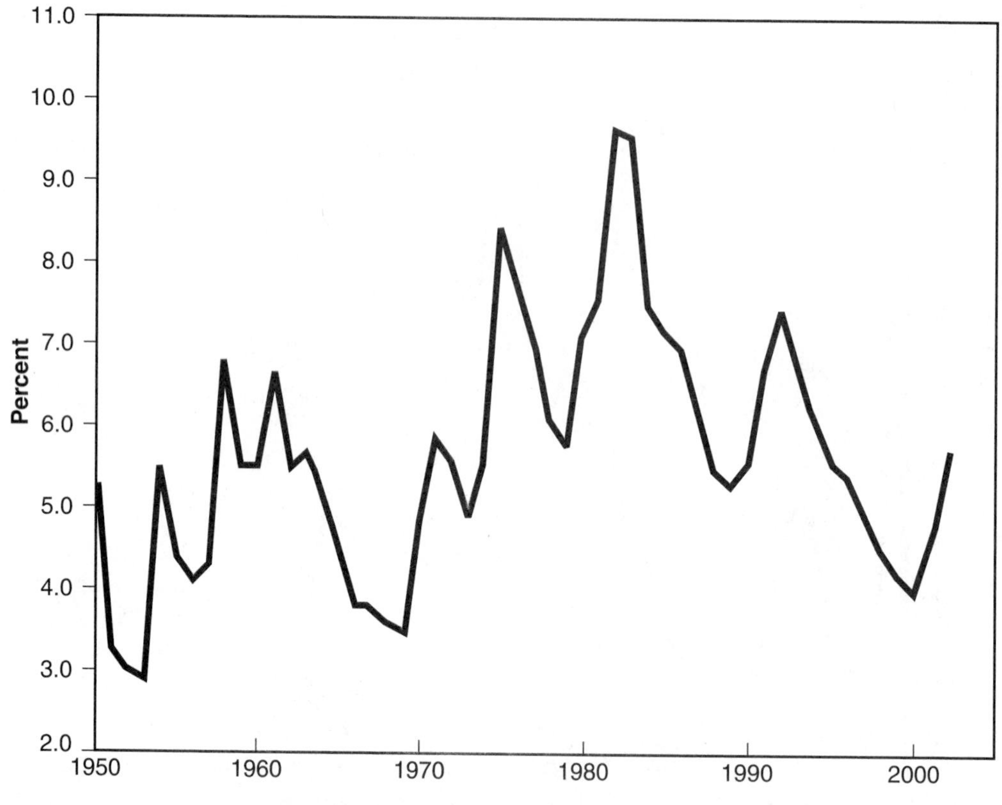

FIGURE 27.2 **The Civilian Unemployment Rate,** 1950–2002

Source: Economic Report of the President, *http://www.access.gpo.gov.*

John Maynard Keynes (1883–1946), architect of the theory that full employment could be maintained by appropriate changes in government spending and taxation and through control of private investment. His theories gained increasing acceptance during the 1940s, 1950s, and 1960s.

© H. ARMSTRONG ROBERTS

recession, which lasted (as shown in Table 27.1) from November 1948 to October 1949. After industrial production dropped 10 percent and the gross domestic product fell 4 percent, the Truman administration moved quickly to award military contracts in "distressed areas," and although unemployment rose above 5 percent for several months, revival came so quickly that public clamor for action never became loud. The Keynesian medicine seemed to work on mild recessions and without creating dangerous side effects requiring other treatments.

The Korean War and the Treasury-Fed Accord

On June 25, 1950, North Korean forces crossed the thirty-eighth parallel and attacked South Korea. President Truman responded immediately by authorizing the use of U.S. forces to repel the attack. Less than five years after the end of World War II, the United States found itself at war again. Consumers responded by stocking up on items that had been scarce during World War II: sugar, automobile tires, consumer durables, and so on. Inflation accelerated. (Figure 27.1) The government responded swiftly; the lesson drawn from World War II was that half-measures don't work. First, the Revenue Act of 1950, which provided for higher personal and corporate tax rates, was enacted in September 1950.The Revenue Act of 1951, although less comprehensive than the Truman administration wanted, provided for additional increases in individual and corporate taxes.

Second the government imposed price and wage controls. A debate quickly developed between those who favored a gradual approach to controlling prices and those who favored an immediate across-the-board freeze on prices. This time, unlike during World War II, the advocates of a freeze won, and a freeze was announced in late January 1951. Michael V. DiSalle, the director of the Office of Price Stabilization and a major advocate of a freeze,

TABLE 27.1 Business Cycles after World War II

PEAK	TROUGH	LENGTH OF THE EXPANSION FROM PREVIOUS TROUGH TO THIS PEAK (months)	LENGTH OF THIS CONTRACTION FROM PEAK TO TROUGH (months)
February 1945	October 1945	80[a]	8
November 1948	October 1949	37	11
July 1953	May 1954	45	10
August 1957	April 1958	39	8
April 1960	February 1961	24	10
December 1969	November 1970	106	11
November 1973	March 1975	36	16
January 1980	July 1980	58	6
July 1981	November 1982	12	16
July 1990	March 1991	92	8
March 2001	November 2001	120	8

[a]*From June 1938—the World War II expansion.*

Note: The National Bureau of Economic Research, a private research group that initiated research on the business cycle, dates peaks and troughs in the business cycle. The precise date is a matter of judgment. Another common definition of a recession, two successive quarters of falling income, usually produces similar dates.

Source: The dates and a description of how they are determined are available from the National Bureau of Economic Research, http://www.nber.org.

explained his position this way. Controlling prices was like "bobbing a cat's tail"—it was better to do it all at once, close to the body; doing it bit by bit produced "a mad cat and a sore tail."

Third, the government imposed a restrictive monetary policy. During World War II, the Fed pegged interest rates (placed a ceiling on them), even though this forced the Fed to purchase more federal debt than it wanted, thus expanding money and credit. Pegging was continued in the early postwar years at the request of the Treasury despite the Fed growing resentment. The Korean War brought the conflict into the open. After discussions conducted at the urging of President Truman, the Fed and the Treasury announced that they had reached an agreement on March 4, 1951.

This agreement came to be known as the Treasury-Fed Accord because the joint statement issued by the two agencies said that they had reached "full accord." The main point of the accord was that the Fed would be allowed to limit its purchase of government debt even if the result were higher interest rates. This was a victory for the Fed, although the Treasury won some minor points. There were predictions that financial markets would be sent into shock by the accord, but financial markets in fact adapted quickly to the new regime. The accord permitted the Fed to follow a noninflationary monetary policy during the war; for the entire period of the war, money per unit of real GDP actually fell slightly.

The anti-inflation program worked well. Consumer prices rose at an annual rate of only 2.1 percent from the price freeze in January 1951 to the termination of controls in February 1953. When controls were terminated, many prices were below their ceilings, and no post-control price explosion occurred. Consumer prices rose at a rate of only 2.6 percent from the termination of controls until the postwar price peak.

As we shall discuss, controls were used again in the 1970s, partly because they had seemed to be such a success in the Korean War. In the 1970s, however, the other parts of the Korean War program—monetary and fiscal restraint—were rejected, and the result was that controls were a failure.

The Eisenhower Years

During 1953, the key economic indicators took an unfavorable turn. In about nine months, industrial production fell 10 percent, the GDP declined 4 percent, and manufacturing employment dropped 10 percent. Keynesian economists had widely forecast this recession. National defense spending and, therefore, total government spending declined $11 billion between the second quarter of 1953 and the second quarter of 1954. There was also a $10 billion drop in gross investment, mostly in inventories. In short, there was a sharp drop in "exogenous" spending, which in the Keynesian model is the source of major fluctuations in the economy as a whole.

This recession aroused great concern. Unemployment in several areas of manufacturing exceeded 10 percent of the local workforce, and many families exhausted their unemployment insurance benefits before any clear signs of improvement were visible.

The administration took no drastic steps to combat the recession. A moderate fiscal deficit, partly the result of a reduction in federal income tax rates effective January 1, 1954, had a stimulating effect, and the Fed adopted the policy of "active ease." The "automatic stabilizers," unemployment insurance payments, a reduction in the total tax bill as incomes declined, and price supports for agriculture also helped to cushion the decline in aggregate spending.

Prices began a steady rise in mid-1955 that continued until early 1957. Inflation became the pressing domestic problem of the day. The Fed responded with a restrictive monetary policy that continued until well past the point of economic downturn in the late summer of 1957. A recession of substantial proportions followed, the deepest of the postwar period thus far. By the spring of 1958, unemployment was at 7.5 percent of the civilian labor force. A rebound began in April 1958, but the recovery through 1959 was disappointing, and when the indicators took another turn for the worse at the end of the year, the frustration of policymakers was evident.

Many liberal economists believed that the performance of the economy in the Eisenhower years could have been improved with more vigorous use of the Keynesian medicine. With this view in mind, the next economic team to assume power attacked unemployment.

The Kennedy-Johnson Years and the New Economics

The economy was a major issue in the election of 1960. Democrat John F. Kennedy promised to get the economy moving, placing more emphasis on full employment and economic growth and (presumably) less on price stability. Although the recession in 1959 and 1960 was mild and short, it was an important factor in Kennedy's narrow 100,000-vote victory over Vice President Richard Nixon.

The economy began its resurgence in February 1961 but at a rate that disappointed the Kennedy team. Therefore, the Council of Economic Advisers, under the guidance of Chairman Walter Heller, laid plans for an experimental tax cut in 1964. After Kennedy's shocking assassination in November 1963, the politically astute Lyndon B. Johnson assumed the presidency and promptly guided the tax cut through Congress and into law.

This tax cut was historic. The federal budget was then in deficit; orthodox economic theory called for tax increases to balance the budget, but President Kennedy's advisers believed in the "new economics" of John Maynard Keynes.[1] They argued that as long as the economy was operating at less than full employment, a tax cut was justified because it would leave more income in the hands of the public, creating more demand for goods and services. As they pointed out, a budget that was in deficit under current conditions might turn out to be balanced or in surplus at full employment because tax revenues tend to rise and certain categories of spending fall as the economy approaches full employment.

In an often-quoted passage from *The General Theory*, Keynes had written the following:

> The ideas of economists and political philosophers, both when they are right and when they are wrong, are more powerful than is commonly understood. Indeed the world is ruled by little else. Practical men, who believe themselves to be quite exempt from any intellectual influences, are usually the slaves of some defunct economist. Madmen in authority, who hear voices in the air, are distilling their frenzy from some academic scribbler of a few years back. I am sure that the power of vested interest is vastly exaggerated compared with the gradual encroachment of ideas.[2]

Less than 30 years after the publication of *The General Theory*, Keynes's ideas were having a profound effect on U.S. fiscal policies. The Kennedy tax cut was widely regarded as a great success. Unemployment fell from 5 percent of the labor force in 1964 to 4.4 percent in 1965 and to 3.7 percent in 1966. The Vietnam War buildup that followed closely on the tax cut had not been part of the calculations, however, when Kennedy's advisers had first planned a cut. The change in conditions encouraged Walter Heller and other creators of the tax cut to urge President Johnson to raise taxes, but he did not take this advice. An important political weakness of the Keynesian system then became apparent. Cutting

---

[1]The influence of Keynesian ideas, as noted, had been growing for some time, but they were still "new" to many Americans untrained in economics.

[2]John Maynard Keynes, *The General Theory of Employment, Interest, and Money* (New York: Harcourt Brace, 1936; first Harbinger ed., 1964), 383. The passage is quoted, it should not surprise us, mostly by economists.

taxes is easy; raising them is hard. Inflationary pressures began to build, and (as Figure 27.1 shows) the rate of inflation turned upward late in 1965. At the time, it was thought that the Kennedy tax cut had ushered in a new era of active fiscal policy; as it turned out, the Kennedy tax cut was the last example of a major change in fiscal policy based on Keynesian ideas.

For a time, the Kennedy administration relied on "wage-price guideposts" to control inflation. In an early and controversial test, President Kennedy publicly castigated the steel industry when it raised prices more than the guideposts allowed, threatening a transfer of federal purchases to companies that remained within the guideposts and other sanctions. Eventually, the steel industry backed down, but the government could not, of course, treat every price increase that violated the guideposts as a major crisis. When inflation accelerated in 1965, the guideposts fell into disuse.

Not until the last quarter of 1969 was there more than a brief pause in the rate of expansion of the economy. Indeed, the expansion from February 1961 to November 1969 was, until that time, the longest sustained rise in the postwar period. The recession that followed the boom, in 1969 and 1970, was brief, with the major indicators showing a trough in the fourth quarter of 1970.

The Nixon Years: Price Controls and the End of Bretton Woods

In 1971, the rate of inflation was around 4 percent per year, and the rate of unemployment around 6 percent. Although inflation was down from the prerecession peak and was probably coming down more, the public was bitter about what seemed a very high price for only a small reduction in inflation. In addition, the United States then was awakening to the seriousness of its international financial position.

After World War II, the world's major trading countries had adopted what came to be known as the *Bretton Woods system*, named after the New Hampshire resort where the meeting to establish the system was held in 1944. At that conference it was decided that the world would adopt a system of fixed exchange rates with all currencies fixed in terms of dollars. Various rules were set up that allowed countries, under certain circumstances, to devalue their currencies. The International Monetary Fund was also set up to provide short-term liquidity for countries experiencing balance-of-payments deficits; and the World Bank was created to provide long-term investment funds.

The system was, in some ways, like the gold standard, except that the base of the world's monetary system was the dollar rather than gold, although the dollar itself was then tied to gold. In the years immediately following World War II, the central problem had been the "dollar shortage": countries devastated by the war had difficulty earning the dollars they desperately needed to buy food and capital equipment. Devaluation could have addressed this problem by making each unit of the domestic currency equal to fewer dollars. Devaluation would have increased the supply of dollars by encouraging exports and decreased the demand by discouraging imports. The belief was, however, that the widespread use of devaluation would impose its own form of pain by pricing people out of the market and that it would undermine the goal of establishing fixed exchange rates.

Gradually, as Europe and Japan recovered from the war, the dollar shortage turned into a dollar surplus. Inflation in the United States worsened the dollar surplus by pricing U.S. goods out of world markets. By the early 1960s, the United States had a balance-of-payments deficit. As a result, foreign countries built up short-term dollar claims on the United States. Foreign central banks held the bulk of these claims. Some of these claims were converted into gold, raising fears that the U.S. balance-of-payments deficit would eventually undermine the world's monetary system. Indeed, conversions into gold would have been even greater had the United States not exerted diplomatic pressures on central banks to hold dollars.

The U.S. balance-of-payments problem became acute in the second half of the 1960s. There were far more dollars in the world than there was gold in Fort Knox, and the possibility of a run on the U.S. gold stock, leading to a collapse of the world financial system, seemed about to happen.

On August 15, 1971, the Nixon administration simultaneously "closed the gold window" and imposed a system of wage and price controls. Closing the gold window meant simply refusing to exchange dollars for gold. A brief attempt to reestablish fixed rates, the Smithsonian Agreement, was reached in December 1971; it called for fixed exchange rates, with the price of gold raised from $35 per ounce to $38 (an 8 percent devaluation of the dollar). The growing worldwide inflation made it difficult to stick to fixed exchange rates, however, and one country after another began to float its currency against the dollar. This sequence of events was reinforced by the ideas of free market economists led by Milton Friedman, who argued that the prices of foreign currencies should be set in the marketplace like the prices of wheat, automobiles, and computers. For a time, some hoped that the world could get back to fixed exchange rates, but this did not happen. The resulting system is frequently described as a "dirty float." Private supplies and demands are the main determinants of exchange rates, but central banks often intervene, buying or selling currencies when the outcome of market forces is not to their liking.

The price controls imposed in 1971 attempted to convince U.S. citizens that something was being done about inflation. Controls also tied in with what was happening to the dollar in international markets. The story was that the balance-of-payments problem was caused primarily by the inflation in the United States because inflation made imports more attractive and exports less attractive. Price controls would buy time while the United States put its house in order.

Price controls went through a series of phases. The first three-month period, known as Phase I, was a price freeze. Because prohibiting all price increases could not work for long without producing shortages and evasions requiring rationing, a system with greater flexibility had to be introduced. In Phase II, prices were set by the Price Commission and wages by the Pay Board. These bureaus were given considerable discretion so that individual markets could be addressed.

Milton Friedman, staunch defender of free markets. His advocacy of slow and steady expansion of the stock of money, flexible exchange rates, an all-volunteer military, and free trade gained increasing acceptance during the 1970s, 1980s, and 1990s.

Inflation in 1972 under Phase II was only 3.3 percent, lower than it had been since 1967, and lower than it would be again until 1983. Price controls got much of the credit, although some economists believe that inflation would have slowed in any case. The time seemed right to begin dismantling controls before they became a permanent part of the economy. In Phase III, which began in January 1973, the rules were eased, and their administration was placed in the hands of businesses. Inflation accelerated from 3.3 percent in 1972 to 6.2 percent in 1973. Worse still, the volatile food index increased at an astonishing 14.5 percent annual rate.

Price controls were subjected to considerable criticism. Conservatives complained that inflation was rising because the inflation repressed in Phases II and I could no longer be kept in check. Liberals complained that the Nixon administration had deliberately undermined the program because it was working all too well.

In response to the critics and to the acceleration of inflation, meat prices were frozen in March 1973 and a freeze on all prices was imposed in June. A shortage of meat resulted; meat counters in many supermarkets were literally empty. The shortage was aggravated by the announcement of a date when controls would be lifted; ranchers held their animals off the market in the almost certain knowledge that they would get a higher price later. This sequence illustrates Economic Reasoning Proposition 3 (incentives matter). Note that here the incentive is the possibility of future large gains.

With meat shortages, distortions in other sectors, evasions, and rising prices, the control program was in a sorry state. Phase IV replaced Freeze II in August 1973. (It was really Phase V, but by that time, no one was counting.) During this phase, prices were decontrolled sector by sector.

What was the control program's overall effect on prices? In 1974, consumer prices rocketed upward at a 12.2 percent annual rate. Some observers have seen this as the release of inflationary pressures built up under controls. Others doubt that much repressed inflation was left after Phase III and look to other factors such as supply-side shocks in oil and food and the lagged response to previous increases in the stock of money—to explain the acceleration of inflation. Most statistical studies agree that controls were successful in repressing inflation for a time, but they differ on how much and for how long.

If the calm created by Freeze I and Phase II had been used to impose restrictive monetary and fiscal policies, the economy might have emerged from this experiment with controls as it had from the Korean War, with stable prices. This, however, was not to be. The stock of money rose at the unprecedented peacetime rate of 13.5 percent from December 1970 to December 1971 and at 13.0 percent from December 1971 to December 1972.[3]

The inflation of 1974 was to some extent the result of these increments to the stock of money working through the economy. Fiscal policy was also inflationary. Deficits of $23 billion and $23.4 billion were run up in 1971 and 1972. In only one previous year during the postwar period had the deficit been larger, but typically it had been far smaller. It is not clear why monetary and fiscal policies were so expansionary in these years, but it is possible that the controls themselves were partly to blame. By creating the false impression that inflation was under control (and creating a new set of people to blame if it accelerated), the existence of controls encouraged the Fed to concentrate on reducing unemployment. In any case, it is clear that an opportunity to return to a stable price level, bought at considerable expense, was lost.

The Carter Years and the Growing Menace of Inflation

When President Jimmy Carter took office, his administration had an excellent opportunity to stamp out the long-building inflationary forces. Instead, it went about the business of

[3]There are various definitions of money, depending on which financial assets are included. Economists are divided on what constitutes the "best" definition. The figures here are for M2, which includes currency and deposits in commercial banks.

stimulating the economy. Political pressure for increases in Social Security benefits, veterans' benefits, farm subsidies, civil service pensions, grants to states, welfare programs, and other spending advances found a warm welcome with the Carter administration and Congress. Meanwhile, monetary policy was strongly expansionary. From 1975 to 1976, the stock of money increased at an annual rate of 13.7 percent, and from 1976 to 1977, it increased at 10.6 percent. By the fall of 1978, inflation was advancing at a rate twice that of two years earlier.

With the polls showing that inflation was "enemy number one," Carter felt compelled to act. Carter's anti-inflation program eventually comprised the following: (1) a commitment to lower the increase in government spending, (2) a commitment to reduce the federal deficit, (3) a call to increase labor productivity and efficiency, and (4) a set of "voluntary guidelines" for wage and price increases. Within a year it was clear that the program was an act of futility. The voluntary controls proved particularly unsettling. Some large corporations and unions were ignored, but other smaller, less politically potent groups were forced to conform. In effect, the voluntary controls became mandatory controls selectively applied. Meanwhile, inflation continued to rise.

An atmosphere of confusion prevailed as key members of the Carter team made conflicting public statements. Upon hearing that prices had risen 1.1 percent in one month, Alfred Kahn the President's "anti-inflation chief" said, "The government can do some things, but not a helluva lot; for the most part it rests with the consumer." Unlike Nixon, who could claim that the Organization of Petroleum Exporting Countries' (OPEC) price increases in oil and other external shocks were behind inflation during the years between 1973 and 1976, the Carter team could find no one to share the blame other than the nation's private sector.[4]

Throughout these years, the news media helped to promote this misplaced emphasis. Routinely, reporters would say that this month, most of the inflation was *caused* by the rise in the price of housing, or food, or energy, or whatever price rose the most that month. Such advances were the result of inflation; however, they did not cause it.

The Great Inflation

In 1979 and 1980, inflation (Figure 27.1) reached double-digit levels, causing widespread fear of economic disaster. Creditors who had not foreseen rising prices lost, and debtors gained, but even many people who gained or kept pace with inflation feared that if they stumbled, inflation would quickly reduce their standard of living.

One of the most troubling aspects of the inflation of 1976 to 1980 was the rise in interest rates. Interest rates had moved irregularly upward after 1965, falling in recessions but then more than making up the lost ground during the subsequent expansions. During the remarkably volatile year of 1980, the prime rate (the rate charged by banks to their lowest-risk customers on short-term unsecured loans) tickled 20 percent in April, fell to 11 percent by midsummer, and reached the all-time record high of 21 percent by Christmas. High interest rates were continued throughout 1981 and into early 1982.

Inflation was clearly an important factor in the rise of interest rates. Economists have long maintained that in a rational world, an inflation premium would be incorporated in the rate of interest. If a lender and a borrower could agree on a rate of 10 percent when no price increases were expected, they should set a rate of 15 percent if prices were expected to rise 5 percent. Inflation would wipe out 5 percent of the value of the principal and interest, leaving

---

[4]Although the large shift in wealth caused by OPEC is beyond dispute, its impact on inflation is less clear. West Germany and Switzerland were far more vulnerable to the real shocks produced by OPEC and failing agricultural crops than was the United States, yet they managed, by a determined effort, to reduce their monetary growth and lower their inflations to the vanishing point between 1972 and 1976.

the lender and borrower in the same real position as when no inflation was expected. Historically, the relationship between inflation and interest rates has not always been as exact as this example suggest, but as inflation persisted year after year, credit markets learned to pay close attention to inflation, and the relationship between inflation and the rate of interest grew closer and closer. Economists were to some extent the teachers in this learning process.

As interest rates and housing prices rose, many people found themselves unable to purchase the new home that had seemed within their grasp only a few years before. In the first decades of the postwar era, the idea that each generation would live a life of increased material comfort than had the preceding generation had come to be taken for granted. Now this view became problematic; many parents feared a bleak future for their children. As the young increasingly found housing difficult to obtain, the old were becoming concerned over the plight of the Social Security system: Would payment increases linked to inflation bankrupt the system?

The inflation is shown in detail in Figure 27.3. The figures may tempt one to blame those sectors revealing the most rapid rise in prices. Clearly, however, the general rise of prices did not stem from any one sector. All sectors, albeit with variation, responded to the underlying inflationary forces.

As during the Great Depression, many government policies were initiated or enlarged in the 1970s to provide relief for needy individuals and families. For instance, as food prices rose, food stamps were distributed more liberally, but these measures could not prevent the public from losing confidence in the ability of the government to protect the future.

The decline in public confidence revealed in the polls would not have surprised John Maynard Keynes. In his 1919 book, *The Economic Consequences of the Peace*, he wrote:

> Lenin is said to have declared that the best way to destroy the Capitalist System was to debauch the currency. By a continuing process of inflation, governments can confiscate, secretly and unobserved, an important part of the wealth of their citizens. By this method they not only confiscate, but they confiscate arbitrarily; and, while the process impoverishes many, it actually enriches some. The sight of this arbitrary rearrangement of riches strikes not only at security, but at confidence in the equity of the existing distribution of wealth. Those to whom the system brings windfalls, beyond their deserts and even beyond their expectations or desires, become "profiteers," who are the object of the hatred of the bourgeoisie, whom the inflation has impoverished, not less than of the proletariat. As the inflation proceeds and the real value of the currency fluctuates wildly from month to month, all permanent relations between debtors and creditors, which form the ultimate foundation of capitalism, become so utterly disordered as to be almost meaningless; and the process of wealth-getting degenerates into a gamble and a lottery.
>
> Lenin was certainly right. There is no subtler, no surer means of overturning the existing basis of society than to debauch the currency. The process engages all the hidden forces of economic law on the side of destruction, and does it in a manner which not one man in a million is able to diagnose.[5]

MONETARISM AND ITS DESCENDANTS

"Stagflation," high unemployment combined with high inflation also undermined economists' confidence in Keynesian economics. In the 1960s, economists had believed in a stable Phillips curve: Unemployment could be permanently lowered at the cost of permanently higher inflation. See Economic Insight 27.1 on page 556. Now they realized that the

[5]John Maynard Keynes, *The Economic Consequences of the Peace* (New York: Harcourt Brace, 1919), 235–236.

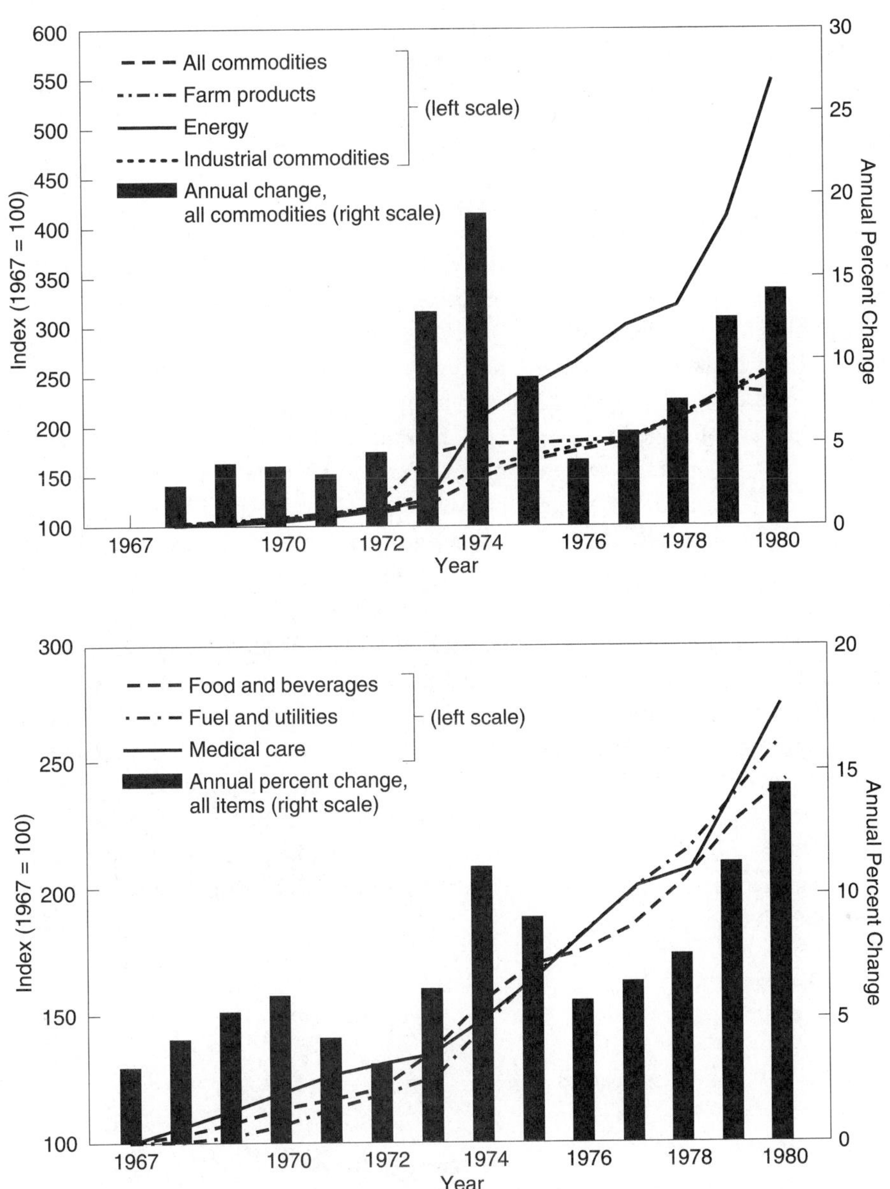

FIGURE 27.3 (top) Producer Price Indexes, 1967–1980 (1967 = 100) (bottom) Consumer Price Indexes, 1967–1980 (1967 = 100)

Source: Charts prepared by the U.S. Bureau of the Census.

Phillips curve represented only a temporary trade-off. Once workers and employers began to adjust to the new higher rate of inflation, unemployment would begin moving back to its "natural" rate.

A number of economists contributed to the new view of the relationship between inflation and unemployment; perhaps most influential was Milton Friedman. His address to the American Economic Association in 1967, "The Role of Monetary Policy," explained that increasing money growth reduced unemployment for a time because prices would initially rise faster than wages, and real wages would fall. Once workers caught on, however, they

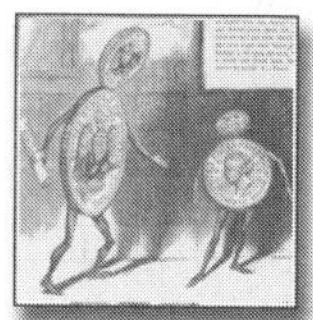

Economic Insight 27.1

The Phillips Curve

The figure below shows the Phillips curve, which describes the relationship between unemployment (on the horizontal axis) and inflation (on the vertical axis). Originally, it was believed that the trade-off was stable. Policymakers, for example, could choose a low level of unemployment. The result would be a high rate of wage increase (unions would naturally be militant when replacement workers were few) and, as wage increases were passed along, a high rate of price increases. Policymakers, in the language of the time, were faced with a stable "menu of choices" and could choose the combination of inflation and unemployment that suited their preferences. Republicans, concerned about the value of the dollar, would choose high unemployment and low inflation; Democrats, concerned about the working poor, would choose low unemployment and high inflation.

The figure shows what happened to this tidy view: The Phillips curve shifted steadily upward. Economists responded with new theories about the curve: Perhaps more young workers were entering the workforce, or perhaps young people were less willing to work. As the shift continued, however, the curve was subjected to a more searching scrutiny. Economists Milton Friedman and Edmund Phelps argued persuasively that not the rate of inflation, but only the gap between actual and expected inflation increases profits and reduces unemployment. Successively higher Phillips curves were produced by successively higher rates of expected inflation. Moreover, because expectations always adapted in the end to actual inflation, no permanent trade-off occurred. Later, economists led by Robert Lucas argued that because people formed their expectations rationally, the trade-off might not exist even in the short run. What had once appeared to be a stable downward-sloping curve had become a cloud surrounding a vertical line.

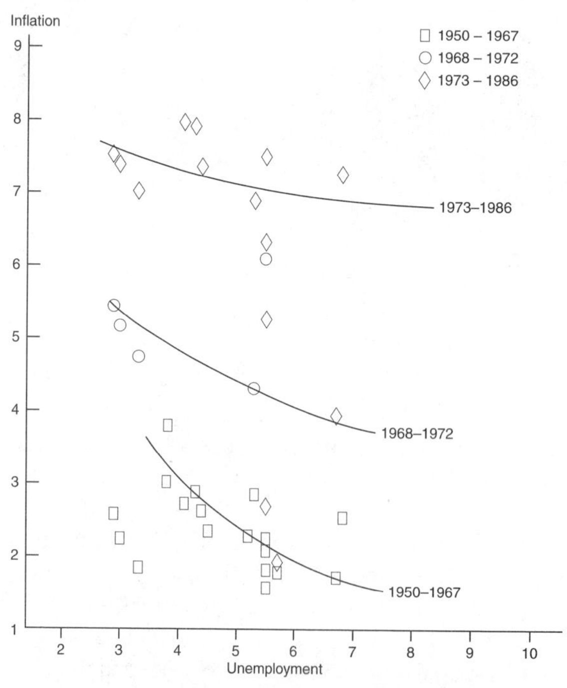

would demand wage increases in line with price increases, and unemployment would return to its "natural rate."[6]

The policy implications were clear. Governments should not try to reduce unemployment to the lowest possible rate through monetary and fiscal policy because that would lead to ever higher rates of inflation. Better would be a stable monetary and fiscal framework. As Keynes noted in the passage just quoted, new ideas are rarely implemented immediately; rather, they gradually encroach upon policymakers.

A Monetarist Experiment?

Recognizing that President Carter's policies were not working and that the American people were becoming increasingly cynical about the prospects of reining in inflation, the Fed finally took dramatic steps. On October 6, 1979, the Fed Board announced a fundamental shift in policy. Henceforth, interest rates were going to assume less importance in their decision making. More attention would be paid to the monetary aggregates (different measures of the money stock), and new techniques would be introduced to control the growth of the money stock.

This shift appeared to be a triumph for the doctrines of Milton Friedman and other monetarists, who had long been making four principal points based on their reading of monetary history: (1) Inflation is primarily a monetary phenomenon— "too much money chasing too few goods." Therefore, to reduce inflation, the Fed had to reduce the growth of the stock of money. (2) Money affects the economy with a long and variable lag. Therefore, the best policy was the simplest: Gradually reduce the rate of growth of the stock of money to a low rate and then hold it. Attempts to fine-tune the economy might end up making matters worse. (3) The tradeoff between inflation and unemployment had been only temporary. Again, the conclusion was not to try to fine-tune the economy. (4) Interest rates are a misleading guide to monetary policy that the Fed cannot control in the long run. During the Great Depression, low interest rates had given the misleading signal that money was easy. The high interest rates of the time were giving the misleading signal that money was tight.

A related but distinct line of thought concerning "rational expectations" held that the costs of disinflation, unemployment, and reduced output were largely the result of mistaken expectations. If workers continued to demand high wage increases based on expectations of high inflation and those expectations were disappointed, the workers would end up pricing themselves out of the market. Remember Economic Reasoning Proposition 2: Choices involve costs. The policy implication of this line of thought was also clear: Even an abrupt change in monetary policy would cause little damage if people truly believed that the Fed would hold true to its new policy.

Once more, policymakers were turning to academic economists for ideas about how to manage the economy. Of course, policymakers could not be forced to carry out the experiment in the way that monetarists would have liked. Monetarists complained that rather than smoothly and slowly reducing the growth rate of the money stock, the fluctuations in the growth rate were becoming greater than ever. As in the Kennedy-Johnson years, policymakers could pay lip service to ideas and adopt the part of the program that suited them while ignoring the advice they did not want to hear. In this case, moreover, adopting a new set of doctrines had the advantage that if the policy did not work or if the costs of disinflation were high, the monetarists could be blamed.

Under the leadership of chairman Paul Volcker, the Fed curtailed the growth rate of the money stock, and inflation dropped dramatically. Inflation had fallen from 13.3 to 8.9 percent between 1980 and 1981, and rates were below 6.0 percent through the first half of 1982. Seizing the opportunity to eradicate inflation, Volcker tenaciously held to his policy

[6]Liberal economists preferred the term "nonaccelerating inflation rate of unemployment" (NAIRU) because it leaves open the question of whether it is a "good" rate. (This is an example of the humor that appeals to economists: the Nehru suit was fashionable at the time.)

© AP/WIDE WORLD PHOTOS

Paul Volcker, the cigar-smoking chairman of the Federal Reserve Board, was one of the principal leaders advocating tight money to reduce double-digit inflation in the 1970s and early 1980s.

throughout 1981 and early 1982. He did so despite an increase in unemployment from 5.8 percent in 1979 to 9.5 percent in 1982, the highest rate since the Great Depression.[7] The political pressure to relax the tight money policy was intense, but the Fed held to its course. In 1982, inflation was 3.9 percent. The cost of disinflation, however, was high, despite the predictions of some economists that once the Fed's commitment to stable prices was taken seriously, the real adjustments would be small. Of course, on this occasion there was little reason based on past experience to take the Fed seriously.

Beginning in 1982, the economy began the longest peacetime expansion up to that time on record. (Refer to Table 27.1) Unemployment gradually declined, and inflation remained at tolerable levels through the remainder of the Ronald Reagan's presidency. After two terms, Reagan left the presidency in 1989 as one of the most popular presidents of the post-war period. Much of that popularity rested on the contrast between economic conditions as he found them and as he left them.

How much of that record was due to monetary policy is difficult to say. One of the ironies of the period is that the economy seemed able to absorb a considerable amount of new money without experiencing a return to high rates of inflation. From December 1980 to December 1986, the stock of money grew at an annual rate of 9.0 percent. Some observers considered this natural as long as the economy was emerging from the deep trough of the early 1980s. Others suggested that deregulation of the banking system and, particularly, the payment of interest on bank deposits had independently increased the demand for money.

In any case, with the stock of money growing rapidly, frequently in excess of the targets proclaimed by the Fed, and with little evidence of unacceptably high rates of inflation, the Fed gradually abandoned its emphasis on monetary growth and began to pay attention again to interest rates.

Ronald Reagan and Supply-Side Economics

Ronald Reagan's landslide victory in the 1980 election and the dramatic shift in power in Congress—particularly in the Senate—to the Republicans provided both a mandate for change and the coalition to realize it. As soon as the Reagan administration was formed, it

[7]The frequent repetition of this fact in the media misled many people into thinking that the unemployment rate was almost as high as it had been during the Great Depression. This, of course, was not the case. See chapter 23.

TABLE 27.2 The Federal Government's Deficit, 1940–2001

YEAR	BILLIONS OF DOLLARS	AS A PERCENTAGE OF FEDERAL EXPENDITURES	AS A PERCENTAGE OF GDP
1940	–2.9	30.53	2.86
1950	–3.1	7.28	1.05
1960	0.3[a]	0.33	0.06
1970	–2.8	1.43	0.27
1980	–73.8	12.49	2.64
1985	–212.3	22.43	5.04
1990	–221.2	17.65	3.81
1995	–164	10.82	2.22
2000	236.4[a]	13.22	2.41
2001	127.3[a]	6.89	1.26

[a]*Surplus*

Source: The Economic Report of the President, 2003 *(Washington, D.C.: Government Printing Office, 2004), Tables B–1and B–80.*

moved swiftly to implement Reagan's economic campaign promises. These centered on a large tax cut achieved by lowering marginal tax rates (especially for very high incomes), elimination of the federal deficit, and a reduction in the role of the federal government in terms of spending and regulation, and a buildup of the armed forces.

Once again, a new school of economic thought was influential in altering the course of economic policy. "Supply-side" economists such as Arthur Laffer argued that high tax rates were inhibiting economic growth. Lowering rates would give people more incentive to work, invest, and innovate. Lowering rates would even produce more tax revenue by expanding the tax base, thus helping to balance the budget. The relationship between tax rates and tax revenues became known as the *Laffer curve*: Over some range, raising rates would increase revenues, but at some other point, additional increases would lead to large reductions in work effort and increases in tax evasion; then total tax revenue would fall. Laffer and other supply-side economists believed that the economy had already entered this range. Although most economists agreed that high tax rates tended in some degree to discourage productive effort, many doubted that the effects of cutting rates would be as large as the supply siders thought. In the campaign for the Republican nomination, George Bush, then Reagan's rival, spoke for many when he denounced the idea of balancing the budget through tax cuts as "voodoo economics," a term that gained wide currency among critics of supply-side theory.

After the election, Congress moved swiftly to reduce income taxes and other taxes by 23 percent over a three-year period, but reductions in spending were much harder to achieve.[8] As David A. Stockman, who was in charge of planning the Reagan spending cuts, tells us in his memoir, *The Triumph of Politics*, even the most commonsense cuts were strongly resisted by an "iron triangle": the direct beneficiaries of government spending in the private sector, the government bureaucrats who administered the program, and the members of Congress who were particularly beholden to the beneficiaries.

Tax cuts, the recession, the failure to make proposed spending cuts, and the increases in the military budget produced deficits in the federal budget unprecedented in peacetime. Table 27.2 reveals both the acceleration of growth in the deficit under president Reagan and the long-term nature of the problem. As the Table 27.2 shows, the deficit reached 5 percent of GDP in 1985 and remained a high, although declining, proportion of GDP for the following decade.

[8]This is usually referred to as a 25 percent decrease, but it was phased in over three years in cuts of 10 percent, 10 percent, and 5 percent. These cumulate to 23 percent: $1 - (1 - 0.10) \times (1 - 0.10) \times (1 - 0.05) = 0.23$.

Alan Greenspan was appointed chairman of the Fed Board in 1987. His deft handling of monetary policy was given much of the credit for the economic expansion of the 1990s.

© REUTERS NEWMEDIA INC./CORBIS

What were the consequences of such deficits? Some economists predicted that large federal deficits would lead to skyrocketing real interest rates (the market rate less inflation) because deficits meant that a much-augmented demand for credit would face the same supply. But the supply of credit proved more elastic than had been anticipated, however. Foreign lenders rushed into the U.S. market, purchasing government bonds, private securities, real estate, and other assets. Real interest rates did not rocket upward, and the dollar remained strong (worth a large number of units of foreign currency) despite a growing gap between exports and imports. There was always the possibility that foreign lenders would some day lose confidence in the U.S. economy, but the "day of reckoning" proved to be longer in coming than many had expected.

Economists warned that the taxes used to finance the deficit were discouraging capital formation. There was, then, much concern about the federal deficit when President George Bush took office in January 1989. During the campaign, Bush had promised to continue Reagan's policies. He laid down the gauntlet to the Democrats by declaring, "Read my lips: no new taxes." He abandoned this pledge, however, when the recession of 1990 and 1991 helped drive the budget deficit higher. The deficit was still a major issue when Bill Clinton took the oath of office in January 1993. Rapid economic growth, however, solved the problem. By 2000, as Table 27.2 shows, there was a large surplus and the new worry that proved to be fleeting was how to spend the surplus rather than how to pay for the deficit.

The Greenspan Era at the Federal Reserve

In 1987 President Ronald Reagan appointed economist Alan Greenspan to head the Federal Reserve Board. Greenspan would go on to serve for the remainder of the century and into the next one, the longest tenure of any chair, and earn an enviable reputation; see *Maestro* a well received biography of Greenspan.[9] He was tested quickly. Only a few months after taking charge, the stock market took a sudden and extreme plunge. Fear was widespread that the entire financial system would collapse. (See New Perspective 27.1) Greenspan arranged a large temporary injection of money into financial markets that

---

[9]Bob Woodward, *Maestro: Greenspan's Fed and the American Boom* (New York: Simon & Schuster, 2000).

Perspective 27.1

Do Stock Market Crashes Cause Depressions?

For reasons that are still not entirely clear, a severe stock market crash occurred in 1987. The Dow Jones Industrial Average, a widely used index (shown in the following figure as the solid line measured against the right value axis) fell 26 percent between September and October 1987. In the immediate aftermath of the crash, many people expected a repeat of the events that had occurred in 1929 and 1930: a rapid slide into severe depression. This did not happen, however; the real economy as represented, for example, by the unemployment rate (shown in the figure as the dashed line measured against the left value axis) remained stable. Alan Greenspan and the Federal Reserve received considerable credit for responding immediately by pumping additional liquidity into financial markets. There is also a lesson to be learned from this case about the danger of jumping to conclusions based on limited evidence. Conclusions such as "stock market crashes cause depressions" cannot be based safely on a hasty reading of one historical event, however compelling. As Economic Reasoning Proposition 5 reminds us, conclusions must be tested by a wide range of facts.

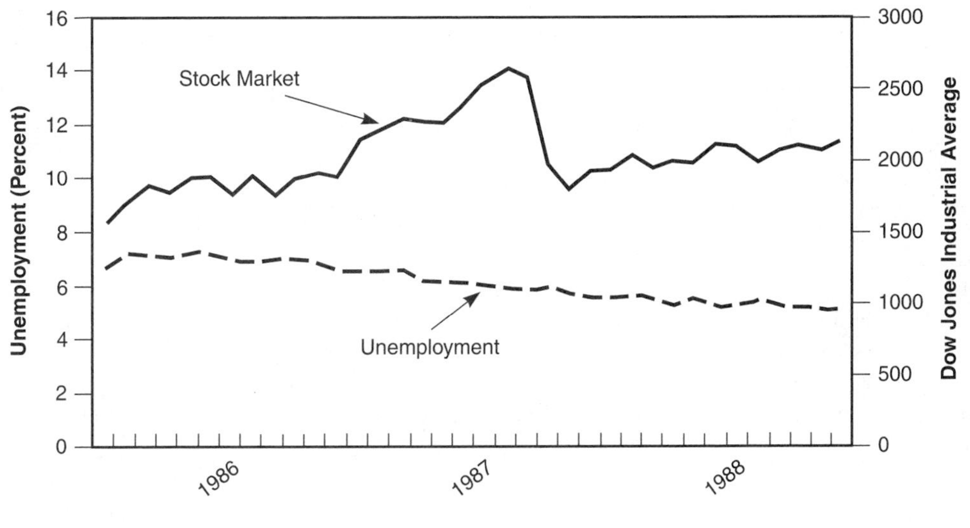

helped quell fears and restore order. There would be other financial crises: a Mexican Debt Crisis in 1995 and an East Asian Debt Crisis in 1997. In both cases, Greenspan supported activist measures to help contain the crisis. In managing the economy, he did not adhere to the view advocated by Milton Friedman that the money supply should grow at precisely the same rate year in and year out, but he did adhere to the older monetarist tradition that stressed price stability as the ultimate goal that the Fed could and should achieve. Indeed, it could be said that Greenspan's policy combined Keynesian means (discretionary control through interest rates) with monetarist ends (price-level stability).

In March 1991 (Table 27.1), the economy reached a trough from which began the longest economic boom in history. It did not end until March 2001, a full decade later. The expansion was driven by a huge investment boom as the use of personal computers and the Internet spread through the economy and changed the way Americans worked and played. To use the colloquial expression, America was "getting wired." A stock market boom was a concomitant with the investment boom, as it had been in earlier investment booms, such as in the 1920s. From a level of 3,018 in March 1991, the Dow Jones Industrial Average nearly quadrupled to a peak of 11,750 in January 2000. The NASDAQ index, which contained more of the high technology stocks that were so much in favor, rose even more.

During this period, Greenspan received considerable credit for keeping the expansion going without driving the economy into an inflationary spiral. Recognizing several factors—increasing productivity growth and a resulting price stability consistent with lower levels of unemployment than had traditionally been the case—Greenspan adjusted monetary policy accordingly. The stock market boom was a continuing worry. Therefore, Greenspan attempted to use some of his immense prestige to talk the market down to what he believed was a more sustainable level. His characterization of the stock market as succumbing to "irrational exuberance" was widely quoted. Nevertheless, for a time the market ignored even the famous chair of the Federal Reserve Board. All good things, at least all economic expansions, must end. The stock market tumbled, real investment tumbled, and unemployment rose. In March 2001, the unemployment rate was 4.2 percent; by the end of the year, it was 5.8 percent. According to the official dating, the recession that followed the great boom of 1990s was not especially long; only eight months from March 2001 to November 2001 (Table 27.1). However, the expansion that followed this interlude, despite a major tax cut pushed through by President George W. Bush, and the turn of the federal budget from surplus to deficit, appears, as this is written, to be somewhat anemic. Unemployment has remained stubbornly high; it has been, to use the term favored by critics of the administration and the Federal Reserve, a "jobless recovery." Whether the new monetary orthodoxy of monetarist ends (price stability) achieved through Keynesian means (targeting interest rates) will prove sufficient for the new economic environment remains to be seen.

WAS THE ECONOMY MORE STABLE AFTER WORLD WAR II THAN BEFORE THE DEPRESSION?

Through most of the postwar era, economists believed that the economy had become more stable, certainly in comparison with the Great Depression but also in comparison with the predepression era. Greater stability was the result, they believed, of changes in the economy's structure (the relative decline of manufacturing and agriculture and the rise of services) and improved monetary and fiscal policy.

Christina Romer challenged this view. She pointed out that the amount and reliability of raw data available in the postwar period on unemployment, GDP, and similar variables was much greater than what it had been earlier in the century. The reduction in the variability of the key macroeconomic indicators, she argued, was merely the result of having better estimates: The improvement was a "figment" of the data. To prove her point, Romer extended the prewar estimates forward in time. In other words, she estimated postwar unemployment, GDP, and so on, as if she had to make do with only the "bad" prewar raw data. An example of what she found can be seen in Table 27.3. The official estimates for 1948–1982 are shown on the second line, and Romer's estimates are shown below them in parentheses. The key change is in the standard deviation of the unemployment rate. The conventional data shows a dramatic fall from 2.38 to 1.58 percent, indicating greater stability. Romer shows that if the prewar technique for estimating unemployment had been used in the postwar period, the fall would have been from 2.38 to 2.24 percent, indicating little improvement in stability. Romer's work has been challenged, but it has made economists more cautious about their claims for modern policymaking.[10]

[10]See David Weir, "The Reliability of Historical Macroeconomic Data," *Journal of Economic History* 46 (June 1986): 353–365, for a criticism of Romer's work.

TABLE 27.3 Alternative Measures of the Unemployment Rate

YEARS	MEAN	STANDARD DEVIATION
1900–1930 (Official)	4.84%	2.38%
1948–1982 (Official)	5.41	1.58
1948–1982 (Romer)	(5.52)	(2.24)

Source: Computed from Christina Romer, "Spurious Volatility in Historical Unemployment Data," Journal of Political Economy *94 (1986): 3, 12.*

Selected References and Suggested Readings

Blinder, Alan S. *Economic Policy and the Great Stagflation.* New York: Academic Press, 1979.

Bordo, Michael D., and Barry Eichengreen. *A Retrospective on the Bretton Woods System: Lessons for International Monetary Reform.* Chicago: University of Chicago Press, 1993.

Brownlee, W. Elliot. "The Public Sector." In *The Cambridge Economic History of the United States,* Vol. III, *The Twentieth Century,* eds. Stanley L. Engerman and Robert E. Gallman. New York: Cambridge University Press, 2000, 1013–1060.

Brunner, Karl, and Allan H. Meltzer, eds. *The Economics of Price and Wage Controls.* Amsterdam: North Holland, 1976.

Eckstein, Otto. *The Great Recession.* Amsterdam: North Holland, 1978.

Federal Reserve Bank of Minneapolis. Materials on the history of the Federal Reserve System. **http://minneapolisfed.org/sylloge/history.html**.

Friedman, Benjamin M. "Postwar Changes in the American Financial Markets." In *The American Economy in Transition,* ed. Martin Feldstein. Chicago: University of Chicago Press, 1980.

Friedman, Milton. "The Role of Monetary Policy." *American Economic Review* 58 (March 1968): 1–17.

Friedman, Milton, and Anna J. Schwartz. *A Monetary History of the United States, 1867–1960.* Princeton, N.J.: Princeton University Press, 1963.

Gordon, Robert J. "Postwar Macroeconomics: The Evolution of Events and Ideas." In *The American Economy in Transition,* ed. Martin Feldstein. Chicago: University of Chicago Press, 1980.

———. "Understanding Inflation in the 1980s." *Brookings Papers on Economic Activity* 16, no. 1 (1985): 263–299.

Heller, Walter W. *New Dimensions of Political Economy.* New York: Norton, 1966.

Lucas, Robert E., Jr. "Econometric Policy Evaluation: A Critique." In *The Phillips Curve and Labor Markets,* eds. K. Brunner and A. H. Meltzer. Carnegie-Rochester Conference Series on Public Policy, Vol. 1. Amsterdam: North Holland, 1976.

———. "Understanding Business Cycles." In *Stabilization of the Domestic and International Economy,* eds. Karl Brunner and Allan Meltzer. Carnegie-Rochester Conference Series, Vol. 5. Amsterdam: North Holland, 1977.

Okun, Arthur M. "Measuring the Impact of the 1964 Tax Reduction." In *Perspectives on Economic Growth,* ed. Walter W. Heller. New York: Random House, 1968.

Phelps, Edmund S. "Phillips Curves, Expectations of Inflation and Optimal Unemployment Policy over Time." *Economica* 34 (1967): 254–281.

Phillips, A.W. "The Relation between Unemployment and the Rate of Change of Money Wage Rates in the United Kingdom, 1861–1957." *Economica* 25 (November 1958): 283–299.

Roberts, Paul Craig. *The Supply-Side Revolution.* Cambridge, Mass.: Harvard University Press, 1984.

Romer, Christina. "Is the Stabilization of the Postwar Economy a Figment of the Data?" *American Economic Review* 76 (1986): 314–334.

———. "Spurious Volatility in Historical Unemployment Data." *Journal of Political Economy* 94 (1986): 1–37.

Sachs, Jeffrey. "The Changing Cyclical Behavior of Wages and Prices, 1890–1976." *American Economic Review* 70 (1980): 78–90.

Schultz, George P., and Kenneth W. Dam. *Economic Policy beyond the Headlines*. New York: Norton, 1977.

Stein, Herbert. *The Fiscal Revolution in America*. Chicago: University of Chicago Press, 1969.

———. *Presidential Economics*. New York: Simon & Schuster, 1984.

Stockman, David A. *The Triumph of Politics: How the Reagan Revolution Failed*. New York: Harper & Row, 1986.

Sundquist, James L. *Politics and Policy: The Eisenhower, Kennedy and Johnson Years*. Washington, D.C.: Brookings Institution, 1968.

Tobin, James. *The New Economics One Decade Older*. Princeton, N.J.: Princeton University Press, 1974.

Weir, David R. "The Reliability of Historical Macroeconomic Data for Comparing Cyclical Stability." *Journal of Economic History* 46 (June 1986): 353–365.

White, Eugene N. "Banking and Finance in the Twentieth Century." In *The Cambridge Economic History of the United States*, Vol. III, *The Twentieth Century*, eds. Stanley L. Engerman and Robert E. Gallman. New York: Cambridge University Press, 2000, 773–802.

Woodward, Bob. *Maestro: Greenspan's Fed and the American Boom*. New York: Simon & Schuster, 2000.

Chapter Twenty-Eight

MANUFACTURING, PRODUCTIVITY, AND LABOR

Although many other nations aspired to increased industrialization, the manufacturing sector in the United States declined (relative to other sectors) throughout much of the twentieth century. U.S. manufacturing employment as shown in Table 28.1 on page 566, was cut in half, from 25.6 percent of the labor force in 1950 to 12.8 percent of the labor force in 2001. The decline in manufacturing employment (in relative terms since the 1950s and absolute terms since the 1980s) was the result of the faster growth in the demand for services, the increasing ability of consumers to purchase manufactured goods more cheaply from abroad, and the increasing productivity in the manufacturing sector.

A portrait of relative decline, however, should not lead to the idea that the sector was stagnant. The manufacturing sector changed dramatically during the postwar era. New industries arose and displaced old ones. New production techniques were adopted. Waves of mergers and acquisitions eliminated old firms and created new giants. An energy crisis forced firms to alter long established practices. "Downsizing" altered the relationship between employer and employee. Antitrust policies were increasingly modified by the ideas of economists.

EMPLOYMENT PATTERNS

The American labor market underwent a profound transformation during the postwar era. On the demand side, the key development was the rise of the service sector. By 1992, two of three workers were in the private service sector or the government. Major changes also occurred on the supply side. A moral awakening in the 1960s vastly reshaped the labor market. Discriminatory barriers that had confined many women, African Americans, and members of other minorities to the margins of American economic life were reduced, and immigration laws were changed to eliminate quotas that restricted immigration from certain parts of the world. In addition, the labor force participation rate of women, including women with young children, rose dramatically.

One consequence of these changes was the decline of the unions, which reached a peak in power and membership in the 1950s only to see their influence wane in the following decades. Finally, in the later part of the century, these changes produced a slowdown in the

TABLE 28.1 The Changing Role of Manufacturing

YEAR	EMPLOYMENT IN MANUFACTURING (millions)	EMPLOYMENT AS A SHARE OF THE LABOR FORCE (percent)	MANUFACTURING OUTPUT AS A SHARE OF GNP (percent)
1950	15.1	25.6%	28.0%
1960	16.2	24.6	26.9
1970	18.9	24.0	23.9
1980	19.8	20.0	20.8
1990	18.7	15.7	17.8
1999	18.3	13.7	16.2
2001	17.3	12.8	14.1

Sources: Labor force: Economic Report of the President, 2003 *(Washington, D.C.: Government Printing Office, 2003), 311; manufacturing employment:* Bureau of Economic Analysis, *NIPA Tables 6.5B, 6.5C; manufacturing output:* Economic Report of the President, 2001 *(Washington, D.C.: Government Printing Office, 2001), 285; GNP:* Bureau of Economic Analysis, *NIPA Table 1.9.*

growth of real wages, particularly for workers with relatively low skills, that threatened to leave a disturbing legacy for the twenty-first century.

GALES OF CREATIVE DESTRUCTION

Long ago, economist Joseph Schumpeter observed that capitalism moves forward, for better or worse, through the introduction of new products that destroy the market for older products in his famous phrase, through "gales of creative destruction".[1]

The postwar era provides abundant evidence for Schumpeter's generalization. In the 1940s and 1950s, the antibiotics industry exhibited the highest average growth rate—a phenomenal 118 percent per year. Output of television sets was almost as great; home freezers and clothes dryers were close behind. At the other end of the spectrum, production of tractors, locomotives, and rayon and acetate slowed. The output of some industries actually declined. Changes in consumer tastes accounted for some of these declines, as in the cases

© D. G. ARNOLD

Plant closings, particularly in the "smokestack industries" of the northeastern and midwestern "rustbelt," produced significant job losses in the 1970s and 1980s.

[1]Joseph Schumpeter, "The Analysis of Economic Change," *The Review of Economic Statistics*, 17 (4), (May, 1935), 2–10. For a critical assessment of Schumpeter's emphasis on major innovations, see Nathan Rosenberg, *Perspectives on Technology* (Cambridge: Cambridge University Press, 1976), chapter 4.

of pipe and chewing tobacco and lamb and mutton. For the most part, however, the retrogressing industries had fallen victim to competition from new products. Television hurt the motion picture industry, changed radio production, raised problems in spectator sports, and affected book sales and restaurant dining. Network television, in turn, has been affected by the growth of cable television, DVDs, and the Internet. Older methods of producing a given commodity may also be displaced by newer methods. Steel-reinforced aluminum cable, which is both stronger and lighter than an electrically equivalent copper cable, captured the high-voltage transmission line business.

After World War II, automatic washing machines, television sets, home freezers, room air conditioners, dehumidifiers, and clothes dryers made their mark. As the 1960s progressed, central air conditioning and electric heating systems vied with color television sets for a rapidly increasing share of household outlays. In the 1970s, recreational and a vocational expenditures on new designs of old products rose spectacularly as families turned to cameras, stereos, boats, campers, and other leisure-time equipment.

Today, as in the past, American manufacturers endlessly strive to develop new products. Schumpeter believed that the central justification for monopolies and oligopolies is that they develop large research departments that institutionalize the process of research and innovation. In Schumpeter's view, a firm with market power would be able to maintain or increase it by introducing new products, whereas competitive firms or independent laboratories may be hard pressed to raise capital to invest in research and development. Subsequent research, however, has challenged the central role of monopolies and oligopolies in research and development. For one thing, it appears that firms with market power often focus on minor innovations designed to protect their monopoly power. New products such as Polaroid cameras and intermittent windshield wipers often come from smaller firms or independent inventors.[2] The Internet and biotechnology sectors have shown that venture capitalists are willing to support new enterprises.

Above all, computers illustrate the role of different types of firms in the innovative process. For a time it looked as if the mainframe computer business dominated by IBM would be the norm. Next the personal computer revolution upset consensus predictions and left IBM scrambling to catch up. Then for a time it looked as if the Apple computer and its operating system would become dominant, but shortly it was overtaken by Microsoft and its Windows operating system. See Perspective 28.1 on page 568 for a comparison of the wealth of Bill Gates, Microsoft founder, and John D. Rockefeller.

Steve Jobs with an early version of the Apple personal computer. Being a pioneer, however, does not ensure one's place in an industry. By the end of the century, rapid technological changes in the industry had left Apple far behind rival Microsoft.

[2]See Frederic M. Scherer, *Innovation and Growth: Schumpeterian Perspectives* (Cambridge, Mass.: MIT Press, 1984), chapter 11, for a review of the evidence.

Perspective 28.1

Is Bill Gates as "Rich as Rockefeller"?

John D. Rockefeller, the founder of Standard Oil, was the richest man of his day. Although estimates differ, it is frequently said that Rockefeller's fortune peaked at about $1 billion in 1913. How does that figure compare with the fortune of Bill Gates, the largest in our day, estimated to be about $43 billion in 2003? Obviously, we cannot directly compare 1913 dollars with 2003 dollars. We need, in economists' words, to inflate the 1913 dollars. The consumer price index is now about 18 times higher than it was in 1913, so by this criterion, Rockefeller's fortune would be worth about $18 billion in today's money. Bill Gates is richer. However, we can make the comparison in other ways. For example, we can compare their fortunes using GDP. Rockefeller's fortune was equal to 2.73 percent of GDP, but Gates's fortune is equal to only .41 percent of GDP. To put it somewhat differently, Gates would need a fortune of $285 billion to have the same wealth today, relative to the size of the economy, that Rockefeller had in 1913. By this criterion, Rockefeller is richer. There is no single "right" way to compare the two fortunes. To understand how much in goods and services could be purchased by philanthropic organizations financed with these fortunes, the consumer price index (CPI) comparison might be a better measuring rod, but to understand how much power and influence each man had, the GDP comparison might be better. The appropriate measure really depends on which focus is chosen.

More information about how to put things into today's money can be found at the Web site of the Economic History Association at **http://www.eh.net**.

Bill Gates, founder of the computer software giant Microsoft. Would the company founded by "the modern Rockefeller" endure? It's hard to say, but note that Exxon is the descendant of Rockefeller's Standard Oil.

© LYNN GOLDSMITH/CORBIS

Economic Insight 28.1

Path Dependence

Sometimes economic historians find it helpful to focus on a simple example that abstracts from many problems surrounding more complex historical processes. For example, many economic historians suspect that the triumph of Microsoft and the Windows operating system was *path dependent*. If Bill Gates had some bad luck early in the computer revolution and Steve Jobs, or some other pioneer, had some good luck, we might have ended up with a different, and possibly better, standard operating system. The problem with discussing path dependence in the context of Microsoft is that one must untangle this issue from so many others, including business practices, intellectual property rights, and so on. For that reason many economic historians have discussed path dependence in the context of a much simpler case. The six keys at the top left of a computer keyboard spell QWERTY. It has been alleged that the keys were originally assigned these letters to slow typists down and prevent the keyboards of the first mechanical typewriters from jamming. Now, according to this story, consumers are stuck with this inefficient design because the wrong path (from our perspective) was chosen in the nineteenth century when computers were unknown. This example was first brought to the attention of economic historians by Paul A. David in his famous paper "Clio and the Economics of Qwerty." Stanley J. Leibowitz and Stephen E. Margolis challenged David's view in a paper entitled "The Fable of the Keys" and other works. Leibowitz and Margolis argued that the advantages of alternative keyboards are not as great as claimed and that the suggestion of some that it would be in the interests of society for the government to force a transition to a new keyboard may well be a mistake. You can read a fascinating discussion among economic historians about path dependence and QWERTY at **http://eh.net/lists/archives/eh.res/**.

Some economic historians believe that these "gales of creative destruction" produce the most efficient allocation of resources. Others argue that the outcome is path dependent. See Economic Insight 28.1. A few chance events determine the path taken and the final destination. Perhaps intervention by government could ensure that the economy would end up in the right place.

Productivity Growth

The wave of new products that hit the market after World War II was accompanied by rapid productivity growth. Indeed, growth was so rapid that some observers began to talk about a second industrial revolution. After about 1970, however, productivity growth slowed. As illustrated in Figure 28.1 on page 570. This figure plots the growth rate of output per labor hour in the nonfarm business sector. To make the graph easier to read, we have plotted a moving three-year average.[3] The exact date when the slowdown began (or the years of transition) are a matter of debate—you can make your own judgment as you look at the diagram—but the contrast between the early years of the postwar era and the middle years is dramatic. The slowdown in productivity growth was a major concern of policymakers because in a market economy, productivity is one of the fundamental determinants of real wages, a theme we will return to later.

[3]The number plotted above 1970 is the average for 1969, 1970, and 1971. Moving averages are used frequently to smooth data so that the viewer can concentrate on long-term trends.

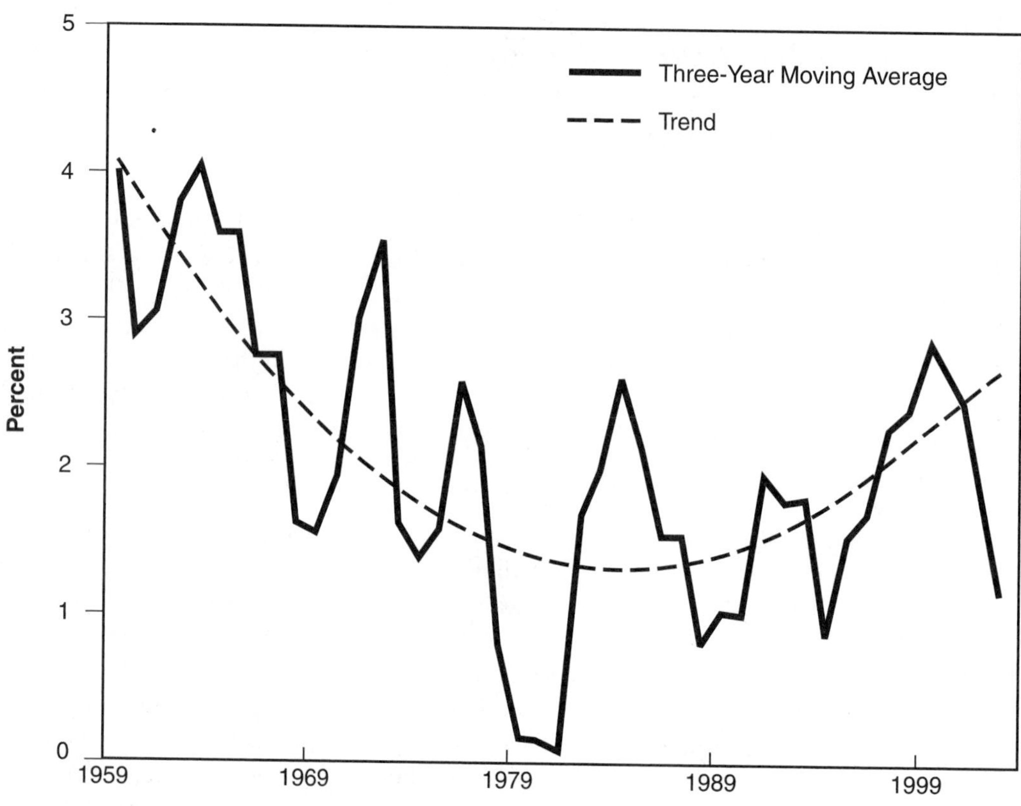

FIGURE 28.1 The Growth of Output per Hour in the Nonfarm Business Sector: Three-Year Moving Average, 1959–2001

Note: The growth of labor productivity slowed to anemic rates in 1970s and the 1980s, but began to increase more rapidly in the 1990s.

Source: Historical Statistics of the United States Colonial Times to 1970 *(Washington, D.C.: Government Printing Office), Series D-684; and* Economic Report of the President 2003 *(Washington, D.C.: Government Printing Office, 2003), Table B–50, 328.*

Why did productivity growth slow down in the 1970s? A number of factors were at work. (1) The shift of production away from manufacturing toward the service sector was one important factor. Quality improvements are extremely difficult to measure in the service sector, so output growth may have been understated. (2) As Michael Darby argued, changes in the structure of the labor force accounted for much of the slowdown. Many young and, therefore, inexperienced workers were entering the labor force for the first time in the 1970s.[4] (3) The growth of capital per unit of labor input also slowed in the 1970s. To some extent, this may have been the result of rising inflation that disrupted financial markets and discouraged saving. (4) The highly variable rate of inflation in the 1970s may also have distorted price signals and prevented the reallocation of resources to their most efficient uses. When inflation varies dramatically from month to month, it is difficult for workers or owners of capital to know whether their real income has fallen because they are in a declining sector or because their nominal income has temporarily lagged behind prices. (5) Some blame should probably be attached to the high cost of complying with new government regulations stemming from legislation passed in the 1960s and even more in the 1970s, perhaps because some credit should be given to deregulation for the rebound of

[4]Michael R. Darby, "The U.S. Productivity Slowdown: A Case of Statistical Myopia," *American Economic Review* 74 (June 1984): 301–322.

manufacturing productivity in the 1980s. (6) When oil prices rose sharply, industries and agricultural producers who had relied on cheap and abundant oil suddenly were forced to adjust to higher prices. Large investments were required to replace older equipment with more energy-efficient equipment, even when the new equipment produced the same output per labor hour. Toward the end of the century, productivity growth began to rise, as is evident in Figure 29.1 on page 593. Adjustment to higher energy prices, the computer revolution, and corporate restructuring all contributed to a rise in productivity growth that was as unexpected as was the preceding decline.

The Energy Crisis

Beginning in 1973, the Organization of Petroleum Exporting Countries (OPEC), which at that time controlled a substantial share of the world oil market, began to flex its muscles. Particularly disruptive was the oil embargo that followed the Arab Israeli war in 1973. When the United States adopted price controls to protect consumers from the price increases, the result was long lines at gas pumps: rationing by waiting time rather than by price.

This experience touched off a fundamental debate on how to meet the "energy crisis." Should it be through government actions—rationing, subsidies for the poor, and federal expenditures for new sources of energy—or through the price mechanism? The bureaucratic approach was tried. A Federal Energy Administration was established in 1974, and a cabinet level Department of Energy followed in 1977. Spending on a wide range of federal energy projects was increased. But in the end, much of the painful adjustment was the response to higher prices. Americans cut their energy consumption by buying smaller cars (many of them from foreign producers), insulating their homes, and investing in more fuel-efficient productive processes. On the supply side, higher prices produced a rapid increase in oil production in countries outside of OPEC, undermining OPEC's monopoly power. The price system worked much as many of its advocates had suggested it would, although not perhaps as quickly and painlessly as some of them had expected.

The dimensions of the energy crisis and its the results can be read from the data in Table 28.2. The first column shows what happened to the price of crude oil. As you can see, it rose dramatically and by 1980 was 6.75 times as high as it had been in 1970. The real price of oil (the price of oil divided by average prices), shown in column 2, however, did not rise as fast. To put it somewhat differently, oil producers were able to lift the price of their product by a factor of 6.3 between 1970 and 1990, but they were able to improve their "terms of trade"

TABLE 28.2 The Energy Crisis

YEAR	PRICE OF CRUDE OIL (current dollars per million BTU)	PRICE OF CRUDE OIL (1996 dollars per million BTU)	AVERAGE PRICE OF ENERGY FROM ALL SOURCES (1996 dollars per million BTU)	ENERGY CONSUMPTION (thousands of BTU per 1996 dollar of GDP)
1970	0.55	1.89	5.67	19.10
1975	1.32	3.30	8.33	17.79
1980	3.72	6.52	12.08	16.10
1985	4.15	5.64	11.36	13.49
1990	3.45	3.99	9.59	12.60
1995	2.52	2.57	8.45	12.07
1999	2.68	2.56	NA	10.85

Source: Statistical Abstract of the United States, 2000, *(Washington, D.C.: Government Printing Office, 2001), Table 954 (price of crude oil), 948 (energy prices), and 945 (energy consumption).*

by only a factor of 2.11.This was a substantial increase, but far from the dire predictions made in the 1970s. Indeed, after 1980, the price of crude oil could not keep pace with inflation. The price of all forms of energy, shown in the third column, also rose as a result of the energy crisis but by a still smaller proportion. The oil price shocks created an incentive to substitute less costly forms of energy for oil, but as demand shifted toward these sources, their prices rose as well.

The result of the increase in the price of energy is shown in the last column of the table, which shows the amount of energy used per dollar of real GDP. This measure fell only 5 percent between 1970 and 1975. In the short run, the number of adjustments that could be made was limited. Perhaps the most a car owner could do was cut out some unnecessary trips. In the long run, however, more adjustments were possible. By 1990, energy use had fallen by almost 30 percent. In the long run, a consumer could buy a smaller, more fuel efficient car, move close to work or public transportation, and so on. The energy crisis is a classical illustration of Economic Reasoning Propositions 2 and 3; choices involve trade-offs and incentives. Making these adjustments took their toll on the economy. Savings that might have financed investments that increased output were used instead to finance investments that conserved energy or developed alternative sources.

CHANGES IN THE ORGANIZATION OF INDUSTRY

Mergers among firms, acquisitions of one firm by another, and divestitures are among the main ways that firms try to increase their productivity and, ultimately, their profitability. A combination of several firms producing the same product, for example, may allow the combined firm to achieve economies of scale that each firm separately could not. Even if the firms are producing different products, it may be more profitable to combine them to take advantage of an elite management. Over the twentieth century, several distinct waves of mergers have made and remade the structure of American industry.

Looking back, we can see that mergers and acquisitions come in waves that crested, typically, during periods of very intense economic activity. The 1920s, for example, brought a wave of business consolidation that was comparable, in some respects, to the great merger movement of 1897 to 1904. These waves, moreover, typically produced a public backlash motivated by fear that giant corporations are taking over the economy. The backlash against the merger movement in the twenties was strengthened by the belief that the existence of widespread monopoly had contributed to the Great Depression.

The postwar period witnessed three waves of mergers: (1) a wave of conglomerate mergers that was particularly marked during 1966 to 1969, (2) a wave of hostile takeovers that was particularly marked during 1977 to 1989, and (3) a wave of mergers to achieve economies of scale that began in the early 1990s and is still in progress.

Conglomerate Mergers

In the first post–World War II wave of mergers, the dominant form was the conglomerate, which combined companies that produced unrelated commodities or services. Between 1964 and 1972, the peak of the wave, about 80 percent of all mergers were conglomerations. This type of merger's fundamental purpose was to reduce the adverse effects of the business cycle or unexpected shocks in individual markets by diversifying the activities the company undertook. A characteristic of the conglomerate was its management organization. A small, elite headquarters staff attended to general matters such as financial planning, capital allocations, legal and accounting tasks, and operations research.

Ling-Temco-Voight (LTV), one of the first and most successful conglomerates, began in 1958 as a small firm called Ling Electronic, with annual sales of less than $7 million. During the next 10 years, Ling acquired or merged with Temco Aircraft, Chance-Voight,

Okonite, Wilson and Company, Wilson Sporting Goods Company, the Greatamerica Corporation, and some 24 other companies. Its revenues in 1968 were nearly $3 billion. When LTV acquired the Jones and Laughlin Steel Company in 1969, the merger meant that two corporations in the list of the nation's 100 largest companies were combining to make LTV the fourteenth-largest company in the United States.

Comparable results were achieved by other conglomerates such as Gulf and Western Industries, International Telephone and Telegraph, Litton Industries, Boise Cascade, and the Automatic Sprinkler Corporation. These and other conglomerate mergers created much of the glamour and fast-paced financial action that characterized the first merger wave. This wave peaked in 1969. During the 1970s, many of the conglomerates failed to perform as expected. Diversified companies proved more difficult to manage than expected, and diversification failed to isolate the conglomerates from the troubles experienced by more conventional companies.

Hostile Takeovers

In the late 1970s and early 1980s, merger activity emerged again. The number of merger and acquisition announcements increased by more than 30 percent between 1975 and 1985, and the value of merged firms rose (at 1975 prices) from $12 billion to $90 billion. New terms such as *junk bonds* and *leveraged buyouts* and new personalities such as T. Boone Pickens, Carl Icahn, and Michael Milken dominated the financial pages.

In the typical case, corporate raiders such as Pickens and Icahn targeted a firm believed to be undervalued. They then issued junk bonds (high-risk and, hence, high yield bonds), offering some combination of these bonds and cash to the holders of the stock of the firm being acquired. Milken (of the investment banking firm of Drexel, Burnham, Lambert) was instrumental in bringing together entrepreneurs who wished to use junk bonds in takeovers with buyers. Milken contended, based on the historical record of junk bonds, that these bonds rarely proved to be as risky in the long run as conventional wisdom would have it. What he and his buyers tended to forget was that through his own actions, Milken had so reshaped the market that his crop of junk bonds could not correctly be compared with those issued in the past.

How could acquiring firms afford to pay more for common stock than it currently sold for in the market? Ultimately, each leveraged buyout (*leverage* is the ratio of debt to equity) depended on the belief that income generated by the firm acquisition could be increased by an amount sufficient to cover the interest on the new debt and still leave an ample return for shareholders. The many ways of increasing income included replacing incompetent management, exploiting underutilized holdings of natural resources, and reducing "excessive" contributions to pension funds.

Defenders of leveraged buyouts and junk bonds argued that these techniques increased economic efficiency. Critics argued that leveraged buyout artists simply stripped firms of valuable assets for short-term gains and gulled foolish purchasers of junk bonds. The critics charged, moreover, that the debt-to-equity ratio for many of the resulting firms was dangerously high and that they would be unable to meet their interest payments during the next recession.

The fall of the junk bond market was as rapid as its ascent. In 1986 Drexel became a target in the ongoing investigation of insider trading by arbitrager Ivan Boesky.[5] In 1989 Drexel was forced to dismiss Milken, who later served time in jail for his part in the scandal. A few months later, Campeau Corporation, a large issuer of junk bonds in the retail field, encountered a liquidity crisis, sending the junk bond market into a tailspin. Legislation prohibiting

[5]"Insider trading" occurs when securities are bought or sold based on information from the management of the firm that has not been released to the public.

U.S. savings institutions from holding junk bonds also contributed to the slide, although only a few savings banks had ever acquired large positions in junk bonds. In 1990 Drexel, which itself held a large inventory of junk bonds, declared bankruptcy. The issuing of new junk bonds and their use in corporate takeovers had ended for a time.

In retrospect, the spectacular rise and fall of the junk bond market was a symptom rather than a cause of the high interest rates and volatile financial markets of the late 1970s and early 1980s, which sent investors in search of new and more flexible forms of finance.

In Search of Economies of Scale and Scope

The third wave of postwar mergers began in the early 1990s. This time, companies sought to achieve economies of scale by merging with or acquiring companies that filled out their "core competencies." The union of Chemical Banking and Chase Manhattan in 1996 produced a leaner firm with a much larger share of the New York consumer market. In other cases, companies sought economies of scale through marketing. This seems to have been the motive behind Gillete's acquisition of Duracell, the battery maker.

What was behind the third wave of mergers? A roaring stock market was one factor. Companies found it relatively easy to raise funds by issuing stock. An indulgent antitrust environment was another.

Antitrust policy has gone through two distinct phases since the Great Depression. In the first, beginning in the late 1930s, the Justice Department and the courts were hostile to mergers and business practices that appeared to limit competition. During this phase, the courts generally followed *per se rules*. For example, they usually held that control of a large share of the market was per se (intrinsically) illegal. It was no excuse that the firm had obtained a large share because it supplied a high-quality product or it had charged "fair" prices.

A second phase of antitrust policy began in the 1970s when the courts began to pay attention to critics of *per se* rules, who argued that they were often inconsistent with sound economic analysis and, because of this, often did more harm than good. Many of the most prominent critics, such as Robert Bork, Harold Demsetz, and Richard Posner, were associated with the famous Law and Economics program at the University of Chicago. The law-and-economics school of antitrust stressed several points. First, large market shares are usually the result of efficient management or innovation. Breaking up such firms may create losses in efficiency that outweigh the benefits from greater competition and (possibly) lower prices. In the *Alcoa* decision, Judge Learned Hand had viewed Alcoa's practice of building new capacity well ahead of demand as a dangerous practice tending toward monopoly. The law-and-economics school viewed it from the other side, as an example of foresight that should be congratulated rather than punished. Second, even if the deconcentrated industry can achieve high efficiency in the long run, high transition costs may be incurred. Such antitrust actions, moreover, may discourage other firms from undertaking product innovation and cost cutting. Third, competition can be effective even when there are few firms in an industry because attempts to collude tend to break down quickly and because the number of potential entrants may be large.

Thus, the wave of mergers at the end of the twentieth century resembled the wave of mergers at the end of the nineteenth century. In both cases, companies sought economies of scale by merging with or acquiring companies in the same or closely related fields. In both cases, a buoyant stock market played a role. And in both cases, regulatory policy was a factor: at the end of the nineteenth century, mergers were driven by the fear that a loose alliance of companies would be attacked under the Sherman Antitrust Act, while at the end of the twentieth century, mergers were driven by confidence that mergers that created more efficient companies would ultimately survive court challenges.

TABLE 28.3 Distribution of Jobs, 1955–2002, as a Percentage of Total Employment

YEAR	AGRICULTURE	MANUFACTURING, MINING, AND CONSTRUCTION	SERVICES	GOVERNMENT
1955	11.3	35.9	40.7	12.1
1960	9.2	34.3	42.6	14.0
1970	4.7	31.7	46.7	16.9
1980	3.6	27.4	51.7	17.3
1990	2.9	22.1	58.8	16.3
2000	2.4	19.0	63.2	15.3
2002	2.4	17.8	63.9	15.9

Source: Economic Report of the President, 2003 *(Washington, D.C.: Government Printing Office, 2003), Table B46.*

THE RISE OF THE SERVICE SECTOR

The most important change in the demand for labor was the growth of the "white-collar" (service) sector, a diverse grouping that includes retail trade, finance, education, medicine, entertainment, and so on. Table 28.3 shows this expansion. In 1955, the service sector provided about 41 percent of all jobs; by 2002, it provided almost 64 percent. The major declining sectors were agriculture, manufacturing, mining, and construction; their combined share fell from 44.5 percent in 1946 to 20.2 percent in 2002. Agriculture declined most rapidly in the period before 1970; manufacturing, on the other hand, held its own until 1970 and then began to decline. As Deirdre McCloskey put it when commenting on this chapter, production of "things" declined relative to production of "words."

The rise and fall in sectors can be explained by the changing structure of demand. As real incomes rose, the demand for certain products, such as consumer durables, increased slowly while demand for certain services increased rapidly. For example, rapid improvements in medical technology and increased federal funding produced rapid growth in the number of health-related jobs. Inflation and deregulation encouraged firms in the financial sector to offer an array of new products.

Productivity growth in the service sector has been slow, compared with that in manufacturing and agriculture.[6] This has contributed to the slowdown in the growth of real wages. This does not mean, however, that the economy would grow faster if the public invested more in other sectors. Expansion of some sectors has favorable effects on others. For example, productivity growth in education may be relatively slow, but the expansion of the education sector contributes to the manufacturing sector by supplying new techniques and better educated workers.

The growth of the service sector has also contributed to economic stability. In the manufacturing sector, a decrease in demand often leads quickly to unemployment. In the white-collar sector, however, employers are often willing to continue to employ workers because they have specialized knowledge or long-term relationships with customers. For this reason, the rise of the service sector has tended to dampen the impact of recessions on employment in the postwar period.

[6]Productivity in the service sector, it should be noted, is notoriously difficult to measure. To illustrate the difficulty, Phillip Coehlo has asked the following question: How much would we pay to use the services of a 2002 dentist in filling a cavity in comparison with a dentist using the techniques applied in 1950 to fill it? (Personal Communication 2003.)

TABLE 28.4 Participation of Men and Women in the Paid Labor Force, 1960–2001

YEAR	MARRIED WOMEN	MARRIED MEN	SINGLE WOMEN	SINGLE MEN	TOTAL
1960	31.9%	89.2%	58.6%	69.8%	59.4%
1970	40.5	86.1	56.8	65.5	60.4
1980	49.8	80.9	64.4	72.6	63.8
1990	58.4	78.6	66.7	74.8	66.5
2000	61.3	77.3	69.0	73.5	67.2
2001	61.4	77.4	68.2	72.6	66.9

Sources: Statistical Abstract of the United States, 2002 *(Washington, D.C.: Government Printing Office, 2003), section 12, table 562, 6; table 568, 10.*

THE CHANGING ROLE OF WOMEN IN THE LABOR FORCE

The most dramatic trend in the supply of labor after the war was the increase in the proportion of women, particularly married women, who participated (worked or actively sought work) in the paid labor force. Table 28.4 above shows the key ratios at decade-long intervals. The proportion of married women participating increased from 32 percent in 1960 to 61 percent in 2001. Among married women with children under six years of age (not shown in Table 28.4), the change was even larger, from 18.6 percent in 1960 to 61.7 percent in 1994. The pundits were fond of pointing out that television comedies, such as *Leave It to Beaver*—originally shown from 1957 to 1963—that portrayed a family in which the mother did not work outside the home no longer represented the typical U.S. family.

The proportion of married men in the labor force fell substantially, in some cases because the additional income earned by their wives made this choice feasible. The proportions of single women and single men participating in the labor force increased. The net result was that the proportion of Americans participating in the paid labor force rose steadily in the postwar period, reaching an all-time peak at the start of the twenty-first century.

★★★ *Economic Reasoning Proposition*

Increased participation of women in the paid labor force was the result of economic, political, and cultural trends. To put it slightly differently, we need both Economic Reasoning Proposition 3, incentives matter, and Economic Reasoning Proposition 4, institutions matter, to explain the change in the role of women in the labor force.[7]

1. *Real wages rose.* Real wages of men rose, which tended to discourage the labor-force participation of married women, but the effect of higher real wages available for women dominated.
2. *Years of schooling increased dramatically over the course of the century.* About 10 percent of the nonwhite women born in 1900 and about 30 percent of the white women in 1900 would graduate from high school; by 1970, those figures had increased to 80 and 90 percent. The increased incomes made possible by additional schooling encouraged women to join the paid labor force. This factor, of course, operated with a long lag. For some women, the full effects of education on labor-force participation were not seen until they had passed the age when child-rearing demands were greatest.

[7] Claudia Goldin, *Understanding the Generation Gap* (New York: Oxford University Press, 1990), 138–149.

New View 28.1

Automation and Downsizing

The implementation of various new technologies of the 1980s resulted in the loss of many jobs. For example, the rapid advances in computer-based technologies enabled telephone companies to increase the number of daily calls from 1.2 billion in 1984 to 9.5 in 1990, while reducing their labor force from 742,000 people in 1984 to 648,000 in 1990. The use of these technologies is one factor in the "downsizing" or reducing of the work force in many other industries. The reduction at General Motors from 1979 to the early 1990s was from 800,000 to 450,000; at General Electric, it was 402,000 to 298,000 during the same time period. As some firms quickly learned, however, the loss of the specialized knowledge provided by experienced laid off employees proved more costly than anticipated.

Are jobs that are lost when new technology is introduced eventually replaced by new jobs? This is one of the oldest questions in economics, and it resurfaces when unemployment rises. In the nineteenth century, David Ricardo, one of the founders of economics, argued that the introduction of the new machines could lead, at least for a considerable period, to higher unemployment, and Karl Marx described the plight of the hand-loom weavers who were displaced by weaving machines. Today, most economists believe that the jobs lost will eventually be replaced because the cost savings that result from technological innovations will be passed on to consumers in the form of lower prices, leaving consumers with more money to spend on other goods and services. Thus, technological progress need not produce mass unemployment. The great economic expansion of the last decade of the twentieth century (the longest on record) in which employment rose from 118 million in 1992 to 135 million in 2000 and unemployment fell from 7.5 percent of the labor force to 4.0 percent, helped to confirm the idea that the economy could create jobs in the face of rapid technological progress.

The confidence that new jobs will replace old ones, however, should not make us insensitive to the suffering that arises from technological progress. Workers whose skills once brought premium rates, typically older workers, may find themselves competing for low-paying jobs. It is little comfort to them to know that in the aggregate the number of jobs is increasing.

3. *The average number of children in a family declined from three or four at the beginning of the century to one or two in the 1980s, and the average life expectancy of women increased.* Together, these demographic trends meant that women had many more years to pursue a career after the burdens of rearing a family moderated.
4. *An increased rate of divorce encouraged women to invest in a career outside the home.* The interaction of these trends was complicated. For example, although a rising divorce rate encouraged women to work outside the home, the rising participation rate of women in the paid labor force encouraged some women to choose divorce who would have been unable to afford it in earlier periods. Causation, in other words, ran both ways.
5. *The rapidly growing service sectors, especially the clerical and educational sectors, were particularly attractive to women.* Until 1950, the growth of these sectors affected mainly the participation rates of white single women due to discrimination against married and minority women. As discriminatory hiring practices were broken, the effects of growth in these sectors spread more widely.

6. *The growing availability and technological sophistication of consumer durables affected labor needs in home maintenance.* Electric washing machines and refrigerators, low-maintenance fabrics, telephone answering machines, and other labor-saving devices reduced the labor input in home maintenance.
7. *The feminist movement helped overcome discrimination against women workers through moral persuasion and political action.* Some barriers were broken during World War II. Before the war, many firms had "marriage bars." These firms simply did not hire married women and forced women who married while on the job to leave. Marriage bars became particularly widespread during the Great Depression as a way to ration scarce jobs. One rationale was that it was unfair for a married woman who might already have a breadwinner in the family to work and thus take a job away from a man who was the sole support of his family. By 1950, marriage bars had virtually disappeared (except for flight attendants), and some personnel managers were singing the praises of married women.

Another burst of activity occurred in the 1960s. President Kennedy's appointment of a Presidential Commission on the Status of Women in 1961, with the venerable Eleanor Roosevelt as its honorary chair, was the starting point. Partly as a result of the commission's recommendations, Congress passed the Equal Pay Act of 1963, which called for equal pay for equal work. Title VII of the Civil Rights Act, passed in the following year, barred discrimination in hiring, promoting, or firing workers on the basis of race, color, religion, national origin, or sex and set up the Equal Employment Opportunity Commission to help enforce the law.[8]

In 1965, President Johnson created the Office of Federal Contract Compliance Program to require the submission of affirmative action plans by employers doing business with the federal government. Affirmative action is more than a color-blind, sex-neutral labor policy; it requires positive efforts to find workers traditionally discriminated against. The National Organization for Women was founded in 1966, partly to pressure the government into vigorous enforcement of its new antidiscriminatory legislation.

During the 1970s the feminist movement experienced further successes. Title IX of the Educational Amendments Act of 1972 extended the Civil Rights Act to educational institutions; one consequence of Title IX was to increase the participation of women in high-school and college sports. In the late 1970s and 1980s, the feminist movement seemed to lose momentum and was unable to win major legislative victories. The institutions created in the 1960s and 1970s continued, however, to press for the removal of discriminatory barriers.

The Gender Gap

Despite federal legislation, increased education and experience, and better understanding by employers of the abilities of women, a considerable gap remained between the earnings of men and women in a variety of occupations. Table 28.5, based on work by Claudia Goldin, one of the leading experts in the field—shows the gender gap in six broad occupational classifications in 1890, 1930, 1970, and, although the data are not strictly comparable, 2001. The surprising thing is the persistence of the gender gap and its tendency to increase in every class of occupations except "professional" between 1930 and 1970. It appears, however, that since 1970, progress toward equal pay has occurred in most sectors except professional. A considerable gap remains.

---

[8]The word *sex* did not appear in the bill until the day before it was passed. It has been claimed that it was originally inserted with the idea of making the bill unacceptable to a majority, but the matter remains unclear. See Claudia Goldin, *Understanding the Gender Gap*, (New York: Oxford University Press, 1990) 201, and the references cited there.

TABLE 28.5 The Gender Gap—Ratios of Female to Male Earnings

OCCUPATION	1890	1930	1970	2001[a]
Professional	0.26	0.38	0.71	0.71
Clerical	0.49	0.71	0.69	0.81
Sales	0.59	0.61	0.44	0.62
Manual	0.54	0.58	0.56	0.74
Service	0.53	0.60	0.56	0.76
Farm	0.53	0.60	0.59	0.84

[a]*Because this column is based on a different source, only rough comparisons can be made with the other columns.*

Sources: 1890–1970: Claudia D. Goldin, Understanding the Gender Gap *(New York: Oxford University Press, 1990), 64; 2001:* Statistical Abstract of the United States: 2002 *(Washington, D.C.: Government Printing Office, 2003), section 12, table 613, 403.*

The main factors that produced the increase in the relative earnings of women over this long period were the increase in the education of women and the breakdown of discriminatory social norms through persuasion and legislation. The increase in the participation rate of women, however, has kept the gender gap from closing even more. Increasing participation means that women's average years of experience in the labor force remains relatively low because so many have just entered the labor force. Moreover, because discrimination often blocks them from entering or advancing in certain fields, women entering the labor force have crowded into areas open to them, thereby preventing wages in those areas from rising as fast as in the rest of the economy. As the labor force participation rate of women stabilizes and the entire array of jobs created by the economy are opened to women, the gender gap should decline even further.

The Baby Boom

Decisions about entering the labor market were closely related to decisions about family formation and child bearing. The birth rate plunged during the Great Depression. For example, for women between the ages of 15 and 44, the prime child-bearing years, the rate fell from 89.3 births per 1,000 women in 1929 to a low of 75.8 in 1936. With the return of prosperity during the war, the rate increased again. In 1942, the birth rate reached 91.5, surpassing 1929, although it fell in 1944 and 1945.

In 1946, the "baby boom" began. Undoubtedly, the baby boom owed part of its existence in its early years to the reuniting of couples separated by war, but it continued long beyond the time when this was an important factor. The baby boom, as shown in Figure 28.2 on page 580 shows, lasted until the late 1950s. The birth rate then plunged to historically low levels. The child dependency ratio (the ratio of children under 14 to women between 20 and 54) peaked somewhat later. The labor force participation rate of women leveled off during the latter part of the period, along with the other variables.

The baby boom was a complex phenomenon, but expectation of future economic conditions were undoubtedly important. The 1950s were the economic reverse of the 1930s: A strong economy and optimism about the future encouraged Americans to start or enlarge families. After the peak, in the late 1950s, the birth rate began a steep decline, reaching very low rates in the 1970s. Indeed, natural fertility rates were so low that in the absence of immigration, the population might have declined.

The birth rate declined for a number of reasons. Again, the rise in uncertainty about the future that prevailed in the 1960s and 1970s, like the uncertainty that prevailed in the 1930s, discouraged family formation and child bearing. The fall in the birth rate was also related, as shown in Figure 28.2, to the increasingly frequent decision by women to enter

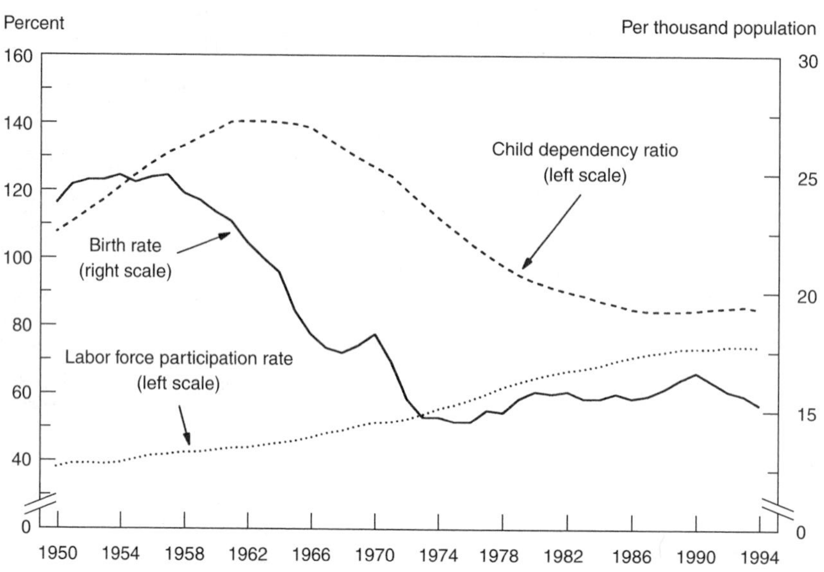

FIGURE 28.2 The Birth Rate, Women's Labor Force Participation Rate, and Child Dependency Rate

Source: Economic Report of the President, 1996 *(Washington, D.C.: Government Printing Office, 1996), 57.*

the paid labor force. Access to highly effective oral contraceptives, beginning in the 1960s, also contributed to the reduction in the birth rate.[9]

MINORITIES

Efforts by African Americans, Hispanic Americans, and other minority workers to move into the economic mainstream met important but limited success during the postwar period. Table 28.6 shows the ratios of median family incomes of African Americans to whites, and Hispanics to whites, at 10-year intervals from 1950 to 2000. These numbers are not adjusted for other differences between the groups that affect earnings: parents' age and work experience, number of children, family's geographic location, and so on. This ratio nevertheless provides a rough indicator of the search for economic equality. For African Americans, surprisingly, increases in the ratio appear to have been confined mainly to the period from 1960 to 1970. For Hispanics also, the change since 1980 has been small.

African Americans

Two factors might have been expected to produce rapid African American progress in the postwar era: (1) their increase in number of years of schooling and (2) the geographic redistribution of the African American labor force. It may be difficult for today's college students, aware of the overcrowding and underfunding of predominantly African American schools, to believe that much progress has been made. The reason is that it is difficult now to imagine how bad things were in, say, 1940. In that year, 80 percent of the African American male workforce had only elementary schooling, and 40 percent had less than five years of schooling.

[9]For a detailed discussion of the complex effects of the availability of oral contraceptives, see Claudia Goldin and Lawrence F. Katz, "The Power of the Pill: Oral Contraceptives and Women's Career and Marriage Decisions," *National Bureau of Economic Research Working Paper 7527*, February 2000, http://www.nber.org.

TABLE 28.6 Ratio of African American and Hispanic Family to White Family Incomes, 1950–2000

YEAR	AFRICAN-AMERICAN	HISPANIC-AMERICAN
1950	0.54[a]	(NA)
1960	0.55[a]	(NA)
1970	0.61	(NA)
1980	0.58	0.73
1990	0.60	0.71
2000	0.69	0.76

[a]*Includes other races.*

Sources: 1950–1965: Statistical Abstract of the United States, 1987*(Washington, D.C.: Government Printing Office, 1988), 436; 1970-1990:* Statistical Abstract of the United States, 2000 *(Washington, D.C.: Government Printing Office, 2001), 466; 2000:* Statistical Abstract of the United States, 2002 *(Washington, D.C.: Government Printing Office, 2003), section 13, table 653, 433.*

As shown in Table 28.7, the gap in the amount of schooling obtained by African American men narrowed considerably during the postwar period. In 1940 only 6.9 percent of African American men over 25 years old had completed high school compared with 24.2 percent of white men. By 2000, 79.1 percent of African American men were high school graduates, compared with 88.5 percent of white men. Similar improvements were recorded for African American women. The gap in quality of education, although more difficult to measure, probably also narrowed substantially.

African Americans also benefited, at least initially, from the geographic redistribution of their population. In 1940, a large gap in the wages for whites and African Americans existed in the North and South and the gap for African Americans was much larger. The rapid migration of African Americans from the low-wage South was motivated by this disparity and tended to lessen it. In 1940, 75 percent of African American men lived in the South; by 1980, that figure had fallen to 53 percent.

TABLE 28.7 Percent of Population Age 25 or More Having Completed 12 or more years of Education by Race or Ethnicity and Gender, 1940–2000

YEAR	WHITE	AFRICAN AMERICAN	HISPANIC
		MALES	
1940	24.2	6.9	NA
1950	34.6	12.6	NA
1960	41.6	20.0	NA
1970	57.2	35.4	NA
1980	72.4	51.2	44.9
1990	81.6	65.8	50.3
2000	88.5	79.1	56.6
		FEMALES	
1940	28.1	8.4	NA
1950	38.2	14.7	NA
1960	44.7	23.1	NA
1970	57.7	36.6	NA
1980	71.5	51.5	44.2
1990	81.3	66.5	51.3
2000	88.4	78.7	57.5

Source: National Center for Education Statistics, Digest of Education Statistics, 2002, *chapter 1, table 8, http://www.nces.ed.gov.*

Despite these trends, gains were slow and halting because of discrimination. The fight against discrimination has been a long and difficult one. In 1947, one of the most famous milestones occurred when Jackie Robinson broke the color barrier in major league baseball. This was important not only for African Americans who would earn their living in professional sports in the postwar period but also for the effect it would have on white stereotypes about African American abilities.

A main goal of the civil rights movement was fair employment laws. These laws, passed after World War II by a number of states, set up commissions that could issue cease and desist orders against firms that discriminated. By the time of the Civil Rights Act of 1964, 98 percent of blacks outside the South were covered by these laws. Recent research by William Collins shows that these laws had some success in improving the wages and working conditions of African American women but little success in improving the wages and working conditions of African American men.

In 1954 the Supreme Court ruled in *Brown v. Board of Education of Topeka* that segregated schools were unconstitutional. This decision would have far-reaching consequences for U.S. education. Although many school districts then claimed that they were providing a separate but equal education for African Americans (a formula ordered by the Supreme Court in *Plessy v. Fergusson* in 1896), this was not actually the case. As Robert Margo documented, African American schools were systematically underfunded, and African Americans entered the labor force with a severe handicap.[10] *Brown v. Board of Education* did not bring about change overnight. Many school districts dragged their feet, and not until the late 1960s, when courts began to order busing to achieve racial integration, was significant progress made in many areas.

Other visible signs of discrimination, such as segregated transportation, were also crumbling as a result of the civil rights movement. The culmination of that movement was the march on Washington in August 1963, where the young leader of the movement, Dr. Martin Luther King, Jr., gave his memorable "I Have a Dream" speech. Less than a year later, the Civil Rights Act was passed, which, among other things (as noted earlier), made it illegal to discriminate in employment. See New View 28.2.

The civil rights movement itself brought about change, as did pressure from the federal government. As Gavin Wright explains in his thoughtful book, *Old South, New South*, southern political and business leaders were trying to attract new businesses to the South; they soon realized that a quick resolution of civil rights turmoil was necessary if they were to continue to compete successfully for outside capital. In 1970, the president of Allis-Chalmers Corporation visited Jackson, Mississippi, and expressed doubts about locating a plant there because of the violent ongoing confrontation between African American students at Jackson State University and local police. As a result, the deadlock over school integration, then seven years old, was broken, and Allis-Chalmers announced construction plans.[11]

In the 1980s and 1990s, however, progress toward equality slowed. One reason is that when the fight against discrimination moved from the South, where the targets were explicit laws, to the North, where the targets were implicit social norms, progress based on legal proceedings proved more difficult to achieve. In addition, as William Julius Wilson shows in *The Truly Disadvantaged*, the loss of manufacturing jobs in a number of older northern cities hit the African American community, which had been drawn to those cities by those jobs, especially hard.

---

[10]See Robert Margo, "Race Differences in Public School Expenditures: Disenfranchisement and School Finance in Louisiana, 1890-1910," *Social Science History* 6 (Winter 1982), and "Educational Achievements in Segregated Schools: The Effects of Separate but Equal," *American Economic Review* 76 (September 1986).

[11]Gavin Wright, *Old South, New South: Revolutions in the Southern Economy since the Civil War* (New York: Basic Books, 1986), 266–267.

New View 28.2

Measuring the Impact of the Civil Rights Act

As John H. Donohue III and James Heckman show, federal pressure to end discrimination was directed at the South, where social norms, backed by state and local legislation, limited employment of African Americans. This pressure was successful. Figure 28.3, showing employment in the South Carolina textile industry, is a dramatic piece of evidence. Notice that the share of African Americans (who were confined to the most menial jobs) was low and stable until 1965. To some extent, employers may have welcomed federal pressure. For example, employers in South Carolina who wanted to take advantage of relatively cheap African American labor could use the threat of federal sanctions as an excuse for breaking with established racial norms.

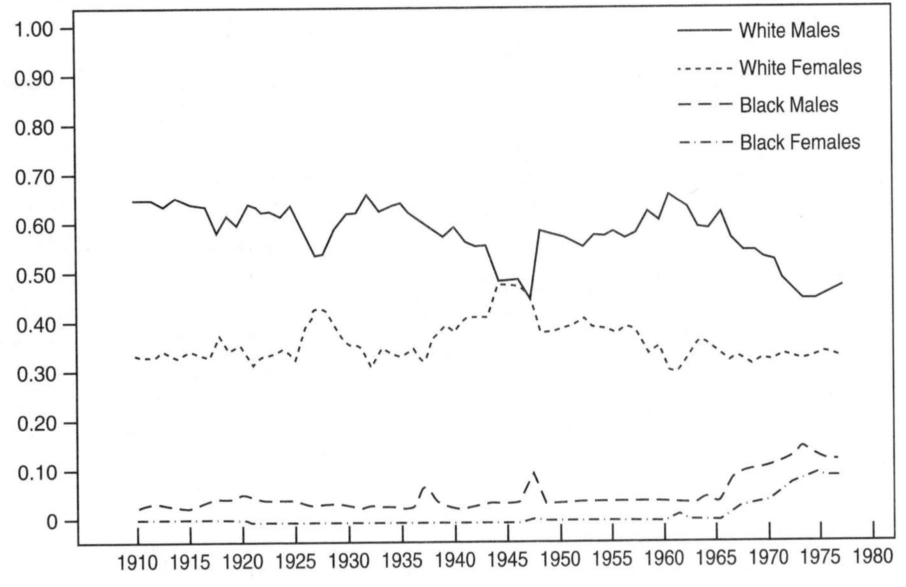

Native Americans

Despite the erosion of discriminatory barriers that followed the moral awakening of the 1960s, the effects of past and present discrimination continue to take a heavy toll. The postwar economic history of Native Americans is a clear illustration.

In the 2000 census, about 4.1 million people, 1.5 percent of the total population, identified themselves (either alone or in combination with other races) as American Indian or Alaskan Native. About 3.1 million identified themselves as belonging to a particular tribe. Median household income was $32,116, and about 800,000 American Indians and Alaskan Natives had incomes that fell below the poverty line.

The current reservation and trust territories are, of course, only a small remnant of even the small amount that still belonged to Native Americans in the nineteenth century. In 1887 Congress passed the Dawes Act, which provided that each registered American Indian would receive 160 acres that would be held in trust for 25 years. In theory, the idea was that by "privatizing" the land, an efficient economy of prosperous farmers could be created. Leonard A. Carlson and a number of other economic historians, however, maintain that the program was structured to hinder the development of farming by Native Americans and to facilitate the transfer of American Indian properties to whites. Between 1887 and 1920, the land held by American Indians fell from 138 million acres to 50 million acres. The allotment program was replaced in 1934 by the Indian Reorganization Act, which finally sought to preserve reservation and trust lands.

Many Native Americans choose to live their lives in accord with traditional values that reject the market, but many examples of an entrepreneurial spirit also exist. Often entrepreneurial initiatives have been deliberately frustrated by government policies intended to benefit white Americans at the expense of Native Americans. Lee Alston and Pablo Spiller have reanalyzed a famous example from the nineteenth century, the *Cherokee Outlet* case. As early as 1867, the Cherokee had leased part of their land to white cattlemen. The leasing arrangement was backed by the federal government, which used the cavalry to keep squatters off the land. In 1888 the government ended the arrangement. The Cherokee were offered $30 million by some of the cattlemen for the land. Instead, the government, acting on behalf of white settlers, forced the Cherokee to sell the land to the government for $8.7 million.

More recently, the most visible sign of American Indian entrepreneurship has been gaming, which has been increasing at a rapid pace. In 2002, about 200 tribes nationwide sponsored gaming. In 1998 gaming revenues were a substantial $8.5 billion; in 2002, they were $14.5 billion, an increase of 13.4 percent per year. However, much of the revenue is generated in a few large facilities. In 2002, the top 12 percent of Indian gaming facilities produced 65 percent of the total revenue.[12] In addition, serious questions have been raised about the extent to which gaming revenues "trickle down" and relieve the economic distress experienced by the entire Native American community. Despite the prominence of gaming, it is wrong to assume that this is the only successful form of Native American entrepreneurship. Native Americans have engaged successfully in manufacturing, agriculture, tourism, and other industries, and have done so in widely diverse parts of the country. The Mississippi Choctaws, the White Mountain Apaches in Arizona, the Salish and Kootenai Tribes of the Flathead Reservation in Montana, and the Cochiti Pueblo in New Mexico have been cited as successful examples of reservation-based economic entrepreneurship.

THE NEW IMMIGRATION

Little change occurred in the immigration laws from the establishment of the quota system in the 1920s until 1965.The major exception to this generalization was a program under which Mexican agricultural workers (*braceros*) could work temporarily in the United States. This program began during World War II (although it is doubtful that it contributed to the war effort) and ended in 1965, another result of the wave of liberal legislation of the mid-1960s.[13]

At that time, a new immigration system was instituted. President John F. Kennedy and his allies in Congress were strongly opposed to national quotas, which they believed reflected racial and ethnic prejudice. The new law, enacted after Kennedy's death, eliminated quotas based on the ethnic composition of the population in favor of a complex system of priorities that gave very high priority to uniting families. A limit was placed on the total number of immigrants, but that limit did not include spouses, minor children, or parents of American citizens. In 1980, a separate program for admitting political refugees was created. As a result of these changes,

---

[12]See the National Indian Gaming Commission at http://www.nigc.gov.

[13]Lee J. Alston and Joseph P. Ferrie, "The Bracero Program and Farm Labor Legislation in World War II," in *Sinews of War: Essays on the Economic History of World War II*, eds. Geofrey T. Mills and Hugh Rockoff (Ames: Iowa State University Press, 1993).

TABLE 28.8 **Immigration, 1901–2000**

YEAR	TOTAL (in thousands)	RATE (annual per thousand U.S. population)
1901–1910	8,795	10.4
1911–1920	5,736	5.7
1921–1930	4,107	3.5
1931–1940	528	0.4
1941–1950	1,035	0.7
1951–1960	2,515	1.5
1961–1970	3,322	1.7
1971–1980	4,493	2.1
1981–1990	7,338	3.1
1991–2000	9,095	3.4

Source: Statistical Abstract of the United States, 2002 *(Washington, D.C.: Government Printing Office, 2003), section 1, 10.*

the number of immigrants increased, many coming from "new" areas—Latin America and the Caribbean. In the 1960s, 37 percent of immigrants came from Europe, 39 percent from Latin America and the Caribbean, and 13 percent from Asia. By 1990, 7 percent came from Europe, 67 percent from Latin America and the Caribbean, and 22 percent from Asia.

Table 28.8 shows total immigration to the United States since 1901. The acceleration of the rate of immigration after the 1965 change in the law is obvious in the table; the rate increased from 1.5 per thousand between 1951 and 1960 to 3.4 between 1991 and 2000. Even the latter rate, however, was still well below the rate of 10.4 averaged between 1901 and 1910.

The figures in Table 28.8 make no allowance for illegal immigration, particularly from Mexico and Latin America. Evidence suggests that the volume of such immigration, although difficult to measure, is large. In 1990, for example, some 1.2 million illegal aliens were apprehended attempting to cross into the United States from Mexico. Some experts believe that the number of illegal immigrants in the 1980s may have totaled as much as 40 percent of the legal immigration. Pressure to do something about illegal immigration led to the Immigration Reform and Control Act of 1986, which put tough new controls on illegal immigration (making it illegal, for example, for employers to hire undocumented workers) while creating an amnesty program for illegal immigrants who had put down roots in this country.

Many Americans benefit from immigration: those who own firms that employ immigrants (including those who own firms indirectly through retirement funds), those who possess special skills that become more valuable when unskilled labor is widely available, those who consume the products and services that immigrants help produce, those who provide the services consumed by immigrants, and those who own property in neighborhoods in which immigrants settle.

On the other hand, native-born workers who compete directly with immigrants in the labor force—unskilled workers in urban areas, for example—face lower real wages and fewer job opportunities. It is difficult to say how large these effects have been. Some labor economists have stressed the substitutability between immigrants and native workers that implies lower wages for native workers.[14] But others have found evidence of complementarity, which

[14]Jean Baldwin Grossman, "The Substitutability of Natives and Immigrants in Production," *Review of Economics and Statistics* 64 (1982): 596–603, and Vernon M. Briggs, "The Imperative of Immigration Reform," in *Essays on Legal and Illegal Immigration*, ed. S. Pozo (Washington, D.C.: W. E. Upjohn Institute, 1986), 43–71.

implies higher wages for native workers.[15] A more recent sophisticated study found evidence of both effects, depending on the group being considered, but stressed that both effects have been small.[16]

The countries from which the United States receives its immigrants also experience a variety of effects. In the first decades after World War II, for example, considerable concern was expressed about the "brain drain," the tendency of the United States to draw down the supply of engineers, scientists, physicians, and similar personnel in developing countries.

In the 1990s, high immigration rates produced much the same political results as high rates of immigration in the early 1900s: exaggerated claims about the impact of immigrants on wages and the social welfare system, met by exaggerated denunciations of even moderate critics of immigration. Whether criticism of immigration will lead to severe restrictions seems to depend on whether the economy can deliver new jobs and rising real incomes.

UNIONS

Membership in labor unions increased sharply during the Great Depression and World War II. The percentage of the unionized labor force rose from 14.7 percent in 1933 to 20.4 percent in nonagricultural 1938, and from 22.5 percent in 1940 to 31.6 percent in 1950, stabilizing in the 1950s. At its peak, near 1953, nearly one third of the nonagricultural labor force was enrolled in labor unions. Since that time, however, there has been a steady decline that has become precipitous since 1970. This can be seen in Table 28.9, which shows the percentage of the labor force unionized. By 1994, the percentage of the labor force enrolled in unions had fallen back to the level of the late 1920s.

A number of factors can account for the deterioration in the strength of organized labor. The rising service sector, where employee groups are usually small, has proved difficult to organize. Moreover, within the goods-producing sector, a steady shift has occurred from blue-collar to white-collar employment that has slowed the pace of union growth because white-collar workers are less prone to organize. The shift of manufacturing to the South and West, areas traditionally hostile to the labor movement, has also undermined union power. Foreign industrial competition, which has made workers in traditional bastions of union strength (such as automobiles) fearful of layoffs and plant closings, has further undermined organized labor. The high rate of immigration of unskilled workers, who tend to fear taking part in union activities and who may oppose union attempts to control the supply of labor, has also undermined union strength.

In addition to these economic trends, changes in the legal environment have worked against the unions. Because of opportunities for legislation established by the Taft-Hartley Act, numerous states passed "right-to-work" laws. In 2003, 19 states, many of them in the South, had right-to-work laws. By making it illegal to enforce the union-shop provisions of an agreement within the state concerned, right-to-work legislation impeded efforts to unionize and were a source of friction between union and nonunion workers.

Intraunion squabbles have also hurt the labor movement. At the peak of union strength, the American Federation of Labor (AFL) and the Congress of Industrial Organizations (CIO) merged in 1955, with George Meany becoming the first president. The radical dream of uniting all workers in one big union seemed near at hand, but harmony could not be maintained. Labor unity suffered a particularly severe blow in 1968 when the United Automobile Workers (UAW), under their dynamic leader Walter Reuther, left the AFL-CIO in a dispute over politics. At the same time, many of the organizational gains were being

---

[15]George J. Borjas, "The Substitutability of Black, Hispanic and White Labor," *Economic Inquiry* 21 (1983): 93–106.

[16]Francisco L. Rivera-Batiz and Selig L. Sechzer, "Substitution and Complementarity between Immigrant and Native Labor in the United States," in *U.S. Immigration Patterns and Policy Reform in the 1980s*, eds. Ira Gang, Francisco L. Rivera-Batiz, and Selig L. Sechzer (New York: Praeger, 1991).

TABLE 28.9 Union Membership, 1950–2001

YEAR	TOTAL UNION MEMBERSHIP (thousands)	PERCENTAGE OF TOTAL CIVILIAN LABOR FORCE
1950	14,294	23.0%
1960	15,516	22.3
1970	20,990	25.4
1980	20,968	19.6
1990	16,740	13.5
2000	16,258	11.5
2001	16,289	11.5

Source: 1950–1980: Leo Troy and Neil Sheflin, U.S.Union Sourcebook *(West Orange, N.J.: Industrial Relations Data and Information Services, 1985); 1990–2001:* Statistical Abstract of the United States, 2002 *(Washington, D.C.: Government Printing Office, 2003), section 12, 367, 411.*

made by independent unions such as the Teamsters, who had been ousted from the AFL-CIO. Thus, it may well be true that critics who blame mainstream union leadership for part of the decline in labor's influence have a point.

Can organized labor regain some of its former influence? The economic trends we have been examining in connection with the union movement seem likely to continue. On the other hand, it has been noted that in Canada, where the industrial structure is in some ways similar to our own—although other policies, such as immigration policies, differ—the labor movement has remained far more influential than in the United States. It is best to remember that unionism in the United States has traditionally grown in spurts that were never predicted by the experts.

REAL WAGES

What was the net result of all the forces—birth rates, immigration, changes in labor force participation, and so on—operating on the labor market throughout the postwar era? Figure 28.4 on page 588 shows what happened to the productivity of labor and to real wages from 1960 to 1995. From the end of the war until the 1970s, both labor productivity and real wages grew steadily, creating dreams of a future characterized by widespread affluence. Then, in the 1970s, as discussed earlier, labor productivity growth and real wage growth shifted to a lower trend.

Figure 28.4 shows 2 real wage series. The higher line looks at the real wage from business's point of view. It plots the ratio of wages and benefits relative to the prices received by businesses. The lower line looks at the real wage from the worker's point of view. It plots the ratio of wages and benefits relative to the prices paid by workers. The two can differ because consumers spend larger proportions of their incomes on certain items than do businesses. Evidently, real wages, especially when measured from a worker's point of view, entered a long period of stagnation in the 1980s and early 1990s. Economic Insight 28.2 on page 588 discusses the close relationship between real wages and the average product of labor over time.

What explains the stagnation in real-wage growth? Some economists have argued that the data are misleading. The price indexes used to measure real wages have been criticized, for example, for not properly considering the quality improvements in electronics, medicine, and other areas. Although this criticism undoubtedly holds some truth, it appears that there is nonetheless a real difference in real wage growth between the years from the end of the war to the 1970s and the years that followed. Some economists, moreover, have claimed that the early postwar decades were exceptional. Perhaps the rates of productivity growth since the 1970s are more typical of what to expect in the long run. This observation is useful for policymakers, but it is cold comfort to workers.

Economic Insight 28.2

Cobb-Douglas Production Function

According to economic theory, the real wage should equal the marginal physical product (MPP) of labor.

(1) Real wage = MPP

The cost of hiring one more worker, measured in goods and services, should equal the additional amount produced. This equation tells us that productivity is an important determinant of wages, but what factors will determine the marginal productivity of labor? Consider the Cobb-Douglas production function:

(2) $Y = AK^aL(1 - a)$

where Y is output, A is the level of technological efficiency, K is the amount of capital, L is the amount of labor, a is the share of capital, and $(1 - a)$ is the share of labor. With this production function, the marginal physical product of labor is given by

(3) $\text{MPP} = (1 - a)\, A\, (K/L)^a$

This equation indicates that the marginal physical product of labor is be determined by A, the general level of efficiency in the economy, and (K/L), the ratio of capital to labor. What is the relationship between the labor productivity measured by the Labor Department and reported in the press (the ratio of the amount of output produced to the amount of labor employed) to the marginal physical product of labor? In this model, the relationship is given by

(4) $\text{MPP} = (1 - a)\,(Y/L)$

In other words, if the a coefficient is stable, a stable relationship exists between the average product of labor, (Y/L), and the marginal product of labor. If equations (1) and (4) both hold, a close relationship should exist over time between real wages and the average product of labor. This is, in fact, what Figure 28.4 indicates.

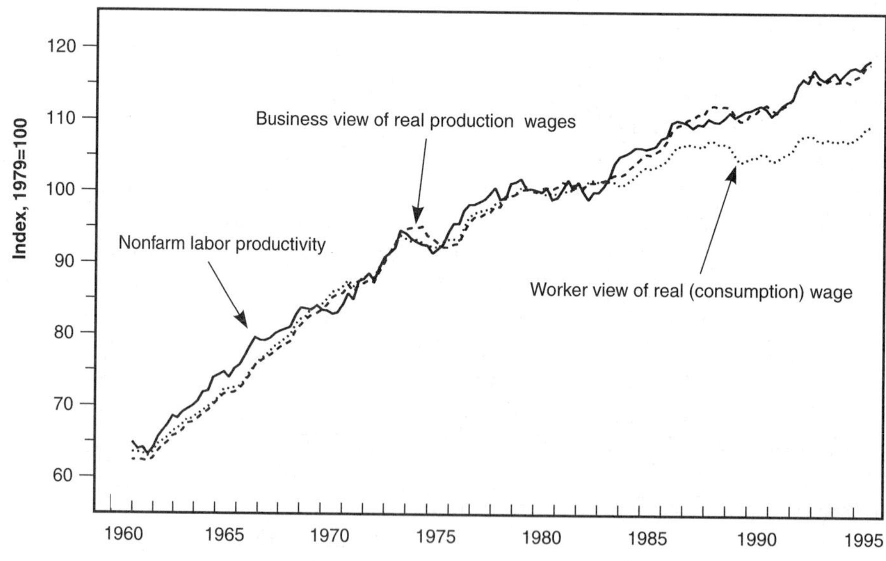

FIGURE 28.4 Measures of Real Compensation and Labor Productivity *The real product wage has kept pace with productivity, whereas the real consumption wage has not.*

Source: Economic Report of the President, 1996 *(Washington, D.C.: Government Printing Office, 1996), 61.*

Many factors, some of which were discussed earlier or in previous chapters, explain the slowdown in real-wage growth. (1) After the 1970s, the savings rate was relatively low, holding down increases in the capital-labor ratio. (2) Changes in the labor market, such as increases in the labor force participation rate, also held down increases in the capital-labor ratio. (3) The shift toward the service sector, the energy crisis, and, some would argue, the cost of complying with government regulations reduced productivity. New View 28.1 discusses two additional factors: automation and downsizing.

Inevitably, stagnant real wage growth produces demands that the government do something. An economic historian is reminded of the end of the nineteenth century and the beginning of the twentieth. In those years, slow growth in real wages produced militant unions and demands from a broad segment of the population that the government break up large corporations and limit immigration. Young people who enter the labor market in the twenty-first century face a very different reality from the future envisioned in the early decades of the postwar era.

Selected References and Suggested Readings

Alston, Lee J., and Joseph P. Ferrie. "The Bracero Program and Farm Labor Legislation in World War II." In *Sinews of War: Essays on the Economic History of World War II*, eds. Geofrey T. Mills and Hugh Rockoff. Ames: Iowa State University Press, 1993.

Alston, Lee, and Pablo Spiller. "A Congressional Theory of Indian Property Rights: The Cherokee Outlet." In *Property Rights and Indian Economies: The Political Economy Forum*, ed. Terry L. Anderson. Baltimore: Rowman & Littlefield, 1992.

Barrington, Linda, ed. *The Other Side of the Frontier: Economic Explorations into Native American History.* Boulder and Oxford: Westview Press, 1999.

Borjas, George J. "Economic Benefits from Immigration." *Journal of Economic Perspectives* 9 (1995): 3–22.

Briggs, Vernon M., Jr. *Immigration Policy and the American Labor Force.* Baltimore: Johns Hopkins University Press, 1984.

Carlson, Leonard A. "Federal Policy and Indian Land: Economic Interests and the Sale of Indian Allotments, 1900–1934." *Agricultural History* 57 (1983): 33–45.

Chiswick, Barry R. "The Effect of Americanization on the Earnings of Foreign-Born Men." *Journal of Political Economy* 86 (October 1978): 897–921.

The Civil Rights Division of the U.S. Department of Justice, a history. **http://www.usdoj.gov/crt/crtann.html**.

Collins, William J. "African-American Economic Mobility in the 1940s: A Portrait from the Palmer Survey." *Journal of Economic History* 60 (September 2000): 756–781.

———. "Race, Roosevelt, and Wartime Production: Fair Employment in World War II Labor Markets." *American Economic Review* 91 (March 2001): 272–286.

David, Paul A. "Clio and the Economics of Qwerty." *American Economic Review* 75 (1985): 332–337.

Donohue, John H., III, and James Heckman. "Continuous versus Episodic Change: The Impact of Civil Rights Policy on the Economic Status of Blacks." *Journal of Economic Literature* 29 (1991): 1603–1643.

Easterlin, Richard. "Twentieth-Century American Population Growth" In *The Cambridge Economic History of the United States*, Vol. III, *The Twentieth Century*, eds. Stanley L. Engerman and Robert E. Gallman. New York: Cambridge University Press, 2000, 505–548.

Fisher, Franklin. *Folded, Spindled, and Mutilated.* Boston: MIT Press, 1983.

Freeman, Richard B. "Unionism Comes to the Public Sector." *Journal of Economic Literature* 24 (March 1986): 41–86.

———. "The Labour Market in the New Information Economy." *Oxford Review of Economic Policy* 18 (2002): 288–305.

Freeman, Richard B., and James L. Medoff. *What Do Unions Do?* New York: Basic Books, 1984.

Galbraith, John Kenneth. *The New Industrial State*. Boston: Houghton Mifflin, 1967.

Goldin, Claudia. "The Changing Economic Role of Women: A Quantitative Approach." *Journal of Interdisciplinary History* 13 (Spring 1983): 707–733.

———. "The Female Labor Force and American Economic Growth, 1890–1980." In *Long Term Factors in the American Economy*, eds. Stanley L. Engerman and Robert Gallman. Chicago: University of Chicago Press, 1986.

———. *Understanding the Gender Gap: An Economic History of American Women*. New York: Oxford University Press, 1990.

———. "Labor Markets in the Twentieth Century." In *The Cambridge Economic History of the United States*, Vol. III, *The Twentieth Century*, eds. Stanley L. Engerman and Robert E. Gallman. New York: Cambridge University Press, 2000, 549–624.

———. "The Human-Capital Century and American Leadership: Virtues of the Past." *The Journal of Economic History* 61 (2001): 263–292.

Jacoway, Elizabeth, and David R. Colburn. *Southern Businessmen and Desegregation*. Baton Rouge: Louisiana State University Press, 1982.

Labor History Sources in the Manuscript Division of the Library of Congress. **http://www.loc.gov/rr/mss/laborlc.html**.

Lamoreaux, Naomi R., Daniel M. G. Raff, and Peter Temin, eds. *Learning by Doing in Markets, Firms, and Countries*. Chicago: University of Chicago Press, 1999.

Liebowitz, S. J., and Stephen E. Margolis. "The Fable of the Keys." *Journal of Law & Economics* 33 (April 1990): 1–25.

———. "Path Dependence, Lock-in, and History." *Journal of Law, Economics, and Organization* 11 (1995): 205–226.

———. *Winners, Losers and Microsoft: Competition and Antitrust in High Technology*. Oakland, Calif.: Independent Institute, 1999.

Mansfield, Edwin. "Technology and Productivity in the United States." In *The American Economy in Transition*, ed. Martin Feldstein. Chicago: University of Chicago Press, National Bureau of Economic Research, 1980.

Margo, Robert. "Race Differences in Public School Expenditures: Disenfranchisement and School Finance in Louisiana, 1890–1910." *Social Science History* 6 (Winter 1982): 9–33.

———. "Educational Achievement in Segregated Schools: The Effects of Separate But Equal." *American Economic Review* 76 (September 1986): 794–801.

———. *Race and Schooling in the South,1880–1950*. Chicago: University of Chicago Press, 1990.

Musoke, Moses S., and Alan L. Olmstead. "The Rise of the Cotton Industry in California: A Comparative Perspective." *Journal of Economic History* 42 (1982): 385–412.

Piore, Michael J. *Birds of Passage*. Cambridge: Cambridge University Press, 1979.

Posner, Richard A. *Antitrust Law*. Chicago: University of Chicago Press, 1976.

Reid, Joseph D., Jr. "Future Unions." *Industrial Relations* 31 (1992): 122–136.

Schumpeter, Joseph. *Capitalism, Socialism, and Democracy*, 3d ed. New York: Harper & Row, 1950.

Simon, Julian C. *The Economic Consequences of Immigration*. Oxford: Basil Blackwell, 1989.

Smith, James P., and Finis R. Welch. "Black Economic Progress after Myrdal." *Journal of Economic Literature* 26 (1989): 519–562.

Stigler, George J. "The Economic Effects of Antitrust Laws." *Journal of Law and Economics* 9 (1966): 225–258.

Temin, Peter with Louis Galambos. *The Fall of the Bell System: A Study in Prices and Politics.* New York: Cambridge University Press, 1987.

Tiffany, Paul A. "The Roots of Decline: Business-Government Relations in the American Steel Industry, 1945–1960." *Journal of Economic History* 44 (1984): 407–419.

Tomlins, Christopher. "Labor Law." In *The Cambridge Economic History of the United States,* Vol. III, *The Twentieth Century,* eds. Stanley L. Engerman and Robert E. Gallman. New York: Cambridge University Press, 2000, 625–692.

Weir, David R. "A Century of U.S. Unemployment, 1890–1990: Revised Estimates and Evidence for Stabilization." *Research in Economic History* 14 (1992): 301–346.

Wilson, William Julius. *The Declining Significance of Race,* 2d ed. Chicago: University of Chicago Press, 1980.

———. *The Truly Disadvantaged: The Inner City, the Underclass, and Public Policy.* Chicago: University of Chicago Press, 1987.

Wright, Gavin. *Old South, New South: Revolutions in the Southern Economy Since the Civil War.* New York: Basic Books, 1986.

Chapter Twenty-Nine

ACHIEVEMENTS OF THE PAST, CHALLENGES FOR THE FUTURE

Chapter Theme

In the first chapter we described some of the incredible changes in the U.S. economy during the twentieth century. To take one fun example, since the early 1900s, you will recall, college football and basketball players at the University of Wisconsin became substantially heavier and taller. Now you realize that constant change characterized every sector of the U.S. economy since colonial times, and you have an idea of how the U.S. economy has gotten from there to here. You know something about British colonial policy, slavery, railroads, tariffs, banking, the Great Depression, stagflation, and many other topics. We will not try to summarize all of those arguments in this chapter. Instead, we will focus on identifying the most important achievements of the U.S. economy and some of the important challenges for the future. History does not provide us with a crystal ball. At best it provides us with lessons that are useful in meeting an unpredictable future. As this is written, the United States faces the enormous uncertainties created by the war in Iraq. There will be events that cannot be forecasted and problems that cannot be solved on the basis of past experience, but the economic history of America's responses to wars and similar forms of adversity provides important lessons to help light the way.

THE ACHIEVEMENTS OF THE PAST

The achievements of the American economy are real and measurable. Here we cannot recount all of the achievements noted in the preceding 28 chapters, but we will describe three developments that are the culmination of those achievements: (1) the rise in real per capita income, the conventional measure of economic success; (2) the convergence of per capita incomes among regions, particularly the integration of the South into the economic mainstream; and (3) the improvement in a variety of biomedical indicators of well-being that have increasingly been used by economic historians to document economic progress.

REAL INCOME HAS GROWN RAPIDLY

We judge the performance of our economy, first of all, by its ability to generate a rising level of real income for the American people. Figure 29.1 reveals the enormous increase in real per capita income since 1870. Although there are several large fluctuations around

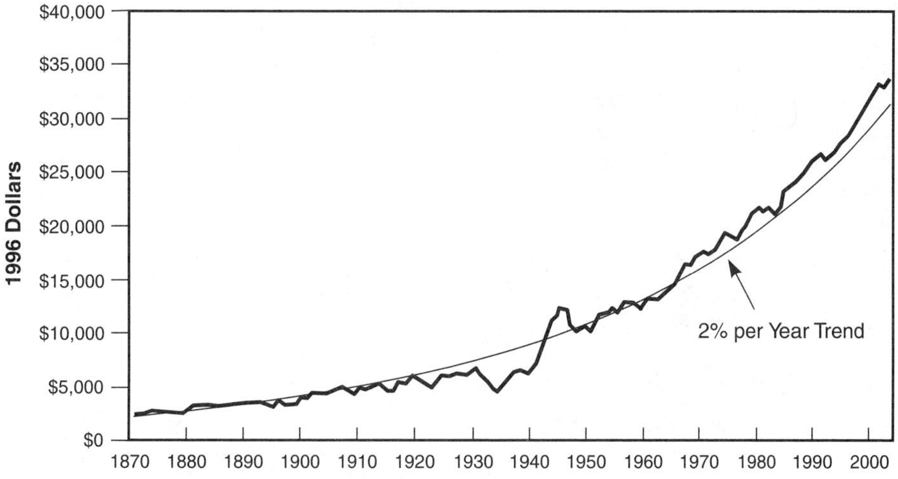

FIGURE 29.1 Real Gross Domestic Product per Capita, 1870–2002

Source: 1870–1928: Louis D. Johnson and Samuel H. Williamson, "Source Note for US GDP," 1789–2002: http:www.eh.net, 1929–2002: Bureau of Economic Analysis (2001) at http://www.bea.gov. All data are in 1996 dollars.

the trend, notably the decrease during the 1930s, the long-term trend is clearly upward. If history is any guide, future generations will be better off than past generations.

Table 29.1 shows real gross domestic product per capita since 1960, real consumption per capita since 1960, and the annual rates of growth. The table indicates that real incomes have risen substantially since the 1960s. Moreover, the figures on real per capita consumption show similar trends. Some economists would argue that real per capita consumption is the best single measure of what the economy is creating for the average citizen. Consumption, after all, is the final product of the economy: You are what you eat. The rates of increase, 2+ percent per year, seem small, but over decades they mount up. In 2001 real per capita income was almost 2.5 times what it was in 1960. Indeed, some economists believe that if full account could be taken of quality improvements—for example, the wide range of electronics that did not exist a generation ago—the current generation would stand even better relative to the past.

TABLE 29.1 Real Gross Domestic Product per Capita and Real Personal Consumption (per capita 1996 dollars)

YEAR	GROSS DOMESTIC PRODUCT (billions)	AVERAGE ANNUAL GROWTH RATE (over the decade)	PERSONAL CONSUMPTION EXPENDITURES	AVERAGE ANNUAL GROWTH RATE (over the decade)
1960	$13,148		$ 8,358	
1970	17,446	2.83%	11,300	3.02%
1980	21,521	2.10	14,021	2.16
1990	26,834	2.21	17,899	2.44
2000	32,579	1.94	22,061	2.09
2001	32,352	1.70[a]	22,390	2.04[a]

[a]*Since 1990.*

Source: Economic Report of the President, 2003 *(Washington, D.C.: Government Printing Office, 2004), Table B-31.*

The United States, moreover, has done about as well as could be expected compared with other industrialized countries. Table 29.2 compares the levels of per capita income in the United States and other leading industrial countries. Such comparisons are inherently difficult, like comparing incomes at very different points in time, but they are, however, an improvement over anecdotal evidence. As you can see, most other industrial nations still have lower per capita real products than the United States, and indeed fell relative to the United States in the 1990s.

The possibility that other countries may surpass the United States worries many Americans. It is important to remember that our own levels of consumption need not fall simply because someone else's are rising. The global economy is not like a football game; in the economic game, all teams can come out ahead.

Lagging Regions Have Caught Up

In the nineteenth and early twentieth centuries, the South lagged far behind other regions. In earlier chapters we discussed some of the institutions that held the South back. Over the long run, however, as shown in Figure 29.2, per capita incomes in different regions of the United States have gradually converged, although some differences remain. Convergence has been brought about mainly by market forces, although government policies that redistributed resources from one region to another played a role. Labor has migrated from labor-abundant regions such as the South to labor-poor regions such as the Pacific Coast, raising the growth rate of per capita income in the labor-exporting regions and lowering the growth rate of per capita income in the labor-importing regions. Similarly, capital has migrated from capital-rich regions such as the Northeast to capital-poor regions such as the South, lowering the growth rate of per capita income in the capital-exporting regions and raising the growth rate of per capita income in the capital-importing regions.

Biomedical Measures of Well-Being Show Improvement

The measures of real income we have been discussing are imperfectly correlated with personal happiness, the ultimate goal of economic activity. One difficulty is what economists call the "index number problem." Typically, real income is computed by dividing money income by a weighted average of prices, where the weights are determined by the amounts consumed in a base period. This works fine for commodities that are consumed in the same amounts now as in the base period. But what happens when consumption of a commodity declines because it is replaced by something new and better? In that case,

TABLE 29.2 Real Gross Domestic Product per Capita—Selected Countries as a Percentage of the United States

COUNTRY	1980	1990	2000
United States	100%	100%	100%
Canada	84	83	80
France	79	76	72
Germany	69	78	73
Italy	71	73	69
Japan	67	87	79
Sweden	78	75	70
United Kingdom	67	71	69

Sources: 1980: Statistical Abstract of the United States, 1996, *section 30, Table 1335, 836; 1990, 2000:* Statistical Abstract of the United States, 2002, *section 30, Table 1319, 833.*

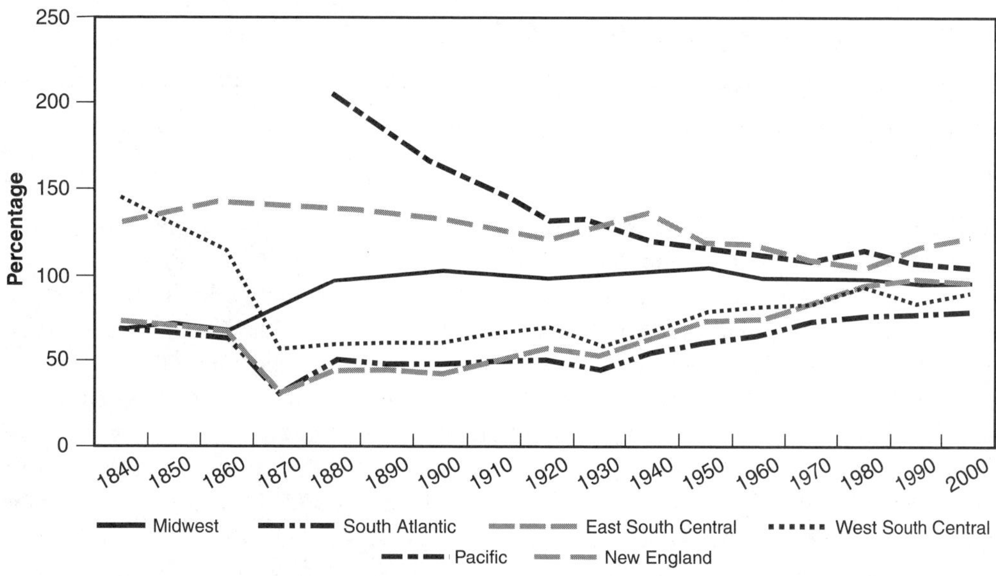

FIGURE 29.2 Convergence of per Capita Incomes in the United States

Sources: Richard A. Easterlin, "Regional Income Trends 1840–1950," The Reinterpretation of American Economic History, *eds. Robert W. Fogel and Stanley L. Engerman (New York: Harper & Row, 1971), 40;* Statistical Abstract of the United States, 2002 *and previous editions.*

the use of the price index based on the old weights tends to understate the increase in real income. The government agencies that compute price indexes are well aware of the problem and have begun using "chain indexes," which update the weights annually, in order to minimize the problem. Nevertheless, it is still difficult to compare real income today with real income decades ago because of the introduction of new products. The computer revolution is a case in point. Pocket digital assistants, personal computers, DVDs, electronic chess partners, video games, cell phones, and so on have added to our well-being but are only imperfectly reflected in our measures of real income, victims of the "index number problem."

Real income, moreover, is only one of many determinants of personal happiness. For that reason economic historians have increasingly turned to biomedical measures of health and well-being to supplement their understanding of the achievements and failures of economic growth. (See Economic Insight 29.1 on page 596 for a discussion of the insights provided by height.) These measures reveal that life in the United States was spent in better physical health in the postwar period as revealed by the statistics on death rates from specific diseases and broader measures of health such as infant mortality and life expectancy.

Striking gains have been made in the postwar period in reducing the death rates from numerous diseases, as shown in Table 29.3 on page 597. For example, the death rate from influenza and pneumonia fell from 70.3 per 100,000 in 1940 to 20.3 in 2000 due in part to the development of antibiotics. Note that the age distribution of the population has a big impact on the death rates. For example, the death rate from major cardiovascular diseases would have fallen from 485.7 per 100,000 in 1940 to 189.8 per 100,000 in 1990, if the proportion of the population in each age group had remained constant. The actual death rate fell only from 485.7 to 368.3. Rapid improvements in medical technology, improved living standards, and for some diseases, the adoption of more healthful lifestyles have produced these improvements. The number of active physicians per 100,000, moreover, climbed

Economic Insight 29.1

Male Height as an Indicator of Well-Being

One of the most sensitive vital statistics is height. Height is the result of a number of factors, including nutrition and disease, and is closely related to the level and distribution of income. Height can supplement income as a measure of well-being and can help us understand periods or places where conventional measures of income are of low quality or not available. Partly through the influence of Robert W. Fogel, John Komlos, Richard Steckel, and other leading scholars, studies of height by age have become a "hot topic" in economic history.

The figure here shows the adult height of white males in the United States by year of birth from colonial times to the present. The data come from a variety of sources. Men are measured, for example, when they enter the military. As you can see, the figure tells an interesting story, one that is different from Figure 29.1, which shows a steady rise in per capita real GDP. Evidently, heights of American men reached a fairly high level, although one below modern standards, during the colonial era. Then heights fell from the 1840s to the turn of the century, when adult male heights began a long climb to modern levels.

The reasons for the depression in heights is not yet well understood. Urbanization does not seem to have been the whole story because heights declined in rural as well as urban areas. Growing inequality of income is one possibility now under study: the poor may not have been able to get enough to eat. Another possibility is that increased movements of people—between urban and rural areas, between regions, and between other countries and the United States—spread infectious childhood diseases that prevented many people from reaching their full adult height.

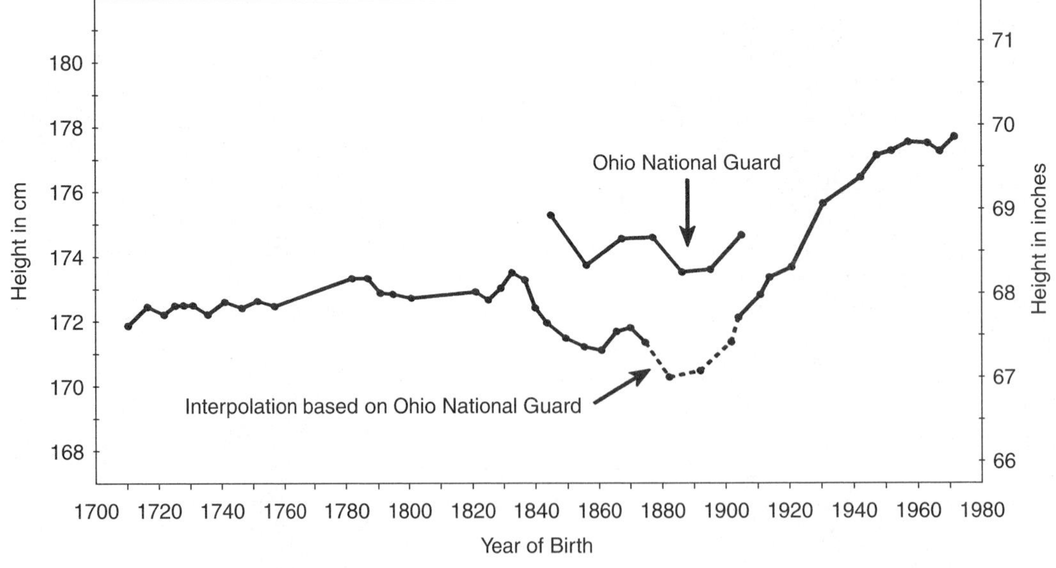

Average Height of Adult, Native Born, White Males by Year of Birth

Source: Richard H. Steckel, "Stature and the Standard of Living," Journal of Economic Literature *33 (1995); 1920.*

Economic Insight 29.1

Male Height as an Indicator of Well-Being, continued

One important lesson we can derive from the study of height by age is that while per capita real GDP is a useful summary measure of how productive the economy is, we need other measures to get a well-rounded picture. Economic historians have long used measures such as industrial production and consumer prices. Now they are beginning to realize that additional measures drawn from other disciplines, such as height by age, can provide important insights.

from 153 in 1970 to 251 in 2000, in part because of the increase in the number of active physicians educated abroad. By the end of the period, physicians were plainly more efficient (if less personal) in treating patients than they had ever been in the history of medical science.

Infant mortality is a sensitive indicator of the overall health of the population. Table 29.4 on page 598 shows infant mortality rates between 1940 and 1999. The decline in infant mortality has been dramatic. Improvements in medicine, such as the development of antibiotics, and improvements in income—because income governs access to nutrition and medical care—account for the downward trend. We are still very far, however, from the lowest levels that could be achieved given the current state of medical knowledge. The infant death rate for African Americans was 11.9 per thousand live births in 1999, more than twice the infant death rate for whites, 5.8. Some foreign countries, moreover, do better than the United States, showing that more progress could be made. In 2001, the infant mortality rate was 4.5 per thousand in France, 5.0 in Canada, and 5.5 in the United Kingdom. Another indicator of the potential for progress is the wide variance in infant mortality rates in the United States, from 4.8 per thousand in Maine in 1999 to a horrendous 15.0 in the District of Columbia.

Life expectancy at birth is another sensitive indicator of the population's health and well-being that inevitably interests college students. This measure also reveals a steady

TABLE 29.3 Deaths from Selected Diseases, 1940–2000 (per 100,000 population: age adjusted figures in parentheses)

	1940	1980		1990		2000[a]
Tuberculosis	45.9	0.6	(0.9)	.5	(0.7)	(0.3)
Chronic liver disease and cirrhosis	8.6	12.2	(13.5)	8.6	(10.4)	(9.5)
Influenza and pneumonia	70.3	12.9	(24.1)	14.0	(32.0)	(24.3)
Diabetes	26.2	10.1	(15.4)	11.7	(19.2)	(24.9)
Major cardiovascular diseases	485.7	256.0	(436.4)	189.8	(368.3)	(339.3)
Human immunodeficiency virus (HIV)	NA	NA	NA	NA	NA	5.2

Note: The first columns for 1980 and 1990 have been "age adjusted" to show what the death rate would have been if the distribution of ages had been the same as it was in 1940. The numbers in parentheses have not been age adjusted. Age-adjusted figures could not be obtained for 2000.

[a]*Preliminary figures*

Sources: Historical Statistics of the United States Colonial Times to 1970, *Series B149, B157, B158, B159, B160, B162; 1980–1990:* Statistical Abstract of the United States, 1995, *section 2, Tables 124, 125, 91–92; 2000:* Statistical Abstract of the United States, 2002, *section 2, Table 101, 80.*

TABLE 29.4 Infant Mortality, 1940–1999 (per one thousand live births)

YEAR	NEONATAL (birth to 28 days)			TOTAL INFANT MORTALITY (birth to one year)		
	TOTAL	WHITE	AFRICAN AMERICAN & OTHER	TOTAL	WHITE	AFRICAN AMERICAN & OTHER
1940	28.8	27.2	39.7	47.0	43.2	73.8
1950	20.5	19.4	27.5	29.2	26.8	44.5
1960	18.7	17.2	26.9	26.0	22.9	43.2
1970	15.1	13.8	21.4	20.0	17.8	30.9
1980	8.5	7.4	13.2	12.6	10.9	20.2
1990	5.8	4.8	9.9	9.2	7.6	15.5
1999	4.7	3.9	7.9	7.1	5.8	11.9

Sources: 1940–1970: Historical Statistics of the United States Colonial Times to 1970, *Series B 136–147. 1980–1990:* Statistical Abstract of the United States, 2000, *section 2, Table 122, 88 and* 1999 Statistical Abstract of the United States, 2002, *section 2, Table 98, 78.*

TABLE 29.5 Life Expectancy at Birth, 1940–2000 (in years)

	TOTAL			AFRICAN AMERICANS[a]		
	TOTAL	MALE	FEMALE	TOTAL	MALE	FEMALE
1940	62.9	60.8	65.2	53.1	51.5	54.9
1950	68.2	65.6	71.1	60.8	59.1	62.9
1960	69.7	66.6	73.1	63.6	61.1	66.3
1970	70.8	67.1	74.7	65.3	61.3	69.4
1980	73.7	70.0	77.4	69.5	65.3	73.6
1990	75.4	71.8	78.8	72.4	68.4	76.3
2000	76.9	74.1	79.5	71.7	68.2	74.9

[a]*The figures for 1940–1960 include other minorities.*

Sources: 1940–1990: Statistical Abstract of the United States, 2000, *section 2, Table 116, 84 and previous editions, 1996–2000:* Statistical Abstract of the United States, 2002, *section 2, Table 91, 71.*

improvement in the standard of living. For the United States, life expectancy in 1850 for a white baby at birth was 40 years; for an African American baby, it was only 23 years. By 1900, life expectancy had risen to 52 years for white babies and to 42 years for African American babies.[1] By 1940, life expectancy was 65 years for whites and 53 years for African Americans. Considerable additional progress has been made since 1940 (see Table 29.5). Between 1940 and 2000, life expectancy at birth for all Americans rose from 63 years to 77 years, an increase of 22 percent. See Perspective 29.1 regarding life expectancy of people with Down Syndrome. Although African Americans still had a lower life expectancy at birth than whites, the increase for African Americans was even larger, from 53 years to 72 years, an increase of 36 percent. This is a testimony to improved public heath, increased access to medical care, and improved standards of living.

The increase in health and well-being in the United States (and the lack of progress when viewed from the perspective of other developed countries or the most successful American states) can be traced to a variety of factors, including nutrition, life style, and

[1]Michael Haines, "The Population of the United States, 1790–1920," in *The Cambridge Economic History of the United States,* Vol. II, eds. Stanley L. Engerman and Robert E. Gallman (New York: Cambridge University Press, 2000), 158.

Perspective 29.1

Gains in the Life Expectancy of the Mentally Retarded

The civil rights movement of the 1960s affected a wide range of groups that traditionally had been excluded from the mainstream of American economic and cultural life. Mentally retarded people were among them. A recent study (J.M. Friedman, "Racial Disparities in Median Age at Death of Persons with Down Syndrome—United States, 1968–1997," *Morbidity and Mortality Weekly Report*, June 8, 2001, 463–465), for example, reveals a startling increase in the life expectancy of people with Down Syndrome, a genetic defect that produces retardation. For white people, the increase in median age at death went from 2 years in 1968 to 50 years in 1997.There was also a startling increase in the life expectancy of African American people with Down Syndrome, but as with other measures of well-being, a gap between the rate for the two groups remained. In 1968, most African Americans born with Down Syndrome died before their first birthday. By 1997, however, median age at death had risen to 25 years. For white people, progress was steady throughout the period. For African Americans, progress began about 1982, with most of the improvement coming after 1992.

Although all reasons for the increase in life expectancy of people with Down Syndrome are not yet known, it seems probable that the increase in the frequency with which children with Down Syndrome are being reared at home rather than being institutionalized has led to improved supervision, nutrition, medical care, and emotional support.

An important component of the improvement in medical care was the development and employment, often at an early age, of surgical techniques for remedying a congenital heart defect that afflicts a significant minority of people with Down Syndrome.

access to medical care. As late as 1940, only about 7 percent of the U.S. population had any kind of hospital insurance (for example, any kind of prepayment of hospital costs that one day nearly everyone must pay). That percentage has risen dramatically in the postwar period as a result of new government programs—the most important being Medicare and Medicaid—and of the extension of private insurance, usually provided by employers. In 2000, 86 percent of the population was covered by private or public heath insurance. However, a worrisome segment of the population concentrated among poor people remained uncovered by health insurance. In 2000, only 70 percent of individuals living in families in which family income fell below the poverty line had any form of health insurance.[2] Many people who had some form of insurance worried about its adequacy. A major concern, for example, was that Medicare had not covered the cost of drugs until 2004.

CHALLENGES FOR THE FUTURE

The achievements of the American economy in the twentieth century would have seemed like science fiction to someone looking forward in the year 1901. However, we also will face challenges in the years ahead. Here, we consider three of the most important: the apparent worsening in the distribution of income, the aging of the population, and the search for a meaningful life.

[2]U.S. Bureau of the Census, *Statistical Abstract of the United States: 2002*, 102.

TABLE 29.6 Distribution of Monetary Income among Families (in percent)

YEAR	LOWEST FIFTH	SECOND FIFTH	THIRD FIFTH	FOURTH FIFTH	HIGHEST FIFTH	TOP 5%
1947	5.0%	11.9%	17.0%	23.1%	43.0%	17.5%
1957	5.1	12.7	18.1	23.8	40.4	15.6
1967	5.5	12.4	17.9	23.9	40.4	15.2
1980	5.2	11.5	17.5	24.3	41.5	15.3
1990	4.6	10.8	16.6	23.8	44.3	17.4
2000	4.3	9.8	15.5	22.8	47.4	20.8

Sources: 1947–1967: U.S. Bureau of the Census, Current Population Reports, *Series P-60, no. 118, Table 13; 1980-1990:* Statistical Abstract of the United States, 2000, *section 14, Table 745, 471; 2000:* Statistical Abstract of the United States, 2002, *section 13, Table 659, 437.*

Improving the Distribution of Income

Many Americans, particularly college students, worry that even though the economy is growing, they may not be able to share in that growth because the distribution of income is becoming less equal. The rich are hogging all the gains. Stories about the fabulous incomes of Internet entrepreneurs or top sports figures seem to confirm the impression that the rich are getting richer and the poor, poorer.

Evidently, the distribution of family incomes has not changed radically over the post-war period—compare the distribution in 2000 with the distribution in 1947. Clearly, the distribution has become less equal since 1967. The share of the lowest fifth has fallen from 5.5 percent to 4.3 percent. To put it more dramatically, the share of the poorest fifth has fallen almost 25 percent.[3] On the other hand, the share of the top five percent has risen from 15.2 percent in 1967 to 20.8 percent in 2000, an increase of 31 percent.

Although the evidence shown in Table 29.6 of a worsening distribution is clear, the reasons for this change, as thoughtful analysts such as Robert W. Fogel have pointed out, are complex.[4] He and other analysts make a number of important points based on their analysis of the underlying determinants of the distribution of income that we will discuss below. Once again, we must remind you of the importance of Economic Reasoning Proposition 5. Opinions must be based on a careful examination of all the evidence. The distribution of income is one of those emotional issues in which people are likely to jump to conclusions from a few examples or a few numbers.

1. A change in the distribution of work hours has had a major effect on the distribution of income. In 1890 poor people generally worked more hours than rich people. Now poor people work fewer hours than the professionals who make up a substantial proportion of the highest fifth. Two-earner families, in which both family members are highly paid professionals, once a rarity, have become commonplace. Table 29.7 shows how different types of families have fared over the past 30 years. Real incomes of families with two earners in the paid labor force have shown the most rapid increases in real income.
2. The mobility of people in moving from one income class to another must be taken into account. Families in the lowest category may be there for temporary reasons: a proprietor of a small business who had a bad year or an executive of a large corporation who was laid off and is temporarily experiencing a low income.

[3] $[(4.3 - 5.5) / (0.5 \times 5.5 + 0.5 \times 4.2)] \times 100 = -24.5$

[4] Robert W. Fogel, *The Fourth Great Awakening and the Future of Egalitarianism* (Chicago: University of Chicago Press, 2000), 217–222.

TABLE 29.7 Median Real Family Income by Type of Family (in 1998 dollars)

FAMILIES	1970	1980	1990	2000[a]	ANNUAL GROWTH RATE 1970-2000
Married couple families	$ 41,504	$ 45,832	$ 49,754	$ 57,141	1.07%
Wife in the paid labor force	48,450	53,235	58,337	67,075	1.08
Wife not in the paid labor force	36,720	37,575	37,744	38,363	0.15
Male householder, no wife present	35,568	34,697	36,224	36,233	0.06
Female householder, no husband present	20,101	20,614	21,116	24,904	0.71
All Families	38,942	41,637	44,090	49,133	0.77

[a]*Preliminary*

Sources: 1970–1990: The Statistical Abstract of the United States, 2000, *section 14, Table 748, 472; 2000:* The Statistical Abstract of the United States, 2002, *section 13, Table 662, 438.*

Highly skilled and ambitious immigrants may enter the lowest category but steadily work their way up.

3. Public policy should focus first on the people who are chronically poor and who year in and year out are unable to consume more than poverty-level incomes. These individuals and families constitute perhaps 4 percent of all households; they are what William Julius Wilson has referred to as "The truly disadvantaged." The capacity of the United States to help these people achieve a decent material standard of living is without question.
4. Almost all observers agree that a major reason for the widening of the gap between rich and poor has been the enormous increase in the demand for highly trained personnel compared with the stagnant demand for personnel with only a high school education. Mostly this was due to changes in the demand for labor: Demands increased for highly trained personnel in medicine, computers, finance, and similar fields. Partly, it was also due to policy mistakes. In the 1970s, fear of oversupply led to cutbacks in government support for the education of highly skilled professionals. The number of medical degrees conferred, for example, declined after 1984. Improving the distribution of income may require a major push by the government to fund additional education.

Caring for an Aging Population

One of the major challenges that Americans face in this new century is caring for an increasingly elderly population. As Table 29.8 on page 602 shows, the percentage of individuals over 65 years of age increased steadily from 1960 to 2000. This trend has created severe strains for the Social Security system and doubts about its future. In 1999, 12.7 percent of the population was 65 and older; projections indicate a rise of the age group eligible for Social Security to 19.4 percent in 2030. Whereas in 1994 there were about 3.2 covered workers per beneficiary, by 2030, it is projected, there will be only 2.0 workers per beneficiary.

Initially, Social Security was an insurance system, based on the principle that an interest-earning fund should be built up from the premiums collected from individuals and that the fund should be adequate to meet future obligations. Taxes were collected beginning in 1937, but no benefits were paid until 1942 in order to accumulate a reserve. The political temptation to increase benefits became too great, however, and in 1939 legislation was passed that converted social security into a pay-as-you-go system, with beneficiaries being supported entirely by those currently paying into the system.

In the ensuing years, social security benefits increased rapidly for several reasons: the population aged, more workers were covered, and benefits were indexed to the price level.

TABLE 29.8 The Elderly Population, 1960–2000

PEOPLE AGED 65 AND OVER	1960	1970	1980	1990	2000
Total in millions	16.7	20.1	25.6	31.1	35
As a percentage of the total population	9.2%	9.8%	11.3%	12.5%	12.4%
As a percentage of the population aged 18-64	17.0%	17.0%	19.0%	20.0%	21.0%

Sources: 1960–1990: The Statistical Abstract of the United States, 2000, *section 1, Table 12, 13; 2000:* The Statistical Abstract of the United States, 2002, *section 1, Table 12, 14.*

Inevitably, the tax rate had to be increased: from 2.0 percent in 1937 to 15.3 percent today. The maximum tax payment rose from $60 in 1937 (about $750 in today's money) to $11,659 today. From a legal point of view, half the tax is paid by the employer, and half by the employee. Economists recognize, however, that the economic locus of the tax may be very different from the legal locus, and many economists believe that in reality workers pay most of the tax through direct contributions or by accepting lower wages. In 1950 there were 43.3 million workers paying into the system and 2.9 million beneficiaries, a ratio of 16.5 workers per beneficiary. By 1975, there were 100.2 million covered workers and 31.1 million beneficiaries, a ratio of 3.2 workers per beneficiary. Today there are 152.9 million covered workers and 45.2 million beneficiaries, for a ratio of 3.4 workers per beneficiary.

The Social Security system has come perilously close to bankruptcy. On April 1, 1982, the system's trustees reported that "Social Security will be unable to pay retirees' and survivors' benefits on time starting in July 1983 unless Congress takes corrective action." Congressman Claude Pepper of Florida, a leading spokesperson for the elderly and chair of the House Select Committee on Aging, said that the trustees' report "confirms my belief that the poor performance of the economy is robbing the Social Security trust funds." For the seventeenth straight year, the combined old age and disability trust funds paid out more than they took in, and soon they would be depleted. Legislation based on a presidential commission headed by Alan Greenspan rescued the system. Nevertheless, concerns about the future of Social Security continue. Proposals to "privatize" Social Security are being considered. Under these proposals, some portion of current Social Security revenues, or perhaps the revenues from a tax increase, could be invested in private securities.

The Search for a Meaningful Life

Many social indicators of well-being began to "deteriorate" in the 1970s. As shown in Table 29.9, the birthrate among unmarried women, the divorce rate, the suicide rate, and the murder rate all rose between 1960 and 1980. Admittedly, the exact meanings of these trends was difficult to determine because of changes in what is socially acceptable. The increase in the proportion of births to unmarried women, for example, may partly reflect changes in social norms. We can see the effect of differences in social norms with respect to births to unmarried women by looking at the international variance in this measure. In 1992, the U.S. proportion stood at 30 percent, less than Sweden (50 percent) but more than the Netherlands (12 percent) or Japan (1 percent). Social norms may also influence the reporting of variables as well as the true levels. Again, international comparisons are instructive. In the early 1990s, age-adjusted suicide rates varied from 12.3 in the United States to 12.9 in Canada, to 20.9 in Denmark (where the social stigma associated with suicide is relatively low), and to 7.1 in Spain (where the social stigma is high). Indeed, in some cases, we could argue that part of the trend represented an increase in well-being—some people may be happier divorcing rather than remaining married merely because of strong social pressures to do so. But in general, these trends also signaled a deterioration in values that many people felt deeply disturbing in society at large and in their own lives.

TABLE 29.9 Changes in Selected Social Indicators, 1950–1999

YEAR	BIRTHS TO UNMARRIED WOMEN (percentage)	DIVORCE RATE (per 1,000 people)	SUICIDE RATE (per 100,000 people)	MURDER RATE (per 100,000 people)
1950	3.9%	2.6	11.4	NA
1960	5.3	2.2	10.6	5.0
1970	10.7	3.5	11.6	8.0
1980	18.4	5.2	11.9	10.2
1990	28.0	4.7	12.4	9.4
1999	33.0	4.1	10.7	6.2

Sources: 1950–1970: Historical Statistics of the United States Colonial Times to 1970, *Series B1, B28, B166, B216, H954; 1980–1990:* Statistical Abstract of the United States, 2000, *section 2, table 86, 70, Table 130, 94; 1999:* Statistical Abstract of the United States, 2002, *section 2, Tables 66, 75,100,108, 59, 63, 79, and 86.*

Indeed, in an important recent book, *The Fourth Great Awakening*, Robert W. Fogel, one of the deans of American economic history, has argued that the attempt to ensure that all citizens have the spiritual resources to achieve a meaningful life may be the greatest challenge of the twenty-first century.[5] By *spiritual* Fogel does not mean only religious values, although they are part of what he has in mind. He means to include as well other values and cultural traditions that help people cope with life and find a meaningful path.

What are some of the issues that we will face that will require spiritual as well as material resources to solve? The truly disadvantaged will require material resources to meet the demands of daily living. Will that be enough? Will they also need help finding a meaningful role in society? Retirement for most people will probably lengthen. How will society provide for meaningful activities for retirees, and how will it address the depression that often afflicts older people? On the other hand, in some sectors of the economy, such as academia, retirement may be delayed. How will young people in these sectors cope with years of delay before they take their place in the sun? As more and more women and minorities enter the workplace, how will society break the glass ceilings that prevent them from reaching the highest rungs in business and government? As Americans become increasingly aware of the world outside the boundaries of the United States, how will Americans cope with the great international disparities in material income? None of these questions is easily answered; all of them require new ways of thinking about our economy and society.

PROPHETS OF DECLINE

What of the future? The slowdown in productivity growth until the past decade along with the rise in various indicators of social malaise such as the murder rate, brought to center stage a series of pundits who claimed that Americans faced a long-term decline in their living standards if they did not quickly shape up. Some focused on the lack of savings and the government deficit; others stressed America's dependence on oil; still others decried the spoiling of the environment.

In his widely acclaimed book, *The Rise and Fall of the Great Powers,* Paul Kennedy, one of the most thoughtful prophets of decline, stressed the tendency of great empires of the past to decline once they had reached a preeminent position because they had exhausted their resources in foreign adventures. It was natural for Americans who had witnessed the destructive domestic consequences of the war in Vietnam to see the force of his point.

[5]The title refers to Fogel's view that the United States is now undergoing a religious revival comparable to similar revivals that have reshaped economic and social institutions in the past.

Most students are familiar with prophecies of decline based on environmental dangers, such as global warming. We do not wish to argue that the problems addressed by the prophets of decline are not real ones or that the solutions they propose might not make things better. It is important to remember that prophecies of decline are not unique to our age. For the British, especially, it is an old story. Writing in 1798, Thomas Robert Malthus, in his celebrated *Essay on Population*, predicted that eventually Britain's growing population would run into its declining ability to produce food (after all, the amount of agricultural land was limited). Wages would eventually fall until they reached the minimum necessary to sustain life.[6] Disaster could be avoided only if population could somehow be held in check. Nearly 200 years later, the population and standard of living of England is far higher than Malthus could have imagined. William Stanley Jevons was another prophet of inevitable decline. In his famous book, *The Coal Question*, written in 1865, Jevons predicted that England would eventually be forced into decline because its reserves of coal (then its chief source of industrial power) would be exhausted. England would face not only economic decline but also "moral and intellectual retrogression."[7] This catastrophe never came to pass: more reserves of coal were found, technological change permitted other sources of power to be used, and the development of world trade made it possible to escape from the confines of a theory based on the premise that Britain was the only industrial nation.

We cannot say that the Jeremiahs of the current generation are wrong. The economic historian, looking at the long record of growth achieved by the American economy, is likely to be skeptical. The point was well put long ago by English historian Thomas Babington Macaulay:

> We cannot absolutely prove that those are in error who tell us that society has reached a turning point, that we have seen our best days. But so said all who came before us, and with just as much apparent reason.[8]

---

[6]Malthus refined his essay a number of times. In later versions he recognized that moral restraints on population growth would prevent the real wage from falling to the minimum needed to sustain life.

[7]Quoted in Stanley Engerman, "Chicken Little, Anna Karenina, and the Economics of Slavery: Two Reflections on Historical Analysis, with Examples Drawn Mostly from the Study of Slavery," *Social Science History* 17 (1993), 163. Engerman points out that both Malthus and Jevons saw the crunch coming far in the future.

[8]"Southey's Colloquies," in *Macaulay's Essays* (1860 ed.; American ed., Boston: 1881; Riverside ed.), Vol. 1, ii, 186. We thank Deirdre McCloskey for suggesting this quotation.

Selected References and Suggested Readings

Abramovitz, Moses. "Catching Up, Forging Ahead, and Falling Behind." *Journal of Economic History* 46 (June 1986): 385–406.

Blinder, Alan S. "The Level and Distribution of Economic Well-Being." In *The American Economy in Transition*, ed. Martin Feldstein. Chicago: University of Chicago Press, 1980, chapter 6.

Browning, Edgar K., and William R. Johnson. "Taxes, Transfers, and Income Equality." In *Regulatory Change in an Atmosphere of Crisis: Current Implications of the Roosevelt Years*, ed. Gary Walton. New York: Academic Press, 1979.

Carter, Susan B. "The Changing Importance of Lifetime Jobs in the U.S. Economy, 189–1978." *Industrial Relations* 27 (1988): 287–300.

Center for Population Economics at the University of Chicago. **http://www.cpe.uchicago.edu**.

Cherlin, Andrew J. *Marriage, Divorce, Remarriage.* Cambridge, Mass.: Harvard University Press, 1981.

Clark, Colin. *The Conditions of Economic Progress*, 3d ed. New York: St. Martin's, 1981.

Cohen, Wilbur J. "Economic Well-Being and Income Distribution." In *The American Economy in Transition*, ed. Martin Feldstein. Chicago: University of Chicago Press, 1980.

Costa, Dora. *The Evolution of Retirement: An American Economic History, 1880–1890.* Chicago: University of Chicago Press, 2000.

Costa, Dora L., and Richard H. Steckel. "Long-Term Trends in Health, Welfare, and Economic Growth in the United States." In *Health and Welfare during Industrialization*, eds. Richard H. Steckel and Roderick Floud. Chicago: University of Chicago Press, 1995.

De Long, J. Bradford. "The Shape of Twentieth Century Economic History." Cambridge, Mass.: National Bureau of Economic Research, working paper 7569, 2000. Available at **http://www.nber.org**.

———. "Cornucopia: The Pace of Economic Growth in the Twentieth Century." Cambridge, Mass.: National Bureau of Economic Research, working paper 7602, 2000. Available at **http://www.nber.org**.

Easterlin, Richard A. "Regional Income Trends, 1840–1950." In *The Reinterpretation of American Economic History*, ed. Robert W. Fogel and Stanley L. Engerman. New York: Harper & Row, 1971.

———. "Does Economic Growth Improve the Human Lot? Some Empirical Evidence." In *Essays in Honor of Moses Abramovitz*, eds. Paul David and Melvin Reder. New York: Academic Press, 1974.

———. *Birth and Fortune*. New York: Basic Books, 1980.

Fogel, Robert W. "Economic Growth, Population Theory, and Physiology: The Bearing of Long-term Processes on the Making of Economic Policy." *American Economic Review* 84 (1994): 369–395.

———. *The Fourth Great Awakening and the Future of Egalitarianism*. Chicago: University of Chicago Press, 2000.

Gershenkron, Alexander. *Economic Backwardness in Historical Perspective*. New York: Praeger, 1962.

Heckman, John J. "The Central Role of the South in Accounting for the Economic Progress of Black Americans." *American Economic Review* 80 (1990): 242–246.

Joyce, Theodore, Hope Corman, and Michael Grossman. "A Cost-Effectiveness Analysis of Strategies to Reduce Infant Mortality." *Medical Care* 26 (April 1988): 348–360.

Kennedy, Paul. *The Rise and Fall of the Great Powers: Economic Change and Military Conflict from 1500 to 2000*. New York: Random House, 1987.

Komlos, John. "The Height and Weight of West Point Cadets: Dietary Change in Antebellum America." *Journal of Economic History* 47 (1987): 897–927.

Krugman, Paul R. *The Age of Diminished Expectations: U. S. Economic Policy in the 1990s*, 3d ed. Cambridge, Mass: MIT Press, 1997.

Lebergott, Stanley. *The American Economy: Income, Wealth and Want.* Princeton, N.J.: Princeton University Press, 1976.

Levy, Frank. *Dollars and Dreams: The Changing American Income Distribution.* New York: Norton, 1988.

Maddison, Angus. *Phases of Capitalist Development.* New York: Oxford University Press, 1982.

Malthus, Thomas R. *An Essay on Population.* London: J. M. Dent, 1914, 2 vols.

National Center for Health Statistics. **http://www.cdc.gov/nchs/**.

Reich, Robert B. *I'll Be Short: Essentials for a Decent Working Society.* Boston: Beacon Press, 2002.

Ruggles, Patricia, and Michael O'Higgins. "The Distribution of Public Expenditure Among Households in the United States." *Review of Income and Wealth* 27 (June 1981): 137–163.

Simon, Julian. *The State of Humanity.* Oxford: Blackwell, 1995.

Rostow, W.W. *The Stages of Economic Growth.* Cambridge: Cambridge University Press, 1960, 1971.

———. *The World Economy: History & Prospect.* Austin: University of Texas Press, 1978.

Steckel, Richard H. "Stature and the Standard of Living." *Journal of Economic Literature* 33 (1995): 1903–1940.

Sundquist, James L. *Politics and Policy, The Eisenhower, Kennedy, and Johnson Years.* Washington, D.C.: Brookings Institution, 1968.

Thurow, Lester. *The Zero-Sum Society.* New York: Basic Books, 1980.

———. *The Zero-Sum Solution.* New York: Simon & Schuster, 1985.

Weaver, Carolyn L. *Understanding the Sources and Dimensions of Crisis in Social Security.* Washington, D.C.: Fiscal Policy Council, 1981.

Wilson, William Julius. *The Truly Disadvantaged: The Inner City, The Underclass, and Public Policy.* Chicago: University of Chicago Press, 1987.

Subject Index

Name Index

NUMBERS EXPRESSED IN SCIENTIFIC NOTATION

1 000 000 =	10 x 10 x 10 x 10 x 10 x 10	$= 10^6$
100 000 =	10 x 10 x 10 x 10 x 10	$= 10^5$
10 000 =	10 x 10 x 10 x 10	$= 10^4$
1000 =	10 x 10 x 10	$= 10^3$
100 =	10 x 10	$= 10^2$
10 =	10	$= 10^1$
1 =	1	$= 10^0$
0.1 =	1/10	$= 10^{-1}$
0.01 =	$1/100 = 1/10^2$	$= 10^{-2}$
0.001 =	$1/1000 = 1/10^3$	$= 10^{-3}$
0.0001 =	$1/10\,000 = 1/10^4$	$= 10^{-4}$
0.000 01 =	$1/100\,000 = 1/10^5$	$= 10^{-5}$
0.000 001 =	$1/1\,000\,000 = 1/10^6$	$= 10^{-6}$

PHYSICAL DATA

Speed of light in a vacuum =	2.9979×10^8 m/s
Speed of sound (20°C, 1 atm) =	343 m/s
Standard atmospheric pressure =	1.01×10^5 Pa
1 astronomical unit (A.U.), (average Earth-Sun distance) =	1.50×10^{11} m
Average Earth-Moon distance =	3.84×10^8 m
Equatorial radius of the Sun =	6.96×10^8 m
Equatorial radius of Jupiter =	7.14×10^7 m
Equatorial radius of the Earth =	6.37×10^6 m
Equatorial radius of the Moon =	1.74×10^6 m
Average radius of hydrogen atom =	5×10^{-11} m
Mass of the Sun =	1.99×10^{30} kg
Mass of Jupiter =	1.90×10^{27} kg
Mass of the Earth =	5.98×10^{24} kg
Mass of the Moon =	7.36×10^{22} kg
Proton mass =	1.6726×10^{-27} kg
Neutron mass =	1.6749×10^{-27} kg
Electron mass =	9.1×10^{-31} kg
Electron charge =	1.602×10^{-19} C

STANDARD ABBREVIATIONS

A	ampere	g	gram	M	molarity
amu	atomic mass unit	h	hour	min	minute
atm	atmosphere	hp	horsepower	mph	mile per hour
Btu	British thermal unit	Hz	Hertz	N	newton
C	coulomb	in.	inch	Pa	pascal
°C	degree Celsius	J	joule	psi	pound per square inch
cal	calorie	K	kelvin	s	second
eV	electron volt	kg	kilogram	V	volt
°F	degree Fahrenheit	lb	pound	W	watt
ft	foot	m	meter	Ω	ohm

Conceptual Physical Science

Third Edition

Paul G. Hewitt
City College of San Francisco

John Suchocki
Saint Michael's College

Leslie A. Hewitt
Westlake School

Executive Editor: Adam Black, Ph.D.
Associate Editor: Liana Allday
Senior Marketing Manager: Christy Lawrence
Managing Producer: Claire Masson
Managing Editor: Joan Marsh
Manufacturing Buyer: Vivian McDougal
Cover Designer: Blakeley Kim
Cover Photo: Art Wolfe/Getty Images

Library of Congress Cataloging-in-Publication Data

Hewitt, Paul G.
Conceptual physical science / Paul G. Hewitt, John Suchocki, Leslie A. Hewitt.—3rd college ed.
p. cm.
Includes bibliographical references and index.
ISBN 0-321-05173-4 (alk. paper)
1. Physical sciences. I. Suchocki, John. II. Hewitt, Leslie A. III. Title.

Q158.5.H48 2003
500.2—dc21 2003051794

ISBN: 0-321-05173-4

www.aw-bc.com/physics

5 6 7 8 9 10-CRK-06 05

To
Megan, Emily,
Ian, Evan, Maitreya,
and
all the other children of the world who wonder

Brief Table of Contents:

Table of contents

The Conceptual Physical Science—Third Edition Photo Album

This is a very personal book, a family undertaking shown in many photographs throughout. The children of authors Leslie and John, to whom this book is dedicated, are seen as follows: Megan Abrams, page 261; and Megan and sister, Emily Abrams, pages 292, and 613. Ian Suchocki (pronounced Su-hock-ee, with a silent c), with his mom Tracy on page 345, Evan Suchocki with his great Uncle Paul on page xvi, and Maitreya Suchocki, page 339.

The late Charlie Spiegel, to whom our first physical science book was dedicated, is shown with the frying-pan mirror on page 286. His optimistic flavor remains in this edition.

The three part opener photos are of family children. Part 1 opens on page 11 with the grandchildren of author Paul, and son and daughter of Paul Jr. and Ludmila Hewitt—Alexander and Grace. Part 2 on page 339 is author John's daughter, Maitreya. Part 3 on page 613 shows the daughters of Leslie—Megan and Emily.

Author Leslie is shown on page 357 in a colored rendition of a black and white photo at the age of 16. This photo has been in all her dad's books since then. Leslie is shown more recently with her dad on page 725, and looking for fossils on page 731. Leslie's husband Bob Abrams is shown on pages 695 and 722. Leslie's mom, Millie, is seen on page 182. Author Paul's brother and his wife, David and Barbara Hewitt, are shown pumping water on page 148. Their son Dave is shown on page 225. Author Paul's other brother, Steve, is shown with daughter Gretchen in the small touching photo on page 62. Son Paul, photographer for several of the photos in this book, is shown in the larger touching photo with his daughter Grace on page 53. He is seen again demonstrating thermodynamics on pages 166 and 181. His lovely wife Ludmila is shown with crossed Polaroids on page 304. Paul and Leslie's younger brother, James, who was killed in an auto accident in 1988, is shown on page 325. He left a son, Manuel, shown on page 278.

Author John, lead guitarist for the *Silent Boys* (www.SilentBoys.com), plays his guitar on page 243 and again on page 373. He is shown again dramatically walking barefoot on hot coals on page 179. John's mom, Marjorie Hewitt Suchocki (a theologian and author of several books), shows the niceties of reflection on page 310. John's nephew Graham Orr is shown enjoying one of this planet's most valued resources on page 432. The Suchocki family dog, Sam, is shown on page 191. Part of John and Tracy's wedding party is shown on page 274; from left to right, Butch Orr, sister Cathy, Tracy and John, sister Joan, Mom Suchocki, Tracy's mother Sharon Hopwood, Tracy's father David Hopwood, Kellie Dipple, Mark Werkmeister, and Uncle Paul. John's cousin George Webster is seen with his scanning electron microscope on page 368. The inverted image of John's son Evan and his wife Tracy enjoying the balmy beaches of Hawaii can be seen on page 556. Several dear friends from Hawaii include Rinchen Trashi on page 363, Jill and Michaela Rabinov on page 420, and Maya Stevens on page 575.

Author Paul's personal friends include, foremost, Lillian Lee, pages 180, 258, and with her pet conure on page 292. Lillian helped with all production stages of this book and its ancillaries (the ninth edition of Conceptual Physics is gratefully dedicated to her). Lillian's dad, Wai Tsan Lee is shown on page 236. Lillian is again shown with friend Sushi Shah in a British supermarket on page 223. The fellow most influential in instilling Paul's love of science is Burl Grey, page 21. Paul's physics mentor, Ken Ford, glider enthusiast, is shown with his noise-canceling earphones in his airplane, page 265. (Two previous books by Paul have been dedicated to Ken Ford.) Paul Ryan, dear friend since early teens, drags his fingers through molten lead on page 197. Close friend Marshall Ellenstein, one of Chicago's finest physics teachers, does his physics on pages 121 and 157. Marshall is the producer of the physics videos and DVDs that complement this book (www.CPro.cc). Howie Brand, dear friend from college days, does his physics on page 70. Paul's buddy Tim Gardner is seen on pages 152 and 815. That's teacher friend Pablo Robinson on page 136, bravely sandwiched between two beds of nails, and again on page 291. Physics chanteuse Lynda Williams is on page 271. Editor and author Suzanne Lyons, good friend and contributor to this book, is shown with children Tristan and Simone on page 307. On page C-2 is a caricature of Paul's cartoonist mentor, Ernie Brown, who designed the title logo on the cover of this book, and on all of Paul's books.

Physics professor friends include Chuck Stone on page 118, Jim Stith showing an impressive Wimshurst generator on page 212, Roy Unruh showing electric cars on page 226, Sheron Snyder generating light on page 247, and Bob Greenler showing a colorful giant soap bubble on page 301.

City College of San Francisco friends include: Will Maynez, pages 74 and 178. Tenny Lim, former teaching assistant to Paul, is seen on page 78. Tenny is now a space engineer at Jet Propulsion Labs. Another of Paul's former teaching assistants who turned to science is Helen Yan, shown on page 186. Helen presently monitors satellite launches for Lockheed Martin. Paul's former student Cassy Cosme nicely severs bricks with her bare hand on page 70. Chelcie Liu shows his novel tracks on page B-4.

Paul's personal friends from Hawaii are Meidor Hu, shown in an electrifying pose on page 210, and her uncle Chiu Man Wu on page 190, whose daughter Andrea is on page 83. Meidor's sister, Mei Tuck and her husband Gabe Vitelli, are shown together on page 193. Also from Hawaii are friends Richard Crowe, page 833, Jean Curtis on page 243, and Praful Shah on page 104.

The inclusion of these people who are so dear to the authors makes this book all the more our labor of love.

To the Students

Physical Science is about the rules of the physical world—physics, chemistry, geology, and astronomy. Just as you can't enjoy a ball game, computer game, or party game until you know its rules, so it is with nature. Nature's rules are beautifully elegant and can be neatly described mathematically. That's why many physical science texts are treated as applied mathematics. But too much emphasis on computation misses something essential—*comprehension*—a gut feeling for the concepts. This book is *conceptual,* focusing on concepts in down-to-earth English rather than in mathematical language. You'll see the mathematical structure in frequent equations, but you'll find them *guides to thinking* rather than recipes for computation.

We enjoy physical science, and you will too—because you'll understand it. Just as a person who knows the rules of botany best appreciates plants, and a person who knows the intricacies of music best appreciates music, you'll better appreciate the physical world about you when you learn its rules.

Enjoy your physical science!

Paul G. Hewitt John Suchocki Leslie A. Hewitt

To the Instructor

Conceptual Physical Science, third edition, with its important ancillaries, provides a first introduction to physics, chemistry, earth science, and astronomy, melded in a manner to captivate student interest. Unlike the eight parts and 30 chapters of the second edition, this edition has 35 chapters, divided into three main parts—Physics, Chemistry, and Earth and Space Science. We begin with physics because we see it as the most basic of the sciences. It reaches up to chemistry, which in turn reaches to the earth and space sciences, and ultimately, beyond this book, to the life sciences.

For the nonscience student, this book provides a base from which to view nature more perceptively—to see that a surprisingly few relationships make up nature's rules. For the science student, it is this as well, but also a springboard to involvement in other sciences, such as biology and the health sciences.

Part One, Physics, treats forces, motion, energy, electricity, heat, sound, and light. Unlike the second edition, the treatment of physics in this edition begins with statics so that students start with forces and vectors rather than with velocity and acceleration. After success with simple forces, chapter 1 progresses to kinematics. Newton's laws of motion pick up the pace, and the conventional order of mechanics topics follow, with heat, thermodynamics, electricity and magnetism, and light.

As in previous editions, physics is not presented as applied mathematics but is treated conceptually, with a focus on qualitative comprehension. Mathematical expression follows in the problem sets. We minimize the mathematical language and mathematical problems that are roadblocks to many students. Although a flip though the pages will show that the equations are there, they are presented as guides to thinking rather than recipes for algebraic manipulation. Their derivations are addressed in the footnotes. The treatment of physics is followed with the realm of the atom—a bridge to chemistry.

The chemistry chapters in this edition were developed from the second edition of Suchocki's *Conceptual Chemistry* rather than from the second edition of *Conceptual Physical Science.* Thus you will find that the chemistry chapters appearing in this third edition have been fully reworked, from the narrative to the photos and illustrations. For example, a new chapter has been dedicated to atomic conceptual models, while acids, bases, and redox reactions have been segregated into two chapters. New sections on the applications of chemistry, such as water treatment facilities and the conservation of metal resources, have been added. Also, the chapter on chemical reactions now begins with a new discussion on chemical kinetics. As with earlier editions, chemistry is related to the students' familiar world—the fluorine in their toothpaste, the Teflon on their frying pans, and the flavors produced by various organic molecules. The environmental aspects of chemistry are also emphasized.

Part Three, Earth and Space Science, is reorganized to encompass both earth science—the sciences of geology, hydrology, oceanography, and meteorology—and astronomy—the science of the cosmos. The study of planet Earth begins with the formation, occurrence, and use of minerals, followed by a chapter on rocks. Both chapters are completely reorganized and restructured, focusing on major processes with special attention given to building on concepts learned in Part Two. Subsequent chapters focus on processes—external and internal—that impact, change, and modify our planet's surface. Elements of hydrology and oceanography are woven into these later chapters to highlight their tight integration within the earth sciences. The cumulative set of concepts is then used as a foundation for understanding the changes that have occurred on earth over geologic time—including the evolution of life. We conclude our study of earth science with a look at how the origin, structure, and behavior of the atmosphere and oceans control the earth's climate and create weather.

The applications of physics, chemistry, and the earth sciences applied to other massive bodies in the universe culminate in astronomy. Astronomy is about "out there," where space and time differ from the students' everyday notions. Discussions of special and general relativity conclude the book in Chapter 35. So our tour of physical science begins with the physics of atoms, then proceeds to the chemistry of molecules, then to the aggregates of molecules in earth science, and finally to the aggregates of matter in the cosmos—astronomy.

This third edition has a greater number of exercises and problems at the ends of all chapters. Another new feature throughout the book is the inclusion of Insight boxes, providing supporting information on most pages. There are also Connections boxes that show the connections of subject matter to real-world applications and phenomena. In the spirit of integrating topics, a new feature is the use of icons throughout the book that show where material integrates with supporting material in other parts of the book.

Pedagogy

At the end of each chapter is a group of pedagogical aids: Summary of Terms, Review Questions, Activities, Exercises, and, in many chapters, Problems. All of the important ideas from each chapter are framed in the relatively easy-to-answer Review Questions, which are grouped by chapter sections. They are, as the name implies, a review of chapter material. Their purpose is simply to provide a structured way to review the chapter. They are not meant to challenge the student's intellect, because, in the vast majority of cases, the answers can simply be looked up. The Exercises, on the other hand, play a different role. Some of these are designed to prompt the application of physical science to everyday situations, while others are more sophisticated and call for considerable critical thinking.

The Problems are mainly simple computations that aid in learning concepts. In order to decrease the likelihood of students focusing on number crunching rather than the conceptual reasoning, there are fewer Problems than Exercises. Exercises call for critical thinking. Although building confidence in math is a worthy goal, it is not the focus of this book.

Students can find the answers to the odd-numbered Exercises and Problems in the back part of the *Conceptual Physical Science Practice Book*. Complete answers to all Exercises and Problems are included in the *Instructor's Manual*.

Units of measurement are not emphasized in this text. When used, they are almost exclusively expressed in SI units. (The few exceptions include such units as calories, grams per centimeter cubed, and light-years). Mathematical derivations are avoided in the main body of the text and appear in footnotes or in the appendices. A new appendix on rotational motion is included in this edition.

Ancillary Materials

More than enough material is included for a one-year course, which allows for a variety of course designs to fit your taste. Helpful to course design is the *Instructor's Manual,* which you'll find to be different from most instructor's manuals. It contains many lecture ideas and topics not treated in the textbook, as well as teaching tips and suggested step-by-step lectures and demonstrations. It has full-page answers to all the Review Questions, Exercises, and Problems in the text.

Answers to the odd-numbered Exercises and Problems are available to students in the student supplement, *Conceptual Physical Science Practice Book.* This very important book, our most creative work, guides your students to a sometimes computational way of developing concepts. It spans a wide use of analogies and intriguing situations, all with a user-friendly tone.

The *Next-Time Questions* book has 141 insightful, full-page questions featuring Hewitt cartoons, with answers provided on the back of each page. Use these as overhead transparencies or for posting. There are Next-Time Questions for every chapter.

The *Test Bank* book has more than 2400 multiple-choice questions, as well as short-answer and essay questions. The questions are categorized by level of difficulty. The *TestGen-EQ Computerized Testing Software* contains everything in the Test Bank, and it allows you to edit and change the order of the questions, to add new questions, and to print different versions of a test. It is available on a dual-platform CD-ROM.

The *Conceptual Physical Science Laboratory Manual* was written by the authors with the help of a new co-author, Dean Baird. In addition to interesting laboratory experiments, it includes a range of activities similar to the activities in the textbook. These guide students to experience various phenomena before they quantify the same phenomena in follow-up laboratory experiments. Answers to the questions in the lab manual are included in the *Instructor's Manual.*

The *Image Library* is a cross-platform CD-ROM which includes JPEGs of nearly every illustration from the book. Transparency acetates of more than 100 important figures from the text are also available from your Addison-Wesley representative. Included with these transparencies is a booklet of questions designed to be shared with your students during class.

An additional instructor supplement is the *Problem-Solving Exercises in Physical Science* book. This new supplement, by Ed Ginoza, is designed for instructors who want to give their students more practice with math. It provides additional, more quantitative and computational, worked examples that encourage students to practice simple algebra, graphing, and scientific notation, and thereby develop their core math skills.

Last, but not least, we three authors have independently produced videos and DVD multimedia that accompany our respective fields: physics, chemistry, and earth science. For more details, please visit us at www.CPro.cc.

Go to it! Your conceptual physical science course really can be the most interesting, informative, and worthwhile science course available to your students.

Acknowledgements

For input to the new coverage of physics in this edition, we are grateful to Dean Baird, Howie Brand, Alexei Cogan, Paul Doherty, Marshall Ellenstein, Ken Ford, Burl Grey, John Hubisz, Dan Johnson, Lillian Lee, Tenny Lim, Anne Linder, Cedric Linder, Ron Perkins, Pablo Robinson, Kenn Sherey, Larry Weinstein, Barbara Wolfe, and Dean Zollman.

For assistance in redeveloping the chemistry chapters of this edition, we are indebted to Hilair Chism, Mark Jackson, Kevin Johnson, Frank Lambert, Robley Light, David Lygre, Irene Matusz, Irene Nunes, Frazier Nyasulu, Michael Reese, Mike Stekoll, Joseph Tausta, Margaret Tolbert, and Bob Widing.

For assistance with the writing and presentation of the earth-science material, we are grateful and indebted to Bob Abrams. We are also indebted to Ann Bykerk-Kauffman, Bonnie Gerstenfeld, Karen Grove, Suzanne Lyons, Lisa White, and Mike Young.

For valued input to the astronomy chapters, we are grateful to Richard Crowe, Björn Davidsson, Michelle Mizuno-Wiedner, Neil de Grasse Tyson, Erik Zackrisson, Joe Wesney, and Lynda Williams.

For editorial help in all stages of production, we are especially grateful to Lillian Lee, Tracy Suchocki, and Bob Abrams.

PROLOGUE

Wow, Great Uncle Paul! Before this chickie exhausted its inner space resources and poked out of its shell, this chickie much have thought it was at its last moments. But what seemed like its end was a new beginning. Are we like chickies, ready to poke through to a new environment and new understanding of our place in the universe?

PROLOGUE
The Nature of Science

Modern civilization is built on science. Nearly all forms of technology—from medicine to space travel—are applications of science. But what exactly *is* science? Where did it originate? How should science be used? What would everyday life be like without it?

Science is an organized body of knowledge about nature. It is the product of observations, common sense, rational thinking, and (sometimes) brilliant insights. Science stems from individuals' discoveries as well as from group efforts. It has been built up over thousands of years and gathered from all parts of the world. Science is an enormous gift to us today, the legacy of countless thinkers and experimenters of the past.

Science is more than a body of knowledge. It is also a *method,* a way of exploring nature and discovering the order within it. Importantly, science is also a tool for solving problems.

The beginnings of science go back before recorded history, when people first discovered repeating patterns in nature. They noted star patterns in the night sky, patterns in the weather, and patterns in animal migration. From these patterns, people learned to make predictions that gave them some control over their surroundings.

A Brief History of Advances in Science

When a light goes out in your room, you ask "How did that happen?" You might check to see if the lamp is plugged in, you might check the bulb, or you might even look at your neighbors' houses to see if there has been a power outage. When you think and act like this, you are searching for *cause-and-effect* relationships—trying to find out what events cause what results. This type of thinking is *rational thinking*. Rational thinking is basic to science.

Today, we use rational thinking so much that it's hard to imagine other ways of interpreting our experiences. But it wasn't always this way. At times, people have relied more on superstition and magic to interpret the world around them. Or they have simply failed to ask, "Why?"

Rational thought became very popular in Greece in the third and fourth centuries B.C. From there, it spread throughout Rome and to other parts of the Mediterranean world. When the Roman Empire fell in the fifth century A.D., advancements in science came to a halt in Europe. Nomadic tribes destroyed much in their paths as they conquered Europe and brought in the Dark Ages. But during this time, science continued to advance in other parts of the world.

Rational thinking of humans from many different parts of the world has contributed to the development of modern science.

Insights

The Chinese and Polynesians were charting the stars and the planets. Arab nations developed mathematics and learned to make glass, paper, metals, and certain chemicals. Finally the Greek philosophy of rational thinking was brought back into Europe by Islamic people who entered through Spain during the tenth, eleventh, and twelfth centuries. Then the university emerged. When the printing press was invented by Johann Gutenberg in the fifteenth century, science made a great leap forward. This invention did much to advance scientific thought, just as computers and the Internet are doing today.

Up until the sixteenth century, most people thought the earth was the center of the universe. They thought the sun circled the stationary earth. This thinking was challenged when the Polish astronomer Nicolaus Copernicus quietly published a book proposing that the sun is stationary and the earth revolves around it. These ideas conflicted with Church teachings and were banned for 200 years.

Modern science began in the sixteenth century, when the Italian physicist Galileo Galilei revived the Copernican view. Galileo used experiments, rather than speculation, to study nature's behavior (we'll say more about Galileo in chapters to follow). Galileo was arrested for popularizing the Copernican theory and for his other contributions to scientific thought. But a century later, his ideas and those of Copernicus were accepted by most educated people.

Scientific discoveries are often opposed, especially if they conflict with what people want to believe. In the early 1800s, geologists were condemned because their findings differed with religious accounts of creation. Later in the same century, geology was accepted, but theories of evolution were condemned. Every age has had its intellectual rebels who were persecuted, vilified, condemned, or suppressed, but later were regarded as harmless and often considered essential to the advancement of civilization and the elevation of the human condition. "At every crossway on the road that leads to the future, each progressive spirit is opposed by a thousand men appointed to guard the past."*

Mathematics and Conceptual Physical Science

Pure mathematics is different from science. Math studies relationships among numbers. When it is used as a tool of science, the results can be astounding. Measurements and calculations are essential parts of the powerful science we practice today. For example, it would not be possible to send missions to Mars if we were unable to measure the positions of spacecraft or to calculate their trajectories.

You will use some math in this course, especially when you make measurements in lab. In this book, we don't make a big deal about math. Our focus is on understanding concepts in everyday language. We use equations as guides to thinking rather than as recipes for "plug-and-chug" math work. We believe that focusing on math too early, especially on math-based problem solving, is a poor substitute for learning the concepts. That's why the emphasis in this book is on building concepts. Only when concepts are understood does solving problems make sense.

You'll see many more conceptual exercises than problems at the ends of the chapters that follow. *Conceptual Physical Science* puts comprehension comfortably before computation.

*From Maurice Maeterlinck's "Our Social Duty."

The Scientific Method—a Classic Tool

There are many paths scientists can follow in doing science. Scientists who explore the ocean floor or who chart new galaxies, for example, are focused only on making and recording new observations.

Insights

The methods of science usually are underscored by keen observations, rational thinking, and experimentation. In the sixteenth century, the Italian physicist Galileo Galilei and the English philosopher Francis Bacon were the first to formalize a particular method for doing science. What they outlined has come to be known as the classic **scientific method.** This method is essentially as follows:

1. Recognize a question or a problem.
2. Make an educated guess—a **hypothesis**—to answer the question.
3. Predict consequences that can be observed if the hypothesis is correct. The consequences should be *absent* if the hypothesis is not correct.
4. Do experiments to see if the consequences you predicted are present.
5. Formulate the simplest general rule that organizes the three ingredients—hypothesis, predicted effects, and experimental findings.

A scientific hypothesis is an educated guess that is testable. When a scientific hypothesis has been tested over and over again and has not been contradicted, it may become known as a **law** or *principle.* A scientific **fact,** on the other hand, is generally something that competent observers can observe and agree to be true. For example, it is a fact that an amputated limb of a salamander can grow back. Anyone can watch it happen. It is not a fact—yet—that a severed limb of a human can grow back.

Scientists use the word *theory* in a way that differs from everyday speech. In everyday speech, a theory is the same as a hypothesis—a statement that hasn't been tested. But scientifically speaking, a **theory** is a synthesis of facts and well-tested hypotheses. Physicists, as we will learn, use quantum theory to explain the behavior of light. Chemists have theories about how atoms bond to form molecules. Geologists use the theory of plate tectonics to show how continents move, and astronomers speak of the theory of the Big Bang to explain how galaxies are presently moving away from one another.

Facts are revisable data about the world. Theories interpret such facts.

Insights

Theories are a foundation of science, but they are not fixed. Rather, they evolve. They pass through stages of refinement. For example, since the theory of the atom was proposed 200 years ago, it has been refined many times in light of new evidence. Those who know only a little about science may argue that scientific theories can't be taken seriously because they are always changing. Those who understand science, however, see it differently. Theories grow stronger as they evolve to include new information.

Scientific Hypotheses

In order for a hypothesis to be scientific, it must be testable. A test, or a series of tests, can determine whether a hypothesis is valid. In scientific work, most hypotheses turn out to be wrong. Scientists must be patient, however, and keep testing their ideas for accuracy.

A well-known scientific hypothesis that was incorrect was that of the greatly respected Greek philosopher Aristotle (384–322 B.C.), who claimed that heavy objects naturally fall faster than light objects. This hypothesis was considered

to be true for nearly 2000 years—mainly because nearly everyone who knew of Aristotle's conclusions had such great respect for him as a thinker that they simply assumed he couldn't be wrong. Also, in Aristotle's time, air resistance was not recognized as an influence on how quickly an object falls. We've all seen that stones fall faster than leaves fluttering in the air. Without investigating further, it is easy to accept false ideas.

Galileo very carefully examined Aristotle's hypothesis. Then he did something that caught on and changed science forever. He *experimented.* Galileo showed the falseness of Aristotle's claim with a single experiment—dropping heavy and light objects from the Leaning Tower of Pisa. Legend tells us that they fell at equal speeds. In the scientific spirit, one experiment that can be reproduced outweighs any authority, regardless of reputation or the number of advocates. Albert Einstein put it well when he stated, "No number of experiments can prove me right; a single experiment can prove me wrong." In science the test of knowledge is experiment.

☑ CHECKPOINT

Which statements are *scientific* hypotheses?

(a) Better stock market decisions are made when the planets Venus, Earth, and Mars are aligned.

(b) Atoms are the smallest particles of matter that exist.

(c) The moon is made of Swiss cheese.

(d) Outer space contains a kind of matter whose existence can't be detected or tested.

(e) Albert Einstein was the greatest physicist of the twentieth century.

Check Your Answer

All statements are hypotheses, but only statements *a, b,* and *c* are scientific hypotheses—because they are testable. Statement *a* can be tested (and proven wrong) by going to the library and researching the performance of the stock market during times when these planets were aligned. Not only can statement *b* be tested, it has been tested. Although the statement has been found to be untrue (many particles smaller than atoms have been discovered), the statement is nevertheless a scientific one. Likewise for statement *c,* where visits to the moon have proven that the statement is wrong. Statement *d,* on the other hand, is easily seen to be unscientific, since it can't be tested. Lastly, statement e is an assertion that has no test. What possible test, beyond collective opinion, could prove Einstein was the greatest physicist? How could we know? Greatness is a quality that cannot be measured in an objective way.

Because the name Einstein is held in high esteem, it is a favorite of quacks (see the box on page 8). So don't be surprised when the name of Einstein—or the name of Jesus, or the names of other highly respected sources—is cited often by quacks who wish to bring respect to themselves and to their points of view. In all fields, we should be skeptical of people who wish to credit themselves by calling upon the authority of others.

While the scientific method is powerful, good science is often done differently, in a less systematic way. Many scientific advances involve trial and error, experimenting without guessing, or just plain accidental discovery. Trained observation, however, is essential for noticing questions in the first place and for making sense of evidence. But more than a particular method, the success of science has to do with an attitude common to scientists. This attitude is one of inquiry, experimentation, and humility before the facts.

A Scientific Attitude Underlies Good Science

Scientists must accept their experimental findings even when they would like them to be different. They must strive to distinguish between the results they see and those they wish to see. This is not easy. Scientists, like most people, are very capable of fooling themselves. People have always tended to adopt general rules, beliefs, creeds, ideas, and hypotheses without thoroughly questioning their validity. And sometimes we retain these ideas long after they have been shown to be meaningless, false, or at least questionable. The most widespread assumptions are often the least questioned. Too often, when an idea is adopted, great attention is given to the instances that support it. Contrary evidence is often distorted, belittled, or ignored.

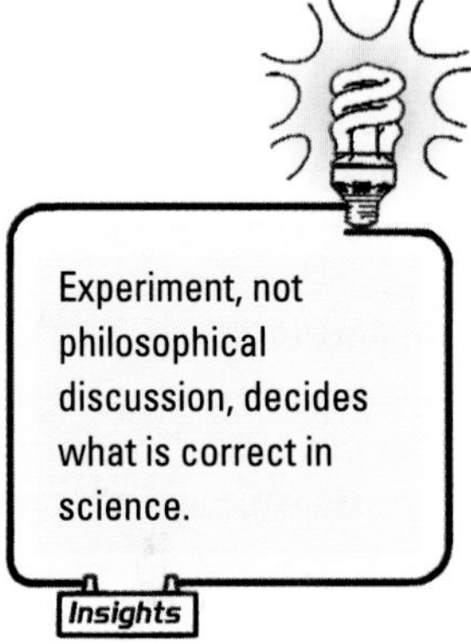

None of us has the time, energy, or resources to test every idea. So most of the time we take somebody's word. How do we know whose word to accept? To reduce the likelihood of error, scientists listen to people whose findings are testable—if not in practice, then at least in principle. Ideas that cannot be tested are regarded as "unscientific."

The fact that scientific statements will be thoroughly tested before being believed helps to keep science honest. Sooner or later, mistakes (or deceptions) are found out. A scientist exposed for cheating doesn't get a second chance in the community of scientists. Honesty, so important to the progress of science, thus becomes a matter of self-interest to scientists. There is relatively little bluffing in a game where all bets are called.

Science Has Limitations

Science deals only with hypotheses that are testable. Its domain is therefore restricted to the observable natural world. While scientific methods can be used to debunk various paranormal claims, they have no way of accounting for testimonies involving the supernatural. The term supernatural literally means "above nature." Science works within nature, not above it. Likewise, science is unable to answer philosophical questions, such as "What is the purpose of life?" or religious questions, such as "What is the nature of the human spirit?" Though these questions are valid and may have great importance to us, they rely on subjective personal experience and do not lead to testable hypotheses. They lie outside the realm of science.

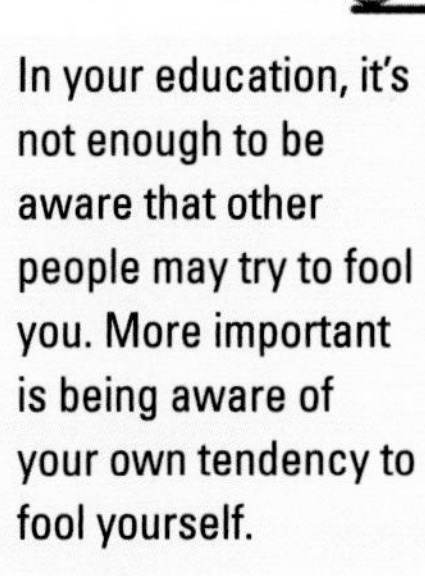

Science, Art, and Religion

The search for a deeper understanding of the world around us has taken different forms, including science, art, and religion. Science is a system by which we discover and record physical phenomena and think about possible explanations for such phenomena. The arts are concerned with personal interpretation and creative expression. Religion addresses the source, purpose, and meaning of it all. Simply put, science asks *how,* art asks *who,* and religion asks *why.*

Pseudoscience

Some belief systems are not scientific but pretend to be. For example, in the nineteenth century, many people in the United States believed in the "science" of phrenology. Phrenology was the study of the surface bumps on a person's head. Phrenologists claimed to predict all sorts of things about a person's health and personality based on the bumps on that person's head. But phrenology was fake science—**pseudoscience.** No experimental findings backed up its claims.

Consider astrology. Astrology tells us that human affairs are influenced by the positions and movements of planets and other celestial bodies. Yet there is no body of experimental evidence to back up this claim. This nonscientific view can be quite appealing. No matter how insignificant we may feel at times, astrologers assure us that we are deeply connected to the workings of the cosmos, which has been created just for us humans. Astrology as ancient magic or entertainment is one thing, but astrology disguised as science is another. When it poses as a science related to astronomy, astrology is full-fledged pseudoscience.

Pseudoscience, like science, makes predictions. The predictions of a dowser, who locates underground water supplies with a dowsing rod, have a very high rate of success—nearly 100%. Whenever the dowser goes through his or her ritual and points to a spot on the ground, a well digger is sure to find water. Dowsing works. Of course, the dowser can hardly miss, because there is ground water within 100 meters of the surface at nearly every spot on Earth. (The real test of a dowser would be finding a place where water wouldn't be found!) Dowsing is another example of pseudoscience.

We humans have learned much since the onset of science four centuries ago. Only by enormous effort did people along the way gain this knowledge and overthrow superstition. We have come far in comprehending nature and in freeing ourselves from ignorance. We should rejoice in what we've learned. We are no longer likely to die whenever an infectious disease strikes. We no longer live in fear of demons. We no longer torture and execute women accused of witchery, as was done for nearly three centuries. Today we have no need to pretend that superstition is anything but superstition, or that junk notions are anything but junk notions—whether voiced by street-corner quacks or by loose thinkers who write promise-heavy health books.

Yet there is reason to fear that what people of one time fight for, a following generation surrenders. The grip that belief in magic and superstition had on people took centuries to overcome. Yet today the same magic and superstition are enchanting a growing number of people. James Randi reports, in his book *Flim-Flam!,* that more than twenty thousand practicing astrologers in the United States service millions of credulous believers. Science writer Martin Gardner reports that a greater percentage of Americans today believe in astrology and occult phenomena than did the citizens of medieval Europe. Few newspapers in the United States carry a daily science column, but nearly all of them provide daily horoscopes. And then there are the flourishing television psychics who gain adherents daily.

Some people believe that the human condition is slipping backward because of growing technology. More likely, however, it is slipping backward because science and technology will too often bow to the irrationality of the past. Watch out for the spokespeople of pseudoscience. It is a huge and lucrative business.

Science and the arts have certain things in common. In the art of literature, we find out about what is possible in human experience. We can learn about emotions from rage to love, even if we haven't yet experienced them. The arts describe these experiences and suggest what may be possible for us. Similarly, a knowledge of science tells us what is possible in nature. Scientific knowledge helps us to predict possibilities in nature even before these possibilities have been experienced. It provides us with a way of connecting things, of seeing relationships between and among them, and of making sense of the great variety of natural events around us. While art broadens our perspective of ourselves, science broadens our perspective of our environment.

Science and religion have similarities also. For example, both are motivated by curiosity and a love for the natural world and all its beauty. Furthermore, they each have great impact on society. Science, for example, leads to useful technological innovations, while religion provides a foothold for many social services. Science and religion, however, are basically different. Science is concerned with understanding the physical universe, while religion is concerned with spiritual matters, such as faith, and the means by which we can achieve basic goodness for ourselves and for our community. In this respect, science and religion are as different as apples and oranges and do not contradict each other.

Ultimately, in learning more about science, art, and religion, we find that they are not mutually exclusive. Rather, they run parallel to each other like strings on a guitar, each resonating at its own frequency. When played together, the chord they produce is a chord of profound richness and the signature of what it means to be human. Learning more about all three of these fields of human activity makes for a wholeness that affects the way we view our world and the decisions we make about it and ourselves. Science, art, and religion can work very well together, which is why we should never feel forced into choosing one over the other. All three are important.

☑ CHECKPOINT

There are certain fundamental questions that scientists are unable to answer. For example, why are apples gravitationally attracted to the earth? Why do electrons repel one another? Why does energy have mass? At the deepest level, scientists don't know the answers to these questions. Why not?

Check Your Answer

A premise of science is that not knowing answers is better than accepting erroneous ones. Most scientists are therefore comfortable about not having the answers to fundamental questions. Can this attitude be applied to other areas as well? Isn't it sometimes acceptable not to know the answers to philosophical and religious questions—to be open minded?

That science and religion can work very well together deserves special emphasis. When we study the nature of light later in this book, we will treat light first as a wave and then as a particle. At first, waves and particles may appear contradictory. You might believe that light can be only one or the other, and that you must choose between them. What scientists have discovered, however, is that light waves and light particles *complement* each other, and that, when these two ideas are taken together, they provide a deeper understanding of light. In a similar way, it is mainly people who are either uninformed or misinformed about the deeper natures of both science and religion who feel that they must choose between believing in religion and believing in science. Unless one has a shallow understanding of either or both, as can occur among extremists, there is no contradiction in being religious and being scientific in one's thinking.

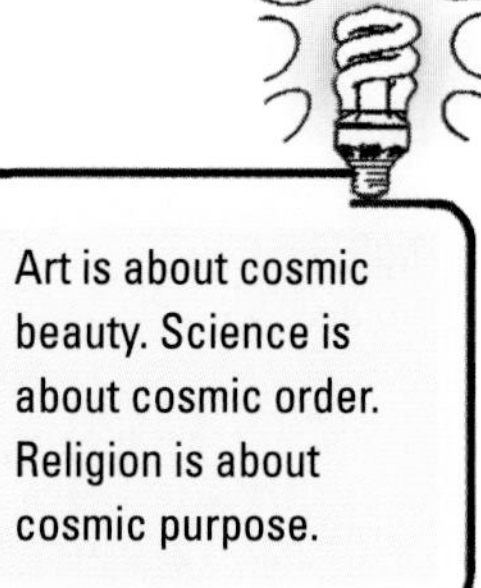

Technology—Practical Use of the Findings of Science

Science and technology are also different from each other. Science is concerned with gathering knowledge and organizing it. **Technology** lets humans use that knowledge for practical purposes, and it provides the instruments scientists need to conduct their investigations.

Technology is a double-edged sword. It can be both helpful and harmful. We have the technology, for example, to extract fossil fuels from the ground and then burn the fossil fuels to produce energy. Energy production from fossil fuels has benefited society in countless ways. On the flip side, the burning of fossil fuels damages the environment. It is tempting to blame technology itself for such problems as pollution, resource depletion, and even overpopulation. These problems, however, are not the fault of technology any more than a stabbing is the fault of the knife. It is humans who use the technology, and humans who are responsible for how it is used.

Remarkably, we already possess the technology to solve many environmental problems. This twenty-first century will likely see a switch from fossil fuels to more sustainable energy sources. We recycle waste products in new and better ways. In some parts of the world, progress is being made toward limiting the human population explosion, a serious threat that worsens almost every problem faced by humans today. Difficulty solving today's problems results more from social inertia than from failing technology. Technology is our tool. What we do with this tool is up to us. The promise of technology is a cleaner and healthier world. Wise applications of technology *can* improve conditions on planet Earth.

The Physical Sciences: Physics, Chemistry, Earth Science, and Astronomy

Science is the present-day equivalent of what used to be called *natural philosophy*. Natural philosophy was the study of unanswered questions about nature. As the answers were found, they became part of what is now called science. The study of science today branches into the study of living things and nonliving things: the life sciences and the physical sciences. The life sciences branch into such areas as biology, zoology, and botany. The *physical sciences* branch into such areas as physics, chemistry, geology, meteorology, and astronomy—the areas addressed in this book. Physics is the study of such basic concepts as motion, force, energy, matter, heat, sound, light, and the components of atoms. Chemistry builds on physics and tells us how matter is put together, how atoms combine to form molecules, and how the molecules combine to make the materials around us. Physics and chemistry, applied to the earth and its processes, make up Earth science—geology, meteorology, and oceanography. When we apply physics, chemistry, and geology to other planets and to the stars, we are speaking about astronomy. Biology is more complex than physical science, for it involves matter that is alive. Underneath biology is chemistry, and underneath chemistry is physics. So physics is basic to both physical science and life science. That is why we

Risk Assessment

Technology comes with risks as well as with benefits. When the benefits are seen to outweigh the risks, a technology can be accepted and applied. X rays, for example, continue to be used to diagnose disease despite their potential risk for causing cancer. The benefits outweigh the risks. Of course, when the risks of a technology outweigh its benefits, it should be used sparingly or not at all.

A difficult ethical problem arises when a technology benefits one group of people but poses a risk to a different group of people. For example, aspirin is useful for adults, but it can cause a potentially fatal condition in children, called *Reye's syndrome.* Are the benefits of aspirin to adults worth the risk that children will die by getting Reye's syndrome? Dumping raw sewage into the local river may pose little risk for a town located upstream, but, for towns downstream, the untreated sewage is a serious health hazard. Technologies involving different risks for different people raise questions that are often hotly debated. Which medications should be sold over the counter to the general public, and how should they be labeled? Should food be irradiated to eliminate the microorganisms that cause food-borne illnesses that kill more than 5000 Americans each year? Or are the unknown potential hazards of food irradiation sufficient cause for banning it?

People seem to have a hard time accepting the fact that zero risk is an impossible goal. Airplanes cannot be made perfectly safe. Processed foods cannot be made completely free of toxicity, for all foods are toxic to some degree. You cannot go to the beach without risking skin cancer, no matter how much sunscreen you apply. You cannot avoid radioactivity, because it's in the air you breathe and the foods you eat, and, as we will discuss in Chapter 16, it has been that way since before humans first walked the earth. Even the cleanest rain contains radioactive carbon-14, as do our bodies. Between each heartbeat in the human body, there have always been about 50,000 naturally occurring radioactive decays. You might hide yourself in the hills, eat the most natural foods, practice obsessive hygiene, and still die from cancer caused by radioactivity. The probability of eventual death is 100 percent. We must accept that. No one is exempt.

Science helps to determine the most probable results. As the tools of science improve, risks can be evaluated more and more accurately. Acceptance of risk, on the other hand, is more of a social issue than a scientific one. If society were to demand zero risk from its technology, this goal would not only be impractical, but selfish as well. Any society striving toward a policy of zero risk would consume all of its present and future economic resources. A society that accepts no risks receives no benefits.

begin with physics, then follow with chemistry and geology, and conclude with astronomy. All are treated conceptually, with the twin goals of enjoyment and understanding.

If it crawls, it's biology. If it smells, it's chemistry. If it doesn't work, it's physics.

Insights

☑ CHECKPOINT

Which of the following activities involves the utmost human expression of passion, talent, and intelligence?
(a) painting and sculpture (b) literature (c) music (d) religion (e) science

Check Your Answer

All of them. In this book, we focus on science, which is an enchanting human activity shared by a wide variety of people. With present-day tools and know-how, scientists are reaching further and finding out more about themselves and their environment than people in the past were ever able to do. The more you know about science, the more passionate you feel toward your surroundings. There is physical science in everything you see, hear, smell, taste, and touch!

We each need a *knowledge filter* to tell the difference between what is true and what only pretends to be true. The best knowledge filter ever invented is science.

Insights

In Perspective

Only a few centuries ago, the most talented and skilled artists, architects, and artisans of the world directed their genius to the construction of the great cathedrals, synagogues, temples, and mosques. Some of these architectural structures took centuries to build. This meant that nobody witnessed both the beginning and the end of construction. The architects and early builders who lived to a ripe old age never saw the finished results of their labors. Entire lifetimes were spent in the shadows of construction that must have seemed without beginning or end. This enormous focus of human energy was inspired by a vision that went beyond worldly concerns—a vision of the cosmos. To the people of that time, the structures they built were their "spaceships of faith," firmly anchored but pointing to the cosmos.

Today, the efforts of many skilled scientists, engineers, artists, and artisans are directed to building the spaceships that already orbit the earth and others that will voyage beyond. The time required to build these spaceships is extremely brief compared with the time spent building the stone structures of the past. Many people working on today's spaceships were alive before the first jetliner aircraft carried passengers. Where will younger lives lead in a comparable time?

We seem to be at the dawn of a major change in human growth. For as little Evan suggests in the photo at the beginning of this book, we may be like the hatching chicken who has exhausted the resources of its inner-egg environment and is about to break through to a whole new range of possibilities. Planet Earth is our cradle and has served us well. But cradles, however comfortable, are one day outgrown. So with the inspiration that in many ways is similar to the inspiration of those who built the early cathedrals, synagogues, temples, and mosques, we aim for the cosmos.

We live in an exciting time!

Summary of Terms

Science The collective findings of humans about nature, and a process of gathering and organizing knowledge about nature.

Scientific method An orderly method for gaining, organizing, and applying new knowledge.

Hypothesis An educated guess or a reasonable explanation. When the hypothesis can be tested by experiment, it qualifies as a *scientific hypothesis.*

Law A general hypothesis or statement about the relationship of natural quantities that has been tested over and over again and has not been contradicted. Also known as a *principle.*

Fact A phenomenon about which competent observers can agree.

Theory A synthesis of a large body of information that encompasses well-tested hypotheses about certain aspects of the natural world.

Pseudoscience A theory or practice that is considered to be without scientific foundation.

Technology The means of solving practical problems by applying the findings of science.

Review Questions

1. What discovery in the fifteenth century greatly advanced progress in science?
2. Why is mathematical problem solving not a major feature of this book?
3. Distinguish among a scientific fact, a hypothesis, a law, and a theory.
4. How many experiments are necessary to invalidate a scientific hypothesis?
5. In science, what kinds of ideas are generally accepted?
6. What is meant by the term *supernatural,* and why does science not deal with it?
7. Why are students of the arts encouraged to learn about science, and why are science students encouraged to learn about the arts?
8. Why is it better to minimize risk than to eliminate it?
9. Clearly distinguish between science and technology.
10. Of physics, chemistry, and biology, which science is the least complex? Which is the most complex? (At your school, which of these is the "easiest," and which is the "hardest" as a science course?)

PART ONE

Physics

CHAPTER 1

Patterns of Motion and Equilibrium

Some two thousand years ago, Greek scientists understood some of the physics we understand today. They had a good grasp of the physics of floating objects and some of the properties of light, but they were confused about motion. One of the first to study motion seriously was Aristotle, the most outstanding philosopher-scientist in ancient Greece. Aristotle attempted to clarify motion by classification.

1.1 Aristotle on Motion

Aristotle classified motion into two kinds of motion: *natural motion* and *violent motion.* We shall briefly consider each, not as study material but as a background to modern ideas about motion.

In Aristotle's view, natural motion proceeds from the "nature" of an object. He believed that all objects were some combination of four elements—earth, water, air, and fire—and he asserted that motion depends on the combination of elements an object contains. He taught that every object in the universe has a proper place, which is determined by this "nature"; any object not in its proper place will "strive" to get there. For example, an unsupported lump of clay, being of the earth, properly falls to the ground; an unimpeded puff of smoke, being of the air, properly rises; a feather properly falls to the ground, but not as rapidly as a lump of clay, because it is a mixture of air and earth. Aristotle stated that heavier objects would strive harder and fall faster than lighter ones.

Do we still think of matter as being some combination of earth, water, air, and fire?

Insights

Natural motion was understood to be either straight up or straight down, as in the case of all things on earth. Natural motion beyond the earth, such as the motion of celestial objects, was circular. Both the sun and the moon continually circle the earth in paths without beginning or end. Aristotle taught that different rules apply in the heavens and that celestial bodies are perfect spheres made of a perfect and unchanging substance, which he called *quintessence.**

Violent motion, Aristotle's other class of motion, is produced by pushes or pulls. Violent motion is imposed motion. A person pushing a cart or lifting a heavy boulder imposes motion, as does someone hurling a stone or winning a tug-of-war. The wind imposes motion on ships. Floodwaters impose it on boulders and tree trunks. Violent motion is externally caused and is imparted to objects, which move not of themselves, not by their nature, but because of impressed *forces*—pushes or pulls.

Figure 1.1
Does a force keep the cannonball moving after it leaves the cannon?

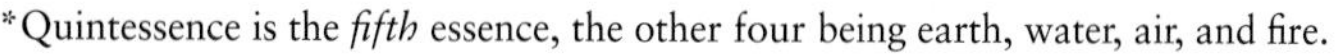

*Quintessence is the *fifth* essence, the other four being earth, water, air, and fire.

The concept of violent motion had its difficulties, because the forces responsible for it were not always evident. For example, Aristotle understood that a bowstring moved an arrow until the arrow left the bow; after that, further explanation of the arrow's motion seemed to require some other pushing agent. Aristotle imagined, therefore, that a parting of the air by the moving arrow resulted in a squeezing effect on the rear of the arrow as the air rushed back to prevent a vacuum from forming behind it. The arrow, he believed, was propelled through the air as a bar of soap is propelled in the bathtub when you squeeze one end of the bar.

To summarize, Aristotle taught that all motions are due either to the nature of the moving object or to a sustained push or pull. Provided that an object is in its proper place, he believed, it will not move unless subjected to a force. Except for celestial objects, the normal state is one of rest.

☑ CHECKPOINT

Isn't it common sense to think of the earth in its proper place, and that a force to move it is inconceivable, as Aristotle held, and that the earth *is* at rest in this universe?

Check Your Answer

Common sense is relative to one's time and place. Aristotle's views were logical and consistent with everyday observations. So, unless you become familiar with the physics to follow in this book, Aristotle's views about motion *do* make common sense (and these views are held by many uneducated people today). But, as you acquire new information about nature's rules, you'll likely discover your common sense progressing beyond Aristotelian thinking.

Aristotle (384–322 BC)

Aristotle was the foremost philosopher, scientist, and educator of his time. Born in Greece, he was the son of a physician who personally served the king of Macedonia. At the age of 17, he entered the Academy of Plato, where he worked and studied for 20 years until Plato's death. He then became the tutor of young Alexander the Great. Eight years later, he formed his own school. Aristotle's aim was to systematize existing knowledge, just as Euclid had systematized geometry. Aristotle made critical observations, collected specimens, and gathered, summarized, and classified almost all of existing knowledge of the physical world. His systematic approach became the method from which Western science later arose. After his death, his voluminous notebooks were preserved in caves near his home and were later sold to the library at Alexandria. Scholarly activity ceased in most of Europe through the Dark Ages, and the works of Aristotle were forgotten and lost in the scholarship that continued in the Byzantine and Islamic empires. Various of his texts were reintroduced to Europe during the eleventh and twelfth centuries and were translated into Latin. The Church, the dominant political and cultural force in Western Europe, at first prohibited the works of Aristotle and then accepted and incorporated them into Christian doctrine.

1.2 Galileo's Concept of Inertia

Aristotle's ideas were accepted as fact for nearly 2000 years. Then, in the early 1500s, the Italian scientist Galileo demolished Aristotle's belief that heavy objects fall faster than light ones. According to legend, Galileo dropped both heavy and light objects from the Leaning Tower of Pisa. He showed that, except for the effects of air friction, objects of different weights fell to the ground in the same amount of time.

Galileo made another huge discovery. He showed that Aristotle was wrong about forces being necessary to keep objects in motion. Although a force is needed to start an object moving, Galileo showed that, once it is moving, no force is needed to keep it moving—except for the force needed to overcome friction. (We will learn more about friction in Section 1.8) When friction is absent, a moving object needs no force to keep it moving. It will remain in motion of itself.

Galileo tested his revolutionary idea by *experiment.* This was the beginning of modern science. He rolled balls down inclined planes and observed and recorded the gain in speed as

Figure 1.2
Galileo's famous demonstration.

Galileo Galilei (1564–1642)

Galileo was born in Pisa, Italy, in the same year in which Shakespeare was born and Michelangelo died. He studied medicine at the University of Pisa and then changed to mathematics. He developed an early interest in motion and was soon in opposition with others around him, who held to Aristotelian ideas about falling bodies. He left Pisa to teach at the University of Padua, where he became an advocate of the new theory of the solar system advanced by the Polish astronomer Copernicus. Galileo was one of the first to build a telescope, and the first to direct it to the nighttime sky and discover mountains on our moon and on the moons of Jupiter. Because he published his findings in Italian instead of in Latin, which was expected of so reputable a scholar, and because of the recent invention of the printing press, his ideas reached many people. He soon ran afoul of the Church, and he was warned not to teach, and not to hold to, Copernican views. He restrained himself publicly for nearly 15 years. Then he defiantly published his observations and conclusions, which opposed Church doctrine. The outcome was a trial in which he was found guilty, and he was forced to renounce his discoveries. By then an old man and broken in health and spirit, he was sentenced to perpetual house arrest. Nevertheless, he completed his studies on motion, and his writings were smuggled out of Italy and published in Holland. His eyes had been damaged years earlier by viewing the sun through a telescope, which led to his blindness at the age of 74. He died 4 years later.

rolling continued (Figure 1.3). On downward-sloping planes, the force of gravity increases a ball's speed. On an upward slope, the force of gravity decreases a ball's speed. What about a ball rolling on a level surface? While rolling level, the ball doesn't roll with nor against the vertical force of gravity—it doesn't speed up or slow down. The rolling ball maintains a constant speed. Galileo reasoned that a ball moving horizontally would move forever, if friction were entirely absent. A ball would move of itself—of its own *inertia*.

Slope downward–
Speed increases

Slope upward–
Speed decreases

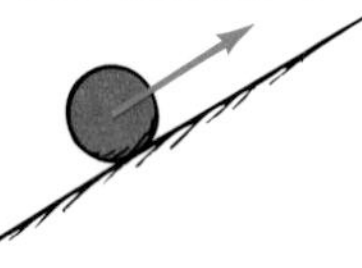

No slope–
Does speed change?

Figure 1.3
The motion of balls on various planes.

☑ **CHECKPOINT**

A ball rolling along a level surface slowly comes to a stop. How would Aristotle explain this behavior? How would Galileo explain it? How would you explain it?

Check Your Answers

Think about the Checkpoint questions throughout this book ***before*** *reading the answers. When you first formulate your own answers, you'll find yourself learning more—much more!*

Aristotle would probably say that the ball stops because it seeks its natural state of rest. Galileo would probably say that friction overcomes the ball's natural tendency to continue rolling—that friction overcomes the ball's *inertia* and brings it to a stop. Only you can answer the last question!

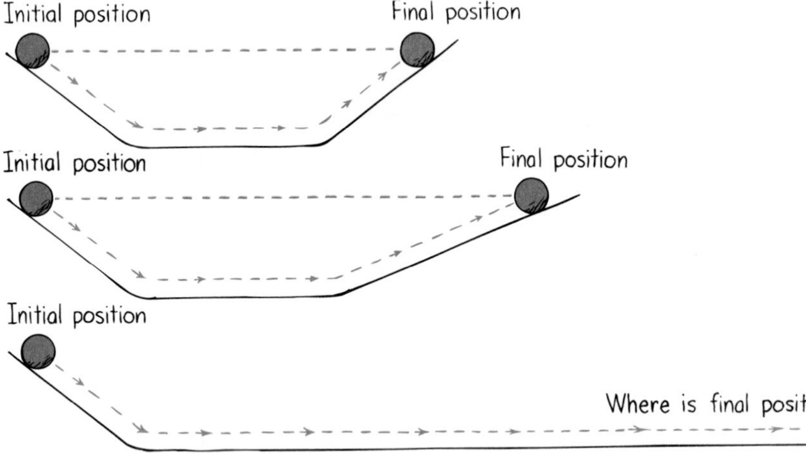

Figure 1.4
A ball rolling down an incline on the left tends to roll up to its initial height on the right. The ball must roll a greater distance as the angle of incline on the right is reduced.

Inertia isn't a kind of *force*; it's a *property* of all matter to resist changes in motion.

Insights

Galileo noted that moving objects tend to remain moving, without the need of an imposed force. Objects at rest tend to remain at rest. This property of objects to maintain their state of motion is called **inertia.**

1.3 Mass—a Measure of Inertia

When an object changes its state of motion—by speeding up, slowing down, or changing course—we say it undergoes *acceleration.* How much acceleration it will undergo will depend on the forces applied to it and on the inertia of the object—how much it resists changes in motion. The amount of inertia an object possesses depends on the amount of matter in the object—the more matter, the more inertia. In speaking of how much matter something has, we use the term *mass.* The greater the mass of an object, the greater its inertia. **Mass** is a measure of the inertia of a material object.

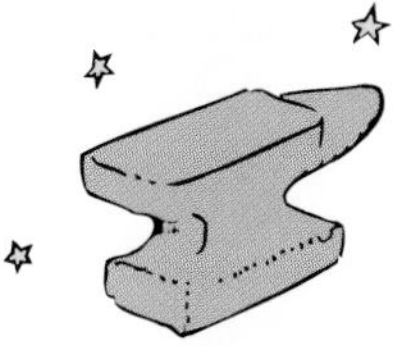

Figure 1.5
An anvil in outer space—beyond the sun, for example—may be weightless, but it still has mass.

Mass corresponds to our intuitive notion of **weight.** We casually say that something contains a lot of matter if it weighs a lot. But there is a difference between mass and weight. We can define each as follows:

> Mass: The quantity of matter in an object. It is also the measure of the inertia or sluggishness that an object exhibits in response to any effort made to start it, stop it, or change its state of motion in any way.
>
> Weight: The force upon an object due to gravity.

Mass and weight are directly proportional to each other.* If the mass of an object is doubled, its weight is also doubled; if the mass is halved, the weight is halved. Because of this, mass and weight are often interchanged. Also, mass and weight are sometimes confused because it is customary to measure the quantity of matter in things (their mass) by their gravitational attraction to the earth (their weight). But mass doesn't depend on gravity. Gravity on the moon, for example, is much less than it is on the earth. Whereas your weight on the surface of the moon would be much less than it is on earth, your mass would be the same in both locations. Mass is a fundamental quantity that completely escapes the notice of most people.

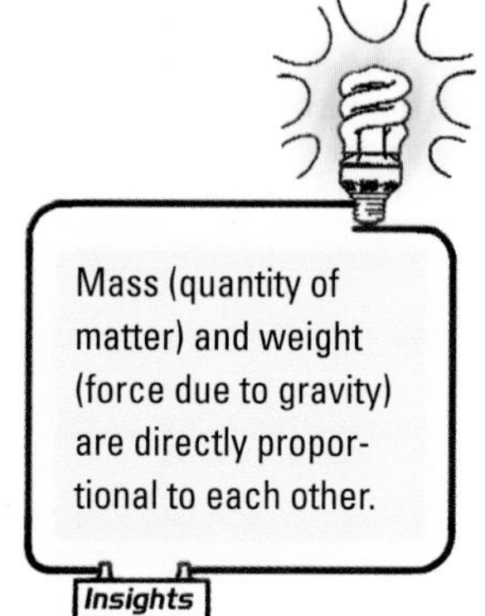

You can sense how much mass is in an object by sensing its inertia. When you shake an object back and forth, you can feel its inertia. If it has a lot of mass, it's difficult to change the object's direction. If it has a small mass, shaking the object is easier. To-and-fro shaking requires the same force even in regions where gravity is different—on the moon, for example. An object's inertia, or mass, is a property of the object itself and not its location.

Mass is measured in **kilograms.** If an object has a large mass, it may or may not have a large volume. Do not confuse mass and volume. Volume is a measure of space, measured in such units as cubic centimeters, cubic meters, or liters. How many kilograms of matter an object contains and how much space the object occupies are two different things. Mass is different from volume.

A nice demonstration that distinguishes mass from weight is the massive ball suspended on the string, shown in Figure 1.7. The top string breaks when the lower string is pulled with a gradual increase in force, but the bottom string breaks when the string is jerked. Which of these cases illustrates the weight of

Figure 1.6
The astronaut in space finds it is just as difficult to shake the "weightless" anvil as it would be on earth. If the anvil is more massive than the astronaut, which shakes more—the anvil or the astronaut?

***Directly proportional* means directly related. If you change one, the other changes proportionally. The constant of proportionality is g, the acceleration due to gravity. As we shall soon see, weight = mg (or mass × acceleration due to gravity), so 9.8 N = (1 kg)(9.8 m/s^2). Later, in Chapter 4, we'll refine our definition of weight to be the gravitational force of a body pressing against a support (like against a weighing scale).

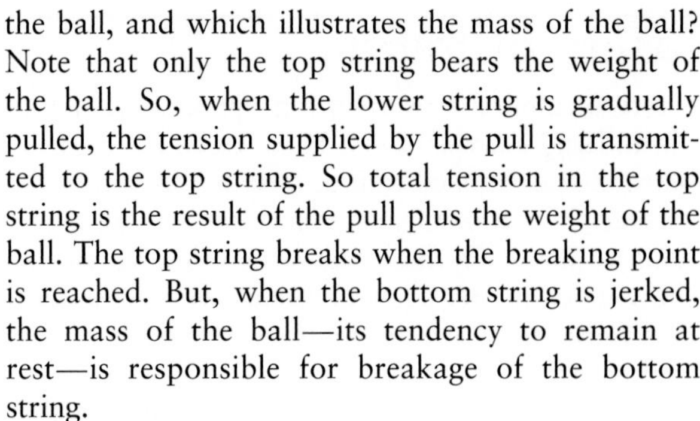
the ball, and which illustrates the mass of the ball? Note that only the top string bears the weight of the ball. So, when the lower string is gradually pulled, the tension supplied by the pull is transmitted to the top string. So total tension in the top string is the result of the pull plus the weight of the ball. The top string breaks when the breaking point is reached. But, when the bottom string is jerked, the mass of the ball—its tendency to remain at rest—is responsible for breakage of the bottom string.

Figure 1.7
Why will a slow continuous increase in downward force break the string above the massive ball, whereas a sudden increase in downward force breaks the lower string?

Figure 1.8
Why does the blow of the hammer not harm her?

☑ **CHECKPOINT**

1. Does a 2-kilogram iron block have twice as much *inertia* as a 1-kilogram iron block? Twice as much *mass*? Twice as much *weight* when weighed in the same location? Twice as much *volume*?
2. Does a 2-kilogram iron block have twice as much *inertia* as a 1-kilogram bunch of bananas? Twice as much *mass*? Twice as much *volume*? Twice as much *weight* when weighed in the same location?
3. How does the mass of a bar of gold vary with location?

Check Your Answers

1. The answer is yes to all questions. A 2-kilogram block of iron has twice as many iron atoms, and therefore twice the amount of inertia, mass, and weight. The blocks consist of the same material, so the 2-kilogram block also has twice the volume.
2. Two kilograms of *anything* has twice the inertia and twice the mass of one kilogram of anything else. Because mass and weight are proportional in the same location, two kilograms of anything will weigh twice as much as one kilogram of anything. Except for volume, the answer to all the questions is yes. Volume and mass are proportional only when the materials are identical—when they have the same *density*. Iron is much more dense than bananas, so two kilograms of iron must occupy less volume than one kilogram of bananas.
3. Not at all! It consists of the same number of atoms no matter what its location. Although its weight may vary with location, it has the same mass everywhere. This is why mass is preferred to weight in scientific studies.

Figure 1.9
One kilogram of nails weighs 9.8 newtons, which is equal to 2.2 pounds.

One Kilogram Weighs 9.8 Newtons

The standard unit of mass is the kilogram, abbreviated kg. The standard unit of force is the newton, abbreviated N. The abbreviation is written with a capital letter because the unit is named after a person. A 1-kg bag of any material at the earth's surface has a weight of 9.8 N in standard units. Away from the earth's surface, where the force of gravity is less (on the moon, for example), the bag would weigh less.

Except in cases where precision is needed, we will round off 9.8 and call it 10. So 1 kilogram of something weighs about 10 newtons. If you know the mass in kilograms and want weight in newtons, multiply the number of kilograms by 10. Or, if you know the weight in newtons, divide by 10 and you'll have the mass in kilograms. Weight and mass are proportional to each other.

The relationship between kilograms and pounds is that 1 kg weighs 2.2 lb at the earth's surface. (That means that 1 lb is the same as 4.45 N.)

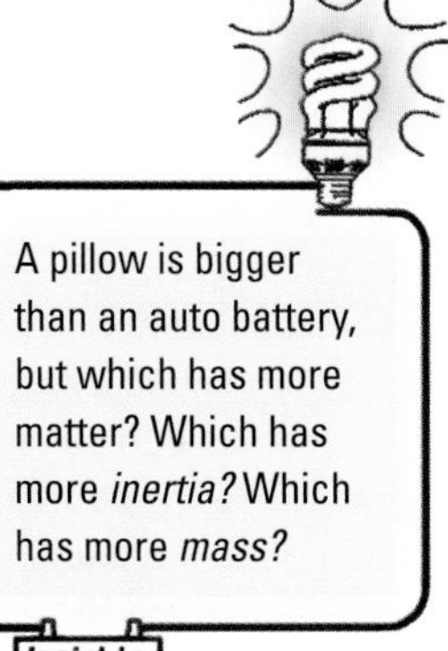

1.4 Net Force

In simplest terms, a force is a push or a pull. An object doesn't speed up, slow down, or change direction unless a force acts upon it. When we say "force," we imply the total force, or *net* force, acting on an object. Often more than one force may be acting on an object. For example, when you throw a baseball, the force of gravity and the pushing force you apply with your muscles both act on the ball. When the ball is sailing through the air, the force of gravity and air resistance both act on it. The **net force** on the ball is the combination of forces. It is the net force that changes an object's state of motion.

For example, suppose you pull on a shoe box with a force of 5 newtons (slightly more than 1 pound). If your friend also pulls with 5 newtons in the same direction, the net force on the box is 10 newtons. If your friend pulls on the box with the same force as you but in the opposite direction, the net force on the box is zero. Now if you increase your pull to 10 newtons and your friend pulls oppositely with a force of 5 newtons, the net force is 5 newtons in the direction of your pull. We see this in Figure 1.10.

The forces in Figure 1.10 are shown by arrows. Forces are vector quantities. A **vector quantity** has both magnitude (how much) and direction (which way). When an arrow represents a vector quantity, the arrow's length represents magnitude and its direction shows the direction of the quantity. Such an arrow is called a **vector.** (You will find more on vectors in the next chapter, in Appendix C, and in the *Conceptual Physical Science Practice Book.*)

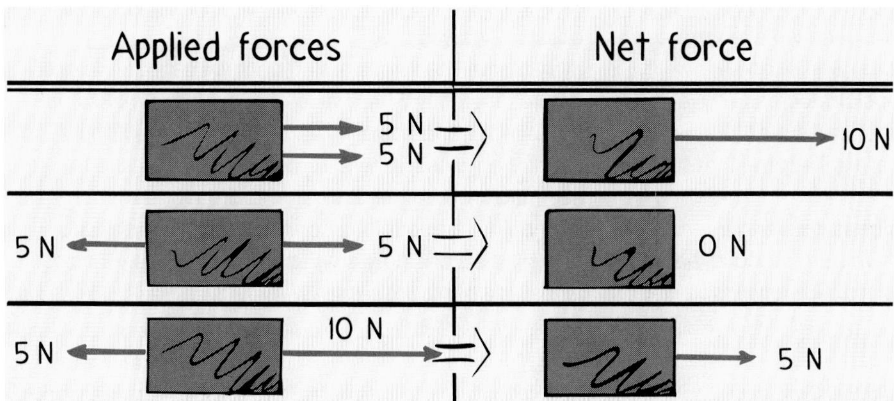

Figure 1.10
Net force.

Paul Hewitt Personal Essay

When I was in high school, my counselor advised me not to enroll in science and math classes but instead to focus on what seemed to be my gift for art. I took this advice. I was then interested in drawing comic strips and in boxing, neither of which earned me much success. After a stint in the army, I tried my luck at sign painting, and the cold Boston winters drove me south to Miami, Florida. There, at age 26, I got a job painting billboards and met my intellectual mentor, Burl Grey. Like me, Burl had never studied physics in high school. But he was passionate about science in general, and he shared his passion with many questions as we painted together.

I remember Burl asking me about the tensions in the ropes that held up the staging we were standing on. The staging was simply a heavy horizontal plank suspended by a pair of ropes. Burl twanged the rope nearest his end of the staging and asked me to do the same with mine. He was comparing the tensions in both ropes—to determine which was greater. Burl was heavier than I was, and he guessed that the tension in his rope was greater. Like a more tightly stretched guitar string, the rope with greater tension twangs at a higher pitch. The finding that Burl's rope had a higher pitch seemed reasonable because his rope supported more of the load.

When I walked toward Burl to borrow one of his brushes, he asked if the tensions in the ropes had changed. Did the tension in his rope increase as I moved closer? We agreed that it should have, because even more of the load was then supported by Burl's rope. How about my rope? Would its tension decrease? We agreed that it would, for it would be supporting less of the total load. I was unaware at the time that I was discussing physics.

Burl and I used exaggeration to bolster our reasoning (just as physicists do). If we both stood at an extreme end of the staging and leaned outward, it was easy to imagine the opposite end of the staging rising like the end of a seesaw, with the opposite rope going limp. Then there would be no tension in that rope. We then reasoned that the tension in my rope would gradually decrease as I walked toward Burl. It was fun posing such questions and seeing if we could answer them.

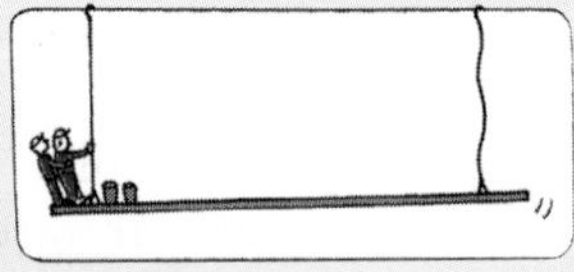

A question that we couldn't answer was whether or not the decrease in tension in my rope when I walked away from it would be *exactly* compensated by a tension increase in Burl's rope. For example, if my rope underwent a decrease of 50 newtons, would Burl's rope gain 50 newtons? (We talked pounds back then, but here we use the scientific unit of force, the *newton*—abbreviated N.) Would the gain be *exactly* 50 N? And if so, would this be a grand coincidence? I didn't know the answer until more than a year later, when Burl's stimulation resulted in my leaving full-time painting and going to college to learn more about science.*

There I learned that any object at rest, such as the sign-painting staging I worked on with Burl, is said to be in equilibrium. That is, all the forces that act on it balance to zero ($\Sigma F = 0$). So the sum of the upward forces supplied by the supporting ropes indeed do add up to our weights plus the weight of the staging. A 50 N loss in one would be accompanied by a 50 N gain in the other.

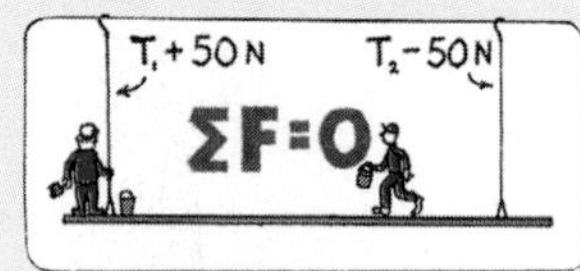

I tell this true story to make the point that one's thinking is very different when there is a rule to guide it. Now, when I look at any motionless object, I know immediately that all the forces acting on it cancel out. We see nature differently when we know its rules. It makes nature simpler and easier to understand. Without the rules of physics, we tend to be superstitious and to see magic where there is none. Quite wonderfully, everything is beautifully connected to everything else by a surprisingly small number of rules. Physics is a study of nature's rules.

*I am forever indebted to Burl Grey for the stimulation he provided, for when I continued with my formal education, it was with great enthusiasm. I lost contact with Burl for 40 years. A student in my class at the Exploratorium in San Francisco, Jayson Wechter, who was a private detective, located him in 1998 and put us back in contact. Our friendship renewed, we continue in our spirited conversations.

1.5 The Equilibrium Rule

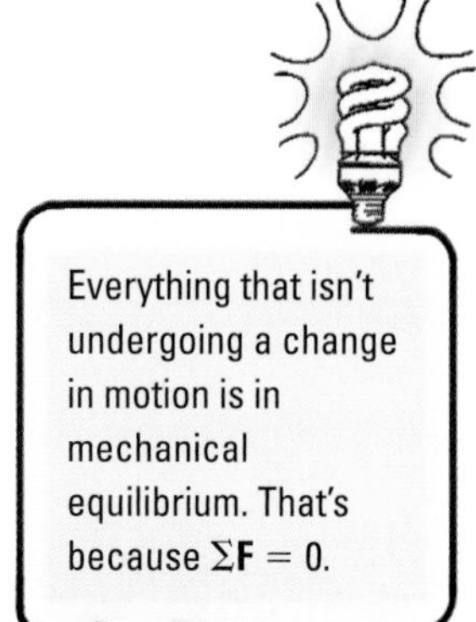

If you tie a string around a 2-pound bag of sugar and suspend it on a weighing scale (Figure 1.11), a spring in the scale stretches until the scale reads 2 pounds. The stretched spring is under a "stretching force" called *tension.* A scale in a science lab is likely calibrated to read the same force as 9 newtons. Both pounds and newtons are units of weight, which, in turn, are units of *force.* The bag of sugar is attracted to the earth with a gravitational force of 2 pounds—or, equivalently, 9 newtons. Suspend twice as much sugar from the scale and the reading will be 18 newtons.

There are two forces acting on the bag of sugar—tension force acting upward and weight acting downward. The two forces on the bag are equal and opposite, and they cancel to zero. Hence the bag remains at rest.

When the net force on something is zero, we say that something is in *mechanical equilibrium.** Anything in mechanical equilibrium obeys an interesting rule: In mathematical notation, the equilibrium rule is

$$\Sigma F = 0$$

The symbol Σ stands for "the vector sum of" and F stands for "forces." For a suspended body at rest, like the bag of sugar, the rule states that the forces acting upward on the body must be balanced by other forces acting

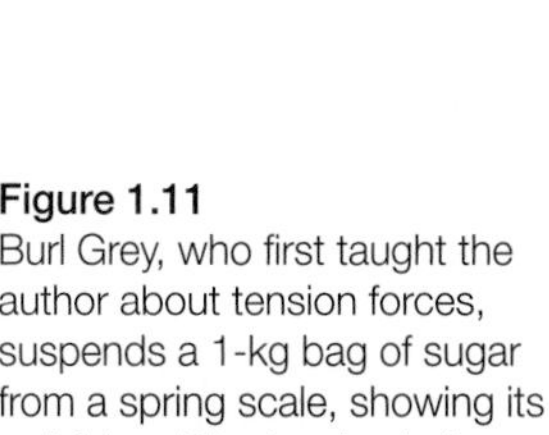

Figure 1.11
Burl Grey, who first taught the author about tension forces, suspends a 1-kg bag of sugar from a spring scale, showing its weight and the tension in the string of nearly 10 newtons.

*We'll see in Appendix B that another condition for mechanical equilibrium is that the net ***torque*** equals zero.

downward to make the vector sum equal zero. (Vector quantities take direction into account, so, if upward forces are positive, downward ones are negative, and when summed they equal zero.)

In Figure 1.12, we see the forces of interest to Burl and Paul on their sign-painting staging. The sum of the upward tensions is equal to the sum of their weights plus the weight of the staging. Note how the magnitudes of the two upward vectors equal the magnitudes of the three downward vectors. Net force on the staging is zero, so we say it is in mechanical equilibrium.

Figuring Physical Science

Practice Box

1. When Burl stands alone in the exact middle of his staging, the left scale reads 500 N. Fill in the reading on the right scale. The total weight of Burl and the staging must be ________ N.

2. Burl stands farther from the left. Fill in the reading on the right scale.

3. In a silly mood, Burl dangles from the right end. Fill in the reading on the right scale.

Practice Box Answers

Do your answers illustrate the equilibrium rule?

1. *The total weight is* **1000 N.** The right rope must be under 500 N of tension because Burl is in the middle, and both ropes support his weight equally. Since the sum of upward tensions is 1000 N, the total weight of Burl and the staging must be 1000 N. Let's call the upward tension forces +1000 N. Then the downward weights are −1000 N. What happens when you add +1000 N and −1000 N? The answer is they equal zero. So we see that $\Sigma \boldsymbol{F} = 0$.

2. *Did you get the correct answer of* **830 N?** Reasoning: We know from Question 1 that the sum of the rope tensions equals 1000 N, and since the left rope has a tension of 170 N, the other rope must make up the difference—that 1000 N − 170 N = 830 N. Get it? If so, great. If not, discuss it with your friends until you do. Then read further.

3. *The answer is* **1000 N.** Do you see that this illustrates $\Sigma \boldsymbol{F} = 0$?

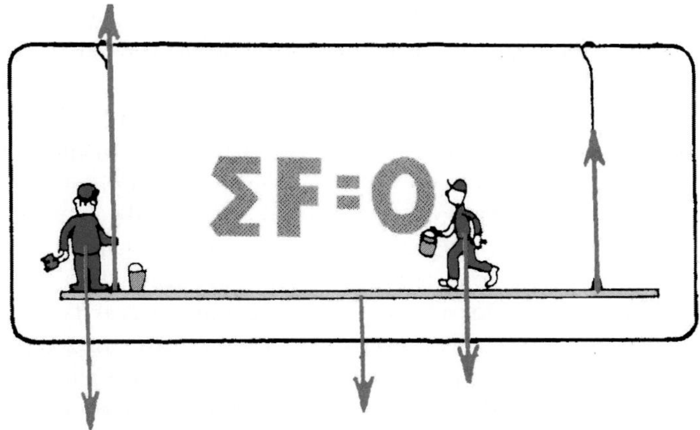

Figure 1.12
The sum of the upward vectors equals the sum of the downward vectors. $\Sigma \boldsymbol{F} = 0$, and the staging is in equilibrium.

☑ CHECKPOINT

Consider the gymnast hanging from the rings.

1. If she hangs with her weight evenly divided between the two rings, how would scale readings in both supporting ropes compare with her weight?
2. Suppose she hangs with slightly more of her weight supported by the left ring. How would a scale on the right read?

Check Your Answers

1. The reading on each scale will be **half her weight.** The sum of the readings on both scales then equals her weight.
2. When more of her weight is supported by the left ring, the reading on the right is ***less than half her weight.*** No matter how she hangs, the sum of the scale readings equals her weight. For example, if one scale reads two-thirds her weight, the other scale will read one-third her weight. Get it?

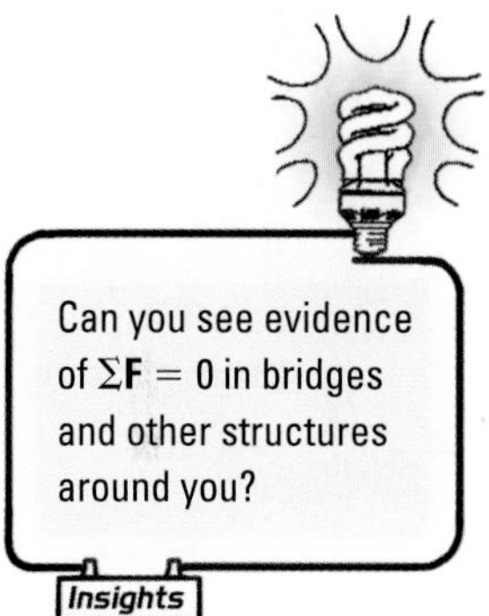

1.6 Support Force

Consider a book lying at rest on a table. It is in equilibrium. What forces act on the book? One is the force due to gravity—the *weight* of the book. Since the book is in equilibrium, there must be another force acting on it to produce a net force of zero—an upward force opposite to the force of gravity. The table exerts this upward force, called the *support force.* This upward support force, often called the *normal force,* must equal the weight of the book.* If we designate the upward force as positive, then the downward force (weight) is negative, and the sum of the two is zero. The net force on the book is zero. Stating it another way, $\Sigma F = 0$.

*This force acts at right angles to the surface. When we say "normal to," we are saying "at right angles to," which is why this force is called a normal force.

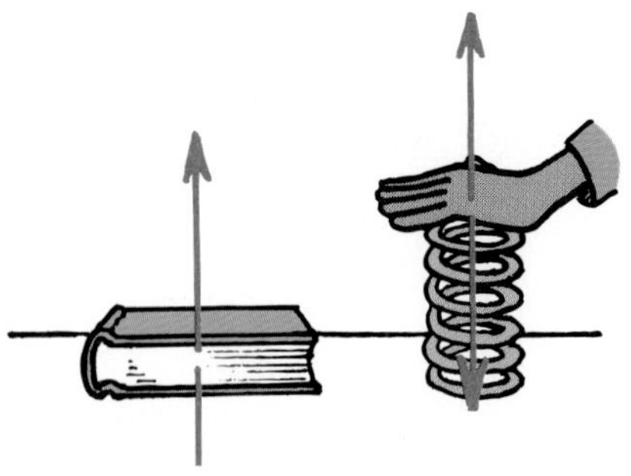

Figure 1.13
The table pushes up on the book with as much force as the downward force of gravity on the book. The spring pushes up on your hand with as much force as you exert to push down on the spring.

To better understand that the table pushes up on the book, compare the case of compressing a spring (Figure 1.13). If you push the spring down, you can feel the spring pushing up on your hand. Similarly, the book lying on the table compresses atoms in the table, which behave like microscopic springs. The weight of the book squeezes downward on the atoms, and they squeeze upward on the book. In this way, the compressed atoms produce the support force.

When you step on a bathroom scale, two forces act on the scale. One is the downward pull of gravity, your weight, and the other is the upward support force of the floor. These forces compress a spring that is calibrated to show your weight (Figure 1.14). In effect, the scale shows the support force. When you weigh yourself on a bathroom scale at rest, the support force and your weight have the same magnitude.

Figure 1.14
The upward support is as much as your weight.

☑ CHECKPOINT

1. What is the net force on a bathroom scale when a 150-pound person stands on it?
2. Suppose you stand on two bathroom scales with your weight evenly distributed between the two scales. What is the reading on each of the scales? What happens when you stand with more of your weight on one foot than the other?

Check Your Answers

1. Zero, because the scale remains at rest. The scale reads the *support force* (which has the same magnitude as weight), not the net force.
2. The reading on each scale is half your weight, because the sum of the scale readings must balance your weight, so the net force on you will be zero. If you lean more on one scale than the other, more than half your weight will be read on that scale but less on the other, so they will still add up to your weight. Like the example of the gymnast hanging by the rings, if one scale reads two-thirds your weight, the other scale will read one-third your weight.

1.7 Equilibrium of Moving Things

Equilibrium is a state of no change. Rest is only one form of equilibrium. An object moving at a constant speed in a straight-line path is also in equilibrium. A bowling ball rolling at a constant speed in a straight line is also in equilibrium—until it hits the pins. Whether at rest or steadily rolling in a straight-line path, $\Sigma F = 0$.

An object under the influence of only one force cannot be in equilibrium. The net force couldn't be zero. Only when two or more forces act on it can the object be in equilibrium. We can test whether or not something is in equilibrium by noting whether or not it undergoes changes in its state of motion.

Consider a crate being pushed horizontally across a factory floor. If it moves at a steady speed in a straight-line path, it is in equilibrium. This indicates that more than one force is acting on the crate. Another force exists—likely the force of friction between the crate and the floor. The fact that the net force on the crate equals zero tells us that the force of friction must be equal and opposite to the pushing force.

There are different forms of equilibrium. In Chapter 7, we'll talk about thermal equilibrium, and in Appendix B, we'll discuss rotational equilibrium.

Figure 1.15
When the push on the crate is as great as the force of friction between the crate and the floor, the net force on the crate is zero, and it slides at an unchanging speed.

1.8 The Force of Friction

Friction occurs when one object rubs against something else.* Friction occurs for solids, liquids, and gases. An important rule of friction is that it always acts in a direction to oppose motion. If you pull a solid block along a floor to the left, the force of friction on the block will be to the right. A boat propelled to the east by its motor experiences water friction to the west. When an object falls downward through the air, the force of friction, **air resistance,** acts upward. Friction always acts in a direction to oppose motion.

☑ CHECKPOINT

An airplane flies through the air at a constant velocity. In other words, it is in equilibrium. Two horizontal forces act on the plane. One is the thrust of the propeller that pushes it forward. The other is the force of air resistance that acts in the opposite direction. Which force is greater?

Check Your Answer

Both forces have the same magnitude. If you call the forward force exerted by the propeller positive, then the air resistance is negative. Since the plane is in equilibrium, can you see that the two forces combine to equal zero?

The amount of friction between two surfaces depends on the kinds of material and how much they are pressed together. Friction is due to tiny surface bumps and also to the "stickiness" of the atoms on the surfaces of the two materials (Figure 1.16). Friction between a crate and a smooth wooden floor is less than that between the same crate and a rough floor. And, if the surface is inclined, the friction is less because the crate doesn't press as much on the inclined surface.

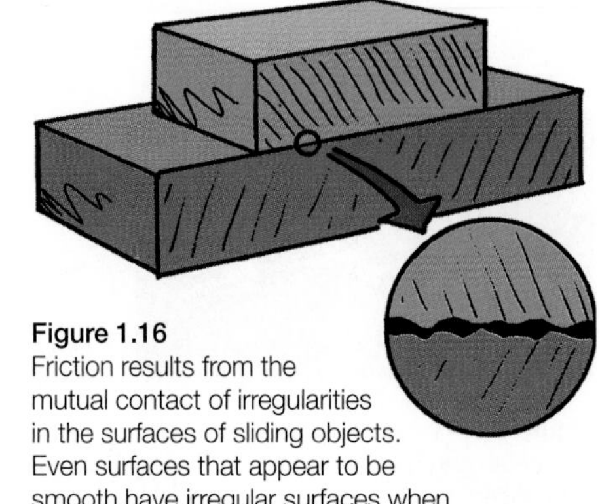

Figure 1.16
Friction results from the mutual contact of irregularities in the surfaces of sliding objects. Even surfaces that appear to be smooth have irregular surfaces when viewed at the microscopic level.

*Even though it may not seem so yet, most of the concepts in physics are not really complicated. But friction is different. Unlike most concepts in physics, it is a very complicated phenomenon. The findings are empirical (gained from a wide range of experiments) and the predictions are approximate (also based on experiment).

When you pull horizontally on a crate and it slides across a factory floor, both your force and the opposite force of friction affect the crate's motion. When you pull hard enough on the crate to match the friction, the net force on the crate is zero, and it slides at a constant velocity. Notice that we are talking about what we recently learned—that no change in motion occurs when $\Sigma F = 0$.

☑ CHECKPOINT

1. Suppose you exert a 100-N horizontal force on a heavy crate resting motionless on a factory floor. The fact that it remains at rest indicates that 100 N isn't great enough to make it slide. How does the force of friction between the crate and the floor compare with your push?
2. You push harder—say, 110 N—and the crate still doesn't slide. How much friction acts on the crate?
3. You push still harder, and the crate moves. Once it is in motion, you push with 115 N, which is just sufficient to keep it sliding at a constant velocity. How much friction acts on the crate?
4. What net force does a sliding crate experience when you exert a force of 125 N and the friction between the crate and the floor is 115 N?

Check Your Answers

1. 100 N in the opposite direction. Friction opposes the motion that would occur otherwise. The fact that the crate is at rest is evidence that $\Sigma \boldsymbol{F} = 0$.
2. Friction increases to 110 N, again $\Sigma \boldsymbol{F} = 0$.
3. 115 N, because, when it is moving at a constant velocity, $\Sigma \boldsymbol{F} = 0$.
4. 10 N, because $\Sigma \boldsymbol{F} = 125\text{ N} - 115\text{ N}$. In this case, the crate accelerates.

1.9 Speed and Velocity

Speed

Before the time of Galileo, people described moving things as simply "slow" or "fast." Such descriptions were vague. Galileo was the first to measure speed by comparing the distance covered with the *time* it takes to move that distance. He defined **speed** as the distance covered per amount of travel time.

Figure 1.17
A cheetah can maintain a very high speed, but only for a short time.

$$\text{Speed} = \frac{\text{distance covered}}{\text{travel time}}$$

For example, if a bicyclist covers 20 kilometers in 1 hour, her speed is 20 km/h. Or, if she runs 6 meters in 1 second, her speed is 6 m/s.

Any combination of units for distance and time can be used for speed—kilometers per hour (km/h), centimeters per day (the speed of a sick snail), or whatever is useful and convenient. The slash symbol (/) is read as "per," and means "divided by." In science, the preferred unit of speed is meters per second (m/s). Table 1.1 compares some speeds in different units.

Figure 1.18
A common automobile speedometer. Note that speed is shown both in km/h and in mi/h.

Table 1.1

Approximate Speeds in Different Units

12 mi/h =	20 km/h =	6 m/s (bowling ball)
25 mi/h =	40 km/h =	11 m/s (very good sprinter)
37 mi/h =	60 km/h =	17 m/s (sprinting rabbit)
50 mi/h =	80 km/h =	22 m/s (tsunami)
62 mi/h =	100 km/h =	28 m/s (sprinting cheetah)
75 mi/h =	120 km/h =	33 m/s (batted softball)
100 mi/h =	160 km/h =	44 m/s (batted baseball)

Instantaneous Speed

Moving things often have variations in speed. A car, for example, may travel along a street at 50 km/h, slow to 0 km/h at a red light, and speed up to only 30 km/h because of traffic. At any instant, you can tell the speed of the car by looking at its speedometer. The speed at any instant is the *instantaneous speed.*

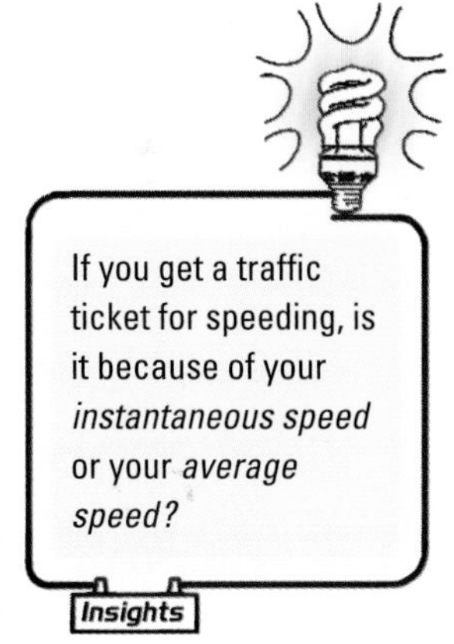

Average Speed

In planning a trip by car, the driver often wants to know the travel time. The driver is concerned with the *average speed* for the trip. How is average speed defined?

$$\text{Average speed} = \frac{\text{total distance covered}}{\text{travel time}}$$

Average speed can be calculated rather easily. For example, if you drive a distance of 80 kilometers in 1 hour, your average speed is 80 kilometers per hour. Likewise, if you travel 320 kilometers in 4 hours,

$$\text{Average speed} = \frac{\text{total distance covered}}{\text{travel time}} = \frac{320\text{ km}}{4\text{ h}} = 80\text{ km/h}$$

Note that, when a distance in kilometers (km) is divided by a time in hours (h), the answer is in kilometers per hour (km/h).

Since average speed is the entire distance covered divided by the total time of travel, it doesn't indicate the various instantaneous speeds that may have occurred along the way. On most trips, the instantaneous speed is often quite different from the average speed.

If we know average speed and travel time, the distance traveled is easy to find. A simple rearrangement of the definition above gives

$$\text{Total distance covered} = \text{average speed} \times \text{travel time}$$

For example, if your average speed on a 4-hour trip is 80 kilometers per hour, then you cover a total distance of 320 kilometers.

☑ CHECKPOINT

1. What is the average speed of a cheetah that sprints 100 m in 4 seconds? How about if it sprints 50 m in 2 s?
2. If a car travels at an average speed of 60 km/h for an hour, it will cover a distance of 60 km. (a) How far would it travel if it moved at this rate for 4 h? (b) For 10 h?
3. In addition to the speedometer on the dashboard of every car, there is an odometer, which records the distance traveled. If the initial reading is set at zero at the beginning of a trip and the reading is 40 km one-half hour later, what was the average speed?
4. Would it be possible to attain this average speed and never go faster than 80 km/h?

Check Your Answers

(Are you reading this before you have reasoned answers in your mind? As mentioned earlier, ***think*** *before you read the answers. You'll not only learn more, you'll enjoy learning more.)*

1. In both cases, the answer is 25 m/s:

$$\text{Average speed} = \frac{\text{total distance covered}}{\text{travel time}} = \frac{100 \text{ meters}}{4 \text{ seconds}} = \frac{50 \text{ meters}}{2 \text{ seconds}} = 25 \text{ m/s}$$

2. The distance traveled is the average speed × time of travel, so

(a) Distance = 60 km/h × 4 h = 240 km
(b) Distance = 60 km/h × 10 hr = 600 km

3. $$\text{Average speed} = \frac{\text{total distance covered}}{\text{travel time}} = \frac{40 \text{ km}}{0.5 \text{ h}} = 80 \text{ km/h}$$

4. No, not if the trip starts from rest and ends at rest. During the trip, there are times when the instantaneous speeds are less than 80 km/h, so the driver must at some time drive faster than 80 km/h in order to average 80 km/h. In practice, average speeds are usually much less than high instantaneous speeds.

Velocity

When we know both the speed and direction of an object, we know its **velocity.** For example, if a vehicle travels at 60 km/h, we know its speed. But, if we say it moves at 60 km/h to the north, we specify its *velocity.* Speed is a description of how fast; velocity is a description of how fast *and* in what direction. Velocity is a vector quantity. (Velocity vectors are developed nicely in the *Conceptual Physical Science Practice Book.*)

Figure 1.19
Although the car can maintain a constant speed along the circular track, it cannot maintain a constant velocity. Why?

Constant speed means steady speed, neither speeding up nor slowing down. Constant velocity, on the other hand, means both constant speed *and* constant direction. Constant direction is a straight line—the object's path doesn't curve. So constant velocity means motion in a straight line at constant speed—motion with no acceleration.

☑ CHECKPOINT

"She moves at a constant speed in a constant direction." Say the same sentence in fewer words.

Check Your Answer

"She moves at constant velocity."

Motion Is Relative

Everything is always moving. Even when you think you're standing still, you're actually speeding through space. You're moving relative to the sun and the stars, although you are at rest relative to the earth. At this moment, your speed relative to the sun is about 100,000 kilometers per hour, and it is even faster relative to the center of our galaxy.

When we discuss the speed or velocity of something, we mean speed or velocity relative to something else. For example, when we say a space shuttle travels at 30,000 kilometers per hour, we mean relative to the earth below. Or when we say a racing car reaches a speed of 300 kilometers per hour, we mean relative to the track. Unless stated otherwise, all speeds discussed in this book are relative to the surface of the earth. Motion is relative.

Figure 1.20
Although you may be at rest relative to the earth's surface, you're moving about 100,000 km/h relative to the sun.

1.10 Acceleration

Most moving things usually experience variations in their motion. We say they undergo *acceleration.* The first to formulate the concept of acceleration was Galileo, who developed the concept in his experiments with inclined planes. He found that balls rolling down inclined planes rolled faster and faster. Their velocity changed as they rolled. Further, the balls gained the same amount of velocity in equal time intervals.

Figure 1.21
A ball gains the same amount of speed in equal intervals of time. It undergoes constant acceleration.

Galileo defined the rate of change of velocity as **acceleration.***

$$\text{Acceleration} = \frac{\text{change of velocity}}{\text{time interval}}$$

Acceleration is experienced when you're in a moving car or bus. When the driver steps on the gas pedal, the vehicle gains speed. We say that the bus

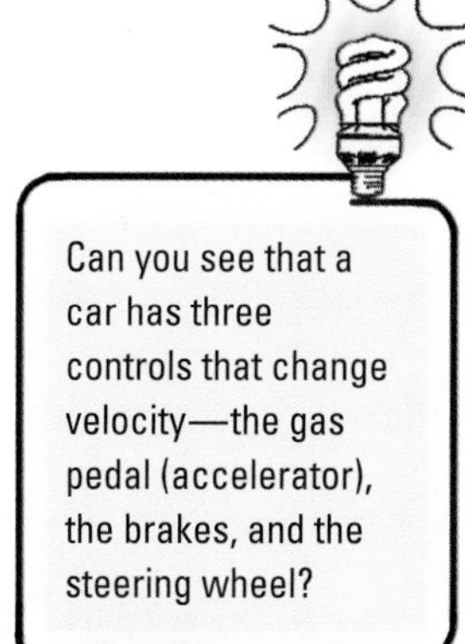

*The Greek letter Δ (delta) is often used as a symbol for "change in" or "difference in." In "delta" notation, $a = \Delta v/\Delta t$, where Δv is the change in velocity and Δt is the change in time (the time interval). From this we can see that $v = at$. See further development of linear motion in Appendix B.

Figure 1.22
We say that a body undergoes acceleration when there is a *change* in its state of motion.

accelerates. We can see why the gas pedal is called the "accelerator"! When the brakes are applied, the vehicle slows. This is also acceleration, because the velocity of the vehicle is changing. When something slows down, we often call this *deceleration,* or *negative acceleration.*

Consider driving in a car that steadily increases in speed. Suppose that in 1 second, you steadily increase your velocity from 30 kilometers per hour to 35 kilometers per hour. In the next second, you go from 35 kilometers per hour to 40 kilometers per hour, and so on. You change your velocity by 5 kilometers per hour each second. Thus, we can see that

$$\text{Acceleration} = \frac{\text{change of velocity}}{\text{time interval}} = \frac{5\text{ km/h}}{1\text{ s}} = 5\text{ km/h·s}$$

In this example, the acceleration is 5 kilometers per hour-second (abbreviated as 5 km/h·s). Note that the unit for time enters twice: once for the unit of velocity and again for the interval of time in which the velocity is changing. Also note that acceleration is not just the change in velocity; it is the *change in velocity per second.* If either speed or direction changes, or if both change, then velocity changes.

When a car makes a turn, even if its speed does not change, it is accelerating. Can you see why? Acceleration occurs because the car's direction is changing. Acceleration refers to a change in velocity. So acceleration involves a change in speed, a change in direction, or a change in both speed *and* direction. Figure 1.22 illustrates this.

☑ CHECKPOINT

In 2.0 seconds, a car increases its speed from 60 km/h to 65 km/h while a bicycle goes from rest to 5 km/h. Which has the greater acceleration?

Check Your Answer

Both have the same acceleration, since both gain the same amount of speed in the same time. Both accelerate at 2.5 km/h·s.

Table 1.2

Free Fall

Time of Fall (s)	Speed of Fall (m/s)	Distance of Fall (m)
0	0	0
1	10	5
2	20	20
3	30	45
4	40	80
5	50	125
.	.	.
.	.	.
.	.	.
t	$10t$	$\frac{1}{2}\,10t^2$

Hold a stone above your head and drop it. It accelerates during its fall. When the only force that acts on a falling object is that due to gravity, when air resistance doesn't affect its motion, we say the object is in **free fall.** All freely-falling objects in the same vicinity undergo the same acceleration. At the earth's surface a freely falling object gains speed at the rate of 10 m/s each second as shown in Table 1.2.

$$\text{Acceleration} = \frac{\text{change of speed}}{\text{time interval}} = \frac{10 \text{ m/s}}{1 \text{ s}} = 10 \text{ m/s}^2$$

We read the acceleration of free fall as 10 meters per second squared. (More precisely, 9.8 m/s^2.) This is the same as saying that acceleration is 10 meters per second per second. Note again that the unit of time, the second, appears twice. It appears once for the unit of velocity and again for the time during which the velocity changes.

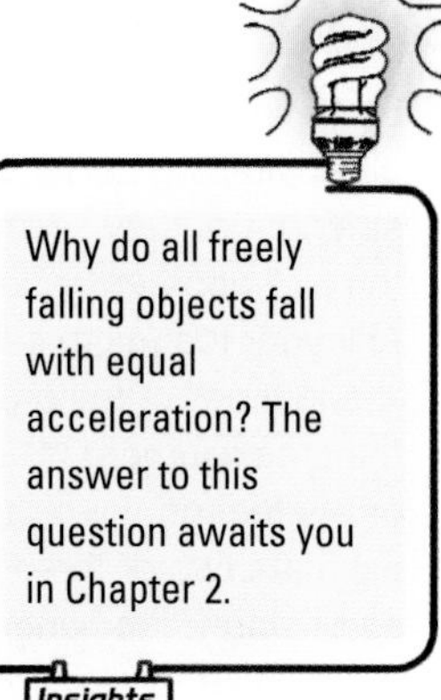

In Figure 1.23, we imagine a freely-falling boulder with a speedometer attached. As the boulder falls, the speedometer shows that the boulder goes 10 m/s faster each second. This 10 m/s gain each second is the boulder's acceleration. (The acceleration of free fall is further developed in Appendix B and in the *Conceptual Physical Science Practice Book.*)

Up-and-down motion is shown in Figure 1.24. The ball leaves the thrower's hand at 30 m/s. Call this the initial velocity. The figure uses the convention of up being + and down being −. Notice that the 1-second interval positions correspond to 10-m/s velocity changes.

Aristotle used logic to establish his ideas of motion. Galileo used experiment. Galileo showed that experiments are superior to logic in testing knowledge. Galileo was concerned with *how* things move rather than *why* they move. The path was paved for Isaac Newton to make further connections of concepts of motion.

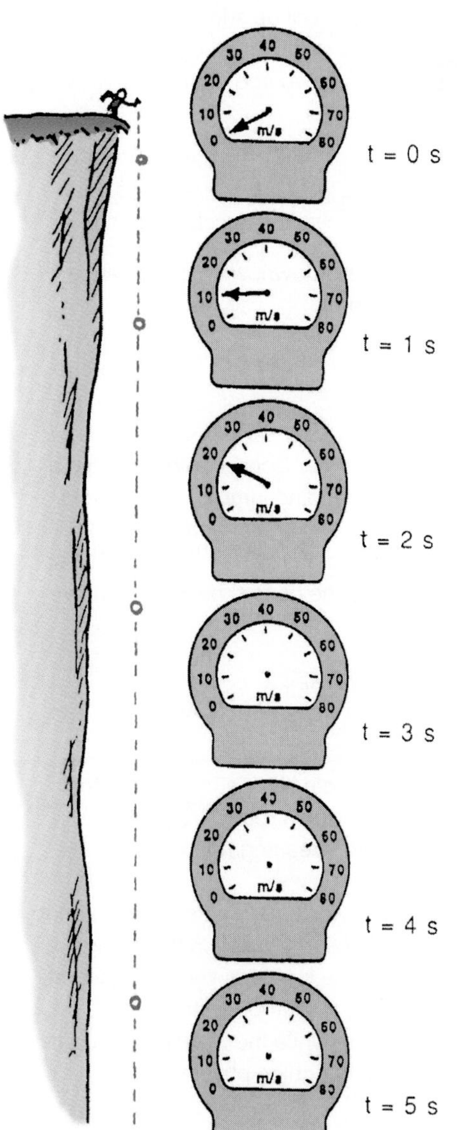

Figure 1.23
Imagine that a falling boulder is equipped with a speedometer. In each succeeding second of fall, you'd find the boulder's speed increasing by the same amount; 10 m/s. Sketch in the missing speedometer needle at t = 3 s, t = 4 s, and t = 5 s.

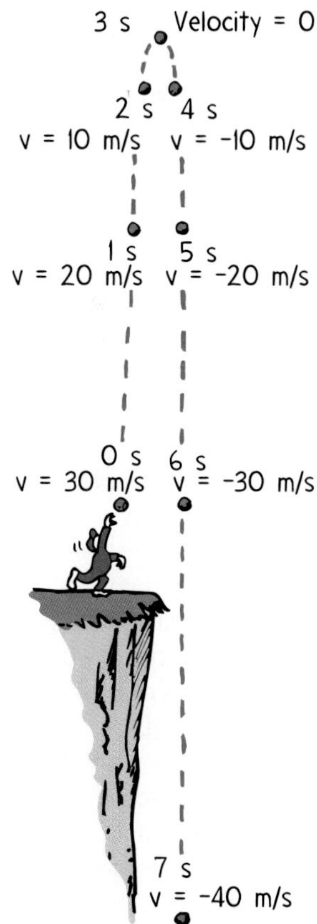

Figure 1.24
The rate at which velocity changes each second is the same.

Hang Time

Some athletes and dancers have great jumping ability. Leaping straight up, they seem to "hang in the air," apparently defying gravity. Ask your friends to estimate the "hang time" of the great jumpers—the time a jumper is airborne with his or her feet off the ground. They may estimate two or three seconds. But, surprisingly, the hang time of the greatest jumpers is most always less than 1 second. The perception of a longer time is one of many illusions we have about nature.

People often have a related illusion about the vertical height a human can jump. Most of your classmates probably cannot jump higher than one-half meter. They can easily step over a 0.5-meter fence, but, in doing so, their bodies rise only slightly. The height of the barrier is different from the height a jumper's "center of gravity" rises. Many people can leap over a 1-meter fence, but only rarely does anybody raise the "center of gravity" of his or her body by 1 meter. Even basketball star Michael Jordan in his prime couldn't raise his body 1.25 meters high, although he could easily reach considerably above the basket, which is more than 3 meters high.

Jumping ability is best measured by a standing vertical jump. Stand facing a wall with your feet flat on the floor and your arms extended upward. Make a mark on the wall at the top of your reach. Then make your jump, and, at the highest point you are able to reach, make another mark. The distance between these two marks measures your vertical leap. If it's more than 0.6 meters (2 feet), you're exceptional.

Here's the physics. When you leap upward, your jumping force is applied only while your feet are still making contact with the ground. The greater the force, the greater your launch speed and the higher your jump. When your feet leave the ground, your upward speed immediately decreases at the steady rate of g, which is 10 m/s^2. At the top of your jump, your upward speed decreases to zero. Then you begin to fall, gaining speed at exactly the same rate, g. If you land as you took off, upright with your legs extended, then your time rising equals your time falling; hang time is time up plus time down. While you are airborne, no amount of leg or arm pumping or other bodily motions can change your hang time.

As will be shown in Appendix B, the relationship between time up or down and vertical height is given by

$$d = \frac{1}{2} gt^2$$

If the vertical height d is known, we can rearrange this expression to read

$$t = \sqrt{\frac{2d}{g}}$$

American basketball star Spud Webb recorded a world-record vertical standing jump of 1.25 meters back in 1986. Let's use his jumping height of 1.25 meters for d, and the more precise value of 9.8 m/s^2 for g. Solving for t, half the hang time (one way), we get

$$t = \sqrt{\frac{2d}{g}} = \sqrt{\frac{2(1.25 \text{ m})}{9.8 \text{ m/s}^2}} = 0.50 \text{ s}$$

Double this amount (because this is the time for one way of an up-and-down round trip) and we see that Spud's record-breaking hang time is 1 second.

We're discussing vertical motion here. How about running jumps? We'll see in Chapter 5 that hang time depends only on the jumper's vertical speed at launch. While airborne, the jumper's horizontal speed remains constant while the vertical speed undergoes acceleration. Intriguing physics!

Summary of Terms

Inertia The property of things to resist changes in motion.

Mass The quantity of matter in an object. More specifically, it is the measure of the inertia or sluggishness that an object exhibits in response to any effort made to start it, stop it, deflect it, or change its state of motion in any way.

Kilogram The unit of mass. One kilogram (symbol kg) is the mass of 1 liter (L) of water at 4°C.

Weight Simply stated, the force due to gravity on an object. More specifically, the gravitational force with which a body presses against a supporting surface.

Force Simply stated, a push or a pull.

Newton The scientific unit of force.

Net Force The combination of all forces that act on an object.

Vector Quantity A quantity that specifies direction as well as magnitude.

Support Force The force that supports an object against gravity, often called the *normal force.*

Equilibrium Rule The vector sum of forces acting on a nonaccelerating object equals zero: $\Sigma F = 0$.

Friction The resistive force that opposes the motion or attempted motion of an object through a fluid or past another object with which it is in contact.

Air Resistance The force of friction acting on an object due to its motion through air.

Speed The distance traveled per time.

Velocity The speed of an object with specification of its direction of motion.

Acceleration The rate at which velocity changes with time; the change in velocity may be in magnitude, or in direction, or in both. It is usually measured in m/s^2.

Hang Time The time that one's feet are off the ground during a vertical jump.

Review Questions

1.1 Aristotle on Motion

1. What were the two main classifications of motion in Aristotle's view of nature?
2. Did Aristotle believe that forces are necessary to keep moving objects moving, or did he believe that, once moving, they'd move of themselves?

1.2 Galileo's Concept of Inertia

3. What two main ideas of Aristotle did Galileo discredit?
4. Which dominated Galileo's way of extending knowledge—philosophical discussion or experiment?
5. What is the name of the property of objects to maintain their states of motion?

1.3 Mass—a Measure of Inertia

6. Which depends on gravity—weight or mass?
7. Where would your weight be greater—on the earth or on the moon? How about your mass?
8. What are the units of measurement for weight and for mass?
9. One kilogram weighs 9.8 newtons on earth. Would it weight more or less on the moon?

1.4 Net Force

10. What is the net force on a box that is being pushed to the left with 50 N of force while it is also being pushed to the right with 60 N of force?
11. What two quantities are necessary to determine a vector quantity?

1.5 The Equilibrium Rule

12. What is the name given to the force that occurs in a rope when both ends are pulled in opposite directions?
13. How much tension is there in a rope that holds a 20-N bag of apples at rest?
14. What does $\Sigma F = 0$ mean?

1.6 Support Force

15. Why is the support force on an object often called the normal force?
16. When you weigh yourself, how does the support force of the scale acting on you compare with the gravitational force between you and the earth?

1.7 Equilibrium of Moving Things

17. A bowling ball rolls along a lane. Another ball rolls down a hill. Which, if either, is in equilibrium? Defend your answer.
18. If we push a crate at a constant velocity, how do we know how much friction acts on the crate compared with our pushing force?

1.8 The Force of Friction

19. How does the direction of a friction force compare with the velocity of a sliding object?
20. If you push on a heavy crate to the right and it slides, what is the direction of friction on the crate?
21. Suppose you push on a heavy crate, but not hard enough to make it slide. Does a friction force act on the crate?

1.9 Speed and Velocity

22. Distinguish between speed and velocity.
23. Why do we say velocity is a vector and speed is not?
24. Does the speedometer on a vehicle show average speed or instantaneous speed?
25. How can you be at rest and also moving at 100,000 km/h at the same time?

1.10 Acceleration

26. Distinguish between velocity and acceleration.
27. What is the acceleration of an object that moves at a constant velocity? What is the net force on the object in this case?
28. What is the acceleration of an object in free fall at the earth's surface?
29. Why does the unit of time appear twice in the definition of acceleration?
30. When you toss a ball upward, by how much does its upward speed decrease each second?

Activities

1. Roll cans of different masses across the floor and notice the effect of inertia on how far each can rolls.
2. By any method you choose, determine both your walking speed and your running speed.
3. Stand flat-footed next to a wall and make a mark on the wall at the highest point you can reach. Then jump vertically and again mark your highest point. The distance between the marks is your vertical jumping distance. Use this to calculate your hang time.

Exercises

Please don't be intimidated by the large number of exercises in this book. If your course work is to cover many chapters, your instructor will likely assign only a few exercises from each.

1. A bowling ball rolling along a lane gradually slows as it rolls. How would Aristotle interpret this observation? How would Galileo interpret it?
2. What Aristotelian idea did Galileo discredit in his fabled Leaning Tower of Pisa experiment? With his inclined plane experiments?
3. When a ball rolls down an inclined plane, it gains speed because of gravity. When rolling up, it loses speed because of gravity. Why doesn't gravity play a role when it rolls on a horizontal surface?
4. What physical quantity is a measure of how much inertia an object has?
5. Which has more mass, a 2-kg fluffy pillow or a 3-kg small piece of iron? More volume? Why are your answers different?
6. Does a dieting person more accurately lose mass or lose weight?
7. A favorite class demonstration by Paul Hewitt is lying on his back with a blacksmith's anvil placed on his chest. When an assistant whacks the anvil with a strong sledge-hammer blow, Hewitt is not hurt. How is the physics here similar to that illustrated in Figure 1.7?
8. What is your own mass in kilograms? Your weight in newtons?
9. Gravitational force on the moon is only 1/6 that of the gravitational force on the earth. What would be the weight of a 10-kg object on the moon and on the earth? What would its mass be on the moon and on the earth?
10. Consider a pair of forces, one with a magnitude of 25 N and the other with a magnitude of 15 N. What maximum net force is possible for these two forces? What is the minimum net force possible?
11. The sketch shows a painter's staging in mechanical equilibrium. The person in the middle weighs 250 N, and the tensions in each rope are 200 N. What is the weight of the staging?
12. A different staging that weighs 300 N supports two painters, one weighing 250 N and the other weighing 300 N. The reading in the left scale is 400 N. What should the reading in the right scale be?

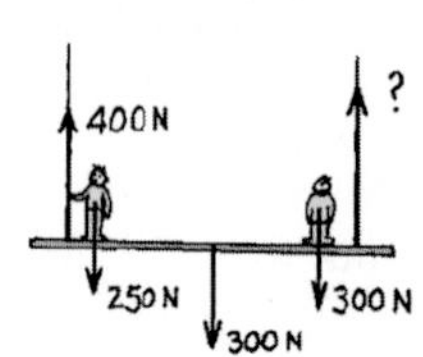

13. Can an object be in mechanical equilibrium when only a single force acts on it? Explain.
14. Nellie Newton hangs at rest from the ends of the rope as shown. How does the reading on the scale compare to her weight?
15. Harry the painter swings year after year from his bosun's chair. His weight is 500 N, and the rope, unknown to him, has a breaking point of 300 N. Why doesn't the rope break when he is supported as shown to the left below? One day, Harry was painting near a flagpole, and, for a change, he tied the free end of the rope to the flagpole instead of to his chair, as shown to the right. Why did Harry end up taking his vacation early?

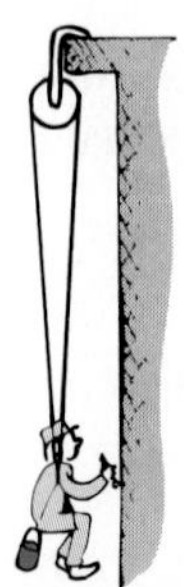

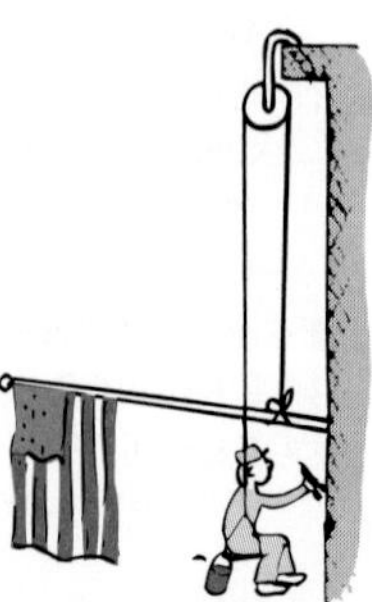

16. Consider the two forces acting on the person who stands still—namely, the downward pull of gravity and the upward support of the floor. Are these forces equal and opposite? Do they form an action-reaction pair? Why or why not?
17. A hockey puck slides across the ice at a constant velocity. Is it in mechanical equilibrium? Why or why not?
18. Can we accurately say that, if something moves at constant velocity, there are no forces acting on it? Explain.
19. At the moment an object that has been tossed upward into the air reaches its highest point, is it in equilibrium? Defend your answer.
20. If you push horizontally on a crate and it slides across the floor, slightly gaining speed, how does the friction acting on the crate compare with your push?
21. When the brakes are applied in a speeding car, how does the direction of the friction force on the car compare with the velocity of the car? With the acceleration of the car?
22. When can an automobile with a velocity toward the north have an acceleration toward the south? Explain.
23. Correct your friend who says, "The dragster rounded the curve at a constant velocity of 100 km/h."
24. What is the impact speed when a car moving at 100 km/h bumps into the rear of another car traveling in the same direction at 98 km/h?
25. Harry Hotshot can paddle a canoe in still water at 8 km/h. How successful will he be at canoeing upstream in a river that flows at 8 km/h?
26. A destination 120 miles away is posted on a highway sign, and the speed limit is 60 miles/hour. If you drive at the posted speed, will you reach the destination in 2 hours? Or in more than 2 hours?
27. Suppose that a freely falling object were somehow equipped with a speedometer. By how much would its speed reading increase with each second of fall?
28. Suppose that the freely falling object in the preceding exercise were also equipped with an odometer. Would the readings of distance fallen each second indicate equal or unequal distances of fall for successive seconds? Explain.
29. Why does a stream of water get narrower as it falls from a faucet?
30. When a ballplayer throws a ball straight up, by how much does the speed of the ball decrease each second while it is ascending? In the absence of air resistance, by how much does its speed increase each second while it is descending? How much time is required for its ascent? How much time is required for its descent?
31. Someone standing at the edge of a cliff (as in Figure 1.24) throws a ball straight up at a certain speed and another ball straight down with the same initial speed. If air resistance is negligible, which ball has the greater speed when it strikes the ground below?
32. What is the acceleration of a car that moves at a steady velocity of 100 km/h for 100 seconds? Explain your answer, and state why this question is an exercise in careful reading as well as in physics.
33. For a freely falling object dropped from rest, what is its acceleration at the end of the fifth second of fall? At the end of the tenth second? Defend your answer (and distinguish between velocity and acceleration).
34. Two balls, A and B, are released simultaneously from rest at the left end of the equal-length tracks A and B, as shown. Which ball will reach the end of its track first?

35. Refer to the tracks above.
    (a) Does ball B roll faster along the lower part of track B than ball A rolls along track A?
    (b) Is the speed gained by ball B going down the extra dip the same as the speed it loses going up near the right-hand end—and doesn't this mean that the speed of balls A and B will be the same at the ends of both tracks?
    (c) On track B, won't the average speed dipping down and up be greater than the average speed of ball A during the same time?
    (d) So, overall, does ball A or ball B have the greater average speed? (Do you wish to change your answer to Exercise 34?)

Problems

1. Find the net force produced by a 30-N force and a 20-N force in each of the following cases:
    (a) Both forces act in the same direction.
    (b) The two act in opposite directions.
2. A horizontal force of 100 N is required to push a box across a floor at a constant velocity.
    (a) What is the net force acting on the box?
    (b) How much is the friction force that acts on the box?

3. A firefighter with a mass of 100 kg slides down a vertical pole at a constant speed. What is the force of friction provided by the pole?
4. The ocean's level is currently rising at about 1.5 mm per year. At this rate, in how many years will sea level be 3 meters higher than it is now?
5. What is the acceleration of a vehicle that changes its velocity from 100 km/h to a dead stop in 10 s?
6. Extend Table 1.2 (which gives values of from 0 to 5 s) to 0 to 10 s, assuming no air resistance.
7. A ball is thrown straight up with an initial speed of 40 m/s. How high does it go, and how long is it in the air (neglecting air resistance)?
8. A ball is thrown straight up with enough speed so that it is in the air for several seconds.
   (a) What is the velocity of the ball when it reaches its highest point?
   (b) What is its velocity 1 s before it reaches its highest point?
   (c) What is the change in its velocity during this 1-s interval?
   (d) What is its velocity 1 s after it reaches its highest point?
   (e) What is the change in velocity during this 1-s interval?
   (f) What is the change in velocity during the 2-s interval from 1 s before the highest point to 1 s after the highest point? (Caution: we are asking for velocity, not speed.)
   (g) What is the acceleration of the ball during any of these time intervals and at the moment the ball has zero velocity?
9. Toss a ball upward. How high should you throw it so that it will be airborne for 1 second? If you ignore air resistance, how fast will it return to your hand (assuming the same tossing and catching distance from the ground)?
10. Surprisingly, very few athletes can jump more than 2 feet (0.6 m) high. Use $d = 1/2\ gt^2$ and solve for the time an athlete spends moving upward in a 2-foot vertical jump. Then double it for the "hang time"—the time one's feet are off the ground.

Chapter 1 Online Resources

Tutorials
- Vectors

Videos
- Newton's Law of Inertia
- The Old Tablecloth Trick
- Toilet Paper Roll
- Inertia of a Ball
- Inertia of a Cylinder
- Inertia of an Anvil
- Vector Representation: How to Add & Subtract
- Geometric Addition of Vectors
- Definition of Speed
- Average Speed
- Velocity
- Changing Velocity
- Definition of Acceleration
- Numerical Example of Acceleration

Quiz
Exercises
Flashcards
Links

CHAPTER 2

Newton's Laws of Motion

Galileo's work set the stage for Isaac Newton, who was born shortly after Galileo's death in 1642. By the time Newton was 23, he had developed his famous three laws of motion, which completed the overthrow of Aristotelian ideas. These three laws first appeared in one of the most famous books of all time, Newton's *Philosophiae Naturalis Principia Mathematica,** often simply known as the *Principia.* The first law is a restatement of Galileo's concept of inertia; the second law relates acceleration to its cause—force; and the third is the law of action and reaction.

2.1 Newton's First Law of Motion

Newton's first law, usually called the **law of inertia,** is a restatement of Galileo's idea.

> **Every object continues in a state of rest, or in a state of motion in a straight line at constant speed, unless it is compelled to change that state by forces exerted upon it.**

You can think of inertia as another word for "laziness" (or resistance to change).

Insights

The key word in this law is *continues:* an object *continues* to do whatever it happens to be doing unless a force is exerted upon it. If the object is at rest, it *continues* in a state of rest. This is nicely demonstrated when a tablecloth is skillfully whipped from beneath dishes sitting on a tabletop, leaving the dishes in their initial state of rest.† On the other hand, if an object

Figure 2.1
Inertia in action.

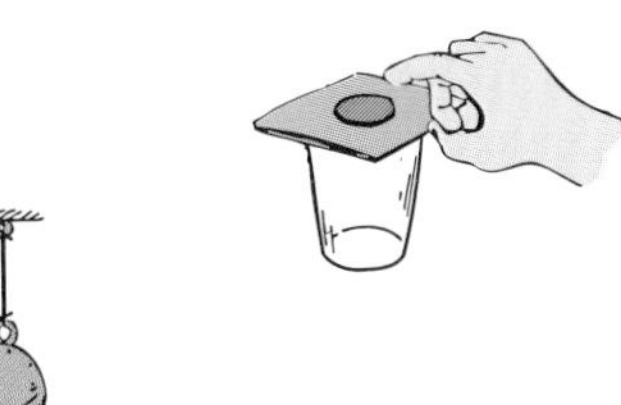

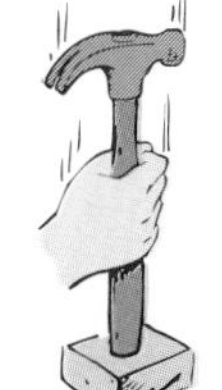

Figure 2.2
Examples of inertia.

*The Latin title means "mathematical principles of natural philosophy." See Newton's biography on page 58.
†Close inspection reveals that brief friction between the dishes and the fast-moving tablecloth starts the dishes moving, but then friction between the dishes and the table stops the dishes before they slide very far. If you try this, use unbreakable dishes!

Figure 2.3
Rapid deceleration is sensed by the driver, who lurches forward—inertia in action!

is moving, it *continues* to move without changing its speed or direction, as evidenced by space probes that continually move in outer space. This property of objects to resist changes in motion is called **inertia.**

☑ CHECKPOINT

When a space shuttle travels in a nearly circular orbit around the earth, is a force required to maintain its high speed? If suddenly the force of gravity were cut off, what type of path would the shuttle follow?

Check Your Answers

No force in the direction of the shuttle's motion exists. The shuttle coasts at a constant speed by its own inertia. The only force acting on it is the force of gravity, which acts at right angles to its motion (toward the earth's center). We'll see later that this right-angled force holds the shuttle in a circular path. If it were cut off, the shuttle would move in a straight line at a constant speed (constant velocity).

The Moving Earth

In 1543, the Polish astronomer Nicolaus Copernicus caused a great controversy when he published a book proposing that the earth revolved around the sun.* This idea conflicted with the popular view that the earth was the center of the universe. Copernicus's concept of a sun-centered solar system was the result of years of studying the motion of the planets. He had kept his theory from the public—for two reasons. The first reason was that he feared persecution: a theory so completely different from common opinion would surely be taken as an attack on the established order. The second reason was that he had reservations about it himself: he could not reconcile the idea of a moving earth with the prevailing ideas of motion. The concept of inertia was unknown to him and to others of his time. In the final days of his life, at the urging of close friends, he sent his manuscript, *De Revolutionibus Orbium Coelestium*†, to the printer. The first copy of his famous exposition reached him on the day he died—May 24, 1543.

The idea of a moving earth was much debated. Europeans thought about the universe much as Aristotle had, and the existence of a force big enough to keep the earth moving was beyond their imagination. They had no idea of the concept of inertia. One of the arguments against a moving earth was the following:

Consider a bird sitting at rest on a branch of a tall tree. On the ground below is a fat, juicy worm. The bird sees the worm and drops vertically below

*Copernicus was certainly not the first to think of a sun-centered solar system. In the fifth century, for example, the Indian astronomer Aryabhatta taught that the earth circles the sun, not the other way around (as the rest of the world believed).

†The Latin title means "On the Revolutions of Heavenly Spheres," by Nicolaus Copernicus.

and catches it. It was argued that this would be impossible if the earth were moving. A moving earth would have to travel at an enormous speed to circle the sun in one year. While the bird would be in the air descending from its branch to the ground below, the worm would be swept far away along with the moving earth. It seemed that catching a worm on a moving earth would be an impossible task. The fact that birds do catch worms from tree branches seemed to be clear evidence that the earth must be at rest.

Can you see the mistake in this argument? You can if you use the concept of inertia. You see, not only is the earth moving at a great speed, but so are the tree, the branch of the tree, the bird that sits on it, the worm below, and even the air in between. Things in motion remain in motion if no unbalanced forces are acting upon them. So when the bird drops from the branch, its initial sideways motion remains unchanged. It catches the worm quite unaffected by the motion of its total environment.

Figure 2.4
Can the bird drop down and catch the worm if the earth moves at 30 km/s?

We live on a moving earth. If you stand next to a wall and jump up so that your feet are no longer in contact with the floor, does the moving wall slam into you? Why not? It doesn't because you are also traveling at the same speed, before, during, and after your jump. The speed of the earth relative to the sun is not the speed of the wall relative to you.

Four hundred years ago, people had difficulty with ideas like these. One reason is that they didn't yet travel in high-speed vehicles. Rather, they experienced slow, bumpy rides in horse-drawn carts. People were less aware of the effects of inertia. Today, we can flip a coin in a high-speed car, bus, or plane and catch the vertically moving coin as easily as we could if the vehicle were at rest. We see evidence of the law of inertia when the horizontal motion of the coin before, during, and after the catch is the same. The coin always keeps up with us.

Figure 2.5
When you flip a coin in a high-speed airplane, it behaves as if the airplane were at rest. The coin keeps up with you—inertia in action!

2.2 Newton's Second Law of Motion

Isaac Newton was the first to recognize the connection between force and mass in producing acceleration, which is one of the most central rules of nature, and he expressed it in his *second law of motion.* **Newton's second law** states:

> **The acceleration produced by a net force on an object is directly proportional to the net force, is in the same direction as the net force, and is inversely proportional to the mass of the object.**

Or, in shorter notation,

$$\text{Acceleration} \sim \frac{\text{net force}}{\text{mass}}$$

By using consistent units such as newtons (N) for force, kilograms (kg) for mass, and meters per second squared (m/s^2) for acceleration, we produce the exact equation:

$$\text{Acceleration} = \frac{\text{net force}}{\text{mass}}$$

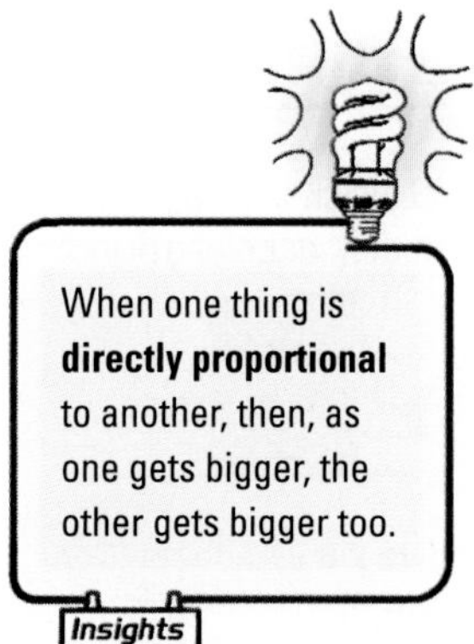

Figure 2.6
Acceleration depends both on the amount of push and on the mass being pushed.

In its briefest form, where a is acceleration, F is net force, and m is mass:

$$a = \frac{F}{m}$$

Acceleration equals the net force divided by the mass. If the net force acting on an object is doubled, the object's acceleration will be doubled. Suppose instead that the mass is doubled. Then the acceleration will be halved. If both the net force and the mass are doubled, then the acceleration will be unchanged. (Now you're ready for "Pulled Over" in the Laboratory Manual.)

An object accelerates in the direction of the net force acting on it. Speed changes when the net force is in the direction of the object's motion. When the net force acts at right angles to motion, then direction changes. Any other direction of application results in a combination of speed change and deflection.

Force of hand accelerates the brick

Twice as much force produces twice as much acceleration

Twice the force on twice the mass gives the same acceleration

Figure 2.7
Acceleration is directly proportional to force.

☑ CHECKPOINT

1. In the previous chapter, we defined acceleration as the time rate of change of velocity; that is, a = (change in v)/time. Are we now saying that acceleration is instead the ratio of force to mass—that is, $a = F/m$? Which is it?
2. A jumbo jet cruises at a constant velocity of 1000 km/h when the thrusting force of its engines is a constant 100,000 N. What is the acceleration of the jet? What is the force of air resistance on the jet?
3. Suppose you apply the same amount of force to two separate carts, one cart with a mass of 1 kg and the other with a mass of 2 kg. Which cart will accelerate more, and how much greater will the acceleration be?

Check Your Answers

1. Acceleration is defined as the time rate of change of velocity, and it is produced by a force. The magnitude of the force/mass (the cause) determines the rate change in velocity/time (the effect). So we must first define acceleration and then define the terms that produce acceleration.
2. The acceleration is zero, as evidenced by the constant velocity. Because the acceleration is zero, it follows from Newton's second law that the net force is zero, which means that the force of air resistance must just equal the thrusting force of 100,000 N and act in the opposite direction. So the air resistance on the jet is 100,000 N. This is in accord with $\Sigma \mathbf{F} = 0$. (Note that we don't need to know the velocity of the jet to answer this question, but only that it is constant—our clue that acceleration, and therefore net force, is zero.)
3. The 1-kg cart will have more acceleration—twice as much, in fact—because it has half as much mass—which means it has half as much resistance to a change in motion.

Force of hand accelerates the brick

The same force accelerates 2 bricks 1/2 as much

3 bricks, 1/3 as much acceleration

Figure 2.8
Acceleration is inversely proportional to mass.

Figure 2.9
When you accelerate in the direction of your velocity, you speed up; against your velocity, you slow down; at an angle to your velocity, your direction changes.

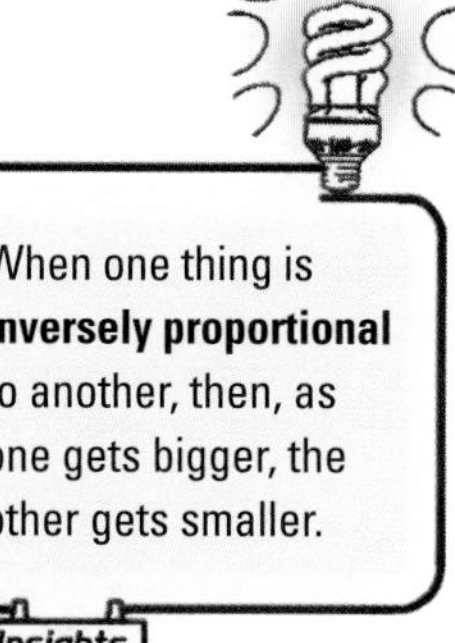

When one thing is **inversely proportional** to another, then, as one gets bigger, the other gets smaller.

Insights

Figuring Physical Science

Problem Solving

If we know the mass of an object in kilograms (kg) and its acceleration in meters per second per second (m/s^2), then the force will be expressed in newtons (N). One newton is the force needed to give a mass of one kilogram an acceleration of one meter per second squared. We can arrange Newton's second law to read

$$\text{force} = \text{mass} \times \text{acceleration}$$
$$1\ \text{N} = (1\ \text{kg}) \times (1\ \text{m/s}^2)$$

We can see that

$$1\ \text{N} = 1\ \text{kg} \cdot \text{m/s}^2$$

The dot between kg and m/s^2 means that the units are multiplied together.

If we know two of the quantities in Newton's second law, we can calculate the third. For example, how much force, or thrust, must a 20,000-kg jet plane develop to achieve an acceleration of 1.5 m/s^2? Using the equation, we can calculate

$$\begin{aligned} F &= ma \\ &= (20{,}000\ \text{kg}) \times (1.5\ \text{m/s}^2) \\ &= 30{,}000\ \text{kg} \cdot \text{m/s}^2 \\ &= 30{,}000\ \text{N} \end{aligned}$$

Suppose we know the force and the mass, and we want to find the acceleration. For example, what acceleration is produced by a force of 2000 N applied to a 1000-kg car? Using Newton's second law, we find that

$$a = \frac{F}{m} = \frac{2000\ \text{N}}{1000\ \text{kg}} = \frac{2000\ \text{kg} \cdot \text{m/s}^2}{1000\ \text{kg}} = 2\ \text{m/s}^2$$

If the force is 4000 N, the acceleration is

$$a = \frac{F}{m} = \frac{4000\ \text{N}}{1000\ \text{kg}} = \frac{4000\ \text{kg} \cdot \text{m/s}^2}{1000\ \text{kg}} = 4\ \text{m/s}^2$$

Doubling the force on the same mass simply doubles the acceleration.

Physics problems are often more complicated than these. We don't focus on solving complicated problems in this book; instead, we emphasize equations as guides to thinking about the relationships of basic physical-science concepts. Remember, mastering concepts first makes problem solving more meaningful.

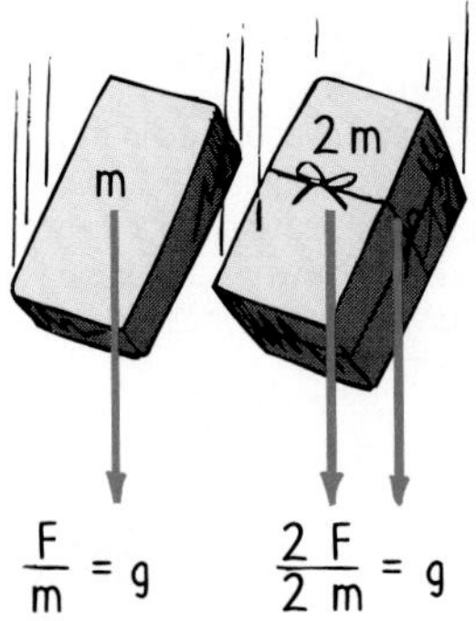

Figure 2.10
The ratio of weight (F) to mass (m) is the same for all objects in the same locality; hence, their accelerations are the same in the absence of air resistance.

When Acceleration Is *g*—Free Fall

Although Galileo articulated both the concept of inertia and the concept of acceleration, and was the first to measure the acceleration of falling objects, he was unable to explain why objects of various masses fall with equal accelerations. Newton's second law provides the explanation.

We know that a falling object accelerates toward the earth because of the gravitational force of attraction between the object and the earth. As mentioned earlier, when the force of gravity is the only force—that is, when air resistance is negligible—we say that the object is in a state of **free fall.** An object in free fall accelerates toward the earth at 10 m/s^2 (or, more precisely, at 9.8 m/s^2.)

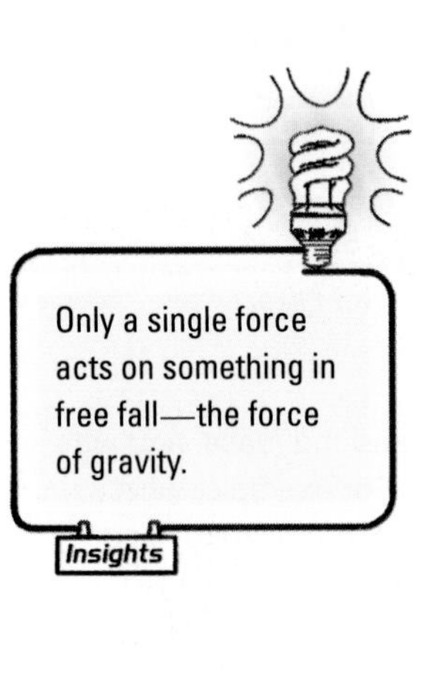

The greater the mass of an object, the stronger is the gravitational pull between it and the earth. The double brick in Figure 2.10, for example, has twice the gravitational attraction to earth as the single brick. Why, then, doesn't the double brick fall twice as fast (as Aristotle supposed it would)? The answer is evident in Newton's second law: the acceleration of an object depends not only on the force (weight, in this case), but on the object's resistance to motion—its inertia. Whereas a force produces an acceleration, inertia is a *resistance* to acceleration. So twice the force exerted on twice the inertia produces the same acceleration as half the force exerted on half the inertia. Both accelerate equally. The acceleration due to gravity is symbolized by *g*. We use the symbol *g*, rather than *a*, to denote that acceleration is due to gravity alone.

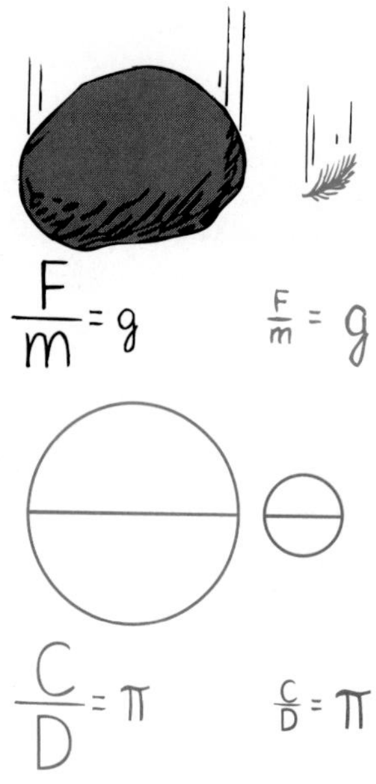

Figure 2.11
The ratio of weight (F) to mass (m) is the same for the large rock and the small feather; similarly, the ratio of circumference (C) to diameter (D) is the same for the large and the small circle.

The ratio of weight to mass for freely falling objects equals a constant, *g*. This is similar to the constant ratio of circumference to diameter for circles, which equals the constant π. The ratio of weight to mass is identical for both heavy and light objects, just as the ratio of circumference to diameter is the same for both large and small circles (Figure 2.11).

Figure 2.12
In a vacuum, a feather and a coin fall at equal accelerations.

We now understand that the acceleration of free fall is independent of an object's mass. A boulder 100 times more massive than a pebble falls at the same acceleration as the pebble because, although the force on the boulder (its weight) is 100 times greater than the weight of the pebble, its resistance to a change in motion (mass) is 100 times that of the pebble. The greater force offsets the equally greater mass.

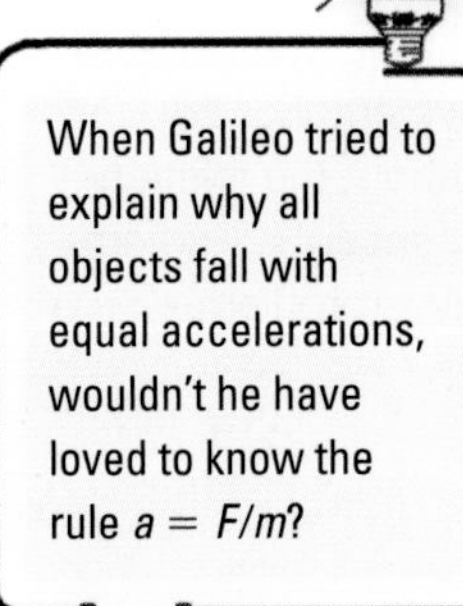

☑ CHECKPOINT

In a vacuum, a coin and a feather fall at an equal rate, side by side. Would it be correct to say that equal forces of gravity act on both the coin and the feather when in a vacuum?

Check Your Answer

No, no, no—a thousand times no! These objects accelerate equally not because of equal forces of gravity on them, but because the *ratios* of their weights to masses are equal. Although air resistance is not present in a vacuum, gravity is. (You'd know this if you placed your hand into a vacuum chamber and a cement truck rolled over it!) If you answered yes to this question, let this be a signal to be more careful when you think physics.

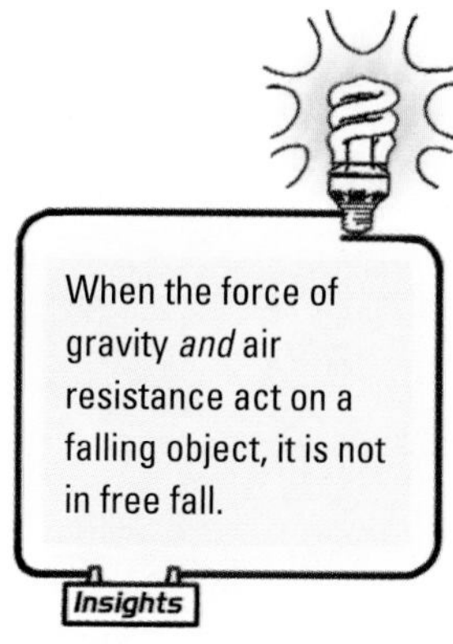

When Acceleration of Fall Is Less Than *g*—Non-free Fall

Most often, air resistance is not negligible for falling objects. Then the acceleration of the object's fall is less. Air resistance depends on two things: speed and surface area. When a skydiver steps from a high-flying plane, the air resistance on the skydiver's body builds up as the falling speed increases. The result is reduced acceleration. The acceleration can be reduced further by increasing the surface area. A skydiver does this by orienting the body so more air is encountered—by spreading out like a flying squirrel. So air resistance depends both on speed and on the surface area encountered by the air.

For free fall, the downward net force is weight—only weight. But when air is present, the downward net force = weight − air resistance. Can you see that the presence of air resistance reduces net force? And that less net force means less acceleration? So, as a skydiver falls faster and faster, the acceleration of fall decreases.* What happens to the net force if air resistance builds up to equal weight? The answer is, net force becomes zero. Here we see $\Sigma F = 0$ again! Then acceleration becomes zero. Does this mean the diver comes to a stop? No! What it means is that the diver no longer gains speed. Acceleration terminates—it no longer occurs. We say the diver has reached **terminal speed.** If we are concerned with direction—down, for falling objects, we say that the diver has reached **terminal velocity.**

Figure 2.13
The heavier parachutist must fall faster than the lighter parachutist for air resistance to cancel her greater weight.

*In mathematical notation,

$$a = \frac{F_{net}}{m} = \frac{mg - R}{m}$$

where mg is the weight and R is the air resistance. Note that, when $R = mg$, $a = 0$; then, with no acceleration, the object falls at a constant velocity. With elementary algebra, we can proceed another step and get

$$a = \frac{F_{net}}{m} = \frac{mg - R}{m} = g - \frac{R}{m}$$

We see that the acceleration a will always be less than g if air resistance R impedes falling. Only when $R = 0$ does $a = g$.

Figure 2.14
A flying squirrel increases its frontal area by spreading out. The result is greater air resistance and a slower fall.

Terminal speed for a human skydiver varies from about 150 to 200 km/h, depending on the weight, size, and orientation of the body. A heavier person has to fall faster for air resistance to balance weight.† The greater weight is more effective in "plowing through" the air, resulting in more terminal speed for a heavier person. Increasing frontal area reduces terminal speed. That's where a parachute is useful. A parachute increases frontal area, which greatly increases air resistance, reducing the terminal speed to a safe 15 to 25 km/h.

Consider the interesting demonstration of the falling coin and feather in the glass tube (Figure 2.12). When air is inside, we see that the feather falls more slowly because of air resis-

Figuring Physical Science

Problem Solving

1. A skydiver jumps from a high-flying helicopter. As she falls faster and faster through the air, does her acceleration increase, decrease, or remain the same?

2. What will be the acceleration of the skydiver when air resistance builds up to be equal to half her weight?

Solutions

1. Acceleration decreases because the net force on her decreases. Net force is equal to her weight minus her air resistance, and because air resistance increases with increasing speed, net force and, therefore, acceleration also decrease. According to Newton's second law,

$$a = \frac{F_{net}}{m} = \frac{mg - R}{m}$$

where mg is her weight and R is the air resistance she encounters. As R increases, a decreases. Note that, if she falls fast enough so that $R = mg$, $a = 0$; then, with no acceleration, she falls at terminal speed.

2. We find the acceleration from

$$a = \frac{F_{net}}{m} = \frac{mg - R}{m} = \frac{mg - mg/2}{m} = \frac{mg/2}{m} = \frac{g}{2}$$

So she accelerates at 1/2 g, 5 m/s^2.

†A skydiver's air resistance is proportional to speed squared.

tance. The feather's weight is very small, so it reaches terminal speed very quickly because it doesn't have to fall very far or fast before air resistance builds up to equal its small weight. The coin, on the other hand, doesn't have a chance to fall fast enough for air resistance to build up to equal its weight. If you were to drop a coin from a very high location, such as from the top of a tall building, its terminal speed would be reached when the speed of the coin would be about 200 km/h. This is a much, much higher terminal speed than that of a falling feather.

When Galileo allegedly dropped objects of different weights from the Leaning Tower of Pisa, they didn't actually hit at the same time. They almost did, but because of air resistance, the heavier one hit slightly before the other. But this contradicted the much longer time difference expected by the followers of Aristotle. The behavior of falling objects was never really understood until Newton announced his second law of motion.

Figure 2.15
A stroboscopic study of a golf ball (left) and a Styrofoam ball (right) falling in air. The air resistance is negligible for the heavier golf ball, and its acceleration is nearly equal to g. Air resistance is not negligible for the lighter Styrofoam ball, which reaches its terminal velocity sooner.

Skydivers and flying squirrels are not alone in increasing their surface areas when falling. When the Paradise Tree Snake *(Chrysopelea paradisi)* jumps from a tree branch it doubles its width by flattening itself. It acquires a slightly concave shape and maneuvers itself by undulating in a graceful S-shape, traveling more than 20 meters in a single leap.

Insights

☑ CHECKPOINT

Consider two parachutists, a heavy person and a light person, who jump from the same altitude with parachutes of the same size.

1. Which person reaches terminal speed first?
2. Which person has the higher terminal speed?
3. Which person reaches the ground first?
4. If there were no air resistance, like on the moon, how would your answers to these questions differ?

Check Your Answers

To answer these questions correctly, think of a coin and a feather falling in air.

1. Just as a feather reaches terminal speed very quickly, the lighter person reaches terminal speed first.
2. Just as a coin falls faster than a feather through air, the heavy person falls faster and reaches a higher terminal speed.
3. Just as in the race between a falling coin and a falling feather, the heavier person falls faster and will reach the ground first.
4. If there were no air resistance, there would be no terminal speed at all. Both would be in free fall, and both would hit the ground at the same time.

2.3 Forces and Interactions

Figure 2.16
When you lean against a wall, you exert a force on the wall. The wall simultaneously exerts an equal and opposite force on you. Hence, you don't topple over.

So far, we've treated force in its simplest sense—as a push or pull. In a broader sense, a force is not a thing in itself but an *interaction* between one thing and another. If you push on a wall with your fingers, more is happening than your pushing on the wall. You're interacting with the wall, and the wall is also pushing on you. The fact that your fingers and the wall push on each other is evident in your bent fingers (Figure 2.16). These two forces are equal in magnitude (amount) and opposite in direction. The pair of forces constitutes a single interaction. In fact, you can't push on the wall unless the wall pushes back.*

In Figure 2.17, we see a boxer's fist hitting a massive punching bag. The fist hits the bag (and dents it) while the bag hits back on the fist (and stops its motion). This force pair is fairly large. But what if the boxer were hitting a piece of tissue paper? The boxer's fist can exert only as much force on the tissue paper as the tissue paper can exert on the boxer's fist. Furthermore, the fist can't exert any force at all unless what is being hit exerts the same amount of reaction force. An interaction requires a *pair* of forces acting on *two* different objects.

Figure 2.17
He can hit the massive bag with considerable force. But, with the same punch, he can exert only a tiny force on the tissue paper in midair.

Figure 2.18
In the interaction between the hammer and the stake, each exerts the same amount of force on the other.

When a hammer hits a stake and drives it into the ground, the stake exerts an equal amount of force on the hammer, and that force brings the hammer to an abrupt halt. And when you pull on a cart and it accelerates, the cart pulls back on you, as evidenced perhaps by the tightening of the rope wrapped around your hand. One thing interacts with another; the hammer interacts with the stake, and you interact with the cart.

*We tend to think of only living things pushing and pulling. But inanimate things can do likewise. So please don't be troubled about the idea of the inanimate wall pushing back on you. It does, just as another person leaning against you would.

Which exerts the force and which receives the force? Isaac Newton's answer to this was that neither force has to be identified as "exerter" or "receiver," and he concluded both objects must be treated equally. For example, when the hammer exerts a force on the stake, it is brought to a halt by the force the stake exerts on the hammer. Both forces are equal and oppositely directed. When you pull the cart, the cart simultaneously pulls on you. This pair of forces, your pull on the cart and the cart's pull on you, make up the single interaction between you and the cart. Such observations led Newton to his third law of motion.

2.4 Newton's Third Law of Motion

Newton's third law states:

> **Whenever one object exerts a force on a second object, the second object exerts an equal and opposite force on the first.**

We can call one force the *action force,* and the other the *reaction force.* Then we can express Newton's Third Law in another form:

> **To every action there is always an opposed equal reaction.**

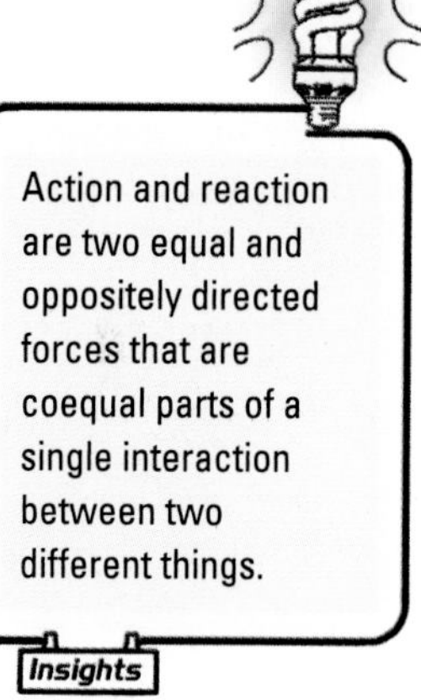

It doesn't matter which force we call the *action* and which we call the *reaction.* The important thing is that they are coequal parts of a single interaction and that neither force exists without the other. Action and reaction forces are equal in strength and opposite in direction. They occur in pairs and make up a single interaction between two things.

When walking, you interact with the floor. Your push against the floor is coupled to the floor's push against you. The pair of forces occurs simultaneously. Likewise, the tires of a car push against the road while the road pushes back on the tires—the tires and road push against each other. In swimming, you interact with the water that you push backward, while the water pushes you forward—you and the water push against each other. The reaction forces are what account for our motion in these cases. These forces depend on friction; a person or a car on ice, for example, may not be able to exert the action force to produce the needed reaction force. Neither force exists without the other.

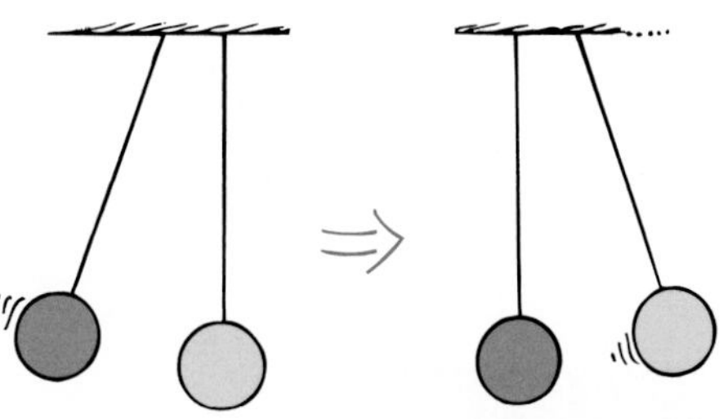

Figure 2.19
The impact forces between the blue and the yellow ball move the yellow ball and stop the blue ball.

Simple Rule to Identify Action and Reaction

There is a simple rule for identifying action and reaction forces. First, identify the interaction—one thing (object A) interacts with another (object B). Then, action and reaction forces can be stated in the following form:

> **Action: Object A exerts a force on object B.**
> **Reaction: Object B exerts a force on object A.**

The rule is easy to remember. If action is A acting on B, reaction is B acting on A. We see that A and B are simply switched around. Consider the case of your hand pushing on the wall. The interaction is between your hand and the wall. We'll say the action is your hand (object A) exerting a force on the wall (object B). Then the reaction is the wall exerting a force on your hand.

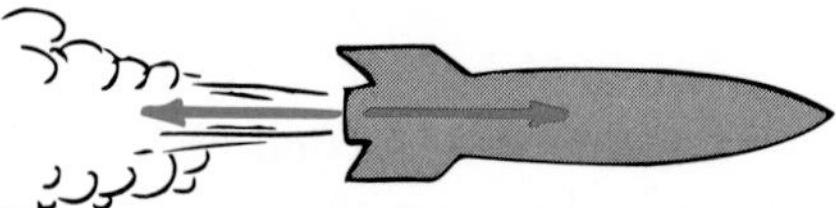

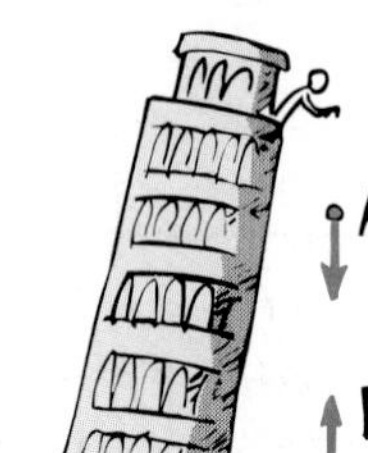

Action: earth pulls on ball

Reaction: ball pulls on earth

Figure 2.20
Action and reaction forces. Note that, when action is "*A* exerts force on *B*," the reaction is then simply "*B* exerts force on *A*."

☑ CHECKPOINT

1. A car accelerates along a road. Identify the force that moves the car.
2. Identify the action and reaction forces for the case of an object in free fall (no air resistance).

Check Your Answers

1. It is the road that pushes the car along. Except for air resistance, only the road provides a horizontal force on the car. How does it do this? The rotating tires of the car push back on the road (action). The road simultaneously pushes forward on the tires (reaction). How about that!
2. To identify a pair of action-reaction forces in any situation, first identify the pair of interacting objects. In this case, the earth interacts with the falling object via the force of gravity. So the earth pulls the falling object downward (call it *action*). Then *reaction* is the falling object pulling the earth upward. It is only because of the earth's enormous mass that you don't notice its upward acceleration.

Figuring Physical Science

Below we see two vectors on the sketch of the hand pushing the wall. The wall also pushes back on the hand. Note that the others show only the action force. Draw appropriate vectors showing the reaction forces. Can you specify the action-reaction pairs in each case?

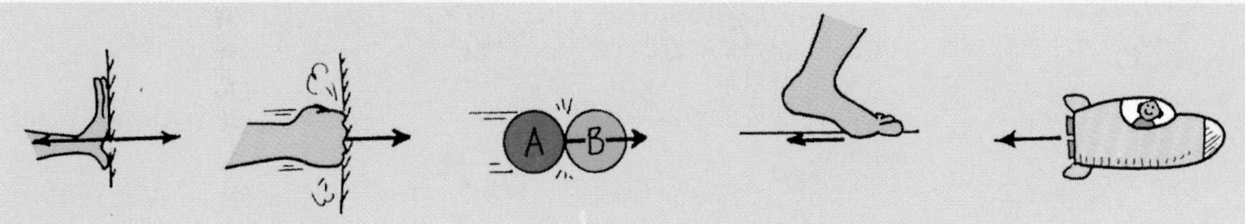

Action and Reaction on Different Masses

Quite interestingly, a falling object pulls upward on the earth with as much force as the earth pulls downward on it. The resulting acceleration of the falling object is evident, while the upward acceleration of the earth is too small to detect.

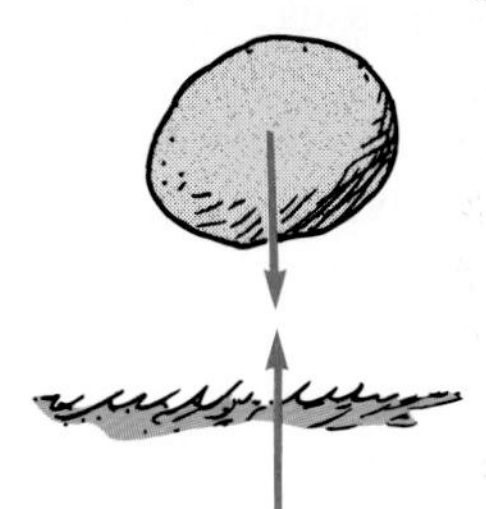

Figure 2.21
The earth is pulled up by the boulder with just as much force as the boulder is pulled down by the earth.

Consider the exaggerated examples of two planetary bodies, *a* through *e* in Figure 2.23. The forces between bodies A and B are equal in magnitude and oppositely directed in each case. If the acceleration of Planet A is unnoticeable in *a,* then it is more noticeable in *b,* where the difference between the masses is less extreme. In *c,* where both bodies have equal mass, the acceleration of Planet A is as evident as it is for B. Continuing, we see that the acceleration of A becomes even more evident in *d* and even more so in *e*. So, strictly speaking, when you step off the curb, the street rises ever so slightly to meet you.

When a cannon is fired, there is an interaction between the cannon and the cannonball. The sudden force that the cannon exerts on the cannonball is exactly equal and opposite to the force the cannonball exerts on the cannon. This is why the cannon recoils (kicks). But the effects of these equal forces are very different. This is because the forces act on different masses. The different accelerations are evident via Newton's second law,

Figure 2.22
The force exerted against the recoiling cannon is just as great as the force that drives the cannonball along the barrel. Why, then, does the cannonball undergo more acceleration than the cannon?

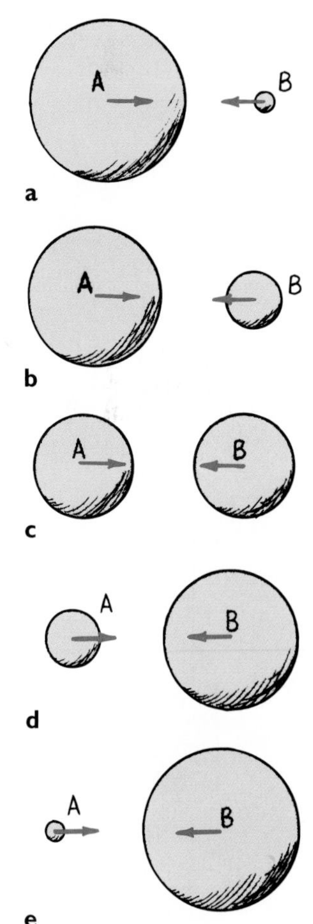

Figure 2.23
Which falls toward the other, A or B? Do the accelerations of each relate to their relative masses?

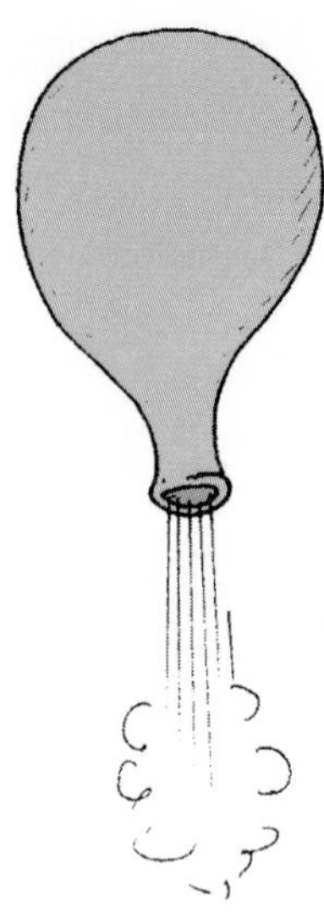

Figure 2.24
The balloon recoils from the escaping air, and it climbs upward.

$$a = \frac{F}{m}$$

Let F represent both the action and reaction forces, $\boldsymbol{m}$ the mass of the cannon, and m the mass of the cannonball. Different sized symbols are used here to indicate the relative masses and the resulting accelerations. Then the accelerations of the cannonball and cannon can be represented in the following way.

$$\text{cannonball: } \frac{F}{m} = \boldsymbol{a}$$

$$\text{cannon: } \frac{F}{\boldsymbol{m}} = a$$

Thus we see why the change in velocity of the cannonball is so large compared with the change in velocity of the cannon. A given force exerted on a small mass produces a large acceleration, while the same force exerted on a large mass produces a small acceleration.

We can extend the idea of a cannon recoiling from the ball it fires to understanding rocket propulsion. Consider an inflated balloon recoiling when air is expelled (Figure 2.24). If the air is expelled downward, the balloon accelerates upward. The same principle applies to a rocket, which continually "recoils" from the ejected exhaust gas. Each molecule of exhaust gas is like a tiny cannonball shot from the rocket (Figure 2.25).

A common misconception is that a rocket is propelled by the impact of exhaust gases against the atmosphere. In fact, before the advent of rockets, it was commonly thought that sending a rocket to the moon was impossible. Why? Because there is no air above the earth's atmosphere for the rocket to push against. But this is like saying a cannon wouldn't recoil unless the cannonball had air to push against. Not true! Both the rocket and recoiling cannon accelerate because of the reaction forces by the material they fire, not because of any pushes on the air. In fact, a rocket operates better above the atmosphere, where there is no air resistance.

Figure 2.25
The rocket recoils from the "molecular cannonballs" it fires, and it rises.

☑ CHECKPOINT

1. We know that the earth pulls on the moon. Does it follow that the moon also pulls on the earth?
2. A high-speed bus and an unfortunate bug have a head-on collision. The force of the bus on the bug splatters it all over the windshield. Is the corresponding force of the bug on the bus greater than, less than, or the same as the force of the bus on the bug? Is the resulting deceleration of the bus greater than, less than, or the same as that of the bug?

Check Your Answers

1. Yes, both pulls make up an action–reaction pair of forces associated with the gravitational interaction between the earth and the moon. We can say that (a) the earth pulls on the moon, and (b) the moon likewise pulls on the earth; but it is more insightful to think of this as a single interaction—the earth and moon simultaneously pulling on each other, each with the *same* amount of force.

2. The magnitudes of the forces are the same, because they constitute an action-reaction ***force pair*** that makes up the interaction between the bus and the bug. The accelerations, however, are very different, because the masses are different. The bug undergoes an enormous and lethal deceleration, while the bus undergoes a very tiny deceleration—so tiny that the very slight slowing of the bus is unnoticed by its passengers. But if the bug were more massive—as massive as another bus, for example—the slowing down would be very apparent.

Defining Your System

An interesting question often arises: since action and reaction forces are equal and opposite, why don't they cancel to zero? To answer this question, we must consider the *system* under consideration. Consider, for example, a system consisting of a single orange, Figure 2.26. The dashed line surrounding the orange encloses and defines the system. The vector that pokes outside the dashed line represents an external force on the system. The system accelerates in accord with Newton's second law. In Figure 2.27, we see that this force is provided by the apple, which doesn't change our analysis. The apple is outside the system. The fact that the orange simultaneously exerts a force on the apple, which is external to the system, may affect the apple (another system), but not the orange. You can't cancel a force on the orange with a force on the apple. So, in this case, the action and reaction forces don't cancel.

Figure 2.26
A force acts on the orange, and the orange accelerates to the right.

Figure 2.27
The force on the orange, provided by the apple, is not cancelled by the reaction force on the apple. The orange still accelerates.

Now let's consider a larger system, enclosing both the orange and the apple. We see the system bounded by the dashed line in Figure 2.28. Notice that the force pair is internal to the orange–apple system. These forces *do* cancel each other. They play no role in accelerating the system. A force external to the system is needed for acceleration. That's where friction with the floor comes in (Figure 2.29). When the apple pushes against the floor, the floor simultaneously pushes on the apple—an external force on the system. The system accelerates to the right.

Figure 2.28
In the larger system of orange + apple, action and reaction forces are internal and cancel. If these are the only horizontal forces, with no external force, no acceleration of the system occurs.

Figure 2.29
An external horizontal force occurs when the floor pushes on the apple (reaction to the apple's push on the floor). The orange–apple system accelerates.

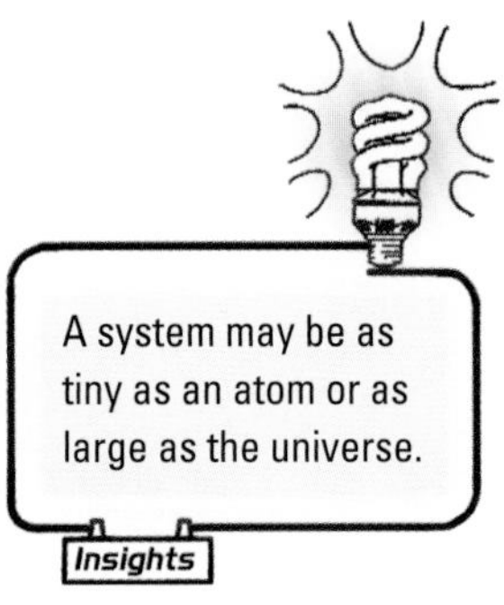

Inside a baseball are trillions and trillions of interatomic forces at play. They hold the ball together, but they play no role in accelerating the ball. Although every one of the interatomic forces is part of an action–reaction pair within the ball, they combine to zero, no matter how many of them there are. A force external to the ball, such as a swinging bat provides, is needed to accelerate the ball.

If this is confusing, it may be well to note that Newton had difficulties with the third law himself.

☑ CHECKPOINT

1. On a cold, rainy day, your car battery is dead, and you must push the car to move it and get it started. Why can't you move the car by remaining comfortably inside and pushing against the dashboard?
2. Does a fast-moving baseball possess force?

Check Your Answers

1. In this case, the system to be accelerated is the car. If you remain inside and push on the dashboard, the force pair you produce acts and reacts within the system. These forces cancel out, as far as any motion of the car is concerned. To accelerate the car, there must be an interaction between the car and something external—for example, you on the outside pushing against the road.
2. No, a force is not something an object *has,* like mass; it is part of an interaction between one object and another. A speeding baseball may possess the capability of exerting a force on another object when interaction occurs, but it does not possess force as a thing in itself. As we will see in the following chapter, moving things possess momentum and kinetic energy.

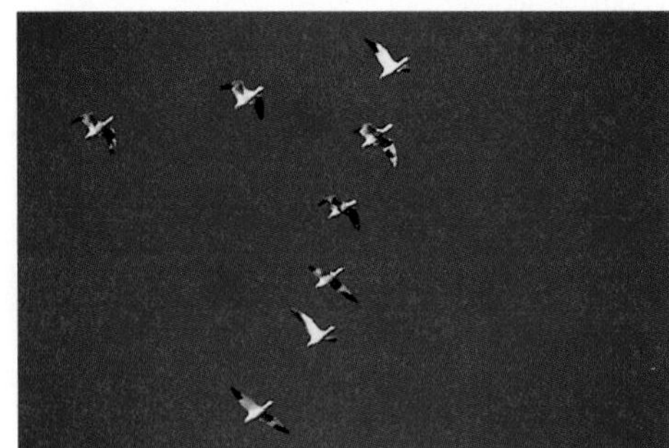

Figure 2.30
Ducks fly in a V formation because air pushed downward at the tips of their wings swirls upward, creating an updraft that is strongest off to the side of the bird. A trailing bird gets added lift by positioning itself in this updraft, pushes air downward, and creates another updraft for the next bird, and so on. The result is a flock flying in a V formation.

Using Newton's third law, we can understand how a helicopter gets its lifting force. The whirling blades are shaped to force air particles down (action), and the air forces the blades up (reaction). This upward reaction force is called *lift.* When lift equals the weight of the craft, the helicopter hovers in midair. When lift is greater, the helicopter climbs upward.

This is true for birds and airplanes. Birds fly by pushing air downward. The air, in turn, pushes the bird upward. When the bird is soaring, the wing must be shaped so that moving air particles are deflected downward. Slightly tilted wings that deflect oncoming air downward produce lift on an airplane. Air that is pushed downward continuously maintains lift. This supply of air is obtained by the forward motion of the aircraft, which results from propellers or jets that push the air backward. When the propellers or jets push the air backward, the air in turn pushes the propellers or jets forward. We will learn in Chapter 6 that the curved surface of a wing is an airfoil, which enhances the lifting force.

We see Newton's third law in action everywhere. A fish propels water backward with its fins, and the water propels the fish forward. The wind caresses the branches of a tree, and the branches caress back on the wind to produce whistling sounds. Forces are interactions between different things. Every contact requires at least a twoness; there is no way that an object can exert a force on nothing. Forces, whether large shoves or slight nudges, always occur in pairs, each opposite to the other. Thus, we cannot touch without being touched.

Figure 2.31
You cannot touch without being touched—Newton's third law.

2.5 Vectors

We have learned that such quantities as velocity, force, and acceleration require both magnitude and direction for a complete description. Such a quantity is a **vector quantity.** By contrast, a quantity that can be described by magnitude only, not involving direction, is called a **scalar quantity.** Mass, volume, and speed are scalar quantities.

A vector quantity is nicely represented by an arrow. When the length of the arrow is scaled to represent the quantity's magnitude and the direction of the arrow indicates the direction of the quantity, we refer to the arrow as a **vector.**

Adding vectors is quite simple when they act along parallel directions: if they are in the same direction, they add; if they are in opposite directions, they subtract. The sum of two or more vectors is called their **resultant.** To find the resultant of nonparallel vectors, we use the *parallelogram rule.** Construct a parallelogram wherein the two vectors are adjacent sides—the diagonal of the parallelogram shows the resultant. In Figure 2.33, the parallelograms are rectangles.

Figure 2.32
This vector, scaled so that 1 cm equals 20 N, represents a force of 60 N to the right.

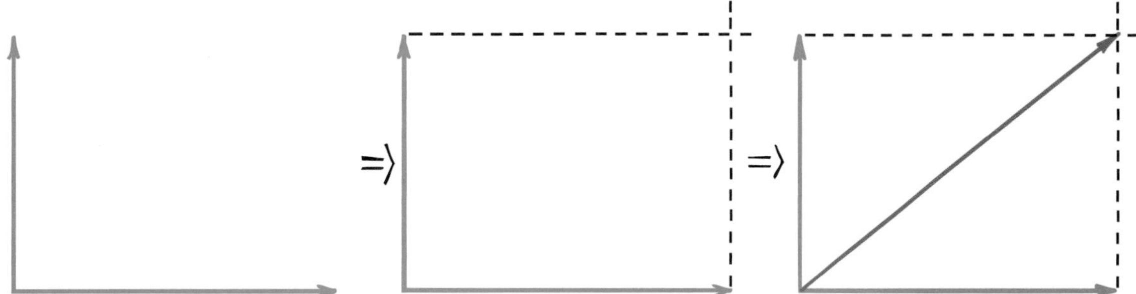

Figure 2.33
The pair of vectors at right angles to each other form two sides of a rectangle, the diagonal of which is their resultant.

* A parallelogram is a four-sided figure with opposite sides equal in length and parallel to each other. You can determine the length of the diagonal by measurement, but, in the special case in which the two vectors V and H are perpendicular, forming a square or rectangle, you can apply the Pythagorean theorem, $R^2 = V^2 + H^2$, to give the resultant: $R = \sqrt{(V^2 + H^2)}$.

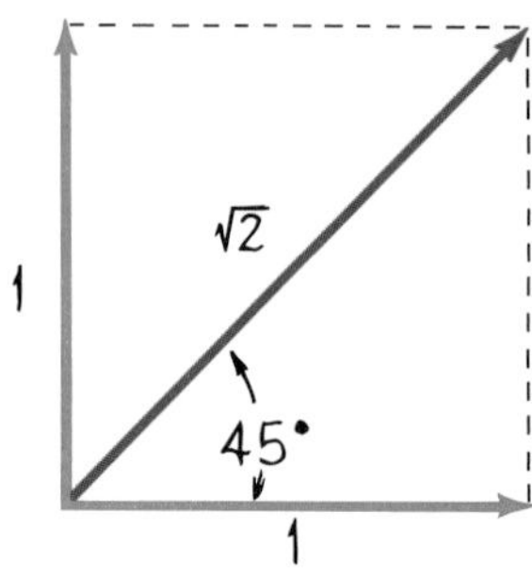

Figure 2.34
When a pair of equal-length vectors at right angles to each other are added, they form a square. The diagonal of the square is the resultant, √2 times the length of either side.

In the special case of two perpendicular vectors that are equal in magnitude, the parallelogram is a square (Figure 2.34). Since for any square the length of a diagonal is $\sqrt{2}$, or 1.41 times one of the sides, the resultant is $\sqrt{2}$ times one of the vectors. For example, the resultant of two equal vectors of magnitude 100 acting at a right angle to each other is 141.

Force Vectors

Figure 2.35 shows the top view of a pair of horizontal forces acting on a box. One is 30 newtons and the other is 40 newtons. Simple measurement shows that the resultant is 50 newtons.

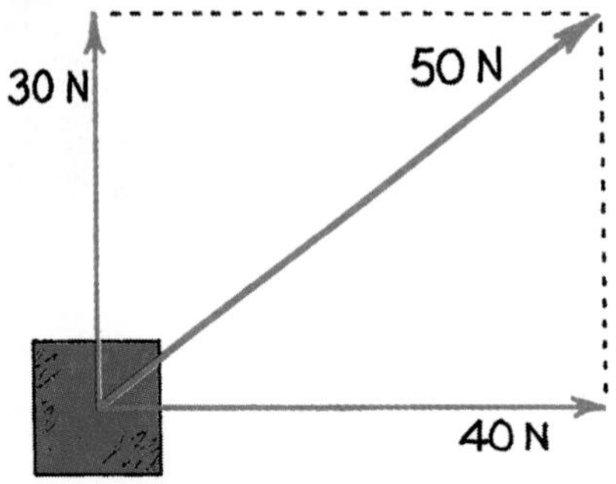

Figure 2.35
The resultant of the 30-N and 40-N forces is 50 N.

Figure 2.36 shows Nellie Newton hanging at rest from a pair of ropes that form different angles with the vertical. Which rope has the greater tension? Investigation will show there are three forces acting on Nellie: her weight, a tension in the left-hand rope, and a tension in the right-hand rope. Because the ropes hang at different angles, the rope tensions will be different from each other.

Figure 2.36
Nellie Newton hangs motionless by one hand from a clothesline. If the line is on the verge of breaking, which side is most likely to break?

Figure 2.37 shows a step-by-step solution. Because Nellie hangs in equilibrium, her weight must be supported by the combination of rope tensions, which must add vectorially to equal her weight. Using the parallelogram rule, we find that the tension in the right-hand rope is greater than the tension in the left-hand rope. By measuring the vectors, you'll see that tension in the right rope is about twice the tension in the left rope. How does tension in the right rope compare with her weight? (Force vectors are treated further in Appendix C, and they are nicely developed in the *Conceptual Physical Science Practice Book*.)

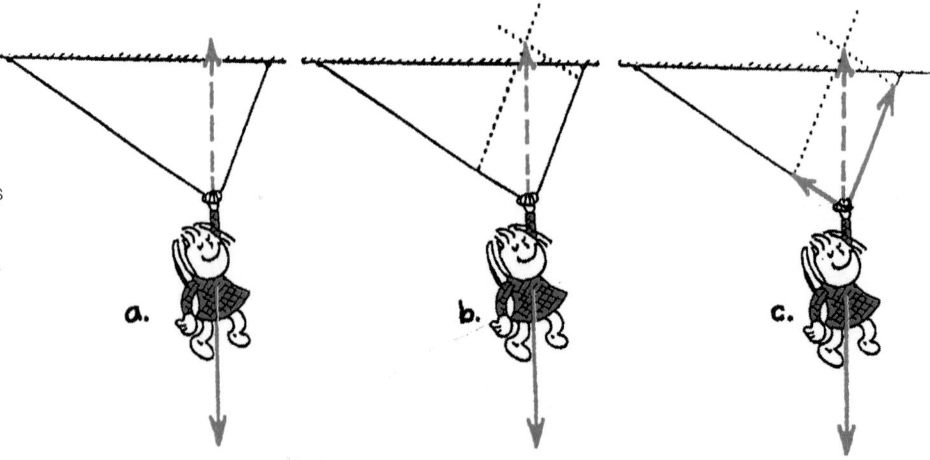

Figure 2.37
(a) Nellie's weight is shown by the downward vertical vector. An equal and opposite vector is needed for equilibrium, shown by the dashed vector.
(b) This dashed vector is the diagonal of a parallelogram defined by the dotted lines.
(c) Both rope tensions are shown by the constructed vectors. Tension is greater in the right rope, the one most likely to break.

Figuring Physical Science

Here we see the top view of an airplane being blown off course by various winds. Using a pencil and employing the parallelogram rule, sketch the vectors that show the resulting velocities for each case. In which case does the airplane travel fastest across the ground? Slowest?

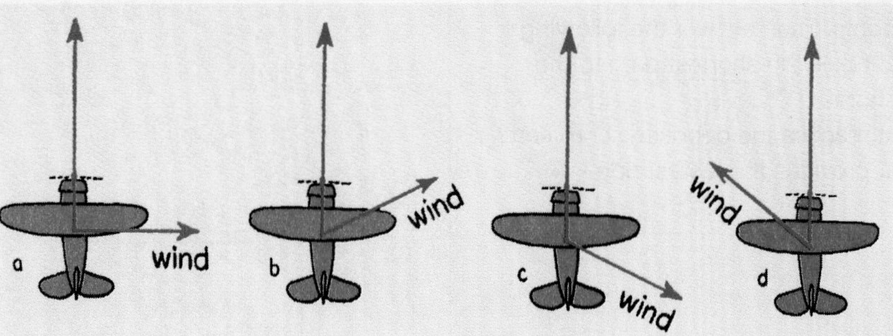

Velocity Vectors

Recall that speed is a measure of "how fast," and that velocity is a measure of "how fast *and* in which direction." If the speedometer in a car reads 100 kilometers per hour, you know your *speed.* If there is also a compass on the dashboard, indicating that the car is moving due north, for example, you know your *velocity*—100 kilometers per hour north. To know your velocity is to know your speed *and* your direction.

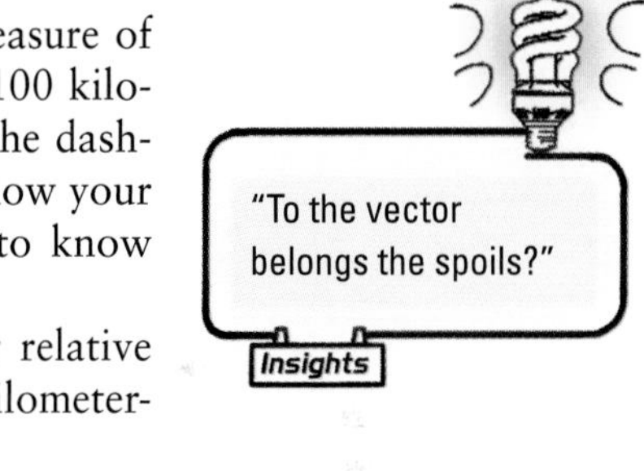

Consider an airplane flying due north at 80 kilometers per hour relative to the surrounding air. Suppose that the plane is caught in a 60-kilometer-per-hour crosswind (wind blowing at right angles to the direction of the airplane) that blows it off its intended course. This example is represented in Figure 2.38 with velocity vectors scaled so that 1 centimeter represents 20 kilometers per hour. Thus, the 80-kilometer-per-hour velocity of the airplane is shown by the 4-centimeter vector, and the 60-kilometer-per-hour tailwind is shown by the 3-centimeter vector. The diagonal of the constructed parallelogram (a rectangle, in this case) measures 5 cm, which represents 100 km/h. So the airplane flies at 100 km/h relative to the ground, in a direction between north and northeast.

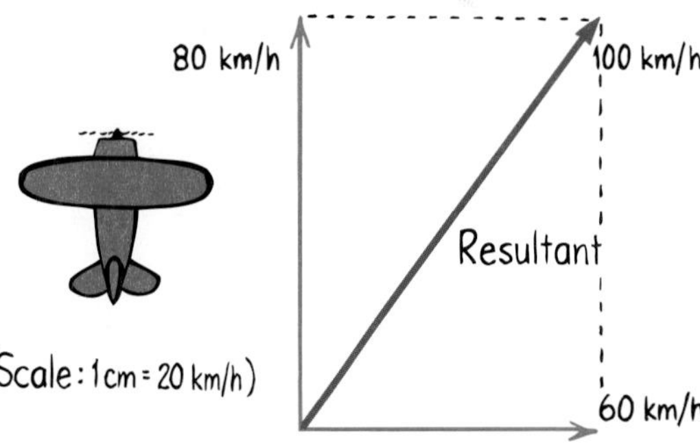

Figure 2.38
The 60-km/h crosswind blows the 80-km/h aircraft off course at 100 km/h.

☑ CHECKPOINT

Consider a motorboat that normally travels 10 km/h in still water. If the boat heads directly across the river, which also flows at a rate of 10 km/h, what will be its velocity relative to the shore?

Check Your Answer

When the boat heads cross-stream (at right angles to the river flow), its velocity is 14.1 km/h, 45 degrees downstream (in accord with the diagram in Figure 2.34).

Figuring Physical Science

Here we see top views of three motorboats crossing a river. All have the same speed relative to the water, and all experience the same water flow. Construct resultant vectors showing the speed and direction of the boats. Then answer the following:

(a) Which boat takes the shortest path to the opposite shore?

(b) Which boat reaches the opposite shore first?

(c) Which boat provides the fastest ride?

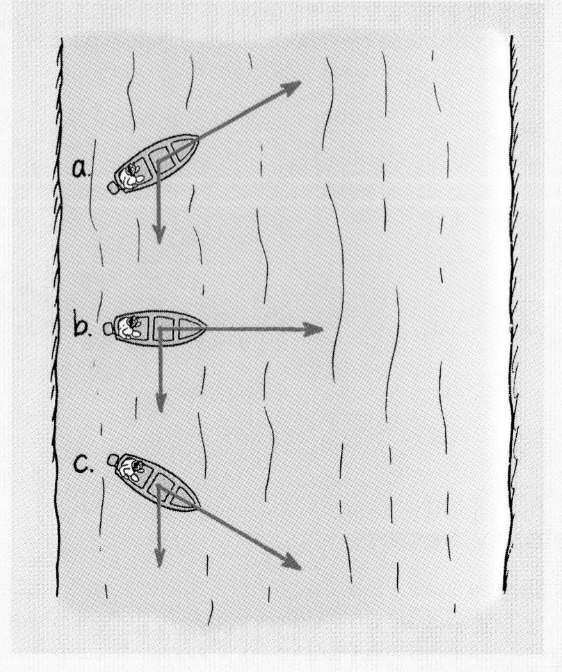

Components of Vectors

Just as two vectors at right angles can be combined into one resultant vector, in reverse any vector can be "resolved" into two *component* vectors perpendicular to each other. These two vectors are known as the components of the given vector they replace (Figure 2.39). The process of determining the components of a vector is called *resolution.* Any vector drawn on a piece of paper can be resolved into a vertical and a horizontal component.

Vector resolution is illustrated in Figure 2.40. A vector ***V*** is drawn in the proper direction to represent a vector quantity. Then vertical and horizontal lines *(axes)* are drawn at the tail of the vector. Next, a rectangle is drawn that has ***V*** as its diagonal. The sides of this rectangle are the desired components, vectors ***X*** and ***Y***. In reverse, note that the vector sum of vectors ***X*** and ***Y*** is ***V***.

We'll return to vector components when we treat projectile motion in Chapter 5.

Figure 2.39
The horizontal and vertical components of a ball's velocity.

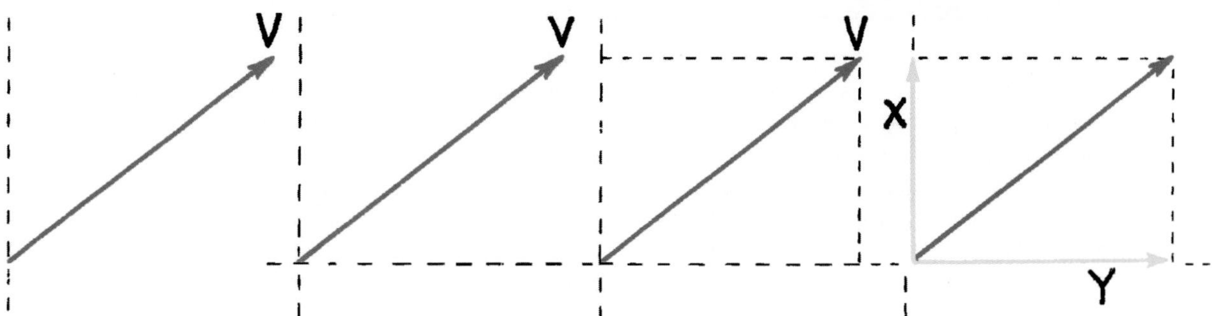

Figure 2.40
Construction of the vertical and horizontal components of a vector.

Exercise

With a ruler, draw the horizontal and vertical components of the two vectors shown. Measure the components before verifying the answers.

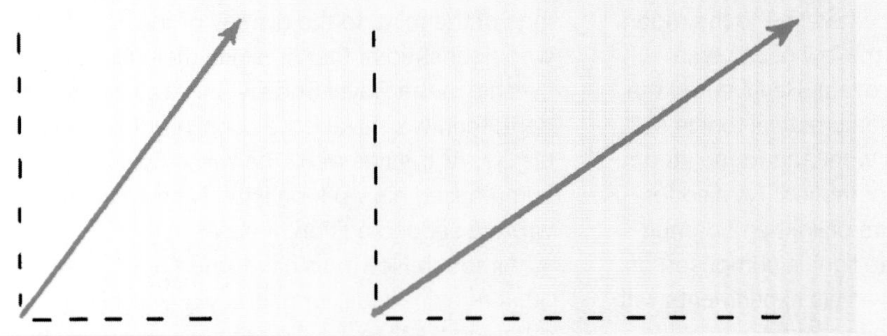

(Left vector: the horizontal component is 2.8 cm; the vertical component is 3.6 cm. Right vector: the horizontal component is 5.3 cm; the vertical component is 3.6 cm.)

2.6 Summary of Newton's Three Laws

Newton's first law, the law of inertia: An object at rest tends to remain at rest; an object in motion tends to remain in motion at constant speed along a straight-line path. This property of objects to resist change in motion is called *inertia*. Mass is a measure of inertia. Objects will undergo changes in motion only in the presence of a net force.

Newton's second law, the law of acceleration: When a net force acts on an object, the object will accelerate. The acceleration is directly proportional to the net force and inversely proportional to the mass. Symbolically, $a \sim F/m$.

Isaac Newton (1642–1727)

Isaac Newton was born prematurely (and barely survived) on Christmas Day, 1642, at his mother's farmhouse in Woolsthorpe, England, the same year that Galileo died. Newton's father had died several months before his birth, and he grew up under the care of his mother and grandmother. As a child, he showed no particular signs of brightness, and at the age of 14½, he was removed from school to work on his mother's farm. As a farmer, he was a failure, preferring to read books he borrowed from a neighboring druggist. An uncle sensed the scholarly potential in young Isaac and prompted him to study at the University of Cambridge, which he did for 5 years, graduating without particular distinction.

A plague swept through London, and Newton retreated to his mother's farm—this time to continue his studies. While at the farm, at age 23, he laid the foundations for the work that was to make him immortal. Seeing an apple fall to the ground led him to consider the force of gravity extending to the moon and beyond. He formulated the law of universal gravitation (which he later proved). He invented the calculus, a very important mathematical tool in science. He extended Galileo's work and formulated the three fundamental laws of motion. He also formulated a theory of the nature of light and demonstrated with prisms that white light is composed of all colors of the rainbow. It was his experiments with prisms that initially brought him fame.

When the plague subsided, Newton returned to Cambridge and soon established a reputation for himself as a first-rate mathematician. His mathematics teacher resigned in his favor, and Newton was appointed the Lucasian professor of mathematics, a post he held for 28 years. In 1672, he was elected to the Royal Society, where he exhibited the world's first reflector telescope. It can still be seen, preserved at the library of the Royal Society in London, with this inscription: "The first reflecting telescope, invented by Sir Isaac Newton, and made with his own hands."

It wasn't until Newton was 42 that he began to write what is generally acknowledged as the greatest scientific book ever written, the *Principia Mathematica Philosophiae Naturalis.* He wrote the work in Latin and completed it in 18 months. It appeared in print in 1687, but an English translation wasn't printed until 1729, two years after his death. When asked how he was able to make so many discoveries, Newton replied that he solved his problems by continually thinking very long and hard about them—and not by sudden insight.

At the age of 46, he was elected a member of Parliament. He attended the sessions in Parliament for two years and never gave a speech. One day he rose and the House fell silent to hear the great man speak. Newton's "speech" was very brief; he simply requested that a window be closed because of a draft.

A further turn from his work in science was his appointment as warden, and then as master, of the mint. Newton resigned his professorship and directed his efforts toward greatly improving the workings of the mint, to the dismay of the counterfeiters who flourished at that time. He maintained his membership in the Royal Society and was elected president, then was re-elected each year for the rest of his life. At the age of 62, he wrote *Opticks,* which summarized his work on light. Nine years later, he wrote a second edition of his *Principia.*

Although Newton's hair turned gray when he was 30, it remained full, long, and wavy all his life. Unlike others in his time, he did not wear a wig. He was a modest man, very sensitive to criticism, and never married. He remained healthy in body and mind into old age. At 80, he still had all his teeth, his eyesight and hearing were sharp, and his mind was alert. In his lifetime, he was regarded by his countrymen as the greatest scientist who ever lived. In 1705, he was knighted by Queen Anne. Newton died at the age of 85, and he was buried in Westminister Abbey, along with England's kings and heroes.

Newton showed that the universe ran according to natural laws—a knowledge that provided hope and inspiration to people of all walks of life and that ushered in the Age of Reason. The ideas and insights of Isaac Newton truly changed the world and elevated the human condition.

Acceleration is always in the direction of the net force. When an object falls in a vacuum, the net force is simply the weight, and the acceleration is g (the symbol g denotes that acceleration is due to gravity alone). When an object falls in air, the net force is equal to the weight minus the force of air resistance, and the acceleration is less than g. If and when the force of air resistance equals the weight of a falling object, acceleration terminates, and the object falls at a constant speed (called the *terminal speed*).

Newton's third law, the law of action–reaction: Whenever one object exerts a force on a second object, the second object exerts an equal and opposite force on the first. Forces occur in pairs: one is an action and the other is a reaction, which together constitute the interaction between one object and the other. Action and reaction always act on different objects. Neither force exists without the other.

There has been a lot of new and exciting physics since the time of Isaac Newton. Nevertheless, and quite interestingly, it was primarily Newton's laws that got us to the moon. Isaac Newton truly changed our way of viewing the world.

Summary of Terms

Newton's first law of motion Every object continues in a state of rest, or in a state of motion in a straight line at a constant speed, unless it is compelled to change that state by forces exerted upon it.

Newton's second law of motion The acceleration produced by a net force on an object is directly proportional to the net force, is in the same direction as the net force, and is inversely proportional to the mass of the object.

Free fall Motion under the influence of gravitational pull only.

Terminal speed The speed at which the acceleration of a falling object terminates when air resistance balances its weight.

Interaction Mutual action between objects in which each one exerts an equal and opposite force on the other.

Force pair The action-and-reaction pair of forces that constitute an interaction.

Newton's third law of motion Whenever one object exerts a force on a second object, the second object exerts an equal and opposite force on the first object.

Force vector An arrow drawn to scale so that its length represents the magnitude of a force and its direction represents the direction of the force.

Velocity vector An arrow drawn to scale so that its length represents the magnitude of a velocity and its direction represents the direction of motion.

Resultant The net result of a combination of two or more vectors.

Vector components Parts into which a vector can be separated and that act in different directions from the vector.

Review Questions

2.1 Newton's First Law of Motion

1. State the law of inertia.
2. Is inertia a property of matter or a force of some kind?
3. What concept was missing from people's minds in the sixteenth century when they couldn't believe the earth was moving?
4. When a bird lets go of a branch and drops to the ground below, why doesn't the moving earth sweep away from the dropping bird?
5. What kind of path would the planets follow if suddenly their attraction to the sun no longer existed?

2.2 Newton's Second Law of Motion

6. State Newton's second law.
7. Is acceleration *directly* proportional to force, or is it *inversely* proportional to force? Give an example.
8. Is acceleration *directly* proportional to mass, or is it *inversely* proportional to mass? Give an example.
9. If the mass of a sliding block is tripled at the same time the net force on it is tripled, how does the resulting acceleration compare to the original acceleration?
10. What is the net force that acts on a 10-N freely falling object?
11. Why doesn't a heavy object accelerate more than a light object when both are freely falling?
12. What is the net force that acts on a 10-N falling object when it encounters 4 N of air resistance? 10 N of air resistance?
13. What two principal factors affect the force of air resistance on a falling object?

14. What is the acceleration of a falling object that has reached its terminal velocity?
15. If two objects of the same size fall through air at different speeds, which encounters the greater air resistance?
16. Why does a heavy parachutist fall faster than a lighter parachutist who wears the same size parachute?

2.3 Forces and Interactions

17. Previously, we said that a force was a push or pull; now we say it is an interaction. Which is it? A push or pull, or an interaction? And what does it mean to say *interaction*?
18. How many forces are required for a single interaction?
19. When you push against a wall with your fingers, they bend because they experience a force. Identify this force.
20. A boxer can hit a heavy bag with great force. Why can't he hit a sheet of newspaper in midair with the same amount of force?

2.4 Newton's Third Law of Motion

21. State Newton's third law.
22. Consider hitting a baseball with a bat. If we call the force on the bat against the ball the *action* force, identify the *reaction* force.
23. If the forces that act on a cannonball and the recoiling cannon from which it is fired are equal in magnitude, why do the cannonball and cannon have very different accelerations?
24. Do action and reaction forces always act on different bodies?
25. Can you cancel a force on Body A with a force that acts on Body B?
26. If Body A and Body B are both within a system, can forces between them affect the acceleration of the system?
27. What is needed to accelerate a system?
28. When do action-and-reaction pairs of forces cancel each other and when do they not?
29. How does a helicopter get its lifting force?
30. What law of physics is inferred when we say you cannot touch without being touched?

2.5 Vectors

31. Cite three examples of a vector quantity. Then cite three examples of a scalar quantity.
32. According to the parallelogram rule, what does the diagonal of a constructed parallelogram represent?
33. Consider Nellie in Figure 2.36. If the ropes were vertical, with no angle involved, what would be the tension in each rope?
34. Can it be said that, when a pair of vectors are at right angles to each other, the resultant is greater than either of the vectors separately?
35. When a vector at an angle is resolved into horizontal and vertical components, can it be said that each component has less magnitude than the original vector?

2.6 Summary of Newton's Three Laws

36. Briefly summarize Newton's three laws of motion.

Activities

1. The net force acting on an object and the resulting acceleration are always in the same direction. You can demonstrate this with a spool. If the spool is pulled horizontally to the right, in which direction will it roll?

2. Hold your hand with the palm down like a flat wing outside the window of a moving automobile. Then slightly tilt the front edge of your hand upward and notice the lifting effect as air bounces from the bottom of your hand. Can you see Newton's laws at work here?
3. If you drop a sheet of paper and a book side by side, the book will fall faster than the paper. Why? The book falls faster because of its greater weight compared with the air resistance it encounters. If you place the paper against the lower surface of the raised book and again drop them at the same time, it will be no surprise that they hit the surface below at the same time. The book simply pushes the paper with it as it falls. Now, repeat this, but with the paper on *top* of the book, and not sticking over its edge. How will the accelerations of the book and paper compare? Will they separate and fall differently? Will they have the same acceleration? Try it and see! Then explain what happens.

Exercises

Again, please do not be intimidated by the large number of exercises and problems in this and other meatier chapters. If your course work is to cover many chapters, your instructor will likely assign only a few exercises and/or problems from each.

1. In the orbiting space shuttle, you are handed two identical closed boxes, one filled with sand and the other filled with feathers. How can you tell which is which without opening the boxes?
2. Your empty hand is not hurt when it bangs lightly against a wall. Why is it hurt if it is carrying a heavy load? Which of Newton's laws is most applicable here?
3. Why is a massive cleaver more effective for chopping vegetables than an equally sharp knife?
4. Each of the vertebrae forming your spine is separated from its neighbors by disks of elastic tissue. What happens, then, when you jump heavily on your feet from an elevated position? Can you think of a reason why you are a little taller in the morning than you are at the end of the day? (Hint: Think about the hammerhead in Figure 2.2.)
5. Before the time of Galileo and Newton, it was thought by many learned scholars that a stone dropped from the top of a tall mast on a moving ship would fall vertically and hit the deck behind the mast by a distance equal to how far the ship had moved forward while the stone was falling. In light of your understanding of Newton's laws, what do you think about this idea?
6. As you stand on a floor, does the floor exert an upward force against your feet? How much force does it exert? Why are you not moved upward by this force?
7. To pull a wagon across a lawn at a constant velocity, you must exert a steady force. Reconcile this fact with Newton's first law, which states that motion with a constant velocity indicates no force.
8. When your car moves along the highway at a constant velocity, the net force on it is zero. Why, then, do you continue running your engine?
9. A rocket becomes progressively easier to accelerate as it travels through space. Why is this so? (Hint: About 90 percent of the mass of a newly launched rocket is fuel.)
10. As you are leaping upward from the ground, how does the force that you exert on the ground compare with your weight?
11. A common saying goes, "It's not the fall that hurts you; it's the sudden stop." Translate this into Newton's laws of motion.
12. On which of these hills does the ball roll down with increasing speed and decreasing acceleration along the path? (Use this example if you wish to explain to someone the difference between speed and acceleration.)

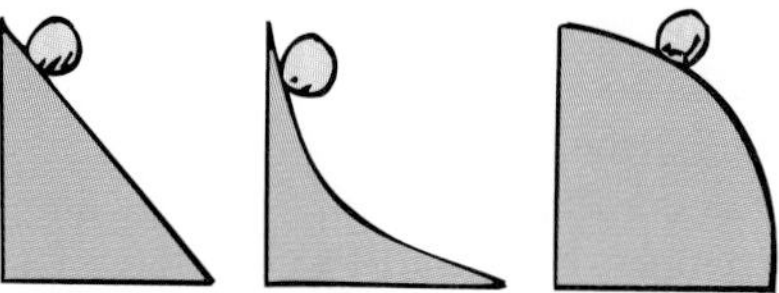

13. If you drop an object, its acceleration toward the ground is 10 m/s^2. If you throw it down instead, would its acceleration after throwing be greater than 10 m/s^2? Why or why not?
14. Can you think of a reason why the acceleration of the object thrown downward through the air in the preceding exercise would actually be less than 10 m/s^2?
15. Two 100-N weights are attached to a spring scale as shown. Does the scale read 0 N, 100 N, or 200 N, or does it give some other reading? (Hint: Would it read any differently if one of the ropes were tied to the wall instead of to the hanging 100-N weight?)

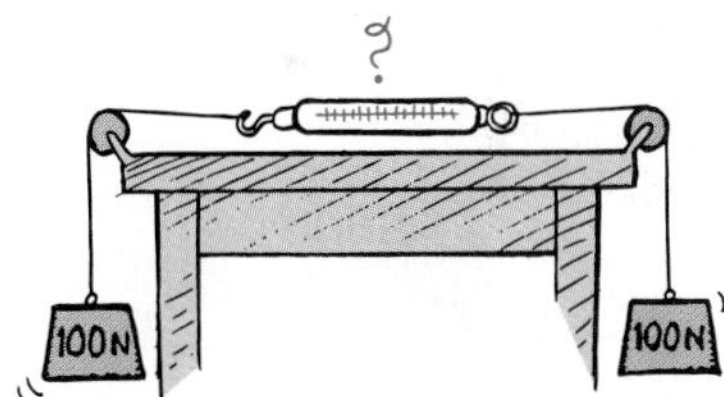

16. You hold an apple over your head. (a) Identify all the forces acting on the apple and their reaction forces. (b) When you drop the apple, identify all the forces acting on it as it falls and the corresponding reaction forces.
17. What is the net force on an apple that weighs 1 N when you hold it at rest above your head? What is the net force on it when you release it?
18. Aristotle claimed that the speed of a falling object depends on its weight. We now know that objects in free fall, whatever their weights, undergo the same gain in speed. Why does weight not affect acceleration?
19. Does a stick of dynamite contain force? Defend your answer.
20. Can a dog wag its tail without the tail in turn "wagging the dog"? (Consider a dog with a relatively massive tail.)

21. When the athlete holds the barbell overhead, the reaction force is the weight of the barbell on his hand. How does this force vary for the case in which the barbell is accelerated upward? Downward?

22. Why can you exert greater force on the pedals of a bicycle if you pull up on the handlebars?
23. If the earth exerts a gravitational force of 1000 N on an orbiting communications satellite, how much force does the satellite exert on the earth?
24. The strong man will push apart the two initially stationary freight cars of equal mass before he himself drops straight to the ground. Is it possible for him to give either of the cars a greater speed than the other? Why or why not?

25. Suppose two carts, one twice as massive as the other, fly apart when the compressed spring that joins them is released. How fast does the heavier cart roll compared with the lighter cart?

26. If you exert a horizontal force of 200 N to slide a crate across a factory floor at a constant velocity, how much friction is exerted by the floor on the crate? Is the force of friction equal and oppositely directed to your 200-N push? Does the force of friction make up the reaction force to your push? Why not?
27. If a Mack truck and a motorcycle have a head-on collision, upon which vehicle is the impact force greater? Which vehicle undergoes the greater change in its motion? Explain your answers.
28. Two people of equal mass attempt a tug-of-war with a 12-m rope while standing on frictionless ice. When they pull on the rope, each person slides toward the other. How do their accelerations compare, and how far does each person slide before they meet?
29. Suppose that one person in the preceding exercise has twice the mass of the other. How far does each person slide before they meet?
30. Which team wins in a tug of war—the team that pulls harder on the rope, or the team that pushes harder against the ground? Explain.
31. The photo shows Steve Hewitt and his daughter Gretchen. Is Gretchen touching her dad, or is he touching her? Explain.

32. When your hand turns the handle of a faucet, water comes out. Do your push on the handle and the water coming out comprise an action–reaction pair? Defend your answer.
33. Why is it that a cat that falls from the top of a 50-story building will hit the ground no faster than if it fell from the twentieth story?

34. Free fall is motion in which gravity is the only force acting. (a) Is a skydiver who has reached terminal speed in free fall? (b) Is a satellite circling the earth above the atmosphere in free fall?
35. How does the weight of a falling body compare with the air resistance it encounters just before it reaches terminal velocity? Just after?
36. You tell your friend that the acceleration of a skydiver decreases as falling progresses. Your friend then asks if this means that the skydiver is slowing down. What is your response?
37. If and when Galileo dropped two balls from the top of the Leaning Tower of Pisa, air resistance was not really negligible. Assuming that both balls were the same size yet one was much heavier than the other, which ball struck the ground first? Why?
38. If you simultaneously drop a pair of tennis balls from the top of a building, they will strike the ground at the same time. If one of the tennis balls is filled with lead pellets, will it fall faster and hit the ground first? Which of the two will encounter more air resistance? Defend your answers.

39. Which is more likely to break, the ropes supporting a hammock stretched tightly between a pair of trees or one that sags more when you sit on it? Defend your answer.
40. When a bird alights on a stretched power line wire, does the tension in the wire change? If so, is the increase more than, less than, or about equal to the bird's weight?
41. When you swim across a river, does the time to reach the opposite shore depend on the rate of flow of the water? Defend your answer.
42. Why does vertically falling rain make slanted streaks on the side windows of a moving automobile? If the streaks make an angle of 45°, what does this tell you about the relative speed of the car and the falling rain?
43. A stone is shown at rest on the ground. (a) The vector shows the weight of the stone. Complete the vector diagram showing another vector that results in zero net force on the stone. (b) What is the conventional name of the vector you have drawn?

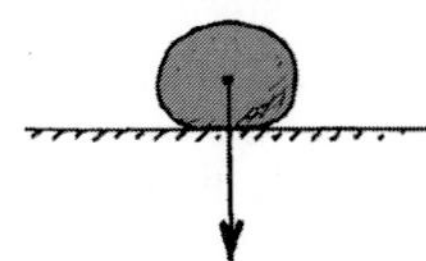

44. Here a stone at rest is suspended by a string. (a) Draw force vectors for all the forces that act on the stone. (b) Should your vectors have a zero resultant? (c) Why, or why not?

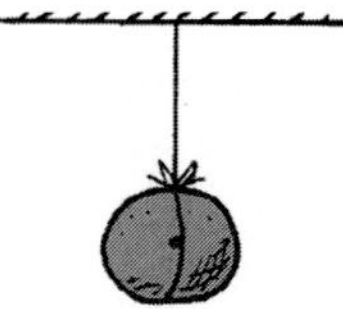

45. Here the same stone is being accelerated vertically upward. (a) Draw force vectors to some suitable scale showing relative forces acting on the stone. (b) Which is the longer vector, and why?
46. Suppose that the string in the preceding exercise breaks and that the stone slows in its upward motion. Draw a force vector diagram of the stone when it reaches the top of its path.
47. What is the net force on the stone in the preceding exercise when it is at the top of its path? What is its instantaneous velocity? Its acceleration?
48. Here is the stone sliding down a friction-free incline. (a) Identify the forces that act on it, and draw appropriate force vectors. (b) By the parallelogram rule, construct the resultant force on the stone (carefully showing that it has a direction parallel to the incline—the same direction as the stone's acceleration).

49. Here is the stone at rest, interacting with both the surface of the incline and the block. (a) Identify all the forces that act on the stone and draw appropriate force vectors. (b) Show that the net force on the stone is zero. (Hint 1: There are two normal forces *on* the stone. Hint 2: Be sure the vectors you draw are for forces that act *on* the stone, not on the surfaces *by* the stone.)

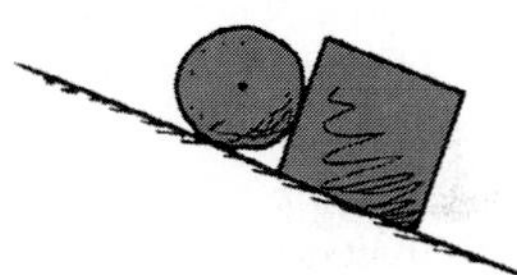

50. Make up three multiple-choice questions, one for each of Newton's laws, that check a classmate's understanding of these laws.

Problems

1. A 400-kg bear grasping a vertical tree slides down at a constant velocity. What is the friction force that acts on the bear?
2. When two horizontal forces are exerted on a cart, 600 N forward and 400 N backward, the cart undergoes acceleration. What additional force is needed to produce nonaccelerated motion?
3. You push with a 20-N horizontal force on a 2-kg mass resting on a horizontal surface against a horizontal friction force of 12 N. What is the acceleration?
4. You push with a 40-N horizontal force on a 4-kg mass resting on a horizontal surface against a horizontal friction force of 24 N. What is the acceleration?
5. If a mass of 1 kg is accelerated 1 m/s^2 by a force of 1 N, what would be the acceleration of 2 kg acted on by a force of 2 N?
6. An astronaut of mass 100 kg recedes from her spacecraft by activating a small propulsion unit attached to her back. If the force generated by a spurt is 25 N, what acceleration will this produce?
7. A rocket of mass 100,000 kg undergoes an acceleration of 2 m/s^2. Calculate the force being developed by the rocket engines.

8. How much acceleration does a 747 jumbo jet of mass 30,000 kg experience in takeoff when the thrust for each of four engines is 30,000 N?
9. A firefighter of mass 80 kg slides down a vertical pole with an acceleration of 4 m/s^2. What is the friction force that acts on the firefighter?
10. A boxer punches a sheet of paper in midair, and thereby brings it from rest up to a speed of 25 m/s in 0.05 second. If the mass of the paper is 0.003 kg, what force does the boxer exert on it?
11. Suppose that you are standing on a skateboard near a wall and that you push on the wall with a force of 30 N. How hard does the wall push on you? If your mass is 60 kg, what's your acceleration?
12. If raindrops fall vertically at a speed of 3 m/s and you are running at 4 m/s, how fast do they hit your face?
13. Forces of 3 N and 4 N act at right angles on a block of mass 5 kg. How much acceleration occurs?
14. Suzie Skydiver with her parachute has a mass of 50 kg.
(a) Before opening her chute, what force of air resistance will she encounter when she reaches terminal velocity?
(b) What force of air resistance will she encounter when she reaches terminal velocity after the chute is open?
(c) Discuss why your answers are the same or different.
15. What is the ground velocity of an airplane that has an air speed of 120 km/h when it is in a 90-km/h crosswind?

Chapter 2 Online Resources

Tutorials
- Parachutes & Newton's Second Law
- Newton's Third Law
- Vectors

Videos
- Newton's Law of Inertia
- The Old Tablecloth Trick
- Toilet Paper Roll
- Inertia of a Ball
- Inertia of a Cylinder
- Inertia of an Anvil
- Newton's Second Law
- Free-Fall Acceleration Explained
- Falling & Air Resistance
- Free Fall: How Fast?
- V = gt
- Air Resistance & Falling Objects
- Free Fall: How Far?
- Forces & Interaction
- Action & Reaction on Different Mass
- Action & Reaction: Rifle & Bullet
- Vector Representation: How to Add & Subtract
- Geometric Addition of Vectors

Quiz
Exercises
Flashcards
Links

CHAPTER 3

Momentum and Energy

Moving objects have a quantity that objects at rest don't have. More than a hundred years ago, this quantity was called *impedo*. A boulder at rest had no impedo, while the same boulder rolling down a steep incline possessed impedo. The faster it moved, the greater the impedo. The change in impedo depended on force and, importantly, on how long the force acted. Apply a force to a cart and you give it impedo. Apply a long force and you give it more impedo. But what do we mean by "long?" Does "long" refer to time or to distance? When this distinction was made, the term impedo gave way to two new terms—*momentum* and *kinetic energy*. This chapter is about both these important concepts.

3.1 Momentum

We all know that a heavy truck is more difficult to stop than a small car moving at the same speed. We state this fact by saying that the truck has more momentum than the car. By **momentum,** we mean inertia in motion—or, more specifically, the product of the mass of an object and its velocity; that is,

Momentum = mass × velocity

Or, in shorthand notation,

Momentum = mv

When direction is not an important factor, we can say momentum = mass × speed, which we still abbreviate mv.

We can see from the definition that a moving object can have a large momentum if either its mass or its velocity is large or if both its mass and its velocity are large. A truck has more momentum than a car moving at the same velocity because it has a greater mass. We can see that a huge ship moving at a small velocity can have a large momentum, as can a small bullet moving at a high velocity. A massive truck rolling down a steep hill with no brakes has a large momentum, whereas the same truck at rest has no momentum at all.

Figure 3.1
The boulder, unfortunately, has more momentum than the runner.

When can a 1000-kg car and a 2000-kg truck have the same momentum?

Check Your Answer

They have the same momentum when the car travels twice as fast as the truck. Then (1000 kg × 2v) for the car equals (2000 kg × v) for the truck. Or, if they were both at rest, they'd certainly have the same momentum—zero.

3.2 Impulse

Changes in momentum may occur when there is a change in the mass of an object, or a change in its velocity, or both. If momentum changes while the mass remains unchanged, as is most often the case, then the velocity changes. Acceleration occurs. And what produces acceleration? The answer is *force.* The greater the force acting on an object, the greater will be the change in velocity and, hence, the change in momentum.

Figure 3.2
When you push with the same force for twice the time, you impart twice the impulse and produce twice the momentum.

But something else is important also: time—how long the force acts. Apply a force briefly to a stalled automobile and you produce a small change in its momentum. Apply the same force over an extended period of time, and a greater change in momentum results. A long sustained force produces more change in momentum than the same force applied briefly. So, for changing an object's momentum, both force and the time interval during which the force acts are important.

The quantity "force × time interval" is called **impulse.**

3.3 Impulse–Momentum Relationship

The greater the impulse exerted on something, the greater will be its change in momentum. This is known as the **impulse–momentum relationship**. Mathematically, the exact relationship is

Impulse = change in momentum

or

Ft = change in mv

which reads, "force multiplied by the time-during-which-it-acts equals change in momentum."*

We can express all terms in this relationship in shorthand notation and use the delta symbol Δ (a letter in the Greek alphabet signifying "change in" or "difference in"):

$$Ft = \Delta mv$$

So, whenever you exert a net force on something, you also exert an impulse. Recall that a net force produces acceleration. Now we are additionally saying that a net force multiplied by the time during which that force acts produces a change in an object's momentum.

*In Newton's second law ($F/m = a$), we can insert the definition of acceleration (a = change in v/t), to get F/m = (change in v)/t. Then multiplying both sides by mt gives Ft = change in (mv), or, in delta notation, $Ft = \Delta(mv)$.

☑ CHECKPOINT

1. Does a moving object *possess* impulse?
2. Does a moving object *possess* momentum?

Check Your Answers

1. No. Recall from the previous chapter that an object cannot *possess* force. Similarly, an object cannot *possess* impulse. Just as a force is something an object can provide when it changes velocity, an impulse is something an object can *provide,* or something it can *experience,* only when it interacts with another object.
2. Yes, but, like velocity, in a relative sense—that is, with respect to a frame of reference, often the earth's surface. For example, a fly inside a fast-moving airplane cabin may have a large momentum relative to the earth below, but very little momentum relative to occupants in the cabin.

Timing is important—especially when you're changing your momentum.

Insights

Impulse may be viewed as causing momentum change, or momentum change may be viewed as causing impulse. It doesn't matter which way you think about it. The important thing is that impulse and change of momentum are always linked. Here we will consider some ordinary examples in which impulse is related (1) to increasing momentum, (2) to decreasing momentum over a long time, and (3) to decreasing momentum over a short time.

Case 1: Increasing Momentum

If you wish to produce the maximum increase in the momentum of something, you not only apply the greatest force, you also extend the time of application as much as possible (hence the different results obtained by pushing briefly on a stalled automobile and by giving it a sustained push).

Figure 3.3
Impact force against a golf ball. Average force multiplied by the time of contact is the impulse.

Long-range cannons have long barrels. The longer the barrel, the greater the velocity of the emerging cannonball or shell. Why? The force of exploding gunpowder in a long barrel acts on the cannonball for a longer time, increasing the impulse on it, which increases its momentum. Of course, the force that acts on the cannonball is not steady—it is strong at first and weaker as the gases expand. Most often the forces involved in impulses vary over time. The force that acts on the golf ball in Figure 3.3, for example, increases rapidly as the ball is distorted and then decreases as the ball comes up to speed and returns to its original shape. When we speak of any force that makes up impulse in this chapter, we mean the *average* force.

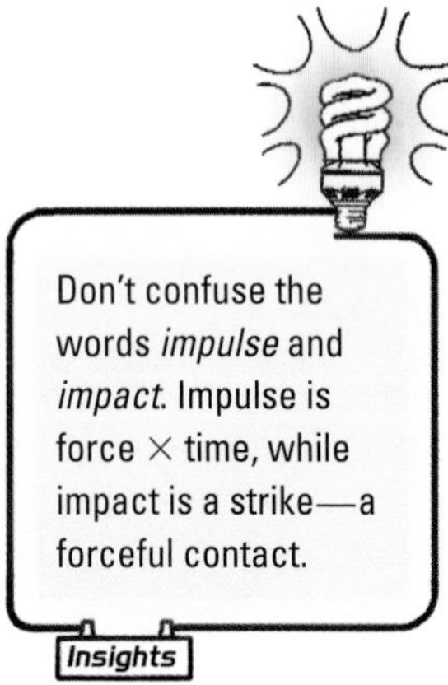

Case 2: Decreasing Momentum over a Long Time

Imagine that you are in a car that is out of control, and you're faced with a choice of slamming into either a concrete wall or a haystack. You don't need much physics knowledge to make the better decision, but knowing some physics aids you in understanding *why* hitting something soft is entirely different from hitting something hard. Whether you hit the wall or the haystack, your momentum will be decreased by the *same* amount, and this means that the impulse required to stop you is the same. The same impulse means the same product of force and time, not the same force or the same time. You have a choice. By hitting the haystack instead of the wall, you extend the time of impact—you extend the time during which your momentum is brought to zero. The longer time is compensated by a lesser force. If you extend the time of impact 100 times, you reduce the force of impact by 100. So, whenever you wish the force of an impact to be small, extend the time of the impact.

Figure 3.4
A large change in momentum over a long time requires a small force.

Figure 3.5
A large change in momentum over a short time requires a large force.

☑ CHECKPOINT

"Whoa," says a friend. "Isn't there a greater impulse in hitting a brick wall than in hitting a haystack?" What is your answer?

Check Your Answer

If, in both cases, your car is brought to a stop, then your change in momentum (to zero) must be the same. This means the impulse that stops you is the same. Of course the forces are *not* the same (but impulse is what the question is about).

A wrestler who is being thrown to the floor tries to prolong his time of arrival on the floor by relaxing his muscles and spreading the crash into a series of impacts, as foot, knee, hip, ribs, and shoulder fold onto the floor in turn. The increased time of impact reduces the force of impact.

When you jump from an elevated position to a floor below, you bend your knees when you land, which extends the time during which your momentum is reduced. This extension of time can be 10 to 20 times more than that of an abrupt, stiff-legged landing. Such knee-bending reduces the forces on your bones by 10 to 20 times. Of course, falling on a mat is preferable to falling on a solid floor, for this also increases the time of impact.

Ballet dancers much prefer a wooden floor with "give" to a hard floor with little or no "give." The wooden floor allows a longer time of impact whenever the dancer lands, thus decreasing the force of impact and reducing the chance of injury. A safety net used by acrobats provides an obvious example of small impact force over a long time to provide the required impulse to reduce the momentum of fall.

Bungee jumping puts the impulse–momentum relationship to a thrilling test. The momentum gained during the fall must be decreased to zero by an impulse equal to the gain in momentum. The long stretching time of the cord insures a small average force to bring the jumper to a safe halt. Bungee cords typically stretch to about twice their original length during the fall.

If you're about to catch a fast baseball with your bare hand, you extend your hand forward so you'll have plenty of space to allow your hand to move backward after making contact with the ball. You extend the time of the impact and thereby reduce the force of the impact. Similarly, a boxer rides or rolls with the punch to reduce the force of the impact (Figure 3.6).

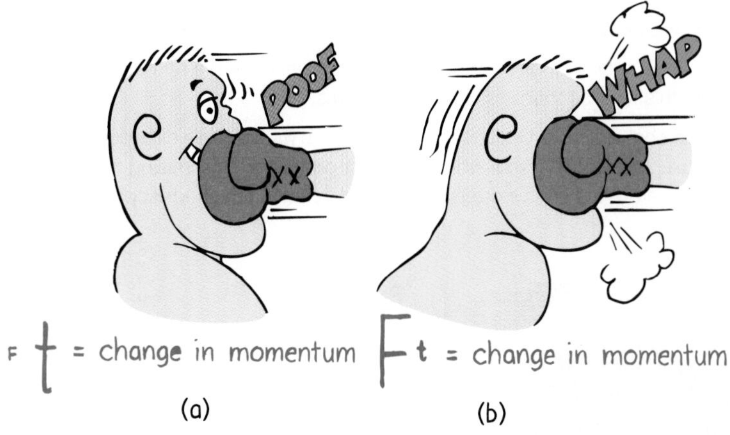

Figure 3.6
In both cases, the boxer's jaw provides an impulse that reduces the momentum of the punch. (a) The boxer is moving away when the glove hits, thereby extending the time of contact. This means the force is less than if the boxer had not moved. (b) The boxer is moving into the glove, thereby lessening the time of contact. This means that the force is greater than if the boxer had not moved.

Case 3: Decreasing Momentum over a Short Time

When boxing, if you move into a punch instead of away from it, you're in trouble. The same is true if you catch a high-speed baseball while your hand is moving toward the ball instead of away from it at the time of contact. Or, when out of control in a car, if you drive it into a concrete wall instead of into a haystack, you're really in trouble. In these cases of short impact times, the impact forces are large. Remember that, for an object brought to rest, the impulse is the same no matter how it is stopped. But, if the time is short, the force will be large.

Figure 3.7
Cassy imparts a large impulse to the bricks in a short time and produces a considerable force.

The idea of short time of contact explains how a karate expert can sever a stack of bricks with the blow of her bare hand (Figure 3.7). She brings her hand swiftly against the bricks with considerable momentum. This momentum is quickly reduced when she delivers an impulse to the bricks. The impulse is the force of her hand against the bricks multiplied by the time her hand makes contact with the bricks. By swift execution, her time of contact is very brief, with a correspondingly huge force of impact. If her hand is made to bounce upon impact, the force is even greater.

☑ CHECKPOINT

1. If the boxer in Figure 3.6 makes the time of contact three times as long by riding with the punch, by how much is the force reduced?
2. If the boxer instead moves into the punch and shortens the contact time by half, by how much is the force increased?
3. A boxer being hit with a punch tries to extend time of contact for best results, whereas a karate expert delivers a blow in a short time for best results. Isn't there a contradiction here?

Check Your Answers

1. The force will be one-third as great as it would have been if he hadn't pulled back.
2. The force will be two times greater than it would have been if he had held his head still. Forces of this kind account for many knockouts.
3. There is no contradiction, because the best results for each are different. The best result for the boxer is reduced force, which is accomplished by maximizing time. The best result for the karate expert is increased force delivered in the shortest possible time.

Figure 3.8
Teacher Howie Brand shows that the block topples when the swinging dart bounces from it. When he removes the rubber head of the dart so it doesn't bounce when it hits the block, no tipping occurs.

Bouncing

You know that, if a flower pot falls from a shelf onto your head, you may be in trouble. If it bounces from your head, you may be in even more trouble. Why? Because impulses are greater when an object bounces. The impulse required to bring an object to a stop and then to "throw it back again" is greater than the impulse required merely to bring it to a stop. Suppose, for example, that you catch the falling pot with your hands. You provide an impulse to reduce its momentum to zero. If you throw the pot upward again, you have to provide additional impulse. It takes more impulse to catch it and throw it back up than merely to catch it. This increased amount of impulse is supplied by your head if the pot bounces from it.

An interesting application of the greater impulse that is provided by bouncing was employed with great success in California during the gold-rush days. The water wheels used in gold-mining operations were not very effective. A man named Lester A. Pelton saw that the problem had to do with their flat paddles. He designed curved-shape paddles that would cause the incident water to make a U-turn—to "bounce." In this way, the impulse exerted on the water wheels was increased. Pelton patented his idea, and he made more money from his invention, the Pelton wheel, than most gold miners earned from gold.

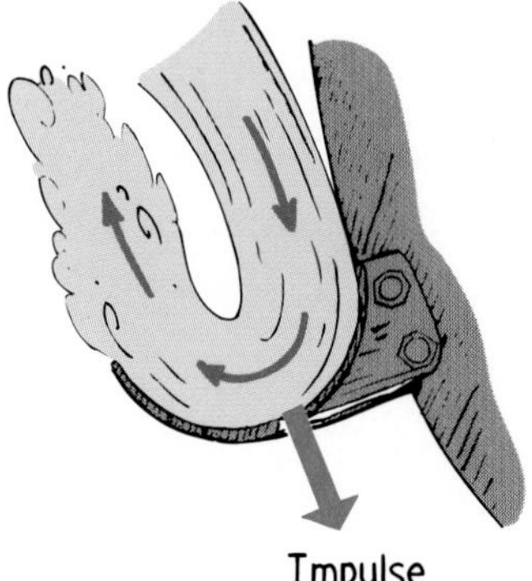

Figure 3.9
The Pelton wheel. The curved blades cause water to bounce and make a U-turn, which produces a greater impulse to turn the wheel.

☑ CHECKPOINT

1. Refer to Figure 3.7. How does the force that Cassy exerts on the bricks compare with the force exerted on her hand?
2. How will the impulse differ if her hand bounces back when striking the bricks?

Check Your Answers

1. In accord with Newton's third law, the forces are equal. Only the resilience of the human hand and the training she has undergone to toughen her hand allow her to perform this without breaking bones.
2. The impulse will be greater if her hand bounces from the bricks. If the time of contact is not increased, a greater force is then exerted on the bricks (and her hand!).

3.4 Conservation of Momentum

Newton's second law tells us that, if we want to accelerate an object, we must apply a force to it. The force must be an external force. If we want to accelerate a car whose engine can't be started, we must push the car from the outside. Inside forces don't qualify—sitting inside the automobile and pushing against the dashboard, with the dashboard pushing back, has no effect in accelerating the automobile. Likewise, if we want to change the momentum of an object, the force must be external. In the impulse–momentum concept, $Ft = \Delta mv$, internal forces have no influence. If no external force is present, then no change in momentum is possible.

Consider a cannon being fired. Both the force that drives the cannonball and the force that makes the cannon recoil are equal and opposite (Newton's third law). To the system consisting of the cannon and the cannonball, they are internal forces. No external net force acts on the cannon–cannonball system, so the momentum of the system undergoes no net change (Figure 3.10). Before

Figure 3.10
The momentum before firing is zero. After firing, the net momentum is still zero, because the momentum of the cannon is equal and opposite to the momentum of the cannonball.

the firing, the momentum is zero; after firing, the *net* momentum is still zero. Like velocity, momentum is a *vector quantity*. The momentum gained by the cannonball is equal and opposite to the momentum gained by the recoiling cannon.* They cancel. No momentum is gained, and no momentum is lost.

Whenever a physical quantity remains unchanged during a process, that quantity is said to be *conserved*. We say momentum is conserved.

The concept that momentum is conserved when no external force acts is so important that it is considered one of the basic laws of mechanics. It is called the **law of conservation of momentum**:

In the absence of an external force, the momentum of a system remains unchanged.

Newton's first law tells us that a body in motion remains in motion when no external forces act. We say the same thing in a different context when we say the momentum of a body doesn't change when no external forces act. Whatever momentum a system may have, in the absence of external force, that momentum remains unchanged. For example, the forces involved in an exploding star are internal forces, which means the net momentum of its flying fragments is the same as the star's momentum before explosion. If the star is initially spinning, the fragments maintain their *rotational momentum* (which we'll treat in Appendix B).

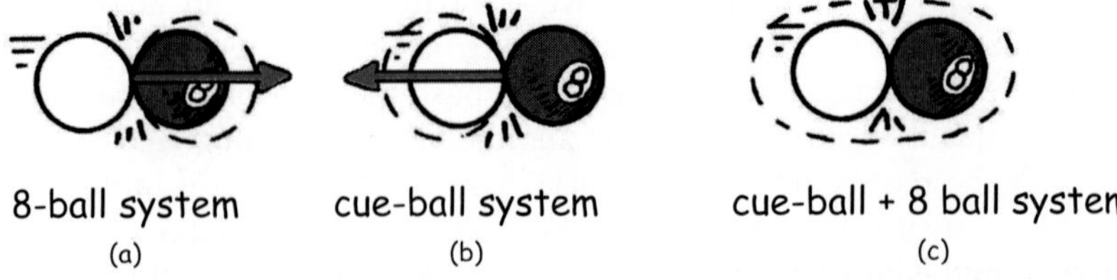

Figure 3.11
A cue ball hits an eight ball head-on. Consider this event in three systems: (a) An external force acts on the eight-ball system, and its momentum increases. (b) An external force acts on the cue-ball system, and its momentum decreases. (c) No external force acts on the cue-ball-plus-eight-ball system, and momentum is conserved (momentum is simply transferred from one part of the system to the other).

*Here we neglect the momentum of ejected gases from the exploding gunpowder, which can be considerable. Firing a gun with blanks at close range is a definite no-no because of the momentum of ejecting gases. More than one person has been killed by close-range firing of blanks. In 1998, a minister in Jacksonville, Florida, dramatizing his sermon before several hundred parishioners, including his family, shot himself in the head with a blank round from a .357-caliber magnum. Although no slug emerged from the gun, exhaust gases did—enough to be lethal. So, strictly speaking, momentum of the bullet (if any) + exhaust gases is equal to the opposite momentum of the recoiling gun.

☑ CHECKPOINT

If you toss a ball horizontally while standing on a skateboard, you'll roll backward with the same amount of momentum given to the ball. Will you roll backward if you go through the motions of tossing the ball but instead hold onto it?

Check Your Answer

No, you'll not roll backward without immediately rolling forward to produce no net rolling. In third-law fashion, if no net force acts on the ball, no net force acts on you. In terms of momentum, if no net momentum is imparted to the ball, no net momentum will be imparted to you. Try it and see!

Collisions

The conservation of momentum is especially useful in collisions, where the forces involved are internal forces. In any collision, we can say that

Net momentum before collision = net momentum after collision.

When a moving billiard ball hits another billiard ball at rest head on, the first ball comes to rest and the second ball moves with the initial velocity of the first ball. We call this an **elastic collision**; the colliding objects rebound without lasting deformation or the generation of heat. In this collision, momentum is transferred from the first ball to the second (Figure 3.12). Momentum is conserved. Billiard balls approximate perfectly elastic collisions, while collisions between molecules in a gas are perfectly elastic.

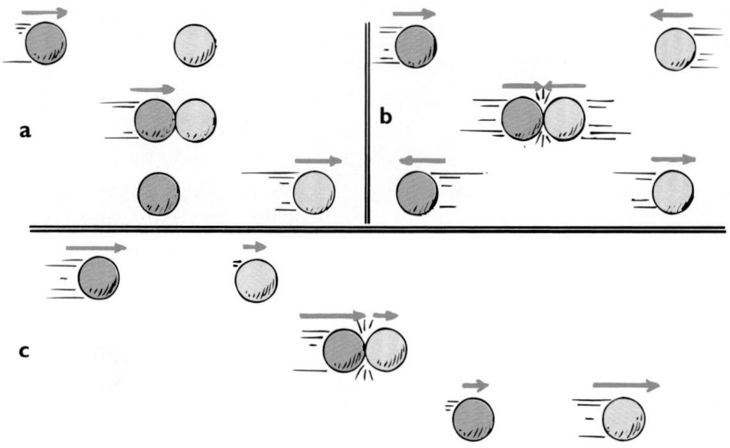

Figure 3.12
Elastic collisions of equally massive balls.
(a) A green ball strikes a yellow ball at rest.
(b) A head-on collision.
(c) A collision of balls moving in the same direction. In each case, the balls exchange roles. Each ball acquires the momentum that the other one had.

Momentum is conserved even when the colliding objects don't rebound. This is an **inelastic collision,** characterized by deformation and/or the generation of heat. Sometimes an inelastic collision results in the coupling of colliding objects. Consider, for example, the case of a freight car moving along a track and colliding with another freight car at rest (Figure 3.13). If the freight cars are of equal mass and are coupled by the collision, can we predict the velocity of the coupled cars after the impact?

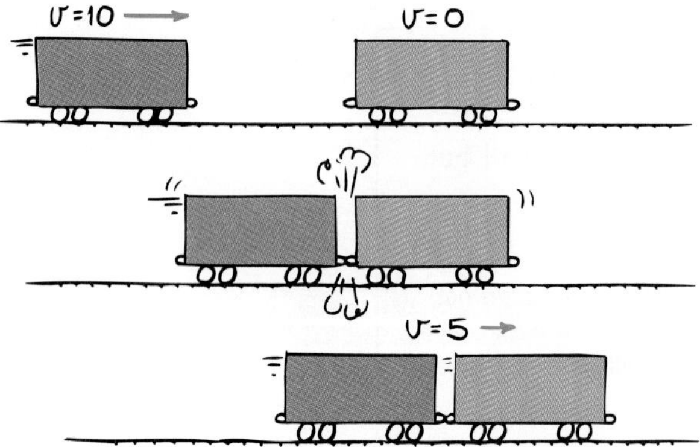

Figure 3.13
Inelastic collision. After the collision, the two cars together have the same momentum that the freight car on the left had before the collision.

Suppose the moving car has a velocity of 10 meters per second, and we consider the mass of each car to be m. Then, from the conservation of momentum,

$$(\text{net } mv)_{\text{before}} = (\text{net } mv)_{\text{after}}$$
$$(m \times 10)_{\text{before}} = (2m \times v)_{\text{after}}$$

By simple algebra, $v = 5$ m/s. This makes sense because, since twice as much mass is moving after the collision, the velocity must be half as much as the velocity before collision. Both sides of the equation are then equal.

Figure 3.14
An air track. Blasts of air from tiny holes provide a friction-free air cushion for the carts to glide upon.

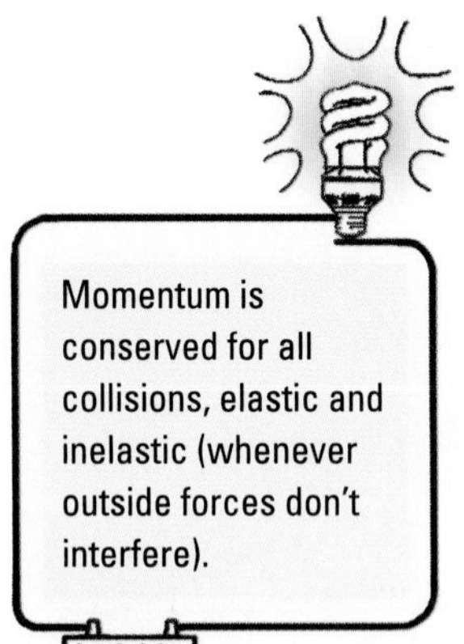

If your instructor has an air track similar to the one shown in Figure 3.14, you may be treated to fascinating demonstrations of momentum conservation. The air that spurts from the tiny holes in the track lets you see an almost friction-free performance. In the everyday world, friction usually shows itself. Ideally, the net momentum of a couple of freight cars that collide is the same before and just after the collision. But, as the combined cars move along the track, friction provides an impulse to decrease momentum.

So we see that changes in an object's motion depend both on force and on how long the force acts. When "how long" means time, we refer to the quantity "force × time" as *impulse*. But "how long" can mean distance also. When we consider the quantity "force × *distance*," we are talking about something entirely different—the concept of *energy*.

Figuring Physical Science

Problem

Consider the air track in Figure 3.14. Suppose that a gliding cart with a mass of 0.5 kg bumps into, and sticks to, a stationary cart that has a mass of 1.5 kg. If the speed of the gliding cart before impact is 4 m/s, how fast will the coupled carts glide after collision?

Solution

According to momentum conservation, the momentum of the cart of mass m and velocity v before the collision will equal the momentum of both carts stuck together after.

$$(\text{total } mv)_{\text{before}} = (\text{total } mv)_{\text{after}}$$
$$0.5 \text{ kg } (4 \text{ m/s}) = (0.5 \text{ kg} + 1.5 \text{ kg})v$$
$$v = [(0.5 \text{ kg})(4 \text{ m/s})/(0.5 \text{ kg} + 1.5 \text{ kg})]$$
$$= [(2.0 \text{ kg}\cdot\text{m/s})/2.0 \text{ kg}] = 1 \text{ m/s}$$

This makes sense, because four times as much mass will be moving after the collision, so the coupled carts will glide more slowly. In keeping the momentum equal, four times the mass glides one-quarter as fast.

3.5 Energy

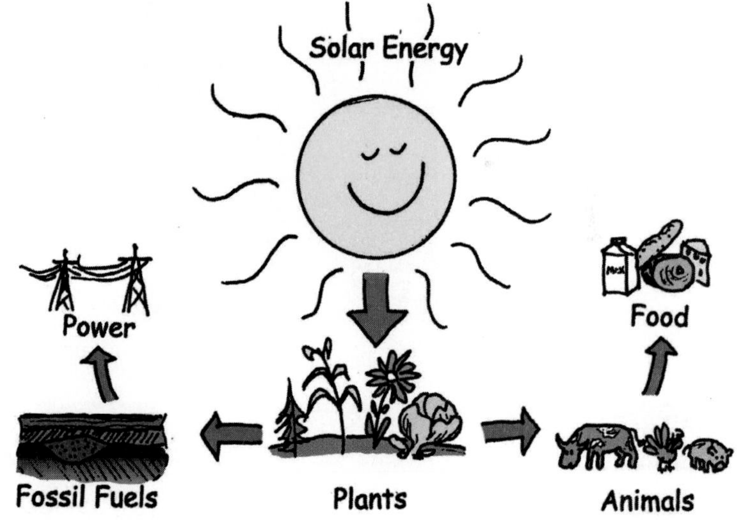

Figure 3.15
Energy transformations.

Energy is perhaps the most central concept in science. The combination of energy and matter makes up the universe: matter is substance, and energy is the mover of substance. The idea of matter is easy to grasp—it is stuff that we can see, smell, and feel. It has mass and it occupies space. Energy, on the other hand, is abstract. We cannot see, smell, or feel most forms of energy. It isn't even noticeable unless it is undergoing a change of some kind—being transferred or being transformed. Surprisingly, the idea of energy was unknown to Isaac Newton, and its existence was still being debated in the 1850s. Energy comes from the sun in the form of sunlight, it is in the food you eat, and it sustains all life. It's in heat, sound, electricity, and radiation. Even matter itself is condensed, bottled-up energy, as set forth in Einstein's famous formula $E = mc^2$, which we'll return to in Chapters 16 and 35. For now, we will begin our study of energy with a related concept: *work*.

First we talked about force × time—impulse. Now we talk about force × distance—work.

Insights

Figure 3.16
The man may expend energy when he pushes on the wall, but, if it doesn't move, no work is performed on the wall.

The word *work,* in common usage, means physical or mental exertion. Don't confuse the physical-science definition of work with the everyday notion of work.

Insights

Work

In Sections 3.2 and 3.3, we learned about impulse—force × time. Now we will consider the quantity force × *distance*, an entirely different quantity—**work.**

Work = force × distance

In every case in which work is done, two things enter: (1) the exertion of a force and (2) the movement of something by that force.* For example, if we lift two loads one story high, we do twice as much work as we do lifting one load the same distance, because the *force* needed to lift twice the weight is twice as much. Similarly, if we lift a load two stories high instead of one story high, we do twice as much work, because the *distance* is twice as much.

When a weightlifter raises a heavy barbell, he does work on the barbell and gives energy to it. Interestingly, when a weightlifter simply holds a barbell overhead, he does no work on it. Work involves not only force but motion as well. He may get tired holding the barbell still, but, if the barbell is not moved by the force he exerts, he does no work *on the barbell.* Work may be done on his muscles, as they stretch and contract, which is force × distance on a biological scale. But this work is not done *on the barbell. Lifting* the barbell is different than *holding* the barbell.

Figure 3.17
Work is done in lifting the barbell. If the weightlifter were taller, he would have to expend proportionally more energy to press the barbell over his head.

The unit of work combines the unit of force (N) with the unit of distance (m), the newton-meter (N·m). We call a newton-meter the *joule* (J), which rhymes with *cool.* One joule of work is done when a force of 1 newton is exerted over a distance of 1 meter in the direction of the force, as in lifting an apple over your head. For larger values, we speak of kilojoules (kJ), thousands of joules, or megajoules (MJ), millions of joules. The weightlifter in Figure 3.17 does work that can be measured in kilojoules. The work done to vertically hoist a heavily loaded truck can be measured in megajoules.

Figuring Physical Science

Problems

1. How much work is needed to lift an object that weighs 500 N to a height of 2 m?
2. How much work is needed to lift it twice as high?
3. How much work is needed to lift a 1000-N object to a height of 4 m?

Solutions

1. $W = F \times d = 500\text{ N} \times 2\text{ m} = 1000\text{ J}$.
2. Twice the height requires twice the work. That is, $W = F \times d = 500\text{ N} \times 4\text{ m} = 2000\text{ J}$.
3. Lifting twice the load twice as high requires four times the work. That is, $F \times d = 1000\text{ N} \times 4\text{ m} = 4000\text{ J}$.

*Force and distance must be in the same direction. When force is not along the direction of motion, then work equals the *component* of force in the direction of motion × distance moved.

3.6 Power

The definition of work says nothing about how long it takes to do the work. The same amount of work is done when carrying a load up a flight of stairs, whether we walk up or run up. So why are we more tired after running upstairs in a few seconds than after walking upstairs in a few minutes? To understand this difference, we need to talk about a measure of how fast the work is done—**power**. Power is the rate at which work is done—the amount of work done divided by the time it takes to do it:

$$\text{power} = \frac{\text{work done}}{\text{time interval}}$$

The work done in climbing stairs requires more power when the worker is running up rapidly than it does when the worker is climbing slowly. A high-power automobile engine does work rapidly. An engine that delivers twice the power of another, however, does not necessarily move a car twice as fast or twice as far. Twice the power means that the engine can do twice the work in the same amount of time—or it can do the same amount of work in half the time. A powerful engine can produce greater acceleration.

Power is also the rate at which energy is changed from one form to another. The unit of power is the joule per second, called the **watt**. This unit was named in honor of James Watt, the eighteenth-century developer of the steam engine. One watt (W) of power is used when one joule of work is done in one second. One kilowatt (kW) equals 1000 watts. One megawatt (MW) equals one million watts.

Figure 3.18
The three main engines of a space shuttle can develop 33,000 MW of power when fuel is burned at the enormous rate of 3400 kg/s. This is like emptying an average-size swimming pool in 20 s.

Figuring Physical Science

Problems

1. How much power is expended when lifting a 1000-N load a vertical distance of 4 m in a time of 2 s?
2. How much power is needed to perform the same job in 1 s?

Solutions

1. Power $= \frac{\text{work done}}{\text{time interval}} = 1000\text{ N} \times 4\text{ m/2 s}$
$= 4000\text{ J/2 s} = 2000\text{ W}$ (or 2 kW).
2. Twice the power is needed to do the same job in half the time. That is,
Power $= \frac{\text{work done}}{\text{time interval}} = 4000\text{ J/1 s}$
$= 4000\text{ W}$ (or 4 kW).

Figure 3.19
The potential energy of Tenny's drawn bow equals the work (average force × distance) she did in drawing the arrow into position. When released, the potential energy of the drawn bow will become the kinetic energy of the arrow.

3.7 Potential Energy

An object can store energy due to its position, shape, or state. Such stored energy is called **potential energy** (PE), because, in the stored state, it has the potential to do work. For example, a stretched or compressed spring has the potential for doing work. Or, when an archer draws an arrow with a bow, energy is stored in the fibers of the bent bow. When the bowstring is released, the energy in the bow is transferred to the arrow.

The chemical energy in fuels is potential energy, for it is energy of position from a microscopic point of view. Such energy characterizes fossil fuels, electric batteries, and the food we eat. This energy is available when atoms are rearranged—that is, when a chemical change occurs. Any substance that can do work through chemical action possesses potential energy.

The easiest-to-visualize form of potential energy is when work is done to elevate objects against the earth's gravity. The potential energy due to elevated positions is called *gravitational potential energy*. Water in an elevated reservoir and the elevated ram of a pile driver have gravitational potential energy. The amount of gravitational potential energy possessed by an elevated object is equal to the work done against gravity in lifting it. The work done equals the force required to move it upward times the vertical distance it is moved ($W = Fd$). The upward force equals the weight mg of the object. So the work done in lifting it to a given height h is given by the product mgh:

$$\text{Gravitational potential energy} = \text{weight} \times \text{height}$$
$$\text{PE} = mgh$$

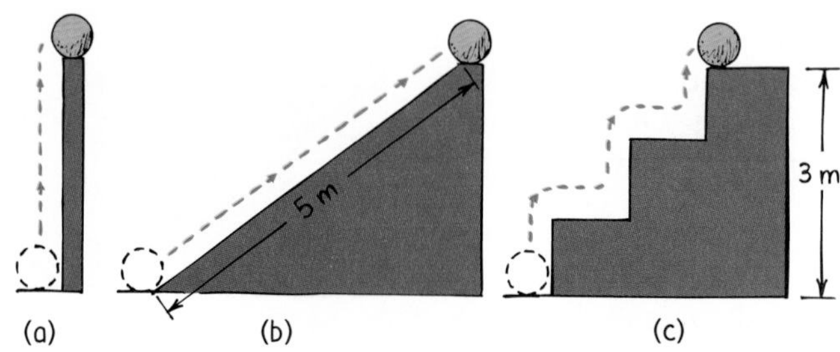

Figure 3.20
The potential energy of the 10-N ball is the same (30 J) in all three cases because the work done in elevating it 3 m is the same whether it is (a) lifted with 10 N of force, (b) pushed with 6 N of force up the 5-m incline, or (c) lifted with 10 N up each 1-m stair. No work is done in moving it horizontally (neglecting friction).

Weight = *mg*, so a 10-kg block of ice weighs 100 N.

Insights

Note that the height h is the distance above some reference level, such as the ground or the floor of a building. The potential energy mgh is relative to that level, and it depends only on mg and the height h. You can see, in Figure 3.20, that the potential energy of the ball at the top of the structure depends on vertical displacement and not on the path taken to get it there.

Figure 3.21
He raises a block of ice by lifting it vertically. She pushes an identical block of ice up the ramp. When both blocks are raised to the same vertical height, both possess the same potential energy.

Figuring Physical Science

Problems

1. How much work is done in lifting the 100-N block of ice a vertical distance of 2 m, as shown in Figure 3.21?
2. How much work is done in pushing the same block of ice up the 4-m-long ramp? The force needed is only 50 N (which is the reason inclines are used).
3. What is the increase in the block's potential energy in each case?

Solutions

1. $W = F \times d = 100\text{ N} \times 2\text{m} = 200\text{ J}$.
2. $W = F \times d = 50\text{ N} \times 4\text{ m} = 200\text{ J}$.
3. Either way increases the block's potential energy by 200 J. The ramp simply makes this work easier to perform.

3.8 Kinetic Energy

If we push on an object, we can set it in motion. More specifically, if we do work on an object, we can change the energy of motion of that object. If an object is moving, then, by virtue of that motion, it is capable of doing work. We call energy of motion **kinetic energy (KE)**. The kinetic energy of an object depends on its mass and its speed. It is equal to half the mass multiplied by the square of the speed.

$$\text{Kinetic energy} = 1/2 \text{ mass} \times \text{speed}^2$$
$$\text{KE} = 1/2\, mv^2$$

A car moving along a road has kinetic energy. A car that is twice as heavy moving at the same speed has twice the kinetic energy. That's because a car that is twice as heavy has twice the mass. Kinetic energy depends on mass. But note that it also depends on speed—not just plain speed, but speed multiplied by itself—*speed squared*. If you double the speed of a car, you'll increase its kinetic energy by *four* ($2^2 = 4$). Or, if you drive three times as fast, you will have *nine*

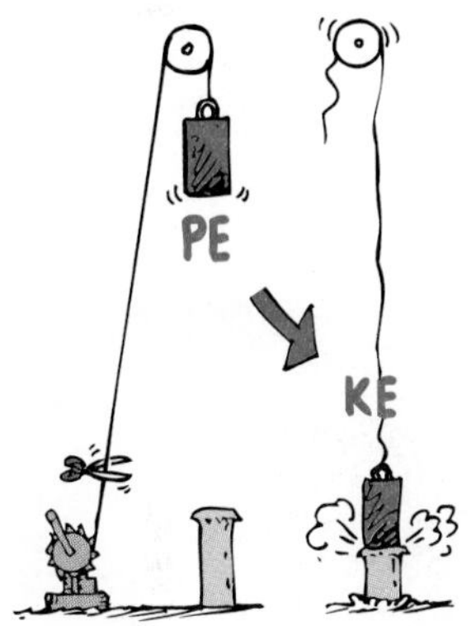

Figure 3.22
The potential energy of the elevated ram is converted to kinetic energy when released.

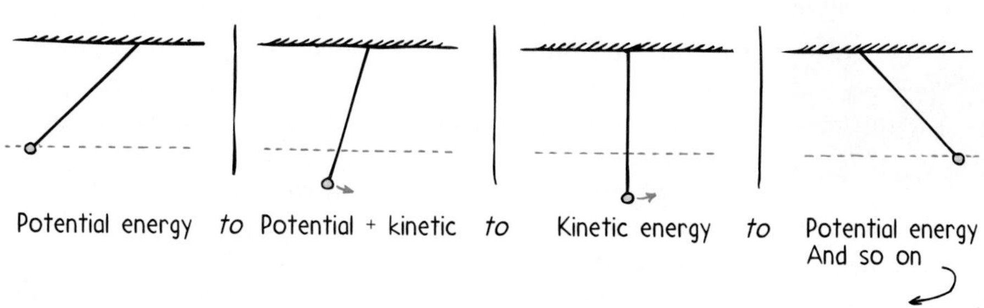

Figure 3.23
Energy transitions in a pendulum.

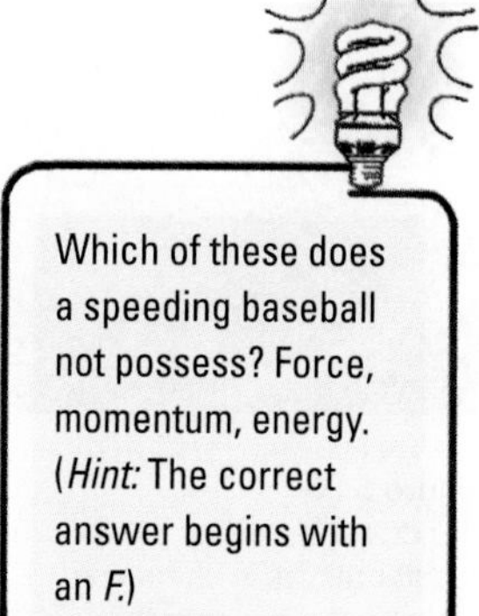

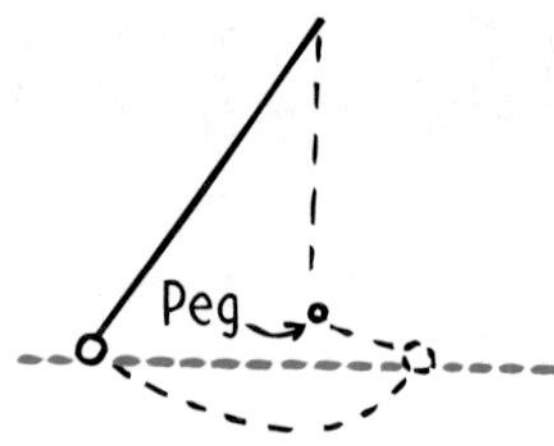

Figure 3.24
The pendulum bob will swing to its original height whether or not the peg is present.

times the kinetic energy ($3^2 = 9$). The fact that kinetic energy depends on the square of the speed means that small changes in speed can produce large changes in kinetic energy. The squaring of speed means that kinetic energy can only be zero or positive—never negative. Now let's relate this to work.

Work–Energy Theorem

To increase the kinetic energy of an object, work must be done on it. The change in kinetic energy is equal to the work done. This important relationship is called the **work–energy theorem**. We abbreviate "change in" with the delta symbol, Δ, and say

$$\text{Work} = \Delta\text{KE}$$

Work equals change in kinetic energy. The work in this equation is the *net* work—that is, the work based on the net force.

Recall that in Section 3.3, a cannonball fired from a cannon with a longer barrel has a greater velocity, because of the longer *time* of the impulse. The greater speed is also evident from the work–energy theorem, because of the longer *distance* through which the force acts. The work done on the cannonball is the force exerted on it multiplied by the distance that force acts: $Fd = \Delta\text{KE}$

The work–energy theorem emphasizes the role of *change*. If there is no change in an object's energy, then we know no net work was done on it. This theorem applies to changes in potential energy also. Recall our previous example of the weightlifter raising the barbell. When work was being done on the barbell, its potential energy was being changed. But when it was held stationary, no further work was being done on the barbell, as evidenced by no further change in its energy.

Figure 3.25
The downhill "fall" of the roller coaster results in its roaring speed in the dip, and this kinetic energy sends it up the track to the next summit.

Similarly, if you push against a box on a floor and it doesn't slide, then you are not doing work on the box. There is no change in kinetic energy. But if you push harder and it slides, then you're doing work on it. When the amount of work done to overcome friction is small, the amount of work done on the box is practically matched by its gain in kinetic energy.

The work–energy theorem applies to decreasing speed as well. Energy is required to reduce the speed of a moving object or to bring it to a halt. When we apply the brakes to slow a moving car, we do work on it. This work is the friction force supplied by the brakes multiplied by the distance over which the friction force acts. The more kinetic energy something has, the more work is required to stop it.

Interestingly, the friction supplied by the brakes is the same whether the car moves slowly or quickly. Friction doesn't depend on speed. The variable that makes a difference is the braking *distance*. A car moving at twice the speed of another takes four times ($2^2 = 4$) as much work to stop. Therefore, it takes four times as much distance to stop. Accident investigators are well aware that an automobile going 100 kilometers per hour has four times the kinetic energy as it would have at 50 kilometers per hour. So a car going 100 kilometers per hour will skid four times as far when its brakes are applied as when going 50 kilometers per hour. Kinetic energy depends on speed *squared.*

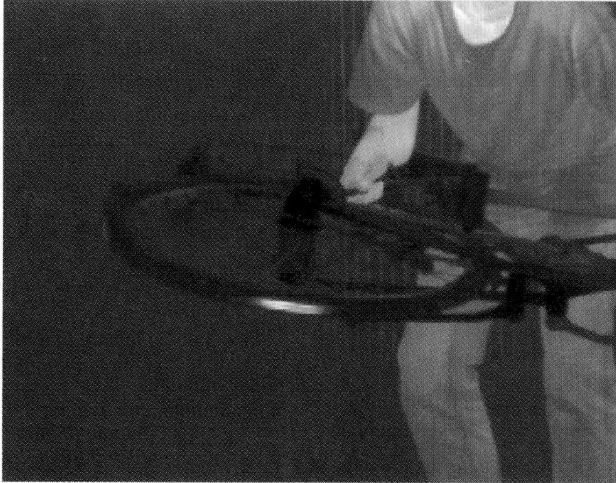

Figure 3.26
Due to the friction, energy is transferred both into the floor and into the tire when the bicycle skids to a stop. An infrared camera reveals (left) the heated tire track (red streak on the floor) and (right) the warmth of the tire. (Courtesy of Michael Vollmer.)

☑ CHECKPOINT

1. When the brakes of a car are locked, the car skids to a stop. How much farther will the car skid if it's moving three times as fast?
2. Can an object possess energy?
3. Can an object possess work?

Check Your Answers

1. Nine times farther. The car has nine times as much energy when it travels three times as fast: $1/2\ m(3v)^2 = 1/2\ m9v^2 = 9(1/2\ mv^2)$. The friction force will ordinarily be the same in either case. Therefore, to do nine times the work to stop requires nine times as much sliding distance.
2. Yes, but only in a relative sense. For example, an elevated object may possess PE relative to the ground, but none relative to a point at the same elevation. Similarly, the kinetic energy of an object is relative to a frame of reference, usually the earth's surface.
3. No, unlike energy, work is not something an object *has*. Work is something an object *does* to some other object. An object can *do* work only if it has energy. Or, stated another way, an object spends energy when it does work on something else.

Kinetic energy underlies other seemingly different forms of energy, such as heat, sound, and light. Random molecular motion is sensed as heat: when fast-moving molecules bump into the molecules in the surface of your skin, they transfer kinetic energy to your molecules, much as the balls in a game of pool or billiards transfer energy to each other. Sound consists of molecules vibrating in rhythmic patterns: shake a group of molecules in one place and, in cascade fashion, they disturb neighboring molecules that, in turn, disturb others, preserving the rhythm of shaking throughout the medium. Electrons in motion produce electric currents. Even light energy originates from the motion of electrons within atoms. Kinetic energy is far-reaching.

Figuring Physical Science

Problems

1. Calculate the change in kinetic energy when a 50-kg shopping cart moving at 2 m/s is pushed to a speed of 6 m/s.
2. How much work is required to make this change in kinetic energy?

Solutions

1. $\Delta KE = 1/2\, m\, (v_f^2 - v_o^2)$
   $= 1/2(50 \text{ kg})[(6 \text{ m/s})^2 - (2 \text{ m/s})^2]$
   $= 800 \text{ J}.$
2. $W = \Delta KE = 800$ J, because the change in KE equals the work done on the shopping cart.

Understanding the distinction between momentum and kinetic energy is high-level physics.

Insights

Comparison of Kinetic Energy and Momentum

Momentum and kinetic energy are properties of moving things, but they differ from each other. Like velocity, momentum is a vector quantity and is therefore directional and capable of being cancelled entirely. But kinetic energy is a nonvector (scalar) quantity, like mass, and can never be cancelled. The momenta (plural of momentum) of two firecrackers approaching each other may cancel, but, when they explode, there is no way their energies can cancel. Energies transform to other forms; momenta do not. Another difference is the velocity dependence of the two. Whereas momentum depends on velocity (mv), kinetic energy depends on the square of velocity ($1/2mv^2$). An object that moves with twice the velocity of another object of the same mass has twice the momentum but four times the kinetic energy. So when a car traveling twice as fast crashes, it crashes with four times the energy.

If the distinction between momentum and kinetic energy isn't really clear to you, you're in good company. Failure to make this distinction, when impedo was in vogue, resulted in disagreements and arguments between the best British and French physicists for two centuries.

3.9 Conservation of Energy

Whenever energy is transformed or transferred, none is lost and none is gained. In the absence of work input or output, the total energy of a system before some process or event is equal to the total energy after.

Consider the system of a bow, arrow, and target. In the process of drawing the arrow in the bow, we do work in bending the bow; we give the arrow and bow potential energy. When the bowstring is released, most of this potential energy is transferred to the arrow as kinetic energy (the rest slightly warms the bow). The arrow, in turn, transfers this energy to its target, perhaps a bale of hay. The distance the arrow penetrates into the hay multiplied by the average force of impact doesn't quite match the kinetic energy of the arrow. The

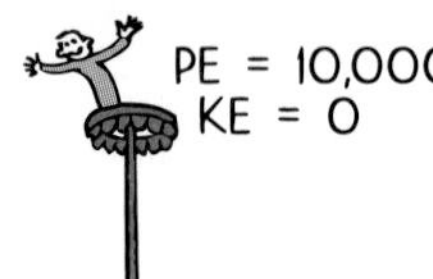

Figure 3.27
A circus diver at the top of a pole has a potential energy of 10,000 J. As he dives, his potential energy converts to kinetic energy. Note that, at successive positions (one-fourth, one-half, three-fourths, and all the way down), the total energy is constant.

The Swinging Wonder

Momentum conservation is nicely demonstrated with the swinging wonder, the novel device shown in the photo. When a single ball is raised and allowed to swing into the array of other identical balls, a single ball from the other side pops out. When two balls are similarly raised and released, presto—two balls on the other side pop out. The number of balls incident on the array is always the same as the number of balls that emerge. We can see that *momentum before* = *momentum after*. That is, $mv = mv$, or $2mv = 2mv$, or $3mv = 3mv$, and so on. An intriguing question arises: When a single ball is raised, released, and makes impact, why cannot two balls emerge with half the speed? Or, if two balls make impact, why cannot one ball emerge with twice the speed? If either of these cases were to occur, the momentum before would still be equal to the momentum after: $mv = 2m(1/2\ v)$; or $2mv = m(2v)$. Intriguingly, this never occurs. Nor can it occur.

Why? Because something besides momentum must be conserved in this interaction—energy. Because the collisions are quite elastic, with very little energy transforming to heat and sound, to a good approximation, the kinetic energy before equals the kinetic energy after. That is, $1/2\ mv^2_{before} = 1/2\ mv^2_{after}$. Consider dropping two balls, with one emerging at twice the speed. Then will $1/2\ 2mv^2 = 1/2\ m(2v)^2$? The answer is *no*. If this case were to occur, there would be more energy after the collision than before. (We'll leave it to you to figure how much more.) Give this some thought and you'll see there is a reason why, for identical balls, the number of balls that make impact will always equal the number of balls that emerge.

In any collision, elastic or inelastic, momentum before collision equals momentum after collision. In the special case of a perfectly elastic collision, where no energy is transformed to other forms, kinetic energy before collision equals kinetic energy after collision.

Why is this device called the swinging wonder? Because the unequal-balls situation and its impossibility has left many people wondering, and wondering, and wondering. But you know the reason why the number of incident and emerging balls must be the same. It's nice to know some physics!

energy score doesn't balance. But, if we investigate further, we discover that both the arrow and the hay are a bit warmer. By how much? By the energy difference. In these transformations of energy, taking the form of thermal energy into account, we find energy transforms without net loss or net gain. Quite remarkable!

The study of various forms of energy and their transformations has led to one of the greatest generalizations in physics—the law of **conservation of energy:**

> **In the absence of external work input or output, the energy of a system remains unchanged. Energy cannot be created or destroyed.**

When we consider any system in its entirety, whether it be as simple as a swinging pendulum or as complex as an exploding galaxy, there is one quantity that doesn't change: energy. It may change form or it may simply be

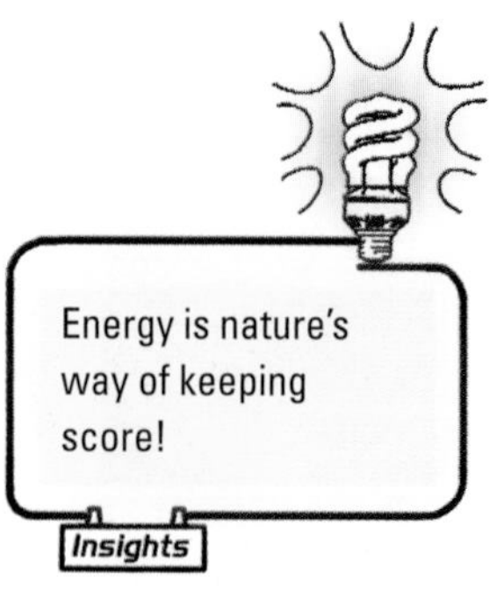

transferred from one part of a system to another, but, as far as we can tell, the total energy score remains the same. This energy score takes into account the fact that the atoms that make up matter are themselves concentrated bundles of energy. When the nuclei (cores) of atoms rearrange themselves, enormous amounts of energy can be released. The sun shines because some of this energy is transformed into radiant energy. In nuclear reactors, much of this energy is transformed into heat. Enormous gravitational forces in the deep hot core of the sun push hydrogen nuclei together to form helium. This welding together of atomic nuclei is called *thermonuclear fusion* (Chapter 16). This process produces radiant energy, some of which reaches the earth. Part of this energy falls on plants, and part of this, in turn, later becomes coal. Another part supports life in the food chain that begins with plants, and part of this energy later becomes oil. Part of the energy from the sun powers the evaporation of water from the ocean, and part of this returns to the earth as rain that may be trapped behind a dam. By virtue of its position, the water behind a dam has energy that may be used to power a generating plant below, where it will be transformed to electric energy. The energy travels through wires to homes, where it is used for lighting, heating, cooking, and operating electric gadgets. How wonderful that energy is transformed from one form to another!

☑ CHECKPOINT

Challenge Questions Rows of wind-powered generators are used in various windy locations to generate electric power. Does the power generated affect the speed of the wind? Would locations behind the windmills be windier if they weren't there?

Answers

Windmills generate power by taking kinetic energy from the wind, so the wind is slowed by interaction with the windmill blades. So yes, it would be windier behind the windmills if they weren't present.

3.10 Machines

A *machine* is a device for multiplying forces or simply changing the direction of forces. Underlying every machine is the *conservation of energy*. Consider one of the simplest machines, the **lever** (Figure 3.28). At the same time we do work on one end of the lever, the other end does work on the load. We see that the direction of force is changed: if we push down, the load is lifted up. If the heat from friction forces is small enough to neglect, the work input will be equal to the work output.

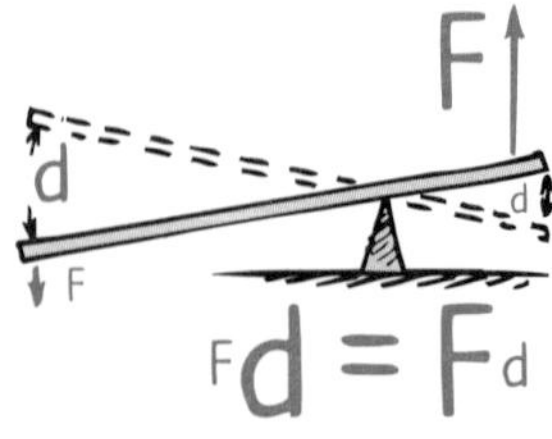

Figure 3.28
The lever.

$$\text{Work input} = \text{work output}$$

Since work equals force times distance

$$(\text{Force} \times \text{distance})_{\text{input}} = (\text{force} \times \text{distance})_{\text{output}}$$

If the pivot point, or *fulcrum,* of the lever is relatively close to the load, then a small input force will produce a large output force. This is because the input force is exerted through a large distance and the load is moved over a correspondingly short distance. In this way, a lever can multiply forces. But no machine can multiply work or multiply energy. That's a conservation-of-energy no-no!

You use the principle of the lever in jacking up the front end of an automobile. By exerting a small force through a large distance, you are able to provide a large force acting through a small distance. Consider the ideal example illustrated in Figure 3.29. Every time the jack handle is pushed down 25 centimeters, the car rises 0.25 centimeters—only a hundredth as far, but with 100 times the force.

Figure 3.29
Applied force × applied distance = output force × output distance.

A block and tackle, or system of pulleys, is a simple machine that multiplies force at the expense of distance. One can exert a relatively small force through a relatively large distance and lift a heavy load through a relatively short distance. With the ideal pulley system shown in Figure 3.32, the man pulls 7 meters of rope with a force of 50 newtons and lifts 350 newtons through a vertical distance of 1 meter. The work done by the man in pulling the rope is numerically equal to the increased potential energy of the 350-newton block.

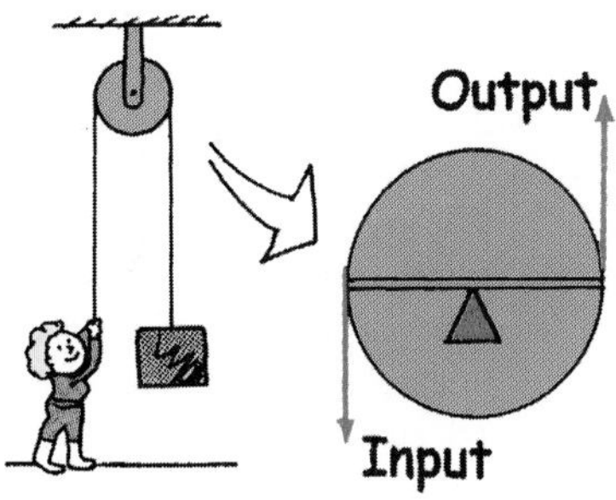

Figure 3.30
This pulley acts like a lever. It changes only the direction of the force.

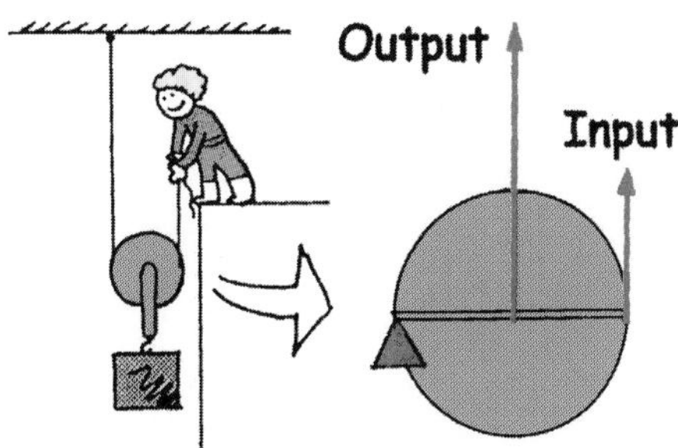

Figure 3.31
In this arrangement, a load can be lifted with half the input force.

Figure 3.32
Applied force × applied distance = output force × output distance.

Any machine that multiplies force does so at the expense of distance. Likewise, any machine that multiplies distance, such as that of your forearm and elbow, does so at the expense of force. No machine or device can put out more energy than is put into it. No machine can create energy; it can only transfer it from one place to another or transform it from one form to another.

☑ CHECKPOINT

If a lever is arranged so that input distance is twice output distance, can we predict that energy output will be doubled?

Check Your Answer

No, no, a thousand times no! We can predict output *force* will be doubled, but never output *energy*. Work and energy remain the same, which means force × distance remains the same. Shorter distance means greater force, and vice versa. Be careful to distinguish between the concepts of *force* and *energy*.

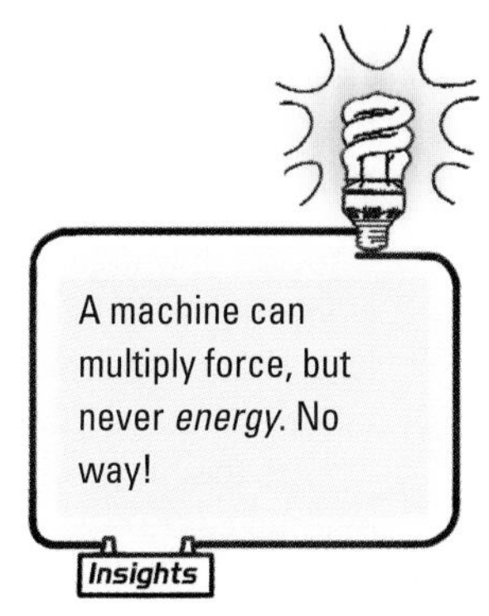

Efficiency

Given the same energy input, some machines can do more work than others. The machines that can perform more work are said to be more efficient. **Efficiency** can be expressed by the ratio,

$$\text{Efficiency} = \frac{\text{work done}}{\text{energy used}}$$

Even a lever converts a small fraction of input energy into heat when it rotates about its fulcrum. We may do 100 joules of work but get out only 98 joules. The lever is then 98% efficient, and we waste 2 joules of work input as heat. In a pulley system, a larger fraction of input energy goes into heat. If we do 100 joules of work, the forces of friction acting through the distances through which the pulleys turn and rub about their axles may dissipate 60 joules of energy as heat. So the work output is only 40 joules, and the pulley system has an efficiency of 40%. The lower the efficiency of a machine, the greater the amount of energy wasted as heat.

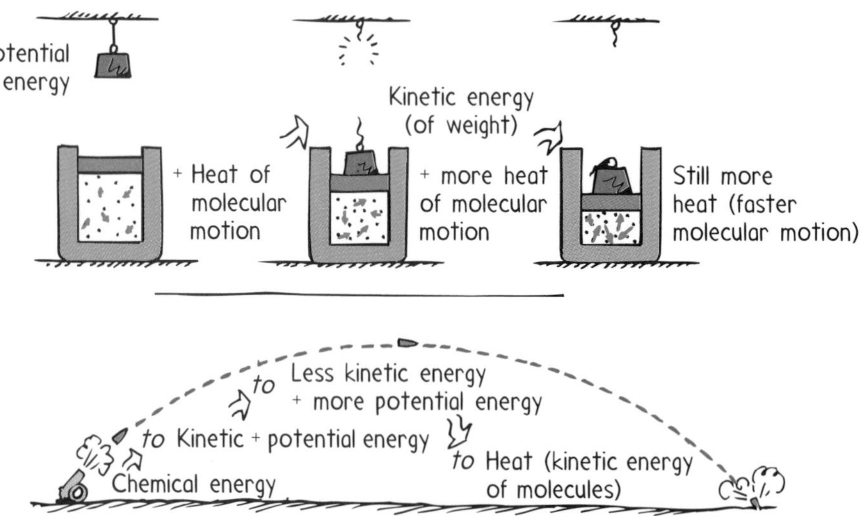

Figure 3.33
Energy transitions. The graveyard of kinetic energy is strewn with heat.

Figuring Physical Science

Problems

1. Consider an imaginary dream car that has a 100% efficient engine and burns fuel that has an energy content of 40 megajoules per liter. If the air resistance plus frictional forces on the car traveling at highway speed is 500 N, what is the maximum distance the car can go on one liter of fuel?

2. One can only dream of a car with a 100% efficient engine. More realistically, a car engine is about 30% efficient. With the same air resistance and same fuel as the car in problem 1, what is the maximum distance per liter for the realistic car?

Solutions

1. From the definition work = force × distance, simple rearrangement gives distance = work/force. If all 40 MJ of energy in 1 liter is used to do the work of overcoming the air resistance and frictional forces, the distance covered is:

$$\text{distance} = \frac{\text{work}}{\text{force}} = \frac{40{,}000{,}000 \text{ J}}{500 \text{ N}} = 80{,}000 \text{ m} = 80 \text{ km}$$

The important point here is that, even with a perfect engine, there is an upper limit of fuel economy dictated by the conservation of energy.

2. The realistic distance per liter is 30% of 80 km = 0.3 (80 km) = 24 km/liter.

An automobile engine is a machine that transforms chemical energy stored in gasoline into mechanical energy. But only a fraction of the energy stored in the fuel actually moves the car. Nearly half is wasted in the friction of the moving engine parts. Some goes out in the hot exhaust gases as waste. In addition to these inefficiencies, some of the fuel doesn't even burn completely and goes unused.

3.11 Sources of Energy

Except for nuclear power, the source of practically all our energy is the sun. Even the energy we obtain from petroleum, coal, natural gas, and wood originally came from the sun. That's because these fuels are created by photosynthesis—the process by which plants trap solar energy and store it as plant tissue.

Figure 3.34
With the exception of nuclear power, all the earth's energy comes from the sun.

Sunlight can be directly transformed into electricity by photovoltaic cells, like those found in solar-powered calculators. Energy from the sun is used to generate electricity indirectly as well. Sunlight evaporates water, which later falls as rain; rainwater flows into rivers and into dams where it is directed to generator turbines. Then it returns to the sea, where the cycle continues.

Wind, caused by unequal warming of the earth's surface, is another form of solar power. The energy of wind can be used to turn generator turbines within specially equipped windmills. Because wind power is unreliable, concentrated energy sources such as fossil and nuclear fuels are the choice contenders for large-scale power production.

The most concentrated form of usable energy is stored in uranium and plutonium, which are nuclear fuels. Public fear about nuclear processes prevents further development of nuclear power. But it is interesting to note that the earth's interior is kept hot because of nuclear power, which has been with us since time zero.

A byproduct of nuclear power in the earth's interior is geothermal energy. Geothermal energy is held in underground reservoirs of hot water. Geothermal energy is predominantly limited to areas of volcanic activity, such as Iceland, New Zealand, Japan, and Hawaii. In these locations, heated water near the earth's surface is tapped to provide steam for driving turbogenerators.

In locations where heat from volcanic activity is near the ground surface and ground water is absent, another method holds promise for producing electricity. That's dry-rock geothermal power (Figure 3.35). With this method, water is put into cavities in deep, dry, hot rock. When the water turns to steam, it is piped to a turbine at the surface. After turning the turbine, it is returned to the cavity for reuse. In this way, electricity is produced inexpensively and cleanly.

Except for geothermal power, methods for obtaining energy have serious environmental consequences. Although nuclear power doesn't pollute the atmosphere, it is controversial because of the nuclear wastes that are generated. The combustion of fossil fuels, on the other hand, leads to increased atmospheric concentrations of carbon dioxide, sulfur dioxide, and other pollutants. Methods of using solar energy are limited, in that they require proper atmospheric conditions.

As the world population increases, so does our need for energy. Common sense dictates that, as alternate sources are being developed, we should continue to optimize present sources and to use what we consume efficiently and wisely.

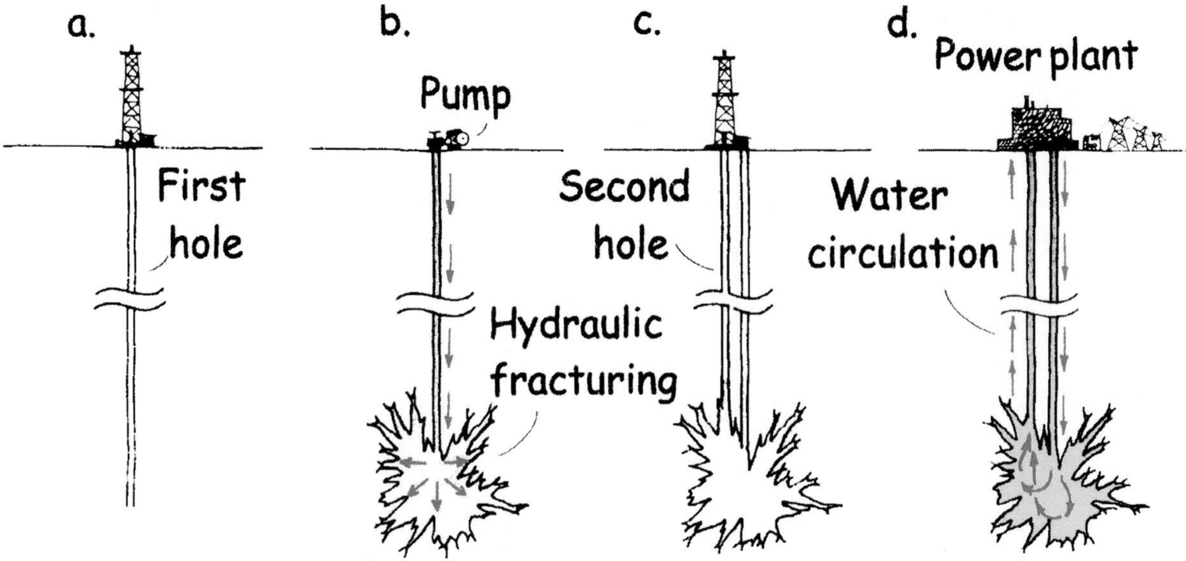

Figure 3.35
Dry-rock geothermal power. (a) A hole is sunk several kilometers into dry granite. (b) Water is pumped into the hole at high pressure, and it fractures the surrounding rock to form a cavity with increased surface area. (c) A second hole is sunk to intercept the cavity. (d) Water is circulated down one hole and through the cavity, where it is superheated, before rising through the second hole. After driving a turbine, it is recirculated into the hot cavity again, making a closed cycle.

Summary of Terms

Momentum The product of the mass of an object and its velocity.

Impulse The product of the force acting on an object and the time during which it acts.

Relationship of impulse and momentum Impulse is equal to the change in the momentum of the object upon which the impulse acts. In symbol notation,

$$Ft = \Delta mv$$

Conservation of momentum In the absence of an external force, the momentum of a system remains unchanged. Hence, the momentum before an event involving only internal forces is equal to the momentum after the event:

$$mv_{\text{(before event)}} = mv_{\text{(after event)}}$$

Elastic collision A collision in which colliding objects rebound without lasting deformation or the generation of heat.

Inelastic collision A collision in which the colliding objects become distorted, generate heat, and possibly stick together.

Work The product of the force and the distance through which the force moves:

$$W = Fd$$

Power The time rate of work:

$$\text{Power} = \frac{\text{work}}{\text{time}}$$

(More generally, power is the rate at which energy is expended.)

Energy The property of a system that enables it to do work.

Potential energy The stored energy that a body possesses because of its position.

Kinetic energy Energy of motion, described by the relationship

$$\text{Kinetic energy} = 1/2\ mv^2$$

Work–Energy Theorem The work done on an object equals the change in kinetic energy of the object.

$$\text{Work} = \Delta\text{KE}$$

Conservation of energy In the absence of external work input or output, the energy of a system remains unchanged. Energy cannot be created or destroyed.

Conservation of energy and machines The work output of any machine cannot exceed the work input. In an ideal machine, where no energy is transformed into heat,

$$\text{work}_{\text{input}} = \text{work}_{\text{output}} \text{ and}$$
$$(Fd)_{\text{input}} = (Fd)_{\text{output}}$$

Efficiency The percentage of the work put into a machine that is converted into useful work output. (More generally, efficiency is useful energy output divided by total energy input.)

Review Questions

3.1 Momentum

1. Which has a greater momentum, a heavy truck at rest or a moving skateboard?
2. How can a huge ship have an enormous momentum when it moves relatively slowly?

3.2 Impulse

3. How does impulse differ from force?
4. What are the two ways in which the impulse exerted on something can be increased?

3.3 Impulse–Momentum Relationship

5. Is the impulse–momentum relationship related to Newton's second law?
6. Why is it incorrect to say that impulse equals momentum?
7. For the same force, which cannon imparts the greater speed to a cannonball—a long cannon or a short one? Explain.
8. Why is it a good idea to have your hand extended forward when you are getting ready to catch a fast-moving baseball with your bare hand?
9. In boxing, why is it advantageous to roll with the punch?
10. In karate, why is it advantageous to apply a force for a very brief time?
11. Consider a baseball that is caught and thrown at the same speed. Which case illustrates the greatest change in momentum: The baseball (1) being caught, (2) being thrown, or (3) being caught and then thrown back?
12. In the preceding question, which case requires the greatest impulse?

3.4 Conservation of Momentum

13. Can you produce a net impulse on an automobile by sitting inside and pushing on the dashboard? Defend your answer.
14. Is it correct to say that, if no net impulse is exerted on an object, there is no change in the object's momentum?
15. What does it mean to say that a quantity is *conserved*?
16. Distinguish between an *elastic* collision and an *inelastic* collision. For which type of collision is momentum conserved?
17. When is momentum conserved—in an elastic collision or in an inelastic collision?
18. Railroad car A rolls at a certain speed and collides elastically with car B of the same mass. After the collision, car A is at rest. How does the speed of B after the collision compare with the initial speed of A?
19. If the equally massive cars of the previous question stick together after colliding inelastically, how does their speed after the collision compare with the initial speed of car A?

3.5 Energy

20. When is energy most evident?
21. What do we call the quantity *force* × *distance,* and what quantity does it change?
22. In what units are work and energy measured?

3.6 Power

23. True or false: One watt is the unit of power equivalent to one joule per second.
24. How many watts of power are expended when a force of 6 N moves a book 2 m in a time interval of 3 s?

3.7 Potential Energy

25. A car is lifted a certain distance in a service station and therefore has potential energy with respect to the floor. If it were lifted twice as high, how much potential energy would it have?
26. Two cars, one twice as heavy as the other, are lifted to the same elevation in a service station. How do their potential energies compare?

3.8 Kinetic Energy

27. When a car travels at 50 km/h, it has kinetic energy. How much more kinetic energy does it have at 100 km/h?
28. Which has the greater kinetic energy—a car traveling at 30 km/h or a car that is half as heavy traveling at 60 km/h?
29. What is the evidence for saying whether or not work is done on an object?
30. The brakes do a certain amount of work to stop a car that is moving at a particular speed. How much work must the brakes do to stop a car that is moving four times as fast?

3.9 Conservation of Energy

31. Cite the law of energy conservation.
32. What is the source of energy that powers a hydroelectric power plant?

3.10 Machines

33. Can a machine multiply input force? Input distance? Input energy? (If your three answers are the same, seek help, for the last question is especially important.)

34. A force of 50 N applied to the end of a lever moves that end a certain distance. If the other end of the lever is moved half as far, how much force does it exert?
35. Is it possible to design a machine that has an efficiency that is greater than 100 percent? Discuss.

3.11 Sources of Energy

36. Explain how the energy that operates an electric toothbrush is actually the energy of sunlight.

Activities

1. When you get a bit ahead in your studies, cut classes some afternoon and visit your local pool or billiards parlor and bone up on momentum conservation. Note that, no matter how complicated the collision of balls, the momentum along the line of action of the cue ball before impact is the same as the combined momentum of all the balls along this direction after impact, and that the components of momenta perpendicular to this line of action cancel to zero after impact, the same value as before impact in this direction. You'll see both the vector nature of momentum and its conservation more clearly when rotational skidding—English—is not imparted to the cue ball. When English is imparted by striking the cue ball off center, rotational momentum, which is also conserved, somewhat complicates the analysis. But, regardless of how the cue ball is struck, in the absence of external forces, both linear and rotational momenta are always conserved. Pool or billiards offers a first-rate exhibition of momentum conservation in action.
2. Pour some dry sand into a tin can with a cover. Compare the temperature of the sand before and after vigorously shaking the can for more than a minute. Explain your observations.
3. Place a small rubber ball on top of a basketball, and then drop them together. How high does the smaller ball bounce. Can you reconcile this with energy conservation? (What if the basketball were not elastic?)

Exercises

1. What is the purpose of a "crumple zone" (which has been manufactured to collapse steadily in a crash) in the front section of an automobile?
2. To bring a supertanker to a stop, its engines are typically cut off about 25 kg from port. Why is it so difficult to stop or turn a supertanker?
3. In terms of impulse and momentum, why are nylon ropes, which stretch considerably under stress, favored by mountain climbers?
4. Why might a wine glass survive a fall onto a carpeted floor but not onto a concrete floor?
5. If you throw an egg against a wall, the egg will break. If you throw an egg at the same speed into a sagging sheet, it won't break. Why?
6. It is generally much more difficult to stop a heavy truck than a light car when they move at the same speed. State a case in which the moving car could require more stopping force. (Consider relative times.)
7. Why is a punch more forceful with a bare fist than with a boxing glove?
8. A boxer can punch a heavy bag for more than an hour without tiring, but will tire quickly when boxing with an opponent for a few minutes. Why? (Hint: When aimed at the bag, what supplies the impulse to stop the punches? When aimed at the opponent, what or who supplies the impulse to stop the punches that are missed?)
9. Railroad cars are loosely coupled so that there is a noticeable time delay from the time the first car is moved and last cars are moved from rest by the locomotive. Discuss the advisability of this loose coupling and slack between cars from an impulse–momentum point of view.

10. A fully dressed person is at rest in the middle of a pond on perfectly frictionless ice and must reach shore. How can this be accomplished?
11. A high-speed bus and an innocent bug have a head-on collision. The sudden change of momentum for the bug spatters it all over the windshield. Is the change in momentum of the bus greater, less, or the same as the change in momentum of the unfortunate bug?
12. Why is it difficult for a firefighter to hold a hose that ejects large quantities of water at a high speed?
13. You're on a small raft next to a dock, and you jump from the raft only to fall into the water. What physics principle did you fail to take into account?
14. Your friend says the conservation of momentum is violated when you step off a chair and gain momentum as you fall. What do you say?
15. If a Mack truck and a Honda Civic have a head-on collision, which vehicle will experience the greater force of impact? The greater impulse? The greater change in its momentum? The greater acceleration?
16. Would a head-on collision between two cars be more damaging to the occupants if the cars stuck together or if the cars rebounded upon impact?

17. In Chapter 2, rocket propulsion was explained in terms of Newton's third law. That is, the force that propels a rocket is from the exhaust gases pushing against the rocket, the reaction to the force the rocket exerts on the exhaust gases. Explain rocket propulsion in terms of momentum conservation.
18. Explain how the conservation of momentum is a consequence of Newton's third law.
19. Suppose there are three astronauts outside a spaceship, and two of them decide to play catch using the third man. All the astronauts weigh the same on earth and are equally strong. The first astronaut throws the second one toward the third one and the game begins. Describe the motion of the astronauts as the game proceeds. How long will the game last?

20. When a stationary uranium nucleus undergoes fission, it breaks into two unequal chunks that fly apart. What can you conclude about the momenta of the chunks? What can you conclude about the speed of the chunks?
21. How is it possible that a flock of birds in flight can have a momentum of zero but not have zero kinetic energy?
22. In determining the potential energy of Tenny's drawn bow (Figure 3.19), would it be an underestimate or an overestimate to multiply the force with which she holds the arrow in its drawn position by the distance she pulled it? Why do we say the work done is the *average* force × distance?
23. When a cannon with a long barrel is fired, the force of expanding gases acts on the cannonball for a longer distance. What effect does this have on the velocity of the emerging cannonball?
24. You and a flight attendant toss a ball back and forth in an airplane in flight. Does the KE of the ball depend on the speed of the airplane? Carefully explain.
25. Can something have energy without having momentum? Explain. Can something have momentum without having energy? Defend your answer.
26. In an effort to combat wasteful habits, we often urge others to "conserve energy" by turning off lights when they are not in use, for example, or by setting thermostats at a moderate level. In this chapter, we also speak of "energy conservation." Distinguish between these two usages.
27. An inefficient machine is said to "waste energy." Does this mean that energy is actually lost? Explain.
28. A friend shows you a light bulb he has just removed from its package. He shows you that it's labeled 100 W, and asks you if it *has* 100 W of power. What's your reply?
29. A child can throw a baseball at 20 mph. Some professional ball players can throw a baseball at 100 mph, which is five times as fast. How much more energy does the pro ball player give to the faster ball?
30. If a golf ball and a Ping-Pong ball both move with the same kinetic energy, can you say which has the greater speed? Explain in terms of KE. Similarly, in a gaseous mixture of massive molecules and light molecules with the same average KE, can you say which has the greater speed?
31. Consider a pendulum swinging to and fro. At what point in its motion is the KE of the pendulum bob at a maximum? At what point is its PE at a maximum? When its KE is half its maximum value, how much PE does it have?
32. A physics instructor demonstrates energy conservation by releasing a heavy pendulum bob, as shown in the sketch, allowing it to swing to and fro. What would happen if, in his exuberance, he gave the bob a slight shove as it left his nose? Why?
33. No work is done on an object unless there is a force, or component of a force, along its direction of motion. This being so, does the string that supports a pendulum bob do work on the bob as it swings to and fro? Explain. Does the force of gravity do work on the bob? Explain.
34. Discuss the design of the roller coaster shown in the sketch in terms of the conservation of energy.
35. Consider the identical balls released from rest on tracks A and B as shown. When each ball has reached the right end of its track, which will have the greater speed? Why is this question easier to answer than the similar question asked in Exercise 34 back in Chapter 1?
36. Strictly speaking, does a car burn more gasoline when its lights are turned on? Does the overall consumption of gasoline depend on whether or not the engine is running? Defend your answer.
37. You tell your friend that no machine can possibly put out more energy than is put into it, and your friend states that a nuclear reactor puts out more energy than is put into it. What do you say?

38. This may seem like an easy question for a physics type to answer: With what force does a rock that weighs 10 N strike the ground if it is dropped from a rest position 10 m high? This question does not have a straightforward numerical answer. Why?
39. If an automobile had a 100-percent-efficient engine, would it be warm to your touch? Would its exhaust heat the surrounding air? Would it make any noise? Would it vibrate? Would any of its fuel go unused?
40. Which requires more work to stop—a light truck or a heavy truck moving with the same momentum?

Problems

1. A car with a mass of 1000 kg moves at 20 m/s. What braking force is needed to bring the car to a halt in 10 s?
2. A railroad diesel engine weighs four times as much as a freight car. If the diesel engine coasts at 5 km per hour into a freight car that is initially at rest, how fast do the two coast after they couple together?
3. A 5-kg fish swimming at 1 m/s swallows an absent-minded 1-kg fish at rest. (a) What is the speed of the larger fish after lunch? (b) What would be its speed if the smaller fish were swimming toward it at 4 m/s?
4. Comic-strip hero Superman meets an asteroid in outer space and hurls it at 800 m/s, as fast as a bullet. The asteroid is a thousand times more massive than Superman. In the strip, Superman is seen at rest after the throw. Taking physics into account, what would be his recoil velocity?
5. Consider the inelastic collision between the two freight cars in Figure 3.13. The momentum before and after the collision is the same. The KE, however, is less after the collision than before the collision. How much less, and what has become of this energy?
6. This question is typical on some driver's license exams: A car moving at 50 km/h skids 15 m with locked brakes. How far will the car skid with locked brakes at 150 km/h?
7. In the hydraulic machine shown, it is observed that, when the small piston is pushed down 10 cm, the large piston is raised 1 cm. If the small piston is pushed down with a force of 100 N, how much force is the large piston capable of exerting?

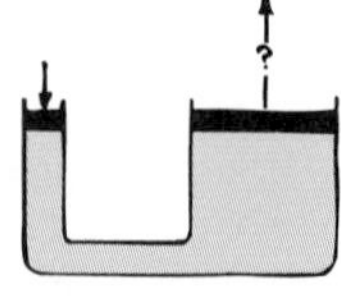

8. How many kilometers per liter will a car obtain if its engine is 25 percent efficient and it encounters an average retarding force of 1000 N? Assume that the energy content of gasoline is 40 MJ/L.
9. What is the efficiency of a pulley system that will raise a 2000-N load a vertical distance of 1 m when 3000 J of effort is involved?
10. What is the efficiency of the body when a cyclist expends 1000 W of power to deliver mechanical energy to her bicycle at the rate of 100 W?
11. The decrease in PE for a freely falling object equals its gain in KE, in accord with the conservation of energy. (a) By simple algebra, find an equation for an object's speed v after falling a vertical distance h. Do this by equating KE to the object's change in PE. (b) Then figure out how much higher a freely falling object must fall to have twice the speed when it hits ground.
12. Using the definitions of momentum and kinetic energy, $p = mv$ and KE $= (1/2)mv^2$, show by algebraic manipulation that you can write KE $= p^2/2m$. This equation tells us that, if two objects have the same momentum, the one of less mass has the greater kinetic energy (see Exercise 40).

Chapter 3 Online Resources

Videos

- Definition of Momentum
- Changing Momentum - Follow Through
- Decreasing Momentum Over a Short Time
- Bowling Ball & Conservation of Energy
- Conservation of Energy: Numerical Example
- Machines: Pulleys

Quiz
Exercises
Flashcards
Links

CHAPTER 4

Newton's Law of Universal Gravitation

It would be erroneous to say that Newton discovered gravity. The discovery of gravity goes back much further than Newton's time, to earlier times when earth dwellers discovered the consequences of tripping and falling. What Newton discovered was that gravity is universal—that it is not a phenomenon unique to earth, as his contemporaries had assumed.

From the time of Aristotle, the circular motions of heavenly bodies were regarded as natural. The ancients believed that the stars, planets, and moon moved in divine circles, free from any impressed forces. As far as the ancients were concerned, this circular motion required no explanation. Isaac Newton, however, recognized that a force of some kind must be acting on the planets; otherwise, their paths would be straight lines. Others of his time, influenced by Aristotle, would say that any force acting on the planets would be directed along the planet's path—in the direction of motion. Newton, however, reasoned a force on the planets must be perpendicular to their motion, directed toward the center of their curved paths—toward the sun. This was the force of gravity, the same force that pulls apples from trees. Newton's stroke of intuition, that the force between the earth and apples is the same force that pulls moons and planets and everything else in our universe, was a revolutionary break with the prevailing notion that there were two sets of natural laws, one for earthly events and another altogether for motions in the heavens. Newton synthesized terrestrial and cosmic laws.

Figure 4.1
Newton realizes that earth's gravity affects both the apple *and* the moon.

4.1 The Law of Universal Gravitation

According to popular legend, Newton was sitting under an apple tree when the idea struck him that gravity extends beyond the earth. Perhaps he looked up through tree branches toward the origin of a falling apple and noticed the moon. In any event, Newton had the insight to see that the force between the earth and a falling apple is the same force that pulls the moon in an orbital path around the earth, a path similar to a planet's path around the sun.

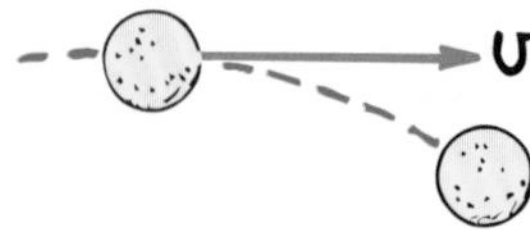

To test his hypothesis, Newton compared the fall of an apple with the fall of the moon. He realized that the moon falls, in the sense that *it falls beneath the straight line that it would follow if there were no forces acting upon it.* Because of its horizontal speed (tangential speed), it "falls around" the round earth. By simple geometry, the moon's distance of fall per second could be compared to the distance that an apple (or anything at that distance) would fall in 1 second. Newton's calculations didn't check. Disappointed, but recognizing that brute fact must always win over a beautiful hypothesis, he placed his papers in a drawer, where they remained for nearly 20 years. During this period, he founded and developed the field of geometric optics, for which he first became famous.

Figure 4.2
If the moon did not fall, it would follow the straight-line path. Because of its attraction to the earth, it falls along a curved path. Its tangential velocity insures that it falls around the earth rather than directly into it.

Newton's interest in mechanics was rekindled with the advent of two spectacular comets, one in 1680 and the other in 1682. He returned to the moon problem at the prodding of his astronomer friend, Edmond Halley, for whom the second comet was later named. He made corrections in his earlier experimental data and obtained excellent results. Only then did he publish what is one of the most far-reaching generalizations of the human mind: the **law of universal gravitation.***

Everything pulls on everything else in a beautifully simple way that involves only mass and distance. According to Newton, every mass attracts every other mass with a force that, for any two masses, is directly proportional to the product of the masses involved and inversely proportional to the square of the distance separating them.

This statement can be expressed as

$$\text{Force} \sim \frac{\text{mass}_1 \times \text{mass}_2}{\text{distance}^2}$$

or symbolically as

$$F \sim \frac{m_1 m_2}{d^2}$$

Figure 4.3
As the rocket gets farther from the earth, gravitational strength between the rocket and the earth decreases.

where m_1 and m_2 are the masses, and d is the distance between their centers. Thus, the greater the masses m_1 and m_2, the greater the force of attraction between them—in direct proportion to the masses.† For example, if the mass of a body is doubled, then the force between it and another body is doubled. If the masses of both bodies are doubled, then the force between them is four times as much. The greater the distance of separation d, the weaker the force of attraction—in inverse proportion to the square of the distance between their centers of mass.

*This is a dramatic example of the painstaking effort and crosschecking that go into the formulation of a scientific theory. Contrast Newton's approach with the failure to "do one's homework," the hasty judgements, and the absence of crosschecking that so often characterize the pronouncements of those who advocate less-than-scientific theories.

†Note the different role of mass here. Thus far, we have treated mass as a measure of inertia, which is called *inertial mass.* Now we see mass as a measure of gravitational force, which, in this context, is called *gravitational mass.* It is experimentally established that the two are equal, and, as a matter of principle, the equivalence of inertial and gravitational mass is the foundation of Einstein's general theory of relativity (Chapter 35).

☑ CHECKPOINT

1. In Figure 4.2, note how the moon falls around the earth rather than straight into it. If the tangential velocity were zero, how would the moon move?
2. According to the equation for gravitational force, what happens to the force between two bodies if the mass of one of the bodies is doubled? If both masses are doubled?
3. Gravitational force acts on all bodies in proportion to their masses. Why, then, doesn't a heavy body fall faster than a light body?

Check Your Answers

1. If the moon's tangential velocity were zero, it would fall straight down and crash into the earth!
2. When one mass is doubled, the force between it and the other one doubles. If both masses double, the force is four times as much.
3. The answer goes back to Chapter 2. Recall Figure 2.10, in which heavy and light bricks fall with the same acceleration because both have the same ratio of weight to mass. Newton's second law ($a = F/m$) reminds us that greater force acting on greater mass does not result in greater acceleration.

4.2 The Universal Gravitational Constant, *G*

The proportionality form of the universal law of gravitation can be expressed as an exact equation when the constant of proportionality G, called the *universal gravitational constant,* is introduced. Then the equation is

$$F = G\frac{m_1 m_2}{d^2}$$

In words, the force of gravity between two objects is found by multiplying their masses, dividing by the square of the distance between their centers, and then multiplying this result by the constant G. The magnitude of G is the same as the magnitude of the force between two masses of 1 kilogram each, 1 meter apart: 0.0000000000667 newton. This small magnitude indicates an extremely weak force. In standard units and in scientific notation,*

$$G = 6.67 \times 10^{-11}\ \text{N}\cdot\text{m}^2/\text{kg}^2$$

G was first measured long after the time of Newton by an English physicist, Henry Cavendish, in the eighteenth century. He accomplished this by measuring the tiny force between lead masses with an extremely sensitive torsion balance. A simpler method was later developed by Philipp von Jolly, who attached a spherical flask of mercury to one arm of a sensitive balance

Just as sheet music guides a musician playing music, equations guide a physical-science student to see how concepts are connected.

Insights

*The numerical value of G depends entirely on the units of measurement we select for mass, distance, and time. The international system of choice is: for mass, the kilogram; for distance, the meter; and for time, the second. Scientific notation is discussed in Appendix A at the end of this book.

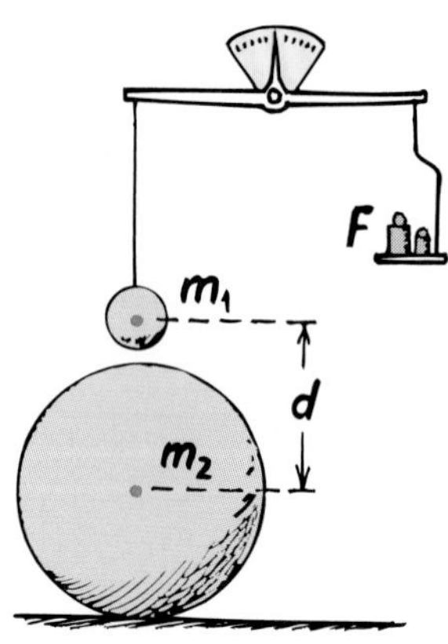

Figure 4.4
Jolly's method of measuring G. Balls m_1 and m_2 attract each other with a force F equal to the weight needed to restore balance.

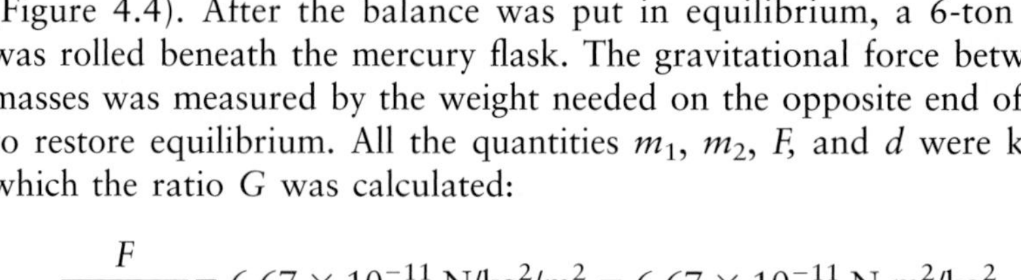

(Figure 4.4). After the balance was put in equilibrium, a 6-ton lead sphere was rolled beneath the mercury flask. The gravitational force between the two masses was measured by the weight needed on the opposite end of the balance to restore equilibrium. All the quantities m_1, m_2, F, and d were known, from which the ratio G was calculated:

$$\frac{F}{m_1 m_2/d^2} = 6.67 \times 10^{-11}\ \text{N/kg}^2/\text{m}^2 = 6.67 \times 10^{-11}\ \text{N}\cdot\text{m}^2/\text{kg}^2$$

The value of G indicates that the force of gravity is a very weak force. It is the weakest of the presently known four fundamental forces. (The other three are the electromagnetic force and two kinds of nuclear forces.) We sense gravitation only when masses like that of the earth are involved. The force of attraction between you and a large ship on which you stand is too weak for ordinary measurement. The force of attraction between you and the earth, however, can be measured. It is your weight.

In addition to your mass, your weight also depends on your distance from the center of the earth. At the top of a mountain, your mass is the same as it is anywhere else, but your weight is slightly less than at ground level. That's because your distance from the center of the earth is greater.

Once the value of G was known, the mass of the earth was easily calculated. The force that the earth exerts on a mass of 1 kilogram at its surface is 9.8 newtons. The distance between the 1-kilogram mass and the center of the earth is the earth's radius, 6.4×10^6 meters. Therefore, from $F = G(m_1 m_2/d^2)$, where m_1 is the mass of the earth,

Just as π relates circumference and diameter for circles, **G** relates gravitational force with mass and distance.

Insights

$$9.8\ \text{N} = 6.67 \times 10^{-11}\ \text{N}\cdot\text{m}^2/\text{kg}^2\ \frac{1\ \text{kg} \times m_1}{(6.4 \times 10^6\ \text{m})^2}$$

from which the mass of the earth is calculated to be $m_1 = 6 \times 10^{24}$ kilograms.

When G was first measured in the eighteenth century, people all over the world were excited about it. That's because newspapers everywhere announced the discovery as one that measured the mass of Planet Earth. How exciting that Newton's formula gives the mass of the entire planet, with all its oceans, mountains, and inner parts yet to be discovered. G and the mass of the earth were measured when a great portion of the earth's surface was still undiscovered.

☑ CHECKPOINT

If there is an attractive force between all objects, why do we not feel ourselves gravitating toward massive buildings in our vicinity?

Check Your Answer

Gravity pulls us to massive buildings and to everything else in the universe. Physicist Paul A. M. Dirac, winner of the 1933 Nobel Prize for physics, put it this way: "Pick a flower on earth and you move the farthest star!" How much we are influenced by buildings or how much interaction there is between flowers and stars is another story. The forces between us and buildings are relatively small because their masses are small compared with the mass of earth. The forces due to the stars are also small because of their great distances from us. These tiny forces escape our notice when they are overwhelmed by the overpowering attraction to earth.

4.3 Gravity and Distance: The Inverse-Square Law

We can better understand how gravity is diluted with distance by considering how paint from a paint gun spreads with increasing distance (Figure 4.5). Suppose we position a paint gun at the center of a sphere with a radius of 1 meter, and a burst of paint spray travels 1 meter to produce a square patch of paint that is 1 millimeter thick. How thick would the patch be if the experiment were done in a sphere with twice the radius? If the same amount of paint travels in straight lines for 2 meters, it will spread to a patch twice as tall and twice as wide. The paint would be spread over an area four times as big, and its thickness would be only ¼ millimeter. Can you see from the figure that, for a sphere of radius 3 meters, the thickness of the paint patch would be only ⅑ millimeter? Can you see that the thickness of the paint decreases as the square of the distance increases? This is known as the **inverse-square law.** The inverse-square law holds for gravity and for all phenomena wherein the effect from a localized source spreads uniformly throughout the surrounding space: the electric field about an isolated electron, the light from a match, the radiation from a piece of uranium, and the sound from a cricket.

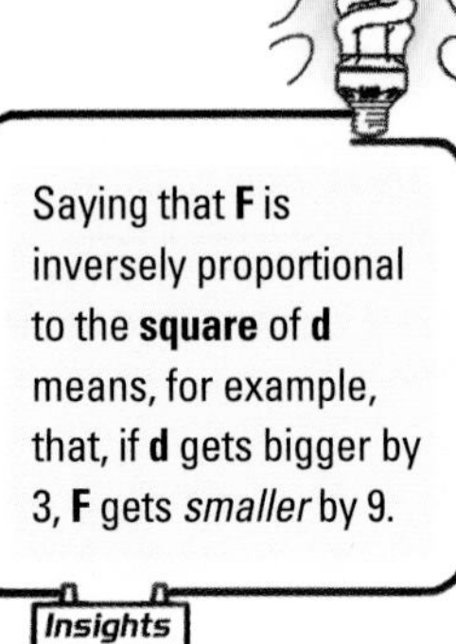

Saying that **F** is inversely proportional to the **square** of **d** means, for example, that, if **d** gets bigger by 3, **F** gets *smaller* by 9.

Insights

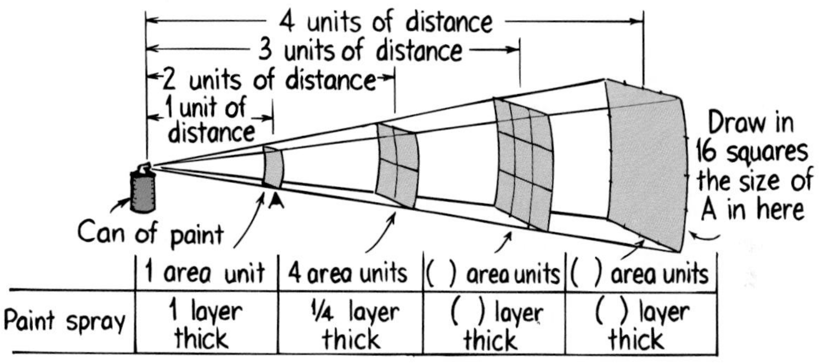

Figure 4.5
The inverse-square law. Paint spray travels radially away from the nozzle of the can in straight lines. Like gravity, the "strength" of the spray obeys the inverse-square law.

Figuring Physical Science

Problems

A 3-kg newborn baby at the earth's surface is gravitationally attracted to earth with a force of about 30 N. (a) Calculate the force of gravity with which the baby on earth is attracted to the planet Mars, when Mars is closest to earth. (The mass of Mars is 6.4×10^{23} kg, and its closest distance is 5.6×10^{10} m). (b) Calculate the force of gravity between the baby and the physician who delivers it. Assume that the physician has a mass of 100 kg and is 0.5 m from the baby. (c) How do the forces compare?

Solutions

(a) Mars: $F = G\frac{mM}{d^2} = 6.67 \times 10^{-11}\frac{(3\text{kg})(6.4 \times 10^{23}\text{kg})}{(5.6 \times 10^{10}\text{m})^2}$

$= 4.1 \times 10^{-8}$ N.

(b) Physician: $F = G\frac{mM}{d^2} = 6.67 \times 10^{-11}\frac{(3\text{kg})(10^2\text{kg})}{(0.5\text{m})^2}$

$= 8.0 \times 10^{-8}$ N.

(c) The gravitational force due to the physician is about twice that due to Mars.

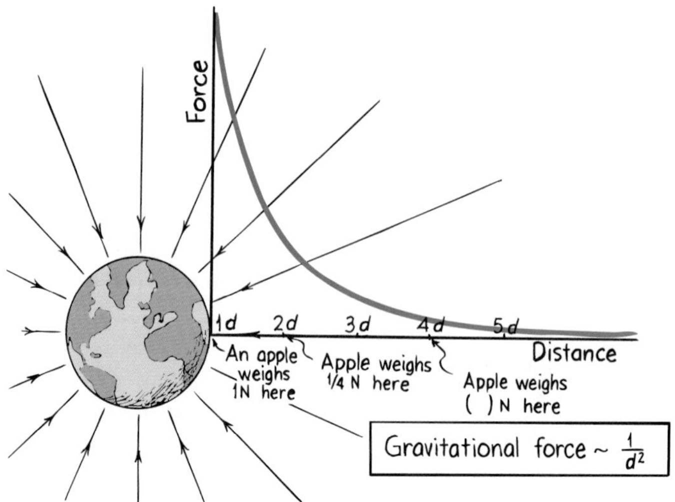

Figure 4.6
If an apple weighs 1 N at the earth's surface, it weighs only 1/4 N twice as far from the center of the earth. At three times the distance, it weighs only 1/9 N. What would it weigh at four times the distance? Five times? Gravitational force versus distance is plotted in color.

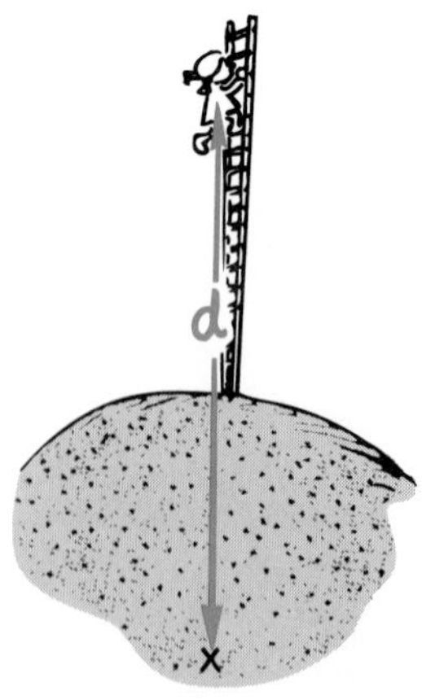

Figure 4.7
According to Newton's equation, her weight (not mass) decreases as she increases her distance from the earth's center (not surface).

In using Newton's equation for gravity, it is important to emphasize that the distance term *d* is the distance between the centers of masses of the objects that are attracted to each other. In Figure 4.6, note that the apple that normally weighs 1 newton at the earth's surface weighs only ¼ as much when it is twice the distance from the earth's center. The greater the distance from the earth's center, the less the weight of an object. A child that weighs 300 newtons at sea level will weigh only 299 newtons atop Mt. Everest. But, no matter how great the distance, the earth's gravitational force approaches, but never reaches, zero. Even if you were transported to the far reaches of the universe, the gravitational influence of home would still remain with you. It may be overwhelmed by the gravitational influences of nearer and/or more massive bodies, but its presence is still there. The gravitational influence of every material object, however small or however far, is exerted through all of space.

Link to Geology

Low-Density Floating Mountains

Gravitation is weaker atop a mountain because of the greater distance from the earth's center, in accord with the law of gravity. Interestingly, the gravitational field at the earth's surface also varies slightly due to varying densities of underlying rock—valued information to geologists and oil prospectors. An additional reason for weaker gravitation atop a mountain has to do with the density of mountain material. Mountains are less dense than the semiliquid portion of the earth they float upon—the mantle. Ice floats on water for the same reason: ice is less dense than water. So, just as the bottom of an iceberg extends far beneath the surface of the water, the bottom of a mountain extends far into the mantle. The result is a greater distance between the top of a mountain and the denser parts of the earth beneath. This increased "gap" further reduces gravitation at the top of a mountain.

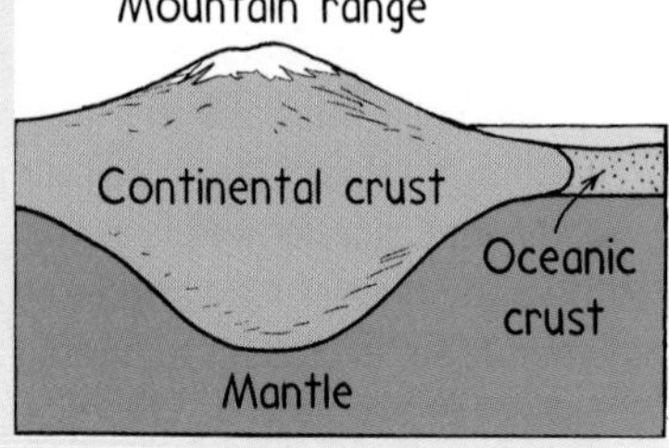

☑ CHECKPOINT

1. By how much does the gravitational force between two objects decrease when the distance between their centers is doubled? Tripled? Increased tenfold?
2. Consider an apple at the top of a tree that is pulled by earth's gravity with a force of 1 N. If the tree were twice as tall, would the force of gravity be only one-quarter as strong? Defend your answer.

Check Your Answers

1. It decreases to one-fourth, one-ninth, and one-hundredth.
2. No, because the twice-as-tall apple tree is not twice as far from earth's center. The tree height for such a reduction of weight would have to equal the radius of earth (6,370 km). Interestingly, before its weight decreases by 1 percent, an apple, or any object, must be raised 32 km—nearly four times the height of Mt. Everest. So, as a practical matter, we disregard the effects of everyday changes in elevation.

Force Fields

We know earth and moon pull on each other. This is *action at a distance,* because both bodies interact with each other without being in contact. But we can look at this in a different way: we can regard the moon as in contact with the *gravitational field* of the earth. A gravitational field is the space surrounding a massive body in which another mass experiences an attractive force. A gravitational field is an example of a **force field,** for any mass in the field space experiences a force. It is common to think of distant space probes being influenced by the gravitational field where they are in space rather than by earth and other planets or stars acting from a distance. The field concept plays an in-between role in our thinking about the forces between different masses.

A more familiar force field is the *magnetic field* of a magnet. Iron filings sprinkled over a sheet of paper on top of the magnet reveal the shape of the magnet's magnetic field. The pattern of filings shows the strength and direction of the magnetic field at different locations around the magnet. Where the filings are close together, the field is strong. The direction of the filings show the direction of the field at each point. Planet earth is a giant magnet, and, like all magnets, it is surrounded by a magnetic field. Evidence of the field is easily seen by the orientation of a magnetic compass.

The pattern of the earth's gravitational field can be represented by field lines. Like the iron filings around a magnet, the field lines are closer together where the gravitational field is stronger. At each point on a field line, the direction of the field at that point is along the line. Arrows show the field direction. A particle, astronaut, spaceship, or any mass in the vicinity of the earth will be accelerated in the direction of the field line at that location. The strength of the earth's gravitational field, like the strength of its force on objects, follows the inverse-square law. It is strongest near the earth's surface and weaker with increased distance from the earth.

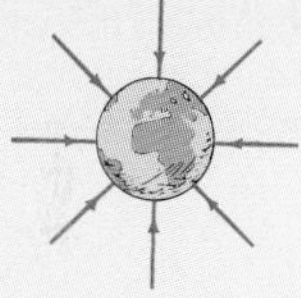

Another example of a force field is the one that surrounds electrical charges—the electric field, which we shall study in Chapter 9. Then, in Chapter 19, we'll learn that atoms align with the electric fields of other atoms and molecules are formed. In Chapter 10, we'll learn how magnets align with the magnetic fields of the earth to become compasses.

And then, in Chapter 33, we'll learn how the moon similarly aligns with the earth's gravitational field, which is why one hemisphere of the moon continually faces the earth. Force fields have far-reaching effects.

4.4 Weight and Weightlessness

When you step on a bathroom scale, you compress a spring inside, which is affixed to a pointer. When the pointer stops moving, the elastic force of the deformed spring balances the gravitational attraction between you and the earth—you and the scale are in equilibrium. The pointer is calibrated to show your weight. If you stand on a bathroom scale in a moving elevator, you'll find variations in your weight. If the elevator accelerates upward, the springs inside the bathroom scale are more compressed and your weight reading is greater. If the elevator accelerates downward, the springs inside the scale are less compressed and your weight reading is less. If the elevator cable breaks and the elevator falls freely, the reading on the scale goes to zero. According to the scale's reading, you would be weightless. Would you really be weightless? We can answer this question only if we agree on what we mean by *weight*.

Figure 4.8
Your weight equals the force with which you press against the supporting floor. If the floor accelerates up or down, your weight varies (even though the gravitational force *mg* that acts on you remains the same).

In Chapters 1 and 2, we defined weight as the force due to gravity on a body, *mg*. Your weight does have the value *mg* if you're not accelerating. To generalize, we now refine this definition by saying that the weight of something is the force it exerts against a supporting floor or a weighing scale. According to this definition, you are as heavy as you feel; so, in an elevator that accelerates downward, the supporting force of the floor is less and you weigh less. If the elevator is in free-fall, your weight is zero (Figure 4.8). Even in this weightless condition, however, there is still a gravitational force acting on you, causing your downward acceleration. But gravity now is not felt as weight because there is no supporting force.

Consider an astronaut in orbit. The astronaut is weightless because he is not supported by anything (Figure 4.9). There would be no compression in the springs of a bathroom scale placed beneath his feet because the bathroom scale is falling as fast as he is. Any objects that are released fall together with him and remain in his vicinity, unlike what occurs on the ground. All the local effects of gravity are eliminated. The body organs respond as if gravity forces were absent, and this gives the sensation of weightlessness. The astronaut experiences the same sensation in orbit that he would feel in a falling elevator—a state of free-fall.

Figure 4.9
Both are weightless.

On the other hand, if the astronaut were in a spacecraft undergoing acceleration, even in deep space and far removed from any attracting objects, he *would* have weight. Like the girl in the accelerating elevator, the astronaut would be pressed against a scale or a supporting surface.

Figure 4.10
The inhabitants in the international space station continually experience weightlessness. They are in free-fall around the earth. Does a force of gravity act on them?

So we see that weight and gravity don't always have to go hand in hand. (This will be discussed further in the section on Einstein's general theory of relativity in Chapter 35). Floating in deep space, far from gravitating objects, is equivalent to "floating" in free-fall near a gravitating object. Weight is not directly a manifestation of gravity. It results when some force other than gravity acts (such as a floor supporting you, or a rocket engine accelerating you).

The international space station in Figure 4.10 provides a weightless environment. The station facility and the astronauts inside all accelerate equally toward earth, at somewhat less than 1 *g* because of their altitude. This acceleration is not sensed at all; with respect to the station, the astronauts experience zero *g*.

Astronauts inside the orbiting space shuttle have no weight, even though the force of gravity between them and Planet Earth is only slightly reduced from what it is at ground level.

Insights

☑ CHECKPOINT

In what sense is drifting in space far away from all celestial bodies like stepping off a chair?

Check Your Answer

In both cases you'd experience weightlessness. When drifting in deep space, you'd remain weightless because no force acts on you. When stepping from a chair, you'd be only momentarily weightless because of a temporary lapse of support force.

Simulated Weight in Space

Occupants in the international space station that presently orbits the earth are weightless because they lack a support force. Over extended periods of time, this causes loss of muscle strength and other detrimental changes in the body.

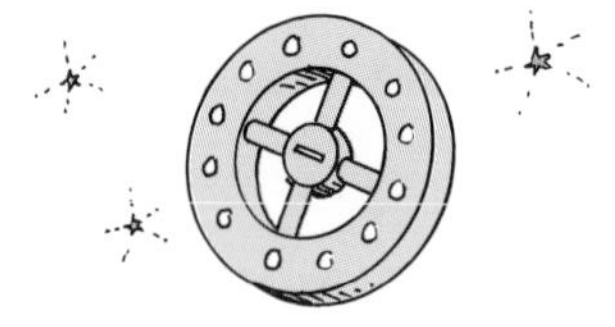

Figure 4.11
Occupants inside the rotating space habitat experience simulated weight and can "stand up" inside. In upright positions, their feet press against the outer rim and their heads point toward the center.

Future space travelers, however, need not be subjected to weightlessness. Lazily rotating giant wheels will likely supplant today's nonrotating space habitats (Figure 4.11). Rotation effectively supplies a support force and nicely simulates weight. Recall, from Chapter 2, that acceleration occurs when you travel in a circle, even though your speed remains constant. Recall also that, when acceleration occurs, there is a force in the direction of the acceleration. Occupants in the rotating habitat travel in circular paths and feel a *centripetal force,* which is directed toward the axis of rotation. This centripetal force is the support force, and it is sensed as weight. At the proper rate of rotation, the support force can simulate normal earth weight.

Figure 4.12
This artist's rendering shows the interior of a fanciful space habitat that can be occupied by thousands of people.

4.5 Tides

Seafaring people have always known there was a connection between the ocean tides and the moon. Newton was the first to show that tides are caused by *differences* in the gravitational pull between the moon and the earth on opposite sides of the earth. Gravitational force between the moon and the earth is stronger on the side of the earth nearest to the moon, and it is weaker on the side of the earth farthest from the moon.

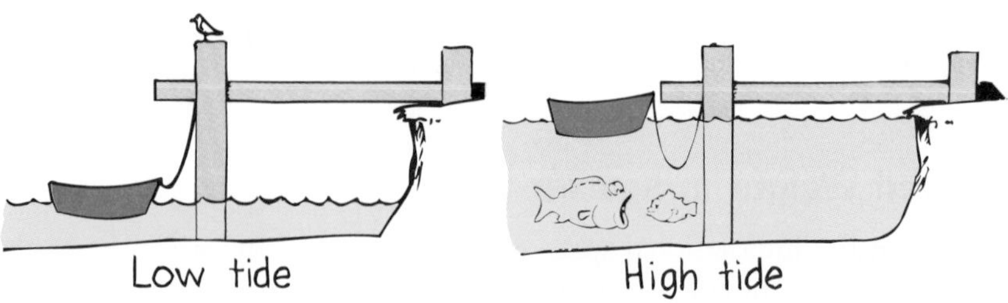

Figure 4.13
Low and high ocean tides.

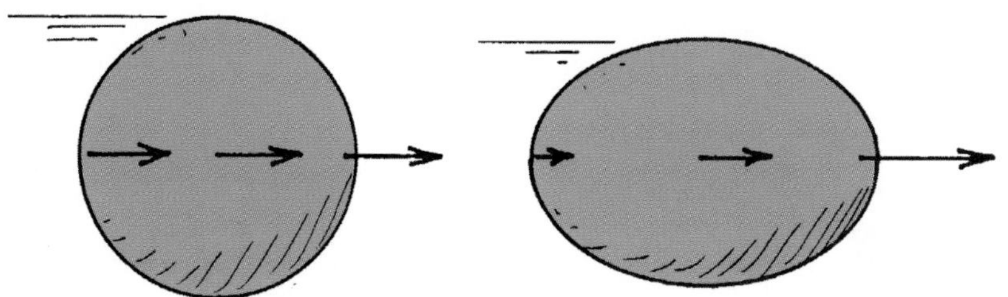

Figure 4.14
A ball of Jell-O would stay spherical if all of its parts were pulled equally in the same direction. If one side were pulled more than another, the shape would be elongated.

To understand why the difference in gravitational pulls produces tides, consider a spherical ball of Jell-O (Figure 4.14). If you were to exert the same force on every part of the ball, it would remain as a sphere as it accelerates. But, if you pulled with more force on one side than on the other, there would be a difference in accelerations, and the ball would become elongated. That's what's happening to this big ball we're living on. The different pulls of the moon stretch the earth, producing ocean bulges that extend nearly one meter above the average surface level of the ocean. The earth spins once per day, so a fixed point on earth passes beneath both of these bulges each day. This produces two sets of ocean tides per day—two high tides and two low tides. Interestingly, while the earth spins, the moon moves along its orbit and appears at the same position in our sky every 24 hours and 50 minutes. Hence, the two-high-tide cycle repeats at 24-hour-and-50-minute intervals. This is why the tides do not occur at the same time every day.

Which pulls with greater force on the earth's oceans, the sun or the moon? Which is more effective in raising tides? (Why do your answers differ?)

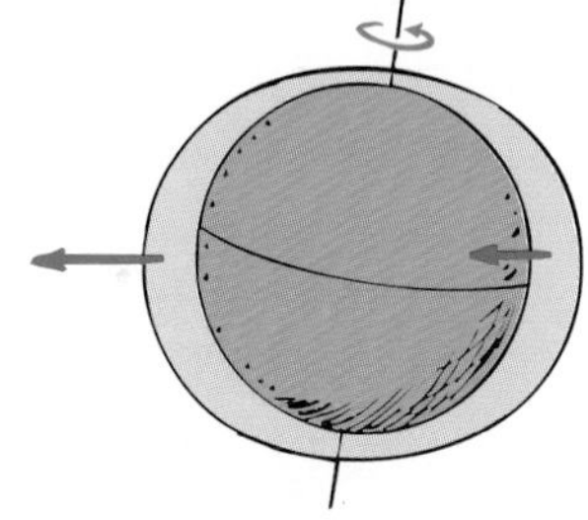

Figure 4.15
Two tidal bulges remain relatively fixed with respect to the moon while the earth spins daily beneath them.

Figure 4.16
Tidal bulges due only to the sun are small because the *differences* in pulls by the sun are small.

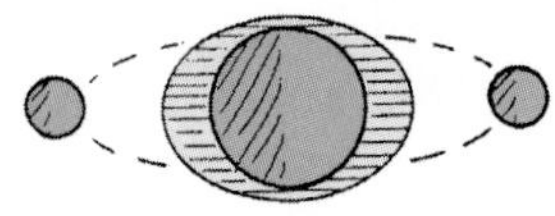

Figure 4.17
When the pulls by the sun and moon are aligned, spring tides occur.

The moon and sun make not only ocean tides, but tides in the earth and atmosphere as well. Does this explain why some of your friends are weird at the time of a full moon?

The sun also contributes to ocean tides, but it is only about half as effective as the moon—even though it pulls 180 times more on the earth than the moon does. Why aren't tides due to the sun 180 times greater than the lunar tides? Because the *difference* in gravitational pulls on opposite sides of the earth is very small (only about 0.017 percent, compared with 6.7 percent across the earth by the moon). When the sun, earth, and moon are all lined up, the tides due to the sun and the moon coincide and we have higher-than-average high tides and lower-than-average low tides. These are called **spring tides.** (Spring tides have nothing to do with the spring season.) Spring tides occur at the times of a new or full moon.

When the moon is halfway between a new moon and a full moon, in either direction, the solar and lunar tides partly cancel each other. Then, the high tides are lower than average, and the low tides are not as low as average low tides. These are called **neap tides.**

Because much of the earth is deformable, we have earth tides, although they are less pronounced than ocean tides. Twice each day, the solid surface of the earth rises and falls as much as one-quarter meter.

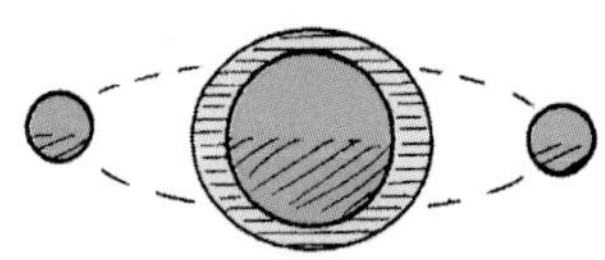

Figure 4.18
When the pulls of the sun and moon are at right angles to each other, neap tides occur.

Figure 4.19
Praful Shah uses a model of the sun, moon, and earth to explain tides. Is he demonstrating a spring tide or a neap tide?

There are also atmospheric tides, which regulate the cosmic rays that reach the earth's surface. Cosmic-ray penetration is evident in subtle changes in the behaviors of living things. Ocean tides, earth tides, and atmospheric tides are greatest when the sun, earth, and moon are aligned—at the time of a full or new moon. Our brief discussion of tides is quite simplified, because the tilt of the earth's axis, interfering land masses, friction with the ocean bottom, and other factors complicate tidal motions. Tides are fascinating.

Figure 4.20
Unequal tides are due to the earth's tilt.

Newton deduced that the difference in pulls decreases as the *cube* of the distance between the centers of the bodies—twice as far away produces one-eighth the tide; three times as far, only 1/27 the tide, and so on. Only relatively close distances result in appreciable tides, and so the nearby moon out-pulls the enormously more massive but farther-away sun. The magnitude of the tide also depends on the size of the body in which the tides are produced. Although the moon produces considerable tides in the earth's oceans, which are thousands of kilometers apart, it produces scarcely any tides in a lake. That's because no part of the lake is significantly closer to the moon than any other part—this means that there is no significant *difference* in moon pulls on the lake. The same is true for the fluids in your body. Any tides in the fluids of your body caused by the moon are negligible. You're not tall enough for tides. What microtides the moon may produce in your body are only about one two-hundredth the magnitude of the tides that would be produced in your body by a one-kilogram melon held one meter above your head!

Figure 4.21
The tidal force difference due to a 1-kg body 1 m over the head of a person of average height is about 60-trillionths N/kg. For an overhead moon, it is about 0.3-trillionths N/kg. So a melon held over your head produces about 200 times as much tidal effect in your body as the moon!

☑ CHECKPOINT

1. If you were able to pull a blob of Jell-O equally on all parts, it would be able to maintain its shape as it moves. But if you were able to pull harder on one end than the other, it would stretch. How does this relate to tides?
2. If the moon didn't exist, would ocean tides occur on the earth? If so, how often?
3. We know that both the moon and the sun produce our ocean tides. And we know that the moon plays the greater role because it is closer. Does its closeness imply that it pulls the oceans with a greater gravitational force than the sun?

Check Your Answers

1. Just as differences in pulls on the Jell-O would distort it, differences in pulls on the oceans distort the oceans and produce tides.
2. Yes, the earth's tides would be due only to the sun. They'd occur twice per day (every 12 hours instead of every 12.4 hours) due to the earth's daily rotation.
3. No, the sun's pull is much stronger. Tides are not caused by gravitational pulls. Tides are caused by *differences* in pulls across a body. Differences in pulls, not pulling strength, is the key to tides. (Amazingly, if the moon were considerably closer to earth, increased tides on the moon could tear the moon into pieces. Astronomers believe that the planetary rings of Saturn and other planets formed in this way.)

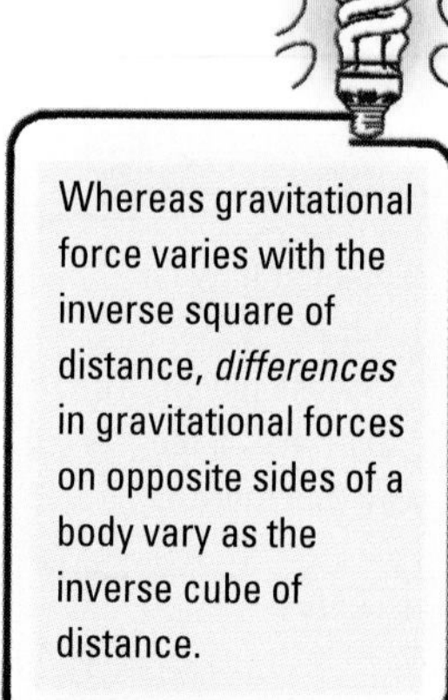

Link to Power Production

Tidal Power

Since 1968, electric power has been produced by ocean tides in Brittany, France. A dam in the estuary at nearby La Rance gets its power from the rising and falling of the daily ocean tides. First, the water is higher on one side of the dam, and its level is maintained at three meters higher than the lower side. It then flows through a tube to the lower side, turning 24 huge turbines in the process. When the tide changes, the water flows in the reverse direction, again turning the turbines. The dam, which supports a highway that allows traffic to cross the estuary, produces more than 200 MW of power for a city of 300,000 people.

4.6 Universal Gravitation

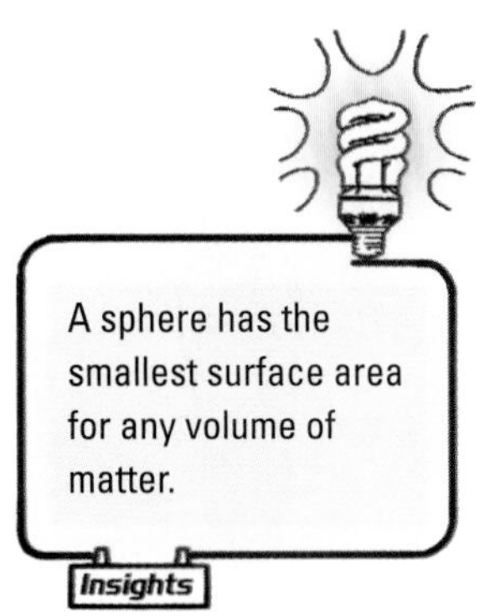

We all know that the earth is round. But why is the earth round? It is round because of gravitation. Everything attracts everything else, and so the earth has attracted itself together as far as it can! Any "corners" of the earth have been pulled in; as a result, every part of the surface is approximately equidistant from the center of gravity. This makes it a sphere. Therefore, we see from the law of gravitation that the sun, the moon, and earth are approximately spherical because they must be. (Rotational effects make them slightly ellipsoidal.)

If everything pulls on everything else, then the planets must pull on each other. The force that controls Jupiter, for example, is not just the force from the sun; there are also the pulls from the other planets. Their effect is small in comparison with the pull of the much more massive sun, but it still shows. When Saturn is near Jupiter, its pull disturbs the otherwise smooth path traced by Jupiter. Both planets "wobble" about their expected orbits. The interplanetary forces causing this wobbling are called *perturbations*. By the 1840s, studies of the most recently discovered planet, Uranus, showed that the deviations of its orbit could not be explained by perturbations from all other known planets. Either the law of gravitation didn't apply at this great distance from the sun, or an unknown eighth planet was perturbing Uranus. An Englishman and a Frenchman, J. C. Adams and Urbain Leverrier, each assumed Newton's law to be valid, and they calculated independently where the eighth planet should be. At about the same time, Adams sent a letter to the Greenwich Observatory in England and Leverrier sent a letter to the Berlin Observatory in Germany, both suggesting that a certain area of the sky be searched for the new planet. The request by Adams was delayed by misunderstandings at Greenwich, but Leverrier's request was heeded immediately. The planet Neptune was discovered that very night!

No matter how far you travel, you can never escape Earth's gravity. It's all the way "out there."

Insights

Studies of the orbit of Neptune and further refinements in calculations of the orbit of Uranus led to the prediction and discovery of Pluto, the ninth planet, in 1930 at the Lowell Observatory in Arizona. Many astronomers regard Pluto as an asteroid and not a true planet. In any event, the object we call Pluto takes 248 years to make a single revolution about the sun, so no one will see it in its discovered position again until the year 2178.*

*Recent evidence suggests the presence of a *dark matter* throughout the universe. This is mysterious matter, unlike the matter we know. We can't see it, but its gravitational presence is sensed by stars and galaxies.

Newton showed that terrestrial laws and celestial laws are one and the same. Few theories have affected science and civilization as much as Newton's theory of gravitation. The successes of Newton's ideas ushered in the so-called Age of Enlightenment, for Newton had demonstrated that, by observation and reason and by employing mechanical models and deducing mathematical laws, people could uncover the very workings of the physical universe. How profound that all the moons and planets and stars and galaxies have such a beautifully simple rule to govern them; namely,

$$F = G\frac{m_1 m_2}{d^2}$$

The formulation of this simple rule is one of the major reasons for the successes in science that followed, for it provided hope that other phenomena of the world might also be described by equally straightforward laws.

This hope nurtured the thinking of many scientists, artists, writers, and philosophers of the 1700s. One of these was the English philosopher John Locke, who argued that observation and reason, as demonstrated by Newton, should be our best judge and guide in all things, and that all of nature and even society should be searched to discover any "natural laws" that might exist. Using Newtonian physics as a model of reason, Locke and his followers modeled a system of government that found adherents in the thirteen British colonies across the Atlantic. These ideas culminated in the Declaration of Independence and the Constitution of the United States of America.

Summary of Terms

The law of universal gravitation Every mass in the universe attracts every other mass with a force that for two masses is directly proportional to the product of their masses and inversely proportional to the square of the distance separating them:

$$F = G\frac{m_1 m_2}{d^2}$$

Inverse-square law A law relating the intensity of an effect to the inverse square of the distance from the cause:

$$\text{Intensity} \sim \frac{1}{\text{distance}^2}$$

Gravity follows an inverse-square law, as do the effects of electric, magnetic, light, sound, and radiation phenomena.

Weightlessness A condition encountered in free-fall wherein a support force is lacking.

Spring tide A high or low tide that occurs when the sun, earth, and moon are aligned so that the tides due to the sun and moon coincide, making high tides higher than average and low tides lower than average.

Neap tide A tide that occurs when the moon is midway between new and full, in either direction. Tides due to the sun and moon partly cancel, making the high tides lower than average and the low tides higher than average.

Review Questions

1. What was it that Newton discovered about gravity?
2. What is the Newtonian synthesis?

4.1 The Law of Universal Gravitation

3. In Newton's insight, what did a falling apple have in common with the moon?
4. In what sense does the moon "fall?"
5. State Newton's law of universal gravitation in words. Then do the same with one equation.
6. How does the force of gravity between two objects depend on their masses?
7. How does the force of gravity depend on the distance between two objects?

4.2 The Universal Gravitational Constant, *G*

8. What is the magnitude of gravitational force between two 1-kilogram bodies that are 1 meter apart?
9. What is the magnitude of the gravitational force between you and the earth?

10. When G was first measured in the eighteenth century, how did newspapers report the experiment?

4.3 Gravity and Distance: The Inverse-Square Law

11. How does the force of gravity between two bodies change when the distance between them is doubled?
12. How does the thickness of paint sprayed on a surface change when the sprayer is held twice as far away?
13. How does the brightness of light change when a point source of light is moved twice as far away?
14. Can you escape from the earth's gravity by getting above the atmosphere? By going to the moon? Defend your answers.
15. At what distance from earth is the gravitational force on an object zero?
16. What is a gravitational field, and how can its presence be detected?

4.4 Weight and Weightlessness

17. Would the springs inside a bathroom scale be more compressed or less compressed if you weighed yourself in an elevator that accelerated upward? Downward?
18. Would the springs inside a bathroom scale be more compressed or less compressed if you weighed yourself in an elevator that moved upward at a constant *velocity*? Downward at a constant *velocity*?
19. When is your weight equal to mg?
20. Give an example of when your weight is more than mg.
21. Give an example of when your weight is zero.
22. How can weight be simulated in a space habitat?

4.5 Tides

23. Do tides depend more on the strength of gravitational pull or on the *difference* in strengths? Explain.
24. Why do both the sun and the moon exert a greater gravitational force on one side of the earth than on the other?
25. Why are all tides greatest at the time of a full or new moon?
26. When would the highest high tides occur, during a spring tide or a neap tide?
27. Do tides occur in the molten interior of the earth for the same reason that tides occur in the oceans?
28. (Fill in the blank.) Whereas gravitational force depends on the inverse square of distance, tidal force, the difference in gravitational forces per unit mass, depends on the inverse ______ of distance.

4.6 Universal Gravitation

29. What was the cause of the perturbations discovered in the orbit of the planet Uranus? What greater discovery did this lead to?
30. What link does the book cite between Newton's law of gravitation and the Declaration of Independence and the Constitution of the United States?

Activities

1. Hold your hands outstretched, one twice as far from your eyes as the other, and make a casual judgment as to which hand looks bigger. Most people see them to be about the same size, while many see the nearer hand as slightly bigger. Almost no one, upon casual inspection, sees the nearer hand as four times as big. But, by the inverse-square law, the nearer hand should appear twice as tall and twice as wide and, therefore, should occupy four times as much of your visual field as the farther hand. Your belief that your hands are the same size is so strong that you likely overrule this information. Now if you overlap your hands slightly and view them with one eye closed, you'll see the nearer hand as clearly bigger. This raises an interesting question: What other illusions do you have that are not so easily checked?

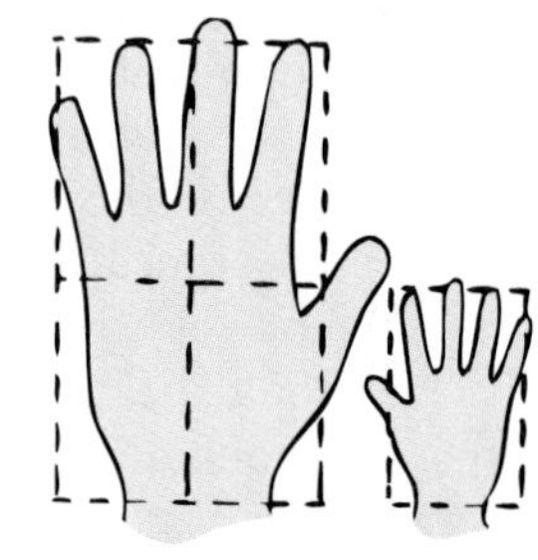

2. Repeat the above eyeballing activity, only this time use two one-dollar bills—one regular, and the other folded along its middle and then again along its width, so it has one-fourth the area. Now hold the two bills in front of your eyes. Where do you hold the folded one so that it looks the same size as the unfolded one? Try this with your friends!

Exercises

1. Comment on whether or not this label on a consumer product should be cause for concern. *CAUTION: The mass of this product pulls on every other mass in the universe, with an attracting force that is proportional to the product of the masses and inversely proportional to the square of the distance between them.*
2. Gravitational force acts on all bodies in proportion to their masses. Why, then, doesn't a heavy body fall faster than a light body?
3. What would be the path of the moon if somehow all gravitational forces on it vanished to zero?
4. Is the force of gravity stronger on a piece of iron than it is on a piece of wood of the same mass? Defend your answer.

5. Is the force of gravity stronger on a crumpled piece of paper than it is on an identical piece of paper that has not been crumpled? Defend your answer.
6. A friend says that, because the earth's gravity is so much stronger than the moon's gravity, rocks on the moon could be dropped from the moon to the earth. What is wrong with this assumption?
7. Another friend says that the moon's gravity would prevent rocks dropping from the moon to the earth, but that, if the moon's gravity somehow vanished to zero, the rocks on the moon would then fall to earth. What is wrong with this assumption?
8. A friend says that astronauts in orbit are weightless because they're beyond the pull of earth's gravity. Correct your friend's ignorance.
9. Somewhere between the earth and the moon, gravity from these two bodies on a space pod would cancel. Is this location nearer to the earth or to the moon?
10. The earth and the moon are attracted to each other by gravitational force. Does the more massive earth attract the less massive moon with a force that is greater, smaller, or the same as the force with which the moon attracts the earth? (With an elastic band stretched between your thumb and forefinger, which is pulled more strongly by the band—your thumb or your forefinger?)
11. If the earth were somehow expanded to a larger radius, with no change in mass, how would your weight be affected? How would it be affected if the earth were shrunk instead? (*Hint:* Let the equation for gravitational force guide your thinking.)
12. The intensity of light from a central source varies inversely as the square of the distance. If you lived on a planet only half as far from the sun as our earth, how would the light intensity compare with that on earth? How would it compare on a planet ten times farther away than the earth?
13. A small light source located 1 m in front of a 1-m^2 opening illuminates a wall behind. If the wall is 1 m behind the opening (2 m from the light source), the illuminated area covers 4 m^2. How many square meters will be illuminated if the wall is 3 m from the light source? 5 m? 10 m?

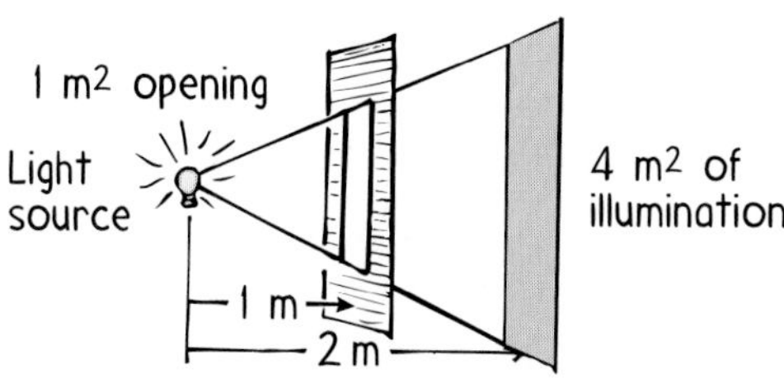

14. The planet Jupiter is more than 300 times as massive as earth, so it might seem that a body on the surface of Jupiter would weigh 300 times as much as on earth. But it so happens that a body would scarcely weigh three times as much on the surface of Jupiter as it would on the surface of the earth. Can you think of an explanation for why this is so? (*Hint:* Let the terms in the equation for gravitational force guide your thinking.)
15. Why do the passengers of high-altitude jet planes feel the sensation of weight while passengers in an orbiting space vehicle such as the space shuttle do not?
16. If you were in a car that drove off the edge of a cliff, why would you be momentarily weightless? Would gravity still be acting on you?
17. Is gravitational force acting on a person who falls off a cliff? On an astronaut inside the orbiting space shuttle?
18. If you were in a freely falling elevator and you dropped a pencil, it would hover in front of you. Is there a force of gravity on the pencil? Defend your answer.
19. How can gravity be simulated in an orbiting space station?
20. If you whirl a stone around and around in a circular path overhead, what is the direction of the force acting on the stone?
21. If you're whirling around and around inside a rotating space station, what is the direction of the force that keeps you in circular motion?
22. Suppose you're in a rotating space facility, and the rate of rotation is such that you press against a scale with as much force as you do on the earth's surface. What happens to your "weight" if the rotation rate is increased?
23. At a constant rotational rate, what happens to your "weight" as you climb a ladder toward the axis of rotation? What is your "weight" at the axis of rotation?
24. Inside a rotating space station, faster rotation results in greater support force. On the surface of a planet, however, faster rotation would result in less support force. Explain.
25. Most people today know that the ocean tides are caused principally by the gravitational influence of the moon. And most people think, therefore, that the gravitational pull of the moon on the earth is greater than the gravitational pull of the sun on the earth. What do you think?
26. If somebody tugged on your shirtsleeve, it might tear. But if all parts of your shirt were tugged equally, no tearing would occur. How does this relate to tidal forces?
27. Would ocean tides exist if the gravitational pull of the moon (and sun) were somehow equal on all parts of the world? Explain.

28. Why aren't high ocean tides exactly 12 hours apart?
29. With respect to spring and neap ocean tides, when are the lowest tides? That is, when is it best for digging clams?
30. Whenever the ocean tide is unusually high, will the following low tide be unusually low? Defend your answer in terms of "conservation of water." (If you slosh water in a tub so it is extra deep at one end, will the other end be extra shallow?)
31. The Mediterranean Sea has very little sediment churned up and suspended in its waters, mainly because of the absence of any substantial ocean tides. Why do you suppose the Mediterranean Sea has practically no tides? Similarly, are there tides in the Black Sea? In the Great Salt Lake? In your county reservoir? In a glass of water? Explain.
32. The human body is composed mostly of water. Why does the moon overhead cause appreciably smaller biological tides in the fluid compartment of your body than does a 1-kg melon held over your head?
33. If the moon didn't exist, would the earth still have ocean tides? If so, how often?
34. What would be the effect on the earth's tides if the diameter of the earth were very much larger than it is? If the earth were as it presently is, but the moon were very much larger and had the same mass?
35. Does the strongest tidal force on our bodies come from the earth, the moon, or the sun?
36. Exactly why do tides occur in the earth's crust and in the earth's atmosphere?
37. Which requires more fuel—a rocket going from the earth to the moon or a rocket returning from the moon to the earth? Why?
38. Some people dismiss the validity of scientific theories by saying they are "only" theories. The law of universal gravitation is a theory. Does this mean that scientists still doubt its validity? Explain.
39. Strictly speaking, you weigh a tiny bit less when you are in the lobby of a massive skyscraper than you do at home. Why is this so?
40. Make up two multiple-choice questions: one that would check a classmate's understanding of the inverse-square law, and another that would check a distinction between weight and weightlessness.

Problems

1. Find the change in the force of gravity between two planets when the distance between them is decreased by five times.
2. Show, by algebraic reasoning, that your gravitational acceleration toward an object of mass M a distance d away is $a = GM/d^2$ and therefore doesn't depend on your mass.
3. Many people mistakenly believe that the astronauts orbiting the earth are "above gravity." Calculate the acceleration due to gravity, g, for space shuttle territory, 200 kilometers above the earth's surface. Earth's mass is 6×10^{24} kg, and its radius is 6.38×10^6m (6380 km). Your answer is what percentage of 9.8 m/s^2?

4. Calculate the force of gravity between the earth (mass = 6×10^{24} kg) and the sun (mass = 2×10^{30} kg, distance = 1.5×10^{11} m).

Chapter 4 Online Resources

Tutorials
- Tides
- Detecting Dark Matter in a Spiral Galaxy

Videos
- Von Jolly's Method of Measuring the Attraction between Two Masses
- Inverse-Square Law
- Weight & Weightlessness
- Apparent Weightlessness
- Gravitational Field Inside a Hollow Planet
- The Weight of an Object Inside a Hollow Planet but Not at its Center
- Discovery of Neptune

Quiz
Exercises
Flashcards
Links

CHAPTER 5

Projectile and Satellite Motion

From the top of the mountain Mauna Kea in Hawaii (or from any high vantage point from which the distant ocean horizon is sharp and clear), you can see the curvature of the earth. To do so, you eyeball the line where ocean and sky meet against a long straightedge held in front of your eyes. Otherwise, you can't be sure whether or not your eyes are playing tricks on you. Line up your sight so that the bottom of the middle of the straightedge just touches the juncture between sky and ocean, and you'll note a space between sky and ocean at the ends. You're seeing the earth's curvature. Now throw a rock horizontally toward the horizon. It quickly falls several meters to the ground below in front of you. It curves as it falls. You'll note that the faster you throw the rock, the wider the curve. Then you wonder how fast Superman would have to throw the rock to clear the horizon ahead—and how fast he'd have to throw it so that its curved path matched the curve of the earth. For if he could do that, and air resistance were somehow eliminated, the rock would follow a curved path completely around the earth and become an earth satellite! A satellite is, after all, no more than a projectile moving fast enough to continually clear the horizon as it falls.

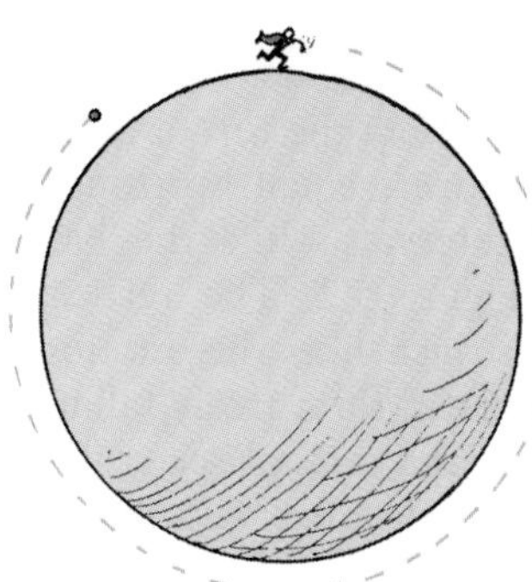

Figure 5.1
If Superman were to throw a rock fast enough, it would orbit the earth if there were no air resistance.

5.1 Projectile Motion

Without gravity, you could toss a rock at an angle skyward and it would follow a straight-line path. But, due to gravity, the path curves. A tossed rock, a cannonball, or any object that is projected by some means and continues in motion by its own inertia is called a **projectile.** To the cannoneers of earlier centuries, the curved paths of projectiles seemed very complex. Today, we see that these paths are surprisingly simple when the horizontal and vertical components of velocity are considered separately.

Projectile motion is nicely analyzed in Figure 5.2, which shows a simulated multiple-flash exposure of a ball rolling off the edge of a table. While on the table, it rolls freely of its own inertia and covers equal distances in equal intervals of time. That's because there's no horizontal force acting on the ball, neglecting friction. In the first box of the figure, we imagine there is no gravity, and we see the horizontal motion continue as the ball rolls off the table's edge. In the second box, we see vertical motion without a horizontal component. In the third and fourth boxes, we see the result of both motions. Notice

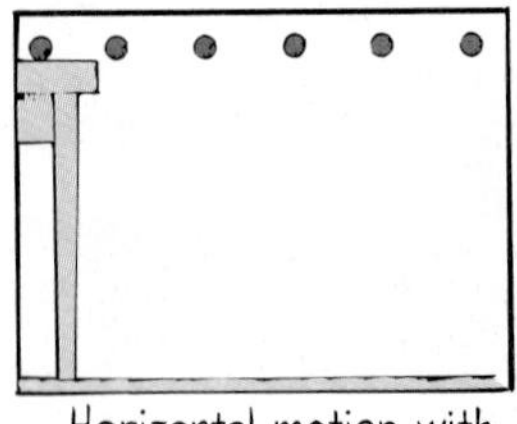

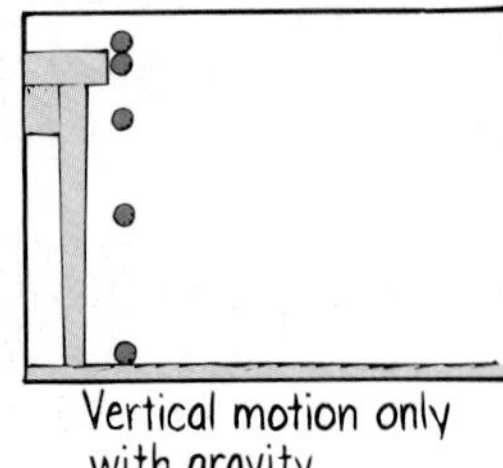

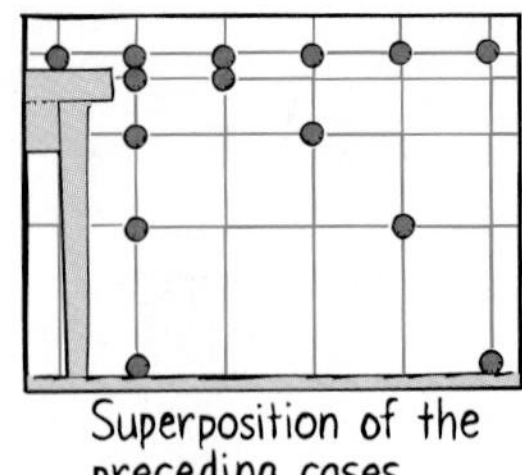

Figure 5.2
Simulated photographs of a moving ball illuminated with a strobe light. Notice that the curved path is a combination of horizontal and vertical motion.

two features. The first is that the ball's horizontal component of velocity doesn't change as the falling ball moves forward. The ball travels the same horizontal distance in equal time intervals because there is no component of gravitational force acting horizontally. Gravity acts only *downward,* so the only acceleration of the ball is *downward.* The second feature to notice is that the vertical positions become farther apart with time. These vertical distances are the same as they would be if the ball were simply dropped. Note that the curvature of the ball's path is the combination of horizontal motion that remains constant and vertical motion that undergoes acceleration due to gravity.

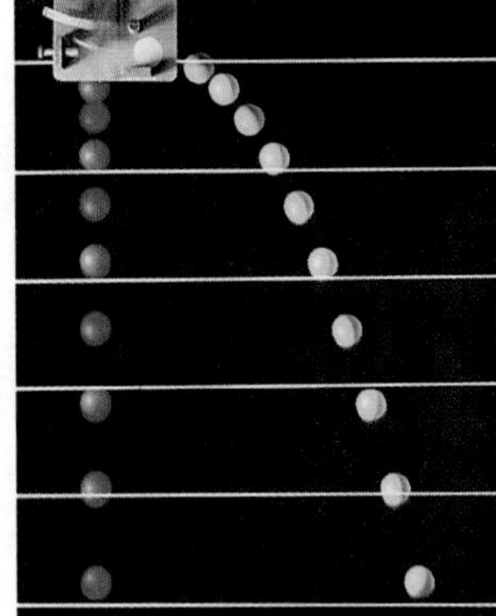

Figure 5.3
A strobe-light photograph of two golf balls released simultaneously from a mechanism that allows one ball to drop freely while the other is projected horizontally.

In Figure 5.4, we can see the same physics for a stone thrown horizontally from the top of a tall cliff. Note that the stone covers equal horizontal distances in equal time intervals—like the ball rolling off the table in Figure 5.2. The vertical component of motion is just like the motion described in Chapter 1 for a freely falling object. The greater the vertical speed, the greater the vertical distance covered in each successive second.

So we see that the horizontal and vertical components of velocity for a projectile are completely independent of each other (when air resistance is small enough to ignore). Each component is independent of the other. Their combined effects produce the curved paths of projectiles. When air resistance is small enough to neglect, as it is for a heavy object that doesn't build up great speed, the trajectory is a parabola.

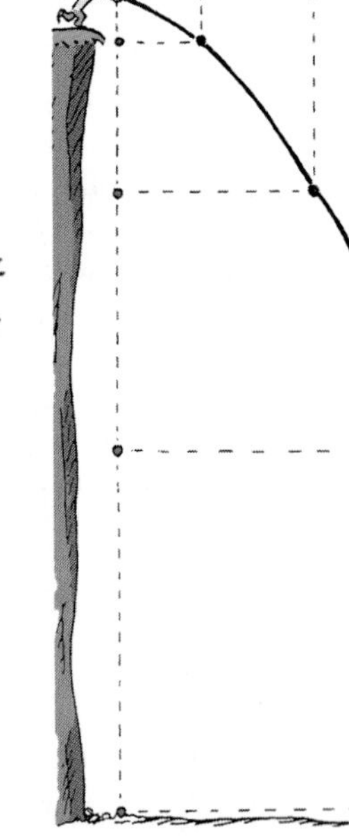

Figure 5.4
The vertical dashed line is the path of a stone dropped from rest. The horizontal dashed line would be its path if there were no gravity. The curved solid line shows the resulting trajectory that combines horizontal and vertical motion.

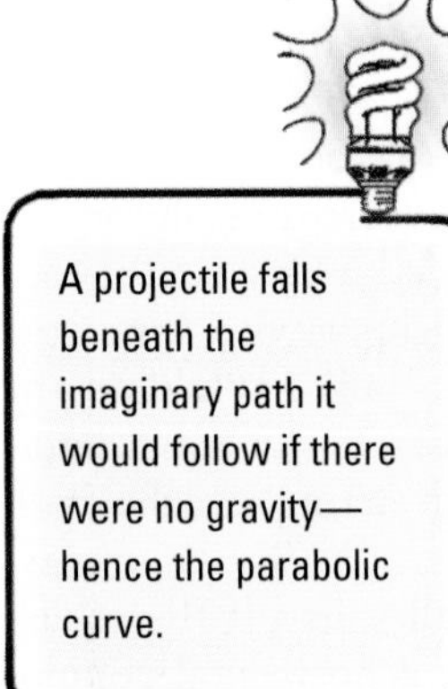

Figure 5.5
One cannonball is fired horizontally at the same time another is simply dropped from rest. Which hits the ground first?

☑ CHECKPOINT

At the instant a cannonball is fired horizontally over a level range, another cannonball held at the side of the cannon is released and drops to the ground. Which ball, the one fired downrange or the one dropped from rest, strikes the ground first?

Check Your Answer

Both cannonballs fall the same vertical distance with the same acceleration *g* and therefore strike the ground at the same time. Can you see that this is consistent with our analysis of Figures 5.2 and 5.4? We can reason this another way by asking which ball would strike the ground first if the cannon were pointed at an upward angle. Then the dropped cannonball would hit the ground first. Suppose the cannon is pointed downward. Then the fired ball would hit first. There must be some angle where both hit at the same time. Can you see it would be when the cannon is neither pointing upward nor downward—that is, when it is pointing horizontally?

Upwardly Launched Projectiles

Consider a cannonball shot at an upward angle (Figure 5.6). Pretend for a moment that there is no gravity; according to the law of inertia, the cannonball would follow the straight-line path shown by the dashed line. But there is gravity, so this doesn't happen. What really happens is that the cannonball continuously falls beneath the imaginary line until it finally strikes the ground. Get this: the vertical distance it falls beneath any point on the dashed line is the same vertical distance it would fall in the same time if it were dropped from rest at that point. This distance, as introduced in Chapter 1, is given by $d = 1/2\ gt^2$, where t is the elapsed time.

We can put it another way: Shoot a projectile skyward at some angle and pretend there is no gravity. After so many seconds t, it should be at a certain point along a straight-line path. But, because of gravity, it isn't. Where is it? The answer is that it's directly below this point. How far below? The answer in meters is $5t^2$ (or, more precisely, $4.9t^2$). How about that!

Note also from Figure 5.6 that the cannonball moves equal horizontal distances in equal time intervals.

Figure 5.6
If there were no gravity, the projectile would follow a straight-line path (dashed line). But, because of gravity, the projectile falls beneath this line by the same vertical distance it would fall if it were released from rest. Compare the distances fallen with those given in Table 1.1 in Chapter 1. (With $g = 9.8\ m/s^2$, these distances are more precisely 4.9 m, 19.6 m, and 44.1 m.)

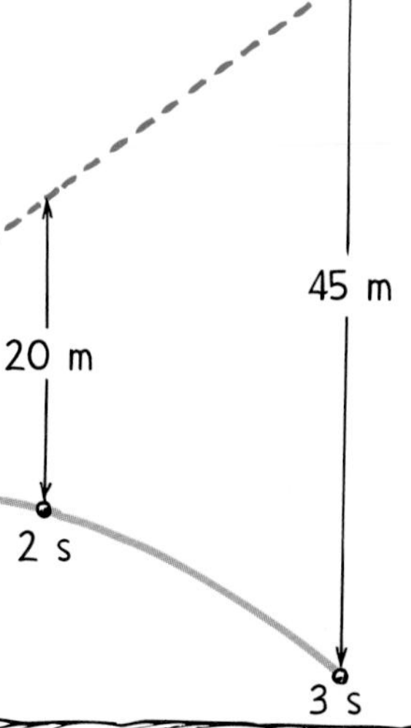

Figuring Physical Science

Problems

1. Suppose the cannonball in Figure 5.6 were fired faster. How many meters below the dashed line would it be at the end of the 5 s?

2. If the horizontal component of the cannonball's velocity were 20 m/s, how far downrange would the cannonball be at the end of 5 s?

Solutions

1. Using $g = 10$ m/s^2, the vertical distance beneath the dashed line at the end of 5 s is 125 m [$d = 5t^2 = 5(5)^2 = 5(25) = 125$ m]. Interestingly enough, this distance doesn't depend on the angle of the cannon. If air resistance is neglected, any projectile will fall $5t^2$ meters below where it would have reached if there were no gravity.

2. With no air resistance, the cannonball will travel a horizontal distance of 100 m [$d = \overline{v}t = (20$ m/s$)(5$ s$) = 100$ m]. With no acceleration in the horizontal direction, the cannonball travels equal horizontal distances in equal times. This distance is simply its horizontal component of velocity multiplied by the time (and not by $5t^2$, which applies only to vertical motion under the acceleration of gravity).

That's because no acceleration occurs horizontally. The only acceleration is vertical, in the direction of earth's gravity. The vertical distance that the cannonball falls below the imaginary straight-line path during equal time intervals continuously increases with time.

In Figure 5.8, we see the trajectories of stones thrown at an angle upward (*left*) and downward (*right*). The dashed straight lines show the ideal paths of the stones if there were no gravity. Notice that the vertical distance beneath the idealized straight-line paths is the same for equal times. This vertical distance is independent of what's happening horizontally.

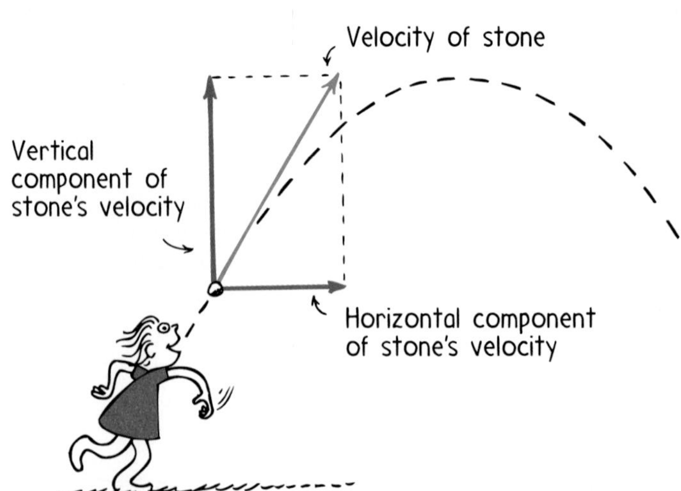

Figure 5.7
Vertical and horizontal components of a stone's velocity. Only the vertical component changes with time—decreasing while rising *against* gravity, and increasing when descending and traveling *with* gravity. Only the horizontal component remains constant, because it goes neither against nor with gravity.

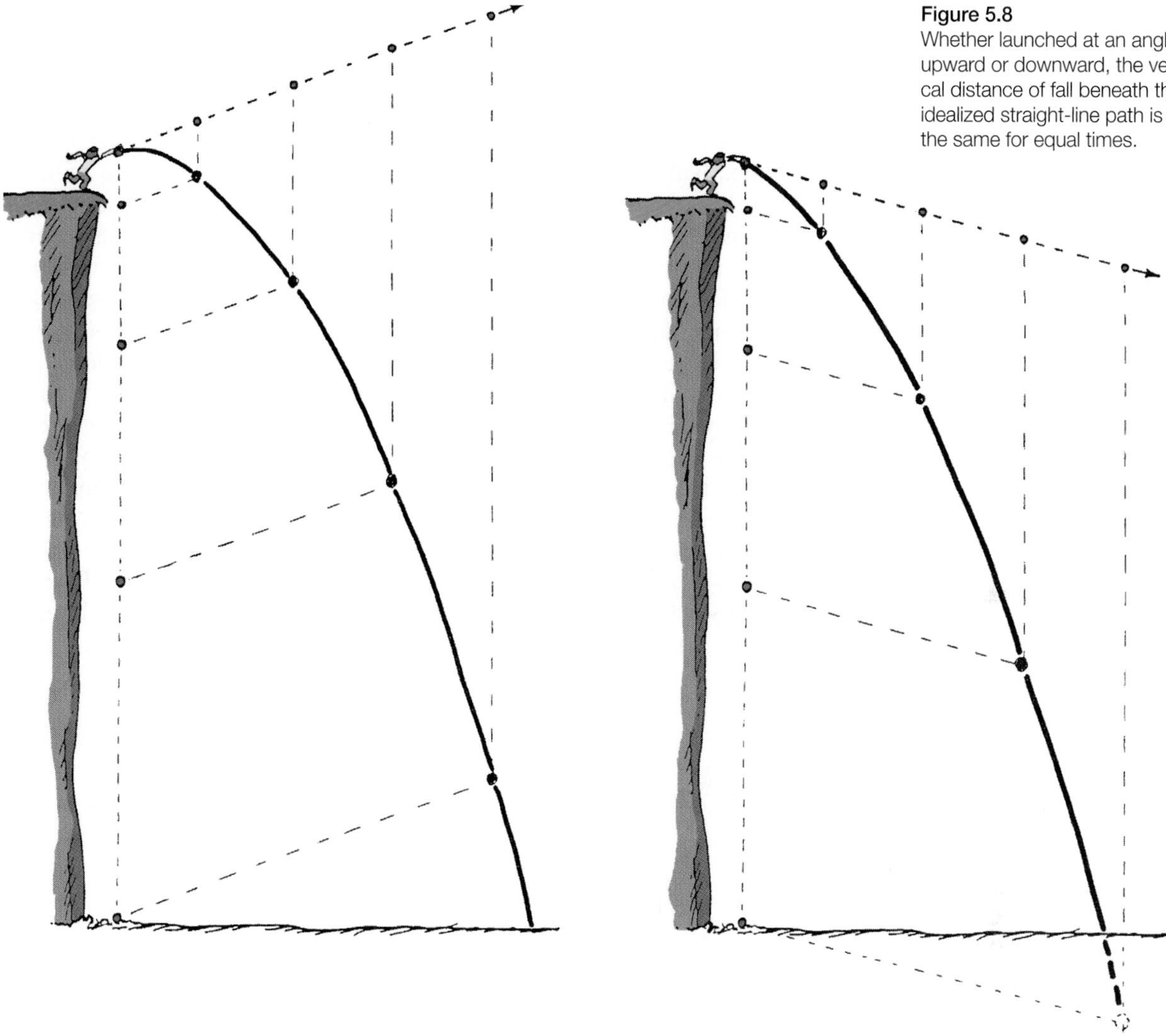

Figure 5.8
Whether launched at an angle upward or downward, the vertical distance of fall beneath the idealized straight-line path is the same for equal times.

Figure 5.9 shows the paths of several projectiles, all with the same initial speed but with different launching angles. With negligible air resistance, the trajectories are all parabolas. Notice that these projectiles reach different *altitudes,* or heights above the ground. They also have different *horizontal ranges,* or distances traveled horizontally. The remarkable thing to note from Figure 5.9 is that the same range is obtained from two different launching angles when the angles add up to 90 degrees! An object thrown into the air at an angle of 60 degrees, for example, has the same range as if it were thrown at the same speed at an angle of 30 degrees. For the smaller angle, of course, the object remains in

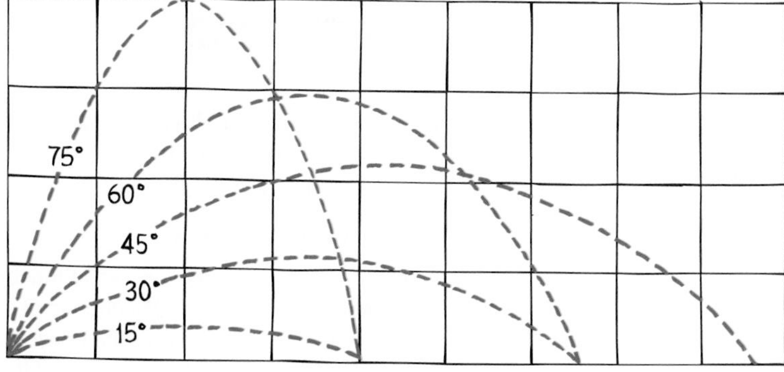

Figure 5.9
Ranges of a projectile shot at the same speed at different projection angles.

Figure 5.10
In the ideal case (same launch speed and no air resistance), maximum range would be attained when a ball is batted at an angle of 45 degrees.

the air for a shorter time. For negligible air resistance, the greatest range occurs when the launching angle is 45 degrees.

Without air resistance and for the same batting force, the maximum range for a baseball can be attained when the ball is batted 45 degrees above the horizontal. Actually, a more forceful ball–bat contact can be made lower on the bat, so a batted ball's speed is greater at a lower angle. This, combined with air resistance, makes about 35 degrees the favored angle for maximum range. Air resistance is more significant for golf balls, where angles of about 38 degrees result in maximum range. For heavier projectiles, such as javelins and the shot, air resistance has less effect on range. A javelin, being heavy and presenting a very small frontal area to the air, follows an almost perfect parabola when thrown. So does the shot. For such a projectile, the maximum range for equal launch speeds would occur for a launch angle of about 45 degrees (slightly less, because the launching height is above ground level). Aha! But launching speeds are not equal for such projectiles thrown at different angles. In throwing a javelin or putting a shot, a significant part of the launching *force* goes into combating gravity—the steeper the angle, the less speed the projectile has when leaving the thrower's hand. You can test this yourself. Throw a heavy boulder horizontally, then vertically—you'll find the horizontal throw to be considerably faster than the vertical throw. So maximum range for heavy projectiles thrown by humans is attained for angles less than 45 degrees—and not because of air resistance.

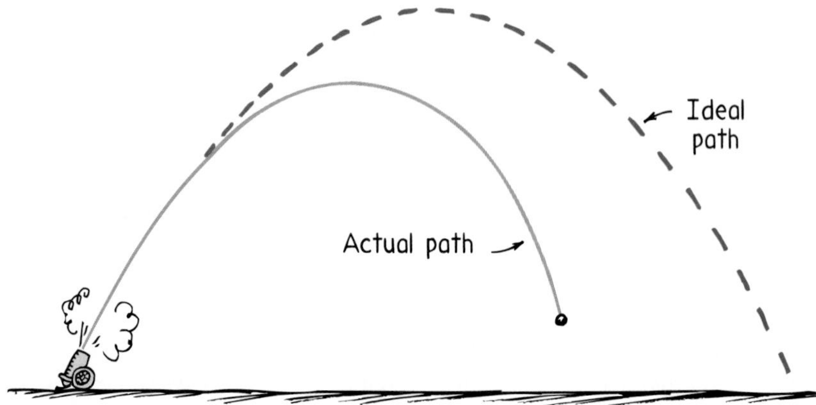

Figure 5.11
In the presence of air resistance, the trajectory of a high-speed projectile falls short of the idealized parabolic path.

☑ CHECKPOINT

1. At what part of its trajectory does a baseball have minimum speed?
2. Consider a batted baseball following a parabolic path on a day when the sun is directly overhead. How does the speed of the ball's shadow across the field compare with the ball's horizontal component of velocity?

Check Your Answers

1. A ball's minimum speed occurs at the top of its trajectory. If it is launched vertically, its speed at the top is zero. If launched at an angle, the vertical component of velocity is zero at the top, leaving only the horizontal component. So the speed at the top is equal to the horizontal component of the ball's velocity at any point. Isn't that nice?
2. They are the same!

Hang Time Revisited

In Chapter 1 we stated that airborne time during a jump is independent of horizontal speed. Now we see why this is so—the horizontal and the vertical components of motion are independent of each other. The rules of projectile motion apply to jumping. Once one's feet are off the ground, only the force of gravity acts on the jumper (neglecting air resistance).

Hang time depends only on the vertical component of lift-off velocity. It turns out that jumping lift-off force can be somewhat increased by the action of running, so hang time for a running jump usually exceeds hang time for a standing jump. But, once the feet are off the ground, only the vertical component of lift-off velocity determines hang time.

When air resistance is small enough to be negligible, a projectile will rise to its maximum height in the same time it takes to fall from that height to the ground (Figure 5.12). This is because its deceleration by gravity while going up is the same as its acceleration by gravity while coming down. The speed it loses while ascending is therefore the same as the speed gained while descending. So the projectile arrives at the ground with the same speed it had when it was initially projected.

Baseball games normally take place on level ground. For the short-range projectile motion on the playing field, the earth can be considered to be flat because the flight of the ball is not affected by the earth's curvature. For very long-range projectiles, however, the curvature of the earth's surface must be taken into account. We'll now see that if an object is projected fast enough, it will fall all the way around the earth and become an earth satellite. We begin by considering the trajectory of a projectile launched horizontally from an elevated position—the baseball thrown from a 5-meter-high tower (Figure 5.13).

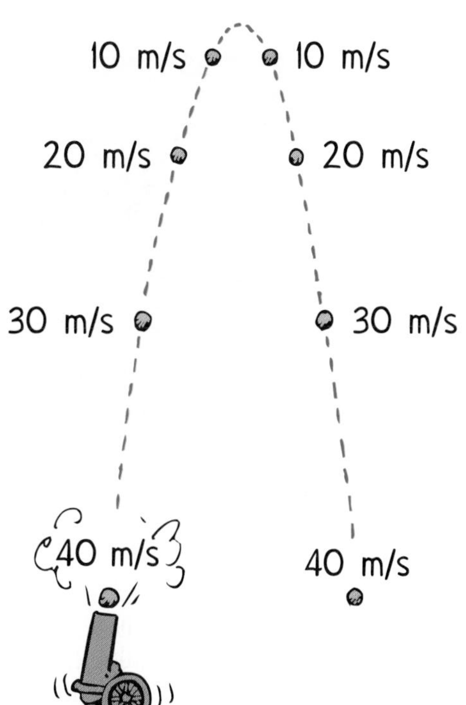

Figure 5.12
Without air resistance, speed lost while going up equals speed gained while coming down: time going up equals time coming down.

> The longest hang time for a standing jump is 1 second, for a record height of 1.25 meters (4 ft). Can anyone in your school jump that high? With their feet 1.25 meters above the ground? Not likely!
>
> *Insights*

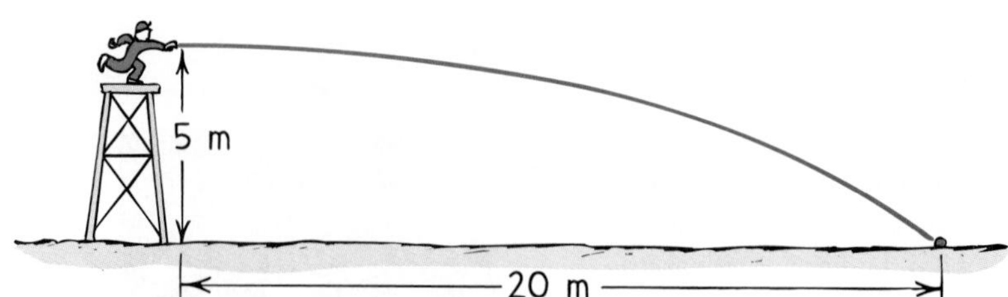

Figure 5.13
How fast is the ball thrown?

Figuring Physical Science

Problem

The boy on the tower throws a ball 20 m downrange, as shown in Figure 5.13. What is his pitching speed?

Solution

The ball is thrown horizontally, so the pitching speed is horizontal distance divided by time. A horizontal distance of 20 m is given, but the time is not stated. However, you can find the time because you know the vertical distance the ball drops—5 m, which takes 1 s. This means it travels horizontally 20 m in 1 s. So its horizontal component of velocity must be 20 m/s. From the equation for constant speed (which applies to horizontal motion), $v = d/t = (20\text{m})/(1\text{s}) = 20$ m/s. It is interesting to note that consideration of the equation for constant speed, $v = d/t$, guides thinking about the crucial factor in this problem—the time.

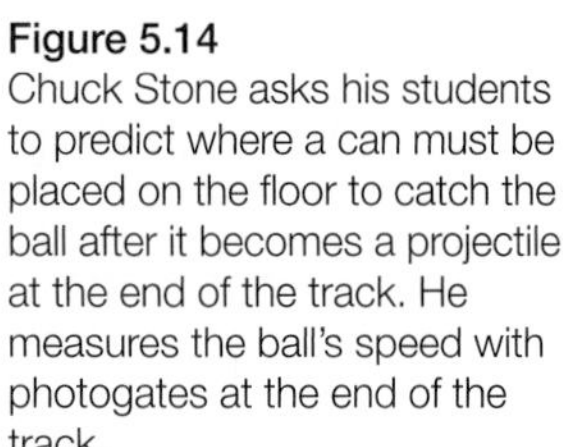

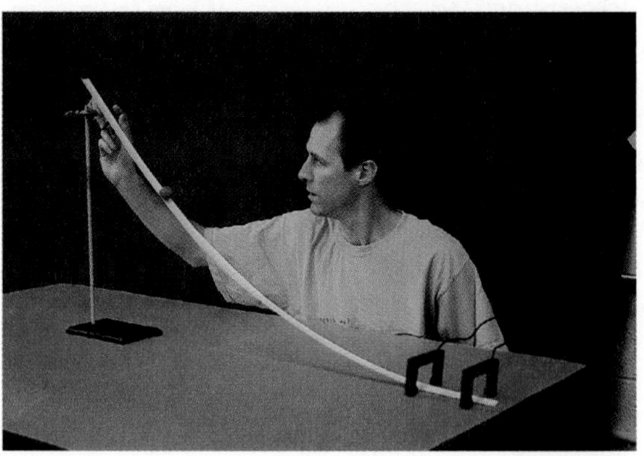

Figure 5.14
Chuck Stone asks his students to predict where a can must be placed on the floor to catch the ball after it becomes a projectile at the end of the track. He measures the ball's speed with photogates at the end of the track.

5.2 Fast-moving Projectiles—Satellites

Consider the baseball pitcher on the cliff in Figure 5.15. If gravity did not act on the ball, the ball would follow a straight-line path shown by the dashed line. But there is gravity, so the ball falls below this straight-line path. In fact, as discussed above, 1 second after the ball leaves the pitcher's hand it will have fallen a vertical distance of 5 meters below the dashed line—whatever the pitching speed. It is important to understand this, for it is the crux of satellite motion.

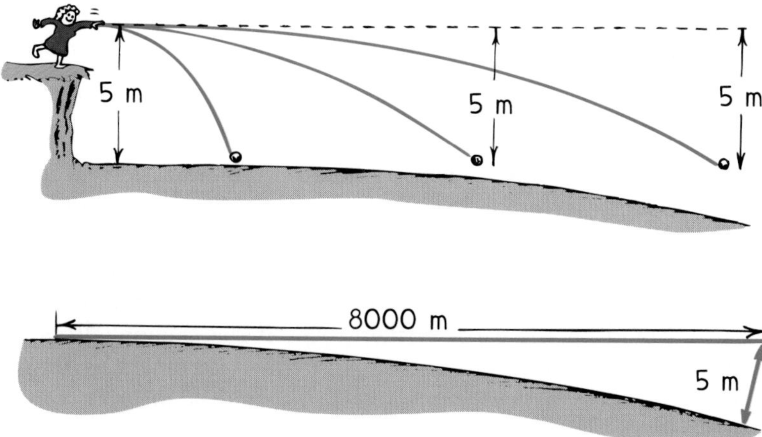

Figure 5.15
Throw a baseball at any speed, and one second later it will have fallen 5 m below where it would have been without gravity.

Figure 5.16
Earth's curvature—not to scale!

An earth satellite is simply a projectile that falls *around* the earth rather than *into* it. The speed of the satellite must be great enough to ensure that its falling distance matches the earth's curvature. A geometrical fact about the curvature of our earth is that its surface drops a vertical distance of 5 meters for every 8000 meters tangent to the surface (Figure 5.16). So, if a baseball could be thrown fast enough to travel a horizontal distance of 8 kilometers during the one second it takes to fall 5 meters, then it would follow the curvature of the earth. This is a speed of 8 kilometers per second. If this doesn't seem fast, convert it to kilometers per hour and you will get an impressive 29,000 kilometers per hour (or 18,000 miles per hour).

At this speed, atmospheric friction would burn the baseball, or even a piece of iron, to a crisp. This is the fate of bits of rock and other meteorites that enter the earth's atmosphere and burn up, appearing as "falling stars." That is why satellites such as the space shuttles are launched to altitudes of 150 kilometers or more—to be above almost all of the atmosphere and nearly free of the friction of air resistance. A common misconception is that satellites orbiting at high altitudes are free from gravity. Nothing could be further from the truth. The force of gravity on a satellite 200 kilometers above the earth's surface is nearly as strong as at the surface. The high altitude is not to place the

Figure 5.17
If the speed of the baseball and the curvature of its trajectory are great enough, the baseball may become a satellite.

Figure 5.18
The space shuttle is a projectile in a constant state of free-fall. Because of its tangential velocity, it falls around the earth rather than vertically into it.

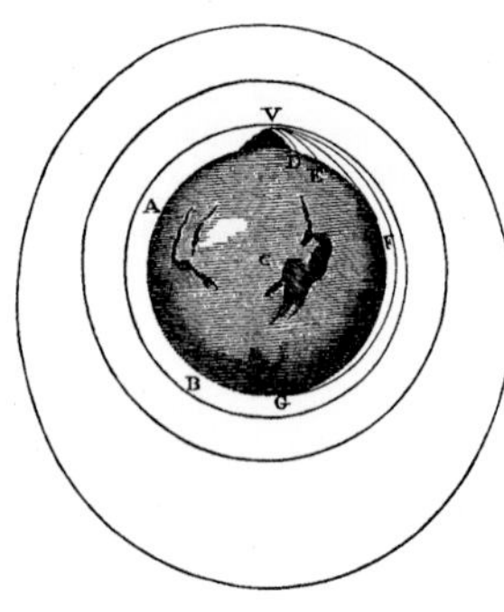

Figure 5.19
"The greater the velocity . . . with which (a stone) is projected, the farther it goes before it falls to the earth. We may therefore suppose the velocity to be so increased, that it would describe an arc of 1, 2, 5, 10, 100, 1000 miles before it arrived at the earth, till at last, exceeding the limits of the earth, it should pass into space without touching."—Isaac Newton, *System of the World.*

satellite beyond the earth's gravity, but beyond the earth's atmosphere, where air resistance is almost totally absent. (If you're using a yellow marker for important statements, yellow in the previous sentence!)

Satellite motion was understood by Isaac Newton, who reasoned that the moon is simply a projectile circling the earth under the attraction of gravity. This concept is illustrated in a drawing by Newton (Figure 5.19). He compared motion of the moon to a cannonball fired from the top of a high mountain—high enough to be above the earth's atmosphere, where air resistance wouldn't impede its motion. A slow-moving cannonball would follow a curved path and would soon hit the earth below. If it were fired faster, its path would be less curved, and it would hit the earth farther away. If the cannonball were fired fast enough, Newton reasoned, the curved path would become a circle, and the cannonball would circle the earth indefinitely. It would be in orbit.

Both cannonball and moon have tangential velocity (parallel to the earth's surface) sufficient to ensure motion *around* the earth rather than *into* it. If there is no resistance to reduce its speed, the moon or any earth satellite "falls" around and around the earth indefinitely. The same is true of the planets that continually fall around the sun in closed paths. Why don't the planets crash into the sun? They don't because of their tangential velocities. What would happen if their tangential velocities were reduced to zero? The answer is simple enough: with zero tangential velocity, they'd fall straight toward the sun and would indeed crash into it. Any objects in the solar system without sufficient tangential velocities have long ago crashed into the sun. What remains is the harmony we observe.

☑ CHECKPOINT

One of the beauties of physics is that there are usually different ways to view and explain a given phenomenon. Is the following explanation valid? Satellites remain in orbit instead of falling to the earth because they are beyond the main pull of earth's gravity.

Check Your Answer

No, no, a thousand times no! If any moving object were beyond the pull of gravity, it would move in a straight line and would not curve around the earth. Satellites remain in orbit because they are in the grip of gravity, not because they are beyond it. For the altitudes of most earth satellites, the earth's gravitational tug is only a few percent weaker than at the earth's surface.

5.3 Circular Satellite Orbits

A cannonball fired horizontally at 8 kilometers per second from Newton's mountain would follow the earth's curvature and glide in a circular path around the earth again and again (provided the cannoneer and the cannon got out of the way). (If it were fired faster, it would overshoot a circular orbit, as we will discuss in the following section.) Newton calculated the speed for a circular orbit, but, because such a cannon-muzzle velocity was clearly impossible (and because he probably didn't consider multistage rockets), he did not foresee humans launching satellites.

Doing Physical Science — The Water Bucket Swing

Swing a bucket of water in a vertical circle, as shown in Figure 5.20. If you swing it sufficiently fast, the water won't spill. The explanation is similar to why satellites don't "fall" to earth. Actually, both the water in the bucket and the satellites *are* falling. The water doesn't spill at the top of the swing because the bucket swings downward at least as fast as the water falls. Similarly, a satellite doesn't get closer to earth because it falls a distance that matches the earth's curvature. Analogies are the way to understand concepts!

Figure 5.20
Teacher Marshall Ellenstein whirls a bucket of water in a vertical circle and asks his class why water doesn't spill at the top of the swing. How does this relate to satellite motion?

Note that, in circular orbit, the speed of a satellite is not changed by gravity: only the direction changes. We can understand this by comparing a satellite in circular orbit with a bowling ball rolling along a bowling alley. Why doesn't the gravitational force that acts on the bowling ball change its speed? The answer is that gravitation pulls straight downward with no component of force acting forward or backward.

Consider a bowling alley that completely surrounds the earth, elevated high enough to be above the atmosphere and air resistance. The bowling ball will roll at constant speed along the alley. If a part of the alley is cut away, the ball would roll off its edge and hit the ground

Figure 5.21
Fired fast enough, the cannonball will go into orbit.

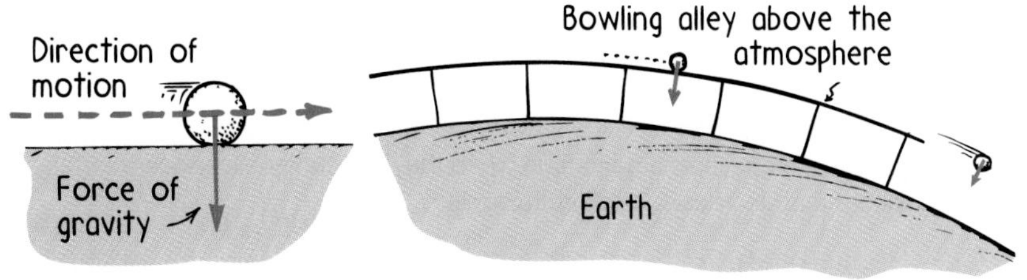

Figure 5.22
(left) The force of gravity on the bowling ball is at 90° to its direction of motion, so it has no component of force to pull it forward or backward, and the ball rolls at constant speed. (right) The same is true even if the bowling alley is larger and remains "level" with the curvature of the earth.

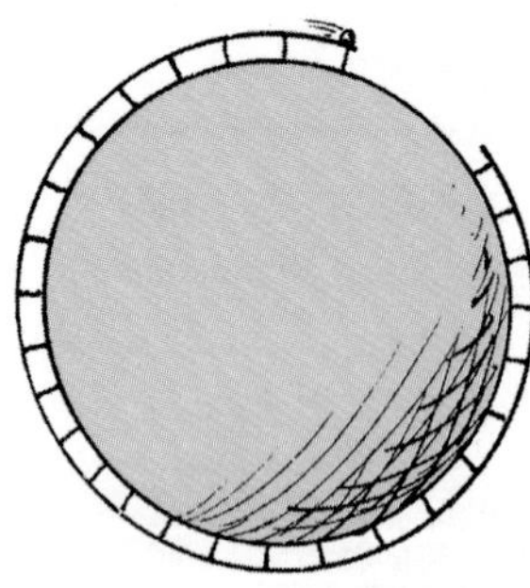

Figure 5.23
What speed will allow the ball to clear the gap?

below. A faster ball encountering the gap would hit the ground farther along the gap. Is there a speed whereby the ball will clear the gap (like a motorcyclist who drives off a ramp and clears a gap to meet a ramp on the other side)? The answer is yes: 8 kilometers per second will clear that gap—and any gap—even a 360-degree gap! It would be in circular orbit.

Note that a satellite in circular orbit is always moving in a direction perpendicular to the force of gravity that acts upon it. The satellite does not move in the direction of the force, which would increase its speed, nor does it move in a direction against the force, which would decrease its speed. Instead, the satellite moves at right angles to the gravitational force that acts upon it. With no component of motion along this force, no change in speed occurs—only change in direction. So we see why a satellite in circular orbit sails parallel to the surface of the earth at constant speed—a very special form of free-fall.

For a satellite close to the earth, the period (the time for a complete orbit around the earth) is about 90 minutes. For higher altitudes, the orbital speed is less, distance is more, and the period is longer. For example, communication satellites located in orbit 5.5 earth radii from earth have a period of 24 hours. This period matches the period of daily earth rotation. For an orbit around the equator, these satellites remain above the same point on the ground (which is why they appear to be motionless). The moon is even farther away and has a period of 27.3 days. The higher the orbit of a satellite, the less its speed, the longer its path, and the longer its period.*

Putting a payload into earth orbit requires control over the speed and direction of the rocket that carries it above the atmosphere. A rocket initially fired vertically is intentionally tipped from the vertical course. Then, once above the

> The initial vertical climb gets a rocket quickly through the denser part of the atmosphere. Eventually, the rocket must acquire enough tangential speed to remain in orbit without thrust, so it must tilt until finally its path is horizontal.
>
> **Insights**

☑ CHECKPOINT

1. True or false: The space shuttle orbits at altitudes in excess of 150 kilometers to be above both gravity and the earth's atmosphere.
2. Satellites in close circular orbit fall about 5 meters during each second of orbit. Why doesn't this distance accumulate and send satellites crashing into the earth's surface?

Check Your Answers

1. False. Satellites are above the atmosphere and air resistance—not gravity! It's important to note that earth's gravity extends throughout the universe in accord with the inverse-square law.
2. In each second, the satellite falls about 5 m below the straight-line tangent it would have taken in the absence of gravity. The earth's surface also curves 5 m beneath a straight-line 8-km tangent. The process of falling with the curvature of the earth continues from tangent line to tangent line, so the curved path of the satellite and the curve of the earth's surface "match" all the way around the earth. Satellites do, in fact, crash to the earth's surface from time to time when they encounter air resistance in the upper atmosphere that decreases their orbital speed.

*The speed of a satellite in a circular orbit is given by $v = \sqrt{GM/d}$, and the period of satellite motion is given by $T = 2\pi\sqrt{d^3/GM}$, where G is the universal gravitational constant (see previous chapter), M is the mass of the earth (or whatever body the satellite orbits), and d is the distance of the satellite from the center of the earth or parent body.

resistance of the atmosphere, it is aimed horizontally, whereupon the payload is given a final thrust to orbital speed. We see this in Figure 5.24, where, for the sake of simplicity, the payload is the entire single-stage rocket. With the proper tangential velocity, it falls around the earth, rather than into it, and it becomes an earth satellite.

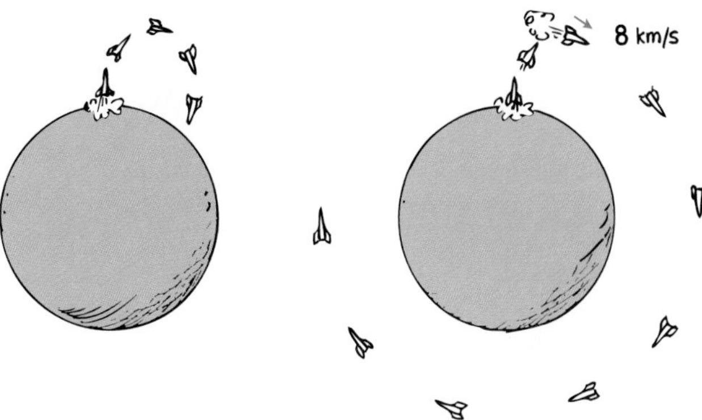

Figure 5.24
The initial thrust of the rocket pushes it up above the atmosphere. Another thrust to a tangential speed of at least 8 km/s is required if the rocket is to fall around (rather than into) the earth.

5.4 Elliptical Orbits

If a projectile just above the resistance of the atmosphere is given a horizontal speed somewhat greater than 8 kilometers per second, it will overshoot a circular path and trace an oval path called an **ellipse.**

An ellipse is a specific curve; the closed path taken by a point that moves in such a way that the sum of its distances from two fixed points (called *foci,* the plural of *focus*) is constant. For a satellite orbiting a planet, one focus is at the center of the planet; the other focus could be inside or outside of the planet. An ellipse can be easily constructed by using a pair of tacks (one at each focus), a loop of string, and a pencil (Figure 5.25). The closer the foci are to each other, the closer the ellipse is to a circle. When both foci are together, the ellipse is a circle. So we see that a circle is a special case of an ellipse.

Whereas the speed of a satellite is constant in a circular orbit, speed varies in an elliptical orbit. When the initial speed is greater than 8 km/s, the satellite overshoots a circular path and moves away from the earth, against the force of gravity. It therefore loses speed. The speed it loses in receding is regained as it falls back toward the earth, and it finally rejoins its original path with the same speed it had initially (Figure 5.27). The procedure repeats over and over, and an ellipse is traced each cycle.

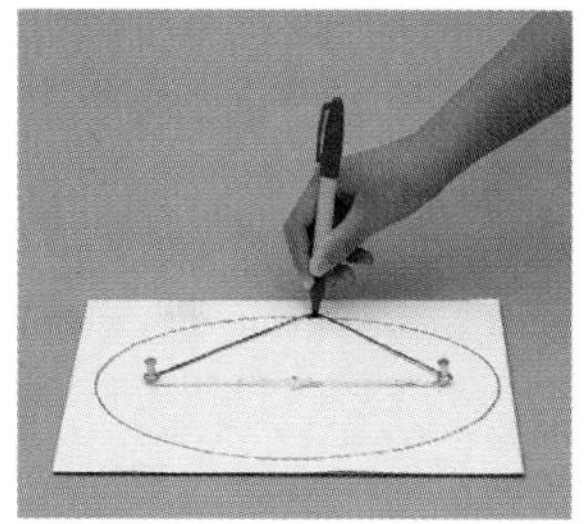

Figure 5.25
A simple method for constructing an ellipse.

Figure 5.26
The shadows cast by the ball are all ellipses, one for each lamp in the room. The point at which the ball makes contact with the table is the common focus of all three ellipses.

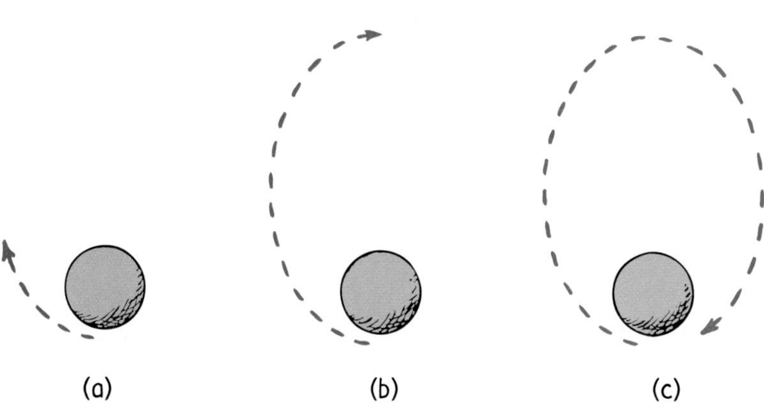

Figure 5.27
Elliptical orbit. An earth satellite that has a speed somewhat greater than 8 km/s overshoots a circular orbit (*a*) and travels away from the earth. Gravitation slows it to a point at which it no longer moves farther from the earth (*b*). It falls toward the earth, gaining the speed it lost in receding (*c*) and it follows the same path as before in a repetitious cycle.

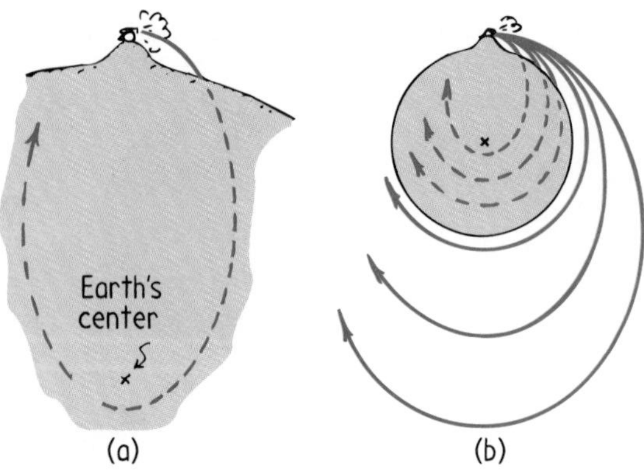

Figure 5.28
(*a*) The parabolic path of the cannonball is part of an ellipse that extends within the earth, with the far focus at the earth's center. (*b*) All paths of the cannonball are ellipses. For less-than-orbital speeds, the center of the earth is the far focus; for a circular orbit, both foci are the earth's center; for greater speeds, the near focus is the earth's center.

Interestingly enough, the parabolic path of a projectile, such as a tossed baseball or a cannonball, is actually a tiny segment of a thin ellipse that extends within and just beyond the center of the earth (Figure 5.28*a*). In Figure 5.28*b*, we see several paths of cannonballs fired from Newton's mountain. All these ellipses have the center of the earth as one focus. As muzzle velocity is increased, the ellipses are less eccentric (more nearly circular); and when muzzle velocity reaches 8 kilometers per second, the ellipse rounds into a circle and doesn't intercept the earth's surface. The cannonball coasts in circular orbit. At greater muzzle velocities, the orbiting cannonball traces the familiar external ellipse.

☑ **CHECKPOINT**

The orbital path of a satellite is shown in the sketch. In which of the marked positions A through D does the satellite have the greatest speed? The lowest speed?

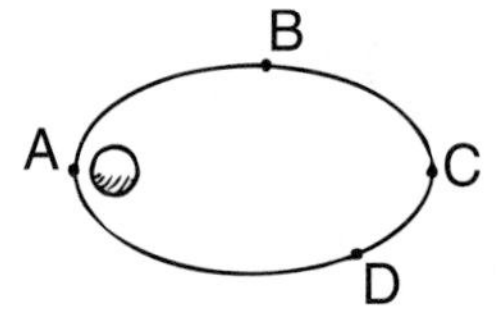

Check Your Answers

The satellite has its greatest speed as it whips around A and has its lowest speed at C. After passing C, it gains speed as it falls back to A to repeat its cycle.

Tycho Brahe (1546–1601)

Johannes Kepler (1571–1630)

5.5 Kepler's Laws of Planetary Motion

Newton's law of gravitation was preceded by three important discoveries about planetary motion by the German astronomer Johannes Kepler, who started as a junior assistant to the famed Danish astronomer Tycho Brahe. Brahe led the world's first great observatory in Denmark, just prior to the advent of the telescope. Using huge brass protractor-like instruments called *quadrants*, Brahe measured the positions of planets over twenty years so accurately that his measurements are still valid today. Brahe entrusted his data to Kepler. After Brahe's death, Kepler converted Brahe's measurements to values that would be obtained by a stationary observer outside the solar system. Kepler's expectation that the planets would move on perfect circles around the sun was shattered after years of effort. He found the paths to be ellipses. This is Kepler's first law of planetary motion:

Each planet moves in an elliptical orbit with the sun at one focus of the ellipse.

Kepler also found that the planets do not go around the sun at a uniform speed but move faster when they are nearer the sun and more slowly when they are farther from the sun. They accomplish this in such a way that an imaginary line or spoke joining the sun and the planet sweeps out equal areas of space in equal times. The triangular-shaped area swept out during a month when a planet is orbiting far from the sun (triangle *ASB* in Figure 5.29) is equal to the triangular area swept out during a month when the planet is orbiting closer to the sun (triangle *CSD* in Figure 5.29). This is Kepler's second law:

The line from the sun to any planet sweeps out equal areas of space in equal time intervals.

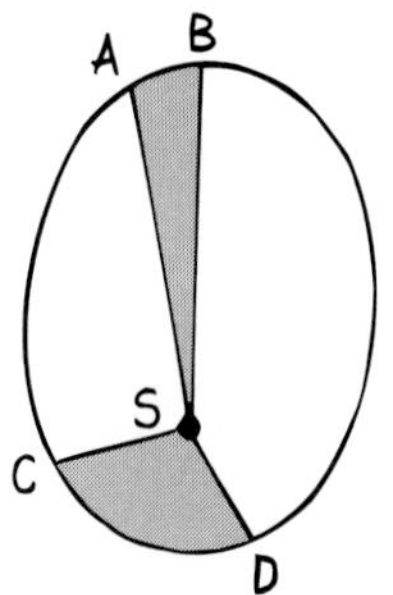

Figure 5.29
Equal areas are swept out in equal intervals of time.

Kepler was the first to coin the word *satellite*. He had no clear idea as to *why* the planets moved as he discovered they did. He lacked a conceptual model. Kepler didn't see that a satellite is simply a projectile under the influence of a gravitational force directed toward the body that the satellite orbits. You know that, if you toss a rock upward, it goes more slowly the higher it rises, because it's going against gravity. And you know that when it returns, it's going with gravity and its speed increases. Kepler never realized that a satellite behaves the same way. Going away from the sun, it slows down. Going toward the sun, it speeds up. A satellite, whether a planet orbiting the sun or one of today's satellites orbiting the earth, moves more slowly against the gravitational field and faster with the field. Kepler wasn't aware of this simplicity, and instead fabricated complex systems of geometrical figures to find sense in his discoveries. These proved to be futile.

Ten years later, Kepler discovered a third law. He had spent these years searching for a connection between the size of a planet's orbit and its period around the sun. From Brahe's data, Kepler found that the square of a period is proportional to the cube of its average distance from the sun. This means that the fraction T^2/R^3 is the same for all the planets, where T is the planet's period and R is the planet's average orbital radius. Law three is:

The squares of the periods (times of revolution) of the planets are proportional to the cubes of their average distances from the sun. ($T^2 \sim R^3$ **for all planets.**)

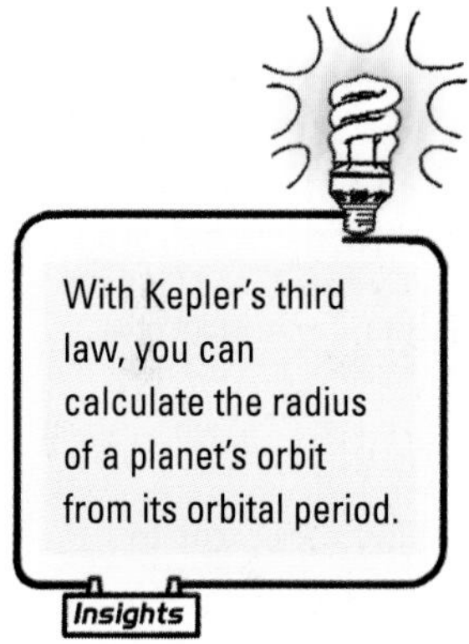

Kepler's laws apply not only to planets but also to moons or any satellite in orbit around any body. The elliptical orbits of the planets are very nearly circular. Only the precise measurements made by Brahe showed the slight differences.

It is interesting to note that Kepler was familiar with Galileo's ideas about inertia and accelerated motion, but he failed to apply them to his own work. Like Aristotle, he thought that the force on a moving body would be in the same direction as the body's motion. Kepler never appreciated the concept of inertia. Galileo, on the other hand, never appreciated Kepler's work, and he held to his conviction that the planets move in circles.* Further understanding of planetary motion required someone who could integrate the findings of these two great scientists.† The rest is history, for this task fell to Isaac Newton.

* It is not easy to look at familiar things through the new insights of others. We tend to see only what we have learned to see or wish to see. Galileo reported that many of his colleagues were unable to see, or refused to see, the moons of Jupiter when they peered skeptically through his telescopes. Galileo's telescopes were a boon to astronomy, but more important than a new instrument to see things better was a new way of understanding what is seen. Isn't this true today?

† Perhaps your instructor will show that Kepler's third law results when Newton's inverse-square formula for gravitational force is equated to centripetal force and how T^2/R^3 equals a constant that depends only on G and M, the mass of the body about which orbiting occurs. Intriguing stuff!

5.6 Energy Conservation and Satellite Motion

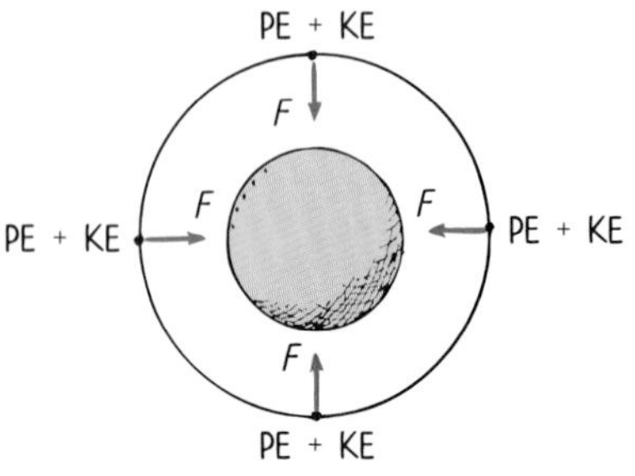

Figure 5.30
The force of gravity on the satellite is always toward the center of the body it orbits. For a satellite in a circular orbit, no component of force acts along the direction of motion. The speed, and thus the KE, do not change.

Recall, from Chapter 3, that a moving object has kinetic energy (KE) because of its motion. An object above the earth's surface has potential energy (PE) because of its position. Everywhere in its orbit, a satellite has both KE and PE relative to the body it orbits. The sum of the KE and PE is a constant all through the orbit. The simplest case occurs for a satellite in a circular orbit.

In circular orbit, the distance between the body's center and the satellite does not change, which means that the satellite's PE is the same everywhere in its orbit. Then, by the conservation of energy, the KE must also be constant. So a satellite in circular orbit coasts at a constant speed with an unchanging PE and KE (Figure 5.30).

In elliptical orbit, the situation is different. Both speed and distance vary. PE is greatest when the satellite is farthest away (at the apogee) and least when the satellite is closest (at the perigee). Note that the KE will be least when the PE is most, and the KE will be most when the PE is least. At every point in the orbit, the *sum* of KE and PE is the same.

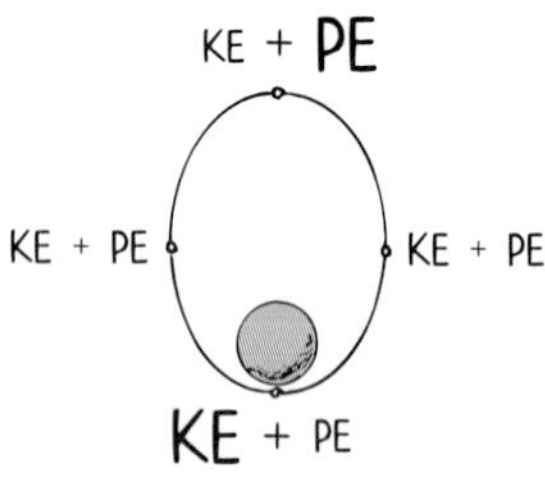

Figure 5.31
The sum of KE and PE for a satellite is a constant at all points along its orbit.

At all points along the elliptical orbit, there is a component of gravitational force in the direction of motion of the satellite (with two exceptions: at the apogee and at the perigee, where the force is perpendicular only). The component of force in the direction of motion changes the speed of the satellite. Or, by the work-energy theorem, we can say (this component of force) $\times$ (distance moved) = ΔKE. Either way, when the satellite gains altitude and moves against this component, its speed and KE decrease. The decrease continues to the apogee. Once past the apogee, the satellite moves in the same direction as the component, and the speed and KE increase. The increase continues until the satellite whips past the perigee and repeats the cycle.

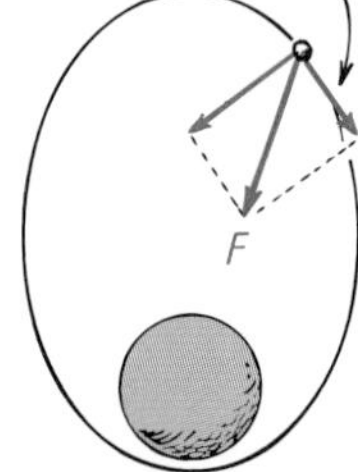

Figure 5.32
In an elliptical orbit, a component of force exists along the direction of the satellite's motion. This component changes the speed and, thus, the KE. (The perpendicular component changes only the direction.)

☑ CHECKPOINT

Why does the force of gravity change the speed of a satellite when it is in an elliptical orbit, but not when it is in a circular orbit?

Check Your Answer

At any point along its path, a satellite's direction of motion is always tangent to the path. If a component of force exists along this tangent, a change of speed occurs. In a circular orbit, the gravitational force is always perpendicular to the satellite's direction of motion, just as every part of the circumference of a circle is perpendicular to the radius. So there is no component of gravitational force along the tangent, and no change in speed (only direction changes). But when the satellite moves in directions that are not perpendicular to the force of gravity, as in an elliptical path, speed changes due to a component of force along the direction of motion. From a work-energy point of view, a component of force along the distance the satellite moves does work to change its KE.

5.7 Escape Speed

We know that a cannonball fired horizontally at 8 kilometers per second from Newton's mountain goes into orbit. But what would happen if the cannonball were instead fired at the same speed *vertically*? It would rise to some maximum height, reverse direction, and then fall back to earth. Then the old saying "What goes up must come down" would hold true, just as surely as a stone tossed skyward will be returned by gravity (unless, as we shall see, its speed is large enough).

In this age of space travel, it is more accurate to say "What goes up *may* come down," for there is a critical starting speed that allows a projectile to outrun gravity and to escape the earth. This critical speed is called the **escape speed** or, if direction is involved, the *escape velocity.* From the surface of the earth, escape speed is 11.2 kilometers per second. Launch a projectile at any speed greater than that and it will leave the earth, traveling slower and slower, never stopping due to the earth's gravity.* We can understand the magnitude of this speed from an energy point of view.

How much work would be required to lift a payload against the force of the earth's gravity to a distance very, very far ("infinitely far") away? We might think that the change of PE would be infinite because the distance is infinite. But gravitation diminishes with distance by the inverse-square law. The force of gravity on the payload would be strong only near the earth. It turns out that the change of PE of a 1-kilogram body moved from the surface of the earth to infinite distance is 62 million joules (62 MJ). So to put a payload infinitely far from the earth's surface requires at least 62 million joules of energy per kilogram of load. We won't go through the calculation here, but 62 million joules per kilogram corresponds to a speed of 11.2 kilometers per second, whatever the total mass involved. This is the escape speed from the surface of the earth.†

If we give a payload any more energy than 62 million joules per kilogram at the surface of the earth or, equivalently, any more speed than 11.2 kilometers per second, then, neglecting air resistance, the payload will escape from the earth, never to return. As it continues outward, its PE increases and its KE decreases. Its speed becomes less and less, although it is never reduced to zero. The payload outruns the gravity of the earth. It escapes.

The escape speeds from various bodies in the solar system are shown in Table 5.1. Note that the escape speed from the surface of the sun is 620 km/s. Even at a 150,000,000-km distance from the sun (earth's distance), the escape speed to break free of the sun's influence is 42.5 km/s—considerably more than the escape speed from the earth. An object projected from the earth at a speed greater than 11.2 km/s but less than 42.5 km/s will escape the earth but not the sun. Rather than recede forever, it will occupy an orbit around the sun.

The first probe to escape the solar system, Pioneer 10, was launched from earth in 1972 with a speed of only 15 km/s. The escape was accomplished by

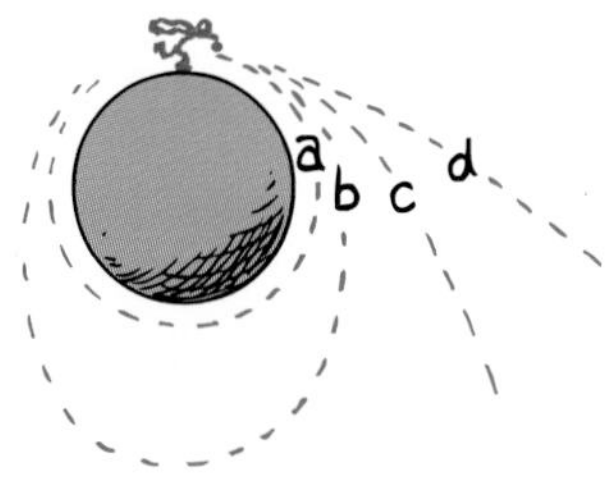

Figure 5.33
If Superman were to toss a ball 8 km/s horizontally from the top of a mountain high enough to be just above air resistance (a), then, about 90 minutes later, he could turn around and catch it (neglecting the earth's rotation). Tossed slightly faster (b), the ball will take an elliptical orbit and return in a slightly longer time. Tossed at more than 11.2 km/s (c), it will escape the earth's gravitational pull. Tossed at more than 42.5 km/s (d), it will escape from the solar system.

If you dropped a candy bar to the earth from a distance as far away from the earth as the earth is from Pluto, wouldn't its speed of impact be about 11.2 km/s?

Insights

*Escape speed from any planet or any body is given by $v = \sqrt{GM/d}$, where G is the universal gravitational constant, M is the mass of the attracting body, and d is the distance from its center. (At the surface of the body, d would simply be the radius of the body.) For a bit more mathematical insight, compare this formula with the one for orbital speed in the footnote on page 122.

†Interestingly enough, this might well be called the *maximum falling speed.* Any object, however far from the earth, if it is released from rest and allowed to fall to earth only under the influence of the earth's gravity, would not exceed 11.2 km/s. (With air resistance, it would be somewhat less.)

Table 5.1

Escape speeds from the surfaces of bodies in the solar system.

Astronomical body	Mass (in earth masses)	Radius (in earth radii)	Escape speed (km/s)
Sun	333,000	109	620
Sun (at a distance of the earth's orbit)		23,500	42.2
Jupiter	318.0	11.0	60.2
Saturn	95.2	9.2	36.0
Neptune	17.3	3.47	24.9
Uranus	14.5	3.7	22.3
Earth	1.00	1.00	11.2
Venus	0.82	0.95	10.4
Mars	0.11	0.53	5.0
Mercury	0.055	0.38	4.3
Moon	0.0123	0.27	2.4

directing the probe into the path of oncoming Jupiter. It was whipped about by Jupiter's great gravitational field, gaining speed in the process—similar to the increase in the speed of a baseball encountering an oncoming bat. Its speed of departure from Jupiter was increased enough to exceed the escape speed from the sun at the distance of Jupiter. Pioneer 10 passed the orbit of Pluto in 1984. Unless it collides with another body, it will wander indefinitely through interstellar space. Like a bottle cast into the sea with a note inside, Pioneer 10 contains information about the earth that might be of interest to extraterrestrials, put there in hopes that it will one day wash up and be found on some distant "seashore."

It is important to point out that the escape speed of a body is the initial speed given by a brief thrust, after which there is no force to assist motion. One could escape the earth at *any* sustained speed more than zero, given enough time. For example, suppose a rocket is launched to a destination such as the moon. If the rocket engines burn out when the rocket is still close to the earth, the rocket needs a minimum speed of 11.2 kilometers per second. But, if the

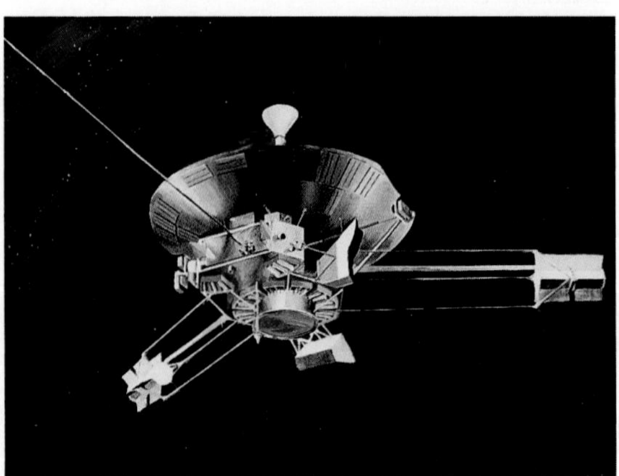

Figure 5.34
Pioneer 10, launched from earth in 1972, passed the outermost planet in 1984 and is now wandering in our galaxy.

rocket engines can be sustained for long periods of time, the rocket could go to the moon without ever attaining 11.2 kilometers per second.

It is interesting to note that the accuracy with which an unmanned rocket reaches its destination is not determined by staying on a preplanned path or by getting back on that path if the rocket strays off course. No attempt is made to return the rocket to its original path. Instead, the control center asks, in effect, "Where is it now and what is its velocity? What is the best way to reach its destination, given its present situation?" With the aid of high-speed computers, the answers to these questions are used in finding a new path. Corrective thrusters put the rocket on this new path. This process is repeated over and over again all the way to the goal.*

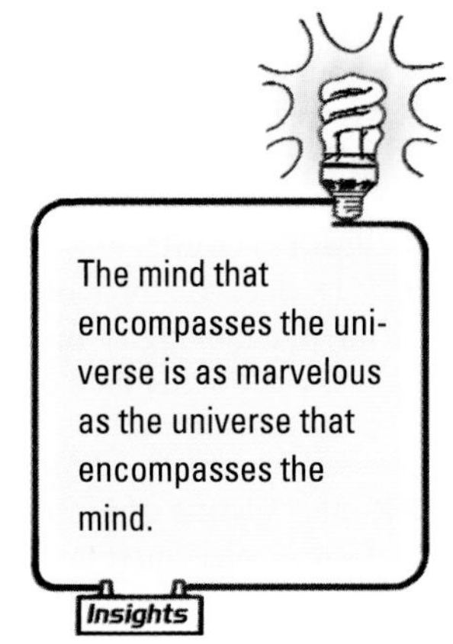

* Is there a personal lesson to be learned here? Suppose you find that you are off course. You may, like the rocket, find it more fruitful to take a course that will lead you to your goal, as best plotted from your present position and circumstances, rather than to try to get back on the course you plotted from a previous position and under, perhaps, different circumstances.

Summary of Terms

Projectile Any object that moves through the air or through space under the influence of gravity.

Parabola The curved path followed by a projectile near the earth under the influence of gravity only.

Satellite A projectile or small celestial body that orbits a larger celestial body.

Ellipse The oval path followed by a satellite. The sum of the distances from any point on the path to two points called foci is a constant. When the foci are together at one point, the ellipse is a circle. As the foci get farther apart, the ellipse gets more "eccentric."

Escape speed The speed that a projectile, a space probe, or a similar object must reach in order to escape the gravitational influence of the earth or of another celestial body to which it is attracted.

Review Questions

1. What does a satellite have in common with a projectile?

5.1 Projectile Motion

2. Why does the horizontal component of a projectile's motion remain constant?
3. Why does the vertical component of a projectile's motion undergo change?
4. How does the vertical distance a projectile falls below an otherwise straight-line path compare with the vertical distance it would fall from rest in the same time?
5. How is the horizontal component of velocity for a projectile affected by the vertical component?
6. What is the name of the curved path of a projectile that accelerates only in the vertical direction while moving at a constant horizontal velocity?
7. What angle from the horizontal gives the greatest range for a projectile launched from ground level?
8. A projectile is launched at an angle of 75 degrees from the horizontal and strikes the ground a certain distance downrange. For what other angle of launch at the same speed would the projectile land just as far away?
9. A projectile is launched vertically at 50 m/s. If air resistance can be neglected, at what speed will it return to its initial level?
10. How does air resistance affect the range of projectiles?

5.2 Fast-moving Projectiles—Satellites

11. In 1 second, how far does a baseball fall beneath the straight-line path it would follow if gravity were nonexistent?
12. In 1 second, how far does an earth satellite in close orbit fall beneath the straight-line path it would follow if gravity were nonexistent?
13. Are satellites placed in orbit at least 150 kilometers high so as to be above the earth's gravity? Or to be above the earth's atmosphere? (Don't say both!)
14. What is *tangential velocity?*

5.3 Circular Satellite Orbits

15. How can a projectile "fall around the earth"?
16. Why doesn't the force of gravity change the speed of a satellite in a circular orbit?

17. How long does it take a satellite in a close orbit around the earth to complete one revolution?
18. For orbits of greater altitude, is the period greater or less than your answer to the previous question?

5.4 Elliptical Orbits

19. Why does the force of gravity change the speed of a satellite moving in an elliptical orbit?
20. Is the parabolic path of a tossed baseball actually part of an ellipse?

5.5 Kepler's Laws of Planetary Motion

21. State Kepler's first law of planetary motion.
22. State Kepler's second law of planetary motion.
23. State Kepler's third law of planetary motion.
24. Did Kepler understand that a planet is simply a fast-moving projectile falling around the sun?

5.6 Energy Conservation and Satellite Motion

25. Why is kinetic energy constant for a satellite in a circular orbit?
26. Why does kinetic energy vary for a satellite in an elliptical orbit?
27. At what part of an elliptical orbit does a satellite have the greatest speed? The least speed?
28. Is the sum of kinetic and potential energies constant for satellites in circular orbits? For satellites in elliptical orbits?

5.7 Escape Speed

29. What is the minimum speed for orbiting the earth in a close orbit? The maximum speed? What happens above this speed?
30. How was Pioneer 10 able to escape the Solar System with an initial speed less than escape speed?

Activities

1. Place a coin at the edge of a table, then slide another coin against it forcefully enough that it knocks the first coin off the edge. Although the knocked coin falls farther from the edge than the coin you slid against it, notice that they both hit the floor at the same time.
2. With a piece of string, a couple of tacks, and a pencil, construct several ellipses, as indicated in Figure 5.25. In a wide (eccentric) ellipse, note how close the perigee is to the focal point representing the center of the body about which orbiting occurs.

Exercises

1. How does the vertical component of a projectile's motion compare with the motion of vertical free-fall?
2. In the absence of air resistance, why does the horizontal component of a projectile's motion not change, while the vertical component does?
3. At what point in its trajectory does a batted baseball have its minimum speed? If air resistance can be neglected, how does this speed compare with the horizontal component of its velocity at other points?
4. A heavy crate accidentally falls from a high-flying airplane just as it flies directly above a shiny red vintage Camaro smartly parked in a car lot. Relative to the Camaro, where will the crate crash?
5. Suppose you drop an object from an airplane traveling at a constant velocity, and further suppose that air resistance doesn't affect the falling object. What will be its falling path as observed by someone at rest on the ground (not directly below, but off to the side, where a clear view can be seen)? What will be the falling path as observed by you looking downward from the airplane? Where will the object strike the ground, relative to you in the airplane? Where will it strike in the more realistic case in which air resistance *does* affect the fall?
6. A friend claims that bullets fired by some high-powered rifles travel for many meters in a straight-line path before they start to fall. Another friend disputes this claim and states that all bullets from any rifle drop beneath a straight-line path a vertical distance given by $1/2\, gt^2$ and that the curved path is apparent for low velocities and less apparent for high velocities. Now it's your turn: Will all bullets drop the same vertical distance in equal times? Explain.
7. For maximum range, a football should be punted at about 45° to the horizontal—or somewhat less, because of air resistance. But punts are often kicked at angles greater than 45°. Can you think of a reason why?
8. Two golfers each hit a ball at the same speed, one at 60° to the horizontal and the other at 30°. Which ball goes farther? Which hits the ground first? (Ignore air resistance.)
9. A park ranger shoots a monkey hanging from a branch of a tree with a tranquilizing dart. The ranger aims directly at the monkey, not realizing that the dart will follow a parabolic path and thus fall below the monkey. The monkey, however, sees the dart leave the gun and lets go of the branch to avoid being hit. Will the monkey be hit anyway? Does the velocity of the dart affect your answer, assuming it is great enough that the dart will travel

the horizontal distance to the tree before hitting the ground? Defend your answer.

10. A projectile is fired straight upward at 141 m/s. How fast is it moving at the instant it reaches the top of its trajectory? Suppose instead that it were fired upward at 45°. What would be its speed at the top of its trajectory?
11. When you jump upward, your hang time is the time your feet are off the ground. Does hang time depend on the vertical component of your velocity when you jump, on the horizontal component of your velocity, or on both? Defend your answer.
12. The hang time of a basketball player who jumps a vertical distance of 2 feet (0.6 m) is about 2/3 second. What will be the hang time if the player reaches the same height while jumping 4 feet (1.2 m) horizontally?
13. If a cannonball is fired from a tall mountain, gravity changes its speed all along its trajectory. But if it is fired fast enough to go into a circular orbit, gravity does not change its speed at all. Explain.
14. Because the moon is gravitationally attracted to the earth, why doesn't it simply crash into the earth?
15. When the space shuttle coasts in a circular orbit at a constant speed about the earth, is it accelerating? If so, in what direction? If not, why not?
16. Which planets have a greater period than 1 earth year, those closer to the sun than to the earth or those farther from the sun than to the earth?
17. Does the speed of a falling object depend on its mass? Does the speed of a satellite in orbit depend on its mass? Defend your answers.
18. If you have ever watched the launching of an earth satellite, you may have noticed that the rocket starts vertically upward, then departs from a vertical course and continues its climb at an angle. Why does it start vertically? Why does it not continue vertically?
19. A satellite can orbit at 5 km above the moon, but not at 5 km above the earth. Why?
20. Would the speed of a satellite in close circular orbit about Jupiter be greater than, equal to, or less than 8 km/s?
21. Why are satellites normally sent into orbit by firing them in an easterly direction, the direction in which the earth spins?
22. When a satellite in a circular orbit slows, perhaps due to the firing of a "retro-rocket," it then gains more speed than it had initially. Why?
23. Of all the states in the United States of America, why is Hawaii the most efficient launching site for nonpolar satellites? (Hint: Look at the spinning earth from above either pole and compare it to a spinning turntable.)
24. What is the shape of the orbit when the velocity of the satellite is everywhere perpendicular to the force of gravity?
25. In the sketch on the left, a ball gains KE when rolling down a hill because work is done by the component of weight (F) that acts in the direction of motion. Sketch in the similar component of gravitational force that does work to change the KE of the satellite on the right.

    F
    WT
26. Why is work done by the force of gravity on a satellite when it moves from one part of an elliptical orbit to another, but not when it moves from one part of a circular orbit to another?
27. If the space shuttle circled the earth at a distance equal to the earth–moon distance, how long would it take for it to make a complete orbit? In other words, what would be its period?
28. Can a satellite coast in a stable orbit in a plane that doesn't intersect the earth's center? Defend your answer.
29. A communications satellite with a 24-h period hovers over a fixed point on the earth. Why is it placed in orbit only in the plane of the earth's equator? (Hint: Think of the satellite's orbit as a ring around the earth.)
30. A "geosynchronous" earth satellite can remain directly overhead in Singapore, but not in San Francisco. Why?
31. Can a satellite maintain an orbit in the plane of the Arctic Circle? Why or why not?
32. If a flight mechanic drops a wrench from a high-flying jumbo jet, it crashes to earth. If an astronaut on the orbiting space shuttle drops a wrench, does it crash to earth also? Defend your answer.
33. A high-orbiting spaceship travels at 7 km/s with respect to the earth. Suppose it projects a capsule at 7 km/s rearward with respect to the ship. Describe the path of the capsule with respect to the earth.
34. A satellite in a circular orbit about the moon fires a small probe in a direction opposite to the velocity of the satellite. If the speed of the probe relative to the satellite is the same as the satellite's speed relative to the moon, describe the motion of the probe. If the probe's relative speed is twice the speed of the satellite, why would it pose a danger to the satellite?

35. The orbital velocity of the earth about the sun is 30 km/s. If the earth were suddenly stopped in its tracks, it would simply fall radially into the sun. Devise a plan whereby a rocket loaded with radioactive wastes could be fired into the sun for permanent disposal. How fast, and in what direction with respect to the earth's orbit, should the rocket be fired?
36. If you stopped an earth satellite dead in its tracks, it would simply crash into the earth. Why, then, don't the communications satellites that "hover motionless" above the same spot on earth crash into the earth?
37. In an accidental explosion, a satellite breaks in half while in a circular orbit about the earth. One half is brought momentarily to rest. What is the fate of the half brought to rest? What happens to the other half?
38. Escape speed from the surface of the earth is 11.2 km/s, but a space vehicle could escape from the earth at half this speed and less. Explain.
39. At which of the indicated positions does the satellite in elliptical orbit experience the greatest gravitational force? Have the greatest speed? The greatest velocity? The greatest momentum? The greatest kinetic energy? The greatest gravitational potential energy? The greatest total energy? The greatest acceleration?
40. Make up two multiple-choice questions that test for a distinction between the characteristics of a satellite in a circular orbit and a satellite in an elliptical orbit.

Problems

1. A ball is thrown horizontally from a cliff at a speed of 10 m/s. What is its speed one second later? (Hint: Think vectors!)
2. An airplane is flying horizontally with a speed of 1000 km/h (280 m/s) when an engine falls off. Ignoring air resistance, if it takes 10 s for the engine to hit the ground,
(a) how high is the airplane and
(b) how far horizontally does the engine travel while it falls?
(c) If the airplane somehow continues to fly as if nothing had happened, where is the engine relative to the airplane at the moment the engine hits the ground?
3. A cannonball shot with an initial velocity of 141 m/s at an angle of 45° follows a parabolic path and hits a balloon at the top of its trajectory. Ignoring air resistance, how fast is the cannonball going when it hits the balloon?
4. Students in a lab measure the speed of a steel ball launched horizontally from a tabletop to be 4 m/s. If the tabletop is 1 m above the floor, where should they place a coffee can that is 20 cm tall to catch the ball when it lands?
5. John and Tracy look from their high-rise balcony, which is 80 m above the ground, to a swimming pool below—not exactly below, but rather 20 m out from the bottom of their building. They wonder how fast they would have to jump horizontally to succeed in reaching the pool. What is the answer?
6. Ignoring air resistance, what is the maximum speed possible for a horizontally moving tennis ball as it clears the net 1 m high and strikes within the court's border, which is 12 m distant?
7. Calculate a person's hang time if he moves horizontally 3 m during a 1.25-m high jump. What is his hang time if he moves 6 m horizontally during this jump?
8. Calculate the speed in m/s at which the earth revolves about the sun. You may assume that the orbit is nearly circular.

Chapter 5 Online Resources

Tutorials
- Projectile Motion
- Orbits & Kepler's Laws

Videos
- Projectile Motion Demonstration
- More Projectile Motion
- Circular Orbits

Quiz
Exercises
Flashcards
Links

CHAPTER 6

Fluid Mechanics

Liquids and gases have the ability to flow; hence, they are called *fluids*. Because they are both fluids, we find that they obey similar mechanical laws.* How is it that iron boats don't sink in water or that helium balloons don't sink from the sky? Why is it impossible to breathe through a snorkel when you're under more than a meter of water? Why do your ears pop when you are riding an elevator in a tall building? How do hydrofoils and airplanes attain lift? To discuss fluids, it is important to introduce two concepts—*density* and *pressure*.

6.1 Density

An important property of materials, whether solid, liquid, or gaseous, is the measure of compactness: **density.** We think of density as the "lightness" or "heaviness" of materials of the same size. It is a measure of how much mass is squeezed into a given space; it is the amount of matter per unit volume:

$$\text{Density} = \frac{\text{mass}}{\text{volume}}$$

Figure 6.1
When the volume of the bread is reduced, its density increases.

The densities of a few materials are listed in Table 6.1. Mass is measured in grams or kilograms, and volume is measured in cubic centimeters (cm^3) or cubic meters (m^3).† A gram of any material has the same mass as 1 cubic centimeter of water at a temperature of 4°C. So water has a density of 1 gram per cubic centimeter. Mercury's density of 13.6 grams per cubic centimeter means that it has 13.6 times as much mass as an equal volume of water. Osmium, a hard, bluish-white metallic element, is the densest solid substance on earth.

*The phases of matter—solid, liquid, gas, and plasma—are described from a chemical point of view in Chapter 19.

†A cubic meter is a sizable volume and contains a million cubic centimeters, so there are a million grams of water in a cubic meter (or, equivalently, a thousand kilograms of water in a cubic meter). Hence, 1 g/cm^3 = 1000 kg/m^3.

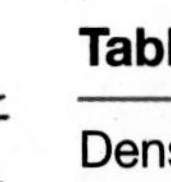

The metals lithium, sodium, and potassium (not in Table 6.1) are all less dense than water and will float in water.

Table 6.1

Densities of some materials

Material	Grams per cubic centimeter	Kilograms per cubic meter
Liquids		
Mercury	13.6	1360
Glycerin	1.26	1260
Seawater	1.03	1025
Water at 4°C	1.00	1000
Benzene	0.90	899
Ethyl alcohol	0.81	806
Solids		
Osmium	22.5	22,480
Platinum	21.5	21,450
Gold	19.3	19,320
Uranium	19.0	19,050
Lead	11.3	11,344
Silver	10.5	10,500
Copper	8.9	8,920
Brass	8.6	8,560
Iron	7.8	7,800
Tin	7.3	7,280
Aluminum	2.7	2,702
Ice	0.92	917
Gases (atmospheric pressure at sea level)		
Dry air:		
at 0°C	0.00129	1.29
at 10°C	0.00125	1.25
at 20°C	0.00121	1.21
at 30°C	0.00116	1.16
Helium	0.000178	0.178
Hydrogen	0.000090	0.090
Oxygen	0.00143	1.43

A quantity known as *weight density,* commonly used when discussing liquid pressure, can be expressed by the amount of weight of a body per unit volume:*

$$\text{Weight density} = \frac{\text{weight}}{\text{volume}}$$

*Weight density is common to USCS units (United States Customary System) in which one cubic foot of fresh water (nearly 7.5 gallons) weighs 62.4 pounds. So fresh water has a weight density of 62.4 lb/ft^3. Salt water is slightly denser, 64 lb/ft^3.

☑ CHECKPOINT

1. Which has the greater density—1 kg of water or 10 kg of water?
2. Which has the greater density—5 kg of lead or 10 kg of aluminum?
3. Which has the greater density—an entire candy bar or half a candy bar?

Check Your Answers

1. The density of any amount of water is the same: 1 g/cm^3 or, equivalently, 1000 kg/m^3, which means that the mass of water that would exactly fill a thimble with a volume 1 cubic centimeter would be 1 gram; or the mass of water that would fill a 1-cubic-meter tank would be 1000 kg. One kg of water would fill a tank only a thousandth as large, 1 liter, whereas 10 kg would fill a 10-liter tank. Nevertheless, the important concept is that the ratio of mass to volume is the same for any amount of water.
2. Density is a *ratio* of weight or mass per volume, and this ratio is greater for any amount of lead than for any amount of aluminum—see Table 6.1.
3. Both the half and the entire candy bar have the same density.

6.2 Pressure

Place a book on a bathroom scale and, whether you place it on its back, on its side, or balanced on a corner, it still exerts the same force. The weight reading is the same. Now balance the book on the palm of your hand and you sense a difference—the *pressure* of the book depends on the area over which the force is distributed. There is a difference between force and pressure. **Pressure** is defined as the force exerted over a unit of area, such as a square meter or square foot:*

$$\text{Pressure} = \frac{\text{force}}{\text{area}}$$

Figure 6.2
Although the weight of both books is the same, the upright book exerts greater pressure against the table.

A dramatic illustration of pressure is shown in Figure 6.3. The physics author applies appreciable force when he breaks the cement block with a sledge hammer. Yet Pablo Robinson, his teaching buddy, who is sandwiched between two beds of sharp nails, is unharmed. This is because the force is distributed over more than 200 nails making contact with his body. The combined surface area of the nails results in a tolerable pressure that does not puncture his skin. Force and pressure are different from each other.

Does a bathroom scale measure weight, pressure, or both?

Check Your Answer

A bathroom scale measures weight, the force that compresses an internal spring or its equivalent. The weight reading is the same whether you stand on one or both feet (although the pressure on the scale is twice as much when you are standing on one foot).

*Pressure may be measured in any unit of force divided by any unit of area. The standard international (SI) unit of pressure, the newton per square meter, is called the *pascal* (Pa), after the seventeenth-century theologian and scientist Blaise Pascal. A pressure of 1 Pa is very small; it is approximately equal to the pressure exerted by a dollar bill resting flat on a table. Science types prefer kilopascals (1 kPa = 1000 Pa).

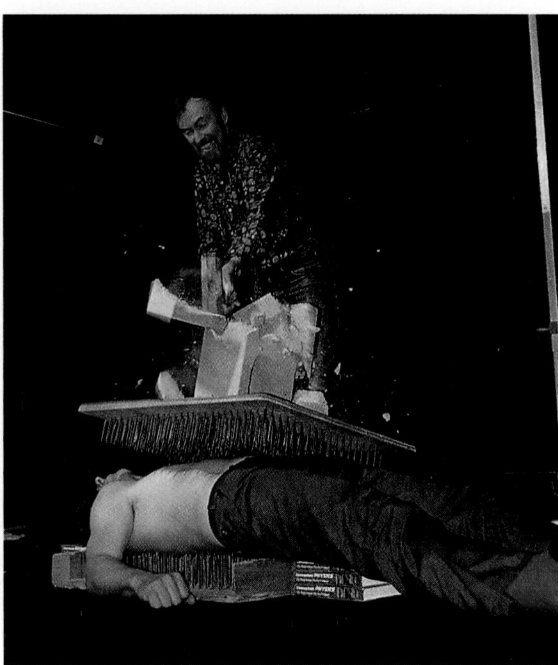

Figure 6.3
Paul Hewitt applies a force to fellow physics teacher Paul Robinson, who is bravely sandwiched between beds of sharp nails. The driving force per nail is not enough to puncture the skin. From an inertia point of view, is Robinson safer if the block is massive? From the point of view of energy, is he safer when the block breaks?

Pressure in a Liquid

When you swim under water, you can feel the water pressure acting against your eardrums. The deeper you swim, the greater the pressure. What causes this pressure? It is simply the weight of the fluids directly above you—water plus air—pushing against you. As you swim deeper, there is more water above you. Therefore, there's more pressure. If you swim twice as deep, there is twice the weight of water above you, so the water's contribution to the pressure you feel is doubled. Added to the water pressure is the pressure of the atmosphere, which is equivalent to an extra 10.3-meter depth of water. Because atmospheric pressure at the earth's surface is nearly constant, the pressure differences you feel under water depend only on changes in depth.

If you were submerged in a liquid denser than water, the pressure would be correspondingly greater. The pressure due to a liquid is precisely equal to the product of weight density and depth:*

$$\text{Liquid pressure} = \text{weight density} \times \text{depth}$$

Figure 6.4
This water tower does more than store water. The depth of water above ground level insures substantial and reliable water pressure to the many homes it serves.

*This is derived from the definitions of pressure and density. Consider an area at the bottom of a vessel of liquid. The weight of the column of liquid directly above this area produces pressure. From the definition Weight density = weight/volume, we can express this weight of liquid as Weight = weight density × volume, where the volume of the column is simply the area multiplied by the depth. Then we get

$$\text{Pressure} = \frac{\text{force}}{\text{area}} = \frac{\text{weight}}{\text{area}} = \frac{\text{weight density} \times \text{volume}}{\text{area}} = \frac{\text{weight density} \times (\cancel{\text{area}} \times \text{depth})}{\cancel{\text{area}}} = \text{weight density} \times \text{depth}$$

Strictly speaking, we should add to this equation the pressure due to the atmosphere on the surface of the liquid.

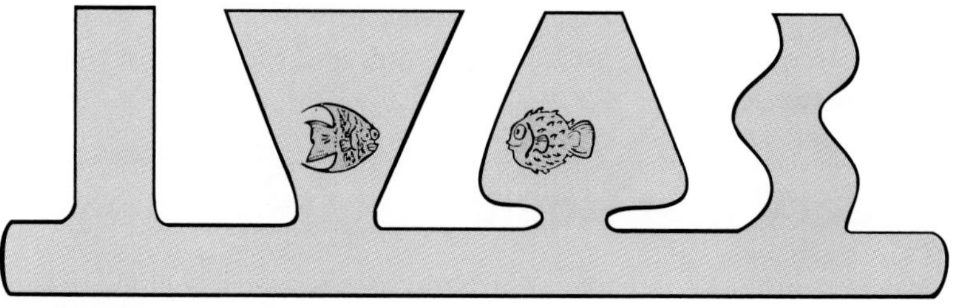

Figure 6.5
Liquid pressure is the same for any given depth below the surface, regardless of the shape of the containing vessel.

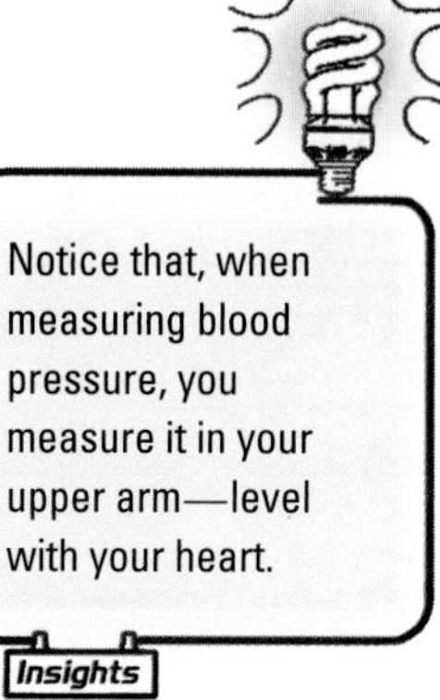

Notice that, when measuring blood pressure, you measure it in your upper arm—level with your heart.

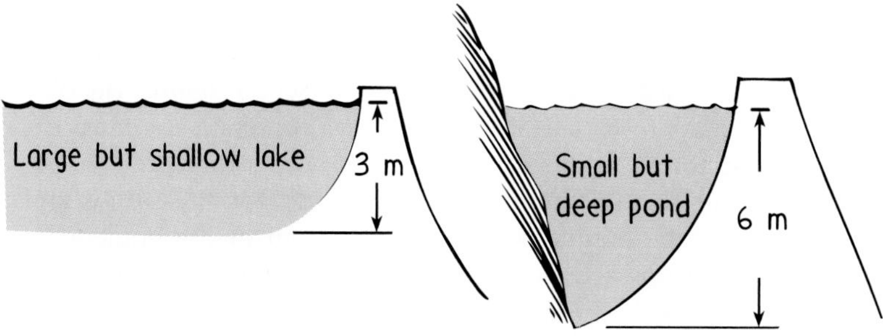

Figure 6.6
The average water pressure acting against the dam depends on the average depth of the water and not on the volume of water held back. The large shallow lake exerts only one-half the average pressure that the small deep pond exerts.

Water in a vessel exerts a pressure proportional to its depth—but this is not so for a vessel of sand or other particles. Hence, sand trickles at a nearly constant rate through the narrow opening separating the two glass bulbs of an hourglass. Contact forces between grains transfer weight to the container's walls.

Insights

It is important to note that pressure does not depend on the volume of the liquid. You feel the same pressure a meter deep in a small pool as you do a meter deep in the middle of the ocean. This is illustrated by the connecting vases shown in Figure 6.5. If the pressure at the bottom of a large vase were greater than the pressure at the bottom of a neighboring, narrower vase, the greater pressure would force water sideways and then up the narrower vase to a higher level. We find, however, that this doesn't happen. Pressure depends on depth, not volume.

Water seeks its own level. This can be demonstrated by filling a garden hose with water and holding the two ends upright. The water levels will be equal whether the ends are held close together or far apart. Pressure is depth dependent, not volume dependent. So we see there is an explanation for why water seeks its own level.

In addition to being depth dependent, liquid pressure is exerted equally in all directions. For example, if we are submerged in water, it makes no difference which way we tilt our heads—our ears feel the same amount of water pressure. Because a liquid can flow, the pressure isn't only downward. We know that pressure acts upward when we try to push a beach ball beneath the water's surface. The bottom of a boat is certainly pushed upward by water pressure. And we know water pressure acts sideways when we see water spurting sideways from a leak in an upright can. Pressure in a liquid at any point is exerted in equal amounts in all directions.

Figure 6.7
Water pressure acts perpendicular to the sides of its container, and it increases with increasing depth.

When liquid presses against a surface, there is a net force directed perpendicular to the surface (Figure 6.7). If there is a hole in the surface, the liquid

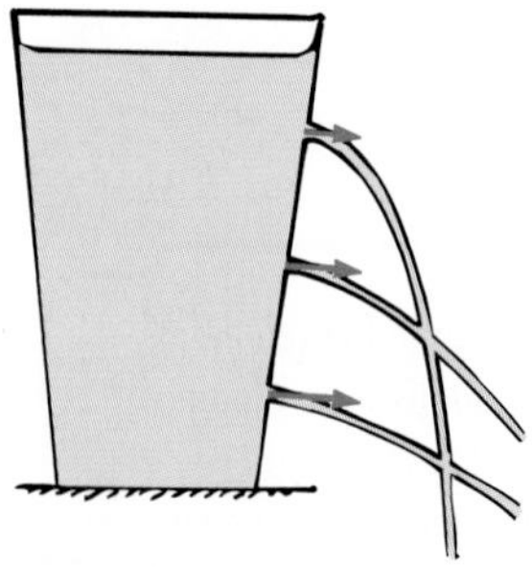
Figure 6.8
The forces due to water pressure are perpendicular to the sides of a container, and they increase with increasing depth.

spurts at right angles to the surface before curving downward due to gravity (Figure 6.8). At greater depths, the pressure is greater and the speed of the outflowing liquid is greater.*

6.3 Buoyancy in a Liquid

Anyone who has ever lifted a submerged object out of the water is familiar with buoyancy, the apparent loss of weight of submerged objects. For example, lifting a large boulder off the bottom of a riverbed is a relatively easy task as long as the boulder is below the surface. When it is lifted above the surface, however, the force required to lift it is considerably more. This is because, when the boulder is submerged, the water exerts an upward force on it that is exactly opposite in direction to gravity. This upward force is called the **buoyant force,** and it is a consequence of pressure increasing with depth. Figure 6.9 shows why the buoyant force acts upward. Pressure is exerted everywhere against the object in a direction perpendicular to its surface. The arrows represent the magnitude and the direction of the forces at different locations. Forces that produce pressures against the sides due to equal depths cancel one another. Pressure is greatest against the bottom of the boulder because the bottom of the boulder is at a greater depth. Since the upward forces against the bottom are greater than the downward forces against the top, the forces do not cancel, and there is a net force upward. This net force is the buoyant force.

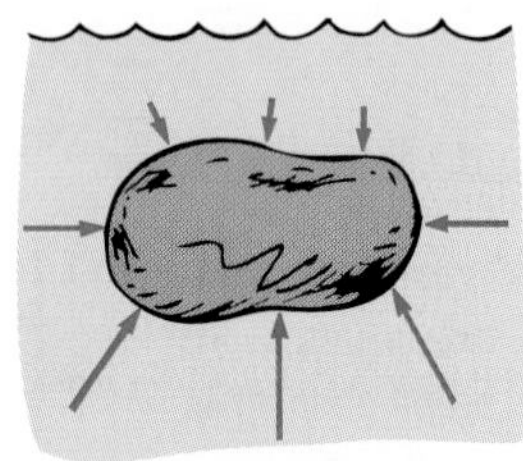
Figure 6.9
The greater pressure against the bottom of a submerged object produces an upward buoyant force.

If the weight of the submerged object is greater than the buoyant force, the object will sink. If the weight is equal to the buoyant force acting up on the submerged object, it will remain at any level, like a fish. If the buoyant force is greater than the weight of the completely submerged object, it will rise to the surface and float.

Understanding buoyancy requires understanding the meaning of the expression "volume of water displaced." If a stone is placed in a container that is brimful of water, some water will overflow (Figure 6.10). Water is *displaced* by the stone. A little thought will tell us that the *volume of the stone*—that is, the amount of space it occupies or its number of cubic centimeters—is equal to the *volume of water displaced.* Place any object in a container partially filled with water, and the level of the surface rises (Figure 6.11). By how much? To exactly the level that would be reached by pouring in a volume of water equal to the volume of the submerged object. This is a good method for determining the volume of irregularly shaped objects: *A completely submerged object always displaces a volume of liquid equal to its own volume.*

Figure 6.10
When a stone is submerged, it displaces a volume of water equal to the volume of the stone.

6.4 Archimedes' Principle

The relationship between buoyancy and displaced liquid was first discovered in the third century BC by the Greek scientist Archimedes. It is stated as follows:

> **An immersed body is buoyed up by a force equal to the weight of the fluid it displaces.**

*The speed of the liquid exiting the hole is $\sqrt{2gh}$, where h is the depth below the free surface. Interestingly, this is the same speed the water or anything else would have if freely falling the same distance h.

This relationship is called **Archimedes' principle.** It applies to liquids and gases, both of which are fluids. If an immersed body displaces 1 kilogram of fluid, the buoyant force acting on it is equal to the weight of 1 kilogram.* By *immersed,* we mean either *completely* or *partially submerged.* If we immerse a sealed 1-liter container halfway into the water, it will displace one-half liter of water and be buoyed up by the weight of one-half liter of water. If we immerse it completely (submerge it), it will be buoyed up by the weight of a full liter (or 1 kilogram) of water. Unless the container is compressed, the buoyant force will equal the weight of 1 kilogram at *any* depth, as long as it is completely submerged. This is because, at any depth, it can displace no greater volume of water than its own volume. And the weight of this volume of water (not the weight of the submerged object!) is equal to the buoyant force.

If a 25-kilogram object displaces 20 kilograms of fluid upon immersion, its apparent weight will equal the weight of 5 kilograms. Notice that, in Figure 6.13, the 3-kilogram block has an apparent weight equal to the weight of 1 kilogram when it is submerged. The *apparent weight* of a submerged object is its weight out of water minus the buoyant force.

Figure 6.11
The raised level is equal to the level that would be reached if a volume of water equal to the stone's volume were poured in.

Figure 6.12
A liter of water occupies a volume of 1000 cm^3, has a mass of 1 kg, and weighs 9.8 N. Its density may therefore be expressed as 1 kg/L and its weight density as 9.8 N/L. (Sea water is slightly denser, about 10 N/L).

☑ CHECKPOINT

1. Does Archimedes' principle tell us that, if an immersed block displaces 10 N of fluid, the buoyant force on the block is 10 N?
2. A 1-liter container completely filled with lead has a mass of 11.3 kg and is submerged in water. What is the buoyant force acting on it?
3. A boulder is thrown into a deep lake. As it sinks deeper and deeper into the water, does the buoyant force on it increase? Decrease?

Check Your Answers

1. Yes. If you look at this question with Newton's third law in mind, you can see that, when the immersed block pushes 10 N of fluid aside, the fluid reacts by pushing back on the block with a force of 10 N.
2. The buoyant force is equal to the weight of 1 kg (9.8 N) because the volume of water displaced is 1 L, which has a mass of 1 kg and a weight of 9.8 N. The 11.3-kg mass of the lead is irrelevant; 1 L of anything submerged in water will displace 1 L and be buoyed upward with a force of 9.8 N, the weight of 1 kg. (Get this straight before going further!)
3. Buoyant force does not change as the boulder sinks because the boulder displaces the same volume of water at any depth. Because water is practically incompressible, its density is very nearly the same at all depths; hence, the weight of water displaced, or the buoyant force, is practically the same at all depths.

*A kilogram is not a unit of force but a unit of mass. So, strictly speaking, the buoyant force is not 1 kg, but the *weight* of 1 kg, which is 9.8 N. We could as well say that the buoyant force is 1 *kilogram weight,* not simply 1 kg.

Figure 6.13
A 3-kg block weighs more in air than in water. When submerged, its loss in weight is the buoyant force, which is equal to the weight of water displaced.

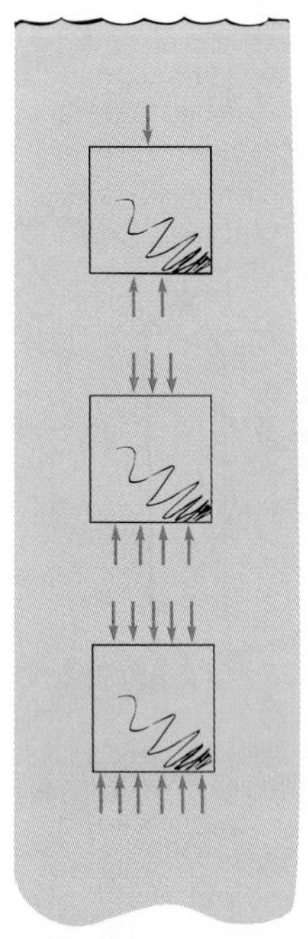

Figure 6.14
The difference in the upward and downward forces acting on the submerged block is the same at any depth.

Perhaps your instructor will summarize Archimedes' principle by way of a numerical example to show the difference between the upward-acting and the downward-acting forces on a submerged cube (due to differences of pressure). You'll see that the force difference is numerically identical to the weight of fluid displaced. It makes no difference how deep the cube is placed because, although the pressures are greater with increasing depths, the *difference* between the pressure exerted upward against the bottom of the cube and the pressure exerted downward against the top of the cube is the same at any depth (Figure 6.14). Whatever the shape of the submerged body, the buoyant force is equal to the weight of fluid displaced.

☑ CHECKPOINT

1. Drop a stone in a tall water-filled container. As it descends beneath the surface, pressure on it increases. Does this imply that buoyant force likewise increases?
2. Because buoyant force is the upward force that a fluid exerts on a body, and as we learned in Chapter 2, forces produce accelerations, why doesn't a submerged body accelerate?

Check Your Answers

1. No! Once the stone is beneath the water's surface, it has displaced all the water it can. This is evidenced by the initial rise of the water level in the container, which corresponds to the volume of the stone (and, hence, to the volume of water displaced by the stone). The level remains the same as the stone descends further, showing that the water displacement, and therefore the buoyant force on the stone, remains the same—even though water pressure on the stone increases with depth. Buoyancy and pressure are different concepts.
2. It does accelerate if the buoyant force is not balanced by other forces that act on it—the force of gravity and fluid resistance. The net force on a submerged body is the result of the force the fluid exerts (buoyant force), the weight of the body, and, if the body is moving, the force of fluid friction. When the net force is zero, the body is in equilibrium.

Link To History

Archimedes and the Gold Crown

According to popular legend, Archimedes (287–212 BC) had been given the task of determining whether a crown made for King Hiero II of Syracuse was of pure gold or whether it contained some less expensive metals, such as silver. Archimedes' problem was to find the density of the crown without destroying it. He could weigh the gold, but determining its volume was a problem. The story has it that Archimedes came to the solution when he noted the rise in water level while immersing his body in the public baths of Syracuse. Legend reports that he excitedly rushed naked through the streets shouting "Eureka! Eureka!" ("I have found it! I have found it!").

What Archimedes had discovered was a simple and accurate method of finding the volume of an irregular object—the displacement method of determining volumes. Once he knew both the weight and volume, he could calculate the density. Then the density of the crown could be compared to the density of gold. Archimedes' insight preceded Newton's laws of motion, from which Archimedes' principle can be derived, by almost 2000 years.

6.5 Flotation

Iron is much denser than water and therefore sinks, but an iron ship floats. Why is this so? Consider a solid 1-ton block of iron. Iron is nearly eight times as dense as water. When it is submerged, it will displace only $\frac{1}{8}$ ton of water, which is certainly not enough to prevent it from sinking. Suppose that we reshape the same iron block into a bowl, as shown in Figure 6.15. Although its surface area is increased, it still weighs 1 ton. When settling in water, it displaces a greater volume of water than before. The deeper it is immersed, the more water it displaces and the greater the buoyant force acting upon it. When the buoyant force equals 1 ton, it will sink no further.

When the iron boat displaces a weight of water equal to its own weight, it floats. This is called the **principle of flotation**, which states:

A floating object displaces a weight of fluid equal to its own weight.

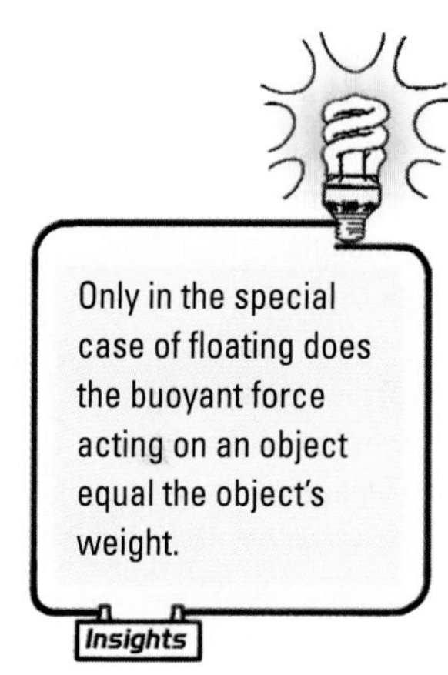

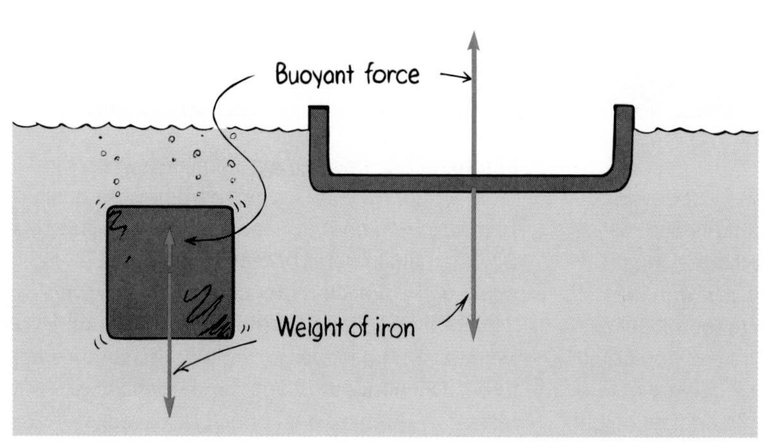

Figure 6.15
An iron block sinks, while the same quantity of iron shaped like a bowl floats.

Figure 6.16
The weight of a floating object equals the weight of the water displaced by the submerged part.

Every ship, submarine, and dirigible must be designed to displace a weight of fluid equal to its own weight. Thus, a 10,000-ton ship must be built wide enough to displace 10,000 tons of water before it sinks too deep in the water. The same applies to vessels in the air. A dirigible or a huge balloon that weighs 100 tons displaces at least 100 tons of air. If it displaces more, it rises; if it displaces less, it descends. If it displaces exactly its weight, it hovers at a constant altitude.

Figure 6.17
A floating object displaces a weight of fluid equal to its own weight.

Since the buoyant force upon a body equals the weight of the fluid it displaces, denser fluids will exert a greater buoyant force upon a body than less dense fluids of the same volume. A ship, therefore, floats higher in salt water than in fresh water because salt water is slightly denser than fresh water. In the same way, a solid chunk of iron will float in mercury even though it sinks in water.

People who can't float are, nine times out of ten, males. Most males are more muscular and slightly denser than most females. Also, cans of diet soda float whereas cans of regular soda sink in water. What does this tell you about their relative densities?

Insights

☑ CHECKPOINT

Fill in the blanks for these statements:

1. The volume of a submerged body is equal to the ___________ of the fluid displaced.
2. The weight of a floating body is equal to the ___________ of the fluid displaced.
3. Why is it easier to float in salt water than in fresh water?

Check Your Answers

1. Volume
2. Weight
3. When you're floating, the weight of water you displace equals your weight. Salt water is denser, so you don't "sink" as far to displace your weight. You'd float even higher in mercury (density 13.6 g/cm^3), and sink completely in alcohol (density 0.8 g/cm^3).

Link to Geology

Floating Mountains

Mountains float on the earth's mantle just as icebergs float on water. Both the mountains and icebergs are less dense than the material they float upon. Just as most of an iceberg is below the water surface (90%), most of a mountain (about 85%) extends into the dense semiliquid mantle. If you could shave off the top of an iceberg, the iceberg would be lighter and be buoyed up to nearly its original height before its top was shaved. Similarly, when mountains erode, they are lighter, and they are pushed up from below to float to nearly their original heights. So when a kilometer of mountain erodes away, some 85% of a kilometer of mountain returns. That's why it takes so long for mountains to weather away. Mountains, like icebergs, are bigger than they appear to be. The concept of floating mountains is *isostacy*—Archimedes' principle for rocks.

Figure 6.18
The same ship empty and loaded. How does the weight of its load compare with the weight of the additional water displaced?

Notice in our discussion of liquids that Archimedes' principle and the principle of flotation were stated in terms of *fluids,* not liquids. That's because, although liquids and gases are different phases of matter, they are both fluids, with much the same mechanical principles. Let's turn our attention to the mechanics of gases in particular.

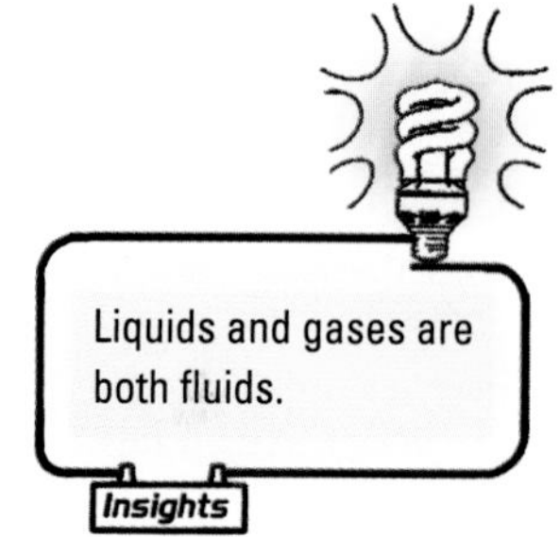

6.6 Pressure in a Gas

The primary difference between a gas and a liquid is the distance between molecules. In a gas, the molecules are far apart and free from the cohesive forces that dominate their motions in the liquid and solid phases. Their motions are less restricted. A gas expands, fills all space available to it, and exerts a pressure against its container. Only when the quantity of gas is very large, as in the earth's atmosphere or in a star, do the gravitational forces limit the size or determine the shape of the mass of gas.

Boyle's Law

The air pressure inside the inflated tires of an automobile is considerably greater than the atmospheric pressure outside. The density of air inside is also more than that of the air outside. To understand the relation between pressure and density, think of the molecules of air (primarily nitrogen and oxygen) inside the tire. The air molecules behave like tiny billiard balls, randomly moving and banging against the inner walls, producing a jittery force that appears to our coarse senses as a steady push. This pushing force, averaged over the wall area, provides the pressure of the enclosed air.

Suppose there are twice as many molecules in the same volume (Figure 6.19). Then the air density is doubled. If the molecules move at the same average speed—or, equivalently, if they have the same temperature—then the number of collisions will be doubled. This means that the pressure is doubled. So pressure is proportional to density.

We double the density of air in the tire by doubling the amount of air. We can also double the density of a *fixed* amount of air by compressing it to half its volume. Consider the cylinder with the movable piston in Figure 6.20. If the piston is pushed downward so that the volume is half the

Figure 6.19
When the density of gas in the tire is increased, the pressure is increased.

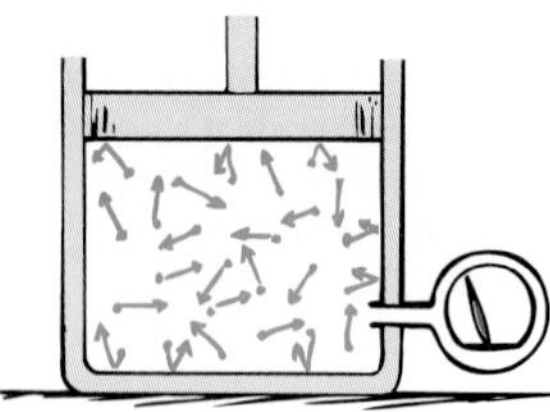

Figure 6.20
When the volume of gas is decreased, the density, and therefore pressure, are increased.

original volume, the density of molecules is doubled, and the pressure is correspondingly doubled. Decrease the volume to a third of its original value, and the pressure is increased by three, and so forth (provided the temperature remains the same).

Notice in these examples with the piston that the product of pressure and volume remains the same. For example, a doubled pressure multiplied by a halved volume gives the same value as a tripled pressure multiplied by a one-third volume. In general, we can state that the product of pressure and volume for a given mass of gas is a constant as long as the temperature does not change. "Pressure × volume" for a quantity of gas at some initial time is equal to any "different pressure × different volume" at some later time. In shorthand notation,

$$P_1V_1 = P_2V_2$$

where P_1 and V_1 represent the original pressure and volume, respectively, and P_2 and V_2 the second pressure and volume. This relationship is called **Boyle's Law**, after Robert Boyle, the seventeenth-century physicist who is credited with its discovery.*

Boyle's law applies to ideal gases. An ideal gas is one in which the disturbing effects of the forces between molecules and the finite size of the individual molecules can be neglected. Air and other gases under normal pressures approach the conditions of ideal gases.

Maybe Boyle's Law is named after Robert Law? Right! Like Washington Street is named after George Street!

Insights

☑ CHECKPOINT

1. A piston in an airtight pump is withdrawn so that the volume of the air chamber is increased three times. What is the change in pressure?
2. A scuba diver breathes compressed air beneath the surface of the water. If she holds her breath while returning to the surface, what happens to the volume of her lungs?

Check Your Answers

1. The pressure in the piston chamber is reduced to one-third. This is the principle that underlies a mechanical vacuum pump.
2. When she rises, the surrounding water pressure decreases, which means the volume of air in her lungs increases—ouch! A first lesson in scuba diving is not to hold your breath when ascending. To do so can be fatal.

6.7 Atmospheric Pressure

We live at the bottom of an ocean of air. The atmosphere, much like the water in a lake, exerts a pressure. One of the most celebrated experiments demonstrating the pressure of the atmosphere was conducted in 1654 by Otto von Gueicke, burgermeister of Magdeburg and inventor of the vacuum pump. Von Gueicke placed together two copper hemispheres about ½ meter in diameter to form a sphere, as shown in Figure 6.21. He set a gasket made of a ring of

*A general law that takes temperature changes into account is $P_1V_1/T_1 = P_2V_2/T_2$, where T_1 and T_2 represent the initial and final *absolute* temperatures, measured in SI units called kelvins (Chapter 7).

Figure 6.21
The famous "Magdeburg hemispheres" experiment of 1654, demonstrating atmospheric pressure. Two teams of horses couldn't pull the evacuated hemispheres apart. Were the hemispheres sucked together or pushed together? By what?

That's right. 99% of the earth's atmosphere is below an altitude of 30 km (only 0.5 % of earth's radius).

Insights

leather soaked in oil and wax between them to make an airtight joint. When he evacuated the sphere with his vacuum pump, two teams of eight horses each were unable to pull the hemispheres apart.

When the air pressure inside a cylinder like that shown in Figure 6.22 is reduced, there is an upward force on the piston. This force is large enough to lift a heavy weight. If the inside diameter of the cylinder is 12 centimeters or greater, a person can be lifted by this force.

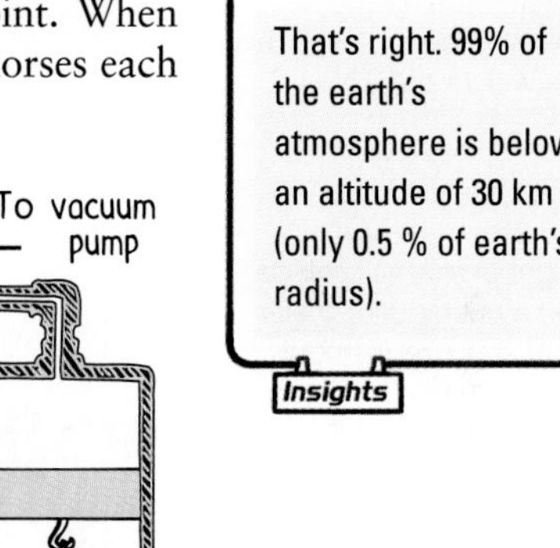

Figure 6.22
Is the piston pulled up or pushed up?

What do the experiments of Figures 6.21 and 6.22 demonstrate? Do they show that air exerts pressure or that there is a "force of suction"? If we say there is a force of suction, then we assume that a vacuum can exert a force. But what is a vacuum? It is an absence of matter; it is a condition of nothingness. How can nothing exert a force? The hemispheres are not sucked together, nor is the piston holding the weight sucked upward. The hemispheres and the piston are being pushed against by the pressure of the atmosphere.

Just as water pressure is caused by the weight of water, **atmospheric pressure** is caused by the weight of air. We have adapted so completely to the invisible air that we sometimes forget it has weight. Perhaps a fish "forgets" about the weight of water in the same way. The reason we don't feel this weight crushing against our bodies is that the pressure inside our bodies equals that of the surrounding air. There is no net force for us to sense.

At sea level, 1 cubic meter of air at 20°C has a mass of about 1.2 kilograms. To estimate the mass of air in your room, estimate the room's number of cubic meters, multiply by 1.2 kg/m^3, and you'll have the mass. Don't be surprised if it's heavier than your kid sister. If your kid sister doesn't believe that air has weight, maybe it's because she's always surrounded by air. Hand her a

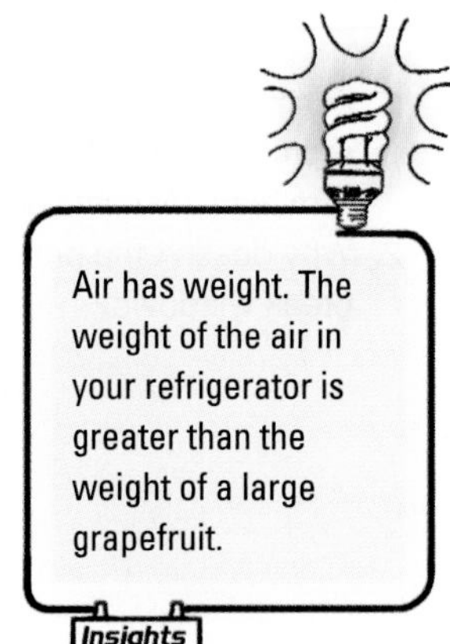

Figure 6.23
You don't notice the weight of a bag of water while you're submerged in water. Similarly, you don't notice that the air around you has weight.

plastic bag of water and she'll tell you it has weight. But hand her the same bag of water while she's submerged in a swimming pool, and she won't feel the weight. We don't notice that air has weight because we're submerged in air.

Unlike the constant density of water in a lake, the density of air in the atmosphere decreases with altitude. At 10 kilometers above the surface of the earth, 1 cubic meter of air has a mass of about 0.4 kilograms. To compensate for this, airplanes are pressurized; the additional air needed to fully pressurize a 747 jumbo jet, for example, is more than 1000 kilograms. Air is heavy, if you have enough of it.

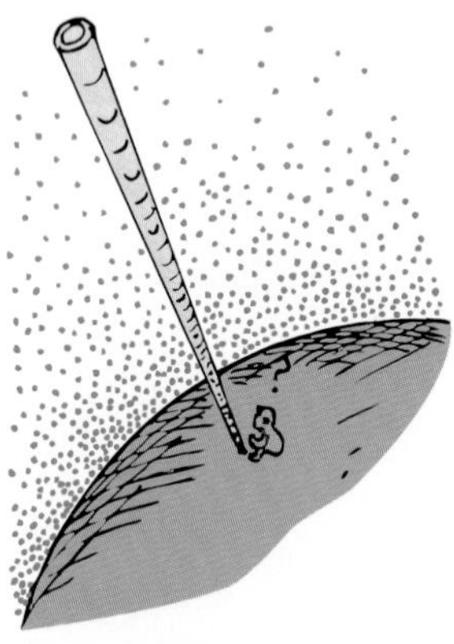

Figure 6.24
The mass of air that would occupy a bamboo pole that extends to the "top" of the atmosphere is about 1 kg. This air has a weight of 10 N.

Consider the mass of air in an upright, 30-kilometer-tall bamboo pole that has an inside cross-sectional area of 1 square centimeter. If the density of air inside the pole matches the density of air outside, the enclosed mass of air would be about one kilogram. The weight of this much air is about 10 newtons. So air pressure at the bottom of the bamboo pole would be about 10 newtons per square centimeter (10 N/cm^2). Of course, the same is true without the bamboo pole. There are 10,000 square centimeters in 1 square meter, so a column of air that has a cross sectional area of 1 square meter and extends up through the atmosphere has a mass of about 10,000 kilograms. The weight of this air is about 100,000 newtons (10^5 N). This weight produces a pressure of 100,000 newtons per square meter—or equivalently, 100,000 pascals, or 100 kilopascals. To be more precise, the average atmospheric pressure at sea level is 101.3 kilopascals (101.3 kPa).*

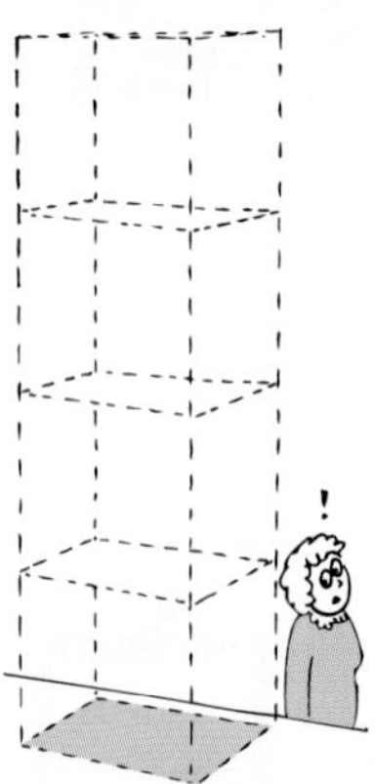

Figure 6.25
The weight of air that presses down on a one-square-meter surface at sea level is about 100,000 newtons. So atmospheric pressure is about 10^5 N/m^2, or about 100 kPa.

The pressure of the atmosphere is not uniform. Besides altitude variations, there are variations in atmospheric pressure at any one locality due to moving fronts and storms. Measurement of changing air pressure is important to meteorologists in predicting weather. (More about weather in Chapter 32.)

Figuring Physical Science

Problems

1. Estimate the mass of air, in kilograms, in a classroom that has a 200-m^2 floor area and a ceiling 4-m high. (Assume a chilly 10°C temperature).
2. Why doesn't the pressure of the atmosphere break windows?

Solutions

1. The mass of air is 1000 kg. The volume of air is 200 m^2 $\times$ 4 m = 800 m^3; each cubic meter of air has a mass of about 1.25 kg, so 800 m^3 $\times$ 1.25 kg/m^3 = 1000 kg.

2. Atmospheric pressure is exerted on both sides of a window, so no net force is exerted on the window. If, for some reason, the pressure is reduced or increased on one side only, as in a strong wind, then watch out!

*The pascal is the SI unit of pressure. The average pressure at sea level (101.3 kPa) is often called 1 atmosphere. In British units, the average atmospheric pressure at sea level is 14.7 lb/in^2 (psi).

Barometers

An instrument used for measuring the pressure of the atmosphere is called a **barometer.** A simple mercury barometer is illustrated in Figure 6.26. A glass tube, longer than 76 centimeters and closed at one end, is filled with mercury and tipped upside down into a dish of mercury. The mercury in the tube flows out of the submerged open bottom until the difference in the mercury levels in the tube and the dish is 76 centimeters. The empty space trapped above, except for some mercury vapor, is a pure vacuum.

Workers in underwater construction work in an environment of compressed air. The air pressure in their underwater chambers is at least as much as the combined pressure of water and atmosphere outside.

Insights

The explanation for the operation of such a barometer is similar to that of children balancing on a seesaw. The barometer "balances" when the weight of liquid in the tube exerts the same pressure as the atmosphere outside. Whatever the width of the tube, a 76-centimeter column of mercury weighs the same as the air that would fill a vertical 30-kilometer tube of the same width. If the atmospheric pressure increases, then the atmosphere pushes down harder on the mercury in the dish and pushes mercury higher in the tube. The increased height of the mercury column exerts an equal balancing pressure.

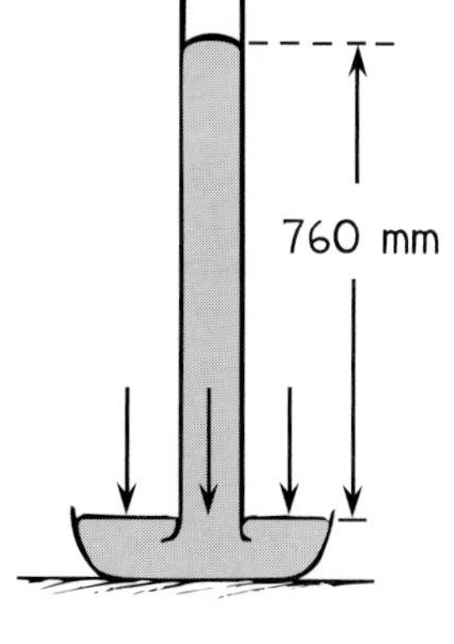

Figure 6.26
A simple mercury barometer. Mercury is pushed up into the tube by atmospheric pressure.

Water could instead be used to make a barometer, but the glass tube would have to be much longer—13.6 times as long, to be exact. The density of mercury is 13.6 the density of water. That's why a tube of water 13.6 times longer than one of mercury (of the same cross section) is needed to provide the same weight as mercury in the tube. A water barometer would have to be 13.6×0.76 meter, or 10.3 meters high—too tall to be practical.

What happens in a barometer is similar to what happens when you are drinking through a straw. By sucking, you reduce the air pressure in the straw when it is placed in a drink. Atmospheric pressure on the drink then pushes the liquid up into the reduced-pressure region. Strictly speaking, the liquid is not sucked up; it is pushed up by the pressure of the atmosphere. If the atmosphere is prevented from pushing on the surface of the drink, as in the party-trick bottle with the straw through an air-tight cork stopper, one can suck and suck and get no drink.

Lower a narrow glass tube or drinking straw in water and place your finger over the top of the tube. Lift the tube and note that the water doesn't fall out. You'll do this often in chemistry lab.

Insights

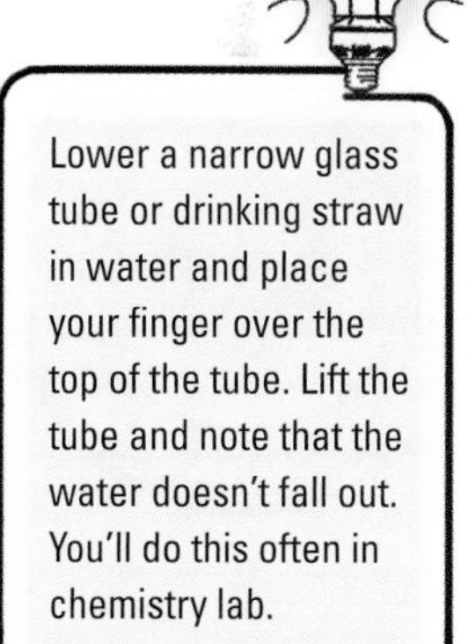

If you understand these ideas, you can understand why there is a 10.3-meter limit on the height water can be lifted with vacuum pumps. The old fashioned farm-type pump, shown in Figure 6.28, operates by producing a partial vacuum in a pipe that extends down into the water below. Atmospheric pressure on the surface of the water simply pushes the water up into the region of reduced pressure inside the pipe. Can you see that, even with a perfect vacuum, the maximum height to which water can be lifted in this way is 10.3 meters?

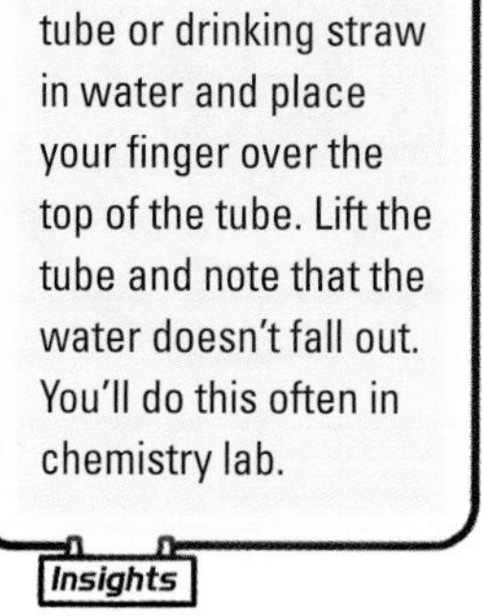

Figure 6.27
Strictly speaking, they do not suck the soda up the straws. They instead reduce the pressure in the straws, which allows the weight of the atmosphere to press the liquid up into the straws. Could they drink a soda this way on the moon?

A small portable instrument that measures atmospheric pressure is the *aneroid barometer* (Figure 6.29). A metal box partially exhausted of

Figure 6.28
The atmosphere pushes water from below up into a pipe that is evacuated of air by the pumping action.

When the pump handle is raised, air in the pipe is "thinned" as it expands to fill a larger volume. Atmospheric pressure on the surface of the water in the well pushes water up the pipe, causing it to overflow at the spout.

Insights

air with a slightly flexible lid bends in or out with changes in atmospheric pressure. Motion of the lid is indicated on a scale by a mechanical spring-and-lever system. Atmospheric pressure decreases with increasing altitude, so a barometer can be used to determine elevation. An aneroid barometer calibrated for altitude is called an altimeter (altitude meter). Some of these instruments are sensitive enough to indicate a change in elevation as you walk up a flight of stairs.*

Reduced air pressures can be produced by pumps, which work by virtue of the tendency of a gas to fill its container. If a space with less pressure is provided, a gas will flow from the region of higher pressure to the one of lower pressure. A vacuum pump simply provides a region of lower pressure into which the normally fast-moving gas molecules randomly move. The air pressure is repeatedly lowered by piston and valve action (Figure 6.30).

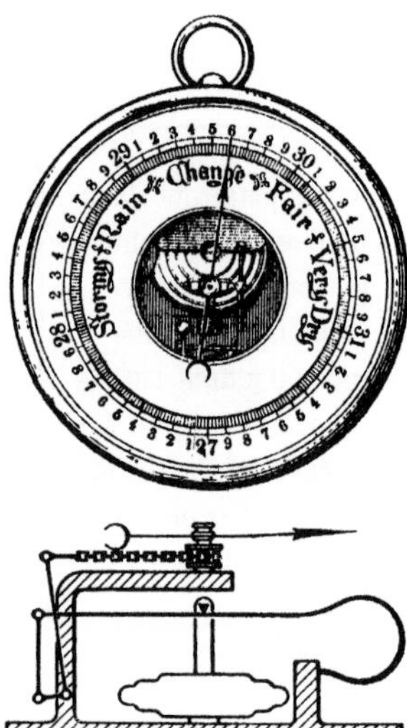

Figure 6.29
The aneroid barometer.

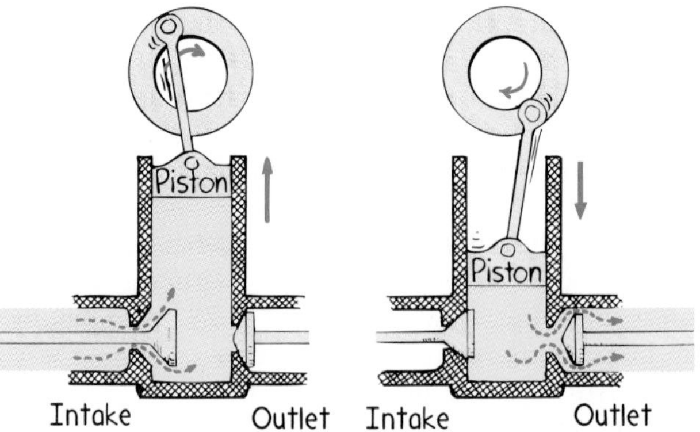

Figure 6.30
A mechanical vacuum pump. When the piston is lifted, the intake valve opens and air moves in to fill the empty space. When the piston is moved downward, the outlet valve opens and the air is pushed out. What changes would you make to convert this pump into an air compressor?

*Evidence of a noticeable pressure difference over a 1-m difference in elevation is provided by any small helium-filled balloon that rises in air. The atmosphere really does push harder against the lower bottom than against the higher top!

6.8 Buoyancy in a Gas

A crab lives on the ocean floor and looks upward at jellyfish and other lighter-than-water marine life drifting above it. Similarly, we live at the bottom of an ocean of air and look upward at balloons and other lighter-than-air objects drifting above us. A balloon is suspended in air and a jellyfish is suspended in water for the same reason: each is buoyed upward by a displaced weight of fluid equal to its own weight. Objects in water are buoyed upward because the pressure acting up against the bottom of the object exceeds the pressure acting down against the top. Likewise, air pressure acting up against an object immersed in air is greater than the pressure above pushing down. The buoyancy in both cases is numerically equal to the weight of fluid displaced. **Archimedes' principle** applies to air just as it does for water:

An object surrounded by air is buoyed up by a force equal to the weight of the air displaced.

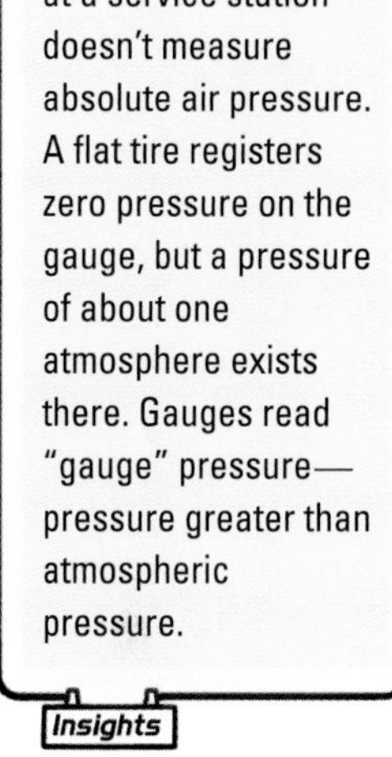

A tire-pressure gauge at a service station doesn't measure absolute air pressure. A flat tire registers zero pressure on the gauge, but a pressure of about one atmosphere exists there. Gauges read "gauge" pressure—pressure greater than atmospheric pressure.

Insights

We know that a cubic meter of air at ordinary atmospheric pressure and room temperature has a mass of about 1.2 kilograms, so its weight is about 12 newtons. Therefore, any 1-cubic-meter object in air is buoyed up with a force of 12 newtons. If the mass of the 1-cubic-meter object is greater than 1.2 kilograms (so that its weight is greater than 12 newtons), it falls to the ground when released. If an object of this size has a mass of less than 1.2 kilograms, buoyant force is greater than weight and it rises in the air. Any object that has a mass that is less than the mass of an equal volume of air rises in the air. Stated another way, any object less dense than air will rise in air. Gas-filled balloons that rise in air are less dense than air.

Any helium-filled balloon that rises in air is evidence that atmospheric pressure is greater below the balloon than above it.

Insights

No gas at all in a balloon would mean no weight, (except for the weight of the balloon's material), but such a balloon would collapse. The gas used in balloons prevents the atmosphere from collapsing them. Hydrogen is the lightest gas, but it is seldom used because it is highly flammable. In sport balloons, the gas is simply heated air. In balloons intended to reach very high altitudes or to remain aloft for a long time, helium is usually used. Its density is small enough that the combined weight of the helium, the balloon, and the cargo is less than the weight of air they displace. Low-density gas is used in a balloon for the same reason that cork is used in life preservers. The cork possesses no strange tendency to be drawn toward the water's surface, and the gas possesses no strange tendency to rise. Cork and gases are buoyed upward like anything else. They are simply light enough for the buoyancy to be significant.

Unlike water, there is no sharp surface at the "top" of the atmosphere. Furthermore, unlike water, the atmosphere becomes less dense with altitude. Whereas cork will float to the surface of the water, a released helium-filled balloon does not rise to any atmospheric surface. Will a lighter-than-air balloon rise indefinitely? How high will a balloon rise? We can state the answer in several ways. A gas-filled balloon will rise only so long as it displaces a weight of air greater than its own

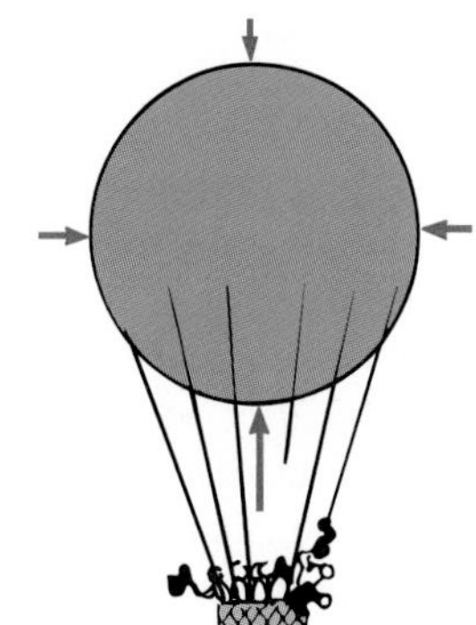

Figure 6.31
All bodies are buoyed up by a force equal to the weight of air they displace. Why, then, don't all objects float like this balloon?

weight. Because air becomes less dense with altitude, a lesser weight of air is displaced per given volume as the balloon rises. When the weight of displaced air equals the total weight of the balloon, upward acceleration of the balloon will cease. We can also say that, when the buoyant force on the balloon equals its weight, the balloon will cease rising. Equivalently, when the density of the balloon (including its load) equals the density of the surrounding air, the balloon will cease rising. Helium-filled toy balloons usually break some time after being released into the air when the expansion of the helium they contain stretches the rubber until it ruptures.

Large dirigible airships are designed so that, when they are loaded, they will slowly rise in the air; that is, their total weight is a little less than the weight of air displaced. When in motion, the airship may be raised or lowered by means of horizontal "elevators."

Thus far, we have treated pressure only as it applies to stationary fluids. Motion produces an additional influence.

☑ CHECKPOINT

1. Is there a buoyant force acting on you? If there is, why are you not buoyed up by this force?
2. How does buoyancy change as a helium-filled balloon ascends?

Check Your Answers

1. There is a buoyant force acting on you, and you are buoyed upward by it. You aren't aware of it only because your weight is so much greater.
2. If the balloon is free to expand as it rises, the increase in volume is counteracted by a decrease in the density of higher-altitude air. So, interestingly, the greater volume of displaced air doesn't weigh more, and buoyancy stays the same. If a balloon is not free to expand, buoyancy will decrease as the balloon rises because of the lesser density of the displaced air. Usually, balloons initially expand when they rise, and, if they don't eventually rupture, fabric stretching reaches a maximum and the balloons settle where buoyancy matches their weight.

6.9 Bernoulli's Principle

Figure 6.32
Because the flow is continuous, water speeds up when it flows through a narrow and/or shallow part of the brook.

Consider a continuous flow of liquid or gas through a pipe: The volume flowing past any cross section of the pipe in a given time is the same as that flowing past any other section of the pipe—even if the pipe widens or narrows. For continuous flow, a fluid speeds up when it goes from a wide part to a narrow part of the pipe. This is evident for a broad, slowly moving river that flows more swiftly as it enters a narrow gorge. It is also evident when water flowing from a garden hose speeds up when you squeeze the end of the hose to make the stream narrower.

The motion of a fluid in steady flow follows imaginary *streamlines,* represented by thin lines in Figure 6.33 and in other figures that follow. Streamlines are the smooth paths of bits of fluid. The lines are closer together in narrower regions, where the flow speed is greater. (Streamlines are visible when smoke or other visible fluids are passed through evenly spaced openings, as in a wind tunnel.)

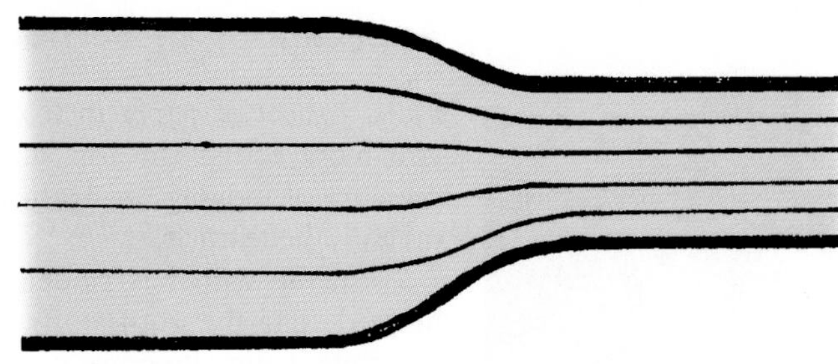

Figure 6.33
Water speeds up when it flows into the narrower pipe. The close-together streamlines indicate increased speed and decreased internal pressure.

Daniel Bernoulli, an eighteenth-century Swiss scientist, studied fluid flow in pipes. His discovery, now called **Bernoulli's principle,** can be stated as follows:

> **Where the speed of a fluid increases, internal pressure in the fluid decreases.**

Where streamlines of a fluid are closer together, flow speed is greater and the pressure within the fluid is less. Changes in internal pressure are evident in water that contains air bubbles. The volume of an air bubble depends on the surrounding water pressure. Where water gains speed, pressure is lowered and bubbles become bigger. In water that slows, pressure is greater and bubbles are squeezed to a smaller size.

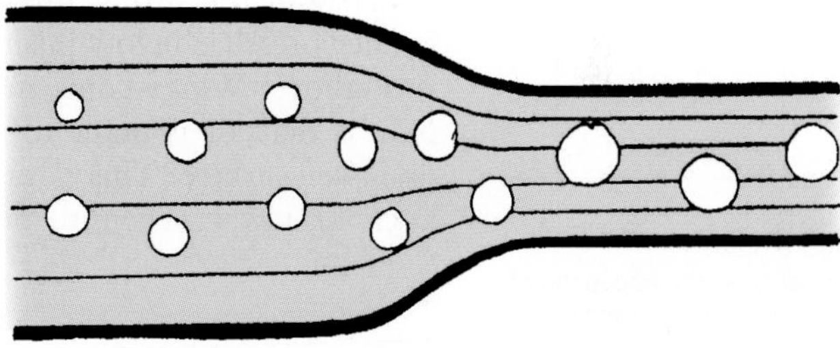

Figure 6.34
Internal pressure is greater in the slower-moving water in the wide part of the pipe, as evidenced by the more compressed air bubbles. The bubbles are bigger in the narrow part because internal pressure there is less.

Bernoulli's principle is a consequence of the conservation of energy, although, surprisingly, he developed it long before the concept of energy became formalized.* The full energy picture for a fluid in motion is quite complicated. Simply stated, more speed and kinetic energy mean less pressure, and more pressure means less speed and kinetic energy.

Bernoulli's principle applies to a smooth, steady flow (called *laminar* flow) of constant-density fluid. At speeds above some critical point, however, the flow may become chaotic (called *turbulent* flow) and follow changing, curling paths called *eddies*. This exerts friction on the fluid and dissipates some of its energy. Then Bernoulli's equation doesn't apply well.

The decrease in fluid pressure with increasing speed may at first seem surprising, particularly if you fail to distinguish between the pressure *within* the fluid, internal pressure, and the pressure *by* the fluid on something that interferes with its flow. Internal pressure within flowing water and the external pressure it can exert on whatever it encounters are two different pressures. When the momentum of moving water or anything else is suddenly reduced, the impulse it exerts is relatively huge. A dramatic example is the use of high-speed jets of water to cut steel in modern machine shops. The water has very little internal pressure, but the pressure the stream exerts on the steel interrupting its flow is enormous.

*In mathematical form: $\frac{1}{2}mv^2 + mgy + pV =$ constant (along a streamline); where m is the mass of some small volume V, v its speed, g the acceleration due to gravity, y its elevation, and p its internal pressure. If mass m is expressed in terms of density ρ, where $\rho = m/V$, and each term is divided by V, Bernoulli's equation takes the form: $\frac{1}{2}\rho v^2 + \rho gy + p =$ constant. Then all three terms have units of pressure. If y does not change, an increase in v means a decrease in p, and vice versa. Note that, when v is zero, Bernoulli's equation reduces to $\Delta p = -\rho g \Delta y$ (weight density × depth).

Applications of Bernoulli's Principle

Figure 6.35
The paper rises when Tim blows air across its top surface.

Hold a sheet of paper in front of your mouth, as shown in Figure 6.35. When you blow across the top surface, the paper rises. That's because the internal pressure of moving air against the top of the paper is less than the atmospheric pressure beneath it.

Anyone who has ridden in a convertible car with the canvas top up has noticed that the roof puffs upward as the car moves. This is the Bernoulli principle again. Pressure outside is less on top of the fabric where air is moving than it is on the inside, where atmospheric pressure is static.

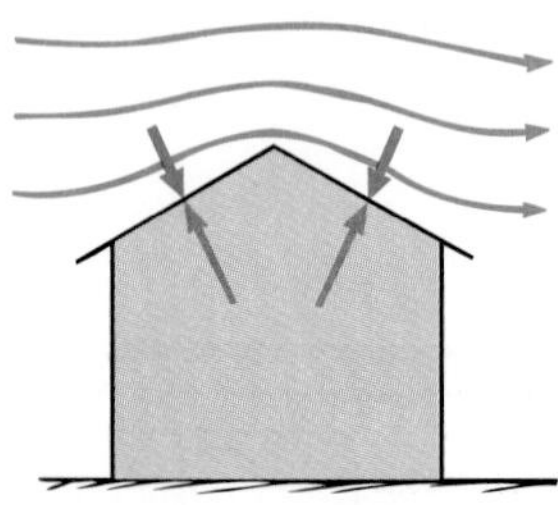

Figure 6.36
The air pressure above the roof is less than the air pressure beneath the roof.

Consider wind blowing across a peaked roof. The wind gains speed as it flows over the roof, as the crowding of streamlines in the sketch indicates. Pressure along the streamlines is reduced where they are closer together. The greater pressure inside the roof can lift it off the house. During a severe storm, the difference between outside and inside pressure doesn't need to be very much. A small pressure difference over a large area produces a force that can be formidable.

If we think of the blown-off roof as an airplane wing, we can better understand the lifting force that supports a heavy aircraft. In both cases, a greater pressure below pushes the roof or the wing into a region of lesser pressure above. Wings come in a variety of designs. What they all have in common is that air is made to flow faster over the wing's top surface than under its lower surface. This is mainly accomplished by a tilt in the wing, called its *angle of attack*. Then air flows faster over the top surface for much the same reason that air flows faster in a narrowed pipe or in any other constricted region. Most often, but not always, different speeds of airflow over and beneath a wing are enhanced by a difference in the curvature *(camber)* of the upper and lower surfaces of the wing. The result is more crowded streamlines along the top wing surface than along the bottom. When the average pressure difference over the wing is multiplied

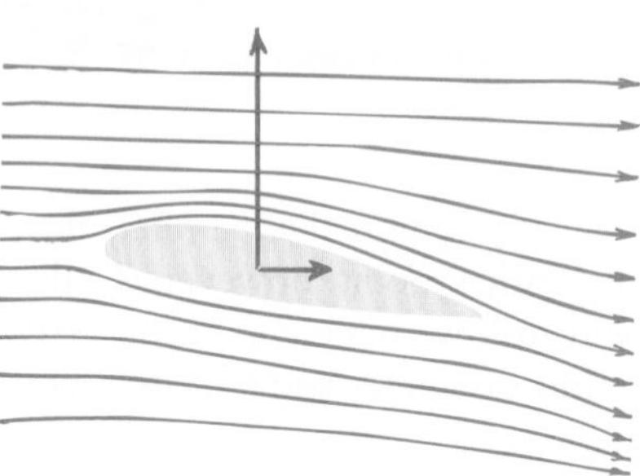

Figure 6.37
The vertical vector represents the net upward force (lift) that results from there being more air pressure below the wing than above the wing. The horizontal vector represents air drag.

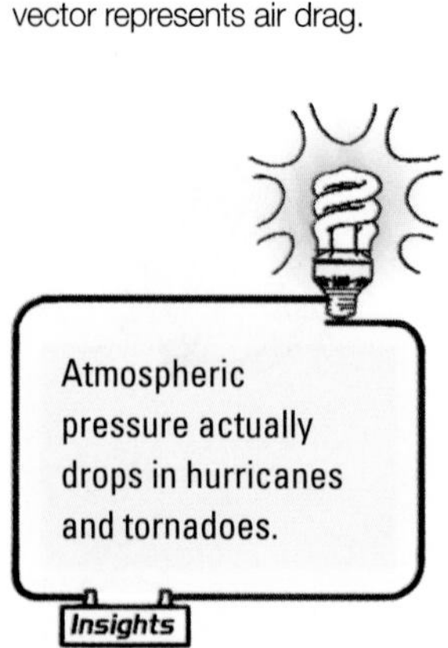

Figure 6.38
Where is air pressure greater—on the top or bottom surface of the hang glider?

by the surface area of the wing, we have a net upward force—lift. Lift is greater when there is a large wing area and when the plane is traveling fast. A glider has a very large wing area relative to its weight, so it does not have to be going very fast for sufficient lift. At the other extreme, a fighter plane designed for high-speed flight has a small wing area relative to its weight. Consequently, it must take off and land at high speeds.

We all know that a baseball pitcher can throw a ball in such a way that it will curve off to one side as it approaches home plate. This is accomplished by imparting a large spin to the ball. Similarly, a tennis player can hit a ball so it curves. A thin layer of air is dragged around the spinning ball by friction, which is enhanced by the baseball's threads or the tennis ball's fuzz. The moving layer of air produces a crowding of streamlines on one side. Note, in Figure 6.39b, that the streamlines are more crowded at B than at A for the direction of spin shown. Air pressure is greater at A, and the ball curves as shown.

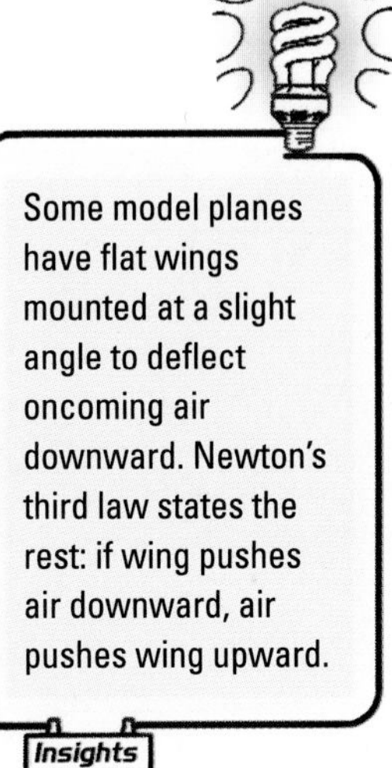

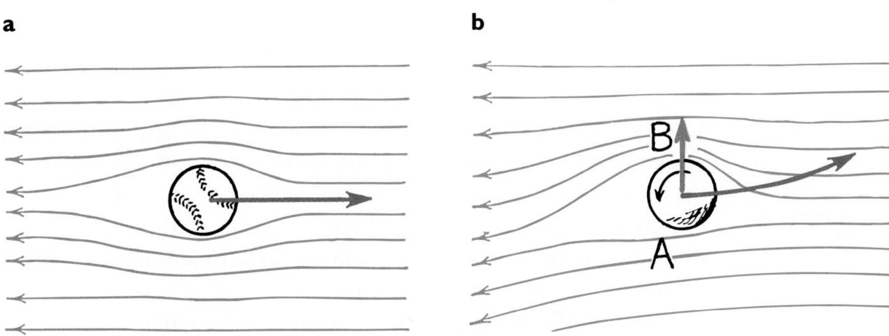

Figure 6.39
(a) The streamlines are the same on either side of a nonspinning baseball. (b) A spinning ball produces a crowding of streamlines. The resulting "lift" (red arrow) causes the ball to curve, as shown by the blue arrow.

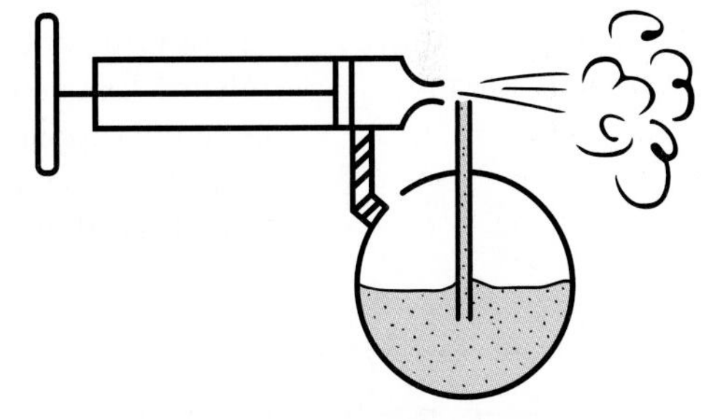

Figure 6.40
Why does the liquid in the reservoir go up the tube?

Recent findings show that many insects increase lift by employing motions similar to those of a curving baseball. Interestingly, most insects do not flap their wings up and down. They flap them forward and backward, with a tilt that provides an angle of attack. Between flaps, their wings make semicircular motions to create lift.

A familiar sprayer, such as a perfume atomizer, utilizes Bernoulli's principle. When you squeeze the bulb, air rushes across the open end of a tube inserted into the perfume. This reduces the pressure in the tube, whereupon atmospheric pressure on the liquid below pushes it up into the tube, where it is carried away by the stream of air.

Bernoulli's principle explains why trucks passing closely on the highway are drawn to each other, and why passing ships run the risk of a sideways collision. Water flowing between the ships travels faster than water flowing past the outer sides.

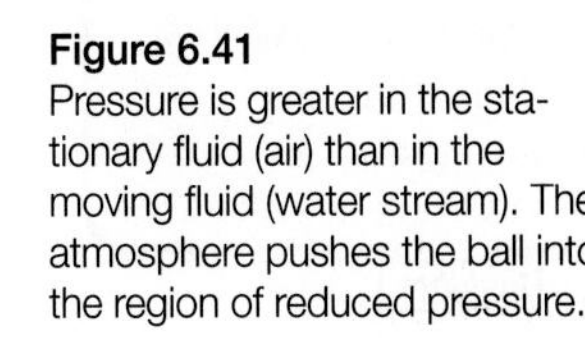

Figure 6.41
Pressure is greater in the stationary fluid (air) than in the moving fluid (water stream). The atmosphere pushes the ball into the region of reduced pressure.

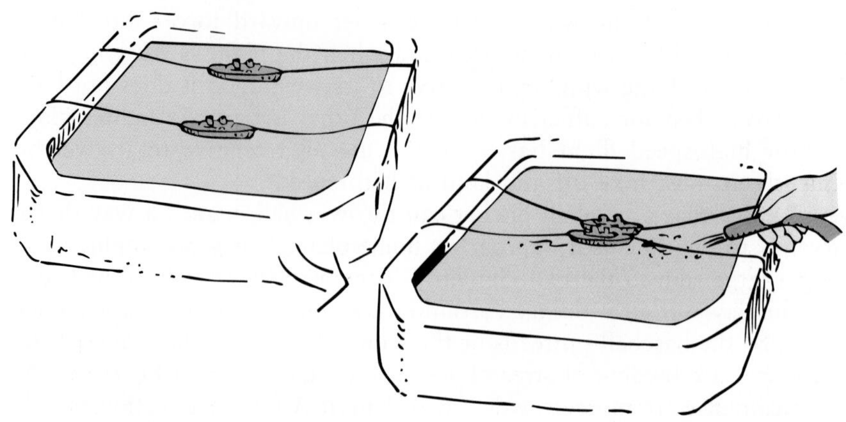

Figure 6.42
Try this in your sink. Loosely moor a pair of toy boats side by side. Then direct a stream of water between them. The boats will draw together and collide. Why?

Figure 6.43
Why can't you blow the bent filing card off the table when you blow through the arch?

Streamlines are closer together between the ships than outside, so water pressure acting against the hulls is reduced between the ships. Unless the ships are steered to compensate for this, the greater pressure against the outer sides of the ships forces them together. The drawing shows how to demonstrate this in your kitchen sink or bathtub.

Bernoulli's principle plays a small role when your bathroom shower curtain swings toward you in the shower when the water is on full blast. The pressure in the shower stall is reduced with fluid in motion, and the relatively greater pressure outside the curtain pushes it inward. Like so much in the complex real world, this is but one physics principle that applies. More important is the convection of air in the shower. In any case, the next time you're taking a shower and the curtain swings in against your legs, think of Daniel Bernoulli.

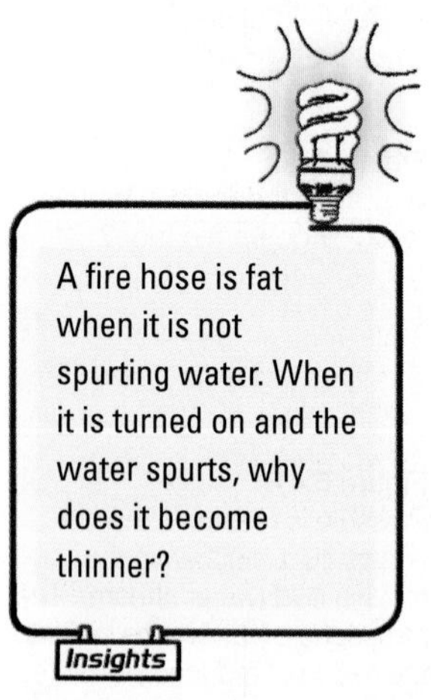

Figure 6.44
The curved shape of an umbrella can be disadvantageous on a windy day.

Summary of Terms

Density The amount of matter per unit volume:

$$\text{Density} = \frac{\text{mass}}{\text{volume}}$$

Weight density is expressed as weight per unit volume.

Pressure The ratio of force to the area over which that force is distributed:

$$\text{Pressure} = \frac{\text{force}}{\text{area}}$$

$$\text{Liquid pressure} = \text{weight density} \times \text{depth}.$$

Buoyant force The net upward force that a fluid exerts on an immersed object.

Archimedes' principle An immersed body is buoyed up by a force equal to the weight of the fluid it displaces.

Principle of flotation A floating object displaces a weight of fluid equal to its own weight.

Boyle's law The product of pressure and volume is a constant for a given mass of confined gas so long as temperature remains unchanged:

$$P_1V_1 = P_2V_2$$

Atmospheric Pressure The pressure exerted against bodies immersed in the atmosphere resulting from the weight of air pressing down from above. At sea level, atmospheric pressure is about 101 kPa.

Barometer Any device that measures atmospheric pressure.

Boyle's law The product of pressure and volume is a constant for a given mass of confined gas regardless of changes either in pressure or in volume individually, so long as temperature remains unchanged:

$$P_1V_1 = P_2V_2$$

Bernoulli's principle The pressure in a fluid moving steadily, without friction or an input of outside energy, decreases when the fluid velocity increases.

Review Questions

1. Give two examples of a fluid.

6.1 Density

2. What happens to the volume of a loaf of bread that is squeezed? What happens to the mass? What happens to the density?
3. Distinguish between *mass density* and *weight density*. What are the mass density and the weight density of water?

6.2 Pressure

4. Distinguish between *force* and *pressure*.
5. How does the pressure exerted by a liquid change with depth in the liquid? How does the pressure exerted by a liquid change as the density of the liquid changes?
6. Discounting the pressure of the atmosphere, if you swim twice as deep in water, how much more water pressure is exerted on your ears? If you swim in salt water, will the pressure be greater than in fresh water at the same depth? Why or why not?
7. How does water pressure one meter below the surface of a small pond compare to water pressure one meter below the surface of a huge lake?
8. If you punch a hole in the side of a container filled with water, in what direction does the water initially flow outward from the container?

6.3 Buoyancy in a Liquid

9. Why does buoyant force act upward on an object submerged in water?
10. How does the volume of a completely submerged object compare with the volume of water displaced?

6.4 Archimedes' Principle

11. Cite Archimedes' principle.
12. What is the difference between *immersed* and *submerged*?
13. How does the buoyant force on a fully submerged object compare with the weight of water displaced?
14. What is the mass in kilograms of 1 L of water? What is its weight in newtons?
15. If a 1-L container is immersed halfway in water, what is the volume of water displaced? What is the buoyant force on the container?
16. Does the buoyant force on a fully submerged object depend on the weight of the object or on the weight of the fluid displaced by the object? Does the force depend on the weight of the object or on its volume? Defend your answer.

6.5 Flotation

17. There is a condition in which the buoyant force on an object does equal the weight of the object. What is this condition?
18. Does the buoyant force on a submerged object depend on the volume of the object?
19. Does the buoyant force on a floating object depend on the weight of the object or on the weight of the fluid displaced by the object? Or are these two weights the same for the special case of floating? Defend your answer.
20. What weight of water is displaced by a 100-ton ship? What is the buoyant force that acts on this ship?

6.6 Pressure in a Gas

21. Describe the primary differences between liquids and gases.
22. By how much does the density of air increase when it is compressed to half its volume?
23. What happens to the air pressure inside a balloon when the balloon is squeezed to half its volume at constant temperature?
24. Define Boyle's law, and give an application.

6.7 Atmospheric Pressure

25. What is the cause of atmospheric pressure?
26. What is the mass in kilograms of a cubic meter of air at room temperature (20°C)?
27. What is the approximate mass in kilograms of a column of air that has a cross-sectional area of 1 cm^2 and extends from sea level to the upper atmosphere? What is the weight in newtons of this amount of air?
28. How does the downward pressure of the 76-cm column of mercury in a barometer compare with the air pressure at the bottom of the atmosphere?
29. How does the weight of mercury in a barometer tube compare with the weight of an equal cross-section of air from sea level to the top of the atmosphere?
30. Why would a water barometer have to be 13.6 times taller than a mercury barometer?
31. When you drink liquid through a straw, is it more accurate to say that the liquid is pushed up the straw rather than sucked up? What exactly does the pushing? Defend your answer.
32. Why will a vacuum pump not operate for a well that is more than 10.3 m deep?

6.8 Buoyancy in a Gas

33. A balloon that weighs 1 N is suspended in air, drifting neither up nor down. How much buoyant force acts upon it? What happens if the buoyant force decreases? Increases?

6.9 Bernoulli's Principle

34. Cite Bernoulli's principle.
35. What are streamlines? Is pressure greater or less in regions of crowded streamlines?
36. Does Bernoulli's principle refer to internal pressure changes in a fluid or to pressures that a fluid can exert on objects it encounters?
37. What do peaked roofs, convertible tops, and airplane wings have in common when air moves faster across their top surfaces?

Activities

1. Try to float an egg in water. Then dissolve salt in the water until the egg floats. How does the density of an egg compare to that of tap water? To salt water?
2. Punch a couple of holes in the bottom of a water-filled container, and water will spurt out because of water pressure. Now drop the container, and, as it freely falls, note that the water no longer spurts out. If your friends don't understand this, could you figure it out and then explain it to them?

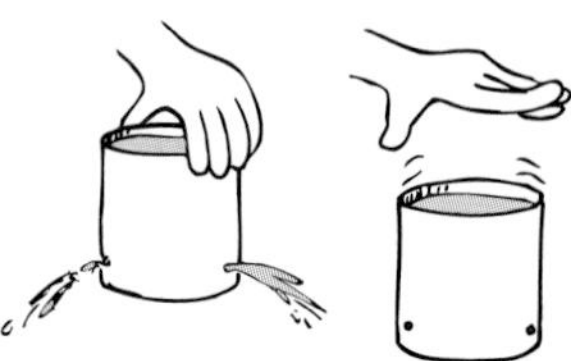

3. Place a wet Ping-Pong ball in a can of water held high above your head. Then drop the can on a rigid floor. Because of surface tension, the ball will be pulled beneath the surface as the can falls. And then what happens when the can comes to an abrupt stop is worth watching!
4. Try this in the bathtub or when you're washing dishes: Lower a drinking glass, mouth downward, over a small floating object. What do you observe? How deep will the glass have to be pushed in order to compress the enclosed air to half its volume? (You won't be able to do this in your bathtub unless it's 10.3 m deep!)
5. You can find the pressure exerted by the tires of your car on the road and compare it with the air pressure in the tires. For this project, you need to get the weight of your car from the manual or a dealer, and then divide by four to get the approximate weight held up by one tire. You can closely approximate the area of contact of a tire with the road by tracing the edges of tire contact on a sheet of paper marked with 1-$inch^2$ squares beneath the tire. After you get the pressure of the tire on the road, compare it with the air pressure in the tire. Are they nearly equal? Which one is greater?

6. You ordinarily pour water from a full glass into an empty glass simply by placing the full glass above the empty glass and tipping. Have you ever poured air from one glass to another? The procedure is similar. Lower two glasses in water, mouths downward. Let one fill with water by tilting its mouth upward. Then hold the water-filled glass mouth downward above the air-filled glass. Slowly tilt the lower glass and let the air escape, filling the upper glass. You will be pouring air from one glass into another!

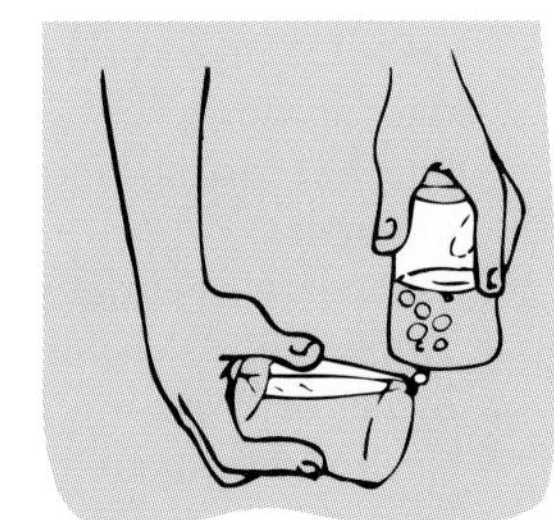

7. Raise a filled glass of water above the waterline, but with its mouth beneath the surface. Why does the water not run out? How tall would a glass have to be before water began to run out? (You won't be able to do this indoors unless you have a ceiling that is at least 10.3m higher than the waterline.)

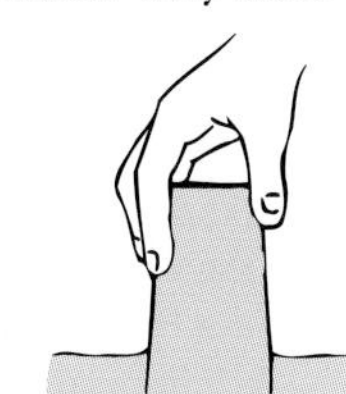

8. Place a card over the open top of a glass filled to the brim with water, and then invert it. Why does the card stay in place? Try it sideways.

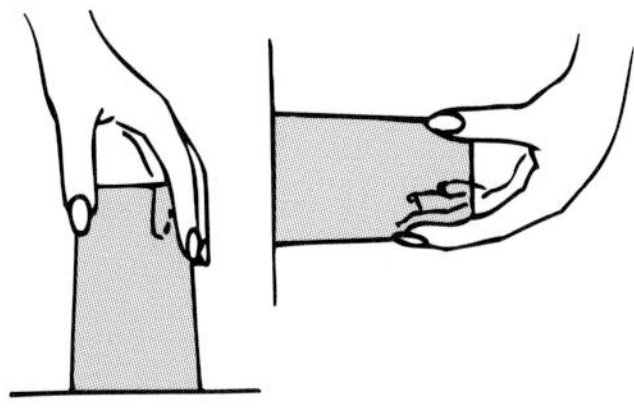

9. Invert a water-filled pop bottle or small-necked jar. Notice that the water doesn't simply fall out, but it gurgles out of the container instead. Air pressure won't allow the water out until some air has pushed its way up inside the bottle to occupy the space above the liquid. How would an inverted, water-filled bottle empty if you tried this on the moon?
10. Heat a small amount of water to boiling in an aluminum soda-pop can, and invert it quickly into a dish of cold water. What happens is surprisingly dramatic!
11. Make a small hole near the bottom of an open tin can. Fill the can with water, which then proceeds to spurt from the hole. If you cover the top of the can firmly with the palm of your hand, the flow stops. Explain.

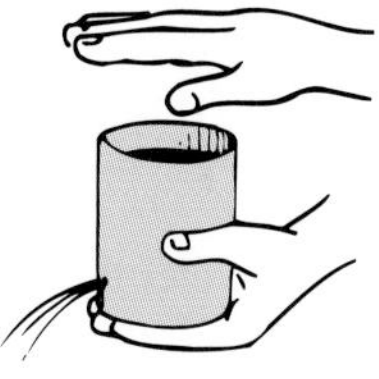

12. Lower a narrow glass tube or drinking straw into water and place your finger over the top of the tube. Lift the tube from the water and then lift your finger from the top of the tube. What happens? (You'll do this often in chemistry experiments.)

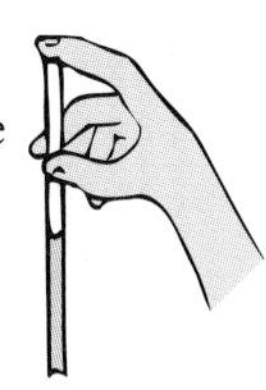

13. Blow across the top of a sheet of paper as Tim does in Figure 6.35. Try this with those of your friends who are not taking a physical science course. Then explain it to them!
14. Push a pin through a small card and place it over the hole of a thread spool. Try to blow the card from the spool by blowing through the hole. Try it in all directions.

15. Hold a spoon in a stream of water as shown and feel the effect of the differences in pressure.

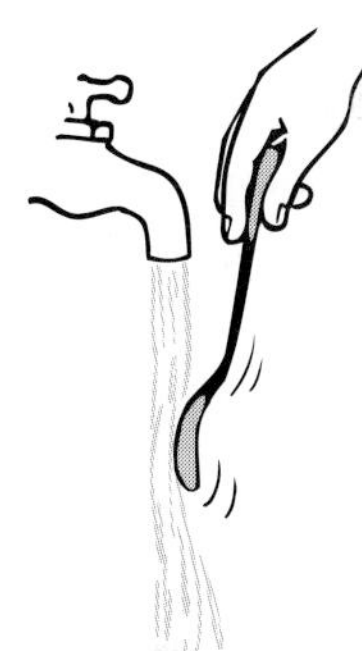

Exercises

1. Stand on a bathroom scale and read your weight. When you lift one foot up so you're standing on one foot, does the reading change? Does a scale read force or pressure?
2. The photo shows physics teacher Marshall Ellenstein walking barefoot on broken glass bottles in his class. What physics concept is Marshall demonstrating, and why is he careful that the broken pieces are small and numerous? (The Band-Aids on his feet are for humor!)

3. In a deep dive, a whale is appreciably compressed by the pressure of the surrounding water. What happens to the whale's density?
4. The density of a rock doesn't change when it is submerged in water. Does your density change when you are submerged in water? Defend your answer.
5. Why are persons who are confined to bed less likely to develop bedsores on their bodies if they use a waterbed rather than an ordinary mattress?
6. If water faucets upstairs and downstairs are turned fully on, will more water per second flow out the downstairs faucet? Or will the flows from the faucets be the same?
7. Which do you suppose exerts more pressure on the ground—an elephant or a woman standing on spike heels? (Which will be more likely to make dents in a linoleum floor?) Can you approximate a rough calculation for each?
8. Suppose you wish to lay a level foundation for a home on hilly and bushy terrain. How can you use a garden hose filled with water to determine equal elevations for distant points?
9. When you are bathing on a stony beach, why do the stones hurt your feet less when you get in deep water?
10. If liquid pressure were the same at all depths, would there be a buoyant force on an object submerged in the liquid? Explain.
11. The Himalaya Mountains are slightly less dense than the mantle material upon which they "float." Do you suppose that, like floating icebergs, they are deeper than they are high?
12. How much force is needed to push a nearly weightless but rigid 1-L carton beneath a surface of water?
13. Why is it inaccurate to say that heavy objects sink and that light objects float? Give exaggerated examples to support your answer.
14. Compared to an empty ship, would a ship loaded with a cargo of Styrofoam sink deeper into water or rise in water? Defend your answer.
15. A barge filled with scrap iron is in a canal lock. If the iron is thrown overboard, does the water level at the side of the lock rise, fall, or remain unchanged? Explain.
16. Would the water level in a canal lock go up or down if a battleship in the lock were to sink?
17. A balloon is weighted so that it is barely able to float in water. If it is pushed beneath the surface, will it come back to the surface, stay at the depth to which it is pushed, or sink? Explain. (Hint: Does the balloon's density change?)

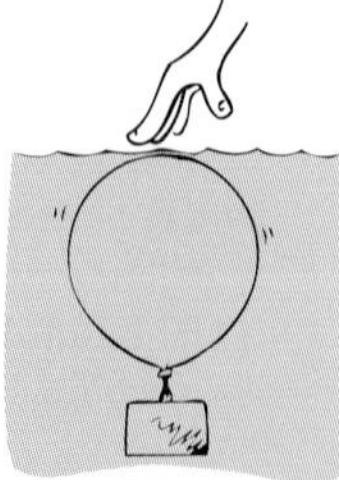

18. A ship sailing from the ocean into a fresh-water harbor sinks slightly deeper into the water. Does the buoyant force on it change? If so, does it increase or decrease?
19. Suppose you are given the choice between two life preservers that are identical in size, the first a light one filled with Styrofoam and the second a very heavy one filled with lead pellets. If you submerge these life preservers in the water, upon which will the buoyant force be greater? Upon which will the buoyant force be ineffective? Why are your answers different?
20. The relative densities of water, ice, and alcohol are 1.0, 0.9, and 0.8, respectively. Do ice cubes float higher or lower in a mixed alcoholic drink? What can you say about a cocktail in which the ice cubes lie submerged at the bottom of the glass?
21. When an ice cube in a glass of water melts, does the water level in the glass rise, fall, or remain unchanged? Does your answer change if the ice cube contains many air bubbles? Does your answer change if the ice cube contains many grains of heavy sand?
22. A half-filled bucket of water is on a spring scale. Will the reading of the scale increase or remain the same if a fish is placed in the bucket? (Will your answer be different if the bucket is initially filled to the brim?)
23. We say that the shape of a liquid is that of its container. But with no container and no gravity, what is the natural shape of a blob of water? Why?
24. If you release a Ping-Pong ball beneath the surface of water, it will rise to the surface. Would it do the same if it were submerged in a big blob of water floating weightless in an orbiting spacecraft?
25. It is said that a gas fills all the space available to it. Why, then, doesn't the atmosphere go off into space?
26. Count the tires on a large-tractor trailer that is unloading food at your local supermarket, and you may be surprised to count 18 tires. Why so many tires? (Hint: See Activity 5.)
27. How does the density of air in a deep mine compare with the air density at the earth's surface?
28. Two teams of eight horses each were unable to pull the Magdeburg hemispheres apart (Figure 6.21). Why? Suppose two teams of nine horses each could pull them apart. Then would one team of nine horses succeed if the other team were replaced with a strong tree? Defend your answer.
29. Before boarding an airplane, you buy a bag of chips (or any item packaged in an airtight foil package) and, while in flight, you notice that the bag is puffed up. Explain why this occurs.
30. Why do you suppose that airplane windows are smaller than bus windows?

31. A half cup or so of water is poured into a 5-L can, which is placed on a source of heat until most of the water has boiled away. Then the top of the can is screwed on tightly and the can is removed from the source of heat and allowed to cool. What happens to the can and why?
32. We can understand how pressure in water depends on depth by considering a stack of bricks. The pressure below the bottom brick is determined by the weight of the entire stack. Halfway up the stack, the pressure is half because the weight of the bricks above is half. To explain atmospheric pressure, we should consider compressible bricks, like foam rubber. Why is this so?

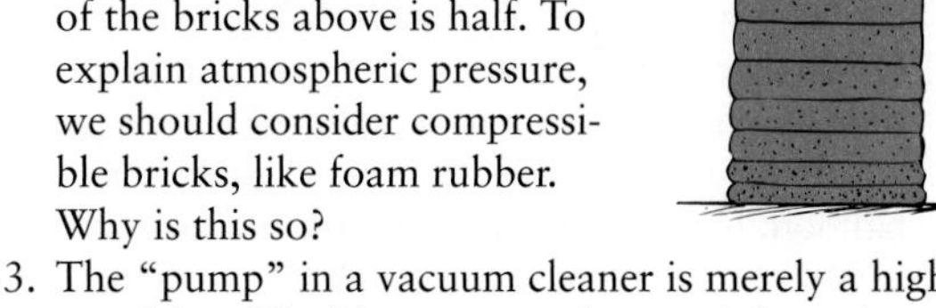

33. The "pump" in a vacuum cleaner is merely a high-speed fan. Would a vacuum cleaner pick up dust from a rug on the moon? Explain.
34. If you could somehow replace the mercury in a mercury barometer with a denser liquid, would the height of the liquid column be greater or less than with mercury? Why?
35. Would it be slightly more difficult to draw soda through a straw at sea level or on top of a very high mountain? Explain.
36. Your friend says that the buoyant force of the atmosphere on an elephant is significantly greater than the buoyant force of the atmosphere on a small helium-filled balloon. What do you say?
37. Why is it so difficult to breathe when snorkeling at a depth of 1 m, and practically impossible at a 2-m depth? Why can't a diver simply breathe through a hose that extends to the surface?
38. When you replace helium in a balloon with hydrogen, which is less dense, does the buoyant force on the balloon change if the balloon remains the same size? Explain.
39. A steel tank filled with helium gas doesn't rise in air, but a balloon containing the same helium easily does? Why?
40. Two identical balloons of the same volume are pumped up with air to more than atmospheric pressure and suspended on the ends of a stick that is horizontally balanced. One of the balloons is then punctured. Is there a change in the stick's balance? If so, which way does it tip?
41. Imagine a huge space colony that consists of a rotating air-filled cylinder. How would the density of air at "ground level" compare to the air densities "above"?
42. Would a helium-filled balloon "rise" in the atmosphere of a rotating space habitat? Defend your answer.
43. The force of the atmosphere at sea level against the outside of a 10-m^2 store window is about a million N. Why does this not shatter the window? Why might the window shatter in a strong wind blowing past the window?
44. In a department store, an airstream from a hose connected to the exhaust of a vacuum cleaner blows upward at an angle and supports a beach ball in midair. Does the air blow mostly under or over the ball to provide support?
45. When a steadily flowing gas flows from a larger-diameter pipe to a smaller-diameter pipe, what happens to (a) its speed, (b) its pressure, and (c) the spacing between its streamlines?
46. How is an airplane able to fly upside down?
47. When a jet plane is cruising at a high altitude, the flight attendants have more of a "hill" to climb as they walk forward along the aisle than when the plane is cruising at a lower altitude. Why does the pilot have to fly with a greater "angle of attack" at a high altitude than at a low one?
48. What physics principle underlies these three observations? When passing an oncoming truck on the highway, your car tends to sway toward the truck. The canvas roof of a convertible automobile bulges upward when the car is traveling at high speeds. The windows of older passenger trains sometimes break when a high-speed train passes by on the next track.
49. A steady wind blows over the waves of an ocean. Why does the wind increase the humps and troughs of the waves?

50. Wharves are made with pilings that permit the free passage of water. Why would a solid-walled wharf be disadvantageous to ships attempting to pull alongside?

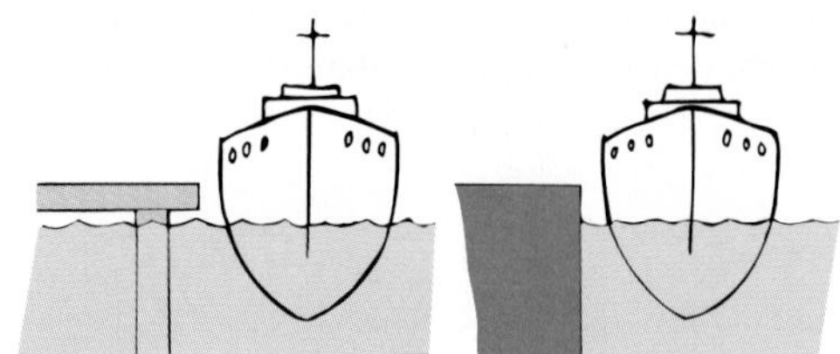

Problems

1. How much pressure do you experience when you balance a 5-kg ball on the tip of your finger, which, let us say, has an area of 1 cm^2?
2. A 6-kg piece of metal displaces 1 liter of water when submerged. What is its density?
3. The depth of water behind the Hoover Dam in Nevada is 220 m. What is the water pressure at the base of this dam? (Ignore the pressure due to the atmosphere.)
4. A rectangular barge, 5 m long and 2 m wide, floats in fresh water. (a) Find how much deeper it floats when its load is a 400-kg horse. (b) If the barge can only be pushed 15 cm deeper into the water before the water overflows to sink it, how many 400-kg horses can it carry?
5. A merchant in Katmandu sells you a solid gold 1-kg statue for a very reasonable price. When you get home, you wonder whether or not you got a bargain, so you lower the statue into a container of water and measure the volume of displaced water. What volume will verify that it's pure gold?
6. When a 2.0-kg object is suspended in water, it "masses" 1.5 kg. What is the density of the object?
7. An ice cube measures 10 cm on a side, and it floats in water. One cm extends above water level. If you shaved off the 1-cm part, how many cm of the remaining ice would extend above water level?
8. A vacationer floats lazily in the ocean with 90 percent of his body below the surface. The density of the ocean water is 1,025 kg/m^3. What is the vacationer's average density?
9. Air in a cylinder is compressed to one-tenth its original volume with no change in temperature. What happens to its pressure?
10. In the previous problem, if a valve is opened to let out enough air to bring the pressure back down to its original value, what percentage of the molecules will escape?
11. Estimate the buoyant force that air exerts on you. (To do this, you can estimate your volume by knowing your weight and by assuming that your weight density is a bit less than that of water.)
12. Nitrogen and oxygen in their liquid states have densities only 0.8 and 0.9 that of water. Atmospheric pressure is due primarily to the weight of nitrogen and oxygen gas in the air. If the atmosphere were liquefied, would its depth be greater or less than 10.3 m?
13. A mountain-climber friend with a mass of 80 kg ponders the idea of attaching a helium-filled balloon to himself to reduce his weight effectively by 25% when he climbs. He wonders what the approximate size of such a balloon would be. Hearing of your physics skills, he asks you. What answer can you come up with, showing your calculations?
14. On a perfect fall day, you are hovering at low altitude in a hot-air balloon, accelerated neither upward nor downward. The total weight of the balloon, including its load and the hot air in it, is 20,000 N. (a) What is the weight of the displaced air? (b) What is the volume of the displaced air?
15. How much lift is exerted on the wings of an airplane that have a total surface area of 100 m^2, when the difference in air pressure below and above the wings is 4% of atmospheric pressure?

Chapter 6 Online Resources

Videos

- Dam Keeps Water in Place
- Buoyancy
- Archimedes' Principle
- Flotation
- Air Has Weight
- Air Is Matter: Pouring Air from One Glass to Another
- Buoyancy of Air
- Air Has Pressure

Quiz
Exercises
Flashcards
Links

CHAPTER 7

Thermal Energy and Thermodynamics

Matter in all forms is made up of constantly jiggling atoms or molecules. When jiggling slowly, the particles form solids. When jiggling faster, they slide over one another and we have a liquid. When atoms and molecules move so fast that they disconnect and fly loose, we have a gas. So whether a substance is a solid, a liquid, or a gas depends on the motion of its particles.

7.1 Thermal Energy

When you strike a penny with a hammer, it becomes warm. Why? Because the hammer's blow causes the coin's atoms to jiggle faster. When you put a flame to a liquid, the liquid becomes warmer. When you rapidly compress air in a tire pump, the air becomes warmer. In these cases, the molecules are made to move faster. They gain kinetic energy. In general, the warmer an object is, the more kinetic energy its atoms and molecules possess. But that's not all. We can also say that the warmer an object becomes, the more thermal energy it contains. The **thermal energy** in a substance is the total energy of all its atoms and molecules. Thermal energy consists of both the potential and kinetic energy of the particles in a substance as they wiggle and jiggle, twist and turn, vibrate, or race back and forth. (Physicists usually refer to thermal energy as *internal energy,* for it is internal to a substance.)

7.2 Temperature

The quantity that indicates how warm or cold an object is with respect to some standard is called **temperature**. We express the temperature of matter by a number that corresponds to the degree of hotness on some chosen scale. A common thermometer measures temperature by means of the expansion and contraction of a liquid, usually mercury or colored alcohol. (You can expect to see mercury thermometers phasing out in coming years because of the health dangers posed by mercury.)

Figure 7.1
Can we trust our sense of hot and cold? Will both fingers feel the same temperature when they are put in the warm water? Try this and see (feel) for yourself.

The most common thermometer in the world is the *Celsius thermometer,* named in honor of the Swedish astronomer Anders Celsius (1701–1744), who first suggested the scale of 100 degrees between the freezing point and boiling point of water. The number 0 is assigned to the temperature at which water freezes, and the number 100 to the temperature at which water boils (at standard atmospheric pressure). In between are 100 equal parts called *degrees*.

In the United States, the number 32 is assigned to the temperature at which water freezes, and the number 212 is assigned to the temperature at which water

Figure 7.2
A testament to Fahrenheit outside his home (now in Gdansk, Poland).

Which has more temperature, a red-hot tack or a cool lake? Which has more thermal energy?

Insights

boils. Such a scale makes up a Fahrenheit thermometer, named after its originator, the German physicist G. D. Fahrenheit (1686–1736). The Fahrenheit scale will become obsolete if and when the United States changes to the metric system.*

Arithmetic formulas used for converting from one temperature scale to the other are common in classroom exams. Because such arithmetic exercises are not really physical science, we won't be concerned with these conversions. (This may be important in a math class, but not here.) Besides, the conversion between Celsius and Fahrenheit temperatures is closely approximated in the side-by-side scales of Figure 7.3.†

Temperature is proportional to the average kinetic energy of molecules in a substance. (As you likely know, atoms make up molecules, and not the reverse. To be brief, from now on in this chapter, we'll simply say *molecules* to mean *atoms and molecules*.) It is important to note that temperature is not a measure of the *total* kinetic energy of molecules in a substance. For example, there is twice as much molecular kinetic energy in 2 liters of boiling water as in 1 liter of boiling water—but the temperatures of both volumes of water are the same because the *average* kinetic energy per molecule in each is the same.

Interestingly, a thermometer actually registers its own temperature. When a thermometer is in thermal contact with something whose temperature we wish to know, thermal energy flows between the two until their temperatures are equal. At this point, thermal equilibrium is established. So, when we look at the temperature of the thermometer, we learn about the temperature of the substance with which it reaches thermal equilibrium.

7.3 Absolute Zero

In principle, there is no upper limit to temperature. As thermal motion increases, a solid object first melts and then vaporizes. As the temperature is further increased, molecules dissociate into atoms, and atoms lose some or all of their electrons, thereby forming a cloud of electrically charged particles—a *plasma*. Plasmas exist in stars, where the temperature is many millions of degrees Celsius. Temperature has no upper limit.

In contrast, there is a definite limit at the opposite end of the temperature scale. Gases expand when heated, and they contract when cooled. Nineteenth-century experiments found that all gases, regardless of their initial pressures or volumes, change by $1/273$ of their volume at 0°C for each degree Celsius change in temperature, provided the pressure is held constant. So, if a gas at 0°C were cooled down by 273°C, it would contract $273/273$ volumes and be reduced to zero volume. Clearly, we cannot have a substance with zero volume.

The same is true of pressure. The pressure of a gas of fixed volume decreases by $1/273$ for each Celsius degree its temperature is lowered. If it is cooled to 273°C below zero, it would have no pressure at all. In practice, every gas

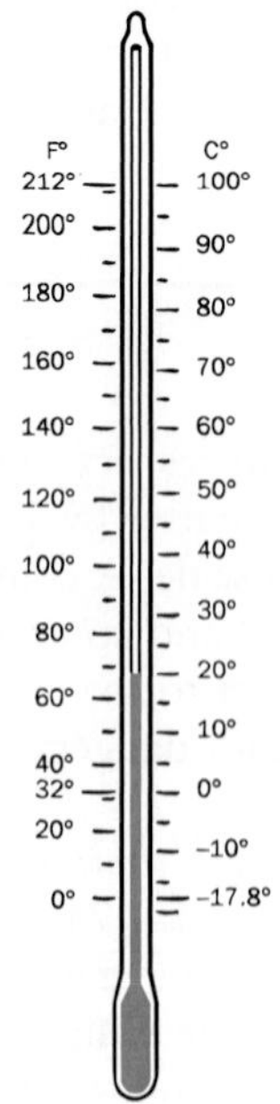

Figure 7.3
Fahrenheit and Celsius scales on a thermometer.

*Changing any long-established custom is difficult, and the Fahrenheit scale does have some advantages in everyday use. For example, its degrees are smaller (1°F = 5/9°C), which gives greater accuracy when reporting the weather in whole-number temperature readings. Then, too, people somehow attribute a special significance to numbers increasing by an extra digit, so that, when the air temperature on a hot day is reported as having reached 100°F, the idea of heat is conveyed more dramatically than it would be by announcing that it is 38°C. Like so much of the British system of measure, the Fahrenheit scale is geared to human beings.
†Okay, if you really want to know, the formulas for temperature conversion are: $C = 5/9\ (F - 32)$; $F = 9/5\ C + 32$, where C is the Celsius temperature and F is the corresponding Fahrenheit temperature.

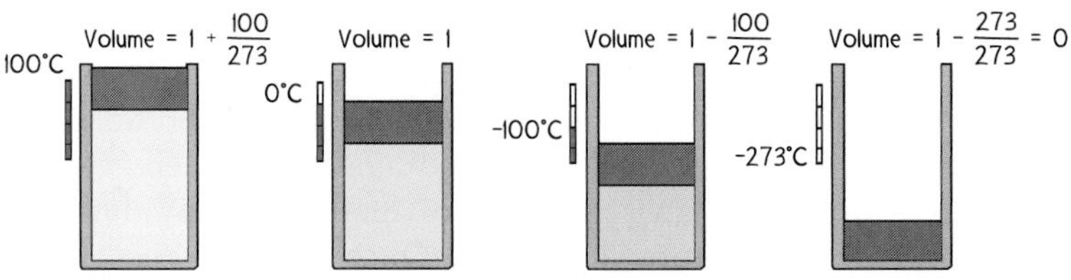

Figure 7.4
When pressure is held constant, the volume of a gas changes by 1/273 of its volume at 0°C with each 1°C change in temperature. At 100°C, the volume is 100/273 greater than it is at 0°C. When the temperature is reduced to −100°C, the volume is reduced by 100/273. At −273°C, the volume of the gas would be reduced by 273/273 and therefore would be zero.

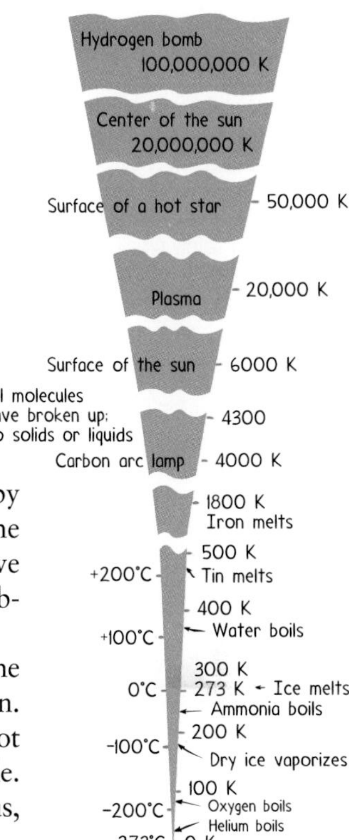

Figure 7.5
Some absolute temperatures.

converts to a liquid before becoming this cold. Nevertheless, these decreases by 1/273 increments suggested the idea of a lowest temperature: −273°C. That's the lower limit of temperature, **absolute zero.** At this temperature, molecules have lost all available kinetic energy.* No more energy can be removed from a substance at absolute zero. It can't get any colder.

The absolute temperature scale is called the Kelvin scale, named after the famous British mathematician and physicist William Thomson, First Baron Kelvin. Absolute zero is 0 K (short for "0 kelvin"; note that the word "degrees" is not used with Kelvin temperatures). There are no negative numbers on the Kelvin scale. Its temperature divisions are identical to the divisions on the Celsius scale. Thus, the melting point of ice is 273 K, and the boiling point of water is 373 K.

☑ CHECKPOINT

1. Which is larger, a Celsius degree or a kelvin?
2. A sample of hydrogen gas has a temperature of 0°C. If it is heated until it has twice the thermal energy, what is its temperature?

Check Your Answers

1. Neither. They are equal.
2. The 0°C gas has an absolute temperature of 273 K. Twice the thermal energy means that it has twice the absolute temperature, or two times 273 K. This would be 546 K, or 273°C.

Absolute zero isn't the coldest you can get. It's the coldest you can hope to approach.

Insights

7.4 Heat

If you touch a hot stove, thermal energy enters your hand because the stove is warmer than your hand. When you touch a piece of ice, however, thermal energy passes out of your hand and into the colder ice. The direction of energy flow is always from a warmer thing to a neighboring cooler thing. A scientist defines

*Even at absolute zero, molecules still possess a small amount of kinetic energy, called the *zero-point energy*. Helium, for example, has enough motion at absolute zero to prevent it from freezing. The explanation for this involves quantum theory.

Figure 7.6
The temperature of the sparks is very high, about 2000°C. That's a lot of thermal energy per molecule of spark. Because there are only a few molecules per spark, however, the total amount of thermal energy in the sparks is safely small. Temperature is one thing; transfer of thermal energy is another.

heat as the thermal energy transferred from one thing to another due to a temperature difference.

According to this definition, matter does not *contain* heat. Matter contains thermal energy, *not heat.* Heat is the flow of thermal energy due to a temperature difference. Once thermal energy has been transferred to an object or substance, it ceases to be heat. Heat is thermal energy in transit.

For substances in thermal contact, thermal energy flows from the higher-temperature substance into the lower-temperature one until thermal equilibrium is reached. This does not mean that thermal energy necessarily flows from a substance with more thermal energy into one with less thermal energy. For example, there is more thermal energy in a bowl of warm water than there is in a red-hot thumbtack. If the tack is placed into the water, thermal energy doesn't flow from the warm water to the tack. Instead, it flows from the hot tack to the cooler water. Thermal energy never flows unassisted from a low-temperature substance into a higher-temperature one.

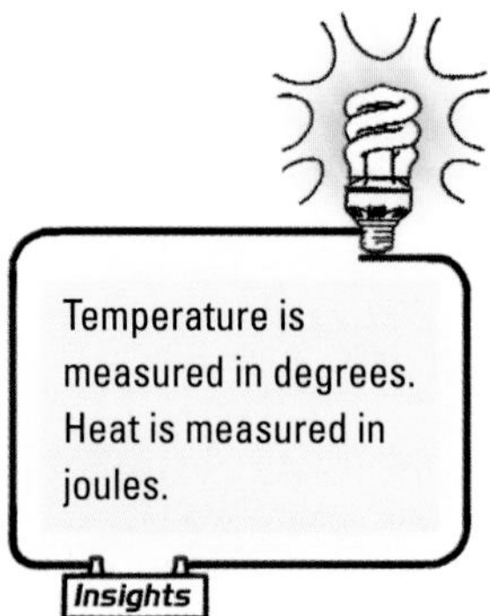

If heat is thermal energy that transfers in a direction from hot to cold, what is cold? Does a cold substance contain something opposite to thermal energy? Not so. An object is cold not because it *contains* something, but because it *lacks* something. It lacks thermal energy. When outdoors on a near-zero winter day, you feel cold not because something called cold gets to you. You feel cold because you lose heat. That's the purpose of your coat—to slow down the heat flow from your body. Cold is not a thing in itself, but the result of reduced thermal energy.

Figure 7.7
The left pot contains 1 liter of water. The right one contains 3 liters. Although both pots absorb the same quantity of heat, the temperature increases three times as much in the pot with the smaller amount of water.

☑ CHECKPOINT

1. Suppose you apply a flame to 1 liter of water for a certain time and its temperature rises by 2°C. If you apply the same flame for the same time to 2 liters of water, by how much will its temperature rise?
2. If a fast marble hits a random scatter of slow marbles, does the fast marble usually speed up or slow down? Which lose(s) kinetic energy and which gain(s) kinetic energy, the initially fast-moving marble or the initially slow ones? How do these questions relate to the direction of heat flow?

Check Your Answers

1. Its temperature will rise by only 1°C, because there are twice as many molecules in 2 liters of water, and each molecule receives only half as much energy on the average. So the average kinetic energy, and thus the temperature, increases by half as much.
2. A fast-moving marble slows when it hits slower-moving marbles. It gives up some of its kinetic energy to the slower ones. Likewise with heat. Molecules with more kinetic energy that make contact with molecules that have lower kinetic energy give up some of their excess kinetic energy to the slower ones. The direction of energy transfer is from hot to cold. For both the marbles and the molecules, however, the total energy before and after contact is the same.

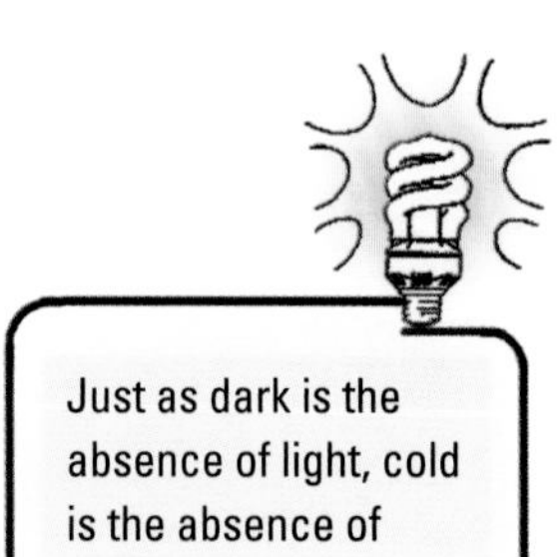

7.5 Quantity of Heat

Heat is a form of energy, and it is measured in joules. It takes about 4.2 joules of heat to change 1 gram of water by 1 Celsius degree. A unit of heat still common in the United States is the **calorie.*** A calorie is defined as the amount of heat needed to change the temperature of 1 gram of water by 1 Celsius degree. (The relationship between calories and joules is that 1 calorie = 4.18 joules.)

The energy ratings of foods and fuels are measured by the energy released when they are burned. (Metabolism is really "burning" at a slow rate). The heat unit for labeling food is the kilocalorie, which is 1000 calories (the heat needed to change the temperature of 1 kilogram of water by 1°C). To differentiate this unit and the smaller calorie, the food unit is usually called a *Calorie,* with a capital C. So 1 Calorie is really 1000 calories.

What we've learned thus far about heat and thermal energy is summed up in the laws of thermodynamics. The word *thermodynamics* stems from Greek words meaning "movement of heat."

Figure 7.8
To the weight watcher, the peanut contains 10 Calories; to the physicist, it releases 10,000 calories (41,800 joules) of energy when burned or digested.

☑ CHECKPOINT

Which will raise the temperature of water more, adding 4.18 joules or 1 calorie?

Check Your Answer

Both the same. This is like asking which is longer, a 1-mile long track or a 1.6-kilometer-long track. They're the same in different units.

7.6 The Laws of Thermodynamics

When thermal energy transfers as heat, it does so without net loss or gain. The energy lost in one place is gained in another. When the conservation of energy (which we discussed back in Chapter 3) is applied to thermal systems, we have the **first law of thermodynamics.**

> **Whenever heat flows into or out of a system, the gain or loss of thermal energy equals the amount of heat transferred.**

A *system* is any substance, device, or well-defined group of atoms or molecules. The system may be the steam in a steam engine, the entire earth's atmosphere, or even the body of a living creature. When heat is added to any of these systems, we increase its thermal energy. The added energy enables the system to do work. The first law makes good sense.

*Another common unit of heat is the British thermal unit (Btu). The Btu is defined as the amount of heat required to change the temperature of 1 lb of water by 1 degree Fahrenheit.

Figure 7.9
When you push down on the piston, you do work on the air inside. What happens to its temperature?

The first law is nicely illustrated when you put an airtight can of air on a hot stove and warm it. The energy put in increases the thermal energy of the enclosed air, so its temperature rises. If the can is fitted with a movable piston, then the heated air can do *mechanical work* as it expands and pushes the piston outward. This ability to do mechanical work is energy that comes from the energy you put in to begin with. The first law says you don't get energy from nothing.

The second law of thermodynamics restates what we've learned about the direction of heat flow.

Heat never spontaneously flows from a cold substance to a hot substance.

When heat flow is spontaneous—that is, without the assistance of external work—the direction of flow is always from hot to cold. In winter, heat flows from inside a warm home to the cold air outside. In summer, heat flows from the hot air outside into the cooler interior. Heat can be made to flow the other way only when work is done on the system or by adding energy from another source. This occurs with heat pumps and air conditioners. In these devices, thermal energy is pumped from a cooler to a warmer region. But without external effort, the direction of heat flow is from hot to cold. The second law, like the first, makes logical sense.*

The third law of thermodynamics restates what we've learned about the lowest limit of temperature.

No system can reach absolute zero.

As investigators attempt to reach this lowest temperature, it becomes more difficult to get closer to it. Physicists have been able to record temperatures that are less than a millionth of 1 kelvin—but never as low as 0 K.

The laws of thermodynamics can be stated this way: You can't win (because you can't get any more energy out of a system than you put into it), you can't break even (because you can't get as much useful energy out as you put in), and you can't get out of the game (entropy in the universe is always increasing).

Insights

7.7 Specific Heat Capacity

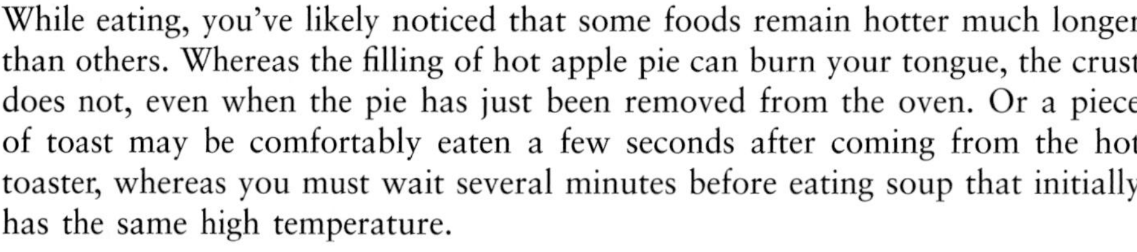

While eating, you've likely noticed that some foods remain hotter much longer than others. Whereas the filling of hot apple pie can burn your tongue, the crust does not, even when the pie has just been removed from the oven. Or a piece of toast may be comfortably eaten a few seconds after coming from the hot toaster, whereas you must wait several minutes before eating soup that initially has the same high temperature.

Figure 7.10
The filling of hot apple pie may be too hot to eat, even though the crust is not.

*The laws of thermodynamics were the rage back in the 1800s. At that time, horses and buggies were yielding to steam-driven locomotives. There is the story of the engineer who explained the operation of a steam engine to a peasant. The engineer cited in detail the operation of the steam cycle, how expanding steam drives a piston that in turn rotates the wheels. After some thought, the peasant asked, "Yes, I understand all that. But where's the horse?" This story illustrates how hard it is to abandon our way of thinking about the world when a newer method comes along to replace established ways. Are we any different today?

Entropy

Organized and concentrated energy disperses to disorganized and diffuse energy. Stated another way, useful energy diffuses to unusable energy. This fits with our everyday experience. The energy of a hot pan, for example, doesn't stay with the pan once it is removed from the stove. Instead, it disperses into the surroundings. Similarly, the energy of gasoline is organized and usable energy. When gasoline burns in a car engine, part of its energy does useful work, part heats the engine and its surroundings, and part goes out the exhaust. When useful energy transforms to unusable forms, it is unavailable for doing the same work again, such as driving another car. Organized forms of energy ultimately degrade into the environment as thermal energy—the graveyard of useful energy.

The second law of thermodynamics can be stated this way: **Natural systems tend to degrade from concentrated and organized-energy states toward diffuse and disorganized states.** Diffuse states are favored in nature—the direction of energy transformations is always toward the diffuse. Transformations that proceed toward concentrated energy states tend *not* to occur—they are not favored. Thermal energy in the room, for example, will not spontaneously move back into the pan and warm it. Likewise, the lower-energy molecules of the car's exhaust won't spontaneously recombine to form higher-energy gasoline molecules. The natural flow of energy is always a one-way trip from where it is organized, concentrated, and useful to where it is disorganized, spread out, and less useful.

The measure of energy dispersal is a quantity known as **entropy.*** More entropy means more degradation of energy. Since energy tends to degrade and to disperse with time, the total amount of entropy in any system tends to increase with time. The same is true for the largest system, the universe. The net entropy in the universe is continually increasing (continually running "downhill"). We say *net* because there are some regions where energy is actually being organized and concentrated. This occurs in living organisms, which survive by concentrating and organizing energy from food sources. The entropy decrease that makes possible the survival of a living organism is ultimately offset by an even greater increase in entropy in the environment upon which the living organism depends—such as through the production of food. But, without energy input, entropy increases.

Work input from outside a system can decrease entropy in the system, with energy proceeding toward organization and concentration. For example, diffuse thermal energy in the air *can* be concentrated in a heat pump. Or low-energy molecules *can* be combined to form higher-energy molecules by energetic chemical processes. But, without some outside energy input, processes in which entropy decreases are not observed in nature.

Interestingly, the direction of time's passage links to increasing entropy. This includes a leaf falling from a tree, leaves burning in a fire, and even the moving hands of a clock. As these occur, energy is dispersed, and we gain the sense that time moves forward. To put it another way, consider the likelihood of a burned leaf in a fire becoming whole, or a leaf on the ground spontaneously moving upward to join the branch from which it came. These cases involve the opposite of the dispersal of energy, which would be perceived as time moving backward. Hence, entropy is both a gauge for the dispersal of energy and time's arrow.†

*Entropy can be expressed mathematically. The increase in entropy ΔS of a thermodynamic system is equal to the amount of heat added to the system ΔQ divided by the temperature T at which the heat is added: $\Delta S = \Delta Q/T$.

†Remember those old movies where a train comes to a stop inches away from a heroine tied to the tracks? This was done by starting with the train at rest, inches away from the heroine, and then moving *backward*, gaining speed. When the film was reversed, the train was seen to move *toward* the heroine. (Next time, watch closely for the telltale smoke that *enters* the smokestack.)

Different substances have different capacities for storing thermal energy. If we heat a pot of water on a stove, we might find that it requires 15 minutes to raise it from room temperature to its boiling temperature. But if we put an equal mass of iron on the same stove, we'd find it would rise through the same temperature range in only about 2 minutes. For silver, the time would be less than a minute. We find that different materials require different quantities of heat to raise the temperature of a given mass of the material by a specified number of degrees. This is because different materials absorb energy in different ways. The energy may increase the jiggling motion of molecules, which raises the temperature; or it may increase the amount of internal vibration or rotation within the molecules and go into potential energy, which does not raise the temperature. Generally, there is a combination of both.

A gram of water requires 1 calorie of energy to raise the temperature 1 degree Celsius. It takes only about one-eighth as much energy to raise the temperature of a gram of iron by the same amount. Water absorbs more heat than iron for the same change in temperature. We say water has a higher **specific heat capacity** (sometimes simply called *specific heat*).*

> **The specific heat capacity of any substance is defined as the quantity of heat required to change the temperature of a unit mass of the substance by 1 degree Celsius.**

We can think of specific heat capacity as thermal inertia. Recall that inertia is a term used in mechanics to signify the resistance of an object to a change in its state of motion. Specific heat capacity is like thermal inertia since it signifies the resistance of a substance to a change in temperature.

☑ CHECKPOINT

Which has a higher specific heat capacity, water or sand? In other words, which takes longer to warm in sunlight (or longer to cool at night)?

Check Your Answer

Water has the higher specific heat capacity. In the same sunlight, the temperature of water increases more slowly than the temperature of sand. And water will cool more slowly at night. The low specific heat capacity of sand and soil, as evidenced by how quickly they warm in the morning sun and how quickly they cool at night, affects local climates.

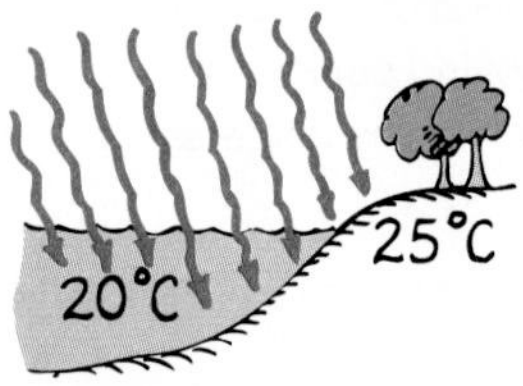

Water has a much higher capacity for storing energy than most all other substances. A lot of heat energy is needed to change the temperature of water. This explains why water is very useful in the cooling systems of automobiles and other engines. It absorbs a great quantity of heat for small increases in temperature. Water also takes longer to cool.

Water's high specific heat capacity changes the world's climate. Look at a world globe and notice the high latitude of Europe. Water's high specific heat keeps Europe's climate appreciably milder than regions of the same latitude in northeastern regions of Canada. Both Europe and Canada receive about the same amount of sunlight per square kilometer. What happens is the Atlantic

Figure 7.11
Because water has a high specific heat capacity and is transparent, it takes more energy to warm the water than to warm the land. Solar energy striking the land is concentrated at the surface, but that striking the water extends beneath the surface and so is "diluted."

*If the specific heat capacity c is known, the formula for the quantity of heat Q involved when a mass m of a substance undergoes a change in temperature ΔT is $Q = cm\Delta T$. In words, heat transferred = specific heat capacity × mass × temperature change.

Ocean current known as the Gulf Stream carries warm water northeast from the Caribbean Sea. It retains much of its thermal energy long enough to reach the North Atlantic Ocean off the coast of Europe. Then it cools, releasing 4.18 joules of energy for each gram of water that cools by 1°C. The released energy is carried by westerly winds over the European continent.

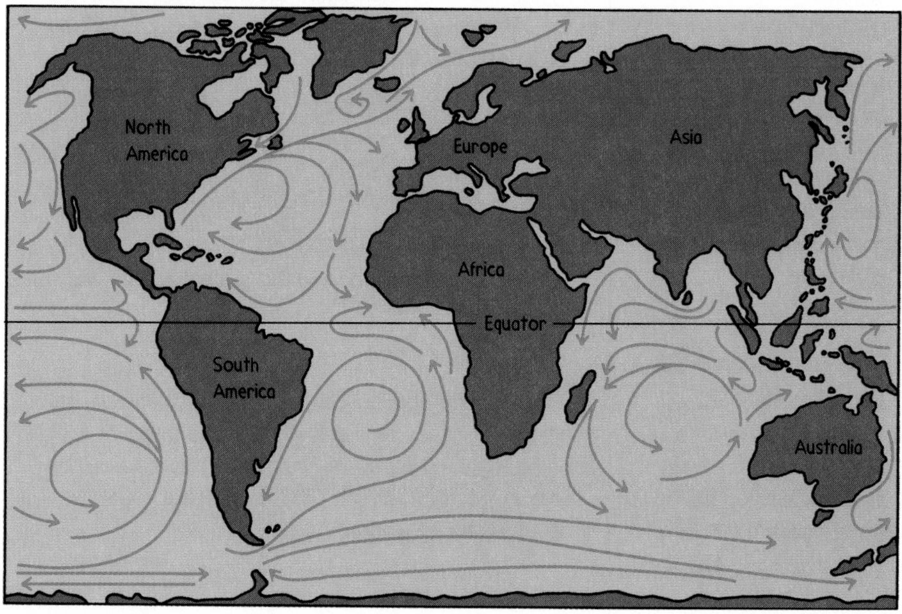

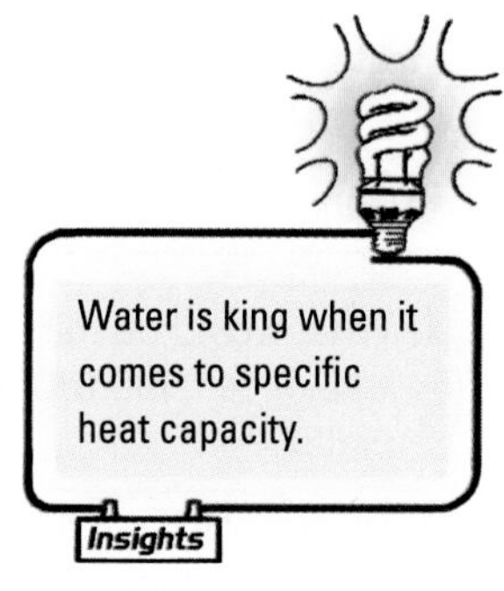

Figure 7.12
Many ocean currents, shown in blue, distribute heat from the warmer equatorial regions to the colder polar regions.

A similar effect occurs in the United States. The winds in North America are mostly westerly. On the West Coast, air moves from the Pacific Ocean to the land. In winter months, the ocean water is warmer than the air. Air blows over the warm water and then moves over the coastal regions. This warms the climate. In summer, the opposite occurs. The water cools the air and the coastal regions are cooled. The East Coast does not benefit from the moderating effects of water because the direction of air is from the land to the Atlantic Ocean. Land, with a lower specific heat capacity, gets hot in the summer but cools rapidly in the winter.

Islands and peninsulas do not have the extremes of temperatures that are common in interior regions of a continent. The high summer and low winter temperatures common in Manitoba and the Dakotas, for example, are largely due to the absence of large bodies of water. Europeans, islanders, and people living near ocean air currents should be glad that water has such a high specific heat capacity. San Franciscans certainly are!

☑ CHECKPOINT

Bermuda is close to North Carolina, but, unlike North Carolina, it has a tropical climate year round. Why?

Check Your Answer

Bermuda is an island. The surrounding water warms it when it might otherwise be too cold, and cools it when it might otherwise be too warm.

Figuring Physical Science

Let's apply the concepts discussed to the transfer of thermal energy when containers of water at different temperatures are mixed together. Each has a quantity of heat, Q, which is equal to the specific heat capacity of the substance c multiplied by its mass m and the temperature change ΔT; that is, $Q = cm\Delta T$.

Problems

1. What would be the final temperature of a mixture of 50 g of 20°C water and 50 g of 40°C water?
2. What would be the final temperature when 100 g of 25°C water is mixed with 75 g of 40°C water?
3. Radioactive decay of granite and other rocks in the earth's interior provides enough energy to keep the interior hot, produce magma, and provide warmth to natural hot springs. This is due to the average release of about 0.03 J per kilogram each year. How many years are required for a chunk of thermally insulated granite to increase 500°C in temperature (assume the specific heat of granite is 800 J/kg·°C)?

Solutions

1. The heat gained by the cooler water = heat lost by the warmer water. Since the masses of water are the same, the final temperature is midway, 30°C. So we'll end up with 100 g of 30°C water.

2. Here we have different masses of water that are mixed together. We equate the heat gained by the cool water to the heat lost by the warm water. We can express this equation formally, and then let the expressed terms lead to a solution:

Heat gained by cool water = heat lost by warm water

$$cm_1\,\Delta T_1 = cm_2\,\Delta T_2$$

ΔT_1 doesn't equal ΔT_2 as in Problem 1 because of different masses of water. We can see that ΔT_1 will be the final temperature T minus 25°, since T will be greater than 25°. ΔT_2 is 40° minus T, because T will be less than 40°. Then,

$$c(100)(T - 25) = c(75)(40 - T)$$

$$100T - 2500 = 3000 - 75T$$

$$T = 31.4°\text{C}.$$

3. Here we switch to rock, but the same concept applies. And we switch to specific heat expressed in joules per kilogram ·°C. No particular mass is specified, so we'll work with quantity of heat/mass (for our answer should be the same for a small chunk of rock or a huge chunk).

From $Q = cm\Delta T$, $Q/m = c\Delta T$ = (800 J/kg·°C) × (500°C) = 400,000 J/kg. The time required is (400,000 J/kg)/(0.03 J/kg·yr) = 13.3 million years. Small wonder it remains hot down there!

7.8 Thermal Expansion

Molecules in a hot substance jiggle faster and move farther apart. The result is **thermal expansion.** Most substances expand when heated and contract when cooled. Sometimes the changes aren't noticed, and sometimes they are. Telephone wires are longer and sag more on a hot summer day than in winter. Railroad tracks that were laid on cold winter days expand and buckle in the hot summer

Figure 7.13
Thermal expansion. Extreme heat on a July day caused the buckling of these railroad tracks.

(Figure 7.13). Metal lids on glass fruit jars can often be loosened by heating them under hot water. If one part of a piece of glass is heated or cooled more rapidly than adjacent parts, the resulting expansion or contraction may break the glass. This is especially true of thick glass. Pyrex glass is an exception because it is specially formulated to expand very little with increasing temperature.

Figure 7.14
One end of the bridge rides on rockers to allow for thermal expansion. The other end (not shown) is anchored.

Thermal expansion must be taken into account in structures and devices of all kinds. A dentist uses filling material that has the same rate of expansion as teeth. A civil engineer uses reinforcing steel with the same expansion rate as concrete. A long steel bridge usually has one end anchored while the other rests on rockers (Figure 7.14). Notice also that many bridges have tongue-and-groove gaps called *expansion joints* (Figure 7.15). Similarly, concrete roadways and sidewalks are intersected by gaps, which are sometimes filled with tar, so that the concrete can expand freely in summer and contract in winter.

Figure 7.15
This gap in the roadway of a bridge is called an expansion joint; it allows the bridge to expand and contract. (Was this photo taken on a warm or a cold day?)

An illustration of the fact that different substances expand at different rates can be provided by a bimetallic strip (Figure 7.16). This device is made of two strips of different metals welded together, one of brass and the other of iron. When heated, the greater expansion of the brass bends the strip. This bending may be used to turn a pointer, to regulate a valve, or to close a switch.

A practical application of a bimetallic strip wrapped into a coil is the thermostat (Figure 7.17). When a room becomes too cold, the coil bends toward the brass side and activates an electrical switch that turns on the heater. When

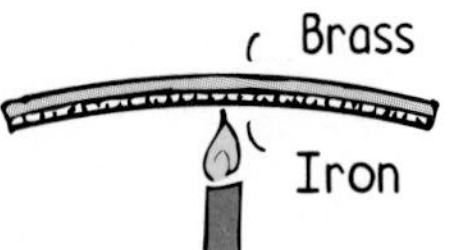

Figure 7.16
A bimetallic strip. Brass expands more when heated than iron does, and it contracts more when cooled. Because of this behavior, the strip bends as shown.

the room gets too warm, the coil bends toward the iron side, which breaks the electrical circuit and turns off the heater. Bimetallic strips are used in oven thermometers, refrigerators, electric toasters, and various other devices.

With increases in temperature, liquids expand more than solids. We notice this when gasoline overflows from a car's tank on a hot day. If the tank and its contents expanded at the same rate, no overflow would occur. This is why a gas tank being filled shouldn't be "topped off," especially on a hot day.

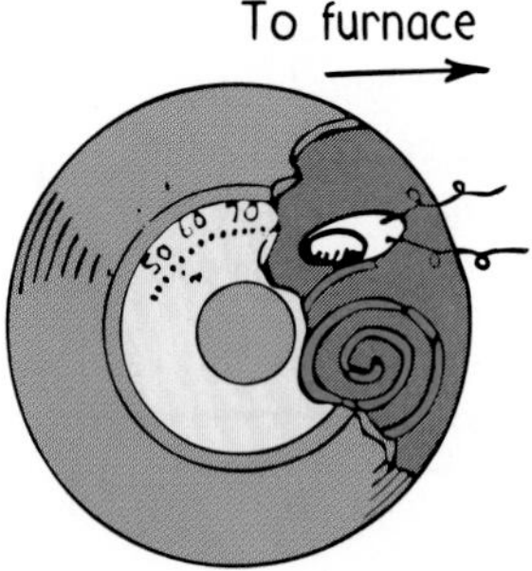

Figure 7.17
A thermostat. When the bimetallic coil expands, the drop of liquid mercury rolls away from the electrical contacts and breaks the electrical circuit. When the coil contracts, the mercury rolls against the contacts and completes the circuit.

☑ CHECKPOINT

A Concorde supersonic airplane is 20 cm longer when in flight than it was before takeoff. Offer an explanation.

Check Your Answer

At cruising speed (faster than the speed of sound), air friction against the Concorde raises its temperature dramatically, resulting in this significant thermal expansion.

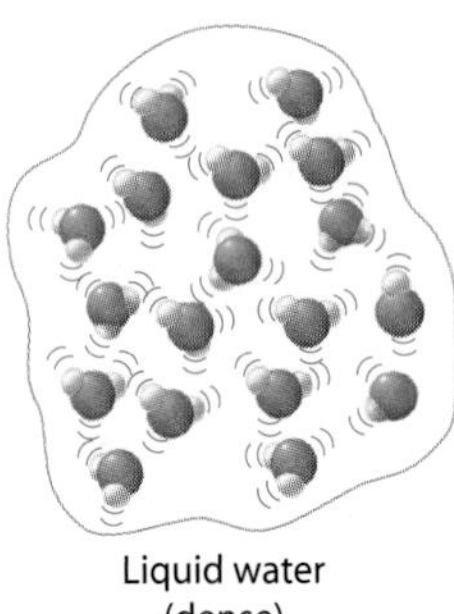

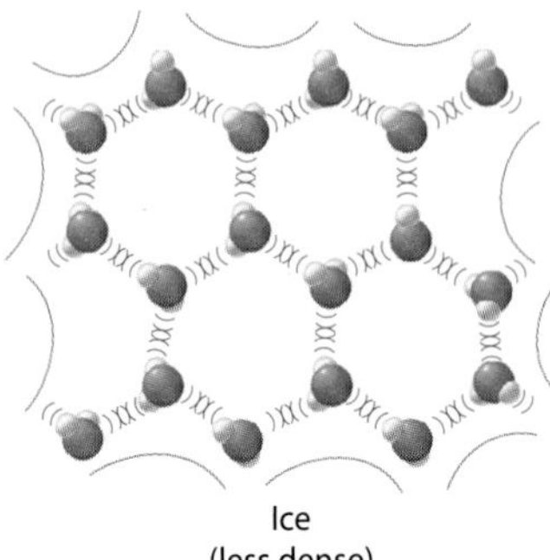

Figure 7.18
Water molecules in a liquid are denser than water molecules frozen in ice, where they have an open crystalline structure.

Figure 7.19
The six-sided structure of a snowflake is a result of the six-sided ice crystals that make it up.

Expansion of Water

Water, like most other substances, expands when it is heated. But it *doesn't* expand in the temperature range between 0°C and 4°C. Something quite fascinating happens in this range. Ice has a crystalline structure, with open-structured crystals. Water molecules in this open structure occupy a greater volume than they do in the liquid phase (Figure 7.18). This means that ice is less dense than water.

When ice melts, not all the six-sided crystals collapse. Some of them remain in the ice–water mixture, making up a microscopic slush that slightly "bloats" the water—increases its volume slightly (Figure 7.20). This results in ice water being less dense than slightly warmer water. As the temperature of water at 0°C is increased, more of the remaining ice crystals collapse. This further decreases the volume of the water. This contraction continues only up to 4°C. That's because two things occur at the same time—contraction and expansion. Volume tends to decrease as ice crystals collapse, while volume tends to increase due to greater molecular motion. The collapsing effect dominates until the temperature reaches 4°C. After that, expansion overrides contraction because most of the ice crystals have melted. (Figure 7.21).

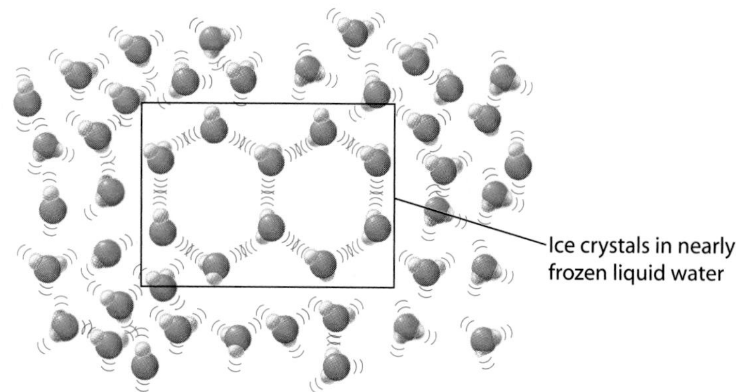

Figure 7.20
Close to 0°C, liquid water contains crystals of ice. The open structure of these crystals increases the volume of the water slightly.

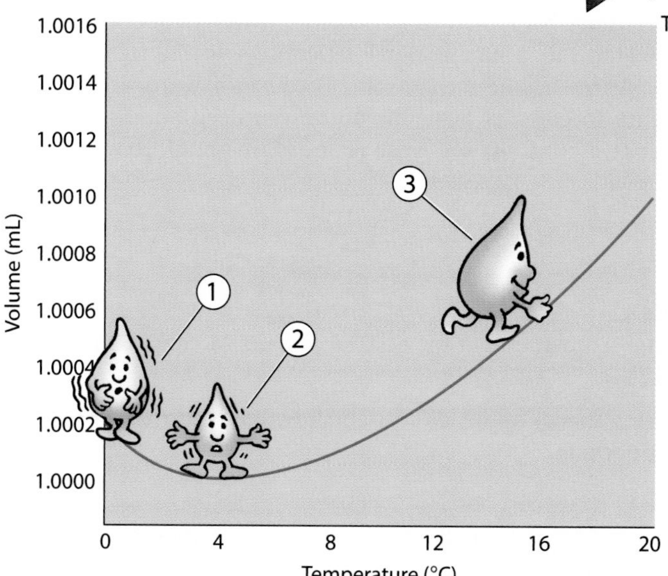

(1) Liquid water below 4°C is bloated with ice crystals.

(2) Upon warming, the crystals collapse, resulting in a smaller volume for the liquid water.

(3) Above 4°C, liquid water expands as it is heated because of greater molecular motion.

Figure 7.21
Between 0°C and 4°C, the volume of liquid water decreases as temperature increases. Above 4°C, water behaves the way other substances do. Its volume increases as its temperature increases. The volumes shown here are for a 1-gram sample.

When ice water freezes to become solid ice, its volume increases tremendously—and its density is therefore much lower. That's why ice floats on water. Like most other substances, solid ice contracts with further cooling. This behavior of water is very important in nature. If water was most dense at 0°C, it would settle to the bottom of a pond or lake. Because water at 0°C is less dense, it floats at the surface. That's why ice forms at the surface.

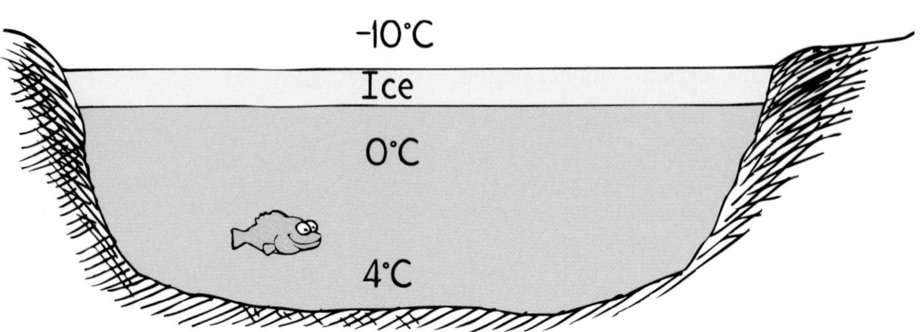

Figure 7.22
As water cools, it sinks until the entire pond is at 4°C. Then, as water at the surface is cooled further, it floats on top and can freeze. Once ice is formed, temperatures lower than 4°C can extend down into the pond.

So a pond freezes from the surface downward. In a cold winter, the ice will be thicker than in a milder winter. Water at the bottom of an ice-covered pond is 4°C, relatively warm for organisms that live there. Interestingly, very deep bodies of water are not ice-covered, even in the coldest of winters. This is because all of the water must be cooled to 4°C before lower temperatures can be reached. For deep water, the winter is not long enough to reduce an entire pond to 4°C. Any 4°C water lies at the bottom. Because of water's high specific heat and poor ability to conduct heat, the bottom of deep bodies of water in cold regions remains at a constant 4°C year round. Fish should be glad that this is so.

☑ CHECKPOINT

1. What was the precise temperature at the bottom of Lake Michigan on New Year's Eve in 1901?
2. What's inside the open spaces of the ice crystals shown in Figure 7.18? Is it air, water vapor, or nothing?

Check Your Answers

1. The temperature at the bottom of any body of water that has 4°C water in it is 4°C at the bottom, for the same reason that rocks are at the bottom. Both 4°C water and rocks are more dense than water at any other temperature. Water is a poor heat conductor, so, if the body of water is deep and in a region of long winters and short summers, the water at the bottom is likely to remain a constant 4°C year round.
2. There's nothing at all in the open spaces. It's empty space—a void. If there were air or vapor in the open spaces, the illustration should show molecules there—oxygen and nitrogen for air and H_2O for water vapor.

Link to Entomology

Life at the Extremes

Some deserts, such as those on the plains of Spain, the Sahara in Africa, and the Gobi Desert in central Asia, reach surface temperatures of 60°C (140°F). Too hot for life? Not for certain species of ants of the genus *Cataglyphis,* which thrive at this searing temperature. At this extremely high temperature, the desert ants can forage for food without the presence of lizards, which would otherwise prey upon them. Resilient to heat, these ants can withstand higher temperatures than any other creatures in the desert. How they are able to do this is currently being researched. They scavenge the desert surface for the corpses of those creatures that did not find cover in time, touching the hot sand as little as possible while often sprinting on four legs with two held high in the air. Although their foraging paths zigzag over the desert floor, their return paths are almost straight lines to their nest holes. They attain speeds of 100 body lengths per second. During an average six-day life, most of these ants retrieve 15 to 20 times their weight in food.

From deserts to glaciers, a variety of creatures have invented ways to survive the harshest corners of the world. A species of worm thrives in the glacial ice in the Arctic. There are insects in the Antarctic ice that pump their bodies full of antifreeze to ward off becoming frozen solid. Some fish that live beneath the ice are able to do the same. Then there are bacteria that thrive in boiling hot springs as a result of having heat-resistant proteins.

An understanding of how creatures survive at the extremes of temperature can provide clues for practical solutions to the physical challenges faced by humans. Astronauts who venture from earth, for example, will need all the techniques available for coping with unfamiliar environments.

Summary of Terms

Thermal energy (or *internal energy*) The total energy (kinetic plus potential) of the submicroscopic particles that make up a substance.

Temperature A measure of the hotness or coldness of substances, related to the average kinetic energy per molecule in a substance, measured in degrees Celsius, or in degrees Fahrenheit, or in kelvins.

Absolute zero The theoretical temperature at which a substance possesses no thermal energy.

Heat The thermal energy that flows from a substance of higher temperature to a substance of lower temperature, commonly measured in calories or joules.

Thermodynamics The study of heat and its transformation to different forms of energy.

First law of thermodynamics A restatement of the law of energy conservation, usually as it applies to systems involving changes in temperature: Whenever heat flows into or out of a system, the gain or loss of thermal energy equals the amount of heat transferred.

Second law of thermodynamics Heat never spontaneously flows from a cold substance to a hot substance. Also, all systems tend to become more and more disordered as time goes by.

Third law of thermodynamics No system can reach absolute zero.

Entropy The measure of energy dispersal of a system. Whenever energy freely transforms from one form to another, the direction of transformation is toward a state of greater disorder and, therefore, toward one of greater entropy.

Specific heat capacity The quantity of heat per unit mass required to raise the temperature of a substance by 1 degree Celsius.

Review Questions

7.1 Thermal Energy

1. Why does a penny become warmer when it is struck by a hammer?
2. What is thermal energy?

7.2 Temperature

3. What are the temperatures for freezing water on the Celsius and Fahrenheit scales? For boiling water?

4. Is the temperature of an object a measure of the total kinetic energy of molecules in the object or a measure of the average kinetic energy per molecule in the object?
5. What is meant by the statement "a thermometer measures its own temperature"?

7.3 Absolute Zero

6. By how much does the pressure of a gas in a rigid vessel decrease when the temperature is decreased by 1°C?
7. What pressure would you expect in a rigid container of 0°C gas if you cooled it by 273 Celsius degrees?
8. What are the temperatures for freezing water and boiling water on the Kelvin temperature scale?
9. How much energy can be taken from a system at 0 K?

7.4 Heat

10. When you touch a cold surface, does cold travel from the surface to your hand or does energy travel from your hand to the cold surface? Explain.
11. Distinguish between temperature and heat.
12. Distinguish between heat and thermal energy.
13. What determines the direction of heat flow?
14. Is cold the opposite of thermal energy or the lack of it?

7.5 Quantity of Heat

15. How is the energy value of foods determined?
16. Distinguish between a calorie and a Calorie.
17. Distinguish between a calorie and a joule.

7.6 The Laws of Thermodynamics

18. Cite the first law of thermodynamics.
19. How does the law of the conservation of energy relate to the first law of thermodynamics?
20. What happens to the thermal energy of a system when mechanical work is done on the system? What happens to the temperature of the system?
21. Cite the second law of thermodynamics.
22. How does the second law of thermodynamics relate to the direction of heat flow?
23. Cite the third law of thermodynamics.
24. What does it mean to say that, when energy is transformed, it becomes less useful?
25. What is the physicist's term for measure of energy dispersal?

7.7 Specific Heat Capacity

26. Which warms up faster when heat is applied—iron or silver?
27. Does a substance that heats up quickly have a high or a low specific heat capacity?
28. How does the specific heat capacity of water compare with the specific heat capacities of other common materials?
29. Northeastern Canada and much of Europe receive about the same amount of sunlight per unit area. Why then is Europe generally warmer in the winter?

7.8 Thermal Expansion

30. Why does a bimetallic strip bend with changes in temperature?
31. Which generally expands more for an equal increase in temperature—solids or liquids?
32. When the temperature of ice-cold water is increased slightly, does it undergo a net expansion or a net contraction?
33. What is the reason for ice being less dense than water?
34. Does "microscopic slush" in water tend to make it more dense or less dense? What happens to it when temperature increases?
35. At what temperature do the combined effects of contraction and expansion produce the smallest volume for water?
36. Why does ice form at the surface of a pond instead of at the bottom?

Activity

How much energy is in a nut? Burn it and find out. The heat of the flame is energy released upon the formation of chemical bonds (carbon dioxide, CO_2, and water, H_2O). Pierce a nut (pecan or walnut halves work best) with a bent paper clip that holds the nut above the table surface. Above this, secure a can of water so that you can measure its temperature change when the nut burns. Use about 10 cubic centimeters (10 milliliters) of water and a Celsius thermometer. As soon as you ignite the nut with a match, place the can of water above it and record the increase in water temperature as soon as the flame burns out. The number of calories released by the burning nut can be calculated by the formula $Q = cm\Delta T$, where m is the mass of water, c is its specific heat (1 cal/kg°C), and ΔT is the change in temperature. The energy in food is expressed in terms of the dietetic Calorie, which is 1000 of the calories you'll measure. So to find the number of dietetic Calories, divide your result by 1000.

Exercises

1. Why wouldn't you expect all the molecules in a gas to have the same speed?
2. In your room, there are things such as tables, chairs, other people, and so forth. Which of these things has a temperature (1) lower than, (2) greater than, and (3) equal to the temperature of the air?
3. Why can't you establish whether you are running a high temperature by touching your own forehead?
4. Which is greater, an increase in temperature of 1°C or one of 1°F?
5. Which has the greater amount of internal energy, an iceberg or a cup of hot coffee? Explain.
6. On which temperature scale does the average kinetic energy of molecules double when the temperature doubles?
7. The temperature of the sun's interior is about 10^7 degrees. Does it matter whether this is degrees Celsius or kelvins? Defend your answer.
8. Use the laws of thermodynamics to defend the statement that 100 percent of the electrical energy that goes into lighting a lamp is converted to thermal energy.
9. When air is rapidly compressed, why does its temperature increase?
10. Which of the laws of thermodynamics has exceptions?
11. If you vigorously shake a can of liquid back and forth for more than a minute, will there be a noticeable temperature increase? (Try it and see.)
12. What happens to the gas pressure within a sealed gallon can when it is heated? Cooled? Why?
13. After driving a car for some distance, why does the air pressure in the tires increase?
14. If you drop a hot rock into a pail of water, the temperature of the rock and the water will change until both are equal. The rock will cool and the water will warm. Does this hold true if the hot rock is dropped into the Atlantic Ocean? Explain.
15. In the old days, on a cold winter night, it was common to bring a hot object to bed with you. Which would be better to keep you warm through the cold night—a 10-kilogram iron brick or a 10-kilogram jug of hot water at the same temperature? Explain.
16. Desert sand is very hot in the day and very cool at night. What does this tell you about its specific heat?
17. Why does adding the same amount of heat to two different objects not necessarily produce the same increase in temperature?
18. Why will a watermelon stay cool for a longer time than sandwiches when both are removed from a cooler on a hot day?
19. Bermuda is about as far north of the Equator as North Carolina, but, unlike North Carolina, it has a tropical climate all year long. Why is this so?
20. Iceland, so named to discourage conquest by expanding empires, is not at all ice-covered like Greenland and parts of Siberia, even though it is nearly on the Arctic Circle. The average winter temperature of Iceland is considerably higher than regions at the same latitude in eastern Greenland and central Siberia. Why is this so?
21. Why does the presence of large bodies of water tend to moderate the climate of nearby land—make it warmer in cold weather, and cooler in hot weather?
22. If the winds at the latitude of San Francisco and Washington, D.C. were from the east rather than from the west, why might San Francisco be able to grow only cherry trees and Washington, D.C. only palm trees?
23. Cite an exception to the claim that all substances expand when heated.
24. Would a bimetallic strip function if the two different metals happened to have the same rates of expansion? Is it important that they expand at different rates? Explain.
25. Steel plates are commonly attached to each other with rivets, which are slipped into holes in the plates and rounded over with hammers. The hotness of the rivets makes them easier to round over, but their hotness has another important advantage in providing a tight fit. What is it?
26. A method for breaking boulders used to be putting them in a hot fire, then dousing them with cold water. Why would this fracture the boulders?
27. An old remedy for a pair of nested drinking glasses that stick together is to run water at different temperatures into the inner glass and over the surface of the outer glass. Which water should be hot, and which cold?
28. Would you or the gas company gain by having gas warmed before it passed through your gas meter?
29. A metal ball is just able to pass through a metal ring. When the ball is heated, however, it will not pass through the ring. What would happen if the ring, rather than the ball, was heated? Does the size of the hole increase, stay the same, or decrease?
30. After a machinist very quickly slips a hot, snugly fitting iron ring over a very cold brass cylinder, there is no way that the two can be separated intact. Can you explain why this is so?

31. Suppose you cut a small gap in a metal ring. If you heat the ring, will the gap become wider or narrower?

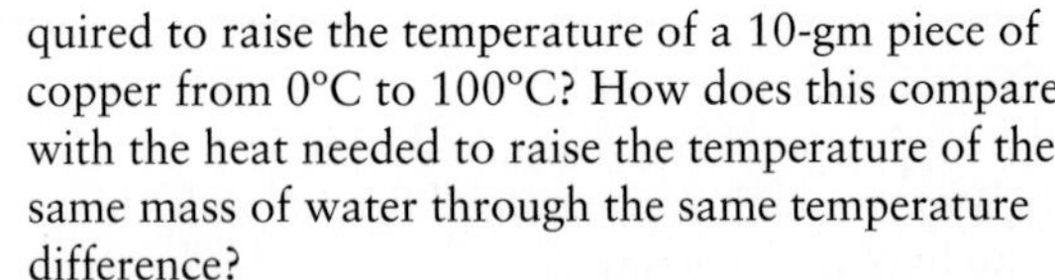

32. One of the reasons the first light bulbs were expensive was that the electrical lead wires into the bulb were made of platinum, which expands at about the same rate as glass when heated. Why is it important that the metal leads and the glass have the same coefficient of expansion?
33. Suppose that water is used in a thermometer instead of mercury. If the temperature is at 4°C and then changes, why can't the thermometer indicate whether the temperature is rising or falling?
34. How does the combined volume of the billions and billions of hexagonal open spaces in the structures of ice crystals in a piece of ice compare with the portion of ice that floats above the water line?
35. State whether water at the following temperatures will expand or contract when warmed a little: 0°C; 4°C; 6°C.
36. Why is it important to protect water pipes so they don't freeze?
37. If cooling occurred at the bottom of a pond instead of at the surface, would a lake freeze from the bottom up? Explain.
38. Make up a multiple-choice question that distinguishes between heat and temperature.

Problems

Quantity of heat, Q, is equal to the specific heat capacity of the substance, c, multiplied by its mass, m, and the temperature change, ΔT; that is, $Q = cm\Delta T$.

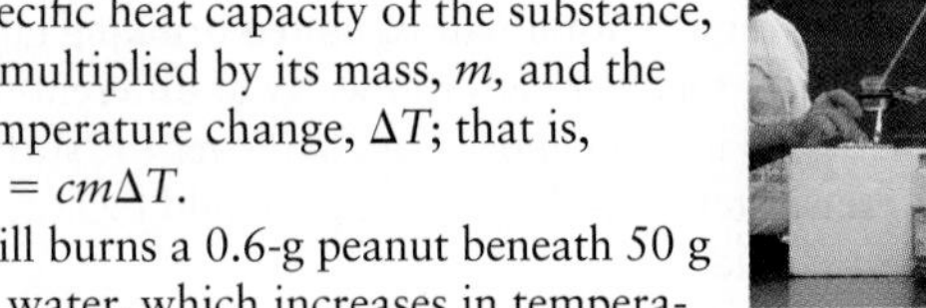

1. Will burns a 0.6-g peanut beneath 50 g of water, which increases in temperature from 22°C to 50°C. (a) Assuming 40% efficiency, what is the food value in calories of the peanut? (b) What is the food value in calories per gram?
2. Pounding a nail into wood makes the nail warmer. Consider a 5-gram steel nail 6 cm long and a hammer that exerts an average force of 500 N on the nail when it is being driven into a piece of wood. The nail becomes hotter. Calculate the increase in the nail's temperature. (Assume that the specific heat capacity of steel is 450 J/kg·°C.)
3. If you wish to warm 100 kg of water by 20°C for your bath, how much heat is required? (Give your answer in calories and joules.)
4. The specific heat capacity of copper is 0.092 calories per gram per degree Celsius. How much heat is required to raise the temperature of a 10-gm piece of copper from 0°C to 100°C? How does this compare with the heat needed to raise the temperature of the same mass of water through the same temperature difference?
5. What will be the final temperature of 100 g of 20°C water when 100 g of 40° iron nails are submerged in it? (The specific heat of iron is 0.12 cal/g·°C. Here you should equate the heat gained by the water to the heat lost by the nails.)

To solve the problems below, you will need to know about the average coefficient of linear expansion, α, which differs for different materials. We define α to be the change in length per unit length—or the fractional change in length—for a temperature change of one degree Celsius. That is, $\alpha = \Delta L/L$ per °C. For aluminum, $\alpha = 24 \times 10^{-6}$/°C, and for steel, $\alpha = 11 \times 10^{-6}$/°C. The change in length ΔL of a material is given by $\Delta L = L\alpha\Delta T$.

6. Suppose that a bar 1 m long expands 0.5 cm when heated. By how much will a bar 100 m long of the same material expand when similarly heated?
7. Suppose that the 1.3-km main span of steel for the Golden Gate Bridge had no expansion joints. How much longer would it be for an increase in temperature of 15°C?
8. Imagine a 40,000-km steel pipe that forms a ring to fit snugly all around the circumference of the earth. Suppose that the people along its length breathe on it so as to raise its temperature by 1°C. The pipe gets longer. It is also no longer snug. How high does it stand above ground level? (To simplify, consider only the expansion of its radial distance from the center of the earth, and apply the geometry formula that relates circumference C and radius r, $C = 2\pi r$. The result is surprising!)

Chapter 7 Online Resources

Videos
- Low Temperatures with Liquid Nitrogen
- How a Thermostat Works

Quiz
Exercises
Flashcards
Links

CHAPTER 8

Heat Transfer and Change of Phase

Heat transfers from warmer to cooler things. If several objects with different temperatures come into contact, those that are warm become cooler and those that are cool become warmer. They tend to reach a common temperature. This process occurs in three ways: by *conduction*, by *convection*, and by *radiation*.

8.1 Conduction

When you hold one end of an iron nail in a flame, it quickly becomes too hot to hold. Thermal energy at the hot end travels along the nail's entire length. This method of heat transfer is called **conduction.** Thermal conduction occurs by means of the movement of particles in a material, mainly electrons. Every atom has electrons, and metal atoms have loosely held electrons that are free to migrate in the metal. We shall see, in Chapter 9, that metals are good electrical conductors for the same reason. Thermal conduction occurs by atomic particles colliding inside the heated object.

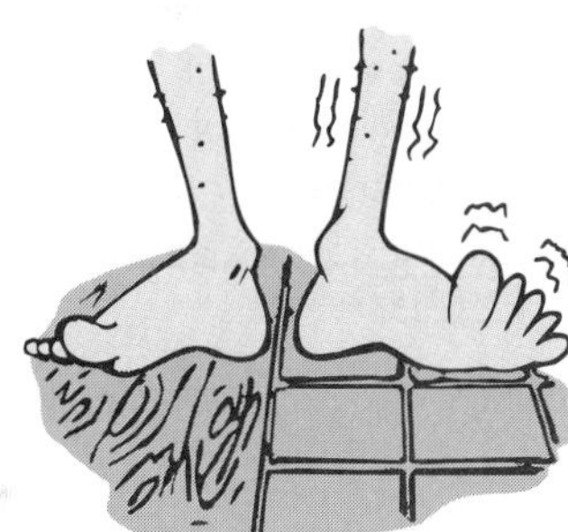

Figure 8.1
The tile floor feels colder than the wooden floor, even though both are at the same temperature. Tile is a better heat conductor than wood, and it more quickly conducts thermal energy from your feet.

Figure 8.2
When you stick a nail into ice, does cold flow from the ice to your hand, or does thermal energy flow from your hand to the ice?

Solids whose atoms or molecules have loosely held electrons are good conductors of heat. Metals have the loosest electrons, and they are excellent conductors of heat. Silver is the best, copper is next, and, among the common metals, aluminum and then iron. Poor conductors include wool, wood, paper, cork, and plastic foam. Molecules in these materials have electrons that are firmly attached to them. Poor conductors are called *insulators*.

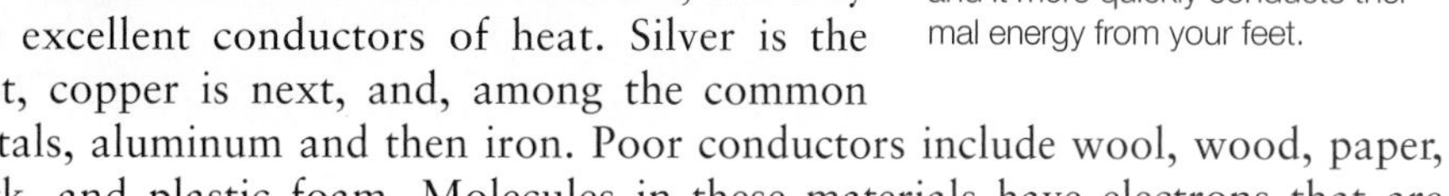

Wood is a good insulator, and it is often used for cookware handles. Even when a pot is hot, you can briefly grasp the wooden handle with your bare hand without harm. An iron handle of the same temperature would surely burn your hand. Wood is a good insulator even when it's red hot. This explains how firewalking coauthor John Suchocki can walk barefoot on red-hot wood coals without burning his feet (see the photo above). (CAUTION: Don't try this on your own; even experienced firewalkers sometimes receive bad burns when conditions aren't just right.) The main factor here is the poor conductivity of wood—even red-hot wood. Although its temperature is high, very little thermal

Figure 8.3
Conduction of heat from Lil's hand to the wine is minimized by the long stem of the wine glass.

energy is conducted to the feet. A firewalker must be careful that no iron nails or other good conductors are among the hot coals. Ouch!

Air is a very poor conductor. Hence, you can briefly put your hand in a hot pizza oven without harm. The hot air doesn't conduct thermal energy well. But don't touch the metal in the hot oven. Ouch again! The good insulating properties of such things as wool, fur, and feathers are largely due to the air spaces they contain. Porous substances are also good insulators because of their many small air spaces. Be glad that air is a poor conductor; if it weren't, you'd feel quite chilly on a 20°C (68°F) day!

What can be both good and poor at the same time? Answer: Any good insulator is a poor conductor. Or any good conductor is a poor insulator.

Insights

Snow is a poor conductor of thermal energy. Snowflakes are formed of crystals that trap air and provide insulation. That's why a blanket of snow keeps the ground warm in winter. Animals in the forest find shelter from the cold in snow banks and in holes in the snow. The snow doesn't provide them with thermal energy—it simply slows down the loss of body heat generated by the animals. Then there are the igloos, Arctic dwellings built from compacted snow to shield those inside from the cold.

Figure 8.4
Snow patterns on the roof of a house show areas of conduction and insulation. Bare parts show where thermal energy from inside has conducted through the roof and melted the snow.

In the United States, many houses are insulated with rock wool or fiberglass. Interestingly, insulation doesn't prevent the flow of thermal energy. Insulation simply slows down the rate at which thermal energy flows. Even a well-insulated warm house gradually cools. Insulation merely delays the transfer of thermal energy from a warmer region to a cooler one. In winter, we wish to slow conduction from inside to outside. But, on hot summer days, we wish to slow conduction in the other direction, from outside to inside. Insulation slows conduction in either direction.

☑ CHECKPOINT

In desert regions that are hot in the day and cold at night, the walls of houses are often made of mud. Why is it important that the mud walls be thick?

Check Your Answer

A wall of appropriate thickness retains the warmth of the house at night by slowing the flow of thermal energy from inside to outside, and it keeps the house cool in the daytime by slowing the flow of thermal energy from outside to inside. Such a wall has "thermal inertia."

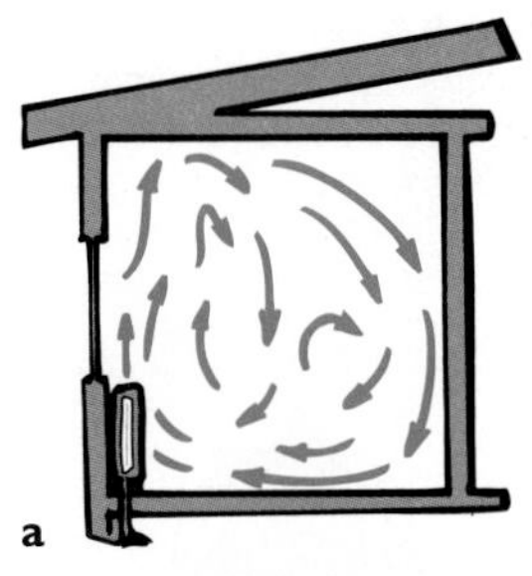

Figure 8.5
Convection currents in a gas (air) and a liquid.

8.2 Convection

Liquids and gases transfer thermal energy mainly by **convection,** which is heat transfer due to the actual motion of the fluid itself. Unlike conduction (in which heat is transferred by successive collisions of electrons and atoms), convection involves motion of a fluid—currents. Convection occurs in all fluids, whether liquids or gases. Whether we heat water in a pan or heat air in a room, the process is the same (Figure 8.5). As the fluid is heated from below, the molecules at the bottom move faster, spread apart more, become less dense, and are buoyed upward. Denser, cooler fluid moves in to take their place. In this way, convection currents keep the fluid stirred up as it heats—warmer fluid moving away from the heat source and cooler fluid moving toward the heat source.

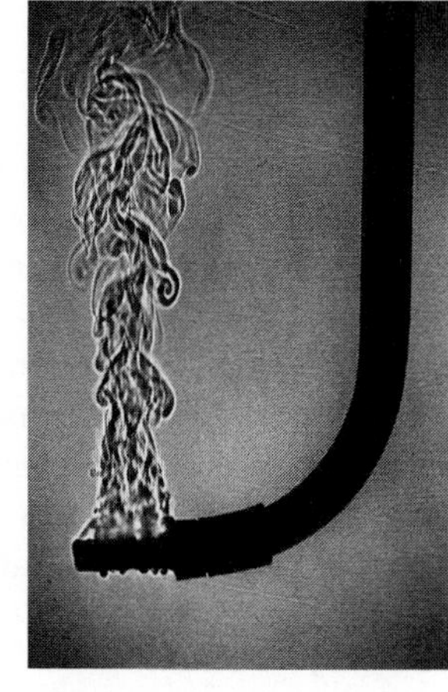

Figure 8.6
The tip of a heater element submerged in water produces convection currents, which are revealed as shadows (caused by deflections of light in water of different temperatures).

Figure 8.7
Blow warm air onto your hand from your wide-open mouth. Now reduce the opening between your lips so the air expands as you blow. Try it now. Do you notice a difference in air temperature?

We can see why warm air rises. When warmed, it expands, becomes less dense, and is buoyed upward in the cooler surrounding air like a balloon buoyed upward. When the rising air reaches an altitude at which the air density is the same, it no longer rises. We see this occurring when smoke from a fire rises and then settles off as it cools and its density matches that of the surrounding air. To see for yourself that expanding air cools, right now do the experiment shown in Figure 8.7. Expanding air really does cool.*

A dramatic example of cooling by expansion occurs with steam expanding through the nozzle of a pressure cooker (Figure 8.8). The combined cooling effects of

*Where does the energy go in this case? It goes into work done on the surrounding air as the expanding air pushes outward.

Figure 8.8
The hot steam expands from the pressure cooker and is cool to Millie's touch.

expansion and rapid mixing with cooler air will allow you to hold your hand comfortably in the jet of condensed vapor. (Caution: If you try this, be sure to place your hand high above the nozzle at first and then lower it slowly to a comfortable distance above the nozzle. If you put your hand directly at the nozzle where no steam is visible, watch out! Steam is invisible, and is clear of the nozzle before it expands and cools. The cloud of "steam" you see is actually condensed water vapor, which is much cooler than live steam.)

Cooling by expansion is the opposite of what occurs when air is compressed. If you've ever compressed air with a tire pump, you probably noticed that both air and pump became quite hot. Compression of air warms it.

As something expands, it spreads its energy over a greater area and, therefore, it cools.

Insights

Convection currents stir the atmosphere and produce winds. Some parts of the earth's surface absorb thermal energy from the sun more readily than others. This results in uneven heating of the air near the ground. We see this effect at the seashore, as Figure 8.9 shows. In the daytime, the ground warms up more than the water. Then warmed air close to the ground rises and is replaced by cooler air that moves in from above the water. The result is a sea breeze. At night, the process reverses because the shore cools off more quickly than the water, and then the warmer air is over the sea. If you build a fire on the beach, you'll see that the smoke sweeps inland during the day and then seaward at night.

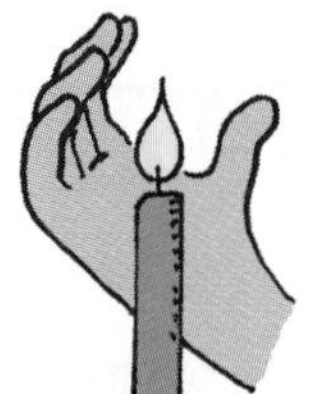

☑ CHECKPOINT

Explain why you can hold your fingers beside the candle flame without harm, but not above the flame.

Check Your Answer

Thermal energy travels upward by air convection. Since air is a poor conductor, very little energy travels sideways to your fingers.

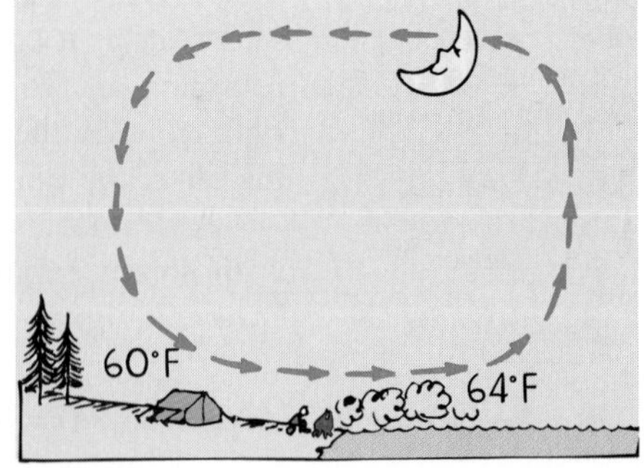

Figure 8.9
Convection currents produced by unequal heating of land and water. During the day, warm air above the land rises, and cooler air over the water moves in to replace it. At night, the direction of air flow is reversed, because now the water is warmer than the land.

Convection Power Tower

Imagine, in a hot desert, a huge greenhouse—a circular, glass-roofed enclosure some several kilometers in diameter, with a kilometer-high chimney in the middle. Such a huge greenhouse preheats the desert air, which flows to the center and rises in the chimney. In the chimney updraft are wind turbines, generating megawatts of clean power. Such power plants are similar to wind turbines, but they are more reliable because they produce their own wind. Watch for the advent of these twenty-first-century clean power sources.

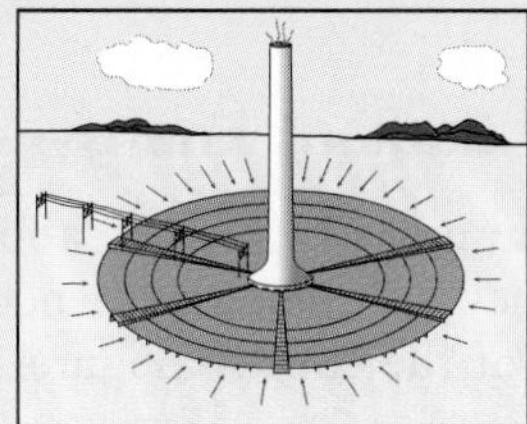

8.3 Radiation

Thermal energy from the sun travels through space and then through the earth's atmosphere and warms the earth's surface. This energy cannot pass through the empty space between the sun and earth by conduction or convection, for there is no medium for doing so. Energy must be transmitted some other way—by **radiation.*** The energy so radiated is called *radiant energy.*

Radiant energy exists in the form of *electromagnetic waves.* It includes a wide span of waves, ranging from longest to shortest: radio waves, microwaves, infrared waves (invisible waves below red in the visible spectrum), visible waves, then to waves that can't be seen by the eye, including ultraviolet waves, x-rays, and gamma rays. We'll treat waves further in Chapters 11 and 12, and electromagnetic waves in Chapter 10.

Figure 8.10
Types of radiant energy (electromagnetic waves).

The wavelength of radiation is related to the frequency of vibration. Frequency is the rate of vibration of a wave source. Nellie Newton in Figure 8.11 shakes a rope at a low frequency (left), and a higher frequency (right). Note that shaking at a low frequency produces a long lazy wave, and the higher-frequency shake produces shorter waves. This is true also with electromagnetic

Figure 8.11
A wave of long wavelength is produced when the rope is shaken gently (at a low frequency). When shaken more vigorously (at a high frequency), a wave of shorter wavelength is produced.

*The radiation we are talking about here is electromagnetic radiation, including visible light. Don't confuse this with radioactivity, a process of the atomic nucleus that we'll discuss in Chapter 16.

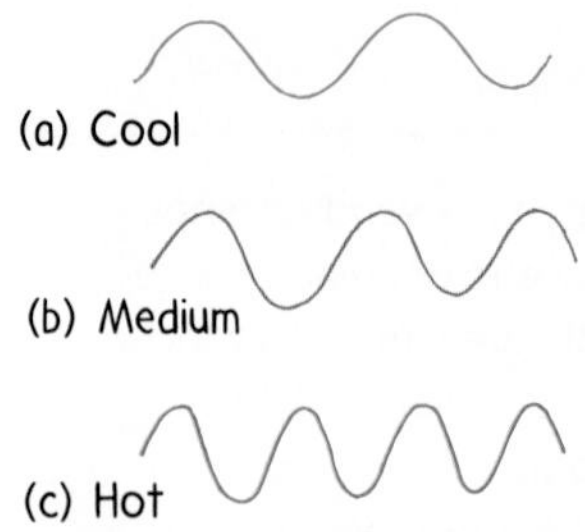

Figure 8.12
(a) A low-temperature (cool) source emits primarily low-frequency, long-wavelength waves. (b) A medium-temperature source emits primarily medium-frequency, medium-wavelength waves. (c) A high-temperature (hot) source emits primarily high-frequency, short-wavelength waves.

waves. We shall see, in Chapter 12, that vibrating electrons emit electromagnetic waves. Low-frequency vibrations produce long waves, and high-frequency vibrations produce shorter waves.

Emission of Radiant Energy

All substances at any temperature above absolute zero emit radiant energy. The average frequency f of the radiant energy is directly proportional to the absolute temperature T of the emitter (Figure 8.13):

$$f \sim T$$

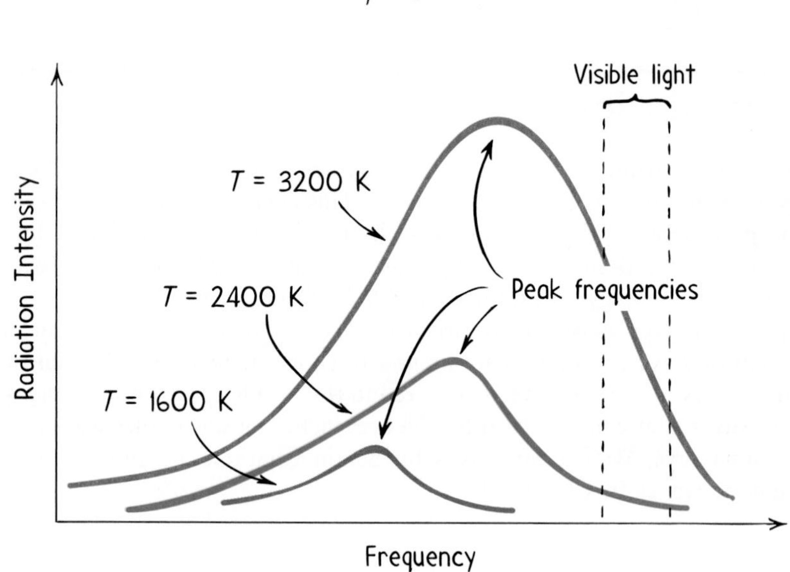

Figure 8.13
Radiation curves for different temperatures. The average frequency of radiant energy is directly proportional to the absolute temperature of the emitter.

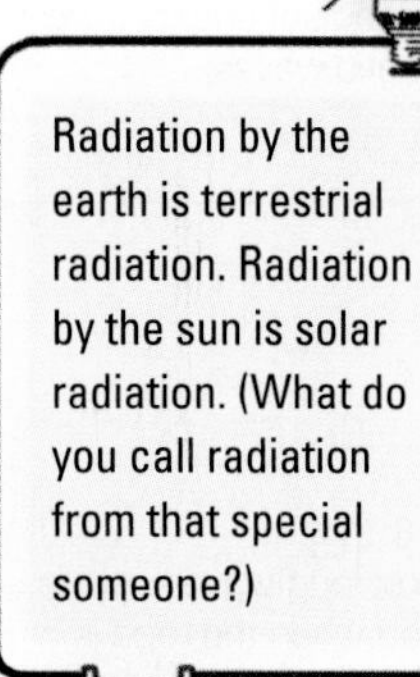

The surface of the sun has a high temperature (by earthly standards) and therefore emits radiant energy at a high frequency—much of it in the visible portion of the electromagnetic spectrum. The surface of the earth, by comparison, is relatively cool, and so the radiant energy it emits has a frequency lower than that of visible light. The radiation emitted by the earth is in the form of infrared waves—below our threshold of sight. Radiant energy emitted by the earth is called **terrestrial radiation.**

Most people know that the sun glows and emits radiant energy. And many educated people know that the source of the sun's radiant energy involves nuclear reactions in its deep interior. However, relatively few people know that the earth also "glows" and emits radiant energy of the same nature. If you visit the depths of any mine you'll find it's warm down there—year-round. Radioactivity in the earth's interior warms the earth. Much of this thermal energy conducts to the surface to become terrestrial radiation. So radiant energy is emitted by both the sun and the earth, and it differs only in the range of frequencies, and the amount. When we study meteorology in Chapter 31, we'll learn how the

Figure 8.14
Both the sun and the earth emit the same kind of radiant energy. The sun's glow is visible to the eye; the earth's glow consists of longer waves and isn't visible to the eye.

atmosphere is transparent to the high-frequency solar radiation but opaque to much of the lower-frequency terrestrial radiation. This produces a *greenhouse effect,* which plays a role in global warming.

All objects—you, your instructor, and everything in your surroundings—continually emit radiant energy in a mixture of frequencies (because temperature corresponds to a mixture of molecular kinetic energies). Objects with everyday temperatures mostly emit low-frequency infrared waves. When the higher-frequency infrared waves are absorbed by your skin, you feel the sensation of heat. So it is common to refer to infrared radiation as *heat radiation.*

Common infrared sources that give the sensation of heat are the burning embers in a fireplace, a lamp filament, and the sun. All of these emit both infrared radiation and visible light. When this radiant energy falls on other objects, it is partly reflected and partly absorbed. The part that is absorbed increases the thermal energy of the objects.

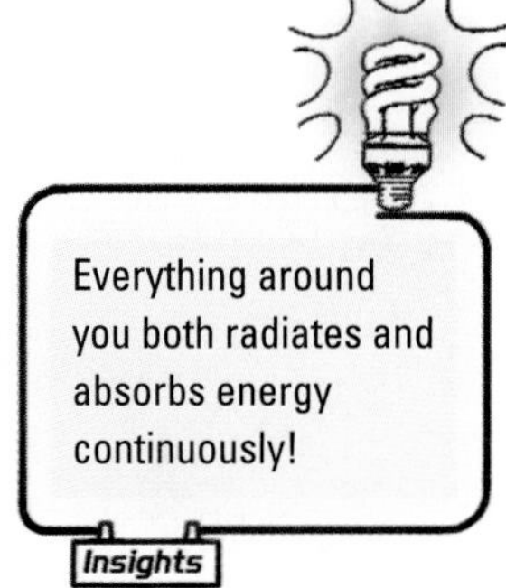

☑ CHECKPOINT

Which of these do *not* emit radiant energy? (a) the sun; (b) lava from a volcano; (c) red-hot coals; (d) this textbook.

Check Your Answer

All the above emit radiant energy—even your textbook, which, like the other substances listed, has a temperature. According to the rule $f \sim T$, the book therefore emits radiation whose average frequency f is quite low compared with the radiation frequencies emitted by the other substances. Everything with any temperature above absolute zero emits radiant energy. That's right—*everything*!

Absorption of Radiant Energy

If everything is radiating energy, why doesn't everything finally run out of it? The answer is, everything is also *absorbing* energy. Good emitters of radiant energy are also good absorbers; poor emitters are poor absorbers. For example, a radio dish antenna constructed to be a good emitter of radio waves is also, by its very design, a good receiver (absorber) of them. A poorly designed transmitting antenna is also a poor receiver.

Figure 8.15
When the black rough-surfaced container and the shiny polished one are filled with hot (or cold) water, the blackened one cools (or warms) faster.

It's interesting to note that, if a good absorber were not also a good emitter, then black objects would remain warmer than lighter-colored objects and the two would never reach a common temperature. Objects in thermal contact, given sufficient time, will reach the same temperature. A blacktop pavement may remain hotter than the surroundings on a hot day, but, at nightfall, it cools faster! Sooner or later, all objects come to thermal equilibrium. So a dark object that absorbs a lot of radiant energy must emit a lot as well.

The surface of any material, hot or cold, both absorbs and emits radiant energy. If the surface absorbs more energy than it emits, it is a net absorber and its temperature rises. If it emits more than it absorbs, it is a net emitter and its temperature drops. Whether a surface plays the role of net emitter or net absorber depends on whether its temperature is above or below that of its surroundings. In short, if it's hotter than its surroundings, the surface will be a net emitter and will cool; if it's colder than its surroundings, it will be a net absorber and will become warmer.

☑ CHECKPOINT

1. If a good absorber of radiant energy were a poor emitter, how would its temperature compare with the temperature of its surroundings?
2. A farmer turns on the propane burner in his barn on a cold morning and heats the air to 20°C (68°F). Why does he still feel cold?

Check Your Answers

1. If a good absorber were not also a good emitter, there would be a net absorption of radiant energy and the temperature of the absorber would remain higher than the temperature of the surroundings. Things around us approach a common temperature only because good absorbers are, by their very nature, also good emitters.
2. The walls of the barn are still cold. He radiates more energy to the walls than the walls radiate back at him, and he feels chilly. (On a winter day, you are comfortable inside your home or classroom only if the walls are warm—not just the air.)

Reflection of Radiant Energy

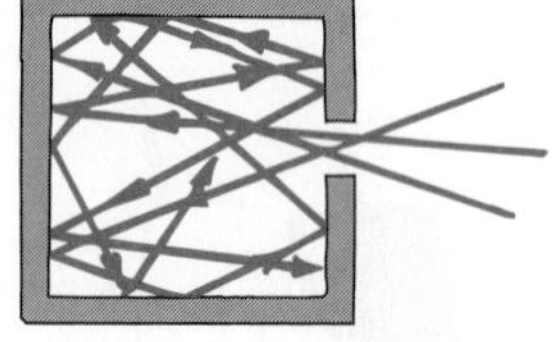

Figure 8.16
Radiation that enters the opening has little chance of leaving because most of it is absorbed. For this reason, the opening to any cavity appears black to us.

Absorption and reflection are opposite processes. A good absorber of radiant energy reflects very little of it, including visible light. Hence, a surface that reflects very little or no radiant energy looks dark. So a good absorber appears dark, and a perfect absorber reflects no radiant energy and appears completely black. The pupil of the eye, for example, allows light to enter with no reflection, which is why it appears black. (An exception occurs in flash photography when pupils appear pink, which occurs when very bright light is reflected off the eye's pink inner surface and back through the pupil.)

Look at the open ends of pipes in a stack; the holes appear black. Look at open doorways or windows of distant houses in the daytime, and they, too, look black. Openings appear black because the light that enters them is reflected back and forth on the inside walls many times and is partly absorbed at each reflection. As a result, very little or none of the light remains to come back out of the opening and travel to your eyes (Figure 8.16).

Figure 8.17
The hole looks perfectly black and indicates a black interior, when in fact the interior has been painted a bright white.

Good reflectors, on the other hand, are poor absorbers. Clean snow is a good reflector and therefore does not melt rapidly in sunlight. If the snow is dirty, it absorbs radiant energy from the sun and melts faster. Dropping black soot from an aircraft onto snow-covered mountains is a technique sometimes used in flood control. Controlled melting at favorable times, rather than a sudden runoff of melted snow, is thereby accomplished.

☑ CHECKPOINT

Is it more efficient to paint the heating radiators in your home black or silver?

Check Your Answer

Interestingly, the color of paint is a small factor, so either color can be used. That's because radiators do very little heating by radiation. Their hot surfaces warm surrounding air by conduction, the warmed air rises, and warmed convection currents heat the room. (A better name for this type of heater would be a *convector*.) Now if you're interested in *optimum* efficiency, a silver-painted radiator will radiate less, become and remain hotter, and do a better job of heating the air.

Emission and absorption in the visible part of the spectrum are affected by color. But emission and absorption in the infrared part of the spectrum are more affected by surface texture. In the infrared, a dull finish emits/absorbs better than a polished one, whatever the color.

Insights

Cooling at Night by Radiation

Bodies that radiate more energy than they receive become cooler. This happens at night when radiation from the sun is absent. An object left out in the open at night radiates energy into space and, because of the absence of any warmer bodies in the vicinity, receives very little energy in return. Thus, it radiates more energy than it receives, and it becomes cooler. But, if the object is a good conductor of thermal energy—such as metal, stone, or concrete—the ground conducts thermal energy to it, which somewhat stabilizes its temperature. On the other hand, poor conductors—such as wood, straw, and grass—receive little energy from the ground. These insulating materials are net radiators, and they become colder than the air. It is common for frost to form on these materials, even when the temperature of the air does not

Figure 8.18
Patches of frost crystals betray the hidden entrances to mouse burrows. Each cluster of crystals is frozen mouse breath!

decrease to freezing. Have you ever seen a frost-covered lawn or field on a chilly but above-freezing morning before the sun is up? The next time you see this, notice that the frost forms only on the grass, straw, or other poor conductors, while none forms on the cement, stone, or other good conductors. Frost will even form on a car, due to the insulation from the ground that is provided by its tires.

The earth itself exchanges radiation with its surroundings. The sun is a dominant part of the earth's surroundings during the day. Then the earth absorbs more radiant energy than it emits. At night, if the air is relatively transparent, the earth radiates more energy to deep space than it receives in return. As the Bell Laboratories researchers Arno Penzias and Robert Wilson learned in 1965, outer space has a temperature—about 2.7 K (2.7 degrees above absolute zero). Space itself emits weak radiation characteristic of that low temperature.*

(In Chapter 31, we'll learn about the effects of heat transfer in the greenhouse effect and on global warming.)

☑ CHECKPOINT

1. Which is likely to be colder, a night when the stars are out or a night with no stars?
2. In winter, why do road surfaces on bridges tend to be more icy than the road surfaces on the land at either side?

Check Your Answers

1. It is colder on the starry night, when the earth radiates directly to frigid deep space. On a cloudy night, net radiation is less, because the clouds radiate energy back to the earth's surface.
2. Energy radiated by roads on land is partially replenished by heat conducted from the warmer ground below the pavement. But there's an absence of thermal contact between the road surfaces of bridges and the ground, so they receive very little if any replenishing energy conducted from the ground. This is why road surfaces on bridges get colder than roads on land, which increases the chance of ice formation. Understanding heat transfer can make you a safer driver!

8.4 Newton's Law of Cooling

Left to themselves, objects hotter than their surroundings eventually cool to match the surrounding temperature. The rate of cooling depends on how much hotter the object is than its surroundings. The temperature change per minute of a hot apple pie will be greater if the hot pie is put in a cold freezer than if

*Penzias and Wilson shared a Nobel prize in physics for this discovery, deemed to be a relic of the big bang. By studying this "cosmic microwave background radiation," scientists are learning much about the early history of the universe.

it is left on the kitchen table. That's because, in the freezer, the temperature difference between the pie and its surroundings is greater. Similarly, the rate at which a warm house leaks thermal energy to the cold outdoors depends on the difference between the inside and outside temperatures.

The rate of cooling of an object—whether by conduction, by convection, or by radiation—is approximately proportional to the temperature difference ΔT between the object and its surroundings.

Rate of cooling ~ ΔT

This is known as **Newton's law of cooling.** (Guess who is credited with discovering this?)

The law applies also to warming. If an object is cooler than its surroundings, its rate of warming up is also proportional to ΔT.* Frozen food will warm up faster in a warm room than in a cold room.

The Thermos Bottle

A common Thermos Bottle, a double-walled glass container with a vacuum between its silvered walls, nicely summarizes heat transfer. When a hot or cold liquid is poured into such a bottle, it remains at very nearly the same temperature for many hours. This is because the transfer of thermal energy by conduction, convection, and radiation is severely inhibited.

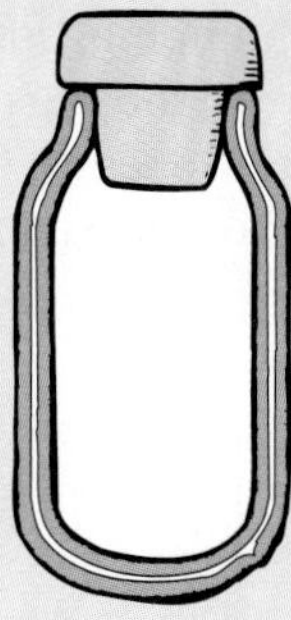

1. Heat transfer by *conduction* through the vacuum is impossible. Some thermal energy escapes by conduction through the glass and stopper, but this is a slow process, because glass and plastic or cork are poor conductors.
2. The vacuum also prevents heat loss through the walls by *convection*.
3. Heat loss by *radiation* is prevented by the silvered surfaces of the walls, which reflect radiant energy back into the bottle.

☑ CHECKPOINT

Since a hot cup of tea loses thermal energy more rapidly than a lukewarm cup of tea, would it be correct to say that a hot cup of tea will cool to room temperature before a lukewarm cup of tea will?

Check Your Answer

No! Although the rate of cooling is greater for the hotter cup, it has further to cool to reach thermal equilibrium. The extra time is equal to the time it takes to cool to the initial temperature of the lukewarm cup of tea. Cooling *rate* and cooling *time* are not the same thing.

*A warm object that contains a *source* of energy may remain warmer than its surroundings indefinitely. The thermal energy it emits doesn't necessarily cool it, and Newton's law of cooling doesn't apply. Thus an automobile engine that is running remains warmer than the automobile's body and the surrounding air. But after the engine is turned off, it cools in accordance with Newton's law of cooling and gradually approaches the same temperature as its surroundings. Likewise the sun will remain hotter than its surroundings as long as its nuclear furnace is functioning—another five billion years or so.

8.5 Heat Transfer and Change of Phase

Matter exists in four common phases (states). Ice, for example, is the *solid* phase of water. When thermal energy is added, the increased molecular motion breaks down the frozen structure and it becomes the *liquid* phase, water. When more energy is added, the liquid changes to the *gaseous* phase. Add still more energy, and the molecules break into ions and electrons, giving the *plasma* phase. Plasma (not to be confused with blood plasma) is the illuminating gas found in fluorescent and other vapor lamps. The sun, stars, and much of the space between them is in the plasma phase. Whenever matter changes phase, a transfer of thermal energy is involved.

8.6 Evaporation

Water changes to the gaseous phase by the process of **evaporation.** In a liquid, molecules move randomly at a wide variety of speeds. Think of the molecules as tiny billiard balls, moving helter-skelter, continually bumping into one another. During their bumping, some gain kinetic energy while others lose kinetic energy. Molecules at the surface that gain kinetic energy by being bumped from below are the ones to break free from the liquid. They leave the surface and escape into the space above the liquid. In this way, they become gas.

Water evaporating from your body takes energy with it, which is why you feel cool when emerging from water on a warm and windy day.

Insights

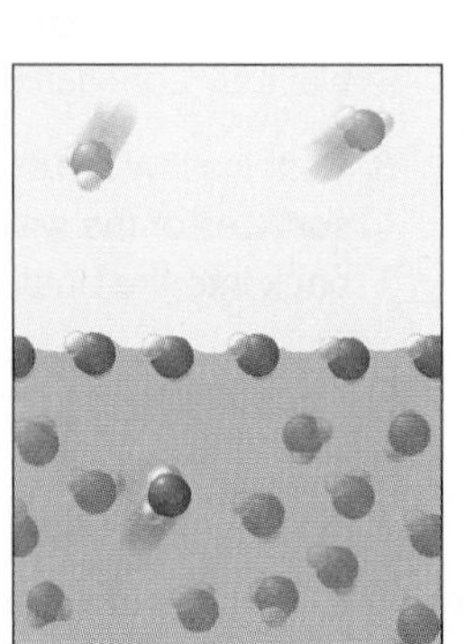

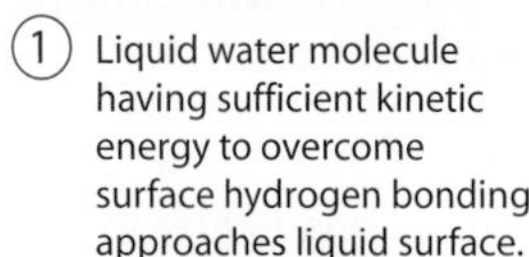
(1) Liquid water molecule having sufficient kinetic energy to overcome surface hydrogen bonding approaches liquid surface.

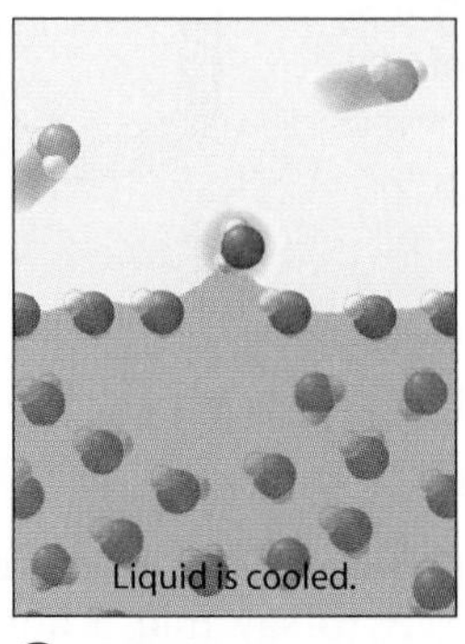

(2) Liquid water is cooled as it loses this high-speed water molecule.

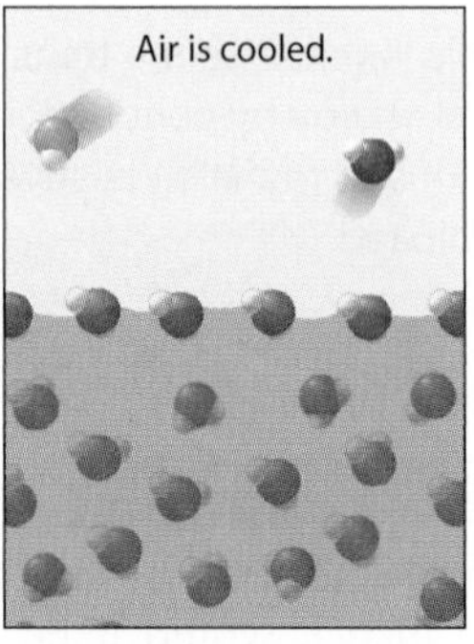

(3) Molecule enters gaseous phase, having lost kinetic energy in overcoming hydrogen bonding at the liquid surface. Air is cooled as it collects these slowly moving gaseous particles.

Figure 8.19
Evaporation is a cooling process.

Figure 8.20
When wet, the cloth covering on the canteen promotes cooling. As the faster-moving water molecules evaporate from the wet cloth, the temperature of the cloth decreases and cools the metal. The metal, in turn, cools the water within. The water in the canteen can become a lot cooler than the air temperature.

When fast-moving molecules leave the water, the molecules left behind are the slow-moving ones. What happens to the overall kinetic energy in a liquid when the high-energy molecules leave? The answer: the average kinetic energy of molecules left in the liquid decreases. The temperature decreases and the water is cooled.

Figure 8.21
Sam has no sweat glands (except between his toes). He cools himself by panting. In this way, evaporation occurs in the mouth and within the bronchial tract.

Figure 8.22
Pigs have no sweat glands and therefore cannot cool by the evaporation of perspiration. Instead, they wallow in the mud to cool themselves.

When our bodies begin to overheat, our sweat glands produce perspiration, and evaporation cools us. This is part of nature's thermostat, for the evaporation of perspiration cools us and helps us maintain a stable body temperature. Many animals do not have sweat glands and must cool themselves by other means (Figures 8.21 and 8.22).

☑ CHECKPOINT

Would evaporation be a cooling process if there were no transfer of molecular kinetic energy from water to the air above?

Check Your Answer

No. A liquid cools only when kinetic energy is carried away by evaporating molecules. This is similar to billiard balls that gain speed at the expense of others that lose speed. Those that leave (evaporate) are gainers, while losers remain behind and lower the temperature of the water.

Even frozen water "evaporates." In this form of evaporation, called **sublimation,** molecules jump directly from the solid to the gaseous phase. Moth balls are well known for their sublimation. Ice also sublimes. Because water molecules are so tightly held in a solid, frozen water sublimes much more slowly than does liquid water. Sublimation accounts for the loss of much snow and ice, especially on high, sunny mountain tops. Sublimation also explains why ice cubes left in the freezer for a long time get smaller.

8.7 Condensation

The opposite of evaporation is **condensation**—the changing of a gas to a liquid. When gas molecules near the surface of a liquid are attracted to the liquid, they strike the surface with increased kinetic energy and become part of the liquid. This kinetic energy is absorbed by the liquid. The result is increased temperature. Condensation is a warming process.

Figure 8.23
The exchange of molecules at the interface between liquid and gaseous water.

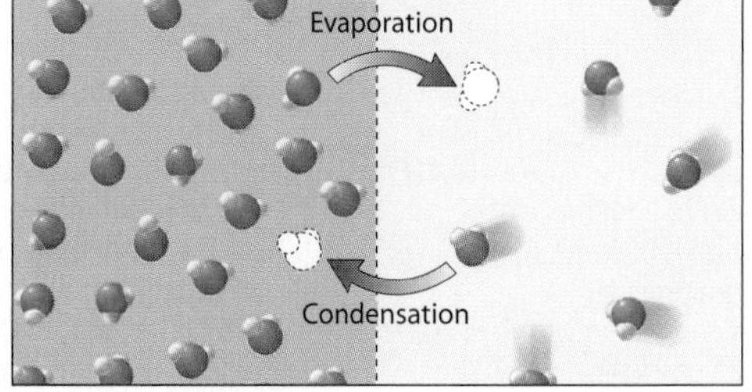

Figure 8.24
Thermal energy is released by steam when it condenses inside the "radiator."

A dramatic example of warming by condensation is the energy released by steam when it condenses. The steam gives up a lot of energy when it condenses to a liquid and moistens the skin. That's why a burn from 100°C steam is much more damaging than a burn from 100°C boiling water. This energy release by condensation is utilized in steam-heating systems.

When taking a shower, you may have noticed that you feel warmer in the moist shower region than outside the shower. This difference is quickly sensed when you step outside. Away from the moisture, the rate of evaporation is much higher than the rate of condensation, and you feel chilly. When you remain in the shower stall where the humidity is higher, the rate of condensation is increased, so that you feel warmer. So now you know why you can dry yourself with a towel much more comfortably if you remain in the shower stall. If you're in a hurry and don't mind the chill, dry yourself off in the hallway.

Figure 8.25
If you're chilly outside the shower stall, step back inside and be warmed by the condensation of the excess water vapor there.

On a July afternoon in dry Phoenix or Santa Fe, you'll feel a lot cooler than in New York City or New Orleans, even when the temperatures are the same. In the drier cities, the rate of evaporation is much greater than the rate of condensation. In humid locations, the rate of condensation is greater than the rate of evaporation. You feel the warming effect as vapor in the air condenses on your skin. You are literally being bombarded by the impact of H_2O molecules in the air slamming into you. (We will explore condensation in the atmosphere when we study meteorology in Chapter 31.)

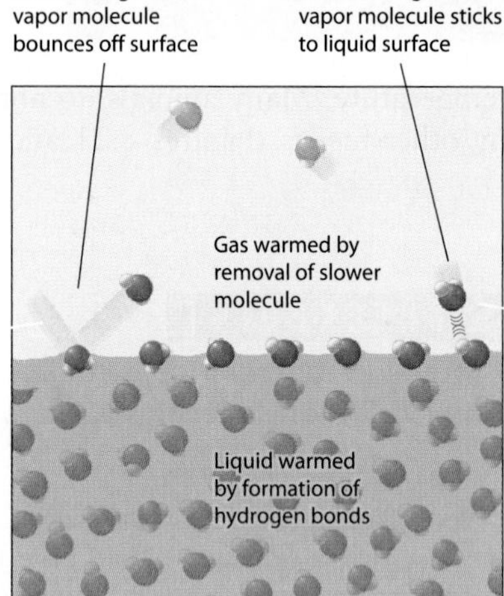

Figure 8.26
Condensation is a warming process.

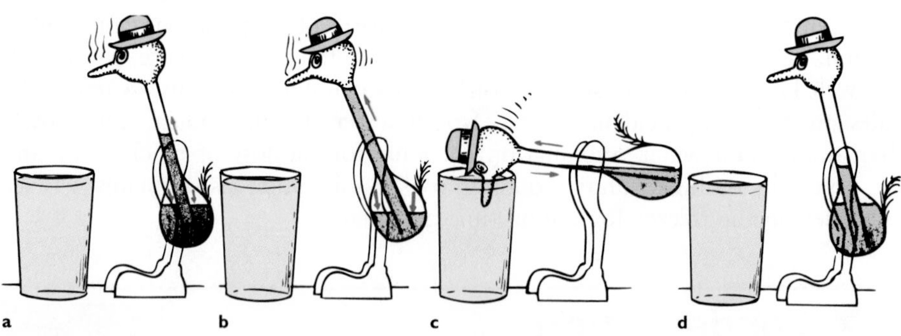

Figure 8.27
The toy drinking bird operates by the evaporation of ether inside its body and by the evaporation of water from the outer surface of its head. The lower body contains liquid ether, which evaporates rapidly at room temperature. As it (a) vaporizes, it (b) creates pressure (inside arrows), which pushes ether up the tube. Ether in the upper part does not vaporize because the head is cooled by the evaporation of water from the outer felt-covered beak and head. When the weight of ether in the head is sufficient, the bird (c) pivots forward, permitting the ether to run back to the body. Each pivot wets the felt surface of the beak and head, and the cycle is repeated.

Condensation Crunch

Put a small amount of water in an aluminum soda pop can and heat it on a stove until steam issues from the opening. When this occurs, air has been driven out and replaced by steam. Then, with a pair of tongs, quickly invert the can into a pan of water. Crunch! The can is crushed by atmospheric pressure! Why? When the molecules of steam in the can encounter water from the pan, condensation occurs, leaving a very low pressure in the can, whereupon the surrounding atmospheric pressure crunches the can. Here we see, dramatically, how pressure is reduced by condensation. (This demo nicely underlies the condensation cycle of a steam engine—perhaps something for future study.)

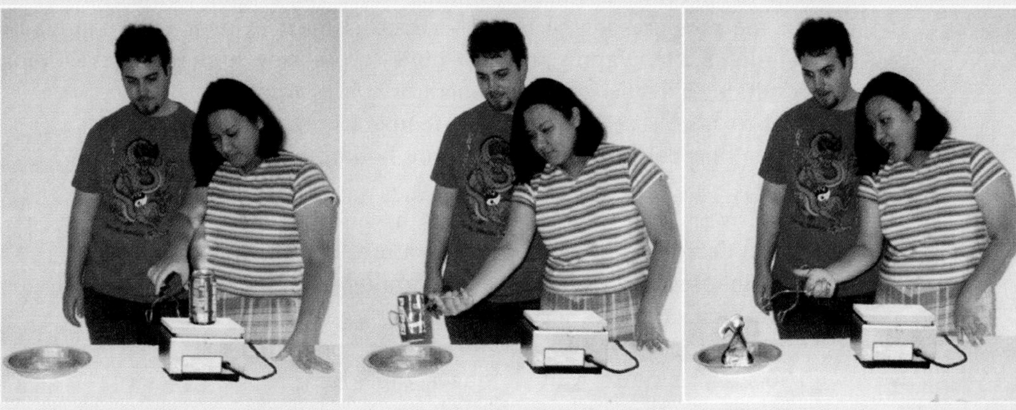

Figure 8.28

☑ CHECKPOINT

If the water level in a dish of water remains unchanged from one day to the next, can you conclude that no evaporation or condensation is occurring?

Check Your Answer

Not at all, for significant evaporation and condensation occur continuously at the molecular level. The fact that the water level remains constant indicates equal rates of evaporation and condensation. (Unless there is extreme humidity, evaporation is normally greater than condensation.)

8.8 Boiling

Evaporation is a surface phenomenon. But evaporation can also occur beneath the surface of a liquid in the process called **boiling.** Bubbles of vapor form in the liquid and are buoyed to the surface, where they escape. Bubbles can form only when the pressure of the vapor within them is great enough to resist the pressure exerted by the surrounding water and atmosphere. This occurs at the boiling temperature of the liquid. At lower temperatures, the vapor pressure in the bubbles is not sufficient, and the surrounding pressure collapses any bubbles that might form.

It is common to say that we boil water, meaning that we add heat to it. Actually, the boiling process cools the water.

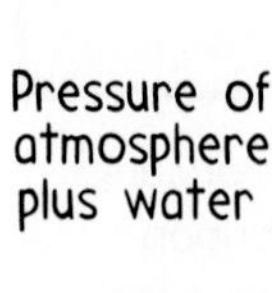

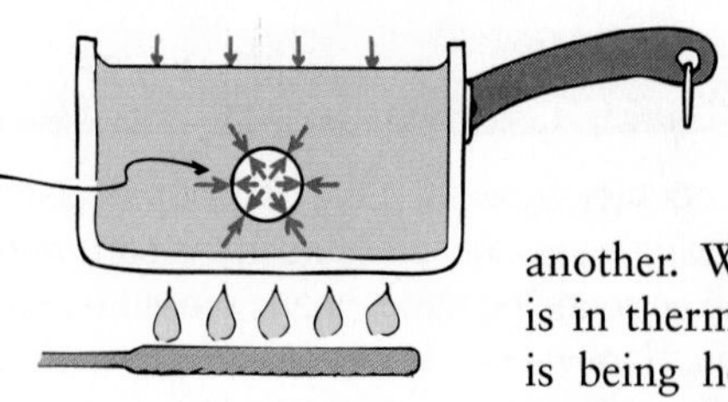

Figure 8.29
The motion of vapor molecules in the bubble of steam (much enlarged) creates a gas pressure (called the *vapor pressure*) that counteracts the atmospheric and water pressure against the bubble.

Boiling, like evaporation, is a cooling process. At first thought, this may seem surprising—perhaps because we usually associate boiling with heating. However, heating water is one thing; boiling it is another. When 100°C water at atmospheric pressure is boiling, it is in thermal equilibrium. It is being cooled by boiling as fast as it is being heated by energy from the heat source (Figure 8.30). If cooling did not occur, continued application of heat to a pot of boiling water would raise its temperature.

When the pressure on the surface of a liquid increases, boiling is hampered. The temperature needed for boiling rises. The boiling point of a liquid depends on the pressure on the liquid—which is most evident with a pressure cooker (Figure 8.31). Vapor pressure builds up inside and prevents boiling, which results in a higher water temperature. It is important to note that it is the high temperature of the water that cooks the food, not the boiling process itself.

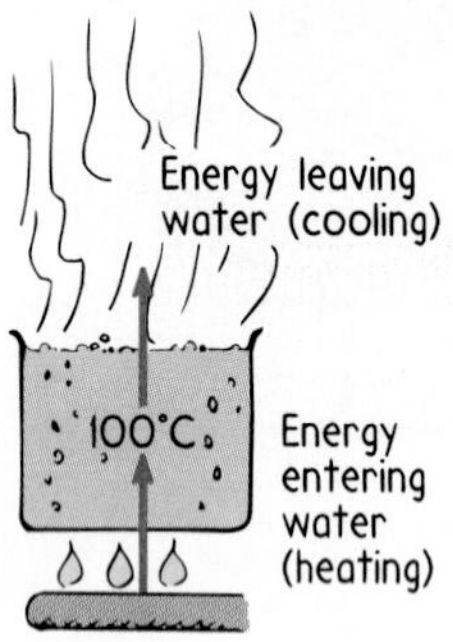

Figure 8.30
Heating warms the water from below, and boiling cools it from above.

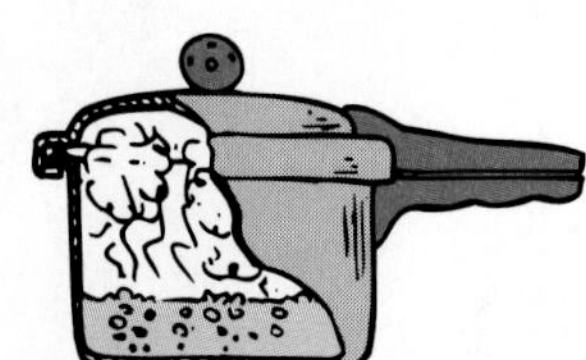

Figure 8.31
The tight lid of a pressure cooker holds pressurized vapor above the water surface, and this inhibits boiling. In this way, the boiling temperature of the water is increased to above 100°C.

Lower atmospheric pressure (as at high altitudes) decreases the boiling temperature. For example, in Denver, Colorado, the "mile-high city," water boils at 95°C, instead of at 100°C. If you try to cook food in boiling water that is cooler than 100°C, you must wait a longer time for proper cooking. A three-minute boiled egg in Denver is yucky. If the temperature of the boiling water is very low, food does not cook at all.

Mountaineering pioneers in the nineteenth century, without altimeters, used the boiling point of water to determine their altitudes.

Insights

☑ CHECKPOINT

1. Since boiling is a cooling process, would it be a good idea to cool your hot, sticky hands by dipping them into boiling water?
2. Why do the directions for cooking spaghetti often call for rapidly boiling water, when simmering water has the same temperature?

Check Your Answers

1. No, no, no! When we say boiling is a cooling process, we mean that the water (not your hands!) is being cooled relative to the higher temperature it would attain otherwise. Because of the cooling effect of the boiling, the water remains at 100°C instead of getting hotter. A dip in 100°C water would be extremely uncomfortable for your hands!
2. Good cooks know that the reason for the rapidly boiling water is not higher temperature, it is simply a way to keep the spaghetti strands from sticking together.

A dramatic demonstration of the cooling effect of evaporation and boiling is shown in Figure 8.32. Here we see a shallow dish of room-temperature water in a vacuum jar. When the pressure in the jar is slowly reduced by a vacuum pump, the water begins to boil. The boiling process removes heat from the water, which cools. As the pressure is further reduced, more and more of the faster-moving molecules boil away until the freezing point of approximately 0°C is reached. Continued cooling by boiling causes ice to form over the surface of the bubbling water. Boiling and freezing occur at the same time! Frozen bubbles of boiling water are a remarkable sight.

If you spray some drops of coffee into a vacuum chamber, they will boil until they freeze. Even after they are frozen, the water molecules continue to evaporate into the vacuum, until little crystals of coffee solids remain. This is how freeze-dried coffee is produced. The low temperature of this process tends to keep the chemical structure of the coffee solids from changing. When hot water is added, much of the original flavor of the coffee is retained.

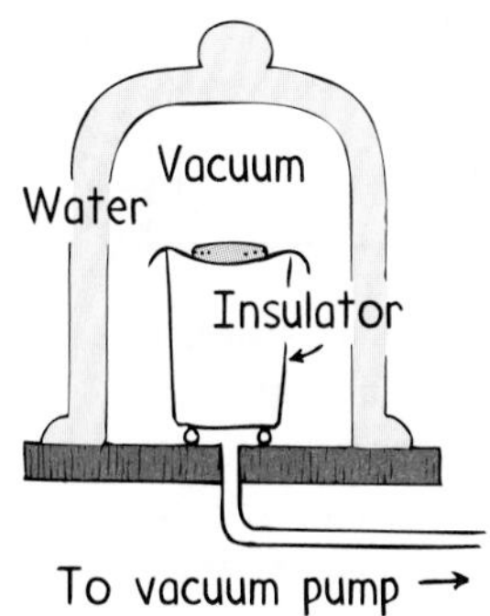

Figure 8.32
Apparatus to demonstrate that water freezes and boils at the same time in a vacuum. A gram or two of water is placed in a dish that is insulated from the base by a polystyrene cup.

8.9 Melting and Freezing

Melting occurs when a substance changes from a solid to a liquid. To visualize what happens, imagine a group of people holding hands and jumping around. The more violent the jumping, the more difficult it is to keep holding hands. If the jumping is violent enough, continuing to hold hands might become impossible. A similar thing happens to the molecules of a solid when it is heated. As heat is absorbed by the solid, its molecules vibrate more and more violently. If enough heat is absorbed, the attractive forces between the molecules no longer hold them together. The solid melts.

Freezing occurs when a liquid changes to a solid—the opposite of melting. As energy is removed from a liquid, molecular motion slows until molecules move so slowly that attractive forces between them bind them together. The liquid freezes when its molecules vibrate about fixed positions and form a solid.

At atmospheric pressure, ice forms at 0°C. With impurities in the water, the freezing point is lowered. "Foreign" molecules get in the way and interfere with crystal formation. In general, adding anything to water lowers its freezing temperature. Antifreeze is a practical application of this process.

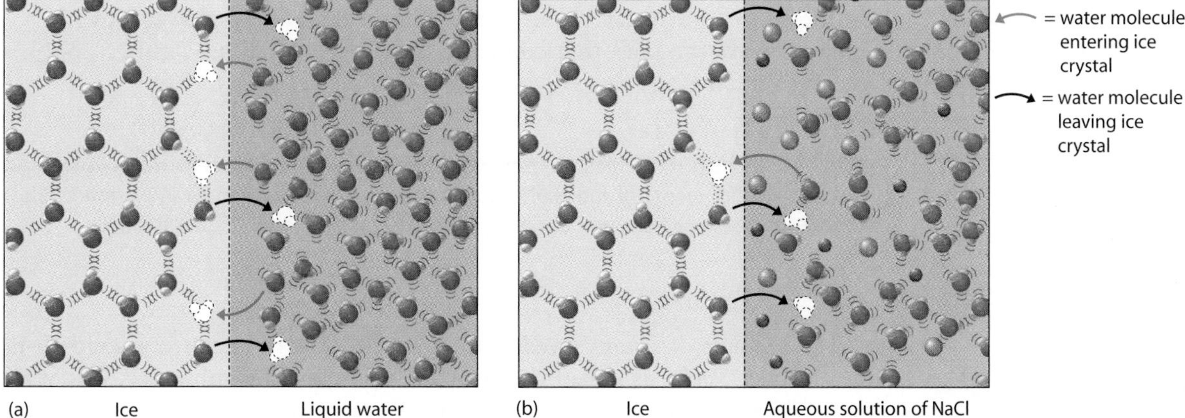

Figure 8.33
(a) In a mixture of ice and water at 0°C, ice crystals gain and lose water molecules at the same time. The ice and water are in thermal equilibrium. (b) When salt is added to the water, there are fewer water molecules entering the ice because there are fewer of them at the interface.

8.10 Energy and Change of Phase

Heat of vaporization is either the energy required to separate molecules from the liquid phase or the energy released when gases condense to the liquid phase.

Insights

Whenever a substance changes phase, a transfer of energy occurs. As just mentioned, energy must be added to melt ice into water or vaporize water into steam. Thermal energy must be removed to condense steam back into water or freeze water into ice (Figure 8.34). In general, a solid absorbs energy in turning to a liquid, and a liquid absorbs energy in turning to a gas. When the phase changes from gas to liquid to solid, energy is taken from the substance.

Energy is absorbed when change of phase is in this direction

Solid ⇄ Liquid ⇄ Gas

Energy is released when change of phase is in this direction

Figure 8.34
Energy changes with change of phase.

The cooling cycle of a refrigerator nicely illustrates these concepts. A motor pumps a special fluid through the system, where it undergoes the cyclic process of vaporization and condensation. In doing so, thermal energy is drawn from things stored inside. The gas that forms, with its added energy, is directed to outside coils in the back—appropriately called condensation coils. The next time you're near a refrigerator, place your hand near the condensation coils in the back and you'll feel the heat that has been extracted from the inside.

An air conditioner uses the same principle and simply pumps heat energy from one part of the unit to another. If the roles of vaporization and condensation were reversed, the air conditioner would become a heater.

Heat of fusion is either the energy needed to separate molecules from the solid phase or the energy released when bonds form in a liquid that changes it to the solid phase.

Insights

☑ CHECKPOINT

In the process of water vapor condensing in the air, the slower-moving molecules are the ones that condense. Does condensation warm or cool the surrounding air?

Check Your Answer

As slower-moving molecules are removed from the air, there is an increase in the average kinetic energy of molecules still in the air. Therefore, the air is warmed. The change of phase is from gas to liquid, which releases energy (Figure 8.34).

The amount of energy needed to change any substance from solid to liquid (and vice versa) is called the **heat of fusion** for the substance. For water, this is 334 joules per gram. The amount of energy required to change any substance from liquid to gas (and vice versa) is called the **heat of vaporization** for the substance. For water, this is a whopping 2256 joules per gram. (We will see later in Chapter 20 that these relatively high values are due to the strong forces between water molecules—hydrogen bonds.)

Figuring Physical Science

The specific heat of water, c, tells us it takes 1 calorie (or 4.18 joules) to change the temperature of 1 gram of water by 1 degree Celsius. The heat of fusion of water, L_f, tells us it takes 334 joules to melt 1 gram of 0°C ice. The heat of vaporization of water, L_v, tells us that it takes 2256 joules to turn 1 gram of 100°C boiling water to steam.

Problem

How much energy must be extracted from 1 kg of 100°C steam to turn it to 0°C ice?

Solution

This change from steam to ice involves three steps: (1) changing steam to boiling water, (2) lowering the temperature of the water by 100°C, and (3) changing 0°C water to ice.

We express the quantity of heat involved in changing temperature as $Q = cm\Delta T$, where m is the mass of water and c is 4.18 J/g°C. We express the quantity of heat in changing 100°C steam to water as $Q = mL_v$, where L_v is 2256 J/g. The quantity of heat to turn 0°C water to ice is $Q = mL_f$, where L_f is 334 J/g. The values are the same whether we go from steam to ice or from ice to steam. Changes of phase occur in either direction.

In three steps, the quantity of heat extracted is

$$Q = mL_v + cm\Delta T + mL_f = m(L_v + c\Delta T + L_f),$$

$$Q = 1000\text{ g }[2256\text{ J/g} + 4.18\text{ J/g°C}(100\text{°C}) + 334\text{ J/g}],$$

$$Q = 3{,}008{,}000\text{ J}.$$

(See more about change of phase on pages 48, 49 of the *Practicing Physical Science* Book.)

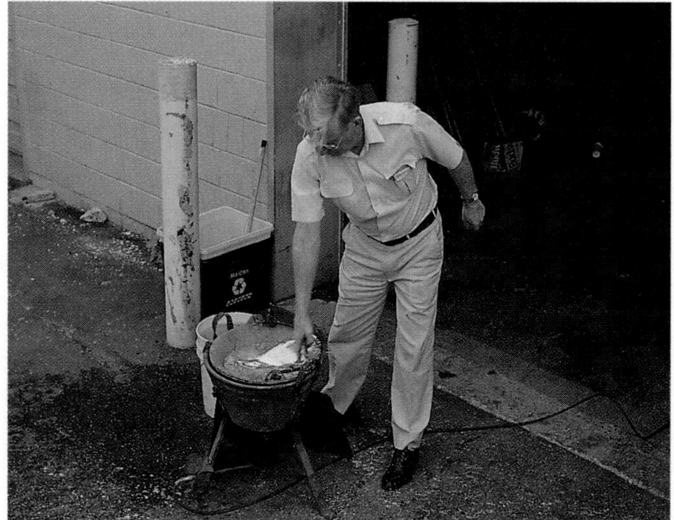

Figure 8.35
Paul Ryan tests the hotness of molten lead by dragging his wetted finger through it.

In premodern times, farmers in cold climates prevented jars of food from freezing by taking advantage of water's high heat of fusion. They simply kept large tubs of water in their cellars. The outside temperature could drop to well below freezing, but not in the cellars where water was releasing thermal energy while undergoing freezing. Canned food requires subzero temperatures to freeze because of its salt or sugar content. So farmers had only to replace frozen tubs of water with unfrozen ones, and the cellar temperatures wouldn't fall below 0°C.

Water's high heat of vaporization allows you to briefly touch your wetted finger to a hot skillet on a hot stove without harm. You can even touch it a few times in succession as long as your finger remains wet. Energy that ordinarily would burn your finger goes instead into changing the phase of the moisture on your finger. Similarly, you are able to judge the hotness of a hot clothes iron.

Paul Ryan, former supervisor in the Department of Public Works in Malden, Massachusetts, has for years used molten lead to seal pipes in certain plumbing operations. He startles onlookers by dragging his finger through molten lead to judge its hotness (Figure 8.35). He is sure that the lead is very hot and his finger is thoroughly wet before he does this. (Do not try this on your own: if the lead is not hot enough, it will stick to your finger—Ouch!)

Summary of Terms

Conduction The transfer of thermal energy by molecular and electronic collisions within a substance (especially a solid).

Convection The transfer of thermal energy in a gas or liquid by means of currents in the heated fluid. The fluid flows, carrying energy with it.

Radiation The transfer of energy by means of electromagnetic waves.

Terrestrial radiation The radiant energy emitted by Planet Earth.

Newton's law of cooling The rate of loss of thermal energy from an object is proportional to the temperature difference between the object and its surroundings.

Evaporation The change of phase at the surface of a liquid as it passes to the gaseous phase.

Sublimation The change of phase directly from solid to gas, bypassing the liquid phase.

Condensation The change of phase from gas to liquid; the opposite of evaporation. Warming of the liquid results.

Boiling A rapid state of evaporation that takes place within the liquid as well as at its surface. As with evaporation, cooling of the liquid results.

Freezing The process of changing state from liquid to solid, as from water to ice.

Heat of fusion The amount of energy needed to change any substance from solid to liquid (and vice versa). For water, this is 334 J/g (or 80 cal/g).

Heat of vaporization The amount of energy required to change any substance from liquid to gas (and vice versa). For water, this is 2256 J/g (or 540 cal/g).

Review Questions

1. What are the three common ways in which heat is transferred?

8.1 Conduction

2. What is the role of "loose" electrons in heat conductors?
3. Distinguish between a heat conductor and a heat insulator.
4. What is the explanation for a barefoot firewalker being able to walk safely on red-hot wooden coals?
5. Why are such materials as wood, fur, feathers, and even snow good insulators?
6. Does a good insulator prevent heat from getting through it, or does it simply slow its passage?

8.2 Convection

7. By what means is heat transferred by convection?
8. How does buoyancy relate to convection?
9. What happens to the temperature of air when it expands?
10. Why is Millie's hand not burned when she holds it above the escape valve of the pressure cooker (Figure 8.8)?
11. Why does the direction of coastal winds change from day to night?

8.3 Radiation

12. What exactly is radiant energy?
13. How does the frequency of radiant energy relate to the absolute temperature of the radiating source?
14. What is *terrestrial radiation*? How does it differ from solar radiation?
15. What is *heat radiation*?
16. Since all objects emit energy to their surroundings, why don't the temperatures of all objects continuously decrease?
17. What determines whether an object at a given time is a net absorber or a net emitter?
18. Can an object be both a good absorber and a good reflector at the same time?
19. Why does the pupil of the eye appear black?
20. An object radiating energy at night is in contact with the relatively warm earth. How does its conductivity affect whether or not it becomes appreciably colder than the air?

8.4 Newton's Law of Cooling

21. If you want a room-temperature can of beverage to cool quickly, should you put it in the freezer compartment or in the main part of your refrigerator? Or does it not matter?

22. Which will undergo the greater rate of cooling, a red-hot poker in a warm oven or a red-hot poker in a cold room? (Or do both cool at the same rate?)
23. Does Newton's law of cooling apply to warming as well as to cooling?

8.5 Heat Transfer and Change of Phase

24. What are the four common phases of matter?

8.6 Evaporation

25. Do all the molecules in a liquid have about the same speed, or do they have a wide variety of speeds?
26. What is evaporation, and why is it a cooling process? Exactly what is it that cools?
27. What is sublimation?

8.7 Condensation

28. What is condensation, and why is it a warming process? Exactly what is it that warms?
29. Why is a steam burn more damaging than a burn from boiling water of the same temperature?
30. Why do you feel uncomfortably warm on a hot and humid day?

8.8 Boiling

31. Distinguish between evaporation and boiling.
32. Why does water not boil at 100°C when it is under greater than normal atmospheric pressure?
33. Is it the boiling of the water or the higher temperature of the water that cooks food faster in a pressure cooker?

8.9 Melting and Freezing

34. Why does increasing the temperature of a solid make it melt?
35. Why does decreasing the temperature of a liquid make it freeze?
36. Why will water not freeze at 0°C when foreign ions are present?

8.10 Energy and Changes of Phase

37. Does a liquid give off energy or absorb energy when it turns into a gas? When it turns into a solid?
38. Does a gas give off energy or absorb energy when it turns into a liquid? How about a solid when it turns to a liquid?
39. Distinguish between heat of fusion and heat of vaporization.
40. Why is it important that your finger be wet if you intend to touch it briefly to a hot clothes iron to test its temperature?

Activities

1. If you live where there is snow, do as Benjamin Franklin did about two hundred years ago: Lay samples of light and dark cloth on the snow and note the differences in the rate of melting beneath the samples of cloth.
2. Hold the bottom end of a test tube full of cold water in your hand. Heat the top part in a flame until the water boils. The fact that you can still hold the bottom shows that water is a poor conductor of heat. This is even more dramatic when you wedge chunks of ice at the bottom; then the water above can be brought to a boil without melting the ice. Try it and see.

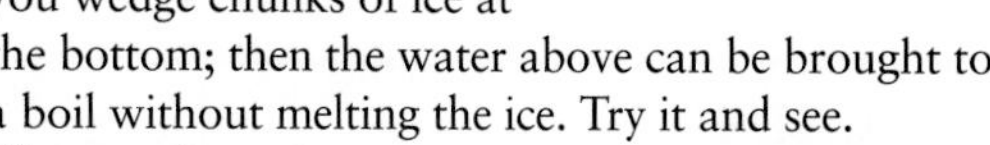

3. Wrap a piece of paper around a thick metal bar and place it in a flame. Note that the paper will not catch fire. Can you figure out why? (Paper generally will not ignite until its temperature reaches 233°C.)
4. Place a Pyrex funnel mouth down in a saucepan full of water so that the straight tube of the funnel sticks above the water. Rest a part of the funnel on a nail or coin so that water can get under it. Place the pan on a stove, and watch the water as it begins to boil. Where do the bubbles form first? Why? As the bubbles rise, they expand rapidly and push water ahead of them. The funnel confines the water, which is forced up the tube and driven out at the top. Now do you know how a geyser and a coffee percolator work?
5. Watch the spout of a teakettle of boiling water. Notice that you cannot see the steam that issues from the spout. The cloud that you see farther away from the spout is not steam, but condensed water droplets. Now hold the flame of a candle in the cloud of condensed steam. Can you explain your observations?
6. You can make rain in your kitchen. Put a cup of water in a Pyrex saucepan or a Silex coffeemaker and heat it slowly over a low flame. When the water is warm, place a saucer filled with ice cubes on top

of the container. As the water below is heated, droplets form at the bottom of the cold saucer and combine until they are large enough to fall, producing a steady "rainfall" as the water below is gently heated. How does this resemble, and how does it differ from, the way in which natural rain is formed?

7. Measure the temperature of boiling water and the temperature of a boiling solution of salt and water. How do they compare?
8. If you suspend an open-topped container of water in a pan of boiling water, with its top above the surface of the boiling water, water in the inner container will reach 100°C but will not boil. Can you figure out why this is so?

Exercises

1. Wrap a fur coat around a thermometer. Will the temperature rise?
2. If you hold one end of a metal nail against a piece of ice, the end in your hand soon becomes cold. Does cold flow from the ice to your hand? Explain.
3. What is the purpose of the layer of copper or aluminum on the bottom of a piece of stainless-steel cookware?
4. In terms of physics, why do restaurants serve baked potatoes wrapped in aluminum foil?
5. Many tongues have been injured by licking a piece of metal on a very cold day. Why would no harm result if a piece of wood were licked on the same day?
6. Wood is a better insulator than glass. Yet fiberglass is commonly used as an insulator in wooden buildings. Explain.
7. Visit a snow-covered cemetery and note that the snow does not slope upward against the gravestones but, instead, forms depressions around them, as shown. Can you think of a reason for this?

8. You can bring water in a paper cup to a boil by placing it over a hot flame. Why doesn't the paper cup burn?
9. Why is it that you can safely hold your bare hand in a hot pizza oven for a few seconds, but, if you were to touch the metal inside, you'd burn yourself?
10. Wood has a very low conductivity. Does it still have a low conductivity if it is very hot—that is, in the stage of smoldering red-hot coals? Could you safely walk across a bed of red-hot wooden coals with bare feet? Although the coals are hot, does much heat conduct from them to your feet if you step quickly? Could you do the same on pieces of red-hot iron? Explain. (Caution: coals can stick to your feet, so OUCH—don't try it!)
11. A friend says that, in a mixture of gases in thermal equilibrium, the molecules have the same average kinetic energy. Do you agree or disagree? Explain.
12. Why would you not expect all of the molecules of air in your room to have the same average speed?
13. In a still room, smoke from a candle will sometimes rise only so far, not reaching the ceiling. Explain why.
14. What does the high specific heat of water have to do with the convection currents in the air at the seashore?
15. How do the average kinetic energies per molecule compare in a mixture of hydrogen and oxygen gases at the same temperature?
16. In a mixture of hydrogen and oxygen gases at the same temperature, which molecules move faster? Why?
17. One container is filled with argon gas and another with krypton gas. If both gases have the same temperature, in which container are the atoms moving faster? Why?
18. Which atoms have the greatest average speed in a mixture, U-238 or U-235? How would this affect diffusion through a porous membrane of otherwise identical gases made from these isotopes?
19. If we warm a volume of air, it expands. Does it then follow that, if we expand a volume of air, it warms? Explain.
20. Machines used for making snow at ski areas blow a mixture of compressed air and water through a nozzle. The temperature of the mixture may initially be well above the freezing temperature of water, yet crystals of snow are formed as the mixture is ejected from the nozzle. Explain how this happens.
21. Turn an incandescent lamp on and off quickly while you are standing near it. You feel its heat, but you find when you touch the bulb that it is not hot. Explain why you felt heat from the lamp.
22. A number of bodies at different temperatures placed in a closed room share radiant energy and ultimately come to the same temperature. Would this thermal equilibrium be possible if good absorbers were poor emitters and poor absorbers were good emitters? Explain.
23. From the rules that a good absorber of radiation is a good radiator and a good reflector is a poor

absorber, state a rule relating the reflecting and radiating properties of a surface.

24. The heat of volcanoes and natural hot springs comes from trace amounts of radioactive minerals in common rock in the earth's interior. Why isn't the same kind of rock at the earth's surface warm to the touch?
25. Suppose that, at a restaurant, you are served coffee before you are ready to drink it. In order that it be hottest when you are ready for it, would you be wiser to add cream to it right away or just before you are ready to drink it?
26. Even though metal is a good conductor, frost can be seen on parked cars in the early morning even when the air temperature is above freezing. Can you explain this?
27. When there is morning frost on the ground in an open park, why is it likely that none is on the ground beneath park benches?
28. Outer space is not "nothingness." It is full of radiation with a temperature of about 3 K. Since this radiation is shining on the earth at night, why does the earth get cold at night?
29. Is it important to convert temperatures to the Kelvin scale when we use Newton's law of cooling? Why or why not?
30. If you wish to save fuel and you're going to leave your warm house for a half hour or so on a very cold day, should you turn your thermostat down a few degrees, turn it off altogether, or let it remain at the room temperature you desire?
31. If you wish to save fuel and you're going to leave your cool house for a half hour or so on a very hot day, should you turn your air conditioning thermostat up a bit, turn it off altogether, or let it remain at the room temperature you desire?
32. You can determine wind direction by wetting your finger and holding it up in the air. Explain.
33. If all the molecules in a liquid had the same speed, and some were able to evaporate, would the remaining liquid be cooled? Explain.
34. Where does the energy come from that keeps the dunking bird in Figure 8.27 operating?
35. Why will wrapping a bottle in a wet cloth at a picnic often produce a cooler bottle than placing the bottle in a bucket of cold water?
36. Why does the temperature of boiling water remain the same as long as the heating and boiling continue?
37. Why do vapor bubbles in a pot of boiling water get larger as they rise in the water?
38. Why does the boiling temperature of water decrease when the water is under reduced pressure, such as it is at a higher altitude?
39. Place a jar of water on a small stand within a saucepan of water so that the bottom of the jar is held above the bottom of the pan. When the pan is put on a stove, the water in the pan will boil, but not the water in the jar. Why?
40. Water will boil spontaneously in a vacuum—on the moon, for example. Could you cook an egg in this boiling water? Explain.
41. Our inventor friend proposes a design for cookware that will allow boiling to take place at a temperature of less than 100°C so that food can be cooked with the consumption of less energy. Comment on this idea.
42. When you boil potatoes, will your cooking time be reduced if the water is vigorously boiling instead of gently boiling?
43. Why does putting a lid over a pot of water on a stove shorten the time it takes for the water to come to a boil, whereas, after the water is boiling, the use of the lid only slightly shortens the cooking time?
44. In the power plant of a nuclear submarine, the temperature of the water in the reactor is above 100°C. How is this possible?
45. A piece of metal and an equal mass of wood are both removed from a hot oven at equal temperatures and dropped onto blocks of ice. The metal has a lower specific heat capacity than the wood. Which will melt more ice before cooling to 0°C?
46. Why is it that, in cold winters, a tub of water placed in a farmer's canning cellar helps prevent canned food from freezing?
47. Why will spraying fruit trees with water before a frost help to protect the fruit from freezing?
48. Why does a dog pant when it is hot?

Problems

1. A 10-kg iron ball is dropped onto a pavement from a height of 100 m. If half of the heat generated goes into warming the ball, find the temperature increase of the ball. (In SI units, the specific heat capacity of iron is 450 J/kg·°C.) Why is the answer the same for an iron ball of any mass?
2. Calculate the height from which a block of ice at 0°C must be dropped for it to completely melt upon impact. Assume that there is no air resistance and that all the energy goes into melting the ice. [Hint: Equate the joules of gravitational potential energy to the product of the mass of ice and its heat of fusion (in SI units, 335,000 J/kg). Do you see why the answer doesn't depend on mass?]
3. The specific heat capacity of ice is about 0.5 cal/g·°C. Supposing that it remains at that value all the way to absolute zero, calculate the number of calories it

would take to change a 1-gram ice cube at absolute zero (−273°C) to 1 gram of boiling water. How does this number of calories compare with the number of calories required to change the same gram of 100°C boiling water to 100°C steam?

4. Find the mass of 0°C ice that 10 g of 100°C steam will melt completely.
5. If 50 grams of hot water at 80°C is poured into a cavity in a very large block of ice at 0°C, what will be the final temperature of the water in the cavity? How much ice must melt in order to cool the hot water down to this temperature?
6. A 50-gram chunk of 80°C iron is dropped into a cavity in a very large block of ice at 0°C. How many grams of ice will melt? (The specific heat capacity of iron is 0.11 cal/g·°C.)
7. The heat of vaporization of ethyl alcohol is about 200 cal/g. If 2 kg of it were allowed to vaporize in a refrigerator, how many grams of ice would be formed from 0°C water?

Chapter 8 Online Resources

Videos

- The Secret to Walking on Hot Coals
- Air Is a Poor Conductor
- Condensation Is a Warming Process
- Boiling Is a Cooling Process
- Pressure Cooker & Boiling & Freezing at the Same Time

Quiz
Exercises
Flashcards
Links

CHAPTER 9
Static and Current Electricity

Electricity underlies just about everything around us. It's in the lightning from the sky, it's in the spark when we strike a match, and it's what holds atoms together to form molecules. The control of electricity is evident in technological devices of many kinds, from lamps to computers. An understanding of electricity requires a step-by-step approach, for one concept is the building block for the next. So please put in extra care in the study of this material. It can be difficult, confusing, and frustrating if you're hasty; but, with careful effort, it can be comprehensible and rewarding. We start with static electricity, electricity at rest, and complete the chapter with current electricity. Let's begin.

9.1 Electric Force and Charge

What if there were a universal force that, like gravity, varies inversely as the square of the distance but that is billions upon billions of times stronger. If there were such a force, and if it were an attractive force like gravity, the universe would be pulled together into a tight ball with all matter pulled as close together as physically possible. But suppose this force were a repelling force, with every bit of matter repelling every other bit of matter. What then? The universe would be an ever-expanding gaseous cloud. Suppose, however, that the universe consisted of two kinds of particles—say, positive and negative. Suppose positives repelled positives but attracted negatives, and that negatives repelled negatives but attracted positives. Like kinds repel and unlike kinds attract (Figure 9.1). Further, suppose there were equal numbers of each so that this strong force was perfectly balanced. What would the universe be like? The answer is simple: it would be like the one we are living in. For there *are* such particles and there *is* such a force. We call it *electrical force.*

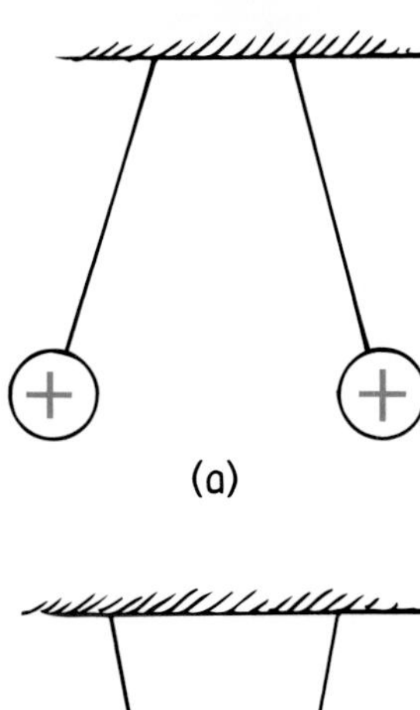

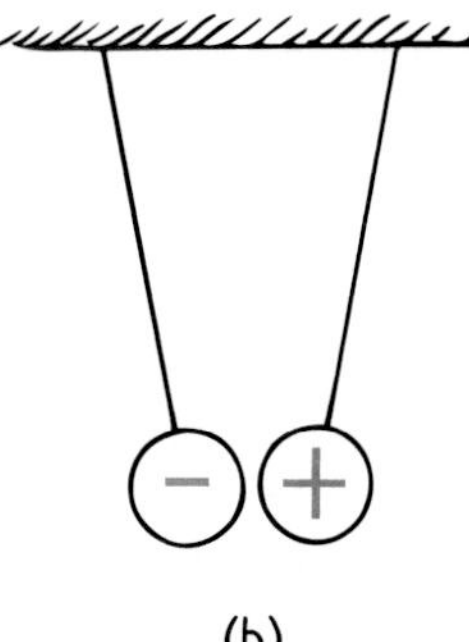

Figure 9.1
(a) Like charges repel.
(b) Unlike charges attract.

The terms *positive* and *negative* refer to electric *charge,* the fundamental quantity that underlies all electrical phenomena. The positively charged particles in ordinary matter are protons, and the negatively charged particles are electrons. The attractive force between these particles causes them to clump together into incredibly small units—atoms. (Atoms also contain neutral particles called *neutrons.*) More interesting details about atoms are presented in Part 2. In order to understand the basic principles of electricity, however, we preview some fundamental facts about atoms:

1. Every atom is composed of a positively charged nucleus surrounded by negatively charged electrons.
2. Each of the electrons in any atom has the same quantity of negative charge and the same mass. Electrons are identical to one another.

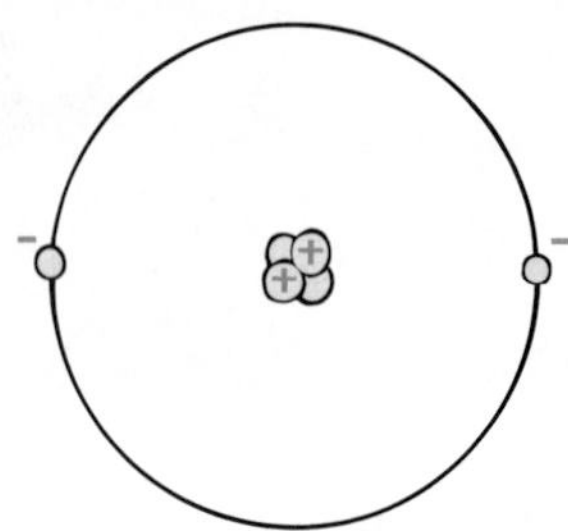

Figure 9.2
Model of a helium atom. The atomic nucleus is made up of two protons and two neutrons. The positively charged protons attract two negatively charged electrons. What is the net charge of this atom?

3. Protons and neutrons compose the nucleus. (The most common form of hydrogen atom, which has no neutrons, is the only exception.) Protons are about 1800 times more massive than electrons, but each one carries an amount of positive charge equal to the negative charge of electrons. Neutrons have slightly more mass than protons and have no net charge.

Normally, an atom has as many electrons as protons. When an atom loses one or more electrons, it has a positive net charge, and when it gains one or more electrons, it has a negative net charge. A charged atom is called an *ion.* A *positive ion* has a net positive charge. A *negative ion,* with one or more extra electrons, has a net negative charge.

Material objects are made of atoms, which means they are composed of electrons and protons (and neutrons as well). Although the innermost electrons in an atom are attracted very strongly to the oppositely charged atomic nucleus, the outermost electrons of many atoms are attracted more loosely and can easily be dislodged. The amount of work required to tear an electron away from an atom varies for different substances. Electrons are held more firmly in rubber or plastic than in your hair, for example. Thus, when you rub a comb against your hair, electrons transfer from the hair to the comb. The comb then has an excess of electrons and is said to be *negatively charged.* Your hair, in turn, has a deficiency of electrons and is said to be positively charged. If you rub a glass or plastic rod with silk, you'll find that the rod becomes positively charged. The silk has a greater affinity for electrons than the glass or plastic rod. Electrons are rubbed off the rod and onto the silk.

So protons attract electrons and we have atoms. Electrons repel electrons and we have matter—because atoms don't mesh into one another. This pair of rules is the guts of electricity.

Negative and *Positive* are just the **names** given to opposite charges. The names chosen could just as well have been "east and west," or "up and down," or "Mary and Larry."

Insights

Figure 9.3
Electrons are transferred from the fur to the rod. The rod is then negatively charged. Is the fur charged? By how much, compared with the rod? Positively or negatively?

Electronics Technology and Sparks

Electric charge can be dangerous. Two hundred years ago, young boys called *powder monkeys* ran barefooted below the decks of warships to bring sacks of black gunpowder to the cannons above. It was ship law that this task be done barefoot. Why? Because it was important that no static charge build up on the powder on their bodies as they ran to and fro. Bare feet scuffed the decks much less than shoes and assured no charge accumulation that might produce an igniting spark and an explosion.

Static charge is a danger in many industries today—not because of explosions, but because delicate electronic circuits may be destroyed by static charges. Some circuit components are sensitive enough to be "fried" by sparks of static electricity. Electronics technicians frequently wear clothing of special fabrics with ground wires between their sleeves and their socks. Some wear special wristbands that are connected to a grounded surface so that static charges will not build up—when moving a chair, for example. The smaller the electronic circuit, the more hazardous are sparks that may short-circuit the circuit elements.

Conservation of Charge

Another basic rule is that, whenever something is charged, no electrons are created or destroyed. Electrons are simply transferred from one material to another. Charge is conserved. In every event, whether large scale or at the atomic and nuclear level, the principle of *conservation of charge* has always been found to apply. No case of the creation or destruction of net electric charge has ever been found. The conservation of charge ranks with the conservation of energy and momentum as a significant fundamental principle in physics.

Figure 9.4
Why will you get a slight shock from the doorknob after scuffing across the carpet?

☑ CHECKPOINT

If you walk across a rug and scuff electrons from your feet, are you negatively or positively charged?

Check Your Answer

You have fewer electrons after you scuff your feet, so you are positively charged (and the rug is negatively charged).

Ionized Bracelets: Science or Pseudoscience?

Surveys indicate that the vast majority of Americans today believe ionized bracelets can reduce joint or muscle pain. Manufacturers make the claim that ionized bracelets relieve such pain. Are they correct? In 2002, the claim was put to a test by researchers at Mayo Clinic in Jacksonville, Florida, who randomly assigned 305 participants to wear an ionized bracelet for 28 days and another 305 participants to wear a placebo bracelet for the same duration. The study volunteers were men and women 18 and older who had self-reported musculoskeletal pain at the beginning of the study.

Neither the researchers nor the participants knew which volunteers wore an ionized bracelet and which wore a placebo bracelet. Both types of bracelets were identical, were supplied by the manufacturer, and were worn according to the manufacturer's recommendations. Interestingly, *both* groups reported significant relief from pain. No difference was found in the amount of self-reported pain relief between the group wearing the ionized bracelets and the group wearing the placebo bracelets. Apparently, just believing that the bracelet relieves pain does the trick!

Interestingly, the brain initiates the creation of endorphins (which bind to opiate receptor sites) when the person expects to get relief from pain. The placebo effect is very real and measurable via blood titrations. So there's some merit in the old adage that wishing hard for something will make it come true. But this has nothing to do with the physics, chemistry, or biological interaction with the bracelet. Hence, ionized bracelets join the ranks of pseudoscientific devices.

In any society that thrives more on capturing attention than on informing, pseudoscience is big business.

9.2 Coulomb's Law

The electrical force, like gravitational force, decreases inversely as the square of the distance between charges. This relationship, which was discovered by Charles Coulomb in the eighteenth century, is called **Coulomb's law.** It states that, for two charged objects that are much smaller than the distance between them, the force between them varies directly as the product of their charges and inversely as the square of the separation distance. The force acts along a straight line from one charge to the other. Coulomb's law can be expressed as

$$F = k\frac{q_1 q_2}{d^2}$$

where d is the distance between the charged particles, q_1 represents the quantity of charge of one particle, q_2 represents the quantity of charge of the second particle, and k is the proportionality constant.

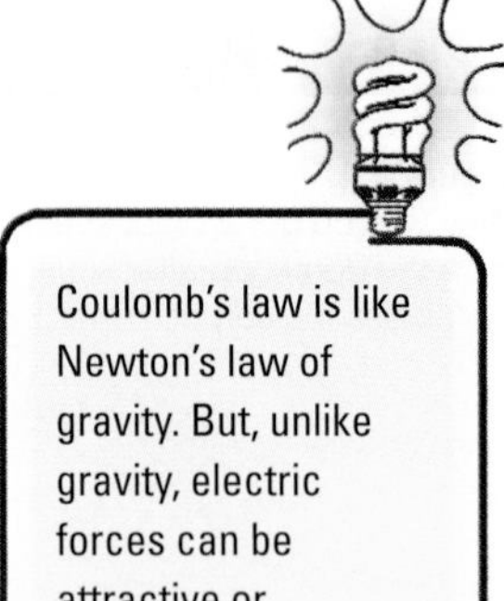

Coulomb's law is like Newton's law of gravity. But, unlike gravity, electric forces can be attractive or repulsive.

Insights

The unit of charge is called the **coulomb,** abbreviated C. It turns out that a charge of 1C is the charge associated with 6.25 billion billion electrons. This might seem like a great number of electrons, but it only represents the amount of charge that flows through a common 100-watt light bulb in a little more than a second.

The proportionality constant k in Coulomb's law is similar to G in Newton's law of gravity. Instead of being a very small number, like G, k is a very large number, approximately

$$k = 9{,}000{,}000{,}000 \text{ N}\cdot\text{m}^2/\text{C}^2$$

In scientific notation, $k = 9.0 \times 10^9 \text{ N}\cdot\text{m}^2/\text{C}^2$. The unit $\text{N}\cdot\text{m}^2/\text{C}^2$ is not central to our interest here; it simply converts the right-hand side of the equation to the unit of force, the newton (N). What is important is the large magnitude of k. If, for example, a pair of like charges of 1 coulomb each were 1 meter apart, the force of repulsion between the two would be 9 billion newtons.* That would be about ten times the weight of a battleship! Obviously, such quantities of net charge do not usually exist in our everyday environment.

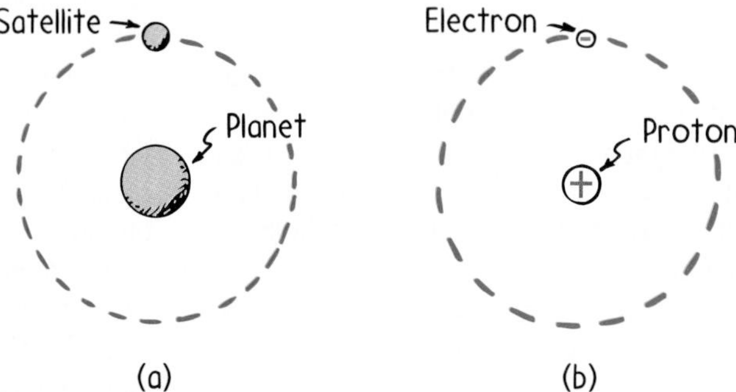

Figure 9.5
(a) A gravitational force holds the satellite in orbit about the planet, and (b), an electrical force holds the electron in orbit about the proton. In both cases, there is no contact between the bodies. We say that the orbiting bodies interact with the *force fields* of the planet and proton and are everywhere in contact with these fields. Thus, the force that one electric charge exerts on another can be described as the interaction between one charge and the field set up by the other.

*Contrast this to the gravitational force of attraction between two 1-kg masses 1 m apart: 6.67×10^{-11} N. This is an extremely small force. For the force to be 1 N, the masses at 1 m apart would have to be nearly 123,000 kg each! Gravitational forces between ordinary objects are exceedingly small, and differences in electrical forces between ordinary objects can be exceedingly huge. We don't sense them because the positives and negatives normally balance out, and, even for highly charged objects, the imbalance of electrons to protons is normally less than one part in a trillion trillion.

So Newton's law of gravitation for masses is similar to Coulomb's law for electrically charged bodies. The most important difference between gravitational and electrical forces is that electrical forces may be either attractive or repulsive, whereas gravitational forces are only attractive. Coulomb's law underlies the bonding forces between molecules that will be covered in our discussion of chemistry (Part 2).

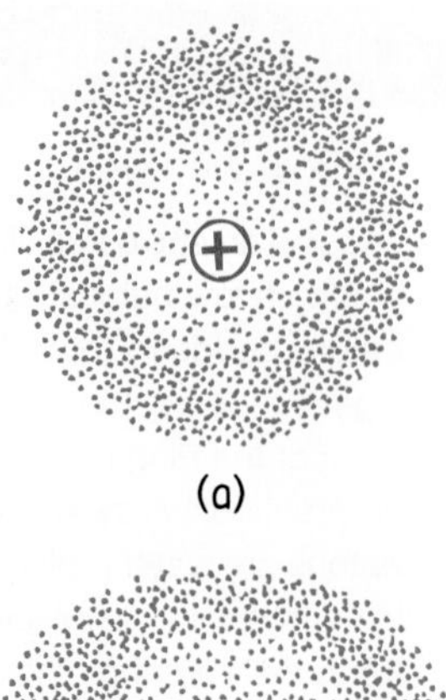

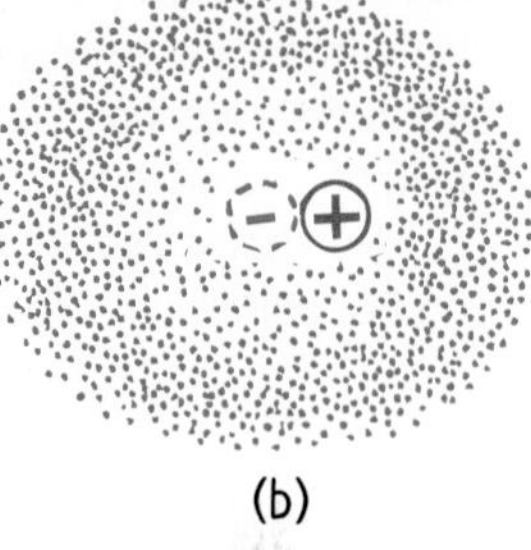

Figure 9.6
(a) The center of the negative "cloud" of electrons coincides with the center of the positive nucleus in an atom. (b) When an external negative charge is brought nearby to the right, as on a charged balloon, the electron cloud is distorted so that the centers of negative and positive charge no longer coincide. The atom is electrically polarized.

☑ CHECKPOINT

1. The proton is the nucleus of the hydrogen atom, and it attracts the electron that orbits it. Relative to this force, does the electron attract the proton with less force, more force, or the same amount of force?
2. If a proton at a particular distance from a charged particle is repelled with a given force, by how much will the force decrease when the proton is three times as distant from the particle? Five times as distant?
3. What is the sign of charge of the particle in this case?

Check Your Answers

1. The same amount of force, in accord with Newton's third law—basic mechanics! Recall that a force is an interaction between two things—in this case, between the proton and the electron. They pull on each other equally.
2. In accord with the inverse-square law, it decreases to $\frac{1}{9}$ its original value. To $\frac{1}{25}$ of its original value.
3. Positive.

Charge Polarization

If you charge an inflated balloon by rubbing it on your hair and then place the balloon against a wall, it sticks. This is because the charge on the balloon alters the charge distribution in the atoms or molecules in the wall, effectively inducing an opposite charge on the wall. The molecules cannot move from their relatively stationary positions, but their "centers of charge" are moved. The positive part of the atom or molecule is attracted toward the balloon while the negative part is repelled. This has the effect of distorting the atom or molecule (Figure 9.6). The atom or molecule is said to be *electrically polarized.* (We will treat electrical polarization further in Chapter 19.)

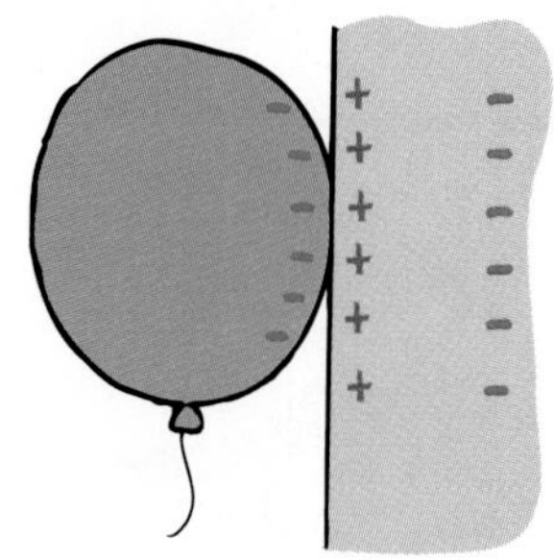

Figure 9.7
The negatively charged balloon polarizes molecules in the wooden wall and creates a positively charged surface, so the balloon sticks to the wall.

☑ CHECKPOINT

You know that a balloon rubbed on your hair will stick to a wall. In a humorous vein, does it follow that your oppositely charged head would also stick to the wall?

Check Your Answer

No, unless you're an airhead (having a head mass about the same as that of an air-filled balloon). The force that holds a balloon to the wall cannot support your heavier head.

Link to Technology

Microwave Oven

Imagine an enclosure filled with Ping Pong balls among a few batons, all at rest. Now imagine that the batons suddenly rotate backward and forward, striking neighboring Ping Pong balls. Almost immediately, most of the Ping Pong balls are energized, vibrating in all directions. A microwave oven works similarly. The batons are water molecules made to rotate to and fro in rhythm with microwaves in the enclosure. The Ping Pong balls are the other molecules that make up the bulk of material being cooked.

H_2O molecules are polar, with opposite charges on opposite sides. When an electric field is imposed on them, they align with the field like a compass needle aligns with a magnetic field. When the field is made to oscillate, the H_2O molecules oscillate also—and quite energetically when the frequency of the waves matches the natural rotational frequency of the H_2O. So food is cooked by converting H_2O molecules into flip-flopping energy sources that impart thermal motion to surrounding food molecules. Without polar molecules in the food, a microwave oven wouldn't work. That's why microwaves pass through foam, paper, or ceramic plates with no effect.

9.3 Electric Field

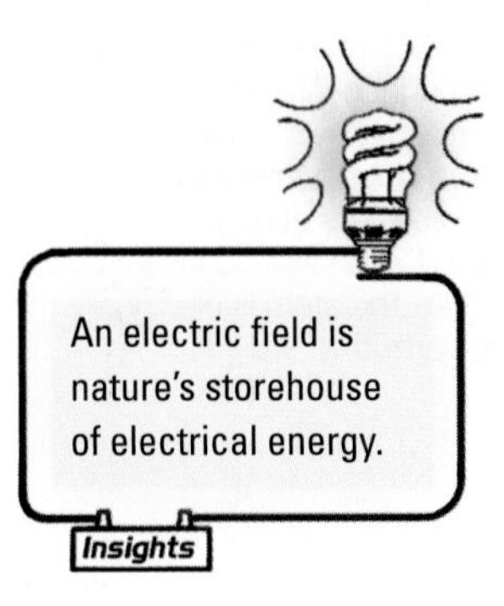

Electrical forces, like gravitational forces, can act between things that are not in contact with each other. Both for electricity and gravity, a *force field* exists that influences distant charges and masses, respectively. Before treating the electric field, we'll first consider the gravitational field (briefly discussed in Chapter 4). The properties of space surrounding any mass are altered such that another mass introduced to this region experiences a force. This "alteration in space" is called its *gravitational field.* We can think of any other mass as interacting with the field and not directly with the mass that produces it. For example, when an apple falls from a tree, we say it is interacting with the mass of the earth, but we can also think of the apple as interacting with the gravitational field of the earth. The field plays an intermediate role in the force between bodies. It is common to think of distant rockets and the like as interacting with gravitational fields rather than with the masses of the earth or other bodies responsible for the fields. Just as the space around a planet and every other mass is filled with a gravitational field, the space around every electric charge is filled with an **electric field**—an energetic aura that extends through space.*

If you place a charged particle in an electric field, it will experience a force. The direction of the force on a positive charge is the same direction as the field. The electric field about a proton extends radially from the proton. About an electron, the field is in the opposite direction (Figure 9.8). As with electric force, the electric field about a particle obeys the inverse-square law. Some electric field configurations are shown in Figure 9.9, and photographs of field patterns are shown in Figure 9.10. In the next chapter, we'll see how bits of iron similarly align with magnetic fields.

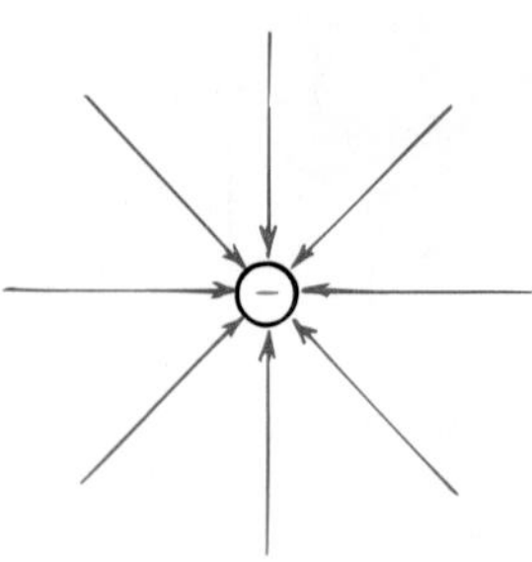

Figure 9.8
Electric field representations about a negative charge.

*An electric field is a vector quantity, having both magnitude and direction. The magnitude of the field at any point is simply the force per unit of charge. If a charge q experiences a force F at some point in space, then the electric field E at that point is

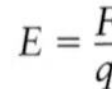

$$E = \frac{F}{q}$$

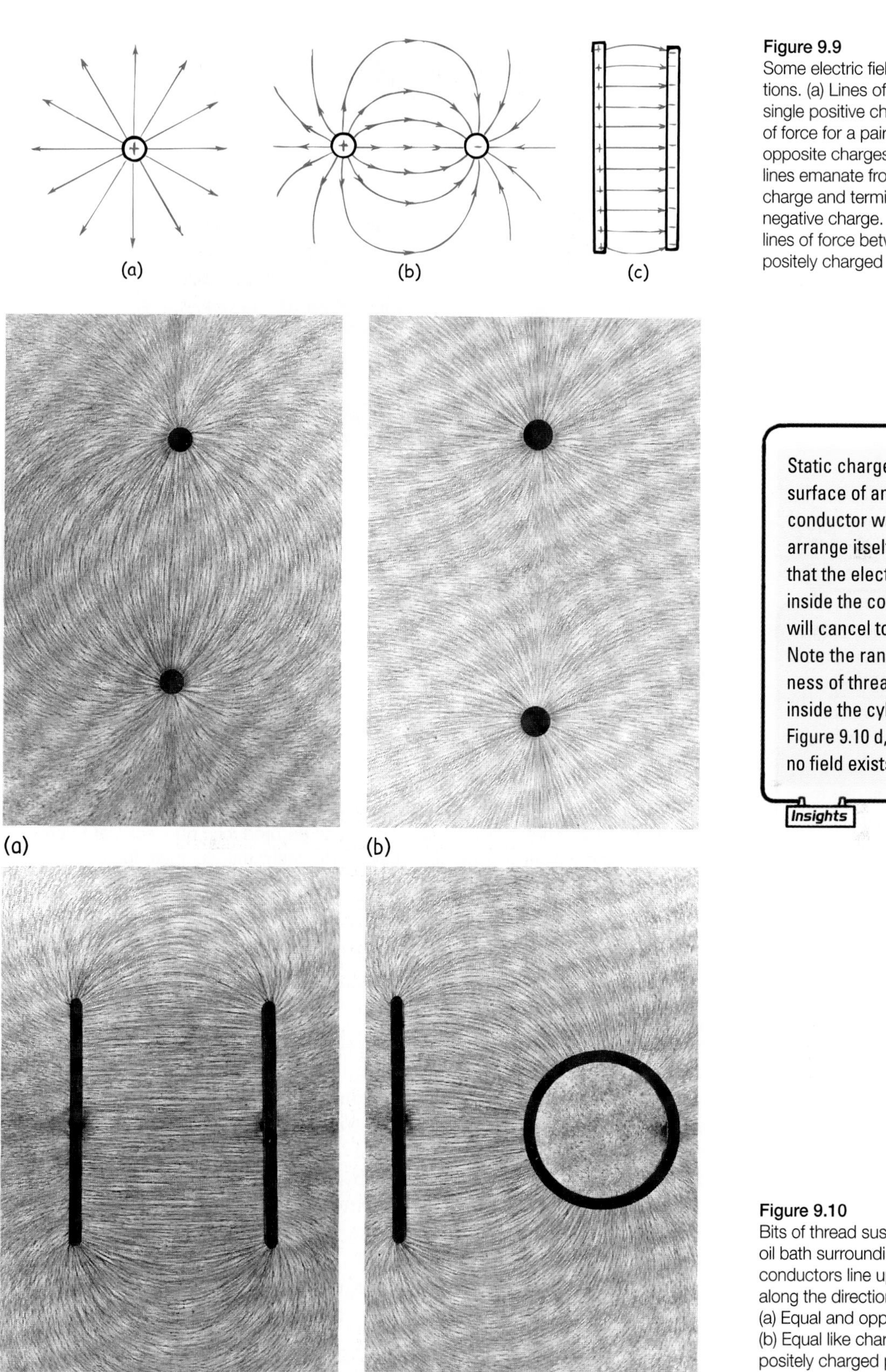

Figure 9.9
Some electric field configurations. (a) Lines of force about a single positive charge. (b) Lines of force for a pair of equal but opposite charges. Note that the lines emanate from the positive charge and terminate on the negative charge. (c) Uniform lines of force between two oppositely charged parallel plates.

Static charge on the surface of any conductor will arrange itself such that the electric field inside the conductor will cancel to zero. Note the randomness of threads inside the cylinder of Figure 9.10 d, where no field exists.

Insights

Figure 9.10
Bits of thread suspended in an oil bath surrounding charged conductors line up end-to-end along the direction of the field. (a) Equal and opposite charges. (b) Equal like charges. (c) Oppositely charged plates. (d) Oppositely charged cylinder and plate.

Figure 9.11
Both Meidor and the spherical dome of the Van de Graaff generator are electrically charged.

Perhaps your instructor will demonstrate the effects of the electric field that surrounds the charged dome of a Van de Graaff generator (Figure 9.11). Charged objects in the field of the dome are either attracted or repelled, depending on their sign of charge.

Whatever the intensity of the electric field about the charged van de Graaff generator, the electric field inside the dome cancels to zero. This is true for the interiors of all conductors carrying static charge.

Insights

☑ CHECKPOINT

Both the young woman and the dome of the Van de Graaff generator in Figure 9.11 are charged. Why does her hair stand out?

Check Your Answer

Meidor and her hair are charged. Each hair is repelled by others around it—evidence that *like charges repel.* Even a small charge produces an electrical force greater than the weight of strands of hair. Fortunately, the electrical force is not great enough to make her arms stand out!

9.4 Electric Potential

In our study of energy in Chapter 3, we learned that an object has gravitational potential energy because of its location in a gravitational field. Similarly, a charged object has potential energy by virtue of its location in an electric field. Just as work is required to lift a massive object against the gravitational field of the earth, work is required to push a charged particle against the electric field of a charged body. This work changes the electric potential energy of the charged particle.* Similarly, work done in compressing a spring increases the potential energy of the spring (Figure 9.13a). Likewise, the work done in pushing a charged particle closer to the charged sphere in Figure 9.13b increases the

*This work is positive if it increases the electric potential energy of the charged particle and negative if it decreases it.

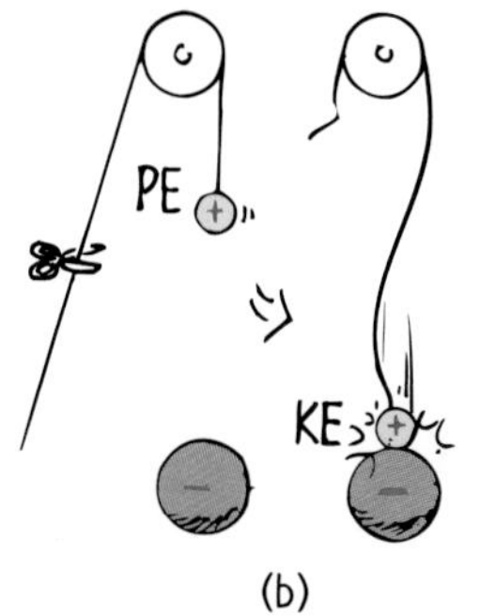

Figure 9.12
(a) The PE (gravitational potential energy) of a mass held in a gravitational field. (b) The PE of a charged particle held in an electric field. When the mass and particle are released, how does the KE (kinetic energy) acquired by each compare with the decrease in PE?

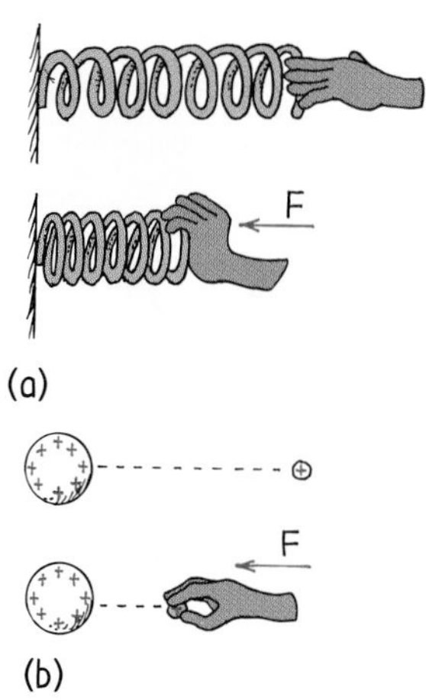

Figure 9.13
(a) The spring has more elastic PE when compressed. (b) The small charge similarly has more PE when pushed closer to the charged sphere. In both cases, the increased PE is the result of work input.

potential energy of the charged particle. We call the energy possessed by the charged particle that is due to its location **electric potential energy.** If the particle is released, it accelerates in a direction away from the sphere, and its electric potential energy changes to kinetic energy.

If we push a particle with twice the charge, we do twice as much work. Twice the charge in the same location has twice the electric potential energy; with three times the charge, there is three times as much potential energy; and so on. When working with electricity, rather than dealing with the total potential energy of a charged body, it is convenient to consider the electric potential energy *per charge.* We simply divide the amount of energy in any case by the amount of charge. The concept of potential energy per charge is called **electric potential;** that is,

$$\text{Electric potential} = \frac{\text{electric potential energy}}{\text{amount of charge}}$$

The unit of measurement for electric potential is the volt, so electric potential is often called *voltage.* A potential of 1 volt (V) equals 1 joule (J) of energy per 1 coulomb (C) of charge.

$$1 \text{ volt} = \frac{1 \text{ joule}}{\text{coulomb}}$$

In a nutshell: *Electric potential* and *potential* mean the same thing—*electrical potential energy per unit charge*—in units of volts. On the other hand, *potential difference* is the same as *voltage*—the difference in electrical potential between two points in a conducting path—in units of volts.

Insights

Thus, a 1.5-volt battery gives 1.5 joules of energy to every 1 coulomb of charge flowing through the battery. *Electric potential* and *voltage* are the same thing, and they are commonly used interchangeably.

The significance of voltage is that a definite value for it can be assigned to a location. We can speak about the voltages at different locations in an electric field whether or not charges occupy those locations. The same is true of voltages at various locations in an electric circuit. Later in this chapter, we will see that the location of the positive terminal of a 12-volt battery is maintained at a voltage 12 volts higher

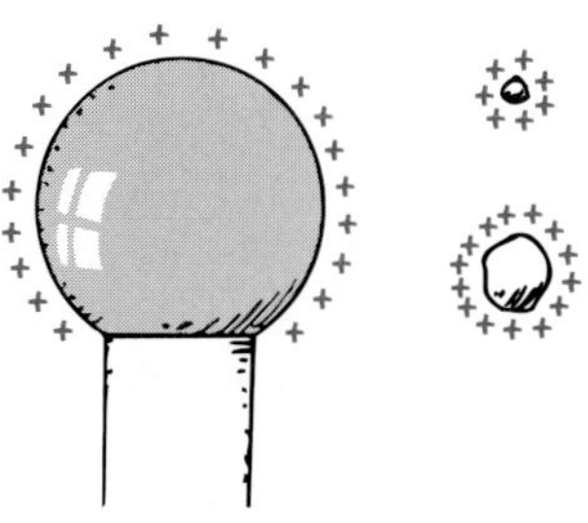

Figure 9.14
The larger test charge has more PE in the field of the charged dome, but the *electric potential* of any amount of charge at the same location is the same.

Figure 9.15
Although the voltage of the charged balloon is high, the electric potential energy is low because of the small amount of charge.

than the location of the negative terminal. When a conducting medium connects this voltage difference, any charges in the medium will move between these locations.

☑ CHECKPOINT

1. If there were twice as many coulombs in the test charge near the charged sphere in Figure 9.14, would the *electric potential energy* of the test charge relative to the charged sphere be the same, or would it be twice as great? Would the *electric potential* of the test charge be the same, or would it be twice as great?
2. What does it mean to say that your car has a 12-volt battery?

Check Your Answers

1. The result of twice as many coulombs is twice as much *electric potential energy* because it takes twice as much work to put the charge there. But the *electric potential* would be the same. Twice the energy divided by twice the charge gives the same potential as one unit of energy divided by one unit of charge. Electric potential is not the same thing as electric potential energy. Be sure you understand this before you study further.
2. It means that one of the battery terminals is 12 V higher in potential than the other one. Soon we'll see that it also means that, when a circuit is connected between these terminals, each coulomb of charge in the resulting current will be given 12 J of energy as it passes through the battery (and 12 J of energy "spent" in the circuit).

High voltage at low energy is very similar to the harmless high-temperature sparks emitted by a Fourth-of-July sparkler. Temperature, the ratio of energy/molecule, means a lot of energy only if a lot of molecules are involved. High voltage means a lot of energy only if a lot of charge is involved.

Insights

Rub a balloon on your hair, and the balloon becomes negatively charged—perhaps to several thousand volts! That would be several thousand joules of energy, if the charge were 1 coulomb. However, 1 coulomb is a fairly respectable amount of charge. The charge on a balloon rubbed on hair is typically much less than a millionth of a coulomb. Therefore, the amount of energy associated with the charged balloon is very, very small. A high voltage means a lot of energy only if a lot of charge is involved. Electrical potential energy differs from electric potential (or voltage).

Figure 9.16
Although the Wimshurst machine can generate thousands of volts, it puts out no more energy than the work that Jim Stith puts into it by cranking the handle.

9.5 Voltage Sources

When the ends of a heat conductor are at different temperatures, heat energy flows from the higher temperature to the lower temperature. The flow ceases when both ends reach the same temperature. Similarly, when the ends of an electrical conductor are at different electric potentials—when there is a **potential difference**—charges in the conductor flow from the higher potential to the lower potential. The flow of charge persists until both ends reach the same potential. Without a potential difference, no flow of charge will occur.

To attain a sustained flow of charge in a conductor, some arrangement must be provided to maintain a difference in potential while charge flows from one end to the other. The situation is analogous to the flow of water from a higher reservoir to a lower one (Figure 9.17a). Water will flow in a pipe that connects the reservoirs only as long as a difference in water level exists. The flow of water in the pipe, like the flow of charge in a wire, will cease when the pressures at each end are equal. (We imply this phenomenon when we say that water seeks its own level.) A continuous flow is possible if the difference in water levels—hence the difference in water pressures—is maintained with the use of a suitable pump (Figure 9.17b).

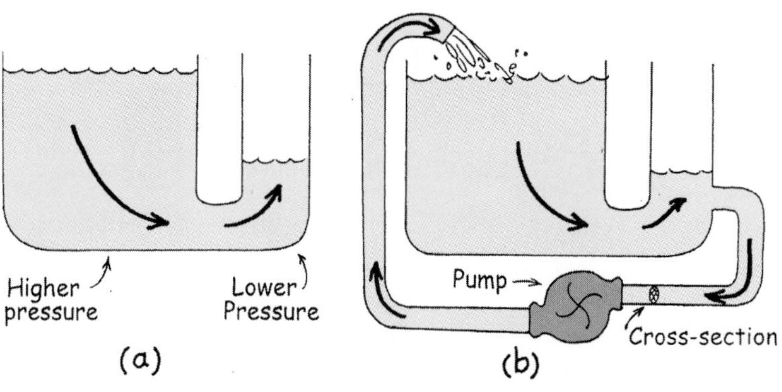

Figure 9.17
(a) Water flows from the reservoir of higher pressure to the reservoir of lower pressure. The flow will cease when the difference in pressure ceases. (b) Water continues to flow because a difference in pressure is maintained with the pump.

Figure 9.18
An unusual source of voltage. The electric potential between the head and tail of the electric eel *(Electrophorus electricus)* can be up to 650 V.

A sustained electric current requires a suitable pumping device to maintain a difference in electric potential—to maintain a voltage. Chemical batteries or generators are "electrical pumps" that can maintain a steady flow of charge. These devices do work to pull negative charges apart from positive ones. In chemical batteries, this work is done by the chemical disintegration of zinc or lead in acid, and the energy stored in the chemical bonds is converted to electric potential energy. (The chemical nature of batteries is described in Chapter 23.)

Generators separate charge by electromagnetic induction, a process we will describe in the next chapter. The work that is done (by whatever means) in separating the opposite charges is available at the terminals of the battery or generator. This energy per charge provides the difference in potential (voltage) that

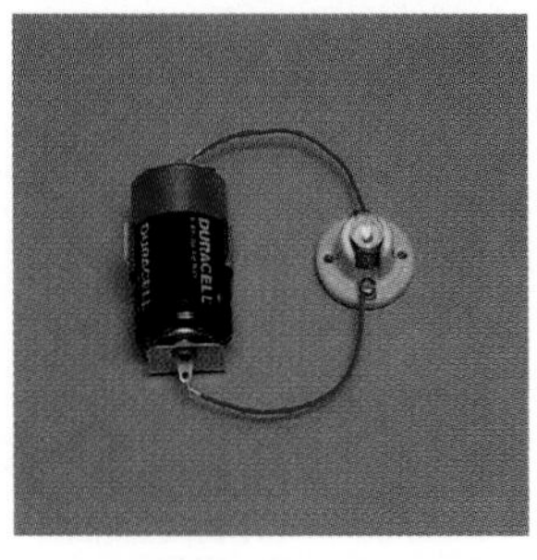

Figure 9.19
Each coulomb of charge that is made to flow in a circuit that connects the ends of this 1.5-V flashlight cell is energized with 1.5 J.

provides the "electrical pressure" to move electrons through a circuit joined to those terminals.

A common automobile battery will provide an electrical pressure of 12 volts to a circuit connected across its terminals. Then 12 joules of energy are supplied to each coulomb of charge that is made to flow in the circuit.

9.6 Electric Current

Just as a water current is a flow of H_2O molecules, **electric current** is a flow of charged particles. In circuits of metal wires, electrons make up the flow of charge. In metals, one or more electrons from each atom are free to move throughout the atomic lattice. These charge carriers are called *conduction electrons*. Protons, on the other hand, do not move because they are bound within the nuclei of atoms that are more or less locked in fixed positions. In fluids, however, positive ions as well as electrons may compose the flow of an electric charge.

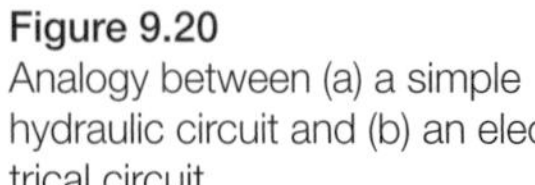

Figure 9.20
Analogy between (a) a simple hydraulic circuit and (b) an electrical circuit.

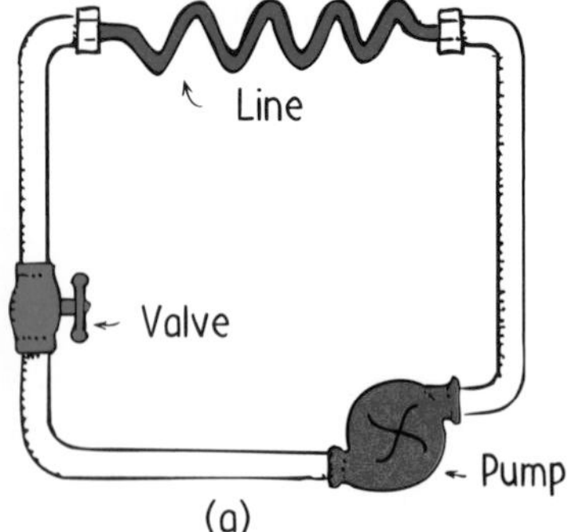

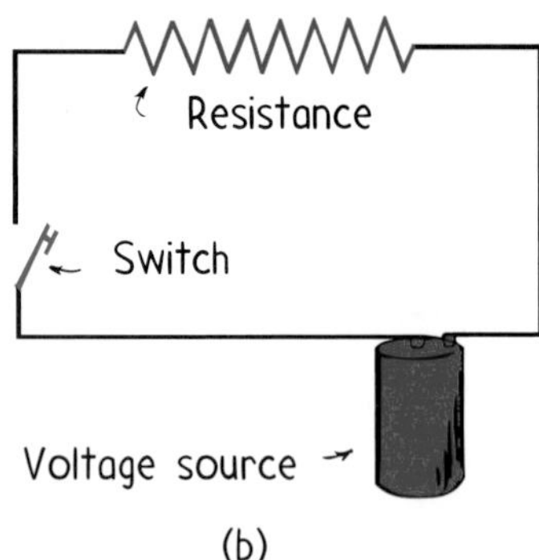

Much effort is expended in building particle accelerators that accelerate electrons to speeds approaching the speed of light. If electrons in a common circuit were to travel that fast, one would only have to bend a wire at a sharp angle to cause those high-momentum electrons to fail to make the turn and to fly off into the air. There'd be no need for accelerators! In fact, electrons in circuits move fairly slowly.

An important difference between water flow and electron flow has to do with their conductors. If you purchase a water pipe at a hardware store, the clerk doesn't sell you the water to flow through it. You provide that yourself. By contrast, when you buy "an electron pipe," an electric wire, you also get the electrons. Every bit of matter, wires included, contains enormous numbers of electrons that swarm about in random directions. When a source of voltage sets them moving, we have an electric current.

The *rate* of electrical flow is measured in **amperes.** An ampere is the rate of flow of 1 coulomb of charge per second. (That's a flow of 6.25 billion billion electrons per second.) In a wire that carries 4 amperes to a car headlight bulb, for example, 4 coulombs of charge flow past any cross section in the wire each second. In a wire that carries 8 amperes, twice as many coulombs flow past any cross section each second.

It is interesting to note that the speed of electrons as they drift through a wire is surprisingly slow. This is because electrons continually bump into atoms in the wire. The net speed, or *drift speed,* of electrons in a typical circuit is much less than one centimeter per second. The electric signal, however, travels at nearly the speed of light. That's the speed at which the electric *field* in the wire is established.

Figure 9.21
The electric field lines between the terminals of a battery are directed through a conductor, which joins the terminals. A thick metal wire is shown here, but the path from one terminal to the other is usually an electric circuit. (If you touch this conducting wire, you won't be shocked, but the wire will heat quickly and may burn your hand!)

Also interesting is that a current-carrying wire is not electrically charged. Under ordinary conditions, there are as many conduction electrons swarming through the atomic lattice as there are positively charged atomic nuclei. The numbers of electrons and protons balance, so, whether a wire carries a current or not, the net charge of the wire is normally zero at every moment.

There is often some confusion between charge flowing *through* a circuit and voltage placed, or impressed, *across* a circuit. We can distinguish between these ideas by considering a long pipe filled with water. Water will flow through the pipe if there is a difference in pressure across (or between) its ends. Water flows from the high-pressure end to the low-pressure end. Only the water flows, not the pressure. Similarly, electric charge flows because of the differences in electrical pressure (voltage). You say that *charges* flow through a circuit because of an applied voltage across the circuit. You don't say that *voltage* flows through a circuit. Voltage doesn't go anywhere, for it is the charges that move. Voltage produces current (if there is a complete circuit).

We often think of current flowing through a circuit; but don't say this around somebody who is picky about grammar, because the expression "current flows" is redundant. More properly, charge flows—which *is* current.

Insights

Direct Current and Alternating Current

Electric current may be DC or AC. By DC, we mean **direct current,** which refers to charges flowing in one direction. A battery produces direct current in a circuit because the terminals of the battery always have the same sign. Electrons move from the repelling negative terminal toward the attracting positive terminal, and they always move through the circuit in the same direction.

Alternating current (AC) acts as the name implies. Electrons in the circuit are moved first in one direction and then in the opposite direction, alternating to and fro about relatively fixed positions. This is accomplished in a generator or alternator by periodically switching the sign at the terminals. Nearly all commercial AC circuits involve currents that alternate back and forth at a frequency of 60 cycles per second. This is 60-hertz current (one cycle per second is called a *hertz*). In some countries, 25-hertz, 30-hertz, or

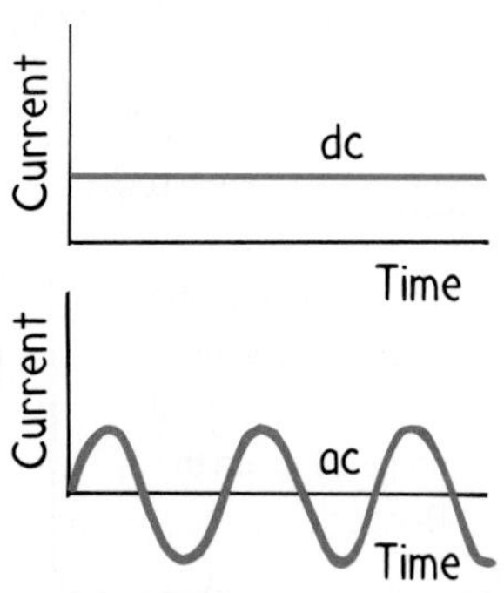

Figure 9.22
Time graphs of DC and AC.

History of 110 Volts

In the early days of electrical lighting, high voltages burned out electric light filaments, so low voltages were more practical. The hundreds of power plants built in the United States prior to 1900 adopted 110 volts (or 115 or 120 volts) as their standard. The tradition of 110 volts was decided upon because it made the bulbs of the day glow as brightly as a gas lamp. By the time electrical lighting became popular in Europe, engineers had figured out how to make light bulbs that would not burn out so fast at higher voltages. Power transmission is more efficient at higher voltages, so Europe adopted 220 volts as their standard. The U.S. remained with 110 volts (today, it is officially 120 volts) because of the initial huge expense in the installation of 110-volt equipment.

In AC circuits, 120 volts is what is called the "root-mean-square" average of the voltage. The actual voltage in a 120-volt AC circuit varies between +170 volts and −170 volts, delivering the same power to an iron or to a toaster as a 120-volt DC circuit.

Insights

50-hertz current is used. Throughout the world, most residential and commercial circuits are AC because electric energy in the form of AC can easily be stepped up to high voltage to be transmitted great distances with small heat losses, then stepped down to convenient voltages where the energy is consumed. Why this occurs is quite fascinating, and it will be touched on in the next chapter.

9.7 Electrical Resistance

How much current is in a circuit depends not only on voltage but also on the **electrical resistance** of the circuit. Just as narrow pipes resist water flow more than wide pipes, thin wires resist electrical current more than thicker wires. And length contributes to resistance also. Just as long pipes have more resistance than short ones, long wires offer more electrical resistance. And most important is the material from which the wires were made. Copper has a low electrical resistance, while a strip of rubber has an enormous resistance. Temperature also affects electrical resistance. The greater the jostling of atoms within a conductor (the higher the temperature), the greater its resistance. The resistance of some materials reaches zero at very low temperatures. These materials are referred to as *superconductors.*

Electrical resistance is measured in units called *ohms.* The Greek letter *omega,* Ω, is commonly used as the symbol for the ohm. This unit was named after Georg Simon Ohm, a German physicist who, in 1826, discovered a simple and very important relationship among voltage, current, and resistance.

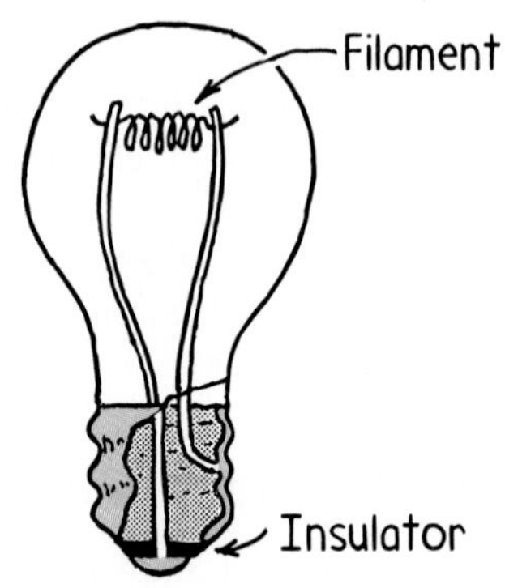

Figure 9.23
The conduction electrons that surge to and fro in the filament of the lamp do not come from the voltage source. They are in the filament to begin with. The voltage source simply provides them with surges of energy. When switched on, the resistance of the very thin tungsten filament heats up to 3000°C and roughly doubles its resistance.

The unit of electrical resistance is the ohm, Ω. Like the old song "Ω, Ω on the Range."

Insights

Superconductors

In common household wiring, flowing electrons collide with atomic nuclei in the wire and convert their kinetic energy to thermal energy in the wire. Early twentieth-century investigators discovered that certain metals in a bath of liquid helium at 4 K lost all electrical resistance. The electrons in these conductors traveled pathways that avoided atomic collisions, permitting them to flow indefinitely. These materials are called **superconductors,** having zero electrical resistance to the flow of charge. No current is lost and no heat is generated in superconductivity. For decades, it was generally thought that zero electrical resistance could occur only in certain metals near absolute zero. Then, in 1986, superconductivity was achieved at 30 K, which spurred hopes of finding superconductivity above 77 K, the point at which nitrogen liquefies. Nitrogen is easier to handle than liquid helium, which is needed for creating colder conditions. The historic leap came in the following year with a nonmetallic compound that lost its resistance at 90 K.

Various ceramic oxides have since been found to be superconducting at temperatures above 100 K. Once electric current is established in a superconductor, the current will flow indefinitely with no voltage source. Steady currents have been observed to persist for years in certain superconductors without apparent loss in energy. There is presently enormous interest in the physics community as to exactly why certain materials acquire superconducting properties. Superconductors are presently being vigorously researched. Explanations generally involve the wave nature of matter—quantum mechanics.

9.8 Ohm's Law

The relationship between voltage, current, and resistance is summarized by a statement called **Ohm's law.** Ohm discovered that the amount of current in a circuit is directly proportional to the voltage established across the circuit and is inversely proportional to the resistance of the circuit:

$$\text{Current} = \frac{\text{voltage}}{\text{resistance}}$$

Or, in units form,

$$\text{Amperes} = \frac{\text{volts}}{\text{ohms}}$$

So, for a given circuit of constant resistance, current and voltage are proportional to each other.* This means we'll get twice the current for twice the voltage. The greater the voltage, the greater the current. But, if the resistance is doubled for a circuit, the current will be half what it would have been otherwise. The greater the resistance, the smaller the current. Ohm's law makes good sense.

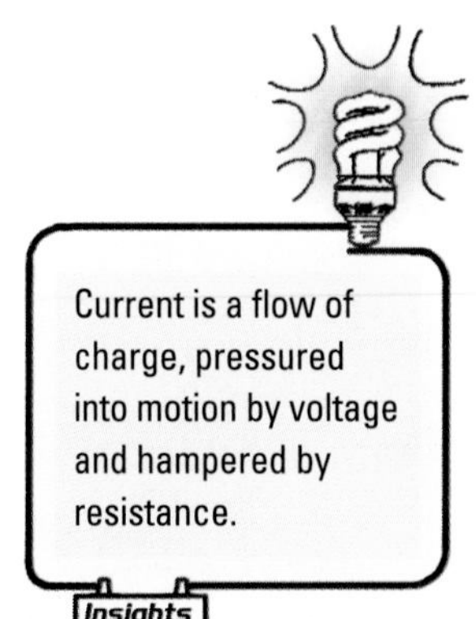

*Many texts use V to stand for voltage, I for current, and R for resistance, and express Ohm's law as $V = IR$. It then follows that $I = V/R$, or $R = V/I$, so that, if any two variables are known, the third can be found. (The names of the units are often abbreviated: V for volts, A for amperes, and Ω (the capital Greek letter omega) for ohms.

Figuring Physical Science

Problems

1. How much current flows through a lamp with a resistance of 60 Ω when the voltage across the lamp is 12 V?

2. What is the resistance of a toaster that draws a current of 12 A when connected to a 120-V circuit?

Solutions

1. From Ohm's law: Current = voltage/resistance = 12 V/60 Ω = 0.2 A.

2. Rearranging Ohm's law:

$$\text{Resistance} = \frac{\text{voltage}}{\text{current}} = \frac{120\text{ V}}{12\text{ A}} = 10\ \Omega$$

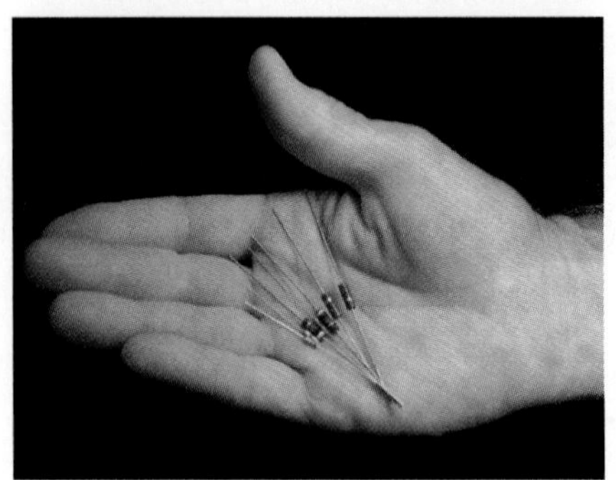

Figure 9.24
Resistors. The symbol of resistance in an electric circuit is -\/\/\/-.

The resistance of a typical lamp cord is much less than 1 ohm, and a typical light bulb has a resistance of more than 100 ohms. An iron or electric toaster has a resistance of 15 to 20 ohms. The current inside these and all other electrical devices is regulated by circuit elements called *resistors* (Figure 9.24), whose resistance may be a few ohms or millions of ohms. Resistors heat up when current flows through them, but for small currents the heating is slight.

Electric Shock

The damaging effects of shock are the result of current passing through the human body. What causes electric shock in the body—current or voltage? From Ohm's law, we can see that this current depends on the voltage that is applied and also on the electrical resistance of the human body. The resistance of one's body depends on its condition, and it ranges from about 100 ohms, if it is soaked with salt water, to about 500,000 ohms, if the skin is very dry. If we touch the two electrodes of a battery with dry fingers, completing the circuit from one hand to the other, we offer a resistance of about 100,000 ohms. We usually cannot feel 12 volts, and 24 volts just barely tingles. If our skin is moist, 24 volts can be quite uncomfortable. Table 9.1 describes the effects that different amounts of current have on the human body.

Table 9.1

Effect of Electric Currents on the Body

Current (A)	Effect
0.001	Can be felt
0.005	Is painful
0.010	Causes involuntary muscle contractions (spasms)
0.015	Causes loss of muscle control
0.070	Goes through the heart; causes serious disruption; probably fatal if current lasts for more than 1 s

Figuring Physical Science

Problems

1. At 100,000 Ω, how much current will flow through your body if you touch the terminals of a 12-V battery?
2. If your skin is very moist, so that your resistance is only 1000 Ω, and you touch the terminals of a 12-V battery, how much current do you receive?

Solutions

1. $\text{Current} = \frac{\text{voltage}}{\text{resistance}} = \frac{12\text{ V}}{100\,000\ \Omega} = 0.00012\text{ A}$
2. $\text{Current} = \frac{\text{voltage}}{\text{resistance}} = \frac{12\text{ V}}{1000\ \Omega} = 0.012\text{ A}$. Ouch!

To receive a shock, there must be a *difference* in electric potential between one part of your body and another part. Most of the current will pass along the path of least electrical resistance connecting these two points. Suppose you fell from a bridge and managed to grab onto a high-voltage power line, halting your fall. So long as you touch nothing else of different potential, you will receive no shock at all. Even if the wire is a few thousand volts above ground potential and you hang by it with two hands, no appreciable charge will flow from one hand to the other. This is because there is no appreciable difference in electric potential between your hands. If, however, you reach over with one hand and grab onto a wire of different potential . . . *zap*! We have all seen birds perched on high-voltage wires. Every part of their bodies is at the same high potential as the wire, so they feel no ill effects.

Figure 9.25
The bird can stand harmlessly on one wire of high potential, but it had better not reach over and touch a neighboring wire! Why not?

Interestingly, the source of electrons in the current that shocks you is your own body. As in all conductors, the electrons are already there. It is the energy given to the electrons that you should be wary of. They are energized when a voltage difference exists across different parts of your body.

Figure 9.26
The third prong connects the body of the appliance directly to ground. Any charge that builds up on an appliance is therefore conducted to the ground.

Most electric plugs and sockets today are wired with three, instead of two, connections. The principal two flat prongs on an electrical plug are for the current-carrying double wire, one part "live" and the other neutral, while the third round prong is grounded—connected directly to the earth (Figure 9.26). Appliances such

Figure 9.27
This table lamp has an insulating body and doesn't need the third (ground) wire.

Electric Shock

Many people are killed each year by current from common 120-volt electric circuits. If your hand touches a faulty 120-volt light fixture while your feet are on the ground, there's likely a 120-volt "electrical pressure" between your hand and the ground. Resistance to current is usually greatest between your feet and the ground, and so the current is usually not enough to do serious harm. But if your feet and the ground are wet, there is a low-resistance electrical path between you and the ground. The 120 volts across this lowered resistance may produce a harmful current in your body.

Pure water is not a good conductor. But the ions that are normally found in water make it a fair conductor. Dissolved materials in water, especially small quantities of salt, lower the resistance even more. There is usually a layer of salt remaining on your skin from perspiration, which, when wet, lowers your skin resistance to a few hundred ohms or less. Handling electrical devices while taking a bath is a definite no-no.

Injury by electric shock occurs in three forms: (1) burning of tissues by heating, (2) contraction of muscles, and (3) disruption of cardiac rhythm. These conditions are caused by the delivery of excessive power for too long a time in critical regions of the body.

Electric shock can upset the nerve center that controls breathing. In rescuing shock victims, the first thing to do is remove them from the source of the electricity. Use a dry wooden stick or some other nonconductor so that you don't get electrocuted yourself. Then apply artificial respiration. It is important to continue artificial respiration. There have been cases of victims of lightning who did not breathe without assistance for several hours, but who were eventually revived and who completely regained good health.

as irons, stoves, washing machines, and dryers are connected with these three wires. If the live wire accidentally comes in contact with the metal surface of the appliance, and you touch the appliance, you could receive a dangerous shock. This won't occur when the appliance casing is grounded via the ground wire, which assures that the appliance casing is at zero ground potential.

☑ CHECKPOINT

What causes electric shock—current or voltage?

Check Your Answer

Electric shock *occurs* when current is produced in the body, but the current is *caused* by an impressed voltage.

9.9 Electric Circuits

Any path along which electrons can flow is a *circuit*. For a continuous flow of electrons, there must be a complete circuit with no gaps. A gap is usually provided by an electric switch that can be opened or closed to either cut off energy or to allow energy to flow. Most circuits have more than one device that receives electric energy. These devices are commonly connected in a circuit in one of two ways, in *series* or in *parallel*. When connected in series, they form a single pathway for electron flow between the terminals of the battery, generator, or wall outlet (which is simply an extension of these terminals). When connected in parallel, they form branches, each of which is a separate path for the flow of electrons. Both series and parallel connections have their own distinctive characteristics. In the following sections, we shall briefly discuss circuits using these two types of connections.

Series Circuits

A simple **series circuit** is shown in Figure 9.28. Three lamps are connected in series with a battery. The same current exists almost immediately in all three lamps when the switch is closed. The current does not "pile up" or accumulate in any lamp but flows *through* each lamp. Electrons that make up this current leave the negative terminal of the battery, pass through each of the resistive filaments in the lamps in turn, and then return to the positive terminal of the battery. (The same amount of current passes through the battery.) This is the only path of the electrons through the circuit. A break anywhere in the path results in an open circuit, and the flow of electrons ceases. Such a break occurs when the switch is opened, when the wire is accidentally cut, or when one of the lamp filaments burns out. The circuit shown in Figure 9.28 illustrates the following characteristics of series connections:

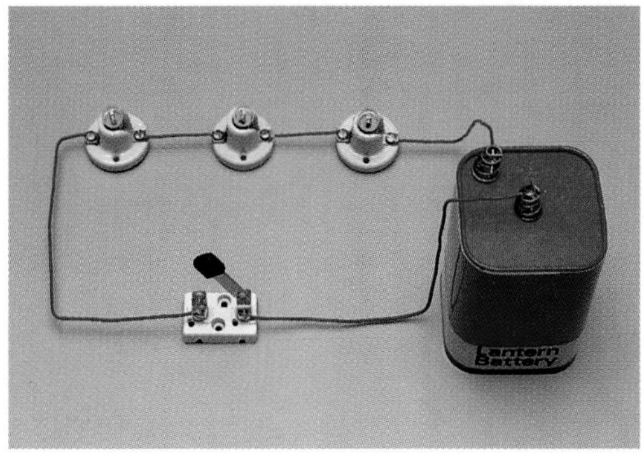

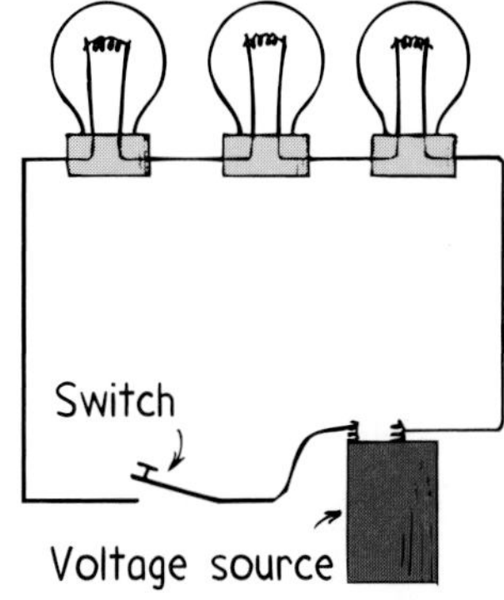

Figure 9.28
A simple series circuit. The 6-V battery provides 2 V across each lamp.

1. Electric current has but a single pathway through the circuit. This means that the current passing through the resistance of each electrical device along the pathway is the same.
2. This current is resisted by the resistance of the first device, the resistance of the second, and that of the third also, so the total resistance to current in the circuit is the sum of the individual resistances along the circuit path.
3. The current in the circuit is numerically equal to the voltage supplied by the source divided by the total resistance of the circuit. This is in accord with Ohm's law.
4. The total voltage impressed across a series circuit divides among the individual electrical devices in the circuit so that the sum of the "voltage drops"

across the resistance of each individual device is equal to the total voltage supplied by the source. This characteristic follows from the fact that the amount of energy given to the total current is equal to the sum of energies given to each device.

5. The voltage drop across each device is proportional to its resistance. This follows from the fact that more energy is dissipated when a current passes through a large resistance than when the same current passes through a small resistance.

☑ CHECKPOINT

1. What happens to current in other lamps if one lamp in a series circuit burns out?
2. What happens to the light intensity of each lamp in a series circuit when more lamps are added to the circuit?

Check Your Answers

1. If one of the lamp filaments burns out, the path connecting the terminals of the voltage source breaks and current ceases. All lamps go out.
2. Adding more lamps in a series circuit produces a greater circuit resistance. This decreases the current in the circuit and therefore in each lamp, which causes dimming of the lamps. Energy is divided among more lamps, so the voltage drop across each lamp is less.

It is easy to see the main disadvantage of a series circuit: if one device fails, current in the entire circuit ceases. Some cheap Christmas tree lights are connected in series. When one bulb burns out, it's fun and games (or frustration) trying to locate which one to replace.

Most circuits are wired so that it is possible to operate several electrical devices, each independently of the other. In your home, for example, a lamp can be turned on or off without affecting the operation of other lamps or electrical devices. This is because these devices are connected not in series but in parallel with one another.

Parallel Circuits

A simple **parallel circuit** is shown in Figure 9.29. Three lamps are connected to the same two points, A and B. Electrical devices connected to the same two points of an electrical circuit are said to be *connected in parallel.* Electrons leaving the negative terminal of the battery need travel through only *one* lamp filament before returning to the positive terminal of the battery. In this case, current branches into three separate pathways from A to B. A break in any one path does not interrupt the flow of charge in the other paths. Each device operates independently of the other devices.

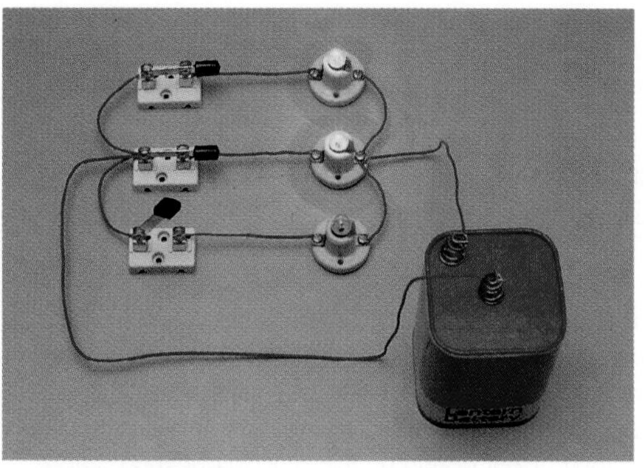

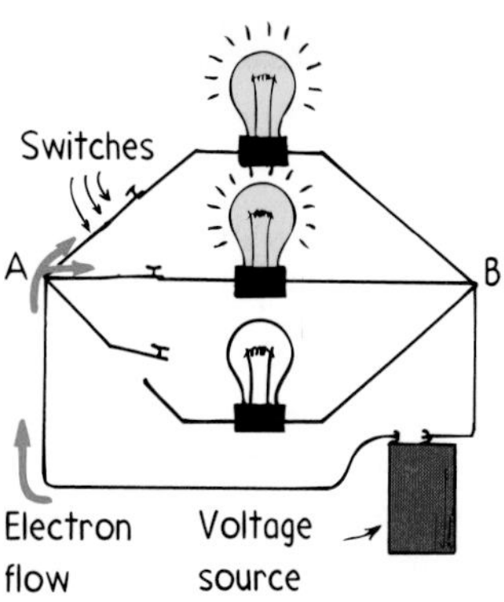

Figure 9.29
A simple parallel circuit. A 6-V battery provides 6 V across each lamp.

The circuit shown in Figure 9.29 illustrates the following major characteristics of parallel connections:

1. Each device connects the same two points, A and B, of the circuit. The voltage is therefore the same across each device.
2. The total current in the circuit divides among the parallel branches. Since the voltage across each branch is the same, the amount of current in each branch is inversely proportional to the resistance of the branch.
3. The total current in the circuit equals the sum of the currents in its parallel branches.
4. As the number of parallel branches is increased, the overall resistance of the circuit is *decreased.* Overall resistance is lowered with each added path between any two points of the circuit. This means the overall resistance of the circuit is less than the resistance of any one of the branches.

Figure 9.30
Just as resistance to checkout is lowered with more lanes in a supermarket, more branches in a parallel circuit lowers total circuit resistance.

☑ CHECKPOINT

1. What happens to the current in other lamps if one of the lamps in a parallel circuit burns out?
2. What happens to the light intensity of each lamp in a parallel circuit when more lamps are added in parallel to the circuit?

Check Your Answers

1. If one lamp burns out, the other lamps will be unaffected. The current in each branch, according to Ohm's law, is equal to voltage/resistance, and since neither voltage nor resistance is affected in the other branches, the current in those branches is unaffected. The total current in the overall circuit (the current through the battery), however, is decreased by an amount equal to the current drawn by the lamp in question before it burned out. But the current in any other single branch is unchanged.
2. The light intensity for each lamp is unchanged as other lamps are introduced (or removed). Only the total resistance and total current in the total circuit changes, which is to say that the current in the battery changes. (There is resistance in a battery also, which we assume is negligible here.) As lamps are introduced, more paths are available between the battery terminals, which effectively decreases total circuit resistance. This decreased resistance is accompanied by an increased current, the same increase that feeds energy to the lamps as they are introduced. Although changes of resistance and current occur for the circuit as a whole, no changes occur in any individual branch in the circuit.

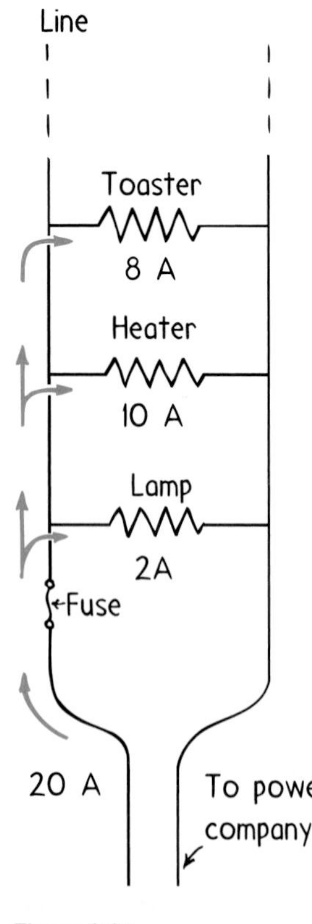

Figure 9.31
Circuit diagram for appliances connected to a household circuit.

Parallel Circuits and Overloading

Electricity is usually fed into a home by way of two wires called *lines.* These lines are very low in resistance and are connected to wall outlets in each room—sometimes through two or more separate circuits. An electric potential of about 110 to 120 volts is applied across these lines by a transformer in the neighborhood. (A transformer is a device that steps down the higher voltage supplied by the power utility.) As more devices are connected to a circuit, more pathways for current result. This lowers the combined resistance of the circuit. Therefore, more current exists in the circuit, which is sometimes a problem. Circuits that carry more than a safe amount of current are said to be *overloaded.*

We can see how overloading occurs in Figure 9.31. The supply line is connected to a toaster that draws 8 amperes, a heater that draws 10 amperes, and a lamp that draws 2 amperes. When only the toaster is operating and drawing 8 amperes, the total line current is 8 amperes. When the heater is also operating, the total line current increases to 18 amperes (8 amperes to the toaster plus 10 amperes to the heater). If you turn on the lamp, the line current increases to 20 amperes. Connecting additional devices increases the current still more. Connecting too many devices into the same circuit results in overheating the wires, which can cause a fire.

Safety Fuses

To prevent overloading in circuits, fuses are connected in series along the supply line. In this way the entire line current must pass through the fuse. The fuse shown in Figure 9.32 is constructed with a wire ribbon that will heat up and melt at a given current. If the fuse is rated at 20 amperes, it will pass 20 amperes, but no more. A current above 20 amperes will melt the fuse, which "blows out" and breaks the circuit. Before a blown fuse is replaced, the cause of overloading should be determined and remedied. Sometimes insulation that separates the wires in a circuit wears away and allows the wires to touch. This greatly reduces the resistance in the circuit and is called a *short circuit*.

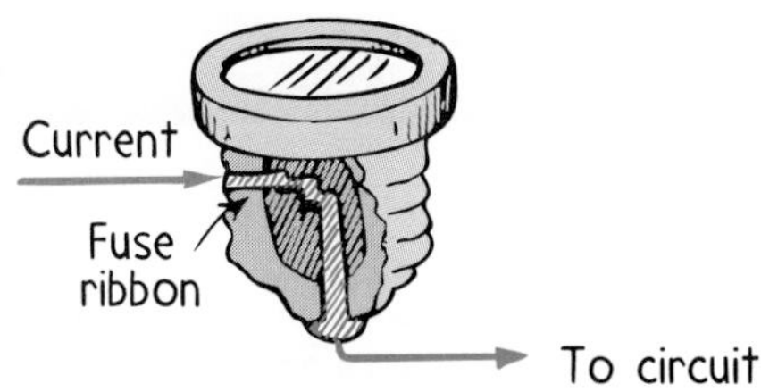

Figure 9.32
A safety fuse.

Figure 9.33
Electrician Dave Hewitt with a safety fuse and a circuit breaker. He favors the old fuses, which he's found more reliable.

In modern buildings, fuses have been largely replaced by circuit breakers, which use magnets or bimetallic strips to open a switch when the current is excessive. Utility companies use circuit breakers to protect their lines all the way back to the generators.

9.10 Electric Power

The moving charges in an electric current do work. This work, for example, can heat a circuit or turn a motor. The rate at which work is done—that is, the rate at which electric energy is converted into another form, such as mechanical energy, heat, or light—is called **electric power.** Electric power is equal to the product of current and voltage.*

Power = current × voltage

*Recall from Chapter 3 that Power = work/time; 1 Watt = 1J/s. Note that the units for mechanical power and electrical power agree (work and energy are both measured in joules):

Power = charge/time × energy/charge = energy/time

Figuring Physical Science

Problems

1. If a 120-V line to a socket is limited to 15 A by a safety fuse, will it operate a 1200-W hair dryer?
2. At 30¢/kWh, what does it cost to operate the 1200-W hair dryer for 1 h?

Solutions

1. Yes. From the expression watts = amperes × volts, we can see that current = 1200 W/120 V = 10 A, so the hair dryer will operate when connected to the circuit. But *two* hair dryers on the same circuit will blow the fuse.
2. 1200 W = 1.2 kW; 1.2 kW × 1 h × 30¢/1 kWh = 36¢.

When 110 volts energizes both a 40-W bulb and a 75-W bulb, which draws more current? Hint: Power = current × voltage.

Insights

If the voltage is expressed in volts and the current in amperes, then the power is expressed in watts. So, in units form,

$$\text{Watts} = \text{amperes} \times \text{volts}$$

If a lamp rated at 120 watts operates on a 120-volt line, you can figure that it will draw a current of 1 ampere (120 watts = 1 ampere × 120 volts). A 60-watt lamp draws ½ ampere on a 120-volt line. This relationship becomes a practical matter when you wish to know the cost of electrical energy, which is usually a small fraction of a dollar per kilowatt-hour, depending on the locality. A kilowatt is 1000 watts, and a kilowatt-hour represents the amount of energy consumed in 1 hour at the rate of 1 kilowatt.* Therefore, in a locality where electric energy costs 25 cents per kilowatt-hour, a 100-watt electric light bulb can operate for 10 hours at a cost of 25 cents, or a half nickel for each hour. A toaster or iron, which draws much more current and therefore much more energy, costs about ten times as much to operate.

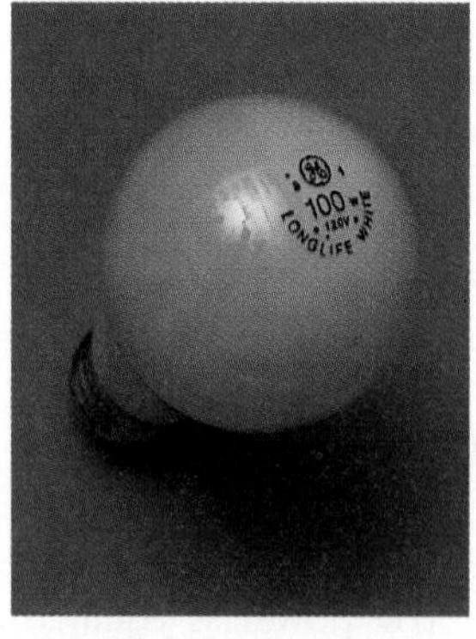

Figure 9.34
The power and voltage on the light bulb read "100 W 120 V." How many amperes will flow though the bulb?

Figure 9.35
Roy Unruh harnesses solar energy to produce electricity, which in turn powers demonstration vehicles.

*Since power = energy/time, simple rearrangement gives energy = power × time; thus, energy can be expressed in the unit *kilowatt-hours* (kWh).

Electrical Energy and Technology

Try to imagine everyday home life before the advent of electrical energy. Think of homes without electric lights, refrigerators, heating and cooling systems, telephones, and radio and TV. We may romanticize a better life without these, but only if we overlook the many hours of daily toil devoted to laundry, cooking, and heating homes. We'd also have to overlook how difficult it was to reach a doctor in times of emergency before the advent of the telephone—when all the doctor had in his bag were laxatives, aspirins, and sugar pills—and when infant death rates were staggering.

We have become so accustomed to the benefits of technology that we are only faintly aware of our dependency on dams, power plants, mass transportation, electrification, modern medicine, and modern agricultural science for our very existence. When we enjoy a good meal, we give little thought to the technology that went into growing, harvesting, and delivering the food on our table. When we turn on a light, we give little thought to the centrally controlled power grid that links the widely separated power stations by long-distance transmission lines. These lines serve as the productive life force of industry, transportation, and the electrification of civilization. Anyone who thinks of science and technology as "inhuman" fails to grasp the ways in which they make our lives more human.

Summary of Terms

Electrostatics The study of electric charge at rest (not *in motion,* as in electric currents).

Coulomb's law The relationship among electrical force, charge, and distance:

$$F = k\frac{q_1 q_2}{d^2}$$

If the charges are alike in sign, the force is repelling; if the charges are unlike, the force is attractive.

Coulomb The SI unit of electrical charge. One coulomb (symbol C) is equal in magnitude to the total charge of 6.25×10^{18} electrons.

Conductor Any material having free charged particles that easily flow through it when an electric force acts on them.

Superconductor Any material with zero electrical resistance, wherein electrons flow without losing energy and without generating heat.

Insulator Any material without free charged particles and through which current does not easily flow.

Electrically polarized Term applied to an atom or molecule in which the charges are aligned so that one side has a slight excess of positive charge and the other side a slight excess of negative charge.

Electric field Defined as force per unit charge, it can be considered to be an energetic "aura" surrounding charged objects. About a charged point, the field decreases with distance according to the inverse-square law, like a gravitational field. Between oppositely charged parallel plates, the electric field is uniform.

Electric potential energy The energy a charge possesses by virtue of its location in an electric field.

Electric potential The electric potential energy per amount of charge, measured in volts, and often called *voltage:*

$$\text{Voltage} = \frac{\text{electric energy}}{\text{amount of charge}}$$

Potential difference The difference in potential between two points, measured in volts, and often called *voltage difference.*

Electric current The flow of electric charge that transports energy from one place to another. It is measured in amperes, where 1 A is the flow of 6.25×10^{18} electrons per second, or 1 coulomb per second.

Electrical resistance The property of a material that resists the flow of an electric current through it. It is measured in ohms (Ω).

Ohm's law The statement that the current in a circuit varies in direct proportion to the potential difference or voltage and inversely with the resistance:

$$\text{Current} = \frac{\text{voltage}}{\text{resistance}}$$

A potential difference of 1 V across a resistance of 1 Ω produces a current of 1 A.

Direct current (DC) An electric current flowing in one direction only.

Alternating current (AC) Electric current that repeatedly reverses its direction; the electric charges vibrate about relatively fixed points. In the United States, the vibrational rate is 60 Hz.

Series circuit An electric circuit with devices connected in such a way that the same electric current flows through each of them.

Parallel circuit An electric circuit with two or more devices connected in such a way that the same voltage acts across each one, and any single one completes the circuit independently of all the others.

Electric power The rate of energy transfer, or the rate of doing work; the amount of energy per unit time, which can be measured by the product of current and voltage:

$$\text{Power} = \text{current} \times \text{voltage}$$

It is measured in watts (or kilowatts), where $1\ \text{A} \times 1\ \text{V} = 1\ \text{W}$.

Review Questions

9.1 Electrical Force and Charge

1. Which part of an atom is *positively* charged, and which part is *negatively* charged?
2. How does the charge of one electron compare with that of another electron?
3. How do the masses of electrons compare with the masses of protons?
4. How does the number of protons in the atomic nucleus normally compare with the number of electrons that orbit the nucleus?
5. What kind of charge does an object acquire when electrons are stripped from it?
6. What is meant by saying that charge is *conserved*?

9.2 Coulomb's Law

7. How is Coulomb's law similar to Newton's law of gravitation? How is it different?
8. How does a *coulomb* of charge compare with the charge of a *single* electron?
9. How does the magnitude of electrical force between a pair of charged particles change when the particles are moved twice as far apart? Three times as far apart?
10. How does an electrically *polarized* object differ from an electrically *charged* object?

9.3 Electric Field

11. Give two examples of common force fields.
12. How is the direction of an electric field defined?

9.4 Electric Potential

13. In terms of the units that measure them, distinguish between *electric potential energy* and *electric potential.*
14. A balloon may easily be charged to several thousand volts. Does that mean it has several thousand joules of energy? Explain.

9.5 Voltage Sources

15. What condition is necessary for heat energy to flow from one end of a metal bar to the other? For an electric charge to flow?
16. What condition is necessary for a sustained flow of electric charge through a conducting medium?
17. How much energy is given to each coulomb of charge passing through a 6-V battery?

9.6 Electric Current

18. Why do electrons, rather than protons, make up the flow of charge in a metal wire?
19. Does electric charge flow *across* a circuit or *through* a circuit? Does voltage *flow* across a circuit or is it *impressed* across a circuit? Explain.
20. Distinguish between *DC* and *AC*.
21. Does a battery produce *DC* or *AC*? Does the generator at a power station produce *DC* or *AC*?

9.7 Electrical Resistance

22. Which has the greater resistance, a thick wire or a thin wire of the same length?
23. What is the unit of electrical resistance?

9.8 Ohm's Law

24. What is the effect on current through a circuit of steady resistance when the voltage is doubled? What if both voltage and resistance are doubled?
25. How much current flows through a radio speaker that has a resistance of 8 Ω when 12 V is impressed across the speaker?
26. Which has the greater electrical resistance, wet skin or dry skin?
27. High voltage by itself does not produce electric shock. What does?
28. What is the function of the third prong on the plug of an electric appliance?
29. What is the source of electrons that makes a shock when you touch a charged conductor?

9.9 Electric Circuits

30. What is an electric circuit, and what is the effect of a gap in such a circuit?
31. In a circuit consisting of two lamps connected in series, if the current in one lamp is 1 A, what is the current in the other lamp?
32. If 6 V were impressed across the circuit in question 31, and the voltage across the first lamp were 2 V, what would be the voltage across the second lamp?
33. In a circuit consisting of two lamps connected in parallel, if there is 6 V across one lamp, what is the voltage across the other lamp?

34. If the current through each of the two branches of a parallel circuit is the same, what does this tell you about the resistance of the two branches?
35. How does the total current through the branches of a parallel circuit compare with the current through the voltage source?
36. As more lines are opened at a fast-food restaurant, the resistance to the motion of people trying to get served is reduced. How is this similar to what happens when more branches are added to a parallel circuit?
37. Are household circuits normally wired in series or in parallel?
38. How does the amount of current in a household circuit differ from the amount of current in a reading lamp?
39. Why will too many electrical devices operating at one time often blow a fuse?

9.10 Electric Power

40. What is the relationship among electric power, current, and voltage?
41. Which draws more current, a 40-W bulb or a 100-W bulb?

Activities

1. Demonstrate charging by friction and discharging from points with a friend who stands at the far end of a carpeted room. With leather shoes, scuff your way across the rug until your noses are close together. This can be a delightfully tingling experience, depending on how dry the air is and how pointed your noses are.
2. Briskly rub a comb against your hair or a woolen garment and bring it near a small but smooth stream of running water. Is the steam of water charged? (Before you say yes, note the behavior of the stream when an opposite charge is brought nearby.)
3. An electric cell is made by placing two plates of different materials that have different affinities for electrons in a conducting solution. You can make a simple 1.5-V cell by placing a strip of copper and a strip of zinc in a tumbler of salt water. The voltage of a cell depends on the materials used and the solution they are placed in, not the size of the plates. A battery is actually a series of cells.

   An easy cell to construct is the citrus cell. Stick a paper clip and a piece of copper wire into a lemon. Hold the ends of the wire close together, but not touching, and place the ends on your tongue. The slight tingle you feel and the metallic taste you experience result from a slight current of electricity pushed by the citrus cell through the wires when your moist tongue closes the circuit.

   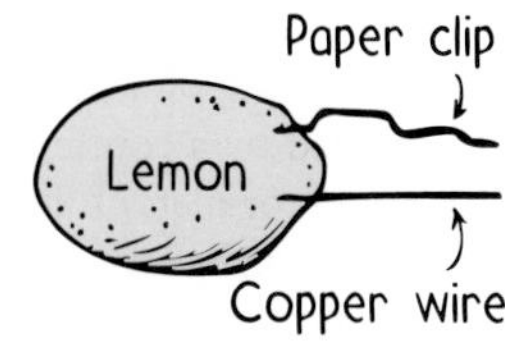

4. Examine the electric meter in your house. (It is probably in the basement or on the outside of your house.) You will see that, in addition to the clock-like dials in the meter, there is a circular aluminum disk that spins between the poles of magnets when electric current goes into the house. The more electric current, the faster the disk turns. The speed of the disk is directly proportional to the number of watts used; for example, it will spin five times as fast for 500 W as for 100 W.

   You can use the meter to determine how many watts an electrical device uses. First, see that all electrical devices in your home are disconnected (you may leave electric clocks connected, for the 2 watts they use will hardly be noticeable). The disk will be practically stationary. Then connect a lamp with a 100-W bulb, turn it on, and note how many seconds it takes for the disk to make five complete revolutions. The black spot painted on the edge of the disk makes this easy. Disconnect the lamp with the 100-W bulb and plug in and turn on a device of unknown wattage. Again, count the seconds for five revolutions. If it takes the same time, it's a 100-W device; if it takes twice the time, it's a 50-W device; if it takes half the time, it's a 200-W device; and so forth. In this way, you can estimate the power consumption of electrical devices fairly accurately.

Exercises

1. We do not feel the gravitational forces between ourselves and the objects around us because these forces are extremely small. Electrical forces, in comparison, are extremely huge. Since we and the objects around us are composed of charged particles, why don't we usually feel electrical forces?
2. With respect to forces, how are electric charge and mass alike? How are they different?
3. When combing your hair, you scuff electrons from your hair onto the comb. Is your hair then positively or negatively charged? How about the comb?

4. An electroscope is a simple device consisting of a metal ball that is attached by a conductor to two thin leaves of metal foil protected from air disturbances in a jar, as shown. When the ball is touched by a charged body, the leaves that normally hang straight down spread apart. Why? (Electroscopes are useful not only as charge detectors but also for measuring the quantity of charge: the greater the charge transferred to the ball, the more the leaves diverge.)
5. The leaves of a charged electroscope collapse in time. At higher altitudes, they collapse more rapidly. Why is this true? (*Hint:* The existence of cosmic rays was first indicated by this observation.)
6. Strictly speaking, will a penny be slightly more massive if it has a negative charge or a positive charge? Explain.
7. When one material is rubbed against another, electrons jump readily from one to the other, but protons do not. Why is this? (Think in atomic terms.)
8. If electrons were positive and protons were negative, would Coulomb's law be written the same or differently?
9. The five thousand billion billion freely moving electrons in a penny repel one another. Why don't they fly out of the penny?
10. Two equal charges exert equal forces on each other. What if one charge has twice the magnitude of the other? How do the forces they exert on each other compare?
11. How does the magnitude of electric force compare with the charge between a pair of charged particles when they are brought to half their original distance of separation? To one-quarter their original distance? To four times their original distance? (What law guides your answers?)
12. Suppose that the strength of the electric field about an isolated point charge has a certain value at a distance of 1 m. How will the electric field strength compare at a distance of 2 m from the point charge? What law guides your answer?
13. Why is a good conductor of electricity also a good conductor of heat?
14. When a car is moved into a painting chamber, a mist of paint is sprayed around it. When the body of the car is given a sudden electric charge and the mist of paint is attracted to it, presto—the car is quickly and uniformly painted. What does the phenomenon of polarization have to do with this?
15. If you place a free electron and a free proton in the same electric field, how will the forces acting on them compare? How will their accelerations compare? Their directions of travel?
16. If you put in 10 joules of work to push 1 coulomb of charge against an electric field, what will be its voltage with respect to its starting position? When released, what will be its kinetic energy if it flies past its starting position?
17. You are not harmed by contact with a charged metal ball, even though its voltage may be very high. Is the reason similar to the reason why you are not harmed by the sparks from a Fourth-of-July sparkler, even though the temperature of each of those sparks is greater than 1000°C? Defend your answer in terms of the energies that are involved.
18. What is the voltage at the location of a 0.0001 C charge that has an electric potential energy of 0.5 J (both voltage and potential relative to the same reference point)?
19. What happens to the brightness of light emitted by a light bulb when the current that flows in it increases?
20. One example of a water system is a garden hose that waters a garden. Another is the cooling system of an automobile. Which of these exhibits behavior more analogous to that of an electric circuit? Why?
21. Is a current-carrying wire electrically charged?
22. Your tutor tells you that an *ampere* and a *volt* really measure the same thing, and the different terms only serve to make a simple concept seem confusing. Why should you consider getting a different tutor?
23. In which of the circuits below does a current exist to light the bulb?

24. Does more current flow out of a battery than into it? Does more current flow into a light bulb than out of it? Explain.
25. Sometimes you hear someone say that a particular appliance "uses up" electricity. What is it that the appliance actually uses up, and what becomes of it?
26. A simple lie detector consists of an electric circuit, one part of which is part of your body, such as a circuit that connects one of your fingers to another of your fingers. A sensitive meter shows the current that flows when a small voltage is applied. How does this technique indicate that a person is lying? (And when does this technique *not* tell when someone is lying?)

27. Only a small percentage of the electric energy fed into a common light bulb is transformed into light. What happens to the rest?
28. Will a lamp with a thick filament draw more current or less current than a lamp with a thin filament?
29. A 1-mile-long copper wire has a resistance of 10 ohms. What will be its new resistance when it is shortened by (a) cutting it in half or by (b) doubling it over and using it as if it were one wire of half the length but twice the cross-sectional area?
30. Will the current in a light bulb connected to a 220-V source be greater or less than that in the same bulb when it is connected to a 110-V source?
31. Which will do less damage—plugging a 110-V appliance into a 220-V circuit or plugging a 220-V appliance into a 110-V circuit? Explain.
32. If a current of one- or two-tenths of an ampere were to flow into one of your hands and out the other, you would probably be electrocuted. But, if the same current were to flow into your hand and out the elbow above the same hand, you could survive, even though the current might be large enough to burn your flesh. Explain.
33. Would you expect to find DC or AC in the filament of a light bulb in your home? How about in the headlight of an automobile?
34. Electric current is generated at 50 Hz in Europe, but at 60 Hz in the United States. If you were to view the signal produced by each of these currents on an oscilloscope screen, which current would produce peaks that are closer together?
35. Are automobile headlights wired in parallel or in series? What is your evidence?
36. A car's headlights dissipate 40 W on low beam and 50 W on high beam. Is there more or less resistance in the high-beam filament?
37. What unit is represented by (a) joule per coulomb, (b) coulomb per second, and (c) watt-second?
38. To connect a pair of resistors so that their equivalent resistance will be greater than the resistance of either one, should you connect them in series or in parallel?
39. To connect a pair of resistors so that their equivalent resistance will be less than the resistance of either one, should you connect them in series or in parallel?
40. Why might the wingspans of birds be a consideration in determining the spacing between parallel wires on power poles?
41. Estimate the number of electrons that a power company delivers annually to the homes of a typical city of 50,000 people.
42. If electrons flow very slowly through a circuit, why does it not take a noticeably long time for a lamp to glow when you turn on a distant switch?
43. Consider a pair of flashlight bulbs connected to a battery. Will they glow brighter if they are connected in series or in parallel? Will the battery run down faster if they are connected in series or in parallel?
44. If several bulbs are connected in series to a battery, they may feel warm to the touch even though they are not visibly glowing. What is your explanation?
45. In the circuit shown, how do the brightnesses of the identical light bulbs compare? Which light bulb draws the most current? What will happen if bulb A is unscrewed? If bulb C is unscrewed?

46. As more and more bulbs are connected in series to a flashlight battery, what happens to the brightness of each bulb? Assuming that the heating inside the battery is negligible, what happens to the brightness of each bulb when more and more bulbs are connected in parallel?
47. Why is there no effect on other branches in a parallel circuit when one branch of the circuit is opened or closed?
48. A battery has internal resistance, so, if the current it supplies goes up, the voltage it supplies goes down. If too many bulbs are connected in parallel across a battery, will their brightness diminish? Explain.
49. Why are devices in household circuits almost never connected in series?
50. If a 60-W bulb and a 100-W bulb are connected in series in a circuit, across which bulb will there be the greater voltage drop? How about if they are connected in parallel?

Problems

1. Two point charges are separated by 6 cm. The attractive force between them is 20 N. Find the force between them when they are separated by 12 cm. (Why can you solve this problem without knowing the magnitudes of the charges?)
2. If the charges attracting each other in the preceding problem have equal magnitudes, what is the magnitude of each charge?
3. Two pellets, each with a charge of 1 microcoulomb (10^{-6} C), are located 3 cm (0.03 m) apart. What is the electric force between them? An object of what mass would experience this same force in the earth's gravitational field?

4. A droplet of ink in an industrial ink-jet printer carries a charge of 1.6×10^{-10} C and is deflected onto paper by a force of 3.2×10^{-4} N. Find the strength of the electric field that is required to produce this force.
5. Find the voltage change when (a) an electric field does 12 J of work on a 0.0001-C charge, and when (b) the same electric field does 24 J of work on a 0.0002-C charge.
6. The wattage marked on a light bulb is not an inherent property of the bulb; rather, it depends on the voltage to which it is connected, usually 110 or 120 V. How many amperes flow through a 60-W bulb connected in a 120-V circuit?
7. Rearrange the equation

   Current = voltage/resistance

   to express *resistance* in terms of current and voltage. Then solve the following: A certain device in a 120-V circuit has a current rating of 20 A. What is the resistance of the device (how many ohms)?
8. Using the formula

   Power = current × voltage

   find the current drawn by a 1200-W hair dryer connected to 120 V. Then, using the method you used in the previous problem, find the resistance of the hair dryer.
9. The total charge that an automobile battery can supply without being recharged is given in terms of ampere-hours. A typical 12-V battery has a rating of 60 ampere-hours (60 A for 1 h, 30 A for 2 h, and so on). Suppose that you forget to turn off the headlights in your parked automobile. If each of the two headlights draws 3 A, how long will it be before your battery is "dead"?
10. How much does it cost to operate a 100-W lamp continuously for 1 week if the power utility rate is 20¢/kWh?
11. A 4-W nightlight is plugged into a 120-V circuit and operates continuously for 1 year. Find the following: (a) the current it draws, (b) the resistance of its filament, (c) the energy consumed in a year, and (d) the cost of its operation for a year at the utility rate of 20¢/kWh.
12. An electric iron connected to a 110-V source draws 9 A of current. How much heat (in joules) does it generate in a minute?
13. How many coulombs of charge flow through the iron in problem 12 in one minute?
14. A certain light bulb with a resistance of 95 ohms is labeled "150 W." Was this bulb designed for use in a 120-V circuit or a 220-V circuit?
15. In periods of peak demand, power companies lower their voltage. This saves them power (and saves you money)! To see the effect, consider a 1200-W toaster that draws 10 A when connected to 120 V. Suppose the voltage is lowered by 10 percent to 108 V. By how much does the current decrease? By how much does the power decrease? (*Caution:* The 1200-W label is valid only when 120 V is applied. When the voltage is lowered, it is the resistance of the toaster, not its power, that remains constant.)

Chapter 9 Online Resources

Tutorials
- Electrostatics

Videos
- Electric Potential
- Van de Graaff Generator
- Alternating Current
- Caution on Handling Electrical Wires
- Birds & High Voltage Wires
- Ohm's Law
- Electric Currents

Quiz
Exercises
Flashcards
Links

CHAPTER 10

Magnetism and Electromagnetic Induction

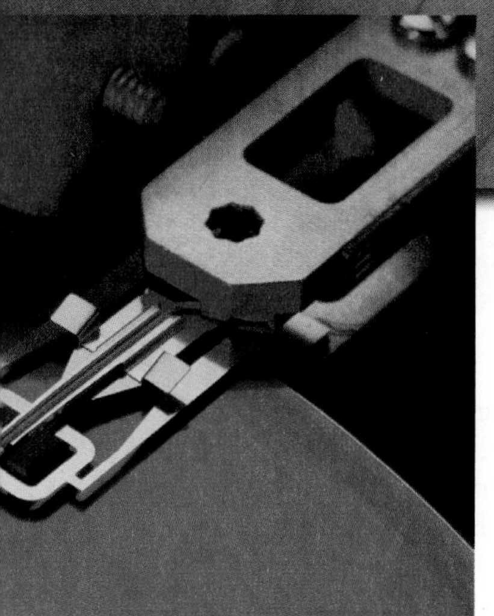

The term *magnetism* comes from Magnesia, the name of an ancient city in Asia Minor, where the Greeks found certain very unusual stones more than 2000 years ago. These stones, called *lodestones,* possess the unusual property of attracting pieces of iron. Such magnets were first fashioned into compasses and used for navigation by the Chinese in the twelfth century A.D.

In the sixteenth century, William Gilbert, Queen Elizabeth's physician, made artificial magnets by rubbing pieces of iron against lodestones. He suggested that a compass always points north and south because the earth itself has magnetic properties. Later, in 1750, John Michell in England found that magnetic poles obey the inverse-square law, and his results were confirmed by Charles Coulomb. The subjects of magnetism and electricity developed almost independently until 1820, when a Danish physicist named Hans Christian Oersted discovered, in a classroom demonstration, that an electric current affects a magnetic compass.* He saw that magnetism was related to electricity. Shortly thereafter, the French physicist André Marie Ampère proposed that electric currents are the source of all magnetic phenomena.

In days gone by, Dick Tracy comic strips, in addition to predicting the advent of cell phones, featured the heading, "He who controls magnetism controls the universe."

Insights

10.1 Magnetic Poles

Anyone who has played around with magnets knows that magnets exert forces on one another. Magnetic forces are similar to electrical forces, in that magnets can both attract and repel without touching (depending on which ends of the magnets are held near one another) and the strength of their interaction depends on the distance between them. Whereas electric charges produce electrical forces, regions called *magnetic poles* give rise to magnetic forces.

If you suspend a bar magnet at its center by a piece of string, you've got a compass. One end, called the *north-seeking pole,* points northward. The opposite end, called the *south-seeking pole,* points southward. More simply, these are called the *north* and *south poles.* All magnets have both a north and a south pole (some have more than one of each). Refrigerator magnets have narrow strips of alternating north and south poles. These magnets are strong enough

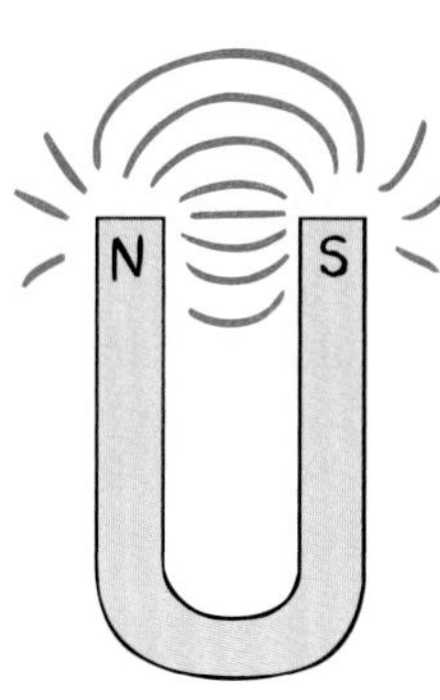

Figure 10.1
A horseshoe magnet.

*We can only speculate about how often such relationships become evident when they "aren't supposed to" and are dismissed as "something wrong with the apparatus." Oersted, however, was keen enough to see that nature was revealing another of its secrets.

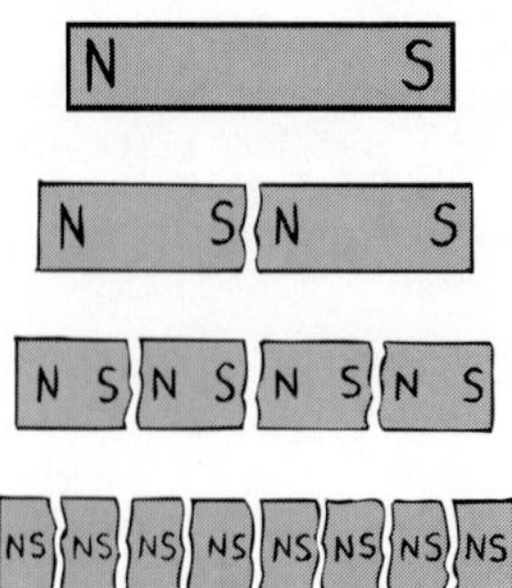

Figure 10.2
If you break a magnet in half, you have two magnets. Break these in half, and you have four magnets, each with a north and south pole. Continue breaking the pieces further and further and you find that you always get the same results. Magnetic poles exist in pairs.

to hold sheets of paper against a refrigerator door, but they have a very short range because the north and south poles cancel a short distance from the magnet. In a simple bar magnet, the magnetic poles are located at the two ends. A common horseshoe magnet is a bar magnet bent into a U shape. Its poles are also located at its two ends.

When the north pole of one magnet is brought near the north pole of another magnet, they repel each other.* The same is true of a south pole near a south pole. If opposite poles are brought together, however, attraction occurs. We find the following rule:

Like poles repel; opposite poles attract.

This rule is similar to the rule for the forces between electric charges, where like charges repel one another and unlike charges attract. But there is a very important difference between magnetic poles and electric charges. Whereas electric charges can be isolated, magnetic poles cannot. Electrons and protons are entities by themselves. A cluster of electrons need not be accompanied by a cluster of protons, and vice versa. But a north magnetic pole never exists without the presence of a south pole, and vice versa. The north and south poles of a magnet are like the head and tail of the same coin.

If you break a bar magnet in half, each half still behaves as a complete magnet. Break the pieces in half again, and you have four complete magnets. You can continue breaking the pieces in half and never isolate a single pole. Even if your pieces were one atom thick, there would still be two poles on each piece, which suggests that the atoms themselves are magnets.

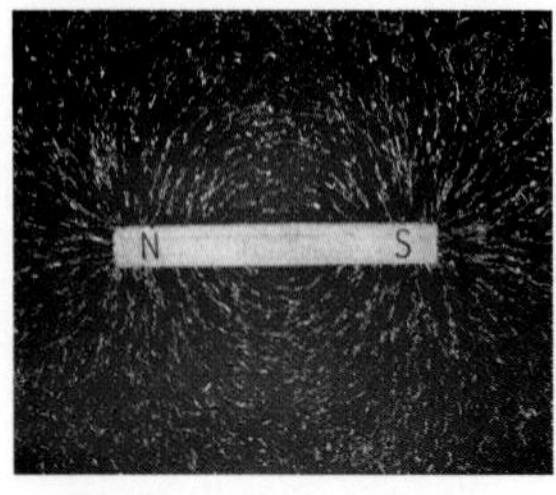

Figure 10.3
Top view of iron filings sprinkled on a sheet of paper on top of a magnet. The filings trace out a pattern of *magnetic field lines* in the surrounding space. Interestingly enough, the magnetic field lines continue inside the magnet (not revealed by the filings) and form closed loops.

☑ CHECKPOINT

Must every magnet necessarily have a north and south pole?

Check Your Answer

Yes, just as every coin has two sides, a head and a tail. Some "trick" magnets may have more than one pair of poles, but, nevertheless, the poles occur in pairs.

10.2 Magnetic Fields

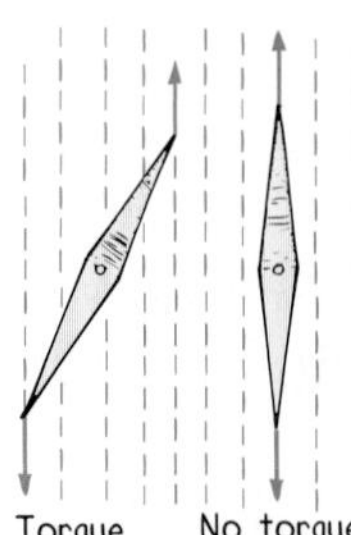

Figure 10.4
When the compass needle is not aligned with the magnetic field, the oppositely directed forces produce a pair of torques (called a *couple*) that twist the needle into alignment.

If you sprinkle some iron filings on a sheet of paper placed on a magnet, you'll see that the filings trace out an orderly pattern of lines that surround the magnet. The space around the magnet contains a **magnetic field.** The shape of the field is revealed by magnetic field lines that spread out from one pole and return to the other pole. It is interesting to compare the field patterns in Figures 10.3 and 10.5 with the electric-field patterns in Figures 9.9 and 9.10 in the previous chapter.

*The force of interaction between magnetic poles is given by $F \sim \frac{p_1 p_2}{d^2}$, where p_1 and p_2 represent magnetic pole strengths and d represents the separation distance between the poles. Note the similarity of this relationship to Coulomb's law and Newton's law of universal gravitation.

The direction of the field outside the magnet is from the north pole to the south pole. Where the lines are closer together, the field is stronger. We can see that the magnetic field strength is greater at the poles. If we place another magnet or a small compass anywhere in the field, its poles will tend to align with the magnetic field.

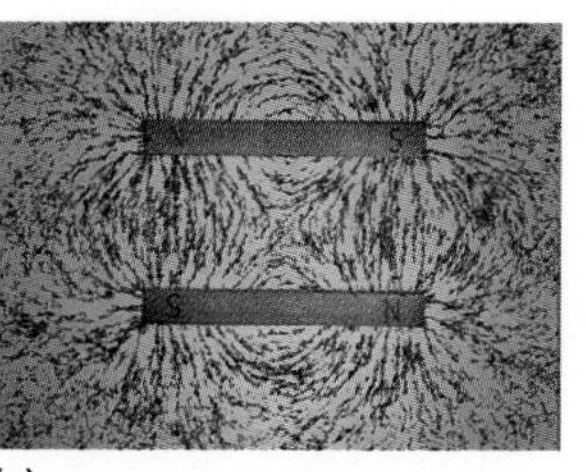
(a)

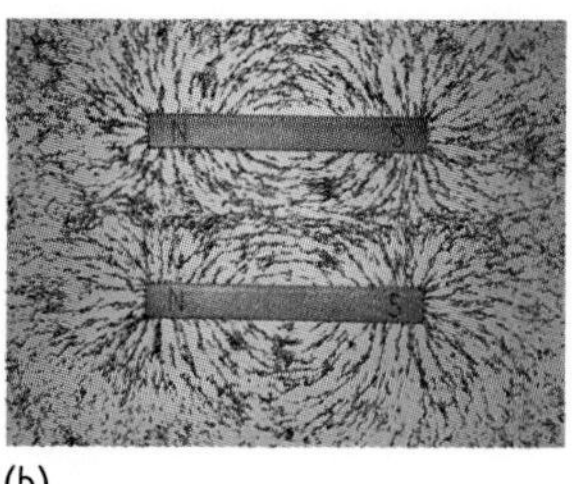
(b)

Figure 10.5
The magnetic field patterns for a pair of magnets. (*a*) Opposite poles are nearest to each other. (*b*) Like poles are nearest to each other.

A magnetic field is produced by the motion of electric charge.* Where, then, is this motion in a common bar magnet? The answer is, in the electrons of the atoms that make up the magnet. These electrons are in constant motion. Two kinds of electron motion produce magnetism: electron spin and electron revolution. Electrons spin about their own axes like tops, and they revolve about the nuclei of their atoms like planets revolving around the sun. In most common magnets, electron spin is the main contributor to magnetism.

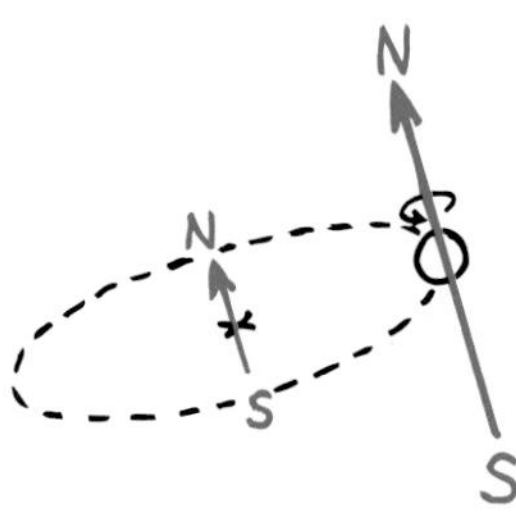

Figure 10.6
Both the spinning motion and the orbital motion of every electron in an atom produce magnetic fields. These fields combine constructively or destructively to produce the magnetic field of the atom. The resulting field is greatest for iron atoms.

Every spinning electron is a tiny magnet. A pair of electrons spinning in the same direction creates a stronger magnet. A pair of electrons spinning in opposite directions, however, work against each other. The magnetic fields cancel. This is why most substances are not magnets. In most atoms, the various fields cancel one another because the electrons spin in opposite directions. In such materials as iron, nickel, and cobalt, however, the fields do not cancel each other entirely. Each iron atom has four electrons whose spin magnetism is uncancelled. Each iron atom, then, is a tiny magnet. The same is true, to a lesser extent, of nickel and cobalt atoms. Most common magnets are therefore made from alloys containing iron, nickel, cobalt, and aluminum in various proportions.

Most of the iron objects around you are magnetized to some degree. A filing cabinet, a refrigerator, or even cans of food on your pantry shelf, have north and south poles induced by the earth's magnetic field. If you pass a compass from their bottoms to their tops, their poles can be easily identified. Then turn the cans upside down and note how many days it takes for the poles to reverse themselves.

Most common magnets are made from alloys containing iron, nickel, cobalt, and aluminum in various proportions. In these, the electron spin contributes virtually all of the magnetic property. In the rare-earth metals, such as gadolinium, the orbital motion is more significant.

Insights

10.3 Magnetic Domains

The magnetic field of an individual iron atom is so strong that interactions among adjacent atoms cause large clusters of them to line up with one another. These clusters of aligned atoms are called **magnetic domains.** Each domain is perfectly magnetized and is made up of billions of aligned atoms. The domains are microscopic (Figure 10.7), and there are many of them in a crystal of iron.

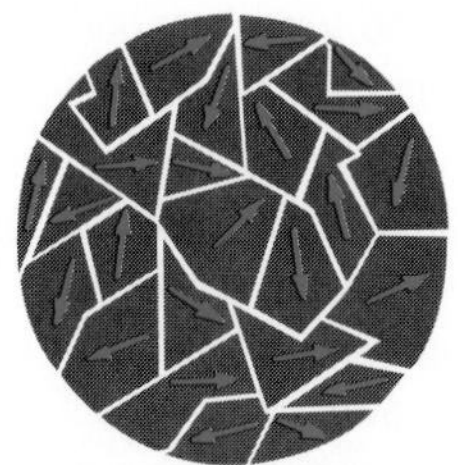

Figure 10.7
A microscopic view of magnetic domains in a crystal of iron. Each domain consists of billions of aligned iron atoms.

*Interestingly, since motion is relative, the magnetic field is relative. For example, when an electron moves by you, there is a definite magnetic field associated with the moving electron. But, if you move along with the electron, so that there is no motion relative to you, you will find no magnetic field associated with the electron. Magnetism is relativistic, as first explained by Albert Einstein when he published his first paper on special relativity, "On the Electrodynamics of Moving Bodies."

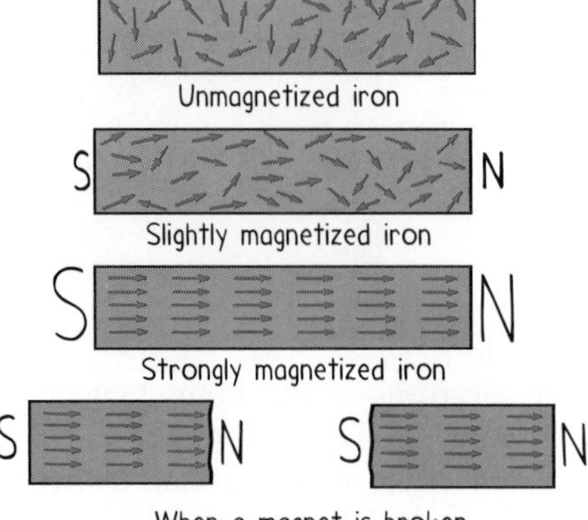

Figure 10.8
Pieces of iron in successive stages of magnetism. The arrows represent domains; the head is a north pole and the tail is a south pole. Poles of neighboring domains neutralize each other's effects, except at the ends.

Not every piece of iron is a magnet, because the domains in ordinary iron are not aligned. In a common iron nail, for example, the domains are randomly oriented. But when you bring a magnet nearby, they can be induced into alignment. (It is interesting to listen, with an amplified stethoscope, to the clickety-clack of domains aligning in a piece of iron when a strong magnet approaches.) The domains align themselves much as electrical charges in a piece of paper align themselves (become polarized) in the presence of a charged rod. When you remove the nail from the magnet, ordinary thermal motion causes most or all of the domains in the nail to return to a random arrangement.

Figure 10.9
Wai Tsan Lee shows iron nails becoming induced magnets.

Permanent magnets can be made by placing pieces of iron or similar magnetic materials in a strong magnetic field. Alloys of iron differ; soft iron is easier to magnetize than steel. It helps to tap the material to nudge any stubborn domains into alignment. Another way is to stroke the material with a magnet. The stroking motion aligns the domains. If a permanent magnet is dropped or heated outside of the strong magnetic field from which it was made, some of the domains are jostled out of alignment and the magnet becomes weaker.

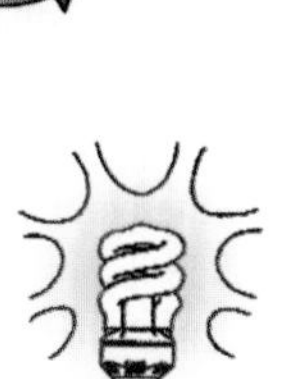

A magstripe on a credit card contains millions of tiny magnetic domains held together by a resin binder. Data is encoded in binary code, with zeros and ones distinguished by the frequency of domain reversals. It is quite amazing how quickly your name pops up when an airline reservationist swipes your card.

Insights

☑ CHECKPOINT

1. Why will a magnet not pick up a penny or a piece of wood?
2. How can a magnet attract a piece of iron that is not magnetized?

Check Your Answers

1. A penny and a piece of wood have no magnetic domains that can be induced into alignment.
2. Like the compass needle in Figure 10.4, domains in the unmagnetized piece of iron are induced into alignment by the magnetic field of the magnet. One domain pole is attracted to the magnet and the other domain pole is repelled. Does this mean the net force is zero? No, because the force is slightly greater on the domain pole closest to the magnet than it is on the farther pole. That's why there is a net attraction. In this way, a magnet attracts unmagnetized pieces of iron (Figure 10.9).

10.4 Electric Currents and Magnetic Fields

A moving charge produces a magnetic field. A current of charges, then, also produces a magnetic field. The magnetic field that surrounds a current-carrying wire can be demonstrated by arranging an assortment of compasses around the wire (Figure 10.10). The magnetic field about the current-carrying wire makes up a pattern of concentric circles. When the current reverses direction, the compass needles turn around, showing that the direction of the magnetic field changes also.*

If the wire is bent into a loop, the magnetic field lines become bunched up inside the loop (Figure 10.11). If the wire is bent into another loop that overlaps the first, the concentration of magnetic field lines inside the loops are doubled. It follows that the magnetic field intensity in this region is increased as the number of loops is increased. The magnetic field intensity is appreciable for a current-carrying coil that has many loops.

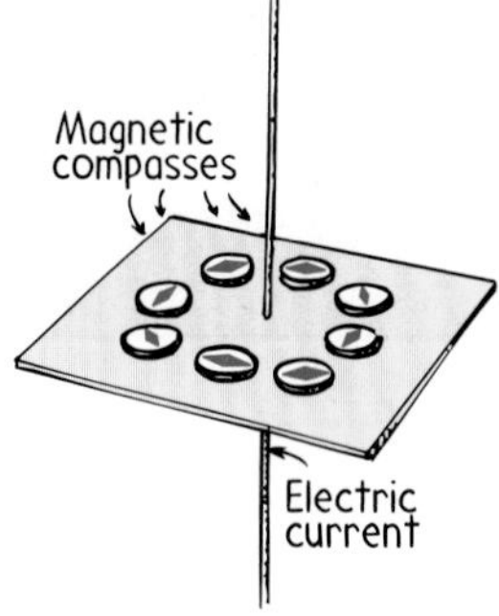

Figure 10.10
The compasses show the circular shape of the magnetic field surrounding the current-carrying wire.

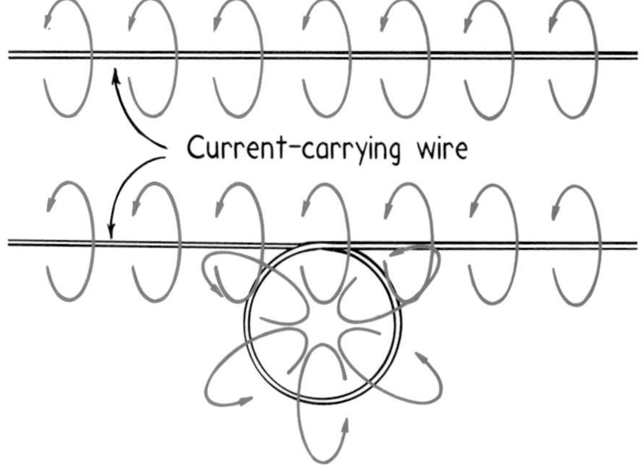

Figure 10.11
Magnetic field lines about a current-carrying wire become bunched up when the wire is bent into a loop.

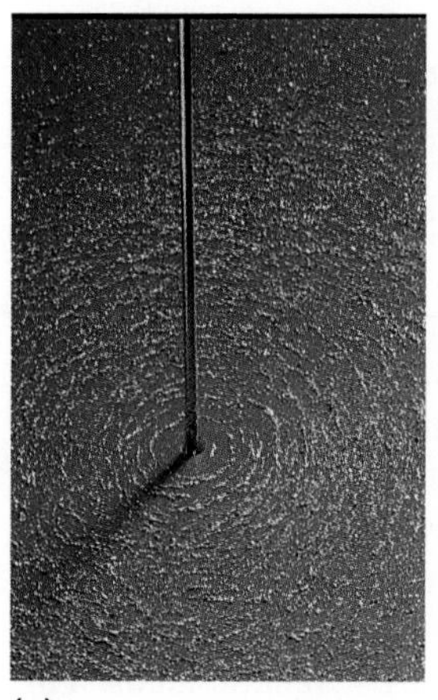
(a)

(b)

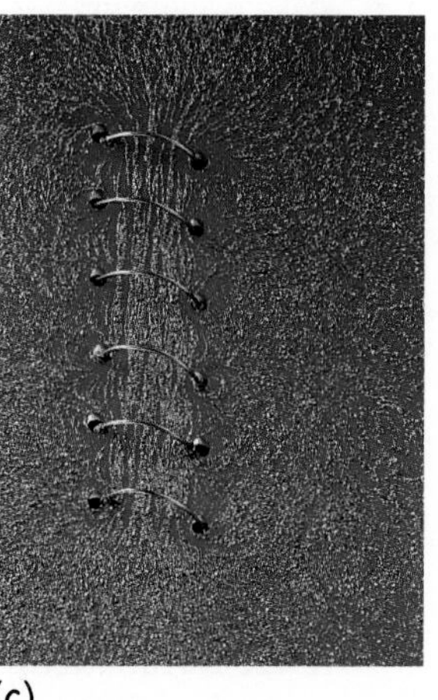
(c)

Figure 10.12
Iron filings sprinkled on paper reveal the magnetic field configurations about (*a*) a current-carrying wire, (*b*) a current-carrying loop, and (*c*) a coil of loops.

*Earth's magnetism is generally accepted as being the result of electric currents that accompany thermal convection in the molten parts of the earth's interior. Earth scientists have found evidence that the earth's poles periodically reverse places—there have been more than 20 reversals in the past 5 million years. This is perhaps the result of changes in the direction of electric currents within the earth. More about this in Chapter 27.

Figure 10.13
A permanent magnet levitates above a superconductor because its magnetic field cannot penetrate the superconducting material.

Figure 10.14
Scale model of a prototype magnetically levitated vehicle—a *magplane.* Whereas conventional trains vibrate as they ride on rails at high speeds, magplanes can travel vibration-free at high speeds because they make no physical contact with the guideway they float above.

Electromagnets

If a piece of iron is placed in a current-carrying coil of wire, the alignment of magnetic domains in the iron produces a particularly strong magnet known as an **electromagnet.** The strength of an electromagnet can be increased simply by increasing the current through the coil. Strong electromagnets are used to control charged-particle beams in high-energy accelerators. They also levitate and propel prototypes of high-speed trains (Figure 10.14).

Electromagnets powerful enough to lift automobiles are a common sight in junkyards. The strength of these electromagnets is limited mainly by overheating of the current-carrying coils. The most powerful electromagnets omit the iron core and employ superconducting coils through which large electrical currents flow with ease.

Superconducting Electromagnets

Ceramic superconductors (Chapter 9) have the interesting property of expelling magnetic fields. Because magnetic fields cannot penetrate the surface of a superconductor, magnets levitate above them. The reasons for this behavior, which are beyond the scope of this book, involve quantum mechanics. One of the more exciting applications of superconducting electromagnets is the levitation of high-speed trains for transportation. Prototype trains have already been demonstrated in the United States, Japan, and Germany. Watch for the growth of this relatively new technology.

10.5 Magnetic Forces on Moving Charges

A charged particle at rest will not interact with a static magnetic field. However, if the charged particle moves in a magnetic field, the magnetic character of a charge in motion becomes evident: The charged particle experiences a deflecting force.* The force is greatest when the particle moves in a direction perpendicular to the magnetic field lines. At other angles, the force is less, and it becomes zero when the particle moves parallel to the field lines. In any case, the direction of the force is always perpendicular to the magnetic field lines and the velocity of the charged particle (Figure 10.15). So a moving charge is deflected when it crosses through a magnetic field, but, when it travels parallel to the field, no deflection occurs.

This deflecting force is very different from the forces that occur in other interactions, such as the gravitational forces between masses, the electric forces between charges, and the magnetic forces between magnetic poles. The force that acts on a moving charged particle, such as an electron in an electron beam, does not act along the line that joins the sources of interaction. Instead, it acts perpendicularly both to the magnetic field and to the electron beam.

We are fortunate that charged particles are deflected by magnetic fields. This fact is employed in guiding electrons onto the inner surface of a television

*When particles of electric charge q and velocity v move perpendicularly into a magnetic field of strength B, the force F on each particle is simply the product of the three variables: $F = qvB$. For nonperpendicular angles, v in this relationship must be the component of velocity perpendicular to B.

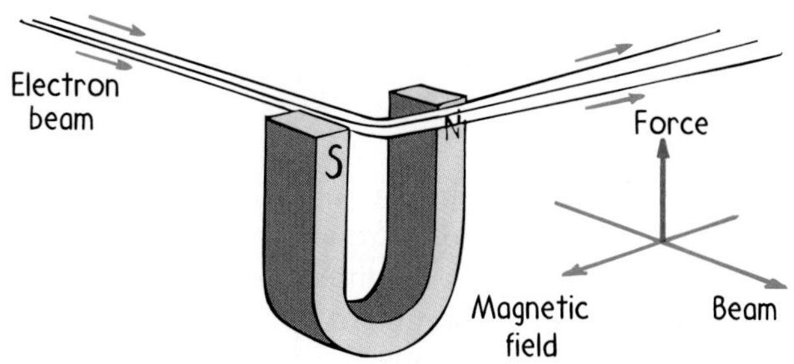

Figure 10.15
A beam of electrons is deflected by a magnetic field.

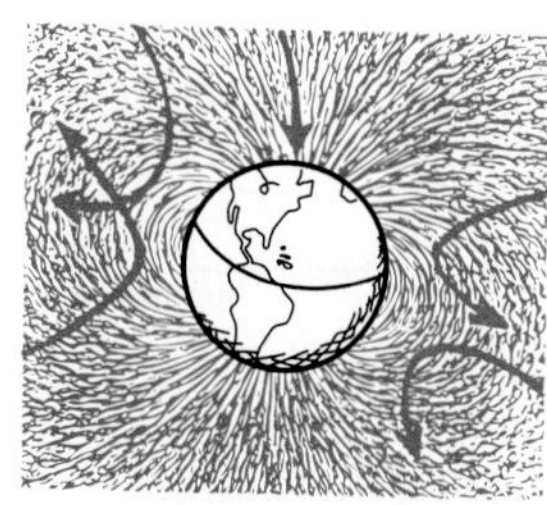

Figure 10.16
The magnetic field of the earth deflects the many charged particles that make up cosmic radiation.

picture tube to produce a picture. Also, charged particles from outer space are deflected by the earth's magnetic field. Otherwise the harmful cosmic rays bombarding the earth's surface would be much more intense.

Magnetic Force on Current-Carrying Wires

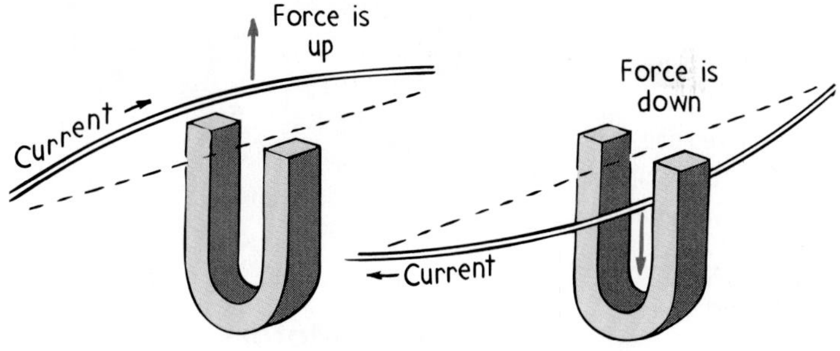

Figure 10.17
A current-carrying wire experiences a force in a magnetic field. (Can you see that this is a simple extension of Figure 10.15?)

Simple logic tells you that if a charged particle moving through a magnetic field experiences a deflecting force, then a current of charged particles moving through a magnetic field also experiences a deflecting force. If the particles are deflected while moving inside a wire, the wire is also deflected (Figure 10.17).

If we reverse the direction of current, the deflecting force acts in the opposite direction. The force is strongest when the current is perpendicular to the magnetic field lines. The direction of force is not along the magnetic field lines nor along the direction of current. The force is perpendicular to both field lines and current. It is a sideways force.

We see that, just as a current-carrying wire will deflect a magnet such as a compass needle (as discovered by Oersted in a physics classroom in 1820), a magnet will deflect a current-carrying wire. When discovered, these complementary links between electricity and magnetism created much excitement. Almost immediately, people began harnessing the electromagnetic force for useful purposes—with great sensitivity in electric meters and with great force in electric motors.

Electric Meters

The simplest meter to detect electric current is a magnetic compass. The next simplest meter is a compass in a coil of wires (Figure 10.18). When an electric current

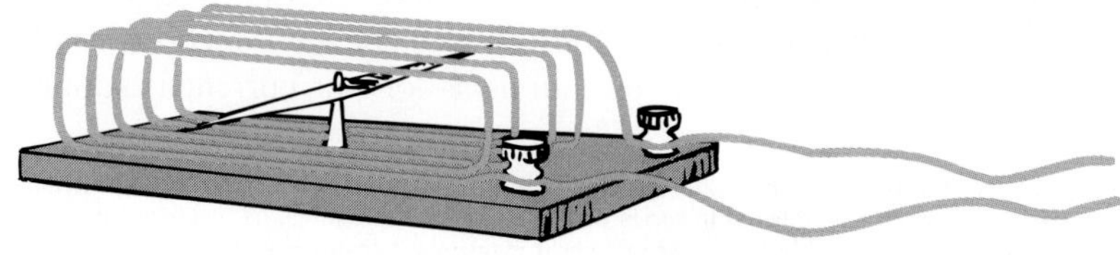

Figure 10.18
A very simple galvanometer.

The galvanometer is named after Luigi Galvani (1737–1798), who, while dissecting a frog's leg, discovered that dissimilar metals touching the leg caused it to twitch. This chance discovery led to the invention of the chemical cell and the battery. The next time you pick up a galvanized pail, think of Luigi Galvani in his anatomy laboratory.

Insights

passes through the coil, each loop produces its own effect on the needle, so even a very small current can be detected. Such a current-indicating instrument is called a *galvanometer.*

A more common design is shown in Figure 10.19. It employs more loops of wire and is therefore more sensitive. The coil is mounted for movement, and the magnet is held stationary. The coil turns against a spring, so the greater the current in its windings, the greater its deflection. A galvanometer may be calibrated to measure current (amperes), in which case it is called an *ammeter.* Or it may be calibrated to measure electric potential (volts), in which case it is called a *voltmeter.**

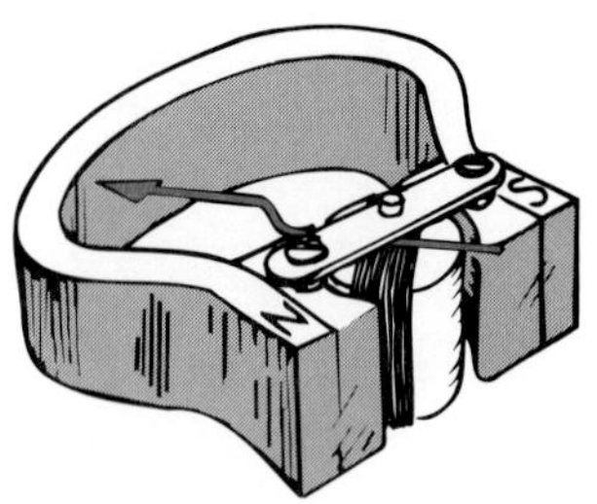

Figure 10.19
A common galvanometer design.

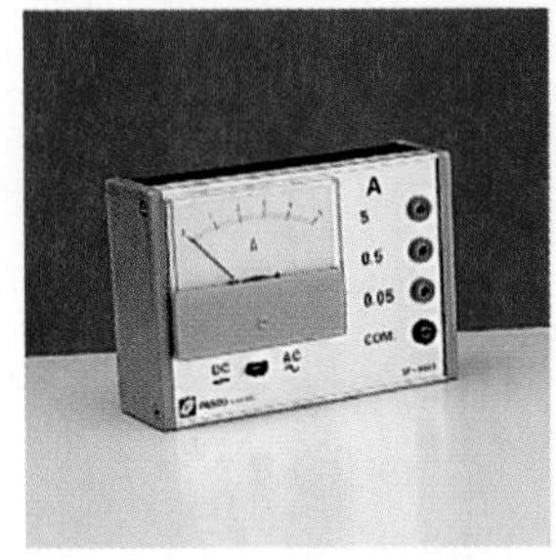

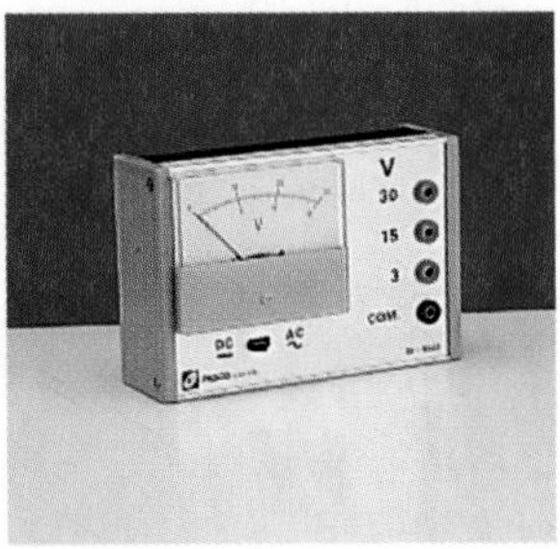

Figure 10.20
Both the ammeter and the voltmeter are basically galvanometers. (The electrical resistance of the instrument is designed to be very low for the ammeter, and very high for the voltmeter.)

Electric Motors

If we change the design of the galvanometer slightly, so that deflection makes a complete turn rather than a partial rotation, we have an **electric motor.** The principal difference is that the current in a motor is made to change direction each time the coil makes a half rotation. This happens in a cyclic fashion to produce continuous rotation, which has been used to run clocks, operate gadgets, and lift heavy loads.

In Figure 10.21 we see the principle of the electric motor in bare outline. A permanent magnet produces a magnetic field in a region where a rectangular loop of wire is mounted to turn about the axis shown by the dashed line. When a current passes through the loop, it flows in opposite directions in the upper and lower sides of the loop. (It must do this because, if charge flows into one end of the loop, it must flow out the other end.) If the upper portion of the loop is forced to the left, then the lower portion is forced to the right, as if it were a galvanometer. But, unlike a galvanometer, the current is reversed during each half revolution by means of stationary contacts on the shaft. The parts of the wire that brush against these contacts are called *brushes.* In this way, the current in the loop alternates so that the forces in the upper and lower regions do not change directions as the loop rotates. The rotation is continuous as long as current is supplied.

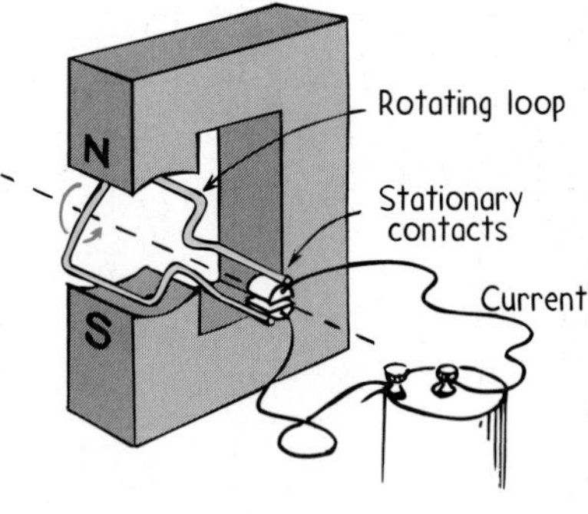

Figure 10.21
A simplified motor.

*To some degree, measuring instruments change what is being measured—ammeters and voltmeters included. Because an ammeter is connected in series with the circuit it measures, its resistance is made very low. That way, it doesn't appreciably lower the current it measures. Because a voltmeter is connected in parallel, its resistance is made very high, so that it draws very little current for its operation.

MRI: Magnetic Resonance Imaging

Magnetic resonance imaging scanners provide high-resolution pictures of the tissues inside a body. Superconducting coils produce a strong magnetic field (up to 60,000 times stronger than the intensity of the earth's magnetic field) that is used to align the protons of hydrogen atoms in the body of the patient.

Like electrons, protons have a "spin" property, so they will align with a magnetic field. Unlike a compass needle that aligns with the earth's magnetic field, the proton's axis wobbles about the applied magnetic field. Wobbling protons are slammed with a burst of radio waves tuned to push the proton's spin axis sideways, perpendicular to the applied magnetic field. When the radio waves pass and the protons quickly return to their wobbling pattern, they emit faint electromagnetic signals whose frequencies depend slightly on the chemical environment in which the proton resides. The signals, which are picked up by sensors, are then analyzed by a computer to reveal varying densities of hydrogen atoms in the body and their interactions with surrounding tissue. The images clearly distinguish between fluid and bone, for example.

It is interesting to note that MRI was formerly called NMRI (nuclear magnetic resonance imaging), because hydrogen nuclei resonate with the applied fields. Because of public phobia about anything "nuclear," this diagnostic technique is now called MRI. (Tell your friends that every atom in their bodies contains a nucleus!)

We have described here only a very simple DC motor. Larger motors, DC or AC, are usually manufactured by replacing the permanent magnet by an electromagnet that is energized by the power source. Of course, more than a single loop is used. Many loops of wire are wound about an iron cylinder, called an *armature,* which then rotates when the wire carries current.

The advent of electric motors brought to an end much human and animal toil in many parts of the world. Electric motors have greatly changed the way people live.

☑ CHECKPOINT

What is the major similarity between a galvanometer and a simple electric motor? What is the major difference?

Check Your Answer

A galvanometer and a motor are similar in that they both use coils positioned in a magnetic field. When a current passes through the coils, forces on the wires rotate the coils. The major difference is that the maximum coil rotation in a galvanometer is one half turn, whereas the coil in a motor (which is wrapped on an armature) rotates through many complete turns. This is accomplished by alternating the direction of the current with each half turn of the armature.

Multiple loops of wire must be insulated, because bare wire loops touching each other make a short circuit. Interestingly, Joseph Henry's wife tearfully sacrificed part of the silk in her wedding gown to cover the wires of Henry's first electromagnets.

Insights

10.6 Electromagnetic Induction

In the early 1800s, the only current-producing devices were voltaic cells, which produced small currents by dissolving metals in acids. These were the forerunners of our present-day batteries. The question arose as to whether electricity could be produced from magnetism. The answer was provided in 1831 by two physicists, Michael Faraday in England and Joseph Henry in the United States—each

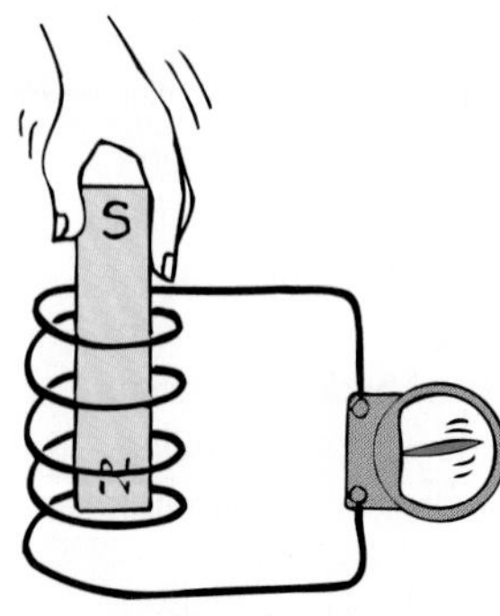

Figure 10.22
When the magnet is plunged into the coil, charges in the coil are set in motion, and voltage is induced in the coil.

working without knowledge of the other. Their discovery changed the world by making electricity commonplace—powering industries by day and lighting up cities at night.

Faraday and Henry both discovered that electric current could be produced in a wire simply by moving a magnet into or out of a coil of wire (Figure 10.22). No battery or other voltage source was needed—only the motion of a magnet in a wire loop. They discovered that voltage is caused, or *induced,* by the relative motion between a wire and a magnetic field. Whether the magnetic field moves near a stationary conductor or vice versa, voltage is induced either way (Figure 10.23).

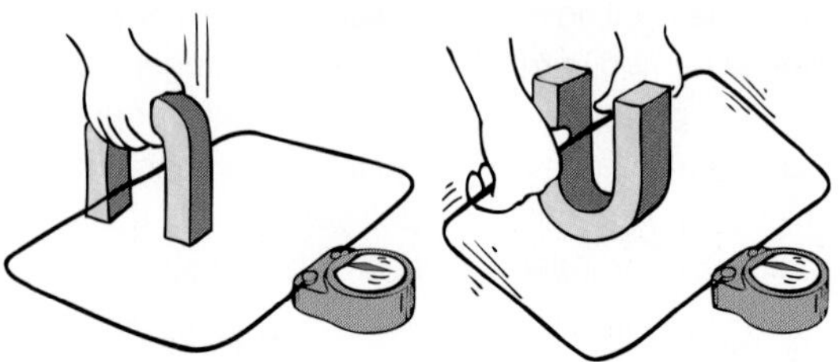

Figure 10.23
Voltage is induced in the wire loop whether the magnetic field moves past the wire or the wire moves through the magnetic field.

The greater the number of loops of wire moving in a magnetic field, the greater the induced voltage (Figure 10.24). Pushing a magnet into a coil with twice as many loops induces twice as much voltage; pushing into a coil with ten times as many loops induces ten times as much voltage; and so on. It may seem that we get something (energy) for nothing simply by increasing the number of loops in a coil of wire, but we don't: We find that it is more difficult to push the magnet into a coil made up of more loops. This is because the induced voltage produces a current, which makes an electromagnet, which repels the magnet in our hand. So we must do more work against this "back force" to induce more voltage (Figure 10.25).

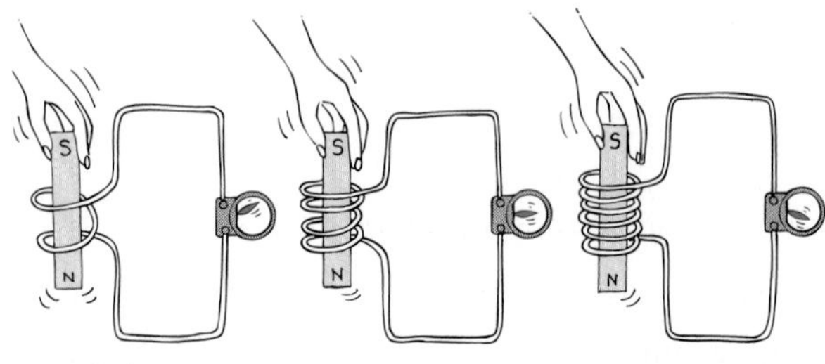

Figure 10.24
When a magnet is plunged into a coil with twice as many loops as another, twice as much voltage is induced. If the magnet is plunged into a coil with three times as many loops, three times as much voltage is induced.

Figure 10.25
It is more difficult to push the magnet into a coil with many loops because the magnetic field of each current loop resists the motion of the magnet.

The amount of voltage induced depends on how fast the magnetic field lines are entering or leaving the coil. Very slow motion produces hardly any voltage at all. Rapid motion induces a greater voltage. This phenomenon of inducing voltage by changing the magnetic field in a coil of wire is called **electromagnetic induction.**

Faraday's Law

Electromagnetic induction is summarized by **Faraday's law:**

> **The induced voltage in a coil is proportional to the number of loops, multiplied by the rate at which the magnetic field changes within those loops.**

The amount of *current* produced by electromagnetic induction depends on the resistance of the coil and the circuit that it connects, as well as the induced voltage.* For example, we can plunge a magnet into and out of a closed rubber loop and into and out of a closed loop of copper. The voltage induced in each is the same, providing the loops are the same size and the magnet moves with the same speed. But the current in each is quite different. The electrons in the rubber sense the same voltage as those in the copper, but their bonding to the fixed atoms prevents the movement of charge that so freely occurs in the copper.

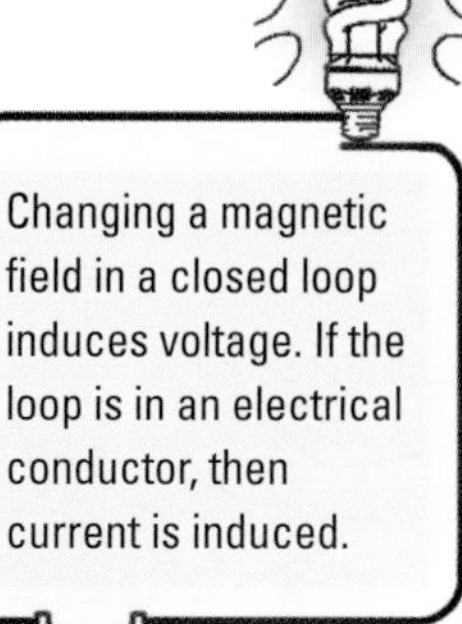

Changing a magnetic field in a closed loop induces voltage. If the loop is in an electrical conductor, then current is induced.

Insights

☑ CHECKPOINT

If you push a magnet into a coil, as shown in Figure 10.25, you'll feel a resistance to your push. Why is this resistance greater in a coil with more loops?

Check Your Answer

Simply put, more work is required to provide more energy. You can also look at it this way: When you push a magnet into a coil, you cause the coil to become an electromagnet. The more loops in the coil, the stronger the electromagnet that you produce and the stronger it pushes back against you. (If the electromagnetic coil attracted your magnet instead of repelling it, energy would have been created from nothing and the law of energy conservation would have been violated. So the coil must repel the magnet.)

Figure 10.26
Guitar pickups are tiny coils with magnets inside them. The magnets magnetize the steel strings. When the strings vibrate, voltage is induced in the coils and boosted by an amplifier, and sound is produced by a speaker.

We have mentioned two ways in which voltage can be induced in a loop of wire: by moving the loop near a magnet, or by moving a magnet near the loop. There is a third way—by changing a current in a nearby loop. All three of these cases possess the same essential ingredient—a changing magnetic field in the loop.

We see electromagnetic induction all around us. On the road, we see it operate when a car drives over buried coils of wire to activate a nearby traffic light. When iron parts of a car move over the buried coils, the effect of earth's magnetic field on the coils is changed, inducing a voltage to trigger the changing of the traffic lights. Similarly, when you walk through the upright coils in the security system at an airport, any metal you carry slightly alters the magnetic field in the coils. This change induces voltage, which sounds an alarm. When the magnetic strip on the back of a credit card is scanned, induced voltage pulses identify the card. Something similar occurs in the recording head of a tape recorder: magnetic domains in the tape are sensed as the tape moves past a current-carrying coil. Electromagnetic induction is everywhere. As we shall see in Chapter 12, it underlies the electromagnetic waves that we call light.

Figure 10.27
When Jean Curtis powers the large coil with AC, an alternating magnetic field is established in the iron bar and thence through the metal ring. Current is therefore induced in the ring, which then establishes its own magnetic field, which always acts in a direction to oppose the field producing it. The result is mutual repulsion—levitation.

*Current also depends on the "inductance" of the coil. Inductance measures the tendency of a coil to resist a change in current because the magnetism produced by one part of the coil acts to oppose the change of current in other parts of the coil. We will not treat inductance in this book.

10.7 Generators and Alternating Current

When a magnet is repeatedly plunged into and back out of a coil of wire, the direction of the induced voltage alternates. As the magnetic field strength inside the coil is increased (as the magnet enters), the induced voltage in the coil is directed one way. When the magnetic field strength diminishes (as the magnet leaves), the voltage is induced in the opposite direction. The frequency of the alternating voltage that is induced is equal to the frequency of the changing magnetic field within the loop.

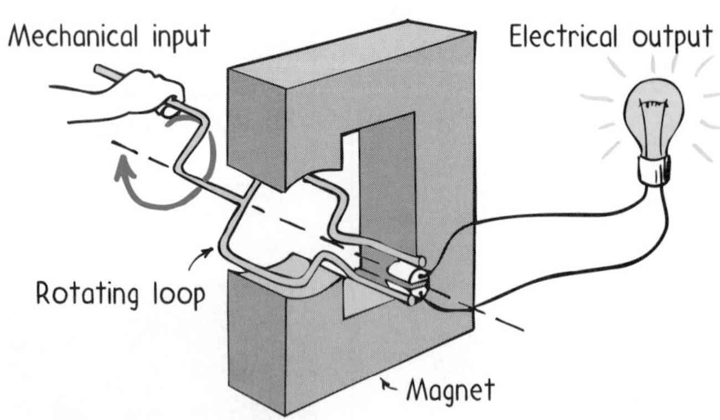

Figure 10.28
A simple generator. Voltage is induced in the loop when it is rotated in the magnetic field.

It is more practical to induce voltage by moving a coil rather than by moving a magnet. This can be done by rotating the coil in a stationary magnetic field (Figure 10.28). Such an arrangement is called a **generator.** A generator is a motor in reverse. The device is much the same, with the roles of input and output reversed. In a motor, electrical energy is the input and mechanical energy is the output. In a generator, mechanical energy is the input and electrical energy is the output. Both devices simply transform energy from one form to another.

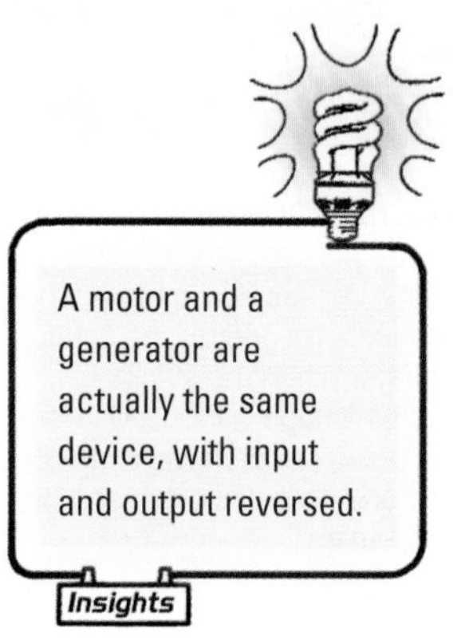

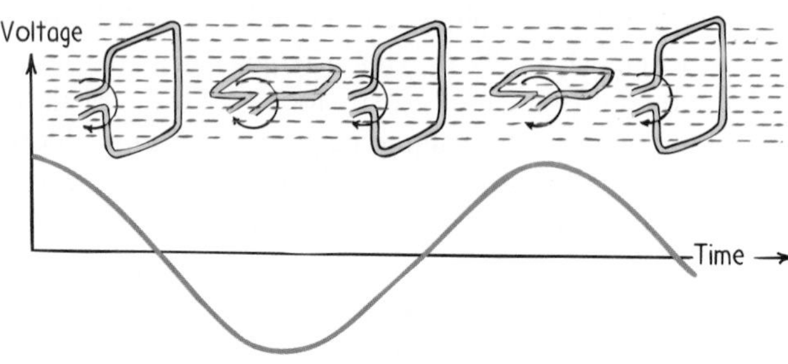

Figure 10.29
As the loop rotates, the magnitude and direction of the induced voltage (and current) changes. One complete rotation of the loop produces one complete cycle in voltage (and current).

Because the voltage induced by the generator alternates, the current produced is AC, an alternating current.* The alternating current in our homes is produced by generators standardized so that the current goes through 60 full cycles of change in magnitude and direction each second—60 hertz.

200 years ago, people got light from whale oil. Whales should be glad that humans discovered electricity!

Insights

10.8 Power Production

Fifty years after Faraday and Henry discovered electromagnetic induction, Nikola Tesla and George Westinghouse put those findings to practical use and showed the world that electricity could be generated reliably and in sufficient quantities to light entire cities.

*With appropriately designed brushes and by other means, the AC in the loop(s) can be taken off as DC to make a DC generator.

Tesla built generators that were much like those still in use, but quite a bit more complicated than the simple model we have discussed. Tesla's generators had armatures consisting of bundles of copper wires that were made to spin within strong magnetic fields by means of a turbine, which, in turn, was spun by the energy of steam or falling water. The rotating loops of wire in the armature cut through the magnetic field of the surrounding electromagnets, thereby inducing alternating voltage and current.

Figure 10.30
Steam drives the turbine, which is connected to the armature of the generator.

We can look at this process from an atomic point of view. When the wires in the spinning armature cut through the magnetic field, oppositely directed electromagnetic forces act on the negative and positive charges. Electrons respond to this force by momentarily swarming relatively freely in one direction throughout the crystalline copper lattice; the copper atoms, which are actually positive ions, are forced in the opposite direction. But the ions are anchored in the lattice, so they barely move at all. Only the electrons move significantly, sloshing back and forth in alternating fashion with each rotation of the armature. The energy produced by this electronic sloshing is tapped at the electrode terminals of the generator.

It's important to know that generators don't produce energy—they simply convert energy from some other form to electric energy. As we discussed in Chapter 3, energy from a source, whether fossil or nuclear fuel or wind or water, is converted to mechanical energy to drive the turbine. The attached generator converts most of this mechanical energy to electrical energy. Some people think that electricity is a primary source of energy. It is not. It is a carrier of energy that requires a source.

Enormous intergalactic magnetic fields that spread far beyond the galaxies have been recently detected. These giant magnetic fields make up an important part of the cosmic energy store and play a significant role in shaping the evolution of galaxies and large-scale grouping of galaxies.

Insights

10.9 The Transformer—Boosting or Lowering Voltage

When changes in the magnetic field of a current-carrying coil of wire are intercepted by a second coil of wire, voltage is induced in the second coil. This is the principle of the **transformer**—a simple electromagnetic-induction device consisting of an input coil of wire (the primary) and an output coil of wire (the secondary). The coils need not physically touch each other, but they are normally wound on a common iron core so that the magnetic field of the primary passes through the secondary. The primary is powered by an AC voltage source, and the secondary is connected to some external circuit. Changes in the primary current produce changes in its magnetic field. These changes extend to the secondary, and, by electromagnetic induction, voltage is induced in the secondary. If the number of turns of wire in both coils is the same, voltage input and voltage output will be the same. Nothing is gained. But, if the secondary has more turns than the primary, then greater voltage will be induced in the

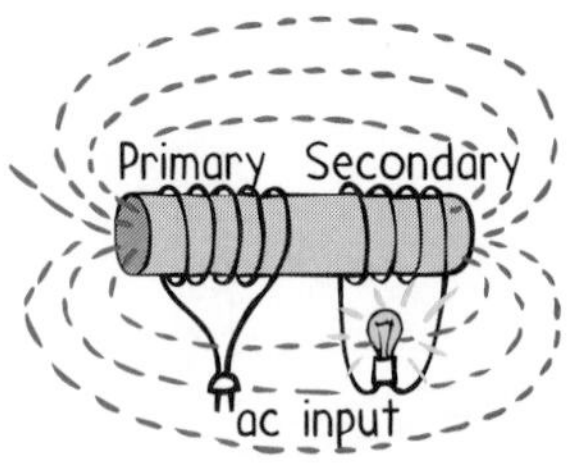

Figure 10.31
A simple transformer.

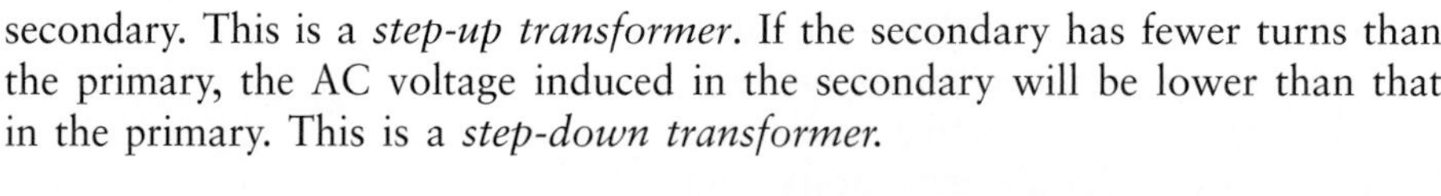
secondary. This is a *step-up transformer*. If the secondary has fewer turns than the primary, the AC voltage induced in the secondary will be lower than that in the primary. This is a *step-down transformer*.

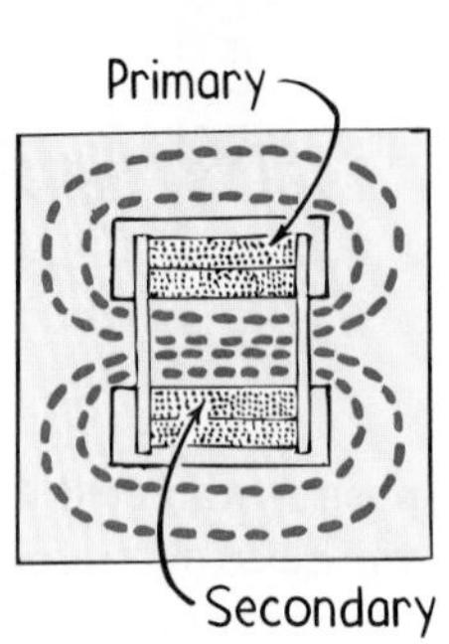

Figure 10.32
A practical transformer. The iron coil guides the changing magnetic field lines.

The relationship between primary and secondary voltages relative to the number of turns is:

$$\frac{\text{Primary voltage}}{\text{Number of primary turns}} = \frac{\text{Secondary voltage}}{\text{Number of secondary turns}}$$

It might seem that we get something for nothing with a transformer that steps up the voltage, but we don't. When voltage is stepped up, current in the secondary is less than in the primary. The transformer actually transfers energy from one coil to the other. The rate of transferring energy is *power*. The power used in the secondary is supplied by the primary. The primary gives no more than the secondary uses, in accord with the law of energy conservation. If the slight power losses due to heating of the core are neglected, then

Power into primary = power out of secondary

Electric power is equal to the product of voltage and current, so we can say that

$$(\text{Voltage} \times \text{current})_{\text{primary}} = (\text{voltage} \times \text{current})_{\text{secondary}}$$

The ease with which voltages can be stepped up or down with a transformer is the principle reason that most electric power is AC rather than DC.

Figure 10.33
Voltage generated in power stations is stepped up with transformers prior to being transferred across country by overhead cables. Then other transformers reduce the voltage before supplying it to homes, offices, and factories.

10.10 Field Induction

Figure 10.34
Electricity and magnetism connect to become light.

Electromagnetic induction explains the induction of voltages and currents. Actually, the more basic concept of *fields* is at the root of both voltages and currents. The modern view of electromagnetic induction states that electric and magnetic fields are induced. These, in turn, produce the voltages we have considered. So induction occurs whether or not a conducting wire or any material medium is present. In this more general sense, Faraday's law states:

> **An electric field is induced in any region of space in which a magnetic field is changing with time.**

There is a second effect, an extension of Faraday's law. It is the same except that the roles of electric and magnetic fields are interchanged. It is one of nature's many symmetries. This effect, which was advanced by the British physicist James Clerk Maxwell in about 1860, is known as **Maxwell's counterpart to Faraday's law:**

> **A magnetic field is induced in any region of space in which an electric field is changing with time.**

In each case, the strength of the induced field is proportional to the rates of change of the inducing field. The induced electric and magnetic fields are at right angles to each other.

Maxwell saw the link between electromagnetic waves and light. If electric charges are set into vibration in the range of frequencies that match those of light, waves are produced that *are* light! Maxwell discovered that light is simply electromagnetic waves in the range of frequencies to which the eye is sensitive.

Figure 10.35
In turning the crank of the generator, Sheron Snyder does work, which is transformed to voltage and current, which, in turn, is transformed into light.

On the eve of his discovery, Maxwell had a date with the young woman he was later to marry. While they were walking in a garden, she remarked about the beauty and wonder of the stars. Maxwell asked her how she would feel if she knew that she was walking with the only person in the world who knew what the starlight really was. In fact, at that time, James Clerk Maxwell was the only person in the entire world to know that light of any kind is energy carried in waves of electric and magnetic fields that continually regenerate each other.

The laws of electromagnetic induction were discovered at about the time the American Civil War was being fought. From a long view of human history, there can be little doubt that events such as the American Civil War will pale into provincial insignificance in comparison with the more significant event of the nineteenth century: the discovery of the electromagnetic laws.

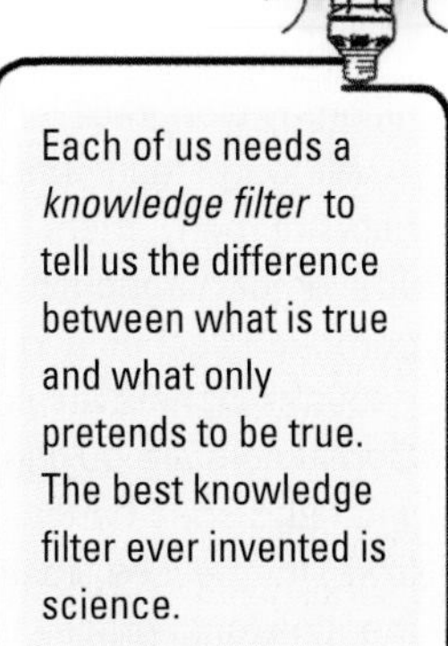

Each of us needs a *knowledge filter* to tell us the difference between what is true and what only pretends to be true. The best knowledge filter ever invented is science.

Insights

Magnetic Therapy

Back in the eighteenth century, a celebrated "magnetizer" from Vienna, Franz Mesmer, brought his magnets to Paris and established himself as a healer in Parisian society. He claimed that he could heal ailing patients simply by waving magnetic wands above their heads.

At that time, Benjamin Franklin, the world's leading authority on electricity, was visiting Paris as a representative of the government of the United States. He suspected that Mesmer's patients did benefit from his ritual—because it kept them away from the bloodletting practices of other physicians. At the urging of the medical establishment, King Louis XVI appointed a royal commission to investigate Mesmer's claims. The commission included Franklin and Antoine Lavoisier, the founder of modern chemistry. The commissioners designed a series of tests in which some subjects thought they were receiving Mesmer's treatment when they weren't, while others received the treatment but were led to believe they had not. The results of these blind experiments established beyond any doubt that Mesmer's success was due solely to the power of suggestion. To this day the report is a model for clarity and reason. Mesmer's reputation was destroyed, and he retired to Austria.

The laws of Faraday and Maxwell are two of the most important statements in physics. They underlie an understanding of the nature of light and of electromagnetic waves in general. In both cases, now, two hundred years later, with all that has been learned about magnetism and physiology, hucksters of magnetism are attracting even larger followings. But there is no government commission of Franklins and Lavoisiers to challenge their claims. Instead, magnetic therapy is another of the untested and unregulated "alternative therapies" given official recognition by Congress in 1992.

Although testimonials about the benefits of magnets are many, there is no scientific evidence whatsoever for magnets boosting body energy or combating aches and pains. Yet millions of "therapeutic" magnets are sold in stores and catalogs. Consumers are buying magnetic bracelets, insoles, wrist and knee bands, back and neck braces, pillows, mattresses, lipstick, and even water (not to mention ionic bracelets, as discussed in the previous chapter.) They are told that magnets have powerful effects on the body, mainly by increasing blood flow to injured areas. The idea that blood is attracted by a magnet is bunk, for the type of iron in blood doesn't respond to a magnet. Furthermore, most therapeutic magnets are the refrigerator type, with a very limited range. To get an idea of how quickly the magnetic field of these magnets drops off, see how many sheets of paper one of these magnets will hold on a refrigerator or any iron surface. The magnet will fall off after a few sheets of paper separate it from the iron surface. The field doesn't extend much more than one millimeter, and it wouldn't penetrate the skin, let alone into muscles. And, even if it did, there is no scientific evidence that magnetism has any beneficial effects on the body at all. But, again, testimonials are another story.

Sometimes an outrageous claim has some truth to it. For example, the practice of bloodletting in previous centuries was in fact beneficial to a small percentage of men. These men suffered the rare genetic disease *hemochromatosis,* which is characterized mainly by excess iron in the blood. (Women may inherit the disease, but they are generally exempt from its most serious effects because menstruation removes the excess iron from the body). Although the number of men who benefited from bloodletting was small, testimonials to its success promoted the spread of the practice, which killed many people.

No claim is so outrageous that testimonials can't be found to support it. Claims such as those for the earth being flat or the existence of flying saucers are quite harmless, and may amuse us. Magnetic therapy may likewise be harmless when used to treat many ailments, but not when used to treat a serious disorder in place of modern medicine. Pseudoscience may be intentionally promoted to deceive, or it may merely be the result of flawed and wishful thinking. In either case, pseudoscience is very big business. The market for therapeutic magnets and other such fruits of unreason is enormous.

Scientists must keep their minds open, must be prepared to accept new findings, and must be ready to be challenged by new evidence. But scientists also have a responsibility to inform the public when the public is being deceived—and, in effect, robbed—by pseudoscientists whose claims do not have any substance.

Summary of Terms

Magnetic force (1) Between magnets, it is the attraction of unlike magnetic poles for each other and the repulsion between like magnetic poles. (2) Between a magnetic field and a moving charge, it is a deflecting force due to the motion of the charge: the deflecting force is perpendicular to the velocity of the charge and perpendicular to the magnetic field lines. This force is greatest when the charge moves perpendicular to the field lines and is smallest (zero) when it moves parallel to the field lines.

Magnetic field The region of magnetic influence around a magnetic pole or a moving charged particle.

Magnetic domains Clustered regions of aligned magnetic atoms. When these regions themselves are aligned with one another, the substance containing them is a magnet.

Electromagnet A magnet whose field is produced by an electric current. It is usually in the form of a wire coil with a piece of iron inside the coil.

Electromagnetic induction The induction of voltage when a magnetic field changes with time. If the magnetic field within a closed loop changes in any way, a voltage is induced in the loop:

$$\text{Voltage induced} \sim \text{number of loops} \times \frac{\text{magnetic field change}}{\text{time}}$$

This is a statement of Faraday's law. (The induction of voltage is actually the result of a more fundamental phenomenon: the induction of an electric *field,* as defined in Maxwell's counterpart to Faraday's law.)

Faraday's law An electric field is induced in any region of space in which a magnetic field is changing with time. The magnitude of the induced electric field is proportional to the rate at which the magnetic field changes. The direction of the induced field is at right angles to the changing magnetic field.

Generator An electromagnetic induction device that produces electric current by rotating a coil within a stationary magnetic field.

Transformer A device for transferring electric power from one coil of wire to another by means of electromagnetic induction.

Maxwell's counterpart to Faraday's law A magnetic field is induced in any region of space in which an electric field is changing with time. The magnitude of the induced magnetic field is proportional to the rate at which the electric field changes. The direction of the induced magnetic field is at right angles to the changing electric field.

Review Questions

1. By whom, and in what setting, was the relationship between electricity and magnetism discovered?

10.1 Magnetic Poles

2. In what way is the rule for the interaction between magnetic poles similar to the rule for the interaction between electric charges?
3. In what way are *magnetic poles very* different from *electric charges*?

10.2 Magnetic Fields

4. What produces a magnetic field?
5. What two kinds of motion are exhibited by electrons in an atom?

10.3 Magnetic Domains

6. What is a magnetic domain?
7. Why is iron magnetic and wood not?
8. Why will dropping an iron magnet on a hard floor make it a weaker magnet?

10.4 Electric Currents and Magnetic Fields

9. What is the shape of a magnetic field about a current-carrying wire?
10. What happens to the direction of the magnetic field about an electric current when the direction of the current is reversed?
11. Why is the magnetic field strength inside a current-carrying loop of wire greater than the field strength about a straight section of wire?
12. How is the strength of a magnetic field in a coil affected when a piece of iron is placed inside?

10.5 Magnetic Force on Moving Charges

13. In what direction relative to a magnetic field does a charged particle move in order to experience maximum deflecting force? Minimum deflecting force?
14. Both gravitational and electrical forces act along the direction of the force fields. How does the direction of the magnetic force on moving charged particles differ?
15. What effect does the earth's magnetic field have on the intensity of cosmic rays striking the earth's surface?
16. Since a magnetic force acts on a moving charged particle, does it make sense that a magnetic force also acts on a current-carrying wire? Defend your answer.
17. What relative direction between a magnetic field and a current-carrying wire results in the greatest force on the wire? In the smallest force?

18. What happens to the direction of the force on a wire when the current in it is reversed?
19. What is a galvanometer called when it is calibrated to read current? To read voltage?
20. Is it correct to say that an electric motor is a simple extension of the physics that underlies a galvanometer?

10.6 Electromagnetic Induction

21. What was the important discovery made by physicists Michael Faraday and Joseph Henry?
22. State Faraday's law.
23. What are the three ways in which voltage can be induced in a wire?

10.7 Generators and Alternating Current

24. How does the frequency of induced voltage compare with how frequently a magnet is plunged into and out of a coil of wire?
25. What is the basic difference between a generator and an electric motor?
26. What is the basic similarity between a generator and an electric motor?
27. Why does the voltage induced in a generator alternate?

10.8 Power Production

28. What commonly supplies the energy input to a turbine?
29. Is it correct to say that a generator produces electric energy?

10.9 The Transformer—Boosting or Lowering Voltage

30. Is it correct to say that a transformer boosts electric energy?
31. Does a step-up transformer step up the voltage, the current, or the power?
32. Does a step-down transformer step up the voltage, the current, or the power?

10.10 Field Induction

33. What is induced by the rapid alternation of a magnetic field?
34. What is induced by the rapid alternation of an electric field?
35. What important connection did Maxwell discover about electric and magnetic fields?

Activities

An iron bar can be magnetized easily by aligning it with the magnetic field lines of the earth and striking it lightly a few times with a hammer. This works best if the bar is tilted down to match the dip of the earth's magnetic field. The hammering jostles the domains so that they can better fall into alignment with the earth's field. The bar can be demagnetized by striking it when it is in an east–west direction.

Exercises

1. Since every iron atom is a tiny magnet, why aren't all iron materials themselves magnets?
2. If you place a chunk of iron near the north pole of a magnet, attraction will occur. Why will attraction also occur if you place the iron near the south pole of the magnet?
3. What is different about the magnetic poles of common refrigerator magnets compared with those of common bar magnets?
4. What surrounds a stationary electric charge? A moving electric charge?
5. "An electron always experiences a force in an electric field, but not always in a magnetic field." Defend this statement.
6. Why will a magnet attract an ordinary nail or paper clip but not a wooden pencil?
7. A friend tells you that a refrigerator door, beneath its layer of white-painted plastic, is made of aluminum. How could you check to see if this is true (without any scraping)?
8. One way to make a compass is to stick a magnetized needle into a piece of cork and to float it in a glass bowl full of water. The needle will align itself with the horizontal component of the earth's magnetic field. Since the north pole of this compass is attracted northward, will the needle float toward the north side of the bowl? Defend your answer.
9. What is the net magnetic force on a compass needle? By what mechanism does a compass needle line up with a magnetic field?
10. Cans of food in your kitchen pantry are likely magnetized. Why?
11. We know a compass points northward because the earth is a giant magnet. Will the northward-pointing needle point northward when the compass is brought to the Southern Hemisphere?
12. Why will a magnet placed in front of a television picture tube distort the picture? (*Note:* Do NOT try this with a color set. If you succeed in magnetizing the metal mask in back of the glass screen, you will have picture distortion even when the magnet is removed!)
13. Magnet A has twice the magnetic field strength of magnet B, and, at a certain distance, it pulls on magnet B with a force of 50 N. With how much force, then, does magnet B pull on magnet A?

14. In Figure 10.17, we see a magnet exerting a force on a current-carrying wire. Does a current-carrying wire exert a force on a magnet? Why or why not?
15. A strong magnet attracts a paper clip to itself with a certain force. Does the paper clip exert a force on the strong magnet? If not, why not? If so, does it exert as much force on the magnet as the magnet exerts on it? Defend your answers.
16. When steel naval ships are built, the location of the shipyard and the orientation in the ship while in the shipyard are recorded on a brass plaque permanently fixed to the ship. Why?
17. Can an electron at rest in a magnetic field be set into motion by the magnetic field? What if it were at rest in an electric field?
18. A cyclotron is a device for accelerating charged particles to high speeds as they follow an expanding spiral path. The charged particles are subjected to both an electric field and a magnetic field. One of these fields increases the speed of the charged particles, and the other field causes them to follow a curved path. Which field performs which function?
19. A magnetic field can deflect a beam of electrons, but it cannot do work on the electrons to change their speed. Why?
20. Two charged particles are projected into a magnetic field that is perpendicular to their velocities. If the charges are deflected in opposite directions, what does this tell you about the particles?
21. A beam of high-energy protons emerges from a cyclotron. Do you suppose there is a magnetic field associated with these particles? Why or why not?
22. Residents of northern Canada are bombarded by more intense cosmic radiation than are residents of Mexico. Why is this so?
23. What changes in cosmic-ray intensity at the earth's surface would you expect during periods in which the earth's magnetic field is passing through a zero phase while undergoing pole reversals?
24. In a mass spectrometer, ions are directed into a magnetic field, where they curve around in the field and strike a detector. If a variety of singly ionized atoms travel at the same speed through the magnetic field, would you expect them all to be deflected by the same amount? Or would you expect different ions to be bent by different amounts?
25. Historically, replacing dirt roads with paved roads reduced friction between vehicles and the surface of the road. Replacing paved roads with steel rails reduced friction further. What will be the next step in reducing friction between vehicles and the surfaces over which they move? What friction will remain after surface friction has been eliminated?
26. Will a pair of parallel current-carrying wires exert forces on each other?
27. Why does an iron core increase the magnetic induction of a coil of wire?
28. Why is a generator armature harder to rotate when it is connected to a circuit and supplying electric current?
29. Will a cyclist coast farther if the lamp connected to his generator is turned off? Explain.
30. If your metal car moves over a wide, closed loop of wire embedded in a road surface, will the magnetic field of the earth within the loop be altered? Will this produce a current pulse? Can you think of a practical application for this at a traffic intersection?
31. At the security area of an airport, you walk through a weak AC magnetic field inside a large coil of wire. What is the result of a small piece of metal on your person that slightly alters the magnetic field in the coil?
32. A piece of plastic tape coated with iron oxide is magnetized more in some parts than in others. When the tape is moved past a small coil of wire, what happens in the coil? What is a practical application of this?
33. What is the primary difference between an electric *motor* and an electric *generator*?
34. Your friend says that, if you crank the shaft of a DC motor manually, the motor becomes a DC generator. Do you agree or disagree?
35. If you place a metal ring in a region in where a magnetic field is rapidly alternating, the ring may become hot to your touch. Why?
36. A magician places an aluminum ring on a table, underneath which is hidden an electromagnet. When the magician says "abracadabra" (and pushes a switch that starts current flowing through the coil under the table), the ring jumps into the air. Explain his "trick."
37. How could a light bulb near, yet not touching, an electromagnet be lit? Is AC or DC required? Defend your answer.
38. Two separate but similar coils of wire are mounted close to each other, as shown below. The first coil is connected to a battery and has a direct current flowing through it. The second coil is connected to a galvanometer. How does the galvanometer respond when the switch in the first circuit is closed? After being closed when the current is steady? When the switch is opened?

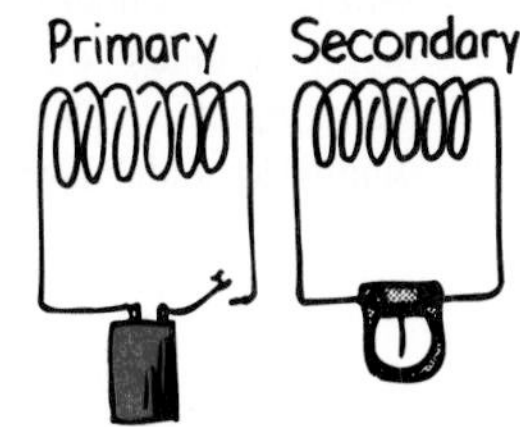

39. Why will more voltage be induced with the apparatus shown above if an iron core is inserted in the coils?
40. Why does a transformer require alternating voltage?
41. How does the current in the secondary of a transformer compare with the current in the primary when the secondary voltage is twice the primary voltage?
42. In what sense can a transformer be thought of as an electrical lever? What does it multiply? What does it *not* multiply?
43. In the circuit shown, how many volts are impressed across, and how many amperes flow through, the light bulb?

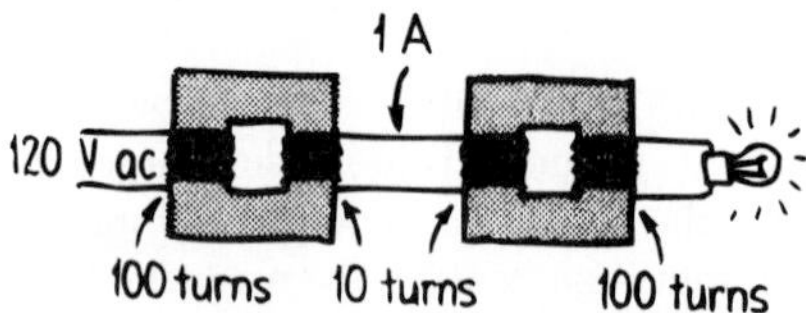

44. In the circuit shown, how many volts are impressed across, and how many amperes flow through, the meter?

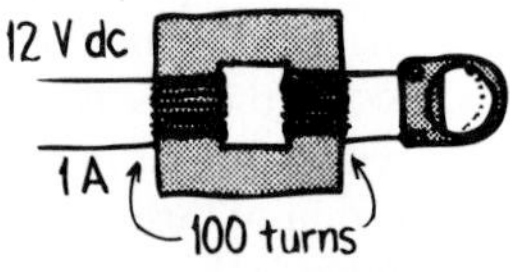

45. How would you answer the previous question if the input were 12-V AC?
46. Can an efficient transformer step up energy? Defend your answer.
47. When a bar magnet is dropped through a vertical length of copper pipe, it falls noticeably more slowly than it does when it is dropped through a vertical length of plastic pipe. If the copper pipe is long enough, the dropped magnet will reach a terminal falling speed. Why?
48. What is wrong with this scheme? To generate electricity without fuel, arrange a motor to run a generator that will produce electricity that is stepped up with transformers so that the generator can run the motor and simultaneously furnish electricity for other uses.
49. A friend says that changing electric and magnetic fields generate one another, and this gives rise to visible light when the frequency of change matches the frequencies of light. Do you agree? Explain.
50. Would electromagnetic waves exist if changing magnetic fields could produce electric fields but changing electric fields could not in turn produce magnetic fields? Explain.

Problems

1. The primary coil of a step-up transformer draws 100 W. Find the power provided by the secondary coil.
2. An ideal transformer has 50 turns in its primary and 250 turns in its secondary. 12-V AC is connected to the primary. Find: (a) the volts AC available at the secondary; (b) the current in a 10-ohm device connected to the secondary; and (c) the power supplied to the primary.
3. A model electric train requires 6 V to operate. If the primary coil of its transformer has 240 windings, how many windings should the secondary have if the primary is connected to a 120-V household circuit?
4. Neon signs require about 12,000 V for their operation. What should be the ratio of the number of loops in the secondary to the number of loops in the primary for a neon-sign transformer that operates off 120-V lines?
5. 100 kW (10^5 W) of power is delivered to the other side of a city by a pair of power lines, between which the voltage is 12,000 V. (a) What current flows in the lines? (b) Each of the two lines has a resistance of 10 ohms. What is the voltage change *along* each line? (Think carefully. This voltage change is along each line, not between the lines.) (c) What power is expended as heat in both lines together (distinct from power delivered to customers)? Do you see why it is so important to step voltages up with transformers for long-distance transmission?

Chapter 10 Online Resources

Videos
- Oersted's Discovery
- Magnetic Forces on Current-Carrying Wires
- Faraday's Law
- Application of E&M Induction

Quiz
Exercises
Flashcards
Links

Waves and Sound

Many things in nature wiggle and jiggle—the surface of a bell, a string on a guitar, the reed in a clarinet, lips on the mouthpiece of a trumpet, and the vocal cords of your larynx when you speak or sing. All these things **vibrate.** When they vibrate in air, they make the air molecules they touch wiggle and jiggle too, in exactly the same way, and these vibrations spread out in all directions, getting weaker, losing energy as heat, until they die out completely. But if these vibrations were to reach your ear instead, they would be transmitted to a part of your brain, and you would hear **sound.**

11.1 Vibrations and Waves

In a general sense, anything that moves back and forth, to and fro, from side to side, in and out, or up and down is vibrating. A **vibration** is a wiggle in time. A wiggle in space and time is a **wave.** A wave extends from one location to another. Light and sound are both vibrations that propagate throughout space as waves, but as waves of two very different kinds. Sound is the propagation of vibrations through a material medium—a solid, a liquid, or a gas. If there is no medium to vibrate, then no sound is possible. Sound cannot travel in a vacuum. But light can, because (as we will discuss in the following chapter) light is a vibration of nonmaterial electric and magnetic fields—a vibration of pure energy. Although light can pass though many materials, it needs none. This is evident when it propagates through the vacuum between the sun and the earth.

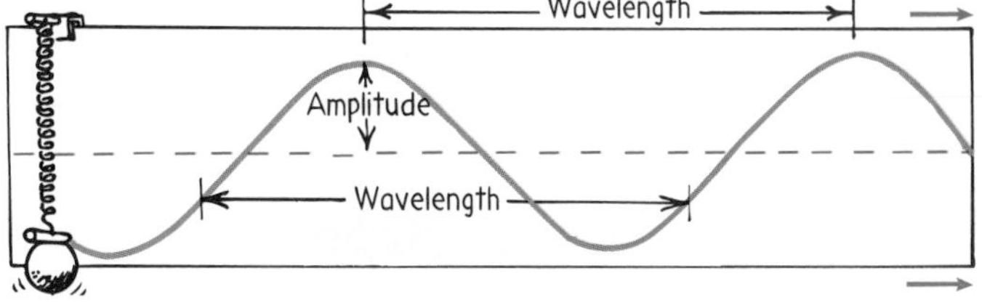

Figure 11.1
When the bob vibrates up and down, a marking pen traces out a sine curve on the paper, which is moved horizontally at constant speed.

The relationship between a vibration and a wave is shown in Figure 11.1. A marking pen on a bob attached to a vertical spring vibrates up and down and traces a wave form on a sheet of paper that is moved horizontally at constant speed. The wave form is actually a *sine curve,* a pictorial representation of a wave. Like a water wave, the high points are called *crests,* and the low points are the *troughs*. The straight dashed line represents the "home" position, or midpoint, of the vibration. The term **amplitude** refers to the distance from

The frequency of a wave matches the frequency of its vibrating source. This is true not only of sound waves, but, as we'll see in the next chapter, of light waves also.

Insights

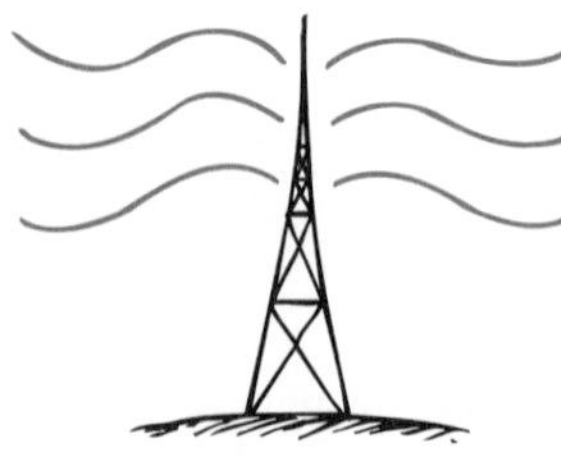

Figure 11.2
The source of any wave is something that vibrates. Electrons in the transmitting antenna vibrate 940,000 times each second and produce 940-kHz radio waves. Radio waves can't be seen or heard, but they send a pattern that tells a radio or a TV set what sounds or pictures to make.

the midpoint to the crest (or to the trough) of the wave. So the amplitude equals the maximum displacement from equilibrium.

The **wavelength** of a wave is the distance from the top of one crest to the top of the next one, or, equivalently, the distance between successive identical parts of the wave. The wavelengths of waves at the beach are measured in meters, the wavelengths of ripples in a pond in centimeters, and the wavelengths of light in billionths of a meter (nanometers). All waves have a vibrating source.

How frequently a vibration occurs is described by its **frequency.** The frequency of a vibrating pendulum, or of an object on a spring, specifies the number of to-and-fro vibrations it makes in a given time (usually in one second). A complete to-and-fro oscillation is one vibration. If it occurs in one second, the frequency is one vibration per second. If two vibrations occur in one second, the frequency is two vibrations per second.

The unit of frequency is called the **hertz** (Hz), after Heinrich Hertz, who demonstrated the existence of radio waves in 1886. One vibration per second is 1 hertz; two vibrations per second is 2 hertz, and so on. Higher frequencies are measured in kilohertz (kHz), and still higher frequencies in megahertz (MHz). AM radio waves are usually measured in kilohertz, while FM radio waves are measured in megahertz. A station at 960 kHz on the AM radio dial, for example, broadcasts radio waves that have a frequency of 960,000 vibrations per second. A station at 101.7 MHz on the FM dial broadcasts radio waves with a frequency of 101,700,000 hertz. These radio-wave frequencies are the frequencies at which electrons are forced to vibrate in the antenna of a radio station's transmitting tower. The frequency of the vibrating electrons and the frequency of the wave produced are the same.

The **period** of a wave or vibration is the time it takes for a complete vibration—for a complete cycle. Period can be calculated from frequency, and vice versa. Suppose, for example, that a pendulum makes two vibrations in one second. Its frequency is 2 Hz. The time needed to complete one vibration—that is, the period of vibration—is 1/2 second. Or if the vibration frequency is 3 Hz, then the period is 1/3 second. The frequency and period are the inverse of each other:

$$\text{Frequency} = \frac{1}{\text{period}}$$

or, vice versa,

$$\text{Period} = \frac{1}{\text{frequency}}$$

☑ CHECKPOINT

1. An electric razor completes 60 cycles every second. What is (a) its frequency? (b) its period?
2. Gusts of wind cause the Sears Building in Chicago to sway back and forth, completing a cycle every ten seconds. What is (a) its frequency: (b) its period?

Check Your Answers

1. (a) 60 cycles per second or 60 Hz; (b) 1/60 second.
2. (a) 1/10 Hz. (b) 10 s.

11.2 Wave Motion

Figure 11.3
Water waves.

If you drop a stone into a calm pond, waves will travel outward in expanding circles. Energy is carried by the wave, traveling from one place to another. The water itself goes nowhere. This can be seen by waves encountering a floating leaf. The leaf bobs up and down, but it doesn't travel with the waves. The waves move along, not the water. Likewise with waves of wind over a field of tall grass on a gusty day. Waves travel across the grass, while the individual grass plants remain in place; instead, they swing to and fro between definite limits, but they go nowhere. When you speak, wave motion through the air travels across the room at about 340 meters per second. The air itself doesn't travel across the room at this speed. In these examples, when the wave motion ceases, the water, the grass, and the air return to their initial positions. It is characteristic of wave motion that the medium transporting the wave returns to its initial condition after the disturbance has passed.

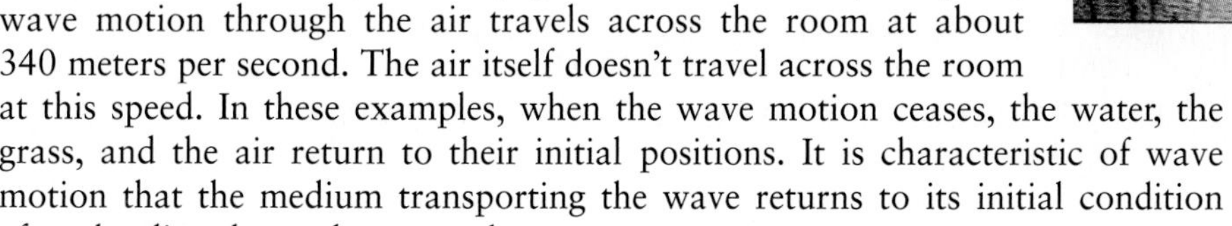

Wave Speed

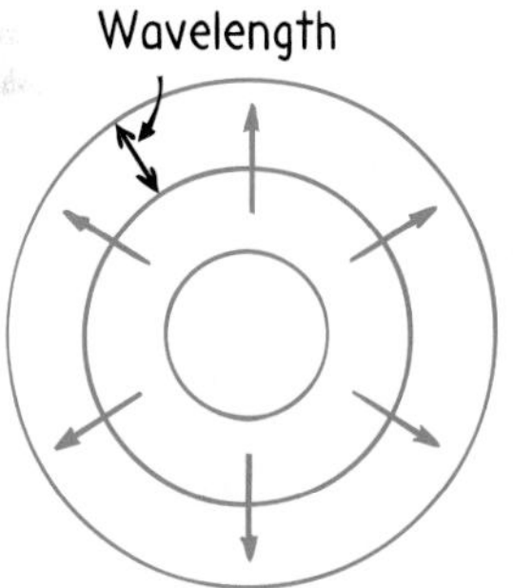

Figure 11.4
A top view of water waves.

The speed of periodic wave motion is related to the frequency and wavelength of the waves. Consider the simple case of water waves (Figures 11.3 and 11.4). Imagine that we fix our eyes on a stationary point on the water's surface and observe the waves passing by that point. We can measure how much time passes between the arrival of one crest and the arrival of the next one (the period), and we can also observe the distance between crests (the wavelength). We know that speed is defined as distance divided by time. In this case, the distance is one wavelength and the time is one period, so wave speed = wavelength/period.

For example, if the wavelength is 10 meters and the time between crests at a point on the surface is 0.5 second, the wave is traveling 10 meters in 0.5 seconds and its speed is 10 meters divided by 0.5 seconds, or 20 meters per second.

Since period is equal to the inverse of frequency, the formula **wave speed** = wavelength/period can also be written,

wave speed = wavelength × frequency

This relationship applies to all kinds of waves, whether they are water waves, sound waves, or light waves.

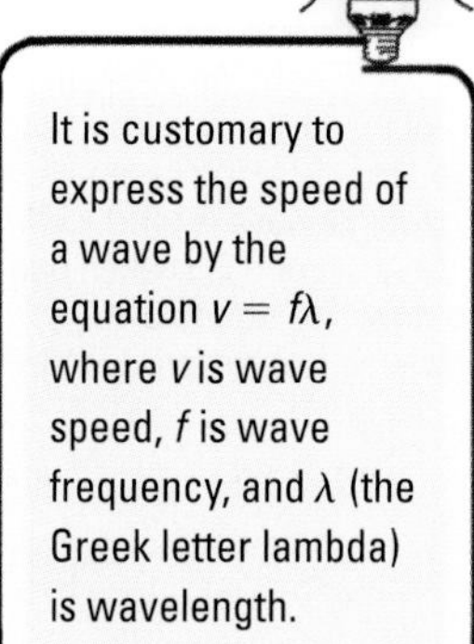

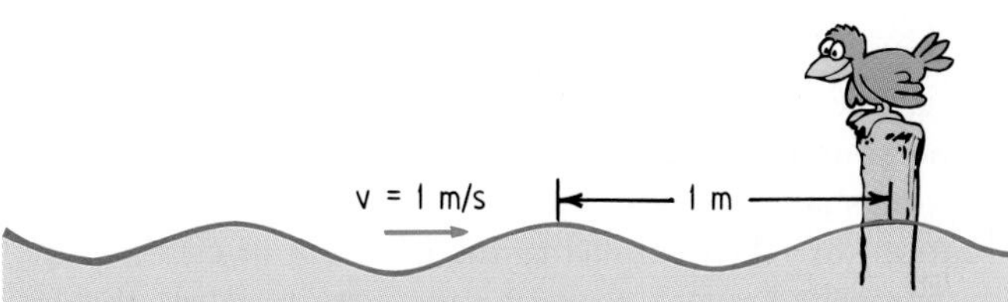

Figure 11.5
If the wavelength is 1 m, and one wavelength per second passes the pole, then the speed of the wave is 1 m/s.

☑ CHECKPOINT

1. If a train of freight cars, each 10 m long, rolls by you at the rate of three cars each second, what is the speed of the train?
2. If a water wave oscillates up and down three times each second and the distance between wave crests is 2 m, (a) what is its frequency? (b) what is its wavelength? (c) what is its wave speed?
3. The sound from a 60-Hz razor spreads out at 340 meters per second. (a) What is the frequency of the sound waves? (b) What is their period? (c) What is their speed? (d) What is their wavelength?

Check Your Answers

1. (a) 30 m/s. We can see this in two ways. According to the definition of speed in Chapter 1, $v = d/t = 3 \times 10$ m/1 s = 30 m/s, since 30 m of train passes you in 1 s.
   (b) If we compare our train to wave motion, where wavelength corresponds to 10 m and frequency is 3 Hz, then

   Speed = frequency × wavelength = 3 Hz × 10 m = 30 m/s
2. (a) 3 Hz; (b) 2 m; (c) Wave speed = frequency × wavelength = 3/s × 2 m = 6 m/s.
3. (a) 60 Hz; (b) 1/60 second; (c) 340 m/s; (d) 5.7 m.

11.3 Transverse and Longitudinal Waves

Fasten one end of a Slinky to a wall and hold the free end in your hand. If you shake the free end up and down, you will produce vibrations that are at right angles to the direction of wave travel. The right-angled, or sideways, motion is called *transverse motion.* This type of wave is called a **transverse wave.** Waves in the stretched strings of musical instruments and upon the surfaces of liquids are transverse waves. We will see later that electromagnetic waves, some of which are radio waves and light waves, are also transverse waves.

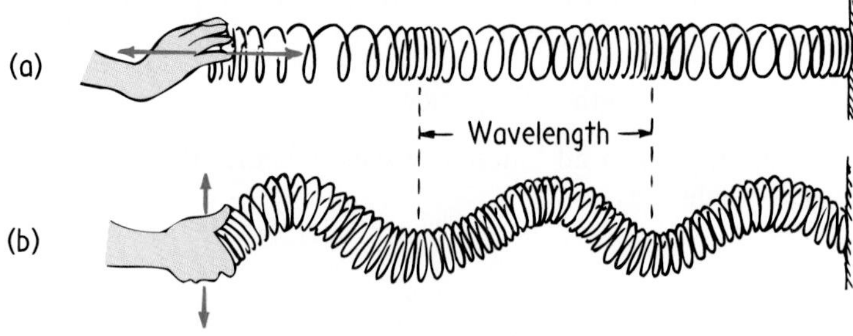

Figure 11.6
Both waves transfer energy from left to right. (a) When the end of the Slinky is pushed and pulled rapidly along its length, a longitudinal wave is produced. (b) When its end is shaken up and down (or side to side), a transverse wave is produced.

A **longitudinal wave** is one in which the direction of wave travel is *along* the direction in which the source vibrates. You produce a longitudinal wave with your Slinky when you shake it back and forth along the Slinky's axis (Figure 11.6a). The vibrations are then parallel to the direction of energy transfer. Part of the Slinky is compressed, and a wave of *compression* travels along it.

In between successive compressions is a stretched region, called a *rarefaction.* Both compressions and rarefactions travel in the same direction along the Slinky. Together they make up the longitudinal wave.

When we study earthquakes in Chapter 27 we'll learn about two types of waves that travel in the ground. One type is longitudinal (P waves), and the other type is transverse (S waves). These travel at different speeds, which provide investigators with a means of determining the source of the waves. Furthermore, the transverse waves cannot travel through liquid matter, while the longitudinal waves can, which provides a means of determining whether matter below ground is molten or solid. More about this later.

11.4 Sound Waves

Think of the air molecules in a room as tiny randomly moving Ping-Pong balls. If you vibrate a Ping-Pong paddle in the midst of the balls, you'll set them vibrating to and fro. The balls will vibrate in rhythm with your vibrating paddle. In some regions, they will be momentarily bunched up (compressions), and in other regions in between, they will be momentarily spread out (rarefactions). The vibrating prongs of a tuning fork do the same to air molecules. Vibrations made up of compressions and rarefactions spread from the tuning fork throughout the air, and a **sound wave** is produced.

Figure 11.7
If you vibrate a Ping-Pong paddle in the midst of a lot of Ping-Pong balls, the balls will vibrate also.

The wavelength of a sound wave is the distance between successive compressions or, equivalently, the distance between successive rarefactions. Each molecule in the air vibrates to and fro about some equilibrium position as the waves move by.

Our subjective impression about the frequency of sound is described as **pitch.** A high-pitched sound, like that from a tiny bell, has a high vibration frequency. Sound from a large bell has a low pitch because its vibrations are of a low frequency.

The human ear can normally hear pitches from sound ranging from about 20 hertz to about 20,000 hertz. As we age, this range shrinks. So, by the time you can afford to trade in your old sound system for an expensive hi-fi one, you may not be able to tell the difference. Sound waves of frequencies below 20 hertz are called *infrasonic waves,* and those of frequencies above 20,000 hertz are called *ultrasonic waves.* We cannot hear infrasonic or ultrasonic sound waves.* But dogs and some other animals can.

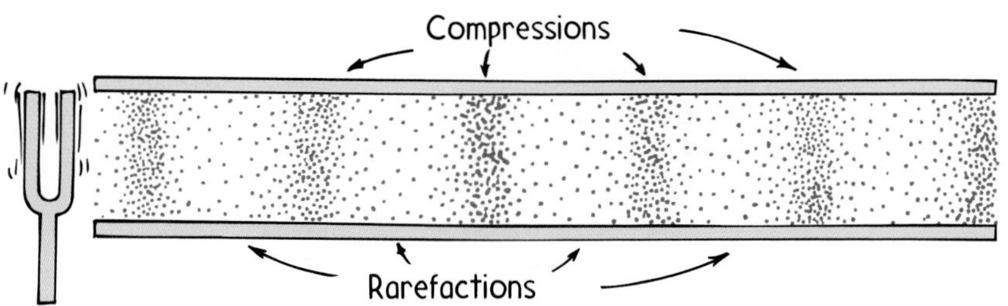

Figure 11.8
Compressions and rarefactions travel (both at the same speed and in the same direction) from the tuning fork through the air in the tube.

*In hospitals, concentrated beams of ultrasound are used to break up kidney stones and gall stones, eliminating the need for surgery.

Most sound is transmitted through air, but any elastic substance—solid, liquid, or gas—can transmit sound.* Air is a poor conductor of sound compared with solids and liquids. You can hear the sound of a distant train clearly by placing your ear against the rail. When swimming, have a friend at a distance click two rocks together beneath the surface of water while you are submerged. Observe how well water conducts the sound. Sound cannot travel in a vacuum because there is nothing to compress and expand. The transmission of sound requires a medium.

Pause to reflect on the physics of sound while you are quietly listening to your radio sometime. The radio loudspeaker is a paper cone that vibrates in rhythm with an electrical signal. Air molecules next to the vibrating cone of the speaker are themselves set into vibration. These, in turn, vibrate against neighboring molecules, which, in turn, do the same, and so on. As a result, rhythmic patterns of compressed and rarefied air emanate from the loudspeaker, showering the entire room with undulating motions. The resulting vibrating air sets your eardrum into vibration, which, in turn, sends cascades of rhythmic electrical impulses along nerves in the cochlea of your inner ear and into the brain. And thus you listen to the sound of music.

Figure 11.10
Waves of compressed and rarefied air, generated by the vibrating cone of the loudspeaker, reproduce the sound of music.

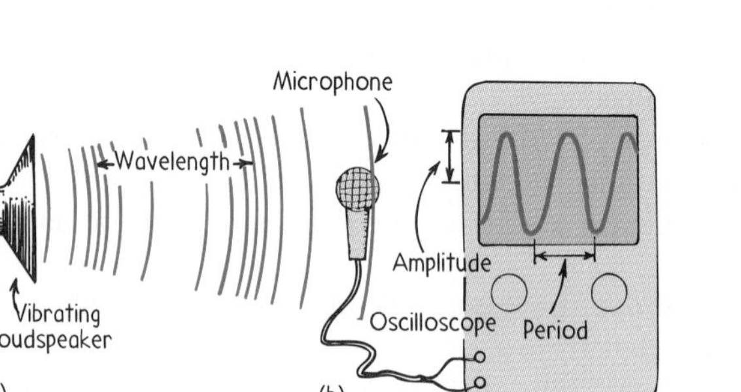

Figure 11.9
(a) The radio loudspeaker is a paper cone that vibrates in rhythm with an electric signal. The sound that is produced sets up similar vibrations in the microphone. The vibrations are displayed on an oscilloscope. (b) The waveform on the oscilloscope screen is a graph of pressure against time, showing how air pressure near the microphone rises and falls as sound waves pass. When the loudness increases, the amplitude of the waveform increases.

Link to Technology

Loudspeaker

The loudspeaker of your radio or other sound-producing systems changes electrical signals into sound waves. The electrical signals pass through a coil wound around the neck of a paper cone. This coil, which acts as an electromagnet, is located near a permanent magnet. When current flows one way, magnetic force pushes the electromagnet toward the permanent magnet, pulling the cone inward. When current flows in the opposite direction, the cone is pushed outward. Vibrations in the electric signal cause the cone to vibrate. Vibrations of the cone then produce sound waves in the air.

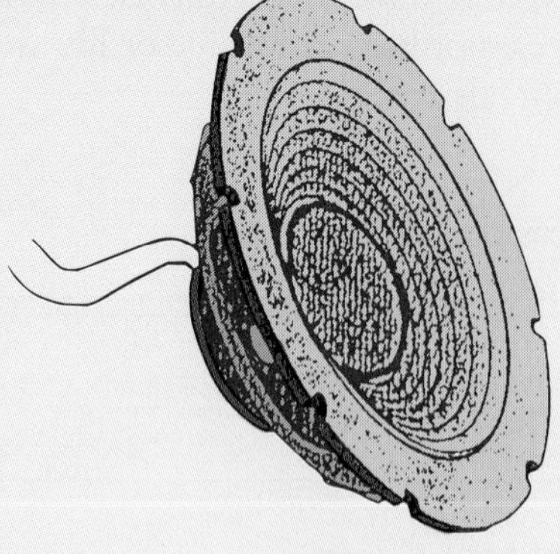

*An elastic substance is "springy," has resilience, and can transmit energy with little loss. Steel, for example, is elastic, while lead and putty are not.

Speed of Sound

If, from a distance, we watch a person chopping wood or hammering, we can easily see that the blow occurs a noticeable time before its sound reaches our ears. Thunder is often heard seconds after a flash of lightning is seen. These common experiences show that sound requires time to travel from one place to another. The speed of sound depends on wind conditions, temperature, and humidity. It does not depend on the loudness or the frequency of the sound; all sounds travel at the same speed in a given medium. The speed of sound in dry air at 0°C is about 330 meters per second, which is nearly 1200 kilometers per hour. Water vapor in the air increases this speed slightly. Sound travels faster through warm air than cold air. This is to be expected, because the faster-moving molecules in warm air bump into each other more frequently and, therefore, can transmit a pulse in less time.* For each degree rise in temperature above 0°C, the speed of sound in air increases by 0.6 meter per second. Thus, in air at a normal room temperature of about 20°C, sound travels at about 340 meters per second. In water, sound speed is about four times its speed in air; in steel, it's about fifteen times its speed in air.

☑ CHECKPOINT

1. Do compressions and rarefactions in a sound wave travel in the same direction or in opposite directions from one another?
2. What is the approximate distance of a thunderstorm when you note a 3-s delay between the flash of lightning and the sound of thunder?

Check Your Answers

1. They travel in the same direction.
2. Assuming the speed of sound in air is about 340 m/s, in 3 s it will travel 340 m/s × 3 s = 1020 m. There is no appreciable time delay for the flash of light, so the storm is slightly more than 1 km away.

11.5 Reflection of Sound

We call the reflection of sound an *echo*. The fraction of sound energy reflected from a surface is large if the surface is rigid and smooth, but it is less if the surface is soft and irregular. The sound energy that is not reflected is transmitted or absorbed.

Sound reflects from a smooth surface in the same way that light does—the angle of incidence is equal to the angle of reflection (Figure 11.11). Sometimes, when sound reflects from the walls, ceiling, and floor of a room, the surfaces are too reflective and the sound becomes garbled. This is due to multiple reflections called **reverberations.** On the other hand, if the reflective surfaces are too absorbent, the sound level is low and the room may sound dull and lifeless. Reflected sound in a room makes it sound lively and full, as you have probably

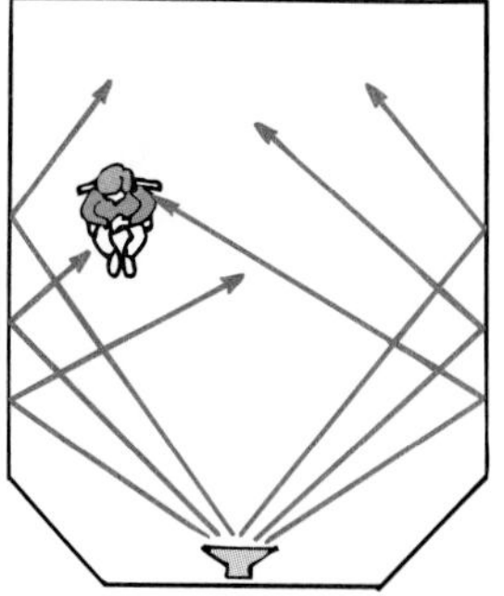

Figure 11.11
The angle of incident sound is equal to the angle of reflected sound.

*The speed of sound in a gas is about 3/4 the average speed of its molecules.

Figure 11.12
The plastic plates above the orchestra reflect both light and sound. Adjusting them is quite simple: what you see is what you hear.

experienced while singing in the shower. In the design of an auditorium or concert hall, a balance must be found between reverberation and absorption. The study of sound properties is called *acoustics.*

It is often advantageous to position highly reflective surfaces behind the stage to direct sound out to the audience. Above the stage, in some concert halls, reflecting surfaces are suspended. The ones in Davies Hall in San Francisco are large shiny plastic surfaces that also reflect light (Figure 11.12). A listener can look up at these reflectors and see the reflected images of the members of the orchestra (the plastic reflectors are somewhat curved, which increases the field of view). Both sound and light obey the same law of reflection. Thus, if a reflector is oriented so that you can see a particular musical instrument, rest assured that you will be able to hear it also. Sound from the instrument will follow the line of sight to the reflector and thence to you. In some halls, absorbers rather than reflectors are used to improve the acoustics.

11.6 Refraction of Sound

Sound waves bend when parts of the wave fronts travel at different speeds. This may happen when sound waves are affected by uneven winds, or when sound is traveling through air of uneven temperatures. This bending of sound is called **refraction.** On a warm day, the air near the ground may be appreciably warmer than the air above, so the speed of sound near the ground increases. Sound waves therefore tend to bend away from the ground, resulting in sound that does not seem to transmit well (Figure 11.13).

The refraction of sound occurs under water, where the speed of sound varies with temperature. This poses a problem for surface vessels that bounce ultrasonic waves off the bottom of the ocean to chart its features. This poses a blessing to submarines that wish to escape detection. Because the ocean has layers of water that are at different temperatures, the refraction of sound leaves gaps

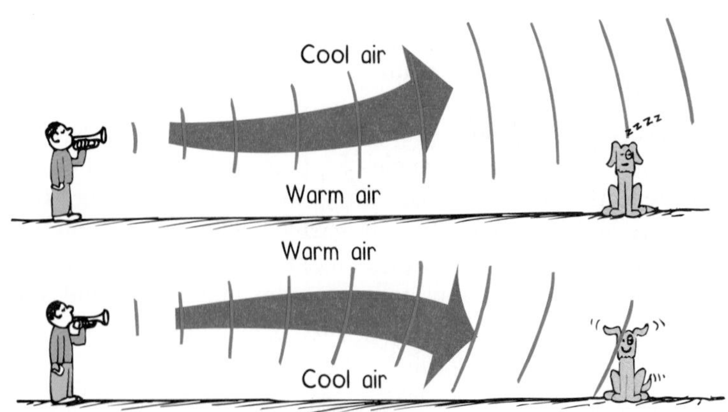

Figure 11.13
Sound waves are bent in air of uneven temperatures.

or "blind spots" in the water. This is where submarines hide. If it weren't for refraction, submarines would be much easier to detect.

The multiple reflections and refractions of ultrasonic waves are used by physicians in a technique for harmlessly "seeing" the interior of the body without the use of x rays. When high-frequency sound (ultrasound) enters the body, it is reflected more strongly from the organs' exteriors than from their interiors, and a picture of the outline of the organs is obtained (Figure 11.14). This ultrasound echo technique may be relatively new to humans, but not to bats and dolphins, who are able to emit ultrasonic squeaks and to locate objects by their echoes.

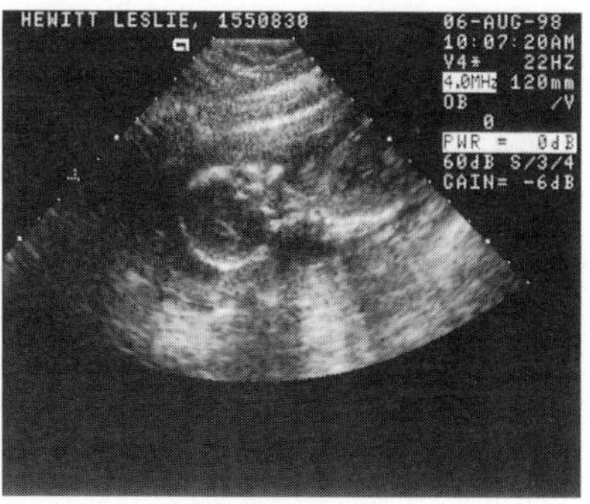

Figure 11.14
The 14-week-old fetus that became Megan Hewitt Abrams, who is more recently seen on page 613.

Figure 11.15
A dolphin emits ultrahigh-frequency sound to locate and identify objects in its environment. Distance is sensed by the time delay between sending sound and receiving its echo, and direction is sensed by differences in time for the echo to reach the dolphin's two ears. A dolphin's main diet is fish. Because fish hear mainly low frequencies, they are not alerted to the fact they are being hunted.

Link to Zoology

Dolphins and Acoustical Imaging

The dominant sense of the dolphin is hearing, for vision is not a very useful sense in the often murky and dark depths of the ocean. Whereas sound is a passive sense for us, it is an active sense for the dolphin, who sends out sounds and then perceives its surroundings by means of the echoes that return. The ultrasonic waves emitted by a dolphin enable it to "see" through the bodies of other animals and people. Skin, muscle, and fat are almost transparent to dolphins, so they "see" a thin outline of the body—but the bones, teeth, and gas-filled cavities are clearly apparent. Physical evidence of cancers, tumors, and heart attacks can all be "seen" by the dolphin—as humans have only recently been capable of doing with ultrasound.

What's more fascinating, the dolphin can reproduce the sonic signals that paint the mental image of its surroundings; thus, it is probably able to communicate its experiences to other dolphins by communicating the full acoustic image of what it has "seen," placing it directly in the minds of other dolphins. It needs no word or symbol for "fish," for example, but it is able to communicate an image of the real thing—perhaps with emphasis highlighted by selective filtering, as we similarly communicate a musical concert to others via various means of sound reproduction. Small wonder that the language of the dolphin is very unlike our own!

Figuring Physical Science

Problem

An oceanic depth-sounding vessel surveys the ocean floor with ultrasonic sound that travels 1530 m/s in seawater. How deep is the water if the time delay of the echo from the ocean floor is 2 s?

Solution

The round trip is 2 s, meaning 1 s down and 1 s up. Then,

$$d = vt = 1530 \text{ m/s} \times 1 \text{ s} = 1530 \text{ m}$$

(Radar works similarly, where microwaves rather than sound waves are sent out.)

11.7 Forced Vibrations

If you strike an unmounted tuning fork, its sound is rather faint. Repeat with the handle of the fork held against a table after striking it, and the sound is louder. This is because the table is forced to vibrate, and its larger surface sets more air in motion. The table is forced into vibration by a fork of any frequency. This is an example of **forced vibration.** The vibration of a factory floor caused by the running of heavy machinery is another example of forced vibration. A more pleasing example is given by the sounding boards of stringed instruments.

If you drop a wrench and a baseball bat on a concrete floor, you will easily notice the difference in their sounds. This is because each vibrates differently when striking the floor. They are not forced to vibrate at a particular frequency, but, instead, each vibrates at its own characteristic frequency. Any object composed of an elastic material will, when disturbed, vibrate at its own special set of frequencies, which together form its special sound. We speak of an object's **natural frequency,** which depends on such factors as the elasticity and shape of the object. Bells and tuning forks, of course, vibrate at their own characteristic frequencies. Interestingly, most things, from atoms to planets and almost everything else in between, have a springiness to them, and they vibrate at one or more natural frequencies.

11.8 Resonance

When the frequency of forced vibrations on an object matches the object's natural frequency, a dramatic increase in amplitude occurs. This phenomenon is called **resonance.** Literally, *resonance* means "resounding," or "sounding again." Putty doesn't resonate, because it isn't elastic, and a dropped handkerchief is too limp to resonate. In order for something to resonate, it needs both a force to pull it back to its starting position and enough energy to maintain its vibration.

A common experience illustrating resonance occurs when you are on a swing. When pumping a swing, you pump in rhythm with the natural frequency of the swing. More important than the force with which you pump is the timing. Even small pumps, or small pushes from someone else, if delivered in rhythm with the frequency of the swinging motion, produce large amplitudes.

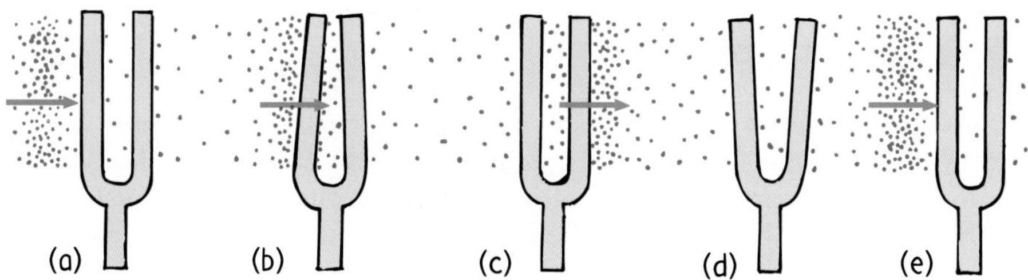

Figure 11.16
Stages of resonance. (a) The first compression meets the fork and gives it a tiny and momentary push; (b) the fork bends and then (c) returns to its initial position just at the time a rarefaction arrives and (d) overshoots in the opposite direction. Just when it returns to its initial position, (e) the next compression arrives to repeat the cycle. Now it bends farther because it is moving.

A common classroom demonstration of resonance is illustrated with a pair of tuning forks adjusted to the same frequency and spaced a meter or so apart. When one of the forks is struck, it sets the other fork into vibration. This is a small-scale version of pushing a friend on a swing—it's the timing that's important. When a series of sound waves impinge on the fork, each compression gives the prong of the fork a tiny push. Since the frequency of these pushes corresponds to the natural frequency of the fork, the pushes will successively increase the amplitude of its vibration. This is because the pushes occur at the right time and repeatedly occur in the same direction as the instantaneous motion of the fork. The motion of the second fork is called a *sympathetic vibration.*

If the forks are not adjusted for matched frequencies, the timing of pushes is off, and resonance doesn't occur. When you tune your radio set, you are similarly adjusting the natural frequency of the electronics in the set to match one of the many surrounding signals. The set then resonates to one station at a time, instead of playing all stations at once.

Resonance is not restricted to wave motion. It occurs whenever successive impulses are applied to a vibrating object in rhythm with its natural frequency. Cavalry troops marching across a footbridge near Manchester, England in 1831 inadvertently caused the bridge to collapse when they marched in rhythm with the bridge's natural frequency. Since then, it is customary to order troops to "break step" when crossing bridges. A more recent bridge disaster was caused by wind-generated resonance (Figure 11.17).

Figure 11.17
In 1940, four months after being completed, the Tacoma Narrows Bridge in the state of Washington was destroyed by wind-generated resonance. The mild gale produced a fluctuating force in resonance with the natural frequency of the bridge, steadily increasing the amplitude until the bridge collapsed.

11.9 Interference

An intriguing property of all waves is **interference.** Consider transverse waves. When the crest of one wave overlaps the crest of another, their individual effects add together. The result is a wave of increased amplitude. This is *constructive interference* (Figure 11.18). When the crest of one wave overlaps the trough of another, their individual effects are reduced. The high part of one wave simply fills in the low part of another. This is *destructive interference.*

Figure 11.18
Constructive and destructive interference in a transverse wave.

Figure 11.19
Two sets of overlapping water waves produce an interference pattern.

Wave interference is easiest to observe in water. In Figure 11.19, we see the interference pattern produced when two vibrating objects touch the surface of water. We can see the regions in which the crest of one wave overlaps the trough of another to produce a region of zero amplitude. At points along such regions, the waves arrive out of step. We say they are *out of phase* with one another.

Interference is a property of all wave motion, whether the waves are water waves, sound waves, or light waves. We see a comparison of interference for transverse waves and for longitudinal waves in Figure 11.20. In the case of sound, the crest of a wave corresponds to a compression and the trough of a wave corresponds to a rarefaction.

Destructive sound interference is at the heart of *antinoise technology.* Noisy devices such as jackhammers are being equipped with microphones that send the sound of the device to electronic microchips, which create mirror-image wave patterns of the sound signals. For the jackhammer, this mirror-image

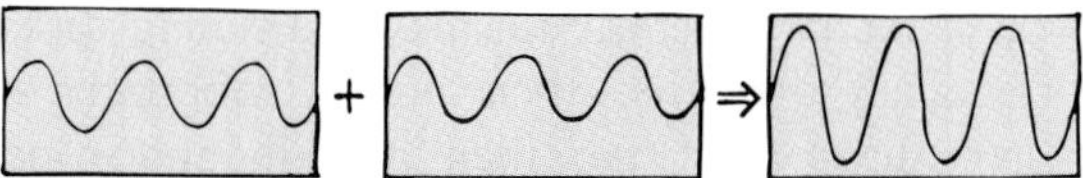

The superposition of two identical transverse waves in phase produces a wave of increased ampitude.

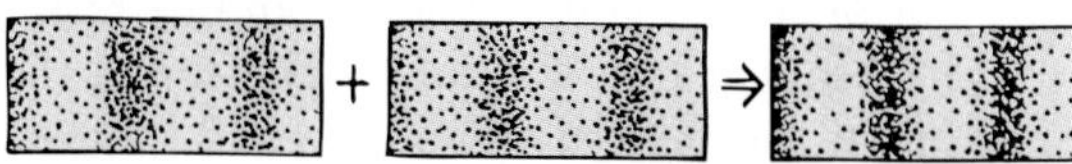

The superposition of two identical longitudinal waves in phase produces a wave of increased intensity.

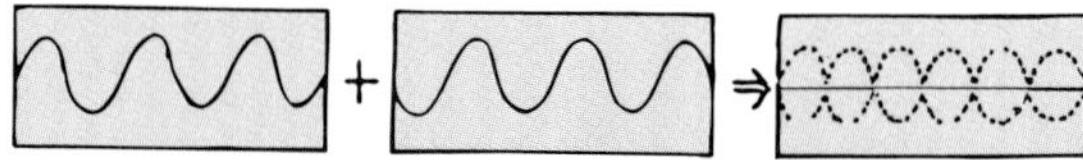

Two identical transverse waves that are out of phase destroy each otherwhen they are superimposed.

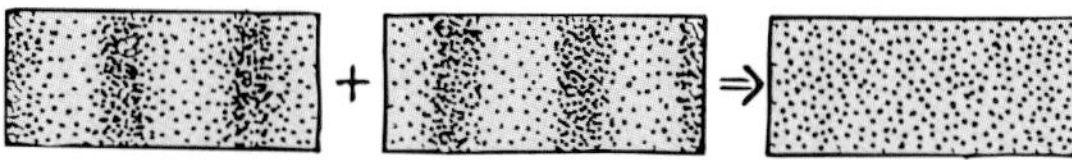

Two identical longitudinal waves that are out of phase destroy each other when they are superimposed.

Figure 11.20
Constructive (top two panels) and destructive (bottom two panels) wave interference in transverse and longitudinal waves.

sound signal is fed to earphones worn by the operator. Sound compressions (or rarefactions) from the hammer are cancelled by mirror image rarefactions (or compressions) in the earphones. The combination of signals cancels the jackhammer noise. Antinoise devices are becoming more common in aircraft, which today are much quieter inside than before this technology was introduced. Are automobiles next, perhaps eliminating the need for mufflers?

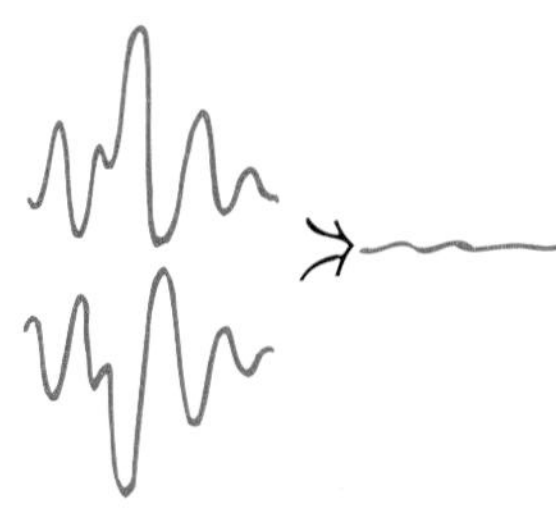

Figure 11.21
When a mirror image of a sound signal combines with the sound itself, the sound is cancelled.

Figure 11.22
When the positive and negative wire inputs to one of the stereo speakers have been interchanged, the speakers are then out of phase. When the speakers are far apart, monaural (not stereo) sound is not as loud as it is from properly phased speakers. When they are brought face to face, very little sound is heard. Interference is nearly complete, as the compressions of one speaker fill in the rarefactions of the other.

Sound interference is dramatically illustrated when monaural sound is played by stereo speakers that are out of phase. Speakers are out of phase when the input wires to one speaker are interchanged (positive and negative wire inputs reversed). For a monaural signal, this means that, when one speaker is sending a compression of sound, the other is sending a rarefaction. The sound produced is not as full and not as loud as from speakers properly connected in phase. The longer waves are cancelled by interference. Shorter waves are cancelled as the speakers are brought closer together, and, when the two speakers are brought face to face against each other, very little sound is heard! Only the highest frequencies survive cancellation. You must try this experiment to appreciate it.

Figure 11.23
Ken Ford tows gliders in quiet comfort when he wears his noise-cancelling earphones. In larger aircraft, sound from the engines is processed and emitted as antinoise from loudspeakers inside the cabin to provide passengers with a quieter ride.

Beats

When two tones of slightly different frequencies are sounded together, a fluctuation in the loudness of the combined sounds is heard; the sound is loud, then faint, then loud, then faint, and so on. This periodic variation in the loudness of sound is called **beats,** and it is due to interference. If you strike two slightly mismatched tuning forks, one fork vibrates at a different frequency than the other, and the vibrations of the forks will be momentarily in step, then out of step, then in again, and so on. When the combined waves reach our ears in step—say, when a compression from one fork overlaps a compression from the other—the sound is at a maximum. A moment later, when the forks are out of step, a compression from one fork is met with a rarefaction from the other, resulting in a minimum. The sound that reaches our ears throbs between maximum and minimum loudness and produces a tremolo effect.

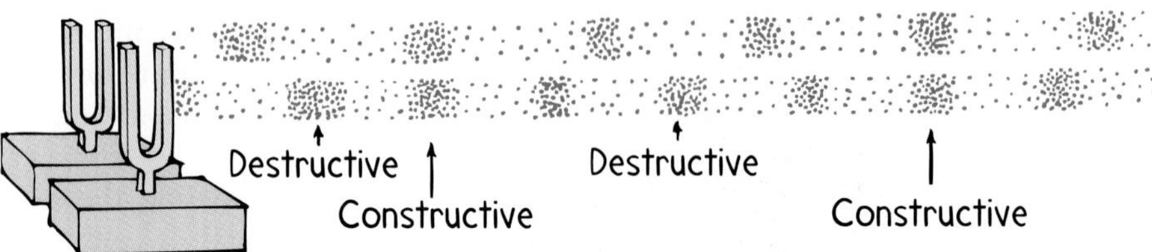

Figure 11.24
The interference of two sound sources of slightly different frequencies produces beats.

Beats can occur with any kind of wave, and they can provide a practical way to compare frequencies. To tune a piano, for example, a piano tuner listens for beats produced between a standard tuning fork and those of a particular string on the piano. When the frequencies are identical, the beats disappear. The members of an orchestra tune up their instruments by listening for beats between their instruments and a standard tone produced by a piano or some other instrument.

Standing Waves

Another fascinating effect of interference is *standing waves*. Tie a rope to a wall and shake the free end up and down. The wall is too rigid to shake, so the waves are reflected back along the rope. By shaking the rope just right, you can cause the incident and reflected waves to interfere and form a **standing wave,** where parts of the rope, called the *nodes,* are stationary. You can hold your fingers on either side of the rope at a node, and the rope doesn't touch them. Other parts of the rope, however, would make contact with your fingers. The positions on a standing wave with the largest displacements are known as *antinodes*. Antinodes occur halfway between nodes.

Standing waves are produced when two sets of waves of equal amplitude and wavelength pass through each other in opposite directions. Then the waves are steadily in and out of phase with each other and produce stable regions of constructive and destructive interference (Figure 11.25).

Standing waves are set up in the strings of musical instruments when plucked, bowed, or struck. They are produced in the air in an organ pipe, a trumpet, or a clarinet—and in the air of a soda-pop bottle when air is blown over the top. Standing waves appear in a tub of water or a cup of coffee when sloshed back and forth at the appropriate frequency. Standing waves can be produced with either transverse or longitudinal vibrations.

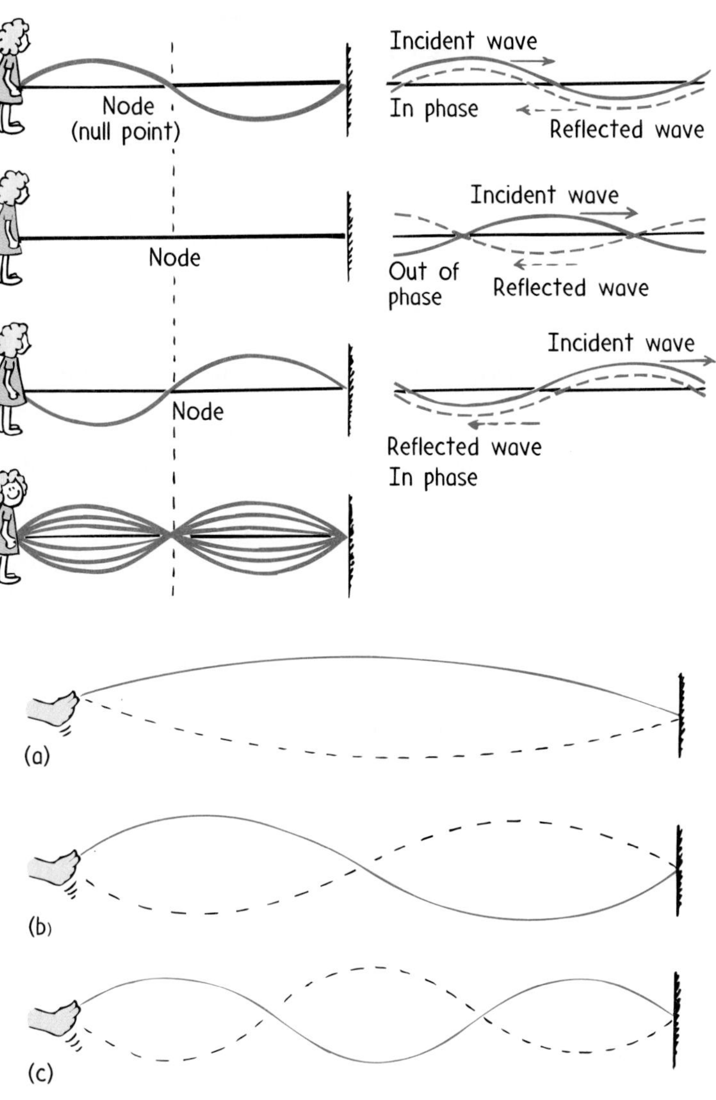

Figure 11.25
The incident and reflected waves interfere to produce a standing wave.

Figure 11.26
(a) Shake the rope until you set up a standing wave of one loop (1/2 wavelength).
(b) Shake with twice the frequency and produce a wave having two loops (1 wavelength).
(c) Shake with three times the frequency and produce three loops (3/2 wavelengths).

☑ CHECKPOINT

1. Is it possible for one wave to cancel another wave so that there is no amplitude remaining.
2. Suppose you set up a standing wave of three segments, as shown in Figure 11.26c. If you shake with a frequency twice as great, how many wave segments will occur in your new standing wave? How many wavelengths?

Check Your Answers

1. Yes. This is called destructive interference. When a standing wave is set up in a rope, for example, parts of the rope have no amplitude—the nodes.
2. If you impart twice the frequency to the rope, you'll produce a standing wave with twice as many segments. You'll have six segments. Since a full wavelength has two segments, you'll have three complete wavelengths in your standing wave.

11.10 Doppler Effect

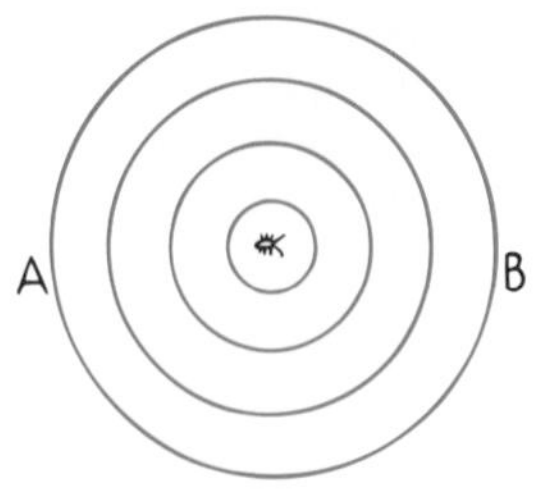

Figure 11.27
Top view of water waves made by a stationary bug jiggling in still water.

Consider a bug in the middle of a quiet puddle. A pattern of water waves is produced when it jiggles its legs and bobs up and down (Figure 11.27). The bug is not traveling anywhere but merely treads water in a stationary position. The waves it creates are concentric circles because wave speed is the same in all directions. If the bug bobs in the water at a constant frequency, the distance between wave crests (the wavelength) is the same in all directions. Waves encounter point A as frequently as they encounter point B. Therefore, the frequency of wave motion is the same at points A and B, or anywhere in the vicinity of the bug. This wave frequency remains the same as the bobbing frequency of the bug.

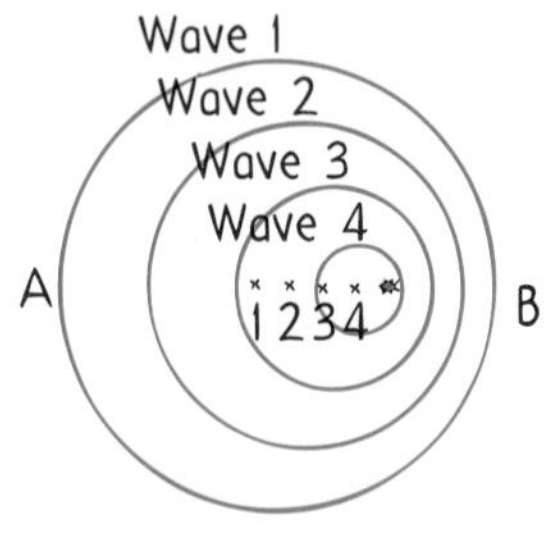

Figure 11.28
Water waves made by a bug swimming in still water toward point B.

Suppose the jiggling bug moves across the water at a speed less than the wave speed. In effect, the bug chases part of the waves it has produced. The wave pattern is distorted and is no longer that of concentric circles (Figure 11.28). The center of the outer wave originated when the bug was at the center of that circle. The center of the next smaller wave originated when the bug was at the center of that circle, and so forth. The centers of the circular waves move in the direction of the swimming bug. Although the bug maintains the same bobbing frequency as before, an observer at B would see the waves coming more often. The observer would measure a higher frequency. This is because each successive wave has a shorter distance to travel and therefore arrives at B sooner than if the bug weren't moving toward B. An observer at A, on the other hand, measures a lower frequency because of the longer time between wave-crest arrivals. This occurs because each successive wave travels farther to A as a result of the bug's motion. This change in frequency due to the motion of the source (or due to the motion of the receiver) is called the **Doppler effect** (after the Austrian physicist and mathematician Christian Johann Doppler, who lived from 1803–1853).

Water waves spread over the flat surface of the water. Sound and light waves, on the other hand, travel in three-dimensional space in all directions like an expanding balloon. Just as circular waves are closer together in front of the swimming bug, spherical sound or light waves ahead of a moving source are closer together and reach an observer more frequently. The Doppler effect holds for all types of waves.

The Doppler effect is evident when you hear the changing pitch of an ambulance or fire-engine siren. When the siren is approaching you, the crests of the sound waves encounter your ear more frequently, and the pitch is higher than normal. And when the siren passes you and moves away, the crests of the waves encounter your ear less frequently, and you hear a drop in pitch.

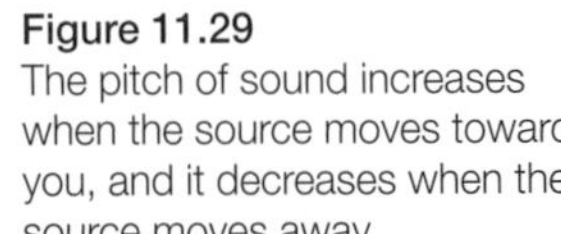

Figure 11.29
The pitch of sound increases when the source moves toward you, and it decreases when the source moves away.

The Doppler effect also occurs for light. When a light source approaches, there is an increase in its measured frequency; when it recedes, there is a decrease in its frequency. An increase in light frequency is called a *blue shift,* because the increase is toward a higher frequency, or toward the blue end of the color spectrum. A decrease in frequency is called a *red shift,* referring to a shift toward a lower frequency, or toward the red end of the color spectrum. The galaxies, for example, show a red shift in the light they emit. A measurement of this shift permits a calculation of their speeds of recession. A rapidly spinning star shows a red shift on the side turning away from us and a relative blue shift on the side turning toward us. This enables us to calculate the star's spin rate.

Be clear about the distinction between *frequency* and *speed.* How frequently a wave vibrates is altogether different from how fast it moves from one location to another.

Insights

☑ CHECKPOINT

When a light or sound source moves toward you, is there an increase or a decrease in the wave speed?

Check Your Answer

Neither! It is the *frequency* of a wave that undergoes a change when the source is moving, not the wave speed.

11.11 Wave Barriers and Bow Waves

When a source of waves travels as fast as the waves it produces, a "wave barrier" is produced. Consider the bug in our previous example. If it swims as fast as the waves it makes, the bug will keep up with the waves it produces. Instead of the waves going ahead of the bug, they superimpose on one another directly, forming a hump in front of the bug (Figure 11.30). Thus, the bug encounters a wave barrier. Much effort is required of the bug to swim over the hump before it can swim faster than wave speed.

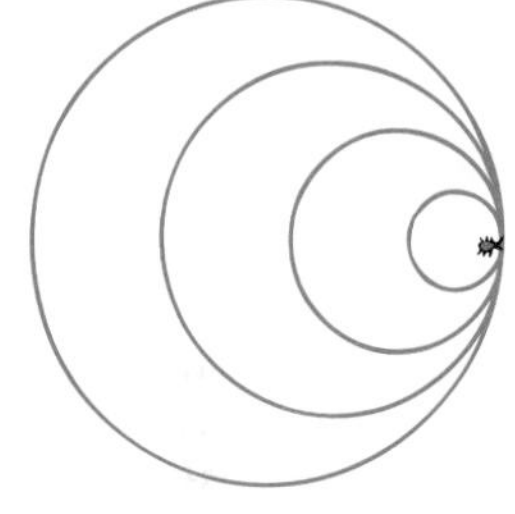

Figure 11.30
The wave pattern made by a bug swimming at wave speed.

The same thing happens when an aircraft travels at the speed of sound. The waves overlap to produce a barrier of compressed air on the leading edges of the wings and on other parts of the aircraft. Considerable thrust is required for the aircraft to push through this barrier (Figure 11.31). Once through, the aircraft can fly faster than the speed of sound without similar opposition. The craft is *supersonic.* It is like the bug, which, once it has passed its wave barrier, finds the medium ahead relatively smooth and undisturbed.

Figure 11.31
Condensation of water vapor by rapid expansion of air about this supersonic craft can be seen in the rarefied region behind the wall of compressed air.

When the bug swims faster than wave speed, it produces a pattern of overlapping waves, ideally shown in Figure 11.32. The bug overtakes and outruns the waves it produces. The overlapping waves form a V shape, called a **bow wave,** which appears to be dragging behind the bug. The familiar bow wave generated by a speedboat knifing through the water is produced by overlapping waves.

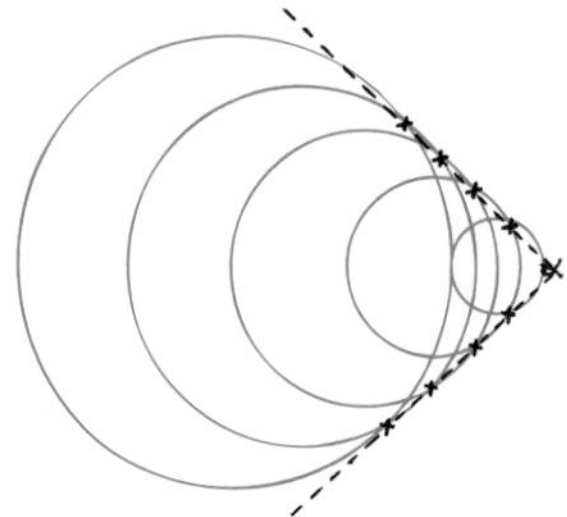

Figure 11.32
Idealized wave pattern made by a bug swimming faster than wave speed.

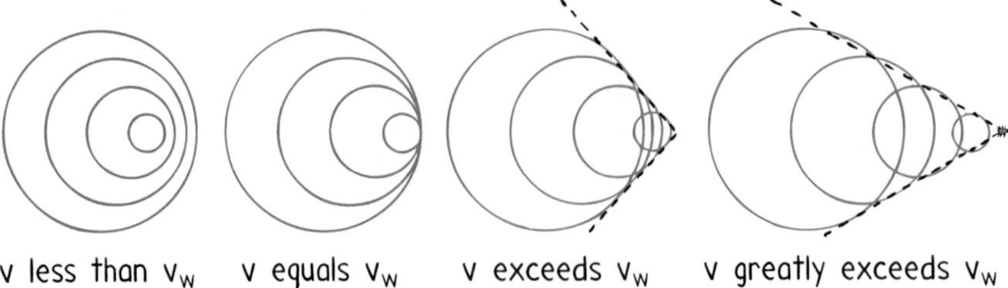

Figure 11.33
Idealized patterns made by a bug swimming at successively greater speeds. Overlapping at the edges occurs only when the bug swims faster than wave speed.

Some wave patterns created by sources moving at various speeds are shown in Figure 11.33. Note that, after the speed of the source exceeds wave speed, increased speed produces a narrower V shape.*

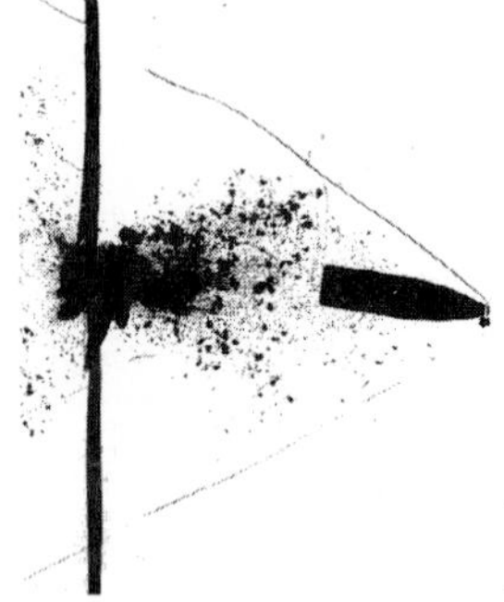

Figure 11.34
The shock wave of a bullet piercing a sheet of Plexiglas. Light is deflected as it passes through the compressed air that makes up the shock wave, making it visible. Look carefully and see the second shock wave originating at the tail of the bullet.

11.12 Shock Waves and the Sonic Boom

Whereas a speedboat knifing through the water generates a two-dimensional bow wave at the surface of the water, a supersonic aircraft similarly generates a three-dimensional **shock wave.** Just as a bow wave is produced by overlapping circles that form a V, a shock wave is produced by overlapping spheres that form a cone. And just as the bow wave of a speedboat spreads until it reaches the shore of a lake, the conical wake generated by a supersonic aircraft spreads until it reaches the ground.

The bow wave of a speedboat that passes by can splash and douse you if you are at the water's edge. You could say that, in a sense, you are hit by a "water boom." In the same way, when the conical shell of compressed air that sweeps behind a supersonic aircraft reaches listeners on the ground below, the sharp crack they hear is described as a **sonic boom.**

We don't hear a sonic boom from slower-than-sound (subsonic) aircraft because the sound waves reach our ears gradually and are perceived as a continuous tone. Only when the craft moves faster than sound do the waves overlap to reach the listener in a single burst. The sudden increase in pressure is much the same in effect as the sudden expansion of air produced by an explosion. Both processes direct a burst of high-pressure air to the listener. The ear is hard pressed to distinguish between the high pressure caused by an explosion and that produced by many overlapping waves.

A water skier is familiar with the fact that, next to the high hump of the V-shaped bow wave, there is a V-shaped depression. The same is true of a shock wave, which consists of two cones: a high-pressure cone generated at the bow of the supersonic aircraft and a low-pressure cone that follows toward (or at) the tail of the aircraft. The edges of these cones are visible in the photograph of the supersonic bullet in Figure 11.34. Between these two cones, the air pressure rises sharply to above atmospheric pressure, then it falls below atmospheric pressure before sharply returning to normal beyond the inner tail cone (Figure 11.35). This overpressure, suddenly followed by underpressure, intensifies the sonic boom.

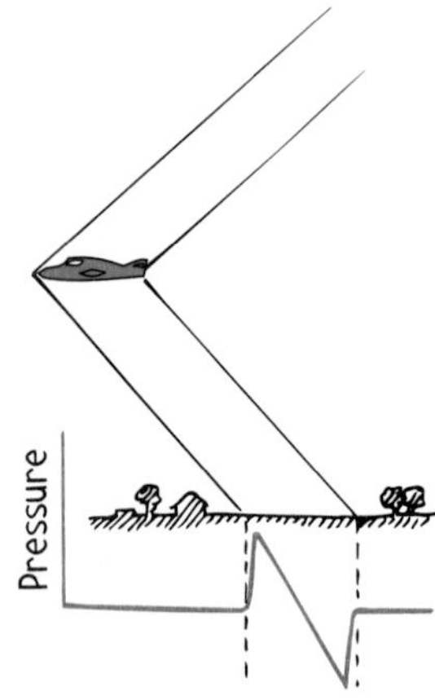

Figure 11.35
A shock wave.

*Bow waves generated by boats in water are more complex than is indicated here. Our idealized treatment serves as an analogy for the production of the less complex shock waves in air.

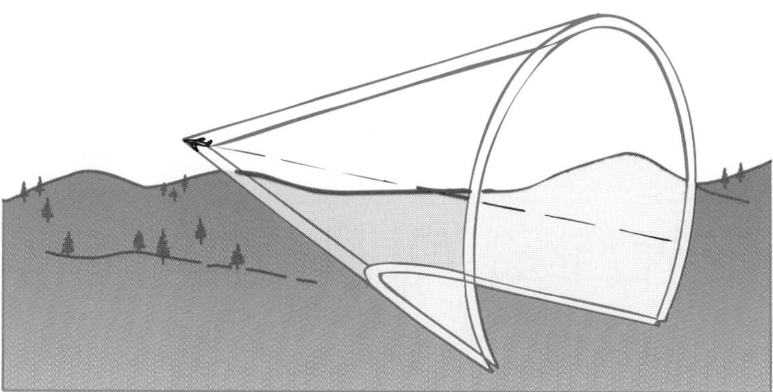

Figure 11.36
The shock wave actually consists of two cones—a high-pressure cone with its apex at the bow and a low-pressure cone with its apex at the tail. A graph of the air pressure at ground level between the cones takes the shape of the letter N.

A common misconception is that sonic booms are produced when an aircraft breaks through the sound barrier—that is, just when the aircraft exceeds the speed of sound. This is essentially the same as saying that a boat produces a bow wave when it overtakes its own waves. This is not so. The fact is that a shock wave and its resulting sonic boom are swept continuously behind an aircraft that is traveling faster than sound, just as a bow wave is swept continuously behind a speedboat. In Figure 11.37, listener B is in the process of hearing a sonic boom. Listener C has already heard it, and listener A will hear it shortly. The aircraft that generated this shock wave may have broken through the sound barrier hours ago!

It is not necessary that the moving source be "noisy" to produce a shock wave. Once an object is moving faster than the speed of sound, it will *make* sound. A supersonic bullet passing overhead produces a crack, which is a small sonic boom. If the bullet were larger and disturbed more air in its path, the crack would be more boomlike. When a lion tamer cracks a circus whip, the cracking sound is actually a sonic boom produced by the tip of the whip traveling faster than the speed of sound. Both the bullet and the whip are not in themselves sound sources, but, when they are traveling at supersonic speeds, they produce their own sound as they generate shock waves.

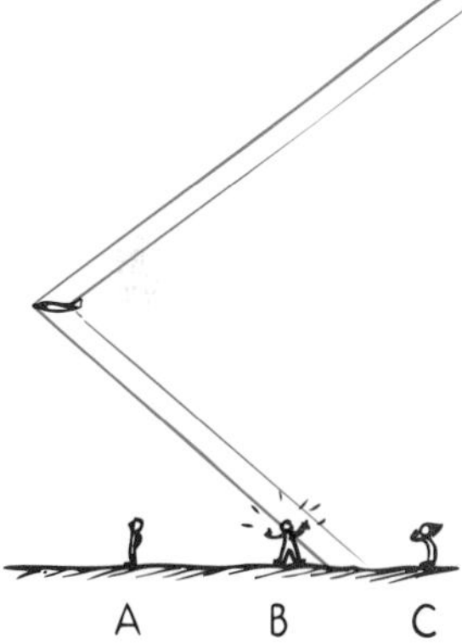

Figure 11.37
The shock wave has not yet reached listener A, but it is now reaching listener B, and it has already reached listener C.

11.13 Musical Sounds

Most of the sounds we hear are noises. The impact of a falling object, the slamming of a door, the roaring of a motorcycle, and most of the sounds from traffic in city streets are noises. Noise corresponds to an irregular vibration of the eardrum produced by an irregularly vibrating source. Graphs that indicate the varying pressure of the air on the eardrum are shown in Figure 11.39. In *a*, we see the erratic pattern of noise. In *b*, the sound of music has shapes that repeat themselves periodically. There are periodic tones, or musical "notes." (But musical instruments can make noise as well!) Such graphs can be displayed on the screen of an oscilloscope when the electrical signal from a microphone is fed into the input terminal of this useful device.

Figure 11.38
Physics chanteuse Lynda Williams, physics instructor at Santa Rosa Junior College, puts herself fully into the physics of music.

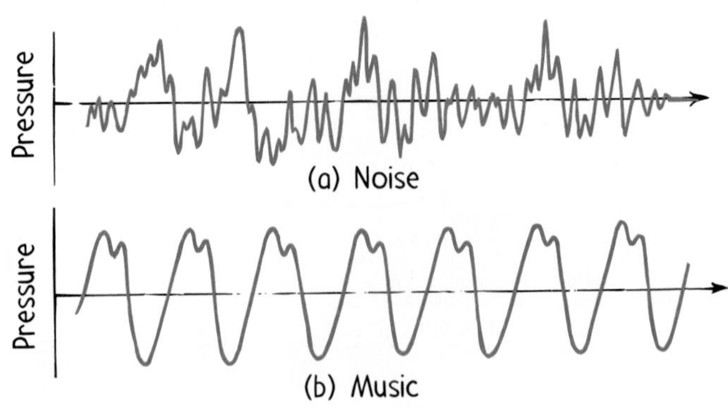

Figure 11.39
Graphical representations of noise and music.

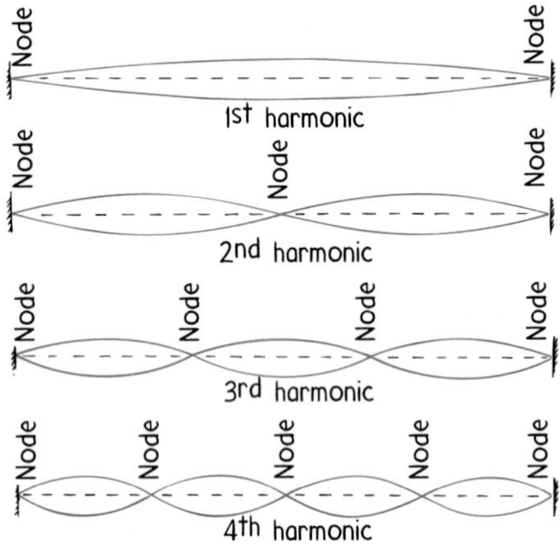

Figure 11.40
Modes of vibration of a guitar string.

We have no trouble distinguishing between the tone from a piano and the tone from a clarinet of the same musical **pitch** (frequency). Each of these tones has a characteristic sound that differs in **quality,** or timbre. Most musical sounds are composed of a superposition of many frequencies called **partial tones,** or simply *partials*. The lowest frequency, called the **fundamental frequency,** determines the pitch of the note. Partial tones that are whole multiples of the fundamental frequency are called **harmonics.** A tone that has twice the frequency of the fundamental is the second harmonic, a tone with three times the fundamental frequency is the third harmonic, and so on (Figure 11.40).* It is the variety of partial tones that gives a musical note its characteristic quality.

Thus, if we strike middle C on the piano, we produce a fundamental tone with a pitch of about 262 hertz and also a blending of partial tones of two, three, four, five, and so on times the frequency of middle C. The number and relative loudness of the partial tones determine the quality of sound associated with the piano. Sound from practically every musical instrument consists of a fundamental and partials. Pure tones, those having only one frequency, can be produced electronically. Electronic synthesizers, for example, produce pure tones and mixtures of these to produce a vast variety of musical sounds.

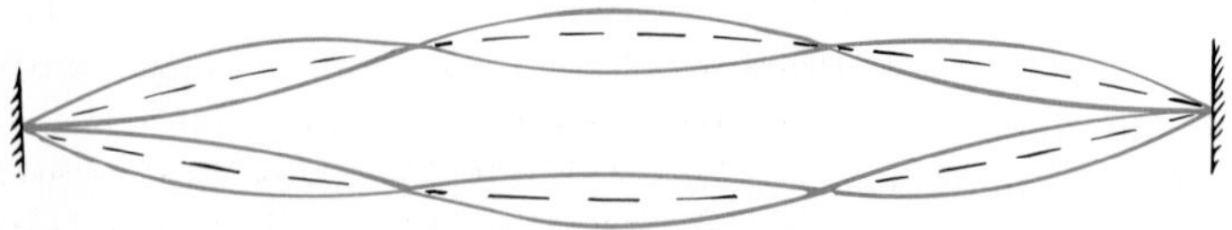

Figure 11.41
A composite vibration of the fundamental mode and the third harmonic.

The quality of a tone is determined by the presence and relative intensity of the various partials. The ear recognizes the different partials and can therefore differentiate the different sounds produced by a piano and a clarinet. A pair of tones of the same pitch with different qualities have either different partials or a difference in the relative intensity of the partials.

*Not all partial tones present in a complex tone are integer multiples of the fundamental. Unlike the harmonics of woodwinds and brasses, stringed instruments, such as the piano, produce "stretched" partial tones that are nearly, but not quite, harmonics.

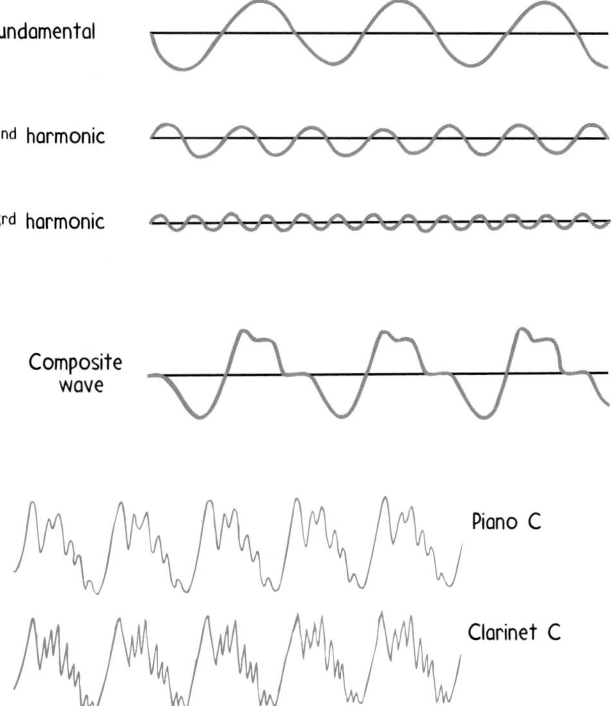

Figure 11.42
Sine waves combine to produce a composite wave.

Figure 11.43
Sounds from the piano and clarinet differ in quality.

Musical Instruments

Sound production from conventional musical instruments can be grouped into three classes: vibrating strings, vibrating air columns, and percussion.

In a stringed instrument, the vibration of the strings is transferred to a sounding board and then to the air, but with low efficiency. To compensate for this effect, we find relatively large string sections in orchestras. A smaller number of the high-efficiency wind instruments sufficiently balances a much larger number of violins.

In a wind instrument, the sound is a vibration of an air column in the instrument. There are various ways to set air columns into vibration. In brass instruments, such as trumpets, French horns, and trombones, vibrations of the player's lips interact with standing waves that are set up by acoustic energy reflected within the instrument by the flared bell. The lengths of the vibrating air columns are manipulated by pushing valves that add or subtract extra segments or by extending or shortening the length of the tube. In woodwinds, such as clarinets, oboes, and saxophones, a stream of air produced by the musician sets a reed vibrating, whereas in fifes, flutes, and piccolos, the musician blows air against the edge of a hole to produce a fluttering stream that sets the air column into vibration.

In percussion instruments, such as drums and cymbals, a two-dimensional membrane or an elastic surface is struck to produce sound. The fundamental tone produced depends on the geometry, the elasticity, and, in some cases, the tension of the surface. Changes in pitch result from changing the tension in the vibrating surface; depressing the edge of a drum membrane with the hand is

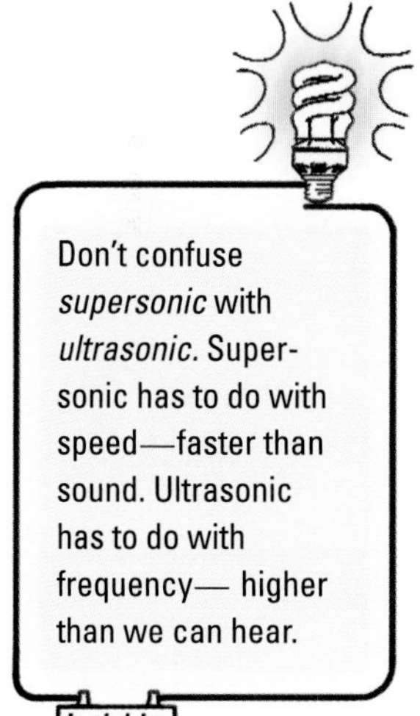

Fourier Analysis

One of the most interesting discoveries about music was made in 1822 by the French mathematician Joseph Fourier. He discovered that wave motion could be reduced to simple sine waves. A sine wave is the simplest of waves, having a single frequency, as shown in Figure 11.42. All periodic waves, however complicated, can be broken down into constituent sine waves of different amplitudes and frequencies. The mathematical operation for doing this is called **Fourier analysis.** We will not explain the mathematics here, but we will simply point out that, by such analysis, one can find the pure sine tones that constitute the tone of, say, a violin. When these pure tones are sounded together, as by striking a number of tuning forks or by selecting the proper keys on an electric organ, they combine to produce the tone of the violin. The lowest-frequency sine wave is the fundamental, and it determines the pitch of the note. The higher-frequency sine waves are the partials, which give the characteristic quality. Thus, the wave form of any musical sound is no more than a sum of simple sine waves.

Since the wave form of music is a multitude of various sine waves, to duplicate sound accurately by radio, tape recorder, or CD player, we should be able to process as large a range of frequencies as possible. The notes of a piano keyboard range from 27 hertz to 4200 hertz, but to duplicate the music of a piano composition accurately, the sound system must have a range of frequencies up to 20,000 hertz. The greater the range of the frequencies of an electrical sound system, the closer the musical output approximates the original sound, hence the wide range of frequencies that can be produced in a high-fidelity sound system.

Our ear performs a sort of Fourier analysis automatically. It sorts out the complex jumble of air pulsations that reach it, and it transforms them into pure tones. And we recombine various groupings of these pure tones when we listen. What combinations of tones we have learned to focus our attention on determines what we hear when we listen to a concert. We can direct our attention to the sounds of the various instruments and discern the faintest tones from the loudest; we can delight in the intricate interplay of instruments and still detect the extraneous noises of others around us. This is a most incredible feat.

Figure 11.44
Does each listener hear the same music?

one way of accomplishing this. Different modes of vibration can be set up by striking the surface in different places. In the kettledrum, the shape of the kettle changes the frequency of the drum. As in all musical sounds, the quality depends on the number and relative loudness of the partial tones.

Electronic musical instruments differ markedly from conventional musical instruments. Instead of strings that must be bowed, plucked, or struck, or reeds over which air must be blown, or diaphragms that must be tapped to produce sounds, some electronic instruments use electrons to generate the signals that make up musical sounds. Others begin with sound from an acoustical instrument and then modify it. Electronic music demands that the composer and the player demonstrate an expertise beyond the knowledge of musicology. It brings a powerful new tool to the hands of the musician.

Summary of Terms

Sine curve A wave form traced by simple harmonic motion, which can be made visible on a moving conveyor belt by a pendulum swinging at right angles above the moving belt.

Amplitude For a wave or vibration, the maximum displacement on either side of the equilibrium (midpoint) position.

Wavelength The distance between successive crests, troughs, or identical parts of a wave.

Frequency For a vibrating body or medium, the number of vibrations per unit time. For a wave, the number of crests that pass a particular point per unit time.

Hertz The SI unit of frequency. One hertz (symbol Hz) equals one vibration per second.

Period The time required for a vibration or a wave to make a complete cycle; equal to 1/frequency.

Wave speed The speed with which waves pass a particular point:

$$\text{wave speed} = \text{frequency} \times \text{wavelength}$$

Transverse wave A wave in which the medium vibrates in a direction perpendicular (transverse) to the direction in which the wave travels. Light consists of transverse waves.

Longitudinal wave A wave in which the medium vibrates in a direction parallel (longitudinal) with the direction in which the wave travels. Sound consists of longitudinal waves.

Compression Condensed region of the medium through which a longitudinal wave travels.

Rarefaction Rarefied region, or region of lessened pressure, of the medium through which a longitudinal wave travels.

Interference pattern The pattern formed by superposition of different sets of waves, which produces mutual reinforcement in some places and cancellation in others.

Standing wave A stationary wave pattern formed in a medium when two sets of identical waves pass through the medium in opposite directions.

Doppler effect The change in frequency of wave motion resulting from motion of the sender or the receiver.

Bow wave The V-shaped wave made by an object moving across a liquid surface at a speed greater than the wave speed.

Shock wave The cone-shaped wave made by an object moving at supersonic speed through a fluid.

Sonic boom The loud sound resulting from a shock wave.

Infrasonic Describes a sound of a frequency too low to be heard by the normal human ear—below 20 hertz.

Ultrasonic Describes a sound of a frequency too high to be heard by the normal human ear—above 20,000 hertz.

Reverberation Reechoed sound.

Refraction The bending of a wave, either through a nonuniform medium or from one medium to another, caused by differences in wave speed.

Forced vibration The setting up of vibrations in an object by a vibrating force.

Natural frequency A frequency at which an elastic object naturally tends to vibrate, so that minimum energy is required to produce a forced vibration or to continue vibration at that frequency.

Fundamental frequency The lowest frequency of vibration, or the first harmonic. In a string, the vibration makes a single segment.

Resonance The response of a body when a forcing frequency matches its natural frequency.

Beats A series of alternate reinforcements and cancellations produced by the interference of two waves of slightly different frequency, heard as a throbbing effect in sound waves.

Quality The characteristic timbre of a musical sound, which is governed by the number and relative intensities of partial tones.

Partial tone One of the frequencies present in a complex tone. When a partial tone is an integer multiple of the lowest frequency, it is a harmonic.

Harmonic A partial tone that is an integer multiple of the fundamental frequency. The vibration that begins with the fundamental vibrating frequency is the first harmonic, twice the fundamental is the second harmonic, and so on in sequence.

Review Questions

11.1 Vibrations and Waves

1. What is a *wiggle in time* called? A *wiggle in space and time*?
2. Distinguish between the propagation of sound waves and the propagation of light waves.
3. What is the source of all waves?
4. Distinguish between these different parts of a wave: period, amplitude, wavelength, and frequency.
5. How many vibrations per second are represented in a radio wave of 101.7 MHz?
6. How do *frequency* and *period* relate to each other?

11.2 Wave Motion

7. In one word, what is it that moves from source to receiver in wave motion?
8. Does the medium in which a wave travels move with the wave? Give examples to support your answer.
9. What is the relationship among frequency, wavelength, and wave speed?

11.3 Transverse and Longitudinal Waves

10. In what direction are the vibrations in a transverse wave, relative to the direction of wave travel?
11. In what direction are the vibrations in a longitudinal wave, relative to the direction of wave travel?
12. Distinguish between a *compression* and a *rarefaction.*

11.4 Sound Waves

13. How does a vibrating tuning fork emit sound?
14. Does sound travel faster in warm air or in cold air? Defend your answer.
15. How does the speed of sound in water compare with the speed of sound in air? How does the speed of sound in steel compare with the speed of sound in air?

11.5 Reflection of Sound

16. What is the law of reflection for sound?
17. What is a *reverberation?*

11.6 Refraction of Sound

18. What causes refraction?
19. Does sound tend to bend upward or downward when its speed near the ground is lower than its speed higher up?
20. There is a difference between the way in which we passively see our surroundings in daylight and the way in which we actively probe our surroundings with a searchlight in the darkness. Which of these ways of perceiving our surroundings is more like the way in which a dolphin perceives its environment?

11.7 Forced Vibrations

21. Why does a struck tuning fork sound louder when its handle is held against a table?
22. Does a blob of putty have a natural frequency? Explain.

11.8 Resonance

23. Distinguish between *forced vibrations* and *resonance.*
24. What is required to make an object resonate?
25. When you listen to a radio, why do you hear only one station at a time instead of all stations at once?
26. Why do troops "break step" when crossing a bridge?

11.9 Interference

27. What kinds of waves exhibit interference?
28. Distinguish between *constructive interference* and *destructive interference.*
29. What does it mean to say that one wave is out of phase with another?
30. What physical phenomenon underlies beats?
31. What causes a standing wave?
32. What is a *node*? What is an *antinode*?

11.10 Doppler Effect

33. In the Doppler effect, does frequency change? Does wavelength change? Does wave speed change?
34. Can the Doppler effect be observed with longitudinal waves, with transverse waves, or with both?

11.11 Wave Barriers and Bow Waves

35. How do the speed of a wave source and the speed of the waves themselves compare when a wave barrier is being produced? How do they compare when a bow wave is being produced?
36. How does the V shape of a bow wave depend on the speed of the wave source?

11.12 Shock Waves and the Sonic Boom

37. True or false: A sonic boom occurs only when an aircraft is breaking through the sound barrier.
38. True or false: In order for an object to produce a sonic boom, it must be "noisy." Give two examples to support your answer.

11.13 Musical Sounds

39. Distinguish between a musical sound and noise.
40. Why are there typically more stringed instruments in an orchestra than wind instruments?

Activities

1. Tie a rubber tube, a spring, or a rope to a fixed support and shake it to produce standing waves. See how many nodes you can produce.
2. Test to see which of your ears has the better hearing by covering one ear and finding how far away your open ear can hear the ticking of a clock; repeat for the other ear. Notice also how the sensitivity of your hearing improves when you cup your hands behind your ears.
3. Do the activity suggested in Figure 11.22 with a stereo sound system. Simply reverse the wire inputs to one of the speakers so the two are out of phase. When monoral sound is played and the speakers are brought face to face, the lowering of volume is truly amazing! If the speakers are well insulated, you will hear almost no sound at all.
4. For this activity, you'll need an isolated loudspeaker (bare of its casing) and a sheet of plywood or cardboard—the bigger the better. Cut a hole in the middle part of the sheet that is about the size of the speaker. Listen to music from the isolated speaker,

then hear the difference when it's placed against the hole. The sheet diminishes the amount of sound from the back of the speaker that interferes with sound coming from the front side, producing a much fuller sound. Now you know why speakers are mounted in enclosures.

5. Wet your finger and rub it slowly around the rim of a thin-rimmed, stemmed glass while you hold the base of the glass firmly to a tabletop with your other hand. The friction of your finger will excite standing waves in the glass, much like the wave made on the strings of a violin by the friction from a violin bow. Try it with a metal bowl.
6. Swing a buzzer of any kind over your head in a circle. You won't hear the Doppler shift, but your friends off to the side will. The pitch will increase as it approaches them, and decrease when it recedes. Then switch places with a friend so you can hear it too.
7. Make the lowest-pitched vocal sound you are capable of; then keep doubling the pitch to see how many octaves your voice can span.

Exercises

1. What is the source of wave motion?
2. If we double the frequency of a vibrating object, what happens to its period?
3. You dip your finger repeatedly into a puddle of water and make waves. What happens to the wavelength if you dip your finger more frequently?
4. How does the frequency of vibration of a small object floating in water compare to the number of waves passing it each second?
5. How far, in terms of wavelength, does a wave travel in one period?
6. What kind of motion should you impart to the nozzle of a garden hose so that the resulting stream of water approximates a sine curve?
7. What kind of motion should you impart to a stretched coiled spring (or to a Slinky) to produce a transverse wave? A longitudinal wave?
8. If a gas tap is turned on for a few seconds, someone a couple of meters away will hear the gas escaping long before he or she smells it. What does this indicate about the speed of sound and the motion of molecules in the sound-carrying medium?
9. A cat can hear sound frequencies up to 70,000 Hz. Bats send and receive ultrahigh-frequency squeaks up to 120,000 Hz. Which hears sound of shorter wavelengths, cats or bats?
10. What does it mean to say that a radio station is "at 101.1 on your FM dial?"
11. Sound from Source A has twice the frequency of sound from Source B. Compare the wavelengths of sound from the two sources.
12. Suppose a sound wave and an electromagnetic wave have the same frequency. Which has the longer wavelength?
13. At the stands of a race track, you notice smoke from the starter's gun before you hear it fire. Explain.
14. In an Olympic competition, a microphone picks up the sound of the starter's gun and sends it electrically to speakers at every runner's starting block. Why?
15. At the instant that a high-pressure region is created just outside the prongs of a vibrating tuning fork, what is being created inside between the prongs?
16. Why is it so quiet after a snowfall?
17. If a bell is ringing inside a bell jar, we can no longer hear it when the air is pumped out, but we can still see it. What differences in the properties of sound and light does this indicate?
18. Why is the moon described as a "silent planet"?
19. As you pour water into a glass, you repeatedly tap the glass with a spoon. As the tapped glass is being filled, does the pitch of the sound increase or decrease? (What should you do to answer this question?)
20. If the speed of sound depended on its frequency, would you enjoy a concert sitting in the second balcony?
21. If the frequency of sound is doubled, what change will occur in its speed? What change will occur in its wavelength?
22. Why does sound travel faster in warm air?
23. Why does sound travel faster in moist air? (Hint: At the same temperature, water-vapor molecules have the same average kinetic energy as the heavier nitrogen and oxygen molecules in the air. How, then, do the average speeds of H_2O molecules compare with those of N_2 and O_2 molecules?)
24. Why is an echo weaker than the original sound?
25. What two physics mistakes occur in a science-fiction movie that shows a distant explosion in outer space, where you see and hear the explosion at the same time?
26. A rule of thumb for estimating the distance in kilometers between an observer and a lightning stroke is to divide the number of seconds in the interval between the flash and the sound by 3. Is this rule correct?
27. If a single disturbance some unknown distance away sends out both transverse and longitudinal waves that travel with distinctly different speeds in the medium, such as in the ground during an earthquake, how could the distance to the disturbance be determined?

28. Why will marchers at the end of a long parade following a band be out of step with marchers near the front?
29. What is the danger posed by people in the balcony of an auditorium stamping their feet in a steady rhythm?
30. Why is the sound of a harp soft in comparison with the sound of a piano?
31. If the handle of a tuning fork is held solidly against a tabletop, the sound from the tuning fork becomes louder. Why? How will this affect the length of time the fork keeps vibrating? Explain.
32. The sitar, an Indian musical instrument, has a set of strings that vibrate and produce music, even though they are never plucked by the player. These "sympathetic strings" are identical to the plucked strings and are mounted below them. What is your explanation?
33. A special device can transmit sound that is out of phase with the sound of a noisy jackhammer to the jackhammer operator by means of earphones. Over the noise of the jackhammer, the operator can easily hear your voice while you are unable to hear his. Explain.
34. Two sound waves of the same frequency can interfere with each other, but two sound waves must have different frequencies in order to make beats. Why?
35. Walking beside you, your friend takes 50 strides per minute while you take 48 strides per minute. If you start in step, when will you be in step again?
36. Suppose a piano tuner hears three beats per second when listening to the combined sound from his tuning fork and the piano note being tuned. After slightly tightening the string, he hears five beats per second. Should the string be loosened or tightened?
37. A railroad locomotive is at rest with its whistle shrieking, and then it starts moving toward you. (a) Does the frequency that you hear increase, decrease, or stay the same? (b) How about the wavelength reaching your ear? (c) How about the speed of sound in the air between you and the locomotive?
38. When you blow your horn while driving toward a stationary listener, an increase in frequency of the horn is heard by the listener. Would the listener hear an increase in the frequency of the horn if he were also in a car traveling at the same speed in the same direction as you are? Explain.
39. Is there an appreciable Doppler effect when the motion of the source is at right angles to a listener? Explain.
40. How does the Doppler effect aid police in detecting speeding motorists?
41. Astronomers find that light emitted by a particular element at one edge of the sun has a slightly higher frequency than light from that element at the opposite edge. What do these measurements tell us about the sun's motion?
42. Would it be correct to say that the Doppler effect is the apparent change in the speed of a wave due to motion of the source? (Why is this question a test of reading comprehension as well as a test of physics knowledge?)
43. Does the conical angle of a shock wave open wider, narrow down, or remain constant as a supersonic aircraft increases its speed?
44. If the sound of an airplane does not originate in the part of the sky where the plane is seen, does this imply that the airplane is traveling faster than the speed of sound? Explain.
45. Does a sonic boom occur at the moment when an aircraft exceeds the speed of sound? Explain.
46. Why is it that a subsonic aircraft, no matter how loud it may be, cannot produce a sonic boom?
47. What physics principle is used by Manuel when he pumps in rhythm with the natural frequency of the swing?

48. Make up two multiple-choice questions that would check a classmate's understanding of the terms that describe a wave.

Problems

1. What is the frequency, in hertz, that corresponds to each of the following periods: (a) 0.10 s, (b) 5 s, (c) 1/60 s?
2. What is the period, in seconds, that corresponds to each of the following frequencies: (a) 10 Hz, (b) 0.2 Hz, (c) 60 Hz?
3. A weight suspended from a spring is seen to bob up and down over a distance of 20 centimeters twice each second. What is its frequency? Its period? Its amplitude?
4. A skipper on a boat notices wave crests passing his anchor chain every 5 s. He estimates the distance between wave crests to be 15 m. He also correctly estimates the speed of the waves. What is this speed?

5. Radio waves travel at the speed of light—300,000 km/s. What is the wavelength of radio waves received at 100.1 MHz on your FM radio dial?
6. A mosquito flaps its wings 600 vibrations per second, which produces an annoying 600-Hz buzz. How far does the sound travel between wing beats? In other words, find the wavelength of the mosquito's sound.
7. On a keyboard, you strike middle C, whose frequency is 256 Hz. (a) What is the period of one vibration of this tone? (b) As the sound leaves the instrument at a speed of 340 m/s, what is its wavelength in air?
8. (a) If you were so foolish as to play your keyboard instrument under water, where the speed of sound is 1,500 m/s, what would be the wavelength of the middle-C tone in water? (b) Explain why middle C (or any other tone) has a longer wavelength in water than in air.
9. For years, marine scientists were mystified by sound waves detected by underwater microphones in the Pacific Ocean. These so-called T waves were among the purest sounds in nature. Eventually the researchers traced the source to underwater volcanoes whose rising columns of bubbles resonated like organ pipes. What is the wavelength of a typical T wave whose frequency is 7 Hz? (The speed of sound in seawater is 1530 m/s.)
10. An oceanic depth-sounding vessel surveys the ocean bottom with ultrasonic waves that travel 1530 m/s in seawater. How deep is the water directly below the vessel if the time delay of the echo to the ocean floor and back is 6 s?
11. A bat flying in a cave emits a sound and receives its echo 0.1 s later. How far away is the cave wall?
12. Susie hammers on a block of wood when she is 85 m from a large brick wall. Each time she hits the block, she hears an echo 0.5 s later. With this information, calculate the speed of sound.
13. Imagine an old hermit type who lives in the mountains. Just before going to sleep, he yells "WAKE UP," and the sound echoes off the nearest mountain and returns 8 hours later. How far away is that mountain?
14. What beat frequencies are possible with tuning forks of frequencies 256, 259, and 261 Hz?
15. As shown in the drawing, the half-angle of the shock-wave cone generated by a supersonic aircraft is 45°. What is the speed of the plane relative to the speed of sound?

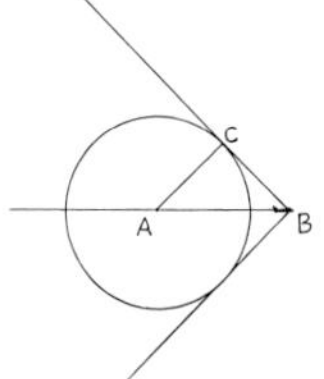

Chapter 11 Online Resources

Tutorials
- Waves
- The Doppler Effect

Videos
- Longitudinal vs. Transverse Waves
- Refraction of Sound
- Doppler Effect

Quiz
Exercises
Flashcards
Links

CHAPTER 12

Light Waves

Light is the only thing we can really see. But what *is* light? We know that, during the day, the primary source of light is the sun, and a secondary source is the brightness of the sky. Other common sources are flames, white-hot filaments in light bulbs, and glowing gases in glass tubes. We find that light originates from the accelerated motion of electrons. Light is an electromagnetic phenomenon, and it is only a tiny part of a larger whole—a wide range of electromagnetic waves called the *electromagnetic spectrum*. We begin our study of light by investigating its electromagnetic properties, how it interacts with materials, and its appearance—color. We see its wave nature in the way it diffracts and interferes and how it aligns to become polarized.

Light is the only thing we see.
Sound is the only thing we hear.

Insights

12.1 Electromagnetic Spectrum

If you shake the end of a stick back and forth in still water, you'll create waves on the water's surface. If you similarly shake an electrically charged rod to and fro in empty space, you'll create electromagnetic waves in space. This is because the moving charge is an electric current. Recall from Chapter 10 that a magnetic field surrounds an electric current and that the field changes as the current changes. Recall also that a changing magnetic field induces an electric field—electromagnetic induction. And what does the

Figure 12.1
If you shake an electrically charged object to and fro, you will produce an electromagnetic wave.

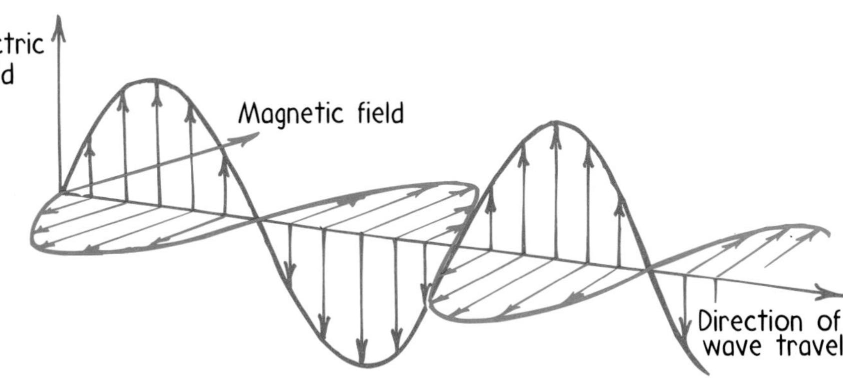

Figure 12.2
The electric and magnetic fields of an electromagnetic wave are perpendicular to each other and to the direction of motion of the wave.

changing electric field do? It induces a changing magnetic field. The vibrating electric and magnetic fields regenerate each other to make up an **electromagnetic wave.**

In a vacuum, all electromagnetic waves move at the same speed. They differ from one another in their frequency. The classification of electromagnetic waves according to frequency is the **electromagnetic spectrum** (Figure 12.3). Electromagnetic waves have been detected with a frequency as low as 0.01 hertz (Hz). Others, with frequencies of several thousand hertz (kHz), are classified as low-frequency radio waves. One million hertz (1 MHz) lies in the middle of the AM radio band. The very high frequency (VHF) television band of waves begins at about 50 million hertz (MHz) and FM radio frequencies are from 88 to 108 MHz. Then come ultrahigh frequencies (UHF), followed by microwaves, beyond which are infrared waves, often called "heat waves." Further still is visible light, which makes up less than a millionth of 1 percent of the electromagnetic spectrum.

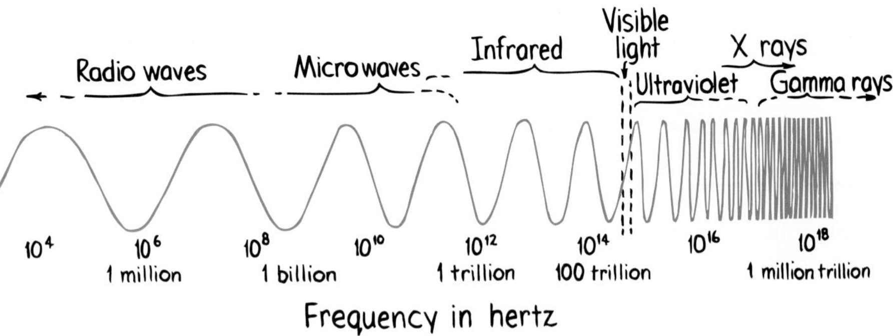

Figure 12.3
The electromagnetic spectrum is a continuous range of waves extending from radio waves to gamma rays. The descriptive names of the sections are merely a historical classification, for all waves are the same in their basic nature, differing principally in frequency and wavelength; all of the waves have the same speed.

Light is energy carried in an electromagnetic wave emitted by vibrating electrons in atoms. In air, light travels a million times faster than sound.

Insights

The lowest frequency of light we can see with our eyes appears red. The highest visible frequencies, which are nearly twice the frequency of red light, appear violet. Still higher frequencies are ultraviolet. These higher-frequency waves are more energetic and can cause sunburns. Beyond ultraviolet light are the x-ray and gamma-ray regions. There is no sharp boundary between regions of the spectrum, for they actually grade continuously into one another. The spectrum is divided into these arbitrary regions for the sake of classification.

The frequency of the electromagnetic wave as it vibrates through space is identical with the frequency of the oscillating electric charge that generates it. Different frequencies result in different wavelengths—low frequencies produce long wavelengths and high frequencies produce short wavelengths. The higher the frequency of the vibrating charge, the shorter the wavelength of the radiation.*

*The relationship is $c = f\lambda$, where c is the speed of light (constant), f is the frequency, and λ is the wavelength. It is common to describe sound and radio by frequency and light by wavelength. In this book, however, we'll favor the single concept of frequency in describing light.

☑ CHECKPOINT

Is it correct to say that a radio wave is a low-frequency light wave? Is a radio wave also a sound wave?

Check Your Answer

Both radio waves and light waves are electromagnetic waves, which originate in the vibrations of electrons. Radio waves have lower frequencies than light waves, so a radio wave might be considered to be a low-frequency light wave (and a light wave might be considered to be a high-frequency radio wave). But a sound wave is a mechanical vibration of matter and is not electromagnetic. A sound wave is fundamentally different from an electromagnetic wave. So a radio wave is definitely not a sound wave. (Don't confuse a radio wave with the sound that a loudspeaker emits.)

12.2 Transparent and Opaque Materials

Light is energy carried in an electromagnetic wave emitted by vibrating electrons in atoms. When light is incident upon matter, some of the electrons in the matter are forced into vibration. In this way, vibrations in the emitter are transmitted to vibrations in the receiver. This is similar to the way that sound is transmitted (Figure 12.4).

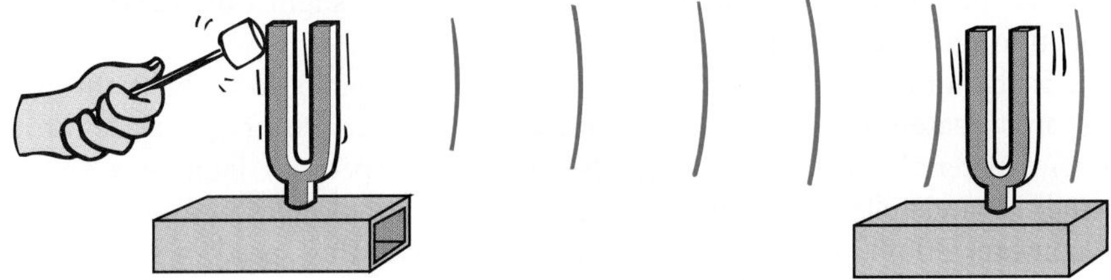

Figure 12.4
Just as a sound wave can force a sound receiver into vibration, a light wave can force the electrons in materials into vibration.

Thus the way a receiving material responds when light is incident upon it depends on the frequency of the light and on the natural frequency of the electrons in the material. Visible light vibrates at a very high rate, some 100 trillion times per second (10^{14} hertz). If a charged object is to respond to these ultrafast vibrations, it must have very, very little inertia. Electrons are light enough to vibrate at this rate.

Such materials as glass and water allow light to pass through in straight lines. We say they are **transparent** to light. To understand how light penetrates a transparent material, visualize the electrons in an atom as if they were connected by springs (Figure 12.5).* When a light wave is incident upon them, the electrons are set into vibration.

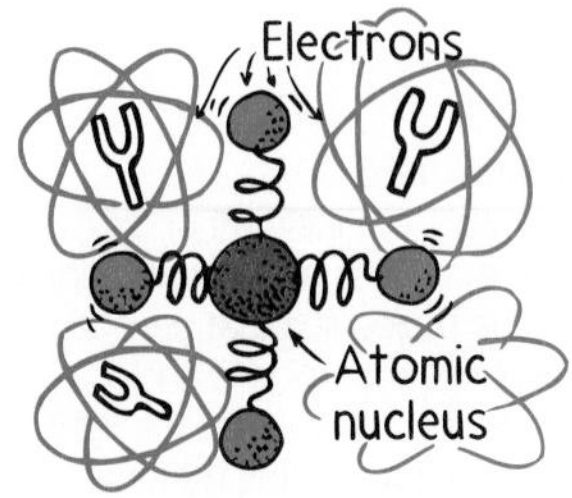

Figure 12.5
The electrons of atoms have certain natural frequencies of vibration, and these can be modeled as particles connected to the atomic nucleus by springs. As a result, atoms and molecules behave somewhat like optical tuning forks.

*Electrons, of course, are not really connected by springs. We are simply presenting a visual "spring model" of the atom to help us understand the interaction of light with matter. Scientists devise such conceptual models to understand nature, particularly at the submicroscopic level. The worth of a model lies not in whether it is "true" but in whether it is useful—in explaining observations and predicting new ones. If predictions are contrary to new observations, the model is usually either refined or abandoned. The simplified model that we present here—of an atom whose electrons vibrate as if on springs, with a time interval between absorbing energy and reemitting it—is quite useful for understanding how light passes through transparent material.

Materials that are springy (elastic) respond more to vibrations at some frequencies than they do to vibrations at other frequencies. Bells ring at a particular frequency, tuning forks vibrate at a particular frequency, and so do the electrons of atoms and molecules. The natural vibration frequencies of an electron depend on how strongly it is attached to its atom or molecule. Different atoms and molecules have different "spring strengths." Electrons in glass have a natural vibration frequency in the ultraviolet range. When ultraviolet rays shine on glass, resonance occurs as the wave builds and maintains a large amplitude of vibration of the electron, just as pushing someone at the resonant frequency on a swing builds a large amplitude. The energy that atoms in the glass receive may be passed on to neighboring atoms by collisions, or the energy may be reemitted. Resonating atoms in the glass can hold onto the energy of the ultraviolet light for quite a long time (about 100 millionths of a second). During this time, the atom makes about 1 million vibrations and collides with neighboring atoms and transfers absorbed energy as heat. Thus, glass is not transparent to ultraviolet. Glass absorbs ultraviolet.

At lower wave frequencies, such as those of visible light, electrons in the glass are forced into vibration at a lower amplitude. The atoms or molecules in the glass hold the energy for less time, with less chance of collision with neighboring atoms and molecules, and less of the energy transformed to heat. The energy of vibrating electrons is reemitted as light. Glass is transparent to all the frequencies of visible light. The frequency of the reemitted light that is passed from molecule to molecule is identical to the frequency of the light that produced the vibration originally. However, there is a slight time delay between absorption and reemission.

It is this time delay that results in a lower average speed of light through a transparent material (Figure 12.6). Light travels at different average speeds through different materials. We say *average speeds,* for the speed of light in a vacuum, whether in interstellar space or in the space between molecules in a piece of glass, is a constant 300,000 kilometers per second. We call this speed of light *c*.* The speed of light in the atmosphere is slightly less than it is in a vacuum, but is usually rounded off as *c*. In water, light travels at 75 percent of its speed in a vacuum, or 0.75 *c*. In glass, light travels about 0.67 *c*, depending on the type of glass. In a diamond, light travels at less than half its speed in a vacuum, only 0.41 *c*. When light emerges from these materials into the air, it travels at its original speed.

Figure 12.6
A light wave incident upon a pane of glass sets up vibrations in the molecules that produce a chain of absorptions and reemissions, which pass the light energy through the material and out the other side. Because of the time delay between absorptions and reemissions, the light travels through the glass more slowly than through empty space.

*The presently accepted value is 299,792 km/s, which is often rounded to 300,000 km/s. (This corresponds to 186,000 mi/s.)

Infrared waves, which have frequencies lower than those of visible light, vibrate not only the electrons but the entire molecules in the structure of the glass and in many other materials. This molecular vibration increases the thermal energy and temperature of the material, which is why infrared waves are often called *heat waves*. Glass is transparent to visible light, but not to ultraviolet and infrared light.

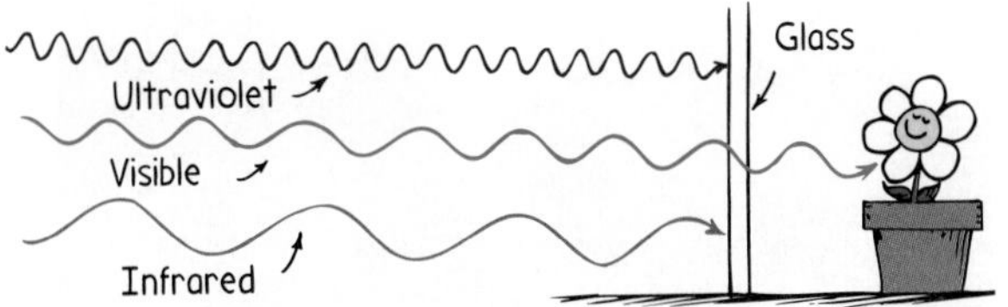

Figure 12.7
Clear glass blocks both infrared and ultraviolet, but it is transparent to all the frequencies of visible light.

☑ CHECKPOINT

1. Why is glass transparent to visible light but opaque to ultraviolet and infrared?
2. Pretend that, while you are at a social gathering, you make several momentary stops across the room to greet people who are "on your wavelength." How is this analogous to light traveling through glass?
3. In what way is it not analogous?

Check Your Answers

1. The natural frequency of vibration for electrons in glass is the same as the frequency of ultraviolet light, so resonance in the glass occurs when ultraviolet waves shine on it. The absorbed energy is transferred to other atoms as heat, not reemitted as light, so the glass is opaque at ultraviolet frequencies. In the range of visible light, the forced vibrations of electrons in the glass are at smaller amplitudes—vibrations are more subtle, reemission of light (rather than the generation of heat) occurs, and the glass is transparent. Lower-frequency infrared causes whole molecules, rather than electrons, to resonate; again, heat is generated and the glass is opaque.
2. Your average speed across the room would be less because of the time delays associated with your momentary stops. Likewise, the speed of light in glass is less because of the time delays in interactions with atoms along its path.
3. In the case of walking across the room, it is you who begin the walk and you who complete the walk. This is not analogous to the similar case of light, for (according to our model for light passing through a transparent material) the light that is absorbed by an electron that has been made to vibrate is not the same light that is reemitted—even though the two, like identical twins, are indistinguishable.

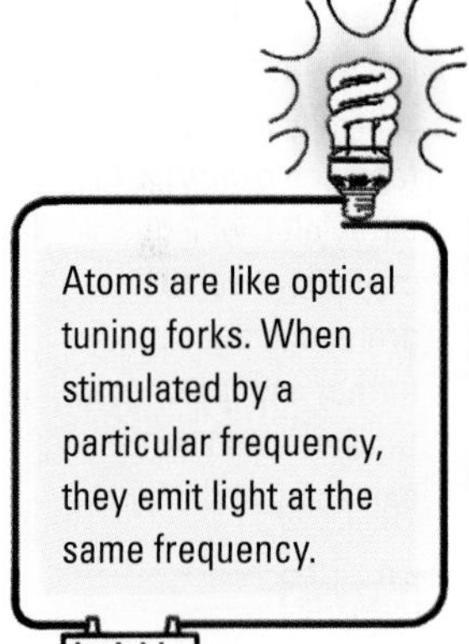

Most things around us are **opaque**—they absorb light without reemission. Books, desks, chairs, and people are opaque. Vibrations given by light to their atoms and molecules are turned into random kinetic energy—into thermal energy. They become slightly warmer.

Metals are opaque. The outer electrons of atoms in metals are not bound to any particular atom. They are loose and free to wander, with very little restraint, throughout the material (which is why metal conducts electricity and heat so well). When light shines on metal and sets these free electrons into vibration, their energy does not "spring" from atom to atom in the material. It is reflected instead. That's why metals are shiny.

Figure 12.8
Metals are shiny because light that shines on them forces free electrons into vibration, which then emit their "own" light waves as reflection.

The earth's atmosphere is transparent to some ultraviolet light, to all visible light, and to some infrared light. But the atmosphere is opaque to high-frequency ultraviolet light. The small amount of ultraviolet that does penetrate causes sunburns. If all ultraviolet light penetrated the atmosphere, we would be fried to a crisp. Clouds are semitransparent to ultraviolet light, which is why you can get a sunburn on a cloudy day. Ultraviolet light is not only harmful to your skin, it is also damaging to tar roofs. Now you know why tarred roofs are often covered with gravel.

Have you noticed that things look darker when they are wet than when they are dry? Light incident on a dry surface, such as sand, bounces directly to your eye. But light incident on a wet surface bounces around inside the transparent wet region before it reaches your eye. What happens with each bounce? Absorption! So sand and other things look darker when wet.

Dark or black skin absorbs ultraviolet radiation before it can penetrate too far. In fair skin, it can travel deeper. Fair skin may develop a tan upon exposure to ultraviolet, which may afford some protection against further exposure. Ultraviolet is also damaging to the eyes.

Insights

12.3 Color

Roses are red and violets are blue; colors intrigue artists and physical-science types too. To the scientist, the colors of objects are not in the substances of the objects themselves or even in the light they emit or reflect. Color is a physiological experience and is in the eye of the beholder. So, when we say that light from a rose is red, in a stricter sense we mean that it appears red. Many organisms, including people with defective color vision, will not see the rose as red at all.

The colors we see depend on the frequency of the light we see. Different frequencies of light are perceived as different colors; the lowest frequency we detect appears, to most people, as the color red, and the highest appears as violet. Between them range the infinite number of hues that make up the color spectrum of the rainbow. By convention, these hues are grouped into the seven colors: red, orange, yellow, green, blue, indigo, and violet. These colors together appear white. The white light from the sun is a composite of all the visible frequencies.

Figure 12.9
Sunlight passing though a prism separates into a color spectrum. The colors of things depend on the colors of the light that illuminates them.

Except for such light sources as lamps, lasers, and gas discharge tubes, most of the objects around us reflect rather than emit light. They reflect only part of the light that is incident upon them, the part that provides their color.

Selective Reflection

A rose, for example, doesn't emit light; it reflects light. If we pass sunlight through a prism and then place a deep-red rose in various parts of the spectrum, the rose will appear brown or black in all regions of the spectrum except in the red region. In the red part of the spectrum, the petal also will appear red, but the green stem and leaves will appear black. This shows that the red rose has the ability to reflect red light, but it cannot reflect other colors; the green leaves have the ability to reflect green light and, likewise, cannot reflect other colors. When the rose is held in white light, the petals appear red and the leaves appear green, because the petals reflect the red part of the white light and the leaves reflect the green part of the white light. To understand why objects reflect specific colors of light, we turn our attention to the atom.

Light is reflected from objects in a manner similar to the way sound is "reflected" from a tuning fork when another tuning fork nearby sets it into vibration. A tuning fork can be made to vibrate even when the frequencies are not matched, although at significantly reduced amplitudes. The same is true of atoms and molecules. Electrons can be forced into vibration (oscillation) by the vibrating (oscillating) electric fields of electromagnetic waves.* Once vibrating, these electrons emit their own electromagnetic waves, just as vibrating acoustical tuning forks emit sound waves.

Figure 12.10
The square on the top *reflects* all the colors illuminating it. In sunlight, it is white. When illuminated with blue light, it is blue. The square on the bottom *absorbs* all the colors illuminating it. In sunlight, it is warmer than the white square.

Usually, a material will absorb light of some frequencies and reflect the rest. If a material absorbs most of the light and reflects red, for example, the material appears red. If it reflects light of all the visible frequencies, like the white part of this page, it will be the same color as the light that shines on it. If a material absorbs light and reflects none, then it is black.

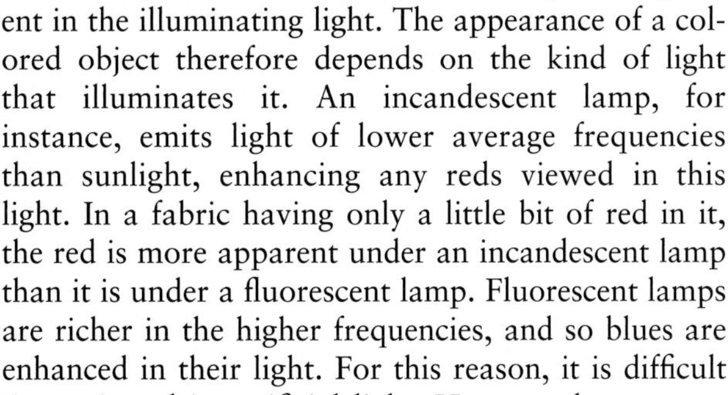

Figure 12.11
The bunny's dark fur absorbs all the radiant energy in incident sunlight and therefore appears black. Light fur on other parts of the body reflects light of all frequencies and therefore appears white.

Interestingly, the petals of most yellow flowers, like daffodils, reflect red and green as well as yellow. Yellow daffodils reflect a broad band of frequencies. The reflected colors of most objects are not pure single-frequency colors but are a mixture of frequencies.

An object can reflect only those frequencies present in the illuminating light. The appearance of a colored object therefore depends on the kind of light that illuminates it. An incandescent lamp, for instance, emits light of lower average frequencies than sunlight, enhancing any reds viewed in this light. In a fabric having only a little bit of red in it, the red is more apparent under an incandescent lamp than it is under a fluorescent lamp. Fluorescent lamps are richer in the higher frequencies, and so blues are enhanced in their light. For this reason, it is difficult to tell the true color of objects viewed in artificial light. How a color appears depends on the light source (Figure 12.12).

Selective Transmission

The color of a transparent object depends on the color of the light it transmits. A red piece of glass appears red because it absorbs all the colors of white light except red, so red light is transmitted. Similarly, a blue piece of glass appears blue because

Figure 12.12
Color depends on the light source.

*We use the words *oscillate* and *vibrate* interchangeably. Also, the words *oscillators* and *vibrators* have the same meaning.

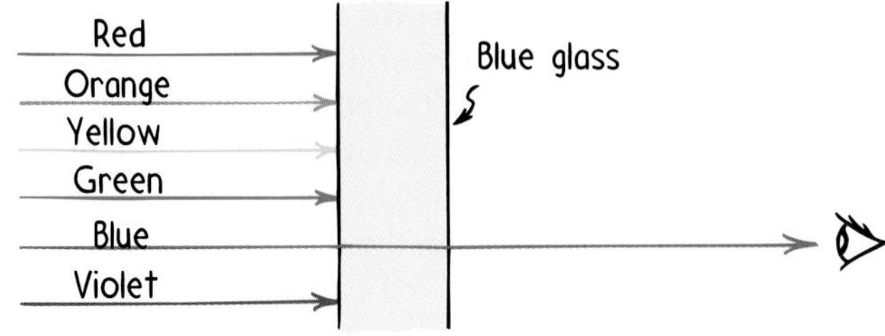

Figure 12.13
Only energy having the frequency of blue light is transmitted; energy of the other frequencies is absorbed and warms the glass.

it transmits primarily blue and absorbs the other colors that illuminate it. These pieces of glass contain dyes or *pigments*—fine particles that selectively absorb light of particular frequencies and selectively transmit others. From an atomic point of view, electrons in the pigment molecules are set into vibration by the illuminating light. Light of some of the frequencies is absorbed by the pigments. The rest is reemitted from atom to atom in the glass. The energy of the absorbed light increases the kinetic energy of the atoms, and the glass is warmed. Ordinary window glass doesn't have a color because it transmits light of all visible frequencies equally well.

☑ CHECKPOINT

1. Why do the leaves of a red rose become warmer than the petals when illuminated with red light?
2. When illuminated with green light, why do the petals of a red rose appear black?
3. If you hold a match, a candle flame, or any small source of white light between you and a piece of red glass, you'll see two reflections from the glass: one from the front surface of the glass and one from the back surface. What color reflections will you see?

Check Your Answers

1. The leaves absorb rather than reflect red light, so the leaves become warmer.
2. The petals absorb rather than reflect the green light. Since green is the only color illuminating the rose, and green contains no red to be reflected, the rose reflects no color at all and appears black.
3. You see white reflected from the top surface. You see red reflected from the back surface because only red reaches the back surface and reflects from there.

Mixing Colored Lights

You can see that white light from the sun is composed of all the visible frequencies when you pass sunlight through a prism. The white light is dispersed into a rainbow-colored spectrum. The distribution of solar frequencies (Figure 12.14) is uneven, and the light is most intense in the yellow-green part of the spectrum. How fascinating it is that our eyes have evolved to have maximum sensitivity in this range. That's why fire engines are painted

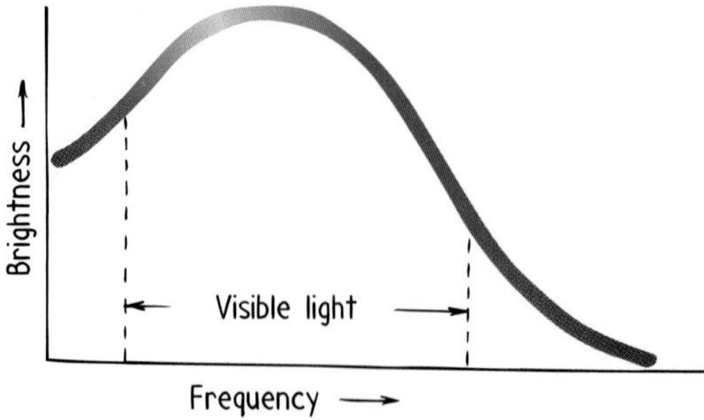

Figure 12.14
The radiation curve of sunlight is a graph of brightness against frequency. Sunlight is brightest in the yellow-green region, which is in the middle of the visible range.

Link to Opthalmology

Color Vision

Light from the world around us focuses upon the retina in our eyes, and we see. The *retina* is composed of tiny antennae of two kinds that resonate to the incoming light—the rods and the cones. As the names imply, the rods are rod-shaped and the cones are cone-shaped. Rods perceive only intensity of light, while cones perceive color. We see color because of the three types of cones—those sensitive to red, those sensitive to green, and those sensitive to blue. Cones are denser toward the region of distinct vision—the *fovea.* The rods are sensitive to intensity rather than to frequency, and they predominate away from the fovea, toward the periphery of the retina. Primates and a species of ground squirrel are the only mammals that have the three types of cones and experience full color vision. The retinas of other mammals consist primarily of rods, which are sensitive only to lightness or darkness, so they capture images like those in black-and-white photographs or movies.

Compared with rods, cones require more energy to "fire" an impulse through the nervous system. If the intensity of light is very low, the things we see have no color. We see low intensities with our rods. That's why it's difficult to identify the color of a car by moonlight. Dark-adapted vision is almost entirely due to the rods, while vision in bright light is due to the cones. Stars, for example, look white to us. Yet most stars are actually brightly colored. A time exposure of the stars with a camera reveals reds and red-oranges for the "cooler" stars and blues and blue-violets for the "hotter" stars. The starlight is too faint, however, to fire the color-perceiving cones in the retina. So we see the stars with our rods and perceive them as white or, at most, as only faintly colored. Females have a slightly lower threshold of firing for the cones, however, and they can see more color in stars than males can. So, if she says she sees colored stars and he says she doesn't, she is probably correct!

yellow-green, particularly at airports, where visibility is vital. Our sensitivity to yellow-green light is also why we see better under the illumination of yellow sodium-vapor lamps at night than we do under incandescent lamps of the same brightness.

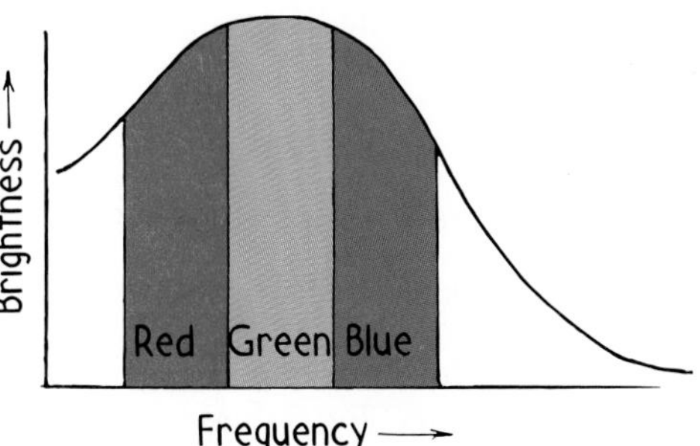

Figure 12.15
The radiation curve of sunlight divided into three regions—red, green, and blue. These are the additive primary colors.

All the colors combined produce white. Interestingly, we see white also from the combination of only red, green, and blue light. We can understand this by dividing the solar radiation curve into three regions, as in Figure 12.15. Three types of cone-shaped receptors in our eyes perceive color. Each is stimulated only by certain frequencies of light. Light of lower visible frequencies stimulates the cones sensitive to low frequencies and appears red. Light of middle frequencies stimulates the mid-frequency-sensitive cones and appears green. Light of higher frequencies stimulates the higher-frequency-sensitive cones and appears blue. When all three types of cones are stimulated equally, we see white.

What takes place in the eye seems to be quite complex. Some color sensations depend on intensity, with both rods and cones responding. As intensity increases, orange appears to become yellower and violet seems to get bluer—with no change in frequency. Yellow, green, and blue, however, are independent of intensity, and are called "psychological primaries." The eye is indeed amazing.

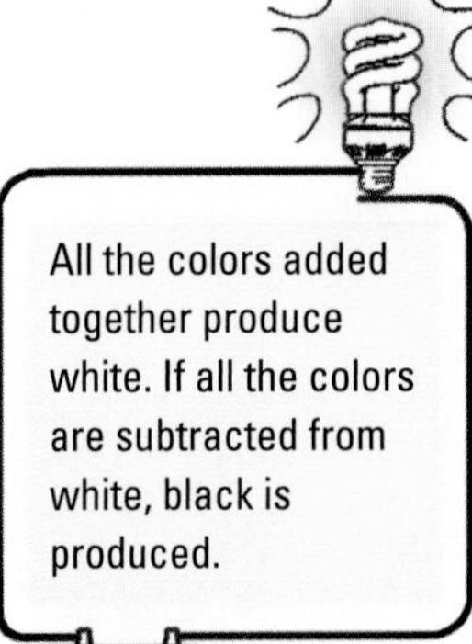

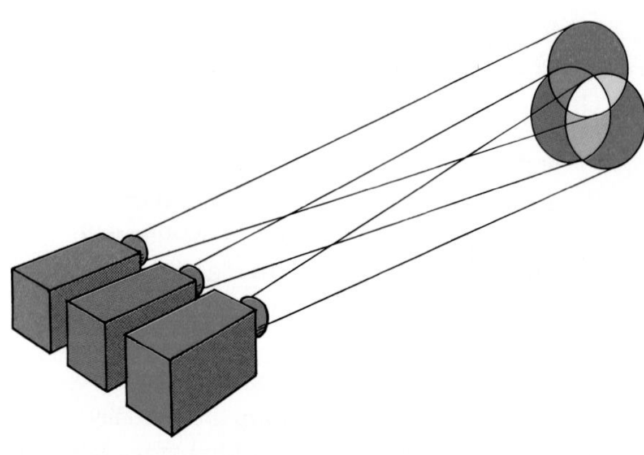

Figure 12.16
Color addition by the mixing of colored lights. When three projectors shine red, green, and blue light on a white screen, the overlapping parts produce different colors. White is produced where all three overlap.

Project red, green, and blue lights on a screen and, where they all overlap, white is produced. If two of the three colors overlap, or are added, then another color sensation will be produced (Figure 12.16). By adding various amounts of red, green, and blue, the colors to which each of our three types of cones are sensitive, we can produce any color in the spectrum. For this reason, red, green, and blue are called the **additive primary colors.** A close examination of the picture on most color television tubes will reveal that the picture is an assemblage of tiny spots, each less than a millimeter across. When the screen is lit, some of the spots are red, some are green, and some are blue; the mixtures of these primary colors at a distance provide a complete range of colors, plus white.

Complementary Colors

Here's what happens when two of the three additive primary colors are combined:

Red + Blue = Magenta

Red + Green = Yellow

Blue + Green = Cyan

It's interesting to note that the "black" you see on the darkest scenes on a TV tube is simply the color of the tube face itself, which is more a light gray than black. Because our eyes are sensitive to the contrast with the illuminated parts of the screen, we see this gray as black.

Insights

We say that magenta is the opposite of green; cyan is opposite red; and yellow is opposite blue. The addition of any color to its opposite color results in white.

Magenta + Green = White (= Red + Blue + Green)

Cyan + Red = White (= Blue + Green + Red)

Yellow + Blue = White (= Red + Green + Blue)

When two colors are added together to produce white, they are called **complementary colors**. Every hue has some complementary color that, when added to it, makes white.

The fact that a color and its complement combine to produce white light is pleasantly used in lighting stage performances. Blue and yellow lights shining on performers, for example, produce the effect of white light—except where one of the two colors is absent, as in the shadows. The shadow of the blue lamp is illuminated by the yellow lamp, and thus it appears yellow. Similarly, the shadow cast by the yellow lamp appears blue. This is a most intriguing effect.

We can see this effect in Figure 12.17, where red, green, and blue lights shine on the golf ball. Note the shadows cast by the ball. The middle shadow is cast by the green spotlight and is not dark because it is illuminated by the red and blue lights, which make magenta. The shadow cast by the blue light appears yellow because it is illuminated by red and green light. Can you see why the shadow cast by the red light appears cyan?

Figuring Physical Science

Exercises

1. From Figure 12.17, find the complements of cyan, of yellow, and of red.
2. Red + cyan = ____.
3. White − cyan = ____.
4. White − red = ____.

Solutions

1. Red, blue, cyan.
2. White.
3. Red.
4. Cyan. Interestingly enough, the cyan color of the sea is the result of the red light having been removed from white sunlight. The natural frequency of water molecules coincides with the frequency of infrared light, so infrared is strongly absorbed by water. To a lesser extent, red light is also absorbed by water—enough to give it the greenish-blue or cyan color.

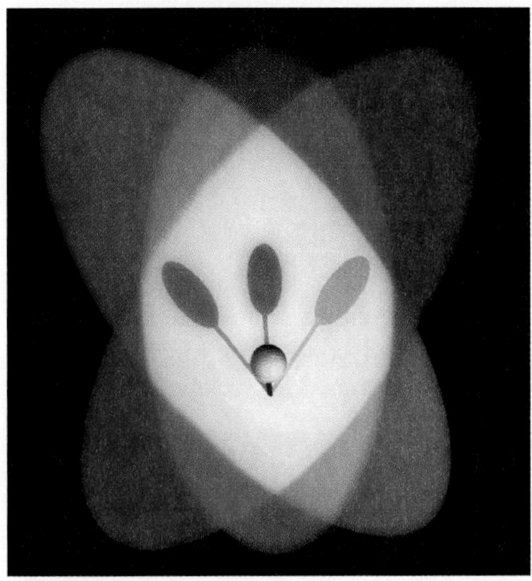

Figure 12.17
The white golf ball appears white when it is illuminated with red, green, and blue lights of equal intensities. Why are the shadows cast by the ball cyan, magenta, and yellow?

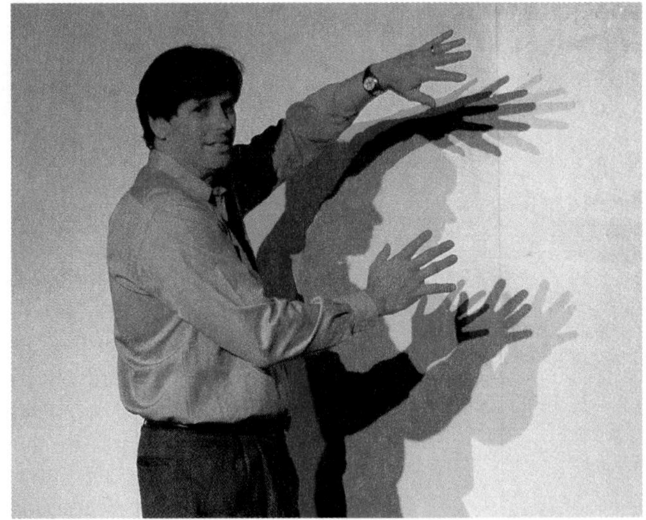

Figure 12.18
Paul Robinson displays a variety of colors when he is illuminated by only a red, green, and blue lamp. Can you account for the other resulting colors that appear?

Mixing Colored Pigments

Every artist knows that, if you mix red, green, and blue paint, the result will not be white but a muddy dark brown. Mixing red and green paint will certainly not produce yellow, so the rule for adding colored lights doesn't apply here. The mixing of pigments in paints and dyes is entirely different from mixing lights. Pigments are tiny particles that absorb specific colors. For example, pigments that produce the color red absorb the complementary color cyan. So something painted

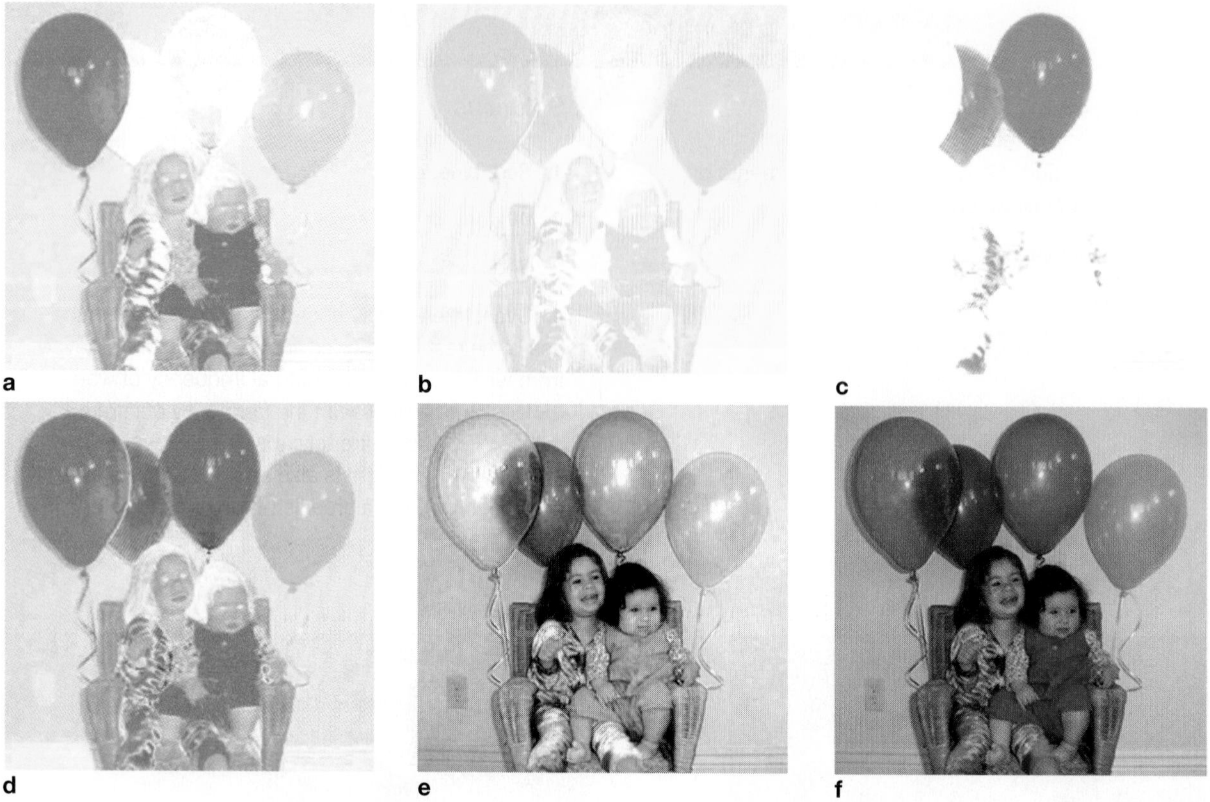

Figure 12.19
Only three colors of ink (plus black) are used to print color photographs—(a) magenta, (b) yellow, (c) cyan, which when combined produce the colors shown in (d). The addition of black (e) produces the finished result (f).

red absorbs cyan, which is why it reflects red. In effect, cyan has been *subtracted* from white light. Something painted blue absorbs yellow, so it reflects all the colors except yellow. Remove yellow from white and you've got blue. The colors magenta, cyan, and yellow are the *subtractive primaries*. The variety of colors that you see in the colored photographs in this or any book are the result of magenta, cyan, and yellow dots. Light illuminates the book, and light of some frequencies is subtracted from the light reflected. The rules of color subtraction differ from the rules of light addition. We leave this topic to the Suggested Reading and Web Sites.

Figure 12.20
Seen through a magnifying glass, the color green on a printed page consists of blue and yellow dots.

Figure 12.21
The vivid colors of Sneezlee represent many frequencies of light. The photo, however, is a mixture of only yellow, magenta, cyan, and black.

Why the Sky Is Blue

Not all colors are the result of the addition or subtraction of light. Some colors, like the blue of the sky, are the result of selective scattering.* Consider the analogous case of sound: If a beam of a particular frequency of sound is directed to a tuning fork of a similar frequency, the tuning fork is set

*This type of scattering, which is called *Rayleigh scattering,* occurs whenever the scattering particles are much smaller than the wavelength of incident light and have resonances at frequencies higher than those of the scattered light.

into vibration and redirects the beam in multiple directions. The tuning fork *scatters* the sound. A similar process occurs with the scattering of light from atoms and particles that are far apart from one another. This is what happens in the atmosphere.

Scattered radiation

Incident beam

Atom

Figure 12.22
A beam of light falls on an atom and increases the vibrational motion of electrons in the atom. The vibrating electrons, in turn, reemit light in various directions. Light is scattered.

We know that atoms behave like tiny optical tuning forks and reemit light waves that shine on them. Very tiny particles act in a similar way. The tinier the particle, the higher the frequency of light it will reemit. This is similar to the way in which small bells ring with higher notes than larger bells. The nitrogen and oxygen molecules that make up most of the atmosphere are like tiny bells that "ring" with high frequencies when they are energized by sunlight. Like sound from the bells, the reemitted light is sent in all directions. When light is reemitted in all directions, we say that the light is *scattered.*

Atmospheric soot heats the earth's atmosphere by absorbing light, while cooling local regions by blocking sunlight from reaching the ground. Soot particles in the air can trigger severe rains in one region and droughts and dust storms in another.

Insights

Of the visible frequencies of sunlight, violet is scattered the most by nitrogen and oxygen in the atmosphere. Then the other colors are scattered in order: blue, green, yellow, orange, and red. Red is scattered only a tenth as much as violet. Although violet light is scattered more than blue, our eyes are not very sensitive to violet light. Therefore, the blue scattered light is what predominates in our vision, so we see a blue sky!

The blue of the sky varies in different locations under various conditions. A main factor is the amount of water vapor in the atmosphere. On clear, dry days, the sky is a much deeper blue than it is on clear, humid days. Places where the upper air is exceptionally dry, such as Italy and Greece, have beautiful blue skies that have inspired painters for centuries. Where the atmosphere contains a lot of particles of dust and other particles larger than oxygen and nitrogen molecules, light of the lower frequencies is also scattered strongly. This causes the sky to appear less blue, with a whitish appearance. After a heavy rainstorm, when the airborne particles have been washed away, the sky becomes a deeper blue.

The grayish haze in the skies over large cities is the result of particles emitted by automobile and truck engines and by factories. Even when idling, a typical automobile engine emits more than 100 billion particles per second. Most are invisible, but they act as tiny centers to which other particles adhere. These are the primary scatterers of lower-frequency light. With the largest of these particles, absorption rather than scattering occurs, and a brownish haze is produced. Yuck!

Figure 12.23
In clean air, the scattering of high-frequency light gives us a blue sky. When the air is full of particles larger than oxygen and nitrogen molecules, light of lower frequencies is also scattered, which adds to the high-frequency scattered light to give us a whitish sky.

Why Sunsets Are Red

Light that isn't scattered is light that is transmitted. Because red, orange, and yellow light are the least scattered by the atmosphere, light of these low frequencies is better transmitted through the air. Red is scattered the least, and it passes through more atmosphere than any other color. So the thicker the atmosphere through which a beam of sunlight travels, the more time there is to scatter all the higher-frequency parts of the light. This means that red light travels

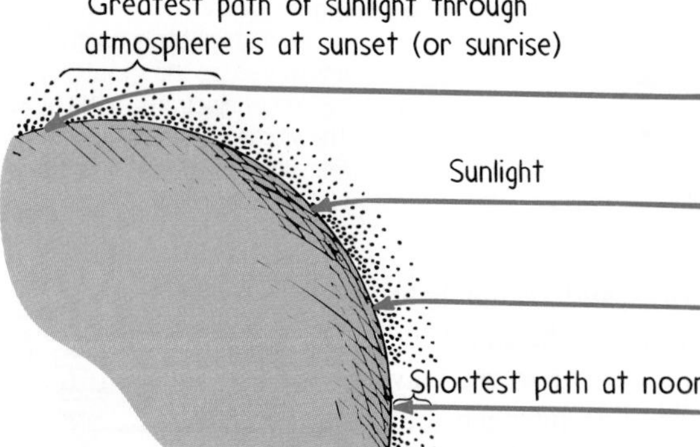

Figure 12.24
A sunbeam must travel through more kilometers of atmosphere at sunset than at noon. As a result, more blue is scattered from the beam at sunset than at noon. By the time a beam of initially white light gets to the ground, only light of the lower frequencies survives to produce a red sunset.

through the atmosphere best. As Figure 12.24 shows, sunlight travels through more atmosphere at sunset, which is why sunsets are red.

At noon, sunlight travels through the least amount of atmosphere to reach the earth's surface. Only a small amount of high-frequency light is scattered from the sunlight, enough to make the sun appear yellowish. As the day progresses and the sun descends lower in the sky, as Figure 12.24 indicates, the path through the atmosphere is longer, and more violet and blue are scattered from the sunlight. The removal of violet and blue leaves the transmitted light redder. The sun becomes progressively redder, going from yellow to orange and finally to a red-orange at sunset. Sunsets and sunrises are unusually colorful following volcanic eruptions because particles larger than atmospheric molecules are more abundant in the air.

The colors of the sunset are consistent with our rules for mixing colors. When blue is subtracted from white light, the complementary color that remains is yellow. When higher-frequency violet is subtracted, the resulting complementary color is orange. When medium-frequency green is subtracted, magenta remains. The combinations of resulting colors vary with atmospheric conditions, which change daily, displaying a variety of sunsets.

☑ CHECKPOINT

1. If molecules in the sky were to scatter low-frequency light more than high-frequency light, what color would the sky be? What color would sunsets be?
2. Distant dark mountains are bluish in color. What is the source of this blueness? (*Hint:* Exactly what is between us and the mountains we see?)
3. Distant snow-covered mountains reflect a lot of light and are bright. But they appear somewhat yellowish, depending on how far away they are. Why do they look yellowish? (*Hint:* What happens to the reflected white light in traveling from the mountain to us?)

Check Your Answers

1. If light of low frequencies were scattered, the noontime sky would appear reddish orange. At sunset, more reds would be scattered by the longer distance traveled by the sunlight, and the sunlight would be predominantly blue and violet. So sunsets would appear blue!
2. If we look at distant dark mountains, very little light from them reaches us, and the blueness of the atmosphere between us and the mountains predominates. The blueness is of the low-altitude "sky" between us and the mountains. That's why distant mountains appear blue.
3. The reason that bright, snow-covered mountains appear yellow is that the blue in the white light from the snowy mountains is scattered on its way to us. So, by the time the light reaches us, it is weak in the high frequencies and strong in the low frequencies—hence, it is yellowish. From much greater distances, from farther away than mountains are usually seen, they would appear orange for the same reason a sunset appears orange.

Why do we see the scattered blue when the background is dark, but not when the background is bright? Because the scattered blue is faint. A faint color will show itself against a dark background, but not against a bright background. For example, when we look from the earth's surface at the atmosphere against the darkness of space, the atmosphere is sky blue. But astronauts above, who look below through the same atmosphere to the bright surface of the earth, do not see the same blueness.

Doesn't knowing why the sky is blue and why sunsets are red actually add to their beauty? Knowledge doesn't subtract.

Insights

Why Clouds Are White

Clouds are made up of clusters of water droplets in a variety of sizes. These clusters of different sizes result in a variety of scattered colors. The tiniest clusters tend to produce blue clouds; slightly larger clusters, green clouds; and still larger clusters, red clouds. The overall result is a white cloud. Electrons close to one another in a cluster vibrate in phase. This results in a greater intensity of scattered light than there would be if the same number of electrons were vibrating separately. Hence, clouds are bright!

Figure 12.25
A cloud is composed of water droplets of various sizes. The tiniest droplets scatter blue light, slightly larger ones scatter green light, and still larger ones scatter red light. The overall result is a white cloud.

Larger clusters of droplets absorb much of the light incident upon them, and so the scattered intensity is less. Therefore, clouds composed of larger clusters are darker. Further increase in the size of the clusters causes them to fall as raindrops, and we have rain.

Colors in distant landscapes are duller, and color contrasts tend to diminish. That's why a color photograph normally conveys more depth than a black-and-white photograph of the same scene.

Insights

The next time you find yourself admiring a crisp blue sky, or delighting in the shapes of bright clouds, or watching a beautiful sunset, think about all those ultratiny optical tuning forks vibrating away. You'll appreciate these daily wonders of nature even more!

Figure 12.26
The wave appears cyan because seawater absorbs red light. The spray at the crest of the wave appears white because, like clouds, it is composed of a variety of tiny water droplets that scatter all the visible frequencies.

12.4 Diffraction

When you touch your finger to the surface of still water, circular ripples are produced. When you touch the surface with a straightedge, such as a horizontally held meterstick, you produce a plane wave. You can produce a series of plane waves by successively dipping a meterstick into the surface of the water (Figure 12.27).

Figure 12.27
The oscillating meterstick makes plane waves in the tank of water. Waves diffract through the opening.

The photographs in Figure 12.28 are top views of water ripples in a shallow glass tank (called a ripple tank). A barrier with an adjustable opening is in the tank. When plane waves meet the barrier, they continue through with some distortion. In the left image, where the opening is wide, the waves continue through the opening almost without change. At the two ends of the opening, however, the waves bend. This bending is called **diffraction.** Any bending of light by means other than reflection and refraction is diffraction. As the width of the opening is narrowed, as in the center image in Figure 12.28, the waves spread more. When the opening is small relative to the wavelength of the incident wave, they spread even more. We see that smaller openings will produce greater diffraction. Diffraction is a property of all kinds of waves, including sound and light waves.

Figure 12.28
Plane waves passing through openings of various sizes. The smaller the opening, the greater the bending of the waves at the edges.

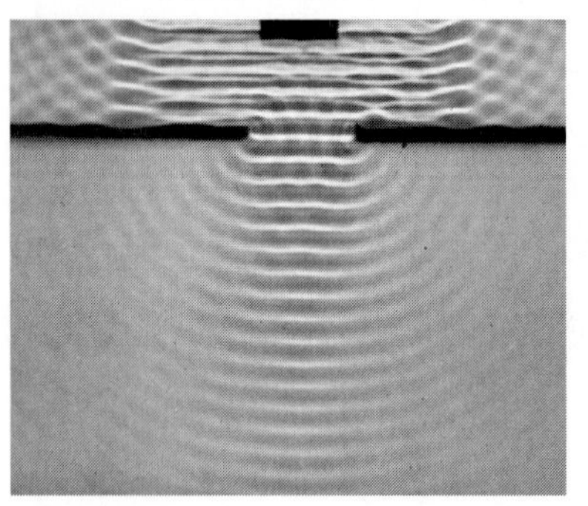

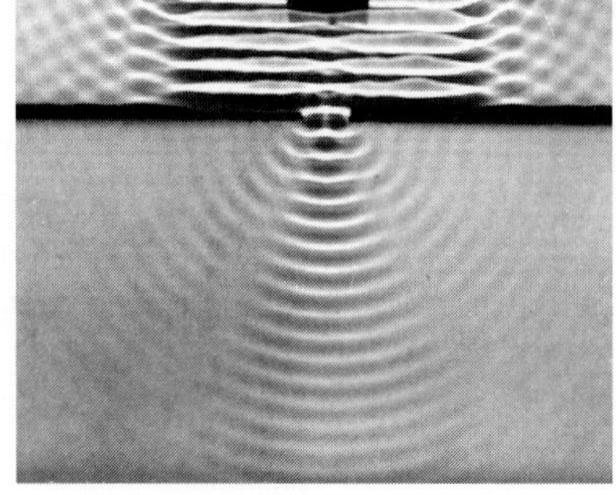

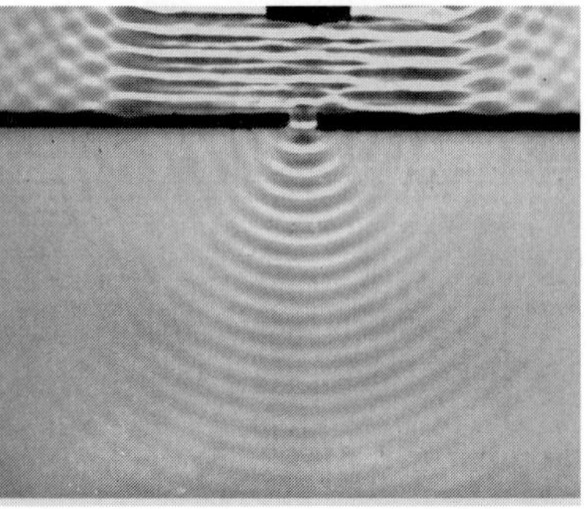

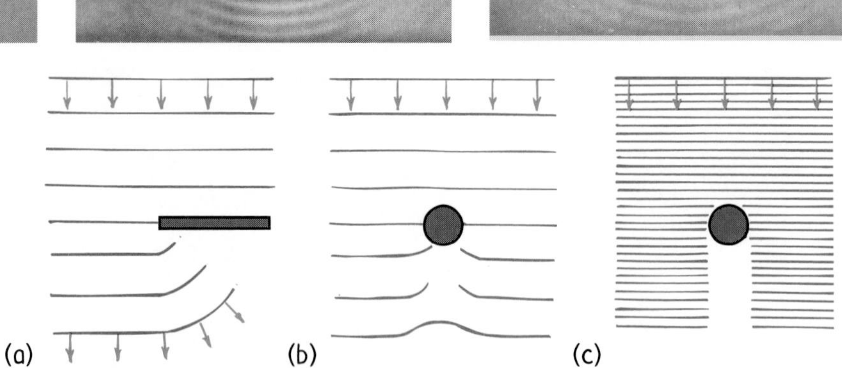

Figure 12.29
(a) Waves tend to spread into the shadow region. (b) When the wavelength is about the size of the object, the shadow is soon filled in. (c) When the wavelength is short compared with the object, a sharp shadow is cast.

Diffraction is not confined to narrow slits or to openings in general but can be seen around the edges of all shadows. On close examination, even the sharpest shadow is blurred slightly at its edges (Figure 12.30).

The amount of diffraction depends on the wavelength of the wave compared with the size of the obstruction that casts the shadow. Long waves are better at filling in shadows, which is why foghorns emit low-frequency sound waves—to fill in any "blind spots." The same is true for radio waves of the standard AM broadcast band, which are very long compared with the sizes of most objects in their path. The wavelength of AM radio waves ranges from 180 to 550 meters, and the waves readily bend around buildings and other objects that might otherwise obstruct them. A long-wavelength radio wave doesn't "see" a relatively small building in its path—but a short-wavelength radio wave does. Because the radio waves of the FM band range from 2.8 to 3.4 meters, they don't bend very well around buildings. This is one of the reasons why FM reception is often poor in localities where AM reception comes in loud and clear. In the case of radio reception, we don't wish to "see" objects in the path of radio waves, so diffraction is welcome.

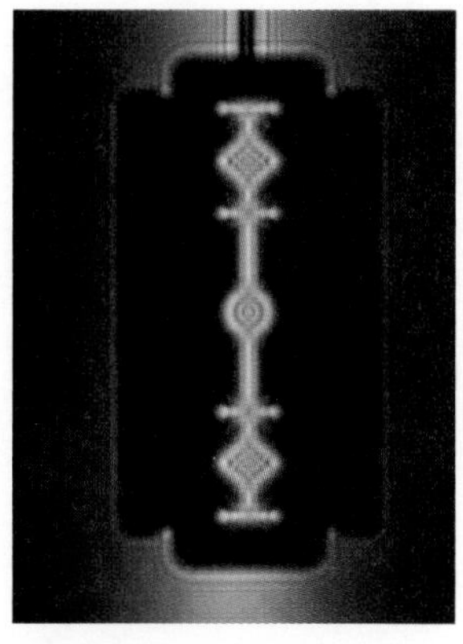

Figure 12.30
Diffraction fringes are evident in the shadows of monochromatic (single-frequency) laser light.

Diffraction is not so welcome when you are viewing very small objects with a microscope. If the size of an object is about the same as the wavelength of light, diffraction blurs the image. If the object is smaller than the wavelength of light, no structure can be seen. The entire image is lost, due to diffraction. No amount of magnification or perfection of microscope design can defeat this fundamental diffraction limit.

To get around this problem, microscopists illuminate very tiny objects with electron beams rather than with light. Compared with light waves, electron beams have extremely short wavelengths. *Electron microscopes* take advantage of the fact that all matter has wave properties. A beam of electrons has a wavelength smaller than the wavelengths of visible light. In an electron microscope, electric and magnetic fields, rather than optical lenses, are used to focus and magnify images.

The use of shorter wavelengths to see finer detail is employed by dolphins, who scan their environment with ultrasound. The echoes of long-wavelength sound give the dolphin an overall image of the objects in its surroundings. To examine them in more detail, the dolphin emits sounds of shorter wavelengths. The dolphin has always done naturally what physicians have only recently been capable of doing with ultrasonic imaging devices.

☑ CHECKPOINT

Why does a microscopist use blue light rather than white light to illuminate objects being viewed?

Check Your Answer

There is less diffraction with blue light. This allows the microscopist to see more detail (just as a dolphin beautifully investigates fine detail in its environment by means of the echoes of ultrashort wavelengths of sound).

12.5 Interference

Note that the diffracted light in Figure 12.30 shows fringes. These fringes are produced by **interference**, which we discussed in the previous chapter. Constructive and destructive interference is reviewed in Figure 12.31. We see that the addition, or *superposition,* of a pair of identical waves in phase with each other produces a wave of the same frequency but with twice the amplitude. If the waves are exactly one-half wavelength out of phase, their superposition results in complete cancellation. If they are out of phase by other amounts, partial cancellation occurs.

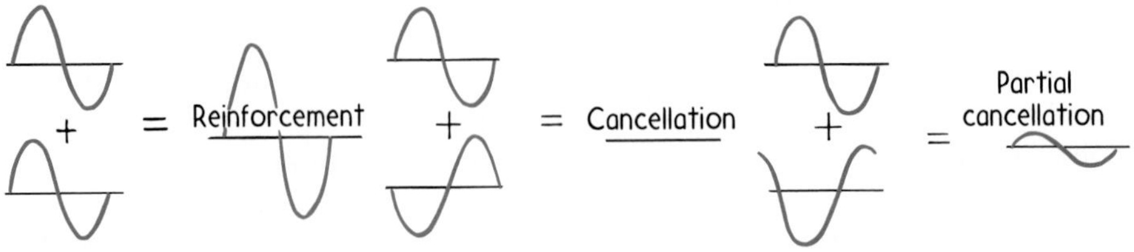

Figure 12.31
Wave interference.

In 1801, the wave nature of light was convincingly demonstrated when the British physicist and physician Thomas Young performed his now famous interference experiment.* Young found that light directed through two closely spaced pinholes recombined to produce fringes of brightness and darkness on a screen behind. The bright fringes of light resulted from light waves from the two holes arriving crest to crest, while the dark areas resulted from light waves arriving trough to crest. Figure 12.32 shows Young's drawing of the pattern of superimposed waves from the two sources. His experiment is now done with two closely spaced slits instead of with pinholes, so the fringe patterns are straight lines (Figure 12.33).

Figure 12.32
Thomas Young's original drawing of a two-source interference pattern. Letters C, D, E, and F mark regions of destructive interference.

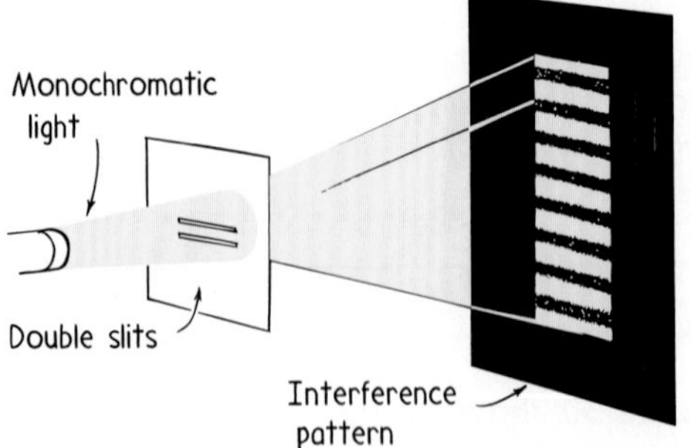

Figure 12.33
When monochromatic light passes through two closely spaced slits, a striped interference pattern is produced.

We see in Figures 12.34 and 12.35 how the series of bright and dark lines results from the different path lengths from the slits to the screen. For the central bright fringe, the paths from each slit are the same length, and the waves arrive in phase and reinforce each other. The dark fringes on either side of the central fringe result from one path

*Thomas Young read fluently at the age of 2; by 4, he had read the Bible twice; by 14, he knew eight languages. In his adult life, he was a physician and scientist, contributing to an understanding of fluids, work and energy, and the elastic properties of materials. He was the first person to make progress in deciphering Egyptian hieroglyphics. There's no doubt about it—Thomas Young was a bright guy!

Figure 12.34
Bright fringes occur when waves from both slits arrive in phase; dark areas result from the overlapping of waves that are out of phase.

being longer (or shorter) by one-half wavelength, where the waves arrive half a wavelength out of phase. The other sets of dark fringes occur where the paths differ by odd multiples of one-half wavelength: 3/2, 5/2, and so on.

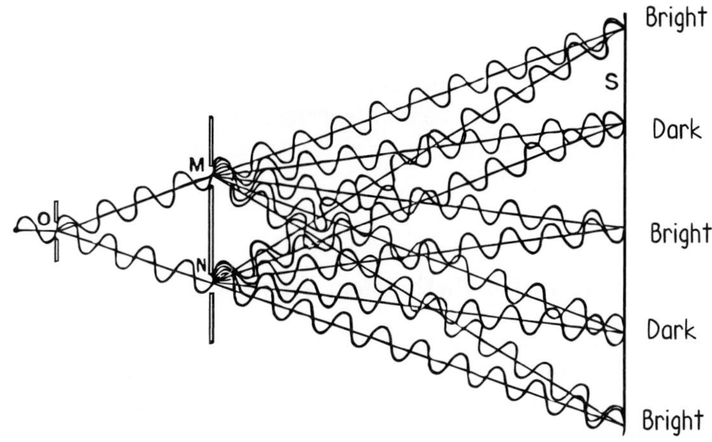

Figure 12.35
Light from O passes through slits M and N and produces an interference pattern on the screen S.

☑ CHECKPOINT

1. If the double slits were illuminated with monochromatic red light, would the fringes be more widely or more closely spaced than if they were illuminated with monochromatic blue light?
2. Why is it important that monochromatic (single-frequency) light be used?

Check Your Answers

1. They would be more widely spaced. Can you see in Figure 12.35 that a slightly longer path—and therefore a slightly more displaced path—from the entrance slit to the screen would result for the longer waves of red light?
2. If light of various wavelengths were diffracted by the slits, dark fringes for one wavelength would be filled in with bright fringes for another, resulting in no distinct fringe pattern. If you haven't seen this, be sure to ask your instructor to demonstrate it.

Interference patterns are not limited to one or two slits. A multitude of closely spaced slits makes up a *diffraction grating.* These devices, like prisms, disperse white light into colors. These are used in devices called *spectrometers,* which we will discuss in Chapter 15. The feathers of some birds act as diffraction gratings and disperse colors. The same is true of the microscopic pits on the reflective surface of a compact disc.

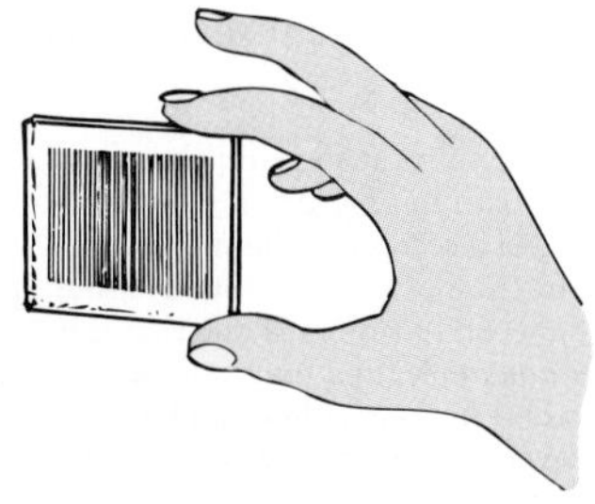

Figure 12.36
A diffraction grating disperses light into colors by interference. It may be used in place of a prism in a spectrometer.

Link to Optometry

Seeing Star-Shaped Stars

Have you wondered why stars are represented with spikes? The stars on the American flag have five spikes, and the Jewish Star of David has six spikes. All through the ages, stars have been drawn with spikes. The reason for this has nothing to do with the actual shapes of the stars, which are merely point sources of light in the night sky; rather, it has to do with imperfect eyesight.

The surfaces of our eyes, the corneas, become scratched for a variety of reasons. These scratches make up a diffraction grating of sorts. A scratched cornea is not a very good diffraction grating, but its effects are evident if you look at a bright point source against a dark background—like a star in the night sky. Instead of seeing a point of light, you see a spiky shape. The spikes will even shimmer and twinkle if there are some temperature differences in the atmosphere to produce some refraction. And, if you live in a windy desert region where sandstorms are frequent, your cornea will be even more scratched and you'll see more vivid star spikes.

So stars don't have spikes. They appear spiked because of scratches on the surfaces of our eyes that behave as diffraction gratings. So there's not only physics in all you see, but in how you see!

Interference Colors by Reflection from Thin Films

We have all noticed the beautiful spectrum of colors reflected from a soap bubble or from gasoline on a wet street. These colors are produced by the interference of light waves. This phenomenon, which is often called *iridescence,* is observed in thin transparent films.

A soap bubble appears iridescent in white light when the thickness of the soap film is about the same as the wavelength of light. Light waves reflected from the outer and inner surfaces of the film to your eye travel different distances. When illuminated by white light, the film may be just the right thickness at one place to cause the destructive interference of, say, red light. When red light is subtracted from white light, the mixture remaining appears as the complementary color—cyan. At another place, where the film is thinner, perhaps blue is canceled. Then the light seen is the complement of blue—yellow. Whatever color is canceled by interference, the light seen is its complementary color.

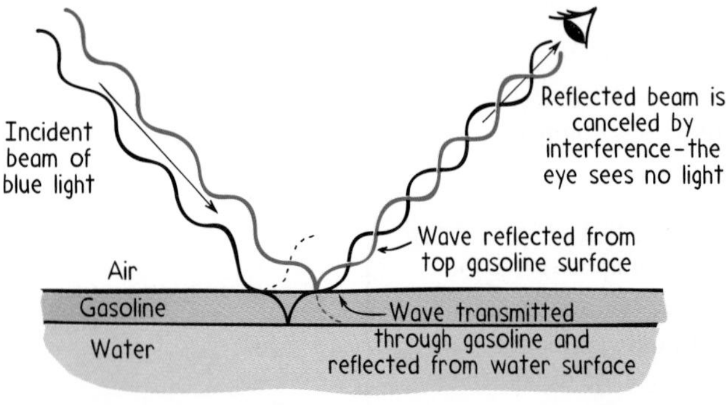

Figure 12.37
The thin film of gasoline is just the right thickness to cancel the reflections of blue light from the top and bottom surfaces. If the film were thinner, perhaps shorter-wavelength violet would be canceled.

This can be seen when some gasoline has been spilled on a wet street (Figure 12.37). Light reflects from two surfaces: the upper, air-gasoline surface and the lower, gasoline-water surface. If the thickness of the gasoline is such as to cancel blue, as the figure suggests, then the gasoline surface appears yellow to the eye.*

*Phase shifts at some reflecting surfaces also contribute to interference. For simplicity and brevity, our concern with this topic will be limited to this footnote: Briefly, when light in a medium is reflected at the surface of a second medium in which the speed of transmitted light is less (when there is a greater index of refraction), there is a 180° phase shift (that is, half a wavelength). No phase shift occurs, however, when the second medium is one that transmits light at a higher speed (and there is a lower index of refraction). For example, in a soap bubble, light reflects from the first surface 180° out of phase. Light reflects from the second surface without a phase change. If the thickness of the soap film is very small compared with the wavelength of light, so that the distance through the film is negligible, the parts of the wave reflected from the two surfaces are out of phase and cancel—for all frequencies. This is why parts of a soap film that are extremely thin appear black. Waves of all frequencies are canceled.

As mentioned earlier, blue subtracted from white leaves yellow. Why are a variety of colors seen in the thin film of gasoline? The answer is that the film thickness is not uniform. Different film thicknesses show a "contour map" of microscopic differences in surface "elevations."

If you view the thin film of gasoline from a lower angle, you'll see different colors. That's because light passing through the film travels a longer path. A longer wave is canceled, and a different color is seen. Different wavelengths of light are canceled for different angles.

Dishes that have been washed in soapy water and poorly rinsed still have a thin film of soap on them. Hold such a dish up to a light source so that *interference colors* can be seen. Then turn the dish to a new position, keeping your eye on the same part of the dish. Do you notice a change in color? Light reflecting from the bottom surface of the transparent soap film cancels light reflecting from the top surface.

Interference techniques can be used to measure the wavelengths of light and other regions of the electromagnetic spectrum. Interference provides a means of measuring extremely small distances with great accuracy. Instruments called *interferometers,* which use the principle of interference, are the most accurate instruments known for measuring small distances.

Soap-bubble colors result from the interference of reflected light from the inside and outside surfaces of the soap film. When a color is canceled, what you see is its complementary color.

Insights

Figure 12.38
Bob Greenler shows interference colors with a big bubble. Note that the colors are secondary primaries—magenta, yellow, and cyan.

☑ CHECKPOINT

1. What color appears to be reflected from a soap bubble in sunlight when its thickness is such that green light is canceled?
2. In the left column are the colors of certain objects. In the right column are various ways in which colors are produced. Match the right column to the left.

(a) yellow daffodil	(1) interference
(b) blue sky	(2) diffraction
(c) rainbow	(3) selective reflection
(d) peacock feathers	(4) refraction
(e) soap bubble	(5) scattering

Check Your Answers

1. The composite of all the visible wavelengths except green is the complementary color, magenta. (Go back and see Figures 12.16 and 12.17.)
2. a–3; b–5; c–4; d–2; e–1.

Figure 12.39
A vertically polarized plane wave and a horizontally polarized plane wave.

12.6 Polarization

Interference and diffraction provide the best evidence that light is wavelike. As we learned in Chapter 11, waves can be either longitudinal or transverse. Sound waves are longitudinal, which means the vibratory motion of the medium is *along* the direction of wave travel. The fact that light waves exhibit **polarization** demonstrates that they are transverse.

If you shake a rope either up and down or from side to side as shown in Figure 12.39, you'll produce a transverse wave along the rope. The plane of vibration is the same as the plane of the wave. If we shake it up and down, the wave vibrates in a vertical plane. If we shake it back and forth, the wave vibrates in a horizontal plane. We say that such a wave is *plane-polarized*—that the waves traveling along the rope are confined to a single plane. Polarization is a property of transverse waves. (Polarization does not occur among longitudinal waves—there is no such thing as polarized sound.)

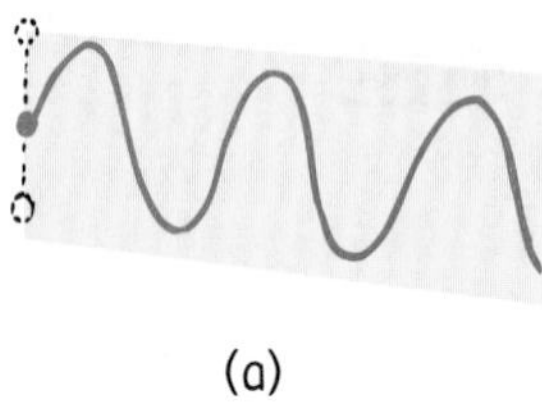

Figure 12.40
(a) A vertically polarized plane wave from a charge vibrating vertically. (b) A horizontally polarized plane wave from a charge vibrating horizontally.

A single vibrating electron can emit an electromagnetic wave that is plane-polarized. The plane of polarization matches the vibrational direction of the electron. That means that a vertically accelerating electron emits light that is vertically polarized. A horizontally accelerating electron emits light that is horizontally polarized (Figure 12.40).*

A common light source, such as an incandescent lamp, a fluorescent lamp, or a candle flame, emits light that is unpolarized. This is because the electrons that emit the light are vibrating in many random directions. There are as many planes of vibration as the vibrating electrons producing them. A few planes are represented in Figure 12.41a. We can represent all these planes by radial lines, shown in Figure 12.41b. (Or, more simply, the planes can be represented by vectors in two mutually perpendicular directions, as shown in Figure 12.41c.) The vertical vector represents all the components of vibration in the vertical direction. The horizontal vector represents all the components of vibration horizontally. The simple model of Figure 12.41c represents unpolarized light. Polarized light would be represented by a single vector.

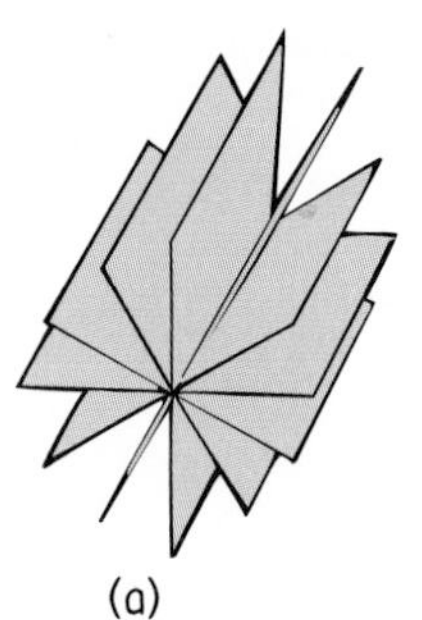

Figure 12.41
Representations of plane-polarized waves.

All transparent crystals having a noncubic natural shape have the property of polarizing light. These crystals divide unpolarized light into two internal beams polarized at right angles to each other. Some crystals strongly absorb one beam while transmitting the other (Figure 12.42). This makes them excellent polarizers. Herapathite is such a crystal. Microscopic herapathite crystals are aligned and embedded between cellulose sheets. They make up Polaroid filters, popular in sunglasses. Other Polaroid sheets consist of certain aligned molecules rather than tiny crystals.

If you look at unpolarized light through a Polaroid filter, you can rotate the filter in any direction and the light appears unchanged. But, if the light is

*Light may also be circularly polarized and elliptically polarized, which are also transverse polarizations. But we will not study these cases.

polarized, rotating the filter allows you to block out more and more of the light until it is completely blocked out. An ideal Polaroid filter transmits 50 percent of incident unpolarized light. That 50 percent is polarized. When two Polaroid filters are arranged so that their polarization axes are aligned, light can pass through both, as shown in the rope analogy (Figure 12.43a). If their axes are at right angles to each other (in this case, we say the filters are *crossed*), almost no light penetrates the pair (Figure 12.43b). (A small amount of shorter wavelengths do get through.) When Polaroid filters are used in pairs like this, the first one is called the *polarizer* and the second one is called the *analyzer.*

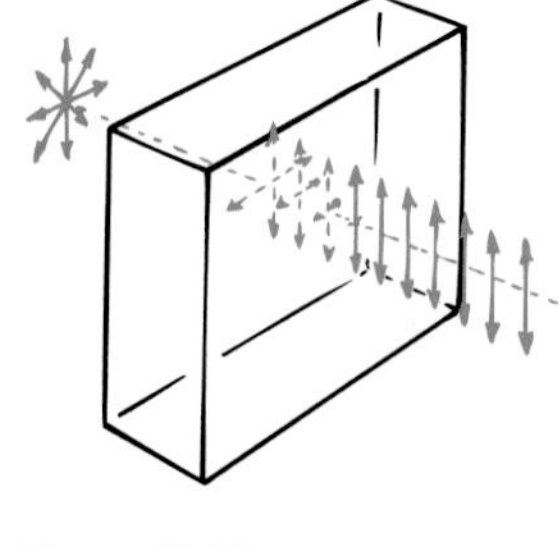

Figure 12.42
One component of the incident nonpolarized light is absorbed, which results in emerging polarized light.

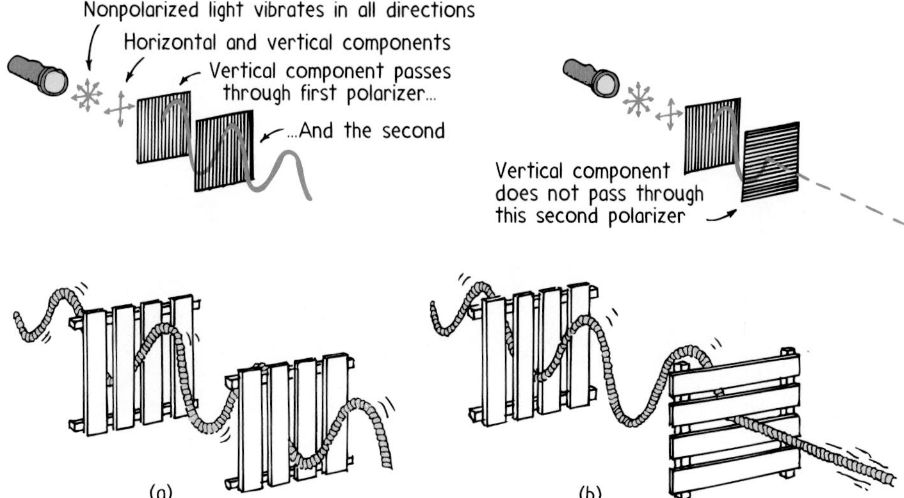

Figure 12.43
A rope analogy illustrates the effect of crossed polaroids.

Much of the light reflected from nonmetallic surfaces is polarized. The glare from glass or water is a good example. Except for light that hits vertically, the reflected ray has more vibrations parallel to the reflecting surface. The part of the ray that penetrates the surface has more vibrations at right angles to the surface (Figure 12.44). Skipping flat rocks off the surface of a pond provides an appropriate analogy. When the rocks hit parallel to the surface, they are easily reflected by the surface. But when they hit with their faces at right angles to the surface, they "refract" into the water. The glare from reflecting surfaces can be dimmed a lot with the use of Polaroid sunglasses. The polarization axes of the lenses are vertical because most of the glare reflects from horizontal surfaces.

Figure 12.44
Polaroid sunglasses block out horizontally vibrating light. When the lenses overlap at right angles, no light gets through.

☑ CHECKPOINT

Which pair of glasses is best suited for automobile drivers? (The polarization axes are shown by the straight lines.)

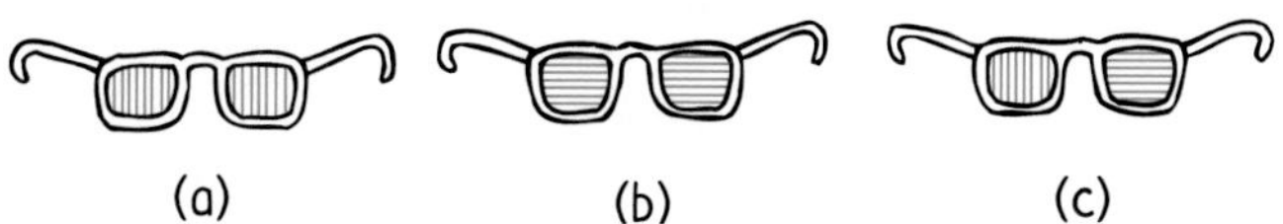

Check Your Answer

Glasses A are best suited because the vertical axis blocks horizontally polarized light, which makes up much of the glare from horizontal surfaces. Glasses C are suited for viewing 3-D movies.

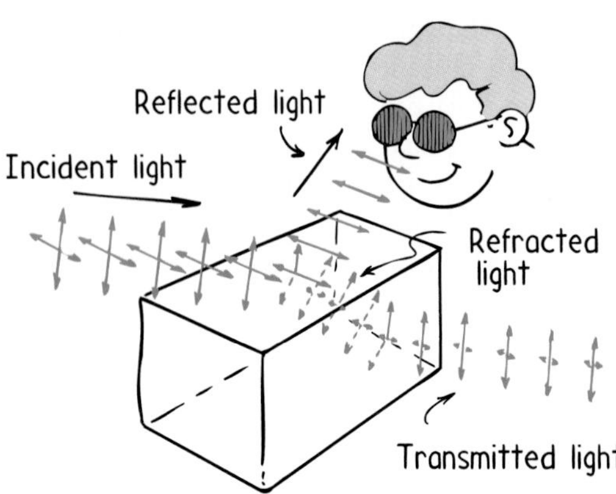

Figure 12.45
Most glare from nonmetallic surfaces is polarized. Here we see that the components of incident light that are parallel to the surface are reflected, while the components that are perpendicular to the surface are refracted into the medium. Since most of the glare that we encounter comes from from horizontal surfaces, the polarization axes of Polaroid sunglasses are vertical.

Beautiful colors similar to interference colors can be seen when certain materials are placed between crossed Polaroid filters. Cellophane works wonderfully. Why these colors are produced is another story—one that is left to the Suggested Reading and Web Sites for this chapter, found at the end of this book.

Figure 12.46
Light is transmitted when the axes of the Polaroid filters are aligned (a), but it is absorbed when Ludmila rotates one so that the axes are at right angles to each other (b). When she inserts a third Polaroid filter at an angle between the crossed ones, light is again transmitted (c). Why?

Summary of Terms

Electromagnetic wave An energy-carrying wave emitted by vibrating electrical charges (often electrons) and composed of oscillating electric and magnetic fields that regenerate one another.

Electromagnetic spectrum The range of electromagnetic waves that extends in frequency from radio waves to gamma rays.

Transparent The term applied to materials through which light can pass in straight lines.

Additive primary colors The three colors—red, blue, and green—that, when added in certain proportions, will produce any color in the spectrum.

Subtractive primary colors The three colors of absorbing pigments—magenta, yellow, and cyan—that, when mixed in certain proportions, will reflect any color in the spectrum.

Complementary colors Any two colors that, when added, will produce white light.

Diffraction The bending of light that passes around an obstacle or through a narrow slit, causing the light to spread and to produce light and dark fringes.

Interference The result of superposing different waves of the same wavelength. Constructive interference results from crest-to-crest reinforcement; destructive interference results from crest-to-trough cancellation. The interference of selected wavelengths of light produces colors known as *interference colors.*

Polarization The alignment of the transverse electric vectors that make up electromagnetic radiation. Such waves of aligned vibrations are said to be *polarized.*

Review Questions

12.1 The Electromagnetic Spectrum

1. Does visible light make up a relatively large part or a relatively small part of the electromagnetic spectrum?
2. What is the principal difference between a radio wave and light? Between light and an X ray?
3. How does the frequency of an electromagnetic wave compare with the frequency of the vibrating electrons that produces it?
4. How is the wavelength of light related to its frequency?

12.2 Transparent and Opaque Materials

5. The sound coming from one tuning fork can force another to vibrate. What is the analogous effect for light?
6. In what region of the electromagnetic spectrum is the resonant frequency of electrons in glass?
7. What is the fate of the energy in ultraviolet light incident on glass?
8. What is the fate of the energy in visible light incident on glass?
9. How does the average speed of light in glass compare with its speed in a vacuum?
10. What part of the electromagnetic spectrum is unable to penetrate the earth's atmosphere?

12.3 Color

11. What is the relationship between the frequency of light and its color?
12. Which has the higher frequency, red light or blue light?
13. Distinguish between the white of this page and the black of this ink, in terms of what happens to the white light that falls on both.
14. How does the color of an object illuminated by an incandescent lamp differ from the color of the same object illuminated by a fluorescent lamp?
15. What is the color of the light that is transmitted through a piece of red glass?
16. Which warms more quickly in sunlight, common window glass or a colored piece of glass? Why?
17. What is the evidence for the statement that white light is a composite of all the colors of the visible part of the electromagnetic spectrum?
18. What is the color of the peak frequency of solar radiation? To what color of light are our eyes most sensitive?
19. What range of frequencies in the radiation curve do red, green, and blue light occupy?
20. Why are red, green, and blue called the *additive primary colors?*
21. Why are red and cyan called *complementary colors?*
22. What are the subtractive primary colors? Why are they so called?
23. What does it mean to say that light is scattered?
24. Why does the sky sometimes appear whitish?
25. Why does the sun look reddish at sunrise and sunset but not at noon?
26. What is the evidence for a cloud being composed of particles having a variety of sizes?

12.4 Diffraction

27. Is diffraction more pronounced through a narrow or a wide opening?
28. For an opening of a given size, is diffraction more pronounced for a longer or a shorter wavelength?
29. What are some of the ways in which diffraction can be useful or troublesome?

12.5 Interference

30. Is interference restricted to only some types of waves, or does it occur for all types of waves?
31. What is monochromatic light?
32. What produces iridescence?
33. What causes the variety of colors seen in gasoline splotches on a wet street? Why are these colors not seen on a dry street?
34. What accounts for the variety of colors in a soap bubble?
35. If you look at a soap bubble from different angles so that you're viewing different apparent thicknesses of soap film, do you see different colors? Explain.

12.6 Polarization

36. What phenomenon distinguishes between longitudinal and transverse waves?
37. How does the direction of polarization of light compare with the direction of vibration of the electrons that produced it?
38. Why does light pass through a pair of Polaroid filters when the axes are aligned but not when the axes are at right angles to each other?
39. How much unpolarized light does an ideal Polaroid filter transmit?
40. When unpolarized light is incident at a grazing angle upon water, what can you say about the reflected light?

Activities

1. Which eye do you use more? To test which you favor, hold a finger up at arm's length. With both eyes open, look past it at a distant object. Now close your right eye. If your finger appears to jump to the right, then you use your right eye more.
2. Stare at a piece of colored paper for 45 seconds or so. Then look at a plain white surface. The cones in your retina receptive to the color of the paper become fatigued, so you see an afterimage of the complementary color when you look at a white area. This is because the fatigued cones send a weaker signal to the brain. All the colors produce white, but all the colors minus one produce the color that is complementary to the missing color. Try it and see!
3. Simulate your own sunset: add a few drops of milk to a glass of water and look at a light bulb through the glass. The bulb appears to be red or pale orange, while light scattered to the side appears blue. Try it and see.

4. With a razor blade, cut a slit in a card and look at a light source through it. You can vary the size of the opening by bending the card slightly. See the interference fringes? Try it with two closely spaced slits.
5. Next time you're in the bathtub, froth up the soapsuds and notice the colors of highlights from the illuminating light overhead on each tiny bubble. Notice that different bubbles reflect different colors, due to the different thicknesses of soap film. If a friend is bathing with you, compare the different colors that you each see reflected from the same bubbles. You'll see that they're different—for what you see depends on your point of view!
6. Do this one at your kitchen sink. Dip a dark-colored coffee cup (dark colors make the best background for viewing interference colors) in dishwashing detergent, and then hold it sideways and look at the reflected light from the detergent film that covers its mouth. Swirling colors appear as the film runs down to form a wedge that grows thicker at the bottom with time. The top becomes thinner, so thin that it appears black. This tells us that its thickness is less than one-fourth the thickness of the shortest waves of visible light. Whatever its wavelength, light reflecting from the inner surface reverses phase, rejoins light reflecting from the outer surface, and cancels. The film soon becomes so thin that it pops.
7. When you're wearing Polaroid sunglasses, view the glare from a nonmetallic surface, such as a road or a body of water. Tip your head from side to side, and see how the glare intensity changes as you vary the magnitude of the electric vector component aligned with the polarization axis of the glasses. Also notice the polarization of different parts of the sky when you hold the sunglasses in your hand and rotate them.
8. Place a bottle of corn syrup between two Polaroid filters. Place a white light source at the back. Then look through the filters and the syrup to view spectacular colors as you rotate one of the filters.
9. See spectacular interference colors with a polarized-light microscope. Any microscope, including an inexpensive toy microscope, can be converted into a polarized-light microscope by fitting a piece of Polaroid filter inside the eyepiece and taping another onto the stage of the microscope. Mix drops of naphthalene and benzene (handle with care, since benzene is toxic!) on a slide and watch the growth of crystals. Rotate the eyepiece and change the colors.
10. Make some slides for a slide projector by sticking some crumpled cellophane onto pieces of slide-sized Polaroid filter. (Also try strips of cellophane tape overlapped at different angles and experiment with different brands of transparent tape.) Project them onto a large screen or a white wall, and rotate a second, slightly larger piece of Polaroid filter in front of the projector lens in rhythm with your favorite music. You'll have your own light show.

Exercises

1. What is the fundamental source of electromagnetic radiation?
2. Which have the longest wavelengths: light waves, X rays, or radio waves?
3. Which has the shorter wavelengths, ultraviolet or infrared? Which has the higher frequencies?
4. We hear people talk of "ultraviolet light" and "infrared light." Why are these terms misleading? Why are we less likely to hear people talk of "radio light" and "X-ray light"?
5. Which requires a physical medium in which to travel, light or sound? Or do both require a physical medium? Explain.
6. Do radio waves travel at the speed of sound, at the speed of light, or at some speed in between?
7. What do radio waves and light have in common? What is different about them?
8. What evidence can you cite to support the idea that light can travel in a vacuum?
9. Short wavelengths of visible light interact more frequently with the atoms in glass than do longer wavelengths. Does this interaction time tend to speed up or to slow down the average speed of light in glass?
10. What determines whether a material is transparent or opaque?
11. You can get a sunburn on a cloudy day, but you can't get a sunburn even on a sunny day if you are behind glass. Explain.
12. Suppose that sunlight falls on both a pair of reading glasses and a pair of dark sunglasses. Which pair of glasses would you expect to become warmer? Defend your answer.
13. In a dress shop with only fluorescent lighting, a customer insists on taking dresses into the daylight at the doorway to check their color. Is she being reasonable? Explain.
14. Fire engines used to be red. Now many of them are yellow-green. Why the change of color?
15. The radiation curve of the sun (Figure 12.14) shows that the brightest light from the sun is yellow-green. Why then do we see the sun as whitish instead of yellow-green?
16. A spotlight is coated so that it won't transmit yellow light from its white-hot filament. What color is the emerging beam of light?

17. How could you use the spotlights at a play to make the yellow clothes of the performers suddenly change to black?
18. Does a color television work by color addition or by color subtraction? Defend your answer.
19. On a TV screen, red, green, and blue spots of fluorescent materials are illuminated at a variety of relative intensities to produce a full spectrum of colors. What dots are activated to produce yellow? To produce magenta? To produce white?
20. What colors of ink do color ink-jet printers use to produce a full range of colors? Do the colors form by color addition or by color subtraction?
21. Below is a photo of physics editor Suzanne Lyons with her son Tristan wearing red and her daughter Simone wearing green. Below that is the negative of the photo, which shows these colors differently. What is your explanation?

22. Check Figure 12.16 to see if the following three statements are accurate. Then provide the missing word in the last statement. (All colors are combined by the addition of light.)
    Red + green + blue = white.
    Red + green = yellow = white − blue.
    Red + blue = magenta = white − green.
    Green + blue = cyan = white − ________.
23. In which of these cases will a ripe banana appear black? When it is illuminated with: (a) red light; (b) yellow light; (c) green light; (d) blue light.
24. When white light is shone on red ink that has dried on a clear glass plate, the color that is transmitted is red. But the color that is reflected is not red. What is it?
25. Stare intently for at least a half minute at an American flag. Then turn your gaze to a white wall. What colors do you see in the image of the flag that appears on the wall?
26. Why can't we see stars in the daytime?
27. Why is the sky a darker blue when you are at high altitudes? (*Hint:* What color is the "sky" on the moon?)
28. Why does smoke from a campfire look bluish against trees near the ground but yellowish against the sky?
29. Tiny particles, like tiny bells, scatter high-frequency waves more than low-frequency waves. Large particles, like large bells, mostly scatter low frequencies. Intermediate-size particles and bells mostly scatter intermediate frequencies. What does this have to do with the whiteness of clouds?
30. Very big particles, like droplets of water, absorb more radiation than they scatter. What does this have to do with the darkness of rain clouds?
31. The atmosphere of Jupiter is more than 1000 km thick. From the surface of this planet, would you expect to see a white sun?
32. You're explaining to a youngster at the seashore why the water is cyan colored. The youngster points to the whitecaps of overturning waves and asks why they are white. What is your answer?
33. Why do *radio waves* diffract around buildings, while *light waves* do not?
34. Light illuminates two thin, closely spaced slits and produces an interference pattern on a screen behind. How will the distance between the fringes of the pattern differ for red light and blue light?
35. Why is Young's experiment more effective if you use slits rather than with the pinholes he first used?
36. A pattern of fringes is produced when monochromatic light passes through a pair of thin slits. Would such a pattern be produced by three thin parallel slits? By thousands of such slits? Give an example to support your answer.
37. The bright colors of peacocks and hummingbirds are the result not of pigments but of ridges in the surface layers of their feathers. By what physical principle do these ridges produce colors?
38. The colored wings of many butterflies are due to pigmentation. In other butterflies, such as the morphos, some of the colors do not result from pigmentation. When the wing is viewed from different angles, the colors change. How are these colors produced?
39. Why do the iridescent colors seen in some seashells (such as abalone shells) change as the shells are viewed from different positions?
40. If you notice the interference patterns of a thin film of oil or gasoline on water, you'll note that the colors form complete rings. How are these rings similar to the lines of equal elevation on a contour map?
41. Because of wave interference, a film of oil on water is seen as yellow by observers directly above in an airplane. What color does the film appear to a scuba diver looking upward from directly below?

42. Some coated lenses appear bluish when seen by reflected light. What color of light do you suppose they are designed to eliminate?
43. What does polarization tell you about the nature of light waves?
44. The digital displays of watches and other devices are normally polarized. What problem occurs with these displays when one is wearing polarized sunglasses?
45. Why will an ideal Polaroid filter transmit 50% of incident nonpolarized light?
46. Why may an ideal Polaroid filter transmit anything from zero to 100% of incident polarized light?
47. What percentage of light is transmitted by two ideal Polaroid filters, one on top of the other with their polarization axes aligned? With their polarization axes at right angles to each other?
48. If you have only a single Polaroid filter, how can you determine its polarization axis?
49. How can a single Polaroid filter be used to show that the sky is partially polarized? (Interestingly enough, unlike humans, bees and many insects can discern polarized light, and they use this ability for navigation.)
50. Light will not pass through a pair of Polaroid filters when they are aligned perpendicularly. But, if a third Polaroid filter is sandwiched between the other two with its alignment halfway between the alignments of the others (that is, with its axis making a 45° angle with each of the other two alignment axes), some light does get through. Why?

Problems

1. How long does it take for a pulse of laser light to reach the moon and bounce back to earth?
2. The nearest star beyond the sun is Alpha Centauri, which is 4.2×10^{16} meters away. If we were to receive a radio message from this star today, how long ago would it have been sent?
3. Blue-green light has a frequency of about 6×10^{14} Hz. Use the relationship $c = f\lambda$ to find the wavelength of this light in air. How does this wavelength compare with the size of an atom, which is about 10^{-10} m?
4. The wavelength of light changes as light goes from one medium to another, while the frequency remains the same. Is the wavelength longer or shorter in water than in air? Explain in terms of the equation Speed = frequency × wavelength.
   A certain blue-green light has a wavelength of 600 nm (6×10^{-7} m) in air. What is its wavelength in water, where light travels at 75 percent of its speed in air? What is its speed in Plexiglas, where light travels at 67 percent of its speed in air?
5. A certain radar installation that is used to track airplanes transmits electromagnetic radiation with a wavelength of 3 cm. (a) What is the frequency of this radiation, measured in billions of hertz (GHz)? (b) What is the time required for a pulse of radar waves to reach an airplane 5 km away and return?

Chapter 12 Online Resources

Tutorials
- Light & Spectroscopy
- Color

Videos
- Light & Transparent Materials
- Colored Shadows
- Yellow-Green Peak of Sunlight
- Why the Sunset Is Red
- Why the Sky Is Blue
- Polarized Light & 3D Viewing

Quiz
Exercises
Flashcards
Links

CHAPTER 13

Properties of Light

Most of the things we see around us do not emit their own light. They are visible because they reemit light reaching their surface from a primary source, such as the sun or a lamp, or from a secondary source, such as the illuminated sky. When light falls on the surface of a material, it is usually either reemitted without change in frequency or is absorbed into the material and turned into heat. Usually, both of these processes occur in varying degrees. When the reemitted light is returned into the medium from which it came, it is *reflected,* and the process is referred to as **reflection.** When the reemitted light bends from its original course and proceeds in straight lines from molecule to molecule into a transparent material, it is *refracted,* and the process is referred to as **refraction.**

13.1 Reflection

When this page is illuminated by sunlight or lamplight, electrons in the atoms of the paper vibrate more energetically in response to the oscillating electric fields of the illuminating light. The energized electrons reemit the light by which we see the page. When the page is illuminated by white light, it appears white, which reveals the fact that the electrons reemit all the visible frequencies. Very little absorption occurs. The ink on the page is a different story. Except for a bit of reflection, the ink absorbs all the visible frequencies and therefore appears black.

Law of Reflection

Anyone who has played pool or billiards knows that, when a ball bounces from a surface, the angle of incidence is equal to the angle of rebound. The same is true of light. This is the **law of reflection,** and it holds for all angles:

The angle of reflection equals the angle of incidence.

Figure 13.1
The law of reflection.

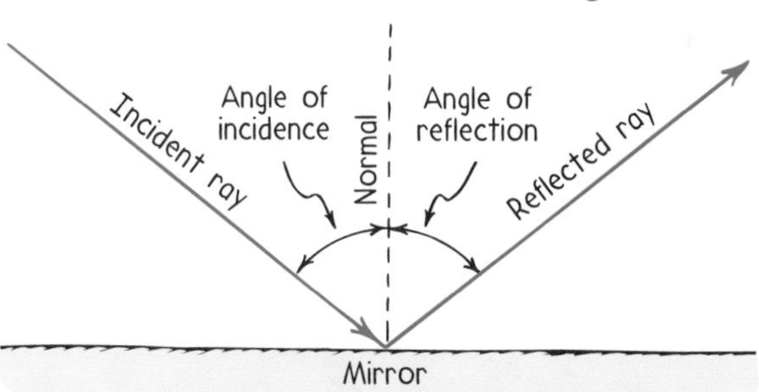

The law of reflection is illustrated with arrows representing light rays in Figure 13.1. Instead of measuring the angles of incident and reflected rays from the reflecting surface, it is customary to measure them from a line perpendicular to the plane of the reflecting surface. This imaginary line is called the *normal.* The incident ray, the normal, and the reflected ray all lie in the same plane.

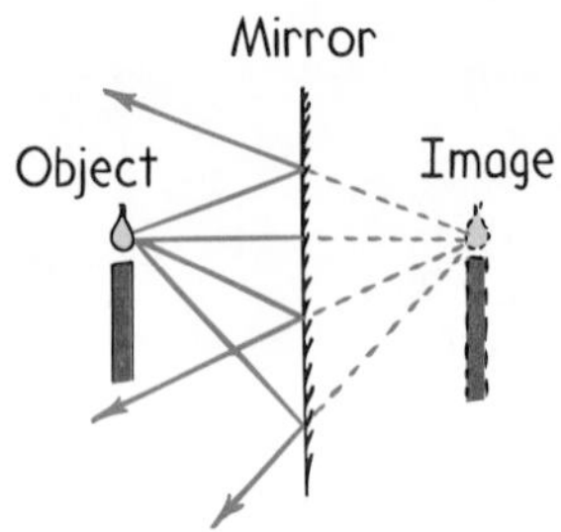

Figure 13.2
A virtual image is formed behind the mirror and is located at the position where the extended reflected rays (dashed lines) converge.

If you place a candle in front of a mirror, rays of light radiate from the flame in all directions. Figure 13.2 shows only four of the infinite number of rays leaving one of the infinite number of points on the candle. When these rays meet the mirror, they reflect at angles equal to their angles of incidence. The rays diverge from the flame. Note that they also diverge when reflecting from the mirror. These divergent rays appear to emanate from behind the mirror (dashed lines). You see an image of the candle at this point. The light rays do not actually come from this point, so the image is called a *virtual image*. The image is as far behind the mirror as the object is in front of the mirror, and image and object have the same size. When you view yourself in a mirror, for example, the size of your image is the same as the size your twin would appear to be, if located as far behind the mirror as you are in front—as long as the mirror is flat. A flat mirror is called a *plane mirror*.

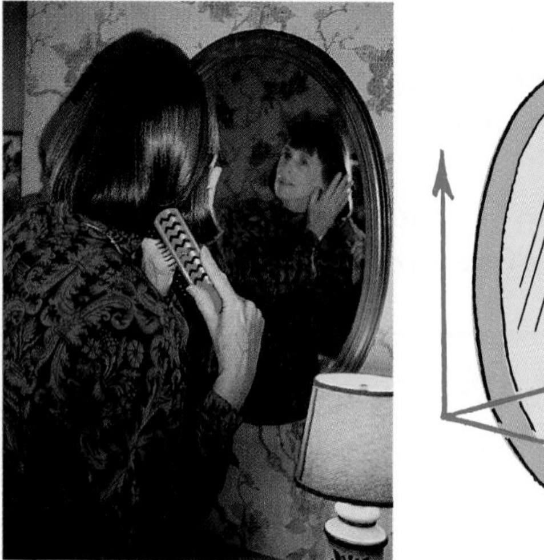

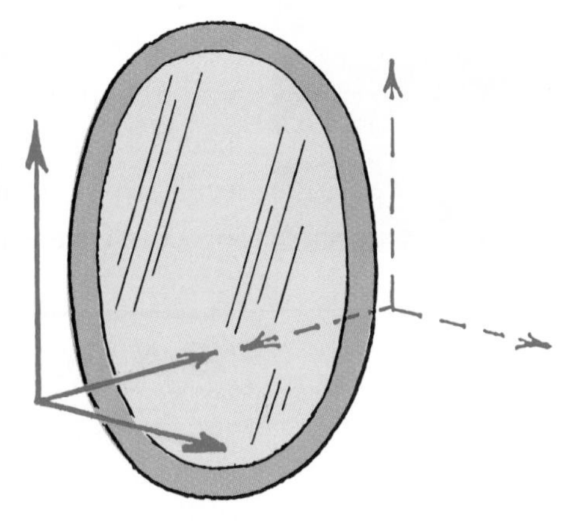

Figure 13.3
Marjorie's image is as far behind the mirror as she is in front of it. Note that she and her image have the same color of clothing—evidence that light doesn't change frequency upon reflection. Interestingly, her left and right axis is no more reversed than her up and down axis. The axis that *is* reversed, as shown to the right, is her front and back axis. That's why it appears that her left hand faces the right hand of her image.

When the mirror is curved, the sizes and distances of object and image are no longer equal. We will not discuss curved mirrors in this text, except to say that the law of reflection still holds. A curved mirror behaves as a succession of flat mirrors, each at a slightly different angular orientation from the one next to it. At each point, the angle of incidence is equal to the angle of reflection (Figure 13.4). Note that, in a curved mirror, unlike in a plane mirror, the normals (shown by the dashed black lines) at different points on the surface are not parallel to one another.

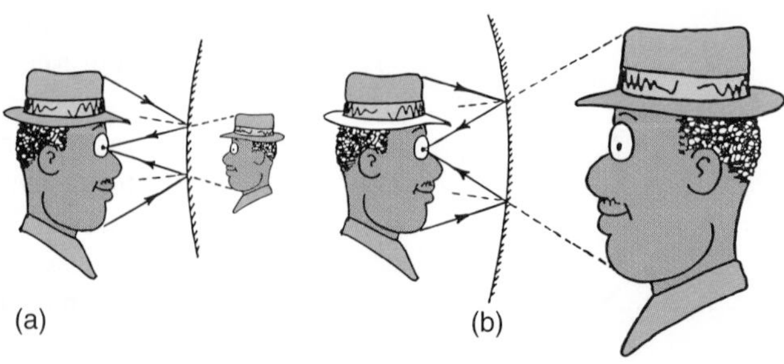

Figure 13.4
(a) The virtual image formed by a *convex* mirror (a mirror that curves outward) is smaller and closer to the mirror than the object. (b) When the object is close to a *concave* mirror (a mirror that curves inward like a "cave"), the virtual image is larger and farther away than the object. In either case, the law of reflection holds for each ray.

Whether the mirror is plane or curved, the eye–brain system cannot ordinarily distinguish between an object and its reflected image. So the illusion that an object exists behind a mirror (or, in some cases, in front of a concave mirror) is merely due to the fact that the light from the object enters the eye in exactly the same manner, physically, as it would have entered if the object really were at the image location.

Your image is as far behind a mirror as you are in front of it—as if your twin stood behind a pane of clear glass at a distance as far behind the glass as you are in front of it.

Insights

☑ **CHECKPOINT**

1. What evidence can you cite to support the claim that the frequency of light does not change upon reflection?
2. If you wish to take a picture of your image while standing 5 m in front of a plane mirror, for what distance should you set your camera to provide the sharpest focus?

Check Your Answers

1. Simply stand in front of a mirror and compare the color of your shirt with the color of its image. The fact that the color is the same is evidence that the frequency of light doesn't change upon reflection.
2. You should set your camera for 10 m; the situation is equivalent to you standing 5 m in front of an open window and viewing your twin standing 5 m in back of the window.

Would you like to become rich? Be the first to invent a surface that will reflect 100% of the light incident upon it.

Insights

Only part of the light that strikes a surface is reflected. For example, on a surface of clear glass and for normal incidence (light perpendicular to the surface), only about 4 percent is reflected from each surface. On a clean and polished aluminum or silver surface, however, about 90 percent of the incident light is reflected.

Diffuse Reflection

When light is incident on a rough surface, it is reflected in many directions. This is called **diffuse reflection** (Figure 13.5). If the surface is so smooth that the distances between successive elevations on the surface are less than about one-eighth the wavelength of the light, there is very little diffuse reflection, and the surface is said to be *polished*. A surface therefore may be polished for radiation of long wavelengths but rough for light of short wavelengths. The wire-mesh "dish" shown in Figure 13.6 is very rough for light waves and is hardly mirrorlike. But, for long-wavelength radio waves, it is "polished" and is an excellent reflector.

Light reflecting from this page is diffuse. The page may be smooth to a radio wave, but, to a light wave, it is rough. Smoothness is relative to the wavelength of the illuminating waves. Rays of light striking this page encounter millions of tiny flat surfaces facing in all directions. The incident light, therefore, is reflected in all directions.

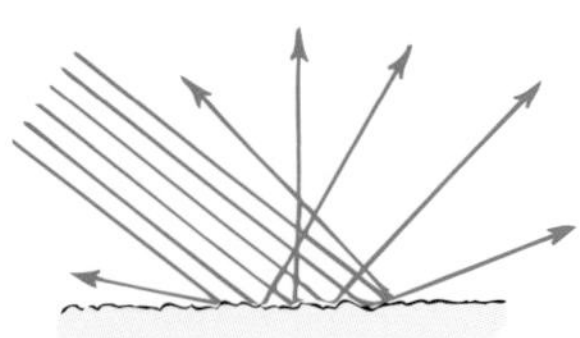

Figure 13.5
Diffuse reflection. Although reflection of each single ray obeys the law of reflection, the many different surface angles that light rays encounter in striking a rough surface produce reflection in many directions.

Figure 13.6
The open-mesh parabolic dish is a diffuse reflector for short-wavelength light but a polished reflector for long-wavelength radio waves.

Figure 13.7
A magnified view of the surface of ordinary paper.

This is a desirable circumstance. It enables us to see objects from any direction or position. You can see the road ahead of your car at night, for instance, because of diffuse reflection by the rough road surface. When the road is wet, however, it is smoother with less diffuse reflection, and therefore more difficult to see. Most of our environment is seen by diffuse reflection.

An undesirable circumstance related to diffuse reflection is the ghost image that occurs on a TV set when the TV signal bounces off buildings and other obstructions. For antenna reception, this difference in path lengths for the direct signal and the reflected signal produces a slight time delay. The ghost image is normally displaced to the right, the direction of scanning in the TV tube, because the reflected signal arrives at the receiving antenna later than the direct signal. Multiple reflections may produce multiple ghosts.

☑ CHECKPOINT

Why is it more dangerous to drive a car on a rainy night?

Check Your Answer

Because the road surface is more mirrored when it is wet, beams from your headlights mostly reflect ahead instead of back to you by diffuse reflection. This makes the road more difficult to see. Furthermore, headlights from oncoming cars reflect from the wet surface full force into your eyes. Glare is much more intense from a mirrored surface.

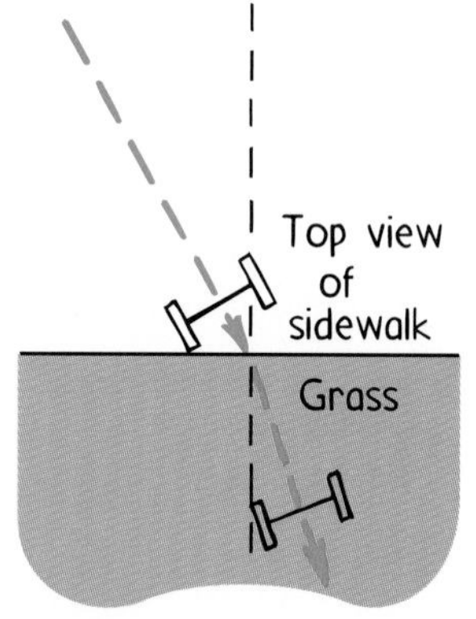

Figure 13.8
The direction of the rolling wheels changes when one wheel slows down before the other does.

13.2 Refraction

Recall, from the previous chapter, that light slows down when it enters glass and that it travels at different speeds in different materials.* It travels at 300,000 km/s in a vacuum, at a slightly lower speed in air, and at about three-fourths that speed in water. In a diamond, light travels at about 40 percent of its speed in a vacuum. As mentioned at the beginning of this chapter, when light passes from one medium to another, we call the process *refraction.* Unless the light is perpendicular to the surface of penetration, bending occurs.

To gain a better understanding of the bending of light in refraction, look at the pair of toy cart wheels in Figure 13.8. The wheels roll from a smooth sidewalk onto a grass lawn. If the wheels meet the grass at an angle, as the figure shows, they are deflected from their straight-line course. Note that the left wheel slows first when it interacts with the grass on the lawn. The right wheel maintains its higher speed while on the sidewalk. It pivots about the slower-moving left wheel because it travels farther in the same time. So the direction of the rolling wheels is bent toward the "normal," the black dashed line perpendicular to the grass-sidewalk border in Figure 13.8.

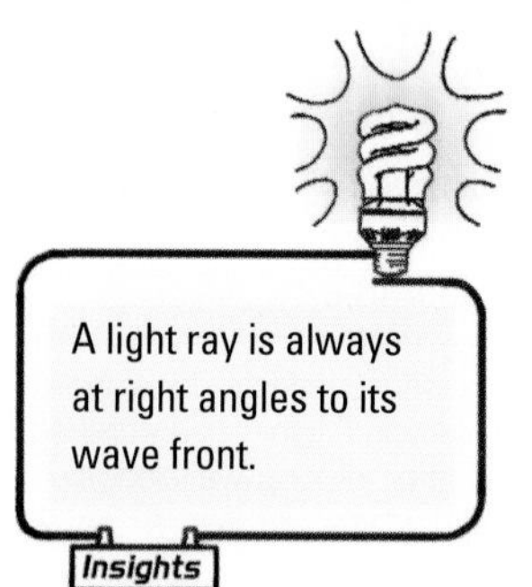

*Just how much the speed of light differs from its speed in a vacuum is given by the index of refraction, n, of the material:

$$n = \frac{\text{speed of light in vacuum}}{\text{speed of light in material}}$$

For example, the speed of light in a diamond is 125,000 km/s, and so the index of refraction for diamond is

$$n = \frac{300{,}000 \text{ km/s}}{125{,}000 \text{ km/s}} = 2.4$$

For a vacuum, $n = 1$.

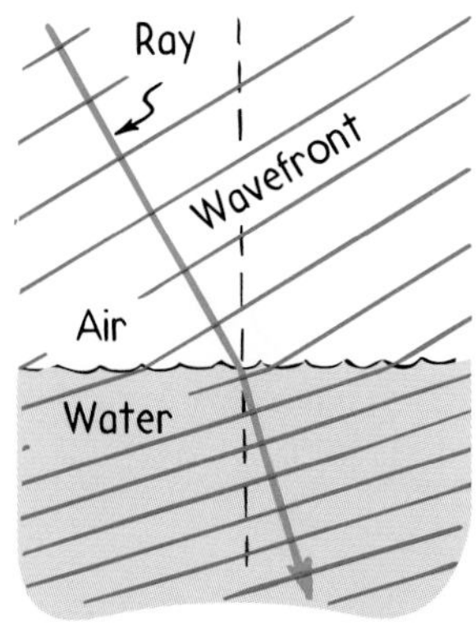

Figure 13.9
The direction of the light waves changes when one part of the wave slows down before the other part.

Figure 13.9 shows how a light wave bends in a similar way. Note the direction of light, indicated by the blue arrow (the light ray). Also note the *wave fronts* drawn at right angles to the ray. (If the light source were close, the wave fronts would appear circular; but, if the distant sun is the source, the wave fronts are practically straight lines.) The wave fronts are everywhere at right angles to the light rays. In the figure, the wave meets the water surface at an angle. This means that the left portion of the wave slows down in the water while the remainder in the air travels at the full speed of light, *c*. The light ray remains perpendicular to the wave front and therefore bends at the surface. It bends like the wheels bend when they roll from the sidewalk onto the grass. In both cases, the bending is caused by a change of speed.*

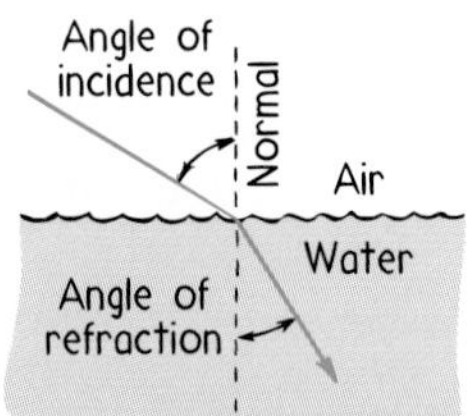

Figure 13.10
Refraction.

Figure 13.11 shows a beam of light entering water at the left and exiting at the right. The path would be the same if the light entered from the right and exited at the left. The light paths are reversible for both reflection and refraction. If you see someone's eyes by way of a reflective or refractive device, such as a mirror or a prism, then that person can see you by way of the device also.

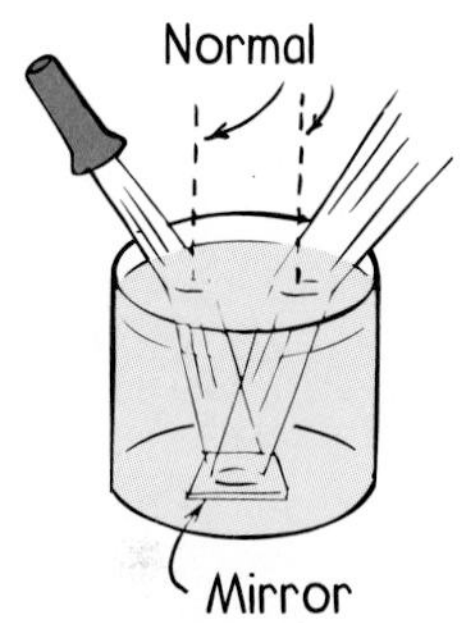

Figure 13.11
When light slows down in going from one medium to another, as it does in going from air to water, it bends toward the normal. When it speeds up in traveling from one medium to another, as it does in going from water to air, it bends away from the normal.

☑ CHECKPOINT

If the speed of light were the same in all media, would refraction still occur when light passes from one medium to another?

Check Your Answer

No.

Refraction causes many illusions. One of them is the apparent bending of a stick that is partially submerged in water. The submerged part appears closer to the surface than it actually is. The same is true when you look at a fish in water. The fish appears nearer to the surface and closer than it really is (Figure 13.12). If we look straight down into water, an object submerged 4 meters beneath the surface appears to be only 3 meters deep. Because of refraction, submerged objects appear to be magnified.

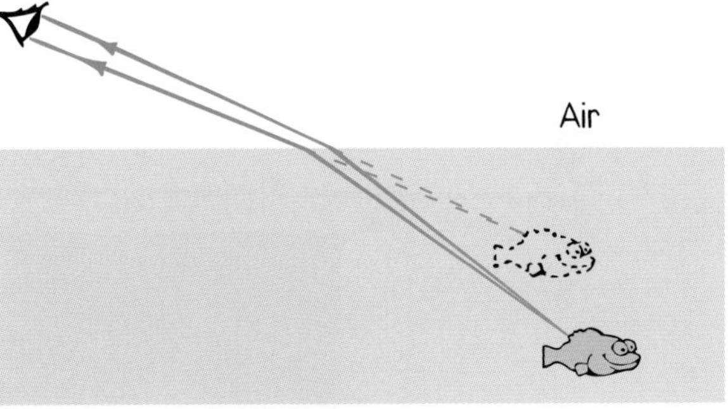

Figure 13.12
Because of refraction, a submerged object appears to be nearer to the surface than it actually is.

Refraction occurs in the earth's atmosphere. Whenever we watch a sunset, we see the sun for several minutes after it has sunk below the horizon (Figure 13.13). The earth's atmosphere is thin at the top and dense at the bottom. Because light travels faster in thin air than in dense air, parts

*The quantitative law of refraction, called *Snell's law*, is credited to Willebrord Snell, a seventeenth-century Dutch astronomer and mathematician: $n_1 \sin \theta_1 = n_2 \sin \theta_2$, where n_1 and n_2 are the indices of refraction of the media on either side of the surface, and θ_1 and θ_2 are the respective angles of incidence and refraction. If three of these values are known, the fourth can be calculated from this relationship.

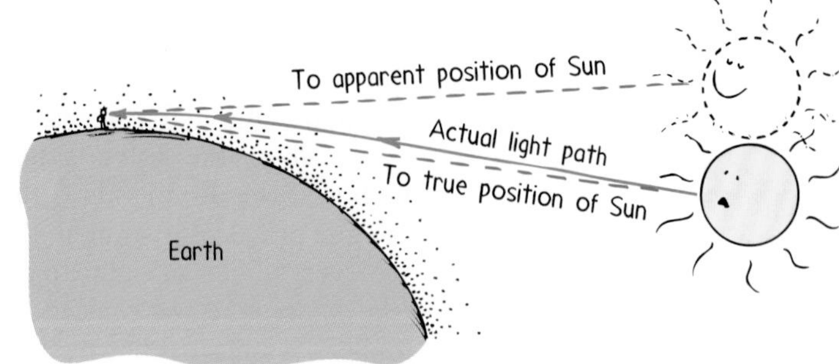

Figure 13.13
Because of atmospheric refraction, when the sun is near the horizon it appears to be higher in the sky.

Figure 13.14
The sun is distorted by differential refraction.

of the wave fronts of sunlight at high altitude travel faster than parts closer to the ground. Light rays bend. The density of the atmosphere changes gradually, so light rays bend gradually and follow a curved path. So we gain additional minutes of daylight each day. Furthermore, when the sun (or moon) is near the horizon, the rays from the lower edge are bent more than the rays from the upper edge. This shortens the vertical diameter, causing the sun to appear elliptical (Figure 13.14).

A mirage occurs when refracted light appears as if it were reflected light. Mirages are a common sight on a desert when the sky appears to be reflected from water on the distant sand. But when you approach what seems to be water, you find dry sand. Why is this so? The air is very hot close to the sand surface and cooler above the sand. Light travels faster through the thinner hot air near the surface than through the denser cool air above. So wave fronts near the ground travel faster than they do above. The result is upward bending (Figure 13.15). So we see an upside-down view that looks as if reflection were occurring from a water surface. We see a mirage, which is formed by real light and can be photographed (Figure 13.16). A mirage is not, as many people think, a trick of the mind.

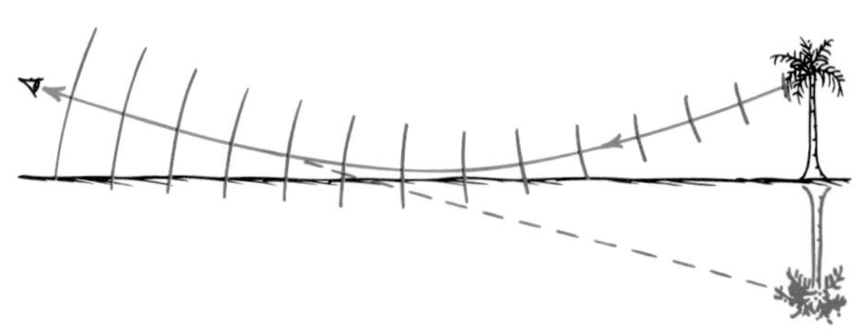

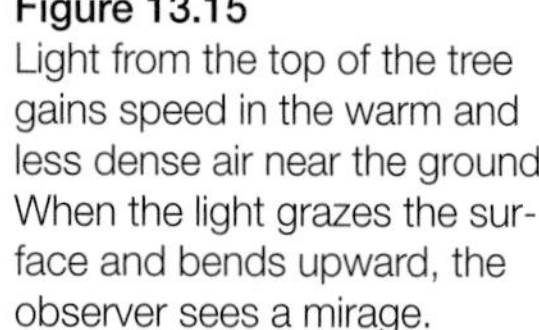

Figure 13.15
Light from the top of the tree gains speed in the warm and less dense air near the ground. When the light grazes the surface and bends upward, the observer sees a mirage.

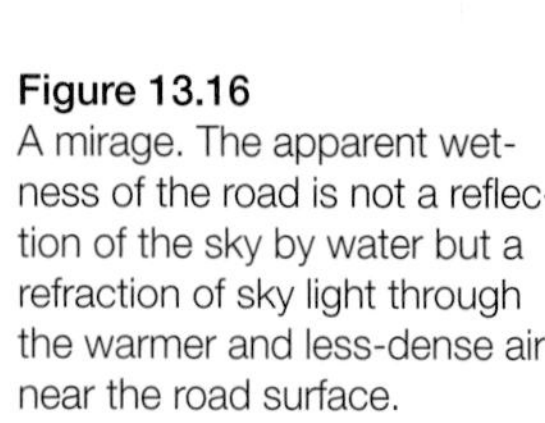

Figure 13.16
A mirage. The apparent wetness of the road is not a reflection of the sky by water but a refraction of sky light through the warmer and less-dense air near the road surface.

When we look at an object over a hot stove or over a hot pavement, we see a wavy, shimmering effect. This is due to varying densities of air caused by changes in temperature. The twinkling of stars results from similar variations in the sky, where light passes through unstable layers in the atmosphere.

☑ CHECKPOINT

If the speed of light were the same in air of various temperatures and densities, would there still be slightly longer daytimes, twinkling stars at night, mirages, and slightly squashed suns at sunset?

Check Your Answer

No.

13.3 Dispersion

Recall, from the previous chapter, that light that resonates with electrons of atoms and molecules in a material is absorbed. Such a material is opaque to light. Also recall that transparency occurs for light of frequencies near (but not at) the resonant frequencies of the material. Light is slowed due to the absorption/reemission sequence, and the closer to the resonant frequencies, the slower the light. This was shown in Figure 12.6. The grand result is that high-frequency light in a transparent medium travels slower than low-frequency light. Violet light travels about 1% slower in ordinary glass than red light. Light of colors between red and violet travel at their own respective speeds in glass.

Because light of various frequencies travels at different speeds in transparent materials, different colors of light refract by different amounts. When white light is refracted twice, as in a prism, the separation of light by colors is quite noticeable. This separation of light into colors arranged by frequency is called *dispersion* (Figure 13.17). Because of dispersion, there are rainbows!

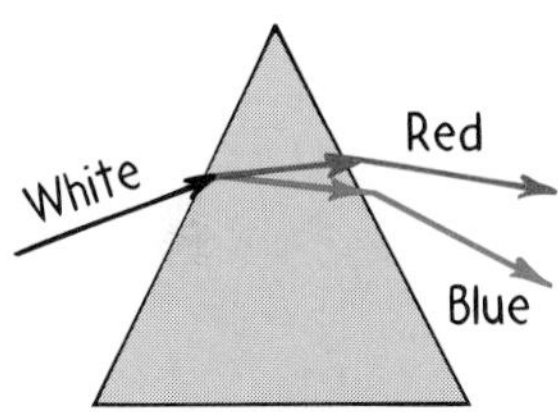

Figure 13.17
Dispersion by a prism makes the components of white light visible.

Rainbows

For you to see a rainbow, the sun must shine on drops of water in a cloud or in falling rain. The drops act as prisms that disperse light. When you face a rainbow, the sun is behind you, in the opposite part of the sky. Seen from an airplane near midday, the bow forms a complete circle. All rainbows would be completely round if the ground were not in the way.

You can see how a raindrop disperses light in Figure 13.18. Follow the ray of sunlight as it enters the drop near its top surface. Some of the light here is reflected (not shown), and the remainder is refracted into the water. At this first refraction, the light is dispersed into its spectrum colors, red being deviated the least and violet the most. When the light reaches the opposite side of the drop, each color is partly refracted out into the air (not shown) and partly reflected back into the water. Arriving at the lower surface of the drop, each color is again partly reflected (not shown) and partly refracted back into the air. This refraction at the second surface, like that in a prism, increases the dispersion already produced at the first surface.*

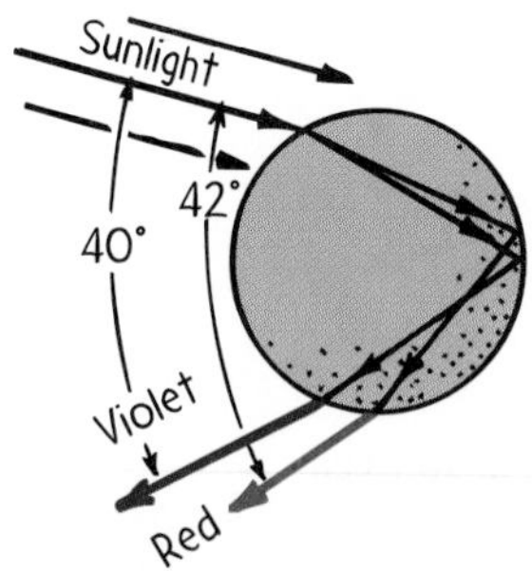

Figure 13.18
Dispersion of sunlight by a single raindrop.

*We're simplifying when we indicate that the red ray disperses at 42°. Actually, the angle between the incoming and outgoing rays can be anywhere between zero and about 42° (zero degrees corresponding to a full 180-degree reversal of the light). The strongest concentration of light intensity for red, however, is near the maximum angle of 42°, as shown in Figures 13.18 and 13.19.

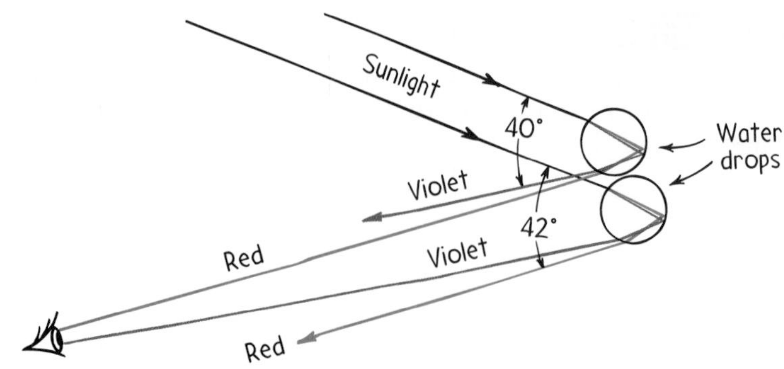

Figure 13.19
Sunlight incident on two raindrops, as shown, emerges from them as dispersed light. The observer sees the red light from the upper drop and the violet light from the lower drop. Millions of drops produce the entire spectrum of visible light.

Although each drop disperses a full spectrum of colors, an observer is in a position to see only a single color from any one drop (Figure 13.19). If violet light from a single drop reaches the eye of an observer, red light from the same drop is incident elsewhere toward the feet. To see red light, one must look to a drop higher in the sky. The color red will be seen when the angle between a beam of sunlight and the dispersed light is 42°. The color violet is seen when the angle between the sunbeams and dispersed light is 40°.

Why does the light dispersed by the raindrops form a bow? The answer to this involves a bit of geometry. First of all, a rainbow is not the flat two-dimensional arc it appears to be. The rainbow you see is actually a three-dimensional cone of dispersed light. The apex of this cone is at your eye. To understand this, consider a glass cone, the shape of those paper cones you sometimes see at drinking fountains. If you held the tip of such a glass cone against your eye, what would you see? You'd see the glass as a circle. Likewise with a rainbow. All the drops that disperse the rainbow's light toward *you* lie in the shape of a cone—a cone of different layers with drops that deflect red to your eye on the outside, orange beneath the red, yellow beneath the orange, and so on, all the way to violet on the inner conical surface (Figure 13.20). The thicker the region containing water drops, the thicker the conical edge you look through and the more vivid the rainbow.

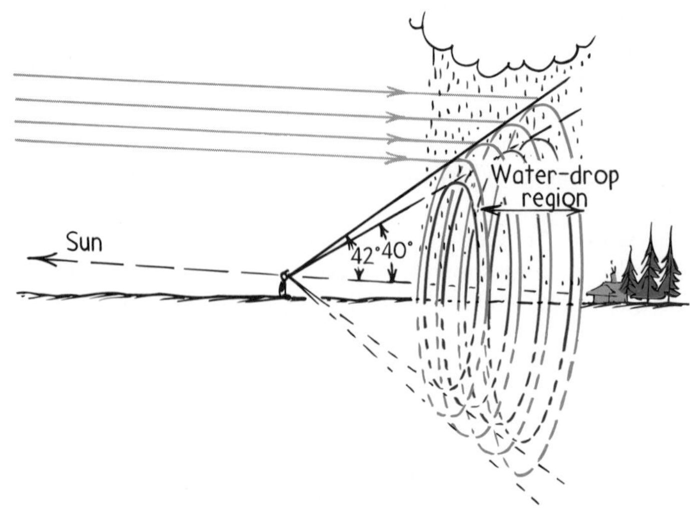

Figure 13.20
When your eye is located between the sun (not shown, off to the left) and the water-drop region, the rainbow you see is the edge of a three-dimensional cone that extends through the water-drop region. Violet is dispersed by drops that form a 40° conical surface; red is seen from drops along a 42° conical surface, with other colors in between. (Innumerable layers of drops form innumerable two-dimensional arcs, like the four suggested here.)

Your cone of vision intersects the cloud of drops and creates your rainbow. It is ever so slightly different from the rainbow seen by a person nearby. So, when a friend says, "Look at the pretty rainbow," you can reply, "Okay, move aside so I can see it, too." Everybody sees his or her own personal rainbow.

Another fact about rainbows: A rainbow always faces you squarely. When you move, your rainbow appears to move with you. So you can never approach the side of a rainbow or see it end-on as in the exaggerated view of Figure 13.20. You *can't* reach its end. Thus the saying "looking for the pot of gold at the end of the rainbow" means pursuing something you can never reach.

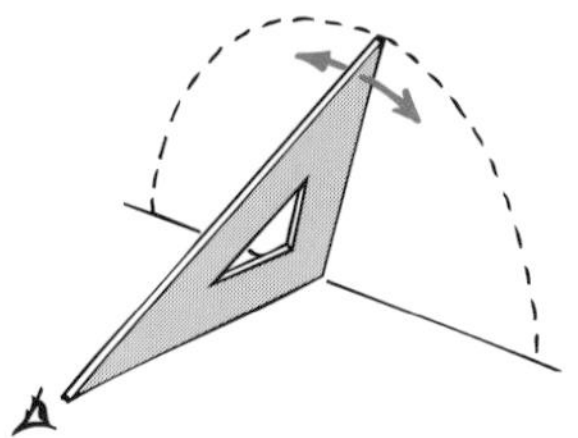

Figure 13.21
Only the raindrops along the dashed line disperse red light to the observer at a 42° angle; hence, the light forms a bow.

Figure 13.22
Two refractions and a reflection in water droplets produce light at all angles up to about 42°, with the intensity concentrated where we see the rainbow at 40° to 42°. Light doesn't exit the water droplet at angles greater than 42° unless it undergoes two or more reflections inside the drop. Thus the sky is brighter inside the rainbow than outside it. Notice the weak secondary rainbow.

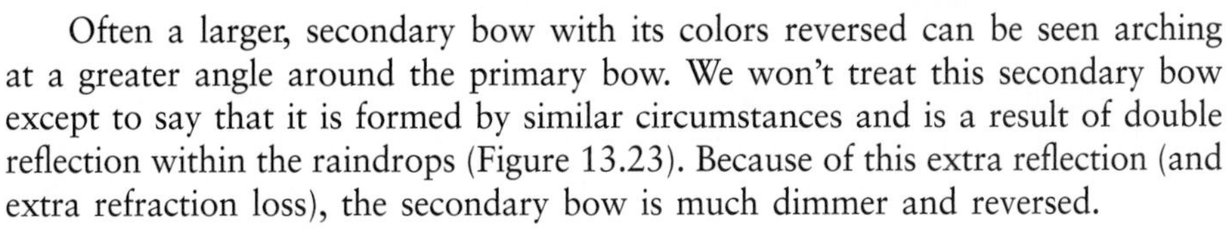

Often a larger, secondary bow with its colors reversed can be seen arching at a greater angle around the primary bow. We won't treat this secondary bow except to say that it is formed by similar circumstances and is a result of double reflection within the raindrops (Figure 13.23). Because of this extra reflection (and extra refraction loss), the secondary bow is much dimmer and reversed.

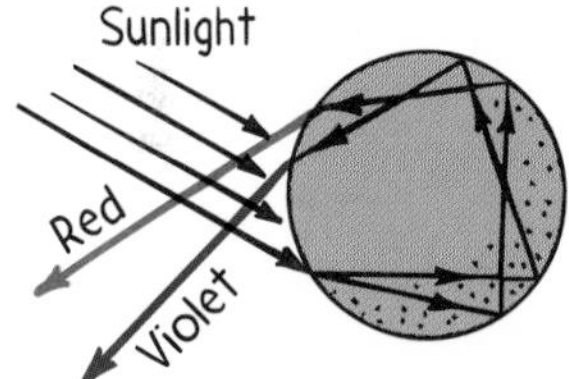

Figure 13.23
Double reflection in a drop produces a secondary bow.

☑ CHECKPOINT

1. Suppose you point to a wall with your arm extended. Then you sweep your arm around, making an angle of about 42° to the wall. If you rotate your arm in a full circle while keeping the same angle, what shape does your arm describe? What shape on the wall does your finger sweep out?
2. If light traveled at the same speed in raindrops as it does in air, would we have rainbows?

Check Your Answers

1. Your arm describes a cone, and your finger sweeps out a circle. Likewise with rainbows.
2. No.

13.4 Total Internal Reflection

Some Saturday night when you're taking your bath, fill the tub extra deep and bring a waterproof flashlight into the tub with you. Turn the bathroom light off. Shine the submerged light straight up and then slowly tip it. Note how the intensity of the emerging beam diminishes and how more light is reflected from the water's surface to the bottom of the tub. When the flashlight is tipped at a certain angle you'll notice that the beam no longer emerges into the air above the surface. This is the **critical angle.** When the flashlight is tipped beyond the critical angle (48° from the normal for water), you'll notice that all the light is reflected back into the tub. This is **total internal reflection.** The light in water striking the air boundary obeys the law of reflection: the angle of incidence is equal to the angle of reflection. The only light emerging from the water's surface is the light that is diffusely reflected from the bottom of the bathtub. This procedure is shown in Figure 13.24. The proportion of light refracted and the proportion of light internally reflected is indicated by the relative lengths of the arrows.

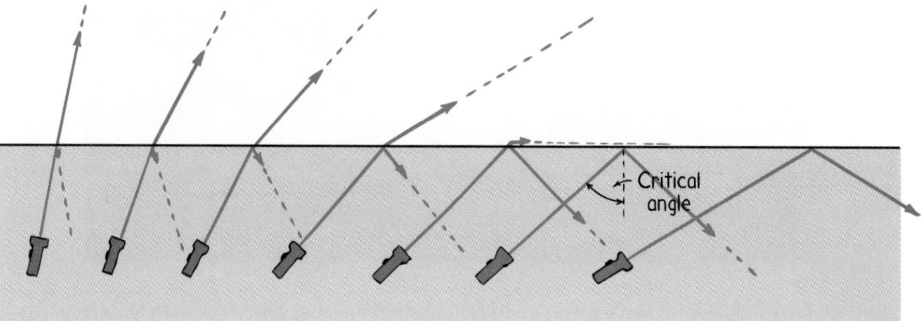

Figure 13.24
Light emitted in the water is partly refracted and partly reflected at the surface, as indicated by the lengths of the arrows. At the critical angle, the emerging beam intensity reduces to zero where it tends to graze the surface. Beyond the critical angle, the beam is totally internally reflected.

Interestingly, total internal reflection occurs only for light striking the boundary of a medium wherein the speed of light is greater. Light travels faster in air than in water, so total internal reflection can occur when light in water meets an air boundary. But it can't occur for light traveling in air that meets a water boundary.

☑ CHECKPOINT

How does the critical angle relate to total internal reflection?

Check Your Answer

Critical angle is the minimum angle of incidence inside a medium for total internal reflection. When a light ray strikes a surface at or beyond the critical angle, total internal reflection occurs.

Your pet goldfish in a large tub looks up to see a compressed view of the outside world (Figure 13.25). The 180° view from horizon to opposite horizon is seen through an angle of 96°—twice the critical angle. A lens that similarly compresses a wide view, called a *fisheye lens,* is used for special-effect photographs.

The critical angle for glass is about 43°, depending on the type of glass. This means that, within glass, light that is incident at angles, at or greater than, 43°

will be totally internally reflected. No light will escape beyond this angle; instead, all of it will be reflected back into the glass. Whereas a silvered or aluminized mirror reflects only about 90 percent of incident light, glass prisms, as shown in Figure 13.26, are more efficient. A little light is lost by reflection before it enters the prism, but, once inside, reflection on the 45°-slanted face is total—100 percent. Moreover, this light is not marred by any dirt or dust on the outside surface, which is the principal reason for the use of prisms instead of mirrors in many optical instruments.

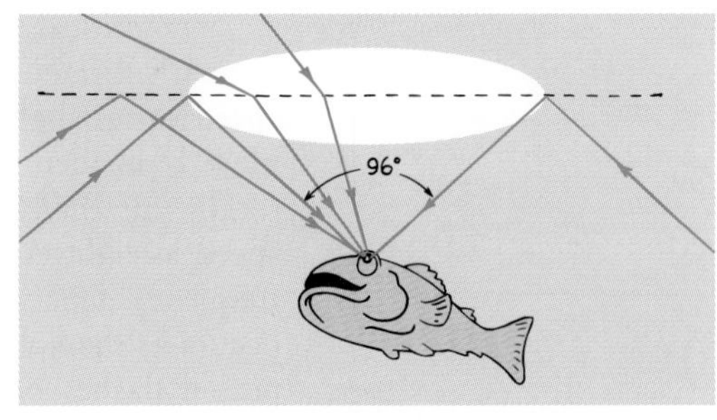

Figure 13.25
An observer underwater sees a circle of light at the still surface. Beyond a cone of 98° (twice the critical angle), an observer sees a reflection of the water interior or bottom.

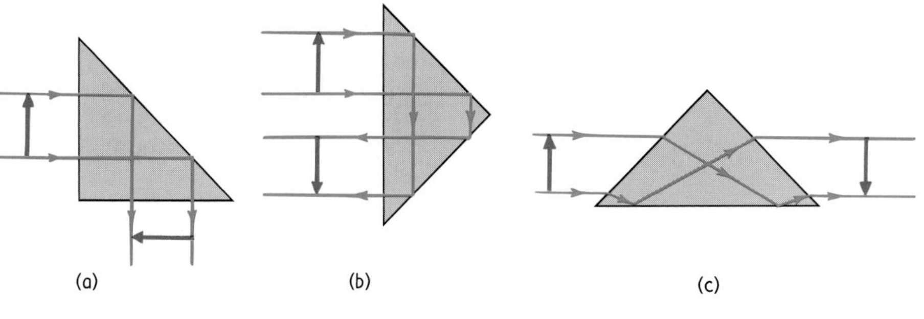

Figure 13.26
Total internal reflection in a prism. In (a), the prism changes the direction of the light beam by 90°; in (b), it changes it by 180°; and in (c), it does not change the direction of the beam but instead turns the image upside down.

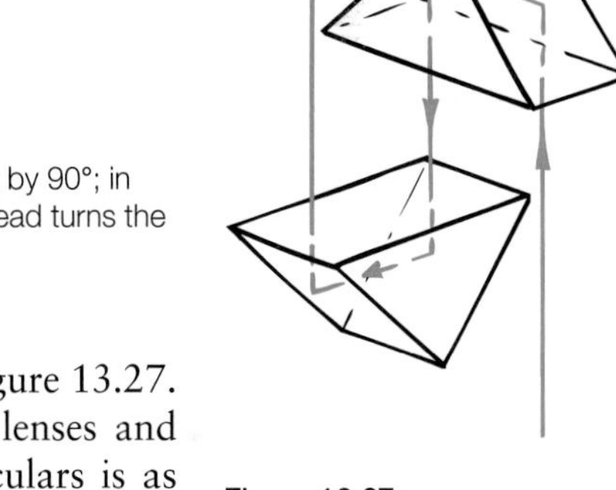

Figure 13.27
Total internal reflection in a pair of prisms.

A pair of prisms each reflecting light through 180° is shown in Figure 13.27. Binoculars use pairs of prisms to lengthen the light path between lenses and thus eliminate the need for long barrels. So a compact set of binoculars is as effective as a longer telescope (Figure 13.28). Another advantage of prisms is that, whereas the image of a straight telescope is upside down, reflection by the prisms in binoculars reinverts the image, so things are seen right-side up.

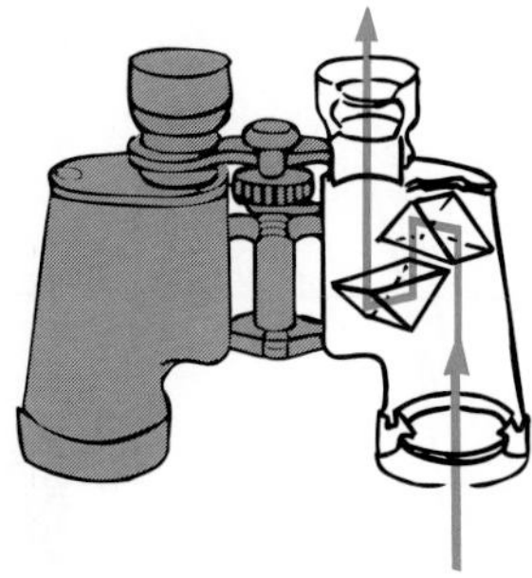

Figure 13.28
Prism binoculars.

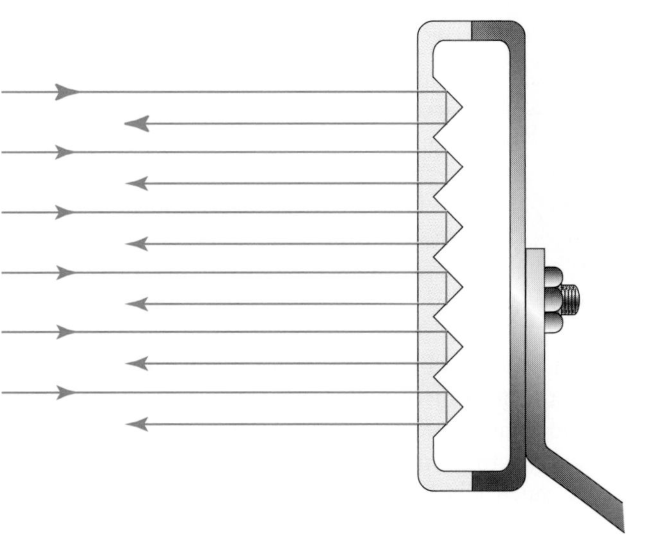

Figure 13.29
The rear reflectors on cars, bicycles, and other vehicles contain arrays of tiny prisms that use total internal reflection to send light back in the opposite direction.

The critical angle for a diamond is about 24.5°, smaller than for any other known substance. The critical angle varies slightly for different colors, because speed varies slightly for different colors. Once light enters a diamond gemstone, most is incident on the sloped backsides at angles greater than 24.5° and is totally internally reflected (Figure 13.30). Because of the great slowdown in speed as light enters a diamond, refraction is pronounced, and, because of the frequency-dependence of the speed, there is great dispersion. Further dispersion occurs as the light exits through the many facets at its face. Hence we see unexpected flashes of a wide array of colors. Interestingly, when these flashes are narrow enough to be seen by only one eye at a time, the diamond "sparkles."

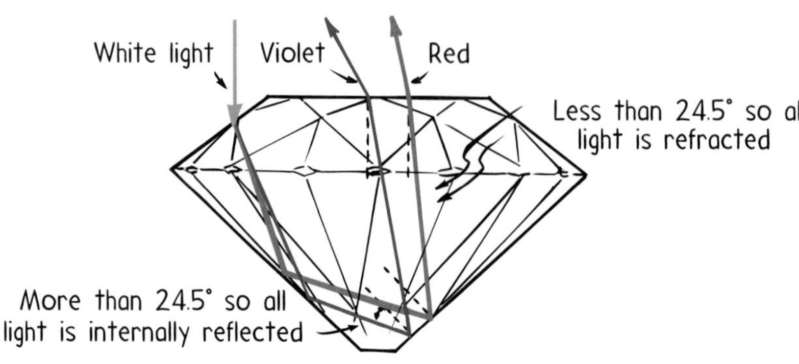

Figure 13.30
Paths of light in a diamond. Rays that strike the inner surface of a diamond at angles greater than the critical angle (about 24.5°, depending on the color of the light) are internally reflected and exit via refraction at the top surface.

Total internal reflection also underlies the operation of optical fibers, or light pipes (Figure 13.31). An optical fiber "pipes" light from one place to another by a series of total internal reflections, much as a bullet ricochets down a steel pipe. Light rays bounce along the inner walls, following the twists and turns of the fiber. Optical fibers are used to illuminate instrument displays on automobile dashboards from a single bulb. Dentists use them with flashlights to get light where they want it. Bundles of thin flexible glass or plastic fibers are used to see what is going on in inaccessible places, such as in the interior of a motor or in a patient's stomach. They can be made small enough to snake through blood vessels or through narrow passages in the body, such as the urethra. Light shines down some of the fibers to illuminate the scene and is reflected back along others.

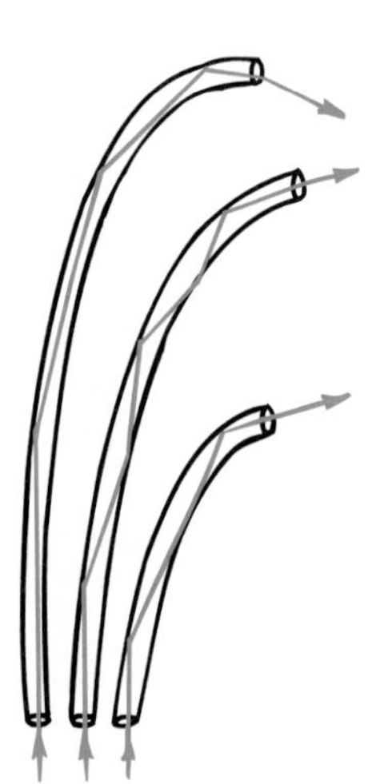

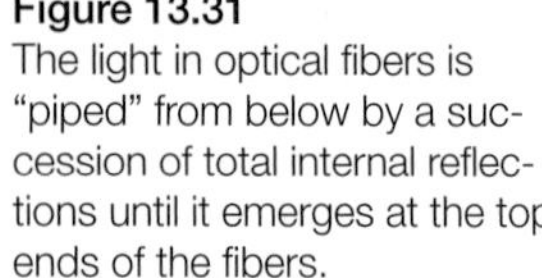

Figure 13.31
The light in optical fibers is "piped" from below by a succession of total internal reflections until it emerges at the top ends of the fibers.

Optical fibers are important in communications because they offer a practical alternative to copper wires and cables. In many places, thin glass fibers now replace thick, bulky, and expensive copper cables to carry thousands of simultaneous telephone messages among the major switching centers. In many aircraft, control signals are fed from the pilot to the control surfaces by means of optical fibers. Signals are carried in the modulations of laser light. Unlike electricity, light is indifferent to temperature and fluctuations in surrounding magnetic fields, so the signal is clearer. Also, it is much less likely to be tapped by eavesdroppers.

13.5 Lenses

When you think of lenses, think of sets of glass prisms arranged as shown in Figure 13.32 They refract incoming parallel light rays so that the rays converge to (or diverge from) a point. The arrangement shown in Figure 13.32a converges the light, and we have a **converging lens.** Notice that it is thicker in the middle. In the arrangement shown in Figure 13.32b, the middle is thinner than the edges. Because this lens diverges the light, we have a **diverging lens.** Note that the prisms in (b) diverge the incident rays in a way that makes them appear to originate from a single point in front of the lens.

In both lenses, the greatest deviation of rays occurs at the outermost prisms, because they have the greatest angle between the two refracting surfaces. No deviation occurs exactly in the middle, for in that region the two surfaces of the glass are parallel to each other (light doesn't deviate when going through glass with parallel surfaces, like window glass). A real lens is not made of prisms, of course. It is made of a solid piece of glass with surfaces ground usually to a circular curve. In Figure 13.33, we see how smooth lenses refract waves.

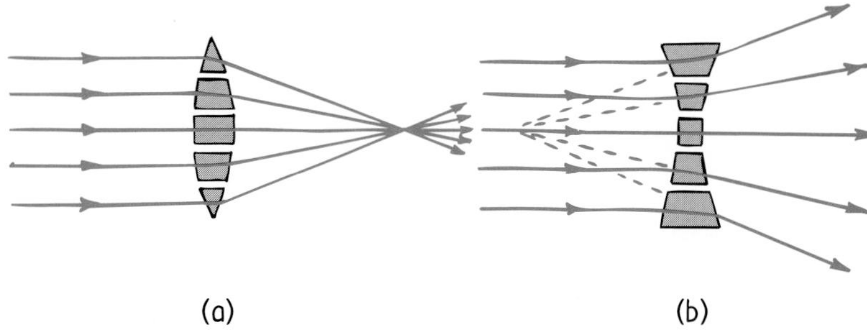

Figure 13.32
A lens may be thought of as a set of prisms.

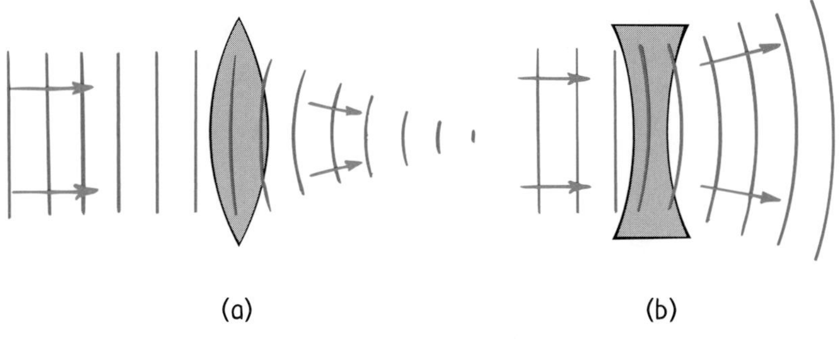

Figure 13.33
Wave fronts travel more slowly in glass than in air. In (a), the waves are retarded more through the center of the lens, and convergence results. In (b), the waves are retarded more at the edges, and divergence results.

Some key features of lenses are shown for a converging lens in Figure 13.35. The *principal axis* is the line joining the centers of curvature of the two lens surfaces. The *focal point* is the point of convergence for light parallel to the principal axis. Incident beams not parallel to the principal axis focus at points above or below the focal point. All such possible points make up a *focal plane* (not shown). Because a lens has two surfaces, it has two focal

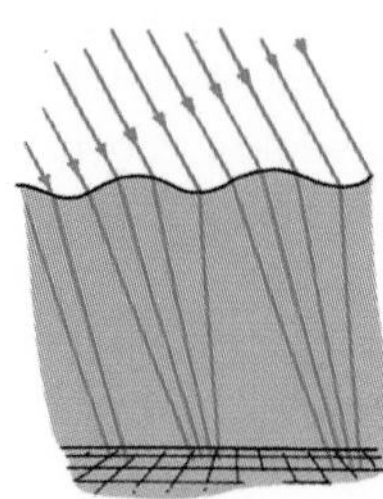

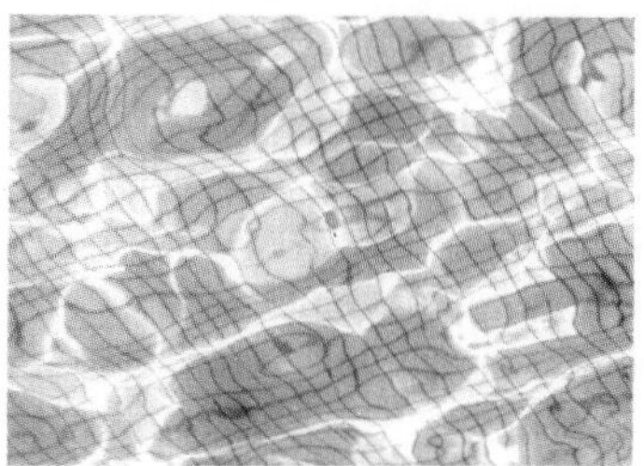

Figure 13.34
The moving patterns of bright and dark areas at the bottom of the pool result from the uneven surface of the water, which behaves like a blanket of undulating lenses. Just as we see the pool bottom shimmering, a fish looking upward at the sun would see it shimmering, too. Because of similar irregularities in the atmosphere, we see the stars twinkle.

points and two focal planes. The *focal length* of the lens is the distance between the center of the lens and either focal point.

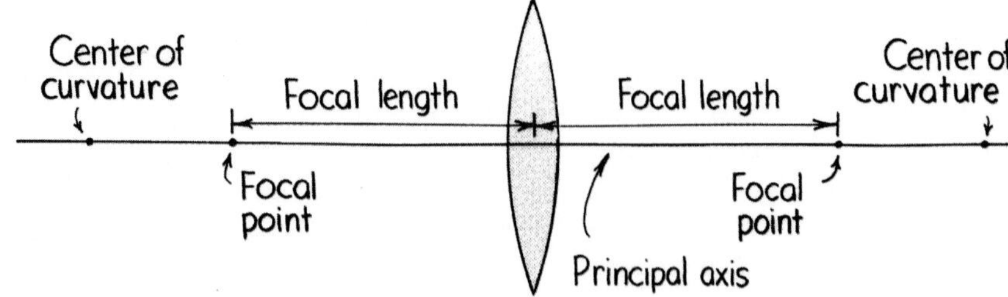

Figure 13.35
Some key features of a converging lens.

Link to Physiology

Your Eye

With all of today's technology, the most remarkable optical instrument known is your eye. Light enters through your *cornea*, which does about 70% of the necessary bending of the light before it passes through your *pupil* (the aperture, or opening, in the iris). Light then passes through your *lens*, which provides the extra bending power needed to focus images of nearby objects on your extremely sensitive *retina.* (Only recently have artificial detectors been made with greater sensitivity to light than the human eye). An image of the visual field outside your eye is spread over the retina. The retina is not uniform. There is a spot in the center of your field of the retina called the *fovea,* which is the region of most acute vision. You see greater detail here than at any other part of your retina. There is also a spot in your retina where the nerves carrying all the information exit the eye on their way to the brain. This is your *blind spot.*

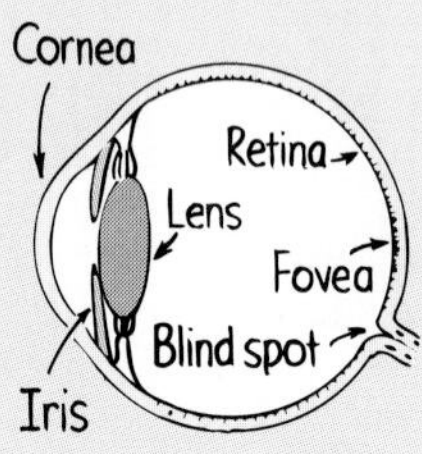

You can demonstrate that you have a blind spot in each eye. Simply hold this book at arm's length, close your left eye, and look at the round dot and X to its right with your right eye only. You can see both the dot and the X at this distance. Now move the book slowly toward your face, with your right eye fixed upon the dot, and you'll reach a position about 20–25 centimeters from your eye where the X disappears. When both eyes are open, one eye "fills in" the part to which your other eye is blind. Now repeat with only the left eye open, looking this time at the X, and the dot will disappear. But note that your brain fills in the two intersecting lines. Amazingly, your brain fills in the "expected" view even with one eye closed. Instead of seeing nothing, your brain graciously fills in the appropriate background. Repeat this for small objects on various backgrounds. You not only see what's there—you see what's not there!

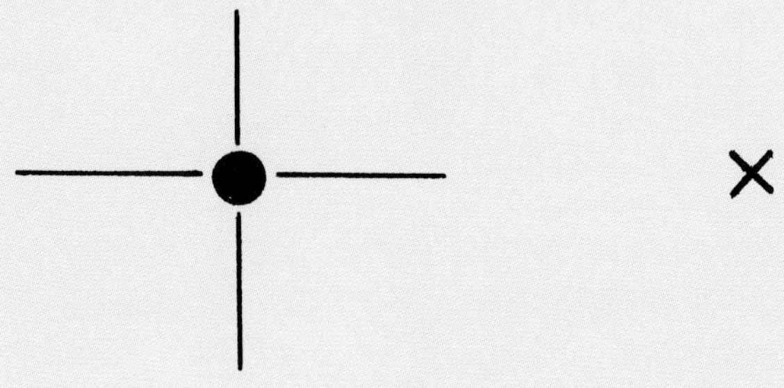

The light receptors in your retina do not connect directly to your optic nerve but are instead interconnected with many other cells. Through these interconnections, a certain amount of information is combined and "digested" in your retina. In this way, the light signal is "thought about" before it goes to the optic nerve and then to the main body of your brain. So some brain functioning occurs in your eye. Amazingly, your eye does some of your "thinking."

In a diverging lens, an incident beam of light parallel to the principal axis is not converged to a point; it is diverged, so the light appears to emerge from a point in front of the lens.

Image Formation by a Lens

At this moment, light is reflecting from your face onto this page. Light that reflects from your forehead, for example, strikes every part of the page. The same is true of the light that reflects from your chin. Every part of the page is illuminated with reflected light from your forehead, your nose, your chin, and every other part of your face. You don't see an image of your face on the page because there is too much overlapping of light. But place a barrier with a pinhole in it between your face and the page, and the light that reaches the page from your forehead does not overlap the light from your chin. Likewise for the rest of your face. Without this overlapping, an image of your face is formed on the page. It will be very dim, for very little light reflected from your face passes through the pinhole. To see the image, you'd have to shield the page from other light sources. The same is true of the vase and flower in Figure 13.36b.

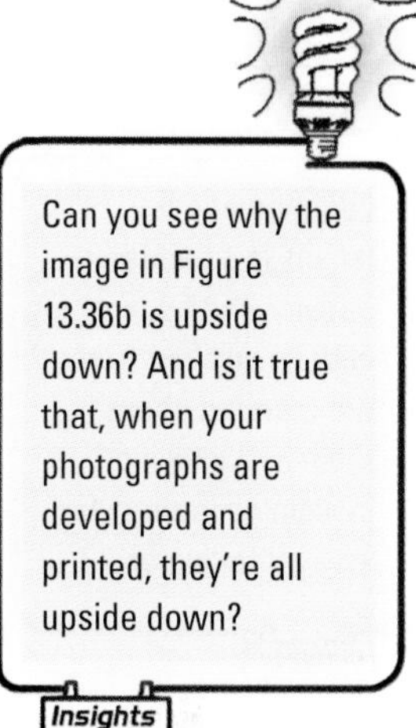

The first cameras had no lenses and admitted light through a small pinhole. Long exposure times were required because of the small amount of light admitted by the pinhole. This meant that subjects being photographed had to remain very still. Motion would produce a blur. If the hole were a bit larger, exposure time would be shorter, but overlapping rays would produce a blurry image. Too large a hole would allow too much overlapping, resulting in no image. That's where a converging lens plays a role (Figure 13.36). The lens converges light onto the film without any overlapping of rays. Moving objects can be taken with the lens camera because of the short exposure time. As mentioned earlier, that's why early photographs taken with lens cameras were called snapshots.

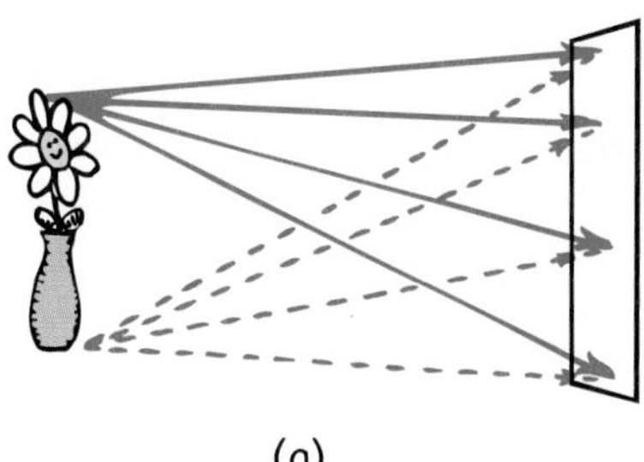

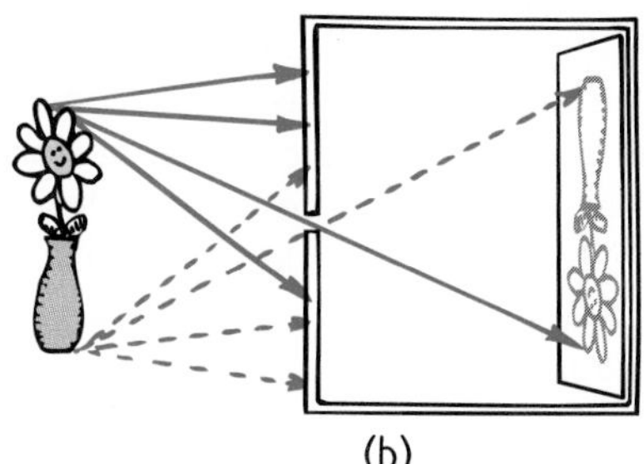

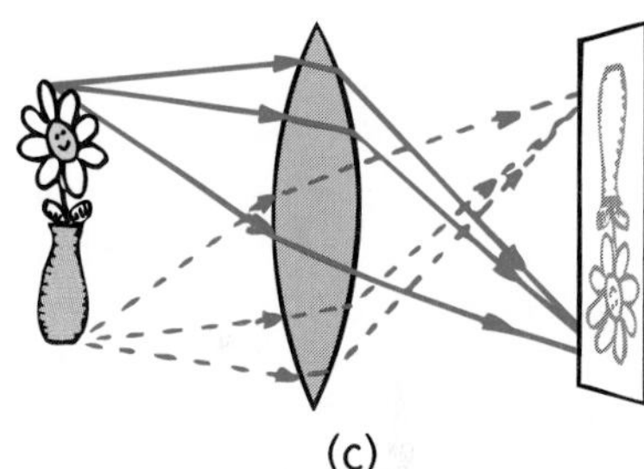

Figure 13.36
Image formation. (a) No image appears on the wall because rays from all parts of the object overlap the entire wall. (b) A single small opening in a barrier prevents overlapping rays from reaching the wall; a dim upside-down image is formed. (c) A lens converges the rays upon the wall without overlapping; more light makes a brighter image.

The simplest application of a converging lens is as a magnifying glass. To understand how it works, think about how you examine objects near and far. With unaided vision, you see a distant object through a relatively narrow angle of view, and you see a close object through a wider angle of view (Figure 13.37). To see the details of a small object, you want to get as close to it as possible for the widest-angle view. But your eye can't focus when it's too close to the object. That's where the magnifying glass is useful. When close to the object, the magnifying glass gives you a clear image that would be blurry without it.

When you use a magnifying glass, you hold it close to the object you wish to examine. This is because a converging lens provides an enlarged image that

Figure 13.37

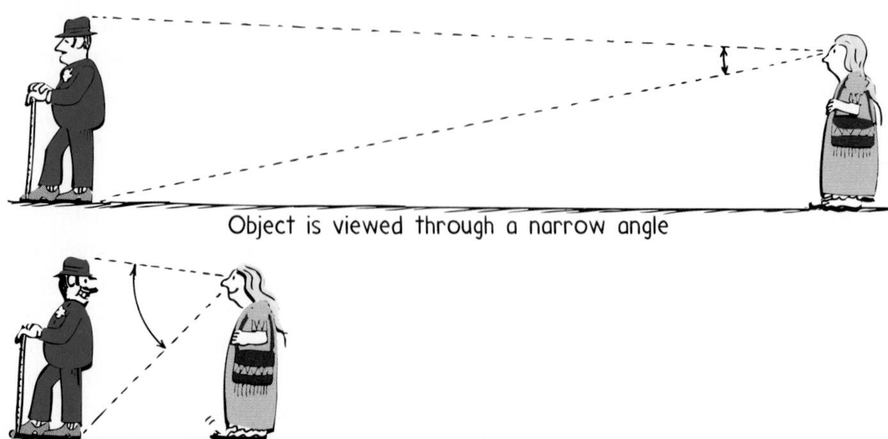

Learning about lenses is a hands-on activity. Not fiddling with lenses while you are learning about them is like taking swimming lessons far away from water.

Insights

is rightside up only when the object is inside the focal point. If a screen is placed at the image distance, no image appears on it because no light is directed to the image position. The rays that reach your eye, however, behave virtually *as if* they originated at the image position. This is called a **virtual image**—one formed by light rays that do not converge at the image location.

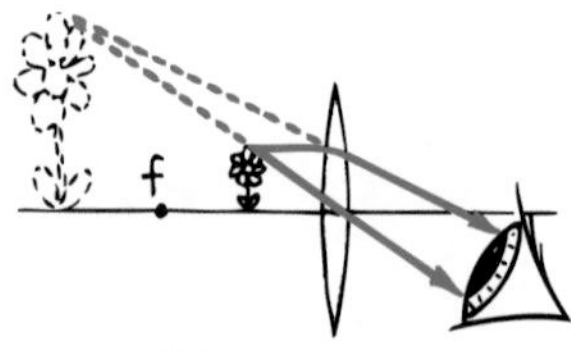

Figure 13.38
When an object is near a converging lens (inside its focal point f), the lens acts as a magnifying glass to produce a virtual image. The image appears larger and farther from the lens than the object.

When the object is distant enough to be outside the focal point of a converging lens, a **real image** is formed instead of a virtual image; Figure 13.39 shows this case. Light rays converge to form a real image that can be displayed on a screen. Real images formed with a single lens are always upside down. That's why, for correct viewing, you must insert slides in a slide projector upside down. The frames of motion pictures are likewise upside down. The same is true for the image in a camera.

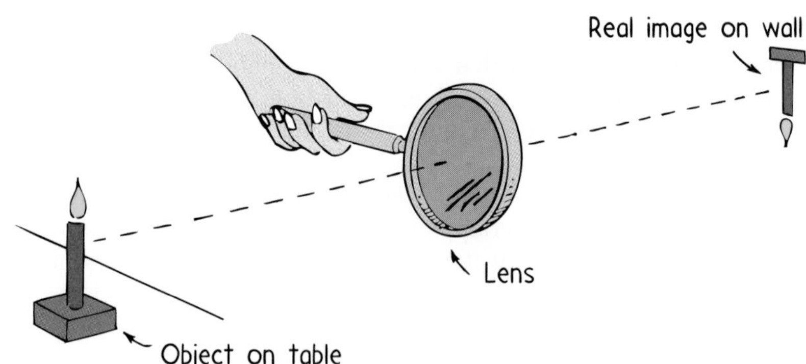

Figure 13.39
When an object is far from a converging lens (beyond its focal point), a real upside-down image is formed.

A diverging lens used alone produces a reduced virtual image. It makes no difference how far or how near the object is. The image is always virtual, rightside up, and smaller than the object. That's why a diverging lens is often used as a "finder" on a camera. When you look at the object to be photographed through such a lens, you see a virtual image that approximates the same proportions as the photograph.

Figure 13.40
A diverging lens forms a virtual, right-side-up image of Jamie and his cat.

☑ CHECKPOINT

Why is the greater part of the photograph in Figure 13.40 out of focus?

Check Your Answer

Both Jamie and his cat and the virtual image of Jamie and his cat are "objects" for the lens of the camera that took this photograph. Since the objects are at different distances from the lens, images are at different distances relative to the film in the camera. So only one can be brought into focus. The same is true of your eyes. You cannot focus on near and far objects at the same time.

Lens Defects

No lens provides a perfect image. A distortion in an image is called an **aberration.** By combining lenses in certain ways, you can minimize aberrations. For this reason, most optical instruments use compound lenses, each consisting of several simple lenses, instead of single lenses.

Spherical aberration results from light passing through the edges of a lens and focusing at a slightly different place from where light passing through the center of the lens focuses (Figure 13.41). This can be remedied by covering the edges of a lens, as with a diaphragm in a camera. Spherical aberration is corrected in good optical instruments by a combination of lenses.

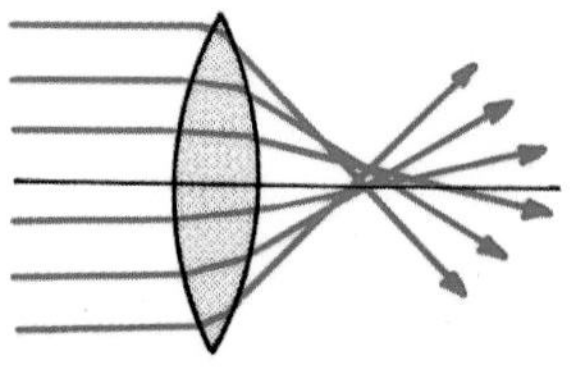

Figure 13.41
Spherical aberration.

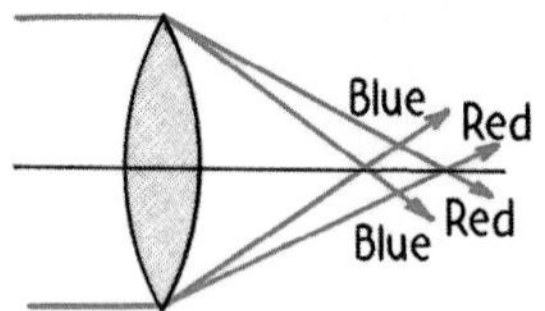

Figure 13.42
Chromatic aberration.

Chromatic aberration is the result of different colors having different speeds and hence different refractions in the lens (Figure 13.42). In a simple lens (as in a prism), red light and blue light do not come to focus in the same place. *Achromatic lenses,* which combine simple lenses of different kinds of glass, correct this defect.

The pupil of the eye regulates the amount of light that enters the eye by changing its size. Vision is sharpest when the pupil is smallest because light then passes through only the center of the eye's lens, where spherical and chromatic aberrations are minimal. Also, the eye then acts more like a pinhole camera, so minimum focusing is required for a sharp image. You see better in bright light because your pupils are smaller.

Astigmatism of the eye is a defect that results when the cornea is curved more in one direction than in another, somewhat like the side of a barrel. Because of this defect, the eye does not form sharp images. The remedy is eyeglasses with cylindrical lenses that have more curvature in one direction than in another.

If you wear glasses and sometimes misplace them, or, if you find it difficult to read small print, as in a telephone book, try squinting—or, even better, try holding a pinhole (in a piece of paper or foil) in front of your eye, close to the page. You'll see the print clearly, and, because you'll be close, it will be magnified. Try it and see!

Insights

☑ CHECKPOINT

1. If light traveled at the same speed in glass and in air, would glass lenses change the direction of light rays?
2. Why is chromatic aberration associated with a lens but not with a mirror?
3. How can chromatic abberation be corrected?
4. There have been reports of round fishbowls starting fires by focusing the sun's rays coming in a window. Can you cite a possible explanation for this occurrence?

Check Your Answers

1. No.
2. Light of different frequencies travels at different speeds in a transparent medium and therefore refracts at different angles. This is the cause of chromatic aberration. The angles of reflected light, however, have no relation to frequency. One color reflects the same as any other color. In telescopes, therefore, mirrors are preferred over lenses because of the absence of chromatic aberration for reflection.
3. This defect can be corrected with a combination of lenses. These are called achromatic lenses.
4. This can certainly happen. The water-filled bowl acts as a converging lens and, like a lens made entirely of glass, can converge rays of sunlight to a focus. If the point of focus is flammable, a fire can occur.

Today the most popular option for those with poor sight is wearing eyeglasses. The advent of eyeglasses probably occurred in Italy late in the thirteenth century. (Curiously, the telescope wasn't invented until some 300 years later. If, in the meantime, anybody viewed objects through a pair of lenses separated along their axes, such as fixed at the ends of a tube, there is no record of it.) Another option today to wearing eyeglasses is contact lenses. And an alternative to both eyeglasses and contacts is laser technology, where eye surgeons reshape the cornea of the eye to allow for normal vision. The wearing of eyeglasses and contact lenses may soon be a thing of the past. We really do live in a rapidly changing world.

Link to Physiology and Psychology

Lateral Inhibition

The human eye can do what no camera film can do: it can perceive degrees of brightness that range from about 500 million to 1. The difference in brightness between the sun and moon, for example, is about 1 million to 1. But, because of an effect called *lateral inhibition*, we don't perceive the actual differences in brightness. The brightest places in our visual field are prevented from outshining the rest, for whenever a receptor cell on our retina sends a strong brightness signal to our brain, it also signals neighboring cells to dim their responses. In this way, we even out our visual field, which allows us to discern detail in very bright areas and in dark areas as well.

Lateral inhibition exaggerates the difference in brightness at the edges of places in our visual field. Edges, by definition, separate one thing from another. So we accentuate differences rather than similarities. This is illustrated in the pair of shaded rectangles to the right. They look to be different shades of brightness because of the edge that separates them. But cover the edge with your pencil or your finger, and they look equally bright (try it now)! That's because both rectangles *are* equally bright; each rectangle is shaded from lighter to darker, moving from left to right. Our eye concentrates on the boundary where the dark edge of the left rectangle joins the light edge of the right rectangle, and our eye–brain system assumes that the rest of the rectangle is the same. We pay attention to the boundary and ignore the rest.

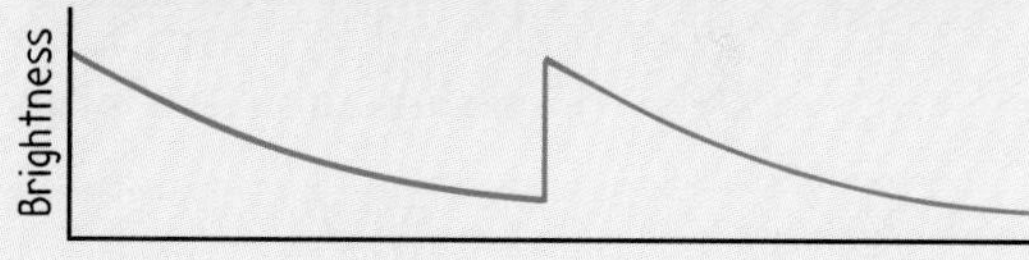

Questions to ponder: Is the way the eye picks out edges and makes assumptions about what lies beyond similar to the way in which we sometimes make judgments about other cultures and other people? Don't we, in the same way, tend to exaggerate the differences on the surface while ignoring the similarities and subtle differences within?

13.6 Wave–Particle Duality

Newton Biography page 58

We have described light as a wave. The earliest ideas about the nature of light, however, were that light was composed of tiny particles. In ancient times, Plato and other Greek philosophers held to a particle view of light—as, in the early 1700s, did Isaac Newton, who first became famous for his experiments with light. A hundred years later, the wave nature of light was demonstrated by Thomas Young in his interference experiments with side-by-side pinholes. The wave view was reinforced in 1862 by Maxwell's finding that light is energy carried in oscillating electric and magnetic fields of electromagnetic waves. The wave view of light was confirmed experimentally by Heinrich Hertz 25 years later.

Then, in 1905, Albert Einstein published a Nobel Prize–winning paper that challenged the wave theory of light. Einstein stated that light in its interactions with matter was confined not in continuous waves, as Maxwell and others had

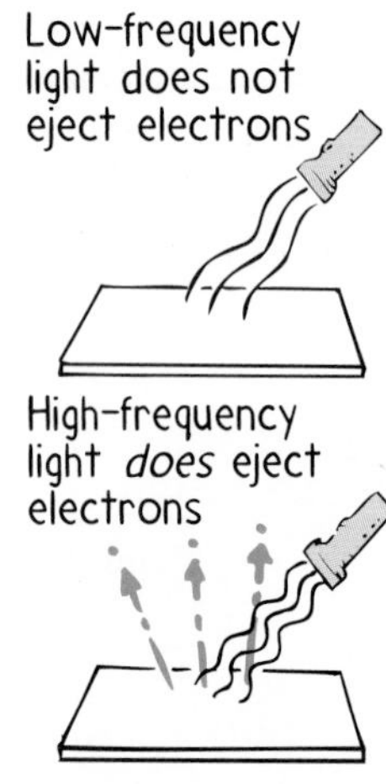

Figure 13.43
The photoelectric effect depends on frequency.

envisioned, but in tiny particles of energy called *photons*. Einstein's particle model of light explained a perplexing phenomenon of that time—the *photoelectric effect*.

The Photoelectric Effect

When light shines on certain metal surfaces, electrons are ejected from those surfaces. This is the **photoelectric effect**, which is put to use in electric eyes, in light meters, and in motion-picture sound tracks. What perplexed investigators at the turn of the twentieth century was that ultraviolet and violet light imparted sufficient energy to knock electrons from those metal surfaces, while lower-frequency light did not—even when the lower-frequency light was very bright. Ejection of electrons depended only on the frequency of light, and the higher the frequency of the light, the greater the kinetic energy of the ejected electrons. Very dim high-frequency light ejected fewer electrons, but it ejected each of them with the same kinetic energy of electrons ejected in brighter light of the same frequency.

Einstein's explanation was that the electrons in the metal were being bombarded by "particles of light"—by **photons.** Einstein stated that the energy of each photon was proportional to its frequency: That is,*

$$E \sim f$$

So Einstein viewed light as a hail of photons, each carrying energy proportional to its frequency. One photon is completely absorbed by each electron ejected from the metal.

All attempts to explain the photoelectric effect by waves failed. A light wave has a broad front, and its energy is spread out along this front. For the light wave to eject a single electron from a metal surface, all its energy would somehow have to be concentrated on that one electron. But this is as improbable as an ocean wave hitting a beach and knocking only one single seashell far inland with an energy equal to the energy of the whole wave. Therefore, the photoelectric effect suggests that, instead of thinking of light encountering a surface as a continuous train of waves, we should conceive of light encountering a surface, or any detector, as a succession of particle-like photons. The energy of each photon is proportional to the frequency of light, and that energy is given completely to a single electron in the metal's surface. The number of ejected electrons has to do with the number of photons—the brightness of the light.

Experimental verification of Einstein's explanation of the photoelectric effect was made 11 years later by the American physicist Robert Millikan. Every aspect of Einstein's interpretation was confirmed. The photoelectric effect proves conclusively that light has particle properties. A wave model of light is

*When the energy of a photon is divided by its frequency, the single number that results is the proportionality constant, called **Planck's constant,** h (6.6×10^{-34} J·s). Planck's constant is a fundamental constant of nature that serves to set a lower limit on the smallness of things. We can insert this constant in the above proportion and express it as an exact equation:

$$E = hf$$

This equation gives the smallest amount of energy that can be converted to light with frequency f. The radiation of light is not emitted continuously but rather, as a stream of photons, each of which throbs at a frequency f and carries an energy hf.

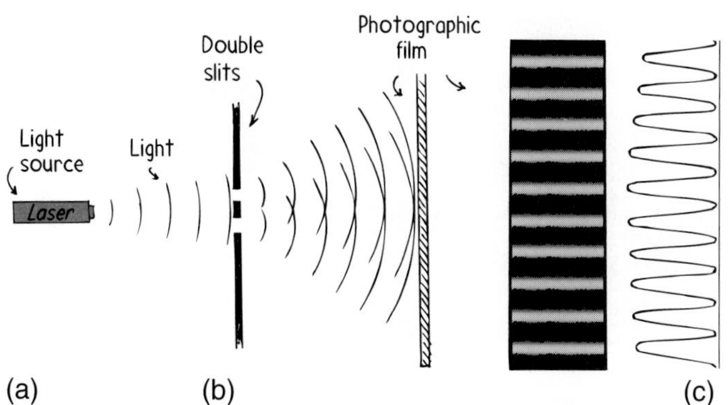

Figure 13.44
(a) The arrangement for the double-slit experiment. (b) A photograph of the interference pattern. (c) A graphic representation of the pattern.

inconsistent with the photoelectric effect. On the other hand, interference demonstrates convincingly that light has wave properties, and a particle model of light is inconsistent with interference.

☑ CHECKPOINT

Why won't a very bright beam of red light impart more energy to an electron than a weak beam of violet light?

Check Your Answer

The brightness of a beam has to do with the number of photons in it, but only one photon in the beam normally hits a single electron at one time. If a red one hits, lower energy is given to it than if a higher-energy violet photon hits it. Energy per photon, not overall energy, is the gist of the photoelectric effect.

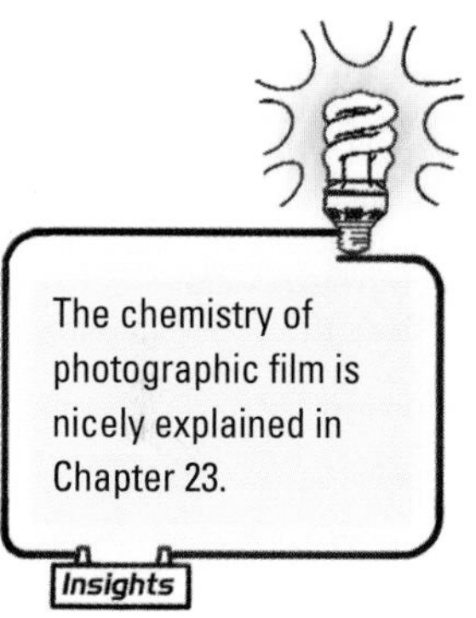

Wave Interference

Recall Thomas Young's double-pinhole interference experiment, which we earlier discussed in terms of waves. When monochromatic light passes through a pair of closely spaced thin slits, an interference pattern is produced on photographic film (Figure 13.44). Now let's consider the experiment in terms of photons. Suppose we dim our light source so that, in effect, only one photon at a time reaches the thin slits. If the film behind the slits is exposed to the light for a very short time, the film becomes exposed, as simulated in Figure 13.45a. Each spot represents the place where the film has been exposed by a photon. If the light is allowed to expose the film for a longer time, a pattern of fringes begins to emerge, as in Figures 13.45b and c. This is quite amazing. Spots on the film are seen to progress, photon by photon, to form the same interference pattern characterized by waves!

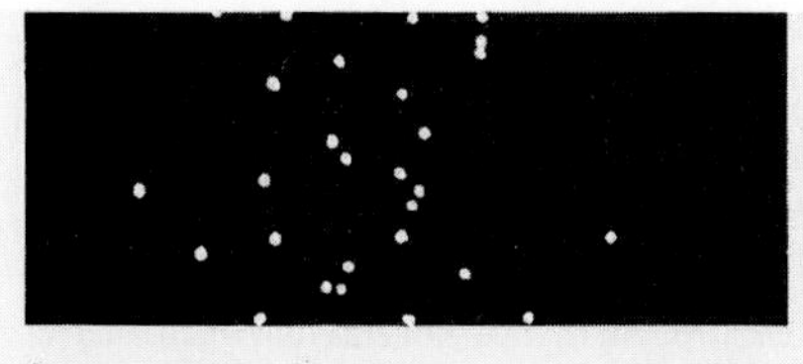
a

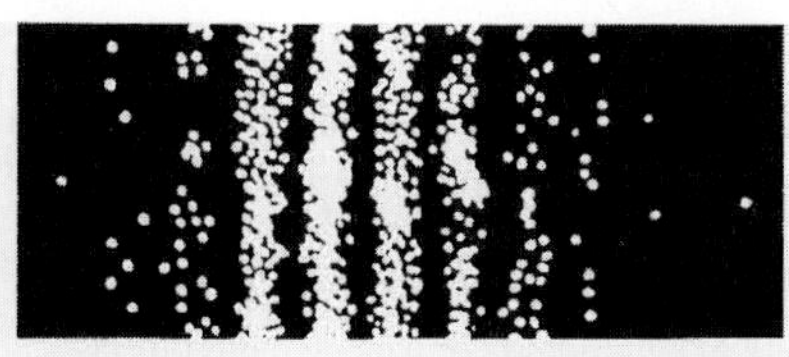
b

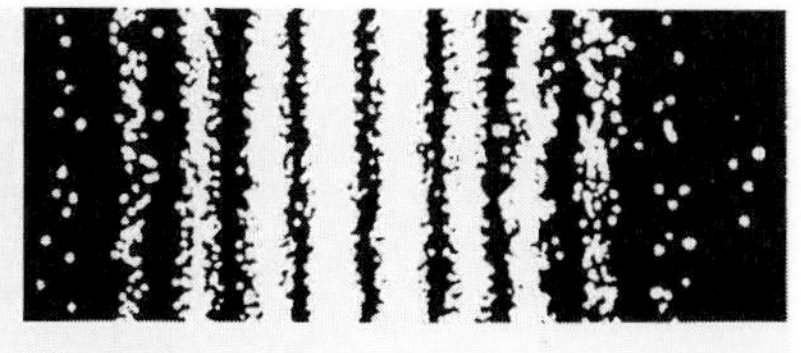
c

Figure 13.45
Stages in the development of a two-slit interference pattern. The pattern of individually exposed grains progresses from (a) 28 photons to (b) 1000 photons to (c) 10,000 photons. As more photons hit the screen, a pattern of interference fringes appears.

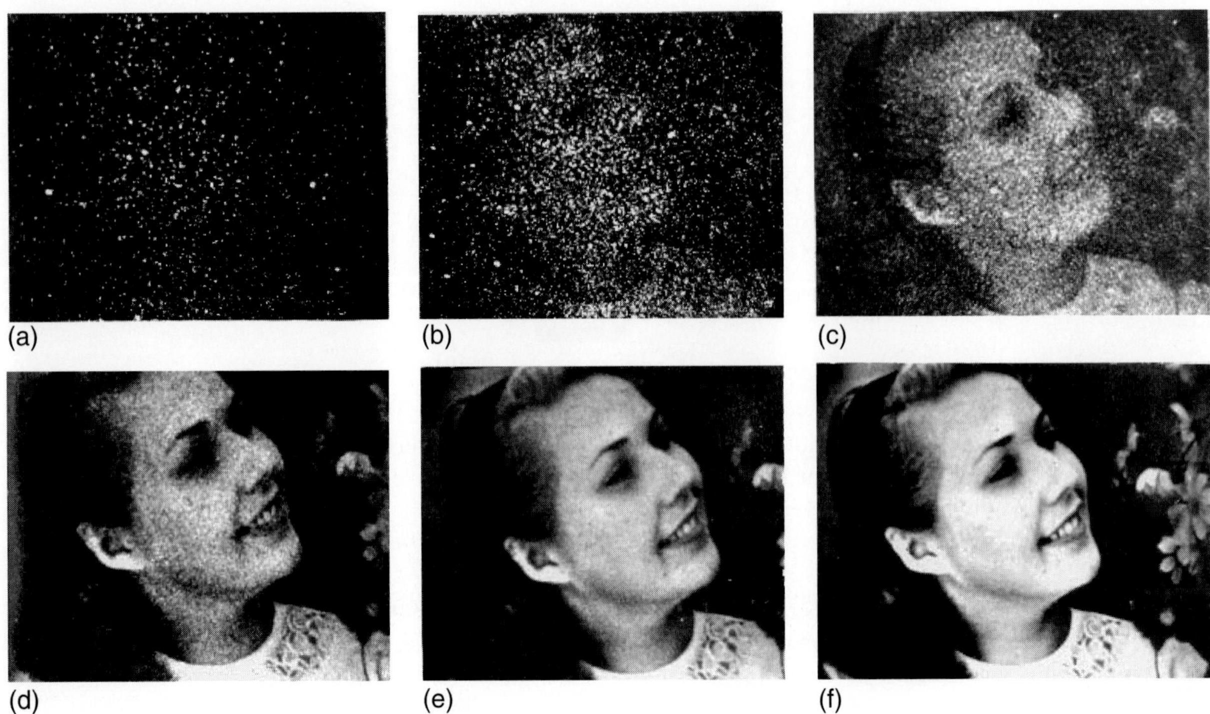

Figure 13.46
Stages of exposure revealing the photon-by-photon production of a photograph. The approximate numbers of photons at each stage were
(a) 3×10^3
(b) 1.2×10^4
(c) 9.3×10^4
(d) 7.6×10^5
(e) 3.6×10^6
(f) 2.8×10^7

Evidently, light has both a wave nature and a particle nature—a wave-particle duality.* This duality is evident in the formation of optical images. We understand the photographic image produced by a camera in terms of light waves, which spread from each point of the object, refract as they pass through the lens system, and converge to focus on the photographic film. The path of light from the object through the lens system and to the focal plane can be calculated using methods developed from the wave theory of light.

But now consider carefully the way in which the photographic image is formed. The photographic film consists of an emulsion that contains grains of silver halide crystal, each grain containing about 10^{10} silver atoms. Each photon that is absorbed gives up its energy to a single grain in the emulsion. This energy activates surrounding crystals in the entire grain and is used in development to complete the photochemical process. Numerous photons activating numerous grains produce the usual photographic exposure. When a photograph is taken with exceedingly feeble light, we find that the image is built up by individual photons that arrive independently and are seemingly random in their distribution. We see this strikingly illustrated in Figure 13.46, which shows how an exposure progresses photon by photon.

*A quantum is the smallest "particle" of something, such as light, electricity, or energy itself. From a pre-quantum point of view, this wave–particle duality is mysterious, leading some people to believe that photons and other "quanta" have some sort of consciousness, with each photon or quantum having "a mind of its own." The mystery, however, is like beauty. It is in the mind of the beholder. We conjure models to understand nature, and then, when inconsistencies arise, we sharpen or change our models. The wave–particle duality of light doesn't fit a model built on classical ideas. An alternative model is that quanta have minds of their own. Another model is quantum physics. We subscribe to the latter.

Figure 13.47
Richard Feynman advanced quantum physics and shared the 1965 Nobel Prize for Physics.

What all this means is that light has both wave and particle properties. Simply stated, *light behaves as a stream of photons when it interacts with photographic film or other detectors, and it behaves as a wave in traveling from a source to the place where it is detected.* Light travels as a wave and hits as a stream of photons. In interference experiments, photons strike the film at places where we would expect to see constructive interference of waves.

The fact that light exhibits both wave and particle behavior is one of the most interesting surprises that physicists discovered in the twentieth century. The finding that light comes in tiny bunches—tiny *quanta,* as they are called—led to a whole new way of perceiving nature, known as wave mechanics, or *quantum mechanics.* An outcome of this new mechanics is that, just as light has particle properties, so do particles have wave properties. First, electrons were found to have wave properties; a beam of electrons passing through slits exhibits the same type of diffraction pattern as light. Then, other particles—even baseballs and orbiting planets—could be described by the new mechanics of waves. Quantum mechanics and Newtonian physics overlap in the macroworld, and both are seen as "correct." But only quantum mechanics, with its emphasis on waves, is wholly accurate in the microworld of the atom—which we will explore in greater detail in Part 2 of this textbook. Onward!

Summary of Terms

Reflection The return of light rays from a surface in such a way that the angle at which a given ray is returned is equal to the angle at which it strikes the surface. When the reflecting surface is irregular, light is returned in irregular directions; this is *diffuse reflection.*

Refraction The bending of an oblique ray of light when it passes from one transparent medium to another. This is caused by a difference in the speed of light in the transparent media. When the change in medium is abrupt (say, from air to water), the bending is abrupt; when the change in medium is gradual (say, from cool air to warm air), the bending is gradual, which accounts for mirages.

Law of reflection The angle of incidence equals the angle of reflection. The incident and reflected rays lie in a plane that is normal to the reflecting surface.

Critical angle The minimum angle of incidence inside a medium at which a light ray is totally reflected.

Total internal reflection The total reflection of light traveling within a medium that strikes the boundary of another medium at an angle at, or greater than, the critical angle.

Converging lens A lens that is thicker in the middle than at the edges and that refracts parallel rays passing through it to a focus.

Diverging lens A lens that is thinner in the middle than at the edges, causing parallel rays passing through it to diverge as if from a point.

Virtual image An image formed by light rays that do not converge at the location of the image. Mirrors, converging lenses used as magnifying glasses, and diverging lenses all produce virtual images.

Real image An image formed by light rays that converge at the location of the image. A real image can be displayed on a screen.

Aberrations Limitations on the formation of perfect images, which are inherent, to some degree, in all optical systems.

Photoelectric effect The emission of electrons from a metal surface when light shines on it.

Review Questions

1. Distinguish between *reflection* and *refraction.*

13.1 Reflection

2. What does incident light that falls on an object do to the electrons in the atoms of the object?
3. What do the electrons in an illuminated object do when they are made to oscillate with greater energy?
4. What is the law of reflection?
5. Relative to the distance of an object in front of a plane mirror, how far behind the mirror is the image?
6. Does the law of reflection hold for curved mirrors? Explain.
7. Does the law of reflection hold for diffuse reflection? Explain.

8. How can a surface be polished for some waves and not for others?

13.2 Refraction

9. What is the angle between a light ray and its wave front?
10. When a wheel rolls from a smooth sidewalk onto grass, the interaction of the wheel with the blades of grass slows the wheel. What slows light when it passes from air into glass or water?
11. What causes the bending of light in refraction?
12. Does light travel faster in thin air or in dense air? What does this difference in speed have to do with the length of daylight?
13. What is a mirage?
14. Why do stars twinkle?

13.3 Dispersion

15. What happens to light of a certain frequency when it is incident on a material whose natural frequency is the same as the frequency of the light?
16. Which travels more slowly in glass, red light or violet light?
17. What is dispersion? Is a rainbow an example of dispersion?
18. What prevents rainbows from being seen as complete circles?
19. Does a single raindrop illuminated by sunlight disperse a spectrum of colors? Does a viewer see a spectrum from a single faraway drop?
20. Is a rainbow flat, or is it three-dimensional?
21. Why is a secondary rainbow dimmer than a primary bow?

13.4 Total Internal Reflection

22. What is meant by *critical angle*?
23. When is light totally reflected in water or glass?
24. When is light totally reflected in a diamond?
25. Light normally travels in straight lines, but it "bends" in an optical fiber. Explain.

13.5 Lenses

26. Distinguish between a *converging lens* and a *diverging lens.*
27. What is the *focal length* of a lens?
28. Distinguish between a *virtual image* and a *real image.*
29. Is a converging lens or a diverging lens used to produce a real image? To produce a virtual image?
30. Distinguish between *spherical aberration* and *chromatic aberration.*
31. What is astigmatism?

13.6 Wave–Particle Duality

32. What evidence can you cite for the wave nature of light? For the particle nature of light?
33. Which are more successful in dislodging electrons from a metal surface, photons of violet light or photons of red light? Why?
34. When does light behave as a particle? When does it behave as a wave?
35. Where do quantum mechanics and Newtonian physics overlap? Where is quantum mechanics wholly accurate?

Activities

1. Make a pinhole camera, as illustrated below. Cut out one end of a small cardboard box, and cover the end with tissue or wax paper. Make a clean-cut pinhole at the other end. (If the cardboard is thick, make it through a piece of aluminum foil placed over an opening in the cardboard.) Aim the camera at a bright object in a darkened room, and you will see an upside-down image on the tissue paper. If, in a dark room, you replace the tissue paper with unexposed photographic film, cover the back so it is light tight, and cover the pinhole with a removable flap, you are ready to take a picture. Exposure times differ, depending principally on the kind of film and the amount of light. Try different exposure times, starting with about 3 seconds. Also try boxes of various lengths. You'll find everything in focus in your photographs, but the pictures will not have clear-cut, sharp outlines. The lens on a commercial camera is much bigger than the pinhole and therefore admits more light in less time—hence the name *snapshots.*

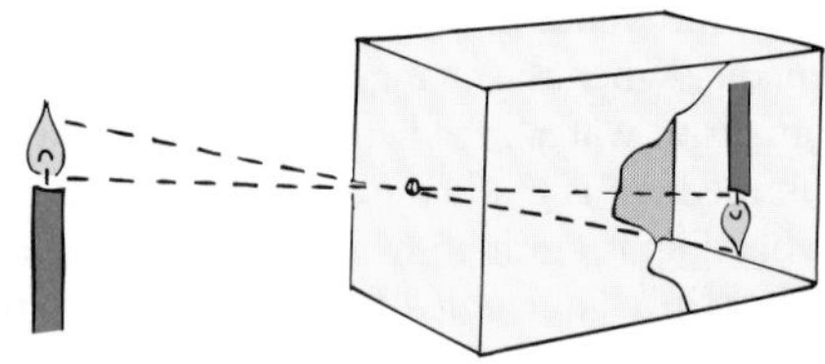

2. Stand a pair of mirrors on edge with the faces parallel to each other. Place an object, such as a coin, between the mirrors, and look at the reflections in each mirror. Nice?
3. Set up two pocket mirrors at right angles, and place a coin between them. You'll see four coins. Change the angle of the mirrors, and see how many images of the coin you can see. With the mirrors at right angles, look at your face. Then wink. What do you see? You now see yourself as others see you. Hold a printed page up to the double mirrors and compare its appearance with the reflection of a single mirror.

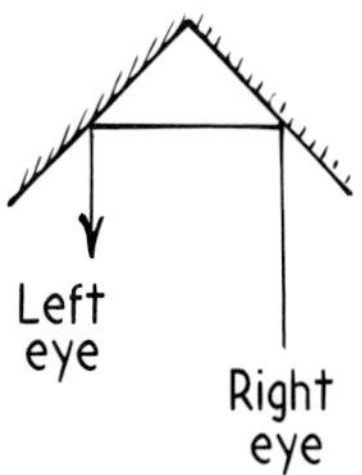

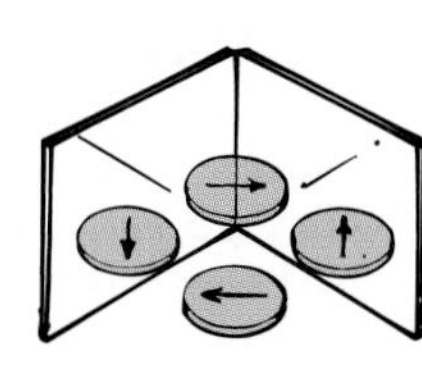

4. Rotate a pair of mirrors, keeping them at right angles to each other. Does your image rotate also? Then place the mirrors 60 degrees apart so that you can see your face. Again rotate the mirrors, and see if your image rotates also. Amazing?

5. Determine the magnifying power of a lens by focusing on the lines of a ruled piece of paper. Count the spaces between the lines that fit into one magnified space, and you have the magnifying power of the lens. You can do the same with binoculars and a distant brick wall. Hold the binoculars so that only one eye looks at the bricks through the eyepiece while the other eye looks directly at the bricks. The number of bricks seen with the unaided eye that will fit into one magnified brick reveals the magnification of the instrument.

6. Look at the reflections of overhead lights from the inner and outer surfaces of eyeglasses, and you will see two fascinatingly different images. Why are they different?

Exercises

1. Her eye at point P looks into the mirror. Which of the numbered cards can she see reflected in the mirror?

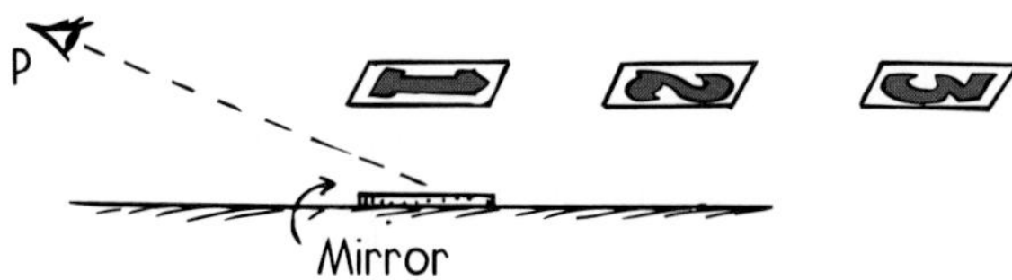

2. Cowboy Joe wishes to shoot his assailant by ricocheting a bullet off a mirrored metal plate. To do so, should he simply aim at the mirrored image of his assailant? Explain.
3. Trucks often have signs on their backs that say, "If you can't see my mirrors, I can't see you." Explain the physics here.
4. Why is the lettering on the front of some vehicles "backward"?

AMBULANCE

5. When you look at yourself in the mirror and wave your right hand, your beautiful image waves its left hand. Then why don't the feet of your image wiggle when you shake your head?
6. Car mirrors are uncoated on the front surface and silvered on the back surface. When the mirror is properly adjusted, light from behind reflects from the silvered surface into the driver's eyes. Good. But this is not so good at nighttime with the glare of headlights behind. This problem is solved by the wedge shape of the mirror (see sketch). When the mirror is tilted slightly upward to the "nighttime" position, glare is directed upward toward the ceiling, away from the driver's eyes. Yet the driver can still see cars behind in the mirror. Explain.

7. To reduce the glare of the surroundings, the windows of some department stores slant inward at the bottom, rather than being vertical. How does this reduce glare?
8. A person in a dark room looking through a window can clearly see a person outside in the daylight, whereas the person outside cannot see the person inside. Explain.
9. Which kind of road surface is easier to see when driving at night, an uneven pebbled surface or a mirror-smooth surface? Explain.
10. Why is it difficult to see the roadway in front of you when driving on a rainy night?
11. We see the bird and its reflection. Why do we not see the bird's feet in the reflection?
12. What must be the minimum length of a plane mirror in order for you to see a full view of yourself?

13. What effect does your distance from the plane mirror have on your answer to the preceding question? (Try it and see!)
14. Hold a pocket mirror almost at arm's length from your face and note the amount of your face you can see. To see more of your face, should you hold the mirror closer or farther, or would you have to have a larger mirror? (Try it and see!)
15. From a steamy mirror, wipe away just enough steam to allow you to see your full face. How tall will the wiped area be compared with the vertical dimension of your face?
16. The diagram shows a person and her twin at equal distances on opposite sides of a thin wall. Suppose that a window were to be cut in the wall so each twin can see a complete view of the other. Show the size and location of the smallest window that could be cut in the wall to do the job. (*Hint:* Draw rays from the top of each twin's head to the other twin's eyes. Do the same from the feet of each to the eyes of the other.)

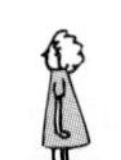

17. Why does reflected light from the sun or moon appear as a column in the body of water as shown? How would it appear if the water's surface were perfectly smooth?

18. What is wrong with the cartoon of the man looking at himself in the mirror? (Have a friend face a mirror as shown, and you'll see.)

19. A pair of toy cart wheels are rolled obliquely from a smooth surface onto two plots of grass, a rectangular plot and a triangular plot, as shown. The ground is on a slight incline, so that, after slowing down in the grass, the wheels will speed up again when emerging onto the smooth surface. Finish the sketches by showing some positions of the wheels inside each plot and on the other side of each plot, thereby indicating their direction of travel.

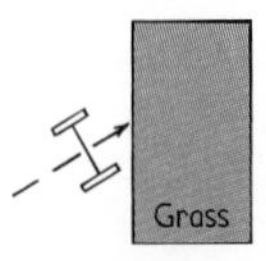

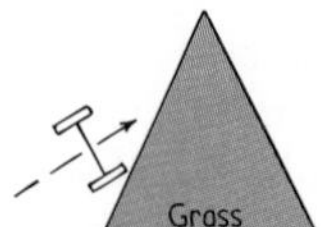

20. A pulse of red light and a pulse of blue light enter a glass block normal to its surface at the same time. Strictly speaking, after passing through the block, which pulse exits first?
21. During a lunar eclipse, the moon is not completely dark, but it is often a deep red in color. Explain this in terms of the refraction of all the sunsets and sunrises around the world.
22. If you place a glass test tube in water, you will be able to see the tube. If you place it in clear soybean oil, you may not be able to see it. What does this tell you about the speed of light in the oil and in the glass?
23. If, while standing on the bank of a stream, you wished to spear a fish swimming in the water out in front of you, would you aim above, below, or directly at the observed fish to make a direct hit? If you decided instead to zap the fish with a laser, would you aim above, below, or directly at the observed fish? Defend your answers.
24. If the fish in the previous exercise were small and blue, and your laser light were red, what corrections should you make? Explain.
25. When a fish looks upward at an angle of 45°, does it see the sky or only the reflection of the bottom? Defend your answer.
26. If you were to send a beam of laser light to a space station above the atmosphere and just above the horizon, would you aim the laser above, below, or directly at the visible space station? Defend your answer.
27. Rays of light in water that shine up to the water–air boundary at angles of more than 48° to the normal are totally reflected. No rays beyond 48° refract outside. How about the other way around? Is there an angle at which light rays in air meeting the air–water boundary will reflect totally? Or will some light be refracted at all angles?
28. When your eye is submerged in water, is the bending of light rays from water to your eyes greater than, less than, or the same as it is in air?
29. When you stand with your back to the sun, you see a rainbow as a circular arc. Could you move off to one side and then see the rainbow as the segment of an ellipse rather than the segment of a circle (such as Figure 13.20 suggests)? Defend your answer.
30. Two observers standing apart from one another do not see the "same" rainbow. Explain.
31. A rainbow viewed from an airplane may form a complete circle. Where will the shadow of the airplane appear? Explain.
32. How is a rainbow similar to the halo sometimes seen around the moon on a frosty night? How are rainbows and halos different?
33. What is responsible for the rainbow-colored fringe commonly seen at the edges of a spot of white light from the beam of a lantern or slide projector?

34. Transparent plastic swimming-pool covers called *solar heat sheets* have thousands of small lenses made up of air-filled bubbles. The lenses in these sheets are advertised to focus heat from the sun into the water and raise its temperature. Do you think the lenses of such sheets direct more solar energy into the water? Defend your answer.
35. Would the average intensity of sunlight measured by a light meter at the bottom of the pool in Figure 13.34 be different if the water were still?
36. What accounts for the large shadows cast by the ends of the thin legs of the water strider? What accounts for the ring of bright light around the shadows on the bottom?

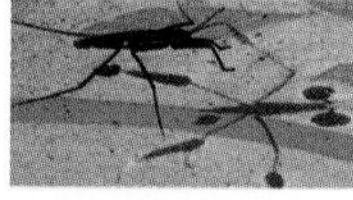

37. Why will goggles allow a swimmer under water to focus more clearly on what he is looking at?
38. Cover the top half of a camera lens. What effect does this have on the pictures taken?
39. Would refracting telescopes and microscopes magnify if light had the same speed in glass as it does in air? Explain.
40. Consider a simple magnifying glass under water. Will it magnify more or less? Explain why.
41. Can you take a photograph of your image in a plane mirror and focus the camera both on your image and on the mirror frame? Explain.
42. Why do you have to put slides into a slide projector upside down?
43. Maps of the moon are upside down. Why?
44. We speak of photons of red light and photons of green light. Can we speak of photons of white light? Why or why not?
45. A beam of red light and a beam of blue light have exactly the same energy. Which beam contains the greater number of photons?
46. Silver bromide (AgBr) is a light-sensitive substance used in some types of photographic film. To cause exposure of the film, it must be illuminated with light having sufficient energy to break apart the molecules. Why do you suppose that this film may be handled without exposure in a darkroom illuminated with red light, but not with blue light? How about very bright red light as compared with very dim blue light?
47. The practice of sunbathing to produce a suntan also produces cell damage in the skin. Ultraviolet radiation, rather than visible radiation, is the culprit. Why is this so?
48. Explain how the photoelectric effect is used to open a door automatically when someone approaches.
49. Explain briefly how the photoelectric effect is used in the operation of at least two of the following: an electric eye, a photographer's light meter, and the sound track of a motion picture.
50. Does the photoelectric effect *prove* that light is made of particles? Do interference experiments *prove* that light is composed of waves? (Is there a distinction between what something *is* and how it *behaves*?)

Problems

1. Show with a simple diagram that, when a mirror with a fixed beam incident on it is rotated through a certain angle, the reflected beam is rotated through an angle twice as large. (This doubling of displacement makes irregularities in ordinary window glass more evident.)
2. A spider hangs by a strand of silk at an eye level 20 cm in front of a plane mirror. You are behind the spider, 50 cm from the mirror. What is the distance between your eye and the image of the spider in the mirror?
3. If you take a photograph of your image in a plane mirror, how many meters away should you set your focus if you are 3 m in front of the mirror?
4. Suppose that you walk toward a mirror at 2 m/s. How rapidly do you and your image approach each other? (The answer is *not* 2 m/s.)
5. When light strikes glass perpendicularly, about 4% of the light is reflected at each surface. Approximately how much light is transmitted through a pane of window glass?
6. The diameter of the sun makes an angle of 0.53° with its apex at the surface of the earth. How many minutes does it take for the sun to move one solar diameter in an overhead sky? (Remember that it takes 24 hours, or 1440 minutes, for the sun to move through 360°.) How does your answer compare with the time it takes for the sun to disappear once its lower edge meets the horizon at sunset? (Does refraction affect your answer?)

Chapter 13 Online Resources

Tutorials
- Waves

Videos
- Image Formation in a Mirror
- Model of Refraction
- The Rainbow

Quiz
Exercises
Flashcards
Links

Sample Exam Questions for Part I—Physics

Choose the BEST answer to each of the following.

1. To be in mechanical equilibrium, an object must be
(a) at rest (b) moving at constant velocity
(c) either of these (d) neither of these
2. If an object moves along a straight-line path, then it must be
(a) accelerating (b) acted on by a force
(c) both of these (d) none of these
3. A heavy rock and a light rock in free fall have the same acceleration. The *reason* the heavy rock does not have more acceleration is because
(a) the force of gravity on each is the same
(b) there is no air resistance
(c) the inertia of both rocks is the same
(d) all of these (e) none of these
4. A ball rolls down a curved ramp as shown. As its speed increases, its rate of gaining speed
(a) increases (b) decreases
(c) remains unchanged
5. An airplane flying directly against the wind moves more slowly across the ground below, and one flying in the same direction as the wind (with the wind) moves faster. When a plane flies across the wind (with the wind coming from the side), its speed across the ground, compared with when there is no wind at all, is
(a) greater (b) less (c) no different
6. A karate chop delivers a force of 3000 N to a board that breaks. The force that acts on the hand during this event is
(a) less than 3000 N (b) 3000 N
(c) more than 3000 N (d) not enough information to say
7. When the brakes are applied in a car traveling at a certain speed, it skids a certain distance to a stop. If the car were traveling three time as fast, skidding distance would be
(a) the same (b) three times longer (c) nine times longer (d) there's no physics principle to guide an answer to this question
8. When a bullet is fired from a rifle, the force that accelerates the bullet is equal in magnitude to the force that makes the rifle recoil. But, compared with the rifle, the bullet has a greater
(a) inertia (b) potential energy
(c) kinetic energy (d) momentum
9. Which pulls with the greater *force* on the earth's oceans?
(a) moon (b) sun (c) both pull the same
10. The space shuttle orbiting the earth is above the earth's
(a) atmosphere (b) gravitational field
(c) both of these (d) neither of these
11. If you squeeze an air-filled balloon to half size, the pressure inside
(a) remains the same (b) halves
(c) doubles (d) quadruples
12. As a weighted air-filled balloon sinks deeper beneath the water surface, the buoyant force on it
(a) increases (b) decreases
(c) remains about the same
13. When scientists discuss kinetic energy per molecule, the concept being discussed is
(a) heat (b) temperature
(c) thermal energy (d) entropy
14. In a mixture of hydrogen gas, oxygen gas, and nitrogen gas, the molecules with the greatest average speed are those of
(a) hydrogen (b) oxygen (c) nitrogen
(d) all have the same speed
15. Consider a sample of water at 2°C. If the temperature is increased slightly—say, by one degree—the volume of water
(a) increases (b) decreases (c) remains unchanged
16. The principle reason one can walk barefoot on red-hot wooden coals without burning the feet has to do with
(a) the low temperature of the coals
(b) the low thermal conductivity of the coals
(c) mind-over-matter techniques
17. Soon after you remove a soda-pop can from a cold refrigerator, it becomes wet. This wetness is primarily due to
(a) conduction (b) convection (c) radiation
(d) evaporation (e) condensation
18. The earth loses heat primarily by
(a) conduction (b) convection
(c) radiation (d) all of these
19. Melting ice actually
(a) tends to warm the surroundings (b) tends to cool the surroundings (c) has no effect on the temperature of the surroundings
20. The interior of the earth is kept hot by
(a) enormous pressure (b) great insulation
(c) radioactivity (d) its own natural heat
21. You can touch and discharge a 10,000-volt Van de Graaff generator with little harm because, although the voltage is high, there is relatively little
(a) resistance (b) energy (c) grounding
(d) all of these (e) none of these
22. The current through a 12-ohm hair dryer connected to a 120-volt power source is
(a) 1 A (b) 10 A (c) 12 A (d) 120 A
(e) none of these

23. Compared with the amount of current in the filament of a lamp, the amount of current in the connecting wire is
    (a) definitely less (b) often less (c) actually more
    (d) the same (e) incredibly, all of these
24. As more lamps are connected to a series circuit, the overall current in the power source
    (a) increases (b) decreases (c) remains the same
25. As more lamps are connected to a parallel circuit, the overall current in the power source
    (a) increases (b) decreases (c) remains the same
26. If you change the magnetic field in a closed loop of wire, you induce in the loop a
    (a) current (b) voltage (c) electric field
    (d) all of these (e) none of these
27. A step-up transformer increases
    (a) power (b) energy (c) both of these
    (d) neither of these
28. A portion of water vibrates up and down two complete cycles in one second as a water wave passes by. The wave's wavelength is 5 meters. What is the wave's speed?
    (a) 2m/s (b) 5m/s (c) 10m/s (d) 15m/s
    (e) none of these
29. When a source of sound approaches you, you detect an increase in its
    (a) speed (b) wavelength
    (c) frequency (d) all of these
30. A sonic boom is typically produced when an aircraft flies
    (a) from subsonic to supersonic speed
    (b) faster than the speed of sound
    (c) neither of these
31. The speed of sound in air depends on
    (a) frequency (b) wavelength (c) air temperature
    (d) all of these (e) none of these
32. A singer holds a high note and shatters a distant crystal wine glass. This phenomenon best demonstrates
    (a) forced vibrations (b) the Doppler effect
    (c) interference (d) resonance
33. Which of the following does not fit in the same family?
    (a) light wave (b) radio wave (c) sound wave
    (d) microwave (e) X ray
34. If water naturally absorbed blue and violet light rather than infrared, water would appear
    (a) greenish blue, as it presently appears
    (b) a more intense greenish blue
    (c) orange-ish yellow (d) to have no color at all
35. The sky is blue because air molecules in the sky act as tiny
    (a) mirrors that reflect primarily blue light
    (b) scatterers of high-frequency light
    (c) diffractors of high-frequency light
    (d) prisms
    (e) none of these
36. If you can't quite see all your face in a pocket mirror, to do so you'll need to
    (a) hold it closer (b) hold it farther away
    (c) get a bigger mirror
37. If different colors of light had the same speed in matter, there would be no
    (a) rainbows (b) dispersion by prisms
    (c) colors from diamonds (d) all of these
38. Lenses work because, in different materials, light has different
    (a) wavelengths (b) frequencies (c) speeds
    (d) energies (e) none of these
39. Which of the photons listed below has the most energy?
    (a) red (b) white (c) blue (d) all the same
40. Light has both a wave nature and a particle nature. Light behaves primarily as a particle when it
    (a) travels from one place to another
    (b) interacts with matter (c) does neither

Answers: 1c, 2d, 3e, 4b, 5a, 6b, 7c, 8c, 9b, 10a, 11c, 12b, 13b, 14a, 15b, 16b, 17e, 18c, 19b, 20c, 21b, 22b, 23d, 24b, 25a, 26d, 27d, 28c, 29c, 30b, 31c, 32d, 33c, 34c, 35b, 36c, 37d, 38c, 39c, 40b

PART TWO

Atoms and Chemistry

Like everyone, I'm made of atoms, which are so small and numerous that I inhale billions of trillions with each breath of air. I exhale some of them right away, but other atoms stay for awhile and become part of me, which I may exhale later. Some of my atoms are in each breath you take, and stay to become part of you (and likewise, yours become part of me). There are way more atoms in a breath of air than the total number of humans since time zero, so in each breath you inhale, you recycle atoms that once were a part of every person who lived. Hey, in this sense, we're all one!

CHAPTER 14

Atoms and the Periodic Table

We humans have long tinkered with the materials around us and used them to our advantage. Once we learned how to control fire, we were able to create many new substances. Moldable wet clay, for example, was found to harden into ceramic when heated by fire. By 5000 B.C., pottery fire pits gave way to furnaces hot enough to refine copper ores to produce metallic copper. By 1200 B.C., even hotter furnaces were converting iron ores to iron. This technology allowed for the mass production of metal tools and weapons and made possible the many achievements of ancient Chinese, Egyptian, and Greek civilizations.

Fast-forward to the twenty-first century, and we've since learned that all the materials around us are made of remarkably small particles called atoms. We have learned how to manipulate these atoms in order to produce a vast array of new and useful modern materials, including pharmaceuticals that help to prolong our lives. We have even learned how to move atoms, one by one, into desired positions. The opening photograph for this chapter, for example, shows a group of titanium atoms that scientists pushed into a circle. This is in the forefront of our present-day technology, which allows us to build nano-devices and new materials atom by atom. In this chapter, we will explore both the nature of atoms and the amazing chart that tells their story—the periodic table.

14.1 The Elements

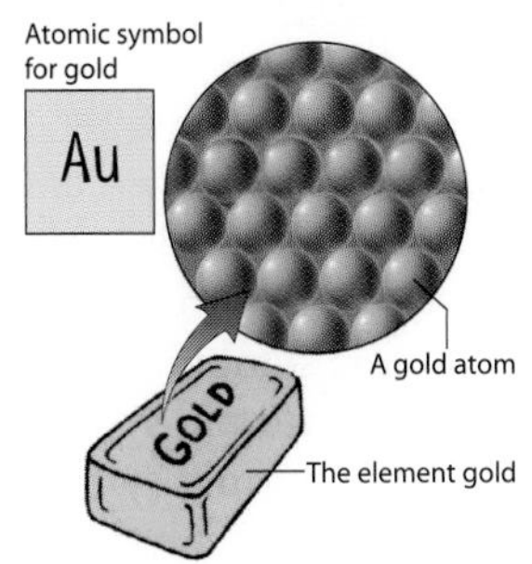

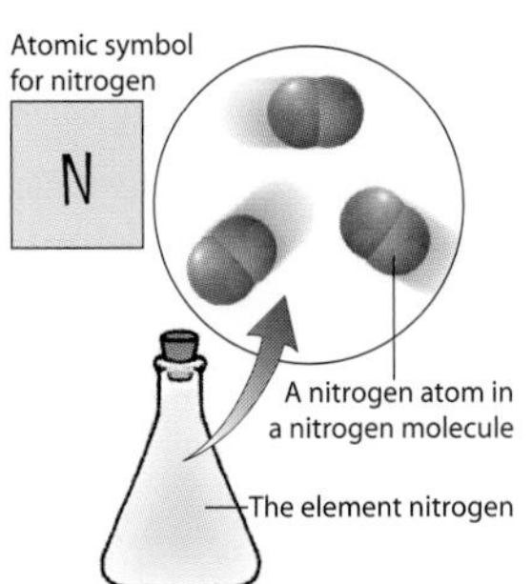

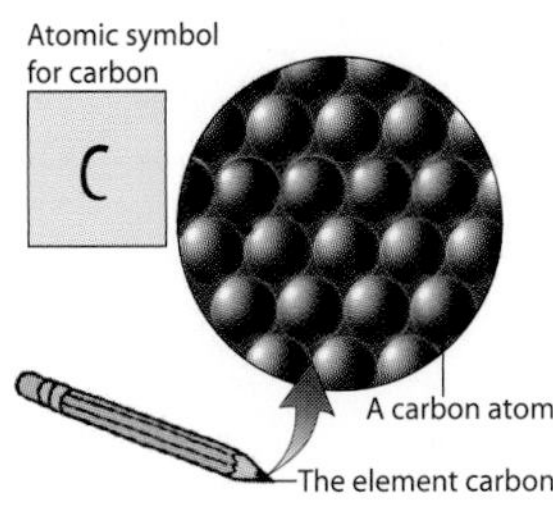

Figure 14.1
Any element consists only of one kind of atom. Gold consists only of gold atoms, a flask of gaseous nitrogen consists only of nitrogen atoms, and the carbon of a graphite pencil consists only of carbon atoms.

You know that atoms make up the matter around you, from stars to steel to chocolate ice cream. Given all these various materials, you might think that there must be many different kinds of atoms. But the number of different kinds of atoms is surprisingly small. The great variety of substances results from the many ways in which a few kinds of atoms can be combined. Just as the three colors red, green, and blue can be combined to form any color on a television screen, or just as the 26 letters of the alphabet make up all the words in a dictionary, only a few kinds of atoms combine in different ways to produce all of the countless substances in the universe. To date, we know of slightly more than 100 distinct kinds of atoms. Of these, about 90 are found in nature. The remaining kinds of atoms have been created in the laboratory.

Any material that is made up of only one type of atom is classified as an **element.** A few examples are shown in Figure 14.1. Pure gold, for example, is an element—it contains only gold atoms. Nitrogen gas is an element because

1 H																	2 He
3 Li	4 Be											5 B	6 C	7 N	8 O	9 F	10 Ne
11 Na	12 Mg											13 Al	14 Si	15 P	16 S	17 Cl	18 Ar
19 K	20 Ca	21 Sc	22 Ti	23 V	24 Cr	25 Mn	26 Fe	27 Co	28 Ni	29 Cu	30 Zn	31 Ga	32 Ge	33 As	34 Se	35 Br	36 Kr
37 Rb	38 Sr	39 Y	40 Zr	41 Nb	42 Mo	43 Tc	44 Ru	45 Rh	46 Pd	47 Ag	48 Cd	49 In	50 Sn	51 Sb	52 Te	53 I	54 Xe
55 Cs	56 Ba	57 La	72 Hf	73 Ta	74 W	75 Re	76 Os	77 Ir	78 Pt	79 Au	80 Hg	81 Tl	82 Pb	83 Bi	84 Po	85 At	86 Rn
87 Fr	88 Ra	89 Ac	104 Rf	105 Db	106 Sg	107 Bh	108 Hs	109 Mt	110 Uun	111 Uuu	112 Uub						
				58 Ce	59 Pr	60 Nd	61 Pm	62 Sm	63 Eu	64 Gd	65 Tb	66 Dy	67 Ho	68 Er	69 Tm	70 Yb	71 Lu
				90 Th	91 Pa	92 U	93 Np	94 Pu	95 Am	96 Cm	97 Bk	98 Cf	99 Es	100 Fm	101 Md	102 No	103 Lr

Figure 14.2
The periodic table lists all the known elements.

"All things are made of atoms—little particles that move around in perpetual motion, attracting each other when they are a little distance apart, but repelling upon being squeezed into one another."
—Richard P. Feynman

Insights

it contains only nitrogen atoms. Likewise, the graphite in your pencil is an element—carbon. Graphite is made up solely of carbon atoms. All of the elements are listed in a chart called the **periodic table,** which is shown in Figure 14.2.

In the periodic table, each element is designated by its **atomic symbol,** which comes from the letters of the element's name. For example, the atomic symbol for carbon is C, and that for chlorine is Cl. In many cases, the atomic symbol is derived from the element's Latin name. Gold has the atomic symbol Au, which comes from its Latin name, *aurum.* Lead has the atomic symbol Pb which comes from its Latin name, *plumbum* (Figure 14.3). Elements having symbols derived from Latin names are usually those that were discovered earliest.

Note that only the first letter of an atomic symbol is capitalized. The symbol for the element cobalt, for instance, is Co, while CO denotes a combination of two elements: carbon, C, and oxygen, O.

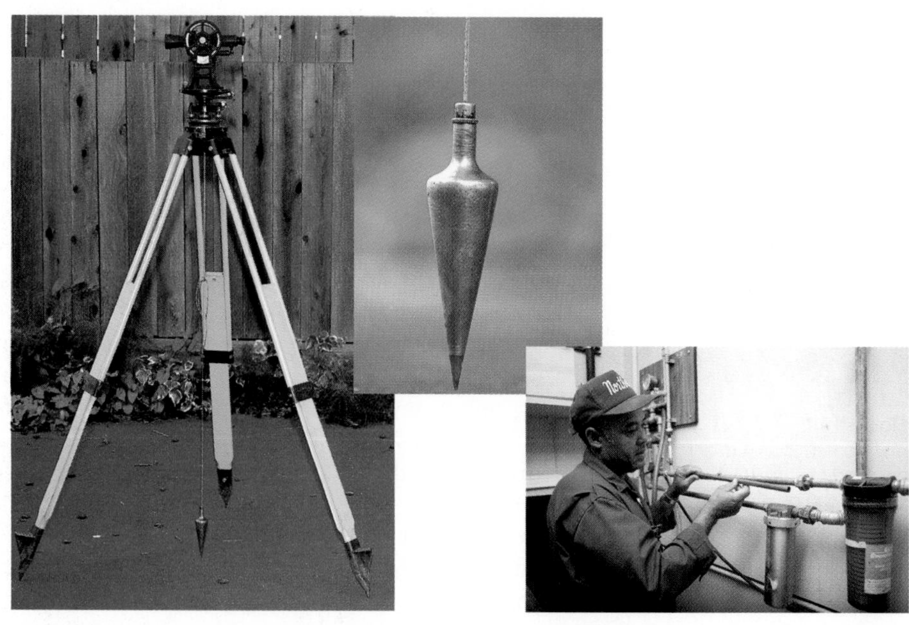

Figure 14.3
The origin of the word *plumb bob,* a heavy weight attached to a string and used by carpenters and surveyors to establish a straight vertical line, is from the Latin word for lead (*plumbum,* Pb). Lead is still sometimes used for the bob. Plumbers got their name because they once worked with lead pipes.

14.2 Atoms Are Ancient and Empty

The origin of most atoms goes back to the birth of the universe. Hydrogen, H, the lightest atom, was also the original atom, and it still makes up more than 90 percent of the atoms in the known universe. The next most abundant element is helium, He. Heavier atoms were produced in stars, which are massive collections of hydrogen and helium atoms pulled together by gravitational forces. Great pressures deep in a star's interior cause hydrogen atoms to fuse and become heavier elements. With the exception of hydrogen, all the atoms that occur naturally on the earth—including those in your body—are the products of stars. A tiny fraction of these atoms came from our own star, the sun, but most are from stars that perished long before our solar system came into existence. You are made of stardust, as is all matter that surrounds you.

So most atoms are ancient. They have existed through imponderable ages, recycling through the universe in innumerable forms, both nonliving and living. In this sense, you don't "own" the atoms that make up your body—you are simply their present caretaker. There will be many caretakers to follow.

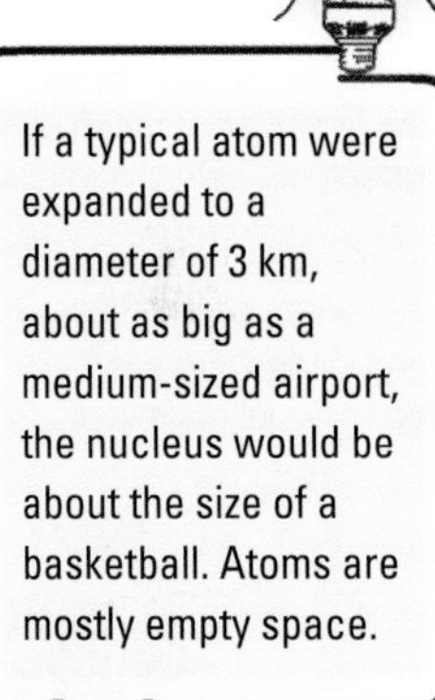

Atoms are in a state of perpetual motion. You can see evidence of this motion when you place a drop of ink into a glass of water. It soon spreads to color the entire glassful. Likewise, if a cupful of the atoms making up DDT is thrown into an ocean, those atoms disperse and are later found in every part of the world's oceans. The same is true of materials released into the atmosphere.

Atoms are so small that there are more than 10 billion trillion of them in each breath you exhale. This is more than the number of breaths in the earth's atmosphere. Within a few years, the atoms of your breath are uniformly mixed throughout the atmosphere. What this means is that anyone anywhere on the earth inhaling a breath of air takes in numerous atoms that were once part of you. And, of course, the reverse is true: you inhale atoms that were once part of everyone who has ever lived. We are literally breathing one another.

Atoms are so small that they can't be seen with visible light. That's because they are smaller than the wavelengths of visible light. We could stack microscope on top of microscope and never "see" an atom. Photographs of atoms, such as in Figure 14.4, are obtained with a scanning tunneling microscope. Discussed further in Chapter 15, this is an imaging device that bypasses the use of light and optics altogether.

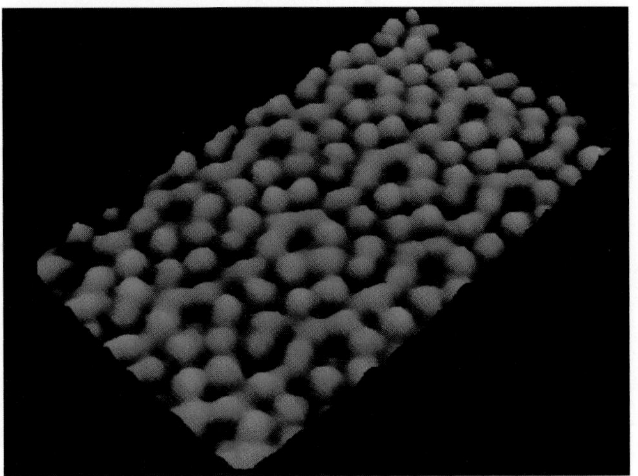

Figure 14.4
An image of carbon atoms obtained with a scanning tunneling microscope.

The first direct evidence for atoms was discovered in 1827 by a Scottish botanist, Robert Brown, while studying grains of pollen in a drop of water under a microscope. He noticed that the grains were continually vibrating. At first he thought that the grains were moving life forms. But later he found that dust particles and grains of soot moved in the same way. This perpetual jiggling of particles—now called *Brownian motion*—results from collisions

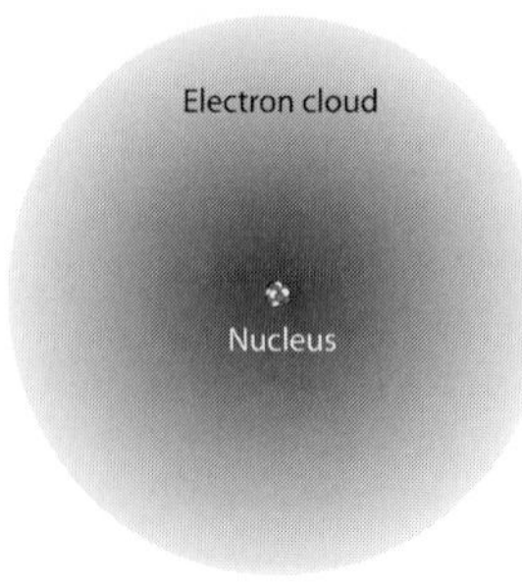

Figure 14.5
Electrons whiz around the atomic nucleus, forming what can be best described as a cloud that is more dense where the electrons tend to spend most of their time. Electrons, however, are invisible to us. Hence, such a cloud can only be imagined. Furthermore, if this illustration were drawn to scale, the atomic nucleus would be too small to be seen. In short, atoms are not well suited to visual depictions.

between visible particles and invisible atoms. Brown's pollen grains were in motion because they were constantly being jostled by the atoms that make up the water.

Since Brown's time, scientific investigation of the atom has been very vigorous and successful. Today we know the atom is made up of smaller, subatomic particles—*electrons, protons,* and *neutrons.* We also know that atoms differ from one another only in the number of these subatomic particles. Protons and neutrons are bound together at the atom's center to form the **atomic nucleus.** The nucleus is much smaller than the atom but it contains most of an atom's mass. Surrounding the nucleus are the tiny **electrons,** as shown in Figure 14.5. When you turn on a light switch, you make electrons flow. As we learned in Chapter 9, these make up the current flowing through a light bulb. The electrons that are so important in electricity are the same electrons that dictate chemical reactions. You will learn more about this in following chapters.

☑ CHECKPOINT

1. Which atoms are older, those in the body of an elderly person or in a baby?
2. A friend claims there are atoms in his brain that were once in the brain of Albert Einstein. Is your friend's claim likely correct or nonsense?

Check Your Answers

1. The age of the atoms in both is the same—most of them manufactured in stars that exploded before the solar system came into being.
2. Your friend is correct! In addition, there are atoms in your friend's and everyone else's body that were once in Mother Theresa, and in everybody else, too! The arrangements of these atoms, however, are now quite different. What's more, the atoms of which you and your friend are composed will live forever in the bodies of all the people on the earth who are yet to be.

Astronomers have recently discovered that stars in galaxies and entire galaxies within clusters move in a way that suggests the existence of much more mass than we can see "out there." Convincing evidence indicates that there is a great deal of "dark matter" in the universe, perhaps amounting to 90 percent of all mass. We thought we could "see" the universe, and now we find that we can't see most of it.

Insights

We and all materials around us are mostly empty space. How can this be? Electrons move about the nucleus in an atom defining the volume of space that the atom occupies. But since electrons are very small, and because they are widely separated from each other and from the nucleus, atoms are indeed mostly empty space.

So what keeps atoms from oozing through one another? How are we supported by a floor despite the empty nature of its atoms? The answer is that, although the space within the atom is mostly devoid of matter, it is filled with electric fields. The range of these fields is several times larger than the atomic volume. Electrons in the outer regions of any atom repel the electrons of neighboring atoms. Any two atoms, therefore, can get only so close to each other before repulsion dominates (provided they don't join in a chemical bond, as discussed in Chapter 19).

When your hand pushes against a wall, you make contact with the wall—at the macroscopic level. At the atomic level, electrical repulsion between electrons in your hand and electrons in the wall prevent contact in the conventional sense—and, furthermore, prevent your hand from passing through the wall. This same electrical repulsion prevents us from falling through a solid floor. So, quite interestingly, when you touch someone, your atoms and those of the other person do not meet. Instead, atoms from the two of you get close enough so that you sense an electrical repulsion. There is still a tiny, though imperceptible, gap between the two of you (Figure 14.6).

Figure 14.6
As close as Tracy and Ian are in this photograph, none of their atoms meet. The closeness between us is in our hearts.

☑ CHECKPOINT

What kind of force prevents atoms from meshing with one another?

Check Your Answer

The kind of force that prevents atoms from meshing with one another is electrical.

14.3 Protons and Neutrons

Let's take a closer look at the atom and investigate the particles found in the atomic nucleus. First, consider protons. A **proton** carries a positive charge and is relatively heavy—nearly 2000 times as massive as the electron. The proton and electron have the same quantity of charge, but the opposite sign. The number of protons in the nucleus of any atom is equal to the number of electrons whirling about the nucleus. So the opposite charges of protons and electrons balance each other, producing a zero net charge. The atom is electrically *neutral.* For example, an electrically balanced oxygen atom has a total of eight electrons and eight protons.

Scientists have agreed to identify elements by **atomic number,** which is the number of protons each atom of a given element contains. The periodic table lists the elements in order of increasing atomic number. Hydrogen, with one proton per atom, has atomic number 1; helium, with two protons per atom, has atomic number 2; and so on.

☑ CHECKPOINT

How many protons are there in an iron atom, Fe (atomic number 26)?

Check Your Answer

The atomic number of an atom and its number of protons are the same. Thus, there are 26 protons in an iron atom. Another way to put this is that all atoms that contain 26 protons are, by definition, iron atoms.

If we compare the electric charges and masses of different atoms, we see that the atomic nucleus must be made up of more than just protons. Helium, for example, has twice the electric charge of hydrogen but four times the mass. The additional mass is due to another subatomic particle found in the nucleus, the *neutron.* The **neutron** has about the same mass as the proton, but it has no electric charge. Any object that has no net electric charge is said to be electrically neutral, which accounts for the neutron's name. In Chapter 16, we will discuss the important role that neutrons play in holding the nucleus of each atom together.

Protons and neutrons are made of still smaller particles, the fundamental particles called *quarks.* Some recent theories suggest that quarks may be made of infinitely thin string loops.

Insights

Table 14.1

Subatomic Particles

	Particle	Charge	Mass Compared to Electron	Actual Mass* (kg)
	Electron	−1	1	9.11×10^{-31}†
Nucleons	Proton	+1	1836	1.673×10^{-27}
	Neutron	0	1841	1.675×10^{-27}

*Not measured directly but calculated from experimental data.
†9.11×10^{-31} kg = 0.000000000000000000000000000000911 kg.

Both protons and neutrons are called **nucleons,** a term that denotes their location in the atomic nucleus. Table 14.1 summarizes the basic facts about our three subatomic particles.

14.4 Isotopes and Atomic Mass

For any element, there is no set number of neutrons in the nucleus. For example, most hydrogen atoms (atomic number 1) have no neutrons. A small percentage, however, have one neutron, and a smaller percentage have two neutrons. Similarly, most iron atoms (atomic number 26) have 30 neutrons, but a small percentage of them have 29 neutrons. Atoms of the same element that contain different numbers of neutrons are referred to as **isotopes** of that element.

We identify an isotope by its **mass number,** which is the total number of protons and neutrons (nucleons) in the nucleus. As Figure 14.7 shows, a hydrogen isotope with only one proton is called hydrogen-1, where 1 is the mass number. A hydrogen isotope with one proton and one neutron is therefore hydrogen-2, and a hydrogen isotope with one proton and two neutrons is hydrogen-3. Similarly, an iron isotope with 26 protons and 30 neutrons is called iron-56, and one with only 29 neutrons is iron-55.

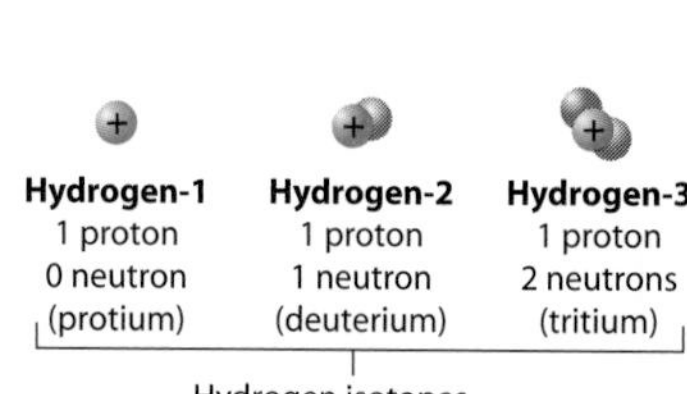

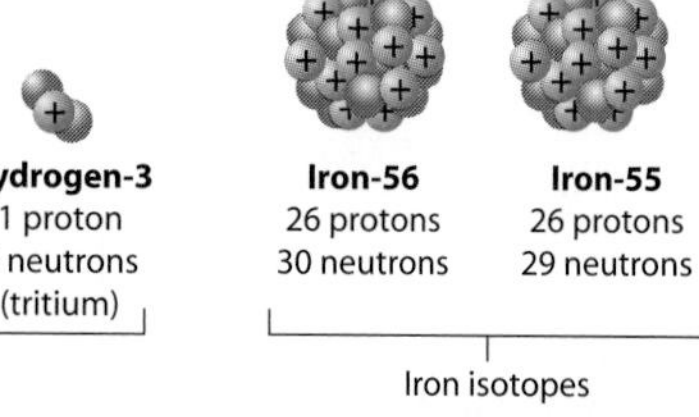

Figure 14.7
Isotopes of an element have the same number of protons but different numbers of neutrons and, therefore, different mass numbers. The three hydrogen isotopes have special names: protium for hydrogen-1 (the most common isotope), deuterium for hydrogen-2, and tritium for hydrogen-3. The isotopes of most elements have no special names and are indicated merely by mass number.

An alternative method of indicating isotopes is to write the mass number as a superscript and the atomic number as a subscript to the left of the atomic symbol. For example, an iron isotope with a mass number of 56 and atomic number of 26 is written:

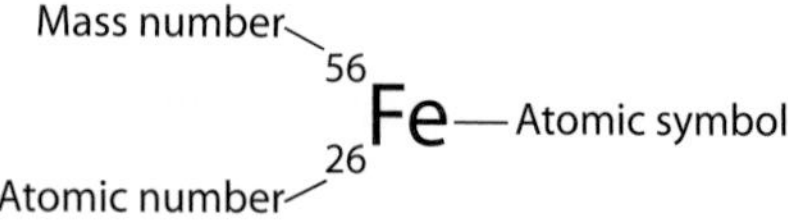

The total number of neutrons in an isotope can be calculated by subtracting its atomic number from its mass number:

$$\begin{array}{l} \text{Mass number} \\ \underline{-\ \text{atomic number}} \\ \text{number of neutrons} \end{array}$$

For example, uranium-238 has 238 nucleons. The atomic number of uranium is 92, which tells us that 92 of these 238 nucleons are protons. The remaining 146 nucleons must be neutrons:

$$\begin{array}{l} \text{238 protons and neutrons} \\ \underline{-\ \text{92 protons}} \\ \text{146 neutrons} \end{array}$$

Atoms interact with one another electrically. Therefore the way any atom behaves in the presence of other atoms is determined largely by the charged particles it contains, especially its electrons. Isotopes of an element differ only in mass, not in electric charge. For this reason, isotopes of an element share many characteristics—in fact, as chemicals they cannot be distinguished from one another. For example, a sugar molecule containing seven neutrons per carbon nucleus is digested no differently from a sugar molecule containing six neutrons per carbon nucleus. Interestingly, about 1 percent of the carbon we eat is the carbon-13 isotope, which contains seven neutrons per nucleus. An even smaller amount is carbon-14 (which we will discuss further when we get to Chapter 16). The remaining nearly 99 percent of the carbon in our diet is the more common carbon-12 isotope, which contains six neutrons per nucleus.

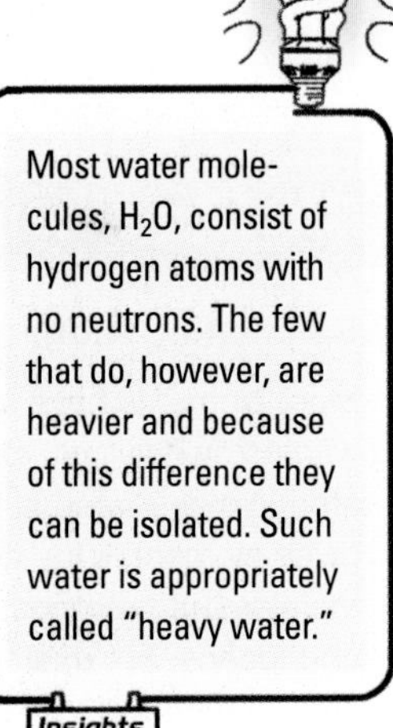

The total mass of an atom is called its **atomic mass.** This is the sum of the masses of all the atom's components (electrons, protons, and neutrons). Because electrons are so much less massive than protons and neutrons, their contribution to atomic mass is negligible. A special unit has been developed for atomic masses. This is the **atomic mass unit,** amu, where 1 atomic mass unit is equal to 1.661×10^{-24}g, which is slightly less than the mass of a single proton. As shown in Figure 14.8, the atomic masses listed in the periodic table are in atomic mass units. As explained in Figuring Physical Science on page 348, the atomic mass of an element as presented in the periodic table is actually the average atomic mass of its various isotopes.

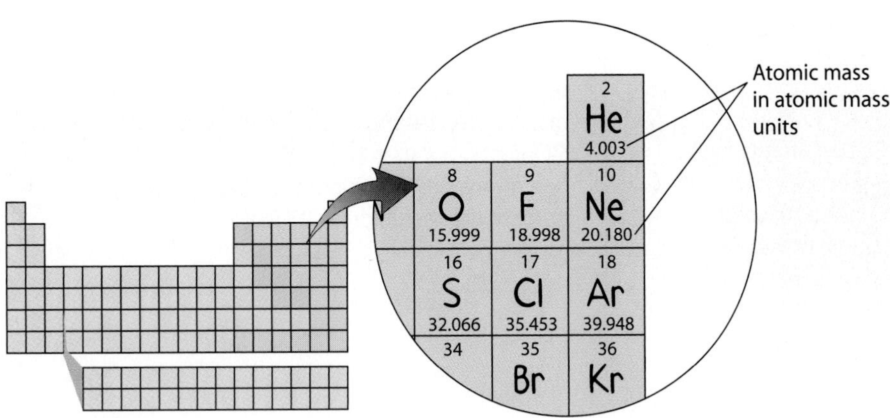

Figure 14.8
Helium, He, has an atomic mass of 4.003 atomic mass units, and neon, Ne, has an atomic mass of 20.180 atomic mass units.

☑ CHECKPOINT

1. Distinguish between mass number and atomic mass.
2. If two atoms are isotopes of the same element, do they have the same *atomic number*? The same *atomic mass*?

Check Your Answers

1. Both terms include the word mass and so are easily confused. Focus your attention on the second word of each term, however, and you'll be correct every time. Mass number is a count of the number of nucleons in an isotope and requires no units because it is simply a count. Atomic mass, however, is a measure of the total mass of an atom, which is given in atomic mass units. For example, the mass number of helium-4 is simply 4, while its atomic mass is 4.003 amu.
2. Both atoms have the same atomic number, but they have different atomic masses (because they have the same number of protons in the nucleus, but different numbers of neutrons).

Figuring Physical Science

Calculating Atomic Mass

Most elements have a variety of isotopes, each with its own atomic mass. For this reason, the atomic mass listed in the periodic table for any given element is the average of the masses of all the element's isotopes based on their relative abundance. For example, about 99 percent of all carbon atoms are atoms of the isotope carbon-12, and most of the remaining 1 percent are atoms of the heavier isotope carbon-13. This small amount of carbon-13 raises the average mass of carbon from 12.000 atomic mass units to the slightly greater value of 12.011 atomic mass units.

To arrive at the atomic mass presented in the periodic table, you must first multiply the mass of each naturally occurring isotope of an element by the fraction of its abundance, and then add up all the fractions.

Example

Carbon-12 has a mass of 12.0000 atomic mass units, and it makes up 98.89 percent of naturally occurring carbon. Carbon-13 has a mass of 13.0034 atomic mass units, and it makes up 1.11 percent of naturally occurring carbon. Use this information to show that the atomic mass of carbon shown in the periodic table, 12.011 atomic mass units, is correct.

Answer

Recognize that 98.89 percent and 1.11 percent expressed as fractions are 0.9889 and 0.0111, respectively.

	Contributing Mass of C^{12}	**Contributing Mass of C^{13}**	
Fraction of Abundance	0.9889	0.0111	step 1
Mass (amu)	× 12.0000	× 13.0034	
	11.867	0.144	

step 2

atomic mass =
11.867 + 0.144 = 12.011

Your Turn

Chlorine-35 has a mass of 34.97 atomic mass units, and chlorine-37 has a mass of 36.95 atomic mass units. Determine the atomic mass of chlorine, Cl (atomic number 17), if 75.53 percent of all chlorine atoms are the chlorine-35 isotope and 24.47 percent are the chlorine-37 isotope.

14.5 The Periodic Table

So the periodic table is a listing of all the known elements with their atomic symbols, atomic numbers, and atomic masses. But there is much more information in this table. The organization of the table tells us a lot about the structures of the elements and how they behave. For instance, let's look at the grouping of elements known as metals, nonmetals, and metalloids.

As shown in Figure 14.9, most elements are metals, which are defined as being shiny, opaque, and good conductors of electricity and heat. Metals are malleable, which means they can be hammered into different shapes or bent without breaking. They are also ductile, which means they can be drawn into wires. All but a few metals are solid at room temperature. The exceptions include mercury, Hg; gallium, Ga; cesium, Cs; and francium, Fr; which are all liquids at a warm room temperature of 30°C (86°F). Another interesting exception is hydrogen, H, which takes on the properties of a liquid metal only at very high pressures (Figure 14.10). Under normal conditions, however, hydrogen behaves as a nonmetallic gas.

Figure 14.9
The periodic table is color-coded to show metals, nonmetals, and metalloids.

Ti
Alloys of **titanium** are relatively strong and resistant to corrosion, which makes them useful for hip implants.

C
About 50,000 pounds of synthetic diamonds are produced from **carbon** each year.

He
Helium is formed underground as a by-product of radioactive decay.

Ag
If this **silver** mug were filled with boiling water, the handle would quickly become too hot to handle because silver is one of the best conductors of heat.

Zn
Zinc has a low melting point and is commonly used in making coins.

Si
Cylinders of 99.9999% pure **silicon** are sliced into wafers for the manufacture of integrated circuits.

Hg
Mercury freezes at −40°C and is a liquid at room temperature.

Br
Bromine is a dark orange liquid that readily vaporizes at room temperature.

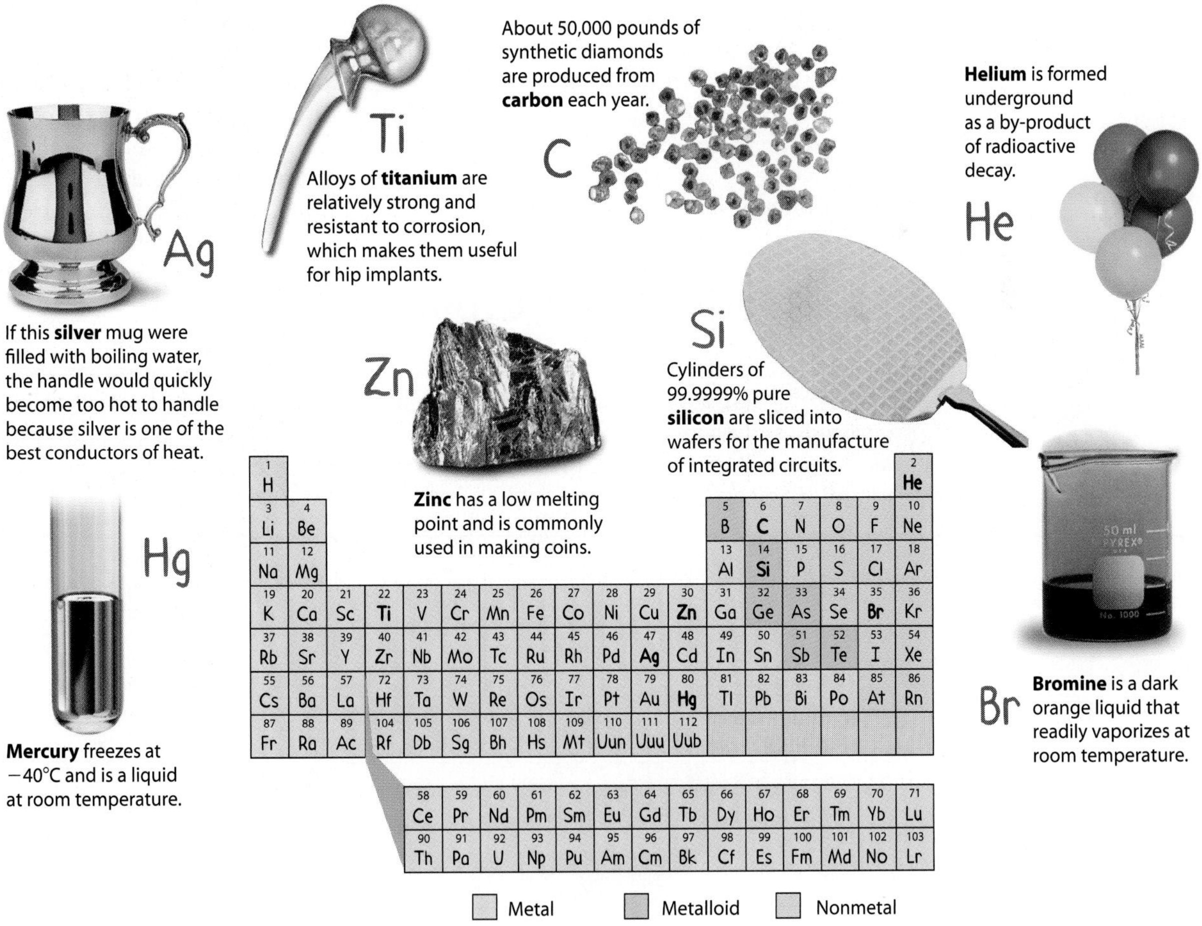

1 H																	2 He
3 Li	4 Be											5 B	6 C	7 N	8 O	9 F	10 Ne
11 Na	12 Mg											13 Al	14 Si	15 P	16 S	17 Cl	18 Ar
19 K	20 Ca	21 Sc	22 Ti	23 V	24 Cr	25 Mn	26 Fe	27 Co	28 Ni	29 Cu	30 Zn	31 Ga	32 Ge	33 As	34 Se	35 Br	36 Kr
37 Rb	38 Sr	39 Y	40 Zr	41 Nb	42 Mo	43 Tc	44 Ru	45 Rh	46 Pd	47 Ag	48 Cd	49 In	50 Sn	51 Sb	52 Te	53 I	54 Xe
55 Cs	56 Ba	57 La	72 Hf	73 Ta	74 W	75 Re	76 Os	77 Ir	78 Pt	79 Au	80 Hg	81 Tl	82 Pb	83 Bi	84 Po	85 At	86 Rn
87 Fr	88 Ra	89 Ac	104 Rf	105 Db	106 Sg	107 Bh	108 Hs	109 Mt	110 Uun	111 Uuu	112 Uub						

58 Ce	59 Pr	60 Nd	61 Pm	62 Sm	63 Eu	64 Gd	65 Tb	66 Dy	67 Ho	68 Er	69 Tm	70 Yb	71 Lu
90 Th	91 Pa	92 U	93 Np	94 Pu	95 Am	96 Cm	97 Bk	98 Cf	99 Es	100 Fm	101 Md	102 No	103 Lr

Metal Metalloid Nonmetal

Figure 14.10
Geoplanetary models suggest that hydrogen exists as a liquid metal deep beneath the surfaces of Jupiter (shown here) and Saturn. These planets are composed mostly of hydrogen. Interior pressures exceed 3 million times the earth's atmospheric pressure. At this tremendously high pressure, hydrogen is pressed to a liquid-metal phase. Back here on the earth, at our relatively low atmospheric pressure, hydrogen exists as a nonmetallic gas.

Please put to rest any fear you may have about needing to memorize the periodic table, or even parts of it—better to focus on the many great concepts behind its organization.

The nonmetallic elements, with the exception of hydrogen, are on the right of the periodic table. Nonmetals are very poor conductors of electricity and heat, and most of them are also transparent. Solid nonmetals are neither malleable nor ductile. Rather, they are brittle and they easily shatter when hammered. At 30°C (86°F), some nonmetals are solid (carbon, C), others are liquid (bromine, Br), and still others are gaseous (helium, He).

Six elements are classified as metalloids: boron, B; silicon, Si; germanium, Ge; arsenic, As; antimony, Sb; and tellurium, Te. Situated between the metals and the nonmetals in the periodic table, the metalloids have both metallic and nonmetallic characteristics. For example, these elements are weak conductors of electricity, which makes them useful as semiconductors in the integrated circuits of computers. Note, from the periodic table, how germanium, Ge (number 32), is closer to the metals than to the nonmetals. Because of this positioning, we can deduce that germanium has more metallic properties than silicon, Si (number 14), and is a slightly better conductor of electricity. So we find that integrated circuits fabricated with germanium operate faster than those fabricated with silicon. Because silicon is much more abundant and less expensive to obtain, however, silicon computer chips remain the industry standard.

14.6 Periods and Groups

Two other important ways in which the elements are organized in the periodic table are by horizontal rows and vertical columns. Each horizontal row is called a **period,** and each vertical column is called a **group** (or sometimes a *family*). As shown in Figure 14.11, there are 7 periods and 18 groups.

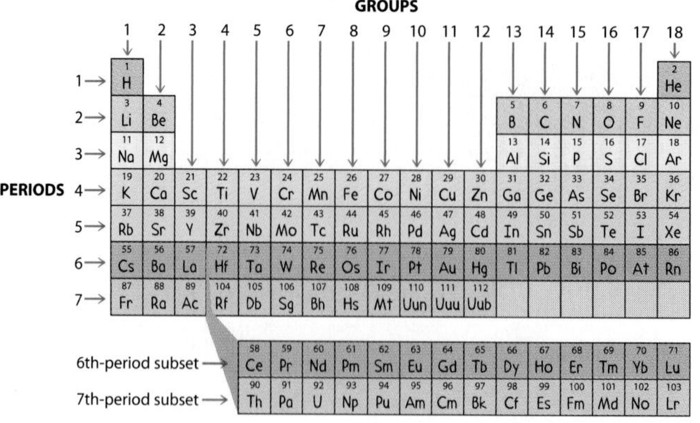

Figure 14.11
The seven periods (horizontal rows) and eighteen groups (vertical columns) of the periodic table. Note that not all periods contain the same number of elements. Also note that, for reasons that will be explained later, the sixth and seventh periods each include a subset of elements that are listed apart from the main body of the table.

Across any period, the properties of elements gradually change. This gradual change is called a periodic trend. As shown in Figure 14.12, one periodic trend is that atomic size tends to decrease as you move from left to right across any period. Note that the trend repeats from one horizontal row to the next. This phenomenon of repeating trends is called periodicity, a term used to indicate that the trends recur in cycles. Each horizontal row is called a period because it corresponds to one full cycle of a trend.

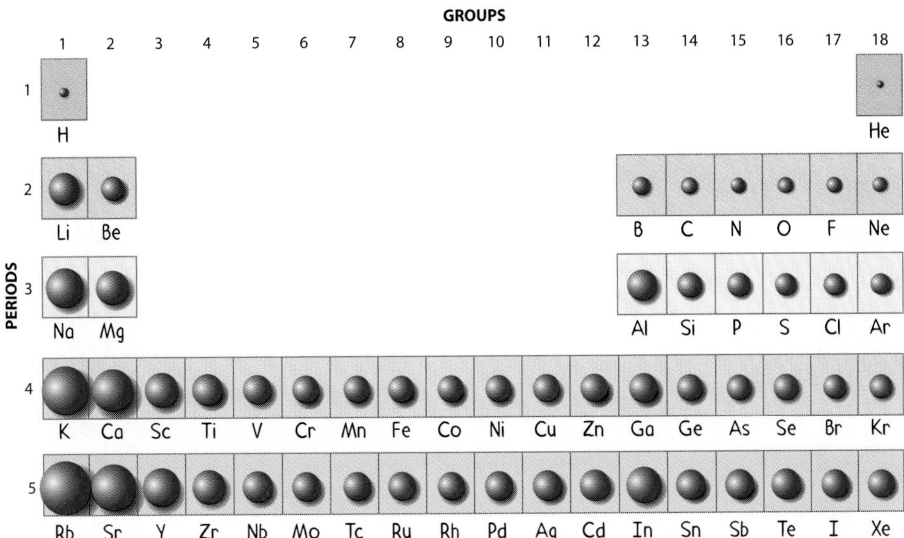

Figure 14.12
The sizes of atoms gradually decrease from left to right across any period. Atomic size is a periodic (repeating) property.

There are many other properties of elements that change gradually in moving from left to right across the periodic table. An important property we'll be discussing in Chapter 19 is the ability of an atom to attract more electrons than it already has. This property goes by the name *electronegativity*. As shown in Figure 14.13, there is a periodic trend such that elements to the lower left of the periodic table have the smallest electronegativities, while elements to the upper right (group 18 elements excluded) have the largest electronegativities.

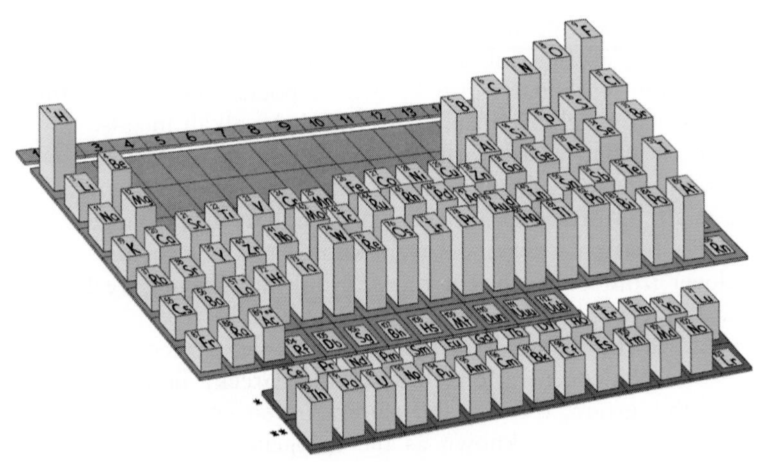

Figure 14.13
Atoms toward the upper right side of the periodic table have a greater ability to attract additional electrons (electronegativity) than do atoms toward the lower left.

☑ CHECKPOINT

Which are larger: atoms of cesium, Cs (number 55), or atoms of radon, Rn (number 86)?

Check Your Answer

Perhaps you tried looking to Figure 14.12 to answer this question and quickly became frustrated because the sixth-period elements are not shown. Well, relax. Look at the trends and you'll see that, in any one period, all atoms to the left are larger than those to the right. Accordingly, cesium is positioned at the far left of period 6, and so you can reasonably predict that its atoms are larger than those of radon, which is positioned at the far right of period 6. The periodic table is a road map to understanding the elements.

A uranium atom is 40 times heavier than a lithium atom, but only slightly larger in size because its more highly charged nucleus pulls harder on its electrons. But it has more electrons to pull, a balancing act that barely changes the atom's size.

Insights

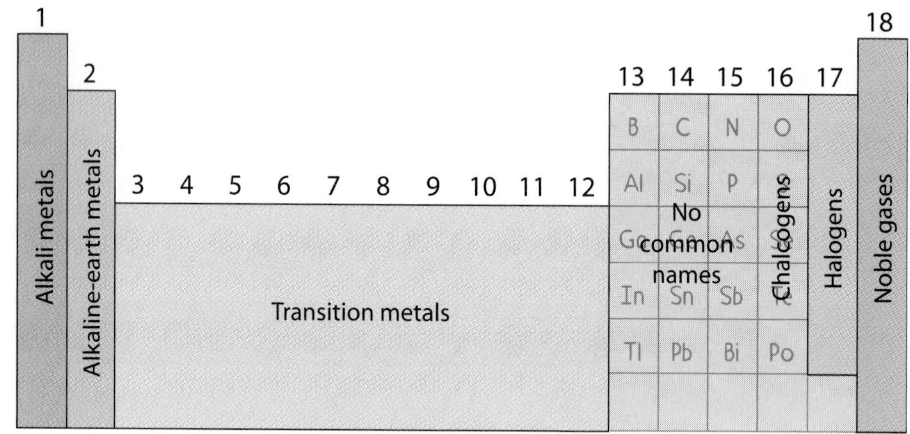

Figure 14.14
The common names for various groups of elements.

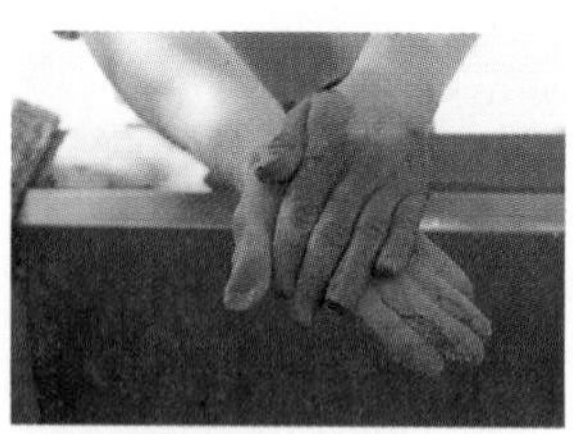

Figure 14.15
Ashes and water make a slippery alkaline solution once used to clean hands.

Down any group (vertical column), the properties of the elements tend to be remarkably similar, which is why these elements are said to be "grouped" or "in a family." As Figure 14.14 shows, several groups have traditional names that describe the properties of their elements. Early in human history, people discovered that ashes mixed with water produce a slippery solution useful for removing grease. By the Middle Ages, such mixtures were described as being alkaline, a term derived from the Arabic al-qily ("the ashes"). Alkaline mixtures found many uses, particularly in the preparation of soaps (Figure 14.15). We now know that alkaline ashes contain compounds of group 1 elements, most notably potassium carbonate, also known as potash. Because of this history, group 1 elements, which are metals, are called the alkali metals.

Elements of group 2 also form alkaline solutions when mixed with water. Furthermore, medieval alchemists noted that certain minerals (which we now know are made up of group 2 elements) do not melt or change when put in fire. These fire-resistant substances were known to the alchemists as "earths." As a holdover from these ancient times, group 2 elements are known as the alkaline-earth metals.

Over toward the right side of the periodic table, elements of group 16 are known as the chalcogens ("ore-forming" in Greek) because the top two elements of this group, oxygen and sulfur, are so commonly found in ores. Elements of group 17 are known as the halogens ("salt-forming" in Greek) because of their tendency to form various salts. Interestingly, a small amount of the halogen iodine or the halogen bromine inside a lamp allows the lamp's tungsten filament to glow more brightly without burning out so quickly. Such lamps are commonly referred to as halogen lamps. Group 18 elements are all unreactive gases that tend not to combine with other elements. For this reason, they are called the noble gases, presumably because the nobility of earlier times were above interacting with common folk.

The elements of groups 3 through 12 are all metals that do not form alkaline solutions with water. These metals tend to be harder than the alkali metals and less reactive with water; hence they are used for structural purposes. Collectively they are known as the transition metals, a name that denotes their central position in the periodic table. The transition metals include some of the most familiar and important elements—iron, Fe; copper, Cu; nickel, Ni; chromium, Cr; silver, Ag; and gold, Au. They also include many lesser-known elements that are nonetheless significant in modern technology. People with hip replacements should appreciate the transition metals—especially titanium, Ti; molybdenum, Mo; and manganese, Mn—because these corrosion-resistant metals are used in artificial hip joints and other implant devices.

☑ CHECKPOINT

The elements copper, Cu; silver, Ag; and gold, Au, are three of the few metals that can be found naturally in their elemental state. These three metals have found great use as currency and jewelry for a number of reasons, including their resistance to corrosion and their remarkable colors. How is the fact that these metals have similar properties reflected in the periodic table?

Check Your Answer

Copper (number 29), silver (number 47), and gold (number 79) are all in the same group in the periodic table (group 11), which suggests they should have similar—though not identical—properties.

Some scientists shake their heads and say they don't know anything. By this they mean that what they *do* know is closer to nothing than to what they *can* know. Scientists know enough to realize they have a relatively small handle on an enormous universe still full of mysteries. Today's scientists know enormously more than their predecessors a century ago, and scientists then knew much more than *their* predecessors. Looking forward, there is so much yet to be learned. Perhaps the next level of science will go beyond *how* to *why*—to meaning. We have scarcely scratched the surface.

Insights

In the sixth period is a subset of 14 metallic elements (numbers 58 to 71) that are quite unlike any of the other transition metals. A similar subset (numbers 90 to 103) is found in the seventh period. These two subsets are the inner transition metals. Inserting the inner transition metals into the main body of the periodic table, as in Figure 14.16, results in a long and cumbersome table. So that the table can fit nicely on a standard paper size, these elements are commonly placed below the main body of the table, as shown on page 354 in Figure 14.17.

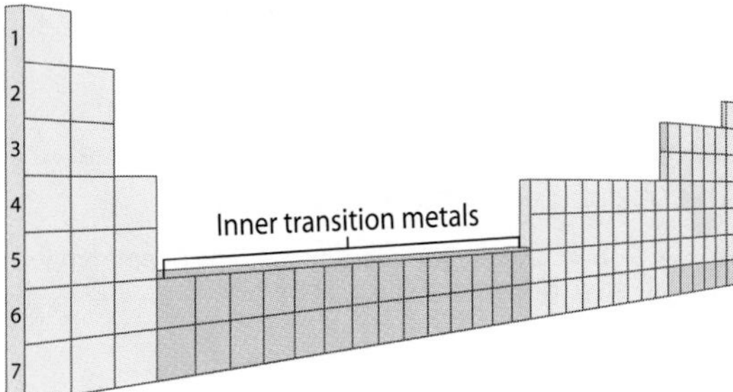

Figure 14.16
Inserting the inner transition metals between atomic groups 3 and 4 results in a periodic table that is not easy to fit on a standard sheet of paper.

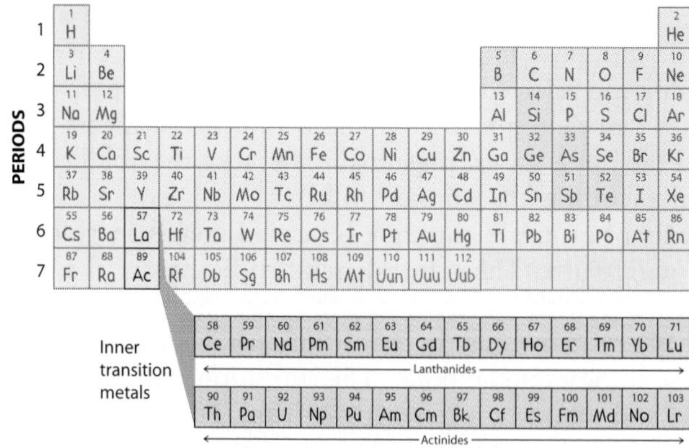

Figure 14.17
The typical display of the inner transition metals. The count of elements in the sixth period goes from lanthanum (La, 57) to cerium (Ce, 58) on through to lutetium (Lu, 71) and then back to hafnium (Hf, 72). A similar jump in numbering occurs in the seventh period.

The Placebo Effect*

Let's take a short break in our study of atoms to examine a scientific phenomenon known as the placebo effect.

People have always sought healers for help with physical pain and fear. As treatment, traditional healers often administer herbs, chant, or wave their hands over a patient's body. And improvement, more often than not, actually occurs! This is the *placebo effect.* A placebo may be a healing practice or a substance (pill) containing elements or molecules that have no medicinal value. But, remarkably, the placebo effect does have a biological basis. It so happens that, when you are fearful or in pain, your brain response is *not* to mobilize your body's healing mechanism—instead, it prepares your body for some external threat. It's an evolutionary adaptation that assigns highest priority to preventing additional injury. Stress hormones released into the bloodstream increase respiration, blood pressure, and heart rate—changes that usually *impede* recovery. The brain prepares your body for action; recovery can wait.

That's why the first objective of a good healer or physician is to relieve stress. Most of us begin feeling better even before leaving the healer or doctor's office. Prior to 1940, most medicine was based on the placebo effect, when about the only medicines doctors had in their bags were laxatives, aspirin, and sugar pills. In about half the cases, a sugar pill is as effective in stopping pain as an aspirin. Here's why. Pain is a signal to the brain that something is wrong and needs attention. The signal is induced at the site of inflammation by prostaglandins released by white blood cells. Aspirin blocks the production of prostaglandins and therefore relieves pain. The mechanism for pain relief by a placebo is altogether different. The placebo fools the brain into thinking that whatever is wrong is being cared for. Then the pain signal is lowered by the release of endorphins, opiate-like proteins produced naturally in the brain. So, instead of blocking the *production* of prostaglandins, the endorphins block their *effect.* With pain alleviated, the body can focus on healing.

The placebo effect has always been employed (and still is!) by healers and others who claim to have wondrous cures that lie outside modern medicine. These healers benefit from the public's tendency to believe that if B follows A, then B is *caused* by A. The cure could be due to the healer, but it could also merely be the body repairing itself. Although the placebo effect can certainly influence the perception of pain, it has not been shown to influence the body's ability to fight infection or repair injury.

Is the placebo effect at work for those who believe that better health is bequeathed to those who wear crystals, magnets, or certain metal bracelets? If so, is there any harm in thinking so—even if there is no scientific evidence for it? Harboring positive beliefs is usually quite harmless—but not always. For serious problems requiring modern medical treatment, reliance on these aids can be disastrous if it is used to the exclusion of modern medical treatment. The placebo effect has real limitations.

*Adapted from Robert L. Park, *Voodoo Science: The Road from Foolishness to Fraud.* New York: Oxford University Press, 2000.

The sixth-period inner transition metals are called the lanthanides because they fall after lanthanum, La. Because of their similar physical and chemical properties, they tend to occur mixed together in the same locations in the earth. Also because of their similarities, lanthanides are unusually difficult to purify. Recently, the commercial use of lanthanides has increased. Several lanthanide elements, for example, are used in the fabrication of the light-emitting diodes (LEDs) of laptop computer monitors.

The seventh-period inner transition metals are called the actinides because they fall after actinium, Ac. They, too, all have similar properties and hence are not easily purified. The nuclear power industry faces this obstacle because it requires purified samples of two of the most publicized actinides: uranium, U, and plutonium, Pu. Actinides heavier than uranium are not found in nature but are synthesized in the laboratory.

Summary of Terms

Atom The smallest particle of an element that has all of the element's chemical properties.

Element Any material that is made up of only one type of atom.

Periodic table A chart in which all known elements are listed in order of atomic number.

Atomic symbol An abbreviation for an element or atom.

Atomic nucleus The core of an atom, consisting of two basic subatomic particles—protons and neutrons.

Electron A negatively charged particle in an atom.

Proton A positively charged particle in an atomic nucleus.

Atomic number The number that designates the identity of an element, which is the number of protons in the nucleus of an atom; in a neutral atom, the atomic number is also the number of electrons in the atom.

Mass number The total number of nucleons in an atomic nucleus.

Neutron An electrically neutral subatomic particle in an atomic nucleus.

Nucleon A nuclear particle; a proton or a neutron in an atomic nucleus.

Isotopes Different forms of an element whose atoms contain the same number of protons but different numbers of neutrons.

Atomic mass The mass of an element's atoms listed in the periodic table as an average value based on the relative abundance of the element's isotopes.

Atomic mass unit (amu) The standard unit of atomic mass, which is equal to one-twelfth the mass of the common atom of carbon, arbitrarily given the value of exactly 12.

Period A horizontal row in the periodic table.

Group A vertical column in the periodic table, also known as a family of elements.

Review Questions

14.1 The Elements

1. How many types of atoms can you expect to find in a sample of any element?
2. Distinguish between an atom and an element.

14.2 Atoms Are Ancient and Empty

3. Which is the oldest element?
4. Why is it not possible to see an atom using visible light?
5. What is the cause of Brownian motion?
6. What is at the center of every atom?
7. If atoms are mostly empty space, why can't we walk through walls?
8. What kind of force prevents atoms from squishing into one another?

14.3 Protons and Neutrons

9. A proton is how much more massive than an electron?
10. Compare the electric charge on a proton with the electric charge on an electron.
11. What is the definition of atomic number?
12. What role does atomic number play in the periodic table?

14.4 Isotopes and Atomic Mass

13. What effect do isotopes of a given element have on the atomic mass calculated for that element?
14. Name two nucleons.
15. Distinguish between atomic number and mass number.
16. Distinguish between mass number and atomic mass.

14.5 The Periodic Table

17. How is the periodic table more than just a listing of the known elements?

18. Are most elements metallic or nonmetallic?
19. Why is hydrogen most often considered a nonmetallic element?
20. How do the physical properties of nonmetals differ from the physical properties of metals?
21. Where are metalloids located in the periodic table?

14.6 Periods and Groups

22. How many periods are there in the periodic table?
23. How many groups are there in the periodic table?
24. What happens to the properties of elements across any period of the periodic table?
25. Why are group 1 elements called alkali metals?
26. Why are group 17 elements called halogens?
27. Which group of elements consists of only gases at room temperature?
28. Why are the inner transition metals not listed in the main body of the periodic table?
29. Why is it difficult to purify an inner transition metal?
30. What two inner transition metals are used to fuel nuclear power plants?

Exercises

1. A cat strolls across your backyard. An hour later, a dog with its nose to the ground follows the trail of the cat. Explain what is going on in terms of atoms.
2. Which of the following is not an element: hydrogen, carbon, oxygen, water?
3. If all the atoms of a body remained part of that body, would the body have any odor?
4. Which are older, the hydrogen atoms in a young star or those in an old star?
5. In what sense can you truthfully say that you are a part of every person around you?
6. Where were the atoms that make up a newborn baby manufactured?
7. Considering how small atoms are, what are the chances that at least one of the atoms exhaled in your first breath will be in your last breath?
8. Computer chips made of germanium, Ge (number 32), operate faster than computer chips made of silicon, Si (number 14). So how might a computer chip made of gallium, Ga (number 31), compare with a germanium chip?
9. Helium, He, is a nonmetallic gas and the second element in the periodic table. Rather than being placed adjacent to hydrogen, H, however, helium is placed on the far right of the table. Why?
10. Name ten elements you have access to in macroscopic quantities as a consumer here on the earth.
11. Radioactive strontium, Sr (number 38), is especially dangerous to humans because it tends to accumulate in calcium-dependent bone marrow tissues (calcium, Ca, number 20). How does this fact relate to what you know about the organization of the periodic table?
12. With the periodic table as your guide, describe the element selenium, Se (number 34), using as many of this chapter's key terms as you can.
13. Which of the following diagrams best represent the size of the atomic nucleus relative to the size of the atom:

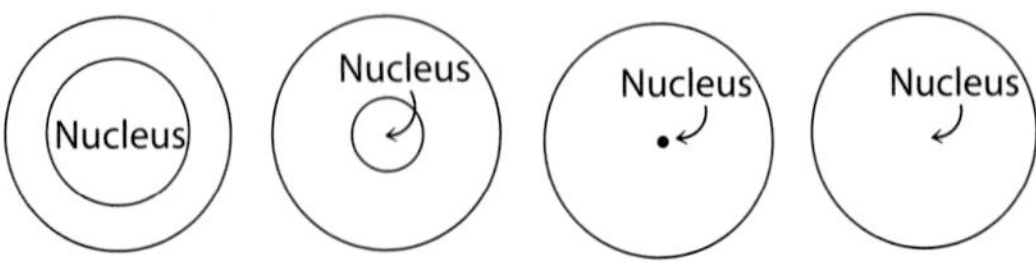

14. Which contributes more to an atom's mass: electrons or protons? Which contributes more to an atom's size?
15. If two protons and two neutrons are removed from the nucleus of an oxygen atom, a nucleus of which element remains?
16. You could swallow a capsule of germanium, Ge (atomic number 32), without ill effects. If a proton were added to each germanium nucleus, however, you would not want to swallow the capsule. Why? (Consult a periodic table of the elements.)
17. Which would be the more valued result: removing one proton from each nucleus of a sample of gold or adding one proton to each gold nucleus? Explain.
18. What element results if one of the neutrons in a nitrogen nucleus is converted by radioactive decay into a proton?
19. What element is produced if you add a pair of protons to the nucleus of mercury?
20. What element results if two protons and two neutrons are ejected from a radium nucleus?
21. The atoms that constitute your body are mostly empty space, and structures such as the chair you're sitting on are composed of atoms that are also mostly empty space. So why don't you fall through the chair?
22. What atoms result when water is chemically decomposed?
23. What happens to the properties of elements across any period of the periodic table?
24. If an atom has 43 electrons, 56 neutrons, and 43 protons, what is its approximate atomic mass? What is the name of this element?
25. The nucleus of an electrically neutral iron atom contains 26 protons. How many electrons does this iron atom have?
26. Evidence for the existence of neutrons did not come until many years after the discoveries of the electron and the proton. Give a possible explanation.

27. Which has more atoms: a 1-gram sample of carbon-12 or a 1-gram sample of carbon-13? Explain.
28. Why are the atomic masses listed in the periodic table not whole numbers?
29. Where did the carbon atoms in Leslie's hair originate? (Shown at right is a photo of coauthor Leslie at age 16.)

30. Make up a multiple-choice question that will test your classmates on the distinction between any two terms in the Summary of Terms list.

Problems

1. The isotope lithium-7 has a mass of 7.0160 atomic mass units, and the isotope lithium-6 has a mass of 6.0151 atomic mass units. Given the information that 92.58 percent of all lithium atoms found in nature are lithium-7 and 7.42 percent are lithium-6, calculate the atomic mass of lithium, Li (atomic number 3).
2. The element bromine, Br (atomic number 35), has two major isotopes of similar abundance, both approximately 50 percent. The atomic mass of bromine is reported in the periodic table as 79.904 atomic mass units. Choose the most likely set of mass numbers for these two bromine isotopes: (a) ^{80}Br, ^{81}Br; (b) ^{79}Br, ^{80}Br; (c) ^{79}Br, ^{81}Br.

Chapter 14 Online Resources

Tutorials
- Atoms & Isotopes
- Periodic Table

Videos
- Evidence for Atoms
- Atoms are Recyclable

Quiz
Exercises
Flashcards
Links

CHAPTER 15

Atomic Models

The elements of many chemical compounds glow with color when heated. Strontium, for example, glows red, sodium glows yellow, and barium glows yellow-green. Package such elements with burning gun powder, and the result is a brilliant fireworks display. Interestingly, the glow of a single element consists of a number of overlapping colors, which can be separated from one another with a prism. Such a separation is shown in the opening photograph of this chapter. In the center of the photograph are the glowing sparks of strontium. The adjacent diagonal stripes, created by a prismlike filter on the camera, reveal its many hues, called a spectral pattern.

Each element emits its own characteristic spectral pattern, which can be used to identify the element just as a fingerprint can be used to identify a person. Scientists of the early 1900s saw these spectral patterns as clues to the internal structure and dynamics of atoms. By studying spectral patterns and by conducting experiments, they were able to develop models of the atom. Through these models, which continue to be refined in present times, chemists gain a powerful understanding of how atoms behave.

15.1 Physical and Conceptual Models

Atoms are so small that the number of them in a baseball is roughly equal to the number of Ping-Pong balls that could fit inside a hollow sphere as big as the earth, as Figure 15.1 illustrates. This number is incredibly large—beyond our intuitive grasp. Atoms are so incredibly small that we can never see them in the usual sense. As mentioned in Chapter 13, light travels in waves, and atoms are smaller than the wavelengths of visible light, the light that humans can see. We could stack microscope on top of microscope and still not see an individual atom. As illustrated in Figure 15.2, the diameter of an object that is visible under the highest magnification must be larger than the wavelengths of visible light.

Although we cannot see atoms *directly*, we can generate images of them *indirectly*. In the mid-1980s, researchers developed the *scanning tunneling microscope* (STM), which produces images by dragging an ultrathin needle back and forth over the surface of a sample. Bumps the size of atoms

Figure 15.1
If the earth were filled with nothing but Ping-Pong balls, the number of balls would be roughly equal to the number of atoms in a baseball. Put differently, if a baseball were the size of the earth, one of its atoms would be the size of a Ping-Pong ball.

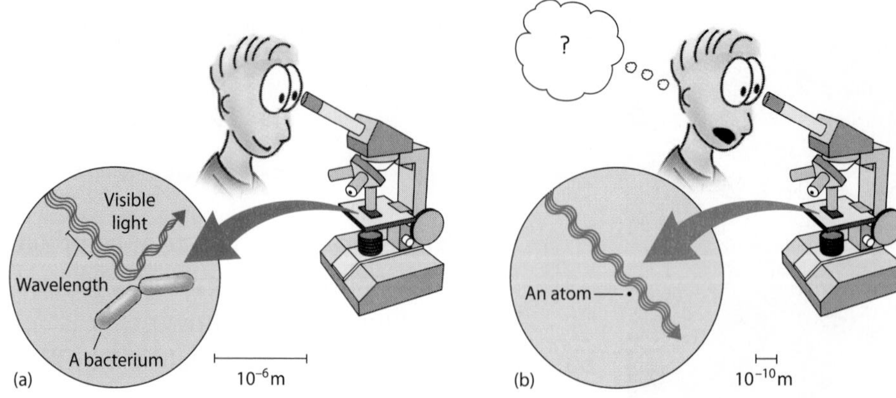

Figure 15.2
Microscopic objects can be seen through a microscope that works with visible light, but submicroscopic particles cannot. (a) A bacterium is visible because it is larger than the wavelengths of visible light. We can see the bacterium through the microscope because the bacterium reflects visible light. (b) An atom is invisible because it is smaller than the wavelengths of visible light, and so it does not reflect the light toward our eyes.

on the surface cause the needle to move up and down. This vertical motion is detected and translated by a computer into a topographical image that corresponds to the positions of atoms on the surface (Figure 15.3). An STM can also be used to push individual atoms into desired positions. This ability opened up the field of nanotechnology, in which incredibly small electronic circuits and motors are built atom by atom.

A machinist makes things by shaving off material. Nature, however, has always done what nanotechnologists are beginning to do—build things atom by atom—the way a tree grows, for example.

☑ CHECKPOINT

Why are atoms invisible?

Check Your Answer

Because an individual atom is smaller than the wavelengths of visible light, it is unable to reflect that light. Atoms are invisible, therefore, because visible light passes right by them. The atomic images generated by STMs are not photographs taken by a camera. Rather, they are computer renditions generated from the movements of an ultrathin needle.

Figure 15.3
(a) Scanning tunneling microscopes are relatively simple devices used to create submicroscopic imagery. (b) An image of gallium and arsenic atoms obtained with an STM. (c) Each dot in the world's tiniest map consists of a few thousand gold atoms, each atom moved into its proper location by an STM.

Visible objects, whether very small or very large, can be represented with a **physical model,** which is a model that replicates the object at a more convenient scale. Figure 15.4a, for instance, shows a large-scale physical model of a microorganism that a biology student uses to study the microorganism's internal structure. Applying a physical model to invisible atoms, however, is ineffective. We cannot simply scale up the atom to a larger size, as we might with a microorganism. (An STM merely shows the *positions* of atoms and not the actual images of atoms, which do not have the solid surfaces implied in the STM images of Figure 15.3.) So, rather than describing the atom with a physical model, chemists use what is known as a **conceptual model** to describe it. The more accurate a conceptual model is, the more accurately it predicts the behavior of the system it is meant to describe. The weather is best described using a conceptual model like the one shown in Figure 15.4b. Such a model shows how the various components of the system—humidity, atmospheric pressure, temperature, electric charge, the motion of large masses of air—interact with one another. Other systems that can be described effectively by conceptual models include the economy, population growth, the spread of diseases, and team sports.

☑ CHECKPOINT

A basketball coach describes a playing strategy to her team by way of sketches on a game card. Do the illustrations represent a physical model or a conceptual model?

Check Your Answer

The sketches are a conceptual model used to describe a system (the players on the court), with the hope of predicting an outcome (winning the game).

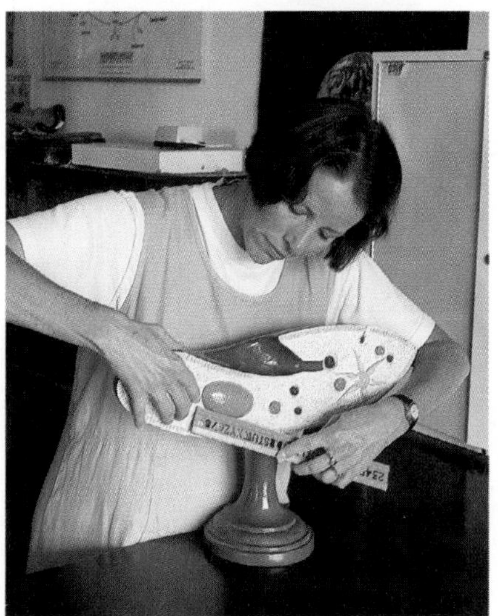

(a)

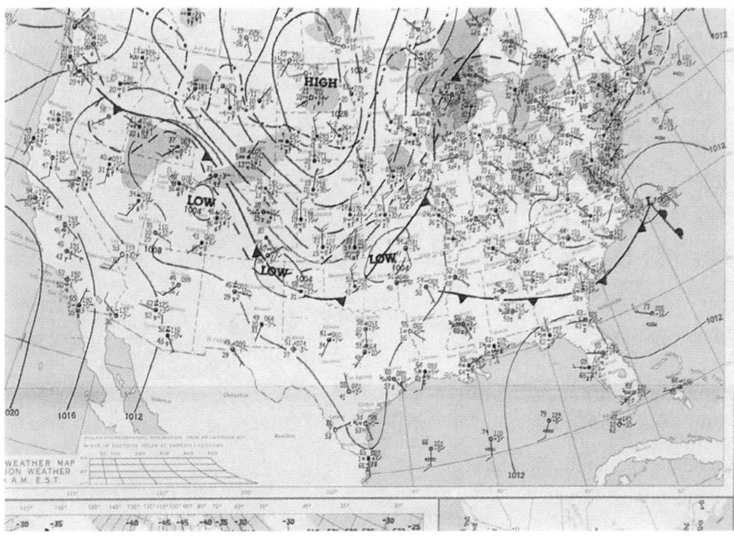

(b)

Figure 15.4
(a) This large-scale model of a microorganism is a physical model. (b) Weather forecasters rely on conceptual models, such as this one, to predict the behavior of weather systems.

We can't "see" an atom because it's too small. We can't see the farthest star either. There's much that we can't see. But that doesn't prevent us from thinking about such things or even collecting indirect evidence.

Insights

Like the weather, the atom is a complex system of interacting components, and it is best described with a conceptual model. You should therefore be careful not to interpret any visual representation of an atomic conceptual model as a re-creation of an actual atom. In following sections of this chapter, for example, you will be introduced to the planetary model of the atom, wherein electrons are shown orbiting the atomic nucleus much as planets orbit the sun. This planetary model is limited, however, in that it fails to explain many properties of atoms. Hence, newer and more accurate (and more complicated) conceptual models of the atom have since been introduced. In these models, electrons appear as a cloud hovering around the atomic nucleus, but even these models have their limitations. Ultimately, the best models of the atom are ones that are purely mathematical.

In this textbook, our focus is on conceptual atomic models that are easily represented by visual images, including the planetary model, the electron-cloud model, and a model in which electrons are grouped in units called shells. Despite their limitations, such images are excellent guides to learning chemistry, especially for the beginning student. As you will see in following sections, these models were developed by scientists to help explain how atoms emit light.

15.2 Identifying Atoms Using the Spectroscope

Recall (from Chapter 12) that, when all frequencies of visible light reach our eye at the same time, we see white light. By passing white light through a prism or through a diffraction grating, the color components of the light can be separated, as shown in Figure 15.5. (Remember that each color of visible light corresponds to a different frequency.) A **spectroscope,** shown in Figure 15.6, is an instrument used to observe the color components of any light source. The spectroscope allows us to analyze the light emitted by elements when they are made to glow.

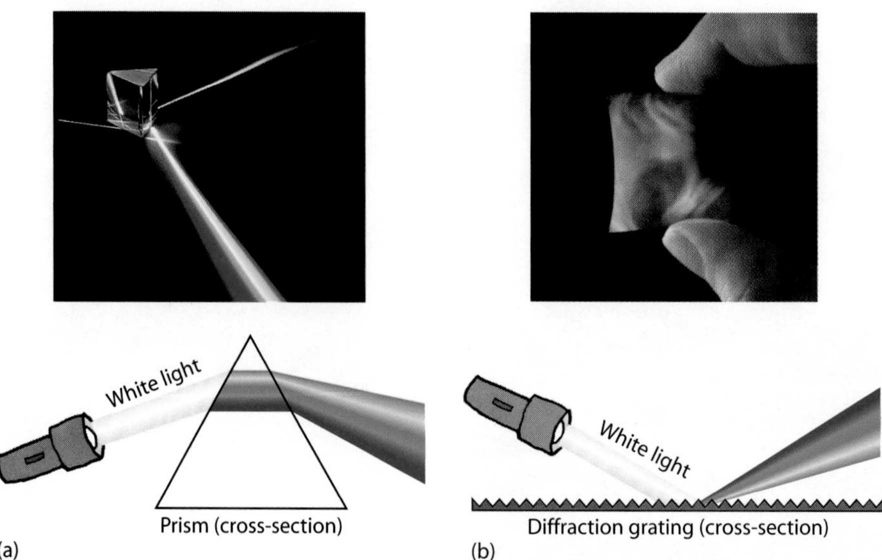

Figure 15.5
White light is separated into its color components by (a) a prism and (b) a diffraction grating.

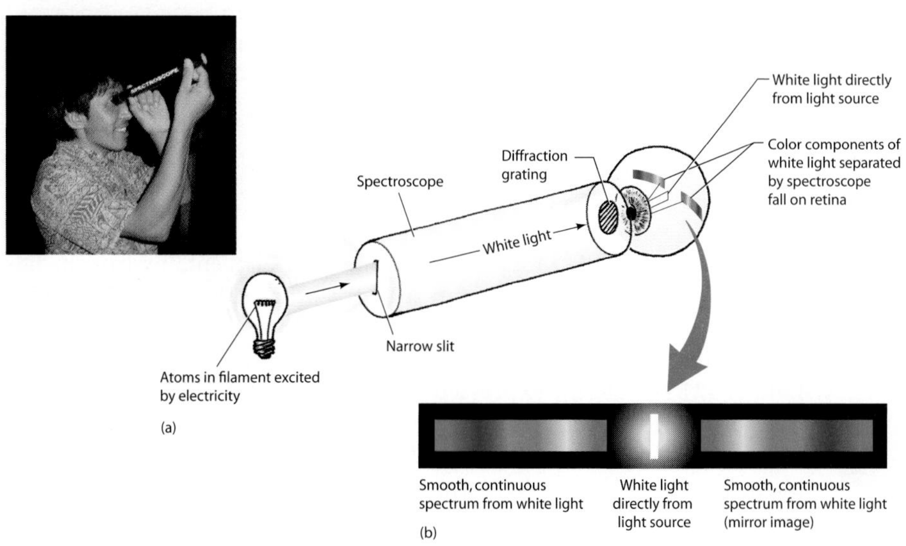

Figure 15.6
(a) In a spectroscope, light emitted by atoms passes through a narrow slit before being separated into particular frequencies by a prism or (as shown here) a diffraction grating. (b) This is what the eye sees when the slit of a diffraction-grating spectroscope is pointed toward a white-light source. Spectra of colors appear to the left and right of the slit.

Insights

Emission spectra are in the shape of lines because they are images of a line-shaped slit through which light is passed before it meets the prism or diffraction grating.

Light is emitted by atoms subjected to various forms of energy, such as heat or electricity. The atoms of a given element emit only certain frequencies of light, however. As a consequence, each element emits a distinctive glow when energized. As mentioned at the beginning of this chapter, sodium atoms emit bright yellow light, which makes them useful as the light source in street lamps, because our eyes are very sensitive to yellow light. Another example is neon atoms, which emit a brilliant red-orange light when used as the light source in neon signs.

When we view the light from glowing atoms through a spectroscope, we see that the light consists of a number of discrete (separate) frequencies rather than a continuous spectrum, like the one shown in Figure 15.6. The pattern of frequencies formed by a given element—some of which are shown in Figure 15.7—is referred to as that element's **atomic spectrum.** The atomic spectrum is an element's fingerprint. You can identify the elements in a light source by analyzing the light through a spectroscope and looking for characteristic patterns. If you don't have the opportunity to work with a spectroscope in your laboratory, check out the activities at the end of this chapter.

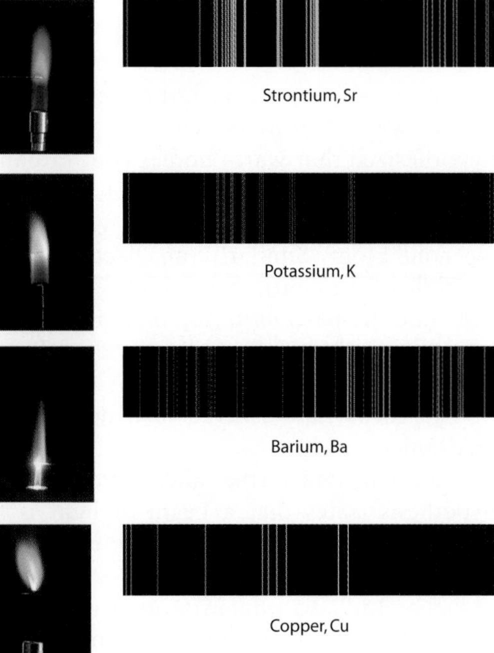

Figure 15.7
Elements heated by a flame glow their characteristic color. This is commonly called a flame test, and it is used to test for the presence of an element in a sample. When viewed through a spectroscope, the color of each element is revealed to consist of a pattern of distinct frequencies known as an atomic spectrum.

☑ CHECKPOINT

How might you deduce the elemental composition of a star?

Check Your Answer

Aim a well-built spectroscope at the star, and study its spectral patterns.

Researchers in the 1800s noted that the lightest element, hydrogen, has a far more orderly atomic spectrum than those of other elements. Figure 15.8 shows a portion of the hydrogen spectrum. Note that the spacing between successive lines decreases in a regular way. A Swiss schoolteacher, Johann Balmer (1825–1898), expressed these line positions by a mathematical formula. Another regularity in hydrogen's atomic spectrum was noticed by Johannes Rydberg (1854–1919)—the sum of the frequencies of two lines often equals the frequency of a third line. For example,

Figure 15.8
A portion of the atomic spectrum for hydrogen. These frequencies are higher than those of visible light, which is why they are not shown in color.

First spectral line 1.6×10^{14} Hz

Second spectral line $+\ 4.6 \times 10^{14}$ Hz

Third spectral line 6.2×10^{14} Hz

The orderliness of hydrogen's atomic spectrum was most intriguing to Balmer, Rydberg, and other investigators of the time. However, these early investigators were unable to formulate any hypothesis as to *why* such orderliness should exist that agreed with any acceptable atomic model of the day.

In the late 1800s, spectroscopes were pointed to the sun. Spectral patterns of hydrogen and some other known elements were observed, in addition to one pattern that couldn't be identified. Scientists concluded that this unidentified pattern belonged to an element not yet discovered on the earth. They named this element *helium* (after *helios,* the Greek word for sun).

Insights

15.3 The Quantum Hypothesis

An important step toward our present-day understanding of atoms and their spectra was taken by the German physicist Max Planck (1858–1947). Planck hypothesized that warm bodies emit radiant energy in discrete bundles, which he called **quanta** (*quanta* is the plural form of *quantum*). The mass of a gold brick, for example, equals some whole number multiple of the mass of a single gold atom. Similarly, an electric charge is always some whole-number multiple of the charge on a single electron. Mass and electric charge are therefore said to be *quantized,* in that they consist of some whole number of fundamental units. According to Planck, the energy in each energy bundle is proportional to the frequency of radiation. His hypothesis began a revolution of ideas that ushered in a new view of the physical world—**quantum mechanics.**

Einstein went further and stated that light itself is quantized. The **quantum hypothesis** states that a beam of light is not the continuous (nonquantized) stream of energy we usually think it is. Instead, the beam consists of countless small, discrete particles of energy, each particle called a **quantum,** as represented in Figure 15.9. To emphasize its particle nature, each quantum of light came to be called a *photon,* a name coined on the model of such words as electron, proton, and neutron.

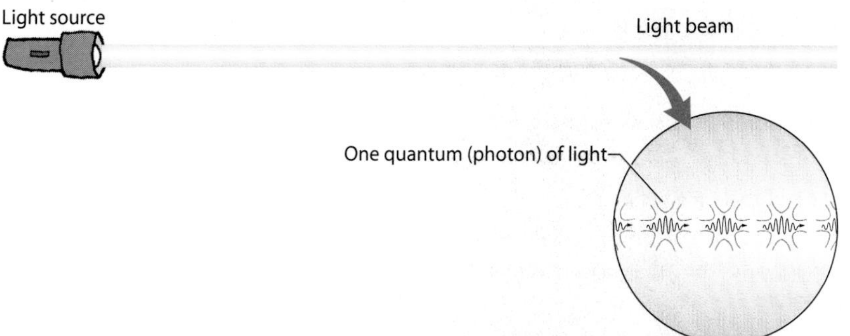

Figure 15.9
Light is quantized, which means it consists of a stream of energy packets. Each packet is called a quantum, also known as a photon.

Recall, from Section 13.6, that light travels as a wave but hits as a stream of photons. So, when scientists study light, they are free to choose the model that best fits their needs—light as a wave or light as a stream of particles. Depending on the model chosen, light has the properties of a wave or the properties of a particle. To represent this duality, photons are illustrated in this text as a burst of light with a wave drawn inside the burst.

Recall, from Chapter 13, that the amount of energy in a photon is directly proportional to the frequency of the light ($E \sim f$). One photon of ultraviolet light, for example, possesses more energy than one photon of infrared light because ultraviolet light has higher frequency than infrared light.

Using Planck's quantum hypothesis, the Danish scientist Niels Bohr (1885–1962) explained the formation of atomic spectra as follows. First, Bohr recognized that the potential energy of an electron in an atom depends on the electron's distance from the nucleus. This is analogous to the potential energy of an object held some distance above the earth's surface. The object has more potential energy when it is held high above the ground than when it is held close to the ground. Likewise, an electron has more potential energy when it is far from the nucleus than when it is close to the nucleus. Second, Bohr recognized that, when an atom absorbs a photon of light, it is absorbing energy. This energy is acquired by one of the electrons surrounding the atom's nucleus. Because this electron has gained energy, it must move away from the nucleus. In other words, absorption of a photon causes a low-potential-energy electron in an atom to become a high-potential-energy electron.

Bohr also realized that the opposite is true: when a high-potential-energy electron in an atom loses some of its energy, the electron moves closer to the nucleus, and the energy lost from the electron is emitted from the atom as a photon of light. Both absorption and emission are illustrated in Figure 15.11.

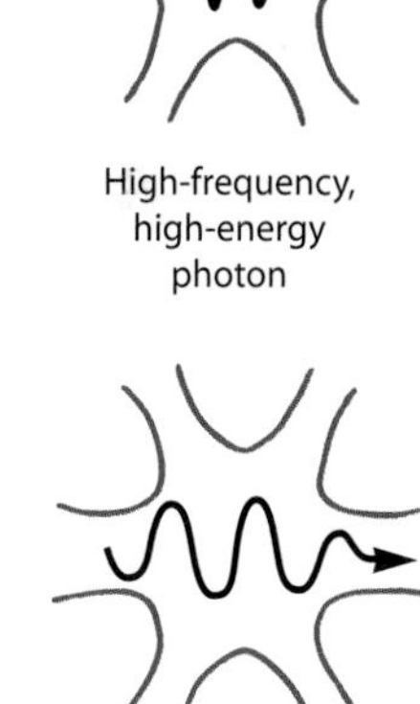

Figure 15.10
The greater the frequency of a photon of light, the greater the energy packed into that photon.

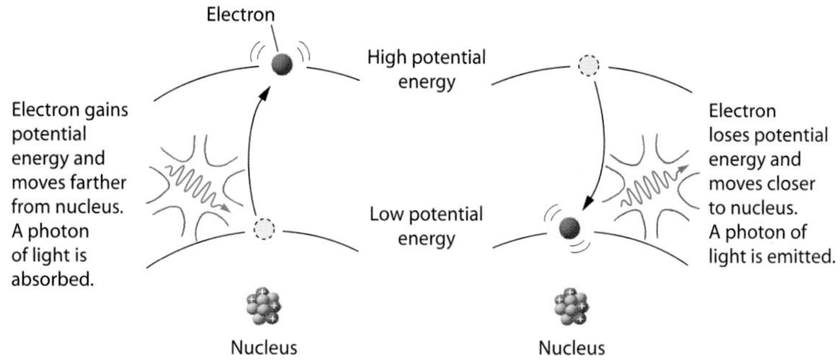

Figure 15.11
An electron is lifted away from the nucleus as the atom it is in absorbs a photon of light, and it drops closer to the nucleus as the atom releases a photon of light.

☑ CHECKPOINT

1. Define the term *quantum.*
2. Which has more energy: a photon of red light or a photon of infrared light?

Check Your Answers

1. A *quantum* is the smallest elemental unit of a quantity. Light (or any form of radiant energy), for example, is composed of many quanta, each of which is called a *photon.*
2. As shown in Figure 15.10, red light has a higher frequency than infrared light, which means a photon of red light has more energy than a photon of infrared light.

For many years, scientists were ambivalent about the particle nature of light. In early textbooks, light was called *corpuscular.* Corpuscles of light have now given way to plain and simple particles.

Insights

Bohr reasoned that, because light energy is quantized, the energy of an electron in an atom must also be quantized. In other words, an electron cannot have just any amount of potential energy. Instead, there must be a number of distinct energy levels within the atom, analogous to steps on a staircase. Where you are on a staircase is restricted to where the steps are—you cannot stand at a height that is, say, halfway between any two adjacent steps. Similarly, there are only a limited number of permitted energy levels in an atom, and an electron can never have an amount of energy between these permitted energy levels. Bohr gave each energy level a **principal quantum number *n*,** where *n* is always some integer. The lowest energy level has a principal quantum number $n = 1$. An electron for which $n = 1$ is as close to the nucleus as possible, and an electron for which $n = 2$, $n = 3$, and so forth, is farther away from the nucleus.

Using these ideas, Bohr developed a conceptual model in which an electron moving around the nucleus is restricted to certain distances from the nucleus, with these distances determined by the amount of energy the electron has. Bohr saw this as similar to how the planets are held in orbit around the sun at given distances from the sun. The allowed energy levels for any atom, therefore, could be graphically represented as orbits around the nucleus, as shown in Figure 15.12. Bohr's quantized model of the atom thus became known as the *planetary model.*

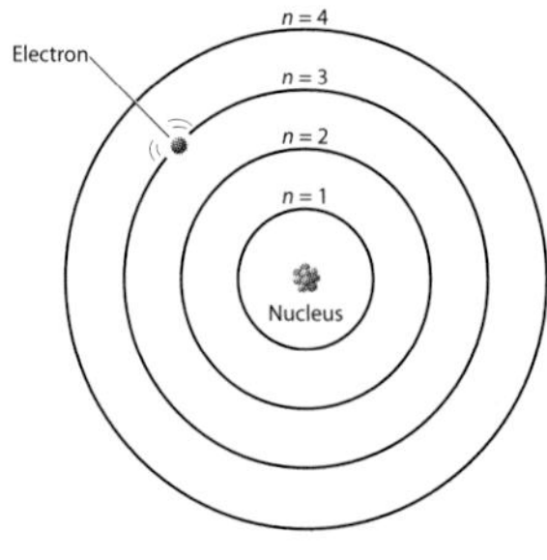

Figure 15.12
Bohr's planetary model of the atom, in which electrons orbit the nucleus much like planets orbit the sun, is a graphical representation that helps us to understand how electrons can possess only certain quantities of energy.

Bohr used his planetary model to explain why atomic spectra contain only a limited number of light frequencies. According to the model, photons are emitted by atoms as electrons move from higher-energy outer orbits to lower-energy inner orbits. The energy of an emitted photon is equal to the difference in energy between the two orbits. Because an electron is restricted to discrete orbits, only particular light frequencies are emitted, as shown in atomic spectra.

Interestingly, any transition between two orbits is always instantaneous. In other words, the electron doesn't "jump" from a higher to lower orbit the way a squirrel jumps from a higher branch in a tree to a lower one. Rather, it takes no time for an electron to move between two orbits. Bohr was serious when he stated that electrons could never exist between the permitted energy levels!

Bohr was also able to explain why the sum of two frequencies of light emitted by an atom often equals a third emitted frequency. If an electron is raised to the third energy level—that is, the third highest orbit, the one for which $n = 3$—it can return to the first orbit by two routes. As shown in Figure 15.13, it can return by a single transition from the third to the first orbit, or it can return by a double transition from the third orbit to the second and then to the first. The single transition emits a photon of frequency C, and the double transition emits two photons, one of frequency A and one of frequency B. These three photons of frequencies A, B, and C are responsible for producing three spectral lines. Note that the energy transition for A plus B is equal to the energy transition for C. Because frequency is proportional to energy, frequency A plus frequency B equals frequency C.

Recall, from Chapter 13, that a photon behaves as a particle when it is being emitted by an atom or being absorbed by photographic film or other detectors, but it behaves as a wave in traveling from a source to the place where it is detected.

Insights

☑ CHECKPOINT

1. Is the Bohr model of the atom a physical model or a conceptual model?
2. Suppose the frequency of light emitted in Figure 15.13 is 5 billion hertz along path A and 7 billion hertz along path B. What frequency of light is emitted when an electron makes a transition along path C?

Check Your Answers

1. The Bohr model is a conceptual model. It is not a scaled-up version of an atom, but instead is a representation that accounts for the atom's behavior.
2. Add the two known frequencies to get the frequency of path C: 5 billion hertz + 7 billion hertz = 12 billion hertz.

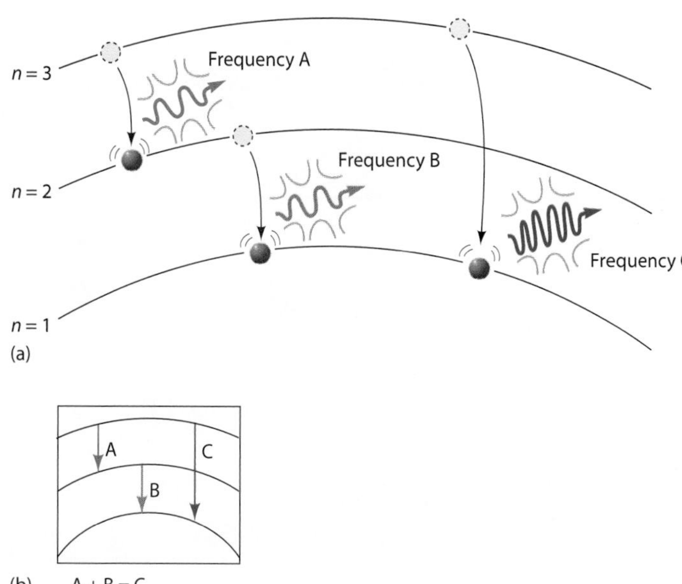

Figure 15.13
(a) The frequency of light emitted (or absorbed) by an atom is proportional to the energy difference between electron orbits. Because the energy differences between orbits are discrete, the frequencies of light emitted (or absorbed) are also discrete. The electron here can emit only three discrete frequencies of light—A, B, and C. The greater the transition, the higher the frequency of the photon emitted. (b) The sum of the energies (and frequencies) for transitions A and B equals the energy (and frequency) of transition C.

Bohr's planetary atomic model proved to be a tremendous success. By utilizing Planck's quantum hypothesis, Bohr's model solved the mystery of atomic spectra. Despite its successes, though, Bohr's model was limited, because it did not explain *why* energy levels in an atom are quantized. Bohr himself was quick to point out that his model was to be interpreted only as a crude beginning, and the picture of electrons whirling about the nucleus like planets about the sun was not to be taken literally (a warning to which popularizers of science paid no heed).

"I think it is safe to say that no one understands quantum mechanics. Do not keep saying to yourself, if you can possibly avoid it, 'But how can it be like that?' because you will go 'down the drain' into a blind alley from which nobody has yet escaped. Nobody knows how it can be like that."—Richard P. Feynman

Insights

15.4 Electron Waves

If light has both wave properties and particle properties, why can't a material particle, such as an electron, also have both? This question was posed by the French physicist Louis de Broglie (1892–1987) while he was still a graduate student in 1924. His revolutionary answer was that every particle of matter is somehow endowed with a wave to guide it as it travels. The more slowly an electron moves, the more its behavior is that of a particle with mass. The more quickly it moves, however, the more its behavior is that of a wave of energy. This duality is an extension of Einstein's famous equation $E = mc^2$, which tells us that matter and energy are interchangeable. We will discuss this relationship further in the next chapter and in Chapter 35.

A practical application of the wave properties of fast-moving electrons is the electron microscope, which focuses electron waves instead of visible light waves. Because electron waves are much shorter than visible-light waves, electron microscopes are able to show far greater detail than optical microscopes, as Figure 15.14 shows.

Figure 15.14
(a) An electron microscope makes practical use of the wave nature of electrons. The wavelengths of electron beams are typically thousands of times shorter than the wavelengths of visible light, and so the electron microscope is able to distinguish detail not visible with optical microscopes. (b) Detail of a female mosquito head as seen with an electron microscope at a "low" magnification of 200 times. Note the remarkable resolution.

(a)

(b)

In an atom, an electron moves at very high speeds—on the order of 2 million meters per second—and therefore exhibits many of the properties of a wave. An electron's wave nature can be used to explain why electrons in an atom are restricted to particular energy levels. Permitted energy levels are a natural consequence of electron waves closing in on themselves in a synchronized manner.

As an analogy, consider the wire loop shown in Figure 15.15. This loop is affixed to a mechanical vibrator that can be adjusted to create waves of different wavelengths in the wire. Waves passing through the wire that convene, as shown in Figure 15.15b, form a stationary wave pattern called a standing wave. This pattern results because the peaks and valleys of successive waves are perfectly matched, which makes the waves reinforce one another. With other wavelengths, as shown in Figure 15.15c, successive waves are not synchronized. As a result, the waves do not build to great amplitude.

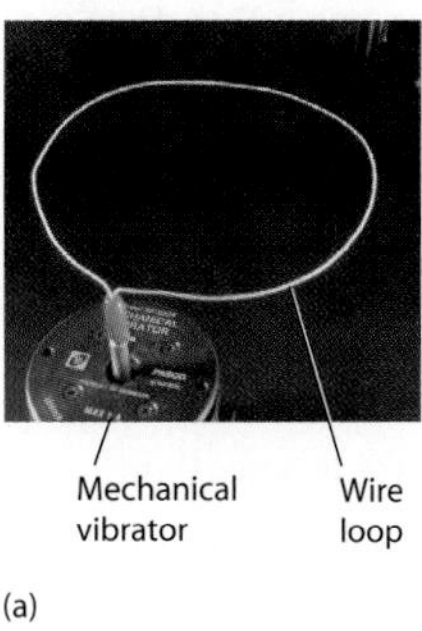

(a)

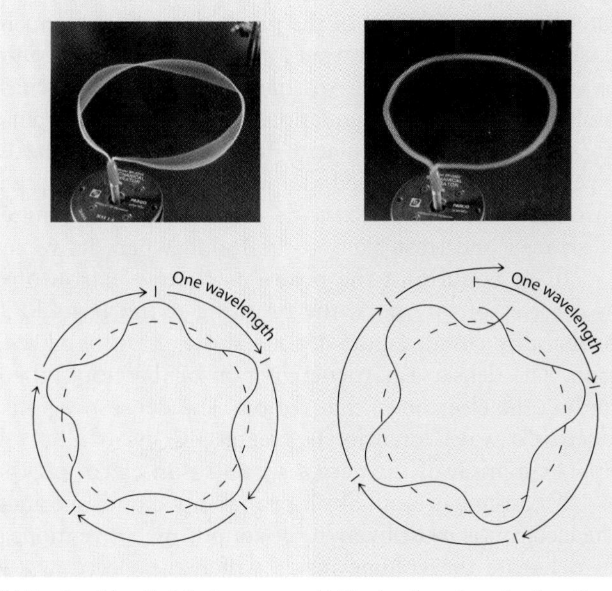

(b) Wavelength is self-reinforcing. (c) Wavelength produces chaotic motion.

Figure 15.15
For the fixed circumference of a wire loop, only some wavelengths are self-reinforcing. (a) The loop affixed to the post of a mechanical vibrator at rest. Waves are sent through the wire when the post vibrates. (b) Waves created by vibration at particular rates are self-reinforcing. (c) Waves created by vibration at other rates are not self-reinforcing.

The only waves that an electron exhibits while confined to an atom are those that are self-reinforcing. These are the ones that resemble a standing wave centered on the atomic nucleus. Each standing wave corresponds to one of the permitted energy levels. Only the frequencies of light that match the difference between any two of these permitted energy levels can be absorbed or emitted by an atom.

The wave nature of electrons also explains why they do not spiral closer and closer to the positive nucleus that attracts them. By viewing each electron orbit as a self-reinforcing wave, we see that the circumference of the smallest orbit can be no smaller than a single wavelength.

☑ CHECKPOINT

What must an electron be doing in order to have wave properties?

Check Your Answer

Moving! According to de Broglie, particles behave as waves by virtue of their motion. The wave nature of electrons in atoms is pronounced because electrons move at speeds of about 2 million meters per second.

15.5 Probability Clouds and Atomic Orbitals

Electron waves are three-dimensional, which makes them difficult to visualize, but scientists have devised two ways of representing them: as probability clouds and as atomic orbitals.

When you pluck a stretched rubber band, the resulting waves are most intense at the midpoint of the plucked length and much weaker at the ends. Similarly, standing electron waves in an atom are more intense in some regions than in others. In 1926, the Austrian scientist Erwin Schrödinger (1887–1961) formulated a remarkable equation from which the intensities of electron waves in an atom could be calculated. It was soon recognized that the intensity at any given location determined the probability of finding the electron at that location. In other words, the electron is most likely to be found where its wave intensity is greatest and least likely to be found where its wave intensity is smallest.

Probability clouds and atomic orbitals are essentially the same thing. They differ only in that atomic orbitals specify an outer limit, which makes them easier to depict graphically.

Insights

If we could plot the positions of an electron of a given energy over time as a series of tiny dots, the resulting pattern would resemble what is called a **probability cloud.** Figure 15.16a shows a probability cloud for hydrogen's electron. The denser a particular region of the cloud, the greater the probability of finding the electron in that region. The densest regions correspond to where the electron's wave intensity is greatest. A probability cloud is therefore a close approximation of the actual shape of an electron's three-dimensional wave.

An atomic orbital, like a probability cloud, specifies a volume of space where the electron is most likely to be found. By convention, **atomic orbitals** are drawn to delineate the volume inside which the electron is located 90 percent of the time. This gives the atomic orbital an apparent border, as shown in Figure 5.16b. This border is arbitrary, however, because the electron may exist on either side of it. Most of the time, though, the electron remains within the border.

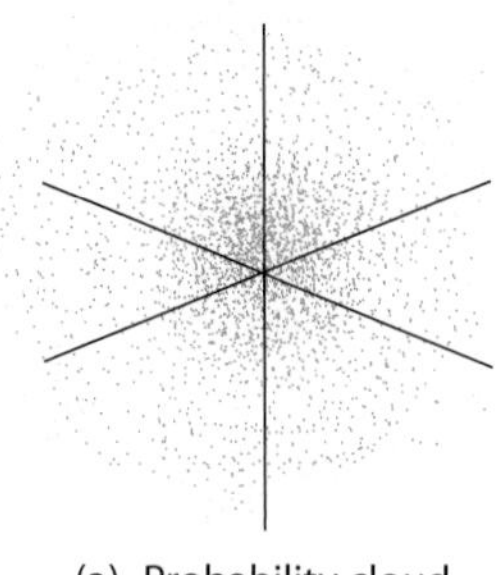

(a) Probability cloud

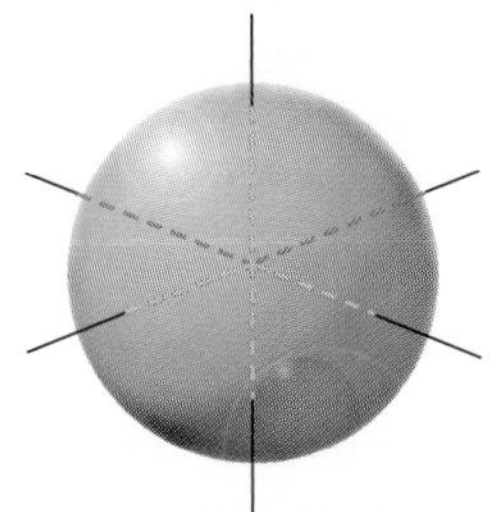

(b) Atomic orbital

Figure 15.16
(a) The probability cloud for hydrogen's electron. The more concentrated the dots, the greater the chance of finding the electron at that location. (b) The atomic orbital for hydrogen's electron. The electron is somewhere inside this spherical volume 90 percent of the time.

As Table 15.1 shows, the first four atomic orbitals are classified by the letters *s, p, d,* and *f,* and they come in a variety of shapes, some quite exquisite. The simplest is the spherical *s* orbital. The *p* orbital consists of two lobes and resembles an hourglass. There are three kinds of *p* orbitals, and they differ from one another only by their orientation in three-dimensional space. The more complex *d* orbitals have five possible shapes, and the *f* orbitals have seven. Please do not feel compelled to memorize all the orbital shapes, especially the *d* and *f* ones. However, you should understand that each orbital represents a different region in which an electron of a given energy is most likely to be found.

Table 15.1

The Four Major Types of Orbitals: *s, p, d, f*

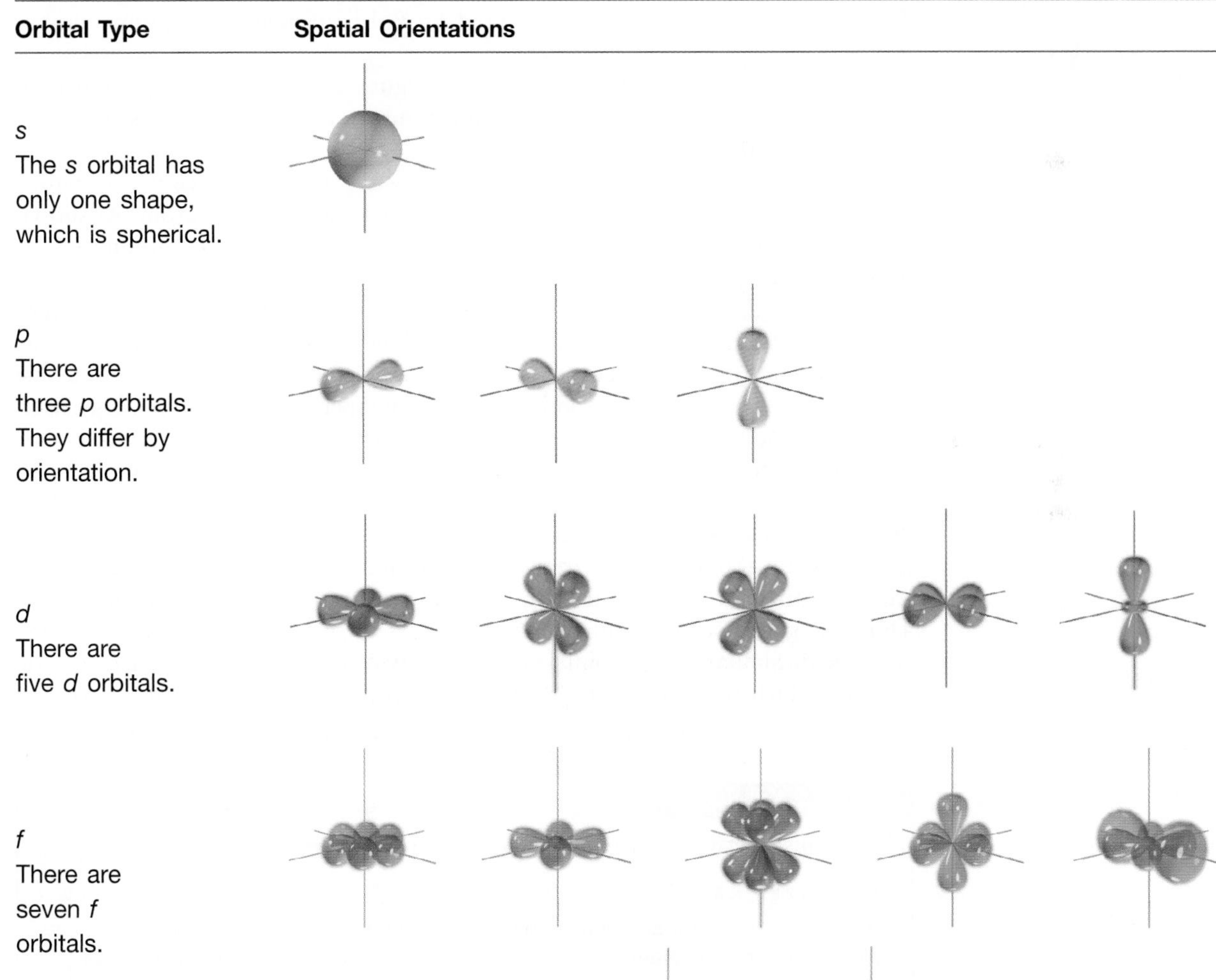

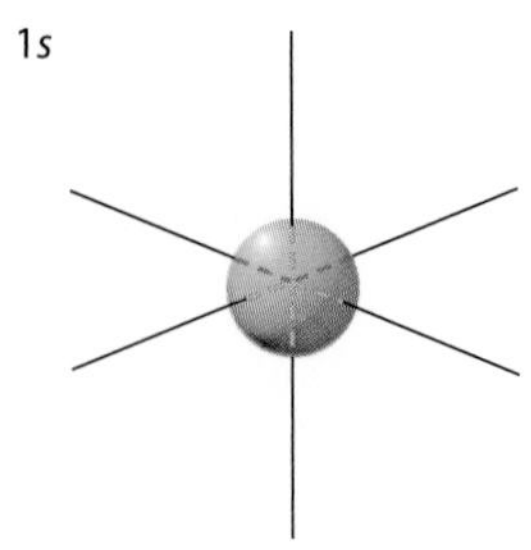

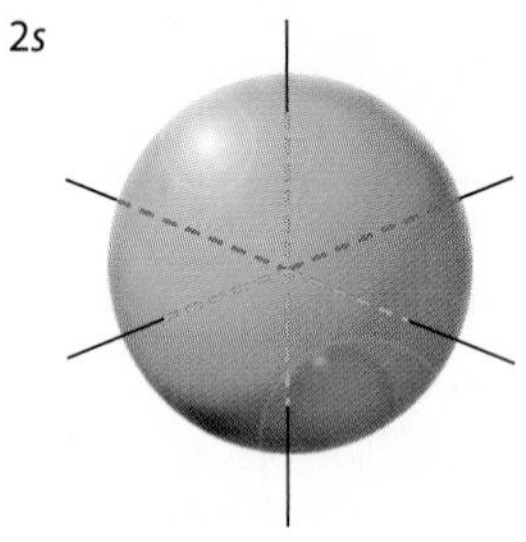

Figure 15.17
The 2*s* orbital is larger than the 1*s* orbital because the 2*s* accommodates electrons of greater energy.

☑ CHECKPOINT

What is the relationship between an electron wave and an atomic orbital?

Check Your Answer

The atomic orbital is an approximation of the shape of the standing electron wave surrounding the atomic nucleus.

In addition to a variety of shapes, atomic orbitals also come in a variety of sizes that correspond to different energy levels. In general, highly energized electrons are able to extend farther away from the attracting nucleus, which means they are distributed over a greater volume of space. The higher the energy of the electron, therefore, the larger its atomic orbital. Because electron energies are quantized, however, the possible sizes of the atomic orbitals are quantized. The size of an orbital is thus indicated by Bohr's principal quantum number $n = 1, 2, 3, 4, 5, 6, 7$, or greater.

The first two *s* orbitals are shown in Figure 15.17. The smallest *s* orbital is 1*s*, where 1 is the principal quantum number. The next largest *s* orbital is 2*s*, and so forth.

So we see that an atomic orbital is simply a volume of space within which an electron may reside. Orbitals may overlap one another in an atom. As shown in Figure 15.18, the electrons of a fluorine atom are distributed among its 1*s*, 2*s*, and three 2*p* orbitals.*

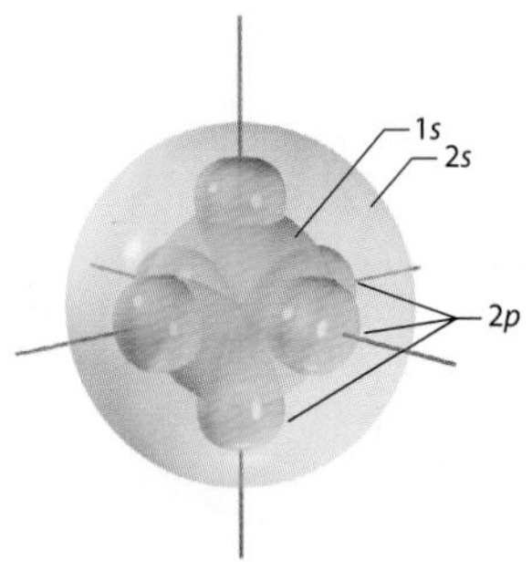

Figure 15.18
The fluorine atom has five overlapping atomic orbitals that contain its nine electrons, which are not shown.

The hourglass-shaped *p* orbital illustrates the significance of the wave nature of the electron. Unlike the case with a real hourglass, the two lobes of this orbital are not open to each other, and yet an electron freely moves from one lobe to the other. To understand how this can happen, consider an analogy from the macroscopic world. A guitar player can gently tap a guitar string at its midpoint (the 12th fret) and pluck it elsewhere at the same time to produce a high-pitched tone called a harmonic. Close inspection of this string, shown in Figure 15.19, reveals that it oscillates everywhere along the string except at the point directly above the 12th fret. This point of zero oscillation is called a *node*. Although there is no motion at the node, waves nonetheless travel through it. Thus, the guitar string oscillates on both sides of the node when only one side is plucked. Similarly, the point between the two lobes of a *p* orbital is a node through which the electron may pass—but only by virtue of its ability to take on the form of a wave.

☑ CHECKPOINT

Distinguish between an orbital and one of Bohr's orbits.

Check Your Answer

An orbit is a distinct path followed by an object in its revolution around another object. In Bohr's planetary model of the atom, he proposed an analogy between electrons orbiting the atomic nucleus and planets orbiting the sun. What orbits and orbitals have in common is that they both use Bohr's principal quantum number to indicate energy levels in an atom.

*For reasons beyond the scope of this text, the 1*p* orbital does not exist. The smallest *p* orbital is therefore the 2*p*. Other nonexistent orbitals are the 1*d*, 2*d*, 1*f*, 2*f*, and 3*f*.

Bohr's planetary atomic model postulated discrete energy values for electrons in order to account for spectral data. The electron-wave model goes further and shows that discrete electron energy values are a natural consequence of the electron's confinement to the atom. While Bohr's planetary model accounts for the generation of light quanta, the wave model takes things a step further by treating light and matter in the same way—both behaving sometimes like a wave and sometimes like a particle. As abstract as the wave model may be, these successes indicate that it presents a more fundamental description of the atom than does Bohr's planetary model.

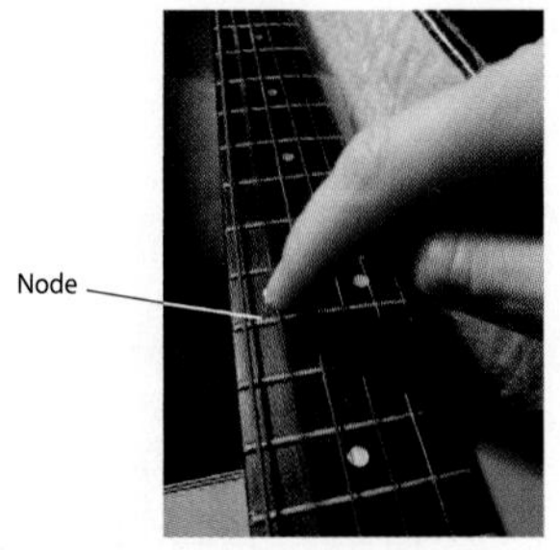

Figure 15.19
The guitar string can oscillate on both sides of the 12th-fret node even when the string is plucked on only one side of the node. This occurs because waves can pass through the node.

15.6 The Shell Model

For the purpose of establishing a cursory understanding of how atoms behave, we turn now to the *shell model*. This model is similar to Bohr's planetary model in that it is highly simplified. We can use it, however, to help explain the organization of the periodic table. Then, in Chapter 19, we'll be using a derivative of this model to show how atoms join together to form chemical bonds.

According to the shell model, electrons behave as if they are arranged in a series of concentric shells. A **shell** is defined as a region of space about the atomic nucleus within which electrons may reside. An important aspect of this model is that there are at least seven shells and that each shell can hold only a limited number of electrons. As shown in Figure 15.20, the innermost shell can hold two; the second and third shells, eight electrons each; the fourth and fifth shells, 18 each; and the sixth and seventh shells, 32 each.

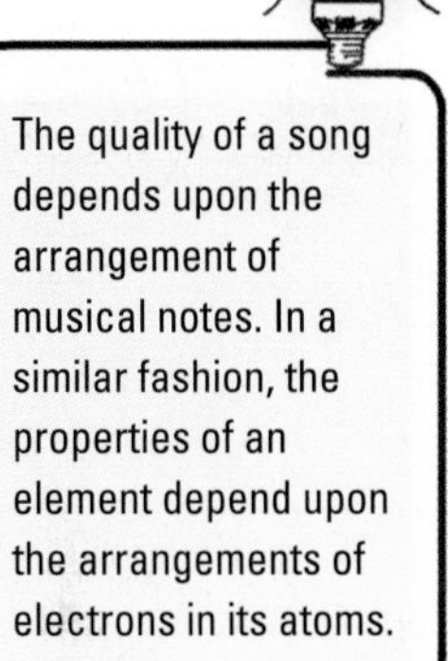

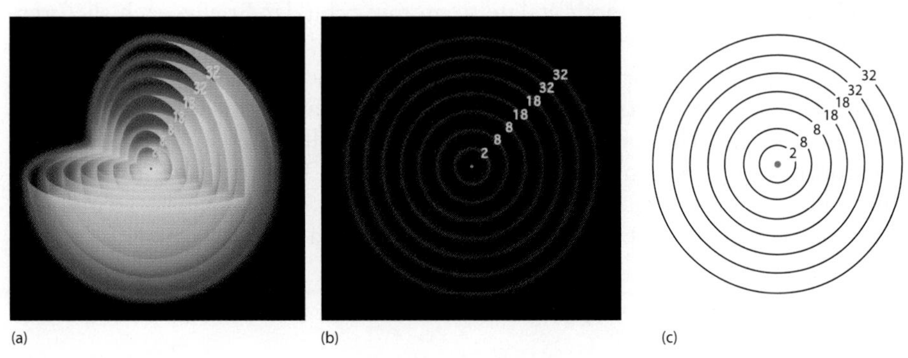

Figure 15.20
(a) A cutaway view of the seven shells, with the number of electrons each shell can hold indicated. (b) A two-dimensional, cross-sectional view of the shells. (c) An easy-to-draw cross-sectional view that resembles Bohr's planetary model.

A series of seven such concentric shells accounts for the seven periods of the periodic table. Furthermore, the number of elements in each period is equal to the shell's capacity for electrons. The first shell, for example, has a capacity for only two electrons. That's why we find only two elements, hydrogen and helium, in the first period (Figure 15.21). The second and third shells each have a capacity for eight electrons, and so eight elements are found in both the second and third periods.

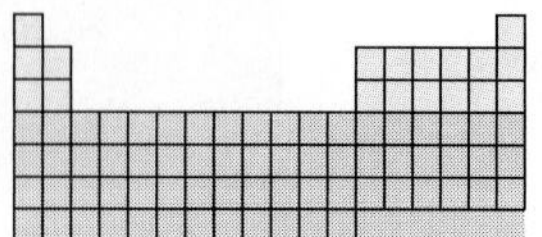

Figure 15.21
The first three periods of the periodic table, according to the shell model. Elements in the same period have electrons in the same shells. Elements in the same period differ from one another by the number of electrons in the outermost shell.

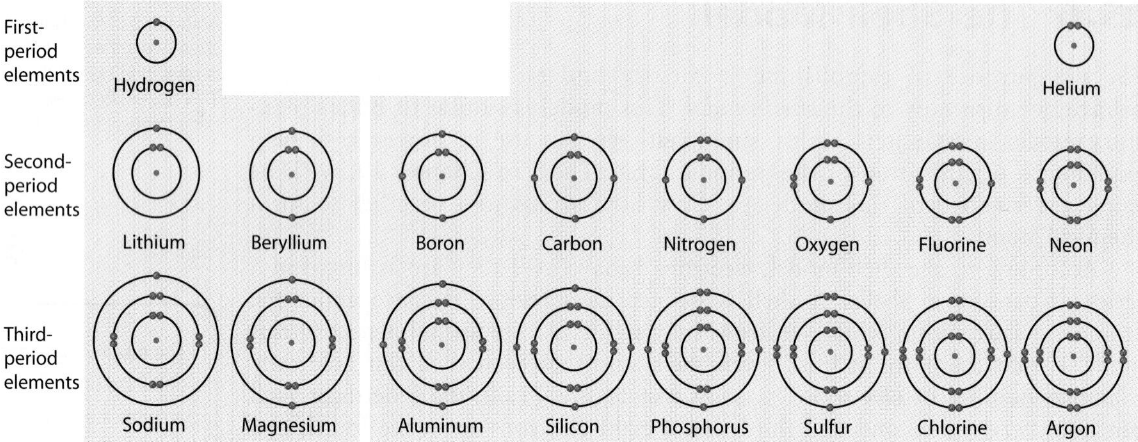

How does this shell model relate to atomic orbitals? Briefly, each shell represents a grouping of orbitals of similar energy levels. The first shell represents only the 1*s* orbital. The second shell represents the 2*s* and three 2*p* orbitals. The third shell represents the 3*s* and three 3*p* orbitals; and so on, as described in Figure 15.22. The limited capacity of each shell arises from the fact that each orbital can hold no more than two electrons. The first shell, representing only one orbital, therefore has a capacity for two electrons. The second and third shells each represent four orbitals, and so each has a capacity to hold eight electrons.

☑ CHECKPOINT

The fourth shell represents the 4*s* orbital, along with five 3*d* orbitals and three 4*p* orbitals. How many orbitals is this altogether? What, then, is the maximum capacity for electrons in the fourth shell? How many elements are found in the fourth period of the periodic table?

Check Your Answer

This adds up to nine orbitals, which have a total capacity of 18 electrons, which is also the number of elements in the fourth period of the periodic table.

High energy

Seventh shell capacity:
32 electrons

7s 7p 6d 5f

Sixth shell capacity:
32 electrons

6s 6p 5d 4f

Fifth shell capacity:
18 electrons

5s 5p 4d

Fourth shell capacity:
18 electrons

4s 4p 3d

Third shell capacity:
8 electrons

3s 3p

Second shell capacity:
8 electrons

2s 2p

First shell capacity:
2 electrons

1s

Low energy

Figure 15.22
In this schematic diagram, each box represents an orbital, and each electron is represented by an arrow. The arrows of two electrons within the same orbital must be shown facing in opposite directions. The higher the orbital, the higher its energy level. Note that orbitals of similar energy are partitioned together and referred to as a "shell" of orbitals.

Two-time Nobel laureate Linus Pauling (1901–1994) was an early proponent of teaching beginning chemistry students by using a shell model to describe the organization of the periodic table. In this model, as is described here, orbitals are grouped according to energy level. However, this shell model differs from those found in advanced physics and chemistry textbooks, which identify a shell as a group of orbitals that all have the same principal quantum number.

The electrons of the outermost occupied shell in any atom are directly exposed to the external environment and are the first to interact with other atoms. Most notably, they are the ones that participate in chemical bonding, as we shall be discussing in Chapter 19. The electrons in the outermost shell, therefore, are quite important. They are called **valence electrons.** The term *valence* is derived from the Latin *valentia,* "strength," and it refers to the "combining power" of an atom.

Predictability and Chaos

We can make predictions about an orderly system when we know the initial conditions of the system. For example, we can state precisely where a launched rocket will land, where a given planet will be at a particular time, or when an eclipse will occur. These are examples of events in the Newtonian macroworld. Similarly, in the quantum microworld, we can predict where an electron is likely to be in an atom and what the probability is that a radioactive particle will decay in a given time interval. Predictability in orderly systems, both Newtonian and quantum, depends on a knowledge of the initial conditions of the system.

Some systems however, whether Newtonian or quantum, are not orderly—they are inherently unpredictable. These are called "chaotic systems." Turbulent water flow is an example. No matter how precisely we know the initial conditions of a piece of floating wood as it flows downstream, we cannot predict its location later downstream. A feature of chaotic systems is that slight differences in initial conditions result in wildly different outcomes later. Two identical pieces of wood just slightly apart at one time are vastly far apart soon thereafter.

Weather is chaotic. Small changes in one day's weather can produce big (and largely unpredictable) changes a week later. Meteorologists try their best, but they are bucking the hard fact of chaos in nature. This barrier to good prediction first led the scientist Edward Lorenz to ask, "Does the flap of a butterfly's wings in Brazil set off a tornado in Texas?" We now talk about the *butterfly effect* when we are dealing with situations where very small influences can amplify into very big effects.

Interestingly, chaos is not all hopeless unpredictability. Even in a chaotic system, there can be patterns of regularity. There is *order in chaos.* Scientists have learned how to treat chaos mathematically and how to find parts of it that are orderly. Artists seek patterns in nature in a different way. Both scientists and artists look for the connections in nature that were always there, but not yet put together in our thinking.

Look carefully at Figure 15.21. Can you see that the valence electrons of atoms above and below one another (within the same group) are similarly organized? For example, atoms of the first group, which includes hydrogen, lithium, and sodium, each have a single valence electron. The atoms of the second group, including beryllium and magnesium, each have two valence electrons. Similarly, atoms of the last group, including helium, neon, and argon, each have their outermost shells filled to capacity with valence electrons—two for helium, and eight each for neon and argon. In general, the valence electrons of atoms in the same group of the periodic table are similarly organized. This explains why elements of the same group have similar properties—a concept first presented in the previous chapter (Section 14.6).

☑ CHECKPOINT

Do atoms really consist of shells that look like those depicted in Figure 15.20?

Check Your Answer

The shell model is *not* a depiction of the "appearance of an atom." Instead, it is a conceptual model that allows us to account for observed behavior. An atom, therefore, does not actually contain a series of concentric shells; it merely behaves as if it does.

In this chapter, a fair amount of detail has been discussed regarding atomic models. We learned how electrons are arranged around an atomic nucleus. Rather than moving in neat orbits like planets around the sun electrons are wavelike entities that swarm in various volumes of space called atomic orbitals. Furthermore, atomic orbitals of similar energy can be grouped together and be represented by a single shell. Such a shell should not be taken literally. Rather, the shell represents a region of space within which electrons of similar energy are most likely to be found.

Remember that these models are not to be interpreted as actual representations of the atom's physical structure. Rather, they serve as tools to help us understand and predict the behavior of atoms. These models, therefore, are the foundation of chemistry and the key to a richer understanding of the atomic and molecular environment that surrounds us.

Summary of Terms

Physical model A representation of an object on some convenient scale.

Conceptual model A representation of a system that helps in making predictions about how the system behaves.

Spectroscope A device that uses a prism or a diffraction grating to separate light into its component colors.

Atomic spectrum The pattern of frequencies of electromagnetic radiation emitted by the atoms of an element, considered to be the element's "fingerprint."

Quantum hypothesis The idea that light energy is contained in discrete packets called quanta.

Quantum A small, discrete packet of light energy.

Principal quantum number, *n* An integer that specifies the quantized energy level of an atomic orbital.

Probability cloud The pattern of electron positions plotted over time to show the likelihood of an electron's being at a given position at a given time.

Atomic orbital A region of space in which an electron in an atom has a 90 percent chance of being located.

Shell A set of overlapping atomic orbitals of similar energy levels; in other words, a region of space in which electrons of similar energy levels in an atom have a 90 percent chance of being located.

Valence electron An electron that is located in the outermost occupied shell of an atom and can participate in chemical bonding.

Review Questions

15.1 Physical and Conceptual Models

1. If a baseball were the size of the earth, about how large would its atoms be?
2. When we use a scanning tunneling microscope, do we see atoms directly or do we see them only indirectly?
3. Why are atoms invisible to visible light?
4. What is the difference between a physical model and a conceptual model?
5. What is the function of an atomic model?

15.2 Identifying Atoms Using the Spectroscope

6. What does a spectroscope do to the light coming from an atom?
7. What occurs in an atom when it emits light?
8. Why do we say atomic spectra are like fingerprints of the elements?
9. What did Rydberg note about the atomic spectrum of hydrogen?

15.3 The Quantum Hypothesis

10. What was Planck's quantum hypothesis?
11. Which has more potential energy: an electron close to an atomic nucleus or one far from an atomic nucleus?
12. What happens to an electron when it absorbs a photon of light?
13. What is the relationship between the light emitted by an atom and the energies of the electrons in the atom?
14. Did Bohr think of his planetary model as an accurate representation of the appearance of an atom?

15.4 Electron Waves

15. About how fast does an electron travel around the atomic nucleus?
16. How does the speed of an electron change its fundamental nature?

15.5 Probability Clouds and Atomic Orbitals

17. Who developed the equation that relates the intensity of an electron's wave to the electron's most probable location?
18. How is an atomic orbital similar to a probability cloud?
19. How many 2*p* orbitals are there within an atom?

15.6 The Shell Model

20. Which electrons are most responsible for the properties of an atom?
21. What do the orbitals in a shell have in common?
22. The shell model presented in this book is not very accurate. Why, then, is it presented here?
23. How many orbitals are present in the third shell?
24. How is the number of shells an atom of a given element contains related to the row of the periodic table in which that element is found?
25. What is the relationship between the maximum number of electrons each shell can hold and the number of elements in each period of the periodic table?

Activities

Spectral Patterns

Purchase some "rainbow" glasses from a nature, toy, or hobby store. The lenses of these glasses are diffraction gratings. Looking through them, you will see light separated into its color components. Certain light sources, such as the moon or a car's headlights, are separated into a continuous spectrum—in other words, all the colors of the rainbow appear in a continuous sequence from red to violet.

Other light sources, however, emit a distinct number of discontinuous colors. Examples include streetlights, neon signs, sparklers, and fireworks. The spectral patterns you see from any of these light sources are the atomic spectra of elements that are heated in the light source. You'll be able to see the patterns best when you are at least 50 meters away from the light source. This distance makes the spectrum appear as a series of dots similar to the series of lines shown in Figure 15.7.

To the naked eye, a glowing element appears as only a single color. However, this color is an average of the many different visible frequencies the element is emitting. Only with a device such as a spectroscope are you able to discern the different frequencies. So when you look at an atomic spectrum, don't get confused and think that each frequency of light (color) corresponds to a different element. Instead, remember that what you are looking at is all the frequencies of light emitted by a single element as its electrons make transitions back and forth between energy levels.

Not all elements produce discrete line patterns in the visible spectrum. Tungsten, for example, produces the full spectrum of colors (white light). This property makes it useful as the glowing component of a car's headlights, as shown in the photograph. Also, the sunlight reflecting off the moon is so bright and contains the glow of so many different elements that it, too, appears as a broad spectrum.

Rubber Waves

Stretch a rubber band between your two thumbs and pluck one length of it. Note that no matter where along the length you pluck, the area of greatest oscillation is always at the midpoint. This is a self-reinforcing wave that occurs as overlapping waves bounce back and forth from thumb to thumb.

Under regular light, it is difficult to see the waves traveling back and forth. For a better view, pluck the rubber band in front of a computer monitor or a television screen that uses a cathode ray tube. The light from these devices, which acts like a strobe light, makes the waves appear to slow down.

Vary the tension in the rubber band to see different effects.

Quantized Whistle

You can "quantize" your whistle by whistling down a long tube, such as the tube from a roll of wrapping paper. First, without the tube: with a single breath, whistle from a high pitch to a low pitch as loud as you can. Next, try the same thing while holding the tube to your lips. Aha! Note that some frequencies simply cannot be whistled, no matter how hard you try. These frequencies are forbidden because their wavelengths are not a multiple of the length of the tube.

Try experimenting with tubes of different lengths. To hear yourself more clearly, use a flexible plastic tube and twist the outer end toward your ear.

When your whistle is confined to the tube, the consequence is a quantization of its frequencies. When an electron wave is confined to an atom, the consequence is a quantization of the electron's energy.

People watching you perform this activity may not believe that the audible "steps" of your whistling down the tube are not intentional. Explain quantization to them before allowing them to attempt this activity for themselves. Try to count the number of steps in your tubular whistle, understanding that each step is analogous to an energy level in an atom. Does a longer tube create fewer or more steps than a shorter tube? Why is it so difficult to whistle down a garden hose?

If you punch a few holes along the tube, you alter the frequencies of the standing waves that can form in the tube, resulting in the production of different pitches. This is the underlying principle in such musical instruments as flutes and saxophones.

Exercises

1. With scanning tunneling microscopy (STM) technology, we don't see actual atoms but, rather, images of them. Explain.
2. Why is it not possible for an STM to make images of the interior of an atom?
3. Would you use a physical model or a conceptual model to describe the following: brain, mind, solar system, birth of universe, stranger, best friend, gold coin, dollar bill, car engine, virus, spread of a cold virus?
4. How might you distinguish a sodium-vapor lamp from a mercury-vapor lamp?
5. How can a hydrogen atom, which has only one electron, create so many spectral lines?
6. Which color of light comes from a greater energy transition, red or blue? Explain.
7. Suppose that a certain atom has four energy levels. Assuming that all transitions between levels are possible, how many spectral lines will this atom exhibit? Which transition corresponds to the highest-energy light emitted? Which corresponds to the lowest-energy light emitted?
8. Which has the greatest energy, a photon of infrared light, a photon of visible light, or a photon of ultraviolet light?
9. If we take a piece of metal at room temperature and begin to heat it continuously in a dark room, it will soon begin to glow visibly. What will be its first visible color, and why?
10. An electron drops from the fourth energy level in an atom to the third level and then to the first level. Two frequencies of light are emitted. How does their combined energy compare with the energy of the single frequency that would have been emitted if the electron had dropped from the fourth level directly to the first level?
11. Figure 15.13 shows three energy-level transitions that produce three spectral lines in a spectroscope. Note that the distance between the $n = 1$ and $n = 2$ levels is greater than the distance between the $n = 2$ and $n = 3$ levels. Would the number of spectral lines produced change if the distance between the $n = 1$ and $n = 2$ levels were exactly the same as the distance between the $n = 2$ and $n = 3$ levels?
12. If light were passed through a round hole instead of a thin slit in a spectroscope, how would the spectral "lines" appear? What is the drawback of a hole relative to a slit?
13. What is the evidence for the claim that iron exists in the relatively cool outer layer of the sun?
14. What does it mean to say that something is quantized?
15. The frequency of violet light is about twice that of red light. Compare the energy of a violet photon with the energy of a red photon.
16. If a beam of red light and a beam of violet light have equal energies, which beam has the greater number of photons?
17. Green light is emitted when electrons in a substance make a particular energy-level transition. If blue light were instead emitted from the same substance, would it correspond to a greater or lesser change of energy in the atom?
18. How does the wave model of electrons orbiting the nucleus account for the fact that the electrons can have only discrete energy values?
19. How might the spectrum of an atom appear if the atom's electrons were not restricted to particular energy levels?
20. How does an electron move from one lobe of a *p* orbital to the other?
21. Light is emitted as an electron transition from a higher-energy orbital to a lower-energy orbital. How long does it take for the transition to take place? At what point in time is the electron found between the two orbitals?
22. Why is there only one spatial orientation for the *s* orbital?
23. Place the proper number of electrons in each shell:

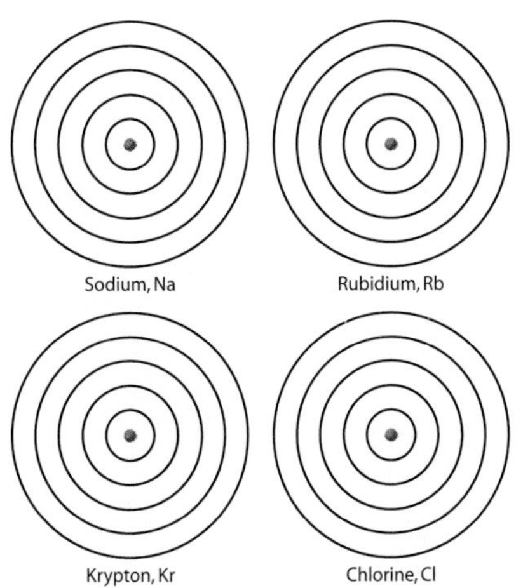

24. Which element is represented in Figure 15.20 if all seven shells are filled to capacity?
25. Does an orbital or shell have to contain electrons in order to exist?
26. Why does an electron occupying a 7*s* orbital have more energy than one in a 1*s* orbital?
27. Use the shell model to explain why a potassium atom, K, is larger than a sodium atom, Na.
28. Use the shell model to explain why a lithium atom, Li, is larger than a beryllium atom, Be.
29. Light has been described as being a wave, and then as being a particle, and then back again. Does this indicate that light's true nature probably lies somewhere in between these models?
30. If a butterfly causes a tornado, does it make sense to eradicate butterflies? Defend your answer.

Chapter 15 Online Resources

Tutorials
- Bohr's Shell Model

Quiz
Exercises
Flashcards
Links

CHAPTER 16

The Atomic Nucleus

When household electricity made its way across the country more than a century ago, it represented a new technology with great potential. But it was not without its hazards. While electric grids could provide cities with a quantity and quality of energy previously unheard of, they could also kill people in ways previously unheard of. Many people opposed the adoption of household electricity because of the inherent dangers. But safeguards were engineered, and society determined that the benefits of electricity outweighed the risks. Similar debates continue today; not over electricity, but over nuclear energy and radioactivity. Proponents tout the benefits, while critics point out the hazards. As a member of society, you will have to make important decisions in these matters. You should do so with an adequate understanding of the atomic nucleus and its inner processes.

16.1 Radioactivity

Atoms are made up of electrons, neutrons, and protons. The neutrons and protons lie at the heart of the atom—in the nucleus. Some atoms have stable nuclei. These nuclei have the right balance of neutrons to protons and the right amount of energy to remain unchanged for a long time. Other atoms don't have the right mix of protons and neutrons or have the wrong amount of energy. The nuclei of these atoms are unstable. Atoms with unstable nuclei are said to be *radioactive*. Sooner or later, they break down and eject energetic particles and emit electromagnetic radiation. This process is **radioactivity,** which, because it involves the decay of the atomic nucleus, is often called *radioactive decay*.

A common misconception is that radioactivity is something new in the environment. Actually, it has been around far longer than the human race. It has always been in the soil we walk on and in the air that we breathe, and it warms the earth's interior. In fact, radioactive decay in the earth's interior is what heats the water that spurts from a geyser or wells up from a natural hot spring. The helium in a child's balloon is nothing more than the products of radioactive decay.

As Figure 16.1 on page 382 shows, most of the radiation we encounter is natural background radiation that originates in the earth and in space and was present long before we humans arrived. Even the cleanest air we breathe is radioactive as a result of bombardment by cosmic rays. These rays originate in the sun and other stars and make up the background radiation in space. Cosmic rays are of two types: high-energy particles or high-frequency electromagnetic

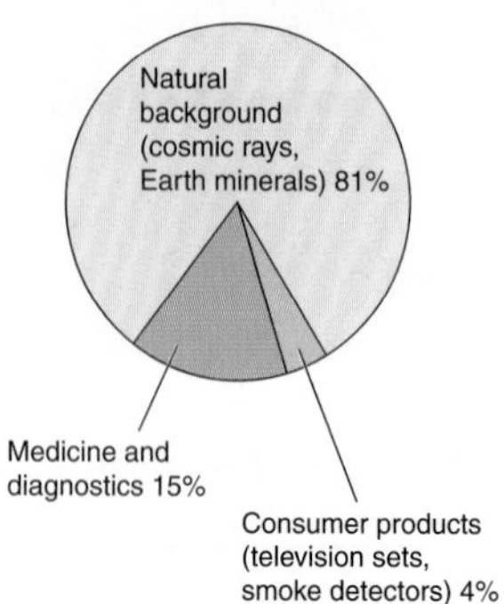

Figure 16.1
Origins of radiation exposure for an average individual in the United States.

radiation (gamma rays). At sea level, the protective blanket of the atmosphere reduces this background radiation, but radiation is more intense at higher altitudes. In Denver, the "mile-high city," a person receives more than twice as much radiation from cosmic rays as someone at sea level. A couple of round-trip flights between New York and San Francisco exposes us to as much radiation as we receive in a chest X ray at the physician's office. Because extended exposure to this level of radiation is dangerous, the flight time of airline personnel is limited.

Cosmic radiation also affects us indirectly, by transforming the nitrogen atoms in the air to radioactive carbon-14, which is incorporated through photosynthesis into the plants we consume. Radioactive potassium from the earth is in our bones. So even our bodies are radioactive.

16.2 Alpha, Beta, and Gamma Rays

All elements having an atomic number greater than 82 (lead) are radioactive. These elements, and others, emit three distinct types of radiation, named by the first three letters of the Greek alphabet, α, β, γ—*alpha*, *beta*, and *gamma*. Alpha rays carry a positive electrical charge, beta rays carry a negative charge, and gamma rays carry no charge. The three rays can be separated by placing a magnetic field across their paths (Figure 16.2).

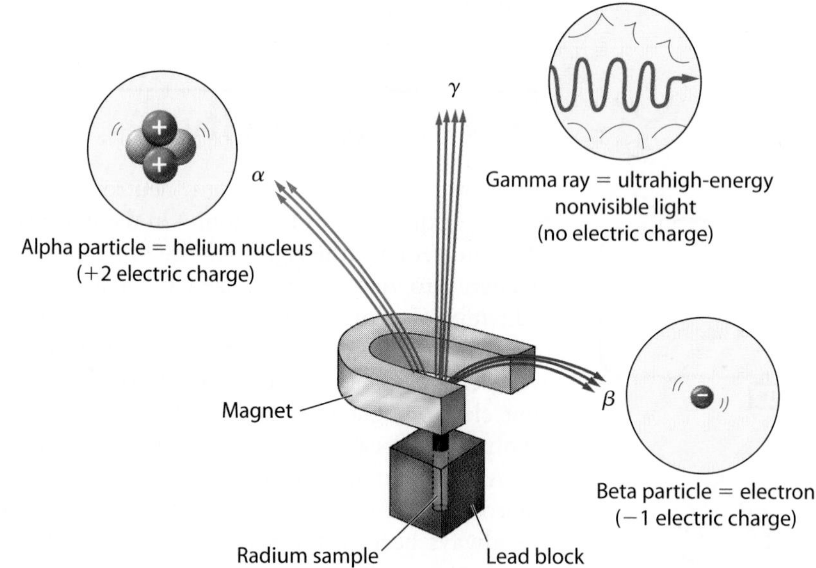

Figure 16.2
In a magnetic field, alpha rays bend one way, beta rays bend the other way, and gamma rays don't bend at all. Note that the alpha rays bend less than beta rays. This occurs because alpha particles have more inertia (mass) than beta particles. The combined beam comes from a radioactive material placed at the bottom of a hole drilled in a lead block.

An **alpha particle** is the combination of two protons and two neutrons (in other words, it is the nucleus of the helium atom, atomic number 2). Alpha particles are relatively easy to shield against because of their relatively large size and their double positive charge (+2). For example, they do not normally penetrate such lightweight materials as paper or clothing. Because of their great kinetic energies, however, alpha particles can cause significant damage to the surface of a material, especially living tissue. When traveling through only a few centimeters of air, alpha particles pick up electrons and become nothing more than harmless helium. As a matter of fact, that's where the helium in a child's balloon comes from—practically all the earth's helium atoms were at one time energetic alpha particles.

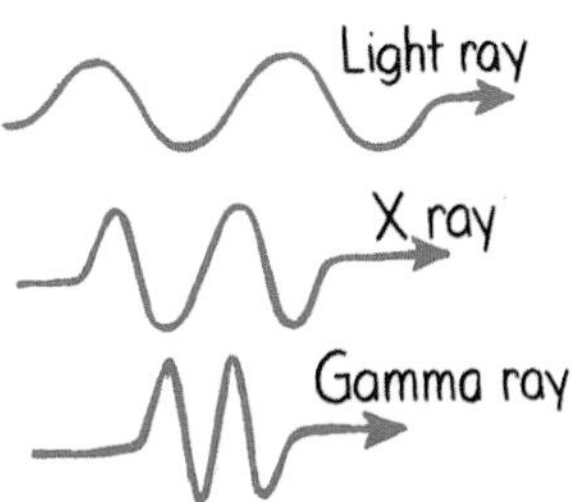

Figure 16.3
A gamma ray is simply electromagnetic radiation, much higher in frequency and energy than light and X rays.

A **beta particle** is an electron ejected from a nucleus. Once ejected, it is indistinguishable from an electron in a cathode ray or in an electrical circuit, or from an electron orbiting the atomic nucleus. The difference is that a beta particle originates inside the nucleus—from a neutron. As we shall soon see, the neutron becomes a proton once it loses the electron that has become a beta particle. A beta particle is normally faster than an alpha particle, and it carries only a single negative charge (-1). Beta particles are not as easy to stop as alpha particles are, and they are able to penetrate such low-mass materials as paper or clothing. They can penetrate fairly deeply into skin, where they have the potential for harming or killing living cells. But they are unable to penetrate even thin sheets of denser materials, such as aluminum. Beta particles, once stopped, simply become a part of the material they are in, like any other electron.

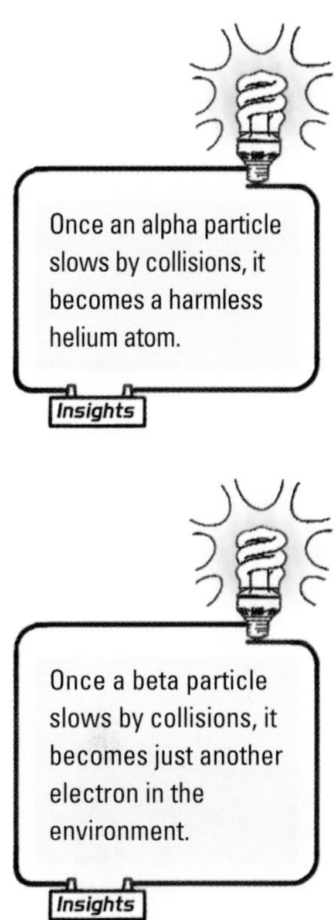

Gamma rays are the high-frequency electromagnetic radiation emitted by radioactive elements. Like photons of visible light, a gamma ray is pure energy. The amount of energy in a gamma ray, however, is much greater per photon than in visible light, ultraviolet light, or even X rays. Because they have no mass or electric charge, and because of their high energies, gamma rays are able to penetrate through most materials. However, they cannot easily penetrate very dense materials, such as lead. Lead is commonly used as a shielding material in laboratories or hospitals where there can be much gamma radiation. Delicate molecules inside cells throughout our bodies that are zapped by gamma rays suffer structural damage. Hence, gamma rays are generally more harmful to us than are alpha or beta particles. However, radioactive materials that emit alpha particles and beta particles *do* pose a significant health risk if they are ingested.

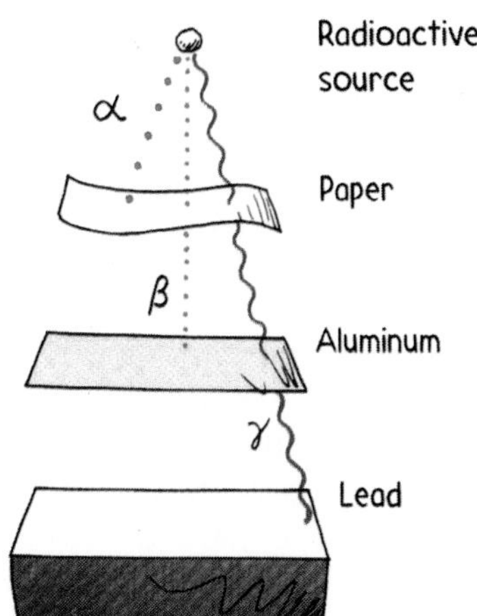

Figure 16.4
Alpha particles are the least penetrating and can be stopped by a few sheets of paper. Beta particles will readily pass through paper, but not through a sheet of aluminum. Gamma rays penetrate several centimeters into solid lead.

Figure 16.5
The shelf-life of fresh strawberries and other perishables is markedly increased when the food is subjected to gamma rays from a radioactive source. The strawberries on the right were treated with gamma radiation, which kills the microorganisms that normally lead to spoilage. The food is only a receiver of radiation and is in no way transformed into an emitter of radiation, as can be confirmed with a radiation detector.

☑ CHECKPOINT

Pretend that you are given three radioactive rocks. One is an alpha emitter, one is a beta emitter, and one is a gamma emitter, and you know which is which. You can throw away one, but, of the remaining two, you must hold one in your hand place one in your pocket. What can you do to minimize your exposure to radiation?

Check Your Answer

Hold the alpha emitter in your hand, because the skin on your hand will shield you. Put the beta emitter in your pocket, because beta particles will likely be stopped by the combined thickness of your clothing and skin. Throw away the gamma emitter, because it would penetrate your body from any of these locations. (Ideally, of course, you should distance yourself as much as possible from all of the rocks.)

16.3 Environmental Radiation

Figure 16.6
A commercially available radon test kit for the home.

Common rocks and minerals in our environment contain significant quantities of radioactive isotopes, because most of them contain trace amounts of uranium. As a matter of fact, people who live in brick, concrete, or stone buildings are exposed to greater amounts of radiation than people who live in wooden buildings.

The leading source of naturally occurring radiation is radon-222, an inert gas arising from uranium deposits. Radon is a heavy gas that tends to accumulate in basements after it seeps up through cracks in the floor. Levels of radon vary from region to region, depending upon local geology. You can check the radon level in your home with a radon detector kit (Figure 16.6). If levels are high, corrective measures, such as sealing the basement floor and walls and maintaining adequate ventilation, should be taken. Radon gas poses a serious health risk.

About 20 percent of our annual exposure to radiation comes from sources outside of nature, primarily medical procedures. Television sets, fallout from nuclear testing, and the coal and nuclear power industries are also contributors. The coal industry far outranks the nuclear power industry as a source of radiation. The global combustion of coal annually releases about 13,000 tons of radioactive thorium and uranium into the atmosphere (in addition to other environmentally damaging molecules). Both of these elements are found naturally in coal deposits, so their release is a natural consequence of burning coal. Worldwide, the nuclear power industries generate about 10,000 tons of radioactive waste each year. Most all of this waste, however, is contained and *not* released into the environment.

The average coal-burning power plant is a far greater source of airborne radioactive material than is a nuclear power plant.

Insights

Units of Radiation

Radiation dosage is commonly measured in *rads* (*r*adiation *a*bsorbed *d*ose), a unit of absorbed energy. One **rad** is equal to 0.01 joule of radiant energy absorbed per kilogram of tissue.

The capacity for nuclear radiation to cause damage is not just a function of its level of energy, however. Some forms of radiation are more harmful than others. For example, suppose you have two arrows, one with a pointed tip and one with a suction cup at its tip. If you shoot each of them at an apple at the same speed, both will have the same kinetic energy. The arrow with the pointed tip, however, will invariably do more damage to the apple than the one with the suction cup. Similarly, some forms of radiation cause greater harm than other forms, even when we receive the same number of rads from both forms.

The unit of measure for radiation dosage based on potential damage is the **rem** (*r*oentgen *e*quivalent *m*an).* In calculating the dosage in rems, we multiply the number of rads by a factor that corresponds to different health effects of different types of radiation as determined by clinical studies. For example, 1 rad of alpha particles has the same biological effect as 10 rads of beta particles.† We call both of these dosages 10 rems:

Particle	Radiation Dosage		Factor		Health Effect
Alpha	1 rad	×	10	=	10 rems
Beta	10 rad	×	1	=	10 rems

☑CHECKPOINT

If you have to decide between the two, would you prefer exposure to 1 rad of alpha particles or 1 rad of beta particles?

Check Your Answer

Multiply these quantities of radiation by the appropriate factor to get the dosages in rems. Alpha: 1 rad × 10 = 10 rems. Beta: 1 rad × 1 = 1 rem. The factors show us that, physiologically speaking, alpha particles are 10 times more damaging than beta particles.

Doses of Radiation

Lethal doses of radiation begin at 500 rems. A person has about a 50 percent chance of surviving a dose of this magnitude received over a short period of time. During radiation therapy, a patient may receive localized doses in excess of 200 rems daily for a period of weeks (Figure 16.7).

All the radiation we receive from natural sources and from medical procedures is only a fraction of 1 rem. For convenience, the smaller unit *millirem* is used, where 1 millirem (mrem) is 1/1000 of a rem.

The average person in the United States is exposed to about 360 mrem a year, as Table 16.1 indicates. About 80 percent of this radiation comes from natural sources, such as cosmic rays and the earth itself. A typical chest X ray exposes a person

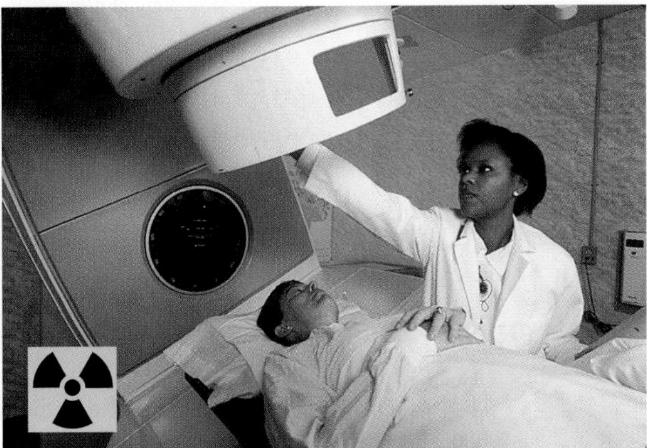

Figure 16.7
Nuclear radiation is focused on harmful tissue, such as a cancerous tumor, to kill cells selectively or to shrink the tissue, in a technique known as *radiation therapy.* This application of nuclear radiation has saved millions of lives—a clear-cut example of the benefits of nuclear technology. The inset shows the internationally used symbol indicating an area where radioactive material is being handled or produced.

*This unit is named for the discoverer of X rays, Wilhelm Roentgen.
†This is true even though beta particles have more penetrating power, as discussed in Section 16.2.

Table 16.1

Annual Radiation Exposure

Source	Typical Annual Dose (mrem)
Natural Origin	
Cosmic radiation	30
Ground	30
Air (radon-222)	200
Human tissues (K-40; Ra-226)	40
Human Origin	
Smoking	280
Medical procedures	
Diagnostic X rays	40
Nuclear medicine	15
TV tubes, other consumer products	11
Weapons-test fallout	1
Coal-burning power plants	<1
Commercial nuclear power plants	$<<1$

to 5 to 30 mrem (0.005 to 0.030 rem), less than one ten-thousandth of the lethal dose. As mentioned earlier, the human body is a significant source of natural radiation, primarily from the potassium we ingest. Our bodies contain about 200 grams of potassium. Of this quantity, about 20 milligrams is the radioactive isotope potassium-40, which is a gamma-ray emitter. Between every heartbeat, about 50,000 potassium-40 isotopes in the average human body undergo spontaneous radioactive decay. Radiation is indeed everywhere.

When radiation encounters the intricately structured molecules in the watery, ion-rich brine that makes up our cells, the radiation can create chaos on the atomic scale. Some molecules are broken, and this change alters other molecules, which can be harmful to our life processes.

Cells are able to repair most kinds of molecular damage caused by radiation, if the radiation is not too severe. A cell can survive an otherwise lethal dose of radiation, if the dose is spread over a long period of time to allow intervals for healing. When radiation is sufficient to kill cells, the dead cells can be replaced by new ones (except for most nerve cells, which are irreplaceable). Sometimes a radiated cell will survive with a damaged DNA molecule. New cells arising from the damaged cell retain the altered genetic information, producing a *mutation*. Usually the effects of a mutation are insignificant, but occasionally the mutation results in cells that do not function as well as unaffected ones, sometimes leading to a cancer. If the damaged DNA is in an individual's reproductive cells, the genetic code of the individual's offspring may retain the mutation.

Radioactive Tracers

In scientific laboratories, radioactive samples of all the elements have been made. This is accomplished by bombardment with neutrons or other particles.

Figure 16.8
Tracking fertilizer uptake with a radioactive isotope.

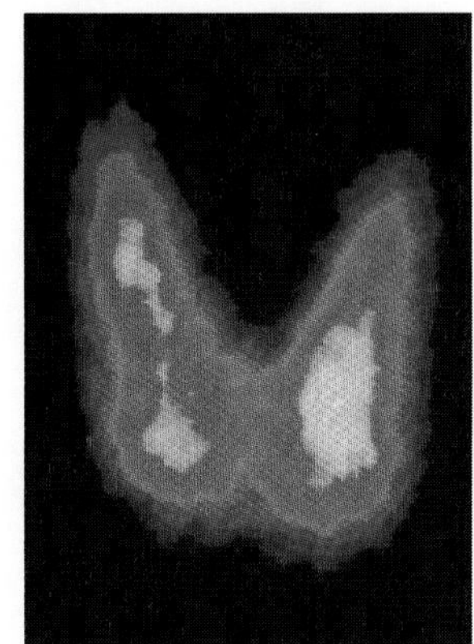

Figure 16.9
The thyroid gland, located in the neck, absorbs much of the iodine that enters the body through food and drink. Images of the thyroid gland, such as the one shown here, can be obtained by giving a patient the radioactive isotope iodine-131. These images are useful in diagnosing metabolic disorders.

Radioactive materials are extremely useful in scientific research and industry. To check the action of a fertilizer, for example, researchers combine a small amount of radioactive material with the fertilizer and then apply the combination to a few plants. The amount of radioactive fertilizer taken up by the plants can easily be measured with radiation detectors. From such measurements, scientists can inform farmers of the proper amount of fertilizer to use. Radioactive isotopes used to trace such pathways are called *tracers.*

In a technique known as medical imaging, tracers are used for the diagnosis of internal disorders. This technique works because the path the tracer takes is influenced only by its physical and chemical properties, not by its radioactivity. The tracer may be introduced alone or along with some other chemical that helps target the tracer to a particular type of tissue in the body.

16.4 The Atomic Nucleus and the Strong Nuclear Force

As described in Chapter 14, the atomic nucleus occupies only a few quadrillionths the volume of the atom, leaving most of the atom as empty space. The nucleus is composed of **nucleons,** which is the collective name for protons and neutrons.

Just as there are energy levels for the orbital electrons of an atom, there are energy levels within the nucleus. Whereas orbiting electrons emit photons when making transitions to lower energy levels, similar energy changes occur in radioactive nuclei that result in the emission of gamma-ray photons. This is gamma radiation.

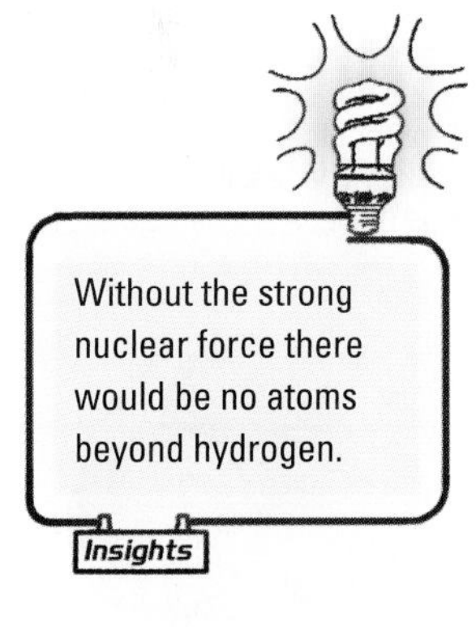

We know that electrical charges of like signs repel one another. So how is it possible that positively charged protons in the nucleus remain clumped together? This question led to the discovery of an attraction called the **strong nuclear force,** which acts between all nucleons. This force is very strong, but only over extremely short distances (about 10^{-15} meters, the diameter of a typical atomic nucleus). Repulsive electrical interactions, on the other hand, have a relatively long range. Figure 16.10 compares the strength of these two forces over distance. For protons that are close together, as in small nuclei, the attractive strong nuclear force easily overcomes the repulsive electrical force. But, for protons that are far apart, such as those on opposite edges of a large nucleus, the attractive strong nuclear force may be weaker than the repulsive electrical force.

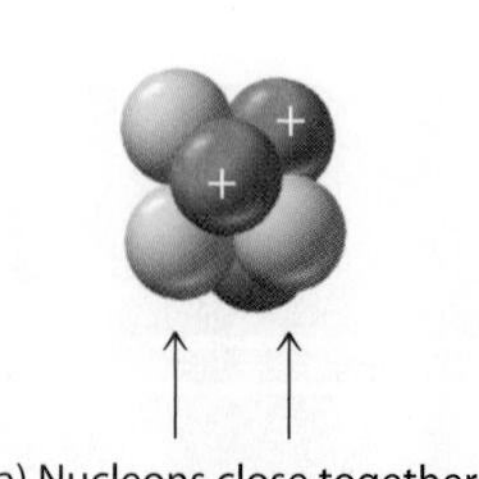

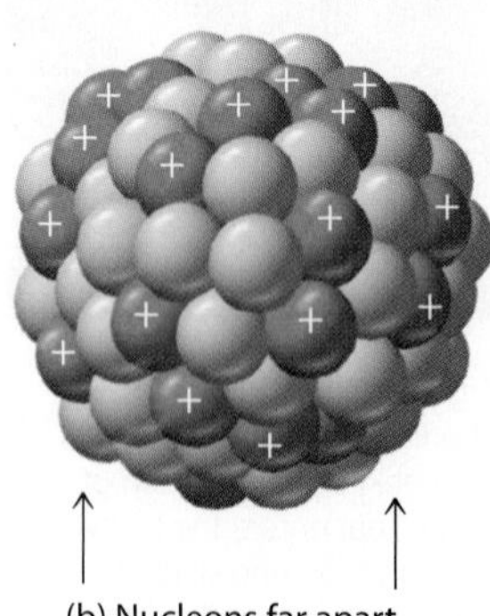

Figure 16.11
(a) All nucleons in a small atomic nucleus are close to one another; hence, they experience an attractive strong nuclear force. (b) Nucleons on opposite sides of a larger nucleus are not as close to one another, and so the attractive strong nuclear forces holding them together are much weaker. The result is that the large nucleus is less stable.

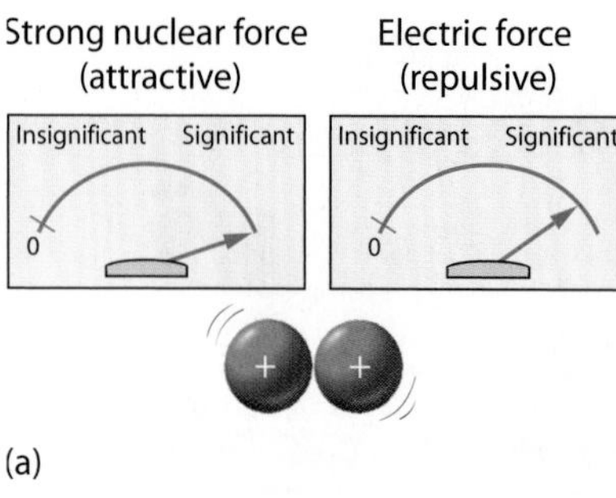

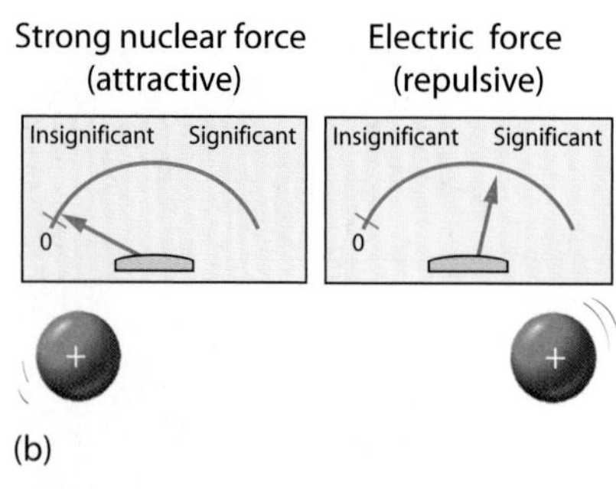

Figure 16.10
(a) Two protons near each other experience both an attractive strong nuclear force and a repulsive electric force. At this tiny separation distance, the strong nuclear force overcomes the electric force, resulting in their remaining together. (b) When the two protons are relatively far from each other, the electric force is more significant. The protons repel each other. This proton–proton repulsion in large atomic nuclei reduces nuclear stability.

A large nucleus is not as stable as a small one. In a helium nucleus, for example, each of the two protons feels the repulsive effect of the other. In a uranium nucleus, each proton feels the repulsive effects of the other 91 protons! The nucleus is unstable. We see that there is a limit to the size of the atomic nucleus. It is for this reason that all nuclei having more than 83 protons are radioactive.

☑ CHECKPOINT

Two protons in the atomic nucleus repel each other, but they are also attracted to each other. Why?

Check Your Answer

While two protons repel each other by the electric force, they also attract each other by the strong nuclear force. Both of these forces act simultaneously. So long as the attractive strong nuclear force is stronger than the repulsive electric force, the protons will remain together. Under conditions in which the electric force overcomes the strong nuclear force, however, the protons fly apart from each other.

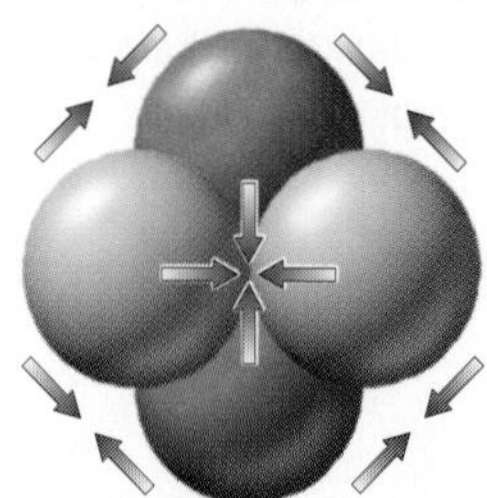

All nucleons, both protons and neutrons, attract one another by the strong nuclear force.

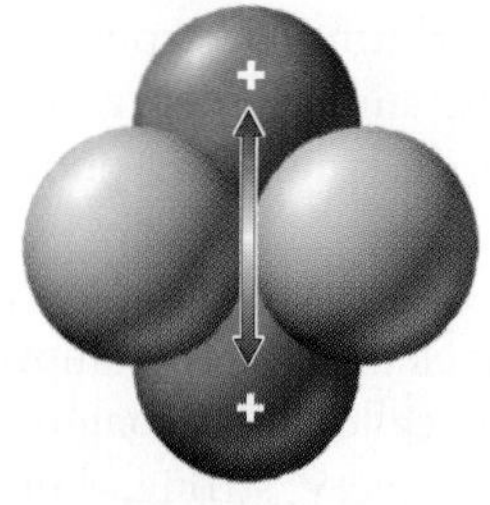

Only protons repel one another by the electric force.

Figure 16.12
The presence of neutrons helps hold the nucleus together by increasing the effect of the strong nuclear force, represented by the single-headed arrows.

Neutrons serve as a "nuclear cement" holding the atomic nucleus together. Protons attract both protons and neutrons by the strong nuclear force. Protons also repel other protons by the electric force. Neutrons, on the other hand, have no electric charge and so only attract other protons and neutrons by the strong nuclear force. The presence of neutrons therefore adds to the attraction among nucleons and helps to hold the nucleus together (Figure 16.12).

The more protons there are in a nucleus, the more neutrons are needed to help balance the repulsive electric forces. For light elements, it is sufficient to have about as many neutrons as protons. For example, the most common isotope of carbon, C-12, has equal numbers of each—six protons and six neutrons. For large nuclei, more neutrons than protons are needed. Because the strong nuclear force diminishes rapidly over distance, nucleons must be practically touching in order for the strong nuclear force to be effective. Nucleons on opposite sides of a large atomic nucleus are not attracted to one another. The electric force, however, diminishes very little across the diameter of a large nucleus, and so it wins out over the strong nuclear force. To compensate for the near absence of the strong nuclear force across the diameter of the nucleus, large nuclei have more neutrons than protons. Lead, for example, has about one and one-half times as many neutrons as protons.

So we see that neutrons have a stabilizing effect, and large nuclei require an abundance of them. But neutrons are not always successful in keeping a nucleus intact. Interestingly, neutrons are unstable when they are by themselves. A lone neutron is radioactive, and it spontaneously transforms to a proton and an electron (Figure 16.13a). A neutron seems to need protons around to keep this from occurring. After the size of a nucleus reaches a certain point, the neutrons so outnumber the protons that there are not sufficient protons in the mix to prevent the neutrons from turning into protons. As neutrons in a nucleus change into protons, the stability of the nucleus decreases because the repulsive electric force becomes increasingly significant. The result is that pieces of the nucleus fragment away in the form of radiation, as indicated in Figure 16.13b.

☑ CHECKPOINT

What role do neutrons serve in the atomic nucleus? What is the fate of a neutron when alone or distant from one or more protons?

Check Your Answers

Neutrons serve as a nuclear cement in nuclei, and they add to nuclear stability. But when alone or away from protons, a neutron becomes radioactive, and it spontaneously transforms to a proton and an electron.

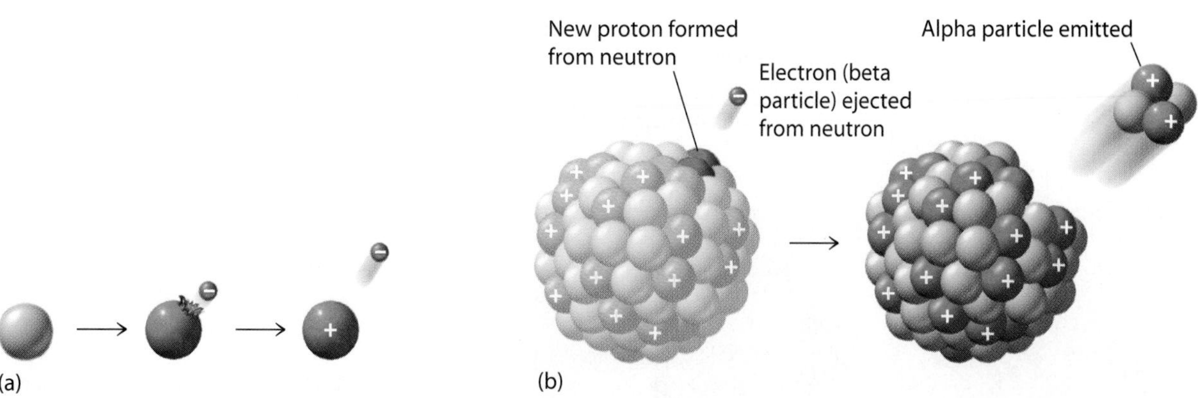

Figure 16.13
(a) A neutron near a proton is stable, but a neutron by itself is unstable and decays to a proton by emitting an electron. (b) Destabilized by an increase in the number of protons, the nucleus begins to shed fragments, such as alpha particles.

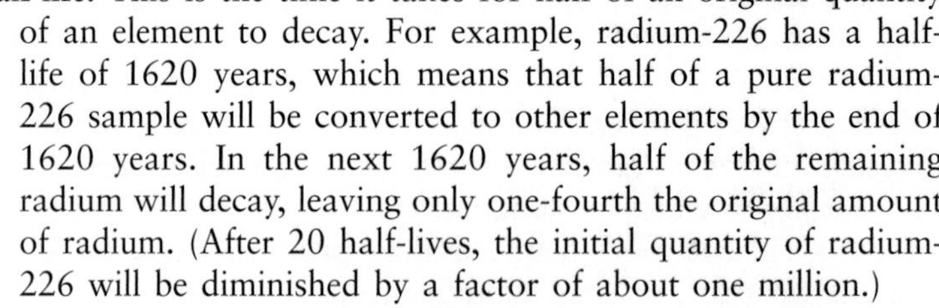

16.5 Half-life

The rate of decay for a radioactive isotope is measured in terms of a characteristic time, the **half-life.** This is the time it takes for half of an original quantity of an element to decay. For example, radium-226 has a half-life of 1620 years, which means that half of a pure radium-226 sample will be converted to other elements by the end of 1620 years. In the next 1620 years, half of the remaining radium will decay, leaving only one-fourth the original amount of radium. (After 20 half-lives, the initial quantity of radium-226 will be diminished by a factor of about one million.)

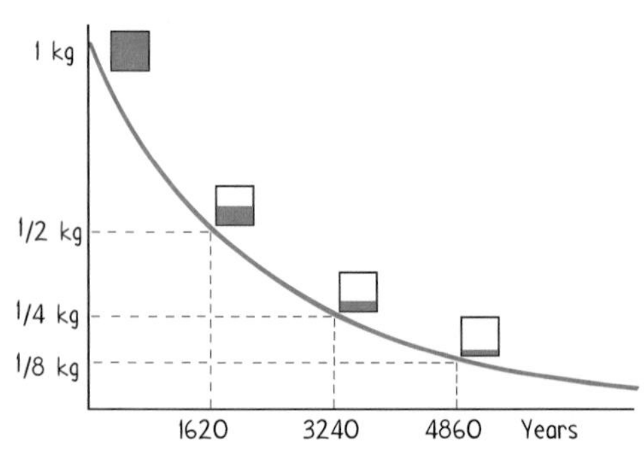

Figure 16.14
Every 1620 years, the amount of radium in a given sample decreases by half.

Half-lives are remarkably constant and not affected by external conditions. Some radioactive isotopes have half-lives that are less than a millionth of a second, while others have half-lives of more than a billion years. Uranium-238 has a half-life of 4.5 billion years. All uranium isotopes eventually decay in a series of steps to become lead.

It is not necessary to wait through the duration of a half-life in order to measure it. The half-life of an element can be calculated at any given moment by measuring the rate of decay of a known quantity. This is easily done using a radiation detector (Figure 16.15). In general, the shorter the half-life of a substance, the faster it disintegrates, and the more radioactivity per amount is detected.

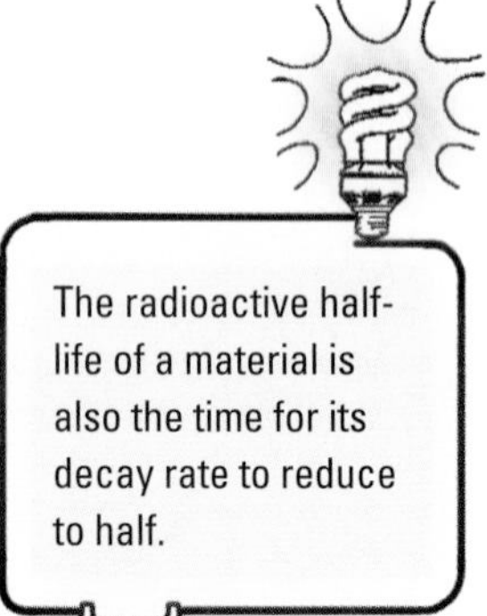

☑ CHECKPOINT

1. If a sample of radioactive isotopes has a half-life of 1 day, how much of the original sample will remain at the end of the second day? The third day?
2. Which will give a higher counting rate on a radiation detector—radioactive material that has a short half-life or a long half-life?

Check Your Answers

1. One-fourth of the original sample will be left—the three-fourths that underwent decay is then a different element altogether. At the end of 3 days, one-eighth of the original sample will remain.
2. The material with the shorter half-life is more active and will show a higher counting rate on a radiation detector.

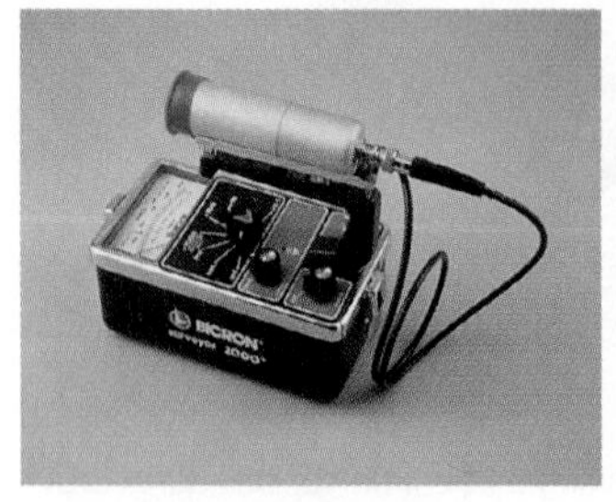

(a)

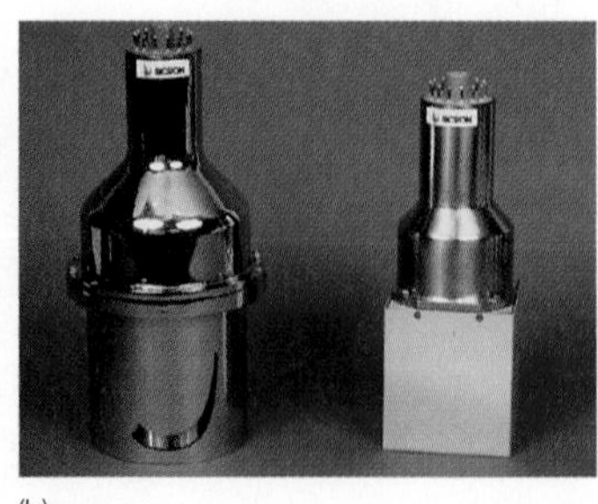

(b)

Figure 16.15
Radiation detectors. (a) A Geiger counter detects incoming radiation by its ionizing effect on enclosed gas in the tube. (b) A scintillation counter detects incoming radiation by flashes of light that are produced when charged particles or gamma rays pass through it.

16.6 Transmutation of the Elements

When a radioactive nucleus emits an alpha or a beta particle, there is a change in atomic number—a different element is formed. The changing of one chemical element to another is called **transmutation.** Transmutation occurs in natural events and is also initiated artificially in the laboratory.

Natural Transmutation

Consider uranium-238, the nucleus of which contains 92 protons and 146 neutrons. When an alpha particle is ejected, the nucleus loses two protons and two neutrons. Because an element is defined by the number of protons in its nucleus, the 90 protons and 144 neutrons left behind are no longer identified as being uranium. What we have is the nucleus of a different element—thorium. This transmutation can be written as a nuclear equation:

$$^{238}_{92}\text{U} \rightarrow {}^{234}_{90}\text{Th} + {}^{4}_{2}\text{He}$$

We see that $^{238}_{92}\text{U}$ transmutes to the two elements written to the right of the arrow. When this transmutation occurs, energy is released, partly in the form of kinetic energy of the alpha particle ($^{4}_{2}\text{He}$), partly in the kinetic energy of the thorium atom, and partly in the form of gamma radiation. In this and all such equations, the mass numbers at the top balance ($238 = 234 + 4$) and the atomic numbers at the bottom also balance ($92 = 90 + 2$).

Thorium-234, the product of this reaction, is also radioactive. When it decays, it emits a beta particle.* Since a beta particle is an electron, the atomic number of the resulting nucleus is *increased* by 1. So, after beta emission by thorium with 90 protons, the resulting element has 91 protons (a neutron ejects the beta and becomes a proton). It is no longer thorium, but has become the element protactinium. Although the atomic number has increased by 1 in this process, the mass number (protons + neutrons) remains the same. The nuclear equation is

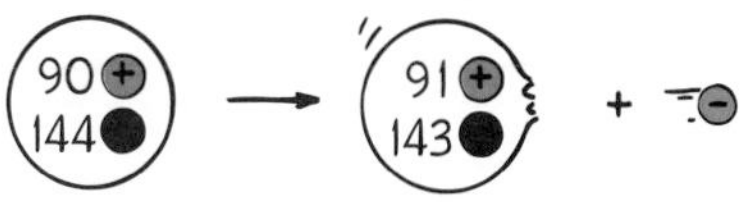

$$^{234}_{90}\text{Th} \rightarrow {}^{234}_{91}\text{Pa} + {}^{0}_{-1}\text{e}$$

*Beta emission is always accompanied by the emission of a neutrino (actually an antineutrino), a neutral particle with nearly zero mass that travels at about the speed of light. The neutrino ("little neutral one") was postulated by Wolfgang Pauli in 1930 and detected in 1956. Neutrinos are difficult to detect because they interact very weakly with matter. Whereas a piece of solid lead a few centimeters thick will stop most gamma rays from a radium source, a piece of lead about 8 light-years thick would be needed to stop half the neutrinos produced in typical nuclear decays. Thousands of neutrinos are flying through you every second of every day, because the universe is filled with them. Only occasionally, one or two times a year or so, does a neutrino or two interact with the matter of your body.

At this writing, the mass of the neutrino is unknown. Neutrinos are so numerous in the universe that, if they have even the tiniest mass, they might constitute most of the mass of the universe. Neutrinos may be the "glue" that holds the universe together.

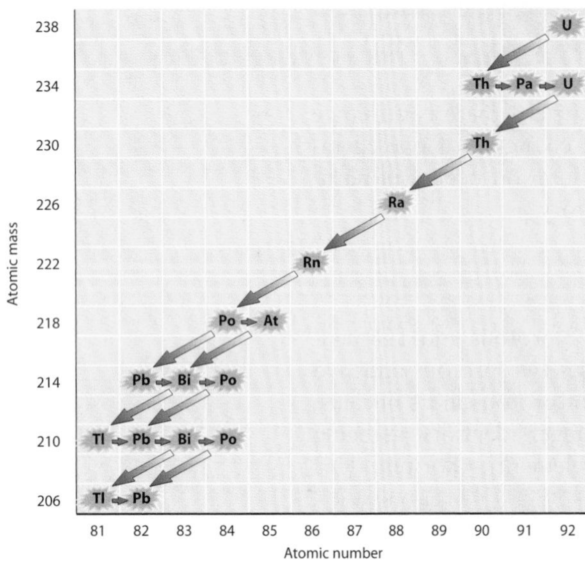

Figure 16.16
U-238 decays to Pb-206 through a series of alpha and beta decays.

We write an electron as $_{-1}^{0}e$. The superscript 0 indicates that the electron's mass is insignificant relative to that of protons and neutrons. The subscript −1 is the electric charge of the electron.

So we see that, when an element ejects an alpha particle from its nucleus, the mass number of the resulting atom is decreased by 4, and its atomic number is decreased by 2. The resulting atom is an element two spaces back in the periodic table of the elements. When an element ejects a beta particle from its nucleus, the mass of the atom is practically unaffected, meaning there is no change in its mass number, but its atomic number increases by 1. The resulting atom belongs to an element one place forward in the periodic table. Gamma emission results in no change in either the mass number or the atomic number. So we see that radioactive elements can decay backward or forward in the periodic table.*

The successions of radioactive decays of $^{238}_{92}U$ to $^{206}_{82}Pb$, an isotope of lead, is shown in Figure 16.16. Each gray arrow shows an alpha decay, and each red arrow shows a beta decay. Notice that some of the nuclei in the series can decay in both ways. This is one of several similar radioactive series that occur in nature.

☑ CHECKPOINT

1. Complete the following nuclear reactions.
   a. $^{226}_{88}Ra \longrightarrow \, ^{?}_{?}? + \, _{-1}^{0}e$
   b. $^{209}_{84}Po \longrightarrow \, ^{205}_{82}Pb + \, ^{?}_{?}?$
2. What finally becomes of all the uranium that undergoes radioactive decay?

Check Your Answers

1. a. $^{226}_{88}Ra \longrightarrow \, ^{226}_{89}Ac + \, _{-1}^{0}e$
   b. $^{209}_{84}Po \longrightarrow \, ^{205}_{82}Pb + \, ^{4}_{2}He$
2. All uranium will ultimately become lead. On the way to becoming lead, it will exist as a series of elements, as indicated in Figure 16.16.

Artificial Transmutation

Ernest Rutherford, in 1919, was the first of many investigators to succeed in transmuting a chemical element. He bombarded nitrogen gas with alpha

*Sometimes a nucleus emits a positron, which is the "antiparticle" of an electron. In this case, a proton becomes a neutron, and the atomic number is decreased.

particles from a piece of radioactive ore. The impact of an alpha particle on a nitrogen nucleus transmutes nitrogen into oxygen:

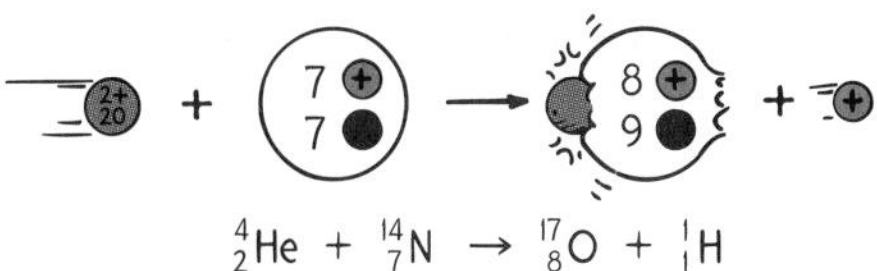

$$^4_2He + ^{14}_7N \rightarrow ^{17}_8O + ^1_1H$$

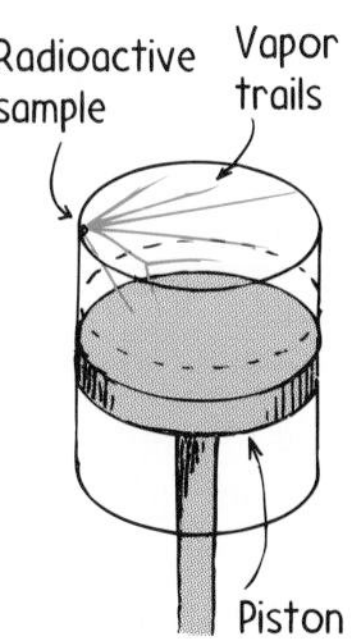

Figure 16.17
A cloud chamber. Charged particles moving through supersaturated vapor leave trails. When the chamber is in a strong electric or magnetic field, bending of the tracks provides information about the charge, mass, and momentum of the particles.

Rutherford used a device called a *cloud chamber* to record this event (Figure 16.17). In a cloud chamber, moving charged particles leave a visible trail of ions along their path, much as a jet plane high in the sky leaves a contrail of water vapor and ice crystals in its wake. From a quarter-million cloud-chamber tracks photographed on movie film, Rutherford showed seven examples of atomic transmutation. Analysis of tracks bent by a strong external magnetic field showed that, when an alpha particle collided with a nitrogen atom, a proton bounced out, and the heavy atom recoiled a short distance. The alpha particle disappeared. The alpha particle was absorbed in the process, transforming nitrogen to oxygen.

Since Rutherford's announcement in 1919, experimenters have carried out many other nuclear reactions, first with natural bombarding projectiles from radioactive ores and then with still more energetic projectiles—protons and electrons hurled by huge particle accelerators. Artificial transmutation is what produces the previously unknown synthetic elements from atomic numbers 93 to 116. All these artificially made elements have short half-lives. If they ever existed naturally when earth was formed, they have long since decayed.

Figure 16.18
Tracks of elementary particles in a bubble chamber, a similar yet more complicated device than a cloud chamber. Two particles have been destroyed at the points where the spirals emanate, and four others have been created in the collision.

The alchemists of old tried vainly for more than two thousand years to cause the transmutation of one element to another. Despite their fervent efforts and rituals, they never came close to succeeding. Ironically, nuclear transmutations were going on all around them, which they never detected. And if they had detected them, they would not have recognized the transmutation process, because they lacked an adequate theory to guide them.

Insights

16.7 Isotopic Dating

The earth's atmosphere is continuously bombarded by cosmic rays, and this bombardment causes many atoms in the upper atmosphere to transmute. These transmutations result in many protons and neutrons being "sprayed out" into the environment. Most of the protons are stopped as they collide with the atoms of the upper atmosphere, stripping electrons from these atoms to become hydrogen

The terms *isotopic dating* and *radiometric dating* (Section 30.2) are interchangeable. Both terms refer to the nuclear decay of naturally occurring radioactive isotopes. Although the terms are interchangeable, for geologic age determination we generally use the term radiometric dating.

Insights

atoms. The neutrons, however, keep going for longer distances because they have no electrical charge and therefore do not interact electrically with matter. Eventually, many of them collide with the nuclei in the denser lower atmosphere. A nitrogen atom that captures a neutron, for example, becomes an isotope of carbon by emitting a proton:

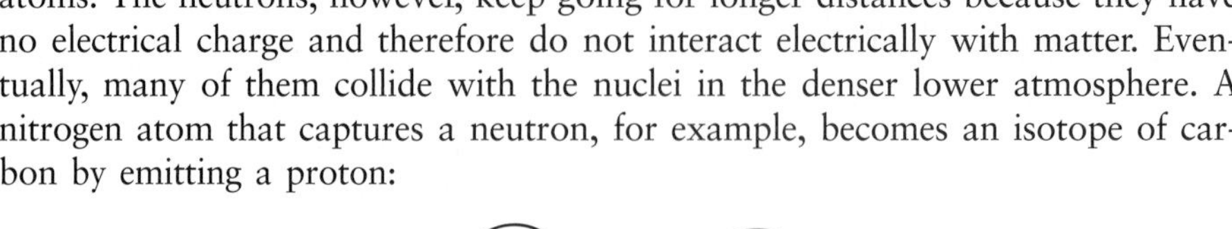

$$^{1}_{0}n + ^{14}_{7}N \rightarrow ^{14}_{6}C + ^{1}_{1}H$$

This carbon-14 isotope, which makes up less than one-millionth of 1 percent of the carbon in the atmosphere, is radioactive and has eight neutrons. (The most common isotope, carbon-12, has six neutrons and is not radioactive). Because both carbon-12 and carbon-14 are forms of carbon, they have the same chemical properties. Both these isotopes can react chemically with oxygen to form carbon dioxide, which is taken in by plants. This means that all plants contain a tiny bit of radioactive carbon-14. All animals eat plants (or at least plant-eating animals) and therefore have a little carbon-14 in them. In short, all living things on earth contain some carbon-14.

Carbon-14 is a beta emitter, and it decays back to nitrogen by the following reaction:

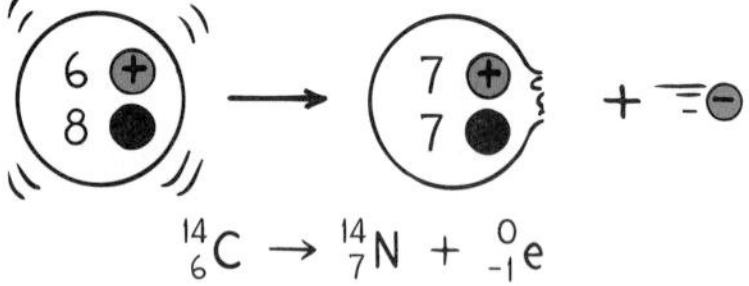

$$^{14}_{6}C \rightarrow ^{14}_{7}N + ^{0}_{-1}e$$

Because plants continue to absorb carbon dioxide as long as they live, any carbon-14 lost by decay is immediately replenished with fresh carbon-14 from the atmosphere. In this way, a radioactive equilibrium is reached where there is a constant ratio of about one carbon-14 atom to every 100 billion carbon-12 atoms. When a plant dies, replenishment of carbon-14 stops. Then the percentage of carbon-14 decreases at a constant rate given by its half-life.* The longer a plant or other organism is dead, therefore, the less carbon-14 it contains relative to the constant amount of carbon-12.

The half-life of carbon-14 is about 5730 years. This means that half of the carbon-14 atoms that are now present in a plant or animal that dies today will decay in the next 5730 years. Half of the remaining carbon-14 atoms will then decay in the following 5730 years, and so forth.

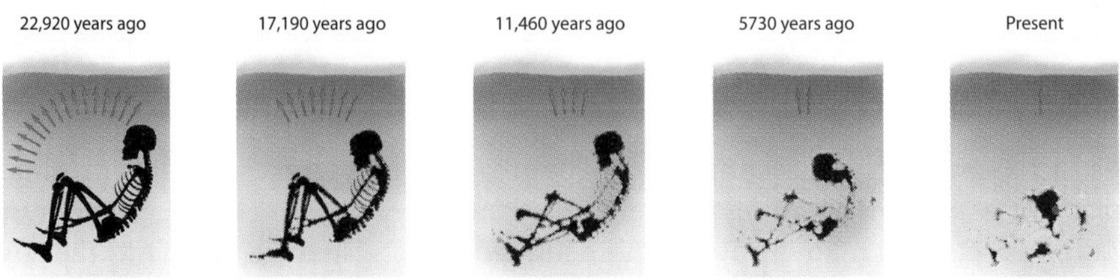

Figure 16.19
The amount of radioactive carbon-14 in the skeleton diminishes by one-half every 5730 years, with the result that the skeleton today contains only a fraction of the carbon-14 it originally had. The red arrows symbolize relative amounts of carbon-14.

*A 1-g sample of contemporary carbon contains about 5×10^{22} atoms, 6.5×10^{10} of which are C-14 atoms. Carbon-14 has a beta disintegration rate of about 13.5 decays per minute.

Link to Section 33.4

With this knowledge, scientists are able to calculate the age of carbon-containing artifacts or remains, such as wooden tools or skeletons, by measuring their current level of radioactivity. This process, known as **carbon-14 dating,** enables us to probe as much as 50,000 years into the past. Beyond this time span, there is too little carbon-14 remaining to permit accurate analysis.

Carbon-14 dating would be an extremely simple and accurate dating method if the amount of radioactive carbon in the atmosphere had been constant over the ages. But it hasn't been. Fluctuations in the sun's magnetic field, as well as changes in the strength of the earth's magnetic field, affect cosmic-ray intensities in the earth's atmosphere, which, in turn, produce fluctuations in the production of C-14. In addition, changes in the earth's climate affect the amount of carbon dioxide in the atmosphere. The oceans are great reservoirs of carbon dioxide. When the oceans are cold, they release less carbon dioxide into the atmosphere than when they are warm. We'll return to the oceans and their interplay with carbon in Chapter 31.

☑ CHECKPOINT

Suppose that an archaeologist extracts a gram of carbon from an ancient ax handle and finds that it is one-fourth as radioactive as a gram of carbon extracted from a freshly cut tree branch. About how old is the ax handle?

Check Your Answer

Assuming the ratio of C-14/C-12 was the same when the ax was made, the ax handle is as old as two half-lives of C-14, or about 11,460 years old.

The dating of older, but inorganic, things is accomplished with radioactive minerals, such as uranium. The naturally occurring isotopes U-238 and U-235 decay very slowly and ultimately become isotopes of lead—but not the common lead isotope Pb-208. For example, U-238 decays through several stages to finally become Pb-206, whereas U-235 finally becomes the isotope Pb-207. Lead isotopes 206 and 207 that now exist were at one time uranium. The older the uranium-bearing rock, the higher the percentage of these remnant isotopes.

From the half-lives of uranium isotopes, and the percentage of lead isotopes in uranium bearing rock, it is possible to calculate the date at which the rock was formed. We'll return to isotopic dating when we investigate the dynamic earth in Chapter 30.

16.8 Nuclear Fission

In 1938, two German scientists, Otto Hahn and Fritz Strassmann, made an accidental discovery that was to change the world. While bombarding a sample of uranium with neutrons in the hope of creating new, heavier elements, they were astonished to discover chemical evidence for the production of barium, an element having about half the mass of uranium. Hahn wrote of this news to his former colleague Lise Meitner, who had fled from Nazi Germany to Sweden because of her Jewish ancestry. From the evidence given to her by

Hahn, Meitner concluded that the uranium nucleus, activated by neutron bombardment, had split in half. Soon thereafter, Meitner, working with her nephew, Otto Frisch, also a physicist, published a paper in which the term *nuclear fission* was first coined.

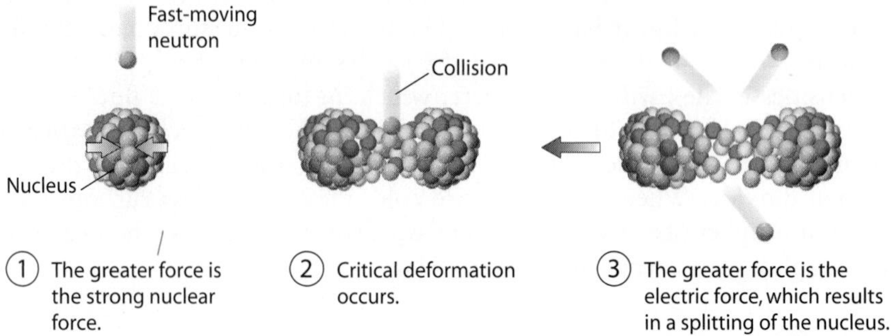

Figure 16.20
Nuclear deformation may result in repulsive electrical forces overcoming attractive nuclear forces, in which case fission takes place.

In the nucleus of every atom, there exists a delicate balance between attractive nuclear forces and repulsive electric forces between protons. In all known nuclei, the nuclear forces dominate. In uranium, however, this domination is tenuous. If a uranium nucleus stretches into an elongated shape (Figure 16.20), the electrical forces may push it into an even more elongated shape. If the elongation passes a certain point, electrical forces overwhelm strong nuclear forces, and the nucleus splits. This is **nuclear fission.**

The energy released by the fission of one U-235 nucleus is relatively enormous—about seven million times the energy released by the combustion of one TNT molecule. This energy is mainly in the form of the kinetic energy of the fission fragments that fly apart from one another, with some energy given to ejected neutrons and the remainder to gamma radiation.

A typical uranium fission reaction is

$$ {}^{1}_{0}n + {}^{235}_{92}\mathrm{U} \rightarrow {}^{91}_{36}\mathrm{Kr} + {}^{142}_{56}\mathrm{Ba} + 3({}^{1}_{0}n) $$

Note that, in this reaction, one neutron starts the fission of a uranium nucleus, and the fission produces three neutrons. (A fission reaction may produce fewer or more than three neutrons.) These product neutrons can cause the fissioning of three other uranium atoms, releasing nine more neutrons. If each of these nine neutrons succeeds in splitting a uranium atom, the next step in the reaction produces 27 neutrons, and so on. Such a sequence, illustrated in Figure 16.21, is called a **chain reaction**—a self-sustaining reaction in which the products of one reaction event stimulate further reaction events.

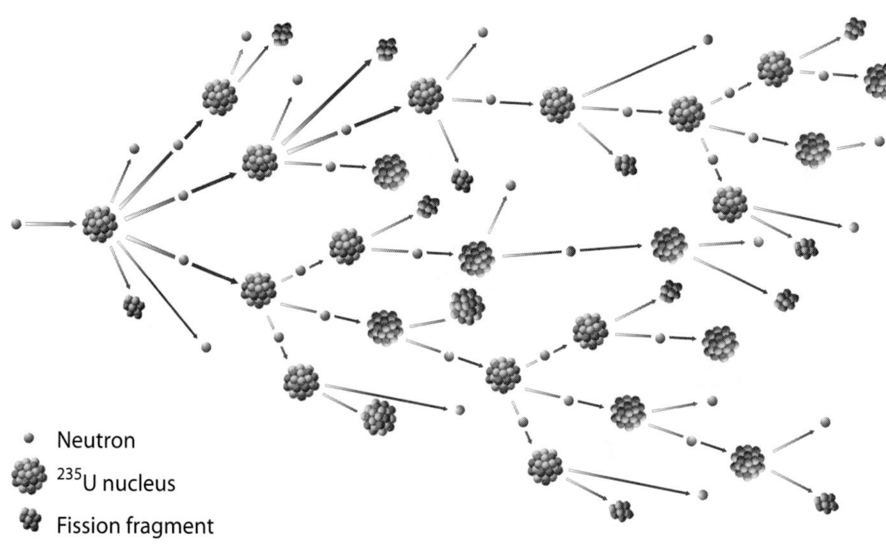

Figure 16.21
A chain reaction.

Why do chain reactions not occur in naturally occurring uranium-ore deposits? They would, if all uranium atoms fissioned so easily. Fission occurs mainly for the rare isotope U-235, which makes up only 0.7 percent of the uranium in pure uranium metal. When the more abundant isotope U-238 absorbs neutrons created by fission of U-235, the U-238 typically does not undergo fission. So any chain reaction is snuffed out by the neutron-absorbing U-238, as well as by the rock in which the ore is imbedded.

If a chain reaction were to occur in a baseball-sized chunk of pure U-235, an enormous explosion would result. If the chain reaction were started in a smaller chunk of pure U-235, however, no explosion would occur. This is because of geometry: The ratio of surface area to mass is larger in a small piece than in a large one (just as there is more skin on six small potatoes having a combined mass of 1 kilogram than there is on a single 1-kilogram potato). So there is more surface area on a bunch of small pieces of uranium than on a large piece. In a small piece of U-235, neutrons leak through the surface before an explosion can occur. In a bigger piece, the chain reaction builds up to enormous energies before the neutrons reach the surface and escape (Figure 16.23). For masses greater than a certain amount, called the **critical mass,** an explosion of enormous magnitude may occur.

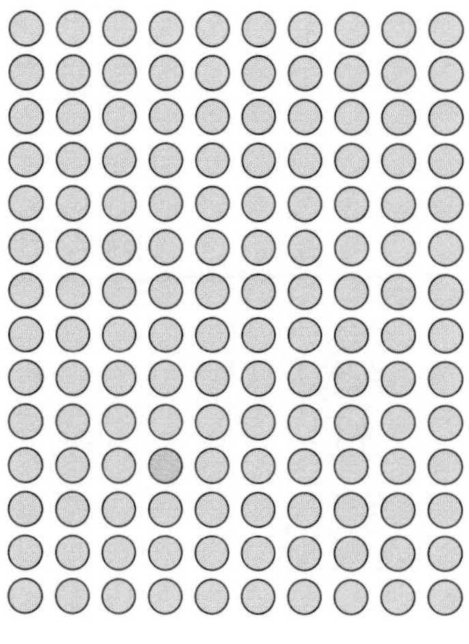

Figure 16.22
Only 1 part in 140 of naturally occurring uranium is U-235.

Consider a large quantity of U-235 divided into two pieces, each having a mass less than critical. The pieces are *subcritical.* Neutrons in either piece readily reach a surface and escape before a sizable chain reaction builds up. But, if the pieces are suddenly driven together, the total surface area decreases. If the timing is

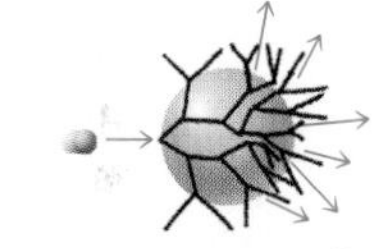

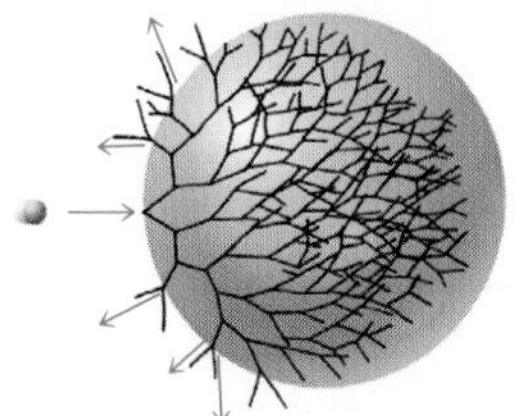

Figure 16.23
The exaggerated view shows that a chain reaction in a small piece of pure U-235 runs its course before it can cause a large explosion because neutrons leak from the surface too soon. The surface area of the small piece is large relative to the mass. In a larger piece, more uranium and less surface is presented to the neutrons.

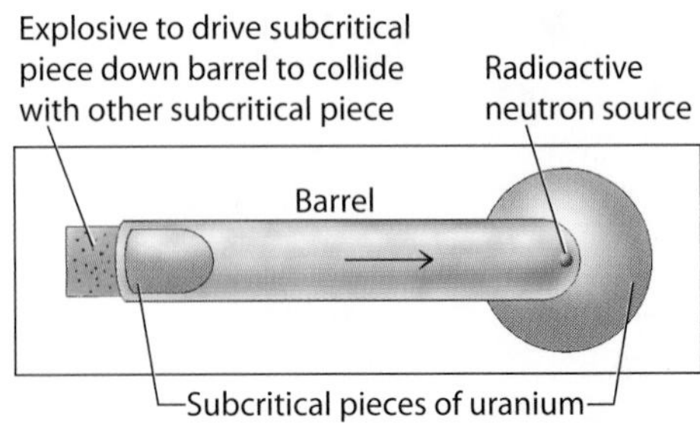

Figure 16.24
Simplified diagram of a uranium fission bomb.

right, and if the combined mass is greater than critical, a violent explosion occurs. This is what happens in a nuclear fission bomb (Figure 16.24).

Constructing a fission bomb is a formidable task. The difficulty consists in separating enough U-235 from the more abundant U-238. Scientists took more than two years to extract enough U-235 from uranium ore to make the bomb that was detonated at Hiroshima in 1945. To this day, uranium isotope separation remains a difficult process.

☑ CHECKPOINT

A 1-kilogram ball of U-235 is critical, but the same ball broken up into small chunks is not. Explain.

Check Your Answer

The small chunks have more combined surface area than the ball from which they came (just as the combined surface area of gravel is greater than the surface area of a boulder of the same mass). Neutrons escape via the surface before a sustained chain reaction can build up.

Nuclear Fission Reactors

The awesome energy of nuclear fission was introduced to the world in the form of nuclear bombs, and this violent image still colors our thinking about nuclear power, making it difficult for many people to recognize its potential usefulness. Currently, about 20 percent of electric energy in the United States is generated by *nuclear fission reactors* (whereas most electric power is nuclear in some other countries—more than 70 percent in France). These reactors are simply nuclear furnaces. They, like fossil-fuel furnaces, do nothing more elegant than boil water to produce steam for a turbine (Figure 16.25). The greatest practical difference is in the amount of fuel required: A mere 1 kilogram of uranium fuel, less than the size of a baseball, yields more energy than 30 freightcar loads of coal.

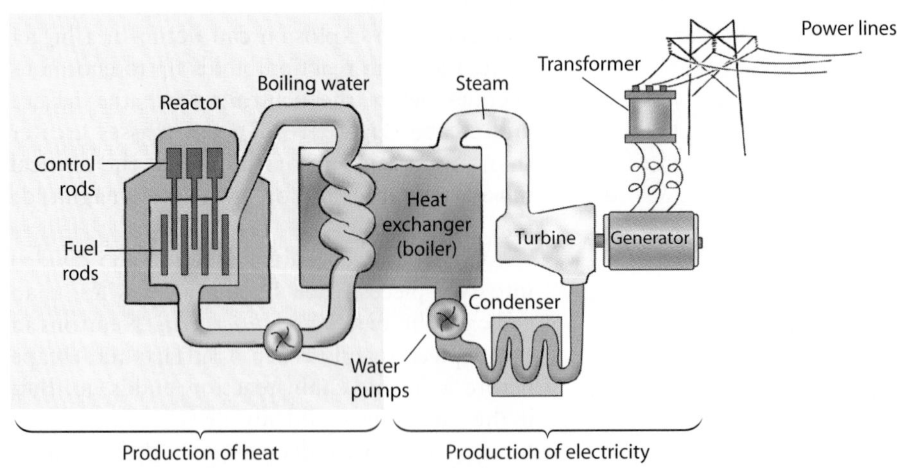

Figure 16.25
Diagram of a nuclear-fission power plant. Note that the water in contact with the fuel rods is completely contained, and radioactive materials are not involved directly in the generation of electricity.

The most common type of fission reactor contains four components: nuclear fuel, control rods, a moderator (to slow the neutrons, which are required for fission),* and a liquid (usually water) to transfer heat from the reactor to the turbine and generator. The nuclear fuel is primarily U-238, plus about 3 percent U-235. Because the U-235 isotopes are so highly diluted with U-238, an explosion like that of a nuclear bomb is not possible.† The reaction rate, which depends on the number of neutrons that initiate the fission of other U-235 nuclei, is controlled by rods inserted into the reactor. The control rods are made of a neutron-absorbing material, usually the metal cadmium or boron.

Figure 16.26
The nuclear reactor is housed within a dome-shaped containment building that is designed to prevent the release of radioactive isotopes in the event of an accident.

Heated water around the nuclear fuel is kept under high pressure to keep it at a high temperature without boiling. It transfers heat to a second water system with lower pressure, which operates the turbine and electric generator in a conventional fashion. In this design, two separate water systems are used so that no radioactivity reaches the turbine or the outside environment.

One disadvantage of fission power is the generation of radioactive waste products. Light atomic nuclei are most stable when composed of equal numbers of protons and neutrons, and mainly heavy nuclei need more neutrons than protons for stability. For example, there are 143 neutrons but only 92 protons in U-235. When uranium fissions into two medium-weight elements, the extra neutrons in their nuclei make them unstable. These elements are radioactive. Most of these elements have very short half-lives, but some have half-lives of thousands of years. Safely disposing of these waste products (as well as materials made radioactive in the production of nuclear fuels) requires special storage casks and procedures. Although fission has been successfully producing electricity for a half century, the search for satisfactory ways of disposing of radioactive wastes in the United States has remained unsuccessful.‡

Know nukes before you say "No nukes"!

Insights

The benefits of fission power are plentiful electricity, conservation of the many billions of tons of fossil fuels that every year are literally turned to heat and smoke (which fuels, in the long run, may be far more precious as sources of organic molecules than as sources of heat), and the elimination of the megatons of sulfur oxides and other poisons that are put into the air each year by the burning of fossil fuels.

*Moderators are graphite, heavy water, or other substances that decrease the speeds of neutrons so they can be captured by the fissionable isotope. Interestingly, although slow neutrons in a reactor maintain the fission process, in a detonated nuclear bomb, slow neutrons couldn't keep up with the explosion and it would fizzle out. So one of the safeguards of commercial reactors is that slow neutrons can't sustain a substantial explosion. Even the 1986 Chernobyl accident was an incomplete explosion in a primitive reactor of a type no longer being manufactured.

†In a worst-case accident, however, heat sufficient to melt the reactor core is possible—and, if the reactor building is not strong enough, a meltdown can indeed spread radioactivity into the environment. Such an accident occurred at the Chernobyl reactor.

‡Whereas Americans deeply bury radioactive wastes, the French do not. Instead, they tend and monitor radioactive wastes in underground storage facilities. Just as the tailings of gold mines and other mines were considered worthless a century ago, but today are being reworked for their commercial value, so today's radioactive wastes may well be valued in coming years. If and when a technology emerges to tap this potential, the French will be prepared.

☑ CHECKPOINT

Coal contains tiny quantities of radioactive materials, enough so there is more environmental radiation surrounding a typical coal-fired power plant than surrounds a fission power plant. What does this indicate about the radioactive safeguards required for the two types of power plants?

Check Your Answer

Coal-fired power plants are as American as apple pie, with no required safeguards for restricting the emissions of radioactive particles. Their radioactive byproducts go unrecognized by the public. Nuclear reactors, on the other hand, are very much in the public spotlight (for good reason), and extensive safeguards are required to ensure strictly low levels of radioactive emissions.

The Breeder Reactor

One of the fascinating features of fission power is the fabrication (breeding) of fission fuel from nonfissionable U-238. This breeding occurs when small amounts of fissionable isotopes are mixed with U-238 in a reactor. Fission liberates neutrons that convert the relatively abundant nonfissionable U-238 to U-239, which beta decays to Np-239, which, in turn, beta decays to fissionable plutonium—Pu-239 (Figure 16.27). So, in addition to the abundant energy produced, fission fuel is bred from the relatively abundant U-238 in the process.

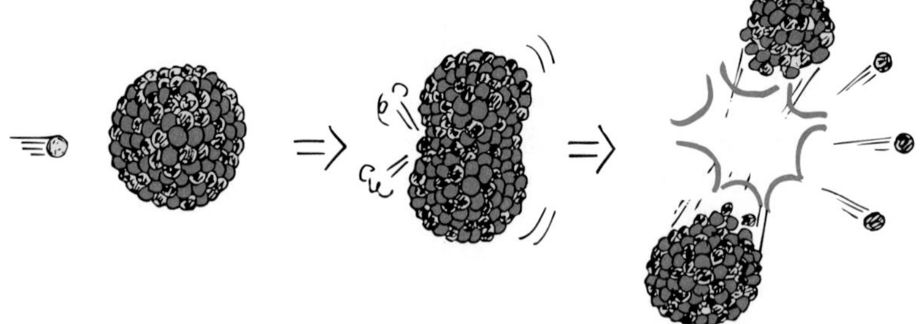

Figure 16.27
Pu-239, like U-235, undergoes fission when it captures a neutron.

Breeding occurs to some extent in all fission reactors, but a reactor specifically designed to breed more fissionable fuel than is put into it is called a **breeder reactor.** Using a breeder reactor is like filling your car's gas tank with water, adding some gasoline, then driving the car—and having more gasoline after the trip than at the beginning! The basic principle of the breeder reactor is very attractive, because, after a few years of operation, a breeder-reactor power plant can produce vast amounts of power while at the same time breeding twice as much fuel as it had at the beginning.

The downside is the enormous complexity of managing successful and safe operation. The United States abandoned breeders nearly two decades ago, and only France and Germany are still investing in them. Officials in these countries point out that the supplies of naturally occurring U-235 are limited. At present rates of consumption, all natural sources of U-235 may be depleted within a century. If countries then decide to turn to breeder reactors, they may well find themselves digging up the radioactive wastes they once buried.*

*Many nuclear scientists disagree with deep burial as a desirable solution to the nuclear-waste problem. Devices are presently being studied that could, in principle, convert long-lived radioactive atoms of spent reactor fuel into short-lived or nonradioactive atoms. (See "Will New Technology Solve the Nuclear Waste Problem?" in *The Physics Teacher,* Vol. 35, February, 1997.) Quite possibly, nuclear wastes may not plague future generations indefinitely, as has been commonly thought.

16.9 The Mass–Energy Relationship—$E = mc^2$

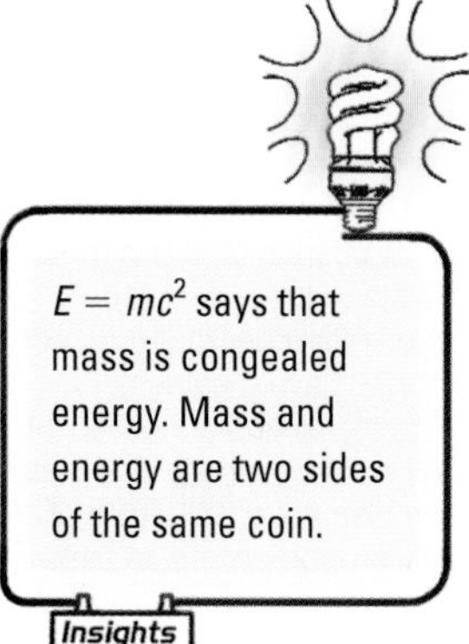

Clearly a lot of energy comes from every gram of nuclear fuel that is fissioned. What is the source of this energy? As we will see, it comes from nucleons losing mass as they undergo nuclear reactions.

Early in the early 1900s, Albert Einstein discovered that mass is actually "congealed" energy. Mass and energy are two sides of the same coin, as stated in his celebrated equation $E = mc^2$. In this equation, E stands for the energy that any mass has at rest, m stands for mass, and c is the speed of light. The quantity c^2 is the proportionality constant of energy and mass. This relationship between energy and mass is the key to understanding why and how energy is released in nuclear reactions.

Figure 16.28
Work is required to pull a nucleon from an atomic nucleus. This work increases the energy, and hence the mass, of the nucleon outside the nucleus.

The more energy associated with a particle, the greater the mass of the particle. Is the mass of a nucleon inside a nucleus the same as that of the same nucleon outside a nucleus? This question can be answered by considering the work that would be required to separate nucleons from a nucleus. From physics, we know that work, which is expended energy, is equal to force × distance. Think of the amount of force required to pull a nucleon out of the nucleus through a sufficient distance to overcome the attractive strong nuclear force, comically indicated in Figure 16.28. Enormous work would be required. This work is energy that is added to the nucleon that is pulled out.

According to Einstein's equation, this newly acquired energy reveals itself as an increase in the nucleon's mass. The mass of a nucleon outside a nucleus is greater than the mass of the same nucleon locked inside a nucleus. As discussed in Chapter 14, the nucleus of a carbon-12 atom, composed of six protons and six neutrons, has a mass of exactly 12.00000 atomic mass units (amu). Therefore, on average, each nucleon contributes a mass of 1 amu. However, outside the nucleus, a proton has a mass of 1.00728 amu and a neutron has a mass of 1.00867 amu. Thus, we see that the combined mass of six free protons and six free neutrons—$(6 \times 1.00728) + (6 \times 1.00867) = 12.09570$—is greater than the mass of one carbon-12 nucleus. The greater mass reflects the energy required to pull the nucleons apart from one another. Thus, what mass a nucleon has depends on where the nucleon is.

The masses of the isotopes of various elements can be very accurately measured with a mass spectrometer (Figure 16.29). This important device uses a magnetic field to deflect ions of these isotopes into circular arcs. The greater the inertia (mass) of the ion, the harder it is to deflect, and the greater the radius of its curved path. The magnetic force sweeps lighter ions into more sharply curved arcs and heavier ions into larger arcs.*

*Interestingly, miniature mass spectrometers are used for detecting molecules associated with explosives at airport security stations. The security agent swabs luggage with a soft cloth that is placed in the device. Molecules on the swab are ionized and scrutinized.

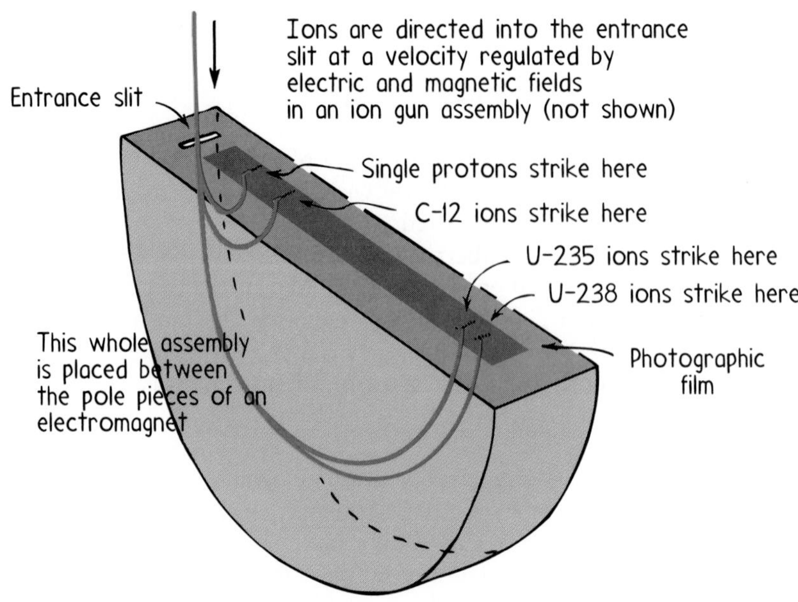

Figure 16.29
The mass spectrometer. Electrically charged isotopes are directed into the semicircular "drum," where they are forced into semicircular paths by a strong magnetic field. Lighter isotopes have less inertia (less mass), change direction more easily, and are pulled into curves of smaller radii. Heavier isotopes have greater inertia (more mass) and are pulled into curves of larger radii. The mass of an isotope, therefore, is directly proportional to its striking distance from the slit.

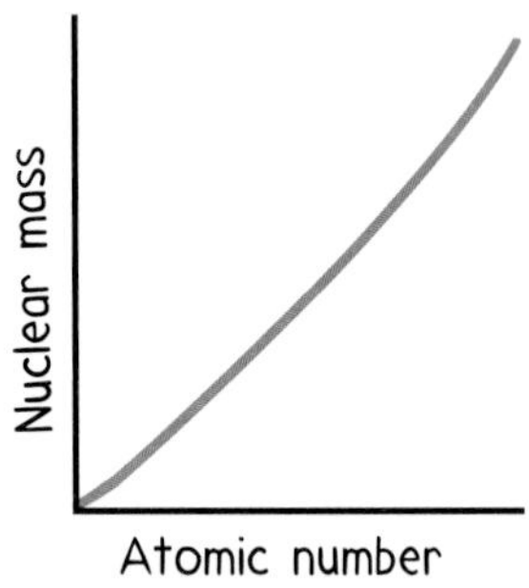

Figure 16.30
The plot shows how nuclear mass increases with increasing atomic number.

A graph of the nuclear masses of the elements ranging from hydrogen through uranium is shown in Figure 16.30. The graph slopes upward with increasing atomic number, as expected: Elements are more massive as atomic number increases. The slope curves because there are proportionally more neutrons in the more massive atoms.

A more important graph results from the plot of nuclear mass *per nucleon* inside each nucleus ranging from hydrogen through uranium (Figure 16.31). This graph is the key to understanding the energy associated with nuclear processes. To obtain the average mass per nucleon, you divide the total mass of a nucleus by the number of nucleons in the nucleus. (Similarly, if you divide the total mass of a roomful of people by the number of people in the room, you get the average mass per person.)

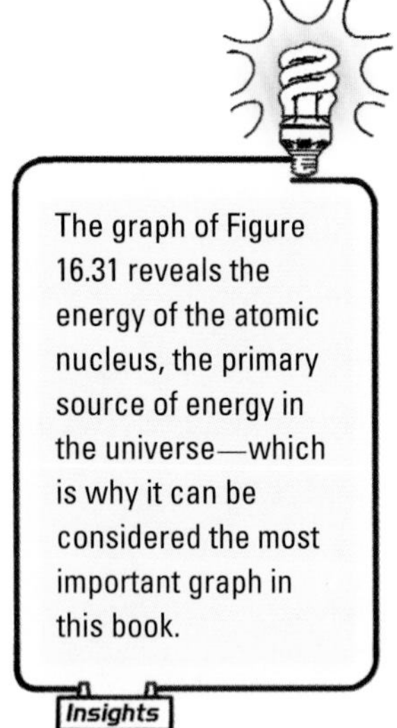

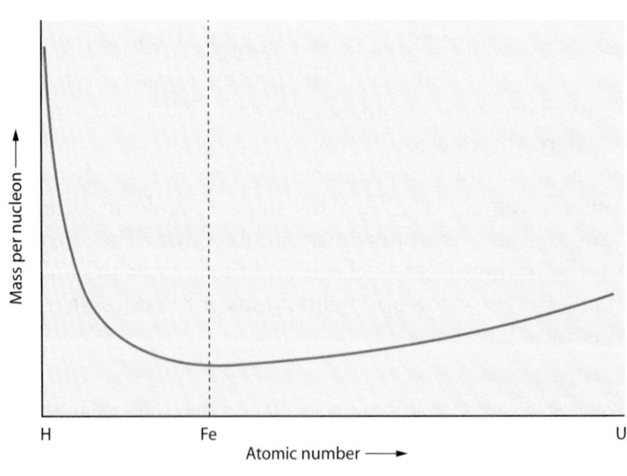

Figure 16.31
This graph shows that the average mass of a nucleon depends on which nucleus it is in. Individual nucleons have the most mass in the lightest (hydrogen) nuclei, the least mass in iron, and intermediate mass in the heaviest (uranium) nuclei.

Note that the masses of the nucleons are different when they are combined in different nuclei. The greatest mass per nucleon occurs for the proton alone, hydrogen, because it has no binding energy to pull its mass down. Progressing beyond hydrogen, the mass per nucleon is smaller, and it is least for a nucleon in the nucleus of the iron atom. Beyond iron, the process reverses itself, as nucleons have progressively more and more mass in atoms of increasing atomic number. This continues all the way to uranium and the transuranic elements.

From Figure 16.31, we can see how energy is released when a uranium nucleus splits into two nuclei of lower atomic number. Uranium, being towards the right-hand side of the graph, is shown to have a relatively large amount of mass per nucleon. When the uranium nucleus splits in half, however, smaller nuclei of lower atomic numbers are formed. As shown in Figure 16.32, these nuclei are lower on the graph than uranium, which means that they have a smaller amount of mass per nucleon. Thus, nucleons lose mass in their transition from being in a uranium nucleus to being in one of its fragments. When this decrease in mass is multiplied by the speed of light squared (c^2 in Einstein's equation), the product is equal to the energy yielded by each uranium nucleus as it undergoes fission.

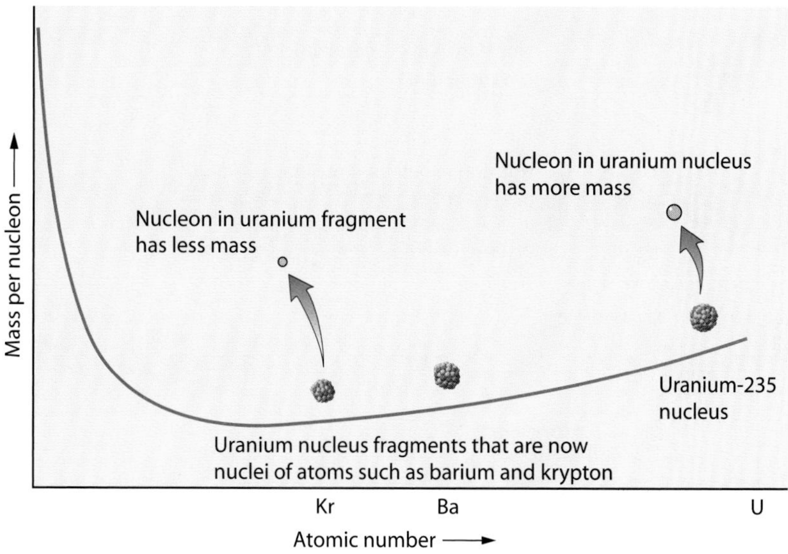

Figure 16.32
The mass of each nucleon in a uranium nucleus is greater than the mass of each nucleon in any one of its nuclear fission fragments. This lost mass is mass that has been transformed into energy, which is why nuclear fission is an energy-releasing process.

☑ CHECKPOINT

Correct the following incorrect statement: When a heavy element such as uranium undergoes fission, there are fewer nucleons after the reaction than before.

Check Your Answer

When a heavy element such as uranium undergoes fission, there aren't fewer nucleons after the reaction. Instead, there's *less mass* in the same number of nucleons.

We can think of the mass-per-nucleon graph as an energy valley that starts at hydrogen (the highest point) and slopes steeply to iron (the lowest point), then slopes gradually up to uranium. Iron is at the bottom of the energy valley and is the most stable nucleus. It is also the most tightly bound nucleus; more energy per nucleon is required to separate nucleons from its nucleus than from any other nucleus.

All nuclear power today is produced by nuclear fission. A more promising long-range source of energy is to be found on the left side of the energy valley.

16.10 Nuclear Fusion

Notice, in the graphs of Figures 16.31 and 16.32, that the steepest part of the energy valley goes from hydrogen to iron. Energy is gained as light nuclei combine. This combining of nuclei is **nuclear fusion**—the opposite of nuclear fission. We can see from Figure 16.33 that, as we move along the list of elements from hydrogen to iron, the average mass per nucleon decreases. Thus, when two small nuclei fuse—say, a pair of hydrogen isotopes—the mass of the resulting helium nucleus is less than the mass of the two small nuclei before fusion. Energy is released as smaller nuclei fuse.*

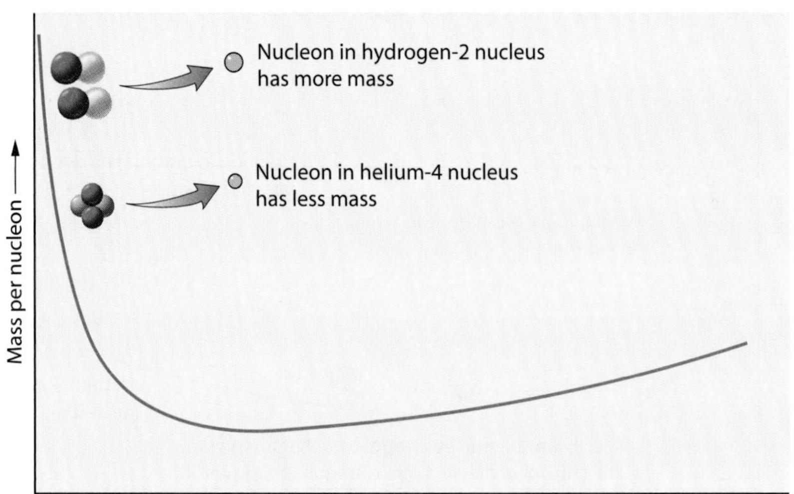

Figure 16.33
The mass of each nucleon in a hydrogen-2 nucleus is greater than the mass of each nucleon in a helium-4 nucleus, which results from the fusion of two hydrogen-2 nuclei. This lost mass is mass that has been converted to energy, which is why nuclear fusion is a process that releases energy.

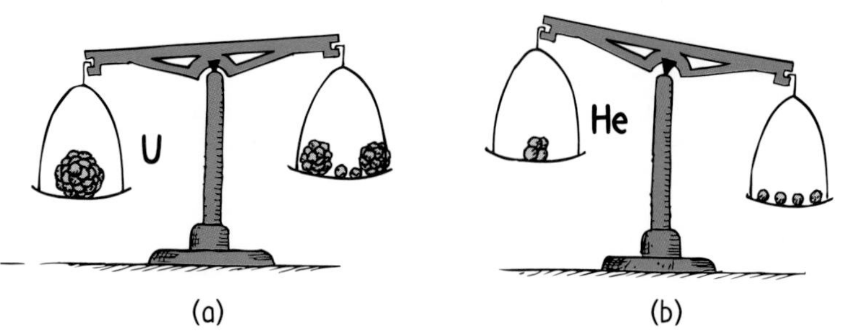

Figure 16.34
The mass of a nucleus is not equal to the sum of the mass of its parts. (a) The fission fragments of a uranium nucleus are less massive than the uranium nucleus. (b) Two protons and two neutrons are more massive in their free states than when they are combined to form a helium nucleus.

*A common reaction is the fusion of a pair of H-2 and H-3 nuclei to become He-4 plus a neutron. Most of the energy released is in the kinetic energy of the ejected neutron. The rest of the energy is in the kinetic energy of the recoiling He-4 nucleus. Interestingly, without the neutron energy carrier, a fusion reaction won't occur. The intensity of fusion reactions is measured by the accompanying neutron flux.

For a fusion reaction to occur, the nuclei must collide at a very high speed in order to overcome their mutual electric repulsion. The required speeds correspond to the extremely high temperatures found in the sun and other stars. Fusion brought about by high temperatures is called **thermonuclear fusion.** In the high temperatures of the sun approximately 657 million tons of hydrogen is converted into 653 million tons of helium *each second.* The missing 4 million tons of mass is discharged as radiant energy.

$$^{2}_{1}H + ^{2}_{1}H \rightarrow ^{3}_{2}He + ^{1}_{0}n + 3.26\ MeV$$

$$^{2}_{1}H + ^{3}_{1}H \rightarrow ^{4}_{2}He + ^{1}_{0}n + 17.6\ MeV$$

Figure 16.35
Fusion reactions of hydrogen isotopes. Most of the energy released is carried by the neutrons ejected at high speeds.

Such reactions are, quite literally, nuclear burning. Thermonuclear fusion is analogous to ordinary chemical combustion. In both chemical and nuclear burning, a high temperature starts the reaction; the release of energy by the reaction maintains a high enough temperature to spread the fire. The net result of the chemical reaction is a combination of atoms into more tightly bound molecules. In nuclear fusion reactions, the net result is more tightly bound nuclei. In both cases, mass decreases as energy is released.

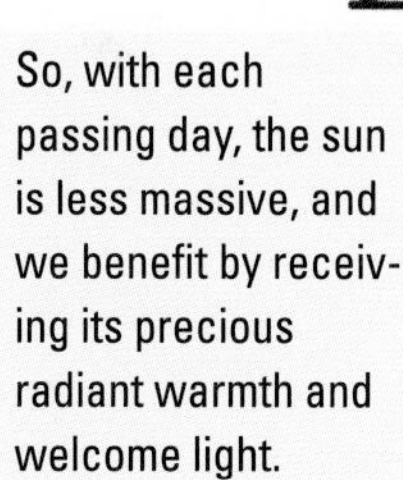

So, with each passing day, the sun is less massive, and we benefit by receiving its precious radiant warmth and welcome light.

Insights

☑ CHECKPOINT

1. Fission and fusion are opposite processes, yet each releases energy. Isn't this contradictory?
2. To get a release of nuclear energy from the element iron, should iron undergo fission or fusion?
3. Predict whether the temperature of the core of a star increases or decreases when iron and elements of higher atomic number than iron in the core are fused.

Check Your Answers

1. No, no, no! This is contradictory only if the same element is said to release energy by both fission and fusion. Only the fusion of light elements and the fission of heavy elements result in a decrease in nucleon mass and a release of energy.
2. Neither, because iron is at the very bottom of the "energy valley." Fusing a pair of iron nuclei produces an element to the right of iron on the curve, where mass per nucleon is higher. If you split an iron nucleus, the products lie to the left of iron on the curve, and also have a higher mass per nucleon. So no energy is released. For energy release, "decrease mass" is the name of the game—*any* game, chemical or nuclear.
3. In the fusion of iron and any nuclei beyond, energy is absorbed and the star core cools at this late stage of its evolution. This, however, leads to the star's collapse, which then greatly increases it temperature. Interestingly, elements beyond iron are not manufactured in normal fusion cycles in stellar sources, but are manufactured when stars violently explode—supernovae.

In a sense, nucleons in the heavy elements wish to lose mass and to be like nucleons in iron. And nucleons in the light elements also wish to lose mass and become more like those in iron.

Insights

Controlling Fusion

Carrying out thermonuclear fusion reactions under controlled conditions requires temperatures of millions of degrees. There are a variety of techniques for attaining high temperatures. No matter how the temperature is produced, a problem is that all materials melt and vaporize at the temperatures required for fusion. One solution to this problem is to confine the reaction in a nonmaterial container.

A nonmaterial container is a magnetic field, which can exist at any temperature and can exert powerful forces on charged particles in motion. "Magnetic walls" of sufficient strength provide a kind of magnetic straightjacket for hot gases called plasmas. Magnetic compression further heats the plasma to fusion temperatures. At this writing, fusion by magnetic confinement has only been partially successful. A sustained and controlled reaction has so far been out of reach.

Another approach bypasses magnetic confinement altogether with high-energy lasers. A promising technique is aiming an array of laser beams at a common point and dropping solid pellets composed of hydrogen isotopes through the synchronous crossfire (Figure 16.36). The energy of the multiple beams should crush pellets to densities 20 times that of lead. Such a fusion "burn" could produce several hundred times more energy than is delivered by the laser beams that compress and ignite the pellets. Like the succession of small fuel–air explosions in an automobile engine's cylinders that convert into a smooth flow of mechanical power, the successive ignition of dropping pellets in a fusion power plant may similarly produce a steady stream of electric power.* The success of this technique requires precise timing, for the necessary compression must occur before a shock wave causes the pellet to disperse. Reliable high-power lasers are vital. Breakeven (where energy output equals energy input) has not yet been achieved with laser fusion.

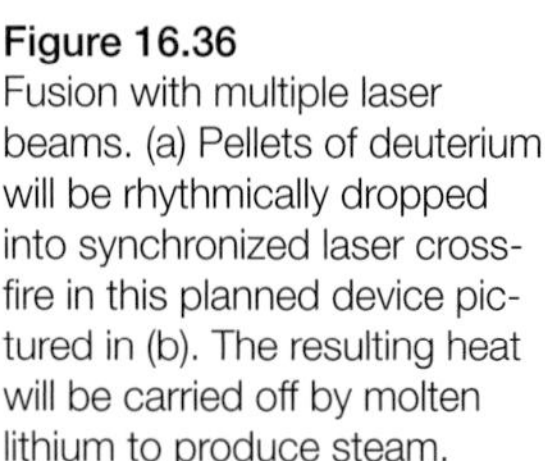

(a)

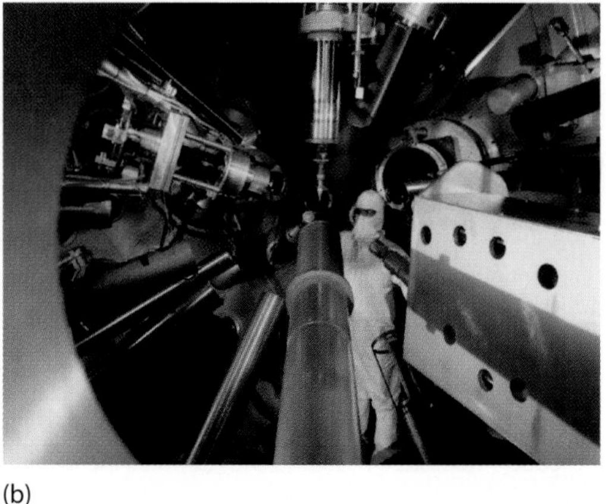

(b)

Figure 16.36
Fusion with multiple laser beams. (a) Pellets of deuterium will be rhythmically dropped into synchronized laser crossfire in this planned device pictured in (b). The resulting heat will be carried off by molten lithium to produce steam.

Other fusion schemes involve the bombardment of fuel pellets not by laser light but by beams of electrons and ions. We await "breakeven day," when one of the techniques for controlled nuclear fusion produces sustained energy.

If people are one day to dart about the universe in the same way we jet about the earth today, their supply of fuel is assured. The fuel for fusion—hydrogen—is found in every part of the universe, not only in the stars but also

*The rate of pellet fusion is 5 per second on the projected Cascade power plant, which is now on the drawing boards at Lawrence Livermore Laboratory. For comparison, about 20 explosions per second occur in each automobile engine cylinder in a car that travels at highway speed. Such a plant could produce 1000 million watts of electric power, enough to supply a city of about 600,000 people. Five fusion burns per second will provide about the same power as 60 liters of fuel oil or 70 kilograms of coal per second from conventional power plants.

in the space between them. About 91 percent of the atoms in the universe are estimated to be hydrogen. For people of the future, the supply of raw materials is also assured, because all the elements known to exist result from the fusing of more and more hydrogen nuclei. Future humans might synthesize their own elements and produce energy in the process, just as the stars have always done.

Summary of Terms

Radioactivity The process whereby unstable atomic nuclei break down and emit radiation.

Alpha particle The nucleus of a helium atom, which consists of two neutrons and two protons, ejected by certain radioactive elements.

Beta particle An electron (or positron) emitted during the radioactive decay of certain nuclei.

Gamma ray High-frequency electromagnetic radiation emitted by the nuclei of radioactive atoms.

Nucleon A nuclear proton or neutron.

Half-life The time required for half the atoms in a sample of a radioactive isotope to decay.

Transmutation The conversion of an atomic nucleus of one element into an atomic nucleus of another element through a loss or gain in the number of protons.

Nuclear fission The splitting of the nucleus of a heavy atom, such as uranium-235, into two main parts, accompanied by the release of much energy.

Chain reaction A self-sustaining reaction in which the products of one reaction event stimulate further reaction events.

Critical mass The minimum mass of fissionable material in a reactor or nuclear bomb that will sustain a chain reaction.

Nuclear fusion The combining of nuclei of light atoms to form heavier nuclei, with the release of much energy.

Thermonuclear fusion Nuclear fusion produced by high temperature.

Review Questions

16.1 Radioactivity

1. Where does most of the radiation you encounter originate?
2. What are cosmic rays, and where do they originate?

16.2 Alpha, Beta, and Gamma Rays

3. How do the electric charges of alpha, beta, and gamma rays differ?
4. Why are alpha and beta rays deflected in opposite directions in a magnetic field? Why are gamma rays undeflected?
5. What is the origin of gamma rays?

16.3 Environmental Radiation

6. What is the leading source of naturally occurring radiation?
7. What type of power plant most exposes us to radioactivity, coal or nuclear plants?
8. Distinguish between a *rad* and a *rem*.
9. Do humans receive more radiation from artificial or from natural sources of radiation?
10. What is the lethal dose of radiation? What is the average radiation dosage per year for the average person in the U.S.? What is an average dose delivered by a typical X ray?
11. Is the human body radioactive?
12. What kinds of cells are in most danger when they are irradiated?
13. What is a radioactive tracer?

16.4 The Atomic Nucleus and the Strong Nuclear Force

14. Name the two different nucleons.
15. Why doesn't the repulsive electric force of protons in the atomic nucleus cause the protons to fly apart?
16. Why is a larger nucleus generally less stable than a smaller nucleus?
17. What is the role of neutrons in the atomic nucleus?
18. Which have more neutrons than protons, large nuclei or small nuclei?

16.5 Half-life

19. What is meant by *radioactive half-life*?
20. What is the half-life of Ra-226? Of a muon?
21. For any radioactive isotope, what is the relationship between decay rate and half-life?

16.6 Transmutation of Elements

22. What is transmutation?
23. When thorium, atomic number 90, decays by emitting an alpha particle, what is the atomic number of the resulting nucleus?
24. When thorium decays by emitting a beta particle, what is the atomic number of the resulting nucleus?
25. What change in atomic mass occurs in the reactions referred to in questions 23 and 24?
26. What change in atomic number occurs when a nucleus emits an alpha particle? When it emits a beta particle? When it emits a gamma ray?

27. What is the long-range fate of all the uranium that exists in the world?
28. When and by whom did the first successful intentional transmutation of an element occur?
29. Why are the elements beyond uranium not common in the earth's crust?

16.7 Isotopic Dating

30. How are radioactive isotopes produced?
31. What occurs when a nitrogen nucleus captures an extra neutron?
32. What does the proportion of lead and uranium in a rock tell us about the age of the rock?

16.8 Nuclear Fission

33. When a nucleus undergoes fission, what role can the ejected neutrons play?
34. Why is a chain reaction more likely in a big piece of uranium than in a small piece?
35. What is a critical mass?
36. Which will leak more neutrons, two separate pieces of uranium or the same two pieces stuck together?
37. What are the four main components of a fission reactor?
38. Why can a reactor not explode like a fission bomb?
39. What is the effect of putting small amounts of fissionable isotopes with large amounts of U-238?
40. How does a breeder reactor breed nuclear fuel?

16.9 The Mass–Energy Relationship—$E = mc^2$

41. Is work required to pull a nucleon out of an atomic nucleus? Does the nucleon, once outside, then have more energy than it did when it was inside the nucleus? In what form is this energy?
42. Which ions are least deflected in a mass spectrometer?
43. What is the basic difference between the graphs of Figure 16.30 and Figure 16.31?
44. In which atomic nucleus do nucleons have the greatest mass? In which do they have the least mass?
45. What becomes of the missing mass when a uranium nucleus undergoes fission?

16.10 Nuclear Fusion

46. If the graph in Figure 16.33 is seen as an energy valley, what can be said of nuclear transformations that progress toward iron?
47. When a pair of hydrogen isotopes is fused, is the mass of the product nucleus more or less than the sum of the masses of the two hydrogen nuclei?
48. For helium to release energy, should it be fissioned or fused?
49. What kind of containers are used to contain plasmas at temperatures of millions of degrees?
50. In what form is energy initially released in nuclear fusion?

Activity

Some watches and clocks have luminous hands that glow continuously. Some of these have traces of radium bromide mixed with zinc sulfide. (Safer clock faces use light rather than radioactive disintegration as a means of excitation, and they become progressively dimmer in the dark.) If you have a luminous watch or clock available, take it into a completely dark room and, after your eyes have become adjusted to the dark, examine the luminous hands with a very strong magnifying glass or the eyepiece of a microscope or telescope. You should be able to see individual tiny flashes, which together seem to be a steady source of light to the unaided eye. Each flash occurs when an alpha particle ejected by a radium nucleus strikes a molecule of zinc sulfide.

Exercises

1. Is radioactivity in the world something relatively new? Defend your answer.
2. Can it be truthfully said that, whenever a nucleus emits an alpha or beta particle, it necessarily becomes the nucleus of a different element?
3. Why is a sample of radium always a little warmer than its surroundings?
4. Some people say that all things are possible. Is it at all possible for a hydrogen nucleus to emit an alpha particle? Defend your answer.
5. Why are alpha and beta rays deflected in opposite directions in a magnetic field? Why are gamma rays undeflected?
6. The alpha particle has twice the electric charge of the beta particle, but it is deflected less than the beta particle in a magnetic field. Why is this so?
7. How would the paths of alpha, beta, and gamma radiations compare in an electric field?
8. In what way is the emission of gamma radiation from a nucleus similar to the emission of light from an atom?
9. Which type of radiation—alpha, beta, or gamma—results in the greatest change in atomic number? In the least change in atomic number?
10. Which type of radiation—alpha, beta, or gamma—produces the greatest change in mass number? The least change in mass number?
11. In bombarding atomic nuclei with proton "bullets," why must the protons be accelerated to high energies to make contact with the target nuclei?
12. Just after an alpha particle leaves the nucleus, would you expect it to speed up? Defend your answer.

13. Within the atomic nucleus, which interaction tends to hold it together and which interaction tends to push it apart?
14. What evidence supports the contention that the strong nuclear force is stronger than the electrical force at short internuclear distances?
15. A friend asks if a radioactive substance with a half life of 1 day will be entirely gone at the end of 2 days. What is your answer?
16. When the isotope bismuth-213 emits an alpha particle, what new element results? What new element results if it instead emits a beta particle?
17. When $^{226}_{84}$Ra decays by emitting an alpha particle, what is the atomic number of the resulting nucleus? What is the resulting atomic mass?
18. When $^{218}_{84}$Po emits a beta particle, it transforms into a new element. What are the atomic number and atomic mass of this new element? What are they if the polonium instead emits an alpha particle?
19. State the number of neutrons and protons in each of the following nuclei: $^{2}_{1}$H, $^{12}_{6}$C, $^{56}_{26}$Fe, $^{197}_{79}$Au, $^{90}_{38}$Sr, and $^{238}_{92}$U.
20. How is it possible for an element to decay "forward in the periodic table"—that is, to decay to an element of higher atomic number?
21. Elements with atomic numbers greater than that of uranium do not exist in any appreciable amounts in nature because they have short half-lives. Yet there are several elements with atomic numbers smaller than that of uranium that have equally short half-lives and that do exist in appreciable amounts in nature. How can you account for this?
22. You and your friend journey to the mountain foothills to get closer to nature and to escape such things as radioactivity. While bathing in the warmth of a natural hot spring, she wonders aloud how the spring gets its heat. What do you tell her?
23. Coal contains minute quantities of radioactive materials, yet there is more environmental radiation surrounding a coal-fired power plant than a fission power plant. What does this indicate about the shielding that typically surrounds these power plants?
24. When we speak of dangerous radiation exposure, are we customarily speaking of alpha radiation, beta radiation, or gamma radiation? Discuss.
25. People who work around radioactivity wear film badges to monitor the amount of radiation that reaches their bodies. These badges consist of small pieces of photographic film enclosed in a light-proof wrapper. What kind of radiation do these devices monitor?
26. A friend produces a Geiger counter to check the local background radiation. It ticks. Another friend, who normally fears most that which is understood least, makes an effort to keep away from the region of the Geiger counter and looks to you for advice. What do you say?
27. When food is irradiated with gamma rays from a cobalt-60 source, does the food become radioactive? Defend your answer.
28. If it were known that cosmic ray intensity was much greater thousands of years ago, how would this affect the ages assigned to ancient samples of once-living matter?
29. The age of the Dead Sea Scrolls was found by carbon dating. Could this technique have worked if they were carved in stone tablets? Explain.
30. Why will nuclear fission probably not be used directly for powering automobiles? How could it be used indirectly?
31. Why does a neutron make a better nuclear bullet than a proton or an electron?
32. Does the average distance that a neutron travels through fissionable material before escaping increase or decrease when two pieces of fissionable material are assembled into one piece? Does this assembly increase or decrease the probability of an explosion?
33. U-235 releases an average of 2.5 neutrons per fission, while Pu-239 releases an average of 2.7 neutrons per fission. Which of these elements might you therefore expect to have the smaller critical mass?
34. Why is lead found in all deposits of uranium ores?
35. Why does plutonium not occur in appreciable amounts in natural ore deposits?
36. Why does a chain reaction not occur in uranium mines?
37. A friend makes the claim that the explosive power of a nuclear bomb is due to static electricity. Do you agree or disagree? Defend your answer.
38. If a nucleus of $^{232}_{90}$Th absorbs a neutron and the resulting nucleus undergoes two successive beta decays (emitting electrons), what nucleus results?
39. The energy release of nuclear fission is tied to the fact that the heaviest nuclei have about 0.1 percent more mass per nucleon than nuclei near the middle of the periodic table of the elements. What would be the effect on energy release if the 0.1 percent figure were instead 1 percent?
40. How does the mass per nucleon in uranium compare with the mass per nucleon in the fission fragments of uranium?
41. How is chemical burning similar to nuclear fusion?
42. To predict the approximate energy release of either a fission or a fusion reaction, explain how a physicist makes use of the curve of Figure 16.31 or a table of nuclear masses and the equation $E = mc^2$.
43. Which process would release energy from gold, fission or fusion? From carbon? From iron?

44. If uranium were to split into three segments of equal size instead of two, would more energy or less energy be released? Defend your answer in terms of Figure 16.31.
45. Explain how radioactive decay has always warmed the earth from the inside, and nuclear fusion has always warmed the earth from the outside.
46. What effect on the mining industry can you foresee in the disposal of urban waste by means of a fusion torch coupled with a mass spectrometer?
47. The world has never been the same since the discovery of electromagnetic induction and its applications to electric motors and generators. Speculate on and list some of the worldwide changes that are likely to follow the advent of successful fusion reactors.
48. Ordinary hydrogen is sometimes called a perfect fuel because there is an almost unlimited supply of it on earth, and, when it burns (oxidizes), harmless water is the combustion product. So why don't we abandon fission energy and fusion energy, not to mention fossil-fuel energy, and just use hydrogen?
49. Referring to the previous exercise, why may it take fusion power or the equivalent to see hydrogen taking the place of gasoline?
50. Discuss and make a comparison of pollution by conventional fossil-fuel power plants and nuclear-fission power plants. Consider thermal pollution, chemical pollution, and radioactive pollution.

Problems

1. Radiation from a point source obeys the inverse-square law. If a Geiger counter 1 meter from a small sample reads 360 counts per minute, what will be its counting rate at 2 meters from the source? At 3 meters from the source?
2. If a sample of a radioactive isotope has a half-life of 1 year, how much of the original sample will be left at the end of the second year? At the end of the third year? At the end of the fourth year?
3. A certain radioactive substance has a half life of one hour. If you start with 1 gram of the material at noon, how much will be left at 3:00 PM? at 6:00 PM? at 10:00 PM?
4. A sample of a particular radioisotope is placed near a Geiger counter, which is observed to register 160 counts per minute. Eight hours later, the detector counts at a rate of 10 counts per minute. What is the half-life of the material?
5. The isotope Cesium-137, which has a half life of 30 years, is a product of nuclear power plants. How long will it take for this isotope to decay to about one-sixteenth its original amount?
6. Suppose that you measure the intensity of radiation from carbon-14 in an ancient piece of wood to be 6 percent of what it would be in a freshly cut piece of wood. How old is this artifact?
7. Suppose that you want to find out how much gasoline is in an underground storage tank. You pour in one gallon of gasoline that contains some radioactive material with a long half-life that gives off 5000 counts per minute. The next day, you remove a gallon from the underground tank and measure its radioactivity to be 10 counts per minute. How much gasoline is in the tank?
8. The kiloton, which is used to measure the energy released in an atomic explosion, is equal to 4.2×10^{12} J (approximately the energy released in the explosion of 1000 tons of TNT). Recalling that 1 kilocalorie of energy raises the temperature of 1 kilogram of water by 1°C and that 4184 joules is equal to 1 kilocalorie, calculate how many kilograms of water can be heated by 50°C by a 20-kiloton atomic bomb.
9. An important fusion reaction is the "DT reaction," in which a deuteron—a deuterium (H-2) nucleus, with a mass of 2 amu—and a triton—a tritium (H-3) nucleus, with a mass of 3 amu—combine to form an alpha particle and a neutron with the release of much energy. Use momentum conservation to find the relative speeds of the neutron and recoiling alpha particle.
10. For the above problem, calculate the relative kinetic energies of the neutron and the recoiling alpha particle.

Chapter 16 Online Resources

Tutorials
- Atoms & Isotopes
- Radiation & its Biological Effects
- Nuclear Chemistry

Videos
- Radioactive Decay
- Half-Life
- Carbon Dating
- Nuclear Fission
- Plutonium
- Nuclear Fusion
- Controlling Nuclear Fusion

Quiz
Exercises
Flashcards
Links

CHAPTER 17

Elements of Chemistry

As you progress through this physical science course, you will note an accumulating list of key terms, which are those terms you'll find in bold print. Why an increase of new terms? Why can't physical science be described in everyday English without the addition of new vocabulary? Consider this: In the laboratory, scientists perform experiments, make many observations, and then draw conclusions. Over time, the result is a growing body of new knowledge that inevitably exceeds the capacity of everyday language. For example, in the language of chemistry, we say that there are more than 100 kinds of *atoms,* and that any material consisting of a single kind of atom is an *element.* (The element gold is shown in this chapter's opening photograph.) Atoms can link together to form a *molecule,* and a molecule consisting of atoms from different elements is a *compound.* And on and on, one term building on another, as we attempt to describe the nature of matter beyond its casual appearance.

Rather than memorizing key terms, you will serve yourself far better by focusing on the underlying concept each term represents. Bear in mind, a term is only a label. It is possible to know the term without understanding the concepts behind it—just as it is possible to understand a concept without knowing the term that labels that concept. So, while this new vocabulary is useful for communication, it does not guarantee conceptual understanding. If you focus first on the concepts, the vocabulary represented will come to you much more naturally.

If you are not doing so already, practice articulating and paraphrasing the concepts represented by the bold-faced terms. Do this aloud to yourself (or to a friend), minimizing looking at the book. When you can express these concepts in your own words—in your own "plain English"—you'll have the insight to do well in this course and beyond.

Insights

17.1 Chemistry: The Central Science

When you wonder what the land, sky, or ocean is made of, you are thinking about chemistry. When you wonder how a rain puddle dries up, how a car acquires energy from gasoline, or how your body extracts energy from the food you eat, you are again thinking about chemistry. By definition, chemistry is the study of matter and the transformations it can undergo. Matter is anything that occupies space. It is the stuff that makes up all material things—anything you can touch, taste, smell, see, or hear is matter. The scope of chemistry, therefore, is very broad.

Chemistry is often described as a central science because it touches all the other sciences. It springs from the principles of physics, and it serves as the

Figure 17.1
Special materials of chemistry, such as rocket fuels, metals for the spaceships, and fabrics for the space suits, were required to allow astronauts to reach and explore the surface of the moon.

Many major advances were made in both the physical sciences and the life sciences over the course of the twentieth century. Advances made in the physical sciences, such as our understanding of the chemistry of life, however, will likely propel the life sciences to even more fantastic advances in this twenty-first century.

Insights

foundation for the most complex science of all—biology. Indeed, many of the great advances in the life sciences today, such as genetic engineering, are applications of some very exotic chemistry. Chemistry sets the foundation for the major earth sciences—geology, oceanography, meteorology—as well as for such related branches as archeology. It is also an important component of space science, as described in Figure 17.1. Just as we learned about the origin of the moon from the chemical analysis of moon rocks in the early 1970s, we are now learning about the history of Mars and other planets from the chemical information gathered by space probes.

Progress in science is made as scientists conduct research. Research is any activity aimed at the systematic discovery and interpretation of new knowledge. Many scientists focus on **basic research**, which leads us to a greater understanding of how the natural world operates. The foundation of knowledge laid down by basic research frequently leads to useful applications. Research that focuses on developing these applications is known as **applied research.** The majority of chemists choose applied research as their major focus. Applied research in chemistry has provided us with medicine, food, water, shelter, and so many of the material goods that characterize modern life. Just a few of a myriad of examples are shown in Figure 17.2.

Over the course of the past century, we excelled at manipulating atoms and molecules to create materials to suit our needs. At the same time, however,

Figure 17.2
Most of the material items in any modern house are shaped by some human-devised chemical process.

mistakes were made when it came to caring for the environment. Waste products were dumped into rivers, buried in the ground, or vented into the air without regard for possible long-term consequences. Many people believed that the earth was so large that its resources were virtually unlimited, and that it could absorb wastes without being significantly harmed.

Most nations now recognize this as a dangerous attitude. As a result, government agencies, industries, and concerned citizens are involved in extensive efforts to clean up toxic-waste sites. Such regulations as the international ban on ozone-destroying chlorofluorocarbons have been enacted to protect the environment. Members of the American Chemistry Council, who, as a group, produce 90 percent of the chemicals manufactured in the United States, have adopted a program called Responsible Care, in which they have pledged to manufacture without causing environmental damage. The Responsible Care program—its emblem is shown in Figure 17.3—is based on a balance between protecting and impairing the environment. By using chemistry wisely, most waste products can be minimized, recycled, engineered into salable commodities, or rendered environmentally benign.

Figure 17.3
The Responsible Care symbol of the American Chemistry Council.

Chemistry has influenced our lives in profound ways, and it will continue to do so in the future. For this reason, it is in everyone's interest to become acquainted with the basic concepts of chemistry.

☑ CHECKPOINT

Chemists have learned how to produce aspirin using petroleum as a starting material. Is this an example of basic or applied research?

Check Your Answer

This is an example of applied research, because the primary goal was to develop a useful commodity. However, the ability to produce aspirin from petroleum depended on an understanding of atoms and molecules developed from many years of basic research.

17.2 The Submicroscopic World

From afar, a sand dune appears to be a smooth, continuous material. Up close, however, the dune reveals itself to be made of tiny particles of sand. In a similar fashion, as discussed in Chapter 14, everything around us—no matter how smooth it may appear—is made of the basic units you know as *atoms.* Atoms are so small, however, that a single grain of sand contains on the order of 125 million trillion of them. There are roughly 250,000 times more atoms in a single grain of sand than there are grains of sand in the dunes shown in Figure 17.4.

As small as atoms are, there is much we have learned about them. We know, for example, that there are more than 100 different types of atoms, and they are listed in the widely recognized periodic table. Some atoms link together to form larger but still incredibly small basic units of matter called **molecules.** As shown in Figure 17.4, for example, two hydrogen atoms and one oxygen atom link together to form a single molecule of water, which you know as H_2O. Water molecules are so small that an 8-ounce glass of water contains about a trillion trillion of them.

How long would it take to count to one million? If each count takes one second, counting nonstop to a million would take 11.6 days. To count to a billion would take 31.7 years. To count to a trillion would take 31,700 years. Counting to a trillion a trillion times would take about 2 million times the estimated age of the universe. In short, a trillion trillion is an inconceivably large number.

Insights

Figure 17.4
There are far more atoms in a glass of water than there are grains of sand within this towering sand dune.

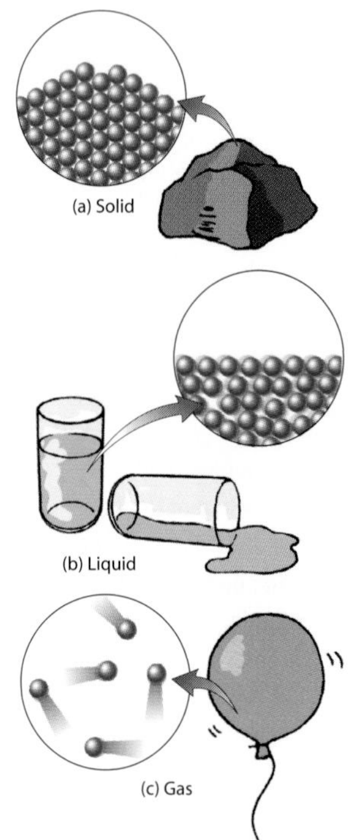

Figure 17.5
The familiar bulk properties of a solid, a liquid, and a gas. (a) The submicroscopic particles of the solid phase vibrate about fixed positions. (b) The submicroscopic particles of the liquid phase slip past one another. (c) The fast-moving submicroscopic particles of the gaseous phase are separated by large average distances.

Our world can be studied at different levels of magnification. At the *macroscopic* level, matter is large enough to be seen, measured, and handled. A handful of sand and a glass of water are macroscopic samples of matter. At the *microscopic* level, physical structure is so fine that it can be seen only with a microscope. A biological cell is microscopic, as is the detail on a dragonfly's wing. Beyond the microscopic level is the **submicroscopic**—the realm of atoms and molecules and an important focus of chemistry.

Recall, from Chapter 8, that matter exists in *phases*. At the submicroscopic level, solid, liquid, and gaseous phases are distinguished by how the submicroscopic particles hold together. This is illustrated in Figure 17.5. In solid matter, such as rock, the attractions between particles are strong enough to hold all the particles together in some fixed three-dimensional arrangement. The particles are able to vibrate about fixed positions, but they cannot move past one another.

The addition of heat causes these vibrations to increase until, at a certain temperature, the vibrations are rapid enough to disrupt the fixed arrangements. Rock will melt into magma (a topic of much discussion in Part 3). Likewise, ice will melt into water. The particles can then slip past one another and tumble around much like a bunch of marbles in a bag. This is the liquid phase of matter, and it is the mobility of the submicroscopic particles that gives rise to the liquid's fluid character—its ability to flow and to assume the shape of its container.

Further heating causes the submicroscopic particles in a liquid to move so fast that the attractions they have for one another are unable to hold them together. They then separate from one another, forming a gas. For magma, this doesn't easily happen, because the particles are strongly attracted to one another. For water, molecules will separate into a gas at 100 °C. For a substance like helium, the submicroscopic particles are already in the gaseous phase at room temperature.

Moving at an average speed of 500 meters per second (1,100 miles per hour), the particles of a gas are widely separated from one another. Matter in the gaseous phase therefore occupies much more volume than it does in the solid or liquid phase. Applying pressure to a gas squeezes the gas particles closer together, which decreases the volume. The amount of air an underwater diver needs to breathe for many minutes, for example, can be squeezed (compressed) into a tank small enough to be carried on the diver's back.

17.3 Physical and Chemical Properties

Properties that describe the look or feel of a substance, such as color, hardness, density, texture, and phase, are called **physical properties.** Every substance has its own set of characteristic physical properties that we can use to identify that substance (Figure 17.6).

Gold
Opacity: opaque
Color: yellowish
Phase at 25°C: solid
Density: 19.3 g/mL

Diamond
Opacity: transparent
Color: colorless
Phase at 25°C: solid
Density: 3.5 g/mL

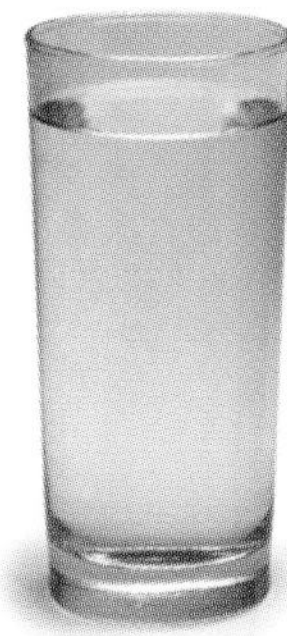

Water
Opacity: transparent
Color: colorless
Phase at 25°C: liquid
Density: 1.0 g/mL

Figure 17.6
Gold, diamond, and water can be identified by their physical properties. If a substance has all the physical properties listed under gold, for example, it must be gold.

The physical properties of a substance can change when conditions change, but that does not mean that a different substance is created. Cooling liquid water to below 0°C causes the water to transform to solid ice, but the substance is still water, no matter what the phase. The only difference is the relative orientation of the H_2O molecules to one another. In the liquid phase, the water molecules tumble around one another, whereas in the ice phase, they vibrate about fixed positions. The freezing of water is an example of what chemists call a physical change. During a **physical change,** a substance changes its phase or some other physical property, but not its chemical composition, as Figure 17.7 shows.

☑ CHECKPOINT

The melting of gold is a physical change. Why?

Check Your Answer

During a physical change, a substance changes only one or more of its physical properties; its chemical identity does not change. Because melted gold is still gold but in a different form, its melting represents only a physical change.

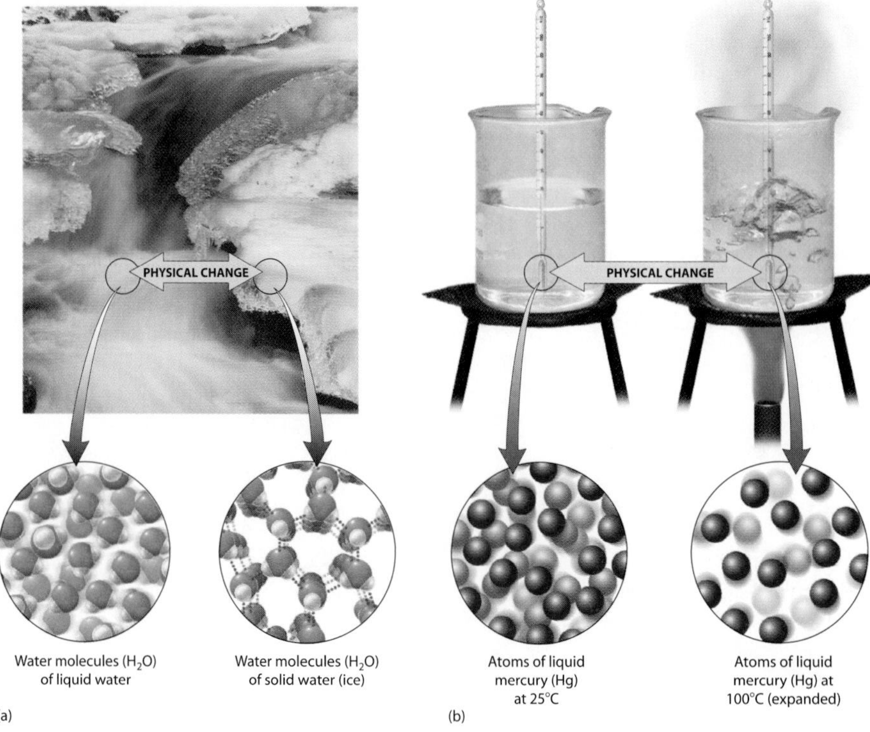

Figure 17.7
Two physical changes. (a) Liquid water and ice might appear to be different substances, but, at the submicroscopic level, it is evident that both consist of water molecules. (b) At 25°C, the atoms in a sample of mercury are a certain distance apart, yielding a density of 13.53 grams per milliliter. At 100°C, the atoms are farther apart, meaning that each milliliter now contains fewer atoms than at 25°C, and the density is now 13.35 grams per milliliter. The physical property we call density has changed with temperature, but the identity of the substance remains unchanged: mercury is mercury.

> A chemical property of a substance is its tendency to change into another substance. For example, it is a chemical property of iron to transform into rust.
>
> Insights

Chemical properties are those that characterize the ability of a substance to react with other substances or to transform from one substance to another. Figure 17.8 shows three examples. The methane of natural gas has the chemical property of reacting with oxygen to produce carbon dioxide and water, along with appreciable heat energy. Similarly, it is a chemical property of baking soda to react with vinegar to produce carbon dioxide and water while absorbing a small amount of heat energy. Copper has the chemical property of reacting with carbon dioxide and water to form a greenish-blue solid known as patina. Copper statues exposed to the carbon dioxide and water in the air become coated with patina. The patina is not copper, it is not carbon dioxide, and it is not water. It is a new substance formed by the reaction of these chemicals with one another.

Methane
Reacts with oxygen to form carbon dioxide and water, giving off lots of heat during the reaction.

Baking soda
Reacts with vinegar to form carbon dioxide and water, absorbing heat during the reaction.

Copper
Reacts with carbon dioxide and water to form the greenish-blue substance called patina.

Figure 17.8
The chemical properties of substances allow them to transform to new substances. Natural gas and baking soda transform to carbon dioxide, water, and heat. Copper transforms to patina.

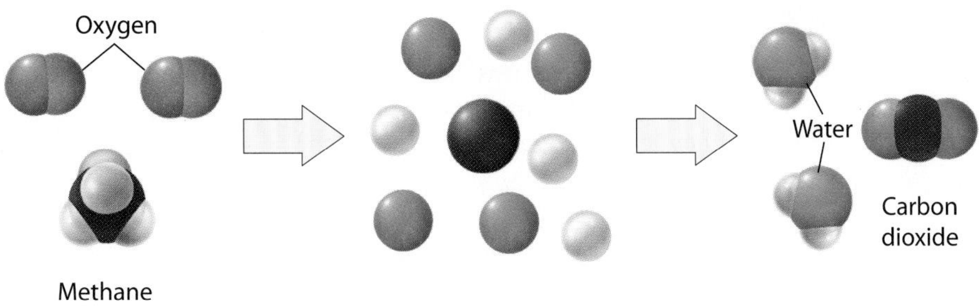

Figure 17.9
The chemical change in which molecules of methane and oxygen transform to molecules of carbon dioxide and water, as atoms break old bonds and form new ones. Although the actual mechanism of this transformation is more complicated than depicted here, the idea that new materials are formed by the rearrangement of atoms is accurate.

All three of these transformations involve a change in the way the atoms in the molecules are *chemically bonded* to one another. A **chemical bond** is the force of attraction between two atoms that holds them together. A methane molecule, for example, is made of a single carbon atom bonded to four hydrogen atoms, and an oxygen molecule is made of two oxygen atoms bonded to each other. Figure 17.9 shows the chemical change in which the atoms in a methane molecule and those in two oxygen molecules first pull apart and then form new bonds with different partners, resulting in the formation of molecules of carbon dioxide and water.

Any change in a substance that involves a rearrangement of the way atoms are bonded is called a **chemical change.** Thus the transformation of methane to carbon dioxide and water is a chemical change, as are the other two transformations shown in Figure 17.8.

The chemical change shown in Figure 17.10 occurs when an electric current is passed through water. The energy of the current causes the water molecules to split into atoms that then form new chemical bonds. Thus, water molecules are changed to molecules of hydrogen and oxygen, two substances that are very different from water. The hydrogen and oxygen are both gases at room temperature, and they can be seen as bubbles rising to the surface.

In the language of chemistry, materials undergoing a chemical change are said to be *reacting*. Methane reacts with oxygen to form carbon dioxide and water. Water reacts when exposed to electricity to form hydrogen gas and oxygen gas. Thus, the term *chemical change* means the same thing as *chemical reaction*. During a **chemical reaction,** new materials are formed by a change in the way atoms are bonded together. We shall explore chemical bonds and the reactions in which they are formed and broken in later chapters 19 and 21.

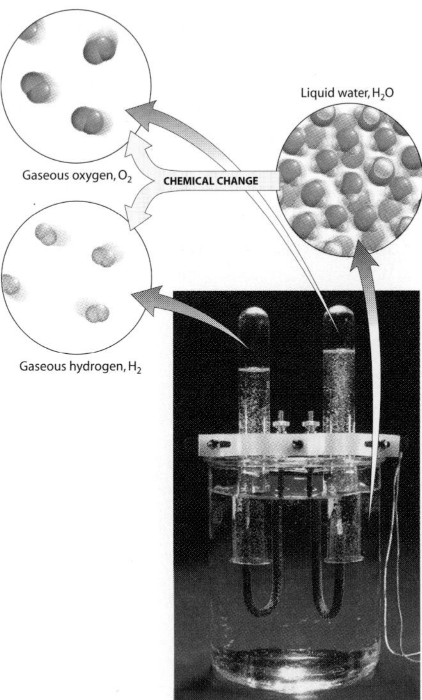

Figure 17.10
Water can be transformed to hydrogen gas and oxygen gas by applying the energy of an electric current. This is a chemical change, because new materials (the two gases) are formed as the atoms originally found in the water molecules are rearranged.

Physical change? Chemical change? It's not always easy to distinguish between the two. Because of many subtleties that are recognized only after years of study and laboratory experience, you'll not soon achieve a firm handle on how to categorize many observed changes. It's okay to learn a little now, and to leave a lot that remains for some future time.

Insights

☑ CHECKPOINT

Each sphere in the following diagrams represents an atom. Joined spheres represent molecules. One set of diagrams shows a physical change, and the other shows a chemical change. Which is which?

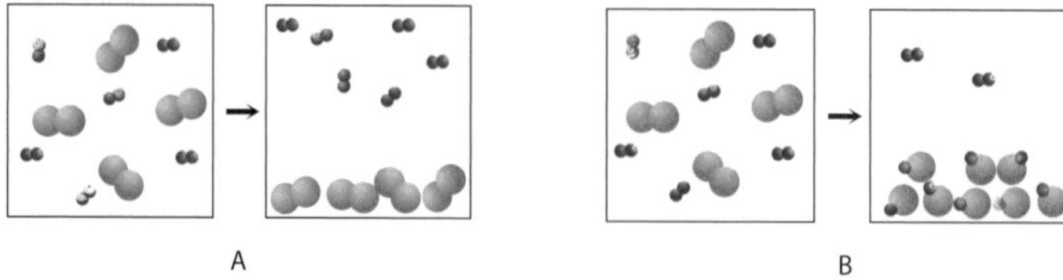

Check Your Answer

Remember that a chemical change (also known as a chemical reaction) involves molecules breaking apart so that the atoms are free to form new bonds with new partners. Be careful to distinguish this breaking apart from a mere change in the relative positions of a group of molecules. In set A, the molecules before and after the change are the same. They differ only in their positions relative to one another. Set A, therefore, represents only a physical change. In set B, new molecules, consisting of bonded red and blue spheres, appear after the change. These molecules represent a new material, and so set B represents a chemical change.

17.4 Determining Physical and Chemical Changes

How can you determine whether an observed change is physical or chemical? This can be tricky because, in both cases, there are changes in physical appearance. Water, for example, looks quite different after it freezes, just as a car looks quite different after it rusts (Figure 17.11). The freezing of water is a physical change because liquid water and frozen water are both forms of water—only the orientation of the water molecules to one another changes. The rusting of a car, by contrast, is the result of the transformation of iron to rust. This is a chemical change because iron and rust are two different materials, each consisting of a different arrangement of atoms. As we shall see in the next two sections, iron is an element, and rust is a compound consisting of iron and oxygen atoms.

Figure 17.11
The transformation of water to ice and the transformation of iron to rust both involve changes in physical appearance. The formation of ice is a physical change, whereas the formation of rust is a chemical change.

There are two powerful guidelines that can assist you in assessing physical and chemical changes. First, in a physical change, a change in appearance is the result of a new set of conditions imposed on the same material. Restoring the original conditions restores the original appearance: frozen water melts upon warming. Second, in a chemical change, a change in appearance is the result of the formation of a new material that has its own unique set of physical properties. The more evidence you have suggesting that a different material has been formed, the greater the likelihood that the change is a chemical change. Iron is a material that can be used to build cars. Rust is not. This suggests that the rusting of iron is a chemical change.

Figure 17.12 shows potassium chromate, a material whose color depends on its temperature. At room temperature, potassium chromate is a bright canary yellow. At higher temperatures, it is a deep reddish orange. Upon cooling, the canary color returns, suggesting that the change is physical. With a chemical change, reverting to the original conditions does not restore the original appearance. Ammonium dichromate, shown in Figure 17.13, is an orange material that, when heated, explodes into ammonia, water vapor, and green chromium(III) oxide. When the test tube is returned to the original temperature, there is no trace of orange ammonium dichromate. In its place are new substances having completely different physical properties.

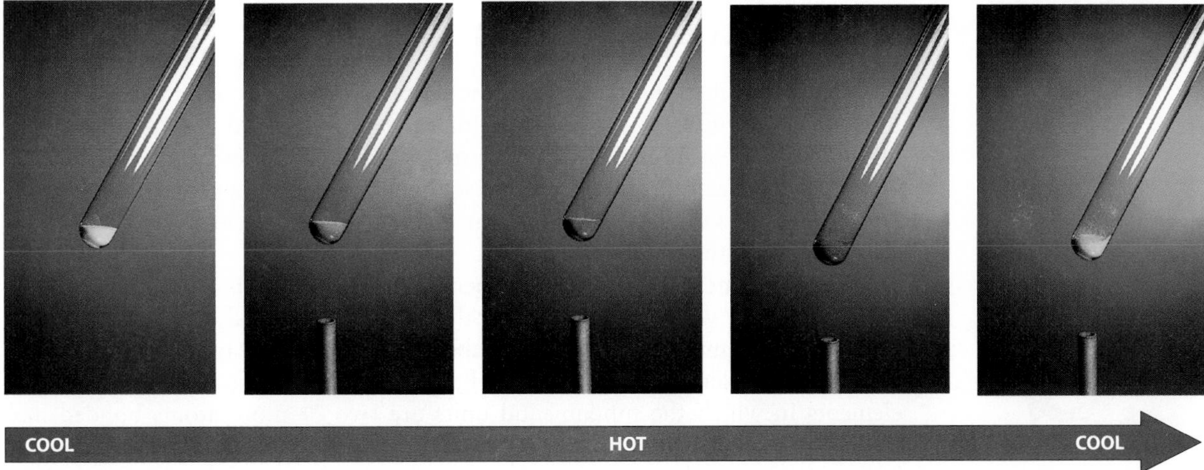

Figure 17.12
Potassium chromate changes color as its temperature changes. This change in color is a physical change. A return to the original temperature restores the original bright yellow color.

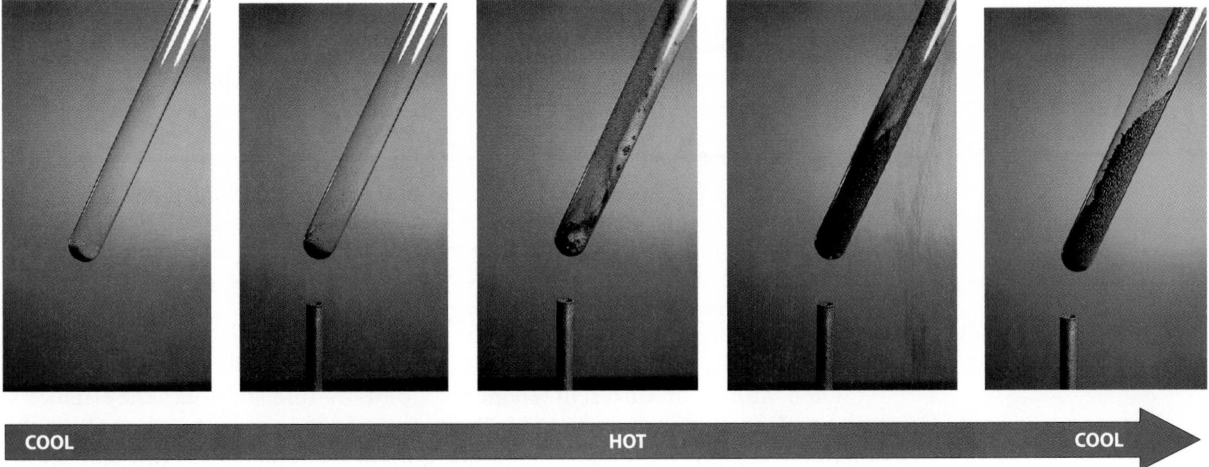

Figure 17.13
When heated, orange ammonium dichromate undergoes a chemical change to ammonia, water vapor, and chromium(III) oxide. A return to the original temperature does not restore the orange color, because the ammonium dichromate is no longer there.

☑ CHECKPOINT

Michaela has grown an inch in height over the past year. Is this best described as a physical or a chemical change?

Check Your Answer

Are new materials being formed as Michaela grows? Absolutely—created out of the food she eats. Her body is very different from, say, the peanut butter sandwich she ate yesterday. Yet, through some very advanced chemistry, her body is able to absorb the atoms of that peanut butter sandwich and rearrange them into new materials. Biological growth, therefore, is best described as a chemical change.

17.5 Elements to Compounds

As briefly described in Chapter 14, the terms *element* and *atom* are often used in a similar context. You might hear, for example, that gold is an element made of gold atoms. Generally, *element* is used in reference to an entire macroscopic or microscopic sample, and *atom* is used when speaking of the submicroscopic particles in the sample. The important distinction is that elements are made of atoms and not the other way around.

The fundamental unit of an element is indicated by its **elemental formula.** For elements in which the fundamental units are individual atoms, the elemental formula is simply the chemical symbol: Au is the elemental formula for gold, and Li is the elemental formula for lithium, to name just two examples. For elements in which the fundamental units are two or more atoms bonded into molecules, the elemental formula is the chemical symbol followed by a subscript indicating the number of atoms in each molecule. For example, elemental nitrogen, as was shown in Figure 14.1 (page 341), commonly consists of molecules containing two nitrogen atoms per molecule. Thus, N_2 is the usual elemental formula given for nitrogen. Similarly, O_2, is the elemental formula for the oxygen we breathe, and S_8 is the elemental formula for sulfur.

☑ CHECKPOINT

The oxygen we breathe, O_2, is converted to ozone, O_3, in the presence of an electric spark. Is this a physical or chemical change?

Check Your Answer

When atoms regroup, the result is an entirely new substance, and that is what happens here. The oxygen we breathe, O_2, is odorless and life-giving. Ozone, O_3, can be toxic, and it has a pungent smell commonly associated with electric motors. The conversion of O_2 to O_3 is therefore a chemical change. However, both O_2 and O_3 are elemental forms of oxygen.

When atoms of different elements bond to one another, they make a **compound.** Sodium atoms and chlorine atoms, for example, bond to make the compound sodium chloride, commonly known as table salt. Nitrogen atoms and hydrogen atoms join to make the compound ammonia, which is a common household cleaner.

A compound is represented by its **chemical formula,** in which the symbols for the elements are written together. The chemical formula for sodium chloride is NaCl, and that for ammonia is NH_3. Numerical subscripts indicate the ratio in which the atoms combine. By convention, the subscript 1 is understood and omitted. So the chemical formula NaCl tells us that, in the compound sodium chloride, there is one sodium atom for every chlorine atom; and the chemical formula NH_3 tells us that, in the compound ammonia, there is one nitrogen atom for every three hydrogen atoms, as Figure 17.14 shows.

Compounds have physical and chemical properties that are completely different from the properties of their elemental components. The sodium chloride, NaCl, shown in Figure 17.15 is very different from the elemental sodium and the elemental chlorine used in its formation. Elemental sodium, Na, consists of nothing but sodium atoms, which form a soft, silvery metal that can be cut easily with a knife. Its melting point is 97.5°C, and it reacts violently with water. Elemental chlorine, Cl_2, consists of chlorine molecules. This material, a yellow-green gas at room temperature, is very toxic, and it was used as a chemical warfare agent during World War I. Its boiling point is −34°C. The compound sodium chloride, NaCl, is a translucent, brittle, colorless crystal having a melting point of 800°C. Sodium chloride does not react chemically with water the way sodium does; and not only is it not toxic to humans, which chlorine is, but the very opposite is true—it is an essential component of all living organisms. Sodium chloride is not sodium, nor is it chlorine; it is uniquely sodium chloride, a tasty chemical when sprinkled lightly over popcorn.

Figure 17.14
The compounds sodium chloride and ammonia are represented by their chemical formulas, NaCl and NH_3. A chemical formula shows the ratio of atoms that constitute the compound.

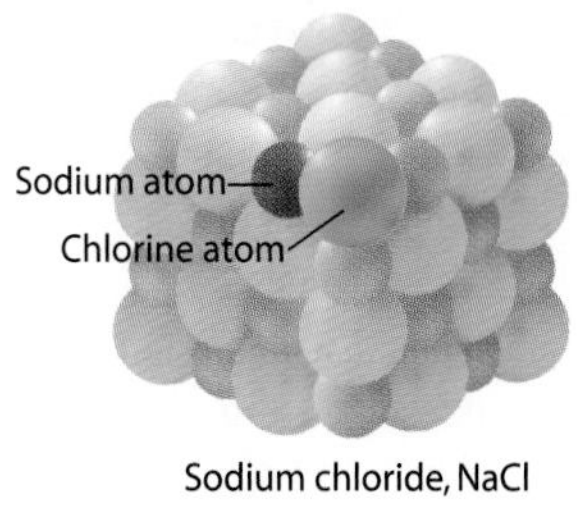

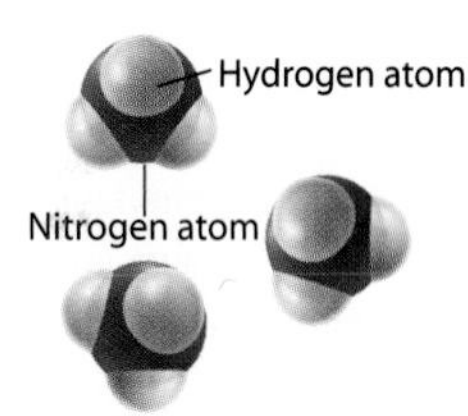

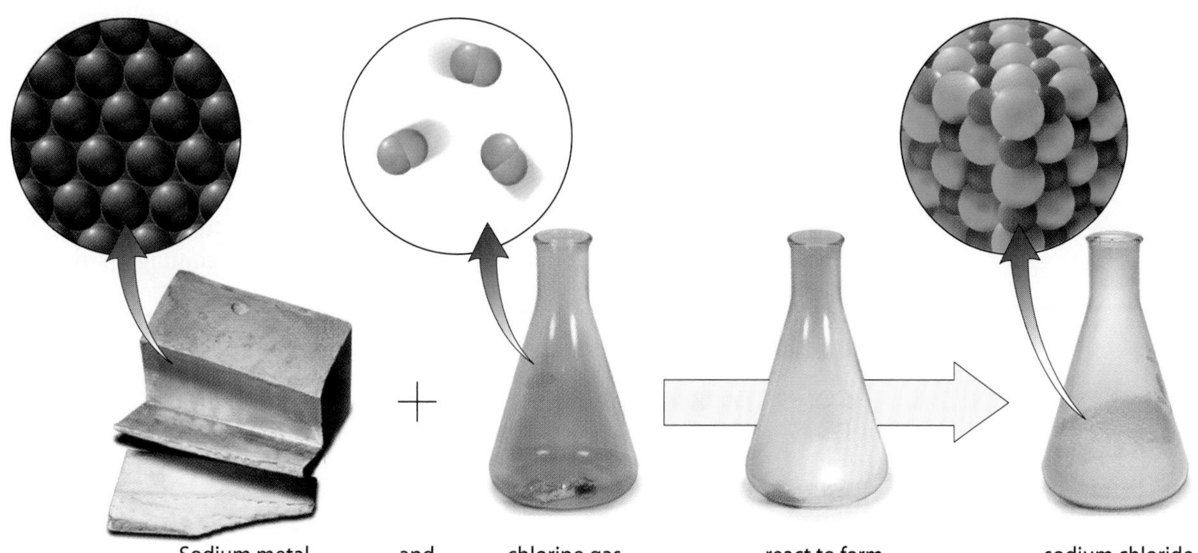

Figure 17.15
Sodium metal and chlorine gas react together to form sodium chloride. Although the compound sodium chloride is composed of sodium and chlorine, the physical and chemical properties of sodium chloride are very different from the physical and chemical properties of either sodium metal or chlorine gas.

A compound is uniquely different from the elements from which it is made. For example, water is a liquid, while the elements that compose it, hydrogen and oxygen, are gases. The harmless compound known as table salt is composed of two very dangerous chemicals: metallic sodium and chlorine gas.

Insights

☑ CHECKPOINT

Hydrogen sulfide, H_2S, is one of the smelliest compounds. Rotten eggs get their characteristic bad smell from the hydrogen sulfide they release. Can you infer from this information that elemental sulfur, S_8, is just as smelly?

Check Your Answer

No, you cannot. In fact, the odor of elemental sulfur is negligible compared with that of hydrogen sulfide. Compounds are truly different from the elements from which they are formed. Hydrogen sulfide, H_2S, is as different from elemental sulfur, S_8, as water, H_2O, is from elemental oxygen, O_2.

17.6 Naming Compounds

A system for naming the countless number of possible compounds has been developed by the International Union for Pure and Applied Chemistry (IUPAC). This system is designed so that a compound's name reflects the elements it contains and how those elements are joined. Anyone familiar with the system, therefore, can deduce the chemical identity of a compound from its systematic name.

As you might imagine, this system is very intricate. However, you need not learn all its rules. But learning some guidelines will prove most helpful. These guidelines alone will not enable you to name every compound. However, they will acquaint you with how the system works for many simple compounds consisting of only two elements.

Guideline 1 The name of the element farther to the left in the periodic table is followed by the name of the element farther to the right, with the suffix "-ide" added to the name of the latter:

NaCl	Sodium chloride	HCl	Hydrogen chloride
Li_2O	Lithium oxide	MgO	Magnesium oxide
CaF_2	Calcium fluoride	Sr_3P_2	Strontium phosphide

Guideline 2 When two or more compounds have different numbers of the same elements, prefixes are added to remove the ambiguity. The first four prefixes are "mono-" (one), "di-" (two), "tri-" (three), and "tetra-" (four). The prefix mono-, however, is commonly omitted from the beginning of the first word of the name:

Carbon and oxygen

CO	Carbon monoxide
CO_2	Carbon dioxide

Nitrogen and oxygen

NO_2	Nitrogen dioxide
N_2O_4	Dinitrogen tetroxide

Sulfur and oxygen

SO_2	Sulfur dioxide
SO_3	Sulfur trioxide

Guideline 3 Many compounds are not usually referred to by their systematic names. Instead, they are assigned common names that are more convenient or have been used traditionally for many years. Some common names are water for H_2O, ammonia for NH_3, and methane for CH_4.

Knowing the name of a chemical is an important step to learning more about the chemical. Similarly, knowing the name of a stranger is an important first step to becoming an acquaintance and then ultimately a friend.

Insights

☑ CHECKPOINT

What is the systematic name for NaF?

Check Your Answer

This compound is a cavity-fighting substance added to some toothpastes—sodium fluoride.

17.7 Chemical Equations

During a chemical reaction, atoms rearrange to create one or more new compounds. This activity is neatly summed up in written form as a **chemical equation.** A chemical equation shows the reacting substances, called **reactants,** to the left of an arrow that points to the newly formed substances, called **products:**

$$\text{reactants} \longrightarrow \text{products}$$

Typically, reactants and products are represented by their elemental or chemical formulas. Sometimes molecular models or, simply, names may be used instead. Phases are also often shown: (*s*) for solid, (*l*) for liquid, and (*g*) for gas. Compounds dissolved in water are designated (*aq*) for aqueous solution. Lastly, numbers are placed in front of the reactants or products to show the ratio in which they either combine or form. These numbers are called *coefficients,* and they represent numbers of individual atoms and molecules. For instance, to represent the chemical reaction in which coal burns in the presence of oxygen to form gaseous carbon dioxide, we write the chemical equation using coefficients of 1:

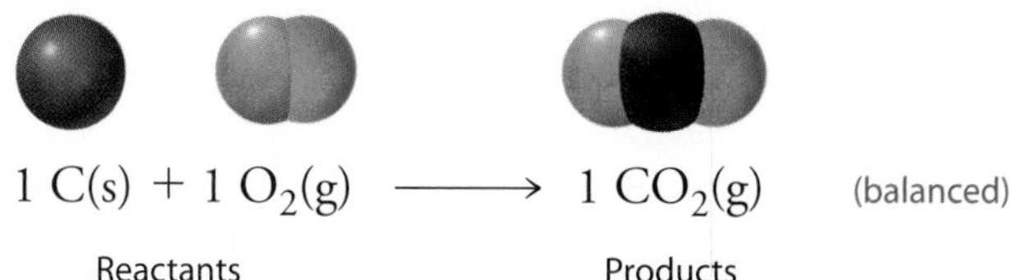

$$1\ C(s) + 1\ O_2(g) \longrightarrow 1\ CO_2(g) \quad \text{(balanced)}$$

Reactants Products

One of the most important principles of chemistry is the **law of mass conservation.** The law of mass conservation states that matter is neither created nor destroyed during a chemical reaction.* The atoms present at the beginning of a reaction merely rearrange to form new molecules. This means that no atoms are lost or gained during any reaction. The chemical equation must therefore be *balanced.* In a balanced equation, each atom must appear on both sides of the arrow

*For all practical purposes this law holds true. Technically, however, any energy that is released or absorbed by a chemical reaction arises from the transformation of matter into energy, or vice versa. The amount of matter lost or gained in a chemical reaction, however, is so small that, for all practical purposes, we can ignore this detail. Not so for the nuclear reaction discussed in Chapter 16. For these reactions, matter/energy conversions are much more pronounced.

the same number of times. The equation for the formation of carbon dioxide is balanced because each side shows one carbon atom and two oxygen atoms. You can count the number of atoms in the models to see this for yourself.

In another chemical reaction, two hydrogen gas molecules, H_2, react with one oxygen gas molecule, O_2, to produce two molecules of water, H_2O, in the gaseous phase:

$$2\ H_2(g) + 1\ O_2(g) \longrightarrow 2\ H_2O(g) \quad \text{(balanced)}$$

This equation for the formation of water is also balanced—there are four hydrogen and two oxygen atoms before and after the arrow.

A coefficient in front of a chemical formula tells us the number of times that element or compound must be counted. For example, 2 H_2O indicates two water molecules, which contain a total of four hydrogen atoms and two oxygen atoms.

By convention, the coefficient 1 is omitted so that the above chemical equations are typically written

$$C(s) + O_2(g) \longrightarrow CO_2(g) \quad \text{(balanced)}$$

$$2\ H_2(g) + O_2(g) \longrightarrow 2\ H_2O(g) \quad \text{(balanced)}$$

☑ CHECKPOINT

How many oxygen atoms are indicated by the following balanced equation?

$$3\ O_2(g) \longrightarrow 2\ O_3(g)$$

Check Your Answer

Before the reaction, these six oxygen atoms are found in three O_2 molecules. After the reaction, these same six atoms are found in two O_3 molecules.

Balancing Unbalanced Equations

An unbalanced chemical equation shows the reactants and products without the correct coefficients. For example, the equation:

$$NO(g) \longrightarrow N_2O(g) + NO_2(g) \quad \text{(not balanced)}$$

is not balanced because there is one nitrogen atom and one oxygen atom before the arrow, but three nitrogen atoms and three oxygen atoms after the arrow.

You can balance unbalanced equations by adding or changing coefficients to produce correct ratios. (It's important not to change subscripts, however, because to do so changes the compound's identity—H_2O is water, but H_2O_2 is hydrogen peroxide!) For example, to balance the equation above, add a 3 before the NO:

$$3\ NO(g) \longrightarrow N_2O(g) + NO_2(g) \quad \text{(balanced)}$$

Now there are three nitrogen atoms and three oxygen atoms on each side of the arrow, and the law of mass conservation is not violated.

There are many methods to balancing equations. For example, consider the following equation in which aluminum oxide, Al_2O_3, and carbon, C, react to form elemental aluminum, Al, and carbon dioxide, CO_2. Here is an unbalanced equation for this reaction:

$$\_\_\_\ Al_2O_3(s) + \_\_\_\ C(s) \longrightarrow \_\_\_\ Al(s) + \_\_\_\ CO_2(g)$$ (not balanced)

Balancing an equation usually proceeds most efficiently when you balance one element at a time, starting with elements in the most complex reactant. For this example, therefore, we can start by balancing the aluminum. This element can be balanced by placing a 2 in front of the product Al, so that there are two aluminum atoms before the arrow and two after:

$$\_\_\_\ Al_2O_3(s) + \_\_\_\ C(s) \longrightarrow 2\ Al(s) + \_\_\_\ CO_2(g)$$

(aluminum balanced)
(oxygen not balanced)
(carbon balanced)

The oxygen can then be balanced by placing a 2 in front of the Al_2O_3 and a 3 in front of the CO_2:

$$2\ Al_2O_3(s) + \_\_\_\ C(s) \longrightarrow \_\_\_\ 2\ Al(s) + 3\ CO_2(g)$$

(aluminum not balanced)
(oxygen balanced)
(carbon not balanced)

Doing this gives six oxygen atoms before and after the arrow. Ignore the fact that adding these coefficients upsets the balance of aluminum and carbon atoms. It is best to focus on one element at a time, and, for the equation above, our focus was on oxygen.

We've now worked with all the elements of the most complex reactant, Al_2O_3, and so it's time to balance the carbon. This can be done by placing a 3 in front of its symbol:

$$2\ Al_2O_3(s) + 3\ C(s) \longrightarrow 2\ Al(s) + 3\ CO_2(g)$$

(aluminum not balanced)
(oxygen balanced)
(carbon balanced)

Go through the equation again, focusing on one element at a time to make sure each is balanced. The number of aluminum atoms, for example, can be balanced by changing the coefficient of Al to 4:

$$2\ Al_2O_3(s) + 3\ C(s) \longrightarrow 4\ Al(s) + 3\ CO_2(g)$$

(aluminum balanced)
(oxygen balanced)
(carbon balanced)

As you will discover, there are often several paths to follow in balancing a chemical equation. For the example above, you could have started by balancing the carbon first, though it's usually wisest to begin with elements in the most complex reactant. If the coefficients start getting very large (beyond 12), you've likely chosen a path that is looping you around to no end. In such an event, it would help to start over.

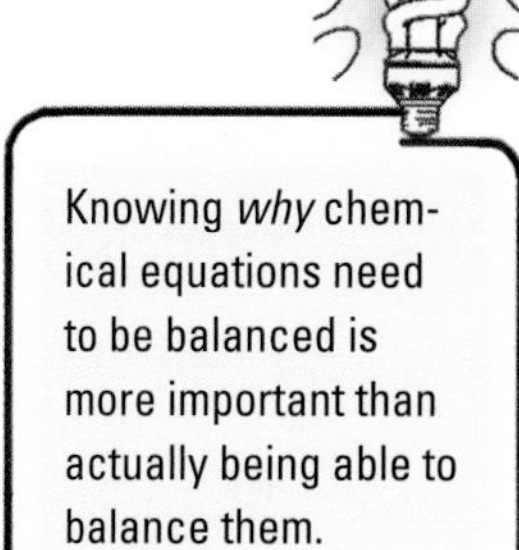

Here is a summary of the steps used in our example:

1. Balance one element at a time. Modify the coefficients to make the element appear the same number of times on both sides of the arrow. Start with the reactant having the most complex formula, and finish with the reactant having the simplest formula.
2. If you incidentally unbalance an element that you worked with previously, leave it alone and come back to it only after you have worked with all the other elements.
3. After you have worked with each element, make another pass through the equation, changing coefficients as needed.
4. Repeat Step 3 until all elements are balanced.
5. If necessary, minimize the coefficients by dividing by the lowest common denominator. The coefficients 2:4:2, for example, should be reduced to 1:2:1 by dividing by the lowest common denominator, which is 2.

Helpful Hints: Never, never, NEVER alter a subscript. Remember that a coefficient must appear before a chemical compound, not within it. Use a pencil so that you can erase coefficients as needed.

☑ CHECKPOINT

Write a balanced equation for the reaction showing hydrogen gas and nitrogen gas forming ammonia gas below:

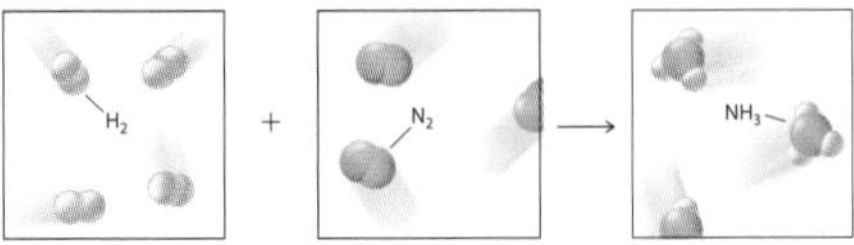

Check Your Answer

Start by writing the equation without the coefficients:

$$\_\_H_2(g) + \_\_N_2(g) \longrightarrow \_\_\ NH_3(g)$$

Then go through the steps outlined above. The balanced equation is

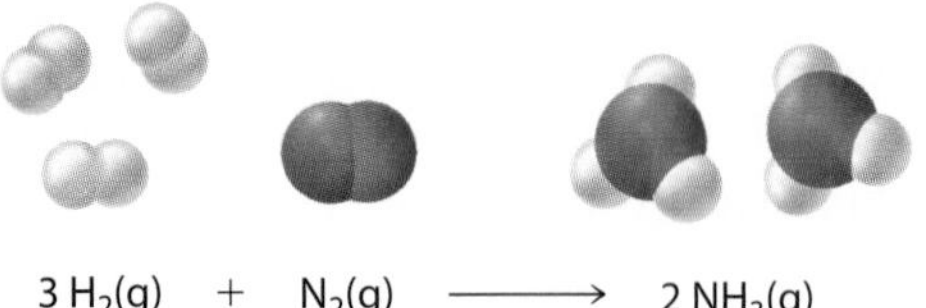

$$3\,H_2(g) \quad + \quad N_2(g) \quad \longrightarrow \quad 2\,NH_3(g)$$

You can see that there are equal numbers of each kind of atom before and after the arrow. For more practice balancing equations, try the ones in the Exercises at the end of this chapter.

Practicing chemists develop a skill for balancing equations. This skill involves creative energy and, like other skills, improves with experience. There are some useful tricks of the trade for balancing equations, and maybe your instructor will share some with you. For brevity, however, this text introduces only the basics. More important than being an expert at balancing equations is knowing why they need to be balanced. And the reason is the law of mass conservation, which tells us that atoms are neither created nor destroyed in a chemical reaction—they are simply rearranged. So every atom present before the reaction must be present after the reaction, even though the groupings of atoms are different.

Summary of Terms

Basic research A branch of scientific research that focuses on a greater understanding of how the natural world operates.

Applied research A branch of scientific research that focuses on developing applications built upon the principles discovered through basic research.

Molecule A submicroscopic particle consisting of a group of atoms.

Submicroscopic Refers to the realm of atoms and molecules, which is a realm so small that we are unable to observe it directly with optical microscopes.

Physical property Any physical attribute of a substance, such as color, density, or hardness.

Physical change A change in which a substance changes one or more of its physical properties without transforming it into a new substance.

Chemical property A property that characterizes the ability of a substance to undergo a change that transforms it into a different substance.

Chemical bond The force of attraction between two atoms that holds them together. As discussed in Chapter 19, the nature of this force is electrical.

Chemical change A change in which the atoms of one or more substances are rearranged into one or more new substances.

Chemical reaction Synonymous with chemical change.

Elemental formula A notation that uses the atomic symbol and (sometimes) a numerical subscript to denote how atoms of the element are bonded together.

Compound A material in which atoms of different elements are bonded to one another.

Chemical formula A notation used to indicate the composition of a compound, consisting of the atomic symbols for the different elements of the compound and numerical subscripts indicating the ratio in which the atoms combine.

Chemical equation A representation of a chemical reaction in which reactants are drawn before an arrow that points to the products.

Reactants The reacting substances in a chemical reaction.

Products The new materials formed in a chemical reaction.

Law of mass conservation Matter is neither created nor destroyed during a chemical reaction—atoms merely rearrange, without any apparent loss or gain of mass, to form new molecules.

Review Questions

17.1 Chemistry: The Central Science

1. What distinguishes basic research and applied research?
2. What is meant by saying that chemistry is the central science?
3. What do members of the Chemical Manufacturers Association pledge in the Responsible Care program?

17.2 The Submicroscopic World

4. Are atoms made of molecules, or are molecules made of atoms?
5. How are the particles in a solid arranged differently from those in a liquid?
6. How does the arrangement of particles in a gas differ from the arrangements in liquids and solids?
7. Which occupies the greatest volume: 1 gram of ice, 1 gram of liquid water, or 1 gram of water vapor?

17.3 Physical and Chemical Properties

8. What is a physical property?
9. What is a chemical property?
10. What doesn't change during a physical change?

17.4 Determining Physical and Chemical Changes

11. Why is it sometimes difficult to decide whether an observed change is physical or chemical?
12. What are some of the clues that help us to determine whether an observed change is physical or chemical?

17.5 Elements to Compounds

13. How many types of atoms can you expect to find in a pure sample of any element?
14. Distinguish between an atom and an element.
15. How many atoms are in a sulfur molecule that has the elemental formula S_8?
16. What is the difference between an element and a compound?

17. How many atoms are there in one molecule of H_3PO_4? How many atoms of each element are there in this molecule?
18. Are the physical and chemical properties of a compound necessarily similar to those of the elements from which it was composed?

17.6 Naming Compounds

19. What is the IUPAC systematic name for the compound KF?
20. What is the chemical formula for the compound titanium dioxide?
21. Why are common names often used for chemical compounds instead of systematic names?

17.7 Chemical Equations

22. What is the purpose of coefficients in a chemical equation?
23. How many chromium atoms and how many oxygen atoms are indicated on the right side of this balanced chemical equation?

$$4\ Cr(s) + 3\ O_2(g) \longrightarrow 2\ Cr_2O_3(g)$$

24. What do the letters (s), (l), (g), and (aq) stand for in a chemical equation?
25. Why is it important that a chemical equation be balanced?
26. Why is it important never to change a subscript in a chemical formula when balancing a chemical equation?
27. Which equations are balanced?
    a. $Mg(s) + 2\ HCl(aq) \longrightarrow MgCl_2(aq) + H_2(g)$
    b. $3\ Al(s) + 3\ Br_2(\ell) \longrightarrow Al_2Br_3(s)$
    c. $2\ HgO(s) \longrightarrow 2\ Hg(\ell) + O_2(g)$

Activities

Fire Water

Place a large pot of cool water on top of a gas stove (or bunsen burner, if performed in the laboratory), and set the flame on high. What product from the combustion of the natural gas do you see condensing on the outside of the pot? Where did it originate? Would more or less of this product form if the pot contained ice water? Where does this product go as the pot gets warmer? What physical and chemical changes can you identify?

Oxygen Bubble Bursts

Compounds can be broken down to their component elements. For example, when you pour a solution of the compound hydrogen peroxide, H_2O_2, over a cut, an enzyme in your blood decomposes it to produce oxygen gas, O_2, as evidenced by the bubbling that occurs. It is this oxygen at high concentrations at the site of the injury that kills off microorganisms. A similar enzyme is found in baker's yeast.

What You Need

Packet of baker's yeast; 3% hydrogen peroxide solution; short, wide drinking glass; tweezers; matches.

Safety Note

Wear safety glasses, and remove all combustibles, such as paper towels, from the area. Keep your fingers well away from the flame because it will glow more brightly as it is exposed to the oxygen.

Procedure

1. Pour the yeast into the glass. Add a couple of capfuls of the hydrogen peroxide and watch the oxygen bubbles form.
2. Test for the presence of oxygen by holding a lighted match with the tweezers and placing the flame near the bubbles. Look for the flame to glow more brightly as the escaping oxygen passes over it. Describe oxygen's physical and chemical properties.

Exercises

1. In what sense is a color computer monitor or television screen similar to our view of matter? Place a drop (and only a drop) of water on your computer monitor or television screen for a closer look.
2. Of these three sciences—physics, chemistry, and biology—which is the most complex?
3. Is chemistry the study of the submicroscopic, the microscopic, the macroscopic, or all three? Defend your answer.
4. Gas particles travel at speeds of up to 500 meters per second. Why, then, does it take so long for gas molecules to travel the length of a room?
5. Which has stronger attractions among its submicroscopic particles: a solid at 25°C or a gas at 25°C? Explain.
6. The leftmost diagram on the next page shows the moving particles of a gaseous material within a rigid container. Which of the three boxes on the right (a, b, or c) best represents this material upon the addition of heat?

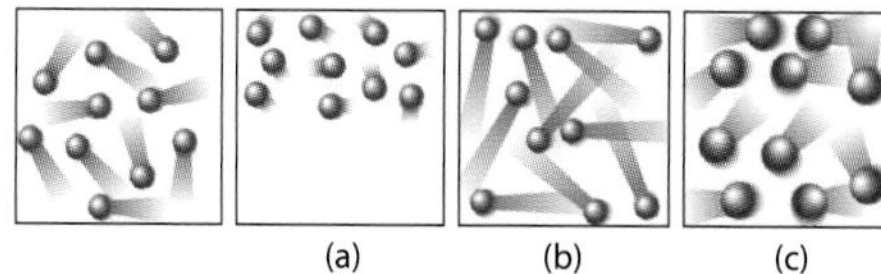

7. The diagram at the left shows two phases of a single substance. In the middle box, sketch these particles as if heat were removed. In the box on the right, show what they would look like if heat were added. If each particle represents a water molecule, what is the likely temperature in the box on the left?

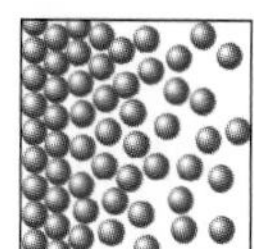  

8. Humidity is a measure of the amount of water vapor in the atmosphere. Why is humidity always very low inside your kitchen freezer?
9. State whether each of the following is an example of a physical or chemical property of matter.
   (a) Graphite conducts electricity.
   (b) Bismuth, Bi, loses its iridescence upon melting.
   (c) A copper penny is smashed to produce an embossed souvenir.
10. State whether each of the following is an example of a physical or chemical property of matter.
    (a) Carbon dioxide escapes when a soda can is opened.
    (b) A bronze statue turns green.
    (c) A silver spoon tarnishes.
11. What is the evidence for the following being examples of chemical change?
    (a) Food spoils.
    (b) An antacid tablet fizzes in water.
    (c) A ring of scum forms around your bathtub.
    (d) Iron rusts.
    (e) A firecracker explodes.
12. Octane is a component of gasoline. It reacts with oxygen, O_2, to form carbon dioxide and water. Is octane an element or a compound? How can you tell?
13. What happens to the density of a gas as the gas is compressed into a smaller volume?
14. What happens to the density of a gas as the gas expands to a larger volume? What normally happens to its temperature in expanding?
15. Each night you measure your height just before going to bed. When you arise each morning, you measure your height again and consistently find that you are appreciably taller than you were the night before but only as tall as you were 24 hours ago! Is what happens to your body in this instance best described as a physical change or a chemical change? Be sure to try this activity if you haven't already.
16. Classify the following changes as physical or chemical. Even if you are incorrect in your assessment, you should be able to defend your choices.
    (a) Grape juice turns to wine. ______________
    (b) Wood burns to ashes. ______________
    (c) Water begins to boil. ______________
17. Classify the following changes as physical or chemical. Defend your choices.
    (a) A broken leg mends itself. ______________
    (b) Grass grows. ______________
    (c) An infant gains 10 pounds. ______________
    (d) A rock is crushed to powder. ______________
18. Is the following transformation representative of a physical change or a chemical change?

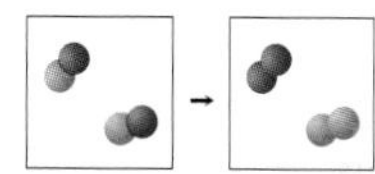

19. Each sphere in the diagrams below represents an atom. Joined spheres represent molecules. Which box contains a liquid? Why can you not assume that box B contains a liquid phase?

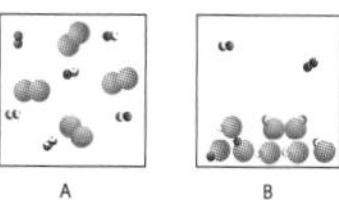

20. In the previous question, why can you not assume that box B represents a lower temperature?
21. Based on the information given in the following diagrams, which substance has the lower boiling point?

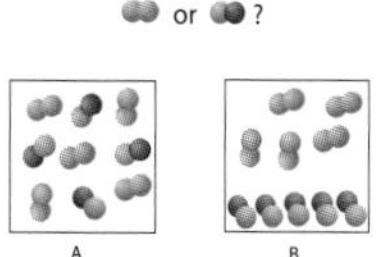

22. What physical and chemical changes occur when a wax candle burns?
23. Which elements are some of the oldest known? What is your evidence?
24. Oxygen atoms are used to make water molecules. Does this mean that oxygen, O_2, and water, H_2O, have similar properties?
25. Why do we drown when we breathe water into our lungs, despite all the oxygen present in water?
26. If you eat metallic sodium or inhale chlorine gas, you stand a very strong chance of dying. Let these two elements react with each other, however, and you can safely sprinkle the resulting compound on your popcorn for better taste. What is going on?

27. Which of these remains constant in a compound?
    (a) The mass of a sample of the compound.
    (b) The compound's phase.
    (c) The compound's density.
    (d) The ratio of elements it contains.
28. Common names of chemical compounds are generally much shorter than the corresponding systematic names. The systematic names for water, ammonia, and methane, for example, are dihydrogen monoxide, H_2O; trihydrogen nitride, NH_3; and tetrahydrogen carbide, CH_4. For these compounds, which would you rather use: common names or systematic names? Which do you find more descriptive?
29. What is the chemical formula for the compound dihydrogen sulfide?
30. What is the chemical name for a compound with the formula Ba_3N_2?
31. What is the common name for dioxygen oxide?
32. What is the common name for oxygen oxide?
33. Is this chemical equation balanced?

    $2\ C_4H_{10}(g) + 13\ O_2(g) \longrightarrow 8\ CO_2(g) + 10\ H_2O(\ell)$
34. Balance these equations:
    (a) __Fe(s) + __ $O_2(g) \longrightarrow$ __ $Fe_2O_3(s)$
    (b) __$H_2(g)$ + __ $N_2(g) \longrightarrow$ __ $NH_3(g)$
    (c) __$Cl_2(g)$ + __ KBr(aq) $\longrightarrow$ __ $Br_2(\ell)$ + __ KCl(aq)
    (d) __$CH_4(g)$ + __ $O_2(g) \longrightarrow$ __ $CO_2(g)$ + __ $H_2O(\ell)$
35. Balance these equations:
    (a) __Fe(s) + __ S(s) $\longrightarrow$ __ $Fe_2S_3(s)$
    (b) __$P_4(s)$ + __ $H_2(g) \longrightarrow$ __ $PH_3(g)$
    (c) __NO(g) + __ $Cl_2(g) \longrightarrow$ __ NOCl(g)
    (d) __$SiCl_4(\ell)$ + __ Mg(s) $\longrightarrow$ __ Si(s) + __ $MgCl_2(s)$
36. In photosynthesis, carbon dioxide, CO_2, is combined with water, H_2O, to form glucose, $C_6H_{12}O_6$ and oxygen, O_2. Balance the following chemical equation for photosynthesis. How many molecules of carbon dioxide are needed to produce one molecule of glucose?

    __CO_2 + __ $H_2O \longrightarrow$ __ $C_6H_{12}O_6$ + __ O_2

Chapter 17 Online Resources

Tutorials
- What is Chemistry?
- Chemical Reactions & Equations

Quiz
Exercises
Flashcards
Links

CHAPTER 18

Mixtures

How can fresh water be prepared from seawater? How is municipal water treated so that it's safe enough to pipe into our homes for consumption? How does a wastewater treatment facility treat wastewater? When you stir sugar into water, the sugar crystals disappear, but where do they go? What are clouds made of, and what do they have in common with the blood that runs through our veins? Is it true that a fish can drown in water? When tap water is left boiling on the stove too long, it evaporates completely but leaves a chalky residue in the pot. What is this residue and where did it originate? The answers to these questions involve an understanding of mixtures.

18.1 Most Materials Are Mixtures

A **mixture** is a combination of two or more substances in which each substance retains its own properties. Most materials we encounter are mixtures: mixtures of elements, mixtures of compounds, or mixtures of elements and compounds. Stainless steel, for example, is a mixture of the elements iron, chromium, nickel, and carbon. Seltzer water is a mixture of a liquid compound, water, and a gaseous compound, carbon dioxide. Our atmosphere, as Figure 18.1 illustrates, is a mixture of the elements nitrogen, oxygen, and argon, plus small amounts of such compounds as carbon dioxide and water vapor.

Figure 18.1
The earth's atmosphere is a mixture of gaseous elements and compounds. Some of them are shown here.

Figure 18.2
Tap water provides us with H_2O as well as a large number of other compounds, many of which are flavorful and healthful. Bottoms up!

Tap water is a mixture containing mostly water but also many other compounds. Depending on your location, your water may contain compounds of calcium, magnesium, chlorine, fluorine, iron, and potassium; trace amounts of compounds of lead, mercury, and cadmium; organic compounds; and dissolved oxygen, nitrogen, and carbon dioxide. While it is surely important to minimize any toxic components in your drinking water, it is unnecessary, undesirable, and impossible to remove all other substances from it. Some of the dissolved solids and gases give water its characteristic taste, and many of them promote human health: fluoride compounds protect teeth, chlorine destroys harmful bacteria, and as much as 10 percent of our daily requirement for iron, potassium, calcium, and magnesium is obtained from drinking water (Figures 18.2 and 18.3).

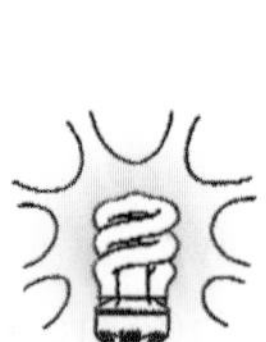

The toxicity of any substance is in the dose. Small concentrations of the fluoride ion serve to prevent tooth decay, for example, while larger concentrations can cause your teeth to mottle. There are also many other nasty side effects of ingesting too much fluoride, which is why dentists urge you to spit after brushing your teeth with fluoridated toothpaste.

Insights

Figure 18.3
Most of the oxygen in the air bubbles produced by an aquarium aerator escapes into the atmosphere. Some of the oxygen, however, mixes with the water. It is this oxygen that fish depend upon to survive. Without this dissolved oxygen, which fish extract from the water with their gills, the fish would promptly drown. So fish don't "breathe" water. They breathe the O_2 that is dissolved in the water.

☑ CHECKPOINT

So far, you have learned about three kinds of matter: elements, compounds, and mixtures. Which box below contains only an element? Which contains only a compound? Which contains a mixture?

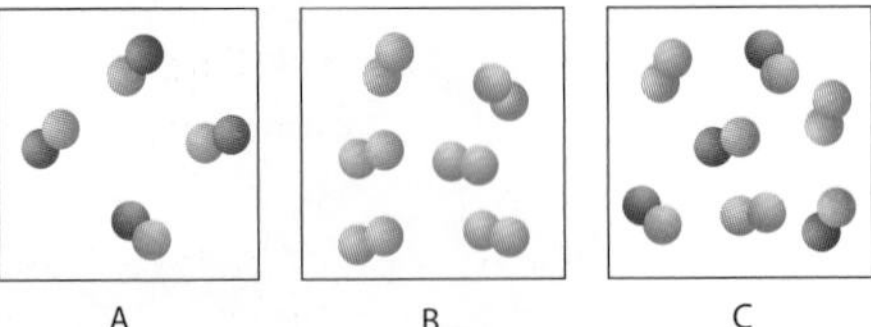

Check Your Answer

The molecules in box A each contain two different types of atoms and so are representative of a compound. The molecules in box B each consist of the same atoms and so are representative of an element. Box C is a mixture of the compound and the element.

Note how the molecules of the compound and those of the element remain intact in the mixture. That is, upon the formation of the mixture, there is no exchange of atoms between the components.

There is a difference between the way substances—either elements or compounds—combine to form mixtures and the way elements combine to form compounds. Each substance in a mixture retains its chemical identity. The sugar molecules in the teaspoon of sugar in Figure 18.4, for example, are identical to the sugar molecules already in the tea. The only difference is that the sugar molecules in the tea are mixed with other substances, mostly water. The formation of a mixture, therefore, is a physical change. In contrast, as discussed in Section 17.5, there is a change in chemical identity when elements join to form compounds. Recall that sodium chloride is not a mixture of sodium and chlorine atoms but is instead a compound, which means it is entirely different from the elements that compose it. The formation of a compound is therefore a chemical change.

Figure 18.4
Table sugar is a compound consisting only of sucrose molecules. Once these molecules are mixed into hot tea, they become interspersed among the water and tea molecules and form a sugar–tea–water mixture. No new compounds are formed, and so this is an example of a physical change.

Mixtures Can Be Separated by Physical Means

The components of mixtures can be separated from one another by taking advantage of differences in the components' physical properties. A mixture of solids and liquids, for example, can be separated using filter paper through which the liquids pass but the solids do not. This is how coffee is often made: the caffeine and flavor molecules in the hot water pass through the filter and into the coffee pot, while the solid coffee grounds remain behind. This method of separating a solid–liquid mixture is called *filtration,* and it is a common technique used by chemists.

Mixtures can also be separated by taking advantage of a difference in boiling or melting points. Seawater is a mixture of water and a variety of compounds, mostly sodium chloride. Whereas water boils at 100°C, sodium chloride doesn't even melt until 800°C. One way to separate water from the mixture we call seawater, therefore, is to heat the seawater to about 100°C. At this temperature, the liquid water readily transforms to water vapor, but the sodium chloride stays behind dissolved in the remaining water. As the water vapor rises, it can be channeled into a cooler container, where it condenses into a liquid without the dissolved solids. This process of collecting a vaporized substance,

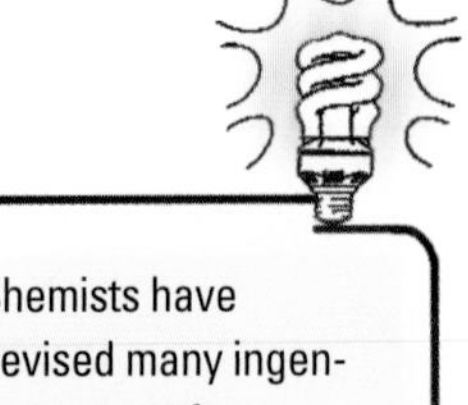

Chemists have devised many ingenious ways of separating the components of a mixture. Most of these techniques employ the simple principle of separating the components by differences in their physical properties.

Insights

called **distillation,** is illustrated in Figure 18.5. Distillation is a very effective, though costly, way of isolating fresh water from seawater. We explore this in further detail in Section 18.5. After all the water has been distilled from seawater, what remains are dry solids. These solids, also a mixture of compounds, contain a variety of commerically valuable compounds, such as sodium chloride and potassium bromide (Figure 18.6).

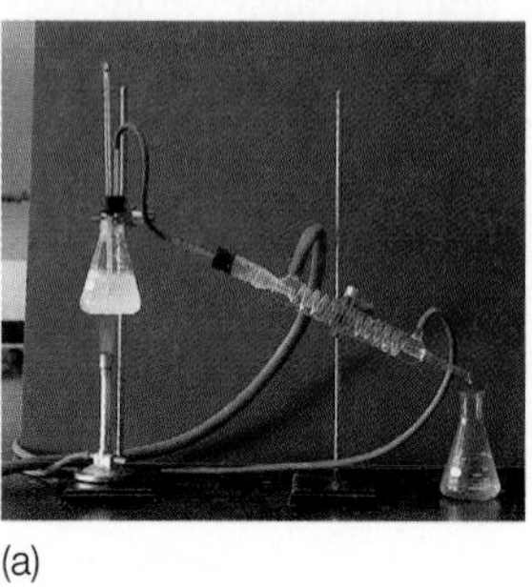

(a)

(b)

Figure 18.5
(a) A simple distillation setup used to separate one component—water—from the mixture we call seawater. The seawater is boiled in the flask on the left. The rising water vapor is channeled into a downward-slanting tube kept cool by cold water flowing across its outer surface. The water vapor inside the cool tube condenses and collects in the flask on the right. (b) A whiskey still functions by the same principle. A mixture containing alcohol is heated to the point where the alcohol, some flavoring molecules, and some water are vaporized. These vapors travel through the copper coils, where they then condense to a liquid.

Figure 18.6
At the southern end of San Francisco Bay, there are areas where the seawater has been partitioned off by earthen dikes. These are evaporation ponds, where the water is allowed to evaporate, leaving behind the solids that were dissolved in the seawater. These solids are further refined for commercial sale. The remarkable color of the ponds results from suspended particles of iron oxide and other minerals, which are easily removed during refining.

18.2 The Chemist's Classification of Matter

If a material is **pure,** it consists of only a single element or a single compound. In pure gold, for example, there is nothing but the element gold. In pure table salt, there is nothing but the compound sodium chloride. If a material is **impure,** it is a mixture and contains two or more elements or compounds. This classification scheme is shown in Figure 18.7.

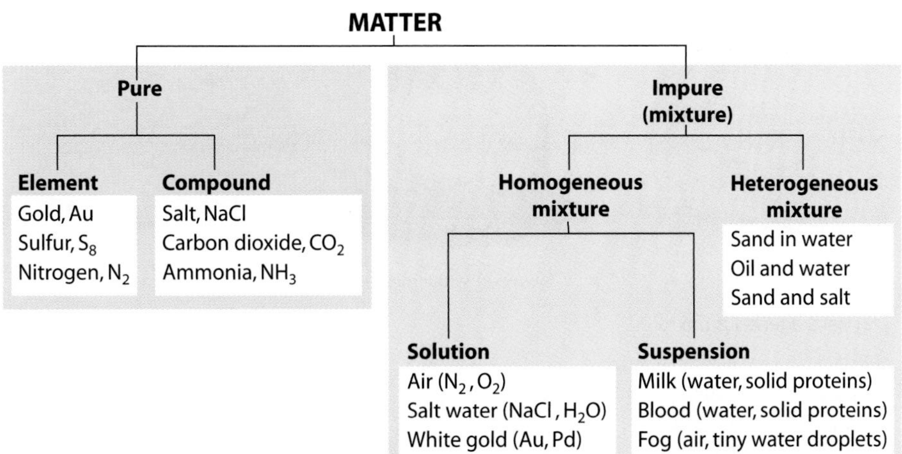

Figure 18.7
A chemical classification of matter.

Because atoms and molecules are so small, it is impractical to prepare a sample that is truly pure—that is, truly 100 percent of a single material. For example, if just one atom or molecule out of a trillion trillion were different, then the 100 percent pure status would be lost. Samples, however, can be "purified" by various methods such as distillation. When we say *pure,* it is understood to be a relative term. Comparing the purity of two samples, the purer one contains fewer impurities. A sample of water that is 99.9 percent pure has a greater proportion of impurities than does a purer sample of water that is 99.9999 percent pure.

Sometimes naturally occurring mixtures are labeled as being pure, as in "pure orange juice." Such a statement merely means that nothing artificial has been added. According to a chemist's definition, however, orange juice is anything but pure, as it contains a wide variety of materials, including water, pulp, flavorings, vitamins, and sugars.

Mixtures may be heterogeneous or homogeneous. In a **heterogeneous mixture,** the different components can be seen as individual substances, such as pulp in orange juice, sand in water, or oil globules dispersed in vinegar. The different components are visible. **Homogeneous mixtures** have the same composition throughout. Any one region of the mixture has the same ratio of substances as does any other region, and the components cannot be seen as individual identifiable entities. The distinction is shown in Figure 18.8.

A homogeneous mixture may be either a solution or a suspension. In a **solution,** all components are in the same phase. The atmosphere we breathe is a gaseous solution consisting of the gaseous elements nitrogen and oxygen as well as minor amounts of other gaseous materials. Salt water is a liquid solution because both the water and the dissolved sodium chloride are found in a single liquid phase. An example of a solid solution is white gold, which is a homogeneous mixture of the elements gold and palladium. We shall be discussing solutions in more detail in the next section.

A **suspension** is a homogeneous mixture in which the different components are in different phases, such as solids in liquids or liquids in gases. In a suspension, the mixing is so thorough that the different phases cannot be readily

Figure 18.8
(a) In heterogeneous mixtures, the different components can be seen with the naked eye. (b) In homogeneous mixtures, the different components are mixed at a much finer level and so are not readily distinguished.

Figure 18.9
The path of light becomes visible when the light passes through a suspension.

distinguished. Milk is a suspension because it is a homogeneous mixture of proteins and fats finely dispersed in water. Blood is a suspension composed of finely dispersed blood cells in water. Another example of a suspension is clouds, which are homogeneous mixtures of tiny water droplets suspended in air. Shining a light through a suspension, as is done in Figure 18.9, results in a visible cone as the light is reflected by the suspended components.

The easiest way to distinguish a suspension from a solution in the laboratory is to spin a sample in a centrifuge. This device, spinning at thousands of revolutions per minute, separates the components of suspensions but not those of solutions, as Figure 18.10 shows.

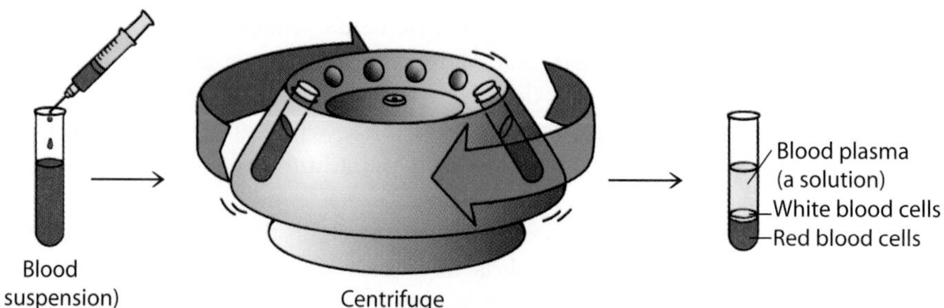

Figure 18.10
Blood, because it is a suspension, can be centrifuged into its components, which include the blood plasma (a yellowish solution) and white and red blood cells. The components of the plasma, however, cannot be separated from one another here because a centrifuge has no effect on solutions.

☑ CHECKPOINT

Impure water can be purified by which of these?

(a) Removing the impure water molecules.

(b) Removing everything that is not water.

(c) Breaking down the water to its simplest components.

(d) Adding some disinfectant such as chlorine.

Check Your Answer

The answer is b: Impure water can be purified by removing everything that isn't water. H_2O is a compound made of the elements hydrogen and oxygen in a 2-to-1 ratio. Every H_2O molecule is exactly the same as every other, and there's no such thing as an impure H_2O molecule. Just about anything, including you, beach balls, rubber ducks, dust particles, and bacteria, can be found in water. When something other than water is found in water, we say that the water is impure. It is important to see that the impurities are in the water and not part of the water, which means that it is possible to remove them by a variety of physical means, such as filtration or distillation.

18.3 Solutions

What happens when table sugar, known chemically as sucrose, is stirred into water? Is the sucrose destroyed? We know it isn't, because it sweetens the water. Does the sucrose disappear because it somehow ceases to occupy space or because it fits within the nooks and crannies of the water? Not so, for the addition of sucrose changes the volume. This may not be noticeable at first, but, if you continue adding sucrose to a glass of water, you'll see that the water level rises, just as it would if you were adding sand.

Sucrose stirred into water loses its crystalline form. Each sucrose crystal consists of billions upon billions of sucrose molecules packed neatly together. When the crystal is exposed to water (as was first shown in Figure 18.4 and is shown again here in Figure 18.11), an even greater number of water molecules pull on the sucrose molecules via hydrogen bonds formed between the sucrose

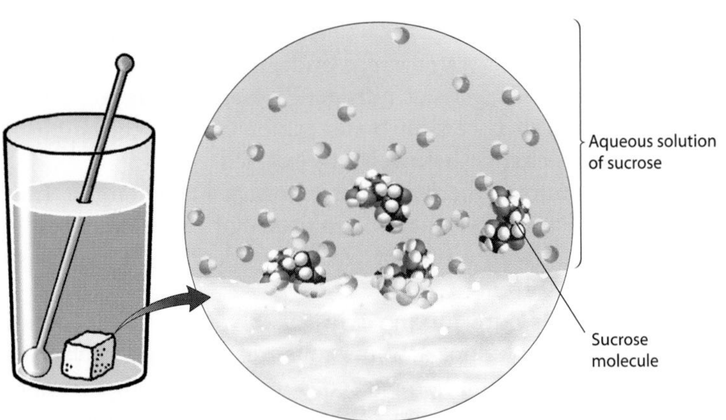

Figure 18.11
Water molecules pull the sucrose molecules in a sucrose crystal away from one another. This pulling away does not, however, affect the covalent bonds within each sucrose molecule, which is why each dissolved sucrose molecule remains intact as a single molecule.

molecules and the water molecules. With a little stirring, the sucrose molecules soon mix throughout the water. In place of sucrose crystals and water, we have a homogeneous mixture of sucrose molecules in water. As discussed earlier, homogeneous means that a sample taken from any part of a mixture is the same as a sample taken from any other part. In our sucrose example, this means that the sweetness of the first sip of the solution is the same as the sweetness of the last sip.

Link to Section 25.3

Recall that a homogeneous mixture consisting of a single phase is called a *solution.* Sugar in water is a solution in the liquid phase. Solutions aren't always liquids, however. They can also be solid or gaseous, as Figure 18.12 shows. Gemstones are solid solutions. A ruby, for example, is a solid solution of trace quantities of red chromium compounds in transparent aluminum oxide. A blue sapphire is a solid solution of trace quantities of light green iron compounds and blue titanium compounds in aluminum oxide. Another important example of solid solutions is metal alloys, which are mixtures of different metallic elements. The alloy known as brass is a solid solution of copper and zinc, for instance, and the alloy stainless steel is a solid solution of iron, chromium, nickel, and carbon.

(a)

(b)

(c)

Figure 18.12
Solutions may occur in (a) the solid phase, (b) the liquid phase, or (c) the gaseous phase.

An example of a gaseous solution is the air we breathe. By volume, this solution is 78 percent nitrogen gas, 21 percent oxygen gas, and 1 percent other gaseous materials, including water vapor and carbon dioxide. The air we exhale is a gaseous solution of 75 percent nitrogen, 14 percent oxygen, 5 percent carbon dioxide, and around 6 percent water vapor. So we see the air we breathe undergoes a chemical change before being exhaled.

To most people, solutions mean finding the answers. To chemists, however, solutions are things that are still all mixed up.

Insights

In describing solutions, the component present in the largest amount is the **solvent,** and any other components are **solutes.** For example, when a teaspoon of table sugar is mixed with 1 liter of water, we identify the sugar as the solute and the water as the solvent.

The process of a solute mixing with a solvent is called **dissolution,** or **dissolving.** To make a solution, a solute must dissolve in a solvent; that is, the solute and solvent must form a homogeneous mixture. Whether or not one material dissolves in another is a function of their electrical attractions for each other.

☑ CHECKPOINT

What is the solvent in the gaseous solution we call air?

Check Your Answer

Nitrogen is the solvent, because it is the component that is present in the greatest quantity.

There is a limit to how much of a given solute can be dissolved in a given solvent, as Figure 18.13 illustrates. We know that when you add table sugar to a glass of water, for example, the sugar rapidly dissolves. As you continue to add sugar, however, there comes a point when it no longer dissolves. Instead, it collects at the bottom of the glass, even after stirring. At this point, the water is saturated with sugar, meaning that the water cannot accept any more sugar. When this happens, we have what is called a **saturated solution,** defined as one in which no more solute can be dissolved. A solution that has not reached the limit of solute that will dissolve is called an **unsaturated solution.**

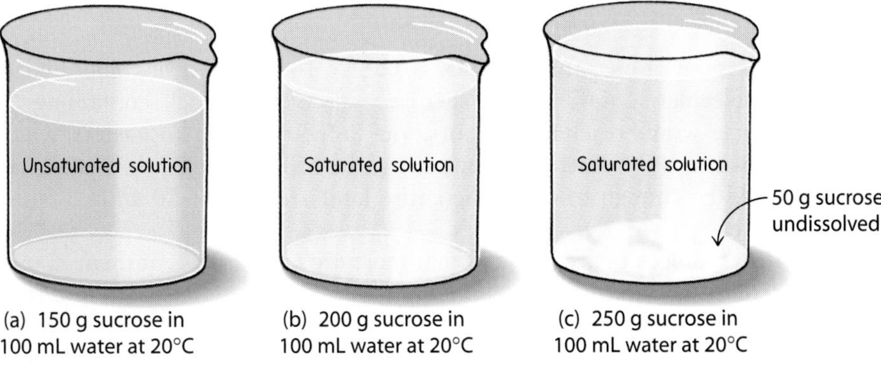

Figure 18.13
A maximum of 200 grams of sucrose dissolves in 100 milliliters of water at 20°C. (a) Mixing 150 grams of sucrose in 100 milliliters of water at 20°C produces an unsaturated solution. (b) Mixing 200 grams of sucrose in 100 milliliters of water at 20°C produces a saturated solution. (c) If 250 grams of sucrose is mixed with 100 milliliters of water at 20°C, 50 grams of sucrose remains undissolved. (As we discuss later, the concentration of a saturated solution varies with temperature.)

The quantity of solute dissolved in a solution is described in mathematical terms by the solution's **concentration,** which is the amount of solute dissolved per amount of solution:

$$\text{Concentration of solution} = \frac{\text{amount of solute}}{\text{amount of solution}}$$

For example, a sucrose–water solution may have a concentration of 1 gram of sucrose for every liter of solution. This can be compared with concentrations of other solutions. A sucrose–water solution containing 2 grams of sucrose per liter of solution, for example, is more concentrated, and one containing only 0.5 gram of sucrose per liter of solution is less concentrated, or more dilute.

Chemists are often more interested in the number of solute particles in a solution than in the number of grams of solute. Submicroscopic particles, however, are so very small that the number of them in any observable sample is incredibly large. To avoid awkwardly large numbers, scientists use a unit called the mole. One **mole** of any type of particle is, by definition, 6.02×10^{23} particles. (This superlarge number is about 602 billion trillion, or 602,000,000,000,000,000,000,000 particles.) (Interestingly, the term mole is derived from the Latin word *moles,* meaning heap, mass, or pile.)

One mole of gold atoms, for example, is 6.02×10^{23} gold atoms, and 1 mole of sucrose molecules is 6.02×10^{23} sucrose molecules.

Even if you've never heard the term mole in your life before now, you are already familiar with the basic idea. Saying "one mole" is just a shorthand way of saying "six point oh two times ten to the twenty-third particles." Just as "a couple of" means two of something and "a dozen of" means 12 of something, "a mole of" means 6.02×10^{23} of some elementary unit, such as atoms, molecules or ions. It's as simple as that:

- a couple of coconuts = 2 coconuts
- a dozen donuts = 12 donuts
- a mole of molecules = 6.02×10^{23} molecules

1 mole of gold atoms, for example, is 6.02×10^{23} gold atoms and 1 mole of sucrose molecules is 6.02×10^{23} sucrose molecules. A stack containing "1 mole" of pennies would reach a height of about 860 quadrillion kilometers, which is roughly equal to the diameter of our galaxy, the Milky Way. And "1 mole" of marbles would be enough to cover the entire land area of the 50 United States to a depth greater than 1.1 kilometers.

But sucrose molecules are so small that there are 6.02×10^{23} of them in only 342 grams of sucrose, which is about a cupful. Thus, because 342 grams of sucrose contains 6.02×10^{23} molecules of sucrose, we can use our shorthand wording and say that 342 grams of sucrose contains 1 mole of sucrose. As Figure 18.14 shows, therefore, an aqueous solution that has a concentration of 342 grams of sucrose per liter of solution also has a concentration of 6.02×10^{23} sucrose molecules per liter of solution or, by definition, a concentration of 1 mole of sucrose per liter of solution. The number of grams tells you the mass of solute

A "mole" of stacked pennies would stretch across our galaxy? Make this estimation yourself. First measure the number of stacked pennies in 1 centimeter. To find the length of one "mole" of stacked pennies, take the number of particles in one mole (6.02×10^{23}) and divide it by the number of pennies in 1 cm. Your answer will be in centimeters. To convert to kilometers, divide by the number of centimeters in a kilometer, which is 100,000. Tall stack!

Insights

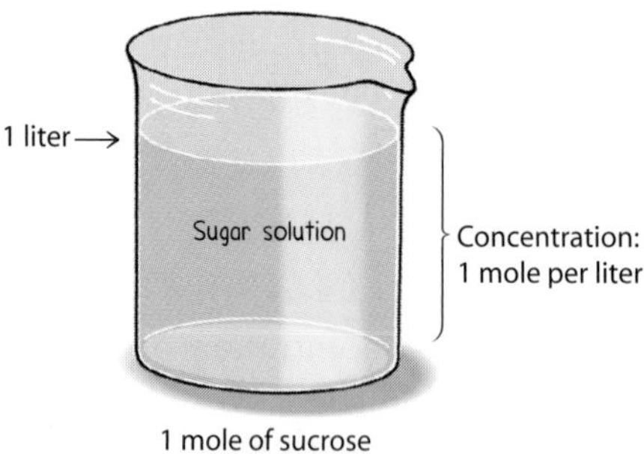

Figure 18.14
An aqueous solution of sucrose that has a concentration of 1 mole of sucrose per liter of solution contains 6.02×10^{23} sucrose molecules (342 grams) in every liter of solution.

in a given solution, and the number of moles indicates the actual number of molecules. Finding the number of molecules in a given mass or the mass of a given number of molecules is something we will further explore in Chapter 21.

A common unit of concentration used by chemists is **molarity,** which is the solution's concentration expressed in moles of solute per liter of solution:

$$\text{Molarity} = \frac{\text{number of moles of solute}}{\text{liters of solution}}$$

A solution that contains 1 mole of solute per liter of solution is a 1 molar solution, which is often abbreviated 1 M. A 2 molar (2 M) solution contains 2 moles of solute per liter of solution.

The difference between referring to the number of molecules of solute and referring to the number of grams of solute can be illustrated by the following question. A saturated aqueous solution of sucrose contains 200 grams of sucrose and 100 grams of water. Which is the solvent: sucrose or water?

As shown in Figure 18.15, there are 3.5×10^{23} molecules of sucrose in 200 grams of sucrose, but there are almost 10 times as many molecules of water in 100 grams of water—3.3×10^{24} molecules. As defined earlier, the solvent is the component present in the largest amount, but what do we mean by amount? If amount means number of molecules, then water is the solvent. If amount means mass, then sucrose is the solvent. So, the answer depends on how you look at it. From a chemist's point of view, amount typically means the number of molecules, and so water is the solvent in this case.

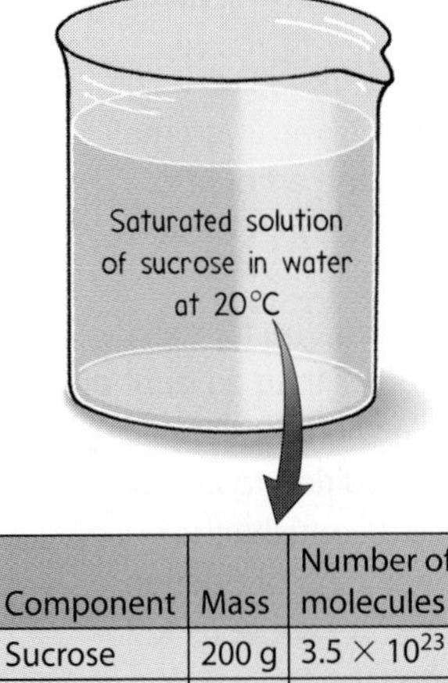

Component	Mass	Number of molecules
Sucrose	200 g	3.5×10^{23}
Water	100 g	3.3×10^{24}

Figure 18.15
Although 200 grams of sucrose is twice as massive as 100 grams of water, there are about 10 times as many water molecules in 100 grams of water as there are sucrose molecules in 200 grams of sucrose. How can this be? Each water molecule is about one-twentieth as massive (and much smaller) than each sucrose molecule, which means that about 10 times as many water molecules can fit within half the mass.

☑ CHECKPOINT

1. How many moles of sucrose are there in 0.5 liter of a 2 molar solution? How many molecules of sucrose is this?
2. Does 1 liter of a 1 molar solution of sucrose in water contain 1 liter of water, less than 1 liter of water, or more than 1 liter of water?

Check Your Answers

1. First you need to understand that 2 molar means 2 moles of sucrose per liter of solution. To obtain the amount of solute, you should multiply solution concentration by amount of solution:

   (2 moles/L)(0.5 L) = 1 mole,

   which is the same as 6.02×10^{23} molecules.
2. The definition of molarity refers to the number of liters of solution, not to the number of liters of solvent. When sucrose is added to a given volume of water, the volume of the solution increases. So, if 1 mole of sucrose is added to 1 liter of water, the result is more than 1 liter of solution. Therefore, 1 liter of a 1 molar solution requires less than 1 liter of water.

Figuring Physical Science

Calculating for Solutions

From the formula for the concentration of a solution, we can derive equations for the amount of solute and the amount of solution:

$$\text{Concentration of solution} = \frac{\text{amount of solute}}{\text{amount of solution}}$$

$$\text{Amount of solute} = \text{concentration of solution} \times \text{volume of solution}$$

$$\text{Amount of solution} = \frac{\text{amount of solute}}{\text{concentration of solution}}$$

In solving for any of these values, the units must always match. If concentration is given in grams per liter of solution, for example, the amount of solute must be in grams and the amount of solution must be in liters.

Note that these equations are set up for calculating the amount of solution rather than amount of solvent. The amount of solution is greater than the amount of solvent because, in addition to containing the solvent, the solution also contains the solute. As discussed at the beginning of Section 18.3, for example, the volume of an aqueous solution of sucrose depends not only on the volume of water but also on the volume of dissolved sucrose.

Example 1
How many grams of sucrose are there in 3 liters of an aqueous solution that has a concentration of 2 grams of sucrose per liter of solution?

Answer 1
This question asks for amount of solute, and so you should use the second of the three formulas given above:

$$\text{Amount of solute} = \frac{2\text{ g}}{1\text{ L}} \times 3\text{ L} = 6\text{ g}$$

Example 2
A solution you are using in an experiment has a concentration of 10 grams of solute per liter of solution. If you pour enough of this solution into an empty laboratory flask to make the flask contain 5 grams of the solute, how many liters of the solution have you poured into the flask?

Answer 2
This question asks for amount of solution, and you will want to use the third formula:

$$\text{Amount of solution} = \frac{5\text{ g}}{10\text{ g/L}} = 0.5\text{ l}$$

Your Turn

1. At 20°C, a saturated solution of sodium chloride in water has a concentration of about 380 grams of sodium chloride per liter of solution. How many grams of sodium chloride are required to make 3 liters of a saturated solution?
2. A student is told to use 20 grams of sodium chloride to make an aqueous solution that has a concentration of 10 grams of sodium chloride per liter of solution. How many liters of solution does she end up with?

Answers
1. Multiply the solution concentration by the final volume of the solution. This provides the amount of solute required: (380 g/L)(3 L) = 1140 g.
2. Divide the amount of solute by the solution concentration to obtain the amount of solution prepared: 20g/10 g/L = 2 L.

18.4 Purifying the Water We Drink

As was discussed earlier, it is impossible to obtain 100 percent pure water. However, we are able to purify water to meet our needs. We do this by taking advantage of the differences in physical properties of water and the solutes or particulates it contains. For the remainder of this chapter, we turn our attention to some of the details involved in the production of drinkable water and the treatment of the wastewater.

Water that is safe for drinking is said to be *potable*. In the United States, potable water is currently used for everything from cooking to flushing our toilets. The first step most public utilities take to produce potable water from natural sources is to remove any dirt particles or pathogens, such as bacteria. This is done by mixing the water with certain minerals, such as slaked lime and aluminum sulfate, which coagulates into a gelatinous material, aluminum hydroxide, that intersperses throughout the water (Figure 18.16). This is done in a large settling basin. Slow stirring causes the gelatinous material to clump together and settle to the bottom of the basin. As these clumps form and settle, they carry with them many of the dirt particles and bacteria. The water is then filtered through sand and gravel.

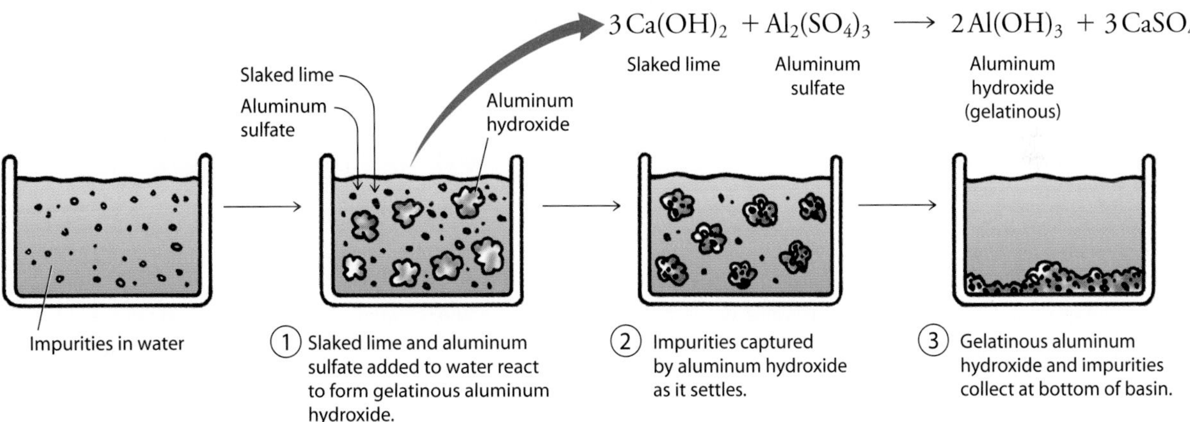

Figure 18.16
Slaked lime, $Ca(OH)_2$, and aluminum sulfate, $Al_2(SO_4)_3$, react to form aluminum hydroxide, $Al(OH)_3$, and calcium sulfate, $CaSO_4$, which together form a gelatinous material.

To improve the odor and flavor of the water, many treatment facilities also *aerate* the water by cascading it through a column of air, as shown in Figure 18.17. Aeration removes many unpleasant-smelling volatile chemicals, such as sulfur compounds. At the same time, air dissolves into the water giving it a better taste—without dissolved air, the water tastes flat. As a final step, the water is treated with a disinfectant, usually chlorine gas, Cl_2, but sometimes ozone, O_3, and then stored in a holding tank that feeds into the city mains.

Figure 18.17
Volatile impurities are removed from drinking water by cascading it through the columns of air within each of these stacks.

Developed countries have the technology and infrastructure to produce vast quantities of water suitable for drinking—as a result, many citizens take their drinking water for granted. The number of public water-treatment facilities in developing nations, however, is relatively small. In these locations, many people drink their water in the form of a hot beverage, such as tea, which is disinfected through boiling. Alternatively, disinfecting iodine tablets can be used.

Fuel for boiling and tablets for disinfecting, however, are not always available. As a result, more than 400 people in the world (mostly children) die every hour from preventable diseases or infections such as cholera, typhoid fever,

dysentery, and hepatitis, which they contract by drinking contaminated water. In response, several American manufacturers have developed tabletop systems that bathe water with pathogen-killing ultraviolet light. One prototype model, shown in Figure 18.18, disinfects 15 gallons per minute, weighs about 15 pounds, and is powered by photovoltaic solar cells, which permit it to run unsupervised in remote locations.

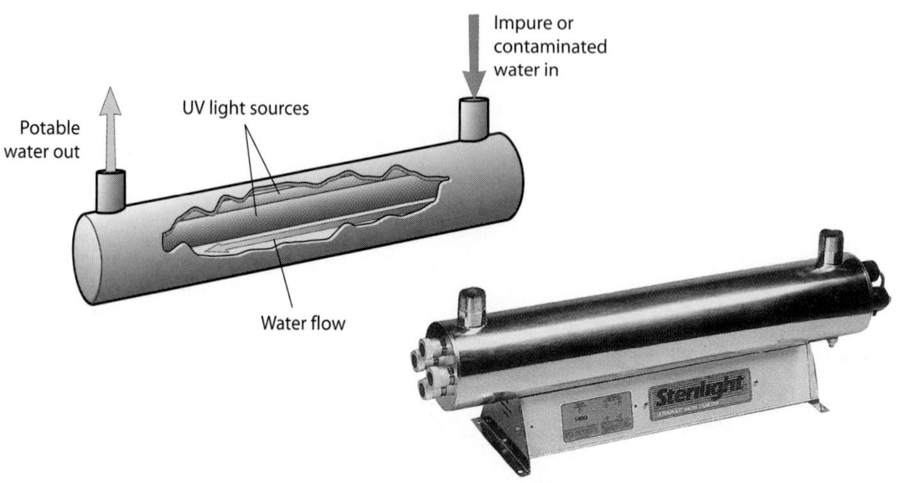

Figure 18.18
Small-scale water-disinfecting units, such as the one shown here, hold great value in regions of the world where potable water is scarce.

Aside from pathogens, untreated water from wells or rivers may contain toxic metals that seep into the water supply from natural geologic formations. Many of the wells in Bangladesh, for example, are made very deep so as to avoid the pathogens that run rampant in the surface waters of this region. The water obtained from these deep wells, however, is highly contaminated with arsenic—a naturally occurring element in the earth's crust. The arsenic is in the underlying rock, which formed from river sediments carried down from the Himalayas. Because this region is so densely populated, as many as 70 million people may be subject to some level of arsenic poisoning, which manifests itself as skin lesions and a higher susceptibility to cancer. Low-cost methods for removing arsenic from well water are greatly needed, as are worldwide recognition of this problem and the political, economic, and social support to overcome it. For one possible technical solution, see the suggested Web sites for this chapter.

☑ CHECKPOINT

At a water-treatment facility, how does adding slaked lime and aluminum sulfate to water purify the water?

Check Your Answer

The water entering a water treatment plant is usually a heterogeneous mixture containing suspended solids. Adding slaked lime and aluminum sulfate serves to capture these suspended solids, which then sink to the bottom, where they are easily removed.

18.5 Desalination

With the depletion of sources of natural fresh water in many regions, there has been growing interest in techniques for generating fresh water from the earth's far larger reserves of seawater or from *brackish* (moderately salty) groundwater. Worldwide, *desalination* plants operate in about 120 countries with a combined capacity to produce about 4.1 billion gallons daily. In many areas of the Caribbean, North Africa, and the Middle East, desalinized water is the main source of municipal supply (Figure 18.19). In the United States, the operation of more than a thousand desalination plants produces a combined capacity of more than 100 million gallons (379 million liters) daily. Most of the treated water in the United States is used for industrial purposes, and it comes from brackish sources or from water that is high in dissolved minerals.

Figure 18.19
Saudi Arabia is the world's leading producer of desalinized water. Its desalination plants, such as the one shown here, have a combined generating capacity of about 4 billion liters per day.

The two primary methods of removing salts from sea water or brackish water are *distillation* and *reverse osmosis*. These techniques are also highly effective in removing a host of other contaminants, such as pathogens, fertilizers, and pesticides. Distillation and reverse osmosis, therefore, are also used to purify naturally occurring fresh water. Many popular brands of bottled water, for example, contain fresh water that has been treated either by distillation or by reverse osmosis.

Distillation involves vaporizing water with heat and then condensing the vapors into purified liquid water (Section 18.1). More than 60 percent of the earth's desalinized water is produced using this technique. Because water has such a high heat of vaporization, however, this technique is energy intensive. Today, most distilling plants heat the water by burning large quantities of fossil fuels, which, unfortunately, generates excessive levels of pollution relative to the volume of fresh water produced. Solar distillers avoid the burning of fuels, but they require about one square meter of surface area to produce 4 liters of fresh water per day, as shown in Figure 18.20. For a single home or a small village, this surface-area requirement may be easily accommodated. For larger urban areas, where open land is scarce, solar distillation is less practical, especially when the maintenance costs of vast fields of solar distillers are taken into account.

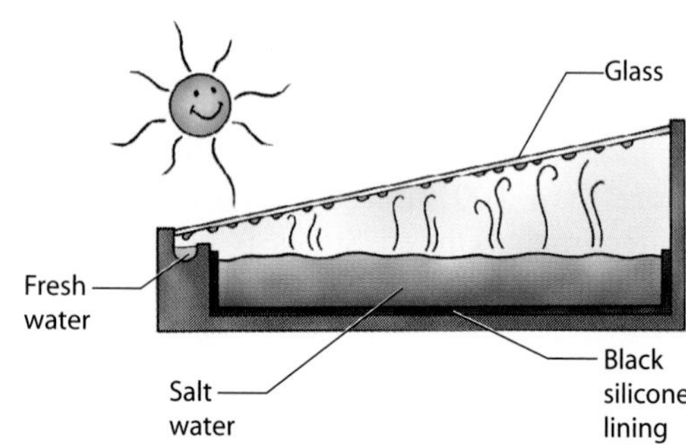

Figure 18.20
These solar distillers are popular in the remote communities along the Texas–Mexico border, where the waters from the Rio Grande basin are saline and tainted by the runoff of agricultural chemicals from upstream irrigation.

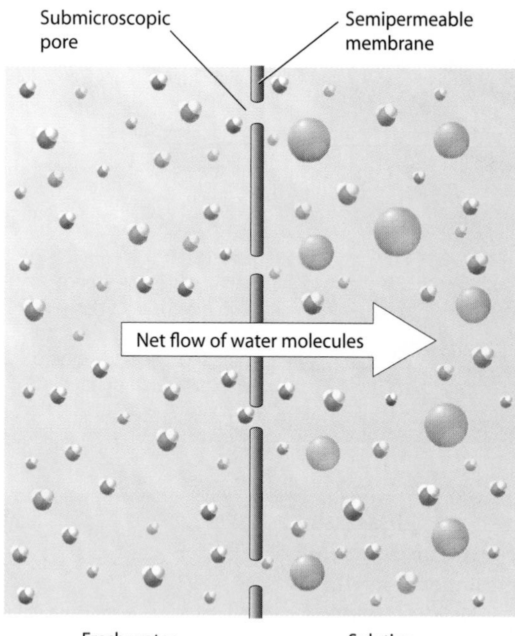

Figure 18.21
Osmosis. The submicroscopic pores of a semipermeable membrane allow only water molecules to pass. Because there are more water molecules along the freshwater face of the membrane than along the solution face, more water molecules are available to migrate into the solution than are available to migrate into the fresh water.

For many regions, *reverse osmosis* is a preferable method of water desalination. In order to understand reverse osmosis, you must first understand osmosis. Osmosis involves a semipermeable membrane. A **semipermeable membrane** contains submicroscopic pores that allow the passage of water molecules but not of larger solute ions or solute molecules. When a body of fresh water is partitioned from a body of salt water by a semipermeable membrane, water molecules pass from the fresh water into the salt water at a higher rate than they pass from the salt water into the fresh water. The reason for this is the presence of more water molecules along the fresh-water face of the membrane than along the salt-water face. The result is a net movement of fresh water into the body of salt water, as illustrated in Figure 18.21. This net flow of water across a semipermeable membrane into a more concentrated solution is called **osmosis.**

The result of osmosis is a buildup in volume of the salt water and a decrease in volume of the fresh water. These changes in volume, in turn, allow for a buildup in pressure, called *osmotic pressure*. For the system in Figure 18.22a, osmotic pressure is the consequence of the salt water's greater height. As osmotic pressure builds, the rate at which water molecules are able to pass from the salt water into the fresh water increases. The water molecules in the salt water are literally being squeezed back across the membrane by the osmotic pressure. Eventually, the rates of water molecules passing in both directions across the membrane are the same and the system reaches equilibrium, as shown in Figure 18.22b. If an external pressure is applied to the salt water, even more water molecules are squeezed across the membrane from the salt water into the fresh water, as

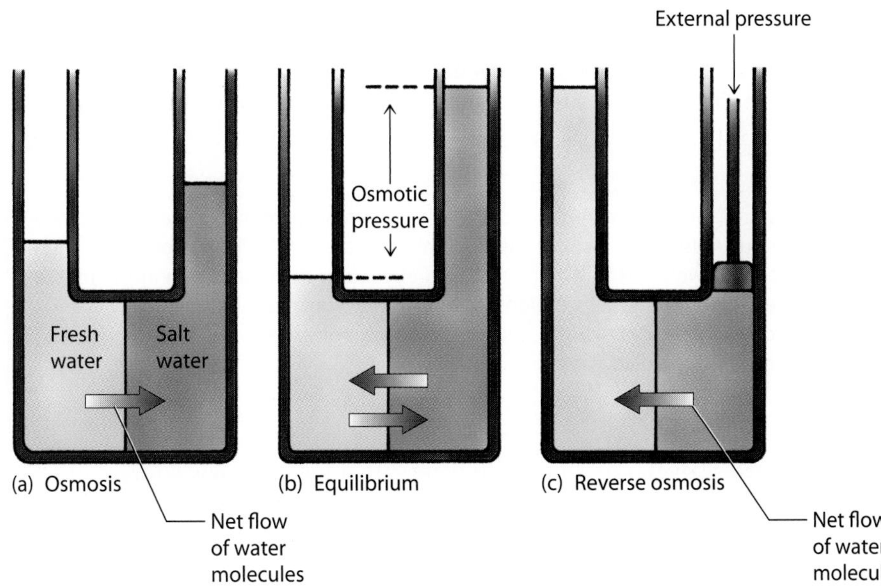

Figure 18.22
(a) Osmosis results in a greater volume of salt water, which causes the pressure to increase on the salt side of the membrane. (b) When the pressure on the salt side becomes high enough, equal numbers of water molecules pass in both directions. (c) The application of external pressure forces water molecules to pass from the salt water to the fresh water, so that now the salt-to-fresh rate exceeds the fresh-to-salt rate.

shown in Figure 18.22c. Water forced across a semipermeable membrane into a less concentrated solution is **reverse osmosis.** So we see that reverse osmosis is a mechanism for generating fresh water from salt water.

The osmotic pressure for seawater, however, is an astounding 24.8 atmospheres (365 pounds per square inch). Generating pressures greater than this has its share of technical difficulties and is an energy-intensive process. Nonetheless, engineers have succeeded in building durable reverse osmosis units, shown in Figure 18.23, that can be networked together to generate fresh water from sea water at rates of millions of gallons per day. Reverse osmosis desalination facilities treating brackish waters, which require much lower external pressures, are proportionately more economical.

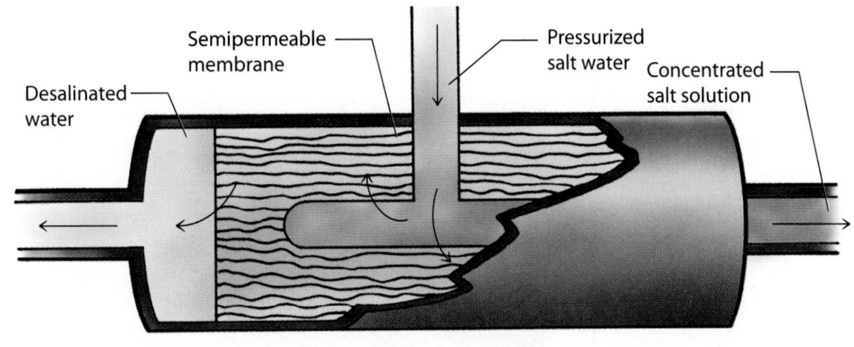

Figure 18.23
An industrial reverse-osmosis unit consists of many semipermeable membranes packed around highly pressurized salt water. As desalinated water is pushed out one side, the remaining salt water, which is now even more concentrated, exits on the other side. A network of reverse osmosis units operating parallel to one another can produce enormous volumes of fresh water from salt water.

☑ CHECKPOINT

Biological membranes, including cucumber membranes, are semipermeable. A cucumber shrivels to a smaller size when it is left in a solution of salt water. Is this an example of osmosis or of reverse osmosis?

Check Your Answer

No external pressure is involved, which rules out reverse osmosis. Instead, the shriveling of the cucumber tells us that the cucumber's cells are losing water to the more concentrated salt water. This is osmosis, whereby water molecules migrate across a semipermeable membrane into regions of higher salt concentrations. If you were to add a few other ingredients to the solution, such as spices and the right kinds of microorganisms, you would have a pickle.

At the microscopic level, naturally occurring water is alive with bacteria, which serve to break down organic matter. *Aerobic bacteria* decompose organic matter only in the presence of O_2, transforming organic matter to such compounds as carbon dioxide, water, nitrates, and sulfates, all of which are odorless in the quantities produced. *Anaerobic bacteria* can decompose organic matter in the absence of oxygen. Anaerobic decomposition, however, results in methane (which is flammable), and foul-smelling nitrogen- and sulfur-containing compounds. Cesspools owe their wretched stink to a lack of dissolved oxygen and the resulting anaerobic decomposition.

Insights

Desalinated seawater and brackish water are important new sources of fresh water. Although this fresh water is more costly than fresh water from natural sources, one could argue that the higher cost reflects fresh water's true value. In the United States, natural sources of fresh water are relatively plentiful, allowing companies to sell fresh water at rates of a fraction of a penny per liter. Nonetheless, consumers are still willing to purchase bottled water at up to $2 per liter! Each year, Americans spend about $400 million dollars on bottled water, and the market continues to grow rapidly. Unless we conserve fresh water, as is discussed in Chapter 28, it is easy to project a growing reliance on distillation and reverse osmosis.

18.6 Wastewater Treatment

The contents of the sewer systems that underlie most municipalities must be treated before being released into a body of water. The level of treatment depends in great part on whether the treated water is to be released into a river or into the ocean. Wastewater destined for a river requires the highest level of treatment for the benefit of communities downstream. However, in a facility located in a region surrounded by very deep ocean water, as is the facility shown in Figure 18.24, treatment requirements are less stringent.

Figure 18.24
In the City of Honolulu, about 280 million liters of wastewater pass through the largest of several wastewater facilities each day. This water can be piped to depths of hundreds of meters below sea level, whence it continues to flow toward the bottom of the ocean. Water-treatment requirements are therefore much less stringent than those at mainland facilities, where the effluent is not so easily discarded.

Human waste loses its form by the time it reaches the wastewater facility, and the wastewater appears as a murky stream. In this stream, however, are many insoluble products—including small plastic items, such as tampon applicators, and gritty material, such as coffee grounds and sand. Hardened balls of grease from discarded cooking fats are also found. The initial step in all wastewater treatments, therefore, involves the screening out of these insolubles. (You should know that wastewater treatment experts point out that these insolubles—even cooking grease—should be disposed of as solid waste and not be washed down the drain or flushed down the toilet.)

After screening, the next level of municipal wastewater treatment is *primary* treatment. In primary treatment, screened wastewater enters a large settling basin, where suspended solids settle out as sludge (Figure 18.25). After a period of time, the sludge is removed from the bottom of the settling basin and is often sent directly to a landfill as solid wastes. Some facilities, however, are equipped with large furnaces in which dried sludge is burned, sometimes along with other municipal wastes, such as paper products. The resulting ash is more compact, and it takes up less space in a landfill.

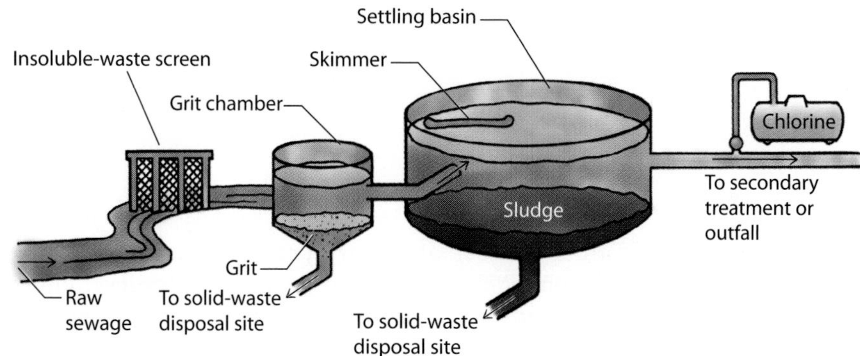

Figure 18.25
A schematic for primary-level wastewater treatment. The rotating skimmer on the settling basin is used to remove buoyant materials and artifacts not captured by the screening process.

Wastewater effluent from primary treatment, as well as higher levels of treatment, is commonly disinfected with either chlorine gas or ozone prior to its release into the environment. A great advantage of using chlorine gas is that it remains in the water for an extended time after leaving the facility. This provides for residual protection against diseases. The chlorine, however, reacts with organic compounds within the effluent to form chlorinated hydrocarbons, many of which are known carcinogens (cancer-causing agents). Also, chlorine only kills bacteria, leaving viruses unharmed. Ozone is more advantageous, in that it kills both bacteria and viruses. Also, there are no carcinogenic by-products that result from treating wastewater effluent with ozone. A disadvantage of ozone, however, is that it provides no residual protection for the effluent once it is released. Most facilities in the United States use chlorine for disinfecting, whereas European facilities tend to favor ozone. In a few locations, chlorine and ozone gases have been replaced by strong ultraviolet lamps, which, like ozone, kill both bacteria and viruses but provide no long-term residual protection.

The potential for pathogens to grow in primary effluent is extremely high and, by virtue of the Clean Water Act of 1972, the release of primary effluent is not permitted in most places. A frequently used *secondary* level of treatment, shown in Figure 18.26, involves passing the primary effluent first through an aeration tank. This supplies the oxygen necessary for continued decomposition of organic matter by oxygen-dependent bacteria, known as *aerobic bacteria*. The effluent is then sent into a tank where any fine particles not removed in primary treatment can settle. Because sludge from this settling step is high in aerobic bacteria, some of it is recycled back to the aeration tank to increase efficiency. The remainder of the sludge is hauled off to the landfill or an incinerator.

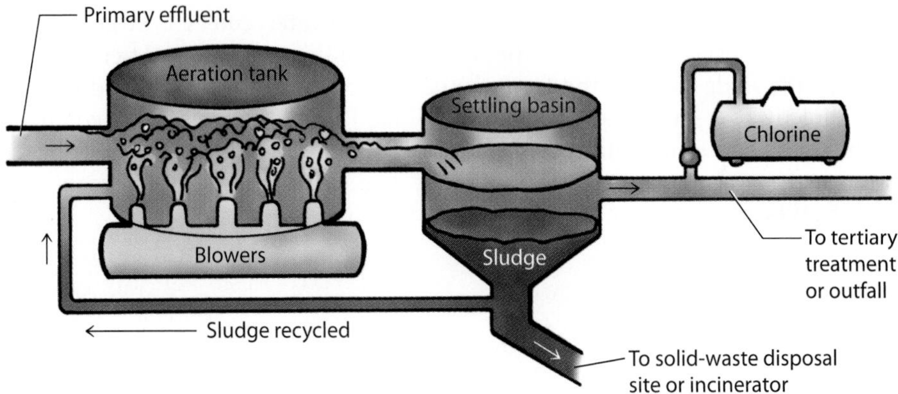

Figure 18.26
A schematic for secondary treatment of wastewater from a municipal system.

Many municipalities also require a third level, a *tertiary* level, of wastewater treatment. There are a number of tertiary processes, and most involve filtrations of some sort. A common method is to pass secondary-level effluent through a bed of finely powdered carbon, which captures most particulate matter and many of the organic molecules not removed in earlier stages. The advantage of tertiary-level treatment is greater protection of our water resources. Unfortunately, tertiary treatment is costly and is normally used only in situations in which the need is deemed vital. Primary and secondary levels of treatment are also not without great cost. Where appropriate, the millions of dollars spent on wastewater treatment might be shifted to alternate methods of waste management, such as advanced integrated pond systems, which are described next.

☑ CHECKPOINT

Distinguish between the main functions of primary, secondary, and tertiary wastewater treatment.

Check Your Answer

Primary wastewater treatment removes the bulk of solid waste and sludge from the sewage effluent using screening devices and large settling basins. Secondary treatment decreases the biochemical oxygen demand of the effluent by aeration. Tertiary treatment removes pathogens and wastes not removed by earlier treatments by filtering the effluent through beds of powdered carbon or other fine particles.

Advanced Integrated Pond Systems

The Advanced Integrated Pond (AIP) system is a method of wastewater treatment that makes sense for many communities of 2,000 to 10,000 people in both advanced and developing nations. Wastewater is channeled into an extensive pond system, where plants use nutrients from the sewage as fertilizer. A system of paddlewheels guarantees constant aeration of the effluent, which is naturally disinfected by ultraviolet light from the sun. The system is equivalent to secondary-level wastewater treatment or better. Researchers at the University of California, Berkeley, designed an AIP-system prototype that costs one-third to one-half as much to build as a conventional facility of equal capacity. A more significant source of savings lies in using solar energy rather than electrical energy for aeration. Conventional secondary plants aerate by using electrical energy to blow or mix air bubbles into the wastewater. This process consumes 60 percent or more of the total electrical energy used in wastewater treatment. In an AIP system, algae and other plants use solar energy and photosynthesis to supersaturate the wastewater with the oxygen that aerobic microbes need in order to break down waste. AIP systems are particularly applicable in sunbelt communities, where solar energy is plentiful, and in developing nations, where the supply of electrical energy is minimal or nonexistent.

Another important advantage of AIP systems is the small amount of sludge they produce. In these ponds, sludge ferments until nothing remains but a small volume. This represents a substantial benefit in terms of satisfying environmental regulations for sludge disposal. Furthermore, harvested plants are a significant source of biomass, which may be fermented for the production of methane fuel (natural gas) or incinerated in gas turbines to produce electrical energy.

Perhaps one of the biggest obstacles to improving waste management lies not in available technology but in our attitudes and our willingness to accept large one-time setup costs. Human waste is not a waste—it is a resource waiting for utilization.

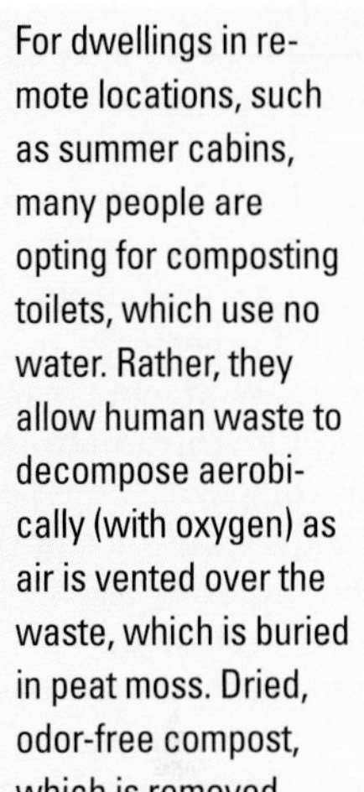

For dwellings in remote locations, such as summer cabins, many people are opting for composting toilets, which use no water. Rather, they allow human waste to decompose aerobically (with oxygen) as air is vented over the waste, which is buried in peat moss. Dried, odor-free compost, which is removed every few months, is useful as a garden fertilizer.

Insights

Figure 18.27
The pilot Advanced Integrated Pond System of St. Helena, California, which has been in operation since the 1960s. There are now more than 85 AIP systems in operation within the United States and in other countries.

Summary of Terms

Mixture A combination of two or more substances in which each substance retains its properties.

Distillation A purifying process in which a vaporized substance is collected by exposing it to cooler temperatures over a receiving flask, which collects the condensed purified liquid.

Pure Having a uniform composition, or being without impurities. In chemistry, the term is used to denote a material that consists of a single element or compound.

Impure In chemistry, this term refers to a material that is a mixture of more than one element or compound.

Heterogeneous mixture A mixture in which the various components can be seen as individual substances.

Homogeneous mixture A mixture in which the components are so finely mixed that the composition is the same throughout.

Solution A homogeneous mixture in which all components are in the same phase.

Suspension A homogeneous mixture in which the various components are in different phases.

Solvent The component in a solution that is present in the largest amount.

Solute Any component in a solution that is not the solvent.

Dissolving The process of mixing a solute in a solvent to produce a homogeneous mixture.

Saturated solution A solution containing the maximum amount of solute that will dissolve in its solvent.

Unsaturated solution A solution that is capable of dissolving additional solute.

Concentration A quantitative measure of the amount of solute in a solution.

Mole The amount of any pure substance that contains as many atoms, molecules, ions, or other elementary units as the number of atoms in 12 grams of carbon-12. This is equal to 6.02×10^{23} particles.

Molarity A unit of concentration equal to the number of moles of a solute per liter of solution.

Semipermeable membrane A membrane that allows only the passage of molecules small enough to fit through its submicroscopic pores.

Osmosis The diffusion of a water or some other fluid through a semipermeable membrane from a solution with a low concentration of solutes to a solution with a higher concentration of solutes.

Reverse osmosis A technique for purifying water by forcing it through a semipermeable membrane.

Review Questions

18.1 Most Materials Are Mixtures

1. What defines a material as being a mixture?
2. How can the components of a mixture be separated from one another?
3. How does distillation separate the components of a mixture?
4. Oxygen, O_2, has a boiling point of 90 K (−183°C), and nitrogen, N_2, has a boiling point of 77 K (−196°C). Which is a liquid and which is a gas at 80 K (−193°C)?

18.2 The Chemist's Classification of Matter

5. Why is it not practical to have a macroscopic sample that is 100 percent pure?
6. Classify the following as (a) homogeneous mixture, (b) heterogeneous mixture, (c) element, or (d) compound:
   milk _____ steel _____
   ocean water _____ blood _____
   sodium _____ planet earth _____
7. How is a solution different from a suspension?
8. How can a solution be distinguished from a suspension?

18.3 Solutions

9. What happens to the volume of a sugar solution as more sugar is dissolved in it?
10. Why is a ruby considered to be a solution?
11. Distinguish between a solute and a solvent.
12. What does it mean to say that a solution is concentrated?
13. Distinguish between a saturated solution and an unsaturated solution.
14. How is the amount of solute in a solution calculated?
15. Is 1 mole of particles a very large number of particles or a very small number?

18.4 Purifying the Water We Drink

16. Why is treated water sprayed into the air prior to being piped to users?
17. What do most water-treatment plants use to filter water?
18. What are two ways in which people disinfect water in areas where municipal treatment facilities are not available?
19. What naturally occurring element has been contaminating the water supply of Bangladesh?

18.5 Desalination

20. What are the two main techniques for desalinizing water?
21. Name one disadvantage of solar distillation.
22. How does a semipermeable membrane allow for the passage of the solvent but not the solute?
23. What reverses with reverse osmosis?

18.6 Wastewater Treatment

24. Why can wastewater treatment requirements in Hawaii be less stringent than those in most locations on the U.S. mainland?
25. What is the first step in treating raw sewage?
26. What is the source of the energy used to aerate wastewater in an advanced integrated pond system?

Activities

Bottoms Up and Bubbles Out

What's in a glass of water? Separate the components of your tap water to find out. *Safety note:* Wear safety glasses for Step 1 because some splattering may occur.

Procedure:

1. Put on your safety glasses and add tap water to a cooking pot. Boil the water to dryness. (Turn off the burner *before* the water is completely gone. The heat from the pot will complete the evaporation.)
2. Examine the resulting residue by scraping it with a knife. These are the solids you ingest with every glass of water you drink.
3. To see the gases dissolved in your water, fill a clean cooking pot with water and let it stand at room temperature for several hours. Note the bubbles that adhere to the inner sides of the pot. Where do the bubbles originate? What do you suppose they contain?

For further experimentation, perform Step 3 in two pots side by side. In one pot, use warm water from the kitchen faucet. In the second pot, use boiled water that has cooled down to the same temperature. You'll find that boiling *deaerates* the water—that is, it removes the atmospheric gases. Chemists sometime need to use deaerated water, which is made by allowing boiled water to cool in a sealed container. Why don't fish live very long in deaerated water?

Micro Water Purifier

You can build a relatively inefficient but fun-to-watch distiller at home. Materials that you'll need include: a deep cooking pot, plastic wrap, ice cube, coffee mug, food coloring, and salt. *Safety note:* Wear safety glasses, and avoid the steam produced in this experiment—steam burns can be particularly harmful.

Procedure:

1. Fill the cooking pot to a depth of about one centimeter. Add several drops of food coloring or some salt (or both) to the water and stir.
2. Place a heavy ceramic coffee mug in the center of the pot. The height of the mug should be at least an inch below the height of the pot.
3. Lay plastic wrap loosely across the top of the pot and secure it with a rubber band. The seal should *not* be airtight. Instead, leave two of the edges open to prevent a buildup of pressure within the pot as the water is brought to a boil. Use scissors to trim away the excess plastic wrap along the perimeter. Place an ice cube at the center of the plastic wrap, which should then sag above the mug.
4. Put on your safety glasses, and turn the burner on low to bring the water in your distiller to a low boil. Look for signs of cloud formation below the ice cube. Once boiling begins, the mug may jostle in the pot. Turn the heat down or off if the jostling becomes too pronounced.
5. Boil the water for only as long as there is still ice present on the plastic wrap. The melted ice can be removed with a sponge. Distillation continues well after the stove has been turned off. Examine the water in the mug. Why isn't the food coloring or the salt carried over into the mug? How much distilled water are you able to collect per ice cube? How might you modify your distiller so that it works well using only sunlight to drive the distillation?

Exercises

1. A sample of water that is 99.9999 percent pure contains 0.0001 percent impurities. A glass of water contains on the order of a trillion trillion (1×10^{24}) molecules. If 0.0001 percent of these molecules were the molecules of some impurity, about how many impurity molecules would this be?
(a) 1000 (one thousand: 1×10^3)
(b) 1,000,000 (one million: 1×10^6)
(c) 1,000,000,000 (one billion: 1×10^9)
(d) 1,000,000,000,000,000,000 (one million trillion: 1×10^{18}) (One million trillion is the same as one quintillion.)
2. How does your answer to the previous exercise make you feel about drinking water that is 99.9999 percent free of some poison, such as a pesticide?
3. Read carefully: Twice as much as one million trillion is two million trillion. One thousand times as much is 1000 million trillion. One million times as much is 1,000,000 million trillion, which is the same as one trillion trillion. Thus, one trillion trillion is one million times greater than one million trillion. Got that? So how many more water molecules than impurity molecules are there in a glass of water that is 99.9999 percent pure?

4. Someone argues that he or she doesn't drink tap water because it contains thousands of molecules of some impurity in each glass. How would you respond in defense of the water's purity, if it indeed contains thousands of molecules of some impurity per glass?
5. Explain what chicken noodle soup and garden soil have in common without using the phrase "heterogeneous mixture."
6. Classify the following as element, compound, or mixture, and justify your classifications: table salt, stainless steel, tap water, table sugar, vanilla extract, and butter.
7. Classify these as element, compound, or mixture, and justify your classifications: maple syrup, aluminum, ice, milk, and cherry-flavored cough drops.
8. Which of the following boxes contains an element? Which one contains a compound? Which one contains a mixture? How many different types of molecules are shown altogether in all three boxes?

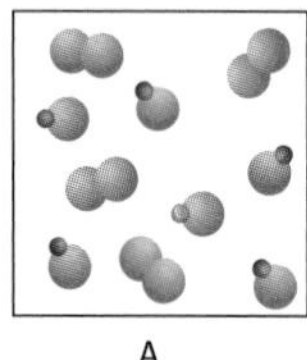
A

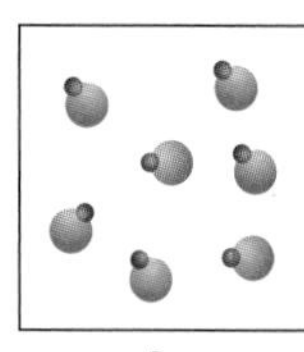
B

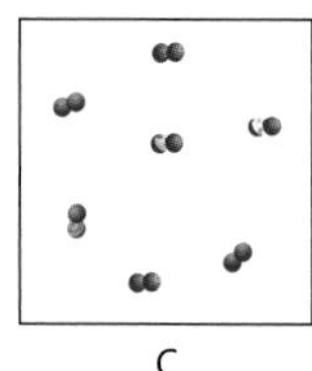
C

9. What is the difference between a compound and a mixture?
10. How might you separate a mixture of sand and salt?
11. How might you separate a mixture of iron and sand?
12. Mixtures can be separated into their components by taking advantage of differences in the chemical properties of the components. Why might this separation method be less convenient than taking advantage of differences in the physical properties of the components?
13. Why can't the elements of a compound be separated from one another by physical means?
14. In lieu of metallic amalgam fillings, which contain mercury, dentists can fill cavities with a dental composite, which is a mixture of organic molecules, silicon and barium oxides, ytterbium trifluoride, and a number of minor components. This mixture is applied to the tooth as a paste, but it quickly hardens as the dentist shines a bright light upon it. Is the hardening of the composite an example of a physical or a chemical change? Explain.
15. Is the air in your house a homogeneous or a heterogeneous mixture? What evidence have you seen?
16. Many dry cereals are fortified with iron, which is added to the cereal in the form of small iron particles. How might these particles be separated from the cereal?
17. Why is half-frozen fruit punch always sweeter than the same fruit punch when it is completely melted?
18. A pain-relieving medicine claims to contain 500 milligrams of pain-relieving acetominophen per pill. You measure the mass of that pill, however, and find that it has a mass of 600 milligrams. What can you conclude about the pill? Is the pharmaceutical company being honest?
19. Describe two ways to determine whether a sugar solution is saturated or not.
20. The volume of many liquid solvents expands with increasing temperature. What happens to the concentration of a solution made with such a solvent as the temperature of the solution is increased?
21. What is an advantage of using chlorine to disinfect drinking-water supplies?
22. What is the advantage of using ozone to disinfect drinking-water supplies?
23. Might reverse osmosis also be used to separate fresh water from a sample of sugar water? Explain.
24. The cells at the top of a tree have a higher concentration of sugars than the cells toward the bottom of the tree. How might this fact assist the tree in moving water upward from its roots?
25. Why is flushing a toilet with clean water from a municipal supply about as wasteful as flushing it with bottled water? Make a rough sketch of a home plumbing system that uses water from an upstairs bathtub to flush a downstairs toilet.
26. Why is it significantly less costly to purify fresh water through reverse osmosis than it is to purify salt water through reverse osmosis?
27. Why do red blood cells, which contain an aqueous solution of dissolved solutes, burst when placed in fresh water?
28. Some people are afraid to drink distilled water because they have heard it leaches minerals from the body. Using your knowledge of chemistry, explain how these fears have no basis, and how distilled water is in fact very good for drinking.
29. How might water be desalinized by freezing?
30. What would be a major advantage and a major disadvantage of desalinizing water by freezing?
31. Where does most of the solid mass of raw sewage end up after being collected at a wastewater-treatment facility?
32. In what ways are the disinfecting properties of ultraviolet light and ozone similar?
33. What prevents an urban or suburban community from developing an advanced integrated pond system?
34. It would be possible to tow huge icebergs to coastal cities as a source of fresh water. What obstacles—

technological, social, environmental, and political—do you foresee for such an endeavor?

35. The lowest point on our planet is the Dead Sea (elevation −413 m), which is located in Israel. The Dead Sea is about 80 kilometers from the Mediterranean Sea and about 175 kilometers from the Red Sea. Plans for building a canal connecting the Dead Sea to either the Mediterranean Sea or the Red Sea are now under consideration. The elevation difference along the canal would provide enough pressure to desalinate sea water by reverse osmosis yielding as much as 800 million cubic meters of fresh water per year to this desert region. Identify some of the pros and cons of such a plan.
36. After considering the plan to build a desalination plant at the Dead Sea (see previous exercise), explain how a long tube with reverse-osmosis filters on one end might be used to extract fresh water from sea water. Sketch a design for such a device, and plan for the technical hurdles and daily operations of your own private fresh-water company.

Problems

1. How many grams of sucrose are there in 5 liters of an aqueous solution of sucrose having a concentration of 0.5 gram of sucrose per liter of solution?
2. How many grams of sodium chloride are needed to make 15 L of a solution that has a concentration of 3.0 grams of sodium chloride per liter of solution?
3. If water is added to 1 mole of sodium chloride in a flask until the volume of the solution is 1 liter, what is the molarity of the solution? What is the molarity when water is added to 2 moles of sodium chloride to make 0.5 liter of solution?
4. A student is told to use 20.0 grams of sodium chloride to make an aqueous solution that has a concentration of 10.0 grams of sodium chloride per liter of solution. Assuming that 20.0 grams of sodium chloride has a volume of 7.5 milliliters, about how much water will she use in making this solution?

Chapter 18 Online Resources

Quiz
Exercises
Flashcards
Links

CHAPTER 19

How Atoms Bond

Millions of years ago, the Great Plains region of what is now the United States was an ocean. As sea levels fell while the North American continent rose, many isolated pockets of seawater, called saline lakes, remained. Over time, these lakes evaporated, leaving behind the solids that had been dissolved in the seawater. Most abundant was sodium chloride, which formed the cubic crystals referred to by mineralogists as the mineral *halite*. When conditions were right, halite crystals like the ones in this chapter's opening photograph grew to be several centimeters across.

Why do halite crystals have such a distinct shape? As we will see in this chapter, the macroscopic properties of any substance can be traced to how its submicroscopic parts are held together. The sodium and chloride ions in a halite crystal, for example, hold together in a cubic orientation, and, as a result, the macroscopic object we know as a halite crystal is also cubic.

Similarly, the macroscopic properties of substances made of molecules are a result of how the atoms in the molecules hold together. For example, many of water's interesting properties result from the angle between the hydrogen and oxygen atoms in the water molecule. Because of this angled orientation, one side of the molecule has a slight negative charge and the opposite side has a slight positive charge. The water molecule is electrically polarized (Chapter 9). The polarization of water molecules gives rise to such phenomena as the inability of water and oil to mix and water's high boiling temperature.

The force of attraction that holds ions or atoms together is the electric force between oppositely charged particles. Chemists refer to this ion-binding or atom-binding force as a chemical bond. In this chapter, we will explore three types of chemical bonds: the *ionic bond,* which holds ions together in a crystal; the *covalent bond,* which holds atoms together in a molecule; and the *metallic bond,* which holds atoms together in a piece of metal.

19.1 Electron-Dot Structures

An atomic model is needed to help us understand how atoms bond. We begin this chapter with a brief overview of the atomic models presented in Chapter 15. Recall how electrons are arranged around an atomic nucleus. Rather than moving in neat orbits like planets around the sun, electrons are wavelike entities that swarm in various volumes of space called *shells.*

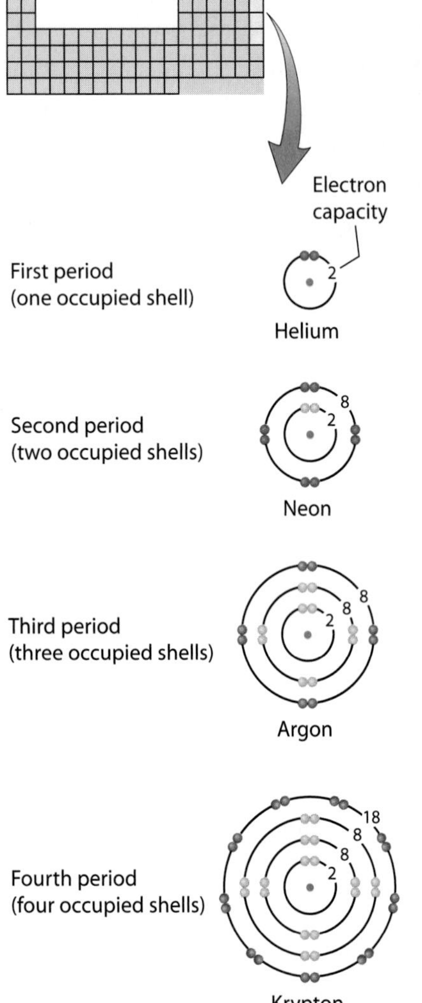

Figure 19.1
Occupied shells in the group 18 elements helium through krypton. Each of these elements has a filled outermost occupied shell, and the number of electrons in each corresponds to the number of elements in the period to which a particular group 18 element belongs.

As was shown in Figure 15.20, there are seven shells available to the electrons in an atom, and the electrons fill these shells in order, from innermost to outermost. Furthermore, the maximum number of electrons allowed in the first shell is 2, and for the second and third shells it is 8. The fourth and fifth shells can each hold 18 electrons, and the sixth and seventh shells can each hold 32 electrons.* These numbers match the number of elements in each period (horizontal row) of the periodic table. Figure 19.1 shows how this model applies to the first four elements of group 18.

Electrons in the outermost occupied shell of any atom may play a significant role in that atom's chemical properties, including its ability to form chemical bonds. To indicate their importance, we call these electrons *valence electrons* (as defined in Section 15.6), and we call the shell they occupy the **valence shell.** Valence electrons can be conveniently represented as a series of dots surrounding an atomic symbol. This notation is called an **electron-dot structure** or, sometimes, a Lewis dot symbol (in honor of the American chemist G. N. Lewis, who first proposed the concepts of shells and valence electrons).

Figure 19.2 shows the electron-dot structures for the atoms important in our discussions of ionic and covalent bonds. For our discussion of metallic bonds at the end of this chapter, we'll focus only on the valence electrons of metal atoms and not on their electron-dot structures.

1	2	13	14	15	16	17	18
H·							He:
Li·	·Be·	·Ḃ·	·Ċ·	·N̈·	:Ö·	:F̈·	:N̈e:
Na·	·Mg·	·Ȧl·	·Ṡi·	·P̈·	:S̈·	:C̈l·	:Ä̤r:
K·	·Ca·	·Ġa·	·Ġe·	·Äs·	:S̈e·	:B̈r·	:K̈r:
Rb·	·Sr·	·İn·	·Ṡn·	·S̈b·	:T̈e·	:Ï·	:Ẍe:
Cs·	·Ba·	·Ṫl·	·Ṗb·	·B̈i·	:P̈o·	:Ät·	:R̈n:

Figure 19.2
The valence electrons of an atom are shown in its electron-dot structure. Note that the first three periods here parallel Figure 15.21. Also note that, for larger atoms, not all the electrons in the valence shell are valence electrons. Krypton, Kr, for example, has 18 electrons in its valence shell, as shown in Figure 19.1, but only 8 of these are classified as valence electrons.

*These are shells of orbitals grouped by similar energy levels rather than by principal quantum number. See Section 15.6.

When you look at the electron-dot structure of an atom, you immediately know two important things about that element. You know how many valence electrons it has and how many of these electrons are *paired.* Chlorine, for example, has three sets of paired electrons and one unpaired electron, and carbon has four unpaired electrons:

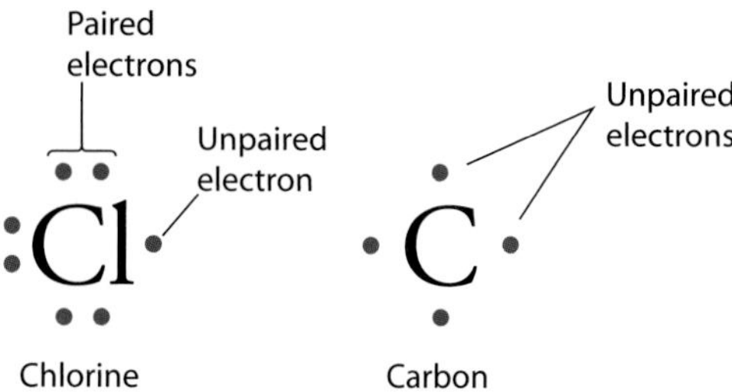

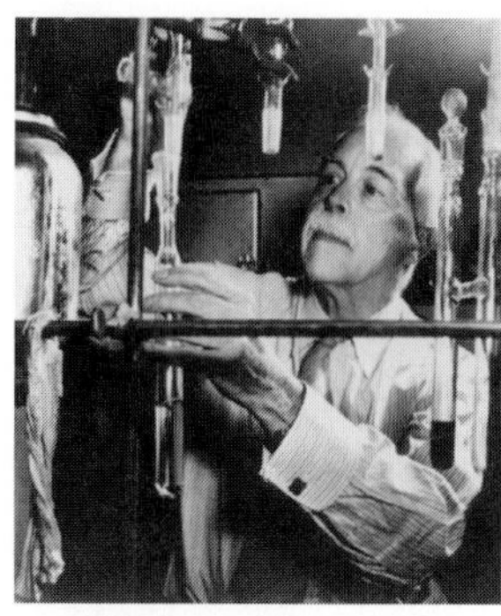

Figure 19.3
Gilbert Newton Lewis (1875–1946) revolutionized chemistry with his theory of chemical bonding, which he published in 1916. He worked most of his life in the chemistry department of the University of California, Berkeley, where he was not only a productive researcher but also an exceptional teacher. Among his teaching innovations was the idea of providing students with problem sets as a follow-up to lectures and readings.

Paired valence electrons are relatively stable. In other words, they usually do not form chemical bonds with other atoms. For this reason, electron pairs in an electron-dot structure are called **nonbonding pairs.** (Do not take this term literally, however, because in Chapter 22 you'll see that, under the right conditions, even "nonbonding" pairs can form a chemical bond.)

Valence electrons that are *unpaired,* by contrast, have a strong tendency to participate in chemical bonding. By doing so, they become paired with an electron from another atom. The ionic and covalent bonds discussed in this chapter all result from either a transfer or a sharing of unpaired valence electrons.

☑ CHECKPOINT

Where are valence electrons located, and why are they important?

Check Your Answer

Valence electrons are located in the outermost occupied shell of an atom. They are important because they play a leading role in determining the chemical properties of the atom.

The electron-dot structure is a simplified version of the shell model presented in Section 15.6. Remember, electrons are incredibly small and they move at high speeds around the atomic nucleus—not in neat circular orbits, but within defined regions of space called orbitals.

Insights

19.2 The Formation of Ions

When the number of protons in the nucleus of an atom equals the number of electrons in the atom, the charges balance and the atom is electrically neutral. If one or more electrons are lost or gained, as illustrated in Figures 19.4 and 19.5, the balance is upset and the atom takes on a net electric charge. Any atom having a net electric charge is an **ion.** When electrons are lost, protons outnumber electrons and the ion has a positive net charge. When electrons are gained, electrons outnumber protons and the ion has a negative net charge.

Chemists use a superscript to the right of the atomic symbol to indicate the magnitude and sign of an ion's charge. Thus, as shown in Figures 19.4 and 19.5, the positive ion formed from the sodium atom is written Na^{1+} and the negative ion formed from the fluorine atom is written F^{1-}. Usually the numeral 1 is omitted when indicating either a 1+ or 1− charge. Hence, these two ions are most frequently written Na^{+} and F^{-}.

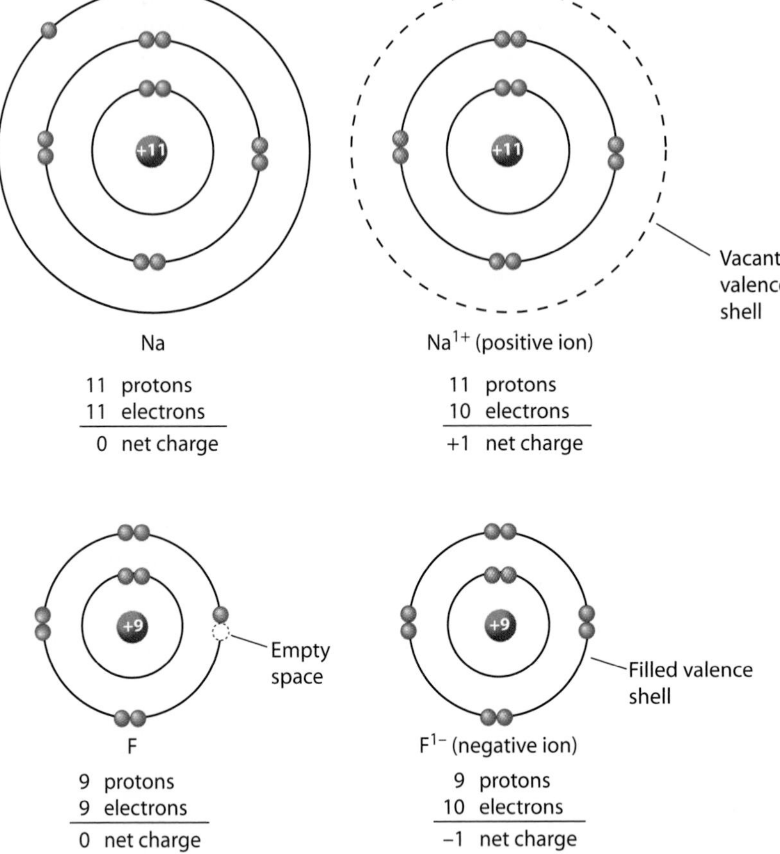

Figure 19.4
An electrically neutral sodium atom contains 11 negatively charged electrons surrounding the 11 positively charged protons of the nucleus. When this atom loses an electron, the result is a positive ion.

Figure 19.5
An electrically neutral fluorine atom contains nine protons and nine electrons. When this atom gains an electron, the result is a negative ion.

To give two more examples, a calcium atom that loses two electrons is written Ca^{2+}, and an oxygen atom that gains two electrons is written O^{2-}. (Note that the convention is to write the numeral before the sign, not after it: 2+, not +2.)

We can use the shell model to deduce the type of ion an atom tends to form. According to this model, *atoms tend to lose or gain electrons that result in an outermost occupied shell filled to capacity.* Let's take a moment to consider this point, looking to Figures 19.4 and 19.5 as visual guides.

If an atom has only one or only a few electrons in its valence shell, it tends to give up (lose) these electrons so that the next shell inward, which is already filled, becomes the outermost occupied shell. The sodium atom of Figure 19.4, for example, has one electron in its valence shell, which is the third shell. In forming an ion, the sodium atom loses this electron, thereby making the second shell, which is already filled to capacity, the outermost occupied shell. Because the sodium atom has only one valence electron to lose, it tends to form the 1+ ion.

If the valence shell of an atom is almost filled, that atom attracts electrons from another atom and so forms a negative ion. The fluorine atom of Figure 19.5, for example, has one space available in its valence shell for an additional electron. After this additional electron is gained, the fluorine atom achieves a filled valence shell. Fluorine therefore tends to form the 1− ion.

You can use the periodic table as a quick reference when determining the type of ion an atom tends to form. As Figure 19.6 shows, each atom of any group 1 element, for example, has only one valence electron and so tends to form the 1+ ion. Each atom of any group 17 element has room for one additional electron in its valence shell and therefore tends to form the 1− ion. Atoms of the noble-gas elements tend not to form ions of any type because their valence shells are already filled to capacity.

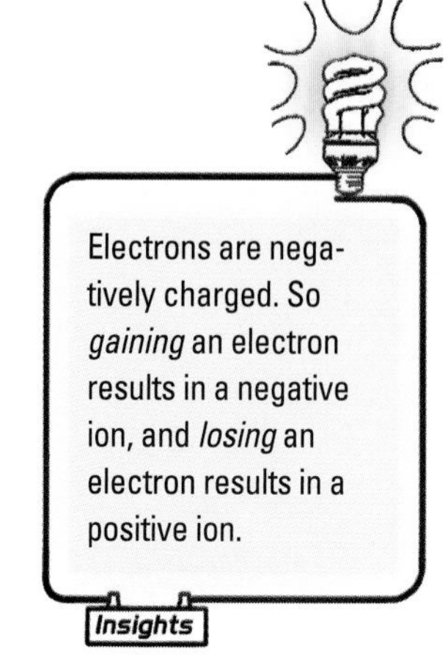

☑ CHECKPOINT

What type of ion does the magnesium atom, Mg, tend to form?

Check Your Answer

The magnesium atom (atomic number 12) is found in group 2 and has two valence electrons to lose (see Figure 19.2). Therefore, it tends to form the 2+ ion.

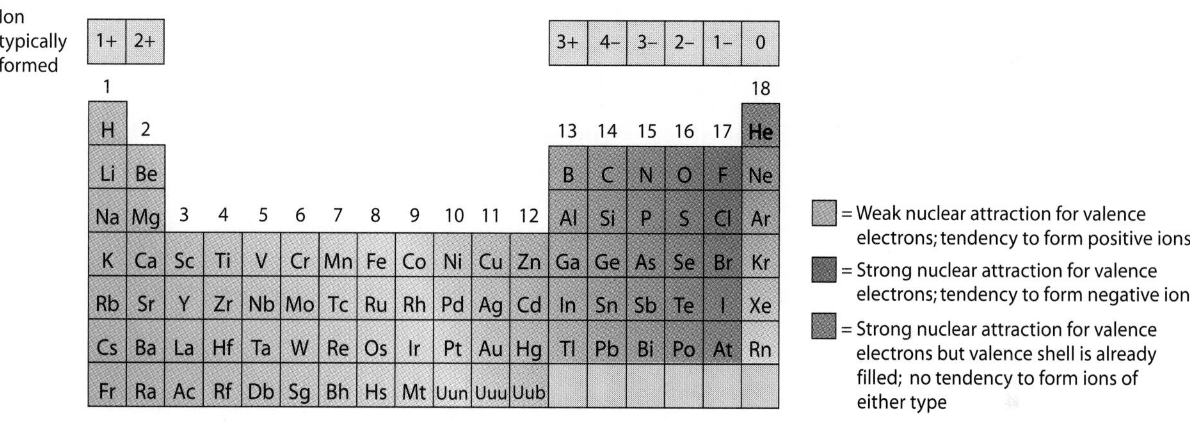

Figure 19.6
The periodic table is your guide to the types of ions that atoms tend to form.

As is indicated in Figure 19.6, the attraction between an atom's nucleus and its valence electrons is weakest for elements on the left in the periodic table and strongest for elements on the right. From sodium's position in the table, we can see that a sodium atom's single valence electron is not held very strongly, which explains why it is so easily lost. The attraction the sodium nucleus has for its second-shell electrons, however, is much stronger, which is why the sodium atom rarely loses more than one electron.

At the other side of the periodic table, the nucleus of a fluorine atom holds strongly onto its valence electrons, which explains why the fluorine atom tends not to lose any electrons to form a positive ion. Instead, fluorine's nuclear pull on the valence electrons is strong enough to accommodate even an additional electron "imported" from some other atom.

The nucleus of a noble-gas atom pulls so strongly on its valence electrons that they are very difficult to remove. Because there is no space available in the valence shell of a noble-gas atom, no additional electrons are gained. Thus, a noble-gas atom tends not to form ions of any sort.

☑ CHECKPOINT

Why does the magnesium atom tend to form the 2+ ion?

Check Your Answer

Magnesium is on the left in the periodic table, and so atoms of this element do not hold onto the two valence electrons very strongly. Because these electrons are not held very tightly, they are easily lost, which is why the magnesium atom tends to form the 2+ ion.

Using our shell model to explain the formation of ions works well for groups 1 and 2 and 13 through 18. This model is too simplified to work well for the transition metals of groups 3 through 12, however, or for the inner transition metals. In general, these metal atoms tend to form positive ions, but the number of electrons lost varies. For example, depending on conditions, an iron atom may lose two electrons to form the Fe^{2+} ion, or it may lose three electrons to form the Fe^{3+} ion.

Molecules Can Form Ions

So we see that atoms form ions by losing or gaining electrons. Interestingly, molecules can also become ions. In most cases, this occurs whenever a molecule loses or gains a proton—equivalent to the hydrogen ion, H^+. (Recall that a hydrogen atom is a proton together with an electron. The hydrogen ion, H^+, therefore, is simply a proton.) For example, a water molecule, H_2O, can gain a hydrogen ion, H^+ (a proton), to form the hydronium ion, H_3O^+:

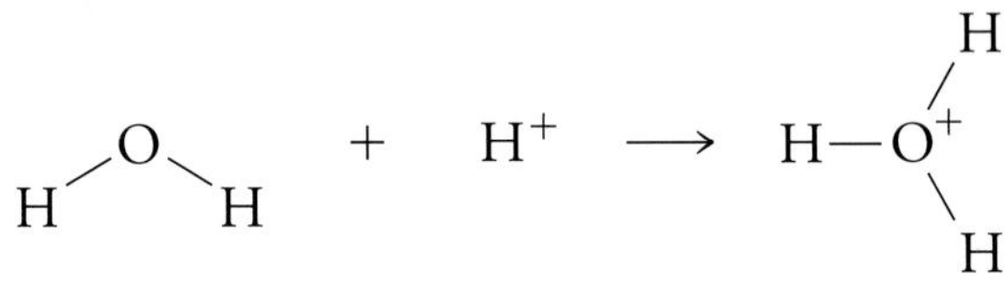

$$\mathrm{H{-}O{-}H} + \mathrm{H^+} \longrightarrow \mathrm{H{-}O^+(H)_2}$$

Water | Hydrogen ion (proton) | Hydronium ion

Similarly, the carbonic acid molecule, H_2CO_3, can lose two protons to form the carbonate ion, CO_3^{2-}:

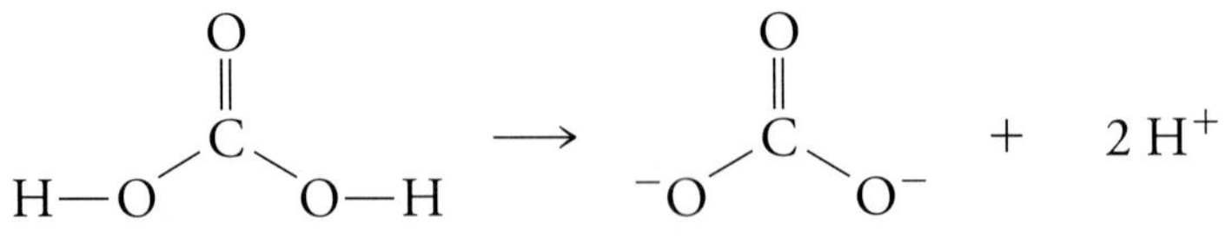

$$\mathrm{H{-}O{-}C({=}O){-}O{-}H} \longrightarrow \mathrm{{}^-O{-}C({=}O){-}O^-} + 2\,\mathrm{H^+}$$

Carbonic acid | Carbonate ion | Hydrogen ions (protons)

How these reactions occur will be explored in later chapters. For now, you should understand that the hydronium and carbonate ions are examples of **polyatomic ions,** which are molecules that carry a net electric charge. Table 19.1 lists some commonly encountered polyatomic ions.

Table 19.1

Common Polyatomic Ions

Name	Formula
Hydronium ion	H_3O^+
Ammonium ion	NH_4^+
Bicarbonate ion	HCO_3^-
Acetate ion	$CH_3CO_2^-$
Nitrate ion	NO_3^-
Cyanide ion	CN^-
Hydroxide ion	OH^-
Carbonate ion	CO_3^{2-}
Sulfate ion	SO_4^{2-}
Phosphate ion	PO_4^{3-}

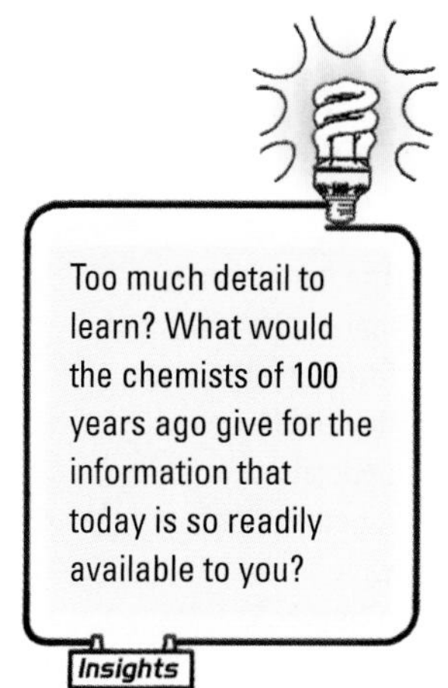

19.3 Ionic Bonds

When an atom that tends to lose electrons is placed in contact with an atom that tends to gain them, the result is an electron transfer and the formation of two oppositely charged ions. This occurs when sodium and chlorine are combined. As shown in Figure 19.7, the sodium atom loses one of its electrons to the chlorine atom, resulting in the formation of a positive sodium ion and a negative chloride ion. The two oppositely charged ions are attracted to each other by the electric force, which holds them close together. This electric force of attraction between two oppositely charged ions is called an **ionic bond.**

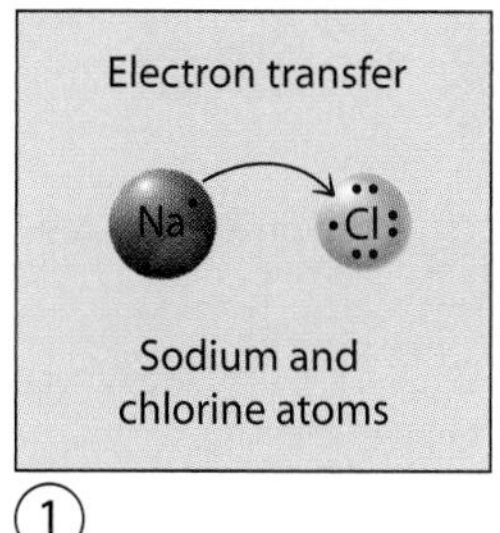

(1)

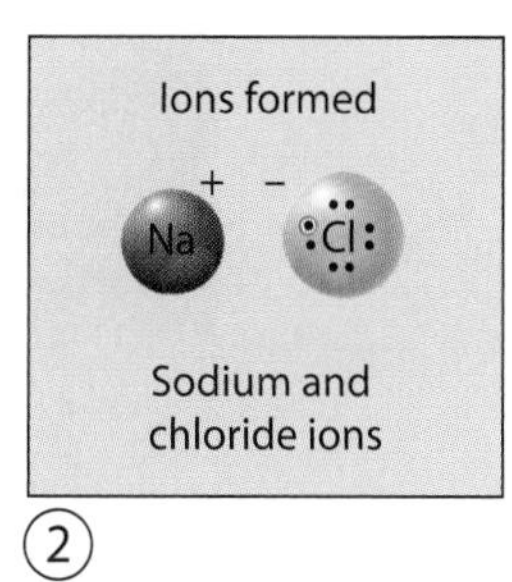

(2)

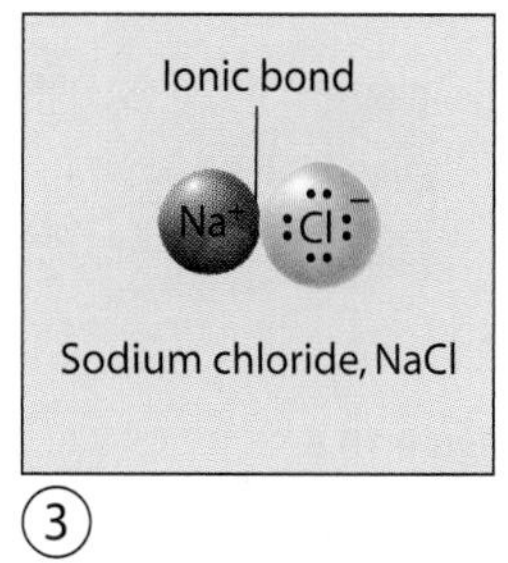

(3)

Figure 19.7
(1) An electrically neutral sodium atom loses its valence electron to an electrically neutral chlorine atom. (2) This electron transfer results in two oppositely charged ions. (3) The ions are then held together by an ionic bond. The spheres drawn around these and subsequent illustrations of electron-dot structures indicate the relative sizes of the atoms and ions. Note that the sodium ion is smaller than the sodium atom because the lone electron in the third shell has gone once the ion forms, leaving the ion with only two occupied shells. The chloride ion is larger than the chlorine atom because the addition of that one electron to the third shell makes the shell expand due to the repulsions among the electrons.

A sodium ion and a chloride ion together make the chemical compound sodium chloride, commonly known as table salt. This and all other chemical compounds containing ions are referred to as **ionic compounds.** All ionic compounds are completely different from the elements from which they are made.

As discussed in Section 17.5, sodium chloride is not sodium, nor is it chlorine. Rather, it is a collection of sodium and chloride ions that form a unique material having its own physical and chemical properties.

The ionic bond is merely the electrical force of attraction that holds ions of opposite charge together, in accord with Coulomb's law (Chapter 9):

$$F = K\frac{q_1 q_2}{d^2}$$

where d is the distance between the charged particles, q_1 represents the quantity of charge of one particle, q_2 represents the quantity of charge of the second particle, and k is the proportionality constant.

Insights

☑ CHECKPOINT

Is the transfer of an electron from a sodium atom to a chlorine atom a physical change or a chemical change?

Check Your Answer

Recall, from Chapter 17, that only a chemical change involves the formation of new material. Thus, this or any other electron transfer, because it results in the formation of a new substance, is a chemical change.

As Figure 19.8 shows, ionic compounds typically consist of elements that are found on opposite sides of the periodic table. Also, because of how the metals and nonmetals are organized in the periodic table, positive ions are generally derived from metallic elements and negative ions are generally derived from nonmetallic elements.

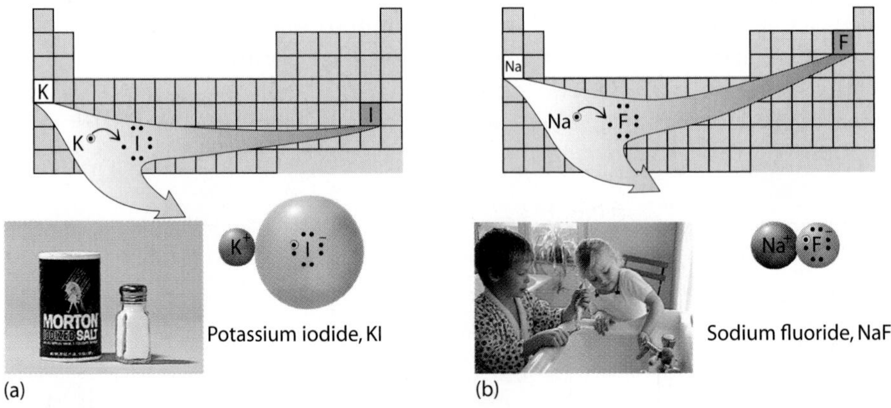

Figure 19.8
(a) The ionic compound potassium iodide, KI, is added in minute quantities to commercial salt because the iodide ion, I−, it contains is an essential dietary mineral. (b) The ionic compound sodium fluoride, NaF, is often added to municipal water supplies and toothpastes because it is a good source of the tooth-strengthening fluoride ion, F−.

For all ionic compounds, positive and negative charges must balance. In sodium chloride, for example, there is one sodium 1+ ion for every chloride 1− ion. Charges must also balance in compounds containing ions that carry multiple charges. The calcium ion, for example, carries a charge of 2+, but the fluoride ion carries a charge of only 1−. Because two fluoride ions are needed to balance each calcium ion, the formula for calcium fluoride is CaF_2, as Figure 19.9 illustrates. Calcium fluoride occurs naturally in the drinking water of some communities, where it is a good source of the tooth-strengthening fluoride ion, F−.

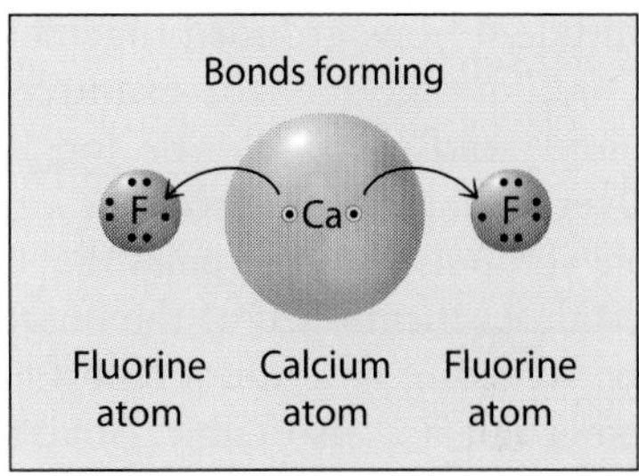

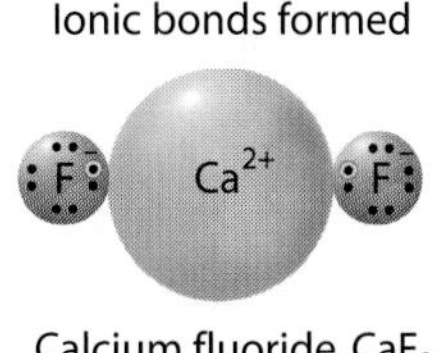

Fluorite

Figure 19.9
A calcium atom loses two electrons to form a calcium ion, Ca^{2+}. These two electrons may be picked up by two fluorine atoms, transforming the atoms to two fluoride ions. Calcium ions and fluoride ions then join to form the ionic compound calcium fluoride, CaF_2, which occurs naturally as the mineral fluorite.

An aluminum ion carries a 3+ charge, and an oxide ion carries a 2− charge. Together, these ions make the ionic compound aluminum oxide, Al_2O_3, the main component of such gemstones as rubies and sapphires. Figure 19.10 illustrates the formation of aluminum oxide. The three oxide ions in Al_2O_3 carry a total charge of 6−, which balances the total 6+ charge of the two aluminum ions. As mentioned earlier, rubies and sapphires differ in color because of the impurities they contain. Rubies are red because of minor amounts of chromium ions, and sapphires are blue because of minor amounts of iron and titanium ions.

☑ CHECKPOINT

What is the chemical formula for the ionic compound magnesium oxide?

Check Your Answer

Because magnesium is a group 2 element, you know a magnesium atom must lose two electrons to form a Mg^{2+} ion. Because oxygen is a group 16 element, an oxygen atom gains two electrons to form an O^{2-} ion. These charges balance in a one-to-one ratio, and so the formula for magnesium oxide is MgO.

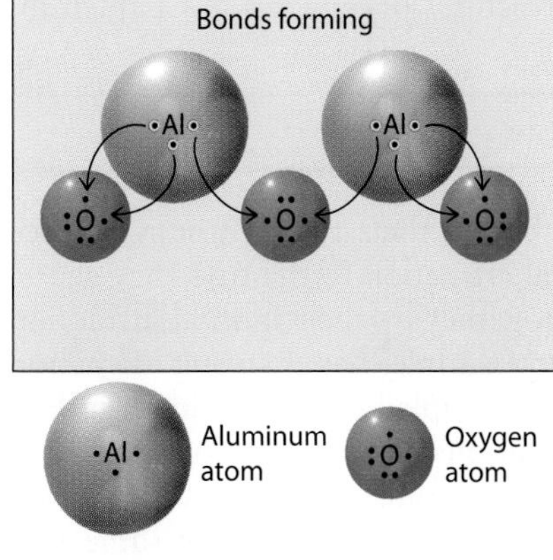

Figure 19.10
Two aluminum atoms lose a total of six electrons to form two aluminum ions, Al^{3+}. These six electrons may be picked up by three oxygen atoms, transforming the atoms to three oxide ions, O^{2-}. The aluminum and oxide ions then join to form the ionic compound aluminum oxide, Al_2O_3.

An ionic compound typically contains a multitude of ions grouped together in a highly ordered three-dimensional array. In sodium chloride, for example, each sodium ion is surrounded by six chloride ions, and each chloride ion is surrounded by six sodium ions (Figure 19.11). Overall, there is one sodium ion for each chloride ion, but there are no identifiable sodium–chloride pairs. Such an orderly array of ions is known as an ionic crystal. As mentioned at the onset of this chapter, on the atomic level, the crystalline structure of sodium chloride is cubic, which is why macroscopic crystals of table salt are also cubic. Smash a large cubic sodium chloride crystal with a hammer, and what do you get? Smaller cubic sodium chloride crystals!

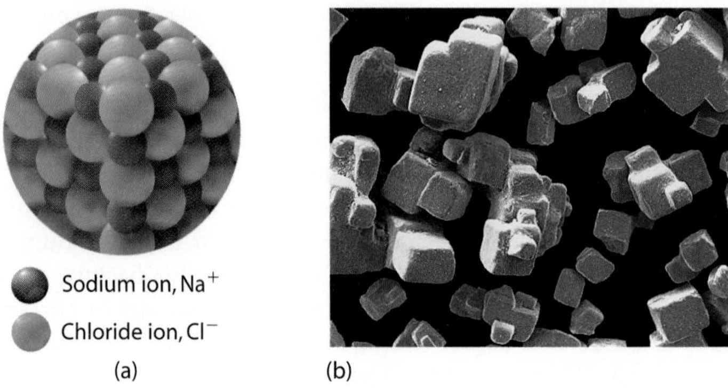

Figure 19.11
(a) Sodium chloride, as well as other ionic compounds, forms ionic crystals in which every internal ion is surrounded by ions of the opposite charge. (For simplicity, only a small portion of the ion array is shown here. A typical NaCl crystal involves millions and millions of ions.) (b) A view of crystals of table salt through a microscope shows their cubic structure. The cubic shape is a consequence of the cubic arrangement of sodium and chloride ions.

Similarly, the crystalline structures of other ionic compounds, such as calcium fluoride and aluminum oxide, are a consequence of how the ions pack together. We go into more detail about the crystalline structures of minerals in Chapter 25.

19.4 Covalent Bonds

Imagine two children playing together and sharing their toys. Perhaps a force that keeps the children together is their mutual attraction to the toys they share. In a similar fashion, two atoms can be held together by their mutual attraction for electrons they share. A fluorine atom, for example, has a strong attraction for one additional electron to fill its outermost occupied shell. As shown in Figure 19.12, a fluorine atom can obtain an additional electron by holding onto the unpaired valence electron of another fluorine atom. This results in a situation in which the two fluorine atoms are mutually attracted to the same two electrons. This type of electrical attraction in which atoms are held together by their mutual attraction for shared electrons is called a **covalent bond,** where *co-* signifies sharing and *-valent* refers to the fact that it is valence electrons that are being shared.

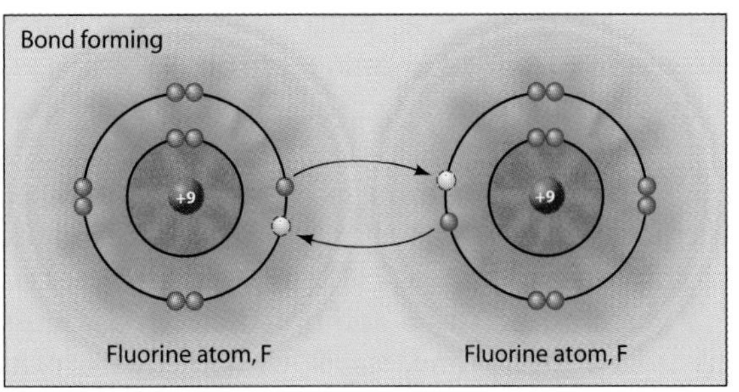

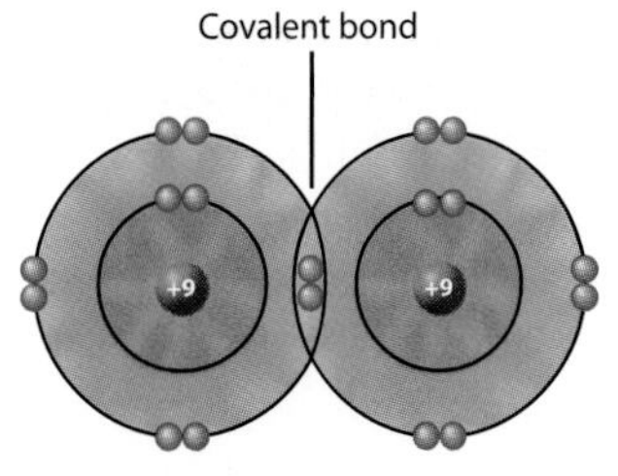

Figure 19.12
The effect of the positive nuclear charge (represented by red shading) of a fluorine atom extends beyond the atom's outermost occupied shell. This positive charge can cause the fluorine atom to become attracted to the unpaired valence electron of a neighboring fluorine atom. Then the two atoms are held together in a fluorine molecule by the attraction they both have for the two shared electrons. Each fluorine atom achieves a filled valence shell.

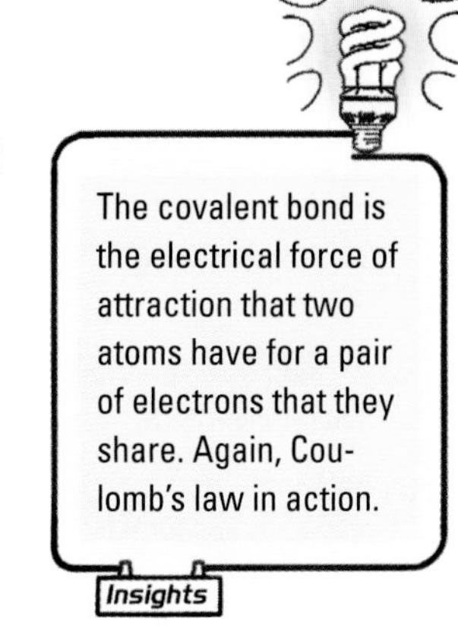

A substance composed of atoms held together by covalent bonds is a **covalent compound.** The fundamental unit of most covalent compounds is a **molecule,** which we can now formally define as any group of atoms held together by covalent bonds. Figure 19.13 uses the element fluorine to illustrate this principle.

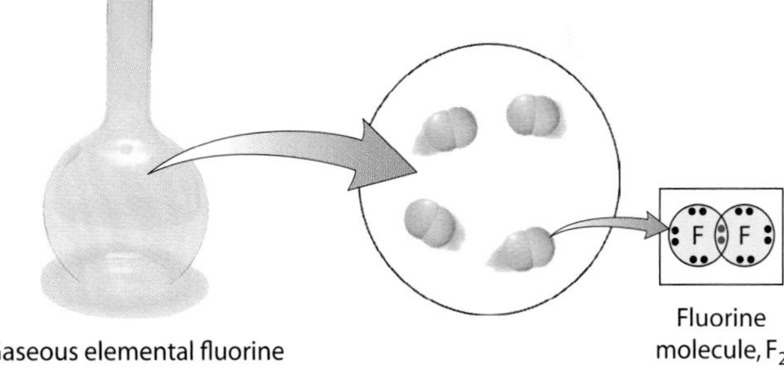

Figure 19.13
Molecules are the fundamental units of the gaseous covalent compound fluorine, F_2. Notice that in this model of a fluorine molecule, the spheres overlap, whereas the spheres shown earlier for ionic compounds do not. Now you know that this difference in representation is because of the difference in bond types.

When writing electron-dot structures for covalent compounds, chemists often use a straight line to represent the two electrons involved in a covalent bond. In some representations, the nonbonding electron pairs are ignored. This occurs in instances where these electrons play no significant role in the process being illustrated. Here are two frequently used ways of showing the electron-dot structure for a fluorine molecule without using spheres to represent the atoms:

$$:\ddot{\underset{\cdot\cdot}{F}}-\ddot{\underset{\cdot\cdot}{F}}: \qquad F-F$$

Remember—the straight line in both versions represents two electrons, one from each atom. Thus, we now have two types of electron pairs to keep track of. The term *nonbonding pair* refers to any pair that exists in the electron-dot structure of an individual atom, and the term *bonding pair* refers to any pair that results from formation of a covalent bond. In a nonbonding pair, both electrons originate in the same atom; in a bonding pair, one electron comes from one of the atoms participating in the covalent bond, and the other electron comes from the other atom participating in the bond.

Recall, from Section 19.3, that an ionic bond is formed when an atom that tends to lose electrons makes contact with an atom that tends to gain them. A covalent bond, by contrast, is formed when two atoms that tend to gain electrons are brought into contact with each other. Atoms that tend to form covalent bonds are therefore primarily atoms of the nonmetallic elements in the upper right corner of the periodic table (with the exception of the noble-gas elements, which are very stable and tend not to form bonds).

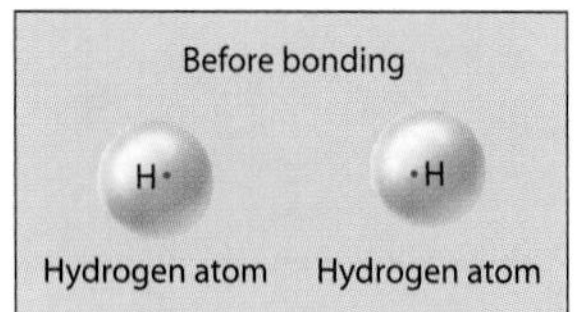

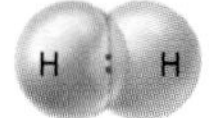

Figure 19.14
Two hydrogen atoms form a covalent bond as they share their unpaired electrons.

Hydrogen tends to form covalent bonds because, unlike the other group 1 elements, it has a fairly strong attraction for an additional electron. Two hydrogen atoms, for example, covalently bond to form a hydrogen molecule, H_2, as shown in Figure 19.14.

The number of covalent bonds an atom can form is equal to the number of additional electrons it can attract, which is the number needed to fill its valence shell. Hydrogen attracts only one additional electron, and so it forms only one covalent bond. Oxygen, which attracts two additional electrons, finds them when it encounters two hydrogen atoms and reacts with them to form water, H_2O, as Figure 19.15 shows. In water, not only does the oxygen atom have access to two additional electrons by covalently bonding to two hydrogen atoms, but each hydrogen atom has access to an additional electron by bonding to the oxygen atom. Each atom thus achieves a filled valence shell.

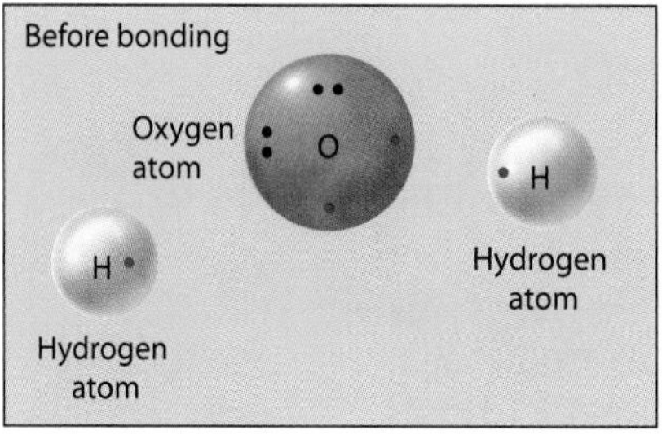

Figure 19.15
The two unpaired valence electrons of oxygen pair with the unpaired valence electrons of two hydrogen atoms to form the covalent compound water.

Nitrogen attracts three additional electrons and is thus able to form three covalent bonds, as occurs in ammonia, NH_3, shown in Figure 19.16. Likewise, a carbon atom can attract four additional electrons and is thus able to form four covalent bonds, as occurs in methane, CH_4. Note that the number of covalent bonds formed by these and other nonmetallic elements parallels the type of negative ions they tend to form (see Figure 19.6). This makes sense because covalent-bond formation and negative-ion formation are both applications of the same concept: nonmetallic atoms tend to gain electrons until their valence shells are filled.

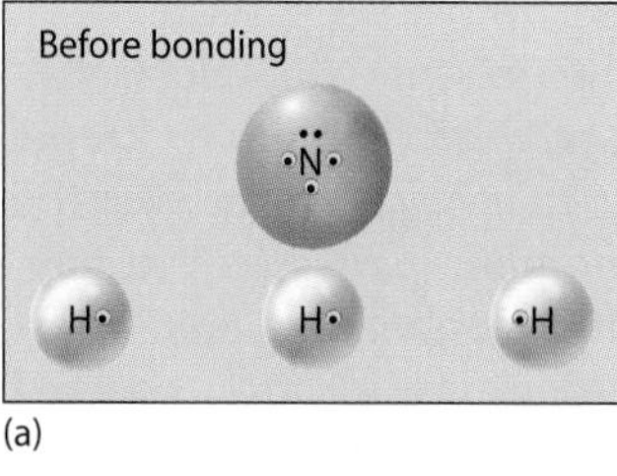

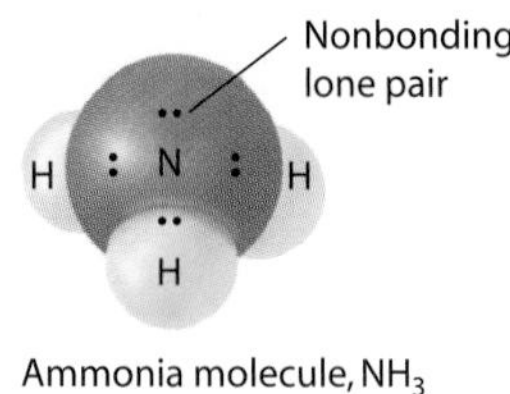

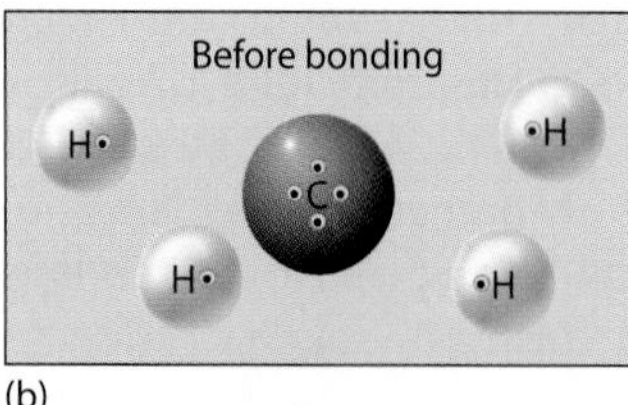

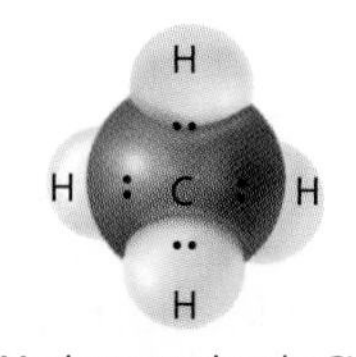

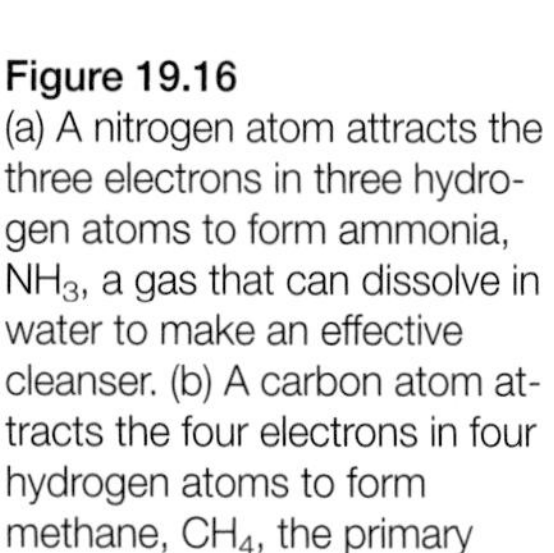

Figure 19.16
(a) A nitrogen atom attracts the three electrons in three hydrogen atoms to form ammonia, NH_3, a gas that can dissolve in water to make an effective cleanser. (b) A carbon atom attracts the four electrons in four hydrogen atoms to form methane, CH_4, the primary component of natural gas. In these and most other cases of covalent-bond formation, the result is a filled valence shell for all the atoms involved.

Diamond is a most unusual covalent compound consisting of carbon atoms covalently bonded to one another in four directions. The result is a covalent crystal, which, as shown in Figure 19.17, is a highly ordered, three-dimensional network of covalently bonded atoms. This network of carbon atoms forms a very strong and rigid structure, which is why diamonds are so hard. Also, because a diamond is a group of atoms held together only by covalent bonds, it can be characterized as a single molecule! Unlike most other molecules, a diamond molecule is large enough to be visible to the naked eye, and so it is more appropriately referred to as a macromolecule.

☑ **CHECKPOINT**

How many electrons make up a covalent bond?

Check Your Answer

Two—one from each participating atom.

Figure 19.17
The crystalline structure of diamond is nicely illustrated with sticks to represent the covalent bonds. The molecular nature of a diamond is responsible for its extreme hardness.

It is possible to have more than two electrons shared between two atoms, and Figure 19.18 shows a few examples. Molecular oxygen, O_2, consists of two oxygen atoms connected by four shared electrons. This arrangement is called a double covalent bond or, for short, a double bond. As another example, the covalent compound carbon dioxide, CO_2, consists of two double bonds connecting two oxygen atoms to a central carbon atom.

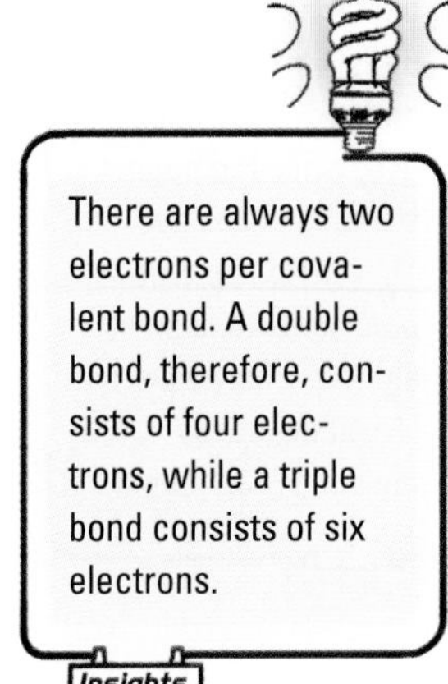

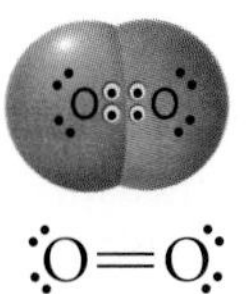

$:\ddot{O}=\ddot{O}:$

Oxygen, O_2

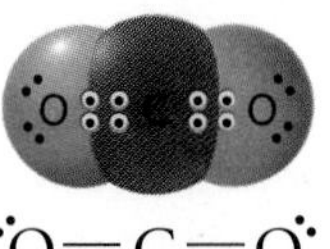

$:\ddot{O}=C=\ddot{O}:$

Carbon dioxide, CO_2

$:N\equiv N:$

Nitrogen, N_2

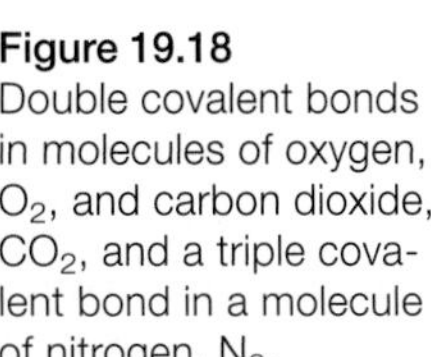

Figure 19.18
Double covalent bonds in molecules of oxygen, O_2, and carbon dioxide, CO_2, and a triple covalent bond in a molecule of nitrogen, N_2.

Some atoms can form triple covalent bonds, in which six electrons—three from each atom—are shared. One example is molecular nitrogen, N_2.

Any double or triple bond is often referred to as a multiple covalent bond. Multiple bonds higher than these, such as the quadruple covalent bond, are not commonly observed.

19.5 Polar Covalent Bonds

If the two atoms in a covalent bond are identical, their nuclei have the same positive charge, and therefore the electrons are shared evenly. We can represent these electrons as being centrally located by using an electron-dot structure with the electrons situated exactly halfway between the two atomic symbols. Alternatively, we can draw a probability cloud (Section 15.5) in which the positions of the two bonding electrons over time are shown as a series of dots. Where the dots are most concentrated is where the electrons have the greatest probability of being located:

H : H   H H

In a covalent bond between nonidentical atoms, the nuclear charges are different, and consequently the bonding electrons may be shared unevenly. This occurs in a hydrogen–fluorine bond, where electrons are more attracted to fluorine's greater nuclear charge:

H : F   H F

One side of the hydrogen–fluorine bond has a greater density of electrons and is slightly negative, while the opposite side is positive. This makes up a *dipole,* an extension of electric-charge polarization, as discussed in Chapter 9.

Insights

The bonding electrons spend more time around the fluorine atom. For this reason, the fluorine side of the bond is slightly negative and, because the bonding electrons have been drawn away from the hydrogen atom, the hydrogen side of the bond is slightly positive. This separation of charge is called a **dipole** (pronounced *die*-pole) and is represented either by the characters $\delta-$ and $\delta+$ (read "slightly negative" and "slightly positive," respectively) or by a crossed arrow pointing to the negative side of the bond:

$$\overset{\delta+}{\text{H}}-\overset{\delta-}{\text{F}} \qquad \overset{\longmapsto}{\text{H}-\text{F}}$$

So atoms forming a chemical bond engage in a tug-of-war for electrons. How strongly an atom is able to tug on bonding electrons has been measured experimentally and quantified as the atom's **electronegativity.** The range of electronegativities runs from 0.7 to 3.98, as Figure 19.19 shows. The greater an atom's electronegativity, the greater its ability to pull electrons toward itself when bonded. Thus, in hydrogen fluoride, fluorine has a greater electronegativity, or pulling power, than hydrogen.

Electronegativity is greatest for elements at the upper right of the periodic table and lowest for elements at the lower left. Noble gases are not considered in electronegativity discussions because, as previously mentioned, they rarely participate in chemical bonding.

H 2.2																	He —
Li 0.98	Be 1.57											B 2.04	C 2.55	N 3.04	O 3.44	F 3.98	Ne —
Na 0.93	Mg 1.31											Al 1.61	Si 1.9	P 2.19	S 2.58	Cl 3.16	Ar —
K 0.82	Ca 1.0	Sc 1.36	Ti 1.54	V 1.63	Cr 1.66	Mn 1.55	Fe 1.83	Co 1.88	Ni 1.91	Cu 1.90	Zn 1.65	Ga 1.81	Ge 2.01	As 2.18	Se 2.55	Br 2.96	Kr —
Rb 0.82	Sr 0.95	Y 1.22	Zr 1.33	Nb 1.6	Mo 2.16	Tc 1.9	Ru 2.2	Rh 2.28	Pd 2.20	Ag 1.93	Cd 1.69	In 1.78	Sn 1.96	Sb 2.05	Te 2.1	I 2.66	Xe —
Cs 0.79	Ba 0.89	La 1.10	Hf 1.3	Ta 1.5	W 2.36	Re 1.9	Os 2.2	Ir 2.20	Pt 2.8	Au 2.54	Hg 2.00	Tl 2.04	Pb 2.33	Bi 2.02	Po 2.0	At 2.2	Rn —
Fr 0.7	Ra 0.9	Ac 1.1	Rf —	Db —	Sg —	Bh —	Hs —	Mt —	Uun —	Uuu —	Uub —						

Figure 19.19
The experimentally measured electronegativities of elements.

When the two atoms in a covalent bond have the same electronegativity, no dipole is formed (as is the case with H_2) and the bond is classified as a **nonpolar** bond. When the electronegativities of the atoms differ, a dipole may form (as with HF) and the bond is classified as a **polar** bond. Just how polar a bond is depends on the difference between the electronegativity values of the two atoms—the greater the difference, the more polar the bond.

As can be seen in Figure 19.19, the greater the distance between two atoms in the periodic table, the greater the difference in their electronegativities, and hence the greater the polarity of the bond between them. So a chemist can predict which bonds are more polar than others without reading the electronegativities. Bond polarity can be inferred by looking at the relative positions of the atoms in the periodic table—the farther apart they are, especially when one is at the lower left and one is at the upper right, the greater the polarity of the bond between them.

☑ CHECKPOINT

List these bonds in order of increasing polarity: P–F, S–F, Ga–F, Ge–F (F, fluorine, atomic number 9; P, phosphorus, atomic number 15; S, sulfur, atomic number 16; Ga, gallium, atomic number 31; Ge, germanium, atomic number 32):
(least polar) ______, ______, ______, ______ (most polar)

Check Your Answer

If you answered the question, or attempted to, before reading this answer, hooray for you! You're doing more than reading the text—you're learning physical science. The greater the difference in electronegativities between two bonded atoms, the greater the polarity of the bond, and so the order of increasing polarity is
S–F < P–F < Ge–F < Ga–F.

Note that this answer can be obtained by looking only at the relative positions of these elements in the periodic table rather than by calculating the differences in their electronegativities.

The magnitude of bond polarity is sometimes indicated by the size of the crossed arrow or the $\delta-$ and $\delta+$ symbols used to depict a dipole, as shown in Figure 19.20.

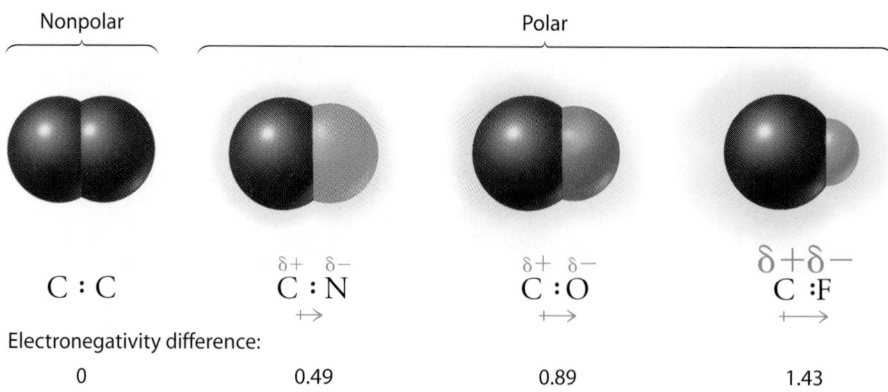

Figure 19.20
These bonds are in order of increasing polarity from left to right, a trend indicated by the larger and larger crossed arrows and $\delta-$ / $\delta+$ symbols. Which of these pairs of elements are farthest apart in the periodic table?

Note that the electronegativity difference between atoms in an ionic bond can also be calculated. For example, the bond in NaCl has an electronegativity difference of 2.23, far greater than the difference of 1.43 shown for the C–F bond in Figure 19.20.

What is important to understand here is that there is no black-and-white distinction between ionic and covalent bonds. Rather, there is a gradual change from one to the other as the atoms that bond are located farther and farther apart in the periodic table. This continuum is illustrated in Figure 19.21. Atoms on opposite sides of the periodic table have great differences in electronegativity, and hence the bonds between them are highly polar—in other words, ionic. Nonmetallic atoms of the same type have the same electronegativities, and so their bonds are nonpolar covalent. The polar covalent bond with its uneven sharing of electrons and slightly charged atoms is between these two extremes.

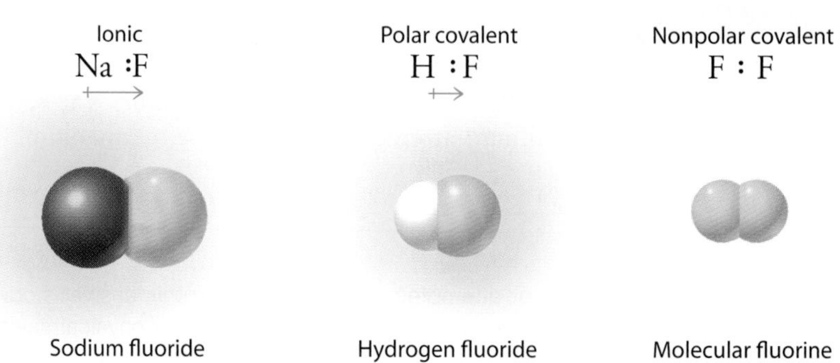

Figure 19.21
The ionic bond and the nonpolar covalent bond represent the two extremes of chemical bonding. The ionic bond involves a transfer of one or more electrons, and the nonpolar covalent bond involves the equitable sharing of electrons. The character of a polar covalent bond falls between these two extremes.

19.6 Molecular Polarity

When all the bonds in a molecule are nonpolar, the molecule as a whole is also nonpolar—as is the case with H_2, O_2, and N_2. When a molecule consists of only two atoms and the bond between them is polar, the polarity of the molecule is the same as the polarity of the bond—as with HF, HCl, and ClF.

Complexities arise when assessing the polarity of a molecule containing more than two atoms. Consider carbon dioxide, CO_2, shown in Figure 19.22. The cause of the dipole in either one of the carbon–oxygen bonds is oxygen's greater pull on the bonding electrons (because oxygen is more electronegative than carbon). At the same time, however, the oxygen atom on the opposite side of the carbon pulls those electrons back to the carbon. The net result is an even distribution of bonding electrons around the entire molecule. So, dipoles that are of equal strength but pull in opposite directions in a molecule effectively cancel each other, with the result that the molecule as a whole is nonpolar.

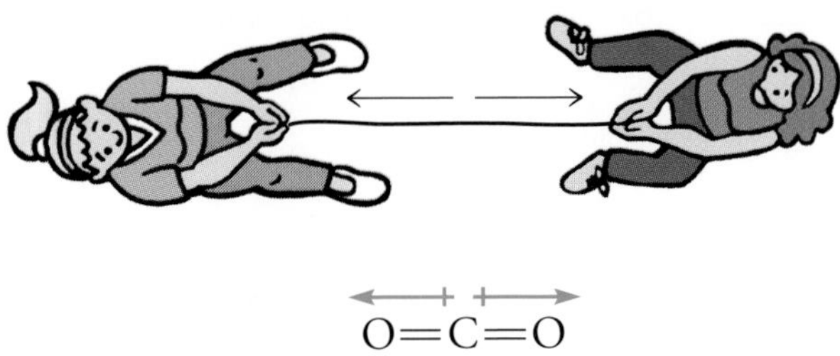

Figure 19.22
There is no net dipole in a carbon dioxide molecule, and so the molecule is nonpolar. This is analogous to two people in a tug-of-war. As long as they pull with equal forces but in opposite directions, the rope remains stationary.

Figure 19.23 illustrates a similar situation in boron trifluoride, BF_3, where three fluorine atoms are oriented 120 degrees from one another around a central boron atom. Because the angles are all the same, and because each fluorine atom pulls on the electrons of its boron–fluorine bond with the same force, the resulting polarity of this molecule is zero.

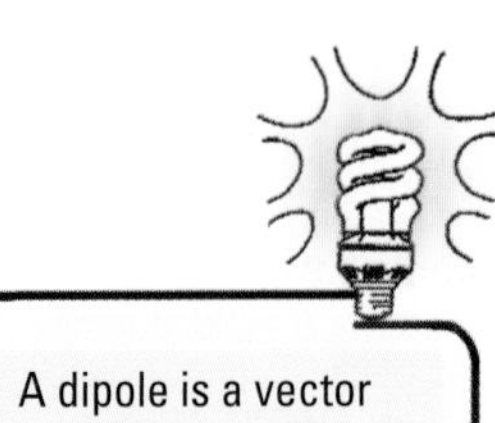

A dipole is a vector quantity possessing both magnitude and direction. When two dipoles are equal and opposite, they effectively cancel each other out.

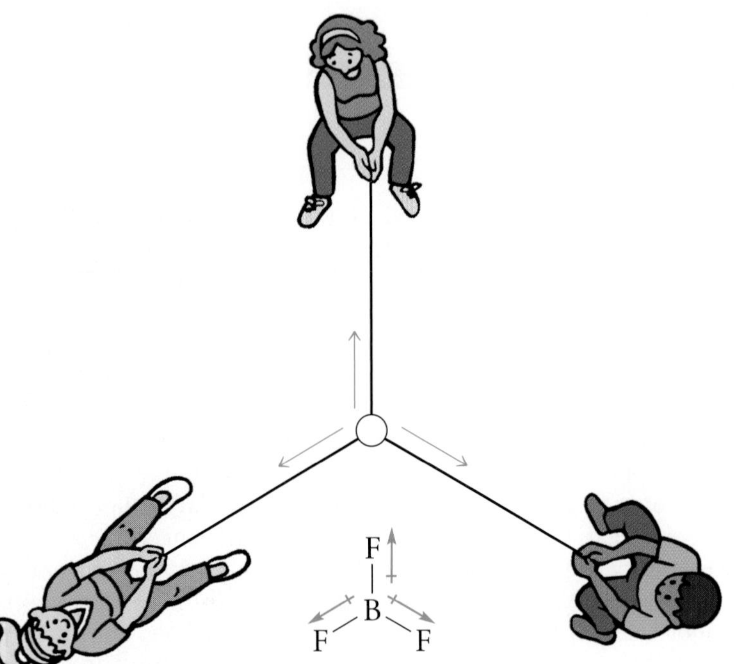

Figure 19.23
The three dipoles of a boron trifluoride molecule oppose one another at 120-degree angles, which makes the overall molecule nonpolar. This is analogous to three people pulling with equal force on ropes attached to a central ring. As long as they all pull with equal force and all maintain the 120-degree angles, the ring will remain stationary.

Nonpolar molecules have only relatively weak attractions to other nonpolar molecules. The covalent bonds in a carbon dioxide molecule, for example, are many times stronger than any forces of attraction that might occur between two adjacent carbon dioxide molecules. This lack of attraction between nonpolar molecules explains the low boiling points of many nonpolar substances. Recall from Section 17.2 that boiling is a process wherein the molecules of a liquid separate from one another as they go into the gaseous phase. When there are only weak attractions between the molecules of a liquid, less heat energy is required to liberate the molecules from one another and allow them to enter the gaseous phase. This translates into a relatively low boiling point for the liquid, as, for example, in the nitrogen, N_2, shown in Figure 19.24. The boiling points of hydrogen, H_2; oxygen, O_2; carbon dioxide, CO_2; and boron trifluoride, BF_3, are also quite low for the same reason.

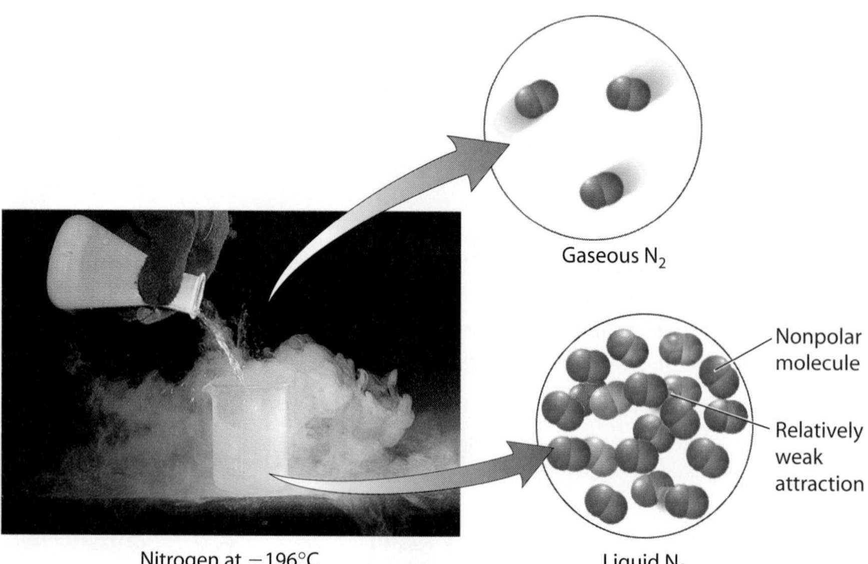

Figure 19.24
Nitrogen is a liquid at temperatures below its chilly boiling point of −196°C. Nitrogen molecules are not very attracted to one another because they are nonpolar. As a result, the small amount of heat energy available at −196°C is enough to separate them and allow them to enter the gaseous phase.

There are many instances in which the dipoles of different bonds in a molecule do not cancel each other. Reconsider the rope analogy of Figure 19.23. As long as everyone pulls equally, the ring stays put. Imagine, however, that one person begins to ease off on the rope. Now the pulls are no longer balanced, and the ring begins to move away from the person who is slacking off, as Figure 19.25 shows. Likewise, if one person began to pull harder, the ring would move away from the other two people.

A similar situation occurs in molecules where polar covalent bonds are not equal and opposite. Perhaps the most relevant example is water, H_2O. Each hydrogen–oxygen covalent bond has a relatively large dipole because of the great electronegativity difference. Because of the bent shape of the molecule, however, the two dipoles, shown in blue in Figure 19.26, do not cancel each other the way the C–O dipoles in Figure 19.22 do. Instead, the dipoles in the water molecule work together to give an overall dipole, shown in purple, for the molecule.

Figure 19.25
If one person eases off in a three-way tug-of-war but the other two continue to pull, the ring moves in the direction of the purple arrow.

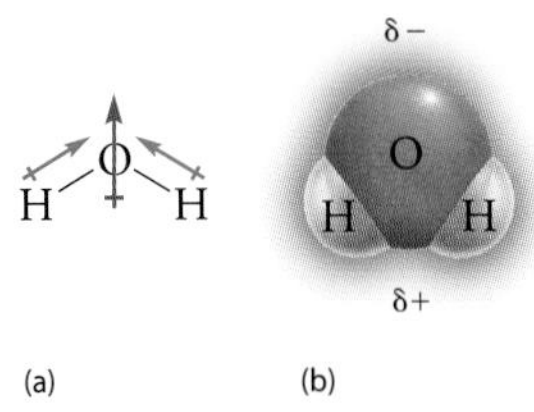

Figure 19.26
(a) The individual dipoles in a water molecule add together to give a large overall dipole for the whole molecule, shown in purple. (b) The region around the oxygen atom is therefore slightly negative, and the region around the two hydrogens is slightly positive.

☑ CHECKPOINT

Which of these molecules is polar and which is nonpolar?

```
F       F          H       F
 \     /            \     /
  C=C                C=C
 /     \            /     \
F       F          H       F
```

Check Your Answer

Symmetry is often the greatest clue for determining polarity. Because the molecule on the left is symmetrical, the dipoles on the two sides cancel each other. This molecule is therefore nonpolar:

```
F       F          H           F
 \     /            \         /
  C=C            δ+  C=C   δ−
 /     \            /         \
F       F          H           F
```

Because the molecule on the right is less symmetrical (more "lopsided"), it is the polar molecule. Because carbon is more electronegative than hydrogen, the dipoles of the two hydrogen–carbon bonds point toward the carbon. Because fluorine is more electronegative than carbon, the dipoles of the carbon–fluorine bonds point toward the fluorines. Because the general direction of all dipole arrows is toward the fluorines, so is the average distribution of the bonding electrons. The fluorine side of the molecule is therefore slightly negative, and the hydrogen side is slightly positive.

Figure 19.27 illustrates how polar molecules electrically attract one another and, as a result, are relatively difficult to separate. In other words, polar molecules can be thought of as being "sticky," which is why it takes more energy

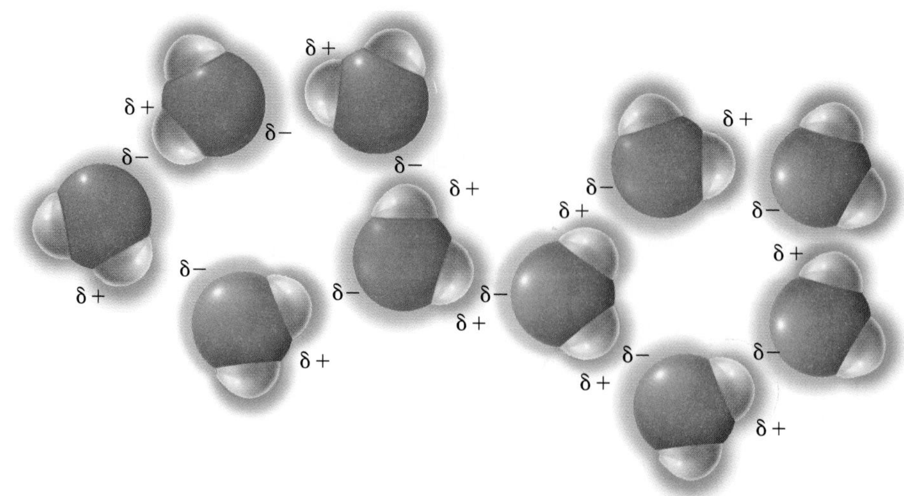

Figure 19.27
Water molecules attract one another because each contains a slightly positive side and a slightly negative side. The molecules position themselves such that the positive side of one faces the negative side of a neighbor.

to separate them—to change phase. For this reason, substances composed of polar molecules typically have higher boiling points than substances composed of nonpolar molecules, as Table 19.2 shows.

We explore the "stickiness" of molecules in much greater detail in Chapter 20.

Insights

Table 19.2

Boiling Points of Some Polar and Nonpolar Substances

Substance	Boiling point (°C)
Polar	
Hydrogen fluoride, HF	20
Water, H_2O	100
Ammonia, NH_3	−33
Nonpolar	
Hydrogen, H_2	−253
Oxygen, O_2	−183
Nitrogen, N_2	−196
Boron trifluoride, BF_3	−100
Carbon dioxide, CO_2	−79

Water boils at 100°C, whereas carbon dioxide boils at −79°C. This 179°C difference is quite dramatic when you consider that a carbon dioxide molecule is more than twice as massive as a water molecule.

Because molecular "stickiness" can play a lead role in determining a substance's macroscopic properties, molecular polarity is a central concept of chemistry. Figure 19.28 describes an interesting example.

Figure 19.28
Oil and water are difficult to mix, as is evident from this oil spill off the coast of Spain in 2002. It's not, however, that oil and water repel each other. Rather, water molecules are so attracted to themselves because of their polarity that they pull themselves together. The nonpolar oil molecules are thus excluded and left to themselves. Being less dense than water, oil floats on the surface, where it poses great danger to birds and other wildlife.

So far, we have explored two types of chemical bonds: ionic and covalent. Ionic bonds form when one or more electrons move from one atom to another. In this way, the atoms become ions—one positive, the other negative—and are held together by the resulting electrical attraction. Covalent bonds form when atoms share electrons. When the sharing is completely equitable, the bond is *nonpolar covalent*. When one atom pulls more strongly on the electrons because of its greater electronegativity, the bond is *polar covalent* and a dipole may be formed. In the next chapter, we will see how these types of chemical bonds affect the macroscopic properties of a material. For the remainder of this chapter, however, we briefly turn our attention to a third type of chemical bonding—the metallic bond.

19.7 Metallic Bonds

In Section 14.5 you learned about the properties of metals. They conduct electricity and heat, are opaque to light, and deform—rather than fracture—under pressure. Because of these properties, metals are used to build homes, appliances, cars, bridges, airplanes, and skyscrapers. Metal wires across the landscape transmit communication signals and electric power. We wear metal jewelry, exchange metal currency, and drink from metal cans. Yet, what is it

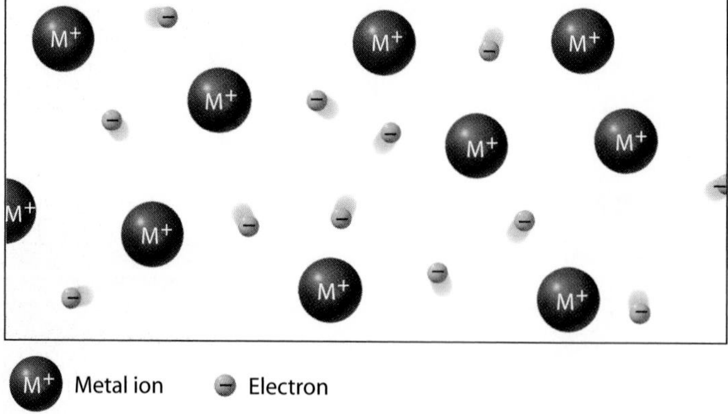

Figure 19.29
Metal ions are held together by freely flowing electrons. These loose electrons form a kind of "electronic fluid," which flows through the lattice of positively charged ions.

that gives a metal its metallic properties? We can answer this question by looking at the behavior of its atoms.

The outer shell electrons of most metal atoms tend to be weakly held to the atomic nucleus. Consequently, these electrons are easily dislodged, leaving behind positively charged metal ions. The many electrons dislodged from a large group of metal atoms flow freely through the resulting metal ions, as is depicted in Figure 19.29. This "fluid" of electrons holds the positively charged metal ions together in the type of chemical bond known as a **metallic bond.**

The mobility of electrons in a metal accounts for the metal's significant ability to conduct electricity and heat. Also, metals are opaque and shiny because the free electrons easily vibrate to the oscillations of any light falling on them, reflecting most of it. Furthermore, the metal ions are not rigidly held to fixed positions, as ions are in an ionic crystal. Rather, because the metal ions are held together by a "fluid" of electrons, these ions can move into various orientations relative to one another, which occurs when a metal is pounded, pulled, or molded into a different shape.

Two or more metals can be bonded to each other by metallic bonds. This occurs, for example, when molten gold and molten palladium are blended to form the homogeneous solution known as white gold. The quality of the white gold can be modified simply by changing the proportions of gold and palladium. White gold is an example of an **alloy,** which is any mixture composed of two or more metallic elements. By playing around with proportions, metal workers can readily modify the properties of an alloy. For example, in designing the Sacagawea dollar coin, shown in Figure 19.30, the U.S. Mint needed a metal having a gold color—so that it would be popular—and also have the same electrical characteristics as the Susan B. Anthony dollar coin—so that the new coin could substitute for the Anthony coin in vending machines.

Only a few metals—gold and platinum are two examples—appear in nature in metallic form. Deposits of these natural metals, also known as *native metals,* are quite rare. For the most part, metals found in nature are chemical compounds. Iron, for example, is most frequently found as iron oxide, Fe_2O_3, and copper is found as chalcopyrite, $CuFeS_2$. Geologic deposits containing relatively high concentrations of metal-containing compounds are called **ores.** The metals industry mines these ores from

Figure 19.30
The gold color of the Sacagawea U.S. dollar coin is achieved by an outer surface made of an alloy of 77 percent copper, 12 percent zinc, 7 percent manganese, and 4 percent nickel. The interior of the coin is pure copper.

Figure 19.31
The world's biggest open-pit mine is the copper mine at Bingham Canyon, Utah.

the ground, as shown in Figure 19.31, and then processes them into metals. Although metal-containing compounds occur just about everywhere, only ores are concentrated enough to make the extraction of the metal economical.

Metal ions bond with only five major types of negatively charged ions, shown in Figure 19.32. Consequently, metal-containing compounds are classified according to which type of negative ion they contain. Iron oxide is classified as an oxide, for instance, and chalcopyrite is classified as a sulfide.

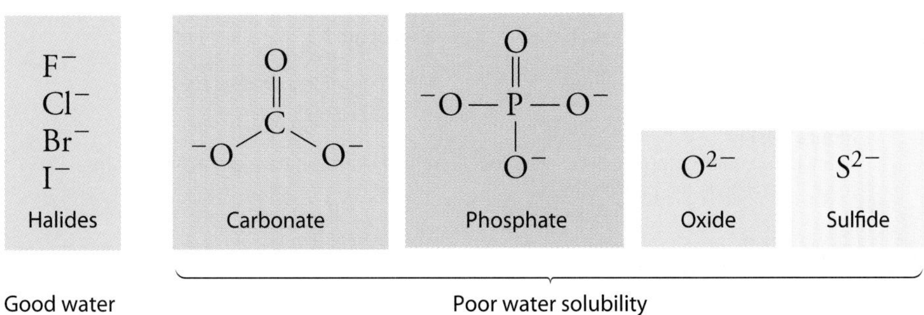

Figure 19.32
Five negatively charged ions to which positively charged metal ions bond.

Halides, such as sodium chloride and magnesium chloride, are commonly referred to as *salts,* which we shall discuss in more detail in Chapter 22. Most salts have good solubility in water and so are readily washed away by the action of either surface water or shallow groundwater. Most of these and other water-soluble metal-containing compounds therefore end up in the ocean. These compounds are recovered by evaporating seawater. Alternatively, water-soluble compounds may end up in land basins, such as the Bonneville salt flats of Utah, where they are readily mined. In some regions, such as along the Gulf of Mexico, vast deposits of halides remain undissolved hundreds of meters below the surface, because salt deposits and the surrounding rock inhibit groundwater flow. The compounds in these deposits are often very pure, which makes deep mining excavations like the one shown in Figure 19.33 worthwhile.

Figure 19.33
This deep subterranean salt deposit contains relatively pure metal-containing compounds. After the deposits are mined, the resulting caverns are very dry and thus make excellent archival storage sites for moisture-sensitive equipment or documents.

In contrast to halides, compounds containing carbonate, phosphate, oxide, or sulfide ions tend to have relatively low solubilities in water. Hence, their ores tend to stay put and are found in more diverse geologic locations.

The form in which a metal is most likely to be found in nature is a function of its position in the periodic table. Figure 19.34 shows that group 1 metals tend to be found mostly as halides, group 2 metals mostly as carbonates, and group 3 metals and lanthanides mostly as phosphates. Most metals from groups 4 to 8, along with aluminum, Al, and tin, Sn, tend to be found as oxides, and most metals from groups 9 to 15, along with molybdenum, Mo, tend to be found as sulfides.

Metal ores are ionic compounds in which the metal atoms have lost electrons to become positively charged ions. To convert the ores to metals requires that electrons be given back to the metal ions. This is done by heating the ore with electron-releasing materials, such as carbon, in hot furnaces that reach about 1500°C. The metal emerges in a molten state that can be cast into a variety of useful shapes.

Insights

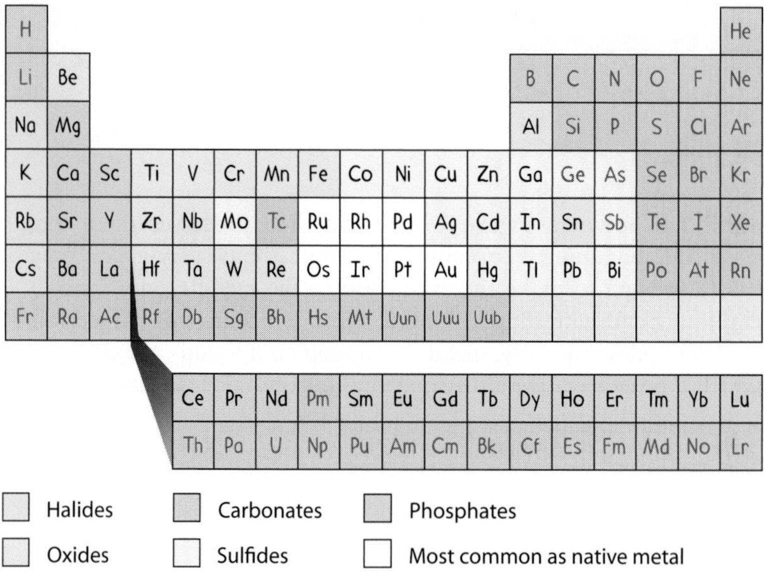

Figure 19.34
The type of metal compound a metal most commonly forms in nature is related to the metal's position in the periodic table.

☑ CHECKPOINT

According to Figure 19.34, which is more abundant in nature: iron oxide, Fe_2O_3, or iron sulfide, FeS?

Check Your Answer

Iron oxide. Figure 19.34 shows that iron is most abundant in the form of iron oxide.

We Should Conserve and Recycle Metals

Because our planet is chock-full of metal-containing compounds, it is difficult to imagine how we could ever incur a shortage of metals. Experts suggest, however, that if we continue with our present rate of consumption, such shortages will occur within the next two centuries. The problem is not a shortage of metal-containing compounds but rather a shortage of ores from which these compounds can be extracted at a reasonable cost.

Consider the recovery of gold. All the gold in the world that has been isolated from nature so far could be placed in a single cube 18 meters on a side, which would have a mass of about 130,000 tons. This includes all the naturally occurring elemental gold we have mined plus all the gold purified from gold-containing ores. Because the rate of gold production is steadily decreasing, one might think we have already isolated a significant portion of the earth's total gold reserves. Our oceans, however, are laden with gold—as much as 2 milligrams per ton of seawater. Given that there are about 1.5×10^{18} tons of seawater on the planet, our oceans contain 3.4 billion tons of gold! As yet, however, no method has been found for recovering gold from seawater profitably—this gold is simply too dilute (Figure 19.35). Like the gold in the ocean, most of the metal-containing compounds in the earth's crust are finely mixed with other stuff, which is to say the compounds are diluted. Ores are, by definition, parts of the earth's crust where, for geological reasons, the compounds have been concentrated. High-grade ores, those containing relatively large concentrations of compounds, are the first to be mined. After these are depleted, we move on to lower-grade ores, which have lower yields that translate into greater costs. Eventually, a nation's ore supplies are depleted, as have been the aluminum oxide ores in the United States, as noted in Figure 19.36, and the nation is forced to import metals or their ores from other countries, which also have finite ore resources.

Figure 19.35
Natural resources are unavailable to us when the energy required to collect them far exceeds their inherent value. For example, most of the world's gold is found in the oceans, but this gold is too dilute for worthwhile extraction.

Figure 19.36
An open-pit aluminum mine in Australia. Aluminum ore is no longer mined in the United States because the reserves of the ore have dwindled to the point where it is less expensive to import high-grade aluminum ore from other countries, including Australia.

We should conserve and recycle metals whenever possible because it is often far cheaper to produce metals from recycled products than from ore. Environmentally sound exploration of new reserves is also required. Ore nodules discovered on the ocean floor, for example, contain as much as 24 percent manganese and 14 percent iron. Significant quantities of copper, nickel, and cobalt have also been found in this submarine terrain. Perhaps mining of the ocean floor may one day replace the mining we now do on land. And in the not too distant future, perhaps the mining of metal-rich asteroids in space will become a reality.

Summary of Terms

Valence shell The outermost occupied shell of an atom.

Electron-dot structure A shorthand notation of the shell model of the atom, in which valence electrons are shown around an atomic symbol.

Nonbonding pairs Two paired valence electrons that tend not to participate in a chemical bond.

Ion An electrically charged particle created when an atom either loses or gains one or more electrons.

Polyatomic ion An ionically charged molecule.

Ionic bond A chemical bond in which an attractive electric force holds ions of opposite charge together.

Ionic compound Any chemical compound containing ions.

Covalent bond A chemical bond in which atoms are held together by their mutual attraction for two or more electrons they share.

Covalent compound An element or chemical compound in which atoms are held together by covalent bonds.

Molecule A group of atoms held tightly together by covalent bonds.

Dipole A separation of charge that occurs in a chemical bond because of differences in the electronegativities of the bonded atoms.

Electronegativity The ability of an atom to attract a bonding pair of electrons to itself when bonded to another atom.

Nonpolar Said of a chemical bond that has no dipole.

Polar Said of a chemical bond that has a dipole.

Review Questions

19.1 Electron-Dot Structures

1. How many shells are needed to account for the seven periods of the periodic table?
2. How many electrons can occupy the first shell? How many can occupy the second shell?
3. How many shells are completely filled in an argon atom, Ar (atomic number 18)?
4. Which electrons are represented by an electron-dot structure?
5. How do the electron-dot structures of elements in the same group in the periodic table compare with one another?
6. How many nonbonding pairs are there in the valence shell of an oxygen atom? How many unpaired valence electrons?

19.2 The Formation of Ions

7. How does an ion differ from an atom?
8. To become a negative ion, does an atom lose or gain electrons?
9. Do metals more readily gain or lose electrons?
10. How many electrons does the calcium atom tend to lose?
11. Why does the fluorine atom tend to gain only one electron?
12. What do molecules lose or gain to become polyatomic ions?

19.3 Ionic Bonds

13. Which elements tend to form ionic bonds?
14. Is an ionic compound an example of a chemical compound, or is a chemical compound an example of an ionic compound?
15. What is the electric charge on the calcium ion in calcium chloride, $CaCl_2$?
16. What is the electric charge on the calcium ion in calcium oxide, CaO?
17. Suppose an oxygen atom gains two electrons to become an oxygen ion. What is its electric charge?
18. What is an ionic crystal?

19.4 Covalent Bonds

19. Which elements tend to form covalent bonds?
20. What force holds two atoms together in a covalent bond?
21. How many electrons are shared in a double covalent bond?
22. How many electrons are shared in a triple covalent bond?
23. How many valence electrons is an oxygen atom able to attract from other atoms?
24. How many covalent bonds is an oxygen atom able to form?

19.5 Polar Covalent Bonds

25. What is a dipole?
26. Which element in the periodic table has the greatest electronegativity? Which has the least electronegativity?
27. Which is more polar: a carbon–oxygen bond or a carbon–nitrogen bond?
28. How is a polar covalent bond similar to an ionic bond?

19.6 Molecular Polarity

29. How can a molecule be nonpolar when it consists of atoms that have different electronegativities?
30. Why do nonpolar substances boil at relatively low temperatures?
31. Which has a greater degree of symmetry: a polar molecule or a nonpolar molecule?
32. Why don't oil and water mix?
33. Which would you describe as "stickier": a polar molecule or a nonpolar one?

19.7 Metallic Bonds

34. How well do metal atoms hold onto their outer shell electrons?

35. What are the five types of negatively charged ions found in metal-containing compounds?
36. Which metal-containing compounds are most soluble in water?

Activities

Up Close with Crystals

View crystals of table salt with a magnifying glass or, better yet, a microscope if one is available. If you do have a microscope, crush the crystals with a spoon and examine the resulting powder. Purchase some sodium-free salt, which is potassium chloride, KCl, and examine these ionic crystals, both intact and crushed. Sodium chloride and potassium chloride both form cubic crystals, but there are significant differences. What are they?

Gumdrop Molecules

Use toothpicks and gumdrops or jelly beans of different colors to build models of the molecules shown below. Choose different colors to represent different elements. Keep in mind that each carbon atom must have four covalent bonds, each oxygen must have two, and each fluorine and hydrogen must have only one. Which should be polar? Which should be nonpolar?

Difluoromethane, CH_2F_2, tetrahedron

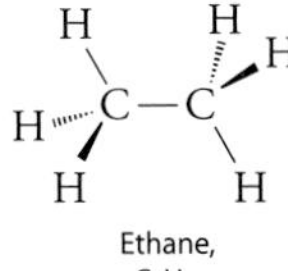

Ethane, C_2H_6, two tetrahedrons

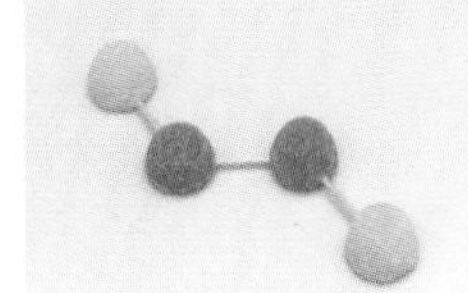

Hydrogen peroxide, H_2O_2, two bent shapes stuck together

H—C≡C—H

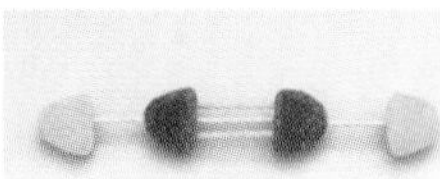

Acetylene, C_2H_2, linear

Exercises

1. An atom loses an electron to another atom. Is this an example of a physical change or a chemical change?
2. Why is it so easy for a magnesium atom to lose two electrons?
3. Why doesn't the sodium atom gain seven electrons so that its third shell becomes the filled outermost occupied shell?
4. Magnesium ions carry a 2+ charge, and chloride ions carry a 1− charge. What is the chemical formula for the ionic compound magnesium chloride?
5. Barium ions carry a 2+ charge, and nitrogen ions carry a 3− charge. What is the chemical formula for the ionic compound barium nitride?
6. Does an ionic bond have a dipole? Defend your answer.
7. What prevents a neon atom from gaining electrons?
8. What prevents a neon atom from losing electrons?
9. Why doesn't a hydrogen atom form more than one covalent bond?
10. What drives an atom to form a covalent bond: its nuclear charge or the need to have a filled valence shell? Explain.
11. Is there an abrupt change or a gradual change between ionic and covalent bonds? Explain.
12. Classify the following bonds as ionic, polar covalent, or nonpolar covalent (O, atomic number 8; F, atomic number 9; Na, atomic number 11; Cl, atomic number 17; Ca, atomic number 20; U, atomic number 92):
    O with F ____________
    Ca with Cl ____________
    Na with Na ____________
    U with Cl ____________
13. Atoms of nonmetallic elements form covalent bonds, but they can also form ionic bonds. How is this possible?
14. Atoms of metallic elements can form ionic bonds, but they are not very good at forming covalent bonds. Why?
15. Phosphine is a covalent compound of phosphorus, P, and hydrogen, H. What is its chemical formula?
16. What is the source of an atom's electronegativity?
17. Which bond is most polar: H–N, N–C, C–O, C–C, O–H, C–H?
18. Which molecule is most polar: S=C=S, O=C=O, O=C=S?
19. In each molecule, which atom carries the greater positive charge: H–Cl, Br–F, C≡O, Br–Br?

20. List the following bonds in order of increasing polarity: N–N, N–F, N–O, H–F

    ______, ______, ______, ______
    (least polar)   (most polar)
21. Which is more polar: a sulfur–bromine bond, S–Br, or a selenium–chlorine bond, Se–Cl?
22. Water, H_2O, and methane, CH_4, have about the same mass and differ by only one type of atom. Why is the boiling point of water so much higher than that of methane?
23. An individual carbon–oxygen bond is polar. Yet carbon dioxide, CO_2, which has two carbon–oxygen bonds, is nonpolar. Explain.
24. In each pair, which compound probably has the higher boiling point? (The atomic numbers of the atoms are: Cl, 17; S, 16; O, 8; C, 6; H, 1.)

```
      Cl    Cl     H     Cl
        \  /        \   /
(a)     C=C          C=C
       /   \        /   \
      H     H     Cl     H

(b) S=C=O         O=C=O

      Cl          Cl     H
        \           \   /
(c)     C=O          C=C
       /            /   \
      Cl          Cl     H
```

25. Why is ammonia, NH_3, more polar than borane, BH_3?
26. Why are ores so valuable?
27. Can only group 1 elements form halides? Explain.
28. Distinguish between a metal and a metal-containing compound.
29. How can we have shortages of the metals we need to run our society, when the planet is essentially made of metals?
30. Why is it so difficult to extract gold from ocean water?

Chapter 19 Online Resources

Tutorials

- Bonds & Bond Polarity
- Covalent Bonds
- Polar Attraction

Quiz
Exercises
Flashcards
Links

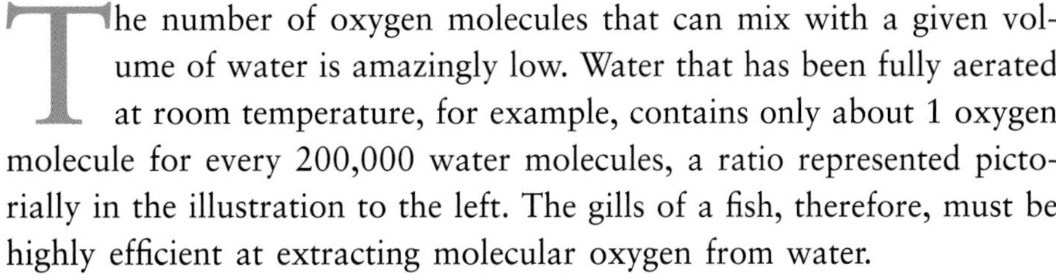

CHAPTER 20

Molecular Attractions

The number of oxygen molecules that can mix with a given volume of water is amazingly low. Water that has been fully aerated at room temperature, for example, contains only about 1 oxygen molecule for every 200,000 water molecules, a ratio represented pictorially in the illustration to the left. The gills of a fish, therefore, must be highly efficient at extracting molecular oxygen from water.

This chapter explains how physical properties of materials are a consequence of attractions among the submicroscopic particles making up the materials. Why only small amounts of oxygen can mix with water, for example, is explained by the weakness of the attractive forces between water molecules and oxygen molecules. We will begin by looking at four types of electrical attractions that take place between submicroscopic particles.

20.1 Types of Attractions

We can think of any pure substance as being made up of a single type of submicroscopic particle. For an ionic compound, that particle is an *ion;* for a covalent compound, it is a *molecule;* and for an element, it is an *atom.*

Table 20.1 lists four types of electrical attractions that can occur between these particles. The strength of even the strongest of these attractions is many times weaker than any chemical bond. The attraction between two adjacent water molecules, for example, is only about one-twentieth as strong as the chemical bonds holding the hydrogen and oxygen atoms together in the water molecules. Although particle-to-particle attractions are relatively weak, their profound effect can be seen on the substances around you.

We will now explore these interparticle attractions in order of relative strength, beginning with the strongest.

Table 20.1

Electrical Attractions Between Submicroscopic Particles

Attraction	Relative Strength
Ion–dipole	Strongest
Dipole–dipole	
Dipole–induced dipole	
Induced dipole–induced dipole	Weakest

Ions and Polar Molecules Attract One Another

Recall, from the previous chapter, that a *polar* molecule is one in which the bonding electrons are unevenly distributed. One side of the molecule carries a slight negative charge, and the opposite side carries a slight positive charge. This separation of charge makes up a *dipole.*

So what happens to polar molecules, such as water molecules, when they are near an ionic compound, such as sodium chloride? The opposite charges electrically attract one another. A positive sodium ion attracts the negative side of a water molecule, and a negative chloride ion attracts the positive side of a water molecule. This phenomenon is illustrated in Figure 20.1. Such an attraction between an ion and the dipole of a polar molecule is called an *ion–dipole* attraction.

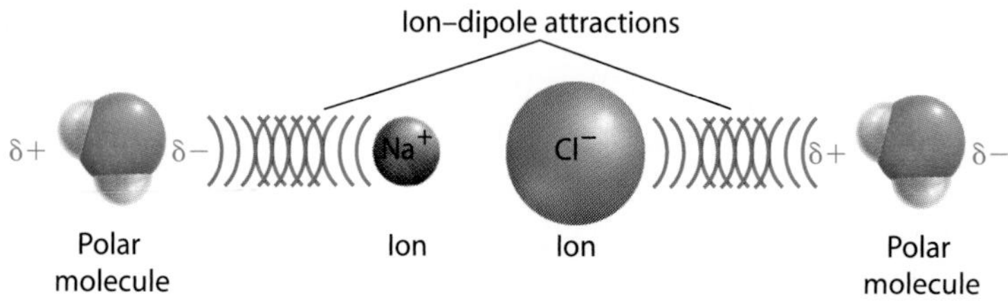

Figure 20.1
Electrical attractions are shown as a series of overlapping arcs. The blue arcs indicate negative charge, and the red arcs indicate positive charge.

A water molecule is a natural dipole—a bit positive on one end and negative on the other. What's the net charge of a dipole?

Insights

Ion–dipole attractions are much weaker than ionic bonds. However, a large number of ion–dipole attractions can act collectively to disrupt ionic bonds. This is what happens to sodium chloride in water. Attractions exerted by the water molecules break the ionic bonds and pull the ions away from one another. The result, represented in Figure 20.2, is a solution of sodium chloride in water. (A solution in water is called an *aqueous solution.*)

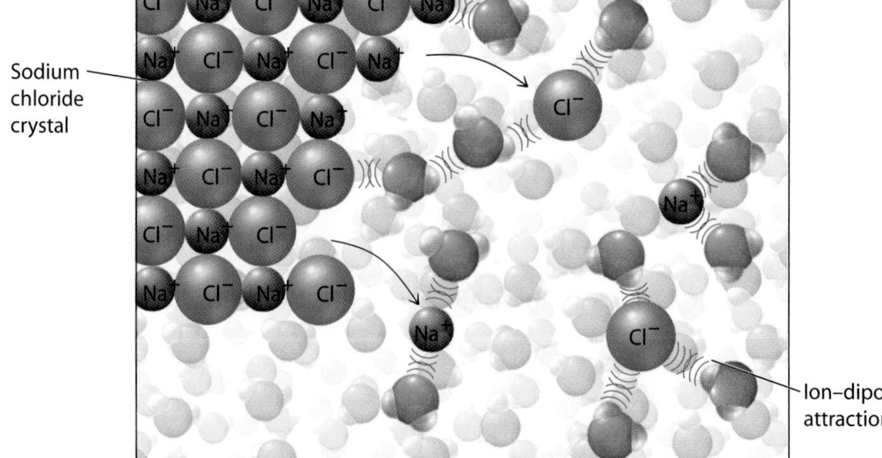

Figure 20.2
Sodium and chloride ions tightly bound in a crystal lattice are separated from one another by the collective attraction exerted by many water molecules to form an aqueous solution of sodium chloride.

Polar Molecules Attract Other Polar Molecules

An attraction between two polar molecules is called a *dipole–dipole* attraction. An unusually strong dipole–dipole attraction is the **hydrogen bond.** This attraction occurs between molecules that have a hydrogen atom covalently bonded to a highly electronegative atom, usually nitrogen, oxygen, or fluorine. Recall, from Chapter 19, that the electronegativity of an atom describes how well that atom is able to pull bonding electrons toward itself. The greater the atom's electronegativity, the better it is able to gain electrons and thus the more negative is its charge.

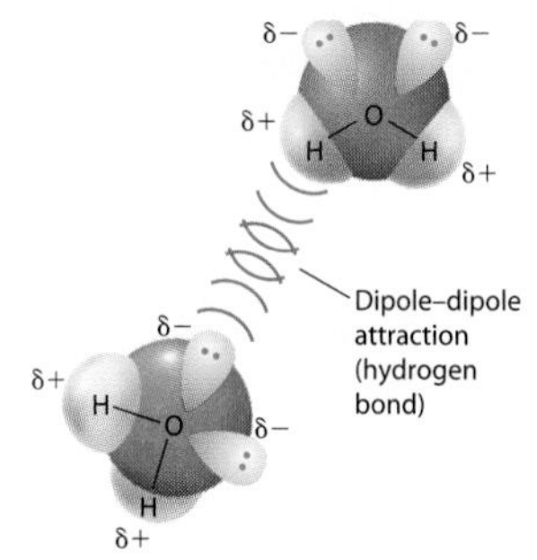

Figure 20.3
The dipole–dipole attraction between two water molecules is a hydrogen bond because it involves hydrogen atoms bonded to highly electronegative oxygen atoms.

Look at Figure 20.3 to see how hydrogen bonding works. The hydrogen side of a polar molecule (water, in this example) has a positive charge because the more electronegative oxygen atom the hydrogen is bonded to tugs on the hydrogen's electron. This hydrogen is therefore electrically attracted to a pair of nonbonding electrons on the negatively charged atom of another molecule (in this case, another water molecule). This mutual attraction between hydrogen and the negatively charged atom of another molecule is a hydrogen bond.

The strength of a hydrogen bond depends on two things: (1) the strength of the dipoles involved (thus, it depends on the difference in electronegativity of the atoms in the polar molecules), and (2) how strongly the nonbonding electrons on one molecule can attract a hydrogen atom on a nearby molecule.

Even though the hydrogen bond is much weaker than any covalent or ionic bond, the effects of hydrogen bonding can be very pronounced. For example, water owes many of its properties to hydrogen bonds. The hydrogen bond is also of great importance in the chemistry of the large molecules, such as DNA and proteins, that are found in living organisms.

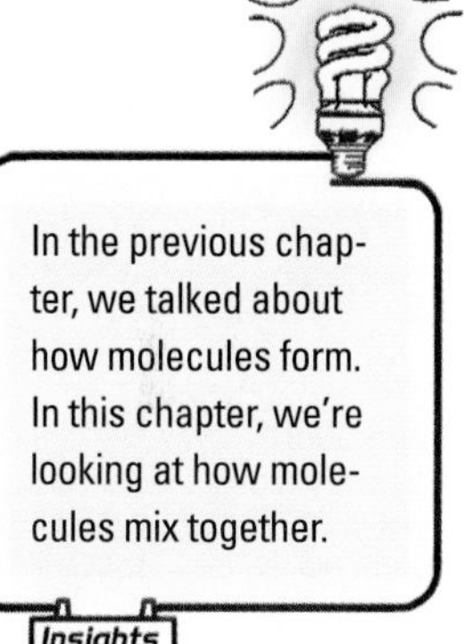

Polar Molecules Can Induce Dipoles in Nonpolar Molecules

In many molecules, the electrons are distributed evenly, and so there is no dipole. The oxygen molecule, O_2, is an example. Such a nonpolar molecule can be induced to become a temporary dipole, however, when it is brought close to a water molecule (or to any other polar molecule), as Figure 20.4 illustrates. The slightly negative side of the water molecule pushes the electrons in the oxygen molecule away. Thus, the oxygen molecule's electrons are pushed to the side that is farthest from the water molecule. The result is a temporarily uneven distribution of electrons called an **induced dipole.** The resulting attraction between the permanent dipole (water) and the induced dipole (oxygen) is a *dipole–induced dipole* attraction.

☑ CHECKPOINT

How does the electron distribution in an oxygen molecule change when the hydrogen side of a water molecule is nearby?

Check Your Answer

Because the hydrogen side of the water molecule is slightly positive, the electrons in the oxygen molecule are pulled toward the water molecule, inducing in the oxygen molecule a temporary dipole in which the larger side is nearest the water molecule (rather than as far away as possible as it was in Figure 20.4).

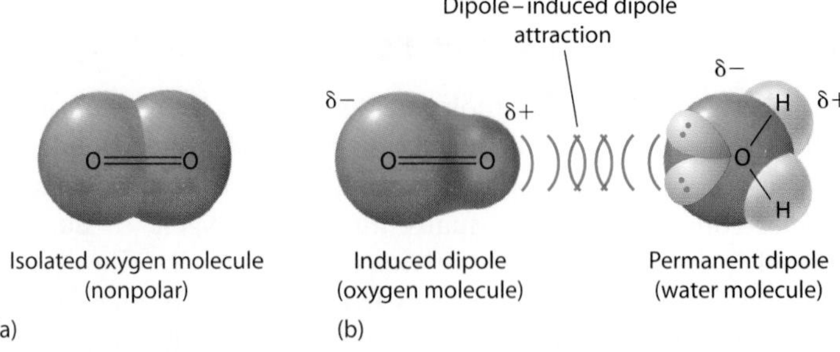

Figure 20.4
(a) An isolated oxygen molecule has no dipole; its electrons are distributed evenly. (b) An adjacent water molecule induces a redistribution of electrons in the oxygen molecule. (The slightly negative side of the oxygen molecule is shown larger than the slightly positive side because the slightly negative side contains more electrons.)

Remember, induced dipoles are only temporary. If the water molecule in Figure 20.4b were removed, the oxygen molecule would return to its normal, nonpolar state. As a consequence, dipole–induced dipole attractions are weaker than dipole–dipole attractions. But dipole–induced dipole attractions are strong enough to hold relatively small quantities of oxygen dissolved in water. As indicated in this chapter's introductory paragraph, this attraction between water and molecular oxygen is vital for fish and other forms of aquatic life that rely on molecular oxygen dissolved in water.

Figure 20.5
Temporary dipoles induced in the normally nonpolar molecules in plastic wrap make it stick to glass.

Dipole–induced dipole attractions also occur between molecules of carbon dioxide, which are nonpolar, and water. It is these attractions that help to keep carbonated beverages (which are largely mixtures of carbon dioxide in water) from losing their fizz too quickly after they've been opened. Dipole–induced dipole attractions are also responsible for holding plastic wrap to glass, as shown in Figure 20.5. These wraps are made of very long nonpolar molecules that are induced to have dipoles when placed in contact with glass, which is highly polar. As we will discuss next, the molecules of a nonpolar material, such as plastic wrap, can also induce dipoles among themselves. This explains why plastic wrap sticks not only to polar materials such as glass but also to itself.

☑ CHECKPOINT

Distinguish between a dipole–dipole attraction and a dipole–induced dipole attraction.

Check Your Answer

The dipole–dipole attraction is stronger and involves two permanent dipoles. The dipole–induced dipole attraction is weaker and involves a permanent dipole and a temporary one.

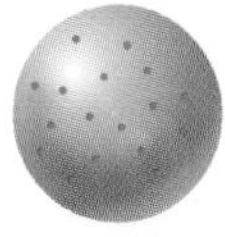
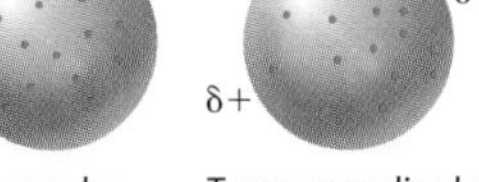

Figure 20.6
The electron distribution in an atom is normally even. At any given moment, however, the electron distribution may be somewhat uneven, resulting in a temporary dipole.

Atoms and Nonpolar Molecules Can Form Temporary Dipoles

Individual atoms and nonpolar molecules, on average, have a fairly even distribution of electrons. Because of the randomness of electron motion, however, at any given moment the electrons in an atom or a nonpolar molecule may be bunched to one side. The result is a temporary dipole, as shown in Figure 20.6.

Just as the permanent dipole of a polar molecule can induce a dipole in a nonpolar molecule, a temporary dipole can do the same thing. This gives rise to the weakest of the particle-to-particle attractions: the *induced dipole–induced dipole* attraction, illustrated in Figure 20.7.

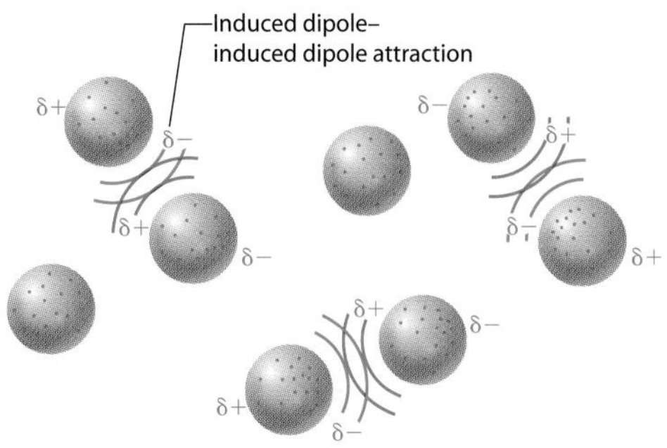

Figure 20.7
Because the normally even distribution of electrons in atoms can momentarily become uneven, atoms can be attracted to one another through induced dipole–induced dipole attractions.

> As an analogy for the temporary dipole, consider a party of people on a boat. They may move about randomly on the deck, but, at any given moment, there may be more people on one side of the boat than the other. As a result, the boat tips slightly to one side.
>
> **Insights**

Temporary dipoles are more significant for larger atoms. This is because the electrons in larger atoms have more space available for random motion and a greater likelihood of bunching together on one side. The electrons in smaller atoms are less able to bunch to one side because they are confined to a smaller space. The resulting greater electrical repulsion tends to keep these electrons evenly spread out. So it is larger atoms—and molecules made of larger atoms—that have the strongest induced dipole–induced dipole attractions.

As shown in Figure 20.8, nonpolar iodine molecules, I_2, are relatively large. Because of this, they have a greater attraction for one another than do relatively small nonpolar fluorine molecules, F_2. This explains why iodine molecules stick together as a solid at room temperature but fluorine molecules at the same temperature drift apart into the gaseous phase.

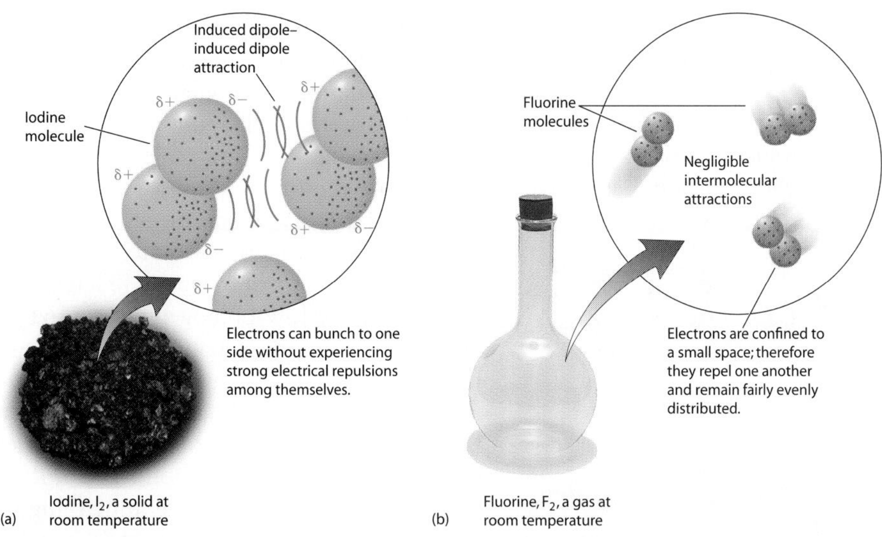

Figure 20.8
(a) Temporary dipoles more readily form in larger atoms, such as those in an iodine molecule, because, in larger atoms, electrons bunched to one side are still relatively far apart from one another and not so repelled by the electric force. (b) In smaller atoms, such as those in a fluorine molecule, electrons cannot bunch to one side as well because the repulsive electric force increases as the electrons bunch closer.

Figure 20.9
Few things stick to Teflon because of the high proportion of fluorine atoms that it contains. The structure depicted here is only a portion of the full length of the molecule.

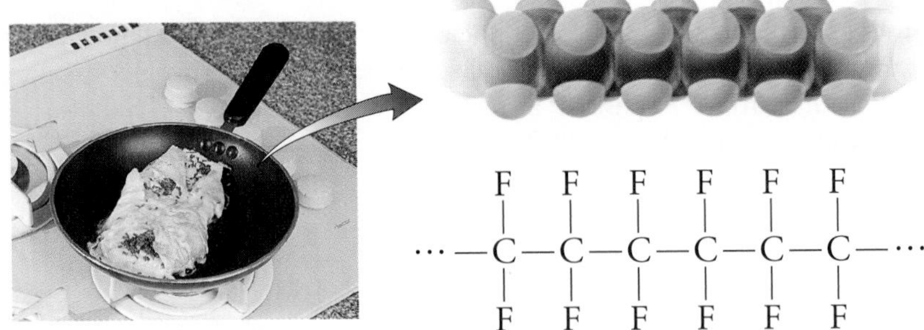

Fluorine is one of the smallest atoms, and nonpolar molecules made with fluorine atoms exhibit only very weak induced dipole–induced dipole attractions. This is the principle behind the Teflon nonstick surface. The Teflon molecule, part of which is shown in Figure 20.9, is a long chain of carbon atoms chemically bonded to fluorine atoms, and the fluorine atoms exert essentially no attractions on any material in contact with the Teflon surface—scrambled eggs in a frying pan, for instance.

☑ CHECKPOINT

What is the distinction between a dipole–induced dipole attraction and an induced dipole–induced dipole attraction.

Check Your Answer

The dipole–induced dipole attraction is stronger and involves a permanent dipole and a temporary one. The induced dipole–induced dipole attraction is weaker and involves two temporary dipoles.

Figure 20.10
(a) Two nonpolar methane molecules are attracted to each other by induced dipole–induced dipole attractions, but there is only one attraction per molecule. (b) Two nonpolar octane molecules are similar to methane, but they are longer. The number of induced dipole–induced dipole attractions between these two molecules is therefore greater.

Induced dipole–induced dipole attractions help explain why natural gas is a gas at room temperature but gasoline is a liquid. The major component of natural gas is methane, CH_4, and one of the major components of gasoline is octane, C_8H_{18}. We can see, in Figure 20.10, that the number of induced dipole–induced dipole attractions between two methane molecules is appreciably less than the number between two octane molecules. You know that two small pieces of Velcro are easier to pull apart than two long pieces. Like short pieces of Velcro, methane molecules can be pulled apart with little effort. That's why methane has a low boiling point, −161°C, and is a gas at room temperature. Octane molecules, like long strips of Velcro, are relatively difficult to pull apart because of the larger number of induced dipole–induced dipole attractions. The boiling point of octane, 125°C, is therefore much higher than that of methane, and octane is a liquid at room temperature. (The greater mass of octane also plays a role in making its boiling point higher.)

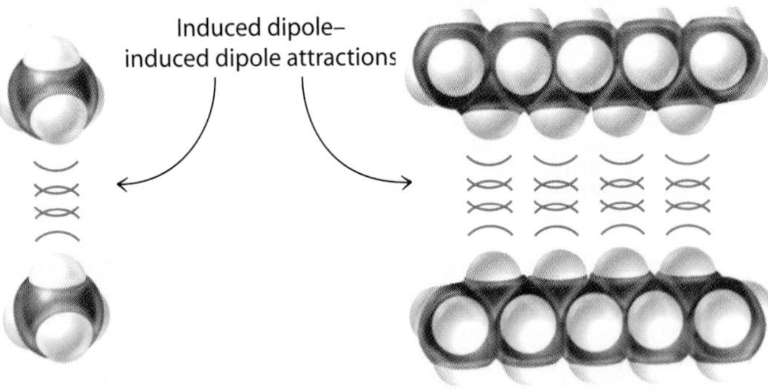

☑ **CHECKPOINT**

Methanol, CH_3OH, which can be used as a fuel, is not much larger than methane, CH_4, but it is a liquid at room temperature. Suggest why.

Check Your Answer

The polar oxygen–hydrogen covalent bond in each methanol molecule leads to hydrogen bonding between molecules. These relatively strong interparticle attractions hold methanol molecules together as a liquid at room temperature.

20.2 Solubility

The **solubility** of a solute is its *ability* to dissolve in a solvent. As can be expected, this ability mainly depends on the submicroscopic attractions between solute particles and solvent particles. If a solute has any appreciable solubility in a solvent, then that solute is said to be **soluble** in that solvent.

Solubility also depends on attractions of solute particles for one another and attractions of solvent particles for one another. As shown in Figure 20.11, for example, there are many polar hydrogen–oxygen bonds in a sucrose molecule. Sucrose molecules, therefore, can form multiple hydrogen bonds with one another. These hydrogen bonds are strong enough to make sucrose a solid at room temperature and to give it the relatively high melting point of 185°C. In order for sucrose to dissolve in water, the water molecules must first pull sucrose molecules away from one another. This puts a limit on the amount of sucrose that can dissolve in water—eventually, a point is reached at which there are not enough water molecules to separate the sucrose molecules from one another. As we discussed in Section 18.3, this is the point of saturation, and any additional sucrose added to the solution does not dissolve.

When the molecule-to-molecule attractions among solute molecules are comparable to the molecule-to-molecule attractions among solvent molecules,

Sucrose

Figure 20.11
A sucrose molecule contains many hydrogen–oxygen covalent bonds, in which the hydrogen atoms are slightly positive and the oxygen atoms are slightly negative. These dipoles in any given sucrose molecule result in the formation of hydrogen bonds with neighboring sucrose molecules.

there is no practical point of saturation. As shown in Figure 20.12, for example, the hydrogen bonds among water molecules are about as strong as those between ethanol molecules. These two liquids therefore mix together quite well and in just about any proportion. We can even add ethanol to water until the ethanol, rather than the water, can be considered the solvent.

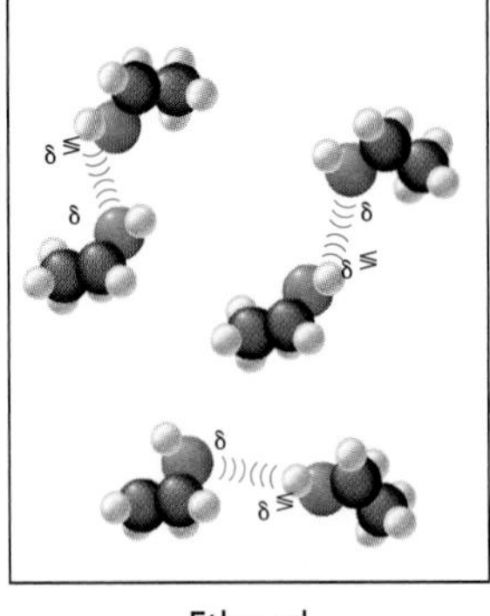

Ethanol

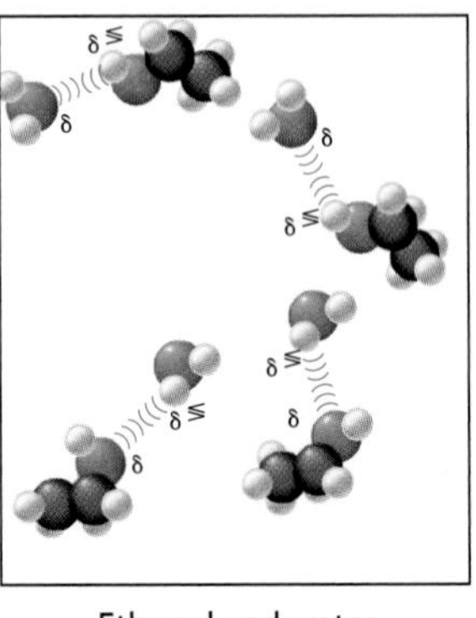

Ethanol and water

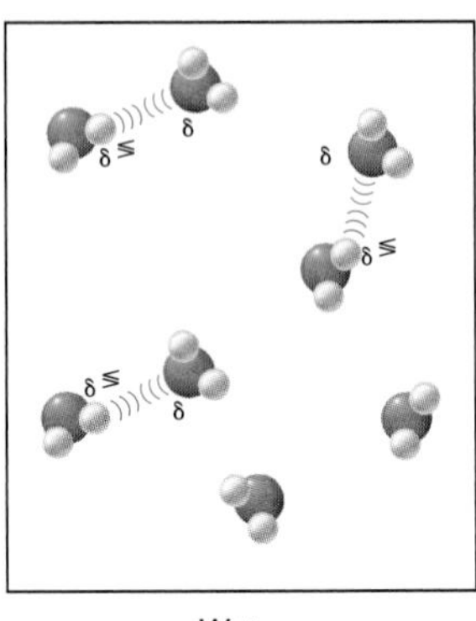

Water

Figure 20.12
Ethanol and water molecules are about the same size, and they both form hydrogen bonds. As a result, ethanol and water will readily mix with each other.

Grease is soluble in paint thinner, which is why paint thinner can be used to clean one's hands of grease. But body oils are also soluble in paint thinner, which is why hands cleaned with paint thinner feel dry and chapped.

Insights

A solute that has no practical point of saturation in a given solvent is said to be *infinitely soluble* in that solvent. Ethanol, for example, is infinitely soluble in water. Also, all gases are generally infinitely soluble in other gases because they can be mixed together in just about any proportion.

Let's now look at the other extreme of solubility, where a solute has very little solubility in a given solvent. An example is oxygen, O_2, in water. In contrast to sucrose, which has a solubility of 200 grams per 100 milliliters of water, only 0.004 gram of oxygen can dissolve in 100 milliliters of water. We can account for oxygen's low solubility in water by noting that the only electrical attractions that occur between oxygen molecules and water molecules are relatively weak dipole–induced dipole attractions. More important, however, is the fact that the stronger attraction of water molecules for one another—through the hydrogen bonds that the water molecules form with one another—effectively excludes oxygen molecules from intermingling.

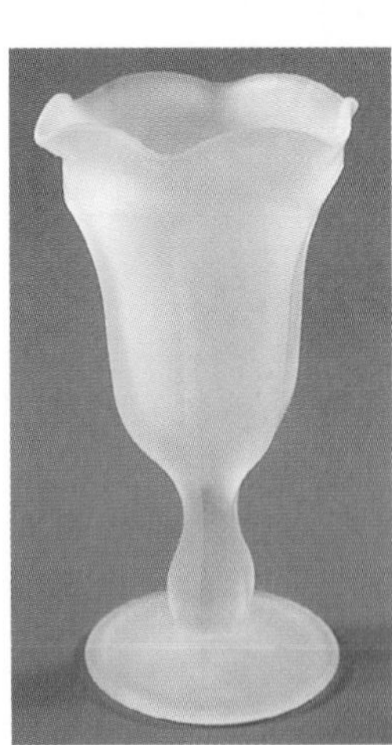

Figure 20.13
Glass is frosted by dissolving its outer surface in hydrofluoric acid.

A material that does not dissolve in a solvent to any appreciable extent is said to be **insoluble** in that solvent. There are many substances we consider to be insoluble in water, including sand and glass. Just because a material is not soluble in one solvent, however, does not mean it won't dissolve in another. Sand and glass, for example, are soluble in hydrofluoric acid, HF, which is used to give glass the decorative frosted look shown in Figure 20.13. Also, although Styrofoam is insoluble in water, it is soluble in acetone, a solvent used in fingernail-polish remover. Pour a little acetone into a Styrofoam cup, and the acetone soon dissolves the Styrofoam, as demonstrated in Figure 20.14.

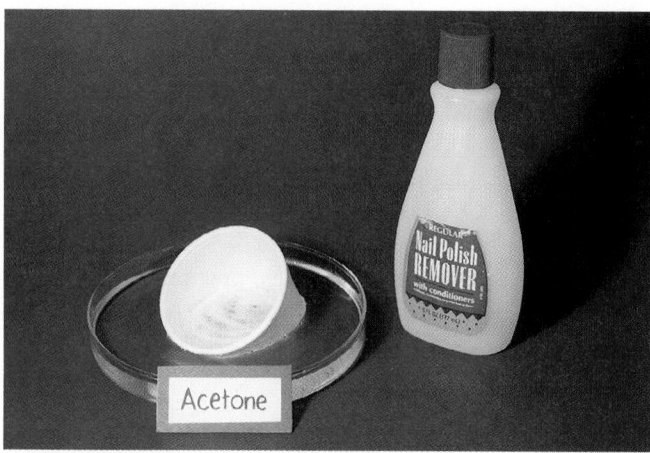

Figure 20.14
Is this cup melting or dissolving?

☑ CHECKPOINT

Why isn't sucrose infinitely soluble in water?

Check Your Answer

The attraction between two sucrose molecules is much stronger than the attraction between a sucrose molecule and a water molecule. Because of this, sucrose dissolves in water only so long as the number of water molecules far exceeds the number of sucrose molecules. When there are too few water molecules to dissolve any additional sucrose, the solution is saturated.

Solubility Changes with Temperature

You probably know from experience that water-soluble solids usually dissolve better in hot water than in cold water. A highly concentrated solution of sucrose in water, for example, can be made by heating the solution almost to the boiling point. This is how syrups and hard candy are made.

Solubility increases with increasing temperature because hot water molecules have greater kinetic energy and therefore are able to collide with the solid solute more vigorously. The vigorous collisions facilitate the disruption of electrical particle-to-particle attractions in the solid.

Although the solubilities of some solid solutes—sucrose, to name just one example—are greatly affected by temperature changes, the solubilities of other solid solutes, such as sodium chloride, are only mildly affected, as Figure 20.15 shows. This difference involves a number of factors, including the strength of the chemical bonds in the solute molecules and the way those molecules are packed together.

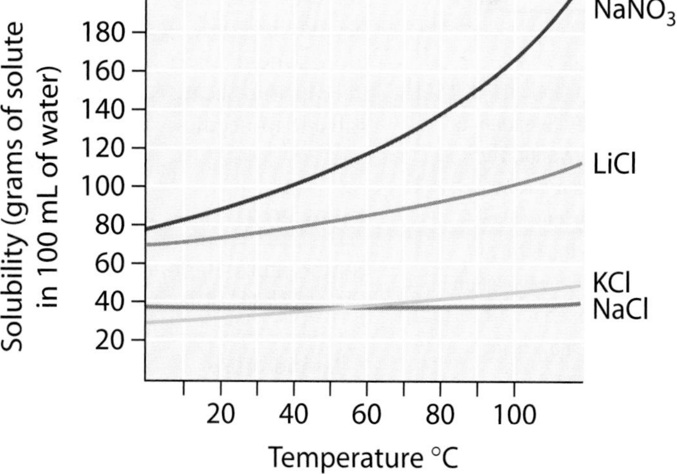

Figure 20.15
The solubility of many water-soluble solids increases with temperature, while the solubility of others is only very slightly affected by temperature.

When a solution saturated at a high temperature is allowed to cool, some of the solute usually comes out of solution and forms what is called a **precipitate.** When this occurs, the solute is said to have *precipitated* from the solution. For example, at 100°C, the solubility of sodium nitrate, $NaNO_3$, in water is 165 grams per 100 milliliters of water. As we cool this solution, the solubility of $NaNO_3$ decreases, as shown in Figure 20.16, and this change in solubility causes some of the dissolved $NaNO_3$ to precipitate (come out of solution). At 20°C, the solubility of $NaNO_3$ is only 87 grams per 100 milliliters of water. So, if we cool the 100°C solution to 20°C, 78 grams (165 grams − 87 grams) precipitates, as shown in Figure 20.16.

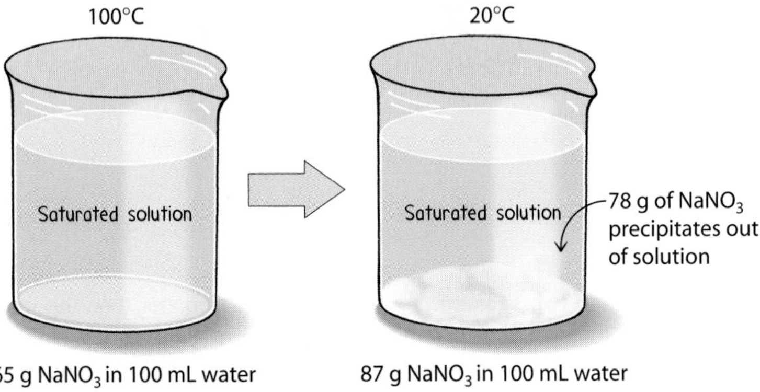

Figure 20.16
The solubility of sodium nitrate is 165 grams per 100 milliliters of water at 100°C but only 87 grams per 100 milliliters at 20°C. Cooling a 100°C saturated solution of $NaNO_3$ to 20°C causes 78 grams of the solute to precipitate.

Gases Are More Soluble at Low Temperatures and High Pressures

In contrast to the solubilities of most solids, the solubilities of gases in liquids *decrease* with increasing temperature, as Table 20.2 shows below. This effect occurs because, with an increase in temperature, the solvent molecules have more kinetic energy. This makes it more difficult for a gaseous solute to remain in solution because the solute molecules are literally ejected by the high-energy solvent molecules.

Air is a gaseous solution, and one of its minor components is water vapor. The process of this water coming "out of solution" in the form of rain or snow is called "precipitation." The rain or snow is the "precipitate."

Insights

Table 20.2

Temperature-Dependent Solubility of Oxygen Gas in Water at a Pressure of 1 Atmosphere

Temperature (°C)	O_2 Solubility ($g\ O_2/L\ H_2O$)
0	0.0141
10	0.0109
20	0.0092
25	0.0083
30	0.0077
35	0.0070
40	0.0065

Perhaps you have noticed that warm carbonated beverages go flat faster than cold ones. The higher temperature causes the molecules of carbon dioxide gas to leave the liquid solvent at a higher rate.

The solubility of a gas in a liquid also depends on the pressure of the gas immediately above the liquid. In general, a higher gas pressure above the liquid means more of the gas dissolves. A gas at a high pressure has many, many gas particles crammed into a given volume. The "empty" space in an unopened soft drink bottle, for example, is crammed with carbon dioxide molecules in the gaseous phase. With nowhere else to go, many of these molecules dissolve in the liquid, as shown in Figure 20.17. Alternatively, we might say that the great pressure forces the carbon dioxide molecules into solution. When the bottle is opened, the "head" of highly pressurized carbon dioxide gas escapes. Now the gas pressure above the liquid is lower than before. As a result, the solubility of the carbon dioxide drops, and the carbon dioxide molecules that were once squeezed into the solution begin to escape into the air above the liquid.

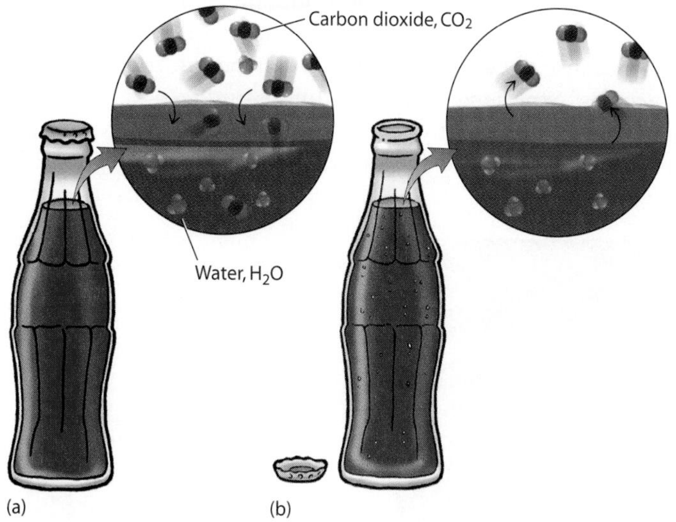

Figure 20.17
(a) The carbon dioxide gas above the liquid in an unopened soft drink bottle consists of many tightly packed carbon dioxide molecules that are forced by pressure into solution. (b) When the bottle is opened, the pressure is released, and carbon dioxide molecules originally dissolved in the liquid can escape into the air.

The rate at which carbon dioxide molecules leave an opened soft drink is relatively slow. You can increase the rate by pouring in granulated sugar, salt, or sand. The microscopic nooks and crannies on the surfaces of the grains serve as *nucleation sites* where carbon dioxide bubbles are able to form rapidly and then to escape by buoyant forces. Shaking the beverage also increases the surface area of the liquid-to-gas interface, making it easier for the carbon dioxide to escape from the solution. Once the solution is shaken, the rate at which carbon dioxide escapes becomes so great that the beverage froths over. You also increase the rate at which carbon dioxide escapes when you pour the beverage into your mouth, which abounds in nucleation sites. You can feel the resulting tingly sensation.

It is not just dipole–induced dipole attractions that keep carbon dioxide dissolved within water. As we'll discuss in Chapter 22, carbon dioxide reacts with water to form carbonic acid, which is much more soluble in water. When a can of carbonated soda is opened, much of this carbonic acid quickly transforms back into water and carbon dioxide, which quickly bubbles out of solution because of its low solubility.

Insights

☑ CHECKPOINT

You open two cans of soft drink, one from a warm kitchen shelf and the other from the coldest depths of your refrigerator. Which provides more bubbles in the first gulp you take, and why?

Check Your Answer

The solubility of carbon dioxide in water decreases with increasing temperature. The warm drink, therefore, will fizz in your mouth more than the cold one will.

Nonpolar Gases Readily Dissolve in Perfluorocarbons

As we discussed earlier, good solubility can result when the particle-to-particle attractions in a solute are comparable to those in a solvent. This was the case with ethanol and water, and it also applies to oxygen and certain *perfluorcarbons,* such as perfluorodecalin, which are molecules consisting only of carbon and fluorine atoms. Oxygen and perfluorodecalin molecules are both nonpolar. Because of the large size of its molecules, perfluorodecalin is a liquid at room temperature. Because they are nonpolar, both perfluorodecalin molecules and oxygen molecules experience induced dipole–induced dipole attractions. At room temperature, consequently, a significant amount of oxygen gas is able to dissolve in liquid perfluorodecalin, as is demonstrated in Figure 20.18.

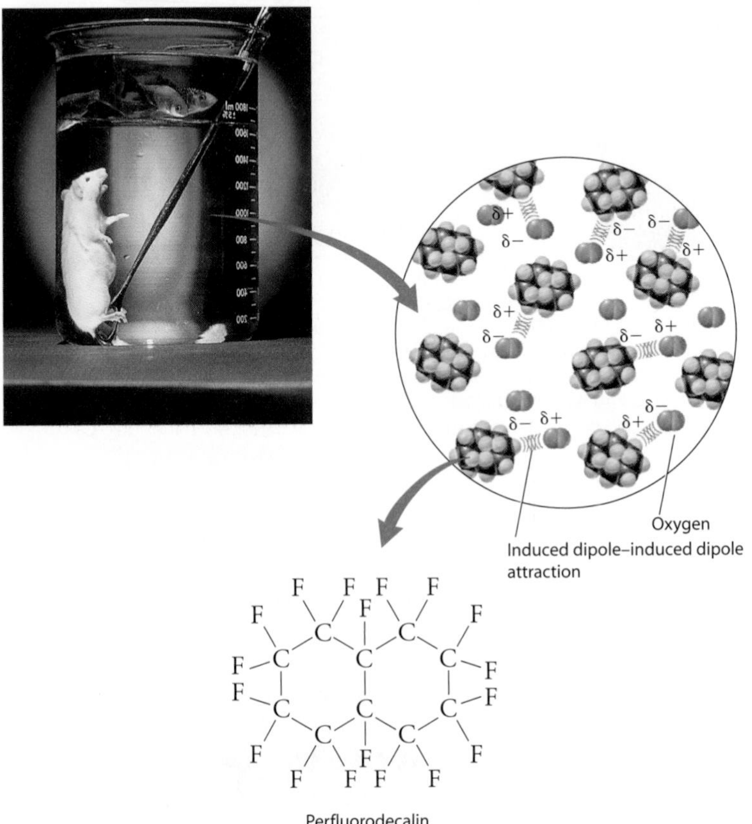

Figure 20.18
This mouse is alive and well, inhaling liquid perfluorodecalin saturated with oxygen gas.

Interestingly, a saturated solution of oxygen in a liquid perfluorocarbon contains about 20 percent more oxygen than does the atmosphere we breathe. When this perfluorocarbon solution is inhaled by a human or other animal, the lungs are able to absorb the oxygen in much the same way that they absorb it from air. Because liquid perfluorocarbons are as inert as Teflon, which is a solid perfluorocarbon, the negative side effects of having these liquids in the lungs are minimal.

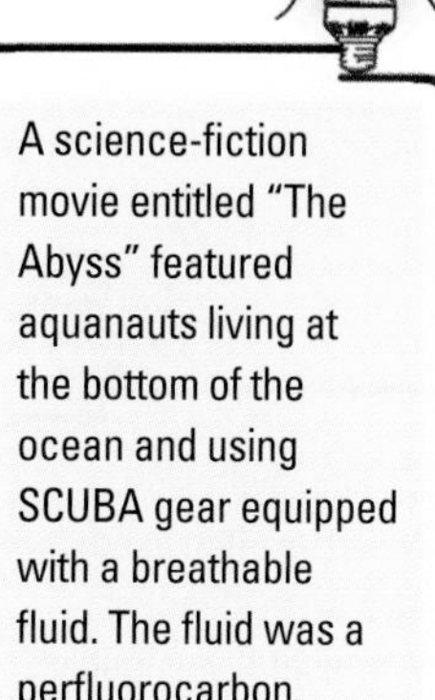

A science-fiction movie entitled "The Abyss" featured aquanauts living at the bottom of the ocean and using SCUBA gear equipped with a breathable fluid. The fluid was a perfluorocarbon.

Insights

Much research is currently being conducted on perfluorocarbons and their potential applications. For example, it is nearly impossible for babies born before seven months of gestation to breathe air. This is because their lungs have yet to develop an inner lining that prevents the moist walls from collapsing and sticking together like wet sheets of plastic food wrap. Researchers have found that premature infants can breathe oxygenated perfluorocarbons quite effectively. Clinical trials are also underway to test the effectiveness of perfluorocarbons in treating pneumonia. Interestingly, the perfluorocarbons are effective at removing foreign matter that has accumulated in the lungs over time. Have you had your lungs cleaned lately?

Another exciting application of perfluorocarbons is their use as a blood substitute. Among the many advantages of *artificial blood* are that it can be stored for long periods of time without deteriorating and that it eliminates the transmission of such diseases as hepatitis and AIDS through blood transfusions. (However, please note that, because of precautionary measures taken by blood banks, our current blood supply is safe from these diseases. For example, over the course of a year, the chance of dying as a result of a blood transfusion is only about 1 in 100,000, whereas the chance of dying in a car accident is about 1 in 7000.)

The need for a reliable blood substitute arises from frequent blood-bank shortages. Currently, less than 5 percent of the population donates blood, and this percentage is dropping as demand increases worldwide by about 7.5 million liters each year. The shortfall could become critical sometime in the next 30 years. Because much research is still needed on perfluorocarbons, donating blood is still a *very* worthwhile thing to do.

20.3 Soaps and Detergents

Dirt and grease together make *grime*. Because grime contains many nonpolar components, it is difficult to remove from hands or clothing with water alone. To remove most grime, we can use a nonpolar solvent, such as turpentine or trichloroethane, which dissolves the grime because of strong induced dipole–induced dipole attractions. Turpentine is good for removing the grime left on hands after such activities as changing a car's motor oil. Trichloroethane is the solvent used to "dry clean" clothes—a process in which dirty clothes are churned in a container full of this nonpolar solvent, which removes the toughest of nonpolar stains without the use of water.

Rather than washing our dirty hands and clothes with nonpolar solvents, however, we have a more pleasant alternative—soap and water. Soap works because soap molecules have both nonpolar and polar properties. A typical soap molecule has two parts: a long, nonpolar tail of carbon and hydrogen atoms and a polar head containing at least one ionic bond.

```
   H   H   H   H   H   H   H   O
   |   |   |   |   |   |   |   ||
H—C—C—C—C—C—C—C—C—O⁻ Na⁺
   |   |   |   |   |   |   |
   H   H   H   H   H   H   H
```

Nonpolar tail   Polar head

Because most of a soap molecule is nonpolar, it attracts nonpolar grime molecules via induced dipole–induced dipole attractions, as Figure 20.19 illustrates. In fact, grime quickly finds itself surrounded in three dimensions by the nonpolar tails of soap molecules. This attraction is usually sufficient to lift the grime away from the surface being cleaned. With the nonpolar tails facing inward toward the grime, the polar heads are all directed outward, where they are attracted to water molecules by relatively strong ion–dipole attractions. If the water is flowing, the whole conglomeration of grime and soap molecules flows with it, away from your hands or clothes and then down the drain.

For the past several centuries, soaps have been prepared by treating animal fats with sodium hydroxide, NaOH, also known as caustic lye. In this reaction, which is still used today, each fat molecule is broken down into three *fatty acid* soap molecules and one glycerol molecule:

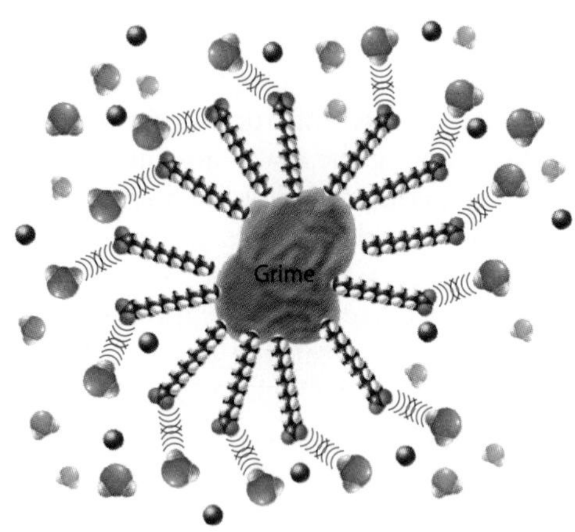

Figure 20.19
Nonpolar grime attracts and is surrounded by the nonpolar tails of soap molecules. The polar heads of the soap molecules are attracted by ion–dipole attractions to water molecules, which then carry the soap–grime combination away.

Sodium hydroxide, NaOH, is often used as a drain cleaner. Warning! If you touch this caustic material with wetted fingers, it transforms the fatty oils of your skin into soap. The result is a slippery feeling, which is a clear warning sign to rinse off with plenty of water. Experienced chemists know to wear rubber gloves (and safety goggles) when working with sodium hydroxide.

Insights

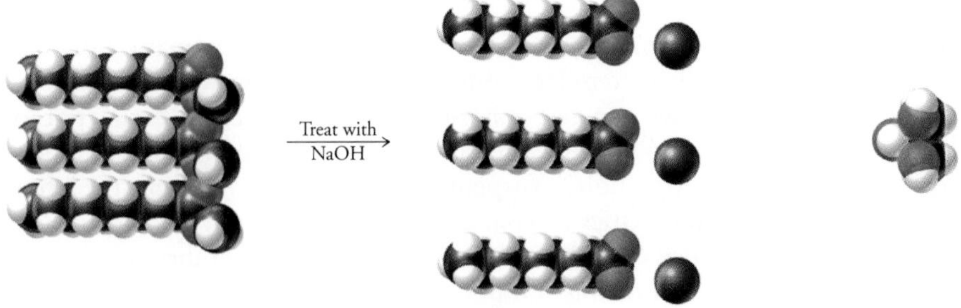

Fat molecule   Three fatty acid soap molecules   Glycerol molecule

In the 1940s, chemists began developing a class of synthetic soaplike compounds known as *detergents,* that offer several advantages over true soaps, such as stronger grease penetration and lower price.

The chemical structure of detergent molecules is similar to that of soap molecules in that both possess a polar head attached to a nonpolar tail. The polar head in a detergent molecule, however, typically consists of either a sulfate group, $-OSO_3^-$, or a sulfonate group, $-SO_3^-$, and the nonpolar tail can have an assortment of structures.

One of the most common sulfate detergents is sodium lauryl sulfate, a main ingredient of many toothpastes. A common sulfonate detergent is sodium dodecyl benzenesulfonate, also known as a linear alkylsulfonate, or LAS, often found in dishwashing liquids. Both of these detergents are biodegradable, which means that microorganisms can break down the molecules once they are released into the environment.

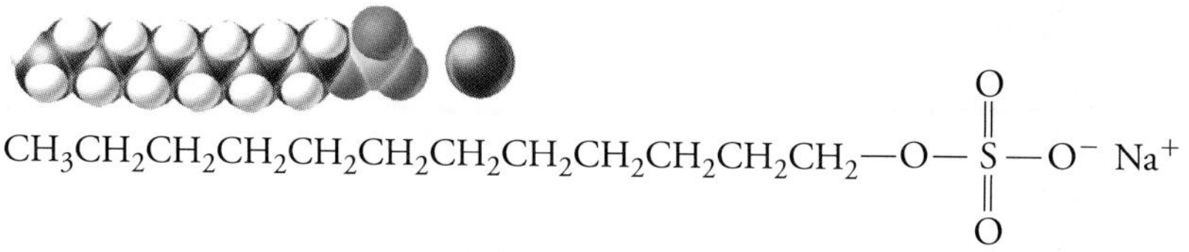

$$CH_3CH_2CH_2CH_2CH_2CH_2CH_2CH_2CH_2CH_2CH_2CH_2{-}O{-}S(=O)_2{-}O^-\ Na^+$$

Sodium lauryl sulfate

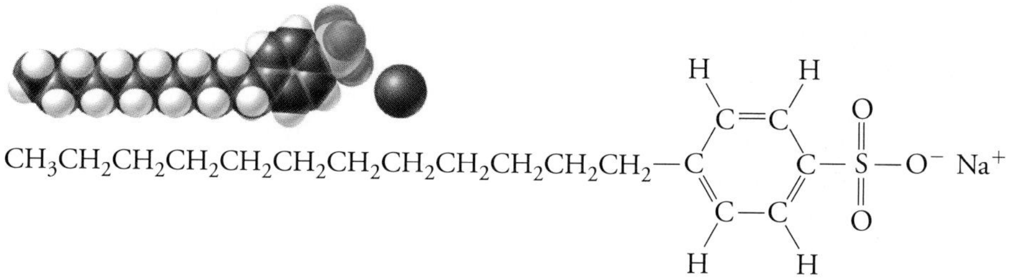

$$CH_3CH_2CH_2CH_2CH_2CH_2CH_2CH_2CH_2CH_2CH_2CH_2{-}C_6H_4{-}S(=O)_2{-}O^-\ Na^+$$

Sodium dodecyl benzenesulfonate

☑ CHECKPOINT

What type of attractions hold soap or detergent molecules to grime?

Check Your Answer

If you haven't yet formulated an answer, why not back up and reread the question? You've got only four choices: ion–dipole, dipole–dipole, dipole–induced dipole, and induced dipole–induced dipole. The answer is induced dipole–induced dipole attractions, because the interaction is between two nonpolar entities—the grime and the nonpolar tail of a soap or detergent molecule.

20.4 Softening Hard Water

Water containing large amounts of calcium and magnesium ions is said to be **hard water,** and it has many undesirable qualities. For example, when hard water is heated, its calcium and magnesium ions tend to bind with negatively

Figure 20.20
Hard water causes calcium and magnesium compounds to build up on the inner surfaces of water pipes, especially those used to carry hot water.

charged ions also found in the water to form solid compounds, like those shown in Figure 20.20. These can clog water heaters and boilers. You'll also find coatings of these calcium and magnesium compounds on the inside surfaces of a well-used teakettle.

Hard water also inhibits the cleansing actions of soaps and, to a lesser extent, detergents. The sodium ions of soap and detergent molecules carry a 1+ charge, and calcium and magnesium ions carry a 2+ charge (note their positions in the periodic table). The negatively charged portion of the polar head of a soap or detergent molecule is more attracted to the double positive charge of calcium and magnesium ions than to the single positive charge of sodium ions. Soap or detergent molecules, therefore, give up their sodium ions to bind selectively with calcium or magnesium ions:

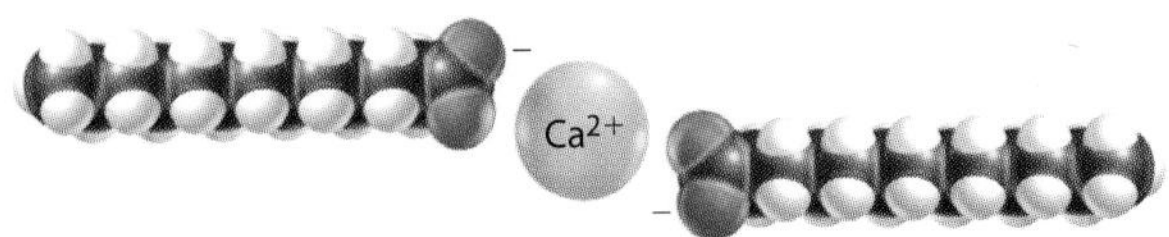

Soap or detergent molecules bound to calcium or magnesium ions tend to be insoluble in water. As they come out of solution, they form a scum, which can appear as a ring around the inside of your bathtub. Because the soap or detergent molecules are tied up with calcium and magnesium ions, more soap or detergent must be added to maintain cleaning effectiveness.

Many detergents today contain sodium carbonate, Na_2CO_3, commonly known as washing soda. The calcium and magnesium ions in hard water are more attracted to the carbonate ion with its two negative charges than they are to a soap or detergent molecule with its single negative charge. With the calcium and magnesium ions bound to the carbonate ion, as shown in Figure 20.21, the soap or detergent is free to do its job. Because it removes the ions that make water hard, sodium carbonate is known as a water-softening agent.

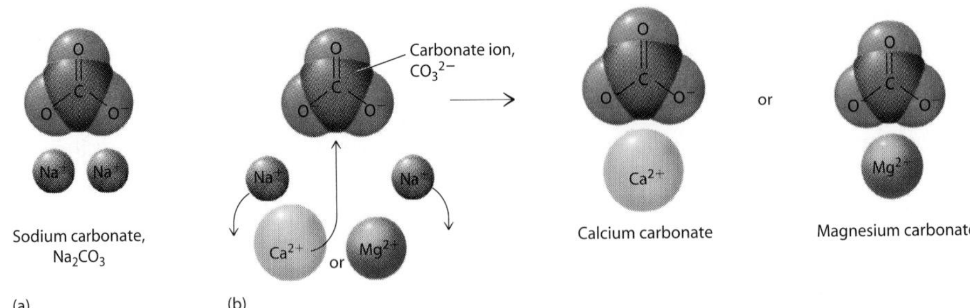

Figure 20.21
(a) Sodium carbonate is added to many detergents as a water-softening agent. (b) The doubly positive calcium and magnesium ions of hard water preferentially bind with the doubly negative carbonate ion, freeing the detergent molecules to do their job.

In some homes, the water is so hard that it must be passed through a *water-softening unit*. In a typical unit, illustrated in Figure 20.22, hard water is passed through a large tank filled with tiny beads of a water-insoluble resin known as an *ion-exchange resin*. The surface of the resin contains many negatively charged ions bound to positively charged sodium ions. As calcium and magnesium ions pass over the resin, the ions displace the sodium ions and thereby become bound to the resin. The calcium and magnesium ions are able to do this because their positive charge (2+) is greater than that of the sodium ions (1+). The calcium and magnesium ions therefore have a greater attraction for the negative sites on the resin. The net result is that, for every one calcium or magnesium ion that binds, two sodium ions are set free. In this way, the resin *exchanges* ions. The water that exits from the unit is now free of calcium and magnesium ions, but it does contain sodium ions in their place.

Eventually, all the sites for calcium and magnesium on the resin are filled, and then the resin needs to be either discarded or recharged. It is recharged by flushing it with a concentrated solution of sodium chloride, NaCl. The abundant sodium ions displace the calcium and magnesium ions (ions are *exchanged* once again), freeing up the binding sites on the resin.

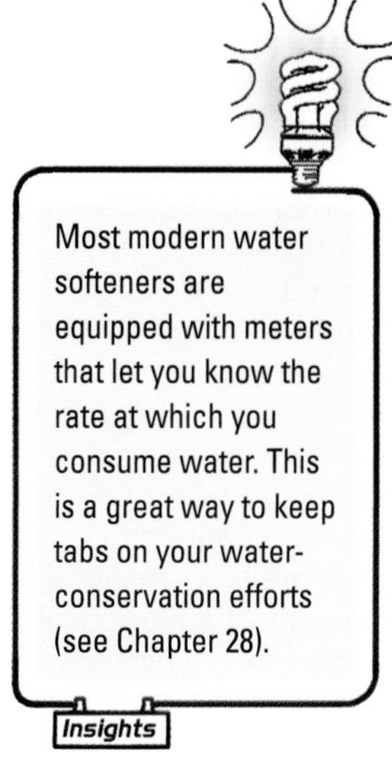

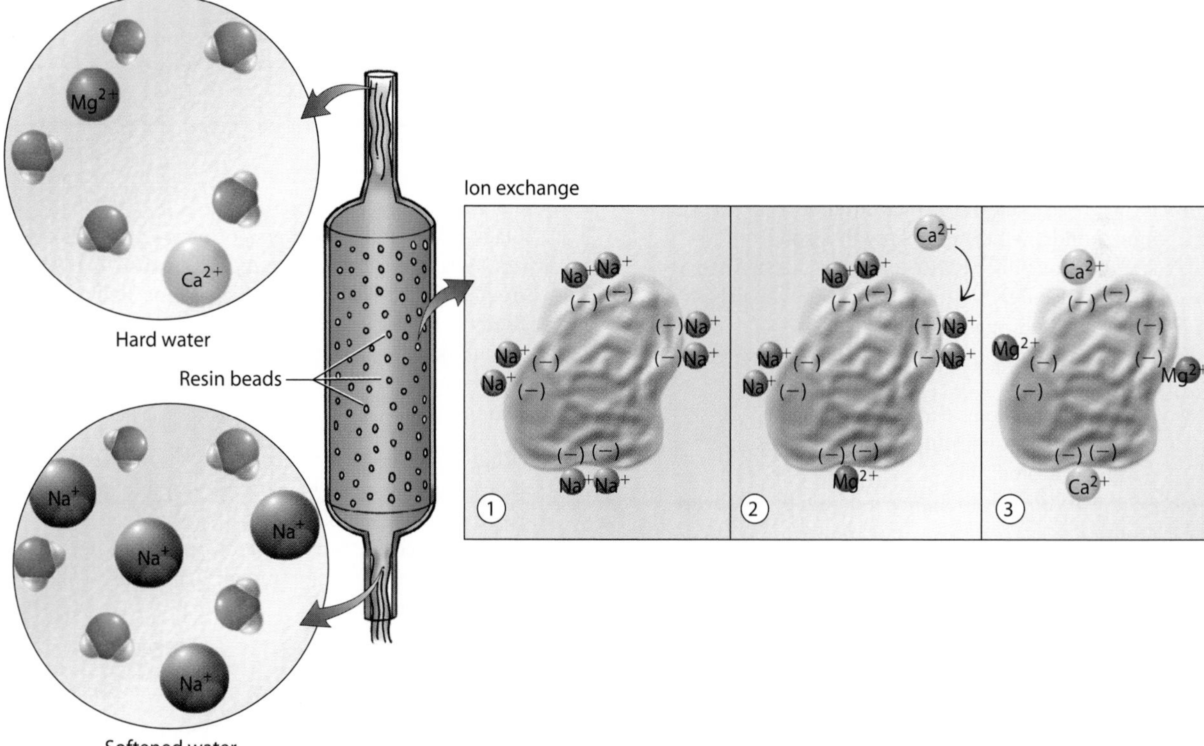

Figure 20.22
(1) Negatively charged sites on the unused ion-exchange resin are occupied by sodium ions. (2) As hard water passes over the resin, sodium ions are displaced by calcium and magnesium ions. (3) After the resin becomes saturated with calcium and magnesium ions, it is no longer effective at softening water.

Summary of Terms

Hydrogen bond A strong dipole–dipole attraction between a slightly positive hydrogen atom on one molecule and a pair of nonbonding electrons on another molecule.

Induced dipole A dipole temporarily created in an otherwise nonpolar molecule, induced by a neighboring charge.

Solubility The ability of a solute to dissolve in a given solvent.

Soluble Capable of dissolving to an appreciable extent in a given solvent.

Insoluble Not capable of dissolving to any appreciable extent in a given solvent.

Precipitate A solute that has come out of solution.

Hard water Water containing large amounts of calcium and magnesium ions.

Review Questions

20.1 Types of Attractions

1. What is the primary difference between a chemical bond and an attraction between two molecules?
2. Which is stronger, the ion–dipole attraction or the induced dipole–induced dipole attraction?
3. Why are water molecules attracted to sodium chloride?
4. How are ion–dipole attractions able to break apart ionic bonds, which are relatively strong?
5. Are electrons distributed evenly or unevenly in a polar molecule?
6. What is a hydrogen bond?
7. How are oxygen molecules attracted to water molecules?
8. Are induced dipoles permanent?
9. How can nonpolar atoms induce dipoles in other nonpolar atoms?
10. Why is it difficult to induce a dipole in a fluorine atom?
11. Why is the boiling point of octane, C_8H_{18}, so much higher than the boiling point of methane, CH_4?

20.2 Solubility

12. Why does oxygen have such a low solubility in water?
13. By what means are ethanol and water molecules attracted to each other?
14. What effect does temperature have on the solubility of a solid solute in a liquid solvent?
15. What effect does temperature have on the solubility of a gas solute in a liquid solvent?
16. How are supersaturated solutions made?
17. What does it mean to say that two materials are infinitely soluble in each other?
18. What type of electrical attraction is responsible for oxygen's ability to dissolve in water?
19. What is the relationship between a precipitate and a solute?
20. Why does the solubility of a gas solute in a liquid solvent decrease with increasing temperature?
21. What do oxygen molecules and perfluorodecane molecules have in common?

20.3 Soaps and Detergents

22. Which portion of a soap molecule is nonpolar?
23. Water and soap are attracted to each other by what type of electrical attraction?
24. Grime molecules are likely attracted to each other by what type of electrical attraction?
25. What is the difference between a soap and a detergent?

20.4 Softening Hard Water

26. What component of hard water makes it hard?
27. Why are soap molecules so attracted to calcium and magnesium ions?
28. Calcium and magnesium ions are more attracted to sodium carbonate than to soap. Why?

Activities

Circular Rainbows

Black ink contains pigments of many different colors. Acting together, these pigments absorb all the frequencies of visible light. Because no light is reflected, the ink appears black. We can use molecular attractions to separate the components of black ink through a technique that is called paper chromatography.

What You Need

Black felt-tip pen or black water-soluble marker; piece of porous paper, such as paper towel, table napkin, or coffee filter; solvent, such as water, acetone (fingernail-polish remover), rubbing alcohol, or white vinegar.

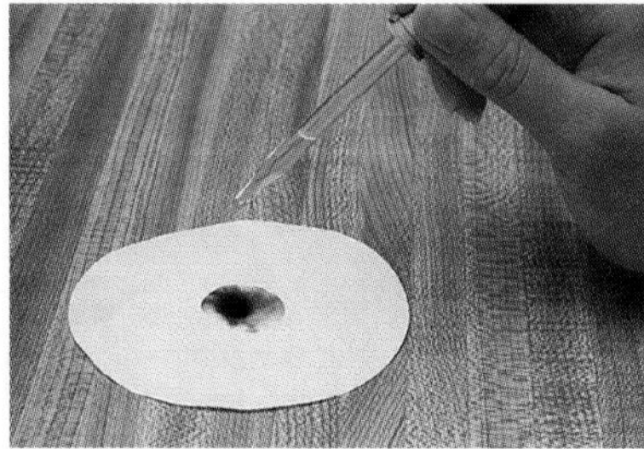

Procedure

1. Place a concentrated dot of ink at the center of the piece of porous paper.
2. Carefully place one drop of solvent on top of the dot, and watch the ink spread radially with the solvent. Because the different components of the ink have different affinities for the solvent (based on the attractions between component molecules and solvent molecules), they travel with the solvent at different rates.
3. Just after the drop of solvent is completely absorbed, add a second drop at the same location as the first one, then a third, and so on until the ink components have separated to your satisfaction.

   How the components separate depends on several factors, including your choice of solvent and your technique. It's also interesting to watch the leading edge of the moving ink under a strong magnifying glass or microscope.

   Paper chromatography was originally developed to separate plant pigments from one another. The separated pigments had different colors, which is how this technique got its name—*chroma* is Latin for "color." Mixtures need not be colored, however, to be separable by chromatography. All that's required is that the components have distinguishable affinities for the moving solvent and the stationary medium, such as paper, through which the solvent will pass.

Overflowing Sweetness

Just because a solid dissolves in a liquid doesn't imply the solid no longer occupies space.

What You Need

Tall glass, warm water, a container larger than the tall glass, 4 tablespoons table sugar.

Procedure

1. Fill the glass to its brim with the warm water, and then carefully pour all the water into the larger container.
2. Add the sugar to the empty glass.
3. Return half of the warm water to the glass and stir to dissolve all the sugar.
4. Return the remaining water, and as you get close to the top, ask a friend to predict whether the water level will be less than before, about the same as before, or more than before so that the water spills over the edge of the glass.

   If your friend doesn't understand the result, ask him or her what would happen if you had added the sugar to the glass when the glass was full of water.

Crystal Crazy

If a hot saturated solution is allowed to cool slowly and without disturbance, the solute may remain in solution. The result is a *supersaturated* solution. Supersaturated aqueous solutions of sucrose (table sugar) are fairly easy to make.

What You Need

A small cooking pot, water, table sugar, a pencil that is longer than the diameter of the pot, string, weight (a nut or bolt works well), and safety glasses to protect eyes from any hot liquid that may splatter.

Procedure

1. Fill the pot no more than 1 inch deep with water, and heat the water to boiling.
2. Lower the heat to medium-low. Slowly pour in sugar, while carefully stirring to avoid splattering. Because sugar is very soluble in hot water, be prepared to add a volume of sugar equal to or greater than the volume of water you began with. Continue to add sugar until no more will dissolve, even with persistent stirring.
3. Allow the solution to return to a boil while stirring carefully. This should help dissolve any excess sugar added in step 2. Do not set the burner on high because doing so may make the sugar solution froth up and spill out of the pot. If the sugar still doesn't fully dissolve after the solution is brought to a slow boil, add more water 1 teaspoon at a time. If the sugar dissolves after being brought to a slow boil, add more sugar 1 tablespoon at a time. Ideally, you want a boiling-hot sugar solution that is just below saturation, which may be difficult to assess without prior experience.
4. Remove the clear (no undissolved sugar) boiling sugar solution from the heat. Tie some string to the weight and lower the weight into the hot solution. Support the string with the pencil set across the rim of the pot so that the weight does not touch the bottom.
5. Leave the mixture undisturbed for about a week, checking it periodically. You will see large sugar crystals, also known as rock candy, form on the string and also along the sides of the pot. The longer you wait, the larger the crystals.

   Interesting crystals can also be made from supersaturated solutions of Epsom salts ($MgSO_4 \cdot 7H_2O$) and alum ($KAl(SO_4)_2 \cdot 12H_2O$), which is used for pickling and is available in the spice sections of some grocery stores.

Exercises

1. Why are ion–dipole attractions stronger than dipole–dipole attractions?
2. Chlorine, Cl_2, is a gas at room temperature, but bromine, Br_2, is a liquid. Why?
3. Plastic wrap is made of nonpolar molecules and is able to stick well to polar surfaces, such as glass, by way of dipole–induced dipole attractions. Why does plastic wrap also stick to itself so well?
4. Dipole–induced dipole attractions exist between molecules of water and molecules of gasoline, and yet these two substances do not mix because water has such a strong attraction for itself. Which of the following compounds might best help these two substances mix into a single liquid phase?

   (a) 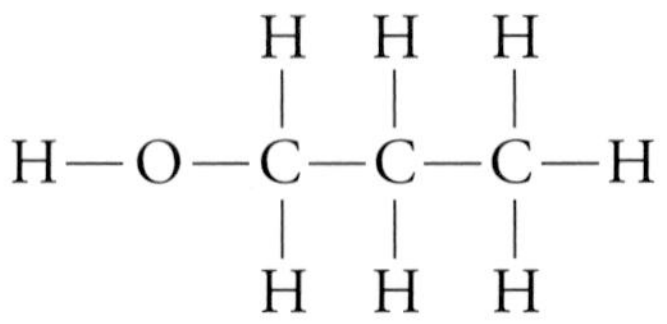

   (b) $Na^+ Cl^-$

   (c) 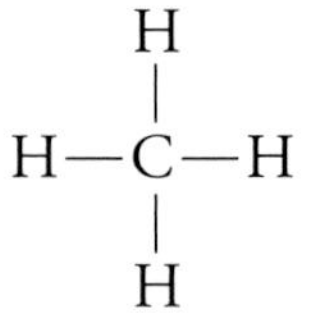

5. Explain why, for the following three substances, the solubility in 20°C water goes down as the molecules get larger but the boiling point goes up?

Substance	**Boiling point/ Solubility**
CH_3-O-H	65°C infinite
$CH_3CH_2CH_2CH_2-O-H$	117°C 8 g/100 mL
$CH_3CH_2CH_2CH_2CH_2-O-H$	138°C 2.3 g/100 mL

6. The boiling point of 1,4-butanediol is 230°C. Would you expect this compound to be soluble or insoluble in room-temperature water? Explain.

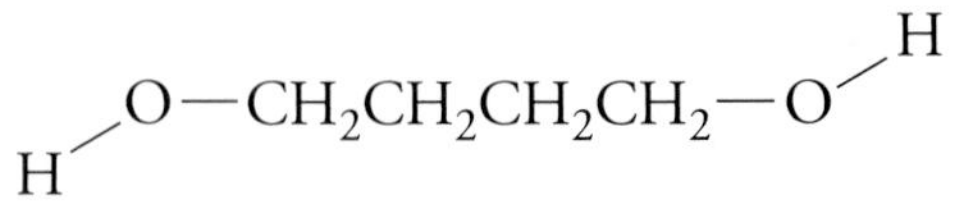

1,4-Butanediol

7. When I_2 dissolves in methanol, CH_3OH, what type of forces must be overcome within the solid I_2 to allow it to dissolve?
8. When I_2 dissolves in methanol, CH_3OH, what type of forces must be disrupted between CH_3OH molecules?
9. When I_2 dissolves in methanol, CH_3OH, what type of forces exist between I_2 and CH_3OH molecules in solution?
10. Based on atomic size, which would you expect to be more soluble in water: helium, He, or nitrogen, N_2?
11. If nitrogen, N_2, were pumped into your lungs at high pressure, what would happen to its solubility in your blood?
12. The air a SCUBA diver breathes is pressurized to counteract the pressure exerted by the water surrounding the diver's body. Breathing the high-pressure air causes excessive amounts of nitrogen to dissolve in body fluids, especially the blood. If a diver ascends to the surface too rapidly, the nitrogen bubbles out of the body fluids (much like the way carbon dioxide bubbles out of a soda immediately after the container is opened). This results in a painful and potentially lethal medical condition known as the bends. Why does breathing a mixture of helium and oxygen rather than air help divers avoid getting the bends?
13. Why are noble gases infinitely soluble in other noble gases?
14. Which solute in Figure 20.15 has a solubility in water that changes the least with increasing temperature?
15. At 10°C, which is more concentrated: a saturated solution of sodium nitrate, $NaNO_3$, or a saturated solution of sodium chloride, NaCl? (See Figure 20.15.)
16. A saturated aqueous solution of compound X has a higher concentration than a saturated aqueous solution of compound Y at the same temperature. Does it follow that compound X is more soluble in water than compound Y is?
17. Suggest why sodium chloride, NaCl, is insoluble in gasoline. Consider the electrical attractions.
18. Recall, from Chapter 14, that the isotopes of an atom differ only in the number of neutrons in the nucleus. Two isotopes of hydrogen are the more common *protium* isotope, which has no neutrons, and the less common *deuterium* isotope, which has one neutron. Either of these hydrogen isotopes can be used to make water molecules. Water made with deuterium is known as heavy water because each molecule is about 11 percent more massive than water made with the more common protium. Would you expect the boiling point of heavy water to be about 11 percent greater than the boiling point of regular water? Draw a picture of these two molecules, if you need help visualizing the difference between them.
19. Which would you expect to have a higher melting point: sodium chloride, NaCl, or aluminum oxide, Al_2O_3? Why?
20. Hydrogen chloride, HCl, is a gas at room temperature. Would you expect this material to be very soluble or not very soluble in water?
21. Would you expect to find more dissolved oxygen in ocean water around the North Pole or in ocean water nearer the equator? Why?
22. Of the two structures shown below, one is a typical gasoline molecule and the other is a typical motor-oil molecule. Which is which? Base your reasoning not on memorization but, rather, on your knowledge of electrical attractions between molecules and the various physical properties of gasoline and motor oil.

```
  H H H H H H H H H H H H H H H H
  | | | | | | | | | | | | | | | |
H-C-C-C-C-C-C-C-C-C-C-C-C-C-C-C-C-H
  | | | | | | | | | | | | | | | |
  H H H H H H H H H H H H H H H H
```

Structure A

```
  H H H H H H H H
  | | | | | | | |
H-C-C-C-C-C-C-C-C-H
  | | | | | | | |
  H H H H H H H H
```

Structure B

23. What is the boiling point of a single water molecule? Why does this question not make sense?
24. Explain the observation of ethanol, C_2H_5OH, dissolving readily in water while dimethyl ether, CH_3OCH_3, having the same number and kinds of atoms, does not.

```
    H   H                     H   H
    |   |       H         H   /   \   H
H — C — C — O /            \ C     C /
    |   |                    / \ O / \
    H   H                   H         H
```

Ethanol   Dimethyl ether

25. Why are the melting points of most ionic compounds far higher than the melting points of most covalent compounds?

26. An inventor claims to have developed a perfume that lasts a long time because it doesn't evaporate. Comment on this claim.
27. How necessary is soap for removing salt from your hands? Why?
28. When you set a pot of tap water on the stove to boil, you'll often see bubbles beginning to form well before boiling temperature is reached. Explain this observation.
29. Fish don't live very long in water that has been boiled and brought back to room temperature. Why?
30. Why might softened water not be good for individuals trying to reduce their dietary sodium-ion intake?

Chapter 20 Online Resources

Tutorials
- Polar Attraction
- Intermolecular Forces
- Solubility

Quiz
Exercises
Flashcards
Links

CHAPTER 21
Chemical Reactions

The heat of a lightning bolt causes multiple chemical reactions in the atmosphere, including one in which nitrogen and oxygen react to form nitrogen monoxide, NO. The nitrogen monoxide that is formed in this manner then reacts with atmospheric oxygen and water vapor to form nitric acid, HNO_3, and nitrous acid, HNO_2. These acids are carried by rain into the ground, where they form ions that are absorbed by growing plants—a process that involves further chemical reactions.

Scientists have learned how to control chemical reactions to produce many useful materials—nitrates and other nitrogen-based fertilizers from atmospheric nitrogen, metals from rocks, and plastics and pharmaceuticals from petroleum. These materials and the thousands of others produced by chemical reactions, as well as the abundant energy released when fossil fuels take part in the chemical reaction called combustion, have dramatically improved our living conditions.

The goal of this chapter is to provide you with a stronger handle on the basics of chemical reactions, which were introduced in Chapter 17. Then, in the following chapters, we'll look at specific classes of chemical reactions.

21.1 Reaction Rates

As we discussed in Section 17.7, the balanced chemical equation helps to determine the amount of products that can be formed from given amounts of reactants. But the equation tells us little about what occurs on the submicroscopic level during the reaction. In this and the following section, we will explore that level to show how the *rate* of a reaction can be changed, either by changing the concentration or the temperature of the reactants or by adding what is known as a *catalyst.*

Some chemical reactions, such as the rusting of iron, are slow, while others, such as the burning of gasoline, are fast. The speed of any reaction is indicated by its reaction rate, which is an indicator of how quickly the reactants transform to products. As shown in Figure 21.1, initially a flask may contain only reactant molecules. Over time, these reactants form product molecules, and, as a result, the concentration of product molecules increases. The **reaction rate**, therefore, can be defined either as how quickly the concentration of products increases or as how quickly the concentration of reactants decreases.

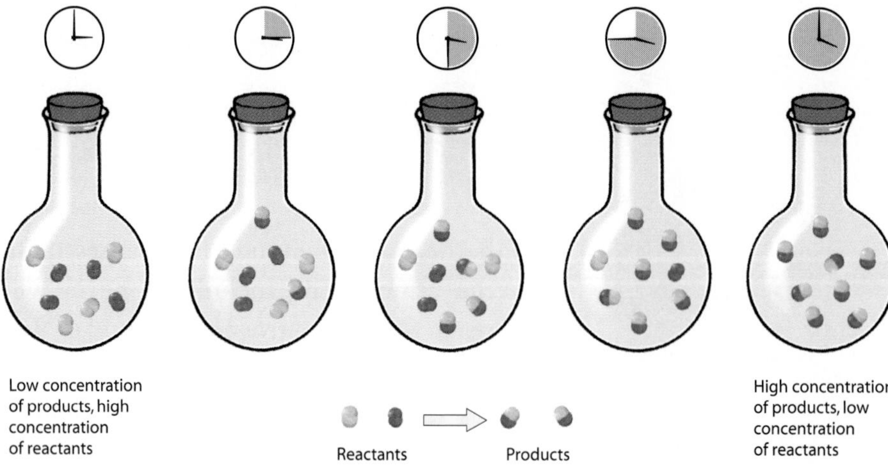

Figure 21.1
Over time, the reactants in this reaction flask may transform to products. If this happens quickly, the reaction rate is high. If this happens slowly, the reaction rate is low.

What determines the rate of a chemical reaction? The answer is complex, but one important factor is that reactant molecules must physically come together. Because molecules move rapidly, this physical contact is appropriately described as a collision. We can illustrate the relationship between molecular collisions and reaction rate by considering the reaction of gaseous nitrogen and gaseous oxygen to form gaseous nitrogen monoxide, as shown in Figure 21.2.

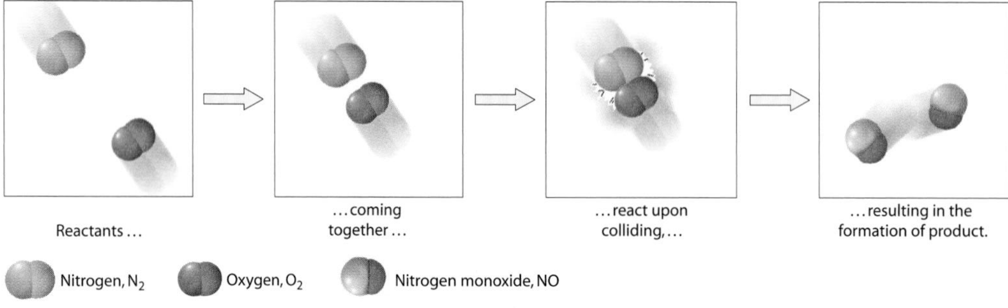

Figure 21.2
During a reaction, reactant molecules collide with one another.

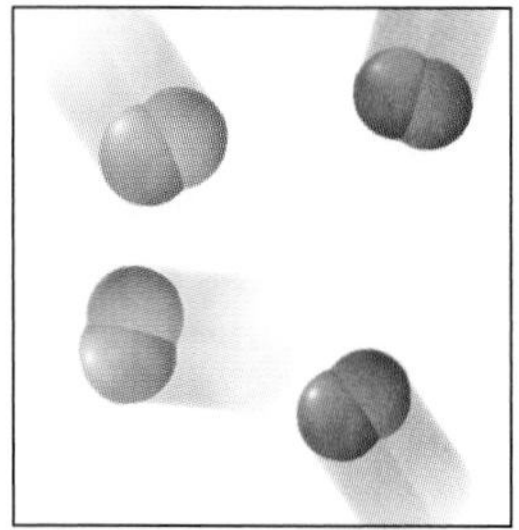

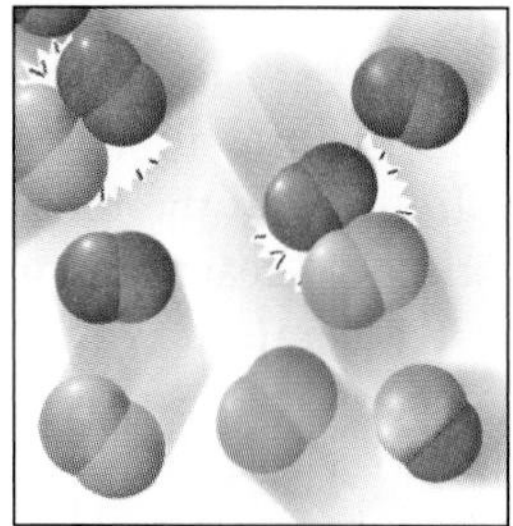

Figure 21.3
The more concentrated a sample of nitrogen and oxygen, the greater the probability that N_2 and O_2 molecules will collide and form nitrogen monoxide.

Because reactant molecules must collide in order for a reaction to occur, the rate of a reaction can be increased by increasing the number of collisions. An effective way to increase the number of collisions is to increase the concentration of the reactants. Figure 21.3 shows that, with higher concentrations, there are more molecules in a given volume, which makes collisions between molecules more probable. As an analogy, consider a group of people on a dance floor—as the number of people increases, so does the rate at which they bump into one another. An increase in the concentration of nitrogen and oxygen molecules, therefore, leads to a greater number of collisions between these molecules—hence, a greater number of nitrogen monoxide molecules will form in a given period of time.

Not all collisions between reactant molecules lead to products, however, because the molecules must collide in a certain orientation in order to react. Nitrogen and oxygen, for example, are much more likely to form nitrogen monoxide when the molecules collide in the parallel orientation shown in Figure 21.2. When they collide in the perpendicular orientation shown in Figure 21.4, nitrogen monoxide does not form. For larger molecules, which can have numerous orientations, this orientation requirement is even more restrictive.

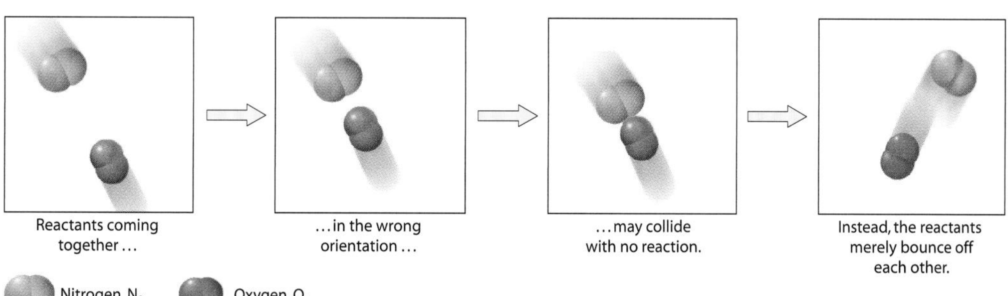

Figure 21.4 The orientation of reactant molecules in a collision can determine whether or not a reaction occurs. A perpendicular collision between N_2 and O_2 tends not to result in formation of a product molecule.

A second reason that not all collisions lead to product formation is that the reactant molecules must also collide with enough kinetic energy to break their bonds. Only then is it possible for the atoms in the reactant molecules to change bonding partners and form product molecules. The bonds in N_2 and O_2 molecules, for example, are quite strong. In order for these bonds to be broken, collisions between the molecules must contain enough energy to break the bonds. As a result, collisions between slow-moving N_2 and O_2 molecules, even those that collide in the proper orientation, may not form NO, as is shown in Figure 21.5.

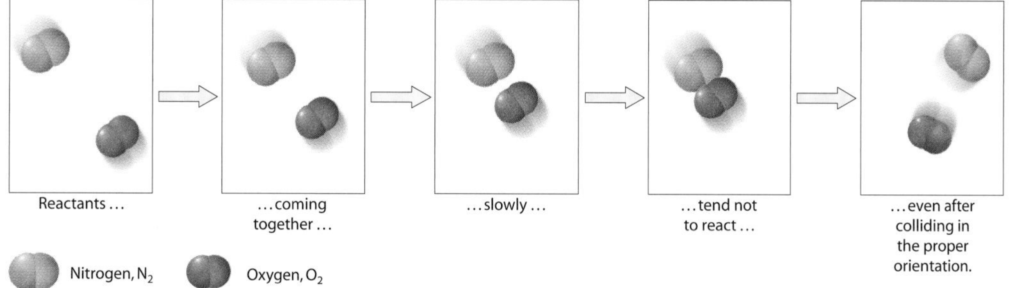

Figure 21.5 Slow-moving molecules may collide with insufficient force to break their bonds. As a result, they cannot react to form product molecules.

The higher the temperature of a material, the faster its molecules move and the more forceful the collisions between them. Higher temperatures, therefore, increase reaction rates. The nitrogen and oxygen molecules that make up our atmosphere, for example, are continually colliding with one another. At the ambient temperatures of our atmosphere, however, these molecules do not generally have sufficient kinetic energy for the formation of nitrogen monoxide. The heat of a lightning bolt, however, dramatically increases the kinetic energy of these molecules to the point that a large portion of the collisions in the vicinity of the bolt result in the formation of nitrogen monoxide. As discussed in the opening of this chapter, the nitrogen monoxide formed in this manner undergoes further atmospheric reactions to form chemicals known as nitrates that plants depend on for survival. This is an example of *nitrogen fixation,* which you may have explored already in a course on the life sciences.

The life sciences involve fantastic applications of the physical sciences, the chemistry of nitrogen fixation being just one example. Others include photosynthesis, cellular respiration, and molecular genetics. So there are distinct advantages to learning about the physical sciences *before* advancing to the life sciences.

Insights

☑ CHECKPOINT

An internal-combustion engine works by drawing a mixture of air and gasoline vapors into a chamber. The action of a piston then compresses these gases into a smaller volume prior to ignition by the spark of a spark plug. What is the advantage of squeezing the vapors to a smaller volume?

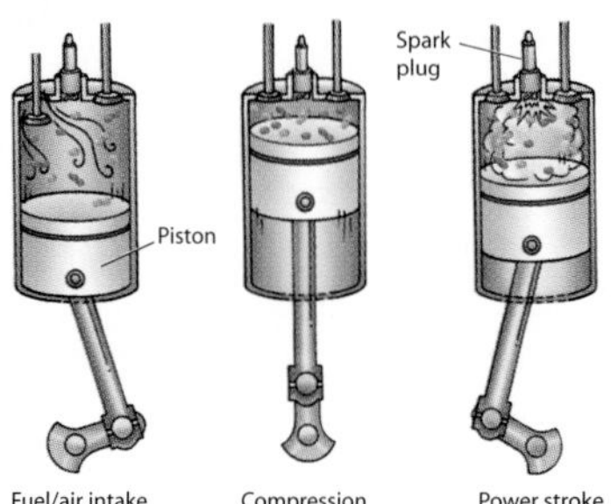

Check Your Answer

Squeezing the vapors to a smaller volume effectively increases their concentration and, hence, the number of collisions between molecules. This, in turn, promotes the chemical reaction.

The energy required to break bonds can also come from the absorption of electromagnetic radiation. As the radiation is absorbed by reactant molecules, the atoms in the molecules may start to vibrate so rapidly that the bonds between them are easily broken. In many instances, the direct absorption of electromagnetic radiation is sufficient to break chemical bonds and to initiate a chemical reaction. The common atmospheric pollutant nitrogen dioxide, NO_2, for example, may transform to nitrogen monoxide and atomic oxygen merely upon exposure to sunlight:

$$NO_2 + \text{sunlight} \longrightarrow NO + O$$

Whether they result from collisions, or from the absorption of electromagnetic radiation, or both, broken bonds are a necessary first step in most chemical reactions. The energy required for this initial breaking of bonds can be viewed as an *energy barrier*. The minimum energy required to overcome this energy barrier is known as the **activation energy** (E_a).

In the reaction between nitrogen and oxygen to form nitrogen monoxide, the activation energy is so high (because the bonds in N_2 and O_2 are strong) that only the fastest-moving nitrogen and oxygen molecules possess sufficient energy to react. Figure 21.6 shows the activation energy in this chemical reaction as a vertical hump.

The activation energy of a chemical reaction is analogous to the energy a car needs to drive over the top of a hill. Without sufficient energy to climb to the top of the hill, it isn't possible for the car to get to the other side. Likewise, reactant

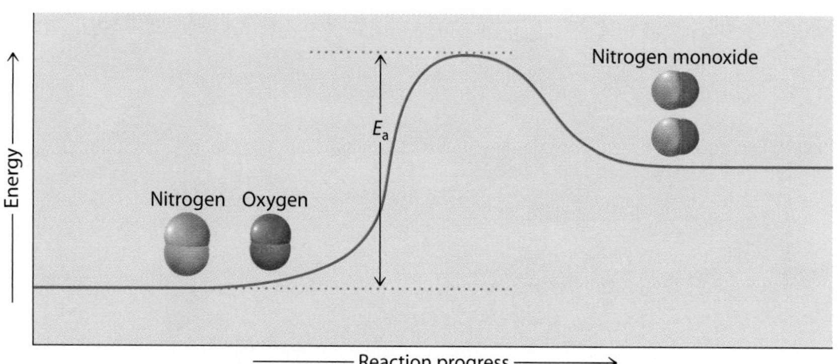

Figure 21.6
Reactant molecules must gain a minimum amount of energy, called the activation energy, E_a, before they can transform to product molecules.

Figure 21.7
Because fast-moving reactant molecules possess sufficient energy to pass over the energy barrier, they are the first ones to transform to product molecules.

Kinetic energies not sufficient to overcome energy barrier

Kinetic energies sufficient to overcome energy barrier

molecules can transform to product molecules only if the reactant molecules possess an amount of energy equal to or greater than the activation energy.

At any given temperature, there is a wide distribution of kinetic energies in reactant molecules. Some are moving slowly, and others are moving quickly. As we discussed in Chapter 7, the temperature of a material is related to the average of all these kinetic energies. The few fast-moving reactant molecules in Figure 21.7 have enough energy to pass over the energy barrier and are the first to transform to product molecules.

When the temperature of the reactants is increased, the number of reactant molecules possessing sufficient energy to pass over the barrier also increases, which is why reactions are generally faster at higher temperatures. Conversely, at lower temperatures, there are fewer molecules having sufficient energy to pass over the barrier. Hence, reactions are generally slower at lower temperatures.

Most chemical reactions are influenced by temperature in this manner, including those reactions occurring in living bodies. The body temperature of animals that regulate their internal temperature, such as humans, is fairly constant. However, the body temperature of some animals, such as the alligator shown in Figure 21.8, rises and falls with the temperature of the environment. On a warm day, the chemical reactions occurring in an alligator are "up to speed," and the animal is more active. On a chilly day, however, the chemical reactions proceed at a lower rate, and, as a consequence, the alligator's movements are unavoidably sluggish.

In order for two chemicals to be able to react, they must first collide in the proper orientation. Second, they must have sufficient kinetic energy to initiate the breaking of chemical bonds so that new bonds can form. These are all aspects of a broad theory known as the *molecular-kinetic theory.*

Insights

☑ CHECKPOINT

What kitchen device is used to lower the rate at which microorganisms grow on food?

Check Your Answer

The refrigerator! Microorganisms, such as bread mold, are everywhere and difficult to avoid. By lowering the temperature of microorganism-contaminated food, the refrigerator decreases the rate of the chemical reactions that these microorganisms depend on for growth, thereby increasing the food's shelf life.

Figure 21.8
This alligator became immobilized on the pavement after being caught in the cold night air. By mid-morning, shown here, the temperature had warmed sufficiently to allow the alligator to get up and walk away.

21.2 Catalysts

As discussed in the previous section, increasing the concentration of the reactants or increasing the temperature can cause a chemical reaction to go faster. A third way to increase the rate of a reaction is to add a **catalyst,** which is any substance that increases the rate of a chemical reaction by lowering its activation energy. The catalyst may participate as a reactant, but it is then regenerated as a product and is thus available to catalyze subsequent reactions.

The conversion of ozone, O_3, to oxygen, O_2, is normally sluggish because the reaction has a relatively high activation energy, as shown in Figure 21.9a. However, when chlorine atoms act as a catalyst, the energy barrier is lowered, as shown in Figure 21.9b, and the reaction is able to proceed faster.

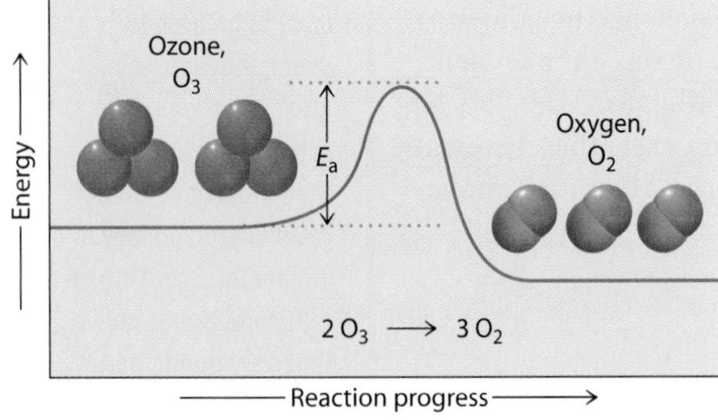

(a) Without catalyst

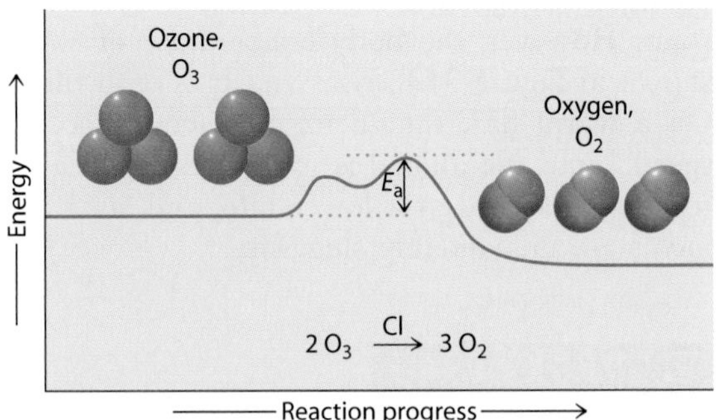

(b) With chlorine catalyst

Figure 21.9
(a) The relatively high activation energy (energy barrier) indicates that only the most energetic ozone molecules can react to form oxygen molecules. (b) The presence of chlorine atoms lowers the activation energy, which means more reactant molecules have sufficient energy to form product. The chlorine allows the reaction to proceed in two steps, and the two smaller activation energies correspond to these steps. (Note that the convention is to write the catalyst above the reaction arrow.)

Atomic chlorine lowers the energy barrier of this reaction by providing an alternate pathway involving intermediate reactions, each having a lower activation energy than the uncatalyzed reaction. This alternate pathway involves two steps. Initially, the chlorine reacts with the ozone to form chlorine monoxide and oxygen:

$$\underset{\text{Chlorine}}{Cl} + \underset{\text{Ozone}}{O_3} \longrightarrow \underset{\text{Chlorine monoxide}}{ClO} + \underset{\text{Oxygen}}{O_2}$$

The chlorine monoxide then reacts with another ozone molecule to re-form the chlorine atom as well as to produce two additional oxygen molecules:

$$\underset{\text{Chlorine monoxide}}{ClO} + \underset{\text{Ozone}}{O_3} \longrightarrow \underset{\text{Chlorine}}{Cl} + \underset{\text{Oxygen}}{2\,O_2}$$

Although chlorine is depleted in the first reaction, it is regenerated in the second reaction. As a result, there is no net consumption of chlorine. At the same time, however, two ozone molecules are rapidly converted to three oxygen molecules. The chlorine is therefore a catalyst for the conversion of ozone to oxygen because the chlorine increases the speed of the reaction while not being consumed by the reaction.

Chlorine atoms in the stratosphere catalyze the destruction of the earth's ozone layer. Evidence indicates that chlorine atoms are generated in the stratosphere as a by-product of human-made chlorofluorocarbons (CFCs), once widely produced as the cooling fluid of refrigerators and air conditioners. Destruction of the ozone layer is a serious concern because of its role in protecting us from the sun's harmful ultraviolet rays. One chlorine atom in the ozone layer is estimated to catalyze the transformation of 100,000 ozone molecules to oxygen molecules in the one or two years before the chlorine atom is removed by natural processes.

Chemists have been able to harness the power of catalysts for numerous beneficial purposes. The exhaust that comes from an automobile engine, for example, contains a wide assortment of pollutants, such as nitrogen monoxide, carbon monoxide, and uncombusted fuel vapors (hydrocarbons). To reduce the amount of these pollutants entering the atmosphere, most automobiles are equipped with *catalytic converters,* as shown in Figure 21.10. Metal catalysts in a converter speed up reactions that convert exhaust pollutants to less toxic substances. Nitrogen monoxide is transformed to nitrogen and oxygen, carbon monoxide is transformed to carbon dioxide, and unburned fuel is converted to carbon dioxide and water vapor. Because catalysts are not consumed by the reactions they facilitate, a single catalytic converter may continue to operate effectively for the lifetime of the car.

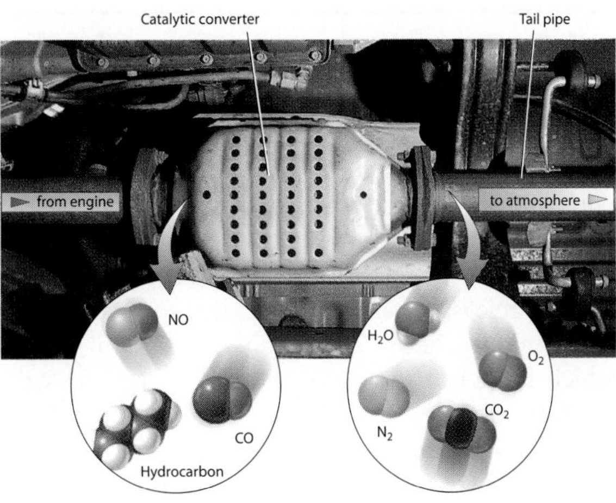

Figure 21.10
A catalytic converter reduces the pollution caused by automobile exhaust by converting such harmful combustion products as NO, CO, and hydrocarbons to harmless N_2, O_2, and CO_2. The catalyst is typically platinum, Pt, palladium, Pd, or rhodium, Rd.

Insights

Before the fall of the Soviet Union, numerous oil-drilling sites in Siberia were allowed to vent natural gas freely into the atmosphere, presumably because the natural gas had no commercial value. After the fall of the Soviet Union, the wells were capped to prevent this venting. Within weeks, instruments at the Moana Loa weather observatory on the other side of the planet noted a significant drop in atmospheric levels of methane and its by-product, carbon dioxide. The effect that we humans have on global atmospheric conditions is very measurable.

Figure 21.11
The exhaust from automobiles today is much cleaner than before the advent of the catalytic converter, but there are many more cars on the road. In 1960, there were 70 million registered motor vehicles in the United States. In 2003, there were more than 200 million.

Catalytic converters, along with microchip-controlled fuel–air ratios, have led to a significant drop in the per-vehicle emission of pollutants. A typical car in 1960 emitted about 11 grams of uncombusted fuel, 4 grams of nitrogen oxide, and 84 grams of carbon monoxide per mile traveled. An improved vehicle in the year 2000 emitted less than 0.5 gram of uncombusted fuel, less than 0.5 gram of nitrogen oxide, and only about 3 grams of carbon monoxide per mile traveled. This improvement, however, has been offset by an increase in the number of cars being driven, as exemplified by the traffic jam shown in Figure 21.11. It is also offset by the growing popularity of SUVs (sport-utility vehicles), which bypass pollution requirements.

The chemical industry depends on catalysts because they lower manufacturing costs by lowering required temperatures and by providing greater product yields without being consumed. Indeed, more than 90 percent of all manufactured goods are produced with the assistance of catalysts. Without catalysts, the price of gasoline would be much higher, as would be the price of such consumer goods as rubber, plastics, pharmaceuticals, automobile parts, clothing, and food grown with chemical fertilizers. Living organisms rely on special types of catalysts known as *enzymes,* which allow exceedingly complex biochemical reactions to occur with ease. You may learn more about the nature and behavior of enzymes in a life-science course.

☑ CHECKPOINT

How does a catalyst lower the activation energy of a chemical reaction?

Check Your Answer

The catalyst provides an alternate and easier-to-achieve pathway, along which the chemical reaction can proceed.

21.3 Energy and Chemical Reactions

As we have discussed in the preceding two sections, reactants must have a certain amount of energy in order to overcome the activation energy so that a chemical reaction can proceed. Once a reaction is complete, however, there may be either a net release or a net absorption of energy. Reactions in which there is a net release of energy are called **exothermic.** Rocket ships lift off into space and campfires glow red hot as a result of exothermic reactions. Reactions in which there is a net absorption of energy are called **endothermic.** Photosynthesis, for example, involves a series of endothermic reactions that are driven by the energy of sunlight. Both exothermic and endothermic reactions, illustrated in Figure 21.12, can be understood through the concept of bond energy.

During a chemical reaction, chemical bonds are broken and atoms rearrange to form new chemical bonds. Such breaking and forming of chemical bonds involves changes in energy. As an analogy, consider a pair of magnets. To

Figure 21.12
For the chemical reactions that occur when wood is burning, there is a net release of energy. For the chemical reactions that occur in a photosynthetic plant, there is a net absorption of energy.

separate them requires an input of "muscle energy." Conversely, when the two separated magnets collide, they become slightly warmer than they were, and this warmth is evidence of energy released. Energy must be absorbed by the magnets if they are to break apart, and energy is released as they come together. The same principle applies to atoms. To pull bonded atoms apart requires an energy input. When atoms combine, there is an energy output, usually in the form of faster-moving atoms and molecules, electromagnetic radiation, or both.

The amount of energy required to pull two bonded atoms apart is the same as the amount released when they are brought together. This energy, whether it is the energy that is absorbed as a bond breaks or the energy that is released as a bond forms, is called **bond energy.** Each chemical bond has its own characteristic bond energy. The hydrogen–hydrogen bond energy, for example, is 436 kilojoules per mole. This means that 436 kilojoules of energy is absorbed as 1 mole of hydrogen–hydrogen bonds break apart, and 436 kilojoules of energy is released upon the formation of 1 mole of hydrogen–hydrogen bonds. Different bonds involving different elements have different bond energies, as Table 21.1 shows. You can refer to the table as you study this section, but please do not memorize these bond energies. Instead, focus on understanding what they mean.

Table 21.1

Selected Bond Energies

Bond	Bond Energy (kJ/mole)	Bond	Bond Energy (kJ/mole)
H–H	436	N–N	159
H–C	414	O–O	138
H–N	389	Cl–Cl	243
H–O	464	C=O	803
H–F	569	N=O	631
H–S	339	O=O	498
H–Cl	431	C≡C	837
C–C	347	N≡N	946

By convention, a positive bond energy represents the amount of energy absorbed as a bond breaks, and a negative bond energy represents the amount of energy released as a bond forms. Thus, when you are calculating the net energy released or absorbed during a reaction, you'll need to be careful about plus and minus signs. It is standard practice when doing such calculations to assign a plus sign to energy absorbed and a minus sign to energy released. For instance, when dealing with a reaction in which 1 mole of H–H bonds are broken, you'll write +436 kilojoules to indicate energy absorbed, and when dealing with the formation of 1 mole of H–H bonds, you'll write −436 kilojoules to indicate energy released. We'll do some sample calculations in a moment.

☑ CHECKPOINT

Do all covalent single bonds have the same bond energy?

Check Your Answer

No. Bond energy depends on the types of atoms bonding. The H–H single bond, for example, has a bond energy of 436 kilojoules per mole, but the H–O single bond has a bond energy of 464 kilojoules per mole. All covalent single bonds do not have the same bond energy.

An Exothermic Reaction Involves a Net Release of Energy

For any chemical reaction, the total amount of energy absorbed in breaking bonds in reactants is always different from the total amount of the energy released as bonds form in the products. Consider the reaction in which hydrogen and oxygen react to form water:

$$\mathrm{H{-}H + H{-}H + O{=}O \longrightarrow H{-}O{-}H + H{-}O{-}H}$$

In the reactants, hydrogen atoms are bonded to hydrogen atoms, and oxygen atoms are double-bonded to oxygen atoms. The total amount of energy absorbed as these bonds break is +1370 kilojoules.

Type of bond	Number of moles	Bond energy	Total Energy
H—H	2	+436 kJ/mole	+872 kJ
O═O	1	+498 kJ/mole	+498 kJ
		Total energy absorbed:	+1370 kJ

In the products there are four hydrogen–oxygen bonds. The total amount of energy released as these bonds form is −1856 kilojoules.

Type of bond	Number of moles	Bond energy	Total Energy
H—O	4	−464 kJ/mole	−1856 kJ
		Total energy released:	−1856 kJ

The amount of energy released in this reaction exceeds the amount of energy absorbed. The net energy of the reaction is found by adding the two quantities:

$$\begin{aligned}\text{Net energy of reaction} &= \text{energy absorbed} + \text{energy released}\\ &= +1370\ \text{kJ} + (-1856\ \text{kJ})\\ &= -486\ \text{kJ}\end{aligned}$$

The negative sign on the net energy indicates that there is a net release of energy, and so the reaction is exothermic. For any exothermic reaction, energy can be considered a product and is thus sometimes included after the arrow of the chemical equation:

$$2\ H_2 + O_2 \longrightarrow 2\ H_2O + \text{energy}$$

In an exothermic reaction, the potential energy of atoms in the product molecules is lower than their potential energy in the reactant molecules. This is illustrated in the reaction profile shown in Figure 21.13. The lowered potential energy of the atoms in the product molecules is due to their being more tightly held together. This is analogous to two attracting magnets, whose potential energy decreases as they come closer together. The loss of potential energy is balanced by a gain in kinetic energy. Like two free-floating magnets coming together and accelerating to higher speeds, the potential energy of the reactants is converted to faster-moving atoms and molecules, electromagnetic radiation, or both. This kinetic energy released by the reaction is equal to the difference between the potential energy of the reactants and the potential energy of the products, as is indicated in Figure 21.13.

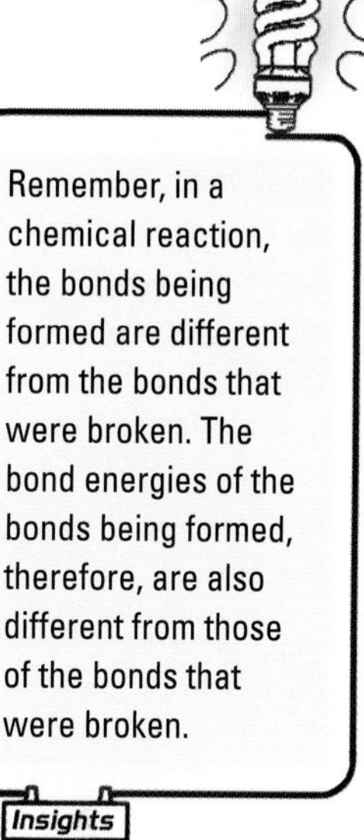

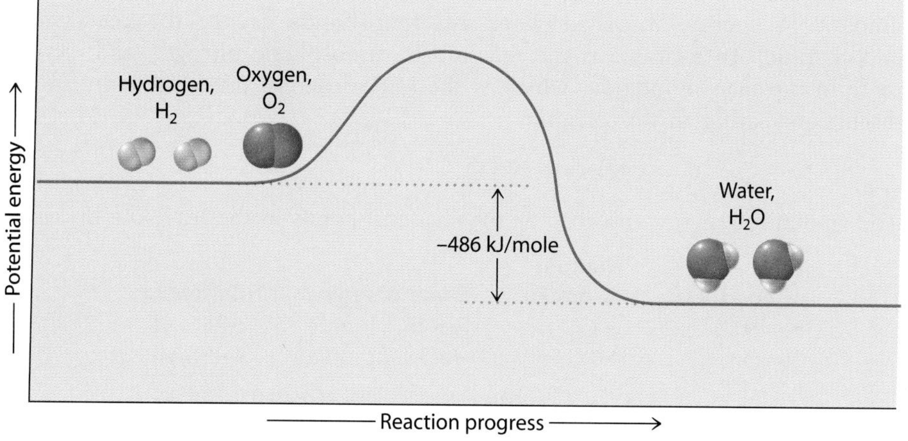

Figure 21.13
In an exothermic reaction, the product molecules are at a lower potential energy than the reactant molecules. The net amount of energy released by the reaction is equal to the difference in potential energies of the reactants and products.

It is important to understand that the energy released by an exothermic reaction is not created by the reaction. This is in accord with the *law of conservation of energy,* which tells us that energy is neither created nor destroyed in a chemical reaction (or any process). Instead, energy is merely converted from one form to another. During an exothermic reaction, energy that was once in the form of the potential energy of chemical bonds is released as the kinetic energy of fast-moving molecules and/or as electromagnetic radiation.

The amount of energy released in an exothermic reaction depends on the amounts of the reactants. The reaction of large amounts of hydrogen and oxygen, for example, provides the energy to lift the space shuttle shown in Figure 21.14 into orbit. There are two compartments in the large central

Recall, from Chapter 2, that for every action there is an opposite and equal reaction. A rocket is thrust upwards, for example, only as its exhaust chemicals are thrust downwards.

Insights

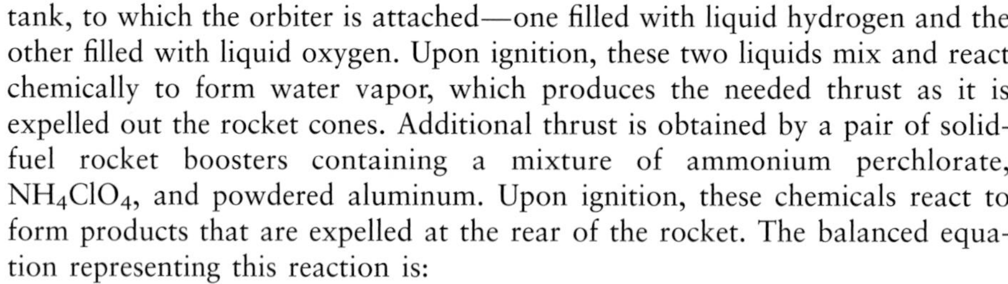

tank, to which the orbiter is attached—one filled with liquid hydrogen and the other filled with liquid oxygen. Upon ignition, these two liquids mix and react chemically to form water vapor, which produces the needed thrust as it is expelled out the rocket cones. Additional thrust is obtained by a pair of solid-fuel rocket boosters containing a mixture of ammonium perchlorate, NH_4ClO_4, and powdered aluminum. Upon ignition, these chemicals react to form products that are expelled at the rear of the rocket. The balanced equation representing this reaction is:

$$3\ NH_4ClO_4 + 3\ Al \longrightarrow Al_2O_3 + AlCl_3 + 3\ NO + 6\ H_2O + \text{energy}$$

☑ CHECKPOINT

Where does the net energy released in an exothermic reaction go?

Check Your Answer

This energy goes into increasing the speeds of reactant atoms and molecules and often into electromagnetic radiation.

Figure 21.14
A space shuttle uses exothermic chemical reactions to lift off from the earth's surface.

An Endothermic Reaction Involves a Net Absorption of Energy

When the amount of energy released in product formation is *less* than the amount of energy absorbed when reactant bonds break, the reaction is endothermic. An example is the reaction of atmospheric nitrogen and oxygen to form nitrogen monoxide, which is the same reaction used for many of the discussions earlier in this chapter:

$$N{\equiv}N + O{=}O \longrightarrow N{=}O + N{=}O$$

The amount of energy absorbed as the chemical bonds in the reactants break is:

Type of bond	Number of moles	Bond energy	Total energy
N≡N	+1	+946 kJ/mole	+946 kJ
O=O	+1	+498 kJ/mole	+498 kJ
		Total energy absorbed:	+1444 kJ

The amount of energy released upon the formation of bonds in the products is:

Type of bond	Number of moles	Bond energy	Total energy
N=O	2	−631 kJ/mole	−1262 kJ
		Total energy released:	−1262 kJ

As before, the net energy of the reaction is found by adding the two quantities:

$$\begin{aligned}\text{Net energy of reaction} &= \text{energy absorbed} + \text{energy released}\\ &= +1444\ \text{kJ} + (-1262\ \text{kJ})\\ &= +182\ \text{kJ}\end{aligned}$$

The positive sign indicates that there is a net *absorption* of energy, meaning the reaction is endothermic. For any endothermic reaction, energy can be considered a reactant and is thus sometimes included before the arrow of the chemical equation:

$$\text{Energy} + N_2 + O_2 \longrightarrow 2\ NO$$

In an endothermic reaction, the potential energy of atoms in the product molecules is higher than their potential energy in the reactant molecules. This is illustrated in the reaction profile shown in Figure 21.15. Raising the potential energy of the atoms in the product molecules requires a net input of energy, which must come from some external source, such as electromagnetic radiation, electricity, or heat. Thus, nitrogen and oxygen react to form nitrogen monoxide only with the application of much heat, as occurs adjacent to a lightning bolt or in an internal-combustion engine.

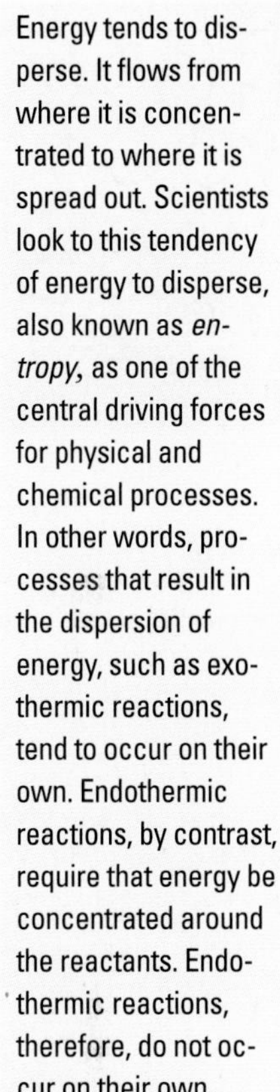

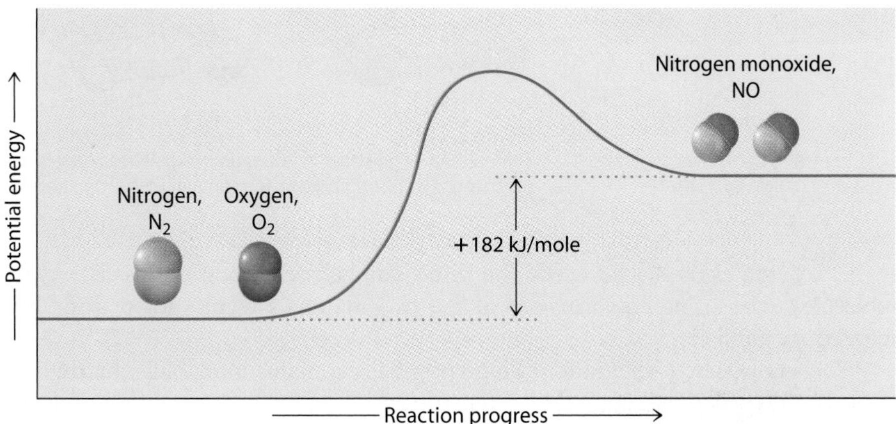

Figure 21.15
In an endothermic reaction, the product molecules are at a higher potential energy than the reactant molecules. The net amount of energy absorbed by the reaction is equal to the difference in potential energies of the reactants and products.

21.4 Relative Masses of Atoms and Molecules

In any chemical reaction, a specific number of reactant atoms or molecules react to form a specific number of product atoms or molecules. For example, when carbon and oxygen combine to form carbon dioxide, they always combine in the ratio of one carbon atom to one oxygen molecule. A chemist who wants to carry out this reaction in the laboratory would be wasting chemicals and money if she were to combine, say, four carbon atoms for every one oxygen molecule. The excess carbon atoms would have no oxygen molecules to react with and would remain unchanged.

How is it possible to measure out a specific number of atoms or molecules? Certainly not by counting these particles individually! Chemists can use a scale that measures the mass of bulk quantities. Because different atoms and molecules have different masses, however, a chemist can't simply measure equal masses of

Figure 21.16
The number of balls in a given mass of Ping-Pong balls is very different from the number of balls in the same mass of golf balls.

Figure 21.17
The number of golf balls in 200 grams of golf balls equals the number of Ping-Pong balls in 10 grams of Ping-Pong balls.

each. Say, for example, he needs the same number of carbon atoms as oxygen molecules. Measuring equal masses of the two materials would not provide him with equal numbers.

You know that 1 kilogram of Ping-Pong balls contains more balls than 1 kilogram of golf balls, as Figure 21.16 illustrates. Likewise, because different atoms and molecules have different masses, there are different numbers of them in a 1-gram sample of each. Because carbon atoms are less massive than oxygen molecules, there are more carbon atoms in 1 gram of carbon than there are oxygen molecules in 1 gram of oxygen. So, clearly, equal masses of these two particles do not yield equal numbers of carbon atoms and oxygen molecules.

If we know the *relative masses* of different materials, we can measure equal numbers. Golf balls, for example, are about 20 times more massive than Ping-Pong balls, which is to say that the relative mass of Ping-Pong balls to golf balls is 20 to 1. Measuring out 20 times as much mass of golf balls as Ping-Pong balls, therefore, gives equal numbers of each, as is shown in Figure 21.17.

☑ CHECKPOINT

A customer wants to purchase a 1:1 mixture of blue and red jelly beans. Each blue bean is twice as massive as each red bean. If the clerk measures out 5 pounds of red beans, how many pounds of blue beans are needed?

Check Your Answer

Because each blue jelly bean has twice the mass of each red one, the clerk needs to measure out twice as much mass of blue beans in order to have the same count, which means 10 pounds of blue beans. If the clerk did not know that the blue beans were twice as massive as the red ones, she would not know what mass of blues was needed for the 1:1 ratio. Likewise, a chemist would be at a loss in setting up a chemical reaction if she did not know the relative masses of the reactants.

The periodic table indicates the relative masses of carbon and molecular oxygen; therefore, we can measure out equal numbers of their fundamental particles—atoms for carbon and molecules for oxygen. Figure 21.18 illustrates this concept. The atomic mass of carbon is 12.011 atomic mass units. (As discussed in Section 14.4, one *atomic mass unit* (amu) = 1.661×10^{-24} gram.) The **formula mass** of a substance is the sum of the atomic masses of the elements in its chemical formula. Therefore, the formula mass of an oxygen molecule, O_2, is 15.999 atomic mass units + 15.999 atomic mass units ≈ 32 atomic mass units. A carbon atom, therefore, is about 12/32 = 3/8 as massive as an oxygen molecule. To measure out equal numbers of carbon atoms and oxygen molecules, we measure out only three-eighths as much carbon. If we started with 8 grams of oxygen, we need 3 grams of carbon to have the same number of particles (because 3 is three-eighths of 8). Alternatively, if we started with 32 grams of oxygen, we need 12 grams of carbon to have the same number of particles (because 12 is three-eighths of 32).

Figure 21.18
To have equal numbers of carbon atoms and oxygen molecules requires measuring out three-eighths as much carbon as oxygen.

☑ CHECKPOINT

1. Reacting 3 grams of carbon, C, with 8 grams of molecular oxygen, O_2, results in 11 grams of carbon dioxide, CO_2. Does it follow that 1.5 grams of carbon (half as much) will react with 4 grams of oxygen to form 5.5 grams of carbon dioxide?
2. Would reacting 5 grams of carbon with 8 grams of oxygen also result in 11 grams of carbon dioxide?

Check Your Answers

1. Yes, for their ratio is the same as when 11 grams of carbon dioxide is formed: 1.5:4:5.5 = 3:8:11.
2. It is a common error of many students to think that no reaction will occur if the proper ratios of reactants are not provided. You should understand, however, that in a 5-gram sample of carbon, 3 grams of carbon is available for reacting. This 3 grams will react with the 8 grams of oxygen to form 11 grams of carbon dioxide. There will be 2 grams of unreacted carbon remaining after the reaction. Reacting this remaining 2 grams of carbon would require more oxygen.

Chemicals react in very specific ratios. Oxygen and hydrogen, for example, always react in a 16:2 ratio by mass to form water. In other words, 16 grams of oxygen and 2 grams of hydrogen can react to form 18 grams of water. What if you were to combine 16 grams of oxygen with 3 grams of hydrogen? Would 19 grams of water form? No! Instead, the 16 grams of oxygen would react with only 2 of the 3 grams of hydrogen to yield 18 grams of water, leaving one gram of hydrogen unreacted. Interestingly, it was this property of chemicals to react only in specific ratios that led scientists of the early 1800s to propose the existence of atoms.

Insights

21.5 Molar Mass

Atoms and molecules react in specific ratios. In the laboratory, however, chemists work with bulk quantities of materials measured by mass. Chemists therefore need to know the relationship between the mass of a given sample and the number of atoms or molecules contained in that mass. The key to this relationship is the *mole*. Recall, from Section 18.3, that the mole is a unit equal to 6.02×10^{23}. This number is known as **Avogadro's number,** in honor of Amedeo Avogadro, an early pioneer in the development of atomic theory.

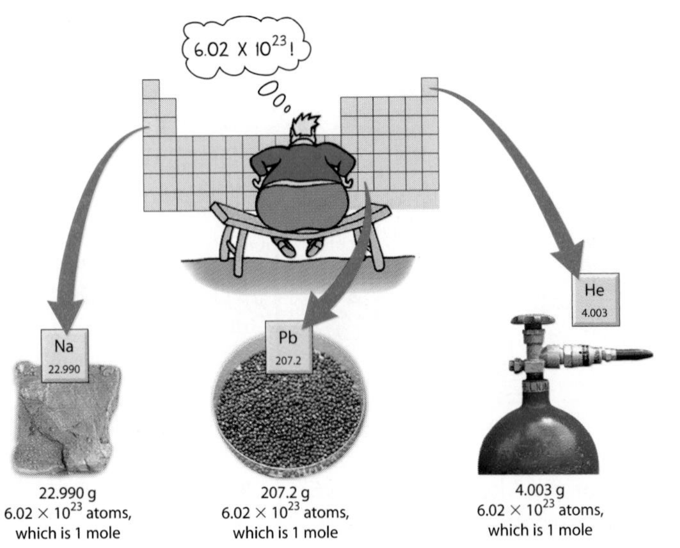

Figure 21.19
When the numeric value of the atomic mass of any element is expressed in grams, that amount of grams contains 6.02×10^{23} atoms.

As Figure 21.19 illustrates, if you express the numeric value of the atomic mass of any element in grams, the number of atoms in a sample of the element having this mass is always 6.02×10^{23}, which is 1 mole. For example, a 22.990-gram sample of sodium metal, Na (atomic mass 22.990 atomic mass units), contains 6.02×10^{23} sodium atoms, and a 207.2-gram sample of lead, Pb (atomic mass 207.2 atomic mass units), contains 6.02×10^{23} lead atoms.

The same concept holds for compounds. Express the numeric value of the formula mass of any compound in grams, and a sample having that mass contains 6.02×10^{23} molecules of that compound. For example, there are 6.02×10^{23} O_2 molecules in 31.998 grams of molecular oxygen, O_2 (formula mass 31.998 atomic mass units), and 6.02×10^{23} CO_2 molecules in 44.009 grams of carbon dioxide, CO_2 (formula mass 44.009 atomic mass units).

☑ **CHECKPOINT**

1. How many atoms are there in a 6.941 gram sample of lithium, Li (atomic mass 6.941 atomic mass units)?
2. How many molecules are there in a 18.015 gram sample of water, H_2O (formula mass 18.015 atomic mass units)?

Check Your Answers

1. Because this number of grams of lithium is numerically equal to the atomic mass, there are 6.02×10^{23} atoms in the sample, which is equal to 1 mole of lithium atoms.
2. Because this number of grams of water is numerically equal to the formula mass, there are 6.02×10^{23} water molecules in the sample, which is equal to 1 mole of water molecules.

The **molar mass** of any substance, be it element or compound, is defined as the mass of 1 mole of the substance. Thus, the units of molar mass are grams per mole. For instance, the atomic mass of carbon is 12.011 atomic mass units, which means that 1 mole of carbon has a mass of 12.011 grams, and we say that the *molar mass* of carbon is 12.011 grams per mole. The molar mass of molecular oxygen, O_2 (formula mass 31.998 atomic mass units), is 31.998 grams per mole. For convenience, values such as these are often rounded off to the nearest whole number. The molar mass of carbon, therefore, might also be presented as 12 grams per mole, and that of molecular oxygen as 32 grams per mole.

☑ CHECKPOINT

What is the molar mass of water (which has a formula mass of 18 atomic mass units)?

Check Your Answer

From the formula mass, you know that 1 mole of water has a mass of 18 grams. Therefore, the molar mass is 18 grams per mole.

Because 1 mole of any substance always contains 6.02×10^{23} particles, the mole is an ideal unit for chemical reactions. For example, 1 mole of carbon (12 grams) reacts with 1 mole of molecular oxygen (32 grams) to give 1 mole of carbon dioxide (44 grams).

In many instances, the ratio in which chemicals react is not 1:1. As shown in Figure 21.20, for example, 2 moles (4 grams) of molecular hydrogen react with 1 mole (32 grams) of molecular oxygen to give 2 moles (36 grams) of water. Note how the coefficients of the balanced chemical equation can be conveniently interpreted as the number of moles of reactants or products. A chemist, therefore, needs only to convert these numbers of moles to grams to determine how much mass of each reactant he or she should measure out to have the proper proportions.

$2\,H_2$	+	$1\,O_2$	$\longrightarrow$	$2\,H_2O$
2 moles		1 mole		2 moles
which is		which is		which is
4 grams		32 grams		36 grams
which is		which is		which is
12.04×10^{23} molecules		6.02×10^{23} molecules		12.04×10^{23} molecules

Figure 21.20
Two moles of H_2 react with 1 mole of O_2 to give 2 moles of H_2O. This is the same as saying 4 grams of H_2 reacts with 32 grams of O_2 to give 36 grams of H_2O or, equivalently, that 12.04×10^{23} H_2 molecules react with 6.02×10^{23} O_2 molecules to give 12.04×10^{23} H_2O molecules.

Cooking and chemistry are similar in that both require measuring ingredients. Just as a cook looks to a recipe to find the necessary quantities measured by the cup or the tablespoon, a chemist looks to the periodic table to find the necessary quantities measured by the number of grams per mole for each element or compound.

Figuring Physical Science

Stoichiometry

Using conversion factors (Appendix A) and the relationship between grams and moles, you can calculate the amount of reactants consumed or products formed in a chemical reaction. For example, what mass of water is produced when 16 grams of methane, CH_4 (formula mass 16 amu), burns in the following reaction?

$$CH_4 + 2\,O_2 \longrightarrow CO_2 + 2\,H_2O$$

Step 1. Convert the given mass to moles:

Conversion factor

$$(16\text{g } \cancel{CH_4})\left(\frac{1 \text{ mole } CH_4}{16\text{g } \cancel{CH_4}}\right) = 1 \text{ mole } CH_4$$

Step 2. Use the coefficients of the balanced equation to find out how many moles of H_2O are produced from this many moles of CH_4:

Conversion factor

$$(1 \text{ } \cancel{\text{mole } CH_4})\left(\frac{2 \text{ moles } H_2O}{1 \text{ } \cancel{\text{mole } CH_4}}\right) = 2 \text{ moles } H_2O$$

Step 3. Now that you know how many moles of H_2O are produced, convert this value to grams of H_2O:

Conversion factor

$$(2 \text{ } \cancel{\text{moles } H_2O})\left(\frac{18\text{g } H_2O}{1 \text{ } \cancel{\text{mole } H_2O}}\right) = 36\text{g } H_2O$$

This method of converting from grams to moles (step 1), then from moles to moles (step 2), and then from moles to grams (step 3) is an important aspect of what is called *stoichiometry*—the science of calculating the amount of reactants or products in any chemical reaction. It is a method that is developed much further in general chemistry courses. For this course, familiarity with stoichiometry is all that is needed—which is keeping tabs on atoms and molecules as they react to form products. Nonetheless, for a special assignment, you might try your analytical thinking skills on the following problems. First try to deduce the answer based on what you know about the law of mass conservation, and then follow the steps given above to check your answers.

Your Turn

1. How many grams of ozone, O_3 (48 amu), can be produced from 64 grams of oxygen, O_2 (32 amu), in the following reaction?

$$3\,O_2 \longrightarrow 2\,O_3$$

2. What mass of nitrogen monoxide, NO (30 amu), is formed when 28 grams of nitrogen, N_2 (28 amu), reacts with 32 grams of oxygen, O_2 (32 amu), in the following reaction?

$$N_2 + O_2 \longrightarrow 2\,NO$$

Answers are found on page 530.

Chemical reactions are truly the heart of chemistry, and their applications abound. For instance, the magician in Figure 21.21 has just ignited a sheet of nitrocellulose, also known as flash paper. In a moment, it will appear to have vanished. You know from the law of mass conservation, however, that materials don't simply vanish. They are instead transformed to new materials. Sometimes we can't see the new materials, but that doesn't mean they don't exist. One of the reactions that occur as flash paper burns is,

$$\underset{\text{A component of nitrocellulose}}{4\,C_6H_7N_5O_{16}(s)} + \underset{\text{Oxygen}}{19\,O_2(g)} \longrightarrow \underset{\text{Carbon dioxide}}{24\,CO_2(g)} + \underset{\text{Nitrogen dioxide}}{20\,NO_2(g)} + \underset{\text{Water}}{14\,H_2O(g)}$$

The equation shows 24 carbon, 28 hydrogen, 20 nitrogen, and 102 oxygen atoms before and after the reaction. The difference is in how these atoms are grouped together. The products formed, in this case, are all gaseous materials that quickly mix into the atmosphere, escaping our notice.

To make the flash paper, the magician would have had to mix the proper proportions of cellulose and nitric acid. He could do this by knowing the formula masses of these two substances. And although the flash paper may be bathed in an atmosphere of oxygen, it will not react with the oxygen until an initial amount of energy (from the spark of the magician's lighter) is provided to overcome the energy barrier. We know the burning of flash paper is exothermic because the amount of energy released as product bonds form is greater than the amount absorbed as reactant bonds break. The energy released is in the form of light and faster-moving molecules, which is why the air where the flash paper once was is now appreciably warmer. No true magic is involved, but it is enchanting all the same.

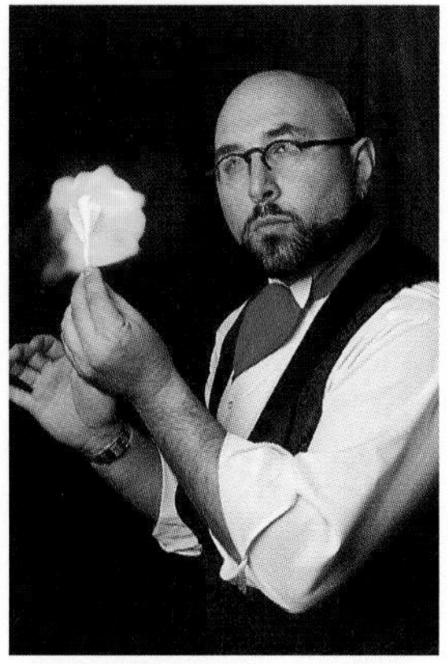

Figure 21.21
Magic often is in the eye of the beholder.

Summary of Terms

Reaction rate A measure of how quickly the concentration of products in a chemical reaction increases or the concentration of reactants decreases.

Activation energy The minimum energy required in order for a chemical reaction to proceed.

Catalyst Any substance that increases the rate of a chemical reaction without itself being consumed by the reaction.

Exothermic A term that describes a chemical reaction in which there is a net release of energy.

Endothermic A term that describes a chemical reaction in which there is a net absorption of energy.

Bond energy The amount of energy that is either absorbed as a chemical bond breaks or is released as a chemical bond forms.

Formula mass The sum of the atomic masses of the atoms in a chemical compound or element.

Avogadro's number The number of particles—6.02×10^{23}—contained in 1 mole of anything.

Molar mass The mass of 1 mole of a substance.

Review Questions

21.1 Reaction Rates

1. Why don't all collisions between reactant molecules lead to product formation?
2. What two aspects of a collision between two reactant molecules determine whether or not the collision results in the formation of product molecules?
3. What generally happens to the rate of a chemical reaction when temperature is increased?
4. Why does food take longer to spoil when it is placed in the refrigerator?
5. Which reactant molecules are the first to pass over the energy barrier?
6. What term is used to describe the minimum amount of energy required in order for a reaction to proceed?
7. Is an energy barrier for reactions synonymous with activation energy?

21.2 Catalysts

8. What catalyst is effective in the destruction of atmospheric ozone, O_3?
9. Can a catalyst react with a reactant?
10. What is the purpose of a catalytic converter?
11. What does a catalyst do to the activation energy of a reaction?
12. What net effect does a chemical reaction have on a catalyst?
13. Why are catalysts so important to our economy?

21.3 Energy and Chemical Reactions

14. If it takes 436 kilojoules of energy to break a bond, how much energy (in kilojoules) is released when the same bond is formed?
15. Is there any energy consumed at any time during an exothermic reaction?
16. What is released by an exothermic reaction?
17. What is absorbed by an endothermic reaction?
18. Which is higher in an endothermic reaction: the potential energy of the reactants or the potential energy of the products?

21.4 Relative Masses of Atoms and Molecules

19. Why don't equal masses of golf balls and Ping-Pong balls contain the same number of balls?

20. Why don't equal masses of carbon atoms and oxygen molecules contain the same number of particles?
21. How does formula mass differ from atomic mass?
22. What is the average mass of a carbon atom in atomic mass units?
23. What is the formula mass of an oxygen molecule in atomic mass units?
24. If you had 1 "mole" of marbles, how many marbles would you have?
25. If you had 2 "moles" of pennies, how many pennies would you have?

21.5 Molar Mass

26. How many moles of carbon are in 12.011 grams of carbon?
27. How many moles of oxygen molecules are in 32 grams of oxygen gas?
28. How many moles of water are there in 18 grams of water?
29. How many molecules of water are there in 18 grams of water?
30. Why is saying that you have 1 mole of water molecules the same as saying that you have 6.02×10^{23} water molecules?

Activities

Warming and Cooling Water Mixtures

Recall, from Section 20.1, that chemical bonds and intermolecular attractions are both consequences of the electric force, the difference being that chemical bonds are generally many times stronger than molecule-to-molecule attractions. So, just as the formation and breaking of chemical bonds involves energy, so does the formation and breaking of molecular attractions. For molecule-to-molecule attractions, the amount of energy absorbed or released per gram of material is relatively small. Physical changes involving the formation or breaking of molecule-to-molecule attractions, therefore, are much safer to perform, which makes them more suitable for an out-of-laboratory activity. Experience the exothermic and endothermic nature of physical changes for yourself by performing the following two activities:

1. Hold some room-temperature water in the cupped palm of your hand over a sink. Pour an equal amount of room-temperature rubbing alcohol into the water. Is this mixing an exothermic or endothermic process? What's going on at the molecular level?

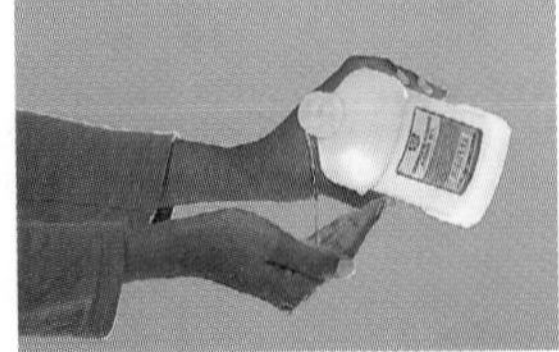

2. Add lukewarm water to two plastic cups. (Do *not* use insulating Styrofoam cups.) Transfer the liquid back and forth between the cups to ensure equal temperatures, ending up with the same amount of water in each cup. Add several tablespoons of table salt to one cup and stir. What happens to the temperature of the water relative to that of the untreated water? (Hold the cups up to your cheeks to tell.) Is this an exothermic or endothermic process? What's going on at the molecular level?

Exercises

1. The yeast used in bread dough feeds on sugar to produce carbon dioxide gas, which causes the dough to rise. Why is bread dough commonly left to rise in a warm area rather than in the refrigerator?
2. Why does food placed in the freezer last longer than food placed in the refrigerator?
3. Why does a glowing splint of wood burn only slowly in air but burst into flames when placed in pure oxygen?
4. Why is heat often added to chemical reactions performed in the laboratory?
5. An Alka-Seltzer antacid tablet bubbles vigorously in room-temperature water but only slowly in a 50:50 mix of alcohol and water, also at room temperature. Propose an explanation involving the relationship between reaction speed and frequency of molecular collisions.
6. What can you deduce about the activation energy of a reaction that takes billions of years to go to completion? How about a reaction that takes only fractions of a second?
7. In the following reaction sequence for the catalytic formation of ozone from molecular oxygen, which chemical compound is the catalyst: nitrogen monoxide or nitrogen dioxide?

$$O_2 + 2\ NO \longrightarrow 2\ NO_2$$

$$2\ NO_2 \longrightarrow 2\ NO + 2\ O$$

$$2\ O + 2\ O_2 \longrightarrow 2\ O_3$$

8. What role do chlorofluorocarbons play in the catalytic destruction of ozone?
9. Many people hear about atmospheric ozone depletion and wonder why we don't simply replace the ozone that has been destroyed. Knowing about chlorofluorocarbons and knowing how catalysts work, explain how this would not be a lasting solution.

10. Use the bond energies in Table 21.1 and the accounting format shown in Section 21.3 to determine whether these reactions are exothermic or endothermic:

$$H_2 + Cl_2 \longrightarrow 2\ HCl$$

$$2\ HC{\equiv}CH + 5\ O_2 \longrightarrow 4\ CO_2 + 2\ H_2O$$

11. Use the bond energies in Table 21.1 and the accounting format shown in Section 21.3 to determine whether these reactions are exothermic or endothermic:

$$N_2H_4 \longrightarrow 2\ H_2 + N_2$$

$$2\ H_2O_2 \longrightarrow O_2 + 2\ H_2O$$

12. Note, in Table 21.1, that bond energy increases going from H–N to H–O to H–F. Provide an explanation for this trend, based on the sizes of these atoms as deduced from their positions in the periodic table. (See Figure 14.12, and remember that, when it comes to the electrical force of attraction, closeness wins.)
13. Are the chemical reactions that take place in a disposable battery exothermic or endothermic? What evidence supports your answer?
14. Is the reaction that is going on in a rechargeable battery while it is recharging exothermic or endothermic?
15. Is the synthesis of ozone from oxygen exothermic or endothermic?
16. Is the synthesis of oxygen from ozone exothermic or endothermic?
17. A commercial "cold pack" consists of a bag within a bag. The inner bag contains a salt, typically ammonium nitrate. The outer bag contains water. Punching the pack breaks an inner seal, which allows the ammonium nitrate to mix with the water. As the ammonium nitrate dissolves, heat is absorbed, and the temperature of anything in contact with the pack—including a sprained ankle—decreases. Is this an example of an exothermic process or an endothermic process? Are the changes physical or chemical?
18. What are the formula masses of the following: water, H_2O; propene, C_3H_6; and 2-propanol, C_3H_8O?
19. What is the formula mass of sulfur dioxide, SO_2?
20. Which has more atoms: 17.031 grams of ammonia, NH_3, or 72.922 grams of hydrogen chloride, HCl?
21. Which has more atoms: 64.058 grams of sulfur dioxide, SO_2, or 72.922 grams of hydrogen chloride, HCl?
22. Which has the greatest number of molecules?
    (a) 28 grams of nitrogen, N_2
    (b) 32 grams of oxygen, O_2
    (c) 32 grams of methane, CH_4
    (d) 38 grams of fluorine, F_2
23. Which has the greatest number of atoms?
    (a) 28 grams of nitrogen, N_2
    (b) 32 grams of oxygen, O_2
    (c) 16 grams of methane, CH_4
    (d) 38 grams of fluorine, F_2
24. Hydrogen and oxygen always react in a 1:8 ratio by mass to form water. Early investigators thought this meant that oxygen was eight times more massive than hydrogen. What did these investigators assume about water's chemical formula?
25. Two atomic mass units equal how many grams?
26. What is the mass of an oxygen atom in atomic mass units?
27. What is the mass of a water molecule in atomic mass units?
28. What is the mass of an oxygen atom in grams?
29. What is the mass of a water molecule in grams?
30. Is it possible to have a sample of oxygen that has a mass of 14 atomic mass units? Explain.
31. Which has more mass: 1.01 amu of hydrogen or 1.01 grams of hydrogen?
32. Which has the greater mass, 1.204×10^{24} molecules of molecular hydrogen or 1.204×10^{24} molecules of water?
33. You are given two samples of elements, and each sample has a mass of 10 grams. If the two samples contain the same number of atoms, what must be true of the two samples?
34. If you had a "mole" of mice, how many mice feet would you have?
35. If you had a "mole" of eggs, how many dozens would you have?

Problems

1. How many molecules of aspirin (which has a formula mass of 180 atomic mass units) are there in a 0.250-gram sample?
2. Small samples of oxygen gas needed in the laboratory can be generated by any number of simple chemical reactions, such as the following:

$$2\ KClO_3(s) \longrightarrow 2\ KCl(s) + 3\ O_2(g)$$

What mass of oxygen (in grams) is produced when 122.55 grams of $KClO_3$ (formula mass 122.55 atomic mass units) takes part in this reaction?

3. How many grams of water, H_2O, and propene, C_3H_6, can be formed from the reaction of 6.0 grams of 2-propanol, C_3H_8O?

$$\begin{array}{c} \text{H}\quad\text{OH}\quad\text{H} \\ |\quad\ |\quad\ | \\ \text{H}-\text{C}-\text{C}-\text{C}-\text{H} \\ |\quad\ |\quad\ | \\ \text{H}\quad\text{H}\quad\text{H} \end{array} \longrightarrow$$

2-Propanol

$$\begin{array}{c} \text{H}\qquad\quad\text{H} \\ |\qquad\quad\ | \\ \text{H}-\text{C}-\text{C}{=}\text{C}-\text{H} \\ |\qquad\ | \\ \text{H}\qquad\text{H} \end{array} + \text{H}-\text{O}-\text{H}$$

Propene Water

4. How many moles of water, H_2O, can be produced from the reaction of 16 grams of methane, CH_4, with an unlimited supply of oxygen, O_2? How many grams of water is this? The reaction is:

$$CH_4 + 2\ O_2 \longrightarrow CO_2 + 2\ H_2O$$

5. How much energy, in kilojoules, is released or absorbed during the reaction of 1 mole of nitrogen, N_2, with 3 moles of molecular hydrogen, H_2, to form 2 moles of ammonia, NH_3? Consult Table 21.1 for bond energies.

$$N{\equiv}N + H{-}H + H{-}H + H{-}H \rightarrow NH_3 + NH_3$$

Figuring Physical Science—Answers

Stoichiometry

1. According to the law of mass conservation, the amount of mass in the products must equal the amount of mass in the reactants. Given that this reaction involves only one reactant and one product, you should not be surprised to learn that 64 grams of reactant produces 64 grams of product:

   Step 1. Convert grams of O_2 to moles of O_2:

$$(64\ \text{g}\ \cancel{O_2})\left(\frac{1\ \text{mole}\ O_2}{32\ \text{g}\ \cancel{O_2}}\right) = 2\ \text{moles}\ O_2$$

   Step 2. Convert moles of O_2 to moles of O_3:

$$(2\ \cancel{\text{moles}\ O_2})\left(\frac{2\ \text{moles}\ O_3}{3\ \cancel{\text{moles}\ O_2}}\right) = 1.33\ \text{moles}\ O_3$$

   Step 3. Convert moles of O_3 to grams of O_3:

$$(1.33\ \cancel{\text{moles}\ O_3})\left(\frac{48\ \text{g}\ O_3}{1\ \cancel{\text{mole}\ O_3}}\right) = 64\ \text{g}\ O_3$$

2. There are several ways to answer this problem. One way would be to recognize that 28 grams of N_2 is 1 mole of N_2 and 32 grams of O_2 is 1 mole of O_2. According to the balanced equation, combining 1 mole of N_2 with 1 mole of O_2 yields 2 moles of NO. The mass of 2 moles of NO is

$$(2\ \cancel{\text{moles NO}})\left(\frac{30\ \text{g NO}}{1\ \cancel{\text{mole NO}}}\right) = 60\ \text{g NO}$$

   which is the sum of the masses of the reactants, as it must be because of the law of mass conservation.

Chapter 21 Online Resources

Tutorials
- Equilibrium
- Chemical Reactions & Equations

Quiz
Exercises
Flashcards
Links

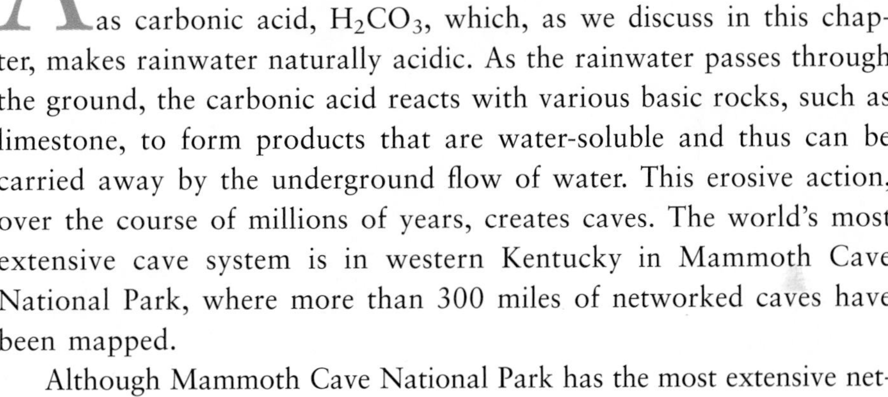

CHAPTER 22

Acids and Bases

As rainwater falls, it absorbs atmospheric carbon dioxide. The carbon dioxide reacts with the water to form an acid known as carbonic acid, H_2CO_3, which, as we discuss in this chapter, makes rainwater naturally acidic. As the rainwater passes through the ground, the carbonic acid reacts with various basic rocks, such as limestone, to form products that are water-soluble and thus can be carried away by the underground flow of water. This erosive action, over the course of millions of years, creates caves. The world's most extensive cave system is in western Kentucky in Mammoth Cave National Park, where more than 300 miles of networked caves have been mapped.

Although Mammoth Cave National Park has the most extensive network of caves, its cave chambers are much smaller than those in Carlsbad Caverns National Park in southeastern New Mexico. The Carlsbad Caverns measure 25 stories high and half a kilometer wide. The great size of the chambers at Carlsbad is due to the "limestone-eating" action of an acid known as sulfuric acid, H_2SO_4, which is much stronger than carbonic acid. This sulfuric acid forms from gaseous hydrogen sulfide, H_2S, and gaseous sulfur dioxide, SO_2, both of which rise up from oil and gas deposits buried deep underground.

In this chapter, we explore acids and bases and the chemical reactions they undergo. We begin with a definition of these two important substances and then explore how some acids and bases are stronger than others. After learning about the pH scale, we close by looking at some environmental and physiological applications of acid–base concepts.

22.1 Acids Donate Protons, Bases Accept Them

The term *acid* comes from the Latin *acidus,* which means "sour." The sour taste of vinegar and citrus fruits is due to the presence of acids. Food is digested in the stomach with the help of acids, and acids are also essential in the chemical industry. Today, for instance, more than 85 billion pounds of sulfuric acid is produced annually in the United States, making this the number-one manufactured chemical. Sulfuric acid is used in fertilizers, detergents, paint dyes, plastics, pharmaceuticals, and storage batteries, as well as in the production of iron and steel. It is so important in the manufacturing of goods that its production is considered a standard measure of a nation's industrial strength. Figure 22.1 shows only a very few of the acids we commonly encounter.

(a)

(b)

(c)

(d)

Figure 22.1
Examples of acids. (a) Citrus fruits contain many types of acids, including ascorbic acid, $C_6H_8O_6$, which is vitamin C. (b) Vinegar contains acetic acid, $C_2H_4O_2$, and can be used to preserve foods. (c) Many toilet-bowl cleaners are formulated with hydrochloric acid, HCl. (d) All carbonated beverages contain carbonic acid, H_2CO_3, while many also contain phosphoric acid, H_3PO_4.

Bases are characterized by their bitter taste and slippery feel. Interestingly, bases themselves are not slippery. Rather, they cause skin oils to transform into slippery solutions of soap. Most commercial preparations for unclogging drains contain sodium hydroxide, NaOH (also known as lye), which is extremely basic and hazardous when concentrated. Bases are also heavily used in industry. Each year in the United States, about 25 billion pounds of sodium hydroxide is manufactured for use in the production of various chemicals and in the pulp and paper industry. Solutions containing bases are often called alkaline, a term derived from the Arabic *al-qali* ("the ashes"), as we found out in Section 14.6. Ashes are slippery when wet because of the presence of the base, potassium carbonate, K_2CO_3. Figure 22.2 shows some familiar bases.

The hydrogen ion, H^+, does not readily exist in water because any hydrogen ion formed is quickly picked up by a water molecule and transformed to the hydronium ion, H_3O^+.

Insights

Acids and bases may be defined in several ways. For our purposes, an appropriate definition is the one suggested in 1923 by the Danish chemist Johannes Brønsted (1879–1947) and the English chemist Thomas Lowry (1874–1936). In the Brønsted–Lowry definition, an **acid** is any chemical that donates a hydrogen ion, H^+, and a **base** is any chemical that accepts a

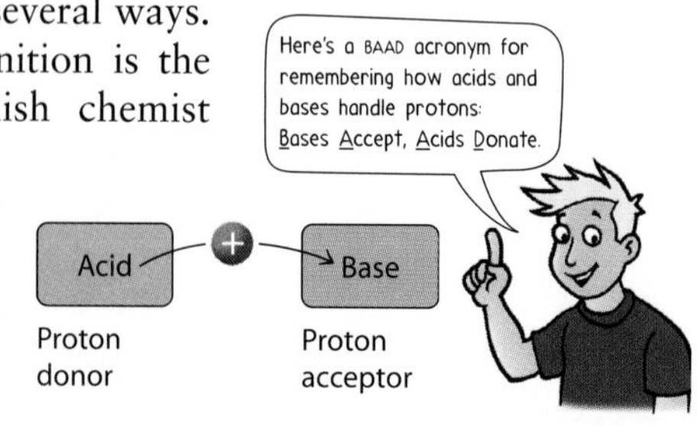

Figure 22.2
Examples of bases. (a) Reactions involving sodium bicarbonate, $NaHCO_3$, cause baked goods to rise. (b) Ashes contain potassium carbonate, K_2CO_3. (c) Soap is made by reacting bases with animal or vegetable oils. The soap itself, then, is slightly alkaline. (d) Powerful bases, such as sodium hydroxide, NaOH, are used in drain cleaners.

hydrogen ion. Recall that a hydrogen atom consists of one electron surrounding a one-proton nucleus. A hydrogen ion, H^+, formed from the loss of an electron, therefore, is nothing more than a lone proton. Thus, it is also sometimes said that an acid is a chemical that donates a proton and a base is a chemical that accepts a proton.

Consider what happens when hydrogen chloride is mixed into water:

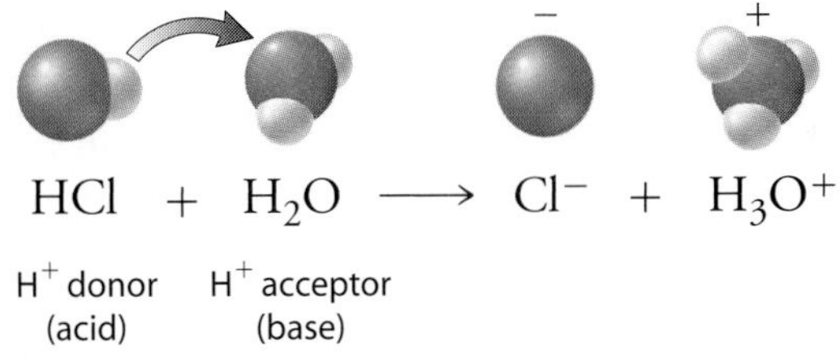

$$HCl + H_2O \longrightarrow Cl^- + H_3O^+$$

Hydrogen chloride donates a hydrogen ion to one of the nonbonding electron pairs on a water molecule, resulting in a third hydrogen bonded to the oxygen. In this case, hydrogen chloride behaves as an acid (proton donor) and water behaves as a base (proton acceptor). The products of this reaction are a chloride ion and a **hydronium ion,** H_3O^+, which, as Figure 22.3 shows, is a water molecule with an extra proton.

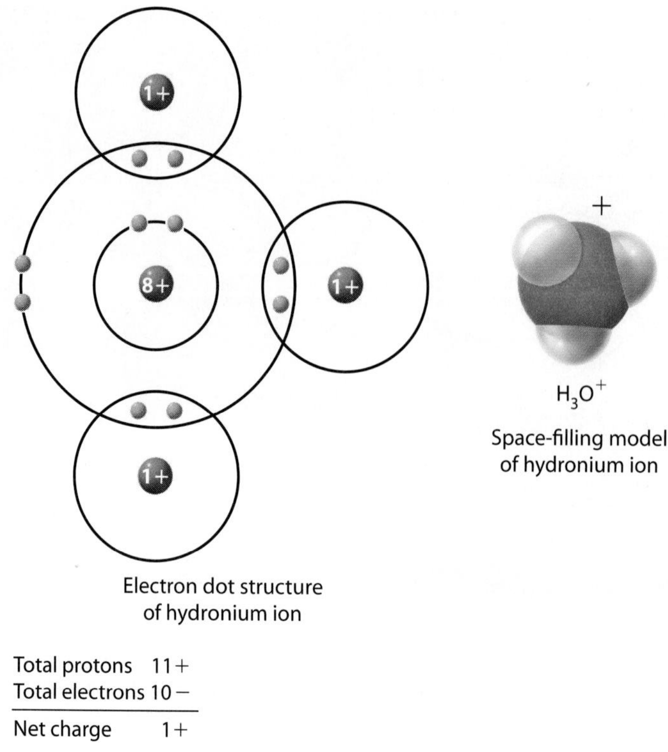

Figure 22.3
The hydronium ion's positive charge is a consequence of the extra proton this molecule has acquired. Hydronium ions, which play a role in many acid–base reactions, are polyatomic ions, which, as mentioned in Section 19.2, are molecules that carry a net electric charge.

When added to water, ammonia behaves as a base as its nonbonding electrons (see Section 19.1) accept a hydrogen ion from water, which, in this case, behaves as an acid:

$$H_2O + NH_3 \longrightarrow OH^- + NH_4^+$$

H^+ donor (acid) H^+ acceptor (base)

Figure 22.4
Hydroxide ions have a net negative charge, which is a consequence of having lost a proton. Like hydronium ions, they play a part in many acid–base reactions.

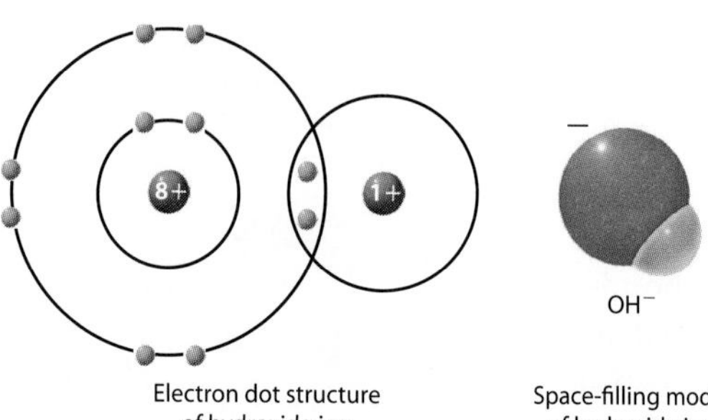

This reaction results in the formation of an ammonium ion and a **hydroxide ion,** which, as shown in Figure 22.4, is a water molecule without the nucleus of one of the hydrogen atoms.

An important aspect of the Brønsted–Lowry definition is that it uses a *behavior* to define a substance as an acid or a base. We say, for example, that hydrogen chloride *behaves* as an acid when mixed with water, which *behaves* as a base. Similarly, ammonia *behaves* as a base when mixed with water, which under this circumstance *behaves* as an acid. Because acid–base is seen as a behavior, there is really no contradiction when a chemical like water behaves as a base in one instance but as an acid in another instance. By analogy, consider yourself. You are who you are, but your behavior changes depending on whom you are with. Likewise, it is a chemical property of water to behave as a base (to accept H^+) when mixed with hydrogen chloride and as an acid (to donate H^+) when mixed with ammonia.

The products of an acid–base reaction can also behave as acids or as bases. An ammonium ion, for example, may donate a hydrogen ion back to a hydroxide ion to re-form ammonia and water:

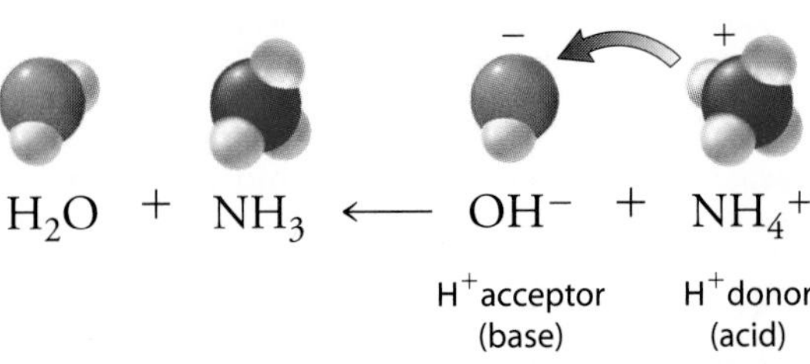

Forward and reverse acid–base reactions proceed simultaneously and can therefore be represented as occurring at the same time by using two oppositely facing arrows:

$$H_2O + NH_3 \rightleftharpoons OH^- + NH_4^+$$

H_2O	NH_3	OH^-	NH_4^+
H^+donor (acid)	H^+acceptor (base)	H^+acceptor (base)	H^+donor (acid)

When the equation is viewed from left to right, the ammonia behaves as a base because it accepts a hydrogen ion from the water, which therefore acts as an acid. Viewed in the reverse direction, the equation shows that the ammonium ion behaves as an acid because it donates a hydrogen ion to the hydroxide ion, which therefore behaves as a base.

☑ CHECKPOINT

Identify the acid or base behavior of each participant in the reaction

$$H_2PO_4^- + H_3O^+ \rightleftharpoons H_3PO_4 + H_2O$$

Check Your Answer

In the forward reaction (left to right), $H_2PO_4^-$ gains a hydrogen ion to become H_3PO_4. In accepting the hydrogen ion, $H_2PO_4^-$ is behaving as a base. It gets the hydrogen ion from the H_3O^+, which is behaving as an acid. In the reverse direction, H_3PO_4 loses a hydrogen ion to become $H_2PO_4^-$ and is thus behaving as an acid. The recipient of the hydrogen ion is the H_2O, which is behaving as a base as it transforms to H_3O^+.

Figure 22.5
"Salt-free" table salt substitutes contain potassium chloride in place of sodium chloride. Caution is advised in using these products, however, because excessive quantities of potassium salts can lead to serious illness. Furthermore, sodium ions are a vital component of our diet and should never be totally excluded. For a good balance of these two important ions, you might inquire about commercially available half-and-half mixtures of sodium chloride and potassium chloride, such as the one shown here.

A Salt Is the Ionic Product of an Acid–Base Reaction

In everyday language, the word *salt* implies sodium chloride, NaCl, table salt. In the language of chemistry, however, **salt** is a general term meaning any ionic compound formed from the reaction between an acid and a base. Hydrogen chloride and sodium hydroxide, for example, react to produce the salt sodium chloride and water:

$$HCl + NaOH \longrightarrow NaCl + H_2O$$

HCl	NaOH	NaCl	H_2O
Hydrogen chloride (acid)	Sodium hydroxide (base)	Sodium chloride (salt)	Water

Similarly, the reaction between hydrogen chloride and potassium hydroxide yields the salt potassium chloride and water:

$$HCl + KOH \longrightarrow KCl + H_2O$$

HCl	KOH	KCl	H_2O
Hydrogen chloride (acid)	Potassium hydroxide (base)	Potassium chloride (salt)	Water

Potassium chloride is the main ingredient in "salt-free" table salt, as noted in Figure 22.5.

Salts are generally far less corrosive than the acids and bases from which they are formed. A corrosive chemical has the power to disintegrate a material or wear away its surface. Hydrogen chloride is a remarkably corrosive acid, which makes it useful for cleaning toilet bowls and etching metal surfaces. Sodium hydroxide is a very corrosive base used for unclogging drains. Mixing hydrogen chloride and sodium hydroxide together in equal portions, however, produces an aqueous solution of sodium chloride—salt water, which is not nearly as destructive as either starting material.

Salts are the products of an acid–base reaction, but a salt itself may be slightly acidic or slightly basic. Acetic acid, CH_3CO_2H, and sodium hydroxide, NaOH, for example, react to form the salt sodium acetate, $CH_3CO_2^-Na^+$, which behaves as a weak base. We treat this further in Section 22.5.

Insights

Table 22.1

Acid–Base Reactions and the Salts Formed

Acid		Base		Salt		Water
HCN	+	NaOH	$\longrightarrow$	NaCN	+	H_2O
Hydrogen cyanide		Sodium hydroxide		Sodium cyanide		
HNO_3	+	KOH	$\longrightarrow$	KNO_3	+	H_2O
Nitric acid		Potassium hydroxide		Potassium nitrate		
2 HCl	+	$Ca(OH)_2$	$\longrightarrow$	$CaCl_2$	+	2 H_2O
Hydrogen chloride		Calcium hydroxide		Calcium chloride		
HF	+	NaOH	$\longrightarrow$	NaF	+	H_2O
Hydrogen fluoride		Sodium hydroxide		Sodium flouride		

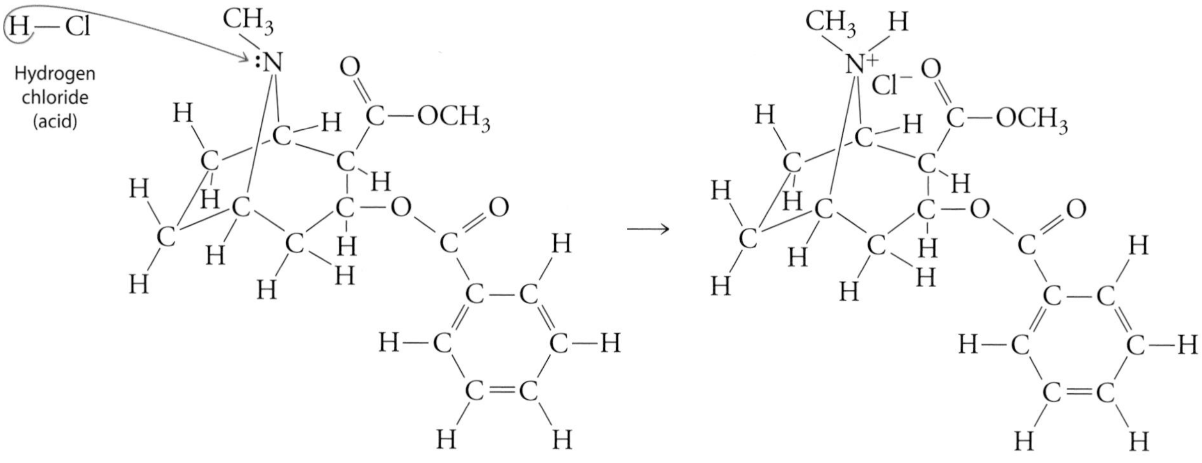

Figure 22.6
Hydrogen chloride and cocaine react to form the salt *cocaine hydrochloride,* which, because of its solubility in water, can be readily absorbed into the body through moist membranes.

There are as many salts as there are acids and bases. Sodium cyanide, NaCN, is a deadly poison. "Saltpeter," which is potassium nitrate, KNO_3, is useful as a fertilizer and in the formulation of gunpowder. Calcium chloride, $CaCl_2$, is commonly used to deice roads, and sodium fluoride, NaF, prevents tooth decay. The acid–base reactions forming these salts are shown in Table 22.1.

The reaction between an acid and a base is called a **neutralization** reaction. As can be seen in the color-coding of the neutralization reactions in Table 22.1, the positive ion of a salt comes from the base and the negative ion comes from the acid. The remaining hydrogen and hydroxide ions join to form water.

Not all neutralization reactions result in the formation of water. In the presence of hydrogen chloride, for example, the drug cocaine behaves as a base by accepting H^+ from a hydrogen chloride. The negative Cl^- then joins the cocaine–H^+ ion to form the salt cocaine hydrochloride, shown in Figure 22.6. This salt of cocaine is soluble in water and can be absorbed through the moist membranes of the nasal or oral passages. The nonsalt form of cocaine, also known as "free-base cocaine" or "crack cocaine," is a nonpolar material that vaporizes easily when heated. When its vapors are inhaled directly into the lungs, the consequence is dangerously high concentrations of cocaine in the bloodstream.

☑ CHECKPOINT

Is a neutralization reaction best described as a physical change or a chemical change?

Check Your Answer

New chemicals are formed during a neutralization reaction, meaning the reaction is a chemical change.

22.2 Relative Strengths of Acids and Bases

In general, the stronger an acid, the more readily it donates hydrogen ions. Likewise, the stronger a base, the more readily it accepts hydrogen ions. An example of a strong acid is hydrogen chloride, HCl, and an example of a strong base is sodium hydroxide, NaOH. The corrosiveness of these materials is a result of their strength.

One way to assess the strength of an acid or base is to measure how much of it remains after it has been added to water. If little remains, the acid or base is strong. If a lot remains, the acid or base is weak. To illustrate this concept, consider what happens when the strong acid hydrogen chloride is added to water and what happens when the weak acid acetic acid, $C_2H_4O_2$ (the active ingredient of vinegar), is added to water.

Being an acid, hydrogen chloride donates hydrogen ions to water, forming chloride ions and hydronium ions. Because HCl is such a strong acid, nearly all of it is converted to these ions, as is shown in Figure 22.7.

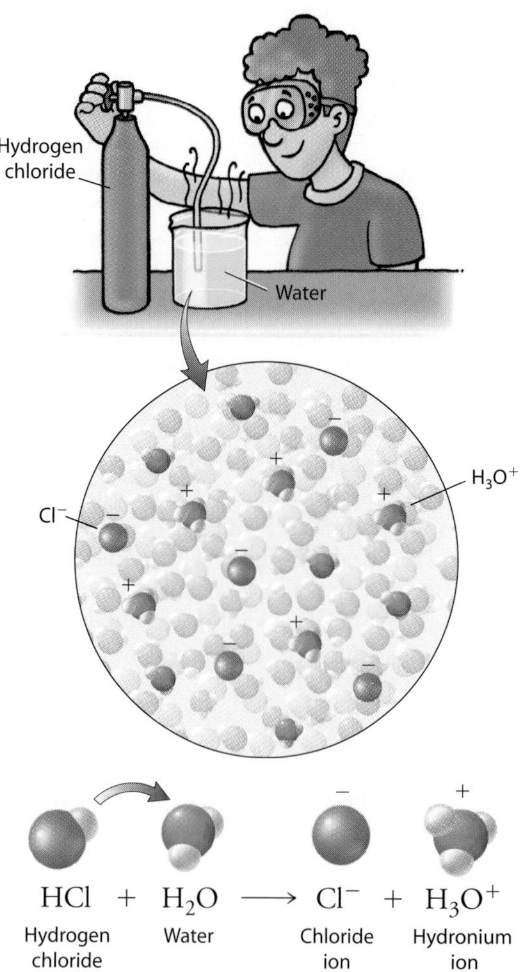

Figure 22.7
Immediately after gaseous hydrogen chloride is added to water, it reacts with the water to form hydronium ions and chloride ions. That very little HCl remains (none shown here) lets us know that HCl acts as a strong acid.

Because acetic acid is a weak acid, it has much less tendency to donate hydrogen ions to water. When this acid is dissolved in water, only a small portion of the acetic acid molecules are converted to ions, a process that occurs as the polar O–H bonds are broken (the C–H bonds of acetic acid are unaffected by the water because of their nonpolarity). The majority of acetic acid molecules remain intact in their original nonionized form, as shown in Figure 22.8.

What makes one acid strong and another weak? A full answer is beyond the scope of this textbook. Briefly, however, it involves the stability of the negative ion that remains after the proton has been donated. Hydrogen chloride is a strong acid because the chloride ion is able to accommodate the negative charge rather well. Acetic acid, however, is a weaker acid because the resulting oxygen ion is less able to accommodate the negative charge.

Insights

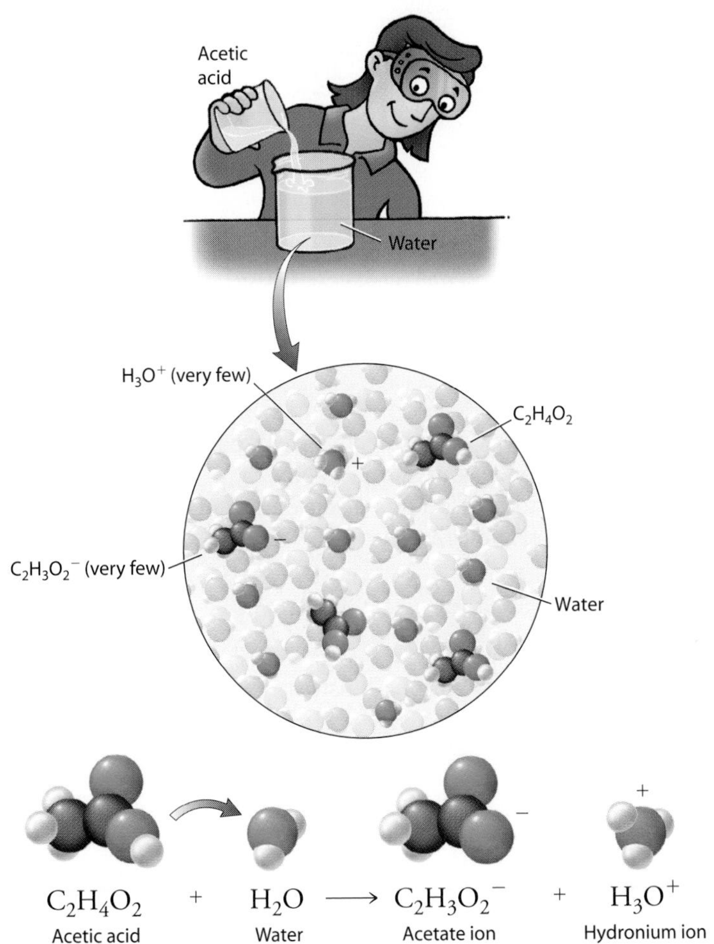

Figure 22.8
When liquid acetic acid is added to water, only a few acetic acid molecules react with water to form ions. The majority of the acetic acid molecules remain in their nonionized form, which implies that acetic acid is a weak acid.

Figures 22.7 and 22.8 show the submicroscopic behavior of strong and weak acids in water. Since molecules and ions are too small to see, how then does a chemist measure the strength of an acid? One way is by measuring a solution's ability to conduct an electric current, as Figure 22.9 illustrates. In pure water there are practically no ions to conduct electricity. When a strong acid is dissolved in water, many ions are generated, as indicated in Figure 22.7. The presence of these ions allows for the flow of a large electric current. A weak acid dissolved in water generates only a few ions, as indicated in Figure 22.8. The presence of fewer ions means there can be only a small electric current.

(a)

(b)

(c)

Figure 22.9
(a) The pure water in this circuit is unable to conduct electricity because it contains practically no ions. The light bulb in the circuit therefore remains unlit. (b) Because HCl is a strong acid, nearly all of its molecules break apart in water, giving a high concentration of ions, which are able to conduct an electric current that lights the bulb. (c) Acetic acid, $C_2H_4O_2$, is a weak acid; in water, only a small portion of its molecules break up into ions. Because fewer ions are generated, only a weak current exists, and the bulb is therefore dimmer.

This same trend is seen with strong and weak bases. Strong bases, for example, tend to accept hydrogen ions more readily than weak bases. In solution, a strong base allows the flow of a large electric current, and a weak base allows the flow of a small electric current.

☑ CHECKPOINT

According to the aqueous solutions illustrated here, which is the stronger base, NH_3 or NaOH?

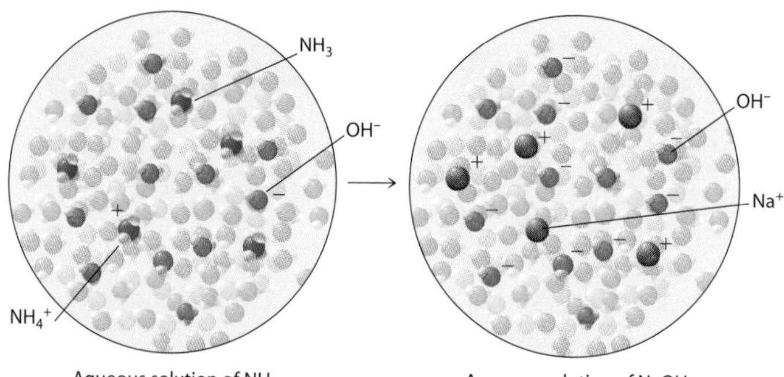

Check Your Answer

The solution on the right contains the greater number of ions, meaning sodium hydroxide, NaOH, is the stronger base. Ammonia, NH_3, is the weaker base, indicated by the relatively few ions in the solution on the left.

Just because an acid or base is strong doesn't mean a solution of that acid or base is corrosive. The corrosive action of an acidic solution is caused by the hydronium ions rather than by the acid that generated those hydronium ions. Similarly, the corrosive action of a basic solution results from the hydroxide ions it contains, regardless of the base that generated those hydroxide ions. A *very* dilute solution of a strong acid or a strong base may have little corrosive action because in such solutions there are only a few hydronium or hydroxide ions. (Almost all the molecules of the strong acid or base break up into ions, but, because the solution is dilute, there are only a few acid or base molecules to begin with. As a result, there are only a few hydronium or hydroxide ions.) You shouldn't be too alarmed, therefore, when you discover that some toothpastes are formulated with small amounts of sodium hydroxide, one of the strongest bases known.

On the other hand, a concentrated solution of a weak acid, such as the acetic acid in vinegar, may be just as corrosive as or may be even more corrosive than a dilute solution of a strong acid, such as hydrogen chloride. The relative strengths of two acids in solution or two bases in solution, therefore, can be compared only when the two solutions have the same concentration.

As an analogy, consider a large room packed full of people, each wearing one hat. At the sound of a bell, five of these people take off their hats and give them to someone nearby who is still wearing one hat. There are now five people with no hats and five people with two hats. Interestingly, no matter how many people give their hats away, the number of people with no hats will always be the same as the number of people with two hats. Likewise, with pure water, the concentration of hydronium and hydroxide ions will always be the same.

Insights

22.3 Acidic, Basic, and Neutral Solutions

A substance whose ability to behave as an acid is about the same as its ability to behave as a base is said to be **amphoteric.** Water is a good example. Because it is amphoteric, water has the ability to react with itself. In behaving as an acid, a water molecule donates a hydrogen ion to a neighboring water molecule, which, in accepting the hydrogen ion, is behaving as a base. This reaction produces a hydroxide ion and a hydronium ion, which react together to re-form the water molecule:

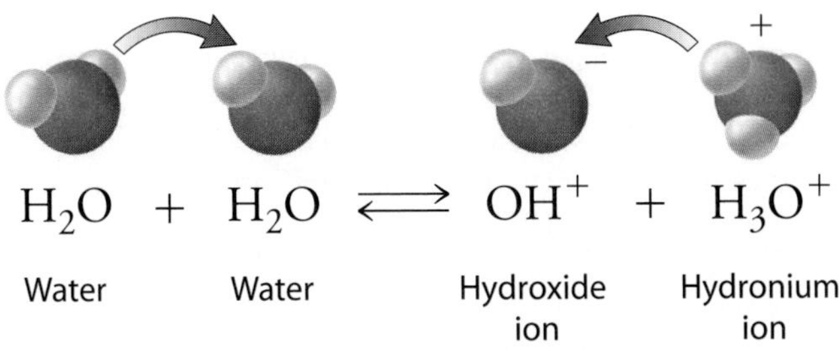

When a water molecule gains a hydrogen ion, a second water molecule must lose a hydrogen ion. So for every one hydronium ion formed, one hydroxide ion also forms. In pure water, therefore, the total number of hydronium ions must be the same as the total number of hydroxide ions. Experiments reveal that the concentration of hydronium and hydroxide ions in pure water is extremely low—about 0.0000001 *M* for each, where *M* stands for molarity or moles per liter (Section 18.3). Water by itself, therefore, is a very weak acid as well as a very weak base, as evidenced by the unlit light bulb in Figure 22.9a.

☑ CHECKPOINT

Do water molecules react with one another?

Check Your Answer

Yes, but not to any large extent. When they do react, they form hydronium and hydroxide ions. (Note: Make sure you understand this point because it serves as a basis for most of the rest of the chapter.)

Further experiments reveal an interesting rule pertaining to the concentrations of hydronium and hydroxide ions in any solution that contains water. The concentration of hydronium ions in any aqueous solution multiplied by the concentration of the hydroxide ions in the solution always equals the constant K_w, which is a very, very small number:

$$\text{Concentration } H_3O^+ \times \text{concentration } OH^- = K_w = 0.00000000000001$$

Concentration is usually given as molarity, which is indicated by abbreviating this equation using brackets:

$$[H_3O^+] \times [OH^-] = K_w = 0.00000000000001$$

The brackets mean this equation is read "the molarity of H_3O^+ times the molarity of OH^- equals K_w." Writing in scientific notation, we have

$$[H_3O^+][OH^-] = K_w = 1.0 \times 10^{-14}$$

For pure water, the value of K_w is the concentration of hydronium ions, 0.0000001 *M*, multiplied by the concentration of hydroxide ions, 0.0000001 *M*, which can be written in scientific notation as

$$[1.0 \times 10^{-7}][1.0 \times 10^{-7}] = K_w = 1.0 \times 10^{-14}$$

The constant value of K_w is quite significant because it means that, *no matter what is dissolved in the water,* the product of the hydronium-ion and hydroxide-ion concentrations always equals 1.0×10^{-14}. So, if the concentration of H_3O^+ goes up, the concentration of OH^- must go down, and the product of the two remains 1.0×10^{-14}.

Suppose, for example, that a small amount of HCl is added to pure water to increase the concentration of hydronium ions to 1.0×10^{-5} *M*. (Be sure to see your instructor if you're confused as to how 10^{-5} is larger than 10^{-7}.) The hydroxide-ion concentration decreases to 1.0×10^{-9} *M*, so that the product of the two remains equal to $K_w = 1.0 \times 10^{-14}$:

$$[H_3O^+][OH^-] = K_w = 1.0 \times 10^{-14}$$

$$\text{pure water } [1.0 \times 10^{-7}][1.0 \times 10^{-7}] = K_w = 1.0 \times 10^{-14}$$

$$\text{HCl added } [1.0 \times 10^{-5}][1.0 \times 10^{-9}] = K_w = 1.0 \times 10^{-14}$$

The hydroxide-ion concentration goes down because some of the hydroxide ions from the water are neutralized by the added hydronium ions from the

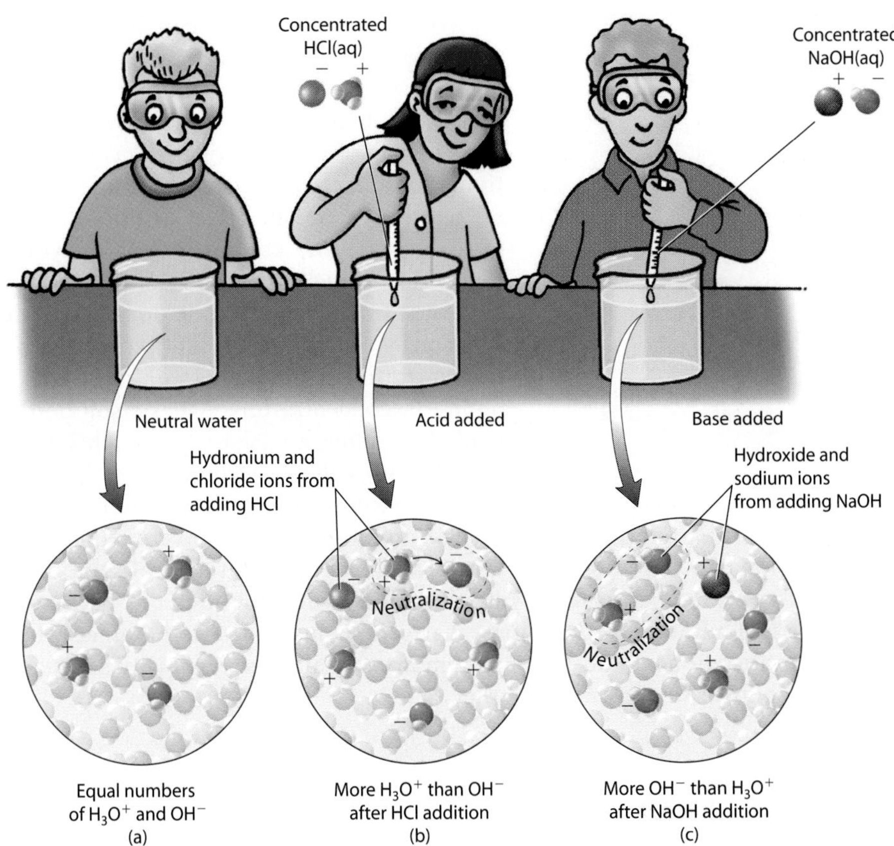

Figure 22.10
(a) Neutral water contains as many hydronium ions as hydroxide ions. (b) When the acid HCl is added to water, hydronium ions from the added HCl neutralize hydroxide ions from the water, thereby decreasing the hydroxide-ion concentration. (c) When the base NaOH is added to water, the added hydroxide ions neutralize hydronium ions from the water, thereby decreasing the hydronium-ion concentration.

HCl, as shown in Figure 22.10b. In a similar manner, adding a base to water increases the hydroxide-ion concentration. The response is a decrease in the hydronium ion concentration as hydronium ions from the water become neutralized by the added hydroxide ions from the base, as shown in Figure 22.10c. The net result is that the product of the hydronium-ion and hydroxide-ion concentrations is always equal to the constant $K_w = 1.0 \times 10^{-14}$.

☑ CHECKPOINT

1. In pure water, the hydroxide-ion concentration is 1.0×10^{-7} *M*. What is the hydronium-ion concentration?
2. What is the concentration of hydronium ions in a solution if the concentration of hydroxide ions is 1.0×10^{-3} *M*?

Check Your Answers

1. 1.0×10^{-7} *M*, because in pure water $[H_3O^+] = [OH^-]$.
2. 1.0×10^{-11} *M*, because $[H_3O^+][OH^-]$ must equal $1.0 \times 10^{-14} = K_w$.

At higher pressures and temperatures, the reaction between two water molecules to form hydronium and hydroxide ions is more favorable. The concentrations of hydronium and hydroxide ions in pure water at higher pressures and temperatures is therefore greater. The product of these concentrations is therefore also greater, which means that K_w is also greater. Thus, K_w is only constant so long as the pressure and temperature of the water is also constant.

Insights

In an **acidic** solution, $[H_3O^+] > [OH^-]$.

In a **basic** solution, $[H_3O^+] < [OH^-]$.

In a **neutral** solution, $[H_3O^+] = [OH^-]$.

Figure 22.11
The relative concentrations of hydronium and hydroxide ions determine whether a solution is acidic, basic, or neutral.

An aqueous solution can be described as acidic, basic, or neutral, as Figure 22.11 summarizes. An **acidic solution** is one in which the hydronium-ion concentration is higher than the hydroxide-ion concentration. An acidic solution is made by adding an acid to water. The effect of this addition is to increase the concentration of hydronium ions, which necessarily decreases the concentration of hydroxide ions. A **basic solution** is one in which the hydroxide-ion concentration is higher than the hydronium-ion concentration. A basic solution is made by adding a base to water. This addition increases the concentration of hydroxide ions, which necessarily decreases the concentration of hydronium ions. A **neutral solution** is one in which the hydronium-ion concentration equals the hydroxide-ion concentration. Pure water is an example of a neutral solution—not because it contains so few hydronium and hydroxide ions but because it contains equal numbers of these ions. A neutral solution is also obtained when equal quantities of acid and base are combined, which explains why acids and bases are said to *neutralize* each other.

☑ CHECKPOINT

How does adding ammonia, NH_3, to water make a basic solution when there are no hydroxide ions in the formula for ammonia?

Check Your Answer

Ammonia indirectly increases the hydroxide ion concentration by reacting with water:

$$NH_3 + H_2O \longrightarrow NH_4^+ + OH^-$$

This reaction raises the hydroxide-ion concentration, which has the effect of lowering the hydronium-ion concentration. With the hydroxide-ion concentration now higher than the hydronium-ion concentration, the solution is basic.

The pH Scale Is Used to Describe Acidity

The *pH scale* is a numeric scale used to express the acidity of a solution. Mathematically, **pH** is equal to the negative logarithm of the hydronium-ion concentration:

$$pH = -\log[H_3O^+]$$

Note again that brackets are used to represent molar concentrations, meaning $[H_3O^+]$ is read "the molar concentration of hydronium ions." For understanding the logarithm function, see the Figuring Physical Science on page 544.

Consider a neutral solution that has a hydronium-ion concentration of 1.0×10^{-7} *M*. To find the pH of this solution, we first take the logarithm of this value, which is -7 (see the Figuring Physical Science on logarithms). The pH is by definition the negative of this value, which means $-(-7) = 7$. Hence, in a neutral solution, where the hydronium-ion concentration equals 1.0×10^{-7} *M*, the pH is 7.

Acidic solutions have pH values less than 7. For an acidic solution in which the hydronium-ion concentration is 1.0×10^{-4} *M*, for example, $\text{pH} = -\log(1.0 \times 10^{-4}) = 4$. The more acidic a solution is, the greater its hydronium-ion concentration and the lower its pH.

Basic solutions have pH values greater than 7. For a basic solution in which the hydronium-ion concentration is 1.0×10^{-8} *M*, for example, $\text{pH} = -\log(1.0 \times 10^{-8}) = 8$. The more basic a solution is, the smaller its hydronium-ion concentration and the higher its pH.

Figure 22.12 shows typical pH values of some familiar solutions, and Figure 22.13 shows two common ways of determining pH values.

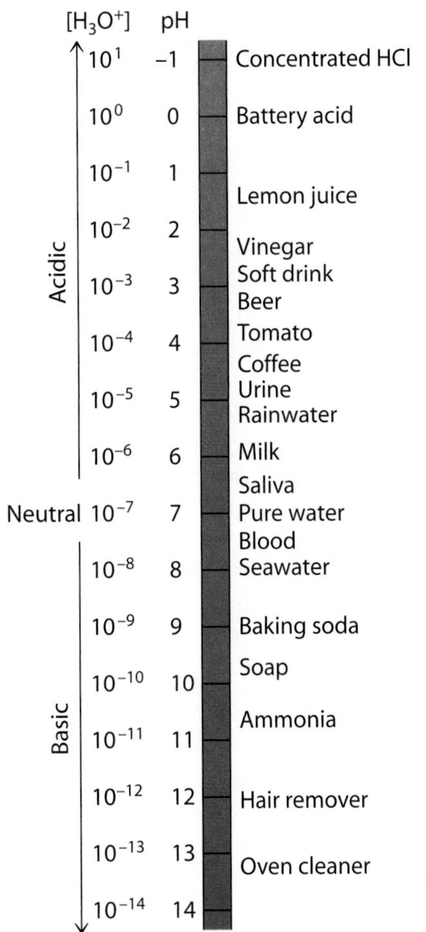

Figure 22.12
The pH values of some common solutions.

Above temperatures of 374°C and pressures of 218 atmospheres, water transforms into a state of matter known as a supercritical fluid, which resembles both a liquid and a gas. For a neutral solution of supercritical water, the pH equals about 2, which means that it is highly corrosive. Research is underway to learn how supercritical water might be used to destroy toxic organic chemicals.

Insights

(a)

(b)

Figure 22.13
(a) The pH of a solution can be measured electronically using a pH meter. (b) A rough estimate of the pH of a solution can be obtained with litmus paper, which is coated with a dye that changes color with pH.

Figuring Physical Science

Logarithms and pH

The logarithm of a number can be found on any scientific calculator by keying in the number and pressing the [log] button. What the calculator does is find the power to which 10 is raised to give the number. The logarithm of 10^2, for example, is 2 because that is the power to which 10 is raised to give the number 10^2. If you know that 10^2 is equal to 100, then you'll understand that the logarithm of 100 also is 2. Check this out on your calculator. Similarly, the logarithm of 1000 is 3 because 10 raised to the third power, 10^3, equals 1000. (Note: we speak here of the base-10 logarithm, not the Napierian logarithm of base *e*.)

Any positive number, including a very small one, has a logarithm. The logarithm of 0.0001, which equals 10^{-4}, for example, is -4 (the power to which 10 is raised to equal this number).

Example

What is the logarithm of 0.01?

Answer

The number 0.01 is 10^{-2}, the logarithm of which is -2 (the power to which 10 is raised).

The concentration of hydronium ions in most solutions is typically much less than 1 *M*. Recall, for example, that in neutral water the hydronium ion concentration is 0.0000001 *M* (10^{-7} *M*). The logarithm of any number smaller than 1 (but greater than zero) is a negative number. The definition of pH includes the minus sign so as to transform the logarithm of the hydronium ion concentration to a positive number.

When a solution has a hydronium ion concentration of 1 *M*, the pH is 0 because 1 *M* = 10^0 *M*. A 10 *M* solution has a pH of -1 because 10 *M* = 10^1 *M*.

Example

What is the pH of a solution that has a hydronium-ion concentration of 0.001 *M*?

Answer

The number 0.001 is 10^{-3}, and so

$$\begin{aligned} pH &= -\log[H_3O^+] \\ &= -\log 10^{-3} \\ &= -(-3) = 3 \end{aligned}$$

Your Turn

1. What is the logarithm of 10^5?
2. What is the logarithm of 100,000?
3. What is the pH of a solution having a hydronium-ion concentration of 10^{-9} *M*? Is this solution acidic, basic, or neutral?

Answers are found on page 554.

22.4 Acidic Rainwater and Basic Ocean Water

As previously mentioned, rainwater is naturally acidic. One source of this acidity is carbon dioxide, the same gas that gives fizz to soda drinks. There are 670 billion tons of CO_2 in the atmosphere, most of it from such natural sources as volcanoes and decaying organic matter and a smaller but growing amount from human activities.

Water in the atmosphere reacts with carbon dioxide to form *carbonic acid:*

$$\underset{\text{Carbon dioxide}}{CO_2(g)} + \underset{\text{Water}}{H_2O(\ell)} \longrightarrow \underset{\text{Carbonic acid}}{H_2CO_3(aq)}$$

Carbonic acid, as its name implies, behaves as an acid and lowers the pH of water. The CO_2 in the atmosphere brings the pH of rainwater to about 5.6—noticeably below the neutral pH value of 7. Because of local fluctuations, the normal pH of rainwater varies between 5 and 7. This natural acidity of rainwater may accelerate the erosion of land and, under certain circumstances, as discussed at the beginning of this chapter, can lead to the formation of underground caves.

By convention, *acid rain* is a term used for rain having a pH lower than 5. Acid rain is created when airborne pollutants, such as sulfur dioxide, are absorbed by atmospheric moisture. Sulfur dioxide is readily converted to sulfur trioxide, which reacts with water to form *sulfuric acid:*

$$\underset{\text{Sulfur dioxide}}{2\ SO_2(g)} + \underset{\text{Oxygen}}{O_2(g)} \longrightarrow \underset{\text{Sulfur trioxide}}{SO_3(g)}$$

$$\underset{\text{Sulfur trioxide}}{SO_3(g)} + \underset{\text{Water}}{H_2O(\ell)} \longrightarrow \underset{\text{Sulfuric acid}}{H_2SO_4(aq)}$$

As noted at the beginning of the chapter, the sulfuric acid that helped create the great chambers of Carlsbad Caverns was generated from sulfur dioxide (and hydrogen sulfide) from subterranean fossil-fuel deposits. When we burn these fossil fuels, the reactants that produce sulfuric acid are dispersed into the atmosphere. Each year about 20 million tons of SO_2 is released into the atmosphere by the combustion of sulfur-containing coal and oil. Sulfuric acid is much stronger than carbonic acid, and, as a result, rain laced with sulfuric acid eventually corrodes metal, paint, and other exposed substances. Each year, the damage costs billions of dollars. The cost to the environment is also high (Figure 22.14). Many rivers and lakes receiving acid rain become less capable of sustaining life. Much vegetation that receives acid rain doesn't survive. This is particularly evident in heavily industrialized regions.

(a)

(b)

Figure 22.14
(a) These two photographs show the same obelisk before and after the effects of acid rain. (b) Many forests downwind from heavily industrialized areas, such as in the northeastern United States and in Europe, have been noticeably hard-hit by acid rain.

☑ CHECKPOINT

When sulfuric acid, H_2SO_4, is added to water, what makes the resulting aqueous solution corrosive?

Check Your Answer

Because H_2SO_4 is a strong acid, it readily forms hydronium ions when dissolved in water. Hydronium ions are responsible for the corrosive action.

The environmental impact of acid rain depends on local geology, as Figure 22.15 illustrates. In certain regions, such as the midwestern United States, the ground contains significant quantities of the alkaline compound calcium carbonate (calcite, which forms limestone), deposited when these lands were submerged under oceans, as has occurred several times over the past 500 million years. Acid rain pouring into these regions is often neutralized by the calcium carbonate before any damage is done. (Figure 22.16 shows calcium carbonate neutralizing an acid.) In the northeastern United States and many other regions, however, the ground contains very little calcium carbonate and is composed primarily of chemically less reactive materials, such as granite. In these regions, the effect of acid rain on lakes and rivers accumulates.

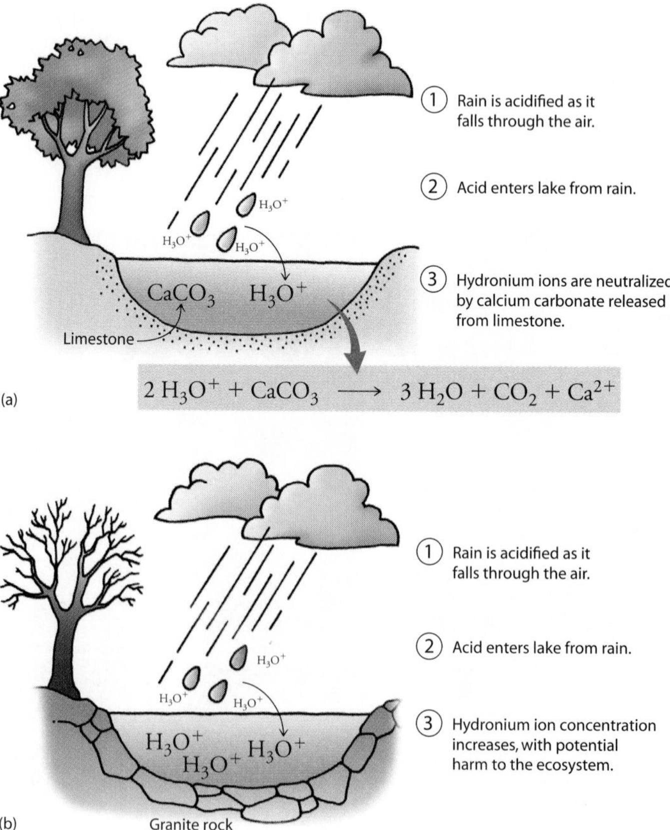

Figure 22.15
(a) The damaging effects of acid rain do not appear in bodies of fresh water lined with calcium carbonate, which neutralizes any acidity. (b) Lakes and rivers lined with inert materials are not protected.

One demonstrated solution to this problem is to raise the pH of acidified lakes and rivers by adding calcium carbonate—a process known as liming. The cost of transporting the calcium carbonate, coupled with the need to monitor treated water systems closely, limits liming to only a small fraction of the vast number of water systems already affected. Furthermore, as acid rain continues to pour into these regions, the need to lime also continues.

A longer-term solution to acid rain is to prevent most of the generated sulfur dioxide and other pollutants from entering the atmosphere in the first place. Toward this end, smokestacks have been designed or retrofitted to minimize the quantities of pollutants released. Though costly, the positive effects of these adjustments have been demonstrated. An ultimate long-term solution, however, would be a shift from fossil fuels to cleaner energy sources, such as nuclear and solar energy.

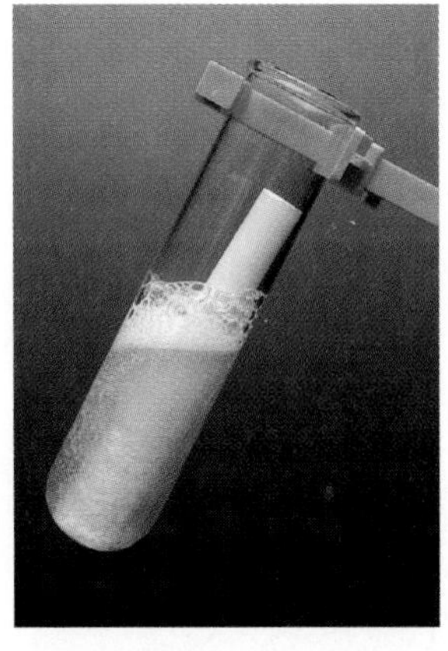

Figure 22.16
Most chalks are made from calcium carbonate, which is the same chemical found in limestone. The addition of even a weak acid, such as the acetic acid of vinegar, produces hydronium ions that react with the calcium carbonate to form several products, the most notable being carbon dioxide, which rapidly bubbles out of solution. Try this for yourself! If the bubbling is not as vigorous as shown here, then the chalk is made of other mineral components.

☑ CHECKPOINT

What kind of lakes are protected against the negative effects of acid rain?

Check Your Answer

Lakes that have a floor consisting of basic minerals, such as limestone, are more resistant to acid rain because the chemicals of the limestone (mostly calcium carbonate, $CaCO_3$) neutralize any incoming acid.

It should come as no surprise that the amount of carbon dioxide put into the atmosphere by human activities is growing. What is surprising, however, is that studies indicate that the atmospheric concentration of CO_2 is not increasing proportionately. A likely explanation has to do with the oceans (Figure 22.17).

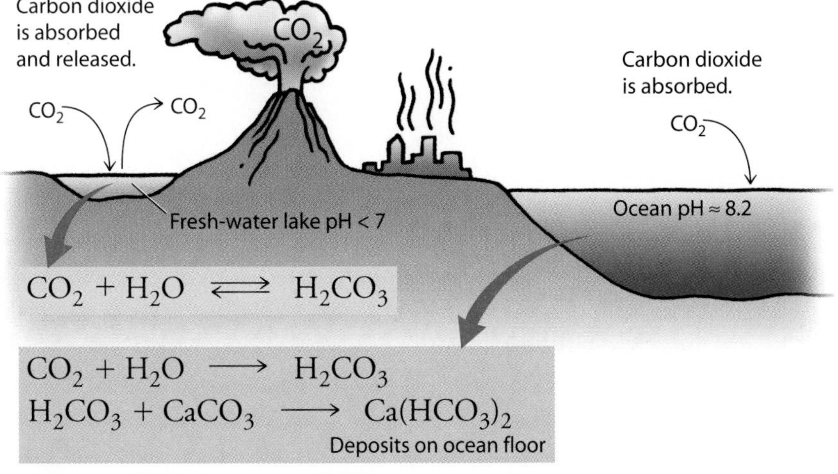

Figure 22.17
Carbon dioxide forms carbonic acid upon entering any body of water. In fresh water, this reaction is reversible, and the carbon dioxide is released back into the atmosphere. In the alkaline ocean, the carbonic acid is neutralized to such compounds as calcium bicarbonate, $Ca(HCO_3)_2$, which precipitate to the ocean floor. As a result, most of the atmospheric carbon dioxide that enters our oceans remains there.

The pollution humans release knows no political boundries. Iron smelters operating in China, for example, release pollutants that are readily detected in Seattle, Washington.

Insights

Scientists have experimented with ways of enhancing the ocean's ability to absorb atmospheric carbon dioxide. Adding powdered iron to a small plot of the ocean, they found, has the effect of fostering the growth of microorganisms that enhance the rate at which carbon dioxide is absorbed. Might this be a solution to the problem of global warming? Might adding too much iron initiate another ice age or alter the ocean's ecology? We don't know.

Insights

When atmospheric CO_2 dissolves in any body of water—a raindrop, a lake, or the ocean—it forms carbonic acid. In fresh water, this carbonic acid transforms back to water and carbon dioxide, which is released back into the atmosphere. Carbonic acid in the ocean, however, is quickly neutralized by dissolved alkaline substances such as calcium carbonate (the ocean is alkaline, pH < 8.2). The products of this neutralization eventually end up on the ocean floor as insoluble solids. Thus, carbonic acid neutralization in the ocean prevents CO_2 from being released back into the atmosphere. The ocean, therefore, is a carbon dioxide *sink*—most of the CO_2 that goes in doesn't come out. So, pushing more CO_2 into our atmosphere means pushing more of it into our vast oceans. This is another of the many ways in which the oceans regulate our global environment.

Nevertheless, as Figure 22.18 shows, the concentration of atmospheric CO_2 is increasing. Carbon dioxide is being produced faster than the ocean can absorb it, and this may alter the earth's environment. Carbon dioxide is a *greenhouse gas*, which means it helps keep the surface of the earth warm by preventing infrared radiation from escaping into outer space. Without greenhouse gases in the atmosphere, the earth's surface would average a frigid $-18°C$. However, with increasing concentration of CO_2 in the atmosphere, we might experience higher average temperatures. Higher temperatures may significantly alter global weather patterns as well as raise the average sea level, as the polar ice caps melt and the volume of seawater increases because of thermal expansion. Global warming is explored in greater detail in Chapter 31.

So the pH of rain depends in great part on the concentration of atmospheric CO_2, which depends on the pH of the oceans. These systems are interconnected with global temperatures, which naturally connect to the countless living systems on the earth. How true it is: All the parts are intricately connected, down to the level of atoms and molecules!

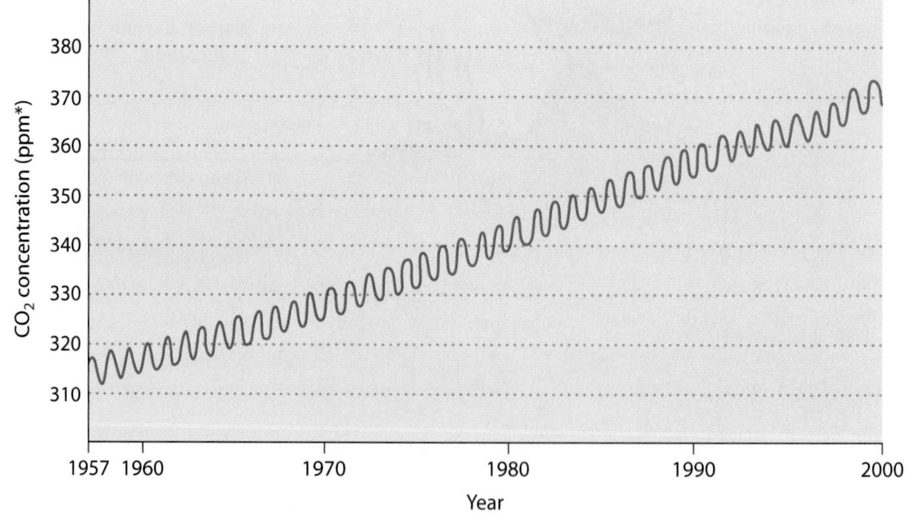

Figure 22.18
Researchers at the Mauna Loa Weather Observatory in Hawaii have recorded increasing concentrations of atmospheric carbon dioxide since they began collecting data in the 1950s. The oscillations of this graph reflect seasonal changes in CO_2 levels.

22.5 Buffer Solutions

A **buffer solution** is any solution that resists large changes in pH. Buffer solutions work by containing two components. One component neutralizes any added base, and the other neutralizes any added acid. Effective buffer solutions can be prepared by mixing a weak acid with a salt of the weak acid. An example would be a mixture of acetic acid, $C_2H_4O_2$, and sodium acetate, $NaC_2H_4O_2$. This salt can be made by reacting acetic acid with sodium hydroxide:

$$H_3C{-}C(=O){-}O{-}H + NaOH \longrightarrow H_3C{-}C(=O){-}O^-Na^+ + H_2O$$

Acetic acid
(weak acid)

Sodium acetate
(salt of weak acid)

To make the buffer solution, a solution of acetic acid and a solution of sodium acetate are combined. To understand how this buffer solution resists changes in pH, first recall what happens when a strong acid is added to plain water, as in Figure 22.10b. The pH of the solution quickly *decreases* because the concentration of hydronium ions increases. Add a strong base to plain water, and you quickly *increase* the pH by decreasing the relative concentration of hydronium ions, as in Figure 22.10c.

Add the strong acid HCl to an acetic acid–sodium acetate buffer solution, however, and the H^+ ions produced by the HCl do not stay in solution to lower the pH because they react with the acetate ions, $C_2H_3O_2^-$, of sodium acetate to form acetic acid, as shown in Figure 22.19. (Remember that acetic acid, being a weak acid, stays mostly in its molecular form, $HC_2H_3O_2$, and so it does not contribute hydronium ions to the solution.) Add the strong base NaOH to the acetic acid–sodium acetate buffer solution, and the OH^- ions produced by the NaOH do not stay in solution to raise the pH because they combine with H^+ ions from the acetic acid to form water, as shown in Figure 22.20.

So, strong bases and acids are neutralized by the components of a buffer solution. This does not mean that the pH remains unchanged, however. When NaOH is added to our buffer system, sodium acetate is produced. Because sodium acetate behaves as a weak base (it accepts hydrogen ions, but not very well), there is a slight increase in pH. When HCl is added, acetic acid is produced. Because acetic acid behaves as a weak acid, there is a slight decrease in pH. Buffer solutions therefore resist only *large* changes in pH.

☑ CHECKPOINT

Why must a buffer solution consist of at least two dissolved components?

Check Your Answer

One component is needed to neutralize any incoming acid, and the second component is needed to neutralize any incoming base.

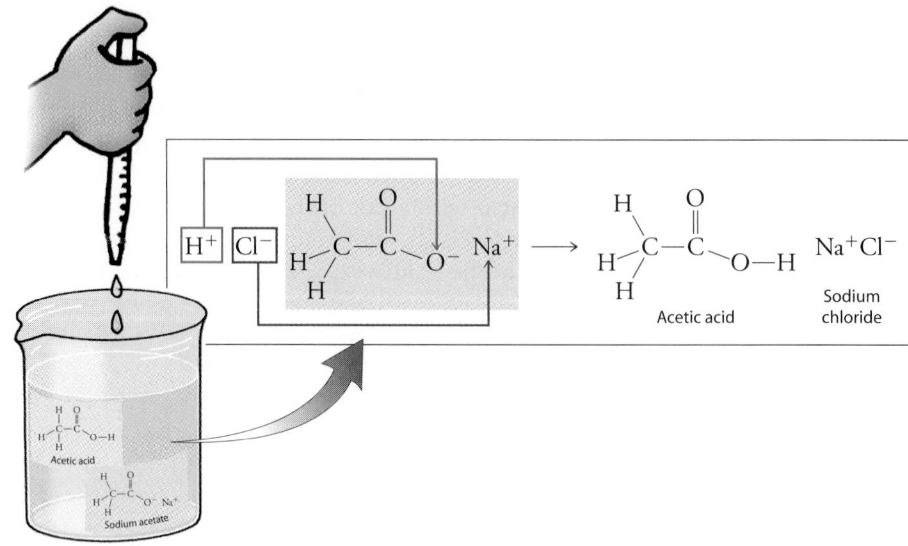

Figure 22.19
Hydrochloric acid added to a solution containing acetic acid and sodium acetate is neutralized by the sodium acetate to form additional acetic acid.

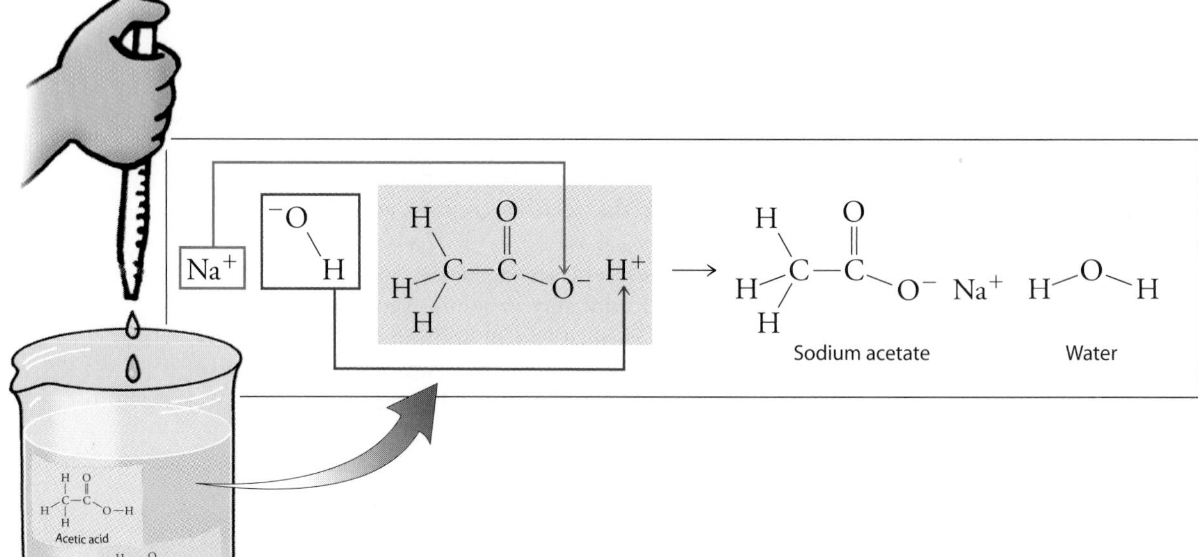

Figure 22.20
Sodium hydroxide added to a solution containing acetic acid and sodium acetate is neutralized by the acetic acid to form additional sodium acetate as well as water.

There are many different buffer systems useful for maintaining particular pH values. The acetic acid–sodium acetate system is good for maintaining a pH around 4.8. Buffer solutions containing equal mixtures of a weak base and a salt of that weak base maintain alkaline pH values. For example, a buffer solution of the weak base ammonia, NH_3, and ammonium chloride, NH_4Cl, is useful for maintaining a pH of about 9.3.

Blood has several buffer systems that work together to maintain a narrow pH range between 7.35 and 7.45. A pH value above or below these levels can be lethal, primarily because cellular proteins become *denatured*, which is what happens to milk when vinegar is added to it.

The primary buffer system of the blood is a combination of carbonic acid and its salt sodium bicarbonate, shown in Figure 22.21. Any acid that builds up in the bloodstream is neutralized by the basic action of sodium bicarbonate, and any base that builds up is neutralized by the carbonic acid.

The carbonic acid in your blood is formed as the carbon dioxide produced by your cells enters the bloodstream and reacts with water—this is the same reaction that occurs in a raindrop, as we discussed earlier. You fine-tune the levels of blood carbonic acid, and hence your blood pH, by your breathing rate, as Figure 22.22 illustrates. Breathe too slowly or hold your breath, and the amount of carbon dioxide (and hence carbonic acid) builds up, causing a slight but significant drop in pH. Hyperventilate and the carbonic acid level decreases, causing a slight but significant increase in pH. Your body uses this mechanism to protect itself from changes in blood pH. One of the symptoms of a severe overdose of aspirin, for example, is hyperventilation. Aspirin, also known as acetylsalicylic acid, is an acidic chemical that, when taken in large amounts, can overwhelm the blood buffering system, causing a dangerous drop in blood pH. As you hyperventilate, however, your body loses carbonic acid, which helps to maintain the proper blood pH, despite the overabundance of the acidic aspirin.

O
‖
H—O—C—O—H

Carbonic acid
(weak acid)

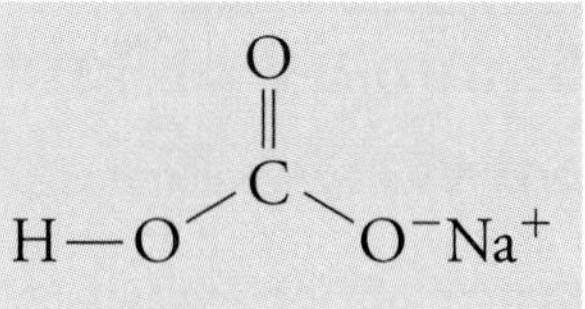

Sodium bicarbonate
(salt)

Figure 22.21
Carbonic acid and sodium bicarbonate.

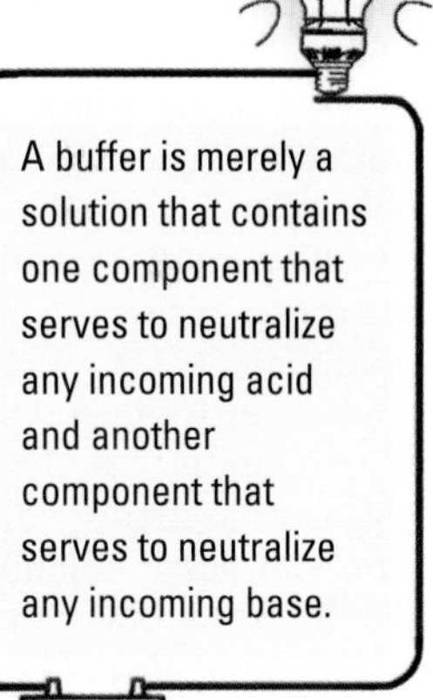

To summarize the concepts of this chapter, consider the gardener shown in Figure 22.23. Using a pH-measuring kit, the gardener has found that the soil pH is unacceptably low, perhaps because of local atmospheric pollutants, which may arise from natural or human-made sources. At this low pH, the soil contains an overabundance of hydronium ions, which react with many of the basic nutrients of the soil, such as ammonia, to form water-soluble salts. Because of their solubility, these nutrients in their salt form are readily washed away with the rainwater, and, as a result, the soil becomes nutrient-poor. The mechanism by which plants absorb whatever nutrients do remain in the soil is also disturbed by the soil's low pH.

Figure 22.22
(a) If you hold your breath, CO_2 builds up in your bloodstream. This increases the amount of carbonic acid, which lowers your blood pH. (b) If you hyperventilate, and the amount of CO_2 in your bloodstream decreases. This decreases the amount of carbonic acid, which raises your blood pH.

As a result of all these factors, most plants do not grow well in acidic soil. To remedy the problem, the gardener spreads powdered limestone, a form of calcium carbonate, $CaCO_3$, which neutralizes the hydronium ions, thus raising the pH toward neutral.

Interestingly, the calcium carbonate reacts with the acidic soil to form carbon dioxide gas, which, in the atmosphere, helps to keep rainwater slightly acidic. This is the same gas that is generated by the cells of our bodies and tends to acidify our blood. The blood pH, however, is kept fairly constant at around 7.4 because it is buffered.

Figure 22.23
Raising the pH of garden soil by the addition of an alkaline mineral is known as liming.

Summary of Terms

Acid A substance that donates hydrogen ions.
Base A substance that accepts hydrogen ions.
Hydronium ion A water molecule after accepting a hydrogen ion.
Hydroxide ion A water molecule after losing a hydrogen ion.
Salt An ionic compound formed from the reaction between an acid and a base.
Neutralization A reaction in which an acid and base combine to form a salt.
Amphoteric A description of a substance that can behave either as an acid or as a base.
Acidic solution A solution in which the hydronium-ion concentration is higher than the hydroxide-ion concentration.
Basic solution A solution in which the hydroxide-ion concentration is higher than the hydronium-ion concentration.
Neutral solution A solution in which the hydronium-ion concentration is equal to the hydroxide-ion concentration.
pH A measure of the acidity of a solution, equal to the negative of the base-10 logarithm of the hydronium-ion concentration.
Buffer solution A solution that resists large changes in pH. It is made either from a weak acid and one of its salts or from a weak base and one of its salts.

Review Questions

22.1 Acids Donate Protons, Bases Accept Them

1. What are the Brønsted–Lowry definitions of acid and base?
2. When an acid is dissolved in water, what ion does the water form?
3. When a chemical loses a hydrogen ion, is it behaving as an acid or a base?
4. Does a salt always contain sodium ions?
5. What two classes of chemicals are involved in a neutralization reaction?

22.2 Relative Strengths of Acids and Bases

6. What does it mean to say that an acid is strong in aqueous solution?
7. What happens to most of the molecules of a strong acid when the acid is mixed with water?
8. Why does a solution of a strong acid conduct electricity better than a solution of a weak acid having the same concentration?
9. Which has a greater ability to accept hydrogen ions: a strong base or a weak base?
10. When can a solution of a weak base be more corrosive than a solution of a strong base?

22.3 Acidic, Basic, and Neutral Solutions

11. Is it possible for a chemical to behave as an acid in one instance and as a base in another instance?
12. Is water a strong acid or a weak acid?
13. Is K_w a very large number or a very small number?
14. As the concentration of H_3O^+ ions in an aqueous solution increases, what happens to the concentration of OH^- ions?
15. What is true about the relative concentrations of hydronium and hydroxide ions in an acidic solution?
16. What is true about the relative concentrations of hydronium and hydroxide ions in a neutral solution?
17. What is true about the relative concentrations of hydronium and hydroxide ions in a basic solution?
18. What does the pH of a solution indicate?
19. As the hydronium-ion concentration of a solution increases, does the pH of the solution increase or decrease?

22.4 Acidic Rainwater and Basic Ocean Water

20. What is the product of the reaction between carbon dioxide and water?
21. How can rain be acidic and yet not qualify as acid rain?
22. What is the relationship between sulfur dioxide and acid rain?
23. How do humans generate the air pollutant sulfur dioxide?
24. How does one lime a lake?
25. Why aren't atmospheric levels of carbon dioxide rising as rapidly as might be expected, based on the increased output of carbon dioxide resulting from human activities?

22.5 Buffer Solutions

26. What is a buffer solution?
27. A strong acid quickly drops the pH when added to water. Not so when added to a buffer solution. Why?
28. Do buffer solutions prevent or inhibit changes in pH?
29. Why is it so important that the pH of our blood be maintained within a narrow range of values?
30. Holding your breath causes the pH of your blood to decrease. Why?

Activity

Rainbow Cabbage

Many pH indicators are found in plants; the pigment of red cabbage is a good example. This pigment is red at low pH values (1 to 5), light purple around neutral pH values (6 to 7), light green at moderately alkaline pH values (8 to 11), and dark green at very alkaline pH values (12 to 14).

Safety Note
Wear safety glasses. Do not use bleach products.

What You Need
A head of red cabbage, a small pot, water, four colorless plastic cups or drinking glasses, toilet-bowl cleaner, vinegar, baking soda, ammonia cleanser.

Procedure
1. Boil a cup of shredded cabbage in 2 cups of water (5 minutes). Strain and collect the broth.
2. Pour one-fourth of the broth into each cup and allow to cool.
3. Add a small amount of toilet-bowl cleaner to the first cup, a small amount of vinegar to the second cup, baking soda to the third, and ammonia solution to the fourth.
4. Use the different colors to estimate the pHs.
5. Mix some of the acidic and basic solutions together and note the rapid change in pH (indicated by the change in color).

   The change in color of a pH indicator is not permanent. To demonstrate this, add a teaspoon of baking soda to the glass/cup to which you originally added the vinegar. (Why does this addition of baking soda also result in bubbling?) Add vinegar again to bring the color back to red.

Exercises

1. Suggest an explanation for why people once washed their hands with ashes.
2. What is the relationship between a hydroxide ion and a water molecule?
3. An acid and a base react to form a salt, which consists of positive and negative ions. Which forms the positive ions, the acid or the base? Which forms the negative ions?
4. Water is formed from the reaction between an acid and a base. Why is water not classified as a salt?
5. Identify the acid or base behavior of each substance in these reactions:

   (a) $H_3O^+ + Cl^- \rightleftharpoons H_2O + HCl$

   (b) $H_2PO_4 + H_2O \rightleftharpoons H_3O^+ + HPO_4^-$

   (c) $HSO_4^- + H_2O \rightleftharpoons H_3O^+ + SO_4^{2-}$
6. Identify the acid or base behavior of each substance in these reactions:

   (a) $HSO_4^- + H_2O \rightleftharpoons OH^- + H_2SO_4$

   (b) $O^{2-} + H_2O \rightleftharpoons OH^- + OH^-$
7. In the following reaction, which of the reactants is the acid and which is the base?

   $$NH_3 + PH_3 \longrightarrow NH_2^- + PH_4^+$$
8. Write a balanced equation for what occurs when gaseous NH_3 is dissolved in water.
9. Does water act as an acid or a base when ammonia is added to it?
10. Sodium hydroxide, NaOH, is a strong base, which means that it readily accepts hydrogen ions. What products are formed when sodium hydroxide accepts a hydrogen ion from a water molecule?
11. What happens to the corrosive properties of an acid and a base after they neutralize each other? Defend your answer.
12. What does the value of K_w indicate about the extent to which water molecules react with one another?
13. Which are always present in aqueous solutions, H_3O^+ or OH^-?
14. Why do we use the pH scale to indicate the acidity of a solution rather than simply stating the concentration of hydronium ions?
15. The amphoteric reaction between two water molecules is endothermic, which means the reaction requires the input of heat energy in order to proceed:

    $$\text{Energy} + H_2O + H_2O \longrightarrow H_3O^+ + OH^-$$

    The warmer the water, the more heat energy is available for this reaction, and the more hydronium and hydroxide ions are formed. Does the value of K_w increase, decrease, or stay the same with increasing temperature?
16. Which has a lower pH: pure water that is hot or pure water that is cold? See question 15.
17. Is it possible for water to be neutral but have a pH less than or greater than 7.0? See question 15.
18. What is your response to a friend who says that there are no ions whatsoever in a glass of pure water?
19. The pOH scale indicates the "basicity" of a solution, where $\text{pOH} = -\log OH^-$. For any solution, what is the sum pH + pOH always equal to?
20. When the hydronium-ion concentration of a solution equals 1 mole per liter, what is the pH of the solution?
21. Is the solution in the previous exercise acidic or basic? Defend your answer.
22. When the hydronium-ion concentration of a solution equals 10 moles per liter, what is the pH of the solution?
23. Is the solution in the previous exercise acidic or basic? Why?
24. What is the concentration of hydronium ions in a solution that has a pH of -3? Why is such a solution impossible to prepare?
25. What happens to the pH of an acidic solution as pure water is added?
26. A weak acid is added to a concentrated solution of hydrochloric acid. Does the solution become more or less acidic?

27. What happens to the pH of soda water as it loses its carbonation?
28. Why might a small piece of chalk be useful for alleviating acid indigestion?
29. How might you determine whether or not your toothpaste contains calcium carbonate, $CaCO_3$, or perhaps baking soda, $NaHCO_3$, without looking at the ingredients label?
30. Why do lakes lying in granite basins tend to become acidified by acid rain more readily than lakes lying in limestone basins?
31. Cutting back on the pollutants that cause acid rain is one solution to the problem of acidified lakes. Suggest another.
32. How might warmer oceans accelerate global warming?
33. Sodium bicarbonate, $NaHCO_3$, is the active ingredient of baking soda. Compare this structure with those of the weak acids and weak bases presented in this chapter and explain how this compound by itself in solution moderates changes in pH.

   H—O—C(=O)—O^-Na^+

   Sodium bicarbonate (salt)

34. Hydrogen chloride is added to a buffer solution of ammonia, NH_3, and ammonium chloride, NH_4Cl. What is the effect on the concentration of ammonia? On the concentration of ammonium chloride?
35. Sodium hydroxide is added to a buffer solution of ammonia, NH_3, and ammonium chloride, NH_4Cl. What is the effect on the concentration of ammonia? On the concentration of ammonium chloride?
36. At what point will a buffer solution cease to resist changes in pH?
37. How does a buffer neutralize an added strong base? How does it neutralize an added strong acid?
38. Sometimes an individual going through a traumatic experience cannot stop hyperventilating. In such a circumstance, it is recommended that the individual breathe into a paper bag or cupped hands as a useful way to avoid an increase in blood pH, which can cause the person to pass out. Explain how this works.
39. You and a friend are cleaning the floors of your grandmother's house. Your friend says to you: "I heard about a cleaner that's supposed to be great at removing embedded salt stains in slate floors. They said it works by 'neutralizing' the salts." You reply that that's impossible because a salt is formed by neutralization. But your friend knows a lot about chemistry and tells you that it is indeed possible. How so?
40. Is it possible for a salt to behave as a base? Explain.

Problems

1. What is the hydroxide-ion concentration in an aqueous solution when the hydronium-ion concentration is 1×10^{-10} mole per liter?
2. When the hydronium ion concentration of a solution is 1×10^{-10} mole per liter, what is the pH of the solution? Is the solution acidic or basic?
3. When the hydronium ion concentration of a solution is 1×10^{-4} mole per liter, what is the pH of the solution? Is the solution acidic or basic?
4. What is the hydroxide ion concentration in an aqueous solution having a pH of 5?
5. When the pH of a solution is 1, the concentration of hydronium ions is $10^{-1}\ M = 0.1M$. Assume that the volume of this solution is 500 mL and that the solution is not buffered. What is the pH after 500 mL of pure water is added? You will need a calculator with a logarithm function to answer this question.

Figuring Physical Science—Answers

Logarithms and pH

1. "What is the logarithm of 10^5?" can be rephrased as "To what power is 10 raised to give the number 10^5?" The answer is 5.
2. You should know that 100,000 is the same as 10^5. Thus the logarithm of 100,000 is 5.
3. The pH is 9, which means this is a basic solution:

$$\begin{aligned} pH &= -\log[H_3O^+] \\ &= -\log 10^{-9} \\ &= -(-9) \\ &= 9 \end{aligned}$$

Chapter 22 Online Resources

Tutorials
- Nature of Acids & Bases
- Strong & Weak Acids & Bases
- The pH Scale

Quiz
Exercises
Flashcards
Links

CHAPTER 23

Oxidation and Reduction

In Chapter 22, we discussed acid–base reactions, which are chemical reactions that involve the transfer of *protons* from one reactant to another. In this chapter, we explore reactions that involve the transfer of one or more *electrons* from one reactant to another. These are called **oxidation–reduction reactions,** and a common example is the burning of wood. Wood is mainly cellulose, a substance made up of carbon, hydrogen, and oxygen atoms. As wood burns, the bonds between these atoms break, and then these atoms form new bonds with each other and with oxygen molecules in the air to create carbon dioxide and water. The formation of these products involves the transfer of electrons from one atom to another, and so it is, by definition, an oxidation–reduction reaction.

We begin by exploring oxidation–reduction reactions by defining necessary terms. With the background on chemical reactions given in Chapter 21, we are then ready to jump right into various applications of oxidation–reduction reactions.

23.1 Losing and Gaining Electrons

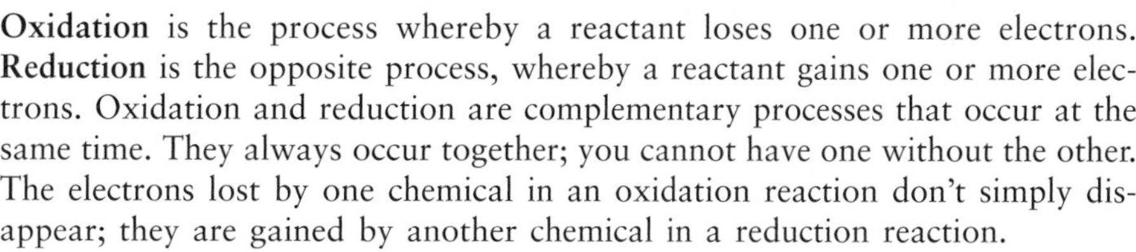

Oxidation is the process whereby a reactant loses one or more electrons. **Reduction** is the opposite process, whereby a reactant gains one or more electrons. Oxidation and reduction are complementary processes that occur at the same time. They always occur together; you cannot have one without the other. The electrons lost by one chemical in an oxidation reaction don't simply disappear; they are gained by another chemical in a reduction reaction.

An oxidation–reduction reaction occurs when sodium and chlorine react to form sodium chloride, as shown in Figure 23.1. The equation for this reaction is

$$2\ Na(s) + Cl_2(g) \longrightarrow 2\ Na^+Cl^-(s)$$

Figure 23.1
In the exothermic formation of sodium chloride, sodium metal is oxidized by chlorine gas, and chlorine gas is reduced by sodium metal.

To see how electrons are transferred in this reaction, we can look at each reactant individually. Each electrically neutral sodium atom changes to a positively charged ion. At the same time, we can say that each atom loses an electron and is therefore oxidized:

$$2\ Na(s) \longrightarrow 2\ Na^+ + 2e^- \qquad \text{Oxidation}$$

Each electrically neutral chlorine molecule changes to two negatively charged ions. Each of these atoms gains an electron and is therefore reduced:

$$Cl_2 + 2e^- \longrightarrow 2Cl^- \qquad \text{Reduction}$$

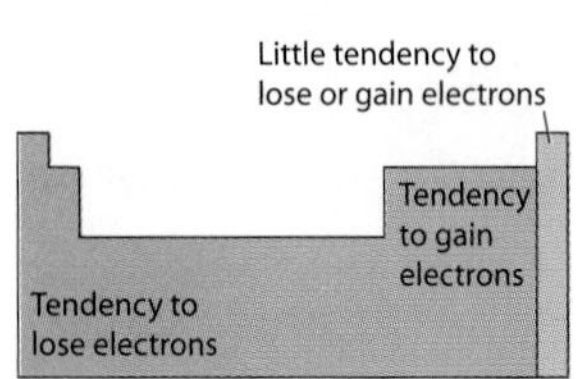

Figure 23.2
The ability of an atom to gain or lose electrons is indicated by its position in the periodic table. Those at the upper right tend to gain electrons, and those at the lower left tend to lose them.

The net result is that the two electrons lost by the sodium atoms are transferred to the chlorine atoms. Therefore, each of the two equations shown above actually represents one half of an entire process, which is why they are each called a **half reaction.** In other words, an electron won't be lost from a sodium atom without the presence of a chlorine atom available to pick up that electron. Both half reactions are required to represent the *whole* oxidation–reduction process. Half reactions are useful for showing which reactant loses electrons and which reactant gains them, which is why half reactions are used throughout this chapter.

As I give you my electron, you become reduced, and so I'm a *reducing agent.*

As I make you lose your electron, you become oxidized, and so I'm an *oxidizing agent.*

Because the sodium causes reduction of the chlorine, the sodium is acting as a *reducing agent.* A reducing agent is any reactant that causes another reactant to be reduced. Note that sodium is oxidized when it behaves as a reducing agent—it loses electrons. Conversely, the chlorine causes oxidation of the sodium and so is acting as an *oxidizing agent.* Because it gains electrons in the process, an oxidizing agent is reduced. Just remember that **l**oss of **e**lectrons is **o**xidation, and **g**ain of **e**lectrons is **r**eduction. Here is a helpful mnemonic adapted from a once-popular children's story: **Leo** the lion went **"ger."**

Different elements have different oxidation and reduction tendencies—some lose electrons more readily, while others gain electrons more readily, as Figure 23.2 illustrates.

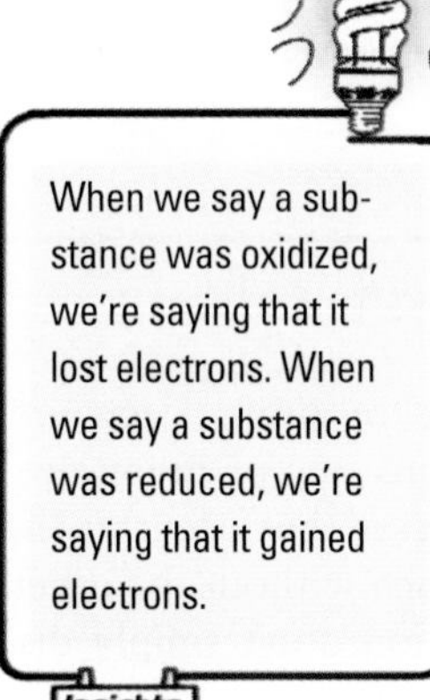

☑ CHECKPOINT

True or false:

1. Reducing agents are oxidized in oxidation–reduction reactions.
2. Oxidizing agents are reduced in oxidation–reduction reactions.

Check Your Answers

Both statements are true.

23.2 Photography

Figure 23.3
A camera can be used to focus an image on wax paper as well as it does on photographic film.

Lay some wax paper on the back of an open, unloaded camera, as shown in Figure 23.3. Hold the shutter open, then focus. Voilà! You have an image. Let the shutter close, however, and the image disappears. This is the same image that forms on the photographic film inside a loaded camera. The difference between the film and the wax paper, of course, is that the film is able to retain the image after the shutter has closed. How does it do that? The answer involves oxidation–reduction chemistry.

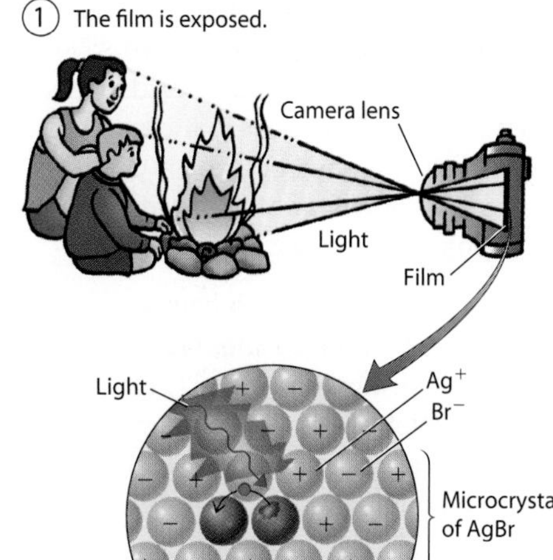

Oxidation $Br^- \longrightarrow Br + e^-$

Reduction $Ag^+ + e^- \longrightarrow Ag$

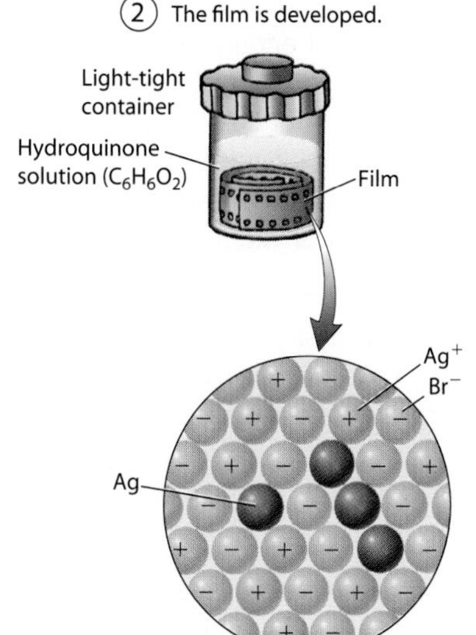

Oxidation $2\,C_6H_6O_2 \longrightarrow 2\,C_6H_4O_2 + 2\,e^- + 2\,H^+$

Reduction $2\,AgBr + 2\,e^- \longrightarrow 2\,Ag + 2\,Br^-$

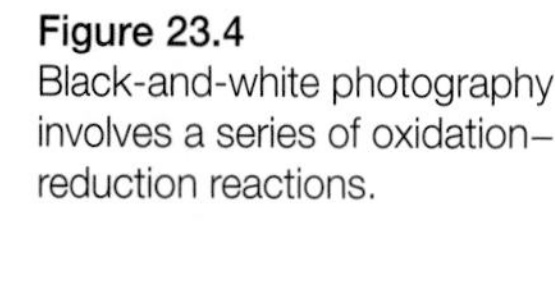

Figure 23.4
Black-and-white photography involves a series of oxidation–reduction reactions.

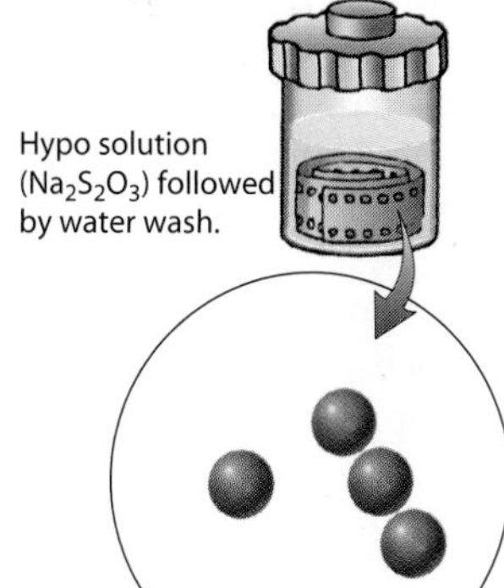

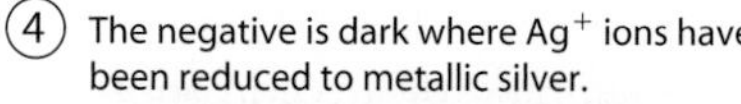

Follow the steps in Figure 23.4 as you read this simplified explanation of how a black-and-white photograph is produced.

1. Unexposed black-and-white photographic film is a transparent strip of plastic coated with a gel containing microcrystals of silver bromide, AgBr. Light reflected from the subject being photographed passes through the camera lens and is focused on these microcrystals. The light causes many of the bromide ions in the microcrystals to oxidize. The electrons set loose by this oxidation are transferred to the silver ions, which are thereby reduced to opaque silver atoms. The more light received by a microcrystal, the greater the number of opaque silver atoms formed. In this way, the photographic image is encoded, and the film is said to have been *exposed*.

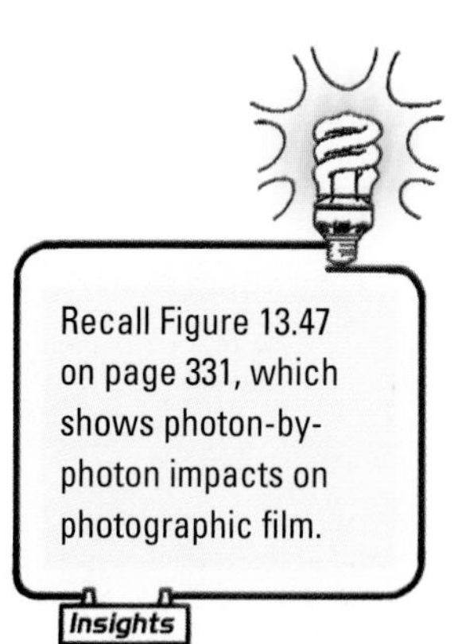

Digital photography also relies on the movement of electrons to generate an image. Basically, photons hit a metalloid chip, dislodging electrons that then travel through an attached wire. The small current so generated flips an on/off switch that determines whether or not a pixel glows. The greater the current, the brighter the pixel.

Insights

2. However, the light reflected from the subject does not typically result in the formation of enough silver atoms to make a visible image. But the more silver atoms a microcrystal contains, the more susceptible it is to further oxidation–reduction reactions. To make a visible image, the photographer in a darkroom treats the exposed film with a reducing agent, such as hydroquinone, $C_6H_6O_2$, which reveals the encoded image by causing the formation of many more opaque silver atoms. Through this step, the image *develops.*
3. The reduction of silver ions by the hydroquinone developing solution is stopped by treating the film with a solution of sodium thiosulfate, $Na_2S_2O_3$, also called either *hypo* or *fixing solution.* The thiosulfate ion, $S_2O_3^{2-}$, binds with any unreduced silver ions to form a water-soluble salt. Subsequent washing with water removes everything except the silver atoms adhering to the film, which are most abundant where the greatest amount of light hit the film when the photograph was taken. The film is now *fixed.*
4. Because the silver atoms are opaque, the film appears as a *negative,* which is dark where the subject was light and light where the subject was dark.
5. Light is projected through the negative onto photographic paper, which is developed using the same reactions that produced the negative. The resulting developed image is a negative of the negative—in other words, a positive print.

Color photographic film is coated with a variety of chemicals that respond to light of different frequencies (colors). There are more oxidation–reduction reactions involved in the developing of a color photograph, but the basic principle is the same—the selective reduction of only those chemicals exposed to light.

☑ CHECKPOINT

Would a photographic negative be mostly transparent or mostly opaque if the camera shutter remained open too long and too much light fell on the film? How would the positive print from this negative appear?

Check Your Answer

The negative would be mostly opaque, because the greater the amount of light that hits the film, the greater the number of silver ions reduced by the bromide ions or hydroquinone. The reduction of the silver ions results in opaque silver atoms that adhere to the film. Such an overexposed negative, therefore, would be mostly opaque, because of the many opaque silver atoms. The positive print would be very light, because there would be very little light passing through the negative to sensitize the silver ions in the photographic paper.

23.3 Harnessing the Energy of Flowing Electrons

Electrochemistry is the study of the relationship between electrical energy and chemical change. It involves either the use of an oxidation–reduction reaction to produce an electric current or the use of an electric current to produce an oxidation–reduction reaction.

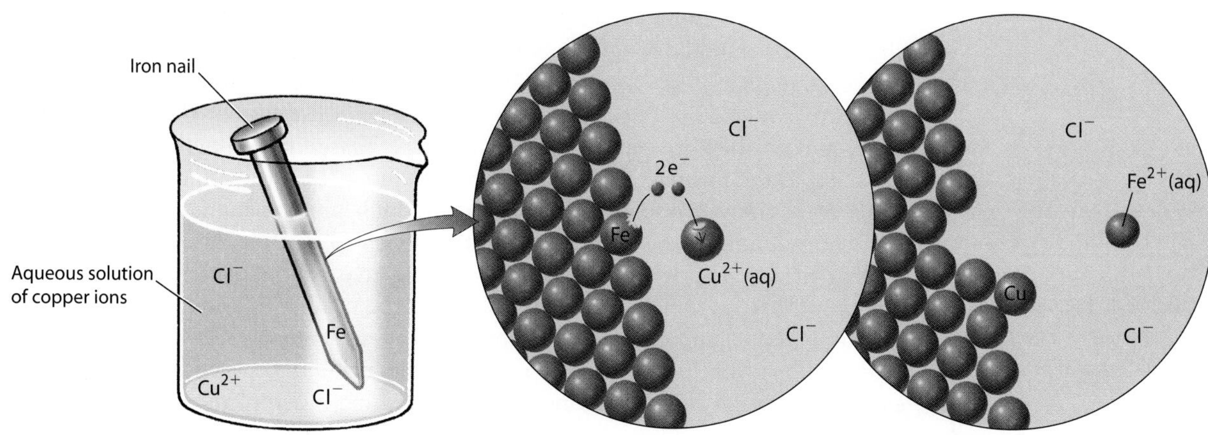

Oxidation $Fe \longrightarrow Fe^{2+} + 2\,e^-$

Reduction $Cu^{2+} + 2\,e^- \longrightarrow Cu$

Figure 23.5
A nail made of iron placed in a solution of Cu^{2+} ions oxidizes to Fe^{2+} ions, which dissolve in the water. At the same time, copper ions are reduced to metallic copper, which coats the nail. (Negatively charged ions, such as chloride ions, Cl^-, must also be present to balance these positively charged ions in solution.)

To understand how an oxidation–reduction reaction can generate an electric current, consider what happens when a reducing agent is placed in direct contact with an oxidizing agent: electrons flow from the reducing agent to the oxidizing agent. This flow of electrons is an electric current, which is a form of kinetic energy that can be harnessed for useful purposes.

Iron atoms, Fe, for example, are better reducing agents than copper ions, Cu^{2+}. So when a piece of iron metal and a solution containing copper ions are placed in contact with each other, electrons flow from the iron to the copper ions, as Figure 23.5 illustrates. The result is the oxidation of iron atoms and the reduction of copper ions.

The elemental iron and copper ions need not be in physical contact for electrons to flow between them. If they are in separate containers but bridged by a conducting wire, the electrons can flow from the iron through the wire to the copper ions. The resulting electric current in the wire can be attached to some useful device, such as a light bulb. But alas, an electric current is not sustained by this arrangement.

The reason the electric current is not sustained is shown in Figure 23.6. An initial flow of electrons through the wire immediately results in a buildup of

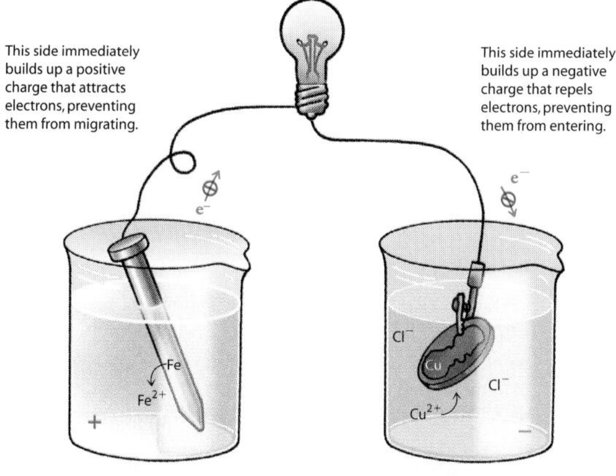

Figure 23.6
An iron nail is placed in water and connected by a conducting wire to a solution of copper ions. Nothing happens, because this arrangement results in a buildup of charge that prevents the further flow of electrons.

electric charge in both containers. The container on the left builds up positive charge as it accumulates Fe^{2+} ions from the nail. The container on the right builds up negative charge as electrons accumulate on this side. This situation prevents any further migration of electrons through the wire. Recall that electrons are negative, and so they are repelled by the negative charge in the right container and attracted to the positive charge in the left container. The net result is that the electrons do not flow through the wire, and the bulb remains unlit.

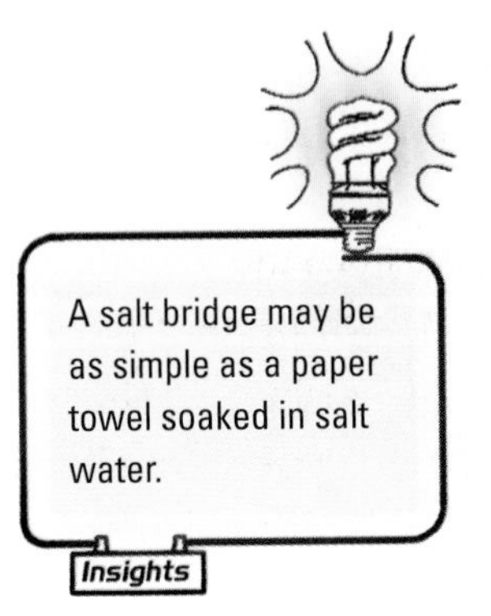

The solution to this problem is to allow ions to migrate into either container so that neither builds up any positive or negative charge. This is accomplished with a *salt bridge,* which may be a U-shaped tube filled with a salt, such as sodium nitrate, $NaNO_3$, and closed with semiporous plugs. Figure 23.7 shows how a salt bridge allows the ions it holds to enter either container, permitting the flow of electrons through the conducting wire and creating a complete electric circuit.

Batteries

So we can see that, with the proper setup, it is possible to harness electrical energy from an oxidation–reduction reaction. The apparatus shown in Figure 23.7 is one example. Such devices are called voltaic cells. Instead of two containers, a *voltaic cell* can be an all-in-one, self-contained unit, in which case it is called a *battery*. Batteries are either disposable or rechargeable, and here we explore some examples of each. Although the two types differ in design and composition, they function by the same principle: two materials that oxidize and reduce each other are connected by a medium through which ions travel to balance an external flow of electrons.

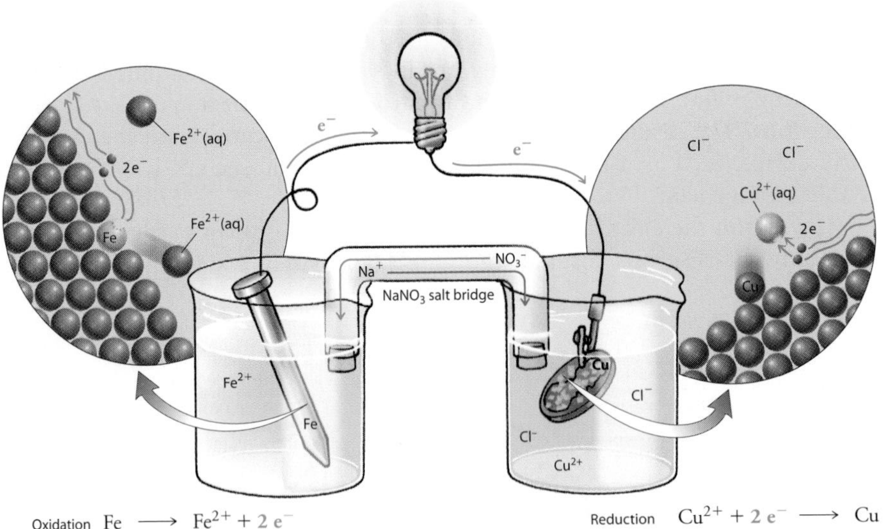

Figure 23.7
The salt bridge completes the electric circuit. Electrons freed as the iron is oxidized pass through the wire to the container on the right. Nitrate ions, NO_3^-, from the salt bridge flow into the left container to balance the positive charges of the Fe^{2+} ions that form, thereby preventing any buildup of positive charge. Meanwhile, Na^+ ions from the salt bridge enter the right container to balance the Cl^- ions "abandoned" by the Cu^{2+} ions as the Cu^{2+} ions pick up electrons to become metallic copper.

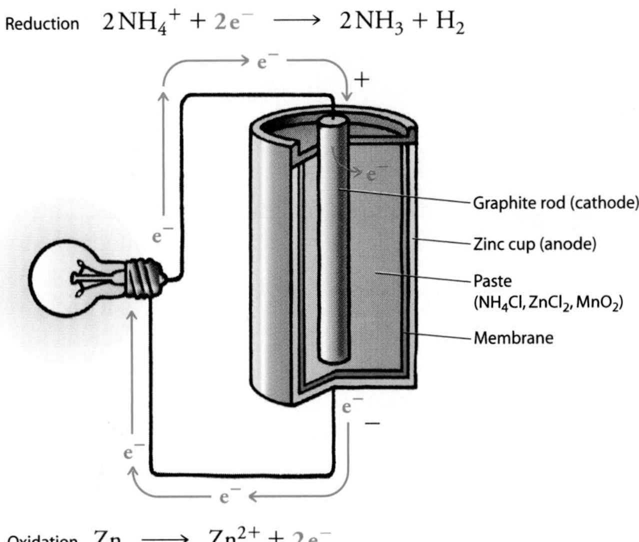

Figure 23.8
A common dry-cell battery with a graphite rod immersed in a paste of ammonium chloride, manganese dioxide, and zinc chloride.

Let's look at disposable batteries first. The common *dry-cell battery,* which was invented in the 1860s, is still used today, and it is probably the cheapest disposable energy source for flashlights, toys, and the like. The basic design consists of a zinc cup filled with a thick paste of ammonium chloride, NH_4Cl, zinc chloride, $ZnCl_2$, and manganese dioxide, MnO_2. Immersed in this paste is a porous stick of graphite that projects to the top of the battery, as shown in Figure 23.8.

Graphite is a good conductor of electricity. Chemicals in the paste receive electrons at the graphite stick and so are reduced. The reaction for the ammonium ions is

$$2NH_4^+(aq) + 2e^- \longrightarrow 2NH_3(g) + H_2(g) \qquad \text{Reduction}$$

An **electrode** is any material that conducts electrons into or out of a medium in which electrochemical reactions are occurring. The electrode where chemicals are reduced is called a **cathode.** For any battery, such as the one shown in Figure 23.8, the cathode is always positive (+), which indicates that electrons are naturally attracted to this location. The electrons gained by chemicals at the cathode originate at the **anode,** which is the electrode where chemicals are oxidized. For any battery, the anode is always negative (−), which indicates that electrons are streaming away from this location. The anode in Figure 23.8 is the zinc cup, where zinc atoms lose electrons to form zinc ions:

$$Zn(s) \longrightarrow Zn^{2+}(aq) + 2\,e^- \qquad \text{Oxidation}$$

The reduction of ammonium ions in a dry-cell battery produces two gases—ammonia, NH_3, and hydrogen, H_2—that need to be removed to avoid a pressure buildup and a potential explosion. Removal is accomplished by having the ammonia and hydrogen react with the zinc chloride and manganese dioxide:

$$ZnCl_2(aq) + 2\,NH_3(g) \longrightarrow Zn(NH_3)_2Cl_2(s)$$

$$2\,MnO_2(s) + H_2(g) \longrightarrow Mn_2O_3(s) + H_2O(\ell)$$

Figure 23.9
Alkaline batteries last a lot longer than dry-cell batteries and give a steadier voltage, but they are more expensive.

The life of a dry-cell battery is relatively short. Oxidation causes the zinc cup to deteriorate, and eventually the contents leak out. Even while the battery is not operating, the zinc corrodes as it reacts with ammonium ions. This zinc corrosion can be inhibited by storing the battery in a refrigerator. As discussed in Chapter 21, chemical reactions slow down with decreasing temperature. Chilling a battery, therefore, slows down the rate at which the zinc corrodes, which increases the life of the battery.

Another type of disposable battery, the more expensive *alkaline battery*, shown in Figure 23.9, avoids many of the problems of dry-cell batteries by operating in a strongly alkaline paste. In the presence of hydroxide ions, the zinc oxidizes to insoluble zinc oxide:

If you store your extra flashlight batteries in the refrigerator, they'll last longer.

Insights

$$Zn(s) + 2\ OH^{-}(aq) \longrightarrow ZnO(s) + H_2O(\ell) + 2e^{-} \qquad \text{Oxidation}$$

At the same time, manganese dioxide is reduced:

$$2\ MnO_2(s) + H_2O(\ell) + 2e^{-} \longrightarrow Mn_2O_3(s) + 2\ H_2O(aq) \qquad \text{Reduction}$$

Note how these two reactions avoid the use of the zinc-corroding ammonium ion (which means alkaline batteries last a lot longer than dry-cell batteries) and also prevent formation of any gaseous products. Furthermore, these reactions are better suited to maintaining a given voltage during longer periods of operation.

The small mercury and lithium disposable batteries used for calculators and cameras are variations of the alkaline battery. In the mercury battery, mercuric oxide, HgO, is reduced rather than manganese dioxide. Manufacturers are phasing out these batteries because of the environmental hazard posed by mercury, which is poisonous. In the lithium battery, lithium metal is used as the source of electrons rather than zinc. Not only is lithium able to maintain a higher voltage than zinc, but also it is about one-thirteenth as dense, which allows for a lighter battery.

Disposable batteries have relatively short lives because electron-producing chemicals are consumed. The main feature of rechargeable batteries is the reversibility of the oxidation and reduction reactions. In your car's rechargeable lead storage battery, for example, electrical energy is produced as lead dioxide, lead, and sulfuric acid are consumed to form lead sulfate and water. The elemental lead is oxidized to Pb^{2+}, and the lead in the lead dioxide is reduced from the Pb^{4+} state to the Pb^{2+} state. Combining the two half reactions gives the complete oxidation–reduction reaction:

$$PbO_2 + Pb + 2\ H_2SO_4 \longrightarrow 2\ PbSO_4 + 2\ H_2O + \text{electrical energy}$$

This reaction can be reversed by supplying electrical energy, as Figure 23.10 shows. This is the task of the car's alternator, which is powered by the engine:

$$\text{Electrical energy} + 2\ PbSO_4 + 2\ H_2O \longrightarrow PbO_2 + Pb + 2\ H_2SO_4$$

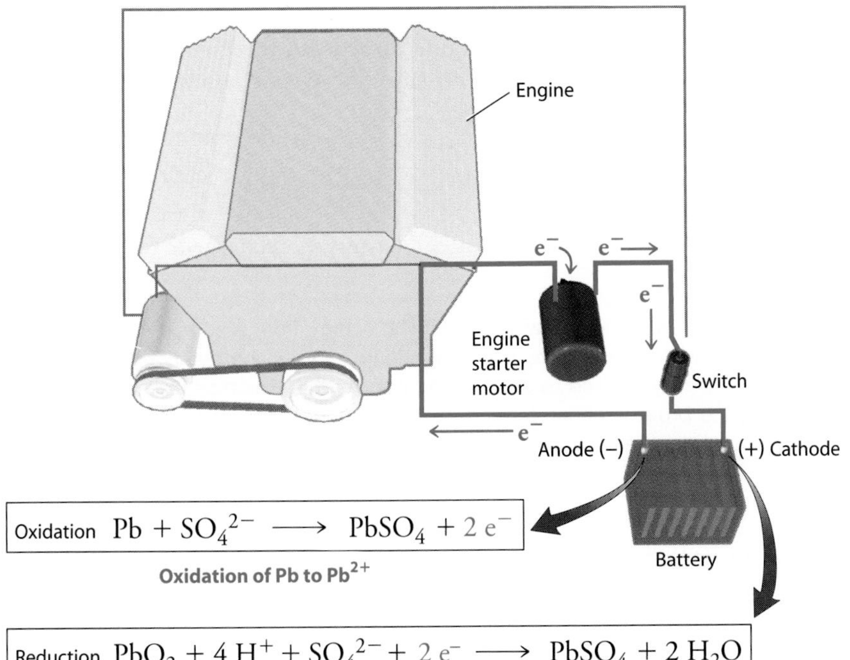

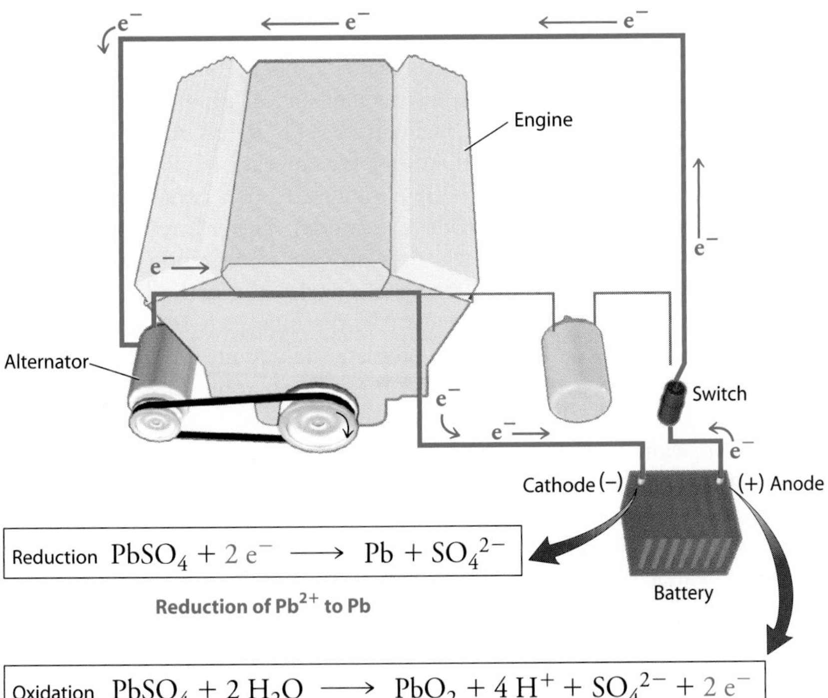

Figure 23.10
(a) Electrical energy from the battery forces the starter motor to start the engine. (b) The combustion of fuel keeps the engine running and provides energy to spin the alternator, which recharges the battery. Note that the battery has a reversed cathode–anode orientation during recharging.

The cathode is where reduction occurs, while the anode is where oxidation occurs. As a battery provides electricity, the cathode is positively charged (electrons move towards it), while the anode is negatively charged (electrons move away from it). These roles are reversed when a rechargable battery is being recharged. What was once the (−) anode now becomes the (−) cathode. Because electrons won't travel to the negative cathode on their own, they must be forced to do so. Hence, recharging is an energy-consuming process.

Insights

Aside from the initial charge of a brand-new battery, the energy in a car battery ultimately comes from fuel in the gas tank through the process of recharging.

Insights

So running the engine maintains concentrations of lead dioxide, lead, and sulfuric acid in the battery. With the engine turned off, these reactants stand ready to supply electric power as needed to start the engine, operate the emergency blinkers, or play the radio.

☑ CHECKPOINT

What chemicals are produced as a car battery is recharged?

Check Your Answer

When the battery is being recharged, electrical energy from a source (the alternator) outside the battery is used to reverse the oxidation–reduction reaction that produced the electrical energy needed to start the engine. As this oxidation–reduction reaction is reversed, the products once formed are transformed back into reactants. The reactants being regenerated are lead dioxide, elemental lead, and sulfuric acid.

Hybrid gasoline–electric automobiles that now channel the energy of braking into charging batteries, which aids the engine in times of acceleration, commonly get some 50 miles per gallon and more.

Insights

Many rechargeable batteries smaller than car batteries are made of compounds of nickel and cadmium (nicad batteries). As with the lead storage battery, nicad reactants are replenished by supplying electrical energy from some external source, such as an electrical wall outlet. Like mercury batteries, nicad batteries pose an environmental hazard because cadmium is toxic to humans and other organisms. For this reason, alkaline batteries designed to be rechargeable are rapidly gaining a place in the market.

Fuel Cells

A *fuel cell* is a device that converts the chemical energy of a fuel to electrical energy. Fuel cells are by far the most efficient means of generating electricity. A hydrogen–oxygen fuel cell is shown in Figure 23.11. It has two compartments, one for entering hydrogen fuel and the other for entering oxygen fuel, separated by a set of porous electrodes. Hydrogen is oxidized upon contact with hydroxide ions at the hydrogen-facing electrode (the anode). The electrons from this oxidation flow through an external circuit and provide electric power before meeting up with oxygen at the oxygen-facing electrode (the cathode). The oxygen readily picks up the electrons (in other words, the oxygen is reduced) and reacts with water to form hydroxide ions. To complete the circuit, these hydroxide ions migrate across the porous electrodes and through an ionic paste of potassium hydroxide, KOH, to join with hydrogen at the hydrogen-facing electrode.

As the oxidation equation shown at the top of Figure 23.11 demonstrates, the hydrogen and hydroxide ions react to produce energetic water molecules that arise in the form of steam. This steam may be used for heating or for generating electricity in a steam turbine. Furthermore, the water that condenses from the steam is pure water, suitable for drinking!

Although fuel cells are similar to dry-cell batteries, they don't run down as long as fuel is supplied. The space shuttle uses hydrogen–oxygen fuel cells to meet its electrical needs. The cells also produce more than 100 gallons of drinking water for the astronauts during a typical week-long mission. Back on the earth, researchers are developing fuel cells for buses and automobiles. As shown in Figure 23.12, experimental fuel-cell buses are already operating in

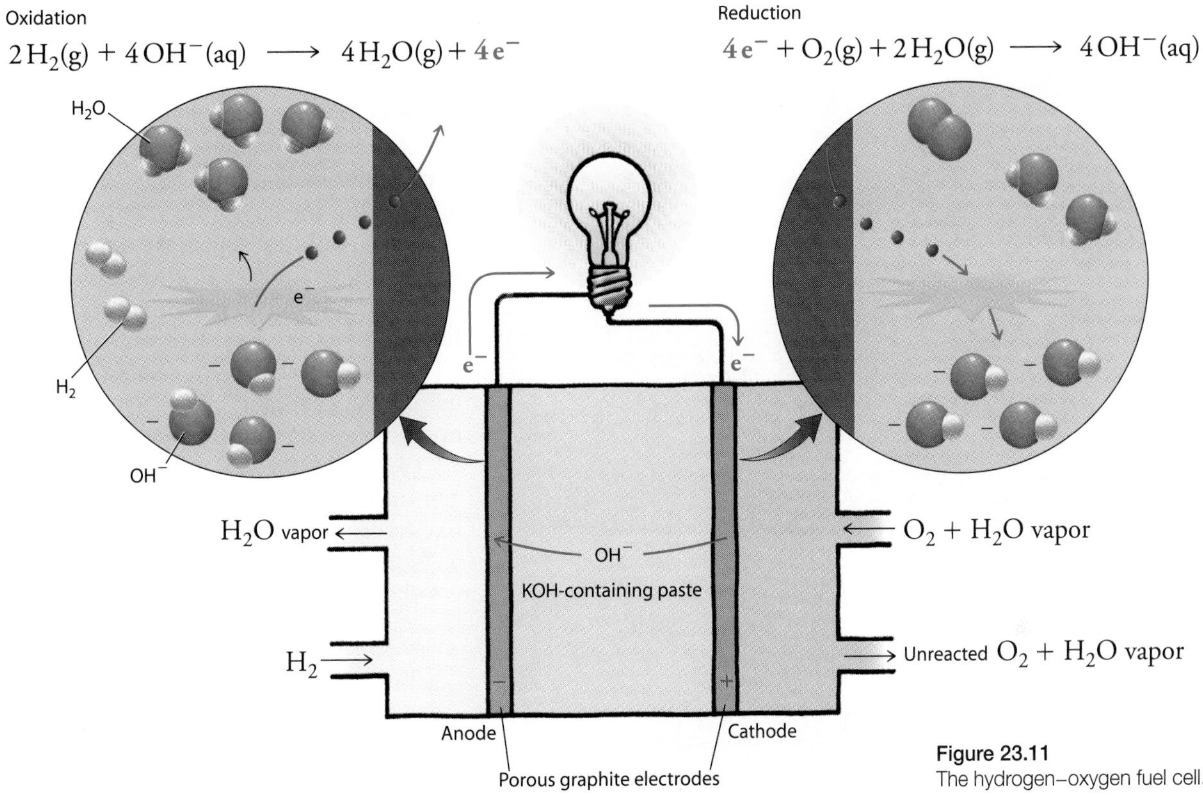

Oxidation

$$2H_2(g) + 4OH^-(aq) \longrightarrow 4H_2O(g) + 4e^-$$

Reduction

$$4e^- + O_2(g) + 2H_2O(g) \longrightarrow 4OH^-(aq)$$

H_2O

H_2

OH^-

e^-

H_2O vapor

H_2

OH^-

KOH-containing paste

$O_2 + H_2O$ vapor

Unreacted $O_2 + H_2O$ vapor

Anode

Cathode

Porous graphite electrodes

Figure 23.11
The hydrogen–oxygen fuel cell.

several cities, such as Vancouver, British Columbia, and Chicago, Illinois. These vehicles produce very few pollutants and can run much more efficiently than vehicles that burn fossil fuels.

In the future, commercial buildings as well as individual homes may be outfitted with fuel cells as an alternative to receiving electricity (and heat) from regional power stations. Researchers are also working on miniature fuel cells that could replace the batteries used for portable electronic devices, such as cellular phones and laptop computers. Such devices could operate for extended periods of time on a single "ampule" of fuel available at your local supermarket.

Figure 23.12
Because this bus is powered by a fuel cell, its tail pipe emits mostly water vapor.

Amazingly, a car powered by a hydrogen–oxygen fuel cell requires only about 3 kilograms of hydrogen to travel 500 kilometers. However, this quantity of hydrogen gas at room temperature and atmospheric pressure would occupy a volume of about 36,000 liters, the volume of about four midsize cars! Thus, the major hurdle to the development of fuel-cell technology lies not with the cell but with the fuel. This volume of gas could be compressed to a much smaller volume, as it is in the experimental buses in Vancouver.

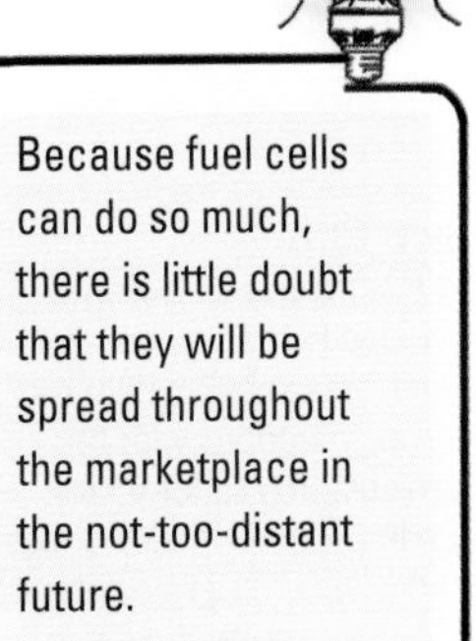

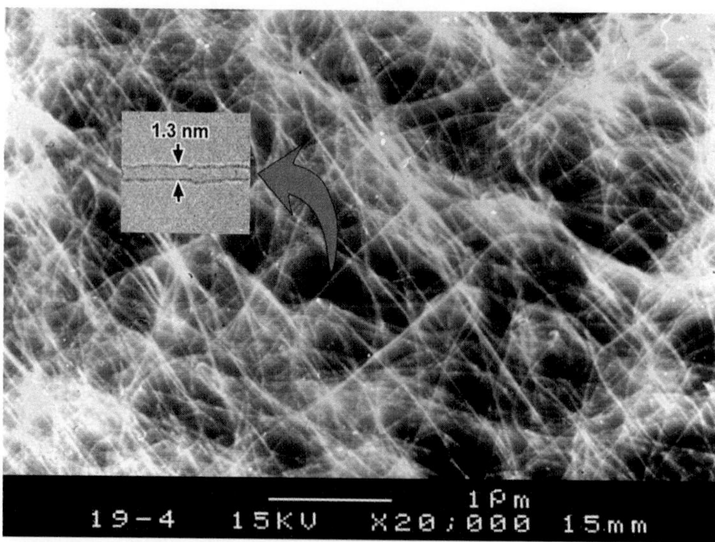

Figure 23.13
Carbon nanofibers consist of near-submicroscopic tubes of carbon atoms. They outclass almost all other known materials in their ability to absorb hydrogen molecules. With carbon nanofibers, a volume of 36,000 liters of hydrogen can be reduced to a mere 35 liters. Carbon nanofibers are a recent discovery, however, and much research is still required to confirm their applicability to hydrogen storage and to develop the technology.

Compressing a gas requires energy, however—and, as a consequence, the inherent efficiency of the fuel cell is lost. Chilling hydrogen to its liquid phase, which occupies much less volume, poses similar problems. Instead, researchers are looking for novel ways of providing fuel cells with hydrogen. In one design, hydrogen is generated within the fuel cell from chemical reactions involving liquid hydrocarbons, such as methanol, CH_3OH. Alternatively, certain porous materials, including the recently developed carbon nanofibers shown in Figure 23.13, can hold large volumes of hydrogen on their surfaces, behaving in effect like hydrogen "sponges." The hydrogen is "squeezed" out of these materials on demand by controlling the temperature—the warmer the material, the more hydrogen that is released.

☑ CHECKPOINT

As long as fuel is available to it, a given fuel cell can supply electrical energy indefinitely. Why can't batteries do the same?

Check Your Answer

Batteries generate electricity as the chemical reactants they contain are reduced and oxidized. Once these reactants are consumed, the battery can no longer generate electricity. A rechargeable battery can be made to operate again, but only after the energy flow is interrupted so that the reactants can be replenished.

23.4 Electrolysis

Electrolysis is the use of electrical energy to produce chemical change. The recharging of a car battery is an example of electrolysis. Another, shown in Figure 23.14, is passing an electric current through water, a process that breaks the water down into its elemental components:

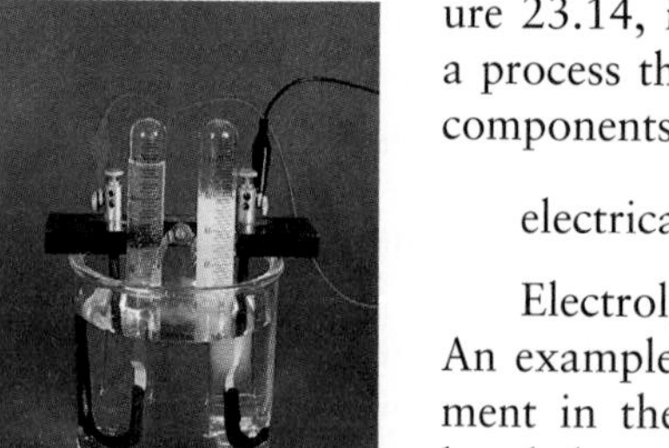

Figure 23.14
The electrolysis of water produces hydrogen gas and oxygen gas in a 2:1 ratio by volume, in accord with the chemical formula for water: H_2O. In order for this process to work, ions must be dissolved in the water so that electric charge can be conducted between the electrodes.

$$\text{electrical energy} + 2H_2O(\ell) \longrightarrow 2\ H_2(g) + O_2(g)$$

Electrolysis is used to purify metals from metal ores. An example is aluminum, the third most abundant element in the earth's crust. Aluminum occurs naturally bonded to oxygen in an ore called bauxite. Aluminum metal wasn't known until about 1827, when it was prepared by reacting bauxite with hydrochloric acid. This reaction gave the aluminum ion, Al^{3+}, which was reduced to aluminum metal, with sodium metal acting as the reducing agent:

$$Al^{3+} + 3Na \longrightarrow Al + 3Na^{+}$$

This chemical process was expensive. The price of aluminum at that time was about \$100,000 per pound, and it was considered a rare and precious metal. In 1855, aluminum dinnerware and other items were exhibited in Paris with the crown jewels of France. Then, in 1886, two men working independently, Charles Hall (1863–1914) in the United States and Paul Heroult (1863–1914) in France, almost simultaneously discovered a process whereby aluminum could be produced from aluminum oxide, Al_2O_3, a main component of bauxite. In what is now known as the Hall–Heroult process, shown in Figure 23.15, a strong electric current is passed through a molten mixture of aluminum oxide and cryolite, Na_3AlF_6, a naturally occurring mineral. The fluoride ions of the cryolite react with the aluminum oxide to form various aluminum fluoride ions, such as $AlOF_3^{2-}$, which are then oxidized to the aluminum hexafluoride ion, AlF_6^{3-}. The Al^{3+} in this ion is then reduced to elemental aluminum, which collects at the bottom of the reaction chamber. This process, which is still in use by manufacturers today, greatly facilitated mass production of aluminum metal, and, by 1890, the price of aluminum had dropped to about \$2 per pound.

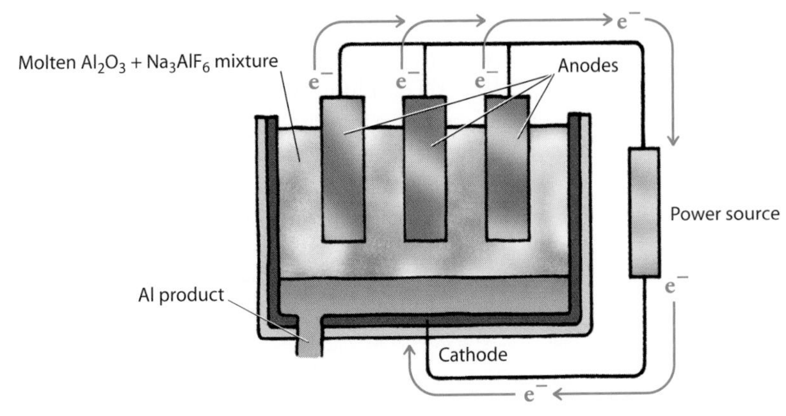

Figure 23.15
The melting point of aluminum oxide (2030°C) is too high for efficiently electrolyzing to aluminum metal. When the oxide is mixed with the mineral cryolite, the melting point of the oxide drops to a more reasonable 980°C. A strong electric current passed through the molten aluminum oxide–cryolite mixture generates aluminum metal at the cathode, where aluminum ions pick up electrons and are thus reduced to elemental aluminum.

Today, worldwide production of aluminum is about 16 million tons annually. For each ton produced from ore, about 16,000 kilowatt-hours of electrical energy is required, as much as a typical American household consumes in 18 months. Processing recycled aluminum, on the other hand, consumes only about 700 kilowatt-hours for every ton. Thus, recycling aluminum not only reduces litter but also helps to reduce the load on power companies, which, in turn, reduces air pollution. Furthermore, as you'll recall from Section 18.6, reserves of high-quality aluminum oxide ores are already depleted in the United States. Recycling aluminum, therefore, also helps to minimize the need for developing new bauxite mines in foreign countries.

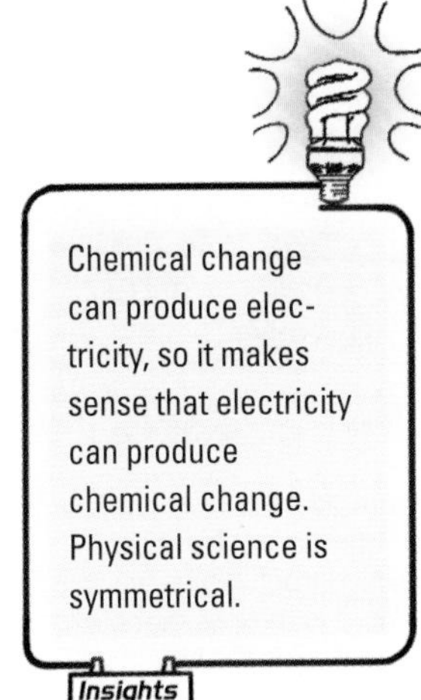

☑ CHECKPOINT

Is the exothermic reaction in a hydrogen–oxygen fuel cell an example of electrolysis?

Check Your Answer

No. During electrolysis, electrical energy is used to produce chemical change. In the hydrogen–oxygen fuel cell, chemical change is used to produce electrical energy.

For a nerve-wracking experience involving the oxidation of elemental aluminum, bite a piece of aluminum foil with a tooth filled with dental amalgam. (If you don't have any dental fillings, hooray for you! You'll need to ask a less fortunate friend how this activity feels.) The aluminum behaves as an anode and releases electrons to the amalgam (a mix of silver, tin, and mercury). The amalgam behaves as a cathode by transferring these electrons to oxygen, which then combines with hydrogen ions to form water. The slight current that results produces a jolt of—Ouch!—Pain.

23.5 Corrosion and Combustion

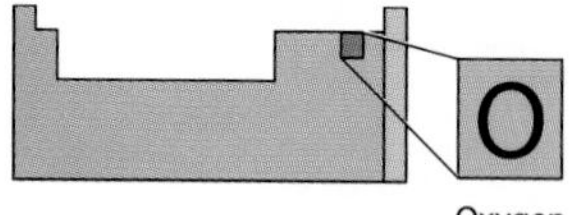

Oxygen

If you look to the upper right of the periodic table, you will find one of the most common oxidizing agents—oxygen. In fact, if you haven't guessed already, the term *oxidation* is derived from the name of this element. Oxygen is able to pluck electrons from many other elements, especially those that lie at the lower left of the periodic table. Two common oxidation–reduction reactions involving oxygen as the oxidizing agent are *corrosion* and *combustion.*

☑ CHECKPOINT

Oxygen is a good oxidizing agent, but so is chlorine. What does this indicate about their relative positions in the periodic table?

Check Your Answer

Chlorine and oxygen must lie in the same area of the periodic table. Both have strong effective nuclear charges and are strong oxidizing agents.

Figure 23.16
Rust itself is not harmful to the iron structures on which it forms. It is the loss of metallic iron that ruins the structural integrity of these objects.

Corrosion is the process whereby a metal deteriorates. Corrosion caused by atmospheric oxygen is a widespread and costly problem. About one-quarter of the steel produced in the United States, for example, goes into replacing corroded iron at a cost of billions of dollars annually. Iron corrodes when it reacts with atmospheric oxygen and water to form iron oxide trihydrate, which is the naturally occurring reddish-brown substance you know as rust, shown in Figure 23.16:

$$\underset{\text{Iron}}{4\,Fe} + \underset{\text{Oxygen}}{3\,O_2} + \underset{\text{Water}}{3\,H_2O} \longrightarrow \underset{\text{Rust}}{2\,Fe_2O_3 \cdot 3\,H_2O}$$

We can better understand rusting by considering this equation in steps, as shown in Figure 23.17. (1) Iron loses electrons to form the Fe^{2+} ion. (2) Oxygen accepts these electrons and then reacts with water to form hydroxide ions, OH^-. (3) Iron ions and hydroxide ions combine to form iron hydroxide, $Fe(OH)_2$, which is further oxidized by oxygen to form rust, $Fe_2O_3 \cdot 3\,H_2O$.

Another common metal oxidized by oxygen is aluminum. The product of aluminum oxidation is aluminum oxide, Al_2O_3, which is not water-soluble.

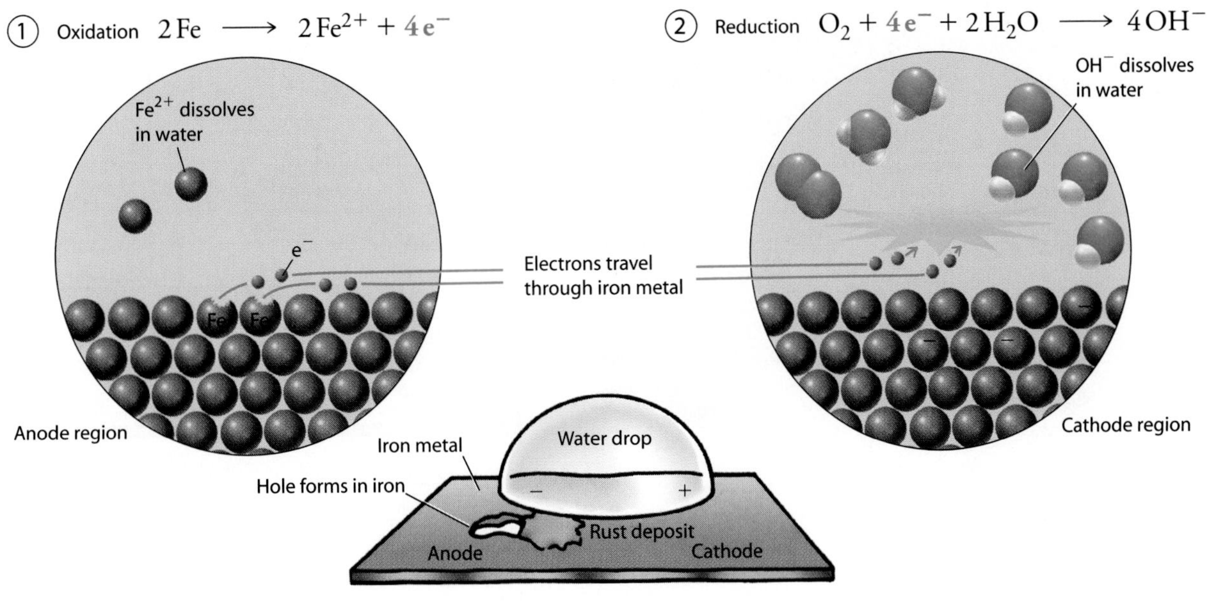

Figure 23.17
A piece of iron metal begins to rust when iron atoms lose electrons to oxygen atoms and form Fe^{2+} ions. The oxygen atoms are reduced to hydroxide ions, OH^-. One region of the piece of iron behaves as the anode while another region behaves as the cathode. Rust forms only in the region of the anode, where iron atoms lose electrons. The loss of elemental iron in this region causes a hole to form in the metal.

Because of its insolubility, aluminum oxide forms a protective coat that shields the metal from further oxidation. This coat is so thin that it's transparent, which is why aluminum maintains its metallic shine.

A protective, water-insoluble oxidized coat is the principle underlying a process called *galvanization*. Zinc has a slightly greater tendency to oxidize than does iron. For this reason, many iron objects, such as the nails pictured in Figure 23.18, are *galvanized* by coating them with a thin layer of zinc. The zinc oxidizes to zinc oxide, an inert, insoluble substance that protects the iron underneath it from rusting.

In a technique called *cathodic protection,* iron structures can be protected from oxidation by placing them in contact with certain metals, such as zinc or magnesium, that have a greater tendency to oxidize. This forces the iron to accept electrons, which means that it is behaving as a cathode. (Recall, from Figure 23.17, that rusting occurs only where iron behaves as an anode). Ocean tankers, for example, are protected from corrosion by strips of zinc affixed to their hulls, as shown in Figure 23.19. Similarly, outdoor steel pipes are protected by being connected to magnesium rods inserted into the ground.

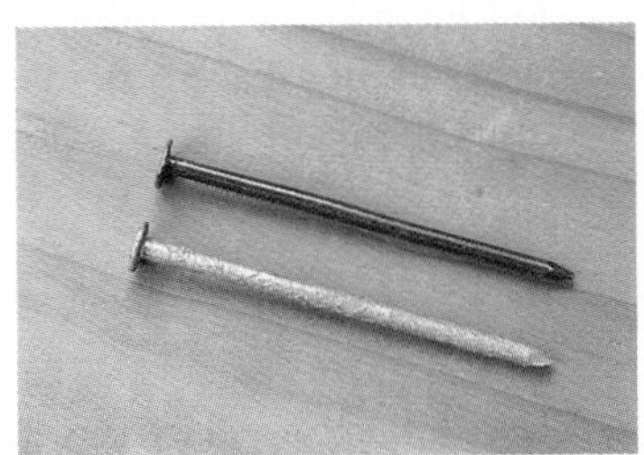

Figure 23.18
The galvanized nail (*bottom*) is protected from rusting by the sacrificial oxidation of zinc.

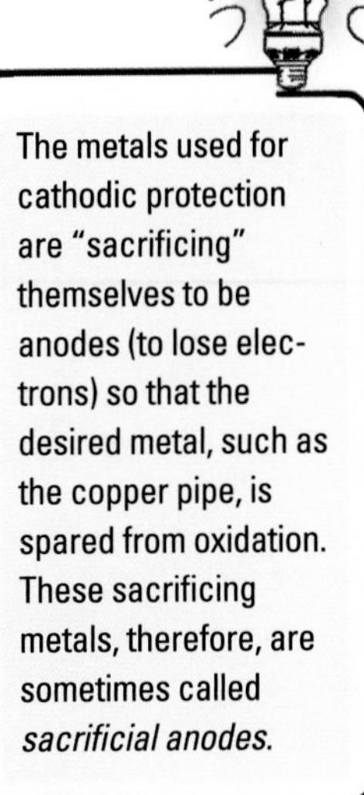

Figure 23.19
Zinc strips help to protect the iron hull of an oil tanker from oxidizing. The zinc strip shown here is attached to the hull's interior surface.

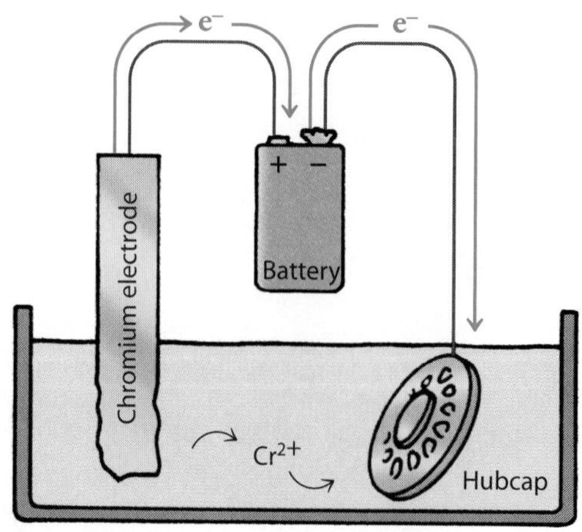

Figure 23.20
As electrons flow into the hubcap and give it a negative charge, positively charged chromium ions move from the solution to the hubcap and are reduced to chromium metal, which deposits as a coating on the hubcap. The solution is supplied with ions as chromium atoms in the cathode are oxidized to Cr^{2+} ions.

Yet another way to protect iron and other metals from oxidation is to coat them with a corrosion-resistant metal, such as chromium, platinum, or gold. *Electroplating* is the operation of coating one metal with another by electrolysis, and it is illustrated in Figure 23.20. The object to be electroplated is connected to a negative battery terminal and then submerged in a solution containing ions of the metal to be used as the coating. The positive terminal of the battery is connected to an electrode made of the coating metal. The circuit is completed when this electrode is submerged in the solution. Dissolved metal ions are attracted to the negatively charged object, where they pick up electrons and are deposited as metal atoms. The ions in solution are replenished by the forced oxidation of the coating metal at the positive electrode.

Combustion is an oxidation–reduction reaction between a nonmetallic material and molecular oxygen. Combustion reactions are characteristically exothermic (energy-releasing). A violent combustion reaction is the formation of water from hydrogen and oxygen. As discussed in Section 21.3, the energy from this reaction is used to power rockets into space. More common examples of combustion include the burning of wood and fossil fuels. The combustion of these and other carbon-based chemicals forms carbon dioxide and water. Consider, for example, the combustion of methane, the major component of natural gas:

$$\underset{\text{Methane}}{CH_4} + \underset{\text{Oxygen}}{2\ O_2} \longrightarrow \underset{\text{Carbon dioxide}}{CO_2} + \underset{\text{Water}}{2\ H_2O} + \text{energy}$$

In combustion, electrons are transferred as polar covalent bonds are formed in place of nonpolar covalent bonds, or vice versa. (This is in contrast with the other examples of oxidation–reduction reactions presented in this chapter, which involve the formation of ions from atoms or, conversely, atoms from ions.) This concept is illustrated in Figure 23.21, which compares the electronic structures of the combustion starting material, molecular oxygen, and the combustion product, water. Molecular oxygen is a nonpolar covalent compound. Although each oxygen atom in the molecule has a fairly strong electronegativity, the four bonding electrons are pulled equally by both atoms and thus are unable to congregate on one side or the other. After combustion, however, the electrons are shared between the oxygen and hydrogen atoms in a water molecule and are pulled to the oxygen. This gives the oxygen a slight negative charge, which is another way of saying it has gained electrons and has thus been reduced. At the same time, the hydrogen atoms in the water molecule develop a slight positive charge, which is another way of saying they have lost electrons and have thus been oxidized. This gain of electrons by oxygen and loss of electrons by hydrogen is an energy-releasing process. Typically, the energy is released either as molecular kinetic energy (heat) or as light (the flame).

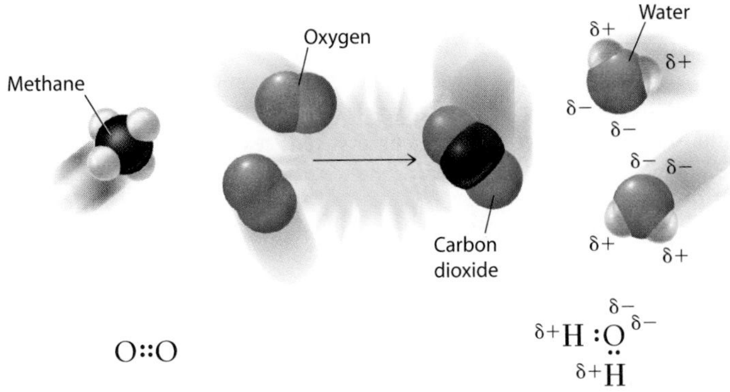

(a) Reactant oxygen atoms share electrons equally in O_2 molecules.

(b) Product oxygen atoms pull electrons away from H atoms in H_2O molecules and are reduced.

Figure 23.21
(a) Neither atom in an oxygen molecule is able to preferentially attract the bonding electrons. (b) The oxygen atom of a water molecule pulls the bonding electrons away from the hydrogen atoms on the water molecule, making the oxygen slightly negative and the two hydrogens slightly positive.

Interestingly, combustion oxidation–reduction reactions occur throughout your body. You can visualize a simplified model of your metabolism by reviewing Figure 23.21 and substituting a food molecule for the methane. Food molecules relinquish their electrons to the oxygen molecules you inhale. The products are carbon dioxide, water vapor, and energy. You exhale the carbon dioxide and water vapor, but much of the energy from the reaction is used to keep your body warm and to drive the many other biochemical reactions necessary for life.

Whereas chemical reactions involving the transfer of protons was the subject of the previous chapter, this chapter has explored reactions involving the transfer of electrons. In the next and final chapter of Part II, we will explore the unique chemistry of carbon atoms.

Summary of Terms

Oxidation The process whereby a reactant loses one or more electrons.

Reduction The process whereby a reactant gains one or more electrons.

Half reaction One portion of an oxidation–reduction reaction, represented by an equation showing electrons as either reactants or products.

Electrochemistry The branch of chemistry concerned with the relationship between electrical energy and chemical change.

Electrode Any material that conducts electrons into or out of a medium in which electrochemical reactions are occurring.

Cathode The electrode where reduction occurs.

Anode The electrode where oxidation occurs.

Electrolysis The use of electrical energy to produce chemical change.

Corrosion The deterioration of a metal, typically caused by atmospheric oxygen.

Combustion An exothermic oxidation–reduction reaction between a nonmetallic material and molecular oxygen.

Review Questions

23.1 Losing and Gaining Electrons

1. Which elements have the greatest tendency to behave as oxidizing agents?
2. Write an equation for the half reaction in which a potassium atom, K, is oxidized.

3. Write an equation for the half reaction in which a bromine atom, Br, is reduced.
4. What is the difference between an oxidizing agent and a reducing agent?
5. What happens to a reducing agent as it reduces?

23.2 Photography

6. What special property of silver bromide makes it so useful for photography?
7. What gets reduced as bromine ions, Br^-, on photographic film are oxidized by light?
8. What role does hydroquinone play in the development of a black-and-white photograph?
9. What is meant by saying that a positive print is the negative of a negative?

23.3 Harnessing the Energy of Flowing Electrons

10. What is electrochemistry?
11. What is the purpose of the manganese dioxide in a dry-cell battery?
12. Distinguish between the anode and cathode of a common battery.
13. What is the effect of temperature on the lifetime of a dry cell?
14. Distinguish between dry cells and alkaline batteries.
15. What is the function of an automobile alternator?
16. What chemical reaction is forced to occur while a car battery is being recharged?
17. What is the primary fuel for a fuel cell?
18. Why don't the electrodes of a fuel cell deteriorate the way the electrodes of a battery do?
19. Why are fuel cells not more prevalent in powering automobiles today?

23.4 Electrolysis

20. What is electrolysis?
21. How does electrolysis differ from what goes on inside a battery?
22. Why was aluminum metal so expensive when it first appeared?
23. Why is the recyling of aluminum products of significant importance?

23.5 Corrosion and Combustion

24. Why is oxygen such a good oxidizing agent?
25. What do the oxidation of zinc and the oxidation of aluminum have in common?
26. What is electroplating, and how is it accomplished?
27. What does it mean to say that an iron product is galvanized?
28. What are some differences between corrosion and combustion?
29. What are some similarities between corrosion and combustion?
30. What is the role of oxidation–reduction reactions in living creatures?

Activities

Silver Lining

Tarnish on silverware is a coating of silver sulfide, Ag_2S, an ionic compound consisting of two silver ions, Ag^+, and one sulfide ion, S^{2-}. Tarnishing begins when silver atoms in the silverware come into contact with airborne hydrogen sulfide, H_2S, a smelly gas produced by the digestion of food in mammals and other organisms. The half reaction for the silver and hydrogen sulfide is

$$4\ Ag + 2\ H_2S \longrightarrow 4\ Ag^+ + 4\ H^+ + 2\ S^{2-} + 4\ e^-$$

Oxidation

The silver ions and sulfide ions combine to form blackish silver sulfide, while, at the same time, the hydrogen ions and electrons combine with atmospheric oxygen to form water:

$$4\ H^+ + 4\ e^- + O_2 \longrightarrow 2\ H_2O$$

Reduction

The balanced chemical equation for the tarnishing of silver is the combination of these two half reactions:

$$4\ Ag + 2\ H_2S + O_2 \longrightarrow 2\ Ag_2S + 2\ H_2O$$

From these equations, we can see that the hydrogen sulfide causes the silver to lose electrons to oxygen. To restore the silver to its shiny elemental state, we need to return the electrons it lost. The oxygen won't relinquish electrons back to silver, but, with the proper connection, aluminum atoms will.

What You Need

A very clean aluminum pot (or a non-aluminum pot and aluminum foil), water, baking soda, and a piece of tarnished silver.

Procedure

1. Place about a liter of water and several heaping tablespoons of baking soda in the aluminum pot (or in the non-aluminum pot containing a piece of aluminum foil).
2. Bring the water to boiling, and then remove the pot from the heat source.
3. Slowly immerse the tarnished silver; you'll see an immediate effect as the silver and aluminum make contact. (Add more baking soda if you don't.) Also, as the silver ions accept electrons from the aluminum and are thereby reduced to shiny silver atoms, the sulfide ions are free to re-form hydrogen sulfide gas, which is released back into the air. You may smell it!

    The baking soda serves as a conductive ionic solution that permits electrons to move from the aluminum atoms to the silver ions. What is the advantage of this approach over polishing the silver with an abrasive paste?

Polishing with an abrasive paste removes both the thin layer of tarnish and some silver atoms. Silver-plated pieces are therefore susceptible to losing their thin coating of silver. The aluminum method, by contrast, restores the silver lost to the tarnishing. For pieces too large to fit in the pot, try rubbing lightly with a paste of baking soda and water, using aluminum foil as your rubbing cloth.

Splitting Water

You can see the electrolysis of water by immersing the top of a disposable 9-volt battery in salt water. The bubbles that form contain hydrogen gas that is produced as the water decomposes. Try this activity with tap water instead of salt water to see the difference that dissolved ions can make—the ions are needed to conduct electricity between the two electrodes.

The primary reaction occurs at the negative electrode (anode), where water molecules accept electrons to form hydrogen gas and hydroxide ions. Recall, from Chapter 22, that an increase in hydroxide-ion concentration causes the pH of the solution to rise. You can track the production of hydroxide ions by adding a pH indicator to the solution. The indicator of choice is phenolphthalein, which you might obtain from your instructor. Alternatively, you might use the red-cabbage extract discussed in Chapter 22. Whichever indicator you use, note the swirls of color forming at the anode as hydroxide ions are generated.

The battery is quickly ruined because placing it in the conducting liquid short-circuits the terminals, which results in a large drain on the battery.

You may be wondering why oxygen gas is not generated along with the hydrogen gas. For reasons beyond the scope of this text, oxygen gas is generated only when the positive electrode (cathode) is made of certain metals, such as gold or platinum. The steel electrode of the 9-volt battery does not suffice.

Exercises

1. Which atom is oxidized, the red one or the blue one?

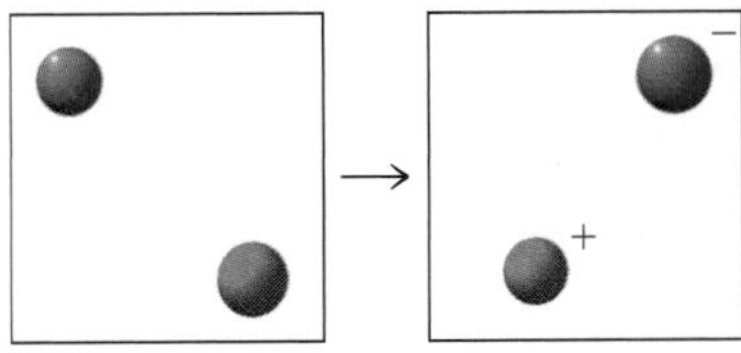

2. In the previous exercise, which atom behaves as the oxidizing agent, the red one or the blue one?
3. What correlation might you expect between an element's electronegativity (Section 19.6) and its ability to behave as an oxidizing agent?
4. What correlation might you expect between an element's electronegativity and its ability to behave as a reducing agent?
5. Ionization energy is the amount of energy required to pull a valence electron away from an atom. What correlation might you expect between an element's ionization energy (Section 5.8) and its ability to behave as an oxidizing agent?
6. What correlation might you expect between an element's ionization energy and its ability to behave as a reducing agent?
7. Based on their relative positions in the periodic table, which might you expect to be a stronger oxidizing agent, chlorine or fluorine? Why?
8. How does an atom's electronegativity relate to its ability to become oxidized?
9. Iron atoms, Fe, are better reducing agents than the copper ion Cu^{2+}. In which direction do electrons flow when an iron nail is submerged in a solution of Cu^{2+} ions?
10. What is the purpose of the salt bridge in Figure 23.7?
11. Why is the anode of a battery indicated with a minus sign?
12. Is sodium metal oxidized or reduced in the production of aluminum?

13. Why is the formation of iron hydroxide, $Fe(OH)_2$, from Fe^{2+} and OH^- not considered an oxidation–reduction reaction?
14. Your car lights were left on while you were shopping, and now your car battery is dead. Has the pH of the battery fluid increased or decreased?
15. Sketch a voltaic cell that uses the oxidation–reduction reaction

$$Mg(s) + Cu^{2+}(aq) \rightleftharpoons Mg^{2+}(aq) + Cu(s)$$

Which atom or ion is reduced? Which atom or ion is oxidized?
16. Jewelry is often manufactured by electroplating an expensive metal such as gold over a cheaper metal. Sketch a setup for this process.
17. Some car batteries require the periodic addition of water. Does adding the water increase or decrease the battery's ability to provide electric power to start the car? Explain.
18. Why does a battery that has thick zinc walls last longer than one that has thin zinc walls?
19. The oxidation of iron to rust is a problem structural engineers need to be concerned about, but the oxidation of aluminum to aluminum oxide is not. Why?
20. Why is rust a greater problem for thin iron rods than for thick iron piles?
21. Why will "steel" wool be more demolished by rust than the same amount of iron in a compact block?
22. How many electrons are transferred from iron atoms to oxygen atoms in the formation of two molecules of iron hydroxide, $Fe(OH)_2$? See Figure 23.17.
23. Why are combustion reactions generally exothermic?
24. Which element is closer to the upper right corner of the periodic table, the red one or the blue one:

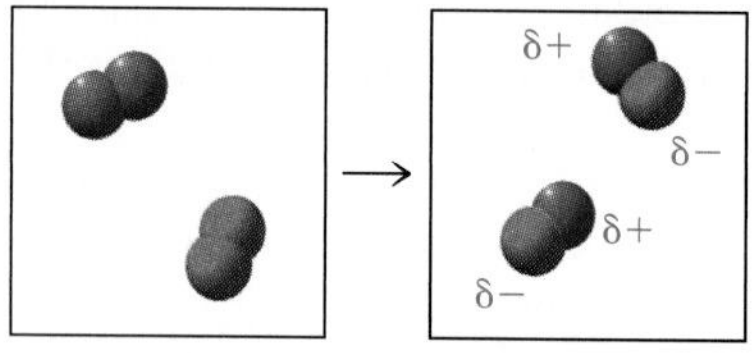

25. Water is 88.88 percent oxygen by mass. Oxygen is exactly what a fire needs to grow brighter and stronger. So why doesn't a fire grow brighter and stronger when water is added to it?
26. Clorox is a laundry bleaching agent used to remove stains from white clothes. Suggest why the name begins with *Clor-* and ends with *-ox*.
27. Iron atoms have a greater tendency to oxidize than copper atoms do. Is this good news or bad news for a home in which much of the plumbing consists of iron and copper pipes connected together? Explain.
28. Copper atoms have a greater tendency to be reduced than iron atoms do. Was this good news or bad news for the Statue of Liberty, whose copper exterior was originally held together by steel rivets?
29. One of the products of combustion is water. Why doesn't this water extinguish the combustion?
30. Shown below is an equation for the production of hydrogen chloride, HCl, from a solution of salt water and sulfuric acid, H_2SO_4. For this reaction, is the chlorine becoming more or less reduced? Explain.

$$NaCl + H_2SO_4 \longrightarrow HCl + NaHSO_4$$

31. Passing an electric current through a solution of salt water results in the formation of sodium hydroxide, NaOH, chlorine gas, Cl_2, plus what other product? Write out the chemical equation.
32. Sodium chlorite, $NaClO_2$, is a powerful bleaching agent that is used in the paper and textile industries. It is prepared by the following reaction:

$$4\ NaOH(aq) + Ca(OH)_2(aq) + C(s) + 4\ ClO_2(g) \longrightarrow 4\ NaClO_2(aq) + CaCO_3(s) + 3\ H_2O(\ell)$$

Which element is oxidized in this reaction: the calcium, Ca, or the carbon, C?
33. How does grease help to prevent the corrosion of iron?
34. What property of zinc and magnesium makes them useful for protecting iron objects from corrosion?

Chapter 23 Online Resources

Tutorials
- EMF Series

Quiz
Exercises
Flashcards
Links

CHAPTER 24

Organic Compounds

Carbon is a unique element. Its ability to connect with other carbon atoms through strong and stable covalent bonds sets it apart from other elements. Whereas no more than three oxygen atoms can bond together, as occurs in ozone, O_3, carbon atoms can form chains more than 100,000 carbon atoms in length. In addition to forming chains, they can link to form a multitude of unusual structures—much like a child's set of Tinkertoys or Legos.

Carbon compounds can be tasty. We perceive the flavor of vanilla, for example, when the compound *vanillin* is absorbed by the sensory organs in the mouth and nose. This compound consists of a ring of carbon atoms with oxygen atoms attached to it. Vanillin is the essential ingredient in anything having the flavor of vanilla—without vanillin, there is no vanilla flavor. The flavor of chocolate, on the other hand, is generated when not just one but a wide assortment of carbon-based molecules are absorbed in the mouth and nose. One of the more significant of these molecules is *tetramethylpyrazine,* which has a ring of nitrogen and carbon atoms attached in a particular fashion.

Life is based on carbon's ability to bond with other carbon atoms to form diverse structures. Reflecting this fact, the branch of chemistry that is the study of carbon-containing compounds is known as **organic chemistry.** (The term *organic* is derived from *organism* and is not necessarily related to the environment-friendly form of farming known as organic farming.) Today, more than 13 million organic compounds are known, and about 100,000 new ones are added to the list each year. This includes those discovered in nature and those synthesized in the laboratory. (By contrast, there are only 200,000 to 300,000 known *inorganic* compounds, those that are based on elements other than carbon.)

You may have trouble pronouncing tetramethylpyrazine, but chances are you love what it does to your ice cream.

Insights

Because organic compounds are so closely tied to living organisms and because they have many applications—from flavorings to fuels, polymers, medicines, agriculture, and more—a basic understanding of them is very important. We will begin with the simplest organic compounds—those consisting of only carbon and hydrogen.

24.1 Hydrocarbons

Organic compounds that contain only carbon and hydrogen are called **hydrocarbons,** which differ from one another by the number of carbon and hydrogen atoms they contain. The simplest hydrocarbon is methane, CH_4, with only one carbon per molecule. Methane is the main component of natural gas. The hydrocarbon octane, C_8H_{18}, has eight carbons per molecule and is a component of gasoline. The hydrocarbon polyethylene contains hundreds of carbon and hydrogen atoms per molecule. Polyethylene is a plastic used to make many familiar items, such as milk containers and plastic bags.

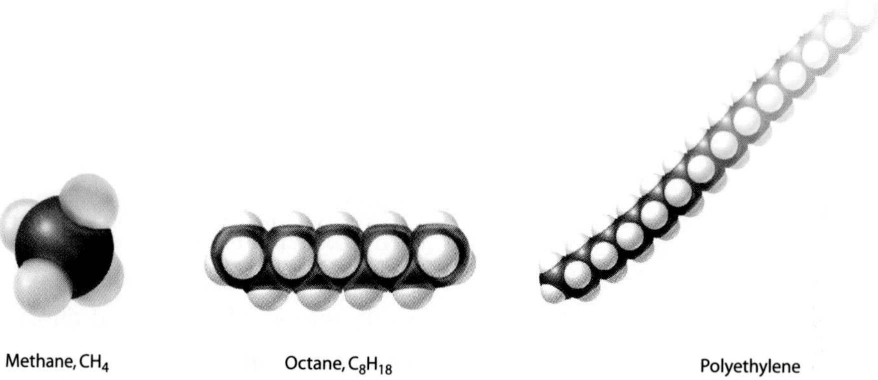

Hydrocarbons also differ in the way the carbon atoms connect to one another. Figure 24.1 shows the three hydrocarbons *n*-pentane, *iso*-pentane, and *neo*-pentane. These hydrocarbons have the same molecular formula, C_5H_{12}, but they are structurally different from one another. The carbon framework of *n*-pentane is a chain of five carbon atoms. In *iso*-pentane, the carbon chain branches, so that the framework is a *four*-carbon chain branched at the second carbon. In *neo*-pentane, a central carbon atom is bonded to four surrounding carbon atoms.

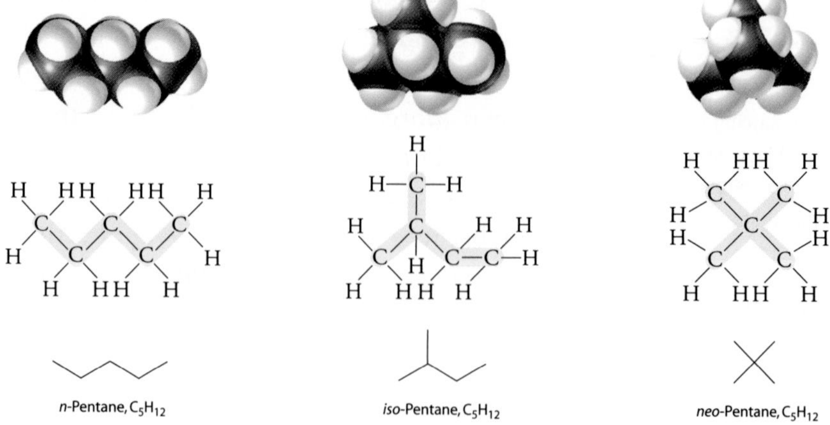

Figure 24.1
These three hydrocarbons all have the same molecular formula. We can see their different structural features by highlighting the carbon framework in two dimensions. Easy-to-draw stick structures that use lines for all carbon–carbon covalent bonds are also useful.

We can see the different structural features of *n*-pentane, *iso*-pentane, and *neo*-pentane more clearly by drawing the molecules in two dimensions, as shown in the middle row of Figure 24.1. Alternatively, we can represent them by the *stick structures* shown in the bottom row. A stick structure is a commonly used, shorthand notation for representing an organic molecule. Each line (stick) represents a covalent bond, and carbon atoms are understood to exist at the end of any line wherever two or more straight lines meet (unless another type of atom is drawn at the end of the line). Any hydrogen atoms bonded to the carbons are also typically not shown. Instead, their presence is only implied, so that the focus can remain on the skeletal structure that is formed by the carbon atoms.

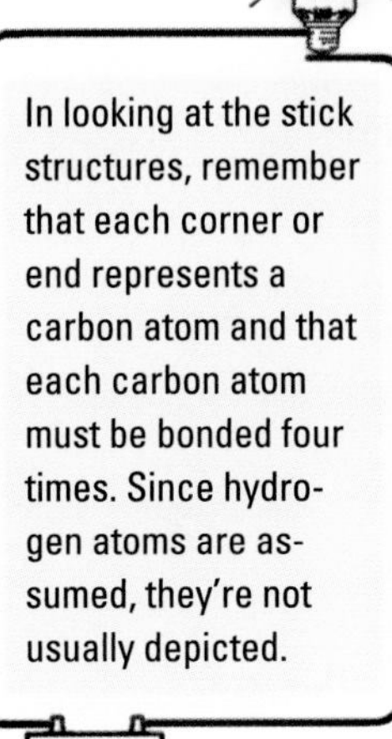

When every carbon atom in a hydrocarbon except the two terminal ones is bonded to only two other carbon atoms, the molecule is called a *straight-chain hydrocarbon.* (Do not take this name literally, for, as the *n*-pentane structures in Figure 24.1 show, this is a straight-chain hydrocarbon despite the zigzag nature of the drawings representing it.) When at least one carbon atom in a hydrocarbon is bonded to either three or four carbon atoms, the molecule is a *branched hydrocarbon.* Therefore, both *iso*-pentane and *neo*-pentane are branched hydrocarbons.

Molecules such as *n*-pentane, *iso*-pentane, and *neo*-pentane, which have the same molecular formula but different structures, are known as **structural isomers.** Structural isomers have different physical and chemical properties. For example, *n*-pentane has a boiling point of 36°C, *iso*-pentane's boiling point is 30°C, and *neo*-pentane's is 10°C.

The number of possible structural isomers for a chemical formula increases rapidly as the number of carbon atoms increases. There are three structural isomers for compounds having the formula C_5H_{12}, 18 for C_8H_{18}, 75 for $C_{10}H_{22}$, and a whopping 366,319 for $C_{20}H_{42}$!

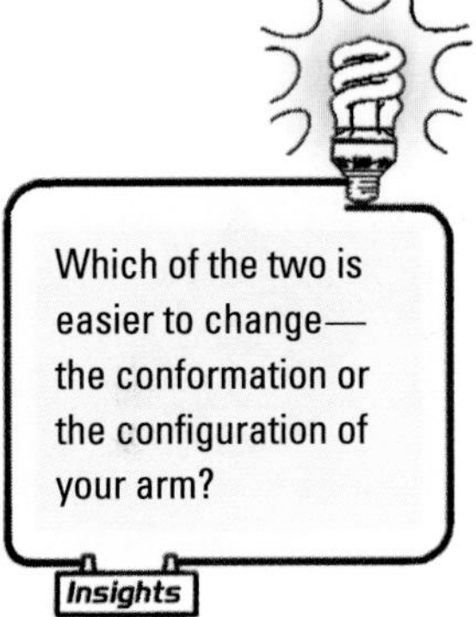

Carbon-based molecules can have different spatial orientations called **conformations.** Flex your wrist, elbow, and shoulder joints, and you'll find your arm passing through a range of conformations. Likewise, organic molecules can twist and turn about their carbon–carbon single bonds and thus have a range of conformations. The structures in Figure 24.2, for example, are different conformations of *n*-pentane.

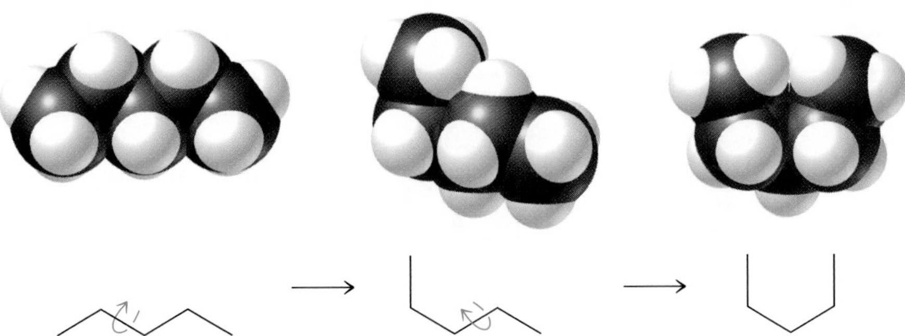

Figure 24.2
Three conformations for a molecule of *n*-pentane. The molecule looks different in each conformation, but the five-carbon framework is the same in all three conformations. In a sample of liquid *n*-pentane, the molecules are found in all conformations—not unlike a bucket of worms.

☑ CHECKPOINT

Which carbon–carbon bond was rotated to go from the "before" conformation of *iso*-pentane to the "after" conformation:

Before After

Check Your Answer

The best way to answer any question about the conformation of a molecule is to play around with molecular models that you can hold in your hand. In this case, bond c rotates in such a way that the carbon at the right end of bond d comes up out of the plane of the page, momentarily points straight at you, and then plops back into the plane of the page below bond c. This rotation is similar to that of the arm of an arm wrestler who, with the arm just above the table while on the brink of losing, suddenly gets a surge of strength and swings the opponent's arm (and his or her own) through a half-circle arc and wins.

Hydrocarbons are obtained primarily from coal and petroleum. Most of the coal and petroleum that exist today were formed between 280 million and 360 million years ago when plant and animal matter decayed in the absence of oxygen. At that time, the earth was covered with extensive swamps that, because they were close to sea level, periodically became submerged. The organic matter of the swamps was buried beneath layers of marine sediments and was eventually transformed to either coal or petroleum.

Coal is a solid material containing many large, complex hydrocarbon molecules. Most of the coal mined today is used for the production of steel and for generating electricity at coal-burning power plants.

Petroleum, also called crude oil, is a liquid readily separated into its hydrocarbon components through a process known as *fractional distillation*, shown in Figure 24.3. The crude oil is heated in a pipe still to a temperature high enough

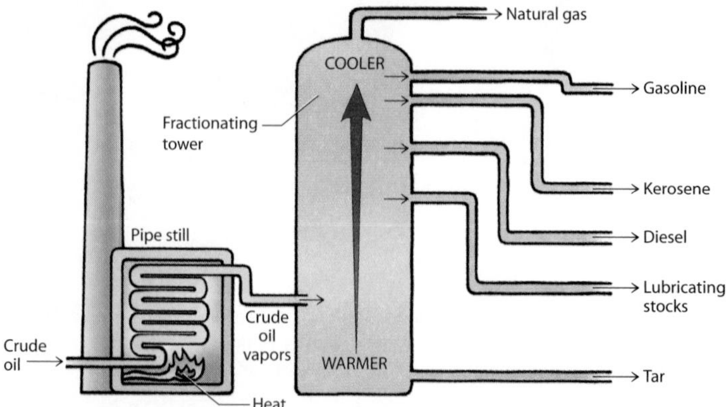

Figure 24.3
A schematic for the fractional distillation of petroleum into its useful hydrocarbon components.

to vaporize most of the components. The hot vapor flows into the bottom of a fractionating tower, which is warmer at the bottom than at the top. As the vapor rises in the tower and cools, the various components begin to condense. Hydrocarbons that have high boiling points, such as tar and lubricating stocks, condense first at warmer temperatures. Hydrocarbons that have low boiling points, such as gasoline, travel to the cooler regions at the top of the tower before condensing. Pipes drain the various liquid hydrocarbon fractions from the tower. Natural gas, which is primarily methane, does not condense. It remains a gas and is collected at the top of the tower.

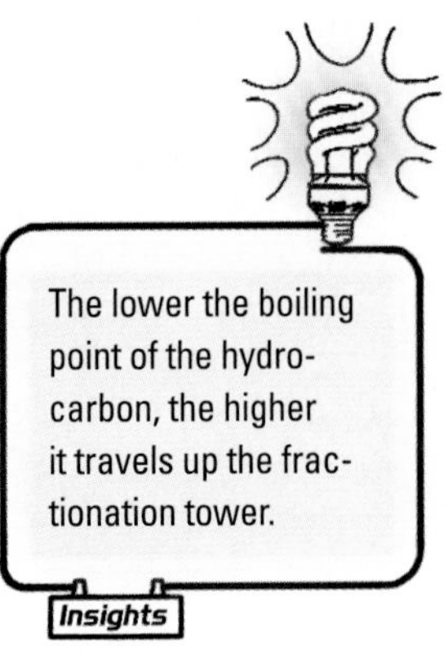

Differences in the strength of molecular attractions explain why different hydrocarbons condense at different temperatures. As discussed in Section 20.1, in our comparison of induced dipole-induced dipole attractions in methane and octane, larger hydrocarbons experience many more of these attractions than smaller hydrocarbons do. For this reason, the larger hydrocarbons condense readily at high temperatures and so are found at the bottom of the tower. Smaller molecules, because they experience fewer attractions to neighbors, condense only at the cooler temperatures found at the top of the tower.

The gasoline obtained from the fractional distillation of petroleum consists of a wide variety of hydrocarbons having similar boiling points. Some of these components burn more efficiently than others in a car engine. The straight-chain hydrocarbons, such as *n*-hexane, burn too quickly, causing what is called *engine knock,* as illustrated in Figure 24.4. Gasoline hydrocarbons that have more

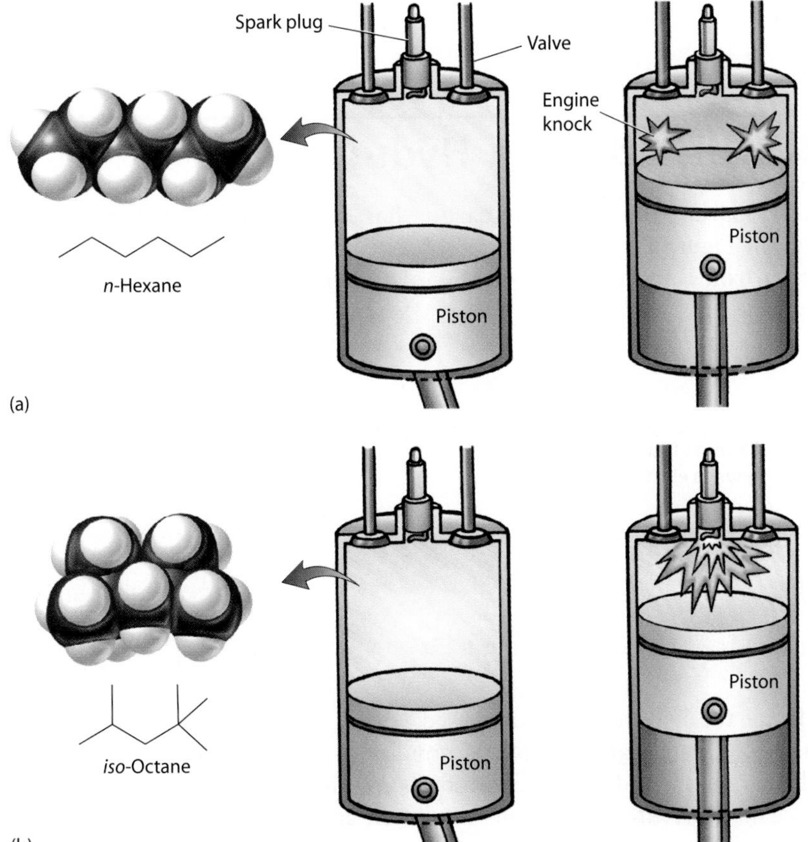

Figure 24.4
(a) A straight-chain hydrocarbon, such as *n*-hexane, can be ignited from the heat generated as gasoline is compressed by the piston—before the spark plug fires. This upsets the timing of the engine cycle, giving rise to a knocking sound. (b) Branched hydrocarbons, such as *iso*-octane, burn less readily and are ignited not by compression alone but only when the spark plug fires.

Figure 24.5
Octane ratings are posted on gasoline pumps.

branching, such as *iso*-octane, burn slowly and result in the engine running more smoothly. These two compounds, *n*-hexane and *iso*-octane, are used as standards in assigning *octane ratings* to gasoline. An octane number of 100 is arbitrarily assigned to *iso*-octane, and *n*-hexane is assigned an octane number of 0. The anti-knock performance of a particular gasoline is compared with that of various mixtures of *iso*-octane and *n*-hexane, and an octane number is assigned. Figure 24.5 shows the octane information appearing on a typical gasoline pump.

☑ CHECKPOINT

Which structural isomer shown in Figure 24.1 should have the highest octane rating?

Check Your Answer

The structural isomer with the greatest amount of branching in the carbon framework will likely have the highest octane rating, making *neo*-pentane the clear winner. For your information, the ratings are

Compound	Octane Rating
n-Pentane	61.7
iso-Pentane	92.3
neo-Pentane	116

24.2 Unsaturated Hydrocarbons

Recall, from Section 19.1, that carbon has four unpaired valence electrons. As shown in Figure 24.6, each of these electrons is available for pairing with an electron from another atom, such as hydrogen, to form a covalent bond.

Carbon's four valence electrons

H· ·C· ·H (with H above and below) ⟶ H:C:H (with H above and below) — Covalent bond

Methane

Also depicted as

H—C—H (with H above and below)

Figure 24.6
Carbon has four valence electrons. Each electron pairs with an electron from a hydrogen atom in the four covalent bonds of methane.

In all the hydrocarbons discussed so far, including the methane shown in Figure 24.6, each carbon atom is bonded to four neighboring atoms by four single covalent bonds. Such hydrocarbons are known as **saturated hydrocarbons.** The term *saturated* means that each carbon has as many atoms bonded to it as possible. We now explore cases where one or more carbon atoms in a hydrocarbon are bonded to fewer than four neighboring atoms. This occurs when at least one of the bonds between a carbon and a neighboring atom is a multiple bond. (See Section 19.4 for a review of multiple bonds.)

A hydrocarbon containing a multiple bond—either double or triple—is known as an **unsaturated hydrocarbon.** Because of the multiple bond, two of the carbons are bonded to fewer than four other atoms. These carbons are thus said to be *unsaturated.*

Figure 24.7 compares the saturated hydrocarbon *n*-butane with the unsaturated hydrocarbon 2-butene. The number of atoms that are bonded to each of the two middle carbons of *n*-butane is four, whereas each of the two middle carbons of 2-butene is bonded to only three other atoms—a hydrogen and two carbons.

Saturated fats in our diet have long carbon chains that contain single bonds. These chains tend to be straight, so they pack well together (like wooden matches in a box). Hence, saturated fats, such as lard, are solid at room temperature. The carbon chains of unsaturated fats have double bonds and take on a bent shape, so they don't pack well together. Unsaturated fats, such as vegetable oils, are liquid at room temperature.

Insights

Saturated hydrocarbon

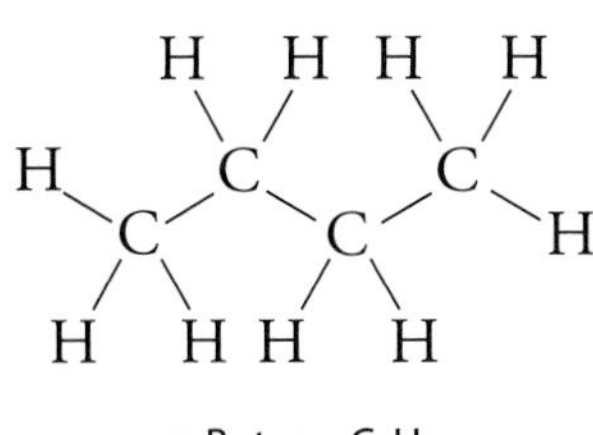

n-Butane, C_4H_{10}

Unsaturated hydrocarbon

2-Butene, C_4H_8

Figure 24.7
The carbons of the hydrocarbon *n*-butane are *saturated,* each being bonded to four other atoms. Because of the double bond, two of the carbons of the unsaturated hydrocarbon 2-butene are bonded to only three other atoms, which makes the molecule an unsaturated hydrocarbon.

An important unsaturated hydrocarbon is benzene, C_6H_6, which may be drawn as three double bonds contained within a flat hexagonal ring, as is shown in Figure 24.8a. Unlike the double-bond electrons in most other unsaturated hydrocarbons, the electrons of the double bonds in benzene are not fixed between any two carbon atoms. Instead, these electrons are able to move freely around the ring. This is commonly represented by drawing a circle within the ring, as shown in Figure 24.8b, rather than by individual double bonds.

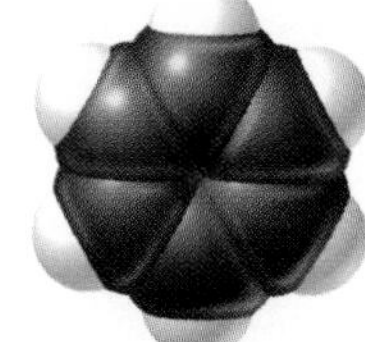

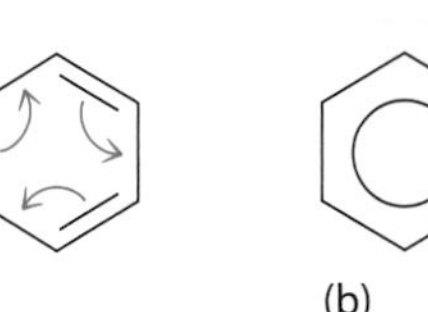

(a) (b)

Figure 24.8
(a) The double bonds of benzene, C_6H_6, are able to migrate around the ring. (b) For this reason, they are often represented by a circle within the ring.

Many organic compounds contain one or more benzene rings in their structure. Because many of these compounds are fragrant, any organic molecule containing a benzene ring is classified as an **aromatic compound** (even if it is not particularly fragrant). Figure 24.9 shows a few examples. Toluene, a common solvent used as a paint thinner, is toxic and gives airplane glue its distinctive odor. Some aromatic compounds, such as naphthalene, contain two or more benzene rings fused together. At one time, mothballs were made of naphthalene. Most mothballs sold today, however, are made of the less toxic 1,4-dichlorobenzene.

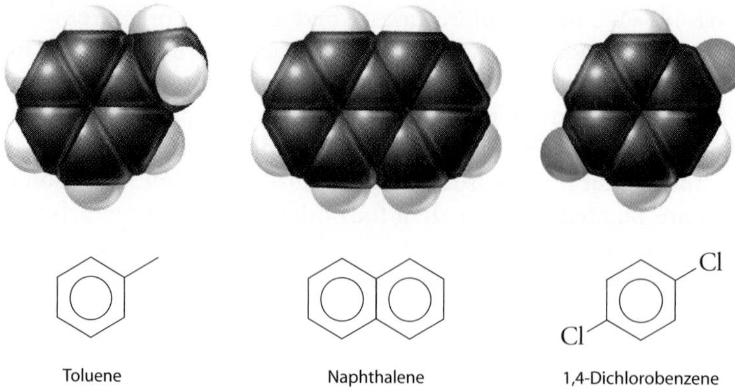

Figure 24.9
The structures for three odoriferous organic compounds containing one or more benzene rings: toluene, naphthalene, and 1,4-dichlorobenzene.

An example of an unsaturated hydrocarbon containing a triple bond is acetylene, C_2H_2. A confined flame of acetylene burning in oxygen is hot enough to melt iron, which makes acetylene a choice fuel for welding (Figure 24.10).

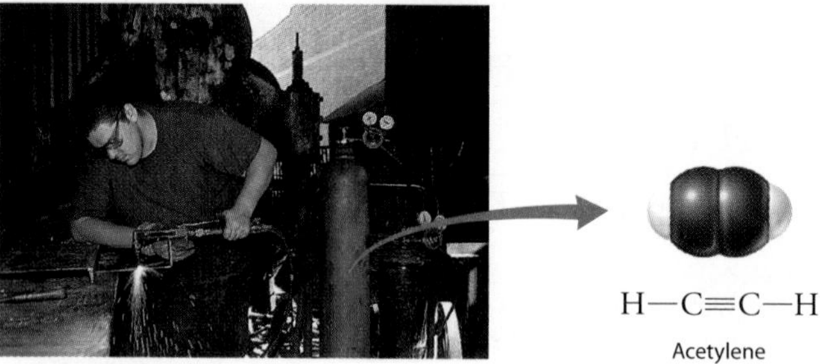

Figure 24.10
The unsaturated hydrocarbon acetylene, C_2H_2, when burned in this torch, produces a flame that is hot enough to melt iron.

☑ CHECKPOINT

Prolonged exposure to benzene increases the risk of developing certain cancers. The structure of aspirin contains a benzene ring. Does this indicate that prolonged exposure to aspirin will increase a person's risk of developing cancer?

Benzene ring

O

OH

O

O

Aspirin

Check Your Answer

No. Although benzene and aspirin both contain a benzene ring, these two molecules have different overall structures and quite different chemical properties. Each carbon-containing organic compound has its own set of unique physical, chemical, and biological properties. While benzene may cause cancer, aspirin work as a safe remedy for headaches.

24.3 Functional Groups

Carbon atoms can bond to one another and to hydrogen atoms in many ways, which results in an incredibly large number of hydrocarbons. But carbon atoms can bond to atoms of other elements as well, further increasing the number of possible organic molecules. In organic chemistry, any atom other than carbon or hydrogen in an organic molecule is called a **heteroatom,** where *hetero-* means "different from either carbon or hydrogen."

Table 24.1

Functional Groups in Organic Molecules

General Structure	Name	Class
—C—OH Hydroxyl group	Hydroxyl group	Alcohols
C=C, —C, C—OH, C—C (ring) Phenolic group	Phenolic group	Phenols
—C—O—C— Ether group	Ether group	Ethers
—C—N Amine group	Amine group	Amines
O, C, —C, C— (C=O between two C) Ketone group	Ketone group	Ketones
O, C, H (C=O bonded to H) Aldehyde group	Aldehyde group	Aldehydes
O, C, N (C=O bonded to N) Amide group	Amide group	Amides
O, C, OH (C=O bonded to OH) Carboxyl group	Carboxyl group	Carboxylic acids
O, C, O—C— (C=O bonded to O—C) Ester group	Ester group	Esters

The chemistry of hydrocarbons is surely interesting, but start adding heteroatoms to these organic molecules and the chemistry becomes extraordinarily interesting. The organic chemicals of living organisms, for example, all contain heteroatoms.

Insights

A hydrocarbon structure can serve as a framework for the attachment of various heteroatoms. This is analogous to a Christmas tree serving as the scaffolding on which ornaments are hung. Just as the ornaments give character to the tree, so do heteroatoms give character to an organic molecule. Heteroatoms have profound effects on the properties of an organic molecule.

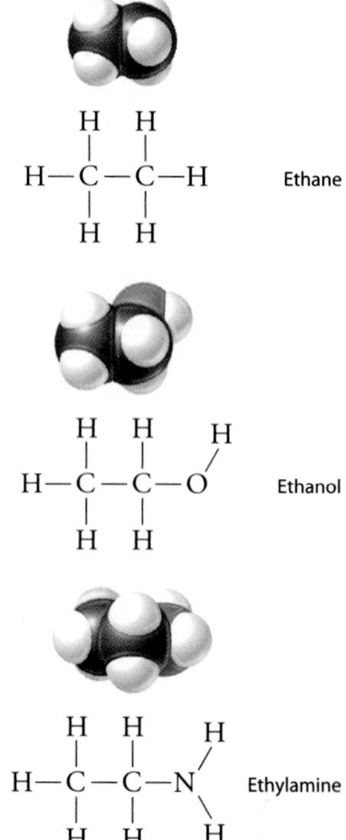

Consider ethane, C_2H_6, and ethanol, C_2H_6O, which differ from each other by only a single oxygen atom. Ethane has a boiling point of −88°C, making it a gas at room temperature, and it does not dissolve in water very well. Ethanol, by contrast, has a boiling point of +78°C, making it a liquid at room temperature. It is infinitely soluble in water, and it is the active ingredient of alcoholic beverages. Consider further ethylamine, C_2H_7N, which has a nitrogen atom on the same basic two-carbon framework. This compound is a corrosive, pungent, highly toxic gas—most unlike either ethane or ethanol.

Organic molecules are classified according to the functional groups they contain, where a **functional group** is defined as a combination of atoms that behave as a unit. Most functional groups are distinguished by the heteroatoms they contain, and some common groups are listed in Table 24.1.

The remainder of this section introduces the classes of organic molecules shown in Table 24.1. The role heteroatoms play in determining the properties of each class is the underlying theme. As you study this material, focus on understanding the chemical and physical properties of the various classes of compounds, for doing so will give you a greater appreciation of the remarkable diversity of organic molecules and their many applications.

☑ CHECKPOINT

What is the significance of heteroatoms in an organic molecule?

Check Your Answer

Heteroatoms largely determine an organic molecule's "personality."

24.4 Alcohols, Phenols, and Ethers

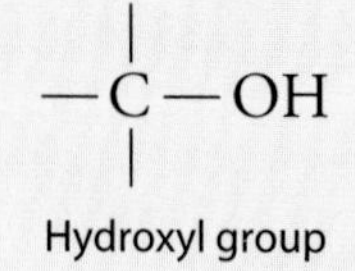

Hydroxyl group

Alcohols are organic molecules in which a *hydroxyl group* is bonded to a saturated carbon. The hydroxyl group consists of an oxygen bonded to a hydrogen. Because of the polarity of the oxygen–hydrogen bond, low-formula-mass alcohols are often soluble in water, which is itself very polar. Some common alcohols and their melting and boiling points are listed in Table 24.2.

Table 24.2

Some Simple Alcohols

Structure	Scientific Name	Common Name	Melting Point (°C)	Boiling Point (°C)
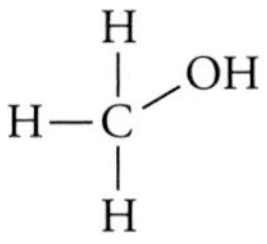 CH_3OH	Methanol	Methyl alcohol	−97	65
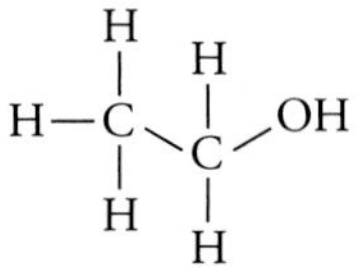 CH_3CH_2OH	Ethanol	Ethyl alcohol	−115	78
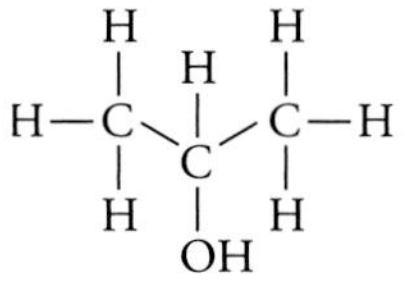 $CH_3CH(OH)CH_3$	2-Propanol	Isopropyl alcohol	−126	97

More than 11 billion pounds of methanol, CH_3OH, is produced annually in the United States. Most of it is used for making formaldehyde and acetic acid, important starting materials in the production of plastics. In addition, methanol is used as a solvent, an octane booster, and an anti-icing agent in gasoline. Sometimes called wood alcohol because it can be obtained from wood, methanol should never be ingested because, in the body, it is metabolized to formaldehyde and formic acid. Formaldehyde is harmful to the eyes, can lead to blindness, and was once used to preserve dead biological specimens. Formic acid, the active ingredient in an ant bite, can lower the pH of the blood to dangerous levels. Methanol itself also has its own inherent toxcities. Ingesting only about 15 milliliters (about 3 tablespoons) of methanol may lead to blindness, and about 30 milliliters can cause death.

Ethanol, C_2H_5OH, on the other hand, is the "alcohol" of alcoholic beverages, and it is one of the oldest chemicals manufactured by humans. Ethanol is prepared by feeding the sugars of various plants to certain yeasts, which produce ethanol through a biological process known as *fermentation*. Ethanol is also widely used as an industrial solvent. For many years, ethanol intended for this purpose was made by fermentation, but today industrial-grade ethanol is more cheaply manufactured from petroleum byproducts, such as ethene, as Figure 24.11 illustrates.

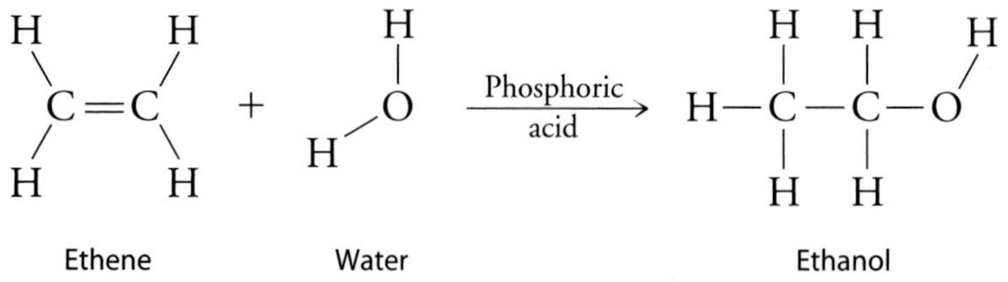

$$H_2C{=}CH_2 + H_2O \xrightarrow[\text{acid}]{\text{Phosphoric}} CH_3CH_2OH$$

Ethene — Water — Ethanol

Figure 24.11
Ethanol can be synthesized from the unsaturated hydrocarbon ethene, with phosphoric acid as a catalyst.

Just as the body metabolizes methanol into formaldehyde, HCOH, it metabolizes ethanol into acetaldehyde, CH_3COH. Acetaldehyde won't cause you to go blind, but it does provide for some painful side effects, which people who drink too much experience as part of their "hangover."

Insights

The liquid produced by fermentation has an ethanol concentration no greater than about 12 percent because, at this concentration, the yeast cells begin to die. This is why most wines have an alcohol content of 11 or 12 percent—they are produced solely by fermentation. To attain the higher ethanol concentrations found in such "hard" alcoholic beverages as gin and vodka, the fermented liquid must be distilled. In the United States, the ethanol content of distilled alcoholic beverages is measured as *proof,* which is twice the percentage of ethanol. An 86-proof whiskey, for example, is 43 percent ethanol by volume. The term *proof* evolved from a crude method once employed to test alcohol content. Gunpowder was wetted with a beverage of suspect alcohol content. If the beverage was primarily water, the powder would not ignite. If the beverage contained a significant amount of ethanol, the powder would burn, thus providing "proof" of the beverage's worth.

A third well-known alcohol is isopropyl alcohol, also called 2-propanol. This is the rubbing alcohol you buy at the drugstore. Although 2-propanol has a relatively high boiling point, it evaporates readily, leading to a pronounced cooling effect when it is applied to skin—an effect once used to reduce fevers. (Isopropyl alcohol is very toxic if ingested. See the activities at the end of this chapter to understand why. In place of isopropyl alcohol, washcloths wetted with cold water are nearly as effective in reducing fever, and they are far safer.) You are probably most familiar with the use of isopropyl alcohol as a topical disinfectant.

```
    \     /
     C=C
    /     \
 —C         C—OH
   \\      //
     C—C
    /     \
```

Phenolic group

Phenols contain a phenolic group, which consists of a hydroxyl group attached to a benzene ring. Because of the presence of the benzene ring, the hydrogen of the hydroxyl group is readily lost in an acid–base reaction, which makes the phenolic group mildly acidic.

The reason for this acidity is illustrated in Figure 24.12. How readily an acid donates a hydrogen ion is a function of how well the acid is able to accommodate the resulting negative charge it gains after donating the hydrogen ion. After phenol donates the hydrogen ion, it becomes a negatively charged phenoxide ion. The negative charge of the phenoxide ion, however, is not restricted to the oxygen atom. Recall that the electrons of the benzene ring are able to migrate around the ring. In a similar manner, the electrons responsible for the negative charge of the phenoxide ion are also able to migrate around the ring, as shown in Figure 24.12. Just as it is easy for several people to hold a hot potato by quickly passing it around, it is easy for the phenoxide ion to hold the negative charge because the charge gets passed around. Because the negative charge of the ion is so nicely accommodated, the phenolic group is more acidic than it would be otherwise.

The simplest phenol, shown in Figure 24.13, is called phenol. In 1867, Joseph Lister (1827–1912) discovered the antiseptic value of phenol, which, when applied to surgical instruments and incisions, greatly increased surgery survival rates. Phenol was the first purposefully used antibacterial solution, or *antiseptic*. Phenol damages healthy tissue, however, and so a number of milder phenols have since been introduced. The phenol 4-*n*-hexylresorcinol, for example, is commonly used in throat lozenges and mouthwashes. This compound has even greater antiseptic properties than phenol, and yet it does not damage tissue. Listerine brand mouthwash (named after Joseph Lister) contains the antiseptic phenols thymol and methyl salicylate.

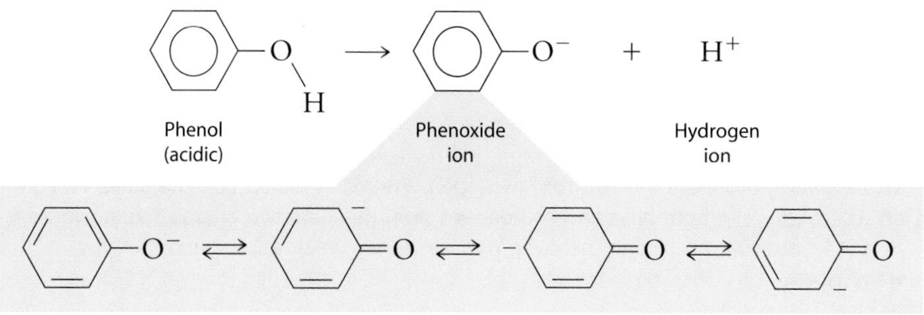

Phenol (acidic) $\longrightarrow$ Phenoxide ion (O^-) + Hydrogen ion (H^+)

$O^- \rightleftarrows\ =O \rightleftarrows\ =O \rightleftarrows\ =O$

Figure 24.12
The negative charge of the phenoxide ion is able to migrate to select positions on the benzene ring. This mobility helps to accommodate the negative charge, which is why the phenolic group readily donates a hydrogen ion.

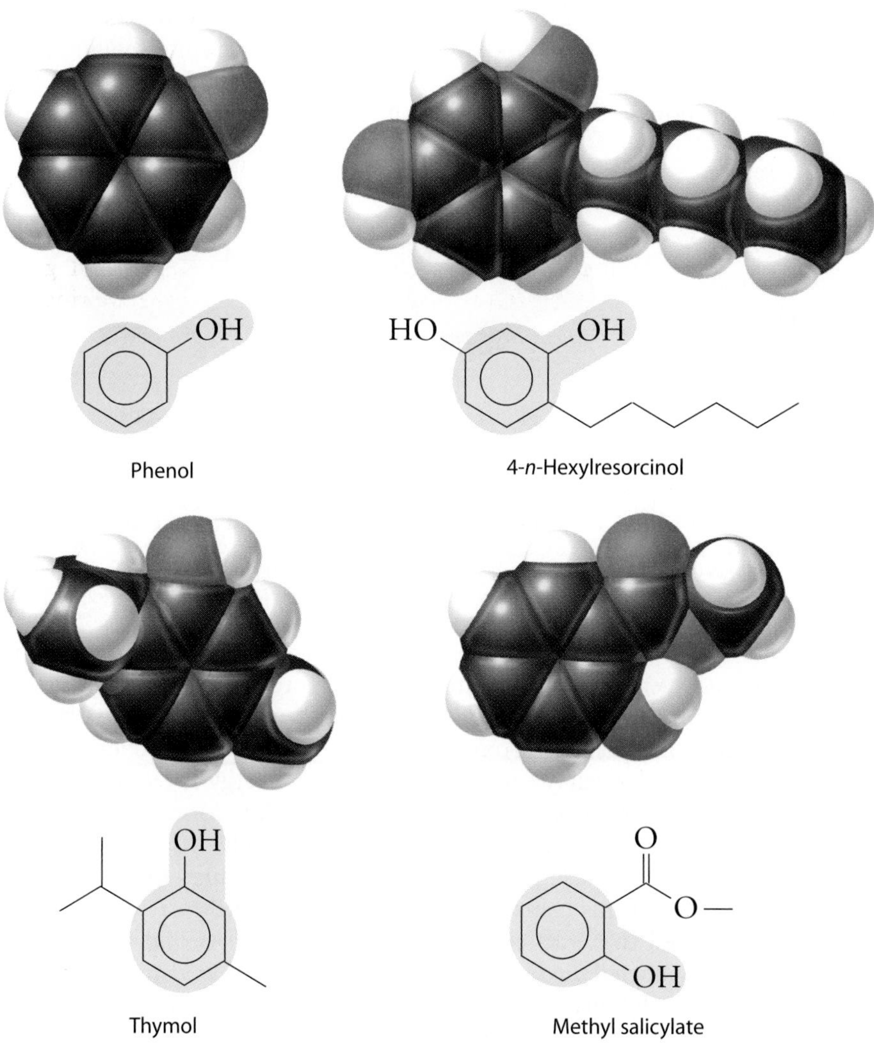

Figure 24.13
Every phenol contains a phenolic group (highlighted in blue).

We're classifying organic molecules based upon the functional groups they contain. As you will see shortly, however, organic molecules may contain more than one type of functional group. A single organic molecule, therefore, might be classified both as a phenol and also as an ether.

Insights

☑ CHECKPOINT

Why are alcohols less acidic than phenols?

Check Your Answer

An alcohol does not contain a benzene ring adjacent to the hydroxyl group. If the alcohol were to donate the hydroxyl hydrogen, the result would be a negative charge on the oxygen. Without an adjacent benzene ring, this negative charge has nowhere to go. As a result, an alcohol behaves only as a very weak acid, much the way water does.

Ethers are organic compounds structurally related to alcohols. The oxygen atom in an ether group, however, is bonded not to a carbon and a hydrogen but rather to two carbons. As we see in Figure 24.14, ethanol and dimethyl ether have the same chemical formula, C_2H_6O, but their physical properties are vastly different. Whereas ethanol is a liquid at room temperature (boiling point 78°C) and mixes quite well with water, dimethyl ether is a gas at room temperature (boiling point −25°C) and is much less soluble in water.

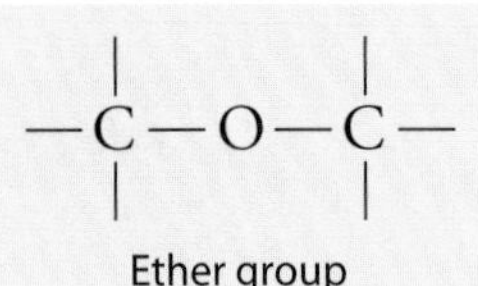

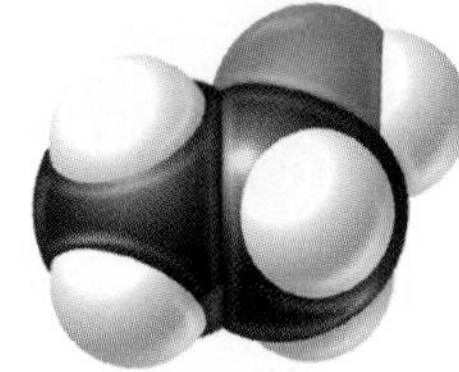

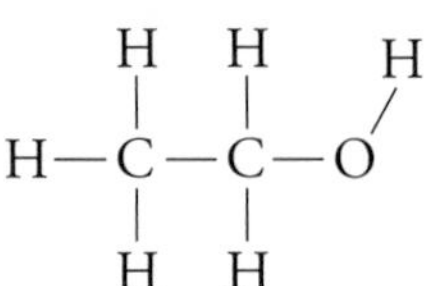

Ethanol: Soluble in water, boiling point 78°C

Dimethyl ether: Insoluble in water, boiling point −25°C

Figure 24.14
The oxygen in an alcohol, such as ethanol, is bonded to one carbon atom and one hydrogen atom. The oxygen in an ether, such as dimethyl ether, is bonded to two carbon atoms. Because of this difference, alcohols and ethers of similar molecular mass have vastly different physical properties.

Ethers are not very soluble in water because, without the hydroxyl group, they are unable to form strong hydrogen bonds with water (Section 20.1). Furthermore, without the polar hydroxyl group, the molecular attractions among ether molecules are relatively weak. As a result, little energy is required to separate ether molecules from one another. This is why low-formula-mass ethers have relatively low boiling points and evaporate so readily.

Diethyl ether, shown in Figure 24.15, was one of the first anesthetics. The anesthetic properties of this compound were discovered in the early 1800s, and its use revolutionized the practice of surgery. Because of its high volatility at room temperature, inhaled diethyl ether rapidly enters the bloodstream. Because this ether has low solubility in water and high volatility, it quickly leaves the bloodstream once introduced. Because of these physical properties, a surgical patient can be brought in and out of anesthesia (a state of unconsciousness) simply by regulating the gases breathed. Modern-day gaseous anesthetics have fewer side effects than diethyl ether, but they operate on the same principle.

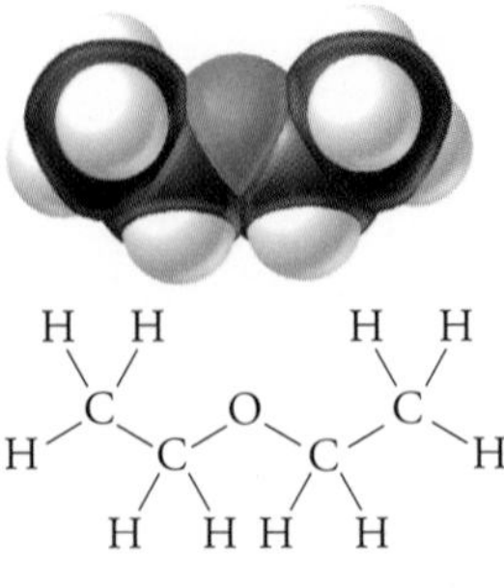

Diethyl ether, boiling point 35°C

Figure 24.15
Diethyl ether is the systematic name for the "ether" historically used as an anesthetic.

24.5 Amines and Alkaline Solutions

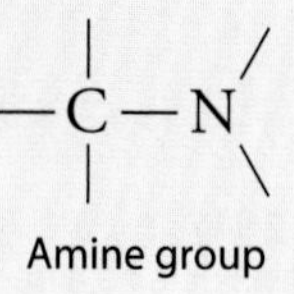

Amines are organic compounds that contain the amine group-a nitrogen atom bonded to one, two, or three saturated carbons. Amines are typically less soluble in water than are alcohols because the nitrogen–hydrogen bond is not quite as polar as the oxygen–hydrogen bond. The lower polarity of amines also means their boiling points are typically somewhat lower than those of alcohols of similar formula mass. Table 24.3 lists three simple amines.

Table 24.3

Three Simple Amines

Structure	Name	Melting Point (°C)	Boiling Point (°C)
H H H H—C—C—N H H H	Ethylamine	−81	17
H H H H H H—C—C—N—C—C—H H H H H	Diethylamine	−50	55
H H H H H—C—C—N—C—C—H H H H H H—C—H H—C—H H	Triethylamine	−7	89

One of the most notable physical properties of many low-formula-mass amines is their offensive odor. Figure 24.16 shows two appropriately named amines, putrescine and cadaverine, which are responsible, in part, for the odor of decaying flesh.

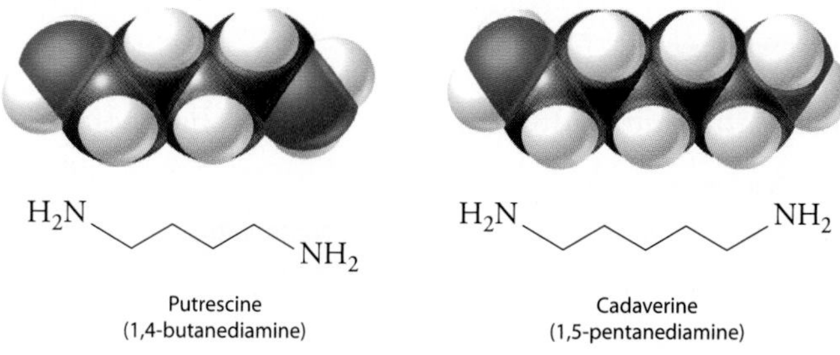

Figure 24.16
Low-formula-mass amines, such as these, tend to have offensive odors.

Amines are typically alkaline because the nitrogen atom readily accepts a hydrogen ion from water, as Figure 24.17 illustrates.

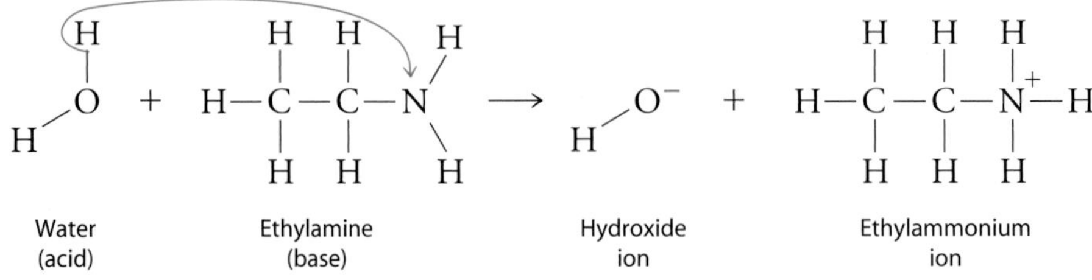

Figure 24.17
Ethylamine acts as a base and accepts a hydrogen ion from water to become the ethylammonium ion. This reaction generates a hydroxide ion, which increases the pH of the solution.

Most all pharmaceuticals that can be administered orally contain nitrogen heteroatoms in the water-soluble salt form.

Insights

A group of naturally occurring complex molecules that are alkaline because they contain nitrogen atoms are often called *alkaloids*. Because many alkaloids have medicinal value, there is great interest in isolating these compounds from plants or marine organisms that contain them. As shown in Figure 24.18, an alkaloid reacts with an acid to form a salt that is usually quite soluble in water. This is in contrast to the nonionized form of the alkaloid, known as a *free base*, which is typically insoluble in water.

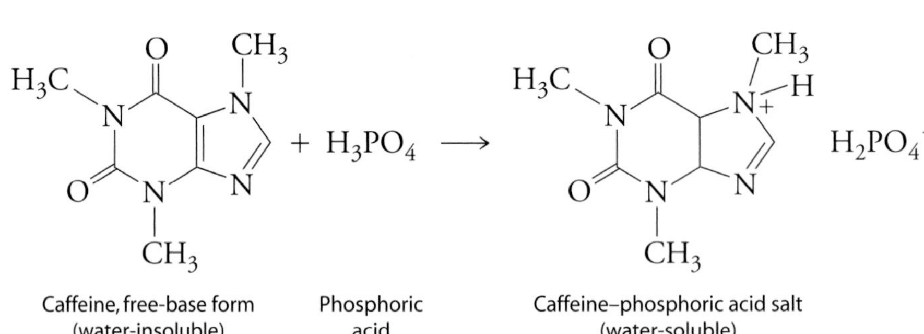

Figure 24.18
All alkaloids are bases that react with acids to form salts. An example is the alkaloid caffeine, shown here reacting with phosphoric acid.

Most alkaloids exist in nature not in their free-base form but rather as the salts of naturally occurring acids known as *tannins*, a group of phenol-based organic acids that have complex structures. The alkaloid salts of these acids are usually much more soluble in hot water than in cold water. The caffeine in coffee and tea exists in the form of the tannin salt, which is why coffee and tea are more effectively brewed in hot water. As Figure 24.19 relates, tannins are also responsible for the stains caused by these beverages.

Figure 24.19
Tannins are responsible for the brown stains in coffee mugs or on a coffee drinker's teeth. Because tannins are acidic, they can be readily removed with an alkaline cleanser. Use a little laundry bleach on the mug, and brush your teeth with baking soda.

☑ CHECKPOINT

Why do most caffeinated soft drinks also contain phosphoric acid?

Check Your Answer

The phosphoric acid, as shown in Figure 24.18, reacts with the caffeine to form the caffeine–phosphoric acid salt, which is much more soluble in cold water than the naturally occurring tannin salt.

24.6 The Carbonyl Functional Group

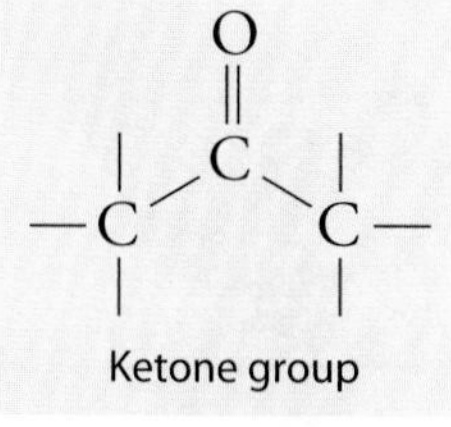

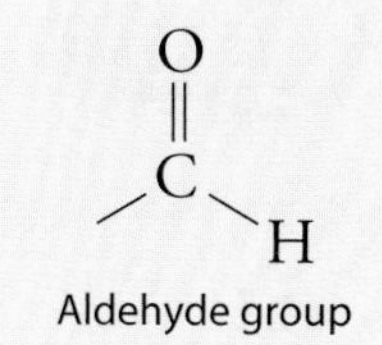

The **carbonyl group** consists of a carbon atom double-bonded to an oxygen atom. It occurs in the organic compounds known as ketones, aldehydes, amides, carboxylic acids, and esters.

A **ketone** is a carbonyl-containing organic molecule in which the carbonyl carbon is bonded to two carbon atoms. A familiar example of a ketone is *acetone,* which is often used in fingernail-polish remover and is shown in Figure 24.20a. In an **aldehyde,** the carbonyl carbon is bonded either to one carbon atom and one hydrogen atom, as in Figure 24.20b, or, in the special case of formaldehyde, to two hydrogen atoms.

Acetone
(a)

Propionaldehyde
(b)

Figure 24.20
(a) When the carbon of a carbonyl group is bonded to two carbon atoms, the result is a ketone. An example is acetone. (b) When the carbon of a carbonyl group is bonded to at least one hydrogen atom, the result is an aldehyde. An example is propionaldehyde.

Many aldehydes are particularly fragrant. A number of flowers, for example, owe their pleasant odor to the presence of simple aldehydes. The smells of lemons, cinnamon, and almonds are due to the aldehydes citral, cinnamaldehyde, and benzaldehyde, respectively. The structures of these three aldehydes are shown in Figure 24.21 on page 592. Another aldehyde, vanillin, which was introduced at the beginning of this chapter, is the key flavoring molecule derived from seed pods of the vanilla orchid. You may have noticed that vanilla seed pods and vanilla extract are fairly expensive. Imitation vanilla flavoring is less expensive because it is merely a solution of the compound vanillin, which is economically synthesized from waste chemicals from the wood-pulp industry. Imitation vanilla does not taste the same as natural vanilla extract, however, because, in addition to vanillin, many other flavorful molecules contribute to the complex taste of natural vanilla. Many books manufactured in the days before "acid-free" paper smell of vanilla because of the vanillin formed and released as the paper ages, a process that is accelerated by the acids the paper contains.

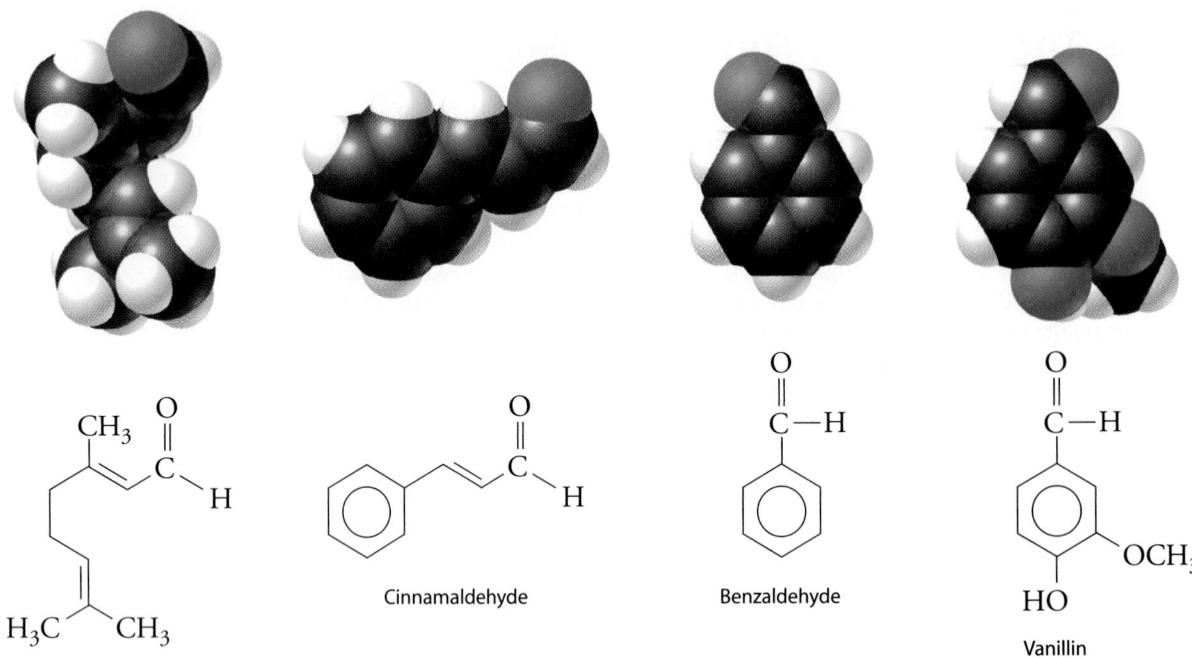

Figure 24.21
Aldehydes are responsible for many familiar fragrances.

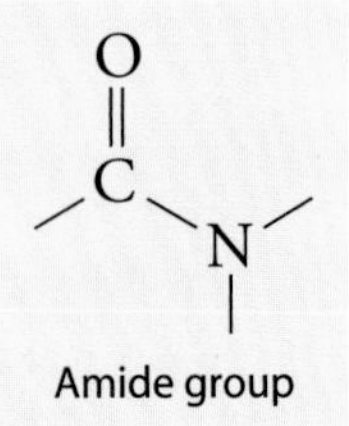

An **amide** is a carbonyl-containing organic molecule in which the carbonyl carbon is bonded to a nitrogen atom. The active ingredient of most mosquito repellents is an amide whose chemical name is *N*,*N*-diethyl-*m*-toluamide but is commercially known as DEET, shown in Figure 24.22. This compound is actually not an insecticide. Rather, it causes certain insects, especially mosquitoes, to lose their sense of direction, which effectively protects DEET wearers from being bitten.

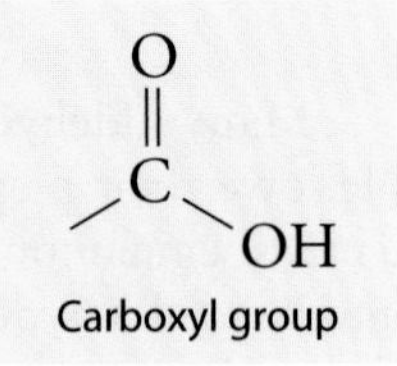

Amide group

A **carboxylic acid** is a carbonyl-containing organic molecule in which the carbonyl carbon is bonded to a hydroxyl group. As its name implies, this functional group is able to donate hydrogen ions. Organic molecules that contain it are therefore acidic. An example is acetic acid, $C_2H_4O_2$, which, after water, is the main ingredient of vinegar. You may recall that this organic compound was used as an example of a weak acid back in Chapter 22.

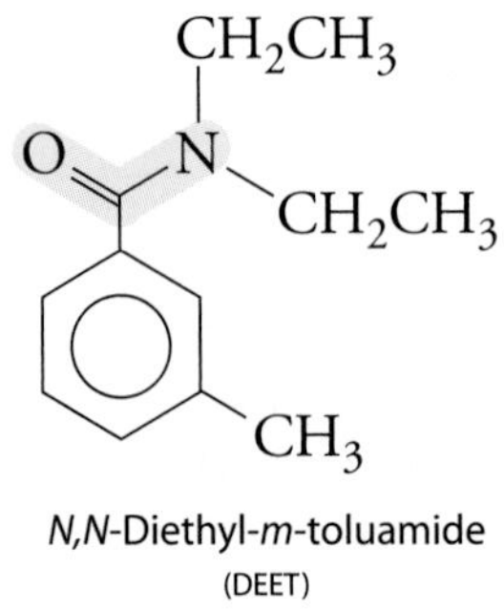

Carboxyl group

N,*N*-Diethyl-*m*-toluamide
(DEET)

Figure 24.22
N,*N*-diethyl-*m*-toluamide is an example of an amide. Amides contain the amide group, shown highlighted in blue.

As with phenols, the acidity of a carboxylic acid results in part from the ability of the functional group to accommodate the negative charge of the ion that forms after the hydrogen ion has been donated. As shown in Figure 24.23, a carboxylic acid transforms to a carboxylate ion as it loses the hydrogen ion. The negative charge of the carboxylate ion then is able to pass back and forth between the two oxygens. This spreading out helps to accommodate the negative charge.

An interesting example of an organic compound that contains both a carboxylic acid and a phenol is salicylic acid, found in the bark of willow trees

Carboxyl group in acetic acid → Carboxylate ion in acetate ion + H^+ Hydrogen ion

Figure 24.23
The negative charge of the carboxylate ion is able to pass back and forth between the two oxygen atoms of the carboxyl group.

and illustrated in Figure 24.24a. At one time brewed for its antipyretic (fever-reducing) effect, salicylic acid is an important analgesic (painkiller), but it causes nausea and stomach upset due to its relatively high acidity, a result of the presence of two acidic functional groups. In 1899, Friederich Bayer and Company, in Germany, introduced a chemically modified version of this compound in which the acidic phenolic group was transformed into an ester functional group. The result was the less acidic and more tolerable acetylsalicylic acid, the chemical name for aspirin, shown in Figure 24.24b.

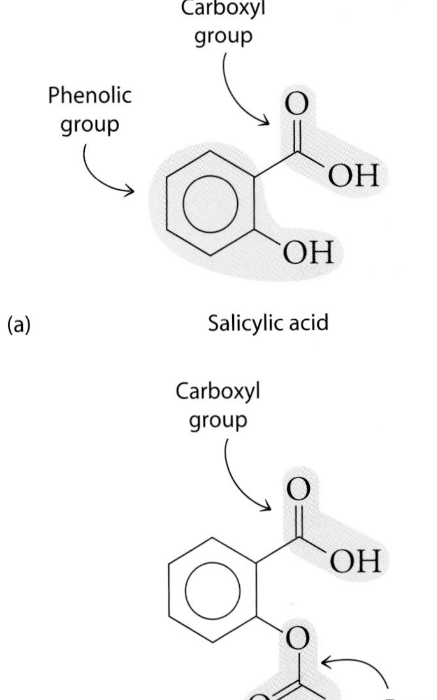

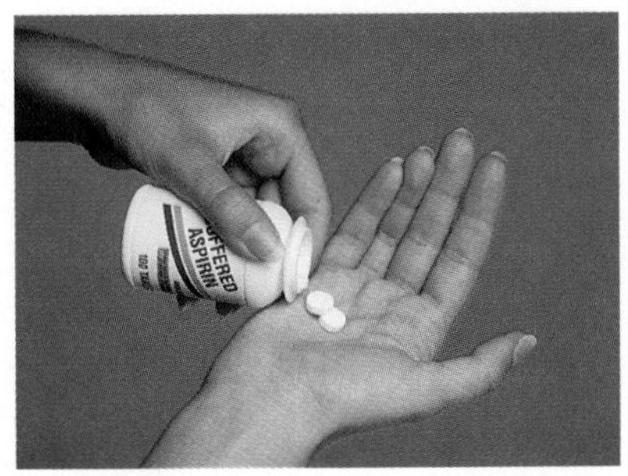

Figure 24.24
(a) Salicylic acid, which is found in the bark of willow trees, is an example of a molecule containing both a carboxyl group and a phenolic group. (b) Aspirin, acetylsalicylic acid, is less acidic than salicylic acid because it no longer contains the acidic phenolic group, which has been converted to an ester.

We eat organic chemicals daily. In fact, organic chemicals are the *only* things we eat, except for some important minerals, such as the ions of sodium and calcium.

Insights

An **ester** is an organic molecule similar to a carboxylic acid except that in the ester, the hydroxyl hydrogen is replaced by a carbon. Unlike carboxylic acids, esters are not acidic because they lack the hydrogen of the hydroxyl group. Like aldehydes, many simple esters have notable fragrances and are often used as flavorings. Some familiar ones are listed in Table 24.4.

$-C(=O)-O-C-$

Ester group

Table 24.4

Some Esters and Their Flavors and Odors

Structure	Name	Flavor/Odor
$H-C(=O)-O-CH_2CH_3$	Ethyl formate	Rum
$H_3C-C(=O)-O-CH_2CH_2-CH(CH_3)_2$	Isopentyl acetate	Banana
$H_3C-C(=O)-O-CH_2(CH_2)_6CH_3$	Octyl acetate	Orange
$CH_3CH_2CH_2-C(=O)-O-CH_2CH_3$	Ethyl butyrate	Pineapple
$CH_3CH_2CH_2-C(=O)-O-CH_3$	Methyl butyrate	Apple
$H-C(=O)-O-CH_2-CH(CH_3)_2$	Isobutyl formate	Raspberry
$C_6H_4(OH)-C(=O)-O-CH_3$	Methyl salicylate	Wintergreen

☑ CHECKPOINT

Identify all the functional groups in these four molecules (ignore the sulfur group in penicillin G):

Acetaldehyde

Penicillin G

Testosterone

Morphine

Check Your Answers

Acetaldehyde: aldehyde. Penicillin G: amide (two amide groups), carboxylic acid. Testosterone: alcohol and ketone. Morphine: alcohol, phenol, ether, and amine.

24.7 Polymers

Polymers are exceedingly long molecules that consist of repeating molecular units called **monomers,** as Figure 24.25 illustrates. Monomers have relatively simple structures consisting of anywhere from 4 to 100 atoms per molecule. When monomers are chained together, they can form polymers consisting of hundreds of thousands of atoms per molecule. These large molecules are still too small to be seen with the unaided eye. They are, however, giants in the submicroscopic world—if a typical polymer molecule were as thick as a kite string, it would be 1 kilometer long.

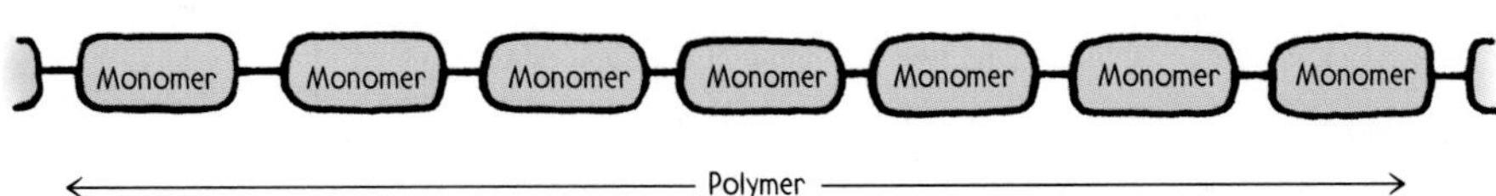

Figure 24.25
A polymer is a long molecule consisting of many smaller monomer molecules linked together.

Table 24.5

Addition and Condensation Polymers

Addition Polymers	Repeating Unit	Common Uses	Recycling Code
Polyethylene (PE)	$\cdots CH_2{-}CH_2 \cdots$	Plastic bags, bottles	2 HDPE, 4 LDPE
Polypropylene (PP)	$\cdots CH_2{-}CH(CH_3) \cdots$	Indoor–outdoor carpets	5 PP
Polystyrene (PS)	$\cdots CH_2{-}CH(C_6H_5) \cdots$	Plastic utensils, insulation	6 PS
Polyvinyl chloride (PVC)	$\cdots CH_2{-}CHCl \cdots$	Shower curtains, tubing	3 V
Polyvinylidene chloride (Saran)	$\cdots CH_2{-}CCl_2 \cdots$	Plastic wrap	—
Polytetrafluoroethylene (Teflon)	$\cdots CF_2{-}CF_2 \cdots$	Nonstick coating	—
Polyacrylonitrile (Orlon)	$\cdots CH_2{-}CH(C{\equiv}N) \cdots$	Yarn, paints	—
Polymethyl methacrylate (Lucite, Plexiglas)	$\cdots CH_2{-}C(CH_3)(C(=O)OCH_3) \cdots$	Windows, bowling balls	—
Polyvinyl acetate (PVA)	$\cdots CH_2{-}CH(O{-}C(=O){-}CH_3) \cdots$	Adhesives, chewing gum	—

(continued)

Table 24.5 (continued)

Addition and Condensation Polymers

Condensation Polymers	Repeating Unit	Common Uses	Recycling Code
Nylon	$\cdots\text{-C(=O)-(CH}_2)_4\text{-C(=O)-N(H)-(CH}_2\text{CH}_2)_3\text{-N(H)-}\cdots$	Carpeting, clothing	—
Polyethylene terephthalate	$\cdots\text{C(=O)-C}_6\text{H}_4\text{-C(=O)-O-CH}_2\text{CH}_2\text{-O}\cdots$	Clothing, plastic bottles	1 PET
Melamine-formaldehyde resin (Melmac, Formica)	triazine ring C_3N_3 with three $\text{-NH-C(=O)}\cdots$ links	Dishes, countertops	—

Many of the molecules that constitute living organisms are polymers, including DNA, proteins, the cellulose of plants, and the complex carbohydrates of starchy foods. For now, we focus on the human-made polymers, also known as synthetic polymers, that make up the class of materials that are commonly known as plastics.

We will begin by exploring the two major types of synthetic polymers used today—*addition polymers* and *condensation polymers.*

As shown in Table 24.5, addition and condensation polymers have a wide variety of uses. Solely the product of human design, these polymers pervade modern living. In the United States, for example, synthetic polymers have surpassed steel as the most widely used material.

Addition Polymers—the Joining Together of Monomers

Addition polymers form simply by the joining together of monomer units. For this to happen, each monomer must contain at least one double bond. As shown in Figure 24.26, polymerization occurs when two of the electrons from each double bond split away from each other to form new covalent bonds with neighboring monomer molecules. During this process, no atoms are lost, so the total mass of the polymer is equal to the sum of the masses of all the monomers.

Nearly 12 million tons of polyethylene is produced annually in the United States; that's about 90 pounds per U.S. citizen. The monomer from which it is synthesized, ethylene, is an unsaturated hydrocarbon produced in large quantities from petroleum.

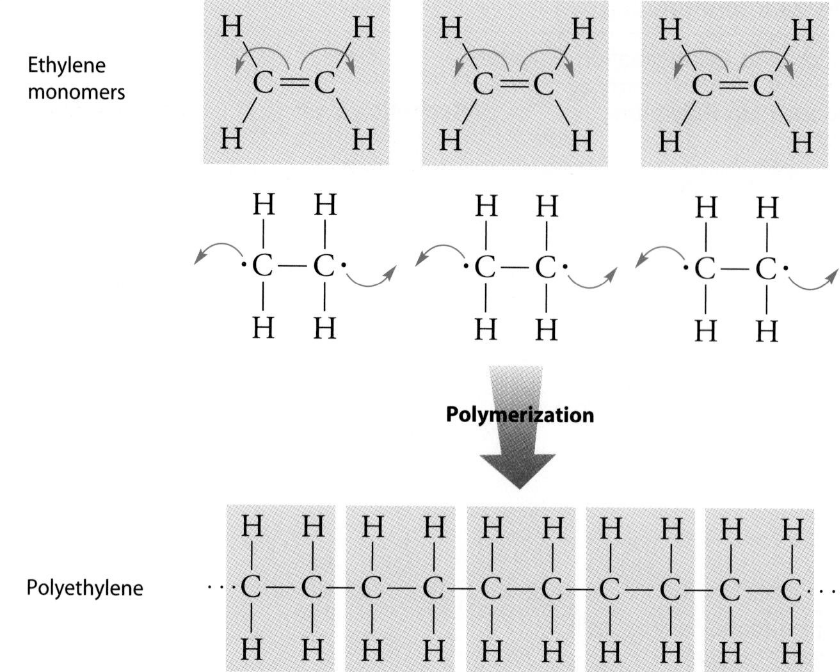

Figure 24.26
The addition polymer polyethylene is formed as electrons from the double bonds of ethylene monomer molecules split away and become unpaired valence electrons. Each unpaired electron then joins with an unpaired electron of a neighboring carbon atom to form a new covalent bond that links two monomer units together.

Two principal forms of polyethylene are produced by using different catalysts and reaction conditions. High-density polyethylene (HDPE), shown schematically in Figure 24.27a, consists of long strands of straight-chain molecules packed closely together. The tight alignment of neighboring strands makes HDPE a relatively rigid, tough plastic useful for such things as bottles and milk jugs. Low-density polyethylene (LDPE), shown in Figure 24.27b, is made of strands of highly branched chains, an architecture that prevents the strands from packing closely together. This makes LDPE more bendable than HDPE and gives it a lower melting point. While HDPE holds its shape in boiling water, LDPE deforms. It is most useful for such items as plastic bags, photographic film, and electrical-wire insulation.

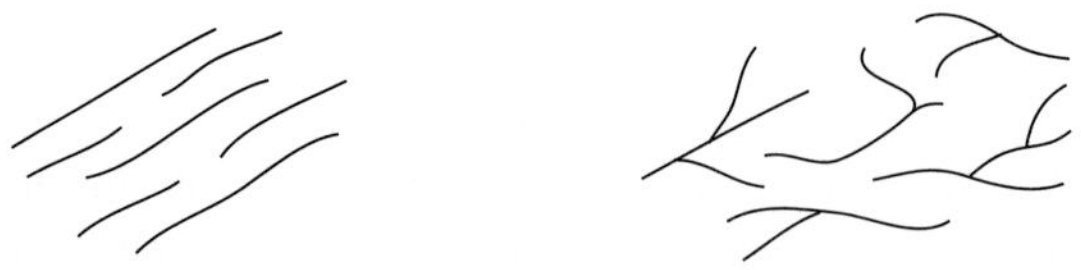

(a) Molecular strands of HDPE

(b) Molecular strands of LDP

Figure 24.27
(a) The polyethylene strands of HDPE are able to pack closely together, much like strands of uncooked spaghetti. (b) The polyethylene strands of LDPE are branched, which prevents the strands from packing well.

Other addition polymers are created by using different monomers. The only requirement is that the monomer must contain a double bond. The monomer propylene, for example, yields polypropylene, as shown in Figure 24.28. Polypropylene is a tough plastic material useful for pipes, hard-shell suitcases, and appliance parts. Fibers of polypropylene are used for upholstery, indoor–outdoor carpets, and even thermal underwear.

Propylene monomers

```
       H       H        H       H        H       H
        \     /          \     /          \     /
··· +    C=C       +      C=C       +      C=C       + ···
        /     \          /     \          /     \
       H       CH3      H       CH3      H       CH3
```

Polymerization

Polypropylene

```
     H  H     H  H     H  H     H  H     H  H
     |  |     |  |     |  |     |  |     |  |
  ···C—C——————C—C——————C—C——————C—C——————C—C···
     |  |     |  |     |  |     |  |     |  |
     H  CH3   H  CH3   H  CH3   H  CH3   H  CH3
```

Figure 24.28
Propylene monomers polymerize to form polypropylene.

Figure 24.29 shows that using styrene as the monomer yields polystyrene. Transparent plastic cups are made of polystyrene, as are thousands of other household items. Blowing gas into liquid polystyrene generates Styrofoam, which is widely used for coffee cups, packing material, and insulation.

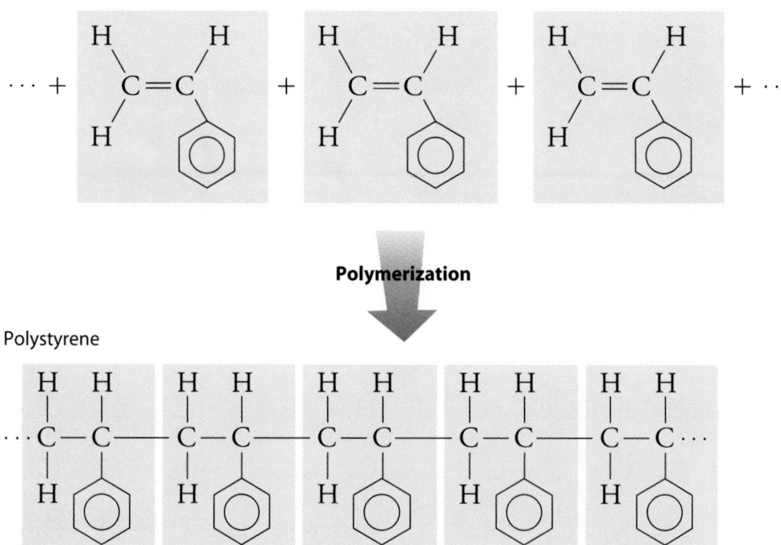

Figure 24.29
Styrene monomers polymerize to form polystyrene.

Another important addition polymer is polyvinylchloride (PVC), which is tough and easily molded. Floor tiles, shower curtains, and pipes are most often made of PVC, shown in Figure 24.30.

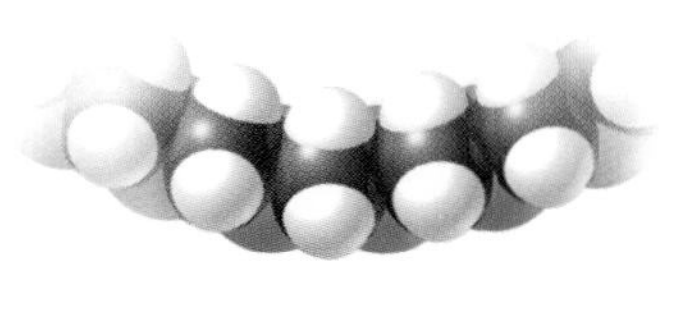

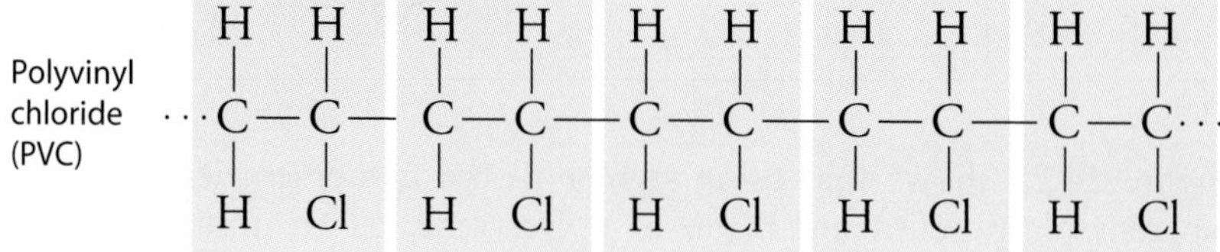

Figure 24.30
PVC is tough and easily molded, which is why it often is used to fabricate many household items.

The addition polymer polyvinylidene chloride (trade name Saran), shown in Figure 24.31, is used to make plastic wrap for food. The large chlorine atoms in this polymer help it to stick to such surfaces as glass by dipole–induced-dipole attractions, as discussed in Section 20.1.

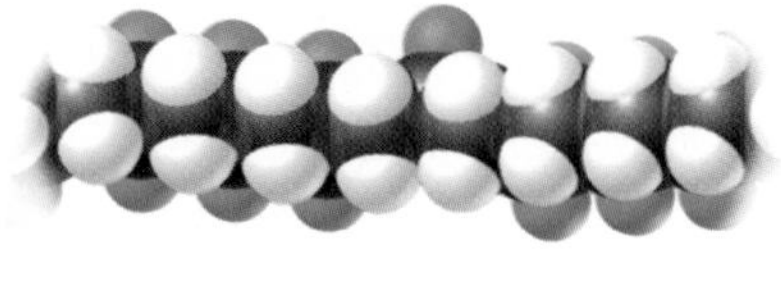

Polyvinylidene chloride (Saran)

H Cl H Cl H Cl H Cl H Cl
···C—C—C—C—C—C—C—C—C—C···
H Cl H Cl H Cl H Cl H Cl

Figure 24.31
The large chlorine atoms in polyvinylidene chloride make this addition polymer sticky.

The addition polymer polytetrafluoroethylene, shown in Figure 24.32, is what you know as Teflon. In contrast to the chlorine-containing Saran, fluorine-containing Teflon has a nonstick surface because the fluorine atoms tend not to experience any molecular attractions. In addition, because carbon–fluorine bonds are unusually strong, Teflon can be heated to high temperatures before decomposing. These properties make Teflon an ideal coating for cooking surfaces. It is also relatively inert, which is why many corrosive chemicals are shipped or stored in Teflon containers.

Polytetra-fluoroethylene (Teflon)

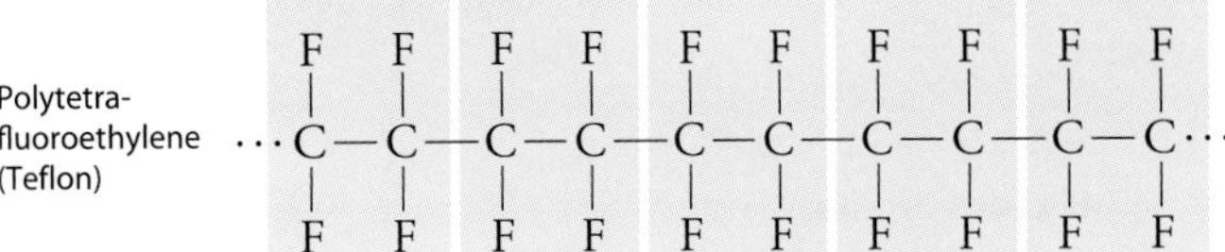

Figure 24.32
The fluorine atoms in polytetrafluoroethylene tend not to experience molecular attractions, which is why this addition polymer is used as a nonstick coating and lubricant.

☑ CHECKPOINT

What do all monomers that are used to make addition polymers have in common?

Check Your Answer

A double covalent bond between two carbon atoms.

Condensation Polymers—the Loss of Small Molecules

A **condensation polymer** is one that is formed when the joining of monomer units is accompanied by the loss of a small molecule, such as water or hydrochloric acid. Any monomer capable of becoming part of a condensation polymer must have a functional group on each end. When two such monomers come together to form a condensation polymer, one functional group of the first monomer links up with one functional group of the other monomer. The result is a two-monomer unit that has two terminal functional groups, one from each of the two original monomers. Each of these terminal functional groups in the two-monomer unit is now free to link with one of the functional groups of a third monomer, and then a fourth, and so on. In this way a polymer chain is built.

Figure 24.33 shows this process for the condensation polymer called nylon, which was created in 1937 by DuPont chemist Wallace Carothers (1896–1937). This polymer is composed of two different monomers, as shown in Figure 24.33, which classifies it as a *copolymer.* One monomer is adipic acid, which contains two reactive end groups, both carboxyl groups. The second monomer is hexamethylenediamine, in which two amine groups are the reactive end groups. One end of an adipic acid molecule and one end of a hexamethylamine molecule can be made to react with each other, splitting off a water molecule in the process. After two monomers have joined, reactive ends still remain for further reactions, which leads to a growing polymer chain. Aside from its use in hosiery, nylon also finds important uses in the manufacture of ropes, parachutes, clothing, and carpets.

So if nothing sticks to Teflon, how is Teflon made to adhere to a pan as a coating? That's a trade secret, but rumor has it that there are microscopic pits in the metal pan that help the Teflon to adhere physically. Of course, we all know that the Teflon is fairly easy to scrape out of the pan, which is why it's recommended that you stir-fry with a wooden utensil.

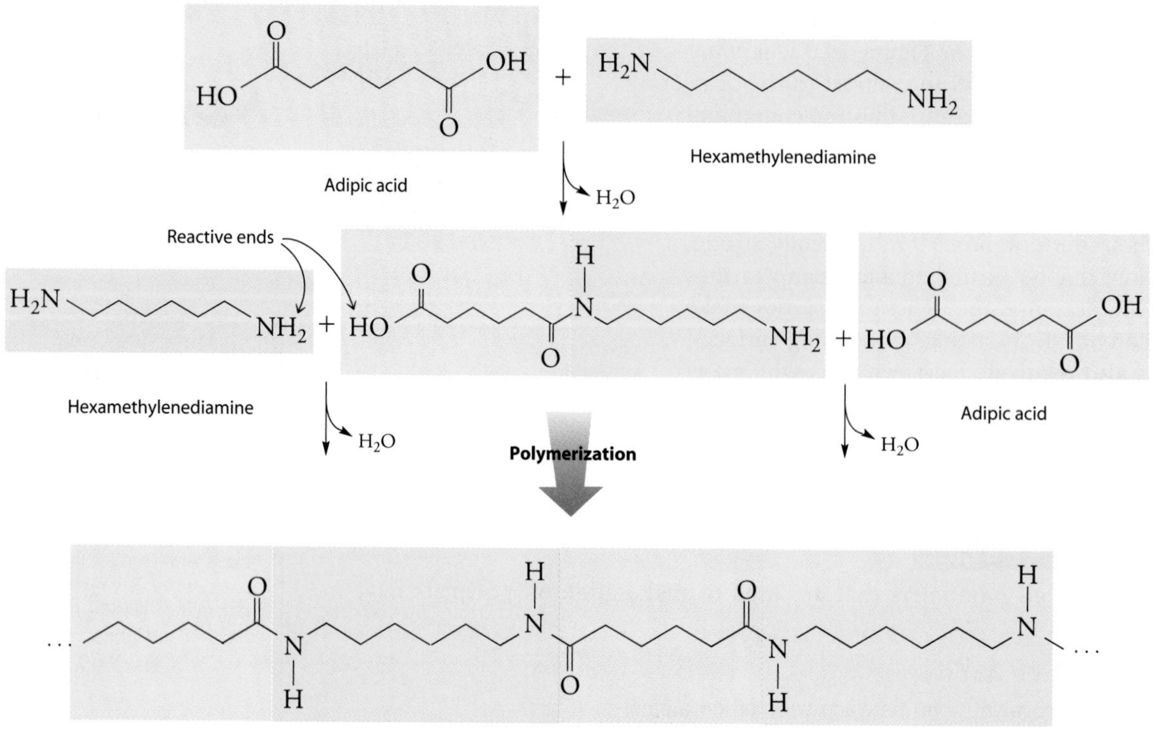

Figure 24.33
Adipic acid and hexamethylenediamine polymerize to form the condensation copolymer nylon.

☑ CHECKPOINT

The structure of 6-aminohexanoic acid is the following:

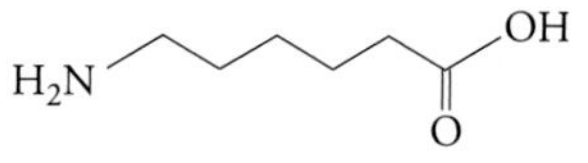

Is this compound a suitable monomer for forming a condensation polymer? If so, what is the structure of the polymer formed, and what small molecule is split off during the condensation?

Check Your Answers

Yes, because the molecule has two reactive ends. You know both ends are reactive because they are the ends shown in Figure 24.33. The only difference here is that both types of reactive ends are on the same molecule. Monomers of 6-aminohexanoic acid combine by splitting off water molecules to form the polymer known as nylon-6:

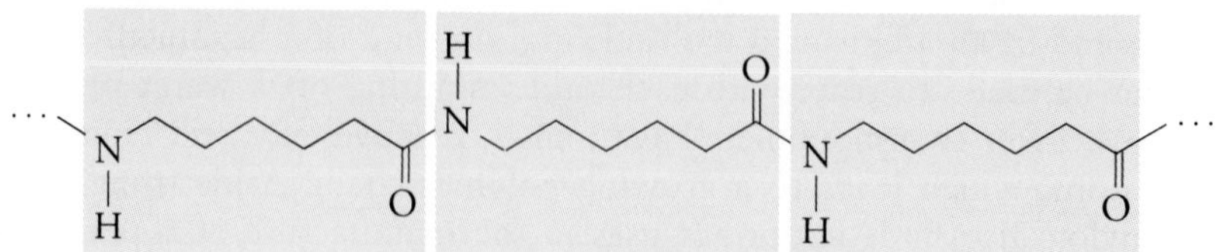

Another widely used condensation polymer is polyethylene terephthalate (PET), which is formed from the copolymerization of ethylene glycol and terephthalic acid, as shown in Figure 24.34. Plastic soda bottles are made from this polymer. Also, PET fibers are sold as Dacron polyester, a product used in clothing and stuffing for pillows and sleeping bags. Thin films of PET, which are called Mylar, can be coated with metal particles to make magnetic recording tape or those metallic-looking balloons you see for sale at most grocery store check-out counters.

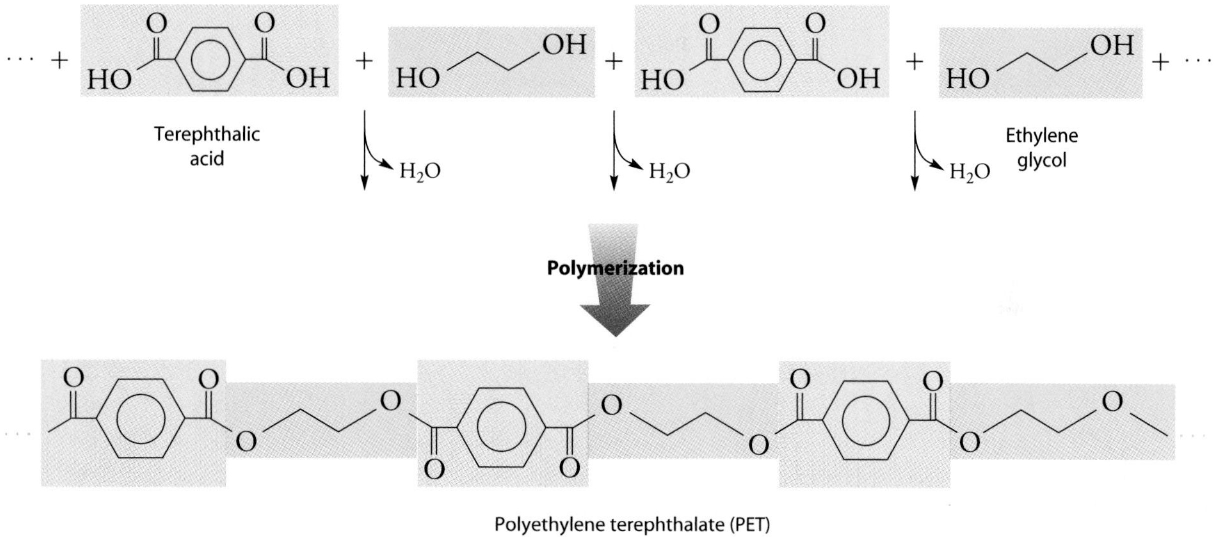

Terephthalic acid

Ethylene glycol

H_2O H_2O H_2O

Polymerization

Polyethylene terephthalate (PET)

Figure 24.34
Terephthalic acid and ethylene glycol polymerize to form the condensation copolymer polyethylene terephthalate.

Monomers that contain three reactive functional groups can also form polymer chains. These chains become interlocked in a rigid three-dimensional network that lends considerable strength and durability to the polymer. Once formed, these condensation polymers cannot be remelted or reshaped, which makes them hard-set, or *thermoset,* polymers. A good example is the thermoset polymer shown in Figure 24.35, formed from the reaction of formaldehyde with melamine. Hard plastic dishes (Melmac) and countertops (Formica) are made of this material. A similar polymer, Bakelite, made from formaldehyde and phenols containing multiple oxygen atoms, is used to bind plywood and particle board. Bakelite was synthesized in the early 1900s, and it was the first widely used polymer.

The synthetic-polymers industry has grown remarkably over the past half century. Annual production of polymers in the United States alone has grown from 3 billion pounds in 1950 to more than 100 billion pounds in 2003. Today, it is a challenge to find any consumer item that does *not* contain a plastic of one sort or another. Try finding one yourself.

In the future, watch for new kinds of polymers having a wide range of remarkable properties. One interesting application is shown in Figure 24.36.

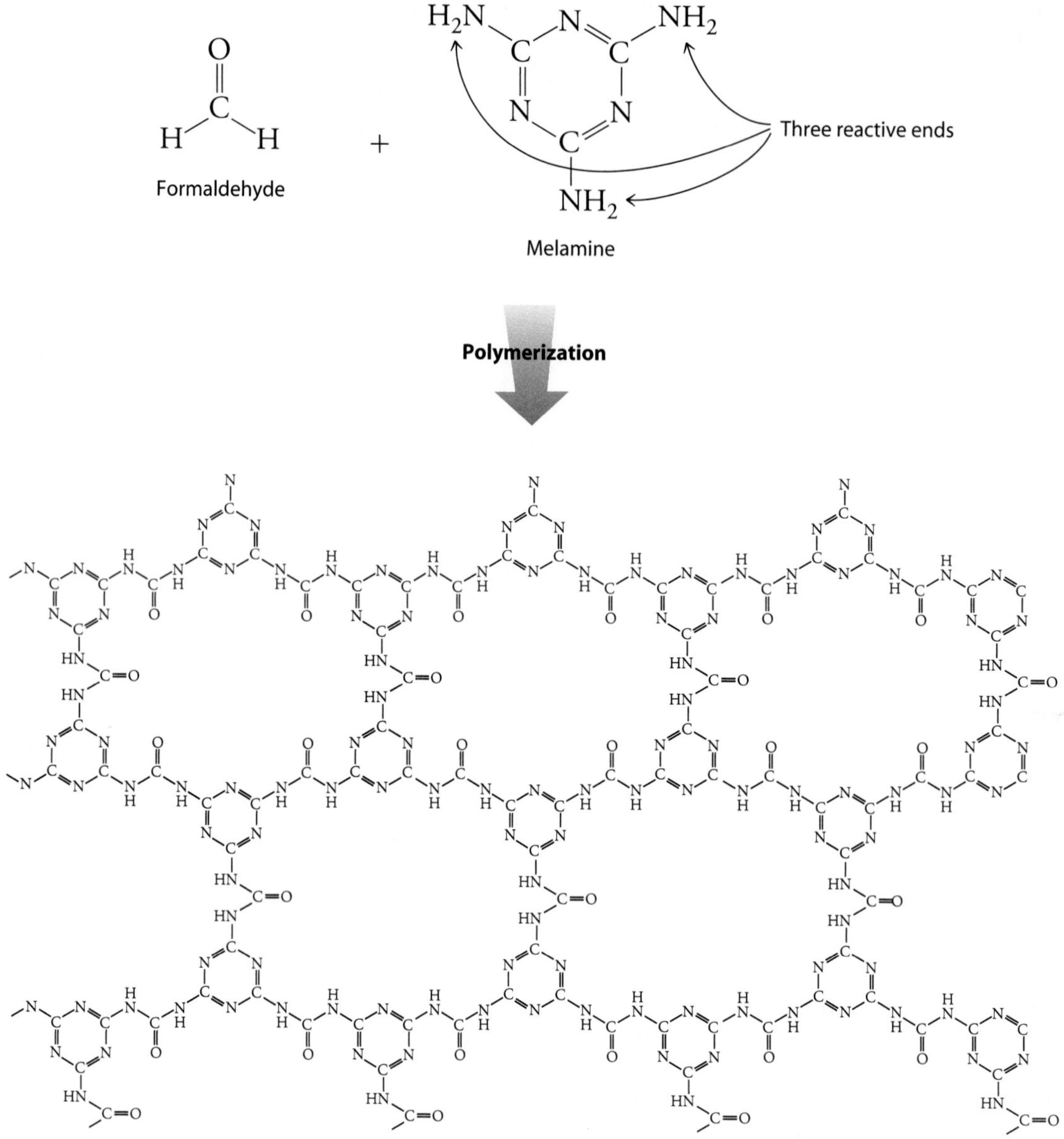

Figure 24.35
The three reactive groups of melamine allow it to polymerize with formaldehyde to form a three-dimensional network.

We already have polymers that conduct electricity, others that emit light, others that replace body parts, and still others that are stronger but much lighter than steel. Imagine synthetic polymers that mimic photosynthesis by transforming solar energy to chemical energy, or that efficiently separate fresh water from the oceans. These are not dreams. They are realities that chemists have already been demonstrating in the laboratory. Polymers hold a clear promise for the future.

Figure 24.36
Flexible and flat video displays can now be fabricated from polymers.

Summary of Terms

Organic chemistry The study of carbon-containing compounds.

Hydrocarbon A chemical compound containing only carbon and hydrogen atoms.

Structural isomers Molecules that have the same molecular formula but different chemical structures.

Conformation One of the possible spatial orientations of a molecule.

Saturated hydrocarbon A hydrocarbon containing no multiple covalent bonds, with each carbon atom bonded to four other atoms.

Unsaturated hydrocarbon A hydrocarbon containing at least one multiple covalent bond.

Aromatic compound Any organic molecule containing a benzene ring.

Heteroatom Any atom other than carbon or hydrogen in an organic molecule.

Functional group A specific combination of atoms that behaves as a unit in an organic molecule.

Alcohol An organic molecule that contains a hydroxyl group bonded to a saturated carbon.

Phenol An organic molecule in which a hydroxyl group is bonded to a benzene ring.

Ether An organic molecule containing an oxygen atom bonded to two carbon atoms.

Amine An organic molecule containing a nitrogen atom bonded to one or more saturated carbon atoms.

Carbonyl group A carbon atom double-bonded to an oxygen atom; found in ketones, aldehydes, amides, carboxylic acids, and esters.

Ketone An organic molecule containing a carbonyl group, the carbon of which is bonded to two carbon atoms.

Aldehyde An organic molecule containing a carbonyl group, the carbon of which is bonded either to one carbon atom and one hydrogen atom or to two hydrogen atoms.

Amide An organic molecule containing a carbonyl group, the carbon of which is bonded to a nitrogen atom.

Carboxylic acid An organic molecule containing a carbonyl group, the carbon of which is bonded to a hydroxyl group.

Ester An organic molecule containing a carbonyl group, the carbon of which is bonded to one carbon atom and one oxygen atom bonded to another carbon atom.

Polymer A long organic molecule made of many repeating units.

Monomers The small molecular units from which a polymer is formed.

Addition polymer A polymer formed by the joining together of monomer units with no atoms being lost as the polymer forms.

Condensation polymer A polymer formed by the joining together of monomer units accompanied by the loss of small molecules, such as water.

Review Questions

24.1 Hydrocarbons

1. What are some examples of hydrocarbons?
2. What are some uses of hydrocarbons?
3. How do two structural isomers differ from each other?
4. How are two structural isomers similar to each other?
5. What physical property of hydrocarbons is used in fractional distillation?
6. What types of hydrocarbons are more abundant in higher-octane gasoline?
7. To how many atoms is a saturated carbon atom bonded?

24.2 Unsaturated Hydrocarbons

8. What is the difference between a saturated hydrocarbon and an unsaturated hydrocarbon?
9. How many multiple bonds must a hydrocarbon have in order to be classified as unsaturated?
10. What kind of ring does an aromatic compound contain?

24.3 Functional Groups

11. What is a heteroatom?
12. Why do heteroatoms make such a difference in the physical and chemical properties of organic molecules?
13. Which of these molecules should have the higher boiling point, and why?

$$CH_3CH_2CH_2CH_3$$
$$CH_3CH_2CH_2CH_2{-}OH$$

24.4 Alcohols, Phenols, and Ethers

14. Why are low-formula-mass alcohols soluble in water?
15. What distinguishes an alcohol from a phenol?
16. What distinguishes an alcohol from an ether?
17. Why do ethers typically have lower boiling points than alcohols?

24.5 Amines and Alkaline Solutions

18. Which heteroatom is characteristic of an amine?
19. Do amines tend to be acidic, neutral, or basic?
20. Are alkaloids found in nature?
21. What are some examples of alkaloids?

24.6 The Carbonyl Functional Group

22. Which elements make up the carbonyl group?
23. How are ketones and aldehydes related to each other? How are they different from each other?
24. What is one commercially useful property of aldehydes?
25. How are amides and carboxylic acids related to each other? How are they different from each other?
26. From what naturally occurring compound is aspirin prepared?
27. Identify each of these molecules as either a hydrocarbon, an alcohol, or a carboxylic acid:

H_3C–(benzene ring)–$C(CH_3)(H)$–$C(=O)OH$

$$CH_3CH_2CH_2CH_3$$
$$CH_3CH_2CH_2CH_2{-}OH$$

24.7 Polymers

28. What happens to the double bond of a monomer participating in the formation of an addition polymer?
29. What are some of the differences between high-density polyethylene (HDPE) and low-density polyethylene (LDPE)?
30. What is released in the formation of a condensation polymer?
31. Why is plastic food wrap a stickier plastic than polyethylene?
32. What is a copolymer?

Activities

Twisting Jellybeans

Two carbon atoms connected by a single bond can rotate relative to each other. As we discussed in Section 24.1, this ability to rotate can give rise to numerous conformations (spatial orientations) of an organic molecule. Is it also possible for two carbon atoms connected by a double bond to rotate relative to each other? Perform this quick activity to see for yourself.

What You Need

Jellybeans (or gumdrops), round toothpicks.

Procedure

1. Attach one jellybean to each end of a single toothpick. Hold one of the jellybeans firmly with one hand while rotating the second jellybean with your other hand. Observe how there is no restriction on the different orientations of the two jellybeans relative to each other.

2. Hold two toothpicks side by side and attach one jellybean to each end such that each jellybean has both toothpicks poked into it. As before, hold one jellybean while rotating the other. What kind of rotations are possible now? Relate what you observe to the carbon—carbon double bond. Which structure of Figure 24.7 do you suppose has more possible conformations: *n*-butane or 2-butene? What do you suppose is true about the ability of atoms connected by a carbon–carbon triple bond to twist relative to each other?

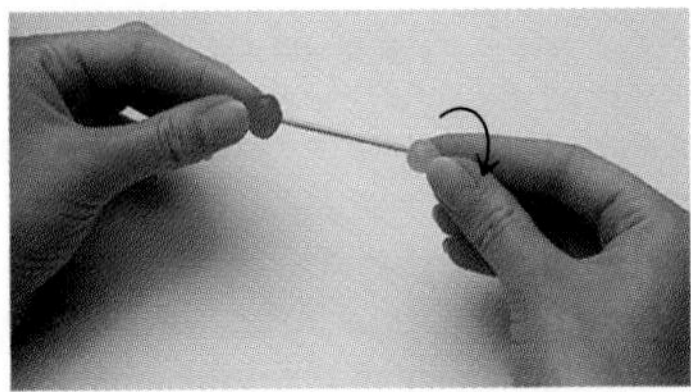

Rubbing Eggs

Isopropyl alcohol, also known as rubbing alcohol, is very toxic if ingested. The reason for this is because it acts to destroy the digestive proteins and other important biomolecules in your stomach. Do this activity to see firsthand the destructive action of isopropyl alcohol on proteins. Crack open an egg and place the egg white and the yolk into two separate bowls. Pour a capful of isopropyl alcohol into the egg white and observe what happens. In the second bowl, stir the yolk with a fork. Add another capful of isopropyl alcohol to the stirred yolk and observe what happens. The same sort of destruction would occur to your own stomach proteins, as well as various tissues, upon ingesting the isopropyl alcohol. Not good! Our skin, however, is more impervious to the destructive powers of isopropyl alcohol, which therefore serves as a good topical antiseptic.

Racing Water Drops

The chemical composition of a polymer has a significant effect on its macroscopic properties. To see this for yourself, place a drop of water on a new plastic sandwich bag, and then tilt the bag vertically so that the drop races off. Observe the behavior of the water carefully. Now race a drop of water off a freshly pulled strip of plastic food wrap. How does the behavior of the drop on the wrap compare with the behavior of the drop on the sandwich bag?

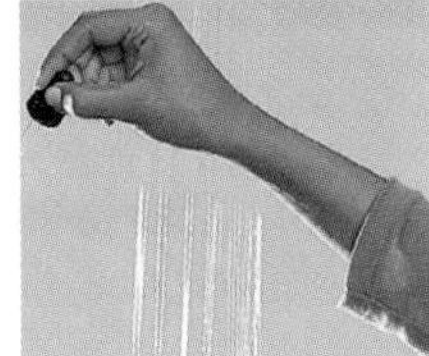

Most brands of sandwich bags are made of polyethylene terephthalate, and most brands of food wrap are made of polyvinylidene chloride. Look carefully at the chemical composition of these polymers, shown in Table 24.5. Which contains larger atoms? Which might be involved in stronger dipole–induced dipole interactions with water? Need help with these questions? Refer back to Section 20.1.

Exercises

1. Which contains more hydrogen atoms: a five-carbon saturated hydrocarbon molecule or a five-carbon unsaturated hydrocarbon molecule?
2. Why does the melting point of hydrocarbons increase as the number of carbon atoms per molecule increases?
3. Draw all the structural isomers for hydrocarbons having the molecular formula C_4H_{10}.
4. Draw all the structural isomers for hydrocarbons having the molecular formula C_6H_{14}.
5. How many structural isomers are shown here?

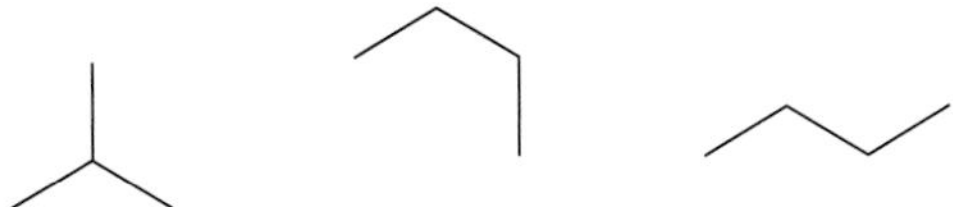

6. Which two of these four structures are of the same structural isomer?

7. The temperatures in a fractionating tower at an oil refinery are important, but so are the pressures. Where might the pressure in a fractionating tower be greatest—at the bottom or at the top? Defend your answer.
8. Heteroatoms make a difference in the physical and chemical properties of an organic molecule because
   (a) they add extra mass to the hydrocarbon structure.
   (b) each heteroatom has its own characteristic chemistry.

(c) they can enhance the polarity of the organic molecule.
(d) all of the above are true.

9. Why might a high-formula-mass alcohol be insoluble in water?
10. What is the percentage by volume of water in 80-proof vodka?
11. How does ingested methanol lead to damaging a person's eyes?
12. One of the skin-irritating components of poison oak is tetrahydrourushiol:

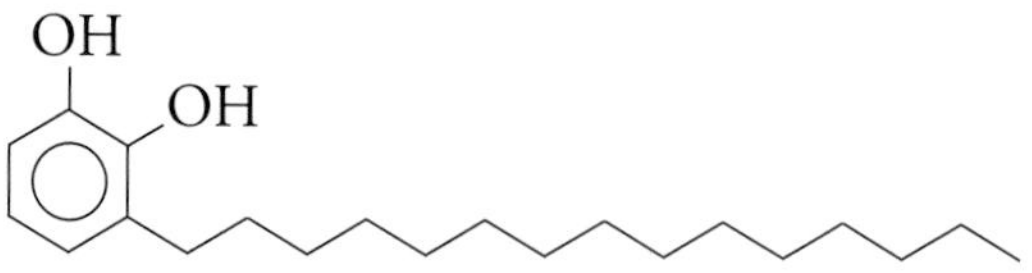

OH OH

The long, nonpolar hydrocarbon tail embeds itself in a person's oily skin, where the molecule initiates an allergic response. Scratching the itch spreads tetrahydrourushiol molecules over a greater surface area, causing the zone of irritation to grow. Is this compound an alcohol or a phenol? Defend your answer.

13. The phosphoric acid salt of caffeine has the structure

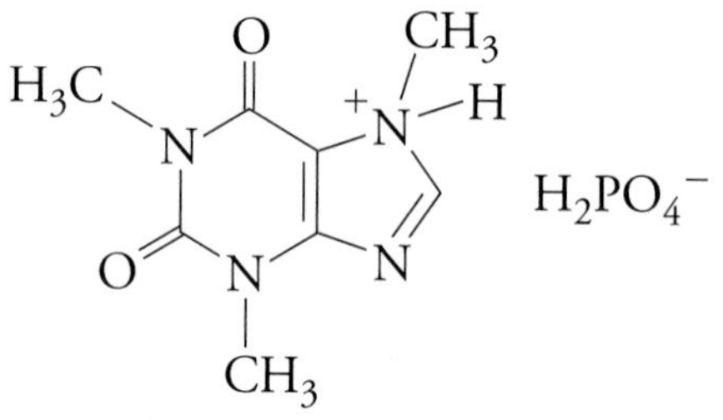

O CH_3 H_3C N ^+N H $H_2PO_4^-$ O N N CH_3

Caffeine–phosphoric acid salt

This molecule behaves as an acid in that it can donate a hydrogen ion, which is created from the hydrogen atom bonded to the positively charged nitrogen atom. What are all the products formed when 1 mole of this salt reacts with 1 mole of sodium hydroxide, NaOH, a strong base?

14. The solvent diethyl ether can be mixed with water but only by shaking the two liquids together. After the shaking is stopped, the liquids separate into two layers, much like oil and vinegar. The free-base form of the alkaloid caffeine is readily soluble in diethyl ether but not in water. Suggest what might happen to the caffeine of a caffeinated beverage if the beverage were first made alkaline with sodium hydroxide and then shaken with some diethyl ether.
15. Alkaloid salts are not very soluble in the organic solvent diethyl ether. What might happen to the free-base form of caffeine dissolved in diethyl ether if gaseous hydrogen chloride, HCl, were bubbled into the solution?

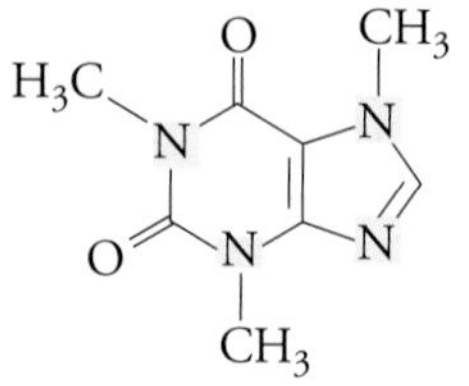

O CH_3 H_3C N N O N N CH_3

Caffeine

16. Draw all the structural isomers for amines having the molecular formula C_3H_9N.
17. Explain why caprylic acid, $CH_3(CH_2)_6COOH$, dissolves in a 5 percent aqueous solution of sodium hydroxide, whereas caprylaldehyde, $CH_3(CH_2)_6CHO$, does not.
18. In water, does the molecule shown below act as an acid, as a base, as neither, or as both?

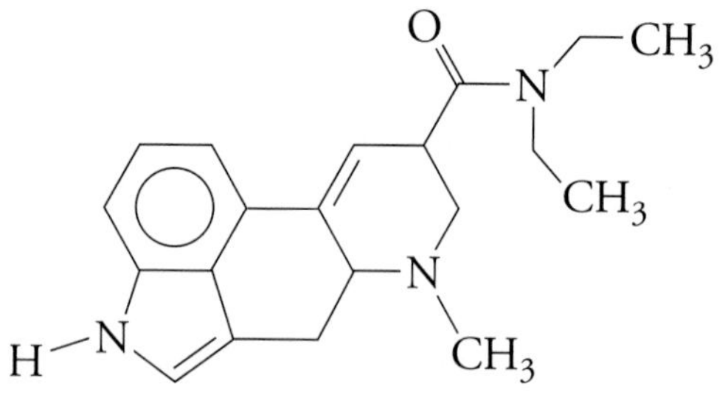

O CH_3 N CH_3 N H N CH_3

Lysergic acid diethylamide

19. If you were to see "phenylephrine·HCl" on the label for a decongestant, would you worry that consuming it would expose you to the strong acid hydrochloric acid? Explain.

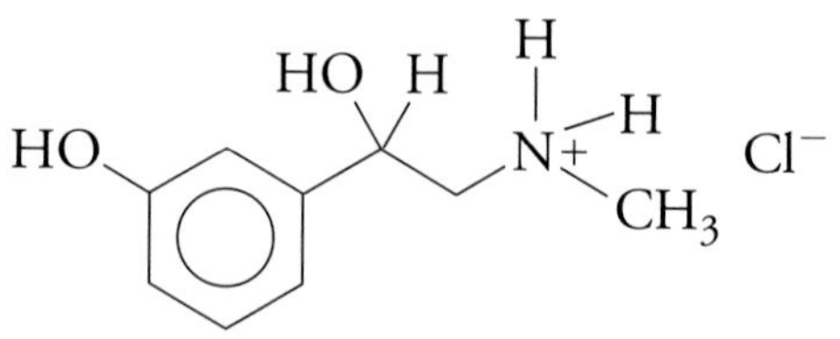

H HO H HO H N+ Cl^- CH_3

Phenylephrine hydrochloride

20. Suggest an explanation for why aspirin has a sour taste.
21. An amino acid is an organic molecule that contains both an amine group and a carboxyl group. At neutral pH, which of the following two structures is more likely?

(a) H_2N-CH_2-COOH

(b) $H_3N^+-CH_2-COO^-$

Explain your answer.

22. An amino acid is an organic molecule that contains both an amine group and a carboxyl group. At an acidic pH, which of these three structures is most likely?

(a) $H_2N-CH_2-COO^-$

(b) H_2N-CH_2-COOH

(c) $H_3N^+-CH_2-COOH$

Explain your answer.

23. Identify the following functional groups in this organic molecule—amide, ester, ketone, ether, alcohol, aldehyde, and amine:

24. Would you expect polypropylene to be denser or less dense than low-density polyethylene? Why?
25. Many polymers emit toxic fumes when burning. Which polymer in Table 24.5 produces hydrogen cyanide, HCN? Which two produce toxic hydrogen chloride gas, HCl?
26. One solution to the problem of our overflowing landfills is to burn plastic objects instead of burying them. What would be some of the advantages and disadvantages of this practice?
27. Which would you expect to be more viscous, a polymer composed of long molecular strands or one made of short molecular stands? Why?
28. Hydrocarbons release a lot of energy when ignited. Where does this energy come from?
29. What type of polymer would be best to use in the manufacture of stain-resistant carpets?
30. As noted in the Checkpoint on page 602, the compound 6-aminohexanoic acid is used to make the condensation polymer nylon-6. Polymerization is not always successful, however, because of a competing side reaction. What is this side reaction? Would polymerization be more likely in a dilute solution of this monomer or in a concentrated solution? Why?

Chapter 24 Online Resources

Tutorials

- Introduction to Organic Molecules
- Organic Molecules & Isomers
- Functional Groups
- Polymers
- Polymers from Monomers

Quiz

Exercises

Flashcards

Links

Sample Exam Questions for Part II—Chemistry

Choose the BEST answer to each of the following.

1. What makes one element distinct from another is the number of
   (a) protons in its nucleus (b) neutrons in its nucleus
   (c) electrons in its nucleus
   (d) total particles in its nucleus
2. In the atomic nucleus of a certain element are 26 protons and 28 neutrons. The atomic number of the element is
   (a) 26 (b) 27 (c) 28 (d) 54 (e) none of these
3. The origin of atoms that constitute the body of a newborn baby is
   (a) tissues from the mother's body
   (b) the father's sperm (c) ancient stars
4. The weight of matter comes mostly from its
   (a) electrons (b) nucleons
5. The volume of matter comes mostly from its
   (a) electrons (b) nucleons
6. The atomic model explaining why electrons orbit at discrete distances from the nucleus involves
   (a) electron wavelengths
   (b) electrons acting like planets orbiting the sun
   (c) the emission of photons from quantized energy levels
   (d) springs connecting electrons to the nucleus
7. Astronomers are able to identify the elements that make up a star by studying its
   (a) Doppler effect (b) structure (c) temperature
   (d) spectra (e) standing waves
8. Which experiences the greatest electrical force in an electrical field?
   (a) alpha particle (b) beta particle (c) gamma ray
   (d) none of these
9. The discovery of radioactivity was a boost to earth scientists, who were then able to know more about
   (a) the ages of various rocks
   (b) why the earth's interior is hot
   (c) both (d) neither
10. There is a greater proportion of C-14/C-12 in
    (a) old bones (b) new bones
    (c) it depends on the organism
    (d) not enough information to say
11. Most of the radioactivity we personally encounter comes from
    (a) fallout from past and present testing of nuclear weapons
    (b) nuclear power plants
    (c) medical X-ray examinations
    (d) the natural environment
12. Electrical forces within the atomic nucleus tend to
    (a) hold the nucleus together
    (b) push the nucleus apart (c) neither of these
13. Fusing a pair of iron nuclei yields a net
    (a) absorption of energy (b) release of energy
    (c) neither of the above (d) both of the above
14. Compared with the energy produced by fissioning a gram of uranium, the energy produced by fusing a gram of deuterium is
    (a) less (b) more (c) about the same
15. Chemical and physical changes
    (a) are virtually indistinguishable on the molecular level
    (b) differ in that only during a chemical change do the atoms of a substance change their identity
    (c) differ in that only during a physical change do the molecules of a substance maintain their identity
    (d) differ in that physical changes usually involve a greater input or output of energy than do chemical changes
16. Solutions and suspensions
    (a) are both examples of heterogeneous mixtures
    (b) are both examples of homogenous mixtures
    (c) cannot be separated into separate components by physical means
    (d) may be either pure or impure
17. Which figure best illustrates the surface of a liquid near its boiling temperature?

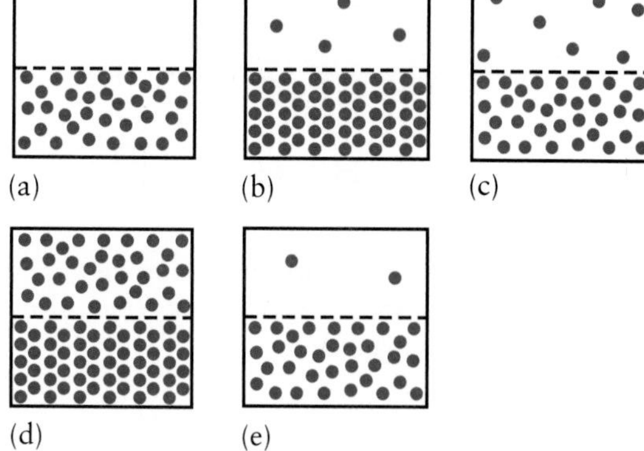

18. Osmosis is a process whereby
    (a) water flows across a semipermeable membrane from regions of high to low solute concentrations
    (b) water flows across a semipermeable membrane from regions of low to high solute concentrations
    (c) solutes flow across a semipermeable membrane from regions of high to low solute concentrations
    (d) solutes flow across a semipermeable membrane from regions of low to high solute concentrations

19. The inner transition elements are placed below the main body of the periodic table because
    (a) these elements do not have as many applications as the elements shown in the main body
    (b) they are the heaviest of all the known elements
    (c) they are not true metals
    (d) such positioning makes the periodic table fit better on a sheet of paper
20. Salts are made of elements found on opposite ends of the periodic table because
    (a) elements on the left tend to form positive ions while those on the right tend to form negative ions
    (b) elements on the left tend to form negative ions while those on the right tend to form positive ions
    (c) elements on opposite ends of the periodic table have similar arrangements of electrons
    (d) False. Salts are generally made of elements found on the same side of the periodic table.
21. The atoms of elements toward the bottom of any group in the periodic table tend to be
    (a) smaller because of the increase in nuclear charge
    (b) smaller because of the decrease in the probability cloud density
    (c) larger because of a greater number of occupied shells
    (d) larger because of a decrease in nuclear charge
22. What type of bonds generally involve nonmetal atoms?
    (a) covalent bonds (b) ionic bonds
    (c) both of the above
23. Electronegativity is an important consideration for assessing the polarity of
    (a) covalent bonds (b) ionic bonds
    (c) both of the above
24. Water is considered a polar compound because
    (a) it is found in its frozen state in both the arctic and antarctic regions of our planet
    (b) it has a strong attraction to magnets
    (c) one side is slightly negative while the other side is slightly positive
    (d) each molecule consists of fewer than 10 atoms
25. Which type of molecular attraction is considered the strongest?
    (a) Ion-dipole (b) dipole-dipole
    (c) dipole-induced dipole
26. Only so much sugar dissolves in water because
    (a) sugar molecules have such a strong attraction to themselves
    (b) water molecules have such a strong attraction to themselves
    (c) sugar is infinitely soluble
    (d) water can only get so hot before it begins to boil
27. Teflon is a flavorless polymer, but sprinkle some sugar on the Teflon and the Teflon will taste
    (a) sweet because the sugar is incorporated into the Teflon polymer
    (b) sweet because of the sugar molecules on it
    (c) flavorless while the sugar molecules taste sweet
    (d) flavorless because the Teflon repels the sweetness of the sugar molecules
28. A razor blade must be lying flat in order to be held up on the surface of water by surface tension because
    (a) the greater the surface area interacting with the water, the greater the surface tension
    (b) the sharp edge of the razor blade disrupts surface tension by slicing through individual water molecules
    (c) a vertically placed razor blade falls sideways and sinks after splashing into the surface
    (d) this minimizes the pressure that the blade exerts on the surface of the liquid
29. Water is described as "hard" when it contains excessive quantities of
    (a) iron ions (b) sodium ions
    (c) lead ions (d) calcium ions
30. Is the following equation balanced or unbalanced?

    $2\ Fe + 2\ Na_2CrO_4 + 2\ H_2O \longrightarrow Fe_2O_3 + Cr_2O_3 + 4\ NaOH$

    (a) balanced (b) unbalanced
31. Energy is required to break apart a chemical bond to overcome
    (a) gravitational forces of attraction
    (b) nuclear forces of attraction
    (c) electrical forces of attraction
    (d) It is not! Energy is actually released when a bond is broken.
32. The higher the activation energy for a chemical reaction
    (a) the more exothermic it is
    (b) the less exothermic it is
    (c) the more energy is required for it to proceed
    (d) the less energy is required for it to proceed
33. How many molecules are there in 34 grams of ammonia, NH_3?
    (a) 6.02×10^{23} (b) 12.04×10^{23}
    (c) 3.01×10^{23} (d) 24.08×10^{23}
34. The pH of a solution is less than zero
    (a) when the concentration of hydronium ions is greater than 10 M
    (b) when the concentration of hydronium ions is less than 10 M
    (c) only after all of the hydroxide ions within a solution have been removed
    (d) Such a solution is not possible because the lower limit of pH is zero

35. A buffer solution prevents rapid changes in pH
    (a) by disintegrating any incoming acid or base
    (b) by increasing the volume of solution
    (c) by neutralizing any incoming acid or base
    (d) by decreasing the volume of solution
36. What do rusting and combustion have in common?
    (a) Neither involve the reduction of a substance
    (b) They are the reverse processes and so they share nothing in common
    (c) They are both impeded by the presence of water
    (d) They are both examples of oxidation
37. Electrolysis is important to the national economy because it
    (a) provides a means of producing electricity
    (b) allows the convenient production of chemicals, especially metals
    (c) promotes clean air
    (d) all of the above
38. How many structural isomers are shown below?
    (a) 0 (b) 1 (c) 2 (d) 3 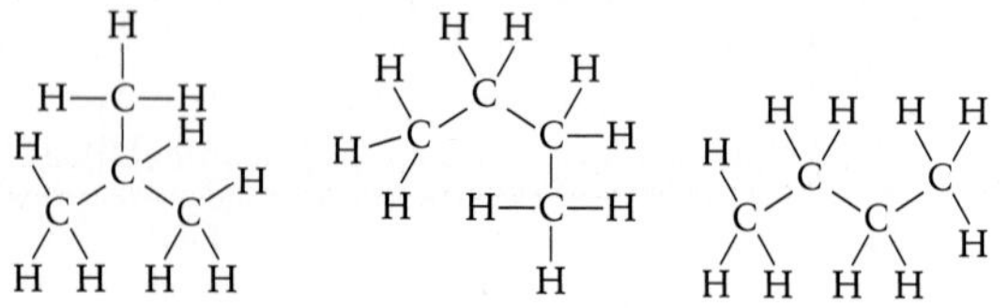
39. Heteroatoms make a difference in the physical and chemical properties of an organic molecule because
    (a) they add extra mass to the hydrocarbon structure
    (b) each heteroatom has its own characteristic chemistry
    (c) they can enhance the polarity of the organic molecule
    (d) all of the above
40. The difference between an addition polymer and a condensation polymer is that
    (a) addition polymers tend to be longer
    (b) condensation polymers form with the loss of a small molecule, such as HCl
    (c) addition polymers are synthetic
    (d) condensation polymers tend to be more highly-branched

Answers: 1a, 2a, 3c, 4b, 5a, 6a, 7d, 8a, 9c, 10b, 11d, 12b, 13a, 14b, 15c, 16b, 17c, 18b, 19d, 20a, 21c, 22c, 23c, 24c, 25a, 26a, 27c, 28d, 29d, 30a, 31c, 32c, 33b, 34a, 35c, 36d, 37b, 38c, 39d, 40b

PART THREE

Earth and Space Science

Hey Megan, I think it's amazing that the sandy bluff we're standing on was once a beach just like the one right below us—until forces generated within the earth's interior caused the land to rise.

You're right Emily, it is amazing. But do you know where the sand on this bluff and the beach below came from? The sand is the remains of mountains long since eroded away. The sand was brought to the ocean by streams flowing over the land. Once in the ocean, wind-driven waves crashing on the beach wore down the sand into smaller and smaller sizes. Earth science in action!

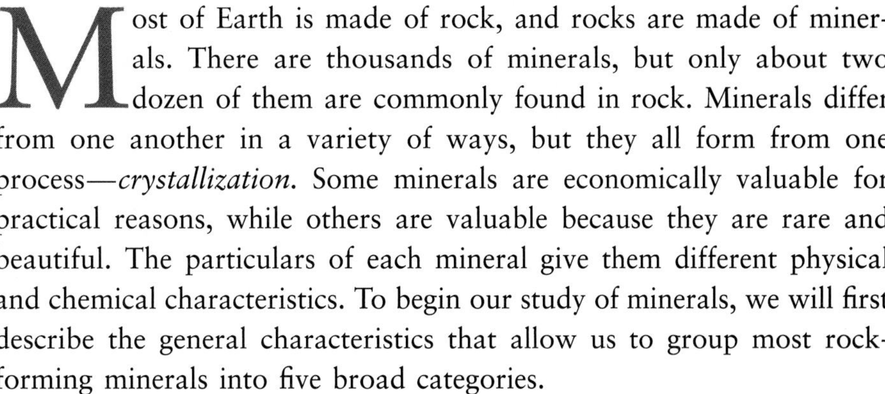

CHAPTER 25

Minerals and How We Use Them

Most of Earth is made of rock, and rocks are made of minerals. There are thousands of minerals, but only about two dozen of them are commonly found in rock. Minerals differ from one another in a variety of ways, but they all form from one process—*crystallization*. Some minerals are economically valuable for practical reasons, while others are valuable because they are rare and beautiful. The particulars of each mineral give them different physical and chemical characteristics. To begin our study of minerals, we will first describe the general characteristics that allow us to group most rock-forming minerals into five broad categories.

Minerals found in rocks and in dietary supplements are similar yet different. The minerals in rocks are naturally occurring, inorganic, crystalline solids, with a definite chemical composition. Minerals found in dietary supplements are human-made inorganic compounds that contain elements necessary for life functions. However, the elements used to make dietary supplements ultimately come from the naturally occurring minerals of the earth's crust.

Insights

25.1 Structure and Distribution of Rock-Forming Minerals

Minerals are the building blocks of rocks, and elements, in turn, are the building blocks of minerals. Most minerals are composed of more than one element. But a few minerals, such as gold, copper, and iron, are composed of single elements. A **mineral** is defined as a naturally formed, inorganic, crystalline solid, composed of an ordered arrangement of atoms with a specific chemical composition.

Just as buildings are made of different materials—some stone, some brick, some wood—minerals are made of different elements. Some minerals, as we shall see, have the same combination of elements, but their atoms are arranged differently, which makes them different minerals. So, carrying our analogy with buildings further, different architecture using the same materials can result in very different minerals.

Of the 112 known elements, 92 occur naturally in the earth's crust. These 92 elements combine to make up nearly 4000 different minerals. And these minerals, like the letters of the alphabet, combine in various ways to create the huge diversity of rocks found on earth.

Although there are thousands of types of minerals on earth, only about two dozen are common. And the two dozen common minerals are chiefly composed of only a dozen elements (Table 25.1). So you can see that very few elements make up the vast majority of the earth's crust. Indeed, the twelve elements found in the two dozen common minerals represent about 99% of the mass of the earth's crust. And almost half of this mass is the element oxygen!

Link to Section 14.1

With few exceptions, all rock-forming minerals are members of five groups. The oxygen in earth's crust is found in such common groups of minerals as the *silicates* and *carbonates*. Other common groups of rock-forming minerals are the *oxides*, *sulfides*, and *sulfates*.

Table 25.1

The Most Common Chemical Elements in the Earth's Crust

Element	Symbol	Percent by Mass
Oxygen	O	46.60
Silicon	Si	27.72
Aluminum	Al	8.13
Iron	Fe	5.00
Calcium	Ca	3.63
Sodium	Na	2.83
Potassium	K	2.59
Magnesium	Mg	2.09
Titanium	Ti	0.44
Hydrogen	H	0.14
Phosphorus	P	0.10
Manganese	Mn	0.09
All other elements		0.64
Total		100.00

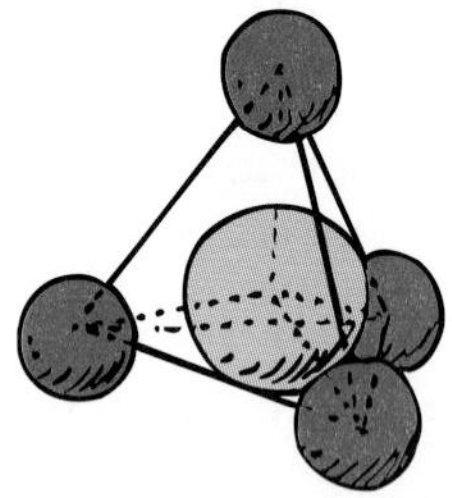

Figure 25.1
The silicon–oxygen tetrahedron consists of four oxygen atoms, which surround a central silicon atom.

The Silicates

Silicon is the second most abundant element in Earth's crust, after oxygen. Silicon and oxygen atoms combine to form the basic structure of the *silicates,* the largest mineral group. Silicon has a great affinity for oxygen. It has such a strong tendency to bond with oxygen that silicon is never found in nature as a pure element; it is always combined with oxygen. All silicates have the same fundamental structure of atoms, the silicon–oxygen tetrahedron (Figure 25.1). But these tetrahedra are not chemically stable until they form organized groups by bonding chemically with one another (Figure 25.2).

Figure 25.2
As silicate tetrahedra link to one another, they polymerize to form chains, sheets, and various network patterns. The complexity of the silicate structure increases down the chart.

Silcate Mineral		Typical Formula	Cleavage	Silicate Structure
Olivine		$(Mg, Fe)_2SiO_4$	None	Single tetrahedron
Pyroxene		$(Mg, Fe)SiO_3$	Two planes at right angles	Chains
Amphibole		$(Ca_2Mg_5)Si_8O_{22}(OH)_2$	Two planes at 60° and 120°	Double chains
Micas	Muscovite	$KAl_3Si_3O_{10}(OH)_2$	One plane	Sheets
	Biotite	$K(Mg, Fe)_3Si_3O_{10}(OH)_2$		
Feldspars	Orthoclase	$KAlSi_3O_8$	Two planes at 90°	Three-dimensional networks
	Plagioclase	$(Ca, Na) AlSi_3O_8$		
Quartz		SiO_2	None	

If you ever collected rocks and minerals, you probably had some quartz specimens in your collection. The silicate known as quartz is the second most common mineral in the earth's crust. Quartz is composed only of oxygen and silicon (SiO_2). Most other silicates, however, contain other elements in addition to oxygen and silicon. For example, feldspar is a silicate that also contains aluminum, sodium, potassium, and/or calcium. Feldspar, which is the most abundant material found in the earth's crust, makes up more than 50% of the crust.

Link to Section 14.5

The Carbonates

The carbonate minerals have a much simpler structure than the silicates. Carbonate structure is triangular, with a central carbon atom bonded to three oxygen atoms, CO_3^{2-}. Groups of carbonate ions are arranged in sheets somewhat like those of the sheet-structured silicates (Figure 25.3). Two common carbonate minerals are calcite and dolomite. Calcite consists of the chemical compound calcium carbonate, $CaCO_3$. Dolomite is a mixture of calcium carbonate and magnesium carbonate, $CaMg(CO_3)_2$. Calcite and dolomite are the main minerals found in the group of rocks called *limestone.*

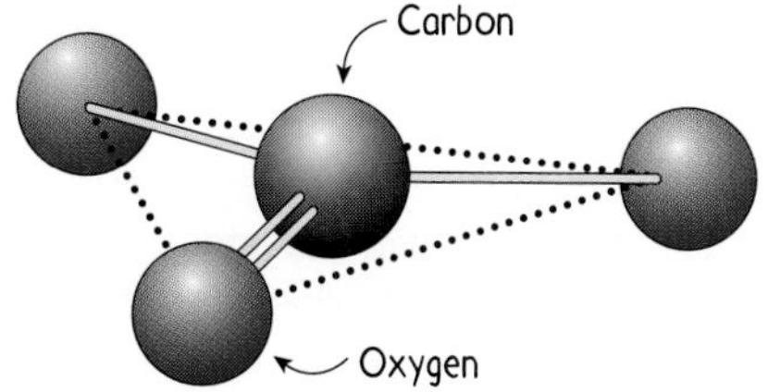

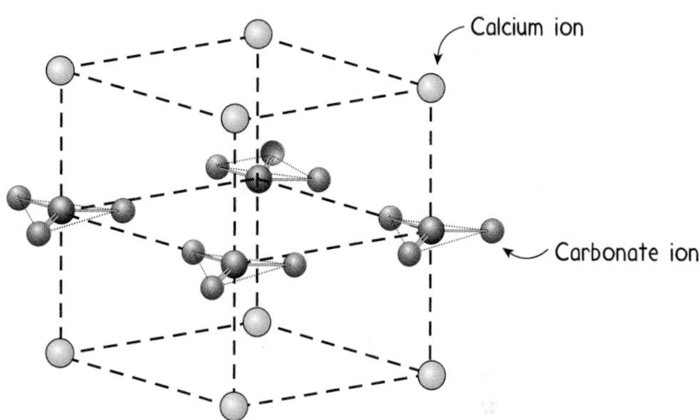

Figure 25.3
(a) The carbonate ion, CO_3^{2-}, has a triangular structure that features a central carbon atom bonded to three oxygen atoms. (b) Carbonate minerals, such as calcite and dolomite, have a layered, sheetlike structure.

The Oxides, Sulfides, and Sulfates

In the oxide group, oxygen is combined with one or more metals. These metals include iron, chromium, manganese, tin, and uranium*. The oxide mineral group is important economically because it contains many useful ores. An **ore** is a mineral deposit that is rich in valuable metals that can be mined for a profit. Many oxide ores are necessary for industrial and technological manufacturing, so they are of great economic importance.

As the names imply, the sulfide and sulfate minerals have sulfur as a main component. In the sulfide group, sulfide ions combine with metallic elements. For this reason, most sulfide minerals look like metals. In fact, the sulfides form an important class of minerals because they, in addition to the oxides, are very useful ores for modern society. The most common sulfide mineral is pyrite (fool's gold), FeS_4.

The sulfates contain sulfur in the form of a sulfate ion, SO_4^{2-}. The sulfate ion is shaped like a tetrahedron, with one sulfur atom and four oxygen atoms. Although not technically considered an ore, many sulfates have economic value as industrial minerals. Gypsum, a hydrated calcium sulfate ($CaSO_4 \cdot 2H_2O$), is one of the most abundant minerals of the sulfate group. It is used for making plaster of Paris and various other construction materials.

*Some common minerals that these metals form are hematite and magnetite (iron), chromite (chromium), pyrolusite (manganese), cassiterite (tin), and uraninite (uranium).

Asbestos: Friend *and* Foe

What do you think when you hear the word *asbestos?* Perhaps you have heard of the lung disease it causes, *asbestosis*. Or maybe images of workers in "space suits" removing asbestos from buildings come to your mind. Today, when we think of asbestos, we first think of its hazards. But it hasn't always been that way.

The first known reference to asbestos goes back to the time of Aristotle. That was when asbestos was discovered to have fireproofing qualities. Since then, the incombustibility and low heat conductivity of asbestos, plus its fibrous, flexible nature, have proven useful in many ways. For example, asbestos has been woven into fabrics (such as theater curtains and fireproof suits). It has been utilized in building materials (as fireproof insulation) and as a flame retardant in plaster, ceiling, and floor tile. It has also been used in automobile brake shoes and clutch facings, air and water filters, military gas masks, and even toothpaste! In the 1970s, the commercial use of asbestos reached an all-time high. But then, asbestos was linked to lung disease. The fibrous nature that makes asbestos so flexible also allows it to penetrate body tissues easily, particularly the tissues of the lungs. The history of asbestos is one of bitter paradox because the unique qualities that allowed it to save lives have also been found to endanger lives.

Asbestos is not really a single mineral. Actually, asbestos is a family of silicate minerals known for their fibrous structures. There are six types of asbestos minerals. Two of these are of commercial importance—chrysotile and crocidolite. The asbestos mineral chrysotile accounts for 95% of asbestos production worldwide, and crocidolite accounts for the remaining 5%.

Chrysotile has a sheet-like silicate structure that makes it soft and flexible (Figure 25.2). Because of its softness, chrysotile is easily broken down in the body, and it produces no apparent damage. This form of asbestos, leached from the ground, is present in many reservoirs whose water is quite safe to drink. Recent medical evidence indicates that people who have been exposed for long periods to moderate amounts of chrysotile show no increase in lung ailments.

Crocidolite is a different story, however. This type of asbestos has a double-chain silicate structure (Figure 25.2). Its structure makes it strong and stiff, and thus more dangerous in the body. People exposed either to high levels of crocidolite for a short time or to moderate levels over a prolonged period of time have been found to develop lung disease. Thus it is crocidolite that is the principal culprit in asbestos-related lung diseases. Despite this knowledge, many reports on the health hazards of asbestos fail to make a distinction between the two types.

This failure to distinguish between harmless and dangerous asbestos has contributed to a public view that any asbestos mineral is fatal. The widely embraced and emotionally volatile premise that "one fiber can kill" has made asbestos one of the most feared contaminants on the earth. It is by far the most expensive pollutant in terms of regulation and removal. The removal of asbestos-containing materials from schools, hospitals, and other public buildings has cost billions of dollars over the past 20 years. But, since only a fraction of the asbestos in use today poses a health problem, many scientists question the practice of eliminating all forms. As with electricity in the 1800s, gasoline-powered vehicles in the early 1900s, and radioactivity in the late 1900s, public fears about asbestos will likely persist longer than the actual threat itself. Ultimately, however, we may view asbestos as both friend (chrysotile) and foe (crocidolite).

25.2 The Formation of Minerals

Minerals are formed by the process of **crystallization.** Crystallization is simply the formation and growth of a solid from a liquid or gas in which the atoms come together in specific chemical compositions and geometric arrangements. Crystallization starts with the formation of single microscopic crystals whose boundaries are flat planar surfaces called *crystal faces*. As more and more atoms bond to the microscopic crystal, the crystal grows. The geometry of crystals ranges from very simple to beautifully complex.

Crystallization starts in a liquid when its temperature drops below its freezing point. A familiar example is ice crystals that begin forming in water when the temperature drops below 0°C. Minerals commonly crystallize from two different sources—from **magma** (which is the molten rock from the earth's interior) and from water solutions. As we shall see in the following chapter, *igneous* rocks are formed from magma, and certain *sedimentary* rocks are formed from water solutions.

Crystallization in Magma

Magma consists primarily of the elements found in the silicate group of minerals—namely, silicon and oxygen, plus aluminum, potassium, sodium, calcium, iron and magnesium. When magma starts to cool, ions in the hot liquid lose kinetic energy. Then the attractive forces among them pull the ions into orderly crystalline structures. Minerals crystallize from magma in a systematic fashion, based upon their respective melting points. Just as ice melts at the same temperature at which water freezes, a mineral's melting point is the same temperature at which it begins to crystallize from magma.

The melting points of silicate minerals are strongly dependent on the amount of silicon they contain. Because silicon in nature is always bonded with oxygen, we use the percentage of *silica* (SiO_2) to measure the amount of silicon in a mineral. The melting point of a mineral is determined mostly by its percentage of silica. The first minerals to crystallize from a cooling magma have the highest melting point and the lowest percentage of silica. And, conversely, the last minerals to crystallize from a cooling magma have the lowest melting points but the highest percentage of silica (Figure 25.4). For example, quartz has a higher percentage of silica (in fact, it is pure silica!) than feldspar, so quartz crystallizes at lower temperatures than feldspar.

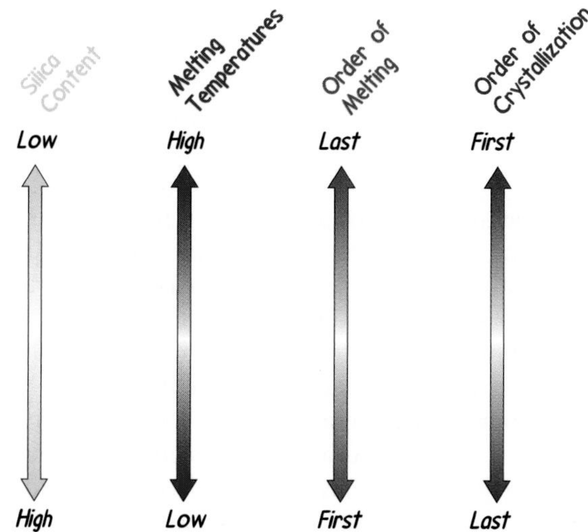

Figure 25.4
Minerals with a high silica content have low melting points. They are the first minerals to melt and the last minerals to crystallize. Minerals with a low silica content have high melting points. They are the last minerals to melt and the first minerals to crystallize.

Figuring Physical Science

Silica Enrichment in Magma

Magma becomes enriched in silica, SiO_2, as crystals such as olivine grow within it. We can express this in exact quantitative terms with a few calculations. Consider this example. Suppose we begin with 1000 kg of magma. Its temperature cools, and 325 kg of olivine crystallizes from it. Before crystallization began, the magma contained the following:

Oxide	Mass (kg)
SiO_2	500
FeO	100
MgO	100
Al_2O_3	150
CaO	100
Na_2O	30
K_2O	20

Before crystallization, the mass percentage of silica in the magma is:

$$\frac{500 \text{ kg silica}}{1000 \text{ kg magma}} \times 100\% = 50\%$$

The chemical formula of olivine is $MgFeSiO_4$. The elements needed to make these crystals within the magma, therefore, come from the MgO, FeO, and SiO_2 components. Specifically, olivine is made from one unit of MgO, plus one unit of FeO, plus one unit of SiO_2, which combine to make $MgFeSiO_4$.

To find the mass percentage of silica in olivine, divide the formula mass of silica (SiO_2), which is 60.0 amu by the formula mass of olivine, $MgFeSiO_4$, which is 172 amu.

The mass percentage of silica in olivine is:

$$\frac{60 \text{ amu}}{172 \text{ amu}} \times 100\% = 34.8\%$$

We can round this off to 35%.

Since we now know the mass percentage of silica in olivine, we can figure out how much silica was removed from the magma when 325 kg of olivine crystallized:

$$325 \text{ kg olivine} \times 0.35 = 114 \text{ kg silica}$$

Now that the olivine has crystallized, the mass percentage of silica in the remaining magma is less than 50%, but how much less? We have:

$$\begin{array}{l} 500 \text{ kg silica in the original magma} \\ -\ 114 \text{ kg silica in olivine} \\ \hline 386 \text{ kg silica in the remaining magma} \end{array}$$

The total mass of magma is different now, too:

$$\begin{array}{l} 1000 \text{ kg magma} \\ -\ 325 \text{ kg olivine} \\ \hline 675 \text{ kg magma} \end{array}$$

So the mass percentage of silica in the remaining magma is:

$$\frac{386 \text{ kg silica}}{675 \text{ kg magma}} \times 100\% = 57\%$$

So the magma has been *enriched* in silica. These concepts are revisited in Problems 1, 2, and 3 at the end of the chapter.

In general, as minerals crystallize in a cooling magma, they settle out from the liquid portion of the magma. Also, some of the remaining liquid can escape from the region where crystallization first occurred. The result is that newly formed crystals become separated from the molten liquid. So, as crystallization proceeds, the composition of the molten liquid changes continuously. It becomes *depleted* in the constituents of minerals that have already crystallized and *enriched* in the constituents of minerals that have yet to crystallize.

The process of crystallization in a cooling magma is actually quite simple. Consider an analogy. Suppose you have all the pieces for a game of checkers—12 red pieces and 12 black ones. All 24 pieces are mixed together to form a single group. So the group as a whole consists of 50% red pieces and 50%

black pieces. Now suppose 3 red and 2 black pieces are removed. There are now 9 red and 10 black pieces remaining from the original group, so the mixture is now roughly 47% red and 53% black. Thus, the large group has become depleted in red and enriched in black. Its composition has changed. Can you now see that the crystallization process acts to enrich magma in silica? The crystallization process allows a single magma to generate several different types of igneous minerals and rock.

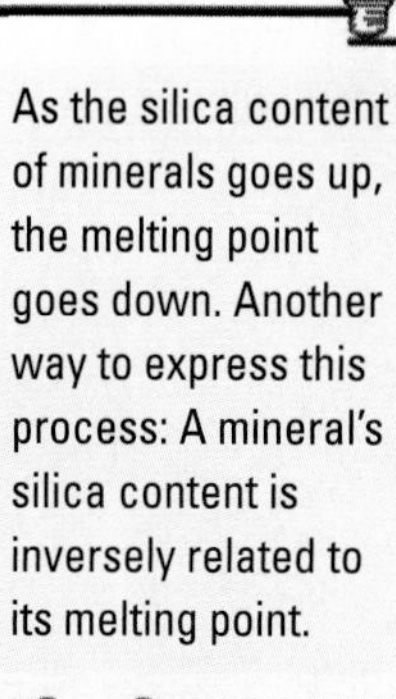

As the silica content of minerals goes up, the melting point goes down. Another way to express this process: A mineral's silica content is inversely related to its melting point.

Insights

Crystallization in Water Solutions

As previously mentioned, crystallization doesn't just happen in magma. It also occurs in water solutions. Often, hydrothermal activity—the circulation of very hot water solutions—occurs in the later stages of crystallization from magmas. While minerals and rock form from magma crystallization, water solutions derived from the magma can circulate through cracks in the newly formed rock. These solutions usually contain many dissolved mineral constituents. Decreasing temperature in the still-hot waters causes the solutions to become chemically saturated, allowing minerals to precipitate. Depending on the composition of the solution, different minerals precipitate and are deposited in the cracks. Sometimes the minerals are deposited within the rock matrix itself. Many of the important ore deposits we find today were formed in this manner.

As with hydrothermal minerals, **chemical sediments** are formed by the precipitation of mineral constituents from water solutions. But chemical sediments form where temperatures are much cooler than the earth's interior, such as in a body of water on the surface of the earth. Chemical sediments fall into two categories: *carbonates* and *evaporites*.

Figure 25.5
Chemical sediments:
(a) calcite, (b) dolomite,
(c) gypsum, (d) and halite.

Figure 25.6
Calcium carbonate precipitating from dripping water in a cave forms icicle-shaped stalactites that hang from the ceiling and cone-shaped stalagmites that protrude upward from the floor.

Carbonates are minerals and rocks that contain the carbonate ion, CO_3^{2-}. Not all carbonates are formed by precipitation directly from a water solution, however. Some carbonates formed as a result of biologic activity. Many living marine organisms grow hard, protective shells from calcium ions and carbonate ions present in seawater. The shells eventually recrystallize to become calcite. This is how limestone, the most abundant carbonate rock, is generally formed. Here's how it works: When organisms with calcium carbonate shells die, their shells accumulate on the sea floor. The shells begin to dissolve, forming a non-crystalline *ooze* of calcium carbonate. This ooze eventually crystallizes into calcite, which forms limestone. Due to compaction, and because calcium carbonate dissolves easily, the original textures and structures of the seashells are often obliterated. Dolomite forms when magnesium chemically replaces some of the calcium.

Some carbonates form without the aid of organisms. Cave dripstones, such as stalactites and stalagmites, provide an interesting example of calcium carbonate precipitating inorganically from dripping water (Figure 25.6). Some limestones also form by inorganic mineral precipitation.

Evaporites are minerals and rocks that are precipitated when a restricted body of seawater, or the water of a salty lake, evaporates. Examples are gypsum, anhydrite, and halite. These names apply both to individual minerals and to rocks made of a single type of evaporite mineral.

Evaporites precipitate out of water solutions in a way that is very similar to the crystallization of minerals from magma. The difference, though, is that solubility rather than melting point determines which minerals form first. Evaporite minerals with the lowest solubility—such as gypsum—precipitate first from water solutions. The low-solubility minerals are followed by minerals that dissolve more easily, such as anhydrite and then halite. Although carbonates make up the bulk of chemical sediments, evaporites comprise just a small but important group.

Hot springs produce hot water that contains various chemicals in solution. When that hot water cools in the open air at the earth's surface, the solution becomes supersaturated. As a result, various types of minerals precipitate, forming the white mineral deposits characteristic of hot springs.

25.3 Mineral Properties

A mineral's observable physical properties depend on its inner microscopic properties. Such microscopic properties as composition, crystal structure, and the strength of chemical bonds determine a mineral's crystal form, hardness, cleavage, color, and specific gravity. Most minerals can be identified by these easily observable physical properties. Other physical properties used to identify minerals are *luster* (the way a mineral reflects light) and *streak* (the color of a mineral in its powdered form). In this section, we discuss the physical properties of minerals as expressions of their inner structures.

Crystal Form

Have you ever seen a halite (table salt) crystal under a magnifying glass? If so, you may have marveled at its perfect geometric form (Figure 25.7). Crystals are well known for the striking geometric shapes that they can exhibit. A crystal's shape, or its **crystal form,** is an expression of the orderly arrangement of its atoms. When you look at a crystal, you are seeing the actual arrangement of atoms in its structure.

Every mineral has its own unique crystal form. In the mineral pyrite (fool's gold), for example, you can see its intergrown cubes. When you look at quartz you can see six-sided prisms that end in a point (Figure 25.8). Asbestos minerals often look like narrow, threadlike fibers. The mineral hematite often has a globular form that resembles a bunch of grapes (Figure 25.9). Unfortunately, well-shaped crystals are rare in nature due to space constraints. Most crystals grow in cramped spaces.

Just as the six sides of a snowflake can reveal the hexagonal pattern of ice crystals, looking closely at mineral crystals can reveal the mineral's arrangement of atoms.

Insights

Figure 25.7
The cubic structure of the mineral halite (common table salt) as seen through a microscope. The cubic shape is a consequence of the cubic arrangement of sodium and chloride ions.

(a)

(b)

Figure 25.8
The unique crystal form exhibited in each mineral is the external expression of the mineral's internal arrangement of atoms. (a) The intergrown cubes of pyrite. (b) The six-sided prisms of quartz.

(a)

(b)

Figure 25.9
Well-shaped crystals do not develop when crystal growth occurs in a confined space. Nevertheless, the distinctive growth patterns of many minerals are apparent. (a) The narrow, threadlike fibers of the asbestos group minerals. (b) The grape-cluster shape of the mineral hematite.

Sometimes, two or more minerals contain the same elements in the same proportions, but their atoms are arranged differently. As a result, their crystalline structure and properties are different. Such minerals are called **polymorphs** of each other. Graphite and diamond are polymorphs because they both consist entirely of the same element, carbon. But the carbon atoms are arranged differently. As a result, graphite and diamond show vastly different properties (Figure 25.10). Because the formation of these similar-yet-different minerals depends on temperature and pressure, a polymorph is a good indicator of the geological conditions at the time and place of its formation.

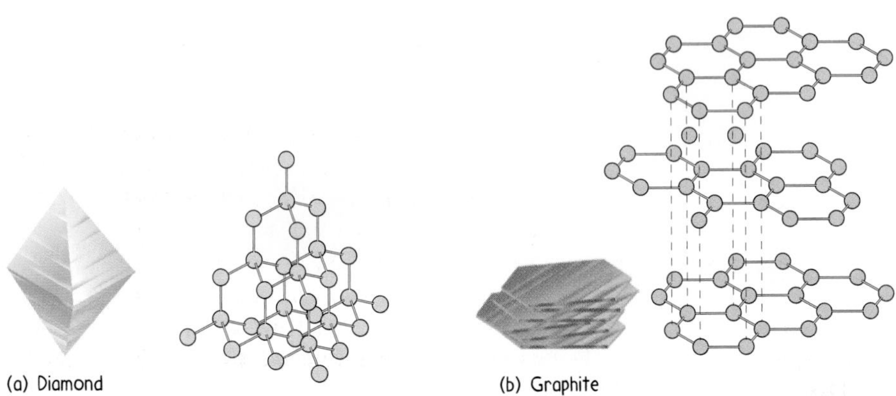

Figure 25.10
Both graphite and diamond are pure carbon. (a) Diamond, the hardest substance known, has a tightly packed, symmetrical structure. (b) Graphite has an open, layered structure. When graphite is rubbed between your fingers, individual graphite molecules glide over one another like cards in a stack, giving it a slippery feel. This slippery effect is why graphite is used as a lubricant. Graphite also glides easily when it is stroked onto paper, where it leaves a mark. Hence its use in pencils. (Graphite is also much less toxic than lead.)

☑ CHECKPOINT

Many minerals can be identified by their physical properties—crystal form, hardness, cleavage, luster, color, streak, and specific gravity. Why is identifying a mineral by its crystal form usually difficult?

Check Your Answer

Well-shaped crystals occur only rarely in nature because minerals typically grow in cramped spaces.

Hardness

Diamond is one of the minerals that can scratch glass. Diamond can do this because it is harder than glass. Similarly, a quartz crystal can scratch a feldspar crystal because quartz is harder than feldspar. The ability of one mineral to scratch another and the resistance of a mineral to being scratched are measures of hardness. We use the **Mohs scale of hardness** (Table 25.2) to compare the hardness of different minerals.

Why are some minerals harder than others? Hardness depends on the strength of a mineral's chemical bonds—the stronger its bonds, the harder the

Table 25.2

Mohs Scale of Hardness

Mineral	Scale Number	Common Objects with Similar Hardnesses
Diamond	10	
Corundum	9	
Topaz	8	
Quartz	7	Steel file
Feldspar	6	Window glass
Apatite	5	Pocket knife
Fluorite	4	
Calcite	3	Copper wire or coin
Gypsum	2	Fingernail
Talc	1	

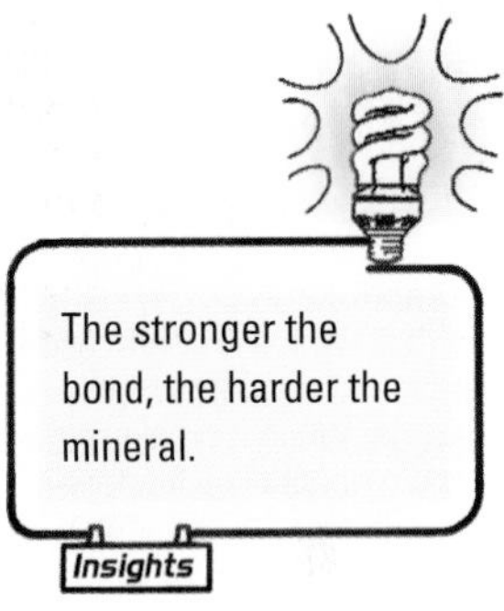

mineral. The factors that influence bond strength are ionic charge, atom (or ion) size, and packing. Each of these factors affects the bond strengths of a mineral and, therefore, its hardness.

Strong bonds are generally found between highly charged ions—the greater the attraction, the stronger the bond. Size affects bond strength as well, because small atoms and ions can generally pack closer together than large atoms and ions. Closely packed atoms and ions have a smaller distance between one another, and thus they form stronger bonds because they attract one another with more force. Gold, with its large atoms, is soft. Its atoms are rather loosely packed and loosely bonded. Diamond, with its small carbon atoms and tightly packed structure, is very hard.

Cleavage and Fracture

If you shatter a sample of the mineral calcite with a hammer, it will tend to break along its *planes of weakness*. These are planes along which chemical bonds are weak or few in number. We refer to the property of a mineral to break along planes of weakness as **cleavage.** Planes of weakness are determined by crystal structure and chemical bond strength.

Some minerals show a greater tendency toward cleavage than others. In general, minerals that have strong bonds between flat (planar) crystal surfaces show poor cleavage, while those with weak bonds along planar surfaces show more developed cleavage. Because the silicon–oxygen bond is strong, silicate minerals tend to cleave between the silicon–oxygen structures rather than across them. For example, muscovite, a sheet-structured silicate, has perfect cleavage in one direction. It breaks apart to form thin, flat sheets (Figures 25.2 and 25.11a). Similarly, in the carbonate mineral calcite, the carbonate ion bond is stronger than the bond between the carbonate ion and the calcium ion. With a layered sheet-like structure and weak bonds between the different layers, calcite has perfect cleavage in three directions. It breaks to produce rhombohedral faces that intersect at 75° angles (Figure 25.3b and 25.11b). In contrast, garnet, whose silicate crystal structure has strong bonds in all directions, shows no cleavage.

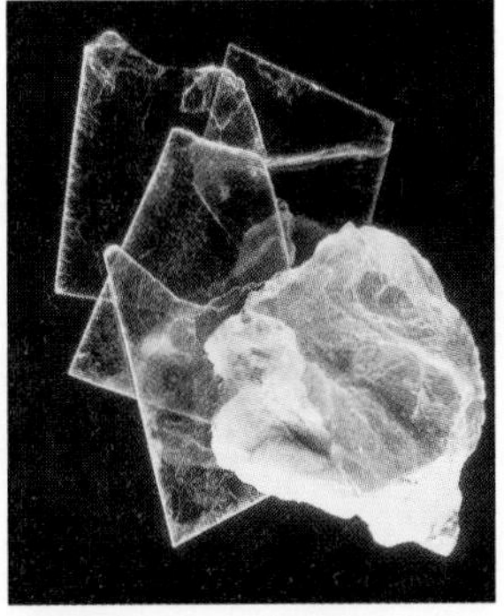
(a)

(b)

Figure 25.11
A mineral's cleavage is very useful in its identification. (a) Muscovite (a mineral of the mica group) has perfect cleavage in one direction. (b) Calcite meanwhile, has perfect cleavage in three directions.

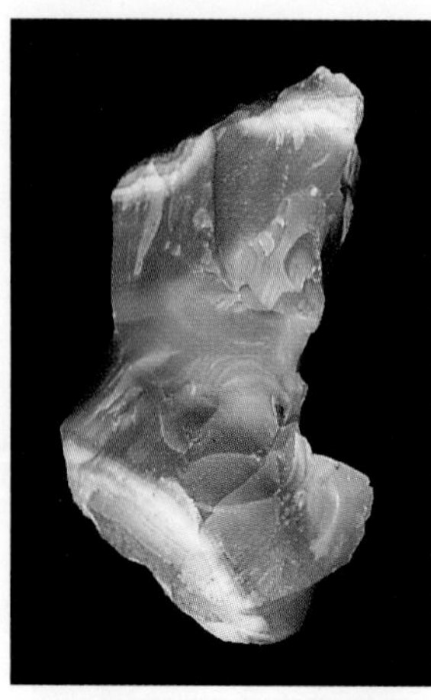

Figure 25.12
This rock, which is composed of quartz, does not exhibit cleavage. When it breaks, it develops a conchoidal fracture—a curved, smooth surface resembling broken glass.

When a mineral with no cleavage breaks, the break is called a **fracture.** A fracture that is smooth and curved, so that it resembles broken glass, is called *conchoidal.* Quartz and olivine display smooth conchoidal fractures. Some minerals, such as hematite and serpentine, break into splinters or fibers. But most minerals fracture irregularly. The degree and type of cleavage or fracture are useful guides for identifying minerals.

☑ CHECKPOINT

1. When pieces of calcite and fluorite are scraped together, which scratches which?
2. The minerals muscovite and calcite display very distinct cleavage, yet the mineral quartz fractures. How does this relate to their crystal structure?

Check Your Answers

1. Looking at Table 25.2, we can see that fluorite is harder than calcite. So fluorite scratches calcite.
2. Calcite and muscovite both form as layered, sheet-like structures. The bonding between the different layers is weaker than the bonds within the individual layers. Therefore, these minerals will cleave between the layers. Quartz has a three-dimensional network structure; it is a more complicated structure with no layering. Therefore, quartz fractures.

Color

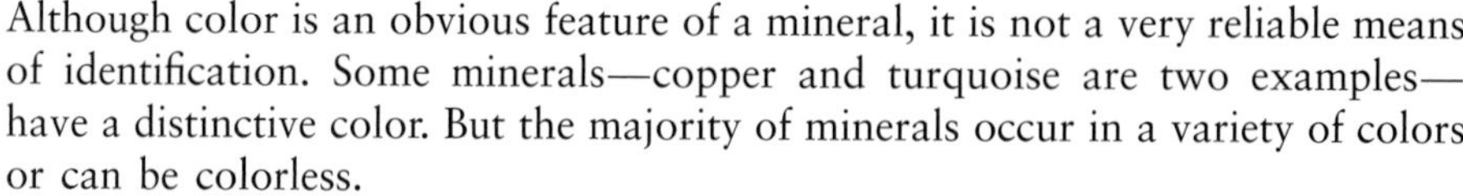

Although color is an obvious feature of a mineral, it is not a very reliable means of identification. Some minerals—copper and turquoise are two examples—have a distinctive color. But the majority of minerals occur in a variety of colors or can be colorless.

Chemical impurities in a mineral affect color. For example, the common mineral quartz, SiO_2, can be found in many colors, depending on slight impurities. It can be clear and colorless if it has no impurities. It can be milky white from tiny fluid inclusions. Rose-colored quartz results from small amounts of titanium, violet quartz (amethyst) results from small amounts of iron, and smoky-gray to black quartz results from radiation damage. The color of the mineral corundum, Al_2O_3, is commonly white or grayish. But impurities in corundum give us rubies and sapphires.

Specific Gravity

Density is a property of all forms of matter, minerals included. In practical terms, the density of a mineral tells us how heavy a mineral feels for its size. One standard measure of density is **specific gravity**—the ratio of the weight of a substance to the weight of an equal volume of water. For example, if 1 cubic centimeter of a mineral weighs three times as much as 1 cubic centimeter of water, its specific gravity is 3. So we can see that specific gravity is simply a ratio of densities. The specific gravities of some minerals are shown in Table 25.3.

The specific gravity of a mineral is determined by a number of factors, including the masses of a mineral's constituent atoms and how well these atoms pack together, which is often a function of the sizes of these atoms. Gold's particularly high specific gravity of 19.3 is nicely taken advantage of by miners panning for gold. Fine gold pieces hidden in a mixture of mud and sand settle to the bottom of the pan when the mixture is swirled in water. Water and less dense materials spill out when the mixture is swirled. After a succession of dousings and swirls, only the substance with the highest specific gravity remains—gold!

Table 25.3

Specific Gravity of Various Minerals

Borax	1.7	Pyrite	5.0
Quartz	2.65	Hematite	5.26
Talc	2.8	Copper	8.9
Mica	3.0	Silver	10.5
Chromite	4.6	Gold	19.3

☑ CHECKPOINT

Why are there no units for specific gravity?

Check Your Answer

Remember, specific gravity is a ratio of densities. Density units divided by density units cancel out. For example, the density of the mineral hematite, Fe_2O_3, is 5.26 g/cm^3, and that of water is 1.0 g/cm^3. Therefore the specific gravity of hematite is (5.26 g/cm^3) ÷ (1.0 g/cm^3) = 5.26.

Figure 25.13
The mineral corundum (Al_2O_3) comes in a variety of colors as a result of chemical impurities. The addition of small amounts of chromium in place of some of the aluminum produces the red gemstone *ruby,* and, with the addition of small amounts of iron and titanium, the result is the blue gemstone *sapphire.*

25.4 Mineral Uses

We have seen what minerals are and the different ways that minerals form, but how do minerals affect our daily lives? Well, first of all, just about everything we use in our daily life comes from the ground. Metallic mineral deposits are the source of the metals we use. Nonmetallic mineral deposits provide salt, clay, gravel, building stone, the limestone from which cement is made, the sand from which glass is made, and many other important products. With so many uses, minerals are a major economic resource.

A few mineral substances can be used just as they are found in the ground. For example, common salt, sand, and gravel don't require special processing to make them useful. Most minerals, however, need some sort of processing before they can be used.

Some mineral resources are readily found—they are abundant. They are either very common throughout the earth's crust or they are less common but can be found in high concentrations in certain places. Other mineral resources are scarce.

Minerals are used in innumerable ways. Modern technology depends on them. Recall that ores are mineral deposits from which valuable metals may be recovered profitably. And other mineral deposits, although they may not be ore

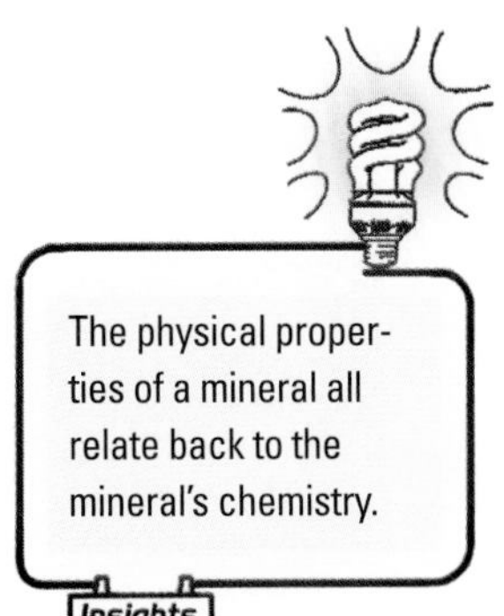

deposits, are important in industry as well. Metallic ores and industrial minerals are mined on every continent. They are mined wherever they are sufficiently concentrated to be economically extracted.

To get a better understanding of mineral usage, let us divide the principal economic minerals into two broad groups: (1) metals—minerals from which metals such as iron, copper, and gold can be recovered; and (2) nonmetals—such minerals as salt, gypsum, and clay, which are used not for the metal they contain but for other chemical properties they possess. These two groups can be further subdivided, as Table 25.4 shows.

Metals

A metal is considered to be abundant if it makes up more than 0.1 percent by weight of the earth's crust. Most of the abundant metals are found in common rock-forming minerals, particularly the oxide and hydroxide minerals. The abundant metals include iron, aluminum, manganese, magnesium, and titanium. The size and number of these ore deposits is so great that we can consider their supplies to be virtually inexhaustible.

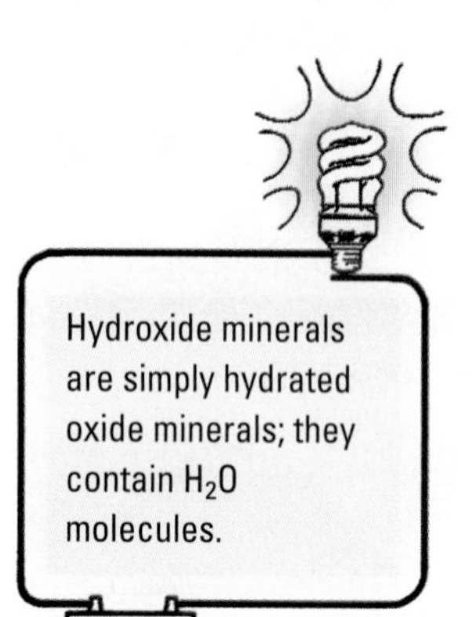

Hydroxide minerals are simply hydrated oxide minerals; they contain H_2O molecules.

Insights

Metals that make up less than 0.1 percent by weight of the earth's crust are considered to be scarce. With the exception of copper, zinc, and chromium, scarce metals are rare in rock-forming minerals. When they do occur in rock-forming minerals, scarce metals do so by *atomic substitution*—ions with similar chemical properties and ions of similar sizes tend to substitute for one another. For example, scarce metallic atoms, such as nickel and cobalt, can readily substitute for more common metallic atoms, such as magnesium and calcium.

Nonmetals

There are many uses for the different nonmetallic substances. Probably the most familiar application is construction materials. Some construction materials can be used just as they come from the ground, such as cut stone, crushed stone, sand, and gravel. Others require a bit of processing—for example; shale and limestone (to make cement), gypsum (used for plaster), clay (used for tile and brick), and asbestos (used for wallboards and insulation).

Other commonly used nonmetallic substances are ceramic and abrasive materials. Ceramic materials have a wide range of uses—as raw materials for making common glass and pottery and as the ingredients for making such exotic materials as the refractory tiles used in coating the hulls of spacecraft. Ceramics are made from certain kinds of clays, and from feldspar and quartz. Abrasive materials are used in industry to grind, shape, and polish machine parts. The principal abrasive materials include such common rock-forming minerals as quartz and garnet and rarer minerals, such as corundum and diamond. Although rare in their natural form, corundum and diamond can be readily produced synthetically.

Another very important use of nonmetallic mineral substances is for fertilizer. As plants draw the chemical elements they need from the soil, those elements are depleted from the soil. To replenish the soil, fertilizer is used. There are three essential elements for fertilizer: (1) nitrogen, recovered from the atmosphere; (2) potassium, recovered from the mineral sylvite (KCl) in marine evaporites; and (3) phosphorus, recovered from apatite $[Ca_5(PO_4)_3(OH,F)]$ in marine sediments.

Table 25.4

Economic Mineral Deposits

Mineral Deposit	Typical Minerals	Uses	Major Deposits
Abundant Metals			
Iron	Hematite, Fe_2O_3 Magnetite, Fe_3O_4	Manufactured materials, construction	Minnesota, Pennsylvania, Sweden
Aluminum	Gibbsite, $Al(OH_3)$ Diaspore, $AlO(OH)$	Bauxite	Jamaica
Magnesium	Dolomite, $CaMg(CO_3)_2$ Magnesite, $MgCO_3$	Alloy metal, insulators, chemical raw material	Extracted from seawater
Titanium	Ilmenite, $FeTiO_3$ Rutile, TiO_2	High temperature alloys, paint pigment	Quebec, India
Chromium	Chromite, $(Mg,Fe)_2CrO_4$	Steel alloys	Bushveldt, S. Africa
Manganese	Pyrolusite, MnO_2	Steelmaking	Ukraine; seafloor resources immense
Scarce Metals			
Copper	Covelite, CuS Chalcocite, Cu_2S	Electrical wire, etc.	Utah, Arizona, Germany, Poland
Lead	Galena, PbS	Storage batteries, gasoline additive	Mississippi, Australia
Zinc	Sphalerite, ZnS	Alloy metal	Mississippi, Australia
Nickel	Pentlandite, $(Ni,Fe)_9S_8$ Garnierite, $Ni_3Si_2O_5(OH)$	Alloy metal	Sudbury, Ontario
Silver	Argentite, Ag_2S	Photographic chemicals, electrical equipment	By-product of copper, lead, and zinc recovery
Mercury	Cinnabar, HgS	Electrical equipment, pharmaceuticals	Almaden, Spain
Platinum	Native metal, Pt	Chemical and electrical industry, alloying metal	Bushveldt, S. Africa
Gold	Native metal, Au	Coinage, dentistry, jewelry	Witwatersrand, S. Africa
Nonmetals			
Salt	Halite, $NaCl$	Food, chemicals	Resources unlimited
Phosphate	Apatite, $Ca_5(PO_4)_3OH$	Fertilizer	Florida
Sulfur	Native sulfur, S	Fertilizer, chemical industry	Texas, Louisiana, Sicily
Potassium	Sylvite, KCl	Fertilizer	New Mexico
Diamond	Diamond, C	Industrial abrasives	Kimberly, S. Africa
Gypsum	Gypsum, $CaSO_4{\cdot}2H_2O$ Anhydrite, $CaSO_4$	Plaster	Resources immense
Limestone	Calcite, $CaCO_3$ Dolomite, $CaMg(CO_3)_2$	Building stone, cement, agricultural lime	Widely distributed
Clay	Kaolinite, $Al_2Si_2O_5(OH)_4$	Ceramics: china Electrical: structural tile	Resources immense
Asbestos	Chrysotile, $Mg_3Si_2O_5(OH)_4$	Nonflammable fibers and products	Southeastern Quebec

Earth's Resources Are Not Unlimited

Although our Earth has many resources, they are not unlimited. This is especially true for the scarce metals. By definition, the scarce metals are a limited resource. Once they are depleted, they are gone. The abundant metals, coming from common rock-forming minerals, are (as the name implies) abundant. The problem is not a shortage of abundant metals, but, rather, a shortage of ores from which these metals can be extracted at a *reasonable* cost. High-grade ores, meaning those containing relatively high concentrations of metals, are the first to be consumed. After these are depleted, we must move on to the lower-grade ores, which have lower yields, and this translates into greater costs. As for the nonmetallic resources, most are plentiful on a worldwide basis. Problems occur when supplies of these resources are beset by geographic restriction and high transportation and processing costs. Eventually, mineral resources within a particular region can become depleted, forcing the people of that region to import resources from other areas. But this isn't always easy. The cost of transporting and processing imported resources may be too great to make it economically feasible.

As the world's population grows, so does its demand for mineral resources. For the most abundant resources, the demand will most likely be met, at least for the foreseeable future. For scarcer resources, demand will exceed supply. In all cases, it is important that we conserve our resources. Eventually, there comes a point when it is far cheaper to extract certain elements from discarded manufactured goods than it is to extract them from mineral deposits. Conservation and recycling will make our natural resources last longer.

25.5 Minerals—the Link to Rocks

Now that we know what minerals are and understand the different ways in which they form, we can begin to learn about the combinations of minerals called *rocks*. As we shall see, the minerals formed from the crystallization of magma are igneous rocks. Minerals formed by precipitation from hot-water solutions are constituents of some igneous rocks. Minerals formed by precipitation from, and evaporation of, surface water are sedimentary rocks. We shall also see that igneous rocks can break down to form sedimentary rocks. And a third rock type—metamorphic rock—is also formed from the modification of previously existing rocks. The minerals, in their many forms, are indeed the building blocks of the many different rocks that constitute the solid portions of the earth.

Summary of Terms

Mineral A naturally formed, inorganic solid composed of an ordered array of atoms chemically bonded to form a particular crystalline structure.

Ore A mineral deposit containing valuable metals that can be economically extracted from the ground to yield a profit.

Crystallization The growth of a solid from a material whose constituent atoms can come together in the proper chemical proportions and geometric arrangements.

Magma Molten rock in the earth's interior.

Chemical sediments Formed by the precipitation of minerals from water on the earth's surface.

Crystal form The outward expression of the orderly internal arrangement of atoms in a crystal.

Polymorphs Two or more minerals that contain the same elements in the same proportions but have different crystal structures.

Mohs scale of hardness A ranking of the hardness of minerals.

Cleavage The tendency of a mineral to break along planes of weakness.

Fracture A break that does not occur along a plane of weakness.

Specific gravity The ratio between the weight of a substance and the weight of an equal volume of water.

Review Questions

25.1 Structure and Distribution of Rock-Forming Minerals

1. What is a mineral?
2. What is the most abundant element in the earth's crust? What is the second most abundant element?
3. What is the most abundant mineral in the earth's crust? What is the second most abundant mineral?
4. Name the five most common rock-forming mineral groups.
5. What is an ore?
6. What is an industrial mineral? Give an example.
7. What are the two most common carbonate minerals?
8. In what ways are the basic carbonate structure and the basic silicate structure similar? In what ways are they different?
9. Which mineral group do the asbestos minerals belong to?
10. The use of asbestos minerals goes back to the time of Aristotle. Name two qualities that have made asbestos so widely used.

25.2 The Formation of Minerals

11. What is the process of crystallization?
12. Briefly describe two sources from which minerals crystallize.
13. As minerals crystallize in a cooling magma, which minerals are the first to crystallize—the minerals with lower percentages of silica, or the minerals with higher percentages of silica?
14. Compare quartz with feldspar. Which of these two minerals will crystallize later than the other? Why?
15. Which of these is a true statement about silicate minerals? (a) Melting point decreases as silica percentage increases. (b) Melting point increases as silica percentage increases.
16. What are three common chemical sediments?
17. When water evaporates from a body of water, what type of sediment is left behind?
18. What is the most common type of chemical sediment?
19. What is the most abundant carbonate rock?
20. How are most of the carbonate minerals and rocks formed?

25.3 Mineral Properties

21. What physical properties are used in the identification of minerals?
22. All minerals are defined by their orderly internal arrangement of their atoms—their crystal forms. Yet, most mineral samples do not display their crystal forms. Why not?
23. The factors that influence bond strength influence mineral hardness. What are these factors?
24. Will topaz scratch quartz, or will quartz scratch topaz? Why?
25. A mineral will cleave (break) along its planes of weakness. What two factors determine a mineral's cleavage?
26. Why does calcite show such distinct cleavage?
27. Although color is an obvious feature of a mineral, it is not a very reliable means of identification. Why not?
28. Silver has a density of 10.5 g/cm^3. What is its specific gravity?
29. What is the relationship of density to specific gravity?

25.4 Mineral Uses

30. Name three minerals that can be used just as they are found in the ground.
31. If we look at the periodic table of elements, we can see that the majority of elements are metallic. As such, most minerals are composed of metallic elements. Why, then, are economic minerals divided into two groups—metals and nonmetals?
32. What are the five most abundant metallic minerals?
33. What is meant by atomic substitution?
34. What are the nonmetals most commonly used for?
35. If abundant metallic minerals are in such great supply, why then do we need to conserve them?

Activity

Look at some crystals of table salt under a microscope or a magnifying glass and observe their generally cubic shapes. There's no machine at the salt factory specifically designed to give salt crystals these cubic shapes, as opposed to round or triangular ones. The cubic shape occurs naturally and is a reflection of how the atoms of salt are organized—cubically. Smash a few of these salt cubes and then look at them again carefully. What you'll see are smaller salt cubes! Use the cleavage properties of crystals to explain these results.

Exercises

1. Describe the difference between a mineral and an element.
2. What do we call minerals that have the same combination of elements but a different arrangement of those elements?
3. What is the difference between the minerals that make up a rock and the minerals we find in common dietary supplements?

4. Look at the periodic table of the elements and you will see that the majority of elements are metallic. Does this mean that most minerals are metallic? Defend your answer.
5. Silicon is essential for the computer industry in making microchips. Can silicon be mined directly from the earth? Defend your answer.
6. What two minerals make up most of the sand in the world?
7. What mineral group provides most of the ore that we, as a society, need?
8. To what class of minerals does galena (PbS) belong?
9. To what class of minerals does anglesite ($PbSO_4$) belong?
10. Why is asbestos in drinking water not particularly harmful to humans, whereas asbestos particles in air may be very harmful?
11. Make an argument that the removal of such asbestos products as ceiling tile and pipe coverings may be more hazardous to humans than simply covering them up.
12. If a rock contains mineral A and mineral B, which would melt first—mineral A with 30% silica, or mineral B with 25% silica?
13. If a magma contains molten forms of mineral A and mineral B, which would crystallize first—mineral A with 30% silica, or mineral B with 25% silica?
14. If a magma contains molten forms of mineral A and mineral B, which would crystallize last—mineral A with 30% silica, or mineral B with 25% silica?
15. If a rock contains mineral A and mineral B, which would melt last—mineral A with 30% silica, or mineral B with 25% silica?
16. Is it possible for crystallization to enrich a magma in more than just silica? Defend your answer.
17. If high-silica magma is the last to cool, why aren't high-silica rocks the last to melt?
18. Why is halite commonly the last mineral to precipitate from evaporating seawater?
19. Would you expect to find any fossils in limestone? Why or why not?
20. How do chemical sediments produce rock? Name two rock types that form by chemical sedimentation.
21. What is a polymorph?
22. Why is color not always the best way to identify a mineral?
23. While you are out hiking in the wilderness, you find a shiny, glassy-looking mineral. What physical test could you use to determine if this mineral is a diamond?
24. What makes gold so soft (easily scratched) while quartz and diamond are so much harder?
25. Imagine that we have a liquid with a specific gravity of 3.5. Knowing that objects of higher specific gravity will sink in the liquid, will a piece of quartz sink or float in the liquid? How about a piece of chromite?
26. Explain why color is not a reliable means for mineral identification. Give an example.
27. Is cleavage the same as crystal form? Why or why not?
28. What might cause a mineral deposit that previously had not been considered an ore to be reclassified as an ore?
29. Name one ore each of lead, of iron, and of copper.
30. The earth's mineral resources are used in many ways. Many of these resources are plentiful, but they are also nonrenewable. Once extracted and used, they do not grow back. What are some possible problems with extracting and using such nonrenewable resources?

Problems

Refer to "Figuring Physical Science: Silica Enrichment in Magma" on page 620 in solving problems 1 through 3.

1. What are the mass percentages of the oxides MgO, FeO, and SiO_2 in pyroxene, $MgFeSi_2O_6$? Give your answers in whole numbers. Hint: Express the formula for pyroxene as a sum of its constituent oxides.
2. How many kilograms of silica are in 225 kg of pyroxene?
3. If 325 kg of olivine and 225 kg of pyroxene have crystallized out of the 1000 kg of magma, what is the mass percentage of silica in the remaining liquid?
4. Gold has a specific gravity of 19.3. A five-gallon pail of water weighs about 40 pounds. How much would a five-gallon pail of gold weigh?

Chapter 25 Online Resources

Quiz
Exercises
Flashcards
Links

CHAPTER 26

Rocks

Rocks are all around us. Wherever we go, we encounter rocks. Whether we are hiking in the mountains, running on the beach, or even strolling down a busy city street—rocks are everywhere. In Chapter 25, we learned about minerals and how each mineral has a unique chemical composition and a unique atomic structure. We learned that minerals are the building blocks of rocks. Rocks are aggregates of minerals that also share common traits. Groupings of rocks are based on how they formed. Each group tells its own part of the story of how earth evolved. The earth is a gigantic recycling plant that continually converts old rock into new. Every cycle reveals its own chapter in earth's history.

26.1 Rock Types

Why study rocks? One reason is that rocks provide clues to the earth's past. If we know how to "read" them, rocks tell us about the processes that have shaped our planet. The earth is not static but is instead continually breaking down, rebuilding, and rearranging itself. As land and rock are formed in one area, they are broken down in another. These processes of change are summed up in the theory of *plate tectonics,* which tells us that the earth's surface is broken into several large, rigid plates. These plates shift because of very slow movements in the earth's interior. The boundaries of these rigid plates are places of intense geological activity. Earthquakes, volcanoes, and young mountain ranges all tend to be concentrated along the edges of plates. For this reason, plate boundaries are where many rocks are created, changed, or destroyed. There will be more about plate tectonics in Chapter 27.

The rocks of the earth are classified into three types according to origin: *igneous, sedimentary,* and *metamorphic.*

Figure 26.1
The three main types of rock. (a) Basalt and granite are igneous rocks. (b) Sandstone and limestone are sedimentary rocks. (c) Marble and slate are metamorphic rocks.

Igneous rocks are formed by the cooling and crystallization of hot, molten rock—magma. The word *igneous* means "formed by fire." Igneous rocks make up about 95 percent of the earth's crust. Basalt and granite are common igneous rocks.

Sedimentary rocks are formed from pieces of other rocks (sediments) carried by water, wind, or ice. Sedimentary rocks are easy to find on the ground beneath our feet—the uppermost portion of earth's crust. In fact, sedimentary rocks cover more than two-thirds of the earth's surface. Sandstone, shale, and limestone are common sedimentary rocks.

Metamorphic rocks are formed from older, preexisting rocks (igneous, sedimentary, or metamorphic) that are transformed by high temperature, high pressure, or both—without melting. The word *metamorphic* means "changed in form." Marble and slate are common metamorphic rocks.

26.2 Igneous Rocks

The earth's crust consists primarily of different kinds of igneous rock. On the continents, the most common igneous rocks are granite and andesite. On the ocean floor, basalt is the most common kind of rock. All igneous rock originated as magma.

Generation of Magma

We learned, in Section 25.2, that many minerals form from cooling magma. But where does magma come from? Do we have magma because the interior of the earth is molten? The answer is *no,* as we will see in Chapter 27. Most of the earth's interior is actually solid, not molten, and magma is derived from rocks that have melted. Just as water cools to form ice, magma cools and solidifies to form the minerals that eventually become rock.

Temperatures recorded in mines and drill holes indicate that the earth's temperature increases with depth. Although the rate of increase varies from place to place, on average it increases about 30°C for each kilometer of depth (Figure 26.2). But this increasing temperature is not enough to cause rocks to melt, even though the temperature at sufficient depth is actually much hotter than that of magma.

If the temperature at depth is hotter than magma, why are the rocks at depth solid? The answer can be found by using water as an analogy. Recall (from Section 8.8) that a change of phase occurs when water is heated to the boiling point. We know that water boils at 100°C at sea level. If we increase the pressure, the temperature needs to be higher for boiling to occur. This is illustrated in Figure 8.32. In other words, phase changes depend on pressure as well as on temperature. When rocks melt, this is of course a phase change. The hot rocks at depth are under enormous pressure from the weight of the rock above—enough pressure to prevent melting.

But rocks *do* sometimes melt to form magma, and there are three reasons why. The dominant reason, in terms of the amount of magma produced, is that rocks actually rise up from depth, which reduces the pressure on them enough to induce melting. Another mechanism is the addition of water to rock. Using the analogy of water again, a "foreign" substance lowers the freezing point—or, conversely, lowers the melting point—of water. This is explained in Section 8.9. In the case of rock, water is the foreign substance that lowers the melting point of rock—enough to cause melting. These two magma-generating mechanisms produce magma that rises upward, sometimes through preexisting rock. This gives us a third mechanism—namely, that rock can melt when it has been heated by magma rising from depth. We will explore the first two mechanisms in more detail in Chapter 27, where we can link them to the model of plate tectonics. For now, we will restrict our discussion to the general formation of magma from melting rock.

Temperature (°C)
0 200 400 600 800 1000
Depth (km)
0 10 20 30 40 50
Geothermal gradient
Melting starts

Figure 26.2
The temperature inside the earth increases about 30°C for each kilometer of depth from the surface. This increase of temperature with depth is known as the *geothermal gradient.*

Keep in mind that rock is usually composed of many different minerals. As rock is heated, the first minerals to melt are those with the lowest melting points. Therefore, the melting of rock into magma occurs over a broad temperature range. This process is similar to the process of crystallization from magma (see Section 25.2), but the changes of phase occur in reverse order. When conditions are such that all minerals within a rock can melt, the composition of the resulting magma is the same as the composition of the original rock. Most often, however, melting is not complete; **partial melting** is the rule. Magma resulting from the partial melting of rock is made from only the constituents of those minerals that have melted, the ones with the lowest melting points. This results in magmas of many different compositions and—because these magmas cool to form igneous rock—many different igneous rocks.

Just as ice melts at the same temperature at which water freezes, the temperature at which a solid mineral begins to melt is the same temperature at which the same mineral in molten form solidifies. So when we discuss the melting temperature of a mineral, we imply that the molten form of that mineral solidifies at the same temperature.

Magmas are classified by the amount of silica they contain. Minerals with a high silica content tend to have lower melting temperatures (they melt more easily) than minerals with less silica. Partial melting thus produces magmas with more silica than the parent rock because the minerals with a high silica content are the first to melt, and the minerals with a lower silica content are left unmelted.

A great way to visualize partial melting is to consider a bowl that contains equal quantities of water, butter (in chunks), and cheese (also in chunks). First, we freeze the mixture. The frozen mixture is now a "rock" whose composition is 33% water. Intuitively, we know that the melting points of ice, butter, and cheese are different. When we add heat to our frozen mixture, the first substance to melt is the water. The substances that are harder to melt—the butter and cheese—remain unmelted in the "rock." We now have a liquid that is 100% water, so the percentage of water in the liquid is higher than the percentage of water that was in the "rock."

There are three major types of magma—*basaltic, andesitic,* and *granitic.* In general, the different magmas occur in different tectonic settings and will be tied to the plate tectonic model in the next chapter. We will also see that the largest region of the earth's interior is a solid, rocky layer called the *mantle.* When mantle rocks that are very low in silica undergo partial melting, basaltic magma is formed. Basaltic magma is still relatively low in silica—it is about 50% silica. When solidified, basaltic magma forms the dark igneous rock known as basalt, which is the kind of rock that makes up the Hawaiian Islands. Andesitic magma is about 60% silica. The rock known as andesite, which is produced from andesitic magma, gets its name from the Andes Mountains in South America, where it is very common. Granitic magma, which is about 70% silica, forms granite and other similar granitic type rocks. Of all the igneous rocks in the crust, oceanic and continental combined, approximately 80% was formed from basaltic magma, 10% from andesitic magma, and 10% from granitic magma.

Partial melting of mantle rocks produces the largest volume of magma. Partial melting of basalt is not thought to occur very often. If basalt is partially melted, andesitic magma is produced. Partial melting of rocks with an andesitic composition is thought to be rare as well. If partial melting of andesitic rocks occurs, granitic magma is produced.

So how is most andesitic and granitic magma produced? As we learned in Section 25.2, crystallization of magma causes an increase in silica content. The key is the amount of time that passes before the magma erupts or solidifies. Magma may travel long distances from where it was generated before it rises to its ultimate destination. The travel time allows the magma to cool and to begin to crystallize. Magma can also stay in one place for a long period of time. Basaltic magma that does not erupt often collects in a *magma chamber,* where it begins to cool and crystallize. Thus, most andesitic magma forms from the crystallization of basaltic magma. If crystallization continues, the composition of the remaining liquid will become granitic. In addition to crystallization, the silica content of a rising magma may increase by incorporating silica-rich rocks. Finally, granitic magma can also be generated when silica-rich rocks are melted by hot basaltic or andesitic magma that rises from regions below.

☑ CHECKPOINT

How is the partial melting of rock similar to the crystallization of magma that produces igneous rock?

Check Your Answer

Both produce temperature-dependent materials, but by opposite processes. Partial melting (solid to liquid) produces *magmas* of various compositions. The magma compositions depend on the melting temperatures of the minerals that constitute the rock that is being melted. Crystallization (liquid to solid) produces *crystals* of various compositions that depend on the solidification temperatures of the minerals in the magma. In both processes, different materials separate at different temperatures.

In ancient times, people used humanized stories and myths to describe and understand nature. Today, we use science.

Insights

Igneous Rocks at the Earth's Surface

Igneous rocks can form either at or below the earth's surface. Igneous rocks that form at the earth's surface are called **extrusive** rock (the word "extrusive" means "pushed out of"). As you now know, partial melting and crystallization produce a variety of magmas with different amounts of silica. Magmas with a high silica content flow more slowly because they are more *viscous* than magmas with a lower silica content. (High-silica magmas are like a spilled milkshake, which flows more slowly than spilled milk.) Basaltic magma is one important example

Link to Mythology

According to Greco-Roman mythology, volcanic activity was caused by Vulcan, the Roman god of fire and metalworking. The word *volcano* may have come from the island of Vulcano off the coast of Sicily. In ancient times, Vulcano was believed to be the metal workshop of Vulcan. The people who lived near Vulcano believed that the lava fragments and glowing ash that erupted from the island were a result of Vulcan's work as he forged thunderbolts for Jupiter, king of the gods, and weapons for Mars, god of war. The people of Polynesia, who attribute volcanic activity to Pele, goddess of volcanoes, tell a similar story.

of a low-silica, fast-flowing magma. The temperature of magma also affects its ability to flow. Hotter magma is less viscous and flows more easily than cooler magma.

Magma that moves upward from inside the earth and flows onto the surface is called **lava.** The term *lava* refers both to the molten rock itself and to the solid rocks that form from it. Lava may be extruded through cracks and fractures in the earth's surface or through a central vent—a **volcano.** Eruptions from a volcano are more familiar to us because they are very exciting to see, but the outpourings of magma from fissures are much more common. Most fissure eruptions occur when fast-flowing basaltic lava erupts at the bottom of the ocean. Such eruptions from underwater fissures form the ocean floors. Fissure eruptions also occur on land. Lava outpourings known as *flood basalts* have flooded large areas and created extensive lava plains. The Columbia Plateau in the Pacific Northwest is the result of extensive flood basalts (Figure 26.3), as is the Deccan Plateau in India.

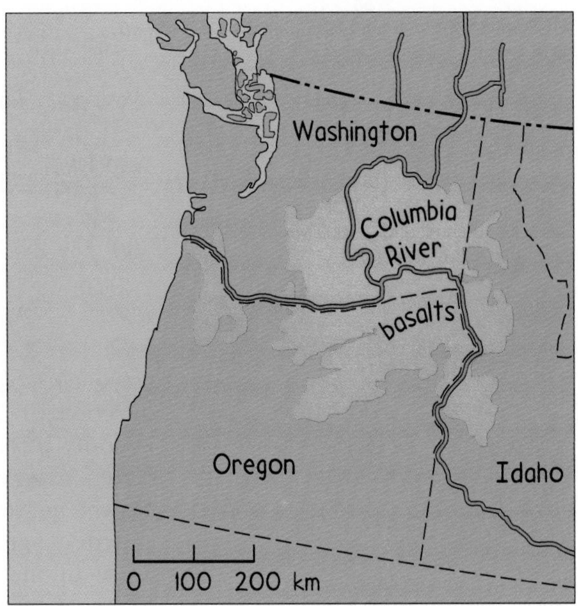

Figure 26.3
The flood basalts that produced the Columbia Plateau covered more than 200,000 km^2 of the preexisting land surface.

☑ **CHECKPOINT**

Is it correct to say that lava and magma with a high silica content are more viscous than those with lower silica content?

Check Your Answer

Yes. A higher silica content in a lava or magma causes it to be more viscous and to flow more slowly. Viscosity is the property of a liquid that describes how well it flows. Molasses flows very slowly (is more viscous) than water (which is less viscous). Therefore, it is correct to say that magmas and lavas with a high silica content are more viscous than those with a lower silica content.

Volcanoes are vents where magma has risen to the earth's surface and erupted as lava. Volcanoes that are built up by a steady supply of easily flowing basaltic lava have a broad, gently sloping cone that resembles a shield. These

Figure 26.4
(a) Mauna Loa, a shield volcano on the island of Hawaii, is the largest volcano on earth. (b) When compared with other large volcanoes, its immense size and volume is dramatic.

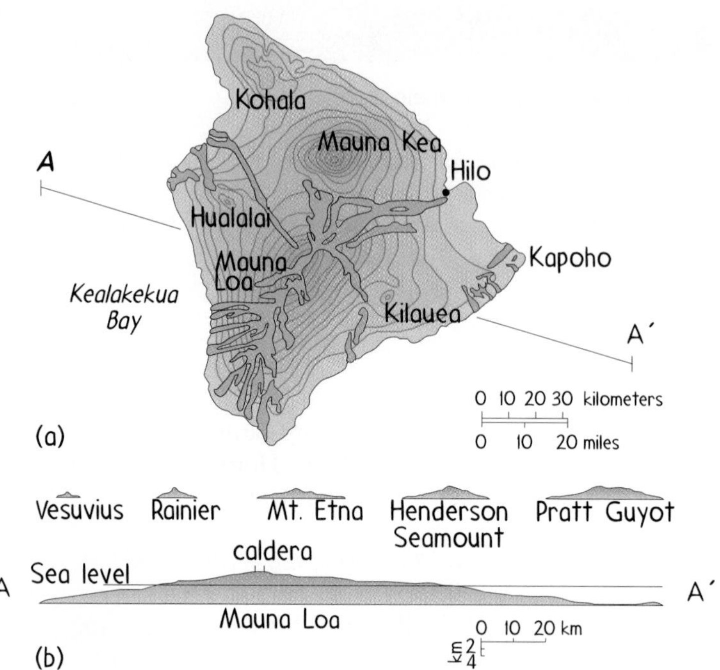

Figure 26.5
The three types of volcanoes. (a) Shield volcanoes, such as Mauna Loa, have broad, gentle slopes that average between 1° and 10° (from the horizontal). (b) Cinder cones, such as Sunset Crater in Arizona, generally have smooth steep slopes of 25° to 40° and bowl-shaped summit craters. (c) Composite cones, such as picturesque Mount Fuji, are also very steep. On average, the slope of a composite cone starts out at 30° at the summit and gradually flattens to 10° at the base.

(a)

(b)

(c)

are *shield volcanoes,* built from many lava flows that pour out in all directions to cool as thin, gently sloping sheets. Because of the low viscosity of basaltic lava, shield volcanoes do not have steep slopes. Here's a way to visualize this. Consider two different still-liquid cement mixtures—one very viscous and the other much less so. It's easy to imagine which cement mixture would be easier to pile up high. Some of the largest volcanoes in the world are shield volcanoes. Mauna Loa in Hawaii is a prime example. It is the largest volcano on Earth, standing 4145 meters above sea level and more than 9750 meters above the deep ocean floor.

Cinder cones are common in many volcanically active areas. They are very steep but rarely rise more than 300 meters or so above ground level. Cinder cones are not restricted to a particular type of lava. They are formed from the piling up of ash, cinders, and rocks that have been explosively erupted from a single vent. As debris showers down, the larger fragments pile up near the top of the cone to form a symmetrical, steep sided cone around the vent. The smaller particles fall farther from the vent to form gentle slopes at the base. Two well-known examples of cinder cones are Sunset Crater in Arizona (Figure 26.5b) and Parícutin in Mexico.

When a volcano erupts both lava and ash, a *composite cone,* with alternating layers of lava, ash, and mud, is produced. (The word "composite" means mixture.) The layers build up to form a volcano with a steep-sided summit and gently sloping lower flanks. Composite cones are usually bigger than cinder cones because the mixture of lava and ash helps to hold the cone together. Mount Fuji (Figure 26.5c) is a classic example of a majestic composite cone.

Composite cones tend to erupt explosively because their magmas and lavas usually do not flow easily. This viscous magma traps volcanic gases, which increases the pressure inside the volcano. We can compare the gases in a magma to gases in a bottle of carbonated soda. If we cover the top of the bottle and shake vigorously, the gases separate from the soda and form bubbles. When we remove the cover, pressure is released and gases and liquid explode from the bottle. The gases in magma behave in much the same way. In a volcanic blast, the pressure

Figuring Physical Science

Volcano Height

Shield volcanoes have gentle slopes, and composite cones have steep slopes, but how high do they grow? We can estimate a volcano's height, if we assume that it is shaped like a cone.

If we know the diameter of the volcano's base and the volume of lava that formed the volcano, we can use the formula for the volume, *V*, of a cone:

$$V = \frac{\pi r^2 h}{3},$$

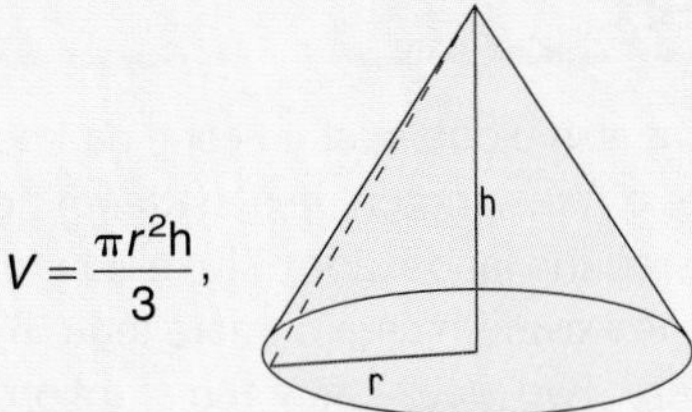

in which *r* is 1/2 the diameter of the base and *h* is the height.

If we know the length of the volcano's slope and the diameter of its base, we can use the Pythagorean theorem. The length of the slope is the distance you'd walk in going from the base of the volcano straight to the top:

$$r^2 + h^2 = s^2,$$

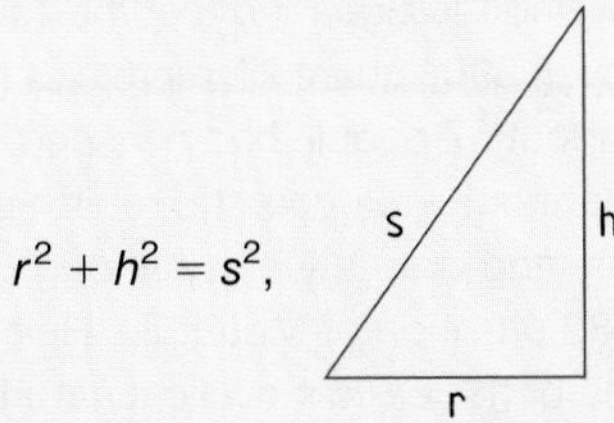

in which *s* is the length of the volcano's slope. The triangle shown is one-half of a cross-section through the cone. Do you see that *h* and *r* represent the same distances in both equations?

Problems

1. If a shield volcano was formed from 1000 km^3 of lava and its base has a diameter of 46 km, what is the volcano's height?
2. If the length of a composite cone's slope is 13.7 km and its base has a diameter of 24 km, what is the volcano's height?
3. What volume of lava was erupted to form the volcano in Problem 2?

Solutions

1. We rearrange the formula for the volume of a cone:

$$h = \frac{3V}{\pi r^2} = \frac{3 \times 1000 \text{ km}^3}{3.14 \times 23 \text{ km} \times 23 \text{ km}}$$
$$= \frac{3000 \text{ km}^3}{1661 \text{ km}^2} = 1.8 \text{ km} \cong 2 \text{ km}$$

2. Solving for *h* in the Pythagorean theorem, we have:

$$h^2 = s^2 - r^2, \text{ which gives}$$
$$h = \sqrt{s^2 - r^2} = \sqrt{187.7 \text{ km}^2 - 144 \text{ km}^2}$$
$$= 6.6 \text{ km} \cong 7 \text{ km}$$

3. We plug the values for the height and 1/2 the diameter into the volume formula:

$$V = \frac{3.14 \times 12 \text{ km} \times 12 \text{ km} \times 6.6 \text{ km}}{3}$$
$$= 994.8 \text{ km}^3 \cong 1000 \text{ km}^3$$

Thus, for 1000 km^3 of lava erupted, the peak of a typical shield volcano would be about 2 km above its base, and the peak of a typical composite cone would be about 7 km above its base.

and temperature increase, and the whole mass of viscous magma and overlying rock explodes into dust and rubble. When combined with abundant volcanic ash, this mixture can expand and destroy everything in its path. Examples of this kind of volcanic activity occurred at Mount Vesuvius in 79 A.D., at Mt. Pelee in 1902, at Mount St. Helens in 1980, and at Mount Pinatubo in 1991.

☑ CHECKPOINT

How are the lavas that form shield volcanoes different from those that form composite cones?

Check Your Answer

Lavas that form shield volcanoes generally have a low silica content, so they tend to flow easily outwards from the vent. This creates a volcano that is wide and gently sloping. Lavas that make up composite cones generally have a higher silica content, so they do not flow out easily from the vent. This may cause explosive eruptions of thick lava and ash that do not flow away but, instead, build a steep composite cone.

Blast from Our Recent Past: Mount St. Helens

Imagine the energy released by dropping 30,000 atomic bombs at a rate of one per second over a period of several hours. Such was the explosive energy released when Mount St. Helens, in the state of Washington, erupted on May 18, 1980. The eruption did not come as a surprise. For months prior to the eruption, earthquake activity beneath the volcano, caused by the upward movement of magma, signaled that the mountain's 123 years of dormancy was over.

To scientists, the dangers of Mount St. Helens were well known. Evidence in the local geologic record showed that, over the past 4500 years, Mount St. Helens had erupted more frequently and more violently than any other volcano in the lower 48 states of the United States.

And so it was on May 18, 1980, when the sleeping giant awoke. Within seconds of a magnitude-5 earthquake, the entire northern flank of the mountain fell apart in a massive landslide. Explosions ripped through the sliding debris, blasting gases, ash, and rock across the land at hurricane speeds. With more than 300 meters of its summit gone, the volcano was like a gigantic pressure cooker suddenly uncorked. Vertical explosions of rapidly expanding ash had been thrust 25 kilometers into the sky (about twice as high as a commercial jet flies). Blown eastward by strong winds, the ash cloud cast an eerie darkness across the state of Washington. In a matter of hours, falling ash covered the landscape; 540 million tons of ash was deposited over an area of more than 57,000 square kilometers. Two weeks after the eruption, large quantities of airborne ash still circled the earth.

As ash particles filled the skies, mudflows scoured the land. Roaring clouds of superheated gas, steam, and ash, traveling at speeds in excess of 565 kilometers per hour, obliterated everything for miles to the north of the volcano. The glowing debris blasted from the volcano quickly melted Mount St. Helens' cover of ice and snow, sending torrents of scalding mudflows down the North Fork and the South Fork of the Toutle River. When it was over, 390 square kilometers of forest lay in ruins and about 57 people had perished.

Even in the face of such violence, the rebirth of life can occur quickly and dramatically. Although devastating, the 1980 eruption of Mount St. Helens provides an example of the earth's cyclical nature. The blast virtually obliterated everything in its path, but, very soon afterwards, life returned to the blast area and now is anchoring itself in the desolate volcanic landscape; pockets of plant and animal life have gained a foothold. Like pioneers moving west, life returns to the mountain.

Igneous Rocks Beneath the Earth's Surface

When magma cools beneath the earth's surface, the resulting rock is called **intrusive** igneous rock (the word "intrusive" means *pushed into*). All intrusive igneous rock bodies are called **plutons.** They occur in a great variety of shapes and sizes, ranging from thin slabs to wide, shapeless blobs (Figure 26.6). It's easy to guess that intrusive rocks can be studied only after they are exposed at the earth's surface.

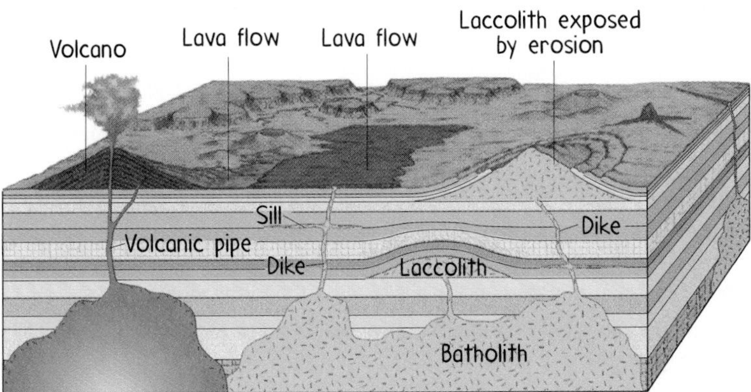

Figure 26.6
Intrusive igneous features in cross-sectional view.

A common type of pluton is a *dike*—formed by the intrusion of magma into fractures that cut across the layers of existing rock. Dikes are old channels for rising magma, and they often occur near volcanic vents. A spectacular example of this can be seen in the radiating dikes around the exposed volcanic neck at Shiprock, New Mexico (Figure 26.7). At Shiprock, the volcanic neck and the dikes are more resistant to erosion than the softer rock they intruded. Erosion has acted to remove the surrounding, softer rock, leaving the harder, volcanic rocks behind as a peak (the volcanic neck) and wall-like ridges (the dikes).

Figure 26.7
Shiprock, New Mexico. Radiating dikes surround the eroded remains of a volcanic vent.

Batholiths, which are the largest of the plutons, are defined as having more than 100 square kilometers of surface exposure. A batholith is usually not generated by a single intrusion. Instead, numerous intrusive events over millions of years create a massive batholith. Batholiths form the cores of many of the major mountain systems of the world. Additionally, many modern mountains are actually the exposed cores of the batholiths of larger mountains that have long since eroded away. Some of the largest batholiths

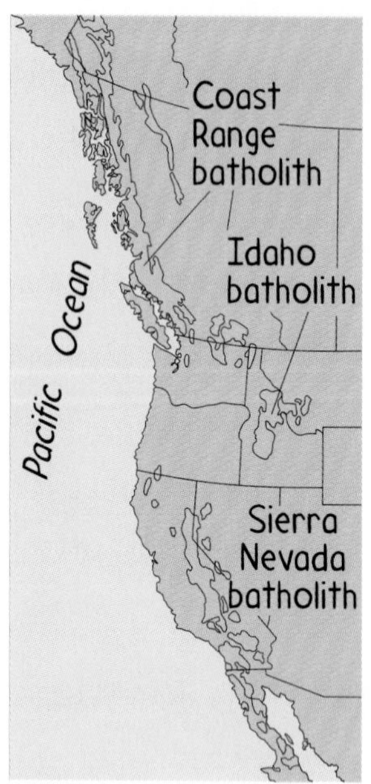

Figure 26.8
Some of the largest batholiths in North America include the Coast Range batholith and the Sierra Nevada batholith.

in North America include the Coast Range batholith and the Sierra Nevada batholith (Figure 26.8). These batholiths continue to push upward even as erosion wears them down. It is interesting to note that the Sierra Nevada is presently gaining height with time because its rate of uplift is greater than its rate of erosion.

☑ CHECKPOINT

1. Why is it incorrect to say that igneous rocks may form from the intrusion of lava?
2. Is it correct to say that igneous rocks may form from the extrusion of lava?

Check Your Answers

1. The terminology in the statement is used incorrectly. The term *intrusion* refers to solidification that occurs in the earth's interior and therefore has nothing to do with lava. Lava is not a synonym for magma; it is the term for magma that has been extruded at the earth's surface in molten form. By definition, there is no lava beneath the earth's surface. Magma is intruded and lava is extruded to form igneous rocks.
2. Yes, once magma is extruded from the earth, it is called lava (which, when solidified, becomes igneous rock).

26.3 Sedimentary Rocks

Sedimentary rocks are the most common rocks in the uppermost part of the crust. They cover two thirds of the earth's surface and form a thin, extensive blanket over igneous and metamorphic rocks. Because sedimentary rocks are the remains of older rocks, they provide information about geological events that have occurred over time at the earth's surface.

Weathering, Erosion, Transportation, and Sedimentation

While the process of volcanism is always generating new rock material at the earth's surface, the opposing process of *weathering* breaks down and decomposes surface rock. There are two kinds of weathering, *mechanical* and *chemical.* Both produce *sediment.* **Mechanical weathering** physically breaks rocks into smaller and smaller pieces. In **chemical weathering,** reactions with water decompose rock into smaller pieces. As rock is weathered, it erodes. **Erosion** is the process by which weathered rock particles are removed and transported away by water, wind, or ice.

Sediments composed of small fragments of other rocks are called *clastic* sediments, whereas those produced by chemical precipitation are called *chemical* sediments. When clastic particles are first produced, they are normally quite angular and jagged. During transportation, especially by water, the particles continuously run into other particles and break. This decreases their size and rounds off their sharp edges. When that transportation stops, deposition and sedimentation begin.

Deposition occurs when a transported particle comes to rest. Sediments are deposited in horizontal layers, with each successive layer younger than the one beneath it. The larger a sediment particle, the stronger a water current must be in order to carry it. Usually, a water current gets weaker as it moves away from its source. As the water slows down, the larger particles are the first to be deposited, while smaller particles are able to remain with the flow. In this way, particles tend to be sorted according to size as they are deposited.

A deposit that contains particles of very similar sizes is called a *well-sorted* deposit, while one that contains particles of various sizes is called a *poorly sorted* deposit. During transportation, sediment is continuously sorted and abraded, and the size, shape, and sorting of particles in a sedimentary deposit provide clues to the distance of transport. In general, poorly sorted, angular particles of various shapes have traveled only a short distance, whereas well-sorted, well-rounded particles have traveled a greater distance. We can also get clues to the method of transportation. Glacial deposits, for example, tend to consist of very poorly sorted and angular particles because they have been moved by ice. Ice can carry very large and very small particles. Being entrained in ice, the sediment particles remain angular because they do not bump into each other as they would in moving water or wind. On the other hand, wind-blown deposits tend to be very well-sorted and to have small particles because wind can only move small particles.

(a)

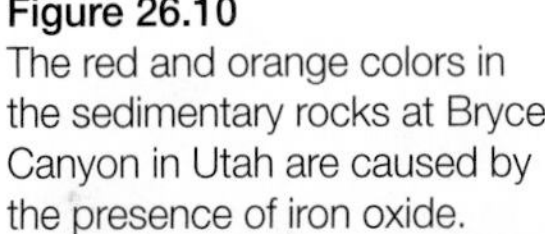

(b)

Figure 26.9
(a) Well-sorted sediment grains. (b) Poorly sorted sediment grains.

In the process of *sedimentation,* sediment particles are deposited horizontally one layer at a time. As the deposited sediment accumulates, it begins to change into *sedimentary rock.* We say that the sediments undergo *lithification,* a term that means "conversion into rock."

Lithification occurs through the processes of *compaction* and *cementation.* Compaction is the first step. As the weight of overlying sediments presses down upon deeper layers, sediment particles are squeezed and compacted together. This compaction squeezes much of the water out of the *pores* between the sediment particles.

The remaining "pore water" often contains dissolved compounds, such as silica, calcium carbonate, and iron oxide. These compounds can precipitate from solution and partially fill the pore spaces with mineral matter. The mineral matter glues the particles together and acts as a cementing agent. This is the process of cementation. Silica cement, the most durable, produces some of the hardest and most resistant sedimentary rocks. When iron oxide acts as a cementing agent, it produces the red or orange stain often seen in sedimentary rocks. The rock colors of Bryce Canyon National Park in Utah provide a beautiful example of iron oxide stain.

Figure 26.10
The red and orange colors in the sedimentary rocks at Bryce Canyon in Utah are caused by the presence of iron oxide.

(a)

(b)

(c)

Figure 26.11
Sedimentary rocks. (a) Shale, which is composed of fine particles; (b) sandstone, which is composed of medium-sized particles; and (c) conglomerate, which is made up of a wide variety of large, rounded particles.

Clastic Sedimentary Rocks

Clastic sedimentary rocks are classified by particle size (Table 26.1). The classification scheme is meaningful because it allows us immediately to visualize the depositional environment in which the rock was formed. The three most abundant clastic sedimentary rocks are *shale,* composed of very fine particles that are too small to be visible with a magnifying hand lens; *sandstone,* composed of medium-sized particles such as those found in typical beach sand; and *conglomerate,* composed mainly of a variety of larger particles, ranging from pebbles to boulders.

Table 26.1

Particle Size Classification of Clastic Sediments and Sedimentary Rocks

	Sediment		Particle Size	Rock
COARSE ↑				
	Gravel	Boulder		Conglomerate
			256 mm	
		Cobble		
			64 mm	
		Pebble		
			2 mm	
		Sand		Sandstone
			0.062 mm	
	Mud	Silt		Siltstone
			0.0039 mm	
		Clay		Mudstone Shale
↓ **FINE**				

Shale is a rock formed by the compaction of superfine silt and clay-sized particles. It is finely layered and has the ability to split into thin layers, or flakes, parallel to the depositional layers. The extremely fine particle size suggests that the particles in shale were deposited in low-energy environments characterized by quiet waters, such as deep ocean basins, flood plains, deltas, lakes, or lagoons. The color of shale ranges from gray to black and from red to brown to green, depending on its environment of formation. Gray to black shale indicates the presence of organic matter in the shale, which can be preserved only in a swampy environment with little or no oxygen. If the depositional environment had had sufficient oxygen, bacteria would have decomposed the organic matter very quickly. Black shale is commercially important, because it is the main source rock for crude oil. Red to brown shale contains ferric oxide (red) or ferric hydroxide (brown). Green shale simply does not contain organic matter, ferric oxide, or ferric hydroxide.

Sandstones can be classified into three types, based on their mineral makeup. When quartz is the primary mineral, the rock is simply called *quartz sandstone*. Quartz sandstone is composed of well-sorted, well-rounded quartz particles. Sandstone that contains considerable amounts of the mineral feldspar is called *arkose*. The particles in arkose tend to be poorly rounded and not as well-sorted as those in quartz sandstone. Sandstone made of a mixture of quartz, feldspar, and angular rock fragments is called *graywacke* (pronounced gray-wack-ee). Sandstones form in a variety of environments, including dunes, beaches, marine sand bars, river channels, canyons, and underwater canyons.

Conglomerates are composed of gravels and rounded rock fragments. The rock fragments are usually large enough for easy identification, which gives us useful information about the areas from which the sediments were eroded. Larger rock fragments must have been transported by water currents strong enough to carry them, which indicate dynamic, high-energy environments, such as rapids and fast-moving streams. Because these strong currents round out the rock fragments, the roundness of their edges and corners is a good indication of the distances they have traveled. Conglomerates are often found in river channels and along rapidly eroding coastlines.

Chemical Sedimentary Rocks

Recall from the previous chapter that chemical sediments are formed by the precipitation of minerals from water. Carbonate rocks, such as limestone, are formed by the precipitation of calcium carbonate. Evaporites, such as halite, are formed by the evaporation of salty waters. In general, chemical sedimentary rocks form where there are no clastic sediments.

Warm climates favor carbonate deposition because carbonates are more soluble in cold water than in warm water. Evaporite deposits require a dry climate that causes the evaporation of lakes or of seawater. As the water dries out, evaporite minerals precipitate and are left behind. Vast carbonate and evaporite deposits on the continents are evidence that expansive, shallow seas have periodically covered the land surfaces in the past. In Chapter 29, we will learn more about the environments in which chemical sedimentary rocks form.

Fossils: Clues to Life in the Past

Because sedimentary rocks (clastic and chemical) are formed at the earth's surface, they often contain the remains of life forms—fossils. Fossils not only tell the story of life on earth, they also give us important clues about the earth's geologic past. As we shall see in Chapter 30, fossils can indicate where and

Living things, especially microorganisms, are unimaginably abundant in rivers, lakes, and oceans. They "drink" the water and use the minerals dissolved in the water to make their shells, skeletons, and cell walls. A great deal of calcite was formed in this way. When these creatures die, they settle to the bottom and form layers of chemical sediment.

Insights

(a)

(b)

(c)

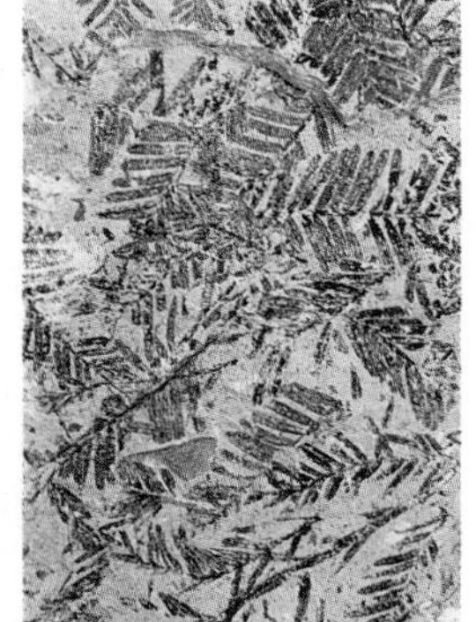
(d)

Figure 26.12
Some of the many processes of fossilization. (a) *Permineralization* occurs when the porous remains of an organism become filled with water that is rich in dissolved minerals. Petrified wood is formed by this process. (b) An *impression* is made by an organism (or part of an organism) that has been buried quickly, before it can decompose, thereby preserving its form. (c) *Replacement* occurs when the remains of organisms are replaced by a mineral. Pyrite has replaced the original shell in this specimen. (d) *Carbonization* occurs when an organism is preserved as a thin film of carbon.

Fossil Fuels

When ancient plants and animals died, most of the organic matter they were made of was quickly decomposed by bacteria and converted to nutrients consumed by other organisms. Material that escaped bacterial decay was either preserved as sparsely distributed organic matter or converted to coal, oil, or gas.

Coal, oil, and gas are all fossils, in the sense that they are the remains of past organisms. However, these remains have been so changed over time that the forms and even the composition of the accumulated organisms are beyond recognition.

The source of oil and gas is fossilized organic matter found in buried sediments. When buried sediment with considerable plant or animal material is subjected to low heat over a long enough period of time, chemical changes take place that create oil. Under the pressure of the overlying sediments, tiny oil droplets are squeezed out of the source rocks and into overlying porous rocks. The porous rocks—commonly sandstones—become oil reservoirs. Just as in the metamorphism of rocks, deeper burial results in higher temperatures. If the temperature gets high enough, natural gas is generated rather than oil.

Coal is formed from plants that do not completely decay but are so altered that the original structure is destroyed. Coal, oil, and natural gas are the primary fuels of our modern economy.

when sediments were deposited. They also help us to match rocks from different places that are of similar geologic age. Some fossils are made of whole organisms, but most fossils are just parts of an organism. Other fossils are simply an impression, or print, made in the rock before it hardened. Plants commonly leave their impression as a thin film of carbon. There are many ways in which organisms have become fossilized (Figure 26.12).

Plants and animals were energized by the sun before they became fossil fuels. So the energy from fossil fuels is delayed solar power.

Insights

☑ CHECKPOINT

1. Why is it incorrect to say that clastic sediments are precipitated out of water?
2. Is it correct to say that evaporites are deposited by water?

Check Your Answers

1. Clastic sediments are made of small fragments of other rocks. Precipitation is a specific chemical reaction in which a solid forms out of a solution. The solid left behind is a chemical sediment, not a clastic sediment. It is correct to say that clastic sediments are deposited by water, air, or ice.
2. Yes, because the word *deposit* is a general term that is applied to all types of sediments.

26.4 Metamorphic Rocks

What happens when a mass of rock is brought to a location that has much higher temperature and pressure than the environment in which it formed? Such changes in the physical and chemical conditions to which rock is exposed can transform rock. New rock is made from old. The new rock is stable under the new conditions, while the preexisting rock was not.

The changes in rocks that happen as physical and chemical conditions change are called **metamorphism.** Preexisting rocks, whether igneous, sedimentary, or metamorphic, can all undergo metamorphism. An everyday example of metamorphism is potter's clay. Potter's clay is soft at room temperature. But, when heated, it becomes a hard ceramic. Similarly, limestone subjected to enough heat and pressure becomes marble. Shale is metamorphosed to slate. Rocks may also be drastically stretched or compressed. It is important to note that, during metamorphism, minerals are not completely melted. Once minerals do melt, metamorphism has ended and igneous activity has begun. In metamorphism, change occurs instead by *recrystallization* of preexisting minerals or by *mechanical deformation* of rock.

Recrystallization occurs when a rock is subjected to higher temperatures and pressures than the conditions under which it formed. The constituents of the metamorphosing minerals actually migrate and recombine to form new minerals. Recrystallization may occur with the exchange of fluid. For example, consider sedimentary rocks containing such fluids as water or carbon dioxide. The fluids in the rock, which are enclosed in pore spaces, can act as catalysts to initiate or speed up metamorphic reactions. If temperature and pressure are high enough, the rock loses pore space as the fluid in the rock is squeezed out. The released fluid can then react chemically with the surrounding rock, contributing constituents to new minerals that are forming. We will see, in Chapter 27, that this fluid plays a strong role in the generation of some types of magma. Metamorphic reactions can also occur without the involvement of fluids. This happens in the case of low-temperature metamorphism.

Mechanical deformation is another mode of metamorphism. It occurs when a rock is subjected to physical stress. It may or may not involve elevated temperatures. For example, surface rocks that become deeply buried are subjected to increased pressure. Such stress may cause the rocks to flow like a plastic, bending them into intricate folds. Or the increased pressure may deform and flatten the rock, or shear it, breaking it and grinding it into fragments. Such physical stress occurs deep in the earth's crust.

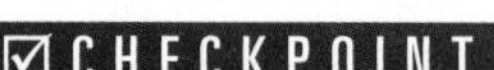

Is recrystallization the opposite of partial melting?

Check Your Answer

No. The process of crystallization, not recrystallization, is the opposite of partial melting. Recrystallization occurs within a rock because of exposure to high temperatures and/or pressures. Rock may not even undergo any chemical changes during recrystallization.

Types of Metamorphism: Contact and Regional

The most common types of metamorphism are *contact metamorphism* and *regional metamorphism.* Each type of metamorphism is characterized by differences in mechanical deformation and recrystallization.

Contact metamorphism occurs when a body of rock is intruded by magma (Figure 26.13). The high temperature of the magma produces a zone of alteration that surrounds the intrusion. The alteration is greatest at the *contact*, which is the surface that separates the intrusive rock from the surrounding rock. The width of the altered zone may range from a few centimeters to several hundred meters. Around a small intrusive body, such as a dike, the altered zone is very narrow and resembles "baked" rock, with a texture and appearance like ordinary brick. But, with a larger intrusive body, such as a batholith, the altered zone may be 100 meters thick or more. One of the most common changes is an increase in crystal size due to recrystallization. The crystal size is greatest at the contact, and it decreases with increasing distance from that point. The water content of the rock also changes with distance from the contact. At the contact, where temperature is high, water content is low. So we find dry, high-temperature minerals, such as garnet and pyroxene, at the contact. Farther away, we find water-rich, low-temperature minerals, such as muscovite and chlorite.

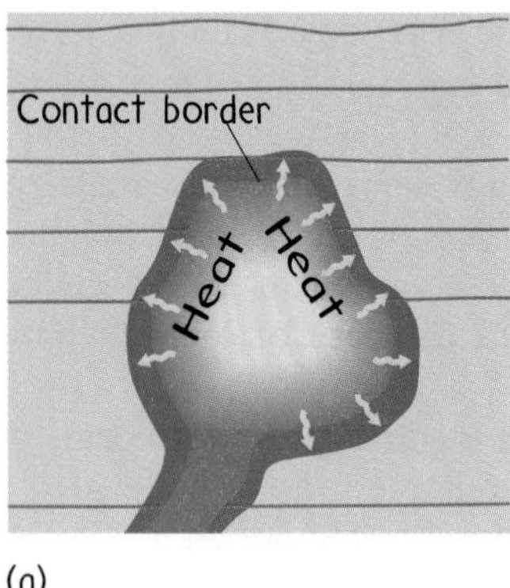

(a)

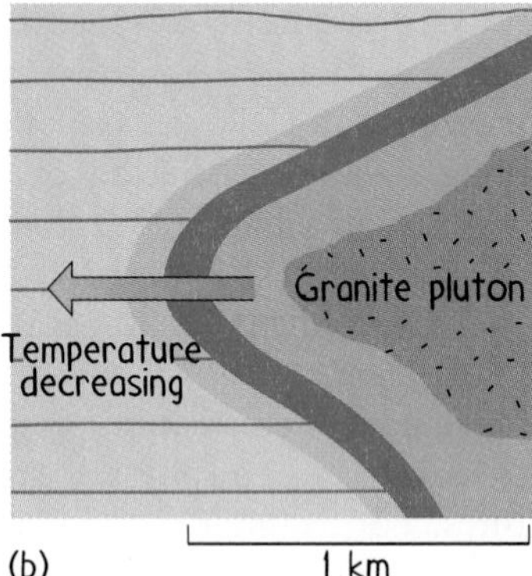

(b)

Figure 26.13
(a) Contact metamorphism is the result of rising molten magma that intrudes a rock body. (b) Surrounding the solidified intrusive rock is a zone of alteration. Alteration is greatest at the contact area, and it decreases farther away from the contact area.

Regional metamorphism is the alteration of rock by both heat and physical stress over an entire region rather than just near a contact. It is more than just recrystallization combined with mechanical deformation. For example, the intrusion of magma is not the only cause of the higher temperatures associated with regional metamorphism. Large sections of rock can be heated if the rock is buried deeply enough, simply because the earth is hotter at greater depths. Regionally metamorphosed rocks are found in all the major mountain belts of the world. During the process of mountain building, the earth's crust is severely compressed into a mass of highly deformed rock. This deformation can be seen in the folded and fractured rock layers in many mountain ranges. The effects of regional metamorphism are most pronounced in the cores of deformed mountains. Rocks develop distinctly "layered" and "foliated" textures and zoned sequences of minerals. Because of the large-scale nature of regional metamorphism, these zones tend to be broad and extensive. Areas of regional metamorphism are the

Figure 26.14
This satellite photo reveals regional-scale folding in the Appalachian Mountains of central Pennsylvania.

hunting grounds of gem prospectors, because the heat and pressure that accompany these changes can produce beautiful minerals.

Metamorphic rocks are defined by their appearance and the minerals they contain. For classification and identification, metamorphic rocks can be divided into two groups: *foliated* and *nonfoliated.*

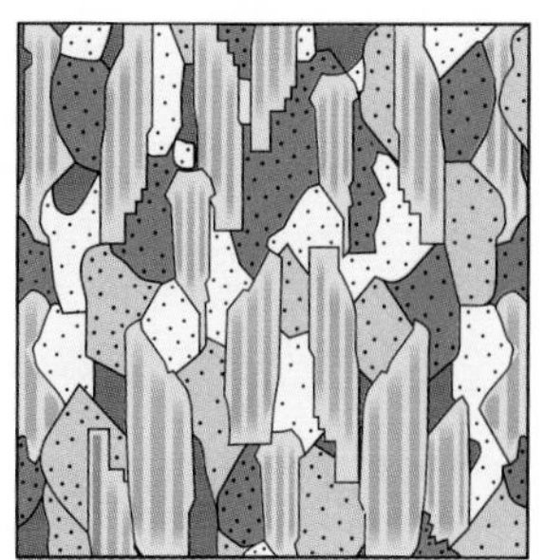

Figure 26.15
As compressive forces squeeze platy and sheet-structured minerals, the grains align themselves perpendicular to the main direction of force. Arrows indicate the direction of compressive force.

Foliated Metamorphic Rocks

When rock is subjected to an increase in temperature and pressure, some of its minerals realign into parallel planes as they recrystallize. The face of each of these parallel planes is perpendicular to the main direction of the compressive force. This leads to a layered appearance called *foliation.* Foliation is a prominent visual feature of regionally metamorphosed rocks, and it is very different from the layering seen in sedimentary rock. For example, sheet-structured minerals, such as the micas, grow and orient themselves with their sheets perpendicular to the direction of maximum pressure (Figure 26.15). The new rock, which now has parallel flakes, or *plates,* of mica, is said to be *foliated.* The most common foliated metamorphic rocks—slate, schist, and gneiss—are derived from sedimentary rocks that have the appropriate chemical composition to favor mica formation.

(a)

(b)

(c)

Figure 26.16
Common foliated metamorphic rocks: (a) slate, (b) schist, and (c) gneiss.

Slate is the "lowest-grade" foliated metamorphic rock, which means that it was formed under relatively low temperature and pressure. Slate, which is metamorphosed shale, is a foliated rock composed of very small particles and tiny mica flakes. The most obvious characteristic of slate is its excellent rock cleavage, which allows it to be split into thin slabs. The best pool tables and chalkboards are made from slate quarried in metamorphic areas where slaty cleavage is well developed. Slate is also commonly used as roofing tile and floor tile.

Schist is one of the most easily recognizable metamorphic rocks because it is shiny. Schist forms under higher temperature and pressure conditions than slate, which causes the mineral grains to grow large enough to be identified with the naked eye. Schists usually contain 50% platy minerals, most commonly muscovite and biotite. The larger mica flakes give the rock a shiny surface that is quite striking. Schists are named according to the major minerals in the rock (biotite schist, staurolite-garnet schist, and so on).

Gneiss (pronounced "nice") is a foliated metamorphic rock that contains alternating layers of dark platy minerals and lighter granular minerals. The layers give this metamorphic rock its characteristic striped appearance. This

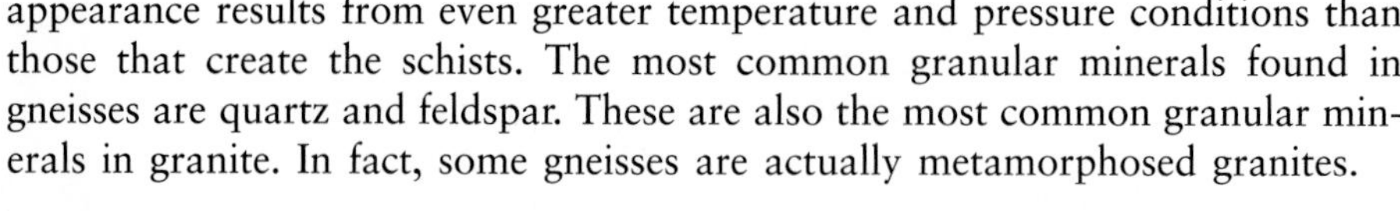

appearance results from even greater temperature and pressure conditions than those that create the schists. The most common granular minerals found in gneisses are quartz and feldspar. These are also the most common granular minerals in granite. In fact, some gneisses are actually metamorphosed granites.

Nonfoliated Metamorphic Rocks

(a)

(b)

Figure 26.17
Nonfoliated metamorphic rocks: (a) marble and (b) quartzite.

Nonfoliated metamorphic rocks can form either in areas of increased temperature and pressure or in areas where only the temperature has increased. Even under high pressure, foliation cannot develop if the rock lacks the chemical composition needed for micas to form. If the chemical composition is correct but the pressure is not high enough, such as in contact metamorphism, foliation cannot develop. Two common nonfoliated rocks that generally do not have the potential for micas to grow in them are marble and quartzite.

Marble (Figure 26.17a) is a crystalline, metamorphosed limestone. Pure marble is white and is virtually 100% calcite. Because of its color and its relative softness (hardness 3), marble is a popular building stone. Often the limestone from which marble was formed contained impurities that produced various colors in the marble. Thus, marble can range from pink to gray, green, or even black.

Quartzite (Figure 26.17b) is metamorphosed quartz sandstone, and it is therefore very hard (hardness 7). The recrystallization of quartzite is so complete that the rock splits across the original quartz particles when it is broken, rather than between them. Although pure quartzite is white, it commonly contains impurities that can cause it to be a variety of colors, such as pink, green, or light gray.

26.5 The Rock Cycle, a Descriptive Key

We have seen that the igneous, sedimentary, and metamorphic rocks of the earth's crust have different origins. Although formed by different processes, the three rock types are related. This relationship is graphically shown in the model of the rock cycle (Figure 26.18). By following the different pathways in the model, we can illustrate the origin of the three basic rock types and the different geologic processes that change one rock type into another. The figure helps to summarize this chapter.

We have learned that igneous rock is formed when magma cools and crystallizes. Magma can crystallize into many different kinds of igneous rock. Although most of the earth's crust is either igneous or derived from rock that was initially igneous, the rock we see at the surface is mainly sedimentary.

We have learned that sedimentary rock is the result of the decomposition and disintegration of other rocks by weathering and erosion. When sedimentary rock is buried deep within the earth or is involved in mountain building, we have seen that great pressures and heat can transform it into metamorphic rock. Fluids released during some types of metamorphism help generate magma or cause further metamorphism. Under the proper conditions, metamorphic rock can melt and become magma, which eventually solidifies as igneous rock to complete the rock cycle.

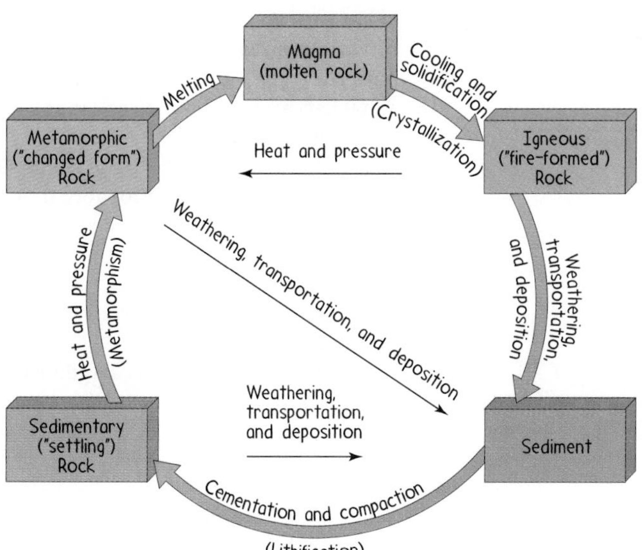

Figure 26.18
The rock cycle: Igneous rock, subjected to heat and pressure far below the earth's surface, may become metamorphic rock; or metamorphic or sedimentary rocks at the earth's surface may decompose to become sediment that in turn becomes new sedimentary rock. Whatever the route, molten rock rises from the depths of the earth, cools, and solidifies to form a crust that, over eons, is reworked by shifting and erosion, only to return eventually to become magma in the earth's interior.

Rocks can follow many different paths around the rock cycle. Sometimes igneous rock, for example, is subjected to heat and pressure far below the earth's surface and becomes metamorphic rock. Or metamorphic or sedimentary rocks at the earth's surface may decompose to become sediment that undergoes compaction and becomes new sedimentary rock. There are many possible variations of the cycle. Cycles within cycles even occur. Whatever the route, the earth's crust is formed when molten rock rises from the depths of the earth, cools, and solidifies to form a crust that, over eons, is reworked by shifting and erosion, and it can eventually be returned to the interior, where it may be completely melted and once again become magma.

Summary of Terms

Igneous rocks Rocks formed by the cooling and crystallization of hot, molten rock material called magma.

Sedimentary rocks Rocks formed from the accumulation of weathered material (sediments) carried by water, wind, or ice.

Metamorphic rocks Rocks formed from preexisting rocks that have been changed or transformed by high temperature, high pressure, or both.

Partial melting The incomplete melting of rocks, resulting in magmas of different compositions.

Extrusive rocks Igneous rocks that form at the earth's surface.

Lava Magma, once it has reached the earth's surface.

Volcano A central vent through which lava, gases, and ash erupt and flow.

Intrusive rocks Igneous rocks that crystallize below the earth's surface.

Pluton A very large intrusive body formed below the earth's surface.

Mechanical weathering The breakdown of rocks on the earth's surface by physical means.

Chemical weathering The breakdown of rocks on the earth's surface by chemical means.

Erosion The wearing away of rocks, and the processes by which rock particles are transported by water, wind, or ice.

Metamorphism The changing of one kind of rock into another kind as a result of high temperature, high pressure, or both.

Recrystallization Occurs when rocks are subjected to high temperatures and pressures and go through a change in mineral assemblage, which is usually accompanied by the loss of H_2O or CO_2.

Mechanical deformation Metamorphism caused by stress, such as increased pressure.

Rock cycle A sequence of events involving the formation, destruction, alteration, and reformation of rocks as a result of the generation and movement of magma; the weathering, erosion, transportation, and deposition of sediment; and the metamorphism of preexisting rocks.

Review Questions

26.1 Rock Types

1. Name the three major types of rocks, and describe the conditions of their origin.

26.2 Igneous Rocks

2. What are the most common igneous rocks, and where do they generally occur?
3. What percentage of the earth's crust is composed of igneous rocks?
4. As rock melts to become magma, which minerals are the first to melt?
5. What is meant by *partial melting*?
6. With respect to the silica content of the parent rock, partial melting will produce what type of magma?
7. What are the three main types of magma? Relate the different magmas to silica content.
8. Which type of volcano produces the most violent eruptions? Which type produces the quietest eruptions?
9. Choose the lettered phrase that best completes the following statement: Magmas with a high silica content flow______________
   (a) more slowly than granitic magmas with a low silica content.
   (b) more quickly than basaltic magmas with a low silica content.
   (c) more slowly than basaltic magmas with a low silica content.
   (d) more quickly than granitic magmas with a low silica content.
10. Where on the earth's surface are lava flows most common?
11. What are the three major types of volcanoes?
12. Name some examples of composite cone volcanoes from around the world.
13. Intrusive igneous rock bodies (plutons) are formed from magma that has cooled beneath the earth's surface. Give two examples of plutonic rock bodies.
14. Shiprock, New Mexico, is an example of what type of igneous formation?

26.3 Sedimentary Rocks

15. How does weathering produce sediment? Distinguish between weathering and erosion.
16. What does roundness tell us about sediment particles?
17. What can we say about a rock that is composed of various sizes of sediments in a disorganized pattern?
18. What can we say about a rock that is composed of very angular sediments?
19. Relate the shape and sorting of sand particles to the way in which they were probably transported.
20. In what two ways does sediment turn into sedimentary rock?
21. What is a clastic sedimentary rock?
22. What are the three most common clastic sedimentary rocks?
23. Name two common chemical sedimentary rocks?
24. What is a fossil? How are fossils used in the study of geology?

26.4 Metamorphic Rocks

25. What is metamorphism? What causes it?
26. What are the two processes by which rock is changed?
27. What patterns of alteration are characteristic of contact metamorphism?
28. Contact metamorphism produces dry, high-temperature minerals nearest to the contact zone. Give two examples of dry, high-temperature minerals.
29. In contact metamorphism, water-rich, low-temperature minerals are found far away from the contact zone. Give two examples of such minerals.
30. What changes are characteristic of regional metamorphism?
31. Why do we find folded and fractured rock layers in zones of regional metamorphism?
32. Distinguish between foliated and nonfoliated metamorphic rocks.
33. How does gneiss differ from granite?
34. Why is schist so easily recognized?

26.5 The Rock Cycle, a Descriptive Key

35. Explain the different cycles of rock formation.

Activity

Rocks never fully melt; they partially melt. So, what happens as a rock partially melts? To understand the partial melting of rocks, let us use the ice, butter, and cheese analogy from the text.

Step 1. Mix cubes of ice, butter, and cheese together with a little water, and put this mixture in the freezer. Once this mixture has frozen, you will have made a "rock."

Step 2. Put this "rock" in a bowl in the refrigerator overnight, and then examine the contents of the bowl the following morning or afternoon.

1. What melts?
2. What does not melt?
3. How would the melt be different from the original "rock"?

For the partial melting of real rocks

1. What melts? What doesn't?
2. How is the melt different from the original rock?
3. Cooling and solidification of the melt: After the melt cools and solidifies into rock, how is the new igneous rock different from the rock that originally melted?

Exercises

1. Name a national park with geologic features that were formed by volcanic or plutonic activity.
2. What type of rock is formed when magma rises slowly and solidifies before reaching the earth's surface? Give an example.
3. Why are minerals in volcanic rocks usually smaller than minerals in plutonic rock?
4. In what parts of the earth's crust (oceanic and/or continental crust) do we find the two most common igneous rocks, basalt and granite?
5. What two primary factors can change a rock's melting point?
6. Are the Hawaiian Islands made up primarily of igneous or of sedimentary or of metamorphic rock?
7. Can metamorphic rocks exist on an island of purely volcanic origin? Defend your answer.
8. What accounts for the differences in lava composition of two volcanoes—Mauna Loa in Hawaii and Mount St. Helens in Washington—that have erupted in recent times?
9. What mainly determines the viscosity of a magma?
10. What mainly determines a rock's initial melting temperature?
11. List some common types of clastic sediments.
12. What general rock feature does a geologist look for in a sedimentary rock to determine the distance the rock has traveled from its place of origin?
13. What feature of clastic sedimentary rock enables the flow of oil after it has been formed?
14. Which of these rocks—granite, sandstone, limestone, or halite—is the first to weather in a wet (humid) climate? Why?
15. In a conglomerate rock, why are pebbles of granite very common and pebbles of marble relatively uncommon?
16. Which type of rock is most sought by petroleum prospectors—igneous, sedimentary, or metamorphic? Why?
17. Cite two examples of sedimentary rocks that provide information about past geologic events at the earth's surface.
18. What kind of weathering is imposed on a rock when it is smashed into small pieces? When it is dissolved in acid?
19. Of the types of rock made from previously existing rock, which one does not require high temperature and pressure for its formation?
20. What properties of slate make it good roofing material?
21. Cite two mica minerals that can give a metamorphic rock its foliation.
22. How is foliation different from sedimentary layering?
23. Can metamorphism caused solely by elevated temperature occur without the presence of magma? Why or why not?
24. Each of the following statements describes one or more characteristics of a particular metamorphic rock. For each statement, name the metamorphic rock being described.
    (a) Foliated rock, sometimes derived from granite.
    (b) Hard, nonfoliated, single-mineral rock, formed under high to moderate pressure.
    (c) Foliated rock possessing excellent rock cleavage; generally used in making blackboards.
    (d) Nonfoliated rock composed of carbonate minerals.
    (e) Foliated rock containing about 50 percent platy minerals; named according to the major minerals in the rock.
25. What feature helps to distinguish schist and gneiss from quartzite and marble?
26. The earth's temperature increases with depth. Why, then, don't all rocks melt in the earth's interior?
27. Is the earth's interior mostly magma?
28. What three factors cause rock to melt?
29. If a rock contains both quartz and pyroxene, which would melt first?
30. If a magma contains molten forms of quartz and olivine, which would crystallize first?

Problems

Refer to "Figuring Physical Science: Volcano Height," on page 639 for the following three problems.

1. A shield volcano was formed by the eruption of 15,000 km^3 of lava. The diameter of the volcano's base is 120 km. Estimate the probable maximum height (from the base to the top) of this volcano.

Assume that all of the now-solidified lava is contained within the volcano.

2. A volcano is 3000 m high and the diameter of the base is 10,400 m. Assuming that the volcano is symmetrical and conical, how many meters would you travel if you were to hike from the base of the volcano *directly* to the top?
3. Topographic maps provide vertical information (elevations) and horizontal information (distances). The vertical information is displayed with *contour lines,* which connect points of equal elevation. Let us assume that we have a topographic map showing a cinder cone with uniform slopes, so that it can be approximated by a cone. The volcano is readily apparent on the map. The contour lines form a series of concentric circles, with each successively smaller circle representing a successively higher elevation. The elevation at the base of the volcano is 1,000 m above sea level. The elevation at the top of the volcano is 1,477 m above sea level. Using the scale bar on the map, we find that the horizontal distance from the peak of the volcano to the circular contour line at the base is 1 km. If the cinder cone was formed from all of the lava that erupted, what was the volume of lava erupted? Give your answer in cubic kilometers.

Chapter 26 Online Resources

Tutorials
- The Rock Cycle Activity

Quiz
Exercises
Flashcards
Links

CHAPTER 27

The Dynamic Earth

If it were possible to dig a hole straight through the earth, what would we find in its interior? Because digging such a hole is impossible, what tools and techniques can we use to explore the interior of earth? Investigation begins with the rocks on the earth's surface, which tell us a great deal about the earth's interior. Earthquakes and volcanic eruptions are a direct link to the inner workings of the planet, so observations and careful measurements of their behavior can offer many clues as well. These features are all external expressions of the earth's internal processes.

27.1 Seismic Waves

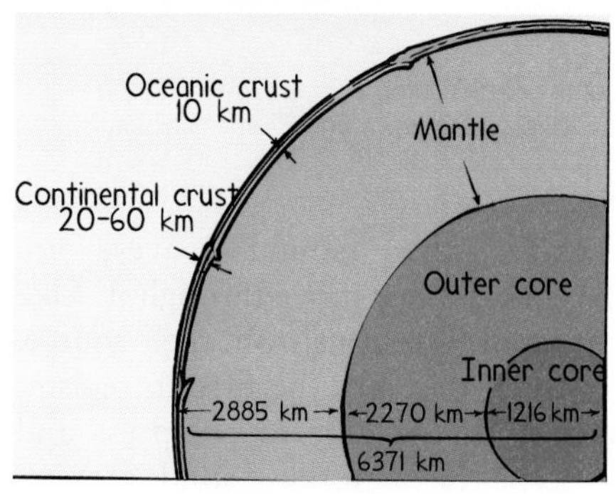

Figure 27.1
Cross section of the earth's interior showing the four major layers and their approximate thickness.

Earthquakes create waves that travel through the earth's interior and across earth's surface. Such earthquake-generated waves are called *seismic waves.* The speed at which these waves travel and the paths they take have provided earth scientists with a view into the earth's interior. What they have discovered is a layered planet. The major layers of the earth consist of the *crust, mantle, outer core,* and *inner core* (Figure 27.1).

Recall, from Chapter 11, that a wave's speed depends on the medium through which it travels. We learned that the sound waves generated by clicking two submerged rocks together travel faster through water than through air. And sound waves travel even faster through a solid. Just like sound waves, the speed of seismic waves depends on the elasticity of the material through which they are traveling. So measuring the speeds of seismic waves provides clues about the composition of the earth.

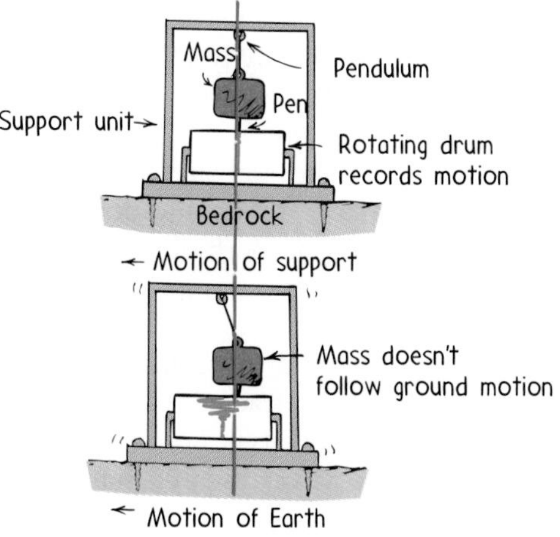

Figure 27.2
Diagram of a seismograph. When the earth moves, the support unit attached to the ground also moves, but, because of inertia, the mass at the end of the pendulum tends to stay in place. A pen attached to the mass marks the relative displacement on the slowly rotating drum beneath. In this way, the seismograph records ground movement.

During an earthquake, energy is released within the earth's interior and radiates in all directions. This energy travels to the earth's surface in the form of seismic waves, which cause the ground to shake and move. This ground movement is recorded on a *seismograph,* providing a map of the earth's interior.

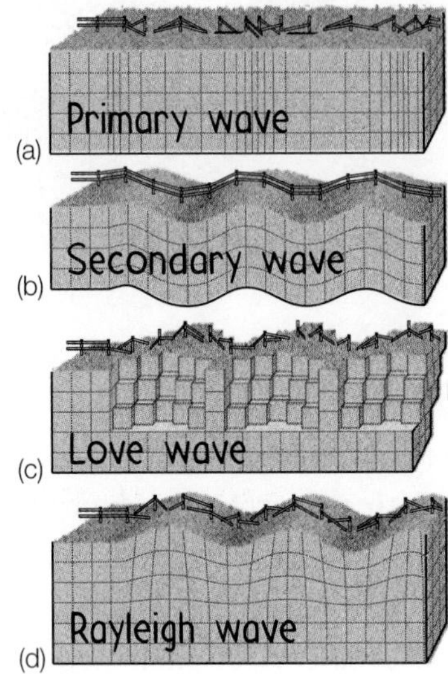

Figure 27.3
Block diagrams show the effects of seismic waves. The yellow portion on the left side of each diagram represents the undisturbed area. (a) Primary body waves alternately compress and expand the earth's crust, as shown by the different spacing between the vertical lines, similar to the action of a spring. (b) Secondary body waves cause the crust to oscillate up and down and from side to side. (c) Love surface waves whip back and forth in horizontal motion. (d) Rayleigh surface waves operate much like secondary body waves but affect only the surface of the earth.

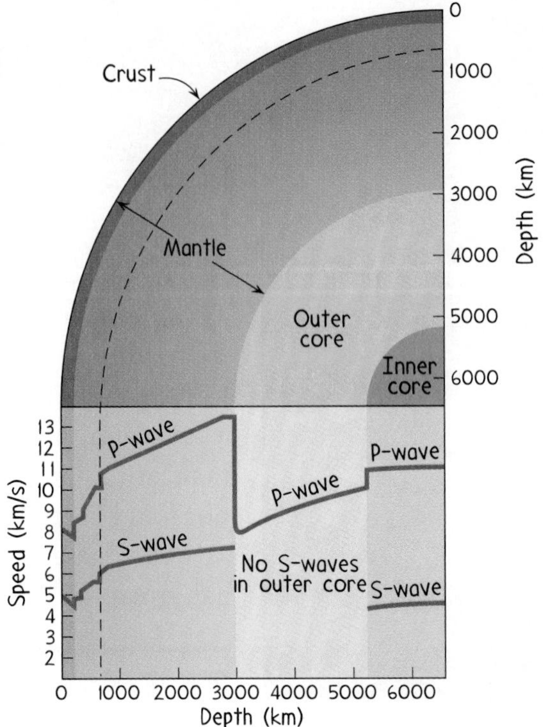

Figure 27.4
Cross section of the earth's internal layers, showing the increases and decreases of P-wave and S-wave velocity in the different layers.

Much that we know about the earth's interior was learned as a result of the Cold War between the United States and the former Soviet Union. In the 1960s, when testing of nuclear weapons was very common, underground nuclear explosions were found to produce seismic waves. Both countries installed sensitive seismographic stations to monitor their opponent's activities. It was the seismograms of this network of stations that revealed details of the unseen structure of our planet.

Insights

There are two types of seismic waves: **body waves,** which travel through the earth's interior, and **surface waves,** which travel on the earth's surface. Body waves are further classified as either **primary waves** (P-waves) or **secondary waves** (S-waves). Primary waves, like sound waves, are longitudinal—they compress and expand the rock as they move through it. Like vibrations in a bell, primary waves move out in all directions from their source. Because they are the fastest of all seismic waves, they are the first to register on a seismograph. Because both solids and fluids are able to compress and expand, P-waves can travel through any type of material—solid granite, magma, water, or air. Secondary waves, like the waves produced by a vibrating violin string, are transverse—they vibrate the particles of their medium up and down and from side-to-side, perpendicular to the direction of wave travel. Because S-waves travel more slowly than P-waves, they are the second waves to register on a seismograph. S-waves cannot move through fluids—they travel only through solids.

There are also two types of surface waves: *Rayleigh waves* and *Love waves.* Rayleigh waves have an up-and-down motion, and Love waves have a side-to-side, whiplike motion. Both of these types of surface waves travel more slowly than P-waves and S-waves, and therefore they are the last to register on a seismograph.

Seismic waves are reflected by surfaces in the earth's interior. Where wave speed changes, they are also refracted. Geoscientists study the reflection, refraction, and speeds of the various types of seismic waves to piece together a story about the earth. Seismic-wave research has revealed the architecture of the earth's internal layers (Figure 27.4).

27.2 Earth's Internal Layers

In 1909, the Croatian seismologist Andrija Mohorovičić presented the first convincing evidence that the earth's "innards" are layered. Studying seismographic data from a recent earthquake, he discovered that the seismic waves generated by the quake suddenly picked up speed at a certain depth below the surface. Knowing that the speeds of these waves depend on the elasticity of the material they pass through, Mohorovičić concluded that the increase in speed was due to density variations within the earth.

So how does density relate to elasticity? Quite different from the common usage of the word elastic, *elasticity* is not an indication of how far a material can be stretched. The elasticity of a substance is related to how rigid and springy it is. It is a measure of a solid's ability to recover its shape once a deforming force is removed from it. Steel, for example, has a high elasticity, while fresh bread has a low elasticity. (A rubber band, interestingly, is called elastic because it returns to its original shape when released.) The density of rock beneath Earth's surface increases because it is compressed by the weight of material above it. The more the rock is compressed, the more rigid and elastic it becomes. So there is a strong connection between density and elasticity within the earth's interior. Thus, increased wave speed indicates denser rock.

Mohorovičić's seismographic data had literally drawn a map of the upper boundary of the earth's mantle, a layer of dense rock underlying the less dense crust. This boundary, known as the **Mohorovičić discontinuity** (called the "Moho" for short), separates the earth's crust from rocks of different composition in the mantle below.

Two years after the discovery of the Moho, the mantle–core boundary was detected. Both P-waves and S-waves are strongly influenced by a pronounced boundary approximately 2900 kilometers deep. When P-waves reach that boundary, they are reflected and refracted so strongly that the boundary actually casts a P-wave *shadow* over part of the earth (Figure 27.5). The shadow is a region where no waves are detected. The wave shadow develops between 105° and 140° from the epicenter of an earthquake and has no direct penetration of seismic waves. Because the boundary is so distinct in the seismographic record, we infer that it marks a very important change in the density of the materials present in the earth's interior. Both the overall density of the earth and the speed with which seismic waves travel through its core suggest that the core is composed of metallic iron, a material that is much more dense than the silicate rocks that make up the mantle.

The sharp boundary between the mantle and core casts an S-wave shadow that is even more extensive than the P-wave shadow, suggesting that S-waves are unable to pass through the core. And since S-waves are transverse and can only travel through solids, we infer that the outer portion of the core is liquid.

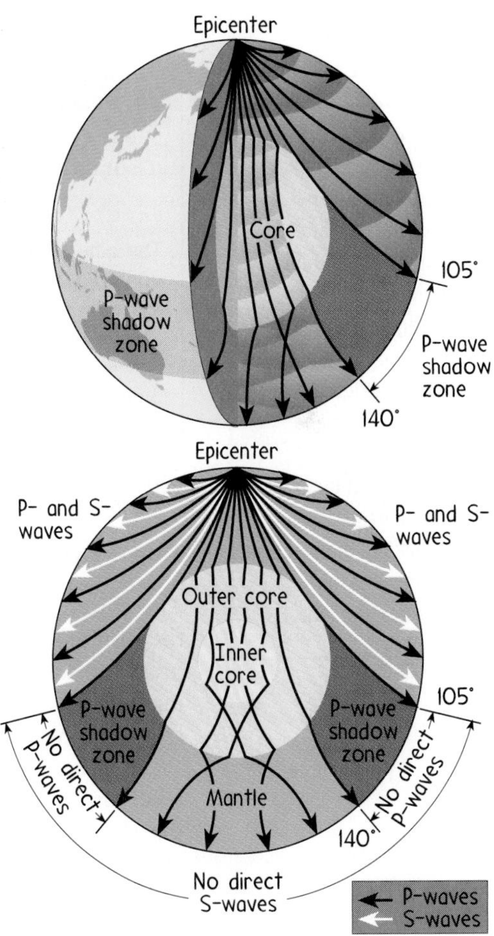

Figure 27.5
Cutaway and cross-sectional diagrams showing the change in wave paths at the major internal boundaries and the P-wave shadow. The P-wave shadow between 105° and 140° from an earthquake's epicenter is caused by the refraction of the P-waves at the core–mantle boundary. Note that any location more than 105° from an earthquake's epicenter does not receive S-waves since the liquid outer core does not transmit S-waves.

The density of rocks at the earth's surface is 2.7–3.0 g/cm^3, whereas the average density of the earth as a whole is 5.5 g/cm^3. Thus, surface rocks are not representative of the planet's interior. To account for the earth's high average density, the density of the core must be at least 10 g/cm^3. This and other reasons suggest that the core is composed of iron and nickel, the most abundant of the heavier elements.

Insights

In 1936, the discovery that some P-waves are reflected from a boundary within the core indicated the existence of yet another layer. Also P-waves passing through the inner portion of the core traveled faster than P-waves passing through the outer core. This change in wave speed tells us that the inner core must be solid.

Do you suppose these layers in the earth's interior influence the geologic changes our planet experiences? The answer is *yes,* as you will now see.

☑ CHECKPOINT

What evidence supports the theory that the earth's inner core is solid and its outer core is liquid?

Check Your Answer

The differences between how P-waves and S-waves move through the earth's interior indicate differences between the earth's inner and outer core. As the waves encounter the boundary at 2900 km below the surface, a very pronounced wave shadow develops. P-waves are both reflected and refracted at that boundary, but S-waves are only reflected. S-waves cannot travel through liquids, implying that the outer core is liquid. As P-waves move through the outer core, there is a depth at which they suddenly increase their speed. Knowing that waves travel faster in solids, we infer the existence of a solid inner core.

The Core

The **core** of the earth is composed mainly of iron and nickel. In the inner core, the iron and nickel are solid. Although the inner core is indeed very hot, intense pressure from the weight of the rest of the earth prevents the material of the inner core from melting (like a pressure cooker prevents high-temperature water from boiling).

Because less weight is exerted on the outer core, the pressure is less there, resulting in a liquid phase of iron and nickel. The molten outer core flows at the very slow rate of several kilometers per year. This flow is evident far outside the earth's surface. The flowing molten outer core produces a flowing electric charge—an electric current. This electric current powers the earth's magnetic field. This magnetic field is not stable but has changed throughout geologic time. Recall, from Chapter 10, that there have been times when the earth's magnetic field has diminished to zero, only to build up again with the poles reversed. These magnetic-pole reversals probably result from changes in the direction of fluid flow in the molten outer core of the earth.

☑ CHECKPOINT

Iron's normal melting point is 1535°C, yet the earth's inner core temperature is greater than 4000°C. Why doesn't the solid inner core melt?

Check Your Answer

The intense pressure from the weight of the earth above crushes atoms together so tightly that even high temperature cannot budge them. In this way, melting is prevented.

The Mantle

Surrounding the core of the planet is the **mantle,** a rocky layer some 2900 kilometers thick. Uniformly composed of hot, iron-rich silicate rocks, the mantle behaves like an elastic solid. Mantle rocks actually flow, even though they are solid—they behave in a *plastic* manner. This is similar to the behavior of Silly Putty: it behaves like a solid under sudden stress (it breaks), but it behaves like a fluid when stress is applied slowly (it flows). Flow in the mantle occurs as *convection currents* that form *convection cells* (Figure 27.6). In other words, hot material in the mantle rises, cools, and then sinks.

Although it is of relatively uniform bulk composition, the mantle is divided into two portions based on their physical properties. The lower mantle extends from the outer core to a depth of about 660 kilometers (the dashed line in Figure 27.4). The lower mantle is completely solid because pressure in the lower mantle is too great for melting to occur.

The upper mantle, which extends from a 660-kilometer depth to the crust–mantle boundary, has two zones (Figure 27.7). The lower part of the upper mantle, called the **asthenosphere,** contains small amounts of liquid derived from the partial melting of mantle rocks. The asthenosphere is especially plastic, and it flows more easily than the lower mantle. Many geologists believe that convection cells in the asthenosphere do not extend below 660 km depth and are separate from convection cells in the lower mantle. But it is equally likely that the convection cells are not separated, extending through the asthenosphere and deep into the mantle, perhaps as deep as the core–mantle boundary. In any case, the constant flowing movements in the asthenosphere greatly affect the surface features of our planet.

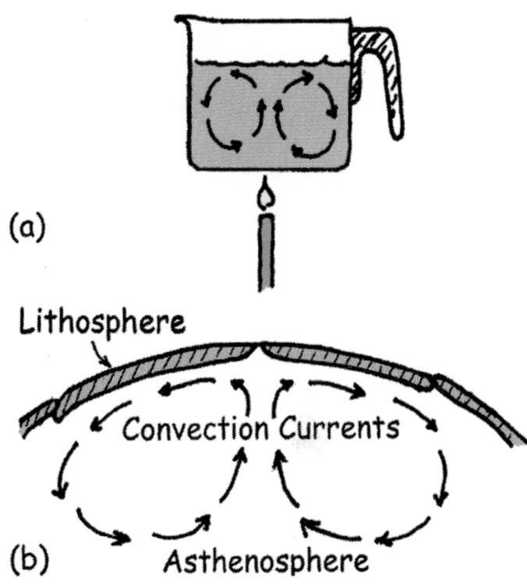

Figure 27.6
(a) A familiar example of convection is seen when water is heated in a pan. (b) A simple model showing convection currents in the asthenosphere.

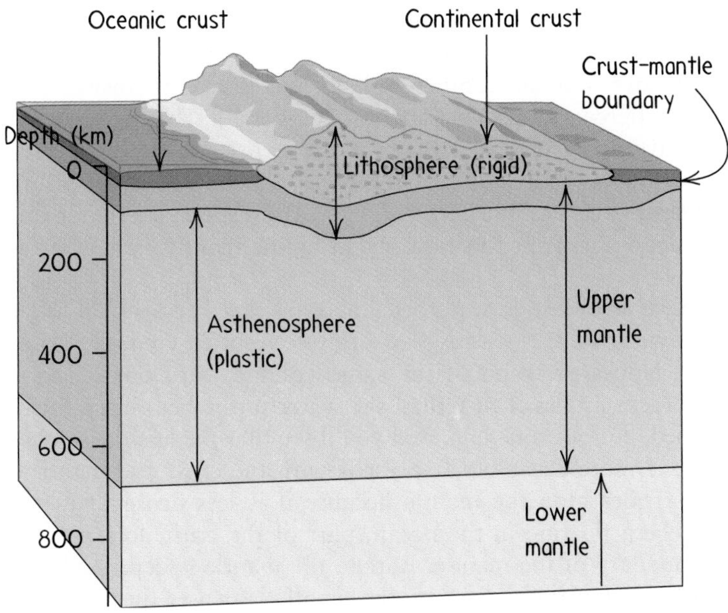

Figure 27.7
The bottom portion of the earth's upper mantle is the plastic asthenosphere. The top portion of the upper mantle plus the crust form the rigid layer called the lithosphere.

Now, we come to the rigid outer layer of Earth, which includes the crust and the upper part of the mantle. This region is called the **lithosphere.** The mantle itself ends at the Moho, but the lithosphere includes the entire crust (Figure 27.7). So, the upper mantle includes the asthenosphere and part of the lithosphere, and the lithosphere is part mantle and part crust. The reason for the strange divisions is the overlap between composition and physical properties, as revealed by seismic waves. The lithosphere behaves as a single unit, but there is a marked change in composition partway through the lithosphere.

Unlike the asthenosphere, the lithosphere is more rigid and brittle and does not flow appreciably. The lithosphere is, in a sense, riding on top of the asthenosphere like a raft on a pond. The lithosphere is carried along by the motions of the material beneath it in the mantle. Motions in the mantle are not uniform, and, because of this (as we shall see later in this chapter), the brittle lithosphere is broken into many individual pieces called *plates.*

The lithospheric plates are always in motion. They ride on the circulating mantle. Although mantle convection currents move at a leisurely pace—taking hundreds of millions of years to complete one loop—they are powerful enough to move continents and to reshape many of our surface features. The movement of the lithospheric plates causes earthquakes, volcanic activity, and the deformation of large masses of rock to create mountains.

The Crustal Surface

The uppermost portion of the lithosphere is the **crust.** Earth's crust is entirely composed of low-density rock. However, the crust is subdivided into two categories: *continental crust* and *oceanic crust.* The density, composition, and thickness of the crust vary markedly from the deep ocean basins to the lofty continental plateaus. The crust of the ocean basins is compact. It's only about 10 kilometers thick, and it is composed of dense basaltic rocks. Continental crust is between 20 and 60 kilometers thick, and it is composed of granitic rocks, which are less dense than basaltic rocks. The lower density keeps most of the continental crust above sea level.

If continental crust is so much thicker than oceanic crust, why are the ocean basins underwater and the continents high and dry? The answer is found in their density differences and buoyancies (Chapter 6). The less dense continental crust always floats higher than the more dense oceanic crust, even if the continental crust has more mass. This is the principle of **isostasy.** Either type of crust reaches an equilibrium height with respect to the mantle when the upward-acting buoyant force, provided by the mantle, equals the weight of the crust.

If you have an old-style waterbed, the type that is essentially a large plastic bag filled with water, you can prove this concept to yourself. Consider two large cubical blocks of wood of the same volume, with one denser than the other. Both blocks are less dense than the water in the bed. Place them side-by-side on the bed, but not touching, and you'll see that the less-dense block stands higher than the more-dense block. So it is with the crust and mantle.

The crust rides atop the mantle because it is less dense than the mantle. Unlike an iceberg floating in the ocean, part of the crust does not sink below the upper boundary of the mantle. Rather, the mantle is depressed beneath the crust, but it still supports it, because the mantle is denser (just as the waterbed is depressed under the wood blocks but still supports them).

On the planetary scale, consider two blocks of crust of equal mass, one composed of oceanic crust and the other of continental crust. The mantle exerts the same buoyant force on both blocks, but the continental block floats higher because it is less dense. If we were to add more crust to the continental block, its upper surface would be higher than before but it would also sink farther into the mantle because of the additional weight. So, the higher the crust floats above the mantle, the deeper its "root" must be to support it.

Link to Section 6.5

Taking these ideas a bit further, blocks of crust come into equilibrium with each other. The weight of the mantle material displaced by a block of floating crust equals the weight of the block. Where does the displaced mantle material go? Because the pressure in the mantle from the overlying crust must be the same at any given depth, the displaced material simply flows away from whatever is pressing down on it until the pressure in the mantle is equalized. This means that the pressure in the mantle underneath the thick (but less dense) continental crust is about the same as the pressure in the mantle beneath the thin (but denser) oceanic crust. To achieve this state of balance, the vertical positions of the different blocks of crust adjust until the pressure in the mantle is balanced.

☑ CHECKPOINT

If you wanted to drill the shortest hole to the mantle, would you drill in western Colorado or in Florida?

Check Your Answer

Put the question another way: If you wanted to drill the shortest hole through ice to the water below, would you drill atop an iceberg or through a slab of ice that hardly extends out of the water? You would drill your hole in the slab, of course; and, likewise, you should drill through the thinner crust of mountain-free Florida. In mountainous western Colorado, the crust is much thicker. (If you really want the shortest hole, you should drill through the ocean floor—exactly what scientists did in the Mohole Project of 1958 to 1966, in the eastern Pacific Ocean.)

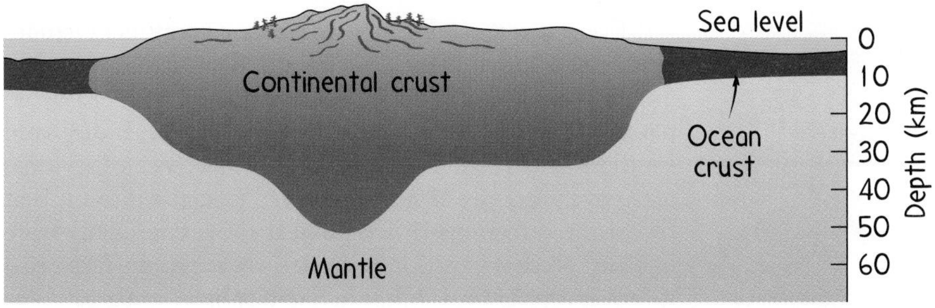

Figure 27.8
Continental crust is thicker and less dense than oceanic crust. As such, continental crust floats higher on the mantle than oceanic crust.

27.3 The Theory of Continental Drift

Scientists of the early twentieth century believed that oceans and continents were geographically fixed. They regarded the surface of the planet as a static skin spread over a molten, gradually cooling interior. They believed that the

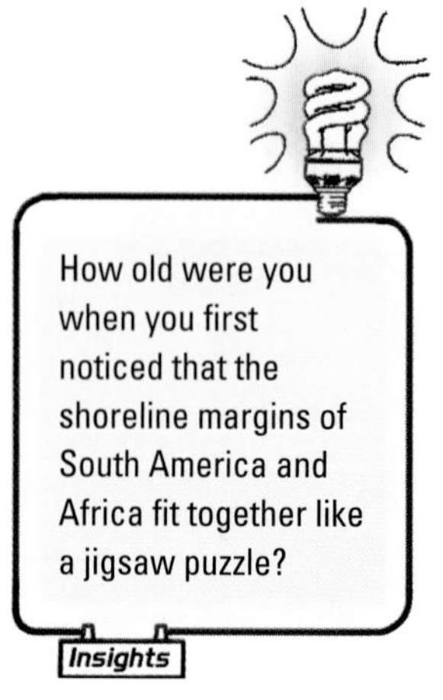

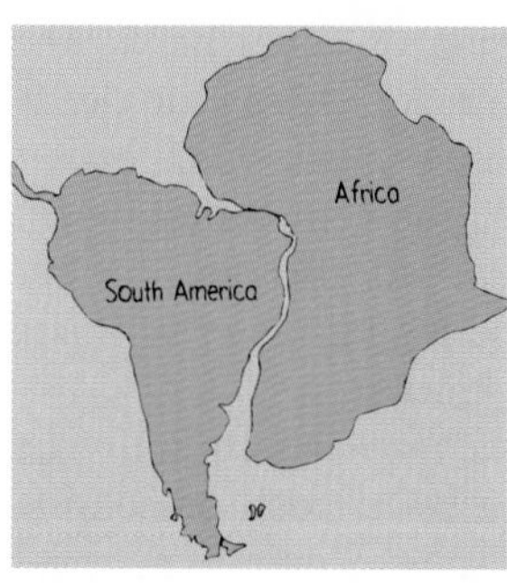

Figure 27.9
When you align the shorelines of South America and Africa, the continents fit together like pieces in a jigsaw puzzle.

cooling of the planet resulted in its contraction, which caused the outer skin to contort and wrinkle into mountains and valleys.

Many people had noticed, however, that the eastern shoreline of South America and the western shoreline of Africa seemed to fit together like pieces of a jigsaw puzzle (Figure 27.9). One Earth scientist who took this observation seriously was Alfred Wegener, who saw the earth as a dynamic planet with the continents in constant motion. He believed that all the continents had once been joined together in one great supercontinent he called **Pangaea,** meaning "all land." His hypothesis was that Pangaea had fractured into a number of pieces, and that South America and Africa had indeed once been joined together as part of a larger land mass.

Wegener supported his hypothesis with impressive geological, biological, and climatological evidence. He proposed that the geological boundary of each continent lay not at its shoreline but at the edge of its *continental shelf* (the gently sloping platform between the shoreline and the steep slope that leads to the deep ocean floor). When Wegener fit Africa and South America together along their continental shelves, the fit was even better than it was at the shorelines (Figure 27.10). Furthermore, rocks on different continents that are brought into juxtaposition when the continental shelves are matched up are virtually identical. In addition, many of the mountain systems in Africa and South America show strong evidence of a previous connection. Similarly, fossils of nearly identical land-dwelling animals are found in South America and Africa but nowhere else. And fossils of nearly identical trees are found in South America, India, Australia, and Antarctica.*

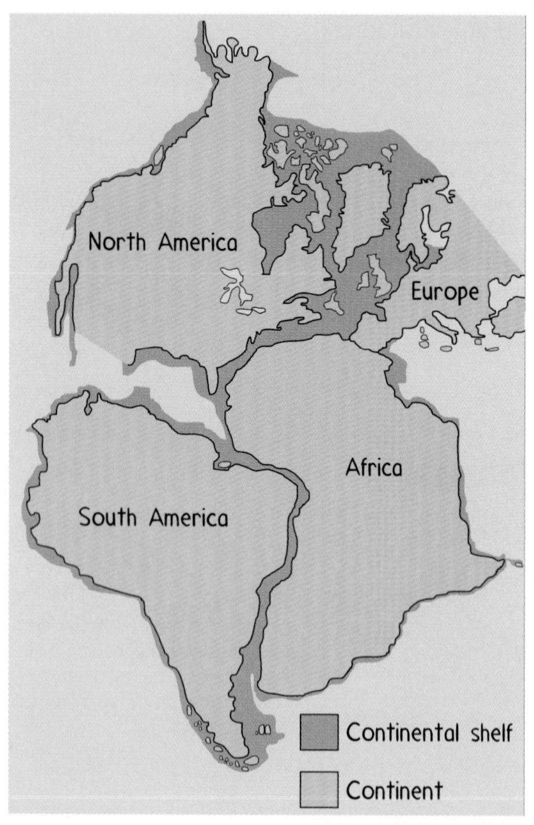

Figure 27.10
The jigsaw-puzzle fit between continents is even better at the continental shelves than at the shorelines of the continents.

Even stronger evidence for a supercontinent comes from paleoclimatic (ancient climate) data. More than 300 million years ago, a huge continental ice sheet covered parts of South America, southern Africa, India, and southern Australia. The ice sheet left evidence of its existence in thousands of well-preserved glacial striations that reveal the directions of ice flow. If these continents were in their present positions, the ice sheet would have had to cover the entire Southern Hemisphere, and, in some places, would have had to cross the equator! If the ice sheet were that extensive, the world climate would have been very cold. But there is no evidence of glaciation in

*One fossil plant assemblage that offers especially strong support for Wegener's idea is the *Glossopteris* flora, which was named after the dominant gymnosperm tree found in the prehistoric southern temperate forests of South America, India, Australia, and Antarctica. Because the seeds from these trees were too large to be distributed by air, the wide distribution of this flora supports Wegener's theory that the continents were once joined together.

the Northern Hemisphere at that time. In fact, the time of glaciation in the Southern Hemisphere was a time of subtropical climate in the Northern Hemisphere. To account for this enigmatic distribution of paleoclimates, Wegener proposed that Pangaea had been in existence 300 million years ago, with South Africa located over the earth's South Pole. This reconstruction brings all the glaciated regions into close proximity in the vicinity of the South Pole and places the modern northern continents nearer the tropics.

Wegener described continental drift in *The Origin of Continents and Oceans,* published in 1915. Although he used evidence from different scientific disciplines, his well-founded hypothesis was ridiculed by the community of earth scientists. Antagonists complained that Wegener failed to provide a suitable driving force to account for the continental movements. (Wegener wrongly proposed that the tidal influence of the moon could produce the needed force. He also proposed that the continents broke through the earth's crust like ice breakers cutting through ice.) Without a convincing explanation for his theory, scientists at that time dismissed his hypothesis. It was only recently, in the light of newfound discoveries, that Wegener's concept became accepted by the scientific community.

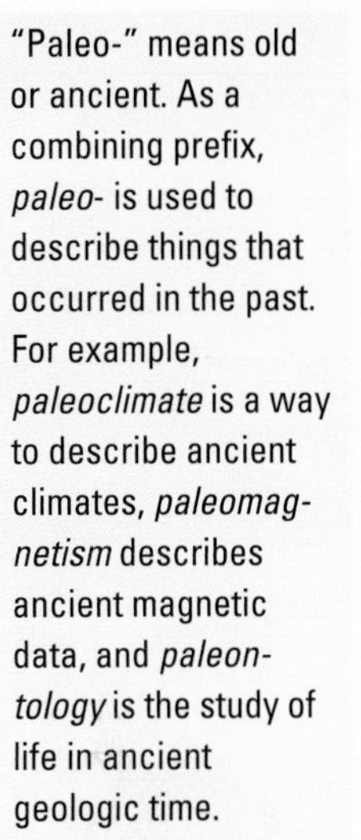
"Paleo-" means old or ancient. As a combining prefix, *paleo-* is used to describe things that occurred in the past. For example, *paleoclimate* is a way to describe ancient climates, *paleomagnetism* describes ancient magnetic data, and *paleontology* is the study of life in ancient geologic time.

Acceptance of the Theory of Continental Drift

One of the first key discoveries in support of continental drift came about through studies of the earth's magnetic field. We know, from Chapter 10, that the earth is a huge magnet and that its magnetic north and south poles are near the geographic poles. Because certain minerals align themselves with the magnetic field when a rock is formed, rocks have a preserved imprint of the changes in the earth's magnetism over the eons of geologic time. This magnetism from the geologic past is known as **paleomagnetism.**

Three essential bits of information are contained in the preserved magnetic record: (1) the polarity of the earth's magnetic field at the time the rock was formed, (2) the direction to the magnetic pole from the rock's location at the time the rock was formed, and (3) the magnetic latitude of the rock's location at the time the rock was formed. Once the magnetic latitude of a rock and the direction of the magnetic poles are known, the position of the magnetic pole at the time of formation can be determined.

Figure 27.11
The path of the magnetic north pole during the last 500 million years. (The unit *m.y.a.* stands for "millions of years ago.") The lower red line is derived from evidence collected in Europe, and the upper red line is derived from evidence collected in North America. One would expect that these two lines would overlie each other. Thus, either the magnetic pole wanders erratically, or the continents have moved. But how could the pole be in more than one place at the same time? This question strongly suggests that the continents have indeed moved relative to each other.

During the 1950s, a plot of the positions of the magnetic north pole through time revealed that, over the past 500 million years, the position of the pole had wandered extensively throughout the world (Figure 27.11). It seemed that either the magnetic poles migrated through time or the continents had drifted. Because the apparent path of polar movement varied from continent to continent, it was more plausible that the continents had moved. Thus the hypothesis of continental drift was revived, but a mechanism to explain how the movement occurred was still lacking.

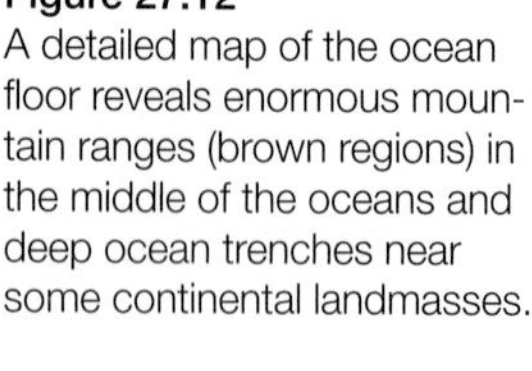
Figure 27.12
A detailed map of the ocean floor reveals enormous mountain ranges (brown regions) in the middle of the oceans and deep ocean trenches near some continental landmasses.

The 1950s were a time of extensive and detailed mapping of ocean floors. Huge mountain ranges running down the middle of the Atlantic, Pacific, and Indian oceans were revealed. A major rift valley along each crest was discovered, and deep ocean trenches near some of the continental landmasses, particularly around the edges of the Pacific (Figure 27.12), were also discovered. So, it was found that some of the deepest parts of the ocean are actually near some of the continents, and that out in the middle of the oceans, the water is relatively shallow because of the underwater mountains. Volcanism and high thermal energies were found to be generated at these undersea ridge systems.

With this new information, H. H. Hess, an American geologist, presented the hypothesis of **seafloor spreading.** Hess proposed that the seafloor is not permanent but is constantly being renewed. He theorized that the ocean ridges are located above upwelling convection cells in the mantle. As rising material from the mantle oozes upward, new lithosphere is formed. The old lithosphere is simultaneously destroyed in the deep ocean trenches near the edges of continents. Thus, in a conveyor-belt fashion, new lithosphere forms at a spreading center and older lithosphere is pushed out from the ridge crest, eventually to be recycled back into the mantle at a deep ocean trench (Figure 27.13).

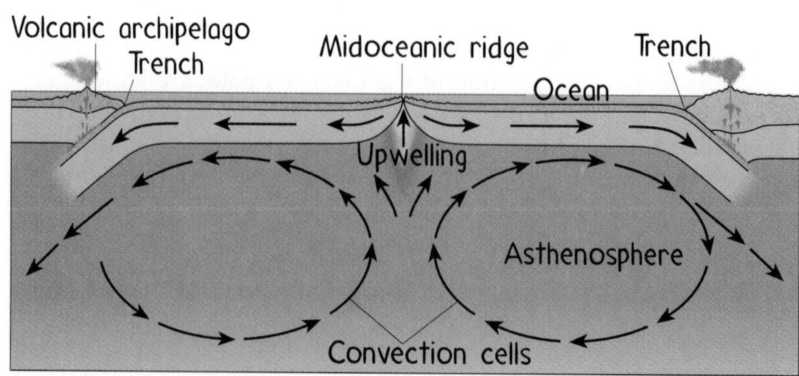

Figure 27.13
In conveyor-belt fashion, new lithosphere is formed at the mid-ocean ridges (also called "spreading centers"), as old lithosphere is recycled back into the asthenosphere at a deep ocean trench.

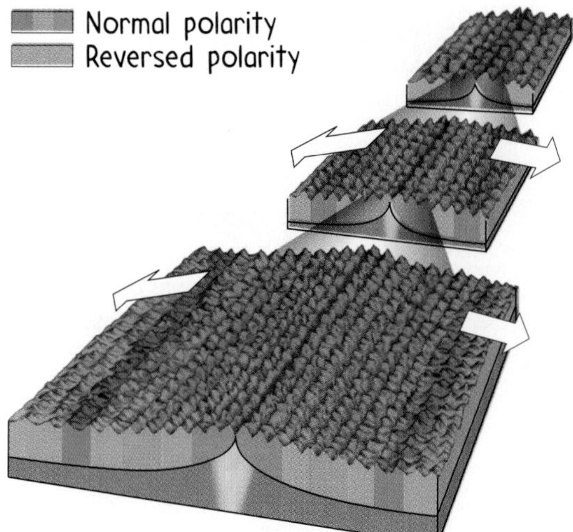

Figure 27.14
As new material is extruded at an oceanic ridge (spreading center), it is magnetized according to the existing magnetic field. Magnetic surveys show alternating strips of normal and reversed polarity paralleling both sides of the rift area. Like a very slow magnetic tape recording, the magnetic history of the earth is thus recorded in the spreading ocean floors.

Support for this theory came from paleomagnetic analysis of the ocean floor. As new basalt is extruded at an oceanic ridge, it is magnetized according to the existing magnetic field. The magnetic surveys of the ocean's floor showed alternating strips of normal and reversed polarity, paralleling either side of the rift areas (Figure 27.14). As in a very slow magnetic tape recording, the magnetic history of the earth is thus recorded in spreading ocean floors. Since the dates of pole reversal can be determined, the magnetic pattern of the spreading seafloor documents both the age of the seafloor and the rate at which it spreads. Thus, the oceanic crust was found to be thin and young near the central ridge region and progressively thicker and older away from the ridge.

The theory of seafloor spreading provided a mechanism for continental drift. The time was right for the revolutionary concepts to follow. The tide of scientific opinion had indeed switched in favor of a mobile earth.

☑ CHECKPOINT

Why was Wegener's theory of continental drift not taken more seriously in the early part of the twentieth century?

Check Your Answer

Wegener failed to produce a suitable driving mechanism to support his theory. Even if he had postulated the role of the convective interior, we can only speculate about how quickly the scientific community would have accepted his hypothesis. Scientists, like all other human beings, tend to identify with the ideas that characterize their time. Do advances in knowledge, scientific or otherwise, occur because they are accepted by those who have supported the status quo or because supporters of the status quo eventually die off? Knowledge that is radical and unacceptable to the old guard is often more easily accepted by newcomers, who use it to push the knowledge frontier further. Hooray for the young (and the young-at-heart)!

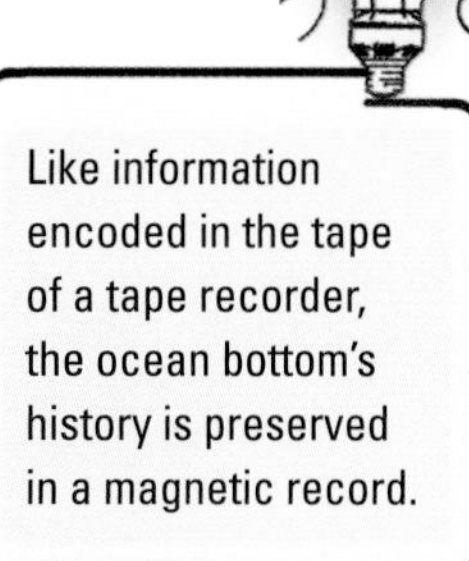
Like information encoded in the tape of a tape recorder, the ocean bottom's history is preserved in a magnetic record.

Hot Spot and Lasers: Measurement of Tectonic Plate Motion

Motion is relative. Whenever we discuss the motion of something, we can only describe its motion relative to something else. We call this something else—the place from which motion is observed and measured—a *reference frame*. Living in a world where everything is in motion, how can we measure rates of plate motion? What do we choose as our reference frame?

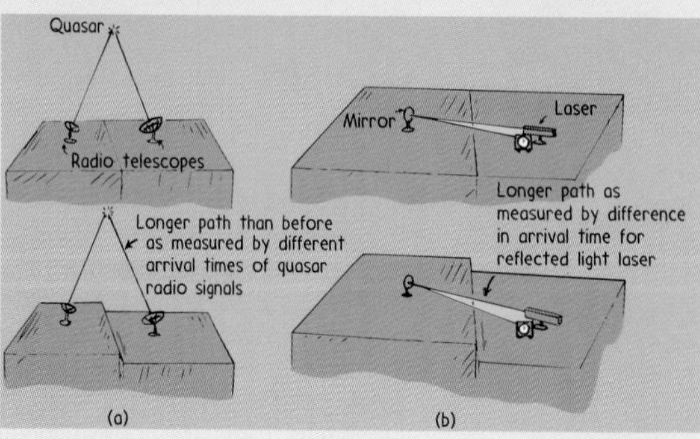

Earth movements are measured by radio telescopes or lasers keyed to a stationary reference point. (a) Broad movements in the range of 1 cm per year are detected using satellites and quasars as reference points. (b) Fault movements are measured by laser beams shot from opposite sides of a fault. The laser flashes a beam off a reflector; the bounce-back time is recorded. Because of light's constant speed, the time of bounce-back will change with Earth movement.

The Canadian geophysicist J. Tuzo Wilson suggested that one measure of Pacific seafloor movement could be found in the ages of the volcanic Hawaiian Islands. Wilson postulated that the islands are the tips of huge volcanoes that formed as the Pacific seafloor moved over a fixed *hot spot*—a magma source rising from the earth's interior. As we learned in Chapter 16, radioactive decay in the earth's interior keeps the earth hot. The concept of a concentrated or fixed hot spot provides a stationary reference point on the surface of the earth against which plate motion can be determined. There are about 100 such reference hot spots around the world, and they are used together to determine rates of plate movements.

There is, however, some debate as to whether the hot spots are truly stationary. A fascinating and more precise way to measure earth movement is by a laser beam reflecting off "mirrors" in outer space. Lasers are used to detect the broad movements of tectonic plates. Laser pulses are beamed from a pair of ground stations located on opposite sides of a plate boundary or a fault to the reference point in space. A laser pulse starts a timer that runs until the reflected pulses are received back at the stations. A computer combines this elapsed time with the known position of the reference point to determine the exact position of the ground station. Any movement of the ground station is registered as a change in the elapsed time.

This type of measurement can also be done with radio signals. Radio telescopes are keyed to a reference point in outer space—a quasar or a satellite—from which relative positions of points on earth can be plotted. Local movements along faults can be measured with lasers as well. In this case, the mirror is placed on the opposite side of the fault from the laser, instead of in outer space. Neat-O!

27.4 The Theory of Plate Tectonics

The framework that allows us to understand how and why the various features of the earth constantly change is called the **theory of plate tectonics.** It describes the forces within the earth that create the continents, ocean basins, mountain ranges, earthquake belts, and other large-scale features of the earth's surface. The theory of plate tectonics states that the earth's outer shell, the lithosphere, is divided into eight relatively large plates and a number of smaller ones (Figure 27.15). These lithospheric plates ride atop the relatively plastic asthenosphere below. Because each plate moves as a single unit in relation to the other plates, the interiors of the plates are generally stable geologically. All major interactions between plates occur along the plate boundaries. Thus, most of the

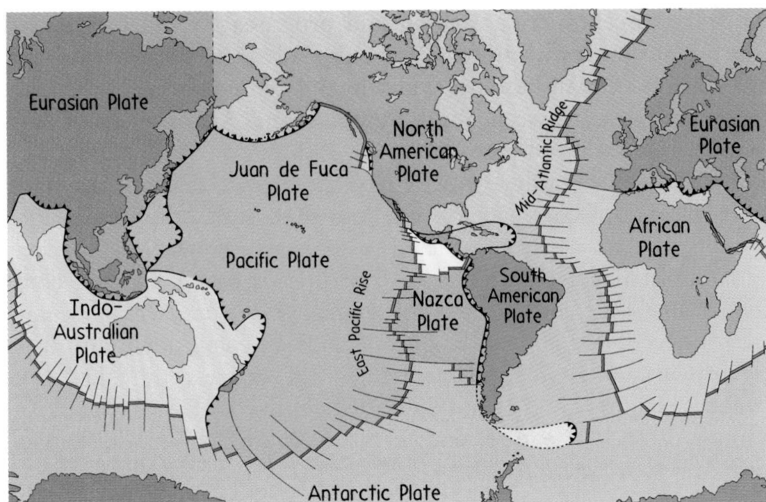

Figure 27.15
The lithosphere is divided into eight large plates and a number of smaller ones.

earth's earthquakes, volcanoes, and mountains occur along these active margins. In fact, the creation and destruction of lithosphere described in Figure 27.13 takes place at such margins.

Moving plates interact at their respective boundaries (Figure 27.16). The first type of plate boundary is a site of magma generation and lithosphere formation. The second type of boundary is a site of magma generation and lithosphere destruction. The third type of plate boundary simply accommodates plate movement at spreading centers (with no magma generation and no formation or destruction of lithosphere).

Divergent Plate Boundaries

Heat-driven convection cells in the mantle operate in loops, with symmetry between adjacent convection cells. The adjacent cell is a mirror image of the first cell, with rising hot rock from great depths in the mantle causing the motion, as shown in Figure 27.13. Where one side of a convection cell is moving toward the earth's surface, the neighboring side of the adjacent cell also moves upward. At the site where these two upward-moving convection currents reach the lithosphere, we find divergent plate boundaries. Also known as spreading centers, divergent boundaries are where plates are moving away from each other—they are *diverging*—as shown in Figure 27.16a. The asthenosphere is very near the surface at divergent boundaries, and the lithosphere is very thin.* New lithosphere forms as the plates move apart, accompanied by voluminous volcanic activity. The lithosphere near the spreading edge is thin and has a relatively low density due to heat and the expansion of rising magma. As it moves away from the spreading center, the new lithosphere cools, contracts, and becomes more dense.

The Mid-Atlantic Ridge is a spreading center that has been producing the floor of the South Atlantic Ocean since South America split off from Africa. The spreading is accompanied by almost continuous earthquake activity that goes largely unnoticed because of its low magnitude and the absence of harm to humans. With the production of lithosphere at the ridge, the continents on opposite sides of the ridge move apart as the ocean floor grows. This happens because the continents are embedded in the lithosphere. The lithosphere is

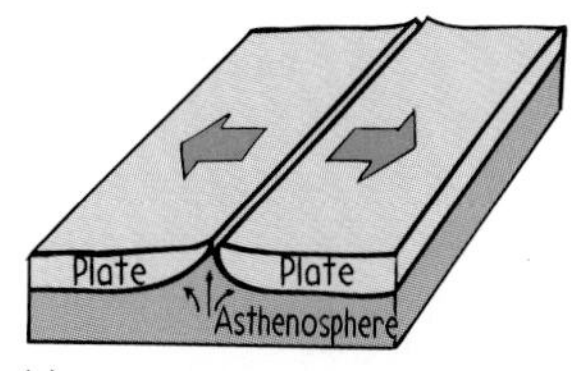

(a)

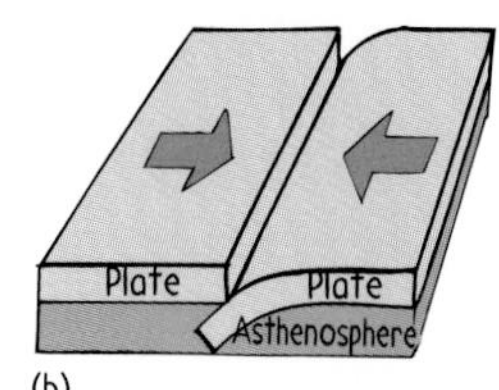

(b)

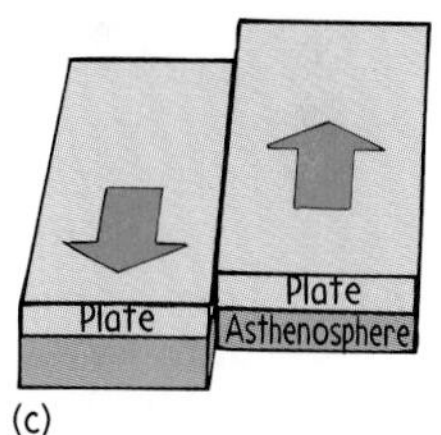

(c)

Figure 27.16
Plate boundaries are often sites of lithospheric formation and destruction. Named for the movement they accommodate, the three types of plate boundaries are (a) divergent, (b) convergent, and (c) transform-fault boundaries.

*Theoretically, the lithosphere has zero thickness at the *exact* location of the divergent boundary.

younger near the central ridge region and progressively older away from the ridge. Each plate moves away from the ridge at a rate of about 1.7 cm/yr, so the South Atlantic Ocean becomes wider by 3.4 centimeters each year. Near the equator, the distance between South America and Africa is about 6500 km. The seemingly slow rate of spreading over 190 million years adds up to about 6500 kilometers. Put another way, it has taken only 190 million years for a fracture in an ancient continent to turn into the South Atlantic Ocean!

Spreading centers are not restricted to the ocean floors but also develop on land. Hot, molten material in the earth's interior rising beneath continental landmasses causes the earth's crust to bend upward *(upwarping)*. Gaps in the crust are produced, and large slabs of rock slide and sink down into these gaps. The large down-faulted valleys generated by this process are called either **rifts** or **rift valleys** (Figure 27.17). The Great Rift Valley of East Africa is an excellent example of such a feature, and, if the spreading continues, it may be the beginning of a new ocean basin.

Magma Generation at Divergent Boundaries

Recall that the lower part of the upper mantle, the asthenosphere, is solid with only a very small amount of molten rock. So where does the magma come from to feed the volcanic activity at the spreading center? The temperature in the asthenosphere is high enough to melt rock at the earth's surface, but rock in the asthenosphere is under enormous pressure created by the weight of the rock above. The pressure raises the melting point of rock and prevents all but the smallest amount of melting. Not so at the spreading center itself. The asthenosphere is nearly at the surface at spreading centers. As mantle rock rises upward by convection, the pressure on the rock steadily decreases, allowing melting to occur. Partial melting of iron-rich mantle rock yields magma with about 10%

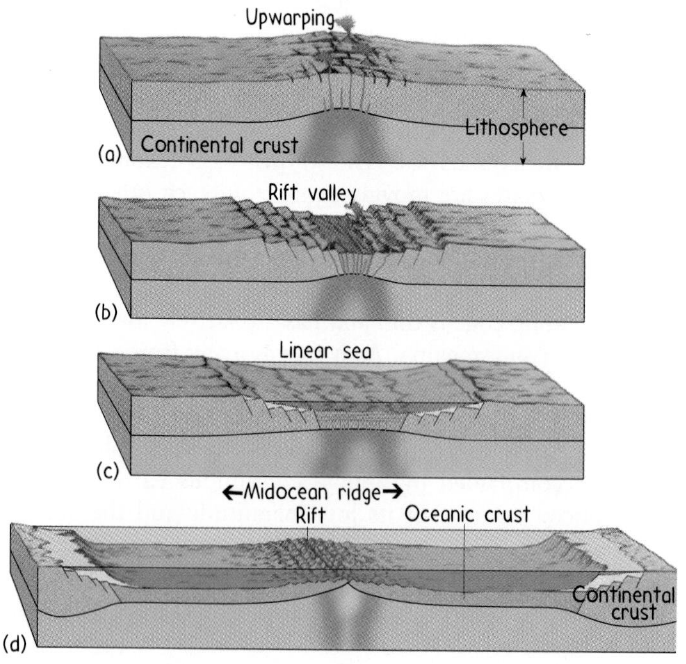

Figure 27.17
Formation of a rift valley and its transformation into an ocean basin. (a) Rising magma uplifts continental crust, causing the surface to crack. (b) Rift valley forms as crust is pulled apart. It is in this stage that we find Africa's Great Rift Valley today. (The two sides of the valley move away from each other because they happen to be located above mantle convection cells that have the same circulation pattern as the cells in Figure 27.13.) (c) Water from the ocean drains in as the rift drops below sea level, forming a linear sea, so called because it is usually long and narrow. (d) Over millions of years, the rift continues to widen and becomes an ocean basin.

iron and 50% silica—the composition of basalt. Huge volumes of basaltic magma are generated this way, forming new oceanic crust.

Convergent Plate Boundaries

Convergent boundaries, as the name suggests, are the boundaries at which plates come together, or *converge*. Where the motion created by convection cells acts to push two plates toward each other, compression either pushes the lithosphere of one plate below the other or shortens the lithosphere by folding and faulting. The regions of plate collisions are regions of great mountain building.

There are three types of plate collisions, each classified by the type of crust involved in the collision: (1) Both plates have an oceanic leading edge, (2) one plate has a continental leading edge and the other has an oceanic leading edge, and (3) both plates have continental leading edges (Figure 27.18).

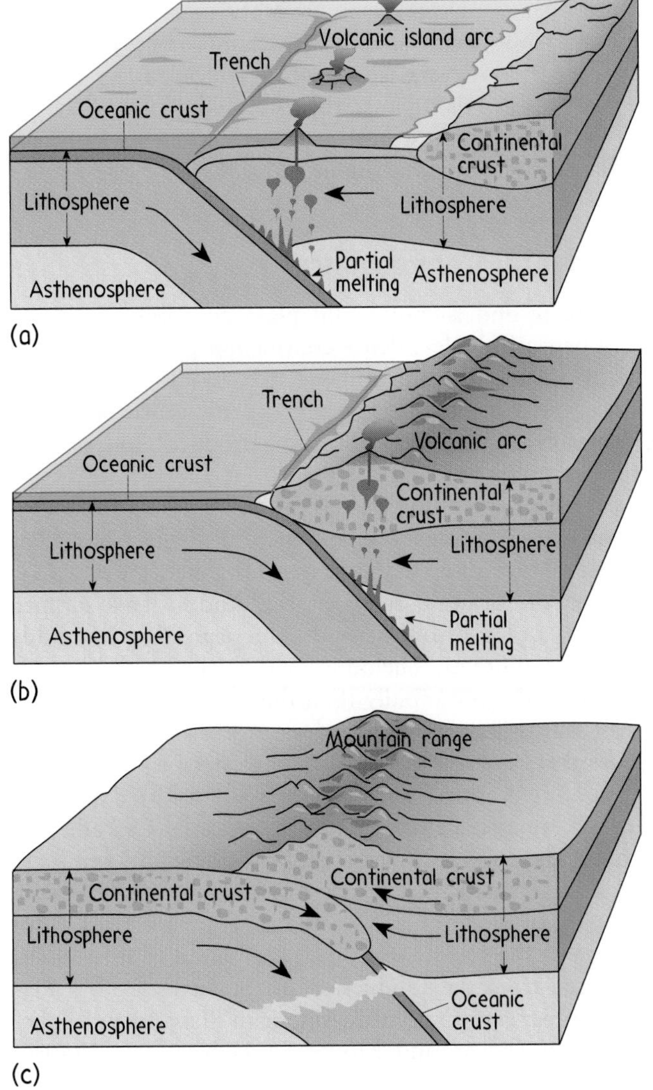

Figure 27.18
The three types of convergent margins: (a) oceanic–oceanic, (b) oceanic–continental, and (c) continental–continental.

Oceanic–Oceanic Convergence

Collision between two oceanic plates can result in *subduction.* Subduction is a process in which one plate bends and descends beneath the other to produce a deep ocean trench. The deepest trench known is the Marianas Trench in the western Pacific Ocean, where the seafloor is as much as 11 kilometers below sea level. Subduction induces the generation of basaltic magma. Eruptions on the ocean floor form the bases of new volcanoes. Crystallization of the basaltic magma causes the volcanoes to begin erupting andesitic magma, which allows them to grow significantly higher. The volcanoes eventually break the surface of the ocean as a series of islands called an *island arc.* The size and elevation of the islands in an island arc increase over time because of continued volcanic activity. Such island arcs have formed the Aleutian Islands, the Marianas Islands, and the Tonga island group in the South Pacific Ocean, as well as the island-arc systems of the Alaskan Peninsula, the Philippines, and Japan.

Deep ocean trenches mark the active subduction zones that border island arcs. Earthquakes occur along the subduction zones as the subducted plate grinds against the overriding plate. The earthquakes become steadily deeper and deeper in the direction of subduction (Figure 27.19).

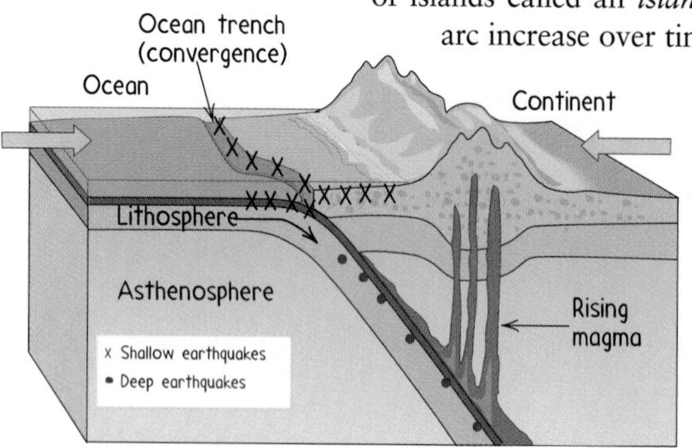

Figure 27.19
Earthquakes at a subduction zone get deeper and deeper in the direction of subduction.

Oceanic–Continental Convergence

When an oceanic plate and a continental plate converge, the denser oceanic plate is subducted beneath the less dense continental plate. A deep ocean trench is formed. As with oceanic–oceanic convergence, basaltic magma is generated. Since continental crust is much thicker than oceanic crust, eruptions of basalt are much less common. Instead, crystallization produces andesitic magma and, given enough time, granitic magma.

The Andes mountain system of western South America formed in this way. The Andes continue to grow higher as subduction of the Nazca Plate beneath the South American Plate causes sediments accumulated on the Nazca Plate to be scraped off onto the granitic roots of the Andes. This scraped material becomes permanently attached to the South American Plate and adds thickness and buoyancy to the mountains. The additional thickness and buoyancy causes the Andes to rise upward more rapidly than they are being eroded by wind and rain. Remnants of the original volcanic chain are the exposed batholiths and metamorphic rocks that flank the Andes on the western coast of South America.

In the western United States, examples of such volcanic activity are found in the Sierra Nevada, an ancient volcanic range, and the Cascade Range, which is currently active. The Sierra Nevada was produced by subduction of the ancient Farallon Plate beneath the North American Plate. The Sierra Nevada batholith is a remnant of the original volcanic range, while the California Coast Range has remnants of the sediments that accumulated in the trench. The Cascade Range, produced from the subduction of the Juan de Fuca Plate (a piece of the Farallon Plate) beneath the North American Plate, includes the volcanoes Mount Rainier, Mount Shasta, and Mount St. Helens. The 1980 eruption of Mount St. Helens gives testimony that the Cascade Range is still quite active.

Earthquakes similar to those in oceanic–oceanic convergence are also characteristic of oceanic–continental convergence.

Continental-Continental Convergence

The collision between two continental landmasses is always preceded by oceanic–continental convergence. Because continental crust, being light and buoyant, doesn't undergo any appreciable subduction, convergence between two continental plates is like a head-on collision (Figure 27.18c). Compression causes the plates to break and fold upon each other, making the crust very thick. Intensely compressed and metamorphosed rock defines the zone where the plates meet. In contrast with convergence involving either two oceanic plates or one continental and one oceanic plate, volcanic activity is not characteristic of continental–continental collisions (although earthquakes are).

The collision between continental plates has produced some of the most famous mountain ranges, one majestic example being the snow-capped Himalayas, the highest mountain range in the world. This chain of towering peaks is still being thrust upward as India continues crunching up against Asia (Figure 27.20). The European Alps were formed in a similar fashion when part of the African Plate collided with the Eurasian Plate 80 million years ago. Relentless pressure between the two plates continues, and it is slowly closing up the Mediterranean Sea. In America, the Appalachian Mountains were produced from a continental–continental collision that ultimately resulted in the formation of the supercontinent Pangaea.

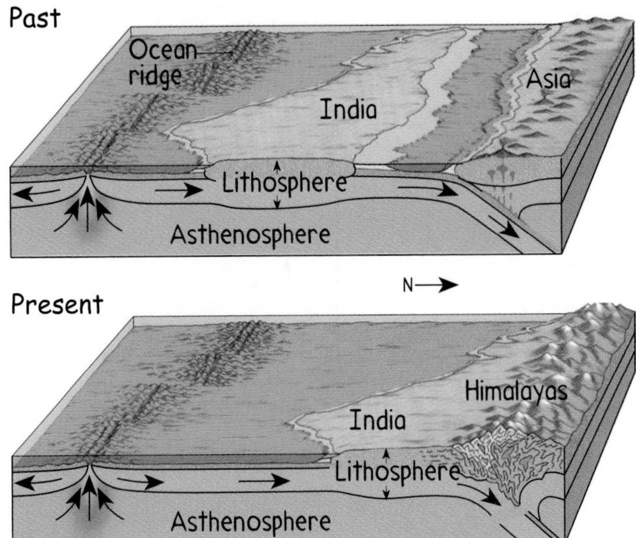

Figure 27.20
The continent-to-continent collision of India with Asia produced—and is still producing—the Himalayas.

Magma Generation at Convergent Boundaries

During subduction, basaltic oceanic crust and water-rich sediments are dragged down to great depths. Such deep burial subjects the rocks to increased temperature and pressure, resulting in the formation of metamorphic rocks. As the sedimentary rocks are converted to slates, schists, and gneisses, large quantities of water and water vapor are released, just as food in a hot oven also dries out.

The water-rich fluid released from the metamorphosing rock is less dense than its surroundings so it rises buoyantly. As this fluid contacts hot mantle rocks in between the subducting and overriding plates, the rock's melting point is sufficiently lowered to allow partial melting (Figures 27.18a and b). Basaltic magma is generated. Some of the magma crystallizes on its way upward, and some of it does not. As eruptions of basaltic lava thicken the crust, upward migration of magma is impeded. And this allows crystallization to occur before eruption, forming andesitic magma.

Continental crust is much thicker than oceanic crust, which allows even more time for crystallization to occur. Some of this magma reaches the surface, where it erupts to form a chain of andesitic volcanoes on the overriding continental plate. Some of the magma crystallizes enough to become very enriched in silica. A large portion of this magma does not erupt but solidifies underground to form granite. Rising magma also incorporates chunks of silica-rich continental rocks, which also increases the magma's silica content.

The main difference between magma generation at convergent and divergent boundaries is the distance between the site of magma generation and the base of the crust. The magma-to-lower-crust distance is shorter at divergent boundaries. This affects the fate of the magma that is produced. Magma generation at divergent boundaries occurs near the earth's surface. Because the lithosphere is essentially absent at divergent boundaries, new basaltic magma moves upward unimpeded. Considerable amounts of magma usually erupt before significant crystallization can occur. At convergent boundaries, magma generation occurs deeper in the mantle, and the rising magma is impeded when it encounters the overlying lithosphere. Both of these factors increase the travel time of the mantle-derived basalt, allowing significant crystallization to occur.

☑ CHECKPOINT

Erosion wears mountains down, and yet the Andes Mountains grow taller each year. Why?

Check Your Answer

Subduction is still occurring, which causes the uplift of the Andes. Because the rate of uplift is greater than the erosion rate, the mountains continue to grow.

Transform-Fault Plate Boundaries

A **transform fault** is a plate boundary that occurs where two plates are neither colliding nor pulling apart but rather sliding horizontally past each other. They occur because spreading ridges are never continuous from one end to the other. For example, look at the Mid-Atlantic Ridge in Figure 27.15. The ridge is broken up into segments, many of which do not appear to be connected. The offset ridge segments actually are connected, but not directly. They are connected by transform faults. The ridge segments are not offset *because* of the transform fault, as was once thought. Rather, each of the faults "transforms" the motion from one ridge segment to another. Between offset ridge segments, lithosphere from one ridge is moving in the opposite direction than the lithosphere coming from the other ridge (Figure 27.21). The two slabs of lithosphere between the ridge segments are separated by the transform fault. Can you see that the two slabs are on different plates? Now look at Figure 27.21 in the area of the fracture zone. The sections of lithosphere on opposite sides of the fracture zone are part of the same plate; both sides are moving in the same direction. Along the transform fault, lithosphere is moving in opposite directions. Can you now see that the transform fault is indeed a plate boundary? Can you also see that fracture zones are former transform faults?

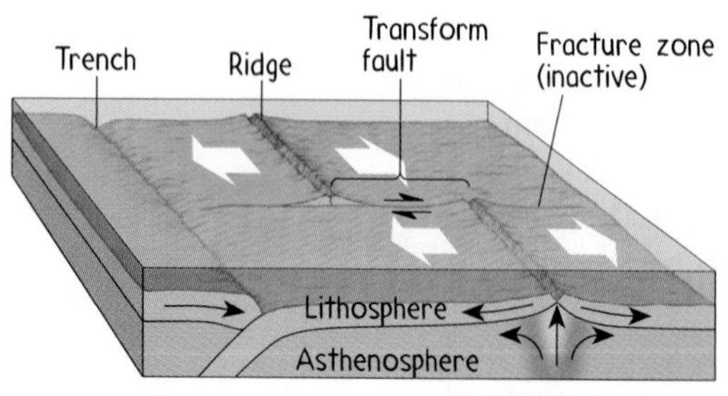

Figure 27.21
Transform faults allow two plates to slide past one another at places where ridge segments are offset.

Because there is no tension or compression between the plates, there is no creation or destruction of the lithosphere. A transform fault is a zone of horizontal accommodation of plate movement, with neither side of the fault moving up or down relative to the other. Transform faults have the same type of motion as *strike-slip faults.*

The San Andreas Fault, one of the most famous transform faults, stretches for 1500 kilometers from Cape Mendocino in northern California to the East Pacific Rise in the Gulf of California. The Pacific Plate is moving northwest at a rate of about 5.0 centimeters per year relative to the North American Plate. The San Andreas Fault accommodates about 70 percent of this motion, or about 3.5 centimeters per year. The rest of the motion occurs along other faults (such as the Hayward Fault). Grinding and crushing take place as the two plates move past each other. When sections of the plates become locked together, stress builds up until it is relieved in the form of an earthquake. On April 18, 1906 the Pacific Plate lurched about 6 meters northward over a 434 kilometer stretch of the fault, releasing the built-up stress, and resulting in the catastrophic San Francisco earthquake.

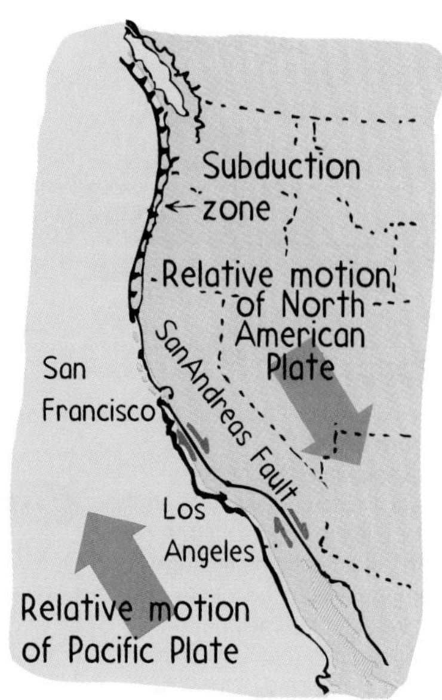

Figure 27.22
The San Andreas Fault shows horizontal offset at the location where the Pacific Plate slides northward past the adjacent North American Plate.

27.5 Continental Evidence for Plate Tectonics

Convection in the earth's mantle causes the overlying lithospheric plates to be in slow but constant motion. Motion in the mantle pushes and pulls on the plates in several directions. The moving plates in turn drag the mantle, and this creates stress within the plates. Rocks subjected to stress begin to deform into intricate and broad *folds.* If enough stress is applied, rocks break and then move along *faults.* Faults come in sizes ranging from small and virtually unnoticeable to large ones loaded with the potential to devastate. Are there any large folds or faults where you live?

Folds

Compressive stresses push rocks together and they begin to buckle and fold. To see what these terms mean, suppose you had a throw rug on your floor, with a friend standing on one end. If you push the rug toward your friend while keeping it on the floor, the rug begins to tilt away from your hand, and a series of ripples, or **folds,** develops. This is what happens to the earth's crust when it is subjected to compressive stress.

We know, from Chapter 26, that sediments settling from water in an ocean or bay are deposited in horizontal layers, with the layer at the bottom deposited first. This bottom layer is therefore the oldest in the sequence of deposited layers. Each new layer is deposited on top of the previous layer, with the youngest at the top. As originally flat sedimentary rock layers are subjected to compressive stress, they tilt and become folded, just as the throw rug became tilted and folded. Each high point and low point in a series of folds is an axis, which you can imagine as a plane extending downward into the earth, as Figure 27.23 shows. When the layers tilt in toward the fold axis, so that if you put a marble on the rock it would roll toward the axis, the fold is called a

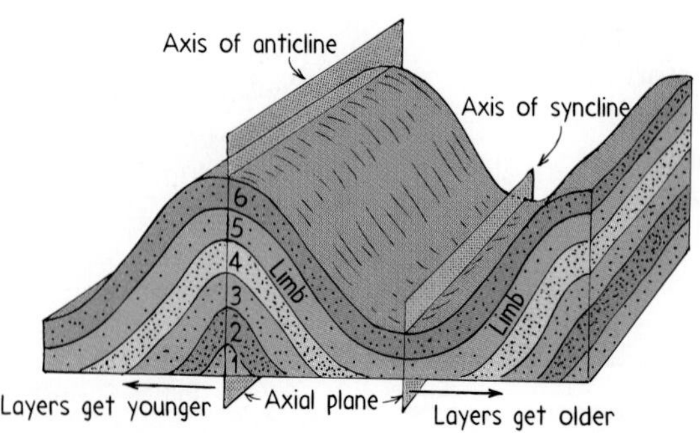

Figure 27.23
Anticline and syncline folds. Layer 1 is the oldest rock, and layer 6 is the youngest. The limbs of an anticline tilt away from the axis of the fold (a marble would roll away from the axis), and the rock layers are oldest at the core of the fold. The limbs of a syncline tilt toward the axis of the fold (a marble would roll toward the axis), and the rocks are youngest at the core.

syncline. The rocks at the center, or *core,* of a syncline are the youngest. As you move horizontally away from the axis, the rocks get older and older. If the fold layers tilt away from the axis, so that if you put a marble on the rock it would roll away from the axis, the fold is called an **anticline.** The rocks in an anticline are oldest at the core, and as you move horizontally away from the axis, the rocks get younger. Another way to think about this concept is that anticlines are pushed upward and synclines are pushed downward.

☑ CHECKPOINT

Why are rocks at the core of a syncline younger than those farther out from the core, while the opposite is true for an anticline?

Check Your Answer

Think of the rug example. Assume the top surface of the rug is younger than the lower surface. When you push the rug, it can (1) fold upward or (2) fold downward. In the first case, the bottom surface makes up the core—an anticline. In the second case, the top surface makes up the core—a syncline. Makes sense!

Faults

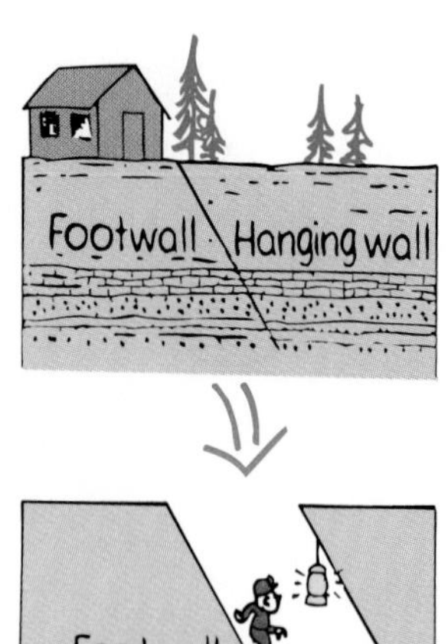

Figure 27.24
The terms *footwall* and *hanging wall* were commonly used by miners because one could hang a lamp on a hanging wall and stand on a footwall.

When compressional stress is stronger than rock, the rock fractures into two parts. If one part then moves relative to the other part, the fracture is called a **fault.**

Note the fault in Figure 27.24 (the oblique line in the top drawing). Imagine that you could pull the block diagram apart at the fault, as shown in the lower drawing. The half containing the fault surface where someone could stand is the *footwall* block. The fault surface of the other half is inclined and would make standing impossible; this is the *hanging wall* block. These terms were coined by miners because one could hang a lamp on a hanging wall and could stand on a footwall.

Once compressional forces have created a fault, these forces cause rocks in the hanging wall to be pushed upward along the fault plane relative to rocks in the footwall, as Figure 27.25 shows. This type of fault is called a *reverse fault.* The Rocky Mountain foreland, the Canadian Rockies, and the Appalachian Mountains, to name a few, were formed in part by the process of reverse faulting.

In addition to compression, stress in rocks can also occur by tension. The opposite of compression forces, which push, tension forces pull at the rocks. Tension causes rocks in a hanging wall to drop downward along the fault plane relative to those in the adjacent footwall, producing a *normal fault* (Figure 27.26). Virtually the entire state of Nevada, eastern California, southern Oregon, southern Idaho, and western Utah are greatly affected by normal faulting.

The faults described so far have mostly vertical up-and-down motion, but some have almost no vertical motion; their motion is horizontal and they are

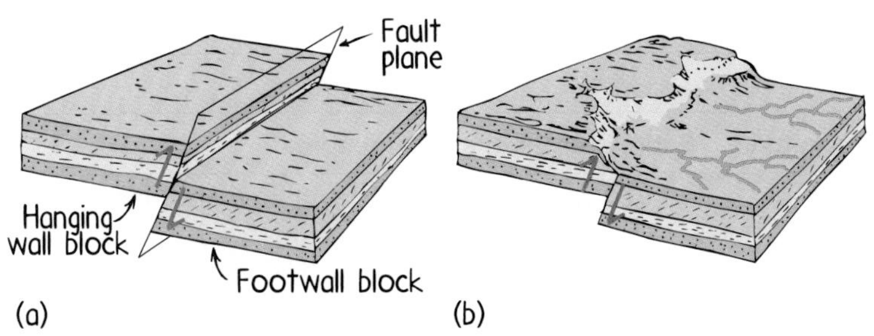

Figure 27.25
A reverse fault. In a zone of compressional faulting, rocks in the hanging wall are pushed up relative to rocks in the footwall. (a) A reverse fault before erosion; (b) the same reverse fault after erosion.

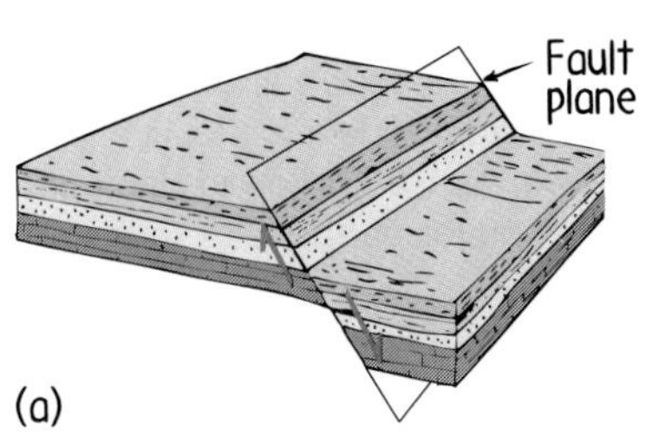

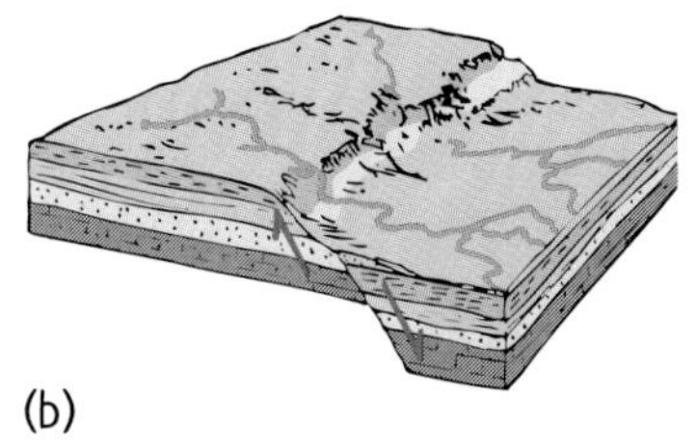

Figure 27.26
A normal fault. In a zone of tensional faulting, rocks in the hanging wall drop down relative to those in the footwall, forming a normal fault. (a) A normal fault before erosion; (b) the same normal fault after erosion.

called *strike-slip* faults. Some of the world's most famous faults, such as the San Andreas Fault in California, are strike-slip faults.

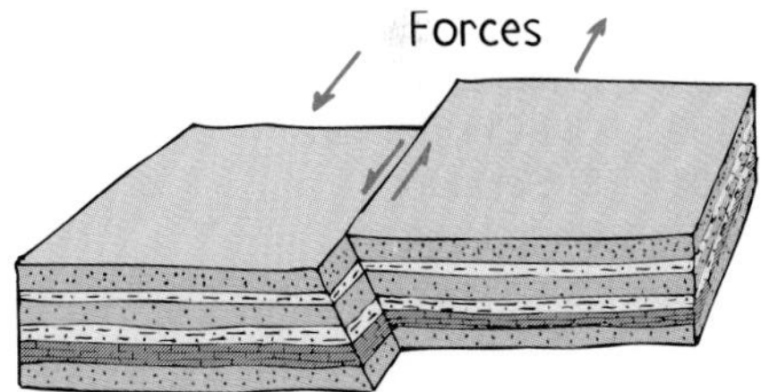

Figure 27.27
The relative movement of a strike-slip fault is horizontal.

Earthquakes

Devastating earthquakes can occur with all three types of faults: reverse, normal or strike-slip. The San Francisco earthquake of 1906 registered near 8.3 on the Richter scale (a measure of ground motion caused by earthquakes). It caused 700 deaths and extensive fire damage. The 1989 Loma Prieta earthquake near Santa Cruz, California, registered 7.1 on the Richter scale, caused 62 deaths, and did more than $6 billion in damage. Strike-slip faulting caused both of these earthquakes. Still larger and more catastrophic

Figuring Physical Science

Moving Faults

If you know the rate of movement along a fault, the amount of *offset* over a period of time can be calculated. The basic relationship is:

$$\text{rate} = \frac{\text{distance}}{\text{time}}$$

Problem

Movement along the San Andreas Fault is about 3.5 centimeters per year. If a fence were built across the fault in 1990, how far apart will the two sections of the now-broken fence be in 2010?

Solution

The time period is:

$$2010 - 1990 = 20 \text{ years}$$

We know time and speed, so we rearrange the basic equation as:

$$\text{distance} = \text{rate} \times \text{time}$$

Thus, the two parts of the fence will be separated by:

$$3.5 \text{ cm/yr} \times 20 \text{ yr} = 70 \text{ cm}$$

Table 27.1

Some Notable Earthquakes

Year	Location	Magnitude	Estimated Deaths	Comments
1556	Shensei, China		830,000	Possibly the greatest natural disaster
1811	New Madrid, Missouri	7.9	few	
1906	San Francisco, California	8.2	700	Fires caused extensive damage
1908	Messina, Italy	7.5	120,000	
1920	Kansu, China	8.5	180,000	
1923	Tokyo, Japan	8.2	150,000	Fire caused extensive destruction
1960	Southern Chile	8.7	5,700	The largest earthquake ever recorded
1964	Anchorage, Alaska	8.5	131	More than $300 million in damage
1970	Peru	7.8	66,000	Great rockslide
1971	San Fernando, California	6.5	65	More than $5 billion in damage
1975	Liaoning, China	7.5	few	First major earthquake to be predicted
1976	Tangshan, China	7.6	500,000	
1985	Mexico City, Mexico	8.1	7,000	Major damage
1989	Loma Prieta, California	6.9	62	More than $6 billion in damage
1994	Northridge, California	6.7	57	More than $25 billion in damage
1995	Kobe, Japan	6.9	5,500	Between $95 and $147 billion in damage
1999	Izmit, Turkey	7.4	17,000	44,000 injured, and 250,000 displaced
1999	Chi-Chi, Taiwan	7.6	2,300	Severe destruction
2001	El Salvador	7.6	1,000	Landslides
2001	Bhuj, India	7.9	20,000	A million people left homeless

Figure 27.28
Offset orchard rows in an orange grove that straddles the right-lateral (an object on the opposite side of the fault moves to the right) San Andreas Fault. Notice that the rows in the background have moved to the right relative to the rows in the foreground.

earthquakes have occurred along reverse faults. The 1964 earthquake in Anchorage, Alaska, registered 8.5 on the Richter scale, and caused 131 deaths and $300 million in damage.* Some of the greatest tragedies of recent times include the August 1999 earthquake in Turkey (7.6 on the Richter scale, 17,000 deaths), the January 2001 earthquake in El Salvador (7.7 on the Richter scale, 844 deaths), and the January 2001 earthquake in India (7.7 on the Richter scale, 20,000 deaths)!

Understanding earthquakes is obviously of major importance to society. Unfortunately, earthquakes and fault movement occur with little or no warning and thus are very difficult to predict. Table 27.1 lists some of the world's most notable earthquakes according to their impact on society. The 1906 San Francisco earthquake is notable because of its damage to the city and its inhabitants. On the other hand, in the winter of 1811–1812, a much greater earthquake on the New Madrid Fault in Missouri changed the landscape beyond recognition, as it shifted the direction and course of the Mississippi River. Fortunately, because the quake occurred in a remote region where there were few settlers, human injuries and deaths were few. Going much, much, further back in time, the presently inactive Appalachian Mountains and parts of the Rocky Mountains were once zones of intense earthquake activity. You can imagine that they were once much like the places listed in Table 27.1 that have recently endured the awesome power of the quaking Earth.

*The death toll was largely due to great seismic sea waves, or *tsunamis*. A tsunami is generated from the displacement of water as a result of an earthquake, a submarine landslide, or an underwater volcanic eruption.

Earthquake Measurements—Mercalli and Richter Scales

Every year, hundreds of thousands of earthquakes occur. Although most are small and go undetected, the danger of large earthquakes certainly exists. Earthquake-prone regions experience large earthquakes about every 50 to 100 years.

The Mercalli scale measures quake intensity in terms of the effects the quake has on the local environment. The scale ranges from an intensity of I (barely detectable) to an intensity of XII (total destruction). The Mercalli intensity at any location depends on (1) how far that location is from where the earthquake occurred, and (2) the nature of the subsurface materials at the location (for example, is the subsurface material solid rock or unconsolidated sediments?).

The Mercalli scale is a valuable yardstick. However, since it is based purely on observation, the Mercalli scale cannot precisely measure quake size. For this reason, seismologists developed a more precise way to estimate the energy released in an earthquake. The Richter scale, which is a magnitude scale, measures quake severity in terms of the amount of energy released and the amount of ground shaking at a standard distance from the location of the quake.

The Richter magnitude scale measures the amplitude of seismic waves recorded by a seismograph. The magnitude is based on the maximum amplitude of all the recorded P-waves and S-waves from an earthquake. The scale is logarithmic. This means that each increase of one unit on the scale is equivalent to a ten-fold increase in the amplitude of ground shaking. So, compared with a magnitude 5 earthquake, a magnitude 6 earthquake produces ground motions 10 times greater, and a magnitude 6 earthquake is 100 times greater than a magnitude 4 earthquake.

But how does Richter magnitude relate to the energy released by an earthquake? The energy released by an earthquake is measured not only by the amplitude of seismic waves but also by their frequencies and wavelengths; and seismic waves occur over a wide range of amplitudes, frequencies, and wavelengths. Through careful analysis of many aspects of earthquakes and faults, scientists find that the energy released by an earthquake increases by about *30 times* for each increase in Richter magnitude. For example, the 1964 Anchorage, Alaska earthquake, which had a magnitude of 8.5, released about 30 times as much energy as, and produced 10 times more ground shaking than, the 1908 Messina earthquake, which had a magnitude of 7.5. The magnitude 8.5 Anchorage quake released 900 times as much energy as, and produced 100 times more ground shaking than, the 1971 magnitude 6.5 quake in San Fernando, California.

The Mercalli Scale of Intensity

I Not felt except by a very few under especially favorable circumstances.

II Felt only by a few persons at rest, especially on upper floors of buildings.

III Felt quite noticeably indoors, especially on upper floors of buildings, but many people do not recognize this as an earthquake.

IV Most people feel it indoors, a few outdoors. Dishes, windows, doors rattle.

V Felt by nearly everyone. Disturbances of trees, poles, and other tall objects.

VI Felt by all; many frightened and run outdoors. Some heavy furniture moved; a few instances of fallen plaster or damaged chimneys. Damage to buildings slight.

VII People run outdoors. Damage negligible in buildings of good design and construction; slight to moderate in well-built structures; considerable in poorly built structures.

VIII Damage slight in specially designed structures; considerable in ordinary substantial buildings, with partial collapse; great in poorly built structures (fall of chimneys, factory stacks, columns, monuments, walls).

IX Damage considerable in specially designed structures. Buildings shifted off foundations. Ground conspicuously cracked.

X Some structures destroyed. Most masonry and frame structures destroyed with foundations. Ground badly cracked.

XI Few, if any, masonry structures remain standing. Bridges destroyed. Broad fissures in ground.

XII Damage total. Waves seen on ground surfaces. Objects thrown up in air.

Source: U.S. Coast Guard and Geodetic Survey

Table 27.2

Richter Magnitude

Magnitude	Number per Year	Maximum Mercalli Intensity	Characteristic Effects
<3.4	800,000	I	Recorded only by seismographs.
3.4–4.4	30,000	II and III	Felt by some people in the area.
4.4–4.8	4,800	IV	Felt by many people in the area.
4.8–5.4	1,400	V	Felt by everyone in the area.
5.4–6.0	500	VI and VII	Slight building damage.
6.0–7.0	100	VIII and IX	Much building damage.
7.0–7.4	15	X	Serious damage, bridges twisted, walls fractured.
7.4–8.0	4	XI	Great damage, buildings collapse.
>8.0	one every 5–10 years	XII	Total damage, waves seen on ground, objects thrown in air.

Source: From B. Gutenberg, 1950

27.6 The Theory That Explains Much

Before the theory of plate tectonics was proposed, such processes as mountain building, folding, and faulting were poorly understood. Without a mechanism to explain a lithosphere that shifts, scientists did the best they could to explain their observations. Plate tectonics offers explanations as to the where and why of many geologic processes. Indeed, it can be thought of as a unifying theory because it links causes and effects.

Why are the Appalachian Mountains located where they are? What about the Sierra Nevada? The Rocky Mountains? The Alps? The plate tectonic model gives an answer: All mountain-building events take place near convergent plate boundaries.

We can also relate the formation of the three different rock types to the plate tectonic theory. Although we are simplifying the discussion of rock formation for the sake of clarity, all rocks are tied to plate interaction in one manner or another.

We can explain the creation of basaltic rocks using the plate tectonic model. Where plates are diverging, such as at a mid-ocean spreading ridge, mantle rocks partially melt to form new oceanic crust—basalt. The intense heat and pressure caused by subduction and continental collisions result in the metamorphism of preexisting rocks. Here is where regional metamorphism occurs. As subducting slabs are heated, they cause the overlying mantle wedge to partially melt, generating basaltic magma that begins to crystallize. Recall, from Chapter 25, that as crystallization proceeds, the remaining liquid contains more silica than the parent magma. Thus, andesite forms from basaltic magma, and we find belts of composite cone volcanoes, like those in the Andes and the Cascade Range.

What about granite? Where does most of that come from? Large volumes of andesitic magma are produced at subduction zones. This magma doesn't all erupt at once but, rather, accumulates in the earth's crust. As the magma bodies cool, they undergo crystallization, which results in a liquid containing more silica than the original liquid. When this silica-enriched magma cools, it forms granite. Where in nature has this occurred? The Sierra Nevada is a largely granitic mountain range in California that formed in such a manner. The large batholiths of granitic rocks are the "roots," or solidified magma bodies, of a once-extensive volcanic belt formed as a result of subduction.

What about sedimentary rocks? As mountains grow by virtue of plate collisions, they also begin to weather and erode. The clastic sediments produced are transported downslope, where they accumulate, layer upon layer, eventually becoming sedimentary rock.

Virtually all earthquake and volcanic activity can be tied directly to plate tectonics. These energetic responses to plate interactions are almost always found where plates interact; earthquakes are found at all types of plate boundaries, and volcanoes are concentrated where plates either collide or pull apart.

So we can see that the tectonic interaction between lithospheric plates, which occurs mostly at their boundaries, provides an explanation to the origin of mountain chains, the development and destruction of the ocean floors, the three types of rocks found on Earth, and the global distribution of earthquakes and volcanoes. The internal motions that change the earth's surface do so in a cycle. In Chapter 30, we shall see the effects of plate tectonic interaction through time. The study of geology uses the processes that are occurring today in order to understand what may have occurred in the past. This concept is commonly stated as "the present is the key to the past." But what has happened in the past provides clues as to what may happen in the future. The earth is indeed a dynamic planet.

Summary of Terms

Body wave A seismic wave that travels through the earth's interior.

Surface wave A seismic wave that travels along the earth's surface.

Primary wave (P-wave) A longitudinal body wave; travels through solids, liquids, and gases and is the fastest seismic wave.

Secondary wave (S-wave) A transverse body wave; cannot travel through liquids and so does not travel through the earth's outer core.

Mohorovičić discontinuity (Moho) The crust-mantle boundary, marking the depth at which the speed of P-waves traveling toward the earth's center increases.

Core The central layer in the earth's interior, divided into an outer liquid core and an inner solid core.

Mantle The middle layer in the earth's interior, between the crust and the core.

Asthenosphere A subdivision of the upper mantle situated below the lithosphere, a zone of plastic, easily deformed rock.

Lithosphere The entire crust plus the portion of the mantle above the asthenosphere.

Crust The earth's outermost layer.

Pangaea A single, large landmass that existed in the geologic past and was composed of all the present-day continents.

Paleomagnetism The study of natural magnetization in a rock to determine the intensity and direction of the earth's magnetic field at the time of the rock's formation.

Seafloor spreading The moving apart of two oceanic plates at a rift in the seafloor.

Theory of plate tectonics The idea that the earth's lithosphere is broken into pieces (plates) that move over the asthenosphere; boundaries between plates are where most earthquakes and volcanoes occur and where lithosphere is created and recycled.

Rift (rift valley) A long, narrow trough that forms as a result of divergence of two plates.

Fold A series of ripples in the crust that result from compressional deformation of the lithosphere.

Syncline A fold in strata that has relatively young rocks at its core, with rock age increasing with increasing horizontal distance from the fold core.

Anticline A fold in strata that has relatively old rocks at its core, with rock age decreasing with increasing horizontal distance from the fold core.

Fault A fracture along which visible displacement can be detected on one side relative to the other.

Transform fault A plate boundary formed by two plates that are sliding horizontally past each other.

Review Questions

27.1 Seismic Waves

1. P-waves and S-waves move through the earth's interior in two ways. What is the difference in their mode of propagation?
2. Can S-waves travel through liquids? Explain.
3. Name the two types of surface waves and describe the motion of each.

27.2 Earth's Internal Layers

4. What was Andrija Mohorovičić's major contribution to Earth science?
5. List the different properties of the four types of seismic waves.
6. How did seismic waves contribute to the discovery of Earth's two deep internal boundaries?
7. What does the wave shadow that develops between 105° and 140° from the origin of an earthquake tell us about the earth's composition?
8. What is the evidence for the solidity of the earth's inner core?
9. Even though the inner and outer cores are both predominantly composed of iron and nickel, the inner core is solid and the outer core is liquid. Why?
10. What is the evidence that the earth's outer core is liquid?
11. Describe the asthenosphere and the lithosphere. In what ways are they different from each other?
12. What convectional movement is responsible for the motion of lithospheric plates?
13. How does continental crust differ from oceanic crust?
14. Why does continental crust stand higher on the mantle than oceanic crust?

27.3 The Theory of Continental Drift

15. What key evidence did Alfred Wegener use to support his idea of continental drift?
16. How does evidence of prehistoric glaciation found in parts of South America, southern Africa, India, and southern Australia support the concept of a supercontinent?
17. What was the stated reason for the scientific community rejecting Wegener's idea of Continental Drift?
18. What information can be learned from a rock's magnetic record?
19. What role did paleomagnetism play in supporting continental drift?
20. Where are the deepest parts of the ocean?
21. What major discovery at the bottom of the ocean did H. H. Hess make?
22. How is the ocean floor similar to a gigantic slow-moving tape recorder?
23. What does the earth's crust have in common with a conveyor belt?
24. In what way does seafloor spreading support continental drift?

27.4 The Theory of Plate Tectonics

25. Name and describe the three types of plate boundaries.
26. How old is the South Atlantic Ocean thought to be? For how many years has lava been extruding at the Mid-Atlantic Ridge?
27. What is a rift?
28. What kind of boundary separates the South American Plate from the African Plate?
29. Describe the three types of plate collisions that occur at convergent boundaries.
30. What is the driving force for mountain building in the Andes?
31. The Appalachian Mountains were produced at what type of plate boundary?
32. What type of lava erupts at divergent boundaries? What types erupt at convergent boundaries?
33. What clues do we use to recognize the boundaries between ancient plates no longer in existence?
34. What is a transform fault?
35. What kind of plate boundary separates the North American Plate from the Pacific Plate?

27.5 Continental Evidence for Plate Tectonics

36. What are folds?
37. Are folded rocks the result of compressional or tensional forces?
38. Distinguish between anticlines and synclines.
39. What is the difference between reverse faults and normal faults?
40. Which kind of fault results primarily from tension in the earth's crust? Primarily from compression?
41. What type of fault is associated with the 1964 earthquake in Alaska?
42. The Mercalli Scale measures earthquake intensity. The Richter Scale measures earthquake magnitude. Which scale is the more precise measurement? Why?

27.6 The Theory That Explains Much

43. At what type of plate boundary is regional metamorphism found?
44. Do you think it is likely to find andesitic rocks close to regionally metamorphosed rock, or should these two rock types be widely separated? Why?

Exercises

1. Compare the relative speeds of primary and secondary seismic waves, and relate speeds of travel to the medium through which the waves travel.
2. Explain how seismic waves indicate whether regions within the earth are solid or liquid.
3. How do seismic waves indicate layering of materials in the earth's interior?
4. What is the evidence that the earth's central core is solid?
5. Speculate on why the lithosphere is rigid and the asthenosphere is plastic, even though they are both part of the mantle.
6. If the earth's mantle is composed of rock, how can we say that the crust floats on the mantle?
7. Why is the earth's crust thicker beneath a mountain range?
8. Which extends farther into the mantle, the continental crust or the oceanic crust? Why?
9. How does erosion and wearing away of a mountain affect the depth to which the crust extends into the lithosphere?
10. Describe how the different paths of polar wandering helped establish that continents move over geologic time.
11. Why are most earthquakes generated near plate boundaries?
12. Why do mountains tend to form in long, narrow ranges?
13. Relate the formation of metamorphic rocks to plate tectonics. Would you expect to find metamorphic rocks at all three types of plate boundaries? Why or why not?
14. Why does granite frequently form at oceanic–continental convergent boundaries but infrequently at oceanic–oceanic convergent boundaries?
15. Cite one line of evidence that suggests that subduction once occurred off the coast of California.
16. Distinguish between continental drift and plate tectonics.
17. Are the present ocean basins a permanent feature on our planet? Discuss why or why not.
18. Are the present continents a permanent feature on our planet? Discuss why or why not.
19. Why is it that the most ancient rocks are found on the continents, not on the ocean floor?
20. Upon crystallization, certain minerals (the most important being magnetite) align themselves in the direction of the surrounding magnetic field, providing a magnetic fossil imprint. How does the seafloor's magnetic record support the theory of continental drift?
21. How are the theories of seafloor spreading and continental drift supported by paleomagnetic data?
22. What kind of boundaries are associated with seafloor spreading centers?
23. What is meant by magnetic pole reversals? What useful information do they tell us about the earth's history?
24. Using a photocopy of Figure 27.15, mark the different boundaries of plate interaction. Draw arrows showing direction of plate movement for convergent, divergent, and transform-fault boundaries.
25. Earthquakes, the result of sudden motion in the earth caused by abrupt release of slowly accumulated stress, causes rock to fracture or fault. Relate such faulting to horizontal movement of plates. Where does this type of movement occur?
26. What is a very likely cause for the existence of the earth's magnetic field?
27. Lithospheric material is continuously created and destroyed. Where does this creation and destruction take place? Do the rates of the two processes balance each other?
28. Subduction is the process of one lithospheric plate descending beneath another. Why does the oceanic portion of the lithosphere undergo subduction while the continental portion does not?
29. What geologic features are explained by plate tectonics?
30. In 1964, a large tsunami struck the Hawaiian Islands without warning, devastating the coastal town of Hilo, Hawaii. Since that time, a tsunami warning station has been established for the coastal areas of the Pacific. Why do you think these stations are located around the Pacific Rim?
31. How did the Himalayas originate? How did the Andes originate?
32. What is the major source of energy responsible for earthquakes in southern California?
33. Describe how the presence of faults and folds supports the idea that lithospheric plates are in motion.
34. Reverse faults are created by compressional forces. Where in the United States do we find evidence of reverse faults?
35. Normal faults are created by tensional forces. Where in the United States do we find evidence of normal faults?
36. Strike-slip faults show horizontal motion. Where in the United States do we find strike-slip faulting?
37. If you found folded beds of sedimentary rock in the field, what detail would you need to know in order to tell if the fold was an anticline or a syncline?
38. Does the fact that the mantle is beneath the crust necessarily mean that the mantle is denser than the crust? Explain.
39. Relate the generation of magma to plate boundaries. What type of magma is dominant at each of

the types of boundaries? What are the mechanisms that drive magma generation?

40. Where is the earth's longest mountain range located?

Activity

Look for a very old window, and note the lens effect in the bottom part of the glass. Glass has both solid and liquid properties; in fact, it is often thought of as a very viscous liquid. Over many years, its downward flow due to gravity is evidenced by the increased thickness near the bottom of the pane. Tie this observation of "plastic" behavior into our discussion of plate tectonics. Which parts of the earth behave plastically? Which parts are rigid? What do these ideas have to do with plate tectonics?

Problems

1. The weight of ocean floor bearing down upon the lithosphere is increased by the weight of ocean water. Relative to the weight of the 10-km-thick basaltic ocean crust (specific gravity 3), how much weight does the 3-km-deep ocean (specific gravity 1) contribute? Express your answer as a percentage of the crust's weight.
2. The Richter scale is logarithmic, meaning that each increase of 1 on the Richter scale corresponds to an increase of 10 in the amplitude of the seismic waves created by an earthquake. An earthquake that measures 8 on the Richter scale has how many times more ground-shaking than a quake that measures 6 on the Richter scale?

Refer to "Figuring Physical Science: Moving Faults" on page 675 for the following two problems.

3. The San Andreas Fault separates the northwest-moving Pacific Plate, on which Los Angeles sits, from the North American Plate, on which San Francisco sits. If the plates slide past one another at a rate of 3.5 cm per year, how long will it take the two cities to form one large city? (The distance between Los Angeles and San Francisco is 600 km.)
4. The San Andreas Fault is really a fault *zone,* meaning that there are several smaller faults running parallel to the main fault. All of the faults in the fault zone accommodate motion between the North American Plate and the Pacific Plate. In the San Francisco area, one of these faults is called the Hayward Fault. A lava flow that is 1.5 million years old and crosses the Hayward fault has been offset by 13.5 kilometers. What is the rate of movement along the Hayward Fault? Give your answer in millimeters.

Chapter 27 Online Resources

Tutorials
- Shaping Planetary Surfaces
- The Earth's Mantle Activity

Quiz
Exercises
Flashcards
Links

CHAPTER 28

Occurrence and Movement of Water

Water is essential to life, and it has been since the first life forms evolved. Virtually all land-dwelling organisms require clean, fresh water. So fresh water is by far the most valuable resource on Earth. It is also a very limited resource—already quite scarce in many parts of the world. Water is used not only for drinking but also for agriculture, industry, sanitation, and transportation. Where does the water we use come from, how does it move, and how can we conserve and preserve it?

28.1 The Hydrologic Cycle

A view of the earth from space shows that our planet is a vast expanse of water interrupted here and there by island-like continents. About 70 percent of the earth's surface is covered with water, and water plays an important role in just about every natural process on the earth's surface.

Slightly more than 97 percent of all the earth's water is in the oceans, and a little more than 2 percent is frozen in the polar icecaps and glaciers. The remainder, less than 1 percent, consists of water vapor in the atmosphere, water in the ground, and water in rivers and lakes.

Water on the earth is constantly circulating, driven by the heat of the sun and the force of gravity. As the sun's energy evaporates ocean water, a cycle begins (Figure 28.2). Evaporation moves water molecules from the earth's surface to

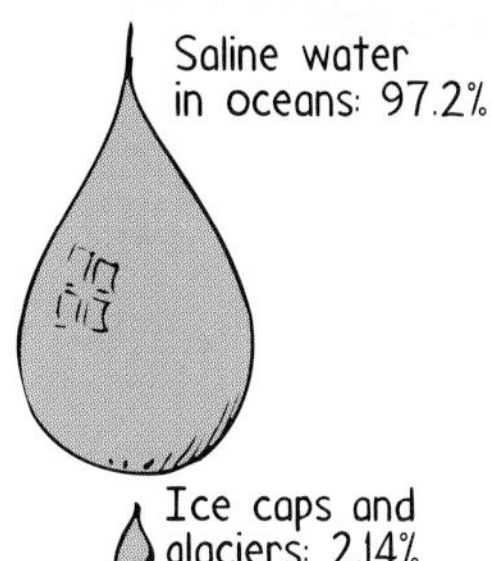

Figure 28.1
Relative distribution of the earth's water supply.

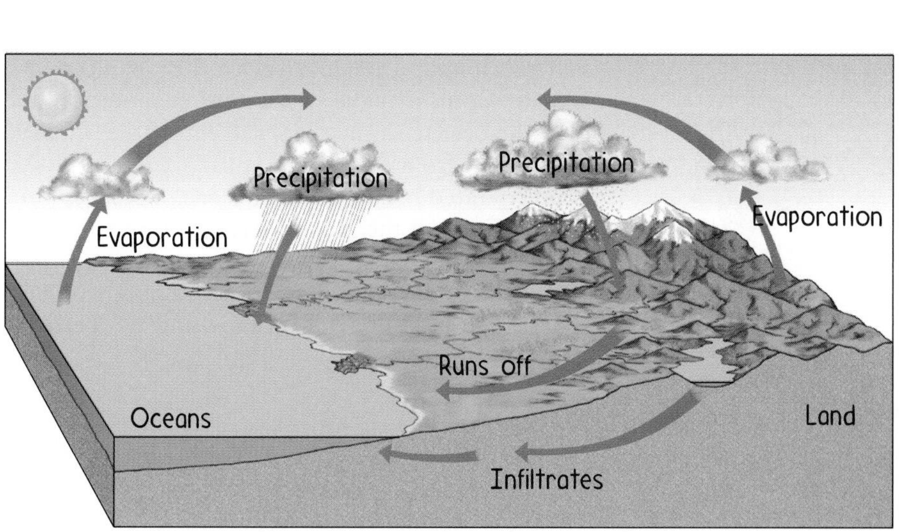

Figure 28.2
The hydrologic cycle. Water evaporated at the earth's surface enters the atmosphere as water vapor, condenses into clouds, precipitates as rain or snow, and falls back to the surface, only to evaporate again and go through the cycle yet another time.

become part of the atmosphere. The resulting moist air may be transported great distances by wind. Some of the water molecules condense to form clouds and then precipitate as rain or snow. If precipitation falls on the ocean, the cycle is complete—from ocean back to ocean.

Completion of the cycle is more complex when precipitation falls on land, for water may drain to streams, then to rivers, and then journey back into the ocean. Or it may percolate into the ground, or evaporate back into the atmosphere before reaching the ocean. Also, water falling on land may become part of a snow pack or glacier. Although snow or ice may lock water up for many years, such water eventually melts or evaporates and returns to the cycle. This natural circulation of water—from the oceans to the air, then to the ground, then to the oceans, and then back to the atmosphere—is called the **hydrologic cycle.***

The time for a certain *parcel* of water to complete the hydrologic cycle is its *residence time*—the *average* length of time a water molecule spends in a particular region. Water residing in polar ice and glaciers has a long residence time. For all practical purposes, the thousands-of-years residence time of deep groundwater means that, if it is withdrawn, it will not be replenished. Water is truly a precious natural resource.

Insights

Table 28.1

Water Resource Residence Times

Location	Average Residence Time
Atmosphere	1–2 weeks
Ocean	
Shallow depths	100–150 years
Deep depths	30,000–40,000 years
Continents	
Rivers	2–3 weeks
Lakes	10–100 years
Shallow groundwater	Up to 100s of years
Deep groundwater	Up to 1000s of years
Glaciers	10,000–20,000 years

Water vapor plays an interesting role in the hydrologic cycle. The total amount of water vapor in the atmosphere remains relatively constant, even though clouds are continually forming. This can occur only if evaporation and precipitation balance each other. Being that most of the earth's surface area is ocean, it makes sense that evaporation and precipitation are greatest over the oceans. In fact, 85 percent of the atmosphere's water vapor is water evaporated from the ocean, and 75 percent of the atmosphere's water vapor is precipitated back into the oceans. On the continents, precipitation exceeds evaporation. Of the atmosphere's water vapor, 15 percent is water evaporated from the continents, and 25 percent is water precipitated back to the land. Balance is maintained between the amount of water taken up into the atmosphere (85 percent from oceans and 15 percent from continents) and the

*This key concept is another conservation principle. Recall that, in Chapter 3, we learned about conservation of momentum and energy; in Chapter 9, we learned about the conservation of electric charge; and in Chapters 16 and 19, we learned about the conservation of nucleons in nuclear reactions. So now we learn that the amount of water on Earth is conserved. A lack of it in one place means an abundance someplace else, which, in most instances, is the ocean.

amount precipitated out of the atmosphere (75 percent to the oceans and 25 percent to the continents).

The rain or snow that falls on the continents is the earth's only natural supply of fresh water. More than three-quarters of the earth's fresh water is locked up in the polar ice caps and glaciers. It is surprising to note that most of the freely flowing fresh water is not in lakes and rivers but, rather, is beneath the earth's surface. As rain falls and sinks into the ground, it percolates downward. Some of the percolating water will fill the open pore spaces between sediment grains. This water is now called **groundwater.**

☑ CHECKPOINT

1. What percentage of the earth's water supply is fresh water?
2. The volume of water evaporated from all of the land surface of the earth is 60,000 km^3 per year, but the volume precipitated over the land surface is 96,000 km^3 per year. Being that the volume that precipitates each year is 36,000 km^3 more than the volume that evaporates, why isn't all the land flooded?

Check Your Answers

1. Less than 3%, as you can see by adding the freshwater values in Figure 28.1: 2.14% (glaciers) + 0.61% (groundwater) + 0.009% (surface water) + 0.005% (soil moisture) = 2.764%.
2. The excess water works its way back to the oceans. Excess water to the oceans does not cause sea level to rise because evaporation (85%) exceeds precipitation (75%) by 10%. Balance is maintained between the amount of water evaporated and precipitated over the oceans (85% − 75% = 10%) and the amount precipitated and evaporated over land (25% − 15% = 10%).

28.2 Groundwater

The liquid water in lakes, ponds, rivers, streams, springs, and puddles is the only fresh water that meets our eye, but all these water sources together hold only about 1.5 percent of the earth's fresh water that is not in the form of ice. The other 98.5 percent resides in porous regions that exist beneath the earth's surface.

Water beneath the ground exists as groundwater and *soil moisture.* Groundwater occurs in the *saturated zone,* the underground region where water has completely filled all open pore spaces (Figure 28.3). Above the saturated zone is the *unsaturated zone*, where soil moisture resides. Pore spaces in the unsaturated zone are not completely filled with water—they contain a significant amount of air. Like water in a swimming pool, the pressure in groundwater increases with depth. Just as we can pump water from a swimming pool, we can pump groundwater from the ground. However, the presence of air in pore spaces prevents us from withdrawing water from the unsaturated zone.

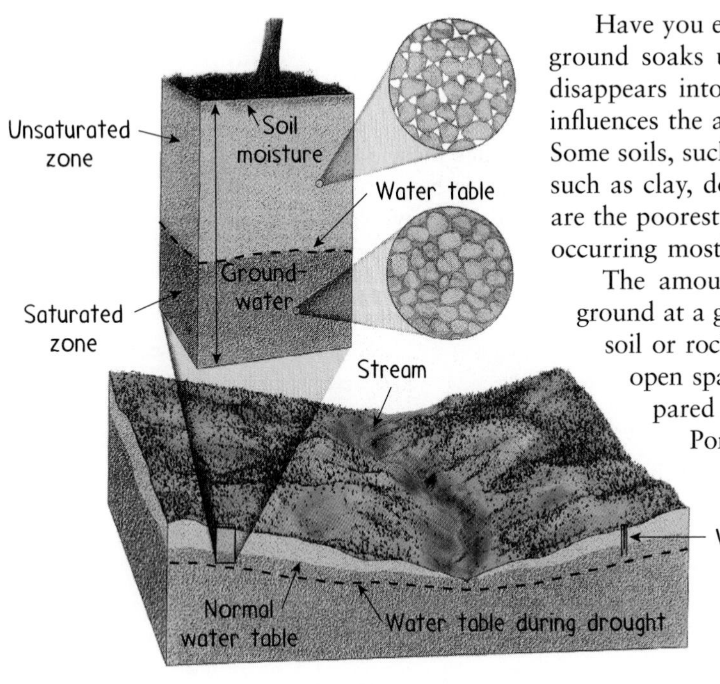

Figure 28.3
The unsaturated zone is above the saturated zone. Water in the unsaturated zone does not completely fill the open pore spaces. This is soil moisture. Water in the saturated zone completely fills all open pore spaces. This is groundwater.

Have you ever noticed how, during a rainstorm, sandy ground soaks up rain like a sponge? The water literally disappears into the ground. The type of surface material influences the amount of water that goes into the ground. Some soils, such as sand, soak up water easily. Other soils, such as clay, do not. Rocky surfaces with little or no soil are the poorest absorbers of water, with water penetration occurring mostly through fractures in the rock.

The amount of water that can be contained underground at a given location depends on the porosity of the soil or rock at that location. **Porosity** is the volume of open space in a soil, sediment, or rock sample compared to the total volume of solids plus voids. Porosity depends on the size and shape of the soil or sediment particles and on how tightly these particles are packed. For example, a soil composed of rounded particles of similar size has a higher porosity than a soil composed of rounded particles of various sizes. This is because the smaller particles fill up the spaces between the larger particles, thereby reducing the overall porosity of the soil.

Porosity is a measure of the volume of open space underground. As such, it represents the maximum *amount* of underground water at a given location. But the porosity does not tell us how groundwater *moves*. The **hydraulic conductivity**—a measure of permeability—tells us the degree to which geologic material can transmit water. If the pores are extremely small and poorly connected (as is the case with flattened clay particles), water may barely move at all. Think of it this way: it's a lot easier to sip soda through a large straw than through one of those very small straws intended for stirring coffee. Likewise, it is difficult for water to move through the pores of clay. The hydraulic conductivity—or permeability—of clay is almost zero, even though the porosity of most clays is very high. In contrast, sand and gravel have large, open, well-connected pore spaces, and water moves freely from one pore space to the next. Thus, sand and gravel are highly porous and highly permeable (Figure 28.4).

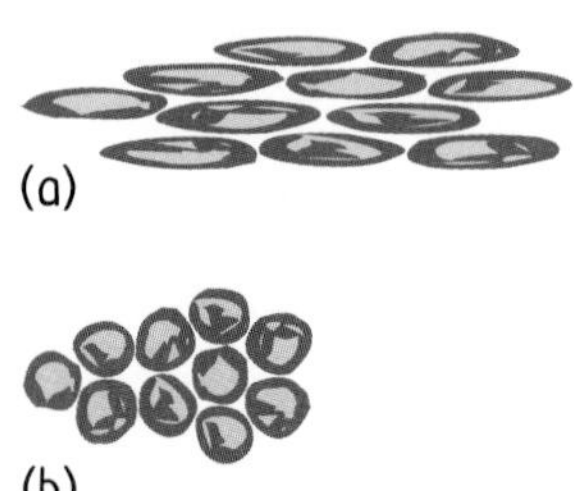

Figure 28.4
Porosity and Permeability.
(a) The sediment particles in clay are small, flat, and tightly packed. Because the sediment particles are flat, the many small pore spaces are poorly connected. Thus, clays have high porosity but low permeability. Low permeability equates to low hydraulic conductivity. (b) Sediment particles in sand or gravel are relatively uniform in size and shape, with large and well-connected pore spaces. This factor allows water to flow freely. Thus, sands and gravels can have both high porosity and high permeability (and high hydraulic conductivity).

☑ CHECKPOINT

Why is a sandy soil better for water flow than a clayey soil?

Check Your Answer

Water flows easily through sandy soil because it is generally composed of rounded particles with pore spaces that are large and well-connected; thus sandy soil is very permeable. We are saying the same thing when we say it has a high hydraulic conductivity. Water doesn't flow very easily through clayey soils because clay is composed of flattened particles with small, poorly connected pore spaces between them. Thus, clayey soils have a low hydraulic conductivity. Water flow is easier in soils with higher hydraulic conductivities.

Figuring Physical Science

Porosity

Porosity tells us the ratio of open space to the total volume of a soil, sediment, or rock sample:

$$\text{Porosity} = \frac{\text{volume of open space}}{\text{volume of open space} + \text{volume of solids}}$$

Problem

The volume of solids in a sediment sample is 975 cm^3, and the volume of open space is 325 cm^3. What is the porosity of the sediment?

Solution

$$\text{Porosity} = \frac{325\ cm^3}{325\ cm^3 + 975\ cm^3} = 0.25$$

So the volume of open space is only one-fourth of the total volume.

The Water Table

When digging a hole in the ground, we find a wetness of the soil that varies with depth. Just below the surface, we encounter the unsaturated zone, where pore spaces are partially filled with water (Figure 28.3). As we descend farther, we enter the saturated zone, where pore spaces are completely filled with water. If our hole is entirely within the unsaturated zone, it will not fill with water. If we dig our hole deeper into the saturated zone, it will partially fill with water. The upper boundary of the saturated zone is called the **water table** (Figure 28.3). The level of the water in our hole will be the same level as the water table. In fact, the level of water in our hole *is* the water table at that location.

Figure 28.5
The water table roughly parallels the surface of the ground. In times of drought, the water table falls, reducing stream flow and drying up wells. The water table also falls if the rate at which water is pumped out of a well exceeds the rate at which the groundwater is replaced.

The depth of the water table beneath the earth's surface varies with precipitation and climate. It ranges from zero in marshes and swamps to hundreds of meters in some parts of the deserts. The water table also tends to rise and fall with the surface topography (Figure 28.5). At lakes and perennial streams (streams that flow all year), the water table is above the land surface.

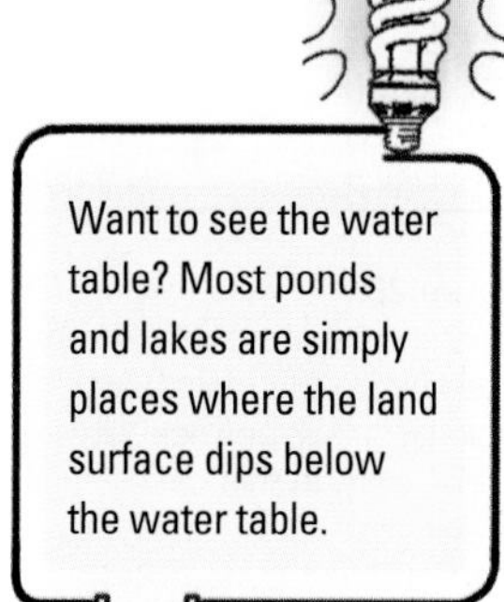

Aquifers and Springs

Any water-bearing underground region through which groundwater can flow is an *aquifer*. These reservoirs underlie the land surface in many places and contain an enormous amount of water. More than half the land area in the United States is underlain by aquifers. One such aquifer is the Ogallala aquifer, which stretches from South Dakota to Texas and from Colorado to Arkansas!

Up to this point, we have been discussing *unconfined* aquifers. In unconfined aquifers, the soil or sediment above the water table is permeable, which allows the *recharge* of water—the process of water soaking into the ground—directly into the aquifer. All aquifers are at least partially unconfined, as illustrated in Figure 28.6.

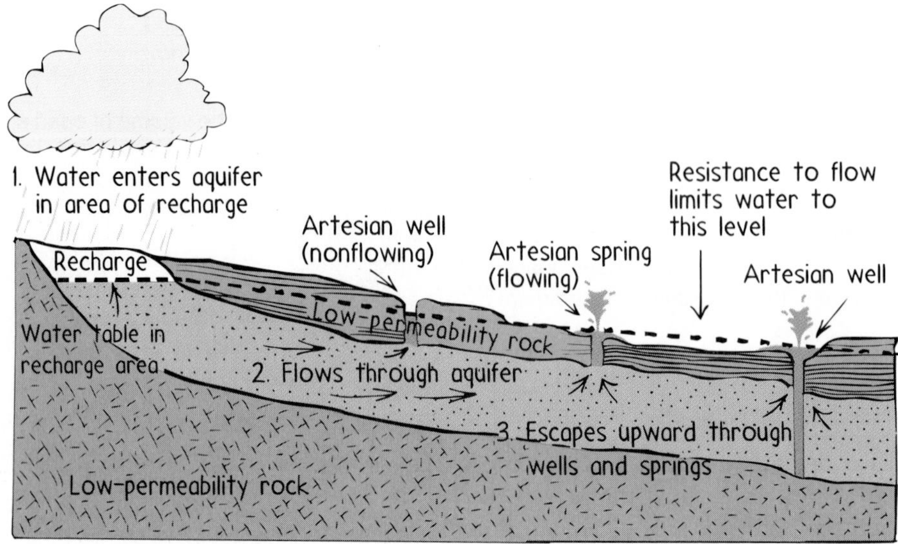

Figure 28.6
An artesian system is formed when groundwater in an aquifer confined between layers of low-permeability rock rises to the surface through any opening that taps the aquifer. Water flows freely if the height of the water table in the recharge area is greater than the height of the opening (flowing artesian well and artesian spring). If the height of the opening is greater than the height of the water table in the recharge area, the water does not flow (nonflowing artesian well).

Another type of aquifer is a *confined* aquifer. An aquifer is considered to be confined if it is sandwiched between continuous low-permeability layers (Figure 28.6). Confining layers* occur in sedimentary deposits that have alternating sand and clay layers, or alternating sandstone and shale layers. In confined aquifers, recharge does not come from directly above—water does not penetrate the confining layer. Natural recharge to confined aquifers comes only from unconfined portions of the aquifer at higher elevation.

As we learned in Chapter 6, pressure in water depends on the height of water above. Water anywhere in the confined portion of an aquifer is below the level of the water table in the recharge area. So groundwater in the confined aquifer—under pressure from water above—flows out through openings at lower elevations. This is an **artesian system.** If the opening is natural and water flows out of the ground, it is an *artesian spring*. If the opening has been drilled, it is an *artesian well.* When first tapped, some artesian wells blast water tens of meters into the air!

Figure 28.7
A perched water table is separated from the main water table by a low-permeability layer—clay, in this case.

Discontinuous low-permeability layers in an unconfined aquifer can intercept downward-percolating water above the water table. When this happens, a perched water table is created (Figure 28.7).

*Geologists call these layers *aquitards*.

Where the water table intersects the land surface, groundwater emerges from an aquifer as either a spring, a stream, or a lake. Springs can generally be found where the water table (or a perched water) table intersects the surface abruptly, such as on a hillside or on a coastal cliff. Because water tends to leak out of the ground through cracks and breaks in rock, springs are often associated with faults. In fact, field geologists can often locate faults by looking for springs.

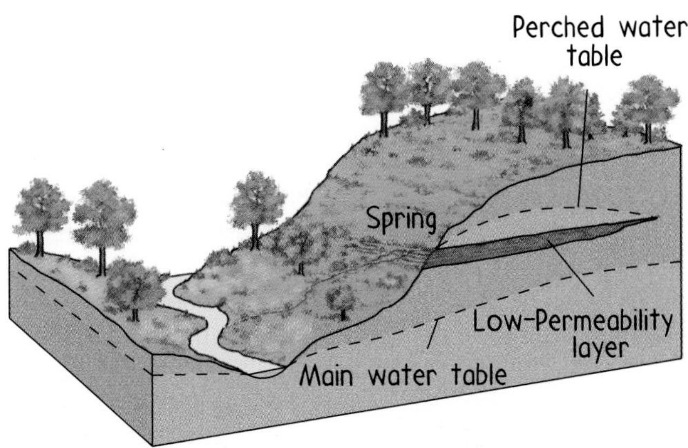

Figure 28.8
When the water table intersects the land surface, groundwater is released. From the perched water table, water is released via a spring; from the main water table, water is released by or into a stream.

☑ CHECKPOINT

1. What is an aquifer?
2. What principal condition is required for an artesian system to occur?

Check Your Answers

1. An aquifer is a body of rock or sediment through which groundwater moves easily.
2. The principal condition required for an artesian system to occur is the presence of confining layers. Confining layers allow groundwater in confined aquifers to be under higher pressure than groundwater in unconfined aquifers. This allows water to rise above the top of the confined aquifer at natural or human-made openings.

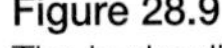

Groundwater Movement

The elevation of a water table above a particular location, usually sea level, is called the *hydraulic head*. This is the same elevation to which water in an unconfined aquifer rises in a well (Figure 28.9). Recall, from Chapter 6, that liquid pressure is directly proportional to depth of liquid. Hence, the higher the hydraulic head above a particular underground location, the greater the water pressure at that location. The downward slope of a water table is the *hydraulic gradient*. It can be expressed like any slope—"rise over run," or, in this case, the difference in hydraulic head between two points divided by the horizontal distance between those points (Figure 28.9).

Figure 28.9
The hydraulic gradient is the difference in hydraulic head between any two locations divided by the horizontal distance between the locations. In this example, we have (440 m − 415 m)/1000 m.

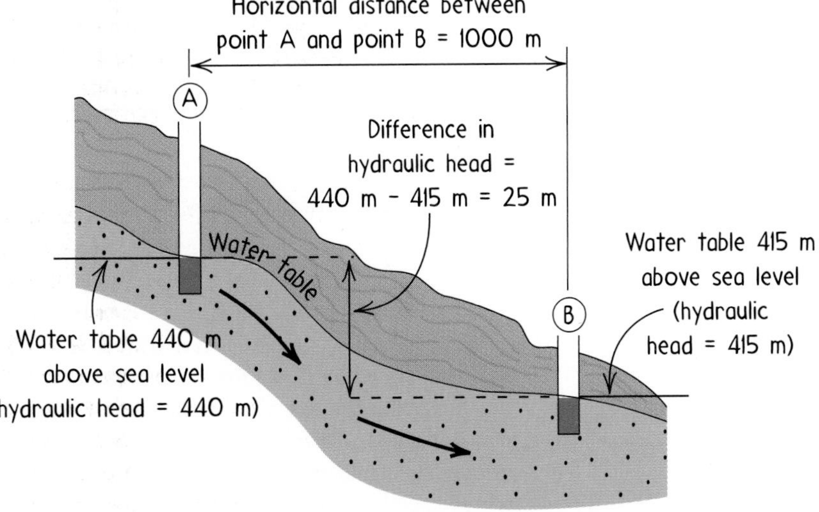

Groundwater flows in response to pressure differences—it flows from high head to low head. Hence, groundwater flow through an aquifer is directly proportional to the hydraulic gradient. This can be expressed as

Groundwater flow rate ~ hydraulic gradient

Flow rate also depends on the hydraulic conductivity of the soil and the cross-sectional area of the aquifer. The cross-sectional area of an aquifer is, by definition, always perpendicular to the flow direction. (The same is true of a water pipe, whose cross-sectional area is a circle defined by the diameter of the pipe.) Hydraulic conductivity values are high for gravel and lower for fine sand or silt. When the hydraulic conductivity and cross-sectional area are introduced, the proportion can be expressed as an exact equation:

Groundwater flow rate
= hydraulic conductivity × cross-sectional area × hydraulic gradient

Groundwater flow, heat, and electric current—all move in response to pressure differences. It's nice when different concepts connect in much the same way.

Insights

This relationship was first recognized by the French engineer Henry Darcy in 1856, and it is aptly termed *Darcy's law*.

Topography plays an equally strong role in groundwater flow because it creates the hydraulic gradient. In unconfined aquifers, the water table tends to be a subdued replica of the topography, as mentioned earlier. Therefore, hydraulic head, which, in unconfined aquifers, equals the elevation of the water table, is generally higher beneath hills and lower beneath stream valleys, as Figure 28.10 shows. So, groundwater moves from regions where the water table is high to regions where the water table is low, essentially flowing "downhill" underground.

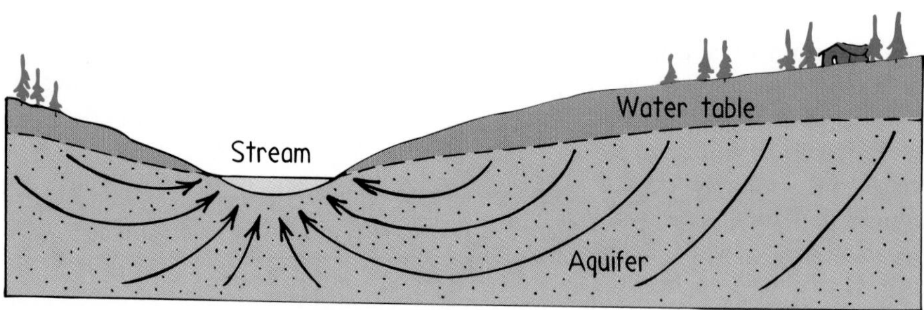

Figure 28.10
Groundwater flows from a high-hydraulic-head area, such as beneath a hill, to a low-hydraulic-head area, such as beneath a stream valley. The curved arrows indicate flow, which show the stream is fed from below.

The speed of groundwater movement is generally very slow compared with the flow speed in rivers and streams. The more permeable the aquifer, the faster the flow; the greater the hydraulic gradient, the faster the flow. The speed and route of groundwater flow can be measured by introducing dye into a well and noting the time it takes to travel to the next well. In most aquifers, groundwater speed is only a few centimeters per day, which is sufficient to keep underground reservoirs full.

Figuring Physical Science

Darcy's Law

Knowing the dimensions and hydraulic conductivity of an aquifer, and the hydraulic head at the beginning and end of the aquifer, we can use Darcy's law to calculate the groundwater flow rate. Again, Darcy's law is stated:

Groundwater flow rate
= hydraulic conductivity × cross-sectional area × hydraulic gradient

Consider an aquifer with a length of 10 km that is between two lakes. Measured perpendicular to the length, a vertical slice of the aquifer has a cross-sectional area of 200,000 m^2. The elevation of the water surface at Lake A is 215 m above sea level. The elevation of the water surface at Lake B is 210 m above sea level. The hydraulic conductivity of the aquifer is 10 meters per day.

Problems

1. What is the hydraulic gradient in the aquifer?
2. What is the groundwater flow rate in the aquifer?

Solutions

1. The lake surfaces give us two locations where we know hydraulic head. First, we need to get the distances and hydraulic heads in the same units:

$$10 \text{ km} \times \frac{1{,}000 \text{ m}}{1 \text{ km}} = 10{,}000 \text{ m}$$

then:

$$\text{hydraulic gradient} = \frac{215 \text{ m} - 210 \text{ m}}{10{,}000 \text{ m}}$$
$$= 0.0005 \text{ (units cancel out)}$$

2. Groundwater flow rate
$= 10 \text{ m/d} \times 200{,}000 \text{ m}^2 \times 0.0005$
$= 1000 \text{ m}^3\text{/d}$

28.3 Surface Water and Drainage Systems

Streams—by which we mean all flowing surface water, from the Mississippi River to the shallowest woodland creek—are dynamic systems that affect both the surface of the land and the people who live on that land. Streams carve out and alter the landscape. They also provide energy, irrigation, and a means of transportation for people.

Stream Speed

As rain falls on land, it begins a complex journey back to the ocean. Some of the rain soaks into the ground, some evaporates back into the atmosphere, and some runs off into streams.

Streams come in a variety of forms—straight or curved, fast or slow. Typically, at their headwaters (the places where streams originate), stream channels are narrow, and water flows quickly through deeply incised, V-shaped mountain valleys. Farther downstream, channels widen so that water flows into and along broad, low valleys.

There are three variables that influence the speed of water in a stream—*stream gradient, stream discharge,* and *channel geometry*. The stream gradient is to surface water what the hydraulic gradient is to groundwater. In a stream,

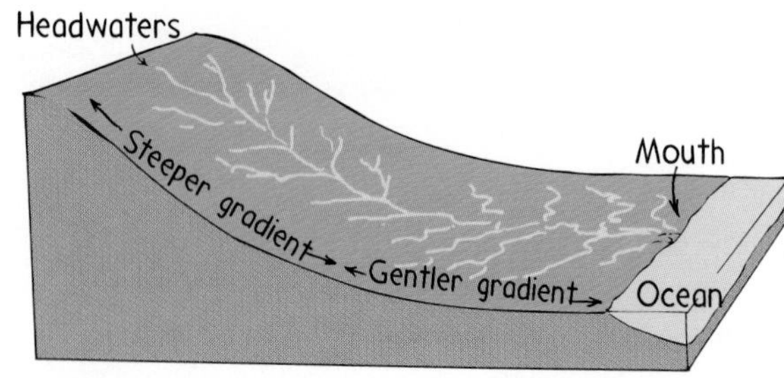

Figure 28.11
The long profile of a stream. At a stream's headwaters, the gradient is high, the channels narrow and shallow, and the stream flow rapid. As the stream progresses downslope, the gradient decreases, the channel widens, and discharge increases.

the gradient is the vertical drop in the elevation of the stream channel divided by the horizontal distance for that drop. If we look at a long profile of a stream (Figure 28.11), we see that the gradient is steep near the stream's headwaters and gentler, almost horizontal, near its mouth. Because of gravity, stream speed tends to be greater where the stream gradient is steep. Downstream, discharge and channel geometry also influence stream speed.

Discharge is the volume of water that passes a given location in a channel in a certain amount of time. It is directly proportional to the cross-sectional area of the channel—the width times the depth—and to the *average* stream speed:

$$\textbf{Discharge} = \textbf{cross-sectional area} \times \textbf{average stream speed}$$

Or put another way,

$$\text{Average stream speed} = \frac{\textbf{discharge}}{\textbf{cross-sectional area}}$$

Stream speed is usually not constant along the length of a stream. In the headwaters of a stream, the gradient is high, so stream speed is also high. In fact, these upland sections of a stream are often called "rapids." As a stream progresses downslope, the gradient gradually decreases, the channel typically widens, and, because tributary streams feed into it, discharge increases.

Because stream speed depends on three variables, downslope changes in stream speed are often counterintuitive. Consider a stream in which discharge doubles downslope, but the channel stays the same size and shape. Looking at the equation for stream speed, we can see that the stream speed also doubles. Now consider a stream in which discharge doubles downslope and the cross-sectional area of the channel also doubles. When friction is insignificant, the speed of this stream will not change, even though discharge has increased. The cross-sectional area of the stream channel increased by the same percentage as the discharge, compensating for the additional water without causing the stream speed to increase. Can you see that stream speed downslope can actually *decrease*?

The shape of the channel also affects stream speed. Now consider two streams that have the same cross-sectional area. Water flowing in the channel touches the channel bottom and sides. Friction between the water and the channel slows stream speed. The cross-sectional shape of a channel determines the amount of water in contact with the channel. The greater the contact area, the greater the friction (Figure 28.12). If the stream channel is rounded and deep,

(a) Rounded, deep channel

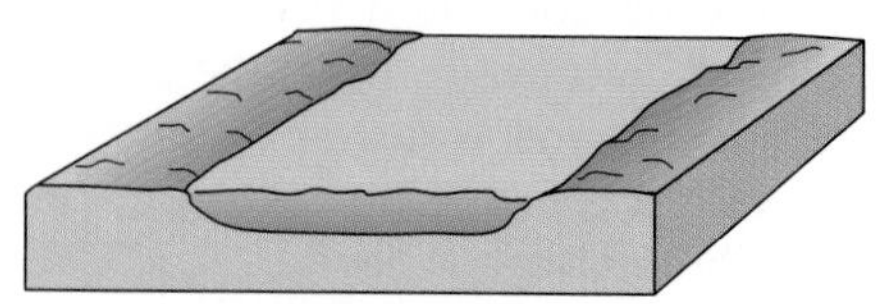

(b) Wide, shallow channel

Figure 28.12
(a) In a rounded, deep channel, the speed of water flow is relatively high because there is relatively less water in contact with the channel (there is less friction). (b) Wide, shallow channels tend to have slower flows because more water is in contact with the channel (there is more friction).

as opposed to flat-bottomed and relatively shallow, the stream speed will be faster because there is less water in contact with the channel.

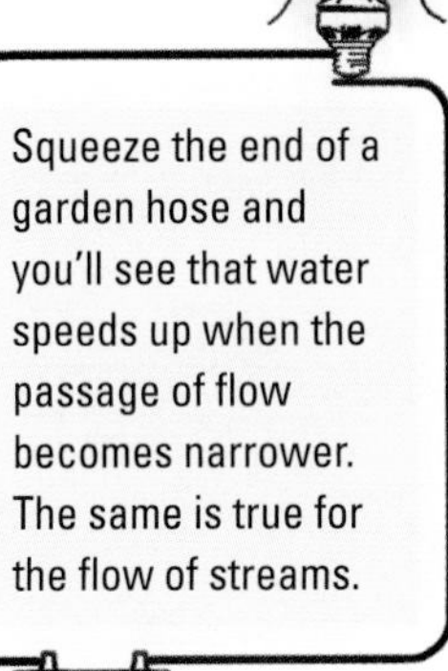

☑ CHECKPOINT

If the gradient of a stream decreases and the cross-sectional area stays the same, will the discharge stay the same? Assume that no water enters from tributaries and friction is insignificant.

Check Your Answer

No, because the decreased gradient will slow the stream speed. The discharge will decrease.

Drainage Basins and Networks

A stream is one small segment of a much larger system called a *drainage basin.* A drainage basin is defined as the total area that contributes water to a given stream. A drainage basin can cover a vast area or be as small as 1 square kilometer. Drainage basins are separated from one another by *divides,* lines tracing out the highest ground between streams. Under most circumstances, the separation is complete—rain that falls on one side of a divide cannot flow to an adjacent basin. A divide can be either very long, if it separates two enormous drainage basins, or a mere ridge separating two small gullies. The *Continental Divide,* a continuous line running north to south down the length of North America, separates the Pacific basin on the west from the Atlantic basin on the east. Water west of the Divide eventually flows to the Pacific Ocean, and water east of it flows to the Atlantic Ocean (Figure 28.13).

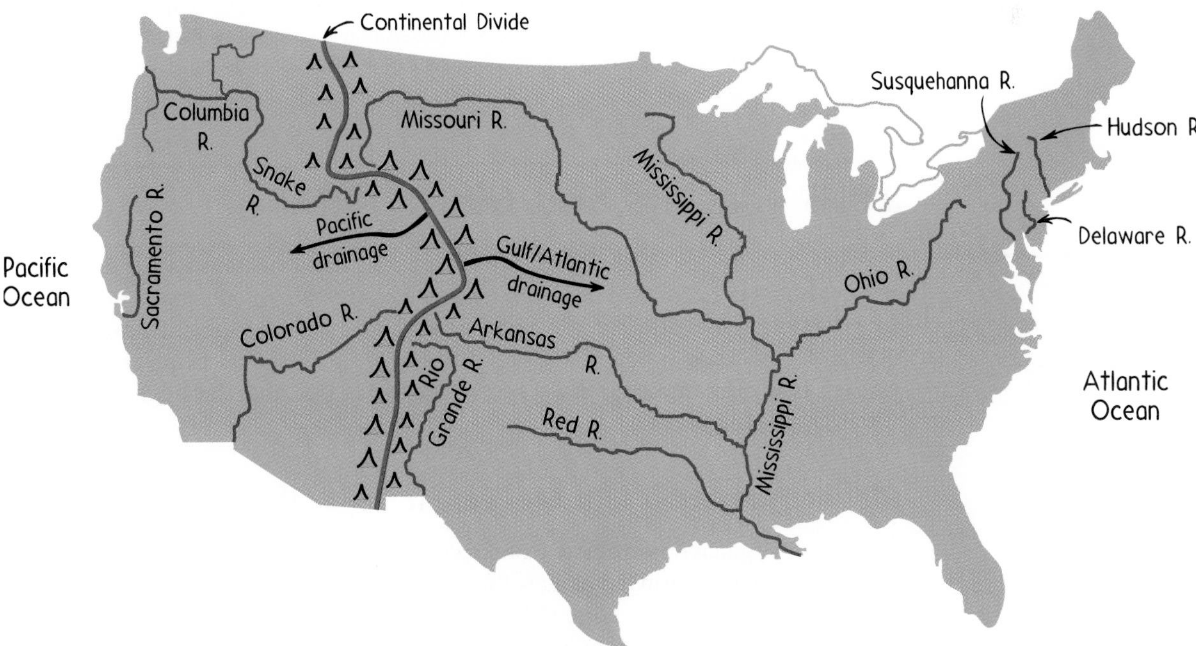

Figure 28.13
The Continental Divide in North America separates the Pacific basin on the west from the Atlantic basin on the east.

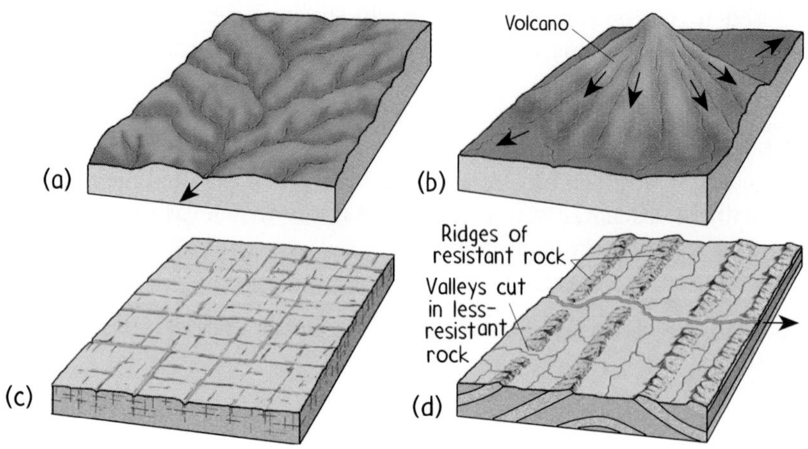

Figure 28.14
Different drainage patterns develop according to surface material and surface structure: (a) dentritic, (b) radial, (c) rectangular, (d) trellis.

As mentioned, streams merge with other streams as they flow downhill, becoming larger and larger. The entire assembly of streams draining a region is called a *drainage network*. A *drainage network* can be characterized by the branching pattern formed by its streams (Figure 28.14). Because streams erode the land surface and hence erode the rocks and rock material on the land, drainage patterns are greatly influenced by the rock type and rock material eroded.

☑ CHECKPOINT

Distinguish between a drainage basin and a drainage network.

Check Your Answer

A drainage basin is the total area that contributes water to a stream. It includes all the streams as well. A drainage network involves only the streams that drain water from the basins. So a drainage network is part of a drainage basin.

28.4 Glaciers and Glaciation

The mightiest rivers on the earth are frozen solid and normally flow a sluggish few centimeters per day. These great icy rivers are called **glaciers.** Glaciers covered significant portions of the earth several times in the distant past. Glaciation is still at work in many regions of the world, its agents being small alpine glaciers in mountainous areas, large alpine ice fields, and the huge Arctic and Antarctic continental ice sheets.

Glacier Formation and Movement

The ice of a glacier is formed from recrystallized snow. After snowflakes fall, their accumulation slowly changes the individual flakes to rounded lumps of icy material. As more snow falls, the pressure exerted on the bottom layers of icy snow compacts and recrystallizes it into glacial ice.

Figure 28.15
When a deck of cards is pushed from one side, the individual playing cards slide past one another, thus shifting the whole deck.

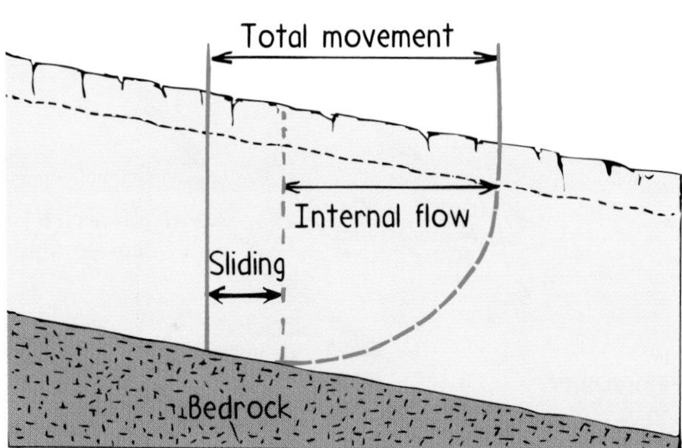

Figure 28.16
Cross section of a glacier. Glacial movement has two components: Internal flow, and sliding resulting from lubrication by meltwater. Movement is slowest at the base, because of frictional drag, and fastest at the surface. The upper parts of the glacier are carried along in piggyback fashion by plastic flow within the ice.

This ice does not become a true glacier, however, until it moves under its own weight. Glacial movement occurs when the ice mass reaches a critical thickness of approximately 50 meters and the pressure exerted by the overlying material causes the ice at the base to deform plastically and flow downslope. This plastic deformation can be likened to what happens to a deck of playing cards. When the deck is pushed from one end, as in Figure 28.15, individual cards slide past one another shifting the entire deck. Plastic deformation of the ice in a glacier is greatest at the base, where pressure is greatest.

Plastic flow from the slippage of ice crystals is not the only component of glacial movement. The melting point of ice decreases as pressure increases. When melted ice—*meltwater*—forms at the base of the glacier, the process called *basal sliding* comes into play.* This second mechanism of glacial movement results in the sliding of the entire glacier downslope, with the meltwater acting as a lubricant. The net speed of the glacial ice increases from the base up, reaching its greatest values at the glacier's surface (Figure 28.16). Overlying layers are carried along in piggyback fashion as plastic deformation and basal sliding occurs in the lowest layers.

The uppermost portion of the glacier, carried along both by basal sliding and by internal plastic deformation, behaves like a rigid, brittle mass that may fracture. Huge, gaping cracks called *crevasses* may develop in this surface ice. These can extend to great depths and can therefore be quite dangerous for people attempting to cross a glacier.

Average glacier speed varies from glacier to glacier, and it can range from only a few centimeters to a few hundred centimeters per day. Such slow speeds are measured by placing a line of markers across the ice and recording their changes in position over a period of time, ranging from days to years. Ice is found to move fastest in the center and more slowly at the edges because of frictional drag (Figure 28.17). Some glaciers experience surges, or periods of much

Glaciers surge when the muddy till below the glacier is warmed by internal heat in the earth. Warmth is retained because insulation against the cold atmosphere is provided by the thick overlying ice. Melting occurs with meltwater seeping into the till, which softens and moves easily under the weight of the overlying ice.

*Meltwater may result from the pressure of the overlying ice (because the melting point of ice decreases as pressure increases), from the internal heat of the Earth, or from the generation of heat from frictional drag as the glacier moves. Whatever the causes of its formation, meltwater contributes to the movement of a glacier.

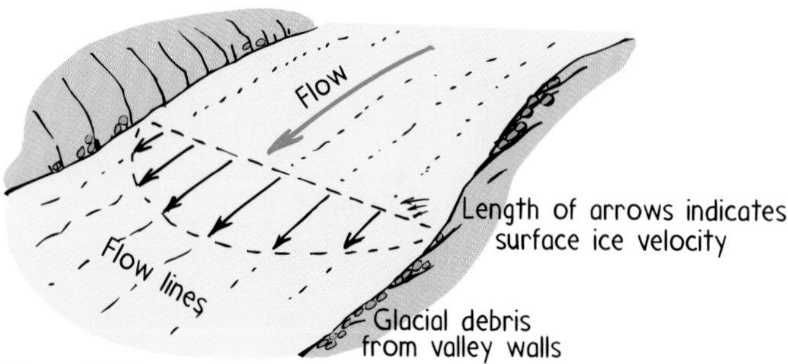

Figure 28.17
Top view of a glacier. Movement is fastest at the center, and it gradually decreases along the edges because of friction.

more rapid movement. These surges are probably caused by periodic melting of the base and sudden redistribution of mass. The flow rate in these relatively brief surges can be 100 times faster than the normal rate. Viewed from above, flow bands of rock debris and ice normally have a parallel pattern, but, during a surge, the flow bands become intricately folded.

(a)

(b)

Figure 28.18
Glacial flows: (a) normal flow and (b) surge flow.

Glacial Mass Balance

From season to season, and over longer periods of time, the mass of a glacier changes. Typically, a glacier grows in the winter as snow accumulates on its surface. The amount of snow added and the process of adding snow to a glacier is aptly termed **accumulation.**

As ice accumulates and begins to flow downhill, it may move to an altitude where temperatures are warmer. Then some ice melts and the glacier loses some of its mass. A glacier may also lose mass as it moves downslope to a shoreline, where ice may break off, or *calve,* to form icebergs that float away to sea. Melting and calving are the two primary mechanisms by which glaciers lose mass. Although less noticeable, glaciers may also lose mass as the ice *sublimates* to water vapor. By whatever means it occurs, the loss of ice by a glacier is called **ablation** (Figure 28.19).

When accumulation equals ablation, the size of the glacier remains constant. For example, in a mountain glacier, accumulation occurs with winter snowfall in the farther-back, higher-elevation parts of the glacier, and most of the ablation occurs in the lower portions, where spring and summer melting is greatest. When accumulation rates and ablation rates are equal, the melting of the lower portions is offset by the downslope flow of ice from higher portions. As a result, the location of the front edge of the glacier does not change. When accumulation exceeds ablation, the glacier advances—it grows. When ablation

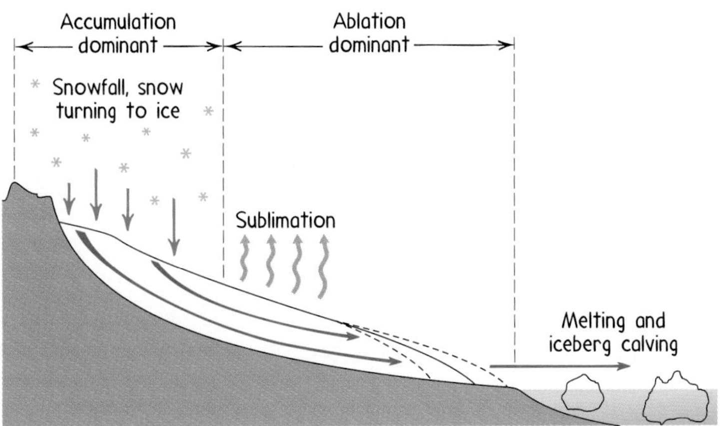

Figure 28.19
Accumulation on a glacier takes place at high elevations as snow falls on the glacier and turns to ice, Ablation takes place at lower, warmer elevations as ice melts, or calves into icebergs, or is lost through sublimation.

exceeds accumulation, the glacier retreats—it shrinks. Naturally, in all these cases, the ice of the glacier is always flowing downslope.

☑ CHECKPOINT

Under what conditions does the front of a glacier remain at the same location from year to year?

Check Your Answer

The front of a glacier remains at the same location when the rate of growth (accumulation) equals the rate of shrinking (ablation). In the spring, as ice at the glacier's front melts away, the glacier retreats upslope. At the same time, the increased mass from the prior winter's accumulation causes the glacier to move forward. When the rate at which this forward movement matches the rate of melting, the location of the front edge doesn't change.

28.5 The Oceans

As we learned in the previous chapter, if we could ever drain the water from the earth's oceans, we'd see enormous mountain ranges in the middle of the ocean basins and deep trenches bordering many of the continents. These features of the ocean bottom are very pronounced. In fact, land rises, on average, about 840 meters above sea level, while the ocean bottom drops on average, about 3800 meters below sea level. If we were to compare the height of Mount Everest in the Himalayas, a majestic 8848 meters above sea level, with the depth of the Marianas Trench in the Pacific Ocean, an astounding 11,035 meters below sea level, we would see that the oceans are much deeper than land mountains are high.

The **continental margin** is the boundary between the continents and the ocean. As Figure 28.20 shows, the continental margin consists of a *continental shelf* (the submerged upper portion of the margin), a *continental slope* (the break point where the shelf steepens as it descends to depths of 2–3 kilometers), and a *continental rise* (the area from the base of the slope seaward to the deep ocean floor). Continental margins are formed by the deposition of continental sediments. Between continental margins, the topography of the ocean floor

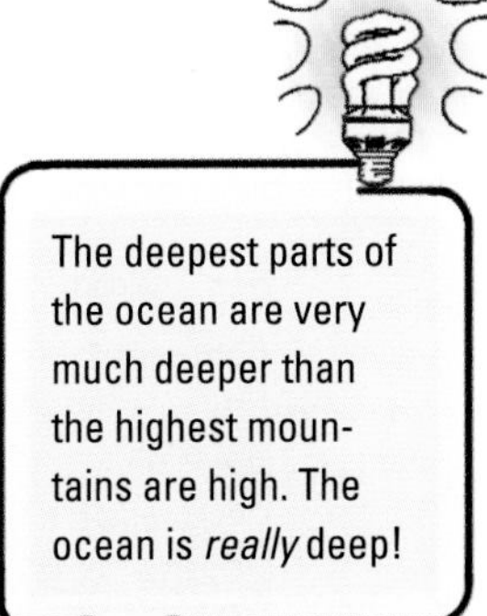

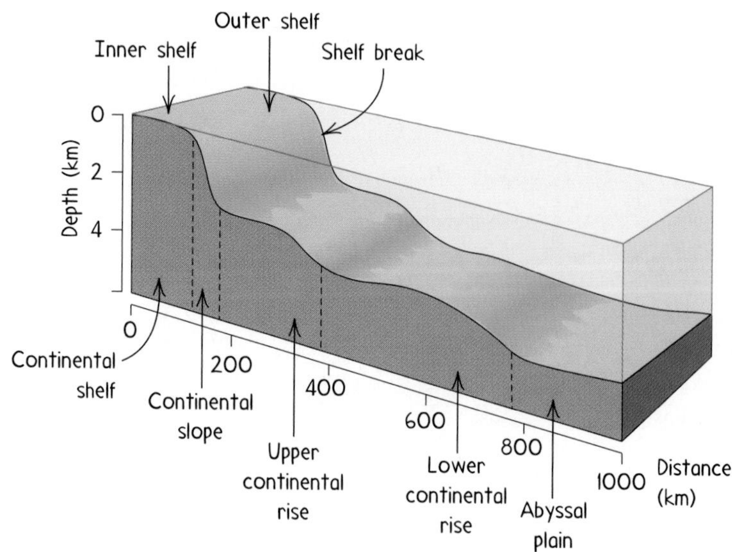

Figure 28.20
Profile of the continental margin going from land to the deep ocean bottom. The vertical dimension is exaggerated for clarity.

varies greatly. The midoceanic ridges that encircle the globe are tall and variable, the sediment-covered ocean bottom is relatively flat, and seafloor trenches near continental margins can be very deep (Figure 28.21).

Ocean Waves

Ocean waves come in a variety of sizes and shapes, from tiny ripples to the gigantic waves powered by hurricanes. Water waves, like all other waves, begin with some kind of disturbance. The most common disturbance that causes ocean waves is the wind. Blow on a bowl filled with water and you'll see a succession of small ripples moving across the water's surface. The generation of ripples in the ocean is similar. As wind speed increases, the ripples grow to full-sized waves; as stronger winds blow, larger waves are created. As waves travel away from their origin, they develop into regular patterns of smooth, rounded waves called *swells*—the mature undulations of the open ocean.

Recall, from our study of waves in Chapter 11, that wave motion can be described in terms of a sine curve (Figure 28.22) and that it is the *disturbance* that is carried by a wave, not the material through which the wave is moving. The waveform travels across the ocean, while the water making up the wave remains, for the most part, in one place.

However, because ocean waves have both transverse and circular components, ocean waves are more complicated than the simple transverse waves discussed in

Figure 28.21
Map of the ocean floor showing variation in topography. (a) Atlantic profile. (b) Pacific profile.

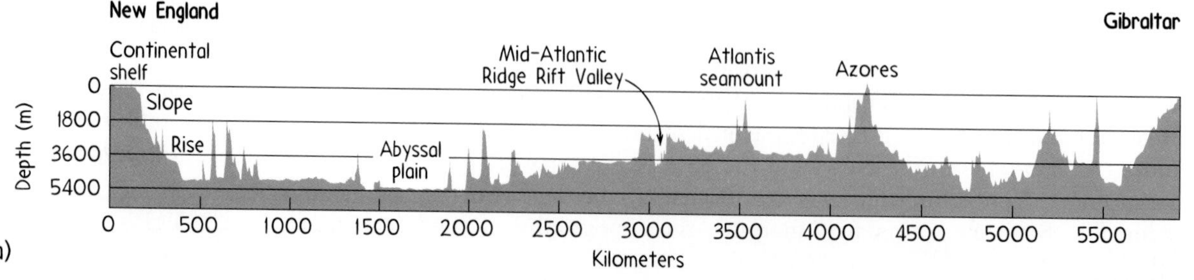

Chapter 11. As a water wave passes a given point, the water particles at that point move in circular paths. This circular motion can be seen by observing the behavior of a floating piece of wood on the ocean surface. The wood sways to and fro while bobbing up and down, actually tracing a circle during each wave cycle. This circular motion occurs near the water surface, and it decreases gradually with depth (Figure 28.23). At a depth of about one-half wavelength, the circular component of the wave is negligible. For this reason, we can say, with reasonable accuracy, that water waves occur mainly at the surface.

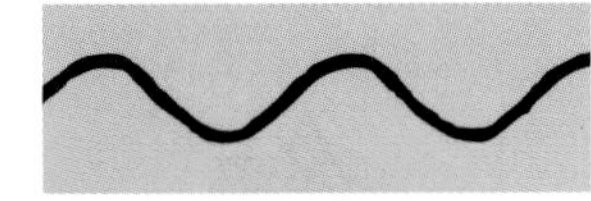

Figure 28.22
Ocean waves have characteristics of simple sine waves.

When a wave approaches the shore, where water depth decreases, the circular motion is interrupted by the ocean bottom. As the water's depth gets shallower and approaches half of the wave's wavelength, the bottom of the circular path flattens, slowing the wave. The wave period remains unchanged because the swells from deeper waters continue to advance. As a result, incoming waves gain on leading slower waves and the distance between waves decreases. This bunching up of waves in a narrower zone produces higher, steeper waves. When wave height steepens to the point where water can no longer support itself, the wave overturns, breaking shoreward with a crash. This breaking water is called *surf*—the area of wave activity between the line of breakers and the shore (Figure 28.24).

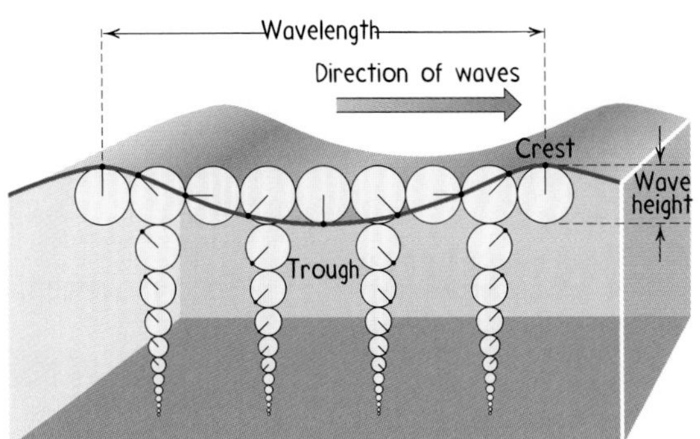

Figure 28.23
Movement of water particles with the passage of a wave. The particles move in a circular orbit. Orbital motion is greatest at the surface and gradually decreases with depth. At depths greater than half a wavelength, orbital motion is negligible.

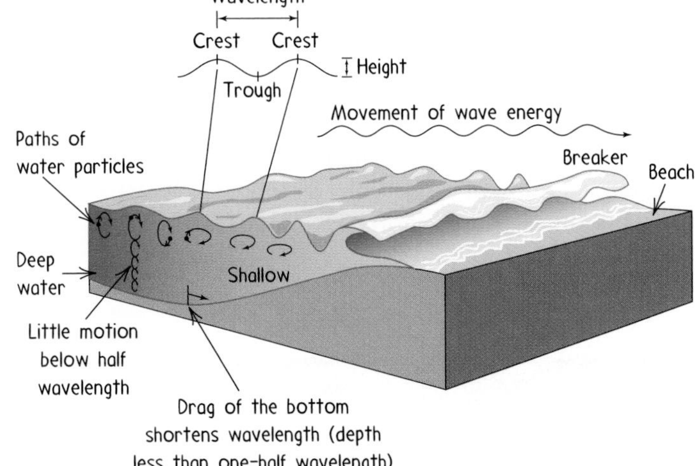

Figure 28.24
Waves change form as they travel from deep water through shallow water to shore. In deep water, orbital motion is circular. In shallow water, orbital motion becomes elliptical as a result of contact of the wave with the bottom. This change decreases the wave speed. As incoming waves continue to advance, the distance between waves decreases, causing wave height to increase. When waves reach a critical height, they break and crash shoreward into the surf zone.

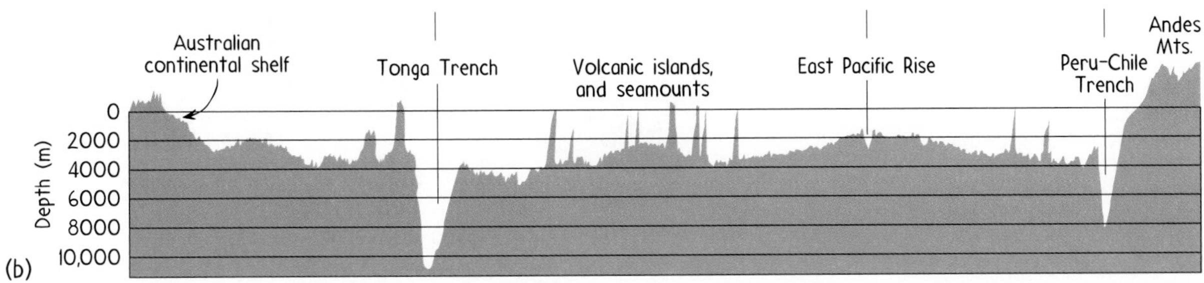

Wave Refraction

As waves enter shallow water, their forward direction changes when they approach the shore at an angle. As the portion of the wave closest to the shore begins touching the ocean bottom, it slows and lags behind the portions of the wave still in deeper water. As the next portion of the wave touches the bottom, it too slows. Thus, in a continuous fashion, the line of the wave crest bends as it moves into shallower water, becoming more nearly parallel to the coastline (Figure 28.25). This is wave refraction. Additionally, the oblique approach of waves causes a *longshore current* that flows parallel to shore.

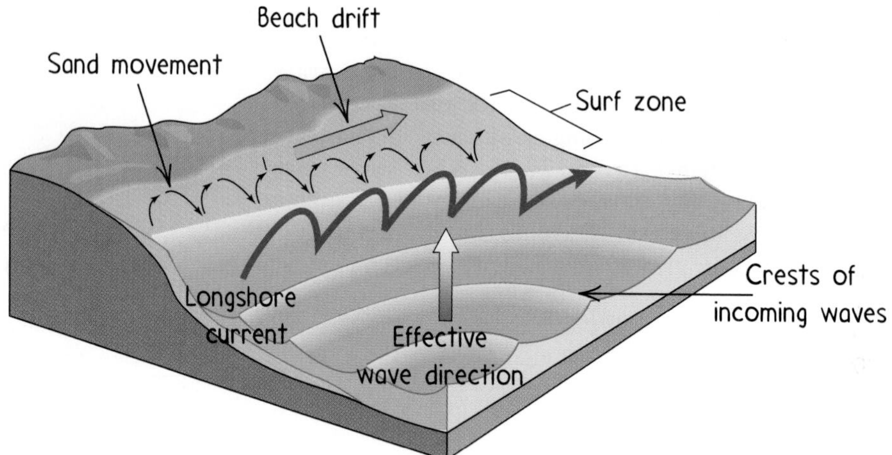

Figure 28.25
When waves approach a shoreline, they refract (bend) so that the crests of the approaching waves become more parallel to the shore as they move into shallower water. Because the overall direction of wave movement is oblique to the shore, a longshore current forms, which causes water and sand to move parallel to the shoreline.

Wave refraction also has a significant impact on irregular shorelines, mainly those on which there are protruding headlands and small bays. Refraction causes wave energy to be unevenly distributed. Wave energy is concentrated at headland areas, where shorelines project into the water, and diluted in adjacent bays (Figure 28.26).

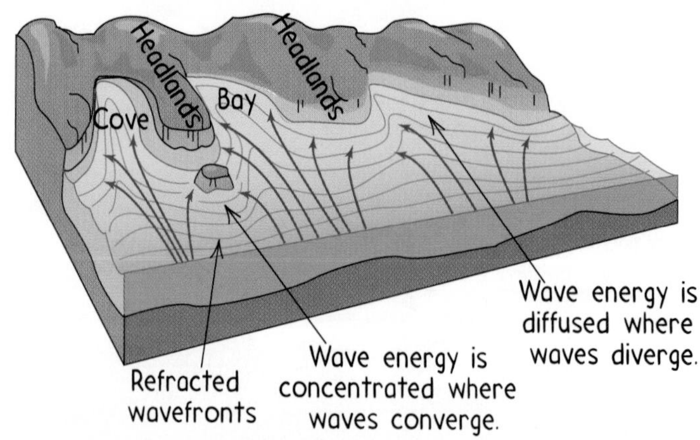

Figure 28.26
On irregular coastlines, wave energy is concentrated as it converges on headlands and is diffused as it diverges in coves and bays.

28.6 The Quality of Water

Water occurs in many environments. The quality of the water we drink, as well as of the water in lakes, streams, rivers, and oceans, is an important factor in the quality of our lives. Rainwater is used as the standard of water purity. Most of our water supply (such as groundwater and water in reservoirs) is of good quality—as good as rainwater. But there are also important variations.

If rain falls through clean air and soaks into nearly pure quartz sand, the quality of the water after filtering through the sand will be about the same as the quality of the rainwater before filtration. On the other hand, rain soaking into carbonate rocks (such as limestone) can become "hard" from dissolved calcium bicarbonate. Limestone dissolution occurs because rainwater is naturally slightly acidic, as we saw in Section 22.5. These dissolved substances can affect the taste of the water as well as its usefulness. For example, hard water does not rinse away detergents very well and therefore is not very useful for washing. Hard water also causes soap scum to form, as described in Section 20.4. So we see that the quality of groundwater depends very much on the type of soil and rock through which it flows.

The amount of dissolved substances in drinking water is generally very small. Water of good quality averages 150 parts per million of total dissolved substances, with an upper limit of 1000 parts per million. The taste of water depends on the type of dissolved substances it contains. Water containing 1000 parts per million of dissolved calcium tastes fine, but water containing 200 parts per million of sodium chloride tastes salty.

Several other dissolved substances, many of them introduced by human activities, have a strong effect on the quality of water; some of these are beneficial to health, while others can be quite dangerous. Added fluoride, for example, helps to reduce tooth decay. Zeolite minerals in water filters soften hard water by chemically exchanging dissolved calcium for sodium. In contrast, lead and arsenic, two elements that occur naturally in some locations, can make water unsafe to drink even if present in small amounts. Bacteria from sewage and other sources may make water unsafe to drink, unless it has been adequately treated.

Figure 28.27
In hard water, dissolved calcium prevents soap from developing a sudsy lather and also from rinsing clean. Bathtub rings are more prevalent in areas that have hard water.

☑ **CHECKPOINT**

How is hard water softened?

Check Your Answer

Hard water is softened by removal of dissolved calcium. This is accomplished by passing it through a zeolite filter, which absorbs calcium ions while releasing an equivalent number of sodium ions. Unlike hard water, soft water allows the formation of soap suds that can readily be rinsed off.

Water-Supply Contamination

The primary cause of water-supply contamination is human activity. As rivers and streams become contaminated by factory and sewage discharge and chemical spills, surface water is polluted. Because surface water is linked to groundwater, what affects one can easily affect the other.

The most common source of groundwater contamination is sewage. Sewage includes both the drainage from septic tanks and inadequate or broken sewer lines, as well as the leaching of barnyard wastes. Sewage water contains bacteria that, if untreated, can cause such waterborne diseases as typhoid, cholera, and infectious hepatitis. Sewage contamination can be treated to some degree naturally. If it travels through sediments that contain small pores, such as sand, sewage-contaminated groundwater can be purified within short distances. The sand filters bacteria and viruses from the water, and chemical reactions remove many other contaminants. Sand is often used in sewage-treatment plants as a step in the water purification process. If, on the other hand, contaminated groundwater travels through sediments that contain large pores, such as gravel, or through rocks having large openings, such as cavernous limestone, it can travel long distances in short periods of time and remain contaminated.

Agricultural areas in which nitrate fertilizers are used extensively can also contribute to groundwater contamination. First of all, nitrates are very soluble in water. Nitrate fertilizer spread over the land is used by plants, but the unused nitrate flows down into the groundwater as a contaminant. Nitrate levels in groundwater must be closely monitored, because these compounds, in amounts as small as 15 parts per million, are toxic to humans. Fertilizers in surface waters can cause damage to the environment as well.

As a population grows, so does its garbage. The most common means of waste and refuse disposal is burial in a landfill. Even radioactive, toxic, and hazardous wastes are buried. The location of underground storage sites is tricky to decide. For a site to be considered safe, it must be located where waste products and their containers cannot be affected chemically by water, physically by Earth movements, or accidentally by human activity. Precipitation infiltrating the site may dissolve a variety of compounds from the solid waste. The resulting liquid, known as **leachate**, can move vertically downward from the landfill to the water table and contaminate the groundwater. When leachate mixes with groundwater, it forms a plume (an area of contaminated groundwater) that spreads in the direction of the flowing groundwater. To reduce the chances of groundwater contamination, the landfill can be capped with layers of compacted clay soil or a synthetic membrane to prevent the generation of leachate. It can also be lined with the same material. Collection systems are often used to catch draining leachate and to prevent its distribution.

Groundwater contamination also occurs as a result of spills and leaks of toxic and hazardous chemicals. These discharges can be sudden, as in a train wreck or a tanker-truck accident, or as a result of slow leakage from a holding container or an underground storage tank.

The way contaminants move through the subsurface depends on the nature of the contaminant. If the contaminant is soluble in water, for example, it dissolves in the groundwater and flows along with it. If it is less dense than water, it floats on the water table (Figure 28.28). If it is more dense than water, it sinks through the water to a low-permeability layer. As we can see in Figure 28.29, groundwater is susceptible to contamination from a wide variety of sources.

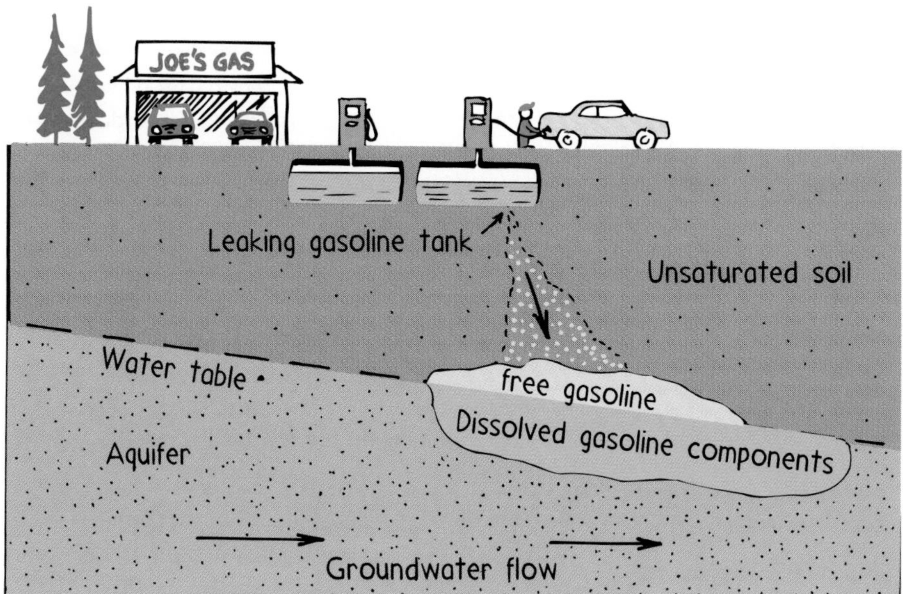

Figure 28.28
A contaminant plume of leachate spreads in the direction of groundwater flow.

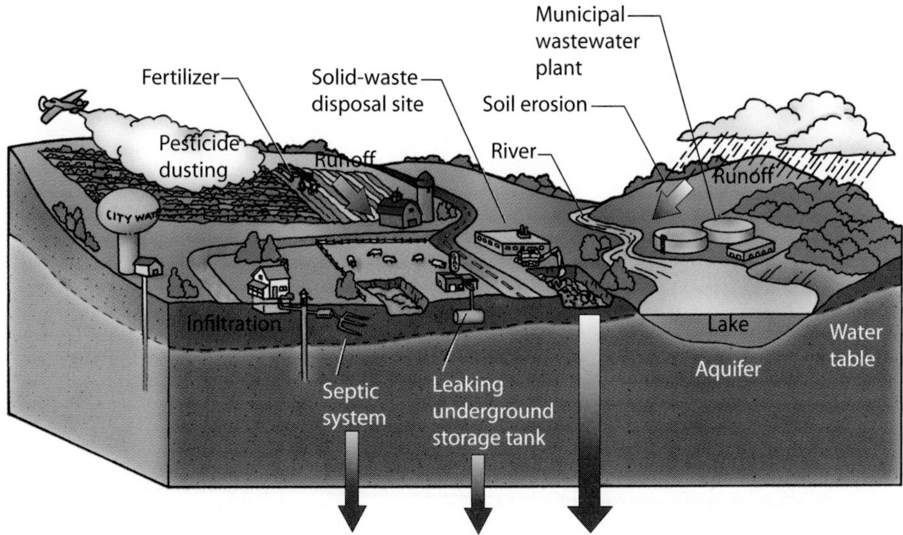

Figure 28.29
Groundwater is susceptible to a wide variety of contamination sources. The arrows indicate some major sources.

Luckily, the problem of human-caused contamination described above is not without hope. Ways in which to prevent such contamination are being used more and more. New technologies are constantly being developed to prevent and to clean up the contamination of water. Our water supply is precious. We, as a society, must do everything we can to protect and to conserve it.

What Can We Do to Conserve Water?

Clean, fresh water is one of the most valuable resources our planet has to offer. Clearly, each of us must be mindful of fresh water's true value, and we must practice conservation measures whenever possible.

Toward this goal, please consider the following guidelines adapted from the American Water and Energy Savers Association.

10 Ways to Save Water

1. Read your water meter before and after a two-hour period when no water is being used. If the reading has changed, there is a leak somewhere in your water system. Get the leak fixed.
2. Fix dripping faucets by replacing the washers in them. If a faucet is dripping at the rate of one drop per second, you can expect to waste 11,000 liters per year!
3. Check for toilet-tank leaks by adding food coloring to the tank. If the toilet is leaking, color will appear in the bowl within 30 minutes.
4. Avoid flushing the toilet unnecessarily.
5. Install a composting toilet, which uses no water. Rather, it allows human wastes to decompose *aerobically* as air is vented over the waste, which is buried in peat moss. Dried, odor-free compost is removed every few months and is useful as a garden fertilizer.
6. Take shorter showers, and don't let the water run unnecessarily while you brush your teeth.
7. When washing dishes by hand, do so in a sink or large pot filled with soapy water. Quickly rinse soapy dishes under a small stream from the faucet.
8. Store drinking water in the refrigerator rather than letting the tap run every time you want a cool glass of water.
9. Always follow all water-conservation and water-shortage rules and restrictions in effect in your area.
10. Encourage family, friends, and neighbors to be part of a water-conscious community.

Summary of Terms

Hydrologic cycle The natural circulation of water from ocean, to atmosphere, to land, and back to ocean.

Groundwater Subsurface water in the saturated zone.

Porosity The volume of open space in rock or sediment compared with the total volume of solids plus open space.

Hydraulic conductivity The ability of a material to transmit water.

Water table The upper boundary of the saturated zone, below which every pore space is filled with water.

Artesian system A system in which confined groundwater under pressure can rise above the level of an aquifer.

Discharge The volume of water that passes a given location in a stream channel in a certain amount of time.

Glacier A large mass of ice, formed by the compaction and recrystallization of snow, that moves downslope under its own weight.

Accumulation The amount of snow added, and the process of adding snow, to a glacier.

Ablation The amount of ice lost, and the process of losing ice, from a glacier.

Continental margin The boundary between continental land and deep ocean basins, consisting of continental shelf, continental slope, and continental rise.

Leachate A solution formed by water that has percolated through soil containing water-soluble substances.

Review Questions

28.1 The Hydrologic Cycle

1. Where does most of the earth's precipitation occur?
2. As water is precipitated onto the land, where does it go? Where does most of the water on land end up?

28.2 Groundwater

3. Distinguish between the terms *porosity* and *hydraulic conductivity*.

4. If a hole is dug in the unsaturated zone, will it fill with water? Why or why not?
5. A kitchen table is usually flat, but the water table is generally not flat. Why?
6. Compare and contrast the unsaturated zone with the saturated zone.
7. What types of soil allow for the greatest infiltration of rainfall?
8. What types of rock can have high porosity but low hydraulic conductivity? Defend your answer.
9. Can an aquifer be composed of igneous rocks? Defend your answer.
10. How does an aquitard differ from an aquifer?
11. What is an artesian system, and how is it formed?
12. What two factors contribute to the ability of an aquifer to recharge?
13. What factors affect the rate of groundwater movement?

28.3 Surface Water and Drainage Systems

14. Rivers are important to human culture. Why?
15. What is meant by stream gradient, and how does it affect stream velocity?
16. What happens to stream speed when the discharge of a stream increases? What happens to discharge when the speed of a stream increases?
17. How does the shape of a stream channel affect flow?
18. What is a continental divide, and what specifically does it divide?
19. What is the significance of the Continental Divide in North America with respect to water flow to the Atlantic Ocean and to the Pacific Ocean?

28.4 Glaciers and Glaciation

20. What conditions are necessary for a glacier to form?
21. What distinguishes a huge block of ice from a glacier?
22. In what two main ways do glaciers flow?
23. What is a glacial surge?
24. Why do crevasses form on the surfaces of glaciers?
25. Does all the ice in a glacier move at the same speed? Explain.
26. Under what conditions does a glacier front advance?
27. Under what conditions does a glacier front retreat?

28.5 The Oceans

28. Why do waves become taller as they approach the shore?
29. What is wave refraction? Why does it occur in ocean waves?
30. Which is greater—the height of Mount Everest or the depth of the deepest part of the ocean?

28.6 The Quality of Water

31. List three ways in which our groundwater supply can be contaminated.
32. What is the most effective material in purifying contaminated groundwater—coarse gravel, sand, or cavernous limestone? Defend your answer.
33. Can groundwater contamination affect the quality of surface water? If so, how? If not, why not?
34. Cite one possible source for high levels of nitrate in groundwater.
35. How does leachate form?

Activity

Water is "hard" if it contains dissolved calcium and magnesium. To test the hardness of the water in your area, collect four water samples from four different local sources—a nearby pond or well, a stream, your kitchen faucet, and bottled distilled water. Add a drop of liquid soap to each water sample and shake. The bottle which has the most suds should be the softest water. Record your observations.

Exercises

1. If you look at a map of any part of the world, you'll see that older cities are located beside rivers, or where rivers existed when the cities were built. What is your explanation?
2. The oceans consist of salt water, yet evaporation over the ocean surface produces clouds that precipitate fresh water. Why no salt?
3. What percentage of the earth's supply of water is fresh water, and where is most of it located?
4. Where does most rainfall on Earth finally end up before becoming rain again?
5. If the water table at location X is lower than the water table at location Y, does groundwater flow from X to Y or from Y to X?
6. Is the infiltration of water into the ground greatest on steep, rocky slopes or on gentle, sandy slopes? Defend your answer.
7. In a confined aquifer, the water in a well can rise above the top of the aquifer. What is this system called?
8. In an unconfined aquifer, how high can water rise in a well that is not pumped?
9. How is the local hydrologic cycle affected by the practice of drawing drinking water from a river and then returning sewage to the same river?

10. Which do earth scientists think is the greater environmental hazard, pollution of groundwater or pollution of surface waters? Why?
11. Some metals can be extremely dangerous to water supplies. Some scientists suspect a link between aluminum and Alzheimer's and Parkinson's diseases; cadmium is known to cause liver damage; and lead affects the circulatory, reproductive, and nervous systems as well as the kidneys. What are the likely ways these metals can get into our water supply?
12. Is water in the unsaturated zone called groundwater? Why or why not?
13. When a water supply becomes overly rich in nitrogen and phosphorus, various aquatic organisms, including algae, may thrive to the point of destruction. The overgrowth of algae causes unsightly scum, unpleasant odors, and robs the water supply of dissolved oxygen. What are the sources of this type of pollution, and how does it affect other aquatic life?
14. What are the major factors that determine the length of time in which a well will produce water?
15. By what means can earth scientists predict the discharge of a stream after a rainstorm?
16. As a population increases, so does the amount of garbage produced by that population. In many areas, the preferred way to deal with increasing wastes is by burial in a landfill or in underground storage facilities. What principal factors must be considered in the planning and building of such sites?
17. With regard to residence time, how may the process of cleaning up groundwater contamination differ from cleaning up surface contamination in a lake?
18. What effect does a dam have on the water table in the vicinity of the dam?
19. What effect does the accumulation of sediments behind a dam have on its capacity for storing water?
20. In an aquifer, if the water table next to a stream is lower than the water level in the stream, does groundwater flow into the stream or does stream water flow into the ground? Explain.
21. As runoff into streams increases, what variables of stream flow (as discussed in the text) increase?
22. What is meant by channel geometry?
23. What change in stream speed occurs if the discharge in a stream doubles while the channel remains the same size and shape?
24. If stream discharge doubles and the cross-sectional area of the channel also doubles, what happens to stream speed?
25. What are the three variables that influence the speed of stream flow?
26. How is a glacier formed?
27. How does "frictional drag" play a role in the external movement of a glacier? How does this drag affect the internal movement?
28. As waves approach shallow water, those with longer wavelengths slow down before those with shorter wavelengths. Why?
29. How can leachate be prevented from entering the groundwater?
30. As a stream progresses downslope, the gradient gradually decreases and the stream channel typically widens. What factors increase the stream's discharge? What factors decrease its discharge?

Problems

1. We know, from Figure 28.1, that 97.2% of the earth's water is in the oceans. The remaining 2.8% is the earth's freshwater supply. Of this freshwater supply, what percentage is found in the polar ice caps? In groundwater? In streams, lakes, and rivers?
2. A particular stream widens as it progresses downstream. Using your answers for parts (a) and (b), briefly describe the changes in discharge.
   (a) If the cross-sectional area of the stream is 1 m^2 and the stream speed is 0.5 m/s, what is the stream's discharge?
   (b) If the cross-sectional area of the stream increases to 2 m^2 and the stream speed remains 0.5 m/s, what is the stream's discharge?

Refer to Figuring Physical Science: Darcy's Law on page 691 for Problems 3, 4, and 5.

3. A pumping well was drilled and completed in a sand aquifer. Before the pump was turned on, the hydraulic gradient and the flow rate were measured to be 0.0001 and 1 m^3/d, respectively. With the pump turned on, the gradient becomes 10 times larger. By how much does the flow rate increase?
4. Darcy's law gives us the *volume flow rate*—volume per time (for example, cubic meters per day, m^3 /d). Sometimes it is not possible to know the value of the cross-sectional area for a Darcy's law calculation. This is especially true if we use a well to estimate flow in an aquifer. The size of a well is much smaller than the cross-sectional area of an entire aquifer, so we can't use the cross-sectional area of the aquifer to calculate the flow rate. Another way to express volume is on a *per unit area* basis. For example, if we have a 1 m^3 cube, we know its base is 1 m^2—the cross-sectional area of the cube—and its height is 1 m. If we fill the cube with water, we can say we have 1 m of water per unit area. Darcy's law can be rearranged to calculate the volume flow rate per unit area. This is called the *specific dis-*

charge, which has units of length per time (for example, meters per day, m/d). Doing the following three problems will illustrate how specific discharge relates to the volume flow rate.

(a) Suppose 1 m^3 of water is pumped from a well into an empty cylindrical tank. If the water level is 2 m above the base, what is the cross-sectional area of the tank?

(b) If it takes a half of a day to pump the 1 m^3 of water into the tank, what is the flow rate in terms of both volume per time and specific discharge?

(c) Write Darcy's law so that it calculates the specific discharge. (Hint: Assume that the units for hydraulic conductivity are m/d and the units for cross-sectional area are m^2.)

5. *Please make sure that you understand Problem 4 before doing this problem.* The hydraulic head at Point A is 209 m. At Point B, which is 300 m from Point A, the hydraulic head is 210 m. The aquifer is composed of sand with a hydraulic conductivity of 150 meters per day. Groundwater flows directly from Point B to Point A. What is the specific discharge?

Chapter 28 Online Resources

Tutorials
- The Hydrologic Cycle Activity

Quiz
Exercises
Flashcards
Links

CHAPTER 29

Surface Processes

We have learned that the earth is an ever-changing planet. Rocks come and go, tectonic plates move, and water is constantly circulating on and in the earth's crust. Change also comes to the earth's surface. The earth's surface is modified by three agents of change—water, wind, and ice. These three agents produce and deposit virtually all the sediment on Earth. After sediments are deposited, they undergo compaction and cementation on their way to becoming sedimentary rock. Knowing the features seen in recent sediment deposits allows us to recognize the same features in ancient sedimentary rocks. What we gain is a knowledge of the environments in which the ancient rocks formed. In this way, the history of the earth is revealed.

29.1 The Work of Air

Water is the dominant agent of change altering our natural landscape, but air plays a role too. If you've ever been in a wind storm or at the beach on a windy day, you may have felt the sandblasting effect of the wind. Once in the air, particles of sediment can be carried great distances by the wind. Red dust from the Sahara is found on glaciers in the Swiss Alps, and on islands in the Caribbean Sea. Fine grains of quartz from central Asia blow onto the Hawaiian Islands.

In the desert, winds move over surfaces of dry sand, picking up the small, more easily transported particles but leaving the large, harder-to-move particles behind. The small particles bounce across the desert floor, knocking more particles into the air, to form *ripple marks,* which are actually tiny sand dunes (Figure 29.1). Ripple marks can also be formed by the movement of sand grains in water currents, as seen in shallow streams or under the waves at beaches.

Figure 29.1
Generated by blowing winds, ripple marks, which are small elongated sand dunes, are narrow ridges of sand separated by wider troughs. Large sand dunes can be seen in the background of the photograph.

A unique feature of sand-dune formation is cross-bedding, which is found on the leeward side of a dune. The direction of cross-bedding indicates the direction of the wind (or water current) that deposited the sediments. A particularly great place to see ancient cross-bedding is in Zion National Park in Utah. Cross-bedding is also a common feature in river deltas and certain stream-channel deposits.

Insights

Sand dunes begin to form when the flow of air is blocked by an obstacle, such as a rock or a clump of vegetation (Figure 29.1). As the wind sweeps over and around the obstacle, wind speed slows and, as a result, sand grains fall out of the air into the wind shadow (Figure 29.2). As more sand falls, mounds form and block the flow of air even more. With more sand and more wind, the mound becomes a dune. As a dune grows, the whole mound of sand starts moving downwind as sand grains on the windward slope move up and over the crest of the dune to fall on the leeward slope. The wind removes sand from the back of the dune and redeposits it on the front of the dune. Over time, this continuous process moves the entire dune.

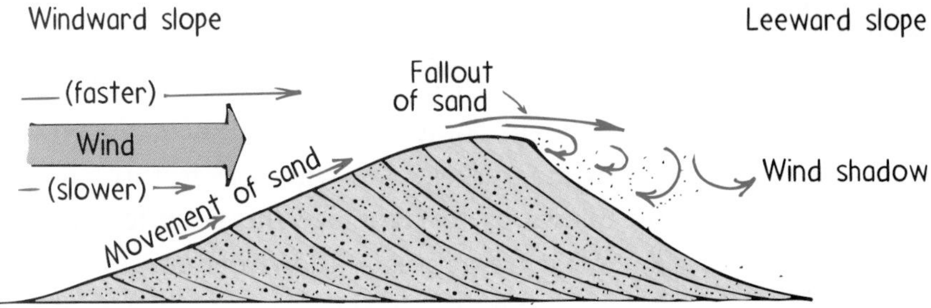

Figure 29.2
Formation of a sand dune. When air flow is obstructed, air speed drops and, as a result, sand grains settle in the wind shadow. With more wind, more sand settles, and a dune is formed. As a dune grows, sand grains on the windward slope move up and over the crest to fall on the leeward slope, which slowly results in the movement of the whole mound downwind.

29.2 The Work of Groundwater

Flowing groundwater—no matter how slow—can cause large changes in landscapes. These impacts can occur because of humans, but, more often, they occur without any human interference.

Land Subsidence

Most wells are drilled so that groundwater can be pumped from the ground. In areas where groundwater withdrawal has been extreme, the land surface is lowered—it *subsides*. The problem of land subsidence is most noticeable where the subsurface consists of a thick sequence of poorly consolidated sediments rather than rock. Such sequences generally have many layers of easily compressed, water-bearing clays sandwiched between a series of sandy aquifers. Recall, from Chapter 28, that clay has a very low hydraulic conductivity. As water is pumped from the aquifers, water slowly leaks out of the clay layers to replenish the aquifers, which usually continue to be pumped. As the clays lose water, they shrink, causing the land surface to subside.

Probably the most well known example of land subsidence is connected with the Leaning Tower of Pisa in Italy, which was built on unconsolidated sediments deposited by the Arno River. Over the years, as groundwater was withdrawn to supply the growing city, the tilt of the tower increased (Figure 29.3). Another place where land subsidence can be seen is Mexico City, which was built in the middle of an ancient shallow lake. The withdrawal of groundwater beneath this city now finds many "street-level" buildings at basement level. Some areas in Mexico City have subsided by as much as 6–7 meters. In the United States, large amounts of groundwater have been pumped for irrigation in the San Joaquin Valley of California. This process has caused the water table to drop 75 meters in 20 years, lowering the land surface by as much as 9 meters (Figure 29.4). Because water for irrigation is now provided by canals, the sandy aquifers are slowly recharging (refilling with water), but most of the land subsidence caused by the compaction of the clay layers cannot be reversed.

Figure 29.3
The Leaning Tower of Pisa. Construction began in about 1173, but it was suspended when builders realized that the foundation was inadequate. Work was later resumed, however, and the 60-m tower was completed 200 years later. The tower's deviation from the vertical is about 4.6 m. The tower's foundation has been recently stabilized by reducing groundwater withdrawal, and so the tower should remain stable for years to come.

Why is land subsidence most evident in regions where the underlying geology is a series of clay layers sandwiched between sandy aquifers?

Check Your Answer

Clay layers lose water and become compacted as water is pumped from the adjacent aquifers. Compaction causes the land to subside. People don't usually drill wells where the underlying ground surface is mostly clay. And when the underlying ground surface is made up mostly of sandy layers, the ground compresses only a little when pumped. That's why subsidence is more noticeable in regions underlain by alternating layers of loosely packed clays and sands.

Carbonate Dissolution

Groundwater occurs in the vast limestone deposits that underlie millions of square kilometers of the earth's surface. But the groundwater slowly "eats away" at the limestone through which it flows. Recall, from Chapters 25 and 26, that limestone is made of the mineral calcite (calcium carbonate, $CaCO_3$). Rainwater chemically reacts with carbon dioxide in the air and soil to produce carbonic acid. When it seeps downward into limestone, the slightly acidic groundwater partially dissolves the rock. As flowing groundwater steadily dissolves the limestone, it creates unusual erosional features, like sinkholes and caverns. It is in limestone that we find the only true underground rivers—in other rocks and soils, underground water is found only in small pore spaces, not in large, open channels.

Figure 29.4
The land surface in California's San Joaquin Valley subsided by more than 9 meters (30 feet) over a 50-year period because of the withdrawal of groundwater and the resulting compaction of sediments.

Caverns and Caves

The dissolving action of underground water has carved out magnificent caves and caverns (a cavern is simply a large cave). Groundwater flow in limestone aquifers occurs mostly through fractures in the rock, rather than through pores. Rainwater (enriched in carbonic acid) soaking into the limestone flows downward through

the fractures toward the water table, dissolving rock as it goes. As groundwater flows toward its outlet—say, a stream—the slightly acidic water continues to dissolve the surrounding limestone, expanding the fractures and forming underground channels and small, water-filled caves (Figure 29.5a). The stream water is also slightly acidic, and it dissolves and deepens the stream channel while groundwater continues to expand the caves. As the water level in the stream and the level of the water table drop, water drains from the first set of channels and caves. Groundwater continues to dissolve the limestone forming a new, lower level of channels and caves (Figures 29.5b and c).

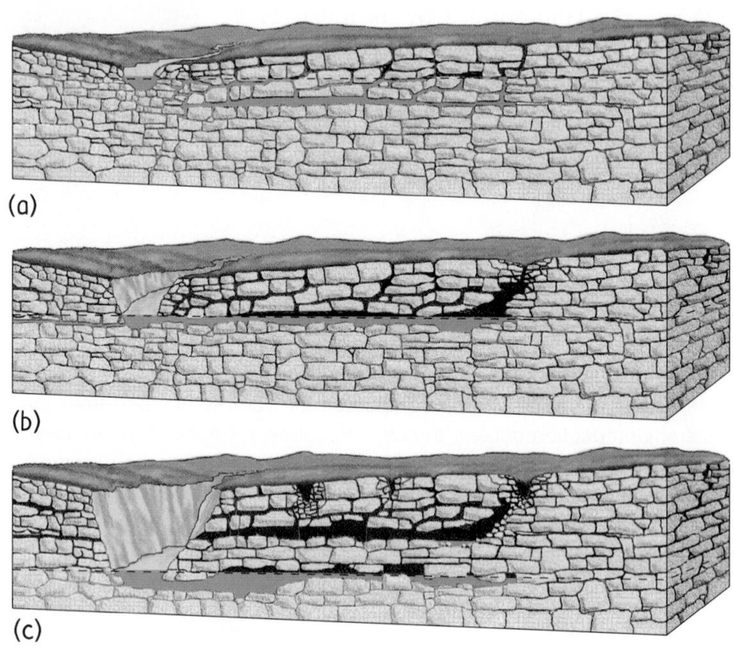

Figure 29.5
The formation of a cave begins with a layer of carbonate rock, mildly acidic groundwater, and an enormous span of time. (a) Groundwater makes its way toward a stream. (b) As the stream valley deepens because of erosion, the water table is lowered. The carbonate rock is eaten away, as acidified water erodes and enlarges the existing fractures into small caves. (c) Further deepening of the stream valley causes the water table to drop even lower; water in the caves seeps downward, leaving empty caves above a lowered groundwater level.

Figure 29.6
Cave dripstone formations at Carlsbad Cavern southwest of Carlsbad, New Mexico.

Water dripping from the cave ceiling, now rich in dissolved calcium carbonate, creates icicle-shaped stalactites as water evaporates and the calcium carbonate precipitates. Some of the water solution drips off the end of the stalactites to build corresponding cone-shaped stalagmites on the cave floor. As caves continue to grow and develop into interconnecting chambers, they are called caverns. One of the most impressive caverns in the United States is Carlsbad Caverns in southeastern New Mexico (Figure 29.6). The cavern descends to a maximum depth of 486 meters. Other famous caves and caverns include Mammoth Cave in Kentucky, Adelsberg Cave in Austria, and Good Luck Cave in Borneo.

Sinkholes

Sinkholes are funnel-shaped cavities in the ground that are open to the sky. They are formed in much the same way as caves. Groundwater dissolves limestone and, eventually, the surface collapses in on itself. Some sinkholes are caves whose roofs have collapsed. Some sinkholes are formed by drought conditions or excessive groundwater pumping.

Figure 29.7
Karst topography covered by vegetation makes up the rolling hills in south central Kentucky.

Karst Regions

When sinkholes, caves, and caverns define the land surface, the terrain is called *karst topography,* named after the Karst region of Yugoslavia, where weathering and erosion of limestone characterizes the landscape. The pattern of streams in this type of landscape is very irregular; streams and rivers disappear into the ground and reappear as springs. Some karst areas appear as soft, rolling hills with large depressions that dot the landscape; the depressions are old sinkholes now covered with vegetation (Figure 29.7). In general, karst areas have sharp, rugged surfaces and thin to nonexistent soils as a result of high runoff and dissolution of surface material.

Karst regions can be found throughout the world: in the Mediterranean basin; in sections of the Alps and the Pyrenees; and in southern China. The beauty of southern China's karst landscape is depicted in Figure 29.8. Karst regions occur in the United States in Kentucky, Missouri, Florida, and Tennessee.

Figure 29.8
The karst landscape of China has been an inspiration to classical Chinese brush artists for centuries.

29.3 The Work of Surface Water

The Grand Canyon is testimony to the mighty erosive power of the Colorado River. For millions of years, the river has been carving out the canyon walls, cutting deeper and deeper into the rock as it makes its way to the ocean. Yet

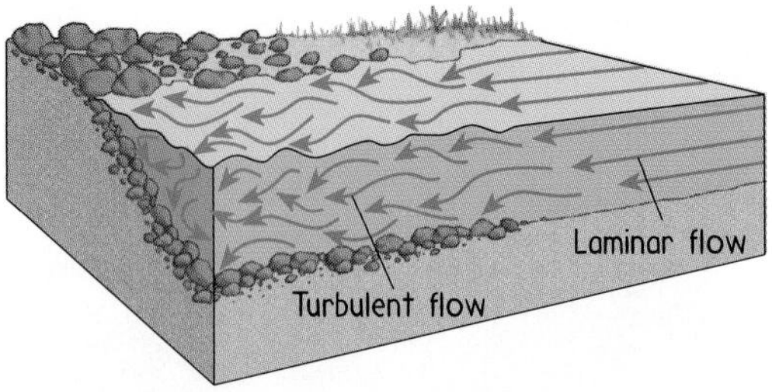

Figure 29.9
Laminar flow is slow and steady, with no mixing of sediment in the channel. Turbulent flow is fast and jumbled, stirring up everything in the flow.

surface water plays another important yet contrasting role as it shapes the landscape—it also deposits sediments. In this way, surface water is both a destroyer and creator of sediments and sedimentary rocks.

Landscape evolution—progressive changes to the earth's surface—is driven by the characteristics of surface water flow. The pattern of flow has a large effect on how the water alters the landscape. The flow pattern of moving water is of two types—turbulent and laminar (Figure 29.9). When water moves erratically downstream, stirring most everything with which it comes in contact, the flow is **turbulent.** When water flows steadily downstream with no mixing of sediment, the flow is **laminar.** In general, slow, shallow flows tend to be laminar and faster moving flows tend to be turbulent. Whether a flow is laminar or turbulent depends on the nature and geometry of the stream channel and the speed of the flow.

Erosion and Transport of Sediment

Figure 29.10
When powered by turbulent circular currents of water, rock particles rotate like drill bits and carve out deep potholes.

We learned, in Chapter 26, that weathering and erosion create and move sediment. Erosion by water is the most common way clastic sediments are carried away from the places in which they formed. Surface water erodes sediment and rocks, transporting them downstream and eventually depositing them in another place. In this way, surface water reshapes our landscape.

Flowing water erodes stream channels in several different ways. First of all, stream water contains many dissolved substances that chemically weather and erode the rocks they encounter. Another powerful mechanism for erosion is hydraulic action—the sheer force of running water. Swiftly flowing streams and streams at flood stage have strong erosive power as they break up and loosen great quantities of sediment and rock. The most powerful type of erosion, however, is abrasion. Abrasion occurs when sediments and particles actually scour a channel, much like sandpaper scraping on wood. When powered by turbulently spiraling water, rock particles rotate like drill bits and carve out deep potholes (Figure 29.10). The faster the current, the greater the turbulence, and the greater the erosion.

Erosion is only the beginning of the story of how surface water alters the earth's surface. Streams carry more than just water—they transport great amounts of sediment from one location to another. In general, laminar flows can lift and carry only the very smallest and lightest particles. A turbulent flow, however, depending on its speed, can move and carry a range of particle sizes—from the smallest particles of clay to large pebbles and cobbles. A turbulent current gathers and moves particles downstream mainly by lifting them into the flow or by rolling and sliding them along the channel bottom. The smaller, finer particles are easily lifted into the flow, and they remain suspended to make the water murky.

As we would expect, the faster the current, the larger the particles that can be carried. Also, the larger the volume of water, the greater the volume of sediment that can be carried. So, streams that have a higher discharge can carry larger volumes of sediment, and streams in which the water is moving fast can carry larger sizes of sediment. The continuous abrasion of sediment in the stream channel breaks up the sediments and thus contributes to the overall decrease in particle size that we see as we move downstream. At the river's mouth, only finer particles of sand, silt, and clay remain. As we shall soon see, these tiny particles are deposited to form a delta when the stream loses speed as it enters the sea.

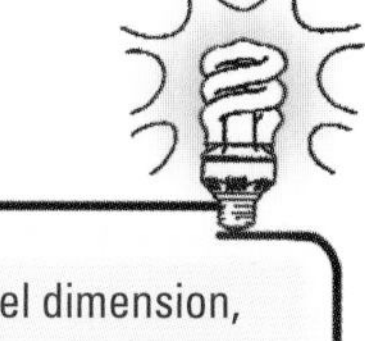

Channel dimension, gradient, discharge, sediment load, and velocity all work together as they influence stream flow. As such, a river is a system of interdependence in which any change in one variable influences change in the entire system.

Insights

☑ CHECKPOINT

Which is more effective in transporting sediment, laminar flow or turbulent flow? Defend your answer.

Check Your Answer

Turbulent flow, because the water's motion is irregular and sediments have a greater tendency to remain in suspension. Turbulent flow carries these sediments because of the energy of its churning water. In laminar flow, water moves steadily in a straight-line path with no mixing of sediment in the channel.

Erosional and Depositional Environments

Eventually, particles that are being transported by surface water drop out of suspension—they are deposited. This happens when the water loses energy and slows. As a river gradually loses energy, larger particles are deposited first and then smaller ones, causing most surface-water deposits to be well-sorted.

The most dominant feature of deposited sediments is the way the particles of sediment are laid down, layer upon horizontal layer. These layers are referred to as *beds*. Varying in both thickness and in area, each bed represents one episode of deposition. For example, flooding in a particular year might produce a layer of sediment next to a river. A flood any time after that produces an overlying layer.

The deposition and erosion of clastic sediments occur in many different environments, including oceans and shorelines, rivers and streams, deserts, and deltas. Each environment in which erosion, transportation, and deposition occur has its own specific characteristics.

Figure 29.11
At a stream's headwaters, high gradients contribute to fast-moving rapids. When there is an abrupt increase in gradient, we see a beautiful cascading waterfall.

Stream Valleys and Floodplains

As rainfall hits the ground, it loosens soil and washes it away. As more and more rain falls and the ground continues to lose soil, gullies form. Once water and soil particles funnel into such a gully, a stream channel is created. This erosive action may be extremely rapid, as in the erosion of unconsolidated sediments, or very slow, as in the erosion of solid rock. Water's erosive power enables a stream to widen and to deepen its channel, to transport sediment away, and, in time, to create a valley. In high mountain areas, the erosive action of a stream cuts down into the underlying rock to form a narrow, V-shaped valley. Because the valley is narrow, the stream channel dominates the whole valley bottom. Fast-moving rapids and beautiful waterfalls are characteristic of V-shaped mountain stream valleys (Figure 29.11).

When a fast-flowing mountain stream leaves its narrow valley, it abruptly emerges onto a broad, relatively flat plain. The speed of the flow drops suddenly, and the stream dumps its load of sediment. Streams of this type often flow no further. The sediment deposits are generally fan-shaped, and they grow outward as additional sediment is deposited (Figure 29.12). The steep, upper slope of such a deposit is dominated by boulders, cobbles, and gravels, while the base area and the adjacent plain are composed of sand, silt, and mud.

Figure 29.12
A fan-shaped clastic sedimentary deposit found in Death Valley, California.

For streams that continue on, stream speed plays an important role in both erosion and deposition. In the previous chapter, we learned about the variations in speed that occur as we follow the water downstream. But water speed also varies at a given location within a channel. Flow speed is slower along the stream bed, where water is in contact with the channel, creating friction; and flow speed is greater near the water surface. In a large stream that is flowing in a straight channel, the maximum flow speed can be found midchannel (Figure 29.13b). In a stream running through a bending, looping channel, the maximum flow speed is found toward the outside of each bend (Figures 29.13a and c).

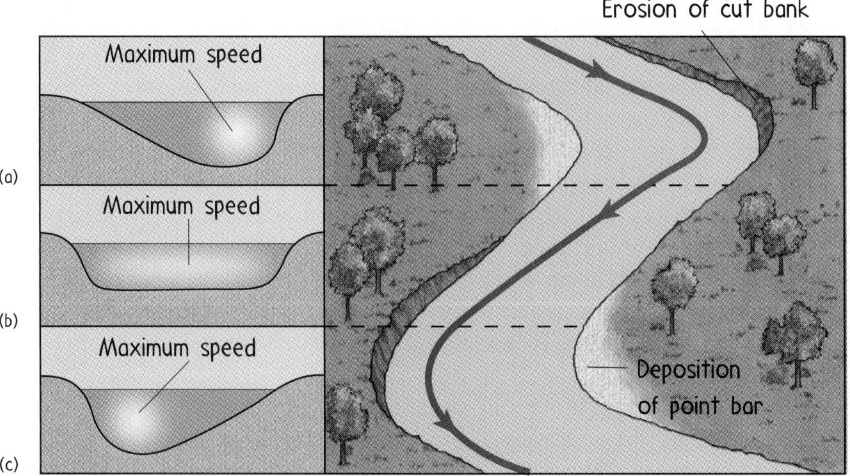

Figure 29.13
In a stream that bends (a and c), maximum flow speed is toward the outside of each bend and slightly below the surface. In a straight-channel stream (b), maximum speed is midchannel and near the water's surface. Erosion of the stream channel occurs where stream speed is greatest (cut bank); deposition occurs where stream flow slows (point bar).

As a stream flows downhill and its gradient becomes gentler and its speed slows, the focus of its energy changes from eroding downward (deepening the channel) to eroding laterally in a side-to-side motion. As a result of this lateral action, the stream develops a more sinuous, *meandering* form (Figure 29.14). As the stream bends and curves, the flow speed in the channel shifts so that the maximum speed is always toward the outside of each bend (Figure 29.13). Rapidly moving water is very effective in eroding material from the outside of the bend, creating a steep bank called a **cut bank.** Material eroded from the cut bank is transported downstream, where it may eventually be deposited in areas where the stream speed decreases. Sandy **point bars** form on the insides of bends by this process.

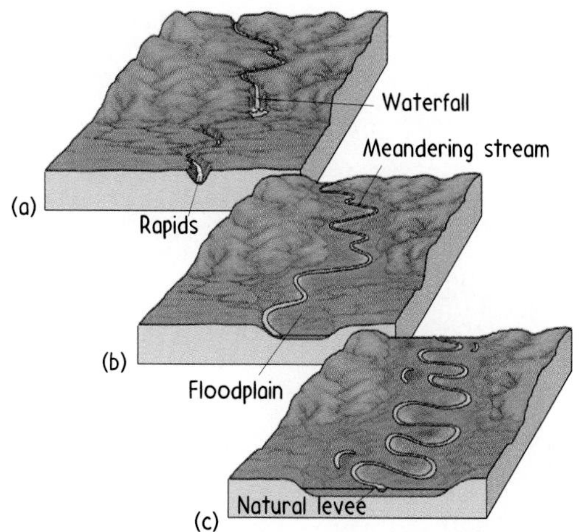

Figure 29.14
The evolution of a stream valley and the development of a floodplain. (a) At the headwaters, the V-shaped stream valley is characterized by steep gradients and fast-moving water that cuts down into the stream channel. Features in this area include cascading rapids and waterfalls. (b) Downstream, with reduced gradient, the stream focuses its erosive action in a side-to-side sinuous manner, thereby widening the stream valley. (c) Farther downstream, meandering increases and further widens the stream valley to form a large floodplain.

Continuing their downhill path, streams meander back and forth across a river valley, depositing sediments as they go (Figure 29.15). The meandering movement creates a wide belt of almost flat land—a **floodplain.** As the name implies, it is this section of the river valley that becomes flooded with water and sediments when a river overflows its banks. In a flood, as discharge and flow speed increase, so does the stream's ability to carry sediment. Thus, when a stream overflows its banks, sediment-rich water spills out onto the floodplain. The speed of the water quickly decreases as it spreads out over the wide, flat floodplain, and a progression of large to small particles is deposited. As expected, larger, coarse-grained sediments are deposited along the edges of the channel and smaller, fine-grained sediments are deposited farther away from the stream channel on the floodplain. The larger particles deposited close to the stream channel form *natural levees* that help to confine future floodwaters (Figure 29.16). The widening of the valley, as shown in Figure 29.15, occurs because sediment deposited by the stream, especially during floods, progressively fills the valley.

You have probably heard the term "100-year-flood." Does this mean that a 100-year flood occurs once every 100 years? Not exactly. In fact, as you probably know, an uncommonly big flood can occur in any year. The term 100-year-flood is a statistical term, indicating there is a 1-in-100 chance that an uncommonly big flood will occur during any given year. Perhaps a better term for this would be the "1-in-100-chance flood."

Insights

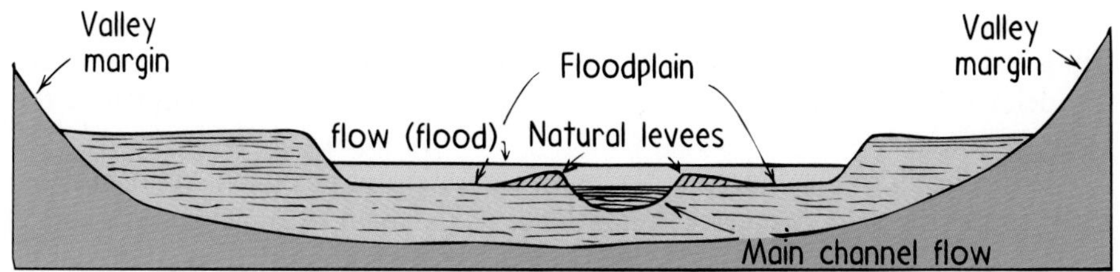

Figure 29.15
Cross section of a river valley. A floodplain is created when a river overflows its banks. Sands and gravels settle out first and act as natural levees to confine the river. Because the finer silt and clay particles are able to flow as a suspended load, they move beyond the levees and settle on the floodplain.

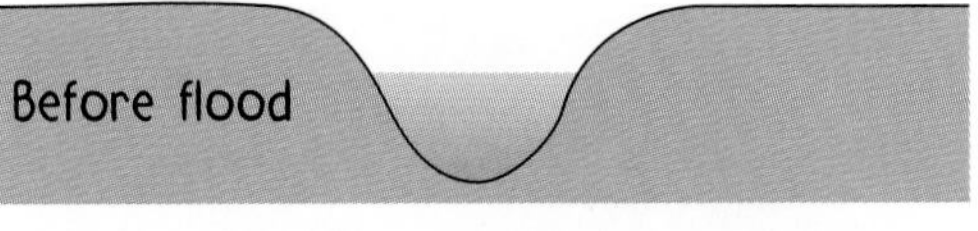

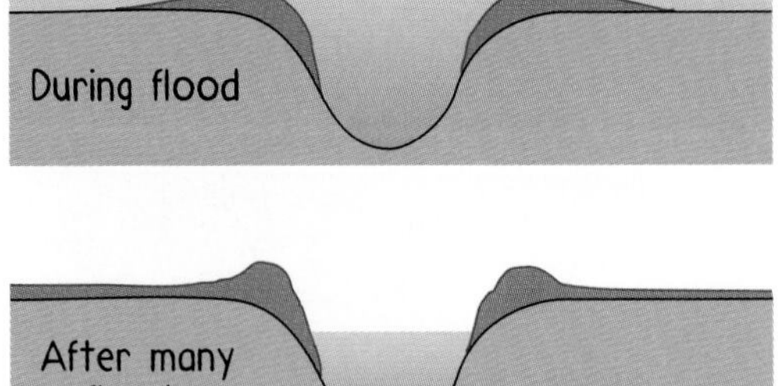

Figure 29.16
In a flood, increased discharge and flow speed help a stream to carry not only a large sediment load but also larger particles. Larger, coarse-grained sediment deposited close to the stream channel forms natural levees that will serve to confine the stream between flood stages. Successive floods increase the height of the levees and may even raise the overall elevation of the channel bed so that it is higher than the surrounding floodplain.

☑ CHECKPOINT

Floodplains are often prime agricultural areas. Why would people want to work and live in areas so prone to flooding?

Check Your Answer

People live and work in floodplain areas because such plains are next to rivers that provide easy access to water, food, and a means of transportation. Also, because of periodic flooding, floodplain soils are often extremely fertile and thus can serve as prime farmland. As for the factor of danger—don't most people associate danger with anyone but themselves?

Some of the world's greatest rivers have huge deltas at their mouths. Millions of years ago, the mouth of the Mississippi River was where Cairo, Illinois, is today. Since that time, the delta has extended 1600 kilometers south to the city of New Orleans. Less than 5,000 years ago, the site of New Orleans was underwater in the Gulf of Mexico!

The Delta—the End of the Line for a River

As a stream flows into a standing body of water, such as a sea, bay, or lake, the moving water gradually loses its forward momentum. With reduced energy, stream speed slows and the stream loses its ability to carry sediment. These changes cause the stream to dump the sediment load it had been transporting. In this way, the mouth of the stream and the area immediately offshore become filled with sediment. The dumped sediment forms a fan-shaped deposit called a **delta.** Sediment is deposited in order of decreasing weight, with heavy, coarse particles deposited first, at and near the shoreline. Light, fine particles are deposited farther offshore. With the continual addition of incoming sediment, the delta progressively builds itself outward as an extension of land into the body of water.

Deltas begin to form underwater, but the addition of incoming sediment eventually causes the delta to emerge as new land. As the main stream channel becomes choked with sediment, more energy is required for water to push through the accumulated sediment than to go around it. So new, smaller channels form off the main channel like branches on a tree. These *distributaries* allow water to flow unimpeded to the standing body of water. As the delta continues to extend outward, the distributaries also become clogged, as sediment continues to arrive from

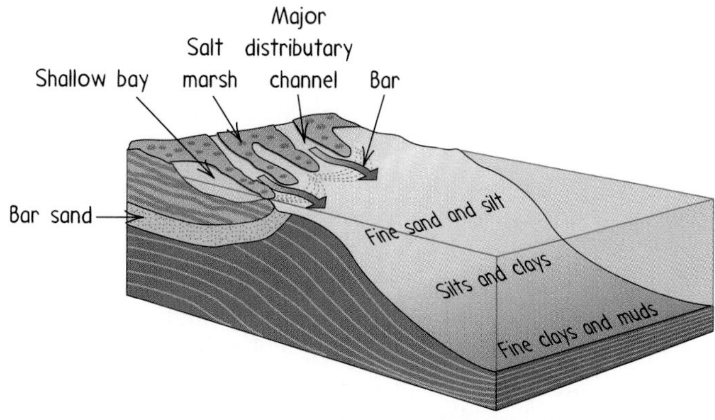

Figure 29.17
Deltas are areas of land generation. As streams flow to the sea, they carry sediments. These sediments are deposited in order of decreasing weight, with heavy, coarse particles settling at or near the shoreline and light, fine particles settling farther offshore. Layer upon layer, the depositional platform called a delta takes form.

Figure 29.18
Satellite image of the Mississippi Delta. Note how smaller streams that branch off from the main river are formed.

upstream. The first set of distributaries thus form distributaries of their own, taking on the appearance of branching fingers (Figure 29.17 and 29.18). When the fingers become clogged, the branching process repeats. As streams continue to flow to the standing water and as successive sediment layers are deposited one on top of the other, the delta continues to build and expand outward (Figure 29.18). Thus, delta environments are areas where new land is continuously created.

Figure 29.19
Desert erosion on a cliff face. A desert has many extremes—scorching daytime heat, chilling night air, and strong winds. Mechanical weathering physically breaks down the rocks to smaller and smaller pieces.

Deserts

We now shift our attention to arid desert environments, with their angular hills, shear canyon walls, and sand dunes. Because such environments lack moisture, mechanical weathering predominates (Figure 29.19). Interestingly, although deserts lack moisture, water is the main cause of erosion and transportation of sediments in deserts. Rare as water is in the

Figure 29.20
Mud cracks, a feature unique to sedimentary rocks, are evidence of alternating wet and dry conditions, often in desert environments.

desert, when a heavy rain falls, the rainwater does not have time to soak into the ground and instead causes powerful flash floods. These flash floods transport and then deposit great quantities of debris and sediment at the bases of mountain slopes and on the floors of wide valleys and basins.

Evidence of alternating wet and dry conditions can be seen in the distinctive sedimentary features called *mud cracks,* which are found in desert basins (Figure 29.20). Flash floods can create temporary lakes that deposit mud as the water disappears. When exposed to air, the mud dries out and shrinks, producing cracks. Mud cracks are also associated with shallow lakes and tidal flats.

The desert environment is also ideal for the formation of evaporites (such as halite) because evaporite deposits require a dry climate that is favorable to the evaporation of lake water or seawater. As the water dries out, evaporite minerals precipitate. Modern-day and ancient evaporites are found in desert basins, tidal flats, and restricted sea basins.

☑ **CHECKPOINT**

What is the ultimate destination of all water flow and, hence, the eventual site of deposition of most sediments?

Check Your Answer

Water flows eventually to the ocean, and sediments settle to the ocean floor.

29.4 The Work of Glaciers

Glacial Erosion and Erosional Landforms

The icy currents called *glaciers* are powerful agents of erosion. Glaciation has created the beautiful landscapes of Tibet, Nepal, and Bhutan in Asia; the Alps of Switzerland; the fjords of Norway; and Yosemite Valley and the Great Lakes in North America. In many ways, a glacier is like a plow, as it scrapes and plucks up rock and sediment. It is also like a sled, as it carries its heavy load to distant places. As it moves across the earth's surface, a glacier loosens and lifts up blocks of rock, incorporating them into the ice. The large rock fragments carried at the bottom of a glacier scrape the underlying bedrock and leave long, parallel scratches (like sled tracks) aligned in the direction of ice flow (Figure 29.21). These scratches are called *striations.*

Figure 29.21
Striations mark the presence of a former glacier.

The two main types of glaciers, *alpine* and *continental,* have different erosional effects and produce dissimilar landforms. Alpine glaciers develop in mountainous areas and are often confined to individual valleys, while continental glaciers cover much larger areas. Alpine glaciers occur in most high mountain chains in the world, such as the Cascades, the Rockies, the Andes, and the Himalayas. The erosional features of alpine glaciation are depicted in Figure 29.22.

Continental glaciers spread over the land surface, smoothing and rounding the underlying topography. Although striations are produced by both alpine and continental glaciers, they have played a larger role in the study of ancient continental glaciers. Since a continental glacier scours very large tracts of land,

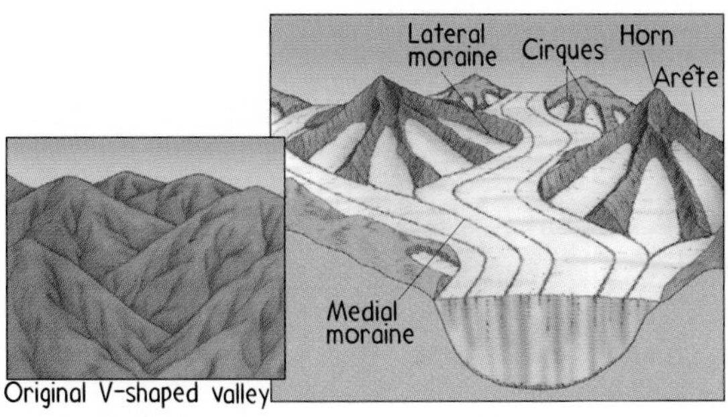

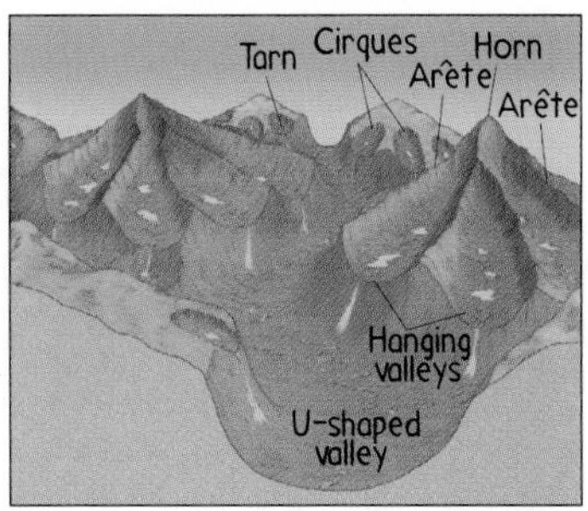

Figure 29.22
The many erosional features of alpine glaciation.

The Matterhorn—named for its characteristic "horn" feature.

Hanging valleys are a spectacular feature found in areas that have been shaped by alpine glacial erosion. Bridalveil Falls in Yosemite National Park spills out of a hanging valley into the larger valley that was once occupied by the main glacier.

it tends to leave behind few obvious valleys (making it difficult to determine the glacier's direction of flow). By mapping striations on land once covered by continental glaciers, geologists can decipher the flow direction of the ice. Flow direction is also indicated by small, asymmetrical hills (Figure 29.23) that are known by the French term *roches moutonnées* (singular, *roche moutonnée*). On the "upsteam" side of the ice flow, the hill's slope is smooth and striated from the abrasion of ice on bedrock. On the "downstream" side, the slope is rough and steep because the moving ice plucked rock fragments away from cracks in the bedrock.

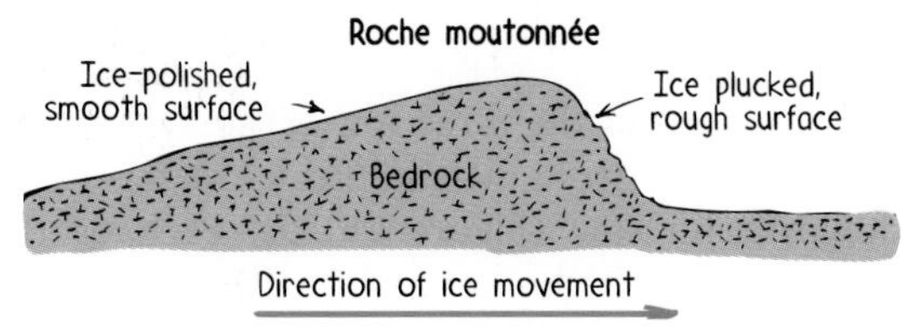

Figure 29.23
Small, asymmetrical hills called *roches moutonnées* show the direction of continental glacial movement. On the side of the hill facing the approaching glacier, the slope is smooth and gentle. On the side facing away from the approaching glacier, the slope is rough and steep, with a plucked appearance.

Glacial Sedimentation and Depositional Landforms

As a glacier advances across the land, it acquires and transports great quantities of debris. When the glacier retreats, this debris is left behind as it is melted out of the ice. Because a glacier abrades and picks up everything in its path, glacial deposits are characteristically composed of unsorted rock fragments in a variety of shapes and sizes. Glacial deposits are collectively called **drift**, a term that dates back to the nineteenth century, when it was conjectured that all such debris had been "drifted in" by the great Biblical Flood.

Geologist Bob Abrams observes the grandeur of the Juneau Ice Field, in Alaska.

Some glacial environments contain elements of several other depositional environments. This is due to the many processes at work, driven by water, wind, and ice. For example, glacial meltwater forms streams that may terminate as deltas in lakes, bays, or seas. Glacial deposits have some unique features, however. When glacial ice melts, it drops a poorly sorted, heterogeneous load of boulders, pebbles, sand, and clay. A wide range of particle sizes is the hallmark that differentiates glacial sediment from the much-better-sorted material deposited solely by streams and winds.

Drift is deposited in two main ways. When glacial sediment is released into meltwater, it is carried and deposited like any other waterborne sediment; thus, it is well-sorted. Material deposited directly by melting ice forms an unsorted mixture of clayey and bouldery rock debris called *till.* Many of the old stone walls and fences of New England are found in areas where the surface material is glacial till. Settlers who tried to farm this land had to remove all the larger boulders before they could plow, and they piled them along the edges of their fields. Oftentimes, large boulders that drastically differ from the local bedrock are found in glacial deposits. The large boulders provide proof of a glacier's ability to transport heavy loads for long distances. If a bedrock outcrop that matches the rock type of the out-of-place boulder can be found, then the distance and direction of glacial transport can be estimated.

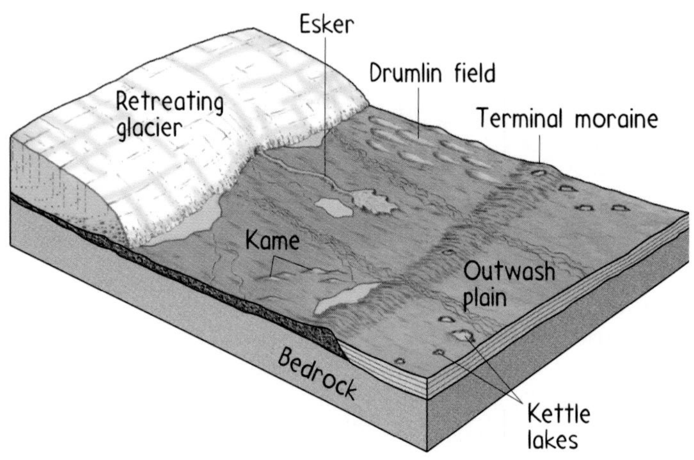

Figure 29.24
Glacial depositional landforms. Of special importance is the terminal moraine, which marks the farthest point of a glacier's advance.

The most common landform created by glaciers is the *moraine*, a ridge-shaped landform that marks the boundaries of ice flow. Of all the different types of moraines, probably the most important is the *terminal moraine,* as it marks the farthest point of a glacier's advance (Figure 29.24).

Another distinctive landform consisting of glacial sediments is the *drumlin,* an elongated hill shaped like the back of a whale. Formed by continental glaciation and lined up in the direction of ice flow, drumlins have a steep, blunt end in the direction from which the ice came and a tapered gentle slope on the downstream side (Figure 29.25). Perhaps the most famous drumlin in the United States is Bunker Hill in Massachusetts.

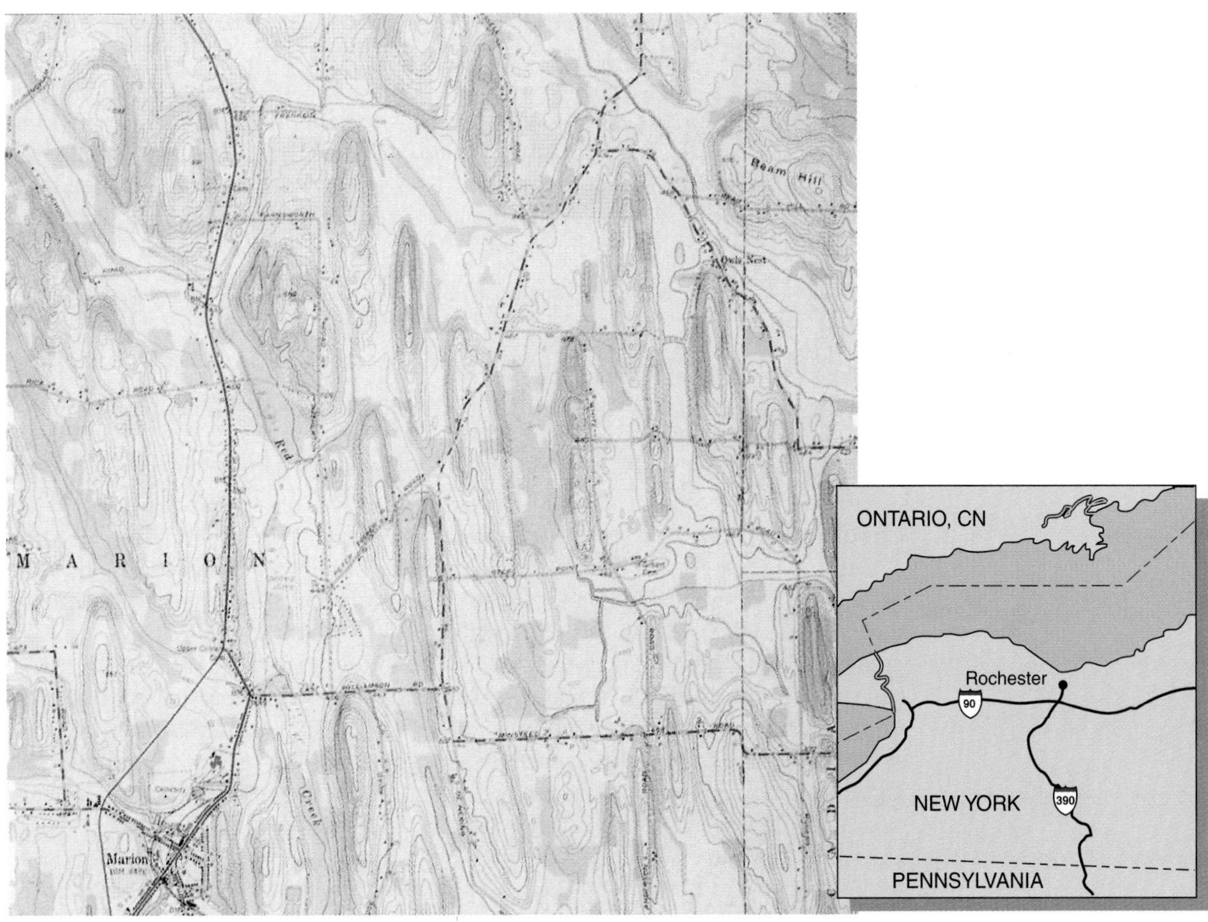

Figure 29.25
Topographic map showing numerous oval-shaped drumlins in upstate New York. Drumlins are steep and blunt on the side that faced the approaching glacier but tapered and gently sloping on the down-flow side. Looking at the map, can you tell the direction of continental ice flow?

Many of the world's lakes, small and large, are the products of glacial action. Glaciers deepened valleys and deposited sediments that acted as dams, blocking stream drainage within some valleys and creating lakes. The Finger Lakes in upstate New York, the "10,000 Lakes" of Minnesota, and the Great Lakes of North America are all products of glacial action.

☑ CHECKPOINT

What land surface forms can be used to determine the direction of ice flow?

Check Your Answer

The direction of ice flow can be known by striations (long, parallel scratches aligned in the direction of ice flow), *roches moutonnées* (small, asymmetrical hills), and *drumlins* (elongated hills shaped like the backs of whales).

29.5 The Work of Oceans

The power of oceans is obvious to anyone who visits the coast. Under normal conditions, some coastlines are quite placid, while others continually endure the ravages of large waves and rough surf. During large storms, all coastlines are at the mercy of the mighty ocean. Quieter realms exist just offshore where the formation of carbonates is dominant.

Offshore

Warm climates favor carbonate deposition because carbonates dissolve more easily in cold water than in warm water. Carbonate depositional environments include coral reefs and carbonate platforms.

Coral reefs are made up of actively growing, individual coral organisms, each of which is only a few millimeters across. The organisms secrete calcium carbonate as they grow. When we see a piece of coral or a coral reef, it is the calcium carbonate that we are seeing, not the organism. Most corals, but not all of them, form colonies, and it is the colony-forming corals that are the major reef-builders. Reefs grow outward with time, but they can also grow upward as new corals cement themselves to the skeletons of dead coral below. Reefs can only survive in shallow water because a major food source for coral is photosynthetic algae, which need bright light to live. The coral and algae live in a symbiotic relationship. The coral provides protection for the algae, and the algae provide oxygen and nutrients for the coral. Corals also require warm, clear, and relatively sediment-free water to flourish.

Coral reefs are partially destroyed by constant, pummeling wave action as the reefs grow and approach the water surface. Carbonate particles adjacent to the reef range in size from blocks several meters across to fine mud. Because ancient coral reefs (which are composed of alternating layers of porous material and impermeable muds) have the potential to act as traps for oil and gas, they are economically important.

Carbonate platforms are much larger than coral reefs, but their existence is also due to organisms. Carbonate platforms are the graveyards of calcium-secreting organisms and are formed in shallow waters either close to or attached to continents. They account for the largest portion of carbonate sediment produced in the ocean.

Shorelines

Shoreline environments are dominated by beaches and barrier islands. In the previous chapter, we learned that winds blowing across the ocean surface generate waves. As the waves approach shallow water near land, they become higher and steeper until they finally collapse, or break. This area is the *surf zone,* where wave activity moves sediment back and forth, both shoreward and seaward. Because the amount of surf at a shoreline varies with time and because the rocks at any shoreline have different degrees of resistance to erosion, surf can form many different erosional features. Soft rocks and highly fractured rocks erode fastest, whereas hard rocks and unfractured ones erode more slowly.

Along shorelines consisting of hard rock, the pounding surf cuts into and notches the base of the land. As erosion proceeds, the notches deepen and the rocks above begin to jut out over the empty space at the base. As the overhanging rocks fall into the surf, the cliff progressively retreats. In time, waves cut into the cliff to form a relatively flat surface known as a *wave cut platform*.

Along some rocky coastlines, *sea caves* form along with cliffs. *Sea arches* can form if two caves, usually on opposite sides of a headland, become connected. When an arch collapses, an isolated remnant called a *sea stack* is left behind. In time, wave action also erodes away the sea stack (Figure 29.26).

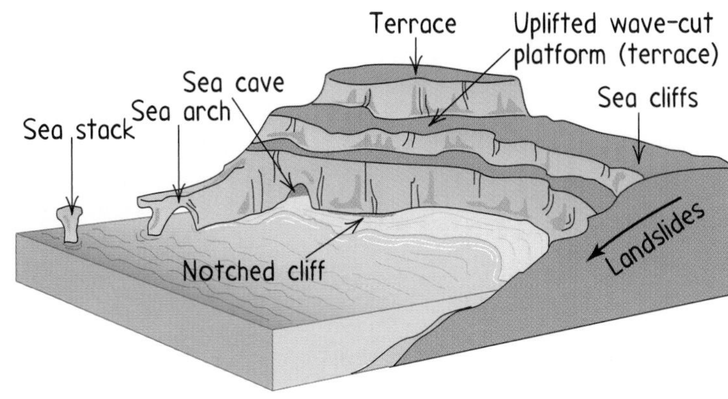

Figure 29.26
Characteristic coastal erosional landforms.

Rock particles eroded from the coast must sooner or later be deposited. Much of the material is deposited in the most common shoreline depositional environment—the beach. Sandy beaches are the result of the turbulent motion of the surf zone. Sand-sized fragments from coral reefs and carbonate platforms make up the white-sand beaches in many island areas, such as Hawaii (Figure 29.27). Look carefully at the sand in such tropical beaches, and you'll see it consists predominantly of shell fragments. In contrast, the sand on the beaches of the continents is mostly composed of silicate minerals. Whereas much of the beach sand in Hawaii is organic in origin, beach sand along the American western coast is largely inorganic.

(a)

(b)

Figure 29.27
(a) The white-sand beaches of California are composed of silicate minerals and are classified as inorganic. (b) The white-sand beaches of Hawaii are composed of carbonate minerals—the sediment remains of tiny shells—and are classified as organic.

Beaches tend to be elongated by longshore currents that form when waves approach the shoreline at an oblique angle. For example, waves approaching a north-south coastline from the northwest would cause a longshore current southward down the beach. These currents move sand down the length of the coast. Where the currents deposit sand, we have the formation of *spits*. Spits begin as submerged ridges of sand. As sand accumulates, the spit rises above the surface and projects from the coast into open water as a continuation of the beach, frequently as a fingerlike piece of land (Figure 29.28).

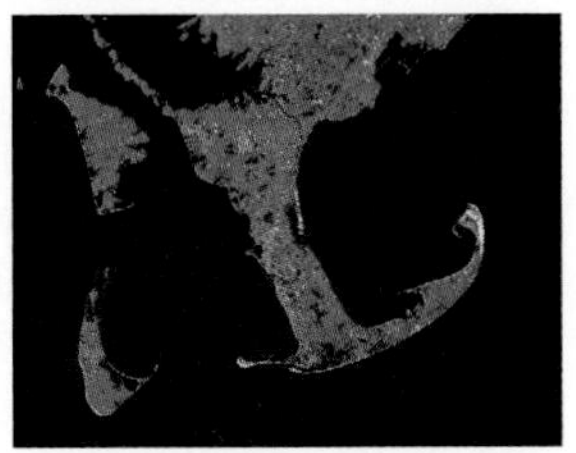

Figure 29.28
A spit forms on the tip of Cape Cod, Massachusetts.

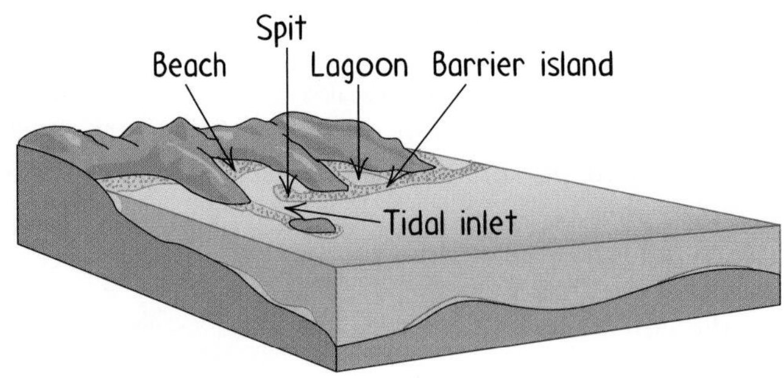

Figure 29.29
Characteristic coastal depositional landforms.

Geologic features are best viewed from an airplane. The next time you are flying in an airplane, request a window seat and enjoy the geology below.

When sand ridges form parallel to the coast, they eventually grow into *barrier islands*. Barrier islands form where ridges of sand break the surface of the water for a long enough period of time that vegetation begins to take hold. During large storms, surf washes over the lowlands, making inlets into the lagoon area between the barrier island and the shore. The lagoon area is a quieter environment. It has finer-grained silts and muds that feature cross-bedding and small ripple marks caused by the oscillating motion of the lagoon water. On shore, smooth stones, rounded pebbles, and/or sand make up the beaches.

Vegetation allows the new barrier island to become resistant to surf and storm erosion. With continued safeguards, the barrier island grows even more. The tidal flats and shallow lagoons that separate barrier islands from the coast form a barricade between the coast and the open ocean (Figure 29.29). The Gulf Coast of the United States and much of the eastern shore south of New York City have abundant barrier islands. Since the lagoons separating these narrow islands from the shore are zones of relatively quiet water, small boats often use the lagoons as a "freeway" between Florida and New York, thus avoiding the potentially rough waters of the open Atlantic.

Summary of Terms

Sand dune Landform created when air flow is blocked by an obstacle, slowing the air speed and therefore promoting the deposition of airborne sand.

Subsidence A lowering of the land surface that results when groundwater is removed from thick aquifers composed of alternating layers of sand and clay.

Cavern A large cave.

Sinkhole A funnel-shaped depression in a karst area that is open to the sky, caused by the dissolution of subsurface limestone by groundwater.

Turbulent flow Water flowing erratically in a jumbled manner, stirring up everything it touches.

Laminar flow Water flowing smoothly and steadily with no mixing of sediment.

Floodplain A wide plain of almost flat land on either side of a stream channel. Submerged during flood stage, the plain is built up by sediments deposited during floods.

Cut bank A steep bank on the outside bend of a river's channel. An area of erosion.

Point bar A sandy, gentle bank on the inside bend of a river's channel. An area of deposition.

Delta An accumulation of sediments, commonly forming a triangular or fan-shaped plain, deposited where a stream flows into a body of water.

Drift A general term for glacial deposits.

Review Questions

29.1 The Work of Air

1. How are sand dunes formed?
2. How do sand dunes migrate?
3. How are ripple marks formed?

29.2 The Work of Groundwater

4. Describe at least one consequence of overpumping groundwater.

5. How does rainwater become acidic? How does this affect limestone?
6. What is karst topography? Where on Earth is it found?
7. How do stalactites and stalagmites form?
8. Name three erosional features caused by groundwater in carbonate rocks.
9. The ground surface above which types of sediments is most prone to subsidence?
10. What is the difference between a cave and a cavern?

29.3 The Work of Surface Water

11. Which is the greater transporter of sediment, a laminar flow or a turbulent flow? Why?
12. Name three ways in which the movement of water erodes a stream channel. Which one creates potholes?
13. What factors are responsible for the formation of a stream valley?
14. Under what conditions do curvy, meandering rivers form along a floodplain?
15. What types of streams and stream valleys do we generally find in high mountainous regions?
16. What is a delta?
17. Deserts are generally dry areas. Why is water still a major factor of erosion in the desert environment?
18. Streams carry more than just water—they carry great quantities of sediment from one place to another. What is the size range of the particles that can be carried by a fast-moving stream?
19. What is the size range of the particles that can be carried in a slowly flowing stream?
20. What is the size of the particles that are the first to be deposited as a river loses energy?
21. In a meandering stream channel, where do we most often find deposition of sediment?
22. In a meandering stream channel, where do we most often find erosive action?

29.4 The Work of Glaciers

23. What are striations? What is their significance?
24. What erosional features are likely found in an area of alpine glaciation? (See Figure 29.22.)
25. What land features are formed from glacial deposits?
26. What is meant by glacial drift? How is glacial drift deposited?
27. What is the significance of the large, out-of-place boulders that are sometimes found in glacial deposits?
28. What is the most common landform created by glaciers?
29. What is a drumlin?
30. Name two glacial drift deposits.

29.5 The Work of Oceans

31. Describe how a sea stack forms.
32. What types of land features are associated with transport of sand from a longshore current?
33. Coral reefs thrive in which kind of climate? Explain.
34. In Hawaii, what type of beach sand predominates?
35. Why is a barrier island's lagoon usually a quiet environment?

Exercises

1. In the formation of a river delta, why are larger particles deposited first, followed by smaller particles farther out? Defend your answer.
2. What causes the formation of branches off the main channel of a river delta?
3. What is a sinkhole? What factors contribute to its formation?
4. The Mississippi Delta has moved south from near Cairo, Illinois, to its present location in Louisiana. Other than the length of time, why has the delta moved so far?
5. Which of the three agents of transportation—wind, water, or ice—transports the largest boulders? Why?
6. Which of the three agents of transportation is limited to transporting small particles? Why?
7. Carbonate rocks are mainly formed in marine environments. Why do we find abundant carbonate deposits on continental land?
8. In what way does a glaciated mountain valley differ from a nonglaciated mountain valley? (See Figure 29.22.)
9. Are underground rivers ever found in nature? Defend your answer.
10. Describe the formation of caves and caverns in limestone.
11. Do you think a stream in which the flow is laminar can become turbulent without increasing the volume of water in the stream? Defend your answer.
12. Name two environments in which cross-bedding occurs. What information does cross-bedding provide?
13. Why is the sand of some beaches composed of small pieces of seashells?
14. Describe the formation of stalactites.
15. Why is surface water both a creator and a destroyer of sediments and sedimentary rocks?
16. Why do point bars form on the inside bends of meandering streams?
17. Name three environments that favor the formation of evaporite deposits. What, if anything, do they have in common?

18. What can we learn from glacial striations? In the context of modern continental glaciation, is there any other way to get the same information about the direction of glacial movement? Would that method help us to learn about ancient continental glaciation?
19. How is a roche moutonée different from a drumlin?
20. What well-known landscapes have been carved by glaciers?
21. How do deposits from glacial ice differ from rocks deposited by rivers?
22. Removal of groundwater can cause subsidence. If removal of groundwater is stopped, will the land likely rise again to its original level? Defend your answer.
23. What is the most dominant feature of deposited sediments?
24. Why do coral-building organisms require clear, shallow water?
25. Suppose a jetty is built perpendicular to the shore. How will this structure affect the longshore current and its transport of sand? Defend your answer.
26. Can a stream erode land that lies below sea level? Explain.
27. Why are headland areas prime areas for erosion?
28. What is the significance of understanding present-day depositional environments?
29. What is landscape evolution? What are the driving forces of landscape evolution?
30. Must a stream's speed increase in order for it to carry more sediment? Defend your answer.

Chapter 29 Online Resources

Quiz
Exercises
Flashcards
Links

CHAPTER 30

A Brief History of the Earth

Earth is some 4.5 billion years old. This vast span of time, called *geologic time,* is difficult to comprehend. But we can try to imagine it with the following thought exercise. Let's imagine that we can compress 4.5 billion years, the age of the earth, into a single year. Then, the Planet Earth would have begun forming from matter surrounding the sun on January 1. The oldest known earth rocks would appear at the end of February. Simple bacterial life would appear in the sea at the end of March, and more complex plants and animals would not emerge until late October or early November. Dinosaurs would rule the earth in mid-December and would disappear by December 26. *Homo sapiens* (humans) would appear at 11:50 P.M. on the evening of December 31. All of recorded human history would take place in the last minute of New Year's Eve!

The earth's history is recorded in the rocks of its crust. Scientists use an assumption called *uniformitarianism* to relate what we know about present-day processes to past events. The present is the key to the past. Simply put, uniformitarianism states that the natural laws (like the laws of physics) we know about today have been constant over the geologic past. The rock record is like a long and detailed diary, containing the history of earth-shaping events. The book is incomplete, however. Many pages, especially in the early part, are missing, and many others are tattered, torn, and difficult to read. But there are enough pages preserved to provide an account of the remarkable events of the earth's 4.5 billion years of history.

30.1 Relative Dating

Sedimentary rock layers and lava flows provide good evidence of relative rock ages. This is because the rock layers were deposited one atop the other. The lower layers were formed before the upper layers, and so they are older than the upper layers. Perhaps the world's most spectacular display of the rock record is the Grand Canyon of the Colorado River in Arizona. The many layers of rock exposed in the canyon walls and the thickness of these layers are testimony to great geologic activity over millions of years. The conditions under which the sedimentary layers were deposited varied widely, changing from season to season and from year to year. Some layers reveal climatic cycles that span centuries,

Figure 30.1
The lowermost layers of the Grand Canyon are older than the uppermost layers, which illustrates the principle of superposition.

other layers indicate times when the land surface became submerged beneath a shallow sea, while still other layers show periods of increased rainfall accompanied by gradual uplift of the entire area. Millions of years after the top layer was deposited, erosion from the Colorado River cut through all these accumulated layers of sedimentary rock like a knife cutting into a layer cake, forming the canyon we see today.

In the Grand Canyon and elsewhere, earth scientists use five common-sense principles to determine the relative ages of the rocks. The principles are:

1. **Original horizontality** Layers of sediment are deposited evenly, with each new layer being laid down nearly horizontally over older sediment. Layers that are inclined at any angle—from very slight to very steep—indicate they were moved into that position by crustal disturbances after deposition.
2. **Superposition** In an undeformed (flat) sequence of sedimentary rocks, each layer is older than the one above and younger than the one below. Like the layers of a huge wedding cake, the rock record was formed from the bottom layer to the top. Upper layers are younger than lower layers.
3. **Cross-cutting** An igneous intrusion or fault that cuts through preexisting rock is younger than the rock through which it cuts (Figure 30.2).

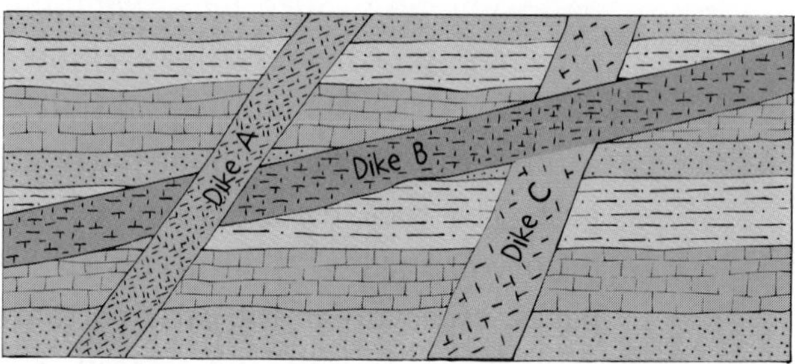

Figure 30.2
Dikes cutting into a rock body are younger than the rock into which they cut. In the diagram, dike A cuts into dike B, and dike B cuts into dike C. From the principle of cross-cutting relationships, A is the youngest dike, B the next youngest, and C the oldest of the three. The horizontal layers, which are cut by all three dikes, are all older than C.

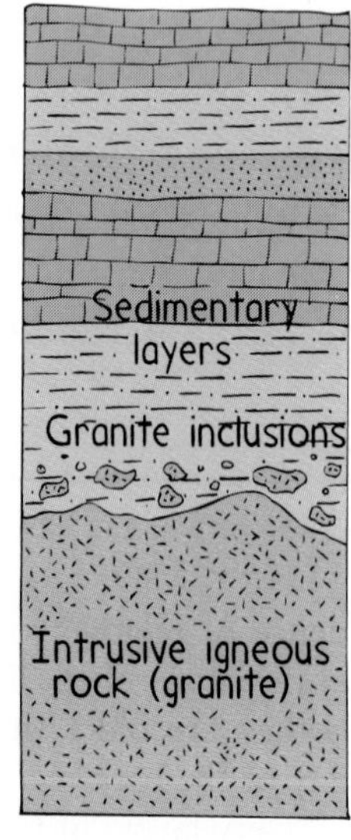

Figure 30.3
The rocks locked in the sedimentary layer existed before the sedimentary layer formed, a situation that illustrates the principle of inclusion.

4. **Inclusion** Inclusions are pieces of one rock type contained within another. Any inclusion is older than the rock containing it; just as small pieces of rock incorporated in a slab of concrete were formed before the concrete was formed (Figure 30.3).
5. **Faunal succession** The evolution of life is recorded in the rock record in the form of fossils. Fossil organisms follow one another in a definite, irreversible time sequence. Fossils provide a great tool for matching up rocks of similar age in different regions because it is possible to recognize any time period by the fossils it contains. Once scientists establish a time period, the fossils in the rocks can be used to identify other rocks of the same age in other regions of the earth.

It comes as a surprise to discover the fossil of an extinct sea animal encased in rock high above sea level. Such fossils are evidence that many of today's land surfaces were yesterday's sea bottoms. Finding fossils is a delight, both to first-time finders and to experienced fossil hunters.

Figure 30.4
Hunting for fossils can be a lot of fun. Finding one is delightful, as the author indicates.

Although most rock layers were deposited without interruption, nowhere is there a continuous sequence from the earth's formation to the present time. Weathering and erosion, crustal uplifts, and other geologic processes interrupt the normal sequence of deposition. So there are breaks or gaps in the rock record, as Figure 30.5 shows. We can find these gaps, called **unconformities,** by observing the relationships of layers and fossils.

The most easily recognized of all unconformities is an **angular unconformity.** In an angular unconformity, tilted or folded sedimentary rocks are overlain by younger, relatively horizontal rock layers. They are easy to recognize because rock layers below the unconformity are at an angle relative to the rock layers on top of the unconformity. An angular unconformity forms when older, previously horizontal rock layers are uplifted and tilted by the earth's movements (Figure 30.6). During and after the uplift, erosion wears down the tilted layers so that rocks at the surface are eroded to a more-or-less even plane, which creates a new, flat land surface. After the period of erosion is over, more sediment layers are deposited over the tilted ones, and these younger layers are horizontal. The angular unconformity is the "surface" that separates the tilted layers from the horizontal layers. It represents the long interval of time during which uplift and erosion took place. The part of the rock record representing this long interval is now missing because of erosion, and the unconformity is the evidence that remains.

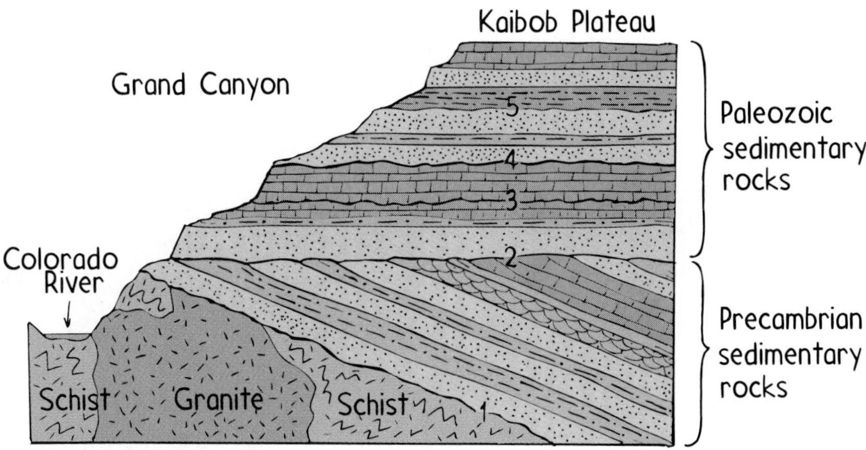

Figure 30.5
The age of the Grand Canyon can be deciphered by its sequence of rock layers. As in other places, the sequence is not continuous, and there are time gaps. (1) A nonconformity separating older metamorphic rocks from sedimentary layers. (2) An angular unconformity separating older tilted layers from horizontal layers. Time gaps are also represented between horizontal sedimentary layers. The unconformities (3)–(5) are difficult to identify, and they often require both a good eye and a knowledge of fossils.

When overlying sedimentary rocks are found on an eroded surface of metamorphic or intrusive igneous rocks, the unconformity is called a **nonconformity.**

Figure 30.6
The sequence of events that create an angular unconformity.

(a) Sediments are deposited layer upon layer beneath the sea.

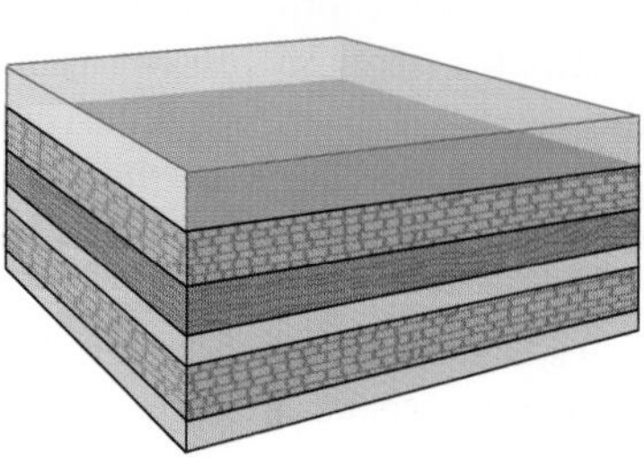

(a)

(b) During mountain building solidified sediment layers become folded and deformed. Erosion begins.

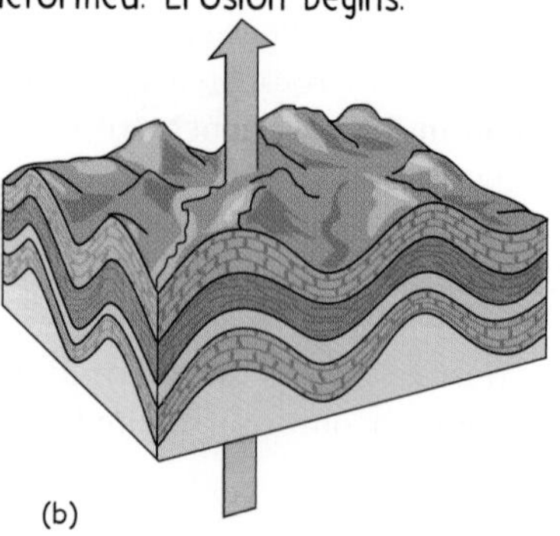

(b)

(c) As mountain building wanes, the exposed surface is eroded to a more or less even plain.

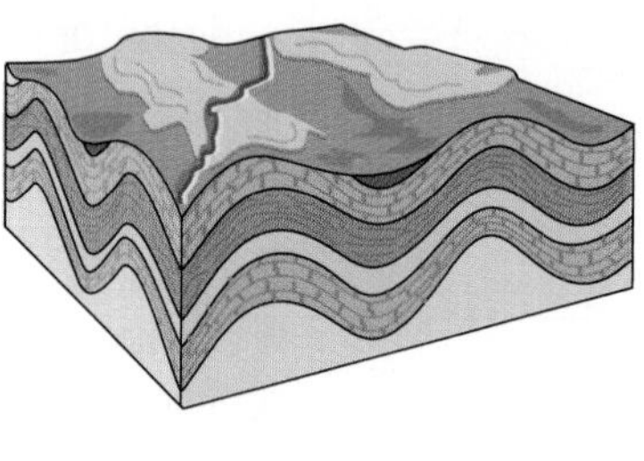

(c)

(d) As the land subsides below sea level, younger sediments are deposited on the former erosional surface.

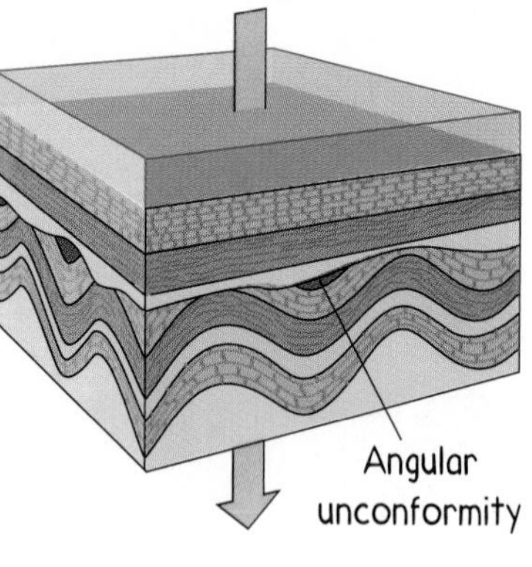

(d)

The older intrusive igneous or metamorphic rocks formed deep beneath the earth's surface but were present at the earth's surface when the overlying sedimentary rocks were deposited on top of them. Therefore, a nonconformity shows that a great deal of uplift and erosion occurred before the sedimentary layers were deposited, with a large stretch of time "missing" from the rock record. Such time gaps are often quite difficult to identify.

☑ CHECKPOINT

If a granitic intrusion—a dike, for example—cuts into or across sedimentary layers, which is older: the granite or the sedimentary layers?

Check Your Answer

The intrusion is new rock in the making. Therefore, the sedimentary layers are older than the intrusions that cut into them.

30.2 Radiometric Dating

Relative dating tells us which parts of the earth's crust are older or younger, but it doesn't tell us the actual age of a rock—the amount of time that has passed since the rock solidified. The actual age of a rock can be determined by **radiometric dating,** a process that measures the ratio of radioactive isotopes to their decay products.

Recall, from Chapter 14, that atoms of the same element that contain different numbers of neutrons are *isotopes;* and recall our discussion of isotopic dating in Chapter 16. Some of the common radioactive isotopes frequently used for dating and estimates of geologic time are shown in Table 30.1.

Table 30.1

Isotopes Most Commonly Used for Radiometric Dating

Radioactive Parent	Stable Daughter Product	Half-life Value
Uranium-238	Lead-206	4.5 billion years
Uranium-235	Lead-207	704 million years
Potassium-40	Argon-40	1.3 billion years
Carbon-14	Nitrogen-14	5730 years

Many rocks contain trace amounts of uranium. In any uranium-bearing rock, there are two naturally occurring radioactive isotopes that can be used for dating. Uranium-238 decays to its stable daughter isotope, lead-206, and uranium-235 decays to the stable isotope, lead-207. Neither uranium isotope decays to the commonest isotope of lead, lead-208. Therefore, any lead-206 and lead-207 found in a rock today were at one time uranium. If, for example, a sample contains equal numbers of uranium-235 and lead-207 atoms, the age of the sample is one uranium-235 half-life—704 million years. If, on the other hand, a sample of uranium ore contains only a relatively small amount of lead-207, it is relatively young.

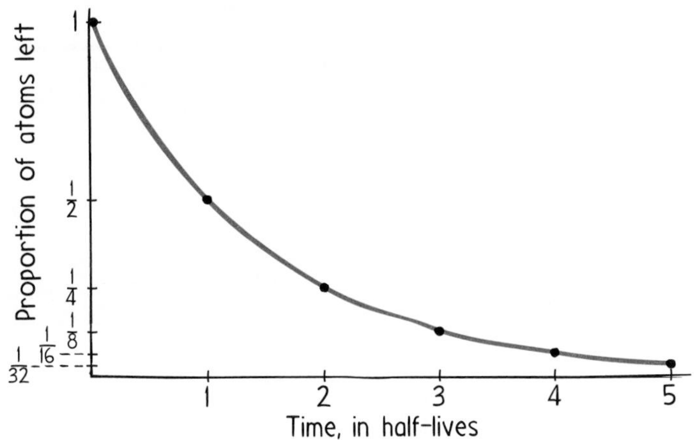

Figure 30.7
The amount of parent material versus the number of half-lives remaining as the radioactive parent decays.

Radiometric dating has shown that the oldest known mineral ever found is an astounding 4.4 billion years old! The oldest whole rock found so far on the earth is 3.8 billion years old.

Insights

Radiometric dating is based on the assumption that, once a mineral has crystallized, any daughter product found within it originates only from the decay of the unstable parent—that is, that there was no daughter product present initially. Another important assumption is that there is no "leakage" of parent or daughter products into or out of the mineral. If a mineral is, for instance, reheated by metamorphism, its "time clock" is reset. For example, if a potassium-bearing mineral is reheated, some or all of the gaseous daughter product argon-40 might diffuse out of the crystalline structure of the mineral. This would reset the time clock for that sample and complicate the estimation of its age. Fortunately, cross checking by different radiometric methods can increase accuracy. Radiometric dating in general is subject to some uncertainty due to the detailed analytical procedures used and the random nature of radioactive decay.

Radiometric dating of organic matter makes use of carbon-14. Because of its short half-life (5730 years), carbon-14 is useful only for dating geologically recent events, within the last 50,000 years or so. Less than one-millionth of 1 percent of the carbon in the atmosphere is carbon-14, but some of this tiny amount enters plants via photosynthesis. Because all animals eat either plants or plant-eating animals, all living things have a little carbon-14 in them. Carbon-14 decays to nitrogen-14, but, because living organisms continuously take in carbon, this decay is accompanied by a replenishment of carbon-14, so that the amount of carbon-14 in a living organism remains constant. When the organism dies, however, the replenishment stops. So the

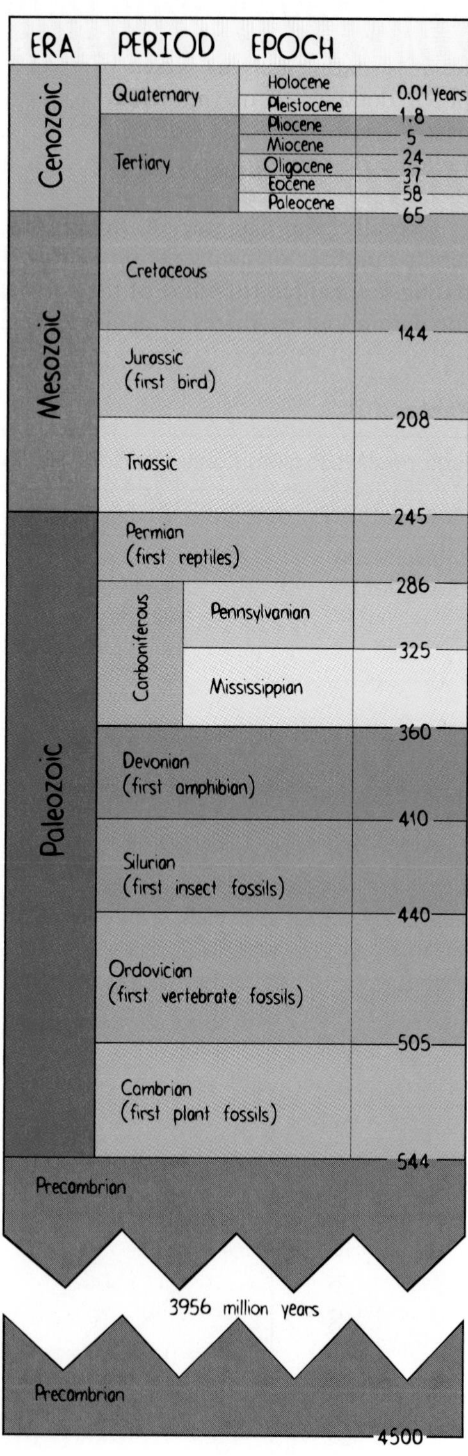

Figure 30.8
The geologic time scale.

amount of carbon-14 remaining in a fossil tells us the amount of time that has elapsed since the time of the organism's death.

The *geologic time scale* was developed through the use of relative dating, and specific dates have been applied to it with radiometric dating. By convention, the geologic time scale is divided into three eras, the **Paleozoic** era, the **Mesozoic** era, and the **Cenozoic** era. These eras are listed in chronological order: Paleozoic means "time of ancient life;" Mesozoic means "time of middle life," and Cenozoic means "time of recent life." Each of the three eras is further divided into periods, which are still further divided into epochs. Note that the vast majority of Earth's history actually occurred before the Paleozoic era. The vast span of time, the time period preceding the Paleozoic, is known as the **Precambrian eon.** The Precambrian encompasses the time prior to the evolution of life forms that left prominent fossils.

Radiometric dating can give us the age of minerals and/or organic matter, but it cannot directly give us the age of sedimentary rocks. Why is this so? Remember, sedimentary rocks are made from the remains of preexisting rocks. Therefore, we can only date the minerals in the rock, but not the sedimentary rock itself. The rock can be no older than the age of the datable minerals within it. So how do we date sedimentary rock layers? We use the principles of relative dating combined with the absolute dates from radiometric dating. The more techniques, the better the date.

Insights

☑ CHECKPOINT

1. Could carbon-14 be used for dating rocks from Precambrian time?
2. How can we determine the age of sedimentary rock layers?

Check Your Answers

1. No. Carbon-14 has a half-life of 5730 years and can be used only to date relatively younger rocks. Any carbon-14 in Precambrian carbonaceous material would have long since been reduced to undetectable amounts.
2. If we know the maximum age (meaning the rock can be no older than the age of the datable minerals within it) of an overlying and an underlying rock layer, we can bracket the age of the sedimentary layer in between by using the principle of superposition.

30.3 Precambrian Time

Precambrian time ranges from about 4.5 billion years ago, when the earth formed, to about 544 million years ago, when abundant macroscopic life appeared. The Precambrian—the time about which we know the least—comprises almost 90 percent of Earth's history! Most of the rocks that formed in this early part of the earth's history have been eroded away, metamorphosed, or recycled into the earth's interior. Relatively few fossils are preserved in Precambrian rocks because organisms of that period did not have any easily fossilized hard body parts, which evolved later in the history of life.

The beginning of the Precambrian was likely a time of considerable volcanic activity and frequent meteorite impact.* Let's imagine the earth as it was at that time: an oceanless planet covered with countless volcanoes belching forth gases and steam from its scorching interior. Huge holes and gashes left by falling meteorites scarred its surface. Intense convection in the mantle, and severe heat escaping from the interior, left the surface of the earth's early

*A meteorite is any solid rock object from interplanetary space that has fallen to the earth's surface without being vaporized during its passage through the atmosphere. We shall learn more about these objects in Chapter 33, when we study the formation of the solar system.

crust in turmoil. The earliest semblances of crust consisted of short-lived, ever-changing, small lithospheric plates. After about 4 billion years, the earth's heat slowly dissipated, large meteorite impacts decreased, and crustal blocks began to survive. All continents were completely devoid of life during this violent time.

Gases brought to the surface of the earth by volcanic processes eventually created both a primitive atmosphere and an ocean. The early atmosphere was rich in water vapor but very poor in free oxygen. The first simple organisms for which fossils have been found are dated at 3.5 billion years old. These fossils, known as stromatolites, are the remains of wavy layers of algae that lived in shallow seas.

During the middle of Precambrian time, such organisms as cyanobacteria evolved a simple version of photosynthesis. Photosynthetic organisms require CO_2 to use the sun's energy. They keep the carbon and expel the oxygen. With the release of free oxygen, a primitive ozone layer began to develop above the earth's surface. The ozone layer reduced the amount of harmful ultraviolet radiation reaching the earth. This protection, and the accumulation of free oxygen in the earth's atmosphere, permitted the emergence of new life.

The primitive cyanobacteria, and other bacteria that lived during this time, were simple cells without nuclei. Reproduction was by simple cell division. The first evidence of single-celled organisms with nuclei (green algae) occurs in rocks dated to approximately 1.5 billion years ago. The discovery of multicellular plants and animals, dated to approximately 700 million years ago, shows evidence of major evolutionary changes that began during the later half of Precambrian time. Some rocks found in southern Australia contain diverse fossils of soft-bodied animals, ranging from jellyfish to wormlike forms. This discovery provides us with the first evidence of an animal community that lived in shallow marine waters.

Figure 30.9
Primitive stromatolites found in Western Australia are dated as roughly 3.5 billion years old. They are very similar in structure to the present-day stromatolites pictured here. Although the first stromatolites evolved in an anaerobic (oxygen-poor) environment, in time they developed the ability to use sunlight to convert carbon dioxide to food, generating oxygen as a waste product. With the production of oxygen, many anaerobic life forms became poisoned by oxygen, while the adaptive stromatolites continued to flourish. Stromatolites thus changed the earth's history as the earth's atmosphere became oxygen-rich.

Precambrian Tectonics

Lithospheric plates began to form during Precambrian time. Evidence from folded and faulted rocks and radiometric ages indicates that the first significant continental crust movements occurred about 2.5 billion years ago. Continents then began to form as small landmasses came together. Scientists speculate that, about 1.5 billion years ago, Siberia merged into the western edge of North America, while Europe was converging with the eastern part of North America. Other continents were converging from the south to form the first documented supercontinent (long before Pangaea).

30.4 The Paleozoic Era

The Paleozoic era is better known than the Precambrian, but it was very short in comparison. The Paleozoic era began about 544 million years ago, and it lasted about 300 million years. During this time, sea levels rose and fell several times worldwide. This allowed shallow seas to cover the continents and marine life to flourish. Changing sea levels greatly influenced the progression and diversification of life forms—marine invertebrates to fishes, amphibians, and reptiles. An important event in the Paleozoic era was the evolution of shelled organisms. In fact, it is because of shelled organisms that we know so much more about the Paleozoic than the Precambrian. Shelled organisms have hard parts that are fairly likely to be preserved as fossils. The Paleozoic era is divided into six periods, each characterized by changes in life forms and changes in tectonics.

Figure 30.10
Trilobites were the dominant fossils of the Cambrian period.

The Cambrian Period

The Cambrian period marks the beginning of the Paleozoic era. Almost all major groups of marine organisms came into existence during this time, as shown by abundant fossil evidence. A most important event in the Cambrian was the evolution of organisms having the ability to secrete calcium carbonate and calcium phosphate for the formation of outer skeletons, or shells. This ability helped organisms to become less vulnerable to predators, and it provided protection against ultraviolet rays, allowing the organisms to move into shallower habitats. In addition, the support provided by a skeleton allowed organisms to grow larger.

The fossil record of the Cambrian period is dominated by the skeletons of shallow marine organisms. A variety of these organisms flourished, including the *trilobite,* the armored "cockroaches" of the Cambrian sea.

Figure 30.11
The hagfish is a descendent of the agnatha, primitive jawless fishes that first appeared in the Cambrian and flourished in the Ordovician periods.

The Ordovician Period

Fossil records show that the Ordovician period was a time of great diversity and abundant marine life. The Ordovician period marks the earliest unquestionable advent of vertebrates, with the appearance in the fossil record of the group of jawless fishes known as the *Agnatha*. The end of the Ordovician brought many extinctions. The extinctions were probably the result of widespread cooling and glaciation. Tropical shallow-water marine groups were the most affected. High-latitude and deep-water organisms were relatively unaffected.

The Silurian Period

During the Silurian period, much of what is now the North American continent was at or above sea level. Thick gypsum and other evaporite minerals accumulated in the vanishing shallow seas. The Silurian period brought the emergence of terrestrial life—plants. The earliest known land plants with a well-developed circulatory system (vascular plants) appeared during the Silurian period. These plants were closely tied to their water origins and inhabited only low wetlands. As plants moved ashore, so did other terrestrial organisms. Air-breathing scorpions and millipedes were common land animals during this period in Earth's history.

The Devonian Period

By the Devonian period, known as the "age of fishes," many dramatic changes had occurred. Plants had spread over the land surfaces. Lowland forests of seed ferns, scale trees, and true ferns flourished. In the seas, fishes diversified into many new groups. Some well adapted groups, such as the sharks and bony fishes, are still present today. Among the bony fishes, the lobe-finned fishes are of particular importance because they led the way for the evolution of land animals. Some lobe-finned fishes evolved internal nostrils, which enabled them to breathe air. Today, the lungfishes and the *coelacanth* (pronounced SEE-la-kanth), a "living fossil," have such internal nostrils and breathe in a similar way. Another important characteristic of the lobe-finned fishes is that their fins were lobed and muscular, with jointed appendages that enabled the animals to walk. Eventually, animal life moved to land. Descended from the lobe-finned fishes, the first amphibians made their appearance during the late Devonian period. The arrival of amphibians was of enormous importance on the evolutionary chain of air-breathing vertebrate land animals. Amphibians, although they are able to live on land, need to return to water to lay their eggs.

Figure 30.12
Life in the Devonian sea. In the front center, a nautiloid (which is related to modern cephalopod molluscs, including the squids), is attacking a trilobite. The colorful organisms on the left are corals.

The coelacanth was thought to have become extinct after the Mesozoic era. However, in 1938, the first living specimen was caught off the coast of East Africa. Since then, other specimens have been discovered in the Madagascar area. The coelacanth is now considered a "living fossil."

Insights

The Carboniferous Period

The Carboniferous period includes both the Mississippian and the Pennsylvanian periods. Warm, moist climatic conditions contributed to lush vegetation and dense swampy forests. These swamps were the source of the extensive coal beds that now lie under parts of North America, Europe, and northern China. In the Carboniferous period, insects underwent rapid changes that led to such diverse forms as giant cockroaches and dragonflies having wingspans of 80 centimeters. The evolution of the first reptiles took place with the arrival of the amniote egg. The amniote egg features a porous shell that contains a membrane, which provides a completely self-contained environment for an embryo. The shell protected the embryo from drying out, allowing animals to complete the transition, begun by amphibians in the Devonian period, from aquatic environments to land. Thanks to the amniote egg, reptiles do not need to lay their eggs in water the way amphibians do.

Figure 30.13
Warm, moist climatic conditions contributed to the lush vegetation and swampy coal forests of the Carboniferous period. These forests produced most of the coal deposits around the world.

The Permian Period

The evolution of reptiles continued in the Permian period. The reptiles must have been well-suited to their environment, for they ruled the earth for 200 million years. (By comparison, modern humans have inhabited the earth for less than 100,000 years.) Two major groups of reptiles appeared during the Permian period: the *diapsids* and the *synapsids*. The synapsids, which include ancestors of the earliest mammals, dominated the Permian. The diapsids were less noticeable than the synapsids in the Permian period, but it was the diapsids that eventually gave rise to the dinosaurs early in the Mesozoic era.

At the end of the Permian period, one of the greatest extinctions of animals in the earth's history occurred. Marine invertebrates were affected more than terrestrial life. Half of all animal families, up to 95 percent of all marine species, and 70 percent of all land species became extinct. The cause of the extinction is not well understood. One hypothesis is that worldwide global cooling resulted in glaciation and an accompanying lowering of sea level. Climatic extremes ranging from glaciers to deserts are clearly recorded in the rocks of this time. The long duration of lowered sea level, about 20–25 million years, undoubtedly placed much stress on the environments of marine organisms. Yet this alone cannot account for the large marine extinction. Whatever happened took a less drastic toll on terrestrial life. Terrestrial life, although affected, continued to evolve, and it expanded rapidly as new land habitats emerged, perhaps due in part to the lowered sea level. As we shall see in the next section, one likely explanation for the Permian extinctions is the tectonic activity that accompanied the formation of Pangaea.

The term *Carboniferous period* originated in England, but it is now used around the world. In North America, the Carboniferous period is divided into the *Mississippian period* and the *Pennsylvanian period.* The names were adopted because many rocks of these periods are found at these locations. Both periods are known for their coal beds.

Insights

Paleozoic Tectonics

The breakup of the Precambrian supercontinent began about 600 million years ago (latest Precambrian) and continued into the Cambrian period (earliest Paleozoic era). This was a time of active sea-floor spreading, with the North American and European plates diverging from each other. This active sea-floor spreading opened up new ocean basins, which resulted in the first of several major worldwide rises in sea level during the Paleozoic era.

Later in the Paleozoic (during the Devonian and Permian periods), the collision of all major land masses resulted in the supercontinent of *Pangaea* (Figure 30.14). Mountain-building activity continued and was widespread throughout the Appalachian Mountains in North America, the Hercynian and

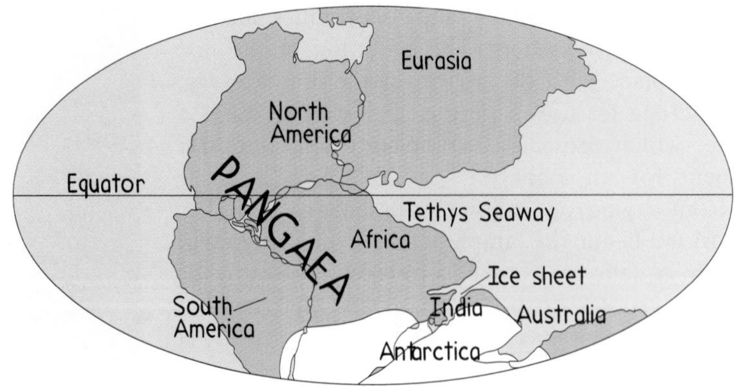

Figure 30.14
With the collision of continental landmasses, the supercontinent Pangaea was formed.

Caledonian Mountains in Europe, and the Ural Mountains in Russia. Crustal disturbances were so great that they affected not only the continental margins but also the inner regions of continents. The ancestral Rocky Mountains, for example, owe their formation to the dramatic collision that produced Pangaea.

The southern climate of Pangaea was dominated by widespread glaciation, owing to the close proximity of Pangaea to the South Pole (Figure 30.15). Paleomagnetic evidence suggests that Pangaea was drifting as a unit across the South Pole, which accounts for the shifts in the centers of glaciation. Pangaea was a very large continent, and its vast and changing climate belts greatly influenced the evolution of terrestrial life.

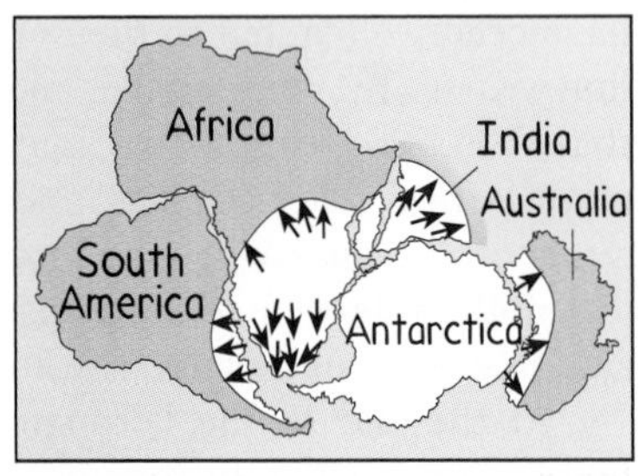

Figure 30.15
The southern climate of Pangaea was dominated by widespread glaciation. Arrows depict direction of glacial movement. Recall, from Chapter 29, that glacial striations provide clues for the positioning of the continents.

New oceanic lithosphere forms as tectonic plates move away from oceanic spreading ridges. When spreading is slow, ocean floors are cold and dense. They "stand" lower on the asthenosphere, so ocean basins are deep. When spreading is fast, ocean floors are warmer and less dense. They stand "higher" on the asthenosphere, so ocean basins are shallow. Because ocean basins are shallow, seawater inundates the lower elevations of continents. In this way, shallow seas form on top of the continental crust.

Insights

30.5 The Mesozoic Era

The Mesozoic era, known as "the age of reptiles," consisted of three periods: *Triassic, Jurassic,* and *Cretaceous.* Reptiles that survived the Permian extinction at the end of the Paleozoic era evolved to become the rulers of the world. The most significant event of the Mesozoic era was the rise of the dinosaurs. Mammals evolved from reptiles early in the Mesozoic, but they were relatively small and insignificant, compared with the dinosaurs.

Land plants greatly diversified during the Mesozoic era. True pines and redwoods appeared, and they rapidly spread throughout the land. Flowering plants arose in the Cretaceous period, and they diversified so quickly that, by the end of the period, they were the dominant plants. The emergence of the flowering plants also accelerated the evolution and specialization of insects.

The end of the Cretaceous period, 65 million years ago, was another time of great extinction. The dinosaurs, flying reptiles, and marine reptiles were completely wiped out, as were many organisms, both on land and in the seas.

The cause of this great extinction is still a source of some debate among scientists. Perhaps the best-documented hypothesis came from Luis and Walter Alvarez. They hypothesized that the extinction was caused by the impact of a very large meteorite. Support for their hypothesis comes from an abundance of the element iridium found in sediments that mark the boundary between the Cretaceous and Tertiary periods. The concentration of iridium in a meteorite is about the same as the concentration of iridium in the earth as a whole. However, the iridium concentration in a meteorite is much higher than the concentration of iridium in the earth's crust. Yet, all over the world the concentration of iridium at the Cretaceous–Tertiary boundary is much greater than it is in sediments above or below the boundary. This strongly suggests that iridium was probably spread worldwide by the impact event. The Cretaceous–Tertiary boundary layer was deposited about 65 million years ago—the time of the great dinosaur extinction.

The Alvarez team hypothesized that a large meteorite hit the earth with such force that a gigantic light-blocking cloud of dust developed. The dust cloud lasted for months, perhaps even longer. The huge cloud stopped photosynthesis, catastrophically reduced the food supply, and chilled the earth. Finally, the dust settled, depositing the layer of iridium-enriched sediment. Other killing mechanisms associated with a meteorite impact of this size would include acid rain, tsunamis, wildfires, and a delayed greenhouse effect. According to recent research, the site of the impact crater is located just offshore of the northern part of the Yucatan peninsula in Mexico.

An alternative to the Alvarez hypothesis suggests that the iridium layer may have been generated from massive volcanic eruptions. The ash and debris from these eruptions also could have blocked out the sun. A third possibility is that large-scale volcanic eruptions could have been caused by the impact of an extraterrestrial object.

Whatever the cause, the Cretaceous extinction dramatically marked the close of the Mesozoic era.

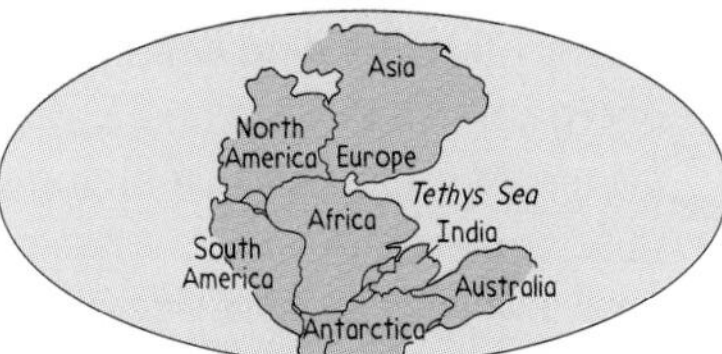

200 million years ago
Mesozoic Era

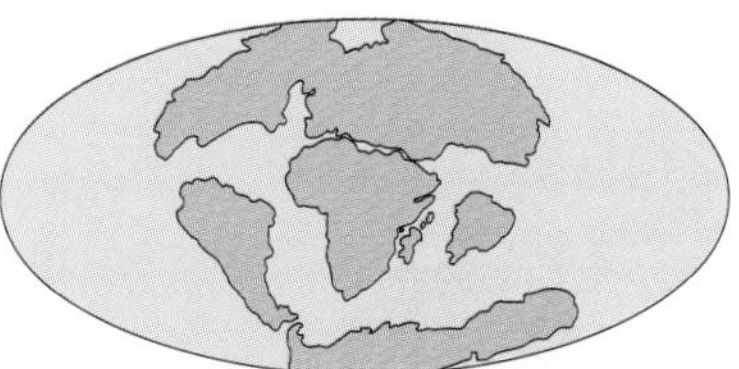

65 million years ago
Cenozoic Era

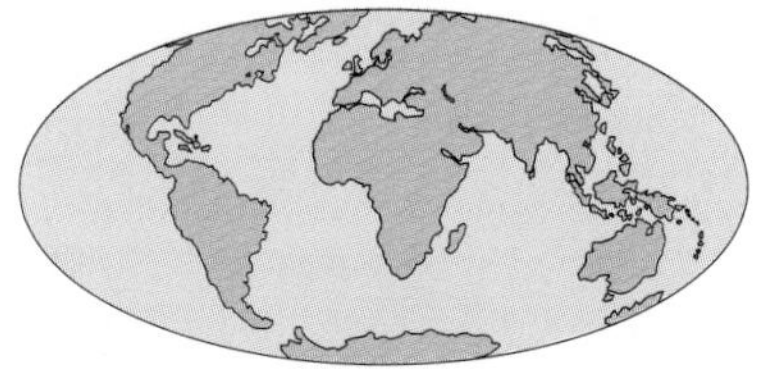

Present

Figure 30.16
Stages during the breakup of Pangaea.

Mesozoic Tectonics

The Mesozoic era witnessed the initial breakup of Pangaea (Figure 30.16). The breakup began at the end of the Triassic period with the eruption of extensive basalt flows associated with two major rift zones. One of these rift zones initiated the separation of North America from Pangaea, thus forming the central Atlantic Ocean basin. During the Jurassic period, India started on a northward journey, while South America/Africa separated from Australia/Antarctica. The south Atlantic Ocean formed after the split of South America and Africa during the Cretaceous period. The breakup of Pangaea occurred during the entire Mesozoic era, which likely caused a worldwide rise in sea level in the Cretaceous. The plate movements that initiated the breakup continue today. Of all the former continental unions that existed in Paleozoic time, only that of Europe and Asia has survived to the present time.

Subduction of the Farallon Plate (Section 27.4) and related tectonic accretions to the North American continent began no later than the Triassic period. Accretions are pieces of one plate that eventually become part of another, and often occur as one plate is subducted beneath another. This activity produced deformation and widespread

Link to Biology

Life Can Thrive in *Very* Inhospitable Places

Recent reports of possible fossil evidence for primitive life on Mars certainly spark the imagination. Here on the earth, we know that life can be found in every nook and cranny of what we term the *biosphere.* We know that simple life forms thrive even in hot springs on land and in the deep ocean near spreading ridges. Whereas we used to think of life as confined to the places on or near the surface of the earth or in its waters, we now find life some 3000 meters beneath the earth's surface—in solid rock! Clearly, there is no photosynthesis at this depth—nor is there free oxygen. And it is very hot: 45–85°C. The bacteria found here, named *Bacillus infernus,* survive under pressures exceeding 3000 pounds per square inch.*

Bacteria need to "breathe" just as we do. The breathing is actually an oxidation/reduction reaction between oxygen (the oxidizing agent) and organic carbon (the reducing agent) that gives the bacterium energy, much in the same way we acquire energy from eating food and breathing air. Not all bacteria utilize oxygen, however. It has been known for some time that near-surface bacteria, such as those found in lakes or shallow aquifers, can use other oxidizing agents, such as iron, manganese, nitrate, and sulfate, to oxidize organic carbon and to gain energy. These bacteria can also utilize a variety of compounds that contain organic carbon, such as gasoline and many industrial solvents. This fact has been a boon to people who are attempting to clean up aquifers contaminated by such compounds.

But it is only very recently that scientists have discovered bacteria that utilize iron surviving at depths as great as 3000 meters. These bacteria were recovered in 1992 and 1994 from deep holes drilled in sedimentary rock in Colorado and Virginia. The colonies appear to be more than 100 million years old (dating from the Jurassic period).

The predecessors of these hearty little creatures could have survived on the surface of the very hot, oxygen-devoid, primitive earth. Because a by-product of their metabolic process is carbon dioxide, related bacteria may even have played a pivotal role in the formation of the early atmosphere. They consumed iron oxide (rust), producing the mineral magnetite in the process. Thus, bacteria such as these may have been responsible for the formation of the earth's very old and poorly understood banded iron deposits.

Amazingly, subsurface life, which includes *Bacillus infernus,* is abundant. Such cryptic life forms may add up to more total weight than all the living things on the earth's surface combined!

volcanism both in the North American and in the Andean mountain belts. The granitic batholiths of the Andes and the Sierra Nevada are what remain from the numerous volcanic arcs that once rimmed the eastern Pacific basin.

30.6 The Cenozoic Era

The Cenozoic era, known as the "age of the mammals," is made up of two periods—the *Tertiary* and the *Quaternary.* From oldest to youngest, these two periods are broken up into the *Paleocene, Eocene, Oligocene, Miocene,* and *Pliocene* epochs (for the Tertiary period) and the *Pleistocene* and *Holocene* epochs (for the Quaternary period). We are currently living in the Holocene epoch.

*Biologists refer to this phenomenon as *adaptive radiation,* because organisms begin to adapt to new environments and radiate, or diversify, away from a smaller set of ancestors.

Link to Global Thermodynamics

Is It Cold Outside?

Yes it is, relatively speaking. For 90 percent of the earth's history, there were no glaciers of continental magnitude anywhere. In fact, because such glaciers exist today, mainly in the polar ice caps and in Greenland, we are technically now in an *ice age.* Because continental-scale glaciers are currently restricted to the polar regions, we are in what is known as an *interglacial* period of an ice age.

Ice ages have occurred five times over the course of Earth's history. The first one of which we have evidence occurred more than 2 billion years ago. Another began about 840 million years ago and lasted an incredible 240 million years! There were two ice ages during the Paleozoic era, but none in the Mesozoic. For the first 50 million years or so of the Cenozoic era, there were also no ice ages. The present ice age actually began 8–10 million years ago, but the extensive glaciation that characterized the Pleistocene epoch began about 1 million years ago.

So what causes ice ages? There is, most likely, no single explanation, but most scientists agree that global-scale cooling leading to ice ages is caused by the right combination of three things: (1) the arrangement of continents around the globe, (2) the amount of sunlight being reflected back into space, and (3) the geometry of the earth's rotation on its axis and revolution around the sun.

The arrangement of continents greatly influences ocean and atmospheric currents, which are the main mechanisms for redistributing ocean and atmospheric thermal energy around the globe. Continents grouped together in one location are easier to warm, as equatorial waters flow with less obstruction toward the poles. For continents which are spread out around the globe, as they are today, circulation "cells" are smaller and heat redistribution is more local and less efficient.

When sea level is lower, for whatever reason, more land area is exposed. The increased amount of land area tends to increase the amount of sunlight reflected back into space. This phenomenon results in cooler temperatures globally. Cloud cover and/or dust in the atmosphere also causes sunlight to be reflected back into space, reducing the absorption of solar radiation.

The *Milankovitch effect* refers to a combination of factors that affects the distribution of solar radiation over the earth's surface during the year: (1) variations in the angle at which the earth's rotational axis is tilted (currently about 23.5 degrees), (2) the wobbling of the earth's rotational axis, and (3) variations in the eccentricity ("ovalness") of the earth's orbit around the sun. Certain combinations of these factors, which recur periodically, lead to reduced solar radiation at high northern latitudes during the summer. If the reduction of that radiation is great enough, then all the snow from the preceding winter does not melt and, if these conditions persist over many years, continental-scale glaciers eventually form. The periodic nature of the Milankovitch effect may be the primary cause of glacial–interglacial cycles. According to this theory, the first two processes—the arrangement of continents and the amount of reflected radiation—make the earth cold enough, and the third—the Milankovitch effect—causes the climate to teeter-totter between glacial and interglacial periods.

So what's next? Large-scale glaciation or global warming? Only further research can provide us with hope of finding an answer. Anything less is pure speculation, at best.

After the mass extinctions at the end of the Mesozoic era, many environmental niches were left vacant. These openings allowed the relatively rapid evolution of mammals in habitats formerly occupied by their extinct predecessors. Flying bats, some large land mammals, and such marine animals as whales and dolphins evolved to occupy niches left vacant by the extinction of many of the Mesozoic reptiles.

Climates cooled during much of the Cenozoic era, culminating in the widespread glaciation that characterized the Pleistocene epoch. Although this *ice age* continues today, there have been many alternations between glacial and interglacial conditions (as the box on the previous page shows). During the glacial episodes, as much as one-third of the present land area was covered by great thicknesses of ice. The huge continental glaciers were very heavy, depressing the land by their weight and altering the courses of many streams and rivers. The glaciers eroded and scratched the land in some places and deposited huge moraines in others, which today show the extent of their former existence.

The Cenozoic era also saw the evolution of humans. The extensive glaciation of the Pleistocene epoch caused sea level to drop because a great deal of water was bound up in glaciers. Even though the distribution of landmasses was essentially the same as it is today, the lowered sea level resulted in "land bridge" connections between landmasses that are now separated by water. One of these land bridges existed across the present-day Bering Strait, and it provided the route for the human migration from Asia to North America. The expansion of humans, not only into North America but also throughout the world, coincided with a period of extinction that occurred during the Pleistocene epoch.

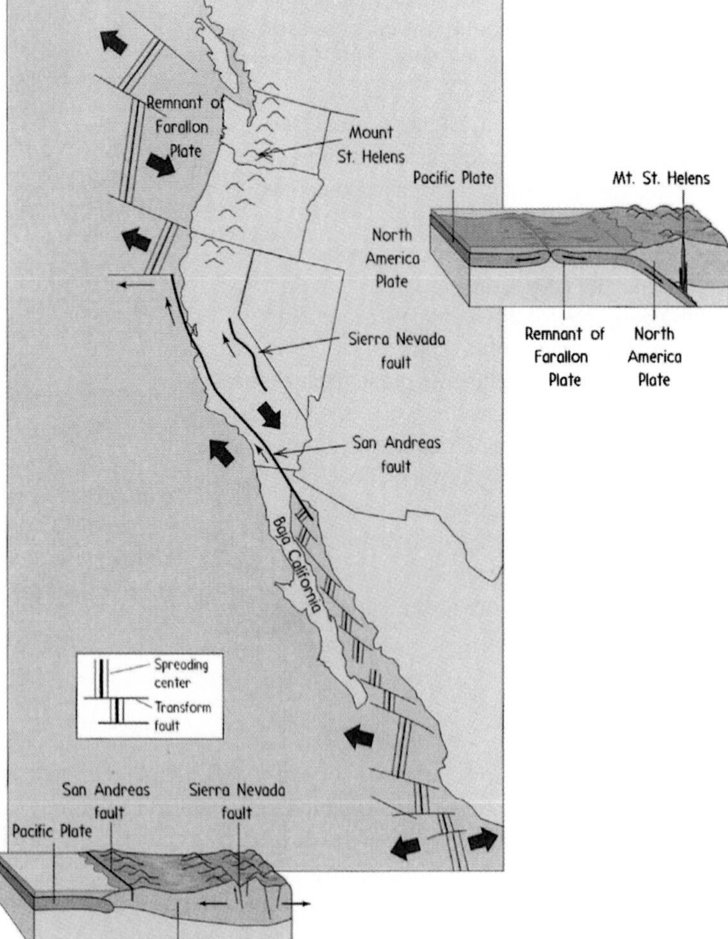

Figure 30.17
The San Andreas Fault is the result of an encounter between the North American Plate and the Pacific Plate. As the fault grew longer, the area of Baja California was torn from the continental margin.

The Pleistocene extinctions primarily involved large terrestrial mammals, while marine animals were for the most part unaffected. In North America, many large mammals became extinct after humans arrived, and in Africa, mammalian extinctions can be related to the appearance of the Stone Age hunters.

The cause of the Pleistocene extinction is a much-debated issue. The extreme climatic variation that existed at the time could have been partly responsible. Even though large-scale glaciation was occurring in some regions, the climate in many areas was relatively mild, leading some scientists to believe that harsh climate likely played only a small role in the Pleistocene extinctions.

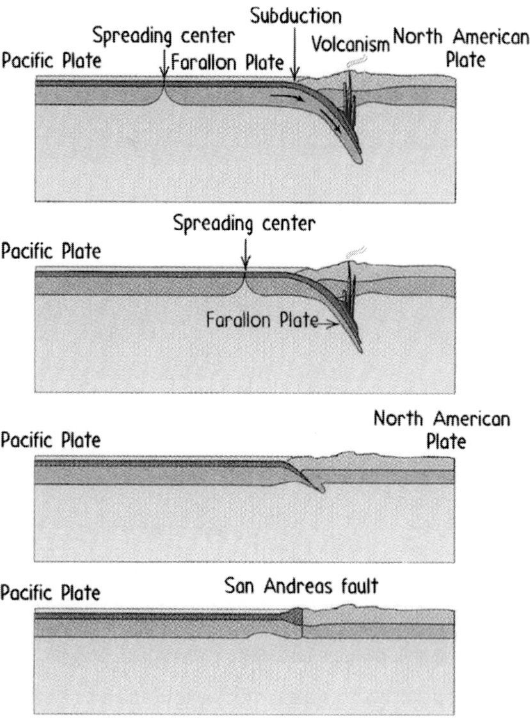

Figure 30.18
Subduction sequence of the Farallon Plate beneath the North American Plate. As the spreading center and the continental margin approached each other, the San Andreas Fault formed as a transform fault between the Pacific Plate and the North American Plate.

Cenozoic Tectonics

Enormous tectonic disturbances occurred rapidly throughout the world during the Tertiary period. In the early Tertiary period, there was a spreading center off the western margin of North America, with the Pacific Plate on the west and the Farallon Plate on the east (Figures 30.17 and 30.18). As the Farallon Plate subducted beneath North America, the spreading center approached the North American continental margin. The collision between the westward moving North American Plate and the Pacific ridge system occurred about 30 million years ago, giving birth to the San Andreas Fault. Baja California was torn away from the Mexican mainland, and, as a result, the Gulf of California was created. Because the plates are still moving, western California and Baja California either will eventually become completely detached from the mainland or will find themselves joined to western Canada.

The Hawaiian Island/Emperor Seamount chain (Figure 30.19) gives evidence of another significant Tertiary tectonic disturbance: the change in direction of the Pacific Plate. The bend in the chain of islands occurred between 30 and

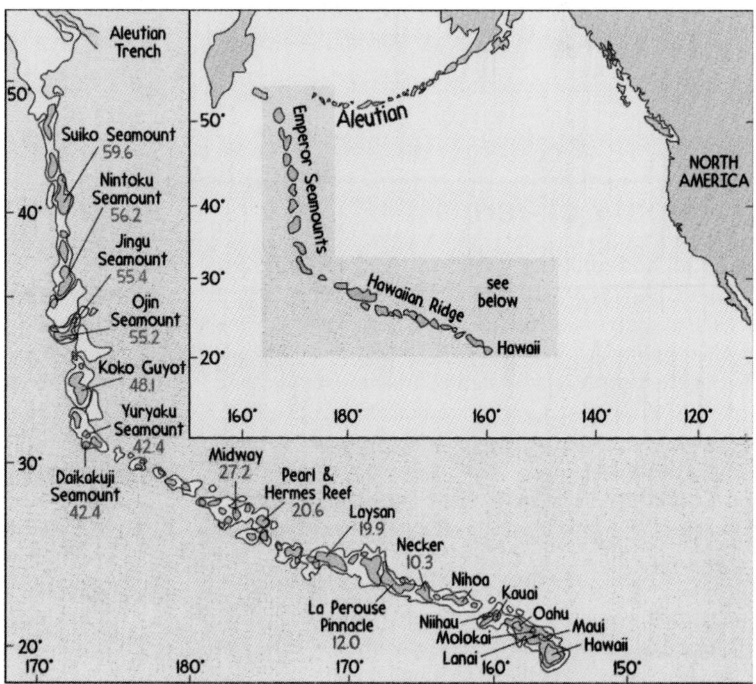

Figure 30.19
The Hawaiian Island/Emperor Seamount chain. The bend in the chain shows the change in direction of the Pacific Plate as a result of the collision of northern Mexico with the Pacific ridge. The red numbers indicate the age (in millions of years) of the individual islands and seamounts.

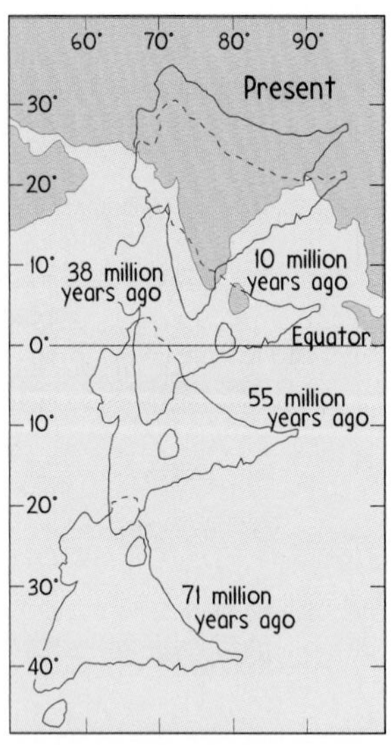

Figure 30.20
The formation of the Himalayas was a result of the collision of India with Asia. Because this was a continent-to-continent collision, the Himalayas have an unusually thick accumulation of continental lithosphere. Like icebergs, the mountains run deeper below the surface than they are high.

40 million years ago (mid-Tertiary) when plate motion changed from nearly due north to northwesterly. The change in direction occurred at about the same time in Earth history as the collision of northern Mexico (the North American Plate) with the Pacific ridge system.

Considerable tectonic activity also occurred in Eurasia during the Tertiary period. The culmination of these activities occurred in the mid-Cenozoic, when Afro-Arabia collided with Europe to produce the Alps and India collided with Asia to produce the Himalayas (Figure 30.20). The leading edge of the Indian Plate was forced partially under Asia, which generated an unusually thick accumulation of continental lithosphere. Due to isostasy, the thick lithosphere provided additional uplift to the Himalayas.

Human Geologic Force

Although the "human age" amounts to only a brief 0.002 percent of geologic time, we are almost certainly the most clever and adaptable organism to have evolved on the planet. All life forms alter their environments. Humans do it more, as we manipulate our environment to meet our needs. We have but to look at the irrigation systems of Mesopotamia, the cultivation of the Nile, the plowing of the prairies in the Great Plains, the invention of machines to further utilize the land, and the dams and locks on the Mississippi, Missouri, and Colorado rivers to illustrate the human role in geologic changes. These geologic changes also include such problems as deterioration of the ozone layer, hydrocarbon pollution, and global warming. Because we have the capacity to affect geologic change, it is imperative that we take care of our terrestrial home. It's the only one we've got!

Summary of Terms

Original horizontality A relative dating principle stating that layers of sediment are deposited evenly, with each new layer laid down almost horizontally over the older sediment.

Superposition A relative dating principle stating that, in an undeformed sequence of sedimentary rocks, each bed or layer is older than the one above and younger than the one below.

Cross-cutting A relative dating principle stating that, where an igneous intrusion or fault cuts through other rocks, the intrusion or fault is younger than the rock it cuts.

Inclusions A relative dating principle stating that any inclusion (a piece of one rock type contained within another) is older than the rock containing it.

Faunal succession A relative dating principle stating that fossil organisms succeed one another in a definite, irreversible, determinable order.

Unconformity A break or gap in the geologic record, caused by an interruption in the sequence of deposition or by erosion of preexisting rock.

Angular unconformity An unconformity in which older, tilted strata are overlain by younger, horizontal beds.

Radiometric dating A method for calculating the age of geologic materials based on the nuclear decay of naturally occurring radioactive isotopes.

Paleozoic era The time of ancient life, from 544 million years ago to 245 million years ago.

Mesozoic era The time of middle life, from 245 million years ago to about 65 million years ago.

Cenozoic era The time of recent life, from 65 million years ago to the present.

Precambrian time The time of hidden life, which began about 4.5 billion years ago when the earth formed, lasted until about 544 million years ago (the beginning of the Paleozoic era), and makes up 85 percent of the earth's history.

Review Questions

30.1 Relative Dating

1. Suppose a certain type of sediment is deposited in all modern streams. On a geologic expedition into unknown territory, we find the same type of deposit in ancient rocks. What can we say about the ancient rocks? What assumption are we making?
2. What five principles are used in relative dating? Describe each one.
3. Where a granitic dike is found in a bed of sandstone, what can be said about the relative ages of the dike and the age of the sandstone? What principle applies here?
4. Why don't all rock formations show a continuous sequence from the beginning of time to the present?
5. How are fossils used in determining geologic time?
6. In a sequence of sedimentary rock layers, the oldest layer is on the bottom and the youngest layer is at the top. What relative dating principle applies here?
7. Explain how fossils of fishes and other marine animals occur at high elevations, such as the Himalayas.
8. In an undeformed sequence of rocks, fossil X is found in a limestone layer at the bottom of the formation, and fossil Y is found in a shale layer at the top of the formation. What can we say about the ages of fossils X and Y?

30.2 Radiometric Dating

9. What is meant by radioactive half-life?
10. What are the half-lives of uranium-238, potassium-40, and carbon-14?
11. What isotope is preferred in dating very old rocks?
12. What isotope is commonly used for dating sediments or organic material from the Pleistocene?

30.3 Precambrian Time

13. Which of the geologic time units spans the greatest length of time?
14. How old is the earth?

30.4 The Paleozoic Era

15. The Paleozoic era experienced several fluctuations in sea level. What effect did this have on life forms?
16. Name the periods of the Paleozoic era.
17. For what is the Silurian period best known?
18. The Devonian period is known as "the age of fishes." What were some of the Devonian life forms?
19. Why is the evolution of internal nostrils in the lobe-finned fishes considered a significant step in the evolution of life on Earth?
20. Why do many geologists consider the lobe-finned fishes especially significant?
21. During what time period were most coal deposits laid down? Why was this period unique?
22. In what area of the United States do we find rich coal deposits?
23. What group evolved from the amphibians with the arrival of the amniote egg?

30.5 The Mesozoic Era

24. By what informal name is the Mesozoic era known?
25. What is the most likely cause of the Cretaceous extinction that wiped out the dinosaurs?
26. What effect did the breakup of Pangaea have on sea level?
27. What Pangaean landmass survives to this day?
28. How does the element iridium relate to the time of the extinction of the dinosaurs?

30.6 The Cenozoic Era

29. Which epochs make up the Tertiary period? The Quaternary period?
30. What geological event resulted in the bending of the Hawaiian Island/Emperor Seamount chain?
31. How did Pleistocene glaciation affect the land surface?
32. What role did tectonic activity play in the formation of the San Andreas Fault?
33. What geologic event allowed the evolution of many mammals early in the Cenozoic era?
34. How was the Gulf of California formed?
35. What important life forms evolved during the Cenozoic era?

Exercises

1. Suppose you see a group of sedimentary rock layers overlaid by a basalt flow. A fault displaces the bedding of the sedimentary rock but does not intersect the basalt flow. Relate the fault to the ages of the two rock types in the formation.
2. If a sedimentary rock contains inclusions of metamorphic rock, which rock is older? Defend your answer.
3. Refer to the figure below. Using the principles of relative dating, determine the relative ages of the

rock bodies and other lettered features. Start with this question: What was there first?

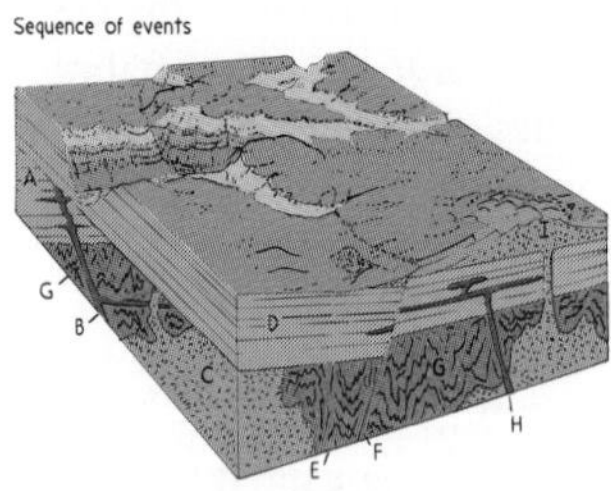

4. Which isotopes are most appropriate for dating rocks from the following ages? (a) Early Precambrian time. (b) The Mesozoic era. (c) The late Pleistocene epoch.
5. Has the amount of uranium in the earth increased over geologic time? Has the amount of lead in the earth increased?
6. Granitic pebbles within a sedimentary rock have a radiometric age of 300 million years. What can you say about the age of the sedimentary rock? Nearby, a dike having a radiometric age of 200 million years intrudes an outcrop of the same sedimentary rock. What can you say about the age of the sedimentary rock?
7. Before the discovery of radioactivity, how did geologists estimate the age of rock layers?
8. In dating a mineral, what is meant by "resetting of the mineral's time clock"?
9. If we divide a number by 2, and then divide the result by 2, and so on indefinitely, the answer will never be zero. Why, then, is carbon dating useful only for materials that are no older than about 50,000 years? (*Hint*: What is the half-life of carbon-14?)
10. Geologists often refer to the early Paleozoic era as the "Cambrian Explosion." What do you think is meant by this phrase?
11. Suppose that, in an undeformed sequence of rocks, you find a trilobite embedded in shale layers at the bottom of the formation and fossil leaves embedded in shale at the top of the formation. From your observation, what can you say about the ages of the formation?
12. In a sequence of sedimentary rock layers, the youngest layer is found at the bottom and the oldest layer at the top. What does this type of layering signify?
13. What is the difference between a nonconformity and an angular unconformity?
14. What key developments in life occurred during Precambrian time?
15. What factors are believed to have contributed to the generation of free oxygen during the early Precambrian? In what way did the increase in oxygen affect our planet?
16. What evidence do we have of Precambrian life?
17. Why are Paleozoic marine sedimentary rocks such as limestone and dolomite found widely distributed in the continental interiors?
18. Coal beds are formed from the accumulation of plant material that has become trapped in swamp floors. Yet coal deposits are found on the continent of Antarctica, where no swamps or vegetation exists. What is your explanation?
19. A radiometric date is determined from mica that has been removed from a rock. What does the date signify if the mica was found in granite? What does the date signify if the mica was found in schist?
20. Most scientists think the iridium-rich sediments found straddling the Cretaceous/Tertiary boundary can be explained by a meteorite impact. Why are high concentrations of iridium significant?
21. During the earth's long history, life has emerged and life has perished. Briefly discuss the emergence of life and the extinction of life for each geologic era.
22. In what ways can sea level be lowered? What effect might the lowering of sea level have on existing life forms?
23. What can cause a rise in sea level? Is this likely to happen in the future? Why or why not?
24. What general assumption must be made in order to understand the processes that occurred throughout the earth's history?
25. If fine muds were laid down at the rate of 1 cm per 1000 years, how long would it take to accumulate a sequence 1 km thick?
26. Why does sea level rise when the rate of seafloor spreading increases?
27. If sea level were to rise today, what land areas would be most affected? What life forms would be in danger of extinction?
28. What circumstances are likely to lead to the formation of continental-scale glaciers?
29. What is a likely cause of glacial–interglacial cycles? Are we currently in an ice age? Explain.
30. How have recent humans affected geological processes?

Chapter 30 Online Resources

Tutorials
- Formation of an Angular Unconformity Activity

Quiz
Exercises
Flashcards
Links

CHAPTER 31

The Atmosphere, the Oceans, and their Interactions

The view of the earth from space shows that our planet is colored distinct shades of blue and silver. The blue is due to the water in the oceans and the silver to clouds in the atmosphere. How did our beautiful, swirling atmosphere and oceans come to be? What is the atmosphere made of? How do the atmosphere and oceans interact? So many questions come to mind.

We begin to answer these questions by learning about the evolution of the atmosphere and the oceans. We then explore important features of these two fluid shells as we investigate the transfer of heat between them and how this transfer affects the earth's climate. We conclude with a look at the mechanisms that influence atmospheric and oceanic circulation patterns and their relationship to changes in the earth's climate. Interactions between the atmosphere and the oceans affect us all.

31.1 Earth's Atmosphere and Oceans

Seventy percent of the earth's surface is covered by water (Figure 31.1). The remaining 30 percent is land, most of which is located in the Northern Hemisphere (Figure 31.2). Although the many oceans are named for their various locations, they are really one big continuous ocean.

As we learned in Section 28.1, the oceans are the reservoir from which water evaporates into the atmosphere, only to precipitate later as rain and snow. The oceans play a major role in moderating the earth's temperature and

Equator

(a) Ocean hemisphere

Figure 31.1
Most of the earth's surface is covered by water. We can divide the earth into (a) an ocean-dominated hemisphere, and (b) a land-dominated hemisphere.

climate. Recall, from Chapter 7, that water has a high specific heat capacity—it is slow to heat up or to cool down. As such, water transfers large amounts of thermal energy to its surroundings when it cools, and it also absorbs large amounts of thermal energy from its surroundings when it warms. This property of water accounts for the moderate temperatures on lands bordering the oceans. The moderating influence of the oceans can be seen when we look at seasonal temperature variations for two cities at the same latitude: coastal San Francisco, California, and continental Wichita, Kansas (Figure 31.3). Whereas temperatures in San Francisco tend to have small seasonal variations, temperatures in Wichita show strong seasonal fluctuations—cold winters and hot summers. The oceans do a great job of moderating climate, both by making summers cooler and by making winters warmer.

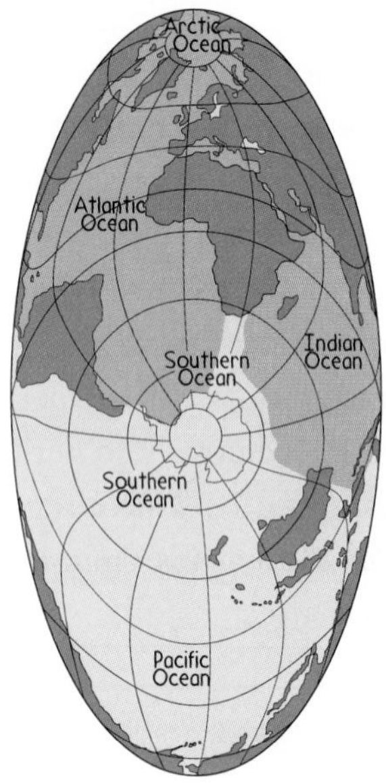

Figure 31.2
When a map is centered over Antarctica, the expanse of the world ocean can be seen. In terms of size and volume, the Pacific Ocean accounts for more than half of the world ocean, and it is thus the largest ocean. In fact, the Atlantic and Indian Oceans combined would easily fit into the space occupied by the Pacific Ocean.

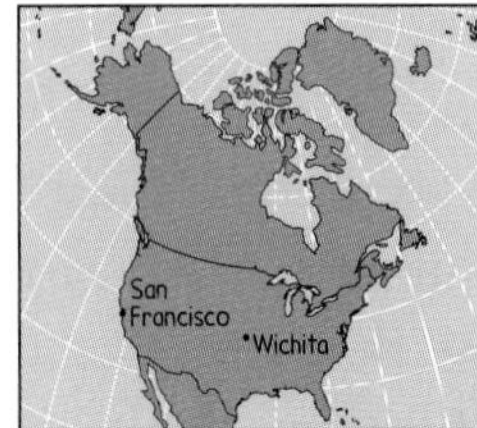

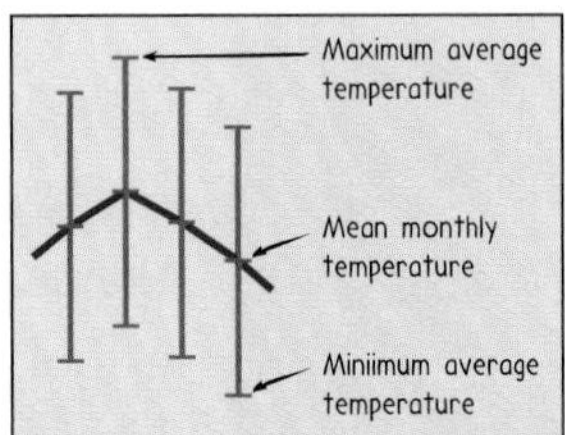

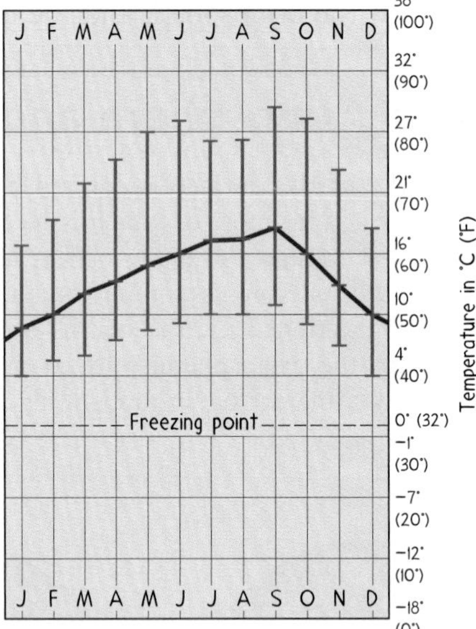

Station: San Francisco, California
Latitude/longtitude: 37°37′ N, 122°23′ W
Average annual temperature: 14°C (57.2°F)
Total annual precipitation: 47.5 cm (18.7 in.)
Elevation: 5 m (16.4 ft)
Population: 750,000
Annual temperature range: 9°C (16.2°F)

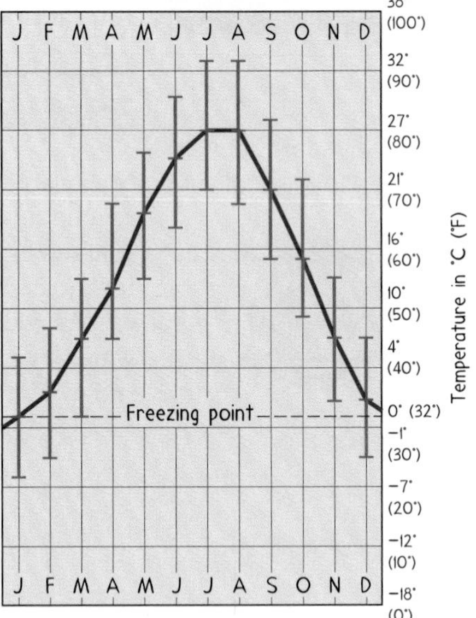

Station: Wichita, Kansas
Latitude/longtitude: 37°39′ N, 97°25′ W
Average annual temperature: 13.7°C (56.6°F)
Total annual precipitation: 72.2 cm (28.4 in.)
Elevation: 402.6 m (1321 ft)
Population: 280,000
Annual temperature range: 27°C (48.6°F)

Figure 31.3
Comparison of seasonal temperature ranges for coastal San Francisco, California, and continental Wichita, Kansas.

Evolution of the Earth's Atmosphere and Oceans

The earth probably had an atmosphere—a blanket of gases surrounding it—before the sun was fully formed. It is possible that this primitive atmosphere was composed only of hydrogen and helium, the two most abundant gases in the universe, along with trace amounts of ammonia and methane. There was no oxygen in the early atmosphere. Then, when the temperature and pressure in the contracting center of the still-forming sun became high enough to ignite thermonuclear reactions, our sun was born. The blast from the sun's formation likely produced a strong outflow of charged particles—an outflow strong enough to sweep the earth of its earliest atmosphere.

But then a new atmosphere likely formed. The first stage in its formation probably occurred when gases trapped in Earth's hot interior escaped through volcanoes and fissures at Earth's surface. The gases spewed out by these early eruptions were probably much like the gases found in the volcanic eruptions of today—about 85 percent water vapor, 10 percent carbon dioxide, and 5 percent nitrogen, by mass. The early atmosphere still had no free oxygen and could not support the type of life we have today.

As we learned in Chapter 30, the production of free oxygen did not occur until primitive bacteria known as blue-green algae appeared. Like all green plants, these organisms used photosynthesis to convert carbon dioxide and water to hydrocarbon and free oxygen:

$$CO_2 + H_2O \xrightarrow{\text{light}} CH_2O + O_2$$

When free oxygen did become available, an ozone (O_3) layer formed in the upper atmosphere. Since the ozone layer acts like a filter to reduce the amount of ultraviolet radiation reaching the earth's surface, the surface was then able to support life.

As the earth cooled, the rich supply of water vapor in the atmosphere condensed to form the oceans. Comet debris from interplanetary space also contributed water to the oceans. These oceans, essential to the evolution of life and ultimately to the development of the present global environment, have remained for the rest of the earth's history.

☑ CHECKPOINT

1. Why are the hottest climates on the earth typically found in the interior sections of continents?
2. Did the ozone layer exist before the earth acquired green plants?

Check Your Answers

1. The large specific heat capacity of water tends to keep coastal areas from experiencing extreme temperatures. Therefore, very hot climates are usually some distance away from the ocean.
2. No. The formation of ozone, O_3, was preceded by the introduction of free oxygen, which came from photosynthesizing plants.

Volcanic eruptions release a great deal of carbon dioxide, yet it is a minor constituent of the earth's atmosphere. That's because most carbon dioxide is gobbled up by the ocean, where it dissolves and ends up as calcium carbonate.

Insights

31.2 Components of the Earth's Atmosphere

If gas molecules in the atmosphere were not continuously moving, gravity would force them to lie on the ground like unpopped popcorn at the bottom of a popcorn machine. But add heat to the popcorn, or to atmospheric gas, and both will bumble their way up to higher altitudes. Popping popcorn attains speeds of perhaps 1 meter per second, and it can rise a meter or two. Air molecules move at speeds of about 450 meters per second, and some of them rise to an altitude of more than 50 kilometers.

If there were no gravity, both popping popcorn and gas molecules in the atmosphere would fly off into outer space. Gases are compressible, which allows the invisible force of gravity to squeeze and hold a great number of gas molecules close to the earth's surface (where gravity is strongest). Thus the density of air molecules is greatest at the earth's surface and gradually decreases with height.

Since air has weight, it exerts pressure on the earth's surface. This pressure is known as *atmospheric pressure* or, simply, *air pressure*. Like the atmosphere's density, air pressure also decreases with increasing height above the earth's surface. The higher up you go, the lower the air pressure. Interestingly, the weight of the air on the ocean's surface keeps the ocean from boiling away. Recall, from Chapter 8, that water will boil at 0°C when no air pressure acts on it. So fish as well as birds should appreciate the existence of the atmosphere.

Table 31.1 shows that the earth's present-day atmosphere is a mixture of various gases—primarily nitrogen and oxygen, with small percentages of water vapor, argon, and carbon dioxide, and trace amounts of other elements and compounds.

Figuring Physical Science

Dense as Air

Knowing the density of air (1.25 kilograms/cubic meter), it's a straight-forward calculation to find the mass of air for any given volume—simply multiply air's density by the volume. The volume of an average-sized room is assumed to be 4.00 meters × 4.00 meters × 3.00 meters = 48.0 cubic meters. Thus the mass of the air in the room is

$$1.25 \text{ kg/m}^3 \times 48.0 \text{ m}^3 = 60.0 \text{ kg}$$

If you're curious to know how many pounds this is, multiply by the conversion factor 2.20 pounds/1 kilogram.

$$60.0 \text{ kg} \times 2.20 \text{ lb/kg} - 132 \text{ lb}$$

Knowing the density of air (1.25 kilograms/cubic meter), it's a straightforward calculation to find the mass of air for any given volume.

Problem

What is the mass in kilograms of the air in a classroom that has a volume of 796 cubic meters?

Answer

Each cubic meter of air has a mass of 1.25 kilograms, and so,

$$796 \text{ m}^3 \times 1.25 \text{ kg/m}^3 = 995 \text{ kg}$$

which is as much as the combined mass of 17 students having a mass of about 60 kilograms each.

Table 31.1

Composition of the Atmosphere

Permanent Gases			Variable Gases		
Gas	**Symbol**	**Percentage by volume**	**Gas**	**Symbol**	**Percentage by volume**
Nitrogen	N_2	78	Water vapor	H_2O	0 to 4
Oxygen	O_2	21	Carbon dioxide	CO_2	0.035
Argon	Ar	0.9	Ozone	O_3	0.000004*
Neon	Ne	0.0018	Carbon monoxide	CO	0.00002*
Helium	He	0.0005	Sulfur dioxide	SO_2	0.000001*
Methane	CH_4	0.0001	Nitrogen dioxide	NO_2	0.000001*
Hydrogen	H_2	0.00005	Particles (dust, pollen)		0.00001*

*Average value in polluted air.

Link to Section 22.4

Vertical Structure of the Atmosphere

Link to Section 6.7

If you have ever gone mountain climbing, you have probably noticed that the air grows cooler and thinner with increasing elevation. At sea level, the air is generally warmer and denser. The greater density near the earth's surface is due to gravity. The density of the air, like the density of a deep pile of feathers, is greatest at the bottom and least at the top. More than half the atmosphere's mass lies below an altitude of 5.6 kilometers, and about 99 percent lies below an altitude of 30 kilometers. Unlike a pile of feathers, however, the atmosphere doesn't have a distinct top. It gradually thins to the near vacuum of outer space.

The atmosphere is classified in layers, each distinct in its characteristics (Figure 31.4). The lowest layer, the **troposphere,** is where weather occurs. The troposphere extends to a height of 16 kilometers over the equatorial region and to a height of 8 kilometers over the polar regions. Commercial jets generally fly at the top of the troposphere to minimize the turbulence caused by weather disturbances. Even though the troposphere is the thinnest atmospheric layer, it contains 90% of the atmosphere's mass and almost all of its water vapor and clouds. Temperature in the troposphere decreases steadily (at 6°C per kilometer) with increasing altitude. At the top of the troposphere, temperature averages a freezing −50°C.

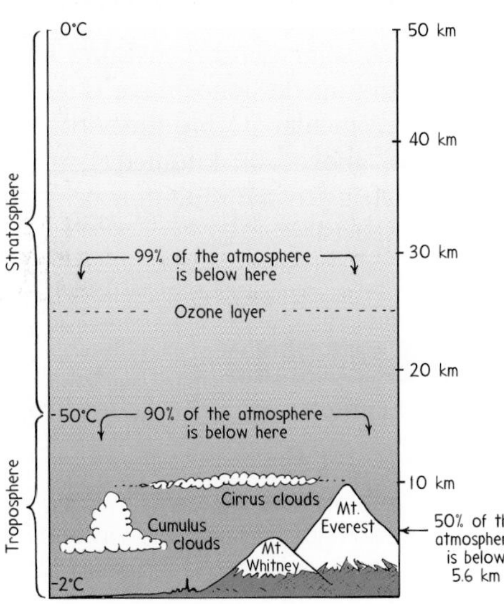

Figure 31.4
The two lowest atmospheric layers, the troposphere and the stratosphere.

Above the troposphere is the **stratosphere,** which reaches a height of 50 kilometers above the ground. Ultraviolet radiation from the sun is absorbed by the ozone layer in the stratosphere, which causes the temperature there to rise from about −50°C at the bottom to about 0°C at the top.

Above the stratosphere, the **mesosphere** extends upward to about 80 kilometers. The gases that make up the mesosphere absorb very little of the sun's radiation. As a result, the temperature decreases again from about 0°C at the bottom of the layer to about −90°C at the top.

The situation is just the opposite in the layer above the mesosphere, the **thermosphere.** Extending upward to 500 kilometers, this layer contains very little air. What air there is absorbs enough solar radiation to reach a temperature of about 2000°C. Because of the low air density, however, this extreme temperature has little significance. Very little heat would be transferred to a slowly moving body in this region.

The **ionosphere** is an ion-rich region within the thermosphere and uppermost mesosphere. The ions in it are produced from the interaction between high-frequency solar radiation and atmospheric atoms. The incoming solar rays strip electrons from nitrogen and oxygen atoms, producing a large concentration of free electrons and positively charged ions in this layer. The degree of ionization in the ionosphere depends on air density and on the amount of solar radiation. Ionization is greatest in the upper part of the ionosphere, where air density is low and solar radiation is high.

Ions in the ionosphere cast a faint glow that prevents moonless nights from becoming stark black. Near the earth's magnetic poles, fiery light displays called *auroras* occur as the solar wind (consisting of high-speed charged particles ejected by the sun) stirs up the ionosphere (Figure 31.5). These auroral displays are particularly spectacular during times of solar flares.

Figure 31.5
The aurora borealis over Alaska is created by solar-charged particles that strike the upper atmosphere and light up the sky (just as similar particles on a smaller scale light up a fluorescent lamp).

Finally, above 500 kilometers, in the **exosphere,** the thinning atmosphere gradually yields to the radiation belts and magnetic fields that belong to interplanetary space.

☑ CHECKPOINT

Why do commercial airliners tend to fly at the top of the troposphere?

Check Your Answer

They fly high because the captain wants to have a smooth ride! Most weather disturbances don't extend past the top of the troposphere. Also, the thinness of the air greatly reduces air drag and increases fuel efficiency.

31.3 Solar Energy

The earth's equatorial regions are warmer than the polar regions. But why? Surface temperatures on Earth depend on the energy each part of the earth receives from the sun each day. And how much energy is received depends on the angle at which the sun's rays strike the earth's surface. This can be seen by holding a flashlight vertically over a table and shining the light directly down on the flat surface (Figure 31.6a). The light produces a bright circle. Now tip the flashlight at various angles and notice that the circle elongates into ellipses, spreading the same amount of energy over a greater area and, therefore, decreasing the intensity of the light. The same is true of sunlight on the earth's surface. High noon in equatorial regions is like the vertically held flashlight; high noon at higher latitudes is like the flashlight held at an angle.

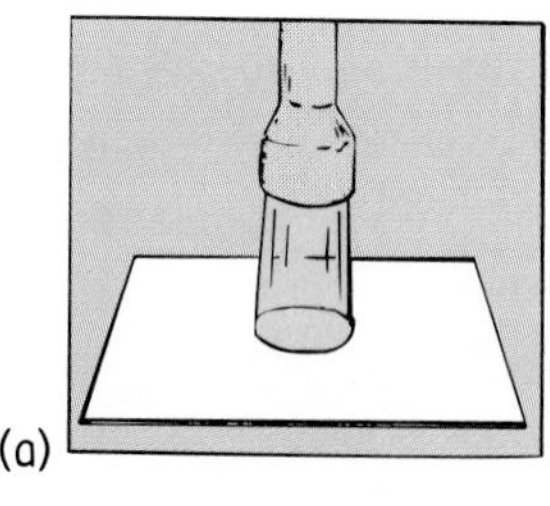

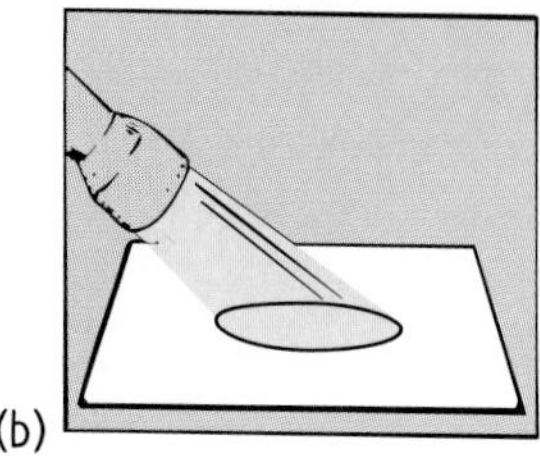

Figure 31.6
(a) When the flashlight is held directly above at a right angle to the surface, the beam of light produces a bright circle. (b) When the light is shone at an angle, the light beam is dispersed over a larger area and is therefore less intense.

The Seasons

The northern United States and Canada, both temperate regions, have distinct summer and winter seasons. These seasons change because the angle at which the sun's rays strike these locations varies over the course of a year. Figure 31.7 shows how the tilt of the earth causes the variation in the rays' angle. Can you see that the rays are more perpendicular to the ground in the United States and Canada when the earth's axis is tilted *toward* the sun? When the sun's rays are closest to perpendicular at any spot on the earth, that region experiences summer. Six months later, the rays fall upon the same region more obliquely, and we have winter. In between are fall and spring.

It is interesting to note that, because the earth follows an elliptical path around the sun, the earth is farthest from the sun when the Northern Hemisphere experiences summer. So the angle of the sun's rays, not the distance from the sun, is most responsible for earth's surface temperatures.

Another effect of the tilting rays is the length of daylight each day. Can you see, in Figure 31.7, that a location in summer has more daylight per daily rotation of the earth than the same location when the earth is on the opposite side of the sun in winter? If you have trouble visualizing this, take a look at the high latitudes near the poles. Consider the special latitude where daylight lasts

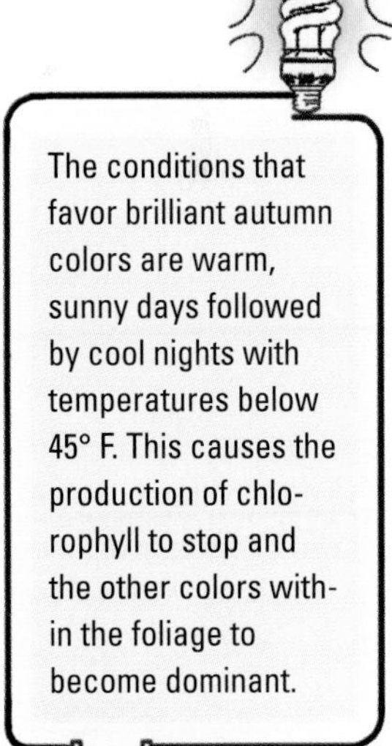

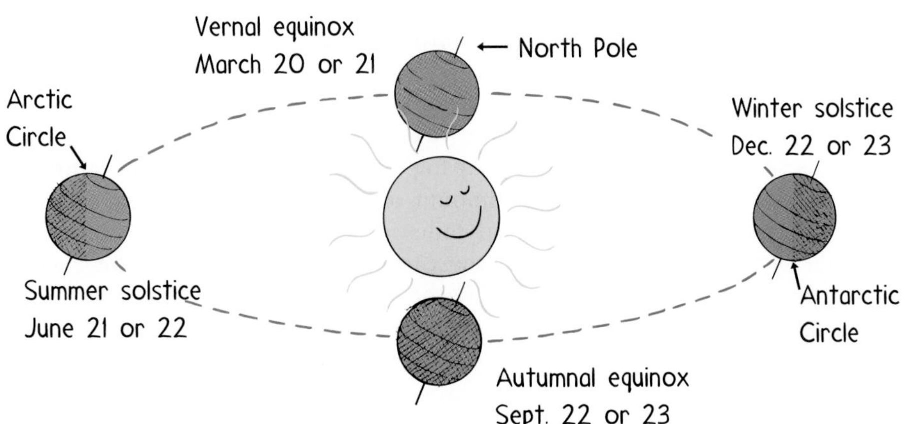

Figure 31.7
The tilt of the earth and the corresponding different spreading of solar radiation produce the yearly cycle of seasons.

nearly 24 hours during the summer solstice (around June 21), and night lasts about 24 hours at the winter solstice (around December 21). This latitude is called the Arctic Circle in the Northern Hemisphere and the Antarctic Circle in the Southern Hemisphere. During the summer solstice, the North Pole leans towards the sun and the South Pole leans away from the sun. (Summer and winter are reversed, of course, in the two hemispheres.)

Halfway between the peaks of the winter and summer solstice, around mid-September and mid-March, the hours of daylight and night are of equal length. These are called the equinoxes (Latin for "equal nights"). The equal hours of day and night during the equinoxes are not restricted to high latitudes but occur all over the world.

Another interesting phenomenon happens as you travel north of the Arctic Circle (or south of the Antarctic Circle). There are more summer days with the sun always above the horizon and more winter days with the sun always below the horizon! At the poles, there is a full six months of continuous sunlight followed by a full six months of continuous night! These 24-hour-long "days" in the polar regions are never very bright because the sun is never very far above the horizon. Likewise, the 24-hour-long "nights" aren't all that dark because the sun never sinks very far below the horizon.

☑ **CHECKPOINT**

Why are daylight hours fewer in winter months?

Check Your Answer

The earth is tilted on its axis, like a top leaning in one direction all the time. As the earth revolves around the sun, the Northern Hemisphere is tilted toward the sun in the summer and away from the sun during the winter. When tilted away, the sun is lower on the horizon. Hence the sun rises later and sets earlier, resulting in shorter days. If it weren't for the 23.5° tilt in the earth's axis, there would be no seasons.

Terrestrial Radiation

Solar radiation covers a wide spectrum of wavelengths, mostly in the visible short-wavelength part of the spectrum. The earth absorbs this energy, and in turn, reradiates part of it back to space. As we learned in Chapter 8, this is *terrestrial radiation,* emitted from the earth's surface (Figure 31.8). Terrestrial radiation is emitted in the infrared long-wavelength part of the spectrum.

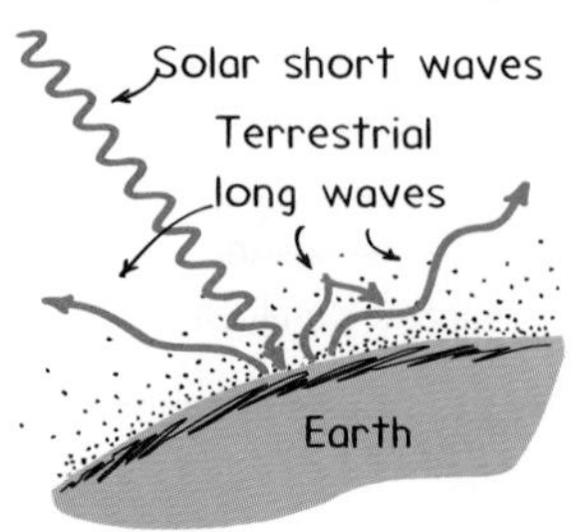

Figure 31.8
The hot sun emits short waves, and the cool earth reemits long waves. Radiation that is emitted from the earth is called terrestrial radiation.

Interestingly, it is terrestrial radiation rather than solar radiation that directly warms the lower atmosphere, which explains why air close to the ground is so much warmer than air at higher elevations. The temperature of the earth's surface depends on the amount of solar radiation coming in compared with the amount of terrestrial radiation going out. In direct sunlight, the net effect is warming, because the earth's surface absorbs more energy from the sun than it emits. At night, the net effect is cooling because the earth's surface emits more energy than it absorbs. Cloud cover blocks both incoming solar radiation and outgoing terrestrial radiation. Hence, cloudy days are much cooler than sunny days, and cloudy nights are generally warmer than clear nights.

The Greenhouse Effect and Global Warming

The earth absorbs short-wavelength radiation from the sun and reradiates it as long-wavelength terrestrial radiation. Incoming short-wavelength solar radiation easily penetrates the atmosphere to reach and warm the earth's surface, but outgoing long-wavelength terrestrial radiation cannot penetrate the atmosphere to escape into space. Instead, atmospheric gases (mainly water vapor and carbon dioxide) absorb the long-wave terrestrial radiation. As a result, this long-wave radiation ends up keeping the earth's surface warmer than it would be if there were no atmosphere. This process is very nice, for the earth would be a frigid −18°C otherwise! Our present environmental concern, however, is that increased levels of carbon dioxide and other gases in the atmosphere may make the earth *too* warm.

Much like the panes of glass in a greenhouse, atmospheric gases trap long-wave terrestrial radiation, thereby warming the lower atmosphere. This warming of the lower atmosphere is called the **greenhouse effect.** The greenhouse effect plays a significant role in global warming. Gases released primarily by volcanic eruptions, but also by the burning of fossil fuels (coal, oil, and gas) and from agricultural and manufacturing industries, add carbon dioxide and other greenhouse

Global Warming

The quantity of CO_2 in the atmosphere amounts to 670 billion tons. This accounts for only about 0.035 percent of the atmosphere, or about 350 parts per million of atmospheric gases. Be glad this is so. Without carbon dioxide, plants could not photosynthesize the biomaterials essential to almost all life forms on our planet. Optimum plant growth occurs at a temperature of 25°C and a CO_2 level of at least 800 parts per million (which is why CO_2 generators are used to elevate the CO_2 level in the air of commercial greenhouses). Concentrations of 5 parts per million CO_2 can barely support certain tropical grasses, while most other plants require a minimum of 50 parts per million.

Human use of fossil fuels has added to the amount of CO_2 in the atmosphere, but atmospheric concentrations of CO_2 haven't increased proportionately, mainly because of oceanic absorption (Section 25.2). Increased amounts of CO_2 accelerate plant growth and also allow plants to grow in drier regions. Animal life, which depends upon plants, also flourishes. So why such an alarm over increased levels of CO_2 in the atmosphere?

Increased CO_2 concentrations heighten the greenhouse effect; that is, sunlight still gets through the atmosphere, but infrared terrestrial waves do not. So atmospheric temperature rises. Interestingly, the gas most responsible for the greenhouse effect is not CO_2, but rather H_2O! There is little concern about water vapor, however, because levels have been fairly constant in recent times. Increased amounts of CO_2 mean a higher average temperature for the planet, which means more melting of polar ice caps and higher sea levels—in short, a different world climate. Does "different" mean better or worse? Although the earth is currently in a long-term warming trend, it has been much warmer during the past 3000 years—without environmental calamities. The earth's average temperature goes through cycles, altered by differences in sunlight and a host of factors other than CO_2 levels. Change one thing and you change another. So, between the extremes of no CO_2 (a world without plants and animals as we know them) and exceedingly high CO_2, as on the planet Venus (a world without life as we know it), lies a favorable balance.

What the favorable balance is and how the earth's climate will change are both questions open to further research.

gases to the atmosphere, changing its composition. This compositional change, in turn, affects atmospheric absorption of both solar and terrestrial energy.

Of all the greenhouse gases, water vapor plays the largest role in confining the earth's heat. As part of the earth's natural hydrologic cycle, water vapor levels have remained relatively constant throughout time. Like water vapor, carbon dioxide occurs naturally in the earth's atmosphere. Unlike water-vapor levels, however, carbon dioxide levels are on the rise. Since the Industrial Revolution of the 1800s, atmospheric carbon dioxide levels have been steadily increasing. This increase may account for the warming of the earth's surface by about 0.6°C since 1850. Some scientists and policy makers believe that further warming will likely occur if carbon dioxide emissions are not held in check. Other gases, such as methane, nitrous oxides, and CFCs (chlolrofluorocarbons) are also on the increase. As such, they too may play a role in changing the earth's atmosphere.

The effects of warming the earth's surface are not fully known. One concern is that warming will cause the polar ice caps to melt. This would raise sea level so that low-lying coastal lands would be flooded. Warming would also likely change rainfall patterns, seriously affecting agricultural industries. The grain-growing regions of North America and Asia might shift northward as local climates warmed and growing seasons lengthened. On the other hand, deserts in the interiors of continents might spread to cover much larger areas. We don't know. What we do know is that the earth has experienced warmer and colder periods in times past and that global-scale climatic changes may have contributed to many of the extinctions discussed in Chapter 30. More research is needed to allow us to understand fully the impacts of global warming.

☑ CHECKPOINT

1. What does it mean to say that the greenhouse effect is like a one-way valve?
2. Which gas in the atmosphere is the greatest contributor to the greenhouse effect?
3. What is the primary contributor to the greenhouse gases in the earth's atmosphere?

Check Your Answers

1. The transparent material—atmosphere for the earth and glass for the florist's greenhouse—passes only incoming short waves and blocks outgoing long waves. In other words, radiation travels only one way.
2. Water vapor.
3. Volcanic eruptions. Interestingly, the volcanic eruption of Mount Pinatubo in 1991 spewed more chlorine into the atmosphere than the combined leakage of CFCs over a century.

31.4 Driving Forces of Air Motion

Link to Section 3.11

We know that, as warm air rises, it expands and cools. As the air rises, cooler air sinks to occupy the region left vacant by the rising warm air. Such motion constitutes a convection cycle and thermal circulation of the air—in other words, a *convection current*. As convection currents stir the atmosphere, the result is *wind*—defined as air with an average horizontal motion. Wind is generated in response to pressure differences in the atmosphere, which are largely the result of temperature differences. A difference in pressure between two different locations is called a *pressure gradient,* and the force that causes air to move is called the **pressure-gradient force.**

To see how temperature affects pressure, consider the two equivalent air columns shown in Figure 31.9a. The two air columns are equivalent because they contain the same number of molecules distributed uniformly. To aid visualization, we make three simplifying assumptions: (1) that there is no change in air density with height (air density is constant), (2) that air cannot enter or leave either column (volume is constant), and (3) that the width of each column remains constant. So, we have a fixed amount of air at constant density that can only move up or down.

When the cities are at the same temperature, the columns are the same height, as in Figure 31.9a. At any elevation—say, the elevation marked X in the drawing—the air columns have the same air pressure, because the number of air molecules above X is the same in both cases. This is true for any elevation. Thus, we have no pressure difference between the two cities at any elevation because we have no temperature difference.

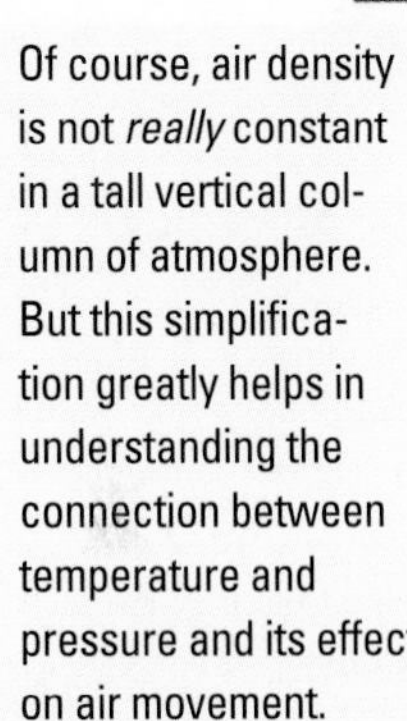

Of course, air density is not *really* constant in a tall vertical column of atmosphere. But this simplification greatly helps in understanding the connection between temperature and pressure and its effect on air movement.

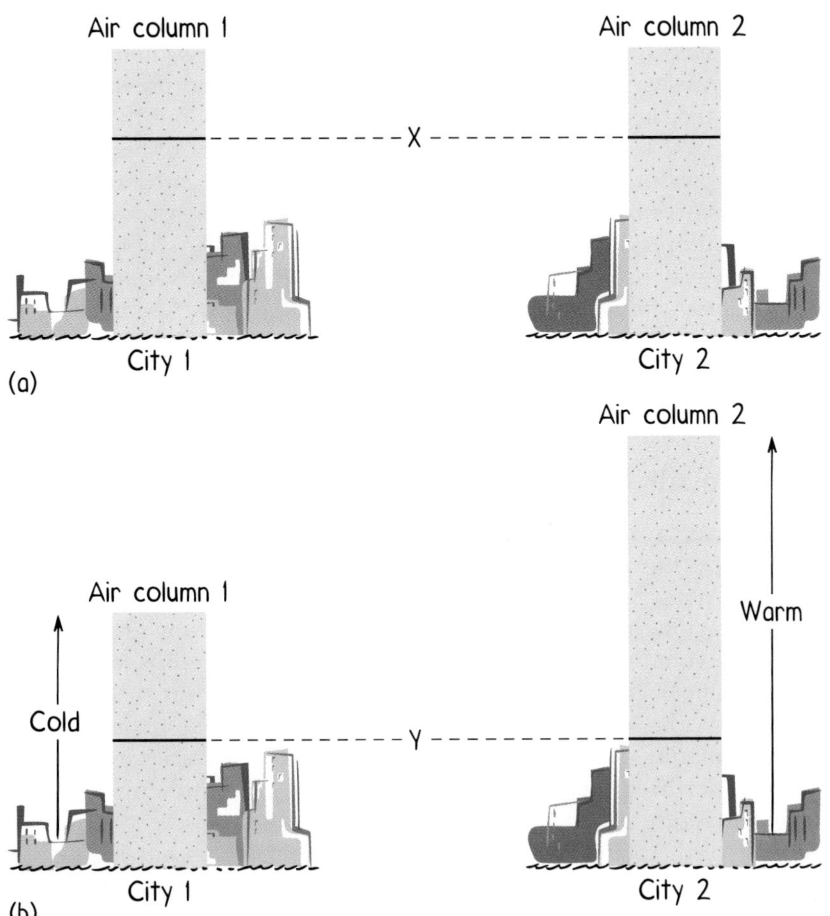

Figure 31.9
(a) Air columns of the same temperature over two cities. Note that the air pressure at any elevation, such as elevation X shown here, is the same for both cities. (b) When City 1 is cold and City 2 is warm, the air column over City 2 is taller due to expansion, which means that, for an equal given elevation, pressure is greater in the taller column. This produces a pressure gradient between the two cities. So wind blows from City 2 to City 1.

Now suppose that the temperature in City 1 drops while the temperature in City 2 rises. In this case, we get the situation shown in Figure 31.9b. The cooling air over City 1 contracts and becomes denser, and the warming air over City 2 expands and becomes less dense. We still have the same number of air molecules over each city, but we have a cool, short air column over city 1 and a warmer, much taller air column over city 2. So, although the ground-level pressure is still the same in the two cities (because equal numbers of air molecules are pressing down on both), we now can see differences in the pressure of the air aloft.

Air aloft is defined as air higher than 1 km above the ground. Consider elevation Y, halfway up air column 1. Because Y is at the midway point, the top half of air column 1 contains half the total number of molecules (again, assuming constant density with height). This same elevation Y must be less than midway up air column 2, and so the part of column 2 above this elevation contains more than half of its air molecules. Because there are more air molecules bearing down at elevation Y in air column 2 than in air column 1, the air *pressure* at Y must be greater in column 2 than it is in column 1. In other words, a difference in temperature has led to a difference in pressure. So, the number of air molecules above any level provides a measure of atmospheric pressure. We come to a very important concept: *Warm air aloft is associated with high atmospheric pressure aloft, and cold air aloft is associated with low atmospheric pressure aloft.*

So what does this pressure difference at elevations of a kilometer or more have to do with wind at the earth's surface? Differences in pressure cause the air to move and, hence, the wind to blow. Let us now allow the air between City 1 and City 2 to mingle. Because air moves from areas of high pressure to areas of low pressure, the wind aloft will blow from City 2 toward City 1. As the air aloft moves from air column 2, air density will decrease and the surface pressure will drop. Meanwhile, as air accumulates in cooler column 1, the surface pressure will rise. Thus we find that *cold days are associated with high surface pressure, and warm days are associated with low surface pressure.* Now that the surface pressure is higher in City 1, surface winds will blow from City 1 to City 2. This, in turn, will change the pressure distribution again, as air moves away from City 1. A dynamic system indeed.

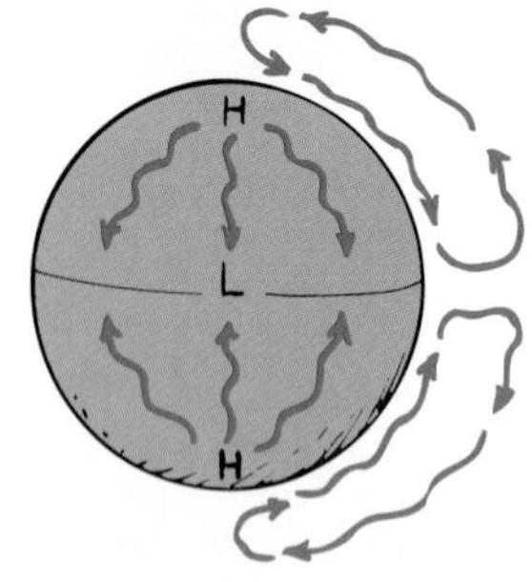

Figure 31.10
If the earth were simply a nonrotating sphere, air circulation would be in a single Northern Hemisphere cell and a single Southern Hemisphere cell. In each cell, heated air would rise at the equator and move toward the polar regions, where it would cool, sink, and be drawn back to the warmer regions of the equator.

Large-Scale Air Movement

The underlying cause of general air circulation is the unequal heating of the earth's surface. On a global level, equatorial regions receive optimum radiant energy from the sun and, as a result, have higher average temperatures than other regions of the world. As air heated by the hot ground (or the ocean) at the equator rises, it moves toward the polar regions, cooling gradually in the upper atmosphere. This cooled air then sinks at the poles and is drawn back to the warmer regions near the equator. If we assume the earth to be a nonrotating sphere, the effect is one simple single-cell circulation pattern in the Northern Hemisphere and another in the Southern Hemisphere, as shown in Figure 31.10.

But the earth rotates, which greatly affects the path of moving air. Think of the earth as a large merry-go-round rotating in a counterclockwise direction (in the same direction as the earth spins, as viewed from above the North

Pole). Pretend that you and a friend are playing catch on this merry-go-round. When you throw the ball to your friend, the circular movement of the merry-go-round affects the direction the ball appears to travel. Although the ball travels in a straight-line path, it appears to curve to the right, as shown in Figure 31.11. (The ball travels straight, but your friend never catches it, because the movement of the merry-go-round causes his position to change.) This apparent curving is similar to what happens on the earth. As the earth spins, all free-moving objects—air and water, aircraft and ballistic missiles, and even snowballs, to a small extent—appear to deviate from their straight-line paths as the earth rotates under them. This apparent deflection due to the rotation of the earth is called the **Coriolis effect.**

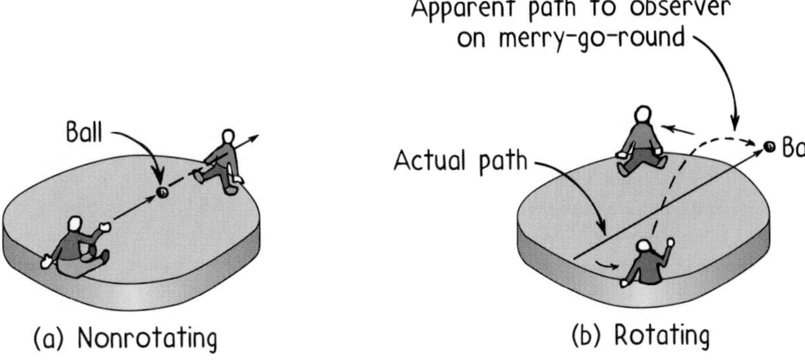

Figure 31.11
(a) On the nonrotating merry-go-round, a thrown ball travels in a straight line. (b) On the counterclockwise-rotating merry-go-round, the ball moves in a straight line. However, because the merry-go-round is rotating, the ball appears to deflect to the right of its intended path.

A significant result of the Coriolis effect is the apparent deflection of winds toward the right in the Northern Hemisphere and toward the left in the Southern Hemisphere (Figure 31.12). The impact of the Coriolis effect varies

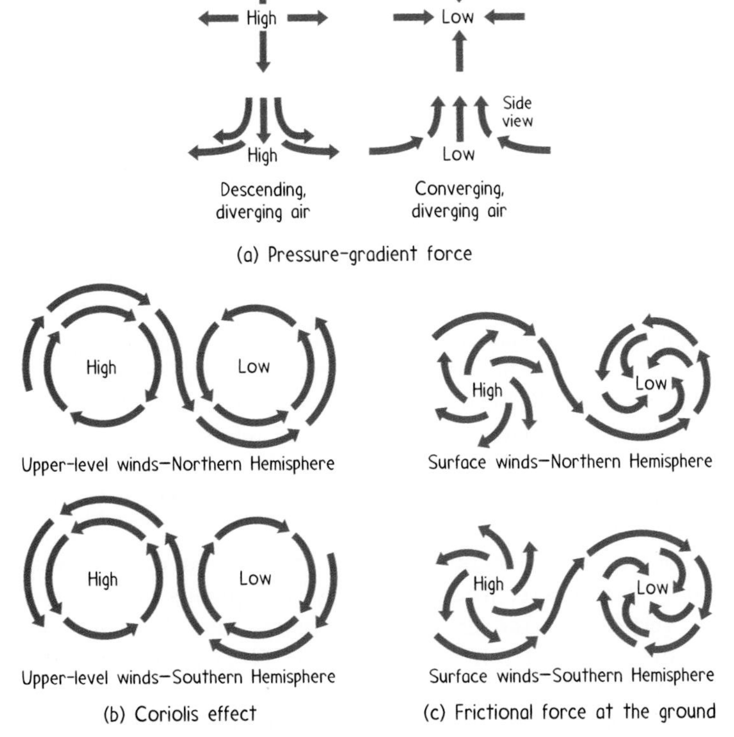

Figure 31.12
The Coriolis effect—the apparent deflection of winds from straight-line paths by the earth's rotation—is a principal force in the production of wind. It is, however, not the only force. (a) First of all, air moves due to pressure differences—the pressure gradient force. (b) Once the air is moving, it is affected by the earth's rotation—the Coriolis effect. (c) As air moves close to the ground, it slows due to frictional force.

Air circulation affects ocean surface currents, as was found during a severe storm in 1990. Five cargo containers of athletic shoes were washed overboard from freighters en route from South Korea to the Pacific Northwest. Thousands of sneakers, hiking boots, and other shoes were picked up along beaches from British Columbia to Oregon and as far into the mid-Pacific as Hawaii. Although months at sea left many shoes mismatched, most shoes were still wearable after washing. Beachcombers formed "swap meets" to search for mates of found shoes!

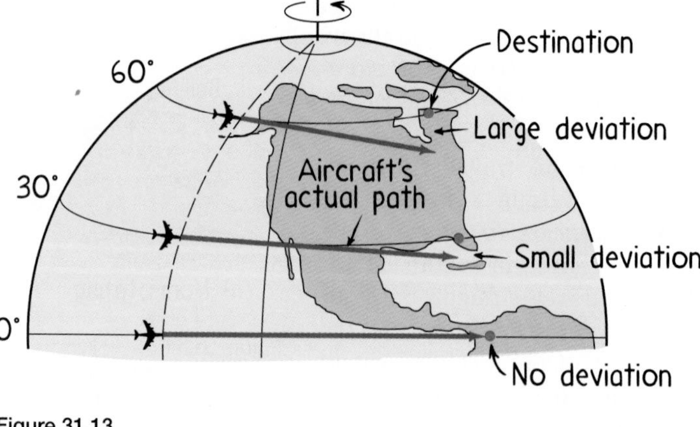

Figure 31.13
Latitude influences the apparent deflection resulting from the Coriolis effect. A free-moving object heading east (or west) appears to deviate from its straight-line path as the earth rotates beneath it. Deflection is greatest at the poles and decreases to zero at the equator.

according to the speed of the wind. The faster the wind, the greater the deflection. Latitude also influences the degree of deflection. Deflection is greatest at the poles and decreases to zero at the equator (Figure 31.13).

Air moving close to the earth's surface encounters a *frictional force.* The rougher the surface, the greater the friction, and so the greater the drag. Because surface friction reduces wind speed, it reduces the effect of the Coriolis force. This causes winds in the Northern Hemisphere to spiral out clockwise from a high-pressure region and spiral counterclockwise into a low-pressure region (top part of Figure 31.12c). In the Southern Hemisphere, these circulation patterns are reversed (bottom part of Figure 31.12c).

The Coriolis effect is evident only for large parcels of air or water, where one part has a greater tangential speed than the other about the earth's axis. Don't believe stories about swirling water in your sink being affected by the Coriolis effect. (Any effect due to difference in speeds of one part of the sink compared with the other are miniscule, and they are masked by thermal motions in the water.)

31.5 Global Circulation Patterns

Cell-like circulation patterns are responsible for the redistribution of heat across the earth's surface and for the global winds (Figure 31.14). At the equator, warmed air flows straight up with very little horizontal movement, resulting in a vast low-pressure zone. This rising motion creates a narrow, windless realm of air that is still, hot, and stagnant. Seamen of long ago cursed the equatorial seas as their ships floated listlessly for lack of wind, and they referred to the area as the *doldrums.* When the moist air from the doldrums rises, it cools and releases torrents of rain. Over land areas, such frequent rains give rise to the tropical rain forests that characterize the equatorial region.

The air of the sweltering doldrums rises to the boundary between the troposphere and stratosphere, where it divides and spreads out to the north and the south. (Very little wind crosses the equator into the neighboring hemisphere.) By the time it has reached about 30°N and 30°S latitudes, this air has cooled enough that it descends toward the surface. The descending air warms as it is compressed. A resulting high-pressure zone girdles the earth, creating a belt of hot, dry surface air. On land, these high-pressure zones account for the world's great deserts—the Sahara in Africa, the Arabian Desert in the Middle East, the Mojave Desert in the United States, and the Great Victoria Desert in Australia. At sea, the hot, descending air produces very weak winds. According to legend, early sailing ships were frequently stalled at these latitudes, both north and south. As food and water supplies dwindled, horses on board were either eaten or cast overboard to conserve fresh water. As a result, this region is now known as the *horse latitudes*. The thermal convection cycle that starts at the equator is completed when air flowing southward from the horse latitudes in the Northern Hemisphere and northward in the Southern Hemisphere is deflected westward to produce the *trade winds*. Air that flows northward from the horse latitudes in the Northern Hemisphere and southward in the Southern Hemisphere is deflected eastward to produce the prevailing *westerlies*.

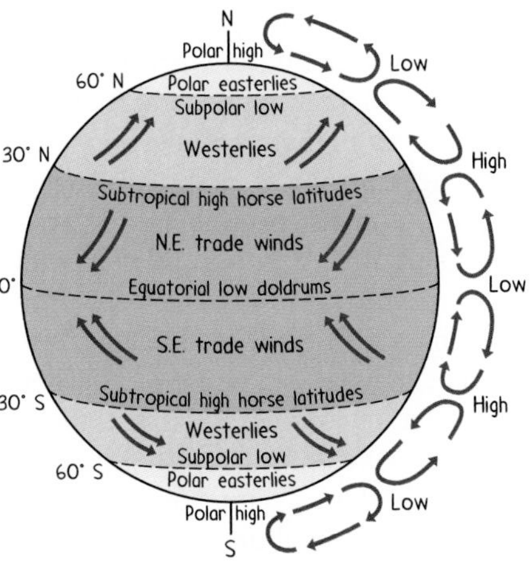

Figure 31.14
Global winds are the result of several cell-like circulation patterns, brought about by unequal heating of the earth's surface and compounded by effects of the earth's rotation.

In the polar regions, frigid air continuously sinks, pushing the surface air outward. The Coriolis effect is quite evident in the polar regions, as the wind deflects to the west to create the *polar easterlies* (Figure 31.14). The cool, dry polar air meets the warm, moist air of the westerlies at latitudes 60°N and 60°S. This boundary, called the *polar front,* is a zone of low pressure where contrasting air masses converge, often resulting in storms.

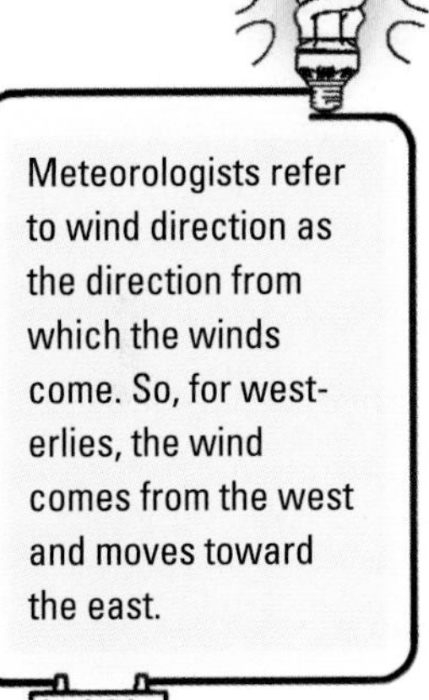

The middle latitudes are noted for their unpredictable weather. Although the winds tend to be westerlies, they are often quite changeable, as the temperature and pressure differences between the subtropical and polar air masses at the polar front produce powerful winds. As air moves from regions of high pressure, where air is denser, toward regions of low pressure, the result is a *cyclone* effect.

Irregularities in the earth's surface also influence wind behavior. Mountains, valleys, deserts, forests, and great bodies of water all play a part in determining which way the wind blows.

Upper Atmospheric Circulation

In the upper troposphere, "rivers" of rapidly moving air meander around the earth at altitudes of 9–14 kilometers. These high-speed winds are the *jet streams*. With wind speeds averaging between 95 and 190 kilometers per hour, the jet streams play an essential role in the global transfer of thermal energy from the equator to the poles.

The two most important jet streams, the *polar jet stream* and the *subtropical jet stream,* form in both the Northern and Southern Hemispheres. The formation of polar jet streams is a result of a temperature gradient at the polar front—at about 60°N and 60°S latitudes—where cool polar air meets warm tropical air. This temperature gradient causes a steep pressure gradient that

(a)

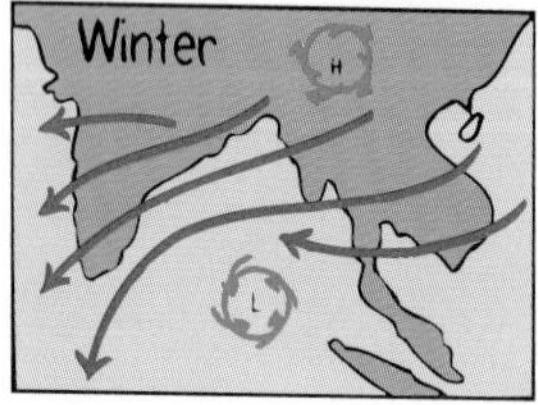

(b)

Figure 31.15
Winds over Southeast Asia. (a) During the summer months, air over the oceans is cooler than the air over land. The summer monsoon brings heavy rains, as the winds blow from sea to land. (b) During the winter months, air over continents is cooler than air over oceans. The winter monsoon generally has clear skies and winds that blow from land to sea.

increases the wind speed. During the winter, the polar jet stream is strong and extensive as it migrates to lower latitudes, bringing strong winter storms and blizzards to the United States. In summer, the polar jet stream is weaker and migrates to higher latitudes.

The subtropical jet stream is generated as warm air is carried from the equator to the poles, producing a sharp temperature gradient along the subtropical front—about 30°N and 30°S latitudes. Once again, a pressure gradient caused by the temperature gradient generates strong winds.

The subtropical jet stream above Southeast Asia, India, and Africa merits special mention (Figure 31.15). The formation of this jet stream is related to the warming of the air above the Tibetan highlands. During the summer, the air above the continental highlands is warmer than the air above the ocean to the south. Thus, temperature and pressure gradients generate strong on-shore winds that contribute to the region's *monsoon* (rainy) climate. During winter, the winds change direction to produce a dry season.

This cycle of winds characterizes the climates of much of Southeast Asia. The predictable rain-bearing summer wind from the sea that moves over the heated land is called the *summer monsoon;* the prevailing wind from land to sea in winter is called the *winter monsoon.*

☑ CHECKPOINT

1. What are the main causes of the trade winds, jet streams, and monsoons?
2. In the middle latitudes, airlines schedule shorter flight times for planes traveling west to east and longer flight times for planes traveling east to west. Why are eastbound planes faster?

Check Your Answers

1. Simply enough, the unequal heating of the earth's surface coupled with the earth's rotation.
2. The upper-level westerly winds of the jet stream account for faster-moving eastbound aircraft. As the jet stream moves from west to east, it carries along everything in its path. To save time and fuel, airline pilots seek the jet stream when traveling west to east and avoid it when traveling east to west.

Oceanic Circulation

The forces that drive the winds also affect the movement of seawater. In the open ocean, the major movement of seawater results from two types of currents: wind-driven surface currents and density-driven, deep-water currents. Near coastlines, water movement is affected not only by surface and deep-water currents but also by coastal boundaries.

The density of seawater is controlled by two things—temperature and salinity. The oceans are "salty." Salts make up more than 99 percent of the ocean's dissolved materials. The principal elements that contribute to the ocean's salinity include chloride, sodium, sulfate, magnesium, calcium, and potassium (Table 31.2). The amount of dissolved salts in seawater is measured as **salinity**—the mass of salts dissolved in 1000 grams of seawater. Although salinity varies from one part of the ocean to another, the overall composition of seawater is about the same from place to place—a mixture of about 96.5 percent water and

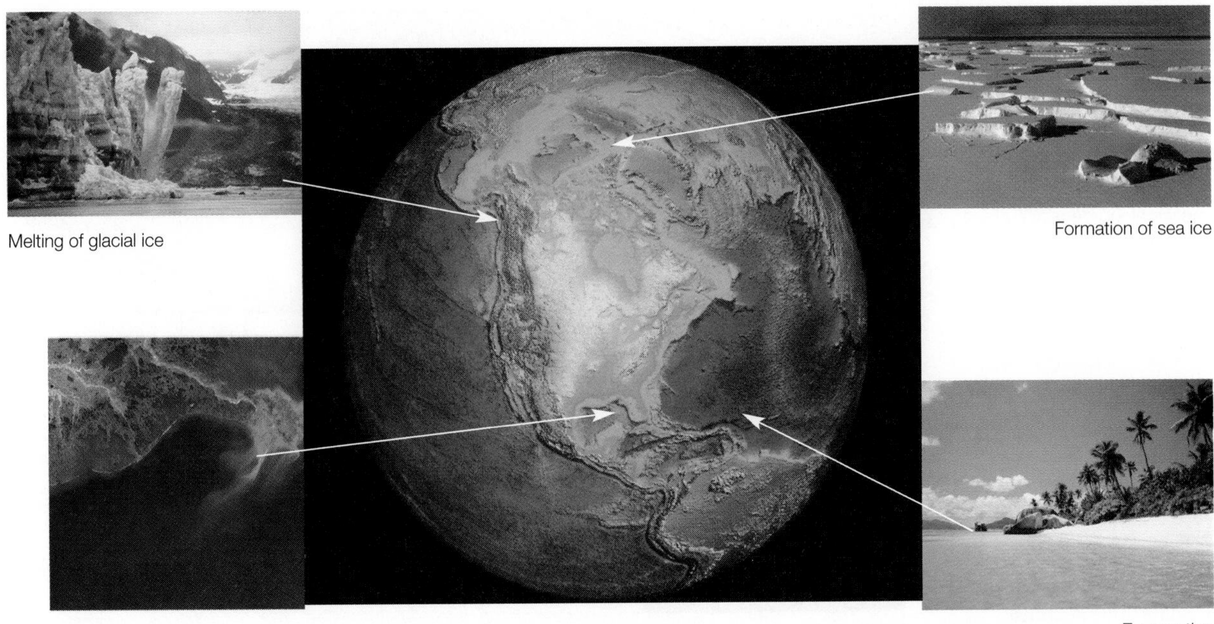

Figure 31.16
Factors that increase salinity include the formation of sea ice and evaporation. Salinity increases as the supply of fresh water decreases. Factors that decrease salinity include the runoff from streams and rivers, precipitation, and the melting of glacial ice and icebergs. Salinity decreases as the supply of fresh water increases.

3.5 percent salts. Variation is, of course, influenced by factors that increase or decrease supplies of fresh water (Figure 31.16). Fresh water enters the ocean in three ways: runoff from streams and rivers, precipitation, and the melting of glacial ice. Fresh water leaves the ocean in two ways: evaporation and the formation of ice. Overall balance is maintained when evaporation is offset by precipitation and runoff, and ice formation is offset by ice melting.

Table 31.2

Principal Elements in Sea Salts

Element	Chemical Symbol	Percentage by Weight
Chloride	Cl^-	55.07
Sodium	Na^+	30.62
Sulfate	SO_4^-	7.72
Magnesium	Mg^{++}	3.68
Calcium	Ca^{++}	1.17
Potassium	K^+	1.10
Total		99.36

Like the atmosphere, the ocean can be divided into several vertical layers—the surface zone, a transition zone, and the deep zone. Scuba divers notice an increase in water pressure when swimming to lower depths. The deeper the descent, the greater the water pressure. The pressure is simply the weight of the water above you pushing against you. Another factor that generally changes as you descend is temperature. Deeper waters are cooler. So, in addition to variations in salinity, seawater also varies in temperature and pressure. Because cold water is denser than warm water, cold seawater sinks below warmer seawater.

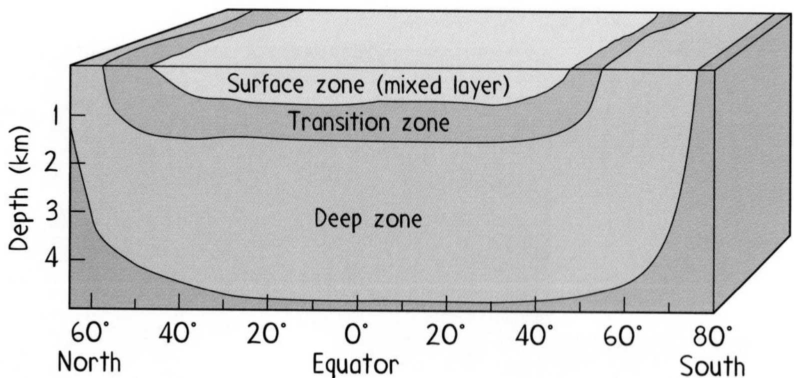

Figure 31.17
The ocean's vertical structure. In the surface zone, water is well-mixed as it moves vertically in response to temperature and density changes, and it moves horizontally in response to wind. Water in the transition zone moves along density surfaces. Water in the deep zone is density-driven, as it circulates from cold polar regions to warmer equatorial regions.

The salinity of the water also affects density: the greater the salinity, the greater the density. These variations are best illustrated when we look at the ocean's vertical structure (Figure 31.17).

From where do the ocean's salts originate? One source is the chemical weathering of continental rocks. As the rocks are weathered, chemicals dissolve in the water. The water carrying these chemicals usually flows downstream and makes its way to the ocean. Another source of salts is the earth's interior. For eons, volcanic eruptions have delivered huge quantities of sodium and chloride ions, as well as water vapor and other gases, to the ocean's waters. Hence the ocean's salty taste.

Insights

☑ CHECKPOINT

Would you expect the pressure 100 m deep in the equatorial Pacific to be the same as it is 100 m deep in the northern Pacific?

Check Your Answer

Probably not. If salinity is the same at both locations (a good assumption, if we are away from coastal areas), the pressure will be slightly higher in the cold northern Pacific. Remember, cold water is denser than warm water, and so a volume of cold water weighs more than an equal volume of warm water. Pressure is the weight per unit of area.

Surface Currents

As winds blow across the ocean, frictional forces set surface waters into motion. If distances are short, the surface waters move in the same direction as the wind. For longer distances, however, other factors come into play. One such factor is the deflective Coriolis effect, which causes surface waters to spiral in a circular whirl pattern called a **gyre.** The circular motion is clockwise in the Northern Hemisphere and counterclockwise in the Southern Hemisphere.

In the tropics, the trade winds drive equatorial ocean currents westward. When the westward flow is blocked by a continental shoreline, the current splits, with some flow going north and some going south. At temperate latitudes, the prevailing westerlies take over to drive the surface currents eastward. In the Northern Hemisphere, huge gyres are created as eastward moving water encounters land boundaries. In the Southern Hemisphere, with fewer land obstructions, the eastward flow is able to encircle the globe (Figure 31.18).

An important consequence of these large gyres is the transport of heat from equatorial regions to higher latitudes. In the North Atlantic Ocean, for example, warm equatorial water flows westward into and around the Gulf of Mexico, then northward along the eastern coast of the United States. This warm-water current is called the *Gulf Stream.* As the Gulf Stream flows northward along the North American coast, the prevailing westerlies steer the warm current eastward toward

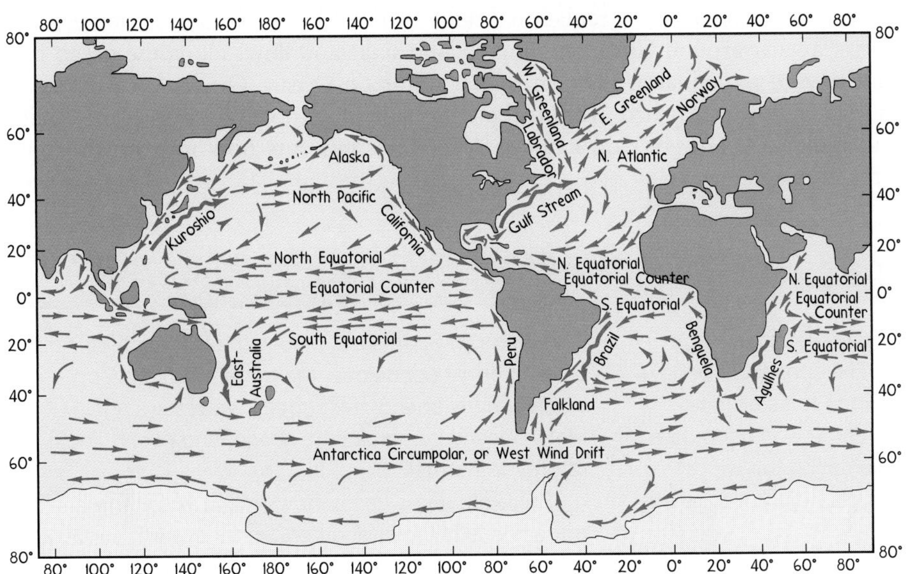

Figure 31.18
The circulation patterns of the ocean's surface waters. The names of the major currents are indicated.

Europe (Figure 31.18). Great Britain and Norway benefit from the warm waters in the Gulf Stream, for lands at this northern latitude would be much colder were they not being warmed by water from the Gulf of Mexico. As the warm current encounters Europe, it is turned southward toward the equator, where it is once again picked up by the trade winds to move westward into the Gulf of Mexico and, once again, to become part of the Gulf Stream.

Oceanic circulation in the North Pacific is similar to that in the North Atlantic. The Pacific counterpart of the Gulf Stream is the warm, northward-flowing current known as the *Kuroshio*. In the Southern Hemisphere, surface oceanic circulation (with the exception of the Antarctica Circumpolar Current) is similar, except that the gyres move counterclockwise.

Deep-Water Currents

Surface waters are driven by winds, but deeper waters are driven by gravity—deep water flows because dense water sinks. Although deep water flows more slowly than surface water, the volume of deep-water flow can be likened to a large global conveyor belt (Figure 31.19).

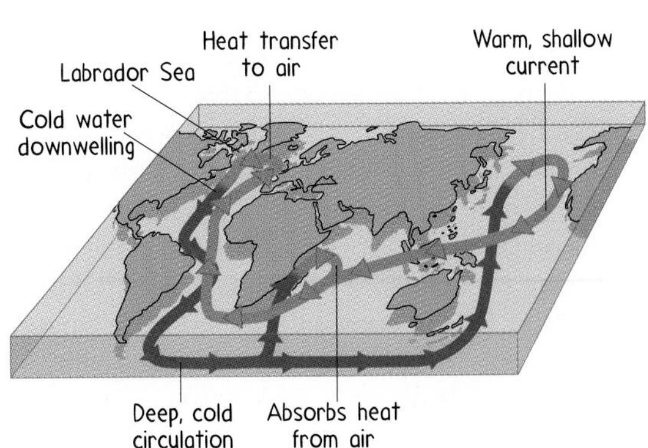

Figure 31.19
Deep-ocean currents act like a conveyor belt, transporting cold water from the North Atlantic to the equator and on to the Antarctic. From the Antarctic, water flows eastward and then northward into the Pacific Ocean and the Indian Ocean.

In the high latitudes, where seawater in the deep zone interacts with seawater in the surface zone, a very slow, worldwide, north–south circulation pattern develops. To understand how this pattern develops, we need to look at what happens when seawater begins to freeze.

Seawater does not freeze easily. When it does, however, only the water freezes and the salt is left behind. Thus, the seawater that does not freeze experiences an increase in salinity, which, in turn, causes an increase in density. The cold, denser, saltier seawater sinks, which sets up a pattern of vertical movement. There is also horizontal movement, as the dense water that sinks in the polar regions flows along the bottom to the deeper parts of the ocean floor.

Thus, conveyor-belt circulation begins in the North Atlantic as dense, cold, salty seawater around Greenland and Iceland sinks and flows along the ocean bottom toward the equator, then on to the Antarctic Ocean. Once near Antarctica, the water flows eastward around the continent, then northward into the Pacific and Indian Oceans. As you can see deep-water currents flow in a north–south circulation pattern.

The El Niño Condition

When weather is measured over time, an *average* weather pattern can be seen. The consistent behavior of weather over time is referred to as climate. There are periods when the *average* weather pattern departs from its norm, thus disrupting the expected climate. A prime example of such a disruption is the El Niño condition.

Under normal conditions, weather patterns in the Pacific are controlled by warm, high-pressure systems located in both hemispheres near the equator. These high-pressure systems cause the trade winds to blow westward along the equator, dragging the warm equatorial surface waters along with them. As warm surface waters move westward, deeper, colder waters to the east rise upward to occupy the space left vacant by the warm surface water. The upwelling cold waters, rich in nutrients, attract a variety of sea life. Upwelling of these cold waters has been especially important to the fishing industry along the west coast of South America, where people earn their living catching anchovies that come to feed in the nutrient-rich waters.

Fishing is not always good, however. Each year in October, the trade winds slacken, reversing the normal westward flow of warm tropical surface waters. As the warm surface waters drift eastward, upwelling decreases and so does the fishing industry. People along the South American coast refer to this occurrence as El Niño because it appears to begin each year around the traditional December celebration of Christmas (in Spanish, *el niño* is the Christ child). Under normal conditions, the trade winds pick up again in early spring, the surface waters are again blown westward across the ocean, and everything returns to normal.

There are some years, however, in which the trade winds fail to strengthen, and the warm surface waters remain off the coast of South America for a year or longer. During these abnormal conditions, upwelling of cold water ceases, and South American fishing industries fail. Although a small El Niño occurs each year, it is this extended El Niño that is referred to as the **El Niño condition.**

The El Niño condition influences climate on both sides of the tropical Pacific Ocean. Under normal conditions, upwelling cold water on the eastern side of the Pacific coincides with dry and cool air, high pressures, and clear skies. On the western side of the Pacific, surface waters—which have been warmed and fueled by their long journey across the ocean—warm the surrounding air. As the warm and moist air rises, low pressures and storms develop on the warm western side of the Pacific.

During an extended El Niño condition, the pattern is reversed. Warm water, rising warm and moist air, low pressures, and storms are found on the eastern side of the Pacific rather than the western side. This exchange of pressure systems and weather patterns between east and west during an El Niño condition is sometimes called the *southern oscillation*.

Summary of Terms

Troposphere The atmospheric layer closest to the earth's surface, 16 km high over the equator and 8 km high over the poles, containing 90 percent of the atmosphere's mass and essentially all of its water vapor and clouds.

Stratosphere The second atmospheric layer above the earth's surface, extending from the top of the troposphere up to 50 km.

Mesosphere The third atmospheric layer above the earth's surface, extending from the top of the stratosphere to 80 km.

Thermosphere The fourth atmospheric layer above the earth's surface, extending from the top of the mesosphere to 500 km.

Ionosphere An electrified region within the thermosphere and uppermost mesosphere, where fairly large concentrations of ions and free electrons exist.

Exosphere The fifth atmospheric layer above the earth's surface, extending from the thermosphere upward and out into interplanetary space.

Greenhouse effect A warming caused by short-wavelength radiant energy from the sun that easily enters the atmosphere and is absorbed by the earth. This energy is then reradiated at longer wavelengths that cannot easily escape the earth's atmosphere.

Pressure-gradient force The force that moves air from a region of high pressure to an adjacent region of low pressure.

Coriolis effect The apparent deflection from a straight-line path observed in any body moving near the earth's surface, caused by the earth's rotation.

Salinity The mass of salts dissolved in 1000 g of seawater.

Gyre A circular or spiral whirl pattern, usually referring to very large current systems in the open ocean.

Review Questions

31.1 Earth's Atmosphere and Oceans

1. Why do we have moderate temperatures on lands bordering the oceans?
2. What were the main components of the earth's first atmosphere? What happened to this atmosphere?
3. The earth's present atmosphere likely developed from gases that escaped from the interior of the earth during volcanic eruptions. What were the three principal atmospheric gases produced by these eruptions?
4. Explain the importance of photosynthesis in the evolution of the atmosphere.

31.2 Components of the Earth's Atmosphere

5. What elements make up today's atmosphere?
6. Being that our atmosphere developed as a result of volcanic eruptions, why aren't there higher traces of atmospheric carbon dioxide, one of the principal volcanic gases?
7. Why doesn't gravity flatten the atmosphere against the earth's surface?
8. Why is the thermosphere so much hotter than the mesosphere?
9. What is the source of the ions that give the ionosphere its name?
10. In which atmospheric layer does all of our weather occur?
11. Does temperature increase or decrease as one moves upward in the troposphere? As one moves upward in the stratosphere?
12. What causes the fiery displays of light called the auroras?

31.3 Solar Energy

13. What does the angle at which light from the sun strikes the earth have to do with the temperate and polar regions?
14. What does the tilt of the earth have to do with the change of seasons?
15. Why are the hours of daylight equal all around the earth on the two equinoxes?
16. When it is winter and January in Chicago, what are the corresponding season and month in Sydney, Australia?
17. How does radiation emitted from the earth differ from that emitted by the sun?
18. How is the atmosphere near the earth's surface heated from below?

31.4 Driving Forces of Air Motion

19. What are the two main driving forces of air motion?
20. What is the underlying cause of air motion?
21. In what direction does the earth spin—west to east, or east to west?
22. What does the Coriolis effect do to winds? To ocean currents?
23. How does the Coriolis effect determine the general path of air circulation?
24. How does the Coriolis effect influence the movement of surface waters?

31.5 Global Circulation Patterns

25. What is the characteristic climate of the doldrums, and why does it occur?
26. Why do winds come predominately from the west in temperate latitudes?
27. Why are most of the world's deserts found in the area known as the horse latitudes?
28. What are the trade winds?
29. In summer, Southeast Asia, India, and Africa experience heavy flooding. Why?
30. What is the name given to the area where cold polar air meets the warm air of the temperate zone?
31. Why are eastbound aircraft flights usually faster than westbound ones?
32. What factors set surface ocean currents into motion?
33. Explain the circulation pattern of the Gulf Stream.
34. How does the density of seawater vary with changes in temperature? How does density change with salinity?
35. Explain why most of the bottom water of the oceans forms in the North Atlantic and near Antarctica.

Exercises

1. It being true that a gas fills all the space available to it, why doesn't the atmosphere go off into space?
2. Explain why your ears pop when you ascend to higher altitudes.
3. How does the density of air in a deep mine compare with the density of air at sea level? Defend your answer.
4. The earth is closest to the sun in January, but January is cold in the Northern Hemisphere. Why?
5. How do the total number of hours of sunlight in a year compare for tropical regions and polar regions of the earth? Why are polar regions so much colder?
6. How do the wavelengths of radiant energy vary with the temperature of the radiating source? How does this affect solar and terrestrial radiation?
7. How is global warming affected by the relative transparencies of the atmosphere to long- and short-wavelength electromagnetic radiation?
8. If the composition of the upper atmosphere were changed so that it permitted a greater amount of terrestrial radiation to escape, what effect would this have on the earth's average temperature? How about if the atmosphere reduced the amount of terrestrial radiation that could escape?
9. As humans consume more energy, the average temperature of the earth's surface tends to rise. Yet, no matter how much energy is consumed, the temperature doesn't rise without limit. By what process is an indefinite rise prevented? Explain.
10. As the world's population increases, the amount of carbon dioxide emissions from fossil fuel combustion also increases. Yet the amount of carbon dioxide emitted is greater than the amount found in the atmosphere. Where is the likely repository of excess atmospheric carbon dioxide?
11. Why is it important that mountain climbers wear sunglasses and use sunblock even when the temperature is below freezing?
12. If there were no water on the earth's surface, would weather occur? Defend your answer.
13. If the earth were not spinning, in what direction would the surface winds blow where you live? In what direction does it blow on the real earth at 15° S latitude and why?
14. What is the relationship between global atmospheric circulation and ocean currents? Relate oceanic gyres to patterns of subtropical high pressure.
15. Relate the jet stream to upper-air circulation. How does this circulation pattern relate to airline schedules from New York to San Francisco and from San Francisco to New York?
16. What are the jet streams, and how do they form?
17. Why are temperature fluctuations greater over land than over water? Explain.
18. Because seawater does not freeze easily, sea ice never gets very thick. This being true, from where do large icebergs originate?
19. The Mediterranean Sea is highly salty. What can you say about the relative rates of evaporation and precipitation over the Mediterranean?
20. What role does the sun play in the circulation of ocean currents?
21. How does the ocean influence weather on land?
22. What happens to the salinity of seawater when evaporation at the ocean's surface exceeds precipitation? When precipitation exceeds evaporation?
23. Why is there more concern about the melting of polar ice caps than there is about the melting of icebergs?
24. Water denser than the surrounding water sinks. With respect to the densities of deeper water, how far does it sink?
25. As a volume of seawater freezes, the salinity of the surrounding water increases. Explain.

Problems

Refer to **Figuring Physical Science: Dense As Air** on page **752** to answer the following two problems.

1. What is the mass in kilograms of the air in an "empty" nonpressurized SCUBA tank that has an internal volume of 0.0100 cubic meter?
2. What is the mass in kilograms of the air in a SCUBA tank that has an internal volume of 0.0100 cubic meter and is pressurized so that the density of the air in the tank is 240 kilograms/cubic meter?

Chapter 31 Online Resources

Tutorials
- Vertical Structure of the Atmosphere Activity
- Surface Temp of Terrestrial Planets
- Seasons

Quiz
Exercises
Flashcards
Links

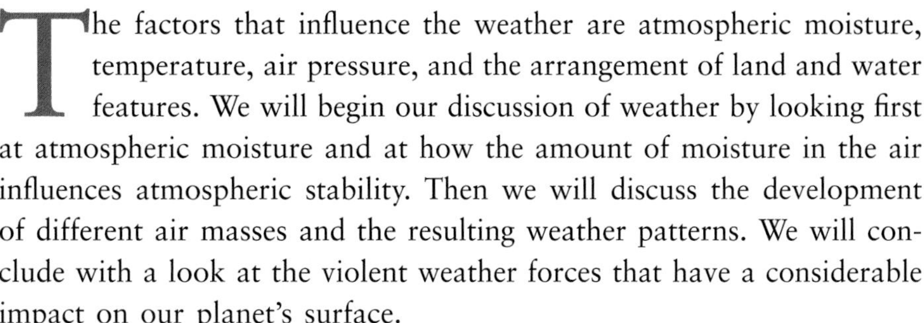

CHAPTER 32 Weather

The factors that influence the weather are atmospheric moisture, temperature, air pressure, and the arrangement of land and water features. We will begin our discussion of weather by looking first at atmospheric moisture and at how the amount of moisture in the air influences atmospheric stability. Then we will discuss the development of different air masses and the resulting weather patterns. We will conclude with a look at the violent weather forces that have a considerable impact on our planet's surface.

32.1 Atmospheric Moisture

Water is certainly vital to life on Earth. But think for a moment about its immense role in the physical processes of the earth. Water shapes earth's surface and governs its weather.

There is always water vapor in the air, measured by the air's **humidity.** Specifically, humidity is the mass of water per volume of air. When you hear TV weather forecasters describing humidity, however, they are probably talking about **relative humidity.** Relative humidity is the ratio of the amount of water vapor currently in the air compared with the largest amount of water vapor that it is possible for the air to contain at that temperature. A relative humidity of 50 percent, for example, means that the water content in the air is half the amount that air can contain at that temperature.*

When air contains as much water vapor as it can, the air is *saturated*. Saturation occurs when the air temperature drops and water vapor molecules in the air begin to condense to form droplets. Because slower-moving molecules characterize lower air temperatures, saturation and condensation are more likely to occur in cool air than in warm air (Figure 32.1). Warm air can contain more water vapor than cold air.

As air rises, it expands. The expansion occurs because air moves to a region of lower air pressure. As we learned in Chapter 8, air cools when it expands. As the air cools, water molecules move slower and condensation occurs. If there are larger and slower-moving particles or ions present in the air, water vapor condenses on these particles, and this creates a cloud. As the size of the cloud droplets grow, they fall to earth and we have rain. Rain is one form of

Most raindrops are nearly perfect spheres, not the teardrop shapes often depicted by artists. The attraction of molecules in a liquid, called *surface tension,* tends to pull the droplet into the shape with the smallest surface area—a sphere. The exceptions are very large raindrops (more than one millimeter in diameter), which air resistance flattens to produce a hamburger-bun shape with a flat bottom and a slightly curved top.

Insights

*Relative humidity is a good indicator of comfort. For most people, conditions are ideal when the temperature is about 20°C and the relative humidity is between 50% and 60%. When the relative humidity is too high, moist air feels "muggy," as condensation counteracts the evaporation of perspiration. Cold air that has a high relative humidity feels colder than dry air of the same temperature because of increased conduction of heat from the body. When the relative humidity is high, hot weather feels hotter, and cold weather feels colder.

Figure 32.1
Condensation of water molecules.

In rainy weather, when your car windshield fogs up, turn on the air conditioner rather than the defroster. What causes window fogging is the humidity in the car caused by rain, by wet clothes, and by the breath of the passengers. Since the air from the air conditioner is very dry, it clears a foggy windshield very nicely in a very short time.

Insights

precipitation. Other familiar forms of precipitation are mist, hail, snow, and sleet. Precipitation comes from water vapor in the air that condenses to make clouds and then falls as liquid water or ice.

Water vapor in the air can condense close to the ground as well. When condensation in the air occurs near the earth's surface, we call it *dew, frost,* or *fog*. On cool, clear nights, objects near the ground cool down more rapidly than the surrounding air. As the air cools below a certain temperature, called the *dew point,* the air cannot hold as much water vapor as when the air was warmer. Water from the now-saturated air condenses on any available surface. This may be a twig, a blade of grass, or the windshield of a car. We often call this type of condensation *early-morning dew*. When the dew point is at or below freezing, we have frost. When a large mass of air cools and reaches its dew point, the relative humidity approaches 100 percent. And this produces a cloud near the ground—fog.

Figure 32.2
San Francisco is well known for its summer fog.

Link to Section 8.5

☑ CHECKPOINT

What is the major difference between fog and a cloud?

Check Your Answer

Altitude.

Figuring Physical Science

Humidity

Humidity is the mass of water vapor per volume of air. Relative humidity is the ratio of the air's water vapor content compared with the air's water vapor capacity at a certain temperature.

For these three problems, consider a small, experimental air mass at 30°C that weighs 90 N.

1. If the air density is 1.25 kg/m^3, what is the volume of the air mass?
2. If there is 0.13 kg of water vapor in the air mass, what is the humidity of the air mass?
3. At 30°C, the maximum amount of water vapor in the air mass is 30 g/m^3. What is the relative humidity of the air mass?

Solutions

1. Newton's second law tells us that

$$a = F/m$$

Rearrange the equation to get

$$\text{mass} = \frac{\text{force}}{\text{acceleration due to gravity}} = \frac{90\ \text{N}}{10\ \text{m/s}^2} = 9\ \text{kg}$$

The volume of 9 kg can be found in this way:

$$9\ \text{kg} \times \frac{1\ \text{m}^3}{1.25\ \text{kg}} = 7.2\ \text{m}^3$$

2. $$\text{Humidity} = \frac{\text{mass of water}}{\text{volume of air}} = \frac{0.13\ \text{kg}}{7.2\ \text{m}^3} = 0.018\ \text{kg/m}^3$$

3. First, we must convert the units:

$$\frac{30\ \text{g}}{\text{m}^3} \times \frac{1\ \text{kg}}{1000\ \text{g}} = 0.03\ \text{kg/m}^3$$

Then,

$$\text{relative humidity} = \frac{\text{amount of water vapor in air}}{\text{maximum amount of water vapor in air at 30°C}} = \frac{0.018\ \text{kg/m}^3}{0.03\ \text{kg/m}^3} \times 100\% = 60\%$$

32.2 Weather Variables

Air pressure, temperature, and density are three key variables that control weather. To understand and predict the weather, we must understand all three. First, consider air pressure. Air is a mixture of molecules that move randomly and collide with one another like billiard balls. When a molecule bumps into something, it exerts a small push on whatever it hits. This push by multiple molecules produces *air pressure*.

The faster the air molecules move, the greater their kinetic energy. The greater the kinetic energy, the greater the impact of molecular collisions and the greater the air pressure. Air composed of fast-moving molecules—warm air—exerts more air pressure on its surroundings than cooler air.

Another factor that affects air pressure is density. The denser the air, the greater the number of molecular collisions that occur, and the greater the air pressure. How air behaves depends on its pressure, temperature, and density.

Adiabatic Processes in Air

The concept of *heat exchange* shows us that air pressure, temperature, and density are interrelated. When heat is added to an air mass, its temperature increases, or its pressure increases, or both increase. Heat can be added to air by solar radiation, by moisture condensation, or by contact with warm ground.

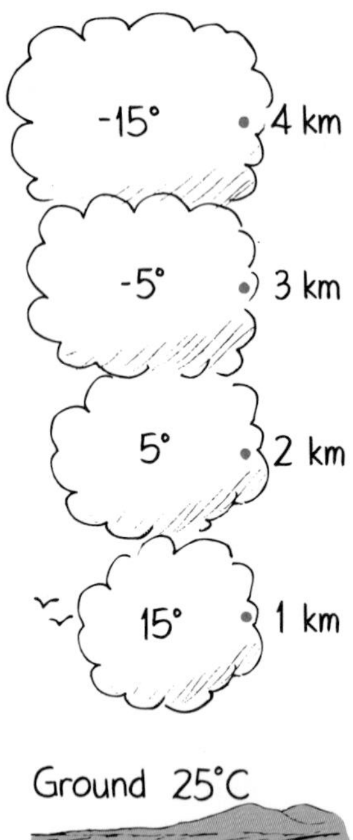

Figure 32.3
The temperature of a parcel of dry air that expands adiabatically changes by about 10°C for each kilometer of elevation.

When heat is subtracted from an air mass, the temperature or the pressure of the air falls. Heat can be subtracted from air by radiation to space, by the evaporation of rain falling through dry air, or by contact with cold surfaces.

Temperature changes can also occur in the atmosphere in the absence of heat transfer. When heat transfer is zero, or nearly zero, we call the atmospheric process *adiabatic*. For example, when air is suddenly compressed or allowed to expand, its temperature changes as its pressure changes. The air was warmed or cooled, even though no heat exchange took place.

Adiabatic processes in the atmosphere are characteristic of large bodies of air. To illustrate how bodies of air behave, imagine a body of air enclosed in a very thin plastic garment bag—an air *parcel*. Like a free-floating balloon, the parcel can expand and contract freely without heat exchange with the air outside the parcel. Air pressure always decreases with increasing height. So, as an air parcel flows up the side of a mountain, air pressure within the parcel decreases, allowing it to expand and cool without any heat exchange.

With adiabatic expansion, the temperature of a dry air parcel decreases about 10°C for each kilometer it rises (Figure 32.3). This rate of cooling for dry air is called the *dry adiabatic rate*. Air flowing up and over tall mountains or rising in thunderstorms may change elevation by several kilometers. Thus, when a dry air parcel at ground level at a comfortable 25°C rises 6 kilometers, its temperature drops to a frigid −35°C. On the other hand, if air at a typical temperature of −20°C at 6 kilometers descends to the ground, its temperature rises to a whopping 40°C.

Adiabatic processes are not restricted to dry air. As rising air cools, its ability to contain water vapor decreases, increasing the relative humidity of the rising air. If the air cools to its dew point, the water vapor condenses and a cloud forms. Because condensation releases heat, the surrounding air is warmed. This added heat offsets the cooling due to expansion, making the air cool at a lesser rate—a *moist adiabatic rate*. Although the moist adiabatic rate varies according to the temperature and the moisture content of the air, on average a moist air parcel cools by 6°C for every kilometer it rises.

> To see that expanding air cools, blow on your hand with your mouth wide open. Notice the warmth of the air. Then repeat this, but pucker your lips so that your mouth opening is very small. This time, your breath expands as it leaves your mouth. Aha! Cool! (Recall this insight from Figure 8.7 earlier in the text.)
>
> **Insights**

Atmospheric Stability

Stable air is air that resists upward movement. When a parcel of rising air is cooler than its surroundings, it is also denser than its surroundings. The denser air tends to sink. The two effects—rising and sinking—balance each other, and the air is stable. Stable air that is forced to rise spreads out horizontally. When clouds develop in stable air, they too spread out into thin horizontal layers having flat tops and bottoms.

On the other hand, when a rising air parcel is warmer than its surroundings, it is less dense, and it continues to move upward until its temperature equals the temperature of its surroundings. In this case, the air is unstable and favors upward movement. Rising dry air cools at the dry adiabatic rate, while air at the surface warms up. When the rising air is moist, billowy, towering clouds develop.

A dramatic example of adiabatic warming is the *Chinook*—a dry wind that blows down from the Rocky Mountains across the Great Plains (Figure 32.4). Cold air moving down a mountain slope is compressed as it moves to lower elevations (where air pressure is greater than at higher elevations), and it becomes much warmer. The effect of expansion or compression of gases is quite impressive.*

Figure 32.4
Chinooks—which are warm, dry winds—occur when high-altitude air descends and is adiabatically warmed.

A rising parcel of air continues to rise as long as it is warmer and less dense than the surrounding air. If it gets cooler and denser than its surroundings, it sinks. Under some conditions, large parcels of cold air sink and remain at a low elevation. This results in air above that is warmer. When the upper regions of the atmosphere are warmer than the lower regions, which is opposite of what normally occurs, we have a **temperature inversion.**† Then most rising air can't pass through the upper layer of warmer air. Evidence of this is commonly seen over a cold lake when visible gases and small particles such as smoke spread out in a flat layer above the lake rather than rising and dissipating higher in the atmosphere (Figure 32.5).

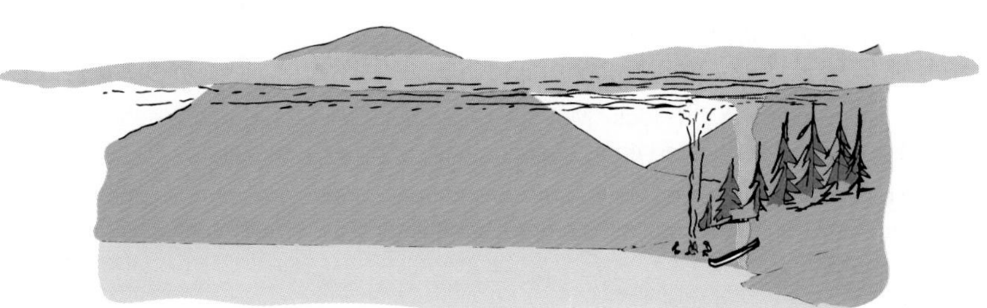

Figure 32.5
The layer of campfire smoke over the lake indicates a temperature inversion. The air above the smoke is warmer than the smoke, and the air below is cooler.

The smog of Los Angeles is trapped by such an inversion, caused by cold air from the ocean being capped by a layer of hot air moving westward over the mountains from the hot Mojave Desert. The west-facing side of the mountains helps to confine the trapped air (Figure 32.6). The Rocky Mountains on

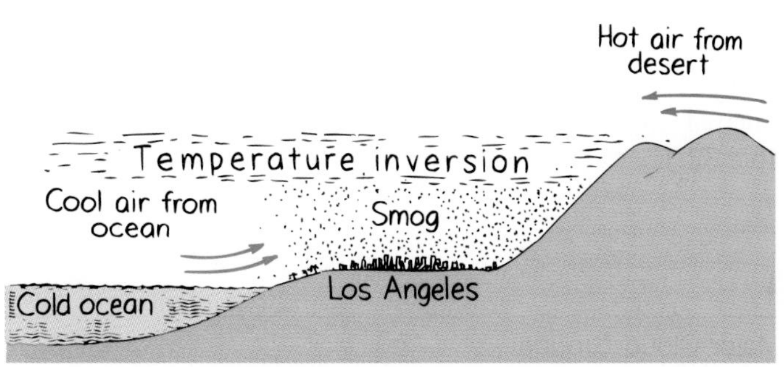

Figure 32.6
Smog in Los Angeles is trapped by the mountains and by a temperature inversion caused by warm air from the Mohave Desert overlying cool air from the Pacific Ocean.

*When you're flying at high altitudes where the outside air temperature is typically −35°C, you're quite comfortable in your warm cabin—but not because of heaters. The process of compressing outside air to maintain a cabin pressure that is nearly the same as the air pressure at sea level normally heats the air to a roasting 55°C (131°F). So air conditioners must be used to extract heat from the pressurized air.

†Strictly speaking, meteorologists refer to any temperature profile that thwarts upward convection as a temperature inversion—including instances in which the upper regions of air are cooler, but not cool enough to allow continued upward convection.

the western edge of Denver play a similar role in trapping smog beneath a temperature inversion.

☑ CHECKPOINT

1. If a parcel of dry air initially at 0°C expands adiabatically while flowing upward alongside a mountain, what is its temperature when it has risen 2 km? When it has risen 5 km?
2. What happens to the air temperature in a valley when dry, cold air blowing across the mountains descends into the valley?
3. Imagine a gigantic dry-cleaner's garment bag full of dry, −10°C air floating 6 km above the ground like a balloon with a string hanging from it. If you were to yank it suddenly to the ground, what would its temperature be?

Check Your Answers

1. The air cools at the dry adiabatic rate of 10°C for each kilometer it rises. When the parcel rises to an elevation of 2 km, its temperature is −20°C. At an elevation of 5 km, its temperature is −50°C.
2. The air is adiabatically compressed, and so its temperature increases. Residents of some valley towns in the Rocky Mountains, such as Salida, Colorado, benefit from this adiabatic compression and enjoy "banana belt" weather in midwinter.
3. If the bag of air were pulled down quickly and heat conduction were negligible, the atmosphere would adiabatically compress the air and its temperature would rise to a piping hot 50°C.

32.3 Cloud Development

A **cloud** is a mixture of suspended water droplets and ice crystals, formed from rising, warm, moist air. As the warm air rises, it cools and therefore becomes less able to retain water vapor. As the water vapor condenses into tiny droplets, clouds are formed.

Clouds are generally classified according to their altitude and shape. There are ten principal cloud forms, each of which belongs to one of four major groups (Table 32.1).

Table 32.1

The Four Major Cloud Groups

1. High clouds (above 6000 m)	**3.** Low clouds (below 2000 m)
Cirrus	Stratus
Cirrostratus	Stratocumulus
Cirrocumulus	Nimbostratus
2. Middle clouds (2000–6000 m)	**4.** Clouds having vertical development
Altostratus	Cumulus
Altocumulus	Cumulonimbus

Figure 32.7
The four cloud groups and representative examples. (a) High clouds—cirrus. (b) Middle clouds—altocumulus. (c) Low clouds—stratocumulus. (d) Clouds with vertical development—cumulus.

High Clouds

High clouds are clouds that form at altitudes above 6000 meters. High clouds (other than cirrus clouds) are denoted by the prefix *cirro-*. The air at this elevation is quite cold and dry, and so clouds this high are made up almost entirely of ice crystals.

The most common high clouds are thin, wispy *cirrus* clouds. Cirrus clouds are blown by high winds into their well-known wispy shapes, such as the classic "mare's tail" or "artist's brush." Cirrus clouds usually indicate fair weather, but they may also indicate approaching rain.

Cirrocumulus clouds are the familiar rounded white puffs. They are found in patches, and they seldom cover more than a small portion of the sky. Small ripples and a wavy appearance make the cirrocumulus clouds look like the markings on the body of a mackerel. Hence, cirrocumulus clouds are often said to make up a *mackerel sky.*

Cirrostratus clouds are thin and sheetlike, and they often cover the entire sky. The ice crystals in these clouds refract light and produce a halo around the sun or the moon. When cirrostratus clouds thicken, they give the sky a white, glary appearance—an indication of coming rain or snow.

Middle Clouds

Middle clouds form at altitudes between 2000 and 6000 meters. Middle clouds are denoted by the prefix *alto-*. These clouds are composed of water droplets and, when temperature allows, ice crystals.

Altostratus clouds are gray to blue-gray, and they often cover the sky for hundreds of square kilometers. Altostratus clouds are often so thick that they diffuse incoming sunlight to the extent that objects on the ground don't produce shadows. Altostratus clouds often form before a storm. Look at the ground the next time you're going on a picnic. If you don't see your shadow there, cancel your plans!

Altocumulus clouds appear as gray, puffy masses in parallel waves or bands. The individual puffs are much larger than those found in cirrocumulus clouds, and the color is also much darker. The appearance of altocumulus clouds on a warm, humid summer morning often indicates thunderstorms by late afternoon.

Cumulus clouds are denser than the surrounding air. So why don't they fall? The answer is, they do fall! They fall at the same speed that the air is rising and, therefore, they remain fixed in elevation. Without updrafts, there would be no cumulus clouds.

Insights

Low Clouds

Low clouds ranging from the surface up to 2000 meters are called *stratus* clouds. They are almost always made up of water droplets, but, in cold weather, they may also contain ice crystals and snow. *Stratus* clouds are uniformly gray, and they often cover the whole sky. They are very common in winter, and they account for the sky's "hazy shade of winter." They resemble a high fog that doesn't touch the ground. Although stratus clouds are not directly associated with falling precipitation, they sometimes generate a light drizzle or mist.

Stratocumulus clouds either form a low, lumpy layer that grows in horizontal rows or patches or, with weak rising motion, appear as rounded masses. Their color is generally light to dark gray. To tell the difference between altocumulus clouds and stratocumulus clouds, hold your hand at arm's length and point toward the cloud in question. An altocumulus cloud commonly appears to be the size of your thumbnail; a stratocumulus cloud appears to be about the size of your fist. Precipitation of rain or snow is not usually produced by stratocumulus clouds.

Nimbostratus clouds are dark and foreboding. They are a wet-looking cloud layer associated with light to moderate rain or snow.

Clouds Having Vertical Development

Rising air currents produce vertical clouds. These are *cumulus* clouds, which are the most familiar of the many cloud types. Cumulus clouds resemble pieces of floating cotton, with sharp outlines and a flat base. They are white to light gray, and they generally occur about 1000 meters above the ground. The tops of cumulus clouds are often in the form of rising towers, showing the upward limit of the rising air. These are the clouds childhood daydreams are made of. Remember the horses, dragons, and magic palaces that you once saw in them?

When cumulus clouds turn dark and are accompanied by precipitation, they are referred to as *cumulonimbus* clouds. In this case, they indicate a coming storm. As we shall see, cumulonimbus clouds often become *thunderheads*.

Although water vapor is less dense than air, once water vapor forms cloud droplets, those droplets are considerably denser than air. The gravitational force pulling the droplets down is enough to make them fall. So why don't all the water droplets in a cloud fall to the ground? The answer involves *updrafts*. An updraft is an upward movement of air. A typical cumulus cloud has an updraft speed of at least 1 meter per second, which is faster than the droplets can fall. So the droplets are supported by the upward-rising air. Without updrafts, the droplets drift so slowly out of the bottom of the cloud and evaporate so quickly that they have no chance of reaching the ground. They are replaced by new droplets forming above.

Raindrops, on the other hand, are huge compared with typical cloud droplets. They fall faster than most updrafts can push them upwards. And raindrops evaporate slowly enough that they can easily reach the ground.

32.4 Air Masses, Fronts, and Storms

An *air mass* is a volume of air much larger than the parcels of air we have discussed. Various distinct air masses cover large portions of the earth's surface. Each has its own characteristics. An air mass formed over water in the tropics is different from one formed over land in the polar regions. Air masses are divided into six general categories, according to what type of land or water they form over and the latitude in which their formation occurs (Table 32.2 and Figure 32.8). The type of surface over which air-mass formation occurs is designated by a lowercase letter (m for maritime, c for continental). The source region in which an air mass forms is designated by a capital letter (A for arctic, P for polar, T for tropical.)

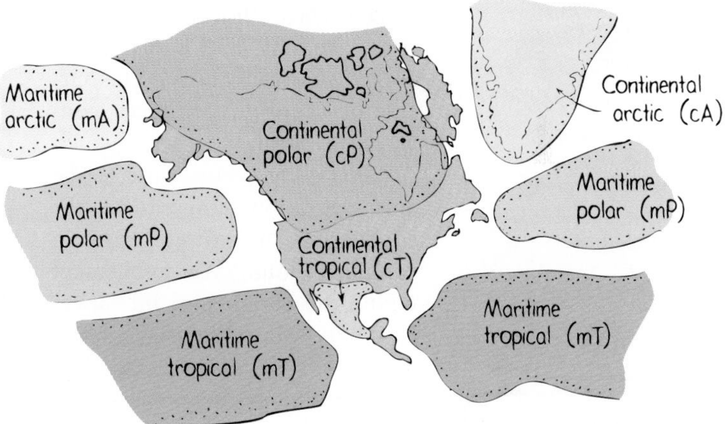

Figure 32.8
Typical source regions of air masses for North America.

Continental polar (cP) and continental arctic (cA) air masses generally produce very cold, dry weather in winter and cool, pleasant weather in summer. Maritime polar (mP) and maritime arctic (mA) air masses, picking up moisture as they travel across the oceans, generally bring cool, moist weather to a region. Continental tropical (cT) air masses are generally responsible for the hot, dry weather of summer, and warm, humid conditions are due to maritime tropical (mT) air masses.

So we see that different types of air masses have their own characteristics. When two different air masses meet, there are a variety of different weather conditions that can develop.

Table 32.2

Classification of Air Masses and Their Characteristics

Typical Source Region	Classification	Symbol	Characteristics
Arctic	maritime arctic	mA	cool, moist, unstable
Greenland	continental arctic	cA	cold, dry, stable
North Atlantic and Pacific Oceans	maritime polar	mP	cool, moist, unstable
Alaska, Canada	continental polar	cP	cold, dry, stable
Caribbean Sea, Gulf of Mexico	maritime tropical	mT	warm, moist; usually unstable
Mexico, southwestern United States	continental tropical	cT	hot, dry, stable aloft; unstable at surface

Atmospheric Lifting

Clouds are great indicators of weather. For clouds to form, air must be lifted. The three principal lifting mechanisms in the atmosphere are convectional lifting, orographic lifting, and frontal lifting.

Convectional Lifting

The earth's surface is heated unequally. Some areas are better absorbers of solar radiation than others, and so they heat up more quickly. The air that touches these surface "hot spots" becomes warmer than the surrounding air, and so it rises, expands, and cools. This rising of air is accompanied by the sinking of cooler air from above. This circulatory motion produces **convectional lifting.**

If cooling occurs close to the air's saturation temperature, the condensing moisture forms a cumulus cloud. Air movement within the cumulus cloud moves in a cycle: Warm air rises, cool air descends. Because descending cool air inhibits the expansion of warm air beneath it, small cumulus clouds usually have a great amount of blue sky between them (Figure 32.9).

Figure 32.9
Cumulus clouds are often found as individual towering white clouds separated from each other by expanses of blue sky.

Cumulus clouds often remain in the places in which they formed, dissipating and reforming many times. As they grow, they shade the ground beneath from the sun. This slows surface heating and inhibits the upward convection of warm air. Without a continuous supply of rising air, any cumulus, cloud begins to dissipate. Once the cloud is gone, the ground reheats, allowing the air above it to warm and rise. Thus, convectional lifting begins again, and another cumulus cloud begins to form at the same location.

As any glider pilot will attest, there is no way in which *all* air can rise. Some of it must come back down. Where air rises, we see clouds; where it descends, we see blue sky between the clouds.

Orographic Lifting

An air mass that is pushed upward over an obstacle, such as a mountain range, undergoes **orographic lifting.** The rising air cools. If the air is humid, clouds form. The types of clouds that form depend on the air's stability and its moisture content. If the air is stable, a layer of stratus clouds may form. If the air is unstable, cumulus clouds may form. As the air mass moves down the other side of the mountain (the leeward slope), it warms adiabatically. This descending air is dry because most of its moisture was removed in the form of clouds and precipitation on the windward (upslope) side of the mountain. Because the dry leeward (downslope) sides of mountain ranges are sheltered from rain and moisture, they are often referred to as regions of *rain shadow* (Figure 32.10).

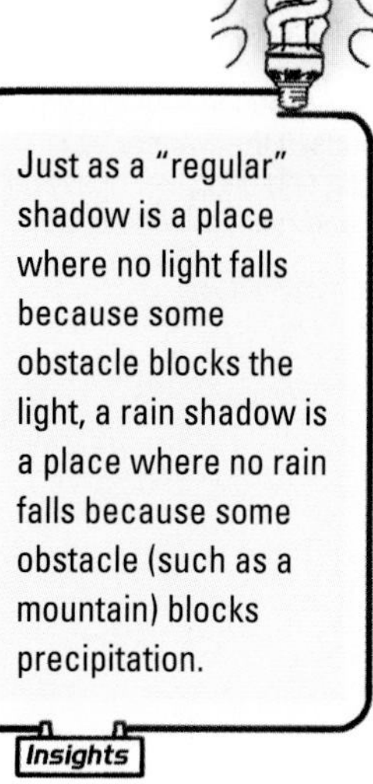

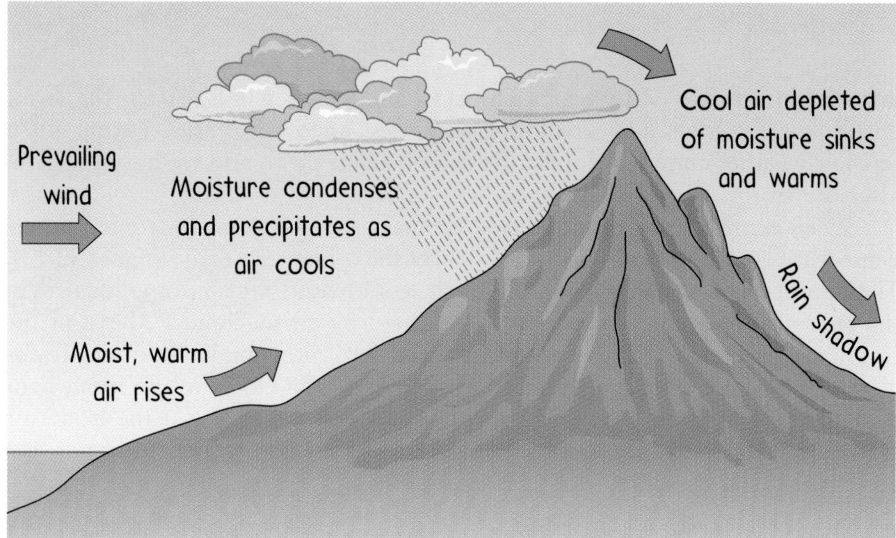

Figure 32.10
A mountain range may produce a rain shadow on its leeward slope. As warm, moist air rises on the windward slope, the air cools and precipitation develops. By the time it reaches the leeward slope, the air is depleted of moisture, so that the leeward side is dry. It lies in a rain shadow.

Frontal Lifting

In weather reports, we often hear about *fronts*. A **front** is the contact zone between two different air masses. When two air masses make contact, differences in temperature, moisture, and pressure can cause one air mass to ride over the other. When this occurs, we have **frontal lifting.** If a cold air mass moves into an area occupied by a nonmoving warm air mass, the contact zone between them is called a *cold front,* and if warm air moves into an area occupied by a nonmoving mass of cold air, the zone of contact is called a *warm front*. If neither of the air masses is moving, the contact zone is called a *stationary front*. Fronts are usually accompanied by wind, clouds, rain, and storms.

Meteorologists and other observers of the sky can often tell when a cold front is approaching by observing high cirrus clouds, a shift in wind direction, a drop in temperature, and a drop in air pressure. As cold air moves into a warm air mass, forming a cold front, the warm air is forced upward (Figure 32.11). As it rises, it cools, and water vapor condenses into a series of cumulonimbus clouds. The advancing wall of clouds at the front develops

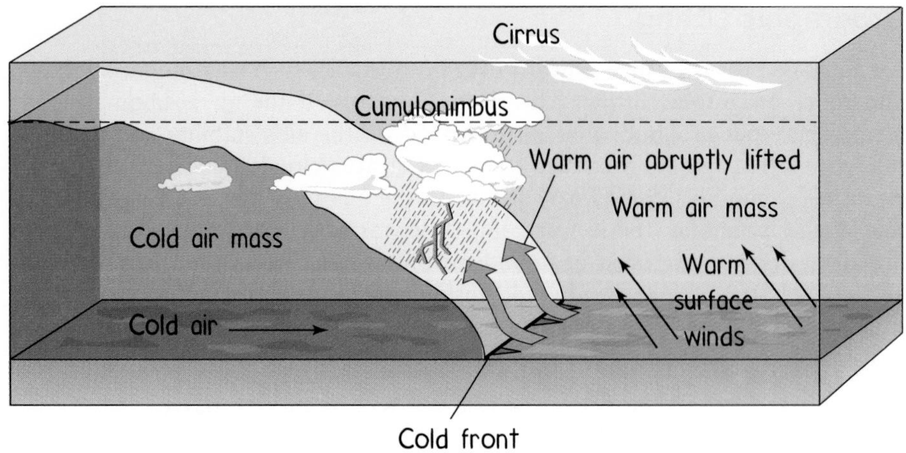

Figure 32.11
A cold front occurs when a cold air mass moves into a warm air mass. The cold air forces the warm air upward, where it condenses to form clouds. If the warmer air is moist and unstable, heavy rainfall and gusty winds develop.

into thunderstorms with heavy showers and gusty winds. After the front passes, the air cools and sinks, pressure rises, and rain ceases. Except for a few fair-weather cumulus clouds, the skies become clear, and we have the calm after the storm.

When warm air moves into a cold air mass, forming a warm front, the less-dense warmer air gradually rides up and over the colder, denser air (Figure 32.12). The approach of a warm front, although less obvious and more gradual than the approach of a cold front, is also indicated by cirrus clouds. Ahead of the front, the cirrus clouds descend and thicken into altocumulus and altostratus clouds that turn the sky an overcast gray. Moving still closer to the front, light to moderate rain or snow develops, and winds become brisk. At the front, air gradually warms, and the rain or snow turns to drizzle. Behind the front, the air is warm and the clouds scatter.

Whereas rising moist air enhances cloud formation, descending moist air has the opposite effect and inhibits cloud formation. That's because downward-moving air warms due to compression by the increased pressure of the surrounding air at lower altitudes. Warmer water molecules move faster with less chance of sticking when they collide.

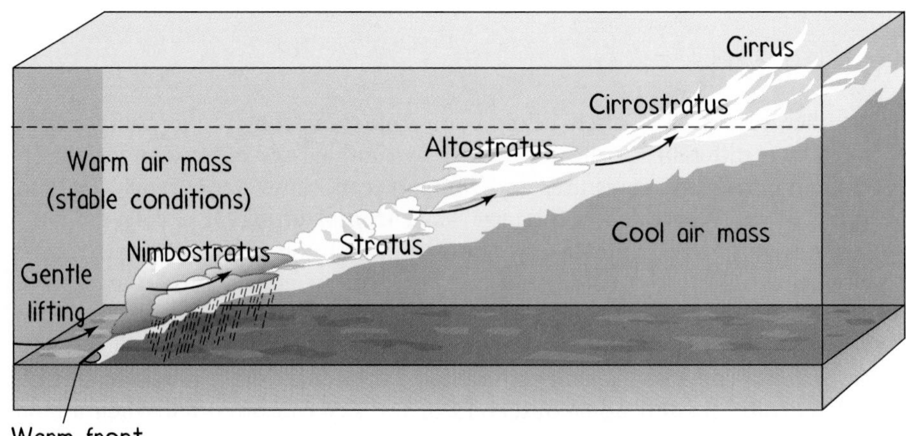

Figure 32.12
A warm front occurs when a warm air mass moves into a cold air mass. The less-dense warmer air rides up and over the colder, denser air, resulting in widespread cloudiness and light to moderate precipitation that can cover great areas.

32.5 Violent Weather

The three types of lifting just discussed bring about many different weather conditions. Weather resulting from air masses in contact depends on the conditions in their source regions. Weather changes can occur slowly or very quickly. The most rapid changes, and the most violent ones occur with three major types of storms: thunderstorms, tornadoes, and hurricanes.

Figure 32.13
The mature stage of a thunderstorm cloud appears as a towering cumulonimbus cloud that reaches up to about 12 km. Strong horizontal winds and icy temperatures flatten and distend the cloud's crown into a characteristic anvil shape.

Thunderstorms

A thunderstorm begins with humid air rising, cooling, and condensing into a single cumulus cloud. This cloud builds and grows upward as long as it is fed by an updraft of rising warm air from below. Cloud droplets grow larger and heavier within the cloud until they eventually begin to fall as rain. The falling rain drags some of the cool air along with it, creating a downdraft. The chilled air is colder and denser than the air around it. Together, the rising warm updraft and the sinking chilled downdraft make up a *storm cell* within the cloud. This is the mature stage, where the thunderstorm cloud appears as a lonely giant—dark and brooding in the sky. It typically has a base several kilometers in diameter, and it can tower to altitudes up to 12 kilometers. At such high altitudes, horizontal winds and lower temperatures flatten and stretch the thunderhead crown into a characteristic anvil shape (Figure 32.13). After the thunderstorm dissipates, it leaves behind the cirrus anvil as a reminder of its once mighty presence.

Figure 32.14
Time exposure of cloud-to-ground lightning during an intense thunderstorm.

At any given time, there are about 1800 thunderstorms in progress in the earth's atmosphere. Wherever thunderstorms occur, there is lightning and thunder. As water droplets in the cloud bump into and rub against one another, the cloud becomes electrically charged—usually positively charged at the top and negatively charged at the bottom. As electrical stresses between the oppositely charged regions build up, the charge becomes great enough that electrical energy is released and passed to other points of opposite charge, which quite often means the ground. The electrical energy flowing from cloud to ground is lightning (Figure 32.14). As lightning heats up the air, the air expands and we hear lightning's noisy companion, thunder. Lightning strikes the earth roughly 100 times every second, with some bolts having an electric potential of as much as 100 million volts. Lightning claims more than 200 human victims per year in the United States alone.

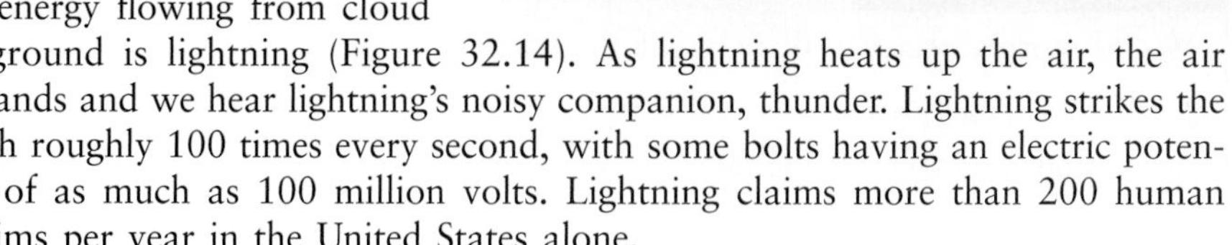

Tornadoes

A revolving object, such as a whirling ball on a string, speeds up when pulled toward its axis of revolution, thus conserving its angular momentum. Similarly, winds slowly rotating over a large area speed up when the radius of rotation decreases. This increase in speed can produce a *tornado,* which is a funnel-shaped cloud that extends downward from a large cumulonimbus cloud. The funnel cloud is called a tornado only after it touches the ground. The winds of a tornado travel at speeds of up to 800 kilometers per hour in a counterclockwise direction (clockwise in the Southern Hemisphere). As a tornado moves across the land, moving at speeds from 45 to 95 kilometers per hour, it may bounce and skip, rising briefly from the ground and then touching down again. A tornado acts like a gigantic vacuum cleaner, picking up everything in its path. It wreaks havoc not only by suction but also by the battering power of its whirling winds. In its wake, a trail of flying dirt and debris is left behind (Figure 32.15).

Figure 32.15
Like a gigantic vacuum cleaner, the strong wind of a tornado can pick up and obliterate everything in its path.

Tornadoes occur in many parts of the world. In the flat central plains of the United States, a tornado zone extends from northern Texas through Oklahoma, Kansas, and Missouri. In this area, more than 300 tornadoes touch down each year. Hence the name for this area: Tornado Alley. Tornadoes are so frequent in this part of the country that some homes are built with underground storm shelters. The power of a tornado is terrifying and devastating.

Hurricanes

In the steamy tropics, where the sun warms the oceans, the transfer of heat to the atmosphere by evaporation and conduction is so thorough that air and water temperatures are about equal. The high humidity in this part of the world favors the development of cumulus clouds and afternoon thunderstorms. Most of the individual storms are not severe. However, as the moisture content and the temperature of the air increase and surface winds collide, a strong vertical wind shear can cause the rising warm, moist air to tilt inward and spiral. This condition produces a more violent storm—a *hurricane*—with wind speeds up to nearly 300 kilometers per hour. Gaining energy from its source area, a hurricane grows as more air rises and increasing winds rotate around a central, relatively calm, low-pressure zone—the *eye* of the storm.

☑ CHECKPOINT

Would storms occur if all parts of the earth's surface were heated evenly?

Check Your Answer

No. The principal factor in the formation of storms is contact between warm air and cool air.

32.6 The Weather—the Number One Topic of Conversation

Meteorologists have the important job of forecasting hurricanes and other storms. Weather forecasting is, in part, a matter of determining air-mass characteristics, predicting how and why the characteristics might change, and in what direction an air mass might move. In the case of hurricanes and tornadoes, such predictions are life-saving. Meteorologists have a long and remarkable record of reducing property loss and saving human lives.

Figure 32.16
On February 23, 1998, El Niño driven tornadoes swept across central Florida. This shot of Kissimmee, Florida shows the destruction as rows of houses lay in ruin. The tornado was catastrophic, with 42 deaths, 260 injured, and many people left homeless. Tornado watches and warnings issued by the National Weather Service have saved countless lives by alerting residents to seek shelter.

We hear weather forecasters talk about short-, medium-, and long-range forecasting. What do these types of forecasting mean? In general, short-range forecasting predicts the first two days with considerable detail about temperature, wind, and weather. Medium-range forecasting predicts weather for the third to seventh days in less detail. Forecasting beyond seven days is considered long-range, and the predictions in such forecasts are in terms of conditions that are expected to be above or below normal.

Insights

Weather forecasting involves great quantities of data from all over the world. Before the 1960s, most of these data were assembled, analyzed, and plotted by hand on weather maps and charts. This took thousands of calculations, a large work force, and long hours. Now, with computers, great quantities of data from around the world can be processed in a matter of minutes. Computers not only plot and analyze data, they also predict the weather. The computer draws maps of projected weather conditions, which the weather forecaster uses as a guide for predicting weather. Even so, the many variables involved often impede the making of accurate predictions, so don't count on an absence of rain on your parade!

And then there's space weather between the sun and the earth—swirling storms and disturbances caused by solar activity. Solar flares, coronal mass ejections, and magnetic storms affect not only Earth satellites but Earth's surface environment as well. Communication systems failures, power blackouts, and brownouts are often attributed to space weather. As our use of space grows, so must our ability to predict its weather.

Insights

Weather Maps

The weather forecaster's primary tool is the surface weather map or chart. A weather map is essentially a representation of the frontal systems and the high-pressure and low-pressure systems that overlie the areas outlined in the map. Symbols on such a map are a shorthand notation to represent data gathered from various observation stations. These symbols are called weather codes.

This shorthand notation compiles 18 items of data into a very small area called a *station model.* The circle at the center describes the overall appearance of the sky. Jutting from the circle is a wind arrow, its tail in the direction from which the wind comes and its feathers indicating wind speed. The other 15 weather elements are in standard position around the circle.

A weather map is covered with lines—*isobars*—that connect points of equal pressure. As air moves from a high-pressure region to a low-pressure region, it rises and cools, and the moisture in it condenses into clouds. In the vicinity of the low (L on map), we see an extensive cloud cover. In the vicinity of the high (H on map), we see clear skies. In a high-pressure region, air sinks and warms adiabatically. Because sinking air does not produce clouds, we find clear skies and fair weather. The heavy lines on a weather map represent fronts. Because fronts generally mean a change in the weather, they are of great importance on weather maps.

Weather Symbols

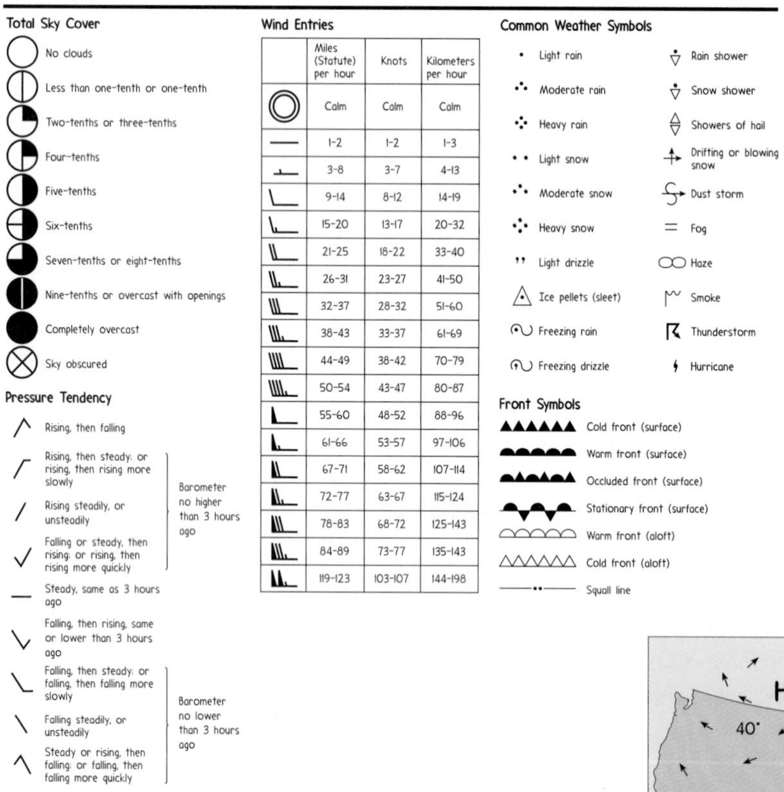

Total Sky Cover

- No clouds
- Less than one-tenth or one-tenth
- Two-tenths or three-tenths
- Four-tenths
- Five-tenths
- Six-tenths
- Seven-tenths or eight-tenths
- Nine-tenths or overcast with openings
- Completely overcast
- Sky obscured

Pressure Tendency

Barometer no higher than 3 hours ago:

- Rising, then falling
- Rising, then steady; or rising, then rising more slowly
- Rising steadily, or unsteadily
- Falling or steady, then rising; or rising, then rising more quickly

- Steady, same as 3 hours ago

Barometer no lower than 3 hours ago:

- Falling, then rising, same or lower than 3 hours ago
- Falling, then steady; or falling, then falling more slowly
- Falling steadily, or unsteadily
- Steady or rising, then falling; or falling, then falling more quickly

Wind Entries

	Miles (Statute) per hour	Knots	Kilometers per hour
	Calm	Calm	Calm
	1-2	1-2	1-3
	3-8	3-7	4-13
	9-14	8-12	14-19
	15-20	13-17	20-32
	21-25	18-22	33-40
	26-31	23-27	41-50
	32-37	28-32	51-60
	38-43	33-37	61-69
	44-49	38-42	70-79
	50-54	43-47	80-87
	55-60	48-52	88-96
	61-66	53-57	97-106
	67-71	58-62	107-114
	72-77	63-67	115-124
	78-83	68-72	125-143
	84-89	73-77	135-143
	119-123	103-107	144-198

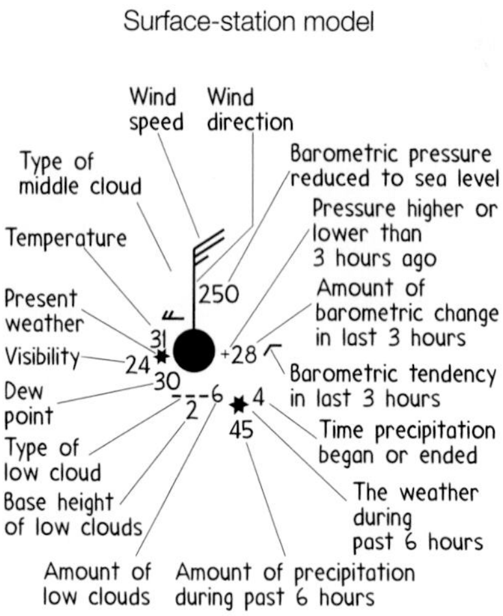

Common Weather Symbols

- Light rain
- Moderate rain
- Heavy rain
- Light snow
- Moderate snow
- Heavy snow
- Light drizzle
- Ice pellets (sleet)
- Freezing rain
- Freezing drizzle
- Rain shower
- Snow shower
- Showers of hail
- Drifting or blowing snow
- Dust storm
- Fog
- Haze
- Smoke
- Thunderstorm
- Hurricane

Front Symbols

- Cold front (surface)
- Warm front (surface)
- Occluded front (surface)
- Stationary front (surface)
- Warm front (aloft)
- Cold front (aloft)
- Squall line

Surface-station model

Wind speed
Wind direction
Type of middle cloud
Barometric pressure reduced to sea level
Pressure higher or lower than 3 hours ago
Temperature
Amount of barometric change in last 3 hours
Present weather
Barometric tendency in last 3 hours
Visibility
Dew point
Time precipitation began or ended
Type of low cloud
The weather during past 6 hours
Base height of low clouds
Amount of low clouds
Amount of precipitation during past 6 hours
250
31
24
+28
30
2
-6
4
45

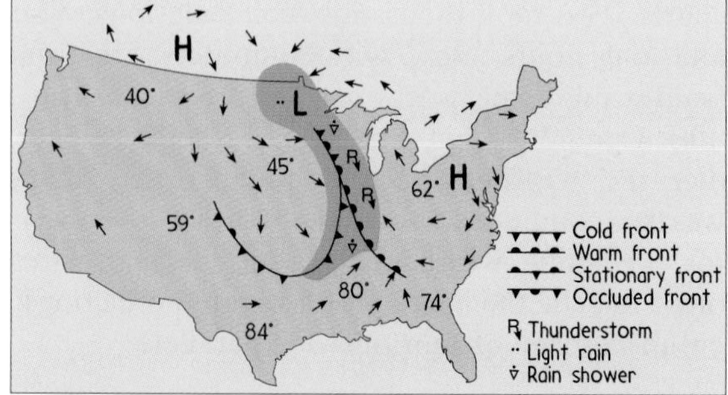

Weather maps show atmospheric conditions. As warm air rises, it expands and chills. As it chills, the water vapor molecules condense to form clouds. Because air moves from a high-pressure region to a low-pressure region, low-pressure zones are accompanied by cloud cover. In a high-pressure zone, air generally sinks. Because sinking air does not usually produce clouds, we find clear skies and fair weather.

Summary of Terms

Humidity A measure of the amount of water vapor in the air.

Relative humidity The amount of water vapor in the air at a given temperature expressed as a percentage of the maximum amount of water vapor the air can hold at that temperature.

Temperature inversion A condition in which the upper regions of the atmosphere are warmer than the lower regions.

Clouds A mixture of suspended water droplets and ice crystals, formed from rising, warm, moist air.

Convectional lifting An air-circulation pattern in which air warmed by the ground rises while cooler air aloft sinks.

Orographic lifting The lifting of an air mass over a topographic barrier, such as a mountain.

Front The contact zone between two different air masses.

Frontal lifting The lifting of one air mass by another as two air masses converge.

Review Questions

32.1 Atmospheric Moisture

1. Distinguish between humidity and relative humidity.
2. Why does relative humidity increase at night?
3. As air temperature decreases, does relative humidity increase, decrease, or stay the same?
4. What does the saturation point have to do with the dew point?
5. What happens to the water vapor in saturated air as the air cools?
6. What factors are responsible for condensation?
7. Does condensation occur more readily at high temperatures or at low temperatures? Explain.
8. Distinguish between dew and frost.
9. When water vapor condenses to liquid water, is heat absorbed or released?
10. Distinguish between condensation and precipitation.

32.2 Weather Variables

11. Explain why warm air rises and cools as it expands.
12. When a parcel of air rises, does it become warmer, cooler, or remain at the same temperature?
13. What is an adiabatic process?
14. Name at least two ways in which the thermal energy of the air can be increased.
15. Name at least two ways in which the thermal energy in the air can be decreased.
16. What is a temperature inversion? Cite at least one location at which such inversions often occur.
17. What happens to the air pressure and temperature of an air parcel as it flows up the side of a mountain?
18. Which cloud form is associated with a stable air mass?

32.3 Cloud Development

19. Explain how clouds form.
20. Name the cloud form associated with (a) the hazy shade of winter, (b) a mackerel sky, (c) floating cotton, and (d) snowfall.
21. Name the cloud group to which each of the following cloud types belongs: (a) altocumulus, (b) cirrostratus, (c) nimbostratus, and (d) cumulus.
22. Rain or snow is most likely to be produced by which of the following cloud forms? (a) cirrostratus, (b) nimbostratus, (c) altocumulus, or (d) stratocumulus.
23. Are clouds that have vertical development characteristic of stable air, of stationary air, of unstable air, or of dry air?
24. Which type of cloud is most likely to become a thunderhead?

32.4 Air Masses, Fronts, and Storms

25. Explain how convectional lifting plays a role in the formation of cumulus clouds.
26. Explain how a convection cycle is generated.
27. Does a rain shadow occur on the windward side of a mountain range or on the leeward side? Explain.
28. Differentiate between a cold front and a warm front.
29. What are the three main atmospheric lifting mechanisms?
30. Under what conditions does orographic precipitation occur?

32.5 Violent Weather

31. What cloud form is associated with thunderstorms?
32. How do downdrafts form in thunderstorms?
33. Briefly describe how thunder and lightning develop.

32.6 The Weather—the Number One Topic of Conversation

34. Cite at least four types of information needed to predict the weather.
35. The accuracy of weather forecasts depends on great quantities of data and on thousands of calculations. If the number of data points were decreased, would accuracy also decrease?

Activity

Open your mouth and blow on your hand. You can feel that your breath is warm. Do it again, only this time pucker your lips to make a small hole so your breath expands as it leaves your mouth. Note that your breath is appreciably cooler! Adiabatic expansion, hooray!

Exercises

1. Distinguish between weather and climate.
2. Which produces precipitation, a rising moist air mass or a descending moist air mass? Or both?
3. Why do clouds tend to form above mountain peaks?
4. Why does warm, moist air blowing over cold water result in fog?
5. Why does dew form on the ground during clear, calm summer nights?
6. Why does a July day in the Gulf of Mexico generally feel appreciably hotter than a July day in Arizona, even when temperatures are the same?
7. Would you expect a glass of water to evaporate more quickly on a windy, warm, dry summer day or on a calm, cold, dry winter day? Defend your answer.
8. Why does the surface temperature of the ground increase on a clear, calm night as a low cloud cover moves overhead?
9. During a summer visit to Cancun, Mexico, you stay in an air-conditioned room. Getting ready to leave your room for the beach, you put on your sunglasses. The minute you step outside, your sunglasses fog up. Why?
10. After a day of skiing in the Rocky Mountains, you decide to go indoors to get a warm cup of cocoa. As you enter the ski lodge, your eyeglasses fog up. Why?
11. Can the temperature of an air mass change if no heat is added or subtracted? Explain.
12. Why is it necessary for an air mass to rise if it is to produce precipitation?
13. As an air mass moves first upslope and then downslope over a mountain, what happens to the air's temperature and moisture content?
14. Why are saturation and condensation more likely to occur on a cold day than on a warm day?
15. The sky is overcast, and it is raining. What cloud type is above you, nimbostratus or cumulonimbus?
16. What accounts for the large spaces of blue sky between cumulus clouds?
17. Why don't cumulus clouds form over cool water?
18. What is the difference between rainfall that accompanies the passage of a warm front and rainfall that accompanies the passage of a cold front?
19. How can a layer of altostratus clouds change into altocumulus clouds?
20. Antarctica is covered by glaciers and large ice sheets. Is the snowfall in Antarctica therefore heavy or light? Why?
21. How do fronts cause clouds and precipitation?
22. Explain why freezing rain is more commonly associated with warm fronts than with cold fronts.
23. How does a rain-shadow desert form?
24. Sinking air warms, and yet the downdrafts in a thunderstorm are cold. Why?
25. Tornadoes form in regions where there is a strong updraft, and yet they descend from the base of a cloud. Explain.
26. Why are hurricanes more likely to occur on the eastern coast of the United States than on the western coast?
27. Why are clouds that form over water more efficient in producing precipitation than clouds that form over land?
28. What is the source of the enormous amount of energy released by a hurricane?

Problems

Refer to Figuring Physical Science: Humidity on page 773 for the following two problems.

1. At 50°F, the maximum amount of water vapor in air is 9 g/m^3. If the relative humidity is 40%, what is the mass of water vapor in 1 m^3 of air?
2. The relative humidity of an air parcel is 50% and the pressure is 1000 millibars (mb). If the pressure increases to 1053 mb without changing the temperature or the water-vapor content of the air, what is the relative humidity? (Hint: Use Boyle's law from Chapter 6.)

Chapter 32 Online Resources

Tutorials
- Rain Shadow Activity
- Cold Front Activity
- Warm Front Activity

Videos
- Adiabatic Process
- Air Has Weight
- Air is Matter: Pouring Air from One Glass to Another
- Buoyancy of Air
- Air Has Pressure

Quiz
Exercises
Flashcards
Links

CHAPTER 33

The Solar System

For thousands of years, people have gazed into the night sky and wondered about the stars. With only the unaided eye, they neither saw nor dreamed that the stars are greater in number than all the grains of sand on all the deserts and beaches of the earth. Nor did they realize that the sun is a star—simply the nearest star of all in the universe. Why do the stars shine? And what is the moon, which, when full, was perceived to be a flat circular disk rather than the three-dimensional sphere we know it to be. Why do we see only one side of the moon? Why does it go through phases, from full to a thin crescent, while the sun remains round? And what makes the sun shine?

These questions seemed unanswerable to the ancients. But, today, men and women on this small planet are able to investigate spots of light in the night sky and, from their investigations, to arrive at a magnificent description of creation, which is quite a remarkable accomplishment.

We begin our study of astronomy with early measurements of the earth, moon, and sun. Then we'll briefly discuss what we know about the moon and the sun today, and how we think our solar system came to be. We'll continue with a brief tour of the planets, and we'll conclude the chapter with the other bodies within the solar system—asteroids, meteoroids, and comets.

> The earth, moon, sun, and planets are all round, or nearly round, because gravity has pulled in any corners that might have been protruding.
>
> Insights

33.1 Early Astronomical Measurements

Unfortunately, school children are taught that Columbus set sail from Europe in 1492 to prove that the earth was round rather than flat, as many people believed. But Columbus and other educated people knew the earth is round. In fact, its circumference had been measured centuries before Columbus's first voyage.

The Size of the Earth

The size of the earth was first measured in Egypt by the geographer and mathematician Eratosthenes about 235 B.C.* Eratosthenes calculated the circumference

*Eratosthenes was second chief librarian at the University of Alexandria in Egypt, which was founded by Alexander the Great. Eratosthenes was one of the foremost scholars of his time, and he wrote on philosophy and on scientific and literary matters. As a mathematician, he invented a method for finding prime numbers. His reputation among his contemporaries was immense—Archimedes dedicated a book to him. As a geographer, he wrote *Geography,* the first book to give geography a mathematical basis and to treat the earth as a globe divided into Frigid, Temperate, and Torrid zones. It long remained a standard work, and it was used a century later by Julius Caesar. Eratosthenes spent most of his life in Alexandria, and he died there in 195 B.C.

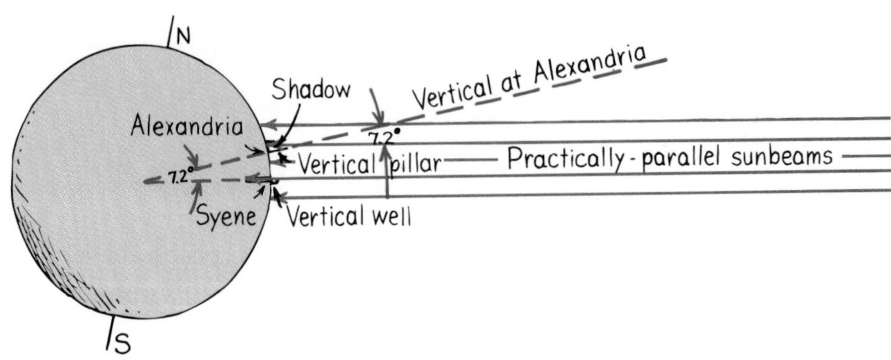

Figure 33.1
When the sun is directly overhead at Syene, it is not directly overhead in Alexandria, 800 km north. When the sun's rays shine directly down a vertical well in Syene, they cast a shadow of a vertical pillar in Alexandria. The verticals at both locations extend to the center of the earth, and they make the same angle that the sun's rays make with the pillar at Alexandria. Eratosthenes measured this angle to be 1/50 of a complete circle. Therefore, the distance between Alexandria and Syene is 1/50 the earth's circumference. (Equivalently, the shadow cast by the pillar is 1/8 the height of the pillar, which means that the distance between the locations is 1/8 the earth's radius.)

of the earth in the following way. He knew that the sun is highest in the sky at noon on the summer solstice (which is June 22 on modern calendars). At this time, a vertical stick casts its shortest shadow. If the sun is directly overhead, a vertical stick casts no shadow at all. This was known to occur in Syene, a city south of Alexandria (where the Aswan High Dam stands today). Eratosthenes learned that the sun was directly overhead in Syene at the summer solstice from library information, which reported that, at this unique time, sunlight shines directly down a deep well in Syene and is reflected back up again. Eratosthenes reasoned that, if the sun's rays were extended into the earth at this point, they would pass through the center. Likewise, a vertical line extended into the earth at Alexandria (or anywhere else) would also pass through the earth's center.

At noon on the summer solstice, Eratosthenes measured the shadow cast by a vertical pillar in Alexandria and found it to be one-eighth the height of the pillar (Figure 33.1). This corresponds to a 7.2-degree angle between the sun's rays and the vertical pillar. Since 7.2° is 7.2/360, or one-fiftieth of a circle, Eratosthenes reasoned that the distance between Alexandria and Syene must be one-fiftieth the circumference of the earth. Thus, the circumference of the earth becomes 50 times the distance between these two cities. This distance, quite flat and frequently traveled, was measured by surveyors to be 5000 stadia (800 kilometers). So Eratosthenes calculated the earth's circumference to be 50×5000 stadia = 250,000 stadia. This is within 5 percent of the currently accepted value of the earth's circumference.

We can get the same result by bypassing degrees altogether and comparing the length of the shadow cast by the pillar to the height of the pillar. Geometrical reasoning shows that, to a close approximation, the ratio *shadow length/pillar height* is the same as the ratio *distance between Alexandria and Syene/Earth's radius.* So, just as the pillar is 8 times greater than its shadow, the radius of the earth must be 8 times greater than the distance between Alexandria and Syene.

Since the circumference of a circle is 2π times its radius ($c = 2\pi r$), the earth's radius is simply its circumference divided by 2π. In modern units the earth's radius is 6370 kilometers, and its circumference is 40,000 km.

The Size of the Moon

Aristarchus was perhaps the first to suggest that the earth spins on a daily axis, which accounts for the daily motion of the stars. He also hypothesized that the earth moves around the sun in a yearly orbit, and that the other planets do likewise.* He correctly measured the moon's diameter and its distance from the earth. He did all this in about 240 B.C., seventeen centuries before his findings became fully accepted.

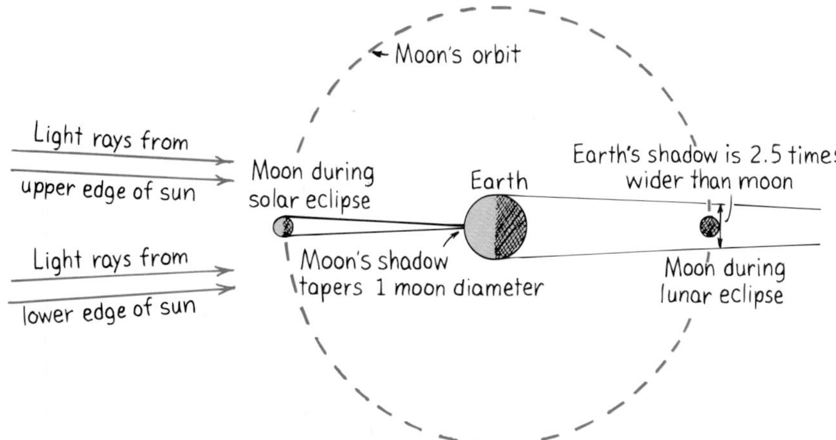

Figure 33.2
During a lunar eclipse, the earth's shadow is observed to be 2.5 times as wide as the moon's diameter. Because of the sun's large size, the earth's shadow must taper. The amount of taper is evident during a solar eclipse, where the moon's shadow tapers a whole moon diameter from moon to earth. So the earth's shadow tapers the same amount in the same distance. Therefore, the earth diameter must be 3.5 moon diameters.

Aristarchus compared the size of the moon with the size of the earth by observing an eclipse of the moon. The earth, like any body in sunlight, casts a shadow. An eclipse of the moon is simply the event wherein the moon passes into this shadow. Aristarchus carefully studied this event and found that the width of the earth's shadow out at the moon was 2.5 moon diameters. This would seem to indicate that the moon's diameter is 2.5 times smaller than the earth's. But, because of the huge size of the sun, the earth's shadow tapers, as evidenced during a solar eclipse. (Figure 33.2 shows this in exaggerated scale.) At that time, the earth intercepts the moon's shadow—but just barely. The moon's shadow tapers almost to a point at the earth's surface, evidence that the taper of the moon's shadow at this distance is one moon diameter. So, during a lunar eclipse, the earth's shadow, covering the same distance, must also taper one moon diameter. Taking the tapering of the sun's rays into account, the earth's diameter must be (2.5 + 1) times the moon's diameter. In this way, Aristarchus showed that the moon's diameter is 1/3.5 (or two-sevenths) that of the earth's. The presently accepted diameter of the moon is 3640 km, which is within 5% of the value calculated by Aristarchus.

Figure 33.3
The correct scale of solar and lunar eclipses, which shows why eclipses are rare. (They are even rarer because the moon's orbit is tilted about 5° from the plane of the earth's orbit about the sun.)

*Aristarchus was unsure of his heliocentric hypothesis, likely because the earth's unequal seasons didn't support the idea that the earth circles the sun. More important, it was noted that the moon's distance from Earth varies—clear evidence that the moon does not perfectly circle the earth. If the moon does not follow a circular path about the earth, it was difficult to argue that the earth follows a circular path about the sun. The explanation, the elliptical paths of planets, was not discovered until centuries later by Johannes Kepler (Chapter 5). In the meantime, the epicycles proposed by other astronomers accounted for these discrepancies. It is interesting to speculate about what the history of astronomy would have been if the moon didn't exist. Its irregular orbit would not have contributed to the early discrediting of the heliocentric theory, which may have taken hold centuries earlier!

The Distance to the Moon

Tape a small coin, such as a dime, to a window and view it with one eye so that it exactly blocks out the full moon. This occurs when your eye is about 110 coin diameters away. Then the ratio *coin diameter/coin distance* is about 1/110. Geometrical reasoning of similar triangles shows this is also the ratio of *moon diameter/moon distance* (Figure 33.4). So the distance to the moon is 110 times the moon's diameter. The early Greeks knew this. Aristarchus's measurement of the moon's diameter was all that was needed to calculate the earth–moon distance. So the early Greeks also knew both the size of the moon and its distance from earth.

With this information, Aristarchus made a measurement of the distance between the earth and the sun.

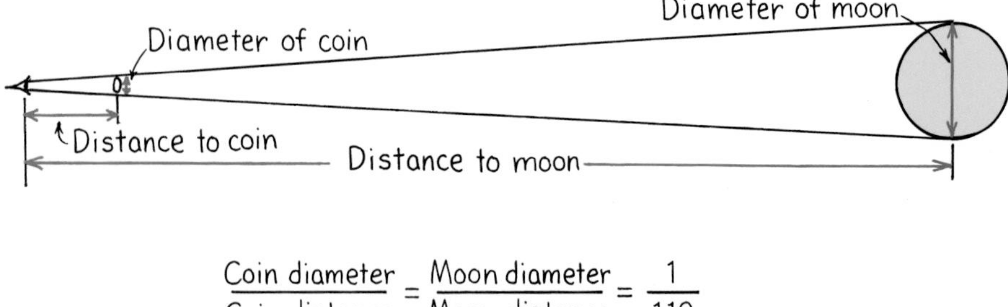

Figure 33.4
An exercise in ratios: When the coin barely "eclipses" the moon, then the ratio of the diameter of the coin to the distance between you and the coin is equal to the ratio of the diameter of the moon to the distance between you and the moon (not to scale here). Measurements give a ratio of 1/110 for both.

The Distance to the Sun

If you were to repeat the coin-on-the-window-and-moon exercise for the sun (which would be dangerous to do, because of the sun's brightness), guess what: The ratio *sun diameter/sun distance* is also 1/110. This is because the sun and moon both appear to be the same size to the eye, tapering at the same angle (about 0.5°). So, although the ratio of diameter to distance was known to the early Greeks, diameter alone or distance alone would have to be determined by some other method. Aristarchus found a means of solving this, and he made a rough estimate. Here's what he did.

Aristarchus watched for the phase of the moon when it was *exactly* half full, with the sun still visible in the sky. Then the sunlight must be falling on the moon at right angles to his line of sight. This meant that the lines between the earth and the moon, between the earth and the sun, and between the moon and the sun form a right triangle (Figure 33.5).

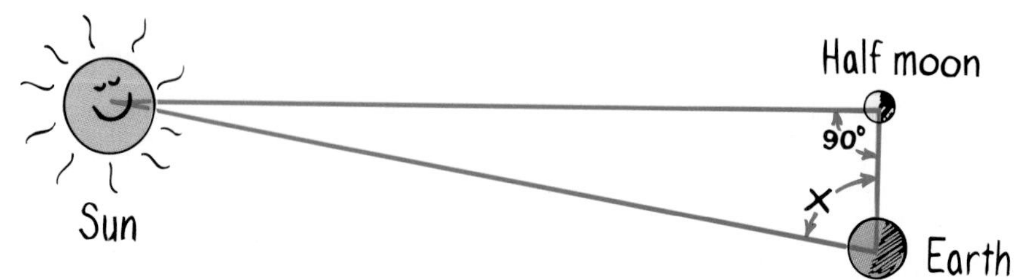

Figure 33.5
When the moon appears exactly half full, the sun, moon, and Earth form a right triangle (not to scale). The hypotenuse is the earth–sun distance. By simple trigonometry, the hypotenuse of a right triangle can be found if you know the value of either of the other two angles and the length of one side. The earth–moon distance is a known side. Measure angle × and you can calculate the earth–sun distance.

A rule of trigonometry states that, if you know all the angles in a right triangle plus the length of any one of its sides, you can calculate the length of any other side. Aristarchus knew the distance from the earth to the moon. At the time of the half moon, he also knew one of the angles, 90°. All he had to do was measure the second angle between the line of sight to the moon and the line of sight to the sun. Then the third angle, a very small one, is 180° minus the sum of the first two angles (the sum of the angles in any triangle = 180°).

Measuring the angle between the lines of sight to the moon and sun is difficult to do without a modern transit. For one thing, both the sun and moon are not points, but are relatively big. Aristarchus had to sight on their centers (or either edge) and measure the angle between them—which was quite large, almost a right angle itself! By modern-day standards, his measurement was very crude. He measured 87°, while the true value was 89.8°. He figured the sun's distance from the earth to be about 20 times the moon's distance, when in fact it is about 400 times as distant. So, although his method was ingenious, his measurements were not. Perhaps Aristarchus found it difficult to believe that the sun was so far away, and he erred on the nearer side. We simply don't know.

Today, we know the sun to be an average of 150,000,000 kilometers away. It is somewhat closer in December (147,000,000 km), and somewhat farther away in June (152,000,000 km).

Poke a hole in a piece of paper, hold it in sunlight so that the solar image is the same size as a coin on the ground, and then determine how many coins would fit between the ground and the pinhole. That's the same number of solar diameters that would fit in the distance from Earth to the sun.

Insights

The Size of the Sun

Once the distance to the sun is known, the 1/110 ratio of diameter/distance enables a measure of the sun's diameter. Another way to measure the 1/110 ratio is to measure the diameter of the sun's image cast through a pinhole opening. You should try this. Poke a hole in a sheet of opaque cardboard and let sunlight shine on it. The round image that is cast on a surface below is actually an image of the sun. You'll see that the size of the image does not depend on the size of the pinhole, but rather on the distance between the pinhole and the image. Bigger holes make brighter images, not bigger ones. Of course, if the hole is very big, no image will be formed. Careful measurement will show the ratio of image size to pinhole distance is 1/110—the same as the ratio of *sun diameter/sun–earth distance* (Figure 33.6).

Have you noticed that the spots of sunlight you see on the ground beneath trees are perfectly round when the sun is overhead, and spread into ellipses when the sun is low in the sky? These are pinhole images of the sun, where light shines through openings in the leaves that are small compared with the distance to the ground below. A round spot 10 cm in diameter is cast by an opening that is 110 × 10 cm above ground. Tall trees make large images; short trees make small images. And, at the time of a partial solar eclipse, the images are crescents (Figure 33.8).

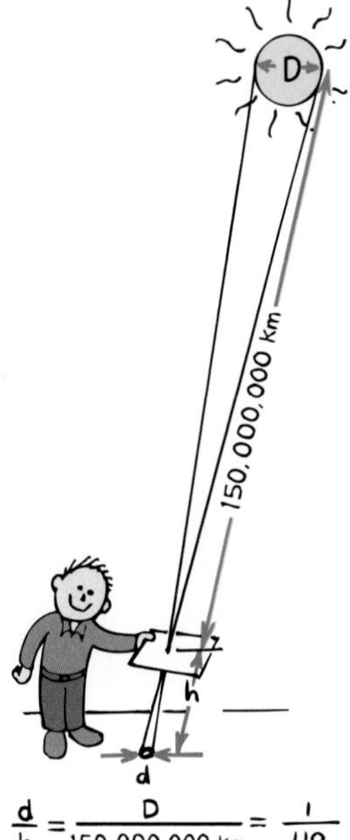

Figure 33.6
The round spot of light cast by the pinhole is an image of the sun. Its *diameter/distance* ratio is the same as the *sun's diameter/sun's distance* ratio, 1/110. The sun's diameter is 1/110 its distance from Earth.

Figure 33.7
Renoir accurately painted the spots of sunlight on his subject's clothing and surroundings—images of the sun cast by relatively small openings in the leaves above.

Figure 33.8
The crescent-shaped spots of sunlight are images of the sun when it is partially eclipsed.

33.2 The Moon

On July 20, 1969, Neil Armstrong was the first human to set foot on the moon. To date, 12 people have stood on the moon. We know more about the moon than any other celestial body. From nearly 400 kilograms of rock and soil samples brought back from lunar landings, we know the moon's age, its composition, and a lot about its history. From its low density (3.36 g/cm^3) we know the moon cannot have a substantial iron core. From its extremely low magnetic field (less than 0.0001 that of Earth's) we know it cannot have a large molten core. But there is so much we don't know about the moon; how it formed, for example. Did it split off from the earth while the earth was forming? Did it materialize somewhere else and then fall into the earth's gravitational grip? Or perhaps the earth and moon are the result of a collision and merger of two very large planets in the making. How the moon formed has been a much-debated subject.

Figure 33.9
Edwin E. Aldrin, Jr., one of the three Apollo 11 astronauts, stands on the dusty lunar surface. Old Glory is rigged to appear to be flapping in the wind, for the moon is too small to have an atmosphere.

The moon is small, with a diameter of about the distance from San Francisco to New York City. It once had a molten surface, but it cooled too rapidly for the establishment of moving crustal plates, like those of the earth. In its early history, it was intensely bombarded by meteoroids. A little more than 3 billion years ago, meteoroid bombardment and volcanic activity filled basins with lava to produce its present surface. It has undergone very little change since then. Its igneous crust is thicker than the earth's. The moon is too small with too little gravitational pull to have an atmosphere, and so, without weather, the only eroding agents have been meteoroid impacts.

Figure 33.10
The earth and moon as photographed in 1977 from the Voyager 1 spacecraft on its way to Jupiter and Saturn. (NASA)

The Phases of the Moon

Sunshine illuminates one-half of the moon's surface. The moon shows different amounts of its sunlit half as it circles around the earth each month. These changes are the **moon's phases** (Figure 33.11). The moon cycle begins with the new moon. In this phase, its dark side faces us and we see darkness. This occurs when the moon is between the earth and sun (position 1 in Figure 33.12).

During the next seven days, we see more and more of the moon's sunlit side (position 2 in Figure 33.12). The moon is going though its *waxing crescent*

Figure 33.11
The moon in its various phases.

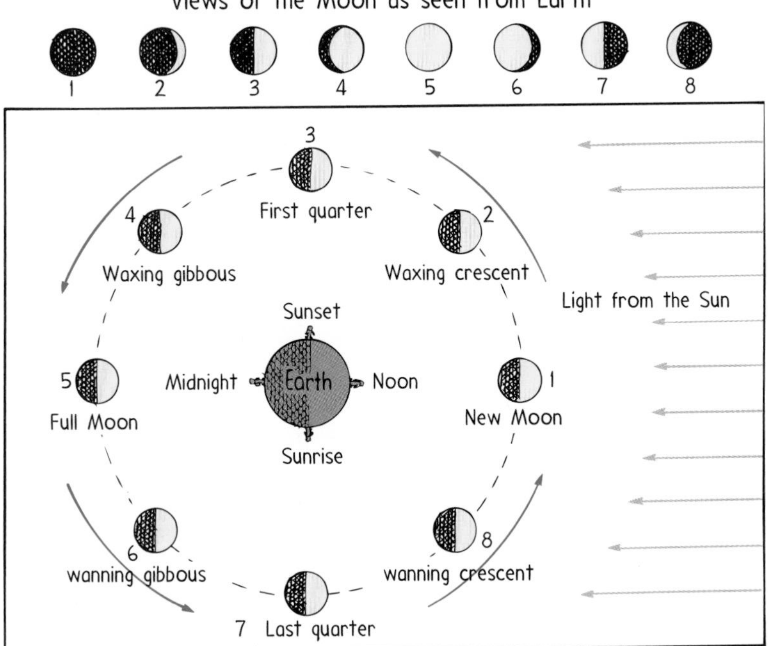

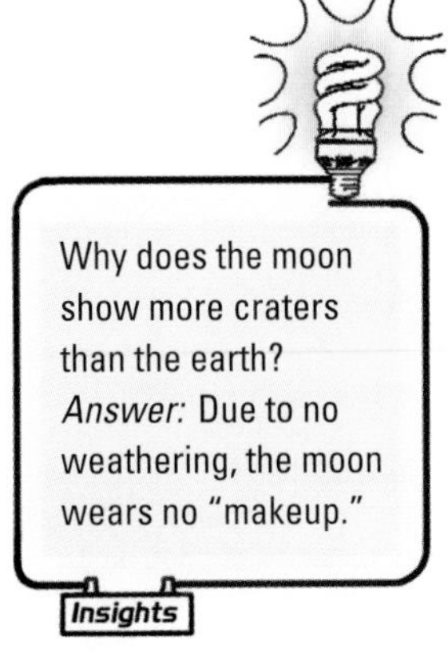

Figure 33.12
Sunlight illuminates only one-half of the moon. As the moon orbits the earth, we see varying amounts of its sunlit side. One lunar phase cycle takes 29.5 days.

If someone shone a flashlight on a ball in a dark room, you could tell where the flashlight was by looking at the illumination on the ball. The same is true of how the moon is lit by the sun.

Insights

phase ("waxing" means increasing). At the *first quarter,* the angle between the sun, moon, and earth is 90°. At this time, we see half the sunlit part of the moon (position 3 in Figure 33.12).

During the next week, we see more and more of the sunlit part. The moon is going through its *waxing gibbous* phase (position 4 in Figure 33.12). ("Gibbous" means more than half.) We see a **full moon** when the sunlit side of the moon faces us squarely (position 5). At this time, the sun, earth, and moon are lined up with the earth in between.

The cycle reverses during the following two weeks, as we see less and less of the sunlit side while the moon continues in its orbit. This movement produces the *waning gibbous, last quarter,* and *waning crescent* phases. ("Waning" means shrinking.) The time for one complete cycle is about 29.5 days.*

☑ CHECKPOINT

1. Can a full moon be seen at noon? Can a new moon be seen at midnight?
2. Astronomers prefer to view the stars when the moon is absent from the night sky. When, and how often, is the moon absent from the night sky?

Check Your Answers

1. Inspection of Figure 33.12 shows that, at noontime, you would be on the wrong side of the earth to view the full moon. Likewise, at midnight, the new moon would be absent. The new moon is in the sky in the daytime, not at night.
2. At the time of the new moon and during the week on either side of the new moon, the night sky does not show the moon. Unless an astronomer wishes to study the moon, these dark nights are the best time for viewing other objects. Astronomers usually view the night skies during two-week periods every two weeks.

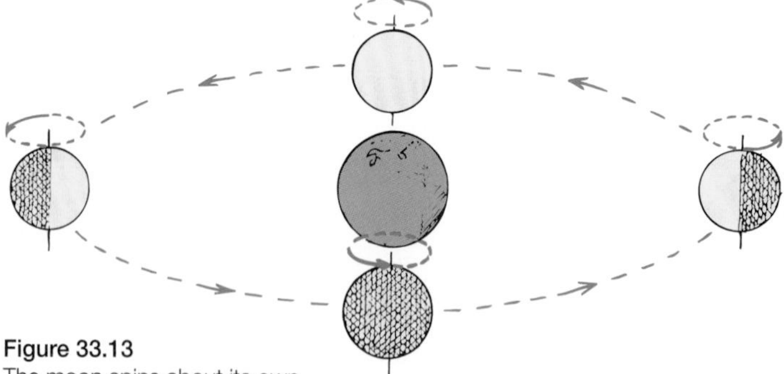

Figure 33.13
The moon spins about its own polar axis just as often as it circles the earth: Once every 29.5 days. So, as the moon circles the earth, it spins so that the same side (shown in yellow) always faces the earth. In each of the four successive positions shown here, the moon has spun 1/4 of a turn.

One Side of the Moon

The first images of the back side of the moon were taken by the unmanned Russian spacecraft Lunik 3 in 1959. The first human witnesses of the moon's back were Apollo 8 astronauts, who orbited the moon in 1968. From Earth, we see only a single lunar side. We can see this is true even with naked-eye observations—the familiar facial features of the "man in the moon" are always turned toward us on Earth. Does this mean that the moon doesn't spin about its axis like the earth does daily? No; but, relative to the stars, the moon in fact does spin, although quite slowly—about once every 27 days. This monthly rate of spin matches the rate at which the moon revolves about the earth. This explains why the same side of the moon always faces the earth (Figure 33.13). This matching of monthly spin rate and orbital revolution rate is not a coincidence. Let's see why.

*The moon actually orbits the earth once every 27.3 days relative to the stars. The 29.5-day cycle is relative to the sun and is due to the motion of the earth–moon system as it revolves about the sun.

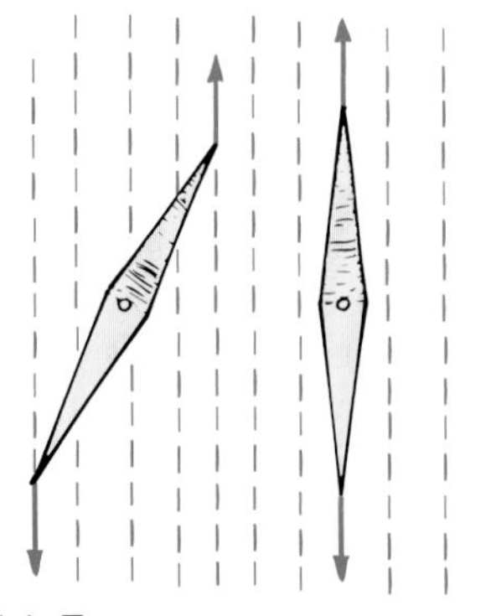

Figure 33.14
(a) When the compass needle is not aligned with the magnetic field (dashed lines), the forces represented by the blue arrows at either end produce a pair of torques that rotate the needle. (b) When the needle is aligned with the magnetic field, the forces no longer produce torques.

Think of a compass needle that lines up with a magnetic field. This lineup is caused by a *torque*—a "turning force with leverage" (like that produced by the weight of a child at the end of a seesaw). The compass needle on the left in Figure 33.14 rotates because of a pair of torques. The needle rotates counterclockwise until it aligns with the magnetic field. In a similar manner, the moon aligns with the earth's gravitational field.

We know that gravity weakens with distance (the inverse-square law, Chapter 4) so the side of the moon nearer to the earth is gravitationally pulled more than the farther side. This stretches the moon out to a football shape (just as the moon does the same to Earth and gives us tides). If its long axis doesn't line up with the earth's gravitational field, a torque acts upon it. (Figure 33.15). Like a compass in a magnetic field, it turns into alignment. So the moon lines up with the earth in its monthly orbit. One hemisphere always faces us.

It's interesting to note that for many moons orbiting other planets, a single hemisphere faces the moon's planet. We say these moons are "tidally locked." The long-range fate of the earth is to be tidally locked to the sun.

The moon has two rotational motions; it spins about its own axis while it revolves about the earth. If the moon were to spin faster or more slowly about its axis, we'd see all its faces instead of the same hemisphere.

Insights

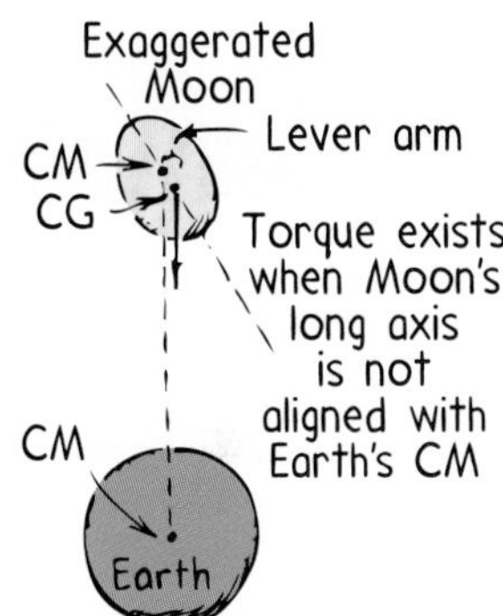

Figure 33.15
When the long axis of the moon is not aligned with the earth's gravitational field, the earth exerts a torque that rotates the moon into alignment.

☑ CHECKPOINT

A friend says that the moon does not spin about its axis, and evidence for a nonspinning moon is the fact that its same side always faces the earth. What do you say?

Check Your Answer

Place a quarter and a penny on a table. Pretend the quarter is the earth and the penny the moon. Keeping the quarter fixed, revolve the penny around it in such a way that Lincoln's head is always pointed to the center of the quarter. Ask your friend to count how many rotations the penny makes in one revolution (orbit) around the quarter. He'll see that it rotates once with each revolution. The key concept is that the moon takes the same amount of time to complete one rotation as it does to revolve around the earth.

33.3 Eclipses

Although the sun is 400 times larger in diameter than the moon, it is also 400 times farther away. So, from Earth, both the sun and moon subtend the same angle (0.5°) and appear to be the same size in the sky. It is this coincidence that allows us to see solar eclipses.

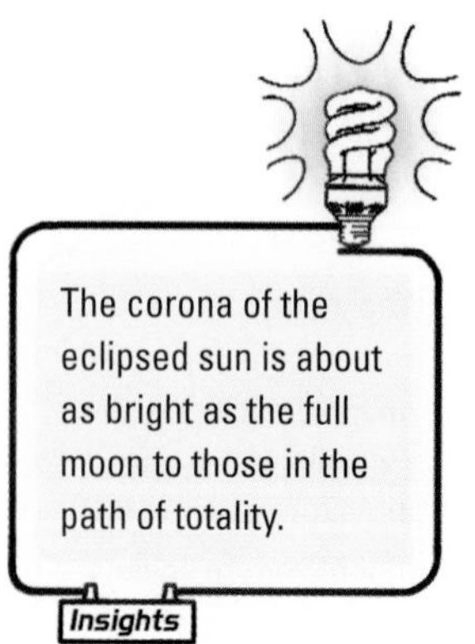

Both the earth and the moon cast shadows when sunlight shines upon them. When the path of either of these bodies crosses into the shadow cast by the other, an eclipse occurs. A **solar eclipse** occurs when the moon's shadow falls on the earth. Because of the large size of the sun, the rays taper to provide an umbra and a surrounding penumbra (Figure 33.16). An observer in the umbra part of the shadow experiences darkness during the day—a total eclipse, *totality.* Totality begins when the sun disappears behind the moon, and ends when the sun reappears on the other edge of the moon. The average time of totality is about 2 or 3 minutes, with a maximum no longer than 7.5 minutes. The eclipse time in any location is brief because of the moon's motion. An observer in the penumbra experiences a partial eclipse, and can still see part of the sun.*

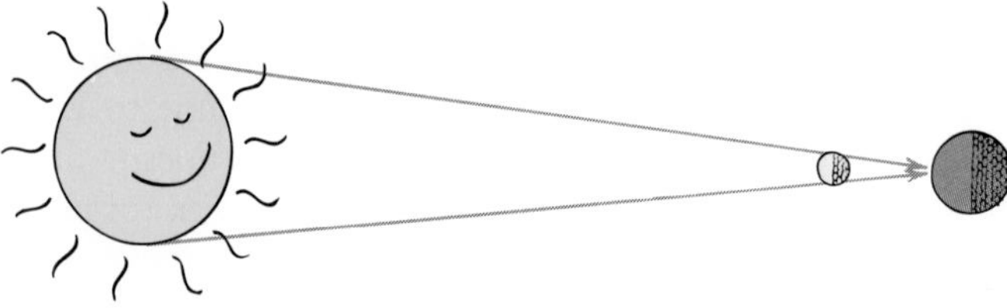

Figure 33.16
A solar eclipse occurs when the moon is directly between the sun and the earth and the moon's shadow is cast on the earth. Because of the small size of the moon and tapering of the solar rays, a solar eclipse occurs only on a small area of the earth.

Figure 33.17
Eclipsed view of the sun, showing the corona, a pearly white halo of solar gases that extends several million kilometers beyond the sun's surface.

Rather surprisingly, the darkness of totality is not complete because of the bright corona that surrounds the sun (Figure 33.17). The corona is not normally seen only because it is overwhelmed by the brightness of the sun's disk.

The alignment of Earth, moon, and sun also produces a **lunar eclipse** when the moon passes into the shadow of the earth (Figure 33.18). Usually a lunar eclipse precedes or follows a solar eclipse by two weeks. Just as all solar eclipses involve a new moon, all lunar eclipses involve a full moon. They may be partial or total. All observers on the dark side of the earth see a lunar eclipse at

During an eclipse, the earth, moon, and sun are exactly lined up. We're in the moon's shadow when we experience a solar eclipse. The moon is in the earth's shadow during a lunar eclipse.

Insights

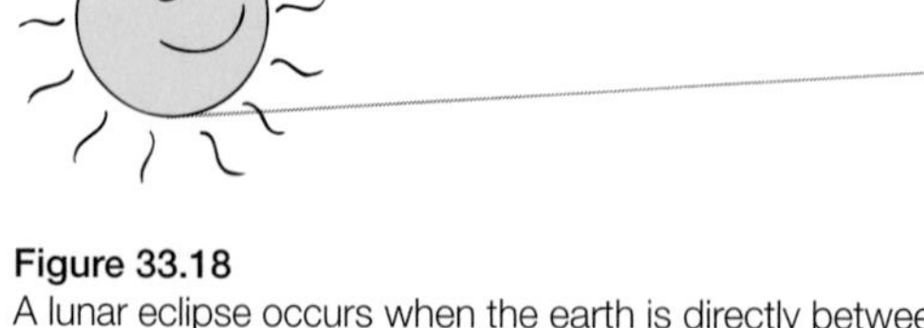

Figure 33.18
A lunar eclipse occurs when the earth is directly between the moon and the sun and the earth's shadow is cast on the moon.

*People are cautioned not to look at the sun at the time of a solar eclipse because the brightness and the ultraviolet light of direct sunlight are damaging to the eyes. This good advice is often misunderstood by those who then think that sunlight is more damaging at this special time. But staring at the sun when it is high in the sky is harmful whether or not an eclipse occurs. In fact, staring at the bare sun is more harmful than when part of the moon blocks it. The reason for special caution at the time of an eclipse is simply that more people are interested in looking at the sun during this time.

Appearance of the Moon During a Lunar Eclipse

A fully eclipsed moon is not completely dark in the shadow of the earth, but is quite visible. This is because the earth's atmosphere acts as a lens and refracts light into the shadow region—sufficient light to faintly illuminate the moon. Also, an eclipsed moon is reddish. To understand why, recall the reason for red sunsets in Chapter 12: The atmosphere scatters high-frequency light from sunlight, and the low frequencies that aren't scattered produce a reddish color (the redness of sunsets). Beams of sunlight through the air travel the longest distance to our eyes when the sun is on the horizon—at sunset or sunrise. The longer "filtering path" at that time produces the red light.

The next time you view a sunset (or sunrise), quickly move your head to one side so that the light that had been meeting your eye instead misses it and continues to the horizon behind you (Figure 33.19). If nothing else is in the way, the light will continue through the atmosphere and refract into space. If the light was reddish when it passed you, it will be even redder by the time it travels the additional distance through the atmosphere before continuing into space. This is the light that shines on the eclipsed moon—hence its deep reddish color (Figure 33.20). So, poetically enough, the redness of the eclipsed moon is the red light from all the world's sunsets and sunrises.

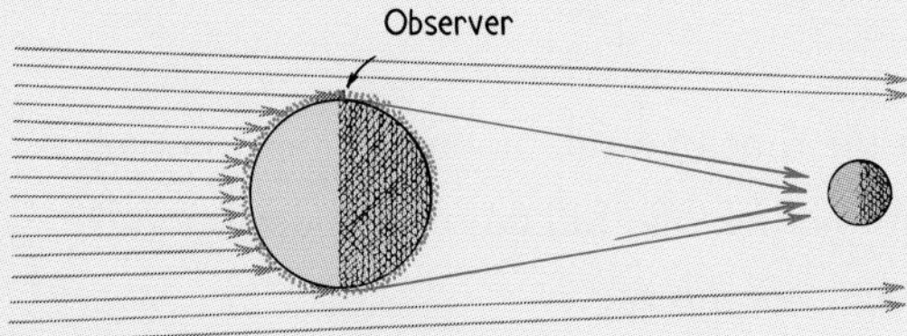

Figure 33.19
When the sun is low in the sky, the long path through the atmosphere to the observer filters blue light to make the sunlight reddish. Hence the red sunset. Light that continues past the observer travels through more atmosphere and is even redder by the time it refracts onto the eclipsed moon. Earth's atmosphere acts as a lens.

Figure 33.20
A fully eclipsed moon most often has a reddish color.

the same time. Interestingly enough, when the moon is fully eclipsed, it is still visible and is reddish in color.

Why are eclipses relatively rare events? This has to do with the different orbital planes of the earth and moon. The earth revolves around the sun in a flat planar orbit. The moon similarly revolves about the earth in a flat planar orbit. But the planes are slightly tipped with respect to each other—a 5.2° tilt (Figure 33.21). If the planes weren't tipped, eclipses would occur monthly. Because of the tip, eclipses occur only when the moon intersects the earth–sun plane at the

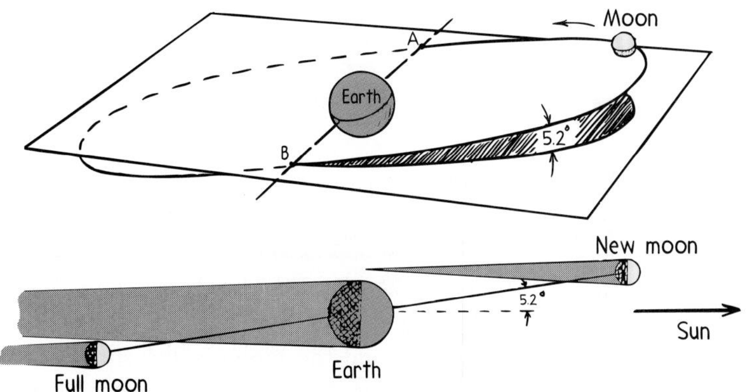

Figure 33.21
The moon orbits the earth in a plane tipped 5.2° relative to the plane of Earth's orbit around the sun. A solar or lunar eclipse occurs only when the moon intersects the earth–sun plane (points A and B) at the precise time of a three-body alignment.

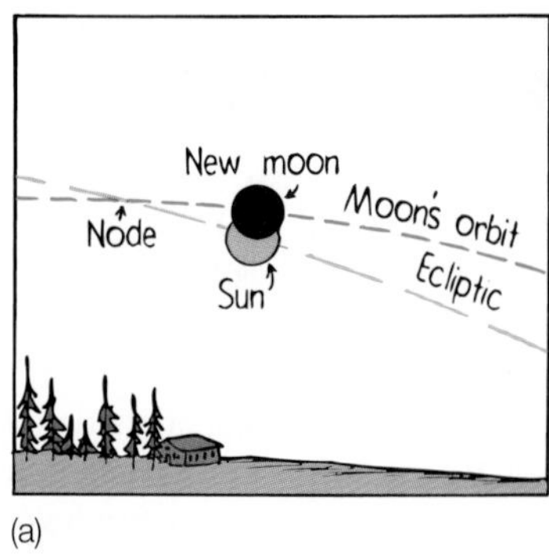

(a)

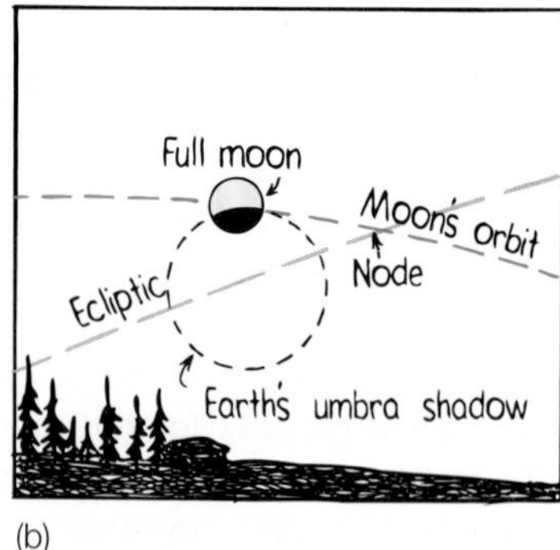

(b)

Figure 33.22
An eclipse can occur only when the earth and moon are near a node (points A and B in Figure 33.21), which is a point where their tipped orbital planes intersect. (a) A partial solar eclipse. (b) A partial lunar eclipse.

time of a three-body alignment (Figure 33.22). This occurs about two times per year, which is why there are at least two solar eclipses per year (visible only from certain locations on earth). Sometimes there are as many as seven solar and lunar eclipses in a year.

☑ CHECKPOINT

1. Does a solar eclipse occur at the time of a full moon or a new moon?
2. Does a lunar eclipse occur at the time of a full moon or a new moon?
3. Why are solar eclipses not seen monthly?
4. Which are more commonly seen—solar or lunar eclipses?

Check Your Answers

1. A solar eclipse occurs at the time of a new moon, when the moon is directly in front of the sun. Then the shadow of the moon falls on part of the earth.
2. A lunar eclipse occurs at the time of a full moon, when the moon and sun are on opposite sides of the earth. Then the shadow of the earth falls on the full moon.
3. Solar eclipses don't occur each month because most of the time the shadow cast by the moon misses the earth (due to the slight tilt of the moon's orbit around the earth). When a solar eclipse does occur, the shadow is very small, due to the tapering of sunlight; so relatively few people are in the shadow to witness the eclipse.
4. Lunar eclipses are more common. That's because the tapered shadow of the earth completely covers the moon. This allows everybody on the night side of the earth to see it at the same time. That's why nearly all your friends have seen a lunar eclipse, while relatively few of them have ever witnessed a solar eclipse.

Figure 33.23
In every second, 4.5 million tons of solar mass is converted to radiant energy in the sun. The sun is so massive, however, that in a period of one million years only one ten-millionth of its mass is consumed.

33.4 The Sun

Beyond the moon is the sun—our nearest star. Ancients who worshipped the sun seem to have realized that it is the source of all life on Earth. We are able to see, hear, touch, feel, and love only because 4.5 million tons of mass in the sun converts to radiant energy every second. A tiny fraction of this energy reaches the earth.

The energy of thermonuclear fusion occurs in the interior of the sun, where hydrogen nuclei are fused to form helium (Chapter 16). The resulting helium has 99.3 percent of the original hydrogen mass. The conversion of hydrogen to helium in the sun has been going on since it formed nearly 5 billion years ago, and it is expected to continue at this rate for another 5 billion years. If all the hydrogen in the sun's core were changed to helium, the core would still have 99.3 percent of its former mass.

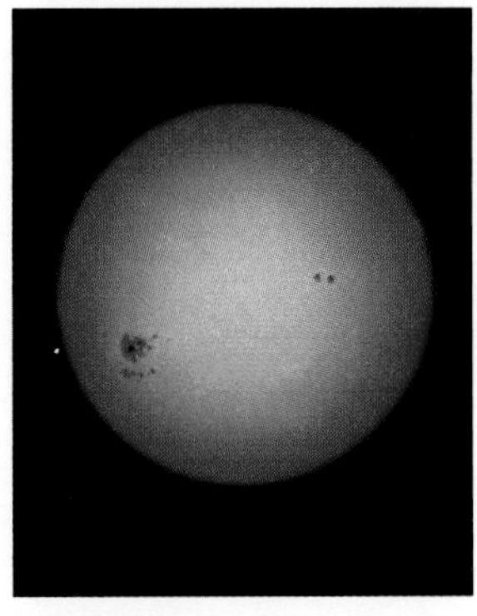

Figure 33.24
Sunspots on the solar surface are relatively cool regions. We say relatively cool because they are hotter than 4000 K. They look dark only in contrast with their 5800-K surroundings.

The visible regions of the sun are its surface and its atmosphere. The sun's tenuous surface is neither solid, nor liquid, nor gas but a glowing 5800-K plasma, probably not more than 500 kilometers thick. At nearly 6000 K, the sun's surface is well above the temperature required to vaporize any known material. This transparent solar surface is the *photosphere* (sphere of light). On this surface are relatively cool regions that appear as **sunspots** when viewed from the earth. Sunspots are cooler and darker than the rest of the sun's surface and are caused by magnetic fields that impede hot gases from rising to the surface and radiating away their heat. These can be seen by the unaided eye through protective filters or when the sun is low enough on the horizon not to damage the eyes. Sunspots are typically twice the size of the earth, they move around due to the sun's rotation, and they last about a week or so. Often, they cluster in groups (Figure 33.24).

The layer of the sun's atmosphere just above the photosphere is a transparent, 10,000-kilometer-thick shell of plasma called the *chromosphere* (sphere of color), seen during an eclipse as a pinkish glow surrounding the eclipsed sun. Beyond the chromosphere are streamers and filaments of outward-moving, high-temperature plasmas curved by the sun's magnetic field. This outermost region of the sun's atmosphere is the *corona* (back in Figure 33.17), extending out several million kilometers to where it merges into a hurricane of high-speed protons and electrons—the *solar wind.* It is the solar wind that powers the aurora borealis on Earth and produces the tails of comets.

The sun spins slowly on its axis. Since the sun is a fluid rather than a solid, different latitudes of the sun spin at different rates. Equatorial regions spin once in 25 days, but higher latitudes take up to 36 days to make a complete rotation. This differential spin means the surface near the equator pulls ahead of the surface farther north or south. The sun's differential spin wraps and distorts the solar magnetic field, which bursts out to form the sunspots mentioned earlier. A reversal of magnetic poles occurs every 11 years, and the number of sunspots also reaches a maximum every 11 years (currently). The complete cycle of solar activity is 22 years.

The Formation of the Solar System

How the sun formed is uncertain. It is generally believed to have originated from the gravitational contraction of a huge amount of interstellar matter nearly 5 billion years ago. The early universe consisted primarily of hydrogen and helium. By the time the solar system formed some 10 billion or so years later, however, it contained small amounts of all the elements known today. All elements beyond hydrogen and helium were formed in the cores of stars that existed before the sun formed. When these stars underwent their death throes, their heavier elements were spewed out into the interstellar mix, providing material for the formation of new stars.

As interstellar matter moves randomly in space, pockets of gas are believed to condense and dissolve repeatedly. They do this like wisps of fog that form and disperse in air. Exploding stars produce pressure waves and compress the gas pockets. Sometimes temporary clumps of condensed gas become permanent because the material within is held together by mutual gravity. A clump adds mass to itself by attracting neighboring material, and then, due to gravity, it falls in upon itself. Gravitational potential energy becomes thermal energy, and the clump's center becomes hotter. Continued gravitational contraction moves concentrated hot matter toward the center. Like an ice skater drawing his or her arms inward when going into a spin, any rotational motion of the contraction speeds up. A faster spin flattens the matter into a disk shape (Figure 33.25), which enhances radiation of its energy into space and causes causes the disk to cool. In the formation of our solar system, this cooling likely led to the condensation of matter in swirling eddies—the birthplaces of the planets.

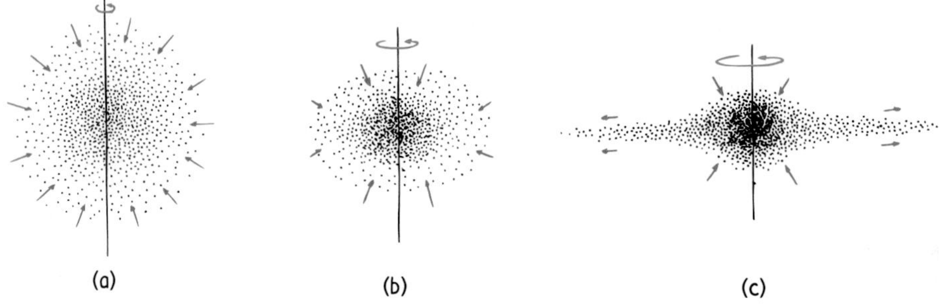

Figure 33.25
(a) A slowly rotating pocket of interstellar gas contracts as a result of the mutual gravitation between all the particles in it. (b) The law of conservation of angular momentum accounts for the pocket speeding up. (c) The increased momentum of individual particles and clusters of particles causes them to move in wider paths about the rotational axis, producing an overall disk shape.

The center of the disk would have been too hot to allow matter to solidify. But, farther out, heavier material probably solidified to become the four inner planets: Mercury, Venus, Earth, and Mars. Farther from the hot center, condensations of larger amounts of lighter matter, mostly hydrogen, formed the giant outer planets: Jupiter, Saturn, Uranus, and Neptune. Small and distant Pluto, as we shall see, is an exception to this creation hypothesis.

So we have a solar system, our home in the universe. Of the countless generations who have wondered about our place in the universe, only those of the past few generations have begun to understand it.

☑ CHECKPOINT

What is the evidence that our sun is a second- or third-generation star?

Check Your Answer

The first stars were made only of hydrogen and helium. Heavy elements appeared after these stars fused lighter elements into heavier elements in their cores. When stars explode, they spew heavy elements into space. These elements mix with others and become the material for the formation of new stars. The abundance of heavy elements in the solar system is evidence of the existence of exploding stars in the past. So the sun is young. There are many stars in our galaxy that are twice as old as the sun. Astronomers are not surprised to learn that these older stars contain lower amounts of the heavier elements.

33.5 The Planets

The ancients could tell the difference between planets and stars because of the differences in their movements in the sky. The stars remain relatively fixed in their patterns in the sky, but the planets wander. The planets were called the *wanderers*. Today we know that planets are relatively cool bodies that orbit the sun. Planets emit no visible light of their own, and, like the moon, they simply reflect sunlight.

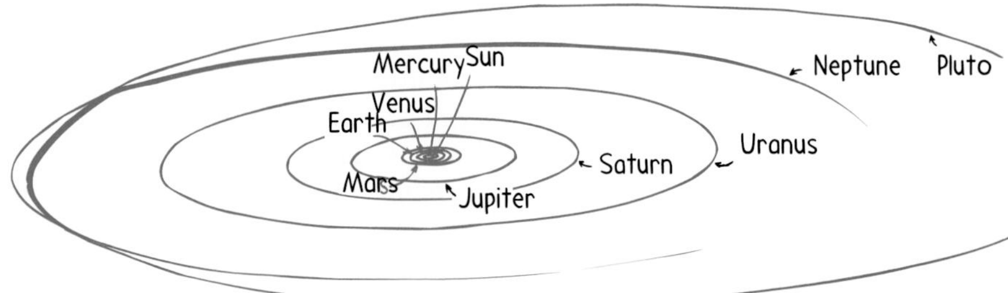

Figure 33.26
Scale drawing of the solar system, showing the orbits of the four inner planets crowded around the sun, with the four outer planets and Pluto orbiting at greater distances.

Very little was known about the planets a century or more ago. Detailed knowledge of the planets today is enormous. How human knowledge advanced—from only knowing planets as starlike spots that cross the nighttime skies to what we understand today—is a fascinating detective story. The journey of discovery was made possible first by careful observation with the naked eye, then with telescopes, and more recently with satellite probes launched from Earth.

Today we know there are five classes of objects that orbit the sun. The inner terrestrial planets, the asteroid belt, the outer gaseous planets, the Kuiper belt of comets, and, much more distant, the Oort cloud of comets. Planets are the major bodies orbiting the sun. They are massive enough for their gravity to make them spherical, but small enough to avoid thermonuclear fusion in their cores.

Table 33.1

	Mean Distance from Sun (Earth-distances, Au)	Orbital Period (years)	Diameter		Mass		Average Density
			(km)	(Earth = 1)	(kg)	(Earth = 1)	(g/cm^3)
Sun			1,392,000	109.1	1.99×10^{30}	3.3×10^{5}	1.41
Mercury	0.39	0.24	4,880	0.38	3.3×10^{23}	0.06	5.4
Venus	0.72	0.62	12,100	0.95	4.9×10^{24}	0.81	5.2
Earth	1.00	1.00	12,760	1.00	6.0×10^{24}	1.00	5.5
Mars	1.52	1.88	6,800	0.53	6.4×10^{23}	0.11	3.9
Jupiter	5.20	11.86	142,800	11.19	1.90×10^{27}	317.73	1.3
Saturn	9.54	29.46	120,700	9.44	5.7×10^{26}	95.15	0.7
Uranus	19.18	84.0	50,800	3.98	8.7×10^{25}	14.65	1.3
Neptune	30.06	164.79	49,600	3.81	1.0×10^{26}	17.23	1.7
Pluto	39.44	247.70	2,300	0.18	10^{22}	0.002	1.9

The Inner Planets

Compared with the outer planets, the four planets nearest the sun are close together. These are Mercury, Venus, Earth, and Mars. These small and dense inner planets all have atmospheres (though Mercury barely has one). They are rocky planets, each with a solid, mineral-containing crust and an earth-like composition. This is why they are called the *terrestrial planets.*

Satellites circling the earth are continually falling due to Earth gravity (Chapter 5). Because of their tangential speeds, they fall *around* (rather than *into*) the earth. The same is true of the planets. Because they continually circle the sun with appropriate tangential speeds, they avoid solar crashing and keep their individual identities.

Insights

Mercury is somewhat larger than the moon and similar in appearance, and it is the closest planet to the sun. Because of its closeness to the sun, it is the fastest planet, circling the sun in only 88 Earth days. Thus one "year" on Mercury lasts for only 88 Earth days. Mercury spins about its axis only three times for each two revolutions about the sun. This makes its "daytime" very long and very hot, with temperatures as high as 430°C.

Because of Mercury's smallness and weak gravitational field, it holds very little atmosphere—about a trillionth as dense as Earth's atmosphere (a better vacuum than laboratories on Earth can produce). So, without a blanket of atmosphere, and because there are no winds to transfer heat from one region to another, nighttime on mercury is very cold, about −170°C. Mercury is a fairly bright object in the nighttime sky, and is best seen as an evening star during March and April, or as a morning star during September and October. It is seen near the sun at sunup or sunset.

Venus is the second planet from the sun. Venus is frequently the first star-like object to appear after the sun sets, so it is often called the evening "star." Nearby Mercury, although less bright, is also seen as an evening and morning "star." Both Mercury and Venus are seen near the sun at either sunup or sunset.

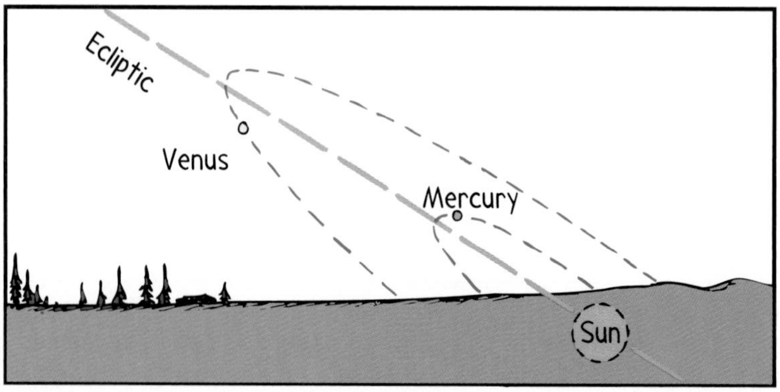

Figure 33.27
Because the orbits of Mercury and Venus lie inside the orbit of Earth, they are always near the sun. Near sunset (or sunrise), they are visible as evening "stars" (or morning "stars").

Compared with the other planets, Venus most closely resembles Earth. It is similar in size, density, and distance from the sun. A major difference is its very dense atmosphere, opaque cloud cover, and high average temperature (460°C)—too hot for oceans. Another difference between Venus and Earth is in how the two planets spin about their axes. Venus takes 243 Earth days to make one full spin, and only 225 Earth days to make one revolution around the sun. This means that a day on Venus lasts longer than a year! Venus spins in a direction opposite to the direction of Earth's spin. A space-traveling observer hovering about the solar system who sees Earth spinning counterclockwise sees Venus spinning clockwise.

Because Venus has been considered as almost an Earth twin, early speculations were that its surface is a steamy swamp inhabited by unfamiliar creatures. Speculations about life there ceased after visits by space probes. In recent years, 17 probes have landed on the surface of Venus. There have been 18 flyby spacecraft (notably Pioneer Venus in 1978 and Magellan in 1993). From spacecraft data, we know that Venus has been very active volcanically and is an extremely harsh place. However, gathered evidence suggests that the surface temperature and the atmosphere of Venus were initially very much like those of Earth. Whereas most of Earth's carbon dioxide is locked up in limestone formations and oceans, with very little in the atmosphere, the greater amount of sunlight on Venus has produced the opposite result on that planet. It now has the hottest planetary surface in the solar system. Much carbon dioxide escaped into its atmosphere, which increased the greenhouse effect and released even more carbon dioxide, which now makes up about 96 percent of the atmosphere. Venus can serve as a model for Earth, for we wonder if a small rise in temperature here on Earth could trigger a similar irreversible greenhouse effect in our atmosphere.

Figure 33.28
The Earth, the blue planet.

Earth is well described in Chapters 25–32, so our treatment here is very brief. In answer to the question of what it must be like to live in outer space, we must not forget that we in fact *are* in outer space—gathered together on a hospitable planet in an inhospitable universe. Planet Earth is our home, and it deserves our greatest respect.

Ours is the blue planet, with more water surface than land. We're not too close to the sun and not too far away, with an average surface temperature delicately balanced between that of freezing and boiling water. And the atmosphere is just dense enough to keep the oceans liquid. The insulating properties of our atmosphere and our relatively high daily spin rate allow only a brief and small lowering of temperature on the nighttime side of the earth. So temperature extremes of day and night are favorable for life on Earth. Considering the harshness of most of the universe, the earth is a very nice place to live. Our activities ought to be consistent with keeping it that way.

Mars captures our fancy as another world, perhaps even as a world with life. This is because of the similarities between Earth and Mars: Mars is a little more than half Earth's size, its mass is about one-ninth that of Earth, and it has a core, mantle, crust, and a thin, nearly cloudless atmosphere. It has polar ice caps and seasons that are nearly twice as long as Earth's because Mars takes nearly two Earth years to orbit the sun. When Mars is closest to Earth, a situation which occurs once every 15 to 17 years, its bright, ruddy color outshines the brightest stars.

The Martian atmosphere is about 95 percent carbon dioxide, with only about 0.15 percent oxygen. So bring your own air supply if you plan to visit there. Also bring warm clothing, for its surface temperature at the equator ranges from a comfortable 30°C in the day to a chilly −130°C at night. Night is only slightly longer than on Earth, for the Martian day lasts 24 hours and 37.4 minutes. Never mind your raincoat, for there is far too little water vapor in the atmosphere for rain. Even the ice at the planet's poles consist primarily of carbon dioxide. And don't give a second thought to waterproof footwear, for the low atmospheric pressure won't permit the existence of any puddles or lakes.

Figure 33.29
Martian canals mapped by astronomer Percival Lowell in the late 1800s. The canals proved to be optical illusions produced by the brain's ability to assemble vague markings into a coherent image (the same ability that enables us to see TV images rather than swarms of incoherent dots).

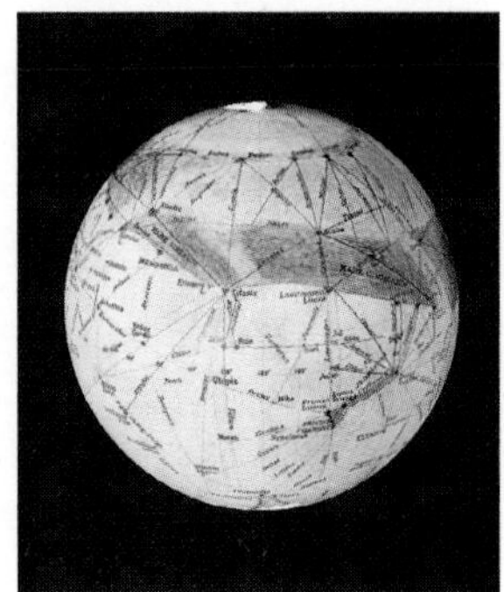

The presence on Mars of features that appear to be dry ocean beds has been taken as an indication that water was once abundant in the Martian past. Channels on the Martian surface that appear to have been carved by water are seen by visiting spacecraft. Although these could not be seen through the telescopes of early investigators, some surface features on Mars were imagined by those early investigators to be canals, reinforcing the notion then of a Martian civilization (Figure 33.29). Although there are questionable traces of life in

Figure 33.30
The rover Sojourner on the surface of Mars before setting out to explore the red planet.

Martian meteorites found in Antarctica, landings on Mars show that it has no life at the surface and no canals. The 1997 Pathfinder Mission showed it to be a very dry and windy place. Since the Martian atmosphere has a very low density, unequal heating produces Martian winds that are about ten times faster than the winds on Earth.

Mars has two small moons—Phobos, the inner one, and Deimos, the outer. Both are potato-shaped and have cratered surfaces. Phobos orbits in the same easterly direction in which Mars spins (like our moon), at a distance of almost 6000 kilometers in a period of 7.5 hours. From Mars it appears about half the size of our moon. Deimos is about half the size of Phobos, and it orbits Mars in 30.3 hours at a distance of 20,000 kilometers from the Martian surface.

The Outer Planets

The more widely spaced outer planets beyond Mars are much different from the inner planets. They're different in size, in composition, and in the way they were formed. Jupiter, Saturn, Uranus, and Neptune are gigantic, gaseous, low-density worlds. Because Saturn, Uranus, and Neptune are similar to Jupiter, the nearest and largest of the outer planets, all four of them are called *Jovian* planets. All have ring systems, Saturn's being the most prominent. Beyond these giants is outermost Pluto, much more dissimilar than any other planet. Pluto is neither terrestrial nor Jovian and is a planet only in a historic sense. We will consider the outer planets in the order of their distance from the sun.

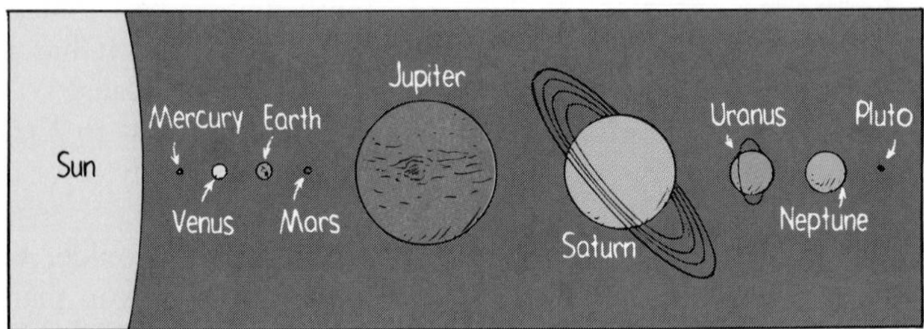

Figure 33.31
Relative sizes of the sun and planets. The sun's diameter extends more than 10 times that of Jupiter.

Jupiter is the largest of all the planets. Its yellow light in the night sky outshines the stars. In prespacecraft years, Jupiter was thought of as a failed star, because its composition is closer to that of the sun than to that of the terrestrial planets. Jupiter is more liquid than gaseous or solid. It spins rapidly about its axis in about ten hours, a speed that flattens it so that its equatorial diameter is about 6 percent greater than its polar diameter. As with the sun, all parts do not rotate in unison. Equatorial regions complete a full revolution several minutes before nearby regions in higher and lower latitudes. Jupiter doesn't have a firm surface crust that an astronaut could walk on. And, even if there were a place to stand, atmospheric pressure would be a crushing experience. The atmospheric pressure at Jupiter's surface is more than a million times more than the atmospheric pressure of Earth. Jupiter's atmosphere is about 82 percent hydrogen, 17 percent helium, and 1 percent methane, ammonia, and other molecules.

The average diameter of Jupiter is about eleven times greater than Earth's, which means Jupiter's volume is more than a thousand times Earth's. Jupiter's mass is greater than the combined masses of all the other planets. Due to its low density, however—about one-fourth of Earth's—Jupiter's mass is barely more than three hundred times Earth's. Jupiter's core is a solid sphere about 20 times as massive as the entire earth, and it is composed of iron, nickel, and other minerals.

Figure 33.32
Jupiter, with its moons Io and Europa, as seen from the Voyager I spacecraft in February 1979. The great red spot (lower left) is a cyclonic weather pattern of high winds and turbulence that is larger than the earth. (Source: NASA)

More than half of Jupiter's volume is an ocean of liquid hydrogen. Beneath the hydrogen ocean lies an inner layer of hydrogen compressed into a sort of liquid metallic state. In it are abundant conduction electrons that flow to produce Jupiter's enormous magnetic field. The strong magnetic field about the planet captures high-energy particles and produces radiation belts 400 million times as energetic as Earth's Van Allen radiation belts. Radiation levels surrounding Jupiter are the highest ever recorded in space.

Surface temperatures are about the same day and night. Jupiter radiates about twice as much heat as it receives from the sun. The excess heat likely comes from internal heat generated long ago by gravitational contraction at the time the planet formed. When forming planets contract, gravitational potential energy is converted to thermal energy.

If you're planning to visit Jupiter, choose one of its moons instead. There are at least 28 of them, in addition to a faint ring orbiting the planet. Among the four largest moons (which were discovered by Galileo in 1610), Io and Europa are about the size of our moon, and Ganymede and Callisto are about as large as Mercury. The most intriguing of Jupiter's moons seems to be Io, which has more volcanic activity than any other body in the solar system.

Saturn is one of the most remarkable objects in the sky, mainly because its rings are clearly visible with a small telescope. It is brighter than all but two stars, and it is second among the planets in mass and size. Saturn is twice as far from Earth as Jupiter. Its diameter, not counting its ring system, is nearly ten times that of Earth, and its mass is nearly 100 times greater. It is composed primarily of hydrogen and helium, and it has the lowest density of any planet, only 0.7 times the density of water. These characteristics mean that Saturn would easily float in a bathtub, if the bathtub were large enough. Its low density and its 10.2-hour rapid spin produce more polar flattening than can be seen in any other planet. Like Jupiter, Saturn radiates about twice as much heat energy as it receives from the sun.

Figure 33.33
Saturn surrounded by its famous rings, which are believed to be composed of rocks and chunks of ice.

Saturn's rings, likely only a few kilometers thick, lie in a plane coincident with Saturn's equator. Four concentric rings have been known for many years, and spacecraft missions have detected others. The rings are composed of chunks of frozen water and rocks, believed to be the material of a moon that never formed or the remnants of a moon torn apart by tidal forces. All the rocks and bits of matter that make up the rings pursue independent orbits about Saturn. The inner parts of the ring travel faster than the outer parts, just as any satellite near a planet travels faster than a more distant satellite.

Saturn has some 24 moons beyond its rings. The largest is Titan, 1.6 times larger than our moon and even larger than Mercury. It spins once every 16 days and has a methane atmosphere with atmospheric pressure that is likely greater than Earth's. Its surface temperature is cold—roughly 170°C. So bring a heavy coat and breathing gear if you plan to visit Titan. If that doesn't work out, try another of Saturn's large moons, Iapetus. One side of Iapetus is very bright and the other very dark. Try the region between these two extremes.

Saturn's entire ring system lies within a critical distance called the Roche limit, equal to about 2.4 Saturn radii. The Roche limit, named after the nineteenth-century French mathematician Edouard Roche, is the distance at which gravitational attraction by a planet on two adjacent orbiting particles is larger than the attraction of the two particles to each other. If our moon came within 2.4 Earth radii, its expected fate would be to be torn apart to form a ring system about the earth.

Insights

Uranus is twice as far from Earth as Saturn is, and it can barely be seen with the naked eye. Uranus was unknown to ancient astronomers. It has a diameter four times larger than Earth's and a density slightly greater than that of water. So, if you were able to place Uranus in a giant bathtub, it would sink. The most unusual feature of Uranus is its tilt. Its axis is tilted 98° to the perpendicular of its orbital plane, so it lies on its side. Unlike Jupiter and Saturn, it appears to have no internal source of heat. Uranus is a cold place.

Uranus has at least 21 moons, in addition to a complicated faint ring system. Recall, from Chapter 4, that perturbations in the planet Uranus led to the discovery in 1846 of a farther planet, Neptune.

Neptune has a diameter about 3.9 times greater than Earth's, its mass is 17 times greater, and its mean density is about a third that of Earth. Its atmosphere is mainly hydrogen and helium, with some methane and ammonia. Like Jupiter and Saturn, it emits about 2.5 times as much heat energy as it receives from the sun.

Neptune has at least eight moons in addition to a ring system. Recent findings suggest a total of eleven moons. The largest moon is Triton, which orbits Neptune in 5.9 days in a direction opposite to the planet's eastward spin. Triton's diameter is three-quarters the size of our moon's diameter, and Triton has twice as much mass as our moon. It has bright polar caps and geysers of liquid nitrogen. A smaller moon, Nereid, takes nearly a year to orbit Neptune in a highly elongated elliptical path.

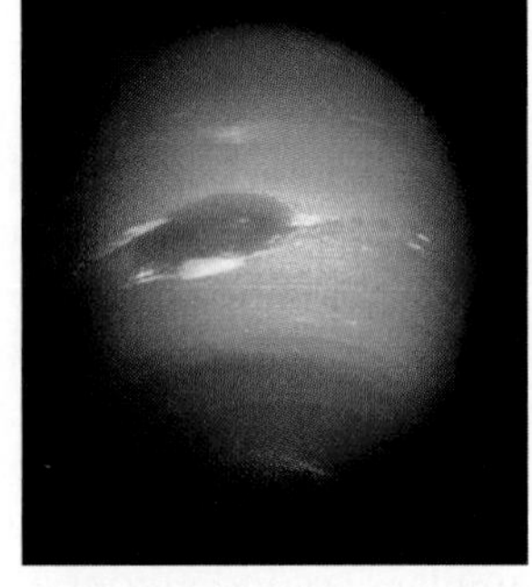

Figure 33.34
Cyclonic disturbances on Neptune in 1989 produced a great dark spot, which was even larger than the earth and similar to Jupiter's great red spot. The spot has now disappeared. (Source: NASA)

Recent studies of Galileo's notebooks show that Galileo saw Neptune in December, 1612 and again in January, 1613. He was interested in Jupiter at the time, and so he merely plotted Neptune as a background star.

Insights

Pluto, to most people today, is the ninth planet. Sorry, it just isn't so anymore. Whatever you learned as a child in school, Pluto doesn't fit into the family of planets. Its misplaced identity began when investigators, excited about the discovery of Neptune, searched the skies for yet another planet. It is well known that we often see what we expect or hope to see, rather than what is there. Finding further perturbations of Uranus prompted astronomers to search a certain region of the sky, and, in 1930, there it was—an object beyond Neptune. The object was named Pluto, and it joined the list of planets.

Today we know that Pluto is smaller than our moon, having a diameter about one-fifth Earth's diameter and a mass of about 1/500 that of Earth. Pluto has bright polar caps that are probably frozen methane. Its rotational period is 6.4 days. It has a moon named Charon that is about 5 to 10 percent the mass of Pluto. Charon also has a period of 6.4 days, so it appears above the same location on Pluto's surface.

Whereas most planets orbit the sun in nearly circular paths, Pluto's path is the most elliptical and most steeply inclined (17°) to the planetary plane. Pluto rotates in a direction opposite that of most of the planets, and, like Uranus, is tipped sideways, with its polar axis nearly in its orbital plane. Pluto's unique, highly elliptical orbit finds it sometimes closer to the sun than Neptune. This occurred for twenty years from 1979 to 1999. Since 1999, it has moved farther from the sun than Neptune.

Pluto's moon, *Charon,* continually faces it, just as Earth's moon faces us. Pluto is not the only body in the Kuiper Belt with a moon. A Pluto-like body discovered in 2002, named *Quaoar,* also has a moon.

Insights

We have always been fascinated about the prospect of finding other planets orbiting other stars in the universe. Today more than 100 stars with planets have been identified. These distant planets are found by wobbles in their parent stars, and more recently, by measuring miniscule reductions in light when they pass between their star and Earth. Most of these discovered planets are giant ones, similar to Jupiter. New telescopes are being devised to detect planets that are similar to Earth, planets that could possibly be home to extraterrestrial life.

A most interesting candidate is a star (47 Ursae Majoris) that is visible with the naked eye in the Great Bear constellation. This star is similar in size and chemical composition to our sun. It has at least two planets sweeping around it in nearly perfect circles, just as Earth moves around the sun. We wait in fascination for more discoveries.

33.6 The Kuiper Belt and the Oort Cloud

The Kuiper Belt

Pluto resides in a disk-shaped region beyond Neptune known as the Kuiper Belt, which is populated by many icy bodies and is considered to be the source of short-period comets. Residents of the Kuiper Belt are called TNOs (Trans-Neptunian Objects). Astronomers estimate there are at least 35,000 TNOs greater than 100 kilometers in diameter, which is several hundred times the number (and mass) of similar-sized objects in the main asteroid belt between the inner and outer planets. Some TNOs have been found that are almost as large as Pluto. Many astronomers expect that TNOs even larger and more distant than Pluto will be discovered. Astronomers are faced with whether to classify the increasing list of Pluto's neighbors as planets, or reclassify Pluto. Rather than classifying Pluto as the pipsqueak of planets, how much more appropriate that it be acknowledged as the king of the Kuiper Belt.

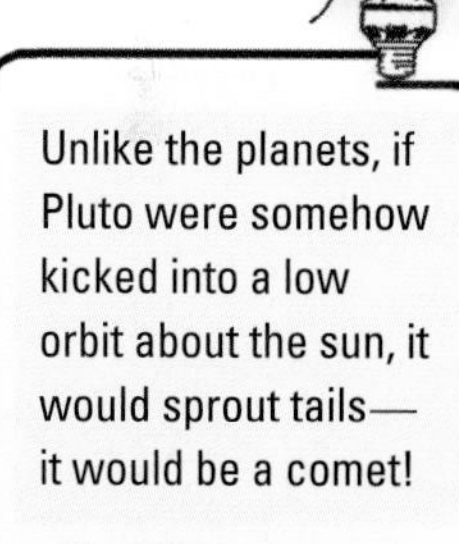

Unlike the planets, if Pluto were somehow kicked into a low orbit about the sun, it would sprout tails—it would be a comet!

Insights

The Oort Cloud

Named for the Dutch astronomer Jan Oort, who first postulated its existence in 1950, the Oort Cloud is a spherical cloud of comets beyond Neptune, extending some 1.5 light-years from the sun near the edge of its gravitational influence. The gravitational effect of passing stars and the rest of our galaxy disturbs some of the comets from the cloud so that they fall in toward the sun on highly elongated orbits, with periods as long as 30 million years. Trillions of comets reside in this far-off region.

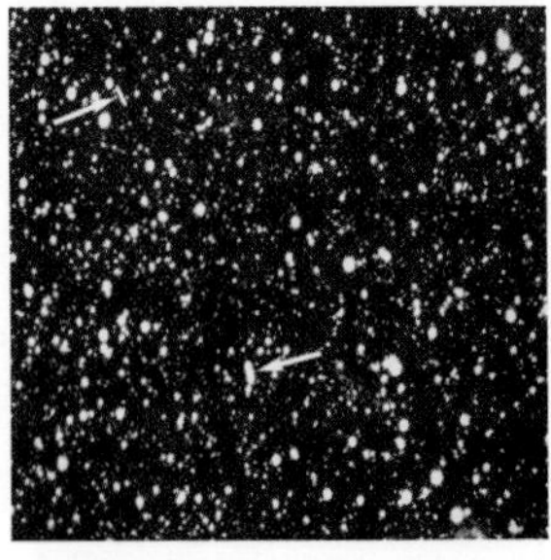

Figure 33.35
Asteroids leave blurred trails on time-exposure photographs of the stars. The images of two asteroids are indicated by the two white arrows.

33.7 Asteroids, Meteoroids, and Comets

There is an unusually large space between Mars and Jupiter. This space contains the *asteroid belt,* which is populated by tens of thousands of small rocky bodies, called **asteroids,** that orbit the sun. The smallest asteroids are irregular in shape, like boulders, and the larger ones are roughly spherical. Asteroids vary in size from grains of sand to rocky chunks hundreds of kilometers in diameter. The largest is Ceres, which is often called a *minor planet* and has a diameter of 750 kilometers. Asteroids are thought to be material that was unsuccessful in accreting to become a planet during the formation of the solar system. If the planet had formed, it would have been small, for the combined mass of all the asteroids is considerably less than the mass of our Earth's moon.

Although many asteroids neatly circle the sun, others do not. Collisions among asteroids are uncommon, but, when they do occur, they send fragments helter-skelter. Some fragments stray toward the earth. Asteroids smaller than a few hundred kilometers in diameter are called **meteoroids.** A **meteor** is a meteoroid that strikes the earth's atmosphere, usually at an altitude of about 80 kilometers, heated white-hot by friction with the atmosphere and seen from the earth as a flash of light—a "falling star." Most meteors we see are very small meteoroids, about the size of a grain of sand. Any meteor that survives its fiery descent through the atmosphere and reaches the ground is called a **meteorite.**

Figure 33.36
A meteor is produced when a meteoroid enters the earth's atmosphere, usually about 80 km high. Most are grains of sand, which are seen as "falling" or "shooting" stars.

Most meteorites are small and strike the earth with no more energy than a falling hailstone. Some are big, however, and evidence of their impact is seen as craters. If the earth were without weather and erosion, its surface would be as cratered as the moon's. Most impact craters on Earth were eroded or covered by geologic processes long ago. More recent impacts, however, leave telltale marks (Figure 33.37). The most dramatic impact on record, though not the largest,* was near the Yucatan Peninsula in Mexico 65 million years ago, which was discussed in Chapter 30. The effects of that impact likely led to the extinction of dinosaurs and half of the other species living at the end of the Cretaceous period.

Figure 33.37
The Barringer Crater in Arizona, made 25,000 years ago by an iron meteorite having a diameter of about 50 meters. The crater extends 1.2 km across and reaches 200 m deep.

☑ CHECKPOINT

Using information about the Mesozoic Era from Chapter 30, how can a meteorite impact on the earth cause mass extinctions of life?

Check Your Answer

Such a huge impact can produce a gigantic light-blocking cloud of dust for months or years. Photosynthesis cannot occur without sunlight, so food supplies diminish and organisms perish. Other killing mechanisms include acid rain, tsunamis, wildfires, and a delayed greenhouse effect. No doubt about it—meteorite impacts are not friendly events.

A **comet** is a chunk of rock, metal, dust, and ice, much like a dirty snowball, that orbits the sun. Each comet has only a tiny solid part, called a *nucleus,* often no bigger than a few kilometers across. The nucleus contains icy chunks

*The Vredefort crater in South Africa, and the Sudbury crater in Canada are both larger than the crater that was found at Yucatan.

and frozen gases packed together with bits of embedded rock, metal, and dust. Interestingly, most of the meteors we see are small particles of comet debris (Figure 33.38). Unlike meteors that shoot briefly across the sky, a comet moves slowly and gracefully to display one of nature's most beautiful astronomical spectacles.

Figure 33.38
When the earth crosses the orbit of a comet, we see a meteor shower.

Whereas asteroids travel between the planets in roughly circular orbits, the orbits of comets are highly elliptical, extending to the Oort Cloud, far beyond the Kuiper Belt. As a comet approaches the sun, solar heat vaporizes the ices. Escaping vapors glow to produce a fuzzy, luminous ball called a *coma.* A coma can be a million kilometers in diameter. Within the bright coma is the solid part of the comet, the nucleus.

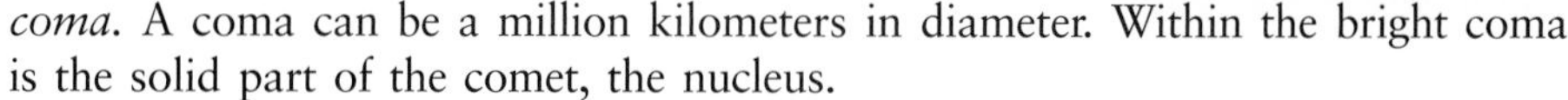

The solar wind and radiation pressure blow luminous vapors from the coma outward, away from the sun. That's why a comet has a long flowing *tail.* This tail can extend over 100 million kilometers. Most often, the sun produces two tails on a comet: an *ion tail* and a *dust tail* (Figure 33.39). The ions are largely the remnants of water vapor, too small to be affected by the pressure of sunlight. They flow with the high-speed solar wind, directly away from the sun. The dust tail is composed of micron-sized dust particles large enough to be affected by radiation pressure. The lower-speed dust tail curves, much as a water stream curves from the nozzle of a moving hose.

Figure 33.39
The two tails of Comet West. A comet is always named after the person who first sees it. Guess who was the first person to see this comet?

The density of the material in a comet's tail is quite low—less than the density of industrial vacuums in Earth laboratories. So compared with the earth's atmosphere, the tails of a comet are "nothing at all." When a tail crosses the earth directly, except for meteor showers high in the atmosphere, nothing at all changes at the earth's surface. The incidence of a comet nucleus, however, is a different story. "Meteor" craters are formed by the impact of comets as well as meteors. Only the impact debris indicates the difference.

Figure 33.40
Comet Hale-Bopp in 1997.

Comets are plentiful. There is almost always a comet in the sky, but most are too faint to be seen without the aid of a good telescope. About a hundred or more new comets are discovered each year, some by amateur astronomers. Most comets have no visible tails, for their supply of ice is eventually exhausted. After about 100 to 1000 passes around the sun, a comet is pretty much burned out.

Summary of Terms

Moon phases The cycles of change of the "face" of the moon, changing from *new,* to *waxing,* to *full,* to *waning,* and back to *new.*

New moon The phase of the moon when darkness covers the side facing Earth.

Full moon The phase of the moon when its sunlit side is the side facing earth.

Solar eclipse The phenomenon whereby the shadow of the moon falls upon the earth, producing a region of darkness in the daytime.

Lunar eclipse The phenomenon whereby the shadow of the earth falls upon the moon, producing relative darkness of the full moon.

Sunspots Temporary, relatively cool and dark regions on the sun's surface.

Planets The major bodies orbiting the sun, which are massive enough for their gravity to make them spherical but small enough to avoid having nuclear fusion in their cores.

Kuiper Belt The disk-shaped region of the sky beyond Neptune that is populated by many icy bodies and is a source of short-period comets.

Oort Cloud The region beyond the Kuiper Belt that is populated by trillions of icy bodies and is a source of long-period comets.

Asteroid A small, rocky, planetlike fragment that orbits the sun. Tens of thousands of these objects make up an asteroid belt between the orbits of Mars and Jupiter.

Meteoroid A small rock in interplanetary space.

Meteor The streak of light produced by a meteoroid burning in the earth's atmosphere; a "shooting star."

Meteorite A meteoroid, or a part of a meteoroid, that has survived passage through the earth's atmosphere to reach the ground.

Comet A body composed of ice and dust that orbits the sun, usually in a very eccentric orbit, and that casts a luminous tail produced by solar radiation pressure when it is close to the sun.

Review Questions

33.1 Early Astronomical Measurements

1. Who measured the size of the earth more than 1700 years before Columbus first set sail for America?
2. If the shadow cast by the pillar in Alexandria had been as long as the pillar itself, would this have meant that the sun's rays would have made an angle of 45° with the pillar? And would this have indicated that the distance between Alexandria and Syene was equal to the earth's radius?
3. When you match the size of a coin with the size of the moon you see in the sky, and when you find that the distance between your eye and the coin is 110 coins long, what does this tell you about how many moon diameters would fit between the moon and earth?
4. Is the distance between the earth and the sun equal to 110 sun diameters?
5. What will be the shape of the light from the sun falling onto a small star-shaped hole instead of a round pin hole in Figure 33.6?

33.2 The Moon

6. Why does the moon have no atmosphere?
7. Where is the sun when you view a full moon?
8. Where are the sun and the moon at the time of a new moon?

33.3 Eclipses

9. In what alignment of sun, moon, and Earth does a solar eclipse occur?
10. In what alignment of sun, moon, and Earth does a lunar eclipse occur?
11. Why is totality during a lunar eclipse not altogether dark?
12. Why don't eclipses occur monthly, or nearly monthly?
13. How does the moon's rate of rotation about its own axis compare with its rate of revolution around the earth?
14. What does the moon have in common with a compass needle?

33.4 The Sun

15. What happens to the amount of the sun's mass as it "burns"?
16. What are sunspots?
17. What is the solar wind?
18. How does the rotation of the sun differ from the rotation of a solid body?
19. What is the age of the sun?
20. What happens to the speed of a spinning mass of gas when it contracts?

33.5 The Planets

21. Why did the ancients call the planets "wanderers"?
22. What are the five classes of objects that orbit the sun?
23. What are the requirements of mass and size to make a body a planet?
24. Why are days on Mercury very hot and the nights very cold?
25. What two planets are evening or morning "stars"?
26. Why is Earth called "the blue planet"?

27. What gas makes up most of the Martian atmosphere?
28. Is there evidence that Mars was at one time wetter than it presently is?
29. What surface feature do Jupiter and the sun have in common?
30. Which move faster, Saturn's inner rings or the outer ones?

33.6 The Kuiper Belt and the Oort Cloud

31. What is the Kuiper Belt?
32. Why was Pluto considered to be a planet for more than 70 years, and why is it now not considered to be one?
33. What is the Oort Cloud, and what is it noted for?

33.7 Asteroids, Meteoroids, and Comets

34. Distinguish between an asteroid, a meteoroid, and a comet.
35. What is a falling star?
36. What causes comet tails to point away from the sun?

Activity

Look at spherical shapes in sunlight: the dome of a building, a ball on the ground, the moon in the sky. From their sunlit parts, determine the location of the sun.

Exercises

1. The shadow cast by a vertical pillar in Alexandria at noon during the summer solstice is found to be one-eighth the height of the pillar. The distance between Alexandria and Syene is one-eighth the earth's radius. What is the geometric connection, if any, between these two 1-to-8 ratios?
2. We know that the sun is much larger than the moon, but both appear the same size in the sky. What is your explanation?
3. Why did Aristarchus make his measurement of the sun's distance at the exact time of a visible half moon?
4. Which is larger, the radius of the sun or the distance between the moon and the earth? (See the inside front cover.)
5. Why are there many more craters on the surface of the moon than on the surface of the earth?
6. What is the main advantage of the Hubble Telescope compared with telescopes on mountaintops?
7. What would be a main advantage of a telescope on the moon compared with telescopes on mountaintops on Earth?
8. Why is there no atmosphere on the moon? Defend your answer.
9. Is the fact that we see only one side of the moon evidence that the moon spins or that it doesn't rotate? Defend your answer.
10. Photograph (a) shows the moon partially lit by the sun. Photograph (b) shows a Ping-Pong ball in sunlight. Compare the positions of the sun in the sky when each photograph was taken. Do the photos support or refute the claim that they were taken on the same day? Defend your answer.

(a)

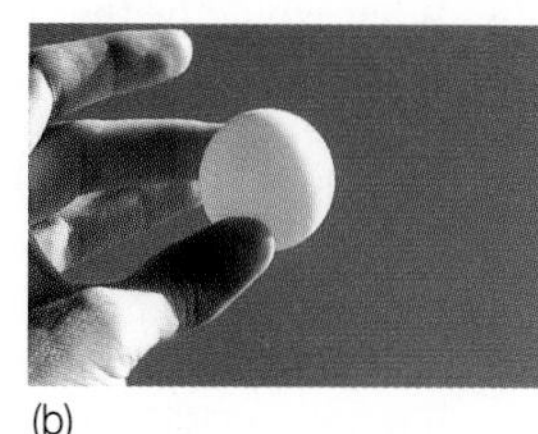
(b)

11. Do star astronomers make stellar observations during the full moon part of the month or during the new moon part of the month? Does it make a difference?
12. Nearly everyone has witnessed a lunar eclipse, but relatively few people have seen a solar eclipse. Why?
13. Because of the earth's shadow, a partially eclipsed moon looks like a cookie with a bite taken out of it. Explain, with a sketch, how the curvature of the bite indicates the size of the earth relative to the size of the moon. How does the tapering of the sun's rays affect the curvature of the bite?
14. Why is it not totally dark in the location where a total solar eclipse occurs?
15. What energy processes make the sun shine? In what sense can it be said that gravity is the prime source of solar energy?
16. A TV screen is normally light gray when it is not illuminated. How is the blackness of sunspots similar to the blackness in images on a TV screen?
17. When a contracting ball of hot gas spins into a disk shape, it cools. Why?
18. The greenhouse effect is very pronounced on Venus, but it doesn't exist on Mercury. Why?
19. Where are the elements heavier than hydrogen and helium formed?
20. What is the cause of winds on Mars (and on almost every other planet, too)?
21. What is the major difference between the terrestrial and Jovian planets?
22. What does Jupiter have in common with the sun that the terrestrial planets don't? What differentiates Jupiter from a star?

23. Why are the seasons on Uranus different from the seasons on any other planet?
24. What were the similar historical circumstances that linked the names of Neptune and Pluto with the elements neptunium and plutonium?
25. How would Pluto appear if it were kicked into a low orbit around the sun?
26. Why are meteorites so much more easily found on Antarctica than on the other continents?
27. A meteor is visible only once, but a comet may be visible at regular intervals throughout its lifetime. Why?
28. What would be the consequence of a comet's tail sweeping across the earth?
29. Chances are about 50–50 that, in any night sky, there is at least one visible comet that has not been discovered. This keeps amateur astronomers busy looking, night after night, because the discoverer of a comet receives the honor of having it named for him or her. With this high probability of comets being visible in the sky, why aren't more of them found?
30. In terms of the conservation of energy, describe why comets eventually burn out.

Chapter 33 Online Resources

Tutorials
- Scale of the Universe
- Phases of the Moon
- Eclipses
- Formation of the Solar System

Quiz
Exercises
Flashcards
Links

CHAPTER 34
The Stars

The roots of astronomy reach back to prehistoric times when humans became familiar with star patterns in the night sky. They divided the night sky into groups of stars, such as the seven stars we now know as the Big Dipper. Star groups in large sections of the sky became the *constellations*. The names of the constellations today carry over mainly from the names assigned to them by early Greek, Babylonian, and Egyptian astronomers. The Greeks, for example, included the stars of the Big Dipper into a larger group of stars that outlined a bear—the large constellation, Ursa Major (the Great Bear). The grouping of stars and the significance given to them varied from culture to culture. Humans in the Southern Hemisphere, of course, saw groups of stars not visible to their northern contemporaries. To some cultures, the constellations stimulated storytelling and the making of great myths; to other cultures, the constellations honored great heroes, such as Hercules and Orion; to others, they served as navigational aids for travelers and sailors; and to still others, they provided a guide for the planting and harvesting of crops, because the constellations were seen to move periodically in the sky, in concert with the seasons. Charts of this periodic movement became some of the first calendars.

Stars were thought to be points of light on a great revolving celestial sphere with the earth at the center. Because positions of the sphere were believed to affect earthly events, they were carefully measured. Keen observations gave birth to both astrology and astronomy. So we find that astronomy and astrology—science and pseudoscience—share the same roots. Today we know that the earth orbits the sun, with its night side always facing away from the sun. We can see, in Figure 34.2, why the background of stars varies in the nighttime sky throughout the year.*

When we look at the stars on a moonless night, we might guess we see many thousands or even millions of them, but the unaided eye sees at most about 3000 stars, horizon to horizon. We see many more stars

The grouping of stars into constellations tells us about the thinking of astronomers of earlier times, but it tells us nothing about the stars themselves.

Insights

* Place a lamp on a table in the middle of your room. Then move around the table, keeping your back to the lamp at all times. You'll see different parts of the room as you walk. Likewise, the night side of the earth is in view of different parts of the sky as the earth orbits about the sun. Looking at Figure 34.2, can you see why the background stars during a midday solar eclipse are of constellations normally seen six months earlier or later?

Figure 34.1
The constellations and Taurus represent figures from Greek mythology.

with a telescope, of course, but, disappointingly, distant stars appear simply as point sources with or without magnification. Only recently have telescopes been able to discern features in the nearest stars. Most stars are really very far away. Many of the brightest stars are 10 to 1000 light-years distant.* Because of their great distance, all appear equally remote from us, as on the celestial sphere imagined by the ancients. This chapter is about stars—how they are born, how they live, and how they die.†

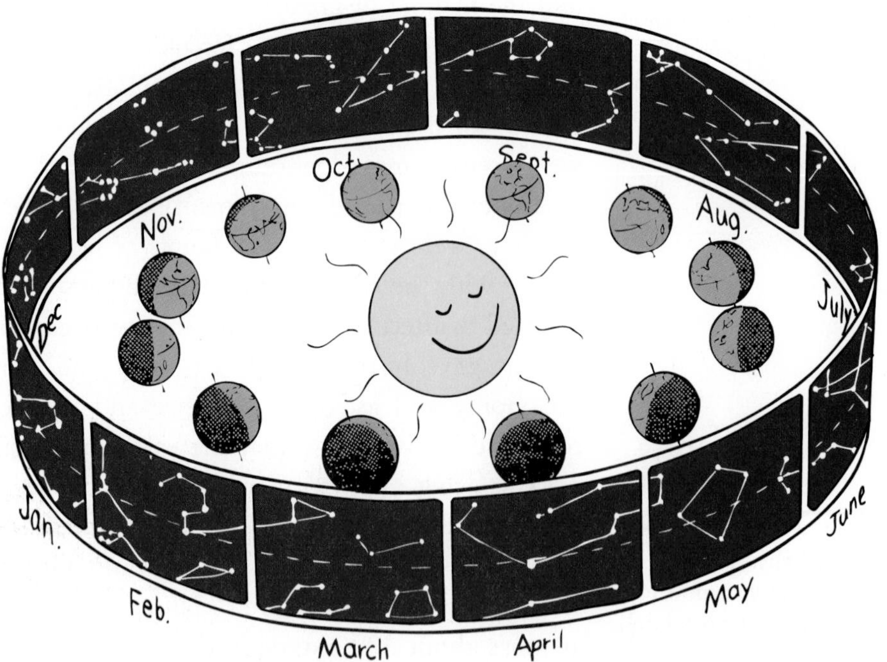

Figure 34.2
The night side of the earth always faces away from the sun. As the earth circles the sun, different parts of the universe are seen in the nighttime sky. Here the circle, representing one year, is divided into twelve parts—the monthly constellations. The stars seen in the nighttime sky change in a yearly cycle.

* One light-year is the distance light travels in one year, about 9.5×10^{12} km. Another unit of distance popular with astronomers is the *parsec,* which is equal to 3.26 light-years.

† This chapter presents a brief "This is how it is" treatment of astronomy. For an expanded "This is how we know this is how it is" treatment, refer to the "Recommended Reading and Web Sites" at the end of this book.

Link to Pseudoscience

Astrology

There is more than one way to view the cosmos and its processes—astronomy is one and astrology is another. Astrology is a belief system that began more than 2000 years ago in Babylonia. Astrology has survived nearly unchanged since the second century A.D., when some revisions were made by Egyptians and Greeks who believed that their gods moved heavenly bodies to influence the lives of people on earth. Astrology today holds that the position of the earth in its orbit around the sun at the time of birth, combined with the relative positions of the planets, has some influence over one's personal life. The stars and planets are said to affect such personal things as one's character, marriage, friendships, wealth, and death.

The question is raised as to whether the force of gravity exerted by these celestial bodies is a legitimate factor in human affairs. After all, the ocean tides are the result of the moon's and sun's positions, and the gravitational pulls between the planets perturb one another's orbits. Since slight variations in gravity produce these effects, might not slight variations in the planetary positions at the time of birth affect a newborn? If the influence of stars and planets is gravitational, then credit must also be given to the effect of the gravitational pull between the newborn and the earth itself. This pull is enormously greater than the combined pull of all the planets, even when lined in a row (as occasionally happens). The gravitational influence of the hospital building on the newborn would surely exceed that of the distant planets. So planetary gravitation cannot be an underlying agent for astrology.

Astrology must seek another realm for its basis, for all attempts to find physical explanations to support it have failed. Astrology is not a science, for it doesn't change with new information as science does, nor are its predictions borne out by fact. So the realm of astrology may be spiritual, a religion of sorts. Or it may be a primitive psychology where the stars serve as a point of departure for musings about personality and personal decisions. Or astrology may be in the realm of numerology or phrenology—a rigid and empty superstition that prevails because of its focus on what is very important to each of us—ourselves. Astrology means different things to different people.

A common position is that astrology is a harmless belief—a little fun at minimum harm. But is it harmless when believers are led to think their personalities are fixed by the stars at birth, that weak people will remain weak, that sad people will remain sad, that one's fate is dictated by the stars? We must also question the harm done to people whose astrological signs are deemed incompatible with the signs of others. Astrology teaches, in a nutshell, that people are hostages to the stars. To say that this is harmless is questionable.

34.1 The Birth of Stars

Interstellar space is not empty. It contains traces of elements, primarily hydrogen, and, to a lesser degree, a wide variety of other molecules, ranging in complexity from ammonia to ethyl alcohol. Among these atoms and molecules are also specks of interstellar dust that are composed of carbon and silicates, sometimes coated with the frozen ices of water, carbon dioxide, methane, and ammonia. Dust particles may play the same condensing role in star formation that similar dust particles play in cloud formation. The density of all this interstellar material is one-millionth the density of the highest vacuum ever achieved in earthbound laboratories.

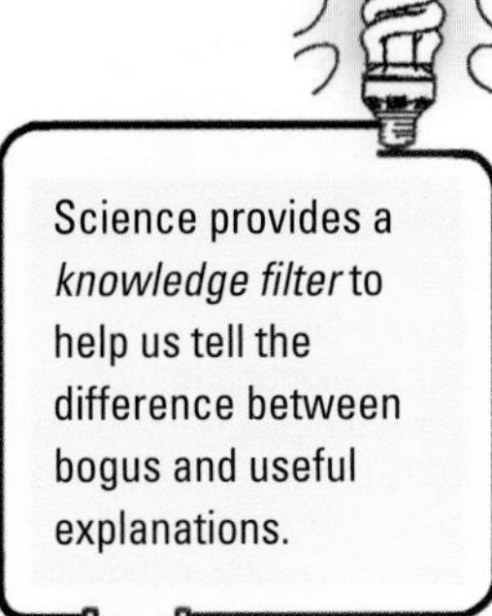

To make a star, begin with a giant cloud of low-temperature interstellar material. The gas will not be perfectly uniform; regions of gas density will differ

The Big Dipper and the North Star

Perhaps the most easily recognized star group in the Northern Hemisphere is the Big Dipper (Figure 34.3). Because of its great distance from us, it seems to form a plane, but its seven stars actually lie at quite different distances from us. The Big Dipper and the larger groups that make up constellations, of course, would take on entirely different patterns if viewed from other locations in the universe. Because of the variety of speeds and directions of the stars, the familiar patterns of all groups slowly move. We can see, in Figure 34.4, how the Big Dipper appeared from earth in the past and how it is projected to look in the future.

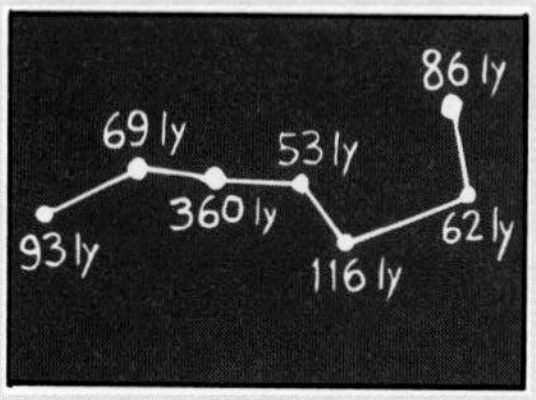

Figure 34.3
The familiar Big Dipper. The sizes of the dots represent the apparent brightness of the stars, which are not all the same distance from Earth. Their distances are noted in light-years.

The Big Dipper is most useful for locating the North Star (Polaris), which happens to lie almost exactly on the earth's rotational axis. It is easily located by drawing a line through the two stars in the end of the bowl of the Big Dipper, and extending the line away from the bowl about five times the distance between these two stars (Figure 34.5). Because the North Star lies very close to the projection of the earth's rotational axis, it appears stationary as the earth rotates.

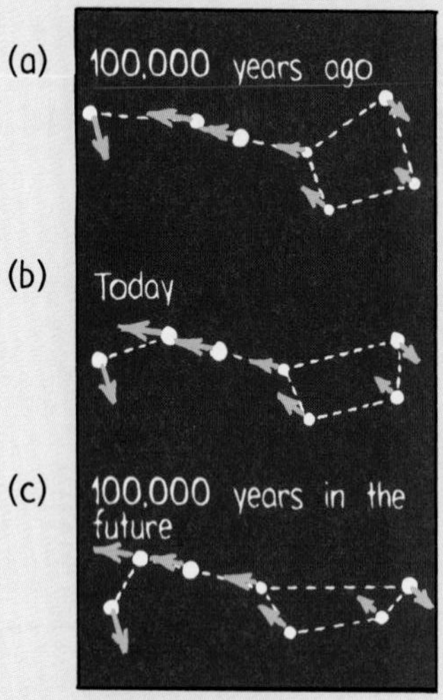

Figure 34.4
The present pattern of the Big Dipper is temporary. Here we can see (a) its pattern 100,000 years ago; (b) as it appears at present; and (c) as it will appear in the future, about 100,000 years from now.

All the surrounding stars appear to move in circles around the North Star, as evidenced in long time exposure photographs (Figure 34.6).

One of the earliest tests of determining good eyesight for centuries has been seeing if you can tell which star in the Big Dipper is actually two closely spaced stars. That star is the next-to-last star in the Big Dipper's handle. Although they seem to be a double star from our point of view, they are actually quite far apart in space. They look close because they happen to lie approximately along the same line of sight from the solar system. Actually, the brighter of these two stars, Mizar, is itself a pair of stars—the first optical binary to be observed by telescope. Without the aid of a good-sized telescope, the double nature of double star Mizar cannot be discerned even by people with the best eyesight.

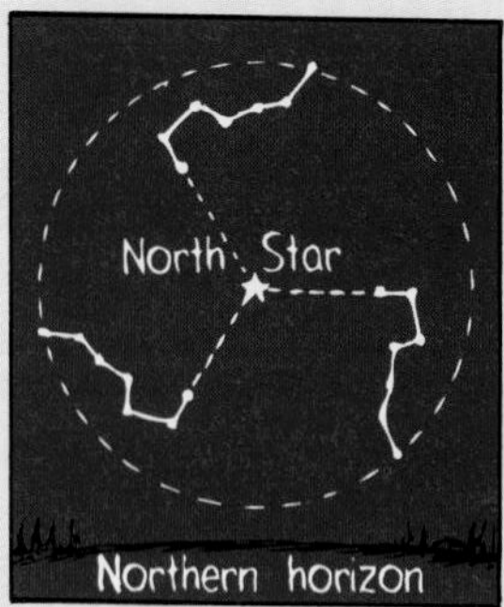

Figure 34.5
The pair of stars in the end of the Big Dipper's bowl point to the North Star. The earth rotates about its axis and therefore about the North Star, so, over a 24-hour period, the Big Dipper (and other surrounding star groups) make a complete revolution.

Figure 34.6
A time exposure of the northern night sky.

from the overall average. Regions of slightly greater gas density will have slightly more mass and a slightly greater gravitational field; therefore, they will more strongly attract neighboring particles. This increases the mass and gravitational field of the region, which then attracts still more particles. In time, there will be an aggregation of matter many times the mass of the sun spreading out over a volume many times larger than the solar system—a forming star; a **protostar.**

Mutual gravitation between the gaseous particles in a protostar results in an overall contraction of this huge ball of gas, and the density at the center increases dramatically as matter is scrunched together with an accompanying rise in pressure and temperature. When the central temperature reaches about 10 million K, some of the hydrogen nuclei *fuse* to form helium nuclei. This **thermonuclear reaction,** converting hydrogen to helium, releases an enormous amount of radiant and thermal energy. This ignition of nuclear fuel marks the change from protostar to star. Outward-moving radiant energy and the gas accompanying it exert an outward pressure on the contracting matter, ultimately becoming strong enough to stop the contraction. Outward radiation and gas pressures balance inward gravitational pressure, resulting in a full-fledged star.

The material composing the star depends on the age of the universe during its formation. The very first protostars had only primordial hydrogen, plus helium, to work with. Stars run their life cycles and, like living things, return their materials to the overall environment. Elements heavier than hydrogen and helium are manufactured in cores of stars, and, when the stars run their life courses, they spew these heavier elements into the interstellar mix. So the protostars that follow are enriched with heavier elements. Heavy elements that make up the sun and its planets are testimony that many stars lived and died before the solar system came to be. All atoms on earth heavier than helium were once part of another star. So we are quite literally made of stardust.

In addition to the multitudes of particles in interstellar space, a montage of electromagnetic waves engulfs the universe. There are also virtual particles, popping in and out of existence. Then there's the dark matter and "vacuum energy," about which we know nothing as yet. Outer space certainly is not empty.

Insights

☑ CHECKPOINT

What do the processes of thermonuclear fusion and gravitational contraction have to do with the physical size of a star?

Check Your Answer

The size of a star is the result of these two continually occurring processes. Energy from thermonuclear fusion tends to blow the star outward like an ongoing hydrogen bomb explosion, and gravitation tends to contract its matter in an ongoing implosion. The outward thermonuclear expansion and inward gravitational contraction produce an equilibrium that accounts for the star's size.

Stars are relentless element factories, transforming hydrogen and helium into heavier elements. Massive elements beyond iron are manufactured in supernova explosions, which spray mixtures of these elements into space.

Insights

34.2 The Life of Stars

Stars have varying life spans that depend on the rate at which they burn their fuel. We are most familiar with stars like our sun, a hydrogen burner with a life expectancy of some 10 billion years. Hydrogen fusion in more massive stars occurs at a more furious rate, and the stars are very bright and have relatively

Figure 34.7
The sun is about 5 billion years old, having completed about half its expected life span of 10 billion years.

short lives. In low-mass stars, hydrogen fusion occurs at a much slower rate, and the stars are dimmer and live longer.

Surprisingly, about half the stars that can be seen in the sky do not live alone but are actually two stars revolving about a common center, just as the earth and the moon revolve about each other. These double stars are **binary stars.** By observing how the two stars in a binary revolve about their common center, their masses can be calculated.[*] Interestingly, the only way to determine the mass of a star is to find it in a binary system. (The sun can be excluded from this generality because its planets provide this information).

There is speculation that our sun does not live a solitary life, but is part of a binary system. If it is, its partner is very small and very distant. This star is thought to travel in a very large elliptical orbit, as far away as three light-years from the sun. At its closest approach, which would occur every 26 to 30 million years, it would pass near the fringes of the outermost planets. Its gravity would perturb billions of comets into the inner solar system, all within a few million years. This star has been named *Nemesis,* after the goddess of divine retribution, because some speculators credit it with triggering the meteorite impact that may have led to the demise of the dinosaurs some 60 million years ago. As intriguing as the Nemesis hypothesis is, such a star hasn't been found and likely doesn't exist.

A star's age is revealed by its elemental makeup. The first and oldest stars were composed of hydrogen and helium. After supernovae formed heavier elements and hurled them into space, later stars incorporated these heavier elements in their formation. Young stars contain greater amounts of these metals.

Insights

With or without a companion star, our sun certainly does not live alone. It has us, seven other planets, and hosts of asteroids, meteoroids, and comets. The sun has 99 percent of all the mass in the solar system, but has only about 2 percent of the solar system's angular momentum.[†] Hence, it has a slow spin, with 98 percent of the solar system's angular momentum in the orbiting planets. Measurements of the spin rates of thousands of stars show that the hot massive stars are spinning at rates 100 times that of the sun, while the cooler, less massive stars spin slowly, like our sun. Perhaps the massive stars spin rapidly because they alone possess angular momentum (without accompanying planets), while the less massive stars have formed planetary systems that absorb most of the system's angular momentum.

Recent findings indicate that our sun is not the only star with a planetary system. We can only wonder if some of these planets, like earth, are at a distance from their respective stars that allow them to be not too hot and not too cold—at a location that would support life perhaps similar to ours. This idea is appealing.[‡] That's why the program Terrestrial Planet Finder (TPF) is presently in progress. Our own civilization is so young that there has hardly

* From Kepler's third law, that the mass of a planet can be found from the ratio of (satellite distance)^3 to (satellite period)^2, R^3/T^2. Likewise for finding the masses of stars that make up a binary system. The sum of the masses of two stars is proportional to R^3/T^2, where R is the average distance between the stars' centers, and T is the period of revolution. Individual star masses are found by their relative distances from their center of revolution, which is somewhere between the two stars. A star four times as massive as its companion, for example, will be four times closer to the center. Equal masses would be equidistant from the center.

† Whereas linear momentum, as studied in Chapter 3, is inertia × velocity, angular momentum is *rotational inertia* × *rotational velocity.* The law of the conservation of angular momentum states that angular momentum is conserved during internal processes. So, just as a spinning figure skater spins faster when her arms are drawn in, a rotating ball of gas spins faster when it contracts (a decreased rotational inertia is compensated for by an increased rotational velocity). And just as the spinning skater slows when her arms are extended, the sun slows as its planets form. (See Appendix B.)

‡ Only one verified contact will prove that intelligent life exists elsewhere. On the negative side, we can never prove that extraterrestrial life *doesn't* exist. However intense our search, it could always be "just around the next corner." If, after centuries of listening and looking, we find no sign of extraterrestrial intelligence, we might then be justified in assuming that we are alone. And if we are the sole heirs to the galaxy, shouldn't our present concern for tending the Planet Earth extend to our being the guardians of the galaxy?

The H-R Diagram

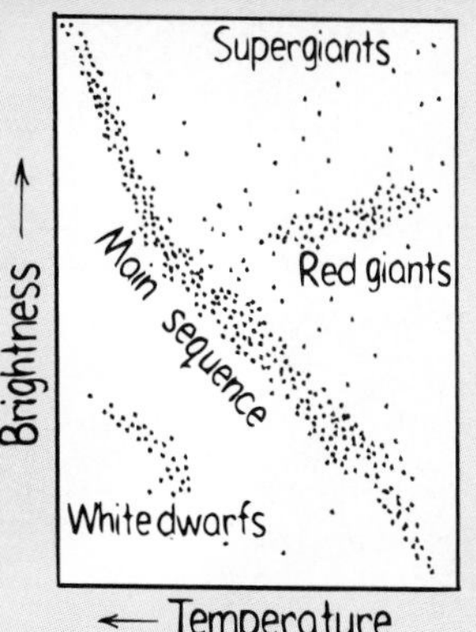

One of the most important tools of astronomers is the **Hertzsprung-Russell diagram,** or **H-R diagram,** developed early in the twentieth century by Danish astronomer Ejnar Hertzsprung and American astronomer Henry Norris Russell. The H-R diagram is a plot of stellar variables equivalent to brightness versus temperature. The temperature of a star is evident by its color. Cooler stars are red, while medium-temperature stars are white, and hotter stars glow bluish-white in color. Each dot in the diagram represents a star whose absolute magnitude of brightness has been determined. Bright stars are near the top of the diagram, and dim stars toward the bottom. Hot stars are toward the left side of the diagram, and cool stars are toward the right side.

The H-R diagram shows several distinct regions of stars. The band that stretches diagonally across the diagram represents a majority of stars seen in the night sky. This band is called the main sequence, and extends from massive, hot, bright, bluish stars in the upper left to less-massive, cool, dim, reddish stars in the lower right of the diagram.

About 90 percent of all stars, including our sun, lie on the main sequence of stars, where they spend the majority of their lives quietly burning hydrogen into helium. The probability of catching any given star in that stage of its life is greatest on the main sequence.

Toward the upper right of the diagram are the group of stars called red giants. They are cooler stars, and they appear reddish in the night sky. Above these are a few rare stars, the supergiants, larger and brighter than the red giants. Toward the lower left are stars both hot and dim, the white dwarfs, which cannot be seen with the unaided eye.

When a spectroscope is attached to a telescope, stars are seen to have a variety of spectral patterns that indicate their elemental makeup and temperatures. Stars are arranged into various *spectral types,* according to their spectra. When brightness versus spectral type is plotted, the same H-R pattern results. The H-R diagram dramatically shows the fundamental fact that different types of stars exist. These stars represent different stages of stellar evolution.

been enough time for it to have come to the attention of others. The most conspicuous evidence of life on the earth—radio, TV, and radar broadcast—has by now reached some 70 light-years into space, a distance encompassing only a few hundred stars.

In a similar way, most of the starlight from faraway stars has not yet reached the earth. That's how far away most of the universe is. And light from most distant stars that does reach us is Doppler-shifted below the visible part of the spectrum and is invisible to us. Hence, the night sky is black instead of ablaze with starlight.

The H-R diagram is to astrophysicists what the periodic table is to chemists—an extremely important tool. A star's location on the H-R diagram can reveal its age. The age of our galaxy can be estimated by looking at the locations of our oldest stars and their white-dwarf remnants.

34.3 The Death of Stars

All luminous stars "burn" nuclear fuel. A star's life begins when it ignites its nuclear fuel, and it ends when its nuclear fires burn out. The first ignition in a star core is the fusion of hydrogen to helium. This hydrogen-fusing process may last from a few million to 50 billion years, depending on the star's mass. In the old age of an average-mass star like our sun, the burned-out hydrogen core that has been converted to helium contracts due to gravity, raising its temperature. This ignites both the helium in the core and the unfused hydrogen outside the

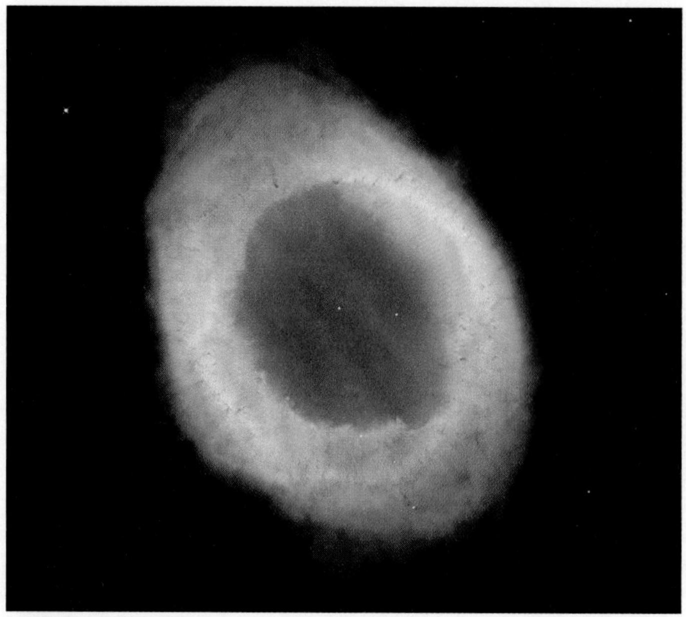

Figure 34.8
The planetary Ring Nebula in the constellation Lyra, which can be seen through a modest telescope.

core, and the star expands to become a **red giant.** Our sun will eventually reach this stage about 5 billion years from now. On the way to reaching this stage, the sun will swell and become more luminous. It will cause temperatures on the earth to escalate, first stripping the earth of its atmosphere and then boiling the oceans dry. Ouch!

The cores of stars of one solar mass or less are not hot enough to fuse carbon, and, lacking a source of nuclear energy, they shrink. In doing so, the outer stellar layers are sometimes ejected, and they form expanding shells that appear smoke-ring-like and that eventually disperse and mix with the interstellar material. Such an expanding shell is a **planetary nebula** (Figure 34.8). The shrunken core that remains blazes white-hot and is known as a **white dwarf.** Its matter is so compressed that a teaspoonful of it weighs tons.

Because the nuclear fires of a white dwarf have burned out, it is not actually a star anymore. It's more accurate to call it a *stellar remnant.* It may continue to radiate energy, changing from white to yellow and then to red, until it slowly but ultimately fades to a cold, black lump of matter—a *black dwarf.* The density of a black dwarf is enormous. Into a volume no more than that of an average-sized planet is concentrated a mass hundreds of thousands of times greater than that of the earth. The black dwarf has a density comparable to that of an aircraft carrier squeezed into a quart jar!

There is another possible fate for a white dwarf, if it is part of a binary and if its partner is close enough. A white dwarf, with its great mass, may gravitationally pull hydrogen from its companion star and deposit this material on its own surface as a very dense hydrogen layer. Continued compacting increases the temperature of this layer, which ignites to embroil the white dwarf's surface in a thermonuclear holocaust that we see as a **nova.** A nova is an event, not a stellar object. After a while, a nova subsides until enough matter again accumulates to repeat the event. A given nova flares up at irregular intervals that may range from decades to hundreds of thousands of years.

The Bigger They Are, the Harder They Fall

How a star evolves depends on its mass. The low- and medium-mass stars become white dwarfs. The fate of more massive stars is different. When a star with mass much greater than the sun's mass contracts, more heat is generated than in the contraction of a small star. Such a star does not shrink to become a white dwarf. Instead, carbon nuclei in its core fuse and liberate energy while synthesizing heavier elements, such as neon and magnesium. Gas and radiation pressure halt further gravitational contraction until all the carbon is fused. Then the core of the star contracts again to produce even greater temperatures and a new fusion series that produces even heavier elements. The fusion cycles repeat until the element iron is formed. The fusion of elements with larger atomic numbers than iron will require energy rather than liberating energy (recall, from Chapter 16, that the fusion of nuclei heavier than iron absorbs energy rather than releasing it). With no energy coming from the iron core, the center of the star collapses without rekindling. The entire star begins its final collapse.

The collapse is catastrophic. When the core density is so great that all the nuclei are compressed against one another, the collapse momentarily comes to a halt. Then it explodes violently, hurling into space the elements previously manufactured over billions of years. The entire episode can last a few minutes. It is during this brief time that the heavy elements beyond iron are synthesized, as protons and neutrons mash into other nuclei to produce such elements as silver, gold, and uranium. Because the time available for synthesizing these heavy elements is so brief, they are not as abundant as iron and the lighter elements.

Such a stellar explosion is a **supernova,** one of nature's most spectacular events. A supernova flares up to millions of times its former brightness. In 1054 A.D., Chinese astronomers recorded their observation of a star so bright that it could be seen by day as well as by night. This was a supernova, its glowing plasma remnants now making up the spectacular Crab Nebula (Figure 34.9). A less spectacular but more recent supernova was witnessed in 1987. This gave astronomers an exciting firsthand look at one of these seldom-seen events. Supernovae are fiery furnaces that generate the elements essential to life, for all the elements beyond iron that make up our bodies originated in far-off, long-ago supernovae.

The inner part of a supernova star implodes to form a core compressed to *neutron density.* Incredibly, protons and electrons compress together to form a core of neutrons just a few kilometers wide. This superdense, central remnant of

The loss of stellar material through stellar winds and pulsations greatly affect a star's evolution. For low-mass stars, the planetary nebula is what we see after a star's "final hiccup." For high-mass stars, the amount of mass lost before running out of nuclear fuel determines whether they become neutron stars or black holes.

Insights

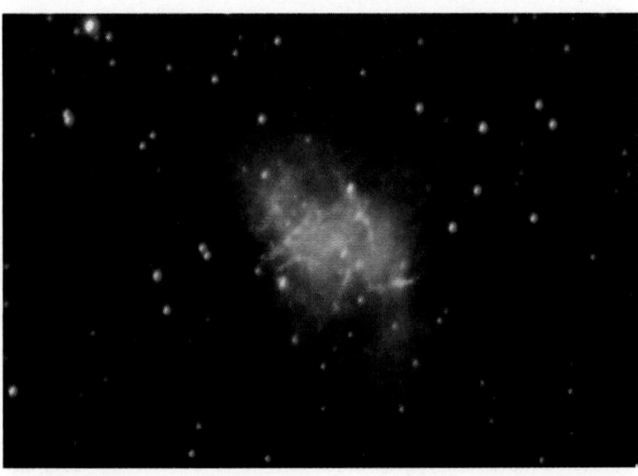

Figure 34.9
The Crab Nebula, the remnant of a supernova explosion that was seen from the earth in 1054 A.D.

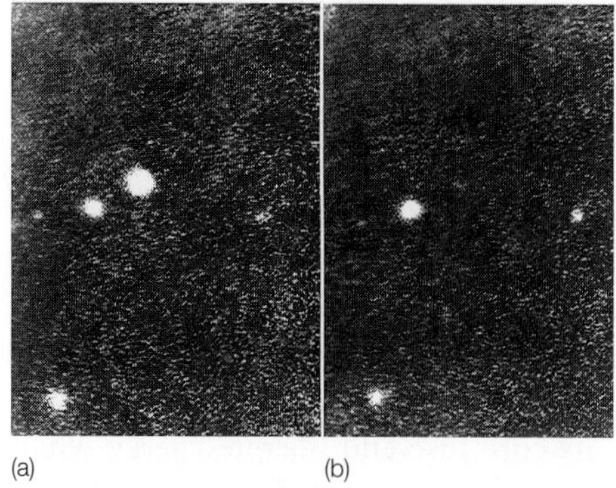

Figure 34.10
The pulsar in the Crab Nebula rotates like a searchlight, beaming light and X rays toward earth about 30 times per second, blinking on and off: (a) pulsar on, (b) pulsar off.

a supernova survives as a **neutron star.** In accord with the law of conservation of angular momentum, these tiny bodies, with densities hundreds of millions times greater than those of white dwarfs, spin at fantastic speeds. Neutron stars provide an explanation for the existence of **pulsars,** which were discovered in 1967 by Jocelyn Bell Bernall, a graduate student of Anthony Hewish. Pulsars, which are, in fact, neutron stars, are rapidly varying sources of low-frequency radio emissions. As a pulsar spins, the beam of radiation it emits sweeps across the sky. If the beam

The 1987 Supernova

Johannes Kepler is credited with spotting, in 1604, the last supernova before the invention of the telescope. Since then, a dozen generations of astronomers have lived and died without ever witnessing such a stellar explosion. Astronomers have contented themselves with studying the remnants of explosions that occurred before their time. This generation is more fortunate, however, for on February 24, 1987, Ian Shelton, graduate school dropout and resident observer at the University of Toronto's telescope in the Andes of northern Chile, stumbled upon a curious blotch in a photograph he had just made of the Large Magellanic Cloud. He stepped outside and confirmed his finding firsthand. He saw a pinpoint of light—less bright than others in the large Magellanic Cloud—that wasn't there the night before. This was Supernova 1987A.

The Supernova 1987A, seen in the southern sky in the Large Magellanic Cloud.

During the first few days after Shelton's sighting, the supernova's brightness increased a thousandfold, much more swiftly than expected, and then its brightness decreased to a level that was dimmer than expected. Although initially very hot and blue, it turned red very quickly, a change that occurred as the shell of debris raced outward at some 80,000,000 km/h and cooled. In March, the supernova brightened again, powered by the decay of radioactive elements in the stellar remains. Enormous quantities of nickel and cobalt that had been forged in the detonation were decaying into iron—enough iron to construct 20,000 Earths. The burst reached its peak toward the end of May, when it was as luminous as billions of suns. This colossal event ran its course during the summer, and, a year later, the visible fireworks were completely over. To the unaided eye, Supernova 1987A had faded into oblivion in the southern sky.

Centuries from now, astronomers will still be studying the wispy, incandescent filaments of Supernova 1987A, just as observers today meticulously examine the remains of the "new stars" observed centuries ago by Kepler and others. Theories rise and fall with each new measurement of the ever-expanding star remnants.

How awe-inspiring it is that men and women on a small planet in the outer reaches of a galaxy are able to investigate spots of light in the night sky and, from their examinations, arrive at a magnificent description of creation. This was well stated in 1948 during the opening of the famous Hale telescope: "In the last analysis, the mind which encompasses the universe is more marvelous than the universe which encompasses the mind."

sweeps over the earth, we detect its pulses. Of the approximately 300 known pulsars, only a few have been found emitting X rays or visible light. One is in the center of the Crab Nebula (Figure 34.10). It has one of the highest rotational speeds of any pulsar studied, rotating more than 30 times per second. This is a relatively young pulsar, for it is theorized that X-radiation and optical radiation are emitted only during a pulsar's early history.

Dying stars with cores greater than three or more solar masses collapse so violently that no physical forces are strong enough to halt continued contraction. The bigger they are, the harder they fall. The enormous gravitational field about the imploding concentration of mass makes explosion impossible. Collapse continues and the star disappears from the observable universe. What is left is a *black hole.*

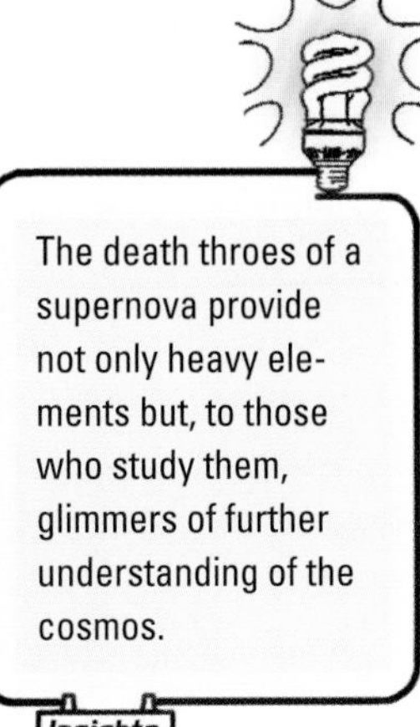

34.4 Black Holes

A **black hole** is the remains of a supergiant star that has collapsed into itself. It is so dense and has such an intense gravitational field that light cannot escape from it. We can see why gravity is so great in the vicinity of a black hole by considering the change in the gravitational field at the surface of any star that collapses. In accord with Newton's law of gravity, any mass at the surface of a star, whether object or particle, has weight that depends both on its mass and on the mass of the star. But, more importantly, weight also depends on the distance between the object and the center of the star. So, if a star collapses, the distance to its center decreases. Weight increases, without a change in total mass. By how much? That depends on the amount of collapse. If a star collapses to half its size, then, in accord with the inverse-square law, the weight of an object at its surface quadruples (Figure 34.11). If a star collapses to a tenth its size, the weight at the surface is 100 times as much. Along with the increase in gravitational field, the escape velocity from the surface of the collapsing star also increases. If a star such as our sun were to collapse to a radius of 3 kilometers, the escape velocity from its surface would exceed the speed of light, and nothing—not even light—could escape!* The sun would be invisible. It would be a black hole.

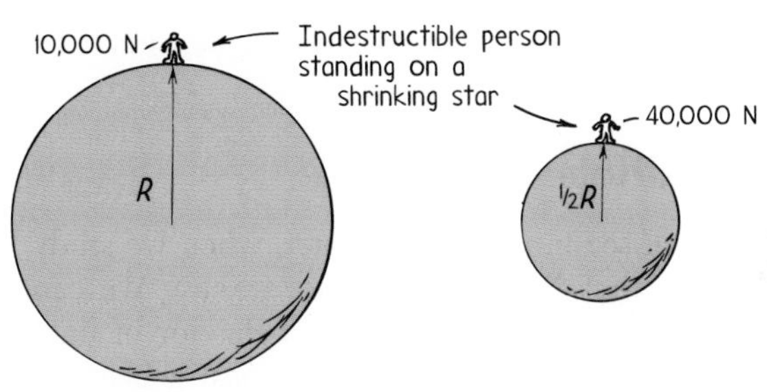

Figure 34.11
If a star collapses to half its radius with no mass change, gravitation at its surface increases by four (in accordance with the inverse-square law). If the star collapses to one-tenth its radius, gravitation at its surface increases 100-fold.

The sun, in fact, has too little mass to experience such a collapse, but when some stars with core masses many times greater than the mass of the sun reach the end of their nuclear resources, they undergo collapse; and, unless their rate of rotation is high enough, their collapse continues until the stars reach infinite densities. Gravitation near the surfaces of these shrunken stars is so enormous that light cannot escape from them. They have crushed themselves out of visible existence.

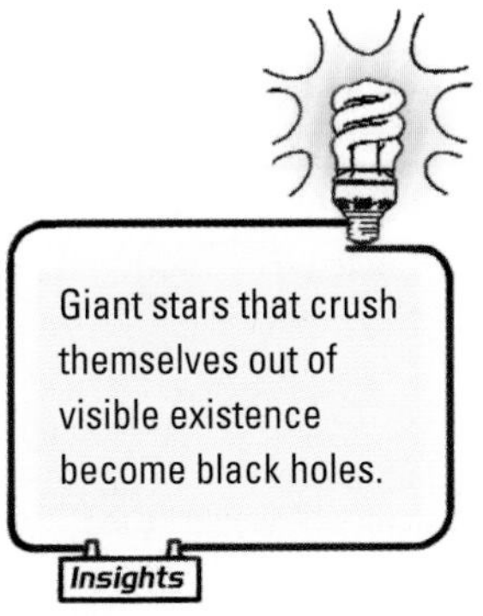

* In the next and final chapter, we'll see that light, just like massive things, is affected by gravity. Just as we fail to see the curvature of a high-speed bullet when viewed along short segments, we most often fail to see the curvature by gravity of even higher-speed light. We'll see that light *does* curve in a gravitational field.

A black hole has the same amount of mass after its collapse as before its collapse, so the gravitational field in regions at and beyond the original star's radius is no different in either case. But closer distances near the vicinity of a black hole are nothing less than the collapse of space itself, with a surrounding warp into which anything that passes too close—light, dust, or a spaceship—is drawn. Astronauts in a powerful spaceship could enter the fringes of this warp and still escape. Below a certain distance, however, they could not, and they would disappear from the observable universe.

☑ CHECKPOINT

1. What determines whether a star becomes a white dwarf, a neutron star, or a black hole?
2. If the sun somehow suddenly collapsed to a black hole, what change would occur in the orbital speed of Earth?

Check Your Answers

1. The mass of a star is the principal factor that determines its fate. Stars that are about as massive as the sun, and those that are less massive, evolve to become white dwarfs; more massive stars evolve to become neutron stars; and enormously massive giant stars ultimately become black holes.
2. None. This is best understood classically; nothing in Newton's law of gravitation, $F = G\frac{mM}{d^2}$, changes. The fact that the sun is compressed doesn't change its mass, M, or its distance, d, from the earth. Because the earth's mass, M, and G don't change either, the force, F, holding the earth in its orbit does not change.

Black-Hole Geometry

We will see in the next chapter, when we study Einstein's general theory of relativity, that light responds to gravity. We can understand the geometry of a black hole by considering the behavior of light in its vicinity.

If we shine a beam of light past a black hole, gravity is intense enough to deflect the beam noticeably. If the beam passes very far from the hole, where gravity is not as strong, the beam bends only slightly (Figure 34.12). The closer the light beam is to a black hole, the more it bends. If we shine a beam toward, but slightly away from, a black hole at precisely the right distance, we can direct the light into *circular orbit* about the hole. This region above the black hole is called the *photon sphere.* The photon sphere is very unstable, however, because the slightest variation in the interaction of a light beam with the gravitational field will send the light beam either spiraling into the hole or back off into space. All beams of light that happen to be incident at this critical distance are captured in the sphere, while beams that are incident at distances within the photon sphere spiral into the black hole and are lost from the outside universe as the black hole literally swallows them up.

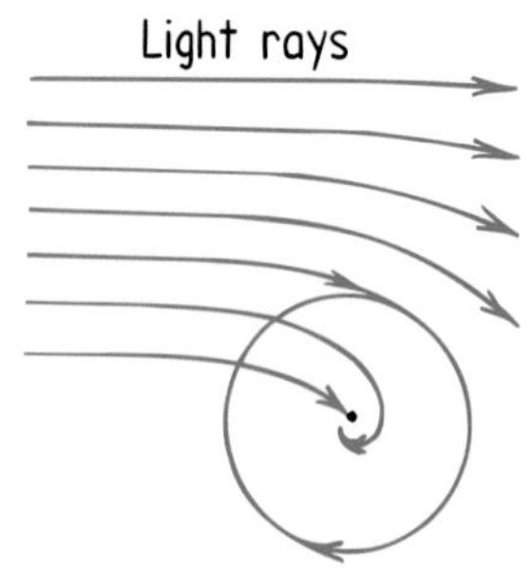

Figure 34.12
Light rays deflected by the gravitational field around a black hole. Light passing far away is bent only slightly; light passing closer can be captured into circular orbit; and light passing closer still is drawn into the hole.

An indestructible astronaut with a powerful enough spaceship could venture into the photon sphere of a black hole and come out again. While inside the photon sphere, she could still send beams of light back into the outside universe (Figure 34.13). If she directed her flashlight in sideways directions and toward the black hole, the light would quickly spiral into the black hole; but

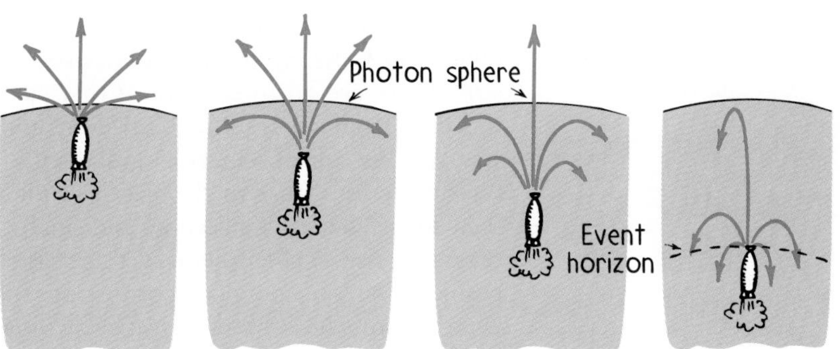

Figure 34.13
Just beneath the photon sphere, an astronaut could still shine light to the outside. But, as she gets closer to the black hole, only light directed nearer to the vertical gets out, until finally even vertically directed light is trapped. This occurs at a distance called the event horizon.

light directed vertically and at angles close to the vertical would still escape. As she gets closer and closer to the black hole, however, she finds she must shine the light beams closer and closer to the vertical for escape. Moving closer still, our astronaut would find a particular distance where *no* light can escape. No matter in what direction the flashlight points, all the beams are deflected into the black hole. Our unfortunate astronaut would have passed within the **event horizon,** the boundary where no light within can escape. Once inside the event horizon, she could no longer communicate with the outside universe; neither light-waves, radio waves, nor any matter could escape from inside the event horizon. Our astronaut would have performed her last experiment in the universe as we conceive it.

The event horizon surrounding a black hole is often called the *surface* of the black hole, the diameter of which depends on the mass of the hole. For example, a black hole resulting from the collapse of a star ten times as massive as the sun has an event-horizon diameter of about 60 kilometers. The radii of event horizons for black holes of various masses are shown in Table 34.1.

Table 34.1

Estimated radii of event horizons for nonrotating black holes of various masses.

Mass of Black Hole	Radius of Event Horizon
1 Earth mass	0.8 centimeter
1 Jupiter mass	2.8 meters
1 solar mass	3 kilometers
2 solar masses	6 kilometers
3 solar masses	9 kilometers
5 solar masses	15 kilometers
10 solar masses	30 kilometers
50 solar masses	148 kilometers
100 solar masses	296 kilometers
1000 solar masses	2961 kilometers

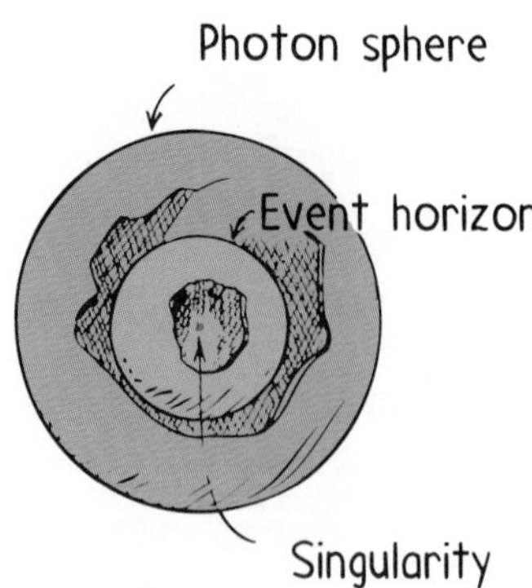

Figure 34.14
Structure of a simple, ideal black hole (uncharged and nonrotating).

When a collapsing star contracts within its own event horizon, the star still has substantial size. There are no forces known that can stop the continued contraction, however, and the star quickly shrinks in size until finally it is crushed, presumably to the size of a pinhead, then to the size of a microbe, and finally to a realm of size smaller than ever measured by humans. At this point, according to theory, what remains has infinite density. This point is the **black-hole singularity.**

The complete description of the simplest kind of black hole is quite straightforward. It has only one property—*mass.* And this can be precisely determined outside the event horizon, for example, by a physicist who measures how much the trajectory of a rocket probe is deflected when in the vicinity of the black hole.

If the black hole has an electric charge (either positive or negative) or a magnetic "charge" (either north pole or south pole), the effects of these charges, like the effects of mass, will also extend beyond the event horizon. A distant physicist could use a sensitive apparatus to detect these charges. So, in addition to mass, a charge on a black hole is not lost to the universe and is an additional physical property. It is unlikely that black holes with appreciable electric charges exist, however. If a black hole did have a substantial charge, its electric field would soon tear apart the atoms in nearby space, and, in a very short time, the black hole's charge would become neutralized by particles of opposite charge.

Contrary to stories about black holes, they're nonaggressive and don't reach out and swallow innocents at a distance. Their gravitational fields are no stronger than the original fields about the stars before their collapse—except at distances smaller than the radius of the original star. Except when they are too close, black holes shouldn't worry future astronauts.

Insights

A more important property is spin, for most stars are rotating and possess angular momentum. If a black hole is formed from a rotating star, the surrounding space and time will be dragged with it. (The connection between space, time, and gravity will be explored in the following and final chapter, when we discuss general relativity.) An observer sitting in a spaceship far from the black hole would notice a gradual pull around the hole in the direction of the black hole's rotation. The closer to the rotating hole, the faster the ship is pulled around. We see that the angular momentum of a black hole is also information that extends beyond the event horizon and is yet another property of black holes.*

Black holes, then, can have only three possible properties: mass, electric charge, and angular momentum. Whereas a complete description of a star involves all sorts of hairy things such as chemical composition, varying pressure, densities, temperatures at different depths, and so on, no such complications are involved in black holes. Physicists put it simply by stating, "*Black holes have no hair*!"

* Science types speculate that material drawn into a black hole may reappear elsewhere through a "white hole." What vanishes in one place might be spewed out at another. The downside to this speculation is that everything that falls into a black hole is reduced to elementary particles, and therefore everything would emerge as particles. If a black hole is a gate from one realm to another—and a temporary gate at that, due to fluctuations—it is a gate through which nothing can pass intact. An upside presents itself, however, if the black hole is spinning fast enough to form a *ring,* whereupon astronauts approaching this ring along the rotational axis of the black hole might travel unharmed through the ring, and perhaps enter another universe! The merits of these intriguing speculations, however, are pretty much confined to science-fiction stories. They're fun to think about!

Observations of Black Holes

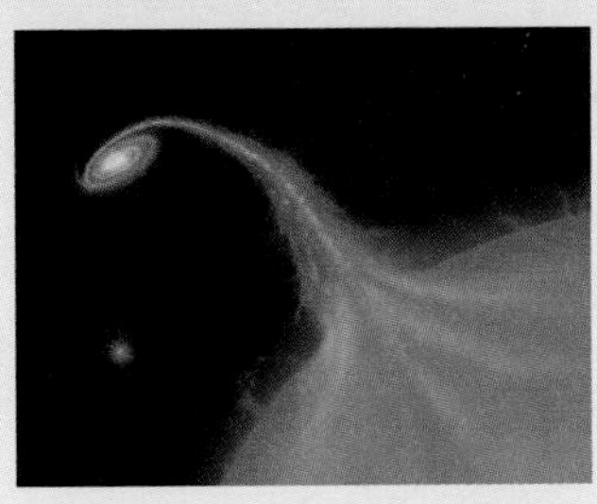

A rendering of a black hole stealing matter from a companion star.

We suspect that all dead stars with core masses greater than about three to five solar masses may be black holes. Locating these invisible star cores, however, is very difficult. One way is to look for a binary system in which a single luminous star appears to orbit about an invisible companion. If they are closely situated, matter ejected by the normal companion and accelerating into the neighboring black hole should emit X rays. The first convincing candidate for a black hole was discovered by astronomers in 1972, the X-ray star Cygnus X-1. Cygnus X-1 is about nine or ten solar masses and is a part of a binary system with a blue supergiant. Material streaming into the supposed black hole from the supergiant companion is found to be emitting X-radiation. Similar radiation patterns have also been found in Circinus X-1, another binary system, and more recently in V404 Cygni, both candidates for black holes. Observations by the NASA satellite *Copernicus* strongly suggest that a star in the constellation Scorpius is a black hole. This star, V861 Sco, is at the relatively close distance of 5000 light-years—slightly nearer than Cygnus X-1. The X-ray source called LMC X-3 in the Large Magellanic Cloud—a dwarf companion galaxy compared to our own—is very likely a black hole. Other massive black holes of 100 to 1000 solar masses are thought to exist at the centers of certain globular clusters (NGC 6624, NGC 1851, and NGC 6440).

More than one black hole can occupy the center of a galaxy. In 2002, the orbiting Chandra X-Ray Observatory discovered a pair of black holes in the center of galaxy NGC 6240. So black holes are not as lonesome as first thought.

34.5 Galaxies

A *galaxy* is a large assemblage of stars, interstellar gas, and dust. Galaxies are the breeding grounds of stars. Our own star, the sun, is an ordinary star among some roughly 200 billion others in an ordinary galaxy known as the **Milky Way.** With unaided eyes, we see the Milky Way as a faint band of light that stretches across the sky. The early Greeks called it the "milky circle" and the Romans called it the "milky road" or "milky way." The latter name has stuck.

Most astronomers believe that, 10 to 15 billion years ago, galaxies formed from huge clouds of primordial gas pulled together by gravity, similar to our description of the solar system's formation in the previous chapter. Formation begins with gravitational attraction between distant particles. Then contraction is accompanied by an increased rotational rate (like a skater who spins faster when her arms are drawn in). In most cases, rotation causes a galaxy to flatten into a disk. This is what happened to the Milky Way. A most striking feature of our galaxy is the spiral arms that wind outward through the disk. These arms are swarms of hot, blue stars and clusters of young stars, amidst clouds of dust and gas.

The masses of galaxies range from about a millionth the mass of our galaxy to some 50 times more. Galaxies are calculated to have much more mass than has been detected. This undetected mass is known as *dark matter.* The nature of this dark matter is still in question. The millions of galaxies visible

Planets in our solar system don't crash into the sun because their tangential velocities are sufficient for orbit; likewise for stars in galaxies. Stars with sufficient tangential velocities orbit about the galactic center. But slower stars are pulled into, and gobbled up by, the galactic nucleus, which, if massive enough is usually a black hole.

Insights

Figure 34.15
A wide-angle photograph of the Milky Way, from the constellation Cassiopeia on the left to the constellation Sagittarius on the right. The dark lanes and blotches are interstellar gas and dust obscuring the light of background stars.

on long-exposure photographs can be separated into three main classes—*elliptical, spiral,* and *irregular.*

Elliptical galaxies are the most common galaxies in the universe. Most contain little gas and dust and cannot make new stars. An exception is the giant elliptical galaxy M87 (Figure 34.16). The largest ellipticals are about five times larger than our galaxy, and the smallest are 100 times smaller. Stars in elliptical galaxies are more crowded toward the center, and the outer parts of some larger ellipticals are occupied by hundreds of globular clusters that contain up to a million old stars.

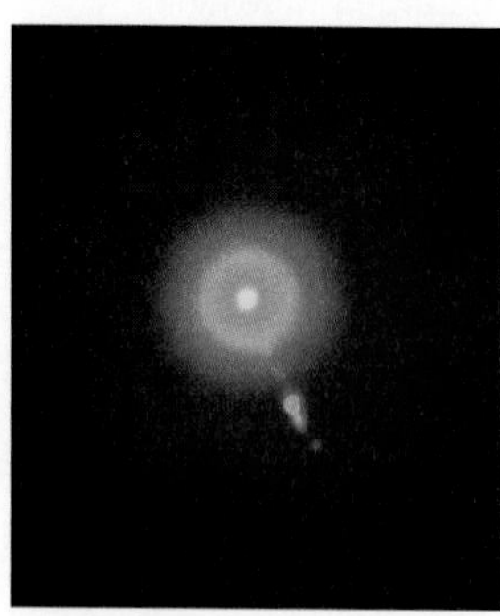

Figure 34.16
The giant elliptical galaxy M87, one of the most luminous galaxies in the sky, is located near the center of the Virgo cluster, some 50 million light-years from earth. It is about 40 times more massive than our own galaxy, the Milky Way.

Irregular galaxies are normally small and faint. They are difficult to detect. They don't have spiral arms or dense centers. They contain large clouds of gas and dust mixed with both young and old stars. The irregular galaxy first described by the navigator on Magellan's voyage around the world in 1521 is our nearest neighboring galaxy—the *Magellanic Clouds.* This galaxy consists of two "clouds," called the Large Magellanic Cloud (LMC) and the Small Magellanic Cloud (SMC). The LMC is dotted with hot young stars having a combined mass of some 20 billion solar masses, and the SMC contains stars having a combined mass of about 2 billion solar masses (Figure 34.17). The combined mass is small for a galaxy. Irregular galaxies are probably as common as spiral galaxies.

Spiral galaxies are perhaps the most beautiful arrangements of stars in the heavens. They are bright with the light of newly formed stars. The brightness

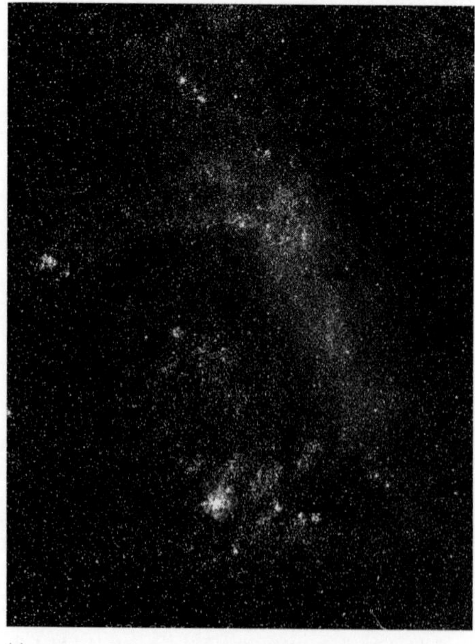

(a)

(b)

Figure 34.17 (a) The Large Magellanic Cloud and (b) the neighboring Small Magellanic Cloud are a pair of irregular galaxies. The Magellanic Clouds are our closest galactic neighbors, about 150,000 light-years distant. They likely orbit the Milky Way.

Figure 34.18
Spiral galaxy M83 in the southern constellation Centaurus, about 12 million light-years from earth.

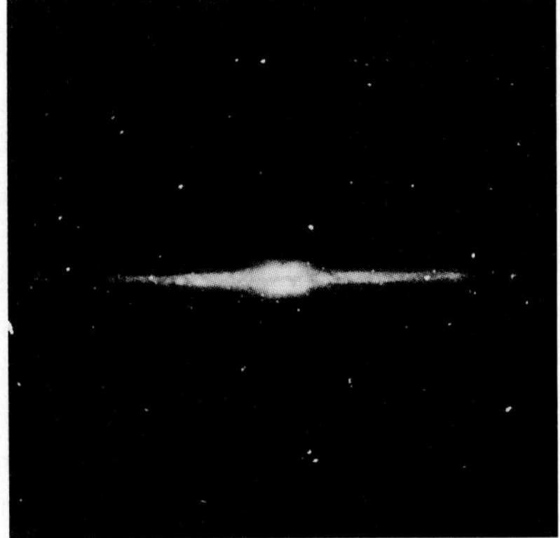

Figure 34.19
An edge-on view of a spiral galaxy, much like our own Milky Way, which makes four rotations every billion years. Our sun is about five-eighths the distance from the center to the outer visible rim.

of most spiral galaxies makes them easy to see at great distances. How their spiral arms form is still being investigated. Perhaps differential rotation of the galaxy stretches star-forming regions into elongated arches of stars and nebulae. Or maybe they are created by density waves that sweep around the galaxy. Investigators are still learning about how spiral arms form. We know that about two-thirds of all known galaxies are spirals, although they probably make up only about 15 to 20 percent of all galaxies. We do not see the greater number of fainter elliptical galaxies that are thought to exist.

We know what it's like to live in a spiral galaxy, for our Milky Way is a typical one. When we look at the Milky Way that crosses the night sky, we are looking through the disk of the galaxy. Interstellar dust obscures our view of most of the visible light that lies along the plane of this disk. Most of our knowledge about our galaxy is via infrared and radio telescopes. Infrared and radio observations reveal many details of the 25,000 light-year distant galactic nucleus, but astronomers are still puzzled by the processes occurring there. The nucleus seems to be crowded with stars and hot dust, and at the very center is thought to be a massive black hole (of about a million solar masses) that generates energy by swallowing surrounding matter. Don't go too near the center of the Milky Way.

Galaxies collide. The stars in a galaxy are normally so far apart, however, that physical collisions of

Figure 34.20
The great spiral nebula in Andromeda, a spiral galaxy about 2.3 million light-years from the earth.

individual stars are highly unlikely. But interstellar gases and dust collide violently, with matter stripped from one galaxy and deposited in another. These collisions also trigger the formation of new stars. Low-speed collisions can result in the merger of two galaxies. There is evidence that the Milky Way may be presently consuming the Magellanic Clouds. At high velocities, colliding galaxies can distort each other through tidal forces and can create tails and bridges. The collisions of spiral galaxies are thought to form huge elliptical galaxies. Many large elliptical galaxies are believed to contain the merged remains of several spiral galaxies. Galaxies are cannibals. Spiral galaxies may have formed by mergers of many small dwarf galaxies.

Galaxies are not the largest things in the universe. Galaxies come in clusters. And **galaxy clusters** appear to be part of even larger clusters, the **galaxy superclusters.** It doesn't stop there; superclusters, in turn, seem to be part of a network of filaments surrounding empty voids. Comprehension of the universe at this scale becomes mind-boggling.

34.6 Quasars

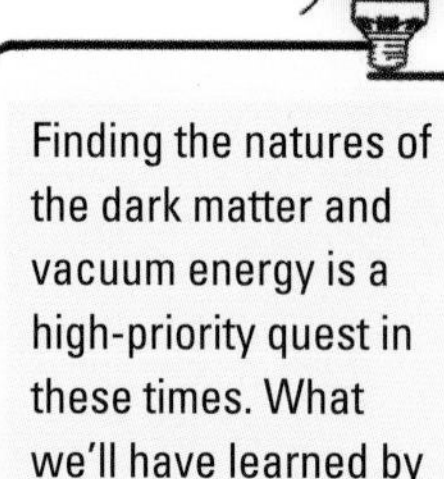

Finding the natures of the dark matter and vacuum energy is a high-priority quest in these times. What we'll have learned by mid-century will likely dwarf all that we've ever known before.

Insights

Galaxies are not the brightest parts of the universe. Brighter still are **quasars.** The energy output of these objects is enormous—hundreds of times that of the entire Milky Way. Quasars were first thought to be relatively faint ordinary stars in our own galaxy, but, in the early 1960s, astronomers found that they emit radio waves. Radio waves are frequently observed coming from galaxies, but no star had been observed to emit strong radio signals. Further investigation revealed that these "radio stars" had a pattern of spectral lines that could not be deciphered. These objects became known as "quasi-stellar sources," soon shortened to **quasars.**

Their unusual spectra turned out to be normal spectra with an extremely large and unprecedented red shift, which indicated enormous recessional velocities—some more than 90 percent the speed of light. Clearly, the objects couldn't be stars in our own galaxy, because we would have noticed a change in their positions against the background of the fixed stars, and quasars had been observed for years as faint stars with no noticeable change in position. At first, some investigators thought that the red shift was not a Doppler shift but a gravitational red shift, which is characteristic of a small body with an enormous mass and a correspondingly enormous gravitational field. But spectra from quasars revealed emission lines from normal atoms with normally orbiting electrons that wouldn't exist in a neutron star, a black hole, or any body with gravitation intense enough to produce such a large red shift.

Figure 34.21
Colorized image of the quasar BR 1202-07, the brightest observed quasar to date.

We do not know what quasars are. They appear to be as much as 15.5 billion light-years distant, placing them back to the beginnings of the universe. They may be gigantic black holes that pull enormous amounts of material toward them with resulting collisions that liberate immense energies. Current findings indicate that quasars are the brilliant cores of very distant spiral galaxies that we see as they were when they were young. Quasars are currently the most puzzling objects known to astronomers.

34.7 The Big Bang

Most astronomers think that the universe began 10 to 15 billion years ago, when a primordial explosion, called the **Big Bang,** occurred. This is the standard model of the universe. The Big Bang marks the beginning of both space and time for our universe. The space formed by the Big Bang was filled by extremely energetic high-frequency radiation called the *primeval fireball.* Today this radiation survives as microwaves, which continually stretch out more and more as the universe expands.

When we look at the stars and faraway galaxies, we are looking backward in time, because it takes a considerable length of time for the light from those galaxies to reach all the way to the earth. The galaxies farthest away are the ones we are seeing as they existed long ago.

The present expansion of the universe is evident in a Doppler red shift in the light that we receive from galaxies. Recall, from Chapter 11, that sound and light-waves are stretched out when the source recedes and compressed when the source approaches. The visible light that we see from distant galaxies is stretched out, which shows an increasing distance between us and the other galaxies in the universe. This does not, however, place the Milky Way in a central location. We can see why by considering ants on a balloon that is expanding (Figure 34.22). As the balloon is inflated, every ant sees every other ant moving farther away. This doesn't imply that each ant is in a central position. In an expanding universe, any observer sees all other galaxies receding.

Recent evidence indicates that the expansion rate of the universe is increasing—that it is accelerating outward. Why this is so is presently unknown. There are indications of the existence of a dark, unseen matter and of a "vacuum energy" unknown to us—not small amounts, but dominant amounts that dwarf the matter and energy with which we are familiar. There is much we have to learn.

We don't view the world in the same way the ancient Egyptians, Greeks, and Chinese did. It is unlikely that people in the future will see the universe as we do. Our view of the universe may be incorrect, but it is most likely less wrong than the views of others before us. Our present view of the universe began with the findings

Figure 34.23
Astronomer Richard Crowe shows his class a model of a celestial sphere.

Telescopes are time devices that let us look only into the past. When we look at the stellar objects that are farthest away from us, we're looking at the objects in the universe that existed furthest back in time. If we understand our past, we are better able to chart our future.

Insights

Figure 34.22
Every ant on the expanding balloon sees every other ant moving farther away. Each ant may therefore think that it is at the center of the expansion. Not so!

of Copernicus, Galileo, and Newton. What they found was very much opposed by others at the time, mainly because established order was based on Aristotle's teachings. These "new" ideas were thought to diminish the role of humans in the universe, to undermine our importance. It was believed that people are important because we are higher than nature—apart from nature. We have expanded our vision since then by enormous effort, painstaking observation, and an ongoing desire to comprehend our surroundings. Seen from today's understanding of the universe, we find our importance not in being apart from nature but in being very much a part of it. We are the part of nature that is becoming more and more conscious of itself.

Summary of Terms

Protostar An aggregation of matter in space that begins the formation of a star.

Thermonuclear reaction A fusion reaction brought about by high temperatures.

Binary star A pair of stars that orbit about a common center of mass.

H-R diagram (Hertzsprung-Russell diagram) A plot of intrinsic brightness versus surface temperature for stars. When so plotted, stars' positions take the form of a main sequence for average stars, with exotic stars above or below the main sequence.

Red giant Cool giant stars above main-sequence stars on the H-R diagram.

Planetary nebula An expanding shell of gas ejected from a low-mass star during the latter stages of its evolution.

White dwarf A dying star that has collapsed to the size of the earth and is slowly cooling off; located at the lower left on the H-R diagram.

Nova An event wherein a white dwarf suddenly brightens and appears as a "new" star.

Supernova The explosion of a massive star caused by gravitational collapse with the emission of enormous quantities of matter.

Neutron star A small, extremely dense star composed of tightly packed neutrons formed by the welding of protons and electrons.

Pulsar A celestial object (most likely a neutron star) that spins rapidly, sending out short, precisely timed bursts of electromagnetic radiation.

Black hole The remains of a giant star that has collapsed upon itself, so dense, and with a gravitational field so intense, that light itself cannot escape from it.

Event horizon The boundary region of a black hole from which no radiation may escape. Any events within the event horizon are invisible to distant observers.

Black-hole singularity The object of zero radius into which the matter of a black hole is compressed.

Milky Way The name of the galaxy to which we belong—our cosmic home.

Elliptical galaxy A galaxy that is round or elliptical in outline. It has little gas and dust, no disk or spiral arms, and few hot, bright stars.

Irregular galaxy A galaxy with a chaotic appearance and with large clouds of gas and dust, but without spiral arms.

Spiral galaxy A disk-shaped galaxy with hot, bright stars and spiral arms. Our Milky Way is a spiral galaxy.

Galaxy cluster A group of two or more galaxies.

Galaxy supercluster A group of an enormous number of galaxies.

Quasar A quasi-stellar object: a small but powerful source of energy believed to be the active core of a very distant galaxy.

Big Bang The primordial explosion of space at the beginning of time.

Review Questions

1. What are constellations?
2. Why does an observer at a given location see one set of constellations in the winter and a different set of constellations in the summer?

34.1 The Birth of Stars

3. It is commonly thought that interstellar space is empty. Is it?
4. What process changes a protostar to a full-fledged star?
5. What are the outward forces that act on a star?
6. What are the inward forces that act on a star?
7. What do the outward and inward forces acting on a star have to do with its size?
8. What is the evidence for believing our sun is a relatively young star in the universe?

34.2 The Life of Stars

9. How common are binaries in the universe?

10. It has been proposed that our sun may be part of a binary system. What is the name that has been given to the sun's supposed companion star?
11. How much of the mass of the solar system is concentrated in the sun?
12. Where is most of the angular momentum of the solar system?
13. What is the goal of the TPF program?

34.3 The Death of Stars

14. What event marks the birth of a star, and what event marks its death?
15. When will our sun reach the red-giant stage?
16. What is the relationship between a planetary nebula and a white dwarf?
17. What is the relationship between a white dwarf and a black dwarf?
18. What is the relationship between a white dwarf and a nova?
19. Compare the lifetimes of high-mass and low-mass stars.
20. What is the relationship between the heavy elements that we find on the earth today and supernovae?
21. What is the relationship between a supernova and a neutron star?
22. What is the relationship between a neutron star and a pulsar?

34.4 Black Holes

23. What is the relationship between a supergiant star and a black hole?
24. Why do we not think the sun will eventually become a black hole?
25. How does the mass of a star before its collapse compare with the mass of the black hole that it becomes?
26. If black holes are invisible, what is the evidence for their existence?
27. What three common properties can a black hole possess?

34.5 Galaxies

28. What type of galaxy is the Milky Way?
29. What kind of force is responsible for pulling stars together to form galaxies?
30. What are the consequences of galaxies colliding?
31. Can it be said that galaxies are the largest bodies known in the universe?

34.6 Quasars

32. How does the brightness of a quasar compare with that of a large galaxy?
33. What is the current speculation as to what quasars are?

34.7 The Big Bang

34. What event is marked by the Big Bang?
35. As the universe expands, is it presently racing outward at a decelerating rate, at a constant rate, or at an accelerating rate?

Exercises

1. Thomas Carlyle wrote, "Why did not somebody teach me the constellations and make me at home in the starry heavens, which are always overhead and which I don't half know to this day?" What besides the names of the constellations did Thomas Carlyle not know?
2. Why do we not see stars in the daytime?
3. Which figure in the chapter best shows that a constellation seen in the background of a solar eclipse is one that will be seen six months later in the night sky?
4. We see the constellations as distinct groups of stars. Discuss why they would look entirely different from some other location in the universe, far distant from the earth.
5. The Big Dipper is sometimes right-side up (as if it could hold water), and at other times upside down (as if it couldn't hold water). What length of time is required for the Big Dipper to change from one position to the other?
6. In what sense are we all made of stardust?
7. How is the gold in your mother's ring evidence of the existence of ancient stars that ran through their life cycles long before the solar system came into being?
8. Would you expect metals to be more abundant in old stars or in new stars? Defend your answer.
9. Why is there a lower limit on the mass of a star? (What can't happen in a low-mass accumulation of hydrogen atoms and other interstellar material?)
10. What ordinarily keeps a star from collapsing?
11. How does a protostar differ from a star?
12. How does the energy of a protostar differ from the energy that powers a star?
13. Why do nuclear fusion reactions not occur on the outer layers of stars?
14. Why are massive stars generally shorter-lived than low-mass stars?
15. What does the spin rate of a star have to do with whether or not it has a system of planets?
16. With respect to stellar evolution, what is meant by the statement "The bigger they are, the harder they fall"?
17. Why will the sun not be able to fuse carbon nuclei in its core?

18. Some stars contain fewer heavy elements than our sun contains. What does this indicate about the age of such stars relative to the age of our sun?
19. Which has the highest surface temperature: a red star, a white star, or a blue star?
20. In what way is a black hole blacker than black ink?
21. If you were to fall into a black hole, you'd likely die as a result of tidal forces. Explain.
22. A black hole is no more massive than the star from which it collapsed. Why, then, is gravitation so intense near a black hole?
23. What happens to the radial distance of the photon sphere of a black hole as more and more mass falls into the black hole?
24. If the nucleus of our galaxy undergoes a gigantic explosion at this very moment, should we be concerned about its possible effects on us during our lifetime? Defend your answer.
25. Are there galaxies other than the Milky Way that can be seen with the unaided eye? Discuss.
26. What does it mean to say that galaxies are cannibals?
27. Quasars are the most distinct objects we know of in the universe. Why do we therefore say their existence goes back to the earliest times in the universe?
28. What is meant by saying that the universe does not exist in space? Change two words around to make the statement agree with the standard model of the universe.
29. Why are the long-wavelength microwaves that permeate the universe considered to be evidence of the Big Bang?
30. In your own opinion, do you have to be at the center of your class to be special? Does the earth have to be at the center of the universe to be special?

Chapter 34 Online Resources

Tutorials
- Stellar Evolution
- Black Holes

Quiz
Exercises
Flashcards
Links

CHAPTER 35

Special and General Relativity

We began this book with the physics concepts of motion, force, and energy in the everyday world. In the chemistry chapters, we studied these concepts in the micro world; and in the earth-science chapters, they were applied to the processes of change on the planet Earth. Then we expanded the discussion of these concepts to our solar system and to the stars beyond. We conclude here with the mechanics that underlie the universe—Einstein's theory of special relativity and his general theory of relativity.

35.1 Space-Time

When we look up at the stars, we realize that we also are looking back in time. Some of the stars we are seeing may actually have perished long ago. Their distances from us are measured in light-years,* which indicates that space and time may be bound together. Einstein showed that space and time are indeed very intimately bound together.

The space we live in is three-dimensional; that is, we can specify any place in space by three dimensions. Loosely speaking, these dimensions are how far over, how far across, and how far up or down. For example, if we are at the corner of a rectangular room and we wish to specify the position of any point in the room, we can do so with three numbers. The first is the number of meters to the point along a line joining the adjacent left wall and the floor; the second is the number of meters to the point along a line joining the adjacent right wall and the floor; and the third is the number of meters the point lies above the floor for the same height above the floor along the vertical line joining the two adjacent walls at the corner. Physicists speak of these three lines as the *coordinate axes* of a reference frame (Figure 35.1). Three numbers—the distances along the x-axis, the y-axis, and the z-axis—specify the position of a point in space.

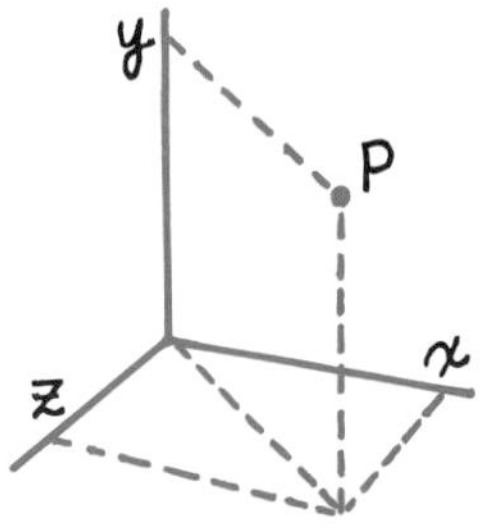

Figure 35.1
Point P can be specified with three numbers: the distances along the *x-axis,* the *y-axis,* and the *z-axis.*

We specify the size of an object with three dimensions. A box, for example, is described by its length, width, and height. But the three dimensions do not give a complete picture. There is a fourth dimension—time. The box was not always a box of a given length, width, and height. It began as a box only at a certain point in time, on the day it was made. Nor will it always be a box. At any moment it may be crushed, burned, or destroyed. So the three dimensions of space are a valid description of the box only during a certain period of time. We cannot speak meaningfully about space without implying time.

*Recall that a light-year is the distance light travels in 1 year, about 10^{16} m.

Things exist in **space-time.** Each atom, object, person, planet, star, or galaxy exists in "the space-time continuum."*

Einstein was 26 in 1905 when he published three major papers that provided the blueprint for much of today's physics. One was on the quantum theory of light and the photoelectric effect, the second on an explanation of Brownian motion, and the third on special relativity. He won the Nobel prize for his quantum explanation of the photoelectric effect—not for relativity.

Insights

35.2 Special Relativity

Einstein's concepts about space and time are part of a larger picture, a revolutionary one that predicts that motion through space causes a "slowing of time," that objects in motion are shorter and more massive than the same objects at rest, and that mass is actually congealed energy. These are the ideas of the **Special Theory of Relativity,** which Einstein developed in 1905. The Special Theory of Relativity is based upon two postulates. The first can be stated:

Observers can never detect their *uniform* motion except relative to other objects.

We've all noticed that, while we are sitting inside a car at a traffic light, we see a nearby car move, only to find that the nearby car is at rest and our car is the one that is moving. We can tell which one is moving by watching the background of trees or other objects. Imagine, however, that we are in a spaceship in interstellar space and another spaceship coasts by at constant velocity. Which spaceship is moving? Without a background, all we can say is that the ships are moving relative to each other. And even with a background, how could we say the background isn't moving? These are Newtonian ideas. Einstein thought about them and added his conclusion: that there is no experiment you can perform to decide which ship is moving and which is not. This means there is no such thing as absolute rest—all motion is relative.

If there is no experiment that can be performed to detect absolute motion through space, the laws of physics must be the same on both spaceships. The more general form of the first postulate is:

All laws of nature are the same in all uniformly moving reference frames.

On a jet airplane going 700 km/h, for example, coffee pours as it does when the plane is at rest; we swing a pendulum and it swings as it would if the plane were on the runway. There is no physical experiment we can perform to determine our state of uniform motion. By uniform motion, we mean nonaccelerated motion. The laws of physics within the uniformly moving cabin (constant velocity; zero acceleration) are the same as those in a stationary laboratory.

According to the first postulate, any measurements of the speed of light would show the same value in uniformly moving reference frames. This constancy of the speed of light is the second postulate of special relativity:

The speed of light in free space will have the same value to all observers, regardless of the motion of the source or the motion of the observer. The speed of light is a constant.

*Points in space and time may be quantized points in a four-dimensional space-time lattice. From the sizes of elementary particles and minimum separation between colliding particles, there seems to be an elemental unit of distance (4.05×10^{-35} m), and the lifetimes of all known elementary particles are consistent with there being an integral number of "chronons" (about 1.35×10^{-43} s). (Chronon is a term for the fundamental unit of time.)

Clockwatching on a Trolleycar Ride

$\frac{\text{SPACE}}{\text{TIME}} = \frac{\text{SPACE}}{\text{TIME}} = c$

Pretend you are Einstein at the turn of the twentieth century riding in a trolleycar, which provided the high-speed travel back then. Suppose that the trolleycar is moving in a direction away from a huge clock displayed in a village square. The clock reads 12 noon. To say it reads 12 noon is to say that light that carries the information "12 noon" is reflected by the clock and travels toward you in the direction of your line of sight. If you suddenly move your head to the side, the light carrying the information, instead of meeting your eye, continues past, presumably out into space. Out there, an observer who *later* receives the light says, "Oh, it's 12 noon on Earth now." But, from your point of view, it isn't. You and the distant observer will see 12 noon at different times. You wonder more about this idea. If the trolleycar traveled as fast as the light, then it would keep up with its information that says "12 noon." Traveling at the speed of light, then, tells you its always 12 noon at the village square. Time at the village square is frozen! So, if the trolleycar is not moving, you see the village-square clock move into the future at the rate of 60 seconds per minute; if you move at the speed of light, you see seconds on the clock taking infinite time. These are the two extremes. What's in between? What happens for speeds that are less than the speed of light? A little thought will show that the clock will be seen to run somewhere between the rate 60 seconds per minute and the rate of 60 seconds per an infinity of time, if your speed is between zero and the speed of light. From your high-speed (but less than *c*) moving frame of reference, the clock and all events in the reference frame of the clock will be seen in slow motion. Time will be stretched. How much depends on speed. This is time dilation.

Every measurement of the speed of light (which we denote as *c*), and there have been many, has confirmed the second postulate. If you move away from a tossed baseball, when you catch it, you'll catch it at a slower speed. Do this for light and you have a different story. Pretend we're in a high-speed rocket moving away from a light source at nearly the speed of light. Good old common sense will tell us that the light that catches up to you and passes you is slower than if you weren't moving. But not so. While moving, we are, in effect, stretching out the space between us and the light source. But Einstein says you can't accomplish that without also stretching out time. How much stretch? Just enough so that, when you divide the space traveled by the time taken, your value for the speed of light is the same as if you weren't moving at all.

Figure 35.2
The speed of light is measured to be the same in all frames of reference.

35.3 Time Dilation

Let's examine this notion that time can be "stretched." Imagine that we are somehow able to observe a flash of light bouncing to and fro between a pair of parallel mirrors, like a ball bouncing to and fro between a floor and ceiling.

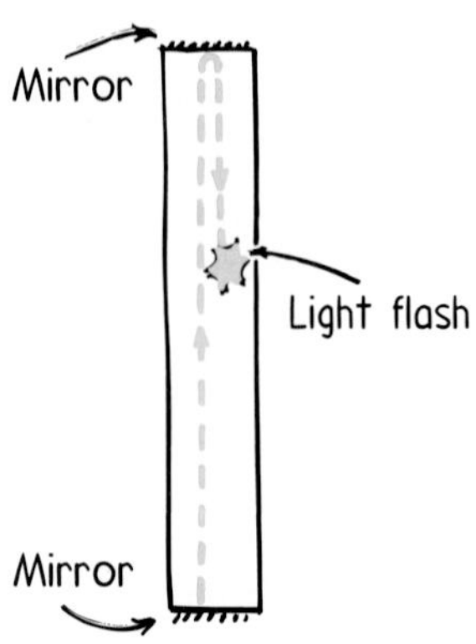

Figure 35.3
A light clock. Light will bounce up and down between parallel mirrors and "tick off" equal intervals of time.

Figure 35.4
(a) An observer moving with the spaceship observes the light flash moving vertically between the mirrors of the light clock. (b) An observer who sees the moving spaceship pass by observes the flash moving along a diagonal path.

If the distance between the mirrors is fixed, then the arrangement constitutes a sort of "light clock," because the back-and-forth trips of the light flash take equal time intervals (Figure 35.3). Suppose our light clock is inside a transparent high-speed spaceship. If we travel along with the ship and watch the light clock (Figure 35.4a), we will see the flash of light reflecting straight up and down between the two mirrors, just as it would if the spaceship were at rest. Our observations will show no unusual effects. Note that there is no relative motion between us and our light clock; we say that we share the same frame of reference in space-time.

If we instead make our observations from some relative rest position as the spaceship whizzes by us at high speed—say, half the speed of light—things are quite different. We will not see the path of light in simple up-and-down motion as before. Because the light flash keeps up with the horizontally moving light clock, we will see the flash follow a diagonal path (Figure 35.4b). Notice that, from our frame of reference, the flash travels a *longer distance* as it moves between the mirrors, considerably longer than it does in the reference frame of an observer riding with the ship. Since the speed of light is the same in all reference frames (Einstein's second postulate), the flash must travel for a correspondingly longer time between the mirrors in our frame than in the reference frame of the on-board observer. This follows from the definition of speed—distance divided by time. *The longer diagonal distance must be divided by a correspondingly longer time interval to yield an unvarying value for the speed of light.* This stretching out of time is referred to as **time dilation.** We have considered a light clock in our

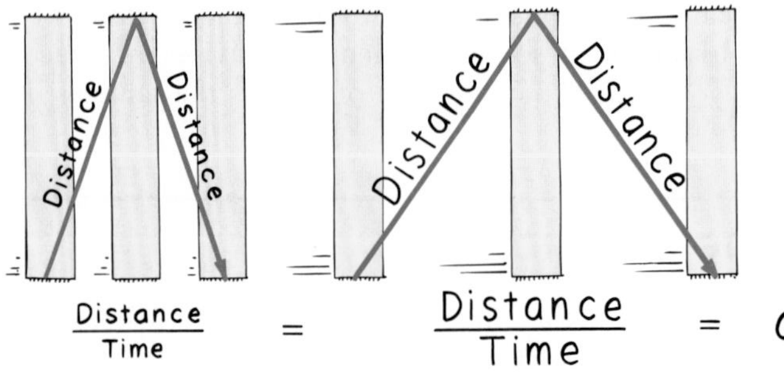

Figure 35.5
The longer distance taken by the light flash in following the diagonal path must be divided by a correspondingly longer time interval to yield an unvarying value for the speed of light.

example, but the same effect is true for any kind of clock. All moving clocks run slow. Time dilation has nothing to do with the mechanics of clocks, but with the nature of time itself.

The relationship of time dilation for different frames of reference in space-time can be derived from Figure 35.5 using simple geometry and algebra.* The relationship between the time t_o (proper time) in the observer's own frame of reference and the relative time t measured in another frame of reference is

$$t = \frac{t_o}{\sqrt{1 - \frac{v^2}{c^2}}}$$

where v represents the relative velocity between the observer and the observed and c is the speed of light. Because no material object can travel at or beyond the speed of light, the ratio v/c is always less than 1; likewise for v^2/c^2. For $v = 0$, this ratio is zero, and for everyday speeds where v is negligibly small compared with c, it's practically zero. Then, $1 - (v^2/c^2)$ has a value of 1, as has $\sqrt{1 - (v^2/c^2)}$, and we find that $t = t_o$, and time intervals appear the same in both systems. For higher speeds, v/c is between zero and 1, and $1 - (v^2/c^2)$ is less than 1; likewise, $\sqrt{1 - (v^2/c^2)}$. So t_o divided by a value less than 1 produces a value greater than t_o, an elongation, a dilation of time.

To consider some numerical values, assume that v is 50 percent the speed of light. Then we substitute 0.5c for v in the time-dilation equation and find, after some arithmetic, that $t = 1.15\ t_o$. This means that, if we viewed a clock on a spaceship traveling at half the speed of light, we would see the second

Figure 35.6
Ken Ford emphasizes the meaning of the time dilation equation in his teaching.

*The light clock is shown in three successive positions in the figure below. The diagonal lines represent the path of the light flash as it starts from the lower mirror at position 1, moves to the upper mirror, at position 2, and then back to the lower mirror at position 3. Distances on the diagram are marked ct, vt, and ct_o, which follows from the fact that distance traveled equals speed multiplied by time.

The symbol t_o represents the time it takes the flash to move between mirrors, as measured from a frame of reference fixed to the light clock. This is the time for straight up or down motion. The speed of light is c, and the path of light is seen to move a vertical distance ct_o. This distance between mirrors is at right angles to the motion of the light clock and is the same in both reference frames.

The symbol t represents the time it takes the flash to move from one mirror to the other, as measured from a frame of reference in which the light clock moves with speed v. Since the speed of the flash is c and the time to go from position 1 to position 2 is t, the diagonal distance traveled is ct. During this time t, the clock (which travels horizontally at speed v) moves a horizontal distance vt from position 1 to position 2.

These three distances make up a right triangle in the figure, in which ct is the hypotenuse and ct_o and vt are legs. A well-known theorem of geometry (the Pythagorean theorem) states that the square of the hypotenuse is equal to the sum of the squares of the two sides. If we apply this to the figure, we obtain:

$$c^2t^2 = c^2t_o^2 + v^2t^2$$
$$c^2t^2 - v^2t^2 = c^2t_o^2$$
$$t^2[1 - (v^2/c^2)] = t_o^2$$
$$t^2 = \frac{t_o^2}{1 - (v^2/c^2)}$$
$$t = \frac{t_o}{\sqrt{1 - (v^2/c^2)}}$$

ct
ct.
vt
Path of light as seen from a position of rest
Mirrors at position 1
Mirrors at position 2
Mirrors at postion 3

Figure 35.7
When we see the rocket at rest, we see it traveling at the maximum rate in time: 24 hours per day. If we see the rocket traveling at the maximum rate through space (the speed of light), we see its time standing still.

hand take 1.15 minutes to make a revolution, whereas, if it were at rest, we would see it take 1 minute. If the spaceship passes us at 87 percent of the speed of light, we find that $t = 2t_o$, and we measure events on the spaceship taking twice the usual time intervals—hands on the spaceship's clock turn only half as fast as those on our own clock. Events on the spaceship are seen in slow motion. At 99.5 percent of the speed of light, $t = 10t_o$, and we see the second hand of the spaceship's clock take 10 minutes to sweep through a revolution requiring 1 minute on our clock.

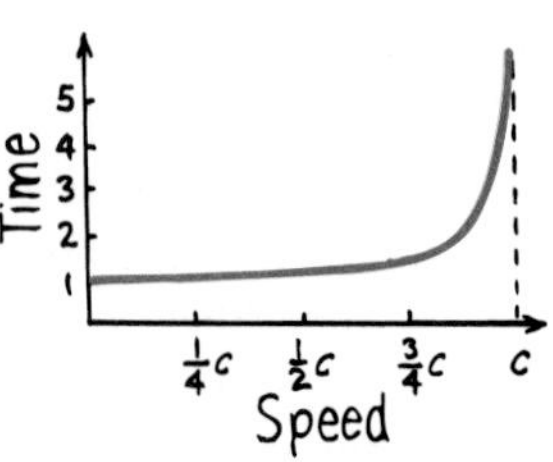

Figure 35.8
The graph shows how 1 second on a stationary clock is stretched out, as measured on a moving clock. Note that the stretching becomes significant only at speeds near the speed of light.

To put these figures in another way, at 99.5 percent of *c*, the moving clock would run at a tenth of our rate; its hands would tick only 6 seconds while our clock's second hand ticks 60 seconds. At 87 percent of *c*, the moving clock ticks at half our rate and shows 30 seconds to our 60 seconds; at 50 percent of *c*, the moving clock ticks 1/1.15 as fast and shows 52 seconds to our 60 seconds. We see that moving clocks run slow.

Nothing is unusual about a moving clock itself; it is simply ticking to the rhythm of a different time. The faster a clock moves, the slower it runs as viewed by an observer not moving with the clock. If it were possible for an observer to watch a clock pass by at the speed of light, the clock would not appear to be running at all. This observer would measure the interval between ticks to be infinite. Time would be frozen and the clock would be ageless! If our observer were moving with the clock, however, the clock would not show any slowing of time at all. This is because there would be no motion between the observer and the observed. The v in the time-dilation equation would then be zero, and $t = t_o$; they share the same reference frame in space-time.

If the person who whizzes past us checked a clock in our reference frame, however, she would find our clock to be running as slowly as we find hers to be. Each sees each other's clock running slow. There is really no contradiction here, for it is physically impossible for two observers moving at different velocities to refer to one and the same realm of space-time. All measurements made in one realm of space-time need not agree with all measurements made in another realm of space-time. The measurement they will always agree upon, however, is the speed of light.

Figure 35.9
From the Earth frame of reference, light takes 25,000 years to travel from the center of the galaxy to our solar system. From the frame of reference of a high-speed spaceship, the trip takes less time. From the frame of reference of light itself, the trip takes no time. There is no time in a speed-of-light frame of reference.

Time dilation has been confirmed in the laboratory innumerable times with atomic particle accelerators. The lifetimes of fast-moving radioactive particles increase as the speed goes up, and the amount of increase is just what Einstein's equation predicts.

Time dilation has been confirmed also for not-so-fast motion. In 1971, to test Einstein's theory, four cesium-beam atomic clocks were twice flown on regularly scheduled commercial jet flights around the earth once eastward and once westward. The clocks indicated different times after their round trips. Relative to the atomic time scale of the U.S. Naval Observatory, the observed time differences, in billionths of a second, were in accord with relativistic prediction.

This all seems very strange to us only because it is not our common experience to deal with measurements made at relativistic speeds or with atomic-clock measurements at ordinary speeds. Because of this inexperience, the theory of relativity does not make common sense. But common sense, according to Einstein, is that layer of prejudices laid down in the mind prior to the age of 18. If you spent your youth zapping through the universe in high-speed spaceships, you would probably be quite comfortable with the results of relativity.

Cosmonaut Sergei Avdeyev spent more than two years orbiting the earth in *Mir,* and, due to time dilation, he is today two-hundredths of a second younger than he would have been if he'd never been in space!

Insights

☑ CHECKPOINT

1. If you are moving in a spaceship at a high speed relative to the earth, would you notice a difference in your pulse rate? In the pulse rate of the people back on Earth?
2. Will observers A and B agree on measurements of time if A moves at half the speed of light relative to B? If both A and B move together at half the speed of light relative to the earth?
3. Does time dilation mean that time really passes more slowly in moving systems or that it only seems to pass more slowly?

Check Your Answers

1. There would be no relative speed between you and your own pulse, which share the same frame of reference, so you would notice no relativistic effects in your own pulse. There would, however, be a relativistic effect between you and people back on Earth. You would find their pulse rate slower than normal (and, likewise, they would find your pulse rate slower than normal). Relativity effects are always attributed to the other guy.
2. When A and B move relative to each other, each observes a slowing of time in the frame of reference of the other. So they will not agree on measurements of time. When they are moving in unison, however, they share the same frame of reference and will agree on measurements of time. They will see each other's time as passing normally, and they will each see events on Earth in the same slow motion.
3. The slowing of time in moving systems is not merely an illusion resulting from motion. Time really does pass more slowly in a moving system compared to one at relative rest. (This is dramatically shown in "The Twin Trip," in the *Conceptual Physical Science Practice Book.)*

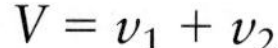

Adding Velocities

Most people know that, if you walk at 1 km/h along the aisle of a train that moves at 60 km/h, your speed relative to the ground is 61 km/h if you walk in the same direction as the moving train and 59 km/h if you walk in the opposite direction. What most people know is *almost* correct. Taking special relativity into account, one's speeds are *very nearly* 61 km/h and very nearly 59 km/h, respectively.

For everyday objects in uniform (nonaccelerating) motion, we ordinarily combine velocities by the simple rule,

$$V = v_1 + v_2$$

Much of nature is built on patterns, and looking for them is the primary preoccupation both of artists and of scientists. We connect things that were always there but never before put together in our thinking.

Insights

But this rule does not apply to light, which always has the same velocity c. Strictly speaking, the above rule is an approximation of the relativistic rule for adding velocities. We'll not treat the long derivation but simply state the rule:

$$V = \frac{v_1 + v_2}{1 + \frac{v_1 v_2}{c^2}}$$

The numerator of this formula makes common sense. But this simple sum of two velocities is altered by the second term in the denominator, which is significant only when both v_1 and v_2 are nearly c.

As an example, consider a spaceship moving away from you at a velocity of $0.5c$. It fires a rocket that thrusts in the same direction, also away from you, at a speed of $0.5c$ relative to itself. How fast does the rocket move relative to you? The nonrelativistic rule would say that the rocket moves at the speed of light in your reference frame. But, in fact,

$$V = \frac{0.5c + 0.5c}{1 + \frac{0.25c^2}{c^2}} = \frac{c}{1.25} = 0.8c$$

which illustrates another consequence of relativity: no material object can travel as fast or faster than light.

Suppose that the spaceship instead fires a pulse of laser light in its direction of travel. How fast does the pulse move in your frame of reference?

$$V = \frac{0.5c + c}{1 + \frac{0.5c^2}{c^2}} = \frac{1.5c}{1.5} = c$$

No matter what the relative velocities between two frames, light moving at c in one frame will be seen to be moving at c in any other frame. You can try chasing light, but you will never catch it.

Space Travel

One of the old arguments advanced against the possibility of human interstellar travel was that the human life span is too short. It was argued, for example, that the nearest star (after the sun), Alpha Centauri, is 4 light-years away, and that a round trip, even at the speed of light, would require at least 8 years. And even a speed-of-light voyage to the center of our galaxy, which is 25,000 light-years distant, would require a 25,000-year lifetime. But these arguments fail to take into account time dilation. Time for a person on Earth and time for a person in a high-speed rocketship are not the same.

A person's heart beats to the rhythm of the realm of space-time it is in, which can be very different for an observer who stands outside the person's frame of reference. For example, astronauts traveling at 99 percent of c could go to the star Procyon (10.4 light-years distant) and back in 21 years. It would take light itself 20.8 years to make the same round trip. Because of time dilation, it would seem to the astronauts that only 3 years had gone by. This is what all their clocks would tell them—and, biologically, they would be only 3 years older. It would be the space officials greeting them on their return who would be 21 years older!

Century Hopping

We can speculate about what human space-faring possibilities would be if the prohibitive problems of radiation and energy were overcome and if space travel were one day to become a routine experience. People would have the option of taking a trip and returning to any future century of their choosing. For example, one might depart from Earth in a high-speed spaceship in the year 2100, travel for 5 years or so, and return in the year 2500. One could live among the Earthlings of that period for a while and depart again to try out the year 3000. People could keep jumping into the future with some expense of their own time—but they could not trip into the past. They could never return to the same era on Earth to which they had bidden farewell. Time, as we know it, travels one way—forward. Here on Earth, we move constantly into the future at the steady rate of 24 hours per day. A deep-space astronaut leaving on a deep-space voyage must live with the fact that, upon return, much more time will have elapsed on Earth than the astronaut has subjectively and physically experienced during voyage. The credo of all star travelers, whatever their physiological condition, will be permanent farewell.

At higher speeds, the results are even more impressive. At a rocket speed of 99.99 percent of c, travelers could travel slightly more than 70 light-years in a single year of their own time; at 99.999 percent of c, the distance traveled would be appreciably farther than 220 light-years. A 5-year trip for them would take them farther than light travels in 1100 years of Earth time.

Present technology does not permit such journeys. The main problems are radiation and energy. Spaceships traveling at relativistic speeds would encounter hails of interstellar particles, just as if the ship were at rest on the launching pad and being bombarded by a steady stream of particles shot by a particle accelerator. No way of shielding against such intense particle bombardment for prolonged periods of time is presently known. And if, somehow, a way were devised to solve this problem, there would be the problem of energy and fuel. Spaceships traveling at relativistic speeds would require billions of times the energy used to put a space shuttle into orbit. To send a shuttle-type craft at 70 percent of c to and from Alpha Centauri, for example, would require some 500,000 times the amount of energy presently consumed in the United States in a year. Even if the spaceship scooped and fused interstellar hydrogen by some kind of interstellar ramjet, it would have to overcome the enormous retarding effect of scooping up the hydrogen at high speeds. The practicalities of such space journeys are enormously prohibitive. So, for the time being, interstellar space travel must be relegated to science fiction.

35.4 Length Contraction

As objects move through space-time, space (as well as time) undergoes changes in measurement. The lengths of objects contract when they move by us at relativistic speeds. This **length contraction** was first proposed by the physicist George F. FitzGerald and mathematically expressed by another physicist, Hendrick A. Lorentz. It is referred to as the *Lorentz-FitzGerald contraction.* We express it mathematically as

$$L = L_o\sqrt{1 - (v^2/c^2)}$$

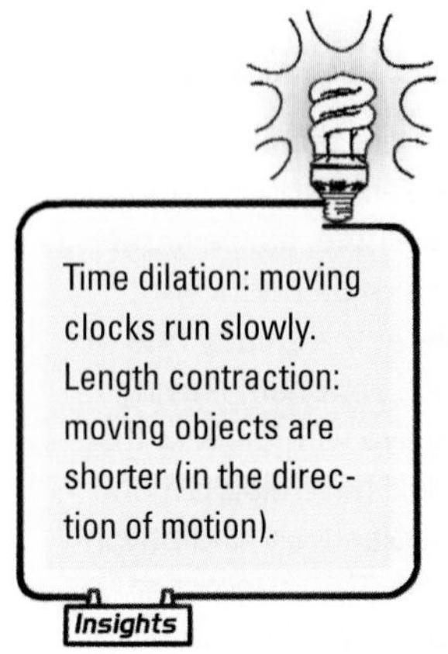

where v is the relative velocity between the observed object and the observer, c is the speed of light, L is the measured length of the moving object, and L_o (the proper length) is the measured length of the object at rest.

Suppose that an object is at rest, so that $v = 0$. Upon substitution of $v = 0$ in the equation, we find that $L = L_o$, as we would expect. At 87 percent of c, an object would be contracted to half its original length. At 99.5 percent of c, it would contract to one-tenth its original length. If the object moved at c, its length would be zero. This is one of the reasons we say that the speed of light is the upper limit for the speed of any moving object. A limerick popular with the science types is:

There was a young fencer named Fisk,
Whose thrust was exceedingly brisk.
So fast was his action
The Lorentz-FitzGerald contraction
Reduced his rapier to a disk.

As Figure 35.10 indicates, contraction takes place only in the direction of motion. If an object is moving horizontally, no contraction takes place vertically.

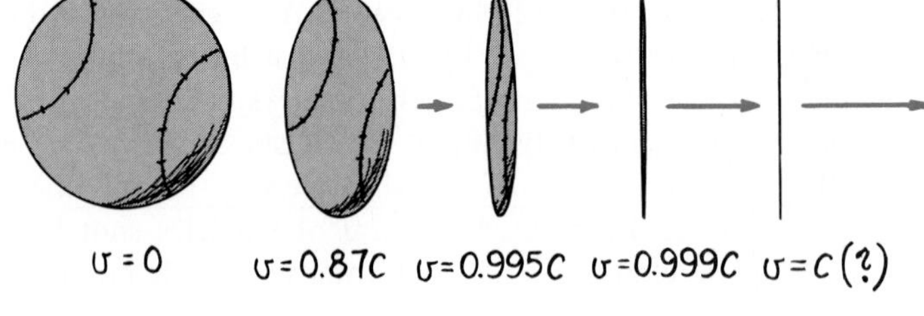

Figure 35.10
The Lorentz-FitzGerald contraction. As speed increases, length in the direction of motion decreases. Lengths in the perpendicular direction do not change.

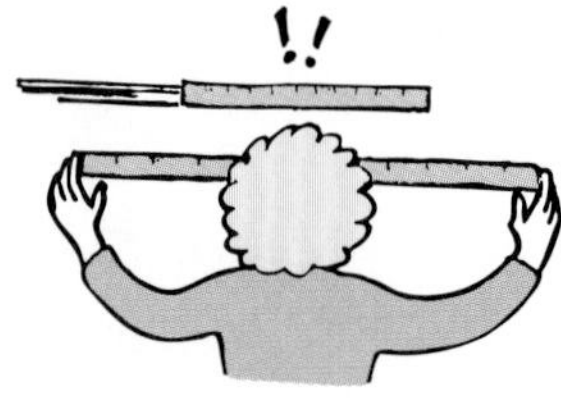

Figure 35.11
The meterstick is measured to be half as long when it is traveling at 87 percent of the speed of light relative to the observer.

Length contraction should be of considerable interest to space voyagers. The center of our Milky Way is some 25,000 light-years distant. Does this mean that, if we were to travel in that direction at the speed of light, it would take 25,000 years to get there? From an Earth frame of reference, yes; but, to the space voyagers themselves, decidedly not! At the speed of light, the 25,000 light-year distance would be contracted to no distance at all. Space voyagers would arrive there instantly!*

For hypothetical travel near the speed of light, length contraction and time dilation are just two faces of the same phenomenon. If astronauts travel so fast that they find the distance to the nearest star to be just 1 light-year instead of the 4 light-years measured from Earth, they make the trip in a little more than a year. But observers back on earth say that the clocks aboard the spaceship have slowed so much that they tick off only 1 year in 4 years of earth time. Both agree on what happens: The astronauts are only a little more than a year older when they reach the star. One set of observers says it's because of length contraction, the other set says it's because of time dilation. Both are correct.

*Did songwriter Leon Russell have this in mind when he sang, "I'll love you in a place where there's no space and time; I'll love you forever, you're a friend of mine."?

Figuring Physical Science

Problem

A rectangular billboard in space has the dimensions 10 m × 20 m. How fast and in what direction with respect to the billboard would a space traveler have to pass for the billboard to appear square?

Solution

For the billboard to be seen as a square, the 20 m side must contract to half its length—10 m. As we have learned, a speed of 87 percent of c produces a contraction of one-half. So the space traveler would have to travel at $0.87c$ in a direction parallel to the longer side of the board.

If space voyagers are ever able to boost themselves to relativistic speeds, they will find distant parts of the universe drawn closer by space contraction, while observers back on Earth will see the astronauts covering more distance because they age more slowly.

35.5 Relativistic Momentum

Recall our study of momentum in Chapter 3. We learned that the change of momentum mv of an object is equal to the impulse Ft applied to it: $Ft = \Delta mv$. For convenience, we can call momentum p. Then, $Ft = \Delta p$ (where $p = mv$). If you apply more impulse to an object that is free to move, the object acquires more momentum. Double the impulse and the momentum doubles. Apply ten times the impulse and the object gains ten times as much momentum. Does this mean that momentum can increase without limit? The answer is *yes*. Does this mean that speed can also increase without limit? The answer is *no*! As previously stated, nature's speed limit for material objects is c.

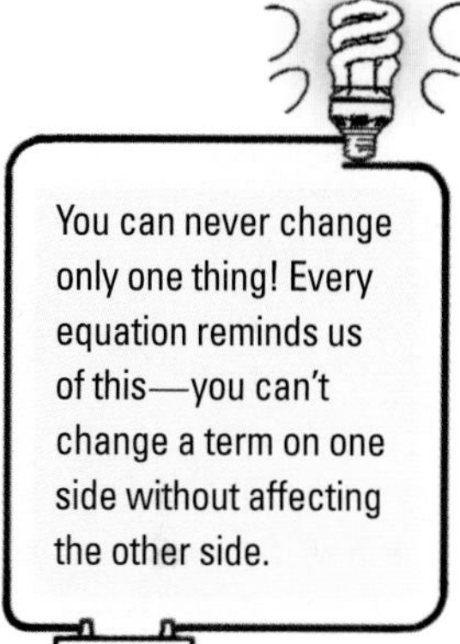

To Newton, infinite momentum would mean infinite mass or infinite speed. But not so in relativity. Einstein showed that a new definition of momentum is required—*relativistic momentum:*

$$p = \frac{mv}{\sqrt{1 - \frac{v^2}{c^2}}}$$

where again we see the familiar term in the denominator, the Lorentz factor. This generalized definition of momentum is valid in all uniformly moving reference frames. Relativistic momentum is larger than mv by a factor of $1/\sqrt{1 - (v^2/c^2)}$. For everyday speeds much less than c, this factor is nearly equal to 1, and so p is nearly equal to mv. So we see that Newton's definition of momentum is valid at low speed.

At higher speeds, the Lorentz factor grows dramatically, and so does relativistic momentum. As speed approaches c, momentum approaches infinity! No matter how close to c an object is pushed, it would still require infinite impulse to give it the last bit of speed it would need to reach c—which is

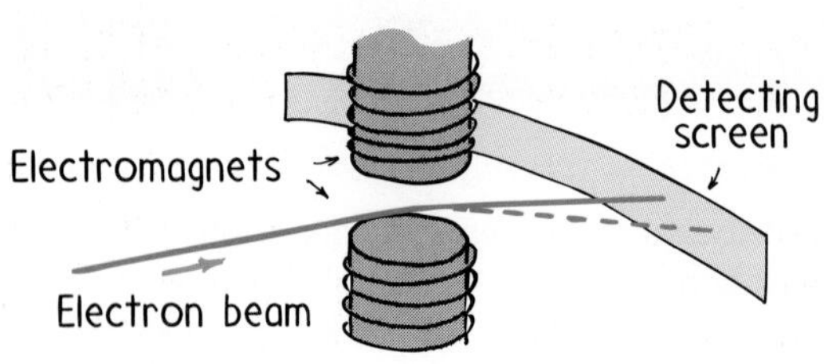

Figure 35.12
If the mass of the electrons did not increase with speed, the beam would follow the dashed line. But, because of the increased inertia, the high-speed electrons in the beam are not deflected as much.

clearly impossible. Hence, we see that no body with any mass at all can be propelled to the speed of light, much less beyond it.

Today, subatomic particles are routinely pushed to *nearly* the speed of light. The momenta of such particles may be thousands of times more than the Newton expression mv predicts. Classically, the particles behave as if their masses increase with speed. Einstein initially favored the increase-of-mass interpretation, but he later changed his mind to keep mass a constant—a property of matter that is the same in all frames of reference. So spacetime changes with speed, not mass.

The increased momentum of a high-speed particle is evident in the increased "stiffness" of its trajectory. The greater its momentum, the stiffer is its trajectory and the harder it is to deflect. We see this when a beam of electrons is directed into a magnetic field. Charged particles moving in a magnetic field experience a force that deflects them from their normal paths. For small momentum, the path curves sharply. For large momentum, there is greater stiffness and the path curves only a little (Figure 35.12). Even though one particle may be moving only a little faster than another one—say, for instance, 99.9 percent of the speed of light instead of 99 percent of the speed of light—its momentum will be considerably greater, and it will follow a straighter path in the magnetic field. This stiffness must be compensated for in circular accelerators such as cyclotrons and synchrotrons, in which momentum dictates the radius of curvature.

So we can see that, as the speed of an object approaches the speed of light, its momentum approaches infinity—which means that there is no way to reach the speed of light. There is, however, at least one thing that reaches the speed of light—light itself! But the photons of light are massless, and the equations that apply to them are different. Light travels always at the same speed. So, interestingly, a material particle can never be brought to the speed of light; and light can never be brought to rest.

35.6 Mass, Energy, and $E = mc^2$

Einstein linked not only space and time, but also mass and energy. A piece of matter, even at rest and not interacting with anything else, has an "energy of being." This is called its *rest energy.* Einstein concluded that it takes energy to make mass and that energy is released if mass disappears. The amount of energy E is related to the amount of mass m by the most celebrated equation of the twentieth century:

$$E = mc^2$$

The c^2 is the conversion factor between energy units and mass units. Because of the large magnitude of c, a small mass corresponds to an enormous quantity of energy.

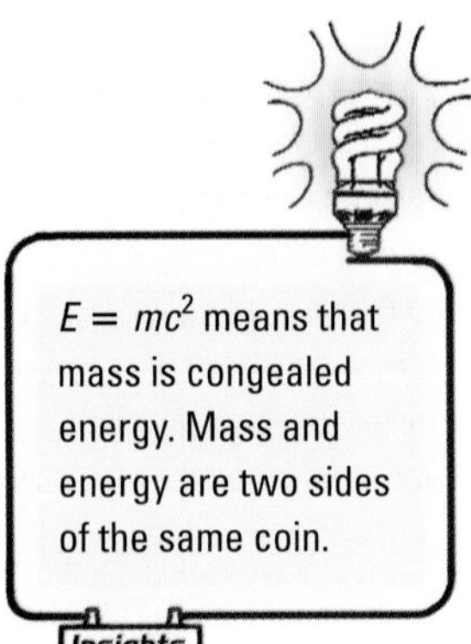

Recall from Chapter 16 that tiny decreases of nuclear mass in both nuclear fission and nuclear fusion produce enormous releases of energy, all in accord with $E = mc^2$. To the general public, $E = mc^2$ is synonymous with nuclear energy. If we were to weigh a fully fueled nuclear power plant, then weigh it again a week later, we'd find that it weighs slightly less. Part of the fuel's mass, about one part

Figure 35.13
Saying that a power plant delivers 90 million megajoules of energy to its consumers is equivalent to saying that it delivers 1 gram of energy to its consumers, because mass and energy are equivalent.

in a thousand, has been converted to energy. Now, interestingly enough, if we were to weigh a coal-burning power plant and all the coal and oxygen it consumes in a week, and then weigh it again with all the carbon dioxide and other combustion products released during the week, we'd also find that it weighs slightly less. Again, mass has been converted to energy. About one part in a billion has been converted. Get this: If both plants produce the same amount of energy, the mass change will be the same for both—whether energy is released by nuclear or chemical mass conversion makes no difference. The chief difference lies in the amount of energy released in each individual reaction and the amount of mass involved. The fissioning of a single uranium nucleus releases 10 million times as much energy as the combustion of carbon to produce a single carbon dioxide molecule. Hence, a few truckloads of uranium fuel will power a fission plant, while a coal-burning plant consumes many hundred-car trainloads of coal.

When we strike a match, phosphorus atoms in the match head rearrange themselves and combine with oxygen in the air to form new molecules. The resulting molecules have very slightly less mass than the separate phosphorus and oxygen molecules. From a mass standpoint, the whole is slightly less than the sum of its parts, by amounts that escape our notice. For all chemical reactions that release energy, there is a corresponding decrease in mass of about one part in a billion.

For nuclear reactions, a decrease in mass by one part in a thousand occurs. This decrease of mass in the sun by thermonuclear fusion bathes the solar system with radiant energy and nourishes life. It's been going on in the sun for 5 billion years, and it is expected to continue for another 5 billion years. It is very nice to have such a big sun!

Figure 35.14
In 1 second, 4.5 million tons of mass is converted to radiant energy in the sun. But the Sun is so massive that, in 1 million years, only one ten-millionth of the sun's mass will have been converted to radiant energy.

The equation $E = mc^2$ is more than a formula for the conversion of mass into other kinds of energy, or vice versa. It states even more—that energy and mass are the *same thing*. Mass is congealed energy. If you want to know how much energy is in a system, measure its mass. For an object at rest, its energy *is* its mass. Energy, like mass, exhibits inertia. Shake a massive object back and forth; it is energy itself that is hard to shake.

☑ CHECKPOINT

Can we look at the equation $E = mc^2$ in another way and say that matter transforms into pure energy when it is traveling at the speed of light squared?

Check Your Answer

No, no, no! Matter cannot be made to move at the speed of light, let alone the speed of light squared (which is not a speed!). The equation $E = mc^2$ simply means that energy and mass are "two sides of the same coin."

The first evidence for the conversion of radiant energy to mass was provided in 1932 by the American physicist Carl Anderson. He and a colleague at the California Institute of Technology (Caltech) discovered the *positron* by the track it left in a cloud chamber. The positron is the *antiparticle* of the electron, equal in mass and spin to the electron but opposite in charge. When a high-frequency photon comes close to an atomic nucleus, it can create an electron and a positron together as a pair, thus creating mass. The created particles fly apart. The positron is not part of normal matter because of its short life span. As soon as it encounters an electron, the pair is annihilated, sending out two gamma rays in the process. Then mass is converted back to radiant energy.

(a)

(b)

Figure 35.15
(a) Everything is weightless on the inside of a nonaccelerating spaceship far away from gravitational influences. (b) When the spaceship accelerates, an occupant inside feels "gravity."

35.7 General Relativity

The special theory of relativity is about uniform motion, which is why it is called special. Einstein's conviction that the laws of nature should be expressed in the same form in every frame of reference, accelerated as well as nonaccelerated, was the primary motivation that led him to the **general theory of relativity**—a new theory of gravitation, where gravity causes space to become curved and time to slow down.

Einstein was led to this new theory of gravity by thinking about observers in accelerated motion. He imagined himself in a spaceship far away from gravitational influences. In such a spaceship at rest or in uniform motion relative to the distant stars, he and everything within the ship would float freely; there would be no "up" and no "down." But if rocket motors were activated to accelerate the ship, things would be different; phenomena similar to gravity would be observed. The wall adjacent to the rocket motors would push up against any occupants and become the floor, while the opposite wall would become the ceiling. Occupants in the ship would be able to stand on the floor and even jump up and down. If the acceleration of the spaceship were equal to g, the occupants could well be convinced the ship was not accelerating but was simply at rest on the surface of the earth.

Einstein concluded that gravity and motion through space-time are related, a conclusion now called the **principle of equivalence:**

Local observations made in an accelerated frame of reference cannot be distinguished from observations made in a Newtonian gravitational field.

To examine this new "gravity" in the accelerating spaceship, Einstein considered the consequence of dropping two balls—say, one of wood and the other of lead. When released, the balls would continue to move upward, side by side, with the velocity of the spaceship at the moment of release. If the spaceship were moving at a *constant velocity* (zero acceleration), the balls would remain suspended in the same place, since both the spaceship and the balls would be moving by the same amount. But, since the spaceship is accelerating, the floor moves upward faster than the balls, which are soon intercepted by the floor (Figure 35.16). Both balls, regardless of their masses, would meet the floor at the same time. Recall the legend of Galileo's demonstration at the Leaning Tower of Pisa. Occupants of the spaceship might be prone to attribute their observations to the force of gravity.

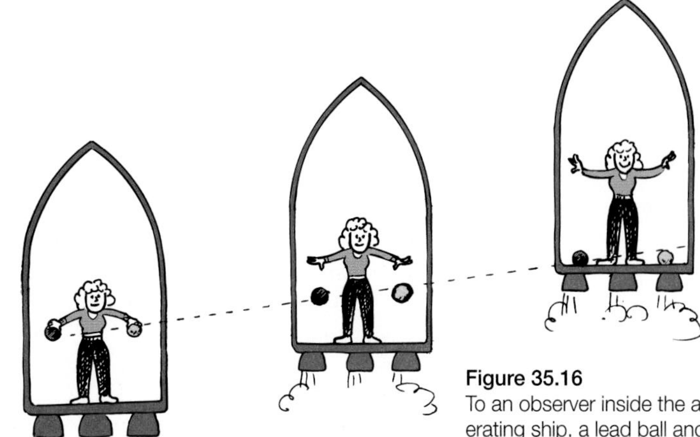

Figure 35.16
To an observer inside the accelerating ship, a lead ball and a wood ball appear to fall together when released.

The two interpretations of the falling balls are equally valid, and Einstein incorporated this equivalence, or the impossibility of distinguishing between gravitation and acceleration, into the foundation of his general theory of relativity. The principle of equivalence states that observations made in an accelerated reference frame are indistinguishable from observations made in a Newtonian gravitational field. This equivalence would be interesting but not revolutionary if it applied only to mechanical phenomena, but Einstein went further and stated that the principle holds for all natural phenomena; it holds for optical and all electromagnetic phenomena as well.

Just as a tossed ball curves in a gravitational field, so does a light beam. Consider a ball thrown sideways in a stationary spaceship in the absence of gravity (Figure 35.17a). The ball will follow a straight-line path relative to both an observer inside the spaceship and to a stationary observer outside the spaceship. But, if the spaceship is accelerating, the floor overtakes the ball and it hits the wall below a point opposite to the window (Figure 35.17b). An observer outside the spaceship still sees a straight-line path, but, to an observer in the accelerating spaceship, the path is curved; it is a parabola. The same result holds true for a beam of light (Figure 35.18). The only difference is the curvatures of both. If the ball were somehow thrown at the speed of light, both curvatures would be the same.

According to Newton, tossed balls curve because of a force of gravity. According to Einstein, both tossed balls and light curve not because of any force but because the space-time in which they travel is curved.

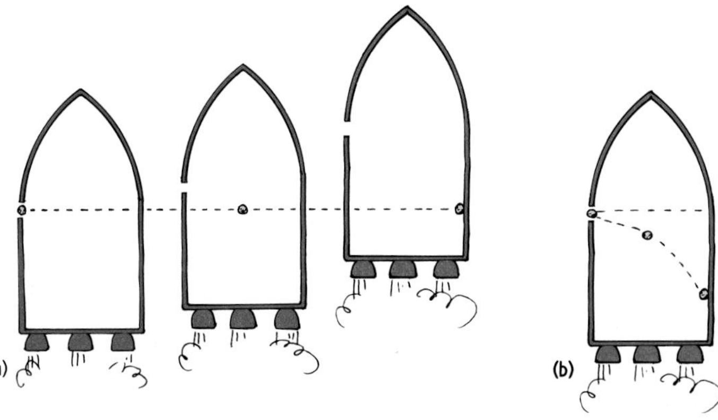

Figure 35.17
(a) An outside observer sees a horizontally thrown ball travel in a straight line, and, since the spaceship is moving upward while the ball travels horizontally, the ball strikes the wall below a point opposite the window. (b) To an inside observer, the ball bends as if in a gravitational field.

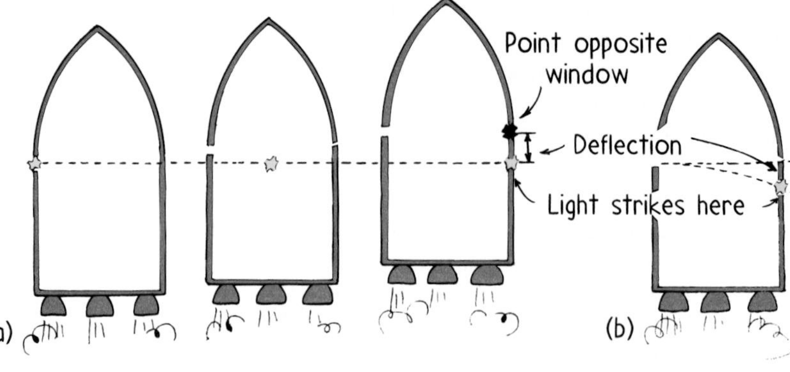

Figure 35.18
(a) An outside observer sees light travel horizontally in a straight line, but, like the ball in the previous figure, it strikes the wall slightly below a point opposite the window. (b) To an inside observer, the light also bends as if responding to a gravitational field.

Figure 35.19
The trajectory of a flashlight beam is identical to the trajectory of a baseball "thrown" at the speed of light. Both paths curve equally in a uniform gravitational field.

☑ CHECKPOINT

Whoa! We learned previously that the pull of gravity is an interaction between masses. And we learned that light has no mass. Now we say that light can be bent by gravity. Isn't this a contradiction?

Check Your Answer

There is no contradiction when the mass–energy equivalence is understood. It's true that light has no mass, but it is not "energyless." The fact that gravity deflects light provides evidence that gravity pulls on the energy of light. Energy indeed is equivalent to mass!

Gravity, Space, and a New Geometry

Einstein perceived a gravitational field as a geometrical warping of four-dimensional space-time. Four-dimensional geometry is altogether different from three-dimensional Euclidean geometry. The laws of Euclidean geometry taught in high school are no longer valid when they are applied to objects in the presence of strong gravitational fields.

The familiar rules of Euclidean geometry pertain to various figures you can draw on a flat surface. The ratio of the circumference of a circle to its diameter is equal to π; all the angles in a triangle add up to 180°; the shortest distance between two points is a straight line. The rules of Euclidean geometry are valid in flat space; but, if you draw these figures on a curved surface like a sphere or a saddle-shaped object, the Euclidean rules no longer hold (Figure 35.20). If you measure the sum of the angles for a triangle in space, you say that the space is flat if the sum is equal to 180°, spherelike or positively curved if the sum is larger than 180°, and saddlelike or negatively curved if it is less than 180°.

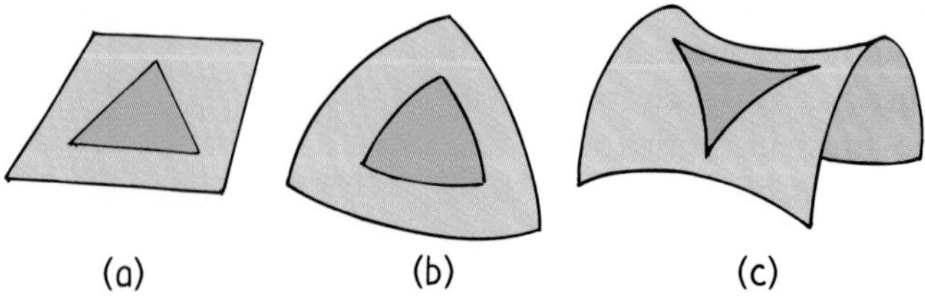

Figure 35.20
The sum of the angles for a triangle drawn (a) on a plane surface = 180°, (b) on a spherical surface is greater than 180°, and (c) on a saddle-shaped surface is less than 180°.

Of course, the lines forming the triangles in Figure 35.20 are not "straight" from the three-dimensional view, but they represent the "straightest" or the *shortest* distances between two points if we are confined to the curved surface. These lines of shortest distance are called *geodesic lines* or simply **geodesics.**

Figure 35.21
The light rays joining the three planets form a triangle. Since light passing near the sun bends, the sum of the angles of the resulting triangle is greater than 180°.

The path of a light beam follows a geodesic. Suppose that three experimenters on Earth, Venus, and Mars measure the angles of a triangle formed by light beams traveling between them. The light beams bend when passing the sun, resulting in the sum of the three angles being larger than 180° (Figure 35.21). So the space around the sun is positively curved. The planets that orbit the sun travel along four-dimensional geodesics in this positively curved space-time. Likewise, freely falling objects, satellites, and light rays all travel along geodesics in four-dimensional space-time.

The whole universe may have an overall curvature. If it is negatively curved, it is open-ended and extends without limit; if it is positively curved, it closes in on itself. The surface of the earth, for example, forms a closed curvature; so, if you travel along a geodesic, you return to your starting point. Similarly, if the universe were positively curved, it would be closed; so, if you could look infinitely into space through an ideal telescope, you would see the back of your own head! (This is assuming that you waited a long enough time or that light traveled infinitely fast.)

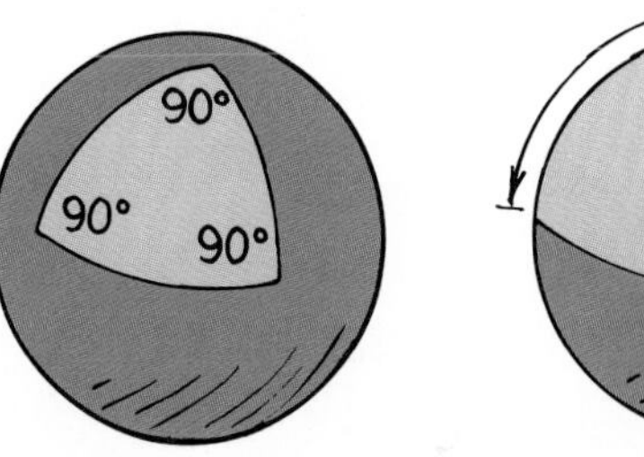

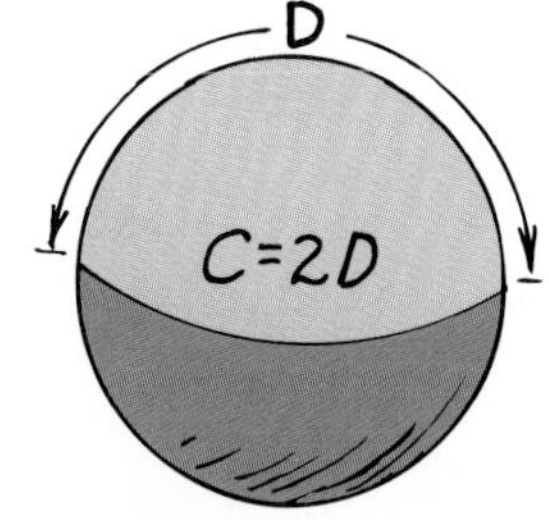

Figure 35.22
The geometry of the curved surface of the earth differs from the Euclidean geometry of flat space. Note that the sum of the angles for an equilateral triangle whose sides equal to one-quarter of the earth's circumference is clearly greater than 180°, and the circumference is only twice its diameter instead of 3.14 times its diameter. Euclidean geometry is also invalid in curved space.

General relativity, then, calls for a new geometry: a geometry not only of curved space but of curved time as well—a geometry of curved four-dimensional space-time.* The mathematics of this geometry is too formidable to present here. The essence, however, is that the presence of mass produces the curvature or warping of space-time; by the same token, a curvature of space-time reveals itself as mass. Instead of visualizing gravitational forces between masses, we abandon altogether the notion of force and instead think of masses responding in their motion to the curvature or warping of the space-time they inhabit. It is the bumps, depressions, and warpings of geometrical space-time that *are* the phenomena of gravity.

We cannot visualize the four-dimensional bumps and depressions in space-time because we are three-dimensional beings. We can get a glimpse of this warping by considering a simplified analogy in two dimensions: a heavy

*Don't be discouraged if you cannot visualize four-dimensional space-time. Einstein himself often told his friends, "Don't try. I can't do it either." Perhaps we are not too different from the great thinkers around Galileo who couldn't think of a moving Earth!

Gravitational Waves

Every object has mass and therefore makes a bump or depression in the surrounding space-time. When an object moves, the surrounding warp of space and time moves to readjust to the new position. These readjustments produce ripples in the overall geometry of space-time. This is similar to moving a ball that rests on the surface of the waterbed. A disturbance ripples across the waterbed surface in waves; if we move a more massive ball, then we get a greater disturbance and the production of even stronger waves. The ripples travel outward from the gravitational sources at the speed of light and are known as **gravitational waves.**

Any moving object produces a gravitational wave. In general, the more massive the moving object and the more violent its motion, the stronger the resulting gravitational wave. But even the strongest waves produced by ordinary astronomical events are extremely weak—the weakest known in nature. For example, the gravitational waves emitted by a vibrating electric charge are a trillion-trillion-trillion times weaker than the electromagnetic waves emitted by the same charge. Detecting gravitational waves is enormously difficult, and no confirmed detection has occurred to date. A new generation of wave detectors, soon to be built, is expected to detect gravitational waves from supernovae, where as much as 0.1 percent of their mass may be radiated away as gravitational waves.

As weak as they are, gravitational waves are everywhere. Shake your hand back and forth: you have just produced a gravitational wave. It is not very strong, but it exists.

ball resting on the middle of a waterbed. The more massive the ball, the greater it dents or warps the two-dimensional surface. A marble rolled across a small-dented surface may trace an elliptical curve and orbit the ball. The planets that orbit the sun similarly travel along four-dimensional geodesics in the warped space-time about the sun.

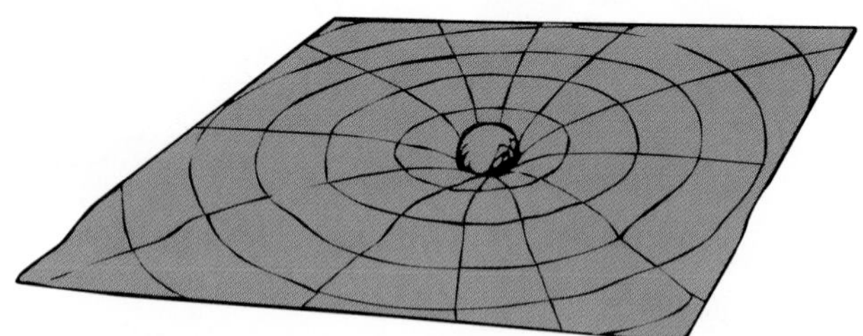

Figure 35.23
A two-dimensional analogy of four-dimensional warped space-time. Space-time near a star is curved in a way similar to the surface of a waterbed when a heavy ball rests upon it.

Tests of General Relativity

Using four-dimensional field equations, Einstein recalculated the orbits of the planets about the sun. Beyond the planets, space is almost flat, and objects travel along nearly straight-line paths. Near the sun, planets and comets travel along curved paths because of the curvature of space. With only one minor exception, his theory gave almost exactly the same results as Newton's law of gravity. The exception was that Einstein's theory predicted that the elliptical orbits of the planets should *precess* (Figure 35.24)—independently of the Newtonian influence of other planets. This precession would be very slight for distant planets and more pronounced for planets close to the sun. Mercury is the only planet close enough to the sun for the curvature of space to produce an effect on it that is not predicted by Newton's law.

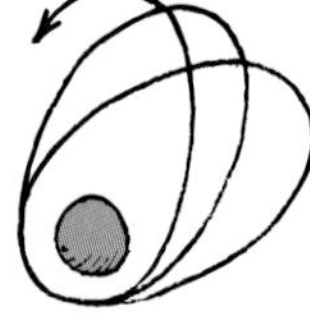

Figure 35.24
A precessing elliptical orbit.

Precession in the orbits of planets caused by perturbations of other planets was well-known. Since the early 1800s, astronomers measured a precession of Mercury's orbit—about 574 seconds of arc per century. Perturbations by the other planets were found to account for the precession—except for 43 seconds of arc per century more than the calculated value. Even after all known corrections due to possible perturbations by other planets had been applied, the calculations of physicists and astronomers failed to account for the extra 43 seconds of arc. Either Venus was extra massive or some other, previously undiscovered planet (tentatively called Vulcan) was pulling on Mercury. And then came the explanation of Einstein, whose general relativity field equations, when applied to Mercury's orbit, predict the extra 43 seconds of arc per century!

As a second test of his theory, Einstein predicted that measurements of starlight passing close to the sun would be deflected by an angle of 1.75 seconds of arc—large enough to be measured. This deflection of starlight can be observed during an eclipse of the sun. (Measuring this deflection has become a standard practice at every total eclipse since the first measurements were made during the total eclipse of 1919.) A photograph taken of the darkened sky around the eclipsed sun reveals the presence of the nearby bright stars. The positions of the stars then are compared with those in other photographs of the same area taken at other times during the night with the same telescope. In every instance, the deflection of starlight has supported Einstein's prediction (Figure 35.25).

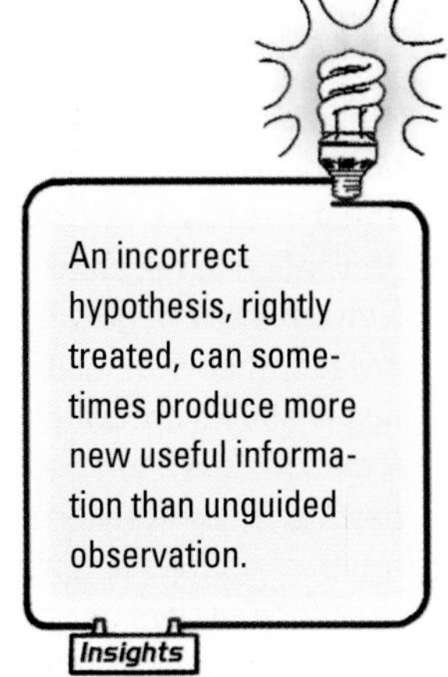

☑ CHECKPOINT

Why do we not notice the bending of light by gravity in our everyday environment?

Check Your Answer

Only because light travels so fast; just as, over a short distance, we do not notice the curved path of a high-speed bullet, we do not notice the curving of a light beam.

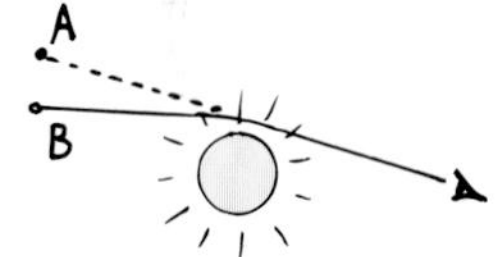

Figure 35.25
Starlight bends as it grazes the sun. Point A shows the apparent position; point B shows the true position.

Einstein made a third prediction—that gravity causes clocks to run slow. He predicted that clocks on the first floor of a building should tick slightly slower than clocks at the top floor, which are farther from the earth and therefore in a location of weaker gravitation. From the top to the bottom of the tallest skyscraper, the difference is very small—only a few millionths of a second per decade—because the difference in the earth's gravitation at the bottom and top of the skyscraper is very small. For larger differences, like those at the surface of the sun compared with the surface of the earth, the clock-slowing effect is more pronounced. A clock at the surface of the sun should run measurably slower than a clock at the surface of the earth. Einstein suggested a way to measure this.

Every atom emits light at specific frequency characteristic of the vibrational rate of the electrons in the atom. Every atom is therefore a "clock," and any slowing down of atomic vibration indicates a slowing down of the clock. An atom on the sun, where gravitation is strong, should emit light of a lower frequency than the light emitted by the same kind of atom on the earth. Because red light is at the low-frequency end of the visible spectrum, a lowering of frequency shifts the color

Figure 35.26
If you move from a distant point down to the surface of the earth, you move in the direction in which the gravitational force acts—toward a location where clocks run more slowly. A clock at the surface of the earth runs slower than a clock that is located farther away.

Newton's and Einstein's Gravity Compared

When Einstein formulated his new theory of gravitation, he realized that, if his theory was valid, his field equations must reduce to Newtonian equations for gravitation in the weak-field limit. He showed that Newton's law of gravitation is a special case of the broader theory of relativity. Newton's law of gravitation is still an accurate description of most of the interactions between bodies in the solar system and beyond. From Newton's law, one can calculate the orbits of comets and asteroids and even predict the existence of undiscovered planets. Even today, when computing the trajectories of space probes throughout the solar system and beyond, only ordinary Newtonian theory is used. This is because the gravitational field of these bodies is very weak, and, from the viewpoint of general relativity, the surrounding space-time is essentially flat. But for regions of more intense gravitation, where space-time is more appreciably curved, Newtonian theory cannot adequately account for various phenomena—such as the precession of Mercury's orbit close to the sun and, in the case of stronger fields, the gravitational red shift and other apparent distortions of space and time. These distortions reach their limit in the case of a star that collapses to a black hole, where space-time completely folds over on itself. Only Einsteinian gravitation reaches into this domain.

of the emitted light toward the red. This effect is the **gravitational red shift.** Although it is weak in the sun, it is stronger in more compact stars because they have a greater surface gravity. An experiment confirming Einstein's prediction was performed in 1960. The gravitational red shift was detected using high-frequency gamma rays sent between the top and bottom floors of a laboratory building at Harvard University.* Incredibly precise measurements confirmed the gravitational slowing of time.

The gravitational red shift can also be understood in terms of the gravitational force acting on photons. As it leaves the surface of a star, a photon is "retarded" by the star's gravity. It loses energy (but not speed). Being that a photon's frequency is proportional to its energy, its frequency decreases as its energy decreases. When we observe the photon, we see that it has a lower frequency than it would have had if it had been emitted by a less massive source. Its time has been slowed, just like the ticking of a clock is slowed.

So measurements of time depend not only on relative motion, as we learned in our discussion of special relativity, but also on gravity. In special relativity, time dilation depends on the *speed* of one frame of reference relative to another one. In general relativity, the gravitational red shift depends on the *location* of one point in a gravitational field relative to another one. It is important to note the relativistic nature of time both in special relativity and in general relativity. In both theories, there is no way that you can extend the duration of your own experience. Others moving at different speeds or in different gravitational fields may attribute a great longevity to you, but your longevity is seen from *their* frame of reference, never from your own. Changes in time and other relativistic effects are always attributed to "the other guy."

*In the late 1950s, shortly after Einstein's death, the German physicist Rudolph Mössbauer discovered a way to use atomic nuclei as atomic clocks, called the *Mössbauer effect,* for which he was awarded the Nobel prize for physics in 1961. In 1960, Professors Pound and Rebka at Harvard University used the Mössbauer effect to perform the confirming experiment.

We saw, in Chapter 13, that Newtonian physics is linked at one end with quantum theory, whose domain is the very light and the very small—tiny particles and atoms. And now we have seen that Newtonian physics is linked at the other end with relativity theory, whose domain includes the very massive and the very large.

Biography: Albert Einstein (1879–1955)

Albert Einstein was born in Ulm, Germany, on March 14, 1879. According to popular legend, he was a slow child and learned to speak at a much later age than average; his parents feared for a while that he might be mentally retarded. Yet his elementary school records show that he was remarkably gifted in mathematics, physics, and playing the violin. He rebelled, however, at the practice of education by regimentation and rote and was expelled just as he was preparing to drop out at the age of 15. Largely because of business reasons, his family moved to Italy. Young Einstein renounced his German citizenship and went to live with family friends in Switzerland. There he was allowed to take the entrance examinations for the renowned Swiss Federal Institute of Technology in Zurich, although he was two years younger than normal age. But, because of difficulties with the French language, he did not pass the examination. He spent a year at a Swiss preparatory school in Aarau, where he was "promoted, with protest, in French." He tried the entrance exam again at Zurich and passed. As a student, he cut many lectures, preferring to study on his own, and, in 1900, he succeeded in passing his examinations by cramming with the help of a friend's meticulous notes. He said later of this, ". . . after I had passed the final examination, I found the consideration of any scientific problem distasteful to me for an entire year." During this year, he became a citizen of Switzerland; he accepted a temporary summer teaching position and tutored two young high school students. He advised their father, a high school teacher himself, to remove the boys from school, where, he maintained, their natural curiosity was being destroyed. Einstein's job as a tutor was short-lived.

It was not until two years after graduation that he got a steady job, as a patent examiner at the Swiss Patent Office in Berne. Einstein held this position for more than seven years. He found the work rather interesting, sometimes stimulating his scientific imagination, but mainly freeing him of financial worries while providing time to ponder the problems in physics that puzzled him.

With no academic connections whatsoever, and with essentially no contact with other physicists, he laid out the main lines along which twentieth-century theoretical physics has developed. In 1905, at the age of 26, he earned his Ph.D. in physics and published three major papers. The first was on the quantum theory of light, including an explanation of the photoelectric effect, for which he won the 1921 Nobel prize in physics. The second paper was on the statistical aspects of molecular theory and Brownian motion, a proof for the existence of atoms. His third and most famous paper was on special relativity. In 1915, he published a paper on the theory of general relativity, which presented a new theory of gravitation that included Newton's theory as a special case. These trailblazing papers have greatly affected the direction of modern physics.

Einstein's concerns were not limited to physics. He lived in Berlin during World War I and denounced the German militarism of his time. He publicly expressed his deeply felt conviction that warfare should be abolished and that an international organization should be founded to govern disputes between nations. In 1933, while Einstein was visiting the United States, Hitler came to power. Einstein spoke out against Hitler's racial and political policies and resigned his position at the University of Berlin.

Biography: Albert Einstein (1879–1955) *continued*

No longer safe in Germany, Einstein came to the United States and accepted a research position at the Institute for Advanced Study in Princeton, New Jersey.

In 1939, one year before Einstein became an American citizen, and after German scientists fissioned the uranium atom, he was urged by several prominent Hungarian-American scientists to write the famous letter to President Roosevelt pointing out the scientific possibilities of a nuclear bomb. Einstein was a pacifist, but the thought of Hitler developing such a bomb prompted his action. The outcome was the development of the first nuclear bombs, which, ironically, were detonated over Japan after the fall of Germany.

Einstein believed that the universe is indifferent to the human condition, and he stated that, if humanity were to continue, it must create a moral order. He intensely advocated world peace through nuclear disarmament. Nuclear bombs, Einstein remarked, had changed everything but our way of thinking.

C.P. Snow, who was acquainted with Einstein, in a review of *The Born–Einstein Letters, 1916–1955,* says this of him: "Einstein was the most powerful mind of the twentieth century, and one of the most powerful that ever lived. He was more than that. He was a man of enormous weight of personality, and perhaps most of all, of normal stature. . . . I have met a number of people whom the world calls great; of these, he was by far, by an order of magnitude, the most impressive. He was—despite the warmth, the humanity, the touch of the comedian—the most different from other men."

Einstein was more than a great scientist; he was a man of unpretentious disposition with a deep concern for the welfare of his fellow beings. The choice of Einstein as the person of the century by *Time* magazine at the end of the 1900s was most appropriate—and noncontroversial.

Summary of Terms

Frame of reference A vantage point (usually a set of coordinate axes), with respect to which position and motion may be described.

Space-time The four-dimensional continuum in which all events take place and all things exist. Three dimensions are the coordinates of space and the fourth dimension is time.

Special theory of relativity The first of Einstein's theories of relativity, which discusses the effects of uniform motion on space, time, energy, and mass.

Postulates of the special theory of relativity (1) All laws of nature are the same in all uniformly moving frames of reference. (2) The speed of light in free space has the same measured value regardless of the motion of the source or the motion of the observer; that is, the speed of light is a constant.

Time dilation The slowing of time as a result of speed.

Length contraction The contraction of objects in their direction of motion as a result of speed.

Mass-energy equivalence The relationship between mass and energy as given by the equation $E = mc^2$.

General theory of relativity The second of Einstein's theories of relativity, which discusses the effects of gravity on space and time.

Geodesic The shortest distance between two points in various models of space.

Gravitational wave The transport of energy by the motion of waves in a gravitational field.

Gravitational red shift The lengthening of the waves of electromagnetic radiation due to escape from a gravitational field.

Review Questions

35.1 Space-Time

1. How many coordinate axes are usually used to describe three-dimensional space? What does the fourth dimension measure?
2. Under what condition will you and a friend share the same realm of space-time? When will you not share the same realm?
3. What is special about the ratio of the distance traveled by a flash of light and the time the light takes to travel this distance?

35.2 Special Relativity

4. Cite at least two examples of Einstein's first postulate.
5. Cite at least one example of Einstein's second postulate.

35.3 Time Dilation

6. What do we call the "stretching out of time"?
7. Suppose the parallel mirrors of a light clock were 150,000 km apart. In the frame of reference of the light clock, how much time would be required for a pulse of light to make a round trip between the mirrors?
8. Suppose that the parallel mirrors of a light clock were 150 km apart. In the frame of reference of the light clock, how much time would be required for a pulse of light to make a round trip between the mirrors?
9. Would your answers to the previous two questions be different if your measurements were made from a frame of reference that is moving relative to the light clock? Defend your answer.
10. Time is required for light to travel along a path from one point to another. If this path is seen to be longer because of motion, what happens to the time it takes for light to travel this longer path?
11. How do measurements of time differ for events in a frame of reference that moves at 50 percent of the speed of light relative to us?
12. How do measurements of time differ for events in a frame of reference that moves at 99.5 percent of the speed of light relative to us?
13. Suppose that a particular clock accurately shows time passing half as fast in a particular frame of reference as in our own. What is the velocity of this frame of reference relative to us?
14. What is the evidence for time dilation?
15. What does Einstein say about common sense?
16. When two velocities v_1 and v_2 are each much less than the speed of light, is the value $\frac{v_1 v_2}{c^2}$ large or small?
17. What is the maximum value of $\frac{v_1 v_2}{c^2}$ in an extreme situation? What is the smallest value?
18. What are the present-day obstacles to interstellar space travel?

35.4 Length Contraction

19. How long would a meterstick appear if it were traveling like a properly thrown spear at 99.5 percent of the speed of light?
20. How long would the meterstick in the previous question appear if it were traveling with its length *perpendicular* to its direction of motion? (Why is your answer different from the previous answer?)
21. If you were traveling in a high-speed rocket ship, would metersticks on board appear to you to be contracted? Defend your answer.

35.5 Relativistic Momentum

22. How does the relativistic momentum of a fast-moving object compare with the momentum described by Newton?
23. What does it mean to say a trajectory is stiffer for particles moving at high speed?
24. What would be the mass of an object if it were somehow propelled to the speed of light?

35.6 Mass, Energy, and $E = mc^2$

25. Does the equation $E = mc^2$ apply only to nuclear and chemical reactions?
26. In what sense can it be said that a power utility sells mass?
27. Why does the mass decrease that occurs in chemical reactions go unnoticed?
28. Compare the relative amounts of mass lost in nuclear reactions and in chemical reactions.

35.7 General Relativity

29. What is the principle difference between *special relativity* and *general relativity*?
30. How would the number of pushups one could perform at the earth's surface compare with the number of pushups one could perform in an elevator accelerating at *g* far from the earth's gravitational field?
31. Compare the bending of the paths of baseballs and the paths of photons by a gravitational field.
32. What does it mean to say that space is curved?
33. What is a *geodesic*?
34. Of all the planets, why is Mercury the best candidate for finding evidence of the relationship of gravitation to space?
35. What is the evidence for light bending near the sun?

36. Which runs faster, a clock at the top of the Sears Tower in Chicago or a clock on the shore of Lake Michigan?
37. What is the effect of a strong gravitational field on the frequency of light? What is the effect on its wavelength?
38. Does Einstein's theory of gravitation invalidate Newton's theory of gravitation? Explain.

Exercises

1. When you switch on the headlights of a car, the light beam moves at a high speed. If the car is moving forward when the lights are switched on, is the speed of the light beam more, less, or the same?
2. A person riding on the roof of a freight car in a train fires a gun pointed forward. (a) Relative to the ground, is the bullet moving faster or slower when the train is moving than when it is standing still? (b) Relative to the freight car, is the bullet moving faster or slower when the train is moving than when the train is standing still?
3. Suppose that the person riding on the roof of the freight car in Exercise 2 shines a searchlight beam in the direction in which the train is traveling. Compare the speed of the light beam relative to the ground when the train is at rest and when it is moving. How does the behavior of the light beam differ from the behavior of the bullet in Exercise 2?
4. When you drive down a highway, you are moving through space. What else are you moving through?
5. In Chapter 12, we learned that light travels more slowly in glass than in air. Does this contradict the special theory of relativity?
6. If we see somebody's clock running slow due to relative motion, will they see our clocks running slow also? Or will they see our clocks running fast?
7. Since there is an upper limit on the speed of a particle, does it follow that there is also an upper limit on its momentum? On its kinetic energy? Explain.
8. Light travels a certain distance in, say, 20,000 years. How is it possible that an astronaut could travel more slowly than the speed of light and travel 20,000 light-years in a 20-year trip?
9. Could a human being who has a life expectancy of 70 years possibly make a round-trip journey to a part of the universe thousands of light-years distant? Explain.
10. A twin who makes a long trip at relativistic speeds returns younger than his stay-at-home twin sister. Could he return before his twin sister was born? Defend your answer.
11. Is it possible for a son or daughter to be biologically older than his or her parents? Explain.
12. If you were in a rocket ship traveling away from the earth at a speed close to the speed of light, what changes would you note in your pulse? In your mass? In your volume? Explain.
13. If you were on Earth monitoring a person in a rocket ship traveling away from the earth at a speed close to the speed of light, what changes would you note in his pulse? In his mass? In his volume? Explain your answer.
14. How does the measured density of a body at rest compare with its density when it is moving?
15. If stationary observers measure the shape of a passing object to be exactly circular, then what is the shape of the object according to observers traveling with it?
16. Is this limerick, which is popular with relativity types, consistent or inconsistent with relativity theory? Defend your answer.

    There was a young lady named Bright
    Who traveled much faster than light.
    She departed one day
    In an Einsteinian way
    And returned on the previous night.
17. As a meterstick that has a rest mass of 1 kg moves past you, your measurements show it to have a mass of 2 kg. If your measurements show it to have a length of 1 m, what is the orientation of the stick?
18. In the preceding exercise, if the stick is moving in a direction along its length (like a properly thrown spear), how long will it appear to you?
19. If a high-speed spaceship appears shrunken to half size, by how much will measurements of its momentum differ from Newtonian momentum?
20. The "2-mile" linear accelerator at Stanford University in California "appears" to be less than a meter long to the electrons that travel in it. Explain.
21. Electrons that are accelerated in the Stanford accelerator gain thousands of times more momentum by the time they reach the end of their trip, as mv dictates. In theory, if you could travel with them, would you notice an increase in relativistic momentum? Explain.
22. Muons are elementary particles that are formed high in the atmosphere by the interactions of cosmic rays with gases in the upper atmosphere. Muons are radioactive and have average lifetimes of about two-millionths of a second. Even though they travel at almost the speed of light, they are so high that very few should be detected at sea level—at least according to classical physics. Laboratory measurements, however, show that muons in great proportions do reach the earth's surface. What is the explanation?
23. When we look into the universe, we see into the past. John Dobson, founder of the San Francisco Sidewalk Astronomers, says that we cannot even see the backs of our own hands *now*—in fact, we can't see anything *now*. Do you agree? Explain.

24. One of the fads of the future might be "century hopping," where occupants of high-speed spaceships would depart from the earth for several years and return centuries later. What are the present-day obstacles to such a practice?
25. An astronaut is provided a "gravity" when the ship's engines are activated to accelerate the ship. This requires the use of fuel. Is there a way to accelerate and provide "gravity" without the sustained use of fuel? Explain. (Hint: Consider Appendix B.)
26. In his famous novel *Journey to the Moon,* Jules Verne stated that the occupants of a spaceship would shift their orientation from up to down when the ship crossed the point where the moon's gravitation became greater than the earth's. Is this correct? Defend your answer.
27. What happens to the separation distance between two people if they both walk north at the same rate from two different places on the earth's equator? And, just for fun, where in the world is a step in any direction a step south?
28. A champion runner who runs at nearly the speed of light holds a mirror in front of herself as she runs. Can she see herself in the mirror? Defend your answer.
29. Why do we say that light travels in straight lines? Is it strictly accurate to say that a laser beam provides a perfectly straight line for purposes of surveying? Explain.
30. Light changes its energy when it "falls" in a gravitational field. This change in energy is not evidenced by a change in speed, however. What is the evidence for this change in energy?
31. How does the rate of ticking of a hypothetical clock on the surface of the massive planet Jupiter compare with the rate of ticking of an identical clock on Earth?
32. If we are splitting hairs, should a person who worries about growing old live at the top or at the bottom of a tall apartment building?
33. If we are splitting hairs, when you shine a beam of colored light at a friend above you in a high tower, will the color of light that friend receives be the same color you send? Explain.
34. Why does the gravitational attraction between the sun and Mercury vary? Would it vary if the orbit of Mercury were perfectly circular?
35. In the astronomical triangle shown in Figure 35.21, with sides defined by light paths, the sum of the interior angles is more than 180°. Is there any astronomical triangle whose interior angles sum to less than 180°?
36. Make up four multiple-choice questions, one each that would check a classmate's understanding of (a) time dilation, (b) length contraction, (c) relativistic momentum, and (d) $E = mc^2$.

Problems

1. You observe a spaceship moving away from you at speed v_1, half the speed of light. A rocket is fired straight ahead from the spaceship so that it also moves away from you. Suppose that, from the spaceship, the rocket is fired at half the speed of light, v_2, relative to the spaceship. Using the relativistic addition of velocities,

$$V = \frac{v_1 + v_2}{1 + \frac{v_1 v_2}{c^2}}$$

substitute $0.5c$ for both v_1 and v_2, and show that the velocity V of the rocket relative to you is $0.8c$.
2. Pretend that the spaceship in the previous question is somehow traveling at c with respect to you and that it fires a rocket at speed c with respect to itself. Use the equation to show that the speed of the rocket with respect to you is still c.
3. Substitute small values of v_1 and v_2 in the preceding equation and show that, for everyday velocities, V is practically equal to $v_1 + v_2$.
4. At the end of 1 s, a horizontally fired bullet has dropped a vertical distance of 4.9 m from its otherwise straight-line path in a gravitational field of 1 *g*. By what distance would a beam of light drop from its otherwise straight-line path if it traveled in a uniform field of 1 *g* for 1 s? For 2 s?
5. The fractional change of mass to energy in a fission reactor is about 0.1 percent, or 1 part in a thousand. For each kilogram of uranium that undergoes fission, how much energy is released? If energy costs three cents per megajoule, how much is this energy worth in dollars?

Chapter 35 Online Resources

Videos
- Space & Time Travel
- The Twin Animation

Quiz
Exercises
Flashcards
Links

Sample Exam Questions for Part 3—Earth and Space Science

Choose the BEST answer to each of the following.

1. The silicates are the largest mineral group because silicon and oxygen are
   (a) the hardest elements on the earth's surface
   (b) the two most abundant elements in the earth's crust
   (c) found in the common mineral quartz
2. Crystal form is the result of
   (a) cleavage
   (b) fracture
   (c) bond strength
   (d) arrangement of atoms
3. Which of the following is *not* an example of a mineral?
   (a) calcite
   (b) graphite
   (c) calcium carbonate shell
   (d) olivine
4. Magma becomes depleted in a mineral constituent when minerals that
   (a) contain it crystallize
   (b) contain it melt
   (c) contain it remain melted
   (d) do not contain it crystallize
5. Low-grade ores are usually mined when
   (a) high-grade ores are gone
   (b) demand exceeds supply
   (c) it is economically reasonable
   (d) extraction technologies improve
6. The addition of water to rock
   (a) decreases the melting point of the rock
   (b) increases the viscosity of the rock
   (c) increases the melting point of the rock
   (d) changes the silica content of the rock
7. Shield volcanoes are composed of
   (a) andesitic magma
   (b) basaltic magma
   (c) granitic magma
   (d) silica-rich magma
8. Plutonic rocks form from
   (a) the eruption of viscous magma
   (b) partial melting of basalt
   (c) solidification of lava
   (d) solidification of magma
9. Well-rounded sediment particles indicate
   (a) a quiet, low-energy environment
   (b) mechanical weathering
   (c) glacial deposits
   (d) long transport distances
10. Compaction and cementation of sediments leads to
    (a) magma generation
    (b) lithification
    (c) formation of porewater
    (d) metamorphism
11. Contact metamorphism usually causes the development of
    (a) altered zones
    (b) foliation
    (c) mechanical deformation
    (d) schist
12. For each increase of one on the Richter scale,
    (a) ground shaking increases 30 times
    (b) the energy released increases 30 times
    (c) the amplitude of the seismic wave doubles
    (d) the energy released increases 10 times
13. At divergent plate boundaries, basaltic magma is generated by the
    (a) crystallization of mantle magma
    (b) partial melting of continental crust
    (c) partial melting of mantle rock
    (d) addition of water to mantle rock
14. The theory of continental drift is *not* supported by
    (a) seafloor spreading
    (b) paleomagnetism
    (c) isostasy
    (d) patterns of ancient glaciation
15. Which of the following statements is false?
    (a) The mantle includes part of the crust.
    (b) The lithosphere includes the entire crust.
    (c) The mantle includes part of the lithosphere.
    (d) The mantle includes the entire asthenosphere.
16. Seismic waves increase in speed when
    (a) they pass through liquid
    (b) rocks become denser and less rigid
    (c) they form a wave shadow
    (d) the elasticity of the rock increases
17. The most common source of groundwater contamination is
    (a) industrial solvents
    (b) sewage
    (c) pesticides
    (d) petroleum refineries
18. Snow converts to glacial ice when subjected to
    (a) decreasing temperature
    (b) pressure
    (c) basal sliding
    (d) plastic deformation
19. Underground water in the saturated zone is called
    (a) groundwater
    (b) soil moisture
    (c) the water table
    (d) an artesian system

20. What factors affect stream speed?
    (a) discharge
    (b) channel length
    (c) stream gradient
    (d) b and c
    (e) a and c
21. Ocean waves refract due to
    (a) wave interference
    (b) ocean swells
    (c) shallow water
    (d) transverse motion
22. Deltas form as
    (a) periodic flooding clogs stream channels
    (b) erosion clogs stream channels
    (c) stream gradient decreases
    (d) streams enter a standing body of water
23. The dominant agent of erosion in a desert environment is
    (a) ice
    (b) water
    (c) heat
    (d) wind
24. The most common shoreline depositional environments are
    (a) beaches
    (b) coral reefs
    (c) carbonate platforms
    (d) barrier islands
25. Uniformitarianism is the assumption that
    (a) ideas across all branches of Earth science are consistent
    (b) certain sedimentary deposits tend to be well-sorted
    (c) present-day processes also occurred in the geologic past
    (d) younger sedimentary rocks are always deposited on top of metamorphic or intrusive igneous rocks
26. The first division of geologic time for which abundant fossils have been found is
    (a) the Precambrian period
    (b) the Silurian period
    (c) the Pliocene epoch
    (d) the Cambrian period
27. The earth's lower atmosphere is kept warm by
    (a) solar radiation
    (b) terrestrial radiation
    (c) short-wave radiation
28. The wind blows in response to
    (a) pressure differences
    (b) the earth's rotation
    (c) temperature differences
    (d) both a and c
    (e) none of the above
29. Air that contains the maximum amount of water vapor is considered to be
    (a) relatively humid
    (b) saturated
    (c) adiabatic
    (d) all of the above
    (e) none of the above
30. As air temperature decreases, relative humidity
    (a) increases
    (b) decreases
    (c) stays the same
    (d) none of the above
31. The first fairly accurate measurements of Earth's size were made
    (a) centuries before the time of Galileo
    (b) at about the time of Galileo
    (c) more than a century after the time of Galileo
32. Immediately before a lunar eclipse, the phase of the moon must be
    (a) first quarter
    (b) half
    (c) full
    (d) new
    (e) none of the above
33. The fact that one hemisphere of the moon continually faces Earth is evidence that the moon
    (a) rotates on its axis
    (b) doesn't rotate on its axis
    (c) reflects rather than emits light
    (d) is distorted in shape
34. The present-day status of Pluto is that it is
    (a) the ninth and farthest planet in the solar system
    (b) the ninth and next to the farthest planet in the solar system
    (c) an object in the Kuiper belt
    (d) merely a large asteroid
35. If the Sun collapsed to become a black hole, Earth would
    (a) likely be sucked into it
    (b) fly off in a straight-line path
    (c) continue in its present orbit
    (d) do none of the above
36. The gold fillings in your grandfather's teeth are most closely related to which of these?
    (a) novae
    (b) supernovae
    (c) white dwarfs
    (d) black holes
    (e) none of the above

37. According to special relativity, if you see a moving spaceship's clocks running slow, observers on the spaceship will see your clocks running
    (a) slow
    (b) fast
    (c) at the same rate that you see your own clock running
38. Since there is an upper limit to the speed of a particle, there is also an upper limit on
    (a) its momentum
    (b) its kinetic energy
    (c) its temperature
    (d) all of the above
    (e) none of the above
39. Compared with special relativity, general relativity is more concerned with
    (a) acceleration
    (b) gravitation
    (c) space-time geometry
    (d) all of the above
    (e) none of the above
40. Which equation is the triumph of the theory of special relativity?
    (a) $E = ma^2$
    (b) $E = mb^2$
    (c) $E = mc^2$
    (d) $E = md^2$
    (e) $E = me^2$

Answers: 1 (b) 2 (d) 3 (c) 4 (a) 5 (c) 6 (a) 7 (b) 8 (d) 9 (d) 10 (b) 11 (a) 12 (b) 13 (c) 14 (c) 15 (a) 16 (d) 17 (b) 18 (b) 19 (a) 20 (e) 21 (c) 22 (d) 23 (b) 24 (a) 25 (c) 26 (d) 27 (b) 28 (d) 29 (b) 30 (a) 31 (a) 32 (c) 33 (a) 34 (c) 35 (c) 36 (b) 37 (a) 38 (e) 39 (d) 40 (c)

APPENDIX A

On Measurement and Unit Conversion

Two major systems of measurement prevail in the world today: the *United States Customary System* (USCS, formerly called the British system of units), used in the United States of America and in Burma, and the *Système International* (SI) (known also as the international system and as the metric system), used everywhere else. Each system has its own standards of length, mass, and time. The units of length, mass, and time are sometimes called the *fundamental units* because, once they are selected, other quantities can be measured in terms of them.

United States Customary System

Based on the British Imperial System, the USCS is familiar to everyone in the United States. It uses the foot as the unit of length, the pound as the unit of weight or force, and the second as the unit of time. The USCS is presently being replaced by the international system—rapidly in science and technology (all 1988 Department of Defense contracts) and some sports (track and swimming), but so slowly in other areas and in some specialties it seems the change may never come. For example, we will continue to buy seats on the 50-yard line. Camera film is in millimeters but computer disks are in inches.

For measuring time, there is no difference between the two systems except that in pure SI the only unit is the second (s, not sec) with prefixes; but in general, minute, hour, day, year, and so on, with two or more lettered abbreviations (h, not hr), are accepted in the USCS.

Systéme International

Table A.1

SI units

Quantity	Unit	Symbol
Length	meter	m
Mass	kilogram	kg
Time	second	s
Force	newton	N
Energy	joule	J
Current	ampere	A
Temperature	kelvin	K

During the 1960 International Conference on Weights and Measures held in Paris, the SI units were defined and given status. Table A.1 shows SI units and their symbols. SI is based on the *metric system,* originated by French scientists after the French Revolution in 1791. The orderliness of this system makes it useful for scientific work, and it is used by scientists all over the world. The metric system branches into two systems of units. In one of these the unit of length is the meter, the unit of mass is the kilogram, and the unit of time is the second. This is called the *meter-kilogram-second* (mks) system and is preferred in physics. The other branch is the *centimeter-gram-second* (cgs) system, which, because of its smaller values, is favored in chemistry. The cgs and mks units are related to each other as follows:

Table A.2

Table Conversions Between Different Units of Length

Unit of Length	Kilometer	Meter	Centimeter	Inch	Foot	Mile
1 kilometer	= 1	1000	100,000	39,370	3280.84	0.62140
1 meter	= 0.00100	1	100	39.370	3.28084	6.21×10^{-4}
1 centimeter	= 1.0×10^{-5}	0.0100	1	0.39370	0.032808	6.21×10^{-6}
1 inch	= 2.54×10^{-5}	0.02540	2.5400	1	0.08333	1.58×10^{-5}
1 foot	= 3.05×10^{-4}	0.30480	30.480	12	1	1.89×10^{-4}
1 mile	= 1.60934	1609.34	160,934	63,360	5280	1

Table A.3

Some Prefixes

Prefix	Definition
micro-	One-millionth: a microsecond is one-millionth of a second
milli-	One-thousandth: a milligram is one-thousandth of a gram
centi-	One-hundredth: a centimeter is one-hundredth of a meter
kilo-	One thousand: a kilogram is 1000 grams
mega-	One million: a megahertz is 1 million hertz

100 centimeters equal 1 meter; 1000 grams equal 1 kilogram. Table A.2 shows several units of length related to each other.

One major advantage of the metric system is that it uses the decimal system, where all units are related to smaller or larger units by dividing or multiplying by 10. The prefixes shown in Table A.3 are commonly used to show the relationship among units.

Meter

The standard of length of the metric system orginally was defined in terms of the distance from the north pole to the equator. This distance was thought at the time to be close to 10,000 kilometers. One ten-millionth of this, the meter, was carefully determined and marked off by means of scratches on a bar of platinum-iridium alloy. This bar is kept at the International Bureau of Weights and Measures in France. The standard meter in France has since been calibrated in terms of the wavelength of light—it is 1,650,763.73 times the wavelength of orange light emitted by the atoms of the gas krypton-86. The meter is now defined as being the length of the path traveled by light in a vacuum during a time interval of 1/299,792,458 of a second.

Figure A.1
The standard kilogram.

Kilogram

The standard unit of mass, the kilogram, is a block of platinum, also preserved at the International Bureau of Weights and Measures located in France (Figure A.1). The kilogram equals 1000 grams. A gram is the mass of 1 cubic centimeter (cc) of water at a temperature of 4°C. (The standard pound is defined in terms of the standard kilogram; the mass of an object that weighs 1 pound is equal to 0.4536 kilogram.)

Second

The official unit of time for both the USCS and the SI is the second. Until 1956, it was defined in terms of the mean solar day, which was divided into 24 hours. Each hour was divided into 60 minutes and each minute into 60 seconds. Thus, there were 86,400 seconds per day, and the second was defined as 1/86,400 of the mean solar day. This proved unsatisfactory because the rate of rotation of the earth is gradually becoming slower. In 1956, the mean solar day of the year 1900 was chosen as the standard on which to base the second. In 1964, the second was officially defined as the time taken by a cesium-133 atom to make 9,192,631,770 vibrations.

Newton

One newton is the force required to accelerate 1 kilogram at 1 meter per second per second. This unit is named after Sir Isaac Newton.

Joule

One joule is equal to the amount of work done by a force of 1 newton acting over a distance of 1 meter. In 1948, the joule was adopted as the unit of energy by the International Conference on Weights and Measures. Therefore, the specific heat of water at 15°C is now given as 4185.5 joules per kilogram Celsius degree. This figure is always associated with the mechanical equivalent of heat—4.1855 joules per calorie.

Ampere

The ampere is defined as the intensity of the constant electric current that, when maintained in two parallel conductors of infinite length and negligible cross section and placed 1 meter apart in a vacuum, would produce between them a force equal to 2×10^{-7} newton per meter length. In our treatment of electric current in this text, we have used the not-so-official but easier-to-comprehend definition of the ampere as being the rate of flow of 1 coulomb of charge per second, where 1 coulomb is the charge of 6.25×10^{18} electrons.

Kelvin

The fundamental unit of temperature is named after the scientist William Thomson, Lord Kelvin. The kelvin is defined to be 1/273.15 the thermodynamic temperature of the triple point of water (the fixed point at which ice, liquid water, and water vapor coexist in equilibrium). This definition was adopted in 1968 when it was decided to change the name *degree Kelvin* (°K) to *kelvin* (K). The temperature of melting ice at atmospheric pressure is 273.15 K. The temperature at which the vapor pressure of pure water is equal to standard atmospheric pressure is 373.15 K (the temperature of boiling water at standard atmospheric pressure).

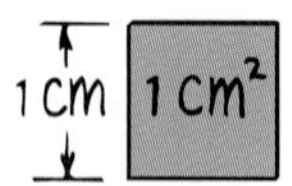

Figure A.2
Unit square.

Area

The unit of area is a square that has a standard unit of length as a side. In the USCS, it is a square with sides that are each 1 foot in length, called 1 square foot and written 1 ft^2. In the international system, it is a square with sides that are 1 meter in length, which makes a unit of area of 1 m^2. In the cgs system it is 1 cm^2. The area of a given surface is specified by the number of square feet, square meters, or square centimeters that would fit into it. The area of a rectangle equals the base times the height. The area of a circle is equal to πr^2, where $\pi = 3.14$ and r is the radius of the circle. Formulas for the surface areas of other objects can be found in geometry textbooks.

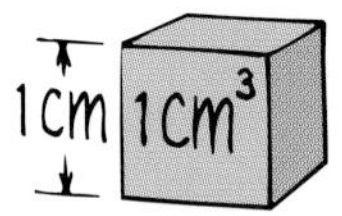

Figure A.3
Unit volume.

Volume

The volume of an object refers to the space it occupies. The unit of volume is the space taken up by a cube that has a standard unit of length for its edge. In the USCS, one unit of volume is the space occupied by a cube 1 foot on an edge and is called 1 cubic foot, written 1 ft^3. In the metric system it is the space occupied by a cube with sides of 1 meter (SI) or 1 centimeter (cgs). It is written 1 m^3 or 1 cm^3 (or cc). The volume of a given space is specified by the number of cubic feet, cubic meters, or cubic centimeters that will fill it.

In the USCS, volumes can also be measured in quarts, gallons, and cubic inches as well as in cubic feet. There are 1728 ($12 \times 12 \times 12$) cubic inches in 1 ft^3. A U.S. gallon is a volume of 231 in^3. Four quarts equal 1 gallon. In the SI volumes are also measured in liters. A liter is equal to 1000 cm^3.

Unit Conversion

Often in science, and especially in a laboratory setting, it is necessary to convert from one unit to another. To do so, you need only multiply the given quantity by the appropriate *conversion factor.*

All conversion factors can be written as ratios in which the numerator and denominator represent the equivalent quantity expressed in different units. Because any quantity divided by itself is equal to 1, all conversion factors are equal to 1. For example, the following two conversion factors are both derived from the relationship 100 centimeters = 1 meter:

$$\frac{100\text{ centimeters}}{1\text{ meter}} = 1 \qquad \frac{1\text{ meter}}{100\text{ centimeters}} = 1$$

Because all conversion factors are equal to 1, multiplying a quantity by a conversion factor does not change the value of the quantity. What does change are the units. Suppose you measured an item to be 60 centimeters in length.

You can convert this measurement to meters by multiplying it by the conversion factor that allows you to cancel centimeters.

Example

Convert 60 centimeters to meters.

Answer

$$(60\ \cancel{\text{centimeters}})\frac{(1\ \text{meter})}{(100\ \cancel{\text{centimeters}})} = 0.6\ \text{meter}$$

↑	↑	↑
quantity in centimeters	conversion factor	quantity in meters

To derive a conversion factor, consult a table that presents unit equalities, such as Table A.2 or on the inside cover of this book. Then multiply the given quantity by the conversion factor, and voilà, the units are converted. Always be careful to write down your units. They are your ultimate guide, telling you what numbers go where and whether you are setting up the equation properly.

☑ CHECKPOINT

Multiply each physical quantity by the appropriate conversion factor to find its numerical value in the new unit indicated. You will need paper, pencil, a calculator, and a table of unit equalities.

a. 7320 grams to kilograms

b. 235 kilograms to pounds

c. 2.61 miles to kilometers.

d. 100 calories to kilocalories.

Check Your Answers

a. 7.32 kg

b. 518 lb

c. 4.20 km

d. 0.1 kcal

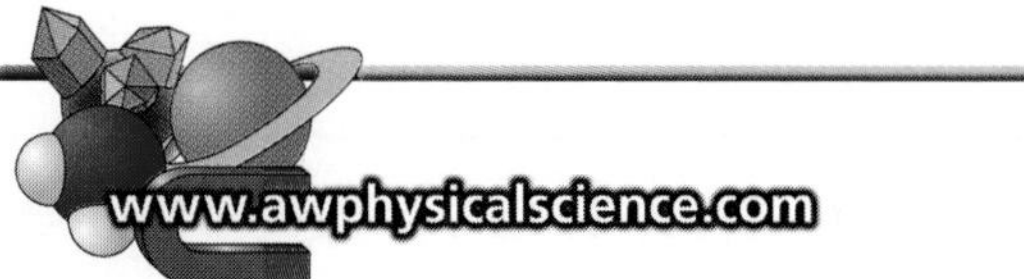

Appendix A Online Resources

Tutorials

- Significant Figures

APPENDIX B

Linear and Rotational Motion

When we describe the motion of something, we say how it moves relative to something else (Chapter 1). In other words, motion requires a reference frame (an observer, origin, and axes). We are free to choose this frame's location and to have it moving relative to another frame. When our frame of motion has zero acceleration, it is called an *inertial frame*. In an inertial frame, force causes an object to accelerate in accord with Newton's laws. When our frame of reference is accelerated, we observe fictitious forces and motions. Observations from a carousel, for example, are different when it is rotating and when it is at rest. Our description of motion and force depends on our "point of view."

We distinguish between *speed* and *velocity* (Chapter 1). Speed is how fast something moves, or the time rate of change of position (excluding direction): a *scalar* quantity. Velocity includes direction of motion: a *vector* quantity whose magnitude is speed. Objects moving at constant velocity move the same distance in the same time in the same direction.

Another distinction between speed and velocity has to do with the difference between distance and net distance, or *displacement*. Speed is *distance per duration* while velocity is *displacement per duration*. Displacement differs from distance. For example, a commuter who travels 10 kilometers to work and back travels 20 kilometers, but has "gone" nowhere. The distance traveled is 20 kilometers and the displacement is zero. Although the instantaneous speed and instantaneous velocity have the same value at the same instant, the average speed and average velocity can be very different. The average speed of this commuter's round-trip is 20 kilometers divided by the total commute time—a value greater than zero. But the average velocity is zero. In science, displacement is often more important than distance. (To avoid information overload, we have not treated this distinction in the text.)

Acceleration is the rate at which velocity changes. This can be a change in speed only, a change in direction only, or both. Negative acceleration is often called *deceleration.*

In Newtonian space and time, space has three dimensions—length, width, and height—each with two directions. We can go, stop, and return in any of them. Time has one dimension, with two directions—past and future. We cannot stop or return, only go. In Einsteinian space-time, these four dimensions merge (Chapter 35).

Computing Velocity and Distance Traveled on an Inclined Plane

Recall from Chapter 1 Galileo's experiments with inclined planes. We considered a plane tilted such that the speed of a rolling ball increases at the rate of 2 meters per second each second—an acceleration of 2 m/s^2. So at the instant it starts moving its velocity is zero, and 1 second later it is rolling at 2 m/s, at the end of the next second 4 m/s, the end of the next second 6 m/s, and so on. The velocity of the ball at any instant is simply Velocity = acceleration × time. Or, in shorthand notation $v = at$. (It is customary to omit the multiplication sign, ×, when expressing relationships in mathematical form. When two symbols are written together, such as the *at* in this case, it is understood that they are multiplied.)

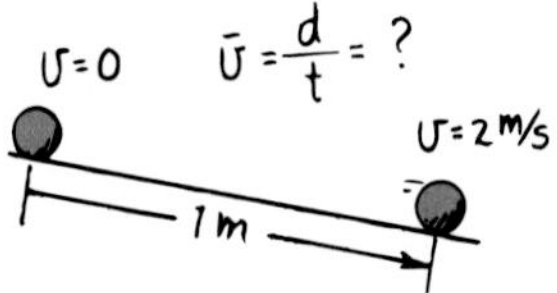

Figure B.1
The ball rolls l m down the incline in l s and reaches a speed of 2 m/s. Its average speed, however, is l m/s. Do you see why?

How fast the ball rolls is one thing; how *far* it rolls is another. To understand the relationship between acceleration and distance traveled, we must first investigate the relationship between instantaneous velocity and *average velocity.* If the ball shown in Figure B.1 starts from rest, it will roll a distance of 1 meter in the first second. What will be its average speed? The answer is 1 m/s (it covered 1 meter in the interval of 1 second). But we have seen that the *instantaneous velocity* at the end of the first second is 2 m/s. Since the acceleration is uniform, the average in any time interval is found the same way we usually find the average of any two numbers: add them and divide by 2. (Be careful not to do this when acceleration is not uniform!) So if we add the initial speed (zero in this case) and the final speed of 2 m/s and then divide by 2, we get 1 m/s for the average velocity.

In each succeeding second we see the ball roll a longer distance down the same slope in Figure B.2. Note the distance covered in the second time interval is 3 meters. This is because the average speed of the ball in this interval is 3 m/s. In the next 1-second interval the average speed is 5 m/s, so the distance covered is 5 meters. It is interesting to see that successive increments of distance increase as a *sequence of odd numbers.* Nature clearly follows mathematical rules!

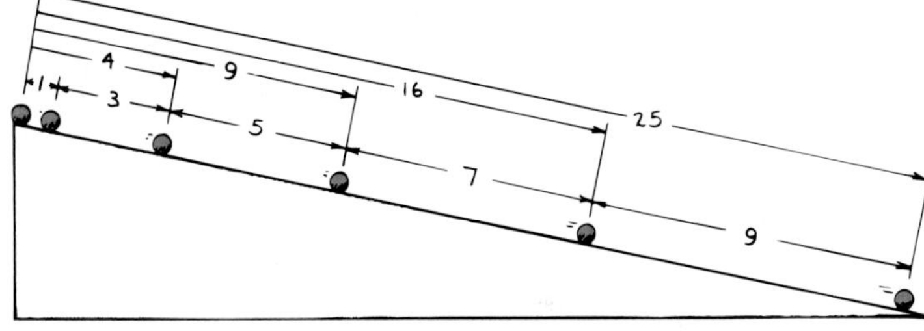

Figure B.2
If the ball covers l m during its first second, then in each successive second it will cover the odd-numbered sequence of 3, 5, 7, 9 m, and so on. Note that the total distance covered increases as the square of the total time.

Investigate Figure B.2 carefully and note the *total* distance covered as the ball accelerates down the plane. The distances go from zero to 1 meter in 1 second, zero to 4 meters in 2 seconds, zero to 9 meters in 3 seconds, zero to 16 meters in 4 seconds, and so on in succeeding seconds. The sequence for *total distances* covered is of the *squares of the time.* We'll investigate the relationship between distance traveled and the square of the time for constant acceleration more closely in the case of free fall.

☑ CHECKPOINT

During the span of the second time interval, the ball begins at 2 m/s and ends at 4 m/s. What is the *average speed* of the ball during this I-s interval? What is its *acceleration?*

Check Your Answers

$$\text{Average speed} = \frac{\text{beginning + final speed}}{2} = \frac{2\text{ m/s} + 4\text{ m/s}}{2} = 3\text{ m/s}$$

$$\text{Acceleration} = \frac{\text{change in velocity}}{\text{time interval}} = \frac{4\text{ m/s} - 2\text{ m/s}}{1\text{ s}} = \frac{2\text{ m/s}}{1\text{ s}} = 2\text{ m/s}^2$$

Computing Distance When Acceleration Is Constant

How far will an object released from rest fall in a given time? To answer this question, let us consider the case in which it falls freely for 3 seconds, starting at rest. Neglecting air resistance, the object will have a constant acceleration of about 10 meters per second each second (actually more like 9.8 m/s^2, but we want to make the numbers easier to follow).

$$\text{Velocity at the } \textit{beginning} = 0 \text{ m/s}$$

$$\text{Velocity at the } \textit{end} \text{ of 3 seconds} = (10 \times 3) \text{ m/s}$$

$$\begin{aligned} \textit{Average} \text{ velocity} &= \frac{1}{2} \text{ the sum of these two speeds} \\ &= \frac{1}{2} \times (0 + 10 \times 3) \text{ m/s} \\ &= \frac{1}{2} \times 10 \times 3 = 15 \text{ m/s} \end{aligned}$$

$$\begin{aligned} \text{Distance traveled} &= \text{average velocity} \times \text{time} \\ &= (\frac{1}{2} \times 10 \times 3) \times 3 \\ &= \frac{1}{2} \times 10 \times 3^2 = 45 \text{ m} \end{aligned}$$

We can see from the meanings of these numbers that

$$\text{Distance traveled} = \frac{1}{2} \times \text{acceleration} \times \text{square of time}$$

This equation is true for an object falling not only for 3 seconds but for any length of time, as long as the acceleration is constant. If we let d stand for the distance traveled, a for the acceleration, and t for the time, the rule may be written, in shorthand notation,

$$d = \frac{1}{2} at^2$$

This relationship was first deduced by Galileo. He reasoned that if an object falls for, say, twice the time, it will fall with *twice the average speed*. Since it falls for *twice* the time at *twice* the average speed, it will fall *four* times as far. Similarly, if an object falls for *three* times the time, it will have an average speed *three* times as great and will fall *nine* times as far. Galileo reasoned that the total distance fallen should be proportional to the *square* of the time.

In the case of objects in free fall, it is customary to use the letter g to represent the acceleration instead of the letter a (g because acceleration is due to *gravity*). While the value of g varies slightly in different parts of the world, it is approximately equal to 9.8 m/s^2 (32 ft/s^2). If we use g for the acceleration of a freely falling object (negligible air resistance), the equations for falling objects starting from a rest position become

$$v = gt$$

$$d = \frac{1}{2} gt^2$$

Much of the difficulty in learning physics, like learning any discipline, has to do with learning the language—the many terms and definitions. Speed is somewhat different from velocity, and acceleration is vastly different from speed or velocity. Please be patient with yourself as you find learning the similarities and the differences among physics concepts is not an easy task.

Figure B.3
When Chelcie Liu releases both balls simultaneously, he asks, "Which will reach the end of the equal-length tracks first?" (Hint: On which track is the average speed of the ball greater? Then, double hint: Which wins, the fast ball or the slow ball?)

☑ CHECKPOINT

1. An auto starting from rest has a constant acceleration of 4 m/s^2. How far will it go in 5 s?
2. How far will an object released from rest fall in 1 s? In this case the acceleration is g = 9.8 m/s^2.
3. If it takes 4 s for an object to freely fall to the water when released from the Golden Gate Bridge, how high is the bridge?

Check Your Answers

1. Distance $= \frac{1}{2} \times 4 \times 5^2 = 50$ m
2. Distance $= \frac{1}{2} \times 9.8 \times 1^2 = 4.9$ m
3. Distance $= \frac{1}{2} \times 9.8 \times 4^2 = 78.4$ m

   Notice that the units of measurement when multiplied give the proper units of meters for distance:

   $$d = \frac{1}{2} \times 9.8 \text{ m} \times 16 = 78.4 \text{ m}$$

Circular Motion

Linear speed is what we have been calling simply *speed*—the distance traveled in meters or kilometers per unit of time. A point on the perimeter of a merry-go-round or turntable moves a greater distance in one complete rotation than a point nearer the center. Moving a greater distance in the same time means a greater speed. The speed of something moving along a circular path is **tangential speed,** because the direction of motion is tangent to the circle.

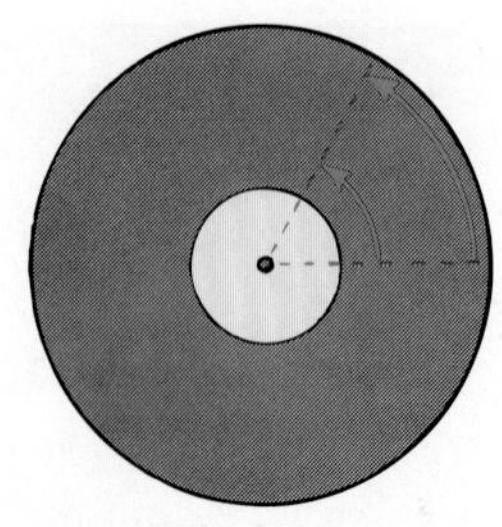

Figure B.4
When a phonograph record turns, a ladybug farther from the center travels a longer path in the same time and has a greater tangential speed.

Rotational speed (sometimes called angular speed) refers to the number of rotations or revolutions per unit of time. All parts of the rigid merry-go-round turn about the axis of rotation *in the same amount of time.* All parts share the same rate of rotation, or *number of rotations or revolutions per unit of time.* It is common to express rotational rates in revolutions per minute (rpm).* Phonograph records that were common a few years ago rotate at 33 1/3 rpm. A ladybug sitting anywhere on the surface of the record revolves at 33 1/3 rpm.

Tangential speed is *directly proportional* to rotational speed (at a fixed radial distance). Unlike rotational speed, tangential speed depends on the distance from the axis (Figure B.5). Something at the center of a rotating platform has no tangential speed at all, and merely rotates. But, approaching the edge of the platform, tangential speed increases. Tangential speed is directly proportional to the distance from the axis (for a given rotational speed). Twice as far from the rotational axis, the speed is twice as great. Three times as far from the rotational axis, there is three times as much tangential speed. When a row of people locked arm in arm at the skating rink makes a turn, the motion of "tail-end Charlie" is evidence of this greater speed. So tangential speed is directly proportional both to rotational speed and to radial distance.†

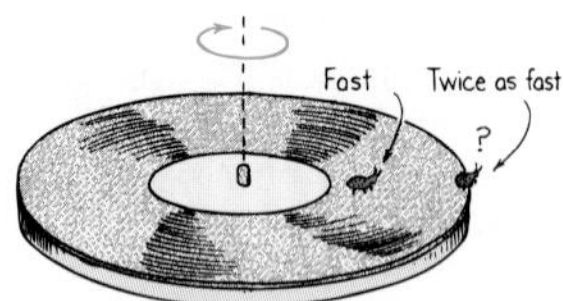

Figure B.5
The entire disk rotates at the same rotational speed, but ladybugs at different distances from the center travel at different tangential speeds. A ladybug twice as far from the center moves twice as fast.

☑ CHECKPOINT

On a rotating platform similar to the disk shown in Figure B.5, if you sit halfway between the rotating axis and the outer edge and have a rotational speed of 20 rpm and a tangential speed of 2 m/s, what will be the rotational and tangential speeds of your friend who sits at the outer edge?

Check Your Answer

Since the rotating platform is rigid, all parts have the same rotational speed, so your friend also rotates at 20 rpm. Tangential speed is a different story; since she is twice as far from the axis of rotation, she moves twice as fast—4 m/s.

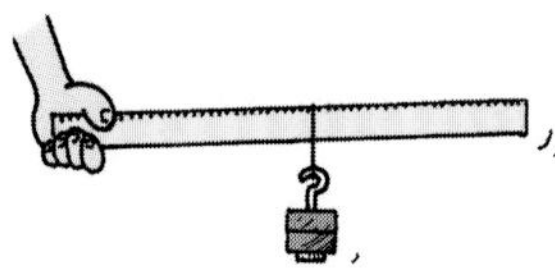

Figure B.6
If you move the weight away from your hand, you will feel the difference between force and torque.

Torque

Whereas force causes changes in speed, *torque* causes changes in rotation. To understand torque (rhymes with *dork*), hold the end of a meterstick horizontally with your hand. If you dangle a weight from the meterstick near your hand, you can feel the meterstick twist. Now if you slide the weight farther from your hand, the twist you feel is greater, although the weight is the same. The force acting on your hand is the same. What's different is the torque.

$$\text{Torque} = \text{lever arm} \times \text{force}$$

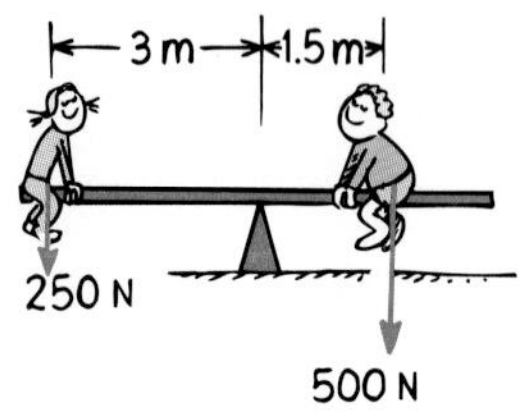

Figure B.7
No rotation is produced when the torques balance each other.

*Physics types usually describe rotational speed in terms of the number of "radians" turned in a unit of time, for which they use the symbol ω (the Greek letter *omega*). There's a little more than 6 radians in a full rotation (2π radians, to be exact).

†When customary units are used for tangential speed v, rotational speed ω, and radial distance r, the direct proportion of v to both r and ω becomes the exact equation $v = r\omega$. So the tangential speed will be directly proportional to r when all parts of a system simultaneously have the same ω, as for a wheel, disk, or rigid wand. (The direct proportionality of v to r is not valid for the planets because planets don't all have the same ω.)

Lever arm is the distance between the point of application of the force and the axis of rotation. It is the shortest distance between the applied force and the rotational axis. Torques are intuitively familiar to youngsters playing on a seesaw. Kids can balance a seesaw even when their weights are unequal. Weight alone doesn't produce rotation. Torque does, and children soon learn that the distance they sit from the pivot point is every bit as important as weight (Figure B.7). When the torques are equal, making the net torque zero, no rotation is produced.

Recall the equilibrium rule in Chapter 1—that the sum of the forces acting on a body or any system must equal zero for mechanical equilibrium. That is, $\Sigma F = 0$. We now see an additional condition. The *net torque* on a body or on a system must also be zero for mechanical equilibrium. Anything in mechanical equilibrium doesn't accelerate—neither linearly nor rotationally.

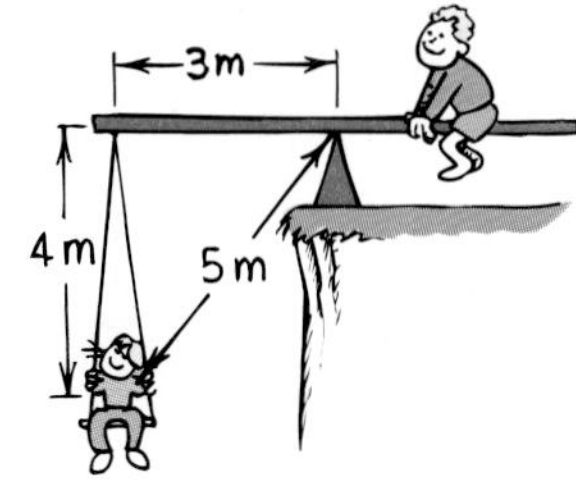

Figure B.8
The lever arm is still 3 m.

Suppose that the seesaw is arranged so that the half-as-heavy girl is suspended from a 4-meter rope hanging from her end of the seesaw (Figure B.8). She is now 5 meters from the fulcrum, and the seesaw is still balanced. We see that the lever-arm distance is 3 meters, not 5 meters. The lever arm about any axis of rotation is the perpendicular distance from the axis to the line along which the force acts. This will always be the shortest distance between the axis of rotation and the line along which the force acts.

This is why the stubborn bolt shown in Figure B.9 is turned more easily when the applied force is perpendicular to the handle, rather than at an oblique angle, as shown in the first figure. In the first figure, the lever arm is shown by the dashed line and is less than the length of the wrench handle. In the second figure, the lever arm is equal to the length of the wrench handle. In the third figure, the lever arm is extended with a pipe to provide more leverage and a greater torque.

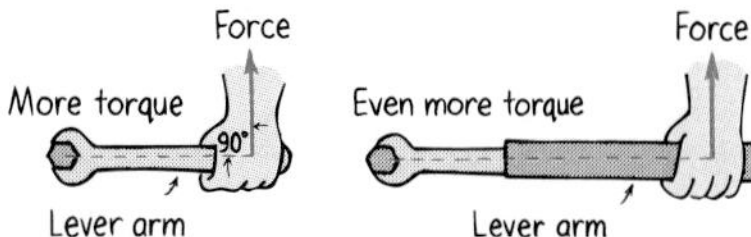

Figure B.9
Although the magnitudes of the force are the same in each case, the torques are different.

☑ **CHECKPOINT**

1. If a pipe effectively extends a wrench handle to three times its length, by how much will the torque increase for the same applied force?
2. Consider the balanced seesaw in Figure B.7. Suppose the girl on the left suddenly gains 50 N, such as by being handed a bag of apples. Where should she sit in order to balance, assuming the heavier boy remains in place?

Check Your Answers

1. Three times more leverage for the same force gives three times more torque. (This method of increasing torque sometimes results in shearing off the bolt!)
2. She should sit $\frac{1}{2}$ m closer to the center. Then her lever arm is 2.5 m. This checks:

   $300\text{ N} \times 2.5\text{ m} = 500\text{ N} \times 1.5\text{ m}$.

Angular Momentum

Things that rotate, whether a cylinder rolling down an incline or an acrobat doing a somersault, keep on rotating until something stops them. A rotating object has an "inertia of rotation." Recall, from Chapter 3, that all moving

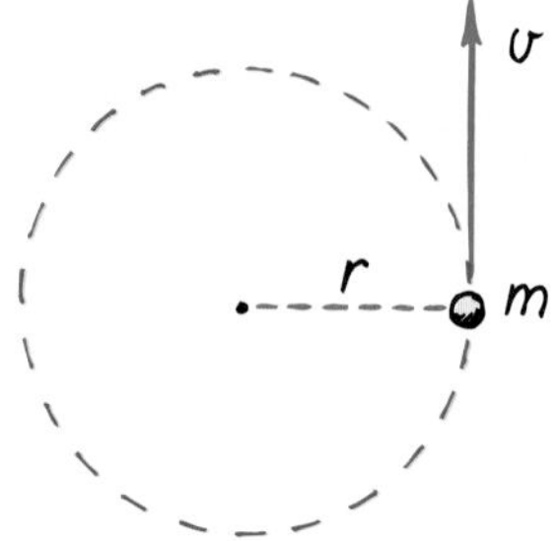

Figure B.10
A small object of mass m whirling in a circular path of radius r with a speed v has angular momentum mvr.

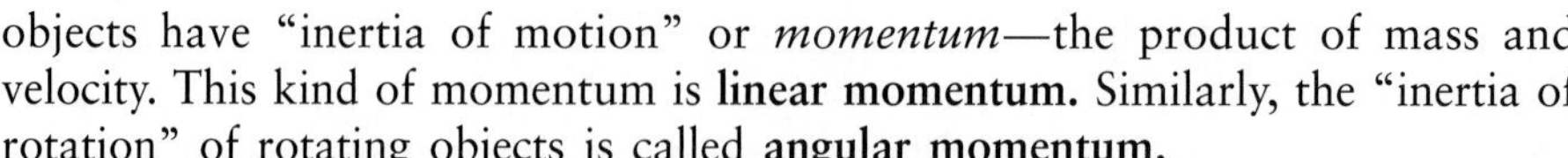

objects have "inertia of motion" or *momentum*—the product of mass and velocity. This kind of momentum is **linear momentum.** Similarly, the "inertia of rotation" of rotating objects is called **angular momentum.**

For the case of an object that is small compared with the radial distance to its axis of rotation, like a tetherball swinging from a long string or a planet orbiting around the sun, the angular momentum can be expressed as the magnitude of its linear momentum, mv, multiplied by the radial distance, r, (Figure B.10).* In shorthand notation, Angular momentum = mvr. Like linear momentum, angular momentum is a vector quantity and has direction as well as magnitude. In this appendix, we won't treat the vector nature of angular momentum (or even of torque, which also is a vector).

Just as an external net force is required to change the linear momentum of an object, an external net torque is required to change the angular momentum of an object. We can state a rotational version of Newton's first law (the law of inertia):

An object or system of objects will maintain its angular momentum unless acted upon by an unbalanced external torque.

We see application of this rule when we look at a spinning top. If friction is low and torque also low, the top tends to remain spinning. The earth and planets spin in torque-free regions, and once they are spinning, they remain so.

Conservation of Angular Momentum

Figure B.11
Conservation of angular momentum. When the man pulls his arms and the whirling weights inward, he decreases the radial distance between the weights and the axis of rotation, and the rotational speed increases correspondingly.

Just as the linear momentum of any system is conserved if no net forces are acting on the system, angular momentum is conserved if no net torque acts on the system. In the absence of an unbalanced external torque, the angular momentum of that system is constant. This means that its angular momentum at any one time will be the same as at any other time.

Conservation of angular momentum is shown in Figure B.11. The man stands on a low-friction turntable with weights extended. To simplify, consider only the weights in his hands. When he is slowly turning with his arms extended, much of the angular momentum is due to the distance between the weights and the rotational axis. When he pulls the weights inward, the distance is considerably reduced. What is the result? His rotational speed increases![†] This example is best appreciated by the turning person, who feels changes in rotational speed that seem to be mysterious. But it's straight physics! This procedure is used by a figure skater who starts to whirl with her arms and perhaps a leg extended and then draws her arms and leg in to obtain a greater rotational speed. Whenever a rotating body contracts, its rotational speed increases.

The law of angular momentum conservation is seen in the motions of the planets and the shape of the galaxies. When a slowly rotating ball of gas in space gravitationally contracts, the result is an increase in its rate of rotation. The conservation of angular momentum is far-reaching.

*For rotating bodies that are large compared with radial distance—for example, a planet rotating about its own axis—the concept of *rotational inertia* must be introduced. Then angular momentum is rotational inertia × rotational speed. See any of Hewitt's *Conceptual Physics* textbooks for more information.

†When a direction is assigned to rotational speed, we call it *rotational velocity* (often called *angular velocity*). By convention, the rotational velocity vector and the angular momentum vector have the same direction and lie along the axis of rotation.

APPENDIX C

Vectors

Vectors and Scalars

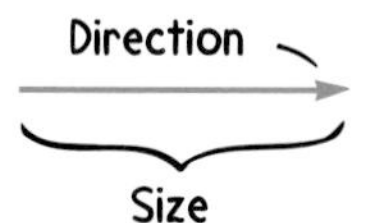

Figure C.1

A *vector* quantity is a directed quantity—one that must be specified not only by magnitude (size) but by direction as well. Recall from Chapter 1 that velocity is a vector quantity. Other examples are force, acceleration, and momentum. In contrast, a *scalar* quantity can be specified by magnitude alone. Some examples of scalar quantities are speed, time, temperature, and energy.

Vector quantities may be represented by arrows. The length of the arrow tells you the magnitude of the vector quantity, and the arrowhead tells you the direction of the vector quantity. Such an arrow drawn to scale and pointing appropriately is called a *vector.*

Adding Vectors

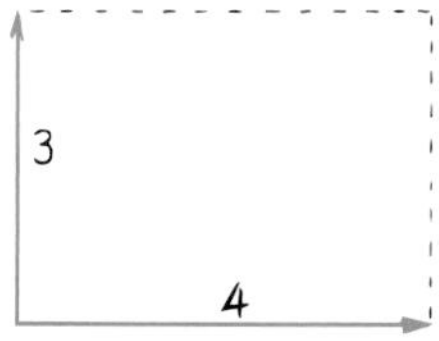

3

4

Figure C.2

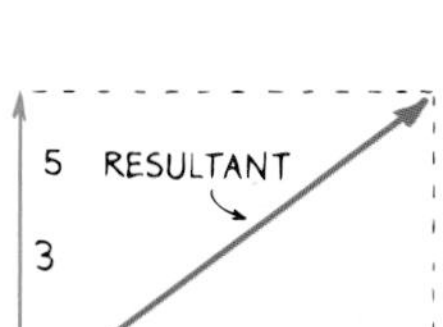

Figure C.3

Vectors that add together are called *component vectors*. The sum of component vectors is called a *resultant.*

To add two vectors, make a parallelogram with two component vectors acting as two of the adjacent sides (Figure C.2). (Here our parallelogram is a rectangle.) Then draw a diagonal from the origin of the vector pair; this is the resultant (Figure C.3).

Caution: Do not try to mix vectors! We cannot add apples and oranges, so velocity vectors combine only with velocity vectors, force vectors combine only with force vectors, and acceleration vectors combine only with acceleration vectors—each on its own vector diagram. If you ever show different kinds of vectors on the same diagram, use different colors or some other method of distinguishing the different kinds of vectors.

Finding Components of Vectors

Recall from Chapter 2 that to find a pair of perpendicular components for a vector, first draw a dashed line through the tail of the vector (in the direction of one of the desired components). Second, draw another dashed line through the tail end of the vector at right angles to the first dashed line. Third, make a rectangle whose diagonal is the given vector. Draw in the two components. Here we let **F** stand for "total force," **U** stand for "upward force," and **S** stand for "sideways force."

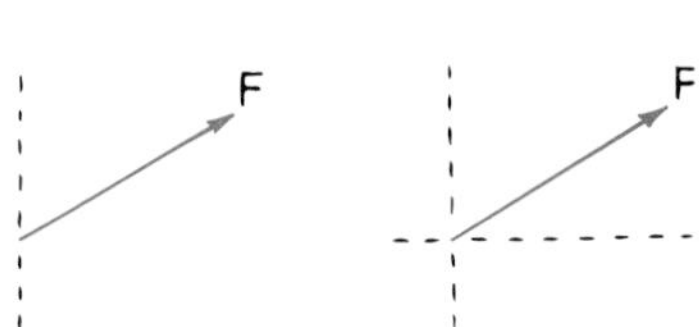

Figure C.4 Figure C.5

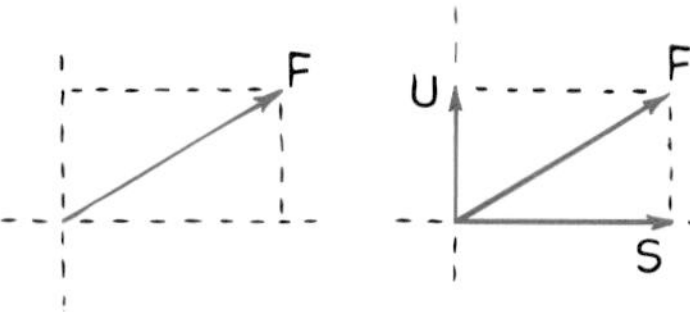

Figure C.6

Examples

1. Ernie Brown pushes a lawnmower and applies a force that pushes it forward and also against the ground. In Figure C.7, **F** represents the force applied by the man. We can separate this force into two components. The vector **D** represents the downward component, and **S** is the sideways component, the force that moves the lawnmower forward. If we know the magnitude and direction of the vector **F**, we can estimate the magnitude of the components from the vector diagram.

Figure C.7

2. Would it be easier to push or pull a wheelbarrow over a step? Figure C.8 shows the force at the wheel's center. When you push a wheelbarrow, part of the force is directed downward, which makes it harder to get over the step. When you pull, however, part of the pulling force is directed upward, which helps to lift the wheel over the step. Note that the vector diagram suggests that pushing the wheelbarrow may not get it over the step at all. Do you see that the height of the step, the radius of the wheel, and the angle of the applied force determine whether the wheelbarrow can be pushed over the step? We see how vectors help us analyze a situation so that we can see just what the problem is!

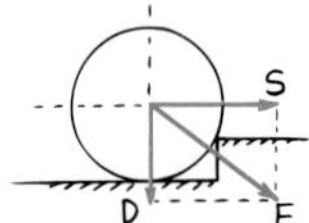

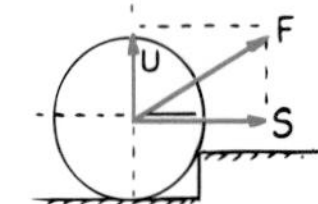

Figure C.8

3. If we consider the components of the weight of an object rolling down an incline, we can see why its speed depends on the angle. Note that the steeper the incline, the greater the component **S** becomes and the faster the object rolls. When the incline is vertical, **S** becomes equal to the weight, and the object attains maximum acceleration, 9.8 m/s^2. There are two more force vectors that are not shown: the normal force **N**, which is equal and oppositely directed to **D**, and the friction force **f**, acting at the barrel-plane contact.

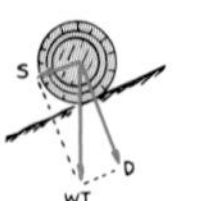
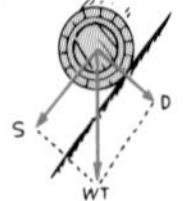

Figure C.9

4. When moving air strikes the underside of an airplane wing, the force of air impact against the wing may be represented by a single vector perpendicular to the plane of the wing (Figure C.10). We represent the force vector as acting midway along the lower wing surface, where the dot is, and pointing above the wing to show the direction of the resulting wind impact force. This force can be broken up into two components, one sideways and the other up. The upward component, **U**, is called *lift*. The sideways component, **S**, is called *drag*. If the aircraft is to fly at constant velocity at constant altitude, then lift must equal the weight of the aircraft and the thrust of the plane's engines must equal drag. The magnitude of lift (and drag) can be altered by changing the speed of the airplane or by changing the angle (called *angle of attack*) between the wing and the horizontal.

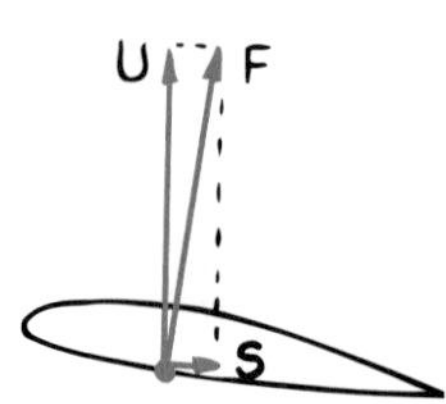

Figure C.10

5. Consider the satellite moving clockwise in Figure C.11. Everywhere in its orbital path, gravitational force **F** pulls it toward the center of the host planet. At position A we see **F** separated into two components: **f**, which is tangent to the path of the projectile, and **f′**, which is perpendicular to the path. The relative magnitudes of these components in comparison to the magnitude of **F** can be seen in the imaginary rectangle they compose: **f** and **f′** are the sides, and **F** is the diagonal. We see that component **f** is along the orbital path but against the direction of motion of the satellite. This force component reduces the speed of the satellite. The other component, **f′**, changes the direction of the satellite's motion and pulls it away from its tendency to go in a straight line. So the path of the satellite curves. The satellite loses speed until it reaches position B. At this farthest point from the planet (apogee), the gravitational force is somewhat weaker but perpendicular to the satellite's motion, and component **f** has reduced to zero. Component **f′**, on the other hand, has increased and is now fully merged to become **F**. Speed at this point is not enough for circular orbit, and the satellite begins to fall toward the planet. It picks up speed because the component **f** reappears and is in the

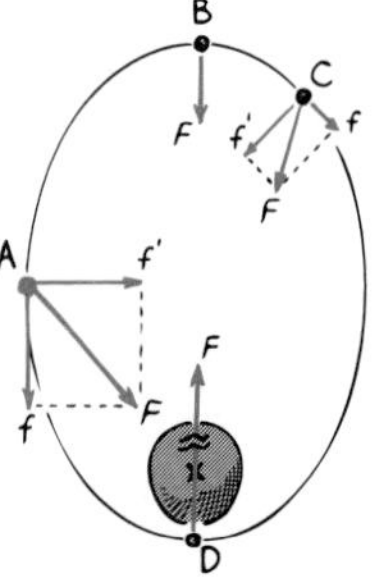

Figure C.11

direction of motion as shown in position C. The satellite picks up speed until it whips around to position D (perigee), where once again the direction of motion is perpendicular to the gravitational force, **f′** blends to full **F**, and **f** is nonexistent. The speed is in excess of that needed for circular orbit at this distance, and it overshoots to repeat the cycle. Its loss in speed in going from D to B equals its gain in speed from B to D. Kepler discovered that planetary paths are elliptical, but never knew why. Do you?

6. Refer to the Polaroids held by Ludmila back in Chapter 12, in Figure 12.46. In the first picture (a), we see that light is transmitted through the pair of Polaroids because their axes are aligned. The emerging light can be represented as a vector aligned with the polarization axes of the Polaroids. When the Polaroids are crossed (b), no light emerges because light passing through the first Polaroid is perpendicular to the polarization axes of the second Polaroid, with no components along its axis. In the third picture (c), we see that light is transmitted when a third Polaroid is sandwiched at an angle between the crossed Polaroids. The explanation for this is shown in Figure C.12.

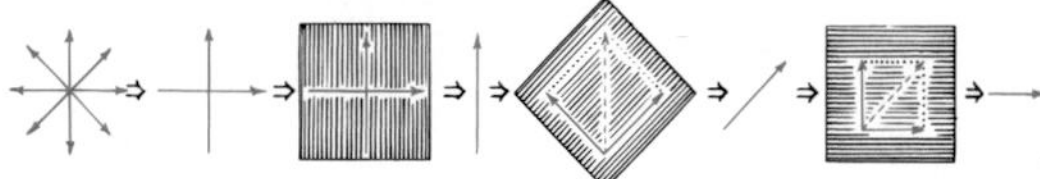

Figure C.12

Sailboats

Sailors have always known that a sailboat can sail downwind, in the direction of the wind. Sailors have not always known, however, that a sailboat can sail upwind, against the wind. One reason for this has to do with a feature that is common only to recent sailboats—a fin-like keel that extends deep beneath the bottom of the boat to ensure that the boat will knife through the water only in a forward (or backward) direction. Without a keel, a sailboat could be blown sideways.

Figure C.13 shows a sailboat sailing directly downwind. The force of wind impact against the sail accelerates the boat. Even if the drag of the water and all other resistance forces are negligible, the maximum speed of the boat is the wind speed. This is because the wind will not make impact against the sail if the boat is moving as fast as the wind. The wind would have no speed relative to the boat and the sail would simply sag. With no force, there is no acceleration. The force vector in Figure C.13 *decreases* as the boat travels faster. The force vector is maximum when the boat is at rest and the full impact of the wind fills the sail, and is minimum when the boat travels as fast as the wind. If the boat is somehow propelled to a speed faster than the wind (by way of a motor, for example), then air resistance against the front side of the sail will produce an oppositely directed force vector. This will slow the boat down. Hence the boat when driven only by the wind cannot exceed wind speed.

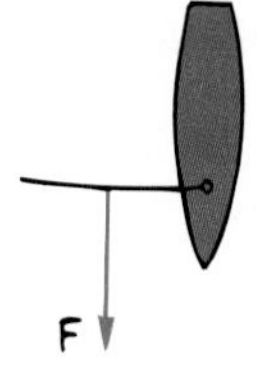

Figure C.13

If the sail is oriented at an angle, as shown in Figure C.14, the boat will move forward, but with less acceleration. There are two reasons for this:

1. The force on the sail is less because the sail does not intercept as much wind in this angular position.

2. The direction of the wind impact force on the sail is not in the direction of the boat's motion, but is perpendicular to the surface of the sail. Generally speaking, whenever any fluid (liquid or gas) interacts with a smooth surface, the force of interaction is perpendicular to the smooth surface.* The boat does not move in the same direction as the perpendicular force on the sail, but is constrained to move in a forward (or backward) direction by its keel.

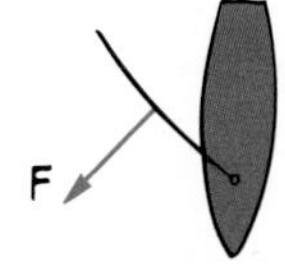

Figure C.14

*You can do a simple exercise to see that this is so. Try bouncing a coin off another on a smooth surface, as shown. Note that the struck coin moves at right angles (perpendicular) to the contact edge. Note also that it makes no difference whether the projected coin moves along path A or path B. See your instructor for a more rigorous explanation, which involves momentum conservation.

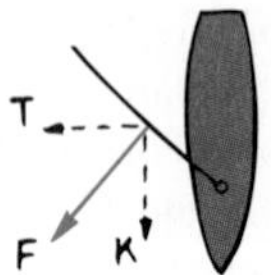

Figure C.15

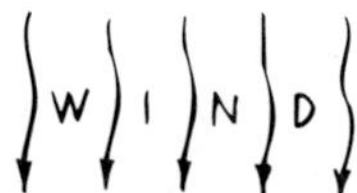

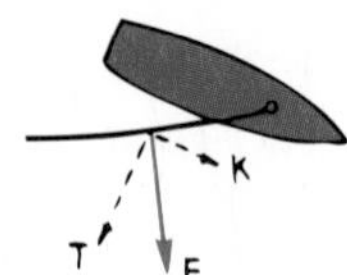

Figure C.16

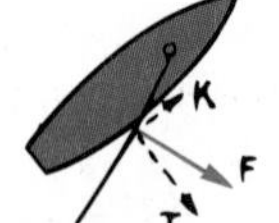

Figure C.17

We can better understand the motion of the boat by resolving the force of wind impact, **F**, into perpendicular components. The important component is that which is parallel to the keel, which we label **K**, and the other component is perpendicular to the keel, which we label **T.** It is the component **K**, as shown in Figure C.15, that is responsible for the forward motion of the boat. Component **T** is a useless force that tends to tip the boat over and move it sideways. This component force is offset by the deep keel. Again, maximum speed of the boat can be no greater than wind speed.

Many sailboats sailing in directions other than exactly downwind (Figure C.16) with their sails properly oriented can exceed wind speed. In the case of a sailboat cutting across the wind, the wind may continue to make impact with the sail even after the boat exceeds wind speed. A surfer, in a similar way, exceeds the velocity of the propelling wave by angling his surfboard across the wave. Greater angles to the propelling medium (wind for the boat, water wave for the surfboard) result in greater speeds. A sailcraft can sail faster cutting across the wind than it can sailing downwind.

As strange as it may seem, maximum speed for most sailcraft is attained by cutting into (against) the wind, that is, by angling the sailcraft in a direction upwind! Although a sailboat cannot sail directly upwind, it can reach a destination upwind by angling back and forth in a zigzag fashion. This is called *tacking*. Suppose the boat and sail are as shown in Figure C.17. Component **K** will push the boat along in a forward direction, angling into the wind. In the position shown, the boat can sail faster than the speed of the wind. This is because as the boat travels faster, the impact of wind is increased. This is similar to running in a rain that comes down at an angle. When you run into the direction of the downpour, the drops strike you harder and more frequently, but when you run away from the direction of the downpour, the drops don't strike you as hard or as frequently. In the same way, a boat sailing upwind experiences greater wind impact force, while a boat sailing downwind experiences a decreased wind impact force. In any case the boat reaches its terminal speed when opposing forces cancel the force of wind impact. The opposing forces consist mainly of water resistance against the hull of the boat. The hulls of racing boats are shaped to minimize this resistive force, which is the principal deterrent to high speeds.

Iceboats (sailcraft equipped with runners for traveling on ice) encounter no water resistance and can travel at several times the speed of the wind when they tack upwind. Although ice friction is nearly absent, an iceboat does not accelerate without limits. The terminal velocity of a sailcraft is determined not only by opposing friction forces but also by the change in relative wind direction. When the boat's orientation and speed are such that the wind seems to shift in direction, so the wind moves parallel to the sail rather than into it, forward acceleration ceases—at least in the case of a flat sail. In practice, sails are curved and produce an airfoil that is as important to sailcraft as it is to aircraft, as discussed in Chapter 6.

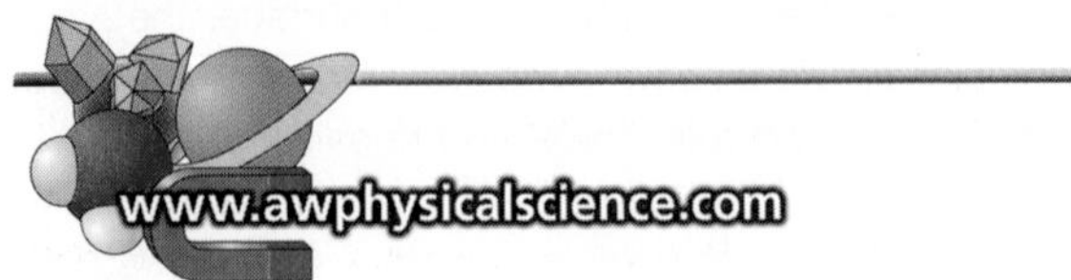

Appendix C Online Resources

Tutorials

- Vectors

APPENDIX D

Exponetial Growth and Doubling Time*

One of the most important things we seem unable to perceive is the process of exponential growth. We think we understand how compound interest works, but we can't get it through our heads that a fine piece of tissue paper folded upon itself 50 times (if that were possible) would be more than 20 million kilometers thick. If we could, we could "see" why our income buys only half of what it did 4 years ago, why the price of everything has doubled in the same time, why populations and pollution proliferate out of control.[†]

When a quantity such as money in the bank, population, or the rate of consumption of a resource steadily grows at a fixed percent per year, we say the growth is exponential. Money in the bank may grow at 4 percent per year; electric power generating capacity in the United States grew at about 7 percent per year for the first three-quarters of the 20th century. The important thing about exponential growth is that the time required for the growing quantity to double in size (increase by 100 percent) is also constant. For example, if the population of a growing city takes 12 years to double from 10,000 to 20,000 inhabitants and its growth remains steady, in the next 12 years the population will double to 40,000, and in the next 10 years to 80,000, and so on.

There is an important relationship between the percent growth rate and its *doubling time,* the time it takes to double a quantity:[‡]

$$\text{Doubling time} = \frac{69.3}{\text{percent growth per unit time}} \approx \frac{70}{\%}$$

So to estimate the doubling time for a steadily growing quantity, we simply divide the number 70 by the percentage growth rate. For example, the 7 percent growth rate of electric power generating capacity in the United States means that in the past the capacity had doubled every 10 years [70%/(7%/year) = 10 years]. A 2 percent growth rate for world population means the population of the world doubles every 35 years [70%/(2%/year) = 35 years]. A city planning commission that accepts what seems like a modest 3.5 percent growth rate may not realize that this means that doubling will occur in 70/3.5 or 20 years; that's double capacity for such things as water supply, sewage-treatment plants, and other municipal services every 20 years.

What happens when you put steady growth in a finite environment? Consider the growth of bacteria that grow by division, so that one bacterium

*This appendix is drawn from material by University of Colorado physics professor Albert A. Bartlett, who strongly asserts, "The greatest shortcoming of the human race is man's inability to understand the exponential function." See Professor Bartlett's still-timely article, "Forgotten Fundamentals in the Energy Crisis" (*American Journal of Physics,* September 1978) or his revised version (*Journal of Geological Education,* January 1980).

[†]K. C. Cole, *Sympathetic Vibrations* (New York: Morrow, 1984).

[‡]For exponential decay we speak about half-life, the time required for a quantity to reduce to half its value. This case is treated in Chapter 16.

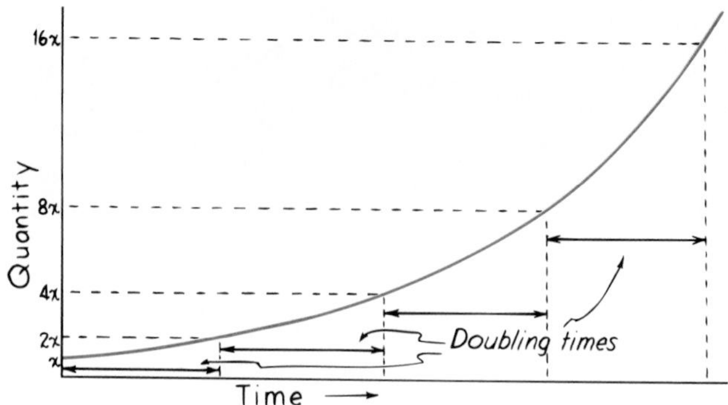

Figure D.1
An exponential curve. Notice that each of the successive equal time intervals noted on the horizontal scale corresponds to a doubling of the quantity indicated on the vertical scale. Such an interval is called the doubling time.

becomes two, the two divide to become four, the four divide to become eight, and so on. Suppose the division time for a certain strain of bacteria is 1 minute. This is then steady growth—the number of bacteria grows exponentially with a doubling time of 1 minute. Further, suppose that one bacterium is put in a bottle at 11:00 A.M. and that growth continues steadily until the bottle becomes full of bacteria at 12 noon. Consider seriously the following question.

Figure D.2

☑ CHECKPOINT

When was the bottle half-full?

Check Your Answer

11:59 A.M.; the bacteria will double in number every minute!

It is startling to note that at 2 minutes before noon the bottle was only 1/4 full. Table D.1 summarizes the amount of space left in the bottle in the last few minutes before noon. If you were an average bacterium in the bottle, at which time would you first realize that you were running out of space? For example, would you sense there was a serious problem at 11:55 A.M., when the bottle was only 3% filled, (1/32), and had 97% of open space (just yearning for development)? The point here is that there isn't much time between the moment that the effects of growth become noticeable and the time when they become overwhelming.

Suppose that at 11:58 A.M. some farsighted bacteria see that they are running out of space and launch a full-scale search for new bottles. Luckily, at 11.59 A.M. they discover three new empty bottles, three times as much space as they had ever known. This quadruples the total resource space ever known to the bacteria, for they now have a total of four bottles, whereas before the discovery they had only one. Further suppose that, thanks to their technological proficiency, they are able to migrate to their new habitats without difficulty. Surely, it seems to most of the bacteria that their problem is solved—and just in time.

Table D.1

The Last Minutes in the Bottle

Time	Part Full (%)	Part Empty
11:54 A.M.	1/64 (1.5%)	63/64
11:55 A.M.	1/32 (3%)	31/32
11:56 A.M.	1/16 (6%)	15/16
11:57 A.M.	1/8 (12%)	7/8
11:58 A.M.	1/4 (25%)	3/4
11:59 A.M.	1/2 (50%)	1/2
12:00 noon	full (100%)	none

☑ CHECKPOINT

If the bacteria growth continues at the unchanged rate, what time will it be when the three new bottles are filled to capacity?

Check Your Answer

12:02 P.M.!

Figure D.3
A single grain of wheat placed on the first square of the chessboard is doubled on the second square, this number is doubled on the third, and so on, presumably for all 64 squares. Note that each square contains one more grain than all the preceding squares combined. Does enough wheat exist in the world to fill all 64 squares in this manner?

We see from Table D.2 that quadrupling the resource extends the life of the resource by only two doubling times. In our example the resource is space—but it could as well be coal, oil, uranium, or any nonrenewable resource.

Table D.2

Effects of the Discovery of Three New Bottles

Time	Effect
11:58 A.M.	Bottle 1 is 1/4 full
11:59 A.M.	Bottle 1 is 1/2 full
12:00 noon	Bottle 1 is full
12:01 P.M.	Bottles 1 and 2 are both full
12:02 P.M.	Bottles 1, 2, 3, and 4 are all full

Continued growth and continued doubling lead to enormous numbers. In two doubling times, a quantity will double twice ($2^2 = 4$; quadruple) in size; in three doubling times, its size will increase eightfold ($2^3 = 8$); in four doubling times, it will increase sixteenfold ($2^4 = 16$); and so on.

This is best illustrated by the story of the court mathematician in India who years ago invented the game of chess for his king. The king was so pleased with the game that he offered to repay the mathematician, whose request seemed modest enough. The mathematician requested a single grain of wheat on the first square of the chessboard, two grains on the second square, four on the third square, and so on, doubling the number of grains on each succeeding square until all squares had been used. At this rate there would be 2^{63} grains of wheat on the 64th square. The king soon saw that he could not fill this "modest" request, which amounted to more wheat than had been harvested in the entire history of the earth!

It is interesting and important to note that the number or grains on any square is one grain more than the total of all grains on the preceding squares. This is true anywhere on the board. Note from Table D.3 that when eight grains are placed on the fourth square, the eight is one more than the total of seven grains that were already on the board. Or the 32 grains placed on the sixth square is one more than the total of 31 grains that were already on the board. We see that in one doubling time we use more than all that had been used in all the preceding growth!

Table D.3

Filling the Squares on the Chessboard

Square Number	Grains on Square	Total Grains Thus Far
1	1	1
2	2	3
3	4	7
4	8	15
5	16	31
6	32	63
7	64	127
.	.	.
.	.	.
.	.	.
64	2^{63}	$2^{64} - 1$

So if we speak of doubling energy consumption in the next however many years, bear in mind that this means in these years we will consume more energy than has heretofore been consumed during the entire preceding period of steady growth. And if power generation continues to use predominantly fossil fuels, then except for some improvements in efficiency, we would burn up in the next doubling time a greater amount of coal, oil, and natural gas than has already been consumed by previous power generation, and except for improvements in pollution control, we can expect to discharge even more toxic wastes into the environment than the millions upon millions of tons already discharged over all the previous years of industrial civilization. We would also expect more human-made calories of heat to be absorbed by the earth's ecosystem than have been absorbed in the entire past! At the previous 7% annual growth rate in energy production, all this would occur in one doubling time of a single decade. If over the coming years the annual growth rate remains at half this value, 3.5 percent, then all this would take place in a doubling time of two decades. Clearly this cannot continue!

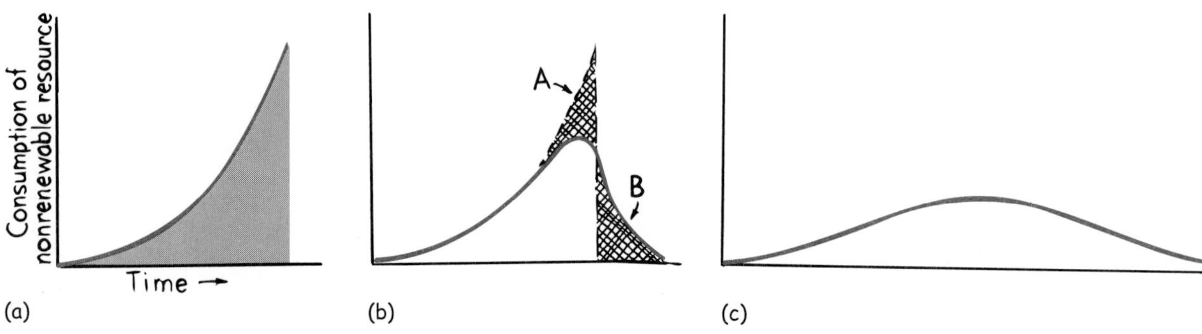

Figure D.4
(a) If the exponential rate of consumption for a nonrenewable resource continues until it is depleted, consumption falls abruptly to zero. The shaded area under this curve represents the total supply of the resource. (b) In practice, the rate of consumption levels off and then falls less abruptly to zero. Note that the crosshatched area A is equal to the crosshatched area B. Why? (c) At lower consumption rates, the same resource lasts a longer time.

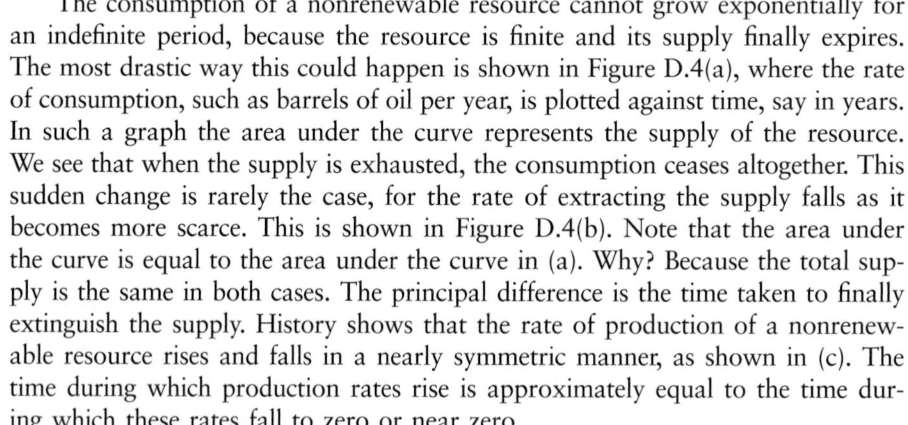

The consumption of a nonrenewable resource cannot grow exponentially for an indefinite period, because the resource is finite and its supply finally expires. The most drastic way this could happen is shown in Figure D.4(a), where the rate of consumption, such as barrels of oil per year, is plotted against time, say in years. In such a graph the area under the curve represents the supply of the resource. We see that when the supply is exhausted, the consumption ceases altogether. This sudden change is rarely the case, for the rate of extracting the supply falls as it becomes more scarce. This is shown in Figure D.4(b). Note that the area under the curve is equal to the area under the curve in (a). Why? Because the total supply is the same in both cases. The principal difference is the time taken to finally extinguish the supply. History shows that the rate of production of a nonrenewable resource rises and falls in a nearly symmetric manner, as shown in (c). The time during which production rates rise is approximately equal to the time during which these rates fall to zero or near zero.

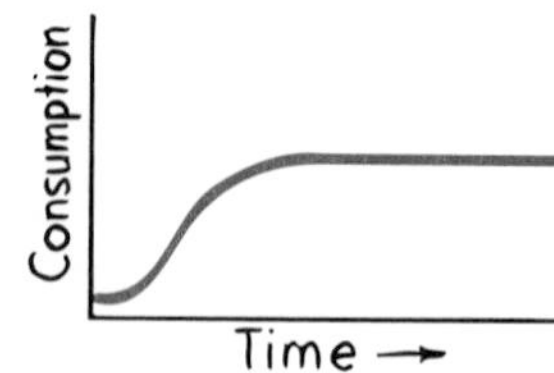

Figure D.5
A curve showing the rate of consumption of a renewable resource such as agricultural or forest products, where a steady rate of production and consumption can be maintained for a long period, provided this production is not dependent upon the use of a nonrenewable resource that is waning in supply.

Production rates for all nonrenewable resources decrease sooner or later. Only production rates for renewable resources, such as agriculture or forest products, can be maintained at steady levels for long periods of time (Figure D.5), provided such production does not depend on waning nonrenewable resources such as petroleum. Much of today's agriculture is so petroleum-dependent that it can be said that modern agriculture is simply the process whereby land is used to convert petroleum into food. The implications of petroleum scarcity go far beyond rationing of gasoline for cars or fuel oil for home heating.

The consequences of unchecked exponential growth are staggering. It is important to ask: Is growth really good? In answering this question, bear in mind that human growth is an early phase of life that continues normally through adolescence. Physical growth stops when physical maturity is reached. What do we say of growth that continues in the period of physical maturity? We say that such growth is obesity—or worse, cancer.

Questions to Ponder

1. According to a French riddle, a lily pond starts with a single leaf. Each day the number of leaves doubles, until the pond is completely covered by leaves on the 30th day. On what day was the pond half covered? One-quarter covered?
2. In an economy that has a steady inflation rate of 7% per year, in how many years does a dollar lose half its value?
3. At a steady inflation rate of 7%, what will be the price every 10 years for the next 50 years for a theater ticket that now costs $20? For a coat that now costs $200? For a car that now costs $20,000? For a home that now costs $200,000?
4. If the sewage treatment plant of a city is just adequate for the city's current population, how many sewage treatment plants will be necessary 42 years later if the city grows steadily at 5% annually?
5. If world population doubles in 40 years and world food production also doubles in 40 years, how many people then will be starving each year compared to now?
6. Suppose you get a prospective employer to agree to hire your services for wages of a single penny for the first day, 2 pennies for the second day, and double each day thereafter providing the employer keeps to the agreement for a month. What will be your total wages for the month?
7. In the preceding exercise, how will your wages for only the 30th day compare to your total wages for the previous 29 days?
8. If fusion power were harnessed today, the abundant energy resulting would probably sustain and even further encourage our present appetite for continued growth and in a relatively few doubling times produce an appreciable fraction of the solar power input to the earth. Make an argument that the current delay in harnessing fusion is a blessing for the human race.

Suggested Reading and Web Sites

Prologue

Hutchings, Edward (Editor), Ralph Leighton, Richard P. Feynman, Albert Hibbs. *"Surely You're Joking, Mr. Feynman!"*: Adventures of a Curious Character. New York: Norton, 1986.

Park, Robert. *Voodoo Science: The Road from Foolishness to Fraud*. New York: Oxford University Press, 2000.

Sagan, Carl. *The Demon-Haunted World: Science As a Candle in the Dark*. New York: Random House, 1996.

Shermer, Michael. *The Borderlands of Science: Where Sense Meets Nonsense*. New York: Oxford University Press, 2001.

http://www.howstuffworks.com
An intriguing website of technological devices.

http://www.csicop.org
Home page for the Committee for the Scientific Investigation of Claims of the Paranormal.

http://www.nsf.gov
Home page of the National Science Foundation, one of the leading sponsors of scientific research and education.

http://www.sciencenews.org/
Archives of *Science News*, a widely read weekly magazine covering current developments in science

Part 1

Chapter 1

Asimov, Isaac. *Understanding Physics*. New York: Barnes and Noble, 1996.
Excellent and accurate introductory physics by a writing master.

Bodanis, David. *$E = mc^2$: A biography of the world's most famous equation*. New York: Berkeley Publishing Group, 2002.
If you want to read a really fascinating book, this is it.

Drake, Stillman. *Galileo at Work: His Scientific Biography*. Chicago, University of Chicago Press, 1978.

Finocchiaro, Maurice A. *The Galileo Affair: A Documentary History.* University of California Press, 1989.

Sharratt, Michael. *Galileo: Decisive Innovator.* Cambridge, Cambridge University Press, 1994.

Sobel, Dava. *Galileo's Daughter: A Historical Memoir of Science, Faith, and Love*. Walker & Company, New York, 1999.

http://www.awphysicalscience.com
Many interactive and animated tutorials that focus on physical science concepts, plus much more.

http://www.fearofphysics.com/
A comprehensive site for beginning physics covering a wide range of mechanics topics plus others. Includes animations and quizzes.

http://www.merlot.org
A rich smorgasbord of teaching and learning materials for the instructor with links to good material in science (and in other fields). Well organized and searchable.

http://www.aw.com
Information on other Hewitt and Suchocki textbooks.

http://www.conceptualphysics.com
Paul Hewitt's personal website.

Chapter 2

Sobel, Dava. *Galileo's Daughter: A Historical Memoir of Science, Faith, and Love*. New York: Walker & Company, 1999.

Waterfall, Richard S. *The Life of Isaac Newton*. Cambridge: Cambridge University Press, 1994.

Westfall, Richard. *Never at Rest: A Biography of Isaac Newton*. New York: Cambridge University Press, 1988.

http://galileo.imss.firenze.it/
Users of this Italian Museum of History of Science website can tour a virtual museum to see scientific instruments, including the telescope used by Galileo.

http://www.learner.org/exhibits/parkphysics/
An extensive site, with information on the physics of amusement parks, including roller coasters, etc.

http://www.explorescience.com
Terminal velocity, as well as many other topics is offered in this rich Exploratorium website.

http://www.fearofphysics.com/
Much more than Newton's laws are on this engaging site.

Chapter 3

Bloomfield, L. A. *How Things Work: The Physics of Everyday Life*. New York: Wiley & Sons, 1997.

Bodanis, David. *$E = mc^2$: A biography of the world's most famous equation*. New York: Berkeley Publishing Group, 2002.
A wonderfully written overview of the history of the concept of energy begins this engaging book.

Brancazio, P. J. *Sport Science*. New York: Simon & Schuster, 1984.
Many goodies on the physics underlying sports.
http://www.energyquest.ca.gov/index.html
A fascinating and entertaining look at energy—all levels.
http://www.explorescience.com
Collisions and air-track physics, as well as many other topics are offered in this rich Exploratorium website.

Chapter 4

Al-Khalili, Jim. *Black Holes, Wormholes & Time Machines*. Philadelphia: IOP, Bristol and Philadelphia, 1999.
Einstein, A., and L. Infeld. *The Evolution of Physics*. New York: Simon & Schuster, 1938.
If you think Einstein's writing is on the difficult side, you'll be in for a pleasant surprise!
Gamow, George. *Gravity*. Science Study Series. Garden City, New York: Doubleday (Anchor), 1962.
This is another oldie but goodie, written by a first-rate scientist who also had a wonderful way with words.
Koestler, Arthur. *The Watershed*. New York: Doubleday (Anchor Books), 1960.
This is a book about Johannes Kepler.

Chapter 5

Clark, A. C. *Rendezvous with Rama*. New York: Harcourt Brace Jovanovich, 1973.
This is the first science fiction novel to seriously consider habitation inside a spinning space facility.
Dyson, Freeman. *From Eros to Gaia*. New York: Pantheon Books, 1992.
Ferris, T., *The Red Limit*, 2nd ed. New York: Morrow, Quill, 1983.
http://www.explorescience.com
Projectiles, independence of horizontal and vertical motion, and many other topics are offered in this rich Exploratorium website.
http://www.fearofphysics.com/
Set tangential speed and see if a projectile becomes a satellite. This and much more. Includes animations and quizzes.
http://www.thetech.org/exhibits/online/satellite/
Satellites check weather, transmit T.V. signals, carry orbiting observatories, and perform other fascinating operations. A construction set helps you assemble three kinds of fully operational satellites! The Satellite Site!
http://liftoff.msfc.nasa.gov/RealTime/JTrack/
Spot the Hubble, the MIR, or another satellite with J-Pass. Sign up, specify your location and the satellite you wish to track. Satellite prediction reports will be emailed to you telling when and where the satellite is coming, its brightness, and more.

Chapter 6

Ball, Philip. Life's Matrix: *A Biography of Water*. New York: Farrar, Straus and Giroux, 1999.
http://www.lerc.nasa.gov/WWW/K-12/airplane/bga.html
Basic information on aerodynamics with enjoyable interactive animations. A good beginner's guide.
http://www.explorescience.com
Labs on density and floatation, as well as many other topics is offered in this rich Exploratorium website.

Chapter 7

Brown, Sanborn C. *Count Rumford*. New York: Doubleday (Anchor Books), 1962.
Campbell, John. *Rutherford: Scientist Supreme*. AAS Publications, 1999.
Krauss, Lawrence. *Fear of Physics*. New York: Basic Books, 1993.

Chapter 8

Cole, K. C. *First You Build a Cloud*. New York: Morrow, 1999.
Delightful and light reading on science and scientists.
http://www.earthsky.com
Click the Skywatching Forecast to find out what you can see in tonight's sky.

Chapter 9

Brands, H. W. *The First American: The Life and Times of Benjamin Franklin*. New York: Doubleday, 2000.
A personal favorite, this is a gripping account of a first-rate scientist and his pivotal role in the formation of the United States.
http://www.fi.edu/Franklin/
"If you would not be forgotten as soon as you are rotten, either write things worth the reading or do things worth the writing." Benjamin Franklin did just that. Click on hypertext links to visit Franklin the scientist, inventor, and philosopher.
http://www.skeptic.com
Publisher of Skeptic magazine and Scientific American columnist, Michael Shermer, champions science as our best filter for identifying pseudoscience.
http://www.nps.gov/edis/home.htm
The Edison National Historic Site features the life of Thomas Edison, his estate, and the forgotten heroes who "mucked" for him.
http://www.iop.org
This appealing site is all about electrons.
http://www.mos.org/sln/toe/toe.html
The Theater of Electricity features the largest air-insulated Van de Graaf generator in the world, with its history and construction.

http://www2.slac.stanford.edu/vvc
Electron beam experiments that go on at SLAC (Stanford Linear Accelerator Complex) and other information about the site.

Chapter 10

MacDonald, D.K.C. *Faraday, Maxwell, and Kelvin*. New York: Doubleday (Anchor Books), 1964.

Park, Robert. *Voodoo Science—The Road from Foolishness to Fraud*. New York: Oxford University Press, 2000.
For a sample, the box on therapeutic magnets was adapted from this book.

Sagan, Carl. *The Demon-Haunted World*. New York: Random House, 1995.
Pseudoscience and its effects are central to this fascinating book.

Shermer, Michael. *The Borderlands of Science: Where Sense Meets Nonsense*. New York: Oxford University Press, 2001.

http://www.colorado.edu/physics/2000/waves_particles/wavpart2.html
Interactive demonstrations of electric charges interacting, force fields, and lines of force.

http://www.explorescience.com
Electricity, magnetism, and much more are offered in this rich Exploratorium website.

http://www.phy6.org/Education/Intro.html
Information about the earth as a magnet and the magnetosphere.

http://www.eskimo.com/~billb/
Built by William Beaty, an electrical engineer and amateur scientist, this entertaining site is rich with information on everything from science fair ideas, to activities, to textbook science myths!

http://www.aip.org/history/electron/
The interesting story of J.J. Thompson, discoverer of the electron, and of the work of other scientists who followed him.

http://www.windows.ucar.edu/spaceweather/
The earth's magnetic field acts as a shield against solar radiation and magnetic fields. QuickTime movies show space storm displays in the atmosphere as you explore the sun-earth system and other basic facts about space weather.

http://jersey.uoregon.edu/vlab/
Experience Ohms Law in a virtual experiment.

Chapter 11

Benade, A. H. "The Physics of Woodwinds," *Scientific American*, October 1960.

Benade, A. H. "The Physics of Brasses," *Scientific American*, July 1973.

Fuller, Robert G., Dean Zollman, and Thomas C. Campbell, *The Puzzle of the Tacoma Narrows Bridge Collapse*, New York: John Wiley & Sons, 1982.

http://www.explorescience.com
Waves and simple harmonic motion, as well as many other topics, are offered in this rich Exploratorium website.

http://bose.com/noise_reduction/qc_headset
Acoustic noise canceling devices for sale.

http://www.lhs.berkeley.edu/whale/osci1.html
One of the best tools for studying sound is the oscilloscope. Learn how to read this instrument that turns sound into pictures. Sound waves of various sources are compared with their oscilloscope images.

http://www.invent.org/index.asp
American inventors who got patents for their inventions are featured. Sound and light technology can be accessed quickly by using the search feature. For sound, search on terms such as audio, amplifier, transmitter and sonar. To research light inventions and inventors, use terms laser, optics, and radar.

http://www.pbs.org/wgbh/nova/barrier/textindex.html
This NOVA Online website is about the test pilots, scientists, and engineers who developed fast-flying jets. It relates their experiences when first breaking the sound barrier.

http://www.pbs.org/wgbh/nova/subsecrets/
Visit the inside of a submarine and its Sonar Room to view equipment that uses sound waves to chart a submarine's path through dark water. A NOVA Online website.

http://asa.aip.org/acou_and_you.html
Careers involving the science of acoustics—designing musical instruments, helping children with hearing problems learn to speak and listen, or finding new ways to reduce noise pollution.

http://www.sv.vt.edu/classes/ESM4714/Student_Proj/class95/physics/chin_sound.html
Featured topics include fundamentals of sound, speed of sound, interference, and the Doppler Effect.

Chapter 12

Bodanis, David. *$E = mc^2$: A biography of the world's most famous equation*. New York: Berkeley Publishing Group, 2002.
Excellent treatment of the speed of light and its history. If you want to read a really fascinating book, this is it.

Falk, D. S., Brill, D. R., and Stork, D. *Seeing the Light: Optics in Nature*. New York: Harper & Row, 1985.

Falk, D. S., Brill, D. R., and Stork, D. G. *Seeing the Light*. New York: J. Wiley & Sons, 1986.

Friedhoffer, Robert. *Light: Book 5*, Scientific Magic Series. New York: Watts, 1992.

Jaffe, Bernard. *Michelson and the Speed of Light*. New York: Doubleday (Anchor Books), 1960.
Lynch, D. K. and Livingston, W. *Color and Light in Nature*. Cambridge and New York: Cambridge University Press, 1955.
Murphy, Pat, and Paul Doherty. *The Color of Nature*. San Francisco: Chronicle Books, 1996.
Rossing, Thomas D., Chiaverina, Christopher J. *Teaching Light and Color*. Maryland: American Association of Physics Teachers, 2001.
http://www.explorescience.com
Click on Optics from the main page for an array of "de-light-ful" online activities. Additive and subtractive colors are a highlight. Check Interference Patterns to view interference patterns created by standing waves.
http://www.exploratorium.edu/light_walk/index.html
The San Francisco Exploratorium's Bob Miller takes you on a virtual walk, showing you how pinhole images reveal properties of light. Quite wonderful.
http://www.explorescience.com
Explore the Waves and Optics features at this interactive science lab. In the Waves section, hear sound pulses and determine mystery frequencies. Click on Simple Prism in Optics to see how changing wavelength affects angle of refraction. Shockwave is required.

Chapter 13

Cole, K. C. *First You Build a Cloud*. New York: Morrow, 1999.
A delightful unraveling of the theories of Bohr, Einstein, and other developers of quantum physics, with emphasis on the human side of physics.
Feynman, Richard P. *QED: The Strange Theory of Light and Matter*. New Jersey: Princeton University Press, 1985.
Greenler, Robert. *Chasing the Rainbow—Recurrences in the Life of a Scientist*. Milwaukee: Elton-Wolf, 2000.
Greenler, R. *Rainbows, Halos, and Glories*. Cambridge: Cambridge University Press, 1980.
Hutchings, Edward (Editor), Ralph Leighton, Richard P. Feynman, Albert Hibbs. *"Surely You're Joking, Mr. Feynman !"*: Adventures of a Curious Character. New York: Norton, 1986.
A best-selling popular book, Feynman's own account of the human and humorous side of being a scientist.
http://www.exploratorium.edu/origins/cern/
Enrichment for students intrigued by particle physics
http://www.fearofphysics.com/
A comprehensive site covering a range of mechanics topics plus some relativity, sound, and atomic models. Includes animations and quizzes.
http://www2.slac.stanford.edu/vvc
The SLAC Virtual Visitor Center gives information about the experiments that go on at SLAC (Stanford Linear Accelerator Complex).

Part 2

Chapter 14

CRC Handbook of Chemistry and Physics, 83rd ed. Boca Raton, FL: CRC Press, 2002. Toward the front of this classic reference book is a section on the history and general properties of each element.
Suchocki, J. *Conceptual Chemistry*, 2nd ed. San Francisco: Benjamin Cummings, 2003. See an expanded treatment of features of the periodic table.
http://www.chemsoc.org/viselements/pages/periodic_table.html
The Visual Elements project of the Royal Society of Chemistry. Provides animations of almost all the elements. A high-speed internet connection is required.
http://www.gsi.de
Web site for the heavy-ion research facility in Darmstadt, Germany, where many of the heaviest but shortest-lived elements are being created.
http://newton.dep.anl.gov/
The Division of Educational Program of the Argonne National Laboratory presents the Newton Bulletin Board Service, which features "Ask a Scientist." Explore the chemistry archives for the answers to more than 1500 student questions compiled since 1991.
http://www.webelements.com/
There are a large number of periodic tables posted on the Web, and this is one of the most popular.
http://www.aip.org/history/electron/jjthomson.htm
An in-depth presentation of the discovery of the electron by J. J. Thomson.
http://www.woodrow.org/teachers/ci/1992/
A series of insightful biographies of historical figures in chemistry, written by participants at the 1992 Institute on the History of Chemistry and sponsored by the Woodrow Wilson National Fellowship Foundation.

Chapter 15

Bodanis, David. *$E = mc^2$: A Biography of the World's Most Famous Equation*. New York: Berkeley Publishing Group, 2000.
A really fascinating book. Wonderful reading.
Gamow George, *Thirty Years That Shook Physics*. New York: Dover, 1985.
A historical tracing of quantum theory by a pioneer of its development.
Milburn Gerard J., Schrödinger's Machines. *The Quantum Technology Shaping Everyday Life*. New York: W. H. Freeman, 1997.
Our understanding of quantum theory has already led to a number of society-shaping inventions, such as the

transistor, a basic component of all computers, and the laser, which scans everything from our groceries to our music. This book presents some of the newer quantum technologies and some of the fantastic quantum technologies that we can expect to see over the next 50 years.

http://home.achilles.net/~jtalbot/
A superb site for learning about the spectral patterns of stars and how they are used to study the universe.

http://home.achilles.net/~jtalbot/data/elements/index.html
Here is where you will find high-resolution spectral patterns of a variety of elements.

http://www.physics.purdue.edu/nanophys
Site of the nanoscale physics laboratory of Purdue University, where they look at things that are really, really, really, really, really, really, really small. Lots of pretty pictures.

http://www.superstringtheory.com
If you think the wave nature of the electron is bizarre, explore this site for information on, and references to, the potentially revolutionary theory that particles, forces, space, and time are merely manifestations of incredibly tiny strings that exist in 10 dimensions.

Chapter 16

For information on radiation exposure, see the following web sites:

http://www.princeton.edu/~ehs/radtrain/Modules/Natbkg.html

http://www.chem.uidaho.edu/

http://www.yankee.com/license_radiation.html

http://www.ornl.gov/ORNLReview/rev26-34/text/colmain.html

http://geology.cr.usgs.gov/energy/factshts/163-97/FS-163-97.html

Chapter 17

CRC Handbook of Chemistry and Physics. Boca Raton, FL: CRC Press, 1996. Toward the front of this classic reference book, you'll find a section on the history and general properties of each element.

http://www.chemsoc.org
Chemistry news updates, an on-line chemistry magazine, and much more at this site managed by the Royal Society of Chemistry.

http://www.chemsoc.org/viselements/pages/periodic_table.html
The Visual Elements project of the Royal Society of Chemistry, providing animations of almost all the elements. A high-speed internet connection is required.

http://www.csc.fi/lul/chem/graphics.html
A virtual art gallery of molecular animations and other cool things, maintained by Finland's Center for Scientific Computing.

http://www.gsi.de
Web site for the heavy-ion research facility in Darmstadt, Germany, where many of the heaviest but shortest-lived elements are being created.

http://newton.dep.anl.gov/
The Division of Educational Program of the Argonne National Laboratory presents the Newton Bulletin Board Service, which features "Ask a Scientist." Explore the chemistry archives for the answers to more than 1500 student questions compiled since 1991.

http://www.shef.ac.uk/~chem/web-elements/
There are a large number of periodic tables posted on the Web, and this is one of the most popular.

Chapter 18

http://www.desalting-ada.org/
Web site for the American Desalination Association, whose mission is to increase the understanding and use of advanced water-treatment technologies to improve municipal, agricultural, and industrial water supplies. These technologies include reverse osmosis and other processes to remove salts, organic materials, microbial contaminants, and other water impurities.

http://www.waterwiser.org/
This web site is a cooperative project of several leading environmental organizations, including the American Water Works Association and the U.S. Environmental Protection Agency. Books, brochures, and papers are available for purchase.

http://www.awwa.org/
Home page for the American Water Works Association, an international nonprofit scientific and educational society dedicated to the improvement of drinking water quality and supply.

http://www.bicn.com/acic
To learn more about the arsenic crisis in Bangladesh, visit this home page for the Arsenic Crisis Information Center.

http://www.eng2.uconn.edu/~nikos/asrt-brochure.html
A detailed description of the chemistry involved in the removal of arsenic using iron filings may be found at this site, which is maintained by Nikolaos P. Nikolaidis, one of the inventors of this technology.

Chapter 19

http://www.ada.org/topics/fluoride.html
Fluoride page of the American Dental Association, with many links to information regarding fluorides and fluoridation of drinking water and toothpastes.

http://www.google.com
Fluoride ions at concentrations of about 1 milligram per liter have proved most effective at preventing tooth decay. At greater concentrations, fluoride ions are toxic. A 10-gram dose of sodium fluoride, for example, is

enough to kill an adult. Use the Google search engine to explore the controversies of fluoride ions in our environment, using such phrases as fluoride ion and tooth decay and fluoride ion toxicity to do your search. As usual, keep in mind that the "loudest" voices on the internet are not necessarily the most accurate.

http://www.saltinstitute.org/idd.htm
Numerous reports in the literature demonstrate the effectiveness of iodized salt in controlling the medical condition called goiter. Check out this site for historical case studies that first pointed to this conclusion.

http://www.soils.wisc.edu/virtual_museum/
Home page of the Virtual Museum of Minerals and Molecules, curated by Phillip Barak of the University of Minnesota and Ed Nater of the University of Wisconsin. Through this site, you will find molecular models that you can manipulate in three dimensions. To do so, your browser will need to be equipped with the Chime plug-in, which you may download by following the hyperlink below.

http://www.mdli.com/download/chimedown.html

http://www.steelnet.org/index.html
Web site for the Steel Manufacturers Association.

Chapter 20

http://www.google.com
Use hard-water magnets as a Web-search keyword to find a large number of Web sites that advertise the use of magnetic fields to prevent calcium buildup in plumbing. The proposed mechanism is that the magnetic field facilitates the formation of calcium carbonate crystals in the water rather than on the pipes. But wait! Calcium ions are not attracted to magnets the way metallic iron is. Does this method really work? Beware and be critical. The Web is chock full of misinformation.

http://www.med.umich.edu/liquid/Research.html
Use perfluorocarbon as a Web-search keyword and you will find references, most of them technical, to a variety of medical and other uses for liquid perfluorocarbons. The site listed here is that of the Liquid Ventilation Program at the University of Michigan. Scroll to the bottom of the home page for a list of useful links.

http://www.sugar.org/
According to this site, the Sugar Association is proud to provide reliable, science-based information about pure, natural sugar. Reliance on sound science has positioned the association as a leader in communicating accurate information about the nutritional and functional uses of sugar to consumers, professionals, and the media.

Chapter 21

http://www.thecatalyst.org/wwwchem.html
This site has been developed as a resource for high-school chemistry teachers, but anyone studying chemistry should find the links helpful. You might follow the link to the history of chemistry, for example, to learn more about Amedeo Avogadro and that huge number named after him.

http://www.wxumac.demon.co.uk/
Nitrogen monoxide, also known as nitric oxide, NO, is a precursor to nitrate fertilizers and a common atmospheric pollutant, but it also plays a multitude of vital roles in our human biology. Use nitric oxide as a keyword in your internet search engine to find a plethora of Web sites devoted to the many roles this small but important molecule plays in our physiology and in diseases, such as Alzheimer's, Parkinson's, asthma, heart disease, and various infections.

http://www.secondlaw.com/

http://www.entropysimple.com/
Chemical reactions are favorable (will proceed on their own) only when they result in an increase in entropy. Recall, from Chapter 7, that entropy is a measure of the dispersal of energy. In general, the more energy is dispersed through a chemical reaction, the more favorable the chemical reaction. You can visit these two Web sites to learn more of the details of the connection between chemical reactions and entropy.

Chapter 22

http://www.nps.gov/cave/

http://www.carlsbad.caverns.national-park.com/info.htm

http://www.nps.gov/maca/

http://www.mammoth.cave.national-park.com/info.htm
Check these official and unofficial sites for Carlsbad Caverns National Park and Mammoth Cave National Park for details on how these underground landmarks formed. Ample travel information is included.

http://www.epa.gov/
Go to this home page for the Environmental Protection Agency and use acid rain as a keyword in the agency's search engine to find numerous articles on this subject.

http://mlso.hao.ucar.edu/cgi-bin/mlso_homepage.cgi
This address itemizes the atmospheric projects of the Climate Monitoring and Diagnostic Laboratory of the Mauna Loa Weather Observatory. Links to the Network for the Detection of Stratospheric Changes are included.

Chapter 23

http://www.aluminum.org/
The Web site of the Aluminum Association, Inc., where you will find basic facts about the aluminum industry, recycling efforts, and the impact of our aluminum use on the environment.

http://www.kodak.com/US/en/corp/aboutKodak/kodakHistory/kodakHistory.shtml
The Eastman Kodak Company was founded in the late 1800s, and it was the first company to offer easy-to-use

photography services to the general public. Explore this site for some of this history, and be sure to check out the link to "About Film and Imaging" to read about the chemistry and engineering required for the manufacture of photographic film.

http://www.internationalfuelcells.com/

http://www.fuelcellworld.org/

Use fuel cells as a search keyword and you will find a number of private companies and organizations, such as the two named here, that are dedicated to improving the efficiency of fuel cells and publicizing their use. Fuel cells are certainly a wave of the future.

Chapter 24

Atkins P. W. *Molecules*. New York: W. H. Freeman, 1987. An enchanting account of some of the more important organic molecules of nature, as well as those produced by chemists. Written for the general public, the dialogue is warm, intriguing, and accompanied by spectacular photographs.

http://www.icco.org/

The home page of the International Cocoa Organization. Through this site, you can find answers to many of the questions you may have regarding the chemistry of chocolate and its path from the cocoa tree to your mouth.

http://www.chevron.com/about/learning_center

Web address for the Learning Zone of the Chevron Texaco Corporation, where you can find information about crude oil and the refining process.

http://www.aw.com/chemplace

Visit The Chemistry Place to learn more about organic compounds.

Part 3

Chapter 25

http://www.usgs.gov/education/

Developed by the U.S. Geological Survey, this lively USGS Learning Web provides extensive information about land, water, plants, animals, and maps. Designed both for students and for teachers, it offers an exciting array of project ideas, homework help, lesson plans, and creative games. Includes downloadable images and "make your own" activities.

http://minerals.usgs.gov/

The Mineral Resources Program Home Page, sponsored by the U.S. Geological Survey. This site provides current, impartial information on the occurrence, quality, quantity, and availability of mineral resources. The site is text intensive, emphasizing research and statistics.

http://webmineral.com/

Winner of the "Rockhounds Informative Site Award," this web site provides an extensive mineralogy database. It contains classification charts and alphabetical reference listings. Check out the beautiful mineral picture gallery, which includes information about mineral origins and compositions.

http://edtech.kennesaw.edu/web/rocks.html

Sponsored by the Educational Technology Center at Kennesaw State University, in Kennesaw, Georgia, this site is an excellent source for both online and offline activities and lesson plans. It also provides links to research and informational sites.

Chapter 26

http://fi.edu/fellows/fellow1/oct98/create/index.html

Part of the Rock Hounds site sponsored by Loogootee Community Schools, in Loogootee, Indiana this page details how rocks are formed. Click back to the main page for more rock facts, along with some suggested teaching resources.

http://wrgis.wr.usgs.gov/docs/parks/rxmin/content.html

A cooperative endeavor of the U.S. Geological Survey's Western Earth Surface Processes Team and the National Park Service, this site provides extensive information about types of rocks. Includes pictures and descriptions, an easy classification chart and some information about minerals.

http://hvo.wr.usgs.gov/

Sponsored by the U.S. Geological Survey, this is the home page for the Hawaiian Volcano Observatory. Find out current information about Hawaii's active volcanoes, along with history of dormant volcanoes. The site also describes the hazards of volcanoes and earthquakes.

Chapter 27

Bolt, Bruce. *Earthquakes*, Revised Edition. New York: W. H. Freeman, 1993.

McPhee, John. *Assembling California*. New York: Farrar, Straus & Giroux, 1993.

Roadside Geology Series. [Many titles covering various parts of North America.] Missoula, Montana: Mountain Press.

Wenkam, Robert. *The Edge of Fire*. San Francisco: Sierra Club Books, 1987.

http://pubs.usgs.gov/publications/text/dynamic.html

Sponsored by the U.S. Geological Survey, "This Dynamic Earth" web page explains plate tectonics, volcanoes, and earthquakes clearly with drawings, maps, and photographs. A great resource for historical information and scientific theory.

http://scign.jpl.nasa.gov/learn/plate1.htm

This is a direct link to the "Structure of the Earth" section of The Southern California Integrated GPS Network Education Module home page. Provides an education module and activities for high-school and college undergraduate students. An interesting and interactive site, it also covers plate tectonics and earthquakes.

http://www.geology.sdsu.edu/visualgeology/geology101/FlashTec/tecintro.htm
This site, designed as a "do it yourself lab," is full of detailed information about the earth's structure and plate tectonics. Includes diagrams and interactive feedback.

http://www.tinynet.com/faults.html
This site describes four different types of faults. It also includes an extensive list of links to interesting geological sites, especially earthquake related sites.

http://earth.leeds.ac.uk/faults/
This link is a good resource for detailed information about the different types of faults. Includes a large picture gallery of various faults. Click the "learn structure" icon to browse additional sections of the site.

http://www.ucmp.berkeley.edu/geology/tectonics.html
This is a direct link to the Geology section of the UC Berkeley Museum of Paleontology web site. This site includes history and descriptions of plate tectonics, and an impressive selection of plate tectonic animations.

http://greenwood.cr.usgs.gov/pub/open-file-reports/ofr-99-0132/
Sponsored by the U.S. Department of the Interior and the U.S. Geological Survey, a good resource for detailed instructions on how to build a model of the outer layers of the Earth. The model can be used to develop a better understanding of the main features of plate tectonics.

Chapter 28

Austin, Mary. *The Land of Little Rain*. New York: Penguin Books, 1988.

Reisner, Mark. *Cadillac Desert*. New York: Penguin Books, 1993.

Reisner, Mark. *Overtapped Oasis*. Washington, D.C.: Island Press, 1990.

Worster, Donald. *Rivers of Empire*. New York: Oxford University Press, 1985.

http://www.groundwater.org/GWBasics/hydro.htm
Home page for the Groundwater Foundation. Full of resources about groundwater, the hydrologic cycle, conservation and water contamination protection. A great resource for programs and freebies.

http://www.epa.gov/kids/water.htm
Sponsored by the U.S. Environmental Protection Agency, this site covers the basics of water treatment and water pollution. Chock full of educational games, activities, and projects!

http://water.usgs.gov/education.html
Educational resource page full of links to excellent sites about water and the environment. Check out the "Water Science for Schools" section, which includes pictures, data, and map resources, along with an interactive center to test your water knowledge.

Chapter 29

Abbey, Edward. *Desert Solitaire*. New York: Ballantine Books, 1968.

Jackson, John Brinckerhoff. *A Sense of Place, A Sense of Time*. New Haven: Yale University Press, 1994.

Leopold, Aldo. *A Sand County Almanac*. New York: Penguin Books, 1988.

McPhee, John. *The Control of Nature*. New York: Farrar, Straus, & Giroux, 1989.

Stegner, Wallace. *Beyond the Hundredth Meridian*. New York: Penguin Books, 1992.

http://www.geocities.com/monte7dco/
This site is a good resource for learning characteristics of world landforms. Contains a descriptive picture glossary of landforms, along with an elementary-level lesson plan and links to additional plans.

http://www.cln.org/themes/glaciers.html
This site, sponsored by the Open Learning Agency, provides a list of links to sites about glaciers, with an emphasis on curricular activities.

http://www.wcc.nrcs.usda.gov/water/quality/common/erosion/erosiontools.html
This site provides links to computer simulation tools to help determine wind and water erosion rates.

http://www.enviroliteracy.org/article.php/244.html
Home page for the Environmental Literacy Council, this site is full of basic information about wind, water, erosion, ecosystems and climate. Text intensive with many resource links and suggestions.

http://spikesworld.spike-jamie.com/science/geology_website/
Need a geology project idea? Visit this site to find a vast number of project suggestions for all areas of geology.

Chapter 30

Gould, Stephen Jay, *Wonderful Life—The Burgess Shale and the Nature of History*. New York: Norton, 1989.

http://www.scotese.com/earth.htm
Winner of the Scientific American's Sci/Tech Web Award in two years running, this is the home page for the PALEOMAP Project. The Earth History section displays a series of full-color paleogeographic maps of past, present and future earth. Click back to the mail page for animations, resource suggestions for software and teaching tools.

http://seaborg.nmu.edu/earth/
An Earth History Resources web page designed for free educational information. Contains text descriptions of geologic time periods and graphic images designed for use in the development of either an on-line Internet or interactive multimedia project related to Earth History. Includes multiple timeline graphs.

http://www.ucmp.berkeley.edu/help/timeform.html
This is a direct link to the Geologic Time Machine page of the UC Berkeley Museum of Paleontology web site.

Provides an easy to use timeline, full of links to detailed descriptions and photographs.

http://www.enchantedlearning.com/subjects/Geologictime.html
Sponsored by Enchanted Learning.com, this page shows a geologic timeline, which includes links to more information about each period. Includes many links to UCBM page listed above.

http://wrgis.wr.usgs.gov/docs/usgsnps/pltec/pltec1.html
A cooperative endeavor of the U.S. Geological Survey Western Earth Surface Processes Team and the National Park Service, this site provides extensive information about plate tectonics and depicts the movement of earth's plates through time.

Chapter 31

http://www.noaa.gov/
The National Oceanic and Atmospheric Association home page is the place to find up to the minute information about climate and weather. Full of articles, satellite photographs, maps, and links, this site should not be missed!

http://www.ncar.ucar.edu/ncar/
Home page for the National Center for Atmospheric Research. From climate modeling to solar-earth interactions to weather prediction, this is an excellent resource for detailed information about climate and weather.

http://response.restoration.noaa.gov/kids/kids.html
If you need elementary-level project ideas to demonstrate the effects of oil spills and other environmental hazards, check out this site.

http://www.geo.nsf.gov/atm/atmkids.htm
This page contains an extensive list of climate and weather-related links. It is aimed primarily at the elementary level.

Chapter 32

http://www.nws.noaa.gov/
The National Weather Service home page provides detailed weather information and forecasts. View maps and pictures and discover historical weather trends. Check out the Education Page for great links to activities and teaching tools.

http://www1.accuweather.com/adcbin/index.asp?partner=accuweather
Get up-to-the-minute weather forecasts here on the Accuweather home page. Includes satellite pictures and interesting weather-related articles.

http://lwf.ncdc.noaa.gov/oa/ncdc.html
If you are looking for an active archive of worldwide weather data, check out this site. There is extensive information here, but the site requires multiple link clicks before you can access data.

http://wildwildweather.com/
This site, which is maintained by a local news meteorologist, is designed for school-age children. A great resource for weather information, games, and activities to capture kids' interest.

Chapter 33

Bronowski, Jacob. *The Ascent of Man*. Boston: Little, Brown. 1973.
This classic is still timely and inspirational.

Ferris, Timothy. *Seeing in the Dark: How Backyard Stargazers Are Probing Deep Space and Guarding Earth from Interplanetary Peril*. New York: Simon & Schuster, 2002.

Morton, Oliver. *Mapping Mars*. New York: Picador USA, 2002. Covers a lot of ground, beginning with the mapping of our planet next door.

Sagan, Carl. *Cosmos*. New York: Random House. 1980.
This historic classic still inspires a passion for understanding the universe.

Weiskopf, Victor. *Knowledge and Wonder: The Natural World as Man Knows It*. Cambridge, Mass: MIT Press, 1979.
Another classic and fascinating reading.

http://www.astro.uva.nl/demo/od95/
Earth's sun is a typical star, it's close, and it's well understood. Take a virtual tour of the sun via this short and engaging solar-science course with movies, diagrams, and first-rate images—and explanations.

http://solar-center.stanford.edu/
This award-winning solar site is a bright spot on the Web. For scientific background, go to About the Sun to link to information about solar physics. Solar Art and Solar Folklore will nicely round out your visit.

http://hubble.stsci.edu/steiner
How are planets created from the huge disks of dust and gas that surround young stars? Click on How to Tune In to step through a series of multimedia presentations that feature images from the Hubble Telescope, video, television, and radio.

http://cannon.sfsu.edu/~gmarcy/cswa/history/history.html
Women have played a "starring" role in astronomy through history, from early observers who catalogued the stars to modern astronauts and research scientists. Click on the names of significant women astronomers, read about their accomplishments, and learn something about their interesting lives. Wonderful archival photos!

http://www.solarviews.com/eng/history.htm
A vast site befitting a vast subject—the history of space exploration. Click on Contents and see an outline and huge array of topic choices. The image index helps you quickly access graphic.

http://sse.jpl.nasa.gov/features/planets/planetsfeat.html
Meteors, meteoroids, meteorites, comets, and much more.

Chaper 34

Comins, Neil F., Kaufmann, and William J. *Discovering the Universe, Sixth Edition.* New York: W. H. Freeman, 2003.
A good solid introductory college textbook, with *Starry Night* CD by Roger Freedman and William J. Kaufmann.

Hawking, Stephen W. *A Brief History of Time: From the Big Bang to Black Holes.* New York: Bantam Books, 1988.
A very popular bestseller.

Taylor, Edwin F., and Wheeler, John Archibald. *Exploring Black Holes.* San Francisco: Addison Wesley Longman, 2000.
All you want to know about black holes and more!

Taylor, Edwin F., and Wheeler, John Archibald. *Spacetime Physics.* New York: W. H. Freeman, 1966.
Wheeler, who coined the term black hole, nicely introduces the concept in this classic book.

Rigden, John. *Hydrogen: The Essential Element.* Cambridge, Mass: Harvard University Press, 2002.
This biography of hydrogen for the general reader is interesting reading, showing the kind and noble side of those who investigated this simplest element.

Weinberg, Steven. *The First Three Minutes: A Modern View of the Origins of the Universe.* New York: Basic Books, 1977.
A readable classic from an astrophysicist who won the Nobel Prize in physics in 1979.

http://www.astro.wisc.edu/~dolan/constellations/constellations.html
A great resource that explains what constellations are and why people have been watching them for more than 6000 years. The alphabetical list shows each constellation, describes its legends and lore, and gives the best viewing time.

http://www.pbs.org/wnet/hawking/html/home.html
Explore such topics as the Big Bang with scientist Stephen Hawking. Click on Universes for historical views of the Universe. Go to Cosmological Stars to meet the scientific superstars who developed present-day astronomy.

http://imagine.gsfc.nasa.gov/docs/homepage.html
Go to Imagine Science for topics ranging from supernovae to black holes. Enjoy clear explanations, great visual effects, and quizzes to test your understanding.

http://windows.ucar.edu/
Much information about stars, galaxies, and all things astronomical. Click on Enter the Site, then, from the main menu, select The Universe or Space Missions. You'll get an array of subtopics to research, many with animations and activities.

http://www.smv.org/hastings/student1.htm
Visit this "stellar" site to learn about galaxies. Step through the on-line lesson, take the quizzes, and follow the links to Galactic News and Activities.

http://oposite.stsci.edu/pubinfo/pictures.html
Beautiful images taken by the Hubble Telescope on its mission of discovery. Animations show stellar fireworks from galactic collisions and other spectacular events.

http://www2.astrobiology.com/astro/how.to.html
How are the building blocks of life formed on earth and elsewhere in the universe, and how do the elements come together to create life? Astrobiologists combine life science with space science to address such questions about the astrobiology web.

http://xml.gsfc.nasa.gov/archive/KeywordIndexG.html#Galaxies%2C

http://nedwww.ipac.caltech.edu/level5/Gallagher/Gall2_2.html
Stars in all galaxies orbit their centers.

Chapter 35

Bodanis, David. $E = mc^2$: *A Biography of the World's Most Famous Equation.* New York: Berkeley Publishing Group, 2000.
A fascinating can't-put-it-down book.

Einstein, Albert. *The Meaning of Relativity.* Princeton, N.J.: Princeton University Press, 1950.
Written for the average person by Einstein himself.

Epstein, Lewis C. *Relativity Visualized.* San Francisco: Insight Press, 1983.
Quite understandable and cleverly written.

Gamow, George. *Mr. Tompkins in Wonderland.* New York: Macmillan, 1940.
An excellent and very interesting little book.

Gardner, Martin. *The Relativity Explosion.* New York: Vintage Books, 1976.

Hewitt, Paul G. *Conceptual Physics,* 9th ed. San Francisco: Addison Wesley Longman, 2002.
For expanded coverage of both special and general relativity.

Hoffmann, Banesh. *Albert Einstein, Creator and Rebel.* New York: Viking, 1972.
Written by a man who knew Einstein as a personal friend.

Scheider, Walter. *A Serious but Not Ponderous Book about Relativity.* Ann Arbor, Mich.: Cavendish Press, 2000.
An award-winning book that is rigorous but readable (www.cavendishscience.org).

Glossary

Aberrations Limitations on the formation of perfect images, which are inherent, to some degree, in all optical systems.

Ablation The amount of ice lost, and the process of losing ice, from a glacier.

Absolute zero The theoretical temperature at which a substance possesses no thermal heat and the temperature at which particles of a substance have their minimum kinetic energy.

Acceleration The rate at which velocity changes with time; the change in velocity may be in magnitude, or in direction, or in both. It is usually measured in m/s^2.

Accumulation The amount of snow added, and the process of adding snow, to a glacier.

Acid A substance that donates hydrogen ions.

Acidic solution A solution in which the hydronium-ion concentration is higher than the hydroxide-ion concentration.

Activation energy The minimum energy required in order for a chemical reaction to proceed.

Addition polymer A polymer formed by the joining together of monomer units with no atoms being lost as the polymer forms.

Additive primary colors The three colors—red, blue, and green—that, when added in certain proportions, will produce any color in the spectrum.

Air resistance The force of friction acting on an object due to its motion through air.

Alcohol An organic molecule that contains a hydroxyl group bonded to a saturated carbon.

Aldehyde An organic molecule containing a carbonyl group, the carbon of which is bonded either to one carbon atom and one hydrogen atom or to two hydrogen atoms.

Alpha particle The nucleus of a helium atom, which consists of two neutrons and two protons, ejected by certain radioactive elements.

Alternating current (AC) Electric current that repeatedly reverses its direction; the electric charges vibrate about relatively fixed points. In the United States, the vibrational rate is 60 Hz.

Amide An organic molecule containing a carbonyl group, the carbon of which is bonded to a nitrogen atom.

Amine An organic molecule containing a nitrogen atom bonded to one or more saturated carbon atoms.

Amphoteric A description of a substance that can behave either as an acid or as a base.

Amplitude For a wave or vibration, the maximum displacement on either side of the equilibrium (midpoint) position.

Angular unconformity An unconformity in which older, tilted strata are overlain by younger, horizontal beds.

Anode The electrode where oxidation occurs.

Anticline A fold in strata that has relatively old rocks at its core, with rock age decreasing with increasing horizontal distance from the fold core.

Applied research A branch of scientific research that focuses on developing applications built upon the principles discovered through basic research.

Archimedes' principle An immersed body is buoyed up by a force equal to the weight of the fluid it displaces.

Aromatic compound Any organic molecule containing a benzene ring.

Artesian system A system in which confined groundwater under pressure can rise above the level of an aquifer.

Asteroid A small rocky planet-like fragment that orbits the sun. Tens of thousands of these objects make up an asteroid belt between the orbits of Mars and Jupiter.

Asthenosphere A subdivision of the upper mantle situated below the lithosphere, a zone of plastic, easily deformed rock.

Atmospheric pressure The pressure exerted against bodies immersed in the atmosphere resulting from the weight of air pressing down from above. At sea level, atmospheric pressure is about 101 kPa.

Atom The smallest particle of an element that has all of the element's chemical properties.

Atomic mass The mass of an element's atoms listed in the periodic table as an average value based on the relative abundance of the element's isotopes.

Atomic mass unit (amu) The standard unit of atomic mass, which is equal to one-twelfth the mass of the common atom of carbon, arbitrarily given the value of exactly 12.

Atomic nucleus The core of an atom, consisting of two basic subatomic particles—protons and neutrons.

Atomic number The number that designates the identity of an element, which is the number of protons in the nucleus of an atom; in a neutral atom, the atomic number is also the number of electrons in the atom.

Atomic orbital A region of space in which an electron in an atom has a 90 percent chance of being located.

Atomic spectrum The pattern of frequencies of electromagnetic radiation emitted by the atoms of an element, considered to be the element's "fingerprint."

Atomic symbol An abbreviation for an element or atom.

Avogadro's number The number of particles—6.02×10^{23}—contained in 1 mole of anything.

Barometer Any device that measures atmospheric pressure.

Base A substance that accepts hydrogen ions.

Basic research A branch of scientific research that focuses on a greater understanding of how the natural world operates.

Basic solution A solution in which the hydroxide-ion concentration is higher than the hydronium-ion concentration.

Beats A series of alternate reinforcements and cancellations produced by the interference of two waves of slightly different frequency, heard as a throbbing effect in sound waves.

Bernoulli's principle The pressure in a fluid moving steadily, without friction or an input of outside energy; decreases when the fluid velocity increases.

Beta particle An electron (or positron) emitted during the radioactive decay of certain nuclei.

Big Bang The primordial explosion of space at the beginning of time.

Binary star Pairs of stars that orbit about a common center of mass.

Black hole The remains of a giant star that has collapsed upon itself, so dense and gravitational field so intense that light itself cannot escape.

Black hole singularity The object of zero radius into which the matter of a black hole is comprised.

Body wave A seismic wave that travels through the earth's interior.

Boiling A rapid state of evaporation that takes place within the liquid as well as at its surface. As with evaporation, cooling of the liquid results.

Bond energy The amount of energy that is either absorbed as a chemical bond breaks or is released as a chemical bond forms.

Bow wave The V-shaped wave made by an object moving across a liquid surface at a speed greater than the wave speed.

Boyle's law The product of pressure and volume is a constant for a given mass of confined gas regardless of changes either in pressure or in volume individually, so long as temperature remains unchanged:

$$P_1V_1 = P_2V_2$$

Buffer solution A solution that resists large changes in pH, made either from a weak acid and one of its salts or from a weak base and one of its salts.

Buoyant force The net upward force that a fluid exerts on an immersed object.

Carbonyl group A carbon atom double-bonded to an oxygen atom; found in ketones, aldehydes, amides, carboxylic acids, and esters.

Carboxylic acid An organic molecule containing a carbonyl group, the carbon of which is bonded to a hydroxyl group.

Catalyst Any substance that increases the rate of a chemical reaction without itself being consumed by the reaction.

Cathode The electrode where reduction occurs.

Cavern A large cave.

Cenozoic era The time of recent life, from 65 million years ago to the present.

Chain reaction A self-sustaining reaction in which the products of one reaction event stimulate further reaction events.

Chemical bond The force of attraction between two atoms that holds them together.

Chemical change A change in which the atoms of one or more substances are rearranged into one or more new substances.

Chemical equation A representation of a chemical reaction in which reactants are drawn before an arrow that points to the products.

Chemical formula A notation used to indicate the composition of a compound, consisting of the atomic symbols for the different elements of the compound and numerical subscripts indicating the ratio in which the atoms combine.

Chemical property A property that characterizes the ability of a substance to undergo a change that transforms it into a different substance.

Chemical reaction Synonymous with chemical change.

Chemical sediments Formed by the precipitation of minerals from water on the earth's surface.

Chemical weathering The breakdown of rocks on the earth's surface by chemical means.

Cleavage The tendency of a mineral to break along planes of weakness.

Clouds The condensation of water droplets above the earth's surface.

Combustion An exothermic oxidation–reduction reaction between a nonmetallic material and molecular oxygen.

Comet A body composed of ice and dust that orbits the sun, usually in a very eccentric orbit, and which casts a luminous tail produced by solar radiation pressure when it is close to the sun.

Complementary colors Any two colors that, when added, will produce white light.

Compound A material in which atoms of different elements are bonded to one another.

Compression Condensed region of the medium through which a longitudinal wave travels.

Concentration A quantitative measure of the amount of solute in a solution.

Conceptual model A representation of a system that helps in making predictions about how the system behaves.

Condensation The change of phase from gas to liquid; the opposite of evaporation. Warming of the liquid results.

Condensation polymer A polymer formed by the joining together of monomer units accompanied by the loss of small molecules, such as water.

Conduction The transfer of thermal energy by molecular and electronic collisions within a substance (especially a solid).

Conductor Any material having free charged particles that easily flow through it when an electric force acts on them.

Conformation One of the possible spatial orientations of a molecule.

Conservation of energy In the absence of external work input or output, the energy of a system remains unchanged. Energy cannot be created or destroyed.

Conservation of energy and machines The work output of any machine cannot exceed the work input. In an ideal machine, where no energy is transformed into heat:

$$\text{work}_{\text{input}} = \text{work}_{\text{output}} \text{ and}$$
$$(Fd)_{\text{input}} = (Fd)_{\text{output}}$$

Conservation of momentum In the absence of an external force, the momentum of a system remains unchanged. Hence, the momentum before an event involving only internal forces is equal to the momentum after the event:

$$mv_{(\text{before event})} = mv_{(\text{after event})}$$

Continental margin The boundary between continental land and deep ocean basins, consisting of continental shelf, continental slope, and continental rise.

Convection The transfer of thermal energy in a gas or liquid by means of currents in the heated fluid. The fluid flows, carrying energy with it.

Convectional lifting An air-circulation pattern in which air warmed by the ground rises while cooler air aloft sinks.

Converging lens A lens that is thicker in the middle than at the edges and that refracts parallel rays passing through it to a focus.

Core The central layer in the earth's interior, divided into an outer liquid core and an inner solid core.

Coriolis effect The apparent deflection from a straight-line path observed in any body moving near the earth's surface, caused by the earth's rotation.

Corrosion The deterioration of a metal, typically caused by atmospheric oxygen

Coulomb The SI unit of electrical charge. One coulomb (symbol C) is equal in magnitude to the total charge of 6.25×10^{18} electrons.

Coulomb's law The relationship among electrical force, charge, and distance. If the charges are alike in sign, the force is repelling; if the charges are unlike, the force is attractive:

$$F = k\frac{q_1 q_2}{d^2}$$

Covalent bond A chemical bond in which atoms are held together by their mutual attraction for two or more electrons they share.

Covalent compound An element or chemical compound in which atoms are held together by covalent bonds.

Critical angle The minimum angle of incidence inside a medium at which a light ray is totally reflected.

Critical mass The minimum mass of fissionable material in a reactor or nuclear bomb that will sustain a chain reaction.

Cross-cutting A relative dating principle stating that, where an igneous intrusion or fault cuts through other rocks, the intrusion or fault is younger than the rock it cuts.

Crust The earth's outermost layer.

Crystal form The outward expression of the orderly internal arrangement of atoms in a crystal.

Crystallization The growth of a solid from a material whose constituent atoms can come together in the proper chemical proportions and geometric arrangements.

Cut bank A steep bank on the outside bend of a river's channel. An area of erosion.

Delta An accumulation of sediments, commonly forming a triangular or fan-shaped plain, deposited where a stream flows into a body of water.

Density The amount of matter per unit volume. *Weight density* is expressed as weight per unit volume:

$$\text{Density} = \frac{\text{mass}}{\text{volume}}$$

Diffraction The bending of light that passes around an obstacle or through a narrow slit, causing the light to spread and to produce light and dark fringes.

Dipole A separation of charge that occurs in a chemical bond because of differences in the electronegativities of the bonded atoms.

Direct current (DC) An electric current flowing in one direction only.

Discharge The volume of water that passes a given location in a stream channel in a certain amount of time.

Dissolving The process of mixing a solute in a solvent to produce a homogeneous mixture.

Distillation A purifying process in which a vaporized substance is collected by exposing it to cooler temperatures over a receiving flask, which collects the condensed purified liquid.

Diverging lens A lens that is thinner in the middle than at the edges, causing parallel rays passing through it to diverge as if from a point.

Doppler effect The change in frequency of wave motion resulting from motion of the sender or the receiver.

Drift A general term for glacial deposits.

Efficiency The percentage of the work put into a machine that is converted into useful work output. (More generally, efficiency is useful energy output divided by total energy input.)

Elastic collision A collision in which colliding objects rebound without lasting deformation or the generation of heat.

Electric current The flow of electric charge that transports energy from one place to another. It is measured in amperes, where 1 A is the flow of 6.25×10^{18} electrons per second, or 1 coulomb per second.

Electric field Defined as force per unit charge, it can be considered to be an energetic "aura" surrounding charged objects. About a charged point, the field decreases with distance according to the inverse-square law, like a gravitational field. Between oppositely charged parallel plates, the electric field is uniform.

Electric potential The electric potential energy per amount of charge, measured in volts, and often called *voltage:*

$$\text{Voltage} = \frac{\text{electric energy}}{\text{amount of charge}}$$

Electric potential energy The energy a charge possesses by virtue of its location in an electric field.

Electric power The rate of energy transfer, or the rate of doing work; the amount of energy per unit time, which can be measured by the product of current and voltage:

$$\text{Power} = \text{current} \times \text{voltage}$$

It is measured in watts (or kilowatts), where $1\text{ A} \times 1\text{ V} = 1\text{ W}$.

Electrical resistance The property of a material that resists the flow of an electric current through it. It is measured in ohms (V).

Electrically polarized Term applied to an atom or molecule in which the charges are aligned so that one side has a slight excess of positive charge and the other side a slight excess of negative charge.

Electrochemistry The branch of chemistry concerned with the relationship between electrical energy and chemical change.

Electrode Any material that conducts electrons into or out of a medium in which electrochemical reactions are occurring.

Electrolysis The use of electrical energy to produce chemical change.

Electromagnet A magnet whose field is produced by an electric current. It is usually in the form of a wire coil with a piece of iron inside the coil.

Electromagnetic induction The induction of voltage when a magnetic field changes with time. If the magnetic field within a closed loop changes in any way, a voltage is induced in the loop. This is a statement of Faraday's law. (The induction of voltage is actually the result of a more fundamental phenomenon: the induction of an electric *field,* as defined in Maxwell's counterpart to Faraday's law.)

Electromagnetic spectrum The range of electromagnetic waves that extends in frequency from radio waves to gamma rays.

Electromagnetic wave An energy-carrying wave emitted by vibrating electrical charges (often electrons) and composed of oscillating electric and magnetic fields that regenerate one another.

Electron A negatively charged particle in an atom.

Electron-dot structure A shorthand notation of the shell model of the atom in which valence electrons are shown around an atomic symbol.

Electronegativity The ability of an atom to attract a bonding pair of electrons to itself when bonded to another atom.

Electrostatics The study of electric charge at rest (not *in motion,* as in electric currents).

Element Any material that is made up of only one type of atom.

Elemental formula A notation that uses the atomic symbol and (sometimes) a numerical subscript to denote how atoms of the element are bonded together.

Ellipse The oval path followed by a satellite. The sum of the distances from any point on the path to two points called foci is a constant. When the foci are together at one point, the ellipse is a circle. As the foci get farther apart, the ellipse gets more "eccentric."

Elliptical galaxy A galaxy that is round or elliptical in outline. It has little gas and dust, no disk or spiral arms, and few hot and bright stars.

Endothermic A term that describes a chemical reaction in which there is a net absorption of energy.

Energy The property of a system that enables it to do work.

Entropy The measure of energy dispersal of a system. Whenever energy freely transforms from one form to another, the direction of transformation is toward a state of greater disorder and, therefore, toward one of greater entropy.

Equilibrium rule The vector sum of forces acting on a nonaccelerating object equals zero: $\Sigma F = 0$.

Erosion The wearing away of rocks, and the processes by which rock particles are transported by water, wind, or ice.

Escape speed The speed that a projectile, a space probe, or a similar object must reach in order to escape the gravitational influence of the earth or of another celestial body to which it is attracted.

Ester An organic molecule containing a carbonyl group, the carbon of which is bonded to one carbon atom and one oxygen atom bonded to another carbon atom.

Ether An organic molecule containing an oxygen atom bonded to two carbon atoms.

Evaporation The change of phase at the surface of a liquid as it passes to the gaseous phase.

Event horizon The boundary region of a black hole from which no radiation may escape. Any events within the event horizon are invisible to distant observers.

Exosphere The fifth atmospheric layer above the earth's surface, extending from the thermosphere upward and out into interplanetary space.

Exothermic A term that describes a chemical reaction in which there is a net release of energy.

Extrusive rocks Igneous rocks that form at the earth's surface.

Fact A phenomenon about which competent observers can agree.

Faraday's law An electric field is induced in any region of space in which a magnetic field is changing with time. The magnitude of the induced electric field is proportional to the rate at which the magnetic field changes. The direction of the induced field is at right angles to the changing magnetic field.

Fault A fracture along which visible displacement can be detected on one side relative to the other.

Faunal succession A relative dating principle stating that fossil organisms succeed one another in a definite, irreversible, determinable order.

First law of thermodynamics A restatement of the law of energy conservation, usually as it applies to systems involving changes in temperature: Whenever heat flows into or out of a system, the gain or loss of thermal energy equals the amount of heat transferred.

Floodplain A wide plain of almost flat land on either side of a stream channel. Submerged during flood stage, the plain is built up by sediments deposited during floods.

Fold A series of ripples in the crust that result from compressional deformation of the lithosphere.

Force Simply stated, a push or a pull.

Force pair The action-and-reaction pair of forces that constitute an interaction.

Force vector An arrow drawn to scale so that its length represents the magnitude of a force and its direction represents the direction of the force.

Forced vibration The setting up of vibrations in an object by a vibrating force.

Formula mass The sum of the atomic masses of the atoms in a chemical compound or element.

Fracture A break that does not occur along a plane of weakness.

Frame of reference A vantage point (usually a set of coordinate axes) with respect to which position and motion may be described.

Free fall Motion under the influence of gravitational pull only.

Freezing The process of changing state from liquid to solid, as from water to ice.

Frequency For a vibrating body or medium, the number of vibrations per unit time. For a wave, the number of crests that pass a particular point per unit time.

Friction The resistive force that opposes the motion or attempted motion of an object through a fluid or past another object with which it is in contact.

Front The contact zone between two different air masses.

Frontal lifting The lifting that occurs as two air masses converge.

Full moon The phase of the moon when its sunlit side is the side facing earth.

Functional group A specific combination of atoms that behaves as a unit in an organic molecule.

Fundamental frequency The lowest frequency of vibration, or the first harmonic. In a string, the vibration makes a single segment.

Galaxy cluster Pertains to a group of more than one galaxy.

Galaxy super cluster A group of an enormous number of galaxies.

Gamma ray High-frequency electromagnetic radiation emitted by the nuclei of radioactive atoms.

General theory of relativity The second of Einstein's theories of relativity, which discusses the effects of gravity on space and time.

Generator An electromagnetic induction device that produces electric current by rotating a coil within a stationary magnetic field.

Geodesic The shortest distance between two points in various models of space.

Glacier A large mass of ice, formed by the compaction and recrystallization of snow, that moves down slope under its own weight.

Gravitational red shift The lengthening of the waves of electromagnetic radiation due to escape from a gravitational field.

Gravitational wave The transport of energy by the motion of waves in a gravitational field.

Greenhouse effect Warming caused by short-wavelength radiant energy from the sun that easily enters the atmosphere and is absorbed by the earth. This energy is then reradiated at longer wavelengths that cannot easily escape the earth's atmosphere.

Groundwater Subsurface water in the saturated zone.

Group A vertical column in the periodic table, also known as a family of elements.

Gyre Circular or spiral whirl pattern, usually referring to very large current systems in the open ocean.

Half-life The time required for half the atoms in a sample of a radioactive isotope to decay.

Half reaction One portion of an oxidation–reduction reaction, represented by an equation showing electrons as either reactants or products.

Hang time The time that one's feet are off the ground during a vertical jump.

Hard water Water containing large amounts of calcium and magnesium ions.

Harmonic A partial tone that is an integer multiple of the fundamental frequency. The vibration that begins with the fundamental vibrating frequency is the first harmonic, twice the fundamental is the second harmonic, and so on in sequence.

Heat The thermal energy that flows from a substance of higher temperature to a substance of lower temperature, commonly measured in calories or joules.

Heat of fusion The amount of energy needed to change any substance from solid to liquid (and vice versa). For water, this is 334 J/g (or 80 cal/g).

Heat of vaporization The amount of energy required to change any substance from liquid to gas (and vice versa). For water, this is 2256 J/g (or 540 cal/g).

Hertz The SI unit of frequency. One hertz (symbol Hz) equals one vibration per second.

Heteroatom Any atom other than carbon or hydrogen in an organic molecule.

Heterogeneous mixture A mixture in which the various components can be seen as individual substances.

Homogeneous mixture A mixture in which the components are so finely mixed that the composition is the same throughout.

H-R diagram (Hertz sprung-Russell diagram) A plot of intrinsic brightness versus surface temperature of stars. When so plotted, stars' positions take the form of a main sequence for average stars, with exotic stars above or below the main sequence.

Humidity A measure of the amount of water vapor in the air.

Hydraulic conductivity The ability of a material to transmit water.

Hydrocarbon A chemical compound containing only carbon and hydrogen atoms.

Hydrogen bond A strong dipole–dipole attraction between a slightly positive hydrogen atom on one molecule and a pair of nonbonding electrons on another molecule.

Hydrologic cycle The natural circulation of water from ocean, to atmosphere, to land, and back to ocean.

Hydronium ion A water molecule after accepting a hydrogen ion.

Hydroxide ion A water molecule after losing a hydrogen ion.

Hypothesis An educated guess or reasonable explanation. When the hypothesis makes a prediction that can be tested by experiment, it qualifies as a scientific hypothesis.

Igneous rocks Rocks formed by the cooling and crystallization of hot, molten rock material called magma.

Impulse The product of the force acting on an object and the time during which it acts.

Impure In chemistry, this term refers to a material that is a mixture of more than one element or compound.

Inclusions A relative dating principle stating that any inclusion (a piece of one rock type contained within another) is older than the rock containing it.

Induced dipole A dipole temporarily created in an otherwise nonpolar molecule, induced by a neighboring charge.

Inelastic collision A collision in which the colliding objects become distorted, generate heat, and possibly stick together.

Inertia The property of things to resist changes in motion.

Infrasonic Describes a sound of a frequency too low to be heard by the normal human ear—below 20 hertz.

Insoluble Not capable of dissolving to any appreciable extent in a given solvent.

Insulator Any material without free charged particles and through which current does not easily flow.

Interaction Mutual action between objects in which each one exerts an equal and opposite force on the other.

Interference The result of superposing different waves of the same wavelength. Constructive interference results from crest-to-crest reinforcement; destructive interference results from crest-to-trough cancellation. The interference of selected wavelengths of light produces colors known as *interference colors.*

Interference pattern The pattern formed by superposition of different sets of waves, which produces mutual reinforcement in some places and cancellation in others.

Intrusive rocks Igneous rocks that crystallize below the earth's surface.

Inverse-square law A law relating the intensity of an effect to the inverse square of the distance from the cause. Gravity follows an inverse-square law, as do the effects of electric, magnetic, light, sound, and radiation phenomena:

$$\text{Intensity} \sim \frac{1}{\text{distance}^2}$$

Ion An electrically charged particle created when an atom either loses or gains one or more electrons.

Ionic bond A chemical bond in which an attractive electric force holds ions of opposite charge together.

Ionic compound Any chemical compound containing ions.

Ionosphere An electrified region within the thermosphere and uppermost mesosphere where fairly large concentrations of ions and free electrons exist.

Irregular Galaxy A galaxy with a chaotic appearance and with large clouds of gas and dust, but without spiral arms.

Isotopes Different forms of an element whose atoms contain the same number of protons but different numbers of neutrons.

Ketone An organic molecule containing a carbonyl group, the carbon of which is bonded to two carbon atoms.

Kilogram The unit of mass. One kilogram (symbol kg) is the mass of 1 liter (L) of water at 4°C.

Kinetic energy Energy of motion, described by the relationship:

$$\text{Kinetic energy} = 1/2\ mv^2$$

Kuiper Belt The disk-shaped region of the sky beyond Neptune populated by many icy bodies, and a source of short-period comets.

Laminar flow Water flowing smoothly and steadily with no mixing of sediment.

Lava Magma, once it has reached the earth's surface.

Law A general hypothesis or statement about the relationship of natural quantities that has been tested over and over again and has not been contradicted. Also known as a *principle*.

Law of mass conservation Matter is neither created nor destroyed during a chemical reaction—atoms merely rearrange, without any apparent loss or gain of mass, to form new molecules.

Law of reflection The angle of incidence equals the angle of reflection. The incident and reflected rays lie in a plane that is normal to the reflecting surface.

Law of universal gravitation Every mass in the universe attracts every other mass with a force that for two masses is directly proportional to the product of their masses and inversely proportional to the square of the distance separating them:

$$F = G\frac{m_1 m_2}{d^2}$$

Leachate A solution formed by water that has percolated through soil containing water-soluble substances.

Length Contraction The contraction of objects in their direction of motion as a result of speed.

Lithosphere The entire crust plus the portion of the mantle above the asthenosphere.

Longitudinal wave A wave in which the medium vibrates in a direction parallel (longitudinal) with the direction in which the wave travels. Sound consists of longitudinal waves.

Lunar eclipse The phenomenon whereby the shadow of the earth falls upon the moon producing relative darkness of the full moon.

Magma Molten rock in the earth's interior.

Magnetic domains Clustered regions of aligned magnetic atoms. When these regions themselves are aligned with one another, the substance containing them is a magnet.

Magnetic field The region of magnetic influence around a magnetic pole or a moving charged particle.

Magnetic force (1) Between magnets, it is the attraction of unlike magnetic poles for each other and the repulsion between like magnetic poles. (2) Between a magnetic field and a moving charge, it is a deflecting force due to the motion of the charge: the deflecting force is perpendicular to the velocity of the charge and perpendicular to the magnetic field lines. This force is greatest when the charge moves perpendicular to the field lines and is smallest (zero) when it moves parallel to the field lines.

Mantle The middle layer in the earth's interior, between the crust and the core.

Mass The quantity of matter in an object. More specifically, it is the measure of the inertia or sluggishness that an object exhibits in response to any effort made to start it, stop it, deflect it, or change its state of motion in any way.

Mass-energy equivalence The relationship between mass and energy as given by the equation $E = mc^2$.

Mass number The total number of nucleons in an atomic nucleus.

Maxwell's counterpart to Faraday's law A magnetic field is induced in any region of space in which an electric field is changing with time. The magnitude of the induced magnetic field is proportional to the rate at which the electric field changes. The direction of the induced magnetic field is at right angles to the changing electric field.

Mechanical deformation Metamorphism caused by stress, such as increased pressure.

Mechanical weathering The breakdown of rocks on the earth's surface by physical means.

Mesosphere The third atmospheric layer above the earth's surface, extending from the top of the stratosphere to 80 km.

Mesozoic era The time of middle life, from 245 million years ago to about 65 million years ago.

Metamorphic rocks Rocks formed from preexisting rocks that have been changed or transformed by high temperature, high pressure, or both.

Metamorphism The changing of one kind of rock into another kind as a result of high temperature, high pressure, or both.

Meteor The streak of light produced by a meteoroid burning in the earth's atmosphere; a "shooting star."

Meteorite A meteoroid or part of a meteoroid that has survived passage through the earth's atmosphere to reach the ground.

Meteoroid A small rock in interplanetary space.

Milky Way The name of the galaxy to which we belong. Our cosmic home.

Mineral A naturally formed, inorganic solid composed of an ordered array of atoms chemically bonded to form a particular crystalline structure.

Mixture A combination of two or more substances in which each substance retains its properties.

Mohorovičić discontinuity (Moho) The crust-mantle boundary, marking the depth at which the speed of P-waves traveling toward the earth's center increases.

Mohs scale of hardness A ranking of the hardness of minerals.

Molarity A unit of concentration equal to the number of moles of a solute per liter of solution.

Molar mass The mass of 1 mole of a substance.

Mole The amount of any pure substance that contains as many atoms, molecules, ions, or other elementary units as the number of atoms in 12 grams of carbon-12. This is equal to 6.02×10^{23} particles.

Molecule A submicroscopic particle consisting of a group of atoms. Also, a group of atoms held tightly together by covalent bonds.

Momentum The product of the mass of an object and its velocity.

Monomers The small molecular units from which a polymer is formed.

Moon phases The cycles of change of the face of the moon, changing from new to waxing, to full, to waning, and back to new.

Natural frequency A frequency at which an elastic object naturally tends to vibrate, so that minimum energy is required to produce a forced vibration or to continue vibration at that frequency.

Neap tide A tide that occurs when the moon is midway between new and full, in either direction. Tides due to the sun and moon partly cancel, making the high tides lower than average and the low tides higher than average.

Net force The combination of all forces that act on an object.

Neutral solution A solution in which the hydronium-ion concentration is equal to the hydroxide-ion concentration.

Neutralization A reaction in which an acid and base combine to form a salt.

Neutron An electrically neutral subatomic particle in an atomic nucleus.

Neutron star A small, highly dense star composed of tightly packed neutrons formed by the welding of protons and electrons.

New moon The phase of the moon when darkness covers the side facing earth.

Newton The scientific unit of force.

Newton's first law of motion Every object continues in a state of rest, or in a state of motion in a straight line at a constant speed, unless it is compelled to change that state by forces exerted upon it.

Newton's law of cooling The rate of loss of thermal energy from an object is proportional to the temperature difference between the object and its surroundings.

Newton's second law of motion The acceleration produced by a net force on an object is directly proportional to the net force, is in the same direction as the net force, and is inversely proportional to the mass of the object.

Newton's third law of motion Whenever one object exerts a force on a second object, the second object exerts an equal and opposite force on the first object.

Nonbonding pairs Two paired valence electrons that tend not to participate in a chemical bond.

Nonpolar Said of a chemical bond that has no dipole.

Nova An event wherein a white dwarf suddenly brightens and appears as a "new" star.

Nuclear fission The splitting of the nucleus of a heavy atom, such as uranium-235, into two main parts, accompanied by the release of much energy.

Nuclear fusion The combining of nuclei of light atoms to form heavier nuclei, with the release of much energy.

Nucleon A nuclear particle; a proton or a neutron in an atomic nucleus.

Ohm's law The statement that the current in a circuit varies in direct proportion to the potential difference or voltage and inversely with the resistance. A potential difference of 1 Ω across a resistance of 1 Ω produces a current of 1 A:

$$\text{Current} = \frac{\text{voltage}}{\text{resistance}}$$

Oort Cloud The region beyond the Kuiper Belt populated by trillions of icy bodies, and a source of long-period comets.

Ore A mineral deposit containing valuable metals that can be economically extracted from the ground to yield a profit.

Organic chemistry The study of carbon-containing compounds.

Original horizontality A relative dating principle stating that layers of sediment are deposited evenly, with each new layer laid down almost horizontally over the older sediment.

Orographic lifting The lifting of an air mass over a topographic barrier such as a mountain.

Osmosis The diffusion of a water or some other fluid through a semipermeable membrane, from a solution with a low concentration of solutes to a solution with a higher concentration of solutes.

Oxidation The process whereby a reactant loses one or more electrons.

Paleomagnetism The study of natural magnetization in a rock to determine the intensity and direction of the earth's magnetic field at the time of the rock's formation.

Paleozoic era The time of ancient life, from 544 million years ago to 245 million years ago.

Pangaea A single, large landmass that existed in the geologic past and was composed of all the present-day continents.

Parabola The curved path followed by a projectile near the earth under the influence of gravity only.

Parallel circuit An electric circuit with two or more devices connected in such a way that the same voltage acts across each one, and any single one completes the circuit independently of all the others.

Partial melting The incomplete melting of rocks, resulting in magmas of different compositions.

Partial tone One of the frequencies present in a complex tone. When a partial tone is an integer multiple of the lowest frequency, it is a harmonic.

Period The time required for a vibration or a wave to make a complete cycle; equal to 1/frequency.

Period A horizontal row in the periodic table.

Periodic table A chart in which all known elements are listed in order of atomic number.

pH A measure of the acidity of a solution, equal to the negative of the base-10 logarithm of the hydronium-ion concentration.

Phenol An organic molecule in which a hydroxyl group is bonded to a benzene ring.

Photoelectric effect The emission of electrons from a metal surface when light shines on it.

Physical change A change in which a substance changes one or more of its physical properties without transforming it into a new substance.

Physical model A representation of an object on some convenient scale.

Physical property Any physical attribute of a substance, such as color, density, or hardness.

Planets The major bodies orbiting the sun, massive enough for their gravity to make them spherical, but small enough to avoid nuclear fusion in their cores.

Planetary nebula An expanding shell of gas ejected from a low-mass star during the latter stages of its evolution.

Pluton A very large intrusive body formed below the earth's surface.

Point bar A sandy, gentle bank on the inside bend of a river's channel. An area of deposition.

Polar Said of a chemical bond that has a dipole.

Polarization The alignment of the transverse electric vectors that make up electromagnetic radiation. Such waves of aligned vibrations are said to be *polarized.*

Polyatomic ion An ionically charged molecule.

Polymer A long, organic molecule made of many repeating units.

Polymorphs Two or more minerals that contain the same elements in the same proportions but have different crystal structures.

Porosity The volume of open space in rock or sediment compared with the total volume of solids plus open space.

Postulates of the special theory of relativity (1) All laws of nature are the same in all uniformly moving frames of reference. (2) The speed of light in free space has the same measured value regardless of the motion of the source or the motion of the observer; that is, the speed of light is a constant.

Potential difference The difference in potential between two points, measured in volts, and often called *voltage difference.*

Potential energy The stored energy that a body possesses because of its position.

Power The time rate of work.

Precambrian time The time of hidden life, which began about 4.5 billion years ago when the earth formed, lasted until about 544 million years ago (the beginning of the Paleozoic era), and which makes up 85 percent of the earth's history.

Precipitate A solute that has come out of solution.

Pressure The ratio of force to the area over which that force is distributed:

$$\text{Pressure} = \frac{\text{force}}{\text{area}}$$

Liquid pressure = weight density × depth.

Pressure-gradient force The force that moves air from a region of high-pressure to an adjacent region of low-pressure air.

Primary wave (P-wave) A longitudinal body wave; travels through solids, liquids, and gases and is the fastest seismic wave.

Principal quantum number, *n* An integer that specifies the quantized energy level of an atomic orbital.

Principle of flotation A floating object displaces a weight of fluid equal to its own weight.

Probability cloud The pattern of electron positions plotted over time to show the likelihood of an electron's being at a given position at a given time.

Products The new materials formed in a chemical reaction.

Projectile Any object that moves through the air or through space under the influence of gravity.

Proton A positively charged particle in an atomic nucleus.

Protostar The aggregation of matter that goes into and precedes the formation of a star.

Pseudoscience A theory or practice that is considered to be without scientific foundation.

Pulsar Likely a neutron star that rapidly spins, sending short precisely timed bursts of electromagnetic radiation.

Pure Having a uniform of homogeneous composition, or being without impurities. In chemistry, the term is used to denote a material that consists of a single element or compound.

Quality The characteristic timbre of a musical sound, which is governed by the number and relative intensities of partial tones.

Quantum A small, discrete packet of light energy.

Quantum hypothesis The idea that light energy is contained in discrete packets called quanta.

Quasar (Quasi-stellar object) A small powerful source of energy believed to be the active core of very distant galaxies.

Radiation The transfer of energy by means of electromagnetic waves.

Radioactivity The process whereby unstable atomic nuclei break down and emit radiation.

Radiometric dating A method for calculating the age of geologic materials based on the nuclear decay of naturally occurring radioactive isotopes.

Rarefaction Rarefied region, or region of lessened pressure, of the medium through which a longitudinal wave travels.

Reactants The reacting substances in a chemical reaction.

Reaction rate A measure of how quickly the concentration of products in a chemical reaction increases or the concentration of reactants decreases.

Real image An image formed by light rays that converge at the location of the image. A real image can be displayed on a screen.

Recrystallization Occurs when rocks are subjected to high temperatures and pressures and go through a change in mineral assemblage, which is usually accompanied by the loss of H_2O or CO_2.

Red giant Cool giant stars above main sequence stars on the H-R Diagram.

Reduction The process whereby a reactant gains one or more electrons.

Reflection The return of light rays from a surface in such a way that the angle at which a given ray is returned is equal to the angle at which it strikes the surface. When the reflecting surface is irregular, light is returned in irregular directions; this is *diffuse reflection.*

Refraction The bending of an oblique ray of light when it passes from one transparent medium to another. This is caused by a difference in the speed of light in the transparent media. When the change in medium is abrupt (say, from air to water), the bending is abrupt; when the change in medium is gradual (say, from cool air to warm air), the bending is gradual, which accounts for mirages.

Refraction The bending of a wave, either through a nonuniform medium or from one medium to another, caused by differences in wave speed.

Relationship of impulse and momentum Impulse is equal to the change in the momentum of the object upon which the impulse acts. In symbol notation, $Ft = \Delta mv$.

Relative humidity The amount of water vapor in the air at a given temperature; expressed as a percentage of the maximum amount of water vapor the air can hold at that temperature.

Resonance The response of a body when a forcing frequency matches its natural frequency.

Resultant The net result of a combination of two or more vectors.

Reverberation Reechoed sound.

Reverse osmosis A technique for purifying water by forcing it through a semipermeable membrane.

Rift (rift valley) A long, narrow trough that forms as a result of the divergence of two plates.

Rock cycle A sequence of events involving the formation, destruction, alteration, and reformation of rocks as a result of the generation and movement of magma; the weathering, erosion, transportation, and deposition of sediment; and the metamorphism of preexisting rocks.

Salinity The mass of salts dissolved in 1000 g of seawater.

Salt An ionic compound formed from the reaction between an acid and a base.

Sand dune Landform created when air flow is blocked by an obstacle, slowing the air speed and therefore promoting the deposition of airborne sand.

Satellite A projectile or small celestial body that orbits a larger celestial body.

Saturated hydrocarbon A hydrocarbon containing no multiple covalent bonds, with each carbon atom bonded to four other atoms.

Saturated solution A solution containing the maximum amount of solute that will dissolve in its solvent.

Science The collective findings of humans about nature, and a process of gathering and organizing knowledge about nature.

Scientific method An orderly method for gaining, organizing, and applying new knowledge.

Seafloor spreading The moving apart of two oceanic plates at a rift in the seafloor.

Second law of thermodynamics Heat never spontaneously flows from a cold substance to a hot substance. Also, all systems tend to become more and more disordered as time goes by.

Secondary wave (S-wave) A transverse body wave; cannot travel through liquids and so does not travel through the earth's outer core.

Sedimentary rocks Rocks formed from the accumulation of weathered material (sediments) carried by water, wind, or ice.

Semipermeable membrane A membrane that allows only the passage of molecules small enough to fit through its submicroscopic pores.

Series circuit An electric circuit with devices connected in such a way that the same electric current flows through each of them.

Shell A set of overlapping atomic orbitals of similar energy levels; in other words, a region of space in which electrons of similar energy levels in an atom have a 90 percent chance of being located.

Shock wave The cone-shaped wave made by an object moving at supersonic speed through a fluid.

Sine curve A wave form traced by simple harmonic motion, which can be made visible on a moving conveyor belt by a pendulum swinging at right angles above the moving belt.

Sinkhole A funnel-shaped depression in a karst area that is open to the sky, caused by the dissolution of subsurface limestone by groundwater.

Solar eclipse The phenomenon whereby the shadow of the moon falls upon the earth producing a region of darkness in the daytime.

Solubility The ability of a solute to dissolve in a given solvent.

Soluble Capable of dissolving to an appreciable extent in a given solvent.

Solute Any component in a solution that is not the solvent.

Solution A homogeneous mixture in which all components are in the same phase.

Solvent The component in a solution that is present in the largest amount.

Sonic boom The loud sound resulting from a shock wave.

Space-time The four-dimensional continuum in which all events take place and all things exist: Three dimensions are the coordinates of space and the fourth is of time.

Special theory of relativity The first of Einstein's theories of relativity, which discusses the effects of uniform motion on space, time, energy, and mass.

Specific gravity The ratio between the weight of a substance and the weight of an equal volume of water.

Specific heat capacity The quantity of heat per unit mass required to raise the temperature of a substance by 1 degree Celsius.

Spectroscope A device that uses a prism or a diffraction grating to separate light into its component colors.

Speed The distance traveled per time.

Spiral galaxy A disk-shaped galaxy with hot bright stars, and spiral arms. Our Milky Way is a spiral galaxy.

Spring tide A high or low tide that occurs when the sun, earth, and moon are aligned so that the tides due to the sun and moon coincide, making the high tides higher than average and the low tides lower than average.

Standing wave A stationary wave pattern formed in a medium when two sets of identical waves pass through the medium in opposite directions.

Stratosphere The second atmospheric layer above the earth's surface, extending from the top of the troposphere up to 50 km.

Structural isomers Molecules that have the same molecular formula but different chemical structures.

Sublimation The change of phase directly from solid to gas, bypassing the liquid phase.

Submicroscopic Refers to the realm of atoms and molecules, which is a realm so small that we are unable to observe it directly with optical microscopes.

Subsidence A lowering of the land surface that results when groundwater is removed from thick aquifers composed of layers of sand and clay.

Subtractive primary colors The three colors of absorbing pigments—magenta, yellow, and cyan—that, when mixed in certain proportions, will reflect any color in the spectrum.

Sunspots Temporary, relatively cool and dark regions on the sun's surface.

Superconductor Any material with zero electrical resistance, wherein electrons flow without losing energy and without generating heat.

Supernova An exploding massive star caused by gravitational collapse with the emission of enormous quantities of matter.

Superposition A relative dating principle stating that, in an undeformed sequence of sedimentary rocks, each bed or layer is older than the one above and younger than the one below.

Support force The force that supports an object against gravity, often called the *normal force*.

Surface wave A seismic wave that travels along the earth's surface.

Suspension A homogeneous mixture in which the various components are in different phases.

Syncline A fold in strata that has relatively young rocks at its core, with rock age increasing with increasing horizontal distance from the fold core.

Technology The means of solving practical problems by applying the findings of science.

Temperature A measure of the hotness or coldness of substances, related to the average kinetic energy per molecule in a substance; measured in degrees Celsius, or in degrees Fahrenheit, or in kelvins.

Temperature inversion A condition in which the upper regions of the atmosphere are warmer than the lower regions.

Terminal speed The speed at which the acceleration of a falling object terminates when air resistance balances its weight.

Terrestrial radiation The radiant energy emitted by Planet Earth.

Theory A synthesis of a large body of information that encompasses well-tested hypotheses about certain aspects of the natural world.

Theory of plate tectonics The idea that the earth's lithosphere is broken into pieces (plates) that move over the asthenosphere; boundaries between plates are where most earthquakes and volcanoes occur and where lithosphere is created and recycled.

Thermal energy (*internal energy*) The total energy (kinetic plus potential) of the submicroscopic particles that make up a substance.

Thermodynamics The study of heat and its transformation to different forms of energy.

Thermonuclear fusion Nuclear fusion produced by high temperature.

Thermonuclear reaction The fusion reaction brought about by high temperatures.

Thermosphere The fourth atmospheric layer above the earth's surface, extending from the top of the mesosphere to 500 km.

Third law of thermodynamics No system can reach absolute zero.

Time dilation The slowing of time as a result of speed.

Total internal reflection The total reflection of light traveling within a medium that strikes the boundary of another medium at an angle at, or greater than, the critical angle.

Transform fault A plate boundary formed by two plates that are sliding horizontally past each other.

Transformer A device for transferring electric power from one coil of wire to another by means of electromagnetic induction.

Transmutation The conversion of an atomic nucleus of one element into an atomic nucleus of another element through a loss or gain in the number of protons.

Transparent The term applied to materials through which light can pass in straight lines.

Transverse wave A wave in which the medium vibrates in a direction perpendicular (transverse) to the direction in which the wave travels. Light consists of transverse waves.

Troposphere The atmospheric layer closest to the earth's surface, 16 km high over the equator and 8 km high over the poles, containing 90% of the atmosphere's mass and essentially all of its water vapor and clouds.

Turbulent flow Water flowing erratically in a jumbled manner, stirring up everything it touches.

Ultrasonic Describes a sound of a frequency too high to be heard by the normal human ear—above 20,000 hertz.

Unconformity A break or gap in the geologic record, caused by an interruption in the sequence of deposition or by erosion of preexisting rock.

Unsaturated hydrocarbon A hydrocarbon containing at least one multiple covalent bond.

Unsaturated solution A solution that is capable of dissolving additional solute.

Valence electron An electron that is located in the outermost occupied shell of an atom and can participate in chemical bonding.

Valence shell The outermost occupied shell of an atom.

Vector component Parts into which a vector can be separated and that act in different directions from the vector.

Vector quantity A quantity that specifies direction as well as magnitude.

Velocity The speed of an object with specification of its direction of motion.

Velocity vector An arrow drawn to scale so that its length represents the magnitude of a velocity and its direction represents the direction of motion.

Virtual image An image formed by light rays that do not converge at the location of the image. Mirrors, converging lenses used as magnifying glasses, and diverging lenses all produce virtual images.

Volcano A central vent through which lava, gases, and ash erupt and flow.

Water table The upper boundary of the saturated zone, below which every pore space is filled with water.

Wave speed The speed with which waves pass a particular point:

$$\text{Wave speed} = \text{frequency} \times \text{wavelength}$$

Wavelength The distance between successive crests, troughs, or identical parts of a wave.

Weight Simply stated, the force due to gravity on an object. More specifically, the gravitational force with which a body presses against a supporting surface.

Weightlessness A condition encountered in free-fall wherein a support force is lacking.

White dwarf Dying star that has collapsed to the size of the earth and is slowly cooling off; located at the lower left of the H-R diagram.

Work The product of the force and the distance through which the force moves:

$$W = Fd$$

Work-Energy Theorum The work done on an object equals the change in kinetic energy of the object:

$$\text{Work} = \Delta\text{KE}$$

Photo Credits

xvii: John Suchocki
1: NASA/Johnson Space Center
11: Paul G. Hewitt III
12: Roger Ressmeyer/Corbis
21: Keith Bardin
26: Terry Murphy/Animals Animals/Earth Scenes
27: Addison Wesley Longman, Inc./San Francisco
37: Larry Sergeant/Comstock Images
44: John Dalton/Photo Researchers, Inc.
52: John Suchocki
53: Paul G. Hewitt
62: Paul G. Hewitt
65: Terje Rakke/Getty Images Inc. - Image Bank
67: Palm Press, Inc.
70: (top) Chris Peacock
71: Paul G. Hewitt
74: Paul G. Hewitt
76: Hubrich/Getty Images Inc. - Image Bank
77: NASA/Goddard Space Flight Center
78: Paul G. Hewitt
80: Paul G. Hewitt
81: Michael Vollmer/Physikalische Ingenieuvwissenschefter FH Brandenburg
83: Meidor Hu
93: P. Wallick/H. Armstrong Roberts
101: NASA/Goddard Space Flight Center
102: NASA/Goddard Space Flight Center
104: Lillian Lee
111: NASA/Johnson Space Center
112: Richard Megna/Fundamental Photographs
119: NASA/Johnson Space Center
123: Diane Schiumo/Fundamental Photographs
128: NASA/Goddard Space Flight Center
133: Alan Becker/Getty Images Inc. - Image Bank
136: Jack Hancock, (bottom) Paul C. Ryan
143: Milo Patterson
145: The Granger Collection
148: David E. Hewitt
152: (top) Lillian Lee, (bottom) William Waterfall/ Corbis/Stock Market
157: Margaret Ellenstein
161: Brad Lewis/Omjalla Images/G. Brad Lewis
162: Kasia Werel
166: Paul G. Hewitt
171: (top) AP/Wide World Photos, (bottom) Paul G. Hewitt, Meidor Hu
172: Nuridsany et Perennou/Photo Researchers, Inc
178: Will Maynez
179: Jim Wallace
180: (top) Paul G. Hewitt, (bottom) Milt and Joan Mann/Cameramann International
181: (right) Nancy Rogers, (left) Paul G. Hewitt
182: Paul G. Hewitt III
186: Robert D. Carey
187: David Cavagnaro
190: Meidor Hu
191: (left) John Suchocki, (right) Pat Crowe/Animals Animals/Earth Scenes
192: Paul G. Hewitt
193: Paul G. Hewitt
197: Paul G. Hewitt
203: Steven Hunt/Getty Images Inc. - Image Bank
209: Princeton University Palmer Physical Laboratory
210: Paul G. Hewitt
212: Jim Stith
213: Zig Leszczynski/Animals Animals/Earth Scenes
214: Addison Wesley Longman, Inc./San Francisco
218: John Lightfoot
219: Lillian Lee
221: Addison Wesley Longman, Inc./San Francisco
223: (top) Addison Wesley Longman, Inc./San Francisco, (bottom) Paul G. Hewitt
225: David E. Hewitt
226: (left) Addison Wesley Longman, Inc./San Francisco, (right) Katia Chtchourova
233: T.S. Florian/Photo Network
234: George Haling/Photo Researchers, Inc.
236: Duane Ackerman
237: Richard Megna/Fundamental Photographs
238: (top) John Suchocki, (bottom) Magplane Technology, Inc.
240: (top) Addison Wesley Longman, Inc./San Francisco
243: (top) John Suchocki, Lillian Lee
246: Will Maynez
247: Lillian Lee
253: Hermann Schlenker/Photo Researchers, Inc.
255: Corbis/Stock Market
258: Paul G. Hewitt
260: San Francisco Symphony
261: (top) Leslie A. Hewitt, (bottom) Eric Meola/Getty Images Inc. - Image Bank
263: (left) AP/Wide World Photos, (middle) CORBIS, (right) AP/Wide World Photos
264: Paul G. Hewitt
265: Norman Synnestvedt
269: U.S. Navy News Photo
271: Dean Baird
274: Meidor Hu
278: Paul G. Hewitt
281: Dr. Jeremy Burges/SPL/Photo Researchers, Inc.
286: Paul G. Hewitt
287: Meidor Hu
291: (left) Dave Vasquez, (right) Brian Robinson
292: (top) Bob Abrams, (bottom) Paul G. Hewitt
293: Meidor Hu
295: (top) Camerique/H. Armstrong Roberts, (bottom) Don King/ Getty Images Inc. - Image Bank
296: Education Development Center, Inc.
297: Ken Kay/Fundamental Photographs
301: Richard Megna
303: Diane Schiumo/Fundamental Photographs
304: Paul G. Hewitt III
307: Suzanne Lyons
309: Nina Leen/Time Picture Service, Time Warner, Inc.
310: Paul G. Hewitt
311: Roger Ressmeyer/Corbis
312: Institute of Paper Science & Technology
314: (top) Ted Mathieu, (bottom) Robert Greenler
317: Robert Greenler
320: Will & Deni McIntyre/Photo Researchers, Inc.
325: Paul G. Hewitt

330: Albert Rose
331: Tamiko Theil
333: Barbara Thomas
334: Armstrong Roberts
335: Milo Patterson
339: John Suchocki
342: (left) Rachel Epstein/Stuart Kenter Associates, (middle) Rachel Epstein/Stuart Kenter Associates, (right) Tony Freeman/PhotoEdit
343: IBM Research, Almaden Research Center
345: John Suchocki
349: (left to right)Getty Images, Inc. - Photodisc, Getty Images, Inc. - Photodisc, Getty Images, Inc. - Photodisc, Getty Images, Inc. - Photodisc Photo Researchers, Inc., Peter Arnold, Inc., Fundamental Photographs
350: Mark Martin/Photo Researchers, Inc.
352: Rachel Epstein/Stuart Kenter Associates
357: Paul G. Hewitt
359: John Suchocki
360: (left) Volker Steger/Peter Arnold, Inc., (middle) IBM/Peter Arnold, Inc., (right) IBM Research, Almaden Research Center
361: (left) Tom Pantages/Stuart Kenter Associates, (right) Rachel Epstein/Stuart Kenter Associates
362: (left) Phototake NYC, (right) John Suchocki
363: (top, left) John Suchocki
363: (top, right) John Suchocki
363: (bottom, left) Tom Pantages/Stuart Kenter Associates
363: (bottom, right) Alan J. Jircitano
364: Science Photo Library/Photo Researchers, Inc.
368: (left) John Suchocki, (right) David Scharf/Peter Arnold, Inc.
369: John Suchocki
373: John Suchocki
375: California Institute of Technology Archives
378: John Suchocki
381: Comstock Images
383: International Atomic Energy Agency
384: Richard Megna/Fundamental Photographs
387: Chris Priest/Photo Researchers, Inc.
393: Lawrence Berkeley National Laboratory
399: Comstock Images
406: Lawrence Livermore National Laboratory
411: Astrid & Hanns Friedler Michler/Photo Researchers, Inc.
412: (top) NASA/Goddard Institute for Space Studies, Getty Images, Inc.
414: John Beatty/Getty Images Inc. - Stone Allstock
415: (left) Fundamental Photographs, (middle) Definitive Stock
416: (left) Getty Images, Inc., (right) Tom Pantages/Stuart Kenter Associates (bottom) Tom Pantages/Stuart Kenter Associates
417: John Suchocki
418: Stephen R. Swinburne/Stock Boston
419: (top) Sharon Hopwood, (bottom) Sharon Hopwood
420: John Suchocki
428: (left) Tom Pantages/Stuart Kenter Associates, (right) Tom Pantages/Stuart Kenter Associates
431: Tim McKenna
431: Getty Images Inc. - Stone Allstock
432: (top) John Suchocki, (middle) Runk Scoenberger/Grant Heilman Photography, Inc.
434: (left) Tom Pantages/Stuart Kenter Associates, (right) Dave Bartruff/Stock Boston (bottom) George Gerster/ Photo Researchers, Inc.
436: (top, left) Kevin Adams/Kevin Adams Nature Photography, (top, middle) Getty Images Inc. - Stone Allstock (top, right) Getty Images, Inc., (middle, left) Science Source/ Photo Researchers, Inc. Getty Images, Inc., (middle) Getty Images, Inc., (middle, right) Brian Yarvin/Photo Researchers, Inc.
438: (top) Fred Ward/Black Star, (middle) Rachel Epstein/ Stuart Kenter Associates, (right) The Image Works
446: SolAqua
447: Ray Pfortner/Peter Arnold, Inc.
448: City of Honolulu
451: City of Helena, CA
457: Charles M. Falco/Photo Researchers, Inc.
459: Science Photo Library/Photo Researchers, Inc.
464: (left) Rachel Epstein/Stuart Kenter Associates, (right) F. Hache/Photo Researchers, Inc.
465: John Suchocki
466: Dee Breger/Photo Researchers, Inc.
469: Vaughan Fleming/Photo Researchers, Inc.
474: David Taylor/Photo Researchers, Inc.
477: AP/Wide World Photos
478: Jeff Daly/Stock Boston
479: (top) Francois Gohier/Photo Researchers, Inc., (bottom) Georg Gerster/Photo Researchers, Inc.
481: (left) Ron Reid/Photo Researchers, Inc., (right) Alcoa Inc.
483: (top) Tom Pantages/Stuart Kenter Associates, (bottom) Tom Pantages/Stuart Kenter Associates
485: Dr. T.S. Schrichte/Photo Resource Hawaii Stock Photography
488: Rachel Epstein/Stuart Kenter Associates
490: Rachel Epstein/Stuart Kenter Associates
492: Leonard Lessin/Peter Arnold, Inc.
493: John Suchocki
500: Sheila Terry/Photo Researchers, Inc.
502: Tom Pantages/Stuart Kenter Associates
503: Tom Pantages/Stuart Kenter Associates
507: DigitalVision
512: CORBIS

513: Rachel Epstein/Stuart Kenter Associates
514: Photo Researchers, Inc.
515: E.R. Degginger/Photo Researchers, Inc.
515: Jon Lemker/Animals Animals/Earth Scenes
518: NASA/Stuart Kenter Associates
525: Rachel Epstein/Stuart Kenter Associates
526: Rachel Epstein/Stuart Kenter Associates
529: J.B. Woolsey and Associates
530: M.P. Gadomski/Photo Researchers, Inc.
530: Rachel Epstein/Stuart Kenter Associates
531: S. Grant/PhotoEdit
531: Rachel Epstein/Stuart Kenter Associates
534: Rachel Epstein/Stuart Kenter Associates
538: Tom Pantages/Stuart Kenter Associates
543: Tom Pantages/Stuart Kenter Associates
545: (left) M. Bleier/Peter Arnold, Inc., (middle) Will McIntyre/ Photo Researchers, Inc., (right) M. Bleier/Peter Arnold, Inc.
547: Tom Pantages/Stuart Kenter Associates
551: Rachel Epstein/Stuart Kenter Associates
555: John-Peter Lahall/Photo Researchers, Inc.
555: Tom Pantages/Stuart Kenter Associates
556: John Suchocki
562: Lennard Lesson/Peter Arnold, Inc.
565: (bottom) Xcellsis Fuel Cell Engines, Inc.
566: (top) C. Liu, John Suchocki
568: Frank Siteman/Stock Boston
569: Rachel Epstein/Stuart Kenter Associates
573: (left) Tom Pantages/Stuart Kenter Associates, (right) Tom Pantages/Stuart Kenter Associates
575: John Suchocki
580: Rachel Epstein/Stuart Kenter Associates
582: Rachel Epstein/Stuart Kenter Associates
593: (top) Bob Gibbons/Photo Researchers, Inc., (bottom) Peter Arnold, Inc.
600: (top) John Suchocki, (bottom) Rachel Epstein/Stuart Kenter Associates
613: Leslie Hewitt
615: California Academy of Sciences
621: (top, left) Visuals Unlimited, (top, right) Paul Silverman/ Fundamental Photographs, (bottom, left) E. R. Degginger/ Animals Animals/Earth Scenes, (bottom, right) Color-Pic, Inc.
622: Color-Pic, Inc.
623: Dee Breger/Photo Researchers, Inc.
623: (bottom) Lee Boltin, (left) E.R. Degginger/Earth Scenes, (right) Breck P. Kent/Earth Scenes
625: (top) Paul Silverman/ Fundamental Photographs, (bottom) Mark A. Schneider/ Visuals Unlimited
626: Color-Pic, Inc.
627: Color-Pic, Inc.
633: Michael Stewart/Lava Images
633: (top, left) Beth Davidson/ Visuals Unlimited, (top, right) California Academy of Sciences, (middle, left) Ken Lucas/Visuals Unlimited (middle, right) California Academy of Sciences, (bottom, left) A. J. Copley/ Visuals Unlimited (bottom, right) California Academy of Sciences
638: (top) Paul Dix/PNI/Cascades Volcano Observatory, U.S. Geological Survey, (middle) Cascades Volcano Observatory, U.S. Geological Survey (bottom) W. H. Hodge/Peter Arnold, Inc.
641: Jim Wark/Peter Arnold, Inc.
643: (top) Dr. Jeremy Burgess/ Science Photo Library/Photo Researchers, Inc., (middle) Dr. Jeremy Burgess/Science Photo Library/Photo Researchers, Inc. (bottom) Grant Heilman Photography, Inc.
644: (top) Runk/Schoenberger/ Grant Heilman Photography, Inc., (middle) Paul Silverman/ Fundamental Photographs (top) Barry L. Runk/Grant Heilman Photography, Inc.
645: (top, left) A. J. Cunningham/ Visuals Unlimited, (bottom, left) Alex Kertish/Visuals Unlimited (middle) Paul Silverman/Fundamental Photographs, (right) Cabisco/ Visuals Unlimited
648: NASA Photo Research/Grant Heilman Photography, Inc.
649: (left) Biological/Phototake NYC, (middle) Gerald & Buff Corsi/Visuals Unlimited, (right) A.J. Copley/Visuals Unlimited
650: (top) Jeffrey A. Scovil, (bottom) Joyce Photo/Photo Researchers, Inc.
655: NASA Earth Observing System
676: John S. Shelton
683: Visuals Unlimited
695: Leslie A. Hewitt
696: (left) EROS Data Center, U.S. Geological Survey, (right) Color-Pic, Inc.
709: Grant Heilman/Grant Heilman Photography, Inc.
709: Steve Linstau/Rainbow
711: (top) Joseph Burke/Rainbow, (bottom) U.S. Geological Survey, Denver
712: David Hiser Photography
713: (top) Paul G. Hewitt III, (bottom) Visuals Unlimited
714: John Lemker/Animals Animals/Earth Scenes
715: Color-Pic, Inc.
716: E.R. Degginger/Color-Pic, Inc.
719: (top) NASA/Color-Pic, Inc., (bottom) Adrienne T. Gibson/ Animals Animals/Earth Scenes
720: (top) Breck P. Kent/Animals Animals/Earth Scenes, (bottom) W.H. Hodge/Peter Arnold, Inc.
721: (left) Color-Pic, Inc., (right) Color-Pic, Inc.
722: Leslie A. Hewitt
725: (left) Paul G. Hewitt, (right) Paul G. HewittI, (bottom) NASA-Photo Research/Grant Heilman Photography, Inc.

729: George H. H. Huey/CORBIS
730: C. Bruce Foster/Getty Images Inc. - Stone Allstock
731: Bob Abrams
736: Roland Seitre/Peter Arnold, Inc.
737: (top) Alex Kertisch/Visuals Unlimited, (bottom) Tom McHugh/Photo Researchers, Inc.
738: American Museum of Natural History
739: American Museum of Natural History
749: NASA/Photo Researchers, Inc.
754: Color-Pic, Inc.
765: (middle) National Geophysical Data Center, (top, left) Mark Newman/Alaska Stock, (bottom, left) EROS Data Center, U.S. Geological Survey, (top, right) B. & C. Alexander/Photo Researchers, Inc., (bottom, right) Manfred Mehlig/Getty Images Inc. - Stone Allstock
771: Michael Townsend/Getty Images Inc. - Stone Allstock
772: Mike J. Howell/Stock Boston
777: (top, left) Mark A. Schneider/ Visuals Unlimited, (bottom, left) Mark A. Schneider/ Visuals Unlimited (top, right) McCutcheon/Visuals Unlimited (bottom, right) E. Webber/Visuals Unlimited
780: H. Armstrong Roberts
783: (top) Thomas Nes/The Stock Market, (bottom) William Bickel/University of Arizona
784: E.R. Degginger/Color-Pic, Inc.
785: AP/Wide World Photos
789: NASA Earth Observing System
794: (top) CORBIS, (middle) Jay M. Pasachoff, (bottom) NASA/Goddard Institute for Space Studies
795: (top) NASA Earth Observing System, (bottom) Lick Observatory Publications Office
798: Roger Ressmeyer/CORBIS
799: Dennis DiCicco
801: Mark Martin/NASA/Photo Researchers, Inc.
805: (top) NASA Earth Observing System, (bottom) NASA/JPL/Phototake NYC
806: Lowell Observatory
807: (top) NASA Earth Observing System, (bottom) NASA Earth Observing System
808: NASA Earth Observing System
810: (top) Yerkes Observatory, (middle) Dennis Milon/ SPL/Photo Researchers, Inc., (bottom) John Sanford/ SPL/Photo Researchers, Inc.
811: A. Behrend/Phototake NYC
815: Paul G. Hewitt III
818: Roger Ressmeyer/CORBIS
822: Hubble Space Telescope/ NASA/Goddard Space Flight Center
823: Ronald Royer/Photo Researchers, Inc.
824: (left) Lick Observatory Publications Office, (right) Lick Observatory Publications Office, (bottom) Photo Researchers, Inc.
829: Julian Baum/New Scientist/ JPL/Photo Researchers, Inc.
830: (middle) Dr. Steve Gull/SPL/Photo Researchers, Inc., (bottom, left) National Optical Astronomy Observatories (bottom, right) Royal Observatory, Edimburg/SPL/ Photo Researchers, Inc.
831: (left) NRAO/SPL/Photo Researchers, Inc., (right) NASA/SS/Photo Researchers, Inc. (bottom) Hale Observatory/Photo Researchers, Inc.
832: Royal Greenwich Observatory/ SPL/Photo Researchers, Inc.
833: Lillian Lee
837: NASA/Johnson Space Center
841: Paul G. Hewitt
842: NOAO/Color-Pic, Inc.
849: Camerique/H. Armstrong Roberts
857: Library of Congress
858: California Institute of Technology Archives

Index

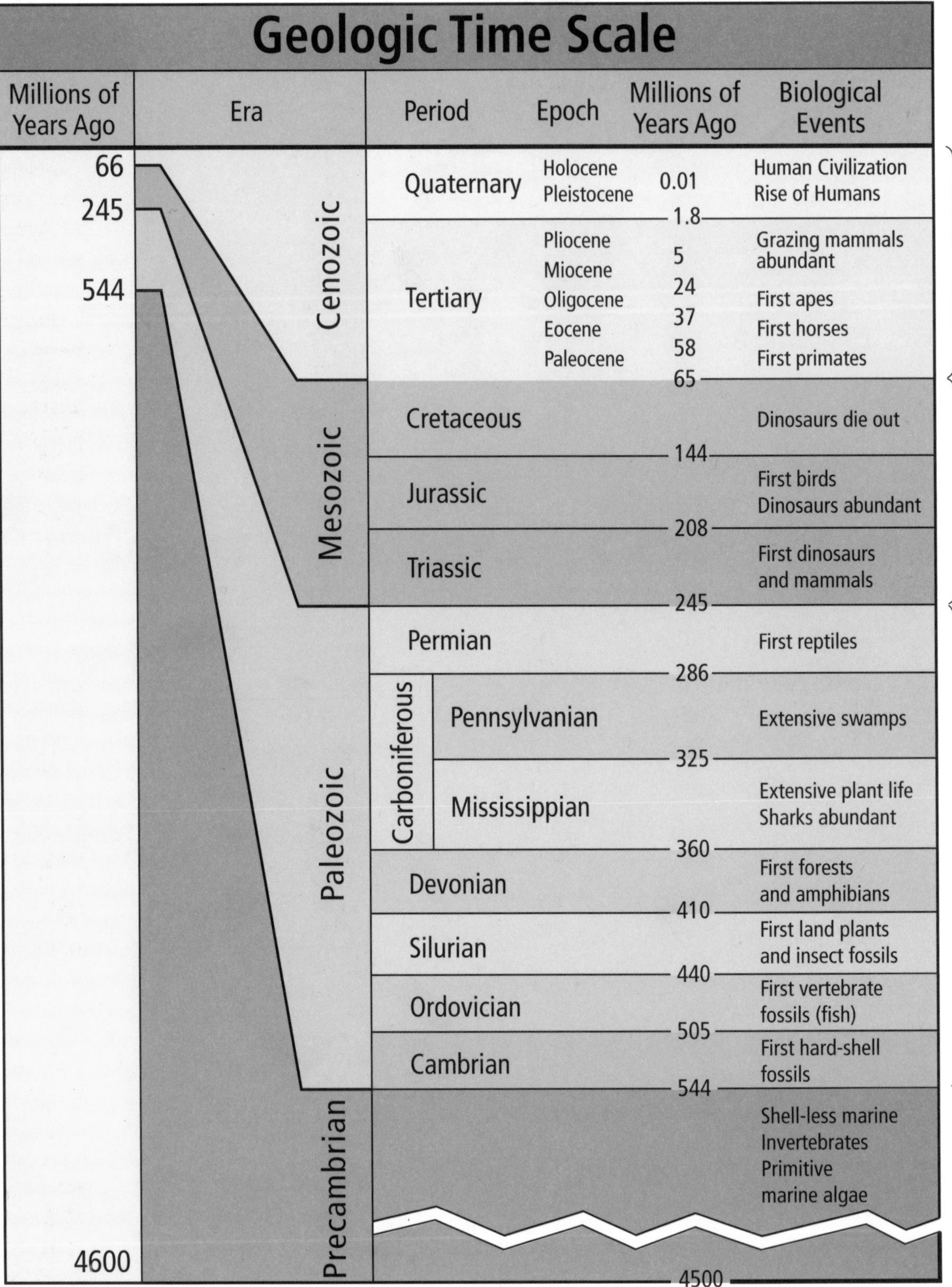

Earth formed about 4500 million (4.5 billion) years ago.